AMERICAN COMPOSERS
A Biographical Dictionary

Some Other Books by David Ewen

The Complete Book of Classical Music
The World of Twentieth Century Music
George Gershwin: His Journey to Greatness
Leonard Bernstein
Richard Rodgers
The World of Jerome Kern
Great Men of American Popular Song
The New Encyclopedia of Opera
Milton Cross' New Encyclopedia of Great Compos-
    ers and Their Music (with Milton Cross)
Dictators of the Baton
Music Comes to America
The Story of America's Musical Theater
David Ewen Introduces Modern Music
Composers of Tomorrow's Music
New Complete Book of the American Musical
    Theater
American Popular Songs: From the Revolutionary
    War to the Present
Composers Since 1900
Musicians Since 1900: Performers in Concert and
    Opera
All the Years of American Popular Music

AMERICAN COMPOSERS

A Biographical Dictionary

David Ewen

G.P. PUTNAM'S SONS   NEW YORK

Library of Congress Cataloging in Publication Data

Ewen, David, date.
American composers.

Includes bibliographies and appendix.
1. Composers—United States—Biography. I. Title.
ML390.E815   780′.92′2 [B]   81-7362
ISBN 0-399-12626-0   AACR2

Printed in the United States of America

Foreword

The aim of this biographical dictionary is to treat each composer, and particularly those living, in depth; to provide heart, flesh and sinews to the bare bones of biographical information available in existing dictionaries and encyclopedias; to gather details and specifics that should, once and for all, be permanently recorded for the present and preserved for the future.

This dictionary also aspires to embrace in each biography a succinct description of each composer's musical style together with a *coup d'oeil* on how that style grew and developed. At the same time, it hopes to provide descriptions (programmatic and/or musical) of some of the composer's major works.

There are between a thousand and fifteen hundred living composers in the United States, most of whom have compiled impressive lists of concert and operatic works. From such a copious reservoir, I have chosen three hundred composers, dating back to William Billings of Colonial days and reaching to young composers of our own day who have already reached artistic fulfillment. These three hundred composers were selected by virtue of the frequency and importance of the performances their compositions have received; the prestigious honors, grants and awards these composers have collected; the significance of their recordings; and other symptoms of success. Only by confining this volume to no more than three hundred entries could each composer receive the kind of comprehensive treatment I felt was needed and valuable. In this process, some productive, talented composers have been sidestepped. I have done so only after having given their lives and works careful study. In some instances, their achievements were circumscribed within the limited boundaries of a University or Conservatory town, or a single city; these composers were not sufficiently well known elsewhere. In brief, the composers represented in this volume are those about whom both the professional and lay music public is most likely to want information.

As a reference book on American composers, the selection was confined almost primarily to those who are native by birth or citizenship. The latter category has caught in its net some composers whose artistic orientation is obviously European rather than American. I allude to such men as Rachmaninoff, Hindemith, Gretchaninoff, Stravinsky and Schoenberg among others. They were included because they were American citizens. Some composers (a small handful) who are Americans neither by birth nor citizenship have also been represented, only because they spent so many years of their life, and produced so much of their basic repertory, in the United States, that to all intents and purposes they should be considered "American" composers. I am thinking, for example, of Gian Carlo Menotti, who has never renounced Italian citizenship. But Menotti lived in the United States for some four decades, received his basic musical training in the United States, wrote most of his major works in the United States, and had most of his world premieres in the United States. It is hardly possible to discuss contemporary American opera without giving him significant consideration. On the other hand there were some other foreign composers (particularly during the years of World War II) who spent a number of years in America where they did some of their composing. I found it difficult to gather such men into the American fold. The American interlude is incidental rather than basic to their overall careers. This is the reason why I did not include Darius Milhaud, Béla Bartók or Bohuslav Martinu, for example.

Only those so-called "popular" composers who have contributed compositions to concert hall and opera house are here represented: Duke Ellington, George Gershwin, Ferde Grofé, Victor Herbert, etc. It is quite true that Stephen Foster's songs have been performed by such eminent concert artists as Lawrence Tibbett, John Charles Thomas and Helen Traubel (of the recent past) or Marilyn Horne and Jan DeGaetani, among others (of the present). It is also true that such "serious" American composers as Ernest Bloch, John Alden Carpenter, Mario Castelnuovo-Tedesco, Aaron Copland, Morton Gould, Percy Grainger and Charles Ives (to single out a few) have used Foster songs as a point of departure for their own concert works. But, in the final analysis, Foster was exclusively a composer of popular songs for mass consumption, most of his classics born in the minstrel show, and for this reason Stephen Foster has been excluded. Similar arguments explain also why John Philip Sousa cannot be found in these pages—no matter that "The Stars and Stripes Forever" was performed by the New York Philharmonic under Leonard Bernstein and other estimable symphonic organizations under eminent conductors! I can go one step further. Within recent years, Itzhak Perlman, the Cleveland Orchestra under Lorin Maazel, and the organist E. Power Biggs, celebrated for his performances of Bach, have carried the rags of Scott Joplin into the concert auditorium. But here, once again, I felt that this was not the proper passport for the admission of Scott Joplin into our territory. After all, it was necessary to draw a sharp line of demarcation to prevent a massive invasion of other similar, if less celebrated, "popular" composers.

The format adopted for the presentation and consolidation of biographical and analytical materials for each composer was planned to cover as wide a spectrum as possible. Each biography begins with a brief, preliminary musical identification, sometimes merely a few lines, sometimes much longer, to individualize him or her, to set him or her apart from their colleagues. Sometimes individual accomplishments are pointed up, but most often their basic musical style is described. It is my feeling that a composer's musical identity set forth without preliminaries could direct illumination on his creative growth as detailed in the long biography that follows. Each such biography has been planned to contain all the salient facts, beginning with the early years and the influences that helped to mold him into a composer. As the biography unfolds, principal compositions are described with additional information provided through copious quotations from newspaper or magazine criticisms. To add another dimension, each biography ends with an artistic statement by the composer quoted verbatim in which often valuable insights are given into his musical thinking. Most of these statements were prepared by the composers themselves for this book. Others were lifted out of published articles, lectures, and occasionally from interviews, with the composer's approval. After that, each biography concludes with a detailed list of principal works, with year of composition, followed by a select bibliography. Three principal reference books are mentioned so consistently in the bibliographical paragraphs that to conserve space it has been found expedient to use for them only identifying initials. Thus *Baker's Biographical Dictionary of Musicians*, 6th edition, edited by Nicolas Slonimsky (N.Y., 1978), is represented by *BBDM*; *Dictionary of Contemporary Music*, edited by John Vinton (N.Y., 1971), by *DCM*; and the *New Grove Dictionary of Music and Musicians*, edited by Stanley Sadie (Washington, D.C., 1980), *NGDMM*.

As far as was possible, every effort was made to get materials from first-hand sources. With this in mind I was in constant communication with some two hundred and twenty-five composers who contributed copious information in response to my detailed questionnaire and subsequent queries. Frequently these composers supplemented the written word with recordings and published music. These composers took exceptional pains to prepare for me an exhaustive *curriculum vitae* of education, academic and musical,

honors received, a list of major works with year of composition and dates and places of world premieres, supplementing this information with programs, newspaper and magazine articles, and reviews. Since submitted facts called for frequent corroboration, in the face of conflicting evidence, these composers were deluged with my persistent questioning. Their patience in most instances was nothing less than saintly. Composers were also given the opportunity to read and correct the first draft of their biographies to ensure accuracy of details and the correctness of my summation of their respective idioms and description of their basic compositions.

The question of accuracy deserves here a brief comment. Throughout this volume there will be found facts and specifics which conflict with those available in existing reference sources. Where discrepancies arose between the facts provided me by the composer and those found in reference books, I made a special effort to verify the accuracy of the composer's submissions by seeking confirmation from printed programs, reviews, published music, publishers' catalogues and similar sources. In all cases where corrections had to be made, the composer gave the final approval.

I have tapped first-hand sources even for composers no longer alive but prominent since the 1920s. This was made possible through my copious files gathered for half a century, files to which composers themselves have contributed exhaustive materials not readily found elsewhere. Though many of these deceased composers are rarely represented on today's concert programs, their presence in this biographical dictionary is warranted, I feel, by their successes and importance during their lifetimes. In many instances, material on them is not easy to come by. The reference value of this volume, I believe, has been greatly enhanced through their inclusion.

Any work on 20th-century music must necessarily employ some technical terminology. I have tried to reduce this to a minimum. Though technical language will be found in this volume, the abstruse and the recondite have been avoided. The intelligent layman, however innocent of Conservatory-taught terminologies, should not have much difficulty in comprehending what these composers have accomplished in their music, and how.

For titles of compositions, I have adopted the expedience of using those most familiar to Americans in order to make this book more serviceable. Sometimes the original foreign language is used if such a title is more familiar than its English translation; sometimes the reverse method is pursued. Where a famous work is equally known both in its original language and in its English translation, both versions are used at initial mention.

Opus numbers have been dispensed with in those rare instances in which contemporary Americans still cling to this practice, except where the opus number is necessary for proper identification, as is often the case with Schoenberg and Hindemith. Opus numbers are also used at times for American composers of the past to arrive at the chronological position of their works where year of composition is not available. One living American composer, John La Montaine, insists on using opus numbers in place of year-of-composition, and his wish has been respected.

In the making of this volume, the help of many people and institutions has been indispensable. My most profound gratitude goes to the composers themselves whose cooperation has been copious, generous, and even enthusiastic. The facilities of the Library of Performing Arts in New York and the Congressional Library in Washington, D.C., have been tapped for valuable information about pre-20th-century Americans. Numerous musical organizations have helped in many different ways. Among these are the American Society of Composers, Authors and Publishers (ASCAP) and Broadcast Music, Inc. (BMI), American Music Center and American Composers Alliance. The publicity departments of some of America's major symphony orchestras and music-publishing houses have also been unsparing in their cooperation. A dozen or so graduate students provided me with their doctoral theses, which often proved to be a rich lode of biographical and critical information not available elsewhere. A final word of gratitude goes to my wife, Hannah, who assumed the thankless chore of attending to all correspondence and of typing the manuscript in its various evolutionary stages. She was my right hand from the very beginning of this project, and it can be said that the right hand always knew what the left hand was doing.

DAVID EWEN

Miami Beach, Fla.
January 1981.

AMERICAN COMPOSERS
A Biographical Dictionary

A

Adler, Samuel Hans, b. Mannheim, Germany, March 4, 1928. American citizen, 1945.

His Judaic background and early parental and home influences left a permanent impression on his creativity. These influences are responsible for his large output of works on biblical subjects and nonliturgical texts of Judaic interest, for his liturgical music for the synagogue, and for the infiltration (though not consciously) of a strong Jewish identity into many of his secular works for the concert hall and operatic stage.

Adler cannot remember a time when music was not an important presence in his life. Both parents were musical. His father, Hugo Chaim, had received a thorough musical training in Germany before becoming a synagogal cantor and a distinguished composer of Jewish liturgical music. His mother had been trained in piano and voice and, though she gave up these studies for marriage, remained preoccupied with the making of music all her life. Samuel's first influences were his father and mother singing German lieder to him, and the chamber music concerts that were regularly held at his home. He was about three when he attended a rehearsal of one of his father's oratorios, an event that stirred him so deeply he then announced that he, too, would become a composer someday.

In kindergarten, Samuel received lessons in solfeggio and in playing the recorder. At seven, he began to study the violin with Albert Levy. During the early years of the Nazi regime he heard his first two operas and attended symphony and chamber concerts arranged by the Jewish community of Mannheim when the Nazis forbade Jewish musicians to perform elsewhere.

The Adler family immigrated to the United States in 1939, settling in Worcester, Mass., where the father was appointed cantor and musical director of Temple Emanu-El. In Worcester, Samuel continued to study violin with Maurice Diamond. While attending the public schools, he played in the school orchestra and sang in the school chorus. At Classical High School in Worcester (1943–46) he came under the influence of Albert W. Wassel, who gave him numerous opportunities to conduct the school orchestra and encouraged him to compose. Adler's creativity was further encouraged by Herbert Fromm, a pupil of Hindemith's, with whom he studied harmony and counterpoint in Boston (1941–45). In 1945, Adler's first serious orchestral composition, *Epitaph for the Young American Soldier,* was premiered by the Worcester Philharmonic (in which Adler had been serving as violinist for two years).

Upon graduating from Classical High School, Adler attended Boston University (1946–48), where he received an intensive musical training from Hugo Norden, Lucia Hershey, Robert King, Karl Geiringer, and Paul Pisk among others. The influence of Hindemith's linear counterpoint and the result of Adler's studies with Fromm are discernible in most of the music Adler wrote during his undergraduate years. Upon receiving his bachelor of arts degree at Boston University in 1948, he continued his musical education at Harvard University (1948–50) with Walter Piston, Randall Thompson, Paul Hindemith, Irving Fine, and others. The summers of 1949 and 1950 were spent at the Berkshire Music Center at Tanglewood in Massachusetts for the study of composition with Aaron Copland and conducting with Serge Koussevitzky.

Soon after earning his master's degree in music from Harvard in 1950, Adler was called into American military service. He served in Germany in the artillery and there he was responsible for organizing the Seventh Army Symphony, which he conducted in public concerts from its inception in April 1952 until he was demobilized later that year with the Medal of Honor for outstanding service, specifically for his achievement in creating the Seventh Army Symphony.

Upon his return to the United States in 1953, Adler was appointed musical director of Temple Emanu-El in Dallas, Tex., retaining this post for the next thirteen years. During this period he was also instructor of fine arts at Hockday School in Dallas (1955–56), professor of composition at North Texas State University in Denton (1957–66) on a Rockefeller grant, conductor of the Lyric Theater in Dallas (1955–59), and conductor of the Dallas Chorale (1954–57).

He completed his first symphony in 1953, in which, still writing within a tonal framework, he began to emulate some of the stylistic mannerisms of Copland and Piston, a tendency he would pursue for the next half dozen years or so. This symphony, which had been commissioned by the University of Texas for the Dallas Symphony, was introduced by that orchestra under Walter Hendl on December 7, 1953; it was awarded the Dallas Symphony Prize. For three years (1954–57) Adler received the Texas

Composer's Prize. Adler's Second Symphony (1957)—in which the composer recalls his Jewish heritage by simulating synagogal cantillations in some of his melodic materials—was given its first hearing on February 12, 1958, in a performance by the Dallas Symphony under Hendl. A one-act opera—*The Outcasts of Poker Flat* (1959), libretto by Judah Stampfer, based on Bret Harte's story—received its world premiere in Denton, Tex., on June 8, 1962.

Under the auspices of the State Department, Adler returned to Europe in 1957–58 to conduct the Seventh Army Symphony at the World's Fair in Brussels and to lecture and conduct in Italy, Austria, Germany, England, Cyprus, and Israel. Once again, in 1960, he made a State Department tour of Europe and Israel, lecturing and conducting in thirteen countries. Between these two tours, on February 14, 1960, he married Carol Ellen Stalker, then a student in philosophy and Near Eastern studies at the University of Michigan, later to become a successful poet and short-story writer. They raised two daughters.

Since 1960, Adler has developed a musical style of his own, combining tonal and nontonal elements. Working within such established frameworks as the symphony, string quartet, concerto, concertino, cantata, sonata, oratorio—and employing contrapuntal and melodic devices dating back several centuries—he nevertheless did not hesitate to use ultramodern practices to broaden his expressiveness. String Quartet no. 4 (1963; Dallas, January 6, 1965) uses the aleatory technique in its fourth-movement cadenza by providing only the notes (based loosely on a twelve-tone row) without specifying time values, rhythm, or dynamics, which were left to the discretion and selectivity of the performers. Concerto for Orchestra (1971; Kalamazoo, Mich., June 24, 1973) has a third movement reminiscent of the modal style of the 13th century, even though the rest of the work is basically atonal. A one-act biblical opera, *The Wrestler* (1971; Dallas, June 22, 1972)—Judah Stampfer's libretto based on the story of Jacob's return to Canaan and his reconciliation with his brother, Esau—abounds with *Sprechstimme* (song-speech) and unresolved discords. And though Adler never wrote for a synthesizer or magnetic tape, he has been affected by synthesized sound since he completed the study of such techniques in the late 1960s. Some of his works of the 1970s reveal the influence electronic music had on his orchestral writing: the Concerto for Orchestra; parts of *The Wrestler;* the Symphony no. 5 (*We Are the Echoes*) (1975; Fort Worth, November 10, 1975); and particularly the first movement of the Concerto for Flute and Orchestra (1977; Rochester, N.Y., December 1977).

Much of his creative productivity has been canalized into ethnic compositions: a library of liturgical music for the synagogue; compositions inspired by and rooted in biblical and Judaic subjects. The one-act biblical opera *The Wrestler* has already been mentioned. In addition, his more significant Judaic works include *The Vision of Isaiah* (1962; Dallas 1963), for bass, chorus, and orchestra, text taken from Isaiah, in which the prophet replies to God's call and in which the words of God are sung by an a cappella chorus; the oratorio *The Binding* (1967; Dallas, May 1968), for five solo voices, chorus, and orchestra describing God's demand that Abraham sacrifice his son, Isaac; Symphony no. 5, for mezzo-soprano and orchestra, a setting of five poems by various poets, each concerned with some aspect of the Jewish experience through the years and the centuries-old joys and sorrows of the Jewish people.

Adler made two contributions to the commemoration of the American bicentennial. *The Disappointment* (1974; Washington, D.C., April 1976) was a recreation of America's earliest ballad opera, written in 1767. Only the libretto, by Andrew Barton, has survived, and for it Adler reconstructed a score made up of the melodies popular in the Colonies (including "Yankee Doodle") together with an overture and orchestral interludes of his own devising. String Quartet no. 6 (1975; Chicago, May 9, 1977)—commissioned for the bicentennial by the Fine Arts Music Foundation of Chicago for the Fine Arts Quartet and Jan DeGaetani—was a setting for mezzo-soprano and string quartet of four poems by Walt Whitman in a modified serial technique.

In 1966, Adler was appointed professor of composition at the Eastman School of Music, and since 1973 he has been chairman of the department. In 1969, he was awarded an honorary doctorate in music from the Southern Methodist University in Dallas. While on leave from Eastman in 1975, he was a lecturer at the Hochschule für Musik in Vienna and the Mozarteum in Salzburg, and under the auspices of the State Department he was lecturer and conductor in Poland, Italy, and Turkey. In 1976, he was invited to Jerusalem to attend the world premiere of his *Nuptial Scene*, for mezzo-soprano and eight instruments (1975), which had been commissioned for that city's "Testimonium" Festival in February. He once again visited Jerusalem, for two months in 1978, to teach at the Rubin Academy of Music.

In 1964, Adler became the first recipient of the Charles Ives Award, which had been instituted at the University of Houston on a grant from Mrs. Charles Ives. (This award has since been given by the American Academy of Arts and Letters.) Between 1966 and 1970, Adler was the eastern regional director of the Contemporary Music Project sponsored jointly by the Music Educators National Conference and the Ford Foundation. The University of Rochester gave him the Lillian Fairchild Award in 1969, presented to an outstanding creative artist in the upstate New York area. In 1973 and in 1977, Adler was awarded National Endowment grants for the writing of *The Lodge of Shadows,* a music drama for baritone, dancers, and orchestra (1973) and *Aeolus, King of the Winds,* for clarinet and piano trio (1977), commissioned for the Aeolian Players, who introduced it in New York in 1978. The Outstanding Educator of the Year Award was presented to Adler by the National Education Association in 1977.

Adler is the editor of *Choral Singing: An Anthology* (1972) and *Sightsinging: Pitch-Interval-Rhythm* (1979).

THE COMPOSER SPEAKS: I have been labeled a composer of the "radical center" and I rather like that classification. I am a happy eclectic who has never been anxious to pursue novelty or the avant-garde, but who tried to be open to all stylistic trends throughout my years as a composer. I was greatly influenced by the classics and have had a longstanding love affair with contrapuntal devices since my father's love for Bach and Handel was transmitted to me early in life. The whole field of liturgical music has also molded my musical thought. My musical ideal is predicated on a solid musical language which is playable and singable even though not necessarily easy to perform and which communicates the major musical and philosophical message I'd like to transmit to audiences; namely, a love of life and mankind, a wonderment of the beauty of creation, and a general excitement I feel about simply being alive.

PRINCIPAL WORKS: 9 cantos for solo instruments or small ensembles (1970–76); 6 string quartets (1945–75); 6 song cycles (1950–76); 5 symphonies (1953–75); 3 violin sonatas (1948, 1956, 1965).

Concert Piece for Orchestra (1946); Praeludium, for brass choir (1947); Divertimento, for brass choir (1948); Horn Sonata (1948); Toccata, for orchestra (1954); Capriccio, for piano (1954); *Summer Stock,* orchestral overture (1955); *A Feast of Light,* orchestral variations on two Chanukah tunes (1955); *Jubilee,* for orchestra (1958); *The Outcasts of Poker Flat,* one-act opera (1959); *Shir Chadash,* synagogue service (1960); Toccata, Recitation, and Postlude, for organ (1960); *Southwestern Sketches,* for wind ensemble (1961); Rhapsody, for violin and orchestra (1961); Elegy, for string orchestra (1962); *The Vision of Isaiah,* cantata for bass, chorus, and orchestra (1962); Five Movements, for brass quintet (1963); *Requiescat in Pace,* in memory of President John F. Kennedy (1963); Sonata Breve, for piano (1963); Piano Trio (1964); *B'sharray T'filah,* synagogue service (1965); Festive Prelude, for wind ensemble (1965); Sonata for Unaccompanied Cello (1966); Seven Epigrams, for woodwind sextet (1966); *Intrada,* for woodwind quintet (1967); *The Binding,* oratorio, for five solo voices, chorus, and orchestra (1967); Five Vignettes, for twelve trombones (1968); Lament, for baritone and chamber orchestra (1968); Concerto for Winds, Brass, and Percussion (1968); *City by the Lake,* a portrait of the city of Rochester, for orchestra (1968); *From Out of Bondage,* cantata for solo voices, chorus and brass quintet, percussion, and organ (1968); *A Whole Bunch of Fun,* secular

cantata for mezzo-soprano or baritone, three choirs, and orchestra (1969); Concerto for Organ (1970); Sinfonietta (1970); Brass Fragments, for twenty brass instruments (1970); *Histrionics,* for brass and percussion (1971); *The Wrestler,* one-act biblical opera (1971); *The Lodge of Shadows,* music drama for baritone, dancers, and orchestra (1973); *The Disappointment,* reconstruction of a 1767 ballad opera (1974); Four Dialogues, for euphonium and marimba (1974); *Déjà vu,* for six recorders (1975); *Nuptial Scene,* for mezzo-soprano and eight instruments (1975); Concertino no. 2, for string orchestra (1976); *Of Saints and Sinners,* for voice and piano (1976); Flute Concerto (1977); *The Waking,* a celebration for dancers, chorus and orchestra (1978); *Line Drawings,* for saxophone quartet (1978); *Aeolus, King of the Winds,* for clarinet and piano trio (1977); *A Little Night and Day Music,* for wind ensemble (1978); Piano Sonatina (1979); *Trumpet Triptych* (1979).

BIBLIOGRAPHY: *DCM;* Rothmuller, A. Marko, *The Music of the Jews,* rev. ed. (N.Y., 1967); *American Music Teacher,* January 1976; *Who's Who in America, 1980–81.*

Aitken, Hugh, b. New York City, September 7, 1924.

Since his student days he has alternated in his compositions between a somewhat tonal idiom, usually in his vocal works, and an almost atonal, more dissonant and complex style in many of his instrumental pieces, with an occasional diversion into wit and satire.

His father, Hugh Walter Aitken, was a professional violinist who had studied at the Juilliard School of Music and who, during the depression years of the 1930s, had to abandon music for business. This experience led him to be less than enthusiastic about having his son pursue music as a profession. Hugh's paternal grandmother, a pianist, encouraged him in his early interest in music and gave him his first piano lessons. While attending Evander Childs High School in New York between 1937 and 1941 he studied the clarinet, played in the school band, sang in its chorus, and made his first efforts at composition. In 1941, he entered New York University, specializing in chemistry. During his two years at college, however, he spent more time playing and composing music than studying chemistry. His first composition to receive a public performance was a piece for men's chorus and piano performed by the N.Y.U. Glee Club in 1943, conducted by Alfred M. Greenfield, a composition Aitken describes as "some overblown Thomas Wolfe made up largely of half-diminished seventh chords."

In July 1943, Aitken joined the Army Air Corps, flying nineteen combat missions as a navigator on a B-17 based in Italy. During his two and a half years of military service he came to the conclusion that he wanted to devote his life to music. Upon separation from the Air Corps he married Laura Tapia (later to become a professor of early childhood education) on September 10, 1946, with whom he had two children. He entered Juilliard in 1946, where he studied clarinet with Arthur Christmann and composition with Bernard Wagenaar, Vincent Persichetti, and, briefly, Robert Ward. As a student, he completed a Piano Sonatina (1947); Short Suite, for winds and piano (1948); Three Motets, for tenor and thirteen instruments (1949); and a Chamber Concerto, for piano and thirteen instruments (1950) among other works. After receiving his bachelor of science degree at Juilliard in 1949, he held a graduate teaching fellowship there in 1949–50 while completing requirements for a master of science degree in 1950. From 1950 to 1963 he was a member of the composition faculty at the Juilliard Preparatory Division and from 1960 to 1970 served in its department of literature and materials of music. For several summers, he served as a professor of composition at the Paris Academy in France (1968, 1973), and composer-in-residence at the Bennington Composers Conference in Vermont (1958, 1965).

In his apprentice compositions, while attending Juilliard as a student, and in his subsequent ones, Aitken never became deeply interested in serial composition, electronic music, or aleatoric devices, feeling that all such methods tended to avoid what he considered the noblest of the composer's problems, namely, to write music dealing with human experience. Nevertheless, in his frequently complex, atonal, harmonically discordant and occasionally percussive style, and in his interest in multiple tempi, his music is thoroughly contemporary.

Cantata no. 2, for tenor and five instruments (1959), to Rilke's poems, was successfully introduced by Charles Bressler and the New York Chamber Soloists (who had commissioned it) at the Library of Congress in Washington, D.C., on November 16, 1962. The Moirai, a ballet score for orchestra (1961), was premiered by the José Limón Dance Company at the American Dance Festival in New London, Conn., on August 18, 1961, Partita, for string quartet and orchestra (1964)—commissioned by the New York Festival Orchestra—was given its first hearing at Carnegie Hall in New York on December 9, 1964, performed by the Juilliard String Quartet and the Festival Orchestra of New York, Thomas Dunn conducting. Piano Fantasy (1966) was premiered on March 20, 1969, at Town Hall, New York, by Santos Ojeda. This was one of several compositions recorded by CRI in an album of Aitken's music released in 1976 that also included Cantata no. 1, on Elizabethan texts, for tenor, oboe and string trio (1958); Cantata no. 3, on poems by Willis Barnstone, for tenor, oboe, and viola (1960); and Cantata no. 4, on Spanish poems by Antonio Machado, for soprano and four instruments (1961). Later works of more

than passing interest include the Trios for Eleven Players (1971; N.Y., April 23, 1972); *Fables*, a satirical and witty chamber opera designated as a "diversion," based on La Fontaine, for four singers and nine instrumentalists, commissioned by the Elizabeth Sprague Coolidge Foundation (1974; Washington, D.C., November 1, 1975), a feature of the Caramoor Festival of Katonah, N.Y., in June 1976; *Johannes*, a homage to the 15th-century Flemish contrapuntist Ockeghem, for five players on Renaissance instruments, commissioned by the W. W. Naumburg Foundation (1977; N.Y., October 27, 1977).

In 1970, Aitken was appointed professor of music at William Paterson College in Wayne, N.J., where he served as chairman of the music department (1970–72) and associate dean of fine and performing arts (1972–73). As a recipient of a grant from the National Endowment for the Arts in 1975 he composed for Gerard Schwartz, trumpet virtuoso, *Tromba*, for string quartet and trumpet (1976), which, in its final and definitive version, was introduced on June 8, 1979, in Great Neck, N.Y.

THE COMPOSER SPEAKS: I draw my strength from the tradition of which I am a part. The desire to destroy the past and start afresh is a symptom of alienation and despair. Of course, this aim is impossible to achieve. Were it doable, it would dehumanize the art I love, the art through which we share in the experience of others and thereby defeat despair.

PRINCIPAL WORKS: 6 partitas for string orchestra or full orchestra (1957–64); 5 cantatas for voice and instruments (1958–62).

Mass, for chorus and chamber orchestra (1950); String Trio (1951); Three Motets, for mixed chorus (1951); Piano Concerto (1953); Short Suite, for string orchestra (1954); Seven Pieces, for chamber orchestra (1957); Seven Bagatelles, for piano (1957); Quintet, for oboes and string quartet (1957); Serenade, for ten instruments (1958); Quartet, for clarinet and string trio (1959); *The Drunkards*, dance score for orchestra (1960); *The Moirai*, ballet score for orchestra (1961); *I, Odysseus,* dance score for chamber group (1962); Mass, for chorus and organ (1964); Piano Fantasy (1966); Trios for Eleven Players (1970); *Fables*, chamber opera (1974); *Tromba*, for trumpet and string quartet (1976); *Johannes*, for five players on Renaissance instruments (1977); *For the Viola*, for solo viola (1978).

BIBLIOGRAPHY: *BBDM; New York Times*, November 2, 1975; *Newark Star-Ledger*, October 23, 1975.

Albert, Stephen, b. New York City, February 6, 1941.

His style has embraced classicism, romanticism, folk music, jazz, but has avoided atonality, the precompositional techniques growing out of the music

and twelve-tone practices of Schoenberg and Webern, and aleatory practices.

There has always been music in the Albert home,
since the mother played the piano well by ear, and
recordings of serious music were regularly heard.
When Stephen was in the third grade in Great Neck,
N.Y., he started studying the trumpet, which he
played in the school band and orchestra. By the time
he reached the sixth grade he was also studying the
French horn and piano. "I enjoyed the brass far more
than the piano," he recalls. "I especially looked forward to marching down Middleneck Road on Memorial Day each year playing Sousa marches for
parents, friends, and hundreds of other faithful on-
lookers lining the sidewalks." At summer camp,
when he was thirteen, he wrote his first composition,
a piano suite. Encouraged by his piano teacher, he
continued composing after he returned home from
camp and that year he told his family firmly he
planned to become a composer. To help bring this
ambition to fruition he studied composition privately
with Elie Siegmeister (1956–58) and, during the
summer of 1958, with Darius Milhaud at Aspen,
Col.

Upon graduating from Great Neck High School in
1958, Albert entered the Eastman School of Music in
Rochester, N.Y., where the study of composition was
continued with Bernard Rogers. As a student at
Eastman, Albert wrote shorter works as part of the
curriculum and began a large four-movement composition for strings, brass, and percussion, *Four Visions,* which he did not complete until 1960. The influence of the language of Bartók and Stravinsky asserted itself in his writing and would continue to do
so for a number of years.

Albert remained at Eastman just a year and a half
because "I found the atmosphere confining and too
geared to music-education programs." Following a
brief period of study with Karl-Birger Blomdahl in
Stockholm during the winter of 1960, Albert entered
the Philadelphia Musical Academy, where for the
two-year period of 1960–62 he studied composition
first with Roy Harris and then with Joseph Castaldo. Castaldo's approach to analysis made a deep impression on young Albert, providing him with a new
direction for his creativity. "He was particularly
fond of demonstrating how an interval or series of
intervals in a motive could dominate and unify a
movement or entire work if handled skillfully," Albert explains. "I later discovered that Stravinsky referred to this perception as 'the weight of an interval.'
While there was nothing new in the idea itself, it was
new to me and I brought it into my own work from
that time to the present. It has since struck me as one
of the most important and deepest organizing principles of Western music since the Middle Ages.
Schoenberg isolated the principle in his serialization
of the twelve tones of our chromatic scale, but this
practice seemed too concentrated for my own musical
needs. But the organization within the context of to-

nality has been my way of writing since my days at
the Philadelphia Musical Academy with Castaldo."
Albert's first mature work written in this manner
was *Illuminations,* for brass, pianos, harps, and percussion (1962), which was performed at the Philadelphia Musical Academy in the spring of 1963.

During his final year at the academy, in 1962,
Albert was awarded first prize in the BMI Hemi-
spheric Competition for *Four Visions,* and a year later he was given the Bearns Prize from Columbia
University. In the fall of 1962 he entered the master's
program at the University of Pennsylvania in Philadelphia, studying counterpoint and analysis for one
semester with George Rochberg. When Rochberg
took a leave of absence from the university, Albert
also decided to withdraw, to concentrate on composition. *Supernatural Songs,* for soprano and chamber
orchestra, came in 1963; *Imitations,* for string quartet, in 1964; and *Winter Songs* (1964–65), for tenor
and orchestra, and *Wedding Songs,* for soprano and
piano, in 1965. All received their first performances
in Rome, where Albert was then (1965–67) residing
on a Prix de Rome. (He had been awarded a Fulbright Fellowship in 1965, but turned it down in favor of the Prix de Rome.) In Rome, on a grant from
the Ford Foundation, he began writing *Bacchae,* for
narrator, chorus, and orchestra, which he completed
in 1968.

Meanwhile, in 1965, he had been given a Huntington Hartford Fellowship and a Martha Baird
Rockefeller grant. On August 7, 1965, Albert married, in New York City, Blanche Silagy, a neuropsy-
chologist. They raised a son and a daughter.

On a grant from the Ford Foundation, Albert became composer-in-residence for the public schools in
Lima, Ohio (1967–68), where *Bacchae* was given its
first performance in the spring of 1968. He received
a Guggenheim Fellowship in 1968–69. From 1969 to
1970 he was a member of the faculty of the Philadelphia Musical Academy. In 1970–71 he was guest
lecturer at Stanford University in California, and
from 1974 to 1976, assistant professor of music at
Smith College in Northampton, Mass.

On a commission from the Seattle Players of the
University of Washington, Albert wrote *Wolf Time,*
for soprano, chamber orchestra, and amplification
(1968). It was introduced in Seattle on December 3,
1970, with Elizabeth Suderburg (for whom it was
written) as soloist. The text comes from the doomsday section of *Volupsa,* a 10th-century Icelandic epic
dealing with the birth, life, death, and rebirth of the
world. This work utilizes half a dozen microphones
placed among the instrumentalists and the singer for
amplification at various points in the composition.

Leaves from the Golden Notebook, for orchestra
(1971), was commissioned by the Chicago Symphony, which introduced it in 1972, Carlo Maria Giulini conducting. A rhapsodic composition in free
form, chromatic in idiom, this orchestral piece emphasizes subtle texture and unusual colorations en-

hanced by a complement of battery and percussion. *Voices Within*, for orchestra and pit band (1975–76), commissioned jointly by the Berkshire Music Center and the Fromm Foundation, was premiered at Tanglewood in August 1975, Gunther Schuller conducting. This is a composition which involves a pit band with the orchestra, the two ensembles in contradiction to each other. The composition is filled with recollections, simulations, or distortions of the composer's experiences with American popular tunes without being explicit about any one particular composer or composition. "It attempted," the composer explains, "to pull out all the stops in this respect while being forged on the anvil of my own style." *To Wake the Dead*, for soprano and instruments (1977–78), written on a grant from the National Endowment for the Arts, uses six excerpts from James Joyce's *Finnegans Wake*, and is the first attempt by a composer to use extended passages from this novel in a musical work. Six of the movements are songs, and a seventh is solely for instruments. The work as a whole is an attempt to translate the dreamstate of Joyce's novel into music that is, as the composer informs us, "something more palpable, less surreal. The music tries to offset the disassociated and fragmented sensibility by speaking in a relatively direct manner which is strongly melodic and tonal throughout. This paradoxical matching of words to music seemed natural and was, in fact, the driving force during the germination of *To Wake the Dead*." Albert's score was largely based on the only tune found in *Finnegans Wake*, which is quoted in its entirety in the second movement, where it receives a music-box setting to Joyce's version of "Humpty-Dumpty." The official premiere took place in New York on March 21, 1979, performed by Sheila Marie Allen and the Pro Musica Moderna of the University of Massachusetts. It was recorded, by means of a grant from the Alice Ditson Fund, in 1980.

THE COMPOSER SPEAKS: What is happening to art is not simply a reaction against a particular decade or a set of aesthetic standards, nor is it an effort to put "paint back into painting," "sound into music," or the like. At its best, it is an attempt by the creative mind to reach out and touch an audience once again; not by cheap compromise but by a convincing multifaceted vision which can stand up to repeated encounters. This attitude may be, in part, a rebellion against a perverse but powerful circle of tastemakers who, for too long, took the fashionable position that the next most innovative idea, no matter how narrow its scope, outrageous its philosophical tenets and antihumanistic its goals, was the most artistically important. Actually, to many of us today, the "cult of the new" seems alien to the workings of the driven artist. He is not concerned with what will be fashionable or topical at next year's cocktail parties but rather what is going on within his own senses and how to record his thoughts and feelings as faithfully and artfully as possible.

In music, particularly, it is an attempt to reexamine ideas and practices that were part of a six-hundred-year continuum, disrupted by the psychological shock and despair of the world wars, one hopeless cold war and two disillusioning wars in Asia. It is a belief that that continuum still moves through our soul as a subterranean river flows faithfully and silently beneath the parched desert.

PRINCIPAL WORKS: *Illuminations,* for brass, pianos, harps, and percussion (1962); *Supernatural Songs*, for soprano and chamber orchestra (1963); *Imitations,* for string quartet (1964); *Winter Songs*, for tenor and orchestra (1964–65); *Wedding Songs*, for soprano and piano (1965); *Bacchae*, for narrator, chorus, and orchestra (1967–68); *Wolf Time*, for soprano, chamber orchestra, and amplification (1968); *Leaves from the Golden Notebook*, for orchestra (1971); *Cathedral Music,* a concerto for four quartets (1973); *Voices Within*, for orchestra and pit band (1975–76); *To Wake the Dead*, for soprano, flute, clarinet, violin, cello, and piano (1977–78); *Winterfire: Music for Seven Players* (1979); *Music from The Stone Harp*, for eight players (1979–80).

BIBLIOGRAPHY: *BBDM.*

Alexander, Josef, b. Boston, Mass., May 15, 1907.

From his beginnings as a composer, Alexander was not influenced by any composer or composers, and as his career progressed he never allied himself with any school or trend. He always drew copiously from the technical and aesthetic reservoir of the past while retaining a 20th-century modernity through discreet dissonances and polytonal writing and robustly propelled rhythms. He has been partial to works with unusual instrumental combinations.

His family traces itself back to the paternal great-great-grandfather, who played the clarinet in the czar's band in the Crimean War. But neither of his parents was a musician, though they did love music deeply and saw to it that each of their children received musical training. Josef became interested in the piano when his older sister began to take piano lessons. When he was eight he started studying the piano with a local teacher; by the time he was twelve he was concertizing; and at thirteen he made an appearance over the radio. With his two brothers, he formed a piano trio which performed regularly at home.

At English High School, in Boston, Alexander played the piano for performances of silent films. Some of his music was compositions he had studied, but most of it was improvisations to suit the mood and emotion of the film. After graduating from high school in 1923, he entered the New England Conservatory, there to study piano with Julius Chaloff, who was influential in directing him toward a career as piano virtuoso, to which he had been aspiring ever since he heard a recital by Paderewski. Later concerts by Rachmaninoff performing his own works sparked Alexander's ambition to become a composer as well. At the conservatory, Alexander concentrated on the piano, without taking any courses in harmony, theory or orchestration, all of which he studied on his own with some supervision by Chaloff. Nevertheless, he graduated from the New England Conservatory in 1925 with special honors in harmony, theory, and analysis, and in 1926 received a postgraduate artist's degree.

From 1926 to 1934, Josef Alexander concertized extensively both in recitals and as guest performer with orchestras. He also taught piano and theory privately, conducted the West Roxbury Symphonietta from 1932 to 1934, and gave courses in music at the St. Rosa Convent in Chelsea and Malden, Mass., and at Boston College.

The turning point in his life, the point where he turned decisively from a career as a virtuoso to that of composer, came at Harvard University, which he entered in 1934. Taking a four-year academic course broadened his intellectual horizon. At the same time he developed musically by studying composition with Walter Piston, orchestration with Edward Burlingame Hill, and musicology with Hugo Leichtentritt and Willi Apel. "My intellect," he reveals, "musical and otherwise, expanded and even exploded in this environment." He received his bachelor of arts degree, *cum laude,* in 1938. That same year he completed writing a piano concerto and *The Ancient Mariner,* a tone poem for orchestra based on Coleridge. The latter work was responsible for his receiving the prestigious Harvard University Fellowship. The piece was first performed on June 8, 1940, in Boston.

Awarded the Paine Traveling Fellowship from Harvard in 1939, Alexander went to Paris and spent several months studying composition with Nadia Boulanger. On January 20, 1940, he married Hannah Margolis in New York. She was a poet and author who worked in Hollywood translating French and German films into English. In time, they raised four sons. Soon after their marriage, they went to Mexico, where Alexander concentrated on compositions, two of which were a string quartet and *Doina,* a Rumanian rhapsody for orchestra (originally for piano), both completed in 1940.

Upon his return to the United States, Alexander spent the summer of 1940 at the Berkshire Music Center at Tanglewood, Mass., on an invitation from Serge Koussevitzky. He studied conducting with Stanley Chapple and composition with Aaron Copland. In 1942, Alexander earned his master of arts degree at Harvard. One year later, he was appointed

to the music faculty of Brooklyn College in New York, where he ultimately rose to the rank of full professor and remained until his retirement in 1977, when he was named professor emeritus.

Compositions for orchestra in the 1940s brought Alexander his first noteworthy performances. *Williamsburg Suite,* for orchestra (1942), was introduced by the NBC Symphony over the NBC radio network on August 19, 1944, Henri Nosoo conducting. *A New England Overture,* for orchestra (1943), commissioned by the Griffith Music Foundation, was premiered by the St. Louis Symphony under Vladimir Golschmann on February 12, 1943. His Symphony no. 1, *Clockwork,* for strings (1947)—so called because each movement is given its exact time duration—was given its first hearing on November 28, 1949, in New York, performed by the Little Orchestra Society under Thomas Scherman. It was written on a grant from the American Music Council.

Alexander's greatest success up to that time came on March 8, 1951, when Dimitri Mitropoulos gave the world premiere of *Epitaphs,* for orchestra (1947). The introduction to this work provides the musical materials from which the ensuing ten epitaphs are evolved (epitaphs for a misfit, politician, maiden lady, a black boy, soldier, child, donkey, preacher, saint, and a conductor). The wide gamut of Alexander's expressivity is here revealed in music that passes flexibly from sardonic wit to sentimentality, from noble and reflective passages to savage utterances. Programmatic literalness was avoided as Alexander, in his own words, sought "to capture an essence and cross section of humanity."

Alexander's gift for effecting an expressive lyricism found in the above compositions continued to be a strong suit of succeeding works. The most important of these are the Andante and Allegro, for string orchestra (1952; St. Louis, February 20, 1953); the Sonata for Cello and Piano (1953; N.Y., April 26, 1954); *Songs for Eve,* a cycle of fifteen songs based on poems by Archibald MacLeish, for soprano and instruments (1957; N.Y., April 14, 1959); Symphony no. 3 (1961; N.Y., April 27, 1970), written on a grant from the International Humanities Foundation in Washington, D.C.; *Quiet Music,* for strings (1966), commissioned by Vladimir Golschmann, who conducted its premiere with the Denver Symphony in February 1966; Symphony no. 4 (1968; N.Y., February 1976); *Gitanjali,* nine songs for soprano, harpsichord and percussion based on texts from Rabindranath Tagore (1973; N.Y., November 14, 1975), written on a grant from the American Music Council; and *Symphonic Odes,* for men's chorus and orchestra (1975), written on a grant from the National Endowment for the Arts.

Alexander's interest in writing music for unusual instrumental combinations is reflected in works such as the Three Diversions for Six Timpani and Piano, the six timpani performed by one player; *Triptych,* for cornet, marimba, and guitar; a work for piccolo and trombone exploiting the extremes of pitch; and the Album for Piano, which can be played on Chinese or toy cymbals.

In 1955, Alexander was awarded a Fulbright Fellowship, enabling him to spend that year in Finland with his family, composing, lecturing, conducting, and concertizing. He has received the Bernard Ravitch Foundation Prize for *Two Geographical Studies,* for two pianos, and the Harvey Gaul Prize in Pittsburgh for some of his songs.

THE COMPOSER SPEAKS: I have never gone in search of an identity or style. Just as my pianism comes from within, so does my composition. I can compose away from the piano, at the piano to test what is in my mind, on ships, airplanes, even while driving or walking. Sometimes ideas are dictated by the chosen medium; at times the reverse is true, in that the idea will suggest the medium. At times, musical problems are solved in my sleep; at times, while half asleep I get up to write down ideas. I've written in the subway, since I have the facility of shutting out or separating inner sounds from those without.

PRINCIPAL WORKS: 4 symphonies (1947–68); 2 piano sonatas (1927, 1948).

Piano Concerto (1938); *The Ancient Mariner,* tone poem for orchestra (1938); String Quartet (1940); Piano Quintet (1942); *Williamsburg Suite,* for orchestra (1942); *A New England Overture,* for orchestra (1943); Piano Trio (1944); *Dialogue spirituale,* for chorus and orchestra (1945); *Epitaphs,* for orchestra (1947); Wind Quintet (1949); Concertino, for trumpet and strings (1950); Piano Quartet (1952); *Canticle of the Night,* for voice and orchestra (1953); Violin Sonata (1953); Flute Sonata (1954); Clarinet Sonata (1957); *Songs for Eve,* song cycle for soprano, harp, English horn, and cello (1957); Four Movements, for brass (1958); Trombone Sonata (1959); *Celebrations,* for orchestra (1960); Nocturne and Scherzo, for violin and piano (1963); *Four for Five,* for brass (1964); Three Pieces, for nine instruments (1965); Duo concertante, for trombone, percussion, and orchestra (1965); *Quiet Music,* for strings (1966); Theme, Variations, and Finale, for string orchestra (1967); *Triptych,* for cornet, marimba, and guitar (1968); *Playthings of the Wind,* for voice, chorus, two trumpets, two horns, two trombones, tuba, and piano (1969–70); Trio for Brass (1971); *Gitanjali,* for soprano, harpsichord, and percussion (1973); *Symphonic Odes,* for voice and orchestra (1976); Album for Piano (1978); Horn Sonata (1979); *Dyad,* for four tubas (1979).

BIBLIOGRAPHY: *BBDM; DCM.*

Amram, David Werner, b. Philadelphia, Pa., November 17, 1930.

Three early influences had a decisive and permanent impact on his future creativity: jazz; his Jewish background and upbringing; and ethnic music and cultures, particularly those of the American Indian. He is, for the most part, a traditionalist. His music is tonal, diatonic, lyrical, occasionally dissonant.

When he was six, his family moved to Pas-a-Grille, Florida, where he began his public school education and acquired his first musical instrument, a bugle. A lifelong addiction to music began, he confesses, when he blew his first notes. In late summer 1937 the Amrams moved to a family farm in Feasterville, Pa. While attending its public schools, David traveled regularly to Philadelphia to study trumpet at the Music School Settlement School. At the same time he acquired the rudiments of playing the piano. A love for jazz was first fostered in 1938 through radio broadcasts of big bands and was soon intensified through jazz recordings, particularly those by Bix Beiderbecke.

When Amram was twelve, his family settled in Washington, D.C. At Gordon Junior High School he played the trumpet and the tuba in the school band and joined a jazz band outside school. Before he reached thirteen, he was playing trumpet professionally with Louis Brown's jazz band, earning a dollar a night. When braces on his teeth made playing the trumpet impossible he shifted to the French horn, from this time on to become his prime instrument.

After graduating from junior high school, he entered the Putney School in Vermont, which had an active music department. In addition to taking the school's music courses he participated in its musical activities. During the summer he studied composition with Wendell Margrave and the French horn with Van Lier Lanning. He also tried his hand at composing a horn trio and some choral pieces, encouraged by Dimitri Mitropoulos, the distinguished conductor, who henceforth became a prime influence in his development.

In 1948 Amram entered Oberlin College Conservatory of Music in Ohio, where he received further instruction on the French horn from Martin Morris. Impatient with institutional life and education where music was concerned, he abandoned the conservatory in June 1948 to matriculate for a bachelor of arts degree at George Washington University in Washington, D.C., majoring in European history. At the same time the study of the French horn was continued with William Klang and Abe Kniaz. For the next two years Amram played the French horn in various amateur and professional orchestras. He also performed in jazz concerts he had organized for public consumption and in private jam sessions in his apartment in which, from time to time, two of his jazz heroes—Charlie ("Bird") Parker and Dizzy Gillespie—participated.

After graduating from George Washington University in 1952, Amram entered military service, playing the French horn in bands before joining the

Seventh Army Symphony Orchestra, which performed in Germany and Austria.

When he was separated from military service in 1954 he remained in Europe to give concerts sponsored by the U.S. Department of State. After that, he made his home in Paris, supporting himself by playing with various jazz combos in night spots and jazz clubs.

The need for further music instruction brought him back to the United States in September 1955, where, for one year, he studied composition with Vittorio Giannini and Ludmilla Ulehla at the Manhattan School of Music. Subsequent music study was pursued privately: composition with Charles Mills and conducting with Jonel Perlea. At the same time, Amram appeared with notable jazz groups at Café Bohemia and at Birdland in New York City. In addition he formed a jazz band of his own, the Amram-Barrow Quartet (later a quintet), which, in addition to public concerts, recorded a Decca album (*Jazz Studio Number 6: The Eastern Scene*). He also composed the background music for *Echo of an Era* (1956), a film documentary about the history of New York's Third Avenue El, and, between 1956 and 1967, wrote the incidental music for twenty-eight Off-Broadway productions of Joseph Papp's New York Shakespearean Theater and for Off-Broadway productions by the Phoenix Theater.

He graduated into the Broadway theater with his incidental music for *Comes a Day* (1958), starring Judith Anderson, the first of several Broadway plays in which his music was heard during the next six years; contributed the music for various significant television productions in 1959–60; and, beginning with *The Young Savages* (1961), starring Burt Lancaster, provided scores for a number of notable films (*Splendor in the Grass,* with Natalie Wood, in 1961; *The Manchurian Candidate,* with Frank Sinatra and Laurence Harvey, in 1962; *The Arrangement,* with Kirk Douglas, in 1969).

His first concert work to be performed professionally was *Autobiography for Strings* (1959) in New York in 1959. This was a tonal recollection of his years as a world traveler and his experience with jazz. On May 8, 1960, an entire evening of Amram's music was given in Town Hall, New York, in which *Shakespearean Concerto,* for oboe, two horns, and strings (1960), was introduced. His Piano Sonata (a tribute to the jazz stylings of Thelonious Monk and Bud Powell), composed in 1960, was first heard in December of that year in New York, followed in 1961 by the writing and premiere of *Sacred Service for Sabbath Eve (Shir l'Erev Shabbat),* commissioned by the Park Avenue Synagogue in New York. As a guest composer at the Marlboro Festival in Vermont in 1961, Amram wrote *Discussion,* for flute, cello, piano, and percussion, and *Three Songs for Marlboro,* for horn and cello. A second all-Amram concert in New York, on February 20, 1962, offered the premiere of his String Quartet (1961). Two other

major works of the early 1960s were *The American Bell,* a cantata for narrator and orchestra with a text by Archibald MacLeish (1961), heard on July 4, 1962, at Independence Hall in Philadelphia, and Dirge and Variations, for violin, cello, and piano (1962), first performed on January 6, 1963, by the Marlboro Trio in Washington, D.C.

A cantata, *A Year in Our Land* (1964), received its first performance on May 13, 1964, in New York. Its text, taken from the writings of James Baldwin, John Dos Passos, Jack Kerouac, John Steinbeck, and Walt Whitman, is descriptive of the four seasons in four parts of the United States. Another cantata, *Let Us Remember,* for vocal soloists, chorus, and orchestra (1965), is a bitter indictment of persecution with text by Langston Hughes. It was commissioned by the Union of American Hebrew Congregations and appeared on a modern Jewish music program at the War Memorial Auditorium in San Francisco, with Edward G. Robinson as narrator, on November 15, 1965.

On April 11, 1965, on the "Directions '65" program over the ABC-TV network, Amram conducted the premiere of his opera *The Final Ingredient* (1965), libretto by Arnold Weinstein, based on a play of Reginald Rose. The setting is a Nazi concentration camp where its Jewish inmates plan a breakout in order to steal an egg from a nest outside the camp for a Passover ceremony. In the *New York World Telegram* Louis Biancolli called it "some of the best operatic writing of our day," adding: "Musically, the work is a compromise between a robust modern idiom and tradition, represented by a moving use of part-writing in the passages of prayer and observance. Amram has a true creative gift . . . *The Final Ingredient* was both an act of faith and a milestone for TV."

In 1966–67, on a Rockefeller Foundation grant, Amram became the first composer-in-residence in the history of the New York Philharmonic, having been selected by the orchestra's music director, Leonard Bernstein. In this office, Amram's *King Lear Variations,* for woodwinds, brass, percussion, and piano (1966), was introduced by the New York Philharmonic on March 23, 1967. The theme used for these variations is a melody (the song of the fool) Amram had written for a production of *King Lear* in 1962. Each variation is an outgrowth of this theme and each contains this theme in one form or another. "I tried," Amram has explained, "to create many varying moods, feelings and attitudes which would sum up a musical experience corresponding to Shakespeare's portrait of human experience."

Amram made his concert hall conducting debut on January 16, 1967, in Corpus Christi, Tex., in a performance of his *Shakespearean Concerto.* His New York concert hall debut followed one month later with his *Sacred Service for Sabbath Eve.*

One of Amram's most successful works in the 1960s was his opera *Twelfth Night* (1968), libretto by the composer and Joseph Papp, based on Shakespeare. It was produced by the Lake George Opera Festival in New York State on August 1, 1968. What aroused particular admiration was Amram's skillful use of a neo-Elizabethan style as well as his gift for comedic writing. Acknowledgment of Amram's importance in American music was further confirmed on April 17, 1969, when the National Education Television network offered an hour-long documentary entitled "The World of David Amram."

Major works in the 1970s added to Amram's continually growing artistic stature. Concerto for Wind, Brass, Jazz Quintets and Orchestra (1970), a modern variation of the baroque concerto grosso, which the composer dedicated "to the spirit of jazz and all who create it," was commissioned by the American Symphony Orchestra in New York, which introduced it on January 10, 1971, under the direction of Kazuyoshi Akyama. *The Trail of Beauty,* for mezzo-soprano, oboe and orchestra (1976), was inspired by Amram's lifelong interest in the American Indian. The Philadelphia Orchestra under Eugene Ormandy (who had commissioned it) premiered it in Philadelphia on March 4, 1977. *Native American Portraits,* for violin, piano, and percussion (1976), was also inspired by the American Indian. It was first heard on March 13, 1977, in New York. *En memoria de Chano Pozo* was written in 1977 for a jazz concert in Cuba by visiting American jazzmen on May 18, 1977—Chano Pozo being a prominent Cuban percussionist who influenced Afro-Cuban jazz. This was the time when the United States first lifted its restrictions against travel to Communist Cuba, thus permitting Amram and his fellow jazz musicians to become the first American musical troupe to set foot on Cuban soil since 1961.

The Cuban visit was only one of many David Amram has made to twenty-five countries as a musical ambassador of goodwill, sometimes self-appointed, sometimes sponsored by the United States Information Agency. In 1975 in Kenya he led programs of international music at the World Council of Churches attended by 104 nations. In October 1977 he toured Central America under the auspices of the State Department. This proved so successful that he was sent by the State Department to tour the Middle East in February 1978. In visiting exotic lands, Amram studied and brought back native music and instruments, which he sometimes used in his compositions and frequently exhibited at his concerts. Such ethnic material was the feature of a David Amram TV documentary presented by the Public Broadcasting Service on its nationwide network in April 1978. At his concerts throughout the world of music, Amram has served as a propagandist not only for his own music but also for jazz, folk music of many lands, and ethnic music of esoteric countries.

In 1979, Amram received an honorary doctorate from Moravian College in Bethlehem, Pa. For the nonmusical Broadway play *Harold and Maude,* Amram contributed "music, lyrics and sounds"; it opened on January 29, 1980.

Amram married Lora Lee Ecobelli on January 7, 1979. They have a daughter, Alana Asha Amram.

THE COMPOSER SPEAKS: True music has always been built to last. All of us who work in music as our life's love try to share it with others. Since I don't believe in separating art and life, or culture and people, I try to perform, conduct and be with musicians and people from all over the world in every kind of musical situation, from concert halls to schools and parks. This keeps me inspired, and everything goes back into my composition that I learn from sharing music in this way. By constantly learning about all forms of music throughout the world, from Eskimo throat music to newly discovered Baroque composers, I am always amazed at what a beautiful language music is.

PRINCIPAL WORKS: Trio, for tenor saxophone, horn, and bassoon (1958); Overture and Allegro, for solo flute (1959); *Autobiography for Strings* (1959); *Shakespearean Concerto,* for oboe, two horns, and strings (1960); Piano Sonata (1960); Violin Sonata (1960); *Discussion,* for flute, cello, piano, and percussion (1961); *Three Songs for Marlboro,* for horn and cello (1961); *Sacred Service for Sabbath Eve (Shir l'Erev Shabbat),* for tenor, chorus, and organ (1961); String Quartet (1961); *The American Bell,* cantata for narrator and orchestra (1961); Dirge and Variations, for piano trio (1962); "May the Word of the Lord," for chorus and organ (1962); "Thou Shalt Love the Lord Thy God," for chorus and organ (1962); *The Wind and the Rain,* for viola and piano (1963); *A Year in Our Land,* cantata for vocal soloists, chorus, and orchestra (1964); Sonata for Solo Violin (1964); *Let Us Remember,* cantata for vocal soloists, chorus, and orchestra (1965); *The Final Ingredient,* opera (1965); *By the Rivers of Babylon,* for soprano and women's voices (1966); *King Lear Variations,* for woodwinds, brass, percussion, and piano (1966); Three Dances, for oboe and strings (1966); Songs from Shakespeare, for voice and piano (1968); Quintet, for winds (1968); *Twelfth Night,* opera (1968); Three Songs for America, for baritone and string quintet (1969); *Triptych,* for solo viola (1969); Concerto for Winds, Brass, Jazz Quintets, and Orchestra (1970); Elegy, for violin and orchestra (1970); Bassoon Concerto (1972); *The Trail of Beauty,* for mezzo-soprano, oboe, and orchestra (1976); *Native American Portraits,* for violin, piano, and percussion (1976); *En memoria de Chano Pozo,* for orchestra (1977); *Zohar,* for unaccompanied flute (1978); Violin Concerto (1980).

BIBLIOGRAPHY: Amram, David, *Vibrations: The Adventures and Musical Times of David Amram*

(N.Y., 1968); *Life,* August 11, 1967; *New York Times,* April 14, 1978; *Who's Who in America, 1980–81.*

Anderson, Thomas Jefferson, b. Coatesville, Pa., August 17, 1928.

Anderson is a black composer who has been influenced by Stravinsky, Alban Berg, and Anton Webern without adhering to a strict twelve-tone technique. His music also shows the adaptation of his environment.

Both his parents were schoolteachers; additionally, his mother was a pianist who became a significant influence in his early musical development. T. J. Anderson received his first music training on the violin from Louis von Jones in Washington, D. C. His academic education took place in public schools in Washington, D. C., Cincinnati, and Coatesville. While attending junior high school in Cincinnati he played professionally with a jazz band. After graduating from Horace Scott High School in Coatesville, he entered West Virginia State College, earning his bachelor of music degree in 1950. In 1951, he received a master's degree in education at Pennsylvania State University in University Park, enabling him to hold a teaching post in instrumental music in public schools in High Point, N. C. (1951–54). During the summer of 1954 he studied with Scott Huston at the Cincinnati Conservatory of Music, and during the year that followed he was an instructor of music at West Virginia State College. At the University of Iowa in Iowa City, where he studied composition with Philip Bezanson and Richard Hervig, he received his doctorate in music in 1958, offering as his doctoral thesis two compositions, *Pyknon,* for orchestra, and his first string quartet. That year (1958) he was appointed professor of music and chairman of the music department at Langston University, Okla., occupying this post for five years. This was a period when his compositions began for the first time to receive significant public performances, though only locally. Introduction and Allegro (1959), for orchestra, New Dances, for orchestra (1960), and Six Pieces for Clarinet and Chamber Orchestra (1962) were all performed by the Oklahoma City Symphony conducted by Guy Fraser Harrison—Introduction and Allegro on October 11, 1959; New Dances on November 13, 1960; and the Six Pieces on March 25, 1962.

From 1963 to 1969, Anderson was professor of music at the Tennessee State University, Nashville, while from 1968 to 1971, on a Rockefeller Foundation grant, he was also composer-in-residence with the Atlanta Symphony in Georgia. In 1964 he wrote his Symphony in Three Movements in Memory of John F. Kennedy, its premiere given by the Oklahoma City Symphony under Harrison on April 10, 1964. That summer was spent in Aspen, Colo.,

studying composition with Darius Milhaud. Five Etudes and a Fancy, for woodwind quintet, was heard at Aspen that same summer. For his achievements in music, Anderson was given the Copley Foundation Award in 1964.

Two commissions in 1965 and 1966 led to the writing of notable compositions. One of these was *Squares,* "an essay for orchestra," written for the seventy-fifth anniversary of West Virginia State College and heard for the first time on February 25, 1966, in Chickasha, Okla., performed by the Oklahoma City Symphony under Harrison. The other was *Personals,* a cantata for narrator, chorus, and brass septet, text by Arna Bontemps, commemorating the centenary of Fisk University. Its premiere was given in Nashville on April 28, 1966, by the Fisk University Choir directed by Robert Jones. Still in 1966, Anderson completed a fantasy for string quintet dedicated to Darius Milhaud—*Connections*—which the Blair String Quartet premiered in Nashville on December 6, 1968. A year later, on November 24, 1969, the Nashville Symphony under Thor Johnson gave the world premiere of Anderson's Chamber Symphony, which Johnson had commissioned. In all these compositions, as in later ones, the writing is atonal and dissonant and the thematic material is fragmented and pointillistic in the style influenced by Webern, with sharp contrasts of color and sonority.

In 1971–72, Anderson served as the Danforth Visiting Professor of Music at Morehouse College in Atlanta, Ga. That summer, on August 2, 1971, *Transitions,* for chamber ensemble, which had been commissioned by the Berkshire Music Center in Massachusetts and the Fromm Music Foundation, received its first performance at the Tanglewood Festival of Contemporary Music (August 2). The large orchestral work *Intervals* was composed in 1970–71, having been commissioned by Robert Shaw, the musical director of the Atlanta Symphony. It is made up of seven sets, with Set I intended for performance before intermission, Sets II through VI during the intermission, and Set VII after the intermission. Sets I and VII can be performed apart from the others under the title of Set VIII, and Sets II through VI can be performed separately.

In 1972, Anderson was appointed professor of music and chairman of the music department at Tufts University in Medford, Mass., a post he has since retained. Among his later compositions are *In Memoriam Malcolm X,* for voice and orchestra (1974), commissioned by the Symphony of the New World in New York for Betty Allen, and receiving its world premiere at the Lincoln Center for the Performing Arts in New York on April 7, 1974; *Horizons '76,* for soprano and orchestra (1975), commissioned by the National Endowment for the Arts for the American bicentennial; Variations on a Theme by Alban Berg, for viola and piano (1977; Cambridge, Mass., September 19, 1978); and *Re-Creation,* for three speakers, dancer, and instruments, commissioned by Richard Hunt (1978; Chicago, June 11, 1978).

A retrospective concert of Anderson's works was heard in Chicago in June 1978. In commemoration of Anderson's fiftieth birthday, another program of his music was performed, this time in Cambridge, Mass., the following September.

Anderson played an important role in the revival of interest in the ragtime music of Scott Joplin in the early 1970s by orchestrating the first complete performance of Joplin's opera, *Treemonisha*, heard in Atlanta, Ga., on January 29, 1972.

Anderson has made numerous appearances as lecturer on music in educational institutions in the United States and Europe. He visited Brazil in 1976 at the invitation of the U. S. State Department. Anderson has also been a prolific contributor of articles to various anthologies on black composers and to magazines.

THE COMPOSER SPEAKS: If humanity was stripped of all support systems but one, I am convinced the one choice would be in the area of communications. And if one had to choose the universal communicators, music would be the adaptable language. It therefore becomes the duty of the composer to unite musical diversity with the personal and thus form an additional link within societies. My music, organized through systematic sets which find adaptability in varying contexts, draws upon sources which are expressed from my contact with people. To date it has been influenced by the African-American music of these United States, European art music, historical traditions, avant-garde styles, and primitive cultures.

PRINCIPAL WORKS: Introduction and Allegro, for orchestra (1959); New Dances, for orchestra (1960); Classical Symphony (1961); Six Pieces for Clarinet and Chamber Orchestra (1962); Five Bagatelles, for oboe, violin, and harpsichord (1963); Five Etudes and a Fancy, for woodwind quintet (1964); Symphony in Three Movements (1964); *Squares*, an essay for orchestra (1965); *Five Portraitures of Two People*, for piano four hands (1965); *Personals*, cantata for chorus, narrator, and brass septet (1966); *Connections*, a fantasy for string quintet (1966); Chamber Symphony (1968); Variations on a Theme by M. B. Tolson, for soprano and instruments (1970); *Intervals*, seven sets for orchestra (1970–71); *Transitions*, for chamber ensemble (1971); *Watermelon*, for piano (1971); *Swing Set*, duo for clarinet and piano (1973); *Beyond Silence*, for tenor and instruments (1973); *In Memoriam Malcolm X*, for voice and orchestra (1974); *Horizons '76*, for soprano and orchestra (1975); *The Shell Fairy*, operetta (1977); Variations on a Theme by Alban Berg, for viola and piano (1977); *Re-Creation*, for three speakers, dancer, and instruments (1978); *Messages, a Creole Fantasy* (1979).

BIBLIOGRAPHY: Baker, David (ed.), *The Black Composer Speaks* (N. Y., 1978); Bruce, Alfred Thompson, "Musical Style and Compositional Techniques in Selected Works by T. J. Anderson" (doctoral thesis, Bloomington, Ind., 1978); Roach, Mildred, *Black American Music* (Boston, 1973); Southern, Eileen, *The Music of Black America: A History* (N. Y., 1971); Walton, Ortiz M., *Music, Black, White and Blue* (N. Y., 1972); *Newsweek*, April 15, 1974.

Antheil, George, b. Trenton, N. J., July 8, 1900; d. New York City, February 12, 1959.

Self-styled "bad boy of music," Antheil first gained notoriety as an iconoclast in the early 1920s. His later works returned to more traditional practices.

His musical education began with lessons on the violin when he was five. Piano lessons started in his tenth year and lessons in harmony two years later. While attending Trenton High School he studied theory for four years (1914–18) with Constantine von Sternberg in Philadelphia. In 1919 he came to New York to become Ernest Bloch's pupil in composition, under whose guidance he completed his first symphony (since withdrawn). In 1922, after a period of piano study with George Boyle at the Philadelphia Settlement School on a scholarship, Antheil went to Europe to launch his career as concert pianist. Part of the attraction at his recitals were his own piano pieces, which freely indulged in unresolved discords used to build up massive sonorities, pieces constructed from epigrammatic and repetitive motives (*Airplane Sonata, Sonate sauvage, Death of the Machines, Mechanisms, Fireworks for the Profane Waltzers*, all written in or about 1922). For a while, in 1922–23, he established residence in Berlin, where he became the first American to hold a conducting post with the Berlin State Opera. In 1922, his Symphony no. 1 was unsuccessfully introduced by the Berlin Philharmonic.

To advance his career as composer, Antheil decided in 1923 to abandon concert tours and make his home permanently in Paris in order to concentrate on composition. There, on October 4, 1925, he married Elizabeth ("Boski") Markus, a niece of the distinguished Viennese novelist and playwright Arthur Schnitzler. (She died in 1978.)

Antheil attracted international attention as music's *enfant terrible* with one of the most provocative and publicized compositions of the 1920s: the *Ballet mécanique*, expressive of the antiromantic and mechanistic aesthetics of that period. This work started out as background music for Fernand Léger's abstract motion picture *Le Ballet mécanique*, which in turn had been inspired by Antheil's *Mechanisms*. Scored for eight pianos, a player piano, and various percussion instruments including anvils, bells, buzzers, and other noisemakers, *Ballet mécanique*, as a concert suite, was introduced in Paris on June 19, 1926, Vladimir Golschmann conducting. (The same program also offered the premiere of Antheil's Symphony in F, actually his second symphony but which he now called his first.) The symphony passed virtually unnoticed, but the *Ballet mécanique* rocked musical Paris. Some, such as Ezra Pound, praised it as the dawn of a new age in music in which the sounds of machines, labor, and factories could be organized into a vibrant 20th-century musical art form. Others were outraged by its endless discords and harsh sonorities.

Despite the title, Antheil had no intention of simulating machine noises or factory sounds for their own sake. Musically, he aimed at a composition of musical abstractions and sound materials based solely on rhythm; he called this device "time-space," comparing his sounds to the colors and shapes splashed on a canvas by a modernist painter. Programmatically, his idea, as he said, was "to warn the age in which I am living of the simultaneous beauty and danger of its unconscious mechanistic philosophy."

Ballet mécanique caused another furor when it was introduced in the United States on April 10, 1927, at Carnegie Hall, New York, Eugene Goossens conducting. Widely promoted, and then presented as a kind of musical circus in which huge airplane propellers were featured on the stage, the work aroused considerable antagonism among serious musicians and critics who deplored its sensationalism. Antheil himself was outraged at the way his work was being abused in blatant publicity and advertising. The attending notoriety did considerable damage to Antheil's career as a composer. A revival of *Ballet mécanique* in New York on February 20, 1954, in a revised and more discreet version, adhered more truthfully to Antheil's original intentions, but by then the work had become a period piece and had lost the power to shock. It did, however, enjoy a substantial success when it was revived at the Holland Festival in 1976 and when the Brooklyn Philharmonia revived it in 1981, Nicholas Kenyon, in *The New Yorker*, called it "stunning," adding: "Its brutality and its naïve sense of excitement make it a nightmarish picture of technology run wild—a supremely unsophisticated version of Edgard Varèse's Sound Structures."

The concert in which *Ballet mécanique* was first performed in New York in 1927 also featured the premiere of Antheil's *Jazz Symphonietta*, for twenty-two instruments, played by a black jazz band. This work revealed another early trend in Antheil's creativity that departed from Stravinskian neoprimitivism to the deployment of elements of American popular music within a serious context. (*Jazz Symphonietta* was actually the finale of Antheil's Symphony in F. Revived and rescored in 1955 for large orchestra and renamed *Jazz Symphony*, it was successfully performed in New York in 1960, at the Holland

Music Festival in 1976, and again in New York in 1978.) Jazz syncopations and rhythms had also appeared in Antheil's Violin Sonata no. 2 (1923). Antheil's most ambitious use of American popularism came with his first opera, *Transatlantic*, produced by the Frankfurt Opera in Germany on May 25, 1930, the first American opera ever premiered by a major German opera company. Writing his own libretto, Antheil used an American presidential campaign to caricature American life. Political meetings, booze parties, a scene in Childs restaurant (Childs was a popular restaurant chain in the United States in the 1920s), an aria sung by the heroine in a bathtub, an attempted suicide by the heroine off the Brooklyn Bridge, and the use of motion picture sequences were some of the ingredients in an opera whose tabloid realism represented a total break with the conventions of romantic grand opera. The music was all of a kind—vividly alive with jazz rhythms and blues harmonies. In the spirit of *Zeitkunst* ("contemporary art") then in vogue in Germany, *Transatlantic* proved a striking success, receiving twenty curtain calls on opening night and accolades from critics. Antheil's second opera, *Helen Retires*, with libretto by John Erskine—written on a Guggenheim Fellowship and first produced on February 28, 1934, in New York—was, on the other hand, a failure.

In the fall of 1933, Antheil left Europe to acquire an apartment in New York, where he earned his living by writing sundry articles for *Esquire* magazine. His protean literary career saw him write articles on endocrinology, an advice-to-the-lovelorn column syndicated in thirty-three newspapers, a mystery novel, *Death in the Dark*, published in London in 1930 under the pseudonym of Stacey Bishop, a political book (*The Shape of the War to Come*) published anonymously in 1940, and an autobiography, *Bad Boy of Music* (1945).

In 1935, Antheil transferred his home to Hollywood, Calif., from then on his permanent residence. He immediately found employment writing music for films. Beginning with *The Plainsman*, starring Gary Cooper (released in 1937; the score composed two years earlier), Antheil contributed scores for twenty-four motion pictures. Among these were *Specter of the Rose* (1946), *Knock on Any Door* (1949), *The Juggler* (1953), *Not as a Stranger* (1955), and *The Pride and the Passion* (1957).

As a serious composer, Antheil arrived at a new and final phase of his creativity in 1937 with the Symphony no. 2 (*American*). Stimulated by a newfound admiration for Mahler and Bruckner, Antheil now adopted values he had formerly rebelled against. "I began to realize," he wrote, "that no young artist starts the world all over again for himself but merely continues . . . the heritage of the past, pushing it if possible on a little further." He now became a neoromantic, concerning himself with well-sounding melodies that received full developmental treatment, richly textured harmonic and polyphonic procedures, and traditional structures. With this new attitude he produced his most important music. Symphony no. 4 (1942) was inspired by World War II (N.Y., February 13, 1944). Concerto for Violin and Orchestra (Dallas, February 9, 1947) was written for and introduced by Werner Gebauer. Symphony no. 5 was subtitled *The Joyous* (Philadelphia, December 31, 1948), and the first movement of Symphony no. 6 (San Francisco, February 10, 1949) was stimulated by Delacroix's painting *Liberty Leading the People*. He also contributed a significant score to the ballet *Capital of the World*, written for television (N. Y., December 6, 1953), and an equally impressive opera, *Volpone*, libretto by Albert Perry (Los Angeles, January 3, 1953), which included infectious waltzes, arias, and ensemble numbers. Antheil's last composition was a cantata, *Cabeza de Vaca*, its premiere given posthumously over the CBS-TV network (June 10, 1962).

THE COMPOSER SPEAKS: Many composers develop a certain style and never change. They are more concerned with maintaining their style than with the music itself. Others write as if music were like a fashion in dressmaking—this year a certain color or fabric, next year another. I used to be like that. I've gone through many things, but now I know there is only one thing that counts: to continue the great art of music. It must follow the grand line.

PRINCIPAL WORKS: 6 symphonies (1922–48); 5 piano sonatas (1922–50); 4 violin sonatas (1923–48); 3 string quartets (1924, 1928, 1948).
Jazz Symphonietta, for twenty-two instruments (1925); *Ballet mécanique*, for eight pianos, a player piano, and various percussion instruments (1926); Piano Concerto (1926); *Transatlantic*, opera (1929); *Helen Retires*, opera (1931); *Dreams*, ballet (1935); Violin Concerto (1947); *McKonkey's Ferry*, orchestral overture (1948); *Over the Plains*, for orchestra (1948); Serenade, for string orchestra (1948); *Songs of Experience*, for voice and piano (1948); *Volpone*, opera (1950); *Tom Sawyer: A Mark Twain Overture*, for orchestra (1950); Piano Trio (1950); Eight Fragments from Shelley, for chorus (1951); *Capital of the World*, ballet (1953); *The Brothers*, opera (1954); *The Wish*, opera (1955); *Cabeza de Vaca*, opera-cantata (1956).

BIBLIOGRAPHY: Antheil, George, *Bad Boy of Music* (N. Y., 1945); Pound, Ezra, *Antheil and the Treatise on Harmony* (Chicago, 1927); *New York Times* (obituary), February 13, 1959; *Opera News*, December 20, 1980; *Who's Who in America, 1958–59*.

Argento, Dominick, b. York, Pa., October 27, 1927.
Though he has used such advanced techniques as serialism, Argento has often turned to past methods and procedures in his search for well-sounding melodies, emotion, dramatic strength and communicability with audiences. He has demonstrated an exceptional gift in writing for the voice and a Verdian respect for the demands of good theater in writing operas. Argento received the Pulitzer Prize in music in 1975.

He had no interest in music until he was fourteen, when he accidentally came upon a biography of George Gershwin in the public library. This and several other musical biographies proved so stimulating that he soon began studying textbooks on harmony and composition. The gift of a piano when he was sixteen led to his first formal music instruction from a local teacher and this, in turn, encouraged him to write his first piece of music, a polka for the piano.

Argento served in the U. S. Army as cryptographer from 1945 to 1947. In 1947, he entered the Peabody Conservatory of Music in Baltimore, where he studied the piano with Alexander Sklarewski and composition with Nicolas Nabokov and, later, with Hugo Weisgall. Nabokov (and the reading of Mozart's letters) encouraged him to be a composer; Hugo Weisgall influenced him to write operas.

In 1951, having received his bachelor of arts degree at Peabody, he was awarded a Fulbright Fellowship, enabling him to attend the Conservatorio Cherubini in Florence, where he studied piano with Pietro Scarpini and composition with Italy's foremost serial composer, Luigi Dallapiccola. Returning to the United States, he continued the study of composition with Henry Cowell at the Peabody Conservatory, receiving a master of arts degree, On September 6, 1954, he married Carolyn Bailey, a soprano who had been a fellow student at Peabody and who later introduced many of his vocal compositions. That same year Argento completed a one-act opera, *Sicilian Limes*, based on Pirandello (since withdrawn).

Between 1955 and 1957 he studied composition with Alan Hovhaness, Howard Hanson, and Bernard Rogers at the Eastman School of Music in Rochester, receiving his doctorate in music in the latter year. Excerpts from his one-act ballet, *The Resurrection of Don Juan* (1956), were performed in Rochester on May 5, 1956. (The premiere of the complete ballet took place in Karlsruhe, Germany, in May 1959.) On April 29, 1957, the Festival of American Music in Rochester, N. Y., presented the premiere of Argento's *Ode to the West Wind*, for soprano and orchestra (1956), text by Shelley. Success first came on May 6, 1957, with the premiere in Rochester of a one-act opera buffa, *The Boor* (1957), based on Chekov's comedy, where Argento first revealed his gift for musical characterization and the buffa style. This one-act opera has frequently been performed throughout the United States and has been televised in Germany.

In 1957, upon receiving the first of two Guggenheim Fellowships (the second came seven years later), Argento returned to Florence to work on a full-length opera, *Colonel Jonathan the Saint* (1958–60), a failure when produced in Denver many years later (1971).

In 1958, Argento was appointed to the music faculty of the University of Minnesota, where he has remained ever since, teaching composition and the history of opera. Impressive indication of increasing articulateness and technical skill was given by the song cycle Six Elizabethan Songs, for voice and piano (1962), and a comic opera, *Christopher Sly* (1962), based on a scene from Shakespeare's *The Taming of the Shrew* (Minneapolis, May 31, 1963).

In 1964, Argento was cofounder of the Center Opera in Minnesota (later renamed Minnesota Opera), whose opening production was Argento's "religious comedy" *The Masque of Angels*, for chorus and small orchestra (1963; January 9, 1964). Between 1965 and 1969 Argento contributed incidental music for plays produced by Tyrone Guthrie at his theater in Minneapolis. There, on June 1, 1967, Argento's opera *The Shoemaker's Holiday* (1967), adapted from Thomas Dekker's Restoration comedy, was premiered successfully. Music for the concert stage was not neglected. In the 1960s, Argento completed *Royal Invitation*, or *Homage to the Queen of Tonga* (1964), a five-part orchestral suite commissioned by the St. Paul Philharmonic (Minneapolis, March 22, 1964); *The Mask of Night*, variations for orchestra (1965; Minneapolis, January 26, 1966); *Letters from Composers*, a seven-song cycle for tenor and guitar based on excerpts from the letters of seven music masters (1968; St. Paul, October 23, 1968); and *Bravo Mozart!*, for violin, oboe, French horn, and chamber orchestra, Argento's musical tribute to one of his favorite composers (1969; Minneapolis, July 3, 1969).

On a commission from the Minnesota Opera, Argento completed *Postcard from Morocco*, a surrealistic fantasy (1971; Minneapolis, October 14, 1971). It proved so successful that it was soon recorded in its entirety and received numerous performances in the United States, Canada, and Germany. Even greater acclaim and more widespread performances came to *From the Diary of Virginia Woolf*, for voice and piano (1974), which received the Pulitzer Prize in music in 1975 after having been introduced in Minneapolis by Dame Janet Baker on January 5, 1975. For his text, Argento went to Virginia Woolf's diary, from which he extracted eight excerpts. Through words and a musical score which though built strictly on the twelve-tone technique made use of a variety of other styles going as far back as the Gregorian chant, the tortured soul of Virginia Woolf was laid bare.

Another distinguished American writer was the stimulus for Argento's most successful opera, *The Voyage of Edgar Allan Poe* (1975–76). Charles M. Nolte's libretto concentrated on Poe's last crazed days when he relived past loves, sins, and misfortunes. Powerful in its dramatic impact, exceptional in word setting and vocal writing, frequently poignant in lyricism, and effective in atmospheric background, *The Voyage of Edgar Allan Poe* was hailed by critics as a major American operatic achievement. Written on a commission from the University of Minnesota to commemorate the American bicentennial, *The Voyage of Edgar Allan Poe* was produced in St. Paul on April 24, 1976. Also noteworthy is *In Praise of Music*, seven songs for orchestra without text, written in 1977 on a commission from the Minnesota Orchestra for its seventy-fifth anniversary. It was first heard in Minneapolis on September 23, 1977.

In 1980, Argento was elected to membership in the American Academy and Institute of Arts and Letters. He had previously (1976) been awarded an honorary doctorate of humane letters from York College in Pennsylvania.

THE COMPOSER SPEAKS: A lot of time is wasted in the analysis of musical styles. So much emphasis is put on manner that matter is forgotten. I'm much more concerned with having the manner follow the matter. . . . I want my work to have emotional impact; I want it to communicate, not obfuscate. I am always thinking of my audience, how they will hear it and what it will mean to them.

PRINCIPAL WORKS: *Songs about Spring*, song cycle for soprano and orchestra (1950, revised 1954, 1960); Divertimento, for piano and strings (1955); *The Resurrection of Don Juan*, ballet (1956); *Ode to the West Wind*, concerto for soprano and orchestra (1956); String Quartet (1956); *The Boor*, opera (1957); *Colonel Jonathan the Saint*, opera (1958–60); Six Elizabethan Songs, for voice and piano (1962); *Christopher Sly*, opera (1962); *The Masque of Angels*, opera (1963); *Royal Invitation*, or *Homage to the Queen of Tonga*, for chamber orchestra (1964); *The Mask of Night*, variations for orchestra (1965); *The Revelation of St. John the Divine*, rhapsody for tenor, men's chorus, brass, and percussion (1966); *The Shoemaker's Holiday*, opera (1967); *A Nation of Cowslips*, song cycle for chorus (1968); *Letters from Composers*, song cycle for tenor and guitar (1968); *Bravo Mozart!*, concerto for oboe, violin, horn, and orchestra (1969); *Tria Carmina Paschalia*, three Latin Easter lyrics, for women's voices, harp, and guitar (1970); *Postcard from Morocco*, one-act opera (1971); *A Ring of Time*, preludes and pageants for orchestra (1972); *To Be Sung upon the Water*, for voice, clarinet, and piano (1973); *Jonah and the Whale*, oratorio for narrator, vocal soloists, chorus, and chamber ensemble (1973); *A Waterbird Talks*, monodrama (1974); *From the Diary of Virginia Woolf*, for voice and piano (1974); *The Voyage of*

Edgar Allan Poe, opera (1975–76); *In Praise of Music*, seven songs for orchestra (1977); *Miss Havisham's Fire*, opera (1977–78).

BIBLIOGRAPHY: *High Fidelity/Musical America*, September 1975; *New York Times*, May 6, 1975; *Opera News*, March 24, 1979.

Austin, Larry Don, b. Duncan, Okla., September 12, 1930.

From a background in both jazz and classical music, Austin developed a compositional approach in which jazz idioms were combined with advanced techniques of atonality, fragmented textures, polyrhythmic structures, and aleatory processes. Extensive experiments with free group improvisation followed, incorporated in a series of works he named "open style," principally involving analog notation techniques and freely evolving formal schemes. Later, work with electronic music and intermedia brought forth a series of works involving technological applications, leading to involvement since 1969 in computer-generated and computer-assisted compositions.

For his ninth birthday, and at his request, Austin was presented with a used trumpet. He proceeded at once to take lessons from Paul Goetze, the local man in Vernon, Tex. "After that," he recalls, "I was singularly dedicated to the instrument and to music. The trumpet became my first medium of personal expression."

While attending public school in Vernon, he played the trumpet with several western bands at dances, barbecues, and at ranches. When he was fifteen he formed his own Dixieland band, the Notecrackers, to perform on a long series of local radio shows. At Vernon High School (1944–47) he occupied the first trumpet chair in the school band. At this time he also studied the piano and made some jazz arrangements. "My primary influence in that small, isolated Texas town was my music, friends, the records we collected (jazz and classical) and live radio broadcasts that included concerts of the New York Philharmonic on Sunday afternoons." At North Texas State University in Denton, during his freshman year (1947–48), his first teacher in theory, Robert Ottman, was also the first to encourage him to compose. "One of his last assignments of that year of common-practice harmony was to 'break any rules you like,' and the first piece I wrote, Quartet for Woodwinds, brought me an A." His five years at Texas State University were culminated with a bachelor of music degree in 1951 and a master's degree in theory and composition in 1952. While there, he came under the influence of Violet Archer, his first teacher in composition. "Having studied with Hindemith and Bartók," Austin explains, "she instilled in me the discipline and care one must have as a composer." His apprentice works, in a Bartókian

idiom, were completed with her encouragement and under her guidance: Violin Sonatina (1951), Duets for Violins (1951), String Trio (1952), and Concertino, for flute, trumpet, and strings (1952), all given their first performances at student composers' concerts in Texas.

Between 1952 and 1955, Austin served in the U.S. Army as one of the composers and arrangers for a weekly radio program in San Antonio, Tex. While in uniform he also attended San Antonio College at night for a three-year period of study of French and German. He composed as well, notably his second orchestral work, *Prosody* (1953), and Fanfare and Procession, for band (1953); the latter was first performed on the army radio network in San Antonio. On October 31, 1953, Austin married Edna Navarro, a registered nurse whom he had met in San Antonio in 1952. During the next ten years they had seven children, one of whom died in infancy and another who died at the age of three.

Upon his discharge from the army, Austin spent the summer of 1955 doing graduate work in composition with Darius Milhaud at Mills College, in Oakland, Calif. "It was Milhaud," he recalls, "who encouraged me to 'let the jazz come through' as well as strengthening my new wife's belief that I was truly talented as a composer."

In 1956, while a graduate student in musicology at the University of California in Berkeley, Austin was appointed teaching assistant. One year later he was made associate in music and administrative assistant to the department chairman. During his three years in Berkeley, Austin served as assistant director of the university band; he studied composition with Andrew Imbrie, counterpoint with Seymour Shifrin, and musicology with David Boyden and Edward Lowinsky.

The jazz idiom, always a part of Austin's personal expression, was now assuming increasing importance in his composition, culminating in the late fifties in a series of works integrating idiomatic jazz and contemporary compositional techniques. His first extended chamber work in which jazz improvisation was used with serious intent and in conjunction with the more progressive techniques of concert music was *Homecoming*, a cantata for soprano and jazz quintet (1959), which set a satirical poem by Peter Viereck. When this piece was heard in San Francisco at the Composers Forum series on May 24, 1960, Alfred Frankenstein remarked in the *San Francisco Chronicle* that the jazz improvisations by the solo instruments were the best part of the entire composition. "Here it got off the ground in proper jazz style."

In the second year of Austin's appointment to the faculty of the University of California at Davis, Gunther Schuller visited the campus for a lecture and saw the scores and heard tapes of Austin's jazz-classical pieces, one of which was the Fantasy on a Theme by Berg, for jazz band (1960). Schuller was impressed and invited Austin to write for him a work for full orchestra and jazz soloists. Broadcast Music Incorporated (BMI) commissioned it for the National Symphony Orchestra in Washington, D.C., which introduced *Improvisations for Orchestra and Jazz Soloists* under Schuller's direction at the International Jazz Festival in Washington on May 31, 1962. On January 12, 1964, the New York Philharmonic under Leonard Bernstein presented a revised version, without violins, at a concert that was televised throughout the United States and Canada. *Improvisations for Orchestra and Jazz Soloists* was Austin's most important work up to that time and his first to make him known nationally. Divided into three uninterrupted sections, the work begins with variants of a twelve-bar blues, followed by a slow and melancholy blues and ending with a *furioso* section in what appears to be a Charleston rhythm. At strategic moments throughout the composition, improvisations by trumpet, bass, and percussion are interspersed, the individual performers called upon to invent rhythmic designs on given pitches within specified time spans.

In 1963, Austin and several of his colleagues in Davis organized the New Music Ensemble, a group of composer-performers specializing in free-group improvisations. With Austin as codirector, this ensemble gave numerous public concerts for the next five years, at many of which Austin's works were performed. In his own music, Austin continued to refine his improvisation techniques in compositions he now designated as "open style." Among them were the *Quartet in Open Style*, for string quartet (1964), which the Lenox String Quartet premiered in Davis on February 7, 1965; *Open Style*, for orchestra with piano soloist (1965), introduced on September 28, 1968, by the Buffalo Philharmonic in Buffalo, N.Y., with the composer conducting and with Yuji Takahashi as soloist; *Catharsis: Open Style for Two Improvisational Ensembles, Tape and Conductor* (1967; Oakland, Calif., February 9, 1967); and *Piano Set in Open Style* (1967; San Francisco, June 2, 1967).

Austin and his family spent the year of 1964–65 in Rome on a $10,000 fellowship and grant from the Institute of Creative Arts at the University of California. In 1967, Austin was cofounder, and for four years coeditor, of *Source*, a publication devoted solely to avant-garde music.

Austin's close professional associations with Karlheinz Stockhausen, David Tudor, and John Cage in Davis, where they had come as resident composers between 1965 and 1969, opened for him new creative vistas, particularly in the areas of live electronic music and multimedia productions. Some of Austin's most ambitious works of these years were multimedia productions or theater-piece portraits. *Roma: A Theater Piece in Open Style* (1965) was introduced in Davis on January 9, 1966. Each instrumentalist was dressed in black attire and a single, white greasepaint pseudo eyepatch. While performing in an im-

provisational manner (which Austin called "movement improvisation") they walked slowly around the stage and disappeared and reappeared through trapdoors. Large Styrofoam sculptures were used to catch and reflect colored spotlights. *The Maze* (1966) is a theater piece for percussionists, dancer, tape, and films, performed in Davis, London, and Oberlin. When it was produced at the University of St. Thomas in Houston, Tex., on March 24, 1968, D. J. Hobdy described it in the *Houston Chronicle* as follows: "Three pajama-clad percussionists . . . ran from stand to stand, up and down that long flight of stairs, hitting, rubbing. Clicking, shaking everything from water-filled glasses to a brake drum. On the balcony wall, a film of the American Brass Quintet using up sixteen minutes for a concert was flashed and on the ceiling a giant projection of a clock face ticked off absurdities. Tying all this together was a dance . . . like some Now Generation in a particularly noisy Wonderland." At this performance in Houston, *Accidents* (1967), for electronically prepared piano, actions, mirrors, and black light, was introduced. The composer, who operated a synthesizer, covered the strings of the piano with little round contact microphones connected to the synthesizer. Large mirrors around the piano revealed this setup to the audience and the pianist, who was glowing in the dark and in front of whom hung a plastic score covered with glowing red and green lines. *The Magicians* (1968; Davis, May 28, 1968) used film projections and iridescent lights flashing on rectangular panels on a darkened stage, mobiles, painted-up children, mimes, and taped electronic sounds. *Agape* (1970) was an "electronic masque or rock mystery play" for soprano and baritone soloists, dancers, rock band, and chorus. It was written to help commemorate the centennial of Canisius College at the Albright-Knox Gallery in Buffalo, N.Y., where it was first produced on February 25, 1970.

In 1969, Austin took a summer course in computer-generated music at Stanford University in California. (A decade later, in 1978, he participated in a workshop in the technology of computer music at the Massachusetts Institute of Technology at Cambridge.) In spring 1971, Austin composed *Quartet Three*, the first of a series of extended electronic compositions for four-channel tape. It was followed by *Quartet Four* (1971), *Primal Hybrid* (1972), *1976* (1973), and *Phoenix* (1974).

During the summer of 1970 Austin was visiting professor of music at Trinity University in San Antonio. Austin left Davis in 1972 to become chairman of the department of music at the University of South Florida in Tampa, where he remained for the next six years, as chairman of the music department in 1972–73 and from 1973 to 1978 director of the System Complex for the Studio and Performing Arts (SYCOM) in its College of Fine Arts. Between 1972 and 1977, Austin completed a series of compositions collectively entitled *Quadrants: Event/Complex,* nos.

1–11. Each Event/Complex can be performed singly—always with the same accompanying four-channel tape—or in combinations with any or all of the
others, simultaneously or successively. Nos. 1 and 2
are for large forces respectively, a sixty-four-
wind/percussion ensemble and a large chorus. Nos.
3 through 11 are for solo instruments. No. 9 received
the Distinguished Composer Award from the Music
Teachers National Association in 1974. A series of
graphic/sonic works was culminated with *Tableaux
vivants* (1973), composed in collaboration with the
graphic artist Charles Ringness. *Phantasmagoria*,
composed between 1974 and 1977, consisted of three
fantasies based on the existing sketches of Charles
Ives's last and uncompleted work, *The Universe
Symphony*, together with Austin's own related but
freely composed materials. The *First Fantasy*, for
brass quintet, narrator, and tape (1975), was performed by the American Brass Quintet (which had
commissioned it) on February 15, 1975; it was then
given at the Muziki Biennale in Zagreb, Yugoslavia,
on May 15, 1975. *Second Fantasy*, for clarinet, viola,
keyboards, percussion, and tape (1976), was premiered in New York in May 1976; it was awarded
first prize by the Florida Festival of New Music and
the Fine Arts Council of Florida in 1976. The third
fantasy, also called *Phantasmagoria* (1977), is for orchestra and tape.

In 1978, Austin was appointed professor of music
at North Texas State University in Denton. Austin
has made numerous tours in the United States, Europe, and South America as performer, conductor,
and lecturer. He has done significant research in the
development of software for hybrid computer systems
for electronic music as well as direct synthesis of music with computers.

THE COMPOSER SPEAKS: I believe that composing,
when approached as a dialectical process rather than
a mysterious phenomenon, is simply a series of musical decisions, the most basic being the decision actually to make decisions. For instance, my own motivation to compose—to make musical decisions—
began with my urge at an early age to improvise
alone and, later, with other people. . . . Composing
was a natural process to me, not at all phenomenal.
What I do years later is not so different from that
first urge: to make music with materials I found appropriate to the music's needs and in a language that
is highly personalized. My deep involvement with
the electronic music medium is simply an extension
of my natural, in-studio music making.

Each compositional project I undertake has to
have its own special reason for existence. While that
may seem a rhetorical statement for a work of art, it
is an important principle to appreciate. To make
each work original art, I must find its essence at the
beginning of the compositional process. Proof of this
lies in the fact that I almost always entitle my pieces
before a single note is written or a single sound ex-

plored. I relate its essence to the title I give it. Those
few pieces I have composed which go nameless until
finished are mainly works which explore some particular compositional technique: they are studies for
my own edification and get their names from the
technique itself or from some extramusical aspect.

PRINCIPAL WORKS: *Homecoming*, cantata for soprano and jazz quintet (1959); Fantasy on a Theme by
Berg, for jazz band (1960); *Improvisations for Orchestra and Jazz Soloists* (1961); *A Broken Consort*,
for seven instruments (1962); *In Memoriam: J. F.
Kennedy*, for band (1963); *Collage*, for assorted instruments (1964); Piano Variations (1964); *Quartet
in Open Style*, for string quartet (1964); *Current*, for
clarinet and piano (1964); *Open Style*, for orchestra
with piano soloist (1965); *Roma: A Theater Piece in
Open Style* (1965); *Catharsis: Open style for Two
Improvisational Ensembles, Tape and Conductor*
(1967); *The Maze*, a theater piece in open style
(1966); *Cyclotron Stew*, for cyclotron with tape montage (1967); *Accidents*, for electronically prepared
piano, mirrors, actions, and black light (1967); *Brass*,
for electronically amplified and modified brass instruments and film slides (1967); *Piano Set*, in open
style (1967); *The Magicians*, a theater piece for children, live and taped electronic sounds, black light,
and slide film (1968); *Transmission One*, video-
audio electronic composition for color-television
broadcast (1969); *Agape*, a "celebration" or "masque"
for soloists, dancers, actors, rock band, and
tapes (1970); *Plastic Surgery*, for electric piano, percussion, magnetic tape, and film (1970); *Walter*, theater piece for viola, viola d'amore, films, and tape
(1971); *Quartet Three*, for four-channel tape (1971);
Quartet Four, for four-channel tape (1971), *J. B.,
Larry and . . .*, for saxophone and tape (1971);
Quadrants: Event/Complex, nos. 1–11 (1971–77);
Primal Hybrid, for four-channel tape (1972); *Tableaux vivants*, a sonograph (1973); *1976*, for four-
channel tape (1973); *Phoenix*, for four-channel tape
(1974); *Phantasmagoria*, 3 fantasies: no. 1, for brass
quintet and tape, no. 2, for clarinet, keyboards, percussion, and tape, no. 3, for orchestra and tape
(1974–77).

BIBLIOGRAPHY: Chase, Gilbert, *America's Music*
(N.Y., 1966); Cope, David, *New Directions in Music*
(Dubuque, Ia., 1971); Gillespie, John, *The Musical
Experience* (N.Y., 1968); Schwartz, Elliott, *Elec-
tronic Music* (N.Y., 1973); Thomson, Virgil, *Ameri-
can Music Since 1910* (N.Y., 1970).

Avshalomov, Jacob, b. Tsingtao, China, March
28, 1919. American citizen, 1944.

His style is conservative, favoring what in the
1940s and 1950s was referred to as a pantonal manner. His works revolve around recognizable, though
shifting, tonal centers. He uses all the traditional ele-

ments of melody, counterpoint, rhythm, harmony, and tonal colors, though with a fresh viewpoint. His father's influence and that of his early years in China have occasionally left their vestiges in pentatonisms and coloristic touches.

His mother was American, his father Russian. The father, Aaron Avshalomov, was a distinguished composer who, for thirty years, lived in China and whose entire compositional output was based on Chinese and other oriental materials. He came to the United States for the first time in 1947, where his last three symphonies were written.

Jacob Avshalomov's musical training began at the piano with an aunt in childhood, and continued with further studies in composition with his father. Watching his father compose, and then hearing his music performed, proved an early inspiration. Jacob's basic academic education took place at the American School (1929–30) and the British Grammar School (1931–34) at Tientsin. After graduating at the age of fifteen he worked for the next three years as a factory supervisor. During this time he was active in such sports as swimming, soccer, water polo, and fancy diving—holding the North China championship in various racquet games for four years. Music had been relegated to an avocation.

Early in 1937, in Shanghai, Avshalomov became involved in musical activities for the first time. He assisted his father in producing a Chinese ballet and in preparing his scores. Such endeavors were interrupted when the Japanese invaded China. For a brief period, he served in the British volunteer corps in Tientsin. Then, in December 1937, he and his mother came to the United States, she for repatriation in San Francisco. By this time, Avshalomov knew he wanted to become a composer.

In 1938, in Los Angeles, he studied composition privately with Ernst Toch, an experience he looks back on as all-important in his development. After that, Avshalomov spent two years at Reed College in Portland, Oreg. (1939–41), where he studied conducting with Jacques Gershkovitch and played in the Junior Symphony. Between 1941 and 1943 he attended the Eastman School of Music in Rochester, N.Y., his study of composition continuing there mainly with Bernard Rogers. In 1942 he wrote incidental music for a Hindu farce, *Cues from the Little Clay Cart,* which was produced that year at Reed College. A suite from that score for a small chamber group in 1949 became Avshalomov's first extended instrumental composition. It was introduced in New York in February 1949. *The Taking of T'ung Khan,* an orchestral tone poem whose subject and musical style were throwbacks to the composer's early years in China, was written in 1943. This was Avshalomov's first symphonic work, notable not only for its esoteric orientalism but also for its dramatic changes of tempi, rhythm, and meter. A decade after it was written, the composer revised it. The new version was introduced by the Detroit Symphony Orchestra

conducted by Leopold Stokowski on November 20, 1953. William Bergsma, writing in the *American Composers Alliance Bulletin,* called it "a thrilling and effective work."

Avshalomov received his bachelor of music degree at the Eastman School in 1942 and his master of arts degree one year later. On August 31, 1943, he married Doris Felde, then a postgraduate student, subsequently a poet and English teacher in high school. Both their sons became professional musicians: David as composer-conductor; Daniel as violist and member of the American String Quartet.

Between 1943 and 1945, during World War II, Avshalomov saw duty in the American army in the European theater of operations as an interpreter. While in London, he made his conducting debut with a performance of Bach's *Passion According to St. John* in April 1944. Also while still in uniform, he composed *Slow Dance,* for orchestra (1945), his first work to get a significant hearing. It was performed by the National Symphony under Richard Bales in Washington, D.C., on August 13, 1945, at which time, writing in the *Times-Herald,* Glenn Dillard Gunn said: "Avshalomov's . . . gravely eloquent melodies are stated in a finely wrought contrapuntal movement. . . . The vitality of this music is in the constantly active bass voice, surely one of the best examples of this important technical element to be found in contemporary art."

Following his discharge from the army, Avshalomov received an Alice M. Ditson Fellowship from Columbia University and spent the summer of 1946 at the Berkshire Music Center at Tanglewood in Massachusetts, studying composition with Aaron Copland. That fall he joined the music faculty of Columbia University. During the next eight years at Columbia, in addition to his teaching assignments, he founded and conducted the university chorus and occasionally conducted the orchestra. There he presented the American premieres of Michael Tippett's *A Child of Our Time,* Bruckner's Mass in D, and Handel's *The Triumph of Time and Truth,* the last given in celebration of the university's bicentennial. In 1946, Avshalomov composed an orchestral sinfonietta which was premiered in New York by the Little Orchestral Society under Thomas Scherman on November 29, 1949. Three years after its revision in 1953 it received the Naumburg Recording Award. *Evocations,* for clarinet and chamber orchestra (1947), was given its first hearing at Saratoga, N.Y., on August 17, 1950, and three years later was conducted in New York by Leopold Stokowski at the Museum of Modern Art. In 1948, Avshalomov was the recipient of the Ernest Bloch Award for the cantata *How Long, O Lord,* for alto, chorus, and orchestra (1948).

Avshalomov received the Guggenheim Fellowship in 1951. Two years later he completed a major choral work, *Tom o' Bedlam,* based on a 17th-century poem about a famous madman. After its premiere on December 15, 1953, in New York, Robert Shaw conducting the Collegiate Chorale, it was awarded the New York Music Critics Circle Award. "Using a simple accompaniment of an oboe and a percussionist with a tambourine and a small drum," reported Ross Parmenter in the *New York Times*, "the composer has managed to evoke a poignant picture of the gentle beggar who felt he was summoned to a journey 'ten leagues beyond the world's end.' . . . Its translations of the text were genuinely inventive." Harriet Johnson, in the *New York Post*, called it an "imaginative piece, provocative of many different moods and a real addition to the choral repertory."

In 1956, Avshalomov completed another major choral work: *Inscriptions at the City of Brass*, for female narrator and orchestra as well as chorus, text based on *The Arabian Nights*. Hugh Ross conducted the premiere performance with the Schola Cantorum in New York in 1958. When it was heard in Boston on February 24, 1960 (this time with the composer conducting), Cyrus Durgin was unqualified in his praise in the *Boston Globe*, calling it "masterly and exciting. . . . This is a truly superb Oriental fantasy, large in subject and scope. . . . It is wrought with a fabulously skilled technique and a sense of choral and instrumental colors altogether rare."

Phases of the Great Land, for orchestra (1958), is a popularist composition in which the composer makes effective use of such favorite popular ballads as "After the Ball," "And the Band Played On," and "A Bird in a Gilded Cage." It was written for the Anchorage Festival in Alaska, where it was introduced on June 13, 1958. *Symphony: The Oregon* (1961) was written in commemoration of the Oregon centennial and first heard in Portland on March 19, 1962, the composer conducting. *City upon a Hill*, for narrator, chorus, orchestra, and "liberty bell" (1964) was introduced at the Boston Winterfest in the year of its composition.

Upon leaving Columbia University in 1954, Avshalomov made his home in Portland, Oreg., where he took over the thirty-year-old Portland Junior Symphony, which he has been conducting since that time with such distinction that in 1965 he was presented with the Ditson Conductor's Award. Under Avshalomov this orchestra toured Europe in 1970, Japan in November 1979, has been heard over the radio and television, and has made recordings. In 1978 its name was changed to Portland Youth Orchestra.

During the summer of 1959 Avshalomov was on the music faculty of the Berkshire Music Center at Tanglewood, and since then has been a visiting professor at the University of Washington in Chestertown, Md., and Northwestern University in Evanston, Ill. He Also has made numerous appearances as guest conductor of orchestras in the American Northwest and Canada. In February 1968, President Johnson appointed him to the National Council on the Humanities, on which he served until 1974. He has also been consultant to the Ford Foundation project for composers in public schools (1958–59) and, in 1974, on the music planning section of the National Endowment for the Arts of which he was cochairman between 1976 and 1978. He received honorary doctorates in music and humane letters from the University of Portland (1966), Reed College (1974), and Linfield College in McMinville, Oreg. (1976). The University of Oregon presented him with the Distinguished Service Award in 1975.

THE COMPOSER SPEAKS: I feel a responsibility to the performer and the listener. I care a lot about the choice of every note I write, and feel accountable for them all. I eschew the recent developments in music where any note will do; and I respect instruments and voices, using them for what is really fitting for them to do. I hope my works touch people's spirit.

PRINCIPAL WORKS: *The Taking of T'ung Khan*, for orchestra (1943); Viola Sonatina (1943); *Slow Dance*, for orchestra (1945); *Prophecy*, for tenor, chorus, and organ (1946); Sinfonietta, for orchestra (1946); *Evocations*, for clarinet and chamber orchestra (1947); *How Long, O Lord*, cantata for alto, chorus, and orchestra (1948); *Tom o' Bedlam*, for chorus and orchestra (1953); *Inscriptions at the City of Brass*, for female narrator, chorus, and orchestra (1956); *Of Man's Moralitie*, for a cappella chorus (1957); *Phases of the Great Land*, for orchestra (1958); *Symphony: The Oregon* (1961); *Wonders*, for a cappella chorus (1961); *Praises from the Corners of the Earth*, for chorus, organ and three percussion (1964); *City upon a Hill*, for narrator, chorus, orchestra, and "liberty bell" (1964); *The Thirteen Clocks*, for two narrators and orchestra (1974); *Quodlibet Montagna*, for brass sextet (1975); *Raptures*, on madrigals of Gesualdo, for orchestra (1975).

BIBLIOGRAPHY: *BBDM; DCM; Who's Who in America, 1978–79.*

B

Babbitt, Milton Byron, b. Philadelphia, Pa., May 10, 1916.

He was the first composer to extend the twelve-tone technique into "total organization," or serialism, and the first composer to write an extended work for the synthesizer.

The son of a professional mathematician, Milton Babbitt began the study of music with the violin when he was five and continued three years later with the clarinet. As a boy he composed songs, words as well as music. Despite such musical preoccupation he was heading toward mathematics. After graduating from Central High School in Jackson, Miss., in 1931, he entered New York University. There, as he explains, he was "appalled at the philistine attitude towards logic and abstract mathematics which I encountered." Having discovered the music of Schoenberg, Berg, and Webern in 1933, and become intrigued with twelve-tonalism, Babbitt transferred his principal major at college from mathematics to music, studying composition, theory, and music history with Marion Bauer, Martin Bernstein, and Philip James. Upon graduating from New York University in 1935, elected a member of Phi Beta Kappa, Babbitt continued to study composition privately with Roger Sessions for three years. The influence of Sessions upon his own musical thinking was far-reaching.

In 1938, Babbitt was appointed to the music faculty of Princeton, where he did his postgraduate work. On December 27, 1939, he married Sylvia Miller, with whom he had a daughter. While at Princeton, he received in 1941 the Bearns Prize from Columbia University for his composition *Music for the Mass* for chorus, which he described as a *pièce d'occasion* which embodied "deliberately idiomatic conservatism." In 1942, Babbitt was a member of the first group to earn the master of fine arts degree at Princeton. In 1942–43, during World War II, he was involved in classified war-related activities. Between 1943 and 1945 he was so busily engaged teaching mathematics at Princeton that he found no time for composition. But he did clarify his ideas on composition, which were set forth in a monograph, "The Function of Set Structure in the Twelve-tone System" (1946), embodying the concept of total organization in which the twelve-tone system applied not only to pitch (Schoenberg) or pitch and tone color (Webern), but also to such other elements as dynamics, rhythm, timbre, and so forth. Putting theory into practice, Babbitt wrote Three Composi-

tions for Piano (1947–48), the first serial work ever written. (Pierre Boulez, the other early prophet of serialism, arrived at the same method later in 1948 with his Piano Sonata no. 2.) This was followed in 1948 by Composition for Four Instruments (which received a citation from the New York Music Critics Circle), Composition for Twelve Instruments, and String Quartet no. 1, and in 1950 by *The Widow's Lament in Springtime,* a setting of a poem by William Carlos Williams. In *All Set* (1957), for two saxophones, trumpet, trombone, bass, drums, vibes and piano—commissioned by Brandeis University—Babbitt successfully applied serialism to jazz. Two Sonnets, for baritone and three instruments (1955), text by Gerard Manley Hopkins, was performed at the festival of the International Society for Contemporary Music in Rome on June 12, 1959.

In 1951, Babbitt was elected president of the United States branch of the International Society for Contemporary Music, and in 1952 he served as member of the faculty of the Salzburg Seminar in American Studies in Austria. During the summers of 1957 and 1958 he taught composition at the Berkshire Music Center in Tanglewood, Mass., and in 1960 he was elevated to the post of professor of music at Princeton.

Babbitt had been interested in electronic music as far back as 1938 when he made his first such experiments. But it was two decades before he took a decisive step in that direction. In January 1958, he was invited by Radio Corporation of America to become actively involved with the Mark II Electronic Sound Synthesizer, which differed from other electronic ways of making music with new sounds by being composed directly on the synthesizer itself instead of being produced through doctored magnetic tape. "Composition and research with this most flexible and vast artifact for the electronic and electromechanical specification, generation, and regulation of the sound event, and the mode of progression from such a so-specified event to the following such event," Babbitt explains, "represent a conjuction of my greatest compositional need and scientific work." A grant by the Rockefeller Foundation led to the establishment of the Electronic Music Center of Columbia and Princeton Universities, of which Babbitt became one of the four members. At this center, Babbitt intensified his explorations of tonal possibilities with the synthesizer. His Composition for Synthesizer (1961) was the first extended work ever produced on that electronic instrument, and *Vision and Prayer,* for soprano and synthesizer (1961), based on a poem by Dylan Thomas and commissioned by the Fromm Music Foundation, was the first work for synthesizer using a human collaborator. *Vision and Prayer* was introduced by Bethany Beardslee at a concert at the Eighth Congress of the International Musicological Society in New York in September 1961.

In 1960–61, Babbitt received a Guggenheim Fellowship for research in electronic music. In 1964 he wrote Ensembles for Synthesizer, heard first at an avant-garde festival at Ojai, Calif., on May 30, 1964. That year, *Philomel,* for soprano, recorded soprano and synthesizer (1964)—text by John Hollander based on a classical legend—was commissioned by the Ford Foundation. It received a citation from the New York Music Critics Circle and was presented at the festival of the International Society for Contemporary Music in Warsaw, Poland, on September 23, 1968.

Babbitt's first work for orchestra was *Relata I* (1965), whose world premiere was given in Cleveland on March 3, 1966, Gunther Schuller conducting the Cleveland Orchestra. (The word *relata* is a term in logic signifying interrelationships.) *Relata II* (1968), also for orchestra, was premiered in New York on January 16, 1969, by the New York Philharmonic (which had commissioned it) under Leonard Bernstein. Both works are in a serial technique, and both are complex in their use of athematic and arhythmic procedures. This was equally true of String Quartet no. 3 (1970; Chicago, May 1970), String Quartet no. 4 (1970; N. Y., February 1970), and *A Solo Requiem* (1977; N. Y., February 10, 1979). Among Babbitt's later electronic compositions are *Phenomena,* for soprano and magnetic tape (1970; N. Y., November 3, 1975), and Occasional Variations, for synthesized tape (1971; Wolf Trap, Va., August 23, 1971).

Babbitt was elected to the National Institute of Arts and Letters in 1965; in 1970 he received the Creative Arts Medal from Brandeis University in Waltham, Mass. He has taught composition at the Juilliard School of Music in New York since 1972. He was lecturer at McMaster University in Hamilton, Ontario in 1972, and he toured the United States and Hawaii as Phi Beta Kappa Visiting Scholar in 1972–73. In 1977, and again in 1979, he gave courses at the Rubin Academy in Jerusalem. He was appointed fellow of the American Academy of Arts and Letters (1974) and received membership to the Elizabeth Sprague Coolidge Foundation Committee (1977). He has been awarded honorary doctorates in music from Swarthmore College in Pennsylvania (1969) and the New England Conservatory of Music in Boston (1972).

THE COMPOSER SPEAKS: The composer expends an enormous amount of time and energy—and, usually considerable money—on the creation of a commodity which has little, none or negative commodity value. He is, in essence, a "vanity" composer. The general public is largely unaware of and uninterested in his music. The majority of performers shun it and resent it. Consequently, the music is little performed, and then primarily at poorly attended concerts before an audience consisting in the main of fellow professionals. At best the music would appear to be for, and of, and by specialists. Toward this condition of musical and societal "isolation," a variety of attitudes has been expressed, usually with the purpose of assigning blame often to the music itself, occasionally to critics or performers, and very occasionally to the public. But to assign blame is to imply that this isolation is unnecessary and undesirable. It is my contention that, on the contrary, this condition is not only inevitable, but potentially advantageous for the composer and his music. From my point of view, the composer would do well to consider means of realizing, consolidating, and extending the advantages. . . .

And so I dare suggest that the composer would do himself and his music an immediate and eventual service by total, resolute and voluntary withdrawal from this public world to one of private performance and electronic media, with its very real possibility of complete elimination of the public and social aspects of musical composition. By so doing, the separation between the domains would be defined beyond any possibility of confusion of categories, and the composer would be free to pursue a private life of professional achievement, as opposed to a public life of unprofessional compromise and exhibitionism.

PRINCIPAL WORKS: 4 string quartets (1948–70).

Three Compositions for Piano (1947–48); Composition for Four Instruments, for flute, clarinet, violin, and cello (1948); Composition for Twelve Instruments (1948); Composition for Viola and Piano (1950); *The Widow's Lament in Springtime,* for soprano and piano (1950); Duo, song cycle for soprano and piano (1951); Woodwind Quartet (1953); Two Sonnets, for baritone, clarinet, viola, and cello (1955); Semi-Simple Variations, for piano (1956); *All Set,* for jazz ensemble (1957); *Partitions,* for piano (1957); *Sounds and Words,* for soprano and piano (1958); Composition, for tenor and 6 instruments (1960); Composition for Synthesizer (1961); *Vision and Prayer,* for soprano and synthesizer (1961); *Philomel,* for soprano, recorded soprano, and synthesized tape (1964); Ensemble, for synthesizer (1964); *Relata I,* for orchestra (1965); *Post-Partitions,* for piano (1966); *Correspondences,* for string orchestra and sythesized sounds on tape (1967); *Relata II,* for orchestra (1968); *Phenomena,* for soprano and magnetic tape (1970); Occasional Variations, for synthesizer (1971); *Tableaux,* for piano (1972); *Arie da capo,* for chamber orchestra (1974); *Reflections,* for piano and synthesized tape (1975); Concerti, for solo violin, orchestra, and synthesized tape (1976); *A*

Solo Requiem, for soprano and two pianos (1977); *More Phenomena,* for chorus (1978); *My Ends Are My Beginnings,* for solo clarinet (1978); *Images,* for saxophone and synthesized tape (1979); *Dual,* for cello and piano (1980).

BIBLIOGRAPHY: *BBDM; NGDMM;* Griffith, Paul, *A Concise History of Avant-Garde Music* (N.Y., 1978); Rosenberg, Deena and Bernard (eds.), *The Music Makers* (N.Y., 1978); Schwartz, Elliott, and Childs, Barney (eds.), *Contemporary Composers on Contemporary Music* (N.Y., 1967); *New York Times Magazine,* January 15, 1967.

Bacon, Ernst, b. Chicago, Ill., May 26, 1898.

Though best known for his art songs, of which he has written over two hundred, Bacon has successfully employed all forms of music. His compositions are rooted in classical and romantic traditions, have persistently avoided avant-garde innovations, and often use materials from American folklore and American folk music, notably those of the mountain regions of the South.

His mother, a good amateur singer and pianist, insisted that all her four children receive musical training. Ernst, who began taking piano lessons with her when he was seven, seriously doubts if he would have turned to music but for her. Hearing a piano recital by Paderewski and a performance of *Il Trovatore* in boyhood first fired his ambition to become a musician, and he continued to study the piano with Glenn Dillard Gunn (1911–16). At the instigation of his father—a physician who was professor at the medical school at the University of Chicago—music was not allowed to interfere with a thorough academic education, which took place at the Lincoln Grammar School and Lane Technical High School, both in Chicago, and at Northwestern University at Evanston, Ill. At Northwestern, while Bacon did not major in music, he studied theory with P.C. Lutkin between 1915 and 1918. Additional academic study took place at the University of Chicago (1919–20) and contrapuntal work with T. Otterstroem, while piano was studied privately with Alexander Raab (1916–21).

In 1924, Bacon went to Vienna for two years, studying composition with Karl Weigl and piano with Malwine Bree and Franz Schmidt. Later, in 1928–29 he attended the classes of Ernest Bloch in San Francisco. In 1935, Bacon received a master's degree in music at the University of California at Berkeley.

A long and distinguished career as teacher of music began in 1925 when he was appointed instructor of piano and coach and assistant conductor of opera at the Eastman School of Music in Rochester, where, at the same time, he attended a conducting seminar with Eugene Goossens. From 1928 to 1930 he was a member of the faculty at the San Francisco Conservatory; in 1937 was acting professor of music at Hamilton College in Clinton, N.Y.; from 1938 to 1945, dean of the School of Music at Converse College in Spartanburg, S.C.; from 1945 to 1947, director of the School of Music there; later, composer-in-residence (1948–60) at Syracuse University in New York, becoming professor emeritus in 1963. During these years he was also visiting professor at Stanford, Denver, and Wyoming universities, was active as a conductor and music critic, was founder of the Bach Festival in Carmel, Calif. (1935), supervisor and conductor of the Federal Music Project in San Francisco (1935–37), and director of the New Spartanburg Festival (1939–45).

He began his career as a composer in 1924 in the field he would henceforth cultivate fruitfully, that of the art song. Here he carried over to American music some of the romantic traditions of the lied, though to songs with American texts; a fresh American flavor is often alloyed through jazz and Anglo-American idioms. Though his early songs, such as Ten Songs (1928), are set to German poets (Goethe, Eichendorff, Rückert, Lenau, and others), some of his finest efforts have been set to poems by Emily Dickinson (*Songs of Eternity* in 1932, Five Poems in 1943, "The Grass" and "Is There Such a Day" in 1944) and to Walt Whitman (*Songs at Parting* in 1930 and a few of the numbers in *Songs of Eternity*). The Bible, Emily Dickinson, and Walt Whitman provided texts for some of his choral works (another area in which he as been productive, revealing an exceptional skill at polyphonic writing that has a closer relation to such old English masters as Purcell and Tallis than to Johann Sebastian Bach). Among his notable choral works are the short oratorios *Ecclesiastes* (1936), *By Blue Ontario* (1953; Boston, May 11, 1969), and *Usania* (1977); the cantata *The Lord Star* (1950); two cycles for solo female voices, women's chorus, and orchestra, *From Emily's Diary* (1947; N.Y., December 13, 1944), and *Nature* (1971); and *The Last Invocation,* a requiem for chorus and orchestra (1968–71) to poems by both Dickinson and Whitman.

In instrumental music, Bacon has favored classical structures thoroughly "romantic" in spirit. His first successful work for orchestra was Symphony no. 1 (1932), which earned a Pulitzer Traveling Fellowship before it was introduced by the San Francisco Symphony under Issai Dobrowen on January 5, 1934. Bacon wrote two additional symphonies: no. 2 (1937; Chicago, February 5, 1940) and *Great River,* a twelve-movement symphony for narrator and orchestra (1956; Dallas, February 11, 1957), text by Paul Horgan, tracing the flow of the Rio Grande from New Mexico to the Gulf of Mexico. Notable orchestral works outside the field of the symphony include *From These States* (1936; N.Y., May 5, 1946), a "cycle of people's song" as seen through the American climate, industry, amusement, travel, and geography; *Fables* (1953; N.Y., December 15, 1953),

Six Fables, for narrator and orchestra, to texts by John Edmunds and Ernst Bacon; *Riolama,* a concerto for piano and orchestra (1962; Syracuse, January 18, 1963), a series of ten paintings of "places real and imagined"; and a second piano concerto, entitled *Voyaging* (1978).

On May 2, 1942, Bacon's opera—or as he prefers to designate it "musical play"—*A Tree on the Plains* (1940), commissioned by the League of Composers, was introduced at the Spartanburg Festival. In 1947 it received the David Bispham medal, and since then it has been widely performed in numerous universities. The subject of Paul Horgan's text was a searing drought in America's Southwest and its impact on an emotionally overwrought family. A second "musical play," *A Drumlin Legend* (1949), commissioned by the Alice M. Ditson Fund of Columbia University, libretto by Helene Carus, was featured none too successfully at the Festival of Contemporary Music at Columbia University on May 9, 1949. Among Bacon's subsequent works for the stage were two ballets—*Jehovah and the Ark* (1968–70) and *The Parliament of Fowls* (1975), both to scenarios by John Edmunds—and a musical play honoring the American bicentennial, *Dr. Franklin* (1976), text by Cornel Lengyel.

Bacon received Guggenheim Fellowships in 1939, 1942, and 1964. A versatile talent outside music composition, he is the author of *Words on Music* (1960) and *Notes on the Piano* (1963) among other books; has written numerous essays; has had a lifelong interest in literature and philosophy; has done painting; and has been a political activist for progressive causes. He has been married four times: to Mary Prentice Lillie in 1927 (divorced); Analee Camp, a cellist, in 1937 (divorced); Moselle Camp, a pianist, in 1955 (deceased); and Ellen Wendt, a musician and teacher, in 1972.

THE COMPOSER SPEAKS: I don't subscribe to a complete break with classical tradition. A classical background is quite in keeping with the expression of any of the diversified facets of the American spirit. Good art calls for honesty in taste as well as deed. One man needs travel, another finds himself by staying home. The king's English is not defunct in music. I believe in the speech and dance origins of music and in their important effect upon musical cadences and melodic directions. Some people have called me a "romantic." Well then, what real music isn't "romantic"? Also they say I'm "eclectic." I am complimented likewise by this designation, just as I am glad to learn of some resemblance to my parents and ancestors. . . . Whether "ahead of my day" or "behind my day" matters little, once that day has passed unless one reasons that art's evolution means more than its actual self. While art invites experiment, its essence is not research, as in science. There remains only the result, enjoyed less for its onetime novelty or known heredity than for its ultimate integrity and beauty.

Among the masters of the past the two directions are fairly balanced.

PRINCIPAL WORKS: 3 symphonies (1932, 1937, 1956); 2 piano concertos (1962, 1978).

Ten Songs, for voice and piano (1928); *Songs at Parting,* song cycle for voice and piano (1930); *Songs of Eternity,* four songs for baritone and orchestra (1932); *Twilight,* three songs for voice and orchestra (1932); *Black and White Songs,* five songs for baritone and orchestra (1932); *Midnight Special,* four songs for voice and orchestra (1932); *My River,* five songs for voice and orchestra (1932); *Ecclesiastes,* oratorio for soprano, bass, chorus, and orchestra (1936); *From These States,* for orchestra (1936); *A Tree on the Plains,* opera (1940, rev. 1962); Six Songs, for voice and piano (1942); Five Poems, for soprano and piano (1943); *Along Unpaved Roads,* for voice and piano (1944); *From Emily's Diary,* for soprano, alto, women's chorus and orchestra (1945); Piano Quintet (1946); Cello Sonata (1946); *A Drumlin Legend,* opera (1949); *Flight,* for piano (1949); *The Lord Star,* cantata, for bass, chorus, brass, strings, and organ (1950); String Quintet (1951); *Fables,* for narrator and orchestra (1953); *The Hootenany,* for piano (1954); *Sassafras,* for piano (1956); *Precepts of Angelus Silesius,* cycle for antiphonal women's voices (1957); *By Blue Ontario,* oratorio for alto, bass, baritone, chorus, and orchestra (1958); *The Animal Christmas,* oratorio for junior chorus, bass and piano (1964); *Byways,* for piano (1965); *Maple Sugaring,* for piano (1965); *Spirits and Places,* for organ (1966); *Jehovah and the Ark,* ballet (1968–70); *The Last Invocation,* requiem for chorus and orchestra (1968–1971); *Nature,* cantata cycle (1971); *Saws,* a suite of canons for chorus and orchestra (1971); *Of a Feather,* for voice and piano (1975); *The Parliament of Fowls,* ballet (1975); *Dr. Franklin,* musical play (1976); *Usania,* oratorio (1977); Fifty Songs, for voice and piano (1977); *Tributaries,* thirty songs for voice and piano (1979).

BIBLIOGRAPHY: *BBDM;* Ewen, David, *American Composers Today* (N.Y., 1949); Howard, John Tasker, *Our American Music* (N.Y., 1946).

Barber, Samuel, b. West Chester, Pa., March 9, 1910; d. New York City, January 23, 1981.

Without abandoning strong lyric elements, for which he had a pronounced gift, Barber dramatized his writing with excursions into dissonance and occasionally through the use of a chromaticism that suggests polytonal and atonal techniques but without abandoning the tonal framework. He received the Pulitzer Prize in music in 1958 and 1963.

Barber was the nephew of the world-famous contralto Louise Homer, and the son of a physician and community leader. Music study began at the piano with William Hatton Green when Barber was six. A year later he wrote his first composition (*Sadness,* for piano) and at ten he made an attempt to write an opera. He was employed as organist in a West Chester church when he was only twelve. In 1924, while attending the West Chester High School, from which he was graduated two years later, he became a charter pupil at the then newly opened Curtis Institute of Music in Philadelphia. There, over a nine-year period, he studied piano with Isabella Vengerova, voice with Emilio de Gogorza, and composition with Rosario Scalero. While attending the Curtis Institute he was awarded the Bearns Prize of Columbia University for his Sonata for Violin and Piano in 1928, and wrote his first composition that would be performed professionally *(Dover Beach,* for soprano and string quartet, a setting of a poem by Matthew Arnold, written in 1931 and first performed on March 5, 1933, in New York). His first orchestral works to be performed were *The School for Scandal,* overture (1933; Philadelphia, August 30, 1933), which brought him a second Bearns Prize, and *Music for a Scene from Shelley* (1933; N.Y., March 24, 1935).

On a Pulitzer Traveling Fellowship and the Prix de Rome (the latter awarded for his Cello Sonata [1932] and *The School for Scandal),* both acquired in 1935, Barber traveled to Europe in 1935. In Vienna he gave several lieder recitals besides making his debut as conductor at a concert at the Workers' Theater. The Prix de Rome entitled him to stay at the American Academy, where, in 1936, he completed his Symphony no. 1 (*In One Movement*). As a composition in which Barber molded the classical structure to his own requirements, rich in lyricism and romantic expressiveness, it foreshadowed characteristics of subsequent Barber compositions. The symphony was introduced on December 13, 1936, in Rome, with Bernardino Molinari conducting the Augusteo Orchestra, received its American premiere five weeks later in Cleveland performed by the Cleveland Orchestra under Artur Rodzinski, and was performed at Salzburg on July 25, 1937, by the Cleveland Orchestra and Rodzinski to become the first American composition ever to be performed at that world-famous Austrian festival. Barber revised the symphony in 1942; the revised version was performed in New York on February 8, 1944.

Further prestige came to Barber in New York on November 5, 1938, when he became the first American to have a work conducted by Toscanini with the NBC Symphony: the *Essay No. 1* (1937) and the Adagio for Strings (1937). The latter—a poetic work with a sustained lyric line, touched with melancholy, subsequently become one of Barber's most frequently played compositions—was an arrangement for string orchestra of the slow movement from his String Quartet in B minor (1936). In 1967, Barber used the music of the Adagio for Strings for a choral work to the text of the *Agnus Dei.*

Upon returning to the United States in 1939, Barber joined the music faculty of the Curtis Institute,

where he remained for the next three years teaching composition and conducting a chorus. During these years he completed his Violin Concerto (1939), which Albert Spalding introduced with the Philadelphia Orchestra on February 7, 1941, and the *Essay No. 2,* for orchestra (1942; N.Y., April 16, 1942).

Between 1943 and 1945, during World War II, Barber served in the U.S. Army Air Corps, where he was assigned to write a work honoring that branch of service. He complied with the Symphony no. 2 (1944), which, in its original version, was a realistic description of air flight, including the sound of a radio beam sending out a code message produced by an electronic instrument invented for this composition. In this version the symphony was introduced by the Boston Symphony Orchestra under Serge Koussevitzky on March 3, 1944. Three weeks later, the Office of War Information transmitted this performance by short wave throughout the free world. In 1947, Barber revised this symphony extensively, omitting all programmatic realism and allowing the work to stand solely as absolute music. This revision was first performed on January 21, 1948, by the Philadelphia Orchestra. This symphony marked a creative development for Barber in that he was now beginning to extend his expressivity through the use of dissonance and the suggestion of polytonal and atonal writing. This is the idiom that Barber favored and mastered in compositions following his separation from the air force in 1945. Concerto for Cello and Orchestra (1945), first performed on April 5, 1944, by Raya Garbousova and the Boston Symphony under Koussevitzky, received the New York Critics Circle Award as the season's best orchestral work. A ballet, *The Serpent Heart* (1946), was commissioned by the Alice M. Ditson Fund of Columbia University for Martha Graham, who introduced it with her troupe on May 10, 1946, in New York. (When Barber revised this score in 1947, and the ballet was again given by Martha Graham, on February 27, 1947, it bore the new title of *Cave of the Heart.* And when Barber adapted this music into a successful orchestral suite, it carried the title of *Medea.*) *Knoxville: Summer of 1915,* for soprano and orchestra (1947), was a setting of a poem by James Agee that Eleanor Steber and the Boston Symphony under Koussevitzky premiered in Boston on April 9, 1948. The Piano Sonata in E-flat Minor, written in 1949 on a commission from the League of Composers to celebrate its twenty-fifth anniversary (with funds provided by Irving Berlin and Richard Rodgers), was introduced by Vladimir Horowitz in New York on January 23, 1950.

Barber's first opera, *Vanessa* (1957), with libretto by Gian Carlo Menotti, was the first American opera produced by the Metropolitan Opera in over a decade, its first performance taking place in New York on January 15, 1958. It proved so successful that it returned to the stage of the Metropolitan the following season, was revived there in 1964–65, was produced in Salzburg during the summer of 1958 to become the first American opera ever performed there, and in 1958 was the recipient of the Pulitzer Prize. Eclectic in style, Barber's score ranged freely from a Puccini-like sentiment and a Wagnerian or Straussian amplitude of orchestration to Bergian discords, atonality and *Sprechstimme* (song-speech). A soaring lyricism often touched with tenderness and melancholy was combined with dramatic power and effective atmospheric writing to make *Vanessa* a compelling theatrical experience. A revised version of this opera was the highlight of the Spoleto Festival at Charleston, S.C., on May 27, 1978, and was filmed for television transmission over the facilities of the Public Broadcasting System the following January.

Barber's second Pulitzer Prize came in 1963 for his Concerto for Piano and Orchestra, completed in 1962 on a commission from the music publishing firm of G. Schirmer to celebrate its centenary. John Browning introduced it with the New York Philharmonic under Erich Leinsdorf on September 24, 1962, during week-long ceremonies attending the opening of the Lincoln Center for the Performing Arts in New York. When the Cleveland Orchestra, with George Szell conducting, toured Europe in the spring of 1965 this concerto was featured widely on its programs (with Browning again as soloist). It has since become recognized as one of Barber's masterworks and one of the most important piano concertos by an American in the post–World War II era.

But Barber's career was not without setbacks, the most serious being the fiasco attending the world premiere of his second opera, *Antony and Cleopatra* (1966), libretto by Franco Zeffirelli based on Shakespeare. This opera had been commissioned by the Metropolitan Opera for the opening of its new auditorium at the Lincoln Center for the Performing Arts on September 16, 1966. The overpretentious production staged by Zeffirelli, the failure of the revolving stage to function properly, together with various stage mishaps and unfortunate last-minute stage adjustments, spelled doom for the opera, which was severely criticized and summarily dropped from the repertoire after that season. But there was much in Barber's score to command respect, such as the first-act ballet music and the deeply affecting closing scene of Cleopatra's death followed by the lament of the people. After Barber revised and shortened the score, and with more economical and felicitous staging, the opera was heard to much better advantage on February 6, 1975, in a performance by the Juilliard American Opera Center in New York, and was praised.

For the opening of Heinz Hall, a new concert auditorium in Pittsburgh, Barber wrote in 1971, on commission from the Alcoa Company, *Fadograph of a Yestern Scene,* title taken from a line in James Joyce's *Finnegans Wake.* It was introduced by the Pittsburgh Symphony under William Steinberg on September 11, 1971. *The Lovers* (1971), a setting of nine love poems by the Chilean poet Pablo Neruda,

for baritone, mixed chorus, and orchestra, was commissioned by the Girard Bank of Philadelphia and premiered by the Philadelphia Orchestra under Eugene Ormandy on September 22, 1971.

There was a five-year hiatus in Barber's productivity between 1972, when he completed Three Songs, for baritone and instruments (1974; New York, April 30, 1974), and 1977. During this period Barber's sole activity as composer was to revise his two operas. The silence ended in 1978 with *Essay No. 3,* for orchestra, whose premiere and the debut of Zubin Mehta as musical director of the New York Philharmonic coincided on September 14, 1978.

In 1945, Barber received a Guggenheim Fellowship; in 1951, he served as vice-president of the International Music Council of UNESCO; in 1958, he was the youngest ever to be elected a member of the American Academy of Arts and Letters; and in 1959, he was awarded an honorary doctorate in music by Harvard University.

Barber's seventieth birthday was commemorated in 1980 with performances of his music by major organizations in the United States and Europe, including two all-Barber programs at the Curtis Institute of Music on March 9, the day of his birth. Two days later, Barber received the Wolf Trap Award from Rosalynn Carter at the White House, and that evening the National Symphony in Washington, D.C., performed the Piano Concerto in his honor. On August 24, 1980, he was presented with the MacDowell medal.

THE COMPOSER SPEAKS: If I'm writing for words, then I immerse myself in those words, and I let the music flow out of them. When I write an abstract piano sonata or concerto, I write what I feel. I'm not a self-conscious composer. . . . One of the physical nurturing components that make my music sound as it does is that I live mostly in the country. . . . I have always believed that I need a circumference of silence. As to what happens when I compose, I really haven't the faintest idea. The point is, I'm not an analyzer, and I don't surround myself with composers. . . . Most composers bore me because most composers are boring. . . . Composers have never helped me. Performers have always helped me.

PRINCIPAL WORKS: 3 *Essays,* for orchestra (1937, 1942, 1978); 2 symphonies (1936, rev. 1942; 1944, rev. 1947).

String Quartet in B minor (1936); Adagio for Strings, adapted from the slow movement of the String Quartet (1937); Violin Concerto (1939); *Capricorn Concerto,* for flute, oboe, trumpet, and strings (1944); Cello Concerto (1945); *Cave of the Heart,* originally entitled *The Serpent Heart,* ballet (1946); *Medea,* suite for orchestra, adapted from score of *Cave of the Heart* (1947); *Knoxville: Summer of 1915,* for soprano and orchestra (1947); Piano Sonata (1949); *Hermit Songs,* for voice and piano (1953);

Prayers of Kierkegaard, for chorus and orchestra (1954); *Vanessa,* opera (1957); *Toccata festiva,* for organ and orchestra (1960); *Die Natali,* for orchestra (1960); *Andromache's Farewell,* for soprano and orchestra (1962); Piano Concerto (1962); *Antony and Cleopatra,* opera (1966); Sonata for Two Violins and Piano (1969); *Despite and Still,* song cycle for voice and piano (1969); *The Lovers,* for baritone, mixed chorus, and orchestra (1971); *Fadograph of a Yestern Scene,* for orchestra (1971); Three Songs, for baritone and instruments (1974); Ballade, for piano (1977); Canzonetta, for oboe and orchestra (1978).

BIBLIOGRAPHY: Broder, Nathan, *Samuel Barber* (N.Y., 1953); Friedewald, R., "A Formal and Stylistic Analysis of the Published Music of Samuel Barber" (doctoral thesis, Ames, Ia., 1957); *New York Times,* October 3, 1971, January 28, 1979, January 24, 1981 (obituary); *New York Times Magazine,* August 28, 1966; *Opera News,* May 1978, March 14, 1981; *Saturday Review/World,* June 1, 1974.

Barlow, Wayne Brewster, b. Elyria, Ohio, September 6, 1912.

Before he became involved with electronic music in the early 1960s, Barlow was a conformist who consistently followed a compositional principle he himself has described as "a balance among the elements of melody, harmony, rhythm, and form."

He began to study the piano with Marjorie Truelove MacKown when he was seven, supplementing this with violin lessons with Effie Knauss four years later. While attending elementary school and Monroe High School in Rochester, N.Y, he was involved in the musical activities. At high school he wrote a number of piano pieces, one of which won a prize in a contest for preparatory students of the Eastman School of Music; he also wrote and scored a composition for piano and orchestra performed at the graduation exercises. After high school, he attended the Eastman School of Music in Rochester, N.Y., where he received his bachelor of music degree in 1934, a master's degree in music in 1935, and the Ph.D. in music composition in 1937. At the Eastman School, Barlow studied with Edward Royce, Bernard Rogers, and Howard Hanson among others. During this time, his orchestral prelude, *De Profundis* (1934), based on a poem by Amy Lowell, was introduced in Rochester on April 18, 1934, Howard Hanson conduting, and a Sinfonietta, for orchestra (1936), was given its premiere in Rochester on April 27, 1936. In 1936 he was awarded the Lillian Fairchild Memorial Prize given annually to a resident of Rochester or its vicinity for outstanding achievement in the arts. During the summer of 1935 he studied composition with Arnold Schoenberg at the University of Southern California in Los Angeles.

While attending the Eastman School, Barlow also

was the organist at the Eastman Baptist Church in Rochester (1932–41). In 1937, he was appointed to the Eastman School faculty where, until his retirement in 1978, in addition to his classroom duties, he was special assistant to the director in charge of American music programs (1938–41), executive secretary of the graduate committee (1947–55), director of graduate studies (1955–57), associate dean for graduate research studies (1957–73), chairman of the department of composition (1968–73), and dean of graduate studies (1973–78).

On August 7, 1937, Barlow married Helen Hurzen, with whom he had two children. Beginning with 1945 he combined his academic studies at Eastman with those of organist and choir director of the St. Thomas Episcopal Church in Rochester, where he remained until 1976. In 1955–56 he served as Fulbright Senior Lecturer at the Royal Danish Conservatory of Music at the University of Copenhagen and the University of Aarbus.

Barlow's first successful composition was an orchestral rhapsody, *The Winter's Passed,* for oboe and strings (1938), which Robert Sprenkle and the Rochester Civic Orchestra under Hanson premiered in April 1938. This is a rarity among Barlow's compositions in that it utilizes American folk material: two melodies of contrasting nature from the Appalachian Mountains region of North Carolina, which are treated in variation form and for the most part harmonized in modal style. *Zion in Exile,* a cantata for vocal soloists, chorus and orchestra (1937), was introduced in Rochester on April 29, 1937. *Songs from the Silence of Amor* (1938; Rochester, April 25, 1939) were settings for soprano and small orchestra of three "prose rhythms" of William Sharp.

Among Barlow's principal works in the 1940s and 1950s were: the score for a ballet, *Three Moods for Dancing* (1940; Rochester, April 25, 1940); Nocturne, for chamber orchestra, inspired by lines from Walt Whitman, written in 1946 on commission from Radio Station WHAM in Rochester (Rochester, April 14, 1946); Mass in G, for vocal soloists, chorus, and orchestra (1951; Rochester, May 10, 1951); *Night Song,* for orchestra (1957; Rochester, May 2, 1958); and *Poems for Music,* for soprano and orchestra (1958; Rochester, June 6, 1958).

In 1963–64, Barlow attended the University of Toronto to study electronic music with Myron Schaeffer. A year later, on a Fulbright research grant, he made further studies in electronic music in Belgium and Holland. Returning to the United States he became director of the Electronic Music Studio at the Eastman School (1968–78). Several of his compositions reflect this new interest in electronics, through his use of magnetic tape: Duo, for harp and tape (1969; N.Y., May 27, 1969); *Soundscapes,* for tape and orchestra (1970; Rochester, March 10, 1972); *Voices of Darkness,* for reader, instruments and tape (1971; Rochester, January 17, 1975); and *Out of the Cradle Endlessly Rocking,* for tenor, chorus, clarinet, viola, piano, and magnetic tape (1978; Rochester, April 4, 1978).

But the bulk of his compositions was in the area outside electronics, the most notable of these being: *Wait for the Promise of the Father,* a cantata for vocal soloists, chorus, and small orchestra (1968; Rochester, December 10, 1968); Concerto for Saxophone and Band (1970; East Stroudsburg, Pa., May 23, 1970); and *Voices of Faith,* a secular cantata for reader, soprano, chorus, and orchestra (1975; Augusta, Ga., February 8, 1976).

Barlow was organist and musical director of the Christ Episcopal Church in Rochester from 1976 to 1978. He has been a guest lecturer, conductor, and composer at colleges and universities throughout the United States. In 1971 he was elected to honorary membership in Phi Beta Kappa, in 1972 was named "Musician of the Year" by the Mu Phi Epsilon Music Fraternity at the University of Rochester, and in 1973 he received a grant from the Exxon Educational Foundation. On July 1, 1978, Barlow was named emeritus professor of composition at the Eastman School.

THE COMPOSER SPEAKS: To me, music is rather indivisible. Which is to say that, while it is impossible to know all about everything involved in the art of music, it is just as impossible to be a totally successful teacher (of an instrument, of history, of theory, or whatever), or composer, or musicologist, or theorist, or performer, or conductor without knowing something about how all these pieces of art fit together. It is no accident that musicologists frequently become skilled performers of the music they study, or vice versa; that many composers make excellent theorists and conductors; or that conductors prosper to the extent that they understand the idiomatic foundations in historical setting of the music they conduct, along with its syntactical complexities. Further, some acquaintance on the part of practicing musicians with the progress of human history and the monuments of human thought, as expressed in literature, the sciences and the arts, is mandatory if the individual is to be an enlightened and effective member of society.

PRINCIPAL WORKS: *De Profundis,* prelude for orchestra (1934); *False Faces,* ballet (1935); Sinfonietta, for chamber orchestra (1936); *Zion in Exile,* cantata for vocal soloists, chorus and orchestra (1937); *The Winter's Passed,* for oboe and strings (1938); *Songs from the Silence of Amor,* for soprano and chamber orchestra (1938); *Three Moods for Dancing,* ballet (1940); *Madrigal for a Bright Morning,* for chorus (1941); 23rd Psalm, for chorus and orchestra (1943); *Lyrical Piece,* for clarinet and strings (1945); Nocturne, for chamber orchestra (1946); Serenade, for orchestra (1946); Rondo-Overture, for orchestra (1947); Piano Sonata (1947); Prelude, Air, and Variations, for bassoon, piano, and string quar-

tet (1949); Sinfonietta in C (1950); Mass in G (1951); Piano Quintet (1951); *Triptych,* for string quartet (1954); Lento and Allegro, for orchestra (1955); *Night Song,* for orchestra (1957); *Poems for Music,* for soprano and orchestra (1958); *Missa Sancti Tomae,* for chorus and organ (1959); Intrada, Fugue, and Postlude, for brass (1959); *Rota,* for piano, also for chamber orchestra (1959); *Images,* for harp and orchestra (1961); *Sinfonia da camera,* for chamber orchestra (1962); Hymn Voluntaries, for the Church Year, for organ (1963–80); *Vistas,* for orchestra (1963); Trio, for oboe, viola, and piano (1964); *We All Believe in One True God,* for chorus (1965); Elegy, for viola and piano, also for viola and orchestra (1967); *Dynamisms,* for two pianos (1967); Two Inventions, for piano, (1968); *Wait for the Promise of the Father,* cantata for vocal soloists, chorus and orchestra (1968); Duo, for harp and magnetic tape (1969); Concerto for Saxophone and Band (1970); *Soundscapes,* for orchestra and magnetic tape (1972); *Voices of Darkness,* for reader, instruments, and magnetic tape (1971); *Voices of Faith,* secular cantata, for reader, soprano, chorus, and orchestra (1975); Vocalise and Canon, for tuba and piano (1976); *Out of the Cradle Endlessly Rocking,* for tenor, chorus, clarinet, viola, piano, and magnetic tape (1978).

BIBLIOGRAPHY: *BBDM*; Ewen, David, *American Composers Today* (N.Y., 1949); Howard, John Tasker, *Our American Music* (N.Y., 1946); Reis, Claire, *Composers in America* (N.Y., 1947); *Who's Who in America, 1980–81.*

Barth, Hans, b. Leipzig, Germany, June 25, 1897; d. Jacksonville, Fla., December 9, 1956. American citizen, 1912.

He was an American pioneer in exploring the potential of microtonal music.

A child prodigy, he began composing and could play the piano competently when he was six. As a child, he earned a scholarship to the Leipzig Conservatory, where he studied composition with Carl Reinecke. In his tenth year, Hans Barth came to the United States, where, two years later, he gave public recitals in New York. By this time he had written about a dozen compositions, one of which was published. As a teenager he returned to Germany to give recitals and to continue music study. He now became intrigued with new scales utilizing less than the half step. (To this writer, Barth once revealed that the idea to break away from standard tonality came to him one night in a dream, even though he had no knowledge of atonality then. The following day he sat down and wrote eight pages using the chromatic scale as a basis.) In this area, Barth received advice and encouragement from Ferruccio Busoni, who was the first to suggest to him that he construct a quarter-tone piano. In 1928, with the collaboration of George

L. Weitz, Barth devised a portable instrument with two keyboards of eighty-eight notes each, the upper tuned to the regular international pitch and the other a quarter-tone lower. On this Barth gave a recital of his own music in Carnegie Hall, New York, on February 3, 1930. Six weeks later, on March 28, he appeared as a soloist with the Philadelphia Orchestra conducted by Leopold Stokowski, in the Concerto for Quarter-tone Piano and Orchestra (1928), believed to be the first quarter-tone concerto ever written. At this time Barth wrote other large-scale works in quarter tones, among these: Suite, for brass, quarter-tone strings, and kettledrums; and Piano Quintet, for quarter-tone strings and quarter-tone piano, both in 1930.

Other of Barth's compositions in succeeding years called for normal tuning. The most ambitious of these was the Symphony no. 1 (*Prince of Peace,* 1940), inspired by the life of Christ, which could be performed with pantomime. Its three movements are respectively subtitled "Accusation," "Crucifixion," and "Resurrection." This was followed by Ten Etudes, for piano and orchestra (1944), and Symphony no. 2 (1948) among other compositions.

Barth was director of the Yonkers Institute of Musical Art in Yonkers, N.Y. He also taught piano at the Mannes School of Music in New York. His last years were spent in Florida, where, from 1948 to 1956, he taught piano at the Miami Conservatory. He was the author of a piano manual, *Technic* (N.Y., 1949).

THE COMPOSER SPEAKS: Rachmaninoff once said to me: "It is not easy to be a pianist, composer, and teacher. One of them is bound to be neglected." Throughout my career I have certainly felt the truth of this statement. My compositions were written at the sacrifice of my playing and my practicing on the piano and at the sacrifice of my duties as teacher which I could not afford to drop. But composition remained always my prime artistic endeavor, and after that came my experiments with quarter-tone music. I have always been convinced that the day of quarter-tone music will inevitably come. It may even be made popular through the medium of jazz or dance music.

PRINCIPAL WORKS: 2 sonatas for piano (1929, 1932); 2 suites for piano (1938, 1941); 2 symphonies (1940, 1948).

Miragia, operetta (1916, rev. 1931); Concerto for Piano and Orchestra (1925, rev. as a concerto for two pianos and orchestra in 1928); Concerto for Quarter-tone Piano and Orchestra (1928); Suite, for brass, quarter-tone strings, and kettledrums (1930); Piano Quintet, for quarter-tone strings and quarter-tone piano (1930); Ten Etudes, for piano and orchestra (1944).

BIBLIOGRAPHY: *BBDM;* Ewen, David, *American Composers Today* (N.Y., 1949); Howard, John Tasker, *This Modern Music* (N.Y., 1942).

Bassett, Leslie Raymond, b. Hanford, Calif., January 22, 1923.

Bassett employs a modern harmonic, rhythmic, and contrapuntal rhetoric, with stress on richness of orchestral color, the colors piled up layer by layer without sacrificing finely balanced instrumental writing. His music is characterized by well-structured forms, with germinal themes given expansive growth, and his musical thoughts have mobility. In some of his compositions in the mid and late 1960s, Bassett utilized serial and electronic methods. He received the Pulitzer Prize in music in 1966.

His mother gave him his first piano lessons when he was five. Two years later his family moved to Fresno, Calif., where he attended its public schools and, in his fourteenth year, started studying the trombone, which from then on was his favorite instrument. While attending Central Union High School in Fresno he played the trombone with various jazz groups. When he was sixteen, his first attempt at composition, a march for band, received several performances. In 1940 he was graduated from high school with an award in music and a scholarship for Fresno State College. His college study was interrupted in 1942, during World War II, when he spent four years in the U.S. Army, playing the trombone with the Thirteenth Armored Division Band in California, Texas, France, and Germany, in addition to performing various military duties during hostilities. In uniform, he began making arrangements for concert groups and dance bands. Separated from the army in 1946, he resumed his studies at Fresno State College, receiving his bachelor of arts degree in music in 1947. While attending college he wrote his first concert work for orchestra, Suite in C, introduced on December 3, 1946, by the Fresno Symphony.

After receiving his master's degree in composition at the university of Michigan in 1949, where his teachers included Ross Lee Finney and Homer Keller, he was appointed a teaching fellow there. On August 21, 1949, he married Anita Denniston, a pianist, with whom he had three children (one deceased). On a Fulbright Fellowship in 1950–51 he studied composition in Paris with Arthur Honegger at the École Normale de Musique and privately with Nadia Boulanger. Subsequent study of composition took place in Michigan with Roberto Gerhard in 1960, and of electronic music with Mario Davidovsky in 1964.

In 1952, Bassett taught instrumental music in public schools in Fresno before being appointed instructor of composition at the University of Michigan School of Music. He has remained there ever since, elevated to full professor in 1965, chairman of composition department in 1970, and in 1977 named Albert A. Stanley Distinguished University Professor.

Though his early chamber music received some recognition through honorable mentions, prizes, and publication awards in the early 1950s, and though he completed two symphonies by 1959, the second written in 1955–56 and introduced in Asilomar, Calif., in July 1959 by the American Symphony Orchestra League, his maturity as a composer was not realized until he lived for two years in Rome (1961–63). As he puts it, he now had "unlimited time to work, an outlet for a large number of works, and a chance to compose for a fine symphony orchestra." Under such circumstances he wrote two important works for orchestra in which his compositorial methods, approaches, and techniques were basically crystalized. Five Movements was introduced in Rome by the RAI Orchestra under Massimo Freccia on July 5, 1962. The American premiere was given by the University of Michigan Symphony in Ann Arbor on February 7, 1964. On July 6, 1963, Ferruccio Scaglia, conducting the RAI Orchestra, gave the premiere of Bassett's Variations for Orchestra in Rome. This was the composition that brought Bassett the Pulitzer Prize in 1966 (together with a recording grant from the National Institute of Arts and Letters), after receiving its first hearing in the United States on October 22, 1965, with Eugene Ormandy conducting the Philadelphia Orchestra. "The variations," the composer explained, "are not based upon a theme. The opening motivic introduction consists of four small areas or phrases, each of which is more memorable as color or mood than as theme, and each of which serves in some respect as the source of one or more variations. . . . Naturally, the early variations expose a significant amount of material that is not directly drawn from the introduction, but which I believed would be able to project and complete the sections. The later variations take up some aspects of the introduction that may have been overlooked or minimized in earlier sections. Some of the variations are attached to those that follow or precede them, others are not. A sizable conclusion, opening rather like the beginning, completes the work, after revealing once again several of the motivic elements in climactic contest."

Bassett was one of six Americans commissioned by the National Endowment for the Arts to write compositions celebrating the American bicentennial, each composition performed by six major American orchestras. While enjoying a sabbatical leave from the university in 1973–74, with the help of a Guggenheim Fellowship, Bassett fulfilled this commission with one of his most famous works, *Echoes from an Invisible World*, for orchestra, whose world premiere was given in Philadelphia on February 27, 1976, with Eugene Ormandy conducting the Philadelphia Orchestra. Soon thereafter it was performed by the principal orchestras of Chicago, Los Angeles, New York, Boston, and Cleveland. In his description of this composition, Bassett wrote: "The title is suggestive, not descriptive. Only a few sounds could, by any stretch of the imagination, be called echoes: quiet tones that remain after a sharp attack in another instrument, repeating sounds that diminish in intensity following a sharp attack, etc. Much of the music springs, instead, from sources that are implanted within the score, yet are comparatively insignificant. One of the more obvious of these is the opening three-chord piano figure whose twelve tones recur in many guises throughout the work and contribute to the formation of other sounds and phrases. The principle of unfolding and growth from small elements is basic to the work, as is the principle of return to them. The musical material came about by very personal means, often prompted by the many exciting possibilities of orchestral texture and gesture. The three movements are similar to the extent that they end quietly, have intense passages as well as quiet ones, fluctuate between metered and unmetered music, and require extensive dividing of the strings. The outer two movements are essentially fast, the middle one slow." In his review in the *Philadelphia Evening Bulletin*, James Felton said: "Bassett uses his tone palette fully, sometimes weaving the brasses or woodwinds in separate meshes of sound, beautiful to the ear,"

In 1974, Bassett earned the Naumburg Foundation Award which made possible a recording of his Sextet (1972), a work introduced in Washington, D.C., on April 27, 1972. He received a citation and grant from the National Council for the Arts in 1978, and a second Guggenheim Fellowship in 1980. In 1981 he was elected membership to the American Academy and Institute of Arts and Letters. Festivals of Bassett's music were held at Drake University in Des Moines, Ia., and at the University of Wisconsin in River Falls, both in 1976.

Bassett was director of the contemporary musical performances project at the University of Michigan between 1969 and 1973, sponsored by the Rockefeller Foundation. From 1967 to 1970 he was a member of the policy committee of the Contemporary Music Project at the same university, sponsored by the Ford Foundation. He was guest composer at the Berkshire Music Center at Tanglewood, Mass., in 1973. In 1978 he was elected senior fellow of the Michigan Society of Fellows and named Distinguished Alumnus of the California State University in Fresno.

THE COMPOSER SPEAKS: The more we know of music and the more we live in it, the more elusive and mysterious it becomes, always changing, capable of a thousand indescribable moods, a strange and somewhat mystical power in our lives, a fascination, a challenge, a craft, a language, a house of cards—the echo from an invisible world.

PRINCIPAL WORKS: Horn Sonata (1952); Trio, for viola, clarinet, and piano (1953); Trio, for trumpet, horn, and trombone (1953); Quintet, for strings and double bass (1954); Trombone Sonata (1954); Toccata, for organ (1955); Symphony no. 2 (1955–56); Viola Sonata (1956); *Out of the Depths*, for chorus (1957); Five Pieces, for string quartet (1957); *Easter Triptych*, for tenor, chorus, brass, and percussion (1958); Woodwind Quintet (1958); Violin Sonata (1959); *Remembrance*, for chorus (1960); *Moonrise*, for women's chorus and nineteen-piece ensemble (1960); Five Movements, for orchestra (1961); "To Music," for solo voice (1962): *Ecologue, Encomium and Evocation*, for chorus (1962); String Quartet no. 3 (1962); Piano Quintet (1962); Variations for Orchestra (1963); *Images and Textures*, for orchestra (1964); *Four Statements*, for organ (1964); Three Studies in Electronic Sound (1965); *Prayers for Divine Service*, for male chorus and organ (1965); Psalm 64, for chorus (1965); Music for Cello and Piano (1966); *Notes in the Silence*, for mixed chorus and piano (1966); *Elaborations*, for piano (1966); *Triform*, for magnetic tape (1966); Nonet, for four winds, four brass, and piano (1967); Music for Alto Saxophone and Piano (1968); *Collect*, for mixed chorus and electronic tape (1969); *Colloquy*, for orchestra (1969); *Moon Canticle*, for narrator, solo cello, and mixed chorus (1969); *Celebration in Praise of Earth*, for narrator, mixed chorus, and orchestra (1970); Sextet, for two violins, two violas, cello, and piano (1971); *Forces*, for solo violin, solo cello, piano, and orchestra (1972); *Sounds Remembered*, for violin and piano (1972); *The Wind and Earth*, for mixed chorus and piano (1973); *The Jade Garden*, for soprano and piano (1973); *Time and Beyond*, for baritone, clarinet and piano (1973); Chamber Music, for four horns (1974); Twelve Duos, for two or four trombones (1974); *Echoes from an Invisible World*, for orchestra (1975); Wind Music, for wind sextet (1975); *Soliloquies*, for solo clarinet (1976); Concerto for Two Pianos and Orchestra (1976); String Quartet no. 4 (1978).

BIBLIOGRAPHY: *Asterisk: A Journal of New Music*, May 1976; BMI, *The Many Worlds of Music*, July 1966; *Bulletin of the National Association of Teachers of Singing*, December 1975.

Bauer, Marion Eugenie, b. Walla Walla, Wash., August 15, 1887; d. South Hadley, Mass., August 9, 1955.

In addition to being a prolific and successful composer of music mainly in impressionist and post-romantic styles and often in shorter forms, Marion Bauer was influential in American music as educator, author, critic, editor, and as a promoter of new music.

Both her parents were French, her mother a linguist and scholar who was a professor of languages at Whitman College in Walla Walla. Her father was a merchant who played in a military band during the Civil War and who possessed a fine singing voice. It

was from her father that Marion inherited both her love and talent for music. Upon his death when she was three, her family moved to Portland, Oreg. There, Marion received her academic education in public schools, then at St. Helen's Hall, where she revealed an equal gift for music, writing, and drawing. By the time she graduated from St. Helen's Hall, just before she was sixteen, she had abandoned her original intention to become a teacher like her mother and to concentrate on music. To achieve this goal, she came to New York, there to study piano and harmony with Henry Holden Huss. "Almost coincidental with my first harmony lesson," she reveals, "I began writing songs." The first was "Light," to a poem by Gouverneur Morris, which was published and sung in the concert hall in 1911 by the renowned diva, Ernestine Schumann-Heink.

Having been hired in 1905 by Raoul Pugno, eminent French pianist on a visit to the United States, to teach his daughter English, Marion Bauer was invited to return with the Pugno family to France and live with them at their country house in Gargenville (Seine et Oise). Pugno gave her lessons in piano. After returning to New York in 1907, Marion Bauer studied theory with Eugene Heffley, who encouraged her to spend more time in composition. Another influential figure at this juncture in her life was the conductor Walter Henry Rothwell, who was so impressed by some of her compositions that he urged her to go to Germany for intensive study. The year of 1910–11 was spent in Berlin, where a concert of her songs was given and where she studied counterpoint and musical form with Paul Ertel. Back in the United States in 1912, she kept on writing songs, some of which were published by Arthur P. Schmidt of Boston, who gave her a seven-year contract. Nine songs were written in 1912 and five more in 1914, in addition to a suite of little piano pieces, *In the Country* (1913), and *Up the Ocklawaha* (1913), for violin and piano, the latter written for and introduced by violin virtuoso Maud Powell, and all were published by Schmidt.

During World War I, Bauer studied composition with Rothwell. After the war, she wrote more piano and chamber music as well as songs and such compositions as *Three Impressions* (1918), Six Preludes (1922), and *From New Hampshire Woods* (1923), all for the piano; *Allegro giocoso*, for eleven instruments (1920); and a Violin Sonata (1921). A movement from *From New Hampshire Woods*—"Indian Piper"—was orchestrated by Martin Bernstein in 1928 and performed that summer in Chautauqua, N.Y.

Feeling the need for additional training, Bauer went back to Europe in May 1923 to spend three years in France. "These were some of the richest years in my life from the standpoint of study and development," she recalled. In addition to meeting and becoming friendly with many prominent musicians in Paris, from whose advice and guidance she profited considerably, she underwent a season of study of the fugue with André Gédalge.

Returning to New York, she joined the music faculty of New York University in 1926, where she remained for the next twenty-five years, becoming assistant professor in 1927 and associate professor and acting head of the music department in 1930. In 1940, she joined the faculty of the Institute of Musical Art, where, after it was combined with the Juilliard School of Music, she stayed until her death. During these years she was also affiliated as teacher with the summer school at Mills College in California, the Carnegie Institute of Technology, Teachers' College of Columbia University, and the New York School of Music among other educational institutions.

Her first affiliation as promoter of new music came in 1921 when she helped to found the short-lived American Music Guild in New York to perform the works of American composers. Despite its brief existence it set the stage for other, similar organizations in New York, the most important being the League of Composers (organized in 1923), of which she became a member of the executive board in 1926. From then on she was a vital force in that organization for the promotion of new music, foreign as well as American. She also used her pen to propagandize modern music: as music critic of the *Evening Mail* in New York; music critic and New York editor of the *Musical Leader*; author of numerous articles published in music journals and encyclopedias and of *Twentieth Century Music* (1933). Outside the field of modern music, with Ethel Peyser as her collaborator, she wrote three other successful books on music: *How Music Grew* (1925), *Music Through the Ages* (1932), and *How Opera Grew* (1955).

In her compositions, which now branched out into ambitious choral and orchestral works, she betrayed the influence of her education and experiences in Paris. Her style was melodically and harmonically oriented to the French tradition, sometimes French postromanticism, occasionally impressionism. Though as a writer, teacher, and member of the League of Composers, she was a strong advocate of the newer trends in music of the 1930s and 1940s, she herself preferred to adopt a more conservative posture, concentrating on solidity of form, emotional, and atmospheric expressiveness and always with an emphasis on what sounded pleasant to the ear. She was best in the smaller forms, the songs and piano pieces, but her lyrical invention, her richly colored harmonic palette, her contrapuntal skill, served her well in some of her larger works, which received significant performances: Sonata for Viola and Piano (1936; N.Y., March 23, 1936); Concertino, for oboe, clarinet, and string quartet (1940), commissioned by the League of Composers for broadcast over the CBS radio network in 1940; Symphonic Suite, for string orchestra (1940; Chautauqua, N.Y., August 20, 1941); *American Youth Concerto*, for piano and or-

chestra (1943; N.Y., May 1943); *China*, a major work for chorus and orchestra (1944), text by Boris Todrin (Worcester Festival, Mass., October 12, 1945); and *Sun Splendor*, written as a piano piece in 1926 and orchestrated by the composer in 1934, performed by the Philadelphia Orchestra under Leopold Stokowski on October 25, 1947.

A concert of her compositions was heard in New York on May 8, 1951, "one of the great events of my professional career," she called it. One month later she was awarded an honorary doctorate in music by the New York College of Music.

PRINCIPAL WORKS: *From New Hamphsire Woods*, suite for piano (1923); Four Songs, for voice and piano (1924); *Sun Splendor*, for piano (1924, orchestrated in 1934), String Quartet (1928); *Fantasia quasi una sonata*, for violin and piano (1928); Songs from *Alice in Wonderland*, for voice and piano, 1928); Three Noëls, for chorus and piano (1929); Four Piano Pieces (1930); Dance Sonata, for piano (1932); Duo, for oboe and clarinet (1932); *Ragpicker's Love*, a cycle of songs for voice and string quartet (1935); Viola Sonata no. 1 (1935); *A Lament*, for orchestra (1935); *Pan,* choreographic sketch for seven instruments (1937); *A Garden Is a Lovesome Thing*, for chorus and piano (1938); *The Thinker*, for chorus and piano (1938); *Five Greek Lyrics,* for solo flute (1938); *Here at High Morning*, for mixed voices and piano (1938); Oboe Sonatina (1939); Concertino for Oboe, Clarinet, and String Quartet (1940); Symphonic Suite (1940); *American Youth Concerto*, for piano and orchestra (1943); *China*, for chorus and orchestra (1944); *Two Aquarelles*, for piano (1945); Prelude and Fugue, for flute and strings (1949); Viola Sonata no. 2 (1950); Symphony (1950); Meditation and Toccata, for organ (1951); Trio no. 2, for flute, cello, and piano (1951); *Death Spreads His Gentle Wings*, for mixed a cappella chorus (1951); *A Foreigner Comes to Earth on Boston Common*, for chorus (1951).

BIBLIOGRAPHY: *BBDM*; Ewen, David, *Composers Since 1900* (N.Y., 1969); Goss, Madeleine, *Modern Music Makers* (N.Y., 1952); Howard, John Tasker, *Our Contemporary Composers* (N.Y., 1941); *Musical America* (obituary), September 1955; *Who's Who in America, 1954–55.*

Bazelon, Irwin Allen, b. Evanston, Ill., June 4, 1922.

As a functional composer, Bazelon has been a contributor of music for television (commercials) and TV and motion picture documentaries. As a serious composer, he has produced a library of highly esteemed concert works. The serious composer has been influenced by the functional one in his expertise in writing for instrumental ensembles, his sensitive ear for unusual instrumental colorations, abstract melodic lines, and in the way popular elements some-times intrude into his serious writing.

He is of American-Russian parentage; his uncle, David L. Bazelon, was chief justice of the United States Court of Appeals in Washington, D.C.

Because in his sixth year an affliction, the conse-quence of scarlet fever, left him permanently with a semideaf left ear, Bazelon was shy and introspective while receiving his academic education in Chicago's public schools. He was, nevertheless, active in sports, played on the baseball team of Senn High School, and dreamed of becoming a big leaguer. Music con-sciousness came comparatively late. When he was about seventeen he heard a concert by the Chicago Symphony and was "seduced" by its sound. "I have been a happy victim of that seduction ever since," he says. His musical activity began with improvisations on the piano, after which he took lessons with Irving Harris. Upon graduating from high school in Chica-go in 1941, he spent almost two years at Northwest-ern University in Evanston, Ill., before entering De Paul University. There he studied piano with Mag-dalen Messmann and composition with Leon Stein, who became a powerful influence in awakening Ba-zelon's ambition to become a composer. At De Paul he received his bachelor of arts degree in 1945 and his master of arts degree one year later.

For six months after that he studied composition at Yale with Paul Hindemith, to whom he did not take favorably. "I could not take his Prussian taskmaster tactics," Bazelon explains. A far more potent in-fluence in his early development as composer was Darius Milhaud, with whom he studied composition between 1946 and 1948 at Mills College in Oakland, Calif. During this time, in 1947, he also studied ad-vanced analysis with Ernest Bloch at the University of California in Berkeley. Bazelon's String Quartet no. 2 (1947) was premiered in New York in 1948 and received a prize in competition conducted by the National Federation of Music Clubs.

In 1948 he came to New York. For the next seven years he earned his living as a railroad reservation clerk. Now with the help of a psychiatrist he was able "to find my true potential." No less important, the psychiatrist sent him to an ear surgeon who oper-ated on Bazelon and cleared up his inner-ear afflic-tion. "The violent, silent world inside me erupted," he recalls. "I came out of my shell." Professionally, he embarked in a new direction by producing func-tional music, becoming the "father of contemporary music commercials" on television. His first commer-cial was for Ipana toothpaste in 1953, followed by similar chores for Buitoni, Noxzema, and others. He also wrote music for television and motion-picture documentaries; and he created the nine-second mu-sical signature used by NBC-TV to end its broad-casts between 1961 and 1971. He wrote the inciden-tal music for two productions of the American Shakespeare Theater in Stratford, Conn., *The Tam-ing of the Shrew* (1958) and *The Merry Wives of Windsor* (1959). In 1959 he provided the back-ground music for the NBC television special *What Makes Sammy Run?*

The writing of compositions with a more serious intent was not neglected. Piano Sonata no. 1 (1947) was performed in New York at a concert of the League of Composers in 1948. Several other compo-sitions were heard at performances of the Interna-tional Society for Contemporary Music in New York: Suite for Clarinet, Cello, and Piano (1947), Piano Sonata no. 2 (1949) and Five Pieces, for piano (1950). A concert of his chamber music was given at Columbia University through the auspices of the Alice Ditson Foundation in 1949.

On a commission from the dancer Valerie Bettis, he wrote Ballet Suite (1949), the score for a ballet produced in New London, Conn., at the summer Dance Festival in 1950. *Movimento da camera*, for harpsichord, bassoon, horn, and flute (1955), com-missioned by the American Associated Gallery, re-ceived its premiere on January 20, 1957, in New York. Chamber Symphony, for seven instruments (1957), commissioned by the New York Philhar-monic Chamber Ensemble, was performed by that group under the aegis of Mitropoulos in New York on December 16, 1956. Piano Sonata no. 3 (1952) was given its first performance on a program devoted to MacDowell Colony composers sponsored by the Julius Hartt School of Music in New Haven.

Bazelon's most successful concert work to this time was also the first time a major orchestra played his music and the first time he appeared as conductor. All this happened with Short Symphony (Symphony no. 2), subtitled *Testimony to a Great City* (1962). With a demonstration record paid for with winnings at a racetrack (for which Bazelon has had a lifelong fascination) Bazelon was able to convince Howard Mitchell, music director of the National Symphony Orchestra in Washington, D.C., to program it. Mit-chell went one step further by inviting Bazelon to conduct the premiere performance on December 4, 1962. Energized by driving rhythmic patterns (a bat-tery of percussion included drum, gongs, cowbells, woodblocks, xylophone, glockenspiel) and a power-ful momentum, this symphony reflected big-city life with music of nervous tensions, dynamic energy and restlessness and infectious exuberance. The Louis-ville Orchestra under Robert Whitney then per-formed this symphony in March 1966 and recorded it two months later, and Sixten Ehrling invited Ba-zelon to conduct two performances of the work with the Detroit Symphony at Meadowbrook, Mich., dur-ing the summer of 1967.

The feverish tempo of the city continued to in-fluence a good deal of Bazelon's music after that. Sometimes he used twelve-tone organization; some-times jazz fragments invaded the texture of his writ-ing. But neither practice was strict, formal, or con-sistent. Rebellious cross rhythms. powerful sonori-ties, contrasting tone colors, occasional discordant harmonies, all brought muscular strength to his music.

Bazelon did not lack important performances after his Short Symphony. His Symphony no. 1, which had preceded the Short Symphony by two years, was finally heard on November 29, 1963, performed by the Kansas City Philharmonic. His Brass Qunitet (1963), commissioned by the American Brass Quintet, was performed by that group in New York on March 22, 1964. On February 21, 1966, *Dramatic Movement*, for orchestra (1965), was premiered in Seattle by the Seattle Symphony under Milton Katims, after which it became a focal point of a one-hour documentary on the Seattle Symphony, *To See a Sound*, telecast throughout the Northwest. *Excursions*, for orchestra (1965), was commissioned by Hans Schwieger, the conductor of the Kansas City Philharmonic, which introduced it in Kansas City on March 5, 1966. Symphony no. 5 (1967) got its initial hearing on May 9, 1969, performed by the Indianapolis Symphony under Izler Solomon. *Symphonie concertante*, for clarinet, trumpet, marimba, and orchestra (1969), was written for Sixten Ehrling, music director of the Detroit Symphony. *Dramatic Fanfare for 1970* (1970) was one of two compositions awarded first prize by the Blossom Festival in a competition for fanfares in which 158 composers submitted pieces; the Cleveland Symphony performed it at the Blossom Festival on June 23, 1970.

Meanwhile, in April 1968, Bazelon had completed the score for a documentary film produced by Jules Dassin with a script by Irwin Shaw about the six-day war in Israel, entitled *Survival 1967*. On a commission from Temple B'nai Jehudah of Kansas City for its centennial commemoration, Bazelon adapted this music into his Symphony no. 6 (1970), which the Kansas City Philharmonic, under the composer's direction, performed on November 17, 1970.

Bazelon's major works since 1970 are the Concerto for Fourteen Players, subtitled *Churchill Downs*, a token of his love for the racetrack (1970; N.Y., May 16, 1971); Woodwind Quintet (1975; N.Y., May 22, 1975); *A Quiet Piece—for a Violent Time* (1975; New Orleans, October 28, 1975), commissioned by the New Orleans Symphony; *Double Crossings*, for trumpet and percussion (1976; Boston and N.Y., December 5, 1976); *Sound Dreams*, for six instruments (1977; Boston, November 13, 1977), inspired by and dedicated to Bazelon's friend, James Jones, the novelist; and *De-Tonations*, for brass quintet and orchestra, commissioned by the American Brass Quintet with a grant from the National Endowment for the Arts (1978; N.Y., April 3, 1979).

On February 5, 1960, Bazelon married Cecile Gray, a professional painter. He was composer-in-residence at Wolf Trap in Virginia in 1974. In 1977, he wrote the music for *Wilma*, an NCB-TV *Movie of the Week*. He is the author of *Knowing the Score: Notes on Film Music* (N.Y., 1975).

THE COMPOSER SPEAKS: I like fast over slow, high over low, loudness to softness. I'm a dramatic composer. My music snarls rather than caresses, but I am not afraid to write a melody.

PRINCIPAL WORKS: 7 symphonies (1960–79); 3 piano sonatas (1947, 1949, 1952); 2 string quartets (1947, 1947).

Ballet Suite, for small ensemble (1949); Concert Overture, for orchestra (1952, revised 1960); *Movimento da camera*, for flute, hassoon, horn, and harpsichord (1955); Adagio and Fugue, for string orchestra (1956); Suite, for small orchestra (1956); Chamber Symphony, for seven instruments (1957); Ballet *Centauri, 17*, for orchestra (1960); Brass Quintet, 1963); *Excursions*, for orchestra (1965); *Symphonie concertante*, for clarinet, trumpet, marimba, and orchestra (1969); *Dramatic Fanfare for 1970* (1970); Duo, for viola and piano (1970); Chamber Concerto, (*Churchill Downs*), for fourteen players (1970); *Propulsions*, concerto for seven percussion players (1974); *A Quiet Piece—for a Violent Time*, for orchestra (1975); Woodwind Quintet (1975); *Double Crossings*, for trumpet and percussion (1976); *Concatenations*, for percussion quartet and viola (1977); *Sound Dreams*, for six instruments (1977); *De-Tonations*, for brass quintet and orchestra (1978); *Imprints on Ivory and Strings*, for piano (1978); *Cross-Currents*, for brass quintet and percussion (1978).

BIBLIOGRAPHY: *Newsweek*, December 17, 1962; *Time*, May 20, 1966.

Beach, H.H.A., Mrs. (originally **Cheney, Amy Marcy**), b. Henniker, N.H., September 5, 1867; d. New York City, December 27, 1944.

She was the most prominent woman composer of her time, one of the first women composers to write in the larger forms, the first American woman to get recognition abroad, and the first American woman musician to receive all her training in the United States. Like her distinguished colleagues of the New England School of Composers of the late 19th and early 20th centuries (Chadwick, Foote, Parker), she was a classicist in her architectonic structures and a romanticist in her melodic and harmonic content.

She was the only child of New Englanders of colonial descent. Highly precocious in music, she would sing tunes on pitch when she was just one year old. By the time she was four she was composing melodies on the piano. Her mother, a trained pianist and singer, began giving her piano lessons when Amy was six. A year later, the child gave a piano recital which featured several of her own waltzes. In 1875, when she was eight, her family moved to Boston, where she attended W. Whittemore's private school for her academic education while studying piano with Ernest Perabo between 1876 and 1882 and, in 1881–82, harmony with Junius W. Hill, the only theoretical instruction she ever received. She subsequently received some coaching at the piano from Carl Baermann.

When she was sixteen, she made her concert debut on October 24. 1883, in Boston, performing a piano concerto by Ignaz Moscheles with orchestra and Chopin's Rondo in E-flat as a solo. This was followed by piano recitals and, on March 28, 1885, by a highly successful appearance with the Boston Symphony conducted by Wilhelm Gericke in Chopin's Concerto in F minor.

When, on December 3, 1885, she married Dr. H.H.A. Beach, a distinguished Boston surgeon and her senior by twenty-four years, she greatly relaxed her concert activity to devote herself more conscientiously to composition. In this she was encouraged by her husband, an excellent amateur musician. From this time on, both in her later concert appearances and in her publications, she assumed the name of "Mrs. H.H.A. Beach" exclusively (initials only). To develop her creative ability she went through an intensive period of autodidactic study and analysis of the music of the masters, and of poring through the theoretical treatises of Gevaert and Berlioz which she translated into English. Her first attempts at composition were small pieces for the piano, but in 1886 she started to work on a major opus, the Mass in E-flat, which took her three years to write. Introduced by the Handel and Haydn Society in Boston on February 18, 1892, the Mass became the first work by a woman to be performed by that historic organization. The premiere of her concert aria "Eilende Wolken" in New York the following winter was the first work by a woman ever given by the New York Symphony Society. A year later, *Festival Jubilate*, for chorus and orchestra, which had been commissioned for the dedication of the Women's Building at the World's Columbia Exposition in Chicago, was premiered. Her most important work for orchestra—the *Gaelic Symphony*, based on Gaelic folk tunes—proved so successful when first performed on October 30, 1896, by the Boston Symphony under Emil Paur that within the next few years it was heard in New York, San Francisco, Buffalo, Kansas City, and Brooklyn. She herself assisted Franz Kneisel in the first performance of her Violin Sonata in New York in January 1897; in 1898 her *Song of Welcome* was heard at the Trans-Mississippi Exposition in Omaha, which had commissioned it; and on April 6, 1900, she was the soloist with the Boston Symphony, Wilhelm Gericke conducting, in the first performance of her Piano Concerto no. 1, which she later performed with major orchestras in Chicago, Pittsburgh, St. Louis, and Los Angeles. She was also highly successful as a composer of songs, producing more than a hundred and fifty settings of French, German, and British poetry. The most popular were "Ah, Love, but a Day," "Ecstasy," and "The Year's at the Spring," all three to poems by Browning and the last of these often sung by the distinguished American soprano Emma Eames. Notable pieces for solo piano included Ballad, Four Sketches, and *Trois morceaux caractéristiques* among her earlier works; *Hermit Thrush at Morn*, and Five Improvisations, among the later ones. Despite her productivity in all areas of music except opera, only three of her compositions failed to get published, a remarkable accomplishment for any composer, let alone a woman of the late 19th and early 20th centuries.

After the death of her husband on June 28, 1910, Mrs. Beach paid her first visit to Europe. She remained abroad from 1911 to 1914, concertizing extensively in recitals in which she often featured her own pieces, appearing as soloist in her Piano Concerto in Berlin, Leipzig, and Hamburg, and participating in presentations of her Violin Sonata and Piano Quintet. She was so warmly acclaimed by critics and public that in Germany she became one of America's most highly esteemed composers.

After returning to the United States in 1914 she made her home in New York City, from which she embarked on numerous concert tours during the next quarter century. All the while she continued to compose. When in her later years she ended her concert work and was no longer able to promote her own music, the popularity of most of her compositions, particularly the larger ones, went into a decline. After her death of a heart attack, her works lapsed into almost total oblivion. But almost four decades after her death, a revival of interest in her music began in the United States in 1976 when Mary Louise Boehm and the American Symphony Orchestra under Morton Gould reintroduced the Piano Concerto no. 1 in New York (its first revival since 1917). A year later, Nonesuch Records released recordings of her Piano Quintet and the Piano Concerto no. 1, and Genesis Records issued an album of her solo piano music. Her Piano Trio, written in 1938 when she was seventy-one, was one of the compositions in the collection *Chamber Music by Woman Composers* in a 1979 Vox album. All this provided testimony that her fame in her own lifetime was well deserved and that she did not deserve her subsequent oblivion. The music in these recordings revealed that she had her own personality in the grace and charm of her expressivity, originality of phrase and a rich imagination in developing her musical thought. One critic (Richard Freed in *Stereo Review*) said of her "Fireflies" for piano from Four Sketches: "a gem, the sort of thing that would immortalize any composer." A critic for *High Fidelity/Musical America* regarded her Piano Concerto no. 1 as superior to the early D-minor Concerto of Edward MacDowell, which had made such a profound impression on Liszt. Peter G. Davis, reviewing the recording of the Piano Trio in the *New York Times*, found it "attractive and distinctively original. . . . [It] has fire, intensity, a striking melodic profile, an interesting impressionistic coloration and not a note is wasted." Davis added: "In fact, the more one hears of this composer the more she appears to be among the leading talents in American music during the early years of the 20th century."

In June 1928, Mrs. Beach was awarded an honorary master of arts degree by the University of New Hampshire. The Beaches were childless.

THE COMPOSER SPEAKS: I have literally lived the life of two people, one a pianist, and the other a writer. Anything more unlike than the state of mind demanded by these two professions I could not imagine! When I do one kind of work, I shut the other up in a closed room and lock the door, unless I happen to be composing for the piano, in which case there is a connecting link. One great advantage, however, in this kind of life is that one never grows stale, but there is always a continual interest and freshness from the change back and forth.

PRINCIPAL WORKS (opus numbers are used where the year of composition is not available): *Valse-Caprice*, for piano, op. 4; Mass in E-flat, for vocal soloists, chorus, orchestra, and organ (1889); Ballad, for piano., op. 6; Four Sketches, for piano, op. 15; *The Minstrel and the King*, cantata for vocal soloists, chorus, and orchestra, op. 16; *Festival Jubilate*, for chorus and orchestra (1892); *Gaelic Symphony* (1896); Violin Sonata in A minor (1896); *Song of Welcome*, for chorus and orchestra (1898); Piano Concerto no. 1 (1900); Piano Quintet (1908); *Panama Hymn*, for chorus and orchestra (1915); *The Chambered Nautilus*, for solo voices, chorus, and orchestra, op. 66; *Te Deum*, for chorus (1922); *Canticles of the Sun*, for vocal soloists, chorus, and orchestra (1925); String Quartet (1929); *Hermit Thrush at Morn*, for piano, op. 92, no. 2; Nocturne, for piano, op. 107; *Christ in the Universe*, for chorus and orchestra (1931); Five Improvisations, for piano, op. 148; Piano Trio (1938).

Also: cantatas, *The Rose of Avontown, Sylvania, The Sea Fairies*; Variations on Balkan Themes, for two pianos; Piano Concerto no. 2; *Bal masqué*, for orchestra; *Cabildo*, one-act opera.

BIBLIOGRAPHY: *BBDM*; Goetschius, Percy, *Mrs. H.H.A. Beach, Analytical Sketch* (Boston, 1906); Howard, John Tasker, *Our American Music* (N.Y., 1946); *Etude*, March 1943; *Musical Quarterly*, July 1940.

Becker, John Joseph, b. Henderson, Ky., January 22, 1886; d. Wilmette, Ill., January 21, 1961.

In the early 1930s he was a potent crusader in the Midwest for the more progressive American composers of the 1920s. As a composer, he anticipated later experiments with multimedia productions besides making a successful rapprochement between the style and techniques of polyphonic composers before Bach and 20th-century America.

He received his academic education in a high school in Evansville, Ind. and at St. Mary's of the Spring, near Columbus, Ohio, where he received his bachelor of arts degree in 1907. At the same time his musical training took place at Kruger Conservatory in Cincinnati, Ohio, from which he graduated in 1905. While serving as professor of piano and composition at Kidd-Key Conservatory at North Texas College for Women in Sherman between 1906 and 1914, he attended the Wisconsin Conservatory of Music in Milwaukee, studying theory, harmony, and conducting with Alexander von Fielitz in 1907–08, composition with Carl Busch in 1908, and, subsequently, counterpoint with Wilhelm Middleschulte, under whose guidance he eventually (1923) earned his doctorate in music. Middleschulte, an outstanding author on the polyphonic era preceding Johann Sebastian Bach and on Bach himself, exerted a profound influence on Becker and encouraged him to do research in early Catholic polyphonic music (Palestrina, Victoria, de Lassus) and in their influence on later centuries. The impact of this research affected Becker's future religious compositions both for the church and for concert hall. Becker combined the polyphonic methods, mysticism, and religiosity of this early Catholic polyphonic art with the strident dissonances of the 20th century, so much so that Becker came to be known as "the 16th-century modernist." In this area lie such compositions as the *Missa Symphonica*, for male chorus (1933), *Mass in Honor of the Sacred Heart* (1944) and *Moments from the Passion* (1945).

From 1918 to 1928 Becker was the head of the department of fine arts and director of the glee club at Notre Dame University, where he continued to do research under Middleschulte. After that, Becker taught in several other Catholic institutions. In 1928–29 he was assistant dean of the college of St. Mary's of the Spring, and from 1928 to 1935 he was chairman of the fine arts department at the College of St. Thomas in St. Paul. He was dismissed from the latter post when that department was disbanded. After a six-year hiatus as Minnesota State director for the Federal Music Project between 1935 and 1941, he served as professor of music at Barat College of the Sacred Heart at Lake Forest, Ill., between 1943 and 1957. He was also on the faculty of the Chicago Musical College in 1949–50.

In the early 1930s, Becker was drawn into the orbit of modern American music through personal associations with such American modernists as Cowell, Ruggles, Ives, and Riegger. Becker allied himself with the new movements in American music by serving between 1936 and 1940 on the editorial board of the *New Music Quarterly*, which had been founded by Cowell to publish and promote new American music. He also did valuable missionary work in the Midwest for new American music by promoting early in 1933 a series of radio broadcasts of "the ultra-modern composers of America." Additionally, as conductor of the St. Paul Chamber Orchestra he presented public concerts of modern American music, much of which was then getting its first hearing in the Midwest. One of these concerts, which had taken place on May 25, 1933, was revived in New York City on May 4, 1975: a program featuring works by Cowell, Ruggles, and Ives in addition to Becker's own *Concerto arabesque,* for piano and orchestra (1931; St. Paul, December 7, 1931).

During this period of close personal and artistic affiliation with ultramoderns in American music, his own writing underwent transformation. In his earliest works he had been alternately romantic or impressionistic. Then discords and polytonal writing began to invade his style. After 1930, his work became discordant, percussive, polytonal at the same time aspiring toward an American identity through its ruggedness and vigor. In a series of eight compositions for various solo instruments or combinations of instruments, collectively entitled *Soundscapes,* he favored abstract forms.

He also began to experiment with dance as an important adjunct of his music. *Abongo* (1932), a primitive dance, was written for a large percussion ensemble, two solo dancers, and a dance group. *Dance Figure* (1932), based on a canto by Ezra Pound, was for a singer, a dance group, and orchestra. In 1932 he evolved a new dramatic form which he called "polyart theater": *Stagework No. 4,* based on the Andreyev drama *The Life of Man.* This was a multimedia production requiring not only theater and music but also poetry, mime, lights, and dance. Becker continued this theatrical experiment three years later with what he himself regarded as his magnum opus: *A Marriage with Space,* or *Stagework No. 3* (1935), requiring for its performance colors, lights, recitations, a solo dancer, a group of dancers and a large orchestra. Later works combining music and dance were *Nostalgic Songs of Earth,* three dances for solo dancer and piano (1938; Northfield, Minn., December 12, 1938) and *Vigilante,* for solo dancer, piano and percussion (1938; Northfield, Minn., December 12, 1938).

Experimentation of a different order is found in other notable works. In his symphonies, he realized new orchestral sounds by juxtaposing contrasting instruments which have no relationship to each other as far as their orchestral color is concerned, and in so doing he brought the science of orchestration to a new advancement. His Symphony no. 1, *Etude Primitive* (1915), was introduced at the University of Minnesota on June 17, 1936; his last symphony, based on *Sermon on the Mount,* was left unfinished. In some of his choral compositions he increased dramatic interest and expressivity by including a spoken text (by a narrator and a chorus) alternating with sung passages, as in *Moments from the Liturgy.*

In 1943 Becker moved to Chicago. By that time his aggressive propagandizing of new American music was over. From this time until his death he continued his career as composer in comparative neglect and obscurity.

THE COMPOSER SPEAKS: The duty of every creative artist is clear. There must be no compromise with mediocrity. There must be a constant striving for perfection. All resources of perfection must be mastered, but this is not enough. The composer must add new resources, evolve new techniques, develop new sound patterns, new harmonies, new contrapuntal procedures, new musical ideals, new approaches to orchestral writing, and he must mold them into new forms of beauty. Accomplishing this, he adds new formulae to the ever-changing laws of artistic creation.

PRINCIPAL WORKS: 8 *Soundscapes,* for various combinations of instruments (1932–59); 7 symphonies (1915–54); 2 piano concertos (1930, 1938).

The Mountain, for orchestra (1912); *Rouge Bouquet,* for male chorus, trumpet, and piano (1917); *Fantasia tragica,* for organ (1920); *A Heine Cycle,* eight songs for high voice and piano (1924); *An American Sonata,* for violin and piano (1926); *Two Poems of Departure,* for soprano and piano (1927); *Out of the Cradle Endlessly Rocking,* cantata for speaker, soprano, tenor, chorus, and orchestra (1929); *Concerto arabesque,* for piano and orchestra (1930); *Dance Figure,* for singer, dance group and orchestra (1932); *Stagework No. 4,* a mixed-media production (1932); *Concertino pastorale, A Forest Rhapsodie,* for two flutes and orchestra (1933); *Abongo, Dance Primitive,* for two solo dancers, dance group, and percussion (1932); Concerto for Horn and Small Orchestra (1933); *Mockery: A Scherzo,* for dance group and piano or chamber orchestra (1933); *Missa Symphonica,* for male chorus (1933); Four Songs from the Japanese, for soprano and piano (1934); *A Marriage with Space (Stagework No. 3),* a mixed-media production (1935); *Psalms of Love,* for soprano and piano (1935); Viola Concerto (1937); *Nostalgic Songs of Earth,* three dances for solo dancer and piano (1938); *Vigilante,* for solo dancer, piano, and percussion (1938); *A Dance,* for percussion orchestra (1938); *Rain Down Death,* Orchestral Suite no. 1 (1939); *Privilege and Private,* "a playful affair with music" (1940); *When the Willow Nods,* Orchestral Suite no. 2 (1940); *Antigone,* symphonic dances (1940); *Lincoln's Gettysburg Address,* for speaker, chorus, and orchestra (1941); *The Snow Goose: A Legend of World War II,* for orchestra (1944); *Mass in Honor of the Sacred Heart,* for female chorus (1944); *Deirdre of the Sorrows,* lyric drama (1945); *Moments from the Liturgy,* for speaker, women's voices, vocal solos, and singing and speaking choruses (1948); Violin Concerto (1948); *Faust,* monodrama (1951).

BIBLIOGRAPHY: *NGDMM;* Chase, Gilbert, *America's Music* (N.Y., 1955); Howard, John Tasker, *Our*

Contemporary Composers (N.Y., 1941); *Musical Quarterly*, April 1976.

Beeson, Jack Hamilton, b. Muncie, Ind., July 15, 1921.

A boyhood passion for opera carried him into an arena in which his creativity came to full power. His writing is tonal and diatonic, consistently lyrical, occasionally witty, and ever fastidious in molding music to the rhythms of English speech patterns.

Born half paralyzed and with a broken left arm, Jack Beeson was given just six months to live when he was six. He managed to confound medical prognoses—in fact, to puzzle even specialists of later years—by surviving. His metabolic disorder led him to an introspective life which helped to nurture his innate love for music and a compulsion to make and invent it, though there was little at home or in his town to provide stimulation. His academic schooling took place at Washington Elementary School, McKinley Junior High School and Central Senior High School, all in Muncie. He was only seven when he asked his parents for a piano, which he then studied privately with Luella Weimer from his seventh to his fifteenth years. Listening to the Saturday afternoon broadcasts of the Metropolitan Opera made him such an opera aficionado that, with his savings, he acquired various piano scores of operatic masterpieces, and when these operas were broadcast he "accompanied" the performances. This fascination for opera led him, when he was about fifteen, to write a rhymed five-act libretto based on Shelley's *Beatrice Cenci*, but by the time he had written the music for the first scene he came to the conclusion that writing an opera was still beyond his capabilities. Nevertheless, in his teenage years he made two more aborted attempts: *Redwing*, based on an Indian legend, and *Manfred*, based on Byron.

In 1936, Luella Weimer turned Beeson over to Percival Owen, a Canadian who had studied with Leschetizky, and who had come to Muncie to teach at Ball State Teachers College. This period of instruction, which included theory and music history with Owen's assistant, lasted three years. At this time Beeson also learned to play clarinet and xylophone.

When Beeson was a high school sophomore, as a grade-A student he was given official permission to attend school only in the morning so that he could spend the rest of the time practicing and composing. At seventeen, on the advice of Percival Owen, Beeson went to Toronto, where he gained certificates in both piano and theory at the Royal Conservatory.

Upon graduating from Central Senior High School in 1939, he entered the Eastman School of Music in Rochester, N.Y., on an honorary fellowship. He studied composition with Bernard Rogers and Burrill Phillips (and later with Howard Hanson) while electing many liberal arts courses. He received a bachelor in music degree in 1942 and a master in music in 1943, and in 1943–44 he worked toward a doctorate in music. Between 1942 and 1944 he was a teaching fellow in theory at Columbia.

When his father died in the spring of 1944, leaving him financially independent for a while, he decided to terminate his studies at the Eastman School without completing the requirements for the doctorate. He came to New York, where, in addition to studying composition with Béla Bartók in 1944–45, he did undergraduate work in conducting and graduate study in musicology at Columbia University between 1945 and 1947. At Columbia, he served as assistant in music (1945–46), associate (1946–47), and assistant professor (1947–51). His dormant interest in opera was reawakened at Columbia when he became involved with its opera workshop and its opera-production setup, serving as coach, assistant, and associate conductor of both the workshop and the opera productions of the Columbia Opera Theater Associates.

On August 20, 1947, Beeson married Nora Beate Sigerist. They had two children, one of whom (a son) was a fatal victim of an automobile accident when he was twenty-five. In 1948–49, the Beesons lived in Rome as a beneficiary of the Prix de Rome of the American Academy, remaining there one year on both a continuation of the Rome prize and a Fulbright Fellowship. During this stay, Beeson completed his first opera, *Jonah* (1950), based on a play by Paul Goodman to Beeson's own libretto. Though it received special mention in the 1951 La Scala International Opera Competition, it was never produced.

Beeson's second completed work for the musical stage, and his first to be produced, was a one-act chamber opera, *Hello, Out There*, adapted by the composer from a play by William Saroyan (1951; New York, May 27, 1954). With just one central plot and two main characters, this little opera already gave evidence of Beeson's natural gift for lyrical and atmospheric writing.

The Sweet Bye and Bye (1956, rev. 1958), though in two acts, was also spare and lean in structure, calling merely for three main characters. This opera—libretto by Kenward Elmslie—was produced by the Juilliard Opera Theater in New York on November 21, 1957. It abounds with singable arias and ensemble pieces, including marching songs, hymns, chants, and dances—a score that proved readily assimilable on first hearing and drew favorable responses from audience and critics. Beeson's reputation as an opera composer gained further momentum with *Lizzie Borden* (1965), which was commissioned by the Ford Foundation for the New York City Opera and was produced by that company on March 25, 1965. Kenward Elmslie's libretto, based on a scenario by Richard Plant, reached back to 1892 and the notorious and much publicized murder trial in Fall River, Mass., of Lizzie Borden, accused of murdering her father and his second wife with an ax, a crime of which the jury finally acquitted her. In a *verismo* style sometimes reminiscent of Puccini, Beeson's score skillfully captured the intense, grim atmosphere of the play and its pervading fabric of evil.

My Heart's in the Highlands (1969) received its first performance by NET (National Education Television) Opera over the NET network on March 17, 1970, with Beeson himself taking on a five-line spoken bit in the production. The composer's libretto had originated first as a short story by William Saroyan that Saroyan later adapted into a one-act, then a two-act play. This is another intimate opera, requiring a cast of seven, a chorus of twelve, and an orchestra of eighteen instrumentalists. Here Beeson continues along the traditional lines he had been pursuing.

Captain Jinks of the Horse Marines (1975) is a "romantic comedy," with libretto by Sheldon Harnick based on a play by Clyde Fitch. It was commissioned for the American bicentennial by the National Endowment for the Arts and was produced by the Kansas City Lyric Theater in Missouri (with additional funds from the Missouri State Council on the Arts) on September 20, 1975. *Dr. Heidigger's Fountain of Youth*—libretto by Sheldon Harnick based on a story by Nathaniel Hawthorne—was produced in New York on November 19, 1978.

Though best known for his operas, Beeson has written a considerable amount of music for the concert stage. Here, as in his operas, he is the traditionalist who shuns avant-garde practices and concentrates on well-sounding melodies, richly conceived harmonies and counterpoint, and expressiveness within well-conceived structures. Over fifty of these compositions were withdrawn and discarded in 1950. His principal works for orchestra since 1950 are the Symphony (1959; N.Y., February 27, 1965) and *Transformations* (1959; Turin, December 1966). He has also written a good deal of choral and vocal music.

Beeson was awarded a Guggenheim Fellowship in 1958–1959, the Marc Blitzstein Award for the Music Theater by the National Institute of Arts and Letters in 1968, and a gold medal for music by the National Arts Club in New York in 1976. He was composer-in-residence in Rome in 1965–66, and in 1976 he was elected to the American Academy and Institute of Arts and Letters. Columbia University presented him with its Great Teachers Award in 1979.

In 1965, he was appointed full professor of music at Columbia University, where, in 1967, he was named MacDowell Professor or Music. He has served as chairman of the music department in the spring of 1964, between 1968 and 1972, and in spring 1976. Since 1962 he has been secretary and officer in charge of the Alice M. Ditson Fund of Columbia University. Between 1969 and 1972 he was a member of the Columbia University Senate.

For many years he has also been in charge of publications of new music by Columbia University Press as well as an active board member and officer of Composers Recordings, Inc. Additionally, he has been a member of the board of Composers Forum (1950–75), officiating as its chairman between 1962 and 1968; of the International Society for Contemporary Music/League of Composers since 1969; and of the Board of Review of the American Society of Authors, Composers, and Publishers (1972–73).

THE COMPOSER SPEAKS: The American scene changes so radically and rapidly that one can suggest only tentatively some of the directions our opera may take in the future. . . . If one believes that American opera will grow directly out of the excitements and simplicities of musical comedy (I do not) one could point out that at the moment the most solvent aspect of the absurd Broadway setup is its musical theater. . . . If our lyric theater is not to be found on Broadway's doorstep, neither will it be found in the foyers of long-established opera houses. These are too stodgy, too snobbish and—for a variety of complicated social and economic reasons—to preoccupied with the polishing of dead composers' tombstones to take part in the present, not to speak of the future. . . . Our numerous university and civic workshops and their audiences cannot yet cope with large-scale operas making use of the more advanced musical idioms. In Germany, audiences, and heavily subsidized opera companies are interested in little else, and within the last years European houses have shown interest in several American works unperformed here. If our situation continues for long, the effect will be to send "advanced" composers back to their symphonies and quartets and to solidify the present conservative personality of American opera, directing it even more strongly toward popular theater.

PRINCIPAL WORKS: Piano Sonata no. 4 (1945, rev. 1951); Piano Sonata no. 5 (1946, rev. 1951); Two Concert Arias, for voice and piano (1951–53); Six Lyrics, for high voice and piano (1952); *Hello, Out There*, one-act chamber opera (1953); Viola Sonata (1953); *The Sweet Bye and Bye*, opera (1956); *Indiana Homecoming*, for baritone and piano (1956); *Leda*, for reciting voice and piano (1957); *The Beat Hunt*, for tenor, baritone, bass, and piano (1957); *Sketches in Black and White*, for piano (1958); Symphony (1959); *Commemoration*, for band and unison chorus (1960); Fanfare, for brass, winds, percussion (1963); *Greener Pastures*, rounds for mixed a cappella voices (1963); *Lizzie Borden*, opera (1965); *My Heart's in the Highlands*, chamber opera (1969); *A Creole Mystery*, for mezzo-soprano or baritone and string quartet (1970); *The Model Housekeeper*, nine rounds and canons for women's voices (1970); *Everyman's Handyman*, nine rounds and canons for unaccompanied men's voices (1970); *The Day's No*

Rounder Than Its Angles, for mezzo-soprano or baritone and string quartet (1971); *Captain Jinks of the Horse Marines*, a romantic comedy in music (1975); *From a Watchtower*, five songs for high voice and piano (1976); *Dr. Heidigger's Fountain of Youth*, one-act chamber opera (1978).

BIBLIOGRAPHY: Schwartz, Elliott, and Childs, Barney (eds.), *Contemporary Composers on Contemporary Music* (N.Y., 1967); *New York Times,* November 1, 1957; *Opera News,* March 21, 1970; *Stereo Review,* December 1975; *Who's Who in America, 1980–81.*

Behrens, Jack, b. Lancaster, Pa., March 25, 1935.

Many of his compositions were written for specific performers or occasions and therefore, to a greater or lesser extent, reflect the personality and virtuosity of the executants or the ambiance and acoustics of the locale. Compositional methods range from serial to indeterminate, although few works are exclusively either.

His father was an ordained minister and his mother a bookbinder. Neither was musical, but his father occasionally played short pieces on the piano, and this was Jack's initiation to music. Listening to phonograph records, of which the family had a modest collection, and to the radio provided other early musical experiences. Jack began studying the piano in Rohrerstown, Pa., with Jeanette Shellenberger when he was seven and, while attending elementary school, continued to study with her until his family moved to Biloxi, Miss., in 1946. Returning to Pennsylvania in 1948, he continued piano study for the next few years with Earle W. Echternach. At Reynolds Junior High School (1948–50) in Lancaster, he received encouragement both as pianist and composer from one of its music teachers, Edna I. Brown. Between 1950 and 1953, while attending J. P. McCaskey High School in Lancaster, he was the piano accompanist for the school orchestra and glee club, the latter performing three chorales he had composed during 1952 and 1953. At high school, initiation into some 20th-century music and further encouragement in his ambition to become a musician came from James E. Zwally.

Behrens entered the Juilliard School of Music in New York in 1953. During the next six years he studied composition with William Bergsma, Vincent Persichetti, and Peter Mennin, conducting with Robert Ward, and music literature with Norman Lloyd. In 1956 he received the Edward Benjamin Award for *Introspection*, for string orchestra (1956), in 1958 his bachelor of science degree in composition and his master of science degree in composition one year later. During these years, several of his youthful compositions were performed at Juilliard, including

the Suite for Piano (1955), on January 31, 1956; *A Baker's Dozen*, for piano (1959), on February 6, 1959; and *Lament*, for brass choir (1959), on May 19, 1959. The influences on these compositions were varied, notably "mainstream" American music of the 1930s, 1940s, and 1950s, Shostakovich, and Vaughan Williams.

Between 1959 and 1961, Behrens taught theory and piano at the Bronx Music School in New York and was a teaching fellow in literature and materials of music at the Juilliard School. During the summers of 1960 and 1961 he taught composition, theory, and piano at the Berkeley Summer Music School in Springvale, Maine, and in 1961–62 he was a member of the music faculty at the Emma Willard School in Troy, N.Y. He spent the summer of 1962 on a Copley Foundation Award studying composition with Darius Milhaud at the Aspen Music Festival in Colorado. From 1962 to 1964 he was instructor of music and, from 1964 to 1966, assistant professor of music at the University of Saskatchewan, Regina Campus, in Canada, where concurrently he also served as head of the theory department in an affiliated conservatory. During the summers of 1964 and 1965 he was codirector of the Emma Lake Composers-Artists Workshop at the University of Saskatchewan, where John Cage, who from then on would have an impact on Behrens's artistic direction, was an invited composer. Meanwhile, on August 31, 1962, in Medford, Oreg., Behrens married Sonja Peterson, a pianist.

At the request of the American Dance Festival in New London, Conn., Behrens prepared the score for a ballet, *Transfigured Season* (1960), choreographed by Ruth Currier in collaboration with Behrens, and introduced at the Bennington College Dance Workshop in Vermont on May 26, 1960, even before it was seen in New London the following August 18. The style of this music was generally lyric, although not without its "darker" aspects. Lighter in character and even humorous in its two outer movements, was the Concertino, for trombone and eight instruments (1961; N.Y., May 4, 1961), written for the trombone virtuoso Davis Shuman. The central lyric slow movement utilized pitches that do not emanate from the bell of the instrument, an effect that Shuman suggested and one that as far as he knew had not been used previously.

While he was in Saskatchewan, further commissions opened up important opportunities for Behrens to write and be heard, his music carefully designed for the performers or the purpose for which it had been intended. For the pianist Stanley Butler, he wrote the Passacaglia, for piano (1963; Saskatchewan, June 28, 1963); for the Saskatchewan House Summer Festival, the ballet *Encounters*, scored for four-hand "prepared piano," choreography by Myrna Smith (1963; Saskatchewan, June 28, 1963), which has been heard as a dramatic concert piece in which one performer frequently plays inside the piano; also for the Saskatchewan House Summer Festival, the incidental music for *A Midsummer Night's Dream* (1964; Saskatchewan, June 17, 1964); for the pianist Adele Marcus, *A Pocket Size Sonata*, for piano (1964; Saskatchewan, July 7, 1965), winner of a prize from the Saskatchewan Diamond Jubilee Committee; and for the Canada Council, for the first convocation at the Regina Campus of the University of Saskatchewan, *Soundings*, for flute, oboe, bassoon, horn, violin, viola, and piano (1965; Saskatchewan, May 17, 1965), a work somewhat in the serial technique and more concerned with texture than previous works.

In 1965, Behrens received a Canada Council Scandinavian Research Grant for research in Viking literature, art, and music in Iceland, Denmark, Sweden, and Norway. As a result of these studies, on a commission from the Canadian Centennial Committee for Festival Canada, he wrote an opera based on the Islandic saga *Thrymskvitha*. He called it *The Lay of Thrym* (1968), libretto by C. Keith Cockburn. It was introduced at the North University of Regina of the University of Saskatchewan on April 15, 1968, the composer conducting. The seventy-minute score called for four leading solo roles, chamber orchestra, and chorus. "Those of us involved in *The Lay of Thrym*," the composer explains, "felt that the boldness and enterprise (sometimes artistic) of the Vikings might serve as an appropriate focus as Canada was about to begin its second century of confederation. As almost nothing is known of Viking music, no attempt was made to incorporate ethnic elements."

Between 1966 and 1970, Behrens was on the music faculty of the Simon Fraser University in Vancouver, British Columbia. There he was director of Visual and Environmental Arts (1966–67), acting chairman of the Center for Communications and Arts (1967), and chairman of the University Works of Art Committee (1967–70). In 1969–70 he was a teaching fellow in music at Harvard University, where he received the Francis Boott Prize for his choral work *How Beautiful Is Night* (1969; Cambridge, Mass., May 17, 1970). He was associate professor of music at California State College in Bakersfield from 1970 to 1973—acting chairman of the Department of Fine Arts (1972–73) and professor and chairman (1973–76). In 1976 he was appointed professor of music and chairman of the Department of Theory and Composition at the University of Western Ontario in London, Ontario, and in 1980 he was named dean of the music faculty. In 1973, Behrens earned his Ph.D. in composition at Harvard University, where he had attended the composition and theory analysis classes of Leon Kirchner and Roger Sessions.

These are Behrens's most significant compositions since 1970: *The Sound of Milo*, for narrator and orchestra (1970), Jack Wasserman's text abounding with puns and subtle literary references, with the music following suit with unusual instrumental effects for the winds, introduced by the New Orleans Symphony on March 4, 1970, and winner of first prize in the New Orleans Symphony contest; Concerto for Clarinet, Violin, Piano, and Orchestra, commissioned by the Kern Philharmonic Society in California (1971; Bakersfield, Calif. November 22, 1971), much of whose central material was derived from Beethoven's String Quartet in F major, op. 135; *The Feast of Life*, for piano (1975; Taos, N.M., August 27, 1975); *Taos Portraits*, for piano (1976; Santa Fe, N.M., April 27, 1977); *Looking Back*, a cycle of songs to poems by Christopher Pratt, for soprano, flute, and piano (1979; London, Ontario, April 28, 1979); and Music for Two Pianos (1979; London, Ontario, January 31, 1980). The idiom in all these is modern, although not necessarily nonmelodic or atonal, with contrast and/or juxtaposition—music without transitions—being a common denominator.

THE COMPOSER SPEAKS: By offering the performers an intriguing challenge (often at their instigation) my hope is that an aura of aural delight will emerge for all who would listen.

PRINCIPAL WORKS: *A Baker's Dozen*, for piano (1959); *Lament*, for brass choir (1959); Divertimento, for flute, clarinet, trumpet, violin, viola, and cello (1959); Rhapsody, for violin and piano (1960); Quartertone Quartet, for string quartet (1960); *Transfigured Season*, ballet (1960); Suite for Strings (1960); Concertino, for trombone and orchestra (1961); Piano Sonata no. 2 (1962); Sonata for Solo Violin (1962); *Encounters*, ballet (1963); Passacaglia, for piano (1963); *Declaration*, for orchestra (1964); Incidental Music for *A Midsummer Night's Dream*, for orchestra (1964); *A Mellow Drama*, for violin, horn, bassoon, and narrator (1964); *Strata*, for percussion ensemble (1964); *A Pocket Size Sonata*, for piano (1964); *Pentad*, for vibraphone and piano (1965); *Soundings*, for flute, bassoon, oboe, horn, violin, viola and piano (1965); *The Lay of Thrym*, opera (1968); Prologue—Serenades—Epilogue, for trumpet, flute, clarinet, violin, cello, and piano (1969); *The Sound of Milo*, for orchestra (1970); Concerto for Clarinet, Piano, and Orchestra (1971); *The Feast of Life*, for piano (1975); *City Life*, on biblical texts, for soprano and piano (1975); Fantasy on Francis Hopkinson's "My Days Have Been So Wondrous Free," for chamber orchestra (1976); *Taos Portraits*, for piano (1976); *A Greeting*, for chamber orchestra (1977); *Looking Back*, a song cycle for soprano, flute, and piano (1979); Music for Two Pianos (1979); *Trees and Skies*, for violin, viola, and cello (1979); *Homage à Chopin*, for piano (1979).

BIBLIOGRAPHY: *BBDM*.

Bennett, Robert Russell, b. Kansas City, Mo., June 15, 1894; d. New York City, August 18, 1981.

Much of Bennett's concert work was deeply rooted in American backgrounds and geography, and just as frequently he drew his material from the reservoir of American popular music. He was consistently tonal and consistently the traditionalist in his harmonic, contrapuntal and structural methods. His style runs the gamut from the dramatic, elegiac, and atmospheric to the satiric and witty. He was a master craftsman in whatever he essayed, and an orchestrator of uncommon endowments.

He came from many generations of Americans, one of his ancestors (on his mother's side) having been William Bradford, governor of Plymouth Colony. Both his parents were musical. His father, George Robert Bennett, was a professional musician who played the violin and trumpet in the Kansas City Philharmonic, and his mother, May (Bradford) Bennett, was a teacher of the piano.

Stricken by infantile paralysis when he was four, Robert Bennett was brought for recovery to a farm forty miles south of Kansas City. There, a year later, his mother began giving him piano lessons. Before long, these were supplemented by instruction from his father in various band instruments. By the time he was ten, Robert Bennett was giving piano recitals and was often called upon to substitute for an absent musician, regardless of the instrument, in the band his father conducted.

The Bennetts returned to Kansas City in 1909. That year Bennett began studying harmony, counterpoint, and composition with Carl Busch. He also began involving himself with popular music by playing the violin, piano, and trombone in theater orchestras, movies and in dance halls. Having accumulated two hundred dollars, he made a move to New York in 1916. Initially he supported himself by working as pianist in restaurants and dance halls. Then he found a job as copyist and arranger for the music publishing house of G. Schirmer. In 1917 he enlisted in the U.S. Army where he was called upon to conduct and make arrangements for army bands. Soon after his demobilization he married Louise Edgerton Merrill on December 29, 1919. They had one child, a daughter.

After a period as orchestrator of popular music for the publishing house of Harms in New York, Bennett embarked in 1922 on an extended and lucrative career as orchestrator of Broadway musicals. He was the first to carry over into this profession the sophistication and the harmonic, contrapuntal, and thematic-development techniques of concert music, lifting such orchestrations to a standard they had never before known. For the next four decades, he remained one of Broadway's most successful orchestrators, producing scores for over two hundred musicals (the work of virtually every important composer Broadway has known). There was hardly a season, except for a period when he dropped orchestration to continue studies abroad, when Bennett did not have four or five productions on Broadway: There was one season when his work was heard in twenty-two theaters. Many of the musicals with which he became involved have become classics in the American musical theater, of which the following is a representative list: Friml's *Rose Marie*, Kern's *Show Boat*, Arthur Schwartz's *The Band Wagon*, Gershwin's *Of Thee I Sing*, Cole Porter's *Kiss Me, Kate*, Burton Lane's *Finian's Rainbow*, Kurt Weill's *Lady in the Dark*, Frederick Loewe's *My Fair Lady* and *Camelot*, and Richard Rodgers's *Oklahoma!, Carousel, South Pacific, The King and I,* and *The Sound of Music.*

Even while filling this role as one of Broadway's most prestigious and sought-after orchestrators and reaping financial harvests, Bennett did not lose sight of a boyhood ambition to become a serious composer. To achieve that goal, he decided, in 1926, to abandon the Broadway scene. On two successive Guggenheim Fellowships, between 1927 and 1929, he lived in Berlin, London, and Paris, studying composition principally with Nadia Boulanger. He also allowed his career as a serious composer to get into full motion. In Europe he completed his first symphony (1926), which received honorable mention in a competition conducted by *Musical America* for American composers; a one-act opera, *An Hour of Delusion* (1927); a second symphony, *Abraham Lincoln* (1927); and an "orchestral entertainment," *Sights and Sounds* (1926). The last two he submitted to a competition for American composers launched by the Radio Corporation of America, the prize being $25,000. When the judges failed to come up with a winner, they decided to divide the prize money equally among the five best compositions submitted. Both of Bennett's works were selected, together with single compositions by Ernest Bloch, Aaron Copland, and Louis Gruenberg. In Bennett's *Abraham Lincoln Symphony*—successfully introduced by the Philadelphia Orchestra conducted by Leopold Stokowski on October 24, 1931—the thematic material for each of its four movements was inspired by Lincoln's outstanding personal attributes, the last movement serving as a proclamation of what Bennett felt to be "a triumph of a great soul, rich, unbending, inevitable." *Sights and Sounds* received its first hearing in Chicago on December 13, 1938, with Izler Solomon conducting the Illinois Symphony.

From this point on, and for the next few decades, Bennett continued to ply the highly profitable trade of making orchestrations for the Broadway theater, while producing numerous works for the concert and operatic stage. His best compositions enjoyed instant approval from both audience and critics because they were so skillfully fashioned and because they were so readily assimilable at first hearing.

Occasionally he brought to his concert work materials and idioms he had mastered on Broadway. Among such compositions we find the Three

Marches, for two pianos and orchestra (1930-50), originally entitled simply March, first performed on July 8, 1930, by the Los Angeles Philharmonic, Karl Krueger conducting; the Concerto Grosso, for jazz band and symphony orchestra (1931), given its initial hearing on December 9, 1932, by the Rochester Philharmonic under Howard Hanson; Variations on a Theme by Jerome Kern (1933), premiered by the Chamber Orchestra of New York under Bernard Herrmann on December 9, 1932; and the Concerto for Violin and Orchestra (1941), initially heard over the NBC radio network on December 26, 1941.

Some compositions touched on different facets of Americana. Symphony in D (1941; N.Y., August 31, 1941) was inspired by baseball, and specifically by the Dodgers team then representing Brooklyn, and so was one of the movements of Eight Etudes, for orchestra (1938; CBS, July 17, 1938), which paid tribute to the pitcher Carl Hubbell. American geography and backgrounds were created tonally in *Hollywood*, a scherzo for orchestra (1936; NBC, November 15, 1936); *Kansas City Album*, for orchestra (1950); *Ohio River Suite* (1959); and *Overture to the Mississippi* (1962; Miami, Fla., February 10, 1963). American college songs provided the material for Symphony on College Tunes (1941). Old American dance music was the source of Suite on Old Dances, for band (1949). He paid tribute to America's musical past in *Stephen Collins Foster*, a commemorative symphony for orchestra and chorus (1959; Pittsburgh, December 30, 1959); and in *The Fun and Faith of William Billings*, for orchestra and chorus (1975), written to commemorate the American bicentennial and introduced by the National Symphony of Washington, D.C., and the University of Maryland chorus at the Kennedy Center of the Performing Arts on April 29, 1975.

Other major works include the opera *Maria Malibran* (1935), libretto by Robert A. Simon, produced by the Juilliard School of Music in New York on April 8, 1935; *The Four Freedoms*, a symphonic suite inspired by four paintings by Norman Rockwell (1943; NBC, September 26, 1943), a work frequently performed by American orchestras during World War II; *Overture to an Imaginary Drama* (1945; Toronto, May 14, 1946); and Symphony no. 2 (1963).

Between 1936 and 1940, Bennett scored more than thirty films in Hollywood, among which were *Show Boat* (1936) and *Rebecca* (1940). He produced music for the screen in later years as well, earning an Oscar from the American Academy of Motion Picture Arts and Sciences in 1955 for his scoring for the motion picture adaptation of *Oklahoma!* He returned to New York City in 1940 and in 1941 he first became affiliated with radio with a weekly program touching on various facets of musical Americana entitled *Russell Bennett's Notebook* over WOR, New York, where he did the arranging, conducting, and composing as well as the commentating, and introduced

"music-box operas" based on American popular songs. This program brought him the Award of Merit from the National Association for American Composers and Conductors in 1942. He promoted American folk music over the radio in a series in 1944-45 in which he wrote and conducted different orchestral fantasies based on such tunes. His first significant assignment for television was the orchestration of Richard Rodgers's music for the documentary series *Victory at Sea* in 1952.

In 1965, Bennett was awarded an honorary doctorate in humane letters from Franklin and Marshall College in Lancaster, Pa. He is the author of a book on orchestration, *Instrumentally Speaking* (New York, 1974).

THE COMPOSER SPEAKS: Although I have made a living at commercial music, I am convinced that the contribution of our lighter composers, authors of what may become American folk songs, is very small. I believe in the deeper thoughts of our better composers to the point of trusting great music to take care of itself against any onslaught of criticism, public reaction, and financial gain for the less cultured (though in many ways equally gifted) writers.

PRINCIPAL WORKS: 4 symphonies (1941–63).

Charleston Rhapsody, for chamber orchestra with piano (1926); *Sights and Sounds,* for orchestra (1926); Violin Sonata (1927); *Paysage*, for orchestra (1927); *Toy Symphony*, for five woodwinds (1928); Three Marches, for two pianos and orchestra (1930–1950); Concerto Grosso, for dance band and orchestra (1931); *Adagio eroico*, for orchestra (1931); Variations on a Theme by Jerome Kern, for orchestra (1933); *Maria Malibran*, opera (1935); *Hollywood*, scherzo for orchestra (1936); *Water Music*, for string quartet (1938); Eight Etudes, for orchestra (1938); Concert Variations, for violin and orchestra (1939); *Hexapoda*, for violin and piano (1941); Violin Concerto (1941); Symphony on College Tunes, for orchestra (1941); Classic Serenade, for string orchestra (1941); A Symphonic Portrait of Gershwin's *Porgy and Bess*, for orchestra (1942); *The Four Freedoms*, suite for orchestra (1943); *The Enchanted Kiss*, opera (1945); *Overture to an Imaginary Drama* (1945); Five Improvisations, for piano trio (1946); *A Dry Weather Legend*, for flute and orchestra (1946); A Symphonic Picture of Jerome Kern (1948); Six Souvenirs, for two flutes and piano (1948); Suite on Old American Dances, for band (1949); *Overture to the Mississippi*, for orchestra (1950); *Kansas City Album*, for orchestra (1950); Concerto Grosso, for wind quartet and wind orchestra (1957): Symphonic Songs, for band (1959); *Stephen Collins Foster*, a commemoration symphony, for orchestra and chorus (1959); *Ohio River Suite*, for orchestra (1959); *Track Meet*, an orchestral suite (1960); Concerto for Violin, Piano, and Orchestra (1963); Guitar Concerto (1963); *The Fun and Faith of William Billings*, for chorus and orchestra (1975); Four Carol Cantatas, for chorus (1976); *The Easter Story*, cantata for chorus and orchestra (1977).

BIBLIOGRAPHY: *BBDM*; Goss, Madeleine, *Modern Music Makers* (N.Y., 1952); Howard, John Tasker, *Our Contemporary Composers* (N.Y., 1941); *New Yorker*, November 17, 1961.

Benson, Warren Frank, b. Detroit, Mich., January 26, 1924.

Virtually all his music has been written for specific performers or ensembles, usually on commission, and many reveal a gift for writing for wind ensemble and percussion, two fields in which Benson has been an innovator. His is a selective technique derived from conservative and modern tonal practices, serial preoccupations, atonalism, highly organized traditional contrapuntal techniques, free writing, elaborate ostinati overlays much influenced by the music of the East and jazz, all employed with economy. The most familiar aspects of his style are harmonic pressure, lyricism, and sparseness. This is not to say his music lacks textural density, but solo playing in large ensembles is one of his most frequently employed expressive means.

From his mother, an amateur singer, and a music-loving father, Benson received his first-remembered musical impressions. At Monnier Elementary School in Detroit, which he attended from 1933 to 1938, he received encouragement and direction in music from one of its teachers, Molly Plotkin. She had him take lessons on the snare drum from Gerry Gerard and, once Benson had acquired some proficiency, she found opportunities for him to perform in the school orchestra and in a small ensemble she had founded to perform monthly at social dances. In his tenth year, Benson also became a member of the Fisher YMCA band, which performed all over the Detroit area; in this ensemble Benson played not only the drums but also the marimba, having begun to study the latter instrument in his twelfth year with Selwyn Alvey. In 1938–39, Benson was percussionist in the All-City Junior High School Orchestra.

At Cass Technical High School (1939–43), Benson studied the French horn with Francis Hellstein, principal horn of the Detroit Symphony and the director of the school band in which Benson played the drums. Taking a class in orchestration, Benson now did his first musical writing by making arrangements for several jazz units within the high school's ensemble program.

Upon graduating from Cass Technical in January 1943, Benson entered the University of Michigan, specializing in music education. Since the University had no teacher in percussion, Benson was recruited to give such a course during the summer of his freshman year. At the university, Benson received a thorough training in theory and orchestration. Two

months after he had entered the university, Benson joined a well-established nineteen-piece jazz band conducted by Wilson Sawyer which performed at the University's Men's Union. For the next six years he played drums in the band and wrote many of its arrangements. He recalls: "This band was the place where I learned how to write music, since everything I wrote I heard almost immediately, performed by first-rate musicians, with adequate time to rehearse." During his junior year, Benson joined the Detroit Symphony as timpanist. (He had played both timpani and horn in the university orchestra.) His university studies were interrupted for a year in 1946–47 because of surgery. But in September 1947 he was back at the university to complete requirements for his bachelor of music degree in theory, which he acquired in 1949; in 1950 he received his master's degree in theory.

The summer of 1949 was spent teaching percussion and performing at the Transylvania Music Camp in Brevard, N.C. The camp director of choral activities, Lester McCoy, commissioned Benson to write a work for the first concert given by the Livonia (Michigan) Civic Chorus, which he had just organized. Benson responded with a set originally entitled *Something of the Sea* (1949), which in later years was published as two separate items under the titles of *A Ship Comes In* and *Two Sea Poems*. This was Benson's first commission and the piece of music he regards as his first "real" composition.

On November 19, 1949, in Ann Arbor, Mich., Benson married Patricia L. Vander Velder. She was an artist who had received a degree in art history and who, additionally, was trained in music. They subsequently had four children. Between 1950 and 1952, on two successive Fulbright Fellowships, Benson lived with his young wife in Greece, teaching music at Anatolia College in Salonica, where he organized the Anatolia College Chorale, the first scholastic co-education choir in that country, and where he designed and initiated a five-year music curriculum. Returning to the United States in 1952, he was appointed director of band and orchestra at Mars Hill College in North Carolina. From 1953 to 1967 he was professor of music and composer-in-residence at Ithaca College, New York, teaching percussion and composition, and organizing the first percussion ensemble in the East, which soon performed successfully in extensive tours and made recordings. During 1953–54 he wrote a work for orchestra, *A Delphic Serenade*, commissioned by the director of the Transylvania Music Camp, which was introduced by the Charlotte Symphony Orchestra in Charlotte, N.C., in spring 1954. Sigurd Rascher, the saxophone virtuoso, was so impressed with this music that he commissioned Benson to write for him a solo saxophone work with band accompaniment. The Concertino for Alto Saxophone and Band (1954) was introduced by Rascher and the West Point Academy Band in West Point, N.Y., in January 1955. Subsequently, Benson wrote several more compositions for Rascher. In Ithaca, on commission, Benson wrote a number of band compositions, beginning with *Night Song* (1958).

An important influence in his later musical life was his residence at the MacDowell Colony in 1955, his first real contact with a large group of other professional artists, particularly poets and painters. At this time he first met such poets as May Swenson, Louise Bogan, and Shirley Schoonover, whose works he later set to music. "It was there," he says, "that I first developed my feelings and concerns for being a professional composer, a professional creative artist."

Benson's full technical and creative maturity as a composer came in the early 1960s with two compositions: Symphony for Drums and Wind Orchestra (1962) and *The Leaves Are Falling*, for wind ensemble (1963). The symphony (introduced in Pittsburgh on July 4, 1964, by the American Wind Symphony, which had commissioned it) reflects the composer's interest in African drum music. But no actual African rhythms are used, the work being centered around various percussion-section ostinati in the outer movements, with the central part being contemplative music which builds to a climax of massive proportions before receding quietly. *The Leaves Are Falling*, title taken from a poem by Rilke, was first heard on April 30, 1964, in Rochester, N.Y., at its American Music Festival, performed by the Eastman Wind Ensemble. Its form deals with montage: superimposition of new material on known material. The tonality is free, at times atonal, even polytonal, as the layers of motives ebb and flow. This work has since become a repertoire staple, one of Benson's most widely played and successfully received compositions.

Benson's style was now crystallized. *Helix*, for solo tuba and wind ensemble (1966), was commissioned by, dedicated to, and introduced by Harvey Phillips, tuba virtuoso; its premiere took place in Ithaca, N.Y., on February 12, 1967, and has since been performed by many tuba virtuosi. *The Solitary Dancer*, for wind ensemble (1967)—which, with *The Leaves Are Falling*, is Benson's most often performed composition—was commissioned by the Clarence, N.Y., High School Band, which introduced it in 1967. This work "deals with the quiet, poised energy of the dancer in repose, alone with her inner music." Though intended solely as band music, it has also served as the background score for several choreographic treatments. *Shadow Wood*, for solo voice and large wind ensemble (1968), is a cycle of five sensitive, romantic songs based on poems by Tennessee Williams touching on the subjects of youth, love, and death. It was commissioned by Baldwin-Wallace College for its seventy-fifth anniversary and its premiere took place in Berea, Ohio, on May 14, 1969.

Since 1970, Benson's most important compositions have been the Concerto for Horn and Orchestra (1971; Quincy, Ill., April 26, 1972), commissioned

by the Quincy Foundation and the Quincy Symphony Orchestra in Illinois; *Meditation, Credo, and Sweet Hallelujah*, for piano and antiphonal choruses written in 1974 on a grant from the National Endowment for the Arts and revised in 1979; *Earth, Sky and Sea*, a programmatic work for chorus, flute, trombone, and marimba (1975), commissioned by the Ohio Music Education Association for the commemoration of the American bicentennial, its text a cycle of poems by Kenneth Rexroth; *Songs of O* (1975; N.Y., April 30, 1976), for large chorus, brass quintet and percussionist, utilizing poems by Shirley Schoonover, Kenneth Patchen, and Langston Hughes, as well as Psalm 47, which begins "O clap your hands," as well as two related poems by Archibald MacLeish and Louise Bogan, commissioned by the New York Choral Society, which introduced it; Five Lyrics of Louise Bogan (1977), a song cycle for mezzo-soprano and flute to poems by Bogan, introduced by Jan DeGaetani and Bonita Boyd (who commissioned the work) in Rochester, N.Y., on January 31, 1978; *Embers*, for trumpet, trombone, and snare drum together with amplified offstage glockenspiel, chimes, and vibraphone (1978; Louisville, Ky., February 20, 1979).

From 1963 to 1973, Benson was involved with the Ford Foundation Contemporary Music Project, lecturing at universities and colleges on the development of a new approach to the teaching of music theory in colleges and universities, and at seminars and workshops throughout the United States. He received Ford Foundation grants in 1963–64 and 1964–65 to develop at Ithaca College the first pilot project in comprehensive musicianship.

Since 1967, Benson has been professor of composition at the Eastman School of Music, becoming Kilbourn Professor of Composition in 1980. In 1970 he traveled to South America to lecture (in Spanish) in Argentina, for which he was awarded the Diploma of Honor from its Ministry of Culture. In 1971 he was presented with the Lillian Fairchild Prize for musical composition; in 1975, a citation from the University of Rochester Alumni Association; and in 1976 a Citation of Excellence from the National Band Association.

THE COMPOSER SPEAKS: My creative process is essentially a layering process. I tend to write a work all the way through in a very sketchy form and then apply a series of overlays to this until the work is completely finished. I usually then put it away for a couple of months to ferment, bringing it back into the harsh light of the new day for appraisal, correction, and final completion. I do not write for competitions or abstract hereafters. I write music for people: family, friends, professionals, and amateurs alike. It is to give us pleasure that we collaborate; not without serious commitment, exposure, and risk, not without striving for genuine expression, new challenge, and fresh solutions worthy of the art.

PRINCIPLE WORKS: *A Delphic Serenade*, for orchestra (1953); Concertino for Alto Saxophone and Band (1954); Trio for Percussion (1956); Psalm 24, for women's voices and string orchestra (1957); *Night Song*, for band (1958); Three Dances, for solo snare drum (1961–62); *Streams*, for percussion septet (1961–62); Symphony for Drums and Wind Orchestra (1962); *Remembrance*, for band (1963); *The Leaves Are Falling*, for wind ensemble (1963); *Badlands*, ballet (1965); *Star Edge*, for alto saxophone (1966), *Helix*, for band and solo tuba (1966); *The Solitary Dancer*, for wind ensemble (1966); *Love*, for antiphonal chorus (1967); *Shadow Wood*, song cycle for soprano and wind ensemble (1968); *The Mask of Night*, for wind ensemble (1968); *Nara*, for soprano, flute, and two percussions (1970); Capriccio, for piano quartet (1971); Horn Concerto (1971); *The Dream Net*, for alto saxophone and string quartet (1972); *The Beaded Leaf*, for solo bass voice and orchestral winds (1973); *Meditation, Credo, and Sweet Hallelujah*, for piano and antiphonal choruses (1974, revised 1979); *The Passing Bell*, for band, 1974); *Songs of O*, song cycle for chorus, brass quintet, and percussion (1975); *Earth, Sky, and Sea*, for chorus, flute, trombone, and marimba (1975); *The Dark Virgin*, for percussion ensemble and large speaking chorus (1976, rev. 1979); Five Lyrics of Louise Bogan, song cycle for mezzo-soprano and flute (1977); *Embers*, for trumpet, trombone, and four percussionists (1978); *Winter Bittersweet*, for six percussionists (1979); *The Man with the Blue Guitar*, for orchestra (1980); *Songs for the End of the World*, song cycle for mezzo-soprano and instruments (1980).

BIBLIOGRAPHY: *Who's Who in America, 1980–81.*

Berezowsky, Nicolai, b. St. Petersburg, Russia, May 17, 1900; d. New York City, August 27, 1953. American citizen, 1928.

While alive, Berezowsky was a highly esteemed composer whose works were performed by some of America's most prestigious organizations and performers. But, following his death, new trends in music made his Russian romanticism old-fashioned and his works were thrown into a desuetude they do not deserve.

When he was eight, he was enrolled at the Imperial Chapel in St. Petersburg, where for the next nine years he studied singing, violin, and piano and for a time was the solo soprano of the choir. During these school years, beginning with 1913, he helped support himself by playing the violin in Russian orchestras in the summer. In 1916 he graduated with honors.

For two years (1917–19) he was concertmaster of the National Opera Orchestra in Saratov. When the local authorities refused to allow him to resign from this position, he borrowed an identification card, disguised himself as a woman, and deserted Saratov for

Moscow. There he played the violin in the orchestra of the Bolshoi Theater and was musical director of the School of Modern Art. In 1920, the Soviet Commission of Education sent him and several other musicians on a tour of southern Russia. He was paid in butter, sugar, and other edibles, which he exchanged for gold pieces to help him escape from the Soviet Union. It took him four months to make the trip on foot from Russia to Poland, his gold pieces serving as the bribe to get him across the border. In Poland he was imprisoned, but through the Near East Relief Agency, which communicated with and received financial aid from his sister then living in the United States, he was freed and allowed to make his way to the United States, arriving in September 1922 on a cattle boat. In New York he found employment as a violinist in the orchestra of the Capitol Theater, then conducted by Erno Rapee and Eugene Ormandy. In October 1923 he became a member of the violin section of the New York Philharmonic, where he remained for the next six years. During this period, on a scholarship, he attended the Juilliard School of Music, studying violin with Paul Kochanski and composition with Rubin Goldmark. On May 3, 1928, he married Alice Newmann, with whom he had two children.

He first attracted interest as a composer with Theme and Variations, a sextet for strings, clarinet, and piano (1926), introduced at a festival of chamber music in Washington, D.C., on October 7, 1926. In 1929 the New York Philharmonic under Willem Mengelberg successfully introduced his *Hebrew Suite*, for orchestra, based on authentic Jewish folk songs and liturgical melodies. (Berezowsky was not Jewish but a member of the Greek Orthodox Church.)

Encouraged by Mengelberg, Berezowsky decided in 1929 to resign from the New York Philharmonic to devote himself to composition. With wisely invested winnings from the chemin de fer tables in Europe, Berezowsky, his wife, and infant daughter were able to live in Europe for two years. His Violin Concerto (1930) so impressed Carl Flesch, the distinguished German violin virtuoso and teacher, that Flesch introduced it in Dresden with the Dresden Philharmonic on April 29, 1930, before it was featured at the Bremen Music Festival in May of the following year, with Berezowsky conducting.

Serge Koussevitzky, musical director of the Boston Symphony Orchestra, became interested in him and was largely responsible for sending Berezowsky's career as composer into high gear as soon as Berezowsky returned to the United States in 1931. Koussevitzky invited Berezowsky to conduct the Boston Symphony in the world premiere of Symphony no. 1 on March 16, 1931. Koussevitzky himself was on the podium with the Boston Symphony when he premiered Berezowsky's Symphony no. 2 (February 16, 1934), Symphony no. 4 (October 22, 1943), which had been commissioned by the Koussevitzky Music Foundation, the *Concerto lirico*, for cello and orchestra, with Gregor Piatigorsky as soloist (February 22, 1935), the Toccata, Variations and Finale, for string quartet and orchestra, with the Coolidge String Quartet as soloist (October 21, 1938), later performed by principal orchestras in Cleveland, Philadelphia, Boston and San Francisco. And though Berezowsky's Symphony no. 3 had been introduced by the Rochester Philharmonic under José Iturbi (January 21, 1937), Koussevitzky did not hesitate to program it with the Boston Symphony soon after its premiere, with the composer conducting.

Berezowsky's music was also being favored by other distinguished American musical organizations. His Sinfonietta, for orchestra (1931), which received a prize in a competition for new American music by the National Broadcasting Company, was given its first hearing over the NBC radio network on May 1, 1932, Eugene Goossens conducting, and then was featured by major orchestras throughout the United States. The New York Philharmonic presented the premiere of *Soldiers on the Town* (1943; November 25, 1943), which the League of Composers had commissioned, the *Christmas Festival Overture* (1943; December 23, 1943), commissioned by Howard Barlow, and Passacaglia, for the theremin and orchestra (1947; February 29, 1948). The Philadelphia Orchestra under Eugene Ormandy gave the first presentation of the Concerto for Harp and Orchestra (1944; January 26, 1945), the soloist being Edna Phillips, for whom it was written. The NBC Symphony under Frank Black gave the initial hearing to Introduction and Waltz (1939; October 15, 1939) and the National Orchestral Association under Leon Barzin, with Vera Brodsky and Harold Triggs soloists, to the Fantasie for two pianos and orchestra (1932; February 12, 1932).

Berezowsky's music was always frankly romantic, occasionally impressionistic. To the end of his life he ignored the new trends in music that were gaining vogue, preferring the musical language he had mastered in Russia in which the expression of human emotions, rather than technical innovations or unusual effects, was the prime concern. His music has a recognizable Russian identity. When Berezowsky once remarked to Koussevitzky that his critics were blaming his music for being so Russian and so little American, Koussevitzky told him: "Of course your music is Russian. What should it be? Creative music must spring from a deep national stream of culture. Only by being true to his inmost atavism can an artist achieve universality."

From 1932 to 1936, and again from 1941 to 1946, Berezowsky was staff violinist and assistant conductor with the Columbia Broadcasting System, and from 1935 to 1940 he was a member of the Coolidge String Quartet. He received awards from the American Academy of Arts and Letters in 1944 in recognition of his "distinguished position in American music" and the Ditson Fund of Columbia University in 1946. In 1948 he was awarded a Guggenheim Fellowship.

PRINCIPAL WORKS: 4 symphonies (1931–42).

Theme and Variations, sextet for clarinet, piano, and strings (1926); *Hebrew Suite*, for orchestra (1929); Violin Concerto (1929–30); Sinfonietta, for orchestra (1931); Duo, for clarinet and viola (1931); Fantasie, for two pianos and orchestra (1932); *Concerto lirico*, for cello and orchestra (1935); Introduction and Allegro, for chamber orchestra (1937); Toccata, Variations, and Finale, for string quartet and orchestra (1938); Music for Seven Brass Instruments (1939); Introduction and Waltz, for orchestra (1939); Woodwind Quintet (1941); Clarinet Concerto (1942); *Christmas Festival Overture*, for orchestra (1943); *Soldiers on the Town*, for orchestra (1943); *Bowdoin Hymn*, for chorus (1944); Harp Concerto (1945); Passacaglia, for theremin and orchestra (1947); *Gilgamesh*, cantata for narrator, vocal quartet, chorus, and orchestra (1947); *Babar and the Elephant*, children's opera (1953); Sextet Concerto, for string orchestra (1953).

BIBLIOGRAPHY: Berezowsky, Alice, *Duet with Nicky* (N.Y., 1943); Howard, John Tasker, *Our Contemporary Composers* (N.Y., 1941); *New York Times*, November 15, 1942.

Berger, Arthur Victor, b. New York City, May 15, 1912.

From the incipient twelve-tone style of his early works, Berger passed on to neoclassicism before turning to serialism. Whatever idiom he has adopted, or however circumscribed it may be, he has been an individualist who has brought to his music the original and idiosyncratic approach of an inventive, thoughtful, highly prinicipled, and technically adroit composer.

His earliest interest in music expressed itself in the singing of popular hit songs heard in vaudeville and on records and in listening to a few classical recordings his family happened to own. His academic schooling began in the public schools in the Bronx (1918–25). When he was about eleven his family acquired a piano, and his older sister was given lessons. Impatient with the way she was preparing her exercises, he proceeded to learn them himself. It would be some time, however, before he received any formal musical instruction. At Townsend Harris Hall (1925–28)—a three-year high school for exceptional students—he organized the Fine Arts Society, which encouraged students to listen to good music through recordings. Most of his musical knowledge was acquired in his high school years from reading books on music and studying scores. Without any instruction, he began writing pieces for the piano, including a sonata.

After two years at the College of the City of New York (1928–30), Berger enrolled in the School of Music Education at New York University to qualify as a teacher of music in secondary schools and to receive his first instruction in composition from Vincent Jones. At New York University, Berger became the friend of two fellow students, Jerome Moross and Bernard Herrmann, both of whom were interested in avant-garde music. Through them, Berger first came to know and admire the music of Charles Ives, Edgard Varèse, and Henry Cowell, whose music he first read about in the writings of Paul Rosenfeld. Berger, Moross, and Herrmann soon drifted into a circle of young creative musicians, later known as the Young Composers Group, of which Aaron Copland was the mentor. In those years, Berger came under the influence of Schoenberg. Two Episodes, for piano (1933)—his only composition of this period to survive—contained some elements of the twelve-tone technique but was basically atonal rather than twelve-tonal. Berger soon found the twelve-tone system as practiced by the Viennese too constricting, and for the time being he abandoned it and composition as well, preferring to turn to other musical directions.

In 1932, Berger embarked upon a career as music critic (which he would pursue fruitfully for the next two decades) by joining the staff of the *New York Daily Mirror*, for which he wrote reviews for the next two years. In 1933, he received his bachelor of science in music degree at the New York University School of Education. A fellowship in the then newly organized Professional School of the Longy School of Music brought him to Cambridge, Mass., in 1934. For two years (1934–36) he was a pupil at the Longy School of Music, and for three years (1934–37) he attended the Harvard Graduate School as a student of Walter Piston, Archibald T. Davison, and Hugo Leichtentritt. In 1936 he was the recipient of a grant from the American Council of Learned Societies and a master of arts degree from Harvard. All this while he continued writing reviews for the *Boston Evening Transcript* (1934–37). He was also the editor of *Musical Mercury* (1934–37), which he had founded.

On May 25, 1937, Berger married Esther Turitz, a teacher of piano and voice. Soon after his marriage Berger (and his young wife) went to Paris on a Paine Traveling Fellowship to study composition for two years with Nadia Boulanger. Returning to the United States in 1939 he became an instructor of music at Mills College in Oakland, Calif. At the same time Berger continued to study composition at Mills College with Darius Milhaud. Milhaud's encouragement gave Berger (who had written little music for five years) the confidence to become a composer. He now turned to a neoclassic approach by writing *Entertainment Piece* (1940), a ballet composition for piano, and two versions of a set of songs based on

poems of Yeats, which both Yeats and Berger called *Words for Music, Perhaps* (1940). The first version of *Words for Music, Perhaps*, for soprano (or mezzo) and piano, was introduced at a concert of the Composers' Forum in San Francisco on March 20, 1941; the second, for soprano (or mezzo) with flute, clarinet, and cello, was heard at the Yaddo Festival at Saratoga, N.Y., in September 1949. His personalized melodic and rhythmic manner was further developed in the Quartet in C major (1941), for woodwinds. This was Berger's first commission, brought about through Milhaud's influence, and it came from Pierre Monteux, then music director of the San Francisco Symphony, for the woodwind ensemble made up of first-desk men from that orchestra. Introduced at Oakland, Calif., on March 5, 1941—and since become one of Berger's most frequently performed works—this quartet was praised by Alfred J. Frankenstein in the *San Francisco Chronicle* for its "firm rhythmic energy," "melodious high spirits" and "formal conciseness and harmonic ingenuity." In the *New York Herald Tribune*, Virgil Thomson wrote a decade later: "The piece was a delight ten years ago, and it has worn well. . . . It is one of the most satisfactory pieces for wind in the whole modern repertory."

For the next decade and a half, Berger continued to be productive as a neoclassicist. The *Serenade concertante*, for violin, woodwind quartet, and orchestra (1944, rev. 1951) was commissioned by the Columbia Broadcasting System but was introduced in Rochester, N.Y., on October 24, 1945, Howard Hanson conducting. Three Pieces for Strings (1945) was first performed in New York on January 26, 1946, Harold Kohon conducting. As Three Pieces for String Quartet (1945), this same work was introduced by the Gordon String Quartet in Washington, D.C., on March 3, 1946. The Duo no. 1, for violin and piano (1948), received its first hearing on October 22, 1949, in New York at the hands of Joseph Fuchs and Leo Smit. Berger's first composition solely for full symphony orchestra, *Ideas of Order* (1952), was commissioned by Dimitri Mitropoulos and first performed by the New York Philharmonic under Mitropoulos on April 11, 1953. *Polyphony*, for orchestra (1955), commissioned by the Louisville Orchestra, received its premiere in Louisville, Ky., on November 17, 1956.

While thus advancing himself as a composer, Berger neglected neither of his two other careers, those of music critic and teacher. Between 1943 and 1946 he wrote music reviews for the *New York Sun* and from 1946 to 1953 for the *New York Hearld Tribune*. He also contributed numerous articles on music to prominent journals. During the summer of 1941 he was an instructor of music at North Texas State College in Denton, and in 1942–43 he was on the music faculty of Brooklyn College in New York.

Chamber Music for Thirteen Players (1956; Los

Angeles, April 4, 1960) is a transition composition—partly neoclassic in the manner of earlier works, and partly in a modified serial procedure. Berger himself described it as "neoclassic twelve tone." The writing is now more chromatic than diatonic, but its rhythmic and harmonic textures and the structure are neoclassic. It was first heard on March 1, 1956, at a concert of "Evenings on the Roof" in Los Angeles conducted by Robert Craft. Berger's serial writing reached its highest development in his String Quartet (1958), which was introduced in Boston by the Boston Fine Arts Quartet on April 14, 1960, and which later, after its premiere in New York by the Lenox String Quartet on January 26, 1962, received a citation from the New York Music Critics Circle. Chamber Concerto, for orchestra (1959, rev. 1978), commissioned by the Fromm Music Foundation, was introduced in New York on May 13, 1962.

Later works are in a postserial idiom, exploiting the total chromatic and basic (intervallic) cells, but not strictly in the twelve-tone system. Most significant have been the Septet (1966), written on a commission from the Koussevitzky Music Foundation, and given its initial hearing on November 25, 1966, at the Library of Congress in Washington, D.C., in a performance by the Contemporary Chamber Ensemble under Arthur Weisberg; Five Pieces, for piano (1969), written for Robert Miller, who both introduced it in New York on October 11, 1968, and recorded it; Trio, for guitar, violin, and piano (1972); and Five Songs, for tenor and piano (1978–79), each song in a different language, texts by Christina Rossetti, Rilke, Valéry, G.G. Bell, and Horace.

In 1953, Berger was appointed Naumburg Professor of Music at Brandeis University in Waltham, Mass. Since 1962 he has been its Irving G. Fine Professor of Music. Berger was composer-in-residence in Tanglewood, Mass., during the summer of 1964, and visiting professor of music at Harvard in 1973–74. In 1960 he received an award from the National Institute of Arts and Letters and a Fulbright Traveling Fellowship, in 1968 the St. Botolph Arts Award in Boston, and in 1975–76 a Guggenheim Fellowship. Berger is a fellow of the National Institute of Arts and Letters and of the American Academy of Arts and Letters.

Between 1957 and 1959, Berger was (and since 1963 has remained) on the board of governors of the American Composers Alliance. In 1962, he was co-founder of the journal *Perspectives of New Music,* which he edited for one year. He is the author of *Aaron Copland* (1953).

Berger's wife, Esther, died in 1960. On December 8, 1967, he married Ellen Phillipsborn Tessman, who has a doctorate in psychology and is a practicing psychologist as well as a painter.

THE COMPOSER SPEAKS: I do not engage in extensive precompositional planning, preferring to find my ideas and even, to a certain extent, to shape the form in the act of composing. For this reason I do not compose rapidly, since I prefer to derive as much pleasure as I can from the creative experience itself. I am satisfied with one work a year, and I like to live with it myself to be sure of its lasting power.

PRINCIPAL WORKS: Quartet in C major, for woodwinds (1941); *Serenade concertante,* for violin, woodwind quartet, and orchestra of strings, two horns, and trumpet (1944, rev. 1951); Three Pieces for String Quartet (1945); Three Pieces for String Orchestra (1945); Psalm 92 (*Tov L'Hodos*), for mixed a cappella chorus (1946); Partita, for piano (1947); Duo no. 1, for violin and piano (1948); Duo no. 2 for violin and piano (1950); Duo, for cello and piano (1951); Duo, for oboe and clarinet (1952); *Ideas of Order,* for orchestra (1952); *Polyphony,* for orchestra (1955); Chamber Music for Thirteen Players (1956); Duo, for clarinet and piano (1957); String Quartet (1958); Chamber Concerto, for orchestra (1959, rev. 1978); Septet, for clarinet, bassoon, flute, violin, viola, cello, and piano (1966); Movement, for orchestra (1969); Five Pieces, for piano (1969); Trio, for guitar, violin, and piano (1972); Composition for Piano, four hands (1977); Five Songs, for tenor and piano (1978–79); Piano Trio (1979).

BIBLIOGRAPHY: *BBDM; NGDMM;* Boretz, Benjamin, and Cone, Edward T. (eds.), *Perspectives on American Composers* (N.Y., 1971); Ewen, David, *American Composers Today* (N.Y., 1949); Thomson, Virgil, *American Music Since 1900* (N.Y., 1970); *American Composers Alliance Bulletin,* Spring 1953; *New York Times,* August 9, 1964; *Perspectives of New Music,* November 1979.

Bergsma, William Laurence, b. Oakland, Calif., April 1, 1921.

Without ever aligning himself with any new school or schools of musical thought, and shunning avant-gardism, Bergsma has consistently kept a middle course between conservatism and 20th-century modernism, drawing from each that which best serves his artistic aims in achieving a personal style.

His mother, Margaret (Doepfner) Bergsma, who had a career as an opera singer, gave William his first music lessons on the piano when he was five. Since he made little progress, mainly because he detested practicing, he was shifted to the violin. In his sixth year, his mother remarried and the family moved to Redwood City, forty miles south of San Francisco. There young Bergsma played the violin in the public school orchestra. He began making significant progress in music while attending Burlingame High School, which has an excellent music department. One of his teachers, Elmer Young (conductor of the school orchestra), gave him lessons in theory which Bergsma put into practice in his senior year by writing his first completed composition, performed by the school orchestra. At high school he was also given frequent opportunities to conduct its orchestra.

Without benefit of a high school diploma, Bergsma enrolled in the University of Southern California in Los Angeles in 1937 to study theory with Howard Hanson. Under such stimulation and with Hanson's encouragement, Bergsma completed, in 1937, the score for a ballet, *Paul Bunyan*, for puppets, solo dancers, and orchestra. After several orchestral numbers from this ballet were introduced by the Burlingame High School Orchestra under Elmer Young in 1938, Howard Hanson conducted a suite from the ballet score with the Rochester Civic Orchester in Rochester, N. Y., on April 29, 1939. As a ballet, the score was performed in San Francisco on June 22, 1939, Pierre Monteux conducting. Twenty-five performances and broadcasts of this suite were heard after that, with many school orchestras subsequently incorporating it into their repertoire.

In 1938 Bergsma entered Stanford University, where he took courses in music. At the same time he composed music for ballet groups in the San Francisco area. From 1940 to 1944 he attended the Eastman School of Music in Rochester, a pupil of Howard Hanson in composition and of Bernard Rogers in orchestration. Bergsma received his bachelor of arts degree from the University of Rochester and his master's degree in music two years later from the Eastman School. While attending the Eastman School he served as a teaching fellow between 1942 and 1944.

While a graduate student at the Eastman School, Bergsma intensified his creativity. His String Quartet no. 1 (1942) was introduced in Rochester by the Gordon String Quartet on April 22, 1943; it was awarded the Bearns Prize of Columbia University in 1943 and the award of the Society for the Publication of American Music in 1945. Here, and in his string Quartet no. 2 (1944; Rochester, N. Y., April 24, 1944), which had been commissioned by the Koussevitzky Music Foundation, Bergsma revealed a breadth of melodic invention that would remain one of the strong points of his creativity, together with an astuteness in contrapuntal writing. A second ballet, *Gold and the Senor Commandante* (1941)—scenario based on Bret Harte's *The Right Eye of the Commander*—was given its first performance on May 1, 1942, with Howard Hanson conducting the Rochester Civic Orchestra. A commission from Town Hall, New York, led to the writing of the Symphony for Chamber Orchestra (1942; Rochester, April 14, 1943). *Music on a Quiet Theme*, for orchestra (1943; Rochester, April 22, 1943), was the winner in a competition sponsored by the Independent Music Publishers in New York. Following its premiere it was performed by the New York Philharmonic and the National Symphony in Washington, D.C. among

other orchestras. *The Fortunate Islands*, for string orchestra (1946), was commissioned by the publishing house of Carl Fischer, Inc., and was introduced over the radio by the CBS Symphony conducted by Sylvan Levin in 1948. It was written as a reaction of the composer against Walter Raleigh's statement that the artist "does not guide the ship . . . nor discover the Fortunate Islands."

In 1944 Bergsma was an instructor in music at Drake University, Des Moines. He came to New York City in 1945, where, that May, he received a grant from the American Academy of Arts and Letters.

On September 1, 1946, Bergsma married Nancy Nickerson. That year Bergsma became the recipient of the first of two Guggenheim Fellowships (the second one coming in 1951). He was appointed to the faculty of the Juilliard School of Music in New York in 1946. He remained at Juilliard until 1963, after having become chairman of the music department and associate dean.

Between 1946 and 1949, Bergsma was involved in writing his first symphony where the contrapuntal emphasis of the first two string quartets was displaced by a rich and at times a modern harmonic treatment and in which Bergsma's mastery of organizing his materials (a characteristic of later works) comes into full focus. Structurally, this work is more of a suite than a classical symphony. It comprises two large sections, the first a Prelude and a March, and the second, an Aria and Epilogue, the two parts linked by a brief interlude. Its world premiere was given on April 18, 1950, over the Netherlands Radio, Erich Leinsdorf conducting, and its American premiere was a feature of the sixth annual Festival of American Music at Columbia University in New York on April 21, 1950, under Izler Solomon's direction.

On a commission from the Louisville Orchestra in Kentucky, Bergsma wrote *A Carol on Twelfth Night*, for orchestra, in 1953, its first performance given by that organization under Robert Whitney on October 31, 1954. String Quartet no. 3 (1953) was also the result of a commission, this one from the Juilliard Music Foundation; the Juilliard String Quartet introduced it in New York on February 17, 1956.

Bergsma's lyrical, dramatic, and organizational talent blossomed in his three-act opera, *The Wife of Martin Guerre* (1955), libretto by Janet Lewis, its first performance given by the Juilliard Opera Theater in New York on February 15, 1956, as part of the commemorative festivities attending the fiftieth anniversary of the school.

When the Lincoln Center for the Performing Arts was opened in New York in 1962, Bergsma was commissioned to write a new work for orchestra for the inaugural week to be performed by the Juilliard Orchestra. He responded with *In Celebration: Toccata for the Sixth Day* (1962; N. Y., September 28, 1962). This was followed by a major choral work based on a text from the book of Job: *Confrontation*, for chorus and twenty-two instruments (1963; Des Moines, Iowa, November 29, 1963).

From 1963 to 1971 Bergsma was director of the School of Music at the University of Washington, after which he held there the post of professor of music. He was visiting professor of music at Brooklyn College, in Brooklyn, N. Y., in 1972–73.

Of his later works, these have been the most significant: String Quartet no. 4 (1970); *The Murder of Comrade Sharik*, an opera (1973); *Wishes, Wonders, Portents, and Charms,* for mixed chorus and instruments (1974; N. Y., February 12, 1975), which the New York State Council of the Arts had commissioned and whose text came from Whitman, Melville, Sir Walter Scott, and Ecclesiastes; Second Symphony: *Voyages,* for orchestra (1975; Great Falls, Mont., May 11, 1976), commissioned by the Great Falls Symphony Orchestra and the Montana Bicentennial Commission; and *Sweet Was the Song the Virgin Sung: Tristan Revisited* (1977; Seattle, Wash., April 10, 1978), commissioned by the Seattle Symphony, the first part being a series of variations on a song by the 17th-century lutenist-composer John Attey, and the second a fantasia using materials (greatly altered) from Wagner's *Tristan and Isolde.*

THE COMPOSER SPEAKS: Everything I have to say *about* music is *in* my music.

PRINCIPAL WORKS: 4 string quartets (1942–70); 2 symphonies (1949, 1976).

Paul Bunyan, ballet (1937); Suite for Brass Quintet (1938); *Gold and the Senor Commandante,* ballet, 1941; Symphony for Chamber Orchestra (1942); *Music on a Quiet Theme,* for orchestra (1943); Three Fantasies, for piano (1943); *In a Glass of Water,* for four-part chorus and piano (1945); Six Songs, for high voice and piano (1945); *On the Beach at Night,* for four-part a cappella chorus (1946); *Black Salt, Black Provender,* for four-part chorus and two pianos (1946); *The Fortunate Islands,* for string orchestra (1946); *Tangents,* Books I and II, for piano (1951); *A Carol on Twelfth Night,* for orchestra (1954); *The Wife of Martin Guerre,* opera (1955); Concerto for Wind Quintet (1958); *Chameleon Variations,* for orchestra (1960); Fantastic Variations on a Theme from *Tristan and Isolde,* for viola and piano (1961); *In Celebration: Toccata for the Sixth Day,* for orchestra (1962); *Confrontation,* for chorus and twenty-two instruments (1963); *Serenade to Await the Moon,* for chamber orchestra (1965); Violin Concerto (1965); *The Sun, the Soaring Eagle, the Turquoise Prince, the God,* for chorus, brass, and percussion (1968); *Illegible Canons,* for clarinet and percussion (1969); *Changes,* for solo woodwind quintet, harp, percussion, and strings (1971); *Clandestine Dialogues,* for cello and percussion (1972); *The Murder of Comrade Sharik,* opera (1973); *Wishes, Wonders, Portents, and Charms,* for chorus

and instruments (1974); *In Space,* for soprano and instruments (1975); *Sweet Was the Song the Virgin Sung: Tristan Revisited,* for viola and orchestra (1977); *Blatant Hypotheses,* for trombone and piano (1977); Quintet, for flute and strings (1979); *Four All,* for three instruments (1979).

BIBLIOGRAPHY: Ewen, David, *Composers Since 1900* N. Y., 1969); Goss, Madeleine, *Modern Music Makers* N. Y., 1952); *Juilliard Review,* Spring 1956; *Who's Who in America 1980–81.*

Ⅹ **Bernstein, Leonard,** b. Lawrenceville, Mass., August 25, 1918.

The same protean genius that brought him success as a composer, conductor, pianist, university lecturer, author, and commentator distinguishes his serious music. It ranges freely over a rich variety of styles and idioms, all of which he handles with consummate technical mastery and articulateness.

Suffering from chronic asthma from birth, and equally victimized by the frequency with which his family moved from one home to another without allowing him to establish roots, he was a lonely, introverted child who sought in music an avenue of escape from his terrors and maladjustments. His first musical experiences were the popular songs he heard on the family phonograph and the religious music of the synagogue. When his family visited friends who owned a piano, he often made a beeline for the keyboard. When he was about ten, an aunt dispatched an old, weatherbeaten upright piano to the Bernstein household. As Bernstein puts it, "I made love to it right away." His first teacher was Frieda Karp, succeeded three years later by Susan Williams at the New England Conservatory of Music in Boston and, in 1932, by Helen Coates, whose influence on his early musical development was decisive. She encouraged him to study symphonies and operas from scores and to go to concerts, particularly those of the Boston Symphony. "He was frighteningly gifted," Helen Coates has recalled. Though he was an outstanding student at the Boston Latin School, which he attended from 1929 to 1935, he insisted that he "didn't exist without music." Music, he also recalls, transformed him from a sickly, frightened child "that everybody could beat up" to "the biggest boy in the class [who could] run faster, jump higher, dive better than anybody."

Upon graduating from the Boston Latin School with honors in 1935, Bernstein entered Harvard University. There he supplemented his academic courses with classes in counterpoint, theory, and music history with Walter Piston and Edward Burlingame Hill, among others. Piano study was pursued privately with Heinrich Gebhard. At Harvard, Bernstein played the piano for glee clubs, at performances of silent motion pictures, and at concerts of the Harvard Music Club. On April 21, 1939, he made his debut as conductor by directing a performance of his own incidental music to Aristophanes' *The Birds* presented at Harvard. A few weeks later, also at Harvard, he directed a production of Marc Blitzstein's *The Cradle Will Rock* in addition to performing the score at the piano. Dimitri Mitropoulos, the noted conductor then in Boston as a guest of the Boston Symphony, took note of Bernstein's talent, advised him to consider a career in conducting and invited him to attend rehearsals of the Boston Symphony.

In 1939, Bernstein graduated from Harvard with a bachelor of arts degree, *cum laude*, in music. Resisting his father's insistence that he enter the business world, Bernstein decided to leave home and try to make his way in music in New York. His first year there was a time of frustrations and physical deprivations as he failed to find any openings, At this juncture, a time of despair, Mitropoulos came to his aid by recommending him for a scholarship to the Curtis Institute of Music in Philadelphia. For two years, Bernstein studied conducting there with Fritz Reiner, orchestration with Randall Thompson, score reading with Renée Longy, and piano with Isabella Vengerova. The last of these once spoke of him as "the most talented, all-around student I ever had."

Bernstein spent the summer of 1940 on a scholarship at the Berkshire Music Center in Tanglewood, Mass., as a conducting student of Serge Koussevitzky's. It was not long before Koussevitzky began looking upon Bernstein as his protégé. After Bernstein received his diploma from Curtis in 1941, Koussevitzky called him back to Tanglewood for the summers of 1942 and 1943 to be his assistant in his conducting classes and with the Boston Symphony.

Bernstein was back in New York in the fall of 1942. He gave piano lessons, played the piano for ballet rehearsals, coached singers, and made arrangements and transcriptions for a music publishing house, some of which were published under the pseudonym of "Lenny Amber." He was also beginning to do some composing. His first composition was in a neoclassic style: a Sonata for Clarinet and Piano (1942), introduced in Boston on April 21, 1942, by David Glazer with the composer at the piano. *I Hate Music: Five Kid Songs*, an amusing song cycle to his own lyrics, was introduced by Jennie Tourel (with whom Bernstein henceforth maintained a close composer-performer relationship) on August 24, 1943, at Tanglewood and was published by Witmark. Bernstein was also working on his first major composition, his first symphony, which he had been sketching since 1939—*Jeremiah*, inspired by the biblical prophet. He completed it by the end of 1942 to submit to a competition held by the New England Conservatory; it did not win.

Though both the Berkshire Music Festival and the Berkshire Music Center at Tanglewood had suspended operations because of World War II, Bernstein was back at Tanglewood in August 1943 to provide musical illustrations at the piano for a series of lecture-recitals given by Koussevitzky for the benefit of the Red Cross. On his birthday, on August 25, Bernstein learned from Artur Rodzinski, music director of the New York Philharmonic, that he had been appointed Rodzinski's assistant with that orchestra—an appointment all the more remarkable in that Bernstein had thus far never conducted a professional orchestra, and no one that young had ever held such a post with the Philharmonic. His debut on the Philharmonic podium was under dramatic circumstances that made him an instant national celebrity. Bruno Walter, scheduled to conduct a Sunday-afternoon performance on November 14, 1943, suddenly fell ill. Just one evening earlier Bernstein was informed that he would be called to substitute—this without the benefit of a single rehearsal, even though the program included a world premiere (Miklos Rózsa's Theme, Variations and Finale). Wearing a gray business suit (the first time such a thing happened with a Philharmonic conductor) and conducting from memory, Bernstein gave a spectacular performance that was relayed by radio throughout the United States and was reported the following day on the front pages of two of New York's leading newspapers; was the subject of an editorial in one of them; and was reported as a major news event in principal newspapers everywhere.

Guest performances with other major American orchestras came in rapid succession. In one of these, with the Pittsburgh Symphony on January 28, 1944, he led the world premiere of his *Jeremiah Symphony*, with Jennie Tourel soloist. This is a work rich with romanticism and rhapsodic lyrical statements, and of ethnic interest in its occasional melodic borrowings from traditional synagogal chants. Its successful premiere led to performances in other American cities—including Boston when Bernstein made his debut with the Boston Symphony on February 18, 1944—and to a recording by RCA Victor. The symphony received the New York Music Critics Circle Award as the "outstanding orchestral work by an American composer" that season.

Bernstein revealed another facet of his creativity the same year when, on April 18, 1944, the Ballet Theater in New York presented the world premiere of his ballet, *Fancy Free* (with which Jerome Robbins made his bow as a choreographer). Bernstein's score was spiced with the rhythms, instrumental colors, and melodies of jazz in contrast to the neoclassic austerity of his clarinet sonata and the racial and romantic idioms of his symphony.

His career as a conductor was now moving at a rapid pace. In less than a year after his momentous debut with the New York Philharmonic he had traveled over fifty thousand miles and conducted over one hundred guest performances. Between 1945 and 1948 he was the musical director of the New York City Symphony. He was a participant at the International Music Festival in Prague in May 1946, conducting the Czech Philharmonic in an all-American program. During the summer of 1947, he led the Boston Symphony at the Berkshire Music Festival, the first time Koussevitzky had ever allowed anyone but himself to officiate over his orchestra during the festival season. In 1948 he made his first tour of Europe and the Middle East, appearing in nine concerts with the Palestine Orchestra in Tel Aviv. Between October 2 and 28, 1948, he directed the Palestine Orchestra during Israel's War of Independence. He conducted the Israel Philharmonic on its first tour of the United States in 1951 and on its tour of Europe in 1955. On October 1, 1957, when the Frederick R. Mann Auditorium was opened in Tel Aviv, he conducted the first concert there. In 1953 he became the first American-born conductor to appear at La Scala in Milan by performing Cherubini's *Medea*. All this was supplemented by numerous guest appearances with virtually every major orchestra in the United States.

By the 1950s he proved himself to be truly a Renaissance man whose gifts reached out in many musical directions other than conducting and the writing of serious music. He entered the popular musical theater triumphantly with his scores for the Broadway musicals *On the Town* (1944), *Wonderful Town* (1953), *Candide* (1956), and *West Side Story* (1957). He invaded motion pictures with his background music for *On the Waterfront*, starring Marlon Brando (1954), a score that received the *Downbeat* Annual Music Award. Between 1951 and 1955 he was head of the orchestra and conducting departments at the Berkshire Music Center at Tanglewood. From 1951 to 1954 he was professor of music at Brandeis University in Waltham, Massachusetts. In 1954, on the *Omnibus* program, he made the first of seven appearances on television, appearing in the dual role of conductor and commentator, and through the years, he has opened new vistas for music appreciation and education for an audience of millions over television. In 1959, he published his first book, *The Joy of Music*.

His serious compositions in the late 1940s and the 1950s consistently revealed new facets in his writing, as well as ever-increasing technical assurance. Many different styles coalesce in his second symphony, *The Age of Anxiety* (1949; Boston, April 8, 1949), commissioned by the Koussevitzky Music Foundation. This symphony was inspired by a "baroque eclogue" by W. H. Auden. In his search for the *mot juste* for each mood, situation, and intellectual concept of Auden's poems, Bernstein used jazz, neoromantic effusions, discordant harmonies and even the twelve-tone system. Yet, despite such disparate idioms, artistic unity is not sacrificed and the symphony impresses itself throughout as music of deep poetic thought and great communicative power. A similar eclecticism and intellectualism are encountered in the Serenade, for violin, strings, and percussion (1954; Venice, Italy, September 12, 1954), commissioned by

the Koussevitzky Music Foundation. This was a five-movement work based on Plato's *Symposium*, devoted to each of the five Greek philosophers or poets engaged in a discussion of love. On the other hand, Bernstein turned to wit and satire in his one-act opera *Trouble in Tahiti* (1952; Waltham, Mass., June 12, 1952), whose text (by Bernstein) concerned the domestic bickerings of a married couple in a suburban community. They escape by going to the movies.

On September 9, 1951, Bernstein married Felicia Montealegre, a Chilean-born girl who had come to America to promote an acting career. They made their home primarily in New York apartments where they raised three children. After twenty-seven years of marriage, Felicia died in East Hampton, Long Island, in 1978.

After serving for one season (1957–58) as codirector of the New York Philharmonic with Mitropoulos, Bernstein assumed full directorship in 1958. He was the youngest conductor to serve as the music director of the Philharmonic; and no musical director in Philharmonic history ever held the post longer than he. Under him, the Philharmonic entered upon a lustrous new chapter in its eventful history. Bernstein's magnetic personal appeal, as well as his uncommon gifts at conducting, were responsible for establishing box-office records and for the far-reaching successes the orchestra enjoyed through recordings and television appearances and on tour. At the same time, Bernstein's vital and progressive programming, which included many world premieres and numerous performances of avant-garde music, made his concerts continually adventurous. With the Philharmonic, Bernstein embarked on numerous tours abroad, conducting the orchestra in seventy cities in thirty-five countries; he was the first conductor to lead the Philharmonic in South America, Denmark, Finland, Holland, Israel, Japan, Mexico, New Zealand, Norway, Poland, the Soviet Union, Sweden, Turkey, and Yugoslavia. When Bernstein resigned as music director in 1969 he received a lifetime appointment as "laureate conductor." He has since continued to appear as a guest conductor with the New York Philharmonic. In addition he has made numerous guest appearances with the world's leading symphony orchestras and opera houses. These guest performances include some historic events. He helped celebrate the centenary of the Vienna State Opera with a performance of Beethoven's *Missa Solemnis* (May 25, 1969) and the bicentenary of Beethoven's birth by directing *Fidelio* (May 14, 1970) at the Theater-an-der-Wien, where the opera had been introduced. He opened a new regime for the Metropolitan Opera with *Carmen* (January 19, 1973). He honored the tenth anniversary of the papacy of Pope Paul VI at the Vatican with a presentation of his own *Chichester Psalms* (June 23, 1973). He opened the United States Bicentennial year on January 6, 1976, with a concert with the National Symphony

Orchestra in Washington, D.C. He performed at the inaugural concert for President Jimmy Carter at the Kennedy Center in Washington, D.C., on January 19, 1977. His performance of *Fidelio* at the Vienna State Opera on January 29, 1978, was the first live telecast from its stage, and it was transmitted to eighteen countries. With the Vienna Philharmonic and the forces of the Vienna State Opera he helped celebrate the two hundredth anniversary of La Scala, in Milan, in February 1978. When the Vienna State Opera paid its first visit to the United States in October 1979, Bernstein conducted it in *Fidelio*. As "laureate conductor," Bernstein conducted his own thousandth concert with the New York Philharmonic on December 15, 1971, something without precedent for a conductor in that orchestra's history.

Despite the exacting and time-consuming demands made upon him by his conductorial obligations the world over, Bernstein did not neglect serious composition in the 1950s. His third symphony, *Kaddish*, for mixed chorus, boys' choir, speaker (a female called Lily of Sharon), soprano, and orchestra, was commissioned by the Koussevitzky Music Foundation eight years before Bernstein completed its writing in 1963. He was working on its closing pages when President John F. Kennedy was assassinated. Since Kaddish is a prayer for the dead in Hebrew liturgy, Bernstein dedicated his threnody to the dead president's memory, conducting its world premiere in Tel Aviv on December 10, 1963. An unconventional text combines passages from the Hebrew prayer, the Kaddish, with interpolated lines of Bernstein's own invention in which he tries to establish a personal relationship between man (or, in this case, a woman, since the narrator is female) and God, addressing God sometimes in angry, belligerent, and familiar terms. The music is equally unconventional. Instead of reaching for an ethnic music with synagogal quotations, the score here makes use of a twelve-tone row (though the work as a whole is basically tonal) and modern rhythms enhanced by the use of an extended percussion group (with members of the chorus sometimes providing its own percussion sounds through the clapping of hands). Thirteen years after its premiere Bernstein revised *Kaddish*, shortening the work by excluding some of the narrative and tightening the structure of the music; in this new version he now assigned the narrator's part to a man to provide a contrast between narrator and the vocal soloist (a mezzo-soprano).

Bernstein's writing became simpler, more serene, and more lyrical in his next choral work, the *Chichester Psalms*, for chorus and orchestra, which had been commissioned by the Chichester Cathedral in England (1965; N.Y., July 15, 1965). For the Mass (1971), written on commission to open the John F. Kennedy Center for the Performing Arts in Washington, D.C., on September 8, 1971, Bernstein pulled out all the dramatic stops in creating a "theater piece for singers, players, and dancers," as he termed it. Here the text combines the basic words of the Catholic Mass with new material written by Bernstein and Stephen Schwartz. The pit orchestra is made up of strings, percussion, and organ, supplemented on the stage by a blues band, a rock group, and a street chorus. Loudspeakers amplified music from prerecorded tapes and spread it throughout the auditorium. A narrator, dressed in blue jeans and a denim work shirt—he was called "Celebrant"—is the central figure in this mammoth production calling for two hundred performers on stage. He personifies youth, the clergy, Everyman, Christ. He comes to the stage after the opening Kyrie to sing a hymn of praise to God ("A Simple Song"), accompanying himself on the guitar. After that, spoken words, dance, dramatics, music, point up the role of religion in a world torn apart by violence and hatred. Along this route, such subjects as the Vietnam War, the assassinations of President Kennedy, Senator Kennedy, and the Reverend Martin Luther King and the persecution of the Berrigan brothers because of their pacifism are commented upon. The Celebrant, disenchanted with religion, goes mad and smashes the sacramental vessels. But hope, love, and peace finally displace frustration and disillusionment. A boys' chorus marches down the aisles of the auditorium to touch members of the audience and encourage them to touch one another. From a recording come the final words, a simple statement (spoken by Bernstein himself): "The Mass is ended. Go in peace." Bernstein's music is an amalgam of folk tunes, church chorales, rock, revivalist hymns, show melodies, and a complex fabric of rhythms and tonalities sometimes reminiscent of Stravinsky and Ives.

The first European opera-house production of the Mass took place in Vienna on February 16, 1981, when it became the first work by an American-born composer to be performed by the Vienna State Opera.

Songfest (1977) is a cycle of twelve songs for six singers and orchestra to poems by various American writers of past and present, traversing three hundred years of American history—a portrait of America as seen from the vantage point of 1976. These songs also represent a personal document on Bernstein's part, commenting as they do on his own life and problems as an artist and a human being. The world premiere of the complete work took place in Washington, D.C., on October 11, 1977, performed by the National Symphony Orchestra under Mstislav Rostropovich in a concert that also included the premieres of two other lesser Bernstein pieces: *Slava!*, a "political overture" written in 1977 as a tribute to Rostropovich (who is affectionately called "Slava" by his closest friends and relatives), and *Three Meditations*, for cello and orchestra (1977), based on material from Bernstein's ill-fated Broadway musical, *1600 Pennsylvania Avenue* (1976).

For the opening concert of its centennial season, on September 25, 1980, the Boston Symphony conducted by Seiji Ozawa presented the world premiere of Bernstein's Divertimento for Orchestra, written on commission for that occasion. Bernstein had originally planned writing simply a fanfare but extended this project into a suite of eight short movements in a popular style that included a waltz, mazurka, sambo, turkey trot, blues, and a march entitled "The BSO Forever." Reporting to the *New York Times* from Boston, Donal Henahan said: "The piece puts its tongue in cheek and keeps it there . . . and does not hesitate to detonate whole arsenals of percussion instruments at climactic points. It is unusually painless to listen to. . . . Mr. Bernstein is a born entertainer of a superior sort, and a score such as his Divertimento is likely to outlive some of the more cerebral pieces that the orchestra's commissioning project will produce."

International recognition of Bernstein's significance as composer has been made in a number of Bernstein festivals covering a wide gamut of his musical creativity, popular as well as serious. One such took place in Israel in March and April 1977, when the Israel Philharmonic, celebrating its fortieth anniversary, presented in Tel Aviv and Jerusalem a two-week retrospective of Bernstein's music. Another retrospective Bernstein festival was held in Carinthia, Austria, in August 1977; a third, at the University of Massachusetts in Amherst between June 29 and July 3, 1978; and a fourth, in Kansas City, Mo., in May 1979.

Honors for Bernstein's overall contributions to music have accumulated through the years. Between 1957 and 1976 he received fifteen honorary doctorates including a doctor of letters from the University of Warwick in England (1974). From Chile, he earned the Order of Merit (1964); from Finland, the Order of the Lion-Commander (1965); from France, Chevalier of the Legion of Honor (1968) and Officier of the Legion of Honor (1978); from Italy, the Order of Merit—Cavaliere (1969); from Austria, the Österreichische Ehrenzeichnen für Wissenschaft und Kunst (1976). Additionally, he received the Albert Einstein Commemorative Award in the Arts from the Albert Einstein College of Medicine in New York; the John H. Finley Medal from New York City; the Alice M. Ditson Award for service to American music; the Institute of International Education Award, which President Nixon presented to him; and, in 1980, the John F. Kennedy Center Honors Award for lifetime contributions to American culture. Bernstein was also the recipient of numerous Grammys from the National Academy of Recording Arts and Sciences for his recordings, and ten Emmy awards from the National Academy of Television Arts and Sciences, as well as George Foster Peabody Awards for his various television programs.

Bernstein was the Charles Eliot Norton Professor of Poetry at Harvard in 1972 when he delivered a series of six lectures, "The Unanswered Question."

These were taped for television transmission over the Public Broadcasting Service network; were recorded by Columbia; and were published as a book. Other books by Bernstein (in addition to the above and the already mentioned *The Joy of Music*) are *Leonard Bernstein's Young People's Concerts for Reading and Listening* (1962) and *The Infinite Variety of Music* (1966).

THE COMPOSER SPEAKS: Of course my music is eclectic; all music is. Any composer's writing is the sum of himself, of all his roots and influences. I have deep roots, each different from one another. They are American, Jewish, and cosmic in the sense they come from the great tradition of all music. I have been as influenced by Handel and Haydn as by jazz, folk songs, Hassidic melodies, or prayers I heard as a child. My music is not one or the other but a mixture of all. I can only hope it adds up to something you could call universal.

PRINCIPAL WORKS: 3 symphonies (1942, 1949, 1963).

Fancy Free, ballet (1944); *Facsimile*, ballet (1946); Brass Music (1948); *Four Anniversaries*, for piano (1948); *Trouble in Tahiti*, one-act opera (1950); *Five Anniversaries*, for piano (1954); Serenade, for solo violin, string orchestra, harp, and percussion (1954); *Chichester Psalms*, for mixed chorus, boy soloist, and orchestra (1965); Mass, a "theater piece for singers, players, and dancers" (1971); *Dybbuk*, ballet (1974); *Three Meditations*, for cello and orchestra (1977); *Songfest*, a cycle of American poems for six singers and orchestra (1977); *Slava!*, a political overture (1977); Divertimento for Orchestra (1980); *Halil*, for flute and orchestra (1980).

BIBLIOGRAPHY: Briggs, John, *Leonard Bernstein: The Man, His Work, and His World* (N.Y., 1961); Ewen, David, *Leonard Bernstein* (N.Y., rev. ed. 1967); Gottlieb, Jack (ed.), *Leonard Bernstein: A Complete Catalogue of His Works* (N.Y., 1978); Gruen, John, and Hyman, Ken, *The Private World of Leonard Bernstein* (N.Y., 1968); *Esquire*, February 1967; *Holiday*, October 1959; *New York Times Magazine*, December 19, 1971; *New Yorker*, January 11 and 18, 1959; *Saturday Evening Post*, June 16, 1956; *Time*, February 4, 1957.

Beversdorf,(Samuel)Thomas, b. Yoakum,Tex., August 8, 1924.

His compositions, which include works for all media from chamber music to opera, are in a variety of 20th-century idioms; but a thread distinctly his can be recognized from his creative beginnings to his full maturity, regardless of changes of approach or style.

He was remarkably precocious in music, something his parents could recognize and develop since both were musical. His father, though employed in the United States postal service, taught music privately, played a number of wind instruments, and helped to found and direct a town band and a town orchestra; his mother was an amateur singer. At the age of two Thomas conducted his father's town band and at about the same time he began to learn to appreciate great music through recordings and the chamber music concerts his father arranged at home. For a brief period, when he was six, Thomas studied the piano, but these lessons had to be halted during the depression. After that, his father taught him the rudiments of a variety of wind instruments, upon which he became sufficiently adept to be able to play in bands and in his father's town orchestra. He also studied the cello (1938–40) with J. M. Brandstetter, director of music at the local high school. In the spring of 1948 he received additional instruction in wind instruments from Bernard Fitzgerald, Emory Remington, and William Bell.

Upon graduating from high school in 1941, Beversdorf attended North Texas Teachers College that summer. Then, on a scholarship, he enrolled at Baylor University in Waco, Tex. When, in 1942, Baylor discontinued all scholarships in music due to the war, Beversdorf transferred to the University of Texas in Austin. After a few months there his studies were temporarily terminated when he enlisted in the air force, where he spent 1942–43 as a member of the Thirty-third Army Air Force Band. Discharged in October 1943 because of asthma, he returned to the University of Texas on a Hoblitzel Fellowship, majoring in theory and compositon with Kent Kennan, Arthur Kreutz, Eric De Lamarter, and Anthony Donato, while at the same time studying cello with Homer Ulrich and trombone with Bernard Fitzgerald. Beversford received his bachelor of music degree, *cum laude,* in 1945. During these undergraduate years he played various instruments with the Austin Symphony, baritone horn with the Austin Municipal Band, first cello and first horn with the university orchestra, and trombone and tuba with the university wind ensemble.

On June 26, 1945, Beversdorf and Norma Beeson were married. She was a pianist who was appointed to the faculty at the University of Texas during the summer of 1945. In time, they raised five children (one of whom is deceased). With his young wife, Beversford left for Rochester, N.Y., in September 1945 to continue his studies in composition at the Eastman School of Music with Bernard Rogers and Howard Hanson, and to receive his master's degree in music in 1946. The summer of 1947 was spent at the Berkshire Music Center at Tanglewood, Mass., where he took supplementary courses in composition with Aaron Copland and Arthur Honegger, and conducting with Serge Koussevitzky and Stanley Chapple. Meanwhile, he had played the trombone with the Rochester Philharmonic in 1945–46. Between 1946 and 1948 he was the first trombonist and com-

poser-in-residence with the Houston Symphony and instructor of music at the University of Houston, and in 1948–49 he played the bass trombone and tenor tuba with the Pittsburgh Symphony. In 1949 he joined the faculty of Indiana University in Bloomington as instructor in music. He has been professor there since 1964.

His earlier works—beginning with his Symphony no. 1 (1945; Rochester, N.Y., 1946), Sonata, for horn and piano (1946), and Suite on Baroque Themes, for clarinet, cello and piano (1947; Houston, 1948)— reveal that strong feeling for musical architecture, that flair for vivid instrumental colorations, and that sense for affecting lyricism that would characterize so much of his later, more mature, compositions. Success came to him first with the *Mexican Portrait,* for orchestra (1948), inspired by and dedicated to Carlos Chávez, which achieved a Mexican identity without resorting to ethnic quotations. It was introduced by the Houston Symphony in April 1948 under the title of *Portrait of Carlos Chávez* and was the recipient of the Houston Symphony Prize. In the Concerto Grosso, for oboe and chamber orchestra (1948; Pittsburgh, April 28, 1950), Beversdorf brings a dissonant harmonic and contrapuntal language into a baroque structure. He becomes increasingly modern in his harmonic, contrapuntal, and rhythmic resources in his compositions in the 1950s. The most significant of these are: *Ode,* for orchestra (1952), suggested by an ode from *The Bacchae* of Euripides, which was commissioned by the Cincinnati Symphony and its musical director, Thor Johnson; the String Quartets no. 1 (1951; Bloomington, Ind., May 1952) and no. 2 (1952; Bloomington, April 1956); both introduced by the Berkshire String Quartet. *New Frontiers,* for orchestra (1953), was commissioned by the Houston Symphony, which introduced it on March 31, 1953, the composer conducting; Symphony no. 3, originally (1954) for winds and percussion, but later (1958) adapted for full orchestra, the orchestral version premiered in Bloomington on October 10, 1958; the oratorio *The Rock* (1958), on a text by T. S. Eliot, introduced in Bloomington on March 16, 1958, and in February 1960 performed by the Danish National Orchestra and Chorus. Part of this oratorio utilizes a twelve-tone row.

In compositions since 1960, Beversdorf has sometimes used a dodecaphonic style though without the Viennese avoidance of tonal regions, and sometimes with a completely tonal one. The Symphony no. 4 (1960; Bloomington, 1960), the Violin Sonata (1964–65; Rochester, 1965), and the Flute Sonata (1966) have no traces of a twelve-tone style, their emphasis being predominantly on lyricism and the projection of sensitive moods. On the other hand, one movement of the Trumpet Sonata (1962) and the Cello Sonata (1967–69; San Francisco, January 7, 1971) are entirely in a twelve-tone series.

In 1970–71, Beversdorf was composer-in-residence at Bucknell University in Lewisburg, Pa. At that time, on a commission from the university, he completed a major twelve-tone work: *Vision of Christ,* a 20th-century mystery play based on the writing of William Langland's 15th-century work, with libretto by John Wheatcroft. It is scored for narrator, vocal soloists, four dancers, chorus, and orchestra with the orchestra dressed in jongleurs' costumes (1971; Lewisburg, Pa., May 1, 1971). Later works in the twelve-tone idiom include the Tuba Concerto (1975), *La petite exposition,* for solo violin or solo clarinet and eleven strings (1976), and the Sonata for Violin and Harp (1977).

In 1977, Beversdorf was lecturer on music at the University of Guadalajara in Mexico. In 1970, the Texas Federation of Music Clubs presented him with the Distinguished Service to Music Award and in 1979 he was the recipient of the International Trombone Associations Artist and Master Teacher Award of the Year.

THE COMPOSER SPEAKS: Is it not possible that a composer is the sum of his musical experiences, filtered through a creative imagination and implemented by brutally hard work? The small recompense or satisfaction for this dedication comes from the conviction that a composer has done his best under this set of circumstances.

PRINCIPAL WORKS: 4 symphonies (1946–60); 2 string quartets (1951, 1955).

Horn Sonata (*Christmas*) (1945); *Reflections,* for small orchestra (1947); Suite, for clarinet, cello, and piano (1947), revised for clarinet, cello and strings (1949); *Mexican Portrait,* for orchestra (1948, rev. 1952); Cathedral Music, for brass choir (1950), revised for brass quartet and organ (1953); Six Short Pieces, for piano (1950); Concerto for Two Pianos and Orchestra (1951); *Ode,* for orchestra (1952); *New Frontiers,* for orchestra (1953); Symphony for Winds and Percussion (1954); Three Epitaphs, for brass quartet (1955); Three Songs, for soprano and piano, on poems of e. e. cummings (1955); Serenade, for small orchestra (1956); Tuba Sonata (1956); Serenade, for winds and percussion (1957); *The Rock,* oratorio, for vocal soloists, chorus, and orchestra (1958); Variations, "A Pretty Maid," for piano (1959); Violin Concerto (*Danforth*) (1959); Trumpet Sonata (1962); Variations for Orchestra—*Threnody: The Funeral of Youth,* for orchestra (1963); Violin Sonata (1964–65); *The Hooligan,* opera (1964–69); *Generation with the Torch,* for young orchestra (1965); Cello Sonata (1967–69); *Divertimento da camera,* for flute or piccolo, oboe or English horn, double bass, and harpsichord (1968); *Visitation of Christ,* a 20th-century mystery play (1971); Seven Short Pieces, for piano (1972); *Walruses, Cheesecake, and Morse Code,* for tuba and piano (1973); *Murals, Tapestries, and Icons,* for symphonic winds with electrified bass and electrified piano (1975); Tuba Concerto (1975); *La petite exposition,* for solo

violin or solo clarinet and eleven strings (1976); Sonata, for violin and harp (1977).

BIBLIOGRAPHY: *BBDM; Who's Who in America, 1980–81.*

Billings, William, b. Boston, Mass., October 7, 1746; d. Boston, Mass., September 26, 1800.

Devoting himself exclusively to vocal music—and primarily to hymns, anthems, and other pieces for the church—Billings became America's first major composer and is reputed to have been its first professional musician.

He was born deformed with one blind eye, one withered arm and one leg shorter than the other. Except for some singing lessons from a local pastor, he had no musical training save what he could learn autodidactically by studying psalm books and musical grammars. Upon his father's death, Billings, age fourteen, was apprenticed to a tanner. His passion for music led him to neglect work and to spend many of his working hours scribbling tunes on the hides of his tannery with chalk. When he was about twenty-one, he decided to make his living solely through music (something with few if any precedents in the colonies) by becoming a singing teacher, his aim being to remedy the musical illiteracy prevailing in the English-speaking churches. Outside the door of his home near the White Horse Tavern he placed a sign reading simply "Billings—Music," the signpost of his new profession.

As he grew older, he compounded his physical deformities with slovenly, outlandish dress, an indifference to cleanliness, boorish manners, and a loud and grating voice made all the more rasping through his continuous use of snuff. Thus he became an easy and frequent target for ridicule, in spite of which he was able to make significant headway in music mainly through his indomitable will and spirit.

When he was twenty-four, he published in Boston *The New England Psalm Singer* (1770). This was the first of six collections of vocal music mainly for the church released between 1770 and 1794. With the hymns, psalms, canons, and anthems for four-part chorus in these volumes, Billings ushered in a new era in American psalmody. His lack of proper schooling in counterpoint and harmony made it all the easier for him to defy textbook rules, and his own innovative and iconoclastic nature led him to a one-man revolution in New England church music. Rebelling against the trim, staid, orderly church pieces of his day, with their neat meters and cliché harmonies, he aimed at a music which, as he put it, was "more than twenty times as powerful as the old tunes." For the most part, he preferred brisk, fast melodies above a striding bass, and a harmony and counterpoint that gained vigor through the inclusion of discords and parallel fifths forbidden by the general practice. In doing so, he created a primitive musical art indigenous to the American colonies and early America rather than the hybrid product that had been imported from England: "Be Glad Then, America," "I Am the Rose of Sharon," "David's Lamentation," "The Lord Is Risen," "Majesty," and "Chester."

In some of his hymns and psalms, Billings was partial to a method known as "fuging tunes" (Billings's own way of spelling fuguing), which he did not invent but which he brought to increased prominence. This technique did not involve any fugal treatment at all, but consisted of a phrase sung by the first voice before it was repeated successively in imitation by the other three voices. Sometimes he used this method to begin a piece, sometimes he placed it in the middle of a composition, and sometimes at the end—preceding and following the "fuging" process with four voices in harmony. "When Jesus Wept," "The Bird," "Kittery," "Creation," are a few of his distinctive fuging tunes.

He was an original who did not hesitate to include dance tunes in religious music or to try simulating extramusical sounds, such as laughter or handclapping, in his music when the text suggested them. And in some of his secular songs, he had the gift of satire. Both in his music and text of "Modern Music" he outlined (with tongue in cheek) the precise process in writing a piece of music in the "author's darling key" of E. When some of his critics hung two cats by their tails on the signpost outside Billings's house—the feline howlings meant to suggest the kind of music Billings was writing—he responded with "Jargon," a piece of secular vocal music filled with discords from beginning to end.

He might be ridiculed and abused, but his influence was far-reaching, and in ways other than in his compositions. In 1774, he founded a singing class in Stoughton, Mass., the first ever organized in the colonies and forerunner of later singing schools which eventually ended the singing by rote in churches. Billings's singing class became, on November 7, 1786, the nucleus of America's first significant musical performing organization: the Stoughton Musical Society. Billings was a founder of the first church choir in America. He directed two of them: one at the Brattle Street Church, the other at the Old South Church. He was the first to use a pitch pipe and a cello in church singing to help establish the correct pitch.

A friend of Paul Revere's and Samuel Adams's, Billings allied himself with the Revolution from its beginnings. He adapted some of his old hymns and psalms as war songs, fitted out with new martial lyrics. "By the Waters of Babylon" became "Lamentation over Boston" written in Watertown when the British occupied Boston. With a touch of gallows humor, the new lyrics began: "By the rivers of Watertown we sat down and wept, yea we wept as we remembered Boston." His most important war song was "Chester," adapted from a hymn in the *Singing Master's Apprentice.* The song was distributed and sung throughout army camps to become a powerful propaganda and morale weapon in the revolution, the "Marseillaise" of the American Revolution, as it has been described. It is the first significant American war song by a native-born composer.

Billings was twice married: to Mary Leonard in 1764, and a decade later to Lucy Swan. With both wives he had six children. In spite of his many activities in music and the frequency with which his psalms were being reprinted in numerous collections throughout New England, Billings was incapable of making a living. He knew abject poverty. Appeals to raise funds to help support him and his family proved fruitless. He died a pauper and was buried in an unidentified grave in Boston Common.

Several 20th-century American composers have incorporated or adapted some of Billings's music into their own compositions. Among these are William Schuman (*A William Billings Overture* and *New England Triptyque*), Robert Russell Bennett (*The Fun and Faith of William Billings*), Ross Lee Finney (*Variations, Fuguing, and Holiday*), and John La Montaine (*Be Glad Then, America*).

THE COMPOSER SPEAKS: Perhaps it may be expected by some, that I should say something concerning Rules for Compositions; to these I answer that Nature is the best Dictator, for all the hard, dry studied rules that ever was prescribed, will not enable any person to form an air. . . . It must be Nature, Nature must lay the Foundation, Nature must inspire the Thought. . . . For my own part, as I don't think myself confin'd to any Rules for composition, laid down by any that went before me, neither should I think (were I to pretend to lay down the Rules) that anyone who came after me were in any way obligated to adhere to them, any further than they should think proper; so in fact, I think it is best for every *Composer* to be his own *Carver.*

PRINCIPAL WORKS: *The New England Psalm Singer* (1770); *The Singing Master's Assistant* (1778); *Music in Miniature* (1779); *The Psalm Singer's Amusement* (1781); *The Suffolk Harmony* (1786); *The Continental Harmony* (1794).

BIBLIOGRAPHY: *NGDMN*; Chase, Gilbert, *America's Music* (N.Y., 1955); McKay, David P., and Crawford, Richard, *William Billings of Boston: 18th-Century Composer* (Princeton, N.J., 1975); Nathan, Hans, *William Billings, Data and Documents* (Detroit, 1970); *American Mercury*, May 1928.

Bird, Arthur H., b. Belmont, Mass., July 23, 1856; d. Berlin, Germany, December 22, 1923. He was the first American to write music for a major ballet, and the first to receive commissions from Germany and France.

He grew up on farms owned jointly by his father and uncle on the Watertown-Cambridge Line. Both were professional musicians, founders of and performers in the Bird Quartet, which gave concerts in the Boston area. Exceptionally musical and precocious, Arthur Bird was early taught by his father to play the organ. When he was fifteen, Arthur succeeded his sister, Helen, as organist of the First Baptist Church in Brookline, Mass. His academic education took place in the public schools of Belmont, including Belmont High School, from which he graduated. In 1875 he went to Berlin, where for the ensuing two years he studied piano with Albert Loeschorn, organ with Karl August Haupt, and composition with E. Rohde. On April 21, 1876, he gave an organ recital in Berlin.

In 1877, he left Berlin for Halifax, Nova Scotia, to serve as organist of the St. Matthew Church, to head the piano department at the Young Ladies' Academy, and to found and direct the Arion Club, the first men's chorus in Nova Scotia. During this period he began composing, mainly short pieces for the piano and chamber music ensembles.

He was back in Berlin in 1881, attending the Kullak School of Music as a pupil of Heinrich Urban's in composition. Bird's first publication appeared in 1882, a set of piano pieces, one of which, "A Witch's Tale," was performed in Boston a year or so later. Bird's op. 2 was also a collection of piano pieces (1882).

His first success as composer came on February 4, 1886, when the Singakademie in Berlin, under his own direction, presented an all-Bird program comprising his Symphony in A major (1885) together with his First Little Suite (1884) and Concert Overture (1885). The symphony was particularly well received, and it was also highly praised in the *New York Times* when it was introduced by the New York Symphony Society under Walter Damrosch on June 3, 1886. The success of Bird's Berlin concert was soon followed by another in Sonderhausen, where, on June 3, 1886, his *Carnival Scene* for orchestra (1884) was introduced. This was a brilliantly orchestrated and vividly pictorial tonal picture of a Mardi Gras. It brought Bird a letter of praise from Liszt, whom Bird first met in April 1884 and with whom he spent several rewarding months in Weimar a year later. The American premiere of *Carnival Scene* followed in Chicago on July 26, 1886, with Theodore Thomas conducting the Chicago Symphony, and was given in New York on April 23, 1887. On June 2, 1974, it was revived in Washington, D.C., in an American music concert by the National Gallery orchestra under Richard Bales, one of the rare occasions when one of Bird's compositions was performed after his death.

At the invitation of the North American Sängerbund in Milwaukee, Bird returned to the United States during the summer of 1886 to fill the post of director of the Milwaukee Music Festival for one year, and to give piano and organ recitals. After that—except for a brief visit to the United States in 1897 for the production of his operetta *The Highwayman* in New York and, in 1911, to explore the possibilities of writing an opera—Bird spent the remainder of his life in Germany, serving for many years as correspondent for the *Musical Leader* and several other American journals. On February 29, 1888, he married Wilhelmine Waldman in Peterboro, England. Since she was a woman of ample financial means, Bird no longer was under any necessity to earn his living through his music, with the result that his activities both as a performer and composer relaxed considerably. The Birds acquired luxurious houses, first in Berlin and then in Grünewald suburb; these became the meeting places of leading Berlin musicians and musical visitors from abroad. The Bird fortune was greatly depleted by the inflation of the post–World War I era in Germany, compelling them to exchange their large house in Grünewald for an apartment on the Kurfürstendamm in Berlin; but they were by no means destitute. Bird was fatally stricken by a heart attack while riding on a suburban train in Berlin: death was instantaneous and was not discovered until after the train had arrived at a station.

Bird's major works were written before 1891—most of them between 1885 and 1887—and enjoyed prominent performances both in Europe and the United States. He allied himself with the musical conservatives of the late 1880s. He was hostile to experiment and innovations, and in his criticisms fiercely attacked the music of Richard Strauss and Debussy.

In his music he combined the late-19th-century German Romanticism wih French refinement and sensitivity. The critics of his time, both in Germany and in the United States, praised him for his facile and infectious lyricism (while noting that it avoided depth of thought or emotion), his flair for color instrumentation, and his talent for musical representations of the kind of scenes and subjects favored by the American Luminist painters, his gift for writing in dance forms, and his occasional expression of a boisterous humor. His score for the ballet *Rübezahl* (1887–88, rev. 1891)—the first full-length ballet by an American—is generally esteemed to be his most important composition in any medium: it had been commissioned by Count Bolko von Hochberg, general manager of the Prussian theaters. (The date and place of the world premiere of the first version is not known, but the revised version was introduced on June 19, 1891, at the New England Conservatory of Music in Boston.) He was also famous for his programmatic music beginning with *A Carnival Scene* and including Second Little Suite, for orchestra (1884–85), Two Episodes for Orchestra (1887–88) and Two Poems, for orchestra (1888). Among his finest nonprogrammatic music are his Symphony in A; the Introduction and Fugue, for orchestra and organ (1886); the Third Little Suite, for orchestra (1890; Chicago, June 12, 1893); Suite in D, for wind instruments (1889): and the Serenade for Wind Instruments (1898). The last of these received the Paderewski Prize in 1901 and was given its initial hearing in Boston on March 31, 1902. One of Bird's few works in the post-1891 period was an operetta, *Daphne*—libretto by Margaurite Merington—which was produced in the ballroom of the Waldorf Astoria Hotel in New York on December 13, 1897. His later compositions include a number of pieces for the harmonium (reed organ). He wrote only two compositions with an American identity: Variations on an American Folk Song, for flute and orchestra 1891), the "folk song" here being Stephen Foster's "Swanee River," and *American Melodies*, a waltz cycle for piano duet (1887).

In the early 1900s Bird stopped composing, although he lived another two decades. Asked in 1907 the reason for his creative abstinence, he replied: "An artist should know when he has said what he had it in him to say."

In 1924, Bird's widow presented many of Bird's manuscripts to the Library of Congress in Washington, D.C.

THE COMPOSER SPEAKS: My aim is to paint ideas skillfully, in glowing, original and perfectly tuned colors . . . [and to be] a successful seeker, finder and opener of new and original effects.

PRINCIPAL WORKS: 3 Little Suites, for orchestra (1884, 1885, 1890).

String Quartet (1880); Four Sonatas, for organ (1882); *A Carnival Scene*, for orchestra (1884); Symphony in A major (1885); Concert Overture, for orchestra (1885); Five Quartets, for men's chorus (1885); Introduction and Fugue in D minor, for orchestra and organ (1886); Eight Sketches, for piano (1886); Seven Pieces, for piano (1887); *American Melodies*, waltz cycle for piano duet (1887); Two Pieces, for flute and small orchestra (1887–88); Two Poems, for orchestra (1888); Two Pieces, for string orchestra (1888); Suite in D major for wind instruments (1889); Theme and Variations, for piano (1889); Theme with Variations, for organ (1889); Two Pieces, for violin and small orchestra (1890); Three Pieces, for piano (1890); Four Pieces, for piano (1890); *Rübezahl*, ballet (1887–91); Variations on an American Folk Song, for flute and orchestra (1891); Five Songs, for women's voices and piano (1894); Serenade for Wind Instruments, for double quartet of woodwinds and two French horns (1898); Three Oriental Sketches, for organ (1898); *Daphne*, operetta (1893–94).

BIBLIOGRAPHY: Elson, Louis Charles, *History of American Music* (N.Y., 1904; reprinted, N.Y., 1971); Loring, William C., *The Music of Arthur Bird* (Washington, D. C. 1974); *Musical America*, February 9, 1924; *Musical Quarterly*, January 1943.

Blackwood, Easley, b. Indianapolis, Ind., April 21, 1933.

Though Blackwood has used serial technique in a modified form, discordant harmonies and even electronics, he never abandoned those romantic and rhapsodic qualities with which he had first gained prominence with his first symphony when he was twenty-six.

His father, Easley Blackwood, was the internationally famous bridge expert who devised the Blackwood Convention. Both parents were musical. From their collection of recordings Blackwood became acquainted with the music of Alban Berg and Schoenberg when he was still a child. When he was four, his mother taught him the names and sounds of pitch and about a year later he received his first piano lesson. Under the instruction of Bomar Cramer, he made such progress that by the time he was nine he performed a Mozart piano concerto at a studio recital. Though he abandoned all formal piano lessons by the time he was thirteen, he continued to develop his technique and repertoire by himself. In his fourteenth year he mastered the complexity of Prokofiev's Piano Sonata no. 7. At about the same time he appeared as a piano soloist with the Indianapolis Symphony, Fabien Sevitzky conducting, in a performance of Tchaikovsky's Piano Concerto no. 1, a performance he repeated soon after that at youth concerts in numerous high schools throughout Indianapolis. When he was fifteen, he gave a piano recital featuring Copland's intricate and lengthy Piano Sonata. The summers between 1948 and 1950 were spent at the Berkshire Music Center at Tanglewood, Mass., studying composition principally with Messiaen and conducting with Lukas Foss and Leonard Bernstein, and singing in the Festival Chorus with the Boston Symphony in performances of Mahler's *Resurrection* Symphony and Stravinsky's *Oedipus Rex*. Between 1949 and 1951, Blackwood studied composition with Bernhard Heiden at Indiana University in Bloomington, commuting sixty miles for each lesson. Then, on Heiden's advice, he entered Yale University to become Paul Hindemith's pupil in composition, to receive his bachelor of music degree in 1953, and his master's degree in music a year later.

Though up to this time Blackwood had written a number of compositions, he discarded everything he had done up to 1953 and began his mature composing career that year with the Sonata for Viola and Piano, which was published by Elkan-Vogel as op. 1. On the strength of this work and the one that followed—Chamber Symphony for fourteen winds (1954)—Blackwood received a Ditson Scholarship for Graduate Study and a Fulbright Fellowship which enabled him to live in France for two years and study composition with Nadia Boulanger both in Paris and at the American Conservatory at Fontainebleau. During the summer of 1955 he was the recipient in France of the Lili Boulanger Memorial Award in composition.

He completed his Symphony no. 1 in France in 1955, which the Boston Symphony, under Charles Munch, introduced in Boston on April 18, 1959. The symphonic structure was here used flexibly, and though the writing was consistently tonal, the tonality was free and fluid. This was music that in its contrapuntal writing and the inexorable logic of its musical thought revealed the influence of Hindemith while also expressing Mahlerlike romantic surges. Munch thought so highly of it that he repeated it in Boston the following November, then performed it in New York. Soon after that, it was also given by the Cleveland Orchestra and the Concertgebouw Orchestra in Amsterdam, both conducted by George Szell, and by the Mexico City Orchestra under Carlos Chávez. Besides being performed by these notable organizations, the symphony was published and, with a grant from the Koussevitzky Music Foundation, was recorded by RCA as a winner among fifty-two competitors. Not yet twenty-six, with only his third opus, Blackwood emerged with his symphony as a composer henceforth to be reckoned with.

After returning to the United States in 1958, Blackwood, on the recommendation of Walter Piston, was appointed assistant professor of music at the University of Chicago even though he lacked a doctorate. He has remained at the university since then, rising to full professorship in 1968.

Soon after returning from Europe, Blackwood was commissioned by the Fromm Music Foundation to write String Quartet no. 1 (1957)—premiered by the Kroll Quartet in 1959, and then performed by the Budapest Quartet and the Fine Arts Quartet. Two more commissions came in 1960, one from the Naumburg Foundation for Fantasy, for cello and piano, and the other from G. Schirmer for the Symphony no. 2 to commemorate the centenary of that publishing house. The symphony, introduced by the Cleveland Orchestra under George Szell in Cleveland on January 5, 1961, had much of the rhapsodic and contrapuntal attributes of the first one, though the harmonic and rhythmic writing and the thematic evolution had become more complex and subtle. In the Concerto for Clarinet and Orchestra (1964)—commissioned for the Cincinnati Symphony by an anonymous patron and given its first performance by that orchestra on November 20, 1964, with Richard Waller conducting—Blackwood pays tribute to the memory of his recently deceased teacher, Paul Hindemith, in the second movement. In this tonal tribute to Hindemith, no themes are actually quoted, but Blackwood builds his own material on some musical elements encountered in Hindemith, with the movement's overall shape and mood suggested by sections

from Hindemith's *Mathis der Maler*, the Violin Concerto (op. 36, no. 4) and the *Kammermusik* (op. 24, no. 1). Blackwood's Symphony no. 3, for small orchestra—written in the same year as the Clarinet Concerto—was given its first hearing in Chicago by the Chicago Symphony under Jean Martinson on March 7, 1965.

Many of Blackwood's later works, in a modified serial technique, became increasingly dissonant and structurally more complex, but without sacrificing earlier dramatic or romantic impulses. Among these are the Symphonic Fantasy (1965), which the Indianpolis Symphony and its musical director, Izler Solomon, commissioned and introduced (October 30, 1965); the Violin Concerto (1967), written on a commission from Yehudi Menuhin, who offered the first performance in Bath, England, on July 4, 1967; and the Concerto for Flute and Orchestra (1968), heard for the first time on July 28, 1968, at the Congregation of the Arts at Hopkins Center, Dartmouth College in Hanover, N.H., where Blackwood was then composer-in-residence. A Piano Concerto (1970)—commissioned by the Illinois Art Council and introduced by the Chicago Symphony under Gunther Schuller at the Ravinia Festival in Illinois on July 26, 1970—looked back to the bravura piano concerto writing of the 19th century, for all its dissonances.

With a multimedia opera, *Four Letters from Gulliver* (1972)—written with the collaboration of Elliot Kaplan and Frank Lewin and with text by Robert Karmon and Louis Phillips based on Jonathan Swift—Blackwood engaged for the first time in writing live electronic music by using the Moog synthesizer. The Minnesota Opera produced it in Milwaukee on February 22, 1975. Three and a half years later, on November 22, 1978, Blackwood's Symphony no. 4 was given its world premiere by the Chicago Symphony under Georg Solti. It took Blackwood six and a half years to complete this work, which had been commissioned by the Chicago Symphony for its eightieth birthday in 1970. Structurally, it was Blackwood's most ambitious work up to then, revealing a remarkable virtuosity in writing for a greatly augmented orchestra and dramatized by sweeping, Mahlerlike romantic climaxes.

In 1968, Blackwood received the Creative Arts Award from Brandeis University in Waltham, Mass. In 1977–78, on leave from the University of Chicago, he served as visiting professor of music in St. Louis on a grant from the National Endowment for the Humanities, to explore nontradiational tuning and other new systems.

THE COMPOSER SPEAKS: A complete understanding of the structure and style of a composition is not necessary to its enjoyment. Indeed, any work which reveals all of its secrets on a single hearing can hardly be considered artistic. The process of discovery and enlightenment upon repeated hearing is an essential part of the true appreciation of any good music. It is the composer's duty, therefore, to make the music such that an intelligent listener will want to hear it again. The listener, in his turn, should focus attention on those aspects which are the most immediately accessible. The purely sensuous nature of the sounds produced is certain to be arresting to most listeners. Beyond this, one must trust the composer to arrange the sounds in a logical, harmonious way, so that the ebb and flow of the music is perceived. Coupled with the logical arrangement should be enough of the irrational and capricious, so that the whole thing does not degenerate into a drearily predictable correctitude. Ideally, something new should be uncovered each time the work is heard, so that each hearing is a fresh and stimulating experience . . . From the composer's standpoint, such a piece is more stimulating to write, both from an intellectual and intuitive point of view, since each problem must be solved on the spot and all are different.

PRINCIPAL WORKS: 5 symphonies (1945–78); 2 string quartets (1958, 1959); 2 violin sonatas (1960, 1975).

Viola Sonata (1953); Chamber Symphony, for fourteen instruments (1954); Concertino, for five instruments (1959); Fantasy for Cello and Piano (1960); Pastorale and Variations, for wind quintet (1961); Clarinet Concerto (1964); Symphonic Fantasy (1965); Fantasy, for flute, clarinet, violin, and piano (1965); Three Short Fantasies, for piano (1965); Symphonic Movement, for organ (1966); *Un voyage à Cythère*, for soprano and ten players (1966); Concerto for Oboe and Strings (1966): Violin Concerto (1967); Piano Trio (1968); Concerto for Flute and String Orchestra (1968); Piano Concerto (1969–70); *Four Letters from Gulliver*, a multimedia opera written with Elliot Kaplan and Frank Lewin (1972).

BIBLIOGRAPHY: Ewen, David, *Composers Since 1900* (N.Y., 1969); *Chicago Symphony Orchestra Program Notes*, November 22, 1978.

Blitzstein, Marc, b. Philadelphia, Pa., March 2, 1905; d. Fort-de-France, Martinique, January 22, 1964.

Blitzstein first became prominent as the musical spokesman for the American political left and the social discontent of the 1930s. Though he never abandoned his political radicalism and his social consciousness, he developed into a powerful musical dramatist, more concerned with the demands of the theater and musico-dramatic writing than with propaganda.

He was born into wealth, both his grandfather and his father being bankers. His mother was an amateur singer. Exceptionally precocious in music, born with perfect pitch, Marc could play the piano when he was three. He began piano lessons at four, at five appeared in a public concert, and at seven performed Mozart's *Coronation Concerto* publicly and made his first attempts at composition. His early music study took place with Constantin von Sternberg, while attending public schools. In 1920 he appeared as piano soloist with the Philadelphia Orchestra.

Upon graduating from high school in 1921, Blitzstein earned a scholarship for the University of Pennsylvania. He remained there only two years, forced out because of persistent absences from the required courses in gymnasium, which he detested. By 1923 he had come to the conviction that henceforth he wanted to develop himself as a musician. With this in mind he enrolled in the Curtis Institute of Music, a student in composition of Rosario Scalero's; at the same time he commuted regularly to New York to take piano lessons with Alexander Siloti. In 1926 he went to Europe to study with Nadia Boulanger in Paris and with Arnold Schoenberg at the Akademie der Kunst in Berlin. In Berlin, in 1928, he wrote the music for an innovative documentary film, *Hands*, made up solely of hand movements.

Returning to the United States in 1928, he supported himself by lecturing on music at women's clubs and various educational institutions. All this while he was writing compositions in the dissonant style then regarded as ultramodern, and they were performed at American modern music concerts (the Copland-Sessions Concerts and those of the League of Composers, both in New York, and at the Yaddo Festival in Saratoga, N.Y.) as well as in Paris and London. These works included *Percussive Music*, for piano (1929), which was discordant from beginning to end and in which the different sections were separated by the banging down of the piano lid. A Serenade, for string quartet (1931), performed at the Yaddo Festival, was unusual in a different way: All of its movements had the tempo marking Largo. Other compositions of this period were thoroughly modern in harmonic and rhythmic idioms; these included a ballet, *Cain* (1930), *Romantic Piece*, for orchestra (1930), String Quartet (1930), Piano Concerto (1931) and a one-act opera commissioned by the League of Composers, *The Harpies* (1931). He also had ventured into the musical theater with *Triple Sec*, a farce with music in a lighter vein than his concert works, produced in Philadelphia on May 6, 1929, interpolated into the Broadway revue *Garrick Gaieties* a year later, and in May 1967 revived posthumously in New York.

The Blitzstein of the early 1930s was described as "a very angry young man, angry with himself, edgy, mettlesome, sharp-tongued [who] looked at everything, listened to everything, and quarreled with everyone." He was affected by the social upheaval taking place in the early years of the Great Depression. Slowly he became convinced that the kind of modern music he had been writing for an elite audience was out of joint with the times. He began to think in terms of music as propaganda.

While trying to crystallize his political thinking and his aims as a composer, he wrote little for the next three years. He traveled to Yugoslavia, Spain, and France in 1932 and 1933, and in March 1933 he married Eva Goldbeck, a writer with pronounced leftist leanings. (She was the daughter of the famous opera singer Lina Abarbanel.) She influenced him in his evolving social and political consciousness. Impressed by the *Zeitkunst* ("contemporary art") of Kurt Weill, Bertolt Brecht, and others—and particularly by the *Threepenny Opera*—with all of which he had become acquainted in Berlin, he began thinking in terms of writing music for a mass public in a popular style, music easy to listen to and comprehend at first hearing, and at the same time serving as a vehicle of left-wing political propaganda. With this in mind, late in 1935, he wrote a song about a prostitute, "The Nickel under My Foot," which he played and sang for Bertolt Brecht when Brecht came to visit him in his Greenwich Village apartment. Brecht liked the song but suggested that Blitzstein work on a broader canvas by writing an opera covering every form of "prostitution"—in politics, religion, business, the press, and so forth. This proved the stimulus Blitzstein needed for the writing of a proletarian musical play for which he prepared his own libretto, and the writing of which brought him the solace and escape he needed after the death of his wife during the summer of 1936. By the end of 1936 he had completed *The Cradle Will Rock*, into which he incorporated "The Nickel under My Foot," which had been its progenitor. It dealt with the efforts to found a union in Steeltown, the unscrupulous methods of the most powerful men of the community to frustrate this attempt, and the final victory of the working people. Though loosely identified as an "opera," *The Cradle Will Rock* was actually a theater piece with music, combining social drama and the Broadway musical stage with elements of opera. Blitzstein's score was a collation of ballads, ditties, patter songs, torch songs, blues, and parodies. Now the music was a basic part of what was transpiring on the stage; now it was a background for satiric commentary; now it was the base upon which spoken dialogue rested; now it was used to point up characterization or to help the dramatic action. All this was done with such compositional skill, theatrical astuteness and imagination that Blitzstein forthwith emerged as a leading American proponent of the left-wing musical theater.

The world premiere of *The Cradle Will Rock* on June 16, 1937, was one of the more dramatic pages in the history of the Broadway theater; it also spontaneously changed the way this music was to be produced. It had been intended for the WPA Federal Theater, an agency subsidized by the government during the depression to find jobs for people in the theater. John Houseman was the producer, and Orson Welles, director—both of them then unknown. By opening night many government officials, objecting to the left-wing subject of this text, successfully brought pressure to bear on the Federal Theater to cancel the production. But this cancellation was made just a few hours before curtain time. Almost at the zero hour, another theater was found nearby to transfer cast and audience to. But a greater problem than finding a theater had to be coped with. Scenery and costumes belonged to the Federal Theater and could not be used. And, with funds denied, there was no money to pay for an orchestra. Thus, through necessity, the production had to be reduced to bare essentials: performed on a totally bare stage with the actors dressed in their everyday clothes. In place of an orchestra, Blitzstein sat at the piano on the stage both to provide the musical accompaniment and to give a brief explanation of some of the stage action. Somehow, this novel approach contributed a new dramatic and emotional appeal to the work. In the *New York Times*, Brooks Atkinson described the production as "the most versatile triumph of the politically insurgent theater," and the music critics, including Virgil Thomson of the *Herald Tribune*, found Blitzstein's music provocative in its satire, delightful in its wit, and fresh in its conception. The show became an instant box-office success; financing was immediately available for an extended Broadway run. Since then, *The Cradle Will Rock* has been intermittently revived both on and off Broadway and at symphony concerts. When it was produced in Miami, Fla., in 1950 it became the first interracial production in that city.

Close on the heels of *The Cradle Will Rock* came Blitzstein's "song play" for radio. *I've Got the Tune* (1937; CBS-Radio, October 24, 1937), a parable of a modern musician who invents a melody and then must find for it some meaningful lyrics, which he ultimately comes upon while watching a May Day parade of workers. With *No for an Answer* (1941; N.Y., January 5, 1941) Blitzstein returned to the stage and to the production procedures that had made *The Cradle Will Rock* famous. Here, too, the story is focused on an attempt to create a union, this time among Greek waiters who are seasonal employees of a summer luxury hotel and the futile efforts of employers to destroy it. Once again the work was given without scenery or costumes, and with Blitzstein at the piano. And, once again, its leftist theme inspired opposition and censorship by the authorities. The license commissioner of New York City prohibited further presentations on the grounds that the auditorium was guilty of "violations," making it unsuitable for operatic presentations—a specious excuse since operas had been frequently mounted there without opposition.

In 1940–41, Blitzstein was the beneficiary of a Guggenheim Fellowship which was renewed one year later. With American's involvement in World War II, Blitzstein enlisted in the army and was assigned to the Eighth Air Force, where he fulfilled various musical commitments. One was the writing of music for a military documentary produced by Garson Kanin, *True Glory* (1945). Another was the composition of *Freedom Morning*, a tone poem for orchestra (1943; London, September 28, 1943) that used thematic materials provided him by other men in uniform; it was dedicated to black soldiers. A third was *The Airborne* (1945; N.Y., April 11, 1946), a symphony scored for narrator, solo voices, male chorus, and orchestra tracing the history of flight from Icarus to the time of World War II and pointing up the futility of war in often vivid programmatic writing. *The Airborne* helped bring Blitzstein a grant from the American Academy of Arts and Letters in 1946 and was responsible for his getting the Page One Award of the Newspaper Guild in 1947.

Blitzstein returned to the Broadway musical stage with *Regina* (1949), commissioned by the Koussevitsky Music Foundation. Here he no longer concerned himself with overt political protest but became a composer ready to use the fullest resources of his creativity and technique to meet the demands of musical drama. He had a powerful play to work with and adapt: Lillian Hellman's *The Little Foxes*, a bitter indictment of a decadent, rapacious southern family torn apart and finally destroyed by hate and avarice. Ragtime, played by a black band, and occasionally a tune reminiscent of Broadway musicals were the carryovers of his former popularism. But with these came expressive recitatives, now of a Handelian breadth and now with the austerity and dramatic thrust of Alban Berg's *Sprechstimme* ("song speech"). There were orchestral interludes of symphonic dimensions to serve as eloquent commentaries on the evils that were transpiring on the stage. Leonard Bernstein said of *Regina* that it was the "apex, a summation of what Blitzstein was trying to do"— and by this he undoubtedly meant that *Regina* was the realization of Blitzstein's ambition to write twentieth-century musical drama. *Regina* opened on Broadway on October 30, 1949. A decade later it passed into the opera house (where it rightfully belonged) in the first of many revivals by the New York City Opera. It was also staged by the Santa Fe Opera in 1959, the Michigan Opera in 1977, and the Houston Opera on April 25, 1980.

In 1959, Blitzstein received a grant from the Ford Foundation to write an opera about the Sacco-Vanzetti case, a political cause célèbre of the 1920s in which two Italian aliens in South Braintree, Mass., were accused of and executed for a murder many believed they had never committed but for which they had been "framed" because of their anarchistic beliefs. This subject had so fascinated Blitzstein as a young radical in 1932 that he then wrote an oratorio about Sacco and Vanzetti entitled *The Condemned*. The writing of an opera on the same subject obsessed him for four years, but all he managed to get down on paper before his death were sketches. He did, however, complete enough of a one-act opera—*Idiots First* based on a story by Bernard Malamud—that it

could be completed by Leonard Lehrman for production in New York on January 22, 1978.

In 1954, Blitzstein made a new adaptation of Bertolt Brecht's libretto for *The Threepenny Opera*, while leaving the Kurt Weill score intact. It opened off Broadway on March 10, 1954, for a six-year run, the longest up to then in the history of the American musical theater. Two national companies toured the United States with it in 1960 and 1961. One of its principal numbers, "Mack the Knife" (originally known as "Moritat"), became a major hit song, in time selling over ten million records in almost fifty different versions.

Between 1931 and 1948, Blitzstein provided the background music for several motion-picture documentaries. He also contributed incidental music to numerous plays in New York and wrote articles on music for leading American journals and newspapers. In 1939 he was founder and vice-president of the Arrow Music Press in New York. In 1962–63 he was composer-playwright-in-residence at Bennington College in Vermont.

Blitzstein was on vacation at Fort-de-France in Martinique in January 1964 when he was so severely attacked by three sailors (under circumstances never explained) that he suffered a fatal brain injury. His body was brought back to the United States and buried in Chelten Hills, Philadelphia. A memorial concert was held in New York on April 20, 1964.

THE COMPOSER SPEAKS: Music in the theater is a powerful, an almost immorally potent weapon. It will do things you could never dream of; it will be fantastically perfect for one scene; it can louse up another scene to an extent that is unbelievable. There is only one rule I know: follow the theater instinct. You discover you have got it very much in the same way you first discovered you were a composer. You may be wrong on both counts, but your inner conviction is all you have got.

Discovering that I am an opera composer and discovering also that I am a rebel, I find myself in perfectly good company—and I am not too upset by it. I do not welcome the sensationalistic aspect of the response that my words get. If you feel I do, let me disabuse your mind immediately. I think it simply turns out that there is perfectly good tradition for this kind of writing and that in all times and all places it has been said to the composer: "You are writing this not because you wish to write music but because you wish to make this kind of statement—because you wish to be sensational in one form or another."

PRINCIPAL WORKS: String Quartet (1930); Serenade, for string quartet (1931); Piano Concerto (1931); *The Harpies*, one-act opera (1931); *The Condemned*, oratorio (1932); *The Cradle Will Rock*, a play with music (1936); *I've Got the Tune*, radio song play (1937); *No for an Answer*, play with music (1940); *Freedom Morning*, tone poem for orchestra

(1943); *The Airborne*, symphony for men's chorus, speaker, solo tenor, solo baritone, and orchestra (1946); *Regina*, opera (1949); *The Guests*, ballet (1949); *Reuben, Reuben*, opera (1955); *Fear*, a study for orchestra (1957); *This Is the Garden*, cantata for chorus and orchestra (1957); *Juno*, opera (1958); *Idiots First*, one-act opera completed by Leonard Lehrman (1964).

BIBLIOGRAPHY: Copland, Aaron, *The New Music: 1900–1960* (N.Y., 1968); Gruen, John, *Close-Up* (N.Y., 1967); *Opera News*, April 12, 1980, *Saturday Review*, May 16, 1959; *Show*, June 1964.

Bloch, Ernest, b. Geneva, Switzerland, July 24, 1880; d. Portland, Oreg., July 15, 1959. American citizen, 1924.

Though most remembered for his racially inspired Jewish compositions, Bloch produced a library of equally impressive nonprogrammatic concert music, usually within traditional structures, with no ethnic implications. It was in the latter category that in 1954 he became the first American to receive top awards from the New York Music Critics Circle in the same year in two different categories (chamber music and orchestral music).

Neither of his parents was musical. They owned a store in Geneva selling clocks, jewelry, handbags, and so forth. Since Ernest's older brother had died of diphtheria at the age of four, Ernest became an overprotected child who betrayed in public schools signs of melancholia, partly because he was victimized by his older schoolmates, and partly because of innate nervousness. His first contact with music came from overhearing his father (who had once planned to study for the rabbinate) sing Jewish folk songs and Hebrew liturgical melodies, and by listening to his sister (five years his senior) playing operatic potpourris and salon pieces on the piano. He was six when his mother presented him with a toy flute on which he improvised melodies. Three years later he acquired a violin and was given lessons by Albert Gos. It was not long afterward that he began to compose melodies for that instrument. When he was about ten and decided to become a composer, he wrote a vow to that effect on a sheet of paper, buried it under a mound of stones, and built a ritual fire.

He had made such rapid progress on the violin that many of his neighbors and friends regarded him as a prodigy. Influenced by their enthusiasm, Bloch's father brought him in December 1894 for testing to Émile Jaques-Dalcroze, professor of theory and composition at the Geneva Conservatory, who forthwith agreed to supervise the boy's training in solfeggio and composition and encouraged him to continue his violin studies with Louis Rey. In 1896 Bloch completed his first ambitious piece of music, a four-movement string quartet (subsequently withdrawn).

Between 1897 and 1899, Bloch resided in Brussels, having come to that city to study violin with Eugène Ysaÿe. At the same time he took lessons in theory and composition from François Rasse. In Brussels, in 1897, he wrote a Fantaisie, for violin and piano, dedicated to Ysaÿe, and a song dedicated to Ysaÿe's wife.

In 1899, Bloch left Brussels to continue his music studies in Germany, where he lived for the next four years, a pupil in composition of Ivan Knorr's at Hoch's Conservatory in Frankfurt (1899–1901) and Ludwig Thuille in Munich (1901–3). In Frankfurt, inspired by a youthful love affair with Marguerite Augusta Schneider, a fellow student at Hoch's Conservatory, he wrote *Vivre-Aimer*, a tone poem in the styles of Liszt and Richard Strauss; its premiere was given at the Festival of Contemporary Swiss Music in Geneva on June 23, 1901. More ambitious still was the Symphony in C-sharp minor (1901–2), an extended work in Mahler's romanticized idiom. This symphony anticipated the direction Bloch's creativity would take a decade later in that one of the themes of the last movement was in the style of a Hassidic dance tune. Bloch himself conducted two movements of this symphony in Basle in 1903. It was not until 1908, in Geneva, that the symphony was given in its entirety for the first time. Romain Rolland, present at the performance, called it "one of the most important works of the modern school."

Following a one-year visit to Paris in 1903—where he met and was influenced by Debussy, and where one of his compositions, *Historiettes au crépuscule*, for mezzo-soprano and piano (1904), became his first publication—Bloch returned to Geneva. There, on August 13, 1904, he married Marguerite Schneider. To support himself and his wife he worked in his father's store as bookkeeper, salesman and traveling merchant. Composition was done in his spare time, mostly in the night: a tone poem, *Hiver-Printemps* (1904–5; Geneva, January 27, 1906); a cycle of songs for mezzo-soprano and piano, *Poèmes d'automne*, in a quasi-impressionistic idiom to texts by Beatrix Rodes (1906) and an opera, *Macbeth*, text by Edmund Fleg based on Shakespeare (1904–9) in which the Wagnerian leitmotif was combined with Debussy-like impressionism. He was also conducting symphony concerts at Lausanne and Neuchâtel (1909–10).

When *Macbeth* was staged for the first time—by the Opéra-Comique in Paris on November 30, 1910—it received a mixed reception and was dropped from the repertoire the following June after fifteen performances. (It was not heard again until March 5, 1938, when the San Carlo Opera in Naples revived it.) Romain Rolland, however, was so strongly impressed by the opera's dramatic power and musical passion that he made a special trip to Geneva to convince Bloch to give up business for composition.

Bloch left his father's business in 1911. For the next four years he earned his living teaching composition and aesthetics at the Geneva Conservatory. He was also intensifying his efforts as a composer while heading toward a new direction. By 1912 he had come to the conviction that if he were to realize his creative powers to their fullest capacities, he would have to express himself as a Jew and use his music to reflect the history, culture, and ideals of his race. As he wrote at that time: "Racial consciousness is absolutely necessary in music, even though nationalism is not. I am a Jew. I aspire to write Jewish music not for the sake of self-advertisement, but because it is the only way in which I can produce music of vitality—if I can do such a thing at all. . . . It is not my purpose or my desire to attempt a 'reconstruction' of Jewish music, or to base my work on melodies more or less authentic. I am not an archaeologist. I hold that it is of first importance to write good, genuine music—my own music. It is the Jewish soul that interests me, the complex, glowing, agitated soul that I feel vibrating through the Bible."

The period from 1912 to 1916—which Bloch designated as his "Jewish cycle"—was one of his most productive, yielding compositions that made him the foremost exponent of concert music with a Hebraic identity as well as a major creative force in early 20th-century music. Behind him lay the postromanticism and impressionism of his earlier works. In their place was rhapsodic music touched by spirituality and mysticism, and identifiably Jewish in its repeated use of augmented-second intervals and in its improvisational character. The following Hebraic works carry Bloch to full maturity: Three Psalms—two of them (nos. 137 and 114) for soprano and orchestra (1912–14), and the third (no. 22) for baritone or alto and orchestra (1914); Three Jewish Poems for orchestra, written in 1913 in memory of his father; the one-movement *Israel Symphony* (1912–16), inspired by the Day of Atonement, the holiest day in the Jewish calendar, and by the festival of thanksgiving (*Succoth*) that comes five days later; and a Rhapsody for orchestra with cello obbligato, *Schelomo* (1916), inspired by King Solomon of the Bible. To this day, *Schelomo* remains one of Bloch's most frequently heard compositions.

The years of World War I made it difficult for Bloch to advance his career further as a composer. Beset by financial problems, he accepted, in 1916, the post of conductor for the dancer Maud Allen on a tour of the United States. The sudden bankruptcy of the Maud Allen troupe in America left Bloch financially stranded in a foreign land. He rented a room in mid-Manhattan, found a job as head of the theory department of the recently organized David Mannes School of Music, and set about the business of making necessary contacts for the performance of his compositions, most of which had not yet been heard anywhere. On December 29, 1916, the Flonzaley Quartet introduced his String Quartet no. 1 (1916). On March 23, 1917, Bloch was the guest conductor of the Boston Symphony in a performance of the pre-

miere of the Three Jewish Poems. On May 3, 1917, he conducted the Society of Friends of Music in the first performance anywhere of *Israel Symphony* and *Schelomo*. Two concerts of his music were given by the Philadelphia Orchestra, with Bloch conducting, on January 25 and 26, 1918. As a guest conductor of the New York Philharmonic he presented the American premiere of his Symphony in C-sharp minor on May 8, 1918. A new work (a departure from his Hebraic writings) won the Coolidge Prize in 1919 and was introduced at the Berkshire Chamber Music Festival in Pittsfield on September 25, 1919: the Suite for Viola and Piano (1919), which he orchestrated a year later.

Now a composer with an established reputation in America, Bloch was appointed, in 1920, to found and become the director of the Cleveland Institute of Music, with which he remained for five years. His best writing during this time was in the field of chamber music, within whose intimacy he brought some of the rhapsodic sweep of thought, passion of feeling and, occasionally, the spiritual exaltation of his Hebraic compositions. There were two violin sonatas, the first in 1920, and the second, subtitled *Mystique*, four years later. There was a momentary return to his Hebraic past with the *Baal Shem Suite*, for violin and piano (1923), three pictures of Hassidic life inspired by the seer Baal Shem, who had founded the cult of Hassidism in Poland in the late 18th century. There was the Piano Quintet (1923, N.Y., November 11, 1923), which was high-tensioned in its simulation of microtonal intervallic structure and which had dark shadows of awe and terror hovering over it through a theme recalling the Dies Irae, which recurred throughout the composition. And there was the neoclassic Concerto Grosso no. 1 (1925; Cleveland, June 1, 1925) in which Bloch proved to his students that one could bring a vibrant 20th-century harmonic and melodic language to even the most traditional of baroque structures.

His high-minded purpose as a teacher who could never accept compromises and his often severe and open criticism of the opportunism of his employers finally brought him into open conflict with the directors of the Cleveland Institute. He left Cleveland in 1925 to become director of the San Francisco Conservatory. In San Francisco, as in Cleveland, he stayed five years. His most ambitious composition during this time was *America* (1926), an epic rhapsody which won first prize by the unanimous decision of a distinguished jury in a competition for music on an American subject conducted by the journal *Musical America*. During the weekend of December 21–22, 1928, six of America's leading orchestras gave the work a simultaneous premiere in their respective cities. The following year, fifteen other American orchestras included it on their programs. Bloch's tribute to the land of his adoption covered three periods: the *Mayflower* and the landing of the Pilgrims; the Civil War; and "the present—the future." The psalm, "The Old Hundredth" is quoted in the first movement. Civil War ballads, Stephen Foster's "Swanee River" and Negro spirituals are briefly heard in the second movement. A patriotic hymn sung not only by a chorus but by the audience as well (music as well as words by Bloch) brings the third part to its climax.

Bloch paid homage to the land of his birth in a "symphonic fresco" entitled *Helvetia* (1928), which received an award of $5,000 in the RCA Victor competition and whose first performance took place in Chicago on February 18, 1932, with Ernest Ansermet conducting the Chicago Symphony.

In 1930, Bloch was the beneficiary of a generous endowment from a San Francisco music patron enabling him to give up his post with the San Francisco Conservatory and dedicate himself completely to composition. That summer, he returned to Switzerland, making his home in Roveredo Capriasco, in the canton of Ticino. There he worked on *Sacred Service (Avodath Hakodish)*, a work of major dimensions intended for the Sabbath morning prayers. "It symbolizes for me far more than a Jewish service," Bloch explained, "but in its great simplicity and variety, it embodies a philosophy acceptable to all men. . . . It has become a cosmic poem, a glorification of the laws of the Universe . . . the very text I was after since the age of ten. . . . It has become a 'private affair' between God and me." At its world premiere in Turin on January 12, 1934, and at its introduction to the United States on April 12, 1934, in New York with Bloch himself conducting, *Sacred Service* was hailed as one of Bloch's major works, music of nobility and grandeur as well as deep religious convictions and encompassing humanity.

After *Sacred Service* (except for one or two minor digressions) Bloch abandoned Hebraic-type compositions. Nevertheless some of his later non-Hebraic works continued to carry reminders of techniques and styles of his Hebraic music. *A Voice in the Wilderness* (1936; Los Angeles, January 21, 1937) was, like *Schelomo*, a work for orchestra with cello obbligato; Bloch referred to each of its six movements as "meditations," and the cello was used as a commentator between sections to discourse on what had just been heard. *Evocations* (1937; San Francisco, February 11, 1938) had an oriental atmosphere reflecting Bloch's lifelong interest in Chinese culture and Far Eastern thought. The Concerto for Violin and Orchestra (1938) was based on themes of American-Indian identity. Joseph Szegeti premiered it in Cleveland on December 15, 1938, as soloist of the Cleveland Symphony conducted by Dimitri Mitropoulos.

From 1943 on, Bloch lived in comparative isolation in a house overlooking the Pacific Ocean at Agate Beach, near Portland, Oreg. He left this retreat each summer to teach classes in composition at the University of California in Berkeley until 1952. Creatively, he remained productive for the rest of his life, even though, in the mid-1950s, he began suffering from cancer. His String Quartet no. 2 (1946; London, October 6, 1946), written basically in a polyphonic style, received the award of the New York Music Critics Circle in the category of chamber music. In 1951 Bloch once again was singled out by the New York Music Critics Circle, this time for awards in two categories: for the String Quartet no. 3 (1951; N.Y., January 4, 1953) in chamber music, and the Concerto Grosso no. 2, for string orchestra (1952; London, April 11, 1953) in orchestral music. Among the other significant works of his later years were *Sinfonia breve* (1952; London, April 11, 1953), in which he turned for the first time to a twelve-tone thematic statement; Symphony for Trombone Solo and Orchestra (1953–54; Houston, Tex., April 4, 1956); Symphony in E-flat (1954–55; London, February 15, 1956); and, in chamber music, his last two string quartets (1953, 1956) and Piano Quintet no. 2 (1956). His seventieth birthday was celebrated in Chicago in 1950 with a six-day festival of his works.

Bloch underwent an operation for cancer in January 1957. While convalescing, he completed two baroque suites for unaccompanied violin which Yehudi Menuhin had commissioned. Bloch also wrote *Two Last Poems (Maybe . . .)*, for flute and orchestra (1958), in which he appeared to have premonitions of imminent death. This is somber, deeply reflective music, the first of its two poems being subtitled "Funeral March."

Bloch was survived by his wife (then age seventy-eight) and their three children: Suzanne, a musical scholar and lutenist; Lucienne, a painter-sculptor; and Lucien, an engineer.

An Ernest Bloch Society was formed in London in 1937 with Albert Einstein as honorary president, to promote performances of Bloch's works. Archives of Bloch's music were established at the University of California in Berkeley in 1962 and at the Library of Congress in Washington, D.C., in July 1975. Among the honors conferred on him were honorary memberships in the Santa Cecilia Academy in Rome and the American Academy of Arts and Letters, the latter presenting him in 1947 with its first gold medal.

The centennial of Bloch's birth was commemorated in spring 1980 with an exhibit of Bloch memorabilia at the Music Museum in Haifa, Israel: this exhibit was transported to the Spoleto, Festival, U.S.A. in Charleston, S.C., in late spring 1980. A centennial program of Bloch's music was heard in New York on April 21, 1980. Throughout the 1980–81 season performances of Bloch's music were given by significant musical organizations and performers in the United States, including a revival of Bloch's Violin Concerto by Yehudi Menuhin.

THE COMPOSER SPEAKS: Music consists, for the most part, of the incomparable legacy left to us by the great masters. When we study their lives and their works, people like Palestrina, Bach, Beethoven, and Wagner appear to us not only as marvelous musicians, but also as human personalities. Their message, comparable to that of Homer and Shakespeare in literature, surpasses infinitely what we commonly conceive as music, the world of sounds. The meaning behind, the spirit of the message, transports us into another world and makes us think, feel, and live differently. It is not because they were great masters of the notes only, but because they were great men first. They expressed their vision through music. . . .

When art is conceived in this way and becomes an expression of a philosophy of life, it is no longer a luxury, a fad, or a cult of big names and virtuosos. Questions of the personalities of interpreters, which seem to play such an important part in the artistic discussions of our day, disappear. It is a storm that carries one away, unites all men in a unit of solidarity, shakes them to the bottom of their souls, waking them to the greatest problems of their common destiny.

PRINCIPAL WORKS: 5 string quartets (1916–56); 3 symphonies (1901, 1912–16, 1954–55); 3 suites for unaccompanied cello (1956, 1956, 1957); 2 piano quintets (1923, 1956); 2 violin sonatas (1920, 1924); 2 concerti grossi (1924–1925, 1952); 2 suites, for unaccompanied violin (1958).

Hiver–Printemps, tone poem for orchestra (1904–5); *Macbeth*, opera (1904–9); Suite for Viola and Piano or Orchestra (1919–1920): Three Jewish Poems, for orchestra (1913); *Schelomo*, rhapsody for orchestra with cello obbligato (1916); *Baal Shem*, suite for violin and piano (1923); *From Jewish Life*, three sketches for cello and piano (1924); Two Suites, for string quartet (1925); *America*, rhapsody for chorus and orchestra (1926); *Helvetia*, tone poem (1926); *Sacred Service*, for baritone, mixed chorus and orchestra (1930–33); Piano Sonata (1935); *Voice in the Wilderness*, for orchestra with cello obbligato (1936); *Evocations*, suite for orchestra (1937); Violin Concerto (1938); Two Pieces, for string quartet (1938–1950); *Suite symphonique*, for orchestra (1944); *Concerto symphonique*, for piano and orchestra (1947–1948); *Scherzo fantastique*, for piano and orchestra (1948); Six Preludes, for organ (1949); *Suite hebraïque*, for viola or violin and orchestra (1951); *In Memoriam*, for orchestra (1951); *Sinfonia breve*, for orchestra (1952); Symphony for Trombone Solo and Orchestra (1953–54); *Proclamation*, for trumpet and orchestra (1955); *Suite modale*, for flutes and strings (1957); *Two Last Poems*, for flute and chamber orchestra (1958).

BIBLIOGRAPHY: Bloch, Suzanne, and Heskes, Irene, *Ernest Bloch: Creative Spirit—A Program Source Book* (N.Y., 1976); Ewen, David (editor), *The New Book of Modern Composers* (N.Y., 1961); Kushner, David Z., *Ernest Bloch and His Music* (Glasgow, 1973); Strasburg, Robert, *Ernest Bloch: Voice in the Wilderness* (Los Angeles, 1977); Tibaldi-Chiesa, Maria, *Ernest Bloch* (Turin, 1933); Weisser, Albert, *The Modern Renaissance of Jewish Music* (N.Y., 1949); *New York Times Magazine*, February 16, 1950, April 20, 1980.

Blumenfeld, Harold, b. Seattle, Wash., October 15, 1923.

Blumenfeld's chief concern as composer lies with vocal music in general, and specifically with opera, an area in which he has been active in a variety of capacities. Following a decade of concentration upon operatic direction in St. Louis during the sixties, he turned his full attention to musical composition, focusing on vocal works involving a wide diversity of accompanying instrumental media and sensitively responsive to the poetic value of his texts.

Both parents were graduates of the University of Washington in St. Louis and both were musical, the father playing the violin and the mother, the piano. He started to study the piano when he was six, but his early training was a hit-and-miss process, finally interrupted by the depression, which found the Blumenfeld family moving from city to city until they settled in Williamsport, Pa. Not until he was sixteen did he become involved in the making of music, resuming piano study in Williamsport with Harold Pries and Magda Glaser, and studying harmony by himself from a textbook by Salomon Jadasohn. By the time he was graduated from University City High School in Williamsport in 1940 he had decided he wanted to become a professional musician. Between 1941 and 1943 he attended the Eastman School of Music in Rochester, N.Y., where he studied composition with Bernard Rogers, piano with Donald Liddell and viola with Samuel Belov. *See Here the Fallen*, a dirge for chorus and orchestra (1941) to a text by George Barker, premiered in Rochester in 1945, is one of his apprentice pieces on which he looks back kindly. "It amazes me for its precocious dramatic sense, and for a certain sincerity and directness which compensated for its technical shortcomings."

Just as he was getting a grip on his writing, World War II took him away from his work. Between 1943 and 1946 he served as a noncommissioned officer with the Eighty-ninth Signal Company, seeing action with General Patton's army in Germany all the way into Thuringia and Saxony. Since he was able to speak German fluently, he also served as division interpreter. Looking back on the war years he says: "What I had gained at Eastman as a young composer fell far into the background against the press of events in three years of war. I emerged with my mind a vacuum, so far as composition was concerned."

When he was demobilized in 1946, he spent several months in occupied Austria. "Those were wonderful months," he recalls. "There were trips to

Vienna, concerts in freezing halls, friendships with emaciated musicians and nobility." Later that year he returned to the United States to spend most of the next three years at Yale University as a composition student of Paul Hindemith's. "This was a period of total immersion. I absorbed a great deal of technical ability from the master and received ideas which I have been elaborating on in the years since. I also acquired the inevitable jugful of his style which took me fifteen years to outgrow." In 1949, Blumenfeld received his bachelor of music degree at Yale. A summer's work in conducting at the Salzburg Mozarteum in Austria and a winter's semester at the University and Conservatory of Zurich for courses in musicology and oboe were followed by his return to Yale, where he received a master of music degree in the spring of 1950. In the meantime, he spent the summers of 1947 and 1949 (and again in 1951) at the Berkshire Music Center at Tanglewood, Mass., studying choral conducting with Robert Shaw, orchestral conducting with Leonard Bernstein, and operatic stage direction with Boris Goldovsky. From this period came Three Scottish Poems, for a cappella chorus (1949) to texts by L. A. G. Strong, and Four Tranquil Poems, for a cappella chorus (1950), to poems by D. H. Lawrence, both stylistically Hindemithian. Manus Sasonkin in the *St. Louis Post-Dispatch* called the Three Scottish Poems "fiendishly difficult . . . although unrelentingly involved, never labored and never obscure." In the *Cleveland Plain Dealer*, Bain Murray described the Four Tranquil Poems as "powerful, expressive, and rich in choral color." In 1951, at the invitation of Boris Goldovsky, Blumenfeld prepared a translation and a realization for original instruments of Monteverdi's *L'incoronazione di Poppea* produced that year at the New England Conservatory in Boston.

In 1951, Blumenfeld joined the music faculty of Washington University in St. Louis, where he has served as professor since then. Though immersed in practical musical activities, he did some composing, but without yet finding his true voice. One such composition was a large-scale cantata, *Elegy for the Nightingale*, for baritone chorus, and orchestra (1954), text taken from Matthew Arnold's *Philomela*. It received the first prize of $2,000 in the Midland Music Foundation national competition and was introduced in St. Louis on April 19, 1959.

Soon after writing *Elegy for the Nightingale*, Blumenfeld took a sabbatical leave from the university to travel in Spain and France. There he worked upon his most ambitious composition up to that time, his first opera, *Amphitryon 4* to his own libretto based on a play by Molière, which he had begun writing in 1956 and completed in 1962. This is a large-scale work calling for a huge cast including chorus and dancers and featuring complex stage situations. This opera has not been produced, but the overture (*Miniature Overture*) received some thirty-five performances by the St. Louis Symphony following its pre-

miere on October 10, 1959, conducted by Edouard van Remoortel. Thirty minutes of orchestral music from this opera, bearing the title of *Symphony Amphitryon 4*, was premiered by the St. Louis Symphony on January 12, 1965, under Eleazar de Carvalho.

In the 1960s, Blumenfeld combined his teaching activities at Washington University with extensive work as conductor and producer of operas. In 1960, he was cofounder of the New Music Circle of St. Louis, of which he was the musical director from 1962 to 1964 in modern programs. In 1963 he founded the Washington University Opera Studio, which, under his direction until 1971, gave significant performances of American premieres of rarely heard foreign operas together with the presentation of works by such 20th-century masters as Hindemith, Berg, Stravinsky, Milhaud, Henze, and Ginastera and by such Americans as Hugo Weisgall and Jack Beeson. In 1964, Blumenfeld founded the St. Louis Opera Theater, which he directed until 1971.

As a composer, he was not prolific in those years, but several works are of more than passing interest. *Transformations*, for piano (1963; St. Louis, September 19, 1967), was Blumenfeld's first work to use a technique he called "expansion," in which linear material is established and then enlarged and contracted laterally without losing basic substance. Movements for Brass, a septet (1965), was commissioned by the New Music Circle for the St. Louis Bicentennial and introduced in St. Louis in November 1966.

It was during the summer of 1970 (spent at Yaddo, a retreat for creative artists in Saratoga, N.Y.) that Blumenfeld felt he had finally found himself as a composer. This came about through the writing of *War Lament*, for a cappella chorus and guitar obbligato, to four poems by Siegfried Sassoon; it was introduced by the Gregg Smith Singers, assisted by the Washington Madrigal Singers, in St. Louis on October 22, 1972. Here Blumenfeld uses the chorus orchestrally, the writing being now in unison, now subdivided into up to more than a dozen parts, all flexibly in keeping with Sassoon's dramatic and expressive requirements.

In 1971–72 Blumenfeld was visiting professor of music at Queens College in Queens, N.Y. There he reorganized the introduction to music courses and revitalized the opera workshop. He returned to Washington University in 1972 partially upon the understanding that he would be permitted completely to withdraw from all opera production activity in order to rededicate himself to musical composition. Sometimes at Yaddo, sometimes at his Osago Beach Studio, which he had built in 1971 as a composing retreat at Lake of the Ozarks in Missouri, he completed several works in which his voice was coming strongly into focus. *Eroscapes* (1971) was for mezzo-coloratura, woodwind quintet, and string trio, a setting of two poems by Isabella Gardner; it was introduced in New York by the Contemporary Chamber Ensemble under Arthur Weisberg, with Janet Steele, soprano, on May 1, 1977. This is a sensuous setting of two evocative and gently erotic poems in which the instrumental part is often quite attenuated, with scattered and intersectional contrapuntal lines and delicate, fleeting woodwind writing. *Song of Innocence* (1973) is a large-scale work in four movements for two vocal soloists, chorus, and orchestra based on five poems by William Blake. Conceived in an overtly lyric-dramatic vein, this work features a large chorus in its outer movements ("To Spring" and "The Evening Star"); a chamber chorus accompanied by only thirteen instruments for its second movement ("Sound the Flute!") and a tenor and mezzo-soprano with men's chorus in its third movement ("Lamentation"). The orchestral part, although lyrical and evocative of the text, makes use of a certain amount of Blumenfeld's expansion technique.

During a sabbatical leave from the university in 1975, Blumenfeld completed three major works. *Rilke* is a setting of three of the poet's poems for voice and guitar, which was widely performed by Rosalind Rees, soprano, and David Starobin, guitarist, in June 1975 in Germany, Austria, and Sweden, and in July 1975 in New York. This music is characterized by a widely leaping vocal line demanding varied but often beautifully legato treatment and virtuoso writing for the guitar. *Circle of the Eye* is a cycle of eleven austere symbolist poems by Tom McKeown, which Rosalind Rees introduced in New York on April 2, 1979. "The songs mirror the rather obvious textual imagery of the words in an economical, pointedly lyrical fashion," reported Peter G. Davis in the *New York Times*, "while the instrumentally conceived vocal line goes it own jaggedly disjuncted way, has a certain pallid charm." *Starfires* is a large cantata for mezzo-soprano, tenor, low strings, brass, and percussion in which whirling galaxies of sound match three electrifying star-poems by Pauline Hanson.

Blumenfeld's largest works since 1975 are *La vie antérieure* (1976) and *Voyages* (1977). The former is a spatial cantata for baritone, strings, piano, guitar, and two percussions on stage, and for contralto, tenor, three percussions, and tapist in the balcony. This is a setting of three quintessential poems by Baudelaire conjuring up profoundly erotic images in the opening "Le jet d'eau," the horror of mortality in "L'horloge," and an epicene remembrance of life, distantly remembered from beyond the grave, in the concluding title poem. The work calls for offstage effects, among them shimmering electronic echoes, the grim tolling of church bells, and the delicate spatial scattering and distancing of chiming silver hand bells.

Voyages, premiered in Brooklyn, N.Y., on November 18, 1977, is a direct setting of five of the six poems of Hart Crane's epic cycle. This audacious work attempts to help illuminate and underline the intent of Crane's headlong, extremely allusive language and its often illusive meaning. The score creates a sonic environment for Crane's saga of immersion in experience, commitment to the "infinite consanguinity" for passion, and follows through with music connoting the drained emptiness following upon the death of passion, and the poet's attempt to come to life again, and to find a meaning for his sufferings. The essential sense of the entire forty-minute work is conveyed by the baritone line alone. Instrumentally, the guitar is almost omnipresent. The viola represents the Voice of the Lover, while the percussionists cope with more than a dozen instruments each, a complete zoo of metal, wood, and skin sounds ranging from raging sea music to the delicate sound bells from a mythic sunken Caribbean city to the transported, transformed mystic ringings of Crane's allegorical and redeeming "Belle Isle."

In 1977, Blumenfeld received a grant from the American Academy and Institute of Arts and Letters to subsidize the recording of Parts I and II of *Voyages*. In 1979, together with his librettist, Charles Kondek, he was awarded a grant from the National Endowment for the Arts for the writing of an opera.

THE COMPOSER SPEAKS: I have become increasingly responsive to the poetic values, more and more in awe of beautiful language. When great poetry is set to music it must be done in reverence. It automatically undergoes much violence. It must consequently compensate in terms of sound for what it causes to be lost in the poetry itself and this is much: much of the sound of painting, assonance, consonance, not to mention rhythm and flow of words, phrases and ideas which become automatically submerged when a spoken line is set to pitch. I have come to look upon such contemporary vocal writing as merely an act of hanging a baggage of sound on words which are treated as a pretext rather than as a casual expressive force. The music must add more than it takes away.

My aim is to find my own way of bringing integrity and meaning to the setting of language to music in this age of the embattled Word; and to contribute some exciting and useful works, in years shortly to come, to the operatic stage.

PRINCIPAL WORKS: *See Here the Fallen*, for chorus and orchestra (1943); Three Scottish Poems, for a cappella chorus (1948); Four Tranquil Poems, for a cappella men's chorus (1949); *Elegy for the Nightingale*, for baritone, chorus, and orchestra (1954); *Miniature Overture*, for orchestra (1958); *Contrasts*, for orchestra (1961); *Symphony Amphitryon 4*, for orchestra (1962); *Amphitryon 4*, comic opera (1962–65); *Transformations*, for piano (1963); *Expansions*, for woodwind quintet (1964); Movements for Brass, for brass septet (1965); *War Lament*, for a cappella chorus and guitar obbligato (1970); *Eroscapes*, for mezzo-coloratura, woodwind quintet and string trio (1971); *Song of Innocence*, for a large chorus, chamber chorus, tenor and mezzo-soprano, and orchestra (1973); *Rilke*, for voice and guitar (1975); *Circle of the Eye*, cycle of eleven songs for voice and piano (1975); *Starfires*, cantata, for mezzo-soprano, tenor, and orchestra of low strings, brasses, and percussion (1975); *La vie antérieure*, spatial cantata for baritone and low strings, guitar, piano and three percussion on the stage and tenor and mezzo-soprano with tape and three percussion in the balcony (1976); *Voyages*, for baritone, viola, guitar and two percussionists (1977); *Fritzi*, one-act opera-bagatelle (1979); *Essence*, for voice and piano (1979); *La voix reconnue*, for tenor with soprano and chamber ensemble (1979–80).

BIBLIOGRAPHY: *BBDM*; *DCM*.

Boatwright, Howard Leake, b. Newport News, Va., March 16, 1918.

With formal classical procedures, Boatwright's mature style combines some of Hindemith's control of dissonance with a twelve-tone (but not serial) idiom, but the sonority is closer to Schoenberg than to Hindemith.

His father was a dentist and his mother a graduate nurse. "It was from my mother and grandmother that my artistic side seems to have come," he explains. Both were musical and both were painters; his mother took a number of prizes in several exhibitions.

Howard began to sing recognizable melodies before he left the cradle. As soon as he could reach it, he tried finding melodies on the piano. A neighborhood teacher gave his first piano lessons when he was six, but these were interrupted three years later due to his father's illness. But when he was ten, Howard entered a violin class in public school; a few months later he shifted to a private teacher with whom he made such rapid progress that a musical career for him was now being seriously contemplated by his parents. In his eleventh year, Jascha Heifetz gave him an audition, playing the accompaniment for him on the piano. Heifetz advised him to continue his violin study in Norfolk with Israel Feldman, a pupil of Franz Kneisel's and a graduate of the Institute of Musical Art in New York. Feldman became Boatwright's only violin teacher, continuing his instruction until 1942. Boatwright, at fourteen, gave his first full-length violin recital in Newport News. The following year he became the first violin in the Feldman Chamber Music Society founded by his teacher, and when he was seventeen Boatwright made his orchestral debut as soloist in Lalo's *Symphonie espagnole* with the Richmond Symphony in Virginia.

When he was graduated from Newport News High School in 1935 the decision was arrived at for

him to concentrate solely on music rather than enter college for an academic education. For seven years, until 1942, he remained in Newport News, riding the ferry twice a week to Norfolk for a two-hour lesson with Feldman and a three-hour rehearsal of the Feldman Chamber Music Society. He also studied theory privately in Norfolk with Virginia Roper. During this period he gave recitals throughout Virginia and appeared as soloist with the Virginia Symphony. In 1941, he performed outside Virginia for the first time and won the district contest of the National Federation of Music Clubs in Washington, going to Los Angeles in the finals. There he met Helen Johanna Strassburger, a soprano who attended Oberlin College and who was also a finalist. Before long they became engaged.

On December 29, 1942, Boatwright made his violin debut in New York at Town Hall. In 1943–44 he toured the United States in joint recitals with the soprano Eileen Farrell, and in joint recitals with Helen Strassburger in Mexico. Meanwhile, in 1943, he was appointed assistant professor of violin at the University of Texas in Austin (1943–45) and on June 25, 1943, he married Helen Strassburger. After giving birth to three children, Helen Boatwright pursued an eminent career as concert singer, often appearing in concerts with her husband.

Though he had done some improvising during his childhood, and had written some violin pieces in his youth, Boatwright did not seriously involve himself with composition until after his career as concert violinist had been successfully launched. While at the University of Texas, he began to show an increasing interest in composition, a fact that led one of his colleagues, Putnam Aldrich, to urge him to acquire more theoretical training and to get it at Yale with Paul Hindemith. With a grant from the Weyman Fund and with the Bradley-Keeler and Horatio Parker fellowships, Boatwright attended Yale between 1945 and 1947, studying composition with Hindemith and receiving his bachelor of music degree in theory in 1947 and his master of music in composition one year later.

In 1948, Boatwright joined the faculty at Yale as assistant professor of theory in the School of Music, serving as associate professor from 1955 to 1964. During these years he was also concertmaster of the New Haven Orchestra (1950–62) and conductor of the Yale University Symphony (1957–60). From 1949 to 1964 he was the director of music at the St. Thomas Church in New Haven where, between 1952 and 1962, notable annual concerts of rarely heard baroque choral music were given; five of these concerts were repeated in New York and several were recorded, one of which (Scarlatti's *Passion According to St. John*) received the Grand Prix du Disque in Paris in 1958.

The summers spent at the camp of the Country Dance Society of America in Massachusetts (1956–61) became a stimulant for the writing of various vocal works based on Anglo-American folk songs, notably: Two English Folk Songs, for voice and violin (1960); *Sinner Man*, for baritone and orchestra, with audience participation (1960), based on an Appalachian folk hymn; and Two Folk Songs, for voice and violin (1961).

He spent 1959–60 in India as a lecturer on a Fulbright Fellowship, and on a Rockefeller Foundation grant that same year he did research on the composer Tyagaraja, South Indian *kritis*, and South Indian violin playing. These Indian studies led to the writing of two monographs: "A Handbook on Staff Notation for Indian Music" and "Indian Classical Music and the Western Listener," both published in Bombay in 1960. In 1960, 1961, and 1962 he conducted the choir of the Kugelkirche in Marburg, Germany, in concerts of baroque music. Under the auspices of the U.S. State Department he toured Germany in 1961 in recitals with Virginia Pleasants, harpsichordist, and his wife.

In New Haven, Boatwright completed a number of chamber-music compositions for various concerts around Yale. These included *Dover Beach*, for soprano and string quartet based on Matthew Arnold (1947), String Quartet (1947), Trio, for two violins and viola (1949), Serenade, for two strings and two winds (1952), and Quartet, for clarinet and strings (1958), the last of which received in 1962 the Society for the Publication of American Music Award. All were dissonant, in the complex linear structure and clear texture of Hindemith's middle period, and with a certain natural lyricism. The church music, modal in its harmonic and melodic construction, fell into two groups. Some were based on pre-existent material: for example, the anthems *Morning Hymn* (1957), a set of variations on the ancient hymn "Jam Lucis Orto Sidere," and *The Star of the East* (1957), in which a Kentucky folk hymn is used; the Mass, A Short Mass in F (1951), utilizing a Merbecke cantus firmus. Other church music is freely composed: for example, the anthems *God Is Our Refuge* (1951) and *Nunc Sanctis Nobis Spiritus* (1954), the Masses A Short Mass for Penitential Seasons (1956) and Mass in C (1958). Larger works to religious texts were: *The Passion According to St. Matthew*, for chorus and organ (1962; New Haven, Conn., April 28, 1962); *Canticle of the Sun*, to a text by St. Francis, for soprano solo, chorus, and full orchestra (1963), commissioned by the New England Association of Secondary Schools for the tenth anniversary of their Spring Choral Festival, first performed on April 28, 1963; and Music for Temple Service, for cantor (baritone), chorus and organ (1964), commissioned by and introduced at The Temple in Cleveland on April 26, 1964.

Boatwright was the dean of the School of Music at Syracuse University between 1964 and 1971, and since 1971, professor of music. On or about 1966 he began to assimilate the twelve-tone idiom into his creative process. This became apparent even in a composition such as *The Lament of Mary Stuart*, a six-movement solo cantata (1968) scored for a typical baroque ensemble (soprano, harpsichord, and a cello continuo) and which stylistically is a combination of baroque sound, texture, and vocal technique with twentieth-century chromatic harmonies. The synthesis of Hindemith and the twelve-tone idiom is even more apparent in the String Quartet no. 2 (1974), which was commissioned by the Society for New Music in Syracuse, N.Y., and first performed in Syracuse on April 20, 1975. The three-movement Symphony (1976), though utilizing classical formal procedures, is also written in an organized (though not serial) type of chromaticism. The first movement is in sonata form; the last is a passacaglia utilizing a recognizable twelve-tone theme (though the order of the notes changes with each repetition). This symphony received its world premiere on January 12, 1979, in a performance by the Syracuse Symphony conducted by Christopher Keene.

Between 1960 and 1963, Boatwright was on the advisory committee of the Performing Arts Program of the Asia Society and he was also a founding member of the Society for Asian Music. He served on the committee on Historical Instruments for the Music Teachers National Association in 1961–62, and was an examiner for the National Association of Schools of Music in 1961–71. He was elected member-at-large for music theory by the College Music Society for the period of 1971–73. In 1970 Boatwright was honored with the Yale School of Music Alumni Award. In 1971–72 he received his second Fulbright Fellowship for travel and research in Rumania, and in 1975 he was elected to the board of directors of the Charles Ives Society.

In addition to writing numerous articles for various publications, Boatwright is the author of *Introduction to the Theory of Music* (1956) and editor of the literary manuscripts of Charles Ives published as *Essays Before a Sonata and Other Writings* (1962).

THE COMPOSER SPEAKS: My composing has been a function of my total musical life, much in the way it used to be before the present fairly common separation into specialist performers and specialist composers. This probably accounted for my compatibility with Paul Hindemith, who, along with Bartók and Prokofiev among 20th-century masters, was both a performing instrumentalist and composer. For me, it has meant a later start and a slow development, but my interests are too diverse to have had it otherwise. Like all pupils of great teachers with positive ideas, it has taken me many years to find my own way without simply negating what I consider a precious heritage. For me, the art I most admire is firmly rooted in the past, yet new in its own time, in its own way. My approach to style and technique is geared to that view; therefore, I have stayed clear of most of the fads of the last thirty years, while at the same time widening my own technique and stylistic postures as much as possible within my own limitations and taste.

PRINCIPAL WORKS: 2 string quartets (1947, 1974). *Dover Beach*, for soprano and string quartet (1947); Trio, for two violins and viola (1948), *A Song for St. Cecilia's Day*, for large string orchestra (1948); Variations, for small orchestra (1949); *The Nativity*, for chorus with vocal soloists and organ (1950); A Short Mass in F, for a cappella chorus (1951); Serenade, for two strings and two winds (1952); *The Women of Trachis*, six choruses for women's voices with chamber orchestra (1955); A Short Mass for Penitential Seasons, for a cappella chorus (1956); Mass in C, for chorus and organ (1958); Clarinet Quartet (1958); *Missa Marialis*, for chorus and organ (1961); *The Passion According to St. Matthew*, for chorus, vocal soloists, and organ (1962); *Canticle of the Sun*, for chorus, soprano solo, and orchestra (1963); Music for Temple Service, for chorus, baritone, and organ (1964); Three Morning Hymns, for soprano and violin (1965); *The Ship of Death*, for vocal quartet and string quartet (1966); Variations, for piano (1966); *The Lament of Mary Stuart*, for soprano, harpsichord, or piano and cello ad libitum (1968); Four Chorale Preludes, for organ (1969–1970); Three Songs of Eternity, for soprano and clarinet (1971); Three Love Songs, for soprano and piano (1971); Three Inventions for Keyboard (1971); Three Christmas Songs, for voice and violin (1971); Three Songs, for soprano, flute, and bassoon (1973); Suite, for solo clarinet (1973); Symphony (1976); Five Songs, for soprano and piano (1977); Twelve Pieces, for solo violin (1977); Six Prayers of Kierkegaard, for soprano and piano (1978).

BIBLIOGRAPHY: *BBDM*; *DCM*; *American Choral Review*, October 1963; *Who's Who in America, 1970–71*.

Bolcom, William Elden, b. Seattle, Wash., May 26, 1938.

Bolcom's fascination for ragtime, jazz, and other American popular idioms is reflected in his serious music combined with some of the techniques and styles of the ultramodern school.

There were no musicians in the Bolcom family, but two members were music lovers. Bolcom's grandfather, a lumber tycoon, raised funds for the Seattle Philharmonic. His compensation was to conduct the orchestra once a year in a concert of march music even though he could not read music. By the time William was born, the grandfather had lost his huge fortune. Bolcom's father became a lumber salesman, and his mother, a schoolteacher. The mother, an amateur pianist, loved music so deeply that when she was pregnant with William she continually played classical music on the phonograph with the hope her child would be born musical. At five, William began

taking piano lessons, and soon after that started writing pieces for his instrument. His mother took him to all the recitals in Seattle by famous visiting pianists. A musical experience that remained indelible came when he was eight: a visit to a local record shop where he heard a recording of Stravinsky's *The Rite of Spring*. At his pleading, the record was bought and he played it continually. Bolcom also acquired and became infatuated with a recording of Charles Ives's *Concord Sonata*. That, and *The Rite of Spring*, he feels were probably the most important influences in his early musical life.

His first significant piano teachers were Evelyn Brandt in Seattle, Gunnar Anderson in Bellingham, Wash., and, beginning with 1949 when his family moved to Everett, Wash., Berthe Poncy Jacobson, head of the piano department at the University of Washington. While attending public school in Everett, Bolcom took a bus once a week to the university to study the piano with Mrs. Jacobson and theory, composition, and orchestration with John Verrall. Bolcolm was only twelve when he wrote his String Quartet no. 1, which harmonically and rhythmically were imitative of Stravinsky and Ives. He wrote several more string quartets after that, most of them dissonant, though the third had a romantic character.

Upon graduating from Everett High School in 1955, Bolcom entered the University of Washington as a regular student. For three years he was the recipient of the General Motors Scholarship, and in 1958 he earned his bachelor of arts degree. Between 1958 and 1959 he attended Mills College in Oakland as a graduate student in composition with Darius Milhaud, with whom he had begun studying at Aspen, Colo., during the summer of 1957. With a Bourse du Gouvernement Français scholarship in hand (given by the French government to foreign students) he attended the Paris Conservatory between 1959 and 1961 as an *élève régulier*, studying composition with Milhaud as well as with Jean Rivier, counterpoint with Mme. Simone Plé-Caussade, and aesthetics with Olivier Messiaen. Attending lectures by Pierre Boulez and others in Darmstadt, Germany, in 1960 interested him in the twelve-tone technique, particularly in the conceptualization of several series built on prominent intervals; but unlike Boulez—and Berio, whom he now came to admire—he was interested in a series not as a means of destroying or replacing tonality but as an ultimate expansion in tonality. This is reflected in the music he was now writing: some piano etudes (1959), the Fantasy-Sonata, for piano (1962), *Décalage*, for cello and piano (1962), and Octet (1962).

Recognition of his talent came through the winning of the William and Norma Copley Award and the Harriet Hale Woolley Award in 1960, and, in 1961, the award of the Kurt Weill Foundation (the Copley and Weill awards had come on Milhaud's recommendation). Back in the United States in 1961, having earned a master of arts degree from

Mills College *in absentia*, Bolcom attended Stanford University in California for two years (1961–63), serving as a teaching assistant while attending the advanced composition class of Leland Smith. He graduated in 1964 with a doctorate of musical arts in composition, the first awarded by Stanford.

In 1963, with Arnold Weinstein as librettist, Bolcom completed *Dynamite Tonite!*, a one-act pop opera that was bitter and at times a madcap satire on war. Since this work was intended more for actors than singers, it was first produced not by an opera company but by the Actors Studio in an off-Broadway production in New York on December 21, 1963, on a grant from the Rockefeller Foundation. In this little opera, Bolcom revealed creatively for the first time his love of American popular music. Thus, while a prisoner from an enemy country is made to sing in an Alban Bergian *Sprechstimme* ("song speech"), everybody else sings in the style of pop tunes of the 1912–15 period. Though *Dynamite Tonite!* was initially received so poorly that it survived only a single performance, it was intermittently revived after that by the Yale Drama School in 1966, the Martinique Theater in New York in 1967, the Stockholm National Opera in Sweden in 1961, and the Yale Repertory Theater in 1975. In 1965 it received the Marc Blitzstein Award for excellence in the musical theater from the American Academy of Arts and Letters.

On December 23, 1963, Bolcom married Fay Levine, a pianist. One year later, having received a Guggenheim Fellowship, he returned to Paris to reenter the Paris Conservatory for a year. In 1965, he was awarded there the Second Prix de Composition for his String Quartet no. 8 (1965), missing first prize because one of the themes in the last movement was in the style of rock 'n' roll.

With his return to the United States in 1966, Bolcom filled a one-year post as assistant professor of music at the University of Washington in Seattle. Between 1966 and 1968 he was lecturer, then assistant professor of music at Queens College in New York. He resigned in 1968 to serve as visiting critic at the Music Theater of the Yale Drama School, part of his salary being paid by a second Guggenheim Fellowship. In 1969–70 he was composer-in-residence on a full-time basis at New York University of the Arts on a Rockefeller Foundation grant, and on a part-time basis for two years after that. Meanwhile, in 1967, he and his wife, Fay, were divorced and on June 8, 1968 he married Katherine Agee Ling, a writer and film maker and niece of James Agee; they were divorced a year later.

A cross between tonal and atonal writing characterized the String Quartets nos. 7 and 8 (1962, 1965), *Oracles*, for orchestra (1964) and *Morning and Evening Poems* (1966). *Oracles* was introduced by the Seattle Symphony under Milton Katims on May 2, 1965, at a Contemporary Arts Festival on a grant from the Rockefeller Foundation and the aus-

pices of the University of Washington School of Music. *Morning and Evening Poems*, a song cycle on texts by William Blake, was given its first hearing at Tanglewood in Massachusetts during the summer of 1966 and in January 1973 was performed at a Prospective Encounters concert in New York, Pierre Boulez conducting. More advanced in its writing was *Session I* (1965), for chamber ensemble, in which a twelve-tone row was counterposed with jazz. It was introduced at a concert of the Domaine Musical in Berlin (which had commissioned it) in May 1965. The Contemporary Chamber Ensemble under Arthur Weisberg performed it during its tour in 1966–67. *Session III* (1966) was commissioned by the Portland, Oreg., Group for New Music, which introduced it in 1967 before taking it on tour in the United States and Europe; at the International Music Festival in Royan, France, in the summer of 1968, it caused a riot, the performance so often interrupted by boos, catcalls, shouts, and fights that the ensemble had to start the piece over from the beginning several times. *Session IV* (1967), which contains quotations from Beethoven's *Eroica Variations* and Schubert waltzes together with a pseudo James Scott rag, was commissioned by the Juilliard Repertory Players, who performed it in London, Berlin, and Paris.

Bolcom feels he reached a turning point in 1967. By then, he says, he no longer took into account what other academic composers were thinking of him but was determined henceforth to strike out on a path all his own wherever it might lead. He broadened his eclecticism by using microtonal music as well as his own personalized serial method, and by drawing more and more copiously from the well of American popular music. Ragtime was prominent in *Black Host*, for organ, percussion and prerecorded tape (1967). Introduced in Ann Arbor, Mich., in 1968, it spoke of laughter on the one hand and fear on the other, while ending on a note of anguish. When given in Paris in 1978, Ed Muller-Moor, writing in the *Tribune de Genève,* compared it to a collage in painting.

Between 1967 and 1970 his interest in ragtime led Bolcom to write fourteen piano rags. In 1970, Duets for Quintet was commissioned by Bowdoin College in Brunswick, Maine, where that summer it was introduced by the Aeolian Chamber Players. A different style is used in each of the two-part dialogues in which the various instruments of the quintet participate. The work is climaxed by a "game section" where four performers literally drive the fifth (the flutist) off the stage. *Whisper Moon* (1971), for piano and small ensemble, introduced by the Aeolian Players at Bowdoin College on April 10, 1973, is "dream music" in which the popular styles of the 1930s are juxtaposed with the romantic outpourings of a Mahler or a Richard Strauss.

Frescoes (1971) is a work for two pianists alternating on a harpsichord and harmonium. Bruce and Pierette Mather introduced it over the radio facilities of the Canadian Broadcasting Company in Toronto on July 21, 1971. Bolcom here carried over to his musical writing the techniques of fresco painting in which the colors and designs are painted on still-wet plaster. This is one of the composer's excursions into programmatic writing. String Quartet no. 9 (*Novella*) (1972), commissioned by Nonesuch Records for the Concord String Quartet, which introduced it in Pittsburgh on May 21, 1973, is a Charles Ivesian combination of discordant harmonies and complex cross rhythms with distorted recollections of old-fashioned salon dance melodies. In *Open House* (1975), a cycle of songs by Theodore Roethke for tenor and orchestra, introduced in St. Paul, Minn., in October 1975, Bolcom shifts from tonal melodies to *Sprechstimme*, from chromatic expressionism to popular-song stylings.

For the American bicentennial, Bolcom wrote the Concerto for Piano and Orchestra (1976) on a commission from the Seattle Symphony. It was introduced in Seattle on March 8, 1976, the composer as soloist and Milton Katims conducting. Here the styles range from Schoenberg and Berg to Gershwin and Joplin, with sprinklings of Charles Ives through brief quotations of American patriotic tunes. The eclecticism of this concerto is found again in the Piano Quartet (1976), commissioned by the Koussevitzky Music Foundation. This is a blending of microtonal writing, John Cagelike silences, Stravinskyan polyrhythms, and Webern's pointillism. Additionally, a Chopin barcarolle alternated with a "*ketjak*" (a Ramayana monkey chant), with a waltz interlude thrown in for good measure. Its premiere took place in New York on October 23, 1977, performed by the Chamber Music Society of Lincoln Center.

Jazz and the blues (the final movement in memory of Joe Venuti) are two elements in the musical make-up of the Violin Sonata no. 2 (1978). It had been commissioned by the McKim Fund of the Library of Congress in Washington, D.C., and was first performed on January 12, 1979, by Sergiu Luca, with the composer at the piano.

Bolcom's interest in ragtime is reflected not only in the way it often intrudes into his musical fabric but also in the way he has promoted it as a pianist. He has, in fact, been a prime mover in the revival of interest in ragtime in the United States in the early 1970s. He has recorded albums of Scott Joplin rags as well as other ragtime classics, and with the collaboration of Robert Kimball, he is the author of *Reminiscing with Noble Sissle and Eubie Blake* (1971). As pianist, Bolcom has also performed and recorded other popular music. With his wife, Joan Morris, a mezzo-soprano he married on November 28, 1975, he has toured the college circuit in concerts of American popular song from the turn of the century to the present. With her, or with other singers, he has recorded songs from the age of vaudeville, the sentimental balladry of the 1890s, and the songs of Henry Clay Work, Henry Russell, George Gershwin, and Irving Berlin.

In 1971 Bolcom received the New York State Council of the Arts Award for participation in experimental theater. In 1973 he was appointed assistant professor at the School of Music at the University of Michigan in Ann Arbor, becoming associate professor four years later. The Henry Russel Award, the highest academic honor the University of Michigan can bestow on a junior professor, was given him in 1977. In 1976–77, Bolcom was a member of the jury of the National Endowment for the Arts.

THE COMPOSER SPEAKS: My explorations in all sorts of music from America's past have been to learn the roots of our musical language so that I can build from them. I believe, despite what is often said, that there always exists a current "common practice"—expressed in many forms our music takes, from concert hall to films, TV, or popular music—and since I also believe that the word *language* applies equally to music and the spoken word, I need all of that common language for my expressive purposes. But I wouldn't want to destroy the diversity of musical language in order to impose a false unity. I prefer to articulate that unity by finding ways for different dialects of our musical language to converse among ourselves. I respect each dialect in order to allow for maximum output; to impose any external system would be anathema to me.

PRINCIPAL WORKS: Twelve Etudes, for piano (1959–66); Concertante, for violin, flute, oboe, and orchestra (1961); String Quartet no. 7 (1962); Octet, for flute, clarinet, bassoon, violin, viola, cello bass, and piano (1962); *Dynamite Tonite!*, pop opera (1963); *Oracles*, for orchestra (1964); Concerto Serenade, for violin and string orchestra (1964); *Dream Music*, for solo piano (1965); String Quartet no. 8 (1965); *Session I*, for chamber ensemble (1965); *Morning and Evening Poems*, for contralto and tenor (or countertenor), soloists, and instruments (1966); *Session II*, for violin and viola (1967); *Session III*, for clarinet, violin, cello, piano, and percussion (1967); *Session IV*, for large chamber ensemble (1967); *Dream Music*, for percussion quartet (1967); *Garden of Eden*, suite for piano (1968); *Dark Music*, for five timpani and cello (1969); Praeludium, for organ and vibraphone (1969); Duets for Quintet (1970); *Satires*, for madrigal group, soprano, tenor (or countertenor), baritone, bass (1970); *Whisper Moon*, for alto and instruments (1971); *Frescoes*, for two keyboard players (1971); *Commedia*, for (almost) 18th-century orchestra (1971); *Hydraulis*, for organ (1971); *Fantasy Tales*, for violin and piano (1972); String Quartet no. 9 (*Novella*) (1972); Duo Fantasy, for violin and piano (1973); *Trauermarsch*, for electrified harpsichord and electrified cello (1973); *Summer Divertimento*, for percussion, harpsichord, piano, and strings (1973); *Mysteries*, for organ (1975); *Open House*, song cycle for tenor and chamber orchestra (1975); Piano Concerto (1976); Piano Quartet (1976); Violin Sonata no. 2 (1978); Symphony (1979); Humoreske, for organ and orchestra (1979).

BIBLIOGRAPHY: *DCM; High Fidelity/Musical America*, September 1976; *Who's Who in America, 1980–81*.

Bowles, Paul Frederic, b. Jamaica, N.Y., December 30, 1910.

Though Bowles has become even more famous as a novelist and short-story writer than as a composer, his music, most of it written in his earlier years, has elegance of style and a personalized profile. Both in literature and in music he has often been influenced by his many visits to and research into the primitive folklore of Morocco and other exotic lands.

His childhood was lonely and unhappy, dominated by a dictatorial and often hostile father, a physician. Until Paul was five he never associated with children. "My idea of the world," he has written, "was a place inhabited exclusively by adults." His childhood and boyhood years were spent in such solitary occupations as drawing, writing, and reading; he made his first attempt at writing when he was four. "Very early I understood that I would always be kept from doing what I enjoyed and forced to that which I did not. The Bowles family took it for granted that pleasure was destructive whereas engaging in an unappealing activity aided in character formation."

His early academic schooling took place at the Jamaica Model School in New York (1917–24). At this time he heard his first music, a recording of Tchaikovsky's Fourth Symphony his father had acquired. When Paul was seven, music study began at the Dunning School of Music with a Miss Chase, who taught him piano, theory, solfeggio and ear training. At nine he tried to write an opera.

He says the "music" that most interested him when he was very young were the sounds produced by spinning a musical top, or sliding a metal object up and down the German zither his grandfather had given him, or the creaking of a rusty door hinge. He reacted to them hypnotically. "They seemed to me the culmination of beauty, and always put me into a nonthinking state which lasted as long as I repeated the sounds."

Graduating from Jamaica Model School in January 1924, Bowles passed on first to Flushing High School (1924–25) and in September 1925 to Jamaica High School. By now he had become a voracious reader and a devotee of literature. He was made president of the school literary society and poetry editor of the school magazine. His musical interests were developed at the Saturday concerts of the New York Philharmonic at Carnegie Hall where a performance of Stravinsky's *The Fire-Bird* proved such an exciting experience that on his way home he stopped off to buy a phonograph recording which he played endlessly on his own portable phonograph.

Upon graduating from Jamaica High School in January 1928 he enrolled in the School of Design and Liberal Arts in New York with some vague idea of trying to become an artist. That spring some of his poems were published in *transition*, a Paris avant-garde literary journal, which went a long way in convincing him that literature and not art was his forte. That fall he entered the University of Virginia, but after a single semester, and without informing his parents, he fled to Europe. In Paris, supporting himself by being employed as a telephone switchboard operator at the office of the *Paris Herald Tribune*, he attended performances of Russian operas at the Théâtre des Champs Elysées and of the Diaghilev Ballet. Back in New York in 1930 he rented a room in Greenwich Village and for a while worked as a clerk in a Fifth Avenue bookshop. Before long, however, on the urging of his father, he returned to the University of Virginia for his second freshman semester. That summer, through a letter of introduction from Henry Cowell, he met Aaron Copland, showed him his Sonata for Oboe and Clarinet (1930), which he had then just written, and was accepted by Copland for daily lessons in composition at Yaddo, in Saratoga, N.Y.

By the fall of 1930, Bowles had had his fill of the stultifying routines of academic life and left college for good. He returned to Europe in Copland's company, with whom he continued to study composition in Berlin. Bowles paid a visit to Morocco, a place that had fascinated him from the time he had heard some Arabic music on recordings. During this visit he fell in love with the place. In ensuing years he returned to it frequently and eventually ended up by establishing residence there; this first visit to Morocco was also the beginnings of his lifelong fascination for Moroccan folk music and barbaric and primitive cultures.

In 1931 he was in Paris attending the École Normale de Musique, studying counterpoint with Nadia Boulanger. During 1932–33 he studied composition intermittently with Virgil Thomson. His music during this period had French refinement and grace, revealing traits reminiscent sometimes of Satie, sometimes of Poulenc, while many of his songs were in a quasi-impressionistic idiom. These compositions included his Piano Sonatina no. 1 (1932); Sonata for Flute and Piano (1932); *Scènes d'Anabase*, five songs for tenor, oboe, and piano (1932); Six Songs (1932); and a cantata, *Par le détroit*, for soprano, male quartet and harmonium (1933). The Six Songs was introduced on April 30, 1932, by Ada MacLeish at the First Festival of Contemporary Music at Yaddo in Saratoga, N.Y. John Kirkpatrick played the Sonatina no. 1 at a concert of the League of Composers in New York in autumn 1933. Bowles's Flute Sonata was given its initial hearing by the Cincinnati Music Society in 1933. And the *Scènes d'Anabase* was featured at the Hartford Music Festival in 1936.

Back in the United States, and settled in New York, Bowles attended a class in harmony given by Roger Sessions. Commissioned by Lincoln Kirstein, director of the American Ballet Caravan, to provide the score of one of his productions, Bowles wrote *Yankee Clipper* (1936), given its initial performance in Philadelphia, with Alexander Smallens conducting, on July 19, 1937.

The year of 1936 also marked his beginnings as a composer of incidental music for the theater, a field in which he proved successful. That year he wrote music for two productions of the WPA Federal Theater, directed by Orson Welles: *Dr. Faustus* and *Horse Eats Hat*. In 1939, the Group Theater assigned him to write music for William Saroyan's play *My Heart's in the Highlands*. From this point on, he showed exceptional skill and imagination in capturing the mood, emotion, and ambience of each play to which he was assigned. "Here," as Bowles has explained, "one can with immunity write climaxless music, hypnotic music in one of the exact senses of the word, in that it makes its effect without the spectator's being aware of it." For the next few years, Bowles devoted a good deal of his creativity to the writing of functional scores for the stage. Among the famous plays in which his incidental music was heard were: Shakespeare's *Twelfth Night* starring Maurice Evans and Helen Hayes (1940); Lillian Hellman's *Watch on the Rhine* (1941); Tennessee Williams's *The Glass Menagerie* (1944); Franz Werfel's *Jacobowsky and the Colonel* (1944); and Tennessee Williams's *Summer and Smoke* (1946).

He did not neglect concert music. During these years he composed, among other works, *Melodia*, for nine instruments (1937); Music for a Farce, for clarinet, trumpet, piano, and percussion (1938); an opera, *Denmark Vesey* (1938), to a libretto by Charles Henri Ford; a ballet, *Pastorela* (1941), which toured South America; and a ballet written for the Ballet International, *Colloque sentimental* (1944), seen in New York in 1944. Together with these he produced a considerable number of songs, song cycles and pieces for the piano. In much of this music, and in the music he would later write, Bowles's style assimilated some of the melodic, rhythmic, and other stylistic elements of African, Mexican, and Central American music. In 1949, on a Rockefeller Foundation grant, he made recordings of Moroccan folk songs, the tapes of which now repose in the Library of Congress in Washington, D.C.

On February 21, 1938, Bowles married Jane Sydney Auer (who, later in her life, became a distinguished short-story writer and novelist; she died in 1973). Since travel had by now become a passion with Bowles, they spent their honeymoon visiting Panama, Central America, ending up in Paris and the French Riviera. A Guggenheim Fellowship in 1941 enabled them to travel to Mexico. There Bowles worked on an opera, *The Wind Remains*, with a surrealistic libretto by Federico García Lorca. It was produced in New York in March 1943 with Leonard Bernstein conducting and Merce Cunningham doing the choreography.

Having for some time contributed articles on music to *Modern Music* and other journals, Bowles, in 1942, was appointed music critic of the *New York Herald Tribune*. He held this job for three years. In 1949, Bowles published his first novel, *The Sheltering Sky*, set in Morocco. It enjoyed considerable critical acclaim. This was the real beginning of an eminent literary career, which has included the writing of other novels, books of short stories, travel books and articles and translations. One of his books is an autobiography, *Without Stopping* (1972). By the mid-1950s, by which time Morocco had become his permanent home, Bowles's deep involvement with literature took precedence over his career as a composer. Several of his letters were used by Peggy Glanville-Hicks as the text for her composition *Letters from Morocco,* for tenor and orchestra (1952). In 1981 Bowles was elected to membership in the American Academy and Institute of Arts and Letters.

PRINCIPAL WORKS: 2 sonatinas, for piano (1932, 1935).

Scènes d'Anabase, five songs for tenor, oboe, and piano (1932); Flute Sonata (1932); *Par le détroit,* cantata for soprano, male quartet, and harmonium (1933); Suite, for orchestra (1933); Violin Sonata (1934); *Yankee Clipper,* ballet (1936); *Melodia,* for flute, clarinet, trumpet, piano, and strings (1937); *Music for a Farce,* for clarinet, trumpet, piano, and percussion (1938); *Denmark Vesey,* opera (1938); *Romantic* Suite, for wind and string instruments, piano, and percussion (1939); *Tornado Blues,* for chorus and piano (1939); Lullaby, for a cappella chorus (1939); *Danza mexicana,* for orchestra (1941); *Pastorela,* ballet (1941); *The Wind Remains,* opera (1943); *Memnon,* suite for voice and piano (1943); *Green Songs,* four songs for voice and piano (1943); *Colloque sentimental,* ballet (1943); Sonata for Two Pianos (1945); Three Pastoral Songs, for tenor, strings, and piano (1945); *Canciones españolas* (1945); Concerto for Piano, Wind, and Percussion (1947); Prelude and Dance, for winds, bass, percussion and piano (1947); *Orosi,* for piano (1948); Concerto for Two Pianos and Orchestra (1949); *Night Waltz,* for two pianos (1949); *A Picnic Cantata,* for women's voices, two pianos and percussion (1953); *Yerma,* opera (1958).

BIBLIOGRAPHY: Bowles, Paul, *Without Stopping* (N.Y., 1971); Thomson, Virgil, *American Music Since 1910* (N.Y., 1970); *High Fidelity/Musical America,* August 1971; *Who's Who in America, 1980–81*.

Boykan, Martin, b. New York City, April 12, 1931.

Though he is a serial composer, he has never subscribed to any single method of composition, permitting each of his works to take its own shape in its own way.

Neither of his parents was a musician, but each loved music. For two years, Martin attended public schools before continuing his academic education at the Ethical Culture School and at Fieldston, both in New York. As far back as he can remember he was interested in music, and particularly in composition. He was almost seven when he started studying the piano with Abby Whiteside (who remained his teacher for the next seven years) and theory with Vivian Fine. In 1943, he attended the Mannes School of Music to study conducting with George Szell. In 1945–46 he continued piano study with Webster Aitken and, one year later, theory with Eduard Steuerman, who introduced him to 20th-century music; the first hearing of atonal music in Steuerman's apartment proved an "electrifying experience." Further study of theory and composition was pursued with Jerzy Fitelberg and Nikolai Lopatnikoff in 1945–46.

After graduating from Fieldston in 1947, Boykan entered Harvard, where he studied composition principally with Walter Piston and where, four years later, he received a bachelor of arts degree, *summa cum laude,* and membership in Phi Beta Kappa. During his Harvard years he spent two summers (1949, 1950) at the Berkshire Music Center at Tanglewood, where he studied composition with Aaron Copland. After graduating from Harvard he was awarded a Paine Traveling Fellowship enabling him to study with Paul Hindemith at the University of Zurich in 1951–52. One year later he continued his study of composition with Hindemith at Yale University, receiving there his master's degree in music in 1953. Between 1953 and 1955 he lived in Vienna on a Fulbright Fellowship. All this while he was composing chamber music, and from his beginnings he was partial to atonal style. These early works include a string quartet (1949), a flute sonata (1950), a violin duo (1951) and a flute quartet (1953), all of which Boykan now regards as his apprenticeship.

Soon after returning from Vienna to the United States, in 1957, Boykan joined the music faculty of Brandeis University in Waltham, Mass., where he has since remained, serving as assistant professor between 1964 and 1967, associate professor between 1967 and 1976, and since 1976 as full professor of composition. He combined his teaching duties with extensive performances as a pianist both in the classical and in the contemporary chamber music repertoires. On June 23, 1963, in New York, he married Constance Berke, a flutist who had then just graduated from Brandeis University. Since their separation in 1973 and their divorce six years later, Boykan has helped to raise their two daughters.

Boykan dates his maturity as a composer from 1967 when he completed the String Quartet no. 1 (the earlier one having been discarded), which was premiered the same year at Brandeis University. It was awarded the Jeunesse Musicale prize, was performed at Expo '67 in Montreal, and was published and recorded. This work is partly in a serial technique. In a fully serial idiom is the Chamber Concerto, for thirteen instruments (1971), given its initial hearing in Boston on November 12, 1972, by the Boston Chamber Players conducted by Joseph Silverstein; subsequent performances were conducted by Gunther Schuller and Arthur Weisberg among others. This is an extended, meditative work whose second movement is a lyrical arioso for the violin. Boykan continued to employ serialism after that, allowing the demands of each successive work to dictate how this serialism could best be used. In his later works, which have become responsive to the experiences through which he has been living, Boykan favored a polyphony of rotating sets. Among his later compositions are: String Quartet no. 2 (1973), which the American String Quartet introduced in Boston in 1974 and which was subsequently performed by the Pro-Arte Quartet in New York and elsewhere and was recorded under a grant from the Martha Baird Rockefeller Fund; and the Piano Trio (1975), commissioned by the Fromm Foundation for the Wheaton Trio who performed it at Wheaton College in Massachusetts, after which it was heard at a concert of the International Society for Contemporary Music in New York.

THE COMPOSER SPEAKS: Somewhere, Simone Weil has written that the spirit is nothing but the capacity for attention. It's not hard to understand why music reaches so small an audience. What is a little harder to understand is the anxiety of so many composers about their work, flooding the market with music about music—music concerned with historical sociological or theoretical points. Perhaps anxiety is responsible also for those currently fashionable pieces that have given up on everything except a sensuous surface, sadly trivializing one of the most powerful aspects of all our experience.

For my part, I have no uneasiness about contemporary language or the opportunities it provides. I do, of course, have enormous anxieties about the specifics of each piece. I want every detail to be vivid (remembering that it takes a lot of context to make a detail vivid), and like every serious composer, I imagine, I hope ultimately for that congruence of notes and shapes that make a musical statement coherent and expressive.

PRINCIPAL WORKS: 2 string quartets (1967, 1973). Psalm, for a capella chorus (1958); Prelude, for organ (1959); Chamber Concerto, for thirteen instruments (1971); Piano Trio (1975); *Elegies,* song cycle for soprano and seven instruments (1979).

BIBLIOGRAPHY: *BBDM*; *Who's Who in America, 1980–81.*

Branscombe, Gena, b. Picton, Ontario, Canada, November 4, 1881; d. New York City, July 26, 1977. American citizen, 1910.

Both as a composer and conductor she made a specialty of choral music. From her beginnings, she favored a German postromantic idiom, at times programmatic, always emotional, richly harmonized and filled with lush melodies.

She dated her American ancestry from 1640. Her pioneer ancestors—John Allison of Edinburgh and Casper Hoover of Holland—landed at New Amsterdam before immigrating to Canada. She was five when she began composing pieces for the piano, and six when she first appeared publicly as pianist. Upon completing her high school education in Toronto in her fifteenth year she was brought to Chicago, where she made her home with her older brother, a minister. On a scholarship, she attended Chicago Musical College for her first serious study of music. Felix Borowski, who was the first to discover she had creative gifts, was her teacher in composition for seven years. She studied piano with Arthur Friedheim and Rudolph Ganz and songwriting with Alexander von Fielitz. In both her graduate and postgraduate years she was awarded gold medals for composition.

Upon receiving her bachelor of music degree, she joined the piano faculty of Chicago Musical College. In 1907 she was appointed director of the piano department at Whitman College in Walla Walla, Wash. Her vacation months in the summer of 1908 were spent in Germany for study and travel. In 1909 she returned to Germany for an extended stay, studying the piano with Rudolph Ganz in Berlin and receiving private lessons in composition and orchestration from Engelbert Humperdinck. In Berlin she gave a number of piano recitals.

Returning to the United States in 1910, she married John Ferguson Tenney, a New York lawyer, in October of that year. She settled in New York City, which remained her home until her death, devoting herself primarily to domesticity and the raising of four daughters (two of them now deceased). Her spare time was spent composing. Her first composition commanding interest was *Festival Prelude,* for orchestra, written in 1913 for a summer pageant at the MacDowell Colony in New Hampshire, following which it was performed in New York and San Francisco. She also wrote some songs, many of her own texts; and, in 1920, she completed two chamber music compositions: a violin sonata and *Carnival Fantasy,* for strings, flute, harp, and piano.

By the middle of the 1920s she was working in that field in which from then on she would be most productive—choral music. Her first successful choral composition was *The Dancer of Fjaard,* for women's voices and orchestra (1926); here, as frequently af-

terwards, she wrote her own text. It was introduced in the year of its composition in New York City and subsequently received performances throughout the United States. Her second successful choral composition was *Pilgrims of Destiny* (1927), for solo voices, chorus, and orchestra, describing dramatic events aboard the *Mayflower* during the last day and night preceding the landing at Plymouth Rock. A partial performance took place in Washington, D.C., in 1928, at which time the National League of American Pen Women awarded it their annual prize for the most distinguished work produced by a woman. In 1929, this composition was heard in its entirety for the first time at historic Plymouth. Performances were subsequently given in many different cities as well as over the radio. Because of *Pilgrims of Destiny,* Branscombe's name was inscribed on the Honor Roll of the National Society in Constitution Hall in Washington, D.C.

Invitations from various choral groups to appear as guest conductor in performances of her own compositions induced Branscombe to study conducting with Warren Erb at New York University and with Frank Damrosch and Chalmers Clifton. Then, from 1931 to 1943, she led the MacDowell Chorus of Mountain Lakes, N.J., and from 1931 to 1934 she was also the conductor of the American Women's Association Choral. When the association decided to disband its chorus in 1934, the members urged her to continue conducting it. Now renamed the Branscombe Choral, and expanded to seventy-five members, it continued giving concerts under Branscombe's direction until 1954. It appeared annually in New York, made numerous broadcasts over major radio networks, and initiated an annual custom of singing Christmas music at the Pennsylvania Station in New York. During World War II, the Branscombe Choral gave numerous performances at army camps and military hospitals. On December 20, 1946, it performed Christmas carols at Security Hall of the United Nations, at Lake Success, N.Y., the first time such a musical event had taken place at the United Nations.

In addition to her conducting chores with the Branscombe Choral, Branscombe led the Jersey State Chorus from 1940 to 1942. In 1940 she directed a performance of *Pilgrims of Destiny* in New York, and one year later she was invited to conduct the National Chorus of one thousand voices in a concert in Atlantic City, N.J., to commemorate the Golden Jubilee Celebration of the General Federation of Music Clubs. In 1945 she became the conductor of the Contemporary Club Chorus in Newark, N.J.

As a composer, she did not confine herself solely to choral music. In the late 1920s she worked on an opera to her own text—*The Bells of Circumstance*—which she did not complete. Three excerpts from that opera ("Prologue," "Baladine," and "Procession") were gathered into an orchestral suite, *Quebec*

(1930), which was performed in 1930 by the Chicago Women's Orchestra under the composer's direction. After that, Branscombe led performances of *Quebec* several times over American and Canadian radio networks. The finale, from the opera's second act, was sung at Town Hall, New York, in 1941 by the Branscombe Choral. In 1937, Branscombe wrote *Élégie*, for orchestra, and *A Lute of Jade*, for woodwinds and soprano. Later instrumental compositions included the *Valse joyeuse,* for orchestra (1946); *Procession,* for trumpet, organ, piano, and instrumental ensemble (1948); *Pacific Suite,* for horn and piano (1957); and *American Suite,* for orchestra (1959). Through the years she was also a prolific composer of concert songs. Those gaining the greatest popularity were "The Morning Wind," "Blow Softly Maple Leaves," "Happiness," "Across the Blue Aegean Sea" and "Serenade."

But choral music remained her favorite and most successful medium. *Youth of the World* (1932) was first performed in 1933 in New York, the composer conducting, before being heard in principal cities of the United States as well as in Toronto, Manila, Paris, and London; it was also broadcast over the NBC radio network and the radio network of the Canadian Broadcasting Corporation. *Coventry's Choir* (1943) was inspired by the Nazi air blitz over Coventry on November 14, 1940, in which the cathedral was completely destroyed; it was introduced in New York in May 1944. *Afar on the Purple Moor* (1948) was based on a fragment of an old Norfolk (Virginia) melody. *Arms That Have Sheltered Me,* for chorus and band (1962), was written for the Canadian Royal Navy and was introduced in Halifax, Nova Scotia, in the year of its composition.

In 1932, Branscombe received an honorary master of arts degree from Whitman College, its citation praising her for her "imaginative genius in words and music [which enabled her] to embody in imperishable beauty the deep spiritual idealism in historic America."

THE COMPOSER SPEAKS: I have a passionate belief in the power of music as one of the greatest healing and regenerative forces operating on this earth. My personal credo is simple: to be constantly developing my technical equipment, to work steadily, to write, as far as I am able, music that brings to its listeners some quality of refreshment, encouragement, entertainment, comfort or illumination.

PRINCIPAL WORKS: *Festival Prelude,* for orchestra (1913); Violin Sonata (1920); *The Dancer of Fjaard,* for female voices and orchestra (1926); *The Phantom Caravan,* for men's voices and orchestra (1926); *See Him in the Bilboes,* for men's voices and orchestra (1926); *Pilgrims of Destiny,* choral drama, for solo voices, chorus and orchestra (1927); *A Wind from the Sea,* for women's voices and orchestra (1927); *Carnival Fantasy,* for violin and piano (1932); *Youth of the World,* for women's voices and orchestra (1932); *Quebec,* suite for orchestra (1935); *Maples,* for small orchestra (1935); *A Lute of Jade,* for soprano and woodwinds (1937); *Élégie,* for orchestra (1937); *Wreathe the Holly, Twine the Bay,* for women's voices and orchestra (1938); *Our Canada from Sea to Sea,* for chorus and orchestra (1939); *Coventry's Choir,* for soprano solo, women's voices, instrumental ensemble, piano and organ (1944); *Sun and Warm Brown Earth,* for women's voices and piano (1945); *Valse joyeuse,* for orchestra (1946); *Our Lord Is Our Fortress,* for chorus and orchestra (1947); *Afar on the Purple Moor,* for mixed chorus and orchestra (1947); *Murmur on Sweet Harp,* for women's voices and orchestra (1948); *Procession,* for trumpet, organ, piano, and instruments (1948); *Prayer for Song,* for women's voices and piano (1952); Psalm 91, for chorus, piano, organ and percussion (1955); *Pacific Suite,* for horn and piano (1957); *Bridesmaid's Song,* for women's voices and piano (1958); *American Suite,* for orchestra (1959); *Arms That Have Sheltered Me,* for chorus and band (1962); *A Joyful Litany,* for chorus and orchestra (1967).

BIBLIOGRAPHY: Goss, Madeleine, *Modern Music Makers* (N.Y., 1952); *Who's Who in America, 1976–77.*

Brant, Henry Dreyfus, b. Montreal, Canada, September 15, 1913.

Brant has been an indefatigable explorer of many areas of avant-garde music, particularly of spatial music.

His parents were American—his father, Saul Brant, a professional violinist who had gone to Canada, where he served on the music faculty of McGill University in Montreal. Henry Brant, who learned the rudiments of music from his father, began composing when he was eight, and at twelve he completed his first string quartet. Already he enjoyed esoteric music by performing on homemade instruments in a backyard orchestra for which he wrote cacophonous pieces. From 1926 to 1929 he continued his music study at McGill University. His fascination for new idioms was reflected in Variations for Four Instruments, written when he was sixteen. In this piece he invented the technique of "oblique harmony," a scheme of harmonic relationships in which the base of one chord, the tenor of a second one, the alto of a third and the soprano of a fourth are combined.

In 1929 his family returned to the United States. From 1930 to 1934 he was a scholarship student at the Institute of Musical Art in New York, studying piano with James Friskin and composition with Leopold Mannes. He supplemented these studies in 1930–31 with private lessons in composition with Wallingford Riegger. Later on (1932–34) he was

Rubin Goldmark's pupil in composition at the Juilliard School of Music. During this period of schooling his talent was recognized through the winning of the Loeb, Seligman and Coolidge prizes in composition. In 1934 and 1935 he continued studying composition with George Antheil and, in 1938–39, conducting with Fritz Mahler.

Early in his studies, Brant became convinced that fledgling composers should be thoroughly schooled in the principal styles of the masters of the past and present. With this in mind, he began writing compositions in the style of Bartók, Hindemith, Prokofiev, Milhaud, Ravel, Richard Strauss, Debussy, Mahler, and others. He divided the lifework of each master into two or three different periods and then went on to analyze and imitate their styles.

Beginning with the 1930s, Brant earned his living by orchestrating and making arrangements for André Kostelanetz and Benny Goodman. In that decade, Brant's serious efforts as a composer were partly along traditional lines, but also partly along unconventional paths through the employment of fanciful titles, unorthodox instruments, and outlandish sounds (to all of which he would henceforth remain partial). The traditionalist is found in Variations for Chamber Orchestra (1930; N.Y., February 7, 1931); Symphony no. 1 (1931); Double Bass Concerto (1932); Lyric Piece for Orchestra (1933; N.Y., October 16, 1933); and Clarinet Concerto (1938). The iconoclast wrote *Five and Ten Cent Store Music*, for violin, piano, and an assortment of kitchenware implements (1933), *Angels and Devils* for an ensemble of "innumerable flutes" (1933, revised in 1948 as *All Day* when it was premiered in New York on January 19, 1948) and *Homages aux Frères Marx* (1938), portraits of Chico, Groucho, and Harpo Marx, scored for whistle and chamber orchestra. Additionally, Brant wrote music for several satiric and burlesque stage and ballet productions, one of which was the ballet *The Great American Goof*, scenario by William Saroyan, described as a "morality-play fantasy" in which the dancers spoke lines as well as danced and which was first produced on January 11, 1940, by the Ballet Theater in New York with Eugene Loring's choreography.

Between 1943 and 1952, Brant was instructor of music at Columbia University. In 1946 he was awarded the first of two Guggenheim fellowships (the second coming in 1953). From 1947 to 1955 he was a member of the music faculty of the Juilliard School of Music, where he taught composition, orchestration, and arranging. During the early years of World War II, he wrote scores for films produced by the Office of War Information for overseas distribution. After the war he found employment as composer and conductor at the three major American radio networks. In 1949 he married Patricia Gorman, a sculptress, with whom he had three children. He had previously (1938) been married to Maxine Picard, whom he divorced.

In the 1940s, many of Brant's compositions were influenced by jazz. One such work was the Concerto for Saxophone and Orchestra (1941), given its initial hearing on May 12, 1945, by Sigurd Rascher and the NBC Symphony. After that, Brant wrote *Statements in Jazz*, for orchestra (1945), Jazz Concerto for Clarinet and Orchestra (1946), and the Symphony in B-flat (1943–46). The last of these was intended to portray the 1930s and the people who grew up in that decade, its four movements respectively entitled "Sermon," "Ballad," "Skit," and "Procession." The second movement featured a prominent jazz melody and a blueslike lament as a basic idea in the finale. The Cincinnati Symphony under Thor Johnson gave the world premiere in Cincinnati on November 19, 1948. Another symphony, *The Promised Land: A Symphony of Palestine* (1947) utilizes not jazz but thematic material derived from authentic liturgical melodies and the work songs, dances, and chants of Palestine in the mid-1940s. The first movement described the Holy Land, the Palestine of the Bible and the great religions. Here a tune made popular in Nazi concentration camps ("*Ani Mamim*") was quoted. The next three movements devoted themselves to a tonal portrait of the mountain and river country and its people. The finale celebrated the building up of modern Palestine with frequent references to popular Palestinian work songs. The Cincinnati Symphony under Thor Johnson gave the first performance in Cincinnati in 1949. Far more unconventional than these, among Brant's compositions of the 1940s, was *Kitchen Music* (1946) written for water glasses, bottles, a tin-can cello and a tin-can bass.

By 1950, as Brant explained, "I had come to feel the single-style music no matter how experimental or full of variety, could no longer evoke the new stresses, layered inanities and multidirectional assaults of contemporary life on the spirit." This is the time when Brant began to explore the possibilities of spatial music with predominantly polytonal and polyrhythmic writing. *Antiphony I* (1953; N.Y., December 6, 1953) was written for five orchestral groups directed by five conductors. One group, the strings, are on the stage with backs to the audience so that they can face Conductor I, who stands upstage facing the auditorium, visible to the conductors of the four other groups scattered through the hall. In *Millennium II* (1954), the various instrumental groups completely surround the audience. Here Brant employs a technique he would follow in some of his later compositions, that of polyphony of tempos; in *Millennium II*, twenty-one different tempi are heard simultaneously. *December*, a cantata for two speakers, soprano, tenor, chorus, a large and small orchestra (1954; N.Y., December 15, 1954) places the trombonists in the boxes, the chorus on both sides of the auditorium, the tenor and soprano soloists on opposite sides of the dress circle, in addition to the performers on the stage. Spatial music took place in the theater with *The Grand Universal Circus*, for eight singing and speaking voices, thirty-two choristers and sixteen instruments (1956; N.Y., May 19, 1956). In different parts of the auditorium musical dramatic episodes took place, one unrelated to the other.

Since 1957, Brant has been on the music faculty of Bennington College in Vermont. In 1955 he had been awarded the Premio Radio Television Italiana Prize and a grant from the National Institute of Arts and Letters. In 1962 he received the Alice M. Ditson Award from Columbia University.

His interest in spatial music has not diminished since the 1950s. The most successful of these works are the following: *Verticals Ascending*, for two orchestral groups and two conductors (1958; Pittsburgh, July 7, 1968), inspired by Watts Towers built by Simon Rodia in Los Angeles; *Voyage 4*, a "spatial concert piece" (1963; New Haven, January 14, 1964), for three orchestras and three conductors; *Immortal Combat* and *American Debate*, both for spatial band, the first written in 1972 and heard in New York on June 4, 1972, and the second coming four years later; *Homage to Ives*, for baritone, orchestra, and three conductors (1974; Denver, February 21, 1975); *An American Requiem*, for soprano and orchestra (1974; Mt. Lebanon, Pa., June 8, 1974), inspired by the Watergate hearings in Washington, D.C., and with text from the Bible descriptive of a holocaust and redemption; and *Spatial Concerto*, for piano and voices (1976).

Off the beaten track in ways other than spatial writing were various other Brant compositions since 1960. The Violin Concerto with Lights (1961; N.Y., April 30, 1961) called for patterns of lights to be created by five musicians pushing appropriate buttons, while the violinist responds with music interpreting the changing light patterns. *Feuerwerk* (1961) is scored for speaker, mixed ensemble and fireworks. *Kingdom Come* (1970; Oakland, Calif., April 14, 1970) has among its instruments sirens, buzzers, bells, whistles, and requires the chorus to sing a wordless text (a singing practice Brant followed in several other choral works) in which vowels and consonants suggested the sound of an imaginary language. *Machinations* (1970) recruited such esoteric instruments as ceramic flute, double ocarina, and double flageolet. In the Desto recording of this composition Brant himself plays all eleven instruments.

In 1972, Brant received a composing fellowship of $15,000 from the Thorne Music Fund, and grants from the New York State Council for Arts (1974) and the National Endowment for the Arts (1976). In 1979 he was elected member of the American Academy and Institute of Arts and Letters.

THE COMPOSER SPEAKS: From my standpoint, a composer's task, now and ever, involves more than the craft of producing original, stimulating or, if you will, compelling patterns in sound. What is needed goes beyond the mere pattern. The composer must evolve a symbolic language of musical sounds in which he can express the sense of what being alive was like during his own time.

PRINCIPAL WORKS: Symphony no. 1 (1931); Double Bass Concerto (1932); Lyric Piece for Orchestra (1933); Prelude and Fugue, for brass and strings (1935); Clarinet Concerto (1938); *The Great American Goof*, ballet (1939); Violin Concerto (1940); Statements in Jazz (1945); Jazz Concerto for Clarinet and Orchestra (1946); Symphony in B-flat (1946); *The Promised Land: A Symphony of Palestine* (1947); *Millennium I*, for eight trumpets, glockenspiel, chimes and cymbals (1950); *Behold the Earth*, a requiem cantata (1951); Symphony for Percussion (1952); *Origins*, percussion symphony (1952); *Antiphony I*, for five separate orchestral groups and five conductors (1953); *Ceremony*, for violin, oboe, cello, soprano, alto, tenor, bass, divided orchestra, piano four hands (1954); *Millennium II*, for soprano, bass, and percussion (1954); *Conclave*, for orchestra (1955); *December*, cantata for two speakers, soprano, tenor, chorus, large and small orchestra (1954); *Labyrinth I*, for two synchronized orchestras (1955); *On the Nature of Things*, for orchestra (1956); *The Grand Universal Circus*, spatial theater for eight singing and speaking voices, thirty-two choristers and sixteen instrumentalists (1956); *Hieroglyphics 3*, for solo viola, timpani, chimes, celesta, harp, optional voice, and organ (1957); *Millennium III*, for percussion and brass (1957); *Mythical Beats*, for mezzo-soprano and chamber orchestra (1958); *The Children's Hour*, for six vocal soloists, chorus, two trumpets, two trombones, organ, jazz drums, and percussion (1958); *Dialogue in the Jungle*, for soprano and tenor voices and declaimers, winds and percussion (1959); *Atlantis*, for speaker, mezzo-soprano, chorus, orchestra, band, and four separate percussion groups (1960); *The Fire Garden*, for soprano, chorus, flute, piccolo, harp, piano, and percussion (1960); Violin Concerto with Lights (1961); *Fire in Cities*, for chorus, orchestra, two pianos, three separated groups, three conductors (1961); *Voyage 4*, for three orchestral groups and three conductors (1963); *Millennium IV*, for voice and five instruments (1964); *September Antiphonies*, for four clarinets and four trumpets (1964); Consort for True Violins and Violins in Eight Sizes (1965); *Verticals Ascending*, for two orchestral groups and two conductors (1968); *Windjammer*, for woodwind quintet (1969); *Kingdom Come*, for two orchestras, two conductors, organ, sirens, slides, buzzers, bells, whistles (1970); *Machinations*, for flute, ceramic flute, double flageolet, double ocarina, organ, harp and percussion (1970); *Immortal Combat*, for spatial band (1972); *Vito de Sancto Hieronymo*, for chorus and instruments (1973); *Divinity*, for harpsichord and brass quintet (1973); *Sixty*, for orchestra (1974); *An American Requiem*, for chorus and orchestra

(1974); *Solomon's Gardens*, for chorus and orchestra (1974); *Prevailing Winds*, for woodwind quintet (1974); *Nomads*, for wordless text, brass and percussion (1974); *Homage to Ives*, for baritone, orchestra and three conductors (1975); *A Plan of the Air*, for singers, percussion, and brass (1975); *American Debate*, for spatial band (1976); *Spatial Concerto*, for piano and voices (1976); *American Weather*, for chorus and orchestra (1976); Piano Sextet (1976); *Antiphonal Responses*, for three bassoons, eight isolated instruments and orchestra (1978); *Trinity of Spheres*, for three orchestras (1978); *Everybody Incorporated*, opera (1980).

BIBLIOGRAPHY: *DCM; NGDMM;* Ewen, David, *Composers Since 1900* (N.Y., 1969); Thomson, Virgil, *American Music Since 1910* (N.Y., 1970); *New York Times,* February 6, 1972; *Who's Who in America, 1980–81.*

Bristow, George Frederick, b. Brooklyn, N.Y., December 19, 1825; d. New York City, December 13, 1898.

He was a pioneer in the writing of native American opera, the composer of one of the first grand operas by a native-born composer on a native subject to be produced. He was also one of the earliest outspoken champions of American music.

His father, William Richard Bristow, a professional musician, came to the United States from Kent, England, one year before George Frederick was born. In the United States the elder Bristow pursued the careers of conductor, pianist, and organist. He gave his son his first music lessons on the violin, later supplementing them with instruction on the organ. George was only eleven when he began his professional career by playing the violin in the orchestra of the Olympic Theater in New York, becoming its concertmaster two years later. He continued studying music (theory and composition) with Henry Christian Timm, one of the founders and the first president of the New York Philharmonic Orchestra, and later counterpoint and orchestration with Sir George Alexander Macfarren and violin with Ole Bull.

When the New York Philharmonic was first organized in 1842, Bristow joined the violin section. He remained with the orchestra for the next forty years, except for a few months in 1854 when he resigned to protest the lack of American music on its programs. As he complained in a letter to the *Musical World* in 1853, "It appears the society's eleven years of promoting art have embraced one whole performance of one whole American overture, one whole rehearsal of one whole American symphony, and the performance of an overture by an Englishman stopping here." However negligent the New York Philharmonic may have been in presenting American music, it did not turn its back to Bristow's composi-

tions. Several of his orchestral works were introduced by the New York Philharmonic, beginning with an early Overture in E-flat in 1842, and continuing with the Concert Overture in 1847, three symphonies (the D minor on March 1, 1856, the F-sharp minor on March 26, 1859, and the *Arcadian Symphony* on February 14, 1874), and the overture *Columbus*, on November 17, 1866. Critics of Bristow's day found his orchestral music pleasant to listen to because of his facile gift at lyricism, tasteful though conventional harmonies and skillful orchestration, but they also found his works so lacking in depth of emotion or dramatic interest to prove monotonous.

Bristow was the concertmaster of the orchestra when Jenny Lind made her sensational American tour in 1850–52, sponsored by P. T. Barnum. He was also in the orchestra when the eccentric and flamboyant French conductor Louis Antoine Julien made his American debut in 1853 in a series of concerts also sponsored by Barnum. Between 1851 and 1862, Bristow was the conductor of the Harmonic Society in New York, where he continued his efforts to promote American music, including his own oratorio, *Praise to God*, in 1861. He also conducted the choruses of the Mendelssohn Union and the St. George Society for a number of years and made some appearances as organist in several churches.

His claim to historic fame rests on his opera *Rip Van Winkle*, libretto by Jonathan Howard Wainwright, based on Washington Irving. The opera was produced at Niblo's Gardens in New York on September 27, 1855, receiving seventeen performances in two months. It was revived in Philadelphia in 1870. One of the earliest grand operas by an American-born composer on a native American text to be produced, it was also the second grand opera produced by an American-born composer, having been preceded in 1845 by William Fry's *Leonora*. The indebtedness of Bristow to Italian bel canto operas of the early 19th century was remarked by the critics who complained that the opera was cluttered with oversentimentalized arias at the expense of ensemble numbers and choruses. These critics also felt that this opera, though occasionally lyrically appealing, lacked expressiveness and dramatic vitality.

After 1854, and up to the time of his death, Bristow was employed as a visiting teacher of music in New York's public schools. His entire life was confined solely to the New York area. In or about 1864, in New York, he married Louise Westervelt Holden, with whom he had a daughter. Bristow was the author of *New and Improved Methods for Reed or Cabinet Organ* (New York, 1888).

PRINCIPAL WORKS: (*Where year of composition is unknown, date of premiere is substituted*): Overture in E-flat (1842); Concert Overture, for orchestra (November 1847); Symphony no. 1 (1848); *Eleutharia*, cantata for solo voices, chorus, and orchestra (1849); *Rip Van Winkle*, opera (September 27,

1855); Symphony in D minor (March 1, 1856); Symphony in F-sharp minor (1858); *Praise to God*, oratorio, for solo voices, chorus, and orchestra (March 2, 1861); *Columbus*, overture for orchestra (November 17, 1866); *Daniel*, oratorio for solo voices, chorus, and orchestra (December 30, 1867); *Arcadian Symphony* (1872); *The Great Republic*, cantata for solo voices, chorus, and orchestra (May 10, 1879); *Winter's Tale*, orchestral overture (1886): *Jibbenainosay*, orchestral overture (March 6, 1889); *Niagara*, cantata for solo voices, chorus, and orchestra (April 11, 1898).

BIBLIOGRAPHY: Chase, Gilbert, *America's Music* (N.Y., 1955); Howard, John Tasker, *Our American Music* (N.Y., 1946); Rogers, D. D., "Nineteenth-Century Music in New York as Reflected in the Career of George Frederick Bristow" (doctoral thesis, Ann Arbor, Mich., 1967); *Musical America*, December 5, 1925; *Musical Quarterly*, April 1920.

Britain, Radie, b. Amarillo, Tex., March 17, 1903.

More than fifty of her compositions received national awards. Some of her most effective writing has been inspired by American geography and backgrounds and these are notable for their descriptive tone painting.

Both of her parents were musical. Her father, a country fiddler, owned a ranch near Amarillo where Radie spent her first years. The family moved to Clarendon, Tex., when Radie was five to provide her with better facilities for her education. Piano study was begun when she was seven at the Clarendon College Conservatory, where the influence of R. Dean Shure led her to become a professional musician, and from which she graduated when she was sixteen. After one year in a finishing school, she continued her musical education at the American Conservatory in Chicago (1922–24), studying piano with Henriot Lévy and organ with Frank Van Dusen and receiving her bachelor of music degree in 1924. Advanced piano study then took place with Leopold Godowsky. For one year (1924–25) she taught music at Clarendon College. During this period she studied organ briefly with Pietro Yon in Dallas and, in Paris, piano with Isidor Phillipp and organ with Marcel Dupré.

A year later, in 1925, she went to Germany to study piano with Joseph Pembauer and composition with Albert Noelte. She became Noelte's protégé: in later years she continued studying composition with him after he had come to live in the United States. In Munich, in 1926, Britain made her debut as composer with public performances of some of her songs (notably "Had I a Cave" and "Withered Flowers," both written in 1926) which were praised by the German critics for the sensitivity of her lyric conception and for her talent in interpreting "the contents

and tension of a poem into music." Six of her songs as well as *Western Suite* and Prelude, both for piano, were published in Germany at this time.

Upon returning to the United States in 1926, she joined the faculty of the Chicago Conservatory of Music, where she remained until 1938. In 1927, she wrote *Epic Poem*, for string quartet, which received first prize in a national competition sponsored by the National League of American Pen Women. In 1928, encouraged by Noelte, she wrote her first compositions for orchestra: *Symphony Intermezzo*, introduced in Chicago in the year of its conception by the Women's Symphony Orchestra conducted by Ethel Leginska, and *Prelude to a Drama*—originally entitled *Pygmalion Overture*, inspired by the Greek legend—premiered in Rochester, N.Y., by the Rochester Philharmonic under Howard Hanson. *Prelude to a Drama* was performed by the Chicago Symphony under Frederick Stock, in 1938, by the Los Angeles Philharmonic under Alfred Wallenstein in 1950, by the United States Air Force Symphony over the radio in Cairo, Egypt, in 1961, and by the Moscow Symphony in Moscow in 1961. *Heroic Poem* (1929), for orchestra, inspired by Lindbergh's flight to Paris in 1927, received a prize in the Hollywood Bowl International Contest in 1930, was premiered in Rochester on March 3, 1932, with Howard Hanson conducting the Rochester Philharmonic, and was given the Juilliard Publications Award in 1946, the first such ever presented to a woman. The Rhapsody for Piano and Orchestra (1933) was performed by the Illinois Symphony in Chicago in 1938. *Drums of Africa* and *Prayer*, both for a cappella chorus (1934), were her first ventures in choral writing, an area in which henceforth she would be highly productive. *Light*, for orchestra, dedicated to Thomas Edison, was heard first on November 29, 1938, in Chicago and won first prize in a contest sponsored by the Boston Women's Symphony Orchestra in 1941. *Prison*, a "lament," for string quartet (1935), inspired by the reading of a poem about the monotony of prison life, was performed at the White House in 1936 at the personal request of Mrs. Franklin D. Roosevelt, from which time on it became one of Britain's best-known compositions. She transcribed the work for small orchestra in 1940. In all of these works Britain was the traditionalist more concerned with emotion, lyricism, and sensitive tone painting than with experimentation and innovation. In some of her later works she experimented with an atonal and a twelve-tone idiom, but these never assumed great significance in her creativity. Emotion, lyricism, atmospheric and pictorial writing, often in contrapuntal structures, have remained her prime interests.

American geography and backgrounds have been the stimuli for some of Britain's finest works. *Southern Symphony* (1935) was premiered in Chicago on March 4, 1940, by the Illinois Symphony under Izler Solomon. *Canyon* (1939), inspired by the Grand Canyon, was first performed in 1941 by the Rochester Philharmonic under Hanson. *Ontonagon Sketches* (1939) are three evocative portraits of scenes in Ontonagon County in Michigan: it won first prize from the San Antonio Music Club. *Jewels of Lake Tahoe* (1945) is a picture of the Lake Tahoe region, and *Red Clay* (1946) depicts the open spaces of Texas cattle country; both are for orchestra. *Cactus Rhapsody*, for orchestra (1953), is a hymn to the American desert; its first performance took place in Washington, D.C., on April 14, 1960. *Paint Horse and Saddle* (1947) and *Cowboy Rhapsody* (1956), both for orchestra, describe the backgrounds of the western cowboy; the latter was given its premiere on October 23, 1956, by the Amarillo Orchestra in Texas.

During the years of World War II, Britain expressed her faith in America and its spiritual values in *We Believe*, a tone poem for orchestra (1942), which, in 1945, was given a national award by the Delta Omicron International Musical Fraternity. Later compositions were also given national awards, including one from the Arizona Cello Society for Barcarolle, for eight cellos and vocalise, and two from the National Society of American Pen Women for *Musical Portrait of Thomas Jefferson*, for string quartet (1967), and *Pyramids of Giza*, for orchestra, 1973.

Radie Britain was married three times. Her first husband was Leslie Moeller, in 1930, an industrialist; they were divorced in 1939. Her second marriage, in 1939, was to Edgardo Simone, a sculptor who died in 1948. In 1959 she married Theodore Morton, a pioneer aviator. Her daughter Lerae, by her first marriage, is an anthropologist.

Britain is the author of *Composer's Corner* (1978). In 1972 she received a citation of achievement from the National Band Association.

THE COMPOSER SPEAKS: I wish to feel in American music the conquest of the pioneer, the determined man of the soil, the gigantic beauty of a sunset, the nobility of the Rockies, the wonder of the Grand Canyon, the serenity of the hidden violet and the purity of the wild flower. American doors are ajar for the musical conquest of unlimited possibilities.

PRINCIPAL WORKS: *Epic Poem*, for string quartet (1927); *Prelude to a Drama*, for orchestra (1928); *Shepherd in the Distance*, ballet (1929); *Heroic Poem*, for orchestra (1929); Rhapsody for Piano and Orchestra (1933); *Wheel of Life*, ballet (1933); Nocturne, for small orchestra (1934); String Quartet (1934); *Infant Suite*, for small orchestra, originally for piano (1935); *Light*, for orchestra (1935); *Southern Symphony* (1935); *Prison*, for string quartet, orchestrated in 1940 (1935); *Ubiquity*, musical drama (1937); *Drouth*, for orchestra (1939); *Canyon*, for orchestra (1939); *Saturnale*, for orchestra (1929); *Ontonagon Sketches*, for orchestra (1939); Suite, for strings (1940); *San Luis Rey*, for orchestra (1941);

Saint Francis of Assisi, for orchestra (1941); Phantasy, for oboe and orchestra (1942); *We Believe*, tone poem for orchestra (1942); *Jewels of Lake Tahoe*, tone poem for orchestra (1945); *Red Clay*, tone poem for orchestra (1946); *Serenata Sorrentina*, for small orchestra (1946); *Umpqua Forest*, tone poem for orchestra (1946); *Paint Horse and Saddle*, for orchestra (1947); *Carillon*, opera (1952); *Cactus Rhapsody*, for orchestra (1953); *Cowboy Rhapsody*, for orchestra (1956); Piano Sonata (1958); Barcarolle, for eight cellos and vocalise (1958); *Kuthara*, chamber opera (1960); *Nissan*, for women's chorus, strings and piano (1961); *Cosmic Mist Symphony* (1962); *Kambu*, ballet (1963); Four Sarabandes, for piano (1963); *Western Testament*, opera (1964); *The Flute Song*, for female voices, flute, and piano (1965); *The Builders*, for mixed chorus (1965); *Musical Portrait of Thomas Jefferson*, for string quartet (1967); *Translunar Cycle*, a song cycle for voice and piano (1969); Fantasy, for flute and piano (1970); *Dance Grotesque*, for two flutes (1970); *Overtones*, for flute and voice (1970); *Pyramids of Giza*, for orchestra (1973); *The Earth Does Not Wish for Beauty*, for chorus and orchestra (1973); *Pastorale*, for flute and harp (1975); *Rhumbando*, for wind ensemble (1975); *Adoration*, for brass quartet (1976); Intermezzo, for five instruments (1976).

BIBLIOGRAPHY: Goss, Madeleine, *Modern Music Makers* (N.Y., 1952); *Who's Who in America, 1980–81*.

Brown, Earle, b. Lunenburg, Mass., December 26, 1926.

Brown had been a pioneer and potent force in the avant-garde movement in American music, having favored advanced idioms from his beginnings as a composer. He was one of the first American composers to use aleatory processes.

Both his parents were musical. His father sang in the church choir and his mother was an excellent amateur pianist. As a boy, Earle took some piano lessons, which he detested. His initial interest in music was focused on jazz and the big bands of the 1930s. While attending elementary school he acquired a trumpet and began taking lessons. At Lunenburg High School he participated in jazz band performances with various groups including one he had founded. His first memorable experience with concert music was hearing Charles Ives's *Concord Sonata*. This in turn led him to listen to some of the music of Bartók, Stravinsky, and Schoenberg.

In 1944, he enrolled in Northeastern University in Boston with the expectation of becoming an aeronautical engineer. One year later, during World War II, he enlisted in the army air force as a pilot officer trainee. Since the war ended before this training could be completed he was shifted to the U.S. Army Air Force Band, where, for a year and a half, he played trumpet. Occasionally he also filled in as trumpet player with the San Antonio Symphony in Texas. During all this time he studied harmony, counterpoint, and arranging from books he borrowed from the library.

After leaving military service, Brown returned to Northeastern University in 1945 to resume his studies. But in 1946 he came to the conclusion that he wanted to be a musician. Leaving the university, he spent the next four years attending the Schillinger School of Music in Boston. At the same time he studied composition, counterpoint and music history with Rosalyn Brogue Henning, trumpet with Fred Berman, and orchestration and arranging with Jesse Smith, all privately.

On June 28, 1950, Brown married Carolyn Rice, a young dancer who later became a member of the Merce Cunningham company. They moved to Denver, where for two years Brown earned his living teaching both arranging and the Schillinger method. His first published works appeared at this time: Three Pieces, for piano (1951), *Perspectives*, for piano (1952) and Music for Violin, Cello and Piano (1952). All revealed the influence of both the Schillinger method and the twelve-tone system. Three Pieces was performed by David Tudor in New York early in 1952.

A meeting with John Cage in Denver was a significant force in Brown's early development as an avant-garde composer. On Cage's invitation, Brown came to New York in 1952 to work for three years on the Project for Music for Magnetic Tape, the first such organization in the United States. This experience led to jobs with Capitol Records and, until 1960, with Time Mainstream Records as recording engineer, producer, and director of artists and repertoire.

Two influences had an impact on Brown's creativity beginning with the fall of 1932. One was jazz improvisation, which would soon be used in a variety of his works. The other was the abstract expressionism of Jackson Pollock's paintings and Alexander Calder's mobiles. "The idea struck Calder of making 'two or more objects find actual relation in space,'" Brown has written. "This was the first feature of his new approach: the organization of contrasting movements and changing relations of form in space. It seemed to me that it might be possible to bring about a similar 'mobility' of sound-objects in time." Brown also wrote about Jackson Pollock: "The dynamic and 'free' look of the work and the artistic and philosophical implications of Pollock's work and working processes seemed completely right and inevitable. In a sense it *looked* like what I wanted to *hear* as sound and seemed to be related to the 'objective' compositional potential of Schoenberg's twelve equal tones related only to one another and Schillinger's mathematical way of generating materials and structures, even though the pointing technique was extremely spontaneous and subjective."

In Brown's attempt to carry over to his own music elements of the art of both Pollock and Calder, he developed the concept of "open forms" in which the conductor or performers are allowed to play pages of a composition in any order they desire; "time-notation," in which pitches, durations, and dynamics are specified, but with the performer exercising his own "time-sense perceptions" of scored relationships; and "graphic notation," in which the written score offers in visual images the relationships between such actions together with the kind of actions musicians might take.

Folio (1952–53) consists of six compositions including "November 1932," "Synergy," "December 1952," and "1953." This was one of the first pieces of classical music ever written in which the performer himself became a partner in the creative process. As the instructions indicated in "December 1952": "The composition may be performed in any direction from any point in the defined space for any length of time and may be performed from any of the four rotational positions in any sequence."

Brown's first composition for magnetic tape came in 1953: the Octet I, a spatial composition for eight loudspeakers which were distributed throughout the auditorium to surround the audience. *25 Pages*, for from one to twenty-five pianos (1953)—introduced by David Tudor in New York on April 14, 1954—consists of twenty-five sheets of music playable in any sequence; the pitches can be performed either side up due to the absence of clefs. *Indices,* for chamber orchestra (1954), first heard in 1954 in Brooklyn, N.Y., at a Merce Cunningham dance concert, and Music for Cello and Piano (1954–55), performed by David Soyer and David Tudor in New York in 1959, are both in "closed form" and "time notation."

During a visit to Europe in 1956, Brown came for the first time into personal contact with some of Europe's leading musical avant-gardists, such as Karlheinz Stockhausen and Bruno Maderna. He also renewed acquaintanceship with Pierre Boulez and Luciano Berio, whom he had previously met in the United States. Their thinking and music further fortified Brown's development along their lines. At Boulez's invitation, Brown wrote *Pentathis*, for nine instruments (1957), first heard during the summer of 1958 at the Darmstadt Festival in Germany, Bruno Maderna conducting.

One of Brown's most significant compositions up to this time was *Available Forms I*, for eighteen instruments (1961), which the city of Darmstadt commissioned and which, following its premiere in that city on September 8, 1961, was given in several other major cities in Europe as well as in Kansas City and twice in New York. The way this composition, which comprises five musical "events," is played is determined by the conductor, who moves an arrow on a numbered board in front of his podium and holds up one or more fingers to indicate to his musicians which "event" he wants played at a given time.

Available Forms II, for ninety-eight instruments and two conductors, followed in 1962, the result of a commission from the Rome Radio Orchestra, which performed it at the Venice Biennale in April 1962. Leonard Bernstein conducted it with the New York Philharmonic in 1964.

The deluge of commissions and grants Brown received from Europe and the United States from the 1960s on testifies to his international reputation. Only a representative few of these need be listed here: *Times Five*, for five instruments and four channels of magnetic tape (1963), from the Service de Recherche de l'O.R.T.F. in Paris; *Corroborée*, for three pianos (1964), from the Bremen Radio in West Germany for the three Kontavsky brothers; String Quartet (1965), from the Baden-Baden Radio for the Donaueschingen Festival, where it was introduced by the La Salle Quartet in 1965; *Modules I and II*, for orchestra (1966), from the Orchestre National in Paris; *Event: Synergy II*, for two chamber groups (1967–68), from the French Radio for the Festival of Royan; *Modules III*, for orchestra (1969), from the Festival de Zagreb in Yugoslavia; *Syntagm III*, for eight instruments (1970), from the Foundation Maeght for the Festival at St. Paul de Vence in France; *New Piece Loops*, for large orchestra and chorus (1972) from the Venice Biennale; *Time Spans*, for large orchestra (1972), from the city of Kiel; and *Centering*, for solo violin and chamber orchestra (1973), from the London Sinfonietta for Paul Zukovsky, who introduced it in London in December 1973. In the United States commissions came for *Sign Sounds*, for chamber orchestra (1972), from the University of New York in Buffalo; for *Cross Sections and Color Fields* (1975), from the Koussevitzky Music Foundation for the Denver Symphony, which introduced it under Brian Priestman's direction in 1975–76; for *Patchen*, for chorus and large orchestra (1979), from the National Endowment for the Arts; and for *Windsor Jambs*, for soprano and chamber orchestra (1979), from the New York State Arts Council.

In one of his commissioned works, this one from Diego Masson for a composition for his Percussion Quartet, which he was then forming in Paris—and under the stimulus of his admiration for Alexander Calder—Brown decided to use a mobile simultaneously as a percussion instrument and as a conductor. He planned such a piece in 1963, calling it *Calder Piece*, but he did not realize it fully until three years later when he renamed it *Chef d'orchestre/Calder Piece* and had it performed for the first time in 1967 in Paris. The four percussionists and their battery of instruments (marimba, cymbals, temple blocks, gongs, drums, bells, vibraphone, and so forth) surrounded the mobile. Though each percussionist was performing from scores clearly notated as to rhythm, pitch, time values, etc., he was required to take his cue from the mobile and play those sections of the score corresponding to the configuration

of the mobile at that given time. Consequently, this piece would be played differently at each performance. The mobile, in addition to being the conductor, was also the principal percussion instrument, producing a wide variety of sounds by being struck by various materials. When *Chef d'orchestre/Calder Piece* received its first American hearing at the Contemporary Music Festival at Valencia, Calif., on March 9, 1980, Joan La Barbara described the performance as follows in *High Fidelity/Musical America*:

"The musicians take their first visual fix on the 'conductor' and then begin with what Brown refers to as 'friction,' rubbing fingernails and stick ends over their traditional instruments . . . producing squeals and chirps at the threshold of audibility, developing gradually into a veritable forest of trills and wails. Superballs are dragged over bells and gongs, then brushes are used and more solid sounds occur. Slowly the musicians approach the mobile for the first time, scraping and tapping on it with drum sticks, setting it in motion, chasing the metal plates as the mobile swings around. One by one they leave the mobile and return to their individual places, this time playing the marimbas, producing hard, sharp, wood sounds, faster moving. On their next approach to the mobile, each carries wrapped mallets and the mobile is transformed into swinging gongs and suspended cymbals. Some rattling is produced by the various metal clips and attachments but mostly one hears the sound of soft, damped gongs, ringing gently. Some of the percussionists chose to chase the mobile in flight, others stand and wait for certain parts to move toward them, hitting them as the objects pass. All movements are dictated by necessity."

Brown has enjoyed successful careers as conductor, lecturer, and teacher. He was guest composer and lecturer at the Darmstadt Summer Courses in Germany in 1964 and 1965 and at the Berkshire Music Center at Tanglewood in Massachusetts in 1968. Between 1968 and 1973 he was composer-in-residence at the Peabody Conservatory in Baltimore. He was composer-in-residence and conductor at the Aspen Music Festival in Colorado in 1971, composer-in-residence with the Rotterdam Philharmonic in Holland in 1974, guest professor at the Basel Conservatory in Switzerland in 1974–75, visiting professor of music at the State University of New York in Buffalo in 1975, visiting professor of music at the University of California in 1976, visiting professor of music at the University of Southern California in Los Angeles in 1978, and visiting professor of composition at the California Institute of the Arts in Valencia, Calif., in 1979.

During the 1960s, Brown and his wife, Carolyn, were separated several years before getting divorced. During his five years at the Peabody Conservatory, Brown met and married Susan Sollins, then curator of education at the Smithsonian National Collection of Fine Arts in Washington, D.C., and since then executive director of Independent Curators, which specialized in traveling exhibitions of contemporary art.

In 1970, Brown received an honorary doctorate in music from the Peabody Conservatory. The American Academy of Arts and Letters, the New York Council on the Arts, and Brandeis University presented him with their awards in 1972, 1974, and 1976 respectively.

THE COMPOSER SPEAKS: It is my responsibility to create and produce sound material, and by verbal and graphic means, making a strong impression on the performers. If I do my job well, I get back varying versions, all acceptable to me. If I have designed the material so that all its potentialities are logical and diverse, and the conducting of it sensible, then the difference of the poetry that the conductor puts in is valid—though I may prefer one performance over another.

I have always worked in search of pure musical sound values, and all different aspects of noise (like blowing wind without pitch through instruments) and with all possibilities, from clear articulation to warming-up or skittering sounds—so one must make a graphic notation, and so varied, to be more inclusive.

Nowadays, performers come to my music more sympathetically; they have seen this kind of notation, they are more confident, and their ears are transformed by all the other music they have heard and played. And different conductors—Japanese, Italian, whatever—also bring something different to my works which won't destroy their built-in composed character. That is all a positive acquisition for me.

PRINCIPAL WORKS: *Folio*, six works for any number of instruments (1952–53); *25 Pages*, for one to twenty-five pianos (1953); *Indices*, for chamber orchestra (1954); *Pentathis*, for nine instruments (1957); *Hodograph I*, for flute, piano and percussion (1959); *Available Forms I*, for chamber orchestra (1961); *Available Forms II*, for ninety-eight musicians and two conductors (1962); *Novara*, for eight instruments (1962); *From Here*, for chamber orchestra and chorus (1964); *Corroborée*, for three pianos (1964); String Quartet (1965); *Modules I and II*, for large orchestra (1966); *Chef d'orchestre/Calder Piece*, for mobile and percussion (1967); *Event: Synergy II*, for two chamber groups (1967–68); *Modules III*, for orchestra (1969); *Syntagm III*, for eight instruments (1970); *New Piece Loops*, for large orchestra and chorus (1971–72); *Time Spans*, for large orchestra (1972); *Sign Sounds*, for chamber orchestra (1972); *Centering*, for solo violin and chamber orchestra (1973); *Cross Sections and Color Fields,* for large orchestra (1975); *Patchen*, for chorus and large orchestra (1979); *Windsor Jambs*, for soprano and chamber orchestra (1979).

BIBLIOGRAPHY: Peyser, Joan, *The New Music* (N.Y., 1971); Rosenberg, Deena and Bernard, *The Music Makers* (N.Y., 1978); Salzman, Eric, *Twentieth-Century Music: An Introduction* (Englewood Cliffs, N.J., 1967); *Baltimore News American*, February 26, 1973; *New York Times*, June 21, 1970; *Time,* January 24, 1969; *Washington Post*, October 19, 1973.

Brubeck, David (Dave) Warren, b. Concord, Calif., December 6, 1920.

As a jazz pianist and as a composer of over one hundred jazz pieces, Dave Brubeck was a powerful, even decisive, force in the progressive jazz movement of the 1950s. In the 1960s he began writing more extended works for orchestra and chorus in an eclectic style, in which jazz remained one of the elements.

He was one of three sons of a father who enjoyed playing cowboy tunes on a harmonica and a mother, a telented pianist and teacher, who had studied with Tobias Matthay in London. Dave's two older brothers became professional musicians: Henry Brubeck, a music educator, is a retired supervisor of music in the public schools of Santa Barbara, and Howard Brubeck combined an academic career with that of a composer of concert works. All three received their initial training in theory and piano from their mother. Dave's first imprcssionable musical experience was hearing his mother play the classical and romantic piano repertoire at home. After his family moved to Ione, Calif., he devoted himself to becoming a skilled cowhand, but from the age of five Dave kept on with his piano and theory studies with his mother through his public school years (1925–38). When he was thirteen he played the piano with several regional Dixieland and swing bands. Upon graduating from the Ione High School, he entered the College of the Pacific in Stockton, Calif., with the expectation of studying veterinary medicine. In his first year at college he began to play in local clubs, and in 1941–42 he organized a twelve-piece band. By his second year he had made music his major, studying composition and theory with J. Russell Bodley (1939–42) and cello with Alexis Brown (1935).

After graduating from the College of the Pacific with a bachelor of music degree in 1942, Brubeck married Iola Whitlock, then a student, on September 21, 1942, at Carson City, Nev. They eventually reared five sons and a daughter. Brubeck entered the army in 1942, first serving with a band unit, then in Europe as a rifleman.

Following his discharge from the army in 1946, Brubeck became a pianist with various small jazz combos. During this period he studied composition with Darius Milhaud from 1946–48 at Mills College in Oakland, Calif., and for an additional year (1948–49) continued as his private student. From 1947–48

Brubeck took private piano lessons from Fred Saatman. Milhaud became, in Brubeck's own words, "the single most important influence in my musical life" by encouraging him to continue to work with jazz and convincing him of the genuine importance of jazz within the framework of music composition. "He told me if I didn't stick to jazz, I'd be working out of my own field and not taking advantage of my heritage." In 1948, with other Milhaud students, he formed an experimental jazz octet. In 1950, he formed the Dave Brubeck Trio, forerunner of the Dave Brubeck Quartet which made jazz history. The appearance of the quartet at the Black Hawk in San Francisco is said to have helped bring about a renaissance of jazz in that city. Through Fantasy Recordings, which he helped establish, and numerous appearances throughout the United States, the quartet rapidly acquired a national following. The first Columbia albums, *Jazz Goes to College* and *Dave Brubeck at Storyville* in 1954–55, invaded the best-selling charts. Brubeck became the "editor's choice" in *Metronome* in 1952; he took top place in the *Down Beat* popularity and critics' poll and in the *Metronome* popularity poll in 1953; he once again won the *Down Beat* popularity poll in 1954 and 1955; and in the *Metronome* all-star poll in 1954 and 1955 he came out on top in the piano category. The group was a continuous winner in jazz polls until it disbanded in 1967. In 1958 the Dave Brubeck Quartet made its first tour outside the United States, playing in eighteen countries during a three-month period.

Both as performer and composer Brubeck stood in the forefront of the progressive movement in jazz which carried some of the techniques of 20th-century music into jazz—atonality, polytonality, and polyrhythm. In performance, the quartet's imaginative flights of improvisation became almost legendary. Brubeck skillfully combined jazz styles and techniques in which he had been influenced by Duke Ellington, Louis Armstrong, Art Tatum, and Fats Waller with baroque polyphony and a modernistic stylistic approach he had learned from the works of Stravinsky, Ives, and Bartók. Of his more than one hundred jazz pieces these are perhaps the most familiar: "Blue Rondo à la Turk," "In Your Own Sweet Way," "The Duke," "Unsquare Dance," "Three to Get Ready," "Raggy Waltz," and "Bossa Nova U.S.A."

In 1966 Brubeck began writing a composition structurally more ambitious than anything he had thus far attempted. It was an oratorio, *The Light in the Wilderness*, with a text by his wife, Iola. For two years he worked on it, on and off, in hotel rooms and airplanes while touring with the quartet.

Following a concert in Pittsburgh on December 26, 1967, Brubeck disbanded the group so that he could work full time on composition. He completed the final scoring of his oratorio in a few weeks in 1968 and on February 29, 1968, it was given its pre-

miere in Cincinnati by the Cincinnati Symphony and the Miami University Chorus, the baritone William Justice and the Dave Brubeck Trio, all conducted by Erich Kunzel. This was an eclectic score, part baroque, part 20th century, partly polyphonic, partly jazz, partly atonal, partly polytonal, music the critic for *Time* described as flowing "with an inner, radiant simplicity . . . with the kind of deeply thought-out stylishness that characterized Brubeck's jazz work at its best." The same forces that had introduced it in Cincinnati brought the oratorio to New York in May 1969. That same year, the work toured Europe and was filmed for television by CBS at the National Cathedral in Washington, D.C.

Since he had a few concert engagements to fill in Mexico, Brubeck formed a new jazz group to play there. The Dave Brubeck Trio with Gerry Mulligan was subsequently heard in leading European capitals and made some notable recordings. In the mid-1970s this group merged with three of Dave's musician sons (Darius, Chris, and Dan) to form the Two Generations of Brubeck.

Brubeck continued to combine his jazz performances with the writing of other ambitious works, all of them eclectic. At times he now employed a twelve-tone technique. *The Gates of Justice* (1969) is a cantata with text by Iola Brubeck based on the Old Testament. It was commissioned by the Corbett Foundation for the Rockdale Temple and the American Hebrew Congregation in Cincinnati, where it was premiered on October 19, 1969. The Cincinnati Symphony commissioned *Fugal Fanfare*, for orchestra and jazz soloists (1970), for its seventy-fifth anniversary and premiered it on February 27, 1970. *Truth Is Fallen* (1971)—Iola Brubeck's text taken from the Biblical books of Isaiah and Jeremiah and the Psalms—is a cantata commissioned by the Midland Center for the Performing Arts for the dedication of its new auditorium. It was first performed on May 1, 1971, in Midland, Mich. The work calls for the usual cantata forces as well as for rock musicians. *La Fiesta de la Posada* (1975)—originally entitled *Song of Bethlehem*—is a Christmas choral pageant with text by Iola Brubeck adapted from the Bible. The Honolulu Symphony commissioned the work and introduced it on December 19, 1975. Adapted for a somewhat smaller orchestra, it was later given over one hundred performances throughout the United States and Canada, with annual presentations heard in New York at the Fifth Avenue Presbyterian Church. *Beloved Son* (1978) is an Easter oratorio commissioned by the American Lutheran Women. It was initially heard in Minneapolis on August 9, 1978 at the American Lutheran Women's Conference, and then was heard in New York in 1979 at the Fifth Avenue Presbyterian Church.

THE COMPOSER SPEAKS: I have long appreciated the relationship of jazz improvisation to the earlier improvised style of the figured bass, and some of my recognition in jazz came from combining Bachlike counterpoint with jazz rhythms. I also draw upon the folk music of the world—with emphasis, of course, on the blues, spirituals, and ragtime—because I've spent my working life as a jazz musician. In composing, as in improvising, I find I often reach back to my earliest, almost subconscious impressions—western folk themes, Mexican dances, American Indian songs—all of which were part of my childhood.

Composing by the rule book of any particular school of thought is anathema to me. I guess because I am fundamentally an improviser, I call upon all the musical resources of my past experience, and in the process of selecting, honing, and developing, that which is basically an improvisation becomes a composition.

PRINCIPAL WORKS: *Points on Jazz*, ballet suite for two pianos (1959; *Elemental*, for orchestra and jazz soloists (1963); *The Light in the Wilderness*, oratorio, for chorus, orchestra, organ, baritone solo, and optional improvising soloists (1966–68); *The Gates of Justice*, cantata for chorus, brass ensemble, percussion and organ, tenor and baritone soloists, and optional improvisation (1969); *Fugal Fanfare*, for orchestra and jazz soloists (1970); *Truth Is Fallen*, cantata, for soprano, chorus, rock group, rock vocalists, and orchestra (1971); *They All Sang "Yankee Doodle*," for orchestra with optional jazz improvisation, also for two pianos and for solo piano (1975); *La Fiesta de la Posada*, a Christmas choral pageant, for soprano, tenor, bass, baritone, chorus, orchestra with added mariachi instruments and optional improvisation (1975); *Glances*, for solo piano, also orchestrated (1976); *Beloved Son*, an Easter oratorio, for baritone, soprano, chorus, orchestra, and optional improvisation (1978); *Tritonis*, for flute and guitar (1978); *Festival Mass*, for solo voices, chorus and orchestra (1979).

BIBLIOGRAPHY: BMI, *The Many Worlds of Music*, Winter 1976; *Contemporary Keyboard*, December 1977; *San Francisco Chronicle*, April 18, 1954; *Time* (cover story), November 8, 1954; *Who's Who in America, 1980–81.*

Brunswick, Mark, b. New York, January 6, 1902, d. London. England, May 26, 1971.

In some of his representative works Brunswick was attracted to classical Greek and Roman subjects and was influenced by 16th-century polyphony.

His first memorable musical experience came when he was eight from hearing his first opera, Wagner's *Das Rheingold*. For a time after that, the world of good music and Wagner's *Der Ring des Nibelungen* were synonymous in his mind. By the time he was fifteen, his musical tastes included Beethoven and Tchaikovsky as well as Wagner. By then,

with no formal instruction behind him, he came to the conclusion he wanted to become a composer. Thus far he had received his academic education at the Horace Mann School in New York and the Phillips Academy in Exeter, N. J. In 1922 he dropped out of school. For the next five years he studied theory and composition with Rubin Goldmark. "I educated myself generally by reading." From 1923 to 1924 he was a pupil of Ernest Bloch's in counterpoint, fugue, and composition in Cleveland, and from 1925 to 1929 he resided in Paris, a student of Nadia Boulanger's.

The composition he numbered opus 1 was Two Movements, for string quartet, written in Paris in 1925–26, "to break the bonds of consonance," as he put it. In a more or less neoclassical idiom, Brunswick's opus 1 seemed to one reviewer (Miriam Gideon in the *American Composers Alliance Bulletin*) "like Venus to have sprung full-blown into existence . . . striking for its command of structure, its instrumental control, and the clear image it gives of its progenitor." This composition had to wait a decade for its first hearing, which took place in Vienna; then, on April 20, 1936, it represented America at the festival of the International Society for Contemporary Music in Barcelona, and in 1939 it was heard for the first time in New York.

In the early 1930s, Brunswick lived in Vienna, where he saturated himself with the music of Mozart. At the same time he became acquainted with the then young school of Viennese twelve-tone composers whose dogmatic rejection of tonality ran counter to his own musical instincts. His own thinking leaned more toward Bartók and Stravinsky on the one hand, and the 16th-century polyphonic masterworks of Palestrina and Orlando de Lasso on the other. Both influences were brought to bear in his Fantasia, for viola (1932), written for and introduced by Marcel Dick. Brunswick's philohellenism was first significantly reflected in his choice of subject matter: *Lysistrata*, a concert suite for mezzo-soprano, women's chorus, and orchestra (1930), and *Eros and Death*, a choral symphony for mezzo-soprano, chorus, and orchestra on texts of Lucretius, Sappho, and Emperor Hadrian (1932–54).

In 1937, Brunswick returned to the United States. One year later he became head of the departments of theory and composition at Greenwich House Music School in New York, where he remained five years. In 1946 he was appointed professor and chairman of the music department at the College of the City of New York; he occupied those posts for the next twenty-one years.

Brunswick's style became crystallized with the Symphony in B-flat (1945), whose world premiere was given by the Minneapolis Symphony under Dimitri Mitropoulos on March 7, 1947. It is dissonant but always clear in its tonal relationships; the thematic statments have a Webernlike epigrammatic character; the work as a whole is basically classic in its organization, though in details not in the traditional concept of the classic symphony.

In the chamber music that followed, Brunswick continued to write dissonantly, his work being characterized by violent contrasts and powerful, sometimes grim, outbursts. His ideas became so concentrated that sometimes single movements last just a few seconds and developments are telescoped into a few measures. All this is found in his seven trios for string quartet (1957); the String Quartet, with doublebass (1957); and the Septet (1958).

When Brunswick retired from the College of the City of New York in 1967, he was named professor emeritus and an annual award for excellence in composition was established in his honor. He spent his last years working on an opera, *The Master Builder*, based on Ibsen, of which he completed only two acts.

In 1938, Brunswick organized, and from 1938 to 1945 administered, the National Committee for Refugee Musicians, which found jobs and provided other assistance to European musicians who had come to America to escape nazism, fascism and World War II. At one time or another, Brunswick held the posts of president of the United States section of the International Society for Contemporary Music, president of the College Music Association, and vice-president of the American Composers Association. He was married to the former Natascha Artin, with whom he had a daughter. Brunswick was vacationing in Europe when he succumbed to a heart attack in London.

THE COMPOSER SPEAKS: Composing for me is very difficult. While I naturally would like it to be easier, I realize that in this musical world of today, with its conflicting and uncertain tendencies and influences, the achieving and maintaining of true individuality and purity of musical thought will always require an intensity of effort and imagination that can never be "easy." If this makes for small creative output, I cannot wish it to be otherwise.

PRINCIPAL WORKS: Two Movements, for string quartet (1925–26); *Lysistrata*, concert suite for mezzo-soprano, women's chorus, and orchestra (1930); Fantasia, for viola (1932); *Eros and Death*, choral symphony for mezzo-soprano, chorus, and orchestra (1932–54); Symphony in B-flat (1945); Seven Trios, for string quartet (1957); Quartet, for violin, viola, cello, and doublebass (1957); Septet, for wind quintet, viola, and cello (1958); Six Bagatelles, for piano (1958); Five Madrigals, for chorus, viola, cello, and doublebass (1958–66); Five Songs (1964); Air with Toccata, for string orchestra (1967).

BIBLIOGRAPHY: Ewen, David, *American Composers Today* (N.Y., 1949); *American Composers Alliance Bulletin*, March 1965; *New York Times* (obituary), May 28, 1971; *Who's Who in America, 1970–71*.

Burleigh, Cecil, b. Wyoming, N. Y., April 17, 1885; d. Madison, Wis., July 30, 1980.

Burleigh was partial to music that was pictorial without being literally programmatic and to a style that was romantic with suggestions of impressionism.

Both his parents played the piano, though not professionally. When Cecil was nine, and living in Omaha, Nebr., he was given a gift of a violin on which he began taking lessons with a local teacher. After his family moved to Bloomington, Ill., Cecil continued to study the violin with L. H. Hersey while taking lessons in theory with O. R. Skinner. Despite his concentration on the violin, Burleigh preferred the piano, at which he would spend hours improvising. While attending high school he made his first attempt at composition. Inspired by reading such classics as *Ivanhoe, Kenilworth,* and *Lady of the Lake*, he wrote a number of sketchy pieces descriptive of scenes that moved him most. He later regarded these and other similar items as so imitative and crude that he discarded them completely, together with everything else he was to write during the next eight years.

For additional music study Burleigh went to Germany in 1903 to attend the Klindworth-Scharwenka Conservatory in Berlin. There his teachers included Anton Witek and Max Grünberg (violin) and Hugo Leichentritt (composition). In 1905, Burleigh returned to the United States to spend the next two years in Chicago studying the violin with Émile Sauret and composition with Felix Borowski at the Chicago Musical College.

From 1909 to 1911, Burleigh was instructor of violin at the Denver Institute of Music and Dramatic Arts in Colorado. In Denver, two events transpired that helped give new direction to his composing career. In 1910, he married Atossa Hopkins, his first wife, who did what she could to encourage her young husband in his creative efforts. Not long after his marriage, Burleigh heard Edward MacDowell's *Woodland Sketches*, which stimulated him to write pictorial pieces inspired by nature, such as *Four Rocky Mountain Sketches*, for violin and piano.

For three years (1911–14) Burleigh lived in Sioux City, Iowa, where he taught violin and composition at Morningside College. This was a period in which he absorbed himself with playing the music of Brahms, Chopin, Schumann, and Grieg and became thoroughly infected with their romanticism. The impact of this total immersion with European romanticism is reflected in works completed between 1911 and 1915: *The Ascension*, a sonata for violin and piano; *Six Winter Evening Tales and Tone Poems*, and *Twelve Short Poems*, both for violin and piano; and his Violin Concerto no. 1, in E minor.

Between 1914 and 1919, Burleigh taught violin and composition at the University of Montana, in Missoula. There he wrote the *Mountain Pictures*, an orchestral suite (1917) that was introduced by Rudolph Ganz and the St. Louis Symphony on January 5, 1923.

In 1919, Burleigh came to New York. During the next two years he studied violin with Leopold Auer, composition with Ernest Bloch, and orchestration with Walter Rothwell. He also did a good deal of concertizing as violinist in recitals, as guest artist with symphony orchestras, and in joint concerts with such notables as Rosa Ponselle, John McCormack, and Rudolph Ganz. Burleigh was heard in the world premieres of his first two violin concertos. He performed the first concerto as soloist with the Minneapolis Symphony under Henri Verbrugghen; and the second (in A minor) on March 13, 1921, with the Cleveland Orchestra under Vladimir Sokoloff.

Burleigh had little sympathy for American composers who tried to achieve a national identity by using musical materials not of their own making—such as jazz or American Indian music, or Negro spirituals. He felt that the work of an American composer should be entirely his own, and that it becomes American music solely by the fact that it is written in America by an American. When on random occasions he wrote compositions inspired by the American Indian (the early *Indian Snake Dance* or the *Five Indian Sketches*, both for violin and piano), he did not actually quote any American Indian melodies or rhythms but, instead, tried to provide an impressionistic portrait of the Indian as seen through his own music. More generally, he preferred writing Mac-Dowell-like little nature tone poems to which he provided programmatic titles as the clue to his inspiration but without ever resorting to literal tone painting.

The late 1930s was a period of creative sterility, from which he emerged in 1940 with his marriage to his second wife, Jessie Meredith Jennings, on May 25, 1940, having divorced his first wife in 1935. He now undertook compositions inspired by ideas and concepts more ambitious than the little scenes he had formerly found so stimulating. *Leaders of Men*

(1940), suite for orchestra, took its title, as the composer himself explained, "from qualities which characterize individuals who, in periods of history, have endeavored to lead humanity out of its confusion and perplexities." *American Processional*, for violin and piano (1941), told of the growth of America from the days of the Indian to 1941. *From the Muses*, for small orchestra (1944), was a tribute to the goddess of flowers and the god of the west wind. *Creation, Prophecy*, and *Revelation* in 1944 were the titles he gave to a trilogy of symphonies, and *Illusion* and *Transition*, to two string quartets in 1945.

THE COMPOSER SPEAKS: To me all composition divides itself into three clases: absolute, impressionistic and realistic. Personally, I greatly favor the first two. In my case, the music must be able to stand alone regardless of its program.

PRINCIPAL WORKS: 3 violin concertos (1915, 1919, 1928).

The Ascension Sonata, for violin and piano (1914); *Mountain Pictures*, for orchestra (1917); *Ballad of New England*, for piano (1924); *From the Life of St. Paul*, sonata for violin and piano (1926); *Three Mood Pictures*, for piano (1926); *Evangeline*, tone poem for orchestra (1929); *Mountain Pictures*, suite for orchestra (1930); *Hymn to the Ancients*, quintet (1940); *Leaders of Men*, suite for orchestra (1940); *From the Muses*, for small orchestra (1944); *Creation, Prophecy*, and *Revelation*, a trilogy of symphonies (1944); *Illusion* and *Transition*, for string quartet (1945). *Also: Translations from Literature*, four volumes for piano; *Two Essays in String Quartet*, for string quartet; *Fragments from Indian Life*, for violin, cello, and piano; *Four Rocky Mountain Sketches*, for violin and piano.

BIBLIOGRAPHY: Howard, John Tasker, *Cecil Burleigh*, a monograph (N. Y., 1929); *Etude*, April 1943.

C

Cadman, Charles Wakefield, b. Johnstown, Pa., December 24, 1881; d. Los Angeles, December 30, 1946.

His first success came with music utilizing American Indian melodies and rhythms. Though later works for the most part abandoned the American Indian, Cadman produced other compositions on American subjects and backgrounds.

Both his parents traced their ancestry back to colonial days. Charles Cadman's great-grandfather, Samuel Wakefield, was a hymnologist who built the first pipe organ west of the Alleghenies. Through his mother, a singer in church choirs, Cadman first became interested in music, but he did not receive any music instruction until he was thirteen. At that time a piano was brought into the Cadman household, and a local teacher was recruited to give him lessons. He later also received instruction in harmony from Leo Oehmler and organ from W. K. Skinner. At sixteen, Cadman served as organist in a suburban Pittsburgh church. At about this time he wrote his first piece of music: a two-step march in the style of Sousa entitled "The Carnegie Library March." It was performed by local bands and sold so well in publication that it provided Cadman with the funds to pay for two years of music study in Pittsburgh with Luigi von Kunits and Emil Paur (orchestration) and Edwin Walker (piano).

In 1903, the Cadman family moved to Duquesne, Pa., where Cadman spent the next three years working as a messenger in a steel plant. Meanwhile, in or about 1901, he became a friend of Nelle Richmond Eberhart, a writer of song lyrics, with whom he soon formed a collaboration in writing songs. About a dozen were published and had only a limited sale. After a few years, they came upon the idea of using the American Indian as song material—the American Indian having fascinated Cadman from his boyhood days and, later on, from his reading of ethnological studies by Alice Fletcher and Francis La Flesche. In 1907, Cadman and Eberhart wrote Four American Indian Songs, a cycle in which for the first time Cadman borrowed or simulated idioms of American Indian music. One of these songs was "The Moon Drops," which won a prize in a competition sponsored by the Carnegie Art Institute. Another was "From the Land of the Sky-Blue Water." The prima donna, Lillian Nordica, featured it so successfully on her concert programs in 1909 that the sheet-music sale rocketed, in time achieving a circulation of about two million copies. It entered the repertoire of American singers everywhere both in the concert hall and on the popular stage. In 1911, "At Dawning" (not of an American Indian identity) became another giant success, made famous by John McCormack.

In 1908, Cadman used the melodies and rhythms of the American Indian in a structure larger than the art song by writing the piano suite *To a Vanishing Race*. In 1909 he spent the summer with the Omaha Indians, witnessing their ritual and listening to and recording their ceremonial songs and flageolet love calls. This experience was the soil from which sprang other ambitious American Indian compositions. In 1912, to a libretto by Nelle Richmond Eberhart, he wrote his first American Indian opera, *Daoma, or The Land of the Misty Water,* and a suite for piano entitled *Idealized Indian Themes*. One year later, he adapted his piano suite *To a Vanishing Race* for strings, and after that for large orchestra, the latter version given its initial hearing on May 17, 1914, in Denver in a performance by the Russian Symphony Orchestra under Modest Altschuler. *Thunderbird* (1916), a suite for orchestra utilizing the melodies and dances of Blackfoot Indians, received its world premiere in Los Angeles on January 9, 1917.

Between 1902 and 1910, Cadman was the music critic of the *Pittsburgh Dispatch*. During that time he was also organist at the East Liberty Presbyterian Church. Illness compelled him to give up both posts early in 1910, to spend most of that year in Colorado for a rest cure. He was back in Pittsburgh before the year was over to attend a testimonial concert devoted entirely to his compositions on December 22, 1910. After that, for the next decade, he continued to study Indian music with the Pima and Isleta tribes of Arizona and New Mexico, and, until 1923, to travel around the United States in lecture-recitals on Indian music with the assistance of the Indian mezzo-soprano Tsianina Redfeather.

Cadman's most important American Indian work was the three-act opera *Shanewis (The Robin Woman)*, libretto by Nelle Richmond Eberhart. In his score, Cadman borrowed liberally from Indian sources, including an Osage ceremonial song and various melodies native to Cheyenne and Omaha tribes. Sometimes spoken of by historians as one of the first truly indigenous American operas—since it was so thoroughly American both in text and in music—*Shanewis* was produced by the Metropolitan

Opera on March 23, 1918, the first American opera at the Metropolitan to be performed for two seasons. Reviewing it in the *New York Sun,* W.J. Henderson praised it for its "good declamation, continuous flow without irrelevant instrumental interruptions, and clear, varied and very discreet orchestration" as well as for its fluent, melodious ideas. *Shewanis* was subsequently heard in Chicago, Denver, San Francisco, Los Angeles, and over the NBC radio network.

On December 5, 1922, Cadman's operatic cantata *The Sunset Trail* was produced in Denver. It was revived in Rochester, N.Y., four years later. This, too, was deeply rooted in the folk music of the American Indian. But with the opera *A Witch of Salem* (1925), libretto by Eberhart, the American Indian was replaced by the colonial New Englander, and Cadman's music was entirely his own, without indigenous borrowings. It was produced by the Chicago Opera on December 8, 1926. Cadman wrote another opera with an Eberhart libretto: *The Willow Tree,* introduced over the NBC radio network on October 3, 1933.

In 1917 Cadman established permanent residence in Los Angeles, where he remained the rest of his life. After writing *The Father of the Waters* for mixed chorus in 1928, Cadman (with one or two minor exceptions) abandoned American Indian music. Many of his most successful later works were rooted in other American backgrounds and experiences. His *Hollywood Suite,* for orchestra (1932), consisted of four tonal portraits, one each of Mary Pickford, Charles Chaplin, Cadman's mother, and the Hollywood Bowl. One of his most popular works for orchestra was a spirited, colorful picture of an American carnival: *Dark Dancers of the Mardi Gras* (1933). Under its original title of *The Dance of Scarlet Sister Mary,* it was premiered in Milwaukee on March 12, 1933. As *Dark Dancers of the Mardi Gras* it was given numerous performances during the next few years, including those by the New York Philharmonic under John Barbirolli in 1937. In *American Suite* (1937), originally for strings but later transcribed for full orchestra, Cadman reached back briefly, and for the last time, to American Indian music for one of its movements, devoting the two others to the American Negro and to country fiddle music. *American Suite* was commissioned for the Saratoga (New York) Music Festival by F. Charles Adler, who conducted the premiere performance there on September 18, 1937. Cadman's only symphony, subtitled *Pennsylvania* (1939), traced the history of that state from its earliest days. After its initial hearing in Los Angeles on March 8, 1940, with Albert Coates conducting the Los Angeles Philharmonic, it was performed by the Chicago Symphony, the Detroit Symphony, the Kansas City Symphony and the Rochester Philharmonic, among other orchestras. *Huckleberry Finn Goes Fishing* (1945) was an "American overture" based on Mark Twain.

In 1923 Cadman was a founder of the Hollywood Bowl summer concerts in Los Angeles. He was also the organizer and chairman of the Congress for the Encouragement of American Music, which held a festival in Los Angeles in June 1915. He received honorary doctorates in music from Wolcott Conservatory of Music in Colorado in 1924 and from the University of California in Los Angeles in 1926.

Throughout his life Cadman adopted a conventional style which scrupulously avoided any suggestion of modernism. The comparative neglect of Cadman's music in his closing years was due for the most part to his conservatism, as performers (as well as critics) were becoming increasingly interested and involved in the more adventurous and innovative writings of so many of Cadman's younger contemporaries.

THE COMPOSER SPEAKS: Though I was the first composer to utilize Indian themes successfully as the basis for song literature, I do not believe that the employment of any style of folk song indigenous to America leads to what is broadly called "American music." I acknowledge the fact that the occasional introduction and use of Negro, Indian, cowboy, and even Kentucky mountain music may add "color" and "locale" at times in the compositions of American composers, but I never believed or declared that the use of this "native material" is at all necessary to significant music.

PRINCIPAL WORKS: Four American Indian Songs, for voice and piano (1907); *The Vision of Sir Launfal,* cantata for female voices and orchestra (1909); "At Dawning," for voice and piano (1911); *Daoma,* opera (1912); *Idealized Indian Themes,* piano suite (1912); *To a Vanishing Race,* for string orchestra or full orchestra, originally for piano (1913); Piano Trio (1914); *The Garden of Mystery,* one-act opera (1915); *Thunderbird,* suite for orchestra (1916); *Shanewis,* opera (1917); String Quartet (1917); *Oriental Rhapsody from Omar Khayyám,* for orchestra (1921); *The Sunset Trail,* operatic cantata (1922); *A Witch of Salem,* opera (1925); *The Willow Tree,* radio opera (1925); *The Father of Waters,* for mixed voices (1928); *Hollywood Suite,* for orchestra (1932); *Dark Dancers of the Mardi Gras,* for orchestra (1933); *American Suite,* for strings, also for full orchestra (1937); Sonata in G, for violin and piano (1937); Symphony, *Pennsylvania* (1939); *Aurora Borealis,* fantasy for piano and orchestra (1942): *A Mad Empress Remembers,* tone drama for cello and orchestra (1944); *Huckleberry Finn Goes Fishing,* an "American overture" (1945).

BIBLIOGRAPHY: Ewen, David, *Composers Since 1900* (N.Y., 1969); Howard, John Tasker, *Our American Music* (N.Y., 1941); Hipsher, E. E., *American Opera and Its Composers* (Philadelphia, 1927).

Cage, John, b. Los Angeles, Calif., September 5, 1912.

Whatever area of avant-garde music Cage has chosen to develop—be it organized sounds and rhythms, chance music, dadaism, electronic music or multimedia productions—he has been an innovator whose influence has been felt and absorbed by composers in both the United States and Europe.

He was the only child of cultured parents, his father being an engineer and inventor and his mother a cub reporter for the *Los Angeles Times*. John gained his first experience in music by studying the piano with his aunt and with neighborhood teachers. Upon graduating from Los Angeles High School in 1928 as class valedictorian, he spent two years at Pomona College in Claremont, Calif., distinguishing himself there by winning a statewide contest in oratory. At this time he continued studying the piano with Fannie Charles Dillon and Richard Buhlig. In 1932, Cage went to Paris for further piano study with Lazare Lévy. Back in the United States in 1933, he made his home in New York, where for one year he was a pupil in composition of Henry Cowell's, whose experiments in tone clusters made a deep impression on him. Six Short Pieces, for seven instruments (1933); Sonata for Two Voices (1933); and Composition for Three Voices (1934) already began to reveal his impatience with the status quo in music through novel tonal procedures.

On Cowell's advice, Cage spent two years (1935–37) studying composition with Arnold Schoenberg and Adolph Weiss. The twelve-tone system Schoenberg and his followers advocated opened up for Cage a new world of composition to which he responded creatively by producing several works in a strict twelve-tone idiom, notably a five-movement suite for piano, *Metamorphosis* (1938). Another strong influence soon brought to bear on Cage was Edgard Varèse and his "organized sounds" in which extramusical sounds and noises were explored for their artistic potential. Stimulated by Varèse, Cage began gravitating more and more to percussion music, which dispensed with melody, harmony, and counterpoint and consisted solely of rhythm and rhythmic units, and in which silences provided significant contrasts to sound. "The theory of percussion is much akin to atonal music," Cage explained at the time. "No sound any more important than any other comes out of atonal music into organized sound."

On June 7, 1935, Cage and Xenia Kashevaroff were married (divorced in 1945). Between 1937 and 1939, Cage was employed at the Cornish School in Seattle, Wash., where he was accompanist to the dance classes. In Seattle, Cage embarked upon his first experiments in percussion music and rhythmic sound by organizing a percussion group that gave regular concerts and for which Cage wrote *First Construction (in metal)* for percussion sextet (1939).

During this period, Cage evolved a method of "preparing" a piano to produce percussive sounds that carried Cowell's earlier experiments in tone clusters and the manipulation of the strings on the piano keyboard several steps further. "Preparing" a piano meant stuffing all kinds of hardware, utensils, and objects between the strings and the soundboard: screws, nuts, wood, felt, spoons, clothespins, bolts and the like. A piano so modified is called a prepared piano. New sonorities were thus produced as the piano suddenly became a one-instrument percussion ensemble for a single performer. Cage's first piece for the prepared piano was *Bacchanal* (1938).

In 1941–42, Cage taught at the School of Design in Chicago. He moved back to New York in 1942, arranged concerts of percussion music there, and, for the first time, formed a collaboration with the dancer Merce Cunningham, with whom for the next two decades he would open new horizons. He often wrote his music totally independent of the choreography and the dancers were often denied a chance of hearing any of his music before their performance. "We do two separate works," he explained, "which are then performed simultaneously."

During the late 1940s, Cage wrote a good deal of music for his prepared piano. The most significant was Sonatas and Interludes (1946–49), a seventy-minute work for which the piano's preparation was so elaborate that it consumed between two and three hours. In these works, as Cage explained, he attempted to express musically "the 'permanent emotions' of Indian tradition: the heroic, the erotic, the wondrous, the mirthful sorrow, fear, anger, the odious, and their common tendency towards tranquillity."

The 1940s also witnessed Cage's experiments in extending his concept of rhythmic sound. *Living Room* (1940) used a speech quartet as well as percussion; in addition, sounds normally encountered at home are reproduced, such as the closing of windows, the banging of doors, the moving about of furniture. *Third Construction* (1941) required rattles, drums, tin cans, claves, cowbells, a lion's roar, cymbal, ratchet, cricket caller, conch shell, and so on. Tin cans, buzzers, a water gong, a metal wastebasket, and an amplified coil of wire is the equipment for *Imaginary Landscape No. 1* (1939); such electronic and mechanical devices as audiofrequency oscillators, a variable speed turntable for the playing of frequency recordings, generator whines and a buzzer are used in *Landscape No. 2* (1942). *Landscape No. 4* (1951) calls on twenty-four players to operate twelve radios, two operators for each radio, whose squeals, static, and other sounds create a new kind of cacophony. In *Water Music* (1952) static produced on radio is combined with the sounds of water poured from a full container into an empty one, a process regulated by a stopwatch, and the riffle of a deck of cards. *Water Music* is Cage's first work of visual as well as aural interest, visual elements henceforth becoming an increasing involvement with Cage.

Whatever ridicule Cage's revolutionary procedures inspired in some quarters was tempered by the recognition he was beginning to receive elsewhere. Virgil Thomson, the music critic of the *New York Herald Tribune* and a distinguished composer, called Cage's music for prepared piano an "original expression of the highest poetic quality." The Guggenheim Foundation presented Cage with a fellowship in 1949, and the National Institute of Arts and Letters gave him an award that year for having extended the "boundaries of music."

In 1952, Cage organized the Project for Music for Magnetic Tape in New York, the first such organization in the United States experimenting with taped music. Cage used magnetic tape in *Williams Mix* (1952) to capture city sounds as well as those produced by the wind. *Fontana Mix* (1958; N.Y., April 26, 1959) amplifies on magnetic tape sounds produced by dropping ashes into an ashtray, scraping wires and microphones on the strings of a piano keyboard, putting on and taking off eyeglasses, swallowing, coughing, grunting, smoking cigarettes, or scraping microphones over glass. "This use of everyday music makes me aware of the world around me" Cage said. "Now I go to a cocktail party. I don't hear noise. I hear music."

But Cage interested himself not only in sounds but also in silences, which dramatically punctuate many of his compositions. Certainly the ultimate in exploiting the value of silence and freedom of expression came with Cage's three-movement *4'33"* (1952; Woodstock, N.Y., August 29, 1952), in which the performer sits in front of the keyboard for four minutes and thirty-three seconds without playing a note.

In the 1950s, Cage turned to aleatory or chance music. One of Cage's chance methods was to write a piano composition on individual sheets, have the performer scatter the sheets haphazardly on the floor and then have him pick up at random one sheet after another until the last sheet has been played. The scattering of these sheets pell-mell at each performance results in a new sequence in which a different composition emerges each time. More frequently, Cage employed a chance method known as *I Ching* (*Chinese Book of Changes*). Here a pair of Chinese dice is employed. Using a prearranged table on which the different numbers a throw of dice is capable of producing is related to various elements in music. Cage throws out the dice and the number coming up instructs him in the kind of music he puts down on paper. *Landscape 4, Water Music,* and *Williams Mix* all use chance, and so does the Concert for Piano and Orchestra (1957–58), which David Tudor introduced in New York on May 15, 1958, and which four months later was broadcast over the Cologne Radio in Germany. Here the solo instrument part consists of eighty-four different compositions that the performer is free to play in any sequence, in whole or in part, and even with one com-

position superimposed upon another. What makes a performance of the Concert further intriguing is the fact that the performer, in addition to participating in the process of composition and playing the keyboard traditionally, is called upon to pluck the strings on the piano or go under the piano to thump its wooden underside or to produce sounds electronically. In Variations I and Variations II (1958), each for players of any kind or number of instruments or sound-producing objects, the performers are permitted to improvise whatever sounds they desire at any given moment: by scraping the microphone up and down the strings of the piano, untangling a pile of wires on the floor, writing a letter, and so forth. Electronics and chance are used to evolve a new chance method in *Reunion* (1968; N.Y., May 27, 1968), where the performers play on an electrified chessboard at which the movements determine the sounds of the composition as they pass through an electronic filter.

Cage spent the summers between 1948 and 1952 at the Black Mountain College in North Carolina as a member of its faculty. There he collaborated with Merce Cunningham in the presentation of multimedia productions, an artistic partnership that would continue successfully for many years after.

In 1961, on a commission from the Montreal Festival Society, Cage completed *Atlas Eclipticalis,* for orchestra and electronics; it was introduced in Montreal on August 3, 1961. Electronic circuits (microphones, amplifiers, loudspeakers) were used in conjunction with the live instruments, operated by an assistant to the conductor. Chance methods were employed, since this work may be performed as a whole or in part or for as long as the conductor desires. Additionally, the conventional instruments of the orchestra and the various unspecified pitched percussion instruments may all be used, or only some.

With Cage, multimedia productions went hand in hand with neodadaism in 1965. Variations V (1965; N.Y., July 23, 1965) recruited dancers and flashed distorted images from television and motion-picture clips on a screen. The principal male dancer, wearing red pants and a gray shirt, rode a bicycle through a mass of electronic transmitters which relayed the sounds of the moving bicycle through loudspeakers. In *Theater Piece* (1965)—introduced on September 11, 1965, in New York—a man wrapped in a black plastic cocoon was hung upside down. While a cellist performed Cage's music, the composer put into and removed from her mouth a cigar. A tiny Japanese waved silken banners from atop huge bamboo poles. Balloons were punctured, buzzers were sounded, and other noises were created electronically.

Between 1967 and 1969, Cage was the recipient of a grant from the Thorne Music Fund. In those years he completed *HPSCHD,* a four-hour multimedia presentation developed with Lejaren Hiller, an expert on computer music. "HPSCHD" is "harpsichord" in computer language, with vowels omitted.

This composition is written for from one to seven amplified harpsichords and one to fifty-one "monaural musicians." The work is used to accompany films and slides, some nonrepresentational, some comprising mere patterns, others of current events such as the Apollo moon landing. Introduced at the University of Illinois in Urbana on May 16, 1969, the work was subsequently performed in Albany (N.Y.), Brooklyn (N.Y.), San Francisco, and abroad in London and Berlin.

A commission from the Koussevitzky Music Foundation led to the orchestration of *Cheap Imitation* in 1972, which Cage had previously (1969) written for piano "in imitation of Erik Satie's *Socrate*." The orchestrated version was first heard on August 28, 1971, in Munich, Germany.

Cage was one of six composers commissioned by the National Endowment for the Arts to honor the American bicentennial with compositions, each to be performed by six major American orchestras. Cage responded with *Renga* and *Apartment House 1776*, "material for a musical happening" inspired by 361 drawings of Thoreau. *Renga* is a score for full symphony orchestra; *Apartment House 1776* (so titled to suggest a number of simultaneous happenings), for an orchestra of twenty-four instruments, or a greatly expanded orchestral ensemble, supplemented by four voices. These voices represent a Protestant, a Sephardi, an American Indian, and a Negro, inhabitants of America two centuries ago. These two works are separate compositions and can be performed independently of each other. They can also be performed simultaneously as a single work, and this is the way the works were first performed on September 19, 1976, by the Boston Symphony under Seiji Ozawa. Chance determines both compositions. In *Renga*, the conductor is given free choice in inserting pauses, changing tempi, and instructing the musicians when they can begin or end their performance. When *Renga* is played conjunctly with *Apartment House 1776* the conductor must decide whether *Renga* is to begin before or after *Apartment House 1776*, and which of these compositions is to end first. *Apartment House 1776* comprises sixty-four pieces that can be played in any sequence and in any superimpositions desired by the conductor.

A concert of Cage's music covering the first quarter century of his creativity was presented in New York on May 15, 1958. To honor his sixty-fifth birthday, a "retrospective concert" of Cage's music was heard in New York on April 24, 1978, its program including eight of the thirty-two etudes in *Études australes* (1974–75) and the world premiere of *Freeman Etudes I–VIII* for solo violin (1978).

In 1963, Cage was invited to the Music Biennale in Zagreb, Yugoslavia, where he lectured and conducted his own music; Gunther Schuller reported from Zagreb that Cage was "unquestionably the most talked about figure at the Biennale." In 1966 and 1967, Cage was composer-in-residence at the University of Cincinnati. In 1968 he was elected a member of the National Institute of Arts and Letters. In 1970, he was appointed Fellow at the Center for Advanced Studies at Wesleyan University in Middletown, Connecticut (where he had also served a decade earlier). Since 1970, Cage has been an Associate at the Center for Advanced Study at the University of Illinois in Urbana where he received the Thorne Music Grant, and was artist-in-residence at the University of California in Davis.

Cage is the author of *Silence* (1961), *A Year from Monday* (1968), *M* (1973), *Writings through Finnegans Wake* (1978), and *Empty Words* (1979). With various collaborators he also wrote *The Life and Works of Virgil Thomson* (1958), *Notations* (1969), *Not Wanting to Say Anything about Marcel A* (1969), and *Mushroom Book* (1974). A collection of Cage's essays, edited by Richard Kostelanetz, was published in New York in 1970.

THE COMPOSER SPEAKS: The writing of music is an affirmation of life, not an attempt to bring order out of chaos nor to suggest improvement in creation but simply a way of waking up to the very life we're living which is so excellent once one gets one's mind and one's desire out of the way and lets it act of its own accord.

PRINCIPAL WORKS: Variations I–VII, for any number of people, action, and sounds (1958–66); *Imaginary Landscapes*, nos. 1–4, for various sound-producing agents and percussion (1939–51); *First, Second*, and *Third Construction (in metal)*, for percussion and sound-producing agents (1939, 1940, 1941).

A Book of Music, for two prepared pianos (1944); *The Seasons*, for orchestra (1947); Sonatas and Interludes, for prepared piano (1946–48); String Quartet in Four Parts (1950); Concerto for Prepared Piano and Chamber Orchestra (1951); *Water Music*, for eight-track tape (1952); *Williams Mix*, for eight-track tape (1952); *Winter Music*, for one to two pianists (1957); Concert for Piano and Orchestra (1957–58); *Fontana Mix*, for prerecorded tape and any kind and number of instruments (1958); *Theater Piece*, for one to eight performers (1960); *Atlas Eclipticalis*, for orchestra and electronics (1961); *Reunion*, for electronic chessboard (1968); *HPSCHD*, for one to seven harpsichords and one to fifty-one "monaural musicians," written with Lejaren Hiller (1967–69); Songs, two books, (1970); *Cheap Imitation*, for piano solo (1969, orchestrated 1972, for violin solo, 1977); *Etcetera*, for chamber orchestra (1973); *Études australes*, for piano solo (1974–75); *Renga*, for orchestra (1976); *Apartment House 1776*, for small orchestra of twenty-four instruments, or an orchestra of forty-two instruments, or an orchestra of ninety-three instruments, and four voices (1976); Quartet I (1976); Quartets V and VI (1977); *Telephones and Birds*, for three performers

(1977); *Forty-nine Waltzes for the Five Boroughs* (1977); *Freeman Etudes*, for violin solo (1978).

BIBLIOGRAPHY: *NGDMM;* Griffith, Paul, *A Concise History of Avant-Garde Music* (N.Y., 1978); Kostelanetz, Richard (editor), *John Cage* (N.Y., 1970); Nyman, M., *Experimental Music, Cage and Beyond* (London, 1974); Yates, Peter, *20th-Century Music* (N.Y., 1967); *High Fidelity/Musical America*, November 1972, June 1980; *Horizon*, December 1980; *Musical Quarterly*, October 1979; *New York Times*, October 22, 1976; *New York Times Magazine*, January 17, 1967; *People*, October 15, 1979; *Saturday Review*, April 30, 1966; *Stereo Review*, May 1969.

Carpenter, John Alden, b. Park Ridge, Ill., February 28, 1876; d. Chicago, April 26, 1951.

Like Charles Ives before him, Carpenter led a double life, that of businessman and composer—and he was highly successful in both. He was a pioneer in using jazz within serious musical contexts. He later distinguished himself in compositions in a romantic or impressionistic style.

A lineal descendant of John Alden of Pilgrim fame, Carpenter was born to wealth, the father being the head of George B. Carpenter & Co., a prosperous mill and railroad and ship supply company. The Carpenter household was musical. The mother, a trained singer who had studied in Paris with Mme. Marchesi, passed on her own interest in music to all four sons. John received his first music lessons on the piano from his mother when he was about five. Before long he started improvising his own melodies. Additional and more formal instruction on the piano took place with Amy Fay (1887–91), and piano and theory with William Charles Ernest Seeboeck (1891–93). After attending Park Ridge Elementary School and High School, both in Illinois, Carpenter entered Harvard University in 1893, where he took courses in music, including composition with John Knowles Paine. Carpenter wrote the music for two productions of the Hasty Pudding Club, and a minuet for orchestra was performed by the Pierian Sodality Orchestra on December 18, 1894. Carpenter graduated with a bachelor of arts degree in 1897 with highest honors. He then entered his father's business, serving as vice-president from 1909 until his retirement in 1936. On November 10, 1900, he married Rue Winterbotham; they had a daughter.

Despite his involvement with a large business establishment, Carpenter was determined not to abandon music. With his wife as colyricist, he wrote a cycle of amusing songs, *Improving Songs for Anxious Children* (1901-2), and Four Negro Songs (1903). In 1904 his first publication appeared, the song "When Little Boys Sing."

During a six-month stay in Italy in 1906 Carpenter studied composition for three months with Edward Elgar. Carpenter completed the study of composition in Chicago with Bernhard Ziehn between 1908 and 1912.

In 1911, Carpenter wrote a violin sonata which was performed by Mischa Elman. Two years later, *Gitanjali*, a song cycle for mezzo-soprano and piano (or orchestra) to poems by Tagore, was praised by Felix Borowski, the noted Chicago music critic, for its "beauty" and "striking a new note in native composition." Two songs from this cycle subsequently became favorites in the concert hall: "When I Bring to You Color'd Toys" and "The Sleep That Flits on Baby's Eyes."

Carpenter scored his first major success with his first composition solely for symphony orchestra: the suite *Adventures in a Perambulator* (1914), given its world premiere in Chicago on March 19, 1915, with Frederick Stock conducting the Chicago Symphony. This is a six-movement programmatic composition that looks through the eyes of a baby as it is being wheeled around in a perambulator by its nurse. Throughout the composition, leitmotifs identify the child, the nurse, and the perambulator to provide unity. Quotations of popular tunes are interwoven into the overall texture (Irving Berlin's "Alexander's Ragtime Band," "Ach du lieber Augustin," and "Where, O Where, Has My Little Dog Gone?") to contribute a wry wit to the musical proceedings. Following its premiere, this suite remained a favorite at symphony concerts for several decades, one of Carpenter's most frequently heard compositions both in the United States and in Europe.

The brief injection of a quotation from an Irving Berlin Tin Pan Alley song was the harbinger of a direction Carpenter would pursue most successfully: the use of popular American idioms—jazz particularly—within the context of serious composition. In carrying over elements of jazz into serious music, Carpenter was a pioneer. Already the sounds of jazz had appeared in his Concertino for Piano and Orchestra (1915), which Percy Grainger introduced in Chicago on March 10, 1916, as soloist with the Chicago Symphony under Stock. Jazz is used even more prominently in *Krazy Kat* (1921)—a ballet pantomime inspired by George Herriman's cartoons then so popular in American newspapers—which was given by the Chicago Symphony in 1921 before it was produced as a ballet by Adolph Bolm and his company in Chicago on December 23, 1921.

Carpenter's principal work in the symphonic-jazz medium was the ballet *Skyscrapers* (1923-24), scenario by the composer. This was the first major ballet descriptive of American big-city life and its tempo. Carpenter wrote it for Serge Diaghilev and the Ballet Russe de Monte Carlo for its projected tour of the United States. (Diaghilev had been so impressed with *Krazy Kat* that he had commissioned Carpenter to write a score for a jazz ballet.) However, the

American tour of the Ballet Russe did not materialize at that time. Negotiations with Diaghilev for production in Monte Carlo were so prolonged and indecisive that Carpenter finally decided to turn his ballet over to the Metropolitan Opera in New York, which produced it on February 19, 1926. The ballet was a resounding success not only in New York but in Munich, where it was mounted two years later. Carpenter himself said of the ballet that "it seeks to reflect some of the many rhythmic movements and sounds of modern American life. It has no story in the usually accepted sense, but proceeds on the simple fact that American life reduces itself essentially to violent alternations of work and play, each with its own peculiar and distinctive rhythmic character." The orchestral suite Carpenter prepared from his ballet score became a frequent item on American symphony programs for many years.

With the Jazz Orchestra Pieces (1925–26) Carpenter's symphonic-jazz period was over. In his Quartet for Strings (1927), first heard at the Elizabeth Sprague Coolidge Festival in Washington, D.C., in April 1928, he was the conformist and the romanticist faithful to conventional patterns and concerned mainly with expressivity of emotion. After 1930 he became increasingly impressionistic, seeking moods, atmosphere, subtle rather than outright suggestions, poetic insight, and tender rather than effusive sentiments.

This impressionist tendency is found in *Song of Faith* (1932), for chorus and orchestra, which uses George Washington's final testament as its text and which had been commissioned by the George Washington Bicentennial; in the tone poem *Sea Drift* (1933), based on Walt Whitman's poems of the sea, which the Chicago Symphony under Frederick Stock premiered in Chicago on November 30, 1933; the Concerto for Violin and Orchestra (1936), first performed on November 18, 1937, by Zlato Balakovic and the Chicago Symphony under Stock; and the Symphony no. 2 (1942), whose finale is colored by Carpenter's recollections of a visit to Algiers and by its native melodies—its world premiere in New York on October 22, 1942, Bruno Walter conducting the New York Philharmonic. Carpenter's most significant works after that were: the tone poem for orchestra *The Anxious Bugler* (1943, N.Y., November 17, 1943); the symphonic suite *The Seven Ages* (1945; N.Y., December 2, 1945), inspired by Jacques's lines in Shakespeare's *As You Like It*, beginning with "All the world's a stage"; and the *Carmel Concerto*, for orchestra (1948; Philadelphia, November 1948).

Carpenter's wife, Rue, died in 1931. On January 31, 1933, he married Ellen Walter Borden. In 1918, Carpenter was elected member of the National Institute of Arts and Letters. He received the ribbon of the French Legion of Honor in 1921, an honorary master of arts degree from Harvard in 1922, and honorary doctorates in music from the University of

Wisconsin in 1935 and Northwestern University in Evanston, Ill., in 1945. In 1942 he was elected a member of the American Academy of Arts and Letters and on February 13, 1947, he was awarded a gold medal by the National Institute of Arts and Letters. On his seventy-fifth birthday in 1951 the then newly founded National Arts Foundation promoted performances of his compositions at special concerts by orchestras, chamber music groups, and individual artists, in the United States, Australia, Great Britain, and several other foreign countries.

THE COMPOSER SPEAKS: The role of music and art is to nourish and sustain people. The day of American leadership has dawned and it is necessary for us to become spiritual leaders. It is not enough to deal with things. In addition, we must express our ideas and ideals. It is the role of music and the arts to be the medium for this expression. I recommend prayer and a return to religion and art as the solution to today's problems. They speak to the best that is in us. These troubled times are not a healthy period for the creator. Artists cannot be afraid of today and afraid for tomorrow but must express themselves freely.

PRINCIPAL WORKS: 2 symphonies (1940, 1942).
Violin Sonata (1911); *Gitanjali*, song cycle for voice and piano, also for voice and orchestra (1913); *Adventures in a Perambulator*, suite for orchestra (1914); Concertino for Piano and Orchestra (1915); *Water Colors*, Four Chinese Songs, for voice and chamber orchestra (1916); *The Birthday of the Infanta*, ballet (1917–18); *A Pilgrim Vision*, for orchestra (1920); *Krazy Kat*, ballet pantomime (1921); *Skyscrapers*, ballet (1923–24); Quartet for Strings (1927); *Patterns*, for piano and orchestra (1932); *Song of Faith*, cantata for chorus and orchestra (1932); *Sea Drift*, tone poem for orchestra (1933); Piano Quintet (1934); Violin Concerto (1936); *Song of Freedom*, cantata for chorus and orchestra (1941); *The Anxious Bugler*, tone poem for orchestra (1943); *The Seven Ages*, suite for orchestra (1945); *Carmel Concerto*, for orchestra (1948).

BIBLIOGRAPHY: Goss, Madeleine, *Modern Music Makers* (N.Y., 1952); Howard, John Tasker, *Our American Music* (N.Y., 1941); Pierson, Thomas C., "John Alden Carpenter" (doctoral thesis, Rochester, N.Y., 1952); *Musical Quarterly*, October 1930; *New York Times* (obituary), April 27, 1951.

Carr, Benjamin, b. London, England, September 12, 1768; d. Philadelphia, May 24, 1831.
Having lived in the United States for his last thirty-eight years, Carr was a major influence in the early musical life of America—as music-shop operator, publisher, performer, founder, or director of new musical organizations, and as a composer.

In his native England he studied music with Samuel Arnold and Charles Wesley; as a performer, he was affiliated with the London Ancient Concerts. His debut as a composer took place in London on October 16, 1792, with a pastoral piece, *Philander and Silvia.*

Benjamin Carr came to the United States in 1793 (followed a few months later by his father and brother). Settling in Philadelphia, he opened one of its first music shops, Carr's Musical Repository. One year later, with his father and brother, he opened branch stores in Baltimore and New York, as well as additional shops in Philadelphia. The significance of Carr's music shops is that they started to publish music in *Musical Journal, Musical Miscellany* and other collections as well as in separate sheets. Carr became probably the first to publish "The Star-Spangled Banner" with all of Francis Scott Key's verses, the patriotic ballad "Columbia the Gem of the Ocean," and Philip Phile's "The President's March." In 1794, Carr published his own *A Federal Overture* in *The Gentleman's Amusement,* a medley of American patriotic airs including "Yankee Doodle," which here and now was published for the first time.

Carr was a talented singer, harpsichordist, pianist, and organist. Soon after arriving in the United States, in the spring of 1793, he appeared as a singer in four concerts of the Amateur and Professional Concerts in Philadelphia, of which he was director. From then on he made numerous appearances in Philadelphia not only as a singer but also as a pianist, some of these made with the City Concerts, which he managed. He also worked for several years as organist of St. Joseph's Church and at the Pennsylvania Tea Gardens.

Between 1794 and 1797, he lived in New York, where he was heard in two different sets of concerts as singer and pianist in 1794, composed music for the theater, played the organ in churches, and sang in opera performances mounted by the Old American Opera Company. Returning to Philadelphia in 1797 he became director of music at St. Augustine's Church and continued his other activities as well. In 1820 he was cofounder of the Musical Fund Society, serving as one of its choral conductors and orchestral arrangers. Its first concert, a historic event in the musical history of Philadelphia, took place on April 24, 1821.

Carr composed numerous songs and ballads in which he was influenced by and imitative of such famous English composers of ballads as Thomas Arne and Samuel Arnold, as well as Handel. He created simple, charming, singable melodies that lay gratefully for the voice. The best of these are: "Ellen, Arise," "Mary Will Smile" and "Noah's Dove." He also wrote numerous hymns, anthems, psalms, motets, masses, and litanies (once again in emulation of the style of English choral composers of the 18th century). In 1799 he wrote *The Dead March and Mon-*

ody, for orchestra, in honor of George Washington, who died that year; it was part of the music selected for the funeral honors.

As a composer, Carr is remembered most often for his ballad opera *The Archers, or Mountaineers of Switzerland.* William Dunlap's libretto was based on Schiller's *William Tell* (thirty-two years before Rossini composed his *William Tell*). Carr's ballad opera was produced by the Old American Opera Company in New York on April 18, 1796, and after that was given twice in Boston. While this is not "the first American opera," as sometimes has been written (it is not even an opera, but belongs in the more popular category of ballad opera), it is one of the first works for the serious American musical stage mounted by a professional company. Not much has survived from Carr's score, just the rondo from the overture, the aria, "Why, Huntress, Why?" and a march.

Following Carr's death, the Musical Fund Society erected a monument to his memory in St. Peter's Church in Philadelphia. The inscription read in part: "Charitable, without ostentation, faithful and true in friendship, with the intelligence of a man, he united the simplicity of a child."

PRINCIPAL WORKS: *Philander and Silvia,* pastoral piece (1792); *The Caledonian Frolic,* ballet (1794); *A Federal Overture,* for orchestra (1794); *The Archers, or Mountaineers of Switzerland,* ballad opera (1796); Six Sonatas, for piano (1796); *Dead March and Monody,* for orchestra (1799); *The Siege of Tripoli: Historical Naval Sonata,* for piano (1804).

BIBLIOGRAPHY: Howard, John Tasker, *Our American Music* (N.Y., 1946); Mates, Julian, *The American Musical Stage Before 1800* (New Brunswick, N.J., 1962); Sprenkle, C. A., "The Life and Works of Benjamin Carr" (doctoral thesis, Baltimore, Md., 1970); *Musical Quarterly,* January 1932.

Carter, Elliott Cook, Jr., b. New York City, December 11, 1908.

One of the most original and complex minds in present-day American music, and one of its most significant composers of chamber music, Carter was twice awarded the Pulitzer Prize for successive string quartets.

His father, a wealthy importer of lace curtains who aspired to bring his son into his prosperous business, never relaxed his stern opposition to a musical career for Elliott. Nevertheless, the privilege of piano lessons in his childhood was not denied. From his beginnings, Elliott revealed unusual musical talent. Before he could read or write he was able to identify all the phonograph records at home, an item reported in the *New York Times.* At Horace Mann High School in New York (1923–26) he found a sympathetic response to his musical interests in several schoolmates, one of whom was Eugene O'Neill, Jr., the son of the famous playwright. They took him to public concerts and brought him into personal contact with such musical avant-gardists as Charles Ives, Edgard Varèse, and Henry Cowell. Ives—to whom Carter had shown some of his youthful compositions—was a particularly important influence. Carter would visit him regularly and play four-hand music with him; he came to know his scores and went with him to concerts of new music. It was mainly through Ives that avant-garde music began to seize Carter's imagination so early; and it was Ives, more than any other person at the time, who encouraged Carter to become a musician. When, in 1926, his father took him to Vienna, Elliott Carter bought all the music of Webern, Schoenberg, and Alban Berg he could find. Thus he versed himself thoroughly in atonal music and the twelve-tone system. At the same time, preoccupied with complex rhythmic practices, he studied and analyzed the polyrhythmic method of Scriabin.

Carter entered Harvard University in 1926. Impatient with the conservatism of the music faculty, he decided to major in English literature rather than music. The study of music (solfeggio and piano) took place elsewhere: at the Longy School of Music at Cambridge with Newton Swift and Hans Ebell. He supplemented these studies by performing with chamber music ensembles in the Boston area and attending concerts of the Boston Symphony. Summers were spent at festivals in Munich, where he was saturated with the music of Wagner, Mozart, and Richard Strauss.

By the time he received his bachelor of arts degree at Harvard in 1930 he was convinced he wanted to become a composer. He spent the next two years as a graduate student at Harvard, taking courses in harmony and counterpoint with Walter Piston, choral composition with A. T. Davison, music history with Edward Burlingame Hill, and composition with Gustav Holst, then a visiting professor. Upon receiving his master of arts degree in 1932, and supported by a five-hundred-dollar-a-year allowance from his father, Carter went to Paris. For three years he studied with Nadia Boulanger and graduated from the École Normale de Musique with a *licence de contrepoint*, sang in a madrigal group conducted by Henri Expert, and directed a chorus he had founded. He was also composing. His incidental music for Sophocles' *Philoctetes* was performed by the Harvard Classical Club in Cambridge in the winter of 1933.

Carter returned to the United States in 1935. Settled in Cambridge, he wrote music for another production of the Harvard Classical Club—Plautus' *Mostelaria*—a "Tarantella" from which was sung by the Harvard Glee Club when it toured in the fall of 1936; another of its excerpts was performed by the Boston Pops Orchestra conducted by G. Wallace Woodworth in May 1937. During the summer of 1936, on a commission from the Ballet Caravan, he

wrote the score of *Pocahontas*, a ballet produced in New York in 1939; in 1940 an orchestral suite from this score received a publication grant from the Juilliard Foundation.

Carter came to New York in 1936. He wrote articles for *Modern Music*, and from 1937 to 1939 was musical director of the Ballet Caravan. As a composer, he was now partial to Hindemithian neoclassicism, with its linear counterpoint, but he also already favored complex rhythmic and metrical structures: in an oratorio, *The Bridge*; in the Madrigal Book for mixed voices; and in the Concerto for English horn, all written in 1937. In 1938, his choral setting of Robert Herrick's *To Music* won a prize in a competition conducted jointly by CBS Radio, Columbia Records and the Works Progress Administration (WPA). In 1939 he wrote the Suite for Alto Saxophones, and *Heart Not So Heavy As Mine* for mixed voices. "I am a radical, having a nature that leads me to perpetual revolt," he said of himself at the time.

On July 6, 1939, Carter married Helen Frost-Jones, a sculptor and art critic; their only child, a son, was born in 1943. Between 1939 and 1941, Carter taught music, Greek, and mathematics at St. John's College in Annapolis, Md., where he evolved a new system of teaching music based on principles of mathematics and physics.

Carter left New York in 1941 for New Mexico to work on his Symphony no. 1 (1942), which was introduced by the Eastman-Rochester Symphony under Howard Hanson on April 27, 1944. Returning east, Carter became a consultant for the office of War Information (1943–45). At this time he wrote *Holiday Overture* (1944; Baltimore, January 7, 1946), which became Carter's first work to be performed in Europe. It won first prize in a competition held by the Independent Music Publishers.

A new direction in Carter's music can be found in his Piano Sonata no. 1 (1946), written on a Guggenheim Fellowship and introduced by Webster Aitken in New York on February 16, 1947. Here Carter broke with his creative past and with neoclassicism, while at the same time departing just as sharply from the music of his contemporaries. He evolved his harmonic material from the overtone series produced through pedaling and the overtone resonance of the piano. He also expanded his metrical diversity, making frequent changes in time signatures, sometimes on the average of every two measures. From here Carter went on to devise "metrical modulation" in his Sonata for Cello and Piano (1948), written for Bernard Greenhouse, who introduced it in New York on February 27, 1950. Continuity is here maintained through a repeated change of tempo, meter and rhythms; secondary rhythms become dominant within a polyrhythmic arrangement; a new tempo is evolved from the development of a cross rhythm in a preceding tempo.

From 1946 to 1948 Carter taught theory and composition at the Peabody Conservatory in Baltimore, and from 1948 to 1950 he was professor of composition at Columbia University. On his second fellowship from the Guggenheim Foundation, and with a grant from the National Institute of Arts and Letters, both in 1950, Carter went to Tucson, Ariz. There he wrote his string Quartet no. 1, in which he further developed his technique of "metrical modulation," which he now used with virtuoso skill and an enriched imagination. Each of the four musicians moved independently of the other three in what Virgil Thomson described as "four intricately integrated solos, all going at the same time." The quartet's world premiere took place in New York in February 1952 in a performance of the Walden String Quartet. Reviewing that concert in the *Herald Tribune*, Paul Henry Lang did not hesitate to describe the work as "an authentic masterpiece by an American composer—one of the handful of truly significant works that open the second half of the twentieth century." The quartet received first prize at the Concours International de Quatuors à Cordes in Lìege, Belgium, in 1953, and in 1954 it scored a major success at the Rome Festival in Italy.

In 1952 Carter was elected president of the U.S. Section of the International Society for Contemporary Music. That year he produced another significant chamber music work, the Sonata for Flute, Oboe, Cello, and Harpsichord, which had been commissioned by the Harpsichord Quartet. The piece was heard in New York on November 19, 1953, and in 1956 received the Naumburg Musical Foundation Award.

As a recipient of the Prix de Rome in 1953, Carter spent a year as fellow of the American Academy of Rome. The following year, on a commission from the Louisville Orchestra in Kentucky, he completed Variations, for orchestra (1955), which the Louisville Orchestra under Robert Whitney introduced on April 21, 1956. Made up of an introduction (Allegro), the statement of the theme (Andante), and ten variations, this work was conceived by its composer as "a series of character studies in various states of interaction with each other both within each variation and between one and the next. . . . Activity, development, type of emphasis, clearness or vagueness of definition, I hoped, would contribute to the characterization. Form, rhythmic and development processes as well as texture and thematic material differ in each for this reason." The Variations received numerous performances in Germany, England, Italy, and Sweden.

Between 1955 and 1956, Carter was professor of composition at Queens College in New York. In 1956 he was elected to membership in the National Institute of Arts and Letters, and during the summer of 1958 he taught composition at the Seminars in Salzburg, Austria. In 1959, on a commission from the Stanley String Quartet, he completed the String Quartet no. 2, with which his international fame became solidly entrenched. More than in his earlier string quartet, each member of the foursome was individualized and acquired his own "behavior patterns." To emphasize this individuality, Carter assigned a descriptive identity to each instrument: the first violin was "fantastic, ornate and mercurial"; the second was "laconic and orderly"; the viola possessed a "repertory of expressive motifs"; the cello was "somewhat impetuous." Additionally, each instrument was given its own specialized intervals: the first violin, thirds and its multiples; the second violin, minor seconds and minor sevenths; the viola, minor sevenths and tritones; the cello, fourths and minor sixths. More and more complex have the composer's use of polyrhythms and changing meters now become. But for all such intricacy, and the severe intellectual processes that are brought into play, the music does not lack humor, fantasy, or passion. "At the end," remarked Howard Taubman in the *New York Times*, "one has completed a momentous journey into a wholly new and magical land."

String Quartet no. 2 was performed for the first time on March 25, 1960, by the Juilliard String Quartet. In 1960 it received the Pulitzer Prize in music and the award of the New York Music Critics Circle. In 1961, it captured first prize from the International Rostrum of Composers sponsored by UNESCO and a nomination from the National Academy of Recording Arts and Sciences as the year's best contemporary classical composition.

While serving as professor of composition at Yale University (1960–62) Carter wrote the Double Concerto, for harpsichord and piano with two chamber orchestras, which had been commissioned by the Fromm Music Foundation. Its premiere took place at the Eighth Congress of the International Society for Musicology in New York on September 8, 1961, performed by Ralph Kirkpatrick and Charles Rosen with an orchestra conducted by Gustave Meier. Once again the New York Critics Circle Award was bestowed on Carter. Within the next four years the piece was well received in London, Berlin, Rome, and Warsaw.

Individualizing different instruments is emphasized even in the Concerto for Piano and Orchestra (1964–65), a work commissioned by Jacob Lateiner on a grant from the Ford Foundation; Lateiner introduced it with the Boston Symphony under Erich Leinsdorf on January 6, 1967. At certain moments, each member of the orchestra is made to play a different note, forming a monumental tone cluster.

In 1968, Carter was commissioned by the New York Philharmonic to write an orchestral work commemorating the orchestra's 125th anniversary. With his writing and organization of materials grown so involved, Carter did not finish his assignment on time. As composer-in-residence at the American Academy in Rome in 1968, Carter worked on the Concerto for Orchestra, but not until February 5, 1970, was it premiered in New York with Leonard Bernstein conducting. Carter's stimulation in writing this concerto was a poem, *Vents*, by the Nobel Prize-winning poet who called himself St. John Perse. The music deals, as Carter himself explained, "primarily with the poetry of change, transformation, reorientation of feelings and thoughts. . . . Each movement comes into focus against a background of the other three, each with its own character and development."

Carter's second Pulitzer Prize in music came for his String Quartet no. 3 (1971), the result of a commission from the Juilliard School of Music for the Juilliard String Quartet, which introduced it in New York on January 23, 1972. The composer divided his four musicians into two pairs, one for violin and cello (playing in a rubato style), and the other for violin and viola (playing in regular rhythm). Each of the duo partners is presented alone and in combination with the other partner. The composer goes on to explain: "The violin-cello duo presents four different musical characters: an angry intense Furioso, a fanciful Leggerisimo, a Pizzicato giocoso with lyrical Andante espressivo, in short sections, one after the other in various orders, sometimes with pauses in between." The violin-viola duo presents seven contrasting "characters" listed as Maestoso; Grazioso; Pizzicato; Giusto mechanico; Scorevole; Largo tranquillo; Appassionato.

Carter was one of the six major American composers chosen by the National Endowment for the Arts to write compositions to honor the American bicentennial, the compositions to be performed by six leading American orchestras. His contribution was the Symphony for Three Orchestras (1977), first heard on February 17, 1977, in New York, with Pierre Boulez conducting the New York Philharmonic, and then performed in Boston, Chicago, Philadelphia, Los Angeles, and Cleveland. In this work the composer recalled the baroque concept of the concerto by splitting up his orchestra into three smaller groups, each of which suggests the "concertino" of the baroque concerto grosso. There are twelve movements (following an introduction and ending with a coda), four each for each of the three smaller ensembles played twice, though not in regular order.

Four concert pianists joined to commission Carter to write a new piano composition, *Night Fantasies*. Carter worked on this project early in 1980 while serving as composer-in-residence at the American Academy in Rome, completing it in March of the same year after his return to the United States. One of the four commissioning pianists—Ursula Oppens–gave the world premiere at the Bath Festival in England on June 2, 1980, and the American premiere in New York City on January 8, 1981. The work is in four sections, its respective tempo markings identified as "Tranquillo," "Fantastico," "Appassionata," and "Capriccio." Writing in the *New Yorker*, Nicholas Kenyon maintained that *Night Fantasies* was "surely the most immediately attractive work that Carter has given us in many years; if it

is not permeated by such a compelling sense of purpose and direction as the Third String Quartet, it has in place of that attribute a passionately expressive quality. . . . What I think distinguishes the sound of the piece from other recent Carter works is that a surprising amount of the material is consonant—based on eloquent thirds and sixths contrasted with bare fourths and fifths. The insistent, angry tritone of the central recitative [marked 'recitative collerico'] is a strident exception."

In 1964 Carter was appointed professor of compostion at the Juilliard School of Music in New York and in 1967–68 he was professor-at-large at Cornell University in Ithaca, N.Y. Since 1960 he has served as American delegate to the East-West Encounter in Tokyo (1960), composer-in-residence at the American Academy in Rome (1963, 1968, and 1980), and, on a grant from the Ford Foundation, composer-in-residence in Berlin (1964). He has been awarded the Sibelius Medal (1961), the Creative Arts Award of Brandeis University in Waltham, Mass. (1965), the Premio delle Muse, "Polimnia," by the Associazione Artistico Letteria Internazionale in Florence (1969) and the gold medal for eminence in music by the National Institute of Arts and Letters (1971). His honorary degrees include those from Princeton (1967), Harvard (1970), and Yale (1970). In 1969 he was elected to membership in the American Academy of Arts and Letters and in 1970 he was given honorary membership to the Akademie der Kunst in Berlin. His seventieth birthday was celebrated with performances of his compositions by major American organizations. These included an all-Carter program in New York on December 19, 1978, when the world premiere was heard of his *Syringa*, for mezzo-soprano, bass, and eleven instruments, based on a poem by John Ashbery with quotations from Plato, Homer, Sappho, Aeschylus, and others. On December 11, 1978, Mayor Koch of New York City presented him with the Handel Medallion, the city's highest cultural award.

The Siemens Music Prize of West Germany, one of the world's largest cash awards for musical achievement ($78,500), was presented to Carter in 1981 for his contributions to orchestral music.

The Writings of Elliott Carter: An American Composer Looks at Music, covering forty years of his critical writings, edited by Else and Kurt Stone, was published in New York in 1977.

THE COMPOSER SPEAKS: I start with a certain poetic idea of what the rhetoric and expression of a piece should be like, and this forces me to find some sort of musical material that will allow this to come out. It's the fight to get the material into shape and that takes a lot of work. The poetic vision of the piece sometimes lasts for years. My pieces have sometimes taken three of four years to write, and the vision is as vivid at the end as it was at the beginning.

It seems to me that the most important and interesting thing that music can do is to deal with the question of continuity. How does it go along? There's been very little novelty in the conception of continuity in contemporary music, generally. On the other hand, there's been a great deal of novelty, especially in recent times, in the use of *sound*. But the concern with special, unusual *sound* is a concern only with momentary effects. These, on the whole, have no future and no past. They can do very little more than produce a sense of surprise.

I'm always concerned with context—with preceding and succeeding ideas. Making things that go along, changing in very slight degrees, bit by bit. Or dealing with things that change abruptly. And making all this *significant*. It seems to me that *this* is the musical language—not just the language of sound itself.

PRINCIPAL WORKS: 3 string quartets (1951, 1959, 1971).

Symphony (1942, revised 1961); *Holiday Overture*, for orchestra (1944, revised 1961); Piano Sonata (1946); *The Minotaur*, ballet (1947); *The Defense of Corinth*, for speaker, male chorus, and piano four hands (1949); Eight Etudes and a Fantasy, for woodwind quintet (1949–50); Sonata for Flute, Oboe, Cello, and Harpsichord (1952); Variations, for orchestra (1955); Double Concerto, for harpsichord, piano and two chamber orchestras (1961); Piano Concerto (1964–66); Concerto for Orchestra (1969); Brass Quintet (1974); Duo, for violin and piano (1974); *A Mirror on Which to Dwell*, a cycle of six songs for soprano and chamber orchestra (1975); Symphony for Three Orchestras (1977); *Syringa*, for mezzo-soprano, bass, and eleven instruments (1978); *Night Fantasies*, for piano (1980).

BIBLIOGRAPHY: Edwards, A. F., *Flawed Words and Stubborn Sounds* (N.Y., 1971); BMI, *The Many Worlds of Music*, Issue 4, 1978; *High Fidelity/Musical America*, May 1968, August 1973; *New York Times*, December 10, 1978; *Stereo Review*, December 1972, February 1975.

Castelnuovo-Tedesco, Mario, b. Florence, Italy, April 3, 1895; d. Los Angeles, Calif., March 16, 1968. American citizen, 1946.

Castelnuovo-Tedesco drew his inspiration from four principal sources: the city of his birth; his Jewish heritage, and, coincidentally, the Bible; Shakespeare and, coincidentally, the English language; and the land of his adoption.

Castelnuovo-Tedesco inherited his love for music from his mother and her family. At the home of his maternal grandfather the child Mario heard synagogue cantillations and Hebrew melodies that haunted him for many years thereafter. It was the grandfather who induced Mario's mother, an excellent amateur pianist, to give the boy his first piano lessons. These took place when Mario was nine, and had to be conducted in secrecy since Mario's father, a wealthy banker, was opposed to raising a musician. When, after a year of such piano instruction, Mario played for his father two Chopin pieces and one of his own, the older man decided to place no further obstacles in the way of his son's musical education. Mario now entered the Cherubini Royal Institute of Music in Florence, where he continued his piano studies with his mother's cousin, Edgardo del Valle de Paz, and composition with Ildebrando Pizzetti. Castelnuovo-Tedesco received his diploma in piano when he was fifteen, and one in composition three years later. His first published composition appeared when he was fifteen, *Cielo di Settembre*, for piano (1910). One year later he wrote the first of numerous works reflecting his love for his native city: *Primavera fiorentina*, for piano (1911). In 1913, his second opus was released, *Questo fu il carro della morte*, for piano. All these were in a quasi-impressionistic style. Impressionistic, too, was his first work in a larger form, *Tre fioretti di Santo Francesco*, for mezzo-soprano and piano or orchestra (1919–20), a setting of verses by St. Francis of Assisi, and his first Florentine-inspired composition to gain recognition, *Cipressi*, for piano (1920), a tonal portrait of the Tuscan hills, fringed with cypresses which the composer could see from his window. In 1921, Castelnuovo-Tedesco orchestrated *Cipressi* for the first time, a version introduced in Florence in 1921 by the Florence Orchestral Society conducted by Pizzetti. A second orchestral version (1940) was performed by the Boston Symphony Orchestra under Serge Koussevitzky on October 25, 1940.

A Florentine-inspired work (his most ambitious up to that time) brought Castelnuovo-Tedesco his first major success: the "Florentine commedia musicale," *La mandragola* (1920–23). Produced in Venice on May 4, 1926, it was an immediate success, with Castelnuovo-Tedesco's light touch and wit coming in for the lion's share of the praise. This opera recieved first prize in the Concorso Lirico Nazionale in 1925.

Castelnouvo-Tedesco's one-act opera, *Bacco in Toscana* (1925–26), is a Tuscan folk opera based on a poem by Francesco Redi about the myth of Ariadne, Theseus, and Bacchus. The little opera was mounted by La Scala in Milan on May 5, 1931. "Redolent of Tuscan fields at vintage, heaped with peasant choruses, saturated with the wine of good Tuscan melody," is the way one writer (Roland von Weber) described this opera.

The shadow of Tuscany hovers over even so late a work as the String Quartet no. 3 (1963). The entire string quartet is descriptive of the hilltop of Vallombrosa above Florence. The first movement tells of a trip to the town: the second movement describes its old abbey; the scherzo is a programmatic picture of a little train that, before World War I, used to whistle its way to and from Vallambrosa; and the finale is a recollection of a conversation between the composer and the art connoisseur Bernhard Berenson, in Vallambrosa.

On March 6, 1924, Castelnuovo-Tedesco married Clara Porti in Florence. They had two sons. One year later, the composer accidentally came upon a notebook hidden in the recesses of his library, in which his grandfather had carefully noted down by hand melodies of Hebrew prayers. "The discovery of this little notebook," Castelnuovo-Tedesco recalled, "was one of the deepest emotions of my life and became for me a precious heritage." It reawakened Castelnuovo-Tedesco's racial consciousness; it recalled to him the spell once cast on him by Hebrew melodies; and it stirred his ambition to write compositions inspired by his race and its music. (One of Castelnuovo-Tedesco's late compositions, *Prayers My Grandfather Wrote*, a set of six preludes for organ, in 1962, was based on some of the melodies in this notebook.)

Castelnuovo-Tedesco's first Hebrew-oriented composition was the rhapsody *Le danze del Re David*, for piano (1925), first performed by Walter Gieseking at the opening concert of the Festival of the International Society for Contemporary Music in Frankfurt, Germany, on June 30, 1927. This work was soon followed by the *Tre corali*, on a Hebrew melody, for piano (1926). Castelnuovo-Tedesco's former impressionistic tendencies were now replaced by a neoromanticism, a vein he would henceforth tap: a neoromanticism that adhered to a basic tonality; which for the most part adopted a conservative posture (though dissonances were sometimes left unresolved, and forbidden consecutive fifths were sometimes not avoided); which is always idiomatic, regardless of the instrument or combination of instruments or voice or combinations of voices, for which he was writing.

He produced a vast library of Hebraic works up to the end of his life, many of them deeply rooted in the Old Testament. One of the most successful was the Concerto for Violin and Orchestra no. 2, *The Prophets* (1931), which Jascha Heifetz introduced in New York on April 12, 1933, as soloist with the New York Philharmonic conducted by Arturo Toscanini. Here the composer provided a tonal characterization of three biblical prophets: Isaiah, Jeremiah, and Elijah. Castelnuovo-Tedesco also produced biblical oratorios (*The Book of Ruth* in 1949; *The Book of Jonah* in 1951; *The Book of Esther* in 1962); a biblical opera, *Saul* (1958–60); *Sacred Service for the Sabbath Eve* (1943), commissioned by the Park Avenue Synagogue in New York, where it was heard on May 19, 1950; and piano music and songs with a Hebraic identity. Late in life he wrote *Divan of Moses-Ibn-Ezra*, a five-part cycle of songs with epilogue, for voice and guitar (1966), based on the writings of the 12th-century Spanish-born Hebraic scholar and poet.

Castelnuovo-Tedesco made his first setting of Shakespeare between 1921 and 1925: Thirty-three Shakespeare Songs, for voice and piano. Much of his music after that owed its inspiration to Shakespeare: eleven overtures, settings of twenty-seven sonnets, and two operas. The opera *The Merchant of Venice* (1958)—first produced on May 25, 1961, at the Florence May Music Festival, then mounted in Los Angeles for its American premiere on April 13, 1966—won first prize among sixty-four entries in an international competition sponsored by La Scala and financed by David Campari. *All's Well That Ends Well*, another Shakespearean opera, was written between 1955 and 1958.

During these years, there were, to be sure, other major works with no Florentine, biblical or Shakespearean associations. The *Concerto italiano*, for violin and orchestra (1924), in which the composer pays tribute to his native country by reaching back to the violinistic styling of Vivaldi and other Italian masters of the 17th and 18th centuries, was performed in Rome on January 31, 1926, by Mario Corti (for whom it was written) with Bernardino Molinari conducting. Jascha Heifetz later gave it its American premiere under Molinari. Castelnuovo-Tedesco's Piano Concerto no. 1 (1927) was given its initial hearing in Rome on December 9, 1928, by E. Consolo, with Molinari conducting again. Symphonic Variations, for violin and orchestra (1928), became the first major work by its composer to be heard in the United States when Toscanini conducted it with the New York Philharmonic for its American premiere on April 9, 1930. (The world premiere had taken place in Rome earlier the same year.) The Concerto for Cello and Orchestra (1932–33) was written for Gregor Piatigorsky and was first performed by him on January 31, 1935, at a New York Philharmonic concert conducted by Toscanini.

With Italy embarked on a program of anti-Semitism in the wake of its alliance with Nazi Germany, Castelnuovo-Tedesco left his native land in 1939 to settle in the United States, first in Larchmont, N.Y., and about a year later, in Beverly Hills, Calif., where he lived his last twenty-eight years. On November 2, 1939, Castelnuovo-Tedesco appeared as soloist in New York in the world premiere of his Piano Concerto no. 2 with the New York Philharmonic under John Barbirolli.

Castelnuovo-Tedesco was extraordinarily productive during his American years in virtually all musical media (except the symphony). At the same time he wrote scores for motion pictures, many under an assumed name, a few under his own. Among the latter were the René Clair film *And Then There Were None* (1945), *The Loves of Carmen* starring Rita Hayworth (1948), and *The Mask of the Avenger* (1951). In California, in addition to his prolific creativity, he was also active as a teacher of composition to many brilliant young musicians writing for the films, including Andre Previn, Henry Mancini, and

Jerry Goldsmith. In 1959, Castelnuovo-Tedesco was visiting professor at Michigan State University in East Lansing, where he gave courses on opera, and from the early 1960s until he died he taught composition at the Los Angeles Conservatory of Music.

In the United States, many of Castelnuovo-Tedesco's compositions were inspired by the backgrounds, geography, or culture of his newly adopted country. In 1947 he wrote the score for a New Orleans ballet, *The Octoroon Ball*. His first American home led to the writing of *Larchmont Hills*, a "poem" for violin and orchestra (1942), and his second and last home was the inspiration for *Nocturne in Hollywood*, for piano (1941). *An American Rhapsody* for orchestra (1943) was based on two popular American folk melodies ("Arkansas Traveler" and "Turkey in the Straw"). Five Humoresques on Foster's Themes, for orchestra (1943), used four Stephen Foster melodies, and *A Lullaby*, for voice and orchestra (1943), developed more Foster music. Though Castelnuovo-Tedesco had interpolated a fox trot in one of his best known pieces for piano, *Alt Wien* (1923), he rarely used popular American idioms. An exception was *The Shadow*, in boogie-woogie piano style, written with tongue in cheek when his teenage son asked him why he never wrote popular songs.

Mention should be made of Castelnuovo-Tedesco's significant contribution to the literature for the guitar. His empathy with Spain and its music had been reflected as early as 1915, when he wrote a cycle of eleven songs for voice and piano (also orchestrated) on Spanish texts entitled *Coplas*, He continued to write songs in a Spanish idiom, and when the classical guitar began to assume increasing importance by the 1920s and the 1930s, and instigated by his friend Andrés Segovia, he began writing for that instrument. In 1939 he completed the Concerto no. 1, for guitar and orchestra at the request of Segovia, who introduced it in Montevideo in the year of its composition. Castelnuovo-Tedesco's guitar works after that included a Serenade, for guitar and orchestra (1943); a Second Concerto (1953; Los Angeles, 1966); a Concerto for Two Guitars and Orchestra (1962); and numerous works for solo guitars and various vocal works calling for the guitar in their accompaniments. Among the most ambitious nonorchestral guitar works are the *Platero y Yo*, twenty-eight pieces for narrator and guitar to texts by Juan Ramón Jiménez (1960), *Caprichos de Goya*, for solo guitar (1961), and *Les guitares bien tempérées,* twenty-four preludes and fugues for two guitars (1962). In 1966, Castelnuovo-Tedesco received the Diploma di Benemerenza from the Italian Association of Guitarists, and in 1973 an international competition for new guitar music was organized in Ancona, Italy, named after Castelnuovo-Tedesco.

In 1966, Castelnuovo-Tedesco received the Academic Diploma of Master Composers from the Reale Accademia Filarmonica in Bologna. Two years earlier, he had been awarded an honorary doctorate of Humane Letters from the Hebrew Union College-Jewish Institute of Religion in Cincinnati, Ohio. His eightieth birthday was remembered in New York with a seven-part festival of his works beginning on February 2, 1975. During the opening performance, two world premieres were given: the opera *The Importance of Being Earnest*, based on Oscar Wilde's play (1962), and the scenic oratorio, *Tobias and the Angel* (1965), the latter written for production by high schools.

Castelnuovo-Tedesco was the author of an unpublished autobiography, *Una vita di musica*.

THE COMPOSER SPEAKS: In my artistic life I have had only one ideal, to write good music without prejudice of any kind. . . . I have never believed in modernism, or in neoclassicism, or any other isms. I believe that music is a form of language capable of progess and renewal. . . . Yet music should not discard what was contributed by preceding generations. Every means of expression can be useful and just, if it is used at the opportune moment (through inner necessity rather than through caprice or fashion). The simplest means are generally the best. . . . What I have sought to do, during my artistic evolution, has been to express myself with means always simpler and more direct, in a language always clearer and more precise.

PRINCIPAL WORKS: 3 string quartets (1929, 1948, 1963); 3 piano trios (1928, 1932, 1950); 3 quintets for piano and strings (1931, 1932, 1951); 3 violin concertos (1924, 1931, 1939); 2 piano concertos (1927, 1937); 2 guitar concertos (1939, 1953).

Cipressi, for piano, also orchestrated (1920); *La mandragola*, opera (1920–23); Thirty-three Shakespeare Songs, for voice and piano (1921–25); *Alt Wien*, for piano (1923); *Le stagione*, suite for piano (1924); *Le danze del Re David*, suite for piano (1925); *Tre corali*, on a Hebrew melody, for piano (1926); Symphonic Variations, for violin and orchestra (1928); Cello Concerto (1932–33); Overture to *The Merchant of Venice* (1933); Overture to *Julius Caesar* (1934); Sonata, *Omaggio a Boccherini*, for guitar (1934); *Leaves of Grass*, for solo voice and piano (1936); Concertino, for harp and orchestra (1937); *Aucassin and Nicolette*, for voice, instruments, and marionettes (1938); Overture to *A Midsummer Night's Dream* (1940); Overture to *King John* (1941); *The Birthday of the Infanta*, ballet (1942); *Sacred Service*, for baritone, chorus, and organ (1943); Serenade, for guitar and orchestra (1943); *Candide*, suite for piano (1944); Shakespeare's Sonnets, for voice and piano (1944–45); Sonata for Violin and Viola (1945); Clarinet Sonata (1945); *The Octoroon Ball*, ballet (1947); Overture to *Antony and Cleopatra* (1947); *Suite nello stile italiano*, for piano (1947); Overture to *Coriolanus* (1947); Three Sephardic Songs, for voice and piano, also for orchestra (1947); *The Book of Ruth*, oratorio for solo voices, chorus and orchestra (1949); Six Canons, for piano (1950); *Concerto da camera*, for oboe and string orchestra (1950); Quintet, for guitar and strings (1950); Sonata for Viola and Cello (1950); Sonata for Violin and Cello (1950); *The Book of Jonah*, oratorio for solo voices, chorus, and orchestra (1951); Six Keats Settings, for a cappella male chorus (1952); Overture to *As You Like It* (1953); *The Song of Songs*, "a rustic wedding Idyll" (1954–55); *The Stories of Joseph*, suite for piano (1955); *All's Well That Ends Well*, opera (1955–58); *The Merchant of Venice*, opera (1956); *Saul*, oratorio for solo voices, chorus, and orchestra (1960); *Platero y Yo*, for narrator and guitar (1960); *Twenty-four Caprichos de Goya*, for guitar (1961); *Sonata canonica*, for two guitars (1961); *The Importance of Being Earnest*, opera (1961–62); *Prayers My Grandfather Wrote*, for organ (1962); *Les guitares bien tempérées*, for two guitars (1962); *The Book of Esther*, oratorio for solo voices, chorus and orchestra (1962); Concerto for Two Guitars and Orchestra (1962); *Tobias and the Angel*, scenic oratorio (1964–65); *The Divan of Moses-Ibn-Ezra*, a cycle of songs for voice and instruments (1966).

BIBLIOGRAPHY: Ewen, David (ed.), *The New Book of Modern Composers* (N.Y., 1961); Rossi, Nick (ed.), *Castelnuovo-Tedesco: Catalogue* (N.Y., 1977); *Who's Who in America, 1966–67*.

Cazden, Norman, b. New York City, September 23, 1914; d. Bangor, Me., August 18, 1980.

Cazden explored a wide expressive range. Without aligning himself with any "school" or movement, and without ever writing music to prove some theory, he remained an individualist in his use of tonality, rhythmic impulses, personalized contrapuntal methods, and melodic shapes.

He was seven when he began to study the piano, which he did privately for six years with Bernard Ravitch while attending public school. Cazden made his first public appearance as pianist when he was ten, and at twelve his official debut took place at Town Hall, New York. He continued to perform publicly and he often served as accompanist for vocal, instrumental, and dance soloists and groups.

Between 1927 and 1932 Cazden continued his study of music on a scholarship at the Institute of Musical Art in New York, majoring in piano with Arthur Newstead and taking courses in theory and the history of music with Leopold Mannes, Charles L. Seeger, and Bernard Wagenaar, among others.

Beginning in 1928, he taught piano and theory privately in New York. Cazden received a regular piano diploma from the institute in 1930, and a teacher's diploma with honors in 1932. At the same time, he attended Morris High School, from which he graduated in 1930. For a seven-year period (1932–39), Cazden attended the Juilliard Gradutate

School on a continuous fellowship basis. There he studied the piano with Ernest Hutcheson and composition with Bernard Wagenaar, combining his studies with the post of instructor in piano between 1934 and 1939. During this time he was receiving his academic education at the College of the City of New York (1938–43) where he earned his bachelor of science degree *cum laude*, with membership in Phi Beta Kappa.

While pursuing his academic and musical studies, Cazden was employed as assistant musical director of radio station WNYC, New York (1941–42) where he was put in charge of its American Music Festival. A year later he was made music director of radio station WLIB in New York and in 1942–43 he became music director of the Humphrey-Weidman Repertory Company in New York.

Cazden's earliest compositions were for the piano, and these included two sonatinas (1932, 1935), and Three Satires (1932–33). The Sonatina no. 2 was performed in New York by the composer on May 12, 1935, followed two years later by the composer's performance of the Sonatina no. 1 also in New York on January 27, 1937. String Quartet (1936) was premiered by the Gordon String Quartet at the Westminster Choir School in Princeton, N.J., on May 20, 1936, receiving the award of its festival. Concerto for Ten Instruments (1937) was first heard on May 4, 1937, at the Juilliard School of Music, Bernard Wagenaar conducting. *On the Death of a Spanish Child*, for symphonic band (1939), a funeral march inspired by the Spanish Civil War, had to wait a decade for its premiere, receiving its first hearing in Louisville, Ky., on May 18, 1948. Three Chamber Sonatas, for clarinet and viola (1938), commissioned by the Juilliard Alumni Association, was first performed on February 26, 1939, in New York. Quartet, for violin, clarinet, viola, and cello (1939), commissioned by the League of Composers, was introduced on May 30, 1940, over radio station WABC in New York by the Dorian String Quartet and Louis de Santis, clarinetist.

In 1943, Cazden entered Harvard University for postgraduate studies with Aaron Copland and Walter Piston (composition), Carroll C. Pratt (psychology of music) and A. T. Davison, A. Tillman Merritt, and G. Wallace Woodworth (musicology). In 1944 he received his master of arts degree, in 1945 the Leverett Saltonstall Fellowship and the George Arthur Knight Prize, in 1945 and 1946 the John Knowles Paine Traveling Fellowship and in 1948 a doctorate, his dissertation being on "Musical Consonance and Dissonance."

An important influence in Cazden's early career as a composer came between 1943 and 1948 when he held the post of music director at Camp Woodland, in Phoenicia, N.Y., and was put in charge of the folk festivals of the Catskill Mountains. (He returned to Camp Woodland between 1954 and 1960.) Together with Herbert Haufrecht, he made numerous field trips collecting, notating, and recording on tapes local folk songs and instrumental music, gathering hundreds of such pieces. Many of these he arranged and had published as *Dances from Woodland* (1945), *A Catskill Songbook* (1955), and *Merry Ditties* (1955). The influence of this research is reflected in some of the music he wrote at the time. In *Stony Hollow*, for orchestra (1944), the strains of square dance music and calls are incorporated; at one point, six different motives are combined polyphonically (including a snatch of "Yankee Doodle"). Sylvan Levin, conducting the WOR Orchestra, introduced it on August 29, 1948, over the Mutual Radio Network. *Three Ballads*, for orchestra (1949), is a symphonic adaptation of three Catskill Mountain folk songs treated in free variation form; its first performance was held in Ann Arbor, Mich., on August 7, 1950, and it has been recorded by the Oslo Philharmonic under Igor Bukhetoff. *Songs from the Catskills*, for symphonic band (1950), which gives a similar treatment to four other Catskill Mountain folk tunes, received its first hearing in Urbana, Ill., on January 11, 1951. In *Dingle Hill*, a cantata for solo voices, chorus and orchestra, with dramatic dialogue (1958), Cazden reached into Catskill Mountain history by dramatizing the attack on rent collectors in northern Catskill Mountains by local farmers masquerading as Indians in protest against the archaic laws on land tenure. In his score, Cazden utilized traditional songs of that period. *Dingle Hill* was produced at the Phoenicia Theatre in New York State on August 17, 1958.

Outside the area of folklore and folk music, Cazden wrote a Symphony (1949), Quintet, for oboe and strings (1960; Lexington, Mass., July 16, 1965), Chamber Concerto for clarinet and strings (1965), a Woodwind Quintet (1969), *The Sunshine Sonata*, for piano (1971; Orono, Me., October 20, 1972), Concerto for Viola and Orchestra (1972), various sonatas for different instruments between 1939 and 1974, Six Preludes and Fugues, for piano (1976; Orono, Me., November 19, 1976), together with numerous other compositions. In his music, Cazden rarely used a key signature, though a feeling of tonality was present; indication of beats of variable duration were often dispensed with. A strong lyricism, sometimes derived from natural modes and sometimes from the prose inflections, was omnipresent. His treatment of thematic material often consists of evolving variations. He was partial to contrapuntal devices from the very simple to the highly complex. His music traversed a wide gamut of expressivity ranging from the astringent to the bucolic, from the highly dramatic to the humorous and sardonic, from the sophisticated to the simple folkloristic or the functional.

In February 1946, Cazden married Courtney Borden. The couple had two children, one of whom, Joanna, is a composer; they were divorced in 1971. In 1947–48 Cazden was assistant professor of music at Vassar College in Poughkeepsie, N.Y. One year later he taught theory at Peabody Conservatory in Baltimore. In 1949–50 he served as assistant professor of music at the University of Michigan School of Music at Ann Arbor, and from 1950 to 1953 he held a similar post at the University of Illinois School of Music in Urbana. From 1953 to 1961 he taught piano and theory privately in Bridgeport, Conn., and from 1961 to 1969 in Lexington, Mass. In 1969 he was appointed associate professor of music at the University of Maine in Orono, where he remained until his death, becoming full professor in 1973. In 1971, Cazden received the Pedro Paz Award in musical composition from Olivet College in Michigan.

Cazden wrote numerous articles on the theoretical aspects of music for various scholarly journals. He was the author of *The Abelard Folksong Book* (1958) and *A Book of Nonsense Songs* (1961), and he was the coauthor of *Folksongs from Maine* (1966), *Lumbering Songs from the Northern Woods* (1970), *Wake Up, Dead Man!* (1972), and several others.

THE COMPOSER SPEAKS: To me, the art of music must be distinguished from any attempted coding into audible signals of nonmusical constructs, however rational, intriguing, or brilliantly conceived, and whether verbalized, diagrammed or programmed. Conversely, I do not envisage the artistic medium called music to be suitable for, adaptable for, restricted to or necessary for rending, or for validating, nonauditory models. Hence, while I favor with amusement the spurt of fascination with and free exploration of musiclike signals that may be obtained via electronic and computerized processing, only such findings would prove relevant to human music as might become imbued with identifiable images belonging to the social communion of music-making.

To me, the source of music proper, of the sonata rather than any mystified fetish formed from acoustical matter, lies in concrete and vivid auditory imagery, an imagery necessarily conditioned by the cultural history of specific human societies, rather than in schematic abstractions. Musical composition to me consists in the ordering and structuring of such auditory images into coherent designs that are evocative of and suffused with human experience whence they arise.

PRINCIPAL WORKS: String Quartet (1936); Concerto for Ten Instruments (1937); Piano Sonata (1938); Three Chamber Sonatas, for clarinet and viola (1938); *On the Death of a Spanish Child*, for symphonic band (1939); Clarinet Quartet (1939); Variations, for piano (1940); Three Dances, for orchestra (1940); String Quintet (1941); Three Modern Dances, for piano (1943); Passacaglia, for piano (1944); *Stony Hollow*, for orchestra (1944); Symphony (1949); *Three Ballads,* for orchestra (1949); Three New Sonatas, for piano (1950); *Songs from the Catskills* for symphonic band (1950); Suite, for brass sextet (1951); *Dingle Hill*, cantata for solo voices, chorus, and orchestra with dramatic dialogue (1958); *Woodland Valley Sketches*, for orchestra (1960); Oboe Quintet (1960); Piano Sonatina (1964); *Elizabethan Suite* no. 1, for brass quintet (1964); *Elizabethan Suite* no. 2, for string quartet (1965); Chamber Concerto, for orchestra (1965); Piano Trio (1969); Woodwind Quintet (1969); *The Sunshine Sonata*, for piano (1971); *Six Sonnets*, for trombone quartet (1971); Bassoon Sonata (1971); Sonata, for alto recorder or flute and harp or harpsichord (1971); Cello Sonata (1971); Viola Concerto (1972); English horn Sonata (1974); Viola Sonata (1974); Clarinet Sonata (1974); Tuba Sonata (1974); Double Bass Sonata (1974); Six Preludes and Fugues, for piano (1976).

BIBLIOGRAPHY: *DCM*; *American Composers Alliance Bulletin*, vol. 8, no. 2, 1959.

Chadwick, George Whitefield, b. Lowell, Mass., November 13, 1854; d. Boston, April 4, 1931.

He was a leading figure in the so-called New England school of composers of the late 19th century which maintained close creative ties with German romanticism.

Both his parents came from New England stock. His mother died eleven days after he was born, and for the first three years he was raised by his grandparents. When the father remarried, the child returned to his parental home in Lowell. In 1860, the Chadwicks moved to Lawrence, Mass., where his father founded an insurance company that soon became successful. Being also a teacher of a singing class and organizer of a local chorus and orchestra, the father brought music into his home and saw to it that each of his sons was trained. George received his first music lessons at the piano from his older brother. These were later supplemented by instruction on the organ. When George was fifteen he substituted for his brother as church organist. His academic education was limited to elementary school and just two years of high school. But music study was allowed to continue. He traveled regularly to Boston, where he studied organ with George E. Whiting and harmony with Stephen A. Emery. Further organ study took place privately between 1874 and 1875 with Dudley Buck and Eugene Thayer.

Meanwhile, in 1873, Chadwick started working in his father's firm. When he was twenty-one, Chadwick decided to abandon business and devote himself entirely to music. He taught privately and gave performances on the organ in 1875–76. In the fall of 1876 he accepted an appointment as head of the music department at Olivet College in Michigan, where his duties included teaching piano, organ, and harmony, giving weekly organ recitals, and conducting a glee club. With his meager savings, and over the stout opposition of his father, he left for Europe in

the fall of 1877 for further music study. At first he was a composition pupil of Karl August Hauptmann's in Berlin. Dissatisfied, Chadwick went on to Leipzig to study counterpoint with Salomon Jadassohn, first privately, then at the conservatory, where he also received instruction in composition from Karl Heinrich Reinecke. In Leipzig, Chadwick wrote his first two string quartets. For his graduation exercises he submitted the first of several concert overtures (a form he would favor through the years): *Rip Van Winkle* (1879), inspired by Washington Irving's story. Performed at the Leipzig Conservatory on June 20, 1879 with the composer conducting, it was enthusiastically received and won a prize. In the fall of 1879, Chadwick left for Munich to continue his study of composition and organ for one year with Josef Rheinberger.

He was back in Boston in 1880 to launch his career as a professional musician. Opening a studio, he gave private lessons in piano, organ, and composition, one of his first students being Horatio Parker, later to become an eminent composer. In addition, Chadwick played the organ at the South Congregational Church from 1883 to 1893 and conducted various local groups. In 1892 he joined the faculty of the New England Conservatory as a teacher of harmony and composition. He remained there for the rest of his life, serving as its director from 1897 on. His influence as a teacher was felt by a generation of American composers. From 1889 to 1899 Chadwick conducted at the Springfield Festival and from 1897 to 1901 at the Worcester Festival, both in Massachusetts. On June 17, 1888, he married Ida Brooks; they had two sons.

He began making his mark as a composer soon after his return from Europe, though a few months earlier, in December 1879, *Rip Van Winkle* had been successfully performed in Boston. On May 6, 1880, he himself conducted another performance of *Rip Van Winkle* with the Handel and Haydn Society. A second concert overture, the lighthearted *Thalia* (1882), was performed in the year of its composition by the Boston Symphony Orchestra under Georg Henschel and soon after that was repeated at a concert of the Handel and Haydn Society. (This was the first of many Chadwick works bearing Greek titles.) In 1882, Chadwick completed the writing of his symphony no. 1 in C major, whose premiere was given by the Harvard Musical Association under the composer's direction on February 23, 1882.

From his compositional beginnings Chadwick was the romanticist strongly affected by German music. Chadwick's love for singing passages echoed Mendelssohn's lyricism; his orchestration was modeled on Wagner's; later on, when he began writing tone poems, he was influenced by Richard Strauss. But Chadwick also had a voice of his own: a wry sense of humor, high Yankee spirits, a vigor, and what Philip Hale once described as "a jaunty irreverence" that was more American than European. He had a pronounced gift for pictorial images and the imitation of natural sounds, for the poetic, and for the creation of subtle atmospheres. He had a superior technique for orchestration. With him, "persons, moods, actions, are translated into orchestral sounds of contour, color, and meaning," as Carl Engel has written.

Chadwick's Symphony, no. 2 in B-flat major was written between 1883 and 1885. At first, only the second movement was heard (Boston, March 8, 1884). Then, on December 11, 1886, the complete symphony was performed at a concert of the Boston Symphony, the composer conducting. His first major success came soon after that with *Melpomene*, a dramatic overture (1886), which the Boston Symphony under Wilhelm Gericke first performed on December 24, 1887. Following its premiere it became such a favorite at the concerts of the Boston Symphony that it was programmed for eight subsequent seasons; it was also popular with the Chicago Symphony, which performed it in six different seasons. The overture was also well received abroad. During the next quarter of a century it was performed by the London Philharmonic, at the Worcester Festival in England, as well as in Paris, Leipzig, Copenhagen, and other European cities.

Chadwick's most popular orchestral work is *Jubilee* (1895). This is the first movement of *Symphonic Sketches*, whose other three movements are *Noël* (1895), *Hobgoblin* (1904) and *A Vagrom Ballad* (1896). The complete suite was given by the Boston Symphony on February 7, 1908, Karl Muck conducting. Brilliantly orchestrated, its thematic material at turns exultant and soaringly lyrical, *Jubilee*, for all its leaning to Germanic romanticism, has a pronounced personal flavor, particularly in the way an Afro-Caribbean beat is combined with Anglo-type melodies. *Noël* is a Christmas pastoral. *Hobgoblin*, a mocking, impish scherzo, has been compared to a vaudeville soft-shoe routine. *A Vagrom Ballad* is vividly programmatic, inspired by an encampment of derelicts. A curious intrusion into this last-named movement is a quotation from Bach's C minor fugue for organ (played by the xylophone), whose unexpected presence has never been explained.

Of his subsequent orchestral works, the most memorable are the following: the Symphony no. 3 in F major (1893–94), which the Boston Symphony, under the composer's direction, presented on October 20, 1894, and which then received the first prize from the National Conservatory of Music in New York; *Adonais*, an elegiac overture based on Keats's poem, written in 1898 as a memorial to a friend and first performed by the Boston Symphony on February 3, 1900; *Tam O'Shanter* (1915; Connecticut Festival, June 3, 1915), based on Robert Burns, a lively ballad for orchestra which quotes the Scottish folk ballad "The Martyrs"; *Suite symphonique* (1910), first performance on March 29, 1911 in Philadelphia, and recipient of first prize from the National Federation of Music Clubs; and *Angel of Death* (1917), a tone poem performed in 1919 by the New York Symphony as a memorial to Theodore Roosevelt.

Chadwick wrote a considerable amount of choral music, some of it for specific occasions. *The Dedication Ode* (1886) was intended for the opening of the New Hollis Street Church in Boston; another Ode (1892), with text by Harriet Monroe, for the opening of the Chicago Columbian Exhibition; and *Ecce, Iam Noctis*, a hymn for male voices (1897), for Yale University when it presented him with an honorary master of arts degree. Of his many compositions for voice and orchestra, the most popular was *A Ballad of Trees and the Master* (1899), on a text by Sidney Lanier.

Chadwick wrote six works for the stage. Three were comic operas: *The Peer and the Pauper* (1884), obviously imitative of Gilbert and Sullivan; *The Quiet Lodging* (1892); and *Tabasco*, performed in Boston on January 29, 1894. *Judith* (1901) was a lyric drama receiving its premiere at the Worcester Festival in Massachusetts on September 26, 1901, and repeated there one year later. On January 29, 1977, it was revived at the Hopkins Center of Dartmouth College in Hanover, N. H., at which time a critic for *High Fidelity/Musical America* praised it for its "admirable workmanship," "moments of inspiration" and "sumptuous orchestral score." *The Padrone* (1915) is a grand opera. *Love's Sacrifice* (1916) is a pastoral opera first mounted in Chicago on February 1, 1923.

In commemoration of Chadwick's fiftieth anniversary as a professional musician (and the fiftieth year since his return from Europe), Chadwick festivals were held at the New England Conservatory in Boston and at the Eastman School of Music in Rochester. In Boston, Chadwick himself conducted *Rip Van Winkle* on May 6, 1930, exactly fifty years after he himself had first directed it in the United States.

In addition to his honorary master of arts degree from Yale, Chadwick received an honorary doctorate from Tufts University in Medford, Mass., in 1905 and a gold medal from the American Academy of Arts and Letters in 1928. He was the author of *Harmony: A Course of Study* (Boston, 1902).

THE COMPOSER SPEAKS: The brain and the heart are one thing and technique is another. You may cultivate the fingers, the throat or whatever else is used, but without brain and heart there is no musical education. . . . If the effect justifies the means, *any rule may be disregarded.*

PRINCIPAL WORKS: 3 symphonies (1882, 1883–85, 1893–94); 5 string quartets (1877–1901).

Rip Van Winkle, concert overture (1879); *The Viking's Last Voyage*, for vocal soloists, chorus, and orchestra (1881); *The Song of the Viking*, for vocal soloists, chorus, and orchestra (1882); *Thalia*, concert overture (1882); *The Miller's Daughter*, concert overture (1884); *Dedication Ode*, for vocal soloists, chorus, and orchestra (1886); *Melpomene*, concert overture (1886); Piano Quintet (1888); *Lovely Rosabel*, choral ballad (1889); Serenade in F, for strings (1890); *A Pastoral Prelude*, for orchestra (1890); *The Pilgrims*, for chorus and orchestra (1891); *Phoenix Expirans*, for solo voices, mixed chorus, and orchestra (1892); *The Lily Nymph*, cantata, for voices, chorus and orchestra (1893); *Symphonic Sketches* (1895–1904); *Lochinvar*, for voice and orchestra (1896); *Ecce Iam Noctis*, hymn for male voices (1897); *Adonais*, elegiac overture for orchestra (1898); *A Ballad of Trees and the Master*, for voice and orchestra (1899); *Judith*, lyric drama (1901); *Euterpe*, concert overture (1904); *Cleopatra*, tone poem for orchestra (1904); Sinfonietta, for orchestra (1904); *Noël*, Christmas pastoral for solo voices, chorus, and orchestra (1908); Theme, Variations, and Fugue, for organ and orchestra (1908); *Joshua*, for voice and orchestra (1909); *Suite symphonique* (1909); *Afar on the Plains of Tigris*, for voice and orchestra (1911); *Aghadoe*, for voice and orchestra (1911); Four Christmas Songs, for voice and orchestra (1912); *Aphrodite*, tone poem for orchestra (1912); *The Voice of Philomel*, for voice and orchestra (1914); *The Padrone*, opera (1915); *Tam O'Shanter*, ballade for orchestra (1915); *Love's Sacrifice*, pastoral opera (1917); *Angel of Death*, tone poem for orchestra (1917); *Land of Our Hearts*, for solo voices, chorus and orchestra (1918); *The Fighting Men*, for voice and orchestra (1918); Elegy, for orchestra (1919); *Drake's Dream*, for voice and orchestra (1920); *Anniversary Overture*, for orchestra (1922); Three Pieces, for orchestra (1923).

BIBLIOGRAPHY: Chase, Gilbert, *America's Music* (N. Y., 1955); Howard, John Tasker. *Our American Music* (N. Y., 1946); Yellin, V., "The Life and Operatic Works of George Whitefield Chadwick" (doctoral thesis, Cambridge, Mass., 1957); *Musical Quarterly*, July 1924, January 1975.

Chanler, Theodore Ward, b. Newport, R. I., April 29, 1902; d. Boston, Mass., July 27, 1961.

Chanler favored the shorter forms of music, particularly the art song, to which he brought a highly expressive gift within a tonal framework.

His father traced his American ancestry to Isaac Chanler, a clergyman who had come from Bristol, England, in 1720 to settle in Charlestown, S. C. In 1906 the Chanler family moved to the Genesee Valley in western New York State where Theodore was raised. In 1911 he was sent to preparatory school in England, but after a year his father decided upon an American schooling and Theodore was enrolled in the Fay School in Southboro, Mass., where he remained two years. Since Theodore showed unmistakable signs of talent for music from the time he began taking piano lessons at six, a family decision

was arrived at to exchange academic schooling for a musical one. In 1914, he was entered in the Institute of Musical Art in New York, but, as he explained, he was then much too young to concentrate "upon such dry and arduous matters as the technics of music, nor was I in any sense a prodigy." This experiment having proved a failure, Chanler was returned to academic schooling at the Middlesex School in Concord, Mass. (1916–18). During this period he made weekly trips to Boston to study piano with Hans Ebell. In 1918, Chanler made his home in Boston to continue piano lessons with Ebell, to study harmony with Arthur Shepherd at the New England Conservatory, and to make his first attempts at composition by writing two songs to poems of William Blake, "Memory" and "The Shepherd" (1919).

In 1919 he returned to New York to divide his efforts between an academic and musical education. The academic training took place at the Browning School (1919–21) and the musical at the Institute of Musical Art with Richard Buhlig (piano) and Percy Goetschius (counterpoint). He expected to enter Harvard University, for which he had taken preparatory examinations, but a meeting with Ernest Bloch in 1920 caused a change of plan. Skipping college, Chanler went to Cleveland to study composition with Bloch at the Institute of Music, of which Bloch had become director. Study with Bloch consumed three years (1920–23). On the urging of his family, Chanler went to England in 1923 to attend Brasenose College at Oxford for two years. During the Christmas vacation in 1923 he took some lessons in composition with Nadia Boulanger in Paris. He found her so stimulating that he returned to Paris the following fall to study harmony and counterpoint with her. He remained her pupil until the spring of 1926; then, after a period of trying to get along by himself, he returned to Paris in the fall of 1927 for one more year of instruction. Under her guidance he wrote a song, "These, My Ophelia," to a poem by Archibald MacLeish (1925) and a Sonata for Violin and Piano (1927), the second movement of which ("Nocturne") was performed in Paris in April 1926.

For the next eight years he wrote almost nothing. This was a period, he said, in which he tried to open for himself "certain inner doors," since "too many outer doors were morally and artistically unacceptable to one brought up with the teachings of the Roman Catholic Church." All the "outer doors," he said, were closed to him when he married Maria de Acosta Sargent on October 19, 1931. The "inner doors" began opening in 1935 with the writing of the first few of *Eight Epitaphs*, a song cycle for voice and piano to poems by Walter De la Mare based on gravestone inscriptions. Chanler completed this cycle in 1937 and it was performed that year in the Library of Congress in Washington, D.C. In 1940, he completed settings of three additional poems by Walter De la Mare. This was the true beginning of his mature career as a composer of art songs—his most fruitful area and the one with which he is most often represented on concert programs. Of special interest are *Four Rhymes from Peacock Pie* (1940), poems by Walter De la Mare, with their fantastic and humorous descriptions of various animals, and *The Children*, a cycle of nine songs for children's chorus or solo voice and piano (1945) to texts by Leonard Feeney. The latter was first performed in May 1945 in Cambridge, Mass., by a group of forty girls aged eight to fourteen who were inmates of the House for Destitute Catholic Children in Boston.

Within a larger framework then the art song, Chanler wrote in 1942 the score for a ballet, *Pas de trois* (for piano and two dancers) performed in New York in May 1942 with choreography by Balanchine. Among his few instrumental pieces is *The Second Joyful Mystery*, a fugue for two pianos (1942–43), title taken from the Roman Catholic Rosary consisting of fifteen Mysteries, the second being the Visitation described in Luke I: 29–56. Later in his career, Chanler wrote a chamber opera, *The Pot of Fat* (1955), text by his sister, Hester Pickman, adapted from a fairy tale of Grimm. Alfred Frankenstein, writing in *High Fidelity Magazine*, called this score "one of the most adroitly written of all American operas, with a genuine vocal line, some exceedingly ingenious writing for a chamber orchestra and—most unusual of all for an American work in this genre—a professional grace in the vocal give and take between the characters." This chamber opera was first produced in Cambridge, Mass., on May 8, 1955 and almost a decade later was recorded.

Chanler never realized a personal identity in his music, much of which is derivative from the French school of Fauré and Poulenc. He had expert craftsmanship, a refinement and sensitivity of style, a charm of expression, and an abundant melodic invention which make the hearing of his best compositions a highly gratifying experience. This became evident at a concert in New York on May 1, 1978, when four of his compositions were given. At that time, Joseph Horowitz commented in the *New York Times*: "What particularly impresses about Chanler's musical thought is its integrity—he sticks to what he really knows and feels, and the means of expression are relevant and concise."

In 1934 Chanler was music critic for the *Boston Herald*. In 1940 he received an Award from the League of Composers in New York, and in 1944, a Guggenheim Fellowship. Between 1945 and 1947 he was a member of the faculty at the Peabody Conservatory in Baltimore.

THE COMPOSER SPEAKS: Songwriting, being a fusion of diverse elements into a single *form*, may be regarded as a species of counterpoint. The text is the *cantus firmus*, something *given* that we are not responsible for, and that, like fate, we can bend to our will only if we accept its terms. The text of a song is its premise; and since a poem is complete without the addition of music, it follows that of all the elements that go into a song, the text is the most self-sufficient. Next, in a descending scale of autonomy, comes the melody. Upon it falls the main burden of achieving the selfhood in self-subservience. Its length, its rhythmic design, even its general contour, are all in one way or another conditioned by the text. Yet in spite of this, if it is to deserve the name of melody it must have a recognizable and relatively independent musical shape. It is a kind of offspring of the text, and, like a human offspring, dependent upon its parent while having an individuality of its own. Next in the hierarchy comes the accompaniment, serving to support the usually frail structure of the melody. Woven into the accompaniment may be ornamental and contrapuntal designs of almost any degree of complexity. But its basic structure should again be clear and solid in itself, having as much autonomy as its doubly conditioned status allows.

PRINCIPAL WORKS: Violin Sonata (1927); Mass, for women's voices or boys' voices and organ (1930); *Five Short Colloquies*, suite for piano (1936); *Eight Epitaphs*, song cycle for voice and piano (1937); Toccata, for piano (1939); *Three Epitaphs*, for voice and piano (1940) *Four Rhymes from Peacock Pie*, for voice and piano (1940); *Pas de trois*, ballet (1942); *The Second Joyful Mystery*, fugue for two pianos (1942–43); *The Children*, for children's chorus or solo voice and piano (1945); Sonata no. 2, for violin and piano (1948); *The Pot of Fat*, chamber opera (1955).

BIBLIOGRAPHY: Ewen, David, *American Composers Today* (N. Y., 1945); *Modern Music*, May–June 1945.

Cheslock, Louis, b. London, England, September 25, 1898; d. Baltimore, Md., July 19, 1981. American citizen, 1913.

For over half a century Cheslock occupied a significant place in the musical life of Baltimore, Md.—as violinist, teacher, author, and composer.

He was three years old when his family came to the United States, settling in Baltimore. Neither parent was musical. When he was twelve, Cheslock expressed a yearning for the violin and for about a year he received instruction from Anna Rodgin. While attending public school in Baltimore he formed a small orchestra (1912) which performed music by Haydn and Mozart and accompanied pupil singing at school assemblies, for which he wrote a little operetta.

While attending Baltimore City College (1913–15), which is actually a high school, Cheslock's musical training took place at Peabody Conservatory in Baltimore, which he entered in 1913. There, he studied the violin with Franz Bornschein, Jan van Hulsteyn, and Frank Gittelson and theory and composition with Gustav Strube, receiving a teaching certificate in violin in 1917, a diploma in harmony in 1919, and a diploma in composition in 1921. Meanwhile, in 1916, he joined the music faculty of Peabody Conservatory as instructor of the violin, adding the teaching of theory and composition to his duties in 1922 and, from 1952 to 1970, serving as chairman of the theory department. Cheslock was on the conservatory faculty for sixty years, retiring in 1976. On May 31, 1926, he married Elise Brown Hamline, with whom he had a son.

While teaching at Peabody, Cheslock played in the violin section of the Baltimore Symphony from 1916 to 1937, the last five years as assistant concertmaster. On several occasions (in 1928, 1944, and 1950) he appeared as composer–guest conductor.

Though Cheslock's works had significant performances in Europe, South America, the Orient, and many parts of the United States, practically every one of them was given its premiere in Baltimore. From the outset he was a neoromantic who basically conformed to traditional methods and idioms, though on occasion he would employ free harmony and unresolved discords. Late in his career he used a modified twelve-tone system—as in *Descant*, for unaccompanied clarinet (1970) and in several twelve-tone pieces for the piano such as *The Five One Page Twelve-tone Pieces* (c. 1958)—but the twelve-tone system did not assume an important role in his creativity.

He achieved his first successes with orchestral music written between 1921 and 1923. The Concerto for Violin and Orchestra (1921) was introduced on February 25, 1926, by Arthur Morgan with Gustav Strube conducting the Peabody Conservatory Symphony. *Three Scenes* (1922) received its first hearing on April 29, 1923, with Nathaniel Finston conducting the Chicago Theater Symphony. Two orchestral dances, *Polish Dance* and *Spanish Dance* (1923), were premiered by the Baltimore Symphony on April 28, 1926, Gustav Strube conducting. These two dances received awards in contests sponsored by the *Chicago Daily News* in 1923 and 1924.

Cheslock's subsequent orchestral works include the *Symphonic Prelude* (1927) which the Baltimore Symphony presented on April 28, 1928, the composer conducting; the Symphony in D major (1932); Suite from *David* (1937), heard on February 19, 1939 with Werner Janssen conducting the Baltimore Symphony; *The Legend of Sleepy Hollow*, a programmatic tone poem based on Washington Irving's tale (1937; Baltimore, May 2, 1978); and *Rhapsody in Red and White*, "an American divertissement" (1948), commissioned by Reginald Stewart for the Baltimore Symphony and first heard on February 8, 1950.

In 1930, Cheslock wrote a one-act, three-character opera, *The Jewel Merchants*, dedicated to H.L. Mencken, libretto by the composer based on a play by James Branch Cabell; it was produced on Febru-

ary 26, 1940. Influenced in part by Wagner and in part by Richard Strauss, this opera has no set arias, and used the orchestra more as a commentary on what is taking place on the stage than as accompaniment. On the suggestion of H. L. Mencken, Cheslock adapted the fairy tale of Cinderella into a ballet (1944) that was produced on May 11, 1946, and was also dedicated to Mencken. In a revised and enlarged format this ballet was presented on May 2, 1958.

Cheslock was awarded first prize—for *The Congo*, for chorus and orchestra (1940), based on the poems of Vachel Lindsay—in a contest for choral compositions sponsored by the Composers Clinic in Akron, Ohio, in 1942. In 1960 he was elected to the Baltimore City College Hall of Fame and in 1964 Peabody Conservatory presented him with an honorary doctorate in music. His seventy-fifth birthday was commemorated in Baltimore on November 12, 1974, with several concerts of his works.

Cheslock is the author of *Introductory Study on Violin Vibrato* (1931) and *Graded List of Violin Music* (1948), and he is the editor of *H. L. Mencken on Music* (1961).

THE COMPOSER SPEAKS: A present-day distinctive style in music, such as classical, baroque, romantic, or impressionistic, has not yet crystallized. This is a period of exploration and experimentation, stimulating and exciting. Yet, within the framework of many-faceted new techniques, I hope to hear more present-day music which might rightfully be regarded as beautiful, or noble, or majestic, or inspirational; I believe deeply that it will come.

PRINCIPAL WORKS: Violin Sonata (1917); Violin Concerto (1921); *Three Scenes*, for orchestra, also for string quintet (1922); Two Dances, for orchestra, also for violin and piano (1923); *Symphonic Prelude*, for orchestra (1927); *Phoenician Dance*, for two violins and viola (1929); *Two Miniatures*, for strings (1930); *Slumber Music and Serenade*, for string orchestra (1930); *The Jewel Merchants*, one-act opera (1930); Psalm 150, for chorus and orchestra (1931); Symphony in D major (1932); *Shire Ami I*, for string quartet and harp (1932); *Shire Ami II*, for violin, cello, and harp (1932); Piano Sonatina (1932); Theme and Variations, for French horn and chamber orchestra (1934); French horn Concerto (1936); Suite from *David*, for orchestra (1937); *The Legend of Sleepy Hollow*, tone poem for orchestra (1937); *The Congo*, for chorus and orchestra (1940); String Quartet (1941); *Cinderella*, ballet for children (1944, revised 1958); *Rhapsody in Red and White*, for orchestra, also for wind band (1948); *The Artist*, for voice and piano (1949); *Set of Six*, for orchestra (1950); Suite, for oboe and strings (1953); Concertinetto, for bass ensemble, piano and percussion, also for two solo pianos (1954); *Homage à Mendelssohn*, for string orchestra (1960); Bagatelle, for cello and piano (1969); *Descant*, for unaccompanied clarinet (1970).

BIBLIOGRAPHY: *BBDM; Who's Who in America, 1980–81*.

Chihara, Paul Seiko, b. Seattle, Wash., July 9, 1938.

Chihara's musical world is a dichotomy of two widely separated epochs. For the most part he is very much of the present moment in his advanced forms of serial techniques and indulgence in aleatory and electronic practices. But his choral music, in its structures and polyphony, reaches back to the baroque era. His style is characterized by sharp and dramatic contrasts of colors, textures, and emotional levels.

He is of Japanese descent. Soon after Pearl Harbor his family was relocated with other Japanese Americans to Minadoka, Idaho. Paul's musical training began in childhood with piano lessons. He continued to study music while attending the public schools in Seattle, but for a long time he had no ambition to become a professional musician. His main interest was English literature, the subject in which he majored at the University of Washington in Seattle where he received his bachelor of arts degree in 1960. He continued to specialize in English literature at Cornell University in Ithaca, N.Y., earning his master of arts degree there in 1961.

He spent the year of 1962–63 in Paris studying composition with Nadia Boulanger. His first compositions to reveal marked talent came in 1963, favoring advanced harmonic and tonal idioms. Concerto for Viola and Orchestra was selected by the Baltimore Symphony at the Rockefeller Foundation Project for Contemporary American Music at Goucher College in Towson, Md. Four Pieces for Orchestra received the Lili Boulanger Memorial Award in 1963 and was premiered a year later in New York.

Chihara continued to study composition with Robert Palmer at Cornell University. There he was awarded the degree of doctor of musical arts in 1965. On a Fulbright fellowship, he returned to Europe in 1965–66, this time to study composition with Ernst Pepping in Berlin.

In 1966, Chihara spent the first of several consecutive summers on a fellowship at the Berkshire Music Center at Tanglewood, Mass., as a student of composition of Gunther Schuller's. There, in 1966, he wrote *Tree Music*, for three violas and three trombones, introduced that summer at Tanglewood. Chihara called this work "a texture study of middle and low range instruments . . . basically an arhythmic composition in which beat or pulse was negated in favor of static or slowly evolving tone colors." *Tree Music* became the first of a series of tone pictures dealing with trees. It was followed by *Branches*, for two bassoons and percussion (1966); *Redwood*, for viola and percussion (1967); *Willow, Willow* for am-

plified bass flute, tuba, and three percussionists (1968); *Logs*, for string bass and electronic tape (1970); *Driftwood*, for violin, two violas and cello (1969); and *Forest Music*, for orchestra (1970). By the time he wrote *Forest Music*, the composer says, "my arboreal world seemed somehow sunnier and warmer. My . . . music has grown relaxed, lyric, and occasionally straight-forward romantic. In general, these lyric passages emerge out of static textures of blocks of sound, like images of rough, natural material." The Los Angeles Philharmonic under Zubin Mehta gave the first performance of *Forest Music* on May 2, 1971, and in 1974 toured with it in Japan. In 1973, this work was featured at the Edinburgh Festival in Scotland.

From 1966 to 1974, Chihara was assistant professor of music at the University of California in Los Angeles. During these years he was the musical adviser and a frequent participant in the "Monday Evening Concerts" in Los Angeles promoting new music. He also toured extensively as composer, performer, and conductor in the United States, Japan, England, and elsewhere; in 1973 he appeared in a series of concerts in Mexico City sponsored by the U.S. Information Agency of the Department of State.

Beginning with 1971, Chihara produced a second extended series of compositions for various instruments, or for orchestra, in an advanced serial technique, characterized by marked contrasts of timbres and textures. He called them *Ceremonies*. The first of these, for oboe, two cellos, double bass, and percussion, was written in 1971 while he was serving as guest composer at Oberlin Conservatory in Ohio; it was premiered at the Marlboro Festival in Vermont in 1971. Chihara planned these compositions as "a series of concert 'meditations' on some basic musical objects, such as the unison, the rhythmic ostinato, the triad, etc.," he explains. During the next two years he completed two more *Ceremonies*, the third of which was written for Neville Marriner and his Los Angeles Chamber Symphony, which introduced it. *Ceremony IV*, for large orchestra, received its first hearing on April 18, 1974, when it was performed by the Los Angeles Philharmonic under Mehta, for whom it was written. This work was intended as a summation of various ideas developed in the earlier pieces. "Perhaps in reaction to the somber, trancelike music of the first three *Ceremonies*," the composer says, "*Ceremony IV* has assumed a festive, thoroughly romantic color." Other musical styles (for example, Wagner, or the big-band sounds of the 1940s) are referred to—"deliberately and respectfully," the composer adds.

The San Francisco Ballet commissioned Chihara to write the music for an oriental ballet, *Shinju* (1973), with which the company toured the United States after having introduced it in San Francisco. An orchestral suite, adapted from this score, was first heard at the Claremont Festival in California in August 1974. Chihara prepared a second ballet score for the San Francisco Ballet in 1978, *Mistletoe Bride*, and in 1980 adapted for the company Henry Purcell's music for *The Tempest*.

In 1974, Chihara resigned from the University of California to devote himself exclusively to composition. On a Guggenheim Fellowship in 1975 he produced music for the ballet *The Infernal Machine*, scenario based on Jean Cocteau's play of the same name on the Oedipus theme.

Commissions led to the writing of other major works. For Jeffrey Solow, cellist, Chihara wrote *Wild Song*, for cello and orchestra (1972), first performance given by Solow in New York on February 2, 1972. *Missa Carminum*, or *Folk-Song Mass* (1975), for a cappella chorus, was a commission from the Roger Wagner Chorale, which first presented it on January 15, 1976, in Los Angeles before recording it. On a commission from the Fromm Music Foundation, Chihara completed *Ceremony V*, "Symphony in Celebration" (1975), and the Houston Symphony gave the world premiere on September 8, 1975. A Naumburg Foundation commission led to the writing of a string quartet, *Primavera* (1977), which the Primavera String Quartet premiered in New York in 1978. A grant from the National Endowment for the Arts resulted in the writing of *Sinfonia concertante*, for nine instruments (1979); the Boston Symphony Chamber Players under Theodore Antoniou introduced it in Boston in 1979 and then performed it in New York on January 28, 1980. Through the Martha Baird Rockefeller Fund, Chihara wrote the Concerto for Saxophone and Orchestra (1980), for the saxophone virtuoso Harvey Pittel, who introduced it in 1980 as soloist with the Boston Symphony, Seiji Ozawa conducting.

Chihara wrote the score for the motion picture *Prince of the City* (1981).

PRINCIPAL WORKS: 5 *Ceremonies*, for various combinations of instruments or chamber orchestra or full orchestra (1971–75); 2 string quartets (1965, 1977).

Viola Concerto (1963); Magnificat, for treble voices (1966); *The 90th Psalm*, choral cantata (1966); *Tree Music*, for three violas and three trombones (1966); *Branches*, for two bassoons and percussion (1966); Nocturne, for twenty-four solo voices (1966); *Redwood*, for viola and percussion (1967); *Willow, Willow*, for amplified bass flute, tuba and three percussionists (1968); *Rain Music*, a tape collage (1968); *Driftwood*, for violin, two violas, and cello (1969); *Forest Music*, for orchestra (1970); *Logs*, for amplified string bass and magnetic tape (1970); *Grass*, concerto for double bass and orchestra (1971); *Wild Song*, for cello and orchestra (1972); *Shinju*, ballet, also orchestral suite (1973); *Missa Carminum*, for a cappella chorus (1975); *The Infernal Machine*, ballet (1978); Guitar Concerto (1976); *Mistletoe Bride*, ballet (1978); *Sinfonia concertante*, for nine instruments (1979); Saxophone Concerto

(1980); *The Tempest*, ballet based on music by Purcell (1980).

BIBLIOGRAPHY: *BBDM*; Anderson, E. Ruth, *Contemporary American Composers* (Boston, 1976).

Childs, Barney Sanford, b. Spokane, Wash., February 13, 1926.

Described by a composer friend as "a square avant-garde composer," Childs does not adhere to a single identifiable style or idiom but writes whatever he thinks will work best at the time and under the circumstances in which he is working. He began as composer with the dissonant contrapuntal and harmonic idioms of Hindemith and Ruggles, from which he progressed to indeterminacy and self-generating musical structures, and from there to non–Western European musical approaches.

Childs wrote his first composition when he was twenty-three, but received no formal training in composition until he was twenty-six. His earliest musical experiences came from singing popular songs with his mother at the piano and from sporadic piano lessons. While attending secondary schools in Spokane and Palo Alto between 1932 and 1943, and in his first college years at Deep Springs College in eastern California, which he attended from 1943 to 1945, his goal was to become an aeronautical engineer; almost all his spare time in high school had been spent with friends building model aircraft. But those years did witness some involvement in music. He enjoyed listening to recordings of popular music, jazz, and occasionally to classical music, and playing boogie-woogie on the piano with friends. At the same time his interest in 20th-century music was awakened through Henry Cowell's *New Musical Quarterly*, copies of which he found in the Palo Alto library, where he was employed in 1941–42.

In the spring of 1944 he was employed as an aircraft tool designer. After serving in the U.S. Army in the infantry between 1943 and 1946, ending up as a sergeant in training corps at Fort Knox, Childs returned to the academic life by entering the University of Nevada at Reno, majoring in English and minoring in mathematics and music; he received his bachelor of arts degree in 1949. At the university his interest in music was stimulated through beginners' courses and by performing with the University Singers. In 1949 he made his initial attempt at composition, a piano trio, his first piece of music which, in his words, was "of any competence and scope."

In 1949, on a Rhodes Scholarship, Childs went to England to attend Oriel College at Oxford University for a bachelor of arts degree in 1951 in English language and literature. At Oxford he was a member of the Oxford University Music Club and Union (as well as serving on its governing committee for several terms) and of the Oriel College Music Society, of which he was the president for a single term. From

1951 to 1954 he did postgraduate work at Stanford University in California, earning a creative writing fellowship in 1954 and receiving his first formal training in composition from Leonard Ratner (1952–54). The summers of 1953 and 1954 were spent on Crofts Fellowships at the Berkshire Music Center at Tanglewood in Massachusetts for additional studies in composition with Carlos Chávez (1953) and Aaron Copland (1954), and in the fall and winter of 1954 the study of composition was further continued in New York with Elliott Carter. Childs was awarded his master's degree in English language and literature at Oxford in 1955, and his doctorate at Stanford in 1959.

"As I hear other music I like," Childs has revealed, "I am influenced by it to avail myself of whatever approaches to making good sounds it can provide me." Thus, having heard and been impressed by the music of Hindemith and Ruggles, he wrote the Solo Clarinet Sonata (1951; Stanford, 1952), the Quartet for Clarinet and Strings (1951–53; San Francisco, 1953), and the Bassoon Sonata (1953; Rochester, N.Y., February 15, 1954)—as well as other chamber music—in a linear counterpoint and dissonant harmonic idiom with structures expanded from conventional ones. Studying with Chávez, Copland, and Carter, and becoming acquainted with their works and with the music of Charles Ives, led him to arrive at a greater complexity and subtlety of polyphonic and harmonic resources. In such a style we find the Symphony no. 2 (1956; N.Y., February 7, 1961), Quartet for Bassoons (1958; Tucson, Ariz., March 22, 1964), Septet, for instruments and voices (1958; Bennington, Vt., June 17, 1959), and the Concerto for English horn, Strings, Harp, and Percussion (1955).

Between 1959 and 1965 Childs was a member of the English faculty at the University of Arizona in Tucson—instructor up to 1961, assistant professor for four years after that. From 1964 to 1971 he was dean at Deep Springs College and in 1969–71 composer-in-residence at Wisconsin College-Conservatory in Milwaukee.

In his music in the 1960s, Childs showed an increasing interest in indeterminacy, beginning with the *Interbalances I–VI* (1961–63) for chamber instrumentations—in employing unconventional materials or using nonpitched sounds for conventional instruments; or occasionally in having performers speak or read aloud as well as play. His electronic music has been limited to the occasional inclusion of pretaped recorded "real" sounds with instrumental groups (such as radio announcements, students practicing, a bowling-show commentary, advertisements). He has never been interested in serialism. "My music," Childs summarized, "is generally 'talking' music rather than 'dancing' music, linear and soloistic rather than chordal. I seem to work best with small and sometimes unorthodox instrumental groupings."

In Music for Two Flute Players (1963; N.Y., December 2, 1963), written for Harvey and Sophie Sollberger, with one player doubling on piccolo and the other on alto flute, Childs used constructional principles he had invented in *Welcome to Whipperginny* (1961; Urbana, Ill., and N.Y., March 1963). Both players have the same number of musical sections, and the abstract content of each is the same for both players, but the order in which each player has these sections is generally different. This means that there are occasional tutti-like passages in which both players are concerned with the same kind of material, sometimes closely related between the players, and other parts of the piece in which what the players will have differ widely. Each player has partial choices of pitch and rhythm within time blocks and without time restrictions and of the order in which composed and notated fragments and lines are played. In Nonet (1967; San Diego, Calif., March 10, 1968) each performer is called upon to assemble and organize his own part before performance from materials provided by the composer.

In the Quartet for Flute, Oboe, Bass, and Percussion (1964; Urbana, Ill., May 1, 1964), any or all of its four movements may be used in any order. Each movement has ten sections, any or all of which may be played, but in the order given. The work ranges from improvisation to completely composed material, with each movement including solos, duos, tuttis, and so forth, so that in the totality of the piece all instrumental combinations are available.

In *The Bayonne Barrel and Drum Company* (1968; Muncie, Ind., 1969), the solo wind player performs improvised sections based on prose suggestions of mood and gesture, preferably in a post-Ornette Coleman jazz idiom. Other players (thirteen winds, piano, percussion, and drum set) play through written parts, each beginning when he pleases and going through to reach that beginning, these parts including player speech. A rather ornate micro- (or out of) tuning is made before the performance.

By the early 1970s, Childs had become disenchanted with the Western European acculturated shape of introduction, gradual complexity, ascent to climax or revelation, denouement and closing. As a result, he began to explore different orderings of movements and material. In Brass Quintet no. 4 (1975; Atlantic City, N.J., 1976)—and in several other works—he experimented with one such ordering of movements and material, with the material being treated differently than any kind of thematic exposition. In the Quintet, a three-note motive, only rarely heard by itself and usually part of solo lines, serves as a kind of germ out of which later and earlier ideas grow, but one is never aware of where and in what fashion it may appear. Moments in the second movement have been loosely influenced by the jazz by John Coltrane and Miles Davis.

Two other works of the early 1970s deserve attention. Trio, for clarinet, cello and piano (1972; Los Angeles, Calif., April 21, 1972), is a work in memoriam for the poet Paul Blackburn. Long intense overlapping solos, austere and large fortissimos, moving to a gentler and almost motionless cello solo, are followed by a section marked "as a grave, quiet dance," the only time all play together in the same tempo. Even this affirmation of music is insufficient to break through the enormity of human isolation, and the players conclude with spoken lines (including some from Blackburn's poetry), fading off into silence.

String Quartet no. 8 (1974; Kent, Ohio, April 30, 1975) is a one-movement work consisting of very long full chords, almost immobile, moving from and to a sort of C major in a long, quiet arch.

Since 1971 Childs has been a member of the faculty in music and literature of the University of Redlands in California—professor of composition and music literature from 1973 on. He has served on both the executive committee and the National Council of the American Society of University Composers and is a member of the National Advisory Committee of the American Composers Alliance and of the advisory board of the American Music Society in England.

Childs is the author of a number of scholarly articles affirming his musical and aesthetic views. With Elliott Schwartz, he edited *Contemporary Composers on Contemporary Music* (1967). He has been married three times: to Charlotte Brown in April 1949 (divorced 1957); Mary Hinson, in December 1961 (divorced 1967); and Virginia Bowling Eckert in August 1967 (divorced 1970).

THE COMPOSER SPEAKS: Music fails if we seek to use it directly to evoke. We can only project similarities of feeling or of senses. Stravinsky is the source of the often cited statement that music is powerless to express anything at all, but later he qualifies this by pointing out that for him "one piece is superior to another essentially only in the quality of its feeling." Actually music can express, or even mean, anything the ear wishes it to, although in the abstract a piece of music is simply a chunk of time you are paying attention to with your ears. But they are *your* ears, and you will thus hear it and do with it as you wish. It may even serve as master metaphor for parts of your experience. When I write a piece I am not being programmatic in dealing with the mountain west; I am simply led to like the music sounds I write because I am myself, and part of this self is the relationship with the land and the past. And most of the new music I admire by my American contemporaries seems to me to work in this manner, with additionally the sense of delight—there is no better word for it—in sound, regardless of whether or not directly as evocation, which comes I think from writing from one's self and one's past.

PRINCIPAL WORKS: 8 string quartets (1951–74); 6 *Interbalances*, for various groups (1961–63); 5 wind quintets (1962–69); 5 brass quintets (1954–75); 2 symphonies (1954, 1956); 2 violin sonatas (1950, 1956).

Piano Trio (1949); *Sonata da camera*, for trumpet and woodwinds (1951); Clarinet Quartet (1953); Sonata, for bassoon and piano (1953); *Four Involutions*, for solo English horn (1955); *Five Considerations*, for solo French horn (1955); Concerto for English horn, Strings, Harp, and Percussion (1955); Quartet, for bassoons (1958); Septet, for instruments and voice (1958); Brass Trio (1959); Flute Sonata (1960); Sonata, for solo trombone (1961); *Welcome to Whipperginny*, for percussion nonet (1961); *Take 5*, for five instruments (1962); Music for Two Flute Players (1963); *Stances*, for flute and silence (1963); Quartet, for flute, oboe, double bass, and percussion (1964); *Any Five*, for five or eight vocal and instrumental parts (1965); *Jack's New Bag*, for ten players (1966); *The Golden Bubble*, for contrabass, sarrusophone, and solo percussion (1967); Nonet, for instruments and voice (1967); *Operation Flabby Sleep*, for any instruments (1968); *The Bayonne Barrel and Drum Company*, for solo wind and sixteen players (1968); Music for Tubas, six players (1969); *Keet Seel*, for a cappella chorus (1970); *Maine Scene*, for baritone and piano (1970); Concerto for Clarinet and Orchestra (1970); *When Lilacs Last in the Dooryard Bloom'd*, for vocal soloists, chorus, and band (1970–71); Trio, for clarinet, cello, and piano (1972); *Of Place*, for five clarinets (1972); Concert Piece, for tuba and band (1973); *The Golden Shore*, for band (1974); *Bowling Again with the Champs*, for six improvisers and tape (1976); *A Question of Summer*, for tuba and harp (1976); Four Pieces, for six winds (1977); *A Continuance*, for band (1979).

BIBLIOGRAPHY: *DCM*; *Proceedings of the American Society of University Composers*, 9/10, 1974–75.

Chou, Wen-Chung, b. Chefoo, China, July 28, 1923. American citizen, 1958.

Chou is the first Chinese-born composer to carry authentic oriental melorhythms to modern Western music. Chinese impressions and Chinese states of mind dominate his musical imagery; pentatonic melodies have been the source of much of his thematic material; Chinese melodies have often been used, adapted to Western harmonic practices but without sacrificing oriental identity; and Chinese poetry, philosophy, and even calligraphy have been a source of continual inspiration. His interest in the controlled flow of sound through organized complexity and ordered interplay of all its properties led him to the philosophy of *I Ching*, the foundation of which is a system of symbolic images that interact with each other in a state of perpetual transformation and superimposition, representing the changing microcosm in the unchanging macrocosm. Following the concept of *I Ching*, he developed a system of mutable modes, each being based upon three disjunct segments of the octave and constantly mutating within itself. These modes are applied not only to the pitch organization but also to duration, intensity, articulation, timbre, register, and contour.

He is one of seven children, each one of whom studied one or another Western musical instrument. Chou's interest in music was first aroused when he was four or five and was attracted to the sound of a Chinese flute (*hsiao*), which one of the household servants played almost daily. At about the same time, Chou often played on a harmonium at the home of a family friend. There was no serious encounter with Western music until he was about ten, when an older brother bought a violin and began studying it. Chou now also acquired a violin, but he experimented with a number of other Western and with some Chinese instruments. At about the age of twelve, he discovered the music for *ch'in*, a zither that is at the same time the most important and least popular of Chinese instruments. He would listen to a radio broadcast of this music early in the morning before going to school. The influence of the unique esthetics of *ch'in* music has never left him.

When the Japanese invaded China in 1937, Chou Wen-Chung's family fled to Shanghai. There Chou's musical training began in earnest. Aside from playing chamber music at home, he also studied harmony, counterpoint, form, and orchestration privately. Among the earliest attempts at composition were two short studies based on the solitary sound of a street peddler hawking his wares to the accompaniment of some percussion, and of the steps of a rickshaw boy Chou heard late at night.

When Shanghai fell to the Japanese, Chou left home and proceeded to Kweilin in southwest China. Bowing to the pressure of the war, Chou decided against a career in music because he realized that the war precluded opportunities for the kind of superior musical education he dreamed of. In line with other Chinese youths who, to help their country, turned to the study of sciences and technology, Chou was persuaded by China's need for modernization to choose engineering as his professional goal. With this aim in mind he attended Kwangsi University in Kweilin. In the wake of the Japanese advance in China, Chou went on to Chungking. There he received a bachelor of science degree in civil engineering at the National Chungking University, where he had been in attendance in 1944 and 1945.

He came to the United States on a scholarship in architecture from Yale University in the fall of 1946. After a week at Yale, he decided to abandon architecture for music. For three years (1946–49) he attended the New England Conservatory of Music in Boston on a Carr Scholarship, studying composition with Carl McKinley and Nicolas Slonimsky. Slonimsky encouraged him to make a serious study of classical Chinese music, which was initiated in 1949. This was the year Chou came to New York, where he studied composition privately with Bohuslav Martinu (1949) and Edgard Varèse (1949–54). The foundation of Chou's musical thinking, the coordination in his music of Eastern and Western elements, was formed in 1949 with the writing of his first mature composition, *Landscapes*, for orchestra, inspired by three poems by three Chinese poets of the 14th, 17th, and 18th centuries. The oriental pentatonic scale was predominant, together with the intervallic structures of Eastern origin. The San Francisco Symphony, conducted by Leopold Stokowski, introduced it on November 19, 1953. At that time, Alfred Frankenstein, writing in the *San Francisco Chronicle*, said: "*Landscapes* made adroit and imaginative use of ancient tunes, are colorful, nostalgic, allusive, and extremely brief. They bridge the gap between Oriental and Occidental music with exceptional success." In *The Nation*, Lester Trimble described this work as "pointillist and as delicately colored as the Chinese poems which inspired them." *Landscapes* was performed by the Chicago Symphony under Fritz Reiner in November 1959 and subsequently was recorded with Thor Johnson conducting.

Chinese melodies and timbres form the basis of two compositions that came soon after that: Suite, for harp, flute, oboe, clarinet, bassoon, and horn (1951; N.Y., February 22, 1952) and Seven Poems of T'ang Dynasty (1951–52). The latter, a setting of Chinese poems of the 8th century for tenor and instruments, was introduced at a concert of the International Society of Contemporary Music in New York on March 16, 1952, and was heard on September 2, 1961 at the Internationale Ferienkurse für Neue Musik in Darmstadt, Germany.

On a Mosenthal Fellowship in 1952, Chou did graduate work in music at Columbia University with Otto Luening, earning his master of arts degree in 1954. As his thesis for this degree, Chou wrote *All in the Spring Wind*, "a rondelet for orchestra" (1952–53; Louisville, Ky., December 7, 1961), which was later recorded by the Louisville Orchestra under Robert Whitney. "The piece," Nicolas Slonimsky wrote in the *American Composers Alliance Bulletin*, "is a tour de force of coloristic brushwork, entirely athematic in structure."

In 1954, Chou completed a "triolet for orchestra," with which he realized his first major success. It was *And the Fallen Petals*, title taken from a poem by Meng-Hao-jan, an 8th-century poet. Commissioned by the Louisville Orchestra, it was premiered in Kentucky on February 9, 1955, Robert Whitney conducting. Chinese thematic materials are here used effectively in terms of the Western orchestra. Reporting to the *Louisville Courier-Journal*, William Mootz called it "a daringly conceived and brilliantly executed piece. The composer frames the composition with a simple melody of Oriental cast, and this haunting tune (or fragments of it) weaves through the work. . . . Chou manipulates the choirs of the orchestra in virtuoso fashion, and frequently uses the strings for percussion effects. The resulting terraced textures and overlapping sonorities achieve devastating effects in sheer sound. . . . [On] its own terms it is a remarkable expressive success." When this work was performed by the Berlin Philharmonic in June 1960, the distinguished German critic H. H. Stuckenschmidt called Chou in the *Frankfurter Allgemeine Zeitung*, "a musical calligrapher, whose pen imitates the subtlest efforts of the painter. . . . The power of atmosphere is irresistible." In addition to this Berlin performance, *And the Fallen Petals* was heard in Hamburg, Germany, on March 25, 1958, and In Tokyo on November 10, 1959.

Between 1955 and 1957, Chou was the director of a research program on classical Chinese music and drama at Columbia University, sponsored by a grant from the Rockefeller Foundation. At the same time he was also technical assistant to Otto Luening and Vladimir Ussachevsky at Columbia's Electronic Music Laboratory, the predecessor of the Electronic Music Center.

Chou's most important work of this period, and characteristic of his best writing, was *The Willows Are New*, for piano (1957; N.Y., February 2, 1958), title taken from Wang We's poem *Yang Kuan*. An adaptation of an old Chinese tune, this work sounded to Alfred Frankenstein in *High Fidelity/Musical America* "like Debussy and Henry Cowell. . . . The music's exoticism is the Debussy facet; its dissonant texture and hard, spare tonal surface is from Cowell."

In 1958–59, Chou was composer-in-residence at the University of Illinois in Urbana. While there, in 1958, he wrote *Soliloquy of a Bhiksuni*, for trumpet with brass and percussion ensemble, introduced at Urbana on December 18, 1958, and *To a Wayfarer*, for clarinet, strings, harp, and percussion, based on a 6th-century Chinese poem. The inspiration for the *Soliloquy* was a scene in a 16th-century Chinese drama representing a Buddhist nun (a Bhiksuni) worshiping before the image of Buddha. Once again, as previously in *The Willows Are New*, a kinship is here established between the music and the art of Chinese calligraphy. *To a Wayfarer* was introduced on December 3, 1958, at a concert of the Contemporary Music Society in New York, Leopold Stokowski conducting. In the *New York Times*, Ross Parmenter described the work as "a combination of sympathetic sadness for a vanished wayfarer, gone probably forever, and the composer's feeling for a willow tree after it had lost its blooms. The feelings were genuinely touching and the music was individual in expression."

Since 1961, Chou has directed a good deal of his energy and talent to teaching. He was lecturer in music at Brooklyn College in Brooklyn, N.Y., in 1961–62 and at Hunter College, N.Y., in 1963–64. In 1964 he was appointed assistant professor of music at Columbia University. He has remained on its faculty since that time, promoted to associate profes-

sor in 1968 and full professor in 1972. Additionally, he served there as chairman of the composition department (1969–74), chairman of the Music Division of the School of Arts (since 1969), coordinator of graduate studies (1974–75), associate dean of the School of Arts (1975–76) and, since 1976, its vicedean for academic affairs. He has been visiting professor of music or composer-in-residence or lecturer in various other educational institutions.

On June 23, 1962, he married Yi-an Chang, the first Chinese student ever to attend the Juilliard School of Music in New York; at the time of her marriage she was chairman of the music department at Abbott Academy in Andover, Mass. They have two sons.

Chung's most important compositions in the 1960s were *Riding the Wind*, for wind instruments (1964; Pittsburgh, June 14, 1964); *Yü Ko*, "Song of the Fisherman," for nine players (1965; N.Y., April 19, 1965); and *Pien*, "Transformations," a concerto for piano, winds, and percussion (1966; N.Y., January 9, 1967). In reviewing a recording of both *Pien* and *YüKo*, Alfred Frankenstein noted in *High Fidelity/Musical America* that *Pien* contained many recollections of both Webern and Varèse but that "what is very much Chou's own—but derived from Chinese tradition—is the composer's way of paying 'minute attention to each tone, providing for numerous ways to attack it; to vary its intensity, pitch and even timbre while the note is continuing, and to conclude it.' Put all these things together . . . and something most striking and exceptional results. The same variety of attacks, 'bending' of pitches and the rest are employed in . . . *Yü Ko*. . . . It is full of the melancholy of Chinese poetry and mysticism that comes out so strongly in Sung Dynasty painting. It is one of the very few musical compositions, indeed, that seem thoroughly equivalent in East-West terms to the great master periods and styles of Chinese literature and visual art."

Chou's research in East Asian music led him to maintain that in Eastern music individual tones are often conceived as musical identities by themselves and that in such cases the so-called deviations in tonal characteristics are an integral part of musical structure. He therefore believes, and has demonstrated in his more recent works, that such deviations are structurable elements that are compositional ideas in their own right and are related to the structure of the work as a whole. On the other hand, Chou believes in the Confucian concept that value in music lies less in the perfection of artistry than in the attainment of *te*, i. e., knowing "that by which things are what they are." He also believes with Chuang Tzu, the Taoist philosopher, that to know *te* means "using things as things, but not being used by things as things." Thus he contends that evolving new concepts and techniques purely as extrinsic procedure and calculation is "being used by things as things" rather than "using things as things."

Since the conclusion of the 1960s, after the completion of *Yün*, for winds, piano, and percussion (1969), Chou has been continually pressed into service in behalf of music education and international arts exchange, taking up major projects one after another. In 1969, Chou took over from Otto Luening the responsibility of developing and overseeing the doctoral program for composers at Columbia University, established less than a year earlier. In 1970, Chou was drafted by the board of directors of the Composers Recordings, Inc., to save the organization from collapsing. During the five years he served as president, he secured the company's independence from the American Composers Alliance, brought the company into fiscal solvency for the first time, and legally converted it from a profit-making status to that of nonprofit, all of which helped to ensure the permanence of CRI's unique service to contemporary music. Since 1977 Chou has also been active in stimulating exchange in the arts between the United States and the People's Republic of China through the Center for United States–China Arts Exchange, which he established in 1978. The center is the only nationwide agency in its field and has, among other things, sent a number of notable American musicians to China for long-term professional activities. Chou has been in much demand for advice and lecturing on music and art in China and in many other Asian countries.

Chou's tireless involvement in so many facets of the art world unfortunately also caused a sharp decline in his productivity as composer. Several works he had begun in the early 1970s remain to be completed. Chou, however, reacts to these circumstances philosophically, regarding what he has been compelled to undertake as obligations he owes to society in return for the opportunities it has offered him, and to history, for the role he has been allowed to play in it. He is also optimistic, believing that once he has met all the demands on his energy, he will be able to concentrate on composing with renewed vigor, greater insight, and more moral strength. Meanwhile, he struggles to find whatever time he can to keep at composing.

Chou has composed music for several documentary films, some of which were produced over television networks, has made numerous appearances as conductor, and has contributed articles to musicological journals, encyclopedias, and dictionaries. In 1972, he edited and completed from the composer's notes and sketches Edgard Varèse's *Nocturnal*, and edited a new version of Varèse's *Amériques*. A revised and corrected edition of Varèse's *Intégrales* prepared by Chou was brought out in 1980.

THE COMPOSER SPEAKS: I try to convey through sound the same emotional qualities of Chinese poetry and landscape painting and to achieve this end with the same economy of means: the maximum expressiveness of a minimum calligraphical brushwork in sound. Thus in all my compositions I am influenced by the same philosophy that governs every Chinese artist, whether he be poet or painter, namely, the affinity to nature in conception, the allusiveness in expression, and the terseness in realization.

PRINCIPAL WORKS: *Landscapes*, for orchestra (1949); Three Folk Songs, for harp and flute (1950); Two Chinese Folk Songs, for harp (1950); Suite, for harp and wind quintet (1951); Seven Poems of T'ang Dynasty, for voice and instrumental ensemble (1951–52); *All in the Spring Wind*, for orchestra (1952–53); *And the Fallen Petals*, for orchestra (1954); *In the Mode of Shang*, for orchestra (1956); *Two Miniatures for T'ang Dynasty*, for chamber ensemble (1957); *The Willows Are New*, for piano (1957); *To a Wayfarer*, for clarinet and strings (1958); *Soliloquy of a Bhiksuni*, for trumpet with brass and percussion ensemble (1958); *Poems of White Stone*, for chorus and instrumental ensemble (1958–59); *Metaphors*, for wind symphony orchestra (1960–61); *Cursive*, for flute and piano (1963); *The Dark and the Light*, for piano, percussion, and strings (1964); *Riding the Wind*, for wind symphony orchestra (1964); *Yü Ko*, for nine players (1965); *Pien*, concerto for piano with percussion and wind (1966); *Yün*, for winds, piano, and percussion (1969).

BIBLIOGRAPHY: DCM; Chase, Gilbert, *America's Music* (rev. ed., N.Y., 1966); Childs, Barney, and Schwartz, Elliott (eds.), *Contemporary Composers on Contemporary Music* (N.Y., 1967); Hitchcock, Wiley, *Music in the United States* (N.Y., 1969); *American Composers Alliance Bulletin*, vol. 9, no. 4, 1961.

Clapp, Philip Greeley, b. Boston, Mass., August 4, 1888; d. Iowa City, Ia., April 9, 1954.

Clapp was a composer who drew creative sustenance from the German romantic school, even while bringing a modern harmonic and rhythmic idiom into his writing.

He was the only son of cultured parents, both of whom loved music; the mother was an excellent singer. The only professional musician in the family was Philip's aunt, Mary Greeley James, who taught piano and gave Philip his first piano lessons in 1895 and remained his teacher for the next four years. Since he was musical, and since his family insisted he receive a thorough academic education, he was channeled in both directions. He studied violin with Jacques Hoffman from 1895 to 1905, and piano, theory, and composition with John P. Marshall from 1899 to 1905, while going to elementary school and high school. From childhood on he profited from the musical guidance and direction given him by George Chadwick and Arthur Foote, among other musical notables in Boston. In the world of academe, he attended the Roxbury Latin School between 1901 and 1905. In 1905 he entered Harvard University, the first two years on a William Merrick Scholarship. There, together with the academic curriculum, he took courses in theory and composition with Walter Raymond Spalding, Edward Burlingame Hill, and Frederick S. Converse. Between 1907 and 1909 he was the conductor of the Pierian Sodality Orchestra. He received his bachelor of arts degree *magna cum laude*, in 1908, his master of arts degree with highest final honors in 1909, and his doctorate in 1911. All this time he was active as a composer, traditional in his choice of structures and in the presentation of his materials. His pastoral Symphony no. 1 in E major was written between 1907 and 1908. (It had to wait a quarter of a century to be performed, and then in a revision made in 1932. This took place at Waterloo, Iowa, on April 27, 1933, the composer conducting.) *Norge*, a tone poem for orchestra with piano obbligato, become one of his popular compositions, was completed in 1908 and premiered by the Pierian Sodality Orchestra in the year of its composition before being heard at a concert of the Boston Symphony on April 29, 1909.

As a graduate student, he received the Frederick Sheldon Traveling Fellowship in 1909, which made it possible for him to spend two years in Europe. During the winter of 1909–10 he studied composition and conducting with Max von Schillings in Stuttgart. Most of the winter of 1910–11 was occupied with research in the British Museum Library in London on his doctoral thesis, "Modern Tendencies in Musical Form." From Europe, Clapp periodically dispatched reviews of European concerts and opera performance to the *Boston Transcript*.

He was back in Boston in 1911, and for one year (1911–12) was a teaching fellow at Harvard, and for two years (1912–14), instructor in music at Middlesex School for Boys in Massachusetts. An important influence in his development as a musician during these years was Karl Muck, the world-famous conductor whom he had first met in Berlin and who was conductor of the Boston Symphony from 1906 to 1908 and again from 1912 to 1918. "The manner in which he brought all of his great knowledge and rich experience to bear in helping me work out my own salvation," Clapp recalled, "could not have been wiser or more generous if I had been his own son." Muck invited Clapp to conduct the Boston Symphony in the premiere of the Symphony no. 2 in E minor (1913) on April 10, 1914. He also urged Clapp to consider developing himself as a full-time conductor, even selecting Clapp to conduct the Cincinnati Symphony on its spring tour in 1913. Muck advised Clapp to go to Europe for a two-year apprenticeship in a German opera house, and Clapp would undoubtedly have followed this suggestion but for the outbreak of World War I.

During 1914–15, Clapp spent a part of each week in Gloucester, Mass., as acting head of its School of Music, and from 1915 to 1918 he was the director of music at Dartmouth College in Hanover, N.H. He returned to Boston every weekend to attend rehearsals and concerts of the Boston Symphony, to lecture at Boston University, and to write articles on music for the *Boston Transcript*.

During World War I, in June 1918, Clapp enlisted in the U.S. Army. While in uniform he served as bandleader, with the rank of second lieutenant, in the Seventy-third Artillery, American Expeditionary Forces. Upon leaving the service in 1919, he was appointed director of music at the School of Fine Arts at State University of Iowa in Iowa City, where he remained for the rest of his life, combining duties as teacher with those of conducting its symphony orchestra in regular seasonal concerts and its chorus. On several leaves of absence he could fill guest appointments: as lecturer at the University of California at Berkeley during the summers of 1926 and 1929 and at the University of California in Los Angeles in 1927; as director of extension at the Juilliard School of Music in New York (1927–28); and as conductor of the American Orchestral Society in New York during the spring of 1929. He married Gladys Elisabeth Chamberlain on December 26, 1919; they were divorced ten years later. On July 21, 1934, he was married a second time, to Mildred Ethel Wright.

The symphony was the medium in which Clapp was most creative as well as prolific, producing twelve such works. The Symphony no. 3 in E-flat major (1916–17) and the Symphony no. 7 in A major (1927–29) were first heard at concerts of the Boston Symphony with the composer conducting—the third, on April 6, 1917, and the seventh, on March 22, 1931. Symphony no. 5 in D major (1926) was given its first performance in Iowa City on July 26, 1944, at a concert commemorating Clapp's twenty-fifth anniversary at the State University of Iowa. Symphony no. 6 in B major (1927–28), subtitled *Golden Gate* (first heard on June 5, 1961, in San Jose, Calif.), is a musical description of sea, sky, and night around San Francisco and the roar and clash of heavy traffic in its streets. The New York Philharmonic under Dimitri Mitropoulos premiered the Symphony no. 8 in C major on February 7, 1952. Symphony no. 9 in E-flat minor, subtitled *The Pioneers*, was commissioned for the Chicago World's Fair in 1933 and introduced in Iowa City on July 16, 1939; it was inspired, as Clapp explained, by "those early settlers who in the face of hardships persisted in pushing on into the unknown until they had conquered a continent." Symphony no. 10 in F major (1935–37), subtitled *Heroic*, was first given in Iowa City on May 23, 1951, the composer conducting.

Clapp produced many shorter works for orchestra, the most famous of which is the *Overture to a Comedy* (1937) which the composer once described as a "chatty trifle to entertain and possibly to amuse." He explained further; "In writing it I had no particular comedy in mind, though characters, scenes, and situatons from diverse sources suggested this and that element in the piece." It was given its first performance on December 28, 1940, by the Cleveland Philharmonic Orchestra under F. Karl Grossman. Within the next few years it was also performed by the St. Louis Symphony under Vladimir Golschmann, the Minneapolis Symphony under Mitropoulos and the New York Philharmonic, again under Mitropoulos.

Outside the field of orchestral music, Clapp's most ambitious works were *A Chant of Darkness*, a cantata for chorus and orchestra (1924; Iowa City, Iowa, April 16, 1935), on a text by Helen Keller, and two operas—*The Taming of the Shrew*, based on Shakespeare (1948) and *The Flaming Brand*, based on the John Brown story—neither of which has been produced.

From the Bruckner Society, Clapp received the Bruckner Medal of Honor in 1940 and the Mahler Medal of Honor in 1942.

THE COMPOSER SPEAKS: As a composer I find myself unable to commit myself to an exclusive theory, program or "ism," and unable to advise others to do so. A composer must study and practice to use and control his tools with as fine workmanship as he can attain, but apparently his best if not his only chance of composing anything of durable worth is to express his own musical ideas as honestly and as clearly as he can. If his ideas are novel, they may at first attract or repel; if on the other hand, he shares some of his ideas with other composers, he may be disparaged as "eclectic" by people who carelessly—or carefully—ignore that Bach and Wagner are the most eclectic of all. Furthermore, the probability that he is no Bach or Wagner must not intimidate him into supposing that any course of treatment in even the elite musical beauty parlor can raise his "ceiling," though it may lower it. He had better write as well as he can the kind of music which he really wants to write; then he may even manage to communicate it.

PRINCIPAL WORKS: 12 symphonies (1908–44).

Norge, tone poem for orchestra (1908, revised 1919); String Quartet in C minor (1909, revised 1924, 1936); *A Song of Youth*, tone poem for orchestra (1910, revised 1935); *Dramatic Poem*, for orchestra with solo trombone (1912, revised 1940); *Summer*, orchestral prelude (1912, revised 1918, 1925); Concerto in B minor, for two pianos and orchestra (1922, revised 1936, 1941); *A Chant of Darkness*, cantata for chorus and orchestra (1924, revised 1929, 1932, 1933); Violin Sonata (1929); *An Academic Diversion*, for chamber orchestra (1931); *Overture to a Comedy*, for orchestra (1933, revised 1937); Suite in E-flat, for brass sextet (1937); Fantasy on an Old Plain Chant, for orchestra with solo cello (1938, revised 1939); Suite, for trombone quartet (1939); *Prologue to a Tragedy*, for orchestra (1939); *Fanfare*

Prelude, for brass choir (1940); *A Hill Rhapsody*, tone poem for orchestra (1945); *The Taming of the Shrew*, opera (1948); *The Flaming Brand*, opera (1949–53).

BIBLIOGRAPHY: Ewen, David, *American Composers Today* (N.Y., 1949); Holcomb, D.R., "Philip Greeley Clapp: His Contribution to the Music of America" (doctoral thesis, Iowa City, Ia., 1972); Howard, John Tasker, *Our American Music* (N.Y., 1946); *Des Moines Register*, May 9, 1948; *Who's Who in America, 1952–53*.

Clarke, Henry Leland, b. Dover, N.H., March 9, 1907.

He has individualized many of his compositions through the invention of special techniques for which a new terminology had to be devised. Other works, inspired by great literature, reveal an exceptional gift for translating words into musical sounds.

The son of a Unitarian minister and a mother who was a college preparatory teacher, Henry received his first music instruction at the piano at the age of four from Louis Hathaway in Montpelier, Vt. The family settled in Saco, Maine, two years later. There, from 1913 to 1924, Henry studied the piano with Ruth Olive Roberts. Encouraged and directed by his teacher, he wrote his first piece of music when he was eight, "Boys and Girls Come Out to Play." In 1917 he completed *Marching As to War*, for violin, piano and drum, inspired by America's entry into World War I. While attending elementary schools (1916–19) and Thornton Academy (1919–24), in Saco, he played the violin in the school orchestra, studying the organ privately with Ruth Olive Roberts and the violin and viola with Bertha L. Nichols.

One of his compositions, *Dance of the Mah Jongg Pieces*, for piano (1923), already revealed an interest in innovative techniques with a device named "intervalescent counterpoint." In the movement "The Winds." one voice was in semitones and another in whole tones. This piano suite reflects the interest of the times in jazz by being marked "tempo di jazz cactico."

At Harvard University, which he entered in 1924, he took music courses with Walter Raymond Spalding, Edward Burlingame Hill, and A. T. Davison; played the viola in the college orchestra; and sang in the choir and glee club with the University Double Quartet. Upon receiving his bachelor of arts degree, *cum laude*, in 1928 and his master of arts degree a year later, he spent two years in Europe on a John Harvard Traveling Fellowship, a pupil in composition of Nadia Boulanger at the École Normale de Musique in Paris. Returning to Harvard for further postgraduate work, he continued to study composition with Gustav Holst while doing some private tutoring.

From 1932 to 1936 Clarke worked as an assistant in the music division of the New York Public Library, and in 1936 he received a grant from the American Council of Learned Societies. At this time (1934) he studied composition privately with Hans Weisse and Hanns Eisler. His *Danza de la muerte*, for oboe and piano (1937), was dedicated to the memory of the Americans who died fighting fascism in Spain. This Spanish dance, with choreography by José Limón, was mounted at the Bennington School of the Dance in Vermont on August 13, 1937. It was revised with a new afterdance as *Danza de la vida* (1975), produced by the Choreographic Workshop of the University of Washington in St. Louis, choreography by Marion Anderson, on May 26, 1976.

In 1936, Clarke initiated a long and eventful career in music education by serving for two years as a teaching fellow at Bennington College in Vermont, and for four years after that (1938–42) as chairman of the graduate faculty at Westminster Choir College in Princeton, N.J. World War II brought a brief interruption to his teaching activities as in 1944 he served in the U.S. Signal Corps. Then, after receiving his doctorate in music at Harvard in 1947, he returned to the academic world as teacher by serving as lecturer at the University of California in Los Angeles (1947–48), assistant professor of music at Vassar College in Poughkeepsie, N.Y. (1948–49), associate professor of music (1949–58), full professor 1975–77) and professor emeritus (1977) at the University of Washington in Seattle. He was a summer visiting professor at Boston University (1949), Harvard University (1956), University of California in Los Angeles (1962), and Columbia University in New York (1963). In 1946 he was given the Washington Music Educators Award.

Several of his most important compositions in the 1950s for the voice provide testimony to his understanding of vocal problems and his skill in declamation of words, choral sonority, and in finding a just relationship between words and music and voice and accompaniment. His *Gloria in the Five Official Languages of the United Nations* was premiered by the choir of the First Unitarian Church of Los Angeles, Earl Robinson conducting, on January 21, 1951. The orchestral version was performed by the Roger Wagner Chorale and members of the Los Angeles Philharmonic Orchestra, conducted by Roger Wagner, at the United Nations Tenth Anniversary Concert, at the University of California in Los Angeles on October 15, 1955. For the dedication ceremonies of the Alfred Hertz Memorial Hall of Music at the University of California in Berkeley on May 9, 1958, he contributed one of his most frequently heard and admired choral works, *No Man Is an Island*, a setting of John Donne's text for men's chorus, piano or band (1951). A one-act chamber opera, *The Loafer and the Loaf* (1953), the text a word-for-word setting of Evelyn Sharp's play, was directed by Jan Popper at the University of California in Los Angeles on

May 1, 1956. Poems by Genevieve Taggard provided the text for *Primavera*, for women's chorus, string quartet, and choreography (1953), and *Love-in-the-World*, for tenor, women's voices, and piano (1953), both first performed on December 5, 1954, by the Radcliffe Chorale Society in Cambridge, Mass. In the latter, in addition to Taggard's poem, the tenor soloist continually repeats a line from Shakespeare: "It looks on tempests and is never shaken."

In instrumental compositions of the 1950s, the innovator developed a method called lipophony, in which certain sounds were systematically omitted. *Monograph,* for orchestra (1952; Los Angeles, May 8, 1955), used only the notes C, D-sharp, E, F, G and A-flat. In *Six Characters,* for piano (1954; Los Angeles, March 22, 1957), the first movement was confined to one pitch class and the second movement to two, and so on. In String Quartet no. 3 (1958; Tucson, Ariz., January 9, 1959) semitones were excluded from both the melodic and harmonic lines.

Subsequent experiments include "word tones," "chain quotations," "homing melody," "transmutation," and "terza rima." In word tones, when any word recurs in a text it is assigned the same pitch in the same octave (little words included). This device appears most notably in Clarke's full-length opera *Lysistrata* (1970), libretto by Janet Stevenson based on the Greek tragedy of Aristophanes. Here word tones are used throughout, except for a few tunes. In chain quotations (for example, *Concatenata,* for French horn and woodwind quartet, written in 1969 and first performed on April 18, 1973, in Seattle, Wash.) the last note of one familiar phrase becomes the first note of the next one. In "homing melody" (as in "Let Me Go Wher'er I Will," for voice and piano, written in 1976 to a text by Emerson) every phrase ends on the same tone (the tonic) with no half-cadence of any kind. *Give and Take*, for two keyboards (1977; British Columbia, November 19, 1977), is an example of Clarke's use of transmutation, in which one ostinato takes over another a measure at a time. Terza rima involves the principles of tercets (ABA, BCB, etc.) applied to individual notes and phrases, a method found in *Terza rima,* for two keyboards (1978; Old Deerfield, Mass., September 4, 1978).

In the 1970s, Clarke also produced notable vocal and choral works that are not experimental. He remembered the tenth anniversary of the first draft card "turn-in" by setting Archibald MacLeish's *The Young Dead Soldiers* (1977), for chorus, introduced in Boston on October 18, 1977, at the Arlington Street Church. "To See the Earth," for bass and piano (1973), once again to a text by Archibald MacLeish, was written for the tercentenary of Old Deerfield in Massachusetts, where it was given its first performance on June 17, 1973. For the commemoration of the American bicentennial he wrote *These Are the Times That Try Men's Souls*, text by Tom Paine, its initial hearing coming at a bicentennial concert at the Kennedy Center for the Performing Arts in Washington, D.C., on September 13, 1976.

In April 1966, Clarke attended in Athens the first Hellenic Week of Contemporary Music promoted by the International Society for Contemporary Music (Greek section) and in July 1977 he participated in the Ninth International Conference of the International Society for Music Education in Moscow.

Clarke married Julia Newbold Keasbey, a nursery-school teacher, in Morristown, N.J., on June 24, 1937. A daughter died in infancy.

THE COMPOSER SPEAKS: My development as a composer has been relatively unaffected by changes in either academic or popular fashion. Within a basically tonal framework the music goes its own way in terms of modality and harmony. Line and, where appropriate, lyricism outweigh the vertical aspects of composition. Fresh procedures arise as alternatives to regular figuration, sequential passages, and overexpected harmonic progressions. When words are used, the music as a rule serves as handmaiden to the rhythms, inflections and intentions of the text. My need to communicate beyond a small circle of specially initiated listeners precludes straying too far from the common language of music. My objective of communication and celebration favors composing for particular occasions, composing what may be distinguished as "celebratory music."

PRINCIPAL WORKS: Gloria, for chorus and orchestra (1950); *No Man Is an Island*, for men's chorus, piano or band (1951); *Monograph*, for orchestra (1952); *Primavera*, for women's chorus and string quartet (1953); *The Loafer and the Loaf*, one-act chamber opera (1953); *Love-in-the-World*, for tenor, women's voices and piano (1953); *Six Characters*, for piano (1954); Nocturne, for viola and piano (1955); *Saraband for the Golden Goose*, for woodwind quintet or orchestra (1957); String Quartet no. 3 (1958); *Points West*, for wind and percussion (1960); *Encounter*, for viola and orchestra (1961); *Four Elements*, for voice and cello (1962); *A Game That Two Can Play*, for flute and clarinet (1966); *Lysistrata*, opera (1970); *Concatenata*, for French horn and woodwind quartet (1969); *Kyrie for All Men*, for chorus (1971); *Look Up and Not Down*, for chorus (1973); *Danza de la vida*, for oboe and piano (1975); *Mass for All Souls*, for chorus (1975); *These Are the Times That Try Men's Souls*, for chorus and piano (1976); "Let Me Go Wher'er I Will," for voice and piano (1976); *The Young Dead Soldiers*, for chorus (1977); *Revelation Is Not Sealed*, for two voices and organ (1977); *Give and Take*, for two keyboards (1978); *Terza rima*, for two keyboards (1978); *The Bounty of Athena*, for chorus (1978); *The Spring*, for chorus (1978); *Opposites*, for voice and cello or viola (1979).

BIBLIOGRAPHY: DCM; *American Composers Alliance Bulletin*, vol. 9, no. 3, 1960; *Who's Who in America, 1980–81.*

Cole, Rossetter Gleason, b. Clyde, Mich., February 5, 1866; d. Lake Bluff, Ill., May 18, 1952.

The composer of 125 compositions, Cole was held in highest esteem in Chicago, where he lived for half a century. He was most famous for some of his choral works, compositions for narrator and orchestra, and organ pieces.

He traces his ancestry back to the 17th century. On his paternal side, John Cole had come to Connecticut from England in or about 1710, while on his maternal side he is descended from Thomas Gleason, who came to Massachusetts from Sulgrave, England, in 1651. Both of Rossetter Cole's parents loved music, the father combining business with teaching music in a small college. When the father died in 1872, the Coles move to Ann Arbor, Mich., to take advantage of its superior educational facilities. While attending high school there, Cole studied harmony with Francis L. York and sang in the Methodist church choir. Upon graduating from high school in 1884 he entered the University of Michigan expecting to become a civil engineer. In his sophomore year he shifted to music by selecting all the courses in musical theory offered by Calvin B. Cady. Through his college years, Cole served as chapel organist and leader of the University Glee Club, which toured the Middle West each year; he also filled the post of organist in local Methodist and Presbyterian churches. During his senior year, as part of his composition course, he wrote a large-scale composition, the lyrical cantata *The Passing of Summer* (1887–88), which was performed on the evening of his graduation by the University Music Society, the first time such a thing had happened at that university.

After graduating from the university with a bachelor of philosophy degree in 1888, Cole spent two years teaching English, German, and Latin in high schools in Ann Arbor. Then, determined to develop himself into a musician, he left for Germany in 1890. In Berlin he met and impressed Joseph Joachim, who advised him to compete for a three-year scholarship at the Royal Master School for Composition. Winning that scholarship enabled Cole to spend two years (1890–92) studying composition with Max Bruch, conducting and score reading with Gustav Kogel, and organ with Wilhelm Middelschulte. Financial problems having made it impossible for him to take advantage of the third year of his scholarship, he returned to the United States in August 1892. Among his compositions in Berlin were the Sonata in D major, for violin and piano (1891), inspired by the composer's visit to the Wartburg castle in Eisenach; the first performance was given by Thomas Spiering in Chicago on April 21, 1898.

Between 1892 and 1894, Cole was director of the School of Music as well as professor at Ripon (Wisconsin) College, and from 1894 to 1901 he was professor of music at Grinnell (Iowa) College. After 1901, with the exception of two years (1907–9) spent in Madison, Wis., as professor of music and director of the School of Music at the University of Wisconsin, Cole lived in Chicago. For many years (1902–7, and from 1909 on) he taught composition privately. From 1915 on he was affiliated with the Cosmopolitan School of Music in Chicago, becoming dean in 1935. Summers between 1908 and 1939 were spent in New York as professor of music at the summer sessions at Columbia University. From 1893 to 1907 Cole was coeditor of the journal *Good Music* with his wife, the former Fannie Louise Gwinner, a professional pianist, whom he married on August 6, 1896.

Cole's first successes as composer came with two compositions for narrator and orchestra utilizing Longfellow's poems as texts: *Hiawatha's Wooing* (1904) and *King Robert of Sicily* (1906). The latter was performed more than five hundred times by David Bispham. *Ballade*, for cello and orchestra (1906), was well received when introduced by the Minneapolis Symphony under Emil Oberhoffer on March 21, 1909, as was the *Symphonic Prelude* (1914) which received its premiere on March 11, 1915, performed by Carlo Fischer as soloist with the Chicago Symphony under Frederick Stock. The *Symphonic Prelude* had originated in 1912 as *Fantaisie symphonique*, for organ, a version performed by numerous organists. The orchestral overture *Pioneer* was written in 1918 at the request of Frederick Stock to commemorate the centennial of the state of Illinois, and was dedicated to Abraham Lincoln. The Chicago Symphony under Stock performed it on March 14, 1919. "This music," the composer explained, "is programmatic only to the extent that it is pervaded by a more or less festival atmosphere . . . and that its material is drawn largely from certain characteristic qualities and typical of the western pioneer-straightforwardness, sincerity, rugged courage and above all a simple faith and an unconquerable optimism." *Heroic Piece,* for orchestra (1938), had started out in 1923 as a work for orchestra and organ but then was revised for orchestra alone. In its original version it was heard at a concert of the Chicago Symphony under Stock on February 11, 1924; the later version was performed on May 14, 1939, by the Illinois Symphony under Izler Solomon.

Two of Cole's most ambitious works were the "pilgrim's ode," *The Rock of Liberty* (1919–20), and the opera *The Maypole Lovers* (1919–31). *The Rock of Liberty* (text by Abbie Farwell Brown) was written on a commission from the publishing house of Arthur P. Schmidt to celebrate the tercentenary of the landing of the Pilgrims at Plymouth Rock, its first performance taking place in Madison, Wis., on December 7, 1920. During the 1920–21 season it was performed twelve times by major choral societies and many times more by smaller choral groups. The

Chicago Apollo Musical Club presented it at its golden jubilee festival in May 1922.

Cole's only opera, *The Maypole Lovers*, a romantic work set in colonial Massachusetts, with libretto by Carty Ranck, was never produced, though it did receive the David Bispham Medal from the Society for American Opera. But a three-movement suite derived from its score was performed by the Chicago Symphony under Frederick Stock on January 9, 1936.

Cole's music for the organ has been represented on numerous organ programs through the years. The *Fantaisie symphonique* (which later became the orchestral *Symphonic Prelude*) was the one performed most often. Also popular with virtuoso organists were: *Meditation,* op. 29, Rhapsody, op. 30, *A Song of Consolation,* op. 34, no. 1, *A Song of Gratitude,* op. 34, no. 2, *Hymnus,* op. 38, no. 1, and *Summer Fancies,* op. 38, no. 2, all of which were written between 1914 and 1925. Of his forty or so art songs for voice and piano, the most popular have been the three found in op. 37 (1922): "Lilacs," "Love's Invocation," and "Halcyon Days."

Though Cole's music has one foot in the 19th century—in its uninhibited romanticism, warm and pleasing lyricism, and sincerely felt emotion—the other foot is in the twentieth century, in its freedom of modulations and from ordinary key limitations, bold harmonic language, and occasional use of cacophony.

Cole served three terms as president of the Music Teachers National Association (1903, 1909, 1910), four terms as dean of the Illinois Chapter of the American Guild of Organists (1912–14, 1929–31), and two terms as president of the Society of American Musicians (1939–41). In 1913, the University of Michigan conferred on him an honorary master of arts degree and in 1934 he received an honorary doctorate from Grinnell College in Iowa. Cole was editor of *Choral and Church Music* (Chicago, 1917).

THE COMPOSER SPEAKS: I have always held the same viewpoint in composition, namely, to make my music a sincere and adequate expression of whatever poetic or imaginative idea or situation may be struggling in my mind for expression. I have never tried to impose upon its expression this or that style as such. My mind has always been open, I think, to the great changes in musical idioms that have appeared since I began and I have been influenced unconsciously by some of these changes, but I have never tried to be "modern" for its own sake nor to adopt any "ism" as such.

PRINCIPAL WORKS: 2 violin sonatas (1891, 1917).
The Passing of Summer, lyrical cantata for vocal soloists, chorus and orchestra (1887–88); *Hiawatha's Wooing,* for narrator and orchestra (1904); *King Robert of Sicily,* for narrator and orchestra, also for narrator and string quartet (1906); *Ballade,* for cello

and orchestra (1906); Rhapsody, for organ (1914, orchestrated 1942); *Fantaisie symphonique*, for organ (1912; orchestrated as *Symphonic Prelude*, 1914); *Legend*, for piano (1916); *The Broken Troth*, cantata for women's voices (1916); *Pioneer*, concert overture for orchestra (1918); *The Maypole Lovers*, opera (1919–31); *The Rock of Liberty*, ode for solo voices, chorus, and orchestra (1920); Three Songs, for voice and piano (1922); *Heroic Piece*, for organ and orchestra (1923; revised in 1938 for orchestra alone).

BIBLIOGRAPHY: Elson, Louis Charles, *History of American Music* (N.Y., 1904); Ewen, David, *American Composers Today* (N.Y., 1949); Howard, John Tasker, *Our Contemporary Composers* (N.Y., 1941); *Who's Who in America, 1950–51*.

Colgrass, Michael Charles, b. Chicago, April 22, 1932.

Colgrass, who was awarded the Pulitzer Prize in music in 1978, has evolved from the complexities of his early percussion and twelve-tone music to tonal, more logical, and more communicable compositions.

Colgrass became fascinated with the drums in childhood when he heard Ray Bauduc, the jazz drummer, perform. Colgrass was ten when he acquired his first set of drums, paid for with fees he earned by caddying at a golf course. Without instruction, he performed drum solos in student programs in public schools, and when he was twelve he formed and played in a jazz band. Jazz continued to be a potent influence upon his early development, particularly that of Charlie ("Bird") Parker and Dizzy Gillespie.

After graduating from Riverside-Brookfield High School in Chicago in 1950, Colgrass entered the University of Illinois in Urbana, where he received his first formal musical instruction: percussion with Paul Price and composition with Eugene Weigel. He also studied composition with Lukas Foss at the Berkshire Music Center at Tanglewood, Mass., and, during the summer of 1953, with Darius Milhaud at Aspen. He played the percussion in the school orchestra of the Berkshire Music Center during the summers of 1952 and 1954.

The necessity to expand the repertoire of percussion music was the stimulus sending him to write his first compositions, all of them chamber music works in which the percussion was predominant. The earliest of these was written while he attended the University of Illinois and performed there. First came *Three Brothers*, for nine percussion (1950–51), followed in 1953 by Percussion Music and Concertino for Timpani and Brass (1953) and in 1954 by *Chamber Music*, for four drums and string quintet. Up to the 1960s he continued to concentrate primarily on percussion music, arriving at a virtuosity in complex

rhythmic and metric structures and in percussion sonorities. One of these compositions, Variations for Four Drums and Viola, was introduced in a New York City café in 1957 with the composer playing the percussion and Emanuel Vardi as violist.

Between 1954 and 1956, Colgrass served in the U.S. Army, performing the percussion in the Seventh Army Symphony Orchestra in Germany. Returning to the United States, he received his bachelor of music degree at the University of Illinois in 1956. Later that year he came to New York, earning his living there for the next decade by playing percussion instruments with dance groups, opera orchestras, and ensembles specializing in new music, also for films, recordings, and in pit orchestras for Broadway musicals and ballets. Studying composition privately with Wallingford Riegger (1958–59) and Ben Weber (1959 and 1962) made him temporarily a confirmed twelve-tone composer. In that idiom he wrote Rhapsody, for clarinet, violin, and piano (1963)—introduced by Arthur Bloom, clarinetist (who had comissioned the work) in February 1963—and *Rhapsodic Fantasy*, for fifteen drums and orchestra, which received its premiere in Copenhagen in October 1965 by the Danish Radio Orchestra conducted by Tamas Vetö with the composer as soloist.

A strange, traumatic experience compelled him to reassess his life and creative values in the mid-1960s. He had just performed at Carnegie Hall and was walking along Fifty-seventh Street when he was suddenly seized by a lapse of memory and could not recall if he had just given a concert or was about to give one. Only the fact that he was walking *away* from Carnegie Hall rather than *toward* it suggested to him that the concert was over. This experience convinced him that he had been doing too many things in music too much of the time, that he had been in a constant state of motion, and that he must henceforth devote himself more to composition. He also came to the conclusion that he had to seek a new direction in his music, away from the twelve-tone system and the intellectualizing of music, away from music slanted solely for avant-garde audiences. He felt he should return to tonality and melody, to the more formal and traditional compositional practices preceding Schoenberg. Most of all, he felt the compulsion to establish contact with a public larger than an elite few. He had been, as he put it, in an "abyss" out of which he had to climb.

In 1965–66 he wrote *As Quiet As*, a suite for orchestra on a commission from the Fromm Music Foundation for the Berkshire Music Center in Tanglewood, where Gunther Schuller conducted its premiere on August 18, 1966. Its text was made up of seven answers to questions posed by a fourth-grade schoolteacher to her children to complete a sentence beginning "let's be as quiet as . . ." The answers were compiled by Constance Fauci in the *New York Times*. Colgrass's music had charm, wit, and a delicate imagination. Two dream sequences quoted a theme from a Beethoven sonatina which then was subjected to adaptations in the style of composers ranging from Haydn to Stravinsky, Webern, and Count Basie. "It is as if one were taking a fleeting glance at music history moving through time," Colgrass said. This composition was the first to bring Colgrass into the limelight, having been performed by virtually all major American orchestras, including the Bostom Symphony under Erich Leinsdorf, who recorded it for RCA.

Having written music about children, Colgrass went on to create a multimedia composition about a child prodigy who is protected by an insurance policy from his dream of success. Entitled *Virgil's Dream*, it was written for four actor-singer-dancers and four instrumentalists, and it drew its overall impact as much from theater and dance as from the music, First produced in Brighton, England, in April 1967, *Virgil's Dream* was soon after that performed throughout the United States.

After marrying Ulla Damgaard Rasmussen on November 25, 1968, Colgrass went to Europe on a Rockefeller grant to study theater arts, including gymnastics, fencing, Yoga, mime, ballet and commedia dell'arte. (He later used this training to give sessions in acting, dance, singing, mime and composing in the United States to high school students, teachers, artists, and laymen and, in 1971, in Fort Wayne, Ind., while he was composer-in-residence with the Fort Wayne Philharmonic.)

In 1968, on a commission from the Boston Symphony Youth Concerts for a composition to be performed by a teenage chorus for a young audience, Colgrass wrote *The Earth's a Baked Apple* to his own poems of American life as seen and reported by a youngster. Once again on commission, this time from the Chamber Music Society of Lincoln Center in New York (their first ever), he wrote *New People* (1969), a setting of his own seven poems for soprano, viola, and piano, which Shirley Verrett helped to introduce on October 17, 1969, in New York. *Image of Man* (1974), to the composer's own ironic text about life on this planet, was written for the opening of a new opera house in Spokane, Wash., during Expo '74, the first performance taking place on May 1, 1974. The unusual scoring called for a car horn, sleigh bells, and various kitchenware together with more traditional instruments.

The year of 1976 brought Colgrass to the forefront of America's significant composers with a succession of important premieres. *Concertmasters* (1975), for three violins and orchestra, was commissioned by the Detroit Symphony, which introduced it on January 29, 1976, with Aldo Ceccato conducting. This work traced the history of the concerto from the baroque era through romanticiam, impressionism, and expressionism, with all three violins required at different times to play in a romantic, impressionistic, or avant-garde idiom. On February 17, 1976, in New York, Ronald Thomas performed *Wolf*, for unaccompanied cello. "Wolf" was the name of an imaginary American-Indian; the music described his various activities (hunting and being hunted, meditating, singing, talking to plants, etc.). *Theater of the Universe* (1975) was a witty, satiric but at times also melancholy work for five vocal soloists, chorus and orchestra (text by the composer) on the subject of "the alienation of human feelings in a fast-changing world," in Colgrass's own words. It was given its first hearing on March 10, 1976, by the Minnesota Orchestra and the Bach Chorus conducted by Stanislaw Skrowaczewski. *Best Wishes, U.S.A.* (commissioned by several eastern orchestras and the National Endowment for the Arts to commemorate the American bicentennial) recruited the services of a black chorus and a white one, a jazz band and an orchestra, folk instruments and solo voices. Its text (mainly by Colgrass) provided a panoramic view of America's social and musical history. Though the music is entirely Colgrass's own, the styles of black-influenced pop tunes and cowboy songs, modern American folk songs and the music of the American Indian are easily identifiable. Its world premiere took place in Springfield, Mass., on March 30, 1976. In *Letter from Mozart*—performed on November 29, 1976, in New York with two conductors, Frederick Waldman and José Serebrier, directing the Musica Aeterna Orchestra—Colgrass paid tribute to Mozart by opening with a subject in the style of that master and then allowing it to develop and change à la Colgrass with suggestions of jazz, percussion music, aleatory music, and twelve-tone music on the way.

Colgrass received the Pulitzer Prize in music in 1978 for *Déjà vu* for percussion quartet and orchestra, commissioned by the New York Philharmonic, which introduced it under Erich Leinsdorf on October 20, 1977. Here the composer created four separate "concertos" for four specific percussion soloists, each soloist getting the kind of music Colgrass felt was best suited to his personality. Writing for the percussion with a variety and mastery that could come only from many years of experimentation and experience, Colgrass here produced music whose favorable impact on audiences proved immediate and inescapable, music which, for all of its discords and rhythmic complexities, always fell pleasantly on the ear.

Flashbacks (1978), described by the composer as "a musical play for five brass," was a fragmented tonal autobiography with the composer providing amusing and always entertaining glimpses into his professional life as a musician and his trip to India that helped make him a product of two cultures. Written for the Canadian Brass, *Flashbacks* was performed in New York City by that group on February 6, 1979.

Colgrass and his wife edit a monthly journal, *Music Magazine*, in Toronto, Canada, where they maintain a residence (a second one being in New York).

THE COMPOSER SPEAKS: I have never seen myself as a part of any group of composers either implicitly or officially. I've never really associated myself with any of my colleagues. I came from a world of music where you improvise, and have close contact with your audience, and the music is not intellectualized. I grew up listening to Charlie Parker and people like that. So my background is different from that of most composers. . . . What impressed me all along, and I got it from the Charlie Parkers and the Dizzy Gillespies, was that the great musicians of any given time communicated with an audience. So I started saying to myself, if you're really a good composer, then you should be able to contact people who are nonspecialists in your art.

PRINCIPAL WORKS: *Three Brothers,* for percussion (1950–51); Concertino, for timpani and brass (1953); Percussion Music (1953); *Chamber Music,* for four drums and string quintet (1954); *Chant,* for vibraphone and chorus (1954); *Chamber Music,* for percussion quintet (1955); *Inventions on a Motive,* for percussion quartet (1956); Variations, for four drums and viola (1957); *Fantasy Variations,* for percussion ensemble (1960); Divertimento, for eight drums, piano and strings (1960); *Seventeen,* for orchestra (1961); Wind Quintet (1962); *Light Spirit,* for flute, viola, guitar, and percussion (1963); Rhapsody, for clarinet, violin, and piano (1963); *Rhapsodic Fantasy,* for solo percussion and orchestra (1965); *As Quiet As,* for orchestra (1965–66); *Sea Shadow,* for orchestra (1966); *Virgil's Dream,* a multimedia production for four actor-singer-dancers and four instrumentalists (1967); *The Earth's a Baked Apple,* for children's chorus and orchestra (1968); *New People,* for mezzo-soprano, viola and piano (1969); *Nightingale, Inc.,* a satiric fantasy for musical theater (1970–71); *Auras,* for harp and orchestra (1973); *Image of Man,* for vocal soloists, chorus and orchestra (1974); *Concertmasters,* for three solo violins and orchestra (1975); *Theater of the Universe,* for vocal soloists, chorus and orchestra (1975); *Wolf,* for solo cello (1976); *Best Wishes, U.S.A.,* for black and white choruses, jazz band, orchestra, folk instruments and vocal soloists (1976); *Letter from Mozart,* for orchestra (1976); *Déjà vu,* for percussion quartet and orchestra (1977); *Flashbacks,* a "musical play for five brass" (1978); *The Tower,* a musical play for child performers (1978); *Mystery Flower of Spring,* for voice and piano (1978); *Delta,* for percussion, violin, clarinet and orchestra (1979); *Night of the Raccoon,* five songs for soprano and four players (1979); *Tales of Power,* for piano (1980).

BIBLIOGRAPHY: *High Fidelity/Musical America,* November 1978; *New York Times,* May 28, 1972; *Who's Who in America, 1980–81.*

Cone, Edward Toner, b. Greensboro, N.C., May 4, 1917.

Cone has favored a chromatic and dissonant idiom that remains basically tonal even when he occasionally employs twelve-tone methods.

Though neither of his parents was musical, Cone cannot remember a time when good music was not vital to him. While attending public school in Greensboro between 1924 and 1933, Cone studied piano privately with Florence Hunt. He also soon received some instruction in harmony and counterpoint. Upon graduating from public school he attended the Riverdale Country School in New York (1933–35), where he took advantage of its courses on music. At the same time he continued to study piano with Geoffrey Stoll (1933–38).

In 1935, Cone entered Princeton University, the year when music was added to the curriculum. At Princeton he studied composition with Roger Sessions (1935–42) and piano with Karl Ulrich Schnabel (1938–42). As an undergraduate, Cone was designated Latin salutatorian of his class. He later became the first at Princeton to have an original composition accepted as a senior thesis: a string quartet (1938–39) that was performed at Princeton in May 1939.

Upon receiving his bachelor of arts degree at Princeton in 1939, Cone went to Columbia University for advanced work in musicology for two years, mainly with Paul Henry Lang. While he was in New York several of his works were performed at concerts of the League of Composers, among these being a Violin Sonata (1939), some piano preludes (1939–40), and a Quintet for Clarinet and Strings (1940–41). In addition he wrote *Lotus Eaters,* a cantata for male chorus, vocal soloists, and orchestra based on Tennyson (1939, revised 1947); *Songs from Housman,* for soprano, alto, baritone, and piano (1941); *Dover Beach,* for baritone and piano or baritone and orchestra (1940–41, text by Matthew Arnold); and *Overture for the War* (1941–42), a nonprogrammatic composition for orchestra whose title was arrived at after the music had been written. Cone subsequently expressed the opinion that all this music was "merely an approximation" of what he was aspiring for, though he also did feel that the overture "most nearly approached my aim."

Cone returned to Princeton in 1941 as a part-time instructor in music and to fulfill requirements for a master of fine arts degree in 1942 (he was one of the first to get such a degree at Princeton). From the fall of 1942 until the winter of 1945–46 he served in the U.S. Army, assigned first to Special Services, and eventually to the Office of Strategic Services in the Mediterranean Theater of Operations. Occasionally, he played the piano with the British army's area orchestra.

Upon his release from army service, Cone became in 1945 one of the first recipients of the Woodrow

Wilson Fellowship at Princeton, serving as a part-time instructor in the music division. In 1946 he was commissioned by the university to write *Let Us Now Praise Famous Men*, for male chorus and organ (1946), text from Ecclesiastes. This was a commemorative anthem for chorus for the university's bicentennial celebration, and was introduced at Princeton on February 28, 1947.

In 1947, a year in which Cone received a Guggenheim Fellowship, he was appointed assistant professor of music at Princeton. He has remained at Princeton since then, becoming associate professor in 1952, full professor in 1960, and serving as acting chairman of the music department in 1955–56 and 1962–63. In 1964–65 he was the Old Dominion Fellow of the Council of Humanities at Princeton and since 1969 a continuing fellow of that council. During his second year as a faculty member at Princeton, (1947–48), Cone studied the piano privately with Eduard Steuermann.

In addition to his teaching commitments at Princeton, Cone has taught and lectured at the Salzburg Seminar in American Studies in Austria in 1953 and 1979, and lectured at Oxford, Leeds, and London in England during 1974, and through the years at Swarthmore College, Rutgers and Indiana universities, the University of Toronto, Peabody Conservatory, the Berkshire Music Center at Tanglewood, and Oberlin College Conservatory. In 1972 he was the Ernest Bloch Professor of Music at the University of California at Berkeley. In 1979 he was elected an Andrew D. White Professor-at-Large at Cornell University in Ithaca, N.Y. This did not conflict with his professorial duties at Princeton.

By the early 1950s, Cone had integrated his style and successfully assimilated that dissonant idiom that would henceforth serve his creative needs. His principal works in the 1950s were: *Elegy,* for orchestra (1953), commissioned by the Princeton Symphony Orchestra which, under Nicholas Harsanyi's direction, introduced it on April 27, 1954; a Symphony (1953); Prelude, Passacaglia, and Fugue, for piano (1957), which the composer himself introduced in New York on April 7, 1959; Nocturne and Rondo, for orchestra and piano (1957; Princeton, January 27, 1962); and Concerto for Violin and Small Orchestra (1959; Princeton, October 26, 1964). Later significant compositions include Music for Strings (1964; Princeton, June 27, 1964), String Sextet (1966; N.Y., February 24, 1975), Variations for Orchestra (1968), and Serenade for Flute and Strings (1975; N.Y., January 11, 1977).

From 1966 to 1972 Cone was an editor of *Perspectives of New Music.* He is the author of *Musical Forms and Musical Performances* (1968) and *The Composer's Voice* (1974) and coeditor, with Benjamin Boretz, of *Perspectives on Schoenberg and Stravinsky* (1968), *Perspectives on American Composers* (1971), *Perspectives on Contemporary Music Theory* (1972) and *Perspectives on Notation and Performance* (1975). *The Composer's Voice* received the Deems Taylor Award of the American Society of Composers, Authors, and Publishers (ASCAP) in 1975. Cone has served on the board of the League of Composers International Society for Contemporary Music and on the board of trustees of the Salzburg Seminar in American Studies. In 1973 the University of Rochester conferred on him an honorary doctorate in music.

THE COMPOSER SPEAKS: One used to hear a great deal of discussion about "systematic" as opposed to "intuitive" composers, of the superiority of one "system" over another, and so on. Fortunately, there seems to be less of that now; most of us realize that the important thing is the music itself, and not the system or nonsystem behind it. Less happily, though, much of the music written today sounds halfhearted—as if the composer himself were not wholly convinced of its value. There is one question that a composer ought always to ask of the music he is writing: Is this music that I want to hear and that I could not otherwise hear? My own most successful compositions have been written when I have kept this in mind.

PRINCIPAL WORKS: *Excursions*, for chorus and orchestra (1946): *Let Us Now Praise Famous Men*, for male chorus and organ (1946); *The Hollow Men*, for male chorus and wind (1950); Symphony (1953); *Elegy*, for orchestra (1953); Around the Year, for madrigal group and string quartet (1956); Prelude, Passacaglia, and Fugue, for piano (1957); Nocturne and Rondo, for piano and orchestra (1957); Concerto for Violin and Small Orchestra (1959); Piano Quintet (1960); *Four Songs from Mythical Story*, for voice and piano (1961); *Silent Noon*, for soprano and piano (1964); Music for Strings (1964); Fantasy, for two pianos (1965); *Stanzas*, for wind quintet (1965); String Sextet (1966); Variations, for orchestra (1968); *Philomela*, three nightingale songs for soprano and chamber group (1970); String Trio (1973); Serenade, for flute and strings (1975); Nine Lyrics from *In Memoriam*, for baritone and piano (1978).

BIBLIOGRAPHY: *DCM;* Ewen, David, *American Composers Today* (N.Y., 1949); Saminsky, Lazare, *Living Music of the Americas* (N.Y., 1949);

Converse, Frederick Shepherd, b. Newton, Mass., January 5, 1871; d. Westwood, Mass., June 8, 1940.

He was the first American composer to have a major choral work performed in Germany, and the first American composer to have an opera introduced at the Metropolitan Opera House.

Descending from New England ancestry, he was the youngest son of a dry-goods merchant. While attending public school in Newton, Converse received instruction on the piano from local teachers. When he entered Harvard University in 1889 it was with the intention of preparing himself for a business career. But his interest in music led him to take courses in composition with John Knowles Paine, and to write popular songs for and play the banjo in Hasty Pudding productions. While at Harvard, he wrote his first composition to see publication, a Sonata for Violin and Piano.

When he was graduated from Harvard in 1893 with highest honors, he joined a stock brokerage firm. Within six months he realized his professional future lay elsewhere. Having decided upon music as a career, he continued his studies with Carl Baermann and George Whitefield Chadwick (1894–96). After marrying Emma Cecil Tudor on June 6, 1894 (with whom in time he raised a family of seven children), he was encouraged by his young wife to go to Europe for additional music study. He did so in 1896, attending the Royal Academy of Music in Munich, where he studied composition with Josef Rheinberger. In 1897, his first concert overture for orchestra, *Youth*, was performed in Munich. When he graduated from the Academy in 1899, his Symphony in D minor (not numbered since he later discarded it) was performed at the graduation ceremonies on July 14, 1898.

He was back in Massachusetts in 1899, settling in Westwood, which remained his home for the rest of his life. He did some part-time farming, while developing his musical career. From 1899 to 1901 he taught harmony at the New England Conservatory. He was an instructor in composition at Harvard University from 1901 to 1907, an assistant professor from 1904 on. In 1907 he withdrew from teaching to concentrate on composition but one year later he accepted the post of vice-president of the Boston Opera Company, in which capacity he went to Europe to scout for singers.

During the first quarter of a century of his composing career, Converse was a child of German romanticism, using traditional classical structures as the mould in which to pour emotion, poetic thoughts, and sensitive moods through broad sweeping melodies, lush harmonies and fulsome orchestrations. For many years, his favorite media were tone poems or other short descriptive works for orchestra, or compositions for voice and orchestra or for chorus. The Boston Symphony, under Wilhelm Gericke, performed his two short works for orchestra inspired by Keats: *Festival of Pan*, "a romance" (1900) on December 21, 1900, and *Endymion's Narrative* (1901), a concert overture, on April 11, 1903. On May 8, 1903, the Boston Pops Orchestra introduced his *Indian Serenade*, for small orchestra (1902). Other successes came with *La belle dame sans merci*, a ballade for baritone and orchestra (1902), written for David Bispham, who performed it widely, and with one of Converse's most famous compositions, *The Mystic Trumpeter*, for orchestra (1903–4) based on Walt

Whitman, its world premiere given by the Philadelphia Orchestra under Fritz Scheel on March 4, 1905, after which it was frequently represented on symphony programs throughout the United States.

In 1905, Converse completed a one-act opera, *The Pipe of Desire*, with which his reputation as an American composer of primary importance was established. The libretto, by George Edward Burton, was a fairy tale about a musical pipe which had magical properties but which, when used for selfish aims, brings doom to the hero and heroine. When the opera was first produced—by the Boston Opera Company on January 31, 1906—H. T. Parker, the critic of the *Boston Transcript*, praised it for its "power of dramatic climax," its ability "to make the vivid, emphasizing, illuminating phrase in voice or orchestra in the poignant moment" and for its skill "in weaving of the voices, instruments, speech and action into a significant moving and musically beautiful whole." When *Pipe of Desire* was mounted by the Metropolitan Opera in New York on March 18, 1910, it became the first opera by an American composer produced by that company. For this opera Converse was awarded the David Bispham Medal by the American Opera Society.

Job was a dramatic poem for vocal soloists, chorus and orchestra (1907) whose premiere took place at the Worcester Festival in Massachusetts on October 2, 1907. When it was performed in Hamburg, Germany, on November 23, 1908, it became the first large-scale choral work by an American to receive a performance in Germany. At that concert, another work of Converse's was also heard: *Hagar in the Desert* (1908), for low voice and orchestra, sung by Ernestine Schumann-Heink.

During World War I, in 1917, Converse became a member of the Motor Corps of the Massachusetts State Guard. He was eventually promoted to the rank of captain, serving in the supply department of the Thirteenth Regiment. In 1918–19, still in uniform, he was also a member of a committee in charge of music for army training camps and the conductor of community choruses. At the invitation of the United States government he prepared a symphonic arrangement of *The Star-Spangled Banner* which was performed regularly by most of America's orchestras during the war period.

Converse returned to the academic life in 1919 by becoming head of the theory department of the New England Conservatory, where, from 1931 to 1938, he served as dean.

With his early symphony discarded, Converse numbered his Symphony in C minor (1920) as no. 1. This one and the Symphony no. 2 in E minor (1921) were performed by the Boston Symphony under Pierre Monteux on January 30, 1920, and April 21, 1922, respectively. The Boston Symphony under Monteux also premiered Converse's tone poem *Song of the Sea* (1923), inspired by Whitman, on April 18, 1924, while the Cleveland Orchestra under Nikolai

Sokoloff offered the first performance of *Elegiac Poem* (1926) on December 2, 1926.

By the middle 1920s, Converse had broken his ties to German romanticism by adopting a modern harmonic and rhythmic language which sidestepped textbook rules; on several occasions he now produced compositions of an American identity. One of these, a short work for orchestra, made news in 1927, more for the provocative and unusual program it was interpreting with literalness than for the quality of the music itself. This work was *Flivver Ten Million*, written in 1926 after Converse had read that the ten-millionth Model-T Ford had left the assembly line. Subtitling his composition "A Joyous Epic Inspired by the Familiar Legend, 'The Ten-Millionth-Ford Is Now Serving Its Owner,' " Converse went on to describe with wry humor and touches of satire one aspect of American life and experience. The composition began with dawn in Detroit with the city beginning to stir and the silence punctuated by sounds of factory whistles and noises. Now we get the "birth of the hero," who emerges from the welter ready for service and goes out into the world seeking adventure. The steel-framed hero meets romance, frolic, and tragedy through a collision. Shaken, but undaunted, this "Phoenix Americanus" proceeds on its way with renewed energy typical of the indomitable spirit of America. In his orchestration, the now-modern Converse introduces nonmusical sounds produced by a muted Ford horn, wind machine, factory whistle, and anvil. The Boston Symphony under Koussevitzky performed *Flivver Ten Million* on April 15, 1927. Proving a novelty that delighted audiences, the work was soon thereafter performed by many other orchestras.

Three later Converse works were also American in orientation. Festival scenes at a fiesta in Santa Barbara, Calif., were responsible for the writing of *California* (1928), which the Boston Symphony under Koussevitzky performed on April 6, 1928. *American Sketches* (1929) was a symphonic suite inspired by Carl Sandburg's *The American Songbag*, first presented by the Boston Symphony under Koussevitzky on February 8, 1935. *Haul Away, Joe* (1939) was a series of variations for small orchestra on a familiar American chantey.

Converse received an honorary doctorate from Boston University in 1933. Four years later he was elected a member of the American Academy of Arts and Letters. His last major work, the Symphony no. 6 (1938–39), was given its world premiere posthumously on November 7, 1940, by the Indianapolis Symphony Orchestra under Fabien Sevitzky.

One of Converse's daughters married the grandson of J. P. Morgan while another was married to the Boston banker Paul Codman Cabot.

PRINCIPAL WORKS: 6 symphonies (1898–1939); 2 string quartets (1902, 1904).

Festival of Pan, romance for orchestra (1900); *En-dymion's Narrative*, concert overture (1901); *Indian Serenade*, for small orchestra (1902); Concerto for Violin, Piano and Orchestra (1902); *La belle dame sans merci*, for baritone and orchestra (1902); *Euphrosyne*, concert overture (1903); *The Mystic Trumpeter*, for orchestra (1903–4); *The Pipe of Desire*, one-act opera (1905); *Jeanne d'Arc*, dramatic scenes for orchestra (1906); *Job*, dramatic poem for vocal soloists, chorus and orchestra (1907); *The Sacrifice*, opera (1911); *Ormazad*, tone poem for orchestra (1911); Violin Sonata (1912); *The Peace Pipe*, cantata for solo voices, chorus and orchestra (1914); *The Immigrants*, opera (1914); *Ave atque Vale*, for orchestra (1916); *Sinbad the Sailor*, opera (1917); *The Answer of the Stars*, cantata for solo voices, chorus and orchestra (1920); Fantasy, for piano and orchestra (1922); *Song of the Sea*, for orchestra (1923); *I Will Praise Thee O Lord*, for chorus (1924); *Elegiac Poem*, for orchestra (1926); *Flivver Ten Million*, "a joyous epic" for orchestra (1926); *California*, festival scenes for orchestra (1928); *American Sketches*, symphonic suite (1929); *The Flight of the Eagle*, for solo voices, chorus and orchestra (1930); Piano Trio (1931); *A Song at Evening*, for orchestra (1937); *Three Old-Fashioned Dances*, for chamber orchestra (1938); Rhapsody, for clarinet and orchestra (1938); *Haul Away, Joe*, variations for small orchestra (1939).

BIBLIOGRAPHY: Howard, John Tasker, *Our Contemporary Composers* (N.Y., 1941); *Harper's Weekly*, February 16, 1907; *Musical America* (obituary), June 1940; *New York Times (obituary)*, June 9, 1940.

Copland, Aaron, b. Brooklyn, N.Y., November 14, 1900.

Winner of a Pulitzer Prize in music, among numerous other prestigious awards, Copland has long been called "the dean of American Music." He wears the title well, for he has occupied a dominant position among American composers for half a century and during that time he has exerted a far-reaching influence on a generation of composers.

Though neither of his parents was musical, they saw to it that their first four children received some musical training. By the time Aaron was born (their fifth and last child) they decided that the money already spent on music had brought meager dividends and they had no intention of paying for any lessons for Aaron. The boy's persistence in wanting to study music broke down their resistance. When he was eleven, while attending public school, he began taking piano lessons with his sister. Two years later, hearing a recital by Paderewski convinced him more than ever that he wanted to study music seriously. A local teacher, Leopold Wolfson, then took over Copland's piano training. Later piano study took place privately with Victor Wittgenstein and Clarence Adler.

Copland was about fifteen, attending Boys' High School in Brooklyn, when "the idea of becoming a composer seems gradually to have dawned upon me." He tried at first to learn harmony through a correspondence course. Then, in the fall of 1917, on Wolfson's suggestion, Copland began to study harmony privately with Rubin Goldmark, who gave him a thorough, disciplined grounding. Goldmark was a musical conservative who looked with disdain upon the indiscretions of modern composers. "That was enough to whet any young man's appetite," Copland writes. "The fact that music was in some sense forbidden only increased its attractiveness." To get to know the "moderns" Copland began studying by himself the scores of Debussy, Ravel, and others, an experience that affected the kind of music he himself was now writing—some songs and piano pieces. Goldmark looked with disfavor upon Copland's attempt to write "modern" music. "The climax came when I brought for his critical approval a piano piece called *The Cat and the Mouse* (1920). He regretfully admitted that he had no criteria by which to judge such music."

When, in 1918, Copland was graduated from Boys' High School (where he found the music classes "a joke" and where he failed to participate in any of its musical activities) he decided his academic education had ended. From this point on he would concentrate exclusively on music. Learning from a musical journal that a music school was being organized for Americans in Fontainebleau, France, he sent in his application with such dispatch that he became the first student to be accepted. In Fontainebleau a course in composition with Paul Vidal proved unsatisfactory because Vidal, like Goldmark, was an ultraconservative. One day, sitting in on one of Nadia Boulanger's classes, Copland sensed that here was the kind of teacher he was looking for. That fall, he visited her at her apartment on rue Ballu in Paris, asked to be her pupil, and was accepted, becoming the first of many Americans to study with her. Copland stayed in Paris three years, profiting not only from Boulanger's teaching, which proved decisive in his early development, but also from the great amount of new music he could hear. He now became familiar with the works of Stravinsky, Schoenberg, Bartók, and Satie, profited from his personal associations with the members of the so-called French Six, and was stimulated by his friendship with Virgil Thomson and George Antheil. In Paris, a Copland composition was published for the first time, *The Cat and the Mouse*, issued by the distinguished firm of Durand. It proved an immediate success and continued to be heard at piano recitals for many years.

During these three years in Paris, Copland wrote several motets for unaccompanied voices, a Passacaglia for piano, and began his first venture with orchestral music, the score for a one-act ballet, *Grohg*.

Here he was adventurous in his use of rhythm, harmony, and structure. "The watchword in those days was 'originality' . . . and I suppose that I was no exception, despite my youth—or possibly because of it."

Copland returned to the United States in June 1924. He spent that summer playing the piano with a trio in a Pennsylvania resort, then, in the fall, opened a studio in New York to teach piano and composition. Not a single pupil showed up. But as a composer, Copland was beginning to make headway. In November 1924 some of his music had its first American hearing when he appeared as pianist at a concert of the League of Composers performing *The Cat and the Mouse* and the Passacaglia. He was also hard at work on a major composing assignment. Nadia Boulanger, planning to tour the United States as organist, had asked Copland to write for her a large work for organ and orchestra. To complete this assignment Copland wrote the Symphony for Organ and Orchestra (1924), which was introduced by the New York Symphony Society under Walter Damrosch, with Boulanger as soloist, on January 11, 1925. It was at this performance that Damrosch made a remark to his audience that was much publicized and quoted and contributed to making Copland's name known. "If a young man can write a piece like that at the age of twenty-three, in five years he will be ready to commit murder." (Commenting on this remark, Ernest Newman, then a visiting critic for the *New York Post*, recalled that the 16th-century-composer Gesualdo had actually gone from dissonance to murder.)

One month after the concert by the New York Symphony Society, Serge Koussevitzky conducted Copland's symphony with the Boston Symphony Orchestra. This was the beginning of a conductor-composer relationship that would go a long way toward bringing Copland to that high station in American music he would henceforth occupy.

Koussevitzky was not the only one to help advance Copland's composing career. Paul Rosenfeld, the eminent critic, found a patron (Alma Wertheim) ready to support Copland. With this help, and by receiving in 1925 the first music fellowship granted by the Guggenheim Foundation (extended for a second year in 1926), Copland was able to write his music without financial problems.

The League of Composers commissioned him to write a new orchestral work for a concert Koussevitzky planned giving at a league concert, this commission having come at Koussevitzky's urging. The new work Copland was planning was to be thoroughly American in style and spirit, a departure from his European-inspired symphony. To realize this Americanism, Copland decided to adopt the jazz idiom symphonically, much as Gershwin had recently done with such success with *Rhapsody in Blue*. Copland spent the summer of 1925 at the MacDowell Colony in Peterboro, N.H. (the first of many such summer visits), working on a five-movement orchestral suite he called *Music for the Theater*. This was a nonprogrammatic composition in which Copland tried to bring to his music some of the dramatic and atmospheric qualities of the theater. Jazz could be heard in the opening solo for the trumpet, in the frenetic rhythms of the second-movement "Dance" and in the blueslike lament in the trumpet in the fourth-movement "Burlesque." Before Koussevitzky conducted this work at a concert of the League of Composers on November 28, 1925, he introduced it in Boston with the Boston Symphony on November 20.

Copland followed *Music for the Theater* with the Concerto for Piano and Orchestra (1926), his second and last attempt to carry jazz into an ambitious symphonic structure. Serge Koussevitzky and the Boston Symphony, with the composer at the piano, premiered it in Boston on January 28, 1927, then brought it to New York on February 3. This concerto has been successfully performed on several occasions since 1964, when Leonard Bernstein and New York Philharmonic first revived it.

With this concerto Copland felt he had exhausted the artistic potential of jazz. He now progressed to a complex and vigorous style making full use of modern tonality, harmony, and rhythms as a replacement for simply stated melodies. Learning in 1929 of a competition for new American music promoted by RCA Victor, Copland labored on a *Symphonic Ode* for possible submission. But finding he could not complete it by the deadline, he hurriedly adapted three movements from his early ballet *Grohg* and called it *Dance Symphony*. It won a prize of $5,000 and was performed by the Philadelphia Orchestra under Leopold Stokowski on April 15, 1931. *Symphonic Ode* (1929) became one of the works with which the Boston Symphony celebrated its fiftieth anniversary when Koussevitzky conducted it on February 19, 1932.

The ode, as Copland has written, "marks the end of a certain period in my development as a composer. The works that follow it are no longer so grandly conceived. Piano Variations (1930; Saratoga, N.Y., April 30, 1932), the *Short Symphony* (1933; Mexico City, November 23, 1934) and the *Statements for Orchestra* (1934; N.Y., January 7, 1942) are more spare in sonority, more lean in texture." These works, however, remained sufficiently complex in harmonic and rhythmic idioms to make them difficult to comprehend at first hearing.

By the middle 1930s, Copland had become dissatisfied that his music was reaching only a small elite audience, that he was failing to communicate with the general music public. He felt that a greater simplicity in his writing was now called for, together with a more readily assimilable style, but without sacrificing sound artistic values. The first work to reach out to a wider listening audience was *El salón México*, for orchestra (1936), inspired by a visit to Mexico and the impressions made on Copland by one of its popular dance halls. Copland set out to write a Mexican work—a "kind of modified potpourri in which Mexican themes and their extensions are sometimes inextricably mixed for use of conciseness and coherence," as he put it—in which tourist Mexico comes to life. Popular Mexican tunes are quoted and elaborated upon, most significantly, "El mosco," and popular Mexican rhythms are used extensively. *El salón México* was introduced in Mexico City on August 27, 1937, with Carlos Chávez conducting the Orquesta Sinfonica de Mexico. Its first American performance followed on May 14, 1938, over the NBC radio network with Adrian Boult conducting the NBC Symphony. It has since been performed and recorded frequently, becoming one of Copland's best-known compositions.

Having used Mexican popular tunes in *El salón México*, Copland went on to draw his inspiration and materials from American folk sources. In his score for the ballet *Billy the Kid* (1938) familiar cowboy songs were quoted, and in *Rodeo* (1942), also a cowboy ballet, other familiar American folk tunes were borrowed. *Billy the Kid*, with choreography by Eugene Loring, was first produced on October 16, 1938, in Chicago, and *Rodeo*, with scenario and choreography by Agnes de Mille, on October 16, 1942, in New York in a production by the Ballet Russe de Monte Carlo. Orchestral suites from both scores have been successfully performed at symphony concerts.

In line with Copland's ambition to reach even larger audiences, is his *Gebrauchsmusik* (functional music) in the 1930s and 1940s. For high school children he wrote a play-opera, *The Second Hurricane* (1937; N.Y., April 2, 1937), and an orchestral piece, *An outdoor Overture* (1938; N.Y., December 16, 1938). For radio he composed *Music for Radio*, subtitled *Saga of the Prairie* (1937; CBS-Radio, July 25, 1937). For the motion picture screen he provided the scores for *The City* (1939), *Of Mice and Men* (1939), *Our Town* (1940), *The Red Pony* (1948), and *The Heiress* (1949), the last of these winning the Academy Award as the year's best original screen music. To the theater he contributed incidental music for *Five Kings* (1939) and *Quiet City* (1939).

In 1941, on an invitation of the Office of Inter-American Affairs headed by Nelson Rockefeller, Copland went to South America for several months to help promote the good-neighbor policy. While in Santiago, Chile, he completed writing the Piano Sonata (1941), a throwback to the more abstruse style of the late 1920s, which he himself introduced in Buenos Aires on October 21, 1941. But he had not abandoned folk and popular idioms. They are present in *Lincoln Portrait* (1942), which was commissioned by André Kostelanetz and which Kostelanetz introduced in Cincinnati on May 14, 1942. Using a text based on Lincoln's letters and speeches, Copland here quotes Stephen Foster's "De Camptown Races" and the folk ballad "Springfield Mountain." Folk elements are also present in the ballet *Appalachian Spring* (1944), the result of a commission from the Elizabeth Sprague Coolidge Foundation for Martha Graham. Martha Graham's scenario described a wedding among the Shakers in the Appalachian Mountain regions. Only one folk melody is quoted directly, "Simple Gifts," but all the rest of the material, though Copland's own, borrows stylistic elements of American mountain folk music, such as the brusque and rapidly changing rhythms and the open-fifth harmonies of country fiddlers. The ballet was mounted on October 30, 1944, in Washington, D.C., and has since become a classic in the modern-ballet repertoire. For his music Copland received the New York Music Critics Award in 1945. The symphonic suite Copland adapted from the ballet score for a large orchestra (first performance on October 4, 1945 by the New York Philharmonic under Artur Rodzinski) brought Copland the Pulitzer Prize in music and gave the concert world a composition that has won a permanent place in the contemporary symphonic repertoire.

There are no actual quotations of American folk music in Copland's Symphony no. 3 (1946), which Koussevitzky commissioned and introduced at a concert of the Boston Symphony on October 18, 1946. But, though all the music is of Copland's invention, there is no mistaking the folk identity of the brusque rhythms and the invigorating and rugged strength of its lyricism. Copland quoted himself in this score, once by employing a tonal device he had favored in *Appalachian Spring* and another time by recalling a subject he had previously used in *Fanfare for the Common Man* (1943; Cincinnati, March 12, 1943). The symphony brought Copland the Boston Symphony Award of Merit and the New York Critics Circle Award. It was one of the works Copland featured when he toured Latin America in 1947.

In 1948, Copland wrote the Concerto for Clarinet and String Orchestra for Benny Goodman (first performed in New York on November, 6, 1950, with Fritz Reiner conducting the NBC Symphony), in which a popular Brazilian melody is basic. And while in Copland's only full-length opera, *The Tender Land* (1954), quotations from any folk or popular sources are scrupulously avoided, the score retains a thoroughly American identity through the simulation of folk styles. With a libretto by Horace Everett set in the farmlands of the Midwest in the early 1930s, *The Tender Land* was produced by the New York City Opera on April 1, 1954, having been commissioned by Richard Rodgers and Oscar Hammerstein II. A revision of the opera was mounted at Oberlin Conservatory in Ohio in 1955, a version since revived elsewhere on several occasions.

Meanwhile Copland had begun to drift into a new creative direction: twelve-tone music. He first employed the technique in the Quartet for Piano and strings (1950; Washington, D.C., October 29, 1950). Among his later works in dodecaphonic style are: *Piano Fantasy* (1957; N.Y., October 29, 1957); *Connotations for Orchestra* (1962), written on commission from the New York Philharmonic for its first concert in its new auditorium in the Lincoln Center for the Performing Arts on September 23, 1962; and *Inscape*, for orchestra (1967), commissioned by the New York Philharmonic for its 125th anniversary but introduced by the Orchestra of the University of Michigan on September 13, 1967; the New York Philharmonic under Leonard Bernstein performed it in New York on October 20, 1967.

Since 1970, Copland's creative productivity has been reduced to a trickle, as he has intensified his activity as a conductor, a career begun in the 1940s in Latin America. In 1956 he made his American baton debut with the Chicago Symphony at Ravinia Park. In 1960 he was guest conductor of the Boston Symphony Orchestra when it paid its first visit to Japan, the Philippines and Australia, and that same year Copland led performances of several of his works in the Soviet Union. For over a decade, beginning with the mid-1960s, he appeared annually with the London Symphony Orchestra. In all he has conducted over one hundred major symphonic organizations in all parts of the world (except Africa and China), mainly in his own music but frequently also in the works of other composers.

As lecturer, writer, teacher, and member or founder of performing organizations, Copland has been indefatigable in promoting American music. He served as chairman of the executive board of directors of the League of Composers; was founder of the Copland-Sessions concerts, which he helped to direct from 1928 to 1931, and of the American Composers Alliance, of which he was the president for eight years; was director of the American Festivals of Contemporary Music at Yaddo in Saratoga, N.Y., and of both the Walter W. Naumburg Musical Foundation and the American Music Center; was a consultant of the Koussevitzky Music Foundation; and was affiliated with the Composers Forum and the United States section of the International Society of Contemporary Music. From 1940 to 1965 he was a member of the faculty of the Berkshire Music Center at Tanglewood, head of the composition department, and from 1957 to 1965 chairman of the faculty. He has taught composition at Harvard University and lectured at the New School for Social Research in New York.

Honors have been heaped upon him abundantly, above and beyond the Pulitzer Prize and the New York Music Critics Circle Awards already mentioned. In 1942 he was elected a member of the National Institute of Arts and Letters and in 1971 he was made president of the American Academy of Arts and Letters. He was awarded the Gold Medal for Music by the American Academy of Arts and Letters (1956), the Creative Arts Medal of Brandeis University in Waltham, Mass. (1960), the Edward MacDowell Medal (1961), the Henry Hadley Medal (1964), the Presidential Medal of Freedom from President Johnson (1964), the Henry Howland Memorial Prize by Yale University (1970), the Commander's Cross of Merit from the Federal Republic of Germany (1970), the Gold Baton from the American Symphony Orchestra League (1978), and the Kennedy Center Award for a "lifetime of significant contribution to American culture in the artistic arts" (1979). He has also been made an honorary member of the Accademia Santa Cecilia in Rome. Additionally, among the many honorary doctorates in music conferred on him were those from Princeton University, Brandeis University, Harvard University, New York University, Rutgers University, Brooklyn College (New York), the University of Portland (Oregon), Columbia University, the University of Rochester (N.Y.), Tulane University and York and Leeds universities in England. In celebration of his seventieth, seventy-fifth, and eightieth birthdays he was saluted with performances of his compositions throughout the United States with numerous commemorative articles in magazines and newspapers.

Copland is the author of *What to Listen for in Music* (1939), *Our New Music* (1941, revised as *The New Music: 1900–1960* in 1968), *Music and the Imagination* (1952), and *Copland on Music* (1960).

THE COMPOSER SPEAKS: The creative mind, in its day-to-day functioning, must be a critical mind. The ideal would be not merely to be aware, but to be "aware of our awareness," as Professor I. A. Richards has put it. In music this self-critical appraisal of the composer's own mind guiding the composition to its inevitable termination is particularly difficult of application, for music is an emotional and comparatively intangible substance. Composers, especially young composers, are not always clear as to the role criticism plays at the instant of creation. They don't seem to be fully aware that each time one note is followed by another note, or one chord by another chord, a decision has been made. They seem even less aware of the psychological and emotional connotations of their music. Instead they appear to be mainly concerned with the purely formal rightness of a general scheme, with a particular care for the note-for-note logic of thematic relationships. In other words, they are partially aware but not fully aware, and not sufficiently cognizant of those factors which have a controlling influence on the success or failure of the composition as a whole. A full and equal appraisal of every smallest contributing factor with an understanding of the controlling and most essential elements in the piece, without allowing this to cramp one's freedom of creative inventiveness—being, as it were, inside and outside the work at the same time; that is how I envisage the "awareness of one's awareness." Beethoven's genius was once attributed by Schubert to what he termed his "superb coolness under the fire of creative fantasy." What a wonderful way to describe the creative mind functioning at its highest potential!

PRINCIPAL WORKS: 3 symphonies (1924, 1933, 1946).

Music for the Theater, for orchestra (1925); Piano Concerto (1926); *Symphonic Ode* (1929, revised 1955); *Vitebsk*, for violin, cello and piano (1929); Piano Variations (1930); *Statements for Orchestra* (1934); *El salón México*, for orchestra (1936); *Billy the Kid*, ballet (1938); Piano Sonata (1941); *Rodeo*, ballet (1942); *Lincoln Portrait*, for narrator and orchestra (1942); *Appalachian Spring*, ballet (1944); Concerto for Clarinet and String Orchestra (1948); Quartet, for piano and strings (1950); Twelve Songs of Emily Dickinson, for medium voice and piano (1950); *The Tender Land*, opera (1954); *Canticle of Freedom*, for mixed chorus and orchestra (1955, revised 1967); Orchestral Variations (1957); *Piano Fantasy* (1957); Nonet, for strings (1960); *Connotations for Orchestra* (1962); *Inscape*, for orchestra (1967); *Threnody I (Igor Stravinsky: In Memoriam)*, for flute, violin, viola, and cello (1971); Duo, for flute and piano (1971); Three Latin Sketches, for small orchestra (1972); *Threnody II (Beatrice Cunningham: In Memoriam)*, for flute, viola, and cello (1973).

BIBLIOGRAPHY: Berger, Arthur, *Aaron Copland* (N.Y., 1953); Copland, Aaron, *The New Music: 1900–1960*, "Composer from Brooklyn: An Autobiographical Sketch," pp. 151-68 (N.Y., 1968); Peare, C.O., *Aaron Copland, His Life* (N.Y., 1969); Smith, Julia, *Aaron Copland* (N.Y., 1955); Thomson, Virgil, *American Music Since 1910* (N.Y., 1970); *New York Times*, November 8, 1970, November 9, 1980; *New York Times Magazine*, November 13, 1960; *Tempo* (Copland Issue), Winter 1970–71; *Stereo Review*, February 1981.

Corigliano, John, b. New York City, February 16, 1938.

His music has avoided the extramusical implications of postromantic music while retaining romantic tendencies. At the same time he has abstained from the laboratory experimentation of avant-gardists.

His father, John Corigliano, Sr., was the concertmaster of the New York Philharmonic from 1943 to 1966. From his mother, a piano teacher, the younger John received his first piano lesson. He later was given some instruction on the clarinet by Stanley Drucker. His first experience in music came at Midwood High School in Brooklyn, N. Y. During his four years there (1951–55) he directed and played for the high school "Sing," performed pop music on the piano, and was influenced by one of the school's music teachers, Bella Tillis, who encouraged him in his music-making and made him think for the first time that he could successfully channel his activities in that direction. He first became interested in symphonic music through a hi-fi set. Discovering Copland in a recording of *Billy the Kid*, he learned to play it on the piano by ear. Soon after that he heard his father perform the William Walton Violin Concerto, which added further to his fascination with contemporary music. Frequent attendance at rehearsals and concerts of the New York Philharmonic fed and nurtured his growing appetite for music.

When he graduated from Midwood High School in 1955 he had no plans to make music a career, his ambition at the time being to become a cartoonist. But at Columbia University, which he entered in 1955, his early interest in music was intensified through courses with Otto Luening. The year he graduated with honors with a bachelor of arts degree (1959) he wrote *Kaleidoscope*, for two pianos, heard at the Festival of Two Worlds in Spoleto, Italy, in July 1961. This was followed in 1961 by *Fern Hill*, for mezzo-soprano, chorus, and orchestra, based on a poem by Dylan Thomas, performed in New York on December 19, 1961. In 1962 he completed *What I Expected Was . . .* , for chorus, brass, and percussion, to a poem by Stephen Spender, performed at Tanglewood in Massachusetts on August 16, 1962, Hugh Ross conducting. In 1962 he continued his study of composition privately with Vittorio Giannini.

His father did not look with favor upon his mounting involvement with composition. "My life was hell for a while," he recalls. "Early on, he did everything he could to discourage me. He knew firsthand that the composer is the lowest man in the musical hierarchy. 'Performers don't want to bother with your work and audiences don't want to hear it. So what are you doing it for?' "

To "buy time to compose," as he himself put it, he worked in a variety of jobs after leaving college. From 1959 to 1961 he was programmer and writer for New York radio station WQXR. From 1963 to 1965 he was the musical director of radio station WBAI, also in New York.

His first success as composer came with the Sonata for Violin and Piano (1963), written for his father, who refused to look at it, let alone play it. The sonata won first prize from among one hundred entries in the 1964 Spoleto Festival Competition for Creative Arts and its world premiere was at the Spoleto Festival on July 10, 1964. Erich Gruenberg introduced it later in London and after that Roman Totenberg gave its American premiere. Only then did the older John Corigliano decide to perform it—in New York in 1966. Though the sonata utilizes nontonal and polytonal sections, together with other resources of 20th-century harmonic, rhythmic, and metric techniques, it adopts a more conservative stance than that usually found in the work of other young American composers. It is basically tonal, melodic and romantic.

The Cloisters (1965) is a cycle of songs for mezzo-soprano and piano to poems by William M. Hoffman. Judith Keller introduced it in New York on November 15, 1965. An orchestral version (without voice) was heard in Miami, performed by the Greater Miami Philharmonic under Pierre Hetu on November 17, 1975, and a version for mezzo-soprano and orchestra was presented at the Kennedy Center for the Performing Arts in Washington, D.C., on May 2, 1976, with Mignon Dunn as vocal soloist.

Further evidence of Corigliano's developing creativity came with the *Elegy*, for orchestra, first performed in San Francisco by the San Francisco Symphony under Verne Sellin on June 1, 1966, and a work for chorus and organ, *Christmas at the Cloisters*, telecast over the NBC network on December 25, 1967.

Corigliano received a Guggenheim Fellowship in 1968. That year he completed his most ambitiously conceived work up to that time: the Concerto for Piano and Orchestra, whose premiere was given by Hilde Somer and the San Antonio Orchestra conducted by Victor Alessandro on April 7, 1968, at the inaugural concert of the San Antonio World's Fair. In 1971 it received the Esther Award as the best contemporary work recorded that year. Irving Kolodin, in the *Saturday Review*, said of it: "It joins the select class of the Ginastera and Carter concertos as one of the more interesting ventures—in its totally different way—in this literature in recent years."

In 1970, Corigliano adapted Bizet's *Carmen* as a multimedia production for singers, pop singers, rock group, the Moog synthesizer, and instruments; it was recorded as *The Naked Carmen*. That same year he was one of ten composers commissioned to write works for the Chamber Music Society of Lincoln Center in New York for its opening season at the center. Corigliano's contribution was *Poem in October*, for tenor and eight instruments (1970), introduced on October 25, 1970. Its text was a poem of the same title by Dylan Thomas in which the poet, on his thirtieth birthday, walks through a Welsh town he had known in boyhood, remembering as he walks a child's forgotten mornings with his mother.

After 1970, Corigliano, more than ever before, became concerned with clarity of design, carrying his musical thoughts to their logical conclusion, achieving effective musical sound and expressivity, and most of all reaching out to his audiences with a directness of speech and a powerful emotional impact.

He achieved full maturity, in total command of his technical and artistic resources, with two concertos. The first was for oboe and orchestra (1975), first performed on November 9, 1975, in New York with Kazuoyoshi Akiyama conducting the American Symphony Orchestra and Bert Lucarelli, soloist. This concerto was commissioned by the New York State Council for the Arts for the American bicentennial year. Each of its five movements was intended to bring out a different quality of the solo instrument.

The other concerto was for clarinet (1977), whose world premiere was given on December 6, 1977, by the New York Philharmonic under Leonard Bernstein with Stanley Drucker, soloist. It received a standing ovation at all five performances. On May 2, 1980, it returned to the program of the New York Philharmonic, in addition to receiving other successful hearings in Los Angeles, Toronto, Kansas City, Syracuse, and elsewhere, and being represented on the programs of the New York Philharmonic on its summer tour of Europe in 1980. "It is indeed a sophisticated work with a complex formal structure and a harmonic base that takes in everything from major/minor tonality to clusters and twelve-tone rows," wrote Allan Kozinn in the *New York Times*. "It also aims for a purely visceral appeal. The orchestration . . . calls for lots of percussion, long sections of melodic strings and wind writing, and antiphonal choirs of brass and wind players stationed in the balconies around the hall. The solo clarinet part is as virtuosic as anything in the instrument's literature, yet it has many lyrical passages too, particularly in the second movement 'Elegy,' which contains a dialogue between the clarinet and a solo violin. Parts of the work are rather theatrical."

On April 24, 1976, at the Washington Cathedral in Washington, D.C., the Cathedral Choral Society offered an all-Corigliano program celebrating both the American bicentennial and the World Congress of the International Shakespeare Association. Three works were performed, bearing the collective title of "A Dylan Thomas Trilogy": *Fern Hill* and *Poem in October*, both previoysly performed and recorded, and the world premiere of *Poem on His Birthday*, which had been commissioned by the Washington Cathedral. In the *Washington Star*, Irving Lowens referred to this work as "a big masterpiece, almost overwhelming in its genius."

Etude Fantasy (1976), thus far the composer's only work for solo piano, must be numbered with his major compositions. Commissioned by the Edyth Bush Foundation, it is a set of five etudes combined into the episodic form and character of a fantasy. James Tocco introduced it on October 9, 1976, at the Kennedy Center for the Performing Arts in Washington, D.C.

Between 1960 and 1973, Corigliano worked with Roger Englander on all the CBS-TV music specials, including Leonard Bernstein's Young People's Concerts, "Horowitz at Carnegie Hall," "Hurok Presents," and so forth. In 1967–68 he was head of the composition department at the College of Church Musicians in Washington, D.C., and between 1969 and 1970 he worked with the Lincoln Center Student Programs in the city high schools. Since 1971 he has been associate professor of music at Lehman College in New York and a member of the composition department of the Manhattan School of Music. He was the producer of Masterwork recordings for Co-

lumbia Records in 1972–73 and music director of the Corfu Music Festival in 1973–74. He made his bow as a composer of music for motion pictures with his score for *Altered States* (1980), for which he was nominated for an "Oscar" by the American Academy of Motion Picture Arts and Sciences.

THE COMPOSER SPEAKS: It has been fashionable for the artist to be misunderstood. My generation of composers has been taught to write music by the book, and not by the ear. Now we have schools of music like schools of fish. I can't blame audiences for feeling that modern music is a dirty word. The establishment that has to be cracked these days is the establishment of incomprehensibility. The composer has to reach out and make his audience understand him with every means at his disposal.

I feel that any great work of art must exist on many levels at the same time, and that very often composers neglect the extreme levels of either visceral communication or cerebral complexity. Thus, when I speak of communication, I do *not* mean a work which only communicates, ignoring the levels and layers of meaning beyond that.

PRINCIPAL WORKS: *Fern Hill*, for mezzo-soprano, chorus, and orchestra (1961); *What I Expected Was . . .* , for mixed voices, brass, and percussion (1962); *The Cloisters*, for voice and orchestra, also for voice and piano (1965); *Elegy*, for orchestra (1965); *Tournaments*, overture for orchestra (1967); Piano Concerto (1968); *Poem in October*, for tenor and orchestra, also tenor and piano (1970); *L'invitation au voyage*, for a cappella chorus (1971); *A Black November Turkey*, for a capella chorus (1972); *Creations*, two scenes from Genesis, for narrator and orchestra (1972); *Gazebo Dances*, for concert band (1973); *Overture to the Imaginary Invalid*, for orchestra (1974); Scherzo, for oboe and percussion (1975); Aria, for oboe and strings (1975); Oboe Concerto (1975); *Poem on His Birthday*, for baritone and chorus (1976); *Soliloquy*, for clarinet and orchestra (1976); *Voyage*, for string orchestra (1976); *Etude Fantasy*, for piano (1976); *Psalm no. 8*, for chorus and organ (1976); Clarinet Concerto (1977); *Wedding Song*, for voice, instruments, and organ (1977); Flute Concerto (1980); *Pied Piper Fantasy*, for flute, orchestra and 100 children (1980).

BIBLIOGRAPHY: *Composers of America*, vol. 9 (Washington, D. C.); *Keynote* (WNCN magazine, N.Y.), December 1977; *New York Times*, April 27, 1980; *Village Voice* (N.Y.), February 21, 1977.

Cowell, Henry Dixon, b. Menlo Park, Calif., March 11, 1897; d. Shady, N.Y., December 10, 1965.

As an innovator, Cowell anticipated many of the techniques and methods adopted by avant-garde composers who followed him. But experimentation was just one phase (and an early one) of a career that produced about a thousand works. Later compositions were influenced by Irish tunes and dances; others were inspired by the Orient and the Middle and Near East; still others were deeply rooted in American hymnology.

His father, Irish by birth, was the son of an Episcopal dean of Kildare; his American-born mother was a poet, author, and early advocate of women's liberation. Since their attitude toward education was progressive, and because Henry had been born frail, he received an informal and desultory education not at school but mainly from his mother. The boy's first musical experiences were the folk songs of Iowa his mother sang to him; the Irish tunes and dances his father liked to perform; and, when he lived near the Chinese district of San Francisco, the oriental tunes he heard Chinese children sing, play, and dance as well as performances of Chinese operas. From childhood on he was sensitive to extramusical sounds around him, which seemed to bring him a music all their own: the noises of the wind and sea, of moving trains, of unusual speech inflections and intonations.

He began studying music formally when he was five by taking violin lessons from Henry Holmes. Cowell made such progress that by the time he was seven he performed Mozart and Beethoven sonatas publicly and gave every indication of being a prodigy. But when, in his eighth year, he revealed symptoms of a nervous disorder, violin lessons were ended. From this point on, Cowell aspired to be a composer. Since no piano was available to him, he would do his composing mentally. As he recalled: "While my friends were practicing the piano for an hour a day, I'd sit in my room and practice composing by listening to all kinds of sounds that came into my head. . . . I was compelled to make my mind a musical instrument . . . I could not attend enough concerts to satisfy the craving for music, so I formed the habit, when I did attend them, of deliberately rehearsing the compositions I heard and liked in order that I might play them over mentally whenever I chose."

Following the San Francisco earthquake, Cowell and his mother (who by this time had divorced her husband) went to live in Des Moines. There Cowell was placed in a public school. But a new seizure of his nervous disorder made him drop out after a year.

When Cowell was ten, he came with his mother to live in New York. A year later, the boy began writing an opera based on Longfellow's *Golden Legend*, which he never finished; one of its completed sections was later rewritten as a piano piece, *Antinomy* (1914). In New York, the Cowells endured such poverty that they became ill through malnutrition and had to be provided food and clothing by the Society for the Improvement of the Condition for the Poor.

Then the Cowells decided to return to Menlo Park in California. To support himself and his mother, Cowell took on such menial jobs as janitor in a high school, cleaning chicken coops, raising and selling plants and herding cows. With the sixty dollars he managed to save he bought a piano in 1910, the first he ever owned, and began taking lessons with a neighbor in exchange for tending her garden. He now began experimenting at the keyboard in producing sounds he had not been taught—chords made up of seconds rather than thirds or fourths—sounds he would soon designate as "tone clusters." Before long he was writing pieces using these cacophonous harmonies, produced by banging fists, palms, and the forearms on the keyboard. His first such piece was *Adventures in Harmony* (1911), which anticipated Cowell's later frequent use of Eastern music in a section called "Oriental." This was followed by *The Tides of Manaunaun* (1912), Manaunaun being an Irish sea-god. Tone clusters were here used in a low register below a Celtic-type melody. Both pieces were on his program when he made his piano debut in San Francisco on March 12, 1912. In 1913 and 1914 Cowell wrote other tone-cluster pieces, among these being *Dynamic Motion* (exploring effects of high, dissonant overtones), *Amiable Conversation* (the musical effect of which came to Cowell by overhearing a conversation between two Chinese, one speaking in a high-pitched voice, the other in a low register), *Advertisement*, and *Antinomy*. Cowell was not the inventor of tone clusters; they had previously been used in Russia by Vladimir Rebikoff and in the United States by Charles Ives. But Cowell was the first to bring this dissonant harmonic method to prominence and to become inextricably identified with it.

In 1914 Cowell began studying harmony and counterpoint with E. G. Strickland and composition with Wallace Sabin at the University of California in Berkeley; also modern composition privately with Charles Seeger. Through Seeger, Cowell was introduced to such then advanced techniques as polytonality, dissonant counterpoint, atonality, all of which fascinated him. In the music he was now writing he was carrying on further experiments of his own. In *Quartet Romantic*, for two flutes, violin, and viola (1914–15), tonal durations and pitches were coordinated to ratios of the overtone series. In *Vestiges*, for large orchestra (1914–42) he worked with elaborate multiple meters. In *Quartet Euphometric*, for strings (1915), a simple harmonic phrase became the source of very complex matric organizations, requiring special note lengths and special notation. Not until 1964 was one movement of *Quartet Romantic* and all of *Quartet Euphometric* performed (by the Griller Quartet in London); the complete *Quartet Romantic* received its world premiere in New York on April 13, 1977.

Cowell was in New York in the fall of 1916, attending the Institute of Musical Art, where he studied composition with Frank Damrosch. Impatient with the restrictions imposed on him by the academic rule book, Cowell left both the institute and New York after a term to return to California to work on a book in which he clarified some of his aims and experiments, the first American book on contemporary musical theory, *New Musical Resources*, which, though written between 1916 and 1919, was not published until 1930.

Cowell remained a student at the University of California in Berkeley until 1917 when he was made an assistant in the music department. A year later, during World War I, he enlisted in the army, serving first as a cook for three months, then as assistant conductor and arranger for the army band. When he was separated from the service in May 1919 he came to New York, spending the next two years studying form, counterpoint, and ensemble music at the Institute of Applied Music.

In 1923, Cowell embarked on the first of five annual tours of Europe, as well as tours of the United States, in piano recitals featuring his provocative compositions. He extended his revolution of keyboard performance by writing new works which adapted conventional violin techniques to the piano strings, such as harmonics, muted tones, pizzicati. In *Aeolian Harp* (1923), *The Banshee* (1925) and *Sinister Resonance* (1925), among other similar items, he bent over the strings of the piano soundboard to produce new sonorities and sounds by manipulating the strings manually, plucking at them, at times (years before John Cage) inserting objects between the strings. Everywhere he played he aroused either furor or ridicule, and sometimes provoked actual riots. But some of Europe's leading musicians took Cowell and his music seriously. Such eminent European critics as Percy Scholes, Henri Prunières, Erwin Felber, Adolph Weissman, and Julius Korngold sprang vigorously to his defense. Artur Schnabel arranged for Cowell's concert in Berlin, Béla Bartók for one in Paris, and Arnold Schoenberg invited Cowell to perform in Vienna at his composition class. In 1928 Cowell became the second American asked to appear in the Soviet Union (the first had been Roland Hayes). Two of Cowell's compositions were published in the Soviet Union, the first time such a thing had happened to American music.

Cowell did not confine his tone-cluster idiom to piano music, applying it as well to orchestral works by assembling massive chords in seconds that moved polyphonically over each other. He did this in Sinfonietta, for small orchestra (1924–28; Paris, November 23, 1931); in the Piano Concerto (1928–1929; Havana, Cuba, December 28, 1929); and in *Synchrony* (1930; Paris, April 12, 1932). The last of these was performed by the Philadelphia Orchestra under Leopold Stokowski on April 12, 1932. Suite, for solo strings, percussion and piano (1928; Boston, March 11, 1929) was an orchestration of three of Cowell's pieces for the piano.

In 1927, Cowell founded the *New Music Quarterly*, a journal devoted to publishing compositions by modern composers (the first to be published was Carl Ruggles's *Men and Mountains*). The journal's coverage soon broadened to include new recordings. He remained active with this project until the early 1960s when the catalogue was taken over by Theodore Presser. In 1928, Cowell was appointed director of musical activities at the New School for Social Research, retaining this post until 1963. In the late 1920s, with several other American composers, and financed by Charles Ives, Cowell helped to form the Pan American Association for the performance of American music in Europe, serving as a member of its executive board; its first concert took place in Paris on June 6, 1931. On a Guggenheim Fellowship in 1931–32, Cowell attended the University of Berlin for the study of non-European systems with Erich von Hornstobel.

In 1932, Cowell devised the rhythmicon, which was built for him by Leon Theremin. This was an instrument capable of performing rhythmic combinations beyond the capabilities of performers. For this instrument, Cowell wrote *Rhythmicana*, for rhythmicon and orchestra (1931), which had to wait forty years to be performed; this took place on December 3, 1971, by the Stanford Symphony in California conducted by Sandor Salgo.

Tragedy struck Cowell in 1937 when, without a trial or the services of a defense attorney, he was sentenced on a "morals" charge in California and incarcerated in San Quentin prison. A traumatic experience that would have completely destroyed others turned out constructively. Without assistance or encouragement, Cowell turned part of the prison into an improvised music school where he gave lessons to fellow inmates, organized a band and pursued his own studies. He was pardoned in 1941 at the request of the prosecuting attorney.

Upon his release from San Quentin, Cowell worked for a short time as Percy Grainger's secretary in White Plains, New York. The year of 1941 proved eventful for Cowell, bringing about radical changes in both his personal and artistic life. On September 27, 1941, he married Miss Sidney Hawkins Robertson, an ethnomusicologist. With the marriage came a restoration of tranquility. Change also came to his musical directions. In 1941 he orchestrated some piano pieces he had written between 1922 and 1930 and called the work *Tales of Our Countryside*. It became Cowell's most successful work for orchestra after Leopold Stokowski directed its premiere in Atlantic City, N. J., on May 11, 1941. Here Cowell departed from the revolutionary practices of the 1920s and 1930s to become diatonic and romantic, and to find nourishment in American backgrounds.

An even more important development in Cowell's interest in creating American music came in 1941 when he discovered *Southern Harmony*, a collection of American hymns by old singing schoolmasters edited by William Walker. These century-old melodies—and particularly the fuguing tunes of 18th-century William Billings—impressed Cowell so deeply that he was now motivated to carry over their styles and techniques into instrumental music. He went on to produce a series of works in a modal style with emphasis on polyphony. His first work in the manner of American rural hymnology was *Hymn and Fuguing Tune* no. 1 for band (1943; N. Y., summer 1943). His first success in this genre was *Hymn and Fuguing Tune* no. 2, for string orchestra (1944), introduced over the NBC network in March 1944 by the NBC Symphony under Henri Nosco, and subsequently receiving numerous performances throughout the United States. Cowell wrote fifteen more hymn and fuguing tune compositions after that, up to 1964. The third, for large orchestra (1944–45) was given its initial hearing in Boston on January 26, 1954, with Pierre Monteux conducting the Boston Symphony. The fifth, for voices (1945), was performed in New York on April 14, 1946. *Hymn, Chorale and Fuguing Tune* no. 8 (1947), written for the Roth String Quartet, was introduced by that ensemble in Tallahassee, Fla., on May 11, 1948. The tenth, for oboe and strings (1955), was given its premiere on September 10, 1955, in Santa Barbara, Calif., with Leopold Stokowski conducting the Pacific Coast Music Festival Orchestra. In the same American rural hymnology category belongs the Sonata for Violin and Piano (1945), which at the same time reveals the Celtic influence in two of its movements ("Ballad" and "Jig"); its second movement is once again in the fuguing style. Written for Joseph Szigeti, this sonata was introduced by him in Los Angeles on November 10, 1947. Old American hymns inspired the writing of *Short Symphony* no. 4 (1946), premiered by the Boston Symphony under Richard Burgin on October 24, 1947. Hymns and fuguing tunes are also part of the fabric of numerous other Cowell compositions, notably the symphonies no. 5 (1949), no. 6 (1951; Houston, Tex., November 14, 1955), no. 7 (1952; Baltimore, Md., November 25, 1952), no. 12 (1956; N. Y., November 5, 1962); and no. 15 (1960; Houston, May 28, 1960); also String Quartet no. 5 (1955–56; Washington, D. C., October 1956) and *Set of Five*, for violin, piano and percussion (1952; N.Y., December 21, 1952).

The Celtic influence on Cowell, reflected in some of his early piano pieces, continued to be felt in his music, particularly in *Irish Suite*, for chamber ensemble (1929), *Celtic Set*, for band or for orchestra (1938–39), *Gaelic Symphony* no. 3 (1942), Violin Sonata (1945) and in the Irish jiglike identity of many of his scherzo movements.

In 1956 and 1957, on a grant from the Rockefeller Foundation, Cowell traveled throughout Asia to survey the music of ten of its countries. Three months were spent in Iran at the request of the State Department, supervising performances of Persian music

over a new Teheran radio station. Ten days were occupied with attendance at the festival at Madras, India. In 1961, Cowell paid another visit to the Far East and Middle East to represent the United States government at the International Music Conference in Teheran and at the East-West Music Encounter in Tokyo.

As a result of these travels, Cowell felt impelled to write a great deal of music utilizing Oriental or Middle Eastern techniques, idioms and instruments. This last phase of Cowell's creativity was as important and as productive as earlier ones. *Persian Set*, for twelve instruments (1957; Minneapolis, Minn., November 1957) used a Persian instrument called the tar. *Ongaku* (1957; Louisville, Ky., March 26, 1958) consisted of two movements built from two different pieces of Japanese classical music. *Homage to Iran* (1957) was a chamber music work for violin, piano and Persian drum. Two concertos for koto and symphony orchestra (1962–63; Philadelphia, December 18, 1964; 1965) were written for a native Japanese instrument, the koto, similar in design to the ancient European table harp.

Over a period of many years, Cowell was involved with teaching, both privately and at renowned colleges and universities (Northwestern University in Evanston, Ill.; Mills College in Oakland, Calif.; University of California at Berkeley; Stanford University in Stanford, Calif.; and Columbia University in New York). He also lectured in numerous other colleges and universities throughout the United States and Europe. He received honorary doctorates from Wilmington College in Ohio (1954) and Monmouth College in Illinois (1963). In 1951 he was elected a member of the National Institute of Arts and Letters, becoming its vice-president a decade later. The fiftieth anniversary of Cowell's debut as composer was remembered in 1962 with concerts of his music throughout the United States. At that time, President Kennedy and Governor Nelson A. Rockefeller of New York sent him congratulatory messages; the National Association for Composers and Conductors presented him with the Henry Hadley medal; and an exhibit of his manuscripts, photographs and memorabilia was displayed at the New York Public Library. A retrospective concert of Cowell's music, covering half a century, was given at Columbia University on April 13, 1977.

Cowell was the editor of the anthology *American Composers on American Music* (1933) and with his wife was the author of *Charles Ives and His Music* (1955)—in addition to the already mentioned *New Musical Resources* (1930).

THE COMPOSER SPEAKS: I place no limitation of period or place on the musical material I may wish to draw on, for the meaning of music does not depend upon the materials themselves. I believe a composer must forge his own forms out of the many influences that play upon him and never close his ears to any part of the world of sound.

Every musical culture, no matter how strange it may sound to us, will yield its systematic organization to study and experience. Underneath the many strange and unexpected and variously appealing regional musical styles, one will always find a fundamental relationship with all the other music in the world. . . . A composer today, and especially in America, should be free to appropriate any forms that he desires. For myself I have always wanted to live in the whole world of music.

PRINCIPAL WORKS: 20 symphonies (1918–65); 18 hymn and fuguing tunes, for various instruments, or for orchestra, or for voices (1943–64); 5 string quartets (1916–56); 2 concertos for koto and orchestra (1962, 1965).

Adventures in Harmony, for piano (1911); *Tides of Manaunaun*, for piano (1912); *Dynamic Motion, Advertisement, Antinomy*, all for piano (1914); *Quartet Romantic*, for two flutes, violin and viola (1914–1915); *Quartet Euphometric*, for strings (1915); Cello Sonata (1915); *Amiable Conversation*, for piano (1917); *Aeolian Harp*, for piano (1923); Sinfonietta, for small orchestra (1924–28); *The Banshee, Lilt of the Reel*, and *Sinister Resonance*, all for piano (1925); *Atlantis*, ballet (1926); Piano Concerto (1928–29); Suite, for solo strings, percussion and piano (1928); *Synchrony*, for orchestra (1929–30); Suite, for woodwind quintet (1930); *Polyphonica*, for orchestra (1930); *Rhythmicana*, for rhythmicon and orchestra (1931); *Old American Country Set*, for orchestra (1937); Toccata, for soprano, flute, cello and piano (1938); *Celtic Set*, for band, also for orchestra (1938–39); *American Melting Pot*, for orchestra (1940); Violin Sonata (1945); *Festival Overture*, for double orchestra (1946); *O'Higgins of Chile*, opera (1947); *Saturday Night at the Firehouse*, for orchestra (1948); *Fiddler's Jig*, for violin and orchestra (1952); *Set of Five*, for violin, piano, and percussion (1952); Variations, for orchestra (1956); *A Thanksgiving Psalm from the Dead Sea Scrolls*, for men's chorus and orchestra (1956–57); *Persian Set*, for twelve instruments (1957); *Music*, for orchestra (1957); *Homage to Iran*, for violin and orchestra (1957); *Ongaku*, for orchestra (1957); *Antiphony*, for two orchestras (1958–59); *Chiaroscuro*, for orchestra (1960); Accordion Concerto (1960); Concerto for Percussion and Orchestra (1960); *The Creator*, for vocal soloists, chorus and orchestra (1963); Harp Concerto (1965); Piano Trio (1965); *Ultima Actio*, for chorus (1965).

BIBLIOGRAPHY: Mead, R. H., "Henry Cowell's New Music" (doctoral thesis, N. Y., 1978); Saylor, B., *The Writings of Henry Cowell: A Descriptive Bibliography* (N. Y., 1977); Thomson, Virgil, *American Music Since 1910* (N. Y., 1970); Yates, Peter, *Twentieth-Century Music* (N. Y., 1967); *Etude*, February 1957; *Musical Quarterly*, October 1959; *New York Times*, May 28, 1978; *Stereo Review*, December 1974.

Crawford, Ruth Porter, b. East Liverpool, Ohio, June 3, 1901; d. Chevy Chase, Md., November 18, 1953.

Though most often remembered for her valuable work in American folk music, Ruth Crawford was the composer of music highly advanced in its idiom for its time, occasionally anticipating procedures of a later avant-garde movement. She was the first woman composer to receive the Guggenheim Fellowship.

She came from Anglo-American stock, the younger of two children of a Methodist minister. Her mother, also the daughter of a minister, was an accomplished pianist who gave Ruth, at age six, her first piano lessons. In Jacksonville, Fla., to which the family had come in 1911, Ruth continued her piano study with Bertha Foster and Mme. Valborg-Collett. Being a precocious child, she advanced so rapidly in classes in elementary school that she could form few friendships. She recalled her schooldays as lonely. "I practiced the piano one to three hours a day, spent study hall periods writing rhymes, was called a bookworm by friends of my older brother who led a more normal social life."

Upon graduating from high school in Jacksonville, and with her father having died in 1913, she was called upon to help support the family. She did so through music, by teaching piano at the School of Musical Art and taking charge of music instruction at a settlement kindergarten. Her own musical experiences were extended by going to concerts of world-famous pianists (Josef Hofmann, Paderewski, Percy Grainger), by studying a harmony book by herself, and by composing some pieces for the piano.

Having saved up enough money to provide for a full year of music instruction, Ruth Crawford came to Chicago in the fall of 1920. At the American Conservatory she studied piano with Heniot Lévy and harmony with John Palmer and Alfred Weidig, receiving a teacher's certificate in 1921 and a bachelor of music degree in 1923. 1923 to 1927 her piano studies were continued with Djan Lavoie-Herz. At the same time, on a scholarship, she continued to study composition, as well as harmony, counterpoint and orchestration, with Weidig. In 1929 she was awarded a Master of Music degree at the American Conservatory, *summa cum laude*. When her money ran out, she worked as usher and in a coat checkroom in various Chicago theaters. Then, from 1925 to 1929 she was a member of the faculty of the American Conservatory and from 1926 to 1929 she taught at the Elmhurst College of Music in Illinois.

Her adult career as composer began in 1924–25

when she completed five preludes for piano which were performed in 1925 by Gitta Gradova in Town Hall, N.Y. Four more preludes came in 1927–28, receiving their first performance by Richard Buhlig at a Copland-Sessions concert in New York in 1928. These last four preludes were published in the *New Music Editions*. All these pieces are homophonic and betray the influence of Debussy and Scriabin. Her writing at that time, as Charles Seeger once wrote, "was embroidered with sudden whirls and snaps of thirty-second notes that give a distinct and characteristic validity to what is often a languid moodiness in her basic choral structure." She became stylistically more advanced in the Suite, for small chamber orchestra (1926), in which she was influenced by Charles Ives in her choice of folklike thematic material and in her now complex polytonal structures. Two movements from this suite were revived in Cambridge, Mass., on February 25, 1975, and were recorded. Alfred J. Frankenstein, the distinguished San Francisco critic, now described this music as "beautifully made and admirably expressive." Another suite, this time for piano and woodwind quintet (1927) was, for its time, so advanced in harmonic and contrapuntal structure that it had to wait half a century to be heard, receiving its world premiere in Cambridge, Mass., on December 14, 1975. Five Songs, for voice and piano (1929), to poems by Carl Sandburg, were declamatory in their melodic line with unvocal intervallic skips and often a bold harmonic background that sometimes called for tone clusters. Three of these songs were among the American works represented at the festival of the International Society for Contemporary Music in Amsterdam on June 15, 1933; they received their first New York hearing on April 24, 1974.

Crawford came East in 1929, spent the summer at the MacDowell Colony in Peterboro, N.H., and the following winter and spring in New York. There she resumed the study of composition with Charles Seeger, the distinguished musicologist, who introduced her to Schoenberg's music and the twelve-tone technique. Speaking of her new teacher, Seeger, she wrote to a friend: "He shared with me his conception of the aspects and as yet untried possibilities, both in form and content, of a new music, and his views as to various means of bringing some organic coordination out of the too often superabundance of materials in use at present. As a result of this study, my work began at last to take a 'handleable' shape, to present itself in some sort of intelligible continuity."

Later in 1930, on a Guggenheim Fellowship, she was able to go to Europe and spend a year wandering about in Paris, Berlin, Vienna, and Budapest, going to museums and concerts and hearing performances in Berlin and Hamburg of her *Diaphonic Suite* no. 3, one of a set of four such suites for bassoon and cello she had written in New York in 1930. After returning to New York in the fall of 1931 she and Charles Seeger were married on November 14, 1931; they raised four children.

Her compositions from 1930 on showed an ever-increasing independence in the use of polymetric, discordant, and heterophonic devices. Her String Quartet (1931; New York, November 13, 1933) was an experiment in dynamic counterpoint, each part having a different alternation of crescendo or diminuendo, or beginning and ending at different times. This composition was also noteworthy for the fact that Crawford here made an attempt to use the twelve-tone system years before other American composers did so. When this quartet was revived by the Fine Arts Quartet in New York on May 13, 1970, Andrew DeRhen wrote in *High Fidelity/Musical America* that it sounded "fresh and original even today. . . . Miss Crawford . . . knew how to communicate directly and with great expressiveness in a dissonant modern idiom. There is no faddishness. . . . Of particular interest was the slow movement, a suspenseful study in tone clusters."

In 1935, the Seeger family moved to Silver Spring, Md., a suburb of Washington, D.C. There, while raising her family, she took charge of music at the Silver Spring Cooperative Nursery School and taught music at the Foxhall Nursery School, the Whitehall County School, and the Potomac School. From 1937 on, Crawford joined her husband in collecting American folk music. She made several thousand transcriptions of songs from recordings in the Library of Congress, composing piano accompaniments for about three hundred of them. She used American folk songs to develop her own method of teaching children music. She edited or arranged eight volumes of folk songs, among which are *American Folk Songs for Children* (1948), *Animal Folk Songs for Children* (1950), *American Folk Songs for Christmas* (1953) and *Let's Build a Railroad* (1954).

She did no composing between 1932 and 1941. This silence was broken in 1941 with *Rissolty Rissolty*, for chamber orchestra, which had been commissioned by the CBS radio network and performed on its "School of the Air" program. This work was based on American and English folk materials: tunes such as the courting song "Rissolty Rissolty," the tea song "Phoebe," and an English ballad, "Last of Callahan." Her next, and last, composition was, by contrast, a return to her earlier abstract, linear, and dissonant style. It was the Suite for Wind Quintet (1952), which earned first prize in a competition sponsored by the District of Columbia chapter of the National Association of American Composers and Conductors and which was given its world premiere in Washington, D.C., on December 2, 1952.

PRINCIPAL WORKS: Nine Preludes, for piano (1924–28); Suite, for small orchestra (1926); Suite, for piano and woodwind quintet (1929); Five Songs, for voice and piano (1929); *Rat Riddles*, for contralto, oboe, percussion, and piano (1930); *Chant*, for a cappella chorus and soprano solo (1930); *Diaphonic Suites*, nos. 1–4, for bassoon and cello, or two cellos (1930); String Quartet (1931); *In Tall Grass*, for contralto, oboe, percussion, and piano (1931); Two Ricercari, for voice and piano (1932); *Prayers of Steel*, for contralto, oboe, percussion and piano (1932); *Rissolty Rissolty*, for small orchestra (1941); Suite for Wind Quintet (1952).

BIBLIOGRAPHY: Cowell, Henry (ed.), *American Composers on American Music* (Stanford, Calif., 1933); Gaume, Mary Matilda, "Ruth Crawford Seeger: Her Life and Works" (doctoral thesis, Bloomington, Ind., 1973); *Composers of Americas*, vol. 2, 1956.

Creston, Paul (originally **Guttoveggio, Giuseppe**), b. New York City, October 10, 1906.

The basis of Creston's music through the years has been the contrast between song and dance, between a strong-fibered and personalized lyricism and variegated rhythms and meters of his own devising. He has never been a revolutionary, never aimed to surprise or shock but rather, as he put it, "to communicate expressions of joy or exhilaration or spirituality" in music that owes as much to the past as to the 20th century.

His father was a house painter who had come to New York from Sicily. The boy Creston learned to love the Italian folk songs his father sang to him to his own guitar accompaniment. When he was six, Paul's mother took him and his brother for a six-month visit to Sicily, where the songs and dances of Sicilian peasants became an indelible memory. When he was back in New York two years later, Paul prevailed on his father to buy him a piano, on which he took lessons for several years from a local teacher whom he recalls as "most mediocre." "Actually," Creston says, "without being aware of it I was teaching myself by reading many books on music fundamentals and piano playing." He stopped taking lessons when he was fourteen, preferring to go his own way in music. He taught himself to play the violin that had been purchased for his brother. Composition had begun as soon as he had acquired the piano, but his ambition for some time was to be a concert pianist rather than a composer.

His academic schooling ended when he was fifteen after two and a half years of high school—terminated because he was forced to help support his family. His first job was as errand boy and receptionist for the MacFadden Publications. After that he worked in the foreign exchange department of the Irving Trust Company, and then as insurance claim examiner for the Metropolitan Life Insurance Company. Early mornings and late into the night he would practice the piano and compose.

On July 1, 1927, he married Louise Gotto, whom he first met at the MacFadden Publications, where she worked as secretary to one of the editors. Later she became a dancer, a member of Martha Graham's first company, but in time she gave up the profession to bear three children and raise two of them (the first died in infancy). When he married, the name of Paul Creston was acquired formally. He chose Creston because, in a high school production he had played the part of Crespino, which led his friends to call him Cress. He expanded Cress to Creston and added Paul to it because he liked the sound.

From 1926 to 1929 Creston worked as organist in a movie house. He lost the job when talkies replaced silent films. In 1934 he was appointed organist of St. Malachy's Church in New York, retaining this post for the next thirty-three years. Meanwhile he continued to study the piano with G. Aldo Randegger and Gaston Dethier, and organ with Pietro Yon. In composition he remained self-taught.

By 1932 he knew he wanted to become a full-time composer. Discarding everything he had written up to this time, he now produced the work he has come to regard as his first opus: *Five Days*, a set of pieces for solo piano (1932). In June 1933 his music was heard publicly for the first time when his incidental music to a play, *Iron Flowers*, was performed in Westchester County, N.Y. That same year he brought *Seven Theses* (1933), for piano, to Henry Cowell, who published it in *New Music Quarterly* (Creston's first publication) and had Creston perform it at a composer's forum at the New School for Social Research. *Out of the Cradle Endlessly Rocking*, for chamber orchestra (1934), based on Walt Whitman, was heard in Rochester, N.Y., on October 19, 1938, Howard Hanson conducting. In 1936, Creston's String Quartet was featured at a festival of American music at Yaddo, in Saratoga, N.Y., where his Partita, for flute, violin and strings (1934, revised 1962), was introduced on September 18, 1937.

Performance by a major organization came on December 2, 1938, with the introduction of Creston's first work for full orchestra, *Threnody*, by the Pittsburgh Symphony conducted by Fritz Reiner. He had written it in 1938, soon after the death of his infant son. The strength of his music lay in its modal lyricism in the style of a Gregorian chant in one instance, and romantically elegiac in another. *Two Choric Dances*, for percussion, piano and strings (1938), introduced in Cleveland on February 20, 1939, is basically rhythmic, since the work was intended to suggest the movements of a group of dancers. It received the award of the Music Library Association.

Though lyricism is not absent from Creston's Symphony no. 1 (1940), which first made him nationally known (it is particularly songful in the third movement), rhythm is predominant, with the rhythmic structure providing the unifying element. After this symphony received its premiere on February 22,

1941, in New York, conducted by Fritz Mahler, the Philadelphia Orchestra under Eugene Ormandy programmed it on March 23, 1943. The work earned the New York Music Critics Circle Award as the season's best orchestral composition and, in 1952, captured the first prize in the Paris Referendum Concert, an international competition conducted in France.

Lyricism and rhythm characterize the Prelude and Dance, for percussion, piano and strings (1941), which was heard over the CBS radio network in a performance by the Columbia Concert Orchestra under Howard Barlow on January 27, 1944; in the two Prelude and Dance compositions for piano (1942); and in Symphony no. 2 (1944), which the composer described as "an apotheosis of the two foundations of all music, song and dance." The symphony is a two-movement work, the first of which is an "Introduction" and "Song," and the second "Interlude" and "Dance." The symphony's two principal themes are heard in the "Introduction," with the "Song" becoming a variation of the first theme and the "Dance" a derivation of the second one. The New York Philharmonic under Arthur Rodzinski presented the first performance in New York on February 15, 1945, after which it received an award from the National Federation of Music Clubs.

Creston's Symphony no. 3, subtitled *Three Mysteries* (1950)—first performed at the Worcester Music Festival in Massachusetts on October 27, 1950, by the Philadelphia Orchestra under Ormandy—is deeply religious, drawing its thematic material out of the storehouse of Gregorian chants and describing the nativity, crucifixion, and resurrection.

Symphony no. 3 had been commissioned by the Worcester Music Festival. From this point on, virtually every major Creston composition was the result of a commission. In the 1950s these included one from Viola Malkin as a memorial to her husband, Joseph D. Malkin (Symphony no. 4, in 1951, performed on January 30, 1952 by the National Symphony Orchestra in Washington, D.C., under Howard Mitchell); from the National Symphony Orchestra of Washington, D.C, for its twenty-fifth anniversary (Symphony no. 5 in 1955, performed on April 4, 1956); from the Cleveland Orchestra for its fortieth anniversary (Toccata in 1957, heard on October 17, 1957); from the Elizabeth Sprague Coolidge Foundation (Suite for the Cello, in 1956); and from the Association of Women's Committees for Symphony Orchestra (*Janus*, for strings, piano, and percussion in 1959, first performed on July 17, 1959 by the Denver Symphony under Saul Caston).

As Creston progressed into the 1960s and 1970s he evolved his own techniques in giving increasing attention to rhythm and meter as opposed to song. In his rhythmic scheme Creston took into account meter, pace, duration, and accent; change in any of these elements altered the entire rhythmic scheme. Creston also developed his own metrical idiom. Rebelling against binary meters, he concocted time signatures of his own (such as 6/12 and 3/9).

Creston's most important compositions of the 1960s were the Violin Concerto no. 2 (1960); *Corinthians XIII*, for orchestra (1963) and *Chthonic Ode* (1966). The Violin Concerto was commissioned by the Ford Foundation for Michael Rabin, who first performed it on November 17, 1960, in Los Angeles with Georg Solti conducting the Los Angeles Philharmonic. *Corinthians XIII*—commissioned for the Phoenix Symphony Orchestra in Arizona by Bruce Irwin and introduced on March 30, 1964—was a tonal representation of the apotheosis of love as expressed in the thirteenth chapter of St. Paul's Epistle to the Corinthians. Creston described his music as "an emotional parallel of three manifestations of love: the love between mother and child, between man and woman, and between man and mankind." *Chthonic Ode* was written in homage to Henry Moore, the sculptor—"chthonic" being a descriptive word Sir Robert Reed had used to describe Moore's art. "In Henry Moore's sculpture," Creston explains, "I see seven qualities which I have striven to incorporate in the music: Vitality, Restraint, Primitiveness, Humanism, Womanhood, Monumentality, and Universality. These qualities determined the form of the piece: free sectional form in four distinct but connected sentences." *Chthonic Ode* had its initial hearing in Detroit on April 6, 1967, with Sixten Ehrling directing the Detroit Symphony.

Among Creston's later compositions the most notable are: *Hyas Illahee* (in Chinook Indian meaning "Great Land"), a work for chorus and orchestra without text, the text being replaced by syllables, Indian words, vowels and geographical names, all selected for their tonal and rhythmic values, written in 1969 and performed in Seattle, Wash., in November of the same year; Concertino for Piano and Woodwind Quintet (1969; Brockport, N.Y., April 15, 1972); *Leaves of Grass*, a cycle of five songs for mixed chorus and piano based on Walt Whitman (1970; Seattle, February 28, 1971); *Jubilee*, for concert band (1971; Washington, D.C., January 24, 1972). To commemorate the American bicentennial Creston completed three works in 1975: *Square Dance '76* for wind symphony orchestra, *Fanfare '76* for full symphony orchestra, and *Liberty Song*, for symphonic band.

Between 1944 and 1950, Creston was the musical director of the "Hour of Faith" program over ABC radio network. In 1956 he was a member of the music faculty at Swarthmore College in Pennsylvania, and from 1963 to 1967 of the New York College of Music. On a grant from the State Department he lectured in Israel and Turkey in 1960. In 1967 he was visiting professor of music at Central Washington State College in Ellensburg and from 1968 to 1975 he served there as professor of music and composer-in-residence. When he retired from the college in 1975, he was named professor emeritus.

He has been the recipient of numerous honors and awards. He was given two consecutive Guggenheim Fellowships (1938, 1939); a citation from the National Association for American Composers and Conductors (1941); the Music Award of the National Institute of Arts and Letters (1943); the Alice M. Ditson Award from Columbia University for *Poem*, for harp and orchestra (1945); the Citation of Honor from the National Catholic Music Educators Association (1956); the Christopher Award for his score to the television production "Revolt in Hungary" (1958); a gold medal from the National Arts Club (1963); an Emmy citation from the National Academy of Television Arts and Sciences for his score to the television documentary "In the American Grain" (1964); the Achievement Award from the New York College of Music (1966); and the Composers Award from the Lancaster Symphony in Pennsylvania (1970).

He was president of the National Association of American Composers and Conductors between 1956 and 1960, a director of the American Society of Composers, Authors, and Publishers (ASCAP) from 1960 to 1968, and was named life fellow of the International Institute of Arts and Letters in 1964. Creston is the author of *Principles of Rhythm* (1964) and *Creative Harmony* (1970), and has explored the world of rhythm in a ten-volume series collectively entitled *Rhythmicon*.

THE COMPOSER SPEAKS: I consider music, and more specifically the writing of it, as a spiritual practice. To me musical composition is as vital to my spiritual welfare as prayer and good deeds, much as good food and exercise are necessities of physical health, and thought and study are requisites of mental being. . . . My philosophic approach to composition is abstract. I am preoccupied with matters of melodic progression, not with imitations of nature, or narrations of fairy tales, or propoundings of sociological ideologies. . . . The intrinsic worth of a composition depends on the integration of musical elements towards a unified whole.

PRINCIPAL WORKS: 5 symphonies (1940–55); 2 violin concertos (1956, 1960).

String Quartet (1936); *Threnody*, for orchestra (1938); *Two Choric Dances*, for orchestra (1938); Saxophone Concerto (1941); Prelude and Dance, for orchestra (1941); Pastorale and Tarantella, for orchestra (1941); Dance Variations, for soprano and orchestra (1942); Fantasy, for piano and orchestra (1943); *Chant of 1942*, for orchestra (1943); *Frontiers*, for orchestra (1943); Six Preludes, for piano (1945); *Poem*, for harp and orchestra (1945); Psalm XXIII, for high voice and piano or orchestra (1947); Fantasy, for trombone and orchestra (1947); *Missa Solemnis*, for chorus and orchestra or organ (1949); Two Motets, for male chorus and organ (1949); Concerto for Two Pianos and Orchestra (1951);

Suite, for flute, violin and piano (1952); *Invocation and Dance*, for orchestra (1953); *The Celestial Vision*, for a cappella male chorus (1954); *Dance Overture*, for orchestra (1954); *Lydian Ode*, for orchestra (1956); Suite, for cello and piano (1956); Toccata, for orchestra (1957); Accordion Concerto (1958); Fantasia, for organ (1958); *Janus*, for orchestra (1959); *Isaiah's Prophecy*, oratorio for vocal soloists, chorus and orchestra (1962); *Three Narratives*, for piano (1962); *Corinthians XIII*, for orchestra (1963); *Metamorphoses*, for piano (1964); Fantasy, for accordion and orchestra (1964); Nocturne, for soprano and eleven instruments (1964); *Choreographic Suite*, for orchestra (1965); *Pavane Variations*, for orchestra (1966); *Chthonic Ode*, for orchestra with piano (1966); *The Psalmist*, for alto and orchestra (1967); *Missa cum Jubilo*, for a cappella chorus and string orchestra (1968); *Hyas Illahee*, for chorus and orchestra (1969); Concertino, for piano and woodwind quintet (1969); *Leaves of Grass*, for chorus and piano (1970); *Thanatopsis*, for orchestra (1971); *Jubilee*, for symphonic band (1971); *Square Dance '76*, for wind orchestra (1975); *Fanfare '76*, for orchestra (1975); *Liberty Song*, for symphonic band (1975); Suite, for string orchestra (1978); *Romanza*, for piano (1978); Piano Trio (1979); *Festive Overture*, for band (1980); *Sadhana*, for chamber orchestra (1981).

BIBLIOGRAPHY: Goss, Madeleine, *Modern Music Makers* (N.Y., 1952); Thomson, Virgil, *American Music Since 1910* (N.Y., 1970); *Music Journal*, December 1976; *Musical America*, October 1944; *Musical Quarterly*, October 1948; *Ovation*, October 1981.

Crumb, George Henry, b. Charleston, W.V., October 24, 1929.

Winner of the Pulitzer Prize in music in 1968, Crumb has had several major influences shape and direct his innovative music: his West Virginian origin, the poetry of Federico García Lorca, and the music of Anton Webern and Charles Ives.

Both his parents were musicians, his father being a clarinetist and bandmaster, and his mother a cellist. Music, omnipresent in the Crumb household, had a strong impact on George from his childhood on. When he was nine he was playing the piano by ear. Not long after that he started composing, an activity that so occupied his time in class at Charleston High School that he was often reprimanded by his teachers.

When he graduated from high school in 1947 he was determined to concentrate henceforth on music. For three years he attended the Mason College, a musical conservatory in Charleston. There he met Elizabeth May Brown, a piano student, whom he married on May 21, 1949 (in time they had three children). After receiving his bachelor of music degree at Mason College in 1950, Crumb did postgraduate work at the University of Illinois in Urbana, where he earned his master's degree in music in 1952, and in 1953 at the University of Michigan in Ann Arbor.

In his early compositions—String Quartet (1954) and Sonata, for solo cello (1955)—Crumb followed the comparatively advanced methods of Bartók, Hindemith, and Alban Berg. Both these compositions brought him the BMI prize in composition in 1937.

After spending a summer in the Berkshire Music Center at Tanglewood, Mass., in 1955, Crumb went to Germany in 1955–56 on a Fulbright Fellowship, attending the Berlin Academy of Music as a pupil in composition of Boris Blacher's. In 1956 he returned to the University of Michigan to complete the study of composition with Ross Lee Finney and to fulfill the requirements for a doctorate in music, received in 1959.

For one year (1958–59) Crumb taught theory at Rollins College of Music in Virginia. For five years after that he was assistant professor of piano at the University of Colorado in Colorado Springs.

In his first work for orchestra, *Variazioni* (1959), Crumb experimented with the twelve-tone system, but using it in a personalized manner that did not preclude lyricism. But he soon became more interested in new sounds, new sonorities, exotic ways of producing percussive effects than in dodecaphony. This tendency first asserted itself in Five Pieces, for piano (1962), which betrayed the impact on him of Webern's pointilism, fragmentation of themes, and economy of materials.

While at the University of Michigan for his doctorate, Crumb came upon a poem of Federico García Lorca in which he found a reflection of his own artistic aims. For the next seven years, Lorca proved a source of and an inspiration for several Crumb compositions, beginning with *Night Music* (1963–64). Described by the composer as "instrumental nocturnes," it consisted of seven pieces, five of them instrumental, and two of them settings of poems by Lorca in a *Sprechstimme* idiom. Unusual sound effects and timbres are realized by having a sounded gong immersed into or withrawn from a tub of water, by requiring the musicians to whistle from time to time, and by producing pattering sounds on a drum head.

Lorca again was the soil from which grew the Madrigals, Books I and II (1965), which the Koussevitzky Music Foundation had commissioned and which was given its initial hearing in July 1968 in New York. Here Lorca's poems deal with life and death, water, rain and earth. In Book I, the mezzo-soprano is supported by vibraphone and contrabass, and in Book II, by percussion and flute. The vocal part sometimes calls for *Sprechstimme*, sometimes for quarter tones, sometimes for coloratura passages, sometimes *senza vibrato*.

Leaving the University of Colorado in 1964, Crumb went to the University of Pennsylvania to teach composition. He was made assistant professor in 1966, and full professor in 1970. In 1965 he received a grant from the Rockefeller Foundation, and in 1967 the first of two Guggenheim Fellowships, the second coming six years later.

Crumb was elevated to national prominence in 1968 when he was awarded the Pulitzer Prize in music for *Echoes of Time and the River* (1967), subtitled "four processionals for orchestra." It had been commissioned by the University of Chicago for the seventy-fifth anniversary of the Chicago Symphony, and its world premiere took place on May 26, 1967. The work is not specifically programmatic, nor (in spite of its title) does it have any relationship with Thomas Wolfe's novel *Of Time and the River*. Time (including psychological and philosophical time) is the unifying theme. To help carry out this concept, Crumb used "processionals" in which members of the orchestra march across the stage while performing a seemingly ritualistic drama. At one point, nine wind players come marching to the front of the orchestra, blowing into their instruments to produce the sound of wind before walking off. (These "processionals" were omitted when the work was first performed, but they have been used in some subsequent performances.) There are other highly unconventional procedures. Members of the orchestra are called upon to whisper or shout certain phrases: for example, the state motto of West Virginia, "Montani semper liberi?" ("Mountaineers are free?") in the first movement, the question mark being a Crumb addition; a phrase by Lorca in the second ("the broken arches where time suffers"); "Krek-tu-dai," a phonetic invention by the composer in the third; and "Koitais," another of the composer's phonetic concoctions in the fourth. At other times, clarinets are asked to play into an open, undamped piano; a small tambourine is placed over the piano's base strings to produce novel metallic sounds; two groups of whistlers are stationed at the right and left of the stage. During the performance, chance methods are also brought into play.

Lorca continued to provide Crumb with creative stimulation. Four Lorca poems are set in *Songs, Drones and Refrains of Death* (1968). Here the vocalist is required to sing much of his music through a cardboard tube while the musicians whisper, shout, or chant as well as perform on their respective instruments. In his search for new sound textures, Crumb uses sleigh bells, a jew's harp, water-tuned crystal glasses, a Chinese temple gong, antique finger cymbals, and a Japanese hand bell together with other sound-producing implements.

Lorca is also the source of *Ancient Voices of Children* (1970), one of Crumb's most highly esteemed and successful works since his Pulitzer Prize-winning composition. *Ancient Voices of Children* was commissioned by the Elizabeth Sprague Coolidge

Foundation for a chamber music festival in Washington, D.C., where it was introduced on October 31, 1970. A mezzo-soprano singing a vocalise into an amplified piano, utilizing only phonetic sounds, is just one of the novel sound effects. Others come from an assortment of exotic instruments such as Tibetan prayer stones, Japanese temple bells, a musical saw, and a toy piano.

The interpolation of the motto of the state of West Virginia in *Echoes of Time and the River* is one of numerous instances in which Crumb's place of birth stimulated or channelized his creativity. In *Makrokosmos II*, for amplified piano (1971), the performer whistles the Appalachian Mountain revival hymn "Will There Be Any Stars in My Crown?" ("Makrokosmos" means "the universe in its entirety," and in the first two books bearing that title Crumb explores every aspect of manipulating the piano strings and keys as well as the entire gamut of harmonic and sonic shadings.) In other compositions, the West Virginian influence on Crumb can be seen in his utilization of such instruments as the musical saw, banjo, jew's harp, all favored in the Appalachian region; also the production of sounds by blowing into the mouth of a stone jug or playing the electric guitar by sliding a glass rod over the frets, devices found in performances of West Virginia mountain music.

The influence of Charles Ives on Crumb can be detected in the way he quotes and distorts familiar music. A distortion of the Negro spiritual "Were You There?" appears in *Echoes from Time and the River*. In *Black Angels* (1970), for electrified string quartet, Schubert's *Death and the Maiden* and Saint-Saëns's *Danse macabre* are referred to; in *Makrokosmos I* (1972) a snatch of Chopin's *Fantaisie Impromptu* is heard; in *Night of the Four Moons* (1969) Ravel's *Bolero* is quoted.

Still in search of the new and the untried, Crumb required the performers to wear masks in *Lux Aeterna* (1971; Philadelphia, April 1972) and *Vox Balaenae* (1972; N.Y., September 30, 1972). *Lux Aeterna* is subtitled "Children of the Night." Five musicians (soprano, bass flute, sitar player and two percussion performers), all masked, group themselves around a burning candle on a stage illuminated solely by a red light. *Vox Balaenae*, or *Voice of the Whale*, was written after Crumb had heard a recording of songs by humpback whales. Crumb simulated these sounds instrumentally through electrified piano, cello, and flute. In order to "efface any sense of human projections," according to the composer, he had the instrumentalists wear masks and perform in a darkened auditorium.

Still other, later works by Crumb are off the beaten track. *Makrokosmos III*, subtitled "Music for a Summer Evening" (1974), calls for the piano strings to be covered by sheets of paper. Commissioned by the Fromm Music Foundation for Swarthmore College, it received its first hearing in Swarthmore, Pa., on March 30, 1974. *Star-Child* (1977) is Crumb's most monumental score, utilizing such immense forces that four conductors are needed. Eight percussionists perform on seventy different instruments or contraptions (pot lids, iron chains, log drums, metal drum sheets, wind machine, and so forth). Three trumpeters and three violins perform from the top balcony while two trumpets are stationed on each side of the auditorium. Two children's choruses are grouped around the conductors, not behind the orchestra. Crumb described the music as having "a sense of progression from darkness (or despair) to light (or joy and spiritual realization)." He uses two medieval texts: "Dies Irae" and "Massacre of the Innocents." Pierre Boulez conducted the New York Philharmonic in its premiere on May 5, 1977.

Apparitions, a song cycle subtitled "Elegiac Songs and Vocalises for Soprano and Amplified Piano," is Crumb's first purely vocal composition in a decade. Crumb here aspired to revert to the traditional idiom of the 19th-century art song. He completed it in 1980, and on January 13, 1981, Jan DeGaetani introduced it in New York. For his text, Crumb used six excerpts from Whitman's *When Lilacs Last in the Dooryard Bloom'd.* The first, third and fourth songs were each followed by a vocalise interlude suggesting phonetically "Sounds of a Summer Evening," "Invocation to the Dark Angel" and "Death Carol." "The musical mood of the cycle is extremely severe and doleful," reported Donal Henahan in the *New York Times.* "Mr. Crumb's ear for delicate sonorities and his way of making these sonorities touchingly allusive to the text were . . . much in evidence. . . . The interweaving of vocalise with words proved to be an effective device."

Crumb received honorary doctorates in music from Norris Harvey College in West Virginia (1969); Marshall University in Huntington, West Virginia (1973); and Oberlin College in Ohio (1978). In 1967 he was elected a member of the National Institute of Arts and Letters.

THE COMPOSER SPEAKS: I have always considered music to be a very strange substance, a substance endowed with magical properties. Music is tangible, almost palpable, and yet unreal, illusive. Music is analyzable only on the most mechanistic level; the important elements—the spiritual impulse, the psychological curve, the metaphysical implications—are understandable only in terms of the music itself. I feel intuitively that music must have been the prime cell from which language, science and religion originated.

PRINCIPAL WORKS: String Quartet (1954); Sonata, for solo cello (1955); *Variazioni,* for orchestra (1959); Five Pieces, for piano (1962); *Night Music I,* for soprano, piano, celesta and percussion (1963); *Night Music II,* for violin and piano (1964); Madrigals, Book I, for soprano, vibraphone, string bass (1965); Madrigals, Book II, for alto flute, flute in C, piccolo and percussion (1965); *Eleven Echoes of Autumn*, 1965, for alto flute, clarinet, piano and violin (1966); *Echoes of Time and the River*, four processionals for orchestra (1967); *Songs, Drones, and Refrains of Death*, for baritone, electric guitar, electric double bass, electrified piano, electrified harpsichord and two percussionists (1968); Madrigals, Book III, for soprano, harp and percussion (1969); Madrigals, Book IV, for soprano, flute, harp, double bass and percussionist (1969); *Night of the Four Moons*, for alto and chamber ensemble (1969); *Ancient Voices of Children*, for soprano, boy soprano, oboe, mandolin, harp, electric piano (or toy piano), musical saw, and percussion (1970); *Black Angels*, "thirteen images from the dark land," for electrified string quartet (1970); *Lux Aeterna*, for soprano, bass flute, sitar and percussion (1971); *Vox Balaenae*, for electrified piano, cello and flute (1972); *Makrokosmos vols. I and II*, for amplified piano (1972, 1973); *Makrokosmos III*, music for a summer evening, for two amplified pianos and two percussion players (1974); *Star-Child*, parable for large orchestra, soprano, two children's choruses, later scored also for male speaking choir and handbells (1977); *Celestial Mechanics, Makrokosmos IV*, for amplified piano, four hands (1978); *Apparitions*, song cycle for soprano and amplified piano (1980).

BIBLIOGRAPHY:*DCM; NGDMM;* BMI, *The Many Worlds of Music*, May 1972; *High Fidelity/Musical America*, September 1968; *New York Times Magazine*, May 11, 1975; *Who's Who in America, 1980–81.*

Custer, Arthur, b. Manchester, Conn., April 21, 1923.

Controlled improvsations and sonorous explorations are prominent in Custer's music, in spite of the fact that much of it is serially ordered. Within such contexts he has arrived at his own idiom and style, which embrace atmospheric evocations and ironic humor as well as strong motor rhythms and provocative subject matter.

He did not have any serious involvement with music study until he was twenty-three. As he has said, he came from a "Lawrence Welkian monotonic family which was never able to explain the existence of that old leaky violin in the attic." When a rich aunt moved to a new house she deposited her piano in the Custer living room. When Arthur was nine he began to explore its musical potential "inside out." Presumably because his autodidactic music making gave him pleasure, he volunteered to be the drummer in the school orchestra when he was in the fifth grade of Manchester Green Grammar School. He continued to play the drums at Manchester High School and in several jazz combos. "Learning from my fellow musicians, my high school teacher, and the jazz greats at Greenwich Village haunts like Nick's, I picked up

trombone, bass, and a little sax." In his last two years of high school and throughout his undergraduate years in college he had his own band, played jazz, and wrote pop tunes.

Despite such musical involvements, he planned to become an engineer. With this aim in view he attended the University of Hartford (1940–42), where he received an associate in science degree. World War II interrupted his academic life. From November 1942 to April 1946 he served with the U.S. Naval Aviation, seeing military service as a carrier-based fighter pilot in the South Pacific.

When he was released from the service, he shifted from engineering to music. In 1946 he entered the University of Connecticut in Storrs for a full baccalaureate program in music education, majoring in trombone and having one of the professors, Robert Yingling, open up for him a world of music he had never known, beginning with symphonies by César Franck and Alexander Borodin. "They took me in, unclean and untutored," he recalls, "and helped me become a musician."

After receiving his bachelor of arts degree in 1949 he attended the University of Redlands in California that year, studying composition with Paul Pisk and receiving his master's degree in 1951. At the University of Iowa in Iowa City (1956–59) he earned his doctorate in music in 1959 after having studied composition with Philip Bezanson. During these postgraduate years he was chairman of the division of fine arts at Kansas Wesleyan in Salina, Kans., (1952–55), then was a member of the music faculty at the University of Omaha in Omaha (1955–58), which later became the University of Nebraska.

In 1957, he discarded everything he had composed up to that time and began his career as composer all over again from scratch. That year, he wrote a Passacaglia, for small orchestra (1957; Chicago, April 14, 1963), together with a few compositions for chamber music combinations. Three Pieces for Brass Quintet (1958) was performed in Madrid on May 3, 1961; *Three Songs on Death* (1958), in New York on November 9, 1964; Concert Piece for Orchestra (1959) at the Inter-American Symposium of Contemporary Music in Austin, Tex., on April 17, 1963, Donald Johanos conducting; and Sextet, for woodwinds and piano (1959), in Madrid on May 3, 1961. All these are atonal, occasionally in a modified serial technique.

In 1959 Custer was appointed supervisor of music for the U.S. Air Force Dependent Schools in Spain. He remained abroad until 1962, serving also from 1960 on as music consultant for the U.S. Information Agency in Madrid, where he lectured, conducted, and organized concerts of American music. During his European stay, he completed the study of composition with Nadia Boulanger in Paris and Fontainebleau between 1960 and 1962.

Upon returning to the United States in 1962, Custer was made assistant dean of fine arts at the University of Rhode Island in Kingston, where he remained three years and received three consecutive grants-in-aid for creative work. Concurrently (1963–65) he was vice-president of the Rhode Island Fine Arts Council, president of the Rhode Island Music Teachers Association, and vice-president of the Eastern Division of the Music Teachers National Association. He was dean of the Philadelphia Musical Academy in Pennsylvania from 1965 to 1967. From 1967 to 1970, under a grant from the U.S. Office of Education, he was director of the Metropolitan Education Center in the Arts in St. Louis, at which time he wrote the program notes for the St. Louis Symphony (1967–69). On a grant from the National Endowment for the Arts, he was director of the Arts in Education Project of the Rhode Island Council of the Arts (1970–73). During the summer of 1973 he was instructor at the Manhattan School of Music in New York, and in the fall of 1975 he taught Multi-Arts Improvisation at Lesley College Graduate School in Cambridge, Mass. Between 1973 and 1975 he was composer-in-residence at the Rhode Island State Council on the Arts.

He completed his first major work, a symphony, in 1961 during his residence in Spain, and it was introduced in Madrid on May 15, 1961 by the Madrid Philharmonic under Odón Alonso. Its American premiere followed in St. Louis on May 9, 1969, with Walter Susskind conducting the St. Louis Symphony This was one of the two works written in 1961 that depended on extramusical impulses. (The other was *Colloquy,* for string quartet, introduced in Madrid on April 28, 1962, and then recipient of a publication award from the Society for the Publication of American Music.) Subtitled *Symphony of Madrid,* this symphony was the composer's emotional response to three places in Madrid that impressed him greatly: Gran Via (Avenida José Antonio), a bustling thoroughfare; Plaza Mayor, the historic main square of the old city; and Casa de Campo, a large bucolic park on the outskirts of the city. "I have not attempted to evoke the essential character of each of these sites," the composer explains, "but rather to offer a simple statement of response to these provocative stimuli. The music, therefore is not programmatic in the sense that it describes or depicts, but merely that the musical materials were worked out within the context of a prevailing mood, or more properly, three different moods."

This symphony is in a dodecaphonic idiom, with a twelve-tone series serving as a basic motive skeleton, the source from which most of the linear and harmonic elements that follow are fashioned. Custer continued to employ serial procedures in the many abstract works that followed, always fashioning these procedures to his own image. He also made significant use of electronic music, most notably in a series of compositions bearing the collective title of *Found Objects.* Here the tone row has been abandoned and live performances are joined with prerecorded tapes

that incorporate instrumental, concrete, and synthesized sounds. The materials which make up each of the *Found Objects,* as the composer informs us, "are chosen, organized and shaped according to fairly common musical impulses, and take into account such standard and conventional elements as melody, counterpoint, texture, and harmony, counterposed with various types of tape manipulations. The intention has been to form an integrated work whose tape component may be thought of as a graciously sonorous partner to the live performance. Composition may be defined as 'putting together.' The putting together of my 'found objects' pieces has never been random. It is always purposeful, though not necessarily serious. The effect may be whimsical, bizarre, startling, provocative. Each piece is 'about' something."

Found Objects I, for chorus and tape (1968), was based on Custer's earlier choral piece, the motet *Ultima Ratio Regum* (1966) with portions of this earlier work quoted and juxtaposed with new material. The singers are asked to whistle, shout, and perform on various kitchen utensils as a way of integrating live sound with tape component. *Found Objects II, Rhapsodality Brass!* for orchestra (1969; N.Y., November 8, 1969), dispenses with prerecorded tape but expands on the device of quotations from earlier Custer material, in this instance his *Rhapsodality Brown!* for piano (1969; Philadelphia, January 5, 1971) and Concerto for Brass Quintet (1968; Kingston, R.I., April 17, 1969) with nonsense syllables chanted by the orchestra players. In his next six *Found Objects* (1971–74) Custer again uses prerecorded tapes with various individual improvising instruments, or as in the case of no. 6 (1973) a group of instruments (flutes).

A Little Sight Music (1973; Providence, R.I., April 14, 1973) is no. 5 in the *Found Objects* set. This is one of several Custer works conceived for performance in museums and galleries, utilizing paintings and sculpture as objects to be rendered into sound by improvising performers. "It's hard for me to pass by something and not think of how it sounds," Custer once said. This work is scored for a pianist-conductor (or, as Custer prefers to designate him, an "artistic referee"), violin, clarinet, trumpet, trombone, and string bass. The players are all expected to have improvisational skill, for they are required to "play" spontaneously the paintings or sculpture in the museum or the sculpture of Styrofoam forms which the audience itself creates. This is a composition to "see" as well as to "hear," a piece intended to entertain and "whose purposeful irony derives from the confluence of serious intentions and playful results," in the composer's words.

Among Custer's other innovative works for prerecorded tape is *Interface I,* for string quartet and two recording engineers (1969; St. Louis, November 23, 1969). The geometrical term "interface" implies the formation of a common boundary of two bodies or spaces by a plane or other surface. In this composition, Custer attempts to create the organization of musical space in which the tape recorder functions as an interface. To achieve this, the recording must be stereophonic with four speakers placed strategically on either side of the stage or elsewhere in the hall. The sounds produced live by the quartet in the first two segments are recorded by the engineers and played back during the performance which also involves the playing of prerecorded tape. In the third segment, the quartet begins to imitate the sounds it has heard on the tape, this third part being performed in a totally dark auditorium.

Custer has written music for numerous documentaries for television and films and for dramatic productions. Two of his educational films were rewarded with the Salerno Festival Grand Award in Italy and the Edinburgh Award of Merit in Scotland. He has lectured extensively, been active as a participant in composition seminars and has served as a visiting composer on various college campuses. With the pianist Dwight Peltzer, he has worked out new methods of music education for children, music students and teachers called *Explorations*. Custer has also written extensively on music for various journals, for the Enciclopedia Internacional published in Madrid and for *Contemporary Music in Europe* (New York, 1965).

Custer was married twice: the first time in Hartford, Conn., on December 27, 1947, to Marilyn Emmons, whom he divorced in 1966; the second time, in Philadelphia, on June 18, 1967, to Dolores Borgaard, a schoolteacher. He had three children from his first marriage, and a daughter from the second.

THE COMPOSER SPEAKS: I would characterize my recent music as highly expressive. The technique is still there, but it is used to communicate something: moods, of course, but also personal concerns and feelings having to do with such things as identity, conflict, fun, striving and so forth. This music is not divorced from me, a clatter in the air; it has me in it.

My recent work has also explored the relationships between visual and aural images. So far, this interest had two different manifestations in my work. One is concerned with the rendering into sound of visual gestures. The other is the exploration of the sonorous implications of visual objects.

PRINCIPAL WORKS: *Colloquy*, for string quartet (1961); Symphony (1961); Cycle for Nine Instruments (1963); *Songs of the Season*, for soprano and small orchestra (1963); Concertino for Second Violin and Strings (1964); String Quartet no. 2 (1964); Two Movements for Woodwind Quintet (1964); *Four Ideas*, for piano (1965); *Ultima Ratio Regum*, motet for chorus (1966); *Permutations*, for violin, clarinet and cello (1967); *Comments on This World*, for contralto and string quartet (1967); Concerto for Quintet (1968); *Found Objects I*, for chorus and tape (1968); *Rhapsodality Brown!*, for piano (1969); *Found Objects II, Rhapsodality Brass!*, for orchestra, (1969); *Songs of Freedom, Love, and War*, for chorus (1969); *Found Objects III*, for contrabass and tape (1971); *Found Objects IV,* for cello and tape (1972); *Rhapsodality Band!*, for wind ensemble (1972); *Doubles*, for violin and small orchestra (1972); *A Little Sight Music, Found Objects V*, for instrumental ensemble (1973); *Found Objects VI*, for flutes and tape (1973); *Found Objects VII*, for piano and tape (1973), *Found Objects VIII*, for violin and tape (1974); *Eyepiece*, for oboe and tape (1974); *The Magic Dragon*, for tuba and tape (1975).

BIBLIOGRAPHY: *BBDM; DCM.*

D

Dahl, Ingolf, b. Hamburg, Germany, June 9, 1912; d. Frutigen, Switzerland, August 7, 1970. American citizen, 1943.

Dahl was a prime mover in Los Angeles in the promotion of new music. His earlier works were in the complex linear style of Hindemith, and in his later ones he turned to the serialization of melodic and harmonic materials.

Of Swedish parentage, Dahl received his early musical training at the piano and in composition with private teachers in Sweden and Switzerland. Between 1930 and 1932 he attended the Music Academy of Cologne in Germany, a pupil in composition of Philip Jarnach's and in conducting of Hermann Abendroth's. Dahl's academic education was continued at the Zurich Conservatory (1932–36), where he took courses in musicology. Concurrently (1932–35) he studied conducting with Volkmar Andreae and piano with Walter Frey at the Zurich Conservatory. While pursuing his academic and musical studies he served as coach and conductor at the Zurich Stadttheater between 1934 and 1938.

He visited the United States in 1935, then returned in 1938 for permanent residence and application for American citizenship. He settled in Los Angeles where, in 1944, he received further instruction in composition from Nadia Boulanger. Between 1942 and 1945 he was employed as a conductor over radio and as an arranger for Hollywood films. From 1945 until the end of his life he was a member of the music faculty of the University of California in Los Angeles, where he conducted the University Symphony between 1945 and 1960 and again in 1968–69. In Los Angeles, over a period of many years, he appeared as a conductor at the Monday "Evenings on the Roof" concerts devoted to new music. Dahl taught composition at the Berkshire Music Center in Tanglewood, Mass., during the summers of 1952 to 1955, and between 1964 and 1965 he was music director of the Ojai Music Festival in California. In 1961–62 he was sent by the U.S. State Department to tour Europe as lecturer and conductor.

Rejecting everything he had composed before 1942 as juvenilia, Dahl looked upon works completed in the early 1940s in the United States as the beginnings of his creative maturity. From then on he was almost exclusively a composer of instrumental music. His first work to command attention was Music for Brass Instruments (1944), which had been commissioned by Arthur Leslie Jacobs of the Church Feder-

ation in Los Angeles, and whose premiere was given at the Festival of Contemporary Music in Los Angeles in May 1944. Though its first movement is based on the original modal version of the Lutheran Easter Chorale *Christ lag in Todesbanden*, the work is atonal. Dahl would continue to use a complex dissonant harmonic and contrapuntal language for the next decade in such compositions as: *Concerto a tre*, for clarinet, violin and cello (1946); Concertino in One Movement, for clarinet, violin and cello (1946); Concerto, for alto saxophone and wind orchestra (1949); *Sonata seria*, for piano (1953); and *The Tower of St. Barbara*, a symphonic legend for orchestra (1954), first performed on January 29, 1955, in Louisville, Ky.

Beginning with the Piano Quartet (1957), Dahl absorbed serialism into his idiom. The most notable of his later works are: *Sonata pastorale*, for piano (1959); Piano Trio (1962); *Aria sinfonico* (1965; Los Angeles, April 15, 1963); and the Variations on a Theme by C. P. E. Bach (1967), commissioned by the American Federation of Musicians Congress of Strings (Western Section) and premiered at the University of Southern California in Los Angeles, Walter Ducloux conducting, on July 12, 1967.

Dahl received a Guggenheim Fellowship, in 1952, and awards from the National Institute of Arts and Letters and the Alice M. Ditson Fund of Columbia University. He was a contributor of numerous articles on music for various journals and the co-translator of Stravinsky's *The Poetics of Music* (Cambridge, Mass. 1947).

PRINCIPAL WORKS: Allegro and Arioso, for woodwind quintet (1942); Music for Brass Instruments, for brass quintet (1944); Variations on a Swedish Folk Tune, for solo flute (1945); *Concerto a tre*, for clarinet, violin and cello (1946); Duo, for cello and piano (1946); Concertino in One Movement, for clarinet, violin and cello (1946); *The Deep Blue Devil's Breakdown*, for two pianos, eight hands (1946); Divertimento, for violin and piano (1948); Concerto, for alto saxophone and wind orchestra (1949); Quodlibet on American Folk Tunes, for two pianos, eight hands (1953, orchestrated 1965); *Sonata seria*, for piano (1953); *Symphonie concertante*, for two clarinets and orchestra (1953); *The Tower of St. Barbara*, symphonic legend for orchestra (1954); Piano Quartet (1957); *Sonata pastorale*, for piano (1959); Serenade, for four flutes (1960); Sinfonietta, for concert band (1961); *Colloquy*, for string quartet (1961); Symphony (1961); Piano Trio (1962); *Elegy Concerto*, for violin and chamber orchestra (1963, completed by Donal Michalsky in 1971); *Aria sinfonica*, for orchestra (1965); *Duo concertante*, for flute and percussion (1966); Variations on a Theme by C.P.E. Bach, for orchestra (1967), A Cycle of Sonnets, for baritone or alto and piano (1968); *Four Intervals*, for piano (1969); *Sonata da camera*, for clarinet and piano (1970); *Little Canonic Suite*, for violin and viola (1970); *A Noiseless, Patient Spider* for female chorus and piano (1970).

BIBLIOGRAPHY: *BBDM; DCM; NGDMM.*

Damrosch, Walter Johannes, b. Breslau, Germany, January 30, 1862; d. New York City, December 22, 1950. American citizen.

Damrosch had such a long eventful career as conductor that his compositions were thrown into the shade. In his music he never released himself from the German romantic music on which he had been nurtured, even when he was producing works on native American subjects, including an American opera with an American text.

His father was Leopold Damrosch, a distinguished musician, friend of such musical greats as Wagner and Liszt, the founder of the Oratorio Society of New York, the New York Symphony Society, and conductor at the Metropolitan Opera. Walter's mother, Helena von Heimburg, was also a professional musician, a successful singer of lieder and opera. Walter's older brother, Frank, became an eminent music educator, the founder of the Institute of Musical Art and the Juilliard School of Music.

Walter spent his first nine years in Germany, where he received his instruction in piano and harmony from his father, and later in theory from Max Draeske and Wilhelm Rischbieter, and piano from Anton Urspruch. In 1871, he was brought to the United States, henceforth to remain his permanent home and the country of his citizenship. While attending public school in the lowest grade because he could not speak English, he continued to study piano with Jean Vogt. During extended return visits to Germany, his study of the piano took place with Ferdinand von Inten, Bernardus Boekelmann, Max Pinner, and Hans von Bülow.

He initiated his professional career in music as organist of the Plymouth Church in Brooklyn, N.Y., and by serving as accompanist for the violinist August Wilhelm when he toured the southern states in 1878; playing the violin in musical organizations conducted by his father; helping his father rehearse a music festival in New York in May 1881; and making his own debut as conductor in 1881 with the Newark (N.J.) Harmonic Society.

The sudden death of his father in 1885 threw the full burden of his father's varied conducting activities squarely on his shoulders. He took over the conductor's posts of the New York Symphony Society and the Oratorio Society of New York, and beginning on February 11, 1885, the direction of the German repertoire of the Metropolitan Opera. When the Metropolitan Opera temporarily lost interest in the production of Wagner's music dramas, Damrosch left the company after the 1890–91 season and four years later organized the Damrosch Opera Company, which toured the United States principally performing a Wagnerian repertoire for four seasons. Earlier, on March 3, 1886, he gave the first presentation of *Parsifal* outside Bayreuth (a concert performance). He was back at the Metropolitan Opera from 1900 to 1902, and made his farewell there on March 6, 1902, with *Die Götterdämmerung*. Between 1895 and 1898 he had conducted the Oratorio Society of New York.

Damrosch's prime significance as conductor, and as shaper of performance history in the United States, rested mainly on his years as conductor of the New York Symphony Society (1885–1926). Through these concerts he gave the United States its first hearings of many European masterworks (Brahms's symphonies nos. 3 and 4, Tchaikovsky's symphonies nos. 4 and 6, Ravel's *Daphnis and Chloé Suite*, Sibelius's Symphony no. 4; and so forth); he brought Tchaikovsky to the United States to participate in ceremonies opening Carnegie Hall, the first time a world-famous foreign composer visited America; and he inaugurated concerts for children, the first such ever undertaken by a leading American orchestra. In 1919 he was the first American invited to tour Europe with an American orchestra.

When the United States became involved in World War I, General Pershing invited Damrosch to organize the American Expeditionary Forces band. Damrosch not only did this but he also formed a school for bandmasters at Chaumont, France, in 1918, out of which grew the American Conservatory of Fontainebleau after the war. During the war he served as president, in France, of the American Friends of Musicians to help destitute French musicians and their families. He also conducted a pickup Parisian orchestra in concerts.

On February 27, 1922, the fiftieth anniversary of Damrosch's arrival in the United States was commemorated with a concert at Carnegie Hall, all proceeds going to help establish the Walter Damrosch Fellowship at the American Academy in Rome. In 1931, Damrosch was a leading figure in establishing the Musicians Emergency Fund Aid, to provide financial assistance to musicians suffering from the depression. To raise funds for this project he conducted a series of concerts at Madison Square Garden in New York. Damrosch's golden jubilee as conductor was celebrated at the Metropolitan Opera House on April 12, 1935, when Damrosch conducted acts from *Fidelio* and *Die Meistersinger*.

When the New York Symphony Society was absorbed by the New York Philharmonic in 1926, Damrosch withdrew as principal conductor. He served as guest conductor for one season and then left for good to devote himself for the next two decades to providing good music over the radio. On November 15, 1926, he conducted the first concert of symphonic music to be given network coverage over NBC. From 1927 to 1947 he was musical adviser to NBC. As such he conducted symphonic music over the radio regularly, as well as a weekly "Music Appreciation Hour" for schoolchildren (1928–42), which was broadcast to schools throughout the United States. When Damrosch resigned from his radio activities on March 31, 1947, he went into retirement.

While thus deeply involved for over half a century in reproducing the music of others, Damrosch was also occupied with creations of his own. He was best known for his operas and a few songs. His first opera was *The Scarlet Letter*, libretto by George Parsons Lathrop, based on the Hawthorne story. Damrosch's own company produced it for the first time on February 10, 1896, in Boston. His writing was so strongly influenced by Wagner in its scoring, chromaticisms and use of the leitmotiv technique that Anton Seidl, a distinguished rival conductor, referred to it as the "New England Nibelung trilogy." The Wagner presence can still be felt in his second opera, though not so obviously: *Cyrano de Bergerac*, libretto by W. J. Henderson derived from Edmond Rostand's play. When its premiere was mounted by the Metropolitan Opera in New York on February 27, 1913, Henry Krehbiel in the *New York Tribune* spoke of it as "a notable artistic achievement and one which reflects credit upon its authors." Damrosch revised this opera in 1939 and conducted the new version in a concert performance with the New York Philharmonic on February 20, 1941. One other Damrosch opera deserves attention, probably his best: *The Man without a Country*, for which Arthur Guiterman provided the libretto derived from the story of Edward Everett Hale. Produced by the Metropolitan Opera House on May 12, 1937 (a performance in which Helen Traubel made her opera debut), it revealed one more step away from Wagner in favor of values favored by Italian grand opera: a warm, engaging lyricism that permitted exploitation of the human voice; an infectious charm; and a continuous consciousness of and responsiveness to stage action.

Damrosch's best works outside the opera house were *Abraham Lincoln Song*, for baritone, chorus, and orchestra (1935), broadcast over the NBC radio network in April 1936; *Dunkirk* (1943), a setting of Robert Nathan's text, for baritone, male chorus and chamber orchestra, first heard on the NBC radio network on May 2, 1943; and the songs "Danny Deever" (1897) and "Death and General Putnam" (1936).

From 1927 to 1929, Damrosch was president of the National Institute of Arts and Letters (which awarded him a gold medal in 1939) and from 1940 to 1948 of the American Academy of Arts and Letters. Among the numerous other honors showered upon him were the following: Chevalier of the Crown of Belgium; Officer of the French Legion of Honor; Officer of the Crown of Italy; a silver medal from the Worshipful Company of Musicians in London; the Banda Communale in Rome; and honorary doctorates from Columbia, Brown, Princeton, Dartmouth, Pennsylvania, and New York universities and Washington and Jefferson College in Washington, Pa. In 1959, a tract at the Lincoln Center for the Performing Arts in New York was named Damrosch Park.

On May 17, 1890, Damrosch married Margaret Blaine, daughter of James G. Blaine, former secretary of state of the United States. Of their four daughters, Gretchen became the wife of the secretary of the air force, Thomas K. Finletter; Leopoldine, the wife of the distinguished playwright Sidney Howard; and Anita, the wife of the eminent writer and editor Robert Littell. Damrosch survived his wife by one year.

Damrosch appeared as himself in the motion picture *The Star Maker* (1939). He was the author of an autobiography, *My Musical Life* (1923).

THE COMPOSER SPEAKS: A composer's fame is not affirmed by professional musicians but by the general public, whose judgment in the end is infallible. A great masterwork that is not destroyed will always eventually be recognized as such whether, like the Venus de Milo, it has lain hidden for centuries beneath the earth or, like the *Matthew Passion* of Bach, equally hidden in the dusty shelves of the Royal Library in Berlin, to be rediscovered by Mendelssohn and pronounced the greatest religious choral work ever written.

Conductors have had their personal convictions and have tried to force them on our audiences, but unless these convictions were based on actual worth, the public has in the end consciously or unconsciously rejected them. Sometimes unworthy composers have had momentary popularity but they were born to dance in the sun for one day and then to die.

PRINCIPAL WORKS: *The Scarlet Letter*, opera (1894); "Danny Deever," song for voice and piano (1897); *Manila Te Deum*, for chorus and orchestra (1898); *The Dove of Peace*, comic opera (1912); *Cyrano de Bergerac*, opera (1913, revised 1939); *Abraham Lincoln Song*, for baritone, chorus, and orchestra (1935); "Death and General Putnam," song for voice and piano (1936); *The Man without a Country*, opera (1937); *The Opera Cloak*, one-act opera (1942), *Dunkirk*, for baritone, male chorus, and chamber orchestra (1943); *Congress and the Elephant*, comic opera (1944).

BIBLIOGRAPHY: Damrosch, Walter, *My Musical Life* (N.Y., 1923); Finletter, Gretchen Damrosch, *From the Top of the Stairs* (Boston, 1946); *Musical*

Quarterly, January 1932; *Opera News*, January 27, 1962; *New York Times* (obituary), December 23, 1950.

Daniels, Mabel Wheeler, b. Swampscott, Mass., November 27, 1878: d. Boston, March 10, 1971.

For the greater part of her composing career, Daniels was a conservative who favored a quasi-impressionistic style, subtle and refined in its expression. The lyricism of her later music (beginning with 1940) had stronger fiber, and her harmonic language became spiced with discords.

She was a New Englander who lived most of her years in or near Boston. Both her parents were musicians, members of the chorus of the Handel and Haydn Society in Boston, of which her father, George F. Daniels, was president. Though Mabel began to study the piano with private teachers early and was composing little pieces for the piano by the time she was ten, she was more interested in literature than music when she attended the Girls Latin School in Boston, writing and publishing several short stories. At Radcliffe College, which she entered in 1896, her latent musical interests were developed. Possessed as she was of an excellent singing voice, she was a member of the college glee club and performed in school productions of operettas, the music for two of which she herself composed. On January 2, 1901, one of her operettas, *The Court of Hearts*, in which she assumed an important singing role, was produced in Cambridge.

After graduating from Radcliffe with a bachelor of arts degree, *magna cum laude*, in 1900, she studied composition and orchestration with George Chadwick. In 1903 she went to Germany, and for two winters studied composition with Ludwig Thuille in Munich. Her girlhood experiences in Germany are described in a charming autobiography, *An American Girl in Munich: Impressions of a Music Student* (1905).

From 1911 to 1913 she was director of the Radcliffe Glee Club, as a result of which she directed her creative energies into choral and vocal music. The National Federation of Music Clubs presented her with prizes in 1911 for two choral works, *The Voice of My Beloved* and *Eastern Song* (1911). Her first significant composition was *The Desolate City* (1913), performed at the MacDowell Colony in Peterboro, N.H., in 1913 during the first of many summers spent there composing. While employed on the music faculty of Simmons College in Boston (1913–18) she continued writing choral music, which was becoming her specialty. *Peace in Liberty, or Peace with a Sword* (1917) was successfully performed by the Handel and Haydn Society in February 1918. Her most famous choral work came a decade later: *Exultate Deo*, written in 1929 for the fiftieth anniversary of the founding of Radcliffe, and introduced in Boston on May 31, 1929. This was subsequently

performed by the Boston Symphony Orchestra under Serge Koussevitzky, at two Worcester Festival concerts in Massachusetts conducted by Hugh Ross and Albert Stoessel, and even in such distant places as Manila. A quarter of a century later, Daniels again wrote a composition for Radcliffe, this time to celebrate its seventy-fifth anniversary: *A Psalm of Praise* (1954), introduced in Cambridge, Mass., on December 3, 1954, then performed by the Boston Symphony under Koussevitzky on April 27, 1956.

She did not confine herself exclusively to choral music, however. Indeed, one of her most frequently performed compositions is orchestral: *Deep Forest* (1931), inspired by the New Hampshire woods at the MacDowell Colony. She wrote it originally for chamber orchestra, and as such it was heard at a concert at the Barrère Little Symphony under George Barrère in New York on June 3, 1931. As rescored for full symphony orchestra, *Deep Forest* was given its initial hearing in Weston, Conn., in a performance by the New York Orchestra under Nikolai Sokoloff on August 7, 1934; and on April 16, 1937, Koussevitzky presented it at a concert of the Boston Symphony. Reviewing the Boston Symphony concert, Redfern Mason wrote in the *Boston Transcript*: "Miss Daniels' piece is a tonal reverie in which she tells us what Mother Nature means to her. In this vein she has something in common with Edward MacDowell, but she is a dryad of the forest, not a faun." *Deep Forest* has received numerous performances throughout the United States since then, including a performance conducted by John Barbirolli with the New York Philharmonic in New York. When the American Society of Composers, Authors, and Publishers (ASCAP) presented a festival of American music at Carnegie Hall, New York, in 1939, *Deep Forest* was the only work by an American woman composer presented at that event.

Pirates' Island (1932), a humorous piece, was another of her successful orchestral compositions. It was first performed on February 19, 1935, by the Harrisburg Symphony in Pennsylvania, and was later programmed by the Cleveland Symphony and the Boston Pops besides serving as the background music for a ballet mounted by Ted Shawn's company at Robin Hood Dell in Philadelphia.

A modern idiom, melodically and harmonically in the manner of Arthur Honegger, began to assert itself by 1940 in one of her major choral works: *Song of Jael*, a cantata for dramatic soprano, mixed voices, and orchestra (1937), which used as text a poem by one of her close friends, Edwin Arlington Robinson. Its premiere was given at the Worcester Festival on October 5, 1940. Warren Storey Smith in the *Boston Post* described it as "a prolonged hymn of triumph that comes to a mighty climax. . . . The outstanding feature of her *Jael* is the striking and frequent highly original handling of the chorus. There are, nevertheless, many effective moments in the orchestral score, while the long soprano solo is dramatic and impressive." She continued to use modern resources in her subsequent works, one of the most successful being the *Pastorale Ode* (1940), first performed by members of the Boston Symphony with George Laurent playing the solo flute, then heard over the NBC radio network in a performance by the NBC Symphony conducted by Frank Black.

In 1926 Daniels received an award from the League of American Penwomen. An honorary degree of master of arts was awarded her in 1933 by Tufts University in Medford, Mass., and in 1939, a doctorate in music by Boston University. The National Association of American Composers and Conductors presented her with an award in 1958. She was an honorary member of Phi Beta Kappa.

In 1945, Daniels was elected trustee of Radcliffe College. There, a loan fund for students majoring in music was established in her name, while she herself created an additional fund named after her to provide assistance to needy music students. To stimulate undergraduate work in music she annually presented a silver cup to the best student in each of the four years. Radcliffe awarded her with an honorary citation in 1954, and in 1966, on the dedication of the Radcliffe Graduate Center, several of her choral works were performed.

PRINCIPAL WORKS: *In the Greenwood*, suite for piano (1908); *In Springtime*, choral cycle for women's voices (1910); Suite, for strings (1910); *The Voice of My Beloved*, for women's chorus with piano and two violins (1911); *Eastern Song*, for women's voices, two violins, and piano (1911); *Veni Creator Spiritus*, for women's voices (1912); *The Desolate City*, for baritone and orchestra (1913); *Fairy Scherzo*, for orchestra (1914); *Peace in Liberty, or Peace with a Sword*, for chorus and orchestra (1917); *Songs of Elfland*, for women's voices and orchestra (1924); *The Rider*, for male chorus (1926); *The Holy Star*, for chorus and orchestra (1928); *Exultate Deo*, for chorus and orchestra (1929); *Deep Forest*, prelude for small or large orchestra (1931); *The Christ Child*, for chorus (1931); *Pirates' Island*, for orchestra (1932); *Christmas in the Wood*, for chorus and orchestra (1934); *Song of Jael*, cantata for dramatic soprano, chorus and orchestra (1937); *Salve, Festa Dies*, for chorus (1938); *Pastorale Ode*, for flute and strings (1940); *Three Observations*, for oboe, clarinet and bassoon (1945); *Flower Wagon*, for women's chorus (1945); *Four Observations*, for four strings (1945); *Digression*, for strings (1947); Two Pieces, for violin and piano (1947); Overture, for orchestra (1951); *A Psalm of Praise*, for vocal soloists, chorus and orchestra (1954); *A Night in Bethlehem*, for chorus (1954).

BIBLIOGRAPHY: Goss, Madeleine, *Modern Music Makers* (N.Y., 1952); Reis, Claire, *Composers in America* (N.Y., 1947); *Who's Who in America, 1970–71*.

Davidovsky, Mario, b. Medanos, Buenos Aires, March 4, 1934. American citizen.

Although Davidovsky has produced notable compositions for traditional instruments, he is perhaps best known for his electronic music. He has created a series of compositions under the title of *Synchronisms* in which one or more standard instruments are combined with electronic sounds. For one of these pieces (no. 6) he was awarded the Pulitzer Prize in music in 1971.

Religion and music were the two most important elements in his early life. Hebraic backgrounds and ritual was a heritage from Davidovsky's grandparents, one of whom was a nonofficiating rabbi, and the other a Hebraic scribe; Davidovsky's mother was a biblical scholar. Music was also basic to the family since Davidovsky's father, Natalio, played the violin and clarinet.

Mario began music study with lessons on the violin when he was seven: two years later he was able to play duets with his father. While continuing to study music, Davidovsky started composing in his thirteenth year. From this time on composition became his prime interest in music. His first important composition teacher, and a major influence in his early development as composer, was Guillermo Graetzer. His other music teachers included Ernesto Epstein, Erwin Leuchter, and Teodoro Fuchs. Music was combined with academic studies, including law, but when Davidovsky was twenty he decided to devote himself entirely to music.

His first success as a composer came with String Quartet no. 1 (1954), which was introduced in Buenos Aires by the Wagnerian Society String Quartet and received first prize from the Asociación Wagneriana. This was followed by String Quartet no. 2 (1957), recipient of a BMI Student Composers Award in 1959, and Concertino for Strings and Percussion (1956), winner of an award from the Society of Friends of Music in Buenos Aires following its premiere in that city. In addition to such concert works, Davidovsky also produced music for the experimental theater and art films. As a promoter of new music he distinguished himself as cofounder of the Sociedad de Jovenes Compositores, which devoted itself to the publicization, performance, and recording of new Argentine music, and as a member of the Asociación Nueva Musica, which gave concerts of new music and sponsored the publication of theoretical works.

Davidovsky first came to the United States in 1958 at the invitation of Aaron Copland in conjunction with a performance of Davidovsky's *Noneto* (1957) at the Berkshire Music Center at Tanglewood, Mass. While in United States he learned from Milton Babbitt that an electronic music center would soon be founded. On the first of two Guggenheim Fellowships (a second following in 1962), and the first of two Rockefeller Foundation grants (the other in 1964), Davidovsky returned to the United States in 1960 to study electronic music at the then newly opened Columbia-Princeton Electronic Music Center in New York. "The amazing thing around the Columbia-Princeton Electronic Music Center," Davidovsky says, "is that you find people working on tremendously different principles and approaches. The differences between anybody within the group are sometimes radical—extremely different and sometimes opposite in techniques. This is one of the great assets of the electronic music center." Since then, Davidovsky has become the Center's associate director.

On November 19, 1961, Davidovsky and Elaine Blaustein were married; they have raised two children. From 1961 to 1965, Davidovsky wrote three *Electronic Studies*. "When I reached a point in which I had enough materials and control over the electronic techniques so as to design a phrase or paragraph," he recalls, "I would then incorporate this into an electronic study. Hence, I was applying techniques that I was discovering myself." *Electronic Study* no. 1 became Davidovsky's first commercial recording, released by Columbia on March 16, 1964. The other two studies have also been recorded.

Contrasts, for strings and electronic sounds, was completed in 1962. That year, Davidovsky produced the first of his *Synchronisms* for a regular instrument and taped sounds, this one for the flute. "One of the points I tried to make," he explained to an interviewer, "is to integrate all levels of sound—both electronic media and the conventional instrumental media—into one single coherent musical space. I try to keep, on the one hand, as much as possible of what is characteristic of the electronic instrument, and on the other what is characteristic of the live performer. At the same time, each extends the other, but essentially there is the integration of the spaces into one." *Synchronisms* no. 2, for flute, clarinet, violin, cello, and tape (1964), was introduced at the Festival of American and Spanish Music in Madrid, Spain, on October 22, 1964, and repeated at the Inter-American Festival in Washington, D.C., on June 20, 1968.

His talent began receiving important recognition in the United States in the 1960s. In 1964 he was given a grant from the Koussevitzky Music Foundation and an award from the National Institute of Arts and Letters. In 1965 he was presented with the Creative Arts Award from Brandeis University in Waltham, Mass.; an award from the Library of Congress in Washington, D.C.; and membership to the American Academy of Arts and Letters. At Tanglewood, he earned the Aaron Copland Award in 1966.

While thus establishing his reputation as composer in the United States, Davidovsky was also advancing his career as teacher. In 1964, he was visiting lecturer at the University of Michigan School of Music at Ann Arbor and, in 1968, visiting professor at the Manhattan School of Music in New York. Since 1969 he has been professor of music at City University of New York. He has also been visiting professor of music at Yale University in 1972, has been director of the Composers Conference at Johnson State College in Vermont, and has been teaching at the Columbia University School of the Arts in the doctor of musical arts program.

After almost five years of devoting himself exclusively to electronic music, Davidovsky returned in 1965 to a purely instrumental composition with the writing of *Inflexions*, for fourteen instruments. This was an outgrowth of a commission from the Fromm Music Foundation to celebrate the seventy-fifth anniversary of the University of Chicago. It was introduced in Chicago in January 24, 1967. *Inflexions* received the Walter Naumburg Foundation Award in 1972 which made possible a recording.

But electronic music was not abandoned. *Synchronisms* no. 5, for percussion and tape, was commissioned by the Thorne Music Foundation and premiered in New York on March 3, 1970. Unusual sounds were produced by the percussion by playing a triangle and tam-tam with a string-bass bow and snapping a sash cord against the timpani for a pizzicato effect. The electronic sounds appeared at the beginning of the second section and slowly developed their sound function, which was also percussive.

Davidovsky received the Pulitzer Prize in music for *Synchronisms* no. 6, for piano and tape (1970), its first performance taking place at the Berkshire Music Festival at Tanglewood on August 17, 1970. "It is shaped," said Elliott Schwartz in *Electronic Music*, "so that the taped sounds, while electronically produced, emerge as subtle analogs of the performers' sounds, creating a real sense of 'duet.' " This composition struck the ears of Donal Henahan, writing in the *New York Times*, "as the finest piece yet heard in the mixed medium. Mr. Davidovsky's taped sounds did not burble along aimlessly, but transformed the piano's ideas, commented on them, echoed them, and otherwise kept the ear and mind involved in his music's progress."

Synchronisms no. 7, which followed in 1974, was for full orchestra and tape, premiered on December 4, 1975, by the New York Philharmonic conducted by Pierre Boulez. "A child of the 1960s, Mr. Davidovsky still writes in the athematic, totally dissonant style favored by so many composers of the time," remarked Harold C. Schonberg in the *New York Times*. "The results are nostalgic if nothing else." In *High Fidelity/Musical America*, a critic said: "The strings drone on in a sequence of tone clusters, the brass and percussion go off on stuttering tangents, the electronic components belch and gurgle cheerfully, and the whole thing is over in less than ten minutes."

Davidovsky has given increasing importance to writing purely instrumental music since the 1970s. In 1973, he completed *Chacona*, for piano trio; in 1975–76, a cantata-opera, *Scenes from Shir Ha-Shirim*, for four voices and chamber ensemble; in 1976

Pennplay, for sixteen instruments, first heard on October 11, 1979, in New York. In his review of the last-named work, Allen Hughes said in the *New York Times* that it featured "contrasts between explosive passages and quiet music, and may represent an attempt to achieve affective juxtapositions or integrations of a disjunct post-Webern style and a variant of neo-Romanticism. . . . The piece made enough favorable impressions along the way to suggest that quality resides there."

String Quartet no. 4 (1979) was premiered in Washington, D.C., on March 30, 1980, by the Emerson String Quartet, for which it was commissioned by the Naumburg Foundation. This one-movement composition, the composer explains, "concerns itself with exploration of regions of extreme dynamics and pitch with the intent of generating continuity of texture and articulation not commonly associated with the string quartet." In his review in *High Fidelity/Musical America*, Kenneth W. Fain said: "Davidovsky juxtaposes soft, somber chordal sections with rhythmically agitated counterpoint. The effect, however, is never disjointed: Everything follows logically from what has come before. Rapid dynamic changes and difficult rhythms make this music complex. But Davidovsky's brand of complexity is consistently exciting. Part of the quartet's beauty derives from its long melodic lines, but the composer never resorts to pretty tunes. There isn't one boring, bewildering note in the entire piece. One was reminded of Bartók's last string quartets. The similarity is not a matter of style, but rather of an ability to writing coherently, lyrically, and dramatically in a contemporary idiom."

THE COMPOSER SPEAKS: One of the points I tried to make is to integrate all levels of sound—both the electronic media and the conventional instrumental media—into one single coherent musical space. I try to keep as much as possible of what is characteristic of both, the living performer and the electronic media. Each media is made to extend and enrich the other, all within a single musical space. . . .

A wide palette of electronic events is stored in my memory, and I can reflect on these events and relate them abstractly. When I write a string quartet, for instance, we assume that the information related to the instruments is also already in the back of my head, so I am able to draw on it. An electronic composer has to work for a few years, like any other kind of composer, in order to create that bank of memory. I work at night on the score and in the morning I go to the laboratory and try to realize the segment I have worked on. So I keep a very tight control.

PRINCIPAL WORKS: 8 *Synchronisms*, for solo instruments, or various instruments, and tape, and no. 7 for symphony orchestra and tape (1962–74); 4 string quartets (1954–79); 3 *Electronic Studies* (1961–65).

Clarinet Quintet (1955); *Suite sinfónica para 'El payaso'* (1955); *Noneto*, two pieces for nine instruments (1957); *Serie sinfónico*, for orchestra (1958); *Pianos*, for orchestra (1960); *Contrasts*, for strings and electronic sound (1962); *Inflexions*, for fourteen instruments (1965); *Chacona*, for piano and two strings (1973); *Scenes from Shir Ha-Shirim*, cantata-opera for four voices and chamber ensemble (1975–76); *Pennplay*, for sixteen instruments (1976).

BIBLIOGRAPHY: *BBDM*; Thomson, Virgil, *American Music Since 1910* (N.Y., 1970); *High Fidelity/Musical America*, August 1971; *Who's Who in America, 1980–81*.

Dawson, William Levi, b. Anniston, Ala., September 26, 1899.

Famous as the conductor of the renowned Tuskegee Choir for almost a quarter of a century, Dawson is also one of the earliest composers to write a symphony based on American-Negro folk music and the first black composer to have a symphony premiered by Leopold Stokowski and the Philadelphia Orchestra.

His father was a popular musician who earned his living playing in honky-tonks and saloons, and who did not look with favor on education. But William's mother was insistent that her children, of whom William was the first of seven, go to school and develop themselves constructively. William attended public school briefly before he was taken out by his father to help support the family. As a child, William was apprenticed to a shoemaker. He learned his trade so well that he was soon able to sew on a pair of soles by hand in twenty minutes. When William expressed a wish to study music, his father discouraged him, but some of the neighbors invervened and succeeded in getting his father's grudging consent to have the boy join a local band led by a former bandmaster at Tuskegee Institute. Now fired with the ambition to attend Tuskegee Institute, William carefully saved his pennies in a small snuffbox hidden in a hole behind his house. In time, it was discovered and stolen by some of his playmates. Temporarily frustrated in his wish to get to Tuskegee, William received private instruction in academic subjects for fifty cents a month from N. W. Carmichael, principal of the local school, soon supplementing this education by attending classes at night school. At the same time he worked for a dry-goods store delivering packages on his secondhand bicycle. By selling the bicycle for six dollars, when he was thirteen, he was able to run away from home and buy transportation for Tuskegee.

At Tuskegee, Dawson was admitted in 1912 as a "special agriculture student," which meant that he was assigned to work at the school's farm to earn his entrance fee and tuition costs. At the institute he was assigned to the band and orchestra, directed by Captain Frank Drye, where he was given a thorough training in the performance of band and orchestral instruments. He also became a member of the institute choir and played the trombone in the school band and orchestra, traveling extensively throughout the northern and southern states with both organizations. All this while he was receiving instruction in piano and harmony privately from Alice Carter Simmons.

He graduated from Tuskegee in 1921. For one year after that he taught band and orchestral instruments and conducted the school band, at the Kansas Vocational College in Topeka, Kans. There, at Washburn College, his own studies continued with Henry V. Stearns (composition and theory). In May 1922, Dawson left the college to play in a concert band in Kansas City that performed in the public park. At this time his first piece of music was published, "Forever Thine," a ballad for voice and piano (1922), copies of which he peddled from door to door.

From 1922 to 1925, Dawson served as director of music at Lincoln High School, a period during which he studied theory and composition with Regina G. Hall and Carl Busch at the Horner Institute of Fine Arts in Kansas City, graduating with honors and a bachelor of music degree in 1925. At the graduation ceremonies, his Piano Trio (1925) was performed, but because of his race Dawson was compelled to sit in the gallery, from which he acknowledged the applause without being allowed to come on the stage.

In 1925 Dawson went to Chicago to attend the American Conservatory as a scholarship student in composition with Adolph Weidig. He was awarded a master's degree in composition with honors in 1927. He remained in Chicago the next three years, employed as an arranger and editor for two publishing companies, conducting the Good Shepherd Congregational Church Choir, working for radio, playing the trombone in a dance band, and, from 1926 to 1930, sitting in the first trombone chair of the Chicago Civic Orchestra conducted by Frederick Stock and Eric de Lamarter. In I929, in a contest conducted by the *Chicago Daily News* for a bandmaster for the 1933 Chicago World's Fair, Dawson won one of the conducting posts after performing in the competition with a sixty-piece band he had organized for that purpose.

Dawson returned to Tuskegee Institute in 1930 to organize its School of Music and serve as its director. One year later he was named conductor of the Tuskegee Choir, with which he made tours of the United States. These included a four-week engagement at the Radio City Music Hall in New York when it opened in 1931, an appearance before President Hoover at the White House in 1932, and a series of radio broadcasts over the NBC network in 1937–38 and the CBS network in 1945. In 1934, under the patronage of the president of the United States, the choir made its first tour of Europe.

In 1930, Dawson received first prizes in a concert sponsored by Rodman Wanamaker for his song "Jump Back, Honey, Jump Back" (1930) and for his first work for orchestra, Scherzo (1930). In 1931 he again won first prize in the Rodman Wanamaker contest for a song, "Lovers Plighted." His greatest success as a composer, and the work for which he is most often remembered, is his *Negro Folk Symphony* (1930–31), its world premiere given in Philadelphia in November 1934 with Leopold Stokowski conducting the Philadelphia Symphony Orchestra. Soon after that it was performed in New York. For his basic melodic material, Dawson utilized the Negro spirituals "Oh, I'm Lit'l Soul, Gwine a Shine," "Oh, Lem-me Shine," and "Hallelujah Lord, I Been Down to the Sea." The introduction of the first movement had a pentatonic leading motive that recurred throughout the symphony to symbolize the link uniting Africa with her descendants in America. The second movement opened with three strokes of a gong to suggest the trinity that guides man's destiny. The symphony is ardently romantic both in its lyricism and in its dramatic climaxes, never diverging from traditional harmonic or rhythmic practices. In the *New York Times*, Olin Downes wrote: "This music has dramatic feeling, a racial sensuousness and directness of melodic speech and a barbaric turbulence," while the critic of the *New York World-Telegram* praised the symphony for its "imagination, warmth, drama . . . [and] sumptuous orchestration." After the premiere performance, the symphony received numerous performances through the Southeast. Following a trip to Africa in 1952, Dawson revised his symphony to incorporate native African rhythms. Stokowski recorded this new version with the American Symphony Orchestra. Among Dawson's later works, all traditional and romantic, are *Negro Work Song*, for orchestra (1940), *Interlude*, for piano and orchestra (1943) and *Behold, the Star*, for chorus (1945).

Dawson retired as conductor of the Tuskegee Choir in 1954 and from his directorial post at the institute a year later when he was given an honorary doctorate in music. In 1956 he was sent by the U.S. State Department to help train and conduct choral groups in Spain. After that Dawson made numerous appearances throughout the United States as guest conductor of choral groups and symphony orchestras and at festivals.

Dawson was twice married, the first time on May 25, 1927, to Cornelia D. Lampton, who died fifteen months later, and after that to Cecile D. Nicholson on September 21, 1935. Both marriages were childless. In 1963 Dawson received an Alumni Achievement Award from the University of Missouri in Kansas City. He was given awards and citations from the University of Pennsylvania Glee Club (1967) and the American Choral Directors Association (1975). In 1976 he was named to the Alabama Hall of Fame.

THE COMPOSER SPEAKS: I believe in God as the father of all mankind; I believe in my race; I believe in myself; I believe in humanity; I believe that to be endowed with a talent to create music is a sacred trust; I believe that a composer should write music which is a part of his spiritual and moral self rather than from those outside influences which are not a part of his own experiences; I believe that the only permanent American music will be that which has its source in the moral, spiritual and industrial ideals of the various ethnic groups that have contributed so much to the development of this country; I believe that one's best teacher is himself, since an instructor, at best, can only be a guide.

PRINCIPAL WORKS: Piano Trio (1925); Violin Sonata (1928); *Out in the Fields*, for soprano and orchestra (1928); *Break, Break, Break*, for chorus (1929); Scherzo, for orchestra (1930); *Negro Folk Symphony* (1931; revised 1952); *Ain't That Good News*, for a cappella chorus (1937); *Negro Work Song*, for orchestra (1940); *Interlude*, for piano and orchestra (1943); *Behold, the Star*, for chorus (1945); *Hail, Mary*, for chorus (1946).

BIBLIOGRAPHY: Ewen, David, *American Composers Today* (N.Y., 1949); Southern, Eileen, *The Music of Black Americans* (N.Y., 1971).

De Lamarter, Eric, b. Lansing, Mich., February 18, 1880; d. Orlando, Fla., May 17, 1953.

For half a century, De Lamarter was a consequential force in Chicago's musical life as church organist, teacher, critic, conductor, and composer. Most of his major orchestral works were introduced by the Chicago Symphony. Although sometimes discreetly dissonant and sometimes spiced with the condiments of American popular idioms, his music scrupulously avoided any 20th-century "school" and any overt display of "modernism." His works, consistently romantic in spirit, were grounded in classical structures.

The son of a minister, Eric De Lamarter received instruction on the piano and organ while he was attending elementary school. By the time he was fifteen, a student at Kalamazoo High School in Michigan, he initiated his professional career in music by becoming a church organist. He continued to study the organ with George Herbert Fairclough in St. Paul and Wilhelm Middelschulte in Chicago, and piano with Mary Wood Chase in Chicago. Upon graduating from Albion College in Michigan in 1900, De Lamarter was appointed organist and choirmaster of the New England Congregational Church in Chicago. In 1901 he took a year's leave of absence to study the organ in Paris with Alexander Guilmant and Charles-Marie Widor.

De Lamarter returned to Chicago in 1902, resuming his duties at the New England Congregational Church where he remained until 1912. He began his career as music critic in 1901 by working for the *Chicago Inter-Ocean*, remaining in this post until 1914. He was also music critic of the *Chicago Record-Herald* (1905–8) and the *Chicago Tribune* (1901–10), all the while serving as music correspondent for the *Boston Transcript*. His career in music education was launched at Olivet College in Michigan (1904–5) and was continued at the Chicago Musical College (1909–10). His first significant attempts at conducting took place with the Musical Art Society where he succeeded Frederick Stock as music director in 1911 and continued to lead its performance for two years. From 1912 to 1914 he was organist at the First Church of Christ Scientist and from 1914 to 1936 at the Fourth Presbyterian Church, both in Chicago. On April 18, 1906, he married Rubee B. Wilson, with whom he had two children.

With *The Faun*, a pictorial concert overture (1913), De Lamarter made his bow as a composer. It was first performed on November 18, 1913, by the Chicago Symphony, Glenn Dillard Gunn conducting. Less than a year later, on January 23, 1914, the Chicago Symphony, directed by Frederick Stock, introduced De Lamarter's Symphony no. 1 in D major (1914). This was the work of a traditionalist who favored the symphonic structure as he had inherited it from Brahms, and who felt that the essential qualities of great music, as he himself put it, are "beauty and nobility of thought and feeling, logic in architecture, and clarity of presentation."

The Chicago Symphony, sometimes under the direction of Frederick Stock and sometimes under that of the composer, continued through the years to promote his works. Since they were easily assimilable they were welcomed by both audiences and critics. Such compositions included the following: *Fable of the Hapless Folktune* (April 6, 1917); the suite *The Betrothal* (March 21, 1919), based on the incidental music De Lamarter had written for the New York production of Maurice Maeterlinck's play, which opened on November 19, 1918; two concertos for organ and orchestra (the first, on April 2, 1920; the second, on February 24, 1922); the suite *The Black Orchid*, derived from the ballet score for *The Dance of Life* (February 27, 1931); and Symphony no. 3 in E minor, with its fleeting excursions into ragtime and the Charleston (February 16, 1933).

The Chicago Symphony was not the only organization providing De Lamarter with significant first hearings of major works. On June 5, 1925, the Philadelphia Orchestra, the composer conducting, presented Symphony no. 2 (1925), inspired by Walt Whitman. Alfred Wallenstein introduced two De Lamarter compositions over the radio: *Serenade near Taos* (1930–38) over WOR, N.Y., on January 11, 1938, and the concert overture *The Giddy Puritan*, originally entitled *They, Too, Went t' Town* (1921), over the NBC network on November 6, 1938, the latter based on two old New England hymns. The music of *The Betrothal* was used for a ballet mounted in Rochester, N.Y., in 1937. The Cincinnati Symphony under Thor Johnson presented the premiere of *Cluny* (1949), "a dialogue for viola and orchestra," on October 22, 1949.

Between 1918 and 1936, Eric De Lamarter was assistant conductor of the Chicago Symphony and the conductor of the Chicago Civic Orchestra. When he retired from his professional duties in Chicago in 1936, De Lamarter joined the musical staff of radio station WOR, New York, for a year of symphonic broadcasts. In the 1940s De Lamarter served on the music faculties of the University of Missouri in Columbus, Mo., Ohio State University in Columbus, Ohio, and the University of Texas in Austin.

De Lamarter's second marriage, on June 9, 1925, was to Alice Young Main. In 1931 he received an honorary degree from Wooster College in Ohio. He was elected a member of the National Institute of Arts and Letters.

THE COMPOSER SPEAKS: Superimposed planes of tonalities, harmonic angularities, distorted and extravagant melodic quips, neurotic rhythms and all the other signboard tricks are not The Formula; they are merely the ingredients. Anyone may use them; anyone *can* use them, if he has a bit of a mathematical mind and some patience and imagination. So, when anyone of us begins the creation of something he hopes will give a little more abstract beauty to an increasingly bewildered world, he must face a decision. Shall he kowtow to "the mode" or shall he use what he finds appropriate to his musical thought from the vernacular, from the orthodox, from some yet unexploited fastness of the musical Far West? After all, his raw material is determined by the idea he wishes to convey. If it be an idea timely only to transitory fancies, he is a fool not to address his audience in the fashionable epigram of the moment. If it be an idea worthy of more serious estimate, he is just as foolish to ignore the modernistic design as to ignore the classic matters of logic of thought and clarity of presentation. After all, a concert of music is something to be heard. It is not a clinic.

PRINCIPAL WORKS: 4 symphonies (1914–32); 2 organ concertos (1920, 1922); 2 string quartets.

The Faun, overture for orchestra (1913); Serenade, for string orchestra (1915); Psalm 144, for baritone and orchestra (1915); Violin Sonata (1915); *Masquerade*, overture for orchestra (1916); *Fable of the Hapless Folktune*, for orchestra (1917); *The Betrothal*, orchestral suite (1918); *The Giddy Puritan*, originally entitled *They, Too, Went t' Town*, for orchestra (1921); *Weaver of Tales*, for organ and chamber orchestra (1926); *Serenade near Taos*, for string orchestra (1930–38); *Dance of Life*, ballet, adapted into the orchestral suite *The Black Orchid* (1931); *Cluny*, "dialogue for viola and orchestra" (1949).

BIBLIOGRAPHY: Ewen, David, *American Composers Today*, (N.Y., 1949); *Chicago Symphony Orchestra Program Book*, February 16, 1933; *Who's Who in America, 1952–53*.

Dello Joio, Norman (originally **Dello Ioio, Norman**), b. New York City, January 24, 1913.

Winner of the Pulitzer Prize in music in 1957, Dello Joio achieved his first major successes in a neoclassical idiom influenced by Hindemith. Modern harmonic and rhythmic styles were carried over into baroque structures, creating a harmonious marriage between the old and the new. Some of his most famous works are on religious subjects. In his instrumental compositions he has been partial to the variation form.

He was descended from three generations of Italian church musicians. His father, Casimir, had come from Italy, had married an American-born woman, and found employment as organist of the Church of Our Lady of Mount Carmel in New York's Manhattan. His organ performances at church and liturgical music awakened not only Dello Joio's love for music but also his interest in Gregorian chants and liturgical music, both of which would influence so many of his compositions. Still another early influence was Italian opera (especially Verdi), with which he first became acquainted through arias sung at home by visiting opera singers.

As a boy, Dello Joio studied organ, piano, and theory with his father, gaining a knowledge of basic musical literature through performances with him of four-hand arrangements of great music. Before long, Dello Joio could play almost any music at sight. When he was twelve, he played the organ well enough to assist his father in church.

For his academic education, Dello Joio was sent to All Hallows Institute in New York (1926–30) and, after that, to the College of the City of New York (1932–34). He continued to study the organ with Pietro Yon (his godfather) between 1930 and 1932. In 1933, Dello Joio entered the Institute of Musical Art, where he remained five years, a student in piano and organ of Gaston Déthier. After his first year at the institute, Dello Joio organized and played the piano in a jazz band that performed throughout the East. This was one of several jazz ensembles with which he had been performing since his sixteenth year, an experience responsible for his subsequent interest in jazz as a creative tool.

Composition began in earnest in 1937 with the completion of several chamber music compositions, and one for voice and piano, including a piano trio, which, two years later, received the Elizabeth Sprague Coolidge Award of one thousand dollars; when it was performed in New York it was praised by the critic for the *New York Times* for its "grace and spirit."

Between 1939 and 1941, on a three-year fellowship, Dello Joio studied composition with Bernard Wagenaar at the Juilliard School of Music. There his first work for orchestra, Sinfonetta (1940), was performed in 1941, after which it was heard over the NBC radio network, conducted by Dean Dixon. It was later used as background music for *Prairie*, a ballet mounted by Eugene Loring and his Dance Players in New York.

In 1940, Dello Joio was one of the first pupils enrolled in the then newly founded Berkshire Music Center at Tanglewood, Mass. He returned to Tanglewood during the summer of 1941 to become Hindemith's pupil in composition. From 1941 to 1943 Dello Joio continued studying composition with Hindemith at Yale University. Hindemith became for Dello Joio a powerful force in opening up new areas of creativity, so much so that he withdrew some of the compositions he had written up to that time, including his prize-winning trio. All this while, Dello Joio helped support himself by playing the organ in various churches, beginning with a short engagement at the Star of the Sea Church in City Island, near New York City.

In 1940, Dello Joio completed the score for a ballet, *The Duke of Sacramento*, which the Dance Players produced in New Hope, Pa., two years later. He served as this dance company's music director from 1941 to 1943. In 1942, he wrote *Magnificat*, for orchestra, which was modal in style, derivative of Gregorian chants; it received the Town Hall Composition Award the same year. Dello Joio looks back on this work as an important step in his development by clarifying and ordering his musical style along Hindemithian lines. "More than once the score recalls the Hindemith of *Mathis der Maler*," wrote Edward Downes in the *Musical Quarterly*, "although the *Magnificat* is not an imitative work. The influence shows first of all in the sturdy craftsmanship and a certain four-square seriousness, which is by no means incompatible with an infectious exuberance in the livelier pages. It shows in the texture of the strongly contrapuntal writing . . . in the frequently organ-like registrations of orchestral sonorities . . . in the careful use of (chiefly diatonic) dissonance . . . in cadential progressions and in the often archaic effects of fourths, fifths and octaves with added seconds." In February 1943, Dello Joio completed writing the Piano Sonata no. 1, a task that took him just four days; this was the composer's first work to be published.

Dello Joio received Guggenheim Fellowships in 1944 and 1945. On June 5, 1942, he married Grace Baumgold, a dancer; they raised three children by the time they were divorced in 1973. Between 1945 and 1950 he taught composition at Sarah Lawrence College in Bronxville, N.Y., and in 1946 he received a grant from the American Academy of Arts and Letters. This was a period in which several major orchestral works helped bring him into the limelight.

Concert Music (1945) was introduced by the Pittsburgh Symphony under Fritz Reiner on January 4, 1946, and after that was performed in three cities in Poland during a European tour of the New York Philharmonic. Ricercari, for piano and orchestra (1946), was first given by the New York Philharmonic on December 19, 1946, with George Szell conducting and the composer at the piano. The latter work reflected Dello Joio's increasing interest both in baroque forms (in this instance that of the ricercare) and in the art and science of variation. In each of its three movements a germinal theme was developed: harmonically in the first, melodically in the second, and rhythmically in the third.

With Variations, Chaconne, and Finale, for orchestra (1947) (originally entitled Three Symphonic Dances), Dello Joio received the New York Music Critics Circle Award for the season's best symphonic work. It was introduced by the Pittsburgh Symphony under Reiner on January 30, 1948, after which it was performed on December 9 of the same year by the New York Philharmonic under Bruno Walter. This work was built on a theme of liturgical character derived from the Kyrie of the *Missa de Angelis*. It received elaborate variation treatment throughout the composition, which, in the opinion of Olin Downes in the *New York Times*, was "the best work that we have heard of Mr. Dello Joio; in it his writing is freer, much more lucid, more released and the flow of ideas genuinely creative."

More secular and more contemporary were some of the compositions that came soon after that. Serenade, for orchestra (1948; Cleveland, October 20, 1949), was partially used in 1955 for *Diversion*, a ballet produced by Martha Graham. *New York Profiles*, for orchestra (1949; La Jolla, Calif., August 21, 1949), was a suite of seven charming vignettes of places in New York. The first was "The Cloisters," in which a religious atmosphere is established with a Gregorian chant. Another, descriptive of Grant's Tomb, quoted "The Battle Hymn of the Republic." The last one was an Italian dance section, once again based on a Gregorian chant, for a movement entitled "Little Italy." Jazz is featured prominently in Concertante for Clarinet and Orchestra (1949). It was written on commission for Artie Shaw, who introduced it in Chautauqua, N.Y., on May 22, 1949.

On a grant fron the Whitney Foundation, Dello Joio wrote his first opera, *The Triumph of St. Joan* (1951), libretto by the composer in collaboration with Joseph Machlis. After it was introduced at Sarah Lawrence College on May 9, 1950, the composer withdrew it, but he used much of his musical score for a three-movement symphony, *The Triumph of St. Joan* (1951), originally called *Seraphic Dialogue*, which had been commissioned by the Louisville Orchestra and which had its initial hearing in Louisville, Ky., under Robert Whitney on December 5, 1951, as music for a dance solo by Martha Graham. After that, without the dance, this work was performed by major American orchestras, becoming the composer's most successful symphonic composition up to this time. But if the opera had been discarded, the subject of St. Joan continued to haunt Dello Joio as material for opera. He finally wrote *The Trial at Rouen* to his own libretto in 1955, and on April 8, 1956, it was produced by the NBC Opera Theater over the NBC television network. At turns lyrical and dramatic, this score was in the tradition of the Italian operas of Verdi and Puccini. "Dello Joio," reported Frank Milburn, Jr., in *Musical America*, "has written an effective score, one that underlines constantly the dramatic implications of the libretto. . . . The music gains in intensity as the drama progresses; in fact, so much so that when Joan denies her voices—the climax of the work—the orchestra can be only silent while she speaks the words. The music's style is mildly dissonant and often Puccinian, but the music seems subordinate to the drama." In a revised version—this time once again bearing the original title of *The Triumph of St. Joan* (but not to be confused with the above-mentioned symphony of the same name)—this opera was produced by the New York City Opera on April 16, 1959, when it brought Dello Joio a New York Music Critics Circle Award for the second time.

Dello Joio received the Pulitzer Prize in music in 1957 for *Meditations on Ecclesiastes*, for string orchestra (1955–56), in which he returned both to liturgical music and to the variation structure. Initially, this score was used as background music for a ballet, *There Is a Time*, which José Limón introduced in New York in May 1956. As a work independent of the dance, it was first performed in Washington, D.C., on December 17, 1957, by the National Symphony Orchestra conducted by Howard Mitchell. Dello Joio's music was an interpretation of the verses from the third chapter of Ecclesiastes ("To everything there is a season and a time for every purpose," etc.). A solemn, simple melody, descriptive of "a time to be born," is subjected to a series of contrasting variations, each describing some phrase of the biblical subject.

On a grant from the Ford Foundation, Dello Joio wrote a three-act opera, *Blood Moon* (1961), which received its world premiere on September 18, 1961, in a performance by the San Francisco Opera. Based on the composer's own scenario adapted into a libretto by Gale Hoffman, *Blood Moon* tells of the amorous adventures of Adah Menken, an actress famous in New Orleans during the Civil War. Reaching back again to the Italian opera of the late 19th century for his operatic approaches, Dello Joio flooded his score with lyricism, emotion, and high-tensioned drama in a style that was basically conservative.

The variation structure and religious subjects continued to fascinate Dello Joio in many of his later works. The most significant of his theme-and-variations compositions are the Fantasy and Variations, for piano and orchestra (1961), and *Colonial Vari-*

ants, for orchestra (1975). The former was commissioned by the Cincinnati Symphony in commemoration of the centenary of the Baldwin Piano Company, the first performance taking place in Cincinnati on March 9, 1962, with Lorin Hollander soloist and Max Rudolph conducting. When this work was given in New York a few weeks later, Harriet Johnson said of it in the *New York Post*: "*Variations* . . . takes a four-note germinal idea and expands its horizon with a far-flung imagination. [Dello Joio] doesn't restrict himself harmonically to any single idiom, using anything that suits his purpose from a simple set of notes to the most involved dissonance. Much of the *Fantasy* is mysterious and sensuous but Dello Joio understands the value of contrast and there is affirmation (especially in a trumpet melody) and strong rhythmic punctuation. In both *Fantasy* and *Variations* there is a terse questioning, never really resolved, never lingering at any point too long. The dialogue between piano and orchestra finds each conversationalist able to hold his own with continued fascination."

Colonial Variants was written to commemorate the American bicentennial as well as to reopen a restored Grand Opera House in Wilmington, Del., as the Delaware Center for the Performing Arts. It used an ancient tune, "Dulci Jubilo," which is developed through thirteen variations, each intended as a profile of one of the original colonies. Writing in the *Wilmington Morning News*, Otto Dekom said: "This music has a very special quality. The emphasis is not . . . so much on the clever turns of musical phrases, but on creating the spirit and mood of the American experience. . . . He makes us see the people."

Among Dello Joio's most important later religious compositions we find the Mass, for chorus, organ, and brass (1968); *Mass to the Blessed Virgin*, for baritone, chorus, and organ (1975; Washington, D.C., December 8, 1975); and *Mass in Honor of the Eucharist*, for chorus, brass, organ, and strings (1976); commissioned by the forty-first International Eucharist Congress and first heard in Philadelphia in August 1976.

In 1958, Dello Joio was appointed professor of composition at the Mannes College of Music in New York. From 1958 to 1972 he was chairman of the Contemporary Music Project sponsored by the Ford Foundation. In 1964 he was sent by the U.S. State Department to tour Rumania, Bulgaria, and the Soviet Union. One year later, the U.S. Office of Education invited him to serve on its research advisory council in Hawaii, and later he was the United States representative to the Festival of the Arts in Hawaii. Early in 1970, he was guest composer at the third Contemporary Festival at Del Mar College in Corpus Christi, Tex., where six of his works were heard. Since 1972 he has been dean of fine arts at Boston University. He received honorary doctorates in music from Lawrence College in Wisconsin (1959), Colby

College in Maine (1963), the University of Cincinnati (1967), and St. Mary's College in South Bend, Ind., (1967).

Dello Joio has written music extensively for television productions, one of which, *Scenes from the Louvre*, was awarded an Emmy from the National Academy of Television Arts and Sciences in 1965. A documentary on Dello Joio, "Profile of a Composer," was televised over the CBS network on February 16, 1958.

Dello Joio married his second wife, Barbara Bolton, in 1974.

THE COMPOSER SPEAKS: There is a generation of musicians growing up that doesn't think that "triad" is a dirty word. I think there is a growing consciousness of the fact that there is a relationship between the music you write and the public that listens. I do not go along with the esoteric approach—you know, "the Philistine public be damned." I think there is a growing return to the idea that you take the trouble to put notes on paper in order to communicate with somebody.

To know music is to become greater in the knowledge and insight and to know many things other than music. It is to develop a sense of values about art and to learn about another dimension of reality previously hidden.

PRINCIPAL WORKS: 3 piano sonatas (1943, 1944, 1948).

Violin Sonata (1938); *The Duke of Sacramento*, ballet (1940); Sinfonietta, for orchestra (1940); Concerto for Two Pianos and Orchestra (1941); *Magnificat*, for orchestra (1942); *The Mystic Trumpeter*, for chorus and French horn (1943); Concert Music, for orchestra (1945); Ricercari, for piano and orchestra (1946); Variations, Chaconne, and Finale, for orchestra (1947); Serenade, for orchestra (1948); *New York Profiles*, for orchestra (1949); *A Psalm of David*, for chorus, strings, brass, and percussion (1950); *The Triumph of St. Joan Symphony* (1951); *Epigraph*, for orchestra (1951); *The Ruby*, one-act opera (1953); *The Trial at Rouen*, opera (1955; revised 1958); *Meditations on Ecclesiastes*, for string orchestra (1956); *Blood Moon*, opera (1961); Fantasy and Variations, for piano and orchestra (1961); Variants on a Medieval Tune, for band (1961); Antiphonal Fantasy on a Theme of Vincenzo Albrici, for organ, brass, and strings (1966); Songs of Walt Whitman, for chorus and orchestra or piano (1967); *Time of Snow*, ballet (1968); *Homage to Haydn*, for orchestra (1968); Mass, for chorus, organ, and brass (1968); *Songs of Abelard*, for band (1969); *Evocations*, for chorus and orchestra (1969); Capriccio on the Interval of a Second, for piano (1969); *Lyric Fantasies*, for viola and strings (1972); *Stage Parodies*, for piano, four hands (1973); *Satiric Dances*, for band (1975); *Colonial Variants*, for orchestra (1975); *Mass to the Blessed Virgin*, for baritone, chorus, and organ

(1975); *Mass in Honor of the Eucharist*, for chorus, brass, organ, and strings (1975); *Songs of Remembrance*, for baritone and orchestra (1977); *As of a Breeze*, masque for narrator, chorus, vocal soloists, orchestra, and dancers (1978).

BIBLIOGRAPHY: Goss, Madeleine, *Modern Music Makers* (N.Y., 1952); BMI, *The Many Worlds of Music*, Winter, 1976; *Musical Quarterly*, April 1962; *New York Times*, July 9, 1972.

Del Tredici, David Walter, b. Cloverdale, Calif., March 16, 1937.

He has made a specialty of writing for the voice (particularly for soprano) and, concurrently, setting poetry to music; and he is most famous for a series of major compositions inspired by Lewis Carroll's *Alice's Adventures in Wonderland*, the eighth of which received the Pulitzer Prize in music in 1980.

After acquiring the elements of the piano by himself from the time he was twelve, Del Tredici received formal instruction from Bernard Abramowitsch between 1953 and 1959. His talent enabled him to give recitals and make several appearances as guest artist with the San Francisco Symphony by the time he was sixteen. He entered the University of Berkeley in 1955, where he studied composition with Seymour Shifrin, Andrew Imbrie, and Arnold Elston, receiving his bachelor of arts degree (and membership in Phi Beta Kappa) in 1959. While attending the Aspen School in Colorado, during the summer of 1958, for further study of the piano with Leonard Schure, Del Tredici composed his first works, pieces for the piano. They were praised by Darius Milhaud, who encouraged him to become a composer rather than a piano virtuoso. Stimulated, Del Tredici now wrote a string trio, a string quartet, Songs on Poems of James Joyce, for voice and piano, and Fantasy Pieces, for piano, between 1959 and 1962. In these works he adopted an atonal and athematic style to which he would remain faithful for the next decade.

In 1959–61, on a Woodrow Wilson Fellowship, Del Tredici attended Princeton University, returning to the university in 1963–64 to complete the requirements for a master of fine arts degree. At Princeton, the study of composition took place with Earl Kim and Roger Sessions. During this period, 1962 to 1964, Del Tredici studied piano with Robert Helps in New York.

Del Tredici spent the summers of 1964 and 1965 as pianist with the Fromm Fellowship Players at Tanglewood, Mass., where, on August 12, 1964, he received for one of his works his first significant performance. That composition was *I Hear an Army*, for soprano and string quartet, based on a poem by James Joyce. Other Joyce poems were the source of *Night Conjure-Verse*, for soprano, mezzo-soprano (or countertenor), woodwind septet, and string quartet, first performed on March 4, 1966, in San Francisco, the composer conducting. Writing in the *San Francisco Chronicle*, Robert Commenday called it "stunning," and said it "confirmed David Del Tredici as a brilliant talent, brimming over with conjured ideas and, more important, the intellect to shape them coherently. . . . His fragmentary melodic snatches were woven into a fabulous and distinctive texture . . . iridescent and as rhythmically alive as a phosphorescent sea. It was fittingly sensuous for James Joyce's two contrasting images of love—romantically idealized and otherwise realized."

On a commission from the Koussevitzky Music Foundation, Del Tredici wrote *Syzygy*, for soprano, French horn, and chamber orchestra in 1966, which received its first hearing on July 6, 1966, in New York. ("Syzygy" is a term in astronomy and several other sciences indicating a strong union or opposition of elements hitherto in no such juxtaposition.) When this work was performed at the Library of Congress in Washington, D.C., some two years after its premiere, Paul Hume, in the *Washington Post*, called it "a fabulous score that, in more ways than one, recalls Mozart's Astrafiammente, the flaming star who is the Queen of the Night. His vocal line is the daughter of Berg's *Lulu*, but far outruns her in explosive shooting stars the singer must fling out. . . . It is music written after Webern, yet more inventive, treasonable though that may sound. It is superb."

Del Tredici was awarded a Guggenheim Fellowship in 1966. In 1966–67 he was resident composer at the Marlboro Festival in Vermont and from 1967 to 1971 he was assistant professor of music at Harvard University.

Two unusual works, in 1967 and 1968, called for amplified soprano, a rock instrumental group consisting of two amplified saxophones and two amplified guitars, together with chorus and orchestra. They were *The Last Gospel* (1967; San Francisco, June 15, 1968) and *Pop-Pourri* (1968; La Jolla, Calif., 1968). The latter was the first of several successive works drawing their textual materials from Lewis Carroll's *Alice's Adventures in Wonderland*. Within the next decade, and without digressing into other material, Del Tredici completed several other compositions, all based on episodes in *Alice*. They were: *The Lobster Quadrille*, for solo folk instrumental group and orchestra with optional soprano or tenor solo (1969; London, England, November 14, 1969); *Vintage Alice*, for amplified soprano solo, solo folk instrumental group, and chamber orchestra (1972; Music at the Vineyards, Calif., August 5, 1972); *Adventures Underground*, for amplified soprano solo with solo folk instrumental group and orchestra (1973; Buffalo, N.Y., April 13, 1975), commissioned by the Buffalo Philharmonic and the New York State Council on the Arts; *In Wonderland*, Part I, for amplified soprano solo with solo folk instrumental group and orchestra (1969–74; Aspen, Colo., July 29, 1975), a commission of the National En-

dowment for the Arts; *In Wonderland*, Part II, for amplified soprano and orchestra (1975); *Final Alice*, for amplified soprano solo, solo folk instrumental group and orchestra (1976); *Annotated Alice*, for amplified soprano solo and solo folk instrumental group and orchestra (1976); and *Child Alice*, for amplified soprano and orchestra (1980–81).

Perhaps the most significant of these *Alice in Wonderland* compositions is *Final Alice*. It is the largest in scope and most imaginative in treatment, calling for huge musical forces and an amplified soprano who not only sings the five arias but also serves as narrator. Aware that at times this work is almost operatic and at other times very much like a concerto for voice and orchestra, Del Tredici preferred to describe it as "an opera written in concert form." This was one of six compositions commissioned by the National Endowment for the Arts from six American composers honoring the American bicentennial, these compositions performed by six major American orchestras. After being introduced by the Chicago Symphony under Sir Georg Solti, with Barbara Hendricks as vocal soloist, on October 7, 1976, *Final Alice* was successfully performed by the New York Philharmonic, the Los Angeles Philharmonic, and the Boston Symphony (in all cases with minor cuts), and (in its entirety) by the St. Louis and Minnesota symphonies. In the *New Yorker*, Andrew Porter called it "a large, generous romantic and melodious score, inspired by love for the book and sensitive to unwritten feelings that lie beneath it. . . . Is this *Final Alice*—and the whole Alice that it crowns—impressive, touching, profound, or slightly absurd? Maybe all four at once."

The eighth of Del Tredici's explorations into the Alice's world—*In Memory of a Summer Day*—brought him the Pulitzer Prize in music in 1980. The St. Louis Symphony had commissioned it for its centennial season and introduced it under Leonard Slatkin's direction on February 23, 1980. The work, which takes its text from the poem opening *Through the Looking Glass*, consists of two large arias, "Simple Alice" and "Ecstatic Alice," the chromatics of the latter, by the composer's own admission, influenced by *Tristan and Isolde*. "Del Tredici's skill in manipulating his theme, and in varying its orchestral colors, is impressive," wrote Frank Peters in *High Fidelity/Musical America*, adding: "Nobody but he could have produced *In Memory of a Summer Day*. . . . It may be slick, clever and ingratiating, but on the other hand it isn't pretentious and boring."

For the opening of the Louise M. Davies Symphony Hall, the new home of the San Francisco Symphony, on September 16, 1980, Del Tredici (on commission from Mrs. Davies) wrote another composition derived from *Alice: Happy Voices* (1980). This was the only American composition on that inaugural gala program. The San Francisco Symphony under Edo de Waart's direction performed it with Judith Blegen as an off-stage (amplified) vocal soloist at the conclusion of the composition. Since this performance was telecast live nationally through the facilities of the Public Broadcasting Service, *Happy Voices* was heard by an audience of several million. *Happy Voices* is an extended orchestral fugue built from five themes. A large percussion ensemble which included ratchets, a wind machine and special bells, is enlisted for grandiose sonoric effects. At the climax of the piece, as the composer explains, "when one theme has struggled to the fore, the other motives, like a gang of howling furies, are not far behind, below or above, seeking to wrest it from its sovereign place. . . . Every possible contrapuntal device is now given full exuberant play." In his review in the *New Yorker*, Andrew Porter said of this work: "The opening stretches of the piece are ingenious and agreeable, and the whole is a remarkable tour de force. The rhythms are playful, beguiling."

The Pulitzer Prize–winning *In Memory of a Summer Day*, and its successor, *Happy Voices*, are parts of a larger work bearing the title *Child Alice*, the third part of which is *All in the Golden Afternoon*, for large orchestra and amplified soprano voice (1981). The last of these was premiered on May 9, 1981, by the Philadelphia Orchestra, Eugene Ormandy conducting.

In 1973—the year in which Del Tredici was recipient of the Creative Arts Citation from Brandeis University in Waltham, Mass.—Del Tredici became teaching associate at Boston University. He served as composer-in-residence at the Aspen Music Festival in Colorado in 1975.

THE COMPOSER SPEAKS: Poetry turns me on, and certain poets force me to write music for them. I know I have to set them to music. When I read a poem, I know before I'm through that I'll set it. It's a feeling of identification. I don't care what it means, whether I connect, whether it turns on the juices or not. In composing songs, the ideal is to want to set the words. But, for me, the reality is that the words are the complete servant to what turns you on to write music. It's the *energy* of the words rather than the sense of the words. It's the mood that's important.

PRINCIPAL WORKS: Four Songs on Poems of James Joyce, for voice and piano (1959); Fantasy Pieces, for piano (1960); *I Hear an Army*, for soprano and string quartet (1964); *Night Conjure-Verse*, for soprano, mezzo-soprano or countertenor, woodwind septet, and string quartet (1965); *Syzygy*, for soprano, French horn, and chamber orchestra (1966); *The Last Gospel*, for amplified soprano, solo rock group, chorus, and orchestra (1967); *Pop-Pourri*, for amplified soprano, solo rock group, chorus, and orchestra (1968); *The Lobster Quadrille*, for solo folk group and orchestra with optional soprano or tenor solo (1969, revised 1974); *Adventures Underground*, for amplified soprano solo with solo folk group and or-

chestra (1971); *Vintage Alice*, for amplified soprano solo with solo folk group and chamber orchestra (1972); *In Wonderland*, Parts I and II, for amplified soprano solo, solo folk instrumental group, and orchestra (1969–75); *Illustrated Alice*, for amplified soprano and orchestra (1975); *Final Alice*, for amplified soprano solo and solo folk instrumental group and orchestra (1976); *Annotated Alice*, for amplified soprano solo with solo folk group and orchestra (1976); *Child Alice* I: *In Memory of a Summer Day*, for amplified soprano and orchestra; II: *Quaint Events*, *Happy Voices*, two instrumental interludes for orchestra with amplified soprano; III: *All in the Golden Afternoon*, for amplified soprano and orchestra (1979–81).

BIBLIOGRAPHY: *BBDM; DCM; Chicago Symphony Program Notes*, October 7, 1976; *High Fidelity/Musical America*, September 1980; *New Yorker*, April 11, 1977; *New York Times*, May 4, 1980, October 26, 1980; *Who's Who in America, 1980–81*.

Dett, (Robert) Nathaniel, b. Drummondsville, Quebec, Canada, October 11, 1882; d. Battle Creek, Mich., October 2, 1943.

Dett dedicated his life to promoting the music of his race—as conductor, teacher, arranger of spirituals and other Negro folk music, and as composer. He is one of the first Americans to use Negro folk music within a large-scale composition.

He was the youngest of four children. His father was a black American, a native of Maryland, who had settled in Canada, where he married a Canadian black woman. Both parents played the piano and sang publicly. Nathaniel early came to love music by listening to them sing and perform, and he came to love Negro folk songs from his maternal grandmother. But it was the mother who supervised his early musical training as well as his reading habits. Dett learned to play the piano by ear "ever since I remember," as he once recalled. "No one taught me. I just 'picked' it up." But before long and before his public school education began, he was given some instruction by a local teacher who was continually upset because he preferred improvising to practicing.

When he was eleven, his family moved to the American side of Niagara Falls, where he attended public school, continued studying the piano (with John Weiss), and attracted attention with his talent for improvisation. To pay for his education, he spent summers working as a bellhop and part-time pianist in a resort hotel. One evening, Fred Butler, a black concert singer, performed in that hotel. That experience convinced Dett that he, too, wanted to become a professional musician. Between 1898 and 1903 he filled various jobs as pianist or organist for church and social functions in Niagara Falls. In 1900, he wrote a ragtime number "After the Cakewalk," which became his first published composition. While attending the Niagara Collegiate Institute, he studied piano with Oliver Willis Halstead (1901–3).

Dett graduated from the institute in 1903. That year he entered the Conservatory of Music at Oberlin College in Ohio, where he remained for the next five years, with composition and piano as his majors. During this period his principal studies took place with Howard Handel Carter and George Carl Hastings (piano), Arthur E. Heacox (theory), J. P. Frampton (organ), and George Whitefield Andrews (composition and organ). He sometimes gave student recitals at the conservatory, including on his program such of his own early pieces as *Cave of the Winds* (1902) and *Inspiration Waltzes* (1903), both of which were published. In 1908 he graduated with a bachelor of music degree to become the first black person ever to complete the five-year course since that conservatory had become an adjunct of Oberlin College. He now settled down to teaching by joining the music faculty at Lane College in Jackson, Tenn. (1908–11). Between 1911 and 1913 he was director of music at Lincoln Institute in Jefferson City, Mo.

Through his intense interest in Negro folk music, Dett came to know Azalia Hackley, a black pianist and singer who devoted her life to helping black music and musicians. In 1913 she successfully recommended Dett for the post of director of music at Hampton Institute in Virginia, which he retained for the next eighteen years. On December 27, 1916, he married Helen Elise Smith, the first black woman to graduate from the piano department at the Insitute of Musical Art in New York. Though they never separated, the marriage was incompatible, and Dett's relationship with his two daughters was equally strained.

These were the years in which he wrote his first structurally ambitious and mature works for the piano: *Magnolia Suite* (1912) and *In the Bottoms* (1913). Without resorting to quotation, both were recognizably racial in their idiom just as they were romantic in style, while portraying Negro life and experiences in the South. "Juba Dance" from *In the Bottoms* became independently popular in 1920 through performances by Percy Grainger in recitals in New York, Chicago, and Boston.

While at Hampton Institute, where the School of Music was formally organized in 1928 with Dett as director, Dett conducted the Hampton Choir in notable concerts of spirituals and other black folk music—not only locally but throughout the northern cities including Washington, D.C. (at the Library of Congress on December 17, 1926, in a concert sponsored by the Elizabeth Sprague Coolidge Foundation), New York (Carnegie Hall on April 16, 1928), and Boston (Symphony Hall on March 11, 1929). In 1930, the choir performed for President Hoover and his guests at the White House. That same year they toured seven European countries, and in 1931 the United States.

While employed at Hampton Institute, Dett also led the American Chorus on radio station WHAM in Virginia (1930–31) and the Negro Community Chorus (1933–34). Many of his summers were spent in continued music study: in 1915 at Columbia University (with G. W. Andrews, R. G. Cole, and Peter Dykema); in 1919, with Nadia Boulanger at the Fontainebleau School of Music in France. On a year's leave of absence from Hampton Institute in 1920, he attended Harvard University, where he was Arthur Foote's pupil in composition and piano. At Harvard he received the Bowdoin Prize for his essay "The Emancipation of Negro Music" and the Francis Boott Prize for his choral work *Don't Be Weary, Traveler* (1921). In 1931 he enrolled in the Eastman School of Music in Rochester, N.Y., studying with Max Landow (piano), Bernard Rogers (composition and orchestration), Edward Royce (counterpoint), and Howard Hanson (modern harmony); he received his master of music degree in 1932.

Dett wrote his first important and successful choral work in order to give black people, as he explained, "something musically which would be peculiarly their own and yet which would bear comparison with the nationalistic utterances of other people's work in art form." That composition was the anthem *Listen to the Lambs* (1914), for a cappella chorus, one of the earliest large-scale American compositions using a Negro spiritual (first two measures of "Listen to the Lambs") as the starting point from which to develop his own folk-style thematic material. This work was extensively performed throughout the United States and Europe. From then on, Dett produced a library of choral music, most of it rooted deeply in the folk music of the American black people. *Chariot Jubilee,* for tenor, chorus, and orchestra (1919) quoted "Swing Low, Sweet Chariot"; it was performed in Boston, Syracuse, Cleveland, and Oberlin. Dett's most ambitious work was the first oratorio ever written by a black man, *The Ordering of Moses,* for vocal soloists, chorus and orchestra (1937), which he subtitled "a biblical folk scene." Based on a biblical text, it made effective use of the spiritual "Go Down, Moses," the first time a Negro spiritual was used in an oratorio. First performed at the Cincinnati May Music Festival on May 7, 1937, it brought its composer the greatest success of his career. After that it was heard at the Worcester Festival in Massachusetts in 1938, was performed by the Oratorio Society of New York in 1939 and in Carnegie Hall in New York in 1941. It was recorded by the Voice of America for radio distribution overseas and in 1969 it was revived in St. Louis at the Golden Jubilee Convention of the National Association of Negro Musicians.

Dett also wrote some music that did not reach into the storehouse of Negro folk music for its material and that was nonracial. One of these was *American Sampler,* for orchestra (1937), commissioned by the Columbia Broadcasting System and introduced over its radio network on October 2, 1938, Howard Hanson conducting.

When Dett resigned from Hampton Institute in 1932, he returned to the Eastman School of Music for an additional year of the study of composition with Howard Hanson and to open a teaching studio in Rochester. One year later he taught music at the Sam Houston State University in Austin, Tex., and from 1937 to 1942 he was on the faculty of Bennett College in Greensboro, N.C. During World War II he was the musical adviser to the United Service Organizations (USO). While serving in this post in Battle Creek, Michigan, he suffered a fatal heart attack.

Dett made numerous arrangements of Negro spirituals for four-voice chorus which were widely performed. He published *Religious Folk-Songs of the Negro as Sung at Hampton Institute* (1927) and *The Dett Collection of Negro Spirituals* in four volumes (1936).

Dett received honorary doctorates in music from Howard University in Washington, D.C. (1924), and Oberlin Conservatory (1926). In 1927 he was presented with the first Harmon Foundation Medal for creative achievement in music. He was president of the National Association of Negro Musicians (1924–26), honorary member of the Coleridge-Taylor Society in England, and life member of Pi Kappa Lambda in Oberlin. By the order of the Queen of Belgium he was awarded the Palm of the Ribbon from the Royal Belgian Band. In 1973, *The Collected Piano Works of R. Nathaniel Dett* was published by Summy-Birchard.

THE COMPOSER SPEAKS: It should be stated that controversies arising from the discussion as to whether or not one ought to try "to improve" the folk song, be it a Negro folk song or whatever its source, are absurd. One might as well talk of "improving" a full grown tree or a rose blossom. We try to preserve the tree or the rose because of its beauty and worth. Either one, through the skill of man, may be made presently to disintegrate later to reappear in other creations of beauty and utility. Even so, the folk song is rich in elements which may be the inspiration of new creations resembling the original as a desk resembles a tree—only in the nature of its material.

PRINCIPAL WORKS: *Magnolia Suite,* for piano (1912); *In the Bottoms,* suite for piano (1913); *Listen to the Lambs,* anthem for chorus (1914); *Music in the Mine,* for chorus (1916); *I'll Never Turn Back,* anthem for chous (1916); *Chariot Jubilee,* for tenor, chorus, and orchestra (1919); *Don't be Weary, Traveler,* for chorus (1921); *Enchantment,* suite for piano (1922); *Gently, Lord, Oh Gently Lead Us,* anthem for chorus (1924); *Let Us Cheer the Weary Traveler,* anthem for chorus (1926); *Cinnamon Grove,* suite for piano (1928); *American Sampler,* for orchestra (1937); *The Ordering of Moses,* oratorio for vocal soloists, chorus, and orchestra (1937); *Tropic Winter,* suite for piano (1938); *Harps of the Willows,* Part II, for piano (1942).

BIBLIOGRAPHY: McBrier, Vivian Flagg, *R. Nathaniel Dett: His Life and Works* (Washington, D. C., 1977); Southern, Eileen, *The Music of Black Americans* (N.Y., 1971).

Diamond, David, b. Rochester, N.Y. July 9, 1915.

For well over forty years Diamond has held a position of eminence as one of the most respected composers of his generation, with a prolific capacity for work of high integrity that has amassed for him a body of compositions as impressive in variety and length as it is in content. His earliest compositions reflect the influences of the tonal Schoenberg and the works of Satie and Ravel. Almost all of his juvenilia is a combination of bitonal and modal harmony with melodic substance of a French-Hebraic cast. His works from 1935 on are complex in contrapuntal textures with long melodic lines and a strong rhythmic drive. His structural concepts are always clear, balanced, often unusual. After 1940 and until 1950 his works were strongly diatonic and modal. Between 1951 and 1960 his style became firmly integrated into what today his critics call an amalgam of classic and neoromantic gestures. But he has also brought an aspect of twelve-note chromaticism into his thematic concepts.

He was the only son, and one of two children, of indigent Austrian-Polish Jewish immigrants, his father being a cabinetmaker, and his mother a dressmaker. In or around 1921, after having seen a violin at a neighbor's home, he was so fascinated by the four strings and the sounds that came from the instrument when he plucked them that he invented a four-line hand-drawn staff (the five lines in printed music confused him when he looked at the four strings) and began to compose curious tunes in scordatura formations. A year or so later, at Public School No. 9 in Rochester, he was given an instrument and free lessons. In classrooms he was often busier writing music and poetry than attending to arithmetic and history.

In 1927, the family's financial difficulties necessitated leaving Rochester for Cleveland, where they lived with relatives. André de Ribaupierre, a Swiss musician who taught music in Cleveland, was so impressed with Diamond's talent that he provided funds for his musical training. Between 1927 and 1929, Diamond studied the violin and some theory with de Ribaupierre at the Cleveland Institute of Music. In 1929, when the Diamond family returned to Rochester, David entered the Eastman School of Music on a scholarship, continuing music study there in the preparatory department with Effie Knauss (violin). He was composing music all the time and his music was brought to the attention of Bernard Rogers, who had joined the Eastman School faculty the same year. By the time Diamond was graduated from Benjamin Franklin High School in 1933 he had written about one hundred compositions, all of which he subsequently withdrew, although they had all been performed.

After an additional year at the Eastman School (1933–34) as a regular undergraduate, dissatisfied with the conservative atmosphere, Diamond left Rochester to come to New York. Once again on a scholarship, he studied Dalcroze subjects with Paul Boepple and composition with Roger Sessions at the New Music School and the Dalcroze Institute for two years (1934–36). He helped support himself, while residing at the YMHA, by accepting whatever menial job was available, including mopping floors. His financial distress was alleviated when he won first prize of $2,500 for a Sinfonietta (1935), inspired by a poem in Carl Sandburg's *Good Morning, America,* in a contest for young composers sponsored by the popular bandleader Paul Whiteman in memory of his mother, Elfrida Whiteman. George Gershwin was one of the judges who was impressed with Diamond's talent and told him so.

In 1935, Diamond was commissioned to write music for a ballet, *Tom,* with scenario by e.e.cummings and choreography by Léonide Massine. With all his expenses paid by the patron, Cary Ross, so that he might confer with Massine, Diamond was sent to Paris. The ballet was completed, but its performance never materialized due to production disagreements.

Diamond was back in Paris a year later through the invitation of Nadia Boulanger to study with her at Fontainebleau. Personal associations with Roussel, Stravinsky, Charles Munch and André Gide proved a maturing experience that brought with it new creative attitudes and perspectives. Under such stimuli Diamond completed in Paris his Violin Concerto no. 1 and a *Psalm,* for orchestra, both in 1936, the latter inspired by a visit to Père Lachaise and Oscar Wilde's grave in that historic Paris cemetery. The concerto was introduced on March 24, 1937, in New York at a WPA concert, the composer conducting and with Nicolai Berezowsky, soloist. The *Psalm,* Diamond's first work to gain him recognition, was premiered by the Rochester Philharmonic under Howard Hanson on December 10, 1936. When this work was performed by the San Francisco Symphony under Pierre Monteux, Alfred J. Frankenstein, the distinguished San Francisco critic, praised it for its "fine, granite seriousness" and its "spare, telling use of the orchestra." The *Psalm* won the Juilliard Publication Award in 1938.

Back in the United States in 1937, Diamond made his home on Perry Street in New York's Greenwich Village. To support himself while composing he worked at nights as clerk behind a soda fountain, and after that as a violinist in the orchestra for the weekly network radio program, "Your Hit Parade." A commission from the League of Composers led to the writing of the Quintet, for flute, string trio and piano (1937; N.Y., March 8, 1938); the death of Maurice Ravel inspired the *Elegy in Memory of Maurice Ravel,* for brass, harps, and percussion (1938; Rochester, N.Y., April 28, 1938). He also wrote at this time, while studying at Fontainebleau with Nadia Boulanger, the *Aria and Hymn,* for orchestra (1937), which was broadcast over the NBC radio network on March 18, 1941, Frank Black conducting, and the Variations, for small orchestra (1937), featured at the American Music Festival in Rochester, N.Y., on April 23, 1940, under Frederick Fennell.

Largely on the strength of his success with the *Psalm,* and the First Violin Concerto, Diamond received the first of three Guggenheim Fellowships in 1938, making it possible for him to make his third visit to Paris to continue his study of composition with Nadia Boulanger. Diamond now remained in Paris until the outbreak of World War II, working hard all the time on new compositions. The most important of these were the Cello Concerto (1938; Rochester, April 30, 1942); *Heroic Piece,* for small orchestra (1938; Zurich, Switz., July 29, 1938); and Concert Piece, for orchestra (1939; N.Y., May 16, 1940).

World War II sent Diamond back to the United States. For a time he made his home at Yaddo, the artists' colony in Saratoga, N.Y. He accelerated his creative activity to write his String Quartet no. 1 (1940), Concerto for Small Orchestra (1940), and his Symphony no. 1 (1940–41), among many other works. The Concerto for Small Orchestra was performed at the Yaddo Festival on September 7, 1940, under the composer's direction, and the Symphony no. 1 on December 21, 1941, by the New York Philharmonic under Dimitri Mitropoulos. On the strength of both the quartet and the symphony, Diamond received a cash grant from the American Academy in Rome in 1942. *The Dream of Audubon* (1941), scenario by Glenway Westcott, was commissioned by the Ballet Guild but rejected for production because Balanchine did not want to adhere to Westcott's scenario.

In 1941, Diamond was awarded his second Guggenheim Fellowship. Two years later, his Piano Quartet (1938) received the Paderewski Prize of $1,000 and on October 13, 1944, his Symphony no. 2 (1942) was introduced by the Boston Symphony under Serge Koussevitzky. In 1944, Diamond wrote incidental music for Margaret Webster's production of *The Tempest,* which the composer conducted (opening on Broadway on January 25, 1945). That year he was given a grant from the National Institute of Arts and Letters "in recognition of his outstanding gifts among the youngest generation of composers, and for the high quality of his achievements."

With *Rounds,* for string orchestra (1944), Diamond realized his greatest success up to that time. Commissioned by Dimitri Mitropoulos, it was first performed on November 24, 1944, by the Minneapolis Symphony under Mitropoulos and in 1945 was the recipient of the New York Music Critics Circle Award as the year's best new symphonic work. Diamond brought a contrapuntal skill to the canonic writing in the first movement and the fugal writing in the closing movement, with the middle expressive Adagio serving as a resting point. Following its premieres in Minneapolis and New York, *Rounds* was prominently featured on programs of major American symphony orchestras.

Another of Diamond's orchestral works of this period to receive numerous performances was the five-movement orchestral suite *Romeo and Juliet* (1947), commissioned by Thomas Scherman, conductor of the Little Orchestral Society, for the orchestra's debut on October 20, 1947. In this music, Diamond aspired, as he said, "to convey as fully and yet as economically as possible the innate beauty and pathos of Shakespeare's great drama without resorting to a large orchestral canvas and a definite musical form."

In between *Rounds* and *Romeo and Juliet* came two symphonies, both written in 1945 and successfully introduced by the Boston Symphony: no. 3, on November 3, 1950, with Charles Munch conducting, and no. 4, commissioned by the Koussevitzky Music Foundation, on January 23, 1948, under Leonard Bernstein. In 1946, Diamond's String Quartet no. 3 (1946) won the New York Music Critics Circle Award following its premiere at a concert of the League of Composers in New York on March 16, 1947.

During the summer of 1949, Diamond was the first lecturer on American music at the seminar of American studies at Schloss Leopoldskron in Salzburg, Austria. There he wrote the symphonic portrait *Timon of Athens* (1949), a commission from the Louisville Orchestra in Kentucky. In 1951, on a Fulbright fellowship, Diamond established residence in Italy, first in Rome, where he was affiliated with the university, then in Florence. He stayed in Italy fourteen years, except for a few return visits to the United States: in 1956 to be with his dying mother, and twice (spring 1961 and fall 1963) to fill the post of Slee Professor of Music at the State University in Buffalo, N.Y., where he gave a series of provocative lectures and taught composition. In 1958, the Guggenheim Fellowship came to him for the third time, in Italy, where he proved highly productive. He completed four symphonies. He labored on no. 5 sporadically over a period of many years and by the time it was completed he had written nos. 6, 7, and 8. Symphony no. 6 (1951–54) was given its initial hearing on March 8, 1957, Charles Munch conducting the Boston Symphony. No. 7 followed in 1959, its first performance taking place on January 26, 1962, by the Philadelphia Orchestra under Eugene Ormandy.

No. 8, in 1960, written to honor Aaron Copland on his sixtieth birthday, was premiered on October 27, 1961, by the New York Philharmonic under Leonard Bernstein.

There were orchestral compositions other than symphonies. *Sinfonia concertante* (1954–56), commissioned by the Rochester Friends of Music, was heard in Rochester, N.Y., on March 7, 1957. *The World of Paul Klee,* for orchestra (1957), commissioned by the Rockefeller Foundation for the Portland Junior Symphony in Oregon, was introduced there on February 15, 1958. *This Sacred Ground,* a setting for baritone, mixed chorus, children's chorus, and orchestra of Lincoln's Gettysburg Address (1962), was written on commission from the *Buffalo Evening News* and the Buffalo radio station WBEN, and was performed in Buffalo on November 17, 1963, under Lukas Foss. *Elegies,* for flute, English horn, and strings (1963), heard in Philadelphia on September 23, 1965, performed by the Philadelphia Orchestra under Ormandy, was written as eulogies to two American writers he admired most, William Faulkner and e. e. cummings.

There was also distinguished chamber music. Diamond completed four later string quartets in Italy (1960–64). The fifth was introduced on February 10, 1961, by the Juilliard Quartet in New York; the sixth (1962; Buffalo, N.Y., December 5, 1963) honored Darius Milhaud's seventieth birthday; and the eighth (1964; Kansas City, Mo., November 18, 1965) received the Rheta Sosland Award. Nonet, for strings (1962), paid tribute to Stravinsky's eightieth birthday and won Diamond the ASCAP-Stravinsky Award.

Diamond returned to the United States in 1965. He spent the summer in Aspen, Colo. as visiting composer where a program of his works was performed on July 9 to celebrate his fiftieth birthday. The performances of *Elegies,* already mentioned, also commemorated his birthday, as did a concert by the New York Philharmonic on April 28, 1966, when Leonard Bernstein introduced the Symphony no. 5 (finally completed in 1964) and David Diamond conducted the world premiere of his Piano Concerto (1950), Thomas Schumacher, soloist.

In 1965, Diamond joined the music faculty of the Manhattan School of Music in New York; he resigned in 1967. When that school dedicated a new auditorium on January 31, 1970, Diamond's *Choral Symphony: To Music* (1969), for tenor and baritone soloists, chorus, and orchestra, was heard, with the composer conducting. The work's texts were the poems "To Music" by John Masefield and Longfellow's "Dedication." The work was commissioned by the Thorne Music Fund for that occasion. As composer-in-residence at the American Academy in Rome (1971–72), Diamond completed the Quintet for Piano and Strings (1969–72), which the Concord Quartet, with Beveridge Webster as pianist, introduced on November 13, 1972, in New York. A Secular Cantata, for vocal soloists, chorus, and small orchestra (1976), a nine-part setting of nine poems by James Agee, was heard in New York on February 5, 1977, by the Collegiate Chorale under Richard Westenburg. Between 1971 and 1975, Diamond wrote his first opera, *The Noblest Game,* libretto by Katie Louccheim, on a commission from the National Opera Institute.

In 1966, Diamond was elected to membership in the National Institute of Arts and Letters. Late in 1967, two concerts of his works were heard at West Virginia University in Morgantown, and on May 30, 1975, at Thorne Hall in Chicago, a program of his music was given by the William Ferris Chorale honoring Diamond on his sixtieth birthday. Since 1973, Diamond has been professor of composition at the Juilliard School of Music in New York. He has continued to lecture both in the United States and Europe.

THE COMPOSER SPEAKS: My emotional life and reactions to certain events and situations have worked hand in hand with purely abstract musical conceptions and manipulations of material; and it was always the material that remained foremostly important to me in my working stages.

To have felt out of step in one's first years confirms one's invalidism in these last years: a sad story, at best, with just a glimmer of hope before the next catastrophe.

PRINCIPAL WORKS: 11 string quartets (1940–68); 8 symphonies (1940–64); 3 violin concertos (1936, 1947, 1968); 2 overtures, for orchestra (1937, 1970); 2 piano sonatas (1947, 1972).

Partita, for oboe, bassoon, and piano (1935); *Four Ladies,* cycle of songs for voice and piano (1935); Vocalise, for soprano and viola (1935); *Psalm,* for orchestra (1936); Concerto, for string quartet (1936); *Tom,* ballet (1936); Variations, for small orchestra (1937); *Heroic Piece,* for small orchestra (1938); Cello Sonata (1938); *Elegy in Memory of Maurice Ravel,* for brass, harps, and percussion (1938); Music, for double string orchestra, brass, and timpani (1938); Cello Concerto (1938); Piano Quartet (1938); Concerto for Small Orchestra (1940); *The Dream of Audubon,* ballet (1942); Concerto for Two Solo Pianos (1942; Music for Shakespeare's *The Tempest,* for orchestra (1944); *Rounds,* for string orchestra (1944); Violin Sonata (1946); Music for Shakespeare's *Romeo and Juliet,* for orchestra (1947); Chaconne, for violin and piano (1948); *L'âme de Debussy,* song cycle for voice and piano (1949); *Timon of Athens,* symphonic portrait (1949); Piano Concerto (1950); Chorale, for a cappella chorus (1950); Quintet, for two violas, two cellos, and clarinet (1950); *Mizmor l'David,* sacred service for tenor, chorus and organ (1951); *The Midnight Meditation,* song cycle for bass-baritone and piano (1951); Piano Trio (1951); *Sinfonia concertante,* for orchestra

(1954–56); Sonata for Solo Violin (1954); Sonata for Solo Cello (1956); *The World of Paul Klee,* for orchestra (1957); Woodwind Quintet (1958); *Mirandola,* musical comedy (1958); *A Private World,* for piano (1959); Nonet, for three violins, three violas, and three cellos (1961); *This Sacred Ground,* for baritone, mixed chorus, children's chorus, and orchestra (1962); Concertino for piano and small orchestra (1965); Hebrew Melodies, song cycle for voice and piano (1967); *Alone at the Piano,* three books for piano (1967); Music for Chamber Orchestra (1969); *Choral Symphony: To Music* (1969); *The Fall,* song cycle for voice and piano (1970); *A Buoyant Overture,* for orchestra (1970); *The Noblest Game,* opera (1971–75); Piano Quintet (1972); Secular Cantata, for vocal soloists, chorus and small orchestra (1976); Concert Piece, for horn and string trio (1978); *Ode to the Morning of Christ's Nativity,* for a cappella chorus (1980).

BIBLIOGRAPHY: *NGDMM;* Ewen, David, *Composers Since 1900* (N.Y., 1969); Goss, Madeleine, *Modern Music Makers* (N.Y., 1952); *Composers of Americas,* vol. 13, Washington, D.C., 1966; *Etude,* November 1947; *New York Times,* April 22, 1965, July 6, 1975.

Dlugoszewski, Lucia, b. Detroit, Mich., June 16, 1931.

She is an avant-garde composer who has been involved with unusual and at times esoteric sonorities and sound textures, for the production of which she has constructed her own percussive instruments.

She was an only child of parents of Polish extraction. "My mother was the artist of the family, actually a painter, but she was oriented traditionally to make wifehood and motherhood her absolutes," Dlugoszewski recalls. "My father was the ferocious intellectual and philosophical personality, a dogmatic atheist. I was brought up not only in an atmosphere of intellectualism but also of isolation: the isolation of the Polish community, a separate island within American culture; the isolation of the winter ambience of the Great Lake country. A further isolation was contributed by the intense poverty brought on by the depression." In such an atmosphere, Lucia began writing little poems and songs when she was three. At about the same time, her mother started her on music study with piano lessons. At about six, Lucia was enrolled at the Detroit Conservatory, where she received further instruction at the piano from Adelgath Morrison. "Curiously I was early singled out as a Bach specialist and gave a small solo recital playing Bach and my own compositions at the time." While attending high school, she began studying composition with Carl Beutel.

Upon graduating from high school, she planned a career not in the arts but in medicine. For this purpose she took a premedical course at Wayne State

University in Detroit from 1946 to 1949, majoring in physics and mathematics. There, a professor of poetry and creative writing became impressed with her literary talent and was influential in luring her away from the science curriculum in favor of the arts. In 1947, Dlugoszewski received the Tomkins Literary Award. Music was not neglected, the study of the piano continuing at the time with Edward Bredshall.

Leaving Wayne State University in 1949 she came to New York for the specific purpose of studying the piano with Grete Sultan, a Bach specialist. Sultan encouraged her to supplement these lessons (1950–53) at the David Mannes School of Music, where she attended the composition class of Felix Salzer in 1950 and 1951. Additional study of composition took place that year privately with Ben Weber. When Salzer recognized that her musical independence and innovative thinking required less orthodox instruction, he had her study composition privately with Edgard Varèse in 1951. Her own interest in the mathematical aspects of music and in nonmusical sounds as a basis for musical creativity was greatly encouraged and stimulated by her studies with Varèse, whose compositions in "organized sound" had fascinated her. She now began experimenting with the sonorific elements of music, with everyday sounds, with sound textures created for their own sake, free of any emotional, intellectual, or programmatic associations. The better to realize these new sounds, she developed in 1951 the "timbre piano," which called for the use of bows (made of glass, felt, metal, wood, or plastic) and plectra on the strings of the piano soundboard. She also experimented with sounds of bouncing balls, pouring water, whistling teakettles and other everyday noises. Sound innovations can already be discovered in her early compositions, in *Moving Space Theater Pieces for Everyday Sounds* (1949), *Transparencies 1–50 for Everyday Sounds* (1951) and *Everyday Sounds for e. e. cummings* (1951).

On April 24, 1951, she gave the first concert of her musical experiments in a loft in New York, using a screen to hide the performers and thus avoid any visual distractions. In 1952 she began providing compositions on commission for the Erick Hawkins Dance Company, for which she produced a series of innovative sound pieces during the next decade, beginning with *Openings of the Eye*, for flute, percussion, and timbre piano (1952). "I was not recognized by the official musical community," she says. "Indeed, it did not recognize me until 1965, when Virgil Thomson began active support of my music, having already charmingly 'adopted' me in 1957 when he first heard *Here and Now with Watchers*, for timbre piano (1954–57). What kept this lonely musical isolation bearable was that I was actively supported by the emerging New York School of painters, poets, and dancers. I met the poets Frank O'Hara and John Ashbery when they were acting at the Living The-

ater in 1953, and the dancer-choreographer Erick Hawkins offered me financial support in the form of commissions."

Another powerful impact on her musical thought came from Taoism, haiku poetry, and the philosopher F.S.C. Northrop, all enabling her to discover the kind of perception and awareness, immediacy, and directness she was aiming for in her own artistic endeavors. "With the meeting of Northrop in 1957, my total initial development as a musical artist had its core finalization and I began my long journey as an independent composer. It is to Northrop that I owe, as does all of modern culture, the valuable insight of enjoying the fruits of both science and art— the independence and intellectual purity of scientific discipline and the intense aesthetic sensitivity that only the oriental cultures dared to make as the extreme goals in the beauty of art (adding such isolated Western figures as James Joyce or Wittgenstein)."

In addition to working on commissions for the Erick Hawkins Dance Company, she also provided music for such organizations as the Living Theater, the Center for Creative and Performing Arts at the State University in Buffalo, and the American Brass Quartet. In 1960, she joined the Foundation of the Modern Dance in New York (sponsor of the Erick Hawkins Dance Company) as teacher and composer, and that same year she lectured on her methods and music at the New School for Social Research in New York.

In the mid-1950s, Dlugoszewski began devising and developing pitched and nonpitched instruments of her own making. They were constructed from all kinds of materials. Most of her compositions—many assuming quixotic titles—were written for those instruments, constructed for her by Ralph Dorazio. These included a whole family of rattles—closed rattles, tangent rattles, unsheltered rattles, and the like—constructed from wood, glass, metal, plastics, or paper to provide a whole gamut of dynamics and sound qualities; square drums, whose pitch is slightly changed by playing in the corners; ladder harps, played by rubbing mallets over pieces of wood, metal, or other materials. She invented so many instruments between 1958 and 1961 that she was able to write *Eight Clear Pieces* (1958–61), for a one-hundred-piece invented percussion orchestra, for the Erick Hawkins Dance Company.

But Dlugoszewski has not confined her creativity to instruments of her own making. Many of her works are also for traditional instruments, but usually performed in an untraditional manner to produce strange, muted effects, eerie glissandi, and novel colorations.

In 1966, Dlugoszewski received an award from the National Institute of Arts and Letters. It was not until the early 1970s that she began gaining recognition among musicians and musical organizations. In 1975, the National Endowment for the Arts, in conjunction with the New York Philharmonic, commissioned her to write *Abyss and Caress* (1975), a concerto for trumpet and seventeen instruments, the world premiere of which was conducted in New York on March 21, 1975, by Pierre Boulez. In 1976 she received the Martha Baird Rockefeller Foundation recording grant for *Fire Fragile Flight*, for orchestra, which she had written in 1973 and which was introduced in New York on April 24, 1974. In 1980, in Stockholm, it received the Koussevitzky Record Award, the first such ever presented to a woman composer. In *SoHo Weekly News*, Jamake Highwater called *Fire Fragile Flight* "an absolutely astonishing piece of music . . . a refined center of energy which moved clearly and dramatically towards a superb climactic resolution." Reviewing a recording of this work, Peter G. Davis said in the *New York Times* it "uses new instrumental techniques to fashion an aural tapestry of arresting originality, poetical vibrancy, compositional energy and visceral impact."

In 1977 Dlugoszewski was the recipient of a Guggenheim Fellowship. In 1978 came another Martha Baird Rockefeller recording grant, this time for *Tender Theatre Flight Nageire*, for brass quintet and orchestra of invented percussion instruments (1978), which was introduced by the Brooklyn Philharmonic in Brooklyn, N.Y., under Lukas Foss on April 28, 1978. In 1979 she received a composition grant from the National Education Association and in 1980 a commission from the Lincoln Center Chamber Society in New York: *Wilderness Elegant Tilt*, for strings, winds, and piano (1981), introduced on November 22, 1981, in New York. Among other late significant world premieres were those of *Strange Tenderness of Naked Leaping*, for string orchestra, two trumpets, and two flutes (1977), by the Orchestra of Santa Fe, William Kirschke conducting, on November 13, 1977; *Amor Elusive Empty August*, for woodwind quintet (1979), commissioned by the Boehm Quintette, and first heard at the Library of Congress in Washington, D.C., on January 11, 1980; and *Swift and Naked*, for string quintet, bass trombone, and timbre piano (1979–80), with the composer performing at timbre piano in New York on March 27, 1980. Virgil Thomson has described Dlugoszewski's works as "far-out music of great delicacy, originality and beauty of sound, almost ingenious with regard to instrumental virtuosities and of unusually high level in its intellectual and poetic aspects."

THE COMPOSER SPEAKS: Music is a ritual whose function is to help imperfect man become identical with "perfect nature." Such music is neither egocentric, romantic self-expression nor artificial common sense, nor selfish pleasure, nor artificial classical order. Such music is not expressing man instead of nature, nor nature instead of man, but man identical with perfect nature—bringing us to our very best: real, alive, free.

Music is the dangerous unexpected universe of our radical empirical immediacy—formally: architecture of speed, a constant leaping into new material. The challenge is always this: leaping for the flexibility of the soul, a hearing whose obligation awakens a sensibility so new that it is forever unique, newborn, antideath surprise—created now and now and now and now.

PRINCIPAL WORKS: 3 piano sonatas (1949, 1950, 1950); *Beauty Music* I, II, and III, for chamber orchestra and invented percussion (1965).

Moving Space Theater Pieces for Everyday Sounds (1949); *Melodic Sonata*, for piano (1950); Sonata, for solo flute (1950); *Transparencies 1–50 for Everyday Sounds* (1951); *Everyday Sounds for e.e. cummings* (1951); *Four Transparencies*, for various solo instruments (1952); *Openings of the Eye*, for flute, percussion, and timbre piano, for dancers (1952); *Orchestra Structure for the Poetry of Everyday Sounds* (1953–70); *Silent Paper Spring and Summer Friend Songs* (1953–70); *Archaic Timbre Piano Music* (1953–56); *Here and Now with Watchers*, for timbre piano, for dancers (1954–57); *Arithmetic Points*, for orchestra (1955); *Instants in Form and Movements*, for timbre piano and chamber orchestra (1957); *Music for Small Centers on Piano* (1958); *Flower Music for Left Ear in a Small Room* (1958); *Eight Clear Pieces*, for one-hundred-piece invented percussion orchestra, for dancers (1958–61); *Delicate Accidents in Space*, for unsheltered rattle quintet (1959); *Concert of Man Rooms and Moving Space*, for flute, clarinet, timbre piano, four unsheltered rattles in various locations (1960); *Suchness Concert*, evening-long orchestra of invented percussion instruments (1960); *Archaic Aggregates* for timbre piano, ladder harps, tangent rattles, unsheltered rattles, and gongs (1961); *Four Attention Spans*, for orchestra (1964); *To Everyone Out There*, for orchestra, for dancers (1964); *Geography of Noon*, for invented percussion orchestra, for dancers (1964); *Cantilever* II, for piano and orchestra, for dancers (1964); *Orchestral Radiant Ground* (1964); *Quick Dichotomies*, for two trumpets, clarinet, invented percussion (1965); *Percussion Kitetails* (1965); *Suchness with Radiant Ground*, for clarinet and percussion duo (1965); *Percussion Flowers* (1965); *Percussion Airplane Hetero* (1965); *Swift Music*, for two timbre pianos (1965); *Music for Left Ear in a Small Room*, for clarinet (1965); *Naked Flight Nageire*, for chamber orchestra (1966); *Hanging Bridges*, for string quartet (1967); *The Heidi Songs*, opera (1967–70); *Tight Rope*, for chamber orchestra, for dancers (1968); *Balanced Naked Flung*, for chamber orchestra (1968); *Hanging Bridges*, for orchestra (1968); *Naked Swift Music*, for violin, timbre piano, invented percussion, and orchestra (1968); *Cicada Skylark Ten*, for chamber orchestra (1969–70); *Suite for Nine Concerts*, for violin, clarinet, timbre piano, invented percussion instruments (1969–70); *Naked Quintet*, for brass quintet (1970); *Space Is a Diamond*, for trumpet (1970); *Sabi Music*, for violin (1970); *Pure Flight*, for string quartet (1970); *John Ashbery Poetry*, for narrator, chamber orchestra, and movement (1970); *Parker Tyler Language*, for voice, chamber orchestra, and movement (1970); *Of Love*, ballet, for brass quintet, invented percussion orchestra (1971); *Kireji: Spring and Tender Speed*, for chamber orchestra (1972); *Naked Point Abyss*, for timbre piano solo (1972–73); *Fire Fragile Flight* (1973); *Densities*, for brass quintet (1974); *Abyss and Caress*, concerto for trumpet and seventeen instruments (1975); *Strange Tenderness of Naked Leaping*, for string orchestra, two trumpets, and two flutes (1977); *Amor Now Tilting Night*, for chamber orchestra (1978); *Tender Theatre Flight Nageire*, for brass quintet and orchestra of invented percussion instruments (1978); *Amor Elusive Empty August*, for woodwind quintet (1979); *Swift and Naked*, for string quintet, bass trombone, and timbre piano (1979–80); *Now Tilting Naked*, for string quintet, bass trombone, and timbre piano (1979–80); *Amor Elusive April Pierce*, for chamber orchestra (1979–80); *Pierce Sever*, for timbre piano solo (1979–80); *Wilderness Elegant Tilt*, for strings, winds and piano (1981).

BIBLIOGRAPHY: *DCM*; Thomson, Virgil, *American Music Since 1910* (N.Y., 1970); *High Fidelity/Musical America*, June 1975; *New York Times*, March 7, 1971; *SoHo Weekly News*, May 11, 1978; *Vogue*, October 1970.

Donato, Anthony, b. Prague, Neb., March 9, 1909.

His music is what he describes as "a modified neoclassical Bartókian type of sound," with occasional excursions into newer techniques. His writing has always been based on a free tonality, often evolving around pitch rather than tonal centers.

His mother, a pianist, brought good music into the Donato household. Anthony took his first music lessons on the violin when he was six, and at twelve made his first attempt at composition. While attending Wahoo High School in Nebraska he played the violin in the school orchestra and the tuba in its band. Upon graduating from high school in 1926 he attended the University of Nebraska in Lincoln for one year; then, in 1927, he entered the Eastman School of Music in Rochester, N.Y., where he remained four years, studying the violin with Gustave Tinlot, composition with Edward Royce, Bernard Rogers, and Howard Hanson, and conducting with Eugene Goossens. At Eastman, Donato received his bachelor of music degree in 1931, the same year in which, on December 30, he married Carolyn C. Scott, a pianist. During these years, Donato played the violin in the Rochester Philharmonic (1927–31) and with the Hochstein Quartet (1929–31) and performed various conducting and performing chores over local radio

stations in Rochester and Des Moines (1929–37). In Des Moines he organized and played in his string quartet and was a member of the Sinfonia Trio.

Between 1931 and 1937, Donato headed the violin department at Drake University in Des Moines, Iowa, and conducted the University Symphony Orchestra. He then was head of the violin department at Iowa State Teachers College (1937–39) and at the University of Texas (1939–46). He earned his master's degree in music in 1937 and his doctorate in music in 1947 at the Eastman School.

His first compositon as a mature composer appeared in 1936. It was the Sinfonietta no. 1, which was first heard in May 1937 in Rochester, N.Y. This is a neoclassic work with a discreet spicing of modern harmonies. Such an idiom also characterized *Elegy*, for strings (1938; Lincoln, Neb., April 23, 1939); the Violin Sonata no. 1 (1938; Ames, Iowa, April 17, 1939); and Divertimento, for orchestra (1939; Rochester, N.Y., October 30, 1941). The Violin Sonata received the first prize from the Iowa Federation of Music Clubs in 1939, and in 1945 the Blue Network Award of the American Composers' Congress.

In the early 1940s, Donato began writing in the neoclassical Hindemith idiom with the infiltration of a Bartók idiom he would henceforth favor, an energetic and varied rhythmic vocabulary, and dissonant harmonies bringing strength to his writing. His String Quartet no. 1 (1941), which received the Society of Publication of American Music Award, was performed at the American Music Festival in Rochester, N.Y., by the Gordon String Quartet on April 29, 1942. His two symphonies (1944, 1945) were introduced in Rochester, both conducted by Howard Hanson, the first on October 23, 1945, and the second on May 1, 1947. *Drag and Run*, for clarinet, two violins, and cello (1946; Evanston, Ill., December 1951), received the Composers Press Publication Award. *Precipitations*, for violin and piano (1946; N.Y., February 17, 1947), was commissioned by the Music Press, Inc., and the String Quartet no. 2 (1947) received its premiere in Rochester, on April 30, 1947, in a performance by the Gordon String Quartet.

In 1947, Donato was appointed professor of theory and composition at Northwestern University in Evanston, Ill. He became conductor of that university's orchestra in 1947, full professor in 1948, and, following his retirement in 1976, professor emeritus. On a Fulbright Fellowship, he took a leave-of-absence from the university to lecture on contemporary American music in England and Scotland.

Donato has been a prolific contributor to orchestral, chamber, choral, and vocal music, his compositions receiving numerous performances throughout the United States and Europe. His only work for the stage is an opera, *The Walker through the Walls* (1964), based on a story by Marcel Aymé, which was produced in Evanston, Ill., on February 26, 1965, with the composer conducting. Among his most successful works are the following: the orchestral overture *Prairie Schooner* (1947; Rochester, October 19, 1948) and *The Plains*, for orchestra (1953; Oklahoma City, Okla., October 31, 1955), both winners of the Composers Press Publication Award; *The Sycophantic Fox and the Gullible Raven*, for chorus and piano (1950), awarded first prize by the Mendelssohn Glee Club in 1955; String Quartet no. 3 (1951; Bloomington, Ill., April 1, 1953), his most frequently performed string quartet; *Solitude in the City*, for narrator and orchestra (1954), based on a poem by John Gould Fletcher, which was commissioned by the Cincinnati Symphony and performed by that orchestra under Thor Johnson on March 25, 1955; *The Congo*, for soprano solo, chorus, and orchestra (1957; Cleveland, Ohio, May 22, 1959), based on Vachel Lindsay's poem of the same name and winner of first prize in a contest sponsored jointly by the Vachel Lindsay Society and the Illinois Federation of Music Clubs; Sinfonietta no. 2 (1959; Fish Creek, Wis., August 12, 1959), which had been commissioned for the 1959 Peninsula Festival directed by Thor Johnson; Serenade, for small orchestra (1961; Traverse City, Mich., March 3, 1962), commissioned and introduced by the Chicago Little Symphony, Thor Johnson conducting; *Centennial Ode*, for orchestra (1967), commissioned by the Nebraska State Centennial for the Omaha Symphony, which premiered it on December 11, 1967, Joseph Levine conducting; *Improvisations*, for orchestra (1968; Kansas City, Mo., May 3, 1969), commissioned by the Kansas City Youth Orchestra; Three Poems from Shelley, for tenor and string quartet (1971; Evanston, Ill., May 1974); and the String Quartet no. 4 (1975; Evanston, Illinois, February 20, 1976), commissioned by the Union League and Civic and Arts Foundation to commemorate the American bicentennial.

Donato has also written many highly successful piano teaching pieces, of which *The Wistful Little Princess, Northern Lights*, and *The Rock Crusher* were voted by the Piano Teachers Information Service as among the best such works in their respective years—1953, 1955, and 1961.

In 1961, Donato was awarded a Huntington Hartford Foundation Fellowship. Donato is the author of *Preparing Music Manuscript* (1963).

THE COMPOSER SPEAKS: This is a remarkable period in music history that has produced a wealth of new material which, along with electronic development, seems to be almost beyond comprehension in its limitless possibilities. It is now time to form this material into something truly significant having wide acceptance in the manner of the tonal period and not just producing works that are "interesting," "clever," or "startling" that appeal only to a limited number of new music enthusiasts. It is worthy of note that even though some leading composers maintain that every-

thing from the past should be discarded, others are backtracking and becoming less concerned with novelty. Everything considered, it is an exciting time for creative music.

PRINCIPAL WORKS: 4 string quartets (1941–75); 2 symphonies (1944, 1945); 2 violin sonatas (1938, 1949); 2 sinfoniettas, for orchestra (1936, 1959).

Elegy, for strings (1938); *Mission San José de Aguaya*, for orchestra (1945); *Drag and Run*, for clarinet, two violins, and cello (1946); *Precipitations*, for violin and piano (1946); Suite, for strings (1948); *March of the Hungry Mountains*, for chorus and orchestra (1949); Sonatina, for three trumpets (1949); Horn Sonata (1950); *The Sycophantic Fox and the Gullible Raven*, for chorus and piano (1950); Piano Sonata (1951); *Solitude in the City*, for narrator and orchestra (1954); *Episode*, for orchestra (1954); Quintet for Winds (1955); *The Congo*, for soprano, chorus, and orchestra (1957); Piano Trio (1959); Serenade, for small orchestra (1961); *The Walker through the Walls*, opera (1964); Clarinet Sonata (1966); *Centennial Ode*, for orchestra (1967); *Improvisation*, for orchestra (1968); *Discourse*, for flute and strings (1969); Three Poems from Shelley, for tenor and string quartet (1971); *Discourse* II, for saxophone and piano (1974).

BIBLIOGRAPHY: *BBDM*; *Who's Who in America, 1980–81*.

Donovan, Richard Frank, b. New Haven, Conn., November 29, 1891; d. Middletown, Conn., August 22, 1970.

His harmonic and polyphonic writing was freely dissonant. His works are characterized by their sonorous balances, variety of color, and complexity of rhythmic invention, and often by their comtemplative and introspective moods.

While attending public schools in New Haven, Donovan studied the piano with private teachers. When he was about seventeen he acquired his first practical knowledge of music by playing the piano in dance bands and in theater-pit orchestras in New Haven, experiences he always regarded as valuable. He soon discovered that there existed a wider world of music when he attended rehearsals of the New Haven Symphony, conducted by Horatio Parker, where local performers, amateur and professional, gathered once a week for a session of music making. On his first visit, Donovan was called on to play the triangle. "My inability to count 214 silent bars, play one note, then count 63 before playing the next," he once recalled, "earned the justified scorn of the short-tempered Dr. Parker and I was dismissed from the stage with appropriate verbal brickbats." He was, however, permitted to remain as a listener and to acquire for the first time, as he said, "the feeling of a symphony orchestra and a glimpse of the world of music."

From 1912 to 1914 (and again in 1922) he attended Yale University, where he received his bachelor of music degree in 1922. From 1914 to 1918 he was a student of the Institute of Musical Art in New York. He also studied the organ privately with Miles Farrow, Walter Henry Hall, and, for a brief period, with Charles-Marie Widor in Paris.

When he returned to the United States from Paris, he earned his living playing the organ in various churches and teaching. He taught music at the Taft School in Watertown, Conn. (1920–23), at Smith College in Northampton, Mass. (1923–28), and at the Institute of Musical Art in New York (1925–28). From 1926 to 1940 he was a lecturer on music at Finch Senior College in New York, where he was also active as a church organist and choral director.

At Smith College Donovan began his composing career officially with the *Poem*, for flute and orchestra (1925), written in an impressionistic idiom. It was performed at Smith College on June 14, 1925, with the composer conducting, at a concert commemorating the school's fiftieth anniversary. This work was revised in 1939, when it was renamed *Wood-Notes*.

In 1928 Donovan was appointed assistant professor of theory at Yale University. He remained there for thirty-two years, becoming associate professor in 1940, full professor in 1947, Battell Professor from 1954 to 1960, and, following his retirement in 1960, Battell Professor emeritus. He conducted the Bach Cantata Club in New Haven (1933–44) and the New Haven Symphony (1936–51); from 1928 to 1965 he also served as organist and choirmaster of the Christ Church in New Haven.

His music first began attracting attention in the 1930s. *Chanson of the Bells of Oseney*, for female chorus (1930), received numerous performances throughout the United States. A Piano Suite (1933) was introduced at Yaddo, the artists' colony at Saratoga, N.Y., in 1934. At Yaddo, Allegro-Fugato, for oboe and strings (1938), was given its premiere on September 11, 1938. In a revision one year later, and under its new and permanent title of Ricercare, this work was performed in Rochester, N.Y., on April 25, 1939. When given at the Cornell Festival of Contemporary American Arts in Ithaca, N.Y., in 1945, a program annotator described it as "a fine example of the resurgence of polyphonic writing."

In subsequent choral works, Donovan revealed his skill in modern contrapuntal writing, while in many of his later instrumental works he combined modern harmonic and rhythmic devices with impressionistic tone painting. Among his works to receive significant performances were: Suite, for oboe and string orchestra (1945), by the Baltimore Little Symphony on March 11, 1945; the orchestral overture *New England Chronicle* (1947) by the NBC Symphony over the NBC radio network, Alfred Wallenstein conducting, on May 17, 1947; Fantasia, for solo bassoon and seven instruments (1960; revised 1961), by the Houston Symphony under Leopold Stokowski on March 18, 1960. For *Design for Radio*, for chamber orchestra (1945), Donovan received the Broadcast Music, Inc. (BMI), Publication Award.

In 1947, Donovan received an honorary master of arts degree from Yale, and in 1962 the Naumburg Recording Award. For many years he was a director of the Yaddo Corporation and a member of the Yaddo Festival Committee. He was a member of the staff of Middlebury College Composers Conference in Vermont (summers, 1946, 1947) and visiting professor of music at the University of Southern California in Los Angeles (summers, 1948, 1964). In 1961–62 he served as president of the American Composers' Alliance.

PRINCIPAL WORKS: 2 symphonies (1936, 1946); 2 piano trios (1937, 1963); 2 piano suites (1932, 1953).

Wood-Notes, for flute, harp and strings (1925; revised 1939); *Chanson of the Bells of Oseney*, for female chorus (1930); Sextet, for wind instruments and piano (1932); *Smoke and Steel*, tone poem for orchestra (1932); Suite, for piano (1933); Clarinet Sonata (1937); Ricercare, for oboe and strings (1938; revised 1939); Three Choruses, for a cappella women's voices (1938); Serenade, for oboe, violin, viola and cello (1939); Fantasy on American Folk Ballads, for men's voices and piano (1940); *Design for Radio*, for chamber orchestra (1945); Suite, for string orchestra and oboe (1945); Overture, for orchestra (1946); Two Chorale Preludes, for organ (1946); *New England Chronicle*, overture for orchestra (1947); *Hymn to the Night*, for women's voices (1947); Passacaglia on Vermont Folk Tunes, for orchestra (1949); Four Songs on Old English Texts, for voice and piano (1950); Woodwind Quartet (1953); Four Songs of Nature, for women's voices and piano (1953); *Sounds*, for trumpet, bassoon, and percussion (1953); Three Madrigals, for a cappella chorus (1954); Mass, for unison voices with organ, three trumpets and timpani (1955); *Forever, O Lord*, for a cappella chorus (1956); Five Elizabethan Lyrics, for voice and string quartet (1957); Fantasia, for solo bassoon and seven instruments (1960, revised 1961); *Music for Six*, for oboe, clarinet, trumpet, piano, violin, and cello (1961); Magnificat, for male chorus and organ, 1961; *Epos*, for orchestra (1963).

BIBLIOGRAPHY: Ewen, David, *American Composers Today* (N.Y., 1949); Reis, Claire, *Composers in America* (N.Y., 1947); *American Composers Alliance Bulletin*, no. 4, 1956; *Composers of America*, vol. 15, 1969.

Doran, Matt Higgins, b. Covington, Ky., September 1, 1921.

Doran has described himself as an "independent" composer, with strong leanings toward the melodic and the lyric and toward contrapuntal textures. Occasionally he composes atonally, but never in the twelve-tone system, and though he has done research in electronic music he has found electronic sounds unsatisfactory as a creative tool.

His father was a teacher of speech at the Los Angeles City College, and his mother, a graduate from the Cincinnati Conservatory, was a competent pianist. His mother began teaching him the piano when he was five. Eight years later he started flute lessons with William E. Hullinger, continuing them with Ary von Leeuwen, Jules Furman, Archie Wade, and Frohman Foster. While continuing with his study of the flute he became, in his sixteenth year, a piano student of George Liebling's; at the same time he took violin lessons from Ferdinand Wismer. In time, he stopped all violin and piano lessons to concentrate on the flute, though he did give some recitals both as pianist and as flutist.

While attending Loyola High School in Los Angeles (1934–39), he played the flute in the school orchestra, the piccolo in the school band, and accompanied the school glee club on the piano. Between 1938 and 1941 he attended Los Angeles City College, where he played flute in its orchestra as well as in the National Youth Administration Orchestra conducted by Alexander Steinert. During World War II he played the flute in a band.

He changed his major musical interest from flute to composition after he entered the University of California in 1944, where he remained for the next ten years. Studying composition with Ernst Toch was the principal reason for the change. "He was my major influence from every musical standpoint—independence of style, craftsmanship, parallels with nature, and so forth," Doran recalls. Among his teachers in music at the university were Ingolf Dahl (orchestra and commercial arranging), Lucien Cailliet (orchestra and orchestration), Gail Kubik (composition), Ernest Kanitz (composition), and Hanns Eisler (composition). Outside the university he also studied composition privately with Peter Korn.

While attending the university he played the flute in Peter Korn's New Orchestra (1945–48), with the Hancock Ensemble (1947–48), and in motion picture studio orchestras. As an undergraduate he completed his Symphony no. 1 (1946), introduced in the year of its composition in Los Angeles by the New Orchestra conducted by Peter Korn. Pauline Alderman in the *International Musician* described it as "a truly serious composition: mature, clearly written, full of the most charming musical ideas and, at times, very moving. It is brilliantly orchestrated. We have listened to many poorer first symphonies by older and more famous men."

Doran received his bachelor of arts degree at the university in 1948, his bachelor of music degree in 1949, the master of music degree in 1951, and his doctorate in music in 1954.

Between 1954 and 1956, Doran taught theory and flute at Del Mar College in Corpus Christi, Tex.; he also played the flute in the Corpus Christi Orchestra conducted by Jacques Singer. In 1954, in Austin, Doran appeared as a soloist in the premiere of his own Flute Concerto at the Austin (Tex.) Symposium, Victor Alessandro conducting.

In 1955 Doran went to Ball State College in Muncie, Ind., to teach music history (1956) as well as to play the flute in the Muncie Symphony. In 1957 he joined the music faculty of Mount St. Mary's College in Los Angeles, where he has remained ever since, teaching theory, composition, music history, and the woodwind instruments; he became full professor in 1966. In 1957 (and again in 1964) he was the recipient of a Huntington Hartford Award in Composition. On August 22, 1957, he married Therese Bernuy, a nurse, with whom he had five children.

Doran tapped a satiric vein with his first opera, *The Committee* (1953), a melodious and witty takeoff on the committee system in academic institutions, libretto by the composer and Trilby Lawrence; its single act is set in "the office of the head of the music department of any large American university." The idea for this opera came to him after he had undergone the grueling oral finals for his doctorate before an academic committee. The opera's premiere took place in Corpus Christi on May 25, 1955. Soon after, it was performed seven times at Western Reserve University in Ohio as well as in Oregon, Kansas, California, and New York City. Following the New York performance, Edward Downes wrote in the *New York Times*: "Mr. Doran has told his story with delicious zest. His music is tuneful, light, humorously reminiscent of Gian Carlo Menotti. . . . Above all, it showed a real flair for the stage."

Since then Doran has written numerous other operas as well as other symphonies, concertos for various solo instruments and orchestra, and sundry other piano and chamber music compositions. In Los Angeles, his Woodwind Quintet was premiered in 1952, Symphony no. 2 (1959) in 1959, the one-act opera *The Marriage Counselor* (1977), on March 12, 1977. *Overture: 1964* (1964) was given its initial hearing at a concert of the Houston Symphony in 1969. In 1968, the soprano Ella Lee featured an aria from Doran's opera *The Little Hand So Obstinate* (1966–70) on her international tour.

In 1964, while taking a sabbatical from Mount St. Mary's College, Doran did research in electronic music in Europe. In 1973 he traveled to the Soviet Union, Rumania, Poland, Czechoslovakia, and Yugoslavia lecturing on aspects of music history.

THE COMPOSER SPEAKS: Composers like Toch, Britten, Barber, have been major influences on me, both by the quality of their music as well as their avoidance of embracing what has come along as new merely because it is new. Hindemith and Vaughan Williams have also influenced me as well as Bartók, Gail Kubik, and other "independent" composers. In the words of Toch, one must be the master, not the slave, of his style. This does not imply any insinuation of insincerity on the part of composers of electronic and total-serialization methods. I believe there is room for more than one or two types of musical composition.

PRINCIPAL WORKS: 3 symphonies (1946, 1959, 1977).

Woodwind Quintet (1951); *The Committee*, one-act opera (1953); *Dramatic Essay*, for band, (1954); Flute Concerto (1955); French horn Concerto (1956); *Overture: 1957*, for orchestra (1957); Symphony, for string orchestra (1960); *Overture: 1964*, for orchestra (1964); *The Little Hand So Obstinate*, opera (1966–70); Piano Concerto (1970); *Sign Here*, opera (1971); *Feet First*, opera (1972); *Faculty Meeting*, opera (1974); *Made by Hand*, opera (1975); Double Concerto, for flute, guitar, and strings (1975); *Eskaton*, oratorio for solo voices, chorus, and orchestra (1976); *The Marriage Counselor*, one-act opera (1977); *The Last Flute Lesson*, opera (1978); *The Registrar*, opera (1979).

BIBLIOGRAPHY: *BBDM*.

Druckman, Jacob Raphael, b. Philadelphia, Pa., June 26, 1928.

Winner of the Pulitzer Prize in music in 1972, Druckman has been interested in the sonorific effects of percussion and occasionally in electronic music. Luminosity of sound and richness of texture characterize his masterful orchestrations. Brief quotations of past music are skillfully woven into the fabric of some of his best compositions.

He was the only son of a manufacturer who was an excellent amateur musician. Jacob began playing the piano when he was three. Formal study of the violin started three years later and continued in earnest in 1938 with Louis Gesensway. When he was fifteen, Druckman was composing without any previous instruction. Then, after a period of the study of harmony and composition in a local settlement school in Philadelphia, he completed his first work to be performed and recorded, a Woodwind Quintet. Impressed by this work, Gesensway decided to teach Druckman composition as well as the violin, with supplementary lessons in solfeggio provided by Renée Longy.

As a teenager, Druckman played the trumpet with various jazz groups, and the violin in string quartets. The summer of 1948 was spent at the Berkshire Music Center at Tanglewood, Mass., studying and playing the violin in an orchestra. He wrote his String Quartet no. 1 in 1948 and, in 1949, a Duo for violin and piano and his first work for orchestra, *Music for the Dance*. By then he had become so discouraged at his failure to make any headway as a composer that he decided to abandon music permanently. But one of his compositions at that time led Aaron Copland to invite Druckman back to Tanglewood as a scholarship student in his class of composition. "This," Druckman recalls, "brought me back to music." After that, from 1949 to 1954, he continued studying composition mainly with Bernard Wagenaar, Vincent Persichetti, and Peter Mennin at the Juilliard School. There, in one of his classes, he met Muriel Helen Topaz, a dance student. They were married on June 6, 1954, and had two children. In time, Muriel Topaz became an authority on dance notation, was on the faculty of the Juilliard School for several years, and then became executive director of the Dance Notation Bureau in New York.

While at Juilliard, Druckman wrote Divertimento, for clarinet, horn, harp, violin, and cello (1950) and *Laude* (1952), songs for baritone, alto flute, viola, and cello on medieval texts. Both were performed at Juilliard in 1953.

In 1952, Druckman received his bachelor of science degree at Juilliard and two years later, the master of science degree. A Fulbright Fellowship in 1954 made it possible for him to go to Paris to attend the École Normale de Musique, a composition pupil of Tony Aubin. Back in the United States, Druckman joined the faculty of Juilliard, in 1957, remaining on its staff until 1972. In 1957 he received the first of two Guggenheim Fellowships (the second coming in 1968). In 1958 he completed Four Madrigals for a cappella chorus, whose premiere was given at the Juilliard School on March 6, 1959. "In completing the Four Madrigals," Druckman said, "I found myself personally involved with the texts in a word by word sense which I had not experienced before. Although the poems come from different authors there is a central theme revolving about a denial of the force of death . . . and a reaffirmation of life."

From 1961 to 1967, Druckman taught music part time at Bard College in Annandale-on-Hudson, N.Y. These were the years when he arrived at full maturity as a composer by reaching back stylistically to the polyphony of the baroque era; but his polyphonic, as well as his harmonic, language, was dissonant. *Dark Upon the Harp*, for mezzo-soprano, brass quintet, and percussion (1962), commissioned by Milton Feist, was a setting of verses from Psalms attributed to David. It was first heard in 1962 in New York, and since has been frequently performed besides being recorded. Raymond Ericson, in the *New York Times*, called it "an ambitious . . . piece . . . well made, with sensitive and not overly obvious musical reflections of the text."

In *Antiphonies* I, II, and III, for two a cappella

choruses (1963), the texts being poems by Gerard Manley Hopkins, Druckman reached back to Renaissance polyphony. The first performance of the first two *Antiphonies* was presented by the Collegiate Chorale, Abraham Kaplan conducting, in New York on February 28, 1964; the third *Antiphony* was performed somewhat later at Tanglewood. These three choral works, as the composer explained, sprang from two sources, the poetry of Gerard Manley Hopkins and "a fascination with the possibilities of spatial distribution of those sounds presented by the two choruses. . . . The two choruses use not only the simple opposition of their Renaissance progenitors, but also 'cross-fading' techniques so that the words seem to float and flash across the space." The *Antiphonies* was followed by *The Sound of Time*, for soprano and orchestra (1965; Provincetown, Mass., July 25, 1965), text by Norman Mailer, and String Quartet no. 2 (1966), which the Juilliard Quartet (for whom it was commissioned by LADO, a music philanthropic organization) premiered on December 13, 1966, in New York. Ricocheting bows and finger tapping are some of the novel features of this quartet.

After attending the Columbia-Princeton Electronic Center at Columbia University in New York to study electronic music (1965–66), Druckman began using electronic devices in some of his compositions, significantly in a series of works bearing the title of *Animus*. These works, Druckman has written, "are involved with the actual presence of the performer theatrically as well as musically, limiting their focus to a particular area of human affections as well as a limited body of musical materials. Each work presumes that the ideal performance of the music already embodies the performance of the drama." *Animus* I, for trombone and tape (1966), which pits man (the live trombone player) against the machine (the recorded tape), received its premiere at Bard College on May 23, 1966, and then was heard at the Inter-American Festival in Washington, D.C., on June 20, 1968. *Animus* II, for mezzo-soprano, two percussionists, and tape (1968), was introduced at a concert of the Domaine Musical in Paris on February 2, 1970. Here the mezzo-soprano walks up the aisle of the stage and both entices and challenges two percussionists. *Animus* III, for clarinet and tape (1969), was commissioned by the Groupe de la Recherche Musicale of Radiodiffusion-Télévision Française and was first heard on October 23, 1969, in Paris. This work was praised by Peter G. Davis in the *New York Times* for "its madcap wit, inventive originality, and sheer creative vitality as the clarinetist . . . jousted heroically against a veritable sonic hailstorm of electronic explosions." Almost a decade later, Druckman completed *Animus* IV, for tenor, instruments, and tape (1977), on a commission from the Institut de Recherche et de la Coordination Acoustique (IRCAM) in Paris, where it was introduced on September 29, 1977, the composer conduct-

ing. Following a practice he would favor in several other works, Druckman here resorted to quotation, in this instance from songs by Chabrier and Liszt.

The work with which Druckman earned the Pulitzer Prize in music in 1972 was *Windows* (1972), his first large composition for orchestra. The title, as the composer informs us, comes "from the original premise of the piece which is that normal sound is a very thick, complex, contemporary structure which occasionally opens up—almost like clouds parting—and that one catches a glimpse of very simple music behind the thick textures. The simple music is, I suppose, a kind of nostalgia flitting on the edge of memory, music that never was but that has the perfume of things remembered." Most of this work consists of "frames" of the "windows." As the windows open up we hear simulations (but not quotations) of waltzes and ragtime, and hinted quotations of music by Debussy, Ravel, and Richard Strauss. *Windows* was commissioned by the Koussevitzky Music Foundation in the Library of Congress in Washington, D.C., and its first performance took place on March 16, 1972, with Bruno Maderna conducting the Chicago Symphony. Soon after that, it was performed by the New York Philharmonic under Pierre Boulez and the Cleveland Orchestra and the Berlin Philharmonic, both under Lorin Maazel. "Any window must have an accompanying wall," wrote Thomas Willis in the *Chicago Tribune*, "and Mr. Druckman has built his out of the plastic musical materials in vogue today. Using an augmented orchestra and a wide range of playing techniques for the individual instruments, he has fashioned planes, layers, and corners of sound. Calling upon the orchestra men to function with more than customary independence, he has found some fascinating, translucent textures of extraordinary vitality."

Quoting the music of other composers is a practice found in several of Druckman's subsequent compositions. In *Lamia*, for mezzo-soprano and orchestra (1974; Albany, N. Y., April 20, 1974), we get a snatch from *Il Giasone*, a 17th-century opera by Cavalli, and a textual reminder of *Tristan and Isolde*. Since Lamia is a mythological Greek sorceress, Druckman sought to evoke the supernatural, utilizing texts in five languages by Ovid, Wagner, and various folk sources involving the occult. In *Mirage*, for orchestra (1975; St. Louis, March 4, 1976)—commissioned by the St. Louis Symphony with a grant from the National Endowment for the Arts for the commemoration of the American bicentennial—Druckman quoted from Debussy's *Sirènes* three times. In both *Lamia* and *Mirage*, Druckman employed two orchestral groups, a larger and a smaller one, each with its own conductor.

Druckman was commissioned by the Cleveland Orchestra, under a grant from the National Endowment for the Arts, to write another composition for the bicentennial. Druckman responded with *Chiaroscuro*, for orchestra (1976), in which the composer carried over into music the Italian Renaissance painting term of "chiaroscuro," denoting a distribution of lights and shades to produce a three-dimensional effect. The composer reveals that this work deals with "the musical equivalents of 'chiaro' ('clear,' 'light') and 'oscuro' ('obscure,' 'dark'); the opening dense dark sound slowly clarifies and reveals simpler sounds within it almost as a dark gem slowly turned will reveal each of its facets in turn. Fragments of bright unison melody are reflected and echoed to the point where they are obscured by their own memory. One image returns several times: that of a bright single note which gradually disintegrates into shimmering dust." A wide gamut of sonorities and sounds was explored by a large orchestra that included an electric piano and an electric organ, and a percussion group which, together with the more formal members, included wood and temple blocks, bell tree, gong, maracas, claves, tam-tam and vibraphone. *Chiaroscuro* was introduced in Cleveland on April 14, 1977, by the Cleveland Orchestra under Lorin Maazel, after which it was performed by major orchestras in the United States as well as by the Berlin Philharmonic.

Novel percussion effects so prominent in *Chiaroscuro* are also encountered in *Aureole*, for orchestra (1979), which employs a large assortment of unusual and foreign percussion instruments. The New York Philharmonic commissioned it and premiered it on June 9, 1979, Leonard Bernstein conducting. Three definitions of the word "aureole" are explored in this composition: a halo; a circle of light over a sacred person's head; the sun's corona seen through a mist. The entire work was based on a monothematic line which, the composer tells us, "accumulated a halo of echoes and refractions which at times spin off and assume a life of their own and at times return to the source." Since Druckman not only wrote this work for Bernstein and the New York Philharmonic but also dedicated it to him, he quotes in his score a subject from Bernstein's symphony *Kaddish*.

Other Voices, for brass quintet (1976), was written to honor the American bicentennial. This one was commissioned by the New York State Council of the Arts and the American Brass Quintet, the latter introducing it in Aspen, Col., on July 10, 1976. In this music we uncover two elements in the composer's makeup: "an adoration of virtuosity," as he himself put it, and a search "for sounds that deal with flesh and blood rather than intellect."

Druckman wrote Concerto for Viola and Orchestra (1978) on a commission from the New York Philharmonic for its first violist, Sol Greitzer, the first performance taking place on November 2, 1978, James Levine conducting. "The theme of my Viola Concerto," Druckman says, "is the transformation of the relationship between the soloist and the orchestra. The beautiful but slightly veiled voice of the viola is surrounded by the terrible power of the full orchestra. There is an insistent pattern: the viola initiates

the activity, the orchestra at first following. The soloist gradually unleashes the force of the orchestra as the orchestra seizes upon moments in his discourse and imitates, underlines, elaborates, and transforms them." Shirley Fleming, in the *New York Post*, described the concerto as "a grand-scaled epic . . . that attains enormous climaxes but never swamps the solo instrument—indeed, caters to its special, dark-hued character in consistently sympathetic ways. . . . The composer, defining the problem of the concerto form in his own provocative terms, has solved it in his own provocative ways."

Druckman was director of the Yale University Electronic Center in 1971-72 and of the Electronic Music Studio at Brooklyn College in Brooklyn, N.Y., from 1972 to 1976. In 1976 he was appointed professor of composition, chairman of the composition department, and director of the Electronic Studio at Yale University.

He has been president of the Koussevitzky Music Foundation since 1972 and on the Musical Advisory Panel of the New York State Council on the Arts from 1975 to 1978. He was the recipient of the Creative Arts Citation for Music from Brandeis University in Waltham, Mass. (1975), was appointed to the board of directors of the American Society of Composers, Authors, and Publishers (ASCAP) in 1976, and was elected member to the American Academy and Institute of Arts and Letters (1978). In 1980 he became cochairman of the National Endowment for the Arts composer-librettist panel.

THE COMPOSER SPEAKS: As a teacher of old music as well as new, I am reminded almost daily that the revolutionary moments in the history of music (the end of the Renaissance, the end of the baroque, etc.) were affected each time by a kind of grass roots movement rising up against the intellectual vanities of the composers. It may be said that each of the uprisings were against the crowning achievements of their respective periods (Palestrina, Bach), but then there is nothing wrong with upstarts like Monteverdi and Haydn.

There is no doubt that we are in the midst of a similar moment of profound change. Look at the world of pop music—the youth culture in general— the resurgence of mysticism, religion, astrology.

We composers begin again to talk about "morality" in music or "uplifting experiences." Being "touched" by musical pieces, we begin once again to use the word "beautiful," which hasn't been used in so many years.

I think many of us are looking once again for that kind of experience. There's no reason why we can't include that with all the sophistication that we have gained in more recent years.

PRINCIPAL WORKS: *Interlude*, ballet (1953); Violin Concerto (1956); Four Madrigals, for chorus (1958); *Performance*, ballet (1960); *Dark upon the Harp*, for mezzo-soprano, brass quintet, and percussion (1962); *Antiphonies* I, II, III, for two a capella choruses (1963); *The Sound of Time*, for soprano and orchestra (1965); *Animus* I, for trombone and tape (1966); String Quartet no. 2 (1966); *Sabbath Eve Service*, for tenor, chorus, and organ (1967); *Incenters*, for thirteen players (1968); *Animus* II, for mezzo-soprano, two percussionists, and tape (1968); *Valentine*, for solo double bass (1969); *Animus* III, for clarinet and tape (1969); *Orison*, for organ and tape (1970); *Synapse*, for tape (1971); *Windows*, for orchestra (1972); *Lamia*, for mezzo-soprano and orchestra (1974, expanded 1975); *Mirage*, for orchestra (1975); *Other Voices*, for brass quintet (1976); *Chiaroscuro*, for orchestra (1977); *Animus* IV, for tenor, six instruments, and tape (1977); Viola Concerto (1978); *Aureole*, for orchestra (1979); *Bo*, for marimba, harp, bass, clarinet and three accompanying voices (1979); *Prism*, for orchestra (1979).

BIBLIOGRAPHY: *ASCAP Today*, January 1974; *DCM*; BMI, *The Many Worlds of Music*, January 1974; *Hi Fi*, August 1972; *New Yorker*, February 10, 1975; *New York Times*, November 4, 1977; *Who's Who in America, 1980–81*.

Dubensky, Arcady, b. Viatka, Russia, October 15, 1890; d. Tenafly, N.J., October 14, 1966. American citizen.

While Dubensky was alive, his compositions were performed widely by prestigious organizations. Whatever subject he chose to write about—be it Armenian, Arabian, oriental, or American—he remained an exponent of the Russian romantic school. His individuality asserted itself in compositions for unusual combinations of instruments (eighteen violins, or four bassoons, or four trumpets, or eighteen toy trumpets, or nine flutes).

Gifted in music from childhood, Dubensky sang in the cathedral choir in Viatka when he was eight and by the time he was thirteen he was supporting himself by playing the violin in a theater orchestra, having previously received instruction from private teachers. In 1904 he went to Moscow Conservatory on a scholarship, studying violin there with Jan Grjimali, composition with Alexander Ilyinsky, and conducting with Arends. In 1908 he received some additional instruction on the violin from César Thomson in Brussels. Upon his graduation from the Mosocw Conservatory in 1909 Dubensky was appointed first violinist of the Moscow Imperial Orchestra, where he remained for the next decade. In 1911 Dubensky married Olympia Lascova; they had one son.

When Dubensky was twenty-six he completed writing Symphony in G minor and a three-act comic opera. *Romance with a Double Bass*, based on Chekov. The symphony was in a classical structure, a homegrown product of the Russian romantic school,

with Tchaikovsky and Glazunov as prime influences. In the opera Dubensky revealed a gift for wit and satire as well as for sentiment and melody. It was introduced in the year of its composition at the Imperial Opera in Moscow. Two decades later, it was successfully revived in New York City (October 31, 1936).

In the wake of the revolution in Russia, Dubensky left his native land in 1919, never to return. For more than a year he lived in Constantinople, where he earned his living playing the violin in hotels and restaurants. In 1921 he came to the United States, henceforth the country of his permanent residence and citizenship. That year he joined the violin section of the New York Symphony Society. When the society was merged with the New York Philharmonic in 1928, Dubensky became a member of the new organization.

Dubensky first attracted attention as composer in the United States in 1927 when, on December 29, he conducted the premiere of his orchestral tone poem *Russian Bells* (1927) with the New York Symphony Society. Becoming interested in him, Leopold Stokowski, during the next two decades, was responsible for introducing several of Dubensky's major works for orchestra with the Philadelphia Orchestra: *Gossips*, for strings (1928), performed on November 24, 1928; *The Raven*, a melo-declamation using the Edgar Allan Poe ballad as text (1931), in the year of its composition; the sonorous and polyphonically skillful Fugue for Eighteen Violins (1932), heard on April 1, 1932; *Tom Sawyer*, a tone poem written in 1935 for the centennial of Mark Twain's birth, given in Philadelphia on November 19, 1935; and Concerto Grosso (1949) which Stokowski premiered with the New York Philharmonic on November 3, 1949. Fugue for Eighteen Violins was Dubensky's most successful composition. Following its premiere in Philadelphia it was performed by numerous major American Symphony orchestras.

Later works by Dubensky received significant premieres from other conductors: Prelude and Fugue, for orchestra (1932), by the Boston Symphony under Serge Koussevitzky on April 12, 1943; *Armenian Dance*, for orchestra (1935), and *Political Suite*, for orchestra (the latter on the subject of monarchism, fascism, and communism), over radio station WOR in New York, Alfred Wallenstein conducting, in 1935 and in 1936 respectively; *Suite Anno, 1600* (1937), for string orchestra, by the New York Philharmonic under John Barbirolli on April 23, 1939; and the Fantasy on a Negro Theme (1938) and *Stephen Foster: Theme, Variations, and Finale*, for orchestra (1940), both by the Indianapolis Symphony under Fabien Sevitzky, in 1938 and 1941 respectively. In addition, Mayor Fiorello H. La Guardia of New York conducted *Fanfare*, an introduction to the "Star-Spangled Banner" (1939), at the opening of the World's Fair in New York.

After twenty-two years of service, Dubensky left

the New York Philharmonic in 1953. He then went into retirement, both as performer and composer.

PRINCIPAL WORKS: Symphony in G minor (1916); *Romance with a Double Bass*, comic opera (1916); *Intermezzo and Complement*, for orchestra (1927); *Tartar Song and Dance*, for orchestra (1927); *From Old Russia*, for orchestra (1927); *Russian Bells*, tone poem for orchestra (1927); Andante and Scherzo, for flute and orchestra (1928); *Gossips*, for strings (1928); *Downtown*, opera (1930); *The Raven*, for narrator and orchestra (1931); *Rajah*, an old Arabian dance (1932); String Quartet in C major (1932); Prelude and Fugue, for orchestra (1932); *Reminiscences*, for orchestra (1932); *Tom Sawyer*, tone poem for orchestra (1935); Suite, for nine flutes, including piccolo and basset horn (1935); *Political Suite*, for orchestra (1936); *On the Highway*, one-act opera (1936); Prelude for String Orchestra (1936); Serenade, for orchestra (1937); *Suite Anno, 1600*, for string orchestra (1937, revised 1940); Fantasy on a Negro Theme (1938); Fanfare and Choral, for four trumpets (1939); *Danse orientale*, for orchestra (1939); *Stephen Foster: Theme, Variations, and Finale*, for orchestra (1940); *Two Yanks in Italy*, one-act opera (1944); *Orientale*, song and dance, for orchestra (1945); Prelude and Fugue, for four bassoons (1946); Concerto Grosso, for orchestra (1949); Trumpet Overture, for eighteen toy trumpets and two bass drums (1949); Trombone Concerto (1953).

BIBLIOGRAPHY: Ewen, David, *American Composers Today* (New York, 1949); Reis, Claire, *Composers in America* (New York, 1947).

Duke, Vernon (originally **Dukelsky, Vladimir**), b. Parfianovka, Russia, October 10, 1893; d. Santa Monica, Calif., January 16, 1969. American citizen, 1936.

He led a dual creative existence for many years. As Vernon Duke he wrote popular songs and scores for Broadway musicals and screen productions that were highly successful. As Vladimir Dukelsky he produced many extended serious works in an eclectic idiom that brought him international fame.

Although a native-born Russian, there was only one-quarter Russian blood in his veins. His mother's father married a woman who was half Viennese and half Spanish, while on his father's side he was half Lithuanian and half Georgian. His paternal grandmother was Princess Daria Toumanov.

He was born in an obscure railroad station because his mother was traveling by train when she was seized by labor pains. Both his parents loved music and practiced it as amateurs. From the time of his birth, they hoped their son would enter the diplomatic service, and with this in mind they began giving him lessons in languages when he was only four

He was a musical child who loved sitting at his mother's feet whenever she played the piano and continually listened to recordings of operatic and Gypsy music. It soon became a practice in the family to lull him to sleep with Italian opera arias. His mother began giving him piano lessons when he was about seven, and at that time he made his first attempt at composition by writing a waltz. It was not long before he branched out creatively to write a ballet in fourteen acts (one page to each act) and a full-length piano sonata. These compositions convinced his mother that he must receive more intensive music instruction. She turned the boy over for piano lessons first to Lubomirsky, then to Josephine Leskevitch. Lessons were supplemented by attendance at opera and symphony performances.

When Duke's father died in 1913, the family settled in Kiev, where the boy attended the conservatory, to study piano with Marian Dombrosky and Bolesav Javorsky, and theory and composition with Reinhold Glière. As a conservatory student Duke was writing music all the time, in the somewhat sentimental and consistently Slavic and romantic style of Glière and Glazunov. One such composition was a four-movement String Sextet (1918), which was performed at the conservatory together with some of his songs and piano pieces.

With the outbreak of the February revolution, the Dukelsky family left Kiev for Odessa. Duke continued his musical training at the conservatory there with Vitold Malishevsky, its director. As the revolution spread to Odessa, the family once again took flight, this time coming to Constantinople, arriving in 1919. Duke worked for the next two years arranging concerts for a refugee branch of the YMCA and playing the piano in cabarets, movie houses, and other public places. It was here and now that he first became acquainted with American popular music, particularly with the songs of Irving Berlin and George Gershwin. These impressed him so deeply that he started to write songs in a similar vein, adopting for them the pseudonym first Ivan Ivin, then Alan Lane. A more serious endeavor was the score for his first ballet, *Tale of a Syrian Night* (which he himself described as "minor-league *Scheherazade*-cum-Glazunov") and which was produced at the Théâtre des Petits-Champs in Paris in 1921.

In the fall of 1921, Duke came to the United States. To earn his keep, he took on various jobs: accompanist for Gypsy music in a restaurant; writing incidental music for vaudeville performers and nightclubs; playing the piano in vaudeville; leading a five-piece band in a burlesque show. He managed to get an introduction to George Gershwin, whose music he now admired inordinately. Gershwin encouraged him to continue writing popular music, did what he could to open some doors for Duke, and was the one who somewhat later coined for him the name of "Vernon Duke" to be used in the popular area.

In serious music, Duke received some encouragement from Eva Gautier, the concert singer, who performed two of his art songs at a concert of the International Composers Guild in New York; from Dirk Foch, the conductor of the then newly founded New York City Symphony, which performed in Carnegie Hall his first orchestral piece, *Gondla*; from the singer Nina Koshetz, who hired him as coach for a concert she was about to give with Leopold Stokowski and the Philadelphia Orchestra; and from the piano virtuoso Artur Rubinstein, who, after hearing some of Duke's piano pieces, urged him to write for him a melodious one-movement piano concerto. That concerto was written in 1924 but Rubinstein never performed it. But he did give Duke some sound advice: go to Paris for further musical development. Gershwin made it possible for Duke to earn the necessary money for the trip in 1924.

In Paris, Duke's Piano Concerto was published. When Duke played it for Diaghilev, the impresario of the Ballet Russe de Monte Carlo commissioned him to write music for one of his forthcoming productions, the ballet *Zéphyr et Flore*, first mounted in Monte Carlo on April 28, 1925, before being brought by the Ballet Russe to London and Paris. It enjoyed an extraordinary success, Duke's music was acclaimed, and he now had his first recognition.

Another event in Paris that would profoundly affect his career as composer was a meeting with Serge Koussevitzky, then the much adulated conductor of the Concerts Koussevitzky. An immediate friendship was struck which soon resulted in having Koussevitzky both publish some of his works and perform at the Concerts Koussevitzky Duke's Sonata for Piano and Orchestra (1927) and Symphony no. 1 (1927), the latter first heard on June 24, 1928, then repeated by Koussevitzky with the Boston Symphony the following March 15.

Others, too, were promoting his music, both serious and popular. In Paris, Vera Vajevska, a singer, devoted half her program to Duke's songs on January 8, 1929. And during a prolonged stay in London, Duke wrote music for an operetta that was a failure, and a musical comedy that had a satisfactory run. Additionally, Duke now published his first popular song, "Try a Little Kiss," an event made significant only because this was the first time that a published piece of music bore the name of Vernon Duke.

He was back in the United States in 1929. For about a year he was employed by Paramount Studios in Astoria, Long Island, writing background music for some of their films. Then some of his songs began to be heard in Broadway revues. In 1932 he wrote his first full score for Broadway, *Walk a Little Faster*, which contained the song classic "April in Paris." Other song hits followed: notably "Autumn in New York" in 1934 and "I Can't Get Started with You" in 1935. Among his most successful Broadway musicals were the *Ziegfeld Follies* in 1934 and 1935 and *Cabin in the Sky* in 1940. He received his first assignment from Hollywood in 1937 when he was

called upon to complete the score of *The Goldwyn Follies*, which had been left unfinished by the sudden death of George Gershwin. For this film Duke wrote two ballets choreographed by Georges Balanchine, one song ("Spring Again"), and missing verses for three Gershwin tunes.

He was also busily occupied as Vladimir Dukelsky, the writer of concert music. His many years of friendship with Prokofiev, combined with his admiration for Prokofiev's music, and his association with Stravinsky in Paris, who advised him to be less formal and correct in his writing and to put more "meat" into it, led him to enter a new phase. He abandoned the Slavic sentiments of his one-time melodies and the lush harmonic and instrumental dress he had provided for them. To his music he now brought a greater rhythmic robustness, a harmonic language that was occasionally dissonant, and a greater economy of means and minimum of resources. He remained diatonic and tonal, but he allowed himself now greater freedom in his expressivity. His Symphony no. 2 (1928) was introduced by the Boston Symphony under Koussevitzky on April 25, 1930. *Epitaph*, a cantata for soprano, chorus, and orchestra written in 1931 in memory of Diaghilev, was also premiered by Koussevitzky and the Boston Symphony, on April 15, 1932, as was *Dédicaces*, for soprano and orchestra (1937) on December 16, 1938. An oratorio, for vocal soloists, chorus, and orchestra, *The End of St. Petersburg* (1938), was given its first hearing on January 12, 1938, performed by the Schola Cantorum in New York. Later he wrote a Violin Concerto for Jascha Heifetz (1942) and a Cello Concerto (1942) for Gregor Piatigorsky. Both were heard at concerts of the Boston Symphony under Koussevitzky with the soloists for whom they were intended—the Violin Concerto on May 19, 1943, and the Cello Concerto on January 4, 1946.

In August 1942, during World War II, Duke enlisted in the Coast Guard with the rating of coxswain. During his three years in service, elevated to the rank of lieutenant commander, he wrote music for a Coast Guard revue, *Tars and Stars* (which was later filmed in Hollywood) and the Coast Guard fighting song "The Silver Shield." For a time he led the Brooklyn Barracks Band in Brooklyn, N.Y. He was discharged in September 1945.

After the war he continued following the dual paths of writing popular music for Broadway and Hollywood as Vernon Duke and serious music for concert hall and the ballet stage as Vladimir Dukelsky. In the latter category we find the *Ode to the Milky Way*, for woodwinds, horns and timpani, first performed on November 18, 1946, in New York, conducted by Leonard Bernstein. Symphony no. 3 (1947) was given its premiere over the Brussels Radio in Belgium on October 10, 1947. His two most successful ballets were *Emperor Norton* (1957), written for the San Francisco Ballet, which produced it in San Francisco on November 8, 1957, and took it on tour to South America, and *Lady Blue* (1961) commissioned by Roland Petit.

Duke spent two years in Europe (1947–49), mainly in Paris, before settling permanently in California. In 1955 he abandoned the name of Vladimir Dukelsky completely, henceforth using only Vernon Duke (which he had acquired legally in 1936) for both his popular and serious creations. In California he founded and was president of the Society for Forgotten Music, devoted to the recording of neglected music of the past. On October 30, 1957, he married Kay McCracken, a young concert singer who had studied with Lotte Lehmann; they made their home in Pacific Palisades. On December 12, 1958, his opera *Mistress into Maid*, first written in 1928 and revised in 1958, received its belated premiere in Santa Barbara.

Duke was the author of an autobiography, *Passport to Paris* (1955) and *Listen Here!* (1963), the latter a critique on "musical depreciation."

THE COMPOSER SPEAKS: There isn't a note of jazz in my serious music, and there are no symphonic overtones in my musical-comedy output. I don't think that's anything to be proud of, and as a matter of fact, the wide gulf between the two styles has proven entirely too wide for most people's comfort, particularly for critics and fellow composers. It has often been said of George Gershwin that his Broadway enemies thought he belonged in Carnegie Hall, and his highbrow detractors kept repeating in print that he should never have left Broadway. This same attempt at pigeonholing has been applied even more severely in my case.

My versatility, far from being a boon, has in reality been infuriating to most musical people. Just why that is I have no way of knowing, but the critical boys seem to think there is something monstrous and unnatural about a composer writing two different kinds of music under two different names. It annoys them not to be able to say that I go slumming when writing jazz, and it annoys them still more not to be able to classify me as an ambitious peasant, gazing at the musical Olympus behind a Lindy's herring.

PRINCIPAL WORKS: 3 symphonies (1927, 1928, 1947).

Zéphyr et Flore, ballet (1925); Piano Sonata (1927); *Mistress into Maid*, opera (1928; revised 1958); Trio, for flute, bassoon, and piano (1930): Ballade, for piano and small orchestra (1931: revised 1943); *Epitaph*, for soprano, chorus, and orchestra (1931); Etude, for bassoon and piano (1932); *Capriccio mexicano*, for violin and piano (1933); *Jardin publique*, ballet (1934); *Dédicaces*, for soprano, piano, and orchestra (1934, revised 1965); Three Caprices, for piano (1937); *Le ciel*, tone poem for orchestra (1938); *Entr'acte*, ballet (1938); *The End of St. Petersburg*, oratorio for vocal soloists, chorus and orchestra (1938); Violin Concerto (1942); Cello Concerto (1942); *Moulin Rouge*, for chorus and orchestra or piano (1943–44); *Surrealist*, suite for piano (1944): *Ode to the Milky Way*, for orchestra (1945); *Le bal des blanchisseuses*, ballet (1946); *The Musical Zoo*, song cycle for voice and piano (1946); *Souvenir de Venise*, for piano (1948); *Souvenir de Monte Carlo*, ballet (1949–56); Violin Sonata (1949); *A Shropshire Lad*, song cycle for voice and piano (1949); Variations on an Old Russian Chant, for oboe and strings (1955); Sonata, for piano or harpsichord (1955); String Quartet (1956); *Serenade to San Francisco*, for piano (1956); *Emperor Norton*, ballet (1957); *Lady Blue*, ballet (1961); *In America*, song cycle (1967).

BIBLIOGRAPHY: Duke, Vernon, *Passport to Paris* (Boston, 1955); Green, Stanley, *The World of Musical Comedy* (New York, 1960); *Christian Science Monitor*, August 21, 1943; *New York Times* (obituary), January 18, 1969.

E

Eaton, John C. (Charles), b. Bryn Mawr, Pa., March 30, 1935.

Eaton is an eclectic centrist who has availed himself of such varied techniques as jazz, serialism, microtonal music, and electronic music. He is the first composer to use an electronic sound synthesizer for live performances.

He is the son of a minister. Both his parents were musical. He first became conscious of music by listening to his brother practice the piano. His own training began when he was seven: piano with Anna Gish. The study of harmony with Numa Snyder came about a year later. While attending East Stroudsburg High School in Pennsylvania he continued to study piano privately with Charles Bodo, besides receiving at school some lessons on every instrument in its band with Clement Wiedinmyer before settling finally on the timpani. Eaton played and sang in the high school band chorus, played the piano in dance bands, and was soloist with a community orchestra. An important early influence was the study of the Schillinger method with Watts Clark in Allentown, Pa. (1948–51).

Upon graduating from East Stroudsburg High School in 1953, Eaton entered Princeton University. There he studied composition with Milton Babbitt, Edward Cone, and Earl Kim before receiving his bachelor of arts degree in 1957. He continued to study composition at Princeton with Roger Sessions between 1957 and 1959, besides taking courses in musicology with Oliver Strunk and Arthur Mendel. In 1959 he earned his master of arts degree. During his years at Princeton, he also received further training at the piano with Louise Strunsky, Eduard Steuerman, Erich Itor-Kahn, and Frank Sheridan.

His earliest compositions included the Song Cycle on Holy Sonnets of John Donne, for voice and piano (1956), which Bethany Beardslee introduced in February 1957; Piano Variations (1957), first heard at Princeton University in the fall of 1958; a one-act opera, *Ma Barker,* in a free jazz style, to a libretto by Arthur Gold (1957); and a String Quartet (1958), premiered at Princeton in the spring of its composition. The three chamber works are in a highly chromatic but still tonal style which flirts with serialism.

In 1962, Eaton received the first of two Guggenheim Fellowships (the second one coming three years later). These were supplemented by three successive American Prix de Rome in 1959, 1960, and 1961. In Rome, at the American Academy, Eaton became interested in a new electronic instrument, a portable sound synthesizer named SynKet, invented by Paul Ketoff. Eaton used it for his *Songs for R.P.B.,* for soprano (1964). Its premiere in Rome on March 1, 1966, was the first *live* performance of synthesizer music. The score of *Songs for R.P.B.* utilized the only notation thus far devised for the SynKet, a notation which Eaton described as "a pictorial representation of the presettings followed by a time scale with the operations to be performed; is curiously almost reminiscent of lute notation."

Spurred on by the success with the SynKet, Eaton had Ketoff build him an instrument similar to the one he had just used for *Songs for R.P.B.* "The implications of the SynKet," Eaton has explained, "are enormous. In the field of electronic music alone, things which would take hours and hosts of different machines and processes can now be done instantaneously. . . . By practicing on it and becoming familiar with the materials of electronic music, the problem becomes the same, more or less, as writing for conventional instruments, or better, for orchestras composed of conventional instruments. By having this music actually performed much is done to supply the element of presence that electronic music has lacked and to avoid many of the mechanical defects of a grinding, impersonal tape recorder."

His first live performance of synthesizer music in the United States took place at Columbia University on March 22, 1966, when a concert of contemporary music that included Eaton's *Songs for R.P.B.* was presented by the John Eaton Microtonal Music Ensemble. "Aside from the philosophical speculations about the need for such new sounds," reported Alan Rich in the *New York Herald Tribune* "the important thing is that it was an evening of solid, intelligent, dedicated innovation, created and presented by a bunch of worthwhile and imaginative musicians."

On a commission from the Fromm Music Foundation, Eaton completed Concert Piece for SynKet and Symphony Orchestra (1966). Its world premiere took place at Tanglewood, Mass., on August 9, 1967, Gunther Schuller conducting. "The SynKet," wrote Joel Chandler in *Electronic Music Review* in discussing the Concert Piece, "moved in and out of the texture, making statements of varying power, and of varying character in relation to the orchestra, so that a kind of scale difference was felt from similarity to dissimilarity. Some of the most effective moments had the SynKet interjecting its own material against the orchestra playing waves of undulating phrases." Concert Piece was subsequently performed by the Los Angeles Philharmonic under Zubin Mehta and the Dallas Symphony under Donald Johanos, among others.

In 1966 Eaton composed a work for voice and an orchestra of synthesizers, *Thoughts on Rilke,* played at the Spoleto Festival in Italy that year. Eaton was commissioned by the Venice Festival in Italy to write a work for its Festival of Contemporary Music in July 1968. Eaton responded with *Blind Man's Cry,* for soprano and an orchestra of electronic synthesizers (1968). For a Koussevitzky Music Foundation commission, he wrote the Mass (1970), for soprano, clarinet, and a chamber group of various electronic instruments played live, including the SynKet. The morning after its world premiere at the Library of Congress in Washington, D.C., on October 31, 1970, it was used as part of the worship service at the Washington Cathedral. In 1970, it represented the United States at the International Rostrum of Composers (UNESCO) in Paris.

In addition to these and other concert works for electronic instruments, Eaton has written several notable operas. The first was *Heracles* (1964), libretto by Michael Fried. A three and a half hour work for large orchestra, chorus, and soloists, it was heard first in a concert performance over the Italian Radio (RAI) in February 1969, the first of many broadcasts in Italy. On April 15, 1972, it was staged in Bloomington, Ind., as the dedicatory performance at the new Musical Arts Center. *Myshkin* (1971), libretto by Patrick Creagh based on Dostoyevsky's *The Idiot,* was commissioned by the Public Broadcasting Service for television transmission, and was first telecast nationally over PBS on April 23, 1973. It is scored for soloists, electronic sounds and chamber orchestra. Since then it was repeated several times on television throughout the United States, was chosen by the United States Information Agency for worldwide exhibition, reaching an audience estimated at fifteen million, and was awarded the Peabody and the Ohio State awards for meritorious achievement in television. His opera *The Lion and Androcles* (1973), written for and involving children, was also shown on national television and given a dozen performances by the Cincinnati Symphony.

Eaton's most successful opera is *Danton and Robespierre,* libretto by Patrick Creagh. It was first produced at Indiana University in Bloomington on April 21, 1978. Tonal arias, a love duet, and choral passages are here juxtaposed with atonal, microtonal, and electronic music. Danton's music is often chromatic and that of Robespierre usually diatonic. The orchestra and some of the singers, including the chorus, are pitched in quarter tones. Throughout, elec-

tronic sounds contribute to the dramatic impact of the text and are skillfully used in climactic scenes. "The results at their best," remarked John Rockwell in his report to the *New York Times,* "had a genuine epic sweep." In the *New Yorker,* Andrew Porter commented: "For all the intricacies of Eaton's score, it is direct and readily comprehensible. No more than Alban Berg is he afraid of big, straightforward, traditional theatrical strokes: ostinatos, sudden outbursts, unisons, firm tonal anchors against which to measure degrees of dissonance and tension. His writing for the orchestra is varied and very colorful. Moreover, and perhaps most important of all, *Danton* is a mellifluous opera, composed with a command of lyrical vocal gestures that reveal character and are also good to sing."

A powerful one-act opera, *The Cry of Clytaemnestra* (1979), libretto by Patrick Creagh based loosely on Aeschylus' tragedy, was given its world premiere at the Indiana University School of Music on March 1, 1980. Though in a single act and scored for a comparatively small orchestra supplemented by electronic sounds, this, as Andrew Porter noted in the *New Yorker,* was "hardly a 'chamber opera.' It makes a big sound. Its gestures are large. It has grandeur and force." The score is partly microtonal, occasionally dissonant, sometimes soaringly lyrical, and charged with calculated electronic effects. The music, wrote John Von Rhein in *Opera News,* "enhances the grim austerity of the drama and gives it an intimate focus. The chamber orchestra wells up with discords of despair and lamentation, pouring its bitter draught over the vocal lines, sometimes at the expense of textual intelligibility. Still, a compelling lyricism lurks just below the scabrous surface . . . and particularly in the high, quasi-shrieked music of Clytaemnestra and Cassandra it weaves an incantatory spell." The West Coast premiere of *The Cry of Clytaemnestra* was given on March 6, 1981, at the Spring Opera Theater in San Francisco.

Eaton has written concert music dispensing with electronic sounds. Since 1964 these have been microtonal. *Sonority Movement,* for flute and nine harps tuned in sixths (1971), was commissioned by the American Harp Society and was first performed by the University of Washington Contemporary Chamber Ensemble in Seattle in 1973. *Trio: In Memoriam Mario Cristini,* for piano trio (1971), written on commission from the Beaux Arts Trio, was introduced in New York by the New Arts Trio in December 1975. *Ajax,* for baritone and orchestra (1972), based on Sophocles, was premiered in Seattle in February 1972. Duo, for chorus (1977), was given its first hearing at the Cork Festival in Ireland (which had commissioned it) in May 1977.

Since 1972, Eaton has been in the department of composition (currently professor) and artistic director of the Center for Electronic and Computer Music at Indiana University in Bloomington. In Bloomington, on May 31, 1975, he married Nelda E. Nelson, a singer, with whom he has two children. Eaton lectured at the Salzburg Center in American Studies in Austria in 1976 and was composer-in-residence at the American Academy in Rome in 1976–77.

Eaton was the recipient of a citation and award from the National Institute of Arts and Letters (1972) and a plaque for community service in music from the Indiana State Arts Council (1975). He has given numerous concerts throughout the United States, Europe, and Latin America. In 1977 he was a guest of the Soviet Composers Society in the Soviet Union.

THE COMPOSER SPEAKS: The basis of music is the need we humans have to sing—it is as natural to us as it is to whales and wolves, for example. For this reason, I am not particularly distressed about the future of music: as long as there are human beings, there will be music. Further, the most significant musical expression of any age will somehow be involved with the intensely human expression stemming from this "song," whatever means are used to realize it.

It is inevitable that we will see a general expansion of our Western pitch materials in the near future. All ethnic and vernacular traditions use the more natural intervals found in the cracks of the piano keyboard. Our creative sensibilities have simply exhausted the chromatic scale. However, I believe the expansion will be based on dividing and extending the materials and instruments we have—we cannot cut ourselves off from our traditional musical experiences. It will also come, I believe, from performers and composers making music from basic musical necessities, not from theoretical or acoustical manipulations.

PRINCIPAL WORKS: Song Cycle on Holy Sonnets of John Donne, for voice and piano (1956); Piano Variations (1957); *Ma Barker,* one-act opera (1957); String Quartet (1958); *Tertullian Overture,* for orchestra (1958); Trumpet Sonata (1959); Adagio and Allegro, for flute, oboe, and strings (1960); *Epigrams,* for clarinet, oboe, and piano (1960); Concert Music for Solo Clarinet (1961); *Heracles,* opera (1964); *Songs for R.P.B.,* for voice, piano, and synthesizer (1964); *Microtonal Fantasy,* for two pianos (1965); Concert Piece for SynKet and Symphony Orchestra (1966); *Thoughts on Rilke,* for voice and an orchestra of synthesizers (1966); *Soliloquy,* for electronic sound synthesizer (1967); *Vibrations,* for two oboes, two clarinets, and flute (1967); *Blind Man's Cry,* for soprano and orchestra of electronic synthesizers (1968); Mass, for soprano, clarinet, and orchestra of electronic synthesizers (1970); *Myshkin,* opera (1971); *Sonority Movement,* for flute and nine harps (1971); *Trio: In Memoriam Mario Cristini,* for piano trio (1971); *Ajax,* for baritone and orchestra (1972); *The Lion and Androcles,* one-act children's opera (1973); *Guillen Songs,* for voice and pi-

ano (1974); *Oro,* for voice and synthesizers (1974); Duo, for mixed chorus (1977); *Danton and Robespierre,* opera (1978); *The Cry of Clytaemnestra,* a one-act opera (1979).

BIBLIOGRAPHY: *BBDM*; *Music Journal,* October 1966; *New York Times,* January 21, 1967; *New Yorker,* May 22, 1978.

Effinger, Cecil, b. Colorado Springs, Colo., July 22, 1914.

The inventor of Musicwriter, a typewriter for music which has had worldwide distribution, Effinger is the composer of one hundred or so compositions in all media, most of them written on commission. Though he has used atonal and polytonal and, in passing, twelve-tone and pointillistic techniques, he regards himself as a comparative conservative who assimilated into his writing the structural and technical procedures of the past, from the polyphony of the baroque era to the melodic idioms of the popular music of the 1930s into later twentieth-century approaches.

His father, Stanley S. Effinger, was supervisor of music in Colorado Springs and a composer of successful songs, the best known of which is the sacred song "I Shall Not Pass Again This Way." Cecil's mother taught Latin in Colorado Springs public schools and, though untrained, was musical. As far back as he can remember Cecil could identify correctly the notes sung or played while his father was giving voice lessons at home or on recordings of classical music on the family phonograph. As a child, while driving around the neighborhood in his uncle's grocery delivery truck, he would attract attention and gather pennies by singing songs of World War I. He also sang solos in church. One of his most memorable boyhood experiences in music came when he was ten and heard his first concert, performed by the Minneapolis Symphony.

While attending Washington Grade School he began receiving lessons on the violin when he was eight, continuing these studies with Edwin Dietrich between 1922 and 1933. At West Junior High School he started to study the oboe, which eventually became his prime instrument. He played the oboe in the school band and orchestra at Colorado Springs High School; the violin in the All-Southwestern High School Orchestra in 1929; the oboe in the National High School Orchestra in Chicago in 1930; and in 1931 he received the Theodore Presser Scholarship for the Interlochen Music Camp in Michigan, where he shared the first oboe desk and continued studying the oboe with André Andraud.

Between 1931 and 1935 Effinger attended the Colorado College in Colorado Springs, majoring in mathematics. The study of music continued in 1934–35 with Frederick Boothroyd (theory, composition, musical analysis). "Through his teaching, his position as conductor of the Colorado Springs Orchestra, which he founded, and his biweekly organ recitals," Effinger recalls, "I found my greatest musical training." Other musical experiences for Effinger in the 1930s came from making arrangements for dance band groups.

After receiving his bachelor of arts degree at Colorado College in 1935, Effinger taught mathematics for one year at Colorado Springs High School. He joined the faculty of Colorado College in 1936 as instructor of music. There he became assistant professor in 1946. He joined the faculty of the University of Colorado in Boulder as associate professor in 1948 and became full professor in 1958. In addition, he was instructor of music at the Colorado School for the Blind (1939–41), first oboist of the Denver Symphony Orchestra (1937–41), and music editor of the *Denver Post* (1946–48).

During the summer of 1937, Effinger studied composition with Bernard Wagenaar in Colorado Springs. That year Effinger wrote his first orchestral composition, Piece for Orchestra, which was followed a year later by a second orchestral work, Nocturne, and a theater work for modern dance entitled *Drum Dance*. During the summer of 1939 Effinger attended the American Conservatory in Fontainebleau, France, a student of composition of Nadia Boulanger's. He was the recipient of the Stoval Prize in composition for *New Horizon,* for orchestra (1939). *105 Degrees West,* for dance, and Prelude and Country Dance, for oboe, were also written in 1939, with Concerto Grosso, for orchestra, and Prelude and Toccata and Pastorale and Scherzo, both for oboe, coming one year later.

During World War II, Effinger was the director and commanding officer of the 506th Army Band at Fort Logan, Colo. (1942–45), holding the rank of Chief Warrant Officer. In 1945–46 he was in France, serving as instructor in composition and orchestration at the American University in Biarritz which was under army jurisdiction. While in uniform, he saw his first published composition, Prelude and Fugue, for organ (1942), in which he attempted to combine the 18th-century textures with the 20th-century harmonic vocabulary. It received its first performance on August 1, 1942, in Washington, D.C., performed by William Strickland. Several other works deserving attention were completed while he was in service. Among them were the scoring of the organ Prelude and Fugue for orchestra (1942), which was heard over the ABC radio network in 1942 with Roy Harris conducting; *Western Overture,* for orchestra (1942); *Fanfare on Chow Call,* for male chorus and brass (1943), which received a performance at the White House in spring 1943; Suite for Strings (1943), introduced by the Colorado Springs Orchestra under Frederick Boothroyd in 1943 before being programmed by the Denver Symphony conducted by the composer on April 23, 1944; Viola Sonata (1944) introduced by Ferenc Molnar,

the violist, in Colorado Springs in summer 1944; Cello Suite (1945); *Variations on a Cowboy Tune,* for orchestra (1945), performed by the Denver Symphony under Saul Caston in fall 1945 at a public concert and in March 1946 over the NBC network; and *Little Symphony* no. 1 (1945), commissioned by the St. Louis Little Symphony, which introduced it under Stanley Chapple's direction in St. Louis on July 10, 1945, and, in 1959, recipient of the Naumburg Recording Award. All these works were classic in form and texture, with somewhat diatonic lyric lines and shifting tonalities.

Effinger's friendship with Roy Harris (a fellow member of the faculty of Colorado College between 1943 and 1948) and hearings of Harris's music gave Effinger the further direction he needed in how best to fuse polyphonic techniques of the baroque era with the harmonic thought of the 20th century. Polyphonic writing is predominant in each of his first two symphonies (the Second Symphony written in 1946, one year before the so-called First Symphony). In the Symphony no. 1 (introduced by the Denver Symphony under Caston on March 11, 1947, this orchestra having commissioned it) the closing movement is a skillfully structured fugue that uses as its theme a subject that had opened the symphony and from which all the later material of the symphony was derived. The Symphony no. 2 (premiered by the Cincinnati Symphony on February 5, 1947, Thor Johnson conducting) opens with a set of forty-seven variations in the polyphonic style and structure of the baroque passacaglia, using as its subject the seven-measure twelve-tone "cell" with which the symphony opens. In both works (as is the case with many of Effinger's later ones) some tonal center or tonal plan and a diatonic-chromatic idiom are operative; and emphasis is placed on extended lyric lines and expressive harmonic movements.

Effinger's most significant works of the 1950s (all at turns broadly lyrical or dramatic, polyphonic or harmonic) include the Symphony for Chorus and Orchestra (1952, Denver, December 2, 1952); Symphony no. 3 (1954); *Tone Poem on the Square Dance* (1955; Denver, October 25, 1955); and the oratorio *The Invisible Fire,* for solo voices, chorus, and orchestra, which became one of Effinger's most frequently performed and highly esteemed compositions. The last of these enjoyed a huge success when it was introduced in Lawrence, Kans., on December 31, 1957. From then on it received numerous performances throughout the United States and was described by some critics as one of the finest sacred oratorios of the 20th century. Symphony no. 5 received its first performance in Iceland in 1959, Thor Johnson conducting.

The following subsequent compositions should be singled out: String Quartet no. 5 (1963), written for, introduced (May 17, 1964) and recorded (1967) by the Hungarian String Quartet; an all-out romantic opera, *Cyrano de Bergerac* (1965), text by Donald

Sutherland, based on the poetical drama of Edmond Rostand, first produced at the University of Colorado in July 21, 1965; *Landscape,* a tone painting for strings and brass (1966; Boulder, Colo., May 26, 1967); *Paul of Tarsus,* a cantata for solo voices, strings and organ (1968) describing three episodes in the life of Paul the Apostle, first performance taking place at the University of Colorado on July 4, 1968; the romantic four-movement Concerto for Violin and Chamber Orchestra (1974), first heard on May 10, 1974, in a performance by Abraham Chavez and the University of Colorado Orchestra conducted by the composer; and Capriccio, for orchestra (1975), the composer's first work solely for orchestra in sixteen years, first performed on March 3, 1975, by the Denver Symphony under Brian Priestman and winner of the Denver Symphony Award.

Effinger received an honorary doctorate in music from Colorado College in 1959, the Governor's Award in Arts and Humanities in Aspen in 1971, and the Award of Merit from the National Federation of Music Clubs in 1975; also, in 1975, the Denver Symphony Trustee Award for contributions to music.

On June 14, 1968, he married Corinne Ann Lindberg, who at that time was a teacher of music in elementary schools. By a previous marriage, to Margaret Wilkins in 1944, divorced in 1958, Effinger has a daughter and a son.

The idea for a musical typewriter (Musicwriter) came to Effinger while he was in Paris, in the army, in 1945, and the way he worked it out then was the way it was patented in 1955. He is also the designer of the Tempowatch, a device for ascertaining tempo as it happens—the opposite of the metronome—in 1969, and in 1974 the inventor of an open-end typewriter for engineers. The latter allows high-quality lettering and other notations on the large documents required by architects, engineers, surveyors, etc.

THE COMPOSER SPEAKS: I feel strongly that harmony (in the broadest sense) and harmonic movement are such powerful expressive and structural elements in music that to do without them is to limit the art seriously. It is like taking color out of painting. And we are far from exhausting the ways of using harmony, simple and complex; the dilemma of the turn of the century which Schoenberg faced should no longer be with us.

Electronic music has influenced me only in that I marvel all the more at the wonderful sounds we already have with which to work. We may now hear all music with different ears, and that is a plus. However, listening to electronic music, I find, gets dull very quickly.

Serialism, logical as it may be theoretically and historically, is, except in brief instances, not useful to me. At least, as we know it so far, it touches only on the lower arithmetic instead of the higher mathematics some would ascribe to it. The quality of unity with variation, which is so important in music, may be its aim, but aside from Berg, Webern, and a few others, I feel it fails as such. Writing it is dull amusement, and it is exceedingly susceptible to relatively successful use by lesser imaginations.

PRINCIPAL WORKS: 5 symphonies (1946–58); 5 string quartets (1944–63); 3 piano sonatas (1946, 1949, 1968); 2 *Little Symphonies* (1945, 1958).

Western Overture, for orchestra (1942); Prelude and Fugue, for organ, also for orchestra, for band, and for two pianos (1942); Concertino, for organ and small orchestra (1943); Suite for Strings (1943); *The Old Chisholm Trail,* for voices and orchestra (1943); Viola Sonata (1944); Suite for Cello (1945); *Variations on a Cowboy Tune,* for orchestra (1945); *Tennessee Variations,* for orchestra (1946); Concerto for Piano and Chamber Orchestra (1946); *Time,* for a cappella chorus (1947); *Lyric Overture,* for orchestra (1949); Divertimento, for violin, viola, and piano (1950); *The St. Luke Christmas Story,* cantata for soloists, chorus, and chamber orchestra (1953); *Symphonie concertante,* for harp, piano, and orchestra (1954); *Tone Poem on the Square Dance,* for orchestra (1955); *Evensong,* for orchestra (1956); *The Invisible Fire,* oratorio for solo voices, chorus, and orchestra (1957); *Fantasia in F-sharp,* for piano (1957); *Symphonic Prelude,* for orchestra (1959); Fantasy, for harpsichord (1960); *Set of Three,* for chorus and brass (1961); *Pandora's Box,* children's opera (1962); Four Pastorales, for oboe and chorus (1962); *Trio concertante,* for trumpet, horn, trombone, and chamber orchestra (1964); *Cyrano de Bergerac,* opera (1965); *Landscape,* for brass and strings (1966); *Paul of Tarsus,* cantata for solo voices, strings, and organ (1968); *Long Dimension,* for baritone, chorus, and orchestra (1970); *Cantata for Easter,* for choir, organ, and orchestra (1971); *Quiet Evening,* for flute, marimba, and strings (1972); Piano Trio (1973); Concerto for Violin and Chamber Orchestra (1974); *This We Believe,* oratorio for vocal soloists, chorus, orchestra or organ (1974); Capriccio, for orchestra (1975); *The Gentleman Desperado,* opera (1976); Suite, for two flutes and voices (1978).

BIBLIOGRAPHY: *BBDM; Who's Who in America, 1980–81.*

Eichheim, Henry, b. Chicago, January 3, 1870; d. Montecito, Calif., August 22, 1942.

His fascination for the Orient influenced everything he wrote. All are on oriental subjects: many utilized native oriental instruments and Korean and Siamese street cries to reconstruct in Western terms the actual music of the East.

His father, Meinhard Eichheim, was a professional cellist who played in the Theodore Thomas Orchestra in Chicago. He gave his son his first music instruction. It was completed at the Chicago Musical College, where Eichheim studied the violin with Carl Beck and Leopold Lichtenberg. Upon graduating, Eichheim received first prize in violin playing.

For one season (1889–90) he played the violin with the Theodore Thomas Orchestra. In 1890 he joined the violin section of the Boston Symphony, where he remained for twenty-two years.

When he retired from the Boston Symphony in 1912 Eichheim devoted himself to concertizing on the violin and to conducting the Winchester (Mass.) Symphony (1913–17). On April 17, 1917, he married Ethel Roe.

In 1915 he paid the first of four visits to the Orient, returning again in 1919, 1922, and 1928. During his first two visits he acquainted himself with oriental music, of which he made copious notes, and with oriental instruments, of which he became a collector. These were the stimulants he needed to become a composer in a serious way.

His first major work was the *Oriental Sketches*, for chamber orchestra (1921), written for the Berkshire Music Festival sponsored by Elizabeth Sprague Coolidge in Pittsfield, Mass., where it was introduced in the year of its composition. A year later Eichheim enlarged this work, renaming it *Oriental Impressions, or The Story of the Bell*, which was introduced by the Boston Symphony under the composer's direction on March 24, 1922. Five of the movements of this seven-movement suite were sketches of Korea, Japan, Siam, China, and Peking at night. One ("Entenraku") was based on an elegy attributed to an 8th-century Chinese emperor, and a seventh was a Japanese nocturne. The movement "Impressions of Peking at Night" (together with Eichheim's *Korea Sketch*, for chamber orchestra, written in 1925) was heard at the International Society for the Contemporary Music Festival in Venice on September 3, 1925. The harmonic language of the suite sprang out of Debussy and Scriabin, but the music remained esoterically oriental, particularly when native instruments were used. The distinguished musicologist Carl Engel described these sketches as "vivid, graphic [abounding] in unusual sonorities which pleasantly impinge upon the ear. . . . To the untraveled, these brief sketches suggest a knowledge of the East as sensitively sympathetic as that of Paul Claudel, tempered as it is—in both cases—with Gallic thought and taste."

Eichheim made numerous appearances as conductor promoting his own music. A ballet, *The Rivals*, whose scenario was based on an ancient Chinese Legend, was produced in Chicago on January 1, 1925; as an orchestral suite named *Chinese Legend* it was performed by the Boston Symphony on April 3, 1925. In both instances Eichheim was the conductor. Eichheim also conducted the premiere performances of several other of his works: *Malay Mosaic*, for chamber orchestra (1924), at a concert of the International Composers Guild in New York on March 1,

1925; the tone poem *Burma* with the Chicago Symphony on February 18, 1927, after it had been heard as incidental music for a play in New York on March 16, 1926; and the tone poem *Java*—which called for a gamelan section of forty-five instruments and was one of Eichheim's works in which he tried to reconstruct oriental music for Western consumption—with the Philadelphia Orchestra on November 8, 1929.

Bali (1932), a series of variations for orchestra on musical themes heard by the composer in a temple court in Denpassar, was given its initial hearing on April 20, 1933, with Leopold Stokowski conducting the Philadelphia Orchestra. When Stokowski repeated this performance the following December in New York, Lawrence Gilman in the *Herald Tribune* called it "a fascinating web of tone, cunningly wrought, perturbing, not easily to be forgotten."

Eichheim made several appearances as lecturer on Western music in Peking and Tokyo, and on oriental music in American cities. He was a fellow of the Asiatic Society of Japan.

PRINCIPAL WORKS: *Oriental Impressions*, for orchestra (1921); *The Rivals*, ballet (1924); *Chinese Legend*, orchestral suite (1924); *Malay Mosaic*, for chamber orchestra (1924); *Korean Sketch*, for orchestra (1925); *Burmese Pwe*, ballet (1926); *The Moon, My Shadow and I*, Chinese ballet (1926), *Burma*, tone poem for orchestra (1926); *Java*, tone poem for orchestra (1928); *Japanese Nocturne*, for chamber orchestra (1930); *Bali*, tone poem (1932); Violin Sonata (1934).

BIBLIOGRAPHY: Howard, John Tasker, *Our American Music* (N.Y., 1946); Reis, Claire, *Composers in America* (N.Y., 1947).

Ellington, Edward Kennedy ("Duke"), b. Washington, D. C., April 29, 1899; d. New York City, May 24, 1974.

Both as a performer and a composer, Duke Ellington is generally accepted as the leading exponent of jazz, whose songs and short jazz pieces have become classics. His presence in this volume is by virtue of his large concert works, all in the jazz idiom.

He was born to a middle-class black family. His father—a butler, caterer, and later employed in the Navy Yard on blueprints—"spent and lived like a man who had money," as Ellington recalled, "and he raised his family as though he were a millionaire." Duke's mother, for whom he bore an extraordinary attachment all his life, played the piano, while his father enjoyed singing opera arias and playing the piano by ear. When their son was seven, he began studying the piano with a local teacher named Mrs. Clinkscales, but initially he was too interested playing and watching baseball to do much practicing. During a visit to Philadelphia, Ellington heard Harvey Brooks play the piano; Brooks became the first musician to arouse his interest in music. While attending public school, and working after school at the Poodle Dog Café, Ellington, aged fourteen, wrote his first piece of music, "Soda Fountain Rag." It was then that he acquired the sobriquet of "Duke," bestowed on him by a friend who, as Ellington said, was "a rather fancy boy who liked to dress well. . . . I think he felt that in order for me to be eligible for his constant companionship I should have a title. So he named me Duke." And the nickname stuck for the rest of Ellington's life to the point of displacing his given names.

Ellington received some further music instruction from Oliver ("Doc") Perry, a jazz musician who first taught him "what I called a system of reading the lead and recognizing the chords. . . . He was my piano parent." While attending Armstrong High School in Washington, Ellington was taught harmony by Henry Grant, the school's music teacher. Still in early boyhood, Ellington acquired such aptitude for playing jazz that he was often called upon to substitute for local musicians at dances and parties.

Both in public and in high school, Ellington revealed a talent for drawing. Winning first prize in a poster competition sponsored by the National Association for the Advancement of Colored People brought him a scholarship to the Pratt Institute of Applied Art in Brooklyn, N.Y., when he was graduated from high school in 1917. He never availed himself of this opportunity. During World War I, he worked as a messenger in the Navy and State departments, then began earning his living by playing in bands, by starting a project called Music-for-All-Occasions, which booked bands for private functions, and by operating a sign-painting business that provided the signs whenever one of his bands was booked. On July 2, 1918, he married Edna Thompson. They had a son, Mercer Kennedy Ellington, who became a successful jazz musician in his own right and took over Ellington's band after his father's death. Duke Ellington's marriage lasted only a few years. Ellington and his wife separated permanently, but they were never divorced. In 1937, Ellington began a relationship with Beatrice ("Evie") Ellis that lasted all his life.

In 1918, Ellington formed a band of his own which filled engagements in the Washington area. In 1922, Ellington paid his first visit to New York, where, for a time, he played the piano in Wilbur Sweatman's band. Listening to such jazz musicians as James P. Johnson, Willie ("the Lion") Smith and Fats Waller proved to be a conservatory in which Ellington learned about jazz at its fountainhead. But, as he remarked many years later, "I never could play anything I heard them play, although they all tried to teach me. So I had to sit down and create something to fit under my fingers." One year later, Ellington formed a five-piece band named the Washingtonians for Barron's, a night spot in Harlem. The

band soon changed clubs, going to midtown to perform at the Hollywood (later renamed the Kentucky), where it remained for four and a half years. Ellington's so-called jungle music of growls, grunts and *wah-wahs*, his improvisations, and the way he fashioned the blues to his own image were here being developed into what came to be known as the Ellington style.

His music attracted the admiration of Irving Mills, a publisher who placed Ellington under an artist's contract. Mills provided the funds to enlarge the band into a twelve-man ensemble and booked it into the Cotton Club in Harlem, an engagement that began on December 4, 1927, and lasted five years. Ellington and the new kind of jazz he was presenting soon grew so famous that jazz aficionados began streaming to the Cotton Club nightly to hear Ellington's performances. His recordings also began to find a welcome market, beginning with two short instrumental numbers in which his creativity was beginning to blossom: "Black and Tan Fantasy" (1927) and "East St. Louis Toodle-oo" (1927), the latter written with Bubber Miles and to become Ellington's radio theme music in the 1930s. "We came in with a new style," Ellington later said. "Our playing was stark and wild and tense. . . . We tried new effects. One of our trombones turned up one night with an ordinary kitchen pot for a sliphorn. It sounded good. We let him keep it until we could get him a handsome gadget that gave him the same effect. We put the Negro feeling and spirit in our music."

Ellington's success continued to soar. He was being heard over radio in nightly broadcasts from the Cotton Club; in the theater (in the George and Ira Gershwin musical *Show Girl* in 1929); in the movies (in *Check and Double Check* in 1930). In 1933 he made his first appearance in Europe—in London, where in addition to his public concerts he gave a command performance at Buckingham Palace. In 1934 he made his first tour of America and in 1939 an extended tour of Europe.

In 1931, Ellington wrote his first composition in a structure more extended than the three- or four-minute pieces he had thus far been producing. It was *Creole Rhapsody*, which spread across both sides of a twelve-inch record, something with few if any precedents in jazz music up to then. The Ellington classics were now coming in rapid succession: "Mood Indigo" (1931), "It Don't Mean a Thing If It Ain't Got That Swing" (1932), "Sophisticated Lady" (1933), "Drop Me Off at Harlem" (1933), "In a Sentimental Mood" (1935), and *Reminiscing in Tempo* (1935). The last of these, written in memory of his mother, was another extended composition, this one calling for four sides of two records. "He gives the same distinction to his genre as Strauss gave to the waltz or Sousa to the march," wrote the English composer Constant Lambert in the *New Statesman*.

Through records, radio appearances, national and foreign tours, the Ellington fame continued to grow in the 1940s. He wrote his first full-length score for the musical stage in 1941—*Jump for Joy*, which opened in Los Angeles. *Beggar's Holiday*, Ellington's jazz adaptation of John Gay's ballad opera *Beggar's Opera*, wss mounted on Broadway on December 26, 1946. Ellington and his band were featured in the motion picture *Reveille with Beverly* in 1943. In 1943 he received the Supreme Award of Merit from George Washington Carver Memorial Institute and the Page One Award of the American Newspaper Guild (a second such award followed two years later). He captured first place among bands in *Down Beat* in 1946 and first place as favorite soloist and favorite band in 1948. *Esquire* selected him for its Gold Award both as arranger and as All-American band in 1945, 1946, and 1947. In 1949, Ellington received his first honorary degree: from Wilberforce University in Ohio.

Ellington emerged as a composer of concert music on January 23, 1943, when he made the first of eight annual appearances in Carnegie Hall, N.Y. For his Carnegie Hall debut he featured a one-hour orchestral suite, *Black, Brown, and Beige* (1943), intended as a symphonic parallel to the history of the American Negro. The first section, "Black," portrayed the black man at labor and in prayer. "Brown" paid tribute to the black heroes of the Revolutionary War. "Beige" described the Negro in Harlem with his songs and dance.

Ellington's Carnegie Hall concerts continued to produce new symphonic works. *New World a-Comin'* (1943)—title taken from Roi Ottley's book—in which the music anticipated a black revolution after the end of World War II, was first heard in December 1943. *The Deep South Suite* (1946), a nostalgic and sentimental portrait of the southland, was first given on December 26, 1947. *Liberian Suite* (1947), written on commission from the Liberian government to commemorate its centenary as a republic, was introduced in 1947. *The Tattooed Bride* (1948) was premiered on November 13, 1948. *Night Creature* (1955) was commissioned by the Symphony of the Air, which, in collaboration with Ellington's band, premiered it in 1955.

Premieres of Ellington's symphonic works were heard elsewhere as well: *Harlem* (1951) at the Metropolitan Opera House in January 1952; *Festival Suite* (1956) and *Toga Brava* (1973) at the Newport Jazz Festival in 1956 and July 1973 respectively; *Suite Thursday* (1960), based on John Steinbeck's story, and *Afro-Eurasian Eclipse* (1970) at the Monterey Jazz Festival on September 23, 1960, and in 1970 respectively. For the hundredth anniversary of the Emancipation Proclamation, Ellington wrote *My People* (1963), initially performed on August 16, 1963, at the Century of Negro Progress Exposition in Chicago. An Ellington concert at the Lincoln Center for the Performing Arts in New York in 1964 featured the premieres of *Golden Broom* and *Green Apple*. Once again at the Lincoln Center he presented the first performance of the *Goutelas Suite* on April 6, 1971.

Between 1962 and 1965, Ellington made five consecutive tours of Europe, that of 1963 to the Near and Middle East being sponsored by the U.S. State Department. In 1966 he performed at the first World Festival of Negro Arts at Senegal, Dakar, under the banner of UNESCO. In September 1971 he made a spectacular one-month tour of the Soviet Union. In the 1950s and 1960s he contributed the scores to several motion pictures, most significantly *Anatomy of a Murder* (1959), *Paris Blues* (1961), and *Assault on a Queen* (1966). He wrote the score for the ballet *The River* (1970), which was produced by the American Ballet Theater with choreography by Alvin Ailey in New York on June 29, 1971. On August 13, 1976, the Alvin Ailey American Dance Theater in New York introduced the ballet *The Black Kings*, in which various Ellington compositions were used as background music. The score of the successful Broadway musical *Sophisticated Ladies* (March 1, 1981) was derived entirely from the repertory of Ellington's popular songs.

Ellington opened new horizons for himself and for jazz at the Grace Cathedral in San Francisco on September 16, 1965, with a concert of his sacred music. This was the first of many such religious services he would give in the United States and Europe—in Europe at St. Sulpice in Paris, Santa Maria del Mar in Barcelona, and Westminster Abbey in London. "These musicians [offered] what they did best—better than any others in the world—to the glory of God," is the way a writer for *Saturday Review* commented on these performances.

Ellington received honors and awards commensurate with his legendary status in American music. He was awarded fifteen honorary doctorates between 1964 and 1973, including doctorates in music from Yale (1967), Washington University in St. Louis (1967), Brown University (1969) and Columbia University (1973). In 1965 he received gold medals from the mayor of the city of New York, the city of Chicago, and the city of Paris. In 1966 in Madrid, Spain, he was presented with the President's Gold Medal in the name of President Lyndon B. Johnson, and in 1969 President Nixon honored him with America's highest civilian award, the Presidential Medal of Freedom. In 1973, President Pompidou of France decorated him with the Legion of Honor. Ellington was elected member of the National Institute of Arts and Letters in 1970, fellow of the American Academy of Arts and Letters in 1971, and member of the Royal Swedish Academy of Music in 1971, the first popular American composer ever to be given this honor in Sweden. In 1972 he received the Highest Award for Distinguished Service from the National Association of Negro Musicians. In 1972, Yale University established the Duke Ellington Fellowship

Program to encourage the study of Afro-American music and perpetuate the tradition of jazz, blues, and gospel. Two African countries, Chad and Togo, issued postage stamps with his picture in 1967. On his seventy-fifth birthday, tributes were beamed around the world in thirty-six languages over radio and television by the United States Information Agency. In Carnegie Hall, thirty-five jazz groups and various distinguished jazz soloists performed his music at a gala birthday concert. On February 11, 1972, CBS-TV honored Ellington with a program covering his productivity over a period of half a century.

There was also a major setback. In 1965 the Pulitzer Prize Committee voted a special citation for the "vitality and originality of his total productivity," but this citation was denied him through a veto of some higher (unidentified) authority.

THE COMPOSER SPEAKS: Music to me is a sound sensation, assimilation, anticipation, adulation, and reputation. It takes me to new places and experiences. It brings me invitations to the most interesting occasions in North and South America, in Europe, Africa, Asia and Australia. I get to smell things in India I couldn't smell anywhere else. I hear distant drums in Africa. I get a compelling urge from the *cuica* in Brazil. I see a flying saucer in Phoenix; a moonbow in Reno; snow and fog together in Toronto; snow and lightning accompanied by thunder in Chicago; four rainbows at once in Stockholm.

Music is thus a key to great rewards in terms of experience. But when someone has to be told that he should study or specialize in music for the purpose of making a career, then I think more harm than good is done. Anyone who loves to make music knows that study is necessary. There are periods when music is a lucrative pursuit, but if money is the only reason for participating in it, then money can be more of a distraction than anything else. And I think this is true of every art form. Music—love it or leave it!

PRINCIPAL WORKS: (all for orchestra except the ballet *The River*): *Creole Rhapsody* (1931); *Reminiscing in Tempo* (1935); *Black, Brown, and Beige* (1943); *New World a-Comin'* (1943); *The Deep South Suite* (1946); *Liberian Suite* (1947); *The Tattooed Bride* (1948); *Harlem* (1950); *Night Creature* (1955); *Festival Suite* (1956); *Such Sweet Thunder* (1957); *Suite Thursday* (1960); *My People* (1963); *Golden Broom* (1964); *Green Apple* (1964); *Far-East Suite* (1964); *Timon of Athens Suite* (1964); *Virgin Island Suite* (1965); *Latin American Suite* (1965); *The River*, ballet (1970); *Afro-Eurasian Eclipse* (1970); *New Orleans Suite* (1970); *Goutelas Suite* (1971); *Toga Brava* (1973).

BIBLIOGRAPHY: Ulanov, Barry, *Duke Ellington* (N.Y., 1946); Dance, Stanley, *The World of Duke Ellington* (N.Y., 1970); Ellington, Edward Kennedy, *Music Is My Mistress* (N.Y., 1973); Grammond, Peter (editor), *Duke Ellington: His Life and Music* (London, 1958); Jewell, Derek, *Duke: A Portrait of Duke Ellington* (N.Y., 1977); Lambert, G.E., *Duke Ellington* (London, 1959).

Elwell, Herbert, b. Minneapolis, Minn., May 10, 1898; d. Cleveland, Ohio, April 17, 1974.

During a long and productive career in music, Elwell divided his energies equally among writing music criticism, teaching, and composing. His music, in a neoromantic style, was influenced by the French school, depending for its effect on an economical use of orchestral and harmonic resources and on a sensitively projected lyricism.

He attended the public schools in Minneapolis before entering the University of Minnesota in Minneapolis in 1916, where he studied piano with Carlyle Scott and theory with Donald N. Ferguson. In 1919 he came to New York, spending the next two years studying composition privately with Ernest Bloch. When the American Conservatory was established in Fontainebleau, France, he was among the first students to attend, an experience that brought him into contact with Nadia Boulanger, with whom he studied composition for the next three years. In 1923 he competed successfully for a three-year fellowship in music at the American Academy in Rome. Since this fellowship combined residence in Rome with travel, he was given the opportunity to visit such centers of music as Vienna, Berlin, and Rome and, in Italy, to come into personal contact with such eminent composers as Respighi, Casella, and Malipiero.

The first works of his maturity were written in Europe. The Piano Quintet (1923) was performed at a concert of the Société Nationale in Paris in 1925, a year later in Rome, and was published in England. In 1925, he completed the score for a ballet, *The Happy Hypocrite*, based on Max Beerbohm's story. A symphonic suite derived from this music was introduced in Rome in a performance by the Augusteo Orchestra in Rome, the composer conducting, on May 21, 1927; subsequently it won the Eastman School of Music Publication Award. The ballet itself was produced and danced by Charles Weidman at the Dance Repertory Theater in New York in 1931, when it proved so successful that Weidman retained it in his repertoire for several years.

Elwell married Maria Cecchini in Europe on July 27, 1927. Upon his return to the United States, he was appointed, in 1928, head of the composition and advanced theory department of the Cleveland Institute of Music and conductor of its orchestra, posts he retained for the next seventeen years. From 1930 to 1936 he was the program annotator of the Cleveland Orchestra and from 1932 to 1965 the music critic of the *Cleveland Plain Dealer*. Beginning with 1940, and continuing for many years, he taught composition at the summer sessions of the Eastman School of

Music and from 1945 on at the summer sessions of Oberlin Conservatory in Ohio.

As a composer, Elwell was a conservative who was less concerned with originality than with possessing the sharp and practical tools with which to work out his musical ideas, and who, as he said, "followed the new trends with interest but not with active participation." His principal works included Introduction and Allegro (1942), introduced by the New York Philharmonic under Efrem Kurtz on July 12, 1942, and recipient of the Juilliard Publication Award; first heard on November 30, 1942, in Cleveland; *Blue Symphony*, for voice and string quartet (1944), introduced on February 2, 1945, in Cleveland; *Lincoln: Requiem Aeternam*, for baritone, chorus, and orchestra (1946), a setting of a poem by John Gould Fletcher, winner of the Paderewski Prize of $1,000, and given its initial hearing on February 16, 1947, in Oberlin and broadcast internationally over the radio facilities of the National Broadcasting Company; Pastorale, for voice and orchestra (1947), written at the request of George Szell, who conducted its premiere with the Cleveland Orchestra on March 25, 1948; *Ode for Orchestra* (1950) premiered in Houston, Tex., by the Houston Symphony Orchestra conducted by Leopold Stokowski; and *The Forever Young*, for voice and orchestra (1953), first performance by the Cleveland Orchestra under Szell on October 29, 1953.

Elwell was awarded honorary doctorates in music by Western Reserve University (1947), the University of Rochester (1950) and Cleveland State University (1970). In 1947 he received the Ohioan Library Association Award; in 1961 the Cleveland Arts Prize; and in 1969 an award from the National Institute of Arts and Letters. He was chairman of the Yaddo Festival in Saratoga Springs, N.Y., in 1952 and for a number of years a member of the Yaddo Corporation.

A Herbert Elwell Archive comprising his scores, articles, program annotations, and various memorabilia was established at Cleveland State University in 1981. Upon the opening of the archive, a concert of Elwell's compositions was given.

THE COMPOSER SPEAKS: For me, the best foundation is in vocal music, where melodic character is paramount, and where music draws it rhythms from the rich diversity of natural speech inflections. The kind of harmony which best promotes the rhythmic character of the phrase is, for me, the right harmony, irrespective of its quality as dissonance or consonance, or its value in contemporary currency. Dissonance, so often associated with "modernism," largely a matter of atmospheric color and therefore of secondary importance. It has always been a relative matter, anyway, and so long as it continues to give harmony to suggestion of unrest moving to repose, it carries out the special and directional feeling which for centuries has been one of the chief and indispens-

able characteristics of the music of western culture. Dissonance can be employed only up to a certain point, however, without bringing into operation the law of diminishing returns as far as motion and space are concerned. Its unrestrained use can easily result in that nonprogressive, or static type of harmony so unnecessarily bewildering to the nonmusician, a type of harmony, incidentally, which forced impressionism up the blind alley from which it has never escaped.

PRINCIPAL WORKS: 2 string quartets (1940, 1944).

Piano Quintet (1923); *The Happy Hypocrite*, ballet (1925); Piano Sonata (1928); Divertimento, for string quartet (1929); *Orchestral Sketches* (1937); *I Was with Him* cantata, for tenor, male chorus, and two pianos (1937); Violin Sonata (1938); Introduction and Allegro, for orchestra (1942); Four Songs, for male voices (1943); *Blue Symphony*, for voice and string quartet (1944); *Lincoln: Requiem Aeternam*, for baritone, chorus, and orchestra (1946); Pastorale, for voice and orchestra (1947); *Ode for Orchestra* (1950); *The Forever Young*, for voice and orchestra (1953); Concert Suite, for violin and orchestra (1957); Pieces, for piano (1962); Three Preludes, for piano (1962); *Cortège*, for piano (1966); Symphony, for small orchestra (1966); *Phoenix Afire*, for voice and piano (1969); *Giorno dei morti*, for voice and piano (1974); Tarantella, for voice and piano (1974); *In a Boat*, for voice and piano (1974).

BIBLIOGRAPHY: Ewen, David, *American Composers Today* (N.Y., 1949); *Bulletin of the National Association of Teachers*, December 30, 1971; *Who's Who in America, 1973–74*.

Epstein, David Mayer, b. New York City, October 3, 1930.

His music is nontonal, reflecting two major concerns: intensity of expression combined with concision in the statement and development of musical ideas.

Both parents were musical. His mother played the piano and she and his father sang in choruses. By growing up in a home where music was loved, practiced, and listened to over radio, phonograph, and at concerts, Epstein came to know good music early and naturally. He was about four when he began improvising at the piano. Piano study started three years later with Augusta Yellin, who, at the same time, gave him some instruction in notation and harmony. In his eighth year Epstein began to compose little pieces for the piano. From his tenth year on, he enjoyed playing jazz. At Woodmere (Long Island) High School, which he attended from 1944 to 1948, he played the clarinet, some alto sax as well as the piano in several small jazz bands, occasionally also making some of their arrangements. His piano study continued with Victor Huttenlocher, a musician who, as Epstein recalls, "guided my interest in jazz toward greater fluency in improvisation while also improving my technique, and subtly revealing the connections between 'classical' composition and jazz." The urge to be a composer of "serious music" and to study it intensively hit him when he was about sixteen, with Huttenlocher providing the necessary stimulus and knowledge. In his senior year, Epstein wrote the music for his high school show.

Upon graduating from high school in 1948, Epstein entered Antioch College in Yellow Springs, Ohio, where he received his bachelor of arts degree in 1952. Piano study during his college years took place with Walter Anderson (1948–51). At the New England Conservatory (1952–53), where he acquired his master of music degree in 1953, the study of composition took place with Francis Judd Cooke and Carl McKinley, and piano with Felix Wolfes and David Barnett. While at the conservatory, Epstein wrote his String Quartet no. 1 (1952), one of hs earliest works to receive wide circulation. Introduced at the Symposium of International Federation of Music Students at the Juilliard School of Music in New York in 1952, it entered the permanent repertoire of the Parrenin Quartet in 1959, which performed it during the next few years in the United States, Europe, Australia, and Asia.

On June 21, 1958, Epstein married Anne Louise Merrick, a writer; they raised two daughters. The first year of his marriage (1953–54) Epstein spent at Brandeis University in Waltham, Mass., on a scholarship and teaching fellowship. There he attended the composition and theory classes of Irving Fine, Harold Shapero, and Arthur Berger. At Brandeis, in 1954, two of Epstein's works were heard: the solo cantata *The Song of Isaiah* (1953), which had been introduced in March 1953 at the Eastman School of Music, in Rochester, N.Y., and the song cycle *Excerpts from a Diary* (1953), whose text was poems from Walter Benton's *This Is My Beloved*. The song cycle won the Friends of Harvey Gaul Composition Award in 1962 and was premiered by Rand Smith in November 1954 in Boston. Movement for Orchestra (1953), which received the award of the Louisville Orchestra, was premiered in Lousiville, Ky., in September 1954 with Sidney Harth conducting.

During the summers of 1955 and 1956, on scholarships, Epstein was Darius Milhaud's pupil in composition at Aspen. There his Symphony no. 1 (1955), winner of the Fromm Music Foundation Award, and the Piano Trio (1955), recipient of an award from Broadcast Music, Inc. (BMI), were introduced in 1955, the trio in July and the symphony in August. From 1954 to 1956, on fellowships, Epstein studied composition and theory with Roger Sessions and Milton Babbitt at Princeton University. The emphasis on linear and formal clarity reflects the influence of Sessions in *The Seasons*, a cycle of songs to poems by Emily Dickinson (1955), which

received its first hearing in Princeton in May 1956.

In 1956–57, Epstein was assistant editor and music critic of *Musical America*. In 1957 he was appointed assistant professor of music at Antioch College, in Yellow Springs, Ohio, where he remained for the next five years, elevated to associate professorship in his last year. During the summers of 1956 and 1959 he studied conducting with Izler Solomon in Aspen, Colo., and in September 1959 he attended the conductors symposium of the Cincinnati Symphony under Max Rudolph.

On a fellowship with the Cleveland Orchestra in 1960–61 he continued to study conducting with George Szell. From 1962 to 1964, Epstein was musical director of the TV station Channel 13/WNET in New York. During 1964–65 he spent a year as a free-lance composer and conductor in New York. During that time he was musical consultant to the United Nations, Office of Film and Television, and to Channel 13, in New York. In 1965 he was appointed associate professor of music at Massachusetts Institute of Technology in Boston, where he has since remained, becoming full professor in 1971. In 1966 and 1967 he received the M.I.T. Humanities Research Grant and in 1968 the Whitings Foundation Research Grant. In 1968, he earned his doctorate in music at Princeton.

In his compositions since 1961, Epstein has shown increasing interest in serialism. His writing revealed a tendency to work with small motives which he allowed to undergo expansions and transformations—the small giving birth to the large, as it were. As these structures grew, so did their expressive qualities and ramifications.

Fantasy Variations, for solo violin (1963), which Sylvia Rosenberg introduced over BBC in London in 1963, is a set of eight contrasting variations on a serial theme. The String Trio (1964), which was commissioned by the Pacific String Trio, who premiered it in New York in November 1964 and which was the recipient of the Arthur Shepherd Award in 1967, is a large-scale serially connected work which uses for its germinal theme an interval (a third) and its inversion, from whose simple material the entire composition was derived. *Sonority-Variations,* for orchestra (1967), dedicated to Milton Babbitt, applied the variation technique to pitch and sonority; the work was premiered by the Baltimore Symphony, the composer conducting, in May 1867. *Vent-ures, Three Pieces for Symphonic Wind Ensemble* (1970) is an excursion into each of three particular worlds of music—tempo, timbre, and sonority—with a Webernlike pointillistic technique. It was written for the Eastman Wind Ensemble, which, under Donald Hunsberger, gave the first performance in Rochester, N.Y., in November 1970. In the String Quartet no. 2 (1971), written on a grant from the Rockefeller Foundation for the Philadelphia String Quartet and given its first hearing in Seattle, Wash., by that group in April 1972, each of the strings acquires its own musical character through its identification with particular intervallic patterns in its theme, through unique timbres, and through the particular use of dynamics and methods of attack. *Night Voices*, for narrator, children's choir, and orchestra (1974), a setting of poems by Anne Epstein, was commissioned by the Boston Symphony for its youth concerts, where it was introduced on November 9, 1974, with the composer conducting. This is a somewhat programmatic, somewhat symbolic composition about an owl, a mouse, a cricket, and a stone. "Their interrelation," wrote Louis Snyder in his review in the *Christian Science Monitor*, "is explored with instrumental and verbal skill and marked by simple strength of means—the words are vivid and the music pungently descriptive, but not too obviously so. The 'weaving' flight of the owl, the mouse's 'twitch of my whiskers,' and the 'high grace of the cricket's leap' provide the needed spring for Mr. Epstein's inventive compositional bent, as does the stone's inertness, 'open to sun and moon.' "

On a commission from the Concord Chorale, Epstein wrote one of his most important compositions: *The Concord Psalter*, for chorus, contralto solo, clarinet, brass clarinet, bass trombone, cello, piano, and a dozen percussion instruments (1979), utilizing as texts Psalms 130, 88, 147, and 148. The first performance took place in Concord, N.H., on December 15, 1979. In *High Fidelity/Musical America*, Stephanie Henkel said it was "a work so free of excess baggage and redundancies, and so profound in its spiritual statement, as to rescue both soul and ear from the high-caloric, tinselled world outside. . . . The three sections are knit together by a pedal point that occurs throughout, bringing to mind the endless Torah scroll with its cyclical accounts of sorrow, exile and redemption. The concision and compression of its musical statement are reminiscent of Webern. . . . The tension, energy, and unremitting forward momentum are pure Epstein. *The Concord Psalter* will shine right through and burn away the fustian of any season."

Through the years, Epstein has made numerous appearances as conductor. Since 1965 he has been the conductor of the M.I.T. Symphony. In 1976 he was appointed music director of the Worcester Orchestra and Worcester Festival in Massachusetts and from 1974 to 1978 he was music director of the Harrisburg Symphony in Pennsylvania. He has made frequent appearances as guest conductor both in the United States and abroad (London, Vienna, Munich, Berlin, Lisbon, Czechoslovakia, Israel).

From 1968 to 1970 Epstein was the director of the Acoustic Research Contemporary Music Project, which devoted itself to recording significant works by American composers on the Deutsche Grammophon/AR label. For other labels, Epstein has conducted the music of many leading 20th-century composers including Hindemith, Walton, Bloch, Copland, Barber, and Perle.

Epstein is the author of *Beyond Orpheus: Studies in Musical Structure* (1979) as well as numerous articles in professional journals.

THE COMPOSER SPEAKS: In recent years I have been increasingly concerned to simplify ("purify" if you like) my musical style, at the same time seeking to write in a musical manner which reduced problems of performance and rehearsal without restricting the imaginative content or approach of the score. It is a difficult problem, but one which many of us, I think, must face. I am disturbed that serious modern music may otherwise find itself in isolation, so difficult to prepare for performance that our performing colleagues cannot afford the investment of time and effort to play it. This amounts to death, and it must not be allowed to happen.

PRINCIPAL WORKS: 2 string quartets (1952, 1971). *The Song of Isaiah*, solo cantata (1953); *Excerpts from a Diary*, song cycle for voice and piano (1953); *Movement for Orchestra* (1953); Piano Trio (1955); Symphony no. 1 (1955); *The Seasons*, song cycle for voice and piano (1955); Five Scenes for Chorus (1958); Four Songs, cycle for soprano, solo French horn and string orchestra (1960); Piano Variations (1961); *Fantasy Variations*, for solo violin (1963); String Trio (1964); *Fancies*, song cycle for voice and clarinet (1966); *Sonority-Variations*, for orchestra (1967); *Vent-ures, Three Pieces for Symphonic Wind Ensemble* (1970); *Night Voices*, for narrator, children's chorus and orchestra (1974); *The Concord Psalter*, a psalm cycle for chorus, contralto solo, and instruments (1979); Cello Concerto (1979).

BIBLIOGRAPHY: *BBDM; Who's Who in America, 1980–81*.

Erb, Donald, b. Youngstown, Ohio, January 17, 1927.

Erb has been deeply involved and become successful with serial and electronic music and has made effective use of unusual timbres and sonorities, shifting rhythms, and fragmented structures.

When Erb was seven his family settled in Cleveland, where he received his early academic education at elementary, junior high school, and Lakewood High School. His first instruction in music came when he was eight from a maiden aunt who gave him some lessons on the trumpet. Soon after that, Erb also received some instruction on a cornet from a local musician who charged him fifteen cents a lesson.

During World War II, Erb served in the navy (1944–46). He entered Kent State University in Ohio in 1946, specializing in trumpet and studying composition with Harold Miles and Kenneth Gaburo. In 1950 he received his bachelor of science degree. All this while he supported himself by playing the trumpet in and making arrangements for dance bands. Serious composition began in 1949 with music in a neoclassical vein influenced mainly by Hindemith, though certain elements of Bartók's rhythmic techniques were also present. Between 1950 and 1952, Erb, as a student at the Cleveland Institute, came under the influence of Marcel Dick, his teacher in composition, who first interested him in the twelve-tone technique as a compositional tool.

After receiving his master of music degree at the Cleveland Institute in 1952, Erb married Lucille Hyman, on June 10 of that year; the first of their four children was born a year later. With funds acquired by pawning their wedding silverware, Erb and his wife went to Paris in 1952 for a period of composition study with Nadia Boulanger which he found unsatisfactory because she was "too regimented." Returning to Cleveland he continued to study composition with Marcel Dick and to become a member of the faculty of the Cleveland Institute in 1953, where he remained for the next eight years. Graduate study was resumed in 1961 at Indiana University in Bloomington with Bernard Heiden, resulting in a doctorate in music in 1964. While working for that doctorate he served for one year as composer-in-residence for the public school system in Bakersfield, Calif., on a Ford Foundation Fellowship (1962–63).

Discarding every composition he had written up to this point, Erb made a fresh start in 1958 with *Dialogue*, for violin and piano (1958), introduced in the year of its composition at the Cleveland Institute; *Correlations*, for piano (1959), frequently performed by the noted Cleveland pianist Arthur Loesser; and *Music for Violin and Piano* (1959), premiered by Max Pollikoff in his "Music in Our Time" series. Erb's most important works in the early 1960s were the String Quartet no. 1 (1960) and *Antipodes*, for string quartet and percussion (1963). *Symphony of Overtures* (1964), written as a dissertation for his doctorate, became his first composition to gain him a wide listening public. After it was introduced in Bloomington, Ind., on February 11, 1965, it was heard later the same year at the Contemporary Music Festival in Seattle under a Rockefeller Foundation grant, and at a concert of the Cleveland Orchestra under Louis Lane. In time it was played by most of America's major orchestras. Each movement in this work is an overture to an off-beat 20th-century play: Jean Gênet's *The Blacks* and *The Maids*, Samuel Beckett's *Endgame*, and Eugene Ionesco's *Rhinoceros*. Reviewing the world premiere in Bloomington, James M. Brody wrote in the *Herald-Telephone*: "The unusual sounds which [Erb] has composed go far beyond mere effect, and the breathless unfolding of ideas covering a great range of expression elicits a profound response on the part of the listener. The remarkable work was so overwhelming that one wished it could have been played a second time."

In 1964–65 Erb was assistant professor of composition at Bowling Green State University in Bowling Green, Ohio. During the summer of 1966 he was composer-in-residence at Roosevelt University in Chicago. Since 1966 he has been on the faculty of the Cleveland Institute of Music as composer-in-residence and, since 1973, as head of the theory and composition departments.

In 1965, Erb was awarded a Guggenheim Fellowship which enabled him to serve as visiting professor for research in electronic music at Case Institute of Technology in Cleveland (now Case Western Reserve University) for two years. Electronic music now became a dominant influence in his creative work. His first electronic composition was *Reticulation* (1965), for symphonic band and tape, followed in rapid succession by *Stargazing* (1966), for symphonic band and tape; *Kyrie* (1967), for chorus, piano, percussion, and tape; and *Reconnaissance*, for violin, string bass, piano, percussion, and two electronic setups (1967). *Kyrie*, introduced in Birmingham, Mich., in fall 1967, featured a collage of sounds on tape taken from the news-of-the-day, from various sounds (such as screams and police whistles), and a quotation from "Deutschland über Alles." For its performance, costuming, slides, and stage movement were required. In *Reconnaissance*, the electronic sounds are produced live on the stage by two Moog synthesizers of different sizes. First heard in New York in 1967, it was soon after that featured at Expo '67 in Montreal and in Los Angeles. Music on tape was supplemented by a soprano saxophone, dancers, and lighting in *Fission* (1968), a multimedia production; by a rock band and a symphony orchestra in *Klangfarbenfunk* (1970), given its world premiere on October 1, 1970, by the Detroit Symphony under Sixten Ehrling; by a wind ensemble in *The Purple Roofed Ethical Suicide Parlor* (1972); by a full orchestra in *Autumnmusic* (1973), which was commissioned by the William Inglis Morse Trust Fund and first performed on November 20, 1973, in Hartford, Conn.; and by forty water-goblet players in *Music for a Festive Occasion* (1975), written to honor the American bicentennial and the seventy-fifth anniversary of the TRW Corporation in Cleveland, which had commissioned it, and premiered by the Cleveland Orchestra under Lorin Maazel on January 11, 1976.

Erb dispensed with electronic music when he was commissioned by the Cleveland Orchestra to write a composition celebrating its fiftieth anniversary. Erb fulfilled this commission with *Christmasmusic* (1967), which was based on the Christmas carol "Come, O Come, Emmanuel." The Cleveland Orchestra under Louis Lane performed it on December 21, 1967, and it was subsequently programmed in Germany by the Leipzig Gewandhaus Orchestra.

Erb's most successful composition, *The Seventh Trumpet*, for orchestra (1969), also dispensed with electronic sounds. It was written on a Rockefeller grant while Erb was composer-in-residence with the Dallas Symphony in 1968–69, and it was given by the Dallas Symphony under Donald Johanos on April 5, 1969. After that it received about two hundred performances by fifty orchestras both in the United States and abroad (Alaska, Helsinki, Luxembourg, Johannesburg, Warsaw, and Mexico), and in 1971 it was given the UNESCO Award. A three-section work in a single movement, it opens with a free cadenza which recurs throughout the composition. The title comes from a section in Revelations, though the composer refused to make any specific comparisons between this text and his music. In the *Cleveland Plain Dealer*, Robert Finn called this work "a piece of tremendous communicative power. . . . It compresses a wealth of imaginative orchestral effects. . . . This is music that grabs one by the throat—powerful, compelling, and eerie."

For sheer structural size, Erb has written nothing more ambitious than *New England's Prospect* (1974), an oratorio for narrator, triple chorus, a children's chorus, and orchestra. The score and its parts require some sixteen thousand pages. This is an eight-section work, each part of which uses a text by some distinguished American talking about America (Thomas Jefferson, Anne Bradford, William Lloyd Garrison, William Carlos Williams, etc.). Under a grant from the Julifs Foundation it was commissioned for the centenary of the Cincinnati May Festival and there it was introduced on May 17, 1974, with James Levine conducting and Julian Bond, the black member of the Georgia House of Representatives, as narrator.

In the *Cincinnati Enquirer,* Gail Stockholm called this work "spellbinding" and in the *Cincinnati Post,* James Wierzbicki opened his review by saying: "Last night patrons of Music Hall heard a piece of music they're not likely to forget for a long time."

Four concertos came after that. The Concerto for Cello and Orchestra (1975) was commissioned by the cellist Lynn Harrell under a grant from the Ford Foundation, and was given its initial performance in Rochester, N.Y., by the Rochester Philharmonic under David Zinman, with Lynn Harrell as soloist, on November 4, 1976. The Trombone Concerto (1976), commissioned by Stuart Dempster under a grant from the Martha Baird Rockefeller Fund for Music, was performed by the St. Louis Symphony under Leonard Slatkin, with Stuart Dempster soloist, on March 11, 1976. Concerto for Keyboards, for piano, electric piano, celesta, and orchestra (1978), was heard in San Francisco in March 1980, performed by the San Francisco Symphony under Edo de Waart with Paul Schenly, soloist. The Concerto for Trumpet and Orchestra was given its premiere on April 29, 1981, by Don Tison (for whom it was written) and the Baltimore Symphony.

Erb was staff composer for the Bennington Composers Conference in Bennington, Vt. (1969–74), visiting professor at Indiana University in Blooming-

ton (1975–76), and Distinguished Professor at California State University in Los Angeles (spring 1977). Between 1973 and 1977 he was on the composer-librettist panel of the National Endowment for the Arts, and from 1977 to 1979 he was its chairman. From 1979 to 1982 he was board member of the American Music Center. He was a fellow at the Bellagio Study and Conference Center in 1979. The state of Ohio presented him with the Ohioana Citation in 1979.

THE COMPOSER SPEAKS: To me, composing is basically an intuitive process. A composer should be able to use what he knows about music in an instinctive manner, flying by the seat of his pants. Neither am I interested in abdicating my responsibility as a composer to factors over which I have little or no control. . . . A craftsman can create entertainment, but you need more than that to create art. You need an emotional, inspirational quality, because craft in and of itself means nothing. There has to be something inside you pushing out or all a man will ever write is a craftsmanlike piece. And that's not quite good enough.

PRINCIPAL WORKS: String Quartet (1960); Chamber Concerto, for Piano and chamber orchestra (1961); *Sonneries*, for brass choir (1961); *Cummings Cycle*, for youth orchestra and chorus (1963); *Hexagon*, for six instruments (1963); *Concertant*, for harpsichord and strings (1963); *Antipodes*, for string quartet and four percussion (1963); *Symphony of Overtures* (1964); *Reticulation*, for symphonic band and tape (1965); Concerto for Solo Percussion and Orchestra (1966); Trio, for violin, cello and electric guitar (1966); *Kyrie*, for chorus, piano percussion and tape (1967); *Christmasmusic*, for orchestra (1967); *Reconnaissance*, for violin, string bass, piano, percussion and two electronic setups (1967); *Fission*, for dancers, lighting, soprano saxophone, and tape (1968); *The Seventh Trumpet*, for orchestra (1969); *Klangfarbenfunk*, for orchestra, rock band, and tape (1970); *. . . And Then, Towards the End*, for trombone and four-track prerecorded trombone (1971); *The Purple Roofed Ethical Suicide Parlor*, for wind ensemble with tape (1972); *Autumnmusic*, for orchestra and tape (1973); *New England's Prospect*, oratorio for narrator, triple chorus, children's chorus, and orchestra (1974); *Music for a Festive Occasion*, for orchestra and tape (1975); Quintet, for violin, cello, flute, clarinet, and piano or electric piano (1976); Trio, for violin, piano, or electric organ, or celesta, or organ, and percussion (1977); *Mirage*, for flute, bassoon, trumpet, trombone, piano or electronic piano or harpsichord or organ, and percussion (1977); Concerto for Keyboards, for piano, electric piano, celesta, and orchestra (1978); Concerto for Trumpet and Orchestra (1980).

BIBLIOGRAPHY: *DCM;* BMI, *The Many Worlds of*

Music, Winter 1976; *Cleveland Plain Dealer,* October 23, 1977; *Who's Who in America, 1980–81.*

Etler, Alvin Derald, b. Battle Creek, Mich., February 19, 1913; d. Northampton, Mass., June 13, 1973.

Many of Etler's later works use serial procedures, sometimes strictly and sometimes loosely, but without abandoning a tonal center. His great successes, however, came with music reaching back to baroque structures and polyphony without becoming neoclassical in the Hindemith definition of that style.

While still in elementary school, Etler learned to play a few instruments and to compose several elementary pieces. In high school, in Urbana, Ill., he continued to learn practically every instrument in the orchestra before he specialized in the oboe, which henceforth became his prime instrument. By the time he graduated from high school in 1930 he had written a number of compositions, one of which (Suite for Wind Quintet) was performed in New York City, and he had made his debut as conductor with the National High School Orchestra in Interlochen, Mich.

He spent a year at the University of Illinois in Urbana (1930–31), where, under the guidance of Austin Harding, he did a considerable amount of arranging for concert bands. In 1931 he went to Cleveland, spending the next five years at the Cleveland Institute of Music studying the oboe with Bert Gassman and Philip Kirchner. At the same time, between 1931 and 1933, he studied composition with Arthur Shepherd at Western Reserve University. The presence of the Walden String Quartet in Cleveland, and its continual performance of new music, provided Etler with a laboratory for his own early creative experiments in chamber music. "Because of the experimental and immature nature of my work at that time," he once recalled, "none of these have survived, but careful consideration for the practical circumstances of each later composition can readily be attributed largely to that invaluable experience." During these formative years (when he worked as a freelance oboist in Cleveland) he wrote a String Trio (1935), a suite for oboe and three strings entitled *Six from Ohio* (1936), and Music for Chamber Orchestra (1938), the last of these introduced at the Yaddo Festival in Saratoga, N.Y., on September 10, 1938. All three were widely performed throughout the United States and on all radio networks.

In 1938 Etler left Cleveland for Indianapolis. For two years he played the oboe with the Indianapolis Symphony. In 1940, he received a Guggenheim Fellowship which made it possible for him to write Symphonietta (1940–41), performed in 1941 by the Pittsburgh Symphony conducted by Fritz Reiner. In 1941, Etler toured Latin America as oboist and composer with the North American Wind Quintet.

Between 1942 and 1946, Etler was band director and woodwind instructor at Yale University, where he studied composition with Paul Hindemith and received his bachelor of music degree in 1944. In 1946–47 he was assistant professor of music at Cornell University in Ithaca, N.Y., and between 1947 and 1949 he was associate professor of music at the University of Illinois in Urbana. In 1948 he inaugurated and planned a festival of contemporary music there. His Concerto for String Quartet and Orchestra (1948) reverted to the baroque structure of the concerto grosso and to baroque polyphonic methods. It was performed in Urbana by the Walden String Quartet in 1949. From 1949 until his death, Etler was professor of composition at Smith College in Northampton, Mass.; in 1968 he was named Henry Dike Sleeper Professor of Music at Smith, and, in 1972, Andrew Mellon Professor of Humanities. He was visiting professor at Mt. Holyoke College in South Hadley, Mass. (1952–53, 1959–60), and Yale University (1965–66), and artist-in-residence at the University of Wisconsin in Madison (summer 1960). He received a second Guggenheim Fellowship in 1963, and from 1968 until his death was chairman of the Hampshire College Electronic Workshop in Amherst, Mass.

In 1947, on a commission from Allen P. Stern, president of Colonial Iron Works in Cleveland, Etler once again returned to the baroque structure and style by writing Passacaglia and Fugue, for orchestra, which soon after its completion was introduced by the Pittsburgh Symphony under Fritz Reiner. Thirty-four variations on a seven-measure theme in the bass culminating in a giant fugue are here worked out with mathematical precision and polyphonic skill without sacrificing expressive content.

Though a good deal of Etler's later music involved serial processes, his most successful work was still a throwback to the age of the baroque. The Concerto in One Movement (1957), commissioned by the Cleveland Orchestra, which premiered it on October 12, 1957, with George Szell conducting, involved a good deal of fugal writing. In the Concerto for Wind Quintet and Orchestra (1960), the solo quintet simulates the concertino of the concerto grosso, though it receives greater solo prominence than in the baroque era to the point of becoming the center of interest in the second movement. A good deal of dissonant harmony brings the concerto grosso into the 20th century. This concerto received its world premiere in Tokyo by the Japan Philharmonic under Akeo Watanabe and the New York Woodwind Quintet on October 18, 1962. Later the same month Leonard Bernstein conducted it with the New York Philharmonic (a concert heard throughout the United States in a radio broadcast), and Erich Leinsdorf presented a revised version with the Boston Symphony on November 23, 1962. In the *New York Times,* Harold C. Schonberg described it as "lively, busy and . . . a good example of modern Kapellmeistermusik."

Etler received the Young Composers Award of the American Federation of Music Clubs in 1954 and

1955, and the Mary Duke Biddle Scholarship Award in 1966. In 1963 he was the first recipient of the Yale Distinguished Alumnus Award. Etler married twice, first to Margo Turner, with whom he had two children, and on May 28, 1967, to Jean Cochran, with whom he had a daughter.

THE COMPOSER SPEAKS: A composer creates music because it is a function of the whole person similar to other spiritual and physical functions. If he is compelled to perform this function with sufficient intensity, and is likewise endowed with certain requisite sensibilities and intellectual vigor, then his work is apt in turn to perform its own function relative to society and to the development of the art he practices. My own work is predicated first on the proposition that much of the highly inventive and imaginative technical innovation which has taken place in the past fifty years is ripe for the gradual integration into the long stream of tradition which has come to us and is continually being renewed, revitalized, and carried forward. In the process, continuity and strength, together with communicability, become paramount.

PRINCIPAL WORKS: 2 woodwind quintets (1955, 1957); 2 clarinet sonatas (1952, 1969); 2 string quartets (1963, 1965).

Music for Chamber Orchestra (1938); Symphonietta (1940–41); Passacaglia and Fugue, for orchestra (1947); Concerto for String Quartet and Orchestra (1948); Symphony (1951); Piano Sonatina (1955); *Dramatic Overture*, for orchestra (1956); Concerto in One Movement, for orchestra (1957); Concerto for Violin and Wind Quintet (1958); Sextet, for winds and strings (1959); *Elegy*, for small orchestra (1959); Sonata for Viola and Harpsichord (1959); *Ode to Pothos*, for mixed chorus (1960); Concerto for Wind Quintet and Orchestra (1960); *Triptych*, for orchestra (1961); Brass Quintet (1963); *Onomatopoësis*, for male chorus, winds, brass, and percussion (1965); Concerto for Brass Quintet, String Orchestra, and Percussion (1967); Concerto for String Quartet and Orchestra (1968); Concerto for Cello and Chamber Orchestra (1970).

BIBLIOGRAPHY: *DCM*; *New York Philharmonic Program Notes*, October 27, 1962; *Who's Who in America, 1972–73*.

F

Farberman, Harold, b. New York City, November 2, 1929.

Refusing to be compartmentalized as a composer, Farberman has investigated all the "isms" of contemporary music and drawn from them whatever he has found valid for his own creative purposes. He avoids purely tonal writing because, as he says, "with the expansion of working materials available to composers, it does not make sense in this day and age to close the door on the immense possibilities available outside the tonal system." But he also rejects those composers who rely on shock, fad or sensation to maintain their status as avant-gardists.

Since his father, brother, and cousins were drummers, there were always percussion instruments in the Farberman household. As far back as Harold can recall he was always playing with drumsticks. When he was about thirteen he began percussion lessons with his cousin, Irving Farberman, and continued to study privately with him for four years. At Seward Park High School in New York (1943–47) Harold Farberman played all the percussion instruments in both the band and orchestra. On a scholarship, Farberman attended the Juilliard School of Music (1947–51), where he studied theory and harmony with Peter Mennin, Robert Ward, and Henry Brant, percussion with Sol Goodman, timpanist of the New York Philharmonic, and received his degree of bachelor of science in 1951. In all this time he never received any formal instruction in composition.

Farberman served as percussionist and first timpanist for the Boston Symphony Orchestra between 1951 and 1963. When he joined that orchestra he was its youngest member. He wrote his first composition in 1954 in eleven days: *Evolution,* scoring it for an "orchestra" of seven percussion instruments, soprano and French horn. "It was my rebellion against the dull amusical percussion writing I had to contend with as a percussion player in the Boston Symphony," he explains. Encouragement came from a small company in Boston, which recorded *Evolution,* and from Aaron Copland, who, on the strength of this composition, advised Farberman to continue writing and to study composition. Farberman entered the New England Conservatory in Boston in 1954, studying composition there for the next three years with Jud Cooke, and receiving his master's degree in composition in 1957. Summers were spent at the Berkshire Music Center in Tanglewood, Mass., where he was able to study with Copland for one

summer and become involved with Lukas Foss and Milton Babbitt, Luciano Berio and others. He also received some valuable criticism and guidance from Walter Piston.

Evolution was the first of a series of compositions for percussion. These included Variations for Percussion with Piano (1954), commissioned by the New York Percussion Trio and performed in 1959 by the Houston Symphony under Leopold Stokowski; *Variations on a Familiar Theme,* for percussion (1955); Symphony for Strings and Seven Percussion Players (1956–57); *Greek Scene,* for mezzo-soprano, piano, and percussion (1957), which represented the United States in the International Composition Competition in Paris in 1959 (later scored for full orchestra and mezzo-soprano); *Music Inn Suite,* for seven percussion (1958); Concerto for Timpani and Orchestra (1958; Boston, November 11, 1958); and *Progressions,* for solo flute and percussion (1961; N. Y., January 1961). His writing for percussion was an outgrowth of a lifelong concern for and interest in the nonmusical use of percussion instruments and was rich in novel sonorific effects and timbres.

After that, Farberman went through a twelve-tone phase, as in his one-act chamber opera *Medea* (1960–61; Boston, March 26, 1961) and in *Elegy, Fanfare, and March,* for chamber orchestra (1963; N. Y., March 15, 1965), which was developed from a single twelve-tone row. At times, Farberman has used jazz instrumentation, coloration, and effects, as in *For Eric and Nick,* for jazz octet (1964), and *If Music Be,* for symphony orchestra, rock group, jazz singer, and films (1968), written on a grant from the National Endowment for the Arts, cocommissioned by the Denver Symphony and the Colorado Springs Symphony, and introduced in Denver on April 30, 1969, by the Denver Symphony. As he developed, Farberman came to the conclusion that form, instrumentation, and performing entities dictate compositional content and that music, freed from systems, will find its own compositional logic.

Stimulated by the civil rights bombings in Alabama, Farberman wrote *New York Times—August 30, 1964,* for mezzo-soprano, piano, and one percussion (1964; N. Y., August 26, 1964), its text taken from actual newspaper stories in the *New York Times.* But this song cycle, far from being totally somber, was sardonic and witty, with numerous humorous suggestions and questions.

On an endowment from the Albert Schweitzer

Chair in the Juilliard School of Music, Farberman wrote a full-length opera, *The Losers* (1971), in which Barbara Fried's libretto describes the emotional, irrational life-style of a motorbike club, "The Losers," in California. The unusual scoring included a jazz quartet and two jazz singers on left stage, an electric guitar, piano, a six-man percussion section, some brass and woodwinds and one violin, one viola, and one cello, all instruments electrically amplified as needed. When the opera was introduced by the American Opera Center at the Juilliard School in New York on March 26, 1971, with the composer conducting, Irving Kolodin wrote in the *Saturday Review*: "*The Losers* operates best, functions finest, and penetrates most profoundly in those episodes when verbal communication is suspended, when attitudes, emotions, and involvements are conveyed by sound and movement."

The Violin Concerto (1974), subtitled *Reflected Realities*, was the result of a commission from the Oakland Symphony Orchestra in California, which introduced it on January 15, 1974. This work was intended by its composer as a "portrait of a violinist," and it was written for Nathan Rubin, who was concertmaster of the Oakland Symphony and soloist at the premiere. It is in one movement with four sections. The first section, "The Violinist as Virtuoso," finds the violinist in a traditional solo role conquering performance difficulties against an accompanying orchestra, harshly dissonant in style. The second, "The Violinist as Studio Musician," calls for an amplified violin and is pop-modern and Hollywood-sweet in style. The third, "The Violinist as Chamber Musician," casts the violinist as a single entity amongst equals in a chamber variation. The fourth, "Trio," pits the soloist playing live against two prerecorded tapes of differing materials (previously heard) against a soft orchestral accompaniment.

War Cry on a Prayer Feather, a song cycle for mezzo-soprano, baritone, and orchestra (1976)—commissioned by the Colorado Springs Symphony Orchestra Association with grants from the Colorado Council on the Arts and Humanities and the Colorado Bicentennial Commission—is set to a text by Nancy Wood of the Taos Indians that attempts to speak for the Indian spirit which has refused to accept the wastefulness of the white man and has retained faith in the traditional Taos way of life. To open the final song, a percussionist rattles chains on a gong to suggest the concrete jungles constructed by the white man within American society.

Farberman has had a long and successful career as a conductor. He was the conductor of the New Arts Orchestra in Boston from 1957 to 1961, which presented the first all-electronic concert in Boston as well as first performances of many young American composers; the Colorado Springs Symphony from 1967 to 1970; and the Oakland Symphony from 1971 to July 1979. In addition, he has made numerous guest appearances with major orchestras throughout the United States and Europe. As a conductor, he has been a pioneer in recording the music of Charles Ives (the only conductor to have recorded all four Ives symphonies). In 1974, the American Academy of Arts and Letters presented him with the Charles Ives Award.

Farberman has written the music for several film documentaries, one of which—*Great American Cowboy*—received the Oscar from the Motion Picture Academy of Arts and Sciences in 1974 as best documentary. He founded the Conductors Guild in 1975, serving as its first chairman until 1979. He married Corinne Curry, a mezzo-soprano, in Brookline, Mass., on June 22, 1958. They have two children.

THE COMPOSER SPEAKS: The quest for compositional and conductorial truth is a lifetime search. Critical reward is welcome, of course, but ultimately unimportant. Self-fulfillment, respect for the character of one's work is the essential ingredient if one is to continue, and hopefully contribute to the Art of Music Making/Making Music.

PRINCIPAL WORKS: *Evolution*, for percussion, soprano, and French horn (1954); Variations for Percussion with Piano (1954); *Variations on a Familiar Theme*, for percussion (1955); Concerto for Bassoon and Strings (1956); Symphony (1956–57); *Greek Scene*, for mezzo-soprano, piano, and one or two percussion, also for mezzo-soprano and orchestra (1957); *Music Inn Suite*, for percussion (1958); Concerto for Timpani and Orchestra (1958); *Impressions for Oboe*, for oboe, string orchestra, and percussion (1959–60); *Medea*, one-act chamber opera (1960–1961); *Progressions*, for flute and piano (1961); String Quartet (1960–1962); *Quintessence*, for woodwind quintet (1962); Trio, for violin, piano and percussion (1962); *New York Times—August 30, 1964*, for mezzo-soprano, piano, and percussion (1964); *For Eric and Nick*, for jazz octet (1964); *Elegy, Fanfare and March*, for orchestra (1965); Concerto for Alto Sax and String Orchestra (1965); *If Music Be*, for symphony orchestra, rock group, jazz singer, and films (1968); *The Losers*, opera (1971); Violin Concerto (1971); *The Preacher*, for electronic trumpet and percussion (1972); *War Cry on a Prayer Feather*, for mezzo-soprano, baritone, and orchestra (1976); *Alea*, for six percussion (1976).

BIBLIOGRAPHY: Anderson, E. Ruth, *Contemporary American Composers* (Boston, 1976); *Who's Who in America, 1980–81*.

Farwell, Arthur, b. St. Paul, Minn., April 23, 1872; d. New York City, January 20, 1952.

At a time when the American composer was being ignored, Farwell was indefatigable in his efforts to promote American music: as publisher, ethnomusicologist, choral conductor, lecturer, organizer of concerts, and one of the earliest composers to use American Indian folk music as a source of concert works.

Though Farwell received violin lessons when he was nine, it was many years before he decided to make music a career. Upon graduating from Baldwin Seminary in St. Paul in 1889, he attended the Massachusetts Institute of Technology in Boston (1889–93), graduating in 1893 with a degree in electrical engineering. During his undergraduate years at the institute, he attended the concerts of the Boston Symphony conducted by Arthur Nikisch, which made such a deep impression on him that, soon after his graduation, he arrived at the decision to make music and not engineering his profession. Between 1893 and 1896 he studied counterpoint, composition, and orchestration with Homer Norris. At the same time he received valuable guidance from Edward MacDowell and George Chadwick. In 1896, Farwell went to Europe to continue his study of composition with Engelbert Humperdinck and Hans Pfitzer in Berlin and organ with Alexandre Guilmant in Paris.

Farwell returned to the United States in 1899. During the next two years he lectured on music at Cornell University in Ithica, N. Y. When Antonín Dvořák, then in the United States, encouraged American composers to use their own native music for serious composition, Farwell began his researches into American Indian music and folklore, making numerous recordings and transcriptions which became the reservoir from which be began to draw material for his own music. His first composition with an American Indian identity was *Dawn*, a fantasy on Indian themes for piano (1901), which was heard at the St. Louis Exposition in 1904. A quarter of a century later he transcribed it for a small orchestra, a version given its first hearing on February 21, 1926, in Pasadena, Calif.

His failure to have his composition published led him in 1901 to found the Wa-Wan Press in Newton Center, Mass., for the publication of "progressive" American music, without respect to its commercial value, and of compositions on American folk themes generally—the first practical enterprise in America for the advancement of native works. During the next eleven years he published the music of thirty-seven Americans (including ten women), among whom were Henry Gilbert, Edgar Stillman Kelley, and Arthur Shepherd, all three then getting their start as composers. In his book *A Birthday Offering* (1943), Edward N. Waters, head of the music division of the Library of Congress in Washington, D.C., called the Wa-Wan Press "an undertaking that is probably without parallel in our nation's music history, certainly so with regard to idealism and self-sacrifice, with no thought of gain attending its

inception, and no evidence of gain ever manifest throughout its existence." In 1912, Farwell turned over the Wa-Wan Press to G. Schirmer.

In September 1903 Farwell published a manifesto for American composers calling for the liberation of American music from German dominance and the creation of an American musical art drawing to itself elements from "ragtime, Negro songs, Indian songs and cowboy songs." In 1904, 1905, and 1907, Farwell made transcontinental tours giving lecture-recitals on American music. In 1905 he established and became president of the American Music Society, a national organization formed to give monthly concerts of American music; by 1909 the society had twenty centers throughout the United States.

He promoted American music—specifically music with American Indian materials—in his own compositions. After *Dawn*, he wrote *The Domain of Huraken*, for piano (1902), performed in an orchestral adaptation by the Volpe Symphony in New York in 1909; also *Pawnee Horses, Navajo War Dance no. 1* and *The Old Man's Love Song*, all for piano (1905). *Pawnee Horses* passed into oblivion soon after its appearance (even though Charles Martin Loeffler then called it "the best composition yet written by an American"), and was not heard again until 1944 when John Kirkpatrick successfully resurrected it at his concerts.

For many years, Farwell was always identified as a composer of American Indian music, something that brought him considerable distress since he wrote much music that had no American Indian identity whatsoever, music ambitious in its artistic intent, gracious lyricism, and harmonic and contrapuntal language, but which was completely overshadowed by his work with American Indian music.

He was basically a conservative composer, even though early in his career he was occasionally involved with discordant harmonies (as in the 1904 *Pawnee Horses*) so that some of his contemporaries regarded him as a musical revolutionary, and late in his career he produced twenty-three polytonal studies for the piano (1940–52). But most of his music is well grounded in classical structures and is thoroughly romantic in spirit. *Symbolistic Study no. 3*, for two pianos (1905)—the title echoing the symbolist movement in literature—was inspired by the Walt Whitman poem "Once I Pass'd Through a Populous City." The first part of Farwell's piece describes the bustle of the city while the second deals with the memory of the woman the poet met there. In its orchestral version (1908) it was introduced in Philadelphia in 1928, at which time it was condemned by some as too reactionary. Writing in the *Philadelphia Public Ledger*, Samuel Laciar said: "While it contains certain moments of great beauty, it leans too heavily upon certain earlier composers, notably Tchaikovsky and Strauss." Farwell revised this work in 1932, its first hearing given on March 30, 1928, by the Philadelphia Orchestra under Pierre Monteux. One other work in this "symbolistic study" category deserves attention. It is the sixth in the series, written in 1912 for two solo pianos and bearing the subtitle of "Mountain Vision." It is concerned with the composer's reflections on his life during a visit to the White Mountains in New Hampshire. In 1929, it received first prize in the State-National Competition of the National Federation of Music Clubs. Farwell orchestrated it in 1932 as a concerto for two pianos and orchestra. As such it was performed on May 28, 1939, conducted by Howard Barlow, with Karl Ulrich Schnabel and Helen Fogel as soloists, over the coast-to-coast network of the CBS radio system.

Other distinguished works by Farwell without any American folk identity include *The Haiko*, a string quartet (1922); the Violin Sonata (1927); the *Rudolph Gott Symphony* (1932–34), so called because it used thematic material by Farwell's friend Gott; Piano Quintet (1937), inspired by the composer's visits to the Far West in 1904 and 1907 when he noted down some of its thematic material descriptive of the loneliness of the western plains and the majesty and ruggedness of its mountains; and the Piano Sonata (1949), which was not performed publicly until 1974.

Farwell wrote a great deal of impressive music for stage or pageant production. In 1913, on a commission from the Kimball Union Academy in Meriden, N. H., Farwell contributed the music for *Pageant Scene*, produced on June 24, 1913, with the composer conducting. For the tercentennary commemoration of Shakespeare's death in 1916, Farwell provided the music for *Caliban by the Yellow Sands*, a pageant written by Percy Mackaye and produced at the Lewisohn Stadium in New York in May of the same year. On a commission from Stuart Walker for the production of Lord Dunsany's play *The Gods of the Mountain*, Farwell prepared music to preface each of the four acts. The original scoring was for harp, violin, and cello, but in 1929 Farwell orchestrated it as a symphonic suite when the Minneapolis Symphony under Henri Verbrugghen introduced it. In 1921, Farwell's music was heard in the *Pilgrimage Play*, the story of Christ, mounted in Hollywood, Calif.

Farwell's inability to get his major works published led him in April 1936 to establish his own handpress in East Lansing, Mich., where he handled the total process of printing his own music, designing its format and cover, and distributing it. He did nothing about his failure to get his important works recorded. The first time one of his larger compositions was recorded was in 1956, four years after his death, when the Karl Krueger Society for the Preservation of the American Music Heritage released the suite *The Gods of the Mountain*, in a performance by the Royal Philharmonic of London with Krueger con-

ducting. Farwell's second recording came more than two decades later, in 1978, in a Musical Heritage album.

In 1910 Farwell went to New York, involving himself there in various musical activities for the next eight years. He was the supervisor of municipal music from 1910 to 1913, providing music in public parks and on recreation piers. In 1916 he founded and conducted the New York Community Chorus, and from 1915 to 1918 he was director of the Music Settlement School. He went to California in 1918, serving for one year (1918-19) as head of the music department of the University of California in Berkeley. He also organized the Santa Barbara Community Chorus (1919-21). In 1925 he organized and directed the Theater of the Stars, in Big Bear Lake, Calif. This was an open-air theater for music and drama in the Sierra Madres.

Between 1921 and 1925 Farwell was the first holder of Composer Fellowships of the Music and Arts Association of Pasadena. He taught composition, theory, and music history at Michigan State College in East Lansing, Mich., from 1927 to 1939. After 1939 he lived in New York, where he devoted himself to composing and teaching composition privately (one of his pupils was Roy Harris). For many years he worked on a book, *Intuition in the World-Making*, which was never published. He was twice married, the first time to Gertrude Everts Brice on June 5, 1917, with whom he had six children, and the second time to Betty Richardson on September 28, 1939, with whom he had a daughter.

THE COMPOSER SPEAKS: My aim in composition is for truth and beauty—truth in what I honestly feel, and the highest beauty which I can sense and capture. Truth and beauty are qualities divine and sacred. When they are applied to music, music must be held equally divine and sacred. In proportion as music becomes a revelation of the spirit of truth and beauty, its worth is greater to man. Music born of the intellect and emotion is not enough. Its matter should spring from intuition, to be moulded into shape by intellect and emotion. Intuition is awakened by asking of the Spirit within.

PRINCIPAL WORKS: *Dawn*, fantasy on Indian themes, for piano (1901, orchestrated 1926); *The Domain of Huraken*, for piano, also for orchestra (1902); *Symbolistic Study* no. 3, for piano (1905, orchestrated 1908, revised 1922); *Pawnee Horses, Navajo War Dance* no. 1, and *The Old Man's Love Song*, all for piano (1905); *Symbolistic Study* no. 6, for two pianos (1912); orchestrated as a concerto for two pianos and orchestra, 1932); *March! March!*, symphonic hymn (1917); *The Haiko*, string quartet (1922); *Mountain Song*, a symphonic song ceremony for chorus calling for audience participation (1924); Violin Sonata (1927, revised 1955); *The Gods of the*

Mountain, a symphonic suite (1929); *Prelude to a Spiritual Drama*, for orchestra (1932); *Rudolph Gott Symphony* (1932–34); Sonata for Solo Violin (1934); Four Choruses on Indian Themes, for a cappella chorus (1937); Piano Quintet (1937); Twenty-three Polytonal Studies, for piano (1940–52); *The Heroic Breed*, for orchestra (1946); Suite for flute and piano (1946); Piano Sonata (1949); Cello Sonata (1950).

BIBLIOGRAPHY: Davis, Evelyn Johnson, *The Significance of Arthur Farwell as an American Music Educator* (College Park, Md., 1972): Farwell, Brice (ed.), *A Guide to the Music of Arthur Farwell and to the Microfilm Collection of His Work* (Briarcliff Manor, N.Y., 1971); Kirk, Edgar L., "Toward American Music: A Study of the Life and Music of Arthur Farwell" (doctoral thesis, Rochester, N.Y., 1959).

Felciano, Richard, b. Santa Rosa, Calif., December 7, 1930.

Many of Felciano's compositions opened new frontiers. His interest in experimental television made him compose the first audience-participation television work and the first musical composition to use the television system as a compositional element. He is generally credited with the introduction of electronic music into the liturgies of the English-speaking world. He has been concerned with the musical implications of the time-space continuum and has created several works exploring this problem. In works employing theatrical elements he has tried subjecting those elements to the same structural discipline as the music itself, indeed, making them an aspect of music. One of his works creates a marriage of the East and West by combining the Western organ with the Javanese gamelan. "The vitality of his invention," wrote Howard Hersh in his program notes for the San Francisco Symphony, "and the depth of his artistic curiosity are clearly enormous. The major thrust of his contribution, however, lies in the power with which he has fused his innovative techniques to that timeless element of dramatic immediacy and his acutely turned sensitivity for the sheer beauty of sound. There has never been any doubt that behind his music—whatever its external form—there stands a human—a humane—sensibility."

Except for Felciano's paternal great-grandfather, who conducted a village band in the Azores, there was no history of professional music making in the Felciano family. But the love of music was deeply ingrained in Richard Felciano's immediate family circle. All five of his father's brothers played musical instruments as amateurs. Richard's father, a gardener, and his mother, the manager of a cafeteria, held good music in highest esteem and stood ready to provide encouragement and direction when Richard began revealing interest in music. He began piano les-

sons when he was six, continuing them intermittently through his high school years. In 1936, during his first year at St. Rosa School, a Catholic institution in Santa Rosa, he conducted a rhythm band. At Analy High School in Sebastopol, Calif. (1944–48), he participated in choral singing and organized a student choral group. At Santa Rosa Junior College (1948–50), he studied harmony, solfeggio, music history, organ, and voice. It was there that he wrote his first compositions, encouraged by his organ teacher, Gordon Dixon.

Between 1950 and 1952 he attended San Francisco State University, where he received his bachelor of arts degree the latter year. For the next year he continued his studies at Mills College in Oakland, Calif. There his principal teacher in composition was Darius Milhaud. Milhaud was so impressed with Felciano's talent that in 1953 he arranged to get him a grant from the French government to enable the young student to continue his lessons with him in Paris for a year. Felciano's work earned him a Woolley Foundation grant from the Cité Universitaire and the American Embassy, enabling him to spend a second year in Paris.

He received his master of arts degree from Mills College, awarded in absentia because he was in Paris at the time, and two diplomas from the Paris Conservatory in 1955. Two grants in 1958—one from the Italian government and the other a Fulbright travel grant—made it possible for him to stay a year in Florence, Italy, studying composition privately with Luigi Dallapiccola. By this time, Felciano had what Dallapiccola described as "the finest preparation of any American who has studied with me." On July 2, 1959, in Switzerland, Felciano married Rita Baumgartner, a student; they have two sons. In the same year he was appointed professor of music at Lone Mountain College in San Francisco. Except for a one-year leave between 1964 and 1965, he remained there until 1967.

A Copley Foundation grant for another period of study with Milhaud, this time in Aspen, Col., and the Fromm Foundation Prize, both in 1963, brought a measure of recognition to the music Felciano had been writing. The Fromm Foundation Prize came for the first scene of a two-act chamber opera, *Sir Gawain and the Green Knight,* selected by a jury that included Roger Sessions and Ernst Krenek. The full-length opera was completed in 1964 and first performed at Lone Mountain College on April 3, 1964, drawing the attention and interest of Joseph Kerman, author of *Opera as Drama,* among others. In the instrumental music he had been producing up to now, Felciano had interested himself with highly refined sonorities and with timbre as a constructive element. This interest led him, in 1963, to work in electronic music at the San Francisco Tape Center. His first major compositions utilizing electronic means came four years later: *Crasis,* for seven instruments and electronic tape, and *Glossolalia,* for organ, baritone voice, percussion and tape. *Crasis* (San Francisco, June 2, 1967) was a response to what Felciano described as "one of the most powerful acoustical experiences of my life." He was referring to a performance of a Noh drama by a visiting Japanese company. "The subtle gradation of the wailing voices . . . and the abrupt and cataclysmic explosions on the part of the drummers, interrupting and yet preserving a strange sense of stasis—all these made an intense impression on me. The appropriateness of these materials to an electronic context seemed clear, and J set about writing a work which would be not programmatic but rather an attempt to build a structure in sound whose acoustical materials are derived from Noh." *Glossolalia* (Pittsburgh, May 21, 1967) is described as a "ritual," for electronic tape, percussion, baritone voice, and organ. It was commissioned for the dedication of a new organ at the St. John Fisher Church in Pittsburgh. With a text phonically derived from Psalm 150—with the organ, timpani, cymbals, strings, and electronic sounds called upon to glorify God in His sanctuary—*Glossolalia* is one of several Felciano works to pioneer the use of electronic sounds in a liturgical context. These works became the forerunner of a body of similar compositions by other composers in which electronic media collaborated with organ or voice in a liturgical setting. When *Glossolalia* was performed at the University of California in Berkeley on May 9, 1969, with the composer conducting, Alexander Fried said in the *San Francisco Examiner*: "Felciano's piece made imaginative use of an abstract, nonmelodic tone-texture idiom. His percussion, organ and voice let go with an uninhibited but thoughtful array of noise, tweets, thumps, scrapes, whistles, thunders, murmurs and more of the same. . . . But its freedom from sense intentionally stimulated its glossolalia—or 'speaking with tongues'—into a degree of subconscious expression even without sense."

In 1964, Felciano was an early participant in a program initiated by the Ford Foundation to provide schools with composers-in-residence. He was assigned to Cass Technical High School in Detroit, where, in an Esterházylike situation for one year, he produced music for performance by local participants. Three years later, in his search for a common electronic basis for acoustical and visual elements, Felciano began experimenting with television by becoming resident composer of the nascent National Center for Experiments in Television in San Francisco. *Linearity*, for harp and electronics (1968; San Francisco, November 22, 1968), became the first musical work to use the television system as a compositional element, and Trio, for speaker, screen and viewer (1968; San Francisco, November 1, 1968), was the first audience-participation television composition.

Felciano was appointed assistant professor of music at the University of California in Berkeley in 1967. He was promoted to associate professorship in 1969 and since 1974 has been full professor. In 1968 he was awarded a Guggenheim Fellowship, and, a year later, he was a Fromm Foundation fellow at the Berkshire Music Center in Tanglewood. With *Background Music* (1969; Oakland, Calif., October 6, 1969), a theater piece for harp, sympathetic piano, stereo tape, FM tuner, and transistor radio, Felciano involved himself with theatrical elements. He attempted to subject those elements to the same structural discipline as the music itself, indeed, to make those elements an aspect of the music. In *Background Music*, the spatially wandering electronic sounds became protagonists in a developing drama with the harpist.

Between 1971 and 1973, on leave from the University of California, Felciano served as composer-in-residence to the city of Boston. In that capacity he produced compositions for various of the city's organizations including an environmental work for Boston's then brand-new City Hall. He called it *The Municipal Box* and it was introduced at City Hall on May 4, 1972. His music took advantage of the building's deployed spaces. "Placed around the hall on different levels were fourteen speakers," reported Louis Snyder in the *Christian Science Monitor*, "each transmitting its own electronic sound, ceaselessly and without hesitation. Heard from the downstairs entrance or from the balcony above the hall, the aural effect was of an impressionistic tonal collage, cloud-borne in Technicolor." The composer explains: "I use static sounds, each coming from different physical locations so that the moving element is not the sound but the listener who makes his own piece by moving his body through the environment."

During his office as composer-in-residence in Boston, Felciano completed a novel orchestral work, *Galactic Rounds*. "For some time," he says, "I have been fascinated by musical applications of the time-space continuum, for although a sound is defined both by time and space, the latter has rarely been used as a structural element. The idea for *Galactic Rounds* came from the motions of celestial bodies, which are essentially interlocking circles of different sizes moving constantly in and out of phase with one another. The musical vehicle for this circular motion is the classical rounds, expressed in terms of 'information banks'—single notes or groups of different lengths which are reiterated according to a variety of rules given in the score. Individual players or sections have considerable autonomy in that they must maintain the circular motion of their sections in constantly shifting and often contradicting environment. The circular approach to time is also applied to space." An element that is both visual and acoustical is injected by having trumpets and trombones, which are dispersed throughout the orchestra, move the bells of the instruments in 360-degree arcs, creating patterns in Dopple shifts (frequency changes caused by approaching and receding sound sources). "I was intrigued with the challenge of creating a work based on the slow unfolding under a variety of guises, of a single harmony, a work which, like the universe, should be full of motion, yet always the same." *Galactic Rounds* was introduced in Boston on March 25, 1973. When the composer conducted this work at a concert of the San Francisco Symphony on May 10, 1978, Michael Walsh wrote in the *San Francisco Examiner*: "Felciano's single-minded development of his idea is strikingly carried out and when he introduces a theatrical element . . . it does not jar, but emerges as a logical extension of what has gone before. . . . With its consistent musical vocabulary consistently employed, its clear development, its apposite orchestration and, not least, its emotional communication, it is an especially successful piece of music."

The confrontation and coexistence—or symbiosis—of the Eastern world and the West, the stasis of the former and the dynamism of the latter, come to the fore in two subsequent Felciano compositions. *Chöd*, for violin, cello, bass, two percussions, piano, and live electronics (1975), was commissioned by the Philadelphia Composers Forum, which introduced it in Berkeley on April 13, 1975. *In Celebration of Golden Rain*, for Indonesian gamelan and organ, was commissioned by Lawrence Moe, organist of the University of California. The title *Chöd* is that of a Tibetan mystery play and it means "cutting off"—"a reference," the composer explains, "to the absorption of personality in the universal order of all created matter." Felciano goes on to say: "In *Chöd* two kinds of motion are apparent: those which manifest a pervasive, slow, quasi-periodic movement in which the five C's of the opening structure move in a single convergence to the central C at the end; and those which, like much of the music of the Occident, are tied to more intermediate time-structures (rhythm and phrase) and to instrumental analogies of the expressive capacities of the human voice, with all its attendant implications and ego manifestations."

Felciano made no attempt to initiate or parody Javanese music in *In Celebration of Golden Rain*, which was introduced at the University of California in Berkeley to open the twelfth World Congress of the International Musicological Society on August 24, 1977; for the gamelan, he produced his own kind of music. "It comes close to suspending all formula, all compositional technique," Charles Shere said in the *Oakland Tribune*. "Objective, free of human egos, it has a hypnotic quality but it is not 'stoned'; it's abstract, like weather. The piece begins with the opposition of organ and gamelan, the former sprinkling thrusting gestures of notes among the serene bells and gongs of the gamelan; gradually the two

forces are brought into a common world, and by the end of a long repetitive figure the gamelan pulls the organ along, setting the scene for the lengthy rhythmic close."

A commission from the San Francisco Symphony and the National Endowment for the Arts led to the writing of Felciano's most ambitious and significant work for symphony orchestra in 1980. He called it simply *Orchestra*, and its world premiere took place on September 24, 1980, Edo de Waart conducting. In writing *Orchestra*, Felciano was "fascinated with the idea of performance space—space within the orchestra in the sense of instrument location—and acoustical space as expressed in frequency, timbre and dyanmics," as he has written. "Each instrument, because of the limitations of its range, attack, and other performance characteristics, occupies a particular portion of that space. In the opposition of sound and silence, acoustical space also has an important existential aspect, for in silence which follows sound, the awareness of *physical* space in which the sound exists becomes paramount. In the minute pauses between notes and the Grand Pauses of the central section of *Orchestra*, the sound is 'listening to the hall,' the hall is 'defining the sound.' " These concerns led the composer to adopt a concertolike approach to his structure, with most of the orchestral sections represented individually, sometimes with solo material. "I wanted the instruments to come and go in a kind of choreography, where solos, *pas de deux*, *trois*, etc., would alternate with larger at first homogeneous and later heterogeneous ensembles." A mammoth percussion section supplements winds and strings. It includes cymbals, timpani, vibraphone, whip, tenor drums, woodblocks, timbales, ratchet, bongos, tomtoms, marimba, claves, chimes, large gongs, bass drum, xylophone, temple blocks, snare drum, lion's roar, cowbells, glockenspiel, celesta, and piano. What impressed Robert Commanday, in his review in the *San Francisco Chronicle*, was not the freshness of the sonorities and textures but the overall "logic, the connective thread of the continuity. . . . While the sound materials may seem 'advanced' to some, the piece is not 'far-out' because the thought, the design is linear. Memory comes into play as Felciano works with and brings back certain building blocks, centrally, the note E and a couple of its neighboring tones that form a kind of armature. . . . The continuity depends importantly on overlapping. Towards the end of an episode for one instrumental family, other instruments enter, mimic the sonorities, then take over. . . . Space is a big factor in the piece, nowhere more effective than in the kind of space illusion that comes with silences. In the middle of a fanciful episode for percussion, there is a grand or total pause for an eternity of five seconds. The absolute quiet in the hall was eloquent."

In 1974, Felciano received an award from the American Academy of Arts and Letters, and a year later, one from the Martha Baird Rockefeller Fund.

THE COMPOSER SPEAKS: I am beginning to realize that the most consistent influence, and one which has become increasingly manifest, is that of my childhood in a small northern California community with substantial oriental and Portuguese populations. From these groups I learned a sense of ritual of structure, of awe and of music as a social function. I am an American with a strong sense of continental Europe (not England) and of the Orient; not a New Englander like Ives but a native Californian—another kind of American. . . . The reality of the world to me is East and West, stasis and dynamism, meditation and dialectics. It is also what California is—the edge where the two meet.

PRINCIPAL WORKS: *Sir Gawain and the Green Knight*, chamber opera (1964); *Gravities*, for piano four hands (1965); *Mutations for Orchestra* (1966); *Aubade*, for string trio, harp and piano (1966); *Spectra*, for piccolo, flute, alto flute, and double bass (1966); *Crasis*, for seven instruments and electronic tape (1967); *Glossolalia*, for organ, baritone voice, percussion and tape (1967); Trio, for speaker, screen and viewer (1968); *Linearity*, a television piece, for harp and live electronics (1968); *Background Music*, theater piece for harp, sympathetic piano, stereo tape, FM tuner, and transistor radio (1969); *God of the Expanding Universe*, for organ and tape (1969); Quintet, for piano, strings, and tape (1970); *Lamentations for Jani Christou*, for twelve instruments and tape (1970); *Signs*, for chorus, tape, and three slide projectors (1971); *The Angels of Turtle Island*, for soprano, violin, flute, percussion, and live electronics (1972); *Galactic Rounds*, for orchestra (1972); Te Deum, for chorus, organ, piano, percussion and three optional trumpets (1974); *Chöd*, for violin, cello, doublebass, two percussion, piano, and live electronics (1975); *In Celebration of Golden Rain*, for Indonesian gamelan and organ (1977); *Orchestra*, for orchestra (1980).

BIBLIOGRAPHY: Anderson, E. Ruth, *Contemporary American Composers* (Boston (1976); *San Francisco Sunday Examiner and Chronicle* (May 7, 1978); *San Francisco Symphony Program Notes,* September 24, 1980.

Feldman, Morton, b. New York City, January 12, 1926.

From his beginnings as a composer, Feldman has stood in the vanguard of the avant-garde movement in American music.

Piano study with Vera Maurina-Press was begun when he was twelve, the study of composition with Wallingford Riegger three years later, and informal instruction in composition with Stefan Wolpe when Feldman was eighteen. But the greatest single influence in his creative development was his friendship with John Cage. They first met during the 1949–50 season in New York at a concert of the New York Philharmonic under Dimitri Mitropoulos which featured Anton Webern's twelve-tone symphony. The hostile reaction of the audience and their own respective enthusiasm was the catalytic agent bringing them together. In subsequent meetings, Cage encouraged Feldman to trust his own musical instincts wherever they might lead. Through Cage, Feldman met and befriended such musical avant-gardists as Earle Brown and Pierre Boulez, whose iconoclastic musical thinking struck in him a responsive chord. But even more influential was his friendship with the abstractionist painters (Jackson Pollock, Philip Guston, Willem de Kooning). Their revolutionary aims and methods pointed out to Feldman the direction he should take as a composer. Feldman wanted to use sound the way the abstractionist painters used color, the sounds providing their own forms, shapes, and designs independent of thought and emotion, self-sufficient as an artistic process. The better to realize sound qualities, Feldman had to devise a new kind of notation that sometimes consisted of graphs which, as he put it, allowed "for the different utterances of the sound unhampered by compositional rhetoric." In projecting sounds, Feldman also emphasized the importance of silences as contrast, and was partial to soft dynamics. At the same time he made a conscious effort to make the performer a collaborator in the creative process through aleatory methods. However, he refused to surrender altogether his prerogatives as a composer, insisting upon certain set controls.

He first developed such concepts in 1950–51 in a series of five chamber music compositions for various instruments or combinations of instruments, collectively entitled *Projections*. Here he indicated the register (high, middle, or low) while leaving the performer or performers to choose the precise pitch within each register. Time values and dynamics (invariably soft) were also indicated. This practice was followed in other chamber music or solo instrumental compositions grouped under other collective titles: *Intermissions* (1950–53), *Extensions* (1951–53), *Intersections* (1951–53), *Durations* (1960–61), and *Vertical Thoughts* (1963).

Feldman extended "chance" elements in *Intersection* I and *Marginal Intersection*, both for orchestra and both written in 1951. In these works performers could decide for themselves not only what pitch to employ in the three indicated registers but also when to enter into the music making.

In . . . *Out of "Last Pieces,"* for orchestra (1961), in addition to earlier aleatory practices, thirty-eight sound units (or "events," as Feldman called them) could be gathered into any combinations, sequences, or juxtapositions of two or more "events" at any moment at the spontaneous direction of the conductor. For this work Feldman devised a notation written on coordinated paper made up of boxes, each measuring 80 mm. Indicated in the score is the number of sounds to be played within each box, with the performer in the orchestra allowed to enter when he wished during the duration of each box. . . . *Out of "Last Pieces,"* first heard in New York in 1961, was successfully performed by the New York Philharmonic under Leonard Bernstein on February 6, 1964.

In *Vertical Thoughts* V, for soprano, violin, tuba, percussion, and celesta (1963; N.Y., October 11, 1963), the musicians were allowed to enter at will. In *The Straits of Magellan*, for seven instruments including amplified guitar (1961; N.Y., October 11, 1963), aleatory methods were combined with predetermined registers, duration of notes, number of sounds within a given time interval, color, and dynamics. Among later Feldman compositions involving all these tried methods were *Mme. Press Died Last Week at 90*, for orchestra (1970; St. Paul au Vence, July 29, 1970); *The Rothko Chapel*, for chorus, viola, and bassoon, written in memory of the artist Mark Rothko (1970; Houston, 1972); and the Concerto for String Quartet and Orchestra, commissioned by the Cleveland Quartet, the Buffalo Philharmonic, and the orchestra's musical director, Michael Tilson Thomas (1973; Buffalo, 1974).

Feldman's first score for the stage was a ballet, *Summerspace*, or *Ixion* (1958), choreography by Merce Cunningham, introduced by the New York City Ballet in New York in April 1966. A decade after this performance, he wrote *Neither* (1976), his first "opera," though in actuality it is a monodrama for soprano and orchestra, to text by Samuel Beckett. The Rome Opera commissioned it and introduced it in spring 1977. When *Neither* was introduced to the United States on November 21, 1978, in New York, John Rockwell, in the *New York Times* explained that "the singer is not a character or narrator so much as a medium for a spectral message." He described Feldman's music as "more a meditation on a poetic idea of isolated ambivalence than an actual setting of specific words. . . . The music consists of more or less steady reiteration of chords. Often there are sustained notes through the chords. Sometimes the chords pulse with shifting dynamics and sometimes their steadiness is deflected for dramatic effect. . . . The result alternated between the quietly gripping—especially as the piece progressed—and the simplistic."

Feldman was the recipient of a Guggenheim Fellowship in 1966, an award from the National Institute of Arts and Letters in 1970, and a commission from the Koussevitzky Music Foundation in 1975. In the 1970s he was on the music faculty of the State University in Buffalo, where he inaugurated and directed an annual festival of contemporary music.

THE COMPOSER SPEAKS: I find that the only way I can work today is not to think of the present, but only to think of the past, the past of my own life, where I worked without being conscious of the ramifications of my own actions in the world. I certainly don't want to create the impression by those religious analogies that I think I was some sort of a deity. But there was a deity in my life, and that was *sound*. Everything else was after the fact. All "realization" was after the fact. Process was after the fact. Of course, what happens in the world when your work starts to become well known is that you have to justify it. You have to make some sort of rationale. And even the most banal rationale is accepted—welcomed—by people who should know better. For example, in some of my music, I leave the rhythmic situation quite free. That is, there are variable degrees of slowness, and the performer has freedom of duration. Several years ago I mentioned to a very renowned colleague that in a certain piece I had made a metronome marking of "between 40 and 70"—which is relatively slow—and it was amazing to me how relieved this brilliant man was.

PRINCIPAL WORKS: *Journey to the End of the Night*, for soprano and instruments (1949); *Intermissions* I–VI, for various instruments, solo or in combinations (1950–53); *Projection* I, for solo cello, *Projections* II–VI, for various solo instruments (1950–53); *Marginal Intersection*, for orchestra (1951); *Structures*, for string quartet (1951); *Extensions* I–IV, for various instruments (1951–53); *Intersection* I, for large orchestra, *Intersections* II–IV, for various instruments (1951–53); Three Pieces, for string quartet (1956); Two Pieces, for seven instruments (1956); *Summerspace*, or *Ixion*, ballet (1958); *Atlantis*, for chamber orchestra (1958); Last Pieces, for piano (1959); *The Swallows of Sanangan*, for large orchestra and twenty-three instruments (1960); *Durations* I–IV, for various instruments (1960–61); *Structures*, for orchestra (1960–62); Two Pieces, for clarinet and string quartet (1961); . . . *Out of "Last Pieces,"* for orchestra (1961); *Intervals*, for bass-baritone and instruments (1961); *The Straits of Magellan*, for seven instruments (1961); *Vertical Thoughts* I–V, for various instruments, solo or in combinations (1963); *Rabbi Akiba*, for soprano and instruments (1963); Chorus and Instruments (1963); *De Kooning*, for horn, percussion, piano, violin, and cello (1963); *Numbers*, for instruments (1964); Four Instruments, for violin, cello, piano, and chimes (1965); Two Pieces, for three pianos (1966); *First Principles*, for instrumental ensemble (1966–67); *In Search of an Orchestration*, for orchestra (1967); Chorus and Instruments II, for chorus, chimes, and tuba (1967); *False Relationships and Extended Ending*, for two chamber music groups (1968); *Between Categories*, for two pianos, two chimes, two violins, two cellos (1969); *The Viola in My Life*, for viola and six instruments (1970); *Rothko's Chapel*, for viola, percussion, and chorus (1970); Concerto for String Quartet and Orchestra (1973); Piano and Orchestra (1975); *Neither*, "opera" (1976); Piano (1977); Oboe and Orchestra (1976); Flute and Orchestra (1978); *Why Patterns*, for violin, piano and percussion (1978); *Spring of Chosroes*, for violin and piano (1978).

BIBLIOGRAPHY: Ewen, David, *Composers of Tomorrow's Music* (N.Y., 1971); Machlis, Joseph, *Introduction to Contemporary Music*, revised edition (N.Y., 1979); Schwartz, Elliott, and Childs, Barney (eds.), *Contemporary Composers on Contemporary Music* (N.Y., 1967).

Fine, Irving Gifford, b. Boston, Mass., December 3, 1914; d. Boston, Mass. August 23, 1962.

Both because he was a slow worker and because he died at the untimely age of forty-seven, Fine left only a handful of compositions. The best of these are of the highest standards in craftsmanship, creative imagination, and in the realization of a personalized style. He started out as a neoclassicist, digressed into the twelve-tone system, which he bent to his own artistic needs, and, finally, fashioned a mature style rich in cohesive melodic, polyphonic, and rhythmic invention.

While attending public schools in Boston and Winthrop, Mass., Fine studied the piano privately with Frances L. Grover. He entered Harvard University in 1933, spending the next five years there acquiring his bachelor of music degree in 1937 and his master's degree in music in 1938. His principal teachers in music at Harvard were Walter Piston, E. Burlingame Hill, A. T. Davison, and A. Tillman Merritt. The study of conducting took place with Serge Koussevitzky at the Berkshire Music Center in Tanglewood, Mass. In 1938, Fine studied composition with Nadia Boulanger in Cambridge, continuing in Paris on a Wyman Foundation grant.

Returning to Harvard later in 1939, Fine became director of its glee club, serving in this post until 1946, and from 1947 to 1950 he was assistant professor of music. He was also on the music faculty of the Berkshire Music Center (1946–47). On June 25, 1941, he married Verna Rudnick; they had three daughters.

His early works were influenced by Hindemith and the neoclassical Stravinsky, while he continually drew creative sustenance from 18th-century forms and polyphony. In this style we find the Violin Sonata (1946), Music for Piano (1947), and *Toccata concertante* (1947), the last, his first work for orchestra and his first to receive more than local attention. To Fine "toccata" indicated a concerted piece of music with a fanfarelike character. "The piece is

roughly in sonata form," the composer explained. "There is a short, fanfarelike introduction containing two motives which generate most of the subsequent thematic material." The Boston Symphony under Charles Munch presented it in Boston on October 22, 1948. Fine continued along his neoclassical ways with the Partita, for wind quintet (1948), which, following its premiere in New York, received the award of the New York Music Critics Circle as the best chamber music work performed that season.

In 1949, Fine did research in France on a Fulbright Fellowship, and in 1950 he was the recipient of the first of two Guggenheim Fellowships (the second coming in 1958). That summer (1950) Fine was codirector of the Salzburg Music Seminar for American Studies in Austria. Later that year he was appointed composer-in-residence, and after that the Walter W. Naumburg Professor of Music and chairman of the school of Creative Arts at Brandeis University in Waltham, Mass., where he remained until his death.

With *Notturno*, for strings and harp (1951), lyric content and romantic feeling began to assume increasing importance in his overall creative scheme. The *Notturno* was written for the Zimbler Sinfonietta and performed by that group with the composer conducting on March 28, 1951. Its Adagio movement was performed by the New York Philharmonic in the fall of 1962 as a memorial to Fine and a few months later, on December 14, the entire *Notturno* was programmed in his memory.

For a period in the 1950s—in the String Quartet (1952) and Fantasy, for string trio (1952)—Fine became interested in the twelve-tone system. In so doing, he became a forerunner of those young composers following him who personalized this method, and for whom the twelve-tone technique was secondary to tonality, form, harmony, and expressiveness. But Fine's concern with an expressive lyricism and romantic feeling soon made him discard the twelve-tone system for a style that henceforth would be his creative identification—strongly lyrical, romantic, transparent in its polyphonic writing, controlled in dissonance, and energetic in its rhythmic force.

Serious Song, or *Lament*, for string orchestra (1955), was commissioned by the Louisville Orchestra in Kentucky, which premiered it in Lousiville on November 16, 1955, Robert Whitney conducting. Symphony (1960–62) is generally conceded to be Fine's most significant work. Here he was a composer in full command of both his technical and artistic resources. The Boston Symphony under Munch premiered it on March 23, 1962. A few months later, Fine himself conducted the symphony at the Berkshire Music Festival in Tanglewood, just eleven days before he died of a heart attack in Beth Israel Hospital in Boston. In a eulogy published in the *Justice*, a publication of Brandeis University, Aaron Copland described Fine's music as follows: "All his compositions, from the lightest to the most serious, 'sound'; they have bounce and thrust and finesse; they are always a *musical* pleasure to hear. . . . For us, his friends and colleagues, they have imbedded in them one of the most cherishable musical natures of our time."

Fine received commissions from the Koussevitzky Music Foundation (1949) and from Rodgers and Hammerstein (1952). In 1952 he was given the Society for Publication of American Music Award and in 1955 an award from the National Institute of Arts and Letters.

PRINCIPAL WORKS: Violin Sonata (1946); Music for Piano (1947); *Toccata concertante*, for orchestra (1947); Partita, for wind quintet (1948); *The Hour Glass*, choral cycle for a cappella chorus (1949); *Notturno*, for string and harp (1951); String Quartet (1952); Fantasy, for string trio (1952); *Mutability*, six songs for mezzo-soprano, piano (1952); *Serious Song*, or *Lament*, for string orchestra (1955); *Children's Songs for Grown-ups*, song cycle for voice and piano (1955); Romanza, for wind quintet (1958); *Diversion,* for orchestra (1960); Symphony (1960–62).

BIBLIOGRAPHY: Ewen, David, *Composers Since 1900* (N.Y., 1969): Thomson, Virgil, *American Music Since 1910* (N.Y., 1970); *Boston Symphony Program Notes* (December 14, 1946); *New York Times*, (obituary), August 24, 1962.

Fine, Vivian, b. Chicago, Ill., September 28, 1913.

Vivian Fine's music is not atonal, but at the same time it is not tonal in the traditional way. There are constantly shifting tones around which the harmony and counterpoint move. In later works, dissonance has been tempered with consonance and there has been a greater concern for structure. But the basic inner qualities of her music have remained unchanged through the years.

When she was five she demanded piano lessons. "I threw one of the few fits of my childhood." she recalls, "screaming that I had to have them, and I was given them." At the age of six she entered Chicago Musical College on a scholarship, where she remained three years. Piano study was continued between 1924 and 1931 with Djane Lavoie-Herz, a pupil of Scriabin's, who subjected her to an extensive repertoire ranging from Bach to the 20th century with particular emphasis on Scriabin's music, which became one of the first significant influences affecting Fine's compositions.

At twelve she started a four-year period of study of harmony and composition with Ruth Crawford (herself a composer of distinction). After the first six months, Crawford asked young Vivian to write a

piece of music. "It had never occurred to me to write music before. I wrote it and could see she liked it. That led to another piece. That somebody felt it was important to encourage a talented little girl played a big role in my becoming a composer. I became so intrigued with composition that I never stopped since then."

In the second semester at Nicholas Senn High School in Chicago she became convinced that going to an academic school was for her a waste of time. Her parents proved sympathetic enough to allow her to drop out. In her music, she received further encouragement when she was fifteen from Henry Cowell and Dane Rudhyar, and additional instruction in composition from Adolph Weidig in Chicago in 1930–31. In her sixteenth year she wrote Solo for Oboe, performed at a concert of the Pan American Association of Composers in New York, on April 21, 1930. A year later she completed Four Pieces for Two Flutes, a composition good enough to receive a brief analysis from Wallingford Riegger in an issue of the *American Composers Alliance Bulletin*; she also wrote a Trio for Strings (1930). Both compositions already revealed a command of dissonant counterpoint, a style she would favor for some time. The Four Pieces for Two Flutes was performed at the Bauhaus in Dessau, Germany, on December 1, 1931, and the Trio in Darmstadt, Germany, on November 23, 1953, by the Herrmann Trio. When she was eighteen the Four Pieces for Two Flutes was featured on a program devoted to women composers in Hamburg, Germany.

She came to New York in 1931, where she became active as composer and accompanist for modern dance and by giving performances of contemporary piano music. Her music study continued in New York for the next fourteen years: privately with Roger Sessions (1933–43); at the Dalcroze School (1935–36); piano with Abby Whiteside (1937–45); and orchestration with George Szell (1943). Her first years in New York saw the writing of Four Polyphonic Pieces, for piano (1931–32); and Four Songs, for voice and piano (1932), to poems by Robert Herrick, James Joyce, and an anonymous poet of the 16th century. The former was heard at the Yaddo Festival at Saratoga, N.Y., on April 30, 1932; the latter, at a concert of the League of Composers in New York on February 5, 1933.

On April 5, 1935, Fine married Benjamin Karp, a sculptor; they raised two daughters.

Fine's second period as composer, beginning in 1937, saw her adopt a more diatonic style. This was the year she wrote her first music for ballets, beginning with *The Race of Life* (1937), choreography by Doris Humphrey, based on drawings by James Thurber, first performed in New York in the original piano version on January 13, 1938, by Doris Humphrey, Charles Weidman, José Limón and the Dance Company. With orchestra, the ballet was mounted by the Juilliard Dance Theater in New York on April 27, 1946. She continued writing music for ballets in 1938 and 1939. *Opus 51* (1938), choreography by Charles Weidman, was introduced by Weidman and his company at the Bennington Dance Festival on August 6, 1938. *Tragic Exodus* (1939), choreography by Hanya Holm, received its first presentation in New York on February 19, 1939, performed by Hanya Holm and her company. *They Too Are Exiles* (1939), choreography once again by Hanya Holm, was premiered by Holm and her company in New York on January 7, 1940.

During the latter half of the 1930s, Vivian Fine wrote various concert works whose performances were beginning to bring her added recognition. Prelude, for string quartet (1937), appeared on a program of the League of Composers in New York on March 26, 1939. Four Elizabethan Songs, for voice and piano, to poems by John Donne, John Lyly, Shakespeare, and Philip Sidney, was completed in 1938. The first and fourth songs ("Daybreak" and "The Bargain") were given a hearing at the composers Forum Laboratory in New York on May 1, 1940; and the second ("Spring Welcome") at the Yaddo Festival in Saratoga on September 10, 1938.

From 1945 to 1948 Vivian Fine was on the music faculty of New York University. In 1948 she taught at the Juilliard School of Music for a semester; in 1951 she taught music at the University College in Potsdam, N.Y.; in 1963–64 at The College School of Dance in Connecticut; and since 1964 at Bennington College in Vermont.

On a Rothschild Foundation commission, Fine wrote *A Guide to the Life Expectancy of a Rose* (1956), text by R. S. Tilley on material published in the garden section of the *New York Times*; its premiere took place in New York City on May 16, 1956. *Alcestis 1960* is a ballet commissioned by Martha Graham, who introduced it with her company in New York on April 29, 1960. *The Confession* (1963), for soprano and instruments (text by Racine), was heard first in New York on March 21, 1963. Concertino, for piano and percussion (1965), was first performed in New York on March 18, 1965. *My Son, My Enemy*, a ballet (1965), was commissioned by the Rockefeller Foundation for José Limón, who introduced it at the Connecticut College in New London, Conn., on August 14, 1965. At a concert in New York devoted entirely to her compositions on April 15, 1973, *Missa Brevis*, for four cellos and taped voice, and the Concerto for Piano, Strings, and Percussion, both completed in 1972, were given their premieres.

A grant from the National Endowment for the Arts led to the writing of *Teisho*, for eight solo singers or small chorus and string quartet (1975), text being Zen sermons or talks from the 10th to the 12th centuries. The first performance took place at Bennington College in Vermont on May 22, 1976. The

American bicentennial commemoration brought Fine a commission from Cooper Union in New York for an oratorio for narrator, soloists, chorus, and orchestra: *Meeting for Equal Rights 1886*, introduced at a concert of the Oratorio Society of New York on April 23, 1976, saluting the American bicentennial. This work promoted the cause of equal rights—sometimes passionately, sometimes in rage, sometimes in compassion—with a text selected by Fine from the writings and spoken words of both men and women.

In 1974, Vivian Fine had received a grant from the National Endowment for the Arts to write an opera. On a visit to San Francisco in 1975, she was encouraged by the Port Costa Players to write a chamber opera for that company. Still on her grant from the National Endowment, she secluded herself in Cuernavaca, Mexico, to write *The Women in the Garden* to her own libretto, and on February 12, 1978, the Port Costa Players produced it in San Francisco. The opera is basically plotless. Four women—Emily Dickinson, Isadora Duncan, Gertrude Stein and Virginia Woolf—meet in a garden, where they soliloquize, meditate, exchange ideas, and quote from their own writings. This, wrote a critic for *High Fidelity/Musical America*, "is an opera of suggestion, of evocation, not of dramatic gesture."

In addition to her teaching obligations at Bennington College, Vivian Fine has lectured on her own music and has given lecture-recitals on 20th-century music at numerous colleges and universities in the United States. She was composer-in-residence at the Panorama of the Arts at the University of Wisconsin at Oshkosh in 1968 and at Skidmore College in Saratoga, N.Y., in 1976. Between 1953 and 1960 she was music director of the Bethsabee de Rothschild Foundation. She was one of the founders of the American Composers Alliance, serving as its vice-president from 1961 to 1965. In 1980 she was elected to membership in the American Academy and Institute of Arts and Letters.

THE COMPOSER SPEAKS: My musical idiom has undergone changes over the years but I feel that there is a common thread in my work. I have always been deeply absorbed by the "intellectual" aspects of composition, but the humanist, feeling side, I hope is always there.

PRINCIPAL WORKS: Four Pieces for Two Flutes (1930); Trio, for strings (1930); Divertimento, for oboe, clarinet, bassoon, piano, and percussion (1933); Prelude, for orchestra, also for string quartet (1937); *The Race of Life*, ballet (1937); Four Elizabethan Songs, for voice and piano (1938); *Opus 51*, ballet (1938); *Tragic Exodus*, ballet (1939); *They Too Are Exiles*, ballet (1939); *Songs of Our Time*, for voice and piano (1943); Concertante, for piano and orchestra (1944); Chaconne, for piano (1947); *The Great Wall of China*, for voice, flute, cello, and piano

(1947); Divertimento, for violin, cello, and percussion (1951); Composition for String Quartet (1951); Violin Sonata (1952); Variations, for piano (1952); Psalm 13, for two sopranos. alto, and bass and piano or organ (1953); *A Guide to the Life Expectancy of a Rose* (1956); String Quartet (1957); *Variations 1959*, for mixed chorus, soprano, tenor, and ten instruments (1959); *Alcestis 1960*, ballet (1960); *Morning*, for mixed chorus, narrator, and organ (1962); Fantasy, for cello and piano (1962); *The Confession*, for soprano, flute, violin, viola, cello, and piano (1963); *Dreamscape*, for percussion ensemble, three flutes, cello, and piano (1964); *My Son, My Enemy*, ballet (1965); Concertino for Piano and Percussion Ensemble (1965); Chamber Concerto for Cello and Six Instruments (1966); Four Piano Pieces (1966); *Epitaph*, for mixed chorus and orchestra (1967); Quintet for String Trio, Trumpet, and Harp (1967); *Paean*, for brass ensemble, female chorus ensemble, narrator (1969); Two Neruda Poems, for voice and piano (1971); *Missa Brevis*, for four cellos and taped voice (1972); Concerto for Piano, Strings, and Percussion (1972); *Teisho*, for eight solo singers or small chorus and string quartet (1975); *Meeting for Equal Rights 1866*, for vocal soloists, narrator, chorus and orchestra (1976); *Romantic Ode*, for string orchestra with solo violin, viola, and cello (1976); *The Women in the Garden*, chamber opera (1977); Quartet for Brass (1978); *Momenti*, for piano (1978); *For a Bust of Erik Satie*, short Mass for soprano, mezzo-soprano, narrator, and six instruments (1979).

BIBLIOGRAPHY: *DCM*; Thomson, Virgil, *Music Since 1910* (N.Y., 1970); *American Composers Alliance Bulletin*, vol. 8, no. 1, 1958; *Oakland (Calif.) Tribune*, July 2, 1975; *San Francisco Examiner and Chronicle*, February 12, 1978.

Finney, Ross Lee, b. Wells, Minn., December 23, 1906.

Finney's early music reflects his interest in American folk song and hymnology and traditional musical structure. He later adopted a principle he called "a method of complementarity," in which the details were ordered by the twelve-tone technique while the large form adhered to tonal organization.

He was born to a cultured middle-class family, his father being a sociologist and writer and his mother a trained musician. His earliest musical training took place in North Dakota during the second decade of this century when that area was still a part of the western frontier. His mother gave him his first instruction in piano and forwarded his interest in composing. He studied cello and played in the local orchestra. His brother Theodore M. Finney (a writer on the history of music) played the violin and his brother Nat S. Finney (a Washington newspaper correspondent) played the cornet. The family orchestra was much in demand. He also sang folk songs with guitar. This midwestern background had a lasting impact on his composition.

In 1918 the family moved to Minneapolis and he began immediately his study of composition with Donald Ferguson and cello with Eggelbert Roentgen. After one year at the University of Minnesota in 1924, he transferred to Carleton College in Northfield, Minn., where he earned his bachelor of arts degree by teaching cello and the history of music. In 1927, by playing in a jazz band, he was able to go to Europe where, on a Johnson Fellowship, he studied composition for one year with Nadia Boulanger in Paris. After a year at Harvard University (1928–29), where he studied with E. Burlingame Hill, Finney was appointed to the music faculty of Smith College in Northampton, Mass. He remained there until 1948, active not only as a teacher but also as the founder of the Smith College Music Archives, a series of scholarly publications of old music for which he edited Francesco Geminiani's violin sonatas, and the Valley Music Press, devoted to the publication of local American composers, and as conductor of the Northampton Chamber Orchestra. In 1935 he taught a course on American music and frequently sang folk songs with guitar. During this period he studied composition privately with Roger Sessions.

On September 3, 1930, Finney married Gretchen Ludke, who later became an author. They had two sons: Ross, a mathematician, and Henry, a sociologist. In 1931, on leave from Smith College, Finney studied composition privately with Alban Berg. Though he then came to admire both Berg and his music, he could not at the time find the theories and practices of dodecaphony applicable to his own musical thinking; such a development would come two decades later. In the 1930s, the roots of his style were still in his midwestern background and in his interest in abstract tonal functions. This blend resulted in the following: Piano Sonatas nos. 1–3 (1933, 1939, 1942), all of which were edited and premiered by John Kirkpatrick; Concerto for Violin and Orchestra (1935); String Quartet no. 1 (1935), which, in 1937, earned a Pulitzer Fellowship and which was performed by the Gordon String Quartet in April 1937; and *Poems by Archibald MacLeish* (1935), for high voice and piano, for which he was awarded the Connecticut Valley Prize and which was introduced by Mabel Garrison and John Duke at the Hartford Festival in February 1936.

On November 4, 1936, a concert devoted entirely to Finney's music was heard in New York. This was one of the first Composers' Forums sponsored by the Works Progress Administration. Finney's music was now also being heard at concerts of the League of Composers in New York and at the Yaddo Festival in Saratoga, N.Y.

A Guggenheim Fellowship in 1937 brought Finney back to Europe to spend a year composing, photographing the manuscripts of Tartini, and studying composition with Gian Francesco Malipiero in Italy. It was during this period that he composed *Bleheris*, for tenor and orchestra, and Sonata in A minor for Viola and Piano.

Between 1940 and 1944, Finney taught not only at Smith College but also at Mt. Holyoke College in South Hadley, Mass., as well as at the Hartt School of Music in Hartford, Conn., where he was head of the theory department. In 1944–45, during World War II, Finney served with the Office of Strategic Services in Paris. He received the Purple Heart for wounds sustained when he stepped on a land mine in southern France; he was also awarded the Certificate of Merit. In 1946–47 he returned to Smith College and also taught at Amherst College in Massachusetts. Immediately after receiving his second Guggenheim Fellowship in 1947, he was appointed composer-in-residence at the University of Michigan at Ann Arbor, where he organized and headed the department of composition, introduced an extensive graduate program in composition, and (on a grant from the Horace H. Rackham School of Graduate Studies) established an electronic music laboratory. He retired from the University in 1973.

The war undermined Finney's interest in nationalism, and he turned from his earlier midwestern influences to a more chromatic style. Nevertheless, several of his most important works that used American folk material date from this period. *Variations, Fuguing, and Holiday,* for orchestra (1943), was based on a hymn by the 18th-century American psalmodist William Billings. After receiving its initial performance in Los Angeles on May 17, 1947, with Alfred Wallenstein conducting, it was the recipient of the Alice M. Ditson Award. Finney revised it in 1956, the new version getting its first hearing in Miami on January 14, 1966, in a performance by the Greater Miami Philharmonic under Fabien Sevitzky. *Pilgrim Psalms*, for solo voices, chorus, and orchestra (1945), was a setting of texts from the Ainsworth Psalter; it was performed at Cornell University in 1946. *Poor Richard*, a song cycle based on texts by Benjamin Franklin, was composed in 1946. Finney's String Quartet no. 4 (1946) was premiered by the Kroll Quartet in Cambridge, Mass., at an Elizabeth Sprague Coolidge concert in December 1947 and has since been widely performed. Two works of this period were influenced by the war: Symphony no. 1 (1943) written immediately after Pearl Harbor, and Piano Sonata no. 4 (1945).

The turning point in Finney's style came with two works composed in 1950: Sonata no. 2, for cello and piano, and String Quartet no. 6 in E. In the string quartet Finney turned to the twelve-tone technique but without abandoning tonal functions or form. This blend he has called "method of complementarity." Finney has continued to adapt the twelve-tone

system to his own technique and requirements ever since, and in this idiom he has produced his most ambitious and important music. Piano Trio no. 2 (1954), commissioned by Sigma Alpha Iota, was introduced by the Alberni Trio in Washington, D.C., in 1955. Yehudi Menuhin commissioned the Fantasy in Two Movements (1958), which he performed at the World's Fair in Brussels on June 1, 1958, before featuring it prominently on his programs in Europe and America. In this work Finney used a twelve-tone row made up of two similar (symmetrical) hexachords, a practice that he continued in later works. On a commission from the Elizabeth Sprague Coolidge Foundation, Finney wrote his String Quintet (1958), first heard at the Library of Congress on October 30, 1959, in Washington, D.C., performed by the Kroll Quartet supplemented by Alan Shulman, cellist. Meanwhile, in 1955, Finney received the Boston Symphony Award; in 1955–56, a grant from the Rockefeller Foundation for study in Europe; in 1956 an award from the Academy of Arts and Letters; and in 1957 an honorary doctorate of humane letters from Carleton College, as well as an honorary membership in Phi Beta Kappa.

In his Symphony no. 2 (1959), commissioned by the Koussevitzky Music Foundation and dedicated to the memory of Serge and Natalie Koussevitzky, Finney used the twelve-tone row to determine not only the pitch but also rhythm, a technique to be found in such later works as Three Pieces for chamber orchestra and tape recorder (1962), *Three Studies in Four*, for solo percussionists (1965), and Concerto for Percussion and Orchestra (1965). Symphony no. 2 was first performed in Philadelphia on November 13, 1959, by the Philadelphia Orchestra under Eugene Ormandy and on their eastern tour in New York City, Baltimore, and Washington. After that it received numerous performances in the United States and Europe, was recorded, and represented the United States at the Rostrum of International Composers at UNESCO in Paris in 1963.

While serving as composer-in-residence at the American Academy in Rome in 1960, Finney completed writing his Symphony no. 3. It differed from its predecessors by being more lyric than dramatic, shorter, less irregular in rhythm and less rigid in its use of serialism. It is based on a tone row that has four variants, each related to a tonal function, and all introduced in the first ten measures. "But," as Harold C. Schonberg noted in the *New York Times*, "Finney has manipulated the line and the intervals of those variants for minimum dissonance. The chances are that few would recognize it as a serial composition without the musical examples printed in the program notes before one's eyes." The Philadelphia Orchestra under Ormandy introduced this symphony on March 6, 1964, in Philadelphia before taking it on its eastern tour to New York City, Baltimore, and Washington, D.C.

In 1960–61, and again in 1977–78, Finney was a traveling scholar for Phi Beta Kappa. During the 1950s and 1960s he toured Germany, Poland, Austria, England, and Greece for the U.S. Information Agency, singing American folk songs to his own accompaniment on the guitar. In 1962 he was elected member of the National Institute of Arts and Letters and in 1967 to the American Academy of Arts and Letters. In the summer of 1962 he worked under Mario Davidovsky's direction at the Columbia-Princeton Electronic Music Laboratory before organizing a similar laboratory at the University of Michigan. In August 1965, Finney was composer-in-residence at the Congregation of the Arts at Dartmouth College N.H., where two weeks of performances of his music were given, including the premiere on August 21 of his only work for the stage, *The Nun's Priest's Tale*, based on Chaucer, for solo voices, chorus, orchestra with percussion (1965). In 1968 he was presented the Brandeis Creative Arts Award by Brandeis University in Waltham, Mass.

During the 1970s Finney turned again to his midwestern American background, finding ways in which to reflect this material within the serial-tonal style that he had developed. *Summer in Valley City* (1969), his first work for concert band, was written to honor his colleague William Revelli, who performed the work with the Michigan Concert Band in Ann Arbor, April 1, 1971, and on tour in New York City. This work and many others written during the 1970s contrasted aleatoric sections with metric sections and quoted from folk songs that the composer sings with guitar. *Two Acts for Three Players* (1970) for clarinet, percussion, and piano was based on memory of the early "flicks" and used the performers as characters. *Spaces* (1971), for large orchestra, was commissioned by the North Dakota Arts Council and premiered on March 26, 1972, by the Fargo-Morehead Orchestra under Sigvald Thompson. Symphony no. 4 (1972), more abstract and still using aleatory practices, was commissioned for the Baltimore Symphony Orchestra and performed by that group on May 9, 1973, under Sergiu Comissiona. *Landscapes Remembered*, for chamber orchestra (1971), was concerned with memory scenes that fade in and out of focus. It was based on hymns and folk songs, one of which was used as the main theme for the Violin Concerto no. 2 (1973), written for the bicentennial programs of the Music Teachers National Association, and given its first performance on March 31, 1976, in Dallas, Tex. Finney's Concerto for Strings (1976) was introduced in New York on December 5, 1977, by the Composers Orchestra Alliance conducted by Dean Dixon.

A choral trilogy, *Earthrise*, for tape voice, soloists, chorus, and orchestra was commissioned by the University of Michigan to celebrate three different occasions: *Still Are New Worlds* (1962), for the fiftieth anniversary of the building of Hill Auditorium (May 10, 1963), concerned with the discovery in the 17th century of new stars that challenged the old concept of a finite universe; *The Martyr's Elegy* (1966), for the sesquicentennial of the founding of the university (April 23, 1967), based on Shelley's *Adonais* and concerned with man's inhumanity to man; *Earthrise* (1978), for the centennial of the founding of the School of Music (December 11, 1979), based on texts by Teilhard de Chardin and Lewis Thomas, concerned with the way in which the view of the fragile earth from the moon undermined man's view of his universe.

Since his retirement from the University of Michigan in 1973, Finney has divided his time between Ann Arbor, Mich., and New York City. He has been active on the editorial boards of New World Records and Composers Records, Inc., on the boards of the Composers' Forum and the Composer Orchestra Alliance, and as head of the music division of the National Institute of Arts and Letters.

THE COMPOSER SPEAKS: I have always wanted my music to "sing," whatever devices or systems I might use in composing it. Beneath the surface, however, is a complexity of memories and functions and abstractions that give depth to the musical experience but only if the music flows and "sings" without interruption from beginning to end.

PRINCIPAL WORKS: 8 string quartets (1935–60); 5 piano sonatas (1933–1961); 4 symphonies (1942–1972); 2 violin sonatas (1951, 1955); 2 piano trios (1938, 1954); 2 viola sonatas (1937, 1953); 2 cello sonatas (1938, 1950); 2 piano quintets (1953, 1961).

Poems by Archibald MacLeish, for voice and piano (1935); *Bleheris,* for tenor and orchestra (1937); *Slow Piece,* for string orchestra (1940); *Pilgrim Psalms,* for solo voices, chorus, and orchestra or organ (1945); *Poor Richard,* for voice and piano (1946); *Nostalgic Waltzes,* for piano (1947); *Three Love Songs,* for voice and piano (1948); Piano Quartet (1948); Chamber Music, thirty-six songs for voice and piano (1952); *Immortal Autumn,* for chorus and tenor solo (1952); *Variations on a Theme by Alban Berg,* for piano (1952); Fantasy, for solo cello (1957); Variations, for orchestra (1957); Fantasy in Two Movements, for solo violin (1958); *Edge of Shadow,* for chorus and two pianos and percussion (1959); Three Pieces, for chamber orchestra and tape recorder (1962); *Still Are New Worlds,* for tape voice, chorus, and orchestra (1962); Divertissement, for clarinet, violin, cello, and piano (1964); *Three Studies in Four,* for four percussion soloists (1965); Concerto for Percussion and Orchestra (1965); *The Nun's Priest's Tale,* for vocal soloist, chorus, folk singer with electric guitar and small orchestra (1965); *The Martyr's Elegy,* for tenor solo, chorus, and orchestra (1966); *Symphony concertante,* for orchestra (1967); Organ Fantasies, (1967); *Thirty-two*

Piano Games (1968); *Summer in Valley City*, for concert band (1969); *Two Acts for Three Players*, for clarinet, percussion, and piano (1970); *Landscape Remembered*, for twelve players (1971); *Spaces*, for orchestra (1971); *Two Ballades*, for flutes and piano (1973); Concerto for Alto Sax and Wind Orchestra (1973); *Variations on a Memory*, for ten players (1975); *Narrative*, for solo cello and chamber orchestra (1975); Concerto for Strings (1976); *Skating on the Sheyenne*, for concert band (1977); *Earthrise*, a choral trilogy, for tape voice, vocal soloists, chorus, and orchestra (1978); Quartet, for oboe, cello, percussion, and piano (1979).

BIBLIOGRAPHY: *DCM*; *Musical Quarterly*, January 1967; *Who's Who in America, 1980–81*.

Flagello, Nicolas, b. New York, March 15, 1928.

Though Flagello's music is an extension of the romanticism of Puccini, Mahler, Rachmaninoff, and Richard Strauss—with a rich and varied melodic content and a constant emotional flow—it is a romanticism with strength and discipline. In his later works, his romantic speech is combined with discords, irregular rhythmic procedures, and a chromatic sense of tonality.

Of Italian extraction, he comes from a musical family. His father, a successful dress designer, was an accomplished musician who performed professionally on the oboe in Italy and the United States; his mother, who assisted her husband in the dress business, was a trained singer. His maternal grandfather, Domenico Casiello, was one of Verdi's last pupils and an esteemed composer and conductor in Naples; and his younger brother by five years, Ezio Flagello, is a renowned opera bass, formerly a resident member of the Metropolitan Opera Company.

Nicolas Flagello began taking piano lessons from his aunt when he was three and a half years old, and started playing publicly a year and a half later. At six, he initiated a six-year period of violin study with Francesco di Giacomo.

Flagello received his academic education in the city public schools and Evander Childs High School in the Bronx, from which he was graduated in 1945. In high school he was active as a violinist in its orchestra, as oboist in the band, and as a soloist on the violin and the piano at various school concerts. Before graduating he was awarded the Gold Medal for excellence in music.

After leaving high school, Flagello played the violin in the All-American Youth Orchestra conducted by Leopold Stokowski (1945–46). He now intensified his musical training with the private study of the piano with Adele Marcus, begun in his senior year in high school and continuing until 1949. At the Manhattan School of Music in New York—which he entered in 1946 and where he received his bachelor of music degree in 1949 and his master of music degree in 1956—his principal teachers were Julius Shaier, Gabor Rejto, Harold Bauer, Hugo Kortschak, Hugh Ross, and Vittorio Giannini—formal study with Giannini from 1935 to 1950, and in a master-apprentice relationship until Giannini's death in 1966. Between 1946 and 1950 he was musical assistant to Friedrich Schorr at the Manhattan School. He also studied the oboe privately with Bruno Labate (1948–50) and, in the late 1940s, conducting with Dimitri Mitropolous.

Beginning with 1947, Flagello was launched on a highly active professional career as pianist. Between 1947 and 1958 he made numerous tours as accompanist for concert singers, among these being Carlo Bergonzi, John Brownlee, Tito Schipa, and Brian Sullivan. In 1950–51, Flagello was also pianist for the Longines Symphonette, which performed over the radio. In all, either as accompanist or solo performer, he gave about two hundred concerts in that eleven-year period.

In 1950, Flagello was appointed to the faculty of the Manhattan School of Music in New York as a teacher of composition. Three years later, on July 18, 1953, he married Dianne Danese, a music educator. After raising two sons, they were divorced in 1978.

Flagello's first mature work for orchestra was the tone poem *Beowulf* (1949); his Piano Concerto no. 1 followed in 1950; in 1953 he completed a Flute Concerto, which had been commissioned by the Columbus (Ohio) Symphony, introduced by Claude Monteux on February 26, 1954, and two operas: *Mirra*, based on a play by Vittorio Alfieri, and *The Wig*, based on Pirandello, both to his own libretti. All these works were tonal, faithful to well-defined traditional structures, more concerned with melody, emotion, clarity of texture and sensitive balances than with innovation or experimentation. Though the two operas are based on a symphonic scale, they do not lose melodic propulsion.

Awarded a Fulbright Fellowship in 1955, Flagello went to Italy to resume music study at the Santa Cecilia Academy in Rome as a composition pupil of Ildebrando Pizzetti. In 1956, Flagello was awarded the Santa Cecilia first prize for musical creativity and a doctorate in superior studies.

After his return to the United States in 1956, Flagello resumed his teaching position at the Manhattan School of Music, which he has since retained, serving as director of the Extension Division between 1969 and 1972. In 1964 he was coordinator with Vittorio Giannini of the North Carolina School of the Performing Arts, and in 1964–65 he headed the composition department at the Curtis Institute of Music in Philadelphia. He was also active as a conductor. In 1960 he was assistant conductor of La Scala Opera in Rome under Antonino Votto; in 1960–61 he conducted the Chicago Lyric Opera; in 1962 he became the musical director of the Orchestra Sinfonica di Roma; and in 1967 he made conducting appearances at the New York City Opera.

Assimilating atonal and harmonically discordant practices into his music and arriving at a more individualized style, Flagello began making his mark as a composer by the late 1950s with *Missa sinfonica,* for orchestra but no voices (1957); the one-act opera *The Sisters* (1958; N.Y., March 23, 1961), libretto by Dean Mundy; the one-act opera *The Judgment of St. Francis* (1959; N.Y., March 18, 1966), libretto by Armand Aulicino; the Concerto for String Orchestra (1959; N.Y., March 12, 1960); and the choral composition *Tristis Est Anima Mea* (1959). Reviewing *The Sisters* in the *New York Herald Tribune,* John Gruen said of Flagello that he possessed "the gift of writing gratefully for the voice," that his music had "melodic sumptuousness," his orchestral texture was "crystal clear," and that he knew how to "underline dramatic events." In the *New Yorker,* Winthrop Sargeant called *The Judgment of St. Francis* "the most vigorous new opera I have come across in a long time. . . . Flagello has shown an unmistakable and a totally unconfused talent for the operatic theater." *The Judgment of St. Francis* received the Vatican's Order of Peter and Paul, in 1960. *Tristis Est Anima Mea* was given an award by the New York Music Critics Circle after having been premiered in New York on February 12, 1961.

Flagello's most important compositions since 1960 have been: Piano Sonata (1962; N.Y., 1963), commissioned by Abbey Simon; *Te Deum for All Mankind,* for chorus and orchestra (1967; N.Y., May 7, 1969), commissioned by the New York Board of Education; the oratorio *Passion of Martin Luther King,* for solo voices, chorus, and orchestra (1968; Washington, D.C., February 19, 1974), commissioned by the London Philharmonic; and the Symphony no. 2 (1970; Ithaca, N.Y., March 4, 1979).

Since 1960, Flagello has been chief conducting consultant for RCA, symphonic Division, in Rome (1961–); chairman of the National Association for American Composers and Conductors (1962–66); chief editor of Lyra Music Publishing (1963–); artistic director of the Festival Musicale di Salerno (1968); and president of the American Artists Ad Astra Foundation (1968). In 1978 he formed Flagello Productions to advance the cause of musical arts in general and, in particular, to develop young performing artists. In 1968 Flagello was awarded the City of Salerno Gold Medal in Italy. On June 29, 1978, he married Maya Armstrong Randolph, soprano.

THE COMPOSER SPEAKS: My entire life has been immersed in the European musical heritage that has surrounded me. I loved that tradition; thus music has been for me the most natural means of expression. The fact that I spent much of my childhood and adolescence in Europe meant that I never felt like an "American" musician, with the isolation from the well-springs of traditions that implies. As a composer, I have never desired or needed to reject or rebel against this heritage. To the contrary, I am proud to make my personal contribution to it, and am not afraid to submit my work alongside that of my predecessors. As unfashionable as such a creed may appear today, I compose to express myself, in a language that is natural and contemporary to me and comprehensible, I believe, to my audience. I have tried to fulfill Mozart's dictum that the greatest task for the composer is to challenge the most sophisticated musician while entertaining the most modest listener.

PRINCIPAL WORKS: 4 piano concertos (1950–75); 2 symphonies (1968, 1970).

Beowulf, tone poem for orchestra (1949); *Symphonic Aria* (1951); *Overture giocosa,* for orchestra (1952); *Mirra,* one-act opera (1953); Flute Concerto (1953); *The Wig,* one-act opera (1953); Theme, Variations, and Fugue, for orchestra (1955); Violin Concerto (1957); *Rip Van Winkle,* children's opera (1957); *Missa sinfonica,* for orchestra, without voices (1957); *The Sisters,* one-act opera (1958); *The Judgment of St. Francis,* one-act opera (1959); Concerto for String Orchestra (1959); *Tristis Est Anima Mea,* for chorus and orchestra (1959); Prelude, Ostinato, and Fugue, for piano (1960); *Burlesca,* for flute and guitar (1961); Harp Sonata (1961); Capriccio, for cello and orchestra (1962); Piano Sonata (1962); *Dante's Farewell,* for soprano and orchestra (1962); Concertino, for piano, brass and timpani (1963); Violin Sonata (1963); *Contemplations,* for soprano and orchestra (1964); *Lautrec,* ballet suite (1965); Suite, for violin, cello and harp (1965); *Elektra,* for piano and percussion (1966); *Declamation,* for violin and piano (1967); *Te Deum for All Mankind,* for chorus (1967); Serenade, for small orchestra (1968); *Passion of Martin Luther King,* for vocal soloists, chorus and orchestra (1968); *The Piper of Hamelin,* children's opera (1970); Ricercare, for brass and percussion (1970); *Remembrance,* for soprano, flute, and string quartet (1972); *Credendum,* for cello and orchestra (1974); *Psalmus Americanus,* for chorus and orchestra (1976); Two Songs, for soprano and piano (1977); *Furama,* for solo flute (1978); *Diptych,* for two trumpets and trombone (1979).

BIBLIOGRAPHY: *BBDM; Who's Who in America, 1978–79.*

Fletcher, Horace Grant, b. Hartsburg, Ill., October 25, 1913.

Fletcher's music combines contrapuntal practices of the baroque era, the traditions of classicism, with the dissonances, chromaticisms, sonorities, and rhythms of the 20th century. It is characterized by lyricism as well as strength, and expressiveness as well as instrumental virtuosity.

Both parents were schoolteachers, and both were musical. His father, a teacher of elocution and physical education, also taught a Kentucky mountain singing class, and his mother, a trained musician, often was her husband's piano accompanist. As a boy, Fletcher sang in a boys' choir. His musical experience began at the age of fourteen with the trumpet and the clarinet, which he learned by trial and error, and continued, two years later, with the piano and violin from instruction books he borrowed from friends. While at Springfield High School in Illinois (1927–32) he studied violin, theory, and choral conducting with E. Carl Lundgren, who provided him with his first opportunities to conduct and encouraged him to make his initial attempts at composing. During the four years in high school, Fletcher sang in its a cappella choir and played the violin in the orchestra. In 1931 his excellence in music brought him a special award from the Springfield High School Honors Society. He spent one year as assistant in its music department.

Between 1932 and 1935, he attended the Illinois Wesleyan University in Bloomington, Ill., on a full music scholarship. There his music study embraced theory with Bessie Louise Smith, conducting and orchestration with Harry K. Lamont, piano with Lucy Brandicon, and viola and composition with William E. Kritch. In 1933–35 he was assistant teacher of theory there and conductor of its Little Symphony of the Phi Mu Alpha Fraternity.

In 1935, Fletcher completed several compositions, romantic and impressionistic in style and with some rhythmic experiments. Rhapsody, for flute and strings, was introduced in Rochester, N.Y., on October 18, 1944, Howard Hanson conducting. *A Rhapsody of Dances*, for chamber orchestra, winner of first prize in the NBC Radio Composers Contest, was heard first on July 25, 1938, in Ann Arbor, Mich. In addition, Fletcher completed two books of Nocturnes, for piano; he orchestrated one of these nocturnes (F minor) and it was premiered in Abilene, Tex., on February 15, 1954.

Upon receiving his bachelor of music degree in 1935, Fletcher was employed as public school instrumental conductor (1936–39), then as teacher of composition and theory at the Illinois Wesleyan Junior College of Music (1939–41). He spent the summer of 1937 and 1938 at the University of Michigan at Ann Arbor in the study of conducting with Thor Johnson. That year he studied composition with Ernst Krenek at the University of Michigan to complete the requirements for a master of music degree in 1939. At the Berkshire Music Center at Tanglewood, Mass., he further studied conducting, served as Paul Hindemith's conducting assistant in 1941 and was offered scholarships as choral conductor assistant to

Hugh Ross in 1943. After serving in the U.S. Army during World War II in 1943, he became Herbert Elwell's student at the Eastman School of Music in Rochester, N.Y., in the summer of 1945; was a student of composition of Bernard Rogers, Burrill Phillips, and Howard Hanson at the Eastman Music School. There in 1948–49 he became instructor of theory and in 1951 was awarded a doctorate in music.

From 1941 to 1943 Fletcher was head of the theory department at Winthrop College in Rock Hill, S.C.; and from 1943 to 1945 he headed the instrumental department and conducted the Little Symphony at Culver-Stockton College in Canton, Mo. In 1945 he expanded his conductorial duties by becoming the musical director of the Akron (Ohio) Symphony, conducting its concerts for the next three years.

Without breaking away from the traditional past, Fletcher began exploring the potentials of 20th-century concepts of harmony, rhythm, atonality, and twelve-tone music in his compositions in the 1940s. *A Song for Warriors* (1944; Rochester, N.Y., October 25, 1945) was based on a Yugoslav poem. *An American Overture* (1945)—notable for its rhythmic dynamism, dramatic use of discords, and modally conceived thematic material—received first prize in a nationwide contest sponsored by the Duluth Symphony in Minnesota, which premiered it on April 23, 1948. *The Crisis*, for chorus and orchestra (1945; Walla Walla, Wash., February 22, 1976), based on a text by Thomas Paine, was the winner of a composers' competition sponsored by the Walla Walla Symphony and the Washington State American Revolution Bicentennial Commission in 1976. *The Carrion Crow* (1948) was a one-act chamber opera, libretto by the composer, based on a radio play by John Jacob Niles. Its overture was given performances by orchestras throughout the United States, including the Los Angeles Philharmonic, the Rochester Philharmonic, the Indianapolis Symphony, and the Chicago Little Symphony. *Panels from a Theater Wall*, suite for orchestra (1949), was introduced in Rochester, N.Y., on April 27, 1949. That year, Serge Koussevitzky invited Fletcher to conduct a program of his works at Tanglewood.

Fletcher was the conductor at the Chicago Musical College Symphonies from 1949 to 1952, and of the Chicago Symphonietta from 1952 to 1956. In 1953 he attended the Cleveland Orchestra Conductors' Symposium on a Kulas Foundation grant where he studied conducting with George Szell. In 1956 he was appointed professor of music at the Arizona University in Tempe, Ariz., where he taught composition, theory, and conducting for the next twenty-two years, retiring as professor emeritus in 1978.

Fletcher's Symphony no. 1 (1950), introduced in Rochester, N.Y., under Hanson on April 24, 1951, was featured at the American Music Festival in

Washington, D.C., on June 3, 1962. In the *Washington Star*, Irving Lowens found it particularly effective "in a broadly elegiac slow movement which ever so often hinted at Bartókian tension." Two Orchestral Pieces (*Sumare* and *Wintare*, titles taken from Chaucerian English) was written in 1956 on a commission from the Door County Festival Concerts in Wisconsin, where it was introduced under Thor Johnson in the year of its composition. The first movement, based on a poem by Hilda Doolittle, was a portrait of the languor and oppressiveness of a hot day in deep summer. The second piece is a series of dance variations on a theme, "The Gonesome Days of Summer," which Fletcher had written in 1954 for the twenty-fifth anniversary of the Rockefeller Carillon Tower at the University of Chicago campus. The general style of these two pieces can best be described as a type of American impressionism. Though based on folklike melody and dance rhythms, it employs chordal parallelisms and the modal character of impressionism.

Among Fletcher's subsequent works, the following are notable: *Seven Cities of Cibola*, for orchestra (1961; Tempe, Ariz., October 20, 1971), a musical picture of the Spanish Conquistadores and their search for the cities of gold in New Mexico and Arizona; *The Sack of Calabasas*, (1964), an opera based on a narrative poem of John Myers, excerpts from which were heard in Phoenix, Ariz., on April 6, 1964; *Diaphony*, for symphonic band (1968; Phoenix, September 1, 1968), which emphasized unusual instrumental effects and sonorities while following the general pattern of the development of the human psyche; *Sōn*, a sonata for cello and piano (1972; Bowling Green State University, Ohio, January 6, 1974); *Cinco de Mayo*, a ballet suite for orchestra (1973; Tempe, Ariz., April 17, 1974), eight scenes based on the Fifth of May Mexican national festival, a work in which the composer embarked upon aleatoric devices; and String Quartet (1975; Philadelphia, April 20, 1979), written on a grant from the Arizona State University Music Department.

Fletcher has received grants from thr Ford Foundation and the National Endowment for the Arts in addition to several grants from Arizona State University. In 1951 he was the Illinois delegate to the International Music Festival in Pittsburg, Pa., and in 1974 and again in 1977 he represented United States Composers at the International Triennial Festliche Musiktage in Uster, Switzerland, where some of his works were heard. In 1976 he was elected to the Illinois Hall of Fame in Springfield. He has made numerous appearances in the United States and abroad as lecturer, commentator over radio and television, and conductor. He is the author of *Syllabus for Advanced Integrated Theory* (1962) and *Fundamental Principles of Counterpoint* (1967). On June 30, 1967, he married Gretchen Anna Walton in Tucson; they have four children.

THE COMPOSER SPEAKS: I hold no brief for simple music or for complex music. I write either or both, as it seems to fit the occasion, adapting the musical and technical concepts to the audiences or commissioning performers. As a musical director of symphonic, operatic, and choral organizations I have been painfully aware of the need to keep audiences excited about music.

It seems to me that contemporary composers have been least interested in melody. Whatever the texture or difficulty, I try to find and work with a melodic idea. This must be welded to fitting rhythmic, timbral, sonorous, and formal elements to create a convincing work. Rhythm has been with me since my first attempts at composition and conducting. In composing large works I have increasingly wrestled with the problems of form, and the invention of shapes and growth techniques.

A major purpose of my continuing creation is to express facets of the human condition in my music. Art, I believe, is a means of leading intelligent individuals to a greater depth of perception while revivifying their human spirit. I would like to write music for intelligent humans whether they are musically experienced or not. I seek a synthesis of craft and spirit.

PRINCIPAL WORKS: 4 sacred cantatas, for solo voices, chorus, and organ (1965–1978); 2 symphonies (1950, 1970); 2 piano concertos (1953, 1966).

A Rhapsody of Dances, for chamber orchestra (1935, revised for large orchestra in 1972); Nocturnes, 2 books for piano (1935); *Four American Dance Pieces*, for piano (1944); *Musicke for Christening*, for string orchestra (1944); *Song of Honor*, for orchestra (1944); *A Song for Warriors*, for orchestra (1944); *The Crisis*, for chorus and orchestra (1945); *An American Overture*, for orchestra (1945); *Panels from a Theater Wall*, for orchestra (1949); *The Pocket Encyclopedia of Orchestral Instruments*, for narrator and orchestra (1953); Two orchestral pieces: *Sumare* and *Wintare* (1956); *Lomatowi*, ballet pantomime (1957); *Tower Music*, for brass choir (1957); Clarinet Sonata (1959); *Seven Cities of Cibola*, for orchestra (1961); *The Sack of Calabasas*, opera 1964; *Dances from the Southwest*, for strings (1966); *Uroboros*, for percussion ensemble (1967); *Glyphs*, for chamber orchestra (1968); Concerto for Winds (1969); *Who Is Sylvia?*, for baritone, lute, oboe, bassoon, and guitar (1969); *Dyad*, for symphonic band (1970); Multiple Concerto, for five solo winds (1970); *Diversion*, for strings (1971); *Octocelli*, for eight solo cellos (1971); Trio, for flute, guitar, and piano (1972); *Sōn*, for cello and piano (1972); *The Dark Hills*, for chorus (1972); *Cinco de Mayo*, ballet suite for orchestra (1973); *Aubade*, for wind instruments (1974); Toccata, for piano (1974); *Quadra*, for percussion ensemble (1975); String Quartet (1975); *Saxson* II, for alto saxophone and string orchestra

(1977); *Zorticos* II, for double bass and piano (1977); *Judas*, cantata for tenor, oboe and viola (1978); Sonata for Violin Alone (1979); *Zorticos* III, for cello and piano (1979); *Zorticos* IV, for bassoon and piano (1979); Serenade, for orchestra (1979); *Symphonic Suite* (1980).

BIBLIOGRAPHY: *BBDM*; *Arizona Music News*, Spring 1978; *Dictionary of International Biography, 1978–79; Men of Achievement* (Cambridge, England, 1973); *Who's Who in the Midwest, 1978–79.*

Floyd, Carlisle Sessions, b. Latta, S.C., June 11, 1926.

One of America's most successful operatic composers, Floyd has carried on the Puccini-Menotti traditions of *verismo*. His operas, for which he has always provided his own librettos, are compelling theater in which plot, stage action, characterization, diction, and music are skillfully coordinated. He generates power in his music through half-spoken declamations that simulate inflections of speech but are regulated in pitch and rhythm and a strong and sometimes dissonant harmonic and polytonal language. But lyricism, emotion, and romantic feelings have not been sacrificed.

His father was a Methodist minister whose French Huguenot ancestors settled in Charleston, S.C, in the late 17th century; his mother, who came from a Scotch-Irish family that immigrated to the Carolinas before the American Revolution, was a trained pianist. Since his father was constantly on the move from one parish to another in South Carolina, Carlisle was transferred from public school to public school in his younger years. His mother started giving him some piano lessons when he was ten, but for some years after that whatever proficiency he acquired as pianist came from a trial-and-error process rather than formal instruction. For a long time music did not occupy a major role in his life, since he was talented in literature and the graphic arts and was a good athlete. At North High School in the town of North in South Carolina he was editor of the school paper and a member of the basketball team.

When he was sixteen he received a scholarship for Converse College in Spartanburg, S.C., where, from 1943–45, he majored in piano with Ernst Bacon and won first prize in a contest for one-act plays. When Bacon was appointed to the music faculty of Syracuse University in New York in 1945, Floyd followed him there for a continuation of piano study with Bacon. Upon receiving his bachelor of music degree at Syracuse in 1946, Floyd became a teacher of piano at Florida State University in Tallahassee in 1947. One year later he initiated there the first accredited course anywhere for composers and librettists covering the problems and techniques of coordinating music and text in operas. He remained at Florida State University for three decades as professor of composition.

On leave from the university in 1948–49, Floyd returned to Syracuse University to complete the requirements for his master of arts degree. In 1949–50 he studied piano privately with Sidney Foster, and during the summers of 1952 and 1955 with Rudolf Firkusny at Aspen, Colo.

Floyd's first serious attempts at composition were in opera, and from the first he wrote his own librettos. *Slow Dusk*, in one act (1949), was produced at Syracuse University in 1949, after which it was performed in several other universities and operatic workshops. *Fugitives*, a musical drama (1951), was seen at Florida State University in 1951 for a single performance, and has since been withdrawn by the composer.

Neither opera gave promise of the kind of artistic fulfillment Floyd would realize with his third opera, *Susannah*, nor hint at the kind of success he would achieve with it. When Floyd decided to make a modern-day setting of the Apocryphal story of Susannah and the Elders, it took him just ten days to write his libretto. The music was completed in 1953–54. Set in a present-day farm in the Tennessee mountains, the plot involved the seduction of Susannah by Reverend Blitch, come to save her soul, and who meets death at the hands of Susannah's avenging brother. To a text of great emotional impact, Floyd provided a score in which Bergian *Sprechstimme* was combined with Puccinilike lyricism and Wagnerian leitmotif technique. Simulation of American hymn tunes, folk songs, and square dances provided American flavoring. The opera was first produced at Florida State University on February 24, 1955. When the New York City Opera produced it a year and a half later (September 27, 1956), it enjoyed one of the greatest successes ever realized there by an American opera. In addition to the acclaim of critics, it received the New York Music Critics Circle Award and on June 25, 1958 represented American opera at the World's Fair in Brussels (its European premiere). Since then, this opera has found a durable place in the American repertoire, being continually revived by opera houses, at universities, colleges, and various opera workshops. On the strength of *Susannah*, Floyd was awarded a Guggenheim Fellowship in 1956, a Citation of Merit from the National Association of American Composers and Conductors in 1957, and was selected in 1959 as one of America's ten outstanding young men by the United States Junior Chamber of Commerce.

Temporarily digressing from the theater, Floyd wrote *Pilgrimage*, a cantata for voice and orchestra (1956) and, for Rudolf Firkusny, a Piano Sonata (1957), which Firkusny performed on October 3, 1959. On November 28, 1957, Carlisle Floyd married Margery Kay Reeder, a graduate student in literature at Florida State University.

When Floyd returned to the musical theater, he selected Emily Brontë's *Wuthering Heights* as the source for his libretto, a rare instance in which his operas did not have an American background and interest. *Wuthering Heights* was written in 1958 on a commission from the Santa Fe Opera. When produced in Santa Fe, N.M., on July 16, 1958, it was criticized for music that was judged uneven in quality and derivative and for a libretto cluttered with clichés. Such a response drove Floyd to make drastic revisions. When the new version was produced by the New York City Opera on April 9, 1959, the reception was far more favorable. In *Musical America*, Robert Sabin called it "a wholly successful and deeply moving opera—one of the best from an American composer," and in the *New York Times*, Howard Taubman found it had "warmth and sincerity . . . the work of a composer whose metier is the lyric theater."

Floyd's next opera, *The Passion of Jonathan Wade* (1962), commissioned by the New York City Opera on a grant from the Ford Foundation, was produced in New York on October 11, 1962. The setting is the post–Civil War period in South Carolina, and its theme, as the composer explained, centered around "a Northern occupation officer caught in a terrible conflict of conscience and duty during the early Reconstruction days in the South." Nobility, integrity, and idealism are destroyed by intolerance and hate. One of the musical highlights in the score is a spiritual sung by a black servant during the marriage ceremonies. There are other memorable pages of lyricism, notably a deeply moving love duet in the same scene. "In fact," remarked Ross Parmenter in his review in the *New York Times*, "there was so much that was pretty and melodious that one was inclined to wish it had been more purely a love story and less encumbered with a sense of dramatic history with philosophical overtones."

Two one-act operas followed. *The Sojourner and Mollie Sinclair* (1963) was commissioned by the Carolina Charter Tercentenary Commission for the 300th anniversary of the state of North Carolina and was intended primarily for television transmission. After being produced live in Raleigh, N.C., on December 2, 1963, it was taped for nationwide television broadcast. *Markheim* (1966), based on Robert Louis Stevenson's story, was written for the baritone Norman Treigle, who sang the title role when the opera was given its premiere in New Orleans on March 3, 1966.

Further growth of Floyd as a musical dramatist and as a portrayer of character was found in *Of Mice and Men* (1969), based on John Steinbeck's novel, written on a grant from the Ford Foundation. The opera concentrated on the relationship between the two migrant ranch hands who dream of owning a farm of their own—Lenny, an idiot, and his protector friend, George—in which both text and music provide probing insights into each character. When it was introduced by the Seattle Opera in Seattle, Wash., on Jaunary 22, 1970, Robert Commanday, reporting to the *New York Times*, found that Floyd's operatic style here made a notable advance in sophistication from *Susannah* and *Wuthering Heights*. "This new score enjoys a rhythmic fluidity that the others do not, a heightened play of asymmetries and changing accentuations and clear textures using light orchestral colors. . . . The vocal writing is fine, as is the structure of the arias assigned each principal, the two excellent duets, and one superb trio when George, Lennie and their new Partner exult over their dream ranch." Since the Seattle premiere, *Of Mice and Men* has been widely produced in the United States and Europe.

To commemorate the American bicentennial, and on a commission from the Houston Opera with a grant from the National Endowment for the Arts, Floyd wrote *Bilby's Doll*, introduced by the Houston Opera on February 27, 1976. Based on Esther Forbes's *A Mirror for Witches*, which Floyd adapted into a libretto, *Bilby's Doll* has a New England setting and a heroine who is a French orphan raised in the Puritan home of a sea captain who is accused by her foster mother of being a witch. To Floyd this drama symbolized "protection in our society—or the need of protection—of the poet, the rebel, the nonconformer, the kind of individual who goes underground when society is repressive. That's what Doll stands for. Here is a girl who refuses to live without magic, the demonic in her life. She won't renounce it." Though the score contains much atonal writing, the work is rich with lyricism. "I've never done anything remotely like it," Floyd has said. "I wanted to write so romantically, so gorgeously, particularly for Doll, because she herself is an archromantic. And in addition to that, the necessity of suggesting otherworldliness, the demonic, has forced me into a different kind of orchestral color. There is an exotic element that's new to me. The orchestra has to work in a Wagnerian sense to underscore what's going on onstage."

Floyd's eleventh opera, *Willie Stark* (1980), was commissioned jointly by the Houston Opera in Texas and the John F. Kennedy Center for the Performing Arts in Washington, D. C. The Houston Opera presented the world premiere on April 24, 1981 as part of a week-long celebration of its twenty-fifth anniversary. Willie Stark is a ruthless, oportunistic American politician who is the central character of Robert Penn Warren's novel *All the King's Men*, which the composer, in collaboration with Harold Prince, adapted into a libretto. "Mr. Floyd's work . . . ," reported Donal Henahan to the *New York Times* from Houston, "retold Mr. Warren's many-leveled tale in a one-dimensional Broadway musical style, which relied for most of its appeal on period flavor and tricky staging ideas. The music was pushed into the background rather effective-ly. . . . The composer . . . has put together a re-markably thin score, in a style that could be heard as a parody of Britten and Menotti."

When Floyd left Florida State University in 1976 he was appointed professor of music at the School of Music at the University of Houston in Texas. He also became codirector of the Houston Opera Studio, formed to provide training ground for young singers. From November 2 to 7, 1977, Floyd was honored for his contributions to American opera at Indiana Uni-versity in Bloomington with performances of his operatic music and presentation of a plaque. For sev-eral years, Floyd has served as chairman of the Opera Musical Theater of the National Endowment for the Arts.

THE COMPOSER SPEAKS: A creative artist isn't likely to be the best judge of his own work: We tend to make very subjective judgments. I quickly lose inter-est in a work of mine once I've seen it onstage, unless I'm involved in the production; I've staged *Susannah* all over the country, for example, but that is already something quite different from having written the work. I revise endlessly before and during the first rehearsals, changing notes, rhythms, cutting, rewrit-ing vocal lines; no vocal line is considered final in my book until the singer has tried it. After that I am willing to leave it alone.

Ten years ago, I'd have had all kinds of answers about the future of opera in America, but now I sim-ply don't know. The trends that seemed to be at work then have either turned in unexpected directions or not turned out at all. If anything, it seems to me that American opera has lost momentum, and composers nowadays face a real dilemma when they write an opera. Where will it be done? Where is the public? The traditional opera audience is inclined to be sus-picious of anything new, of opera in English, of opera as a dramatic presentation. . . . There are many discouraging aspects in this business of writing new operas, not the least of which is the Broadway economic bind that has afflicted our opera houses and created the necessity for a critical and popular smash the first time around. And I am not particularly hopeful that things will get better in the foreseeable future. But despite these far from satisfactory condi-tions, I know that I am never happier than when I am involved in the production of a new opera of mine.

PRINCIPAL WORKS: *Slow Dusk*, one-act opera (1949); *Lost Eden*, ballet (1952); *Susannah*, opera (1953–54); *Pilgrimage*, cantata for voice and orches-tra (1956); Piano Sonata (1957); *Wuthering Heights*, opera (1958); *The Mystery*, song cycle for voice and orchestra (1960); *Five Songs of Mother-hood*, for soprano and orchestra (1960); *The Passion of Jonathan Wade*, opera (1962); *The Sojourner and*

Mollie Sinclair, one-act opera (1963); *Markheim*, one-act opera (1966); Introduction, Aria, and Dance, for orchestra (1967); *Of Mice and Men*, opera (1969); *Flower and the Hawk*, monodrama for so-prano and orchestra (1972); *Bilby's Doll*, opera (1975); *In Celebration*, an overture for orchestra (1978); *Willie Stark*, opera (1980).

BIBLIOGRAPHY: *Musical America/High Fidelity*, February 1976; *New York Times*, May 28, 1972; *Opera News*, September 6, 1969; February 7, 1976.

Foote, Arthur William, b. Salem, Mass., March 5, 1853; d. Boston, April 8, 1937.

Foote was one of the few Americans of his time to receive his complete musical education in the United States. In spite of this he, like his colleagues of the New England school of composers, was thoroughly oriented to European music. Foote was a disciple of Brahms in the classical structures and romanticism of his instrumental music, and of Wagner in the or-chestration and chromaticism of his large choral works.

Both his parents were Anglo-Saxon from an old New England family, his father the editor of the *Sal-em Gazette*. When Arhtur's mother died in 1857, the four-year-old child was put in the care of his older sister, Mary Wilder Tiletson, an author. While at-tending Salem High School, Foote, aged fourteen, re-ceived his first music lessons: instruction on the piano with Fanny Paine. This was supplemented two years later by lessons in harmony from Stephen A. Emery at the New England Conservatory of Music in Bos-ton. In 1870 Foote entered Harvard University, where he conducted the Harvard Glee Club for two years (1872–74), took courses in music with John Knowles Paine, received his bachelor of music degree in 1874 and was elected to Phi Beta Kappa. Though he had no intention of becoming a musician, plan-ning a career in business, he took some lessons in organ during the summer of 1874 with Benjamin Lang. Convinced of Foote's talent, Lang used his in-fluence to steer Foote away from business toward a professional career in music. In 1874–75, Foote did graduate work at Harvard, acquiring the degree of master of arts in 1875, the first such degree given by an American university. In August 1875, Foote opened a studio for the teaching of the piano, an ac-tivity that would occupy him for the next half cen-tury. The following year he made his piano recital debut in Boston and became the organist of the Church of the Disciples in Boston.

He spent the summer of 1876 at the Bayreuth Fes-tival in Germany where he heard the first complete performance of the *Ring des Nibelungen*, an experi-ence that started him on his lifelong admiration for Wagner's music. One year later, on May 12, 1877, one of his compositions (Gavotte, for piano), received a public performance for the first time when Annette Essipoff presented it in Boston. In October 1878, Foote was appointed organist and choirmaster of the First Unitarian Church in Boston, a post he held until 1910.

On March 10, 1880, Foote initiated in Boston a series of chamber music concerts in which he often participated as pianist, and which gave concerts annually in Boston until the end of the century. Three Pieces, for cello and piano (1882), made its appearance in publication in 1882, Foote's first.

The Boston Symphony Orchestra, which for many years would be the showcase for his works, introduced his first significant work for orchestra, *In the Mountains* (1886), on February 5, 1887, Wilhelm Gericke conducting. This work proved so successful that it was repeated by the Boston Symphony the following season and on July 12, 1889, was featured at the Paris Exposition. The period 1885 to 1886 saw the writing of the Serenade in E, for strings, in which the composer reverted to a partially baroque structure and which the Boston Symphony premiered on May 15, 1886; and two large choral works greatly influenced by Wagner: *The Farewell of Hiawatha*, for men's voices and orchestra, and *The Wreck of the Hesperus*, a cantata for mixed voices and orchestra, both based on poems by Longfellow. On November 22, 1889, the Boston Symphony under Arthur Nikisch premiered Foote's Suite no. 2 in D, for strings (1889).

The style of the above works was one Foote would use for the rest of his life: thoroughly lyrical, with broad and stately melodies; romantic in rhapsodic moods; classical in structure; a reflection of his lifelong adoration of Brahms and Wagner. One of his best works for orchestra—the symphonic prologue *Francesca da Rimini* (1890), which received its premiere at a Boston Symphony concert on January 24, 1891—is characteristic. In its realistic and dramatic description of the Inferno, it sprang from both Liszt and (in its orchestration) Wagner; in its passionate love music, from Brahms.

Foote's main orchestrral and choral compositions in the 1890s included *The Skeleton in Armor*, a cantata for mixed voices and orchestra (1891); Cello Concerto (1893; Chicago, November 30, 1894); and the Orchestral Suite in D minor No. 1 (1896; Boston, March 7, 1896). But his main creative interest that decade was chamber music. To that field he contributed the Violin Sonata (1889), a piano quartet (1890), the String Quartet No. 2 (1894) and the Piano Quintet (1897). Between 1890 and 1910 he made numerous appearances as assisting artist with the Kneisel Quartet in performances of his chamber works requiring a piano.

Three of Foote's most famous works from the period 1907–18 were frequently performed in his lifetime and have been revived since his death. The first of these is perhaps his most famous composition, the Suite in E major, for strings (1907) a neoromantic work within a baroque structure that begins and ends with a fugue. Foote himself regarded this as one of his best creations. The first performance was given by the Boston Symphony Orchestra under Max Fiedler on April 16, 1909, after which it became so basic to that orchestra's repertoire that, during the composer's lifetime, it was repeated in 1921, 1925, 1929, and 1936. One day after Foote's death the Boston Symphony performed it as a memorial.

Then there was the *Four Character Pieces after Omar Khayyám*, for orchestra (c. 1907) episodes arranged from *The Five Poems after Omar Khayyám*, for piano, based on Omar Khayyám's verses. This is perhaps the most haunting and evocative music he ever wrote. The Chicago Symphony under Frederick Stock introduced in on December 13, 1907. *A Night Piece* (1918) was originally written for flute and string quartet for the San Francisco Chamber Music Society, which performed it on January 28, 1919, and then transcribed for flute and orchestra, a version introduced by the Boston Symphony under Pierre Monteux on April 13, 1923.

Foote wrote a considerable amount of other music: for organ, piano, chorus, solo voice. His finest piece for organ is the Suite in D (1904). He published over one hundred songs, the most popular of which are "The Night Has a Thousand Eyes," "I Know a Little Garden Patch," "Constancy," and "Ashes of Roses."

Foote received honorary doctorates in music from Trinity College in Hartford, Conn. (1919), and Dartmouth College in Hanover, N.H. (1925). In 1898 he was elected member of the National Institute of Arts and Letters and in 1913 made a fellow of the American Academy of Arts and Letters. From 1909 to 1912 he was president of the American Guild of Organists, which he helped organize. He was also the president of the Cecilia Society in Boston and of the Oliver Ditson Society for the Relief of Needy Musicians. He wrote the following manuals: *Modern Harmony in Theory and Practice*, in collaboration with W. R. Spalding (1905, revised 1959, republished as *Harmony* in 1969); *Some Practical Things in Piano Playing* (1909); and *Modulation and Related Harmonic Questions* (1919). *An Autobiography* was published privately and posthumously by his daughter in Norwood, Mass., in 1946, and reprinted in New York in 1978.

His eightieth birthday was celebrated by the Boston Symphony in 1933 with a concert of his works. He spent the summer before his death memorizing or relearning the piano literature of Bach and Beethoven and trying to limber up his fingers.

In 1950, a bust of Foote, the work of Bashka Paeff, was placed in the entrance hall of Jordan Hall in Boston.

Foote's three string quartets, Piano Quintet, first

Violin Sonata no. 1, Piano Sonata no. 1, Suite in D, for organ, and *Francesca da Rimini* were all revived in recordings in the 1970s.

THE COMPOSER SPEAKS: It is not easy to keep an open mind for changes and new developments, especially when these fly in the face of all that one has cared for. But we should pray not to become so hardened in tradition as not to be honest towards what may seem to be new and perhaps not of value.

It must be confessed, however, that since 1910, a severe strain has been put upon one's willingness to be hospitable to new ideas. There has been beyond doubt a sweeping away of a lot of rubbish, such as the uncompromising doctrines as to consecutive fifths, cross-relations, etc.; our ideas as to key relationships have been broadened (chiefly through Wagner); our feeling about form has become more elastic; knowledge of the orchestra is infinitely greater, and so on. Theory has always lagged behind practice. In fact, theory amounts to a registering of what has been accomplished (often without set purpose) by men bigger than their book knowledge.

Dissonance and consonance seem to me to be complementary; while music entirely consonant becomes monotonous, that which is constantly dissonant is not only tiresome, but, worse than this, unpleasant. Dissonance is not undesirable in itself, but often becomes so because of the unskillful way in which it is used.

PRINCIPAL WORKS: 4 suites for orchestra (1886–1908); 3 string quartets (1883, 1894, 1910); 2 piano trios (1883, 1909).

The Farewell of Hiawatha, a cantata for men's voices and orchestra (1885); *In the Mountains*, overture for orchestra (1886, revised 1910); Serenade in E, for strings (1886); *The Wreck of the Hesperus*, cantata for chorus (1887); Violin Sonata (1889); *Francesca da Rimini*, symphonic prologue (1890); Piano Quartet (1890); *The Skeleton in Armor*, cantata for chorus and orchestra (1891); Cello Concerto (1893); Piano Quintet (1897); Music for the Synagogue, for chorus (1900); Suite in D, for organ (1904); *Four Character Pieces after Omar Khayyâm*, for orchestra, also for piano (c. 1907); Suite in E major (1907); Cello Sonata (c. 1912); *In the Gateway of Ispaham*, for women's voices and orchestra (1914); *A Night Piece*, for flute and string quartet, also for flute and orchestra (1918).

BIBLIOGRAPHY: Chase, Gilbert, *America's Music* (N.Y., 1955); Foote, Arthur, *An Autobiography* (Norwood, Mass., 1946, reprinted 1978); Howard, John Tasker, *Our American Music* (N.Y., 1946); Kopp, F. "Arthur Foote, American Composer and Theorist" (doctoral thesis, Rochester, N.Y., 1957); *Modern Music*, May–June 1937; *Musical Quarter-ly*, January 1937; *New York Times*, April 18, 1937.

Foss, Lukas (originally Fuchs, Lukas), b. Berlin, Germany, August 15, 1922. American citizen, 1942.

As a young student, Foss was influenced by Hindemith's counterpoint. His first success came with a classic-romantic and consonant style, inspired either by American or biblical texts. After the late 1950s, he became a leading figure in the avant-garde movement, with particular emphasis for a while on aleatory and improvisatory methods.

He was one of two children of highly cultured parents, his father being a professor of philosophy and his mother a painter. Given an accordion when he was six, Lukas was soon able to accompany himself singing German folk songs. When he was seven he began to study piano with Julius Goldstein-Herford, who, in 1929, supplemented this with lessons in theory. Having become interested in the music of Bach, Haydn, and Mozart, among the older masters, Lukas, age seven, began writing music in emulation of their style. A performance of *The Marriage of Figaro* when he was nine convinced him that he wanted to become a professional musician. He acquired the score and learned the entire second-act finale by heart, a performance of which at the piano often entertained his family and its friends.

Foss was ten when Hitler came to power in Germany. Sensing the menace of the rising tide of nazism, the father left with his family in 1933 for Paris, where they stayed for the next four years. In Paris Foss attended the Lycée Pasteur for his academic education, while studying piano with Lazare Lévy, composition with Noël Gallon, flute with Marcel Moyse, and orchestration with Felix Wolfes. In his last year in Paris he attended the Paris Conservatory briefly.

In 1937, the Foss family migrated to the United States, henceforth its permanent home and land of citizenship. That year, the fifteen-year-old Foss had his first publication: Four Two-Voice Inventions, for piano. From 1937 to 1940 he attended the Curtis Institute of Music in Philadelphia, where his teachers included Rosario Scalero (composition), Isabelle Vengerova (piano) and Fritz Reiner (conducting). During the summer of 1940 he was one of the first students registered for the newly opened Berkshire Music Center at Tanglewood, Mass. There he studied conducting with Serge Koussevitzky (whose protégé he soon became as well as his assistant in the conducting class in 1942) and composition with Paul Hindemith. Piano pieces, a violin sonata, and some songs represented a gradual attempt to break with the more formalized techniques of classical music toward greater independence of harmonic and contrapuntal thought along Hindemithian neoclassical lines. On a commission he wrote incidental music for a New York children's production of Shakespeare's *The Tempest* in 1940, which opened on March 31, 1940, and which a critic for *Time* described as "remarkably workmanlike . . . archaic in mood, making deft use of a small orchestra." In 1939, Foss made his conducting debut by appearing as a guest with the Pittsburgh Symphony.

In 1940–41, Foss continued his study of composition with Hindemith at Yale University. But by 1941 he was beginning to break loose from Hindemith's influence, demonstrated in his Two Pieces for Orchestra (1941), in which a romantic approach and a greater concern for harmonic interest replaced his former linear idiom. The second of these pieces, *Allegro concertante*, was performed in Philadelphia and New York in 1941. In 1942, Foss was awarded a Pulitzer traveling fellowship on the strength of his music to *The Tempest*.

Conducting a performance of Aaron Copland's *Billy the Kid* at the Berkshire Music Center during the summer of 1941 fired Foss with the ambition to write music inspired by the country of his adoption. A reading of Carl Sandburg's poem "The Prairie" provided Foss with the inspiration and material for his first American-oriented composition, and the most ambitious he had thus far attempted. With *The Prairie*, a cantata for solo voices, chorus, and orchestra (1942), Foss realized his first success as a composer. Without attempting to quote or even simulate American folk music, he managed to achieve an American musical identity through broad, sweeping melodies and sonorities suggestive of vast open spaces. This work was first heard as an orchestral suite, performed by the Boston Symphony under Koussevitzky on October 15, 1943. A half year later, on May 15, 1944, the complete work (with the vocal and choral sections) was introduced by the Collegiate Chorale under Robert Shaw in New York where it was awarded the New York Music Critics Circle Award. The following season Artur Rodzinski programmed it for a concert of the New York Philharmonic.

For a number of years after that, Foss continued to favor a classic-romantic style. In 1944 he wrote three ballet scores and two orchestral compositions. The ballets were *The Heart Remembers*, produced in New York on April 2, 1944; *The Gift of the Magi*, based on the O. Henry story, performed by the Ballet Theater in Boston on October 5, 1945; and *Within These Walls*. The two orchestral works were contrasts in mood. Symphony in G, music of high, joyous spirits, was introduced by the Pittsburgh Symphony Orchestra under Reiner on February 4, 1945. *Ode* was a threnody dedicated to "those who will not return" and inspired by the line of John Donne reading "any man's death diminishes me." Though it has no specific program, its music was intended to suggest, as Foss explained, "crisis, war, and ultimately

faith." *Ode* was given its premiere on March 15, 1945, by the New York Philharmonic under George Szell. Thirteen years later Foss revised *Ode*, the new version getting its first performance in October 1958 in Philadelphia by the Philadelphia Orchestra under Eugene Ormandy.

All this while, Foss was also achieving note as a concert pianist by appearing as a soloist with major American orchestras. In 1944, he was appointed official pianist of the Boston Symphony Orchestra, remaining in this post for the next six years. In 1946 he initiated his career as teacher through an appointment to the Berkshire Music Center.

On a Guggenheim Fellowship in 1945 (the youngest composer ever to get it) Foss went to work on two biblical cantatas as "an inner metamorphosis" began taking place. "I started studying 17th- and 18th-century music with renewed intensity, because it became apparent to me that the late 19th- and 20th- century composer commands an increasingly limited field of expression." *The Song of Anguish*, for baritone and orchestra (1945), text from Isaiah, was commissioned by the Kulas Foundation in Cleveland. This music received its initial hearing as a background for a dance performed by Pauline Kohner at Jacob's Pillow in Massachusetts during the summer of 1948. The first concert presentation followed on March 10, 1950, at a concert of the Boston Symphony with the composer conducting and Marko Rothmuller, soloist. *Song of Songs*, for soprano and orchestra (1946), a setting of four of Solomon's songs, was commissioned by the League of Composers for the soprano Ellabelle Davis, who introduced it with the Boston Symphony under Koussevitzky on March 7, 1947. Koussevitzky's enthusiasm for this work led him to break Boston Symphony precedent by performing it eight times in nine days. Both biblical cantatas are songful, sensuous in style, with page upon page of great emotional intensity.

On the day of Gandhi's death on January 30, 1948, Foss began writing an orchestral work, *Recordare*, using for his title a term from the traditional Requiem Mass connoting remembrance. The funereal music of the first and third parts is contrasted with the agitation of the middle section. The Boston Symphony under Koussevitzky introduced it on December 31, 1948. In 1949 came Foss's Piano Concerto no. 2, which he himself performed at its world premiere on October 7, 1951, in Venice; after receiving its American premiere in Boston in November 1951, it was awarded the Horblit-Boston Symphony Award. A revision of this concerto in 1953 earned Foss the New York Music Critics Circle Award again. The year of 1949 also witnessed Foss's first attempt at writing opera. *The Jumping Frog of Calaveras County*—libretto by Jean Karsavina based on Mark Twain's story—was produced at Indiana University in Bloomington on May 18, 1950. Three weeks later it was seen in New York, and in 1956 it received its German premiere in Cologne. This score is in a pronounced American idiom, with one cowboy tune interpolated.

Between 1950 and 1952, Foss lived in Rome on a Fulbright fellowship and as fellow of the American Academy and in October 1951 he married Cornelia Brendel, an artist, with whom he has had a son and a daughter. One year after his return to the United States, Foss succeeded Arnold Schoenberg as professor of composition at the University of California in Los Angeles. There, in 1957, he founded the Improvisation Chamber Ensemble made up of four virtuosos who toured the United States in spontaneous performances of improvised music. "It all started very modestly as a means of helping the students," Foss recalls, "but suddenly a door opened for me and I saw a vast new territory to explore." He also explained these improvisation performances as follows: "Improvisation is not composition. It relates to composition, much in the same way a sketch relates to the finished work of art. . . . It is . . . a spontaneous sketchlike and—incidentally—unrepeatable expression full of surprises for the listener and for the performer as well."

Improvisation and other processes of indeterminacy would give Foss's creativity a new direction in the 1960s. But before that happened he continued in the 1950s to produce compositions along the more traditional route they had thus far been traveling. Commissioned by the Louisville Orchestra in Kentucky, he completed in 1952 a cantata for narrator, tenor, and chorus, *A Parable of Death*, which used a story and several poems of Rainer Maria Rilke as text. The narrator, Foss says, tells "quietly and intimately what appears to be an old legend about a man, a woman. Chorus and solo tenor comment on the story, their lines taken from Rilke's poems." This cantata was premiered on March 11, 1953, by the Louisville Orchestra under Robert Whitney, with Vera Zorina (for whom it was written) as narrator.

Between 1953 and 1955, Foss wrote on a commission from the NBC Opera Company his only full-length opera to date, *Griffelkin*, a fantasy with a text by Alastair Reid based on a Grimm fairy tale. It was televised over the national network of NBC on November 6, 1955. For this tale for children, Foss created music simple and direct in its approach, tuneful in its arias, duets, choruses, and instrumental pages and in its digressions into popular-music idioms, engagingly witty in the way a bravura aria is parodied and a Mozart piano sonata is quoted. Before the 1950s ended, Foss completed a delightful little opera, this one requiring only nine minutes for performance. It was called *Introductions and Goodbyes* (1959), libretto by Gian-Carlo Menotti, and enlisting just one leading character (a baritone), who is the host at a cocktail party, and a chorus, which represents his guests. Commissioned for the Festival of Two Worlds in Spoleto, Italy, of which Menotti was

founder and director, *Introductions and Goodbyes* was produced there in June 1960; but one month earlier, on May 6, it was heard for the first time anywhere in a concert performance by the New York Philharmonic with Leonard Bernstein conducting.

Between these two operas came the *Symphony of Chorales* (1955–58), an orchestral work written on commission from the Koussevitzky Music Foundation at the invitation of the Friends of Albert Schweitzer in Boston to honor Schweitzer; its first performance was given by the Pittsburgh Symphony under William Steinberg on October 24, 1958. This work is entirely based on chorales by Johann Sebastian Bach.

In 1960, Foss received his second Guggenheim Fellowship. That year he toured the Soviet Union under the auspices of the U. S. State Department, conducting and performing his own works. In 1964–65, Foss directed in New York "Evenings for New Music," a series of four chamber music concerts devoted primarily to avant-garde music, and was director of the Franco-American Festival held by the New York Philharmonic at the Lincoln Center for the Performing Arts in New York. In 1965 he was the director-conductor of the Stravinsky Festival at Lincoln Center.

In the 1960s, Foss was embracing and becoming a major force in the avant-garde movement by developing the improvisational and aleatory methods in provocative and innovative compositions. In collaboration with two of his students he wrote Concerto for Improvising Instruments and Orchestra in 1960 for a tour of the East and Middle West by the Improvisation Chamber Ensemble, which performed it for the first time on October 7, 1960, with the Philadelphia Orchestra under Eugene Ormandy. For this work, Foss prepared a chart suggesting germ motives, rhythmic patterns, entrances, and exits of each individual instrumentalist and other basic ideas which the soloists could select at will and elaborate upon spontaneously during the actual performance.

Two weeks later, the New York Philharmonic under Leonard Bernstein offered the premiere of Foss's *Time Cycle*, for soprano and orchestra (1960), Foss's most significant composition to that time and one of the greatest successes he has enjoyed as composer. Written on a grant from the Ford Foundation for the soprano Adele Addison, *Time Cycle* is made up of four songs using poems by W. H. Auden and A. E. Housman as texts for the first two, some lines of Kafka's diaries for the third, and a poem from Nietzsche's *Thus Spake Zarathustra* for the fourth. Each of these textual items makes some reference to time or clocks or bells. As a unifying factor in his score, Foss continually repeated a single chord (C-sharp, A, B, D-sharp) in various inversions. Indeterminacy appeared in interludes (since discarded) between one song and the next for piano, clarinet, cello and percussion, intended to serve as a spontaneously arrived-at commentary on time; during the rendition of each song the improvising instruments were silent as the orchestra became the accompaniment. When *Time Cycle* was introduced on October 20, 1960, at a concert of the New York Philharmonic under Bernstein, the entire work was repeated to enhance the audience's comprehension. About two years later, at the Stratford Festival in Ontario, it inspired an ovation, and Glenn Gould, the festival director, described it as "the most important work in at least ten years." The New York Music Critics Circle presented the composition with its award in 1961; and two different recording versions were released, the second without the improvised interludes and without the orchestra, the accompaniment provided solely by the quartet of instruments. This shorter version received its first hearing at Tanglewood on July 10, 1961. The music of *Time Cycle* was used for a ballet of the same name, produced by the New Contemporary Ballet and choreographed by William Forsyth. That company premiered the ballet in Stuttgart, Germany, in 1979 and in the United States on November 26, 1980 in New York.

Indeterminacy entered into the Concert for Cello, Orchestra and Tape (1966), which Mstislav Rostropovich introduced in New York on March 5, 1967, by allowing the soloist to select any one of three composed orchestral accompaniments he wishes. This was also Foss's first composition for an electronically amplified solo instrument.

Avant-garde methods other than indeterminacy are encountered in other Foss compositions. In *Echoi*, for piano, percussion, clarinet, and cello (1963; N.Y., November 11, 1963), the percussion group includes a garbage can, and the percussionist controls the action of his fellow musicians. In *Elytres*, for flute, two violins, and ensemble (1964; Los Angeles, December 8, 1964) a percussionist plays "*à la mandoline*" with mallets on the strings of the piano soundboard, and all the instruments play only in high register and solely in the G clef. In *Ni bruit, ni vitesse*, for two pianos (1973), the pianists perform on the keyboard and percussionists on the piano strings.

Elytres is one of three compositions which, while they can be played differently at different performances, are nevertheless not aleatory but written out. The other two works are *The Fragments of Archilochos*, for countertenor, speakers, chorus, mandolin, guitar, and percussion (1965), and *For Twenty-four Winds* (1966). In each case the full score is written out. But an accompanying diagram is so marked that only a small amount of possible combinations is heard at any given time. Different combinations can be used at different concerts, so that actually it is possible to create hundreds of different works from any single composition.

Still another unusual practice for Foss has been to use the music of others as the starting point for his own compositions. *Phorion*, for strings, electronic organ, electronically amplified harpsichord or piano, and amplified harp or electric guitar (1966), which the Women's Committee for Symphony Orchestra commissioned, used the notes of the Prelude of Bach's E major Partita for solo violin, adapted and distorted at Foss's discretion. *Phorion* was first performed on April 27, 1967, by the New York Philharmonic under Bernstein. In *Non Improvisation*, for four players (1967), material from Bach's Concerto in D minor, for clavier and orchestra, was juxtaposed to sounds created by an electric organ and gong. *Baroque Variations*, for orchestra (1967), commissioned by the Lincoln Center for the Performing Arts, borrowed music from Handel and Domenico Scarlatti as well as incorporating the earlier *Phorion*, with its Bach quotation. *Geod* (1969; Hamburg, Germany, December 6, 1969)—which divided the orchestra into four groups, each with its own conductor, and expanding on the *Elytres* idea of every performance selecting from the total—is an Ivesian recall of folk songs (the songs chosen by the performer). American tunes are also fragmented in *Folksong for Orchestra* (1975; Baltimore, Md., January 21, 1976). Reviewing *Folksong for Orchestra* for the *Baltimore Morning Sun*, Elliott W. Galkin wrote: "What . . . Foss has done is recall nostalgically those folk tunes which he learned during his youth ('On Top of Old Smokey' is the most familiar) and exploit them in a manner brilliant in terms of its echoes and antiphonies. . . . Not only as in Ives' music, are there effects of little bands emerging and fading away, each with a snippet of popular song, but there are moments when the mutations of phrases and color are dependent on the element of ever-shifting gradations of loudness and softness. . . . This is, as a result, impressionistic music in the most contemporary terms." *The American Cantata*, for tenor, soprano, two speakers, chorus, and orchestra (1976), quotes or fragmentizes seven folk tunes and one Negro spiritual. Commissioned by the American Choral Directors Association and the National Endowment for the Arts—and with text assembled by Arien Sachs and Lukas Foss consisting exclusively of quotes—it was first introduced in Interlochen, Mich., on July 24, 1976, and then, following an elaborate revision, performed by the New York Philharmonic under Leonard Bernstein on December 1, 1977.

MAP, acronym for "men at play" (1973), is a multimedia production in which game rules were set for the five musicians, each playing several instruments, each moving about the stage and auditorium. *Orpheus* is a programmatic concerto for viola or guitar or cello, and orchestra (1972), premiered at the Ojai Festival in California in 1973, Michael Tilson Thomas conducting and Jesse Levine, soloist. String Quartet no. 3 (1975)—commissioned by the New York State Council for the Arts in conjunction with the Brooklyn Philharmonia—became *Quartet Plus* in 1977 (Brooklyn, N.Y., April 29, 1977) when a narrator, videotape, and second string quartet were added. Quintets for Orchestra (1978) originated as a quintet for brass before it was rewritten for orchestra. It called for five groups of five voices each with a five-note chord endlessly repeated, varied, transposed, and inverted dominating the entire composition; its world premiere took place on May 2, 1979, with the composer conducting the Cleveland Orchestra.

From 1963 to 1970, Foss was the conductor of the Buffalo Symphony, where he often introduced innovative programs of avant-garde music. There, in 1963, with funds from the Rockefeller Foundation, he developed (with Allen Sapp) the Center for the Creative and Performing Arts at Buffalo University as a laboratory in which musicians could come to do experimental work. Foss was also the director-conductor of the Festival of Arts Today in Buffalo in 1966 and 1967. Since 1971 Foss has been the conductor of the Brooklyn (N.Y.) Philharmonia, and from 1972 to 1975, conductor and musical adviser of the Jerusalem Symphony Orchestra. In 1981-82 he assumed the post of music director of the Milwaukee Symphony. His appearances as guest conductor have been worldwide.

Foss was visiting professor of music at Harvard (1969-1970) and the Manhattan School of Music in New York (1972-73), and composer-in-residence at the University of Cincinnati Conservatory of Music (1975). He has also lectured extensively in colleges and universities throughout the United States and Canada.

He was awarded an honorary doctorate in letters from Los Angeles Conservatory of Music in 1956, and in 1957 he received a Creative Music Grant from the National Institute of Arts and Letters, of which he became a member in 1963. In 1976, he was given the New York City Award for special contributions to the arts and, in 1979, an award from the American Society of Composers, Authors, and Publishers (ASCAP) for "adventurous programming."

THE COMPOSER SPEAKS: I think that, if you are going to have a big foot in the future, you've got to have a big foot in the past. That creates real strength. Then you stand well balanced. I think that's healthy. Don't burn the past in you—the people who ignore the past become dabblers.

The artist who feels that art is not an escape from the world but a direct expression of it . . . always has the urge to come to grips with the problems of his time and seeks their solution in his particular field of endeavor. Time can thus become a great incentive.

PRINCIPAL WORKS: 3 string quartets (1947, 1973, 1975); 2 piano concertos (1942; 1949, revised 1953).

The Prairie, cantata for vocal soloists, chorus, and

orchestra (1942); Symphony in G (1944); *Ode*, for orchestra (1944); *The Song of Anguish*, cantata for baritone and orchestra, or chamber orchestra, or piano (1945); *Song of Songs*, cantata for soprano and orchestra (1946); *Recordare*, for orchestra (1948); Oboe Concerto (1948); *The Jumping Frog of Calaveras County*, opera (1949); *A Parable of Death*, for narrator, tenor, chorus, and orchestra or chamber orchestra (1952); *Griffelkin*, opera (1953-55); Psalms, for chorus and orchestra (1955-56); *Symphony of Chorales*, for orchestra (1958); *Introductions and Goodbyes*, one-act opera (1959); Concerto for Improvising Instruments and Orchestra (1960); *Time Cycle*, four songs for soprano and orchestra or chamber orchestra (1959-60); *Echoi*, for clarinet, cello, percussion and piano (1961-63); *Elytres*, for flute, two violins, and ensemble (1964); *The Fragments of Archilochos*, for countertenor, speakers, chorus and chamber ensemble (1965); *Phorion*, for electric guitar, electric piano, electric organ (1966); Concert for Cello, Orchestra, and Tape (1966); *Baroque Variations*, for orchestra (1967); *Paradigm*, for five instruments and percussion (1968); *Geod*, for orchestra with optional voices (1969); *Orpheus*, concerto for viola, or cello or guitar and orchestra (1972); *Ni bruit, ni vitesse*, for two pianos and two percussion (1973); *MAP*, "a musical game," a multimedia production with any five players (1973); Fanfare, for orchestra (1973); Concerto for Solo Percussion and Orchestra (1974); *Folk Song for Orchestra* (1975); *Salomone Rossi*, suite for orchestra (1975); *American Cantata*, for tenor, chorus, and orchestra (1976); Music for Six, for any six instruments (1977); *Quartet Plus*, for narrator and double string quartet (1977); Brass Quintet (1978); *Thirteen Ways of Looking at a Blackbird*, for voice, distant flute, piano and percussion (1978); Quintets for Orchestra (1978); *Round a Common Center*, for piano, three or four strings and optional voice (1979).

BIBLIOGRAPHY: Goss, Madeleine, *Modern Music Makers* (N.Y., 1952); Thomson, Virgil, *American Music Since 1910* (N.Y., 1970); *High Fidelity/Musical America*, January 1981; *New Yorker*, January 30, 1965; *New York Times*, October 13, 1971, January 27, 1978, October 21, 1979; *Saturday Review*, February 26, 1967.

Franco, Johan Henri Gustav, b. Zaandam, Holland, July 12, 1908. American citizen, 1942.

Franco is unique among contemporary composers in his predilection for the carillon, to which he has brought artistic significance in over a hundred compositions, both soloistically and as part of the instrumentation for larger works. But he has also written extensively for the more conventional instruments and virtually in every musical medium except opera. He is a modern mystic, a spiritual descendant of the

Dutch contrapuntists of the baroque era who, nevertheless, speaks very much with a 20th-century vocabulary.

His father was an architect, and his mother an artist who was highly musical both as singer and pianist. Johan's interest in music reaches back to his earliest years. He started improvising on the piano when he was four, and in 1918 began receiving piano instruction from Eva van Dantzig. At the first Municipal High School in the Hague he played with the school orchestra and performed with it concertos by Bach and Mozart. Upon graduating from high school in 1928, he started a five-year period of the study of harmony, counterpoint, orchestration, and composition with one of Holland's foremost composers and teachers, Willem Pijper. At the same time, Franco studied law at the University of Amsterdam for two years (1929–31), then from 1931–1934 attended the Kunstnijverheid Institute for the study of architecture and furniture designing. At that time, he designed and supervised the construction of three houses in Amstelreen, a suburb of Amsterdam, for three composers.

By 1931 he had become deeply involved in composition. Under the influence of his teacher, Pijper, and Bertus van Lier, a Pijper student who became an esteemed composer in his own right, Franco wrote his String Quartet no. 1 (1931); the Sinfonia, for chamber orchestra (1932), which was performed in Utrecht on March 6, 1933; and his Symphony no. 1 (1933), introduced by the Rotterdam Philharmonic on October 6, 1934.

Later that year (1934) Franco immigrated to the United States, making his home for the next fourteen years in New York City, where several of his works were performed: *In Memoriam (Elegy)* for string orchestra (1932–36), heard in New York on November 16, 1941, Dean Dixon conducting; *Serenata concertante*, for piano and chamber orchestra (1938), first heard on March 11, 1940, performed by William Masselos; and Symphony no. 3, for piano and orchestra (1940), conducted by Leon Barzin on March 17, 1941, with William Masselos, soloist. Abroad, his *Concerto lirico* no. 1, for violin and orchestra (the first of six concertos for various solo instruments bearing the title "lirico"), which he had written in 1937, was introduced by the violinist Olly Folge Fonden, the first wife of Henk Badings, the eminent Dutch composer.

In 1941, Franco wrote *Baconiana*, a tone poem inspired by the life of Francis Bacon. A descending motive in this work representing Bacon was later used by Franco in several other compositions based on the subject of Bacon, such as *The Virgin Queen's Dream Monologue*, an aria for dramatic soprano and orchestra (1947), originally planned as an aria for an opera and in 1952 made into a concert aria which was given its first performance at the Southeastern Composers League Forum at the University of Ala-

bama. This motive can also be found in the *Four Miniatures and Encore* for solo flute (1942–43), in the nonprogrammatic Suite for Violin and Piano (1947) and in the Symphony no. 5, *The Cosmos* (1958).

During World War II, in 1942–43, Franco served as company clerk in the U. S. Army and later in the air force. On March 28, 1948, in Washington, D.C., he married Eloise Bauder Lavrischeff, a successful author and poet who, in succeeding years, provided texts for some of Franco's compositions. Upon their marriage, the Francos settled in Virginia Beach, Virginia, which has remained their home ever since.

In his later symphonies and other orchestral works, string quartets, various compositions for piano and other solo instruments, for solo voice, and the incidental music for five stage productions of the Everyman Players under Orlin Corey between 1963 and 1972, Franco developed his personal style. It is characterized by understatement. Franco has a deep respect for the tonal functions of tonic, dominant, and subdominant. He is frequently lyrical, he often dramatizes his writing with rapidly changing moods, and he maintains a 20th-century posture through his polymodal, polytonal, and polyrhythmic idioms. This is the basic language of his last four quartets (1949, 1950, 1953, 1960), his last two symphonies (1950, 1958), and the "lirico concertos" for cello (1962), piano (1967), percussion (1970), guitar (1971), and flute (1974).

Franco wrote his first composition for the carillon in 1949—*Hymn to the Sun*. "I recall a visit as a child to the Jef Denijn carillon recital in Mechlin," he recalls, "and I distinctly remember the reverent atmosphere and complete silence in the area surrounding the great St. Rombouts tower. . . . As a rule, however, the carillon in Europe is not a concert instrument yet. . . . In Europe, the objections could be that the old and familiar carillons were so 'delightfully' out of tune and the claviers hopelessly obsolete before World War II. Anyway, it never occurred to me while I lived and grew up in the Netherlands that the carillon was a living instrument, ready to reproduce the creative children of living composers. . . . I lived in the United States almost twenty years before I fully realized that here the carillons were 'in tune' and were played from highly efficient claviers." From 1953 on, Franco wrote twelve partitas, two fantasies, forty preludes and toccatas, many nocturnes, "seven biblical sketches" and sundry other solo pieces for the carillon. He also used the carillon extensively as part of the instrumentation of such larger works as the cantata *As the Prophets Foretold*, for solo voices, chorus, brass, and carillon (1956), and the carillon-ballet with narrator *The Ways of Water* (1978), both to texts by his wife; also the incidental music to *Romans by St. Paul*, for a cappella voices and carillon (1963; Los Angeles, October 10, 1963), a production that toured Europe in 1966 and was videotaped by CBS-TV in 1970.

Franco has also worked successfully with the guitar, beginning with *Three Prayers* (1959), three two-voice inventions in which Franco concentrated on the expressive quality of that instrument while emphasizing its vocal character. After 1970, when he met and was influenced by the guitarist and composer Angelo Gilardino in Milan, Franco grew increasingly ambitious in his guitar compositions, producing works such as the *American Folk Song Suite*, for guitar (1970), and the *Concerto lirico* no. 5, for guitar and chamber orchestra (1971).

In 1974, Franco was awarded first prize at the Delius Festival in Jacksonville, Fla., for his Ode, for male chorus and symphonic band (1969; Jacksonville, 1974), on a text by his wife.

THE COMPOSER SPEAKS: I have learned to trust inspiration exclusively for my compositions. All else is merely scaffolding.

PRINCIPAL WORKS: 40 toccatas, for carillon (1953–1979); 12 partitas, for carillon (1953–76); 7 biblical sketches, for carillon (1977–78); 6 partitas for piano (1940–52); 6 string quartets (1931–60); 5 symphonies (1933–58); 3 nocturnes for piano (1941, 1949, 1959); 2 sonatas for solo cello (1950, 1951).

In Memoriam (*Elegy*), for string orchestra (1932–36); *Péripétie*, tone poem for orchestra (1935–36); *Concerto lirico* no. 1, for violin and orchestra (1937); *Serenata concertante*, for piano and chamber orchestra (1938); *Baconiana*, tone poem for orchestra (1941); Sonata for Solo Violin (1944); Theme and Variations, for piano (1944); Suite, for string orchestra (1945); Divertimento, for flute and strings (1947); *Three Temple Dances*, for piano (1948); Fantasy, for cello and orchestra (1951); Viola Sonata (1951); *American Folk Song Suite*, for carillon (1952); *As the Prophets Foretold*, cantata for vocal soloists, chorus, brass, and carillon (1956); Suite no. 2, for organ (1956); *Three Prayers*, for guitar (1959); *Songs of the Spirit*, for voice, wind quintet or piano (1960); *Supplication, Revelation, and Triumph*, for orchestra (1961–67); *Concerto lirico* no. 2, for cello and orchestra (1962); *Suite of Prayers*, for organ (1962); Suite, for solo tenor and saxophone (1964); *Twelve Words*, for voice and piano (1965); *Concerto lirico* no. 3, for piano and chamber orchestra (1967); *Sayings of the Word*, for voice and piano (1968); *The Bells of Zion*, for carillon (1968); Ode, for male chorus and symphonic band (1969); *Concerto lirico* no. 4, for percussion and chamber orchestra (1970); *American Folk Song Suite*, for guitar (1970); Four Pieces, for guitar (1970); *Concerto lirico* no. 5, for guitar and orchestra (1971); Passacaglia, for carillon (1971); *Diptych*, for flute and electronic tape (1972); *Concerto lirico* no. 6, for flute and chamber orchestra (1974); Twelve Preludes, for piano (1975); Twelve Miniatures, for carillon (1976).

BIBLIOGRAPHY: *DCM*; *American Composers Alliance Bulletin*, vol. 8, no. 3, 1959; *Who's Who in America, 1980–81*.

Fry, William Henry, b. Philadelphia, Pa., August 10, 1813; d. Santa Cruz, West Indies, September 21, 1864.

As a journalist and lecturer, Fry was a passionate promoter of American music, the American composer, and American operas produced in English.

He was one of five sons of William Fry, the founder and publisher of the *National Gazette* in Philadelphia. Three of William Henry Fry's brothers had an interest in drama. Joseph was the librettist for Fry's operas and two others wrote plays that were produced. William Henry received his academic education in Philadelphia's public schools and at Mount St. Mary's College in Emmitsburg, Md. Musically, he was self-taught except for some lessons in theory with Leopold Meignen. Fry learned to play the piano by listening to the lessons given to his older brother, Joseph. When William Henry was fourteen he wrote his first orchestral overture and by the time he was twenty-one he had written several more, one of which was performed by the Philharmonic Society of Philadelphia, which awarded him a gold medal for it. Another of his overtures was given by the orchestra of the Italian Opera Company, and a third, *Pastoral Overture*, by the Philharmonic Society of Philadelphia in December 1836.

Since he planned a career in journalism rather than music, Fry began working in his father's office, writing unsigned music criticisms for the *National Gazette* from 1836 on, and becoming a full-ranking member of the editorial staff in 1839. In 1844, he was made the editor of the *Philadelphia Ledger*. But all this time he remained deeply involved with music as an amateur. He steeped himself in the operas of Bellini, Donizetti, Rossini and Balfe. On January 11, 1841, he was the musical director of a performance of Bellini's *Norma* in Philadelphia. *Norma* was his model when he wrote his first completed opera in 1841, *Aurelia, the Vestal*, his brother's libretto developing the familiar theme of the love of a vestal virgin for a Roman Christian nobleman. In this opera, Fry used some fragments from an earlier unfinished opera, *Cristiani e pagani*. *Aurelia, the Vestal* was never produced.

In 1845, Fry completed *Leonora*, for which his brother Joseph once again provided the libretto, this time based on Bulwer-Lytton's novel *The Lady of Lyons*. When the opera was produced—at the Chestnut Street Theater in Philadelphia on June 4, 1845, where it received sixteen performances—*Leonora* was said to be the first grand opera by an American to reach the stage. The production, given in English, was lavish (paid for by the composer). It received a mixed reaction from the critics, all of whom recognized the influence of Bellini and Donizetti in the bel canto arias, the suave ensemble numbers, and the rousing choruses. "It has many flowing melodies, many pretty effects, much that should encourage its author to renewed efforts," wrote the critic of the *Tribune*. "But, like all early efforts, it is full of reminiscences. . . . The peculiarities which most strongly distinguish his production are sweetness of melody and lack of dramatic characterization." The critic of the *Philadelphia Times* said: "*Leonora* is Fry's first operatic effort for the public, and like all first works, it contains much that is admirable, and much that might be better. Its principal characteristic is melody. The fertility of Mr. Fry's invention in this respect is remarkable. . . . There is a certain suggestiveness in the opening bars of some of the melodies which carries out memory to past pleasures afforded by other composers." Leopold Meignen conducted a concert performance of *Leonora* in Philadelphia on June 20, 1845. The opera itself was revived in Philadelphia on December 8, 1846, and, in 1858, by an Italian company at the New York Academy of Music, sung in Italian. Portions of the opera were resuscitated on February 27, 1929, in a concert performance in New York at which time the critical consensus was that the music was sadly derivative and dated and that its rightful place was in historical archives and not in the opera house.

In 1846, Fry went to Europe as a correspondent for the *New York Tribune*. He spent six years in London and Paris, coming into contact with some of its leading composers (including Berlioz) and attending numerous opera performances (including the world premiere of Meyerbeer's *Le prophète*). When he returned to the United States in 1852, he was appointed editorial writer and music critic for the *New York Tribune*. Beginning with November 30, 1852 (and at a personal loss of four thousand dollars), he initiated a series of ten lectures on music at the Metropolitan Hall in New York which recruited the services of "a crop of principal Italian vocalists," as a news item then reported, "a grand chorus of 100 singers, an orchestra of 80 performers, and a military band of 50 performers to provide extensive illustrations." Both as a music critic and as lecturer he was a potent advocate of American music. In his last series-lecture, in 1853, he called for a declaration of independence in art on the part of the American composer, urging him to dedicate himself to the writing of American music. In 1853, Fry dispatched a virulent letter to the New York Philharmonic, published in the *Musical World*, in which he called the orchestra "an incubus on Art, never having asked for or performed a single American composition during the eleven years of its existence."

When Antoine Jullien, the flamboyant French conductor, toured the United States with his orchestra in 1853 under the auspices of P.T. Barnum, he premiered four Fry "symphonies" (they were not symphonies at all in the classical sense but lengthy, programmatic one-movement orchestral pieces): *A Day in the Country* on September 20; *The Breaking Heart* on December 7; *Santa Claus, a Christmas Symphony* on December 24; and *Childe Harold*, based on Byron, on May 31, 1854. The naïve realism with which Fry translated nonmusical experiences and sounds into music in all these "symphonies" is illustrated in *Santa Claus*, with its musical recreation of a snow storm and howling winds, trotting horses, cracking whips, the sound of sleigh bells, and so forth. This composition ends with a climactic presentation of the Christmas hymn "Adeste Fideles." Fry's "symphony," *Niagara*, first performed on May 4, 1854, was also vividly programmatic.

Fry suffered two setbacks in 1855. First, his Stabat Mater, which had been scheduled for performance on April 7 and after that on April 19, was canceled. He suffered a second blow that year through the death of his father.

Despite deteriorating health, Fry received a diplomatic appointment, that of secretary of legation at Turin. Between 1860 and 1862 he wrote his two finest orchestral overtures, *Evangeline* in 1860 and *Macbeth* in 1862. On May 3, 1864, his last opera, *Notre Dame de Paris* (1864)—his brother's libretto based on Victor Hugo—was introduced in Philadelphia, and soon after that was also heard in New York. The critics were unanimous in their praises. The critic for the *Philadelphia Evening Bulletin* went so far as to say that "we do not hesitate to put it in the very front rank of modern operas—better than some of Verdi's, Donizetti's, and Bellini's." The critic for the *New York Tribune* wrote: "No one could deny that *Notre Dame* stands well . . . beside the acknowledged works of modern writers of repute. . . . The stride from his *Leonora* to *Notre Dame* is prodigious."

Long suffering from tuberculosis, Fry succumbed to that disease in the West Indies, where he had gone for an indeterminate stay to improve his health. He was working on his last composition, a Mass, nine days before his death; it remained incomplete.

Fry was the author of *Artificial Fish-Breeding* (1858).

THE COMPOSER SPEAKS: The public is totally oblivious of and indifferent to the huge and repulsive obstacles which every aspirant to composition beyond the parlor music or organ details has in this country now to test his efforts—to find out whether in his own opinion and of his master he has composed really sound and well-balanced effects for masses of instruments. Twenty years ago there were in some cities, perhaps in New York, half amateur, half professional societies who were glad to play original compositions; and in one or two instances struck medals in honor of the composer. But all that is now changed. Art is degraded to the level of soap and cheese, and there is never a word of cheer or a thousand dollars of assistance for the young composer—though pictures good, bad, and indifferent are freely bought of American artists—generally with the same spirit that money is laid out for furniture or horses.

Nothing by any chance is ever done for musical art as a public thing, an entity to be encouraged by private purses in default of any government or class support such as it receives in Europe. Hence being artistic barbarians, our effects are exactly measured by our causes in this regard.

Occasionally, a composer, once in ten or fifteen years, is found enterprising enough to do something, but always at his own cost. Consequently, the art that the public knows anything of, if American, is as scarce in New York as on the western prairies.

PRINCIPAL WORKS: *Aurelia, the Vestal*, opera (1841); *Leonora*, opera (1845); *Santa Claus, a Christmas Symphony* (1853); *Hagar in the Wilderness*, a sacred "symphony" (1854); *Niagara*, "symphony" (1854); Stabat Mater, or *The Crucifixion of Christ*, for vocal soloists, chorus and orchestra (1855); *Evangeline*, overture for orchestra (1860); *Overture to Macbeth* (1862); *Notre Dame de Paris*, opera (1864); Mass, incomplete, for vocal soloists, chorus, and orchestra (1864); *Also: Esmeralda*, lyrical drama; ten string quartets: the "symphonies," *The Breaking Heart, Childe Harold, A Day in the Country*, and *The Dying Soldier*.

BIBLIOGRAPHY: Howard, John Tasker, *Our American Music* (N.Y., 1946); Lowens, Irving, *Music and Musicians in Early America* (N.Y., 1964); Upton, William Treat, *The Musical Works of William Henry Fry* (Philadelphia, 1946); Upton, William Treat, *William Henry Fry: American Journalist and Composer-Critic* (N.Y., 1954).

Fuleihan, Anis, b. Kyrenia, Cyprus, April 2, 1900; d. Palo Alto, Calif., October 11, 1970. American citizen, 1925.

Many of Fuleihan's mature works were influenced by his fascination for and research in eastern Mediterranean folk music.

His father was a physician. Both parents were born in Lebanon of Arab descent, but though most Syrian-Arab families are Muhammedan, that of the Fuleihans had been Christian for several centuries. In time, Fuleihan's parents became British subjects. When the British government, which had leased the island of Cyprus from Turkey, sent a call for physicians, Fuleihan's family settled in Cyprus toward the end of the 19th century. In Cyprus, Anis Fuleihan attended the English School. He also took some lessons on the piano and early demonstrated a talent for it. But, as he once recalled, "fortunately, the lack of good musical instruction on the island, plus the good sense of my parents, saved me from the fate of a child prodigy."

When he was fifteen his family came to the United States. In Brooklyn, N.Y., Fuleihan continued his academic education at the Polytechnic School; his musical training took place at the Van Ende School of Music in New York in 1915–16, where he received instruction in theory. Piano was later studied privately with Alberto Jonas. When he was nineteen, Fuleihan made his debut as pianist in Aeolian Hall, N.Y., including on his program several of his own compositions. These, he explained, "were written in the sort of synthetic orientalism dear to hearts of some Russian and French composers of the period." At a later recital the same year, in the same hall, he played more of his compositions, none of them any longer of the pseudo-oriental variety but in the discordant harmonic style of what then was considered "modernism." Though his pseudo-oriental pieces were well received by critics and audiences, and were published, Fuleihan decided a few years later to withdraw them completely because they "sickened me," and he even convinced his publishers to destroy the plates. Throughout the 1920s he continued to write in a discordant modern style, but early in the 1930s he decided to abandon it because "I had become fed up with the idiom and no longer derived any pleasure from it."

To support himself while trying to make progress as a virtuoso, Fuleihan became affiliated with a company manufacturing piano rolls. He promoted these piano rolls through so-called comparison concerts. "For some four years I went into every nook and cranny of the New England states exhibiting myself as a pianist and bowing low to the reproducing piano which, at some point in the recital, took a deep electrical breath and imitated my playing. The perfection of the imitation depended very much on the electrical current and the condition of the rubber tubing that made up the innards of the instrument. As many of our best pianists engaged in this sort of enterprise, I did not feel ashamed of myself."

When his father died in 1925, Fuleihan went to live in Cairo, Egypt, to which his family had immigrated. During his three years in Cairo he gave concerts throughout the Near East, did a good deal of composing, and, what proved most important for his further development, came into contact with and made an intensive study of the folk music of the eastern Mediterranean. "I realized then that the synthetic product which had been fed to the occidental public over a number of years as 'oriental music' by occidental composers (not excluding myself) served only to give an impression of the weakest and most undesirable characteristic of the cheap phases of that music." In his own compositions, he now began incorporating the melodic, intervallic and harmonic structures of eastern Mediterranean folk music in compositions for voice and piano.

He returned to the United States in 1928, devoting himself to lecturing, conducting over the radio, and, beginning with 1932, promoting for the next seven years publications of G. Schirmer.

His first success as a composer came with *Mediterranean*, a suite for orchestra (1930) whose five movements respectively gave tonal images of shepherds, peasants, priests and priestesses, musicians and dancers. *Mediterranean* was introduced on March 15, 1935, by the Cincinnati Symphony under Eugene Goossens. Goossens was so enthusiastic about it that he acquired a publisher for it, whose promotion resulted in performances by numerous orchestras in the United States and England.

Important performances of Fuleihan's major works were now growing increasingly frequent. Leon Barzin conducted the premiere of *Preface to a Child's Storybook*, for orchestra (1932), in New York in 1936. Fuleihan's Concerto no. 1, for piano and string orchestra (1937), commissioned by F. Charles Adler for the Saratoga Festival in Saratoga, N.Y., was first heard on September 11, 1937, with the composer as soloist. Piano Concerto no. 2 (1938) received its first hearing in 1938 at a concert of the New York Philharmonic under John Barbirolli, with Eugene List as soloist. On December 1, 1939, the Indianapolis Symphony under Fabien Sevitzky presented the first performance of *Fiesta* (1939), which it had commissioned. The *Symphonie concertante*, for string quartet and orchestra (1939), was premiered by the New York Philharmonic under John Barbirolli on April 25, 1940. In the early part of 1939, the BBC Symphony in London performed three of his major works within a two-month period. In his programmatic and abstract compositions the simple folklike melodies and the harmonic and instrumental coloration of eastern Mediterranean music were prominent.

In 1939, Fuleihan was the recipient of a Guggenheim Fellowship. He resigned his position at Schirmer's to spend the Guggenheim year of 1940 writing copiously. These compositions included the Concerto for Two Pianos and Orchestra, commissioned by the Nassau Philharmonic and heard in Hempstead, N.Y., on January 10, 1941; his Piano Sonata no. 1, subtitled *Cipriana*, in recollection of his birthplace; his string quartet no. 1; *Invocation for Isis*, for orchestra, commissioned by the Indianapolis Symphony and performed by that orchestra under Sevitzky on February 28, 1941; and *Epithalamium*, for piano and string orchestra, a series of variations on a traditional Lebanese wedding song, performed on February 6, 1941, by the Philadelphia Chamber String Sinfonietta under Sevitzky, which had commissioned it.

Later in the 1940s, among other works, came *Three Cyprus Serenades* (1941), introduced by the Philadelphia Orchestra under Eugene Ormandy on December 13, 1946; Concerto for Violin, Piano, and

Orchestra (1943); Rhapsody, for cello and string orchestra (1945; Saratoga, N.Y., September 12, 1946); Overture for Five Winds (1946; N.Y., May 17, 1947). In addition, he completed a concerto for Theremin and orchestra (1945), the Theremin being an electronic instrument invented by Leon Theremin that produced sounds through the movement of hands in front of, but without touching, the instrument. Leopold Stokowski introduced it with the New York City Symphony on February 26, 1945, and on July 30, 1947, it was repeated by the New York Philharmonic, this time under Bernard Herrmann, at a Lewisohn Stadium concert.

In the early 1940s, Fuleihan taught piano privately in New York City. Between 1947 and 1951 he taught piano and composition at Indiana University in Bloomington. He did further research in east Mediterranean music in Egypt on a Fulbright Fellowship in 1952. From 1953 to 1960 he was director of the Beirut National Conservatory, and from 1956 to 1960 consultant for the Baalbeck Festival in Lebanon. Between 1962 and 1965 he lived in Tunis, where, under the auspices of the U.S. State Department, he founded and conducted the Orchestra Classique, which gave concerts every two weeks and served as musical consultant for the International Cultural Center and the Tunis Festival. In 1967–68 he was visiting lecturer of music at the University of Illinois in Urbana.

Until the end of his life, Fuleihan remained prolific as a composer, his large output including additional piano sonatas, string quartets, concertos, Symphony no. 2, shorter works for orchestra, and an opera. His music was performed worldwide. Symphony no. 2 (1966) was introduced on February 16, 1967, by the New York Philharmonic with the composer conducting. "There is much to admire in the strong melodies, the clarity of the presentation and the orthodox but effective scoring." Harold C. Schonberg said of it in the *New York Times*.

THE COMPOSER SPEAKS: I labor under the conviction that music is a pleasurable art rather than a mathematical science. Musical mathematics is comparatively easy, and so is design. Formulae are neither difficult to construct nor to put into operation, and there is no trick in compounding complicated rhythms, counterpoint, or sound combinations.

PRINCIPAL WORKS: 14 piano sonatas (1940–70); 5 string quartets (1940–65); 3 piano concertos (1936, 1938, 1963); 2 symphonies (1936, 1962), 2 violin concertos (1930, 1965); 2 piano sonatinas (1940, 1945).

Mediterranean, suite for orchestra (1930); *Preface to a Child's Storybook*, for orchestra (1932); Fantasy, for viola and orchestra (1938); *Fiesta*, for orchestra (1939); *Symphonie concertante*, for string quartet and orchestra (1939); *Epithalamium*, for piano and string orchestra (1940); *Invocation to Isis*, for orchestra (1941); *Three Cyprus Serenades*, for orchestra, (1941); Divertimento no. 2, for orchestra (1941); Concerto for Violin, Piano, and Orchestra (1943); Concerto for Theremin and Orchestra (1945); Rhapsody, for cello and string orchestra (1945); Overture for Five Winds (1947); *The Pyramids of Giza*, tone poem for orchestra (1952); *Duo concertante*, for violin, viola and orchestra (1958); *Vasco*, opera (1958); Toccata, for piano and orchestra (1959); *Islands Suite*, for orchestra (1961); *Pour les cordes*, for string orchestra (1961); Violin Sonata (1961); Cello Concerto (1963); Viola Concerto (1963); Piano Trio (1968).

BIBLIOGRAPHY: Ewen, David, *American Composers Today* (N.Y., 1949); *New York Times*, August 8, 1965 (obituary), October 13, 1970; *Who's Who in America, 1968–69*.

G

Gaburo, Kenneth Louis, b. Somerville, N.J., July 5, 1926.

Virgil Thomsom has described Gaburo's earlier music for orthodox instruments as "ravishing in sound on account of its high sensitivity to interval relations," and his works using electronics as "among the most original that exist." Gaburo's lifelong fascination for the human voice, both in music and language, and his researches into the science of verbal and nonverbal language/linguistics, is reflected in his compositions dating from 1960 for the concert stage and the experimental theater.

Both of Gaburo's parents loved music. His father, a skilled electrician, carpenter, and proprietor of a laundry business, was a devotee of Italian opera, and his mother sang, played the piano, and directed a church choir. Kenneth Gaburo was the younger of two children; his sister was an accomplished pianist.

Kenneth began studying the piano with one of his mother's friends when he was five, having become stimulated by attending a student recital. From the time he was eight through high school he continued piano study privately with Kathryn Griscom. Since the public school Gaburo attended—Bridgewater Township Elementary School in Raritan, N.J. (1930–38)—had a full music program, he was able to attend music classes daily. "We mostly sang from books such as *Twice 55*, but Mrs. Rinehart, our teacher, always insisted that we sing in the 'spirit' of a given song and frequently provided storylike details of elementary music theory and the lives of composers whose music we were singing. From that first expression of interest, I started to improvise, although I used to refer to those improvisations as compositions. I did not begin to actually notate anything until I entered high school." At Somerville High School in New Jersey (1939–43) he was a member of the school orchestra, concert choir, and jazz band. There he received encouragement in his musical interests from Claude Chappell, who taught him conducting, helped him make jazz arrangements, and occasionally made available the school organizations for the readings of his compositional "exercises."

His early education was enriched with cultural experiences other than music, in all of which he became involved: literature, creative writing, arts and crafts, mathematics, languages. During his four years in high school he was a member of its debating team. Here he gained invaluable insights with regard to logic, discourse and the nature of argument. And due to his proximity to New York City, he was able to make frequent visits to its art galleries and theaters as well as live concerts.

By the time he graduated from high school in 1943 he had completed a number of works including a piano concerto, a symphony, a choral work with string orchestra, some love songs to his own texts, and several piano pieces. "They were not very good," he concedes, "since I didn't know anything about music composition."

In 1943 Gaburo entered the Eastman School of Music in Rochester, N.Y. He stayed there only a single academic year since in the spring of 1944, during World War II, he was inducted into the army. In uniform, after a brief period in the Army Specialized Training Program at the University of Delaware, where he studied radio electronics and physics, he joined the air force as an aerial gunner on B-17, B-24, and B-29 bombers in the Pacific theater. When the war ended, but before he was discharged, he played the piano in the Seventy-sixth AAF Jazz Band, for which he also made arrangements and with which he toured Japan, Australia, certain areas of mainland China, and the Philippines.

Upon his discharge in August 1946, Gaburo returned to Eastman to complete his music study: composition with Bernard Rogers, piano with Cecile Genhart, theory with Allan McHose, counterpoint with Gustave Soderlund, and music history with Charles Warren Fox. Gaburo gained the bachelor of music degree in composition and piano in 1948 and his master of music degree in composition a year later. While attending Eastman, he married Yvonne Stevens (September 14, 1947), with whom he raised two sons. That marriage ended in divorce in 1962, Also while at Eastman, Gaburo completed several works advanced in their harmonic and tonal idioms. These included Five Postludes, for piano (1948; Macon, Ga., December 8, 1948), Three Interludes, for string orchestra (1948; Rochester, April 27, 1948), and *Sinfonia concertante*, for piano and orchestra (1949; Rochester, April 29, 1949). The critic of the *Rochester Democrat Chronicle* (Norman Nairn) considered the music of the *Sinfonia concertante* so far-out in its dissonances and atonality that he wrote: "From its absolutely weird string opening . . . through its cacophonous distortions, distortions sounding like the illegitimate offspring of some hideous monster . . . it seemed like a conglomeration of Schoenberg, Satie, Stravinsky, and Bartók, all at their worst."

In 1949–50, Gaburo was a member of the music faculty at Kent State University in Ohio, and from 1950 to 1954 at McNeese State College in Lake Charles, La. At the latter place, in 1950, Gaburo wrote his first work to gain more than localized attention. It was *On a Quiet Theme*, for full orchestra, which received the George Gershwin Memorial Award and was introduced on February 26, 1955, in New York by the New York Philharmonic, Dimitri Mitropoulos conducting. Among other works completed at McNeese was a three-act opera, *The Snow Queen* (1951–52), his first work for the stage, libretto by Marjory Wilson. It had been commissioned by the Lake Charles Little Theater, which presented the premiere (with the help of community performers) on May 5, 1952.

Gaburo launched his career as a confirmed twelve-tone composer with Four Inventions, for clarinet and piano (1954), and Music for Five Instruments (1954). The latter was commissioned by Victor Alessandro under the auspices of the University of Texas and was premiered at the Southwestern Symposium of Contemporary American Music in Austin on April 5, 1954.

In 1954, Gaburo received the Award of the Eastman School Alumni and a Fulbright Fellowship. The latter enabled him to travel to Rome and study composition with Goffredo Petrassi at the Santa Cecilia Academy. Upon his return to the United States, the study of composition was continued at the University of Illinois in Urbana (1955–62) with Burrill Phillips and Hubert Kessler, where Gaburo acquired a doctor of musical arts degree in 1962. Between 1955 and 1968, Gaburo was on the music faculty of that university and an active member of the Festival of Contemporary Arts Committee. This festival achieved recognition, particularly due to its innovative programs and excellence in performance of new and difficult works. Gaburo recalls: "The arts at Illinois had an immense flowering and impact on the world community during that period." In 1967–68 he served as associate fellow at its Institute for Advanced Study. On July 15, 1964, he married Virginia Hommel, a pianist and poet, who subsequently collaborated with him in performances of his works and provided some of his vocal compositions with texts; they have a daughter.

Gaburo spent the summer of 1956 at the Berkshire Music Center at Tanglewood, Mass. There he wrote *Elegy for Small Orchestra* (1956) under the stimulus of his father's death. The idiom here is twelve tone, but Gaburo had now learned to personalize and humanize it. The New York Philharmonic, under Leonard Bernstein, gave the premiere on April 3, 1959. "It has a grave intensity of feeling," said Howard Taubman in the *New York Times*. "But it is not obvious lamentation. It conveys a sense of starkness and hesitation, as of sorrow beyond words or tears. . . . In *Elegy* . . . he . . . takes account of an advanced idiom but does not lose sight of the fact that music is human communication." *Elegy* was the recipient of the Raphael Sagalyn Award.

Gaburo's most advanced conception of the twelve-tone row compositional procedure up to that time came with *Line Studies* (1957). The performance took place in New York on December 15, 1957. Here, as the composer has explained, he imagined the twelve-tone series "as a linear body of independent factors; a single series of tones, each of which occupies a fixed, unalterable position in the sequence." This composition has five titled movements, each, the composer says, reflecting "an essential technique used to create a particular type of line out of a single series of fixed tones. They may be basically defined as follows: (1) 'Projection,' the initial primitive series as a single line; (2) 'Extraction,' the fragmentation of the series to create more lines; (3) 'Displacement,' spatial arrangement of fixed series; (4) 'Density,' lines with harmonic emphasis, and (5) 'Expansion,' the series as a simultaneous definition of the total space offered by the instruments." In reviewing a recording of *Line Studies* in *High Fidelity/Musical America*, Eric Salzman wrote: "This is purified and elegant twelve-tone music, executed and elaborated with the most carefully simple and cunningly economical means. . . . The music often suggests a kind of tonal, diatonic Webern. Interestingly enough, this gives the impression neither of jarring inconsistency nor of accidental irrelevancy; rather it emerges as an aspect of the fundamental clarity and simplicity of the musical communication."

Gaburo first utilized electronics in 1955–56 with *Bodies*, "an opera for actors and tape," whose world premiere took place at the University of Illinois on November 7, 1956. He became increasingly involved with electronics in a series of compositions collectively called *Antiphony*, the first of which, for three string groups and tape, was completed in 1958. These *Antiphonies* were compositions for voices or instruments, electronic sounds and tape transformations. *Antiphony* II, "variations on a poem of Cavafy," was created in 1962 for large chorus, soprano solo, and two-channel audio tape; it was premiered at the University of Illinois on July 31, 1966. *Antiphony* III, "Pearl White Moments," for chamber chorus and two-channel tape, text by Virginia Hommel Gaburo, was commissioned by the Fromm Music Foundation and introduced at the University of Chicago on February 21, 1967. In *High Fidelity/Musical America*, Eric Salzman said of it: "*Antiphony* III . . . uses live voices in such a way that you can hardly tell where they leave off and the electronics begin." *Antiphony* IV, "Poised," for piccolo, trombone, double bass, and two-channel tape (1967), text by Gaburo's wife, was commissioned by the University of Illinois Chamber Players, the first performance taking place at Smith College in Northampton, Mass., on January 24, 1968. "In both of these works," Salzman continues in his comment on *Antiphony* III and *Antiphony* IV, "There is a complex interplay between the sounds of language and the human voice on the one hand and abstract sound, instrumental and electronic, on the other. The result is a very precise, evocative, and original poetics." *Antiphony* VI, "Cogito," for string quartet, slides, and tape (1971), was commissioned by the New Age Quartet in Los Angeles and introduced on April 10, 1972. This work consists primarily of a reading of a poem by Gaburo's wife, the speech sounds integrated with the string quartet performances (the musicians required to hum, whistle, and make tongue-clicking sounds as well as perform on their instruments) and with slides showing photographs of members of the New Age Quartet in various settings and the words of the poem synchronized in speech with the tape sounds. "The whole piece hangs together beautifully," reported Allen B. Skei in the *Fresno Bee*. "It seems to proceed with ineluctible logic from its quiet but sure beginnings to its almost tentative conclusion. . . . The total effect was marvelous."

In the late 1950s and early 1960s, Gaburo was also producing music for the stage. In a theatrical vein was *Tiger Rag* (1957), a play by Seyril Schochen in which the Greek legend of Oedipus and Jocasta receives a modern setting and treatment as a social commentary on the 1920s, 1930s, and 1940s. For this play, Gaburo provided a sophisticated score generously spiced with the condiments of popularism: a tango, rag, waltzes, blues, rhumba, and so forth. Its premiere took place at the University of Illinois Festival of Contemporary Arts on March 6, 1957. On January 16, 1961, it was brought for a limited run to the Cherry Lane Theater, off Broadway. "Several of the musical numbers have verve and charm," said Howard Taubman in the *New York Times*. "A seedy fortune teller, presumably to be equated with the oracle, has a 'Tiger Rag Blues' that makes an impressive effect. There are brash turns for the girlies, and there is a sinuous 'Apache.' "

More exploratory in its musical content is *The Widow* (1961), a one-act opera adapted by the composer from *The Encantadas*, the searing psychological story of Herman Melville. The opera was commissioned for the opening of the Festival of Contemporary Arts at the University of Illinois on February 26, 1961. "The music to his libretto," David Ward-Steinman has written "is flexible, expressive, and sensuous and is eminently suitable for the varying demands of the text. The scoring is for a chamber orchestra, and Gaburo's handling of this medium is masterly."

Gaburo began his formal studies in linguistics in 1959, leading to the formulation of the expression "compositional linguistics." From this point on, he became growingly concerned with music-as-language and language-as-music in many of his compositions. In 1965, at the University of Illinois, he founded the New Music Choral Ensemble for the performance of avant-garde choral music. Within three years, its repertoire ranged from improvisation to strictly serial pieces, and from microtonal to performer-electronic sound media. The New Music Choral Ensemble was re-formed several times under various grants including those from the Rockefeller and Ford foundations. Under Gaburo's leadership, it has performed extensively throughout the United States and abroad. By the time New Music Choral Ensemble III was formed, its compositions included synchronization of vocal transmission with body movements as well as the development of its own brand of theater through "gesture music," "action music," "talk music and/or theater music." Improvisation was combined with electronics, linguistics, computers, dance mime, films, and taped music. Within a decade of its founding, this group has performed over a hundred works ranging from the avant-garde choral music of Schoenberg, Luigi Nono, Pauline Oliveros, and others to theater music (Maurice Kagel, etc.), theater itself (Beckett and Albee), and linguistic compositions.

In 1967, Gaburo received a Guggenheim Fellowship. One year later he left the University of Illinois to join the music faculty of the University of California in San Diego, where he remained until 1975. There he produced a rich repertoire of theater pieces, begun at the University of Illinois, engaging the resources of poetry, music, theater, body movements, electronics, linguistics, projections, and film. Some of these bore the collective title of *Lingua* (1965–70), a title derived from the composer's concern with body linguistics as well as verbal. *Lingua* is divided into four broad and connected sections, namely, *Lingua* I–IV. Taken as a whole, *Lingua* comprises a "massive" six-hour theater. The first of these sections, *Lingua* I, consists of seven parts entitled "Poems and Poesies," "Mouth-Piece," "Inside," "Dante's Joynte," "The Flight of Sparrow," "Cantilena III," and "Glass." The first composition, "Poesies" (for seven or more sculpted humans and tape), had been created in 1965 but was not produced until March 3, 1970, after Gaburo had come to San Diego. The composer here, as well as elsewhere in *Lingua*, wrote his own text and designed his own stage sets and lighting. Of "Dante's Joynte" (composition for six shouting voices, overhead amber spot, 16mm film, tape), Andrew DeRhen, reporting in *High Fidelity/Musical America*, noted: "The spasmodic gestures and shouted interjections of the performers who advanced menacingly toward the audience, combined with a sinister, pulsating taped score and a color film of malignant cell growth, all produced a strangely overwhelming impression. Also admirable from a performance standpoint was 'The Flight of Sparrow' . . . a pantomimist responding to a set of increasingly demanding and contradictory instructions from an unseen speaker . . . Two other movements ('Inside' and 'Mouth-Piece') . . . involved the not exactly new or entertaining gimmick of a single performer doing multiple-duty as instrumentalist, vocalist, percussionist and sound effects man."

Lingua II, "Maledetto" (composition for seven virtuoso speakers), written in 1967–69, was first performed at the San Diego Ballet Studio on October 31, 1969. After a performance of "Maledetto" at the Smithsonian Institution in March 1971, Alan Kriegsman, writing in the *Washington Post*, thus described the proceedings: "The performers were mostly blue-jeaned and barefoot. . . . Members of the audience were asked to sit on stage, while the ensemble gathered in front of them in a kind of makeshift living room . . . [one] 'virtuoso speaker' read a technical disquisition on the mechanical device known as the screw, replete with obvious double-entendres, while the rest of the group intermittently drowned him out with a doggedly salacious hubbub. It was pretty sophomoric."

Lingua III, "In the Can," called "a dialectic mix in three rounds," for forty actors, slides, film, and tape (1970), involved the sense of smell. "We let the performers pick from four types of perfume," Gaburo explains, "then introduced them into the air conditioning ducts at appropriate times . . . the desired effect was that of perfumed toilet paper." This work was written on commission from the University of Oregon in Eugene, where it was premiered on April 17, 1970.

Among Gaburo's significant theater pieces in the 1970s was — — —*Ringings* (1976), for three choruses, slides, tape, films, and lighting effects. It was commissioned by the Michigan State Council for the Arts and the New Vocal Arts Ensemble in commemoration of the American bicentennial. The three dashes preceding the title suggested, the composer says, that the history of America is a continuing process that has not ended nor been resolved. In creating this work, Gaburo kept in mind the environment of a planetarium in which it was to receive its premiere (Abrams Planetarium in East Lansing, Mich., on April 9, 1976) and took into account the materials available to him there. The work as a whole, the composer says, "was influenced by the writings of three individuals at the time of the Revolution: the poetry of a frontierswoman whose child was killed in the war; the writing of a conservative intellectual at Princeton; and the poetry of a liberated black slave which was widely read at the time. The piece itself is based on a poem by the frontierswoman and a 'beat' poem written in 1970."

Other late theater pieces include the following: *My, My, My, What a Wonderful Fall* (1975), for dancers, acrobats, sculpted light, and four-channel audio, commissioned for the opening of the Mandeville Center of the Arts at the University of California in San Diego on March 6, 1975; *Serious Music-Making in San Diego and Other Happy Memories* (1977), for live performers, tape, text, and slides, a radio project commissioned by the New Mexico Arts Council and introduced by community performers over KUNM in Albuquerque, N.M., on September 25, 1977; and *Subito*, for voice, trumpet, viola, and double bass (1977–78), commissioned by the Koussevitzky Music Foundation.

In 1975, after resigning his position at the University of California in San Diego, Gaburo founded Lingua Press, a publishing house for innovative new works in music, the arts and the humanities.

THE COMPOSER SPEAKS: I am in love with serious music making as *idea*, and love some instances of idea's music, and how it speaks. I neither exalt nor condemn current-day society for its seeming neglect or insensitivity to such music's presence.

Serious music making as idea has always been, and is, experimental; so have been, and are, some of its instances. I do not think such music, per se, can instruct (i.e., its intrinsic complexities are not, nor have they ever been, self-evident). Thus I cannot imagine it to be sufficient to say: 'Let Music Speak.' Sooner or later, societies—if they do anything at all—consume the work of experimenters; but they do not generate experiments and thus have no easy way to embrace idea's music, how it speaks, or exactly what it is they consume.

A self-recognized biological *need* to find my idea's music has enabled me to compose; the need to help music's ideas speak has enabled me to compose; the need to help music's ideas speak has enabled me to teach, to perform and to publish. If society finds that it, too, needs music and its idea, we can begin speaking to each other. For that to occur we shall have to recognize the need for appropriate language as well. Until then, music and its idea remain private matters.

PRINCIPAL WORKS: Piano Concerto (1949); *On a Quiet Theme*, for orchestra (1950); *The Snow Queen*, opera (1951–1952); Music for Five Instruments, for flute, clarinet, trumpet, trombone, and piano (1954); Four Inventions for Clarinet and Piano (1954); *Elegy for Small Orchestra* (1956); String Quartet in One Movement (1956); *Line Studies*, for flute, clarinet, viola, and trombone (1957); *Tiger Rag*, play with music (1957); *Antiphony* I, "Voices," for three string groups and tape (1958); *Shapes and Sounds*, for orchestra (1960); *The Widow*, one-act opera (1961); *Antiphony* II, "Variations on a Poem of Cavafy," for chorus, soprano solo, and tape (1962); *Antiphony* III, "Pearl White Moments," for chamber chorus and tape (1963); *The Hydrogen Jukebox*, play with electronic score (1964); *Lingua* I: *Poems and Other Theaters* (1965–70); Psalm, for chorus (1965); *Never*, for four groups of male voices (1966); *Antiphony* IV, "Poised," for piccolo, trombone, double bass, and tape (1968); *December 8*, for forty male voices (1967); *Lingua* II "Maledetto," for seven virtuoso speakers (1967–69); *Antiphony* V, for solo piano and tape (1968); *Carissima* I and II, for women's chorus (1968); *Lingua* III, "In the Can," a dialectic mix in three rounds, for forty actors, slides, film, and tape (1970); *Lingua* IV, for assorted phenomena (1970); *Antiphony* VI "Cogito," for string quartet, slides and tape (1971); *Antiphony* VII, "— — —And," composition with video systems and audio tape (1974); *My, My, My, What a Wonderful Fall*, for five dancers/acrobats, text, sculpted light, and four-channel audio (1975); — — — *Ringings*, for three choruses, tape, slides, and film (1976); *Serious Music-Making in San Diego and Other Happy Memories*, for live performers, tape, text, and slides (1977); *Subito*, theater for voice, trumpet, viola, and double bass (1977–78).

BIBLIOGRAPHY: *DCM;* Cage, John, *Notations* (N.Y., 1967); Salzman, Eric, *Twentieth-Century Music* (Englewood Cliffs, N.J. 1967); Schwartz, Elliott, *Electronic Music* (N.Y., 1975); Thomson, Virgil, *American Music Since 1910* (N.Y., 1970); *Who's Who in America, 1980–81.*

George, Earl, b. Milwaukee, Wis., May 1, 1924.

He is a neoclassical composer who draws his material from a wide range of sources, often nationalistic.

His father did some semiprofessional singing as a young man, and his mother had studied piano in her childhood, but good music was not a strong presence in the George household. Earl showed a gift for singing as a child, and was occasionally called upon to perform at amateur gatherings. While attending Garden Homes School in Milwaukee (1930–37) he began to study piano. At Rufus King High School in Milwaukee (1938–42) he studied clarinet and was a member of the school band, orchestra, and chorus; he also made his first attempts at composition, with several works being performed. George further studied piano in Milwaukee with Irma Schenuit Hall, who, along with his high school music teachers Ellen Sargeant and Arthur Zahorik, was influential in directing him to a career in music.

Upon graduating from high school in 1942 he entered the Eastman School of Music in Rochester, N.Y., majoring in composition wtih Bernard Rogers and Howard Hanson and with a minor in piano with Donald Liddell. He received his bachelor of music degree in 1946 and his master of music a year later. While attending Eastman, he served as a teaching assistant in theory (1946–47). He was also involved with composition, completing among other works a Passacaglia (1944) and an Adagietto (1946), both for orchestra and both introduced by the Eastman-Rochester Symphony Orchestra conducted by Hanson.

The summer of 1946 was spent at the Berkshire Music Center at Tanglewood in Massachusetts for the study of composition with Bohuslav Martinu and Nikolai Lopatnikoff. At the Berkshire Music Center he began to write Introduction and Allegro, for orchestra, his first composition to focus attention on his talent. He completed it in the fall of the same year, and it was performed on October 21, 1946, by the Eastman-Rochester Symphony under Hanson. In 1947 it received the George Gershwin Memorial Award, which brought it a performance by the New York City Symphony conducted by Leonard Bernstein on March 31, 1947, in Brooklyn, N.Y. Soon after this, Introduction and Allegro was performed by the New York Philharmonic, with Charles Munch conducting, a concert that was broadcast by CBS radio network and relayed abroad by the Voice of America.

In 1947, George studied composition privately with Martinu. That year George received the Koussevitzky Music Foundation commission which led to the writing of *Arioso*, for cello and piano, introduced in Town Hall, New York, on March 14, 1950. *Four American Portraits* (Thomas Jefferson, John Quincy Adams, Daniel Boone, and Abraham Lincoln) for a cappella chorus (1941–47), performed on March 19, 1947, in Decatur, Ill., was awarded the James Millikin University Choral Prize.

On September 11, 1948, Earl George married Margaret Heidner, a piano graduate of the Eastman School; they have one son. That year (1948), George became instructor at the Hartt College of Music in Hartford, Conn., and during the summer of 1948 he was assistant professor of composition at the University of Texas in Austin. In the fall of 1948 he was appointed instructor of theory and composition at the University of Minnesota in Milwaukee, retaining this post eight years. At the university, George did graduate work in Elizabethan drama and held the Dorati Graduate Scholarship in conducting.

George received two awards in 1950. The National Federation of Music Clubs Prize came to *Missa Brevis*, for vocal soloists, chorus, and orchestra (1948), first heard on May 10, 1953, in Minneapolis with the composer conducting. The Boosey and Hawkes–University of Illinois Publication Prize went to *A Thanksgiving Overture*, for orchestra (1949)—first performance in Urbana, Ill., on March 3, 1950. During the next dozen years or so this overture was frequently performed throughout the United States, notably by the Minneapolis Symphony under Antal Dorati, the Hartford Symphony under Fritz Mahler, and the University of Miami Symphony under Fabien Sevitzky. In 1954, the University of Minnesota provided funds for George to write a violin concerto for Rafael Druian, then concertmaster of the Minneapolis Symphony. It was first performed on November 16, 1954, by Druian and the Minneapolis Symphony conducted by Dorati. Druian played it again with the Minneapolis Symphony in 1955, and in 1957 he performed it in New York with the Symphony of the Air, Howard Mitchell conducting.

In 1955–56, on a Fulbright Fellowship, George

lectured on 20th-century music at the University of Oslo, in Norway. In 1957 he was awarded a Guggenheim Fellowship which enabled him to spend that year in Florence, Italy, composing. Since 1959 George has been professor of theory and composition at Syracuse University in Syracuse, N.Y. There, in 1963 he founded, and from 1963 to 1969 directed, the Syracuse University Singers in performances of Renaissance and 20th-century choral works. He also was guest conductor of the Syracuse Symphony Orchestra and in 1965–66 was appointed conductor of the Syracuse University Orchestra. Since 1961 George has been the music and dance critic of the *Syracuse Herald-Journal*. In 1963–69 he was a commentator for sponsored radio and television concerts of the Syracuse Symphony as he had been in 1954–55 for the Minneapolis Symphony, and from 1961 to 1965 he was the program annotator for the Syracuse Symphony. In addition to all this, he appeared with the Syracuse Symphony as piano soloist (Beethoven's Triple Concerto), narrator (Prokofiev's *Peter and the Wolf*) and commentator for youth concerts.

From the mid-1940s on, George has been partial to the neoclassical idiom, endowing the classical structures with a discreet discordant harmonic and polyphonic vocabulary, and always bringing to his writing a warmth of lyricism and emotions and transparency and lucidity of texture. Among his more important later works are: Piano Concerto (1958; Syracuse, N.Y., April 22, 1966); the String Quartet (1961), commissioned by Louis Krasner and first performed by the Krasner Quartet on October 5, 1961; and two one-act operas bearing the single title of *Birthdays* (1975), for which he wrote the librettos. These two little operas were premiered at the Festival of the Arts at Syracuse University on April 23, 1976. They had one thing in common: The protagonist of each work was born on the Fourth of July. The first opera, *Pursuing Happiness*, took place on July 4, 1777; the second, *Another Fourth of July*, in or about 1912. A review for *High Fidelity/Musical America* described the first opera as a "brilliantly contrived, clever, and timeless cameo" and the second as "a surrealistic two-scene opera full of haunting melody and rich orchestration . . . a joyful bit of Americana." Dances, simulation of American folk and popular tunes, the interpolation of "Yankee Doodle," the tinny sound of a player piano all contributed to provide George's score with a pronounced American flavor.

THE COMPOSER SPEAKS: I believe that the function of serious music is undergoing a serious transformation governed by the needs of an ever-more egalitarian society. This is a direction not necessarily good, but one hardly likely to be reversed by the work of any individual composer.

PRINCIPAL WORKS: *Four American Portraits*, for a cappella chorus (1941–47); Adagietto, for orchestra (1946); Introduction and Allegro, for orchestra (1946); Concerto for Strings (1948); *Missa Brevis*, for vocal soloists, chorus, and orchestra or band (1948); *A Thanksgiving Overture*, for orchestra (1949); *Abraham Lincoln Walks at Midnight*, for vocal soloists, chorus, and orchestra (1949); Piano Sonata (1950); Three Pieces, for violin, piano, and cello (1951); *Songs of Innocence*, for a cappella chorus (1951); *Five Sonnets of Edna St. Vincent Millay*, for voice and piano (1954); Violin Concerto (1954); Introduction, Variations, and Finale, for orchestra (1957); Piano Concerto (1958); *A Definition*, for women's chorus (1960); *William Wordsworth*, for narrator, chorus, and piano (1961); String Quartet (1961); *Voyages*, for narrator, soprano, alto flute, percussion, piano, harp, organ, and chorus (1967); Three Songs, for voice and piano (1967); *Voices*, for soprano, chorus, piano, and percussion (1974); *Three Pieces about Marches*, for piano (1974); *Birthdays*, two one-act operas (1975); *Hum-Drum Heaven,* for soprano, chorus, and percussion (1978).

BIBLIOGRAPHY: Anderson, E. Ruth (ed.), *Contemporary American Composers* (Boston, 1976); *American Society of Composers, Authors and Publishers Biographical Dictionary* (N.Y., 1966); *Dictionary of International Biography* (London, 1969).

Gershwin, George (originally **Gershvin, Jacob**), b. Brooklyn, N.Y., September 25, 1898; d. Hollywood, Cal., July 11, 1937.

From his youthful years, Gershwin set himself a dual goal as composer: to bring the fullest resources of concert music to the popular song; and to carry over into serious compositions the idioms of popular music (ragtime, the blues, the Tin Pan Alley ballad). In achieving both goals he became (in the picturesque imagery of Isaac Goldberg) a Colossus bestriding the world of music, one foot in Tin Pan Alley, the other in Carnegie Hall—a composer who, since his death, has become a legend the world over.

He was born to a middle-class family, the second of four children, the oldest of whom, Ira Gershwin, became his lyricist. Both parents had come to New York from Russia, and neither was musical. The father became an entrepreneur involved in numerous business ventures; in good times or during financial reverses, he always managed to provide for his family. At public school, in New York City's East Side, George was no scholar. He was far more interested in the pleasures of the city streets—street hockey, punch ball, roller skating—than in schoolbooks. Good music, which was nonexistent in the Gershwin household, made its first impact on George when he was six and heard Anton Rubinstein's *Melody in F* in a penny arcade. "The peculiar jumps in the music held me rooted," he later recalled. Not long after that he would roller-skate to Harlem to listen to the jazz of Jim Europe and his band performing at the Baron Wilkins Club. He would drink in the sounds as he sat outside on the sidewalk curb. One day, when he was ten, while playing ball in the schoolyard of P. S. 25, he heard, through an open window, the strains of Dvořák's *Humoresque* played on a violin. The performer was a prodigy named Maxie Rosenzweig (later to become a concert violinist under the name of Max Rosen). Gershwin sought him out, became his friend, and learned from him for the first time about the world of great composers and great music. Under such a stimulus Gershwin tried inventing melodies of his own, one of which he sang to his violin-playing friend. Maxie told him firmly: "I'm sorry, but you have no talent for music, and you haven't got it in you to become a musician."

In 1910, a piano came into the Gershwin household, brought there so that George's older brother, Ira, could take lessons. But it was George who monopolized the instrument. He now began to seek instruction from several incompetent local teachers. But in Charles Hambitzer, with whom he began studying the piano in 1912, Gershwin found a teacher who could give him proper instruction. He now received an intelligent initiation into the literature of the classics and the moderns, as well as lessons in theory, harmony, and composition. Gershwin was also encouraged to go to concerts. Hambitzer was the right teacher at the right time. Gershwin devoted himself passionately to music study and made remarkable progress. Hambitzer took note of his zeal and talent. He wrote to his sister: "I have a new pupil who will make his mark in music if anybody will. The boy is a genius, without a doubt. He's just crazy about music and can't wait until it is time to take his lesson." At the High School of Commerce, which Gershwin entered in 1912, he played the piano in the school assembly. During the summer of 1913 he found a piano job in a resort hotel in the Catskill Mountains. That year he wrote his first ballad and a piano rag. "He wants to go in for this modern stuff, jazz and whatnot," Hambitzer wrote to his sister. "But I'm not going to let him for a while. I'll see that he gets a firm foundation in the standard music first."

In May 1916 Gershwin found employment as staff pianist in Tin Pan Alley, at the publishing house of Remick, for a salary of fifteen dollars a week. He was the youngest piano demonstrator in the song industry and the first inexperienced employee Remick ever engaged. As a Tin Pan Alley employee, Gershwin wrote his first song to get published and another that marked his entrance into the Broadway musical theater, both in 1916. In 1917, with Will Donaldson, he wrote his first published piano rag ("Rialto Ripples"). At this time he also played the piano for piano-roll recordings, making thirty of them in 1916.

All this while, study continued, not only with Hambitzer but theory and composition with Edward Kilenyi. "He had an extraordinary faculty or genius to absorb everything and to apply what he learned to his own music," Kilenyi later recalled. Subsequent study of composition took place with Rubin Goldmark, Henry Cowell, and Joseph Schillinger.

In 1917, Gershwin left Remick to develop a career as a composer. The publishing house of Harms, headed by Max Dreyfus, provided him with a regular weekly salary (thirty-five dollars) to write songs at his convenience. Through Dreyfus's influence more of Gershwin's songs were interpolated into Broadway musicals until 1919, when Gershwin was contracted to write his own first full score for a Broadway show *La, La, Lucille,* which opened on Broadway on May 26, 1919. In 1919 Gershwin also made his first attempt at writing a concert work. It was *Lullaby,* for string quartet, whose world premiere had to wait almost half a century—in Washington, D.C., on December 19, 1967. Still in 1919, Gershwin had his first resounding hit song in "Swanee," made popular by Al Jolson at the Winter Garden. And from 1920 to 1924 Gershwin was under contract to provide songs for George White's annual Broadway revue, the *Scandals,* out of which came two of Gershwin's earliest song classics: "I'll Build a Stairway to Paradise" and "Somebody Loves Me." For the *Scandals* he also wrote a one-act jazz opera called *Blue Monday,* introduced on August 29, 1922, and dropped from the show the next day because it was regarded as too somber. Later, under the title of *135th Street,* it was intermittently revived in the concert hall, in motion pictures, and over television.

Several serious musicians were becoming aware of the extraordinary rhythmic and harmonic inventiveness, and the fresh lyricism, of Gershwin's popular songs. Beryl Rubinstein, concert pianist and member of the faculty of the Cleveland Institute, told an interviewer in 1922 that Gershwin was "a great composer. The young fellow has the spark of musical genius. . . . When we speak of American composers George Gershwin's name will be prominent." In the esoteric literary journal *Dial,* Gilbert Seldes wrote in August 1923: "Delicacy, even dreaminess, is the quality [Gershwin] alone brings to jazz music." And on November 1, 1923, the concert singer Eva Gauthier gave a recital featuring the music of old and contemporary masters from Bellini to Schoenberg and Hindemith with a closing group of popular numbers including three Gershwin songs for which Gershwin himself served as accompanist. "I consider this one of the very important events in American musical history," wrote Carl van Vechten.

Gershwin's emergence as a serious composer came on February 12, 1924, when Paul Whiteman and his orchestra presented a concert of American music in Aeolian Hall, New York, the highlight of which was the world premiere of Gershwin's *Rhapsody in Blue,* with Gershwin at the piano. This, of course, was not the first time jazz had been used with serious intent in a concert work, Gershwin having been preceded by Erik Satie, Darius Milhaud, Stravinsky, and John Alden Carpenter. But this was the most successful of this species, a work brash in its youth, infectious in its spirit, muscular in its energy, an appropriate reflection and voice of the 1920s, the jazz age of "flappers" and "cake eaters," hip flasks, companionate marriage, and a soaring stock market. Though the *Rhapsody in Blue* inspired an ovation at the concert hall, the critical reaction the next morning was a mixed one, running the gamut from outright denunciation and hostility to an excessive praise which placed the work on a higher level of artistic achievement than anything by Stravinsky, Schoenberg, and Milhaud.

The success of *Rhapsody in Blue* has few if any parallels in the history of serious American music. In a short period it was heard in arrangements for jazz band, solo piano, two pianos, solo harmonica, harmonica orchestra, mandolin orchestra and chorus; it was used as background music for tap dancers and ballet companies; it was featured in a motion picture; the rhapsodic main theme was adopted by Paul Whiteman as his permanent signature; the Roxy Theater in New York paid Gershwin $10,000 a week (an unprecedented sum at the time for such an appearance) to perform it on the stage; the Paul Whiteman Victor recording became an instant best-seller. After that, and for the next half century and more, *Rhapsody in Blue* was heard throughout the civilized world, and was recorded in innumerable releases, to become the most frequently performed concert composition by an American composer. Its title was used in 1946 for George Gershwin's screen biography.

Now a world figure, as well as a man of considerable financial means, all resulting from the *Rhapsody in Blue*, Gershwin continued to divide his activity between writing popular music for stage and screen, and music for the concert hall and opera house. Among his best scores for the musical theater were *Tip Toes* (1925), *Oh, Kay!* (1926), *Funny Face* (1927), *Strike Up the Band* (1929), *Girl Crazy* (1929), and *Of Thee I Sing!* (1931), the last becoming the first musical comedy ever to win the Pulitzer Prize in drama and the first musical to have its text published in book form. For motion pictures, Gershwin contributed the songs for *Delicious* (1931), *A Damsel in Distress* (1937), *Shall We Dance* (1937), and *The Goldwyn Follies* (1938). Out of these Broadway and Hollywood productions came some of the most inventive and innovative popular songs of the era, songs which survived to become classics in American popular music, all the lyrics for which were provided by his brother Ira, beginning with the musical *Lady Be Good!* (1924). Some of them provided the scores for such ballets as *The New Yorkers*, produced by the Ballet Russe de Monte Carlo in New York City on October 18, 1940, and *Who Cares?*, a New York City Ballet production with choreography by George Balanchine, produced on

February 5, 1970, in New York. The songs also contributed the basic material for innumerable radio and television specials, one of which, *'S Wonderful, 'S Marvelous, 'S Gershwin*, received an Emmy in 1972 from the National Academy of Television Arts and Sciences after being produced over NBC-TV. An hour and a half of Gershwin songs broadcast by radio from London to twenty-one countries in 1969 elicited the following comment from Ronald Stevenson in *The Listener* in London: "The total impression was of a prodigality of melody matched only by Schubert and Johann Strauss."

Gershwin was also successful and productive in the world of concert music. In 1924 he was commissioned by Walter Damrosch and the New York Symphony to write a piano concerto, the Concerto in F (1925), which Gershwin himself introduced under Damrosch's direction on December 3, 1925. The European premiere followed in Paris on May 29, 1928. Since then, the concerto has been second in popularity only to *Rhapsody in Blue* among Gershwin's concert compositions, certainly the most frequently performed concerto written by an American. Its score was used for a ballet mounted at the Volksoper in Vienna on March 24, 1969. When in 1930 the conductor Albert Coates compiled a list of the fifty of the foremost musical works of the 20th century, he included only a single American composition, Gershwin's Concerto in F.

On December 4, 1926, Gershwin introduced Three Piano Preludes (1926) at a concert in New York which he shared with the singer Marguerite d'Alvarez. These preludes have been transcribed for orchestra several times, and Jascha Heifetz arranged them for violin and piano.

In 1928 Gershwin took a vacation in Europe. There he completed writing a programmatic tone poem, *An American in Paris*, whose premiere was given by the New York Philharmonic under Walter Damrosch on December 13, 1928. A vividly descriptive piece of a walk taken by an American on Parisian boulevards, this composition is novel in its orchestration by employing in its percussion section actual Parisian taxihorns, an early example of the utilization of nonmusical sounds with serious artistic intent. *An American in Paris* has also become a staple in 20th-century American orchestral literature. It provided the title for a motion picture in 1952 where a twenty-minute ballet to its music was the climax; this motion picture received the Academy Award.

For his first assignment to write music for the films, *Delicious* in 1930, Gershwin prepared a six-minute orchestral sequence descriptive of the movements of city life and the sounds and rhythms of riveting. When five minutes of this sequence had to be discarded, Gershwin decided to expand it into an orchestral piece. He completed it in May 1931, initially calling it *Rhapsody in Rivets*. By the time it was performed the title was changed to *Second Rhapsody*. It was premiered at a concert of the Boston Symphony under Serge Koussevitzky on January 29, 1932. The sound of riveting is simulated in the opening measures for solo piano.

During a visit to Cuba in 1932, Gershwin became fascinated with Cuban music and Cuban instruments. The idea was then born to write an overture using such material, first named *Rhumba*, and then officially to be known as *Cuban Overture*. Its first performance was conducted by Albert Coates at the Lewisohn Stadium in New York on August 16, 1932—a historic date for Gershwin since this was the first all-Gershwin program ever given, the forerunner of hundreds such the world over since that time. In his orchestration for *Cuban Overture*, Gershwin utilized such Cuban instruments as the Cuban stick, the bongo drum, the gourd, and the maracas; in his score Gershwin suggested that these Cuban instruments be placed in a row in front of the conductor's stand.

Gershwin's last work for orchestra was the *Variations on I Got Rhythm*, for piano and orchestra. He wrote it for an extended tour of one-night stands in all-Gershwin concerts which he was making with the Leo Reisman orchestra in 1934. The theme on which this series of variations is based is the hit song, "I Got Rhythm" from the musical *Girl Crazy*, introduced and first made famous by Ethel Merman. The world premiere of *Variations* took place in Boston on January 13, 1934.

Gershwin's magnum opus is the American folk opera *Porgy and Bess*—libretto by DuBose Heyward based on his novel, *Porgy*, and the play of the same name he later wrote with his wife, Dorothy. Ira Gershwin collaborated with DuBose Heyward in writing the lyrics. The Theater Guild presented *Porgy and Bess* in Boston on September 30, 1935, before opening on Broadway on October 10.

It took Gershwin twenty months to write and orchestrate the huge score, part of which he developed in Charleston, S.C., where he spent several weeks making a firsthand study of the music and ritual of Gullah Negroes. Writing this opera was a labor of love, and in the process he was in a continuous state of euphoria. The score became for Gershwin the final meeting ground of the popular and the serious, both poised on the highest planes of artistic excellence. Popular-type songs that have the identity of show tunes are combined with folklike hymns and expressive tone speech; choral and ensemble numbers of operatic dimension with street cries. But there is no feeling of incongruity in this blending of the popular and the serious, as each becomes basic to the overall dramatic and artistic design.

At first, *Porgy and Bess* was hardly a success. The reaction of the critics was mainly negative in their belief that this was neither opera nor musical comedy. The opera stayed on the boards for 124 performances, entailing a financial loss for all concerned. Gershwin's folk opera had every appearance of repeating the sad fate of so many other American op-

eras, that of being produced, severely critized, and then discarded. But *Porgy and Bess* refused to die. In 1937 it received the David Bispham Medal for distinguished contribution to American opera. It returned to the stage in Los Angeles and San Francisco in 1938. A revival in New York in 1942 resulted in the longest run of any revival in the history of the American musical theater. Between 1952 and 1956 an American black company brought the opera throughout the United States, Latin America, Europe, the Middle East, the Soviet Union, and countries behind the iron curtain (and after that to the Far East), scoring a triumph wherever they went. It became the first American opera ever to be seen on the stage of La Scala in Milan, and this company was the first from America to tour the Soviet Union. In 1959, the opera was made into a motion picture produced by Samuel Goldwyn. In 1965 *Porgy and Bess* entered the repertoire of the Volksoper in Vienna. In the years that followed, the opera was also produced by native opera companies in Turkey, Bulgaria, France, Hungary, Germany, Czechoslovakia, Sweden, and Norway. The year of 1970 began with a production by the Komische Oper in East Berlin and ended with a Danish production by the Copenhagen Opera. When, in 1970, the opera was given in its setting of Charleston, S.C., to commemorate the 300th anniversary of the founding of the city, social history was made in America, for this was the first time in Charleston that whites and blacks were allowed to mingle both in the auditorium and at the gala party that followed.

The opera that had been produced in all these places, beginning with the world premiere, was not the opera Gershwin had originally written. It was truncated through the omission of some salient sections to reduce the running time and to make the role of Porgy less exacting. In addition, the opera had been presented with spoken dialogue whereas originally, true to grand opera tradition, recitatives were used. On August 16, 1975—after more than forty years following its premiere—*Porgy and Bess* was finally heard the way the original score demanded, though heard in a concert version, by the Cleveland Orchestra, soloists and chorus conducted by Lorin Maazel at the Blossom Music Center in Cleveland. The first stage production of the complete score, and with the recitatives, followed in the spring of 1976 at the Houston Grand Opera in Texas, which then took it on tour throughout the United States and in Europe. The critical consensus was that, given this way, as Gershwin had originally intended, the opera gained dimension and stature. Edward Greenfield, writing in *Gramophone* in London, said that the "bigness" of the opera could now be perceived fully for the first time and that now it ranked with *Wozzeck* and *Peter Grimes* as a revealing and moving operatic portrait of human nature.

Gershwin was working on the music for *The Goldwyn Follies* in Beverly Hills, Calif., in 1937 when he collapsed. After an exploratory operation at the Cedars of Lebanon Hospital it was discovered that he was suffering from cystic tumor in the right temporal lobe. He died in the hospital the following morning.

Since his death, performances of his compositions and all-Gershwin concerts have kept his music vibrantly alive in all parts of the civilized world. He is the only American, and one of the few composers of the 20th century, whose works continually occupy complete programs everywhere, a fact made all the more remarkable when it is recalled how few in number are his serious compositions. He is also the only American composer to have his biography written by foreign authors for publication in their own countries: Germany and Holland each released two such biographies; Austria, France, Italy, Hungary and Poland, one each. This does not take into account the sixteen languages into which my own biography of Gershwin was translated (including Chinese, Japanese, Vietnamese and Hebrew).

In 1937, while he was still alive, Gershwin was elected to the Royal Academy of Santa Cecilia in Rome, the highest honor Italy could bestow on a foreign composer. Gershwin's name was used for a Liberty Ship during World War II; a competition for young American composers in New York (1943) and Los Angeles (1947); a collection of music and music literature at Fisk University in Nashville, Tenn., (1946); a workshop at Boston University (1950); a junior high school in Brooklyn, N.Y. (1957); for an elementary school in the black section of Chicago (1966); and one of the colleges at the State University at Stony Brook, Long Island (1970). Mayor Robert F. Wagner of New York proclaimed George Gershwin Week in March 1957 in anticipation of the twentieth anniversary of his death and in October 1959, to honor his sixtieth birthday retrospectively, Gershwin was honored throughout the United States with concerts of his music, study sessions in schools, radio and television programs, and a Gershwin exhibit at the library of Congress in Washington, D.C. In 1963, the borough president of Brooklyn, N.Y., named September 26 George Gershwin Day. In 1968, A Gershwin Week was proclaimed by Mayor Lindsay of New York in conjunction with the opening, at the Museum of the City of New York, of the most comprehensive retrospective exhibition of Gershwiniana ever attempted. A three-day Gershwin festival, organized by the School of Music of the University of Miami in Florida on October 27, 28, and 29, 1970, was the first anywhere to offer every concert work ever written by Gershwin, including some that had not been heard in decades. In 1973, an eight-cent stamp bearing the Gershwin likeness was issued by the U. S. Post Office; one year later, Gershwin became one of the first inducted into the Entertainment Hall of Fame.

THE COMPOSER SPEAKS: Jazz I regard as an Ameri-

can folk music; not the only one, but a very powerful one that is probably in the blood and feeling of the American people more than any other style of folk music. I believe that it can be made the basis of serious symphonic works of lasting value, in the hands of a composer with talent for both jazz and symphonic music. . . .

Jazz has contributed an enduring value to America in the sense that it has expressed ourselves. It is an original American achievement that will endure, not as jazz perhaps, and will leave its mark on future music in one form or another. The only kinds of music that endure are those which possess form in the universal sense and folk music. All else dies. But unquestionably folk songs are being written and have been written that contain enduring elements of jazz. To be sure, that is only an element; it is not the whole. An entire composition written in jazz could not live.

PRINCIPAL WORKS: *Lullaby*, for string quartet (1919); *135th Street*, one-act opera (1922); *Rhapsody in Blue*, for piano and orchestra (1924); Concerto in F, for piano and orchestra; (1925); Three Piano Preludes (1926); *An American in Paris*, tone poem for orchestra (1928); *Second Rhapsody*, for piano and orchestra (1931); *Cuban Overture*, for orchestra and Cuban percussion instruments (1932); *Variations on I Got Rhythm*, for piano and orchestra (1934); *Porgy and Bess*, opera (1935).

BIBLIOGRAPHY: Armitage, Merle (ed.), *George Gershwin* (N.Y., 1938); Ewen, David, *George Gershwin: His Journey to Greatness* (Englewood Cliffs, N.J., 1970); Goldberg, Isaac, *George Gershwin* (N.Y., 1931); Jablonski, Edward and Stewart, Lawrence D., *The Gershwin Years* (N.Y., 1973); Schwartz, Charles, *George Gershwin: His Life and Music* (N.Y., 1973).

Ghent, Emmanuel, b. Montreal, Canada, May 15, 1925. American citizen, 1962.

Since 1969, Ghent has made extensive use of the GROOVE Computer System, which generates, edits, and stores functions of time which in turn provide the controls for the real-time synthesis of electronically generated music, and/or theatrical lighting effects. While most of the music Ghent composed before 1969 was for acoustic instruments, all his music since then has been composed for computer-generated tape either alone or in conjunction with live instruments. Some of his pieces involve computer-composed theatrical lighting scores. He has explored a multiplicity of rhythmic avenues suggested by a harmonic-melodic kernel. After some experimentation with his "polynome" in the early 1960s, Ghent devised the "coordinome," a paper tape device whose signals were recorded on magnetic tape, with or without synchronized electronic music. The aggregate of signals on tape was separately decoded, enabling each performer equipped with an earphone to have his own "conductor."

His early boyhood passion for playing hockey vanished suddenly when, at the age of fourteen, he became passionately interested in music. At Montreal High School, he played the timpani in the school orchestra and made arrangements of sonatas by Mozart and Beethoven for a small chamber ensemble he conducted there. While at high school he composed some chamber music, including a quartet for string trio and flute; all this early music has been lost.

Between 1942 and 1946 he attended McGill University, where he majored in biochemistry. Through his college years he took courses in music with many teachers at the McGill Conservatory. He studied the bassoon with R. de H. Tupper and performed it with the McGill Orchestra. He also played the sousaphone in the McGill Canadian Officers' Training Corps Military Marching Band.

Upon graduating from McGill University with a bachelor of science degree, he spent four years at the McGill University Faculty of Medicine. He received the Holmes Gold Medal for the highest standing throughout these years in medical school and was graduated in 1950 with an M.D. degree. Between June and September 1948 he was sent as a McGill representative to the UNESCO-sponsored International Student Seminar in Plön, Germany.

In 1951, he made his permanent address in New York City. During the next four years he attended the W. A. White Institute of Psychoanalysis, receiving in 1956 his diploma in psychoanalysis.

He composed little music between 1946 and 1960, and the works he wrote were confined exclusively to chamber music. These included three duos for flutes (1944), *Movement*, for wind quintet (1944) and *Lament*, for string quartet (1958). Composition came to the foreground in 1960 with the completion of a quartet for woodwinds, sketches of which had been gathering dust for years. It was after completing this composition that his main career as composer began. Between 1961 and 1963 he studied composition privately with Ralph Shapey, whose influence (together with that of Edgard Varèse and Stravinsky) were strongly brought to bear on the music he was now writing: Two Duos, for flute and clarinet (1962; N.Y., March 21, 1974), *Dance Movements*, for trumpet and string quartet (1962): *Entelechy*, for viola and piano (1963; Bennington, Vt., August 29, 1964), and *Triality* I and II, for violin, trumpet, bassoon, and the polynome (1964; N.Y., February 24, 1965). "Beginning with *Entelechy*," Ghent explains, "most of the instrumental music I have written has made use of intervallic groupings as the basis for pitch structure both melodically and vertically." A sense of excitement was realized rhythmically through the use of conflicting multitempo relationships. In *Entelechy* these were notated as occurring at a single tempo. But in *Dithyrambos*, for brass

quintet (1965) and in *Hex* (1966), for trumpet, eleven instruments, and four-track tape (one track used to transmit signals to the performer) a frankly multitempo multimeter notation was used. "Performability was assured through the assistance of a programmed signal track on a single magnetic track," Ghent says. "Those signals were decoded by a rather simple pitch-filtering device that enabled each performer or group of performers to hear only the signals intended for him (them). This technique has the further advantage of permitting absolutely precise synchronization of performers with pre-recorded electronic music on three other tracks of a four-channel tape, as in *Hex*." After a concert at the Composers Forum in New York on January 15, 1966, where *Entelechy* was performed and *Dithyrambos* was premiered, a critic for *The Village Voice* wrote: "*Entelechy* is an intelligent and intense work that showed Mr. Ghent to be a composer of serious rhythmic interest . . . Ghent's brass piece utilized . . . a coordinome which fed varying tempos and rhythmic references through earphones to the performers, who were scattered about the auditorium. It is to his credit that he didn't use this device as a toy but as a sincere aid to the execution of a very musically conceived work." Closely related to *Entelechy* is *Entelechy* II (1976; N.Y., April 22, 1976), in which the viola part is identical to the one in *Entelechy* but the piano part replaced by an "orchestration" for computer.

Hex, "an ellipsis for trumpet, instruments, and tape" (1966; N.Y., September 27, 1966)—which may be thought of as a chamber symphony in four sections—was commissioned by the trumpeter Ronald Anderson, who introduced it with Arthur Bloom conducting. It was based on six harmonic structures which made their first appearance in linear or melodic form right at the outset. A unique feature of this piece is that at all times the live performers and tape were precisely synchronized, ensured by the use of four-track magnetic tape, the electronic music recorded in three tracks and the fourth used for signals to the performers. "This wild excursion into the beyond of electronic music," noted Howard Klein in the *New York Times* after the premiere, "may be the most successful combination of live musicians and tape so far."

On a commission from the violinist Paul Zukofsky, Ghent wrote *Helices*, for violin, piano, and tape, early in 1969, and it received its world premiere in New York on March 26, 1969. "This work," the composer explains, "derives its name from the structural notion of unfolding spirals in which the same material returns with each twist of the helix. Each new turn, however, is different by virtue of its own structural development as well as its new relationship with other unfolding elements."

In the 1960s Ghent was associated with the Columbia Princeton Electronic Music Center and, since 1969, he has worked at the computer-controlled electronic music studio of the Bell Telephone Laboratories in Murray Hill, N.J. He received a Guggenheim Fellowship in 1967.

With *Phosphones* (1971), commissioned by the Mimi Garrard Dance Company, Ghent initiated his collaboration with James Seawright, a kinetic sculptor, and his wife, the dancer Mimi Garrard, in developing a computer-composed theatrical lighting score by means of the GROOVE program in conjunction with a Honeywell DDP-224 computer. This, the composer informs us, "allows the most subtle, complex, and hitherto impossible effects to be exactly synchronized with music and live dance. This system affords the most refined control of nuance in lighting and makes it possible to treat the lighting, if so desired, as another contrapuntal element in the compositional fabric." The score of *Phosphones* consists of two compositions, one of music on magnetic tape (which is not always precisely synchronized with the lighting) and the other of lighting on punched-paper tape. The music may be played either alone or in conjunction with a dance composition. The premiere took place in New York on April 13, 1971, choreographed by Mimi Garrard and performed by the Mimi Garrard Dance Company. As described by Vicki Smith in the *Fullerton* (Calif.) *Register*, in *Phosphones* "the dancers interact with the light's undulations and rhythmic fluctuation to form a counterpoint with the rhythms of the music. As the music changes from the slow, rhythmic patterns of the first section to the jazz patterns of later sections, the lights change to the corresponding cool colors of blue and green to the hot colors of red, orange, amber and magenta. In *Phosphones*, the light, music, and dance were exquisitely executed."

Later computer-generated music, synchronized with a computer-generated lighting score by Mimi Garrard and played in conjunction with dance patterns choreographed by her, include *Dualities* (1972; Jackson, Miss., April 25, 1972); *Oith* (1972, N.Y., March 23, 1973); and *Brazen* (1975; N.Y., May 15, 1975), commissioned by the New York State Council on the Arts. The last of these was a fully computerized version of *Lustrum*, a concerto grosso for electronic string quintet, brass quintet, and computer-generated tape (1974; Chicago, April 4, 1974) which the Fromm Music Foundation had commissioned.

In 1974, Ghent's focus in computer music shifted to making use of the computer as a kind of compositional associate. "I, as composer, would write programs which both made 'intelligent' pitch and rhythmic choices and yet afforded me, as composer, a vast variety of choices both precompositionally as well as in real-time, through the manipulation of every conceivable compositional parameter." The first experiments intentionally oriented to a tonal center (in order to more easily "hear" what the computer was doing in real-time) was the already mentioned *Lustrum* together with the *Divertimento for Electronic Violin and Computer Brass* (1973; N.Y. February 2,

1975). In the *New York Times* Joseph Horowitz called the *Divertimento* "a delight. Mr. Ghent has juxtaposed taped sounds suggesting idealized horns and trombones with the livelier, more personalized elaborations of a plugged-in violinist. The tape's handsome slabs of tone are linked in a chugging, harmonically static ostinato."

Ghent's most recent phase of computer music represents a kind of return to the earlier concern with intervallic groupings. But this time the focus has been on "teaching the computer how to collaborate with my overall intentions." This effort resulted in a series of compositions entitled *Program Music 1 through 29* (1977-79), twenty-nine computer-music pieces varying in duration from two to twenty-seven minutes. *Baobab* (1979) is computer music with computer-graphic film, images created by Ken Knowlton. It was first shown at the Composers Forum Festival (which commissioned it) in New York on April 2, 1979.

Ghent received grants from the National Endowment for the Arts in 1974 and 1975, and a Special Projects Grant from the same foundation with Mimi Garrard and James Seawright. He has given lecture-demonstrations through the years in many of America's leading colleges, universities, and conservatories and has written numerous articles and papers.

He maintains a part-time practice in New York as psychoanalytic therapist, is involved in the training of other analysts, and is on the teaching faculty of New York University Post-Doctoral Program for Psychoanalysis. He was married three times: to Lila Rosenzweig, an experimental psychologist, in Montreal on October 6, 1946, whom he divorced in 1956; Natalie Gudkov, a violinist, in New York on September 22, 1962, divorced in 1974; and Karen Weiss, a teacher, in New York on December 7, 1978. Ghent's two daughters and a stepdaughter are all from his second marriage.

PRINCIPAL WORKS: *Entelechy*, for violin and piano (1963); *Triality* I and II, for violin, trumpet, bassoon, and special equipment (1964); *Dithyrambos*, for brass quintet and special equipment (1965); *Hex*, an ellipsis for trumpet, chamber ensemble, four-track tape, and special equipment (1966); *Helices*, for violin, piano, and tape (1969); *L'après midi d'un Summit Meeting*, for computer-generated electronic tape (1970); *Our Daily Bread*, for electronic tape (1970); *Innerness*, for computer-generated electronic tape (1970); *Fission*, for computer-generated electronic tape (1971); *Phosphones*, computer-generated electronic music with or without synchronized computer-generated electronic lighting (1971); *Dualities*, computer-generated electronic music with a computer-generated lighting score (1972); *Divertimento for Electronic Violin and Computer Bass*, a piece for electronic or amplified violin and tape (1973); *Lustrum*, concerto grosso for electronic string quintet, brass quintet, and computer-generated tape (1974);

Brazen, a fully computerized version of *Lustrum* (1975); *Entelechy* II, for viola and computer-generated tape (1976); *Program Music 1 through 29,* a series of computer music pieces (1977–79); *Baobab,* computer music and computer-graphic film (1979); *A Little Hammerpiece,* for two mallet players (1979).

BIBLIOGRAPHY: *BBDM; DCM; High Fidelity/Musical America,* June 1979.

Giannini, Vittorio, b. Philadelphia, Pa., October 19, 1903; d. New York November 28, 1966.

Though he wrote a considerable amount of concert music, Giannini is perhaps best remembered for his operas, of which he wrote a dozen. He carried on the traditions of the Italian opera from 18th-century bel canto and the 19th-century opera buffa through the verismo works of Puccini.

His grandfather was a poet and song composer who had come to New York from Tuscany as a political refugee. Both of Vittorio's parents were musicians. His father, Vittorio Giannini, was a tenor of the Metropolitan Opera who became the first man to record on the modern flat phonograph disk in the late 1890s; his mother was a trained violinist; and his sister, Dusolina, his senior by a year, became a celebrated prima donna. Vittorio's mother was his first music teacher, giving him violin lessons in early childhood. He made such progress that when he was nine he won a scholarship to the Verdi Conservatory in Milan, where he remained four years (1913–17). In Milan, when he was fourteen, he made his first attempt at writing opera.

Upon returning to the United States he received further instruction in violin as well as in composition from private teachers in New York. On fellowships in violin and composition he entered the Juilliard School of Music in 1925, where he remained for the next five years, a student of Rubin Goldmark's in composition and Hans Letz's in violin. He graduated from Juilliard in 1930. On June 1, 1931, he married Lucia Avella; they were divorced in 1951.

In 1932, Giannini was awarded the Prix de Rome, which brought him to the American Academy in Rome for a three-year residence. Because of his exceptional work, he was invited to stay there for a fourth year.

His first works revealed a conservative posture, a composer ready to submit to the structural demands of baroque or classical music, while bringing to them a romantic and melodic gift influenced by Brahms and Fauré. These initial works included the String Quartet (1930), which received the Juilliard School Publication Award in 1931, and the Piano Quintet (1930), recipient of the Society for the Publication of American Music Award in 1932. His first orchestral work was the Suite (1931), its first performance taking place in New York on June 23, 1940. In 1934,

the Trustees of the New York State Theodore Roosevelt Memorial invited Giannini to write a symphonic work honoring Roosevelt. He complied with the *Symphony: In Memoriam Theodore Roosevelt* (1935), which was broadcast by NBC radio network from the American Museum of Natural History in New York on January 19, 1936; its first public performance followed in Rochester, N.Y., on April 30, 1936, by the Rochester Philharmonic under Howard Hanson. In 1939 Giannini wrote the *IBM Symphony* for the inauguration of IBM's new world headquarters building.

Giannini's first opera, *Lucedia* (1934), was produced in Munich, Germany, on October 10, 1934. His next opera was *The Scarlet Letter* (1937), his own libretto based on Nathaniel Hawthorne. When it was first presented—Hamburg, Germany, on June 2, 1938—his sister, Dusolina, assumed the principal soprano role. Before the 1930s were over, Giannini wrote two more operas, both intended for radio transmission and both commissioned by CBS: *Beauty and the Beast* (1938; November 24, 1938) and *Blennerhasset* (1939; November 24, 1939). Here Giannini revealed a strong gift for mobile Italian lyricism and a deft hand in the writing of ensemble and choral numbers very much in the 19th-century tradition.

Giannini's most successful opera—indeed, his most successful work in any medium—was *The Taming of the Shrew* (1950), libretto by Giannini and Dorothy Fee based on the Shakespeare comedy with supplementary material from the sonnets and *Romeo and Juliet.* Its first performance was given by the Cincinnati Music Drama Guild and the Cincinnati Symphony on January 31, 1953, Thor Johnson conducting. It had originally been intended for television, and on March 13, 1954, it was produced by the NBC Opera Theater over the NBC-TV network, when it received the Music Critics Circle Award. On April 13, 1956, it was successfully staged by the New York City Opera, and on August 9, 1979, it was revived by the Houston Grand Opera in Texas. To a text of exceptional beauty, offered in Shakespeare's own words, Giannini created an ebullient, witty, insouciant score, skillfull in its contrasts and climaxes and spilling over with gay or poignant Italianate melodies, sprightly ensemble numbers in the tradition of opera buffa and Verdi's *Falstaff,* and sensitive in its balance between voices and orchestra. In the *New York Times,* Howard Taubman said: "There is crispness and point in this music as it speeds the action, and it does not hesitate to pause and sing with sentiment in a shamelessly old-fashioned way. . . . The score is instinct with the spirit of Italian lyricism."

The Taming of the Shrew was written on a commission from NBC-TV. Many of Giannini's compositions outside the theater in the 1950s were also the result of commissions. For the Cincinnati Symphony and its conductor, Thor Johnson, he wrote the Symphony no. 1 (1950), performed on April 6, 1951, and the *Canticle for Christmas*, for baritone, chorus and orchestra (1951), heard in the year of its composition. For the 500th anniversary of the Moravian Church he wrote *Canticle of the Martyrs* (1957), given at the Moravian Festival at Bethlehem, Pa., in 1957. Prelude and Fugue, for string orchestra (1955), was written for the Juilliard School of Music, and the Symphony no. 3, for band (1959) for Duke University in North Carolina.

In 1939 Giannini became a faculty member of the Juilliard School of Music, where he taught composition, orchestration, and theory until his death. Concurrently, he taught composition, fugue, and orchestration and was head of the theory department at the Manhattan School of Music beginning in 1941, and from 1956 until 1964 he was professor of composition at the Curtis Institute in Philadelphia. During the summer of 1962 he served as dean of the Advance Division at Brevard Music Center in North Carolina. In 1953 he married his second wife, Joan Adler, this marriage ending in divorce ten years later.

Giannini wrote *The Medead* (1960), a monodrama for soprano and orchestra, text based on Euripides, on a commission from the Ford Foundation, and it was premiered by Irene Jordan and the Atlanta Symphony in Atlanta, Ga., on October 20, 1960. Once again under the auspices of the Ford Foundation he wrote the opera *The Harvest* (1961). Its libretto, by the composer and Karl Flaster, used the setting of an American farm on or about 1900 to relate a story of lust and tragedy. *The Harvest* was produced by the Lyric Opera of Chicago on November 25, 1961. In the vein of the opera buffa was *Rehearsal Call* (1951), commissioned by the Juilliard School of Music, where it was first performed on February 15, 1962. The libretto was by Francis Swann and Robert A. Simon, based on Swann's play. Giannini's last opera, *The Servant of Two Masters* (1966), was also an opera buffa, Bernard Stambler preparing a libretto adapted from the comedy of Goldoni. Commissioned by the New York City Opera with a grant from the Ford Foundation, it was premiered in New York on March 9, 1967.

In 1964, Giannini was appointed president of the North Carolina School of the Arts at Winston-Salem, N.C., where he created a summer school affiliated with the Chigi Academy in Siena, Italy. At the same time, Giannini continued his affiliation with the Juilliard School by taking the office of director of a special repertoire project financed by the U.S. Office of Education. Giannini was not destined to hold either position long. He was found dead in bed in his apartment in New York City.

Giannini was awarded honorary doctorates in music from the New York College of Music (1939), the Curtis Institute in Philadelphia (1957), and the Cincinnati Conservatory of Music (1961).

THE COMPOSER SPEAKS: There's a tremendous difference between "writing music" and composing. Anyone who has had the proper amount of technical training, which anyone can get if he works hard enough, is able to write music. But to compose, one has to wait for inspiration. The composer's duty is to express what is in him with the utmost sincerity, with no thought of whether it is "original" and no desire to make an impression by doing startling things. It may sound trite to say it, but there's no denying that beauty must still be the ultimate goal of composition. A composer can say to himself, "I'm going to write a canon," or "I'm going to write a fugue," and do it. But he can't say, "I'm going to write a melody," and do that. You have to wait for a melody—and it has to come to you. Those composers who make a point of avoiding melody are those who, in most instances, couldn't [write one] if they wanted to, because it never comes to them.

PRINCIPAL WORKS: 4 (numbered) symphonies (1950–60); 3 divertimentos, for orchestra (1953, 1961, 1964); 2 violin sonatas (1926, 1945).

String Quartet (1930); Suite, for orchestra (1931); Piano Quintet (1931); Woodwind Quintet (1933); Piano Trio (1933); Piano Sonata (1933); *Lucedia*, opera (1934); *Symphony: In Memoriam Theodore Roosevelt* (1935); Piano Concerto (1935); Requiem, for vocal soloists, chorus, and orchestra (1936); Organ Concerto (1937); *The Scarlet Letter*, opera (1937); *Beauty and the Beast*, radio opera (1938); *Blennerhasset*, radio opera (1939); *IBM Symphony* (1939); Violin Concerto (1940); Concerto, for two pianos and orchestra (1940); Concerto Grosso, for string quartet and string orchestra (1946); Trumpet Concerto (1947); *Variations on a Cantus Firmus*, for piano (1947); *Frescobaldia*, for orchestra (1948); *The Taming of the Shrew*, opera (1950); Canticle for Christmas, for baritone, chorus, and orchestra (1951); Prelude and Fugue, for string orchestra (1955); *Canticle of the Martyrs*, for vocal soloists, chorus, and orchestra (1957); Praeludium and Allegro, for band (1959); *The Medead*, monodrama for soprano and orchestra (1960); *The Harvest*, opera (1961); Psalm 130, concerto for double bass or cello and orchestra (1963); *The Servant of Two Masters*, opera (1966).

BIBLIOGRAPHY: Ewen, David, *Composers Since 1900* (N.Y., 1969). *Juilliard Review*, Spring 1957; *New York City Opera Program Book*, March 9, 1967; *New York Times*, November 28, 1966 (obituary); *Opera News*, April 11, 1964; *Who's Who in America, 1966–67*.

Gideon, Miriam, b. Greeley, Colo., October 23, 1906.

Since the early 1940s, Gideon has used both the refractory twelve-tone method and expressionism in virtually all her representative works, making them, as Lester Trimble once wrote, "the servant of a very personal imagery. Hers is an American expressionism, not central European."

Her father, Abram Gideon, was a distinguished linguist, a professor at Colorado State Teachers College. In spite of the cultural atmosphere in which she grew up, there was no musical instrument or music of any kind in the household. She was fascinated, however, by any music she heard or sang in school and was transported with delight when at the age of nine she began piano lessons with a cousin in Chicago, where the family moved in 1915. An uncle, Henry Gideon, a prominent choral conductor and organist in Boston who was musical director of Temple Israel, took notice of her interest in music, and her ability to read music at sight, transpose, and improvise. These same gifts were recognized by the pianist Hans Barth after the Gideon family had moved to New York in 1916. Miriam studied with him for the next three years, during which time she was invited to play short solo recitals every few weeks at the Music Conservatory in Yonkers, where her lessons took place.

In 1921, Henry Gideon persuaded her parents to allow him to take charge of her musical education in Boston. There she was graduated from Girls High School in 1922. She then attended Boston University, College of Liberal Arts, receiving a bachelor of arts degree in 1926. During the Boston sojourn she studied piano with Felix Fox, a pupil of Isidor Philipp's, but her interest in the piano as a career gave way to a greater interest in composing. She acquired a solid theoretical background in music at the university, but the most profound influence during these years came from the environment in her uncle's home and that of her colleagues, where she became acquainted with choral and art-song literature as well as that of the synagogue.

In 1926, after graduation from Boston University, she returned to New York City where she has lived ever since. She studied briefly at New York University with Martin Bernstein, Marion Bauer, Charles Haubiel, and Jacques Pillois. These studies reinforced her enthusiasm for composing. She spent the next few years (1931–34) as a student of Lazare Saminsky's, who consolidated her previous theoretical training and helped her find a more personal style. At his suggestion she decided to work with Roger Sessions, who had just returned from several years' stay in Europe, and the next years (1935–43) were spent in concentrated study with him. It was under his tutelage that she wrote her first representative works, and she considers him her most important influence as a teacher.

In 1939 she went to France and Switzerland with the intention of staying there indefinitely to devote herself to further study and composition. The outbreak of World War II frustrated these plans.

After her return to the United States she entered Columbia University in 1942, studying medieval music with Eric Herzmann and musicology with Paul Henry Lang; in 1946 she received a master of arts degree in musicology. In 1944 she was appointed to the music faculty of Brooklyn College in New York, where she remained for the next decade; concurrently, beginning with 1947, she was also on the music faculty of the College of the City of New York. One of her colleagues at Brooklyn College was Frederic Ewen, writer and professor of English literature; they were married in New York on December 16, 1949.

Among her earliest compositions, the most important is *Lyric Piece*, for string quartet (1941; Baltimore, Md., January 14, 1962). Arranged for orchestra, it was introduced by the London Symphony Orchestra under Hugo Weisgall on April 9, 1944, and was subsequently recorded by the Imperial Orchestra of Tokyo, William Strickland conducting.

With *The Hound of Heaven* (1945; N.Y., March 23, 1945) Gideon achieved a personal style. Inspired by several lines from a poem of the same name by Francis Thompson, the work is scored for medium voice, oboe, and string trio. Here Gideon explores areas of dissonant counterpoint and concerns herself with intervals as generating forces for larger statements. In the *American Composers Alliance Bulletin* George Perle describes this music as "strikingly personal, characterized by lightness, the sudden exposure of individual notes, constantly shifting octave relationships. . . . This is a technique that imposes economy and the exclusion of irrelevancies."

Her skill in writing for the voice and making the sensitive adjustment between solo voice and a small group of instruments, as demonstrated in *The Hound of Heaven*, was further revealed in two succeeding song cycles: *Five Sonnets from Shakespeare*, for voice, trumpet, and string quartet or string orchestra (1950; N.Y., April 1, 1951), and *Three Sonnets from "Fatal Interview"* on poems of Edna St. Vincent Millay, for voice and piano (1952), later arranged for voice and string trio (1955; N.Y., January 14, 1956).

Gideon was also developing as an instrumental composer, showing increasing subtlety in her rhythmic invention and a more striking use of dissonant harmonies and dramatic contrast. This first became evident in Quartet for Strings (1946), introduced by the Walden String Quartet at Yaddo in Saratoga, N.Y., on September 14, 1956. Other works of this period include the Sonata for Viola and Piano (1940; N.Y., November 21, 1948); Divertimento, for woodwind quartet (1940; N.Y., March 21, 1949); *Symphonia Brevis*, for orchestra (1953), commissioned by the orchestra of the College of the City of New York, which introduced it on May 16, 1953, later recorded by the Zurich Radio Orchestra conducted by Jacques Monod; and Sonata for Cello and Piano (1948; N.Y., April 14, 1961).

Fantasy on a Javanese Motive, for cello and piano (1948; N.Y., January 14, 1956), was the first of several of her excursions into ethnic territory; in it the intervallic structure of a gamelan melody and the sonorities of a gamelan orchestra were suggested. This work anticipated some of Gideon's subsequent ambitious compositions in which she was attracted to various national identities.

In her opera *Fortunato* (1954–56), based on the Spanish play by Serafín and Joaquín Quintero, libretto by the composer, authentic folk songs of the Madrid area (the locale of the play) were fused with the composer's style. In the "Hiroshima" section of *The Condemned Playground* (1963, N.Y., May 16, 1963), for soprano, tenor, flute, bassoon, and string quartet, a poem by Gary Spokes is set first in English, then in a Japanese translation by Satoka Akiya. The remainder of the work is also bilingual: the first part, "Pyrrya," a setting of an ode by Horace, is first sung in the English translation by John Milton and then in the original Latin; the third section, based on *The Litanies of Satan* by Baudelaire, is sung mainly in the English translation by Edna St. Vincent Millay, with refrains in the original French.

Japanese poetry is featured prominently in *The Seasons of Time*, for voice, flute, cello, celesta, and piano (1969; N.Y., February 13, 1970). These are ten songs based on ancient Japanese Tanka poetry, in which the delicacy of the text, as Paul Hume noted in *Book World*, "is mirrored in the sounds [of the instruments], each used with a shimmer like that of a silk screening." On the other hand, Gideon reaches to German poetry in *Spiritual Madrigals*, for men's voices, viola, cello, and bassoon (1965; N.Y., May 22, 1968), also arranged for solo voice and instrumental ensemble; in *Rhymes from the Hill*, for voice, clarinet, cello, and marimba (1968; N.Y., May 22, 1968); and in *Songs of Youth and Madness*, for voice and orchestra (1977; N.Y., December 5, 1977), written on a grant from the National Endowment for the Arts. *Spiritual Madrigals* derived its texts from poems by Frederic Ewen, Heinrich Heine, and a 13th-century Minnisinger. *Rhymes from the Hill* utilized five poems from the *Galgenlieder*, or *Gallows Songs* of Christian Morgenstern. *Songs of Youth and Madness* set four poems by Friedrich Hölderlin, in which each song is heard twice, first in English translation and then in the original German.

An interest in Irish folk material, which looks back on Gideon's years in Boston, when she made the acquaintance of folk songs from the British Isles and elsewhere, is evident in her *Fantasy on Irish Folk Motives*, for oboe, viola, bassoon or cello, vibraphone, glockenspiel, and tam-tam, commissioned by the New York State Music Teachers Association (1975; Albany, N.Y., October 26, 1975). *Voices from Elysium*, for voice, flute, clarinet, violin, cello, and piano (1979; N.Y., April 18, 1979)—commissioned by the Da Capo Players, who introduced it—is an evocation of Greek antiquity, as it reflects tenderly and at times whimsically upon life and death.

The first setting Gideon made for a Hebrew prayer was *Adon Olom*, for mixed chorus, solo voices,

and instruments or organ (1954; Baltimore, Md., May 23, 1954). During her years in Boston and subsequently as professor of music at the Cantors Institute of the Jewish Theological Seminary, Gideon became closely acquainted with synagogal music. Thus when in 1970 David Gooding, music director of the temple in Cleveland, commissioned her to write a Sabbath Morning Service (the first woman to be commissioned to write a complete service), she was no stranger to the music of the synagogue. This service—*Sacred Service for the Sabbath Morning* (1970)—was introduced in Cleveland on April 18, 1971, scored for vocal soloists, choir and flute, oboe, bassoon, trumpet, viola, cello, and organ. Though her musical style here remains freely atonal, her writing so conveys the spirit of the Hebrew Liturgy that in the *Congress Bi-Weekly*, the organ of the American Jewish Congress, Albert Weisser called it "the finest service yet composed by a native-born American-Jewish composer, and very probably the most important advance in the form since Darius Milhaud's *Service sacré* (1947)."

Two years later, Gideon was commissioned by Cantor David Putterman and the Park Avenue Synagogue to write a Friday Evening Service, *Shirat Miriam L'Shabbat (Miriam's Song for the Sabbath)*, for cantor, choir and organ. Written in 1973 and presented at the Park Avenue Synagogue on May 3, 1974, it differs from its predecessor in its harmonic language, which is less dissonant, and in its use of cantillation motives, transformed and elaborated. Albert Weisser, in a review for the *Journal of Synagogue Music*, called it "a work of such deceptive simplicity that only a master could have fashioned it."

Also related to biblical cantillation is a work for organ: *Three Biblical Masks* (1957; N.Y., January 26, 1958). These are portraits of the main characters in the story of Purim in the Old Testament, for which cantillation motives from Esther are suggested and exploited; this work was later arranged for violin and piano. Drawing also on biblical sources is *The Habitable Earth* (1965; N.Y., May 10, 1965), a cantata for soloists, chorus, piano, and oboe, based on Proverbs.

Among Gideon's settings for solo voice and instrumental group is *Questions on Nature*, for voice, oboe, piano, glockenspiel, and tam-tam (1964; N.Y., April 26, 1964), a setting of the questions propounded by Adelard of Bath, the 12th-century English philosopher. "The instrumental sonorities as well as the character of the vocal lines," the composer explains, "are intended to convey the mystery and childlike directness of the topics contemplated, such as: 'How the earth moves,' 'What food the stars eat if they are animals,' and 'Why men universally die.'" Nocturnes, for voices and instrumental ensemble (1975), written on commission for a young girl's eighteenth birthday, set three poems respectively by Shelley, Jean Starr Untermeyer, and Frank Dempster Sherman. Each poem and its transmutation into music seemed to her "an appropriate evocation of youth and its awakening to the magical forces of Nature." Judith Raskin and the Saint Paul Chamber Orchestra gave the premiere in St. Paul, Minn., on February 21, 1976.

Two works involving the clarinet, commissioned by the composer-clarinetist Meyer Kupferman, are the Suite, for clarinet and piano (1972; N.Y., January 31, 1973) and the Trio, for clarinet, cello, and piano (1978; N.Y., April 3, 1979). "In recognition of the high achievement of one of our outstanding composers," Miriam Gideon received a commission from the Elizabeth Sprague Coolidge Foundation of the Library of Congress in Washington, D.C., in 1979. Her response was *Spirit Above the Dust* (1980), a song cycle of American poetry for solo voice and eight instruments. The world premiere took place at Yale University on February 11, 1981, followed by repeat performances at the Library of Congress on September 25, 1981, and at a concert of the International Society for Contemporary Music in New York on October 15, 1981.

In 1969, Gideon received an award from the National Federation of Music Clubs and the American Society of Composers, Authors, and Publishers (ASCAP), given to an American woman composer for notable contributions to symphonic literature. In 1970 she was awarded a doctorate of sacred music in composition and in 1980 an honorary doctorate in music from the Jewish Theological Seminary. In 1975 she was elected to membership in the American Academy of Arts and Letters—the second woman composer to be thus honored. She has served on the board of governors of the American Composers Alliance, the American Music Center, and the National Society of Contemporary Music.

THE COMPOSER SPEAKS: If I were to use a technical term to describe my music it would be "free atonality." I am not primarily concerned with sonorities or precompositional devices, but rather with whether my ideas come from a genuine impulse to which I can respond. My ideas have to seem new to me . . . I have to be surprised by them.

One aspect of my music that has aroused interest and at times controversy is my dual setting within the same work of poems in the original language and in English translation. I can explain my attraction for this way of composing by my fascination with language as such, and by the challenge of finding an appropriate musical garb for the same poetic idea in a different language, at the same time resolving this diversity into an integrated whole.

PRINCIPAL WORKS: *Lyric Piece*, for string quartet or string orchestra (1941); Canzona, for piano (1945); *The Hound of Heaven*, for voice, oboe and string trio (1945); String Quartet (1946); Viola Sonata (1948); *Fantasy on a Javanese Motive*, for cello and piano (1948); Divertimento, for woodwind quartet (1949);

Air for Violin and Piano (1950); *Five Sonnets from Shakespeare*, for voice, trumpet, and string quartet (1950); *Three Sonnets from "Fatal Interview,"* for voice and piano, also for voice and string trio (1952); *Epitaphs from Robert Burns*, for voice and piano (1952); *Symphonia Brevis*, for orchestra (1953); *Adon Olom*, for solo voices, mixed chorus, instruments or organ (1954); *Fortunato,* opera (1954–56); *Three Biblical Masks*, for organ, also for violin and piano (1957); *To Music*, for voice and piano (1957); *Mixco*, for voice and piano (1957); *The Adorable Mouse*, a French folk tale, for voice and chamber group (1960); Cello Sonata (1961); *Songs of Voyage*, for voice and piano (1961); *The Condemned Playground*, for soprano, tenor, flute, bassoon, string quartet (1963); *Spiritual Madrigals*, for men's voices, viola, cello, bassoon (1965), later arranged as *Spiritual Airs*, for solo voice and instrumental ensemble; *The Habitable Earth*, for vocal soloists, chorus, piano, oboe (1965); *Of Shadows Numberless*, suite for piano, (1966); *Rhymes from the Hill*, for voice, clarinet, cello, marimba (1968); *The Seasons of Time*, for voice, flute, cello, celesta alternating with piano (1969); *Sacred Service for Sabbath Morning*, for soloists, choir, organ, and instrumental ensemble (1970); Suite for Clarinet and Piano (1972); *Shirat Miriam L'Shabbat*, Friday Evening Service, for cantor, choir, organ (1973); *Fantasy on Irish Folk Motives*, for oboe, viola, bassoon or cello, vibraphone, glockenspiel, tam-tam (1975); Nocturnes, for voice, flute, oboe, violin, cello, and vibraphone (1976); *Songs of Youth and Madness*, for voice and orchestra (1977); Piano Sonata (1977); Trio, for clarinet, cello and piano (1978); *Voices from Elysium*, for voice, flute, clarinet, violin, cello, and piano (1979); *Spirit above the Dust*, song cycle of American poetry for solo voice and eight instruments (1980); *Ayelet Hashakar*, "Morning Star," for voice and piano (1980).

BIBLIOGRAPHY: Rosenberg, Deena and Bernard (eds.), *The Music Makers* (N.Y., 1978); *American Composers Alliance Bulletin*, vol. 7, no. 4, 1958; *Ear*, Magazine East, April-May 1981; *Music Journal*, April 1976; *Who's Who in America, 1980–81*.

Gilbert, Henry Franklin Belknap, b. Somerville, Mass., September 26, 1868; d. Cambridge, Mass., May 19, 1928.

Gilbert belonged to those early 20th-century romantic composers striving for an American identity in composition. In this group he was probably the leading creative figure. He was one of the few musicians of his time to receive his entire musical education in the United States.

His ancestry reached back to the Revolutionary War. One of his uncles (James L. Gilbert) was the composer of the famous ballad "Bonnie Sweet Bessie," and one of his cousins was an eminent actor.

Both his parents were musical. His father, a bank clerk, was a church organist, singer, and composer of anthems, and his mother was a professional singer. Henry F. Gilbert was born with the right ventricle of his heart larger than normal, which sent an unusual amount of blood through his skin capillaries. This brought him a rich red complexion and, more dangerously, a heart deformity that made doctors predict he would not outlive his thirtieth birthday.

When he was ten, Henry F. Gilbert was so moved by a violin recital by Ole Bull, visiting Norwegian virtuoso, that he built for himself a violin from a cigar box and learned to play tunes on it. He received formal music instruction in grammar school, from which he was graduated in 1884, and from local teachers. In 1886 he entered the New England Conservatory in Boston, where he studied the violin with Emil Mollenhauer and harmony with Arthur Batelle Whiting. Between 1889 and 1892 he studied the piano with Edward MacDowell in Boston, becoming MacDowell's first American pupil. All this while, Gilbert earned his living by playing the violin for dances, in resort hotels, and in theater orchestras.

Unhappy with playing the violin for popular consumption, Gilbert decided in 1892 to abandon music altogether and earn his living elsewhere. For three years he supported himself by working in his uncle's printing plant, as a real estate agent, as a factory foreman, as an engraver and arranger for a Boston music publisher, by raising silkworms and collecting butterflies. In 1893 he worked as a bread-and-pie cutter at the World's Fair in Chicago. There he met a Russian prince who was a friend of Rimsky-Korsakov's. What the prince told him about the Russian nationalist school fired Gilbert's ambition to create a national music for America, an ideal that was further stimulated when he read the encouragement that Antonín Dvořák gave to American composers to seek out native material for their compositions, and from hearing Dvořák's *Symphony from the New World*. Under such a stimulus, he wrote *Two Episodes*, for orchestra (1895), one of which was based on Negro folk music; its first performance took place in Boston on January 13, 1896.

A small inheritance made it possible for Gilbert to give up work and, in 1894, go to Europe for travel and absorption of musical experiences. He collected scores for the library of Josiah D. Whitney which, in time, became the nucleus of the music library at Harvard University. He was back in Europe in 1900, working his way across on a cattle boat, in order to hear the world premiere of Charpentier's *Louise*. Its naturalism and thoroughly Parisian identity made such a profound impression on Gilbert that he now decided to devote himself completely to composition. Returning to the United States after having suffered from typhoid fever in Paris, he made his home in a barn in Quincy, Mass., where he lived and worked for many years in poverty and poor health, tending to horses and a cow in return for his board, acquiring a

weatherbeaten piano, and using a breadboard atop a flour barrel on which to compose. In 1902, he helped Arthur Farwell found the Wa-Wan Press for the publication of American music. Gilbert also did a considerable amount of study of folk music; he helped organize concerts of Slavic music at Harvard University. And in his own music he was tapping native sources, sometimes that of the American Indian, sometimes ragtime, but most often that of the American Negro.

Gilbert's first work of any consequence was *Humoresque on Negro-Minstrel Tunes* (1902), which did not get performed until May 24, 1911, when it appeared at a concert of the Boston Pops. Originally named *Americanesque*, this work was a symphonic treatment of three songs popularized in minstrel shows: "Zip Coon" (or "Turkey in the Straw"), "Dearest May," and "Don't Be So Foolish, Joe." Gilbert explained: "I have tried to bind together a few scraps into an art form very much in the manner of Edvard Grieg and the folk music of Norway."

In 1904, Gilbert temporarily left the American nationalist camp to write a prelude, for small orchestra, which used the fragment of an Old Irish tune. Gilbert rescored this work for full orchestra in 1914 and renamed it *Symphonic Prologue for Riders to the Sea*, an orchestral preface to the play of J. M. Synge. After getting performed at Peterboro, N. H., on August 20, 1914, this revised version was performed by the New York Philharmonic on November 11, 1917.

Gilbert's first success came with the *Comedy Overture on Negro Themes*, for orchestra (1905), though he had to wait about five years after its completion for that acclaim. Into this work Gilbert incorporated three Negro melodies, two in fragments, one in full. In the lighthearted first section, the initial theme is developed from two four-measure phrases from "I's Gwine to Alabamy," which Gilbert had come upon in Charles L. Edwards's book *Bahama Songs and Stories*. This is followed by a complete statement of a working song of roustabouts and stevedores on the Mississippi River. The third part is a fugue whose theme comes from the first four measures of the spiritual "Old Ship of Zion." The composition ends in a comic vein with ragtime music.

This composition had been intended as the overture to an opera based on the Uncle Remus stories of Joel Chandler Harris upon which Gilbert was long at work. He had written most of the opera when he learned that he was denied permission to the text because it had already been assigned to another composer. This setback proved a severe blow, particularly since at that time performances of Gilbert's music were infrequent and he was working in almost complete obscurity and neglect.

Comedy Overture on Negro Themes was first performed at a municipal concert in a public park in New York on August 17, 1910. Its success, however, dates from the time the Boston Symphony presented it on April 13, 1911. Reinhold Glière successfully conducted it in the Crimea and Odessa during the summer of 1914 to make Gilbert the first American composer to become known and popular in Russia. "In its rhythmic impulse born of the fragment of the spiritual," wrote Olin Downes at this time, "its shrewd wit, its infectious laughter, it announces itself as a piece of craft which could have come from nowhere but America."

In 1906 (the year he married Helen Kalischer on June 4, with whom he had two daughters) Gilbert completed writing his most famous work, the orchestral tone poem *The Dance in Place Congo*, which had been inspired by an article by George W. Cable in *Century Magazine* describing exotic dances in Place Congo in New Orleans and the tunes of its Negro and Creole population. "It has been for a long time an ideal of mine to write some music which should be in its inspiration native to America." Gilbert wrote in his forward to the published score. "The efforts of my compatriots, though frequently very fine technically, failed to satisfy me. To my mind, they leaned far too heavily upon the tradition of Europe, and seemed to me to ignore too completely the very genuine touches of inspiration which exist in *our* history, *our* temperment and *our* national life. I was therefore moved to strike out boldly on a different course." He took his basic melodic materials from five Creole dance tunes, one of which is a bamboula. As he stated further in his preface, he was using them "much in the manner of Grieg or Tchaikovsky." The subject of the revels of Place Congo seemed so dramatic and colorful to Gilbert that after completing his tone poem he wrote a scenario for his music which became a ballet-pantomime. As such it was first performed on March 23, 1918, at the Metropolitan Opera, Pierre Monteux conducting (on the same afternoon of the premiere of Charles Wakefield Cadman's American opera *Shanewis*). Only after that was the tone poem performed solely as an orchestral work, at a concert of the Boston Symphony. The tone poem was one of two works representing American music at the festival of the International Society for Contemporary Music in Frankfurt, Germany, on July 1, 1927. Though now an invalid, Gilbert made the trip to Europe to attend this performance.

On a commission from the Norfolk Music Festival in Connecticut, Gilbert wrote the *Negro Rhapsody*, for orchestra (1912), where it was premiered on June 5, 1913, the composer conducting. In this work Gilbert aspired to portray the contrasts between the spiritual and barbaric facets of Negro music, the latter represented by a "Shout." This work was followed in 1914 by the *Indian Sketches*, for orchestra, first performed on March 4, 1921, by the Boston Symphony. Once again on commission, Gilbert provided the score for the Pilgrim Tercentenary Pageant at Plymouth, Mass. (1921), a suite that was performed by the Boston Symphony on March 31, 1922.

Gilbert's last compositions were: *Symphonic Piece* (1925; Boston, February 26, 1926); Nocturne (1926), a "symphonic mood," for orchestra, inspired by Walt Whitman, which brought its composer a standing ovation when it was introduced by the Philadelphia Orchestra under Monteux on March 16, 1928; and the Suite, for chamber orchestra (1927; Boston, April 28, 1928), commissioned by the Elizabeth Sprague Coolidge Foundation. In all these later works, Gilbert avoided drawing his thematic material from American folk music as he had done heretofore; but he continued to aim for a thoroughly American art that embodied the spirit of America and its national characteristics.

Several of Gilbert's compositions made effective use of such American popular idioms as ragtime and jazz, among these being the five *Negro Dances*, for piano (1915), and *Jazz Study* (1924). He also wrote some art songs that gained wide circulation. The best known of these are "The Pirate Song" (1902) based on Robert Louis Stevenson's "Fifteen Men on a Dead Man's Chest," and "The Fish Wharf Rhapsody" (1909), both popularized by David Bispham at his concerts. In 1909, Gilbert edited *One Hundred Folk Songs*.

THE COMPOSER SPEAKS: It has been my ideal not to allow any composer or school of music to influence me to the point of imitating them. I have striven to express my own individuality, good, bad, or indifferent. I prefer my own hat to a borrowed crown. Of course, I have had many admirations and have absorbed musical nutriment from many sources. . . . More than the music of any individual composer; more than the music of any particular school, the folk tunes of the world, of all nationalities, races and peoples have been to me a never-failing source of delight, wonder, and inspiration. In them I can hear the spirit of all great music. In them I can feel the very heartbeat of humanity. Simple as these folk melodies are in structure, they yet speak to me so poignantly, and with such deep sincerity of expression, as to be (for myself, at least) more pregnant with inspirational suggestion than the music of any *one* composer.

PRINCIPAL WORKS: *Two Episodes*, for orchestra (1895); "The Pirate Song," for voice and piano (1902); *Humoresque on Negro-Minstrel Tunes*, for orchestra (1902); *Two Verlaine Moods*, for piano (1903); *Symphonic Prologue for Riders to the Sea*, for chamber orchestra, also for full orchestra (1904); *Celtic Songs*, a song cycle for voice and piano (1905); *Comedy Overture on Negro Themes*, for orchestra (1905); *Salammbô's Invocation to Tanith*, aria for soprano and orchestra (1905); *Two South American Gypsy Songs*, for voice and piano (1906); *The Dance in Place Congo*, tone poem for orchestra, also a ballet (1906); "The Fish Wharf Rhapsody," for voice and piano (1909); *Strife*, for orchestra (1910); *American*

Dances, for orchestra (1911); *Negro Rhapsody*, for orchestra (1912); *The Fantasy in Delft*, a one-act opera (1915); *The Island of the Fay*, tone poem for orchestra, also for piano (1923); *Symphonic Piece* (1925); Nocturne, a "symphonic mood" (1926); Suite, for chamber orchestra (1927).

BIBLIOGRAPHY: Chase, Gilbert, *America's Music* (N.Y., 1955); Engel, Carl (ed.), *A Birthday Greeting* (N.Y., 1943); Howard, John Tasker, *Our American Music* (N.Y., 1946); Longyear, K. M. E., "Henry F. Gilbert: His Life and Works" (doctoral dissertation, Rochester, N.Y., 1968); *American Mercury*, November 1928; *Musical Quarterly*, January 1918.

Gillis, Don, b. Cameron, Miss., June 17, 1912; d. Columbia, S.C., January 10, 1978.

Gillis was most beguiling when he brought fun and laughter into his music, with his whimsical titles and tongue-in-the-cheek programmatic contents. He also wrote music of greater sobriety, much of it on American subjects and backgrounds. He was a traditionalist whose prime concern was pleasing and readily assimilable melodies. He did not hesitate to use popular American idioms, and his music consistently sought to appeal to heart rather than mind.

Gillis's childhood was influenced musically by listening to performances at home by members of his family. As a boy he studied the trumpet and trombone with William E. Tracy and Ray Neff, and performed in the Cameron Rotary Boys Club band and in his high school orchestra. While attending high school, he formed a jazz band for which he prepared arrangements and wrote music. During his boyhood years he helped support himself by working as a soda jerk, in a drugstore, in a bakery, and by delivering newspapers.

When his family moved to Fort Worth, Tex., in 1931, Gillis enrolled in Texas Christian University. There, on a scholarship, he studied composition with Keith Mixson and played the trombone in and was assistant director of the university band. He also wrote music for two musical comedies produced at the university. From 1932 to 1935 he served as trombonist in the staff orchestra of radio station WBAP and in 1935 he organized a symphony orchestra at the Polytechnic Baptist Church, which he conducted until 1942. In 1935 he received a bachelor of music degree. In 1942 he did postgraduate work in composition with Roy T. Willis, Wilfred Bain, and Floyd Graham at North Texas University in Denton where he was awarded his master of music degree in 1943. In 1942 he also joined the staff of radio station WBAP as production director.

From his earliest compositions he favored the status quo in music, faithful to traditional structures and idioms and always seeking a musical speech communicable through its simplicity, directness, and melodic interest. This was true of his String Quartet

no. 1 (1936); *The Raven*, for narrator and orchestra (1937), which, after being performed by the WBAP Staff Orchestra, was broadcast twice by the NBC Symphony Orchestra over the radio facilities of NBC, the first time conducted by Frank Black, and the second time by Roy Shield; *The Crucifixion*, a cantata for solo voices, narrator, chorus, and orchestra (1937), which was introduced by the WBAP Staff Orchestra and Chorus; and *The Panhandle*, a symphonic suite (1937) that described the cowboy country and cowboy scenes in Texas.

His first three symphonies, which formed a trilogy of America and its way of life, written under the stimulation of World War II, reflected what would become a lifetime interest: interpreting American backgrounds, experiences, and events in his music. His first symphony was entitled *An American Symphony* (1939–40); his second, *Symphony of Faith* (1940); his third, *Symphony of Free Men* (1940–41). Also inspired by World War II was the cantata *This Is Our America*, for baritone, orchestra, and organ (1941). *Portrait of a Frontier Town*, for orchestra (1940), evoked scenes and sights in Fort Worth, Tex. It was widely performed by such distinguished orchestras as the Cincinnati Symphony, the NBC Symphony, the Dallas Symphony, and the Boston Pops and was part of an all-Gillis program presented in Forth Worth in 1948 at the seventy-fifth anniversary of Texas Christian University.

The Woolyworm, for orchestra (1937), and *Thoughts Provoked on Becoming a Prospective Papa*, a symphonic suite (1937), were two of his earliest excursions into musical humor and satire. "I feel that music is largely an emotional experience," he once explained, "and since the laugh is even more common than the tear, perhaps it may be logically used in writing."

In December 1943, Gillis became production director of the NBC radio outlet in Chicago. One year later he was transferred to the New York offices of NBC to assume the post of producer of, and scriptwriter and commentator for, the NBC Symphony, of which Toscanini was music director. Gillis also served as producer of numerous other NBC radio presentations including *Music for Tomorrow* and *Air Music Programs*. When Toscanini retired in 1954, Gillis became a prime mover in the effort to save the NBC Symphony, becoming president of the Symphony Foundation of America which formed the Symphony of the Air with members of the NBC Symphony. The Symphony of the Air gave public concerts in New York and toured the Far East in 1955.

Gillis's most famous composition carries the jocular title of *Symphony No. 5½* because of its brevity; it is subtitled "A Symphony for Fun." The entire work was based on jazz themes treated in a burlesque manner. Each of the four movements bears a whimsical title: "Perpetual Emotion," "Spiritual?," "Scherzophrenia," and "Conclusion!" Well-known Tin Pan Alley tunes are alluded to. After being introduced by the Boston Pops under Arthur Fiedler in May 1947, this work was performed by the NBC Symphony conducted by Toscanini over the NBC radio network, was heard on the programs of numerous other major symphony orchestras, and in 1952 was used as the background music for a ballet presented by the Festival Ballet in London, Antal Dorati conducting.

In some of his later compositions Gillis continued to explore Americana successfully. *The Alamo* was written in 1944; *Dude Ranch* in 1947; *Saga of the Prairie School* (Symphony no. 7) in 1948; and *Tulsa; a Symphonic Portrait in Oil*, in 1950. When the last of these was recorded in 1978, Paul Kershe said in *Stereo Review*: "Like Gillis' other breezy, light-hearted scores, *Tulsa* is a vivid rouser. There is a pastoral episode evoking the American landscape before it was cluttered up with cities, a section bristling with bugles and cannon fire depicting the struggle for the territories, a movement marking the 'bringing in' of an oil well, and a patriotic finale complete with parade and square dance." After that, Gillis continued to tap Amaricana for his subject matter with *The Land of Wheat*, a suite for band (1959), *Ceremony of Allegiance*, for narrator and band (1964), and Symphony no. 10, *Big D* (1967). To commemorate the American bicentennial, he wrote *The Secret History of the Birth of a Nation*, for narrator, chorus, and orchestra (1976), which was introduced in York, Pa., on November 14, 1976.

His bent for whimsy and humor surfaced in several of his operas, among which were *The Park Avenue Kids* (1957; Elkhart, Ind., May 12, 1957), *The Libretto* (1958; Norman, Okla., December 1, 1961), and *World Premiere* (1966; Fort Worth, December 1, 1965). A full-length serious opera, *The Legend of Star Valley Junction* (1961–62), was produced in New York on January 7, 1969.

From 1958 to 1961 Gillis was vice-president of the Interlochen Music Camp in Michigan, and from 1968 to 1972 he was chairman of the arts at Dallas Baptist College in Texas. In 1973 he was appointed composer-in-residence and chairman of the Institute of Media Arts at the University of South Carolina, the posts he was holding when he died suddenly of a heart attack. Gillis was the author of *The Unfinished Symphony Conductor* (1967). He received an honorary doctorate from Texas Christian University and the Christopher Award.

THE COMPOSER SPEAKS: I think it is unimportant for a composer to wonder about what posterity thinks of him. It is more important that he be faithful to his own beliefs in music. He must be the final critic, and he must write what is his own, regardless of current trends or popularity. If his music reflects folk quality, it must be because it is a natural thing, not a contrived use of folk material merely to be "American." Honesty, above all things, is the important ingredient a composer needs.

As to basic American folk music, I have long held that American jazz has been and is the most positive influence in this country—not the jazz we call "popular music" but rather the traditional feeling that is the result of years of improvisation. For certainly in the traditional rhythmic, melodic and harmonic patterns which have grown from the spontaneous utterances of jazz musicians, there is a real folklore which has been but little exploited in serious composition.

PRINCIPAL WORKS: 10 symphonies (1939–67); 6 string quartets (1936–47); 3 suites for woodwind quintet (1938, 1939, 1939).

The Panhandle, symphonic suite (1937); *The Crucifixion*, for vocal soloists, narrator, chorus, and orchestra (1937); *The Woolyworm*, symphonic satire (1937); *Thoughts Provoked on Becoming a Prospective Papa*, symphonic suite (1937); *The Raven*, tone poem for narrator and orchestra (1937); *Intermission—Ten Minutes*, symphonic sketch (1940); *The Night Before Christmas*, for narrator and orchestra (1941); *Three Sketches*, for strings (1942); *Prairie Poem*, tone poem for orchestra (1943); *The Alamo*, tone poem for orchestra (1944); *A Short Overture to an Unwritten Opera* (1944); *To an Unknown Soldier*, tone poem for orchestra (1945); *This Is Our America*, cantata for baritone and orchestra (1945); Rhapsody, for harp and orchestra (1946); *Dude Ranch*, symphonic suite (1967); *Symphony No. 5 ½*, "a symphony for fun" (1947); *Shindig*, ballet (1949); *Tulsa: A Symphonic Portrait in Oil* (1950); *The Coming of the King*, for chorus (1954); *Pep-Rally*, opera for band (1956); *The Park Avenue Kids*, opera (1957); *Five Acre Pond*, poem for oboe and orchestra (1957); *The Libretto*, one-act comic opera (1958); *Men of Music*, for band (1958); *The Land of Wheat*, suite for band (1959); *The Legend of Star Valley Junction*, opera (1961–62); *Ceremony of Allegiance*, for narrator and band (1964); *Seven Golden Texts*, for narrator, chorus, band or orchestra (1965); *World Premiere*, one-act comic opera (1966–67); *The Gift of the Magi*, one-act opera (1966); Piano Concerto, no. 2 (1966); *The Nazarene*, one-act opera (1967–68); *Toscanini: A Portrait of a Century*, for narrator and orchestra (1967); Rhapsody, for trumpet and orchestra (1969); *Behold the Man*, opera (1973); *The Secret History of the Birth of a Nation*, for narrator, chorus, and orchestra (1976).

BIBLIOGRAPHY: Ewen, David, *American Composers Today* (N.Y., 1949); Reis, Clare, *Composers in America* (N.Y., 1947).

Glanville-Hicks, Peggy, b. Melbourne, Australia, December 29, 1912. American citizen, 1948.

Many of her works have an exotic appeal through the application of Middle Eastern or oriental idioms and through the relationship of some of her compositions to Greek antiquity.

She was fifteen when she started receiving her first lessons in piano and composition. From 1927 to 1931 she attended the Melbourne Conservatory, continuing her composition studies there with its director, Fritz Hart. In 1931 she came to London, attending the Royal College of Music for four years on a Carlotta Rowe Scholarship; her teachers there included Ralph Vaughan Williams (composition), Arthur Benjamin and Constant Lambert (piano), R. O. Morris (theory), and Gordon Jacob and Sir Malcolm Sargent (conducting). During these years at the Academy she completed among other works, two song cycles to poems by A. E. Housman—*Frolic* and *Rest*, both in 1931—a *Poem*, for chorus and orchestra (1933), a Sinfonietta, for orchestra (1934) and an opera, *Caedmon*, to her own libretto (1934).

Awarded the Octavia Traveling Scholarship in 1935, she wandered about Europe, spending time in Paris studying composition with Nadia Boulanger and, in Vienna, studying advanced composition and musicology with Egon Wellesz. Her first successful composition was written in 1937: *Choral Suite*, for women's voices, oboe, and strings; two of its movements were heard at the festival of the International Society for Contemporary Music in London on June 20, 1938, the first time the work of an Australian composer had been performed at any of these festivals.

On November 7, 1938, Glanville-Hicks married the English composer Stanley Richard Bate (they were divorced eight years later). In 1940 she helped her husband organize Les Trois Arts, a ballet company in London, for which she served as assistant manager, publicity director, and assistant conductor.

In 1942, Peggy Glanville-Hicks and her husband came to the United States, making their home in New York City. She soon became affiliated with the League of Composers, serving on a committee that arranged free public concerts in Central Park. After World War II, she helped establish the International Music Fund to help displaced European musicians reestablish themselves. As a delegate to the festival of the International Society of Contemporary Music in Amsterdam in 1948 she was present, on June 10, at a performance of her *Concertino da camera*, for flute, clarinet, bassoon, and piano (1945). From 1948 to 1958 she was the music critic for the *New York Herald Tribune*. During these years she helped organize concerts of avant-garde and other new music in New York, including those given by the Composers Forum of which she was director. In 1953 she was awarded a grant from the American Academy of Arts and Letters.

By the early 1950s she had abandoned the neoclassic or atonal idioms she had previously favored for a consonant, melodic-rhythmic structure that came close to the musical patterns of the antique or Middle Eastern world, in which melody and rhythm gained almost total ascendancy over harmony, which had been demoted to a minor, even occasional, role. (Harmony, as such, had not existed in the music of ancient times.) She also became interested in Middle Eastern or oriental subjects for her compositions. *Letters from Morocco*, for tenor and orchestra (1952), used for its text some letters about Morocco written to her by Paul Bowles, the composer-writer. This composition was given its first hearing on February 22, 1953, in New York, with William Hess as vocal soloist and Leopold Stokowski conducting. Without resorting to oriental or esoteric devices or idioms, Glanville-Hicks here succeeded in capturing the mood, the feel, the atmosphere of Morocco through her emphathetic recreation in music of Bowles's richly descriptive letters. *The Transposed Heads* (1953) was an opera, the first ever commissioned by the Louisville Orchestra in Kentucky and written with a grant from the Rockefeller Foundation; its first performance was held on April 4, 1954, in Kentucky with Robert Whitney conducting. Its libretto, prepared by the composer from a story by Thomas Mann, is set in India, and for it Glanville-Hicks assimilated into her style Hindu tunes and scale patterns besides incorporating into her score dances derived from Hindu folklore. "It required no great amendment of my own writing method to plan the structure of the work so as to include Indian materials," Glanville-Hicks explained. "It was possible with a certain selectivity in regard to scales used to incorporate Indian folk themes without doing any violence to their unique character, or without altering my own way of writing." *The Transposed Heads* was given its American premiere in New York in February 1958. *Three Gymnopédies* (1953)—the first for string orchestra with oboe and harp; the second for string orchestra alone; the third for string orchestra, celesta and harp—gave a musical description (even as Erik Satie had done sixty-five years earlier) of the ancient Spartan festival in which naked youths celebrated their gods with song and dance. The *Etruscan Concerto*, for piano and orchestra (1954; N.Y., January 25, 1956)—written for the Italian pianist Carlo Bussotti—was inspired by D. H. Lawrence's *Etruscan Places and Painted Tombs of Tarquinia*; the music is a warm and vivid portrait of ancient Mediterranean people.

In 1956, Glanville-Hicks was awarded a Guggenheim Fellowship (renewed for a second year in 1957) which made it possible for her to go to Greece to study Greek folk music. In 1958, on a commission, she completed the score for the ballet *The Masque of the Wild Man*, produced at the first Festival of the Two Worlds in Spoleto, Italy, in June 1958. A year later, once again on commission, this time from CBS-TV, she prepared the music for the ballet *Saul and the Witch of Endor*, produced on television in the year of its composition with choreography by John Butler. On a Rockefeller grant in 1960 and a Fulbright research grant in 1961 she not only continued her former studies in Greek folk music but also did research in other musical styles of the Middle East and India.

Glanville-Hicks established permanent residence in Athens, Greece, in 1959 in a house situated on the slopes of the Acropolis. There, on August 19, 1961, at the Athens Festival, her most important work was produced: the opera *Nausicaa* (1960). The libretto—by the composer based on Robert Graves's novel *Homer's Daughter*—was a version of the Homeric legend of Odysseus and Penelope in which Penelope becomes the Princess Nausicaa, and Odysseus, a shipwrecked Cretan sailor-nobelman named Aethon, and in which it is suggested that *The Odyssey* was actually the work of Princess Nausicaa and not of Homer. Melodic ideas from various Greek regions are here used bountifully in a score in which a melody-rhythm structure (raga-tala in oriental terminology) is almost totally devoid of any harmonic element. "It is an opera," wrote Peter Gradenwitz in the *Frankfurter Allgemeine Zeitung*, "with an individuality all its own—a work opening vistas to new modern roads in ancient spirit never trodden on before."

After being operated on for a brain tumor at the New York Medical Center in 1969, Peggy Glanville-Hicks went temporarily blind. She returned to Greece, where her vision was partly restored; but her career as a composer was over. She went back to her native Australia in 1976 on an invitation from the Australian Arts Council to help establish the East-West Department at the Australian Music Center in Sydney. When Queen Elizabeth II of the United Kingdom visited Australia in 1977, she decorated Glanville-Hicks with the Royal Medal.

THE COMPOSER SPEAKS: I don't believe in "style" as such, or "personalized" materials. Personality, if one has it, should be able to shine through neutral materials. . . . To me both atonalism and neoclassicism as such seem old-fashioned and a bore. Nothing is guaranteed to alienate the affections of audiences so fast as the acid and despairing sounds of a twelve-toner, while neoclassicism is at best a chromium-plated brownstone, a snappy resurfacing job that fools no real modern who has perceived the soundness of organized architecture, and the form which flows from grace within, and from the nature of materials without.

PRINCIPAL WORKS: Sinfonietta, for orchestra (1934); *Caedmon*, opera (1934); *In Midwood Silence*, for soprano, oboe and string quartet (1935); *Song in Summer*, for chorus and orchestra (1935); *Hylas and Nymos*, ballet (1935); *Spanish Suite*, for orchestra (1935); Piano Concerto (1936); Flute Concerto (1937); *Choral Suite*, for women's voices, oboe, and strings (1937); String Quartet (1937); *Postman's Knock*, ballet (1938); Sonatina, for flute (1939); *Concertino da camera*, for flute, clarinet, bassoon and piano (1945); *Profile from China*, for tenor and piano

(1945); *Songs of A. E. Housman*, for voice and piano (1945); *Killer of Enemies*, ballet (1946); *Dance Cantata*, for tenor, spoken chorus, and orchestra (1946); Harp Sonata (1950); Sonata for Piano and Percussion (1951); *Letters from Morocco*, for tenor and orchestra (1952); *Sinfonica da Pacifica* (1952–53); *The Transposed Heads*, opera (1953); *Three Gymnopédies*, for chamber orchestra (1953); *Etruscan Concerto*, for piano and orchestra (1954); *Concerto romantico*, for viola and orchestra (1956); *Tapestry*, for orchestra (1956); *The Masque of the Wild Man*, ballet (1958); *Saul and the Witch of Endor*, ballet (1959); *The Glittering Gate*, opera (1959); *Nausicaa*, opera (1960); *Sappho*, opera (1963); *Prelude for a Pensive Pupil*, for piano (1963); *A Season in Hell*, ballet (1965); *Tragic Celebration*, ballet (1966).

BIBLIOGRAPHY: Ewen, David, *Composers Since 1900* (N.Y., 1969); Murdoch, J., *Australia's Contemporary Composers* (Melbourne, 1972); *American Composers Alliance Bulletin*. vol. 4, no. 1, 1954; *Opera News*, December 16, 1961.

Glass, Philip, b. Baltimore, Md., January 31, 1937.

One of the most provocative and successful of music's extreme avant-gardists, Glass has devised a musical art form of his own (sometimes called "minimalism" and sometimes "solid state") by combining Hindu rhythmic cycles and other idiomatic devices of non-Western music with abstract intervallic structures, Western harmonic or modulatory practices reduced to their barest essentials, and rock—sometimes in Gargantuan-sized compositions requiring four or more hours for performance.

His father was the owner of a small record shop in Baltimore, and his mother was a teacher and librarian. Music study for Glass began on the violin when he was six but, unhappy with that instrument, he soon shifted to the flute. When he was eight he studied the flute at the Peabody Conservatory with Britton Johnson, who remained his teacher until 1952. At Baltimore City College (a high school) Glass played the flute in the school band and orchestra. When he was fourteen, he passed an early-entrance examination at the University of Chicago, which he entered in 1952, and from which he received a bachelor of arts degree four years later. During the summer of 1955 he studied harmony with Louis Cheslock.

In 1958, Glass entered the Juilliard School of Music in New York. He remained there four years, studying composition with William Bergsma and Vincent Persichetti, and earning a master of science degree in composition in 1962. The summer of 1960 was spent at Aspen, Colo., for the study of composition with Darius Milhaud. In these student days Glass was a prolific composer of instrumental music, all of it either in the twelve-tone technique or in the then advanced rhythmic and harmonic idioms favored by many Juilliard students. Some seventy-five of Glass's works were performed at Juilliard and twenty of them were published. In addition, he received a Broadcast Music Industry (BMI) Award in 1960, the Lado Prize in 1961, and in 1961 and 1962 two Benjamin Awards.

On a Ford Foundation grant, Glass served as composer-in-residence for the Pittsburgh public schools between 1962 and 1964. About twenty more of Glass's compositions, which he wrote in Pittsburgh, were now published. In 1964 the Ford Foundation presented him with the Young Composers' Award of $10,000.

In spite of his success as composer, Glass was dissatisfied with what he had written, As he put it: "I had reached a kind of dead end. I just didn't believe in my music anymore." He felt strongly that he had to seek out new avenues of creativity, and that the best way this could be achieved was by going to Europe for more study. He was able to do so on a Fulbright Fellowship in 1964, which brought him to Paris, where he studied harmony and counterpoint with Nadia Boulanger. He also did a good deal of traveling to Eastern countries—India, Tunisia, Tibet—and by becoming acquainted with Eastern music he felt he had discovered for himself a new world of sound which he was determined to explore further.

In Paris, in 1965, met Ravi Shankar, the Indian virtuoso of the sitar, who had come to France to make a film. Since Glass was trained musically and could speak French, Shankar hired him to notate Eastern music for French musicians. Working with Shankar—and doing additional study of Indian music with Alla Rakha—revolutionzied Glass's musical thinking. "I saw," he told an interviewer, "there was a whole different tradition of music that I knew nothing about." Glass now discarded all his previous concepts of composition in the Western tradition to embrace a new system based on the modular-form style and repetitive structure of Indian music in which short rhythmic phrases were joined together in additive combinations of beats. For a time, Glass concentrated in his music solely on the rhythmic structure, but after 1970 he began adding harmony and modulation but to only a minimal degree. His harmony, for example, consisted of just a few single basic static chords.

One year after his return to the United States in 1967, he formed the Philip Glass Ensemble for the performance of his works. This was a seven-man unit, with three saxophonists doubling on flutes, three electric organists (of which Glass was one), and a sound engineer. The ensemble gave its first concert at Queens College, in Queens, N.Y., on April 13, 1968, and in 1969 it made the first of several European tours. With this ensemble Glass introduced his unique brand of music. *Pieces in the Shape of a Square* (1968), which was introduced in New York on May 19, 1968, was followed by such works as *Music in Fifths* (1969; N.Y., January 16, 1970), *Music with Changing Parts* (1970; N.Y. October 10, 1970), *Music for Voices* (1972; N.Y., November 10, 1972); and *Music in Twelve Parts* (1971–74). The last of these required over four hours for complete performance, the first such taking place in New York on June 1, 1974, when the concert started at 6:00 P.M., ended at midnight, and allowed an hour and a half for dinner. *Music with Changing Parts* was the first release of Chatham Records, which Glass had founded in 1971.

Glass's exploratory methods with simplified harmony as an element of his sytem were pursued in four compositions entitled *Another Look at Harmony:* Parts 1 and 2 written in 1975 and performed in New York on May 6, 1975; Part 3 in 1975; and Part 4, in 1977, a commission of the Holland Festival, where it was presented in June 1977.

By the 1970s Glass was able to appeal not only to devotees of avant-garde music but also to the advanced rock set. Some of its leading figures became acquainted with his music when his ensemble performed it at the Royal College of Art in London in 1970. His influence with the progressive rock set was advanced further in 1974 when Virgin Records, an English outfit specializing in rock, recorded and released the first parts of *Music in Twelve Parts.*

With *Einstein on the Beach* (1976) Glass grew into something of a worldwide cult figure. This was a huge, four-and-a-half-hour multimedia production (referred to by its authors as an "opera," though it was basically a series of "events"), which he devised with Robert Wilson, architect, painter, and leader in the theatrical avant-garde. They conceived an abstract work without libretto, story line, lyrics for the singing, but which included action, dancing, pantomime, music, but no singing principals. All the singing was assigned to the chorus, and that was done with syllables, numerical counts or outright clichés. Episodes had a surrealistic quality: a little boy shooting paper airplanes from a tower; an entire scene with one of the characters just walking back and forth across the stage; another in which the walking was done in slow motion; a monologue about the sight of bathing caps in an air-conditioned supermarket. One scene used as its setting a space ship on a journey to outer space. Another scene, about justice, transpired in a courtroom with the accused lying on a huge bed in front of the judge's bench. Throughout the production several characters appeared as Albert Einstein, one of them called upon to play a solo on the violin in the orchestra pit, another serving as a symbol of science, and a third writing mathematical formulas on an imaginary blackboard. "Go to *Einstein* and enjoy the sights and sounds," advised Robert Wilson, "feel the feelings they evoke. Listen to the Pictures."

Einstein on the Beach was a sensation when given its world premiere at the Avignon Festival in France on July 25, 1976. From Avignon it went to Venice (the Biennale), Belgrade, Brussels, Paris, Hamburg, Rotterdam, and Amsterdam (everywhere a success of the first magnitude) before reaching the United States on the stage of the Metropolitan Opera in New York on November 21, 1976. In New York, the demand for admission far exceeded the auditorium's seating capacity and a second performance had to be scheduled a week later (also completely sold out). Reporting from Avignon to *High Fidelity/Musical America*, Dale Harris wrote: "The succession of dreamlike images that make up *Einstein* is beautifully realized. . . . Such visions, unconnected by logic or sequential narrative, make a great and disturbing impact upon one's imagination. Yet at the same time they bring illumination to it." As for Glass's score, Harris added: "All the music is reiterative and rhythmically complex, forcing itself upon the listener's attention with such assurance—and such beauty of texture—that one quickly capitulated to its hypnotic power."

Glass continued to work productively for the stage following his success with *Einstein on the Beach*. In 1978 he provided the score for a ballet, *Dance* (which used films as background for the dancing), for which Lucinda Childs provided the choreography. This consisted of five solo and ensemble dance numbers which Childs premiered in Amsterdam, Holland, on October 19, 1979. On November 29, 1979, it was given its first American presentation in Brooklyn N.Y. And, in 1980, he finished writing the music for an opera which had been commissioned by the Netherlands Opera in Rotterdam, introduced on September 5, 1980. This was *Satyagraha*, which can be regarded as Glass's first opera since it has libretto with full narrative and was composed directly for an opera house contingent of singers and orchestra players. But as John Rockwell pointed out in the *New York Times* in reviewing the premiere performance, this was not "an opera in the conventional sense of a melodramatic tale with beefy high notes. Nor is it a stereotypical 'modern opera,' all dissonant and abrasive. It is, instead, a mythical ritual, reminiscent in mood of Wagner's *Parsifal* and Hans Pfitzner's *Palestrina*." Constance De Jong's libretto consisted of a series of tableaux tracing the early life of Gandhi, the opera's title coming from Gandhi's term for his nonviolent political beliefs and his spiritual philosophy. Before each of the three acts, a silent figure stands on top of a central podium, surveying the scene and evoking episodes from Gandhi's life. The silent figures represent Tolstoy, Tagore, and Martin Luther King, Jr. The text was entirely derived from the *Bhagavad Gita*, and the entire opera was sung in Sanskrit. "Mr. Glass's music," Rockwell continues, "grows out of his familiar style: harmonically static and sweetly consonant, with small melodic and rhythmic units strung together and repeated hypnotically, the shapes of the larger structures changing through addition and subtraction of

the modules. Each scene is basically a passacaglia, harmonically speaking, with all manner of arpeggiated figurations on top. What is new is first of all the use of the orchestra—fifty-one instruments, in this case, with full strings, winds in threes, electric keyboard, but no percussion. There are also . . . intensely lyrical vocal lines that arrive out of the instrumental texture. And there is a considerable amount of slow contemplative music along with Mr. Glass's more familiar busily burbling, motoric style. But the last impression is of a floating lyricism, cushioned in soft strings and dulcet winds." The American premiere was given in Lewiston, N.Y., on July 29, 1981.

In 1970 and again in 1973, Glass revisited India. In 1976 the Off-Broadway award, Obie, was twice presented to him by the *Village Voice*, once for his *Another Look at Harmony*, Part 3, used for a production by the experimental theatrical company Mabou Mines, and the other for his music for *Einstein on the Beach*. Commissions, grants, and fellowships have come to him from the Foundation for Contemporary Performance Arts (1970–71), Changes, Inc. (1971–72), the National Endowment for the Arts (1974, 1975, 1978–79), and the Mentil Foundation to match the 1974 National Endowment grant (1974). In 1981, Glass received one of the largest individual art awards in the history of the Rockefeller Foundation: a three-year grant of $90,000 which did not involve any specific commissions.

In 1975, Glass contributed music to *North Star*, a documentary film study of the sculptor Mark de Suvero. In 1978, Glass organized Tomato Records for the recording of his own music or that of his ensemble members. A concert of Glass's music was heard in Carnegie Hall, in New York, on June 1, 1978, and on February 28, 1979, he made the first of two appearances with his music at the Bottom Line, a New York rock club. Thus Glass earned the distinction of being the only composer ever to receive standing ovations in three such varied locations as Carnegie Hall, the Metropolitan Opera House, and a rock club. A four-concert retrospective of Glass's most significant works was given in New York by his own ensemble between February 12 and 15, 1981.

Glass makes a dozen or so annual appearances as a solo organist in programs of his own music. He married Luba Burtyk, an internist, in October 1980. This is his second marriage. His first wife, with whom he had two sons, was Jo Anne Akalaitis, an actress and theatrical director.

THE COMPOSER SPEAKS: At most music schools, Eastern music was called primitive, but if you study ragas and other Indian music you find it a highly evolved art that is based upon different premises from our own.

The use of time is the big thing. In Western music, we take time and divide it—whole notes into half notes into quarter notes—but in Eastern music they take very small units and add them together. They form rhythmic structures out of an additive process. We divide. They add. Then there's the cyclical process, where you have something that lasts maybe thirty-five beats and then the cycle begins. Then you join cycles of different beats, like wheels inside wheels, everything going at the same time and always changing.

PRINCIPAL WORKS (*all for chamber ensemble unless otherwise identified*): *Pieces in the Shape of a Square* (1968); *Music in Contrary Motion*, for organ (1969); *Music in Fifths* (1969); *Music in Eight Parts* (1970); *Music in Similar Motion* (1970); *Music with Changing Parts* (1970); *Music in Twelve Parts*, Parts 1–6 (1971); *Music for Voices* (1972); *Music in Twelve Parts*, Parts 7–9 (1973); *Music in Twelve Parts*, Parts 10–12 (1974); *Another Look at Harmony*, Parts 1–2 (1975); *Another Look at Harmony*, Part 3 (1975); *Einstein on the Beach*, a multimedia production (1976); *Fourth Series*, for organ (1977–79); *Another Look at Harmony*, Part 4 (1977); *Dance*, ballet (1978); *Geometry of Circles* (1979); *Satyagraha*, opera (1980); *The Panther*, theater piece for six singers, six actors, two musicians, and a panther.

BIBLIOGRAPHY: *BBDM*; *DCM*; *Time*, June 19, 1978; *DCM*; *High Fidelity/Musical America*, April 1979; *Horizon*, March 1980; *People*, October 6, 1980; *Quest*, November 1980; *Who's Who in America, 1980–81*.

Goeb, Roger, b. Cherokee, Ia., October 9, 1914. Before family problems struck and interrupted his professional career, Goeb produced a sizable repertoire of music notable for its sensitive instrumental timbres, effective contrasting sounds and rhythms, and a fine-grained lyricism.

Though he received some training in piano and trumpet while attending grade school and high school in Cherokee, he was not subjected to any significant musical influence until he entered the University of Wisconsin in 1932 for the study of chemistry, graduating in 1936 with the degree of bachelor of science and agriculture. He then heard for the first time music performed for a purpose other than accompaniment to dancing and beer drinking and realized he wanted to make music and not chemistry his life's work. He spent the next two years working in factories and playing in jazz bands to raise enough money to go to Europe for music study. In 1938 he came to Paris, where for one year he studied solfeggio and craft with two assistants of Nadia Boulanger's at the École Normale de Musique, receiving a *licence de contrepoint* in 1939.

Back in the United States later in 1939, he spent the next two years in intensive private study of composition with Otto Luening. On February 15, 1941, he married Janey Hoy Price, a dancer and teacher of

the dance who subsequently was a departmental head at Adelphi College in Garden City, N.Y., and became the mother of his son and daughter.

In 1942, Goeb received his master of music degree in composition at the Cleveland Institute. That same year he completed several compositions, among which were his String Quartet no. 1, a sonata for solo viola, and a piano sonata.

After two years as music director of the radio station of the University of Oklahoma in Norman, Goeb joined the music faculty of the State University of Iowa in Ames in 1944–45, where he taught harmony, counterpoint, and orchestration and was assistant to Philip G. Clapp, department head. At the same time he received training in all woodwind instruments from Himie Voxman and studied acoustics with George W. Stewart while completing requirements for his doctorate in music in 1945, in partial fulfillment for which he submitted his Symphony no. 1 (1945). During the next few years he taught all orchestral instruments and coached and conducted ensembles at Bard College in Annandale, N.Y. (1945–47). Between 1946 and 1962 he spent two weeks each summer at the Bennington Composers Conference in Vermont, first under Otto Luening and subsequently directing it by himself.

Goeb's compositions began reaching a wider audience and receiving greater public approbation than heretofore in the latter part of the 1940s, with *Prairie Songs* (originally scored for woodwind quintet—in which form it was played by woodwind students throughout the United States and Europe—but later transcribed for small orchestra) and *Lyric Pieces*, for trumpet and orchestra, both written in 1946. His Woodwind Quintet no. 1 (1949) was performed in New York on February 27, 1950, at a concert of the National Association of American Composers and Conductors when it was called by Arthur Berger in the *New York Herald Tribune* "the most absorbing work on the program." The trombonist Davis Shuman featured Goeb's Quintet, for trombone and string quartet (1949), at his concert in New York in February 1950. At a concert of the Composers Forum in New York in November 1950, several other Goeb compositions were heard, including the Suite, for woodwind trio (1945), a Fantasy, for solo piano (1948) and two Divertimentos, for flutes (1950). In these works Goeb's musical style was already crystallized: occasionally percussive and dissonant, with harmonic and melodic control basically chromatic, its intervallic structure dominated by fourths in various inversions, and with lyricism and rhythmic contrasts a continuous presence.

In 1950 Goeb received a Guggenheim Fellowship (renewed for another year in 1951) which made it possible for him to concentrate on the writing of his most successful composition to that time: the Symphony no. 3 (1951), performed by the CBS Symphony under Leopold Stokowski over the CBS radio network during the Contemporary American Music

Festival on April 3, 1952 (and subsequently recorded by that orchestra under Stokowski for RCA Victor). In the *Saturday Review*, Irving Kolodin was "particularly impressed by Goeb's sense of instrumental color, his facility in juxtaposing timbres and accents in a way that made new sounds of the familiar combinations. This is no matter, in the old sense, of orchestration or instrumentation; it is rather a keen sense of creating directly in terms of the elements involved. . . . It is a skill so highly developed that one might well suspend judgment on how far he might eventually go."

The homespun *Five American Dances*, for string orchestra, was written in 1952; three of these dances received their first hearing over the CBS radio network in 1952, and all five were heard in St. Louis in June 1953. This was followed in the 1950s by his Violin Concerto (1953), which Maurice Wilk introduced in New York in February 1954; the Symphony no. 4 (1954), successfully premiered by the Pittsburgh Symphony under William Steinberg on February 24, 1956, and later performed by the Japan Philharmonic under Akeo Watanabe; the Woodwind Quintet no. 2 (1955), written for the New Art Wind Quintet, which performed it in New York in April 1957; and the Concertino no. 2 for orchestra (1956), commissioned by the Louisville Orchestra, and receiving its first hearing in Louisville, with Robert Whitney conducting, on November 28, 1956.

In 1953, Goeb received an award from the American Academy of Arts and Letters. He was assistant professor at Stanford University, in California, in 1954–55, teaching theory and composition, and on the faculty of Adelphi College between 1956 and 1958. From 1956 to 1962 he was the director of the American Composers Alliance, and for several years he was also secretary-treasurer of Composers Recording, Inc.

The prolonged illness both of his wife and son (multiple sclerosis) between 1955 and 1974, which terminated with the death of his wife in 1967 and that on his son in 1974, ended Goeb's involvement in music in 1964.

THE COMPOSER SPEAKS: I am basically a craftsman with some imagination in sound and with a willingness to pay attention to detail. One prominent detail in my pieces is the effort to make music challinging for the performers. My hope is that if I can concentrate the performers' interest, the music itself will gain. Since I have never had much sympathy with preset schemes of composition, whether they be called "twelve-tone" or "neoclassic" or anything else, I have had to pay especial attention to the second basic element in music besides sound, which is time. In temporal art, one has to coax the audience into remembering what has first been presented in order to elaborate it later to a more complete significance. This makes me conscious of the sanctity of the dictum of Noel Coward: Don't bore the customers.

PRINCIPAL WORKS: 4 symphonies (1945–54); 4 concertantes, for various instruments and orchestra (1948–51); 3 string quartets (1942, 1948, 1954); 2 concertinos, for orchestra (1949, 1956); 2 sinfonias (1957, 1962); 2 quintets for woodwinds (1949, 1955).

Sonata for Solo Viola (1942); Piano Sonata (1942); *Suite in Folk Style*, for four clarinets (1944); String Trio (1945); Suite, for woodwind trio (1946); *Lyric Piece*, for trumpet and orchestra (1946); *Prairie Songs*, for woodwind quintet, also for chamber orchestra (1946); Fantasy, for oboe and strings (1947); Romanza, for string orchestra (1948); Quartet, for four clarinets (1948); Brass Septet (1949); Quintet, for trombone and string quartet (1949); Two Divertimentos, for flutes (1950); Processionals, for organ and brass quintet (1951); *Five American Dances*, for string orchestra (1952); Violin Concerto (1953); Piano Concerto (1954); Sonata for Solo Violin (1957); *Encomium*, for woodwinds, brass, and percussion (1958); *Iowa Concerto*, for chamber orchestra (1959); *Running Colors*, for string quartet (1961); *Declarations*, for cello, flute, oboe, clarinet, bassoon, and horn (1961); Quartet, for oboe and strings (1964).

BIBLIOGRAPHY: *BBDM*; *American Composers Alliance Bulletin*, vol. 2 no. 2, June 1952.

Goldmark, Rubin, b. New York City, August 15, 1872; d. New York City, March 6, 1936.

Goldmark was a conservative composer who never allowed himself to digress from the lessons he had learned so well, and the music he had come to admire, in his younger days in Vienna and New York. His music belongs more in the late 19th century than in Goldmark's own time, and however well structured and pleasingly melodic, it remains an anachronism in the 20th century.

He was the nephew of Karl Goldmark, the eminent Hungarian-born Viennese romantic composer of the late 19th century. Rubin Goldmark's father had been a high school teacher in Austria before coming to the United States, where he practiced law. An enthusiastic music lover, Goldmark's father was prominent in the musical life of New York as one of the founders of and performers in the Oratorio Society of New York and one of the founding fathers and a director of the New York Symphony Society. His home was a favorite rendezvous for the city's leading musicians; their music making being Rubin's earliest indelible recollections.

Rubin Goldmark studied the piano privately with Alfred von Livonius while attending the New York City public schools. For a year he was a student at the College of the City of New York. Then, in 1889, he went to Europe to enroll in the Vienna Conservatory, and study piano with Anton Door and composition with Robert Ruchs and Johann Nepomuk

Fuchs. When Goldmark returned to the United States in 1891 he continued his music study for two years at the National Conservatory of which Antonín Dvořák was director; piano with Rafael Joseffy and composition with Dvořák. When Dvořák heard one of Goldmark's compositions performed at the conservatory (Piano Trio in B minor), he exclaimed: "Now there are *two* Goldmarks!"

In 1893–94, Goldmark taught piano and theory at the National Conservatory. Failing health compelled him to leave New York and, in 1894, settle in Colorado, where he served as director of the Conservatory founded for him at Colorado College in Colorado Springs. In 1900, Goldmark made his first bid for attention as composer when his orchestral tone poem *Hiawatha*, based on Longfellow, was introduced by the Boston Symphony on January 13. James Gibbons Huneker wrote of it after that performance: "It was bewilderingly luscious and Goldmarkian—a young Goldmark come to judgment. The family gifts are color and rhythm. The youth has them, and he also has brains. . . . The overture, which though not Indian, is full of good things. . . . There is life, and while there's life there's rhythm. . . . The Allegro has one stout tune, and the rush and dynamic glow last."

With his health improved, Goldmark was back in New York in 1902, spending the next two decades teaching piano and composition privately, and giving lecture-recitals on Wagner throughout the United States and Canada. In 1909, his Piano Quartet (1909) won the Paderewski Prize and was introduced in New York on December 3, 1910. A tone poem, *Samson*, was premiered by the Boston Symphony Orchestra on March 14, 1914. *Call of the Plains*, for violin and piano, was written in 1915 for the violin virtuoso Mischa Elman; Goldmark orchestrated it in 1922, a version performed in or about 1923 by the New York Symphony under Walter Damrosch. Goldmark's most famous works came in 1919 and 1922 respectively. They were the *Requiem*, for orchestra, inspired by the Gettysburg Address, and *A Negro Rhapsody*, based on seven melodies of Negro origin including "Sometimes I Feel Like a Motherless Child" and "Nobody Knows de Trouble I've Seen." Both were premiered by the New York Philharmonic, the former on January 30, 1919, and the latter on January 18, 1923.

In 1924, Goldmark was appointed director of composition at the Juilliard School of Music in New York. He retained this post until his death. Though some of his students chafed under his conservatism, they profited from the sound groundings he gave them in the compositional craft.

In 1907, Goldmark was one of the founders of the Bohemians, a New York Club for musicians, serving as its president from 1907 to 1910 and again from 1926 to 1936. He was also founder and an officer of the Society for the Publication of American Music, and president of the Musicians Foundation, Inc. In

1900 Colorado College presented him with an honorary master of arts degree. The Associate Alumni of the College of the City of New York awarded him the Townsend Harris Medal in 1935 and in 1956 a new music building at that college was named after him.

PRINCIPAL WORKS: *Hiawatha*, tone poem for orchestra (1900); Piano Quartet (1909); *Samson*, tone poem for orchestra (1914); *Call of the Plains*, for violin and piano (1915; orchestrated 1922); *Requiem*, for orchestra (1919); *A Negro Rhapsody*, for orchestra (1922). Also: Piano Trio in D minor; Violin Sonata in B minor; String Quartet in A.

BIBLIOGRAPHY: Howard, John Tasker, *Our American Music* (N.Y., 1946); *Modern Music*, March–April 1936; *New York Times* (obituary), March 7, 1936; *Dictionary of American Biography*, Supplement 2.

Gottlieb, Jack, b. New Rochelle, N.Y., October 12, 1930.

The works of Jack Gottlieb embrace a wide musical spectrum—ranging from show tunes to Hebrew liturgical settings, from art songs to operas, and from chamber music to orchestral pieces.

Both parents immigrated to the United States from the Russian-Polish Pale of Settlement, near Pinsk, just prior to World War I. Since the only so-called professional musicians they had encountered until then were either Gypsies or lowly *klesmer* performers, they had little tolerance for any of their three children making careers in music. His father was untutored but musically gifted. He played violin and mandolin, and wrote tunes for Yiddish texts. Recognizing the value of music for a well-rounded education, his father saw to it that Jack's older sister, Irene, received piano lessons; and this became Jack's first direct contact with music. At her instigation, he began listening to Saturday afternoon Metropolitan Opera broadcasts. An early radio performance of *Daphnis and Chloë* by the Boston Symphony Orchestra also was memorable: "I was spellbound by the ravishing sounds which had a palpable effect on me."

Music lessons for Jack began on the tonette while he was attending Stevenson Elementary School in New Rochelle (1936–42); but he soon advanced to the more legitimate clarinet, on which he received instruction from Bryant Minot. With Minot's guidance in instrumental music continuing through high school, and that of Walter Poyntz in vocal music, Gottlieb's musical abilities began to develop at Isaac E. Young Junior and Senior High School (1943–48), from which he was graduated in 1948. He played clarinet throughout his secondary school years in concert and marching bands; participated in choral concerts and student variety shows (for one of which he wrote a song) as a singer; and also performed at various Hebrew School musical events. The first piece he wrote, words and music, was in 1948, a popular ballad called "Moonlight Escapade," in the then prevalent style of songs promoted on radio by the program *Your Hit Parade*. The popular music and the motion pictures of the time were, he says, "seductively conditioning agents, affecting some of my later works."

About 1946, Gottlieb began to teach himself the piano. Formal piano lessons were undertaken in 1948, for two years, with Sylvia Roseman, a friend of the family. He studied later (1952–53) with Rebecca Davidson in New York City. Despite all his musical activity in high school, Gottlieb nevertheless aspired to become a journalist, like his brother David, rather than a musician. The testing given him by high school guidance counselors, however, revealed inescapably that music was his strongest asset. Impressed by this evidence, he enrolled in summer courses at the Juilliard School of Music, where one of his instructors, Johannes Smit, introduced him to the "magical world" of harmony.

Upon graduating from high school in 1948, Gottlieb began his college studies in the fall at the Washington Square division of New York University. The teachers there who made impact on him were Marion Bauer in music history and Luther W. Goodhart, conductor of the chorus. After a year and a half, Gottlieb transferred to Queens College, Flushing, N.Y., studying composition with Karol Rathaus, under whose benign but disciplined tutelage he completed his first successful composition. It was a setting of a children's story by Dr. Seuss, called *Horton Hatches the Egg*, for narrator and chamber orchestra (1951), first performed at Queens College on January 6, 1952.

At Queens College, Gottlieb sang in the college choir under John Castellini, but he also was a member of the New York Schola Cantorum under Hugh Ross, participating in several major concerts at Carnegie Hall. In 1952, Gottlieb was elected to Phi Beta Kappa at Queens, and in 1953 he received a bachelor of arts degree, *cum laude*.

He spent his summers during these college years as a camp music counselor and several more as a camper himself at the Brandeis Camp Institute in California, where he was instilled with Jewish value systems and arts. This was where he became an apprentice to Max Helfman, an eminent composer of synagogue music. Gottlieb studied informally with Helfman, who really was his first composer-model, and Helfman led him to a more formal private teacher, Robert Strassberg (1949). In 1950, as a result of his Brandeis Camp experiences, Gottlieb wrote his first instrumental composition, *Variations on a Hebrew Dance Theme*, for seven instruments, which had its one and only performance at Queens, N.Y., on April 17, 1951.

He went on to graduate work at Brandeis University in Waltham, Mass., in the fall of 1953. His teacher in composition was Irving Fine. Other instructors were Harold Shapero and Arthur Berger, who, with Fine, helped him discover the unique sounds of Stravinsky and Copland, two all-important influences on his further musical progress. At Brandeis, Gottlieb also attended composition seminars given by Leonard Bernstein, who, in a few years, would play a decisive role in Gottlieb's career. In 1955, Gottlieb earned his master of fine arts degree at Brandeis, and was honored by being selected marshal for the first graduating class of the graduate school. The summers of 1954 and 1955 were devoted to studies at the Berkshire Music Center at Tanglewood, Mass., as a composition student first of Aaron Copland and then of Boris Blacher.

In 1954, Gottlieb wrote a string quartet which won an award from Broadcast Music, Inc. (BMI), first performed at Brandeis University on April 25, 1955, by members of the Boston Symphony. In 1954 he also completed a song cycle to poems by Tennessee Williams, later revised into two separate groups: *Two Blues*, for female voice and clarinet, and *Hoofprints*, three songs for soprano and piano. The latter led John Rockwell to write in the *New York Times* in 1973: "What is most appealing about the piece is the way it treads the line between popular inspiration and serious aspiration."

A one-act opera was completed in 1955, with libretto by Erik Johns: *Tea Party*, the first of four one-act operas collectively entitled *A Symphony of Operas*, each libretto reflecting the structures of classical symphonic movements. *Tea Party*, in sonata form, was the winner of the Ohio University Opera Competition and the Nadworney Memorial Award of the National Federation of Music Clubs, both in 1957. It was premiered in Athens, Ohio, on August 4, 1957. The second opera (or movement) of the tetralogy of one-acters is a set of variations called *Public Dance* (1964). The last two "movements," a scherzo and a rondo, are still unfinished.

From 1955 to 1958 Gottlieb was in residence at the University of Illinois in Urbana. In addition to teaching as a graduate fellow, he led a choir at the university's Hillel Foundation and served as music director for several theatrical productions both in Urbana and in Fort Wayne, Ind. His "quodlibet for chorus and piano," *Kids' Calls* (1957; Urbana, Ill., February 23, 1958), was given first prize by the National Federation of Music Clubs in 1957. He continued his composition studies, first with Burrill Phillips, then with Robert Palmer. Gottlieb earned the degree of doctor of musical arts in 1964; the subject of his doctoral thesis was the music of Leonard Bernstein.

When Bernstein became the music director of the New York Philharmonic in 1958, he asked Gottlieb to join him as his liaison assistant. For the next eight years, Gottlieb acted as go-between in planning concerts, examining scores for possible performance, and helping in the writing and production of Bernstein's television shows. "Indeed," says Gottlieb, "much of my professional life has been linked to Bernstein's career. I have benefited immensely from sharing his musical example and philosophy. Yet, at the same time, he is such a powerful personality that it has been necessary for me to keep close checks on myself in order to guard my own creative identity."

On a grant from the Ford Foundation in 1959, Gottlieb was invited to attend an opera workshop at the New York City Center. In 1960 he completed a Piano Sonata, dedicated to Bernstein, first performed by Herbert Rogers in New York on February 9, 1963. Another work, a cantata entitled *In Memory of . . .* , on texts by the medieval poet Moses Ibn Ezra, for high voice, choir, and organ, was awarded first prize in the Brown University Choral Contest of 1961 and was introduced on March 18, 1960, at the Park Avenue Synagogue of New York.

Although he had written only a small amount of liturgical music up to 1964, that year Gottlieb was given a special citation by the Park Avenue Synagogue for his "outstanding contributions" to the field. From this point on, his accomplishments in contemporary synagogue music are impressive. The first of these is a Friday Evening Service, *Love Songs for Sabbath*, for cantor, choir, organ, percussion, and female reader (1965; N.Y., May 7, 1965). In 1967 this work was given a controversial performance in a church on the campus of the College of St. Catherine in St. Paul, Minn., making performance history by becoming the first complete Hebrew service to be given under Catholic auspices.

Other choral works include: *Shout for Joy*, settings of Psalms 95, 84, and 81 for mostly unison choir, piano, two flutes and three drums (1967; N.Y., January 19, 1969); *New Year's Service for Young People* (1970; St. Louis, October 1, 1970); and *Verses from Psalm 118* (1973), one of seventeen works commissioned by the Union of American Hebrew Congregations in its centennial year.

In observance of the American bicentennial, Gottlieb received two commissions. The first was from the Board of Jewish Education of Greater New York for *Sharing the Prophets*, "a musical encounter for singers, piano, bass, and percussion," fourteen individual numbers with texts by the composer (1975; N.Y., March 14, 1976). The second commission came from Temple Emanu-El of New York, for *Four Affirmations*, a choral work with soloist and brass sextet (1976; N.Y., April 17, 1976).

The Song of Songs, Which Is Solomon's (1976) is an "operatorio" completed with the assistance of a grant from the National Endowment for the Arts. Written for soprano, tenor, and baritone soloists with women's chorus, it is a setting of the entire Jerusalem Bible translation.

Among Gottlieb's secular works there is a woodwind quintet, *Twilight Crane*, a fantasy based on a Japanese folk tale (1961), premiered by the New York Philharmonic Quintet on NBC television on March 24, 1962. In 1962 came *Pieces of Seven*, overture for orchestra, given its first performance by the Jacksonville Symphony in Florida, October 23, 1962, the title derived from the principal meter of 7/8. *Songs of Loneliness*, a large cycle for baritone and piano to poems of Constantine Cavafy (1962), was introduced by John Reardon and Bliss Hebert in Washington, D.C., on March 7, 1964.

Downtown Blues for Uptown Halls (1967, revised 1978; N.Y., March 28, 1978), three songs for soprano, clarinet, and piano, with words by the composer, was inspired by the *cinéma noir* films of the 1940s. *Flickers*, in two versions (1968), is another film-inspired work. One set is scored for woodwind quintet, cello, and percussion. The other, an expanded version, is for piano, four hands. *Articles of Faith for Orchestra and Memorble Voices* is a work that uses the actual voices of statesmen, with emphasis on Franklin Roosevelt and John Kennedy. Commissioned by André Kostelanetz, it was premiered by the Detroit Symphony under Sixten Ehrling on April 14, 1966.

Two vocal works, written as a direct result of Gottlieb's association with Bernstein, are *Haiku Souvenirs* (1967), a song cycle, set to Bernstein's words (Elmont, N.Y., November 22, 1969); and *I Think Continually* (1978), poem by Stephen Spender, written in response to the death of Bernstein's wife, Felicia Montealegre, who had performed the role of the Reader in Gottlieb's *Love Songs for Sabbath*.

A small inheritance, received after his mother's death, enabled Gottlieb to move to a country home in upstate New York. For the next four years he freelanced, still working part-time on Bernstein's television programs, but also becoming active in several projects that cut across religious denominational boundary lines. This included the teaching of Jewish music to Catholic students at Loyola University in New Orleans (June 1966). "My move to Dutchess County was like retiring to a monastery after the jungle of Manhattan," he recalls, "and it proved too hermetic a life." Consequently in 1970 he accepted a post as organist and choir director of Temple Israel, St. Louis, Mo., one of the nation's largest reform congregations, where he remained for three years.

In 1972, he devised a multimedia lecture-entertainment called *From Shtetl to Stage Door, A Melting Pot-pourri Showing the Jewish Influence on the American Musical Theater*. Since its first performance at the Indianapolis Museum of Art on November 27, 1972, it has been successfully presented numerous times nationwide.

In the fall of 1973 Gottlieb was named composer-in-residence at the Hebrew Union College–Jewish Institute of Religion in New York, which prepares candidates for cantorial careers. Two years later he was promoted to the rank of assistant professor of music, the first such appointment in the history of the School of Sacred Music. But, in 1977, Gottlieb came full circle by rejoining Bernstein in his company, Amberson Enterprises, Inc. In 1979, Gottlieb formed his own publishing outlet, Theophilous Music, Inc., in association with G. Schirmer, Inc., which distributes his works.

In celebration of Jack Gottlieb's fiftieth birthday, fifty musicians (including Leonard Bernstein) gathered on the stage of the Abraham Goodman House in New York City on October 12, 1980, to present a concert of his vocal music. The program featured the world premiere of Gottlieb's *Psalmistry* (1979). This is a forty-minute setting of various psalms for four singers, chorus, and eleven players, Seymour Lipkin conducting. "The work," said Peter G. Davis in the *New York Times*, "provided an apt summary of Mr. Gottlieb's musical concerns as expressed in his songs: a fluent eclectic mix praising the Lord in terms of Broadway, blues, jazz, and an all-purpose popsy Americana that does not disdain liberal helpings of Continental dissonances for added spice. It is a combination that has worked well in the past for Mr. Bernstein . . . and so it did in this ebullient, deftly contrived concoction."

In 1965, Gottlieb recorded the celesta "chimes" that precede concerts and recall audiences after intermissions at Avery Fisher Hall (formerly called Philharmonic Hall) at the Lincoln Center for the Performing Arts in New York. These chimes consist of five sets of three twelve-tone rows selected by Gottlieb. By virtue of these musical summonses, Gottlieb laughingly refers to himself as a composer who has been performed at every concert in that auditorium since its opening in 1965.

THE COMPOSER SPEAKS: I am convinced, this late in the 20th century, that avant-garde practices will never make inroads on synagogue music; and this is one reason (but by no means the only one) why I am a musical conservative. I favor tonality, I do not hesitate to allow popular idioms to infiltrate my writings. This does not mean that I am opposed to nontonal music, especially when used in unmechanical ways, but I do not regard such music as an end in itself. Rather, it is for me a tool, useful for conveying feeling of tension and irresolution. When Webern's music was the rage in the 1950s and 1960s, the music establishment made me feel I was on the outside since I did not flow with the tide. In fact, some of my music was accused of being too "Broadway." But I never understood why this necessarily had to be a critique of opprobrium. Although this kind of influence was then dismissed as "selling out" or as "commercial trash," I believe the attitudinal climate these days has changed. Instead of allowing surface style, rather than inner content, to determine value judgments, now such sounds are regarded as possible source materials as much as any other musical stuff.

PRINCIPAL WORKS: *Hoofprints* and *Two Blues*,

songs (1954; revised 1963); String Quartet (1954); *Tea Party*, one-act opera (1955); *Kids' Calls*, for chorus (1957); Piano Sonata (1960); *In Memory of . . .*, cantata for high voice, choir and organ (1960); *Twilight Crane*, woodwind quintet (1961); *Pieces of Seven*, overture for orchestra (1962); *Songs of Loneliness*, cycle for voice and piano (1962); *Public Dance*, one-act opera (1964); *Love Songs for Sabbath*, Friday Evening Service (1965); *Articles of Faith*, for orchestra (1965); *Downtown Blues for Uptown Halls*, songs for soprano, clarinet, and piano (1967); *Haiku Souvenirs*, song cycle for voice and piano (1967); *Shout for Joy*, for chorus (1967); *Flickers*, two versions (1968); *New Year's Service for Young People* (1970); *Three Candle Blessings*, for choir (1970); *Verses from Psalm 118*, for choir (1973); *Tefilot Sheva*, liturgical song cycle for voice and piano (1974); *Judge of the World*, for organ (1975); *Sharing the Prophets*, for singers, piano, bass, and percussion (1975); *Four Affirmations*, for chorus, soloists, and brass sextet or keyboard (1976); *The Song of Songs, Which Is Solomon's*, operatorio (1976); *Psalmistry*, for four singers, chorus, and eleven instruments (1979).

BIBLIOGRAPHY: *BBDM; DCM; Composers of America*, vol. 9, 1963.

Gottschalk, Louis Moreau, b. New Orleans, La., May 8, 1829; d. Rio de Janiero, Brazil, December 18, 1869.

He was the first American-born concert pianist and composer of international renown, and America's earliest nationalist composer.

He was the oldest of seven children of a wealthy and cultured English broker who had immigrated to New Orleans when he was twenty-five and married a Creole beauty of noble French descent who was a well-trained singer.

When Louis was three he was discovered at the piano playing by ear an aria from Meyerbeer's *Robert le diable* he had just heard his mother sing. He began to study the piano one year later with François Letellier, who subsequently supplemented this with lessons on the organ; he was also trained in the violin by Félix Miolan. When Gottschalk was seven, on short notice, he substituted for Letellier at the organ of the Saint-Louis Church in New Orleans, where he played all the music for the High Mass at sight, an accomplishment that led the New Orleans press to hail him as a prodigy. By the time Gottschalk was eleven, Letellier said there was nothing more he could teach him and insisted that the boy go to Paris for further instruction. Gottschalk gave a concert, billed as his "farewell appearance," on April 23, 1841, in the St. Louis Ballroom in New Orleans. But, because of his mother's reluctance to part with her son, it was still almost two years before young Gottschalk was sent abroad. During this interim he was often heard in performances at various soirées. Finally, on May 17, 1842, placed in the care of the ship's captain, the thirteen-year-old Gottschalk set sail for France by himself. There he studied the piano privately with Charles Hallé and Camille Stamaty, and harmony with Pierre Maleden. In addition, he acquired instruction in Latin, Greek, the modern classics, horsemanship, and fencing. He was constantly brought into a circle of French writers and musicians who provided him with further intellectual cultivation. Before long, he became the darling of the Parisian salon, the doors to which had been opened for him by his mother's influential Parisian relatives and friends. An informal concert in Paris in April 1844 was attended by Chopin, who then predicted Gottschalk would become a "king of pianists." Chopin later spoke favorably of one of Gottschalk's early piano works: *Ossian*, two ballades, published in 1848. Berlioz also spoke rhapsodically of Gottschalk's talent, became Gottschalk's mentor in the writing of his first compositions, and, beginning with 1846, had him appear as soloist at concerts Berlioz conducted. Writing in the *Journal des débats*, Berlioz called Gottschalk "one of the very small number who possess all the different elements of a consummate pianist—all the faculties which surround him with an irresible prestige and give him a sovereign power."

In his performances in Paris Gottschalk was featuring his own piano pieces in which he recalled his boyhood in New Orleans through recollections of songs and dances of the Creoles and the blacks. *Bamboula* (a Negro dance in New Orleans's Place Congo), *Le Bananier* (a Negro song), *La savane* (a Creole ballad)—all written in 1845 or 1846—and *Le mancenillier* (a serenade) in 1849, were, pianistically speaking, influenced by Chopin and Liszt. But the voice was the voice of Gottschalk in the rhythmic impulses, unusual harmonic colors, and the popular turns of phrases. This was the first serious music to use American popular tunes so successfully, and Europe welcomed it warmly. Everywhere in Europe pianists were including it in their repertoires, and pirated editions began sprouting up in different countries.

Serious financial reverses in the family made it necessary for Gottschalk for the first time to depend exclusively on his own music and music making for a livelihood. He now intensified his performing schedule. Between 1850 and 1852 he toured Switzerland, France, and Spain in public concerts and appearances in provincial salons, always featuring his own compositions. Many of these were functional pieces for a distinguished person or a special occasion. A tour de force was *El sitio de Zaragoza* (1851), written for his Spanish appearances, programmed as "a grand symphony for ten pianos," in which the sound and fury of battle were realistically recreated and the Spanish national anthem and other popular Spanish tunes interpolated. In other Spanish pieces—*Souvenirs d'Andalousie* (1851), for example, whose fan-

dango movement developed a Spanish dance tune made famous a century later by Ernesto Lecuona in his popular *Malagueña*, or *La jota aragonesa* (1852), a Spanish caprice—the sounds of plucking guitars and clicking castenets were simulated. His triumphant tour of Spain was climaxed by a concert in Madrid in 1851, given at the invitation of the queen of Spain, where he was given a tumultuous ovation and following which the queen conferred on him the Order of Isabella. (In 1856, Gottschalk was again honored in Spain, this time with the title of chevalier of the Royal Order of Charles III.) By 1853, Gottschalk's fame both as pianist and composer covered most of Europe, something that had never happened before to an American-born musician.

His march of triumph brought him back to the United States in 1853, his first return concert given at Niblo's Gardens in New York on February 11, followed by a highly successful tour. Everyone seems intoxicated with his performances. William Mason, an eminent pianist, described Gottschalk's playing as "full of brilliancy and bravura. His strong, rhythmic accent, his vigor and dash, were exciting and always aroused enthusiasm. He was the perfection of his school and his effects had the sparkle and effervescence of champagne." At his concerts Gottschalk never hesitated to include special potpourris, *pièces d'occasion*, and display pieces calculated to arouse and excite audience response. At one time, the once-Spanish *El sitio de Zaragoza* was transformed into *Bunker's Hill*, a "grand national symphony for ten pianos" which he rewrote to include such native American items as "Yankee Doodle" and "The Star-Spangled Banner." As a piece for solo piano he called it *American Reminiscences of Old Glory*, now adding to the score quotations from Stephen Foster's "Swanee River" and "Oh! Susannah." He also conceived display items (polkas, mazurkas, galops, caprices) to enchant his audiences with harplike effects, glissandos, tremolos and soulful material which have since become identified as Gottschalk's "style pianola"; choice pieces of Americana such as "The Banjo" (1855); and sentimental salon music. Of the last, the most celebrated by far was *The Last Hope* (1853–54), probably the most famous American salon composition of its time, a fixture of pianos of American households, beloved by young females performing for relatives and friends and, toward the end of the century, a standby in the repertoire of pianists accompanying silent films.

Such was Gottschalk's public appeal that P. T. Barnum offered him the then-munificent fee of $20,000 and expenses to perform under his management for a year. Gottschalk declined only because his father regarded any affiliation with Barnum as undignified. Instead, Gottschalk continued to tour on his own, covering small cities as well as large ones, and sometimes playing in mining camps.

Between 1856 and 1861 he toured the West Indies. This led to the writing of works inspired by native melodies and rhythms such as in *Souvenir de Puerto Rico*, a march (1857), *Souvenir de la Havane, "a grand caprice"* (1859), and his most famous work for orchestra, the two-movement fantasy *Night of the Tropics* (1858–59), which Gottschalk introduced in Havana on April 17, 1861. This composition, scored for large orchestra supplemented by a band of winds, was an exceptional exercise in the use of unusual subtle and instrumental effects, dynamic shadings, and blendings of massed colors. (The Andante movement was reconstructed by Quinto Maganini in 1932, who directed its American premiere in New York on January 30, 1933. The first modern performance of the entire work, as well as its American premiere, was given on May 5, 1955, in New York, conducted by Howard Shanet, who had reconstructed the work from random manuscripts.)

In Havana, on February 17, 1860, Gottschalk promoted and directed a giant festival enlisting the services of nine hundred musicians including choristers, solo singers, fifty drums and eighty trumpets. For this event he wrote *Escenas campestres*, for soprano, tenor, baritone and full orchestra, a work overflowing with popular Latin American and North American tunes.

There was an interruption in Gottschalk's professional life between 1860 and 1862 when he deserted music to wander about the West Indies and succumb to its geographical and amatory allurements. Finally weary of his indolence, and guilty of having neglected music, he came back to the United States to resume his concert life in 1862. Under the management of Max Strakosch, he toured the United States, traveling fifteen thousand miles and giving eleven hundred concerts in a three-year period. During the Civil War, though he was of Southern birth, he allied himself with the Northern cause. To promote Northern morale and to fire the martial spirit he wrote, in 1862, a rabble-rousing piano piece, *Union*, in which massive loud chords and chromatic passages brought up the sounds of warfare and included quotations and paraphrases of such anthems as "Yankee Doodle," "The Star-Spangled Banner," and "Hail, Columbia." A contrasting composition written in 1863–64 was *The Dying Poet*, described as a "meditation," still another salon piece to gain worldwide favor.

A scandal involving him with a young seminary schoolgirl in San Francisco forced him to flee the United States under cover of darkness on a boat bound for South America in 1865. He remained in exile for the rest of his life, concertizing in Peru, Chile, Argentina, and Uruguay, organizing and conducting monster festivals and producing more and more compositions. In 1868 came his orchestral tone poem *Montevideo* (in which Uruguayan melodies were incongruously combined with "Yankee Doodle" and "Hail, Columbia") and the lamentation *Morte!* in the "style pianola." In 1869 he wrote the *Grand Tarantelle*, for piano and orchestra. He was also bringing to completion two operas—*Isaura di Salerno* and *Charles IX*—neither of which was ever performed.

He was participating in a festival of his music in Rio de Janiero, which opened on November 26, 1869, when he was stricken by yellow fever. Though ill, he tried to perform at the second concert but collapsed before the first number. Removed to Tijuca, a suburb of Rio de Janiero, he died a month later. His remains were brought back to the United States in 1870. After a service on October 3, Gottschalk was buried in Greenwood Cemetery in Brooklyn, N.Y.

By the turn of the 20th century, Gottschalk's music had all but disappeared from the concert repertoire. But since 1950 there has been a vigorous Gottschalk revival, beginning on June 12, 1951, with the production of the ballet *Cakewalk* by the New York City Ballet, with choreography by Ruthanna Boris, in which several of Gottschalk's compositions were adapted orchestrally by Hershey Kay. In 1964, Gottschalk's diaries, *Notes of a Pianist* (originally published in Philadelphia in 1881), were reissued in New York, edited by Jeanne Behrend. The first official honor New Orleans paid its native son took place in January 1969 when a commemorative plaque was placed in the Municipal Theater, an event inspiring an all-Gottschalk program by the New Orleans Philharmonic. *The Piano Works of Louis Moreau Gottschalk*, edited in five volumes by Vera L. Brodsky, was released in New York in 1969, and in 1970 in New York *The Centennial Catalogue of the Published and Unpublished Compositions of Louis Moreau Gottschalk*, edited by Robert Offergeld, was published. Later in the early 1970s, comprehensive albums of Gottschalk's piano compositions were recorded by Alan Mandel, Leonard Pennario, and Eugene List, among others, and Gottschalk's music began reappearing on the programs of American concert pianists. On May 2, 1979, a three-hour "Gottschalk Extravaganza," produced by Eugene List, presented forty-two pianists on ten Steinway pianos. "With its saucy rhythms, gaudy colors and catchy tunes," reported Joseph Horowitz in the *New York Times*, "Gottschalk's music certainly deserves the revival Mr. List has helped motivate. By mixing plantation, West Indian and Latin American strains with the elegance of the salon, and the polished showmanship of the concert hall, Gottschalk was an inspired purveyor of cultivated naivete, and characteristically American."

THE COMPOSER SPEAKS: Music is a thing eminently sensuous. Certain combinations move us, not because they are ingenious, but because they move our nervous systems in a certain way. I have a horror of musical Puritans. They are arid natures, deprived of sensibility, generally hypocrites, incapable of understanding two phrases in music. They never judge until they are assured that it is proper, like those tasters who do not esteem a wine until they have seen the seal, and who can be made to drink execrable wine imperturbably which they will announce excellent if it is served to them in a bottle powdered with age.

PRINCIPAL WORKS: *(unless otherwise indicated all are for solo piano)*: *Bamboula*, Negro dance (1845); *Le Bananier*, Negro song (1846); *La savane*, Creole ballad (1846); *La mêlancolie* (1847); *La moisson- neuse* (1847); *Le mancenillier*, serenade (1849); *Sov- enirs d'Andalousie* (1851); *El sito de Zaragoza*, "grand symphony for ten pianos" (1851); *La jota aragonesa* (1852); *The Last Hope*, "religious medita- tion" (1854); *The Banjo*, "an American sketch" (1855); *Manchega*, concert etude (1856); *Minuit à Seville*, caprice (1865); *Souvenir de Puerto Rico*, march (1857); *Danza* (1857); *Night of the Tropics*, orchestral fantasy (1858–59); *Souvenir de la Havane*, grand caprice (1859); *Ojos criollos*, Cuban dance for piano, four hands (1859); *Escenas campestres*, for soprano, tenor, baritone, and orchestra (1860); Ber- ceuse, for voice and piano (1861); *Union*, concert paraphrase of national airs (1862); *La gallina*, for piano, four hands (1863); *The Dying Poet*, a "medi- tation" (1864); *Charles IX*, opera (1865–69); *Isaura de Salerno*, opera (1865–69); *Morte!*, "a lamenta- tion" (1868); *Montevideo*, orchestral tone poem (1868); *Grande Tarantelle*, or *Célèbre Tarantelle*, for piano and orchestra (1868); Grand Scherzo (1869).

BIBLIOGRAPHY: Behrend, Jeanne (ed.), *Notes of a Pianist* (N.Y., 1964); Loggins, Vernon, *Where the World Ends: The Life of Louis Moreau Gottschalk* (Baton Rouge, La., 1958); *Etude*, January 1957; *Stereo Review*, September 1968, March 1970; *Inter- American Music Bulletin*, July–October 1970; *Mu- sical America*, February 1959; *New York Times*, April 23, 1961, February 25, 1968, January 29, 1969, February 22, 1970, April 22, 1979.

Gould, Morton, b. Richmond Hill, N.Y., Decem- ber 10, 1913.

His first successes came as a popularist who skill- fully carried idioms of American popular music into the concert hall. Later works occasionally remind us of his interest in popular music but many are more complex and abstract with advanced contrapuntal and harmonic procedures.

His father (a real estate broker who later became his business manager) had come from Vienna and his mother was of Russian extraction; he was the oldest of four sons. A musical prodigy, he sat at the piano at the age of four and a half and correctly played "The Stars and Stripes Forever," which he had just heard played by an American Legion post band. From then on he was continually recreating on the piano what- ever piece of music he heard, mostly from piano rolls. He also improvised and composed his first published composition at the age of six: a piano waltz entitled *Just Six*. "Not until then," his father recalls, "did I

realize fully that I had a musician in the family. But how and when Morton learned music is a myste- ry."

Gould received some local instruction on the piano before he was given a scholarship at the Institute of Musical Art in his eighth year. He remained there a year, after which he studied piano privately with Jo- seph Kardos. When he was thirteen Gould acquired a new piano teacher, Abby Whiteside, who had a far-reaching influence on his musical development both as composer and pianist. At the same time he studied composition at New York University with Vincent Jones. When he was fifteen, the prestigious publishing house of G. Schirmer issued his piano suite *Three Conservative Sketches*. One year later, a concert of his works was given at New York Univer- sity. All this while, he combined music study with an academic education in the city public schools.

The early depression years so greatly affected the family finances that, in 1930, Gould had to drop out of Richmond High School to help support the family. He played the piano in motion picture and vaudeville theaters and jazz bands; toured the vaudeville circuit with the two-piano team of Gould and Shefter; was an accompanist to the De Marcos, dancers; lectured in colleges and conservatories where he demonstrated his gift at improvisation by requesting the audience to provide him with musical notes or a phrase that he would spontaneously build into a fugue.

In 1931–32 he found employment as staff pianist at the newly opened Radio City Music Hall in New York, and one year after that he joined the staff of NBC radio as pianist and a partner with Shefter in duos. From this he progressed in 1934 to a weekly assignment to conduct, compose, and make arrange- ments on a weekly orchestral radio program over sta- tion WOR and the Mutual network for a series enti- tled *Music for Today*, a post he retained for the next eight years. In 1943 Gould became the musical direc- tor of the *Cresta Blanca Carnival* and the *Chrysler Hour* on the CBS radio network, becoming thereby one of radio's outstanding musical personalities of the time. Many of his earlier, lighter compositions were introduced on these programs. Drawing from his rich and varied experiences in popular music, he wrote *American Symphonette* no. 1 (1933), which he introduced on his radio program, in which a popular style and popular material are given serious concert treatment. A similar marriage between the popular and the serious took place with *Chorale and Fugue in Jazz*, for two pianos and orchestra (1934), intro- duced by the Philadelphia Orchestra under Leopold Stokowski on January 2, 1936. These were followed by other works serious in intent but popular in con- tent, and among them were: three more symphon- ettes (1935, 1938, 1941, the last of which contains the popular "Pavane"); *A Foster Gallery*, based on several well-loved or little known Stephen Foster songs (1940), which was premiered by the Pitts- burgh Symphony under Fritz Reiner on January 12,

1940; the *Latin-American Symphonette* (1940; N.Y., February 21, 1941), whose four movements are respectively a rhumba, tango, guaracha, and conga, music subsequently used by the San Francisco Ballet for *Parranda*; *American Salute*, a symphonic treatment of Civil War songs and the Civil War and Spanish-American War favorite, "When Johnny Comes Marching Home" (1942); *American Concertette*, for piano and orchestra (1943); which contains a "blues" movement, introduced on Gould's radio program with José Iturbi as soloist on August 23, 1943, then used as the background music for a Jerome Robbins ballet, *Interplay*; *Boogie-Woogie Etude*, for piano (1943), written for and introduced by José Iturbi; the Concerto for Orchestra (1944), whose finale is in a boogie-woogie style, first performed on February 1, 1945, by the Cleveland Orchestra (which had commissioned it) conducted by Vladimir Golschmann; and the Symphony no. 2 (1944; N.Y., June 4, 1944), made up of marching tunes and war songs including "The Battle Hymn of the Republic" and "When Johnny Comes Marching Home."

Other Gould compositions of the 1940s revealed his interest in using American subjects, backgrounds, and experiences as material. One of his greatest successes up to this time falls in this category. It is the *Spirituals*, for string choir and orchestra (1941), first heard under the composer's direction at the New York City Festival of American Music on February 9, 1941, and soon after that programmed by many of America's major orchestras, including the Cleveland Orchestra and the New York Philharmonic. Here the composer tried to convey the overall mood and the general idiom of spirituals, both white and black, without quoting any specific ones at length. "My starting premise was that our spirituals develop a wide game of emotions musically," Gould explains. "These emotions are specifically American. The songs range from ones that are escapist in feelings, or light and gay, to those having tremendous depth and tragic impact. There are five moods, widely contrasted in feeling." Gould uses the strings as if they were a vocal choir, with the rest of the orchestra as a kind of accompaniment, similar to a group singing with antiphonal responses. The titles of the five movements provide a clue to their programmatic intent: "Proclamation," "Sermon," "A Little Bit of Sin," "Protest," and "Jubilee." Other works of this period exploiting Americana included *A Lincoln Legend* (1941), introduced by the NBC Symphony under Arturo Toscanini on November 1, 1942; *Cowboy Rhapsody* (1943), a symphonic treatment of such well-known cowboy tunes as "Trail to Mexico," "Home on the Range," and "Good-bye, Old Paint," which originated as a work for concert band but which he later orchestrated, the later version presented by the St. Louis Symphony in March 1944; the Symphony no. 1 (1943), which attempted to cap-

ture the mood and spirit of America during the years of World War II, a work introduced by the Pittsburgh Symphony under Fritz Reiner on March 5, 1943; *Minstrel Show*, written in 1946 for Fabien Sevitzky and the Indianapolis Symphony and performed by them on December 21, 1946, a work in which no literal use of minstrel show tunes is made, but in which sliding trombone and banjo effects and the sounds and tempo of the soft-shoe dance, all so favored in minstrel shows, are simulated.

Gould's rapidly mounting importance in American music was underlined in December 1945 when he was invited to conduct the Boston Symphony in an all-Gould program which included some of his now well established favorites together with a new work, *Harvest*, for vibraphone, harp, and strings (1945), which had been introduced in St. Louis two months earlier (October 21). Gould was invited by Antal Dorati, the music director of the Dallas Symphony, to conduct that orchestra on February 16, 1947, in the premiere of Symphony no. 3 (1946–47), in which elements of the blues and jazz are integrated into the symphonic texture. Gould revised this symphony, providing it with a new third movement (a passacaglia and fugue), which the New York Philharmonic under Dimitri Mitropoulos performed on October 28, 1948.

Gould's most famous ballet, *Fall River Legend* (1947)—scenario and choreography by Agnes De Mille based on the sensational Lizzie Borden trial for the murder of her father and his second wife in Fall River, Mass., in which she was acquitted—was produced by the Ballet Theater in New York on April 22, 1948. The six-movement orchestral suite derived by the composer from his ballet score was first heard on March 29, 1952, performed by the New York Philharmonic under Mitropoulos. On November 16, 1948, the New York Philharmonic under Mitropoulos premiered the *Philharmonic Waltzes* (1947), which Gould had been commissioned to write for the annual Pension Ball of the New York Philharmonic; its three movements portrayed three different types of waltzes, beginning with a "sweet" waltz from the Gay Nineties, continuing with a romantic waltz, and concluding with a continental waltz.

Gould's inordinate skill and originality in orchestration, his sensitivity for color and texture, his mastery of architectonic structure, and his articulateness were now being widely recognized and acclaimed. Writing in the *American Mercury*, Schima Kaufman praised Gould for carrying "the American idiom to its highest development," and for evolving "an individual native musical language which is not a mixture of classical and jive, but rather jazz-become-classical."

Time and again, since 1950, Gould continued to write popular-styled and American-oriented works for the concert platform. The ingeniously contrived

Concerto for Tap Dancer and Orchestra (1952), introduced by Danny Daniels in Rochester, N.Y., on November 16, 1952, was a full-length three-movement concerto which places the varied rhythmic beats of tap-dancing feet against a symphonic background. In *Derivations for Clarinet and Jazz Band* (1954), written for Benny Goodman and introduced by him on July 14, 1956, the baroque structure of the concerto grosso was combined with the jazz vernacular. George Balanchine used this music for a ballet, *Clarinade*, in April 1964, and Eliot Field for the ballet *Jive* later on. *Declaration* (1957), commissioned by the NBC affiliate in Washington, D.C., was a setting of the Declaration of Independence. The first performance took place at the Eisenhower Inaugural Concert in Washington, D.C., on January 20, 1957, Howard Mitchell conducting the National Symphony Orchestra. *Symphony of Spirituals* (1976), commissioned by the National Endowment for the Arts for the American bicentennial, was a successor to the 1940 *Spirituals* in recreating the sound and style of the spiritual. Its premiere took place on April 1, 1976, in a performance by the Detroit Symphony under Aldo Ceccato. *American Ballads* (1976; Queens, N.Y., April 24, 1976), commissioned by the New York State Council for the Arts and the United States Historical Society, was a work for orchestra providing symphonic dress to such national or popular ballads as "America the Beautiful," "The Star-Spangled Banner," "Taps," "The Girl I Left Behind Me," and "We Shall Overcome."

But many of Gould's compositions since 1950 sidestepped both popular music and Americana to provide music more complicated and sophisticated, its interest centered on the enlargement of its musical ideas, its structure, and enriched harmonic and contrapuntal resources. Among these works are the following: *Showpiece for Orchestra* (1954), which was introduced by the Philadelphia Orchestra under Eugene Ormandy on May 7, 1954, and then presented at the Edinburgh Festival in Scotland in 1955; *Jekyll and Hyde Variations*, for orchestra (1955), premiered by the New York Philharmonic under Mitropoulos on February 2, 1957; *Dialogues*, for piano and strings (1956), written for and introduced by Thomas Scherman and the Little Orchestra Society on November 2, 1958; *Venice*, an "audiograph" for two orchestras and brass bands (1966; Seattle, Wash., May 2, 1967); *Vivaldi Gallery*, for string quartet and divided orchestra (1967; Seattle, Wash., March 25, 1968); *Soundings*, two threnodies for orchestra (1969; Atlanta, Ga., September 18, 1969).

For the Broadway musical theater Gould provided the music for *Billion Dollar Baby* (1945) and *Arms and the Girl* (1950); for the Hollywood screen, scores to *Delightfully Dangerous* (1944); *Cinerama Holiday* (1955), and *Windjammer* (1958); for television, music for documentaries or television dramas—*The Secret of Freedom* (1960), *The Turn of the Century*

(1960), *Verdun* (1963), *World War I*, a twenty-six-week series (1964–65), *The World of Music* (1965), *F. Scott Figzgerald in Hollywood* (1976), and *Holocaust* (1978).

Gould's appearances as conductor have been worldwide, and he has made numerous recordings, one of which, that of Charles Ives's Symphony no. 1, was presented with a Grammy by the National Academy of Recording Arts and Sciences. In 1967 Gould received the Henry Hadley Medal from the National Association for American Composers and Conductors for his outstanding service to American music. In 1977 he toured Australia, and in 1979 Japan. Gould has been a member of the board of directors of the American Society of Composers, Authors, and Publishers (ASCAP), American Symphony League, and American Music Center. In June 1944, he married Shirley Bank, a schoolteacher; they have two sons and two daughters.

THE COMPOSER SPEAKS: My artistic statements should be in my music. I have experienced and explored various facets of music and I am sure that the combination of my experiences and particular abilities, plus circumstances in time and place, have shaped my creative character the way any artist is shaped by these elements. I have always been and still am stimulated by the vernacular, by the sound of spirituals, jazz, etc. I am that kind of composer and I would imagine that although I might venture into more complicated abstractions, there is always present in one form or another, at least the residue of these influences. I would hope that I am true to myself, rather than to trends or fads.

PRINCIPAL WORKS: 4 *American Symphonettes* (1933–41); 3 symphonies (1943, 1946–47, 1951); 3 piano sonatas (1930–36).

Choral and Fugue in Jazz, for two pianos and orchestra (1934); *Little Symphony* (1936); Piano Concerto (1937); Violin Concerto (1938); *A Foster Gallery*, for orchestra (1940); *Spirituals*, for orchestra (1940); *Latin-American Symphonette*, for orchestra (1940); *A Lincoln Legend*, for orchestra (1941); *Cowboy Rhapsody*, for concert band, also for orchestra (1943); *American Concertette*, or *Interplay*, ballet (1943); Viola Concerto (1944); Concerto for Orchestra (1944); *Harvest*, for vibraphone, harp and strings (1945); *Ballad*, for concert band (1945); *Minstrel Show*, for orchestra (1946); *Philharmonic Waltzes*, for orchestra (1947); *Fall River Legend*, ballet (1947); *Serenade of Carols*, for orchestra (1948); *Family Album*, for orchestra (1950); Symphony for concert band, *West Point* (1951); *Dance Variations*, for two pianos and orchestra (1952); *Concerto for Tap Dancer and Orchestra* (1952); Inventions, for four pianos and orchestra (1953); *Jekyll and Hyde Variations*, for orchestra (1955); *Santa Fe Saga*, for concert band (1953); *Derivations, for Clar-*

inet and *Jazz Band* (1954); *Dialogues*, for piano and strings (1956); *Declaration*, for two speakers, male chorus, and orchestra (1957); *Rhythm Gallery*, for narrator and orchestra (1958); *St. Lawrence Suite*, for concert band (1958); *Prisms*, for concert band (1962); *Festive Music*, for off-stage trumpet and orchestra (1964); *Venice*, "audiograph" for two orchestras and brass bands (1966); *Vivaldi Gallery*, for string quartet and divided orchestra (1967); *Troubadour Music*, for four guitars and orchestra (1968); *Soundings*, for orchestra (1969); *Symphony of Spirituals*, for orchestra (1976); *American Ballads*, for orchestra (1976); *Burchfield Gallery*, for orchestra (1979).

BIBLIOGRAPHY: Evans, Lee, "Morton Gould: His Life and Music" (doctoral thesis, N.Y., 1978); Ewen, David, *Composers Since 1900* (N.Y., 1969); Goss, Madeleine, *Modern Music Makers* (N.Y., 1952); *American Mercury*, July 1949; *New York Times*, April 14, 1978.

Grainger, (George) Percy Aldridge, b. Brighton, Melbourne, Australia, July 8, 1882; d. White Plains, N.Y., February 20, 1961. American citizen 1919.

Those simple, charming English folk tunes Grainger recreated for orchestra and with which he gained his passport for survival are only one facet of his creativity. Throughout his career as a composer he was the restless, searching innovator who used avant-garde idioms sometimes far in advance of his time—indeterminacy, microtones, polyrhythms, polytonality, and, toward the end of his life, electronic devices. His goal was "free music," that is, music more free in rhythms than was traditional, gliding intervals within traditional scales, more dissonances. He also sought to free music from its slavery to German and Italian tempo or dynamic markings by using colloquial English expressions instead.

His mother, a piano teacher, early detected in Percy signs of musical talent. From the time Percy was five, and for the next five years, she gave him piano lessons, and toward the end of that period instruction and guidance in composition. By the time Percy Granger was ten, he was giving public concerts. Further piano study took place with Louis Pabst (1893–95).

In 1895 Grainger went to Germany for additional musical training: piano with James Kwast (1895–99) and composition with Ivan Knorr (1895–97) and again in 1899. He had been composing music from his early boyhood days, and when he was sixteen he was an experimenter who tried to develop "beatless music."

In 1900 Grainger settled in London, where he made a successful debut as pianist before touring Great Britain and Germany, New Zealand, Australia, and South Africa. Among his compositions of this period was *Hill Song,* no. 1, for chamber orchestra (1902; rescored 1921), unusual because of its highly complex rhythmic patterns.

In 1906, in London, Grainger met Edvard Grieg, who was so impressed with Grainger's talent as pianist and his innovative ideas that he invited Grainger to visit him at his home Troldhaugen, in Norway, during the summer of 1907. There Grieg played for Grainger his Piano Concerto in A minor, then invited him to perform the work under his own direction at the Leeds Festival in England later in 1907. Though Grieg died two months before the festival, Grainger fulfilled his obligations to Grieg by performing his concerto and enjoying a triumph. Since then Grainger was universally recognized as one of the most notable interpreters of the Grieg concerto.

Grainger's personal association with Grieg, Grieg's infectious enthusiasm for Norwegian folk music and the successful way in which Grieg exploited it in some of his works, directed Grainger's interest toward the folk music of England. He embarked on a research project in which (with the aid of a wax cylinder phonograph, the first time it was being used for research in England) he gathered some five hundred British folk songs which he then harmonized and adapted for orchestra. *Irish Tune from County Derry*, for strings (1902), is a version of the famous Irish melody "Londonderry Air." *Brigg Fair,* for tenor and chorus (1906), used a pastoral melody from the district of Lincolnshire. (When Delius wrote his orchestral rhapsody *Brigg Fair* at about the same time, he dedicated it to Grainger.) *Molly on the Shore* (1907) was first written for the piano, then for orchestra. *Mock Morris,* for orchestra (1910), originated as a composition for piano, and only then was orchestrated, the orchestral version introduced under the composer's direction at a Balfour Gardiner concert in London in 1912. (Mock Morris is an old English dance popular during the reign of Henry VIII and since become associated with festivities attending May Day.) *Handel in the Strand*, for orchestra (1912), is a clog dance. *Shepherd's Hey*, for orchestra (1913), is another "Mock Morris" and comprises four tunes, two of them fiddle tunes and two folk songs. The bucolic *Country Gardens*, for orchestra (1918), is once again a Mock Morris. The resuscitation and modernization of these and other English folk songs won instant recognition in England and elsewhere. "Grainger was a folklorist who netted tunes and pinned them to paper with the precision and art of a lepidopterist," wrote John Ardoin in the *New York Times*. "What resulted was more than an arrangement: his pieces are too richly varied and too individual." "Even when he keeps the folk songs within their original dimensions," wrote Cyril Scott in *Musical Quarterly*, "he has a way of dealing with them which is entirely new, yet at the same time never lacking in taste."

In 1914, Grainger immigrated to the United

States. From that time on, America remained his permanent homeland and the country of his citizenship. His American debut as pianist took place in New York on February 11, 1915, his program including his own *Colonial Song* (1912) and *Mock Morris.* In the *New York Times,* Richard Aldrich called him "a pianist of altogether uncommon quality and accomplishment. . . . He possesses an intensely musical feeling that vitalizes all he does." The following March 13 he scored an even greater success as a guest artist with the New York Philharmonic in the Grieg concerto. His concerts after that, both in the United States and abroad, placed him in the highest rank of living pianists. In London he became known as the "trotting pianist" because, due to his fetish for exercise, he often trotted from his hotel to the concert hall. He sometimes walked for miles from one city to another (with knapsack on back) rather than use motor or rail transportation. He usually made his concerts as informal as possible by including informative and at times amusing comments about the music he was playing and including on his programs improvisations which he liked to call "rambles."

During World War I, Grainger enlisted as a bandman in the U.S. Army, where he first played oboe and saxophone in the Fifteenth Coast Artillery Band at Fort Hamilton, in Brooklyn, N.Y., and then served as instructor in the Army Music School. One of his compositions during the war was the "Children's March: Over the Hills and Far Away" (1918), written for the United States Band. "This march," composer said, "is structurally of a complicated build, on account of the large number of different themes and tunes employed and of the varied and irregular interplay of many contrasted sections. Tonally speaking, it is a study in the blend of piano, wind, and percussion instruments." After the war, from 1919 to 1931, he taught the piano at the summer sessions at the Chicago Musical College. In 1921, he settled in White Plains, N.Y., which remained his home until his death. In 1932–33 he was chairman of the music department at New York University.

The demands made on him by his concert tours notwithstanding, Grainger was composing music all the time, producing a prolific output for band (an area in which he exerted a powerful influence), orchestra, small instrumental ensembles, and voice. Many of his original compositions absorbed folk song influences. *Youthful Suite,* for orchestra, begun in 1902 and completed in 1945, is a five-section work, the first movement of which derives its character from the melodic and rhythmic traits of the folk music of northern England and Scotland. *Green Bushes,* a passacaglia for chamber orchestra (1906), is based on the English folk melody "Green Bushes," which remains unchanged in key, line and rhythm throughout the work (except for eight measures in the free passage work near the beginning and forty measures

at the end). Against this melody move several folklike melodies of Grainger's own invention.

But much of what he wrote was in pursuit of the untried in his continual effort to expand the boundaries of music. He used polytonality in "Gumsucker's March" (1914) and suggested a "chance" process in *Random Round* (1914). His harmonic and rhythmic language and his instrumentation were continually innovative, as in such works as *The Warriors,* for orchestra and three pianos (1916), which called for three conductors and mallet percussion, and *The Marching Song of Democracy,* for chorus, orchestra and organ, or chorus and band (1917), introduced at the Worcester Festival in Massachusetts the year of its composition. The instrumentation for *Tribute to Foster* (1916: Worcester Festival 1930) called for "musical glasses," in addition to solo voices, piano, chorus, and orchestra. *Free Music,* for string quartet (1935), employs not only microtonal music but other innovations with which Grainger had long hoped to "free music." As he explained: "The composer freely uses all intervals, mostly gliding, without being controlled by existing limitations of scale and tonality, and in which all rhythms are free, without beat cohesion between the various polyphonic parts."

In 1928, Grainger married Ella Viola Ström, a Swedish painter and poet, in a spectacular ceremony held at the Hollywood Bowl in California before an audience of 22,000. During the ceremonies, Grainger conducted his orchestral work *To a Nordic Princess,* which he had composed as a gift to his bride. She survived her husband by eighteen years, her death coming in White Plains, N.Y., in 1979 in her ninetieth year.

Grainger founded a Grainger Museum in Melbourne, Australia, in 1935 as a repository for his manuscripts, souvenirs, and other memorabilia. In his will he expressed the wish that after his death his skeleton be on permanent display at this museum, but his wish was never carried out.

THE COMPOSER SPEAKS: The big object of the modern composer is to bring music more and more into line with the irregularities and complexities of nature and away from the straight lines and simplifications imposed by man. . . . We should follow nature and allow ourselves every possible freedom of expression.

PRINCIPAL WORKS: *Jungle Book,* cycle of fourteen songs for small chorus and chamber orchestra (1898–1945); *Love Verses from the Song of Solomon,* for mezzo-soprano, tenor, and chamber orchestra (1900); *Hill Song* no. 1, for chamber orchestra (1902, rescored 1921); *English Dance,* for orchestra (1901–9); *Irish Tune from County Derry,* for strings, or band, or small orchestra (1902); *Youthful Suite,* for orchestra (1902); *Walking Tune,* for woodwind quintet (1905); *Brigg Fair,* for tenor and chorus (1906); *Green Bushes,* passacaglia for chamber orchestra (1906); *Hill Song* no. 2, for twenty-two winds (1907); *Molly on the Shore*, for piano, also for orchestra (1907); *Mock Morris*, for piano, also for orchestra (1910); *Colonial Song*, for piano or band or orchestra (1912); *Handel on the Strand*, for orchestra (1912) *Shepherd's Hey*, for orchestra (1913); *In a Nutshell*, suite for orchestra, piano, and percussion (1916); *Tribute to Foster*, for five solo voices, piano, chorus, orchestra, and musical glasses (1916): *The Warriors*, music for orchestra and three pianos for an imaginary ballet (1916); *The Marching Song of Democracy*, for chorus and band or orchestra (1917); "Children's March: Over the Hills and Far Away," for piano and band (1918); *Country Gardens*, for orchestra (1918); *Spoon River*, for various instrumental combinations (1919–22); *To a Nordic Princess*, for orchestra (1928); *The Nightingale and the Two Sisters*, for from four to eighteen instruments (1930); *Suite on Danish Folksongs*, for orchestra (1930); *Harvest Hymns*, for from three to twenty instruments (1932); *Free Music,* for string quartet (1935); *English Gothic Music,* thirteen pieces for chorus, optional organ, and instruments (1930–50); *Lincolnshire Posy*, for band (1937).

BIBLIOGRAPHY: Balough, Teresa (ed.), *A Complete Catalogue of Works by Percy Grainger* (U. of Australia, 1975): Bird, John, *Percy Grainger* (London, 1976): Parker, D. C., *Percy A. Grainger: A Study* (N.Y., 1918); Slattery, T. C., *Percy Grainger: The Inveterate Inventor* (Evanston, Ill., 1974); Taylor, R. L., *The Running Pianist* (N.Y., 1959); *Musical Quarterly*, April 1937; *New York Times* (obituary), February 21, 1961, July 13, 1980.

Green, Ray, b. Cavendish, Mo., September 13, 1908.

The common denominator of Green's music is its Americanism, as many of the titles of his compositions reveal. Green's lifetime ideal in music has been the creation of American music rooted in American experiences and largely influenced by his early preoccupation with jazz and American hymnology. Additionally, an intensive study in counterpoint led him to bring polyphonic practices into his writing.

Green's ancestry reaches back to the American Revolution. He was the youngest of eight children, the son of a wealthy farmer and breeder of cattle. Both parents were musical. His father trained and rehearsed the local choir and wrote music for it, and his mother, a former schoolteacher, was the possessor of a good voice. The singing of hymns from the Methodist hymn book was a family practice, so early in life, Green learned "to sight-read inner parts, or melody, or anything else," as he recalls, "before I could do the multiplication tables." When he was three and a half, his father sold his properties in Missouri for a ranch in eastern Montana, where his

investment proved so disastrous that he lost his fortune in one year's time, and after an interval was reduced to living the last three years in Montana on the ranch on a sharecropper basis.

Though Green received no formal training in music in his boyhood years in Montana, he was able, in addition to reading music at sight, to notate music by the time he was ten. Musical stimulation came not only from the singing sessions at home but also from listening to ragtime recordings. In 1921, the family moved to San Joaquin in California. There, while completing grade school, Green occupied himself at home with the creation of pieces at the piano. When he was fourteen, his formal instruction began with lessons at the piano from Mrs. John Crooker. At Tranquillity Union High School, in Tranquillity, Calif., Green played leading roles in school productions of operettas. In California, he had his first experience listening to live performances in nearby Fresno, and they were unforgettable.

By the time he was graduated from high school in 1926 Green knew he wanted to become a professional musician. To get enough money to enter a conservatory he moved to San Francisco, where, for one year, he worked as a clerk and general timekeeper in a small business firm. Then he entered the San Francisco Conservatory of Music in 1927, receiving his first instruction in harmony and ear training from Lillian Hodghead, while studying the piano privately with one of the conservatory staff members. He made such progress that in 1928 he earned scholarships to study composition, form, and harmony based on Bach chorales with Ernest Bloch, director of the conservatory. Additional scholarships, and a Carnegie Foundation Award, enabled him to continue at the conservatory until 1933. In his last two years at the conservatory, Green studied the Gregorian chant with Giulio Silva, which intensified his growing fascination for polyphony. In 1930–31, he studied composition privately with Albert Elkus, also on a special scholarship. During these formative school years, jazz remained a significant interest through the stimulus of hearing live, in San Francisco, such big-name bands as those of Duke Ellington, Benny Goodman, and Glen Gray.

Between 1929 and 1935, Green taught the piano privately in his studio in San Francisco, where he first began producing his own teaching methods. From 1933 to 1935 he attended the University of California, at Berkeley, as a special student at the postgraduate level, studying fugue with E. G. Stricklen (the fugue soon to become one of Green's favored creative tools) and composition with Albert Elkus.

In his aim to develop a uniquely American style in his compositions, Green early became disturbed by the tendency of so many of his colleagues to imitate 20th-century modernists. This dissatisfaction led him, in 1929, to write *Suite ironico*, for violin and piano, in which the Stravinsky cult was satirized, and, in 1930, *Rondo patetico*, which similarly mocked imitators of Prokofiev. *Set of Piano Pieces for a Man Puppet: Peeannie Soot Yerself* in 1932 was, as he said, "about the culmination of my indignation at the false elements I felt that there were in the sounds of the music that was prevailing at the time"; its minuet movement was written in a typical Prokofiev style, Green's last satiric thrust. From satire, he soon progressed to the kind of Americanism to which he would henceforth be partial, beginning with *An American Agon*, his first sonata for piano (1933), and continuing with *Festival Fugues*, for solo piano (1934–36), which he subtitled "American Toccata." In April 1934, *New Music*, edited by Henry Cowell, published an entire issue of Green's piano and vocal music. At about this time, too, Green (never forgetting his early experiences with hymnology) became interested in old American hymns published in such collections as *The Sacred Harp, The Southern Harmony*, and *The Missouri Harmony*. He spent considerable time studying their idiomatic methods and incorporated some of them into compositions to provide his writing with a stronger American identity—such as the pentatonic scale, parallel fourths, fifths, and octaves, and the fuguing style.

By winning the George Ladd Prix de Paris in the spring of 1935, Green was able to spend two years in Paris. He hoped to study composition with either Milhaud or Nadia Boulanger but was dissatisfied with each and decided to go his own way without instruction; but he did manage to study conducting with Pierre Monteux. In Paris in 1936 Green completed *Festival Fugues,* for piano (begun in 1934), introduced at a meeting of the Southeastern Chapter of the American Musicological Society at the Library of Congress in Washington, D.C. on June 1, 1948, Margaret Tolson pianist. In 1936 he also completed *Holiday for Four*, for viola, clarinet, bassoon and piano, premiered by the San Francisco Woodwind Quintet, of which Pierre Monteux was artistic director, on March 18, 1940. In both these works he used a jazz idiom. Reviewing the premiere performance of *Festival Fugues*, Glenn Dillard Gunn, in the *Washington Times-Herald*, called the work "exciting, novel, eloquent of many moods. The ancient and honorable fugal pattern still serves: but its content is an effervescent compound of new tonalities, new rhythmical pulses and new sounds. . . . Quite certainly this is great new music. It marks a turning of the art into a new direction." In *Holiday for Four*, according to Alexander Fried in the *San Francisco Examiner*, Green "used melodies of rustic native spirit to make up the vigorous exhilaration of his snappy, loose-jointed rhythm. For interlude, he spun out a fine mood of pastoral reflection." Two concerts in Paris in 1936 presented some of Green's compositions. He added to his musical experiences by becoming acquainted with several foreign musicians and composers and by sending reports on music in Paris and at the Salzburg Festival in Austria to the *San Francisco Chronicle*. All this helped to rid him of that provincialism that had clung to him when he first arrived in Europe.

He was back in San Francisco in June 1937. That fall he assumed a teaching post in the department of music at the University of California in Berkeley. A meeting with May O'Donnell in 1937, then a dancer with the Martha Graham Company, led to the writing of *Of Pioneer Women*. This work was incorporated into her debut solo concert, *So Proudly We Hail*, at the Veterans' Auditorium, San Francisco, on February 15, 1940.

In February 1938 Green moved to New York, there to write *Processional Dance for Symphonic Band* (1938) for Martha Graham on commission for the official opening of the New York World's Fair in 1939. In the summer of 1938 he was commissioned to write *American Document*, scored for two pianos and drums, for Martha Graham and her company.

Ray Green and May O'Donnell were married in Santa Fe, New Mexico, on September 12, 1938. This was an artistic as well as marital partnership since from this point on Green would provide the music for numerous works choreographed by O'Donnell for her company. They set up a dance studio in San Francisco and began putting together a May O'Donnell solo dance concert in San Francisco featuring *So Proudly We Hail* (1940). During the summer of 1940, José Limón invited O'Donnell to appear in his new work, *War Lyrics*; Limón subsequently collaborated with Green on a new work, *On American Themes* (1940), premiered in San Francisco May 1, 1941.

During this period, outside the world of dance, Green wrote *Three Inventories of Casey Jones*, for piano and orchestra (1939), commissioned by the Golden Gate International Exposition; with Green as soloist it was premiered over NBC radio on September 6, 1939.

Between 1939 and 1941 Green worked first as arranger for the WPA and after two assignments as arranger was appointed director of the Federal Chorus of San Francisco, with which he gave numerous performances in schools, colleges and universities, hospitals, and other public institutions. His programming for music in hospitals was his first experience in this setting and led, later, into his prominent role in the establishment of the use of music in therapy. He was a key organizer of the National Association of Music Therapy and served as first president for two years. During World War II, from February 1943 to June 1945, Green served in the U. S. Army and Air Corps. Just prior to his induction into the armed forces he and his wife completed what was to become her most famous dance work, *Suspension . . . "at the still point of the turning world, there the dance is . . . ,"* introduced at their studio in San Francisco in February 1943. In military service he organized and led soldiers' choral groups. One of these, the Fort Logan Singers, at Fort Logan in Denver, was heard on the famous wartime radio program *The Army Hour*. Green was brought back from Texas, where he was serving in an artillery unit, to head up as instructor and direct the Music Reconditioning Program at the Fort Logan Convalescent Hospital of the Air Corps in Denver. In uniform, Green gave a course in music appreciation and music history at the University of Denver.

While still in the service, Green participated in an all-day hymn-singing session in a small country church in Texas. This experience led him to complete perhaps his most famous composition, *Sunday Sing Symphony*, with trio concertante for flute, clarinet, and bassoon (1939–46), which he had begun sketching in 1942. Its premiere took place at the biennial Convention of the National Federation of Music Clubs in Kansas City on April 21, 1961, when the Kansas City Philharmonic under Hans Schweiger performed it to May O'Donnell's dance. This work drew its style and idiom from American hymnology, particularly its modality and the technique of the fuguing tune. Reviewing it in the *San Francisco Chronicle*, Alfred Frankenstein wrote, "The modal character of the old melodies is beautifully preserved and so is their characteristic harmony. . . . It stands in a direct line of descent from the music of Charles Ives." Regional American folk music, rather than hymnology, was the source of several notable Green compositions for band: *Kentucky Mountain Running Set* (1946), *Jig Theme and Six Changes* (1948) and *Folksong Fantasies*, for trumpet and band (1949).

In 1945, on the GI Bill of Rights, Green took courses at Columbia University, leading to a bachelor of arts degree. From 1946 to 1948 he was chief of the music division of the Veterans Administration in Washington, D.C., a newly created post to organize and administer the music recreation program which led to the establishment of music therapy for veterans' hospitals in the United States, Alaska, Puerto Rico, and Hawaii. While in Washington, his evening hours were spent composing and giving courses on music and teaching the piano in the King-Smith School. In 1947 he was appointed instructor in music in the School of Education at New York University and for the next five years he gave courses in community music and the use of music in recreation. From 1948 to 1961 he was executive secretary of the American Music Edition. In 1960 Green installed an electronic studio at his home in New York City, electronic music having become a major interest a few years earlier.

His later dance scores included the *Dance Sonata*, for two pianos (1953); *Dance Energies* (1950, 1956, 1960), for solo flute, solo piano, and Chinese and Javanese gongs and Hindu tabla; and *The Queen's Obsession* (1952–59) based on *Macbeth*, for piano solo with other sounds produced by mallets, strikers, picks, iron bar and sweeps of the hand directly on the strings of the piano.

The acquisition in 1963 of a house in New York was the beginning of some real estate involvement. He wrote nothing from then until 1970. This creative silence ended when he reworked "I Love My Friend" (1935–70) to a poem by Langston Hughes, prepared for inclusion in a new song anthology published by Galaxy Music Corporation in New York.

THE COMPOSER SPEAKS: Thematics are among the motivating factors in the makeup of a style. The criteria of a style are its indigenous thematics. These may be summated as a distillation of those native elements that go into the makeup of a culture and a civilization. By thematics I mean the theme of a Bach fugue, or his B minor Mass, Mozart's G minor Symphony, Beethoven's Fifth, Chopin's soaring melodies, Debussy's works as evocations, Stravinsky's *Rite of Spring*, the fantastic Classical Hindu music of India, the uniqueness of Charles Ives and Carl Ruggles. Today our earth civilization is an amalgam of national and international currents, symbols and thematics. Nowadays, the parameters of sounds and sound resources are as broad as the spectrum of a world civilization. I believe that a dynamic, evocative, meaningful music geared to the human ear and imagination can result from the concatenation of today's world culture on the composer and listeners. I abjure the fantasies of other isms of the space age and choose to follow my own seasoned instincts in what to use or not to use in my music.

PRINCIPAL WORKS: *Quartet*, four preludes for piano solo (1927); "Hey Nonny No!," madrigal (1931); "Break of Day," madrigal (1931); *Five Epigrammatic Portraits*, for string quartet (1933); String Quartet (1933); *An American Agon*, sonata for piano (1933); Wind Quintet (1933); Five-part Canons (1933); "Sea Calm," madrigal for five men's voices (1933); *Sonata Brevis*, for piano (1933); *Festival Fugues*, an "American Toccata," for piano (1934–36); Four Short Songs, for voice and piano (1934); *Holiday for Four*, for clarinet, bassoon, viola, and piano (1936; revised 1939); *Dance Set*, for piano (1936–41); *Adam Lay I-Bowndyn*, for chorus (1937); *Three Inventories of Casey Jones*, for piano and percussion or piano and orchestra (1939); *Hymn Tune Set*, for two pianos (1937, revised 1960); *Of Pioneer Women*, ballet (1937); *American Document*, ballet (1938); *Sunday Sing Symphony* (1939–46); *So Proudly We Hail*, ballet (1940); *Dance Theme and Variations*, for piano (1940); *On American Themes*, ballet (1941); *Suspension* ". . . at the still point of the turning world, there the dance is . . . ,*"* ballet (1942); Short Symphony in A (1945–53); Concertante for Viola and Orchestra (1946); *Kentucky Mountain Running Set*, for band (1946); *Jig Theme and Six Changes*, for band (1948); Short Sonata in F, for piano (1948); *Folksong Fantasies*, for trumpet and band (1949); *Duo concertante*, for violin and piano (1950); Rhapsody, for Harp and Orchestra

(1950); *Corpus Christi*, for chorus (1950); *The Queen's Obsession*, ballet (1952–59); *Dance Sonata*, for two pianos (1953); Twelve Inventions, for piano solo (1955); Short Sonata in D, for piano solo (1957; revised 1973–74); *Dedications for Piano (1956—continuing series); Dance Energies*, ballet (1959); *Hymn Tune Set for Two Pianos* (1960); Short Sonata in C, for piano solo (1962, revised 1972); Short Symphony in C (1974–80); Short Sonata in B-flat (1980); Concerto for Piano and Orchestra no. 3 (1980–81).

BIBLIOGRAPHY: *BBDM; DCM*; Vise, Sidney, "Ray Green: His Life and Stylistic Elements of His Music from 1935 to 1962" (doctoral thesis, University of Missouri, Kansas City, 1975).

Gretchaninoff, Alexander, b. Moscow, Russia, October 25, 1864; d. New York., January 3, 1956. American citizen, 1946.

He carried the traditions of late-19th-century Russian music into the 20th century, but with his own ramifications and refinements. He was most important in his choral and vocal music. His Russian church music, to which he brought revolutionary practices, is among the finest of such music in the 20th century, and his art songs contributed several durable masterpieces to that repertoire.

He was one of eleven children of a father, the owner of a successful grocery store, who was partly illiterate and a mother who was totally so. But both were innately musical. Alexander's earliest musical recollections were hearing his mother sing sentimental ballads and his father, religious songs. When Alexander was twelve, his father presented him with a cylindrical music box, to which the boy would listen for hours. "Unfortunately," as he recalled, "these songs were vulgar tavern ballads and factory songs." When he heard his cousin play the guitar, he begged his father to buy him one but was turned down. By saving his lunch money for two months Alexander accumulated the three rubles needed for the purchase of the instrument, on which he would accompany himself and his parents in singing.

He saw his first piano when he was fourteen when one was brought into his house so that a younger sister might take lessons. "The piano became my constant companion." He received his first lessons from his sister-in-law, a conservatory student. Other musical activities included singing in a chorus, and sometimes taking solo parts at the Fifth High School, and participating in an amateur church choir.

By the time he was ready to leave high school, Gretchaninoff knew he wanted to devote his life to music. Opposing the wishes of his father, who wanted him to become a doctor, he successfully passed the entrance examinations for the Moscow Conservatory in 1881, receiving a partial scholarship. He remained there nine years, studying the pi-

ano with Nikolai Kashkin and Vassily Safanov, counterpoint with Hermann Laroche and composition with Taneiev and Arensky. Gretchaninoff combined music study with enriching experiences outside the conservatory: singing in the chorus at a performance of Liszt's oratorio *St. Elizabeth* performed by the Russian Musical Society; hearing a series of historic piano recitals by Anton Rubinstein; playing the glockenspiel in a performance of Tchaikovsky's *Mozartiana* conducted by that master; and attending the world premieres of Tchaikovsky's operas *Eugen Onegin* and *Pique Dame*. Under such stimuli he was beginning to compose songs, one of which is the popular "Cradle Song," to a poem by Lermontov. Though his teacher, Taneiev, thought little of it, it was published in 1892 by Belaiev in a volume of *Five Melodies* that became Gretchaninoff's first opus; in time the song grew popular throughout the world and has remained one of its composer's most frequently performed songs.

An altercation with one of his teachers, Arensky, over the writing of a fugue, firmed Gretchaninoff's decision to leave the Moscow Conservatory in 1890 and, on a scholarship, to enter the St. Petersburg Conservatory, where he studied with Rimsky-Korsakov. During his two years at this conservatory he continued writing songs, including "On the Steppe" and "Night," which became famous. He also completed a concert overture for large orchestra (1892; St. Petersburg, March 1893) and *Samson*, a cantata for solo voices, chorus, and orchestra (1893), whose first performance was given at a gala concert at the Michael Palace with the composer conducting on May 30, 1893. Meanwhile, on February 21, 1891, Gretchaninoff married his childhood sweetheart, Vera Ivanova Röhrberg, a pianist, in a ceremony in which Rimsky-Korsakov was best man. They had no children, and separated permanently in the spring of 1911, when Gretchaninoff became emotionally involved with Maria Grigorievna Aksakous, who, from 1912 until her death in 1947, remained his permanent mate.

Upon leaving the St. Petersburg Conservatory in 1893, Gretchaninoff spent the next eight years in St. Petersburg composing, supporting himself and his wife by giving piano lessons. His first work in a large form was the String Quartet no. 1 (1894), which won a Belaiev prize, and was premiered at a Belaiev concert in St. Petersburg on December 7, 1894, and published by Belaiev to become Gretchaninoff's second opus. He also completed his Symphony no. 1 (1893), a work markedly influenced by Rimsky-Korsakov and Tchaikovsky, its first performance conducted by Rimsky-Korsakov in St. Petersburg on January 14, 1895. This symphony was received apathetically. But Gretchaninoff's first significant work for unaccompanied chorus, *North and South* (1895), to a poem by Alexei Tolstoy, was such a success when introduced in St. Petersburg on March 19, 1895, that it had to be repeated on the same program.

(Up to then choral music was virtually nonexistent in Russia.) With his first *Liturgy of St. John Chrysostom*, for unaccompanied voices (1897; Moscow, October 19, 1898), which did not satisfy him, and the *Two Sacred Choruses*, for a cappella voices (1896), which did, Gretchaninoff made his first inroad into that area in which he would henceforth prove highly productive—liturgical music. The *Two Sacred Choruses* set the foundation for the style he would henceforth employ in his religious music. He explained: "I made use for the first time of old Russian church chants. In my treatment of these chants I tried to observe the modal character of the melodies, avoiding chromatic leads and large melodic skips, and keeping clear of sentimental Italianisms." This practice, then novel for Russian liturgical music, would become standard procedure with Gretchaninoff.

In 1901, Gretchaninoff left St. Petersburg to return to Moscow, there to complete the writing of his first opera, *Dobrinya Nikitisch*, produced by the Bolshoi Theater on October 27, 1903, with Feodor Chaliapin in the leading male role. "It was a triumphant success," wrote Gretchaninoff in his autobiography, "such as rarely happens in a composer's life." Soon after its premiere this opera was repeated in St. Petersburg at the People's Opera House and then was given in Moscow and Kiev. It has since been intermittently revived.

In 1902, Gretchaninoff completed the *Second Liturgy of St. John Chrysostom*, for a cappella chorus. When first performed on March 2, 1902, in Moscow it was acclaimed as a major contribution to Russian church music in spite of its stylistic divergence from the liturgical norm. Nikolai Kashkin wrote of it as "a work of genius in its inventiveness, its simplicity and its superb poetic spirit." From this point on, Gretchaninoff would continue to cover all the services of the Greek Orthodox Church to become, as the historian Leonid Sabaneyev described him, "a perfect master of choral orchestration, if one may use this expression, knowing ideally and to perfection the properties of the human voice . . . extracting from the choral masses utterly unexpected and frequently overpowering effects." In writing liturgical music for voices with orchestral accompaniment, instead of solely for a cappella voices, Gretchaninoff once again proved himself the innovator, since instrumental music was not admitted in the church of the Russian Orthodox faith. His first religious composition with orchestral accompaniment was *Laudate Deum*, three psalms for tenor, chorus, orchestra, and organ (1914); Serge Koussevitzky conducted its premiere in Moscow on November 24, 1915.

By 1907, with *Autumnal Sketches*, for voice and piano, Gretchaninoff was also moving in a new direction in his songwriting, away from his dependence on Russian folk song and Tchaikovsky and heading toward Debussy, Ravel, and impressionism. He continued in this vein with *Les fleurs du mal* to Baudelaire's poems (1909) and *Poème dramatique*, to texts by Heine and Vladimir Soloviev (1910). But these, and others of his subsequent impressionist songs, are generally conceded to hold second place to his Russian-styled songs, which are some of the finest in the literature.

Gretchaninoff's high station in Russian music was confirmed in 1910 when the czar gave him a life pension. With the outbreak of the February 1917 revolution in Russia, Gretchaninoff was in full sympathy with it to the point of writing *A Hymn to Free Russia* for the provisional government of Prince Lvov. But he was bitterly opposed to the Bolshevik takeover in October 1917. During the next few years he gave lecture-recitals for children, played in sanitariums and conducted children's choruses. He also managed to arrange professional tours in various Russian cities in the performance of his songs and chamber music. In 1922 he gave concerts in London, Prague, and Berlin. On May 29, 1924, he conducted the world premiere of his Symphony no. 3 in E major (1920–23).

In 1925, Gretchaninoff—leaving behind all his possessions, music library, and archives—escaped from Russia with Maria Grigorievna and settled in Paris. There for the next few years he was active as composer, conductor, and teacher of singing. He also toured the music world outside the Soviet Union, making his American debut in New York on January 17, 1929, in a concert of his songs performed by Nina Koshetz with himself at the piano. Two months later, on March 25, he conducted in New York a performance of his *Domestic Liturgy*, or the *Third Liturgy of St. John Chrysostom* (1917; Moscow, March 30, 1918). He made four more tours of the United States after that. The fifth, in 1939, had been planned as a three-month stay, but the outbreak of World War II made it permanent. He made his home in an apartment in New York.

Among his later works the most significant were his last two symphonies and the *Missa Oecumenica*. The Symphony no. 4 in C major (1923–24), dedicated to the memory of Tchaikovsky, and the Symphony no. 5 (1936) were stylistically more strongly dependent on the German postromantic movement than upon the Russian national school. The Fourth Symphony was given its first hearing on April 9, 1942, by the New York Philharmonic under John Barbirolli; the Fifth was introduced on April 5, 1939 with Leopold Stokowski conducting the Philadelphia Orchestra. The *Missa Oecumenica* (1936)—a giant work for vocal soloists, chorus, orchestra, and organ—was not planned as a religious service for the Russian Orthodox Church or for any other single church, but as a service embodying the universal service of all churches. Gretchaninoff explained he wanted his Mass to combine the musical character of the Eastern and Western churches. Its Latin text, however, was one used in Catholic churches. Though this work calls for solo singers, there are no set numbers for any of them; their music sometimes alternates with the chorus and sometimes is integrated with it. Serge Koussevitzky directed the world premiere in Boston on February 25, 1944. In his autobiography, Gretchaninoff claimed that this Mass was his most important achievement in sacred music.

Though in old age his productivity slackened, he continued composing. After his eightieth year he completed, among other works, several short compositions for orchestra including the *Poème élégiaque* (1944; Boston, March 29, 1946), and *Festival Overture* (1946; Indianapolis, November 15, 1946); the Piano Sonata no. 2 (1944), and the *Petits tableaux musicaux*, twelve miniatures for piano (1947). A three-act opera, *The Marriage* (1946), based on Gogol's play, was produced in Paris on October 8, 1950. A concert of his works was performed in New York on October 26, 1954, to honor his ninetieth birthday, at which he was present.

THE COMPOSER SPEAKS: What was the influence of modernism on my own creative work? Have I joined the modernists, or have I kept myself outside the sphere of their influence? The multiplicity of musical genres demands different modes of expression. The advanced idioms of the string quartet, and of the ballet, do not fit the mood of sacred music. . . .

One wonders how long musicians will go on discussing modernism, or lack of modernism, in contemporary music. This debate opened a century ago, and reached the heights of acrimony early in this century; it has now all but subsided. Yet is has served its purpose; the horizons of harmony have been broadened; the excessive infatuation with dissonance has abated. Somehow, one can breathe a little more freely, listening to the latest brand of modern music.

The early modernists paid too much attention to the concrete materials of music, forgetting that music is the expression of human emotion. Blessed is the composer who can faithfully communicate his inner emotion to the performer and to the listener! Then, leaving this beautiful world, he can say to himself: "I have fulfilled my life's task."

PRINCIPAL WORKS: 48 melodies, for voice and piano, including "Cradle Song," "Night," "On the Steppe," and "My Land" (1887–1945); 41 sacred choruses, for a cappella choruses (1898–1940); 11 *morceaux*, for piano (1905–1947); 5 symphonies (1893–1936); 5 miniatures, for piano (1950); 4 string quartets (1894–1919); 4 mazurkas, for piano (1911); 3 *Liturgies of St. John Chrysostom* (1897, 1902, 1917); 2 violin sonatas (1919, 1933); 2 piano sonatas (1931, 1944); 2 piano trios (1906, 1931); 2 clarinet sonatas (1940, 1943); 2 albums, *Pastels*, for piano (1893, 1912); 2 sonatinas for piano (1927).

Dobrinya Nikitisch, opera (1895–1901); *At the Crossroads*, a musical scene for bass and orchestra (1901); *Ne m'oubliez pas*, concert aria for voice and orchestra (1903); *La lettre*, concert aria for voice and orchestra (1907); *Sister Beatrice*, opera (1908–10); *Snowflakes*, ten children's songs (1908); *Les fleurs du mal*, for voice and piano (1909); *Feuilles mortes*, three sketches for contralto and string quartet (1910); *Poème dramatique*, for voice and piano (1910); *Passions*, for chorus (1911); *Laudate Deum*, three psalms for tenor, chorus, orchestra, and organ (1914); *Two Tableaux musicaux*, for soprano and orchestra (1914); *Moments lyriques*, three miniatures for piano (1917); Suite, for cello and orchestra, also for cello and piano (1919–29); *Les fleurs d'automne*, for voice and piano (1926); Cello Sonata (1927); *Pensées fugitives*, fifteen sketches for piano (1927); Violin Concerto in C minor (1932); *Aquarelles*, for piano (1935); Three *Chants élégiaques* (1936), *Missa Oecumenica*, for solo voices, chorus, orchestra and organ (1936); *Missa Festiva*, for chorus and organ (1937); *Concerto da camera*, for flute and chamber orchestra (1938); *Sonetti romani*, for voice and piano (1939); Viola Sonata (1940); *Rhapsody on a Russian Theme*, for violin and orchestra, or violin and piano (1940); *Six Russian Folk Songs*, suite for orchestra (1940); *Triptyque*, suite for string orchestra (1940); Mass, for women's voices or children's chorus and organ (1942); *Sancti Spiritus*, mass for chorus and organ (1943); *Poème élégiaque*, for orchestra (1944); *The Marriage*, opera (1945–46); *The Lord Reigneth*, cantata for chorus and organ (1946); *Festival Overture*, for orchestra (1946); Septet, for clarinet, bassoon and string quintet (1948).

BIBLIOGRAPHY: Gretchaninoff, Alexander, *My Life* (N.Y., 1952); Sabaneyev, Leonid, *Modern Russian Composers* (N.Y., 1927); *Musical Quarterly*, July 1942; *New York Times*, October 16, 1949, January 5, 1956 (obituary).

Griffes, Charles Tomlinson, b. Elmira, N.Y., September 17, 1884; d. New York City April 8, 1920.

Griffes was only thirty-six when he died. Most of his works were written within a six-year period, his three masterworks coming in his last five years. Considering his consistent artistic growth, there is little doubt that his premature death robbed America of a major composer. Even as it is, he remains an important one. He tapped two veins successfully, the exoticism of the Orient on the one hand and impressionism on the other. To these he added the influence of the harmonic language of Scriabin and Mussorgsky and his own ultrasensitivity to tonal colors and an uncommon gift at descriptive writing.

He was the third of five children in a family tracing its antecedents back to the American Revolution. Both his father (a manufacturer) and his mother had received instruction at the piano. They saw to it that their children had musical training. Griffes's sister gave Charles some piano lessons when he was eight but, since he despised practicing, these were soon dropped. He was much more interested in water colors, pen-and-ink drawings and copper plate etchings—particularly in water colors, a fact not without significance in view of his later preoccupation with color as related to music and his tendency to associate certain colors with keys in music. He also early interested himself in poetry, books, and photography.

The first significant impact of music on him came when he was eleven, recovering from an attack of typhoid fever. From his bed he heard his sister playing some Beethoven downstairs, music that affected him so strongly that he insisted on learning it. Piano study was now resumed in earnest with his sister as his teacher for the next three years, supplemented by lessons on the organ. When he was fifteen, he was turned over for more professional instruction to Mary Selena Broughton, who played an influential, possibly decisive, role in his early musical growth. She gave him a thorough grounding in piano technique and literature. It was not long before Griffes began making public appearances: as accompanist for a YMCA chorus; organist at the Lutheran church; and piano virtuoso in concerts arranged by his teacher at random engagements. During the summer of 1902 he was a member of a trio providing dinnner music at a resort hotel.

His boyhood was a lonely one. Since he was introspective and made aware that he was a social misfit through his homosexuality, he kept much to himself while attending the public schools in Elmira. He found his diversions in such solitary pursuits as reading, taking long walks to enjoy nature, in art, and in music.

In 1903, when he was graduated from Elmira Free Academy, his teacher, Mary Broughton, became convinced of his talent and insisted he go to Germany for additional training, providing all the necessary funds. After appearing at a farewell concert in Elmira on May 21, 1903, in which three of his earliest songs composed in 1901 were performed, Griffes left for Berlin for a four-year stay. At first he attended the Stern Conservatory, studying piano with Ernst Jedliczka, composition with Philippe Rüfer, and theory with Max Julius Lowengard. Later study in Berlin took place with Gottfried Galston (piano), Wilhelm Klatte (theory), and Engelbert Humperdinck (composition). His musical life was further enriched through attendance at numerous concerts and theater productions. To help support himself he took on several students and occasionally performed the piano publicly, including a recital on July 29, 1906. He also did some composing, including an orchestral overture, a symphonic fantasy, and some songs.

He returned to the United States in 1907. From that year to the time of his death he was employed as music teacher at the Hackley School in Tarryton, N.Y., at a salary of thirty-six dollars a week with room and board. There was not a time in those thirteen years when he did not find the work detestable

and the boys boring. To supplement his meager income he later gave piano lessons in his studio in New York City and wrote study pieces for the piano, published under the pseudonym of Arthur Tomlinson.

Studying (particularly the music of the Russian nationalist school) and composing provided a refuge. In 1909 the publishing house of G. Schirmer signed him to a contract for the publication of five German songs to texts by Lenau, Heine, Mosen, and Geibel. The songs were uniformly in a Teutonic style, influenced by and imitative of the lieder of Brahms and Richard Strauss. Over a two-year period, these songs earned him a royalty of $33.10; a few of them were sung at informal concerts in Elmira. This Teutonic period was followed, in 1921, by songs with English texts, mainly taken from Oscar Wilde's poetry, in which Griffes was beginning to free himself from Germanic influences. At the same time, between 1911 and 1912, he was writing pieces for the piano, some of which were performed publicly by Leslie Hodgson.

Griffes now put German romanticism behind him completely to embrace a style that was much better attuned to his sensitive nature: impressionism. He had originally rejected it but was finally won over after hearing a performance of Ravel's *Jeux d'eau*. In this vein he completed writing one of three of his most famous compositions: "The White Peacock" (1917). This became the first movement of a suite for piano collectively entitled *Four Roman Sketches* (1915—17), which was introduced in New York on February 26, 1918, by the composer on the same program in which he also offered the premiere of his Piano Sonata (1917). The peacock had always fascinated Griffes; he used to clip out and save pictures of them. Reading the poem "The White Peacock" by William Sharp (who used the pseudonym of Fiona Macleod) moved him so deeply that set himself the task of interpreting in music a peacock that moved in silence "as the breath, as the soul of beauty." His tone poem is a sustained mood picture dominated by a haunting melody over undulating figures. In 1919 Griffes orchestrated it for a choreographic production at the Rivoli Theater in New York staged by Adolph Bolm, the first performance taking place on June 22. On December 19, 1919, the orchestral version was performed by the Philadelphia Orchestra under Leopold Stokowski.

Griffes's fascination for the exotic led to the writing of *Two Sketches* for string quartet (1916–18), based on Indian themes. But the Orient and its music was an even more potent influence on him. In 1916 he wrote the music for *The Kairn of Koridwen*, a dance drama with text by Edouard Schure, scored for five woodwinds, celesta, harp, and piano produced in New York on February 10, 1917, Nikolai Sokoloff conducting. In 1917 came *Five Poems of Ancient China and Japan* to oriental texts in which he used the oriental pentatonic and six-note scales as well as rhythmic devices of oriental music. Eva Gauthier introduced this cycle in New York on November 1, 1917, with the composer at the piano. Then, on a commission from Adolph Bolm, who had formed his own dance company, Griffes prepared the score for *Sho-Jo* (1917), a Japanese dance pantomime starring Michio Ito, first produced in Atlantic City, N.J., on August 5, 1917. Provided by Eva Gauthier with melodies she had copied in Japan, (supplemented by his own researches into Japanese music), Griffes here produced his most unusual score in which three Japanese folk themes are developed in an identifiable Far Eastern harmonic, rhythmic, and instrumental language. As Griffes himself explained: "My harmonization is all in octaves, fifths, fourths, and seconds—consonant major thirds and sixths are omitted. The orchestration is as Japanese as possible: thin and delicate, and the muted strings *points d'orgue* serve as a neutral tinted background, like the empty spaces in a Japanese print. The whole thematic material is given to the flute, clarinet, and oboe—akin to the Japanese reed instruments; the harp suggests the koto."

Impressionism is the prevailing style in the second of the three Griffes works to survive in the orchestral repertoire: the *Poem*, for flute and orchestra (1918), written for the flutist Georges Barrère, who introduced it with the New York Symphony under Walter Damrosch on November 16, 1919. And impressionism is combined with orientalism in Griffes's third surviving orchestral work, *The Pleasure Dome of Kubla Khan* (1917), based on Coleridge's poem but concentrating on those lines describing the stately pleasure dome with caves of ice. "I have given my imagination free reign in the description of this strange place," Griffes explained, "as well as of purely imaginary revelry which might take place there. The vague, foggy beginning suggests the sacred river, running 'through caverns measureless to man down to a sunless sea.' Then gradually rise the outlines of the palace with 'walls and towers . . . girdled round.' The gardens with fountains and 'sunny spots of greenery' are next suggested. From inside come sounds of dancing and revelry which increase to a wild climax, and then suddenly break off. There is a return to the original mood suggesting the sacred river and 'caves of ice.' "

The world premiere of *The Pleasure Dome of Kubla Khan* by the Boston Symphony under Pierre Monteux on November 28, 1919, brought Griffes his greatest success. The audience gave him an ovation. The critic of the *Boston Globe* maintained that with this composition Griffes had joined the hallowed company of Ravel, Rachmaninoff, and Stravinsky among leading 20th-century composers. Characteristic of this critical acclaim was the review of Philip Hale, dean of Boston music critics, in the *Boston Herald*: "No one hearing this music of Mr. Griffes will feel that the poem has been belittled; that its splendor has been tarnished; for this composer is blessed with what is rare among American musi-

cians, imagination. His gift of expression is pronounced. . . . He has succeeded in being musically, aesthetically and successfully unusual. . . . He has found an Oriental expression that is his own, as he has found new harmonic and orchestral colors. . . . The music, from the strange unearthly opening, which at once arrests attention, to the exquisitely fanciful ending, is fascinating throughout."

The physical strain of copying the orchestral parts for this premiere (he was too poor to pay for a copyist), superimposed on his teaching duties, took its toll. A month after the premiere, Griffes collapsed, a victim of pleurisy. After that he suffered emphysema and abscesses of the lungs resulting from influenza. He died three days after being operated upon.

A Griffes Memorial Concert was given in New York on April 11, 1952, when *The Kairn of Koridwen* was revived for the first time since 1917. In posthumous remembrance of his eightieth birthday, a three-day festival of his works was presented at Elmira College in Elmira, N.Y., from November 20 to 22, 1964.

PRINCIPAL WORKS: *Tone Images*, for mezzo-soprano and piano (1912); *Three Tone Pictures*, for piano (1912); Fantasy Pieces, for piano (1912); *Four Roman Sketches*, for piano (1915–17); *Two Sketches*, for string quartet (1916–18); *The Kairn of Koridwen*, dance drama for five woodwinds, celesta, harp, and piano (1916); Piano Sonata (1917); *Five Poems of Ancient China and Japan* (1917); *The Pleasure Dome of Kubla Khan*, tone poem for orchestra (1917); *Sho-Jo*, dance pantomime for four woodwinds, four strings, harp, and percussion (1917); *Three Poems by Fiona Macleod*, for voice and piano (1918); *Poem*, for flute and orchestra (1918); Nocturne, for orchestra (1919); Three Preludes, for piano (1919).

BIBLIOGRAPHY: Chase, Gilbert, *America's Music* (N.Y., 1955); Maisel, Edward M., *Charles T. Griffes* (N.Y., 1942); *Musical America*, May 12, 1920; *Musical Quarterly*, July 1943; *New York Times*, April 8, 10, 25, 1920.

Grofé, Ferde (originally **Grofé, Ferdinand Rudolph Von**), b. New York City, March 27, 1892; d. Santa Monica, Calif., April 3, 1972.

Grofé was the highly esteemed popular-music arranger for the Paul Whiteman Orchestra when he made his transition to serious music. He used the rhythms, harmonies, and thematic idioms of jazz in symphonic orchestral suites, many of which were graphic portrayals of American geography.

Both parents, who were of French Huguenot and German extraction, were musical. His father was an actor and singer in operettas and his mother a trained cellist. Other members of the family were similarly musical. Grofé's grandfather, Bernard Bierlich, was first cellist of the Los Angeles Philharmonic for a quarter of a century, and one of his uncles, Julius Bierlich, was that orchestra's concertmaster.

When Grofé was an infant, his family moved to Los Angeles, where, when he was five, his mother began teaching him to read music. He received at that time some lessons on the violin and piano. In 1900, one year after his father's death, Grofé was brought by his mother to Germany so that she could spend the next three years as a student at the Leipzig Conservatory. When they returned to Los Angeles in 1906, she set up a studio to teach the cello (one of her students was Alfred Wallenstein, later to become the distinguished cellist and conductor). She also remarried.

Grofé was thirteen when he began writing popular songs. Since his stepfather discouraged his musical interests, hoping the boy would train himself as a lawyer or engineer, young Grofé ran away from home in 1907. For the next few years, while continuing to study the violin, piano, and drums by himself, he supported himself by taking any job he could find. He worked as a bookbinder, truckdriver, usher, newsboy, elevator operator, steel worker, and milk salesman. By 1908 he was accepting random musical engagements by performing on the piano or violin at dances and playing brass instruments and drums at picnics and parades. At one time he teamed with Albert Jerome, a dancing teacher, to tour the California mining camps. They operated a pressing and cleaning establishment by day. At night, Grofé played the piano for Jerome's ballet pupils, and on Saturday nights, at a grand ball arranged for the entire town, Grofé performed on whatever instrument was needed.

In 1909, on his first commission, Grofé wrote "The Elks Grand Reunion March" for an Elks' convention in Los Angeles; this was Grofé's first published composition. The year of 1909 also saw a reconciliation between himself and his family, making it possible for him to settle in Los Angeles in further pursuit of his musical career. He then joined the viola section of the Los Angeles Philharmonic, holding this post for the next ten years. He also taught in his mother's studio. At the same time, he briefly attended St. Vincent's College, studied the piano privately with Homer Grunn, and harmony and counterpoint with C. E. Pemberton at the University of Southern California in Los Angeles. (Years later he also studied the piano with Herman Wasserman in New York.) When he was not required to perform in the symphony hall, he played at the Horseshoe Pier in Ocean Park, California's first nickel-a-dance hall and, for two years, was pianist and violist in the orchestra of the Majestic Theater.

He was in San Francisco in 1914, performing on the Old Barbary Coast in dance halls and hotels. He played the banjo in what is believed to have been the first ragtime band to play in San Francisco. Grofé then formed a jazz band of his own which was heard regularly at the Portola Louvre. Jazz musicians in San Francisco habitually visited the Portola Louvre to hear Grofé's orchestrations and jazz improvisations.

In 1920, Grofé joined the Paul Whiteman Orchestra as pianist and arranger. For the next twelve years he made the arrangements for every number featured by this world-famous popular orchestra, the very first of which, "Whispering," sold more than a million and a half records. Grofé combined the technical knowledge of numerous instruments he had acquired by performing them with an innovative technique in achieving unusual sounds and timbres. He soon proved himself to be one of the ace arrangers in the business, something that was forcefully confirmed when his arrangement for the Paul Whiteman Orchestra of George Gershwin's *Rhapsody in Blue* made music history at Aeolian Hall, N.Y., on February 12, 1924.

The success of *Rhapsody in Blue* encouraged Grofé to outgrow the three-minute popular songs he had thus far been favoring and attempt writing concert works, still popular in style, but in ambitious structures. In 1924 he withdrew as the pianist of the Paul Whiteman Orchestra, while remaining its arranger for another seven years, to devote more time to composition. His first extended work was *Broadway at Night*, for orchestra (1924), which went unnoticed. But *Mississippi Suite* (1925), which the Paul Whiteman Orchestra introduced in Carnegie Hall, N.Y., on December 29, 1925, gave him status in concert music for the first time. Its skillful orchestration, jaunty popular idioms, and facile lyricism made it an immediate favorite. Two of its movements ("Mardi Gras" and "Huckleberry Finn") became popular independently of the suite. *Mississippi Suite* was filmed as a documentary in 1933.

On May 11, 1929, Grofé married his first wife, Ruth Harriet MacGloan, with whom he had two children. Through the late 1920s and into the 1930s, Grofé made numerous appearances as guest conductor at nightclubs and on radio programs. In 1929 he prepared the score for the motion picture *King of Jazz*, starring Paul Whiteman and his orchestra.

In 1931 Grofé permanently severed affiliation with the Paul Whiteman Orchestra as arranger. That year he completed his most famous composition, *Grand Canyon Suite*, which Whiteman introduced in Chicago on November 22, 1931. Now more discreet than heretofore in his use of jazz idioms, though the style remained in a popular vein, Grofé here became more subtle in his rhythmic and melodic language, and more vivid in his pictorial writing. A travelog in tones, *Grand Canyon Suite* provided five tonal pictures of the canyon in all its varied beauty and majesty. The most famous of the five movements is the third, "On the Trail," in which a hesitant rhythm suggests the halting gait of a burro down the rim of the canyon, a rhythm against which a cowboy tune is introduced contrapuntally. Since its premiere, *Grand Canyon Suite* has been widely performed and recorded by major symphony orchestras; in 1946, the NBC Symphony under Arturo Toscanini recorded it for RCA Victor, his first appearance on disks in a work by an American composer.

In many of his subsequent works, Grofé continued to assume the role of musical interpreter of American scenes and settings: *Hollywood Suite* (1935); *Kentucky Derby Suite* (1938); *Metropolis* (1941); *Death Valley Suite* (1950); *Hudson River Suite* (1955), which was introduced by the New York Philharmonic under André Kostelanetz on February 6, 1955; *Yellowstone Suite* (1960), premiered by the Utah Symphony under Maurice Abravanel at Yellowstone National Park on June 18, 1960; *San Francisco Suite* (1960; San Francisco, April 23, 1960); *Niagara Falls Suite* (1960; Buffalo, N.Y., February 1961), commissioned by the New York State Power Authority to celebrate the opening of the Niagara Power Porject at Niagara Falls, N.Y.; and *Virginia City: Requiem for a Ghost Town* (1968; Virginia City, Nev., August 10, 1968). Of American interest, even though not about an American locale, is *Lincoln's Gettysburg Address* (1953), which was first heard on February 6, 1955, over the CBS radio network.

In some of his compositions Grofé achieved unique sonorous and timbre effects and arrived at programmatic realism through the use of nonmusical implements as part of his orchestration. His first such effort was *Tabloid*, a portrait of a great city newspaper in four movements (1933; N.Y., January 25, 1933). Here the musical sounds are supplemented by those from a battery of typewriters, a police siren and whistle, machine guns, and a pneumatic drill. A locomotive bell, sirens, pneumatic drills, and two brooms are used in *Symphony in Steel* (1935; NBC radio, February 1, 1936), which had been commissioned by the American Rolling Mill Corporation. *Hollywood Suite* reproduced the sounds of the banging of carpenters, scraping of electricians, shouts of movie directors, and a rhythmic beat pounded by shoes to suggest a tap dance routine. *San Francisco Suite* introduced a solo for cable-car bells as well as foghorns, old fire bells, and the simulated explosions attending the great earthquake.

Through the years, Grofé continued to make numerous appearances as conductor in the concert hall and over the radio, both in guest appearances and at the head of his own orchestra and on his own radio programs. In January 1937 he made his Carnegie Hall conducting debut in an all-Grofé program. From 1939 to 1942 Grofé taught orchestration at the Juilliard School of Music in New York. During World War II he toured service camps, veterans'

hospitals, and USOs, besides conducting the army, navy and Marine Corps bands in Washington, D.C. As a salute to Detroit's war effort, he wrote *Aviation Suite* (1944).

On January 12, 1952, Grofé married his second wife, the former Anna May Lempton, a pianist, with whom he formed a two-piano team which made its debut in Las Vegas in 1954. In 1964, Grofé was commissioned by the New York World's Fair to write the *New York World's Fair Suite*, introduced on April 22, 1964.

Grofé wrote music for two ballets. In *Hollywood Ballet* (1935), produced at the Hollywood Bowl in 1935, he portrayed the great of the cinematic world tonally by using the trombone to represent Greta Garbo, a muted trumpet for Katharine Hepburn, a tuba for Gary Cooper, and a harp, flute, and clarinet for Grace Moore. His second ballet, *Café Society* (1938), was introduced in Philadelphia by Catherine Littlefield and the Philadelphia Ballet. Among his later scores for motion pictures were *Thousands Cheer* (1943) and *The Return of Jesse James* (1950). His music for the documentary *Minstrel Man* was awarded an Oscar by the Academy of Motion Picture Arts and Sciences. In 1946, Grofé received an honorary doctorate from Illinois Wesleyan University in Bloomington.

PRINCIPAL WORKS: *(all for orchestra unless otherwise designated)*: *Mississippi Suite* (1925); *Three Shades of Blue* (1928); *Free Air* (1929); *Grand Canyon Suite* (1931); *Tabloid* (1933); *Hollywood Ballet*, a ballet (1935); *Symphony in Steel* (1935); *Hollywood Suite* (1935); *Killarney Irish Fantasy* (1937); *Café Society*, ballet (1938); *Kentucky Derby Suite* (1938); *Metropolis* (1941); *Table d'hôte*, for flute, violin and viola (1942); *Aviation Suite* (1944); *Deep Nocturne* (1947); *Death Valley Suite* (1950); *Lincoln's Gettysburg Address* (1953); *Hudson River Suite* (1955); *San Francisco Suite* (1960); *Yellowstone Suite* (1960); *Niagara Falls Suite* (1960); *Virginia City: Requiem for a Ghost Town* (1968).

BIBLIOGRAPHY: Ewen, David, *Popular American Composers* (N.Y., 1962); *New Yorker*, May 25, 1940; *New York Times*, April 4, 1972 (obituary); *Time*, May 9, 1960; *Who's Who in America, 1970–71*.

Gruenberg, Louis, b. Brest-Litovsk, Poland, August 3, 1884; d. Los Angeles, Calif., June 9, 1964. American citizen.

He was one of the earliest serious American composers using jazz in concert works, and with some of this music he realized his first successes. The music of the American Negro also significantly influenced some of his later major works.

He was of Russian parentage, son of a professional violinist who came to the United States in 1884, sent for his wife and son to join him in 1885, and later became an American citizen. Gruenberg cannot remember a time when music was not an important element in his life. His father began giving him violin lessons. Gruenberg then attended the National Conservatory of Music in New York. Between 1892 and 1903 he studied the piano privately with Adele Margolies. By the time he was ten, he was giving concerts throughout the United States besides appearing on the Keith vaudeville circuit.

His determination to become a concert pianist sent him to Berlin, Germany, in 1903, where he studied the piano with Friederick E. Koch and, for six years, piano and composition with Ferruccio Busoni. Intermittently, during these years, he took courses at the Vienna Conservatory before becoming there a private tutor in piano (1912–18). In 1912, Gruenberg made his debut as pianist with the Berlin Philharmonic, which led to a two-year concert tour of Europe. In 1912 he wrote a children's opera, *The Witch of Brocken*, and his first violin sonata. At that time one of his compositions received a prize in a contest sponsored by the German periodical *Signale* in which almost seven hundred other composers competed.

He was in London trying to arrange for the production of his children's opera when World War I broke out. He found himself with no passport, no money, a German name, and no way of proving he was an American citizen. When a friend was able to identify him, he was finally provided by the American consul with steerage passage.

Now settled permanently in the United States, Gruenberg abandoned any further intention of promoting his career as a concert pianist in order to devote himself to composition. In a style influenced by French impressionism, he wrote the orchestral tone poem *Hill of Dreams* (1919), which was awarded the Flagler Prize and was introduced on October 23, 1921, by the New York Symphony Society under Walter Damrosch. Gruenberg completed an opera, *The Dumb Wife*, in 1921, its libretto based on Anatole France's play, only to discover he could not get it produced because he had failed to clear the rights with France's executors.

Early in the 1920s, Gruenberg became interested in jazz as a serious artistic medium. "I asked myself," he said, "what would be real American music—the Indians in the West, the Puritans in the East, the Negroes in the South, the Jews in New York? . . . I landed at Jazz. Although jazz perhaps originated with the cakewalk, I don't think that in its present form it is the music only of the Negro. Something else has emerged from it which is very American in its significance, its sentiments, its inborn nervous tension. It is the musical expression of black, red, and white people—the American race." Gruenberg's first success as a composer came with one of his jazz-oriented compositions: *Daniel Jazz*, for vocal soloists and eight instruments (1923), using poems by Vachel Lindsay as text. It was first heard in New York on February 22, 1925, at a concert of the League of Composers, then a young organization promoting new music of which Gruenberg was a cofounder and on which he served as board member. On September 8, 1925, *Daniel Jazz* was heard in Venice at the festival of the International Society for Contemporary Music. Combining the rhythmic vitality and the blues harmonies of jazz with compositional skill and harmonic inventiveness, Gruenberg here produced a musical composition which, as the Viennese musicologist and composer Egon Wellesz noted in *Anbruch*, "in its inner tempo and vital originality and strength is the perfect expression of an art that can only come from the New World. . . . *Daniel Jazz* is a landmark in the history of American music." Reporting to *Modern Music* from Venice, the distinguished Italian composer Alfredo Casella described this music as "very lively and dynamic, full of delicious humor, and, what is most important, thoroughly American in its general spirit." He added: "It was the first time that Broadway made an authentic appearance at a festival of the society."

Gruenberg continued employing jazz during the next few years in works such as the *Jazz Suite*, for orchestra (1925), which the Cincinnati Symphony under Fritz Reiner premiered on March 22, 1929; *Creation*, a "Negro sermon," for vocal soloist and eight instruments (1925; N.Y., November 27, 1926), text taken from a Negro spiritual; and *Jazzettes*, for violin and piano (1926).

Creation and *Twenty Negro Spirituals*, for voice and piano (1926), revealed Gruenberg's interest in spirituals and the music of the Negro; Negro folk music would be prominent in some later works. But other early works drew their material from neither jazz nor the Negro but from either romanticism or impressionism. *The Enchanted Isle*, a tone poem for orchestra (1927), was first performed on October 3, 1929, at the Worcester Festival in Massachusetts under Albert Stoessel; it received second prize in a contest sponsored by Columbia Phonograph Company and the Juilliard Foundation Award. Gruenberg's Piano Quintet no. 1 (1929) won the first prize of $1,000 in a contest sponsored by the Lake Placid Club in New York. In 1930 Gruenberg revised his Symphony no. 1 (1919) and entered it in an RCA Victor competition to win a prize of $5,000; it was introduced on February 10, 1934, by the Boston Symphony under Serge Koussevitzky. A children's opera, *Jack and the Beanstalk* (1930), libretto by John Erskine, was performed in New York on November 19, 1931, and was the recipient of the Juilliard Award and the David Bispham Memorial Medal. This little opera was transferred to a Broadway theater in December 1931, was revived in Chicago in 1936, and went on tour in 1959. *Four Diversions*, for string quartet (1930), was given the Elizabeth Sprague Coolidge Medal.

The limelight of national attention was focused on Gruenberg with the world premiere of his opera *The Emperor Jones* (1932), libretto by Kathleen de Jaffa based on Eugene O'Neill's drama. It took place at the Metropolitan Opera House on January 7, 1933. Though the principal character was an American black man, Gruenberg only once reached back to the style of the spiritual, one of his own invention, when at a climactic point in the opera Emperor Jones sings "Standin' in the Need of Prayer." Otherwise, Gruenberg's tonal translation of the tensions, mounting terrors, and the final tragedy was harmonically discordant, rhythmically complex, with a melodic line that sometimes approximated the *Sprechstimme* of the atonal school. "The composer," wrote Marion Bauer, "has lost all sense of personality in the primitive force of his music. Short-breathed phrases follow each other in rapid succession. The deeper-toned instruments are used to create a somber, sinister web over which the highest registers of the woodwinds and violins flare up shriekingly." *The Emperor Jones* remained in the Metropolitan Opera repertoire two seasons, was produced in San Francisco in 1933, in Philadelphia in a concert presentation in 1940, and in Rome in 1951 (in the last of these productions Emperor Jones was transformed from an American into an Italian Emperor). A modern-day revival was given by the Michigan Opera Company on February 9, 1979. This opera brought Gruenberg the David Bispham Memorial Medal for the second time.

More concerned with American Negro folk music than this opera is the Concerto for Violin and Orchestra (1944), commissioned by Jascha Heifetz, who gave the premiere performance on December 1, 1944, as soloist with the Philadelphia Orchestra under Eugene Ormandy. In the second movement, two Negro Spirituals are quoted: "Oh, Holy Lord" and "Master Jesus." In the third movement, a picture of rural America, another facet of American folk music is uncovered. Here a hillbilly fiddler is heard in snatches of "The Arkansas Traveler" intermingled with some jazz. The sounds of a harmonica contribute further rural color. A revival tent meeting in which a frenzied sinner seeks salvation follows in music that grows increasingly animated, the orchestration energized by the sounds of clappers, tambourine, and gong.

In December 1930, Gruenberg married Irma Pickora, a Czechoslovakian physician, with whom he had a daughter. Between 1933 and 1936 he taught composition at the Chicago Musical College. In 1940 he and his family left for California, settling in Santa Monica, his home for the rest of his life. He now wrote music for the movies, beginning with a documentary, *Fight for Life* (1940), produced by Pare Lorentz. Among the films to which Gruenberg subsequently contributed notable scores were *So Ends Our Night* (1941), *Commandos Strike at Dawn* (1943), *Counter-Attack* (1945) and *The Arch of Triumph* (1948). He received Oscars from the American Academy of Motion Picture Arts and Sciences for *The Fight for Life, So Ends Our Night* and *Commandos Strike at Dawn*.

Gruenberg spent his last years in bitterness. He felt he had been forgotten by publishers, record companies, and performers. Two of his later operas, which he placed with his most important works, could not get produced: *Volpone* (1948–50) and *Anthony and Cleopatra* (1940–60). His later symphonies and chamber music were ignored. "The world of yesterday seems to have forgotten me," he lamented to a friend, "and the world of today does not know me." When an effort was made to present a concert of his works in honor of his eightieth birthday he refused to cooperate, and the project was stillborn. "I was forgotten on my seventieth, sixtieth, and fiftieth birthdays (where in hell was everybody when I needed this kind of treatment?)," he wrote to the sponsors. "But now I don't need anybody. If my stuff is to be played, it will be because it is worthy of being played, and not because I am an old dog being thrown a bone."

Gruenberg was elected a member of the National Institute of Arts and Letters in 1947. For several years he served as president of the American section of the International Society for Contemporary Music.

THE COMPOSER SPEAKS: Why do I write so much music? Is it for posterity? Well, what will posterity do for me? I write because nothing else gives me a sense of joy, of power, when I succeed; of frustration when I fail; beauty when I am inspired. And when I take pains, I can create in my brain and in my heart all things the world has to offer. Where else can I get this just sitting at my desk?

PRINCIPAL WORKS: 5 symphonies (1919–48); 3 violin sonatas (1912, 1924, 1950); 2 piano concertos (1914; 1938, revised 1963); 2 piano quintets (1929, 1937).

Hill of Dreams, tone poem for orchestra (1919); *The Dumb Wife*, opera (1921); *Four Indiscretions*, for string quartet (1922); *Daniel Jazz*, for vocal soloists and eight instruments (1923); *Polychromatics*, for piano (1924); *Insects*, for voice and piano (1924); *Jazz Suite*, for orchestra (1925); Four Songs, for voice and piano (1925); *Creation*, a "Negro sermon," for voice and eight instruments (1925); *Jazzettes*, for violin and piano (1926); *The Enchanted Isle*, tone poem for orchestra (1927, revised 1933); *Nine Moods*, for orchestra (1929); *Jack and the Beanstalk*, children's opera (1930); *Four Diversions*, for string quartet (1930); *The Emperor Jones*, opera (1932); *Serenade to a Beauteous Lady*, for orchestra (1934); *Queen Helena*, opera (1936); *Green Mansions*, radio opera (1938): *Five Variations on a Popular Theme*, for string quartet (1942); Violin Concerto (1944); *Music to an Imaginary Ballet*, Set II, for orchestra (1944); *Music to an Imaginary Legend*, for orchestra (1945); *Americana*, suite for orchestra (1945); *Volpone*, opera (1948–50); *Antony and Cleopatra*, opera (1940–60); *A Song of Faith*, oratorio for narrator, vocal soloists, chorus, and orchestra (1952–62); *Six Winter Songs*, for voice and piano (1963); *Prose Songs*, for voice and piano (1963).

BIBLIOGRAPHY: Ewen, David, *Composers Since 1900* (N.Y., 1969); Goss, Madeleine, *Modern Music Makers* (N.Y., 1952); Howard, John Tasker, *Our Contemporary Composers* (N.Y., 1941); Reis, Claire, *Composers in America* (N..Y., 1947); *Opera News*, February 10, 1979; *Who's Who in America, 1962–63,*

Gutchë, Gene (originally **Gutsche, Romeo Maximilian Eugene Ludwig**), b. Berlin, Germany, July 3, 1907.

Though he has written a considerable amount of abstract music, Gutchë is best known for programmatic orchestral compositions within integrated structures which exploit fully the resources of modern techniques without sacrificing romanticism, thereby arriving at "romantic expressionism."

He was one of two children of a successful merchant who maintained homes in Berlin and Zurich, where Gutchë was raised. He began piano lessons in Zurich with Marie Magnian when he was four, and later continued them with Ferdinand Conrad and Ferruccio Busoni in Switzerland. A broken wrist suffered while roller skating put an end to an early ambition to become a concert pianist. He now concentrated on his academic education as preparation for a business career, attending universities in Heidelberg, Lausanne, and Padua, where he majored in business and economics. He ended these studies, and at the same time broke ties with his family, in 1925, by escaping to the United States, supporting himself by shocking wheat in Texas and as a migrant worker. Settling in St. Paul, Minn., in the late 1920s, he gave piano lessons, made arrangements for jazz bands and performed as church organist. At the same time he studied theory with Donald Ferguson.

On December 1, 1935, he married Marion Frances Buchan. They made their home in New York. For the next eight years he was employed as a foreign correspondent, purchasing agent and later vice-president in public relations for an oil company. The outbreak of World War II ended this business affiliation. Gutchë now decided to study music more seriously than ever. Two benefactors in New York provided scholarship funds for the University of Minnesota. There, from 1947 to 1950, he studied with Donald Ferguson (basic theory and music history) and James Aliferis (harmony and counterpoint), and in 1950 was awarded a master's degree in

music after submitting his Symphony no. 1 (1951) and his String Quartet no. 3, *The Centennial* (1950). The symphony was introduced by the Minneapolis Symphony under James Aliferis on April 11, 1950; the string quartet was heard in Minneapolis on May 16, 1958, and was awarded the Minnesota State Prize. In these works and those that followed immediately—Symphony no. 2 (1950–54), Symphony no. 3 (1952), and the *Rondo capriccioso*, for orchestra (1953)—Gutchë outgrew the romanticism of his earliest works to adopt such modern techniques as polytonality, polyrhythm, discordant harmonies, the twelve-tone system, and microtonal music.

Gutchë continued studying composition, as well as conducting, with Philip Greeley Clapp at the University of Iowa (1950–53), where he was awarded a doctorate in music in 1953 with his Symphony no. 3 as his doctoral thesis. Beginning with 1953, Gutchë became a full-time composer and he has remained a full-time composer ever since, refusing to accept any outside occupations and relying solely on his music for his income. The first three years were difficult, as he worked in obscurity, supported by several benefactors. Much of what he wrote he later destroyed, but the Piano Concerto (1955) has survived. Performed for the first time on June 19, 1956, with James Aliferis conducting the Minneapolis Symphony, and with Bernhard Weiser as soloist, it received the Louis Moreau Gottschalk Gold Medal in 1970.

By the end of the 1950s, Gutchë was beginning to break new ground for his music. *Holofernes* (1958), which originated as an overture to the opera *Yodi* but which had acquired a separate identity as a concert overture, was given an award in the Luria Competition. It took Gutchë to a new direction in serialism, breaking the barrier of dodechism by using the twelve-tone row motivically and implementing the row to the degree that a feeling for polarity was manifested. It is with this work that Gutchë arrived at "romantic expressionism." It was introduced by the Minneapolis Symphony under Antal Dorati on November 27, 1959, and was performed even more successfully on October 26, 1960, by the National Symphony under Howard Mitchell in Washington, D.C.

Awards in the 1960s added further dimensions to Gutchë's stature. His Symphony no. 4 (1960; Albuquerque, N.M., March 8, 1962) received the Albuquerque Composition Prize. Symphony no. 5, for strings (1962; Chautauqua, N.Y., July 29, 1962), earned the Oscar Espla International Award and was telecast by the National Educational Television in 1964. Concerto for Violin and Orchestra (1962; Trieste, October 24, 1969) was the recipient of the XVI Premio Città di Trieste Prize.

Gutchë was awarded two successive Guggenheim Fellowships between 1963 and 1965. Beginning with *Ghengis Khan*, for orchestra (1963), which the Minneapolis Symphony introduced on December 3, 1963, under Stanislaw Skrowaczewski, Gutchë began to concentrate his efforts on programmatic music. Scored solely for winds and string basses, *Ghengis Khan* described the exploits and barbarism of the conqueror of the Mongolian tribes and the subjugator of all Europe. Though thoroughly modern in idiom, this music made an immediate contact with audiences everywhere through the vivid realism of its programmatic writing, its brilliant orchestration, and the power of its expression. Effective, too, were some of the programmatic orchestral compositions that followed, notably *Raquel* (1963; Tulsa, Okla., December 2, 1963), which narrates the tale of the beautiful Jewess of Toledo and Alfonso VIII, king of Castile; *Hsiang Fei*, for orchestra (1965; Cincinnati, October 21, 1966), based on an oriental tale about a beautiful young oriental girl who threatens suicide rather than submit to the emperor; *Epimetheus U.S.A.* (1968; Detroit, November 13, 1968), based on a legend of Greek mythology in which Epimetheus, husband of Pandora, fails to prevent his wife from opening the box that releases evil for themselves and the world. The last of these programmatic pieces had been commissioned by the Detroit Symphony, which, after the premiere performance, presented it eighteen times on a tour of the Midwest; Sixten Ehrling introduced it to Europe in December 1969 with the Stockholm Philharmonic.

Three of Gutchë's later programmatic orchestral works were written to commemorate the American bicentennial, all three with grants from the National Endowment for the Arts: *Icarus* (1975; Washington, D.C., October 26, 1976), commissioned by the National Symphony of Washington, D.C.; *Bi-Centurion* (1976; Rochester, N.Y., January 8, 1977), commissioned by the Rochester Philharmonic and its conductor David Zinman; and *Perseus and Andromeda XX* (1976; Cincinnati, February 25, 1977), commissioned by the Cincinnati Symphony. Meanwhile, on October 7, 1971, the Detroit Symphony under Sixten Ehrling introduced the Symphony no. 6 (1971)—Gutchë's first symphony in eight years—which, structurally, is more of a concerto grosso than a symphony. The first movement was scored for brass alone; the second, for strings; the third, for woodwinds; and the finale for the entire orchestra. "Each family of the orchestra," the composer explains, "is asked to excel against each other. Indeed that is as it should be, and there is rhyme to the mad-

ness. For a fundamental concept is reestablished: A symphony orchestra is a body of virtuosi."

THE COMPOSER SPEAKS: Programmatic music can be meaningful when the listener involved provides his own image. I like to think in each of us a greatness resides. For every man is his own alter ego. Music is a reflection of what we are. In this sense also we herald a quality of greatness in man, which is there.

Every artist is compelled to egomania—a delusion of grandeur—which hypnotizes him to express his ideas in the grand manner. His art combines the expression and techniques which are the style or manner of his time. The basis element of humanity is also involved, for even the noblest ideas resolve in futility unless coupled with the "psyche" of its people. Humanity is a deep well. The artist throws a pebble into the well. Despairingly he turns when, suddenly, he hears a splash. So our artists in the creation of a culture search for a response in the deep well of the American people.

PRINCIPAL WORKS: 6 symphonies (1951–71); 4 string quartets (1948–60); 4 piano sonatas (1948–62).

Rondo capriccioso, for chamber orchestra (1953); Piano Concerto (1955); Cello Concerto (1957); *Holofernes*, for orchestra (1958); *Judith*, prologue for speaker and strings (1959); Concertino, for orchestra (1959); *Timpani concertante*, for timpani and orchestra (1961); *Bongo Divertimento*, for percussion and orchestra (1962); Violin Concerto (1962); *Genghis Khan*, for orchestra (1963); *Raquel*, for orchestra (1963); *Rites in Tehnochtitlàn*, for piano and orchestra (1965); *Hsiang Fei*, for orchestra (1965); *Gemini*, for piano four hands and orchestra (1965); *Aesop's Fables*, suite for orchestra (1967); *Classic Concerto*, for orchestra (1967); *Epimetheus U.S.A.*, for orchestra (1968); *Icarus*, for orchestra (1975); *Bi-Centurion*, for orchestra (1976); *Perseus and Andromeda XX* (1976); *Helios Kenetic* (1977); *Akhenaten*, for orchestra (1978).

BIBLIOGRAPHY: BMI, *Many Worlds of Music*, December 1966; *Christian Science Monitor*, September 9, 1964; *Composers of the Americas*, vol. 15, 1969; *Who's Who in America, 1980–81*.

H

Hadley, Henry Kimball, b. Somerville, Mass., December 20, 1871; d. New York City., September 6, 1937.

He was a prolific composer in all media whose works had outstanding success in his own time in both the United States and Europe but which since his death have fallen into discard. The best of these are so skillfully structured, so brilliantly orchestrated, and so richly endowed with a spirited vitality that they compensate for the lack of any depth or originality of musical thought. Hadley was a romanticist and a conservative whose finest achievements were programmatic works for orchestra, graphic in their pictorial detail.

His father, director of music in several of Boston's schools, gave him his first lessons on violin and the piano after he was found trying to scrawl some waltzes on paper. More thorough music study followed at the New England Conservatory: piano with Stephen Emery and composition with George W. Chadwick. When he was seventeen, Hadley wrote the music for *Happy Jack*, an operetta that received numerous performances in schools and colleges. One year later, on December 9, 1889, a concert of his works was heard at the Franklin Church in Somerville. In 1891, Walter Damrosch directed in New York the premiere of Hadley's first concert overture: *Hector and Andromache*. In 1893, Hadley was appointed assistant conductor and violinist of the Laura Schirmer-Mapleson Opera Company, which went into bankruptcy following a tour.

Dissatisfied with his technical equipment, Hadley decided to go to Europe for further instruction. For about a year, he studied theory and composition with Eusebius Mandyczewski in Vienna.

Having returned to the United States in 1895, Hadley served for the next seven years as director of music at St. Paul's School in Garden City, N.Y. He soon began attracting attention to his creative talent. His programmatic Symphony no. 1, *Youth and Life* (1897), was introduced in New York by the New York Philharmonic under Anton Seidl's direction on December 2, 1897. A cantata, *In Music's Praise* (1899), was awarded the Oliver Ditson Prize. His first successful tone poem was written in 1900 at the request of the Bohemian Club in San Francisco. He named it *In Bohemia*, referring not to any country but to "that Elysium where true artists dwell." Its world premiere was given by the Boston Symphony on December 16, 1901, after which it was performed in Queen's Hall in London in 1913. The contrasting melodic ideas—a vigorous and joyous opening subject followed by a quiet and introspective second theme—suggested to one London critic that "the artist's life is . . . a mixture of stern endeavor and dream pleasure."

Hadley's Symphony no. 2, *The Four Seasons* (1901), was premiered by the New York Philharmonic under Emil Paur on December 20, 1901. It received the Paderewski Prize and awards from the New York Philharmonic, the Chicago Symphony, and the New England Conservatory.

Hadley spent the years between 1904 and 1909 in Europe, studying composition with Ludwig Thuille in Munich, composing, and conducting throughout Germany, mainly in performances of his own compositions. Among the compositions completed in Europe were: the tone poem *Salome* (1905), inspired by the Oscar Wilde drama but written before Richard Strauss's opera was produced, which the Boston Symphony, with Karl Muck conducting, introduced on April 12, 1907; and the nonprogrammatic Symphony no. 3 (1906), whose first performance was given by the Berlin Philharmonic with the composer conducting on December 27, 1907. In 1908–9 Hadley served as conductor of the Stadttheater in Mainz where, under his direction, his one-act opera, *Safié*—English libretto by Edward Oxenford translated into German—was produced on April 4, 1909.

Back in the United States in 1909, Hadley now divided his energies equally between conducting and composing. In 1909 he was conductor of the Seattle Symphony for one year, and from 1920 to 1927 was associate conductor of the New York Philharmonic. Hadley conducted the New York Philharmonic in a short sound film presented by Vitaphone films on August 6, 1926, as the first public demonstration of talking pictures. He also conducted the New York Philharmonic for several summer seasons at the Lewisohn Stadium. In 1929 he founded, and for three years directed, the Manhattan Symphony, his programs featuring thirty-six native American compositions (eight his own). Earlier, in 1924, he was the conductor of the Worcester Festival in Massachusetts and toured Europe; in 1927 he led concerts in Buenos Aires and in 1930 in Japan; and in August 1934 he conducted three concerts with which the Berkshire Music Festival was inaugurated in Stockbridge, Mass., returning to this summer festival for three more concerts in August 1935.

He continued composing, oblivious of the new trends in music being explored in Europe. He remained consistently true to the postromantic traditions he had learned to admire in Europe. What Richard Aldrich said in the *New York Times* of his Symphony no. 3 in 1910 applied to most of Hadley's other works. "It is, at its best, really charming music, and it shows skill in orchestration and frequently in structure, and in the exposition of fine and subtle detail. . . . As such it is quite worthwhile, for Mr. Hadley's musical ideals, his treatment of them are quite able to stand by themselves. Nor has he been afraid to think in terms of . . . the melodic. His feeling for harmony is rich, free and untrammeled."

An orchestral rhapsody, *The Culprit Fay* (1909), inspired by a poem of Joseph Rodman Drake, received the $1,000 prize of the National Federation of Music Clubs after being introduced by the Chicago Symphony, the composer conducting, in Grand Rapids, Mich., on May 28, 1909. In 1911, Hadley completed writing Symphony no. 4, *North, East, South and West*, which was commissioned for and heard at the festival at Norfolk, Conn., on June 6, 1911, with the composer conducting. The orchestral tone poem *Lucifer* (1913) was also written for the Norfolk Festival, where it was given on June 2, 1914. *Azora, The Daughter of Montezuma* (1915)—a full-length opera with libretto by David Stevens set in 15th-century Mexico—was mounted in Chicago on December 26, 1917, and in New York a month later. *Bianca* (1916; N.Y., October 18, 1918) was an opera with a libretto by Grant Stewart based on Goldoni's comedy *The Mistress of the Inn*; it won the Hinshaw Prize of $1,000 from the Society of American Singers in New York. One of Hadley's finest choral works, *Ode to Music*, for solo voices, chorus, children's voices, and orchestra (1917)—to a poem by Henry van Dyke—was featured at the Worcester Festival in Massachusetts in 1917, having been written on commission to commemorate the festival's sixtieth anniversary.

Hadley's most successful opera was *Cleopatra's Night* (1918), libretto by Alice Neal Pollock derived from Gautier's *Une nuit de Cléopâtre*. Its premiere at the Metropolitan Opera in New York on January 31, 1920, with Frances Alda as Cleopatra, was so successful that it was retained in the repertoire the following season. The oriental exoticism that Hadley introduced into his melodic, harmonic, and instrumental writing, and its dramatic effectiveness, proved particularly appealing. To Richard Aldrich in the *New York Times* this opera "seemed in certain ways the most successful of the ten or dozen compositions that have been given at the Metropolitan. . . . The composer seems to have succeeded better than his predecessors in making an opera that is 'practicable' for the stage."

Among Hadley's subsequent compositions, the most important were: the concert overture *Othello* 1919; Philadelphia, December 26, 1919); the tone poem *The Ocean* (1920–21; N.Y., November 17, 1921); *Resurgam*, for solo voices, chorus, and orchestra (1922) to a text by Louise Ayres Garnett, its premiere taking place at the Cincinnati May Festival in May 1923 after which it was performed abroad; the descriptive and esoterically styled orchestral suite *Streets of Pekin* (1930; Tokyo, September 24, 1930); *Silhouettes, San Francisco*, a suite for orchestra (1931; Philadelphia, July 17, 1932); and the Symphony no. 5, subtitled *Connecticut* (1935; Norfolk, Conn., 1935), portraying three different centuries in the life of Connecticut and written on commission for the tercentenary celebration of that state.

On September 2, 1918, Hadley married the concert singer Inez Barbour. In 1925, Hadley received an honorary doctorate from Tufts University in Medford, Mass. He was elected member of the National Institute of Arts and Letters and the American Academy of Arts and Letters and was decorated with the Order of Merit by the French government. In 1932, Hadley founded the National Association of American Composers and Conductors, which subsequently sponsored the Henry Hadley Memorial Library of works by American composers and the Henry Hadley Medal to deserving American composers. A Henry Hadley Foundation for the Advancement of American Music was organized in 1938.

PRINCIPAL WORKS: 5 symphonies (1897–1935); 2 string quartets (1896, 1934); 2 piano trios (1897, 1933).

Violin Sonata (1896); *In Music's Praise*, cantata (1899); *In Bohemia*, concert overture (1900); *Oriental Suite*, for orchestra (1903); *Salome*, tone poem for orchestra (1905); *Concert Piece*, for cello and orchestra (1907); *Safié*, one-act opera (1909); *Elegy*, for cello and piano, or cello and orchestra (1910); *The Atonement of Pan*, festival play (1912); *Lucifer*, tone poem for orchestra (1913); *Azora*, opera (1915); *The Fairy Thorn*, for women's voices and orchestra (1915); *Bianca*, opera (1916); *Ode to Music*, for solo voices, chorus, and orchestra (1917); *Ode to the New Earth*, for solo voices, chorus, and orchestra (1917); *Cleopatra's Night*, opera (1918); *Othello*, concert overture for orchestra (1919); Piano Quintet (1920); *Ballet of the Flowers*, orchestral suite (1920); *The Ocean*, tone poem for orchestra (1921); *Resurgam*, for solo voices, chorus, and orchestra (1922); *A Night in Old Paris*, radio opera (1925); *Suite ancienne*, for orchestra (1926); *Mirtil in Arcadia*, for solo voices, narrator, chorus, and orchestra (1927); *Streets of Pekin*, suite for orchestra (1930); *Herod*, concert overture for orchestra (1931); *Youth Triumphant*, concert overture for orchestra (1931); *Aurora Borealis*, concert overture for orchestra (1931); *Silhouettes, San Francisco*, suite for orchestra (1931); *Alma Mater*, tone poem for orchestra (1932); *Belshazzar*, for solo voices, chorus, and orchestra (1932); *Scherzo diabolique*, for orchestra (1934); Concertino, for orchestra (1937).

BIBLIOGRAPHY: Berthoud, Paul B., *The Musical Works of Dr. Henry Hadley* (N.Y., 1942); Boardman, H. R., *Henry Hadley, Ambassador of Harmony* (Emory University, Ga., 1932).

Haieff, Alexei, b. Blagoveshchensk, Siberia, Russia, August 25, 1914. American citizen, 1939.

The compositions that brought Haieff success were in a neoclassical style, lean and precise in structure, tonal and diatonic, with a meticulous attention to detail and with effects produced more often by understatement than by powerful sonorities or emotionalism. Nevertheless, romanticism and a free spirit are not lacking. In *Music in a New Found Land*, Wilfred Mellers stated that Haieff liked to " 'build' his pieces geometrically from tiny figures, so that the mosaic metaphor is freqently applicable to his forms."

He was the youngest of seven children of Russian parents, both of whom were musical, the father through listening and the mother as an amateur pianist. When Alexei was six, his family fled from Communist Russia to Harbin, Manchuria. There (unlike so many of the other "white" Russian refugees) the Haieffs were financially comfortable. "We had a very good gramophone and collected records of good music," Haieff recalls. "The discovery of the moderns—Milhaud, Hindemith, and especially Stravinsky—opened my ears forever."

Though most of the other Haieff children received music lessons early, Alexei Haieff did not begin formal piano study until he was fourteen. "I somehow resisted to be taught, till most of them left home in their different pursuits. The moment they were gone I started piano lessons. The trouble appeared almost immediately—improvising became more interesting than practice. Within a year, my mind was made up to be a composer."

The first academic school Haieff attended (1923–24) was run by the Chinese-Eastern Railroad, one half of which was owned by the Russian government, the other half by the Chinese government. When the Soviets took over the Russian half, Haieff was removed from the school by his parents, who disapproved of the change in educational policies. The next three years (1924–27), he was tutored at home until, in 1927, he was able to enter a newly organized school with more advanced educational principles, sponsored by the local branch of the YMCA. There, a history professor, who was exceptionally musical, gave an important lift to Haieff's early musical growth. That growth was beginning to take place through piano lessons with Boris M. Lazareff and later, and more importantly, with Eugenia M. Glikin. Haieff also received his first lessons in harmony and theory from a young conservatory graduate whose name he has forgotten.

Haieff graduated from the YMCA school in 1931 "with very fond memories." In May 1932 he appeared at a concert of Mme. Glikin's pupils in a program that included a movement of his own juvenile piano concerto with a fellow student providing the accompaniment on a second piano.

Haieff immigrated to the United States in the fall of 1932, settling in New York City. In New York, he became acquainted with Rachmaninoff, who soon became for him a rich source of encouragement and guidance. At Rachmaninoff's recommendation, Haieff studied composition with Constantin Shvedoff, "a brilliant teacher and a very strict one."

In 1934, Haieff was accepted at, and received a fellowship from, the Juilliard School of Music. He spent the next three and a half years at Juilliard in the study of composition with Rubin Goldmark (and, after Goldmark's death, with Frederick Jacobi) and orchestration with Bernard Wagenaar. Further study of composition took place with Nadia Boulanger in Cambridge, Mass. (1938–39), Haieff discontinuing his fellowship at Juilliard to move to Boston to work with her. Meanwhile, in 1937, he had served his apprenticeship as composer by writing the Sonatina, for string quartet (1937), which was followed two years later by Three Bagatelles, for oboe and bassoon.

In the fall of 1939, Haieff left for Paris. A meeting with Stravinsky, and the friendship that followed, had a powerful impact on Haieff's creative development. By 1942, Haieff outgrew apprenticeship, a fact officially recognized that year when he was awarded a medal from the American Academy in Rome and First Award from the Lili Boulanger Memorial.

Haieff's first success came with Divertimento, for orchestra (1944), introduced in New York on April 5, 1946, by the Barone Little Symphony and after that programmed by major orchestra in the United States and abroad, including the Boston Symphony under Richard Burgin on October 29, 1946. This is a five-movement composition (three movements of which had originated as pieces for the piano), each dedicated to one of Haieff's friends, except for a "lullaby" movement composed "for my friends' babies, who were being born in abundance in 1944." George Balanchine was so taken with this music that he choreographed it; his production was introduced by the Ballet Society of New York on January 13, 1947.

Haieff was awarded a medal from the American Academy of Arts and Letters in 1945. That year, on a commission from the two-piano team of Gold and Fizdale, he wrote Sonata for Two Pianos, which they introduced in February 1946 in New York and then recorded for Columbia. This music was choreographed a decade later by Paul Taylor in a production mounted at the Spoleto Festival in Italy during the summer of 1966. In 1977, Haieff "rearranged" this two-piano sonata for piano and orchestra as Piano Concerto no. 2.

In 1946, Haieff received the first of two Guggenheim Fellowships, the second following in 1949. Between 1947 and 1949 he was a fellow at the American Academy in Rome. In 1947, he received a grant from the National Institute of Arts and Letters. On January 12, 1947, Benar Heifetz introduced Haieff's *Eclogue*, for cello and piano (1945), in New York.

Haieff's neoclassical style became crystallized between 1948 and 1950 with the writing of two concertos, one for violin (1948) and the other for piano (1950). The Violin Concerto was composed for Fredell Lack and the Little Orchestra Society conducted by Thomas Scherman, who introduced it in New York soon after its composition. Nicolas Slonimsky, in his program notes for that concert, described this work as "a characteristic product of the time. It is economically compressed into a single movement. It is entirely tonal, with a definite key signature of three sharps in the beginning and in the end, and with modulatory interludes in the middle section. The rhythm is firm and almost severe in its unambiguous pattern. The solo part is treated functionally. The orchestral accompaniment is differentiated into groups of several instruments that form a counterpart of the classical concertino. The percussion section serves to accentuate the important connectives of the musical current."

Before Haieff's Piano Concerto no. 1 (1950) was given its first public performance it had been recorded in Vienna and, on April 27, 1952, was heard over the CBS radio network in a performance by Leo Smit and the CBS Symphony conducted by Leopold Stokowski. The first public performance followed on October 31, 1952, with Leo Smit, soloist, and the Boston Symphony directed by Charles Munch. It now received the New York Music Critics Circle Award. In 1953, this concerto was heard both at the Venice Festival and in Rome, and on June 10, 1956, it represented the United States at the festival of the International Society for Contemporary Music in Stockholm.

On a commission from the Ojai Festival in California, Haieff completed his String Quartet in 1951. It was given its initial hearing at that festival in September of that year and was subsequently recorded by the Juilliard String Quartet.

In 1952–53, Haieff was composer-in-residence at the American Academy in Rome. He returned to the American Academy for another year's residence in 1958–59. Meanwhile, in 1957, he orchestrated his Piano Sonata as a symphony. In making this adaptation, Haieff explained, "I tried to preserve the transparency of the original writing by avoiding any unnecessary doubling or introducing any new contrapuntal voices, and the discipline of the restriction was inspiring and very gratifying. The only structural change in the whole piece is the final chord which, instead of being on the first beat as in the sonata, now in the symphony comes on the second." This symphony (Haieff's second) opens with a slow fantasialike introduction followed by a fugal Allegro. A free-fantasia second movement Andante, romantically

conceived, is succeeded by the concluding Maestoso which recalls the subject of the opening Maestoso before proceeding to a new fugal subject. The symphony was given its world premiere by the Boston Symphony on April 11, 1958, Charles Munch conducting. It then received the UNESCO International Award. The New York Philharmonic, under Josef Krips, performed it in the fall of 1963, when Harold C. Schonberg, in the *New York Times*, described it as "delicately turned and exquisitely jeweled. Haieff does not go in for the big utterance. This symphony is a very personal melange of neoclassicism in general (and Stravinsky in particular), the elements of the French school and a few suggestions of something Russian lurking in the background. It is a very civilized piece of writing."

On January 9, 1958, the New York Philharmonic under Leonard Bernstein offered the New York premiere of *Ballet in E*, for orchestra (1955). This work had been commissioned by the Louisville Orchestra, which had premiered it in Kentucky under Robert Whitney on October 29, 1955. On April 1, 1961, Symphony no. 3 (1961) was introduced in New Haven, Conn., having been commissioned by the New Haven Symphony; it was performed in 1962 by the Boston Symphony under Charles Munch both in Boston and at the Berkshire Music Festival at Tanglewood, Mass. A Ford commission led to the writing of the Cello Sonata for Zara Nelsova (1963; N.Y., November 1963), and a Koussevitzky Music Foundation commission, to that of *Eloge*, for nine instruments (1967; Washington, D.C., 1968). *Caligula*, for baritone and orchestra, on a text by Robert Lowell, written in 1970 on a commission from the Manhattan School of Music in New York, was premiered in New York on November 5, 1971.

In 1962, and again in 1964–65, Haieff was Visiting Slee Professor at the State University of New York in Buffalo; in 1962–63 he was Distinguished Visiting Mellon Professor of Music at Carnegie Mellon University in Pittsburgh; in 1965–66, he was visiting professor of music at Brandeis University in Waltham, Mass.; and from 1968 to 1970, he was composer-in-residence at the University of Utah in Salt Lake City.

THE COMPOSER SPEAKS: I believe that the general desire of composers (whether or not for a larger public) lately has been on a theatrical form of attraction. The future trend (I believe) is to be again in the love of surprising combination of notes, outside the joys of the magic of the stage.

PRINCIPAL WORKS: 3 symphonies (1942, 1957, 1961); 2 piano concertos, the second rearranged from Sonata for Two Pianos (1950, 1977).

Divertimento, for chamber orchestra (1944); Sonata for Two Pianos (1945); *Eclogue*, for cello and piano (1945); *The Princess Zondilda and Her Entourage*, ballet (1946); *Beauty and the Beast*, ballet

(1947); Violin Concerto (1948); String Quartet (1951); *Eclogue*, for harp and string orchestra, originally for harp and string quartet (1954); Piano Sonata (1955); *Ballet in E*, for orchestra (1955); *Saints' Wheel*, for piano (1960); Cello Sonata (1963); *La nouvelle Heloïse*, for harp and strings (1963); *Eloge*, for nine instruments (1967); *Holy Week Liturgy*, for chorus (1969); *Caligula*, for baritone and orchestra (1970); Rhapsodies, for guitar and harpsichord (1980).

BIBLIOGRAPHY: *BBDM*; *DCM*; Mellers, Wilfrid, *Music in a New Found Land* (N.Y., 1965); *Who's Who in America, 1980–81*.

Hannay, Roger Durham, b. Plattsburg, N.Y., September 22, 1930.

His music has passed from the neoclassic, twelve-tone and atonal, through multimedia productions and electronic music, to a new expressivity and lyricism in which the quotations and recompositions of thematic materials from other composers have been prominent.

He is the son of an itinerant rural Methodist minister whose musical interests embraced singing, playing the piano by ear, and composing sacred songs and instrumental pieces. Roger's mother was an amateur musician who played hymns on the piano. His first significant experience in music came from hearing a recording of Bach's music transcribed for orchestra and performed by Leopold Stokowski and the American Youth Orchestra. "It was simply an instantaneous religious conversion for me," he recalls. Two weeks later he received his first piano lesson and made his initial attempt at composition by writing a little piano prelude. "My father responded with delight and appreciation to my steady flow of adolescent compositions and piano practicing but remained steadfastly innocent of my potentially fatal flaw, my utter inability to sight-read." At Schoharie Central High School, which he entered in 1944, he was a member of the school chorus both as singer and piano accompanist. During his four years in high school, he studied the piano privately with Orpha Gage Quay, who "patiently, perhaps too patiently for my own good, tolerated my piano thumping and pounding and my attempts to play pieces far in advance of my beginner's technique."

After graduating from high school with honors in 1948, he entered Syracuse University where his studies in music continued with Dika Newlin, Ernst Bacon, and Franklin Morris; there he earned his bachelor of music degree in 1952. On June 2, 1951, at the chapel of the university, Hannay married Jane Roberts, a graduate student in music at the university who later became a teacher; their only child, a daughter, Dawn, became a professional violist and member of the New York Philharmonic.

In 1952–53, Hannay pursued graduate studies with Karl Geiringer, Gardner Read, and Hugo Norden at Boston University, receiving a master of music degree in 1953. To get additional funds for further graduate work, Hannay spent the next year traveling about to various rural public schools in New York State, teaching singing and conducting community and school choruses; at the same time his wife helped him with the finances by teaching school. Then, between 1954 and 1956, Hannay attended the Eastman School of Music, in Rochester, N.Y., a student of Howard Hanson, Bernard Rogers, and Harold Gleason, acquiring his doctorate in 1956. Postdoctoral studies took place with Lukas Foss and Aaron Copland at the Berkshire Music Center in Tanglewood, Mass., during the summer of 1959, and at the Seminar for Advanced Studies at Princeton University during the summer of 1960 with Roger Sessions and Elliott Carter.

After holding various teaching posts in music between 1956 and 1960 at the State University of New York at Cortland, N.Y., at the University of Wyoming at Laramie, and Concordia College at Moorhead, Minn., Hannay was appointed to the music faculty at the University of North Carolina in Chapel Hill in 1966, where he has since remained. There, in addition to his activities in the department of theory and of composition, he founded and conducted the New Music Ensemble; he also organized and directed Thursday evening series of concerts and festivals of new music emphasizing the works of young composers. In 1979 Hannay was made chairman of the fine arts division.

His career as composer began in 1952 with Rhapsody, for flute and piano, and a cantata, for chorus, tenor, and orchestra. The compositions that followed in the next dozen years represented the first of three clearly separated creative eras. That was the time when he sought to express formal and quasi-classical procedures (not necessarily those normally associated with neoclassicism) but in terms of attention to technical control factors of musical experiences. During this period, while favoring classic forms, he began using twelve-tone and atonal techniques, his first use of a twelve-tone row occurring in the Symphony no. 1 (1953; Chapel Hill, April 4, 1974) and developed in its full expressive technique in *A Dramatic Overture*, for orchestra (1955), written in homage to Arnold Schoenberg. This twelve-tone phase ended in 1967 with *Fantôme*, a highly structured serial work which contained improvisation and his first use of quotation. Other significant works of this period included the Symphony no. 2 (1955); the chamber operas, *Two Tickets to Omaha* (1960) and *The Fortune of St. Macabre* (1964); *Requiem*, for soprano solo, chorus, and orchestra (1961), based on Walt Whitman's "When Lilacs Last in the Dooryard Bloom'd," commissioned by the Civil War Centennial Committee of Concordia College; two string quartets (1962); and the String Quartet no. 3, *Designs* (1963). When the last of these was first heard in New York on February 9, 1964, the *New York Times* described it as "an attractive series of clearly marked moods from snappy to aching to assertive to wan."

Beginning with 1964, Hannay moved to new directions: to electronic music, percussion music, and multimedia productions. This period started with *Structure*, for percussion ensemble (1965); *America Sing!*, for electronic tape and with visuals by Donald Evans (1967); and *Marshall's Medium Message*, for percussion quartet and female announcer (1967). Involvement in social commentary through multimedia productions also characterized some of his more ambitious efforts. One of these was *The Inter-Planetary Aleatoric Serial Factory* (1969), a huge work performed in a university gymnasium, scored for electronic tape, films, slides, dancers, actors, string quartet, soprano solo, and rock band, text by Donald Evans. Another such multimedia production was an angry, anti-Vietnam war, anti-military-industrial complex, work for chorus and orchestra, *Sayings for Our Time* (1968; Winston Salem, N.C., August 2, 1968), text taken from newspaper items. With the exception of *Structure*, all the above works were introduced at the University of North Carolina in the year of their composition.

Some of Hannay's major works since 1967 have quoted the music of other composers, frequently rewritten or distorted as collage-synthesis very different from that of Charles Ives, whose music has been a major factor in Hannay's later compositions. The spectral appearance of Berlioz can be found in the already mentioned *Fantôme*, for viola, clarinet, and piano (1967), which received the Hilda Honigman Composer's Cup from the North Carolina Federation of Music Clubs and which was heard in New York on September 18, 1968. In the *New York Times*, Allen Hughes called it one of the two "most compelling" works heard on that program. The scores for the viola and clarinet had to be stretched across two rows of twelve stands each with the performers required to walk across the stage to read the music as they performed. *Listen*, for orchestra (1971), first performed on July 7, 1973, by the Eastern Philharmonic in North Carolina, was described by its composer as a "time-filtered collage" of music of the 19th-century he had heard in earlier years and it uses material from a wide range of 19th-century "classics." "My intention," the composer explains further, "was not merely to quote the 19th century. The work consists of simultaneous recomposition and decomposition of the original material into frequently unrecognizable components." *Celebration*, for tape and orchestra (1975), commissioned by the Composers Theatre in New York and featured at the sixth annual May Festival of Contemporary American Music in New York on May 19, 1975, alludes to music by Ives, Debussy, William Billings, and even to some of Hannay's own earlier orchestral compositions. Symphony no. 3, *The Great American Novel*,

for chorus, orchestra, and optional tape-recorded sound, and the Symphony no. 4, *American Classic*, both completed in 1977, were constructed entirely of 19th-century and 20th-century American symphonic music, literally quoted or style-referenced. The Symphony no. 3 was written on a grant from the National Endowment for the Arts, and the Symphony no. 4 on a grant from the Kennan Foundation; the latter work was introduced in Chapel Hill on April 27, 1978, following which it was televised for statewide broadcast.

In 1971 Hannay has entered what for him was a new sphere in which his main concern has been with lyricism, splendor of musical sound, and the expression of beauty rather than innovation and experimentation.

On a grant from the University Research Council of the University of North Carolina, Hanny compiled, transcribed, and edited the *Anthology of American Symphonic Music* (1974). In 1975 and 1979 he received the North Carolina Federation of Music Clubs Composers Publishing Awards.

THE COMPOSER SPEAKS: My compositional method is not a method at all, just a blind groping within a vague, usually nonverbal intention, feeling, or attitude. My pieces usually start from nothing, rapidly grow, and I'm often surprised at the final result. There is no precompositional brain-strain for me, just the heavy weight of spiritual waiting and distrust and the ever haunting question of whether I can tap the Muse again. When I write, I write rapidly. I'm a great believer in the necessity to be able to grasp the propitious gift of the unexpected moment (surprise, accidental, unplanned) and am absolutely convinced that most art is the result of the unpredictable alignment and collision of events which the wary artist seizes upon and makes tangible.

PRINCIPAL WORKS: 4 symphonies (1953–77); 4 string quartets (1962–74).

A Dramatic Overture, for orchestra (1955); Concertino for Organ and Strings (1952, revised 1957); Sonata for Brass Ensemble (1957); *Lament*, for oboe and strings (1957); *Summer Festival Overture*, for orchestra (1958); *Concerto da camera*, for soprano and chamber orchestra (1958, revised 1975); Divertimento, for woodwind quintet (1958); Prelude and Dance, for orchestra (1959, revised 1974); *Two Tickets to Omaha*, chamber opera (1960); *Requiem*, for soprano solo, chorus and orchestra (1961); *Abstractions*, for piano (1962); Symphony for Band (1963); *The Fortune of St. Macabre*, chamber opera (1964); Piano Sonata (1964); *The Fruit of Love*, song cycle for soprano and piano or chamber ensemble (1964); *Spectrum*, for brass quintet (1964); *Structure*, for percussion (1965, revised 1974); *Sonorities*, for piano (1966); *America Sing!*, for electronic tape and visuals (1967); *Marshall's Medium Message*, for percussion quartet and female announcer (1967);

Fantôme, for viola, clarinet, and piano (1967); *Live and In Color*, for electronic tape, percussion quartet, films, slides, and female announcer (1967); *Sonorous Image*, for orchestra (1968); *Sayings in Our Time*, for chorus and orchestra (1968); *The Inter-Planetary Aleatoric Serial Factory*, for electronic tape, films, slides, dancers, actors, string quartet, soprano solo, and rock band (1969); *Fragmentation*, for orchestra, also for chamber orchestra (1969); *Confrontation*, for electronic tape and percussion solo (1969); *Elegy—Peace for Dawn*, for electronic tape and viola (1970); *Choral Fantasies* I, II, and III, for chorus (1970); *Listen*, for orchestra (1971); *Tuonelan Joutsen*, for electronic tape, English horn, and film (1971); *Chanson sombre*, for flute, viola, and harp (1972–74); *The Prophecy of Despair*, for male voices and percussion (1972); Vocalise, for soprano, electronic tape, and optional brass (1972); *Grande concerte*, for solo violin (1972); Concerto Music for Solo Cello (1973); *Sphinx*, for electronic tape and solo trumpet (1973); *Four for Five*, for brass quintet (1973); *Celebration*, for orchestra and electronic tape (1975); *Pied Piper*, for clarinet and tape (1975); *Phantom of the Opera*, for organ and soprano (1975); *Guitar Set* (1975); *Suite Billings*, for youth orchestra (1975); *Oh, Friends!*, for chamber winds and pitch percussion (1976); *ARP*, for dancers, visuals, and electronic tape (1977); *Mere Bagatelle*, for piano four hands and synthesizer (1978); *Festival Trumpets*, for ten trumpets and conductor (1978); Serenade, for piano and synthesizer (1978–79); Duo, for solo percussion and electronic tape (1979); Nocturnes, for woodwind quintet (1979); *American Colonial*, suite for band arranged from *Suite Billings* (1979);

BIBLIOGRAPHY: *BBDM*; *NGDMM*; *Musical Quarterly*, July 1969.

Hanson, Howard, b. Wahoo, Neb., October 28, 1896; d. Rochester, N.Y., February 26, 1981.

For four decades, both as educator and as the conductor of the annual American Music Festival in Rochester, Hanson was the mentor and indefatigable promoter of new American music, however advanced the methods or ideology. But as a composer, Hanson consistently avoided the avant-garde, always remaining true to his romantic principles and frequently nurtured by his spiritual kinship with his Swedish ancestry. He was awarded the Pulitzer Prize in music in 1944.

He came from Swedish parents who had immigrated to the United States in their youth and settled in the Swedish American community in Wahoo. He was six when his mother began teaching him the piano, lessons soon supplemented by instruction on the cello. In his eighth year Hanson wrote his first composition, a piano trio influenced by Grieg; when he was nine he played the cello in a string quartet. While attending Wahoo High School, and the School

of Music at Luther College (a junior college), where he took courses in harmony, counterpoint, piano, and cello, Hanson played the piano and organ in town churches, sang in the church choir, and conducted the high school orchestra. In 1911 he received his diploma with highest honors from Luther College and in 1912 he graduated from Wahoo High School as class valedictorian. For one year after that he attended the University of Nebraska School of Music in Lincoln.

With his eyes fixed on New York for additional music study, Hanson spent a year and a half playing the cello in popular orchestras to accumulate the needed money. He spent one year (1914) at the Institute of Musical Art in New York as a student of Percy Goetshius's in composition and of James Friskin's in piano. An additional summer of playing in popular orchestras provided the financial means with which to enroll in Northwestern University in Evanston, Ill., for a continuation of both academic and music studies. As a student there he completed Prelude and Double Fugue for two pianos (1915), a Piano Quintet (1916), and *Symphonic Prelude*, for orchestra (1916). The last of these was performed by the Chicago Symphony, with Frederick Stock conducting.

In 1916, upon graduating from Northwestern University (where in 1915–16 he served as an assistant in the music department) with a bachelor of arts degree, Hanson was appointed professor of theory and composition at the College of the Pacific in San Jose, Calif. Between 1919 and 1921 he held the post of dean at the Conservatory of Fine Arts at the College of the Pacific. Among the compositions he had completed by this time were *Symphonic Legend* (1917) and *Symphonic Rhapsody* (1919), both for orchestra, introduced in their years of composition respectively in San Francisco and Los Angeles with Hanson making his first appearances as conductor. *Scandinavian Suite*, for piano (1918–19), was his first work to be influenced by his Swedish heredity and American Swedish environment. In 1919, Hanson also wrote the music for the *California Forest Play of 1920* scored for solo voices, mixed chorus, ballet, and orchestra.

When the American Prix de Rome competition was initiated in 1921, Hanson submitted a tone poem, *Before the Dawn* (1920, and was one of the three winners for the prescribed three-year residence at the American Academy in Rome. Hanson now made significant strides as composer. In the year of 1923 he wrote two orchestral tone poems—*Lux Aeterna*, which was performed in Rome in 1923 and subsequently recipient of the award of the Society for the Publication of American Music, and *North and West*, for orchestra and chorus; a string quartet, commissioned for the Coolidge Festival in Washington, D.C.; and his Symphony no. 1, *Nordic*, whose world premiere he conducted with the Augusteo Orchestra in Rome on May 30, 1923. As its title suggests, this symphony is strongly Nordic in personality—singing, as the composer explained, "of the solemnity, austerity and grandeur of the North, of its restless surging and strife, and of its somberness and melancholy." Some of the characteristics of Hanson's fully mature style can be detected here: his preference for classical, and at times cyclical, structure; his broad, sweeping themes; his partiality for somber moods produced by low instrumental registers and the occasional austere instrumentation; the alternation between introspection and restless agitation; the bleakness of the tonal landscapes. Some of these compositional traits could also be found in the music of Sibelius, the reason Hanson soon came to be known as "the American Sibelius." But when he wrote the *Nordic Symphony*, Hanson had no acquaintance with Sibelius's music.

In 1923, Walter Damrosch invited Hanson to come to New York to conduct the premiere of *North and West*. Hanson was then called to Rochester, N.Y., to direct the American premiere of his *Nordic Symphony*. A fateful meeting in Rochester with George Eastman, the industrialist and philanthropist who had founded the Eastman School of Music at the University of Rochester in 1919, brought Hanson in 1924 the appointment of director of the Eastman School of Music. He held this post for forty years, elevating that school to a topmost rank among American conservatories. An entire generation of young composers studied under and were influenced by him. On May 1, 1925, Hanson inaugurated the first annual festival of American music in Rochester, which was to become perhaps the most significant forum for the presentation of first hearings of works by living Americans. By the time Hanson retired in 1964, he had conducted at these festivals more than fifteen hundred compositions by seven hundred composers.

If he was active on behalf of his students both as teacher and conductor, he was not idle as composer. *The Lament of Beowulf*, for chorus and orchestra (1925), is based on the Old English (Anglo-Saxon) saga translated into modern English by William Morris and A. J. Wyatt, its first performance taking place at the Ann Arbor Festival in Michigan in 1926. *Pan and the Priest*, a tone poem with piano obbligato (1926), was premiered at Queen's Hall in London in October 1926, Henry J. Wood conducting. *Heroic Elegy*, for chorus and orchestra (but with no verbal text), was written in 1927 in commemoration of the centennial of Beethoven's death.

Hanson's most significant writing can be found in his symphonies, of which he produced six after the *Nordic*. He gave his romanticism free play in the Symphony no. 2, subtitled *Romantic* (1930), which he wrote on commission from the Boston Symphony for its fiftieth anniversary and which enjoyed an extraordinary success when that orchestra introduced it under Serge Koussevitzky on November 28, 1930. As Hanson explained, this work was "an escape from

the rather bitter type of modern musical realism . . . [aiming to be] young in spirit, lyrical, and romantic in temperament, and simple and direct in expression." A Nordic presence is found in Symphony no. 3 (1936–37), which pays tribute to the epic qualities of the pioneers who had founded the first Swedish settlement on the Delaware in 1638 before opening up new territory in the West. Commissioned by the Columbia Broadcasting System, it was first heard in part (three movements) over the CBS network on September 10, 1937, then given in its entirety over the NBC radio network on March 26, 1938, with the composer conducting both performances. Symphony no. 4, subtitled *The Requiem* (1943), is an elegiac work inspired by the death of the composer's father; the usual tempo markings of the four movements are here replaced by the subtitles from the Requiem Mass (Kyrie, Requiescat, Dies Irae, Lux Aeterna). The Boston Symphony under the composer's direction introduced it on December 3, 1943, after which, in 1944, it was awarded the Pulitzer Prize in music. Symphony no. 5 is a one-movement work entitled *Sinfonia Sacra* (1954). It is a musical interpretation of the story of the first Easter as narrated in the Gospel According to St. John. This is not programmatic music but, as the composer informs us, an attempt "to invoke some of the atmosphere of tragedy and triumph, mysticism and affirmation of this story which is the essential symbol of the Christian faith." Eugene Ormandy directed its premiere with the Philadelphia Orchestra on February 18, 1955. Symphony no. 6 (1967) was commissioned by Leonard Bernstein and the New York Philharmonic to commemorate the orchestra's 125th anniversary; they first performed it on February 29, 1968. Symphony no. 7, *A Sea Symphony*, based on Walt Whitman, for chorus and orchestra, was written in 1977 to commemorate the fiftieth anniversary of the National Music Camp at Interlochen, Mich., where it received its first hearing on August 7, 1977.

His orchestral literature also embraces the Piano Concerto in C major (1948)—which the Koussevitzky Music Foundation had commissioned and which Rudolf Firkusny and the Boston Symphony under the composer's direction premiered on December 31, 1948—together with numerous shorter works. The most important of these shorter compositions are: *Elegy in Memory of Serge Koussevitzky* (1955; Boston, January 20, 1956), which the Boston Symphony commissioned for its seventy-fifth anniversary; *Mosaics* (1957; Cleveland, January 23, 1958), commissioned by the Cleveland Orchestra for its fortieth anniversary; *Summer Seascape* (1958; New Orleans, March 10, 1959), commissioned by the New Orleans Symphony, a tonal picture of a beautiful summer day on an island off the coast of Maine; *Bold Island Suite* (1959–61; Cleveland, January 25, 1962), commissioned by George Szell and the Cleveland Orchestra; and *Dies Natalis* (1967; Omaha, November 1967), a set of orchestral variations on a Lutheran Christmas chorale, written on commission for the centennial celebration of the state of Nebraska.

Some of Hanson's major works for chorus have an American identity. These include the *Three Songs from Drum Taps* for baritone, chorus, and orchestra (1935), based on Walt Whitman, featured at the Ann Arbor Festival in 1935; *The Song of Democracy*, for vocal soloists, chorus, and orchestra (1957; Philadelphia, April 9, 1957); *The Mystic Trumpeter*, for narrator, chorus, and orchestra (1969; Kansas City, Mo., April 26, 1970), based on Walt Whitman; and *New Land, New Covenant* (1976; Rochester, N.Y., May 2, 1976), an oratorio for solo voices, chorus, and orchestra to words by Isaac Watts, T. S. Eliot, John Newton, the Bible and the Declaration of Independence in which a parallel is drawn between the founding of America and the biblical origins of Israel.

American, too, is Hanson's only opera, *Merry Mount* (1933), produced on February 10, 1934, by the Metropolitan Opera, which had commissioned it. Its text, by Richard L. Stokes based on Nathaniel Hawthorne's *The Maypole of Merry Mount*, used colonial England as a setting. This is a lyrical work making extensive use of broad melodic passages, many in the traditional arioso style, with the lyrical high point coming in the third-act love duet. Some of the writing is modal, particularly when the music is called upon to identify the Puritans, and some of the most effective moments are achieved in choruses and orchestral dances.

When measured by the music of so many of his students and contemporaries, Hanson may appear conservative. But he frequently energizes his lyricism and romanticism with a discordant harmony, bitonal writing, asymmetrical rhythms and compound meters. All this brings to his writing a strong fiber which places his music solidly in 20th-century America.

Hanson retired from the Eastman School of Music in 1964, when he was made director of the newly founded Institute of American Music at the University of Rochester. A new auditorium was named after him at the Eastman School of Music, dedicated on February 19, 1976. Later the same year, in October, his eightieth birthday was celebrated in Rochester with two concerts, a highlight of which was *Nine by Nine: Variations on a Theme by Howard Hanson* in which nine faculty members of the Eastman School each wrote a variation on a theme from Hanson's *Nordic Symphony*.

In addition to his baton activities with the annual American Music Festival, and in performances of his own works elsewhere, Hanson has appeared as guest conductor of major orchestras throughout the United States and Europe. From November 1961 to February 1962 he toured Europe, the Middle East, and the Soviet Union with the Eastman School Philharmonic under the auspices of the State Department.

Hanson was the recipient of the Alice M. Ditson Award for outstanding contributions to American music in 1945; the George Foster Peabody Award in 1946 for his radio broadcasts; the Award of Merit from Northwestern University in 1951; a citation from the National Federation of Music and the Laurel Leaf Award from the American Composers Alliance, both in 1957; the Huntington Hartford Foundation Award in 1959; and the Medal of Honor from the National Arts Club in 1962. His more than twenty honorary degrees include doctorates in music from Northwestern University (1924), Syracuse University (1928), University of Nebraska (1935), Columbia University (1946), New England Conservatory (1956) and University of Michigan (1960).

In 1935, Hanson was elected to membership in the National Institute of Arts and Letters; in 1938 he was named fellow of the Royal Academy of Music in Sweden; in 1950 he was made a member of the American Philosophical Society; and in 1961 he became a fellow of the American Academy of Arts and Letters. In 1980 he was elevated to the fifty-member American Academy and Institute of Arts and Letters.

He served as president of the National Association of Schools of Music, National Music Council, and Music Teachers National Association; as a member of the examining jury of the American Academy in Rome and the United States Commission for UNESCO; on the advisory committee on the arts of the American Cultural Center in Washington, D.C., and on the advisory panel of the New York State Council of the Arts. He was also a consultant to the U.S. Department of State.

Hanson married Margaret Elizabeth Nelson, an excellent amateur musician, on July 24, 1946. He is the author of *Harmonic Materials of Modern Music* (1960).

THE COMPOSER SPEAKS: I recognize, of course, that romanticism is at the present time the poor stepchild without the social standing of her elder sister, neoclassicism. Nevertheless, I embrace her all the more fervently, believing as I do that romanticism will find in this country rich soil for a new, young and vigorous growth. . . .

I am a "natural" composer. I write music because I have to write. Though I have a profound interest in theoretical problems, my own music comes "from the heart" and is a direct expression of my own emotional reactions.

PRINCIPAL WORKS: 7 symphonies (1923–77).
Concerto, for organ, strings, harp, and orchestra (1921); String Quartet (1923); *Lux Aeterna*, tone poem with viola obbligato (1923); *North and West*, tone poem with chorus (1923); *The Lament of Beowulf*, for chorus and orchestra (1925); *Pan and the Priest*, tone poem with piano obbligato (1926); Concerto for Organ and Orchestra (1926) *Heroic Elegy*,

for chorus and orchestra, without text (1927); *Merry Mount*, opera (1933); *Three Songs from Drum Taps*, for baritone solo, chorus and orchestra (1935); *Hymn for Pioneers*, for men's voices (1938); *Fantasy Variations on a Theme of Youth*, for piano and strings (1941); *Serenade*, for flute, strings, harp, and orchestra (1945); Piano Concerto in C major (1948); *Pastorale*, for solo oboe, strings, and harp (1949); *The Cherubic Hymn*, for chorus and orchestra (1949); *Elegy in Memory of Serge Koussevitzky*, for orchestra (1955); *The Song of Democracy*, for vocal soloists, chorus, and orchestra (1957); *Mosaics*, for orchestra (1957); *Summer Seascape*, for orchestra (1958); *Bold Island Suite*, for orchestra (1959–61); *Song of Human Rights*, cantata for solo voices, chorus, and orchestra (1963); Four Psalms, for baritone solo, cello, and string sextet (1964); *Dies Natalis*, for orchestra (1967); Psalms 121 and 150, for chorus and orchestra (1968); *Streams in the Desert*, for chorus and orchestra (1969); *The Mystic Trumpeter*, for narrator, chorus, and orchestra (1969); Laude, for wind ensemble (1974); *New Land, New Covenant*, oratorio for solo voices, children's chorus, adult chorus, and orchestra (1976); *Prayer for the Middle Ages*, for a cappella chorus (1976); *Nymph and Satyr*, ballet (1978).

BIBLIOGRAPHY: Ewen, David, *Composers Since 1900* (N.Y., 1969); Goss, Madeleine, *Modern Music Makers* (N..Y., 1952); Thomson, Virgil, *American Music Since 1900* (N.Y., 1970); *ASCAP Today*, March 1971; *High Fidelity*, December 1966; *New York Times*, February 26, 1981 (obituary); *Saturday Review*, January 30, 1954; *Stereo Review*, June 1968.

Harbison, John Harris, b. Orange, N.J., December 20, 1938.

After composing a number of pieces of virtuoso chamber music in the 1960s, often based on the contrapuntal ideas he had developed as a jazz improviser, Harbison moved steadily toward choral and operatic music, often of a ritual character, and of increasingly larger dimensions, with simplicity, economy, and directness as primary values.

His father, E. Harris Harbison, professor of history at Princeton University, had studied musical composition in his younger years, composed some serious compositions and popular tunes, and played both classical and popular music on the piano. John's mother, Janet German Harbison, a writer of magazine articles, played show tunes and was adept at improvising alto parts in Christmas part-singing. John was improvising on the piano before he could read notes. When he was about five, his father simplified for him piano arrangements of the Bach chorale preludes as adapted by Busoni and also taught him the progressions of popular songs. John attended concerts early, "hoarding progressions I had heard as

precious new possessions." Other musical experiences came from recordings and the radio. At about nine he listened continually to opera performances broadcast from the Metropolitan Opera. Before long, practical experience in playing jazz and string chamber music joined concerts, records and radio as avenues to music. By the time he was thirteen, he was playing piano in jazz groups with established musicians.

Between 1952 and 1956 he attended Princeton High School. These years found him studying the violin with Chapell White, Peter Marsh, and Sandor Salzo, viola with Nicholas Harsanyi, piano and composition with Mathilde McKinney, tuba with Walter Homer, and voice with Thomas Hilbish. He was solo tubist with the Princeton High School band and, encouraged by Thomas Hilbish, conductor of the school choir, he was given opportunities to conduct as well as hear some of his compositions performed. Some encouragement came in 1954 with the winning of a Broadcast Music, Inc. (BMI), award for his Capriccio, for trumpet and piano.

He attended Harvard University from 1956 to 1960, and was awarded in 1960 the Chorus Musical Composition Prize, the Bohemian Prize, and the Knight Prize as well as the Academy of American Poets Prize and the Hatch Prize, the last two for poetry. In 1960 he received at Harvard his bachelor of arts degree. As the recipient of a Paine Traveling Fellowship from Harvard he spent 1960–61 in Berlin as a student of composition of Boris Blacher's, who, Harbison explains, "was willing to start from the beginning with me." In Berlin, Harbison sang in a choir conducted by Hans-Martin Schneidt. Upon his return to the United States, on a Naumburg Fellowship, Harbison attended Princeton University (1961–63), to study composition with Roger Sessions and Earl Kim. "Sessions," Harbison recalls, "was best at conveying an attitude. He was then preoccupied with 'the long line' of a piece. He was very good at getting across to people that they had to *do* it. 'Get it out,' he'd insist. 'Come out with it; don't beat around the bush.' Earl Kim, on the other hand, would give advice and criticism about details, and it was very helpful to have someone who would take the trouble with, for example, the structure of a particular chord. I felt fortunate to have these complementary influences. To have one without the other would have been a loss of far more than half."

Harbison was awarded the degree of master of fine arts at Princeton in 1963. That year, on August 30, he married Rose Mary Pedersen, a violinist. She was the soloist with the Bach Society Orchestra under Gregory Biss when Harbison's Sinfonia for Violin and Double Orchestra (1963) was introduced at Harvard in March 1964.

Between 1963 and 1966, and again from 1966 to 1968, Harbison held a junior fellowship from the Society of Fellows at Harvard, a nonteaching fellowship designed to give time for individual work. These were years in which he was becoming increasingly productive as a composer. *Confinement*, for twelve players (1965), was heard in New York in February 1967 performed by the Contemporary Chamber Ensemble, Arthur Weisberg conducting. *Shakespeare Series*, for mezzo-soprano and piano (1965), was introduced by Janice Harsanyi in Cambridge, Mass., in November 1965. Two cantatas for soprano and orchestra to poems by Emily Dickinson (1965, 1967) were performed at Columbia University in New York by the Group for Contemporary Music under Harvey Sollerberg, with Valarie Lamoree soloist, in February 1966 and May 1967 respectively. Music for Mixed Chorus (1966), to poems by Shelley, was heard in Cambridge in April 1971. These earlier works, of which *Confinement* was the most characteristic, deal with symmetrical, closed forms and twelve-tone structures, processes which virtually disappear in the works of the next decade.

On a grant from the Rockefeller Foundation, Harbison served as composer-in-residence at Reed College in Portland, Oreg. (1968–69). In 1969 he joined the faculty of the Massachusetts Institute of Technology in Cambridge, where he has since remained, serving as associate professor in 1972, a year in which he received there the Old Dominion Fellowship which provided for a leave-of-absence, and as full professor since 1979. Harbison combined classroom duties with those of conducting by serving as music director of the Cantata Singers from 1969 to 1973; this group gave notable performances of baroque music and particularly of Johann Sebastian Bach and Heinrich Schütz.

In 1970, on a commission from the Rockefeller Foundation, Harbison wrote for the New York Camerata the *Bermuda Triangle*, for amplified cello, tenor saxophone, and electric organ. It was premiered in New York in April 1973. A Fromm Music Foundation commission then led to the writing of *Elegiac Songs*, for mezzo-soprano and chamber orchestra (1974), to poems by Emily Dickinson. These songs were intended for Jan DeGaetani, who introduced them in New York on January 12, 1975.

Harbison's most important work up to this time came about as the result of a grant from the National Endowment for the Arts. It was his first opera, *Winter's Tale* (1974), libretto by the composer based on Shakespeare. "Opera is my favorite medium," says Harbison. "Speaking through the characters and situations cuts through reticence. I am not much interested in expression of personality, which seems lately to lead to mannerism and empty gesture. Composition can be an escape from self-absorption—an actualization of something larger and more interesting than personality." An innovation in *A Winter's Tale* is the use of six "dumbshows" with which the Shakespeare plot is carried forward through pantomime. Since Harbison felt that these dumbshows required a different kind of musical sound, he used recordings (performed by members of the Boston Music Viva) instead of live music. The opera is split into two different sequences. The first, dissonant and partly atonal, is a portrait of King Leontes, who is anguished because he feels his wife has been unfaithful and who suspects that his children are not really his. The second, more lyrical and tranquil, describes the love of Perdita (Leontes' daughter) for Florizel. "The first act," reported Richard Dyer in the *Boston Globe*, "is full of uncompleted gestures, of arias interrupted, of ensembles without climax, and that is what gives the resolution of the second act its measure and weight. Leontes' great line, 'Welcome hither, as is the spring to earth'—which Harbison sets with a sublime simplicity—gains eloquence from our memory of the earlier hysteria." Excerpts from this opera were heard first in Cambridge on October 8, 1974. The complete opera was produced five years later by the American Opera Project of the San Francisco Opera on August 20, 1979.

Diotima, for full orchestra (1976), was also a commissioned work, this one from the Koussevitzky Music Foundation. The Boston Symphony under Joseph Silverstein introduced it on March 10, 1977. It is based on a poem of the same name by Hölderlin invoking the Platonic muse to return to a chaotic world to restore order. A hymnal melody, heard at the outset over a lean and austere accompaniment, dominates the entire composition. It is frequently interrupted only to return refurbished harmonically and with embellished figuration, each reappearance receiving a continually enriched background.

The Flower-Fed Buffaloes, for baritone and chorus (1976), which the Emmanuel Choir premiered at a concert of Speculum Musicae in Boston under the composer's direction in February 1978, was inspired by *The Spirit of Liberty*, a speech by Judge Hand. Reading the speech, Harbison explains, "two binding threads emerged and gave rise to the sequence of texts I used. The first thread is the American paradox—the dualistic nature of the country, its capacity for generosity and selfishness. The second is the continuous engagement with a frontier, once a physical wilderness, recently a spiritual wilderness." With such thoughts in mind, Harbison selected for his texts poems by Vachel Lindsay, Hart Crane, Michael Fried, and Gary Snyder. In his music, Harbison intended the opening motive to represent the metaphor of travel to new places—in time, space, body or mind—with which all four poems are concerned. Throughout, Harbison draws on the American vernacular for his musical language. "It embraces," he says, "the possibility (so available to music) of making rhythmic and harmonic connections below the verbal surface."

Harbison described his thirty-five minute one-act opera, *Full Moon in March* (1977), as an "emblematic ritual opera." Based on a short symbolic verse-play by W. B. Yeats, this opera calls for merely two characters (soprano and tenor), a chorus of just two singers and an "orchestra" of eight instruments, including a "prepared" piano. Harbison wrote this music, as he reveals, "in a nonreflective state, well before any effort had been made to understand the matter, beyond the absorption of the images." In the *New Yorker*, Andrew Porter commented: "The music sounds as if it had been written without preconceptions, under the inspiration of the play, directly and fluently, and had then been carefully refined in its work. *Full Moon in March* is an opera that holds the ear and stirs the mind. It moves surely and it sounds beautiful." The harmonic writing is Western, but the sonorities from the prepared piano, the incantational rhythmic patterns, and the high-pitched vocalism contributed an Eastern identity. The opera ends suddenly, like an awakening from a troubled dream.

On May 12, 1980, Harbison's Piano Concerto—which subsequently received the Kennedy Center-Friedheim Award—was premiered by the American Composers Orchestra in New York, Gunther Schuller conducting, and with Robert Miller, soloist. "His score," reported Donal Henahan in the *New York Times*, "is a brave effort to break free of contemporary cliches, an engrossing piece filled with strange yearnings for the past while anchoring itself solidly in the atonal present."

In the early Spring 1981, Harbison was composer-in-residence at the American Academy of Rome. Later that year, as composer-in-residence at the Santa Fe Chamber Music Festival in New Mexico, he received, in August, the premieres of two works. One was a twenty-song cycle, *Mottetti di Montale* (1981), for mezzo-soprano and piano, a setting of Eugenio Montale's sombre *Le Occasioni*. Quotations from the music of other composers—the "Bell Song" from *Lakmé*, a rigaudon by Ravel, Schoenberg's *Pierrot lunaire*, as well as such extramusical effects as the tick-tock of a watch—intrude to make the textual content more vivid. Harbison's second work introduced in Santa Fe was the Piano Quintet (1981) which the Chamber Music Festival had commissioned.

In 1971, Harbison received the Creative Arts Award from Brandeis University in Waltham, Mass.; in 1973 he was given an award from the American Academy of Arts and Letters; and in 1977–78 he was the recipient of a Guggenheim Fellowship.

THE COMPOSER SPEAKS: In composing I try to make room for the unavoidable and the involuntary. I am happiest when the piece takes its own way, insists on its own shape. But there are always times when the will has to take over.

Often I attack a project head-on only to find that another piece is growing in the margins, better and less calculated. This association between illicitness and artistic impulse is probably due to a background filled with inarticulate religious imperatives.

I try to hold on to the forces which carried me into music, the fascination of harmonic progressions, the directness of melody, the magic of sonorities. Since there is so much drudgery involved, copying and proofing and organizing, it is essential to keep the first instincts alive.

The invention of fresh large designs seems the best hold on the future. No amount of up-to-date detail will make a piece unless the formal impulse is generating and ordering everything.

PRINCIPAL WORKS: Sinfonia for Violin and Double Orchestra (1963); *Autumnal*, for mezzo-soprano and piano (1964); *Confinement*, for twelve players (1965); *Shakespeare Series*, for mezzo-soprano and piano (1965); Cantata I, for soprano and orchestra (1965); Music for Mixed Chorus (1966); Cantata II, for soprano and orchestra (1967); Serenade, for six players (1969); Cantata III, for soprano and string quartet (1968); Piano Trio (1969); *Die Kürze*, for piano and four players (1970); *Bermuda Triangle*, for amplified cello, tenor saxophone, and electric organ (1970); *Five Songs of Experience*, for chorus, string quartet, and percussion (1971); Incidental Music for *The Merchant of Venice*, for string orchestra (1971); *Elegiac Songs*, for mezzo-soprano and chamber orchestra (1974); *The Winter's Tale*, opera (1974); *Three Harp Songs*, for tenor and harp (1975); *Book of Hours and Seasons*, for mezzo-soprano or tenor and flute, cello, and piano (1975); *Diotima*, for large orchestra (1976); *The Flower-Fed Buffaloes*, for baritone and chorus (1976); *Descant Nocturne*, on a lullaby by Seymour Shifrin, for orchestra (1976); *Full Moon in March*, one-act opera (1977); *Samuel Chapter*, for high voice, flute, clarinet, viola, cello, piano, and percussion (1978); Quintet, for flute, oboe, clarinet, horn and bassoon (1978); Piano Concerto (1979); Piano Quintet (1981); *Mottetti di Montale*, for mezzo-soprano and piano (1981).

BIBLIOGRAPHY: *DCM*; *Boston Phoenix*, October 23, 1979; *New Yorker*, May 28, 1979; *Who's Who in America, 1980–81*; *New York Times*, August 16, 1981.

Harris, Donald, b. St. Paul, Minn., April 7, 1931.

Though he is not a strict serialist, his musical idiom has been influenced by the Viennese school, also by France and French music. The poetic but measured French approach to culture is more akin to his nature than extreme expressionism.

His father had come from Russia and became the head of a manufacturing firm in St. Paul; his mother was an accomplished violinist. When Donald was five he began to study the piano with Alice Rosenfield Ruskin. He was about twelve when he gave up the piano to begin learning the saxophone, a hand-me-down instrument he had acquired from his brother. Once he had mastered the elements of saxo-

phone playing he devoted himself to jazz performances in various bands, one of which he led. In his
senior year at St. Paul's Academy, a high school, the
ambition to write jazz arrangements sent him to
study harmony and composition with Paul Wilkinson. Wilkinson changed Harris's focus away from
jazz back to concert music and aroused his interest in
Stravinsky. Though Harris did produce at this time
an arrangement for jazz ensembles, he also completed a work for a string quartet, some piano pieces,
and a composition for male glee club and brass ensemble. On the strength of these, he gained admission
to the University of Michigan in 1948, where he
studied theory and composition with Homer Keller,
Ross Lee Finney, and again with Paul Wilkinson,
the latter two becoming the decisive influences in his
musical growth. In 1952, Harris received his bachelor of music degree in composition, following it in
1954 with his master of music degree, also in composition. During this period (the summers from 1953 to
1955), he attended the Berkshire Music Center at
Tanglewood, Mass., where his teachers in composition were Boris Blacher and Lukas Foss.

As his thesis for his master's degree, Harris presented music for a ballet, *The Legend of John Henry*
(1954), scenario freely adapted from the folk legend.
It was first produced at Ann Arbor, Mich., on May
8, 1954. The following July it was performed by the
Louisville Orchestra in Kentucky, when it won the
Louisville Award, and was performed by the Cincinnati Symphony under Thor Johnson. It had originally been scored for chamber orchestra and piano, and
Harris adapted it for full orchestra in 1979 for the
Greater Hartford Young Orchestra, which introduced it that year.

A Fulbright Fellowship in 1956 enabled Harris to
go to France for further study of composition with
Max Deutsch and Nadia Boulanger in Paris and
André Jolivet in Aix-en-Provence. His studies with
Max Deutsch were of special consequence. "With
him," Harris recalls, "I studied Mahler and Wagner
in addition to Schoenberg, Alban Berg, and Webern.
I did not learn a lot of twelve-tone theory from
Deutsch. I learned that from others. I did get to know
the late 19th century, however, and this was perhaps
more decisive for my musical formation than were
formal studies in twelve-tone and serial techniques."
The first composition Harris completed in Paris was
the Piano Sonata (1956), introduced in Paris on
June 11, 1961 by Geneviève Joy and represented at
the second Biennale de Paris that same year. Here,
the emerging characteristics of Harris's adult style
began to take form and substance; a penchant for
brevity and a reaction against too much repetition:
the beginnings in the use of angular melodic lines
and densely constructed harmonies which were to become increasingly frequent in later works; a developing interest in rhythmic and metric variation as well
as some exploitation of extreme registral contrast.
Though classic in structure and basically tonal, this

sonata revealed at the same time the influence of the
twelve-tone technique in that a row, repeated again
and again melodically and most often from different
starting points within the same transposition, was
used, though hardly in strict Schonbergian terms.
Another aspect of this piano sonata which would recur in Harris's subsequent music was its French
orientation, such as the use of a waltz in the last
movement similar to the style of French waltzes written in homage to Ravel, and the lighthearted, whimsical mood of the Scherzo movement reminiscent of
the music of the "French Six," and particularly of
Milhaud and Poulenc. When Pierre Boulez saw the
manuscript of this sonata he commented: "It recalls
the past too much." But, Harris says in his own defense, "what Boulez saw as a fault, I perceived and
continue to perceive as perhaps its chief virtue,
namely its deliberate attempt to provide a link with
the tradition from which it sprang." This sonata was
Harris's last tonal composition, a transition between
his earlier music and that of his mature years.

Progressing further toward a fully crystallized and
mature style were two works in which a rich, expressive polyphonic idiom is developed: Fantasy, for violin and piano, or violin and orchestra (1957), first
heard at a concert of the Société Nationale de Musique in Paris on April 11, 1962, performed by Maurice Crut, and String Quartet (1965), commissioned
for the Festival of Contemporary Music at Tanglewood, where its premiere took place on August 18,
1965. Rhythmic and metric virtuosity, but without
sacrificing lyric values, can be found in the Symphony in Two Movements (1961), awarded the Prix du
Concours Prince Rainier de Monaco in 1962, first
performed on October 7, 1964, over the Strasbourg
radio by the Strasbourg Radio Orchestra conducted
by Charles Bruck and a feature of the Semaines musicales internationales de Paris on October 25,
1966.

The last work of this period in Harris's creativity
is *Ludus* I, for ten instruments (1966), in which he
arrived at an ever greater musical freedom and expressivity. "*Ludus*," the composer has explained, "is
the term derived from the Latin which refers to play
or games. It is thus intended to relate directly to the
players for whom it was written, and to how performers view their interpretative styles. . . . There
is no doubling in *Ludus*, as occurs so frequently in
music of today where a player is often called upon to
play several instruments during the course of the
same piece. I have attempted . . . to exploit as
much as possible the different ranges of instrumental
color and timbre which have been recently discovered, so as to give the illusion of as much variety as if
there were a good deal of doubling. *Ludus*, in my
own mind, therefore ought to suggest a virtuosity in
instrumental writing, an idea that today seems almost more related to timbral velocity and difficulty.
A . . . final set of rules . . . result[s] in the constantly changing rhythmic and melodic patterns."

The world premiere of *Ludus* I was given by the St. Paul Chamber Orchestra in Minnesota in 1966. When it was heard in Boston on May 29, 1973, David Noble wrote in the *Boston Herald American*: "The 'games' of the title . . . seem to come out when intense nervous textures hanging motionless as they do in Schoenberg or Webern are broken up by slashing, angular outbursts of sound made by instruments suddenly designated by the composer to act as gadflies. The writing, at these moments, is quirky, amusing but somehow hysterical."

During his prolonged stay in Paris, Harris was active in many of its musical activities. He served as a member of the music committee of the Royaumont Foundation; founded the International Music Competition Prize presided over by a jury from Eastern and Western Europe as well as the United States; for four successive years served as the United States delegate to the International Rostrum of Composers at UNESCO, where he arranged public concerts and radio performances of new music; was music consultant for the American Cultural Center of the USIS; and served on the international jury of the Biennale of Paris. In Paris, on June 23, 1959, he married Nadine Claire Oppert; they were separated in 1978 after raising two sons. In 1965, Harris received a Guggenheim Fellowship.

After an absence of more than a decade, Harris was back in the United States in 1967. Between 1967 and 1977 he was a member of the departments of composition and musical literature at the New England Conservatory—assistant to the president for academic affairs between 1969 and 1971, vice-president for administrative affairs from 1971 to 1974 and executive vice-president between 1974 and 1977. Since 1977 he has been composer-in-residence and professor at the Hartt College of Music of the University of Hartford in Connecticut, serving as chairman of the department of composition and theory and member of the department of history and literature of music. In 1968 he was made director of the New England Conservatory Institute at Tanglewood devoted exclusively to jazz and non-Western music. From 1974 to 1976 he served on the committee on independent schools of the National Association of Schools of Music; in 1974 he was appointed to the visiting committee in humanities of the Massachusetts Institute of Technology, reappointed for a three-year term in 1977; and in 1975 he became coordinator of the conference of the American Society of University Composers. In 1978 he was given a three-year appointment to the trustees visiting committee for the humanities of the Suffolk University College of Liberal Arts in Boston.

Ludus II (1973), world premiere in Boston by Musica Viva (which had commissioned it) on May 8, 1973, is scored for violin, cello, flute, clarinet, and piano. Germane to the entire composition is a chorale which comes in the middle, inspired by the death of someone close to the composer. The sorrowful mood projected by this chorale is sustained for the rest of the work, which ends with isolated melodic lines and notes in unusual timbres that come close to expressing bitterness. Since its premiere, *Ludis* II has been performed in England, Portugal, Quebec, and Germany and was presented by Pierre Boulez at the Prospective Encounter concert in New York on January 17, 1975.

On Variations, for chamber orchestra (1976), was commissioned by the Musical Arts Association of Cleveland for the Cleveland Orchestra to commemorate the American bicentennial; its first performance took place on October 13, 1976. Conscious of both the American celebration and the fact that he was writing for a chamber rather than full orchestra, Harris decided to exploit the jazz idiom, with extended use of alto and tenor saxophones and instruments such as the vibraphone, marimba, and xylophone, which helped evoke sounds and moods associated with jazz. "The entire composition," the composer says, "is intended to evoke a festive and 'airy' mood, one not devoid of lyricism, in which an atmosphere of spirited movement alternates with passages of a more intense and oppressive nature." The work is a virtuoso piece for the conductor with constant variation and rhythmic strettos.

A commission from the Elizabeth Sprague Coolidge Foundation led to the writing of *For the Night to Wear*, for mezzo-soprano and an instrumental ensemble (1978), first heard on February 3, 1978, performed by Beverly Morgan and the Boston Musica Viva at the Library of Congress in Washington, D.C. The text is a two-stanza poem by Hortense Flexner, and the music is correspondingly in two parts, the first slow, the second fast. The work was repeated at a concert of the International Society for Contemporary Music in New York on April 5, 1979.

In honor of the centennial of the birth of the poet Wallace Stevens, Harris composed *Of Hartford in a Purple Light*, for soprano and piano (1979), commissioned by the Connecticut Public Radio and utilizing a text by Stevens. It was first heard over the stations of the Eastern Public Radio Network on October 2, 1979, performed by Susan Davenny Wyner, during a one-and-one-half-hour documentary on Stevens for which Harris also wrote the incidental music.

Harris received grants-in-aid from the Rockefeller Foundation in 1969 and the Chapelbrook Foundation in 1970 to prepare an edition of the correspondence between Schoenberg and Alban Berg. The National Endowment for the Arts presented him with a grant in composition in 1974. Commissions from the Koussevitzky Music Foundation and the Goethe Institute came in 1977 and 1978 respectively, the latter for the writing of *Balladen*, for piano. On March 6, 1974, a concert devoted exclusively to Harris's music took place in Paris. On an invitation from the National Council of Culture and Art, the Faculty of the Arts at the University of Tel Aviv, the Israel Composers League and the Israel Festival, Harris spent three weeks in Israel in July 1977.

THE COMPOSER SPEAKS: My music is sensual, at least in conception. Its forms are today principally *sui generis*; its harmonic content is rich and dense consciously; the same is true of its polyphonic content. I believe in the emotional content of my music, and this content is what I intend to communicate to the listener, the structural content being secondary.

PRINCIPAL WORKS: Piano Sonata (1956); Fantasy, for violin and piano, also violin and orchestra (1957); Symphony in Two Movements (1961); String Quartet (1965); *Ludus* I, for ten instruments (1966); *Ludus* II, for flute, clarinet, violin, cello, and piano (1973); *On Variations*, for chamber orchestra (1976); *For the Night to Wear*, for mezzo-soprano and instrumental ensemble (1978); *Charmes*, for soprano and orchestra (1978); *Balladen*, for piano (1979); *Of Hartford in a Purple Light*, for voice and piano (1979).

BIBLIOGRAPHY: *BBDM: Who's Who in America, 1980–81.*

Harris, Roy Ellsworth (originally **Harris, Leroy Ellsworth**), b. Chandler, Lincoln County, Okla. February 12, 1898; d. Santa Monica, Calif., October 1, 1979.

Though Harris was basically not a nationalist composer and though much of his music is abstract, he and his compositions are American homespun products. His style—tonal, diatonic, occasionally modal and polyphonic, with a partiality for classic and sometimes even baroque structures—is thoroughly American in its breadth, dynamic sweep, rugged power. This is the reason why he has long come to be identified as the "Walt Whitman of music," above and beyond the fact that Whitman and his poetry were the inspiration and source of some of his compositions.

Harris's parents were of Irish and Scottish descent. His father had participated in the last frontier land rush, staking a claim in Nebraska, cutting down the trees, and building a log cabin where Roy Harris was born on Lincoln's birthday in Lincoln County. "Father," Harris once recalled, "loved music, especially the guitar playing and folk singing of his wife." When Roy was five, his family had to leave Nebraska for California because of his mother's delicate health. They settled on a farm in Covina in the San Gabriel Valley. There Roy attended the public schools, distinguishing himself in sports and for his exceptional interest in literature and music. He received some preliminary instruction on the piano from his mother before being turned over to local teachers for lessons in piano and clarinet. This contact with music was supplemented with listening to

recordings on an old Edison phonograph. "Each new record," Harris said, "was an event in our family. We played them nearly every evening—even in the later summer evening after a long day's work."

While still in school, Harris made some appearances in public both as pianist and as clarinetist. During his high school years he belonged to what he described as a "semisecret group of nonconformists" which included a painter-poet, two chemists, a pianist, and a Scotchman who played the organ. "We discussed philosophy, drama, and literature. We went on long hikes together, played chess, and listened to records, went to opera and symphony concerts in the nearby city of Los Angeles." As Harris finished high school his own "secret world" consisted, as he has said, of "music, philosophy, poetry, the wonder of clouds, mountain bird songs, and sunsets."

When he left high school, Harris worked on his own farm for two years, coupling work with the study of Greek philosophy. He then rented out his farm and earned his living by driving a truck. At night, he studied organ and theory by himself. With the money he saved, he was able to enroll in the Los Angeles Normal School, where he received further instruction in theory. When America declared war on Germany during World War I, Harris, now nineteen, enlisted in the Student Army Training Corps at the University of Southern California in Berkeley. After the war he continued to support himself as a truck driver, at the same time attending the University of California at Berkeley as a special student in philosophy and economics (1919–20). He broadened his musical horizon with the study of organ with Charles Demarest and piano with Fannie Charles Dillon. He was now beginning for the first time to think of becoming a composer. Fired by this ambition and "in the fullness of my ignorance," he completed a large work for chorus and orchestra, which his philosophy teacher at the university brought to the attention of Alfred Hertz, conductor of the San Francisco Symphony. "He [Hertz] inspired me to believe that I might become a composer and suggested that I leave anything faintly resembling a university as quickly as possible." Harris followed this suggestion and for two years studied composition privately with Arthur Farwell in Los Angeles. "I was convinced," Farwell later wrote, "that he would one day challenge the world."

Under Farwell's guidance, and with Farwell's encouragement, Harris made his first steps as a composer: Andante, for strings (1925), and *Impressions of a Rainy Day*, for string quartet (1926). The string quartet was performed in Los Angeles on March 15, 1926. Andante was introduced in Rochester, N.Y., with Howard Hanson conducting, on April 23, 1926, and then won first prize in a contest sponsored by the New York Philharmonic at the Stadium Concerts, where it was performed during the summer of 1926. Borrowing a hundred dollars, and giving up his job as truck driver, Harris came East to hear his Andante performed, intending to return to California two weeks later. He stayed away some four years.

From New York, Harris went on to Paris on the advice of Aaron Copland, who encouraged him to study with Nadia Boulanger, with funds provided by a benefactor. "I rejected Boulanger's formal teaching of counterpoint, harmony and solfeggio," Harris has said. "I was all for immediate action. I was like the rookie who came to France to win the war." He studied by himself all the string quartets of Beethoven, the last ones of which became something of a revelation to him. He also came to know the contrapuntal music of the pre-Bach and Bach eras, which later would have a significant impact on his writing.

His first major work completed in Paris was Concerto for String Quartet, Piano, and Clarinet (1927), successfully introduced at a concert of the Société nationale de musique in Paris on May 8, 1927, by the Roth Quartet with Nadia Boulanger at the piano and Monsieur Cahuzac at the clarinet. One French critic praised its "warmth, life, a rhythm, an accent which denotes a nature of the first order." This concerto was first heard in the United States over a national radio network in 1933, and soon after that was both published and recorded. On the strength of the talent revealed in this work Harris was awarded a Guggenheim Fellowship in 1927, which was renewed one year after that. Another composition in 1927 was the *Whitman Triptyque,* for women's voices and piano, which has significance only in that it was the first of a number of compositions yet to be written which reached to Walt Whitman for text and inspiration.

Upon the termination of his second Guggenheim Fellowship, Harris suffered a serious accident which was to prove providential in his creative growth. He fell down a flight of stairs, broke his spine, and became an invalid. For five months he was in a plaster cast, then, after partial recovery, had to return to New York for a dangerous operation which proved successful. Bedridden in the hospital, he continued composing, but this time without the aid of a piano. Freed from the keyboard, he no longer thought exclusively in terms of harmony but allowed his musical imagination to move with greater freedom in his melodic and rhythmic invention, to think in terms of instruments other than the piano, and to indulge his fascination for polyphony. Out of this long period of recuperation came Harris's contrapuntal style—and his use of such baroque forms as the passacaglia, fugue, toccata, and chorale—with which he arrived at an individuality which placed him in the vanguard of American composers.

Relieved of financial pressures through the Creative Fellowship of the Pasadena Music and Arts Association in 1930–31, Harris completed String Quartet no. 1 (1930) and Toccata, for orchestra (1931), following them with the *Chorale,* for strings (1932; Los Angeles, February 23, 1933), String Sextet (1932), and his first symphony, *Symphony: 1933.*

The last of these had been commissioned by Koussevitzky, who introduced it with the Boston Symphony on January 26, 1934. This work, which Koussevitzky described as "the first truly tragic symphony by an American," became the first American symphony ever to be recorded commercially.

Already in these early works, Harris was arriving at an indigenously American style through his broad and sweeping melodic lines, which often owed their derivations to rural American folk music and Anglo-Saxon hymns, vigorous use of asymmetrical rhythms and unusual accentations, dissonant chordal combinations, and overall energy and drive. Harris's Americanism is what impressed Aaron Copland when he wrote: "It is American in rhythm, especially in the fast parts, with a jerky, nervous quality that is peculiarly our own. It is crude and unabashed at times, with occasional blobs and yawps of sound that Whitman would have approved of." Harris's Americanism became obvious in two early works based on Walt Whitman in which he matched musically the metric and rhythmic power of Whitman's free verse: *A Song for Occupations* (1934) and the *Symphony for Voices* (1936), both for a cappella chorus. Harris's Americanism was also pronounced in the orchestral overture commissioned by RCA Victor (the first time an American recording company commissioned a musical work), the orchestral overture, *When Johnny Comes Marching Home* (1934; Minneapolis, January 13, 1935). This was a symphonic treatment of the popular Civil War song reputedly by Patrick S. Gilmore that was revived so successfully during the Spanish American War.

Harris assumed the first of many later teaching posts at the Juilliard School of Music, where, from 1932 to 1940, he taught composition during the summer. From 1934 to 1938 he was director of festivals and the composition department at the Westminster Choir School in Princeton, N.J. On October 10, 1936, he married Beula Duffy, a concert pianist, who then assumed the professional name of Johana Harris. They raised five children, three of whom formed a rock group for some recordings.

By 1940, Harris's fame as a composer had soared. He was now overwhelmed with commissions and was one of the most widely performed American composers of his day, and one of the most highly esteemed. A nationwide poll among radio listeners of the New York Philharmonic in 1935 gave Harris first place among American composers, a distinction repeated two years later in a poll taken by *Scribner's* magazine. He justified such accolades and distinctions with the writing of three important works, the first two completed in 1937 and generally numbered among the best chamber music works written by an American up to that time: String Quartet no. 3 and Piano Quintet. The other work is one of the most successful and often performed of any Harris composition, whose permanent place in the American symphonic reportoire seems assured: Symphony no 3

(1938). The String Quartet, modal in harmonic and melodic idiom, consists of four preludes and fugues that have a medieval character and which reveal an uncommon gift at contrapuntal writing. It was introduced by the Roth Quartet in Washington, D.C., on September 11, 1939; that same year the Roth Quartet selected it as the only American contemporary work to be featured at the International Congress of Musicologists in New York. Also modal and contrapuntal is the Piano Quintet, which begins with a passacaglia, continues with a cadenza and ends with a fugue; it was introduced in New York City on February 12, 1937.

The consensus is that Harris's Symphony no. 3 is one of the best works of its kind by an American. As one critic wrote in *Modern Music* when the symphony was first heard: "For significance of material, breadth of treatment, and depth of meaning; for tragic implication, dramatic intensity and concentration; for moving beauty, glowing sound, it can find no peer in the musical art of America." Many years later (1980), William Schuman could say of it: "For me the sounds were like no others I had ever heard—his wholly 'autogenetic' concept of form, the free and strong orchestration, the extraordinary beauty and sweep of the melodic material. . . . His was a new voice, and between that time and now that voice, as it matured, underwent enormous change and growth, yet all discernibly evolving from the youthful kernel." In a single movement, this symphony is in five sections, each of which is identified either emotionally or structurally as "Tragic," "Lyric," "Pastoral," "Fugue," and "Dramatic-Tragic." Serge Koussevitzky, who called it "the greatest orchestral work yet written by an American," introduced it with the Boston Symphony on February 24, 1939. After that it was performed by virtually every major American orchestra and by many in Europe; this was the first American symphony Toscanini conducted, in a performance with the NBC Symphony. During the early years of World War II, a London writer suggested that recordings of one hundred works of music be preserved as a heritage for future generations, and the only American work on the list was this Harris symphony. Leonard Bernstein conducted it with the New York Philharmonic when he toured the United States and Europe in 1976 in all-American programs commemorating the American bicentennial. And, still in 1976, this symphony became the first work by an American to be heard in China when that country was toured by the Philadelphia Orchestra under Eugene Ormandy.

Symphony no. 4 (1939) was subtitled *Folk-Song Symphony*. Here Harris gave voice to his Americanism by using American folk-song and popular-song materials: western fiddle tunes; the cowboy song "Oh, Bury Me Not on the Lone Prairie"; such popular ditties as "When Johnny Comes Marching Home," "Jump Up, My Lady," and "The Blackbird

and the Crow." Parts of this symphony were first heard in Rochester, N.Y., on April 25, 1940, conducted by Howard Hanson. The entire symphony was given in Cleveland on December 26, 1940, under Rudolf Ringwall; and a revised version was performed by the New York Philharmonic under Dimitri Mitropoulos on December 31, 1942. After the Cleveland performance the symphony was awarded a prize of $500 from the National Federation of Music Clubs as the year's best symphonic work. It also received first honors from the Committee for the Appreciation of American Music.

Symphony no. 6 (1944) was also rooted in the American soil, a programmatic work inspired by and giving a tonal representation to the Gettysburg Address. Commissioned by the National Broadcasting Company, it received its world premiere on April 14, 1944, performed by the Boston Symphony under Koussevitzky.

Between 1940 and 1942 Harris was composer-in-residence at Cornell University on a Carnegie Creative Grant. In 1945, during World War II, he served as the musical head of the overseas branch of the Office of War Information. The long shadow of the war hovered over some of the compositions Harris completed in the early 1940s: *American Creed*, for chorus and orchestra (1940; Chicago, October 30, 1940); the score to the ballet *What So Proudly We Hail* (1942); and Symphony no. 5 (1942). The last of these, consisting of a prelude, chorale, and fugue, was inspired by the Soviet resistance to the Nazi invasion. Its premiere was given by the Boston Symphony under Koussevitzky on February 26, 1943, a performance transmitted by short wave to the Soviet Union. During the remaining war years it was beamed eleven times by short wave to American armed forces throughout the world. Harris conducted a performance of this symphony over the Moscow radio during a visit to the Soviet Union on October 15, 1958, becoming the first American to conduct his own music in that country.

There was little change in Harris's style in his later works. His writing remained sometimes modal and contrapuntal, sometimes dissonant, always tonal and diatonic, and usually alive with American identity. If he occasionally ventured into a new field—such as the twelve-tone technique in Symphony no. 7 (1951; Chicago, November 20, 1952—revised in 1955; Copenhagen, September 15, 1955), recipient of the Naumburg Prize—he soon deserted it for those areas in which he was most at ease and most himself. His output was prolific in all media except the opera, and particularly in symphonies. A commission from the San Francisco Symphony for its fiftieth anniversary led to the writing of the Symphony no. 8, *San Francisco Symphony* (1961) in which five dominant periods in the life of St. Francis were described since St. Francis is the patron saint of the city of San Francisco; the San Francisco Symphony premiered it on

January 17, 1962. Symphony no. 9—*1963* (1962) was commissioned by the Philadelphia Orchestra, which introduced it under Eugene Ormandy on January 18, 1963. The preamble to the American Constitution provided the stimulus for its writing, with three thematic subjects becoming the musical counterpart to three inscriptions by Walt Whitman which served as the symphony's principle mottos: "Of Life, Immense in Passion, Pulse and Power," "Cheerful for Freest Action Formed," and "The Modern Man I Sing." Symphony no. 10, *Abraham Lincoln Symphony*, for women's chorus, men's chorus, mixed chorus, brass choir, two amplified pianos, and percussion (1965; Los Angeles, April 14, 1965), was written to commemorate the centenary of Lincoln's assassination. This five-movement work, influenced by Carl Sandburg's biography of Lincoln, recreates two moods from Lincoln's youth together with three other moods expressing Lincoln's profound concern for the destiny of American democracy. Harris himself provided the text for the first, second, and fifth movements, while that of the third comes from Lincoln's writings and speeches, and that of the fourth makes use of the Gettysburg Address. Symphony no. 11 (1967) was commissioned by the New York Philharmonic for its 125th anniversary, the first performance given by that orchestra under Leonard Bernstein on February 8, 1968. A two-part symphony, it drew its programmatic content from the subjects of war and peace. "My theme," Harris explained, "is the conflict facing the entire world. We are about to decide whether or not civilization can save itself, whether problems can be solved through silence." Harris described his music as "highly dramatic, almost operatic. It begins in a mood of nervous agitation, dips downward, and ends in an expansive affirmation and optimism." Symphony no. 12 (1968; Milwaukee, February 24, 1968) was written at the request of Father Marquette Tercentenary Commission to commemorate the 300th anniversary of the voyages of Father Jacques Marquette in North America, the first white man to see the confluence of the Mississippi and the Wisconsin Rivers. Symphony no. 14, for speaker, chorus, and orchestra, came in 1974 to honor the American bicentennial and was premiered by Antal Dorati and the National Symphony Orchestra in Washington, D.C. (which had commissioned it), on February 10, 1976.

Other significant work outside the sphere of the symphony included: *Kentucky Spring*, for orchestra (1949), which the Louisville Orchestra commissioned and introduced on April 5, 1949, a tone poem paying tribute both to Kentucky and the springtime with Stephen Foster's "My Old Kentucky Home" briefly quoted; the Piano Concerto no. 2 (1952; Louisville, December 9, 1953); a chamber cantata, *Abraham Lincoln Walks at Midnight* (1953), text by Vachel Lindsay; a cantata, *Canticle to the Sun*, for coloratura soprano and chamber orchestra based on

St. Francis (1961; Washington, D.C., September 21, 1961); *Epilogue to Profiles in Courage: J. F. K.* (1963; Los Angeles, May 10, 1964), written in memory of President Kennedy following his assassination; Piano Sextet (1968); and the Concerto, for amplified piano, brass, and percussion (1968).

Through the years Harris was affiliated with numerous educational institutions as professor of composition: Colorado College in Colorado Springs (1943–48) on an El Pomar Creative Grant; Peabody College for Teachers at Nashville, Tenn. (1949–51), and Sewanee, Tenn. (1951); Pennsylvania College for Women (1951–56) on a five-year grant from the Mellon Educational Trust; University of Southern Illinois in Carbondale (1956–57); Indiana University in Bloomington (1957–60); Inter-American University in Puerto Rico (1960–61); University of California in Los Angeles (1961–73). He was composer-in-residence at Utah State College in Salt Lake City (1948–49) and at California State University in Los Angeles (1973–76).

From 1946 to 1950 Harris was the national director of the National Composers Alliance. In 1952 he served as executive director of the Pittsburgh International Contemporary Music Festival and from 1958 to 1961 he was director of the International String Congress, which he had founded.

The list of honors conferred on him included: certificate of honor from the National Association for American Composers and Conductors (1940); the Elizabeth Sprague Coolidge Medal for "eminent service to chamber music" (1942); membership to the National Institute of Arts and Letters (1942); the decoration of the Military Order of S. Saviour and S. Bridget by Sweden (1965); Letter of Distinction Award from the American Music Council (1973); and appointment as composer laureate of the state of California and the city of Covina in California (1975). He was given honorary doctorates in music by Rutgers University (1941) and the University of Rochester (1946). In 1975–76 he was awarded his third Guggenheim Fellowship. On his eightieth birthday, in 1978, the town of Chandler, Okla., where he was born, dedicated a commemorative sign to him and presented an all-Harris concert; performances of Harris's music were heard in many American cities on that occasion.

A Roy Harris Archive was founded in the library of the California State University in Los Angeles in 1973 as a storehouse of his recordings, manuscripts, letters, various memorabilia, and sketches.

THE COMPOSER SPEAKS: I have become increasingly convinced that music is a fluid architecture of sound and all the elements of music—melody, harmony, counterpoint, dynamics, orchestration—must be coordinated into a swift-moving form that fulfills itself from the root idea to its complete flowering in organic ornamentation. . . . Nature surrounds us constantly with the most beautiful examples of craftsmanship. We ourselves could not live and enjoy life if we did not embody that wonderful coordination of craftsmanship which makes us a functioning organism.

I believe that music has been steadily running downhill since Beethoven, because orchestral color has been exploited at the expense of all the other elements of music. This sort of romantic attitude has governed man for more than two hundred years and has brought us to a sorry pass. We have constantly exploited personal ambition at the expense of the body politic. So the romanticists have done in music. It really is an attitude of supreme egoism wherein the individual assumes a *summum bonum* of all widsom and beneficence in his own self. One generation is not long enough for man to become wise; and so we have suffered greatly in losing the wisdom of tradition. And so the romantic composer who thinks he can in one lifetime offset the sum total of all the highest and best that all other composers in all times and periods preceding him have sifted out through experience is condemned to produce an unbalanced and immature expression.

PRINCIPAL WORKS: 15 symphonies, one for band (1933–78); 3 string quartets (1930, 1933, 1937).

Concerto for Clarinet, Piano, and String Quartet (1927); Piano Sonata (1928); Toccata, for orchestra (1931); *Chorale*, for strings (1932); Fantasy, for piano, flute, oboe, clarinet, bassoon, and horn (1932); *When Johnny Comes Marching Home*, overture for orchestra (1934); *A Song for Occupations*, for a cappella chorus (1934); Piano Trio (1934); *Farewell to Pioneers*, symphonic elegy (1935); Prelude and Fugue, for string orchestra (1936); *Symphony for Voices*, for a cappella chorus (1936); Piano Quintet (1936); *Soliloquy and Dance*, for viola and piano (1938); *Variations on an Irish Theme*, for piano (1938); String Quintet (1939); *Challenge*, for baritone, chorus and orchestra (1940); *Western Landscape*, ballet (1940); *American Creed*, for chorus and orchestra (1940); *Evening Piece*, for orchestra (1941); *From This Earth*, ballet (1941); *Ode to Truth*, for orchestra (1941); *What So Proudly We Hail*, ballet (1942); *American Ballads*, for piano (1942); Violin Sonata (1942); Cantata, for chorus, organ, and brass (1943); Piano Concerto (1945); Accordion Concerto (1946); Concerto for Two Pianos and Orchestra (1946); Mass, for men's voices and organ (1947); *Quest*, for orchestra (1947); *Elegy and Paean*, for viola and orchestra (1948); *Kentucky Spring*, for orchestra (1949); *Cumberland Concerto*, for orchestra (1951); *Abraham Lincoln Walks at Midnight*, chamber cantata (1953); Fantasy, for piano and orchestra (1954); *Folk Fantasy for Festivals*, for piano and chorus (1956); *Canticle to the Sun*, cantata for coloratura soprano and chamber orchestra (1961); *Epilogue to Profiles in Courage: J. F. K.*, for orchestra (1963); *Salute to Youth*, for orchestra

(1963); *Jubilation*, for chorus, brass, and piano (1964); Duo, for cello and piano (1964); *Horn of Plenty*, for orchestra (1964); Piano Sextet (1968); Concerto, for amplified piano, brass, and percussion (1968); *Peace and Good Will to All*, cantata for chorus, brasses, organ, and percussion (1970); *Folk Song Suite*, for harp, winds, and percussion (1973); *Life*, cantata for soprano, winds, and percussion (1973); *Rejoice and Sing*, cantata for soprano or bass, string quartet, and piano (1976).

BIBLIOGRAPHY: Copland, Aaron, *The New Music: 1900–1960* (N.Y., 1968); Ewen, David (ed), *The New Book of Modern Composers* (N.Y., 1967); Mellers, Wilfrid, *Music in a New Found Land* (N.Y., 1964); Strassburg, Robert, *Roy Harris: A Catalogue of his Works* (Los Angeles, 1974); BMI, *The Many Worlds of Music*, Winter 1976; *High Fidelity/Musical America*, June 1978, August 1980; *Musical Quarterly*, January 1947; *New York Times*, February 4, 1968, October 4, 1979 (obituary); *Stereo Review*, December 1968.

Harrison, Lou Silver, b. Portland, Oreg., May 14, 1917.

Harrison is an avant-garde composer who has written twelve-tone music, percussion music exploiting nonmusical sounds from nonmusical implements, and music utilizing the modes, rhythms, and instruments of the Orient.

From his mother he received not only his first piano lessons but also his love for oriental things, since she was a collector of Chinese art and Persian rugs. When he was nine his family moved to Stockton, Calif. There he continued his piano lessons with private teachers and began composing sentimental pieces for the piano. Since the family was continually on the move, there were frequent changes in Harrison's early academic and musical education. At Sequoia High School, in Redlands City, he was often called upon to sing in the school auditorium; in addition, he was a member of the local church choir. During his last three semesters at Burlingame High School, from which he graduated in December 1934, he studied piano and composition with Howard Cooper; the first of Harrison's six sonatas for cembalo (or piano) was written in 1934.

Between 1934 and 1936, Harrison attended San Francisco State College. This was a period when he studied the French horn, clarinet, recorder, harpsichord, and percussion instruments; sang in a madrigal group; was a piano accompanist for several dance groups for which he wrote music. As a composer he was innovative by writing a piece in microtones. Through Henry Cowell, with whom he was then studying composition, he became interested in writing music for percussion instruments. Also through Cowell, he came to know the music of Charles Ives for the first time. It had a powerful impact upon him and sent him further in the direction of musical experimentation.

Harrison was on the music faculty of Mills College in Oakland, Calif., between 1936 and 1939. He supplemented his teaching duties by working once again as accompanist and composer for dance groups and also by taking on a part-time job as a clerk in a music shop. In 1937 he wrote *France 1917—Spain 1937*, for strings and percussion. A year later, a Saraband and a Prelude (1937), both for piano, were published in *New Music Quarterly*, a journal of new music edited by Cowell. A new major influence in Harrison's development as composer came about through John Cage, whom he met in San Francisco at this time on Cowell's suggestion, and who soon became a valuable colleague and friend.

Harrison's fascination for the Orient, which would affect so much of his later music, was revealed early in the Canticle no. 3, for flute, guitar, and seven percussion instruments (1941). "The most instantaneously recognizable effects," reported Virgil Thomson in the *Herald Tribune* when this work was performed in New York in February 1953, "came from the Far East, but one . . . cannot call it a piece about Java or Bali or India. It is Western in its drama and structure, though many of its rhythmic and instrumental devices have been learned from the lands where percussive orchestration is the norm of music."

In 1941, Harrison went to Los Angeles to attend Arnold Schoenberg's seminars at the University of Southern California, where Harrison found employment in the dance department. The twelve-tone technique now became an important compositional tool for Harrison, beginning with a piano suite which Schoenberg praised.

The years between 1943 and 1949 were spent in New York in varied involvements including writing music articles for magazines and music reviews for the *Herald Tribune* and editing *New Music Quarterly* (1945–46). In 1947 he received a grant from the American Academy of Arts and Letters. He did not react favorably to life in a metropolis, being particularly sensitive to its noises. Consequently he wrote little music. The continual wear and tear of city life on his nervous system brought on a nervous breakdown which sent him to the hospital for nine months and to psychotherapy for some years more.

In the summer of 1949 he left New York for Portland, Oreg., to work in the dance, music, and drama workshop at Reed College. There he wrote the music in a twelve-tone idiom for two ballets: *The Marriage at the Eiffel Tower* (1949), text by Jean Cocteau translated into English, and *The Only Jealousy of Emer* (1949), based on a poetic drama by Yeats. Back in New York that fall, he became a faculty member at the Greenwich Settlement Music School for two years. He now wrote several chamber music works in the twelve-tone system, among these being Suite for Cello and Harp (1949), Suite no. 2, for

string quartet (1949) and Four Pastorales, for orchestra (1950).

On John Cage's recommendation, Harrison was appointed to the music faculty of Black Mountain College in North Carolina in 1951. During his two years there Harrison was active as a composer and wrote music for such dancers as Shirley Broughton, Merce Cunningham, and Jean Erdman. He also completed Suite for Violin, Piano, and Small Orchestra (1951), for Mario and Anahid Ajemian, who premiered it in New York on January 11, 1952, with the composer conducting; an opera, *Rapunzel* (1952), to a text by William Morris, which was produced in New York on May 14, 1959; Mass (to St. Anthony) for chorus, trumpet, harp, and strings begun in 1939 and completed in 1952; and *Symphony on G*, a serial work, though tonally centered, begun in 1947 and completed in 1953, first performed in Aptos, Calif., in August 1964 and, in a revised version, in Oakland, Calif., on February 8, 1966. The Mass was inspired by the music of early California missions and, as opposed to the twelve-tonal method of other Harrison works of this period, is modal in its melodic and harmonic content and dissonant in its polyphony. Its first public performance took place in New York in February 1954. One year later it was given a Fromm Music Foundation grant for a recording.

Harrison came to Rome in April 1953 to compete in an international composers' contest sponsored by the Committee for Cultural Freedom. He submitted a scene from his opera *Rapunzel*, which was sung by Leontyne Price and which was awarded first prize in the category of music for voice and chamber orchestra. The cash award, supplemented by a second Guggenheim Fellowship, enabled Harrison to linger on in Rome for a while.

When he returned to California in 1954, he settled in Aptos, which has since remained his home. On a commission from the Louisville Orchestra he wrote *Four Strict Songs*, for eight baritones and orchestra (1955), to his own text, introduced by the Louisville Orchestra under Robert Whitney in January 1956 and then recorded. This was one of Harrison's compositions in "just intonation," a tuning method in mathematically pure intervals with which Harrison had become interested by reading Harry Partch's *Genesis of a Music*. Each song is tuned to a different five-note scale, calling for special tuning for piano and harp; the rest of the instruments of the orchestra—two trombones, percussion, and strings—do not have fixed pitch.

The summer of 1956 was spent fighting fires with the Forestry Service; a year or so after that, Harrison worked in an animal hospital. While thus employed he completed the Concerto for Violin, Percussion and Orchestra (1959), which carries a title in Esperanto, *Koncerto por la violono kun porkuna orkestro*, because of Harrison's lifelong interest in and knowledge of that international language. This concerto

was first performed in Town Hall, New York, by
Anahaid Ajemian soon after it was completed, was
featured at the Cabrillo Festival in Aptos in August
1965, and then was heard in Buffalo, N.Y., on November 19, 1959, during a week devoted entirely to
Harrison's works. Reviewing the concerto in the *San
Francisco Chronicle*, Dean Wallace noted that Harrison "is an absolute master in the employment of
one elusive element which renders music meaningful:
silence."

Through a Rockefeller Foundation grant in 1961–
62 Harrison visited Japan, Korea, and Taiwan to
study oriental modes, rhythms, and instruments. The
fruits of this research could be found in *Novo Odo*
(1961–63), a protest against nuclear war, for which
the composer wrote his own text. Special oriental instruments are here used for Japanese ceremonial
music. *Novo Odo* was first heard in 1963 in Aptos,
Calif., at the Cabrillo Festival.

An invitation in 1963 to serve as senior-scholar-
in-residence at the University of Hawaii and the
East-West Center of the university brought Harrison
to Hawaii. *Pacifika Rondo*, Esperanto for *The Pacific Circle* (1963), for an orchestra made up of Western and oriental instruments, was written there on
commission from the University and the East/West
Center and was premiered in Hawaii in May 1963
at the Festival of Arts of the 20th Century. Each of
the seven movements refers to a section of the Pacific
basin except for the sixth, which is a protest against
the atomic bomb and the way it destroyed life in the
Pacific. Pentatonic scales, oriental rhythmic patterns,
and an array of esoteric eastern instruments all provided an oriental character to each of these movements.

A generous grant from the Phoebe Ketchum
Thorne Foundation enabled Harrison to abandon
his job in the animal hospital in 1965 and concentrate more fully on composition. A year spent in
Mexico resulted in the writing of *A Political Primer*,
for vocal soloists, chorus, and orchestra (1967). Returning to California in 1967, Harrison joined the
music faculty of the San Jose State College (now
University), where he has remained ever since, devoting himself to teaching, lecturing and giving concerts. Premieres of several of Harrison's works were
given at the college. These included: *Music for Violin
with Various European, Asian, and African Instruments* (1967), which Gary Beswick (for whom it was
written) introduced in 1967; *Orpheus—For Singer to
the Dance*, for chorus, percussion, and orchestra
(1969), written for Anthony Cirone, who helped to
introduce it with the San Francisco Orchestra in
1969; and the Organ Concerto (1973) written for
and introduced by Philip Simpson on April 30,
1973.

Other Harrison premieres were heard off the college campus. *Young Caesar* (1971), a chamber opera
for puppets with text by Robert Gordon, was premiered at Aptos on August 5, 1971. *Peace Piece* IV,

or, in Esperanto, *La Koro Sutro*, for chorus and
American gamelan, with a text in Esperanto (1972),
was commissioned by the Thorne Music Fund and
performed for the first time on November 13, 1972,
at the Lincoln Center for the Performing Arts by the
Aeolian Players. *Elegiac Symphony* (1974) was commissioned by the Koussevitzky Music Foundation
and premiered in Oakland, Calif., on December 7,
1975. The symphony, which had its gestation period
in 1942 but was not completed until thirty-two years
later, bears a quotation from Horace: "Bitter sorrows
will grow milder with music." Some of this music is
modal, some in a twelve-tone technique, and some in
a functional harmony. Serenade, for the suling (Far
Eastern flute) with gamelan degung (1977), was
heard for the first time in 1978 at the Cabrillo Festival in Aptos.

Harrison spent many years building instruments,
beginning with two clavichords, along new principles. He subsequently constructed a Phrygian aulos
and Javanese-styled gamelans. His protean talent
further included painting, calligraphy, the writing of
plays and poetry, a scholarly knowledge of world religious philosophies, and his aforementioned fluency
with Esperanto.

In 1968, Harrison served as panel member of the
World Music Council and UNESCO Conference in
New York City. He was appointed a member of the
National Institute of Arts and Letters in 1973.

THE COMPOSER SPEAKS: I have felt for a long time,
and still do, that the real problem, the real interest in
music is the conflict, the friction, the pulls and responses between what is coming along spontaneously
as the material and the intellectual superimposition
of the whole form the shape of the entire movement.
It's the friction between those two that produces interesting music. At least, I keep feeling that that's it.
It's a balancing act, a juggling act between what bub-
bles up spontaneously and has continuity of its own
and a general form which you know that you want to
use. It's a constant juggle right up to the last joint
between the final section and that other that comes
out. And that's interesting juggling; it makes for
what I think is exciting music. . . . There are very
few, except small pieces, that I would write out spontaneously to the end. Mostly, I have decided what the
general shape of the movement is going to be. This is
the more precise form.

PRINCIPAL WORKS: 6 cembalo sonatas (1934–43); 2
suites for string orchestra (1947, 1948).

Flute Concerto (1939); Mass, for vocal soloists,
trumpet, harp, and strings (1939–49); Canticles nos.
1 and 3, for percussion (1940, 1941); *Orpheus—For
Singer to the Dance*, for chorus, percussion and orchestra (1941–69); Fugue, for percussion (1942); Piano Suite (1943); *Easter Cantata*, for vocal soloists,
chorus, and small orchestra (1943–66); *Schoenber-
giana*, for string sextet (1945); *Alleluia*, for orchestra

(1946); *The Open Road, or Western Dance*, ballet (1947); *Praises for Michael the Archangel*, for piano (1947); *Pied Beauty*, for voice, trombone, cello, flute, and percussion (1948); *Symphony on G* (1948–61); Suite, for cello and harp (1949); *The Marriage at the Eiffel Tower*, ballet (1949); *The Only Jealousy of Emer*, ballet (1949); *Little Suite*, for piano (1949); *Solstice*, for flute, oboe, trumpet, celesta, tack piano, two cellos, and double bass (1950); *An Almanac of the Seasons*, ballet (1950); Suite for Violin, Piano, and Small Orchestra (1951); Mass (to St. Anthony), for chorus, trumpet, harp, and strings (1952); *Rapunzel*, opera (1952); *Peace Piece* III, for voice, violin, harp, and drone strings (1953–68); *Four Strict Songs*, for eight baritones and orchestra (1955); *Simfony from Simfonies*, in free style, for orchestra (1956); Concerto for Violin, Percussion, and Orchestra, or *Koncerto por la violono kun porkuna orkestro* (1959); *Suite for Symphonic Strings* (1960); *Concerto in Slendro*, for violin and orchestra (1961); *Novo Odo*, for orchestra, chorus, and special instruments (1961–63); *A Joyous Occasion and a Solemn Procession*, for high and low voices, trombone, and percussion (1962); *At the Tomb of Charles Ives*, for chamber ensemble (1963); *Pacifika Rondo*, for chamber orchestra of Western and Asian instruments (1963); *Political Power*, for vocal soloists, chorus, and orchestra (1965); Symphony in G (1966); *Music for Violin with Various European, Asian, and African Instruments* (1967); *Peace Piece* I, for chorus and instruments (1968); *Young Caesar*, puppet opera (1971); *Peace Piece* IV, or *La Koro Sutro*, for chorus and American gamelan (1972); Concerto for Organ and Orchestra (1973); Suite for Violin with American Gamelan (1974); *Elegiac Symphony*, for orchestra (1974); Serenade, for suling and gamelan degung (1977).

BIBLIOGRAPHY: Thomson, Virgil, *American Music Since 1910* (N.Y., 1971); Yates, Peter, *Twentieth Century Music* (N.Y., 1968); *American Record Guide*, November 1979; *New York Times*, October 26, 1969.

Haubiel, Charles Trowbridge (originally **Pratt, Charles Trowbridge**), b. Delta, Ohio, January 30, 1892, d. Los Angeles, August 26, 1978.

Haubiel first gained recognition as a neobaroque composer who reached back to the 16th and 17th centuries for his polyphonic style and structures. Subsequently he favored either a romantic or an impressionistic idiom, influenced on the one hand by Brahms and on the other by Debussy. Some of his later works are American in subject matter or folk idiom.

Though his father was named Pratt, Haubiel early assumed his mother's maiden name of Haubiel as his own. He revealed an interest and talent for music from childhood but he did not receive his first in-struction until he was ten. At that time, the family moved to New York, where, while attending public school, he was given lessons on the piano by his sister, Florence Pratt, a pupil of Leschetizky's. When he was fifteen, Haubiel gave his first public recital.

In 1909 he went to Europe for further music study, mainly the piano with Rudolph Ganz in Berlin between 1911 and 1913. Though he was already composing, Haubiel had thus far had no systematic training in theory or composition.

Returning to the United States in 1913, Haubiel toured the country as pianist in joint recitals with the Bohemian violinist Jaroslav Kocián. Between 1913 and 1915 Haubiel taught piano, harmony, and the history of music at Kingfisher College in Oklahoma, and from 1915 to 1917 he taught piano at the Musical Art Institute in Oklahoma City. In 1916, he wrote a composition for piano solo in which he already revealed his later interest in baroque structures and style: the *Suite passacaille*, consisting of a chorale prelude, air and variations, and fugue. He arranged it for orchestra in 1930, and for two pianos in 1932; the orchestral version was introduced in Los Angeles on January 31, 1936.

Soon after the United States became involved in World War I, Haubiel enlisted in the army, seeing service for the next two years in Texas and France and in the field artillery and in the field hospital. Upon his discharge with the rank of second lieutenant in 1919, he settled in New York to continue music study and composing. At the Mannes School of Music in New York, he studied composition with Rosario Scalero (1919–24), who gave him a thorough training in polyphonic music of the baroque era. Between 1920 and 1926 Haubiel continued his piano study with Rosina and Josef Lhevinne.

Haubiel's fascination for polyphony and baroque music led to the writing of such early works as the *Gothic Variations*, for violin and piano (1919), which he revised in 1942, and adapted for full orchestra in 1968, the last of these versions performed first in Los Angeles on June 9, 1970; *L'amore spirituale*, three songs in canonic form for women's voices and two pianos (1924), using poetic texts by Oscar Wilde, adapted for women's voices and orchestra in 1933, when it was premiered in New York; and *Vox Cathedralis*, chorale variations and fugue for organ (1925), adapted for two pianos in 1928, and for orchestra in 1934, the orchestral version introduced in New York on May 6, 1938.

For a decade, from 1921 to 1931, Haubiel was a member of the faculty of the Institute of Musical Art in New York and from 1923 to 1947 he taught the history of music at New York University.

Haubiel favored a consonant polyphonic style mainly influenced by Bach in the composition that first brought him into the national limelight. This work was *Karma*, symphonic variations for orchestra (1928), with which Haubiel captured first prize in a competition conducted by Columbia Records to commemorate the centenary of Schubert's death. *Karma* was intended to illustrate some of the philosophic concepts of the Hindu Bible (Bhagavad Gita) as translated into English by Sir Edwin Arnold. The following quotation appears at the head of the published score: "I Brahma am! The one eternal God. And Soul of Souls. What goeth forth from me Causing All Life to live is Karma called." This work is divided into four uninterrupted cycles, each bearing descriptive programmatic titles to suggest its emotional or pictorial content, and the third of which is a psychic recapitulation in the form of variation-fugue.

By the early 1930s, Haubiel began moving from polyphony to a more harmonic idiom, as he increasingly came to realize that romanticism or impressionism was creatively more satisfying to him. Adaptation for orchestra from his early piano works brought Haubiel several more awards and honors in the 1940s. In 1934 he received second prize in the Swift and Company Symphonic Contest for *Rittrati* (1934), which was an adaptation for orchestra of a movement from his *Portraits*, for piano (1919), in which the composer describes several of his friends; the Chicago Symphony under Frederick Stock introduced *Rittrati* on December 12, 1935. Still in 1934, Haubiel won honorable mention in the Paderewski Prize for *Mars Ascending* (1923), a transcription for orchestra of a piano piece written in 1917. The New York Philharmonic Award came in 1936 for *Solari* (1936), an arrangement of a piano suite of three pieces describing three periods in a man's life, written between 1932 and 1934; as a work for orchestra it was premiered in 1938 by the New York Philharmonic under the composer's direction.

Haubiel brought his romanticism and impressionism to a number of works deriving either their subject matter from American backgrounds or their musical materials from American folk or popular music. *Metamorphosis*, for orchestra (1926), was an adroit and at times amusing set of twenty-nine variations on Stephen Foster's "Swanee River," each variation simulating the style of composers from the time of Gregory I to Gershwin. This work was filmed as a short, entitled *Swanee River Goes Hi-Hat* by Paramount Pictures. *1865 A.D.*, for orchestra (1943), started out as scenes from the Civil War. In a revision in 1958 it acquired the new title of *Mississippi Story*, when it was heard in Los Angeles on April 24, 1959. *Pioneers* was a symphonic saga of Ohio (1947, revised 1956; Los Angeles, February 19, 1960), made up of American Indian and American folk thematic materials. *American Rhapsody* was a work for orchestra, or for soprano, men's chorus and band, written in 1948. *Ohioana* was a cycle for violin and piano (1966).

Haubiel's only work for the stage is a Mexican folk opera called *Sunday Costs Five Pesos*, libretto by Josephine Nigli (1949). It was produced in Charlotte, N.C., on November 6, 1950, and was revised in 1954.

In 1935, Haubiel founded Composers Press, Inc., to promote American music, serving as its president until 1966. In 1953, Haubiel received the Distinguished Service to Music Award from the International Piano Teachers Association and the Martha Kinney Cooper Citation from the Ohioanan Library Association. The National Federation of Music Clubs presented him with the Three Star Award of Merit in 1965. In 1967, Haubiel received the Pegasus award for outstanding contributions to culture and in 1977 the Johann Award from the Viennese Culture Society. He was the recipient of an honorary doctorate in music from Southwestern Conservatory. Haubiel married Mary Rice Storke in 1954.

THE COMPOSER SPEAKS: My beliefs in music have changed greatly since I first began composing. In 1920, Rudolph Ganz laughingly called me the Bolshevist composer. If I had followed my revolutionary tendencies of that period, I certainly would write and feel differently about the music today. But . . . I have become a pure classicist. Every day my conviction becomes firmer that any music that does not stem from classic tradition will have no success with musical audiences of future generations. In other words, polytonality, atonality, duo modality, the quarter-tone system and all other isms, are psychologically unsound.

PRINCIPAL WORKS: *Suite passacaille*, for solo piano, also for two pianos and for orchestra (1916); *Mars Ascending*, for piano, also for orchestra (1917); *Gothic Variations*, for violin and piano, also for orchestra (1919, revised 1942); *Portraits*, for piano (1919); *L'amore spirituale*, three songs in canonic form for women's chorus and two pianos (1924); *Ecchi classici*, for string quartet (1924); *Vox Cathedralis*, for organ, also for two pianos, and for orchestra (1925); *Metamorphosis*, twenty-nine variations on "Swanee River" for orchestra (1926); *Karma*, symphonic variations (1928, revised 1933, 1968); *Duo Forms*, for cello and piano (1929–31); *Sea Songs*, for chorus (1931); *Cryptics*, for bassoon and piano (1932); *Lodando la danza*, for oboe, violin, cello, and piano (1932); *Solari*, suite for piano, also for orchestra (1932–34); *The Cosmic Christ*, cantata for high voice and piano, also for voice and orchestra (1937); *Symphony in Variation Form* (1937); *Miniatures*, suite for piano, also for orchestra (1937); *Nuances*, suite for flute and piano, also flute and orchestra (1938); *1865 A.D.*, for piano, also for orchestra under the title of *Mississippi Story* (1939); *Vision of St. Joan*, for soprano, alto, boys' chorus, adult chorus, and orchestra (1939); Cello Sonata (1941); *In the French Manner*, for flute, cello, and piano, also for orchestra (1942); String Trio (1943); *Jungle Tale*, for chorus (1943); *Father Abraham*, for chorus (1943); Violin Sonata (1945); *Pioneers*, symphonic saga of Ohio, for orchestra (1947, revised 1956); *Shadows*, for violin and piano (1947); *American*

Rhapsody, for orchestra, also for soprano, men's chorus and band (1948); *Pastoral Trio*, for flute, cello, and piano (1949); *Sunday Costs Five Pesos*, Mexican folk opera (1949); *Epochs*, for violin and piano (1954–55); *Threnody for Love*, for six instruments (1965); *Heroic Elegy*, for orchestra (1965); *Ohioana*, cycle for violin and piano (1966); Trio, for clarinet, cellos, and piano (1969); *Cryptics*, for cello and piano (1973).

BIBLIOGRAPHY: *BBDM;* Ewen, David, *American Composers Today* (N.Y., 1949); *Who's Who in America, 1978–79.*

Heinrich, Anthony Philip (Anton Philipp), b. Schönbüchel, Bohemia, March 11, 1781; d. New York, May 3, 1861.

Affectionately called "Father Heinrich" and with far less justification described by one of his contemporaries as "America's Beethoven," Heinrich was an extraordinarily prolific composer who made a specialty of writing large works to elaborately contrived programs bearing quixotic titles. Whatever his shortcomings, and they are considerable, they are more than compensated for by his historic importance. He was one of the earliest American nationalists, one of the first to use American ballads in seriously contrived concert works, and the first to employ American Indian subjects and motives within large-scale compositions.

Little is known of his early life in Bohemia beyond the fact that he was born to wealth, that he responded sensitively to music from childhood on, and that as a boy he studied the violin and piano by himself. He was adopted by his wealthy uncle upon whose death in 1800 he inherited his foster father's elegant house, a thriving business that dealt with linen, wine, and other commodities, as well as manufacturing plants and warehouses throughout Europe. Heinrich ran these business ventures successfully, adding to them a large banking and exchange operation. During one of his business trips he acquired a Cremona violin in Malta to which he applied himself industriously until he could play it well and which became his constant companion on his travels. Another of his trips, in 1805, brought him for his first visit to the United States.

By the time he came to the United States for permanent residence in 1810, music had assumed in his life a more dominant role than business. He accepted a post (without pay) as musical director of the Southwark Theater in Philadelphia, and soon settled down to domesticity by marrying "a lady of superior personal and mental endowments" (his words), her name and the date of their marriage unknown. The Napoleonic wars and the financial crash in Austria that followed brought about the downfall of his business empire in 1811, reducing him to total poverty,

which made it necessary for him henceforth to depend upon music making for a livelihood.

By 1813 he managed to accumulate enough funds to take his wife for a trip to his native Bohemia, where their daughter, Antonia, was born. When Heinrich and his wife returned to Boston in 1816 they left their daughter in Bohemia in the care of a distant relative, probably because of the mother's precarious health. Almost as soon as the Heinrichs were back in America, she died.

In 1817, Heinrich found a short-lived post as musical director of a theater in Pittsburgh, making the long and arduous journey from Boston mainly on foot. After that, he proceeded westward, coming to Lexington, Ky., where a concert was given for his benefit on November 12, 1817, in which he appeared as conductor in a program that included what may have been the first performance of a Beethoven symphony in the United States. In Lexington, Heinrich taught music, played the violin and conducted orchestras.

In the spring of 1818 he left Lexington for Bardstown, an early Kentucky settlement, where he lived the life of a recluse in a log cabin. It was now that he made his first foray into composition, without ever having had a lesson in theory, by writing a song, "How Sleep the Brave" (1818), which was subsequently published. Other songs, as well as pieces for the piano, followed in rapid succession, some of these titles already revealing his musical Americanism: "Hail to Kentucky," "Yankee Doodle Waltz," "Ode to the Memory of Commodore O. H. Perry," "The Birthday of Washington," and "Sons of the Woods," the last of these an Indian war song. In 1820, he gathered his songs and pieces for piano or violin into an album published in Philadelphia under the elaborate title of *The Dawning of Music in Kentucky, or The Pleasures of Harmony in the Solitudes of Nature.* This was followed that same year by the publication of a second album of song and solo instrumental pieces, *The Western Minstrel.* "Amateur in music as he was," commented William Treat Upton in his biography of the composer, "Heinrich . . . produced a work unique in American music annals. . . . In the way of a general collection of musical works expressive of varying moods, *The Dawning* cannot have had its equal in America. . . . These excerpts show plainly authentic evidence of an inherent musicianship, of a feeling for the appropriate expression of varying moods, and—even at this time—of a technique in composition which, while not always dependable, is yet often apparently quite adequate to the task at hand."

By the early spring of 1820, Heinrich had returned East. A melodrama, to which he contributed songs and instrumental pieces—*Child of the Mountain, or The Deserted Mother*—was produced at the Chestnut Street Theater in Philadelphia on March 7, 1821; none of this music has survived. A month later, on April 19, a concert devoted principally to his songs was given at the Masonic Hall. In the spring of 1823 Heinrich came to Boston, where he was welcomed with still another Heinrich concert on May 19, appearing as conductor, composer, pianist, and organist.

He was back in Europe in 1826. In London he played the violin in the orchestra at Drury Lane and did a considerable amount of composing. In April 1831 he completed his first work for orchestra, and also the first large-scale composition about the American Indian: *Pushmataha—A Venerable Chief of a Western Tribe of Indians*, a "fantasia instrumentale" for an orchestra of thirty-three players. Upton described this work as "monumental in conception but ofentimes weak in execution . . . verbose and rhetorical."

Heinrich spent five years in London before returning to Boston in 1831. The year of 1833 found him again in London, busily occupied with teaching, occasionally playing the violin at Drury Lane and Covent Garden, and composing on a grander scale than ever. With aspirations far greater than his technical capabilities, he now worked with what (for that period) was an oversized orchestra in large-scale compositions cluttered with extended and explicit programs bearing unusual titles. Eight were completed in 1834, including *The Tower of Babel*, or *The Languages Confounded*, "a grand oratorical divertissement"; *Complaint of Logan the Mingo Chief, the Last of his Race*, which he described as a "fantasia agitato dolorsa"; *Schiller*, a "grande sinfonia dramatica"; *The Treaty of William Penn with the Indians*, a "concerto grosso"; *The Fair Daughters of the Western World*, a "capriccio scherzevole for grand orchestra," which he subsequently retitled *The Mocking Bird to the Nightingale*, one of several of his compositions on an ornithological subject. In 1835 he completed the orchestral work he regarded most highly, *The Ornithological Combat of Kings*, or *The Condor of the Andes and the Eagle of the Cordilleras*, which quoted American ballads.

A yearning to visit his daughter, whom he had not seen since her infancy and who was now twenty, induced Heinrich to revisit his homeland in 1835. But upon his arrival in northern Bohemia he discovered she no longer was there, having departed for America in search of him. (It was not until many years later that their paths finally crossed.) At this time, in Graz, Austria, the first performance of *The Ornithological Combat of Kings* was performed on June 9, 1836. "Your reviewer," wrote August Mandel in *Musik*, "dares not maintain that this composition will please every ear. Something peculiar in its design and treatment distinguishes it from everything that has yet come into our sphere of enjoyment."

Between 1837 and 1857, Heinrich lived in New York. In April 1842 he participated in the founding of the Philharmonic Society of New York. Later the same year, on June 16, a grand Heinrich Musical Festival enlisted probably the largest orchestra assembled up to that time on an American stage, over one hundred men. The opening number was the overture to *Oratorio of the Pilgrim Fathers*, whose four movements depicted "the genius of Freedom slumbering in the Forest shades of America," her awakening to melodies "with which Nature regales her solitudes," the attempt of Power to clip the wing of "the young Eagle of Liberty," and the "joyous reign of universal Intelligence and universal Freedom." Another all-Heinrich program was given on May 6, 1846, featuring, among other works, *To the Spirit of Beethoven* and other parts of the *Oratorio of the Pilgrim Fathers*. An autobiographical symphony, *The Wildwood Troubadour*, was the opening number of an all-Heinrich concert in New York on April 21, 1853.

He toured Europe in 1857–58, offering an all-Heinrich concert in Prague on March 22, 1857 that included another of his ornithologically inspired compositions, *The Migration of Wild Passenger Pigeons*. This work, too, was overprogrammed, the music too often a literal and naïve interpretation of his pompous text. Its finale interpolated the strains of "Yankee Doodle" and "Hail, Columbia."

He came back to the United States for the last time in October 1859 to spend his last two years in New York in appalling poverty and with the failure of both his eyesight and hearing.

In 1917, the Library of Congress in Washington, D. C., acquired many of Heinrich's published works and almost all of his orchestral scores together with memorabilia. Heinrich's *The Ornithological Combat of the Kings* was revived in the United States in 1979 in a New World recording.

THE COMPOSER SPEAKS: The many and severe animadversions so long and repeatedly cast on the talent for music in this country has been one of the chief motives of the author, in the exercise of his abilities, and should he be able, by this effort, to create but one single *Star* in the *West*, no one would ever be more proud than himself to be called an American Musician. He, however, is fully aware of the dangers which, at the present day, attend talent on the crowded and difficult road of eminence; but fears of just criticism, by "competent masters" should never retard the enthusiasm of genius, when ambitious of producing works more lasting than the "Butterfly-effusions" of the present age. He, therefore, will rely on the candor of the public, will rest confident that justice will be done, by due comparison with works of other authors (celebrated for their merit, especially as regards instrumental execution) but who have never, like him, been thrown, as it were, by discordant events, far from the emporiums of musical science, into the isolated wilds of nature, where he invoked the Muse, tutored only by Alma Mater.

PRINCIPAL WORKS: *The Dawning of Music in Kentucky*, or *The Pleasures of Harmony in the Solitudes* *of Nature*, a collection of songs and pieces for the piano and for the violin (1820); *The Western Minstrel*, a collection of songs and pieces for the piano and for the violin (1820); *Pushmataha—A Venerable Chief of a Western Tribe of Indians*, for orchestra (1831); *The Tower of Babel*, or *The Languages Confounded*, for orchestra (1834); *Complaint of Logan the Mingo Chief, the Last of His Race*, for orchestra (1834); *Schiller*, for orchestra (1834); *The Treaty of William Penn with the Indians*, concerto grosso for orchestra (1834); Concerto for the Kent Bugle, or Klappenflügel (1834); *The Mocking Bird to the Nightingale*, for orchestra (1834); *The Indian War Council*, "concerto bellico" for orchestra (1834); *Gran sinfonia Eroica* (1835); *The Jäger's Adieu*, for orchestra (1835); *The Ornithological Combat of Kings*, or *The Condor of the Andes and the Eagle of the Cordilleras* (1836); *The Columbiad*, "grand American National Chivalrous Symphony" (1837); *Elegia Impromptu*, for piano (1837); *Bohemia*, "sinfonia romantico" (1837); *The Jubilee*, "Grand National Song of Triumph," for chorus and orchestra (1841); *Oratorio of the Pilgrim Fathers* (c. 1842); *To the Spirit of Beethoven*, a "monumental symphony" (1846); *The Wildwood Troubadour*, an autobiographical symphony (c. 1853); *The Mastodon*, a grand symphony (1857); *Maria Theresa*, symphony (1857); *The Migration of Wild Passenger Pigeons*, "grande capriccio volante" for orchestra (1857).

BIBLIOGRAPHY: *NGDMM*; Barron, D. M., *The Vocal Works of Anthony Philips Heinrich* (Urbana, Ill., 1973); Maust, W. R., *The Symphonies of Anthony Philip Heinrich* (Urbana, Ill., 1973); Upton, William Treat, *Anthony Philip Heinrich* (N.Y. 1939); *Musical Quarterly*, April 1920.

Herbert, Victor August, b. Dublin, Ireland, February 1, 1859; d. New York, May 26, 1924. American citizen, 1902.

Herbert's name and music survive through his operettas for the popular American musical stage and through the numerous songs he wrote for them. But he is also a composer of concert music and two grand operas, all in the romantic style he had studied and assimilated during his extended musical apprenticeship in Germany.

His father, an artist, died when Victor was three. At that time, his widowed mother took him to England to live with his grandfather, Samuel Lover, a distinguished novelist, poet, and dramatist, the author of the popular *Handy Andy*. At his home, The Vine, in Sevenoaks, twenty miles outside London, Lover maintained a salon which attracted many world-famous writers, artists, and musicians. It was under such intellectual stimulation that Victor spent his childhood and early boyhood. He was seven when his mother recognized he had a bent for music and gave him his first piano lessons. His progress was so

rapid that the Lover household soon decided to send him to Germany for intensive musical training. This was facilitated by the fact that, in 1866, his mother married Dr. Wilhelm Schmid, a German physician whose home was in Stuttgart. There, Victor attended public school and high school, specializing in Latin and Greek. At the same time, he continued studying music—not only the piano but the flute and piccolo, which he played in the school orchestra, and the cello. Family reverses compelled him to leave high school when he was fifteen. It was now that he decided to become a professional musician. Between 1874 and 1876 he studied the cello privately with Bernhard Cossmann, a celebrated cellist at that time. "These lessons," Herbert once said, "were no fifteen-minute affairs. I was under the constant eye of the master." Herbert supplemented cello study with attendance at numerous concerts; memories of the piano recitals of Hans von Bülow and Anton Rubinstein remained indelible.

From 1876 to 1880 Herbert earned his living playing the cello in solo appearances and in orchestras conducted by Brahms, Saint-Saëns, Anton Rubinstein, and Eduard Strauss (the last, the brother of the waltz king).

In 1881 Herbert became first cellist in the Court Orchestra in Stuttgart conducted by Max Seyfritz, and on October 25 of that year Herbert appeared with that orchestra as cello soloist. Impressed by his young cellist, Seyfritz encouraged Herbert to become a composer, in preparation for which he gave him valuable instruction in theory, composition, and orchestration. "Under this system of corrective criticism, I . . . learned to distinguish well-sounding from poorly sounding harmony, and by degrees was developing a sound musical judgment." Under Seyfritz's watchful eye, Herbert completed his first large-scale work: Suite for Cello and Orchestra (1883) which he himself introduced with the Stuttgart Orchestra under Seyfritz on October 23, 1883. Each of its five movements, writes Edward N. Waters in his biography of Herbert, "is rich in melody, sharply rhythmic, finely orchestrated. Each has a distinctive character, maintained from beginning to end. The music is romantic—Herbert never learned or wished to write any other kind—but cleanly so, with none of the contemporary exaggeration of pathos or *Schwärmerei* which was so typical." The fourth movement, a serenade, became popular throughout Europe independent of the suite and brought Herbert his first bid for fame.

While serving in the Court Orchestra, Herbert made numerous appearances in performances of chamber music. Additionally, in the fall of 1885, he joined the faculty of the newly founded Neue Stuttgarter Musikschule. Another of its teachers was Therese Förster, a distinguished dramatic soprano who sang with the Stuttgart Opera and Vienna Royal Opera. Herbert and Therese Förster were married on August 14, 1886, in Vienna and in the fall of that year both set sail for the United States, Therese Förster to sing with the Metropolitan Opera in New York, and Herbert to play the cello in its orchestra.

Therese Förster stayed with the Metropolitan Opera only one full season, and so did Herbert. After leaving the Metropolitan Opera he began making numerous appearances as solo cellist and as guest artist with orchestras. On January 8, 1887, he appeared as soloist with the New York Symphony Society under Walter Damrosch in three movements of his Suite for Cello and Orchestra. A few days later he was heard in a joint recital with a pianist in Brooklyn, N.Y., playing two of his own smaller pieces, Berceuse and Polonaise, which he probably had written before coming to America.

Later in 1887 Herbert founded an orchestra of his own, which he conducted in New York and Boston in programs of classical and semiclassical music. A season later he helped form and played in the New York String Quartet, which gave the first of several concerts on December 8, 1887, in New York. On the afternoon of December 10, 1887, Herbert was heard in the world premiere of his Concerto for Cello and Orchestra (1887) with the Theodore Thomas Orchestra, and that same evening he played the concerto again, this time with the New York Philharmonic conducted by Theodore Thomas. "Though far from profound," remarked a critic for the *New York Times*, "[it] contains many good ideas and some delightful effects. The final movement is humoresque in spirit and moves with briskness."

As a composer, Herbert was not confining himself exclusively to his own instrument. His Serenade, for string orchestra (1888), was performed on December 1, 1888, by an orchestra conducted by Anton Seidl. On September 24, 1891, at the Worcester Festival in Massachusetts, of which he was associate conductor (1889–91), he presented the premiere of a major work for solo voices, chorus, and orchestra. It was *The Captive* (1891), its text a poem by Rudolf Baumbach. James Gibbons Huneker, the noted New York critic, described it as an "extremely strong work, picturesque in coloring and incident and extremely dramatic." Herbert's *An American Fantasy* (1893), a symphonic medley of American patriotic ballads culminating with a grandiose setting of "The Star-Spangled Banner," was first performed on November 26, 1893, by the band of the Twenty-second Regiment of the National Guard of the state of New York, of which Herbert had that year become conductor in succession to Patrick S. Gilmore.

Herbert's most significant concert work was the Concerto no. 2, for cello and orchestra (1894), which he himself introduced as soloist with the New York Philharmonic on March 9, 1894. Writing in *The World*, Reginald de Koven called it "an interesting and effective composition; effective in the organic whole rather than a mere accompaniment, and effective also for the solo instrument." After suffering

many years of total neglect, this concerto was revived in New York on January 28, 1980, by Lorne Munroe and the American Composers Orchestra under Ainslee Cox. At that time, in the *New York Times*, Harold C. Schonberg called it "an expertly composed bravura piece, full of good tunes, and certainly worth revival once in a while."

Herbert was also active outside the areas of composer and cellist. In the fall of 1889 he was appointed to the faculty of the National Conservatory of Music in New York, which had been founded four years earlier and of which Antonín Dvořák became director a few years later. He remained the bandmaster of the Twenty-second Regiment until 1898 after having served five years. Between 1898 and 1904 he was the conductor of the Pittsburgh Symphony Orchestra, where he introduced several of his own symphonic works. Among these were: *Suite romantique* (1899; February 2, 1900), *Hero and Leander* (1900; January 18, 1901), and *Columbus* (1902; January 2, 1903). In 1904 he formed the Victor Herbert Orchestra as a successor to one he had founded in 1887, which gave concerts of semiclassics.

As a composer of American operettas, the field in which he gained preeminence, Herbert made his official bow with *Prince Ananias*, first produced in Boston on November 20, 1894. His first success came with *The Wizard of the Nile*, which opened at the Casino Theater in New York on November 4, 1895. His first operetta to gain a foothold in the permanent repertoire was *The Fortune Teller* on September 26, 1898. After that came a prolific output, the classics of which were *Babes in Toyland* (October 13, 1903); *Mlle. Modiste* (December 25, 1905), *The Red Mill* (September 24, 1906), and *Naughty Marietta* (November 7, 1910). Each was made into a motion picture in addition to being intermittently revived on the popular musical stage and occasionally even in the opera house. Among the songs to come from these productions, a veritable cornucopia of pure melody and affecting sentiments, are: "Gypsy Love Song" (*The Fortune Teller*), "The March of the Toys" (*Babes in Toyland*), "Kiss Me Again" (*Mlle. Modiste*), "Moonbeams" (*The Red Mill*), "Ah, Sweet Mystery of Life" and "I'm Falling in Love with Someone" (*Naughty Marietta*).

He graduated from the popular musical theater into grand opera with *Natoma* (1911), libretto by Joseph Deighn Redding. This opera had been offered to and rejected by the Metropolitan Opera in New York before being produced by the Philadelphia-Chicago Opera Company in Philadelphia and a little later by the same company in New York. Mary Garden played the title role of the pure-blooded American Indian girl, and Cleofante Campanini was the conductor. "I have composed all of Natoma's music, at least the greater part of it," Herbert explained, "out of Indian music which I have collected and studied for some time past. . . . If I used Indian music with all its original intervals and cadences, it would have become very monotonous and so, of course, I have adapted it. But I have fashioned melodies by using fragments of this and that Indian theme." The libretto was severely attacked by the critics as "undramatic," "antimusical," and even "non-American," the last of these accusations because the setting was in and off the coast of California, at the time (1820) under Spanish rule. The *New York Tribune* called that libretto "one of the most futile, fatuous, halting, impotent, inane and puerile ever written." Herbert's music came off far batter, particularly his skillful and tasteful use of American Indian musical materials. Arthur Farwell, an authority on the subject, said in the *American Review of Reviews*: "He has shown remarkable sympathy in devising a scheme for these themes which retain their peculiar character and 'color' and his music in this genre is both impressive and convincing." In *Harper's Weekly*, Lawrence Gilman described Herbert's music as "smoothly constructed, the work of a deft and well-trained musician. It betrays a true instinct for the stage, a keen sense of theatrical effect." *Natoma* remained a favorite with American opera audiences for several years.

Herbert's second grand opera, *Madeleine* (1913), had French characters and setting. When it was produced by the Metropolitan Opera on January 24, 1914, it proved such a failure that it was removed from the repertoire after six performances. "It was not grateful to listen to," explains Edward N. Waters, "and it was very artificially contrived."

Herbert never again wrote a grand opera, but up to the time of his death he continued to provide scores for Broadway productions, but without the kind of success he had formerly enjoyed. In his last years he complained to a friend: "My day is over. They are forgetting poor old Herbert." But neither his best operettas, nor their finest songs died with him when he suddenly succumbed to a heart attack in a New York City street soon after having enjoyed a hearty lunch at the Lambs Club in New York.

In 1914, Herbert was one of the founders of the American Society of Composers, Authors, and Publishers (ASCAP), serving as vice-president up to the time of his death. He was a member of the National Institute of Arts and Letters. In 1916, he wrote one of the first original scores ever created for motion pictures, *The Fall of a Nation*. Since this was still the time of silent movies, the score was performed by a pit orchestra to synchronize with the screen production. Herbert's screen biography, *The Great Victor Herbert*, with Allan Jones portraying the composer, was released in 1939.

THE COMPOSER SPEAKS: Good criticism is courted by the composer and musician. It is necessary; but the critic should tell what happened in his review, which should be a real review and not pick to pieces one or two sections of an opera which displease him. He should take into account the hard work that is done by the composer and the librettist. . . . I do not want flattery nor . . . honeyed words. Many critics are men of splendid education and can point out the defects in a score that the composer never thought of. But this should be done kindly.

PRINCIPAL WORKS: 2 cello concertos (1887, 1894).

The Captive, for solo voices, chorus, and orchestra (1891); *The Vision of Columbus*, for orchestra (1893); *An American Fantasy*, for band or orchestra (1893); *Suite romantique*, for orchestra (1899); *Hero and Leander*, tone poem for orchestra (1900); *Punchinello*, for piano (1900); *Pan-Americana*, for piano, also for orchestra (1901); *Columbus*, for orchestra (1902); *Christ Is Arisen*, an Easter oratorio, for chorus and piano (1904); *Al fresco*, an intermezzo for piano (1904); *Spanish Rhapsody*, for orchestra (c. 1905); *Natoma*, opera (1911); *Madeleine*, opera (1913); *Whispering Willows*, for piano (1915); *Indian Lullaby*, for orchestra (1922); *Star of the North*, overture for orchestra (1923); Prelude, for orchestra (1923); *Dramatic Overture*, or *Under the Red Robe*, for orchestra (1923); *Golden Days Overture*, or *The Great White Way*, for orchestra (1923); *A Suite of Serenades*, for orchestra (1924); *Chant d'amour*, for organ (1924).

BIBLIOGRAPHY: Kaye Joseph, *Victor Herbert* (N.Y., 1931); Waters, Edward N., *Victor Herbert* (N.Y., 1955); *Musical America*, May 1931; *New York World*, June 1, 1924; *New York Times* (obituary), May 27, 1924, November 18, 1979, May 31, 1981.

Herrmann, Bernard, b., New York, June 29, 1911; d. Los Angeles, Calif., December 24, 1975.

Most often, Herrmann is remembered as one of the most prolific, successful, and innovative composers motion pictures have known. Less often is he recalled as the composer of excellent concert music that had significant performances in his time. He who, as conductor, promoted the cause of new music, however advanced, and who was one of the first to recognize and promote the music of Charles Ives, became an unashamed neoromanticist when he turned to composition, untouched by any of the styles that so beguiled many of his colleagues. Herrmann often used this neoromantic style to interpret various aspects of Americana.

He was born to a nonmusical family, the son of an optometrist. While attending public school, Herrmann studied the piano with local teachers. At thirteen, as a student at De Witt Clinton High School, he wrote a song, "The Bells," to a poem by Paul Verlaine, which won first prize of $100 in a competition. At New York University, he studied composition with Philip James and Percy Grainger. His now awakened interest in the new music and new idioms of such composers as Ives, Cowell, and Varèse was nurtured during the college years through association with two classmates, Arthur V. Berger and Jerome Moross. They soon became members of the Young Composers Group, made up of several progressive-minded young musicians who were stimulated and inspired by their mentor, Aaron Copland.

As a scholarship student at the Juilliard School of Music in New York, Herrmann studied composition with Bernard Wagenaar and conducting with Albert Stoessel. He remained at Juilliard just two years, leaving without graduating because the formal academic musical training he was getting there seemed to him stultified in comparison to the brave new music he was espousing. While at Juilliard, he completed a string quartet (1932).

In 1929, Herrmann made his conducting debut by leading an orchestra in ballet music he had written for one of the scenes in the Broadway intimate revue *Americana*. In 1933 he founded and directed the New Chamber Orchestra, which gave concerts in New York and Washington, D.C. That same year he became affiliated with radio for the first time by preparing the background music for poetic readings (called "melodramas") by David Ross over the Columbia Broadcasting System. Among his scores for these radio broadcasts were *The City of Brass*, *La belle dame sans merci*, *The Shropshire Lad* and *Annabel Lee* written in 1933–34. His first orchestral work for the concert stage was Nocturne and Scherzo (1935), premiered over the radio by the CBS Symphony with Howard Barlow conducting in the year of its composition. Hewing to a convervative line in this music, Herrmann fastidiously sidestepped the modern harmonic, rhythmic, and tonal devices he so favored in the music of others to produce music that was tonal, lyrical, and emotional.

In 1934 Herrmann was appointed assistant to John Green as composer and director of music for radio productions over the Columbia Broadcasting System network. During the next half dozen years he selected, arranged and conducted music for about 1,200 programs, writing original scores for 125 of them. One of the radio programs for which he served both as composer and conductor was the Orson Welles Mercury Theater presentations, including that historic broadcast of *The War of the Worlds* dramatizing a Martian attack on the United States that proved so realistic as to terrify an entire nation in 1938. As staff conductor for CBS, Herrmann directed performances of such musical programs as *Exploring Music* and *Invitation to Music*. Between 1940 and 1945 he was the conductor of the CBS Symphony, offering numerous performances of new music by Americans, including works by Ives, then little known and rarely played. Herrmann also led concerts of American music over the BBC network in London and with the Hallé Orchestra in Manchester.

As a composer, Herrmann early sought Americana subjects for his music. *The Skating Rink* (1934) was a five-movement ballet score whose scenario was inspired by the 19th-century prints and lithographs of American life, character and history by Currier and Ives. This ballet music, scored for vocal soloists, chorus, and orchestra, was written for the Radio City Music Hall in New York but was premiered in 1936 by the NBC Symphony with Erno Rapee conducting. *Moby Dick* (1937) was a cantata for solo voices, chorus, and orchestra, text by W. Clark Harrington based on Herman Melville's novel. It was successfully introduced by the New York Philharmonic and the Westminster Choir, John Barbirolli conducting, on April 11, 1930. Reviewing it in the *New York Herald Tribune*, Francis D. Perkins wrote: "It reveals a remarkable command of the resources of instrumental color and timbre, an exceptional ability to depict with convincing vividness a wide variety of emotional hues and atmospheres. . . . Mr. Herrmann's power for dramatic suggestion is best revealed in his instruments, although both the singers and the orchestra contributed to the sense of impending tragedy which marked the work as a whole." *Johnny Appleseed* (1940) was also a cantata for solo voices, chorus, and orchestra, lifting its principal character out of American folklore.

In 1939, Orson Welles called Herrmann to Hollywood to write the music for his first film, *Citizen Kane* (1941). This score, with which Herrmann made his debut as a composer for the screen, moved flexibly from the romantic to the dramatic while capturing the character of both Kane and the times in which he lived. Here, as in all his subsequent scores for the movies, Herrmann insisted on doing his own orchestrations, one of a rare few to do so in Hollywood. Out of this score, and out of the one he wrote for *The Magnificent Ambersons* (1942), Herrmann extracted some of the basic musical episodes for an orchestral suite entitled *Welles Raises Kane* (1943), which the CBS Symphony premiered the year of its composition under the direction of its composer.

In his music for the motion picture *All That Money Can Buy* (1941)—to meet the demands of Stephen Vincent Benét's short story *The Devil and Daniel Webster*, on which it was based—Herrmann incorporated into his music such authentic New Hampshire folk songs as "Springfield Mountain," "Lady McLeod's Reel" and "Devil's Dream." This is the score that brought him in 1941 his only Oscar from the American Academy of Motion Picture Arts and Sciences, though he was nominated for three others. This score was the source of an orchestral concert suite, *The Devil and Daniel Webster* (1942), first performed in 1942 by the CBS Symphony under the composer's direction over the radio and given its first concert hall presentation in 1944 by the Philadelphia Orchestra under Eugene Ormandy.

Herrmann's technical skill and grasp of a great variety of styles made it possible for him to meet the needs of each of his screen plays on its own terms. For *Anna and the King of Siam* (1946) he used the scales and melodic intervallic and the rhythmic structures of Siamese instruments, while confining himself to Western instruments. In this instance, as he explained, he wanted his music "to serve as musical scenery" rather than as "a commentary, or an emotional counterpart of the drama." For *The Day the Earth Stood Still* (1951), an early science-fiction film, Herrmann suggested the sounds of electronic music without actually using electronic instruments. He enlisted bizarre instrumental timbres, discordant harmonies and a dramatic use of percussion instruments to suggest the eerie atmosphere surrounding such Alfred Hitchcock suspense films as *Vertigo* (1958), *Psycho* (1960), and *The Birds* (1963). In all, Herrmann provided music for sixty-one films, among the most successful of which (besides those already mentioned) were *The Snows of Kilimanjaro* (1952), *The Trouble with Harry* (1955), *The Man Who Knew Too Much* (1956), *North by Northwest* (1959), *Sisters* (1973), *Obsession* (1975), and *Taxi Driver* (1975).

Despite his deep involvement with the screen, Herrmann did not neglect concert music. Symphony (1941) was introduced by the CBS Symphony under the composer's direction in 1941 and was performed by the New York Philharmonic under Howard Barlow on November 12, 1942. *The Fantasticks* (1944) was a song cycle for four vocal soloists and orchestra, first performed in 1942 by the CBS Symphony under the composer. *For the Fallen* (1944) was a tone poem inspired by World War II in which a melodic fragment of "He Shall Feed His Flock" from Handel's *Messiah* is quoted. It was commissioned by the League of Composers, was introduced by the New York Philharmonic under the composer's direction on December 16, 1943, and in 1945 was the recipient of the Juilliard Foundation Publication Award. *Wuthering Heights* (1948–50) was an opera, text based on the celebrated novel by Emily Brontë. It was never produced, but in 1966 it was recorded in its entirety in England. *A Christmas Carol* (1954) was an opera for television, produced over the CBS-TV network on December 23, 1954.

With a radical change in values in the writing of screen music taking place in Hollywood in the early 1960s, in which the hit songs and the sounds of rock took precedence over symphonically conceived scores, Herrmann abandoned California. The last ten years of his life were spent in England, where he was involved in making recordings and where he did the score for the François Truffaut motion picture *Fahrenheit 451* (1966). He returned to Hollywood in 1975 to write the music for the motion picture *Taxi Driver*. He completed this score the evening before he was found dead of a heart attack in his bed. Herrmann was survived by his third wife, Nora, a British journalist, and two children from his first marriage on October 2, 1939, to Lucille Fletcher. After divorcing his first wife, Herrmann married Lucille Anderson.

In 1942, Herrmann received a grant from the National Institute of Arts and Letters and the American Academy of Arts and Letters for his contributions to radio and films. He won two awards in 1947, one from Lord and Taylor, the department store, for his success in expanding the musical repertoire over the radio, and the other from the Society of American Composers for his overall services to American music.

THE COMPOSER SPEAKS: Musically I count myself an individualist. I believe that only music which springs out of genuine personal emotion is alive and important. I hate all cults, fads, and circles. I feel that a composer should be true to his own innate instincts and tastes, and develop these to the best of his ability, no matter what the present vogue may be. . . . I am not interested in music, or any work of art, that fails to stimulate appreciation of life and, more importantly, pride in life.

PRINCIPAL WORKS: Sinfonietta, for strings (1935); Nocturne and Scherzo, for orchestra (1935); *Moby Dick*, cantata for solo voices, chorus, and orchestra (1937); *Johnny Appleseed*, cantata for solo voices, chorus, and orchestra (1940); Symphony (1940); *Welles Raises Kane*, suite for orchestra (1943); *For the Fallen*, tone poem for orchestra (1943); *The Devil and Daniel Webster*, suite for orchestra (1942); *The Fantasticks*, for vocal quartet and orchestra (1944); *Wuthering Heights*, opera (1948–50); *A Christmas Carol*, TV opera (1954); *Echoes*, for string quartet and two dancers (1965); *Souvenirs de voyage*, for clarinet quintet (1967).

BIBLIOGRAPHY: Ewen, David, *American Composers Today* (N.Y., 1949); Howard, John Tasker, *Our Contemporary Composers* (N.Y., 1941); Thomas, Tony, *Music for the Movies* (Cranbury, N.J., 1973); *New York Times*, December 26, 1975 (obituary); *Saturday Review*, July 13, 1968.

Hewitt, James, b. Dartmoor, England, June 4, 1770; d. Boston, Mass., August 1, 1827.

He made a significant contribution to the musical culture of early America as a violinist, organist, impresario of concerts, conductor, teacher, and publisher. He was also a prolific composer of art songs and ballads, of instrumental compositions which often were naïvely literal in translating a given program into music, and of the first American opera on an American Indian subject.

He was the son of Capt. John Hewitt of the British navy. As a boy, James Hewitt followed in his father's footsteps by entering the navy, but left it in rebellion against the cruelty inflicted on British seamen. Apparently he was also musical and was encouraged by his father to pursue the study of the violin and music history. His professional involvement in music in London included leading the court orchestra of George III. In or about 1790 he married Louisa Lamb, but a year later both his wife and infant child died.

In 1792 he came to the United States for permanent residence, settling in New York, where he remained until 1812. With the support of several other English musicians who had arrived in America with him on his ship, Hewitt presented a concert in New York on September 21, 1792, which included one of the compositions he had undoubtedly written in England, an *Overture in Nine Movements*, "expressive of a Battle," in which battle scenes were created vividly in detail.

Hewitt made several more concert appearances in New York in 1793, including a series of six subscription concerts at Corre's Hotel between January and April 1793, the fifth of which (March 25, 1793) offered the American premiere of Haydn's *The Seven Last Words of the Savior on the Cross*. He also conducted the orchestra of the Old American Company, and in 1794 he published a volume of songs, *A Book of Songs*, in collaboration with Mary Ann Pownall, an English singer and actress. Later in 1794 he wrote the music for a political opera, *Tammany, or the Indian Chief*, produced by the Old American Company in New York that same year under the auspices of the Tammany Society, the first opera in America on an American Indian subject. It caused considerable controversy not for its music but for the political slant of its libretto by Anne Julia Hatton, which expressed Republican protest against the Federalist party, which was either highly praised or bitterly denounced, depending upon the political affiliation of the critics. It received performances in Philadelphia and Boston as well as in New York. Both the libretto and the score have been lost except for a single song, "The Death Song of the Cherokee Indian."

On December 10, 1795, Hewitt married one of his pupils, Eliza King. Each of their six children was active in the musical life of America, either as impresario, or concert pianist, or composer, or teacher, or publisher. The most celebrated was the firstborn son, John Hill Hewitt (1801—90), the composer of some three hundred popular songs and known as "the father of the American ballad" by virtue of such Civil War classics as "The Minstrel's Return from the War" and "All Quiet Along the Potomac."

While giving and arranging concerts both in and out of New York, Hewitt continued to be productive as a composer. He published three piano sonatas, probably in 1796, stylistically influenced by the early Beethoven. In 1796 he wrote *The New Federal Overture*, a potpourri of popular melodies of that day which was transcribed for small orchestra by R. D. Ward in 1975 and performed that way in Richmond, Va., on December 15 of that year. One of Hewitt's most famous instrumental pieces was *The Battle of Trenton*, for piano, dedicated to George Washington, written in 1792. Its subtitles provide the program which Hewitt's music described so graphically: "The

Army in Motion," "Attack—Cannons—Bombs," "Flight of the Hessians," "General Confusion," "Articles of Capitulation Signed," Trumpets of Victory," and "General Rejoicing" —all this topped off with a meretricious rendering of "Yankee Doodle." John W. Wagner described Hewitt's instrumental works, particularly his programmatic ones and his marches, as "bombastic, trite, and generally lacking in good taste," and this proved particularly true of his "battle music." In 1950–51, Richard Bales provided an orchestral adaptation of *The Battle of Trenton* which he performed in Washington, D.C., on April 22, 1951.

Hewitt's later instrumental compositions included a "grand military sonata" for piano, published sometime between 1801 and 1811, and the *Grand Sinfonie, Characteristic of the Peace of the French Republic*, performed by his orchestra in 1802 and greatly admired in its time. He also wrote numerous ballad operas, most of which have been lost except for some of their vocal numbers, and a library of songs which reveal a simplicity of approach and a freshness of lyricism not often encountered in his other compositions. His finest vocal music included such sentimental ballads as "The Music of the Harp of Love," "The Wounded Hussar," "How Happy Was My Humble Lot," "When the Shades of Night Pursuing," "Song of the Waving Willow," and "In a Far Distant Clime I Have Left a Sweet Rose." The last of these was favorably compared by William Treat Upton in *The Art Song in America* to Mozart's songs for its harmonic and melodic invention. Hewitt also wrote patriotic ballads. The most celebrated of these was "The Federal Constitution and Liberty Forever," in which he quoted "Yankee Doodle" and "Washington's March." R. D. Ward adapted this song for small orchestra in 1975, introducing it in Richmond, Va., on December 15, 1975. Hewitt provided a new musical setting for Francis Scott Key's words to "The Star-Spangled Banner" in 1816, but this found little favor and was soon forgotten.

In 1798, Hewitt acquired the New York branch of Carr's Musical Repository and used it as a publishing house of his own. After 1812, Hewitt's home base was Boston, where he was organist at the Trinity Church and the director of musical activities at the Federal Street Theater. He was back in New York in 1824 to arrange the orchestral accompaniments for Micah Hawkins's ballad opera *The Sawmill*, or *A Yankee Trick*, produced at the Chatham Square Theater on November 29, 1824.

During his last two years, Hewitt was afflicted with a facial cancer that brought on total blindness. His burial place is no longer known.

PRINCIPAL WORKS: *The Battle of Trenton*, for piano (1792); *Battle Overture*, for orchestra (1792); *Tammany*, opera (1794); *A Patriot*, or *Liberty Asserted*, opera (1794); *Storm Overture*, for orchestra (1795); Three Piano Sonatas (1795–96); *The Mysterious*

Marriage, opera (1799); *Columbus*, opera (1799); *Pizarro*, opera (1800); *Robin Hood*, opera (1800); *The Wild Goose Chase*, opera (1800); *The Fourth of July*, a grand military sonata for piano (published between 1801 and 1811); *Grand Sinfonie, Characteristic of the Peace of the French Republic*, for orchestra (c. 1802); *Theme and Variations*, for piano (1803–06).

BIBLIOGRAPHY: Howard, John Tasker, *Our American Music* (N.Y., 1946); Upton, William Treat, *The Art Song in America* (Boston, 1930); Wagner, John W., *James Hewitt: His Life and Works* (doctoral thesis, Bloomington, Ind., 1969); *Musical Quarterly*, April 1972.

Hill, Edward Burlingame, b. Cambridge, Mass., September 9, 1872; d. Francestown, N.H., July 9, 1960.

Hill practiced what he preached: As a distinguished professor of composition and orchestration at Harvard for thirty-two years he taught the structural and stylistic values of musical conservatism. As a composer, his own "modernism" consisted primarily of impressionistic writing; otherwise, he was the complete conservative. His best works were instrumental. He was partial to wind instruments in his chamber music, and to the orchestra.

He seemed predestined for an academic career—and specifically for a career at Harvard both as student and as professor—since his grandfather, Thomas Hill, was president of Harvard just before Charles Williams Eliot, and his father, Henry B. Hill, was professor of organic chemistry at this university. "My father sang the songs of Schubert and Robert Franz," Edward Burlingame Hill once recalled, "and was a great admirer of Bach. Thus at an early age I was imbued with a deep love for serious music. I wasted many years in trying to play the piano with only one good result: a sound knowledge of its literature." Two of his father's friends were important in Edward Hill's early musical development: John Knowles Paine, who had established at Harvard the first music department in any American college, and the noted music critic William F. Apthorp.

Hill went to Harvard, "as a matter of course," for his academic education in 1890, where he took all of the music courses given by Paine. Hill graduated with a bachelor of arts degree, *summa cum laude*, in 1894. The next two years were spent in New York studying the piano with B. J. Lang and Arthur Whiting—a time, he added, "chiefly valuable for acquiring independence." Returning to Boston, he began earning his living by teaching piano and harmony. He spent the summer of 1898 in Paris studying composition with Charles Widor. On June 12, 1900, he married Alison Bixby, with whom he raised four sons.

His first compositions to outgrow creative apprenticeship were suites for the piano: *Poetical Sketches* (1902) and *Country Idyls*, a set of six pieces written at about the same time. Both were attempts to imitate the style of MacDowell's delicate tonal pictures of nature which then impressed Hill greatly. A course in orchestration with George Chadwick at the New England Conservatory in 1902 turned Hill to writing orchestral works, henceforth to become an all-important medium for him, while further study of composition with Frederick Field Bullard provided him with the technique he needed to grapple with forms more ambitious than pieces for the piano or songs. Thus, in 1907, he completed writing *Nuns of Perpetual Adoration*, a cantata for women's voices and orchestra, which enjoyed a marked success in Birmingham, England, in 1912 when it was performed there under the direction of Sir Granville Bantock.

In 1908 Hill was appointed instructor of music at Harvard as a substitute for Professor Spalding, then on leave. Hill remained at Harvard for the next three decades, becoming associate professor in 1918, full professor in 1928, and James F. Ditson Professor in 1937. He retired in 1940.

He found his first significant opportunity to write for orchestra in 1908 when the Boston artist Joseph Lindon Smith asked him to prepare the music for *Jack Frost in Midsummer*, a pantomime-ballet scheduled for a benefit concert of the Chicago Orchestra that year. "I had the valuable experience of having this somewhat tentative music carefully rehearsed by Frederick Stock," Hill said, "and learned much as to orchestral effect." He wrote the music for a second ballet-pantomime six years later, *Pan and the Star*.

Influenced by the modern French school and impressionism, Hill turned to the writing of program music with the tone poem *The Parting of Lancelot and Guinevere* (1915), introduced in St. Louis on December 31, 1915, then performed by the Boston Symphony Orchestra on March 24, 1916. *The Fall of the House of Usher* (1920), another programmatic tone poem, this one based on Edgar Allan Poe's story, was given its initial hearing on October 29, 1920, by the Boston Symphony.

With two *Stevensoniana* suites for orchestra (1917, 1922), inspired by Robert Louis Stevenson's *A Child's Garden of Verses*, and in his most celebrated orchestral work, *Lilacs* (1926), Hill strove for atmospheric verity within an impressionist style but with no concern for specific descriptive details. The suites were introduced by the New York Symphony under Walter Damrosch on January 27, 1918, and March 25, 1923, respectively before being programmed by the Boston Symphony. *Lilacs*, suggested by a poem by Amy Lowell, was premiered in Cambridge, Mass., on March 31, 1927, and was heard in four different seasons on the programs of the Boston Symphony under Serge Koussevitzky, beginning with April 1, 1927. The Boston Symphony, under

Koussevitzky, was responsible for the premiere of Waltzes (1921; February 24, 1922) and Scherzo, for two pianos and orchestra (1924; December 19, 1924).

After 1927, Hill turned permanently away from his former programmatic style in favor of more abstract music still in an impressionist vein. "In this," he confesses, "I was doubtless affected by the attitudes of younger composers." This abstract approach is found in three symphonies, all given their premieres by the Boston Symphony under Koussevitzky: Symphony no. 1 in B-flat major (1927) on March 30, 1928; Symphony no. 2 in C major (1929) on February 27, 1931; and Symphony no. 3 in G major (1937) on December 3, 1937. An Ode, for chorus and orchestra to a text by Robert Hillyer, was written to commemorate the fiftieth anniversary of the Boston Symphony, which performed it on October 17, 1930. In addition to the above works, the Boston Symphony also offered the world premieres of the Sinfonietta, for string orchestra (1932; Brooklyn, N.Y., April 3, 1936); Violin Concerto (1933–37; November 10, 1938); Concertino for String Orchestra (1940; April 19, 1940); Music for English horn and Orchestra (1943; March 2, 1945); and Prelude, for orchestra (1953; N.Y., March 29, 1953).

After 1926, Hill also produced a good deal of chamber music in much of which he used wind instruments whose expressive personalities had a special appeal for him. A sonata for flute (1926) was followed a year later by a clarinet sonata. On a commission from Elizabeth Sprague Coolidge he completed in 1934 a Sextet for five winds (flute, oboe, clarinet, bassoon and horn) and piano, successfully performed at the Pittsfield Music Festival in Massachusetts on September 20, 1934. After that he wrote a String Quartet (1935), Piano Quartet (1937), Sonata for Two Clarinets (1938), a Clarinet Quintet (1945), and a Bassoon Sonata (1948) among other chamber music compositions.

In 1921, Hill lectured on French music at the universities of Strasbourg and Lyons, and in 1924 he served on the International Jury for Musical Composition at the Olympic Games in Paris. He was a member of the National Institute of Arts and Letters and of the American Academy of Arts and Letters. France decorated him as a chevalier of the Legion of Honor. Hill was the author of *French Music* (1924).

THE COMPOSER SPEAKS: My method of composition? Orchestral works are always composed in sketch and then orchestrated with many changes necessary for orchestral style. I am unfortunately addicted to the use of a piano when composing. Being devoted to the country, I do my best work there. The location of my small workshop in the woods is most conducive to composition. I seldom compose except in the morning. I believe the eraser an all-important adjunct to composition. I think I get better results from a few

hours of concentration, followed by relaxation, which brings a fresh viewpoint the following morning.

PRINCIPAL WORKS: 3 symphonies (1927, 1929, 1937); 2 *Stevensoniana* suites for orchestra (1917, 1922).

The Parting of Lancelot and Guinevere, tone poem for orchestra (1915); *The Fall of the House of Usher*, tone poem for orchestra (1920); Waltzes, for orchestra (1921); Scherzo, for two pianos and orchestra (1924); *Jazz Study*, for two pianos (1924); *Lilacs*, tone poem for orchestra (1926); Flute Sonata (1926); Clarinet Sonata (1927); Ode, for chorus and orchestra (1930); Piano Concertino (1931); Sinfonietta, for string orchestra (1932); Violin Concerto (1933–37); Sextet, for flute, oboe, clarinet, bassoon, horn, and piano (1934); String Quartet (1935); Piano Quartet (1937); Sonata for Two Clarinets (1938); Concertino for String Orchestra (1940); Music for English horn and Orchestra (1943); Clarinet Quintet (1945); Diversion, for small ensemble (1946); Concerto for Two Flutes and Small Orchestra (1947); Bassoon Sonata (1948); Four Pieces, for small orchestra (1948); Cello Sonatina (1949); Violin Sonatina (1951); Prelude, for orchestra (1953).

BIBLIOGRAPHY: Ewen, David, *American Composers Today* (N.Y., 1949); Howard, John Tasker, *Our Contemporary Composers* (N.Y., 1941); Thomson, Virgil, *American Music Since 1910* (N.Y., 1970).

Hiller, Lejaren Arthur, Jr., b. New York City, February 23, 1924.

Hiller began his career as composer with abstract music for traditional instruments within traditional structures and in traditional idioms. He then became involved with electronic music and was one of the first to write computer-made music. In addition to electronic music, he has interested himself in multimedia productions, twelve-tone and serial music, microtonal music, aleatory music, and music expressive of Americana. However wide the diversity of style and resources, his music through the years has shown a consistent profile and a logical development.

In his early years he anticipated the duality of his later professional life by becoming interested in both science and music. "My parents," he recalls, "owned a Duo-art player piano. I often fooled around at the keyboard and even often tried to jot down my own tunes. I found, however, that I could obtain highly satisfying effects by cutting designs and punching holes into the piano roles." To canalize his musical impulses more constructively, and into a more socially acceptable form, his parents had him take formal piano lessons with Harvey Brown (1938–41). Though Hiller made significant progress at the keyboard, his main interest lay not in playing the piano but in composing. From Harvey Officer, he received instruction in harmony from 1939 to 1941, and was given constructive guidance in the pieces he was now beginning to compose. During this same period, Hiller also learned to play the clarinet and saxophone.

From the first through the twelfth grades, Hiller attended Friends Seminary, a Quaker-run private school in New York, from which he graduated in 1941. In his high school years he sang in choral groups and played in a percussion ensemble. He also earned his first money through music by singing the jingle in a pet-food commercial for a radio station.

With the intention of specializing in chemistry—he had long shown both an interest in and a talent for that science—Hiller entered Princeton University in 1941. While concentrating on the sciences and specializing in chemistry, he attended the classes of Milton Babbitt in strict counterpoint, ear training, and composition (1941–42) and those of Roger Sessions in composition and analysis (1942–45). Outside the university, he took lessons in oboe playing from Joseph Marx (1941–43). As a woodwind performer, Hiller participated in many of the regular concerts heard at Princeton in addition to playing with and managing a college dance band for several years. He now also wrote the earliest works that he chose to save and sometimes to revise: his first two piano sonatas (1946–47) and his first chamber music work, a Trio for Violin, Cello, and Piano (1947). All were conservative in style and idiom. "I was more interested in acquiring technique and fluency before breaking ground," he explains.

On April 18, 1945, in Elkton, Md., Hiller married Elizabeth Halsey, an actress, with whom he had two children. At Princeton, Hiller received his bachelor of arts degree in 1944, his master of arts degree in 1946 and his doctorate in 1947, all in chemistry. Sessions strongly suggested that he now continue to study music exclusively towards a career, but for the time being science took precedence over music as a profession. Between 1947 and 1952, Hiller was employed by E. I. Du Pont de Nemours and Company in Waynesboro, Va., to do research in cellulose chemistry, reaction rate studies, and dyestuff chemistry; his final research work led to the discovery of the successful method for dyeing such acrylic fibers as Orlon with cationic "basic" dyes. While thus employed, Hiller did not neglect composition. Among other works he completed were *Seven Artifacts,* for piano (1948), his first attempt at experimentation by investigating somewhat novel scales, structures, and harmonic systems, and *Jesse James,* for vocal quartet and upright piano (1950), to a text by William Rose Benét, an early reflection of Hiller's later interest in Americana. In addition he produced his first two string quartets (1949, 1951), a Piano Concerto (1949), his Violin Sonata no. 1 (1949), the third and fourth piano sonatas (1949, 1950), and Suite, for small orchestra (1951). The Piano Concerto and Suite were Hiller's first works to be performed, at a concert of the Virginia Symphony Orchestra in Waynesboro on April 17, 1951. All these compositions may be regarded as transitional works between his conservative past and his innovative future.

In 1952, Hiller left the Du Pont Company to assume the post of research associate in physical chemistry at the University of Illinois at Urbana. His assignment was to work on a problem of statistical mechanics requiring the use of ILLIAC I (acronym of Illinois Accumulator), a digital computer at the university which enabled him to generate and evaluate the necessary data. "I soon saw analogies between what I was doing (restricted random flights) and processes for music composition." During 1955 and 1956, with the collaboration of Leonard Isaacson, he wrote a number of programs for the ILLIAC I which they fed into the computer and which, once the computer language had been translated into notes, became the *ILLIAC Suite,* for string quartet (1957)—now listed as String Quartet No. 4—probably the first composition to have been produced through a computer. "The problem was," Hiller has explained, "to restate music values in terms of mathematics. We put the rules of counterpoint . . . into language the computer could handle. The computer went to work on it and we obtained as an end product a score which could be played. The computer works just like a composer, by trial and error—more trial than error. It will erase notes that don't fit in, and like a human composer it can write itself into a box where whole sections of the composition have to be rewritten." the *ILLIAC Suite* was introduced at Urbana on August 9, 1956. In *Experimental Music* (1959) Hiller and Isaacson described the processes involved in the preparation of the *ILLIAC Suite.*

In the music for traditional instruments that Hiller was producing at this time he was entering other new worlds of sound textures and techniques. The *Twelve-Tone Variations* for piano (1954; Buffalo, N.Y., April 12, 1969) is one of Hiller's earliest works composed according to serial techniques. But the strict style of the Viennese school is not adhered to. In this work, the theme is a combination of six tone rows instead of a single row, and the six rows bear no particular relationship to one another. Nevertheless, they are combined to form a melodic phrase several bars long that constitutes the actual "theme" of the whole set of variations. The first movement consists of four presentations of this theme, and the remaining four movements are all variations derived from this basic material. Divertimento, for eleven instruments including Theremin (1959), ranges from tonal and serial structures to chance music. Microtonal music is explored in String Quartet no. 5, "In Quarter Tones" (1962; Binghamton, N.Y., September 25, 1971), in which the four instrumentalists had to learn a completely new playing technique and develop new listening habits. "To assist in this," the composer explains, "in the score I have consistently notated all quarter tones by inserting small downward pointing arrows following notes written in ordinary notation. Thus the performer has at his disposal in effect two twelve-tone scales tuned a quarter tone apart from each other."

While at the University of Illinois, Hiller studied the Heinrich Schenker theory of composition with Hubert Kessler (1953–55) and took other courses in music that enabled him to obtain a master of music degree in 1958. That year he accepted a position to found an electronic music studio for the School of Music at the university; it was at this juncture in his life that he changed his profession permanently from chemistry to music. He served as assistant professor of music from 1961 to 1965 and full professor from 1965 to 1968. Although members of the old guard on the music faculty made no effort to hide their hostility to the electronic studio, their influence gradually declined and the studio became accepted as an integral part of the local scene. During this period, Hiller also organized with Jack McKenzie the University of Illinois Contemporary Chamber Players, a group that toured Europe in 1966 and which still exists.

With the establishment of that studio, Hiller became deeply involved in the writing of electronic music. He completed *Blue Is the Antecedent of It,* an electronic theater fantasy in 1959. This is a tape score made up of ten sections for a one-act play by Jack Leckel. Some sections were recorded by groups of actors in the studio before the production, while others accompany the action as incidental music. This production was introduced at the University of Illinois on March 18, 1959, to an outraged audience. Almost a decade later, at an all-Hiller concert in New York, it was seen in a revised version as a dance production without text. In 1960, Hiller once again applied the resources of electronic music for the stage in *Cuthbert Bound,* chamber music for four actors and tape, performed at Urbana on January 14, 1960. It used a text by Christopher Newton. Away from the theater, Hiller prepared the *Seven Electronic Studies,* for two-channel tape (1963), and the *Computer Cantata,* for live soprano and chamber ensemble and tape (1963), the latter written in collaboration with Robert Baker. This cantata was the first of a proposed series of compositions to be prepared by means of a generalized programming procedure called MUSICOMP written for the IBM-7094 electronic digital computer. But the *Computer Cantata* was actually prepared with three different computers. The text (by Lee Hultzén, Joseph Allen, and Murray Miron, consisting of five stochastic approximations to spoken English), was generated with ILLIAC I; the musical score was done by means of MUSICOMP with IBM-7090; and two examples of computer-generated sounds were prepared with the CSX-1 computer of the Coordinated Science Laboratory. This cantata was introduced at Urbana on December 8, 1963, and soon after that was recorded by the same group that had performed it originally. Reviewing the recording in *Hi-Fi Stereo,* Eric Salz-

man considered the final result "an impressive web of sound," adding: "The vocal text is based on a kind of imaginary English invented by the computer out of the actual sounds of English. Fields of pitched sound and unpitched rhythmic percussion are played in big patches—something like a colorfield painting or certain aspects of abstract expressionism in which the big form is controlled but details fall in random but perfectly consistent patterns." The last electronic composition Hiller worked upon in Illinois was *HPSCHD* (in computer language, "harpsichord" without the vowels), for one to seven harpsichords and one to fifty-one tapes (1968). This was a multimedia production composed in collaboration with John Cage. All soloists except one were generated by a computer program based on Mozart's *Musical Dicegame* (K. 294-d) and an aleatory method arrived at through the *I-Ching Book of Changes.* When the first complete performance was given in Urbana on May 16, 1969, in a circular 18,000-seat assembly hall, and including massive amounts of additional audio-visual effects, Richard Kostelanetz called it, in the *New York Times,* "the multimedia event of the decade."

In 1968, Hiller left Urbana to occupy the Frederick B. Slee Chair in composition at the State University of New York in Buffalo. Not long after his arrival, this appointment was made permanent and included an arrangement whereby he could also serve with Lukas Foss as codirector of the Center of Creative and Performing Arts. In 1974, Hiller relinquished this codirectorship to Morton Feldman in order to take over and build up the Experimental Studio at Buffalo. Under his direction, it became one of the few "in houses" of computer systems for digital-to-analog sound synthesis and other up-to-date technology.

Among Hiller's later electronic works is a series of compositions collectively entitled *Algorithms,* composed entirely with a computer, and the direct descendants of the *ILLIAC Suite* and the *Computer Cantata.* These *Algorithms* were prepared to demonstrate in successive movements how compositional modules expressed as closed subroutines can impose musical order upon a stochastically chosen musical matrix. "My objective in creating these works is didactic," Hiller explains. "Here I am continuing to investigate the logic of musical composition for its own sake rather than to have it serve other expressive purposes." There are four alternate versions for each of these *Algorithms,* any of which may be chosen for a given performance. *Algorithms* I (1968) and *Algorithms* IV (1970) were introduced in Buffalo, N.Y., on February 8, 1970, the composer conducting; the second at St. Paul de Vence in France on July 20, 1970; the third, in Rochester, N.Y., on March 17, 1973. Two succeeding *Algorithms* were prepared in 1972 and 1980 respectively. *Algorithms* II was written in collaboration with Ravi Kumra.

Hiller's later works outside the field of electronics

include a curiosity: the Piano Sonata no. 6, subtitled "Rage Over the Lost Beethoven" and inspired by a "museum piece" by Frank Parman with that same title. Its first movement is a musical search for Beethoven and his style from his youth to full maturity, composed in sonata form with an introduction, two complete expositions, development and recapitulation; materials from Beethoven's piano works are tapped. This sonata can be performed as a theatrical work and was so produced in Buffalo, N.Y., on February 10, 1972. It can also be heard as a concert work for solo piano; as such it was premiered by Goeffrey Madge in Middleburg, Holland, on July 1, 1978.

String Quartet no. 6 (1972) was written for the Concord String Quartet, which presented it first on January 24, 1973, in New York. This is mildly programmatic in that it is a commentary on environmental soundscapes, both pleasant and offensive. Much of the musical material comes from sound patterns Hiller heard, jotted down, and sometimes recorded—sounds that originated in the racket and noise of commercial and industrial areas, or sounds from relatively peaceful circumstances.

On a Fulbright lectureship, Hiller spent 1973–74 in Warsaw, Poland, giving courses in experimental and American music and working in the Experimental Studio of the Polish Radio. On a commission from the Polish Radio, he wrote *A Portfolio for Diverse Performers and Tapes* (1975). Hiller describes this piece as "a portfolio containing many diverse elements intended for use in a variety of situations." In one long movement, slow in pace, it becomes increasingly more complex as new elements are added until a climax is reached halfway through. Then it gradually recedes to its original state to reach at its end a perfectly symmetrical arch. *Portfolio* was given its initial hearing on September 20, 1975, in Reykjavik, Iceland.

Hiller paid a return visit to Warsaw in January 1978. At that time, he came upon a homemade instrument labeled "devil's fiddle" (*diabelskie skrzypce*). Taking it back with him to Malta, where he was then living for a time, he had it built to make the tuning similar to that of a cello. For it he wrote *Diabelskie Skrzypce,* for stringed instrument and harpsichord (1978), given its first hearing at a festival in Middleburg, Holland, on June 30, 1978.

THE COMPOSER SPEAKS: I have always gone my own way, basically a lone wolf. I write what I want to write and in the final analysis never have been much concerned whether other people (other composers, critics, audiences, anyone) approve or disapprove. It is not that I am arrogant, hostile or embattled. Not at all! It's just that I get wrapped up in each successive compositional (or research) project and its necessities seem (to me) to override other considerations. So usually, especially more recently, I have been thoroughly innovative and provocative; other times, however, I have most assuredly been "après-garde," if

you will accept the term, rather than "avant-garde," if the circumstances require it.

Some composers find that they work most effectively by steadily and slowly progressing from one piece to the next in a clearly perceived evolution of style and idea. The consistency seems necessary to their development. With me, I seem to need to address each new compositional project as something that should differ, even radically, from previous efforts, that should have its own identity and gesture. Hence, everything is grist for the mill—from the abstract experimentation of computer pieces to multimedia extravaganzas, to expressions of Americana, to twelve-tone and serial music, to microtone, to popular musical comedy style, to classical romantic mainstream, to folk-music sources."

PRINCIPAL WORKS: 7 string quartets (1949–79); 6 piano sonatas (1946–72); 5 *Algorithms,* for nine instruments and tape (1968–80); 3 violin sonatas (1949, 1955, 1970); 2 symphonies (1953, 1960).

Piano Trio (1947); *Seven Artifacts,* for piano (1948, revised 1973); Piano Concerto (1949); *Jesse James,* for vocal quartet and piano (1950); Suite, for small orchestra (1951); Fantasy, for three pianos (1951); *Twelve-Tone Variations,* for piano (1954); Two Theater Pieces, for piano (1956); Scherzo, for piano (1958); *Five Appalachian Ballads,* for voice and guitar or harpsichord (1958); Divertimento, for chamber ensemble (1959); *Blue Is the Antecedent of It,* for tape (1959); *Cuthbert Bound,* chamber music for four actors and tape (1960); *Amplification,* for tape and theater band (1962); *Seven Electronic Studies,* for tape (1963); *Computer Cantata,* for soprano, chamber ensemble, and tape, written with Robert Baker (1963); *Machine Music,* for piano, percussion, and tape (1964); *A Triptych for Hieronymus,* a multimedia production for actors, dancers, acrobats, projections, tape, and orchestra (1966); Suite for Two Pianos and Tape (1966); *HPSCHD,* for one to seven harpsichords and one to fifty-one tapes, written with John Cage (1968); *Computer Music for Percussion and Tape,* written with G. Allen O'Connor (1968); *Three Rituals,* for two percussion, film, and lights (1969); *A Cenotaph,* for two pianos (1971); *A Portfolio for Diverse Performers and Tapes* (1975); *Malta,* for tuba and tape (1975); *A Preview of Coming Attractions,* for orchestra (1975); *Electronic Sonata,* for four-channel tape (1976); *Midnight Carnival,* for numerous tapes in an urban environment (1976); *Persiflage,* for flute, oboe, and percussion (1977); *Ponteach,* a melodrama for narrator and piano (1977); *Diabelskie Skrzypce,* for stringed instrument and harpsichord (1978); *An Apotheosis of Achaeopterix,* for piccolo and Berimbau (1979).

BIBLIOGRAPHY: Lincoln, H.B. (editor), *The Computer and Music* (Ithaca, N.Y., 1970); *DCM; Schwartz, Elliott, Electronic Music* (N.Y., 1973); Thomson, Virgil, *American Music Since 1910*

(N.Y., 1970); *Who's Who in America, 1980–81.*

Hindemith, Paul, b. Hanau, Germany, November 16, 1895; d. Frankfurt, Germany, December 28, 1963. American citizen, 1946.

One of the giants of 20th-century music, Hindemith was a neoclassicist. Marching under the banner of *Neue Sachlichkeit* ("New Objectivity"), a "back to Bach" movement launched by Max Reger and Ferruccio Busoni, Hindemith favored a polyphonic style within the classical structures in which the voices in the polyphonic web moved independently of harmonic relationships, a practice that came to be known as linear counterpoint. His music is dissonant, intense, subtle in its intellectual processes, inexorable in its structural logic, and objective in its expressivity.

A descendant of Silesian artisans, Hindemith was the oldest of three children, one of whom, Rudolf, became a concert cellist. Their father was a decorator and house painter. In 1902, the family moved to Mühlhausen. There, two years later, Hindemith received his first instruction in music by taking violin lessons with Eugen Reinhardt. He commuted daily to Frankfurt to complete his academic education in elementary school; while so doing, he continued violin study in Frankfurt with Anna Hegner. Two years later, Hegner turned him over to Adolf Rebner, who said: "I immediately recognized the boy's remarkable talent."

When Hindemith completed his elementary schooling in 1908 he entered Rebner's violin class at Hoch's Conservatory in Frankfurt on a scholarship. He had also received some instruction in harmony but none in composition when he began a prolific output of music, including a string quartet, two piano trios, three violin sonatas, and an extended work for cello, none of which has survived.

At Hoch's Conservatory, Hindemith began studying composition with Arnold Mendelssohn. Later he continued these lessons with Bernhard Sekles while also attending the conducting class of Fritz Basserman. To help support himself, Hindemith played the violin in taverns, cafés, and movie theaters and during the summers in minor Swiss orchestras. His first composition to get a public hearing was a set of piano variations performed at the conservatory on July 15, 1913.

In 1915, while still a student at the conservatory, Hindemith was appointed violinist in the Frankfurt Opera Orchestra. Three months later he was elevated to the post of concertmaster. He supplemented his income by teaching, playing the violin (later, viola) in the Adolf Rebner Quartet, and performing on the violin in the orchestra at the Museum Concerts conducted by Willem Mengelberg.

By the time he was nineteen he had completed more chamber music, including his first published work, Andante and Scherzo, for clarinet, horn, and piano (1914), and String Quartet no. 1 (1918), the latter awarded the Mendelssohn Prize. These and several later compositions—including a Cello Concerto (1915) and a Sinfonietta, for small orchestra (1916), influenced mainly by Brahms and Richard Strauss—were thoroughly conventional in structure and harmonic idiom. A Piano Quintet op. 7 (1917), was his first work to head toward a direction of his own. As he wrote in explanation: "The piece must never sound like an orthodox quintet with a first and second theme. It should give the impression of a colorful improvisation." Of one of his piano pieces written in 1917 he wrote: "It sounds thoroughly degenerate; has no rhythm, key, or harmony of any recognizable sort. If I go on in this vein I shall come to a territory beyond good and evil where it will be impossible for me to know whether I have written a higher sort of music or just a substitute for music."

In 1917, he was called into military service. A year later he was stationed in France, where he played the drum in a military band and the violin in a string quartet performing for the commanding officer. Released from military duty in 1919, he returned to his various musical commitments in Frankfurt. On June 2, 1919, an all-Hindemith program was presented by the Society of Theatrical and Musical Culture in Frankfurt in which his String Quartet no. 1, the Piano Quintet and two sonatas, one for violin (1918) and the other for viola (1919), were heard. "The composer's remarkable melodic invention, his surprisingly assured mastery of form and the powerful impetus of his works entitle us to speak of a creative talent far beyond the average," reported Karl Holl in the *Frankfurter Zeitung.* The success of this concert helped bring him the publisher with whom he remained for the rest of his life, Schott und Söhne.

He was moving further away from the compositional norm of his day, causing some of his closest friends and admirers to raise questioning and at times critical eyebrows. Commenting on Hindemith's *Three Hymns by Walt Whitman*, for baritone and piano (1919), and the Piano Sonata op. 17 (1919), his friend Willy Strecker wrote him: "You have given us a hard nut to crack with your new piano sonata and songs. We are completely puzzled by your sudden change of direction. Your new radical style seems to us to obscure those individual characteristics we so much admire in you." Hindemith's reply was: "It is all true and natural music, not in the least bit 'forced' . . . I could not write this way before because I was still too undeveloped technically."

In 1922, he helped found the Amar String Quartet, in which he played viola; for the next seven years he toured with this group in concerts favoring new music, including some of his own compositions. Among the places where the Amar String Quartet was heard was the Donaueschingen Festival in

Germany, which Hindemith had helped to organize to provide a hearing of new composers and new music, particularly experimental music. When, at the first festival in August 1921, Richard Strauss heard the Amar String Quartet perform Hindemith's String Quartet no. 2, he asked Hindemith: "Why do you compose atonal music? You have plenty of talent." Hindemith replied sternly: "Herr Professor, you make your music, and I'll make mine." This reply is particularly significant in pointing up how far Hindemith had already traveled from the Straussian neoromanticism that in his earlier years had been a fetish.

At the beginning of his rebellion against romanticism Hindemith produced several works in which comdey, satire, and grotesquerie were significant elements. *Kammermusik* no. 1, op. 24, for chamber orchestra (1922; Donauenschingen Festival, July 31, 1922) had a finale entitled "1921," which reflected the bitterness and despair in postwar Germany through a sardonic interpolation of a German fox trot, *Fuchstanz.*" Good humor, mockery, and irony are present in *Kleine Kammermusik* op. 24, no. 2, for flute, oboe, clarinet, and bassoon (1922), one of Hindemith's most popular early works, in which a delightful parody of dance hall music is heard. These qualities can also be found in two one-act operas produced in Stuttgart, Germany, on June 4, 1921: *Mörder, Hoffnung der Frauen* (1919), to an expressionist text by Kokoschka, and *Das Nunsch-Nuschi*, a little opera for Burmese marionettes to an expressionist text by Franz Blei (1919); in the latter, Hindemith makes an amusing interpolation of a theme from *Tristan and Isolde.*

But his rebellion took another and more significant direction as well: toward the kind of classicism and objectivity that Busoni had promoted which denied the importance of any individual element in the music and which, as Hindemith himself put it, "purified music from all the elements not deriving from its inner being." Modern idiomatic innovations, however, are not sacrificed. Hindemith now began paying increasing attention to contrapuntal writing. By freeing the polyphonic voices from harmonic relationships, Hindemith arrived at linear counterpoint that was dissonant, which deserted tonal principles of construction and arrived at new techniques of tonality of his own devising. This style appears forcefully in two string quartets—no. 3, op. 22 (1922: Donauenschingen Festival, November 4, 1922) and no. 4, op. 32 (1922). In both, the key signature is dispensed with and in the first movement of Quartet no. 3 an atonal fugato allows each of its voices to move independently. *Das Marienleben*, a song cycle for soprano and piano (1923; Donauenschingen Festival, June 17, 1923), is an early example of Hindemith's growing interest in the polyphonic music of the early 18th century (and particularly that of Johann Sebastian Bach) as well as a directness and purity of style

and simplicity of form. Hindemith revised this cycle extensively between 1936 and 1948, the new version heard first on November 3, 1948 in Hanover, Germany.

On May 15, 1924, Hindemith married Gertrud Rottenberg, daughter of the conductor of the Frankfurt opera. Two years later he completed writing his first full-length opera, in which his antiromanticism and his ideal of objectivity were once again successfully realized. This was *Cardillac*, libretto by Ferdinand Lion based on E.T.A. Hoffmann, first produced on November 9, 1926, in Dresden. Reverting to a Handel-like operatic structure made up of separate musical numbers and, at the same time, taking a cue from Alban Berg's *Wozzeck* by applying instrumental forms to opera, Hindemith realized a style consistently economical and austere, linear in its contrapuntal writing, and spare in its resources. In 1952, Hindemith thoroughly overhauled the opera by providing it with a new libretto, rewriting some of the original music and supplementing it with new material, and emphasizing dramatic and psychological interest over musical ones. This revision was premiered in Zurich, Switzerland, on June 20, 1952.

In 1927, Hindemith left Frankfurt for Berlin to become professor of composition at the Berlin High School for Music and later to be made a member of the German Academy. In Berlin, Hindemith began an eventful career as a teacher of composition who influenced a generation of composers. Hindemith's teaching methods were elaborated on in *The Craft of Musical Composition* (1937–39) and *A Composer's World: Horizons and Limitations* (1954), with which his position as one of the foremost musical theoreticians of the 20th century was solidified.

In Berlin, Hindemith became infected with the spirit of *Zeitkunst* ("contemporary art") that pervaded so much of Berlin music and theater at the time. This movement favored modern subjects filled with contemporary allusions and references, set to timely, popular-styled music, sometimes jazz. To *Zeitkunst* Hindemith contributed the opera *Neues vom Tage* (1929), introduced in Berlin on June 8, 1929. The text by Marcellus Schiffer involved a marital dispute that hit the front pages and ended up in divorce courts. One of its provocative scenes had a nude woman singing an aria in the bathtub. Hindemith's score is realistic, witty, and spiced with jazz idioms. Also in the spirit of *Zeitkunst* is a one-act "sketch with music," *Hin und Zurück* (1929), libretto by Marcellus Schiffer based on an English revue sketch; it was performed in Baden-Baden, Germany, on July 17, 1927.

At this same period, Hindemith began feeling that the composer had a responsibility to society by producing functional music reaching a larger public. His works in this vein included music for radio, brass bands, popular theater, motion pictures and a delightful opera for and about children, *Wir bauen eine*

Stadt (1930; Berlin, June 21, 1930). The term *Gebrauchmusic* ("functional music") was coined to identify such efforts. In line with functional music, Hindemith produced a number of compositions intended for amateur performance at home (*Hausmusik*).

But Hindemith's involvement with *Zeitkunst, Gebrauchmusik* or *Hausmusik* did not mean a retreat from the complex, cerebral music in a linear idiom he was writing for the concert stage. This is the style of *Kammermusik*, nos. 6 and 7, op. 46, nos. 1 and 2 (1928); *Konzertmusik*, for brass and strings, op. 50, written in 1930 on commission to commemorate the fiftieth anniversary of the Boston Symphony, which introduced it on April 3, 1931, Serge Koussevitzky conducting; the oratorio *Das Unaufhörliche* (1931; Berlin, November 21, 1931); and the *Philharmonic Concerto* (1932), which the Berlin Philharmonic commissioned and premiered on April 15, 1932, with Wilhelm Furtwaengler conducting.

By 1933, Hindemith was one of Germany's most prestigious and influential musicians, second in importance only to Richard Strauss. But with the rise of the Third Reich his position grew uncomfortable. He himself was pure Aryan but his wife was Jewish, and he refused to disavow her. In addition, the Nazis did not ignore the fact that Hindemith never gave the Nazi salute when he entered his class at the Academy of Music or that he had openly expressed dissent with Nazi ideology. They had still other things to grumble about. He insisted upon giving public performances and making recordings with such Jewish artists as Emanuel Feuermann and Szymon Goldberg. The *Kulturkammer* (Chamber of Culture) condemned his *Zeitkunst* as typical of postwar decadence and degeneracy and regarded his concert music as out of step with the spirit of the great social and political upheaval now taking place in Germany. Accusing him of being a "musical Bolshevik," the Nazi press proceeded to denigrate him and his music, while officialdom used pressure to keep his music from being broadcast.

It was not long before Hindemith became the center of violent political storm. Early in 1934, Wilhelm Furtwaengler, musical director of the Berlin State Opera and the Berlin Philharmonic, announced he would stage Hindemith's new opera, *Mathis der Maler* (1934). This was an act of both courage and defiance to Nazi authority, which did not favor a world premiere by Hindemith and was also critical of the politically sensitive subject of the text prepared by Hindemith himself. Its central character was Mathias (Mathis) Grünewald, a 16th-century painter who led a peasant revolt against the church. Nazi officials considered the theme of rebellion by the people against authority as highly incendiary. They consequently ordered Furtwaengler to abandon the project. As an immediate countermove, at a concert of the Berlin Philharmonic on March 12, 1934, Furtwaengler performed the world premiere of a sym-

phony Hindemith had adapted from his opera score. It was made up of three extended orchestral episodes, each representing a panel on Grünewald's famous paintings on the Isenheim altar. This concert was an overwhelming success, first, because this was a resplendent score, one of Hindemith's finest, and subsequently to become his most famous work for orchestra, and second, because the ovation was a safe and vocal way of demonstrating against the Nazi regime. This public reaction led Furtwaengler to reintensify his efforts to get the opera staged the following winter. When the pressure against him from highest political sources mounted, Furtwaengler published a defiant letter in the *Deutsche Allgemeine Zeitung* on November 25, 1934, in defense of Hindemith and his opera. This act, with which Furtwaengler intended to win Hitler over to Hindemith and his opera, had an instant and unexpected response. That same night, Hitler himself issued the order to cancel the forthcoming production of *Mathis der Maler*, while at the same time Furtwaengler was relieved of all his musical posts, had his passport confiscated, and was sent into musical exile that lasted almost a year. The opera was first performed not in Germany but in Zurich on May 28, 1938, to outstanding acclaim. It was first heard in the United States on February 17, 1956, in Boston, but by then it had already been mounted in Germany, in Stuttgart in 1946.

With his music banned in Germany, Hindemith had to seek performances for his new works elsewhere. On November 14, 1935, as viola soloist with the Concertgebouw Orchestra in Amsterdam, Willem Mengelberg conducting, he introduced *Der Schwanendreher*, a concerto for viola and orchestra (1935) based on old folk melodies, one of them, "Seid ihr nicht der Schwanendreher," used in the third movement for a set of variations. *Trauermusik*, for solo viola and orchestra, was written in 1936 as a memorial to King George V and was first heard on January 22, 1936, in London with the composer as soloist. *Symphonic Dances*, for orchestra (1937), was also premiered in London on December 5, 1937.

Between 1935 and 1937, while still living in Berlin, Hindemith paid several visits to Turkey on an invitation from that government to help reorganize and modernize its musical life. When, in 1937, Hindemith was removed from his professorial post at the Berlin Academy of Music and from his membership in the German Academy, he knew the time had come for him to leave his native land. That spring he came to the United States for the first time, making his American debut at the Coolidge Festival in Washington, D. C., on April 10, 1937, in a performance of his own Sonata for Unaccompanied Viola (1923). This was one of several appearances throughout the United States including one with orchestra in the American premiere of *Der Schwanendreher*. Hindemith returned for a second season of American appearances in 1938–39 when, that summer, he held a master class in composition at the Berkshire Music Center at Tanglewood, Mass.

Hindemith's home was now in Switzerland, and there he continued producing major works. On a commission from the Ballet Russe de Monte Carlo, Hindemith prepared the score of *St. Francis* (1937), which, with scenario and choreography by Leonid Massine, was produced in London on July 21, 1938. A year later, Hindemith lifted several sections from this score and developed them into one of his orchestral masterworks. Now renamed *Nobilissima Visione* (1938), it was given its world premiere at the Venice Festival in September 1938. In 1939, Hindemith wrote the Concerto for Violin and Chamber Orchestra, premiered in Amsterdam on March 14, 1940.

With war breaking out in Europe, Hindemith came to the United States in 1940 for permanent residence. That fall he was appointed to the music faculty of Yale University to teach theory and composition and to overhaul the music curriculum. In 1947 he was named Battell Professor of theory. While maintaining his post at Yale he also served as Charles Eliot Norton Lecturer at Harvard in 1950–51.

As an American citizen, Hindemith remained in the United States, retaining his professorial post at Yale, until 1953. Those were years of great creative productivity. Some of the works completed in America, each of the highest order, are: Symphony in E-flat (1940; Minneapolis, November 21, 1941), which uses a key signature on the title page but not within the work itself; *Theme with Variations According to the Four Temperaments,* for piano and strings (1940; Boston, September 3, 1943), expressing the four different moods of melancholic, sanguine, phlegmatic, and choleric people: *Symphonic Metamorphosis on Themes by Carl Maria von Weber,* for orchestra (1943; N.Y., January 20, 1944), constructed from melodies taken from comparatively little known works of Weber; *Ludus Tonalis,* for piano (1943; Chicago, February 15, 1944), sometimes described as Hindemith's *Art of the Fugue,* since, like that work of Bach's, it is a giant exercise in polyphonic, and specifically fugal, writing; the Piano Concerto (1945), commissioned by the virtuoso Jesú Maria Sanromá, who introduced it in Cleveland on February 27, 1947, with George Szell conducting; *Symphonia serena,* for orchestra (1946), commissioned by Antal Dorati for the Dallas Symphony and first heard in Dallas on February 2, 1947; the opera *Die Harmonie der Welt* (1957), text built around the character of the renowned astronomer and mathematician Johannes Kepler, an opera introduced in Munich on August 11, 1957, while the symphony extracted from its score was premiered in Basle, Switzerland, on January 24, 1952. Two of his works received the awards of the New York Music Critics Circle: Septet, for winds (1948), in 1953 and Twelve Madri-

gals, for chorus (1958; Pittsburgh, January 30, 1959), in 1960. Two others have an American identity: *When Lilacs Last in the Dooryard Bloom'd,* subtitled "a requiem for those we love," for soprano, contralto, chorus, and orchestra (1945; N.Y., May 14, 1946), used the poem of Walt Whitman as text. *A Frog He Would a-Wooing Go,* for cello and piano (1946), was a set of variations on an American folk song. A later Hindemith work is also of American interest since it uses a text by the American playwright Thornton Wilder. It was the one-act opera *The Long Christmas Dinner* (1960), first produced on December 17, 1961, in Mannheim.

Hindemith paid his first return visit to Europe in 1947 to conduct guest performances of his works in Italy, England, and Holland. In 1948 he was appointed to the music faculty at the University of Zurich in Switzerland, but without severing his ties to Yale. In 1949, Hindemith stepped foot on German soil for the first time since his departure almost two decades earlier when he conducted a program of his music with the Berlin Philharmonic. At that time the West German government made overtures to him to return permanently to Germany but he declined on the grounds that he was now an American.

But in 1953 he finally broke his ties to the United States. He now decided to live permanently in Zurich and concentrate on his duties there as professor of composition at the university until 1956. He remained a Swiss resident for the rest of his life. He was back in the United States to attend the world premiere of his *Pittsburgh Symphony* (1958) on January 31, 1959, which he had written on commission for the Pittsburgh Symphony. In 1963 he participated in a four-day festival of his music in New York at which time the American premiere of *The Long Christmas Dinner* was given on March 13. Later the same year, on April 25, when he was guest conductor of the New York Philharmonic, he led the world premiere of his Organ Concerto (1962), which the New York Philharmonic had commissioned him to write for the opening of Lincoln Center. His last public appearance, and his last composition, came simultaneously on November 12, 1963, when he directed the premiere of his Mass, for a cappella voices, in Vienna.

In 1947, Hindemith was made a member of the National Institute of Arts and Letters. He received the Bach Prize of the city of Hamburg in 1947, the Sibelius Prize from Finland in 1955, and the Balzan Prize from Italy in 1962. Just before her death of cancer in 1967, Hindemith's wife left the entire Hindemith estate for the establishment of a Hindemith Foundation "to promote music in the spirit of Paul Hindemith, and most particularly contemporary music."

THE COMPOSER SPEAKS: If there is anything remaining in this world that is on the side basically aristocratic and individualistic, and on the other hand as brutal as the flight of wild animals, it is artistic creation: individualistic, because it is as private as your dreams; brutal, because works that have no strength are eliminated and forgotten; and no reasoning, no excuse can prolong their life or protect them against the crude power of the stronger work.

PRINCIPAL WORKS: *Kammermusik*, nos. 1–7, for various instrumental combinations (1922–27); 3 piano sonatas (1936); 6 string quartets (1918–65); 3 organ sonatas, (1927, 1927, 1940); 2 symphonies (1940–58) other than those extracted from operas; 2 violin sonatas (1935, 1939); 2 string trios (1924, 1933); 2 sonatas for solo violin (1924); 2 piano concertos (1924, 1945).

Die junge Magd, song cycle for alto, flute, clarinet, and string quartet (1922); *Suite 1922*, for piano (1923); Clarinet Quintet (1923); *Das Marienleben*, song cycle for soprano and piano (1923; revised 1936–38); *Die Serenaden*, cantata for soprano, oboe, viola, and cello (1924); Concerto for Orchestra (1925); *Cardillac*, opera (1926, revised 1952); *Konzertmusik*, for wind instruments (1926); *Spielmusik*, for strings, flute, and oboes (1926); *Hin und Zurück*, one-act opera (1927); *Neues vom Tage*, one-act opera (1929, revised 1953): *Konzertmusik*, for viola and large chamber orchestra (1930); *Konzertmusik*, for viola, piano, brass, and harp (1930); *Das Unaufhörliche*, oratorio for solo voices, chorus, and orchestra (1932); *Mathis der Maler*, symphony (1934); *Mathis der Maler*, opera (1934); *Der Schwanendreher*, concerto for viola and orchestra (1935); Flute Sonata (1936); *Trauermusik*, for viola and orchestra (1936); *Symphonic Dances*, for orchestra (1937); Oboe Sonata (1938); Bassoon Sonata (1938); Quartet, for piano, clarinet, violin, and cello (1938): *Nobilissima Visione*, ballet and orchestral suite (1938); Violin Concerto (1939); Six Chansons, for a cappella chorus (1939); Viola Sonata (1939): Clarinet Sonata (1939); Horn Sonata (1939); Trumpet Sonata (1939); English horn Sonata (1939); *The Four Temperaments*, ballet and suite for piano and string orchestra (1940): Cello Concerto (1940); Trombone Sonata (1941); *A Frog He Would a-Wooing Go*, variations for cello and piano (1941); *Ludus Tonalis*, for piano (1942); Suite, for two pianos (1941); *Symphonic Metamorphosis on Themes of Carl Maria von Weber*, for orchestra (1943); *Hérodiade*, recitation for narrator and chamber orchestra, also a ballet (1944); *Symphonia serena*, for orchestra (1946); *When Lilacs Last in the Dooryard Bloom'd*, requiem for chorus and orchestra (1946); Clarinet Concerto (1947); Cello Sonata (1948); Septet, for winds (1948); Concerto for four winds, harp, and orchestra (1949); Horn Concerto (1949); Concerto, for trumpet, bassoon, and string orchestra (1949); Double bass Sonata (1949); Sinfonietta, for orchestra (1950); *Die Harmonie der Welt*, symphony (1951); Sonata for Four Horns (1952); Tuba Sonata (1955); *Die*

Harmonie der Welt, opera (1957); Octet, for clarinet, bassoon, horn, violin, two violas, cello, and double bass (1958); Twelve Madrigals, for chorus (1958); *The Long Christmas Dinner*, one-act opera (1960); Organ Concerto (1962); Mass, for a cappela chorus (1963).

BIBLIOGRAPHY: Briner, Andreas, *Paul Hindemith* (Zurich, 1971); Kemp, I., *Hindemith* (London, 1970); Skelton, Geoffrey, *Hindemith: The Man Behind the Music* (London, 1975); Strobel, Heinrich, *Paul Hindemith*, 3rd ed. (Mainz, 1948); *Musical America*, January 1964; *Musical Quarterly*, January 1944, July 1964; *New York Times*, December 30, 1963 (obituary), August 14, 1977.

Hoiby, Lee, b. Madison, Wis., February 17, 1926.

Whatever his medium, Hoiby is a romanticist who has assumed a conservative stance. From Samuel Barber, whom he admires inordinately, he has learned to write a lyric line with expressivity, and from Menotti he acquired a respect for the demands of the stage and learned the musical means with which to write opera with a powerful theatrical impact.

Both his parents pursued music as amateurs. His mother played the piano by ear, and his father performed on the guitar and ukulele. When Hoiby was five he began studying the piano with Olive Endres. From his childhood on, Hoiby would make up tunes for nursery rhymes. He enjoyed improvising at the piano, but not until he was fifteen did he commit music to paper. From that time on he wrote music constantly, but it was some time before he knew he wanted to become a full-time composer.

His early academic training took place mostly in Madison, first at Doty School, then at Central High School, and after that at West High School, from which he graduated in 1944. From his grade school years on, he occasionally performed as pianist in assemblies. In high school, when he was about sixteen, he was heard in the Grieg Piano Concerto and as soloist in Vincent d'Indy's *Symphony on a French Mountain Air*. A music appreciation course with Lillian Sargent when he was sixteen further "opened the doors of music to me."

With the ambition of becoming a concert pianist, Hoiby went through an intensive period of study with Gunnar Johansen between 1941 and 1946. "Gunnar Johansen," Hoiby says, "was the first great musical influence of my life. It was he who introduced me to the world of piano literature."

Upon graduating from high school, Hoiby entered the University of Wisconsin, where he received his bachelor of music degree in 1947. During the summer of 1944, at the instigation of Johansen, he went to Ithaca, N.Y., to attend Egon Petri's master class in piano. At the University of Wisconsin, Hoiby often participated in the May Music Festival organized by Johansen, sometimes performing his own compositions, sometimes the works of other 20th-century composers. From the University of Wisconsin, Hoiby went on to Mills College, in Oakland, Calif., expressly to continue piano study with Egon Petri, who was on its faculty. "He was and still is my idol." During the summer of 1951, at Mills College, Hoiby studied composition with Darius Milhaud, and in 1952 he received there his master's degree in music.

Though he still had not abandoned the aim of becoming a concert pianist, with composition relegated to a position of secondary importance, he did complete a number of works at Mills College. A Toccata, for piano (1949), was his op. 1. This was followed by a Nocturne, for orchestra (1949), premiered in New York by the NBC Symphony under Thomas Schippers in October 1950; *Pastoral Dances*, for flute and orchestra (1950); a ballet, *Hearts, Meadows, and Flags* (1950), introduced in Rochester, N.Y., on November 6, 1952, with Erich Leinsdorf conducting; and a Violin Sonata (1951).

Between 1949 and 1952, Hoiby attended the Curtis Institute of Music as a composition pupil of Menotti's. It was at this time that Hoiby decided to devote his life henceforth to composition. "It was Menotti who encouraged me to write for the orchestra (which, at first, did not interest me at all) and to try my hand at opera (which interested me even less). When I resisted, he pressured me into trying and to my great surprise, I discovered my love for the orchestra and my own gift for opera. Without his insistence, I doubt if I would ever have tried." As Menotti's pupil, Hoiby completed Second Suite, for orchestra (1953), which received its first performance in Baltimore in 1960, and an untitled and never performed opera.

The opera Hoiby now recognizes as his first real effort in that field was *The Scarf*, in one act (1955), based on Chekhov's story "The Witch." It was first produced at the Festival of Two Worlds in Spoleto, Italy, on June 20, 1958. When this work was performed at the Boston Arts Festival on June 5, 1959, Cyrus Durgin said in *Musical America*: "Despite the amorphous nature of the story, *The Scarf* has a powerful musical tissue and emotional punch."

In 1957, Hoiby received an award from the National Institute of Arts and Letters, and in the same year he contributed incidental music to the play *The Duchess of Malfi*, which opened at the Phoenix Theater in New York on March 19, 1957. In 1958 he received a Guggenheim Fellowship that enabled him to complete a a piano concerto. In 1959, on a commission from the Louisville Opera Company in Kentucky, he wrote a three-act opera, *Beatrice*, based on Maurice Maeterlinck's *Sister Beatrice*, libretto by Marcia Nardi. In the production by the Louisville Opera, *Beatrice* opened a new radio and TV center in Louisville, Kentucky (WAVE), on October 23,

1959, followed by the first stage production on October 30 in that city.

Natalia Petrovna (1964) was a two-act opera with William Ball's libretto based on Turgenev's tempestuous love story, *A Month in the Country*. The opera received its premiere performance at the New York City Opera on October 8, 1964. Here, as in earlier operas, Hoiby's style, as Harold C. Schonberg pointed out in the *New York Times*, "is simple, romantic, traditional, and cosmopolitan." Hoiby subsequently retitled his opera *A Month in the Country*, and under that name it was revived in Boston in January 1981.

At about the time *Natalia Petrovna* was being produced by the New York City Opera, Hoiby wrote incidental music for *A Slapstick Tragedy*, a play by Tennessee Williams produced Off Broadway in 1964. Williams was so impressed by Hoiby's music score for his play and with *Natalia Petrovna* that he urged Hoiby to set one of his plays to music. Hoiby chose *Summer and Smoke*, for which Lanford Wilson provided the libretto. This was the first time Tennessee Williams had given permission for one of his major plays to be made into an opera.

Summer and Smoke was a success when it received its world premiere in St. Paul, Minn., by the St. Paul Opera on June 19, 1971. Writing in the *New York Times*, Raymond Ericson said, "The composer sets the English language to music as well as anyone today and is able to give it musical shape. He uses speech a good deal and makes the transitions back and forth to song smoothly and adroitly. . . . Hoiby sets the hesitations and silences of the characters' speeches as well as their impassioned outbursts." The New York City Opera produced it in New York in 1972. Following a revival in Chicago in June 1980, *Summer and Smoke* was filmed for nationwide television transmission.

In or about 1971, Hoiby began once again to take playing the piano seriously. On January 17, 1978, he made his debut as concert pianist at the Lincoln Center for the Performing Arts in New York, probably the first time in performing history that a fifty-two-year-old virtuoso was making a professional bow. He was the soloist in the premiere of his own Piano Concerto no. 2 (1979), with the American Chamber Orchestra under Robert Frisbie, in Chicago, on June 6, 1980, a performance that was filmed for television. In the traditional three-movement concerto structure, this music was, reported Philip Huscher in *High Fidelity/Musical America*, "unabashedly Romantic in spirit. . . . The slow movement, lush and lyrical, recalled Rachmaninoff, and in the more aggressive, percussive outer movements, the shadows of many early twentieth-century figures (notably Prokofiev and Stravinsky) hovered uncomfortably. . . . The score fits squarely in the virtuoso-showpiece tradition, and the piano part is nearly omnipresent, weaving filigree around orchestral statements, or taking the lead in long cadenza-like stretches."

THE COMPOSER SPEAKS: I love melody. For me, music has got to sing and dance. My music is lyrical, it's traditional, it's real. It may be hopelessly out of fashion. I began writing music at a time when the atonal revolution was in full swing. Now, atonality is an expressive device of some limited usefulness, and it is perhaps understandable that its discoverers were inordinately fascinated by it. But what then happened is this: the great modern premise, that one can do anything one wants for expressive purposes, was too much for musicians, and an austere tyranny of revolt set in. Not merely the tyranny of serialism, but the idea that anything goes, so long as it doesn't remind one of the 19th century. Well, thank God, this is coming to an end. But with what opprobrium has the tonal composer struggled in our time! Time will sort this out, but I have sometimes felt like a man on a dying limb; also, sometimes, when writing down a signature, like a freedom fighter.

PRINCIPAL WORKS: 2 piano concertos (1958, 1979). Toccata, for piano (1949); Nocturne, for orchestra (1949); *Hearts, Meadows, and Flags*, ballet (1950); Violin Sonata (1951); Five Preludes, for piano (1952); Second Suite, for orchestra (1953); *Diversions*, for woodwind quartet (1953); *The Scarf*, one-act opera (1955); Overture to *Twelfth Night*, for orchestra (1957); *Beatrice*, opera (1959); *A Hymn of the Nativity*, for soprano, baritone, and orchestra (1960); *The Tides of Sleep*, for voice and orchestra (1961); *Capriccio on Five Notes*, for piano (1962); *A Month in the Country*, originally *Natalia Petrovna*, opera (1964); *After Eden*, ballet (1966); *Landscape*, ballet (1968); *Summer and Smoke*, opera (1970); Piano Sextet (1974); *Music for a Celebration*, for orchestra (1975); *Galileo Galilei*, for soprano, mezzo-soprano, two baritones, two or three tenors, chorus, and orchestra (1975); *Something New for the Zoo*, one-act opera buffa (1980).

BIBLIOGRAPHY: *BBDM; DCM; High Fidelity/Musical America*, July 1971; *New York Times*, June 13, 1971, October 19, 1980.

Hopkinson, Francis, b. Philadelphia, Pa., September 21, 1737; d. Philadelphia, May 9, 1791.

Lawyer, jurist, statesman, poet, writer, inventor, and a signer of the Declaration of Independence, Hopkinson was also a dedicated musical amateur who composed the first piece of music written by an American that is still extant.

His father, Thomas Hopkinson, had migrated to Philadelphia in or about 1731, where he became a lawyer and judge of the vice-admiralty for the province. Little is known of Francis Hopkinson's early years beyond the fact that music was a tradition in the Hopkinson household to which he was subjected from his first years. He appears to have started studying the harpsichord when he was seventeen, eventually acquiring considerable proficiency. In 1754 he wrote words and music for one of the earliest compositions by an American, *Ode to Music*. Earlier, in 1751, he was the first student to enroll in the Academy of Philadelphia for his academic education, and in 1757 he became a member of the first class receiving bachelor's degrees at the College of Philadelphia (now the University of Pennsylvania). At college he was known not only for his harpsichord playing but also for his poetry. His first public appearance as a performer took place at the college in January 1757 in a presentation of Thomas Arne's *Masque of Alfred the Great*, for which he served as harpsichord accompanist for the vocal solos and choruses. He also helped arrange Arne's score for this occasion; he even interpolated into it some of his own music.

Upon his graduation from College he studied law with Benjamin Chew. While involved in law study, and while serving as secretary of the Library Company of Philadelphia, he composed, in 1759, the song for which he is most often remembered, "My Days Have Been So Wondrous Free," a setting of Thomas Parnell's poem "Love and Innocence." This is the earliest example of a secular art song by an American that has survived. It is one of several numbers found in a manuscript collection entitled *Songs* reposing in the Library of Congress in Washington, D. C. The other pieces by Hopkinson in this collection are: "The Garland," "Oh, Come to Mason Borough's Grove," and "With Pleasure Have I Past My Days," together with "The 23rd Psalm" and "An Anthem from the 114th Psalm." The melodic style was modeled after that of the English songs by Purcell and Arne.

In 1760, Hopkinson earned his master of arts degree at the college. At the commencement exercises Hopkinson played the organ, including a few of his own compositions, and contributed a vocal piece, an *Ode to the Sacred Memory of Our Late Gracious Sovereign George II*. In April 1761, Hopkinson was admitted to the Supreme Court of Pennsylvania. He was appointed the collector of customs at Salem, N.J., in November 1763. This same year he is reputed to have published a collection of psalm tunes (together with a few anthems and hymns) and one year later he initiated and managed a series of subscription concerts in Philadelphia at which he often officiated as the harpsichordist. At about this time, too, he began studying the organ with James Bremner.

Hopkinson spent the year of 1766–67 in England. After returning to the Colonies, he married Ann Borden, daughter of a leading citizen in Bordentown, N.J., on September 1, 1768, and soon thereafter became proprietor of a dry-goods shop. In 1770, when Bremner took leave of absence as organist of Christ Church, Hopkinson substituted for him.

In 1772, Hopkinson became collector of customs at the Port of New Castle in Delaware, but he soon left this post to practice law in Bordentown. In 1774 he was appointed to a seat in the Provincial Council of New Jersey. He resigned all offices requiring allegiance to George III in 1776 to align himself with the Revolution. He was a delegate from New Jersey to the Continental Congress, and then was one of the signers of the Declaration of Independence. From November 1776 to August 1778 he served as chairman of the Continental Navy Board, and from July 1778 to July 1781 he held the office of treasurer of loans. He served as judge of the Admiralty in Pennsylvania from 1779 to 1789. During all these years he was highly active as a literary man, as political pamphleteer and as writer of satirical verses. Of the last, the most famous is "The Battle of the Kegs." Sung to the tune of "Yankee Doodle," it mocked the efforts of the British, who were firing wildly from their ships at approaching powder-filled kegs.

In 1780, Hopkinson composed an *Ode to the Memory of James Bremner*. A year later he wrote the libretto and contributed an overture, arias, ensemble numbers, and choruses (none any longer extant) for *The Temple of Minerva*, an "oratorial entertainment" produced in Philadelphia in 1781. This was an allegorical political opera or dramatic cantata in praise of America's alliance with France. In 1788, Hopkinson published *Seven Songs* (they were actually eight in number) described in the publication as pieces "for harpsichord or forte piano" but which in actuality were pieces of music with lyrics, the latter also by Hopkinson. Dedicated to George Washington, this is often considered the first such volume published in America. "I will not tell you how much they have pleased me," wrote Thomas Jefferson after receiving this volume, "nor how well the last of them merits praise for its pathos, but relate a fact only, which is that while my elder daughter was playing it on the harpsichord, I happened to look toward the fire and saw the younger one all in tears. I asked her if she was sick. She said, 'No, but the tune was so mournful.'"

In 1789, Hopkinson was appointed judge of the United States court of the eastern district of Pennsylvania, a post he retained until the end of his life. His last composition was *A New Song* in 1791. Hopkinson was the compiler of *Collection of Psalm Tunes* (1763) and *The Psalms of David* (1767). Just before his death of apoplexy he collected his literary works, published in 1792 under the title *The Miscellaneous Essays and Occasional Writings of Francis Hopkinson*.

In addition to all his other achievements, Hopkinson was also an inventor. He provided Benjamin Franklin's glass harmonica with a keyboard, introduced improvements in the quilling of harpsichords, and devised the Bellarmonic, an instrument constructed of steel bells. Hopkinson's son, Joseph, wrote the words for "Hail, Columbia."

THE COMPOSER SPEAKS: With respect to this little work [*Seven Songs*] . . . I can only say, that it is such as a Lover, not a Master of the Arts can furnish. I am neither a Profess'd poet, nor a Profess'd Musician; and yet venture to appear in those characters united; for which, I confess, the censure of Temerity may justly be brought against me.

If these Songs should not be so fortunate as to please the young Performers for whom they are intended, they will at least not occasion much Trouble in learning to perform them; and this will, I hope, be some Alleviation to their Disappointment.

However small the Reputation may be that I shall derive from this Work, I cannot, I believe, be refused the Credit of being the first Native of the United States who has produced a Musical Composition. If this attempt should not be too severely treated, others may be encouraged to venture on a path, yet untrodden in America, and the Arts in succession will take root and flourish amongst us.

PRINCIPAL WORKS: *Ode to Music*, for voice and harpsichord (1754); Songs, including "My Days Have Been So Wondrous Free," for voice and harpsichord (c. 1759); *Ode to the Memory of James Bremner*, for voice and harpsichord (1780); *The Temple of Minerva*, an "oratorial entertainment" (1781); Seven Songs, for voice and harpsichord (1788); *A New Song*, for voice and harpsichord (1791).

BIBLIOGRAPHY: Albrecht, O. E., *Francis Hopkinson, Musician, Poet, Patriot* (Philadelphia, 1938); Hastings, G. E., *The Life and Works of Francis Hopkinson* (Chicago, 1926); Howard, John Tasker, *Our American Music* (N.Y., 1946); Sonneck, O. G., *Francis Hopkinson, The First American Poet-Composer* (Washington, D. C., 1905, reprinted 1969).

Hovhaness, Alan (originally **Chakmakjian, Alan Vaness**), b. Somerville, Mass., March 8, 1911.

One of the most prolific composers of the 20th century, with some three hundred compositions in all media and most in large structures to his credit, Hovhaness has arrived at an individuality of style by synthesizing the music of the Western world with that of the East.

His father, a professor of chemistry, was Armenian, and his mother was Scottish. Alan Hovhaness reveals that music "kept running through my head" long before he received formal instruction. He learned to improvise on the piano before he took his first lesson. He made his first attempt at composition when he was four, writing a short organ piece on an eleven-line staff which his mother refused to play on the family's small harmonium. "I gave up music until I was seven years old," he reveals. "At that time I composed on regular staff notation, but at night when I was supposed to sleep I made another notation which I could see in the dark. This system of writing music without being able to see it resembled a vocal Armenian notation of around the 1820 period which I learned later." By then his family had moved to Arlington, a suburb of Boston, where Alan was raised and received his preliminary academic education at its public schools and at Arlington High School. When he was nine he began taking piano lessons from Adelaide Proctor, who encouraged him to compose. He completed two operas as well as numerous shorter compositions by the time he was thirteen. In 1929 piano study took place with Heinrich Gebhard. When Hovhaness graduated from high school that year, he entered Tufts University, where he remained a year and a half. In 1932, on a scholarship, he was admitted to the New England Conservatory. During the next two years, he studied composition there with Frederick S. Converse. An important influence in his early life was the music of Gomidas Vartabed, an Armenian composer-priest who lost his mind in 1917 in the Turkish massacres of Armenians and died in a Parisian asylum in 1936. Having become interested in Armenian music through Vartabed, Hovhaness proceeded to learn what he could about Armenia, its background and its music, which in turn brought about an interest in the music and culture of other Eastern countries.

When he was seventeen, Hovhaness completed writing several successful compositions. These included a piano quintet, *Oror* (a lullaby for violin and piano), and *Watchman, Tell Us of the Night* (a Christmas song for solo bass, chorus and organ). A symphony (1933) was performed by the New England Conservatory and received the Samuel Endicott Prize. (He withdrew the symphony soon thereafter.) What officially became Symphony no. 1, subtitled *Exile*, was written in 1936 and introduced on May 26, 1939, in England in a performance by the BBC Symphony conducted by Leslie Heward. Earlier, in 1935, Hovhaness completed, among other works, *Missa Brevis*, for bass, chorus, strings, and organ; Sonata Ricercare, for piano; Fantasy, for piano; and Prelude and Fugue, for oboe and bassoon. His String Quartet no. 1 came in 1936. Some of these works were influenced largely by Bartók. But the invasion of the East had also begun, if only tentatively: in *Layla*, for voice and piano, based on a Persian text, the two *ghazalas* (love songs) for piano, and the *Love Songs of Háfiz*, for voice and piano—early version text by Háfiz, later version by the composer—all written in 1935.

Between 1940 and 1947, Hovhaness earned his living in Boston by teaching, working as piano accompanist, and as organist at the Armenian Church of St. James in Watertown. Playing Armenian liturgical music, with its monodic and modal styles, further stirred his interest in the land and music of his father's birth. A second major influence about this time was attending a performance in Boston by Uday Shankar and his company of Indian musicians and dancers, which opened up for Hovhaness the world of Indian music and culture. To penetrate more deeply in the world of the East, Hovhaness began mastering the Armenian language and Armenian music as well as the music of other Eastern countries. At the same time he delved into a study of Eastern religions and philosophies.

This imersion into the East made him dissatisfied with the kind of music he had been writing thus far. Hovhaness destroyed most of what he had written before 1940—several hundred compositions including his first seven symphonies, five string quartets, some operas, sonatas and sundry piano works. Experiencing a musical rebirth, he began developing a style combining important elements of Eastern music with Western materials and resources. His melodies began simulating the improvisational character of Armenian cantillations. He adopted Eastern modes and rhythmic practices. To advance himself technically, Hovhaness went, on a scholarship, to the Berkshire Music Center at Tanglewood, Mass., during the summer of 1942 to study composition with Bohuslav Martinu.

By 1945, the Eastern influence on his music became a pervading presence. In 1943, *Twelve Armenian Folk Songs*, for piano, were based on Armenian mountain village melodies. *Armenian Rhapsodies*, for strings (1944–45), used Armenian dance tunes and an Armenian feast-day melody (*dagh*); the first of these rhapsodies was introduced in Boston under the composer's direction on February 4, 1944. On this same program was also heard *Lousadzak* (*Coming of Light*), a concerto for piano and orchestra (1944), in which aleatory processes were used for the first time. Here the sounds of Eastern instruments were reproduced on Western instruments. Melodies were decorated with fanciful figurations, chordal harmonies were dispensed with, and climaxes were achieved by melodies spiraling toward a point of silence—all in the Eastern manner. *Elibris* (Elibris being the god of dawn worshiped by Uraraduans) is a concerto for flute and orchestra (1944) in which Hindu ragas were used. At times several different melodies in the same or different ragas were sounded simultaneously, but not contrapuntally, or two former lines were combined to create a new melody. When Hovhaness made his debut in New York on June 17, 1945, in an all-Hovhaness program at the invitation of the arts committee of the Armenian Students Association of America, he performed *Elibris*, as well as the two *Armenian Rhapsodies*, *Lousadzak* and *Varak* (a monastery in Armenia), for violin and piano (1944), and *Khrimian Hairig* (a heroic Armenian priest), for trumpet and string orchestra (1944). In 1948, Hovhaness revised *Elibris*, the new version getting its first hearing on January 26, 1950, in a performance by the San Francisco Symphony under Pierre Monteux.

In *Mihr*, for two pianos (1945)—named after the

Armenian fire god—Hovhaness used the Eastern method of repetitive tones to achieve tension, the modal melodies and arabesque figurations over a cantus. *Anahid*, a fantasy for flute, English horn, trumpet, timpani, percussion, and strings (1945), was inspired by the goddess of pre-Christian Armenia. Though using a program based on a Hindu story, the Symphony no. 8, *Arjuna*, modeled its melodic material after the patterns of Armenian folk songs; after being introduced in Madras, India, on February 1, 1960, *Arjuna* was performed in Germany, France, Korea, Japan, Vancouver, and Hawaii. In 1949, Hovhaness contributed a score to his first ballet, *Is There Survival?*, whose scenario was based on the exploits of King Vakhaken, the legendary Armenian warrior-king; it was produced in 1950 with choreography by Jan Keen.

Eastern history, geography, legends, continued to fascinate Hovhaness in the 1950s while he was further refining and perfecting his personalized Eastern-oriented idiom. Symphony no. 9, *St. Vartan* (1950), was inspired by an Armenian folk hero who was martyred in A.D. 451. The New York Philharmonic premiered it on March 11, 1951, the composer conducting. The writing of *Artik*, a concerto for horn and orchestra (1950; Rochester, N.Y., May 7, 1954), was stimulated by a 7th-century Armenian church, and that of *Talin*, a concerto for viola and orchestra (1950; Colorado Springs, 1952), by a 7th-century Armenian ruin.

One of Hovhaness's most successful works up to this time was his Symphony no. 2, *The Mysterious Mountain* (1955), its world premiere given by the Houston Symphony under Leopold Stokowski on October 31, 1955. In describing this work, the composer explained that to him the mountains represented "symbols, like pyramids, of man's attempt to know God. Mountains are symbolic meeting places between the mundane and spiritual worlds. To some, Mysterious Mountain may be the phantom peak, unmeasured, thought to be higher than Everest, as seen from great distances by fliers in Tibet. To some it may be the solitary mountain, the tower of strength over a countryside."

Hovhaness remained a resident of Boston until 1951, serving on the faculty of the Boston Conservatory of Music since 1948. After receiving a grant from the National Institute of Arts and Letters in 1951, Hovhaness transferred his home to New York City. In addition to other compositions, he wrote incidental music for Clifford Odets's *The Flowering Peach*, which opened on Broadway on December 29, 1954; provided the score for a ballet, *Ardent Song*, which Martha Graham and her company introduced in London in 1954 and with which they toured the Far East in 1955–56; and prepared the music for two film documentaries commissioned and produced by NBC-TV, *Assignment India* (1956) and *Assignment Southeast Asia* (1957). In 1953, and again in 1954

and 1958, he was awarded Guggenheim Fellowships, and in 1959, honorary doctorates in music from the University of Rochester, N.Y, and Bates College in Lewiston, Me.

On a Fulbright Fellowship in 1959, he was able to embark on a world tour that brought him for the first time to India and Japan for research into their native music and for the presentation of some of his works. He became the first western composer invited to participate in the musical festival of Madras in South India, where, in addition to the premiere of his *Arjuna Symphony*, he presented the first performance of *Madras Sonata*, for piano, which he had written in 1946 but, on commission, revised for this event. At the request of All-India Radio, he wrote *Nagooran*, a work honoring the patron saint of Madras, using only South Indian musical instruments.

Great as his success was in India, it was even more formidable in Japan. He was welcomed at the airport by newsmen and photographers; in Tokyo he was lionized; he made appearances on television; the Tokyo Symphony invited him to conduct that orchestra in performances of some of his works; and he was the beneficiary of several commissions. Among his new compositions to be heard were *Fuji*, a cantata for Japanese female chorus, flute, harp, and string orchestra (1960), and *Koke No Niwa (Moss Garden)* for English horn or clarinet, two percussion players and harp, which he had written in 1954 but revised in 1960.

In May 1961, Hovhaness toured France and Germany, performing his music. During the first six months of 1962 he was composer-in-residence at the University of Hawaii. On a commission from the East-West Center in Hawaii, he wrote *Wind Drum*, a "music-dance drama," which used Indian scales. It was introduced in Hawaii in May 1962, with a New York premiere following three years later. *The Burning House*, a one-act opera with libretto by the composer, which he had written in 1960 and revised two years later, was given its initial hearing at the newly founded summer music festival at Gatlinburg, Tenn., in August 1964.

A Rockefeller grant in 1962 brought Hovhaness back to the East for research in ancient court music of Japan (*gagaku*) and ancient court music of Korea (*ah-ak*). In Korea, Symphony no. 16, for strings and Korean instruments (1962), was premiered in Seoul on January 26, 1963, the composer conducting. It was inspired by "the beauty of Korean mountains," in the composer's words, "the sublimity of Korean traditional music, the wisdom and nobility of Korean people." The sound textures were stimulated by paintings of "Mountains and Rivers Without End" in the Korean National Museum. In Tokyo, Hovhaness's one-act opera *Spirit of the Avalanche* (1962), to his own libretto, was produced for the first time on February 15, 1963.

With Hovhaness's remarkable productivity it is

possible to mention only a few of his other important compositions since 1960. Symphony no. 15, *Silver Pilgrimage* (1963), was given its initial performance by the Orchestra of the Americas in New York in December 1963, Stokowski conducting. The ballet *Circe* (1963) was performed by Martha Graham and her company in London and New York. *Meditation on Zeami*, for orchestra (1964), named after the father of the Japanese Noh drama, was introduced in New York by the American Symphony Orchestra under Stokowski on October 5, 1964. *Ukiyo—Floating World*, ballade for orchestra (1964), was heard for the first time on January 30, 1965, in Salt Lake City, Utah. "Floating World," the composer explained, "is an old Japanese Buddhist concept of uncertainty, change, undependability, insubstantial qualities of the world, the only joy being the hope of salvation in the next world. However, a new concept was superimposed during the prosperity of the 17th century, when the transitory world became associated with ideas of pleasure, delight and adventure. These two ideas became united. This music is an abstraction of these thoughts, inspired by the genius of the great Japanese playwright Chikamatsu." *Fantasy on Japanese Woodprints*, for xylophone and orchestra (1964), is a set of mood pictures reflecting the composer's love of Japan and for its ancient woodblock prints. The Chicago Symphony under Seiji Ozawa, with Yoichi Hiraoka as soloist, first performed it on July 4, 1964. Soon after this it was heard in Japan. *Fra Angelico*, fantasy for orchestra (1967), was commissioned by the Detroit Symphony, which premiered it under Sixten Ehrling's direction on March 21, 1968. This music paid tribute to the early 15th-century artist "who painted in the Eastern spirit." *And God Created Whales*, for orchestra (1969; N.Y., June 11, 1970), was written after the composer had heard songs of humpback whales whose voices are reproduced on tape in the score. *A Rose for Emily* (1970) is a ballet based on a William Faulkner story that was first mounted at the North Carolina School for the Arts in October 1970, then produced the following December in New York by the American ballet. *The Way of Jesus* is an oratorio (1974; N.Y., March 7, 1975), and *Ode to Freedom* (1976) is a concerto for violin and orchestra honoring the American bicentennial. The *Ode to Freedom* was performed by Yehudi Menuhin and the National Symphony Orchestra of Washington, D. C., under André Kostelanetz at Wolf Trap Farm in Virginia on July 3, 1976. Kostelanetz also introduced *Rubáiyát*, for narrator, accordion, and orchestra (1977), utilizing texts by Omar Khayyám, at a Promenade Concert in New York on May 20, 1977. Symphony no. 35, for a full symphony orchestra and an ancient orchestra of ah-ak instruments (1978), was commissioned by Korea for the opening of the Seoul Art Center, where it was introduced on June 9, 1978. Symphony no. 36 (1978), for solo flute and orchestra, was given its first performance on January 18, 1979,

in Washington, D. C., performed by the National Symphony under Mstislav Rostropovich with Jean-Pierre Rampal, soloist. A seventy-minute cantata for soprano, tenor, baritone, chorus and orchestra—*Revelations of St. Paul* (1980)—was first heard on January 28, 1981, in New York performed by Musica Sacra, which had commissioned it, Richard Westenburg conducting. The text, prepared by Donald V. R. Thompson, was derived from the writings of St. Paul. "This twenty-six section work exploits many familiar Hovhaness devices," reported Donal Henahan in the *New York Times*. "It is frequently reminiscent of the ancient church modes. Its textures are generally uncluttered and plain. . . . As in previous Hovhaness music, *St. Paul* makes considerable use of simple instrumental motives played off against solo voices."

Hovhaness was married twice, the first time to the former Elizabeth Whittington on March 9, 1959. After their divorce, he married Hinako Fujihara, a coloratura soprano on June 17, 1977. In 1977, Hovhaness was elected to the American Academy and Institute of Arts and Letters.

THE COMPOSER SPEAKS: To me, atonality is against nature. There is a center to everything that exists. The planets have the sun, the moon, the earth. The reason I like oriental music is that everything has a firm center. All music with a center is tonal. Music without a center is fine for a minute or two, but it soon sounds all the same.

Things which are very complicated tend to disappear and get lost. Simplicity is difficult, not easy. Beauty is simple. All unnecessary elements are removed—only essence remains.

PRINCIPAL WORKS: 43 symphonies (1936–79); 5 string quartets (1936–77).

Elibris, concerto for flute and string orchestra (1944, revised 1949); *Lousadzak*, concerto for piano and orchestra (1944); *Return and Rebuild the Desolate Places*, concerto for trumpet solo and winds (1944); *Armenian Rhapsodies*, for orchestra (1944–45); *Tzaikerk*, for chamber orchestra (1945); *Anahid*, fantasy for flute, English horn, trumpet, timpani, percussion, and strings (1945); *Etchmiadzin*, opera for vocal soloists, chorus, and orchestra (1946); *Madras Sonata*, for piano (1946, revised 1960); *Haroutiun*, for trumpet and string orchestra (1948); *Zartik Parkim*, concerto for piano and chamber orchestra (1949); *Artik*, concerto for horn and orchestra (1949); *Is There Survival?*, ballet (1949); *Shalimar*, for piano (1949, revised 1960); *Janabar*, five hymns for violin, trumpet, piano, and strings (1959); *Arevakal*, concerto for orchestra (1951); *Talin*, concerto for viola and string orchestra (1952); Concerto no. 7, for orchestra (1953–54); *Koke No Kiwa*, for English horn or clarinet, two percussion players, and harp (1954, revised 1960); *Ardent Song*, ballet (1955); Prelude and Quadruple Fugue, for orchestra

(1955); *Ad Lyram*, for solo voices, double chorus, and chamber chamber orchestra (1955); Magnificat, for solo voices, chorus, and chamber orchestra (1957); *The Blue Flame*, opera (1959); Accordion Concerto (1959); *The Burning House*, one-act opera (1960); *Nagooran*, for south Indian instruments (1960); *Fuji*, cantata for female voices, flute, harp, and string orchestra (1960); *Wind Drum*, a music-dance drama (1962); Trio, for violin, viola, and cello (1962); *Spirit of the Avalanche*, opera (1962); *In the Beginning Was the Word*, for vocal soloists, chorus, and orchestra (1963); *Pilate*, one-act opera (1963); *Circe*, ballet (1963); Variations and Fugue, for orchestra (1964); *Meditation on Zeami*, tone poem for orchestra (1964); *Dark River and Distant Bell*, for harpsichord (1964); *Fantasy on Japanese Woodprints*, for xylophone and orchestra (1964); *Ukiyo—Floating World*, tone poem for orchestra (1965); *The Holy City*, for orchestra (1966); *Pilate*, opera (1966); *Fra Angelico*, tone poem for orchestra (1967); *The Traveler*, opera (1967); *Mountains and Rivers Without End*, for ten instruments (1968); *Requiem and Resurrection*, for brass choir and percussion (1968); *Lady of Light*, for solo voices, chorus, and chamber orchestra (1969); *And God Created Whales*, for humpback whale solo on tape, and orchestra (1969); *A Rose for Emily*, ballet (1970); *Saturn*, twelve pieces for clarinet, soprano, and piano (1971); *The Way of Jesus*, oratorio for solo voices, chorus, and orchestra (1974); *Fanfare for the New Atlantic*, for orchestra (1976); *Ode to Freedom*, concerto for violin and orchestra (1976); *Rubáiyát*, for narrator, accordion, and orchestra (1977); Euphonium Concerto (1977); *Tale of the Sun Goddess Going into the Stone House*, opera (1979); Guitar Concerto (1979); *Revelations of St. Paul*, cantata for soprano, tenor, baritone, chorus, and orchestra (1980).

BIBLIOGRAPHY: Mellers, Wilfrid, *Music in a New Found Land* (N.Y., 1964); Rosner, A., "An Analytical Survey of the Music of Alan Hovhaness" (doctoral thesis, Buffalo, N.Y., 1972); BMI, *The Many Worlds of Music*, Winter 1976; *New York Times*, November 12, 1978; *Saturday Review*, February 22, 1959; *Time*, March 29, 1968.

Husa, Karel, b. Prague, Czechoslovakia, August 7, 1921. American citizen, 1959. Awarded the Pulitzer Prize in music in 1969.

Husa's music is a link between the past and the present. He has written in many different styles with equal facility and artistic value, including impressionism, neoprimitivism, serialism, microtonal music, music of the American Indian, and music carrying reminders of his Czech heritage in its lyricism and rhythms.

Since his parents wanted him to become an engineer, he was sent to technical school in 1938 where he specialized in civil engineering. He began his mu-

sic instruction on the violin when he was eight, supplementing this with piano lessons five years later. But despite this musical activity, he did not hear his first concert until he was seventeen.

The Nazi occupation of Czechoslovakia in 1939 resulted in the closing of universities there, but a few months later conservatories of music and art schools were reopened. To escape possible deportation, Husa decided to seek admission to the Prague Conservatory. As preparation, since he had no previous theoretical instruction, he studied theory privately with Jaroslav Řídký for one year. Then, at the conservatory (1941–45), Husa studied composition with Řídký and conducting with Pavel Dědeček. At the same time he began going to concerts and for the first time showed genuine interest in composition. His first work was a piano sonatina in classical structure (1943) that was published and was heard in Prague in April 1945 at a concert of the International Society for Contemporary Music, Czech section. In 1945, Husa received his diploma in composition, *summa cum laude*, and a master's degree. To fulfill the requirements for that degree, he wrote his first work for orchestra, an overture, stylistically influenced by such Czech composers as Janáček and Suk. It was performed in 1945 by the Prague Symphony with the composer conducting.

Husa did graduate work in composition at the Academy of Musical Arts in Prague (1945–46). In 1946 he went to Paris, attending the École Normale de Musique as a pupil in composition of Arthur Honegger's and of Jean Fournet's in conducting. He also studied composition privately with Nadia Boulanger and conducting with André Cluytens. Because of this year of study in Paris, the Academy of Musical Arts conferred on him a doctorate when he returned to Prague in the summer of 1947. For this doctorate, Husa submitted a sinfonietta, for orchestra (1947), which was successfully performed by the Radio Orchestra in Prague, Karel Ancerl conducting, on April 25, 1947, and received in 1948 the Czech Academy of Sciences and Arts Award.

On a scholarship, Husa returned to Paris in the fall of 1947, reentered the École Normale where he received a *diplome licence* in conducting. His study of conducting ended with Eugène Bigot at the Paris Conservatory. When this schooling was done in 1949, Husa decided to remain in France. On February 2, 1952, in Paris, he married Simone Perault, with whom he had four daughters.

As a student of composition in Paris, Husa produced several works that revealed not only technical growth but also increasing articulateness. In a style that was basically tonal and consonant, lyrical and expressive, and skillful in its voice leading, he produced the String Quartet no. 1 (1948), commissioned by the Smetana Quartet and premiered at the Spring Festival in Prague on May 23, 1948. It was then heard at a concert of the International Society for Contemporary Music Festival in Brussels on June

20, 1950, and given further performances in Germany, Austria, Sweden, and Holland. The work received the Lili Boulanger Award in 1950 and the Bilthoven Festival Prize in Holland in 1952.

Conducting as well as composing occupied Husa's interests. In the early 1950s he made numerous appearances as guest conductor of symphony orchestras in Switzerland and Paris, both in public concerts and on records. Additionally, between 1952 and 1953 he served as a member of the jury of the Paris Conservatory and in 1953 held a similar post at the Fontainebleau School of Music and Fine Arts.

In his compositions he was developing and refining an eclectic style that began moving ever closer to dissonance and atonality and which occasionally borrowed Slavic melodies and rhythms. *Evocations of Slovakia*, for clarinet, viola, and cello (1951), drew some of its material for "imaginary" variation treatment from Slavic folk songs in all its three movements, subtitled "Mountain," "Night," and "Dance." The three instruments here were carefully chosen to recreate the colors, sonorities, and instrumental combinations of Slovakian folk-dance ensembles. Its first hearing took place on May 4, 1957, over the French Radio in Paris.

On a commission from UNESCO, Husa wrote *Musique d'amateurs*, a functional work for oboe, trumpet, percussion, and strings (1953) made up of five easy pieces. A commission from the Donaueschingen Festival in Germany led to the writing of *Portrait*, for orchestra (1953; Baden-Baden, October 10, 1953). On October 23, 1953, in Paris, String Quartet no. 2 (1953) was introduced by the Parrenin Quartet, for whom it was written. Symphony no. 1, Husa's most ambitious work up to this time, was given its world premiere over Radio Brussels on March 4, 1954, before being heard throughout Europe and, in April 1965, being introduced to the United States by the Baltimore Symphony under the composer's direction. This symphony follows in the postromantic tradition of Mahler, Vaughan Williams, and Sibelius.

Husa came to the United States in 1954 to join the music faculty in the department of theory at Cornell University in Ithaca, N.Y. He has remained there ever since—appointed associate professor in 1957, full professor in 1967, and from 1973 on, holding the distinguished Kappa Alpha Professorship. At Cornell, Husa was musical director of the university orchestra (1956–75) and conductor of the Ithaca Chamber Orchestra (1957–62). Since 1978 he has been music director of the fully professional Cayuga Chamber Orchestra in Ithaca.

His first significant compositions after coming to the United States were the three Fantasies, for orchestra (1956; Ithaca, N.Y., April 28, 1975), consisting of an "Aria," "Capriccio," and "Nocturne," and *Poem*, for viola and orchestra (1959), constructed from a twelve-tone row. The latter received its premiere at the festival of the International Society for Contemporary Music in Cologne on June 12, 1960. In *Mosaïques*, for orchestra (1961; Hamburg, Germany, November 7, 1961), some parts are in a strict serial technique while others are constructed more freely.

The work that brought Husa the Pulitzer Prize in music in 1969 was the String Quartet no. 3 (1968), commissioned by the Fine Arts Quartet, which first performed it on October 14, 1968, in Chicago. In this work, Husa explores new sonorities and timbres for the four stringed instruments by having bows bounce freely on the strings, having strings plucked with the fingernail, exploiting novel harmonics and quarter-tone intervals. Individual prominence is given to each of the four instruments: the viola being spotlighted in the first movement, the cello in the second, and the two violins in the third, while the last movement has all four instruments treated as equals. The forms of each movement are freer than those Husa had previously employed in string quartet writing, with interest centered on contrasting colors and inner tensions.

Another of Husa's highly successful compositions of the late 1960s was *Music for Prague 1968* (1968), inspired by the political upheavals in Czechoslovakia in August 1968 that resulted in the Soviet coup. Written on commission from the director of bands of Ithaca College, *Music for Prague 1968* was originally scored for band. This version was first heard in January 1969 in Washington, D.C., after which it entered the repertoire of bands throughout the United States to receive between four and five thousand performances. Husa then adapted the work for orchestra, its world premiere heard in Munich on January 31, 1970, with Husa conducting the Munich Philharmonic. Its first American presentation was given by the Cleveland Orchestra under Louis Lane in Cleveland on February 26, 1971. An old Hussite religious song is quoted in the first movement as a symbol of resistance to tyranny. It returns in later movements in various guises and becomes the material for a stirring closing climax. A piccolo suggests Czech bird calls of liberty, and the ringing of bells recalls the churches of Prague.

War, hunger, everyday murders, and, most of all, the pollution that despoils the blessings of nature— the ever present problems of the 1960s—led to the writing of *Apotheosis of This Earth*, originally (1970) for wind band, then (1973) rewritten for chorus and orchestra. The chorus is also called upon to hum, howl, speak, whisper, stamp its feet, clap its hands. The writing throughout is graphically programmatic. Commissioned by the Michigan School Band and Orchestra, it was heard in its original band version at Ann Arbor, Mich., on April 1, 1971, the composer conducting.

Sonata for Violin and Piano (1972–73) was written on a commission from the Koussevitzky Music Foundation. Virtuoso writing for each of the two instruments, which retain their respective independence, characterizes this music. Ani Kavafian, violinist, and Richard Goode, pianist, gave the premiere performance on March 31, 1974, in New York at a concert of the Chamber Music Society of Lincoln Center.

Husa produced two works in commemoration of the American bicentennial. One of these—the ballet *Monodrama*, choreography by Bud Kerwin (1975)—was written on a grant from the National Endowment for the Arts and was sponsored by Jordan College of Music of Butler University of Indianapolis, Ind. Its first performance was given by the Butler Ballet in Indianapolis on March 26, 1976. *Monodrama*, which utilizes verbal quotations from James Baldwin's *The Creative Process*, portrays the solitude of the American artist in a society that does not understand him.

Husa's second work for the American bicentennial, which was also intended to celebrate the 125th anniversary of the founding of Coe College at Cedar Rapids, Iowa, was *An American Te Deum*, for baritone, chorus, and band, the first performance taking place on December 5, 1976. For a text that concentrated on the Midwest, the composer used poems by Paul Engle, some material from Ole Edvart Rølvaag's novel *Giants in the Earth*, some writings of Henry David Thoreau, etc. American-Indian material is incorporated into the score through quotations of a motive from Dvořák's Quintet in E major and an Indian melody entitled "Chippewa Lullaby." Two hymn tunes from the Amana Song Book, a Moravian folk song and a Swedish emigrant ballad are also tapped. "I have tried," Husa explains, "to 'praise' nature and men together with God on this festive occasion, at the time that this country celebrated its bicentennial." *An American Te Deum* was rescored for chorus and orchestra in 1977 and introduced at the Kennedy Center for the Performing Arts in Washington, D. C., on May 10, 1978, the composer conducting.

In 1964 and 1965, Husa received two consecutive Guggenheim Fellowships. For his fiftieth birthday, numerous colleges and universities throughout the United States presented performances of his compositions in 1971–72. These commemorative festivities included a Husa festival during a week in March 1972 at the University of Wisconsin in Madison, when examples of his work through the years were offered with eleven compositions. In 1974, Husa was elected associate member of the Royal Belgian Academy of Arts and Sciences, and in 1976 he was awarded an honorary doctorate in music by Coe College.

THE COMPOSER SPEAKS: I have been trying to preserve what little is still visible and useful from the past, but mostly my concern is to write music of today and, also, find some new paths for tomorrow. Most of the works of the past and present mirror the period in which they were composed, so I hope my music can reflect the exciting, passionate and also tragic times of today.

PRINCIPAL WORKS: 3 string quartets (1948, 1953, 1968); 2 piano sonatas (1949, 1975).

Fresques, for orchestra (1946; revised 1963); Divertimento, for string orchestra (1948); Piano Concertino (1949); *Evocations of Slovakia*, for clarinet, viola, and cello (1951); *Musique d'amateurs*, for orchestra (1953); *Portrait*, for orchestra (1953); Symphony (1953); Four Little Pieces, for strings (1955); Fantasies, for orchestra (1956): Twelve Moravian Songs, for voice and piano (1956): Divertimento for Brass and Percussion (1959); *Poem*, for viola and chamber orchestra (1959); *Élégie et Rondeau*, for alto saxophone and orchestra (1961); *Mosaïques*, for orchestra (1961); Serenade, for woodwind quintet, string orchestra, xylophone, and harp (1963); Concerto for Brass Quintet and String Orchestra (1965); *Festive Ode*, for chorus and orchestra (1965); Concerto for Alto Saxophone and Concert Band (1967); *Music for Prague 1968*, for band, also for orchestra (1968); Divertimento, for brass quintet (1968): *Apotheosis of This Earth*, for band, also for orchestra (1970); Concerto for Percussion and Wind Ensemble (1970–71); Two Sonnets from Michelangelo, for orchestra (1971); Violin Sonata (1972–73); Trumpet Concerto (1973); *Al fresco*, for wind ensemble (1973); *The Steadfast Tin Soldier*, for narrator and orchestra (1974); *Monodrama*, ballet (1975); *An American Te Deum*, for baritone solo, chorus, and band (1976; revised for baritone solo, chorus, and orchestra, 1977); Concerto for Trumpet and Piano (1977); *Landscapes,* for brass quintet (1977); Three Dance Sketches, for percussion (1979); Pastoral, for strings (1979); *Intradas and Interludes*, for trumpet ensemble and timpani (1980).

BIBLIOGRAPHY: BMI, *The Many Worlds of Music*, winter 1976; *High Fidelity/Musical America*, August 1969; *Musical Quarterly*, January 1976; *Who's Who in America, 1980–81*.

Huston, (Thomas) Scott Jr., b. Tacoma, Wash., October 10, 1916.

Scott explains that as a composer he has never favored any "method, be it mathematical, numerical, layered, calculated, logarithmic or placental." He likes to design each work on its own terms, proceeding from the original germinating seed to a logical result.

Both parents loved music and practiced it as amateurs. Huston's father, a clothing salesman, sang, and his mother, a former schoolteacher, played the piano. Sunday evenings were devoted to musicals at home in which the family, including brother Robert, gathered around the piano to sing or take turns playing solos or duets.

Scott became interested in music at the age of five

through these home concerts. He soon began receiving piano lessons from his mother, and after that from a cousin, an aunt, and, most significantly, from Myrtle Murdoch Smith, who not only developed his technique but also gave him insights into the music he was studying. Another important early musical influence was a teacher at the Sherman Grade School in Tacoma he attended between 1922 and 1928. She forced her students to learn the different clefs and taught them to identify basic themes from the masterworks. At Allen C. Mason Junior High School (1928–31) Huston played piano solos in the assembly and percussion in the small school orchestra. Later on, at Stadium High School (1931–34), he continued to perform on the piano at assemblies besides singing in the men's glee club. He was active outside the school as well by performing on the organ and singing in the choir of the Mason Methodist Church.

Upon graduating from high school in 1934, Huston spent a year at the College of Puget Sound in the state of Washington. Having by now arrived at the decision to devote himself to music, he left the college in 1938 to enter the Eastman School of Music in Rochester, N.Y., where his study of composition took place with Burrill Phillips, Bernard Rogers, Edward Royce, and Howard Hanson. He received his bachelor of music degree in 1941, his master of music degree in 1942, and his doctorate in composition in 1952. In 1941, his orchestral tone poem *Columbia: Saga of a River* (1941) won first prize in the Northwest Composers Contest; it was introduced by the Rochester Civic Orchestra under Howard Hanson in April 1941, and in 1942 was performed by the Seattle Symphony under Sir Thomas Beecham.

During World War II, Huston served in the U.S. Navy from 1942 to 1946, as chief petty officer aboard an aircraft carrier. In 1946–47, Huston taught piano and theory at the University of Redlands in California. From 1947 to 1950, he was assistant professor of piano and theory at Kearney State Teachers College in Nebraska. At Kearney, Huston married Natalie Joy Maser, a college voice major, on July 30, 1950; they have five children.

Huston was associate professor of composition and theory from 1952 to 1962, and, from 1955 to 1957, dean at the Conservatory of Music in Cincinnati. When the College-Conservatory became part of the University of Cincinnati, Huston continued as associate professor of composition and theory from 1957 to 1962, and since 1967 he served there as full professor.

Huston began his mature years as composer with Toccata, for piano and orchestra (1951), given its premiere in Rochester on May 30, 1951, Hanson conducting. The Cincinnati Symphony under Max Rudolf featured this work on one of its programs in 1964, but before then, this orchestra, under Thor Johnson, offered the world premiere of *Abstract*, for large orchestra (1954) on November 20, 1955. Hus-

ton's most ambitious work in the 1950s was *The Eighth Word of Christ*, a sacred cantata for solo voices, chorus, and organ. It was introduced on April 6, 1959, at The Walnut Hills Christian Church in Cincinnati, with the composer conducting.

After 1960, Huston began developing an individualized style. His works revealed a fascination for color, but never for its own sake. Huston is intrigued with translating architectural designs and shapes into sounds, never losing sight of the musical results, and he prefers through-composed rather than closed or ritornello forms. He has scrupulously avoided strict serialism, pointillism, aleatory methods and electronic means, in spite of which his music remains thoroughly "modern" in harmonic, rhythmic, contrapuntal, and structural procedures.

Four Phantasms, for orchestra (1964), was a programmatic symphony inspired by four abstract paintings of Fridtjof Schroder. It is numbered Symphony no. 3 but in actuality it is the composer's first symphony, since Symphony no. 1, written when he was a student, was never finished, and Symphony no. 2 was discarded almost as soon as he had completed it. While not basically an atonal work, *Four Phantasms* was not written for any fixed tonality. Each of its four movements ("Image V," "The Mystic," "Face of Anger," and "Image IV") has an individual character of its own. The writing ranges from the pictorial to the mystic to the highly dramatic. The Cincinnati Symphony under Max Rudolf premiered it on February 2, 1968. Since then, it has had numerous performances by other orchestras in the United States, Scandinavia, and France.

Phenomena, for baroque quartet (flute, oboe, string bass, and harpsichord), written in 1967, was commissioned by the Heritage Chamber Quartet, which introduced it in Cincinnati on February 22, 1968. Subsequently, it was heard in Washington, D.C., Rochester, and abroad in England, France, Sweden, and Norway.

On a commission from the American Federation of Musicians, Huston wrote Symphony no. 4, for strings, in 1972. In two movements, subtitled "Fragile, Elusive, Passionate" and "Reflective, Agitated, and Vigorous," this symphony, which has no key signature, is built out of recurring sonorities, with certain note patterns unilized and repeated in both the harmonic and melodic structures. The subtitles, the composer explains, refer to personalities and moods. Only one of the movements was given when this symphony was introduced by the Congress of Strings under Henry Mazer on August 10, 1972. Huston's Symphony no. 5 (1975) received its World Premiere in a performance by the St. Louis Symphony under Jerzy Semkov on April 18, 1978, having been written on a grant from that orchestra. It is entitled *The Human Condition*, exploiting the composer's favorite pastime of observing the strengths, weaknesses, powers, and foibles of humans. It attempts to portray in sound the wide and fasinating variances among his friends. This work bears a resemblance to, and in fact is partly drawn from, the composer's Symphony no. 4, for strings.

Shadowy Waters, for clarinet, piano, and cello (1977), based on a poem by William Butler Yeats, reflects in tones the shadows of the mind, the conflicts among dreams, ideals and reality. Sonos III Trio introduced it at the Walker Art Center in Minneapolis on October 10, 1977. It was heard in New York on November 22, 1978.

On October 24, 1978, *Ecstasies of Janus*, a song cycle for countertenor and seven instruments (1978) and using for its text three poems by Jeannie Elizabeth Lloyd, received its world premiere in Columbus, Ohio. In the *Cincinnati Enquirer*, Nancy Malitz reported: "Huston's settings of all three poems were filled with intense and varied imagery. In fact, his treatment of words such as 'scream' and 'mock' and 'leap' and 'sleep' was often downright madrigalistic. But the real effectiveness of *Ecstasies* stemmed from Huston's ability to fit poetic passages with appropriate increments of musical intensity often through his manipulation of the unusual color and capability of the countertenor voice."

While on the faculty of the College-Conservatory of Music in Cincinnati, Huston has frequently been invited as composer-in-residence to colleges and universities throughout the United States to lecture and present his compositions. At Tufts University in Boston on April 11, 1976, five of his works were performed, including the world premiere of *Intensity* II, for wind ensemble (1975). In 1976, Huston received the Ernest N. Glover Award for excellence in teaching. He has also received grants from the National Endowment for the Arts for copying parts of his Symphony no. 5 in 1975 and from the Cincinnati Symphony for *Fanfare for the Two Hundredth* (1975) in 1976.

THE COMPOSER SPEAKS: I like to move my listeners, stir their imagination, make them aware of discriminating pacing of events and heightened impact of human emotions by combining long lines with brief cellular motives in intense counterpoint, by using a harmonic language derived from the twelve-tone vocabulary and intervallic coconstructions; add rhythmic procedures juxtaposed with clear and precise rhythmic patterns and elements of unpredictability alternating with clear formal designs crammed with much seeming extraneous material so that the constant freshness (thus, no ennui) results.

PRINCIPAL WORKS: 3 symphonies, two earlier ones having been discarded (1964, 1972, 1975); *Intensity* nos. I and II, for wind ensemble (1962, 1975).

Toccata, for piano and orchestra (1951); *Abstract*, for large orchestra (1954); *Trimurti*, for trombone quartet (1957); Piano Sonata (1958); *The Eighth Word of Christ*, sacred cantata for solo voices, chorus, and organ (1959); Organ Sonata (1960); Three Biblical Songs, for alto voice and piano (1961); Trumpet Concerto, for trumpet, string orchestra, harp, and timpani (1963): *Lamentations of Jeremiah*, for a cappella chorus (1964): *Four Conversations*, for woodwind quintet (1965); *Mass in English*, for chorus and organ (1965); *Planta-Tholoi*, for piano (1966); Three Psalms, for a cappella chorus (1966); *Venus and Mercury*, sonata for violin and piano (1967); *Phenomena*, for baroque quartet (1967): *Autumn Evening and Evening Ebb*, song cycle for soprano and piano (1968); *Idioms*, for violin, clarinet, and French horn (1968): *The Song of Deborah*, for narrator, chorus, and orchestra (1969); *Love and Marriage*, cantata for soprano and bass soli and chamber ensemble (1969): *The Oratorio of Understanding*, for 8 soloists, chorus, and orchestra (1969): *Divinely Superfluous Beauty, Natural Music*, song cycle for lyric soprano and chamber ensemble (1971); *Sounds at Night*, for brass choir (1971): *Life Styles*, I, II, III, and IV, for piano trio (1972); *Life Styles* I, II, III, and IV, for clarinet, cello, and piano (1972); *Quintessence*, for brass quintet (1973); *Tamar*, monodrama for soprano and prepared piano (1974); *Eleataron*, for viola and piano (1975); *Fanfare for the Two Hundredth*, for orchestra (1975); *Impressions from Life*, for eleven chamber instruments (1976); *Shadowy Waters*, for clarinet, piano, and cello (1977); *Ecstasies of Janus*, song cycle for countertenor and chamber ensemble (1978); *Time/Reflections*, "cantata enigmatica" for chorus and chamber orchestra (1978), *Variables for the Rascher Saxophone Quartet* (1979).

BIBLIOGRAPHY: Anderson, E. Ruth, *Contemporary American Composers: A Biographical Dictionary* (Boston, 1976); Machlis, Joseph, *Introduction to Contemporary Music*, revised ed. (N.Y., 1979); *Cincinnati Symphony Program Notes*, February 2, 1968: *Cincinnati Enquirer*, February 6, 1972.

Imbrie, Andrew Welsh, b. New York City, April 6, 1921.

Imbrie favors a complex linear and a dissonantly harmonic idiom. To his writing he brings lyrical, dramatic, poetic and expressive interest. "Imbrie's musical ideas," Robert Commanday has written in the *San Francisco Chronicle*, "seems self-actuating. . . . Once set into motion, these ideas determine a musical course that is both fanciful and insistent. The fulfillment of these ideas projects a genuine sense of life in movement."

Both Imbrie's parents were of Scottish descent. When Andrew was five he began taking piano lessons from Ann Abajian, who was the first to encourage him to become a composer. A year later, his family moved to Princeton, N.J. While attending private schools he commuted regularly to Philadelphia to study the piano with Leo Ornstein first at the Philadelphia Conservatory, then at the Ornstein School of Music. At the conservatory, Imbrie performed piano concertos with its orchestra. In 1933, he appeared as one of the two pianists performing the Saint-Saëns *Carnival of Animals* with the Philadelphia Orchestra.

After graduating from the Princeton Country Day School in 1935, he entered Lawrenceville School to continue academic study. By this time he had come to the decision that in music he wanted to develop himself as composer rather than pianist. The summer of 1937 was spent in Fontainebleau, France, studying composition with Nadia Boulanger. That fall, in the United States, he studied harmony and counterpoint privately with Roger Sessions.

In 1938, upon graduating from Lawrenceville School, he entered Princeton University. There, as a freshman, he took courses in fugue, analysis, and composition, later continuing his study of composition at Princeton with Sessions. In his senior year, he completed a work of exceptional merit, in a motivic idiom, occasionally lyrical and energized by rhythmic strength. It was String Quartet no. 1 (1942), introduced in Princeton in June 1942 and then performed by several string quartets. Following a performance by the Bennington Quartet in New York on April 10, 1944, it received the New York Music Critics Circle Award as the best chamber music composition of the season and was recorded by the Juilliard Quartet.

Graduating from Princeton in 1942, Imbrie joined the Armed Forces. He served in the U.S. Army Sig-

nal Corps in Washington, D. C., where his duties consisted of making translations from the Japanese. As an extracurricular activity, he provided original music (which he would improvise on the piano) for army-produced musicals.

After being discharged from military service in 1946, Imbrie continued to study composition with Sessions on an Alice M. Ditson Fellowship at the University of California in Berkeley, where he received his master's degree in music in 1947. That year he was appointed instructor of music at the university, but he was given permission to delay classroom duties for two years to spend them at the American Academy of Rome on a Prix de Rome. In Rome he completed the Piano Sonata (1947); *Ballad*, for orchestra (1947), first heard over the Rome radio (RAI) before receiving its first public hearing in Florence on June 20, 1949; *Divertimento*, for six instruments (1949; Rome, May 4, 1949); and *On the Beach at Night*, for chorus and strings (1949; Berkeley, Calif., April 1952).

In 1949, Imbrie became a member of the music faculty at the University of California at Berkeley, where he has remained ever since, becoming assistant professor in 1951, associate professor in 1957, and full professor in 1960. He also served as chairman of the department of composition at the San Francisco Conservatory of Music in 1970. In 1950 he received a grant from the National Institute of Arts and Letters. On January 31, 1953, he married Barbara Cushing, with whom he has had two sons. In 1953 and again in 1960 he was awarded Guggenheim Fellowships.

His individuality as a composer began emerging and receiving national recognition in the 1950s, notably with the String Quartet no. 2 (1951; Cambridge, Mass., May 12, 1953), the Violin Concerto (1954; Berkeley, Calif., April 22, 1958) and the String Quartet no. 3 (1957; Urbana, Ill., March 29, 1957). What Ingolf Dahl said in *Musical Quarterly* about these two string quartets applies as well to his other works both of this and of a later period. They combined "clear, classically oriented forms with the spontaneity of those welcome comments in which the music bursts out of the established patterns in free declamation." The lyrical and contrapuntal elements are virile and pronounced, the dissonant harmonies expressively dramatic. In recognition of his growing stature, the Boston Symphony presented Imbrie with its Merit Award (1955), the Brandeis University at

Waltham, Mass., with the Creative Arts Award (1958), and the Naumburg Foundation with its award (1960), the last of these subsidizing the recording of his Violin Concerto (1954).

Imbrie's major compositions in the 1960s were *Drum Taps*, for chorus and orchestra (1960; N.Y., spring 1961), based on Walt Whitman; Symphony no. 1 (1966; San Francisco, May 11, 1966); Symphony no. 2 (1969; San Francisco, May 21, 1970); and String Quartet no. 4 (1969; Madison, Wis., November 12, 1969). *Drum Taps* was commissioned by the Interracial Chorus of New York, which introduced it. The two symphonies were written for Josef Krips, musical director of the San Francisco Symphony, that orchestra and conductor providing the world premieres. The String Quartet no. 4, recognized not only as Imbrie's finest work in that medium but also a major contribution to contemporary chamber music, was commissioned by the group that introduced it, the Pro Arte Quartet. Passion, power, intensity, and a kind of toughness, generated by inner forces, are qualities that predominate in all this music, and in much of what Imbrie has written since. In 1967–68 Imbrie was awarded a grant by the National Foundation on Arts and Humanities that helped to subsidize a sabbatical leave from the university and allow him to serve as composer-in-residence at the American Academy in Rome.

Though Imbrie completed a symphony, his third, in the 1970s (1970; Manchester, England, December 3, 1970), which received the Walter Hinrichson Award providing for its recording, the form that Imbrie seemed most partial to in that decade was the concerto. He completed two piano concertos, the first in 1973 (Saratoga, Calif., August 4, 1973), and the second, a commission from the Ford Foundation, in 1974 (Indianapolis, Ind., January 29, 1976); a Cello Concerto (1973; Oakland, Calif., April 24, 1973); and a Flute Concerto (1977), commissioned by the New York Philharmonic for its first flutist, Julius Baker, and orchestra, its premiere taking place on October 13, 1977, Erich Leinsdorf conducting.

In commemoration of the American bicentenary, Imbrie produced *Angle of Repose* (1976), his first full-length opera. This was only his second work for the stage, the first having been a fantasy (libretto by Richard Wincor) about the abolition of Christmas called *Three Against Christmas*, or *Christmas in Peebles Town*, (1960; Berkeley, Calif., December 3, 1964). *Angle of Repose* (1976), based on Wallace Stegner's novel of that name, with libretto by Oakley Hall, was produced in San Francisco on November 6, 1976. The score, while written in the composer's mature idiom, includes such American folk elements as Virginia reels and banjo tunes with attempts to reconcile these elements with the prevailing style.

Imbrie was elected a member of the American Academy of Arts and Letters in 1969.

THE COMPOSER SPEAKS: Music isn't really *about* any-

thing. Music just *is*. Words can describe, paintings can depict. But in music, things actually do happen in and of themselves. Music is different because the things that happen in it are musical things. They strike us, not as make-believe, but as real. The dominant chord, a melodic phrase, a roll on the timpani—all of these things have a concrete existence of their own: They are true experiences, they really take place. So you see, composing is fun because it makes things happen.

But the things that happen are more than just sensations, pleasant or unpleasant or in between. They have a kind of syntax, they make a kind of sense, which we recognize because the sounds appear to move from one point to another. It is this effect of *movement* in *time* that forges the link between raw stimulus and human response.

So if I want my music to make sense to you, I have to make the music move in a way that resembles the movements of your body and mind—the tensions, the releases of your nerves, muscles, and feelings. Yet, remember, I do not have to tell you stories or give examples. What I *do* have to do is somehow to get under your skin and reach that responsive chord which connects us together as human beings even though perhaps we have never met or shared the same specific experiences.

PRINCIPAL WORKS: 4 string quartets (1942–69); 3 symphonies (1966, 1969, 1970); 2 piano concertos (1973, 1974).

Piano Sonata (1947); *Ballad*, for orchestra (1947); Piano Trio (1947); *On the Beach at Night*, for chorus and string orchestra (1949); Three Songs, for soprano and small orchestra (1949); Divertimento, for flute, bassoon, trumpet, violin, cello, and piano (1949); Serenade, for flute, viola, and piano (1952); Violin Concerto (1954); Introit, Gradual and Offertory, for chorus and organ (1956); *Legend*, for orchestra (1959); *Drum Taps*, for chorus and orchestra (1960); *Little Concerto*, for piano four hands and orchestra (1960); Impromptu, for violin and piano (1960); *Three Against Christmas* or *Christmas in Peebles Town*, operatic fantasy for five singers, double chorus, and orchestra (1960); Psalm 42, for male chorus and organ (1962); *Tell Me Where Is Fancy Bred*, for soprano, clarinet, and guitar (1964); *Love Distills Desire upon the Eyes*, for chorus and piano (1966); *The Serpent*, for chorus and piano (1966); *The Wind Has Blown the Rain Away*, for chorus and piano (1966); Cello Sonata (1966); *Dandelion Wine*, for oboe, clarinet, piano, and string quartet (1967); *Chamber Symphony* (1968); *Let All the World*, for chorus, two horns, two trumpets, two trombones, tuba, percussion, and organ (1971); *To a Traveler*, for violin, cello, and piano (1971); *Fancy for Five*, for five trombones (1972); Cello Concerto (1973); *Angle of Repose*, opera (1976); Flute Concerto (1977); Waltz, for piano (1977); *O Moment's Reflection*, for piano (1978); *Prometheus Bound*, dance cantata for three singers, double chorus, and orchestra with dancers (1979–80); *Roethke Songs*, for soprano and piano (1980).

BIBLIOGRAPHY: *DCM*; Thomson, Virgil, *American Music Since 1910* (N.Y., 1970); *Musical Journal*, February 1977; Oakland (Calif.) *Tribune*, December 4, 1977; *Who's Who in America, 1980–81*.

Ives, Charles Edward, b. Danbury, Conn., October 20, 1874; d. New York City, May 19, 1954.

When Ives received the Pulitzer Prize in music in 1947 for a symphony he had written forty years earlier, he was getting belated recognition not merely for a symphony but for the fact that he was a major creative and germinative force in American music. Most of his music was written before 1920. Yet in spite of its early vintage, in it he not only anticipated but profoundly influenced the avant-garde movement in music that came into focus decades later. The ingrained iconoclast in him led him to use atonality, polytonality, arhythmic, and polyrhythmic procedures, tone clusters, unresolved discords, quarter-tone music, and aleatory practices long before the composers who became identified with those techniques. But Ives was not merely an innovator. At the same time, he created a thoroughly indigenous musical art that could have come from nowhere but the United States. That art derived its subject, inspiration, and materials from American history, politics, geography, holidays and sundry other native experiences as well as from American folk, popular, and church music, which he quoted so copiously.

He was the son of a man who was also a musical visionary. The father, George Ives, was the bandmaster of the First Connecticut Heavy Artillery in the army of General Ulysses S. Grant. George Ives preceded his son in experimenting with polytonal, directional, and even microtonal music. From his father, Charles received his first instruction in music: in theory, composition, sight-reading, ear training, orchestration, piano, cornet, and organ. When he was twelve, Charles played the drums in his father's band. Bands so fascinated the boy that whenever one came to town he would follow it, listening rapturously. What he seemed to like most of all was when two bands marched into town from opposite directions, playing as they went, their respective sounds mingling into cacophony. This discordant effect of two meeting bands playing two different melodies was a device he would later reproduce in some of his works.

His interest in unorthodox, discordant sound patterns was something his father inculcated in him. Time and again his father would play for him on the piano two different melodies in two different keys at the same time. "You must learn to stretch your ears!" his father told him.

His father also encouraged him in his early creative attempts. When Charles was thirteen he completed his first orchestral work, *Holiday Quickstep*, which his father's band performed in Danbury three weeks after it was written. In 1898, Charles Ives wrote the song "Slow March," whose accompaniment consisted of tone clusters to be played with the help of a wooden ruler, the first piece of published music to use such a discordant harmonic device. On August 31, 1889, Ives's orchestral overture *The American Woods* was heard at one of his father's band concerts. In 1891, Ives arranged "America" for organ in a bitonal idiom, the first time this was being used. This is also the earliest of Ives's compositions to have survived in public favor both as a work for solo organ and in a transcription for orchestra by William Schuman (1963).

Ives's early academic schooling took place at the Danbury High School, where he was captain of the football team. In 1893 he went to New Haven to continue his academic studies at the Hopkins Preparatory School, for whose baseball team he was a pitcher. He supported himself by playing the organ at St. Thomas Church, and then in the Second Baptist Church and the Center Church. At Yale he attended the composition classes of Horatio W. Parker, while outside Yale he studied the organ with Dudley Buck and Harry Rowe Shelley. He was also busy composing: eighty works in all during his four years at college including church music, organ pieces, songs, and his String Quartet no. 1 (1896). Much of this music was still traditional, but in some of it the rebel began to stir. When he showed the opening movement of his symphony to Horatio W. Parker, the teacher was appalled to find that the first subject progressed through eight different keys.

Upon being graduated from Yale in 1898, with a bachelor of arts degree, Ives moved to New York. He found a clerking job at Mutual Life Insurance Company for five dollars a week, supplementing this by playing the organ at the First Presbyterian Church in Bloomfield, N.J., and in 1900, as organist of the Central Presbyterian Church in New York City. This marked the beginnings of Ives's dual existence: as an insurance man, work in which he ultimately became highly successful; and as a composer, working laboriously and in total obscurity on compositions that shattered existing traditions.

In two remarkable works, in 1901–2, Ives took a giant leap into music's future. *From the Steeples and the Mountains* was scored for two sets of church bells and chimes (each sounding tones in different keys), four trumpets, and four trombones, each group playing in unison. The effect Ives was trying to achieve was the discordant and polytonal sounds realized when bells from different steeples are sounded simultaneously. At the end of his score, Ives appended the following printed comment: "After the brass stops, the chimes sound on until they die away! . . . From the Steeples—the Bells!—then the Rocks on the

Mountains begin to shout!" So far in advance of its time was this music that it had to wait sixty-four years before being performed. This happened on July 30, 1965, when Lukas Foss conducted the New York Philharmonic during a French-American festival.

Symphony no. 2—begun in 1897 but completed in 1902—was Ives's first work to indulge in what henceforth would become one of his identifiable practices: quoting popular American tunes, in snatches (sometimes distorted), often in dissonant conjunction with other types of quoted or original melodies. Ives's own description of this symphony is that it "expresses the musical feelings of the Connecticut country around here in the 1890s, the music of the country folk. It is full of the tunes they sang and played then." In the first movement, a fragment of "Columbia, the Gem of the Ocean" became a countersubject in the horns to a virile theme of Ives's own invention. The music of a village band on the green is suggested in the second movement. In the third, American church music of the 1860s, 1870s, and 1880s was remembered and parodied. In the fourth, the hurried strains of country dances, barn melodies, and Stephen Foster's "De Camptown Races" and "Old Black Joe" were interpolated. "Columbia, the Gem of the Ocean" returned to bring the symphony to a triumphant culmination in the final movement. The overall effect of the symphony is that of a complex, polytonal, polyrhythmic, tone-clustered fabric in which the thematic materials, quoted and original, jostle one another when they do not come into outright collision. Ivesian whimsy, a recurrent trait in so many of his subsequent works, was also present in the way (as a gesture of mock defiance against traditional music) Ives juxtaposed popular tunes discordantly with quotations from Bach, Wagner, Bruckner, Brahms, and Dvořák. It took fifty years for this symphony to be heard for the first time, Leonard Bernstein conducting its premiere with the New York Philharmonic on February 22, 1951.

The orchestral suite *Three Places in New England* (1903–14) was Ives's first major work for orchestra to be heard in its entirety. This happened when Nicolas Slonimsky conducted the Chamber Orchestra of Boston on January 10, 1931, in New York. The version Slonimsky conducted was for chamber orchestra, which the composer had prepared in 1914, and this is the way the work has become popular. But Ives originally scored it for a large orchestra, the original manuscript of which went astray. Working at the Yale University Ives Collection beginning with 1972, James Sinclair was able to restore Ives's original scoring with the help of the completely scored first movement discovered in the personal library of Goddard Lieberson, president of Columbia Records. By January 1974, the work of restoration was completed, and *Three Places in New England* received its second "premiere," this time for

full orchestra, in New Haven on February 9, 1974. The inspiration for this Ives masterwork is the geography and history of New England. We are given a picture of Saint-Gaudens in the Boston Common in the first movement, the second part of which recalls the era of the Civil War. The middle movement is set in a small park near Redding, Conn., where General Putnam encamped in 1778–79. Here there takes place a Fourth of July picnic where children are at play. One of them tries to envision what had happened in this very place many years ago. Revolutionary War marches and songs are quoted. A violent discord is achieved when two marches, in different keys and in different rhythms, are played simultaneously by two bands. A tonal scenic picture of the Housatonic River at Stockbridge, Mass., concludes the suite, a movement Paul Rosenfeld, the noted critic, described as "easily the jewel of the suite, and one of the thrilling American compositions."

In 1947, Ives received the Pulitzer Prize in music for Symphony no. 3 (1901–4), into which he brought both the spirit and the tunes of American camp meetings of 19th-century Connecticut. Two old hymn tunes provide the principal thematic material: "O for a Thousand Tongues," treated fugally in the first movement, and "Just As I Am," heard in the third. The middle movement describes a children's game at camp meetings. On April 5, 1946, Lou Harrison conducted the New York Little Symphony in the symphony's world premiere, and, on May 11, 1946, it attracted further attention when it was repeated in New York in an all-Ives program. In addition to the Pulitzer Prize, the symphony was awarded a special citation by the New York Music Critics Circle.

Holidays (1904–13), described as "a symphony of New England holidays," represents the composer's boyhood recollections of the Connecticut country. It consists of four descriptive orchestral pieces that can be played as a suite or independently. Opening with "Washington's Birthday" (1909; San Francisco, September 3, 1913), it continued with "Decoration Day" (1912), "The Fourth of July" (1913; Paris, France, February 21, 1932) and "Thanksgiving Day and/or Forefather's Day" (1904). As in his symphonies, this work is a montage of original and quoted tunes piled on one another in a rhythmic, harmonic and polyphonic network: marches, quick steps, barn dances, "Adeste Fideles," "Taps," etc.

Central Park in the Dark, for orchestra (1907), is, as the composer explained, "a picture of sounds of nature and of happenings that men would hear . . . when sitting on a bench in Central Park on a hot summer night." The sounds, presented almost at random, pierce through the darkness of the park and include popular tunes of the day as sung by street singers, the whistling of a "freshman march" by some passing "night owl," newsboys crying out their "extras," a ragtime tune from a distant pianola, noises of fire engines and streetcars, the *oompahs* of a street band, and so forth. "Again in the darkness is heard . . . an echo over the pond . . . and we walk home," Ives concludes.

In 1906, Ives left the Mutual Insurance Company to establish Ives and Company, which was dissolved a year later. On January 1, 1909, it reemerged as Ives and Myrick Insurance Company, which achieved outstanding success and provided Ives with economic stability for the rest of his life. On June 9, 1908, he married Harmony Twichell, daughter of a Hartford (Conn.) clergyman. In two houses—one in New York City, the other in West Redding, Conn.— they raised their only child, an adopted daughter.

By day, a practical, conservative, and well-trained businessman, Ives turned to his alter ego—the composer—at nighttime and on holidays. He scrupulously avoided social functions whether in his own home or elsewhere. He almost never went to concerts. To avoid distractions at home, he never owned a phonograph or radio, and never subscribed to a newspaper. He kept to himself most of his free time, his composing having become a strictly private function, a secret to all except his family and a few personal friends. In all this he had the stout cooperation of his wife. "Mrs. Ives," he once revealed, "never once said or suggested or looked or thought there must be something wrong with me. She never said, 'Now why don't you be good and write something nice, the way they like it?' Never. She urged me on my way to be myself and gave me her confidence." He would write his strange music and then put it in a closet and forget about it, never trying to get it published or performed. Apparently, the mere writing of it was all the satisfaction he needed. Only comparatively late in his creative career did he take the trouble to publish two of his works at his own expense, doing so only to be able to distribute them to personal friends.

He kept on producing remarkable, revolutionary compositions up to about 1918. One of the most philosophical and enigmatic is *The Unanswered Question* (1908), subtitled "a cosmic landscape." Rhythmic coordination is dispensed with as muted strings, playing pianissimo throughout without any change in tempo, and representing "Silences of the Druids, who Know, See and Hear nothing," find contrast in the atonal sounds of a solo trumpet as it propounds the "perennial question of existence." The woodwinds respond dissonantly as they search for "the invisible answer." But, in the end, after the trumpet asks the question for the last time, there is only silence.

Piano Sonata no. 2, subtitled *Concord* (1909–15), is one of the most difficult piano works ever written. This music was intended, as Ives explained, to recreate "the spirit of literature, the philosophy, and the men of Concord, Mass., of over half a century." The prose and poetry of Ralph Waldo Emerson provided the inspiration for the first movement. Here the tempo is not indicated but left to the decision of the performer, because "the same essay or poem by Emerson may bring a slightly different feeling when

read at sunrise or when read at sunset." Nathaniel Hawthorne was the subject of the second movement, in which Ives used a ruler or strip of wood to cover a two-octave tone cluster. In the last movement we are in the world of the Alcotts, one of whom (Louisa May) was the author of *Little Women*. The first four notes of Beethoven's Fifth Symphony made a sudden presence because the Alcott children were always practicing Beethoven's music on the piano. The sonata ended with a musical tribute to Thoreau in idyllic music in which, seemingly out of nowhere, we suddenly hear the sounds of a brief flute solo (optional); Thoreau always enjoyed flute music at dusk at Walden. When John Kirkpatrick gave the first complete performance of this sonata in New York on January 20, 1939, Lawrence Gilman called it, in the *New York Herald Tribune*, "the greatest music composed by an American, and the most deeply and essentially American in pulse and implication."

Ives's most monumental symphony was his fourth and last (1910–16). In the first movement, in which the spirit of a man questions the "what" and "why" of life, Ives quotes three hymns: "The Sweet Bye-and-Bye," "Nearer, My God, to Thee" and "Watchman, Tell Us of the Night." Popular tunes weave their way into the fabric of the second movement: "Marching through Georgia," "Yankee Doodle," "Turkey in the Straw," and "Columbia, the Gem of the Ocean." Sometimes these are recognizable, sometimes they are fragmented, sometimes they are completely distorted. The third movement is an orchestral transcription of the opening movement from Ives's String Quartet no. 1 (1896). Two hymns— "From Greenland's Icy Mountains" and "All Hail the Power"—provide the subjects for a giant double fugue. Such immense forces are required for the performance of this symphony (a huge orchestra, a greatly expanded percussion section, a chorus and a brass band), and so involved is the musical texture (twenty-seven different rhythms are heard simultaneously in one section) that three conductors are required. This is the way the symphony was premiered by Leopold Stokowski and the American Symphony Orchestra on April 25, 1965, in New York. Since then, a simplified version, demanding a single conductor, has been favored.

In 1919, Ives privately published the *Concord Sonata,* following it in 1920 with an explanatory volume entitled *Essays Before a Sonata*. He explained the raison d'être for these publications as follows: "These prefatory essays were written by the composer for those who can't read music, and the music for those who can't stand his essays; to those who can't stand either, the whole is respectfully dedicated."

The whimsy inspiring such a statement recurs again and again in annotations in various of his compositions. In one of his piano sonatas he added this verbal comment: "Back to the first theme—all nice sonatas must have first themes." The second violin in one of his string quartets was given the name of

"Rollo"; during a pause in the music he informs Rollo that it is "too hard to play, so it just can't be good music." In one of his songs, he remarked in an aside that it was written "to clear up the long-disputed point, namely, which is worse, the music or the words?" In an orchestral score he stopped the bassoon midway to inform him: "From here on, the bassoon may play anything at all." A trumpet solo appeared inexplicably in a violin sonata and a violin obbligato intruded into a song for voice and piano.

In 1921 Ives privately published *114 Songs,* an anthology of songs he had written since 1888. They are presented in reverse chronological order, beginning with "Majority," which he had completed in 1921, and ending with "Slow March" of 1888. A wide gamut of style was traversed here, from the romantic to the satiric. We encounter ballads, war songs, protest songs, hymns, cowboy tunes, street songs, even ragtime. The styles were equally varied. Some songs were atonal, some had tone clusters, Some were syncopated, some were in folklike idiom, and some were simple and direct in their emotional appeal. In these songs, Aaron Copland has written, "one knows oneself to be in the presence of a composer of imagination, a real creator."

Ives's most ambitious project was never realized: the *Universe Symphony,* begun in 1911, whose overall plan was "presentation and contemplation in tones, rather than in music, of the mysterious creation of the earth and the firmament, the evolution of all life in nature, in humanity, to the Divine." The project collapsed under the weight of its vast concept. Ives abandoned it in 1916 after producing just a few sketches. This venture, as Henry and Sidney Cowell explain in their biography of Ives (written while Ives was still alive) was "so gigantic, so inclusive, and so exalted that he [Ives] feels its complete realization is beyond any single man. . . . Ives has never intended that *Universe Symphony* be brought to an end, for it represents aspects of life about which there is always something more to be said." Never again was Ives to attempt a work of major proportions.

Ives's most important work was done by 1918, a year in which he suffered a heart attack. For the next decade he produced only a few random, unimportant pieces. Diabetes, a disturbed nervous system, and a trembling hand forced him to give up composition in 1928. Further physical problems, including cataracts of both eyes, compelled him to withdraw from his prosperous insurance business in 1930. Retiring to his home in West Redding, he became a recluse, refusing to emerge when, in 1946, he was elected to the National Institute of Arts and Letters, and in 1947, when he was awarded the Pulitzer Prize. Then, as before, he avoided meeting interviewers, photographers, or admirers. He never answered the mail that now flooded his door. He stubbornly refused to attend performances of any of his works. When Bernstein offered the world premiere of the Symphony no. 2, Ives not only would not come to the concert but

even declined Berstein's invitation to a private performance given for him alone. But when Berstein's performance was broadcast over the radio, Ives sneaked into the kitchen to listen to the cook's radio; and when the concert was over, he came into the living room doing a jig.

His fame has grown prodigiously since his death. Performances and recordings of his works have become abundant in the United States and abroad. The centenary of his birth inspired a series of commemorations which included festivals of Ives's music in different parts of the country; performances of his major and even minor works by leading symphony orchestras, chamber music ensembles and solo performers; the release of a five-disk album of his works by Columbia Records, which included examples of Ives playing the piano, improvising, and singing; several television documentaries; symposiums and lectures in colleges and universities; the publication of numerous articles in leading newspapers and magazines and several new biographies.

On August 18, 1980, a Charles Ives Center for American Music was inaugurated at New Milford, Conn., funded by a grant from the Connecticut Commission on the Arts.

THE COMPOSER SPEAKS: The hope of all music—of the future, of the past, to say nothing of the present—will not lie with the partialist who raves about an ultramodern opera (if there is such a thing) but despises Schubert, or with the party man who viciously maintains the opposite assumption. Nor will it lie in any cult or any idiom or in any artist or any composer. "All things in their variety are of one essence and are limited only by themselves."

The future of music many not lie entirely with music itself, but rather in the way it encourages and extends, rather than limits, the aspirations and ideals of the people, in the way it makes itself a part with the finer things that humanity does and dreams of. Or to put it the other way around, what music is and is to be may lie somewhere in the belief of an unknown philosopher of half a century ago who said: "How can there be any bad music? All music is from heaven. If there is anything bad in it, I put it there—by my implications and limitations. Nature builds the mountains and meadows and man puts in the fences and labels." He may have been nearer right than we think.

PRINCIPAL WORKS: 114 songs (1884–21); 6 *Sets,* for orchestra (1907–22); 5 violin sonatas (1908–15); 4 symphonies (1898–1916); 2 string quartets (1896, 1913); 2 piano sonatas (1902–10, 1909–15).

From the Steeples and the Mountains, for church bells, chimes, four trumpets, and four trombones (1901); Trio, for violin, clarinet, and piano (1902); *Three Places in New England,* suite for orchestra (1903–14); *Three Quarter-tone Piano Pieces* (1903–24); *Central Park in the Dark,* for orchestra (1907); *Holidays,* suite for orchestra (1904–13); *The Unan-*

swered Question, for orchestra (1908); Trio, for violin, cello, and piano (1911); *Browning*, overture for orchestra (1911); *Tone Roads*, for chamber orchestra (1911–15); *Lincoln, the Great Commoner*, for chorus and orchestra (1912); *Set*, for string quartet and piano (1914); *General William Booth Enters into Heaven*, for chorus and brass band (1914); *Three Protests*, for piano (1914).

BIBLIOGRAPHY: Cowell, Henry and Sidney, *Charles Ives and His Music*, revised ed. (N.Y., 1969); Hitchcock, H. Wiley, *Charles Ives* (London, 1977); Perlis, Vivian, *Ives Remembered: An Oral History* (New Haven, Conn., 1974); Rossiter, Frank R., *Charles Ives and His America* (N.Y., 1955); Woolridge, David, *From the Steeples and Mountains: A Study of Charles Ives* (N.Y., 1974); *Musical America*, February 15, 1954; *Musical Quarterly*, January 1933; *New York Times Magazine*, April 21, 1974; *Perspectives of New Music*, spring–summer, 1968.

J

Jacobi, Frederick, b. San Francisco, Calif., May 4, 1891; d. New York City, October 24, 1952.

Jacobi is remembered for both his American Indian and his Hebraic music, but he also produced many works without ethnic interest. His style is a skillful synthesis of the classic and the romantic with some modern harmonic and rhythmic approaches.

In his childhood, his family moved to New York. There he received his academic education at the Ethical Culture School. His musical training took place in New York and Berlin: in New York with Rubin Goldmark and Ernest Bloch (composition), and Paolo Gallico and Rafael Joseffy (piano); in Berlin, at the High School of Music, with Paul Juon (composition).

Between 1913 and 1917 Jacobi was assistant conductor of the Metropolitan Opera in New York. He wrote several works during this period, all in a romantic idiom. Three Songs, for voice and piano (1914), and *Three Songs to Poems by Sarojini Naidu*, for voice and piano (1916), were his first to be published. *A California Suite*, for orchestra (1917), was his first to receive a significant hearing, introduced in San Francisco on December 6, 1917.

On May 29, 1917, Jacobi married Irene Schwarz, a concert pianist who, in later years, introduced many of his piano works. They had three children. In 1917–18, during World War I, Jacobi served in the armed forces and he played the saxophone in army bands.

After the war Jacobi spent several years doing research in American Indian music among the Pueblo and Navajo Indians of New Mexico and Arizona. His first successful compositions were the result of this period of investigation. *String Quartet on Indian Themes* (1924) was introduced by the Flonzaley Quartet, received the Society for the Publication of American Music Award, won honorable mention in the Elizabeth Sprague Coolidge competition, represented the United States at the festival of the International Society for Contemporary Music at Zurich on June 19, 1926, and was performed by various chamber music groups. Another major work utilizing authentic American Indian melodies and rhythms came in 1927: *Indian Dances*, a four-movement suite which the Boston Symphony under Serge Koussevitzky introduced on November 8, 1928. Soon after

that, it was performed by the Philadelphia Orchestra under Leopold Stokowski, the San Francisco Symphony under Alfred Hertz, as well as in Warsaw and Copenhagen.

In some of Jacobi's later works the musical idioms of the American Indian continue to be used effectively, particularly in the Concerto for Piano and Orchestra (1934–35), which his wife introduced at a WPA Festival in New York with Chalmers Clifton conducting, and *Yebiche*, a set of variations for orchestra on an American Indian theme (1949).

Two other works of the 1920s, however, are of Assyrian rather than American Indian interest: Symphony no. 1, subtitled *Assyrian* (1922), and *Two Assyrian Prayers*, for voice and orchestra (1923). The symphony was given its premiere on November 14, 1924, by the San Francisco Symphony under Alfred Hertz. It went into neglect after that, except for the second movement. In 1926, Jacobi adapted it for flute and small orchestra and called it Nocturne (Rochester, N.Y., December 30, 1926); in 1941 he revised it again, renaming it *Night Music* (San Diego, Calif., July 21, 1941).

Beginning with the *Sabbath Evening Service*, for baritone and a cappella chorus (1930–31)—commissioned and introduced by Temple Emanu-El in New York—Jacobi produced several notable racially oriented compositions which assimilated the intervallic and modal characteristics of Hebrew music. The most significant of these were *Hagiographa*, three biblical narratives for string quartet and piano (1938); *Saadia*, a hymn for men's chorus (1942); *From the Prophet Nehemiah*, three excerpts for voice and two pianos (1942); *Two Pieces in Sabbath Mood*, for orchestra (1946; Indianapolis, Ind., February 13, 1946), which had originated as two pieces for organ named *Kaddish* and Toccata; *Oneg Shabbat*, a Friday Evening Service, for baritone, chorus, and orchestra, which was completed just before his death and which he referred to as his "last will and testament"; and settings of individual synagogal prayers.

Many of Jacobi's works, however, have no ethnic source. They are the absolute music of a modern romantic nature, usually in traditional structures. String Quartet no. 2 (1933), extensively performed by such prestigious chamber music groups as the Pro Arte, the Gordon String Quartet, and the Budapest

String Quartet, among others, received the Society for the Publication of American Music Award. Albert Spalding and the Chicago Symphony under Frederick Stock introduced the Violin Concerto (1936–37) on March 14, 1939. After the San Francisco Symphony premiered the *Ode*, for orchestra (1941), on February 12, 1943, a critic for *Modern Music* reported: "Jacobi's work, no mistake, has stuff, fibre, and structure. It is no mere sketch, no experiment in form, no excursion into strange realms of sonority. It has a consistent style. It masters the situation in which it finds itself. . . . It is music possessing heart and voice. It says what I have not heard before and want to hear again." Symphony in C (1947) was written for Pierre Monteux and the San Francisco Symphony, which presented its world premiere on April 1, 1948. *Music Hall*, for orchestra (1948), which, in the composer's words, was descriptive of "the evanescent tinsel world of vaudeville," was heard first on July 2, 1949, at the Lewisohn Stadium in New York, Alexander Smallens conducting.

Jacobi wrote only one work for the stage, a full-length opera, *The Prodigal Son* (1944). The libretto, by Herman Voaden, was based on four early American prints recreating the biblical story of the Prodigal Son, but placing it in the setting of early-19th-century America. A concert performance was given in Chicago by the American National Opera Society and the second act was staged at Stanford University in California on August 19, 1949. Soon afterwards, it was heard in Chicago, where the Opera Society presented it with the David Bispham medal.

In 1927, Jacobi was appointed to the composition faculty at the Master School of Arts in New York, where he remained several years. He was a member of the music faculty at the Juilliard School of Music in New York from 1936 to 1950 and a lecturer at the Julius Hartt School of Music in Hartford, Conn., from 1946 on. He also lectured at the University of California at Berkeley during the summers of 1939 and 1940. He was a director of the International Society for Contemporary Music, a member of the executive board of the League of Composers, and a charter member of the American Music Guild.

THE COMPOSER SPEAKS: My conscious aim has been to write music that is clear, definite, and concise; I am an antiobstructionist! I am a great believer in melody, a believer, too, that music should give pleasure and not try to solve philosophical problems. I believe that art and craft have much in common and that art, to be valid, must be more than the manifestation of a passing mode: in short, that there are eternal values which transcend period and time. . . .

My personal feeling is that there is perhaps an overemphasis these days on several aspects of music: on originality, on modernism, on Americanism. . . . Let the composer try to be himself: clear, honest, natural, and direct. And I think that, if he has the stuff within him, he will have a greater chance of attaining originality, Americanism, "todayism," than if he tries too hard to labor these special points.

PRINCIPAL WORKS: 3 string quartets (1924, 1933, 1945); 2 symphonies (1922, 1947).

A California Suite, for orchestra (1917); *The Eve of St. Agnes*, tone poem (1919); *Two Assyrian Prayers*, for voice and orchestra (1923); *The Poet in the Desert*, for baritone, chorus, and orchestra (1925); *Indian Dances*, suite for orchestra (1927–28); *Sabbath Evening Service*, for baritone and a cappella chorus (1930–31); Cello Concerto (1932); Six Pieces for Organ, for use in the synagogue (1933); Piano Concerto (1934–35); Violin Concerto (1936–37); *Hagiographa*, three biblical narratives for string quartet and piano (1938); *Ave Rota*, three pieces in multiple style for small orchestra and piano, also for large orchestra and piano (1939); Rhapsody for Harp and String Orchestra (1940); Fantasy, for viola and piano (1941); *Ode*, for orchestra (1941); *Night Piece*, an adaptation for flute and small orchestra of the second movement of the 1922 Symphony no. 1 (1941); Ballade, for violin and piano (1942); *Saadia*, hymn for men's chorus (1942); *From the Prophet Nehemiah*, three excerpts for voice and two pianos (1942); *The Prodigal Son*, opera (1943–44); *Ahavas Olem*, for tenor, chorus, and organ (1945); *Music for Monticello*, for flute, cello, and piano (1945); *Two Pieces in Sabbath Mood*, for orchestra, originally for organ solo (1946); *Moods*, for piano (1946); Introduction and Toccata, for piano (1946); Concertino, for piano and string orchestra (1947); *Impressions from the Odyssey*, for violin and piano (1947); *Contemplations*, for chorus and piano (1947); *Ode to Zion*, for mixed voices, and two harps (1948); *Music Hall*, overture for orchestra (1948); *Suite fantastique*, for piano (1948); Three Songs, for voice and piano (1948); *Yebiche*, variations on an American Indian theme, for orchestra (1949); *Friday Evening Service*, for baritone, chorus, and orchestra (1952); *Night Piece and Dance*, for flute and piano (1953).

BIBLIOGRAPHY: *DCM*; Ewen, David, *American Composers Today* (N.Y., 1949); *Modern Music*, March 1937; *New York Times*, November 2, 1952; *Who's Who in America, 1950–51*.

James, Philip Frederick Wright, b. Jersey City, N.J., May 17, 1890; d. Southampton, Long Island, N.Y., November 1, 1975.

James's compositions cover a wide territory. He has tapped American, French, Italian, Hebraic, and Irish backgrounds, all with equal facility and grace. To whatever subject matter he addressed himself he aimed to please ear and heart, to emphasize melodic interest and well-sounding harmonic and orchestral textures, and to leave the exploration of new sounds, idioms, and media to others.

His early academic and musical education took place in his native city. While attending elementary and high school in Jersey City, he received instruction on the piano from private teachers. Later on, in New York City, he received a bachelor of arts degree from the College of the City of New York. At the same time he underwent intensive instruction in composition with Rubin Goldmark and Rosario Scalero, among others.

In 1915–16, James was the conductor of the Winthrop Ames Theatrical productions in New York. On September 7, 1916, he married Millicent Eady. In 1917 he began his career as composer by writing two works for solo voices, chorus and orchestra: *The Nightingale of Bethlehem* and *Spring in Vienna*.

For two years, during World War I, he served in the American armed forces in the infantry. After the armistice, he was made commanding officer and the bandmaster of the American Expeditionary Forces General Headquarters Band.

Between 1919 and 1922, James was the musical director of the Victor Herbert Opera Company. From 1922 to 1929 he conducted the New Jersey Symphony; from 1927 to 1930, the Brooklyn Orchestral Society; and from 1929 to 1936, the Bamberger Little Symphony over radio station WOR, in New Jersey. He subsequently made numerous appearances as guest conductor of major American orchestras, including the Philadelphia Orchestra, the New York Philharmonic, the National Symphony in Washington, D. C., the NBC Symphony and the CBS Symphony.

He combined these varied conducting assignments with a long, productive career as teacher, joining the music faculty of New York University in 1923, and serving as chairman of that department from 1933 until 1965, when he retired and was named professor emeritus.

While on a trip to Venice, in 1924, James completed a string quartet which, though sometimes referred to as the *Venetian Quartet*, is entirely abstract within a thoroughly conventional structure, with no attempt to portray Venetian life or scenes. It was not performed until sixteen years after being written—in New York on May 15, 1940. In 1926, James wrote his first successful work for orchestra: *Overture in Olden Style in French Noëls*, first heard in Montclair, N.J., on December 14, 1926.

The winning of several awards in the 1920s and 1930s helped draw attention to his music and provide some of his works with significant performances. A sacred hymn for chorus was awarded first prize in 1927 in a contest sponsored by the *Homiletic Review*. In 1932, in a contest for American compositions conducted by NBC radio, James emerged with the first prize of $5,000 for a satirical orchestral piece about radio broadcasting: *Station WGZBK*, introduced by an orchestra under Eugene Goossens over the NBC radio network on May 8, 1932. An orchestral overture, *Bret Harte*, earned honorable mention in a contest held by the New York Philharmonic, which premiered it under John Barbirolli's direction on December 20, 1936. "The recklessness, the humor, and the adventurous flavor of the place and period are there," wrote Olin Downes in the *New York Times* of this overture. This was actually the third of three overtures James wrote under the title of *Bret Harte* in which, as he said, he sought to capture "the romance, the animation and many other abstract qualities of the people of Bret Harte and the West . . . whose glamour has been bedimmed through the eyes of Hollywood as well as by the mawkishness of the radio 'hillbilly' singer." Suite, for string orchestra (1934), was the recipient of the Juilliard Publication Award in 1937, and *Song of the Night*, a tone poem for orchestra (1930), was given a prize of $500 by the Women's Symphony Orchestra in New York in 1938 and performed by that orchestra under Antonia Brico on March 15, 1938.

A wide gamut of backgrounds and nationalities continued to stimulate James. *Il riposo* (1934) was a symphonic suite taking its name from a 16th-century religious style in painting. The three movements were respectively tonal representations of a Jan van Eyck altarpiece (*The March of the Magi*), a Byzantine mosaic in the basilica of Saint Apollinaire-Nuevo in Ravenna and Anton van Dyck's riposo-styled paintings. *Il riposo* had originated as part of *Stabat Mater Speciosa*, an elaborate work for chorus and orchestra (1921), but was adapted into an orchestral suite in 1934 and as such was introduced over radio station WOR on May 7, 1934. *Gwalia*, for orchestra, was a Welsh rhapsody (1937; N. Y., February 18, 1940). *Brennan on the Moor*, for orchestra, commissioned by CBS radio, was based on an Irish ballad (1939; N.Y., November 28, 1939). *Shirat Ha-Yam*, for chorus and orchestra (1944), used a Hebraic text. *Miniver Cheever*, for orchestra, and *Richard Corey*, for narrator and orchestra (1947; Saratoga, N.Y., September 9, 1947), used as texts two of the most famous poems of Edward Arlington Robinson. *Chaumont*, a tone poem for orchestra (1948; N. Y., May 2, 1951), was inspired by the hills outside the town of Chaumont, Haute-Marne, France. Passacaglia, for organ (1951), adapted for band six years later, utilized an old Cambrian ground bass.

James was elected to membership in the National Institute of Arts and Letters in 1933, for which he later served as vice-president. He was also vice-president of the Llangollen International Musical Eistedfod in North Wales, and fellow of Trinity College in London. In 1946, the New York College of Music conferred on him an honorary doctorate in music. His first wife, Millicent, died in 1945, and on February 3, 1952, James married Helga Boyer, with whom he had two children.

PRINCIPAL WORKS: 3 *Bret Harte* overtures (1925,

1933, 1934); 2 symphonies (1943, 1949); 2 suites for strings, (1934, 1943).

Stabat Mater Speciosa, for chorus and orchestra (1921, revised 1930); *Song of the Future*, for a cappella chorus (1922); Suite, for chamber orchestra (1924); String Quartet (1924); *Overture in Olden Style on French Noëls*, for orchestra (1926); *Judith*, dramatic reading with ballet and small orchestra (1927); *Hymn*, for chorus (1927); *Sea Symphony*, for bass-baritone and orchestra (1928); *Missa Imaginum*, for chorus and orchestra (1929); *Song of the Night*, tone poem for orchestra (1930); *Station WGZBX*, satirical suite for orchestra (1931); *General William Booth Enters into Heaven*, for tenor, male voices, and small orchestra (1932); *The Triumph of Israel*, for chorus and orchestra (1934); *Il riposo*, suite for orchestra (1934); Suite, for flute, oboe, clarinet, bassoon, and horn (1936); *Gwalia*, a Welsh rhapsody for orchestra (1937); Piano Quartet (1938); *World of Tomorrow*, for chorus and orchestra (1938); Sinfonietta, for orchestra (1938); *Brennan on the Moor*, for orchestra (1939); *Shirat Ha-Yam*, for chorus and orchestra (1944); *Miniver Cheever*, for orchestra, and *Richard Corey*, for narrator and orchestra (1947); *Chaumont*, tone poem for orchestra (1948); Passacaglia on an Old Cambrian ground bass, for organ, also for band (1951); *Overture to a Greek Play* (1952); *Mass of the Pictures*, for chorus and orchestra (1965); *To Cecilia*, cantata for chorus and small orchestra (1965); *Mass in Honor of St. Mark*, for chorus and orchestra (1966).

BIBLIOGRAPHY: Ewen, David, *American Composers Today* (N.Y., 1949); Howard John Tasker, *Our Contemporary Composers* (N.Y., 1941); *Who's Who in America*, 1972–73.

Johnston, Ben (Benjamin), Burwell, b. Macon, Ga., March 15, 1926.

Since he does not like to be identified with any single position in music, Johnston has cultivated a rather diverse range of stylistic approaches. Nevertheless, some of his most important compositions, and those revealing his most identifiable stylistic traits, are those utilizing microtonal just intonation. Occasionally, he has combined such nonstandard tunings with serial techniques.

Neither parent was musical; his father was a newspaper editor in Macon. Piano study for Ben Johnston began in his sixth year in Macon. In 1938, the family moved to Richmond, Va. There during the next four years he continued piano study with Mrs. Eleanor K. Greenwalt and Florence Robertson; at the same time he received occasional master lessons from John Powell. Eleanor Greenwalt encouraged him to play popular music by ear, a practice that soon led him to invent melodies of his own. This preoccupation assumed a more serious character as his taste and sophistication improved.

Upon graduating from Thomas Jefferson High School in Richmond in 1944, where he had played in the school orchestra and band, he spent a year at Catholic University (U. S. Naval School of Music) in Washington, D. C., and four more years (1945–49) at the College of William and Mary at Williamsburg, Va. At Catholic University he studied trombone and piano, and at the College of William and Mary, piano and theory. Between 1946 and 1948 he played the piano in various dance bands and theater pit orchestras. He returned to William and Mary in 1948, graduating with a bachelor of arts degree in 1949. In 1949–50, he attended the Cincinnati Conservatory for the study of piano with Oliver Manning, composition with Hugo Grimm, and atonal counterpoint with Mrs. Mary Leighton, the last of whom was an all-important influence on his early development. In 1950 he received his master of music degree. During this period he confined his creativity solely to piano pieces.

By 1950, having become interested in the artistic potential of just intonation, Johnston worked under Harry Partch in microtonal theory and instruments at Gualala, Calif. Johnston collaborated with Partch in writing incidental music for Wilford Leach's *The Wooden Bird* (1950), which was performed at the University of Virginia in 1950. "After I left his studio in 1951," Johnston says, "I spent a little over ten years building skill and reputation in other stylistic areas until I felt ready to attack the problem of how to make microtonal just intonation practical for performers."

In 1951, Johnston joined the music faculty of the University of Illinois in Urbana, where he has remained since that time, becoming assistant professor in 1958, associate professor in 1961, and full professor in 1965. For one year (1951–52) he attended Mills College in Oakland, Calif. There he was a student of composition, orchestration and musical analysis of Darius Milhaud's and piano, of Alexander Liebermann's and received a master of arts degree in 1952. After that, while teaching full time at the University of Illinois, he took courses in music there, including piano with Claire Richards and composition with Burrill Phillips.

In his compositions of the 1950s, Johnston employed standard tuning and traditional styles. Much of what he wrote in those years was either for the theater or ballet. In 1952, on a commission from the University of Illinois Festival of Contemporary Music, he prepared the music for Arthur Gregory's *Fire*. In 1954 he wrote the songs, dance music, and instrumental interludes for Leach's *The Zodiac of Memphis Street (Trapdoors of the Moon)*; in 1955, he contributed a piano score for the ballet *St. Joan* for the dancer Sybil Shearer; in 1956, a Tango, for Anouilh's *Ring around the Moon*; and in 1957 the dance score of *Of Burden and of Mercy*, commissioned by Margret Dietz for the American Dance Festival and introduced in New London, Conn., in the summer of 1957; and, in 1959, music for *Gambit for Dancers and Orchestra*, commissioned for Merce Cunningham and Company by the University of Illinois Festival of the Arts. The last of these was adapted into a concert work bearing the new title of *Ludes for Twelve Instruments* (1959). Other Johnston compositions outside the world of theater and dance in the 1950s included a Concerto, for brass ensemble and timpani (1951); *Dirge*, for percussion ensemble (1952); Variations, for piano (1954); a cantata, *Night*, for baritone, women's chorus, and chamber ensemble to a text by Robinson Jeffers (1955), commissioned by the University of Illinois Festival of Contemporary Arts; and Nine Variations, for string quartet (1959), premiered at a Composers Forum Concert in New York and later frequently performed by the La Salle Quartet.

Johnston made his first efforts at arriving at microtonal just-intonation music through electronics. Upon receiving a Guggenheim Fellowship in 1959, he entered the Columbia-Princeton Music Center to study the theory and techniques of electronic music with Otto Luening and Vladimir Ussachevsky (1959–60). That year he also studied privately with John Cage. "I tried to work out a way of arriving at microtonal just intonation electronically, but regrettably neither the means available to me at the time nor my talents were equal to the problem." After returning to the University of Illinois, he made his first experiment at indeterminacy in the *Sonata for Two*, for violin and piano (1960), in which an entire movement was improvised within some set rules. He also composed Duo, for flute and string bass (1963), a serial work using microtonal embellishments. But just intonation continued to absorb his interests. One of his first approaches in this direction involved a rapprochement between twelve-tone serial techniques and just intonation. String Quartet no. 2 (1964; Urbana, Ill., 1964), which was commissioned by the La Salle Quartet but introduced by the Composers Quartet; *Sonata for Microtonal Piano*, commissioned by Claire Richards (1965; Urbana, Ill., 1965), which was so complex in structure and ambitious in scope that it had taken him five years to write; and *Quintet for Groups*, for orchestra (1966), which received its world premiere in March 1967, performed by the St. Louis Symphony, which had commissioned it. In this work for orchestra, Johnston seized as his principal precompositional determinant the same kind of microtonally modulating just-tuned twelve-tone sets that had served him as the generative basis of the opening movement of his String Quartet no. 2.

Johnston explains that behind his interest in just intonation lay "a rejection of the intonational compromises of equal temperament. The multiplicity of tones is an incidental side benefit, but an important one. The restoration of a significant, perceptible palette of consonance and dissonance and a clear-cut harmonic hierarchy of relationships is a central aspect

of this type of systematics. Just intonation provides not a system of harmony but an infinite number of infinitely extensive systems of harmony." First in 1966 with *Ci-Gît Satie*, for chorus, double bass and drums, written on a commission from the Swingle Singers but introduced and recorded by Kenneth Gaburo's New Music Choral Ensemble, and then in *Rose*, for chorus (1971), and Mass, for chorus, eight trombones, and rhythm section (1972), Johnston became actively concerned with a type of music which approached the problem of establishing new concepts of tonality and a bridge to a wider and less elite audience. The rock chamber opera, *Carmilla* (1970; Urbana, Ill., 1973), was a related effort even though it was not concerned with microtones or with just intonation. This chamber opera has a text by Wilford Leach based upon a supernatural novella by J. S. Le Fanu. It describes the hysteria and sexual repression in a Victorian setting of two girls and their developing attachment for each other. Dream sequences are significant in developing this theme, and motion pictures are used to flash paintings, photographs, abstractions, and films on a screen to comment on what is taking place. "*Carmilla*," reported Gerald Rabkin in *After Dark*, "is a dense, intense work of theatrical complexity which is almost totally sung. . . . [Johnston's] score is excellent, moving in and out of different styles without any sense of facile pastiche. Although the music varies from Gregorian chant to Arabian wail to rock ballad to Stravinskian percussiveness to a cappella lyricism, it is remarkably of a piece. . . . Above all, it works theatrically, underlining mood and theme, creating a world of musical resonance which amplifies the chilling universe of the presentation."

One of Johnston's most complex works in microtonal just intonation is *SEVEN*, for soprano, two soprano instruments, and two percussionists (1971), which utilizes the 142-tone scale based upon the prime numbers 1, 2, 3, 5, 7. Its rhythmic proportions form an exact simultaneous analogue to its pitch intervals. *Crossings*, for string quartet, is a provocative composition since it is a hybrid product. Introduced in New York on March 15, 1976, by the Concord String Quartet in commemoration of the fiftieth anniversary of the Namburg Foundation, it is actually made up of two already completed one-movement string quartets separated by a two-minute pause entitled in the score "Silence." The first of these compositions is the romantic, contemplative, and serially conceived String Quartet no. 3, *Vergings* (1966), which was now receiving its world premiere. After the two-minute silence came String Quartet no. 4, *Ascent* (1973), a series of rhythmically complex variations with ever shifting intonations on the old hymn "Amazing Grace"; this quartet had first been heard on April 21, 1973, in New York performed by the Fine Arts Quartet, which had commissioned it. "New or old," reported John Rockwell in the *New York Times*, "it made an attractive package. . . . The Third Quartet is an exactly colored tapestry of pitch relationships in which ostensibly identical intervals expand and contract depending on the context. The Fourth Quartet . . . [is] beautiful."

In 1949, Johnston was awarded an honorary membership to Phi Beta Kappa. He has received grants from the University of Illinois Research Board (1965), the National Foundation on the Arts and Humanities (1966) and the Center for Music Experiment at the University of California in San Diego (1975), among others.

In 1968–69, with Jaap Spek, Johnston created the background music for *Museum Piece*, a Smithsonian Institution orientation film. He has appeared as lecturer, guest composer, and clinician at numerous American colleges, universities, and educational societies. He was composer-in-residence at the American University in Washington, D. C. (1974), and the University of Wisconsin in Milwaukee (1974). He has contributed numerous articles to musicological and other journals. On April 14, 1950, he married Betty Ruth Hall, a teacher of art in college, in Covington, Ky. They have three children.

THE COMPOSER SPEAKS: In my opinion, art cannot spring from such shallow sources as the projection of ideological or political doctrines. It *may* project such content, but this is a side effect. The basic content is always more fundamental than such ideas: myths, beyond ready conscious and verbal expression. This is especially true of music. Art has some of the same functions and values as dreams: it puts us into contact with less superficial aspects of ourselves than waking ego-consciousness ideas do. An artist cannot dictate to these sources what he wants to say. He can only dry them up by such effort.

The power of art lies precisely in its ability to transcend natural thoughts and put us in a mode of symbolism which interconnects all of us in an exploration of the unknown in ourselves. It is only incidentally "psychiatric" or "social" or "ideological" since it transcends such categories. Such issues can be addressed artistically only by getting beyond them to the basic form of experience of which they are simply examples. This cannot be achieved merely by intellectual effort.

Symbols of important aspects of human expression can be expressed by the very forms of organization used in artistic expression. In using extended just intonation as a basis for the pitch usage in my music, I am making a statement about the role of order in human life. The extension of the boundaries of perception and understanding of complexity in experience is the burden of this symbol. I am interested in complexity which results from subtleties of relationship more than in the complexity of multiplicity and statistical averages.

PRINCIPAL WORKS: 6 string quartets (1959–79).

Night, cantata for baritone, women's chorus, chamber ensemble (1955); *Gertrude*, or *Would She Be Pleased to Receive It?*, dance-opera for alto, tenor, soprano, small chorus, chamber ensemble (1956); Septet, for woodwind quintet, cello, and bass (1956–58); *Gambit for Dancers and Orchestra*, ballet, concert version entitled *Ludes for Twelve Instruments* (1959); Nine Variations, for string quartet (1959); *Five Fragments*, for alto, oboe, cello, and bassoon (1960); *Sonata for Two*, for violin and piano (1960); *A Sea Dirge*, for mezzo-soprano, flute, violin, and oboe (1962); *Knocking Piece*, for two percussionists and piano (1962); Duo, for flute and double bass (1963); *Sonata for Microtonal Piano* (1965); *Lament*, for flute, trumpet, trombone, viola, cello, and bass (1966); *Quintet for Groups*, for orchestra (1966); *Ci-Gît Satie*, for chorus, double bass, and drums (1967); *One Man*, for trombone and percussion (1967); *Knocking Piece Collage*, for tape (1969); *Carmilla*, opera (1970); *Seven*, for soprano, two soprano instruments, and two percussionists (1971); *Rose*, for chorus (1971); Mass, for chorus, eight trombones, and rhythm section (1972); Twelve Psalms, for chorus (1977); Duo, for two violins (1978); *Strata*, for tape (1978); *Suite for Microtonal Piano* (1978); Two Sonnets of Shakespeare, for bass-baritone and chamber ensemble (1978); *Diversion*, for chamber ensemble (1979).

BIBLIOGRAPHY: *BBDM; DCM; Perspectives of New Music*, vol. 7, no. 1, 1968; vol. 15, no. 2, 1977.

Jones, Charles, b. Tamworth, Ontario, Canada, June 21, 1910.

Jones is a "modern" composer who has avoided the accoutrements of the avant-garde school for a style that is partial to extended, smooth, flowing, melodic lines, long-range contours, and chromatic and jagged intervallic leaps. Lyricism and craftsmanship are his strong suits.

He was born to American parents. His father, a bank manager who was born and raised in Brooklyn, N.Y., played the violin, and it was from him that Charles got his first musical impressions. When his father died in 1919, the family moved to Toronto. There Jones began formal study of music by taking lessons on the violin with Leo Smith.

In 1928, Jones came to New York, entering the Institute of Musical Art, where he majored in the violin with Sascha Jacobsen and Samuel Gardner, graduating in 1932. On a fellowship, he entered the Juilliard School of Music in 1935, working in composition mainly with Bernard Wagenaar. At Juilliard, he produced numerous works including his String Quartet no. 1 (1936); a Suite, for string orchestra (1937), performed at Juilliard in March 1939; a Suite for small orchestra (1937), which was introduced by the Wallenstein Sinfonietta over radio Station WOR in New Jersey in July 1937 and since played frequently by various orchestras including the St. Louis Symphony under Vladimir Golschmann in November 1941; and his Symphony no. 1 (1939). "I think the Suite, for small orchestra, is probably the best of these student works," says Jones, "and I still enjoy hearing it."

Jones graduated from Juilliard in 1939. In the summer of 1940, when the Berkshire Music Center was opened at Tanglewood, Mass., he studied composition with Aaron Copland. In 1939, Jones joined the music faculty at Mills College in Oakland, Calif., where he remained five years, "teaching all manner of musical subjects to fair young ladies." There he began an artistic association with Darius Milhaud that lasted thirty years. "His interest, encouragement, and broad sympathies with the problems of a young composer have been of the greatest help," Jones reveals; but Milhaud had little influence on his own compositional style. Pierre Monteux was still another musician in San Francisco whose influence on Jones's early career was valuable. "He gave me my first opportunity to conduct an orchestra and twice invited me to conduct my works with his orchestra, the San Francisco Symphony." On September 2, 1943, in San Francisco, Jones married Sally Pickrell, a writer.

Jones's first successful works for orchestra came in 1940 and 1941: *Gallop*, for full orchestra (1940) and *Cowboy Song*, for oboe, piano, and strings (1941). "By spelling 'Galop' with two l's instead of one," the composer explains, "we change the meaning of the piece from a 19th-century two-step to what is known in Hollywood parlance as a 'chase' in which our hero is found to be a gay, hard-riding hombre." That "hero" is the cowboy of *Cowboy Song*, whose melody came from a southern Negro who had never seen a cowboy. "However," the composer says, "its feeling of pathos and nostalgia is so akin to that of the best cowboy music that, while making certain changes, I have based this work upon it." The *Gallop*, together with a Pastorale, for chamber orchestra (1940), was introduced in San Francisco in July 1941 and Werner Janssen premiered *Cowboy Song* over the radio in June 1942. In December 1943 the St. Louis Symphony under Vladimir Golschmann presented *Cowboy Song* as a companion piece to *Gallop*.

A Sonatina, for violin and piano (1942), was premiered by Sascha Jacobsen and Maxim Shapiro at the festival of the International Society for Contemporary Music at Berkeley, Calif., on August 7, 1942. One year after that, Jones provided the music for a ballet, *Down with the Drink*, its score for women's voices, piano, and percussion (1943) based on American temperance songs. With choreography by Marian van Tuyl, it was produced in Oakland, Calif., in March 1943.

Soon after leaving Mills College, Jones wrote another successful work for orchestra, *Five Melodies for Orchestra* (1945). This five-movement suite, he informs us, was "the result of my wishing to write music for a ballet. However, as no opportunity to write a ballet arose, I wrote some music anyway—music which, I think, has the elements of theater and ballet but which, because there is no story or plot, must be considered simply as abstract music." When it was first heard in January 1946 in San Francisco, the composer once again was the conductor of the San Francisco Symphony. In June 1947, *Five Melodies for Orchestra* was given its European premiere in Brussels, Belgium.

In the late 1940s Jones spent several years traveling in the United States and Europe before settling down in New York. Since the summer of 1951, Jones has taught composition, counterpoint, orchestration, and fugue at Aspen, Colo., where, beginning 1951, he shared the composer-in-residence post with Milhaud. On Milhaud's retirement in 1969, Jones continued as composer-in-residence and teacher, posts he has held since that time. From 1954 on he has been on the faculty of the Juilliard School of Music in New York. He has also been director of the Seminar in American Studies in Salzburg, Austria (1950), a faculty member of the Bryanston Summer School in England (1951), and since 1973 chairman of the composition department of the Mannes College of Music in New York.

Jones regards his seven string quartets "as a musical diary which I have kept through the years." He goes on to explain: "The first one dates from student days, the second (1944) is already concerned with the special sonorities possible in this medium, the third (1951) is more complex in texture and probably the most dissonant, the fourth (1954) is more simple and lyrical, the fifth (1961) again is much taken up with special sonorities, the sixth (1970) is in a large and general way concerned with two diverse elements, fanfare and a kind of lyricism normally associated with the voice, and the seventh (1978) is dedicated to the memory of Milhaud and quotes from his String Quartet no. 18." The Ford Foundation gave Jones a grant for the recording of String Quartet no. 6.

Other significant works include three settings of the Middle English text of William Langland's *Piers Plowman*, for tenor, chorus and orchestra (1963), *I Am a Mynstral*, cantata for tenor and five players (1967), and *Anima*, a cycle of songs for soprano, piano, and viola (1968). Additionally, among Jones's later works are four symphonies (1939, 1957, 1962, 1965), together with the *Little Symphony for the New Year* (1953), commissioned by the Canadian Broadcasting Company and introduced over its facilities on January 4, 1954; *Masque*, for speaker and twelve players (1968), text taken from Alexander Pope's *The Rape of the Lock*; Concerto for Four Violins and Orchestra (1963); *Allegory*, for divided orchestra (1970); Serenade, for flute, violin, cello, and harpsichord (1973); and *Triptychon*, for violin, viola, and piano (1975). He received the Copley Award in 1956, in fulfillment of which he wrote his Symphony no. 2.

THE COMPOSER SPEAKS: In planning the construction of a work so many considerations have to be taken into account that one has to find the proper technical approach for each individual composition. This makes most of the accepted systems of composing only partially useful in each given instance, and, as the concentration has to be on the problem of the work in hand, this may very well bring about new methods of composition which work best perhaps only for the particular piece of the moment.

I continue to think of music in terms of poetry rather than prose.

PRINCIPAL WORKS: 7 string quartets (1936–78); 4 symphonies (1939–65); 2 piano sonatas (1946, 1950).

Gallop, for orchestra (1940); *Cowboy Song*, for oboe and strings (1941); Violin Sonatina (1942); *Down with the Drink*, ballet (1943); *Five Melodies for Orchestra* (1945); Suite, for violin and piano (1945); *Threnody*, for solo viola (1947); Sonata for Two Pianos (1947); *Lyric Waltz Suite*, for woodwind quartet (1948); *Hymn*, for orchestra (1949); *Sonata a tre*, for piano trio (1952); *Epiphany*, for speaker and four instruments (1952); *On the Morning of Christ's Nativity*, for chorus (1953); *Little Symphony for the New Year* (1953); Toccata, for piano (1955); Duo, for violin and viola (1956); Introduction and Rondo, for strings (1957); *Suite after a Notebook of 1762*, for chamber orchestra (1957); Violin Sonata (1958); Chorale Prelude, for solo violin (1958); *The Season*, cantata for soprano, baritone, speaker, and six instruments (1959); *Sonata piccola*, for piccolo and harpsichord (1961); Ballade, for piano (1961); *Piers Plowman*, oratorio for tenor, chorus, and orchestra (1963); Concerto for Four Violins and Orchestra (1963); Sonata, for oboe and harpsichord (1965); *Music for Two Violinists* (1966); *I Am a Mynstrel*, for tenor, violin, harpsichord, piano, and percussion (1967); String Trio (1968); *Masque*, for speaker and twelve instruments (1968); *Anima*, cycle for voice, piano, and viola (1968); *Allegory*, for divided orchestra (1970); *In Nomine*, for violin and piano (1972); Serenade, for flute, violin, cello, and harpsichord (1973); *Triptychon*, for violin, viola, and piano (1975); *Psalm*, for piano (1976); *The Fond Observer*, song cycle for voice and piano (1977).

BIBLIOGRAPHY: *BBDM; DCM;* Ewen, David, *American Composers Today* (N.Y., 1949); Machlis, Joseph, *Introduction to Contemporary Music*, revised ed. (N.Y., 1979).

Josten, Werner Eric, b. Elberfeld, Germany, June 12, 1885; d. New York City, February 6, 1963. American citizen, 1933.

Josten was a neoromantic whose works were richly textured in harmonic and polyphonic style, abundant in their lyricism, and occasionally touched with religious feeling and mysticism.

His parents intended him for a business career, for which he received training in Munich schools. But he also studied piano with private teachers, eventually supplementing this with lessons in harmony and counterpoint with Rudolph Siegel in Munich, and composition with Émile Jaques-Dalcroze in Geneva. After five years in business in Munich, Josten decided to engage solely in music. He did some conducting in Munich and Paris, making his home in the French capital from 1912 to 1914. At the outbreak of World War I, he returned to Germany. During the war years he did some composing, including a work for bass and chorus, *Crucifixion* (1915), the first of several of his works to reveal his interest in religious subjects. He was assistant conductor of the Munich Opera from 1918 to 1920.

He came to the United States in 1920, making his home for the next three years in New York and supporting himself by serving as piano accompanist for singers. Soon after his arrival in the United States he married Margaret R. Fatman on December 1, 1920; they had two children.

In 1923 Josten was appointed professor of counterpoint and composition at Smith College in Northampton, Mass. He remained at Smith College until 1949, when he retired. During these years, in addition to his teaching assignments, he conducted the joint orchestra of Amherst and Smith colleges and was director of the Northampton Opera Festival. This festival was responsible for the revival of 17th- and 18th-century operas, many of them being heard in the United States for the first time. Among the operas performed under his direction were Monteverdi's *L'incoronazione di Poppea* and *Orfeo*, Handel's *Julius Caesar, Xerxes, Florindo e Dafne* and *Rodelinda*; and Fux's *Costanza e Fortezza,* the performance of 1938 being the first anywhere since that opera was heard two hundred years earlier.

As a composer, Josten first made his mark in the latter part of the 1920s. *Ode for St. Cecilia's Day*, for soprano, baritone, chorus, and orchestra (1925), was introduced at the Worcester Festival in Massachusetts. He was acclaimed for the deep religious feeling and mysticism of his *Concerto sacro*, nos. 1 and 2 (1925). Lawrence Gilman said of them in the *New York Herald Tribune:* "The flame of devotional tenderness and exaltation burns with singular purity." These two works were inspired by Mathias Grünewald's altar triptych at Colmar, Alsace. After Josten revised both concertos in 1927, they were introduced in New York on March 27, 1929, Albert Stoessel conducting. After that the Boston Symphony under Serge Koussevitzky performed the second of these concertos in 1929, and the Philadelphia Orchestra under Leopold Stokowski, the first concerto in 1933. The concertos received the Juilliard Publication Award.

Jungle, a symphonic movement for orchestra

(1928), a tonal representation of Henri Rousseau's painting *Forêt exotique*, was premiered by the Boston Symphony under Koussevitzky on October 25, 1929, before it was heard at concerts of the Philadelphia Orchestra and the Chicago Symphony. To emphasize primitivism, Josten added African drums to the percussion, as well as a "lion's roar" produced on a drum with a rosined cord drawn through the drumhead.

A religious presence is again found in the ballet *Joseph and His Brethren* (1932), first performed in New York in 1936. Two other ballets were, respectively, of African and classic Greek interest. The former is *Batoula*, a ballet calling for chorus as well as orchestra (1930–31), written in collaboration with the French black author René Maran, and the first ballet to give an authentic account of an African voodoo ceremonial. An orchestral suite from this score was introduced under the title of *Suite nègre* in Northampton, Mass., on November 10, 1963. *Endymion* (1933) used a classic Greek subject. Here, too, the ballet score provided a concert suite, first performed in New York on October 28, 1936.

Still in a pronounced romantic idiom are: String Quartet (1934), given its initial hearing in 1936 by the Gordon String Quartet, then entering the repertoire of other chamber music groups including the Pro Arte and Roth quartets; Serenade, for orchestra (1934), written for the conductor Artur Rodzinski, who directed its first performance with the Cleveland Orchestra in 1934; Sonata for Violin and Piano (1936), which Albert Spalding performed at the festival of the International Society for Contemporary Music in London on June 18, 1938; Symphony in F (1936), introduced on November 13, 1936, by the Boston Symphony under Koussevitzky, and recipient of the Juilliard Publication Award; *Canzona Seria*, for low strings (1937; Rochester, N.Y., 1942); and

Sonatina, for violin and piano (1939), premiered in New York in 1941 by Eudice Shapiro. Josten's later chamber music works and the *Rhapsody*, for orchestra (1957), are leaner in texture, more restrained in emotion and more classical in style.

THE COMPOSER SPEAKS: In my opinion, an artist's work is largely directed by influences received during his early childhood and formative years. In my father's house, the Bible played a major role at all occasions and influenced considerably my mind and soul. A no lesser influence—and of my own choosing—came from the study of Greek mythological and Mediterranean culture. A third powerful magnet was Africa on which I devoured every available book since I learned to read.

PRINCIPAL WORKS: *Ode for St. Cecilia's Day*, for soprano, baritone, chorus, and orchestra (1925); *Concerto sacro*, nos. 1 and 2, for piano and string orchestra (1925); *Jungle*, symphonic movement for orchestra (1928); *Batoula*, ballet with chorus (1930–31); *Joseph and His Brethren*, ballet (1932); *Endymion*, ballet (1933); Serenade, for small orchestra (1934); String Quartet (1934); *Symphony for Strings* (1935); Violin Sonata (1936); Symphony in F (1936); *Canzona seria*, for low strings (1937); Piano Sonata (1937); Cello Sonata (1938); Violin Sonatina (1939); Trio, for woodwinds (1941); String Trio (1942); Trio, for flute, cello, and piano (1943); Horn Sonata (1944); *Canzona seria*, "A Hamlet Monologue," for flute, oboe, clarinet, bassoon, and piano (1957); Rhapsody, for orchestra (1958).

BIBLIOGRAPHY: Howard, John Tasker, *Our Contemporary Composers* (N.Y., 1941); *Werner Josten: A Summary of His Compositions with Press Reviews* (N.Y., 1964); *Opera News*, December 1, 1958.

K

Karlins, Martin William, b. New York City, February 25, 1932.

Influenced by his early teacher, Frederick Piket, and later by Stefan Wolpe and some of Stravinsky's music, Karlins initially developed a personal style synthesizing the free manipulation of the basic elements of serial composition, especially where it concerned pitch; but none of these works were in a strict serial technique. Subsequently he became even more interested in tonality and centrality: working at times with some emphasis on tone centers but in a new manner.

Both his parents were interested in music as amateurs. His father, a lawyer, was a jazz aficionado, and his mother played the violin and piano. From boyhood on, Karlins was interested in music but not until he was thirteen did he begin its study by taking lessons on the clarinet. At that time jazz was his prime interest, particularly the big band sound of Stan Kenton, which turned Karlins to making jazz arrangements. When he was fifteen he started to take some private lessons in harmony and when he was seventeen he studied the Schillinger System of Musical Composition.

He attended Erasmus Hall High School in Brooklyn, N.Y., between 1946 and 1950 where he played in the school orchestra, band, and jazz band. Upon graduating from high school, he went to work in his father's law office. On April 6, 1952, he married Mickey Cutler, then an accounting supervisor, with whom he has had two children. Music was not being neglected. In 1953 he began writing his first nonjazz piece. Aware of his lack of technique, he studied composition privately with Frederick Piket between 1954 and 1957. It was at Piket's suggestion that Karlins finally gave up all thought of law as a possible profession to immerse himself totally in music. He attended the Manhattan School of Music (1958–61), a pupil in composition of Vittorio Giannini's. During these years he also studied composition briefly with Gunther Schuller (1960) and Stefan Wolpe (1960–61).

While studying with Giannini he completed two atonal works in a modified and personalized serial technique in 1959. One was *Concert Music* I, for orchestra; another, the Concerto Grosso no. 1, for nine instruments. When the latter was given its premiere on April 4, 1960 in New York, Eric Salzman said of it in the *New York Times*: "It lives up to its title with some baroque touches, but in the slow sec-

tions particularly it is shaped with a great deal of intensity and color that is very much the composer's own."

During the summers of 1959 and 1961, Karlins received scholarships to the Bennington Composers Conference in Vermont, where he was given the opportunity to study composition further with Roger Goeb and Lester Trimble. In 1960 he was invited to attend the Princeton Seminar for advanced Musical Studies at Princeton, N.J., where he worked with Roger Sessions, Elliott Carter, Karl Birger-Blomdahl, and Milton Babbitt.

In May 1961, Karlins recieved his bachelor of music and master of music degrees concurrently at the Manhattan School of Music. Performance of his compositions between 1961 and 1963 focused the limelight on his burgeoning talent. Among the more notable of these works, more concerned with a new working out of tonality than with serial manipulation, were Quartet, for strings and soprano (1960, N.Y., June 2, 1962), which has some serial sections; *Concert Music* II, for chorus and orchestra (1960; Milwaukee, Wis., February 14, 1971); and Concerto Grosso no. II, for seven solo instruments (1961; N.Y., March 21, 1962), which was influenced by the Stravinsky of *Symphony of Psalms* and *Threni*. Also freely manipulative of serial elements were *Birthday Music* I for flute, bass clarinet, and double bass (1962; N.Y., July 17, 1962): *Birthday Music* II, for flute and double bass (1962; Hartford, Conn., December 29, 1963); and String Trio (1962–63; N.Y., March 22, 1964).

Karlins left New York in 1963 to attend the University of Iowa, there to study composition with Philip Bezanson and Richard Hervig on a tuition grant and assistantship, and to earn his doctorate in composition in June 1965. From 1965 to 1967 he was assistant professor of theory and composition at Western Illinois University at Macomb. In 1967 he was appointed associate professor of composition of Northwestern University in Evanston, where he has remained since, having become a full professor in 1973. At Northwestern University his *Concert Music* IV, for orchestra (1964), was introduced on April 14, 1965, Anthony Donato conducting. This work was performed by the Chicago Symphony on June 1, 1978. It is a short three-movement composition which creates "a sort of (1) statement, (2) working out with climax, and the last movement acts as a coda," in the composer's words. Like so many of his compositions, careful use of pitch and octave placement of pitch is made here. The final movement is a case in point. "Every pitch of the chromatic scale has its own octave in which to sound and none other," explains the composer. "The highest and lowest pitches are held throughout by the contrabasses and as a harmonic in the first violins. The other pitches are used mostly as held tone in differing combinations with each other, thus highlighting the pitch arrangement. Each instrument, except the tuned percussion and piano, has its own pitch to play (some instruments sharing the same pitch)." *Concert Music* IV, together with its predecessor, *Concert Music* III, was chosen to represent the University of Iowa at the Midwest Composers Symposium in 1964–65. Quartet for Saxophones (1966–67; Chicago, Ill., April 14, 1968) was awarded a prize in the Northwestern University Saxophone Quartet Competition.

Since then, Karlins has continued to be concerned with the problem of centrality in 20th-century music. By the end of the 1960s, Karlins revealed still further interest in tonality and centrality as in the Music for Tenor, Saxophone, and Piano (1969; Evanston, Ill., December 3, 1969). On December 20, 1973, the Chicago Symphony under Henry Mazer presented the world premiere of *Concert Music* V, for orchestra (1972–73). The scoring included a trio of saxophones, a piano, and a large percussion contingent in addition to the other instruments of the orchestra. Writing in the *Chicago Daily News*, Karen Monson said: "Quite snobbishly, the instruments stick with their own kinds during the work's six connected sections, forming distinct ensembles of brass, winds, strings and percussion. Karlins ingeniously contrasts these blocks of sounds; to keep the effect from becoming square, he gives the players imitative lines that suggest games of musical tag." Monson goes on further to describe the music: "*Concert Music* V opens with an evocatively elegiac passage, then accelerates to a percussion cadenza and a tutti climax. The last minute of the work's eleven recalls the mood of the opening with a haunting trio for oboes and English horn."

Among Karlins's subsequent notable works are *Reflux*, a concerto for double bass and wind ensemble (1971–72); Quintet, for alto saxophone and string quartet (1973–74; Wichita, Kan., February 6, 1975); Woodwind Quintet no. 2, *And All Our World Is Dew* (1977–78); *Infinity*, for oboe d'amore, clarinet, viola, and female voice (1978); and Symphony no. 1 (1979–80; Chicago, May 10, 1980). This symphony is a two-movement work inspired by three poems of Henry Chapin. The composer explains that these poems serve well as a program for each of the movements: "The Artist" for the movement marked "Exposition" and "One Swift Glance" and "Hark to the Piper" for "Outgrowths." The composer further indicated that these poems may be read aloud on the stage, or silently by the audience, before each movement is performed. In the "Exposition" part all the material dealt with throughout the symphony is exposed, including an opening fanfare section and a fugal part for all winds and brass. The composer named the second part "Outgrowths" to symbolize something more complex than variations, something in the nature of a metamorphosis of earlier material used in such a way as to sound new, as to take on a world of its own, and yet inwardly related to the whole." In the *Chicago Sun-Times*, Robert C. Marsh spoke of this symphony as "a well-crafted, well-scored imaginative work."

Karlins was composer-in-residence at the American Society of University Composers summer institute at the University of Illinois in Urbana (1970); composer-in-residence and panel member of the World Saxophone Congress in Bordeaux, France (1974), and London, England (1976). In 1979 he received a grant from the National Endowment for the Arts and in 1980 the "Meet the Composer" grant. He is the first president of the Chicago Society of Composers.

THE COMPOSER SPEAKS: From the very beginning my compositions have always focused on material which I thought would communicate with people in my culture. I have, therefore, tried to employ what I think of as my human gestures in my music. The gestures which I have learned through experience communicate with me as well as with the serious audience are a result of empirical knowledge in its best sense.

I think it goes without saying that technique (an almost saturating knowledge of the possibilities offered up by the materials being used in a piece) is a prerequisite to any attempt to communicate.

It is not difficult to imagine what one would like a piece to do, but, to have the technique to proceed with it especially as it metamorphosized and the original images change, is the only way the material being used, no matter how experimental, can be fulfilled on an artistic level. One can only take risks if one is in control.

Since every composer, whatever his idiom or purpose, is an experimenter, he must depend upon this technique, experience and, last but by no means least, his fantasy to guide him to his goal.

PRINCIPAL WORKS: 3 piano sonatas (1959, 1962, 1965); 2 woodwind quintets (1970, 1977–78); 2 Music for Solo Cello (1966, 1969).

Concert Music I, for orchestra (1959); Concerto Grosso no. 1, for orchestra (1959); String Quartet, with soprano (1960); *Concert Music* II, for chorus and orchestra (1960); Concerto Grosso no. II, for seven solo instruments (1961); Fantasy and Passacaglia, for flute, viola, bassoon, and double bass (1961); *Outgrowths—Variations*, for piano (1961); String Trio (1962–63); *Birthday Music* I, for flute, bass clarinet, and double bass (1962); *Birthday Music* II, for flute and double bass (1962); Variations, for clarinet and string trio (1963); *Concert Music* III, for woodwinds, brass, piano, and percussion (1963–64); *Concert Music* IV, for orchestra (1964); Solo Piece with Passacaglia, for clarinet (1964); *Variations on Obiter Dictum*, for cello, piano, and percussion (1965); Music for Oboe, Bassoon, Clarinet, and Piano (1966); Three Songs, for soprano, flute and piano (1967); *Variations and Outgrowths*, for bassoon and piano (1967); *Lamentations—In Memoriam*, for narrator and chamber group (1968); Music for Saxophone and Piano (1969); *Graphic Mobile*, for any three or multiple of three instruments (1969); *Celebration*, for flute, oboe, and harpsichord (1970); Passacaglia and Rounds, for band (1970); *Reflux*, concerto for double bass and wind ensemble (1971–72); *Fantasy on My Mother's Name*, for flute (1971); *Concert Music* V, for orchestra (1972–73); Quintet, for saxophone and string quartet (1973–74); Four Etudes, for double bass and tape or three double basses (1974); *Infinity*, for oboe d'amore, clarinet, viola, and female voice (1978); Fantasia, for tenor, saxophone, and percussion (1979); Symphony no. 1, (1979–80).

BIBLIOGRAPHY: *BBDM;* Machlis, Joseph; *Introduction to Contemporary Music*, revised ed. (N.Y., 1979); *Chicagoan Magazine*, August 1974; *Chicago Orchestra Program Notes*, December 20, 1973, June 1978; *Saxophone Symposium*, Fall, 1977.

Kay, Ulysses Simpson, b. Tucson, Ariz., January 7, 1917.

The first black man to receive the American Prix de Rome, Kay is one of America's most frequently performed and most often commissioned composers, as well as the recipient of numerous awards. Though he has quoted Negro spirituals in several compositions, his music is more than ethnic. Occasionally it taps the resources of earlier periods of music, occasionally it is traditional in style, and occasionally it avails itself of 20th-century neoclassicism, and harmonically dissonant and linear devices.

Kay is the nephew of the New Orleans cornet player Joe ("King") Oliver, who has become a legend in jazz history. The members of Ulysses' immediate family also loved music and made it as amateurs. His father, a barber, sang, and his mother played the piano. "The earliest musical experiences which I recall," he says, "are the ballads, work songs, hymns and 'non-sense' songs which my father always sang to entertain or pacify me. The most striking pieces which I heard during those early days were some of the piano pieces my sister played. Later I learned they were Chopin waltzes and polonaises."

When Kay's parents asked King Oliver to teach the boy the trumpet, the jazzman insisted that the boy first be trained at the piano. When he was eight, Kay began receiving piano lessons from William A. Ferguson. Then he started learning to play the violin in school. At Dunbar Junior High School, when he

was twelve, he learned to make music on the saxophone, an instrument his sister had given him. "What followed," he recalls, "was the usual round of practice, disgust, more practice, class recitals, and a few solo recitals." His love for jazz led him to neglect the violin and piano in favor of the saxophone, which, during his high school years, he played in the school marching band and, outside school, in dance orchestras.

Upon graduating from the Tucson Senior High School in 1934, he entered the University of Arizona in Tucson for a liberal arts course, but he soon changed directions by majoring in public-school music and receiving his bachelor of music degree in 1938. At the university, "piano study with Julia Rebeil introduced me to the works of Béla Bartók and other contemporaries. Music theory with John L. Lowell gave me a completely new world to conjure with." On their encouragement, he was enrolled in 1938 in the Eastman School of Music in Rochester, N.Y., on a scholarship, studying composition there with Bernard Rogers and Howard Hanson (1938–41) and earning a master's degree in composition in 1940. In Rochester he had the opportunity to hear his first orchestral works performed publicly. Among these were Sinfonietta (1939; April 18, 1939), winner of the first prize in the Phi Mu Alpha Sinfonia contest; an Oboe Concerto (1940; April 16, 1940); and, most significantly, *Dance Calinda*, "first scene for orchestra" (1941; April 23, 1941), based on a story by Ridgley Torrence. (In 1947 Kay wrote a "second scene" for *Dance Calinda*. It was introduced in New York on May 23, 1947, and was the recipient of the Anna Bobbit Gardner Award.)

During the summer of 1941, on a scholarship, Kay studied composition with Paul Hindemith at the Berkshire Music Center at Tanglewood, Mass., continuing these studies with Hindemith at Yale University in 1941–42. World War II interrupted his studies, but not his musical activities. Serving in the U.S. Navy from 1942 to 1946, Kay spent the war years as musician 2nd class, stationed at Quonset Point, R.I., playing the flute, saxophone, and piccolo in the navy band, the piano in a dance orchestra, and doing some arranging and composing.

Upon separation from military service in 1946, he was awarded the Alice M. Ditson Fellowship for a year of creative work. In 1947–48 he was also the beneficiary of the Julius Rosenwald Fellowship which enabled him to travel to Europe. He spent the years between 1946 and 1949 attending Columbia University as a sporadic student in composition of Otto Luening's. On August 20, 1949, Kay married Barbara Harrison; they raised three children.

Awards in the 1940s brought him his first recognition as composer while adding several impressive works to his list. The orchestral overture *Of New Horizons* (1944), in a neoclassic idiom, received first prize in a contest sponsored jointly by the Fellowship of American Composers and the American Broadcasting Company; it was given its initial hearing at the Lewisohn Stadium in New York on July 9, 1944, Thor Johnson conducting the New York Philharmonic. When the distinguished Soviet composer Yuri Shaporin heard this overture performed in Moscow on October 17, 1958, he commented: "This . . . work is testimony of the genuine artistic talent of the composer. He, who took part in the second World War, believed that with the arrival of peace there would open new, bright horizons of which the overture speaks so eloquently."

Suite for Orchestra (1945) was awarded a prize by Broadcast Music, Inc. (BMI). *A Short Overture*, for orchestra (1946), received the George Gershwin Memorial Award, its first performance taking place in Brooklyn, N.Y., on March 31, 1947, conducted by Leonard Bernstein. *Portrait Suite*, for orchestra (1948; Erie, Pa., April 22, 1964), was presented the Phoenix Symphony Orchestra Award by the Arizona Musicians Club in 1948. This suite was inspired by "recent sculptures" by Henry Moore, Jacob Lipschitz, and Wilhelm Lehmbruch.

Outside the concert hall, Kay earned high praise (though no awards) for his score to the motion picture *The Quiet One* (1948); a concert suite from that score was first heard on November 19, 1948, in New York.

In 1947, Kay received a grant from the National Institute of Arts and Letters. Between 1949 and 1952 he lived in Italy on two Prix de Rome fellowships and a Fulbright grant. In Italy, his Concerto for Orchestra (1948) was premiered by the Teatro La Fenice Orchestra, conducted by Jonel Perlea in Venice in 1953. A new major work was completed in Italy: Sinfonia, or Symphony, in E (1950; Rochester, N.Y., May 2, 1951), which on April 1, 1954, was featured in Cleveland by the Cleveland Orchestra under George Szell. Reviewing the Cleveland performance in the *New England News*, Elmore Bacon wrote: "It is a remarkable work in which the intent and purpose are clearly kept to the front despite the intricate and clever orchestral design in which there is 'modern' angularity."

Kay was the music consultant for Broadcast Music Incorporated (BMI) between 1953 and 1968. In 1958 he was selected as a member of the first delegation of American composers sent on a cultural exchange mission to the Soviet Union. A Guggenheim Fellowship was awarded him in 1964. In 1965 he was visiting professor at Boston University and in 1966–67 at the University of California at Los Angeles. In 1968 he was appointed to the music faculty of the Herbert H. Lehman College of the City University of New York, where, in 1972, he was named Distinguished Professor of Music.

Commissions continued to play a significant role in the writing of major works and in getting significant performances. *Umbrian Scene* (1963) was written for the project instituted by Edward B. Benjamin for the writing and performance of "tranquil music."

An introspective, gentle, transparently scored mood picture, *Umbrian Scene*, drew its inspiration from the Festival of Sacred Music near Perugia, which the composer attended in the fall of 1950. In writing *Umbrian Scene*, "I recalled the antiphonal instrumental music, the glorious choral singing there in the old chapel of Umbria . . . I thought of my visit to the historic towns of Assisi and Narni, of the rugged hills and beautiful valleys." *Umbrian Scene* was introduced in New Orleans on March 31, 1964; the following August it was heard in New York.

Markings (1966), an "essay for orchestra," took its title from Dag Hammarskjöld's posthumously published book and was dedicated to the UN secretary general. Kay composed it on a commission from the Detroit Symphony for the Meadow Brook Festival, the first performance taking place in Rochester, Mich., on August 18, 1966, with Sixten Ehrling conducting. This is elegiac music of great intensity and at times agitation. *Theater Set* (1968) was written through a commission from the Atlanta Symphony in Georgia and its conductor, Robert Shaw; it was premiered in Atlanta on September 26, 1968, the opening night concert of the season. This work was the composer's tribute to "show music without quoting any popular theater tunes." *Facets*, a sextet for woodwinds and piano (1970), which places as much importance on silence as on instrumental timbres, was written on commission to help celebrate the golden jubilee season of the Eastman School of Music, the first performance taking place in Rochester on October 19, 1971. *Quintet Concerto*, for five brass soloists and orchestra (1973; New York, March 14, 1975), was commissioned by the Juilliard School of Music, and *Chariots*, for orchestra (1978; Saratoga, N.Y., August 8, 1979), by the Saratoga Performing Arts Center, where it was performed by the Philadelphia Orchestra with the composer conducting.

Four works were commissioned for the commemoration of the American bicentennial. *Western Paradise*, for narrator and orchestra (1975; Washington, D.C., October 12, 1976), was written for the National Symphony Orchestra. A text by Donald Dorr focussed on the break between the colonies and the British as seen from the British point of view. *Southern Harmony*, "four aspects for orchestra" (1975), was commissioned by the Southern Regional Metropolitan Orchestras Managers Association with a grant from the National Endowment for the Arts. Premiered by the North Carolina Orchestra on February 10, 1976, this music was based on American hymn tunes of the mid-19th century as collected by William Walker. *Epigrams and Hymn* (1976; N.Y., May 16, 1976) was commissioned by the Princeton (N.J.) Theological Seminary and Presbyterian Church. And Kay's first full-length opera, *Jubilee*, was written at the request of Opera/South in Jackson, Miss. (1975; Jackson, November 20, 1976). Based on a novel by Margaret Walker and adapted for the operatic stage by Donald Dorr, this opera was set in Georgia during the post–Civil War and Reconstruction eras. Though Kay's score is largely atonal, it includes spirituallike melodies and folk hymns together with choral passages. "The work emphasizes lyric and meditative rather than epic dimensions," reported Richard Freis in the *Jackson Clarion-Ledger*. "One might say it has more of the lightness of a watercolor than the density and richness of oils. This is especially noticeable in Kay's orchestration, which eschews lushness in favor of spareness and precision."

In describing Kay's eclecticism, Robert D. Herrema wrote in *The Choral Journal*: "A marvelous dichotomy exists in the music of Ulysses Kay: craftsmanship and romanticism, reason and emotion. Occasionally, one will give way to the other, but usually both are present in equal amounts. His craft is at once Hindemithian, classical, and Netherlandish; his expressiveness is incredibly romantic and madrigalian. His music cannot—and therefore should not—be labeled stylistically, technically, or racially. It is modern in the sense that it is contemporary."

Kay provided the scores for numerous television documentaries including the CBS series *The Twentieth Century*, and the TV Special *An Essay on Death*, the latter a tribute to John F. Kennedy, telecast over WNET in New York on November 19, 1964. Kay has received honorary doctorates in music from Lincoln College in Lincoln, Ill. (1963), Bucknell University in Lewisburg, Pa. (1966), University of Arizona in Tucson (1969), and Dickinson College in Carlisle, Pa. (1978); also an honorary doctorate of humane letters from Illinois Wesleyan University in Bloomington, Ill. (1969). In 1979, Kay was voted to membership in the American Institute of Arts and Letters.

THE COMPOSER SPEAKS: For me music is a means of communication and self-expression through the medium of sound.

PRINCIPAL WORKS: 3 string quartets (1953, 1956, 1961).

Dance Calinda, two scenes for orchestra (1941–47); *Of New Horizons*, overture for orchestra (1944); Suite for Orchestra (1945); *Brief Elegy*, for oboe and strings (1946); *A Short Overture*, for orchestra (1946); Suite, for strings (1947); Concerto for Orchestra (1948); *Portrait Suite*, for orchestra (1948); Sinfonia, or Symphony, in E (1950); *Three Pieces after Blake*, for soprano and orchestra (1952); Six Dances, for string orchestra (1954); Serenade, for orchestra (1954); *The Boor*, one-act opera (1955); *The Juggler of Our Lady*, one-act opera (1956); *Phoebus, Arise*, for soprano, baritone, chorus, and orchestra (1959); *Choral Triptych*, for chorus and string orchestra (1962); *Fantasy Variations*, for orchestra (1963); *Inscriptions from Whitman*, for chorus and orchestra (1963); *Umbrian Scene*, for orchestra (1963); *Emily Dickinson Set*, for women's chorus and piano (1964); *Markings*, essay for orchestra (1966); Symphony (1967); *Stephen Crane Set*, for chorus and thirteen instruments (1967); *Theater Set*, for orchestra (1968); *Aulos*, for flute and chamber orchestra (1970); *Facets*, sexet for woodwinds and piano (1970); *The Capitoline Venus*, one-act opera (1970); *Scherzi musicali*, for chamber orchestra (1971); *Five Portraits*, for violin and piano (1973); *Quintet Concerto*, for five brass soloists and orchestra (1975); *Western Paradise*, for orchestra (1975); *Southern Harmony*, for orchestra (1975); *Epigrams and Hymn*, for chorus and organ (1975); *Jubilee*, opera (1976); *Chariots*, for orchestra (1978); *Jersey Hours*, three poems for voice and three harps (1979).

BIBLIOGRAPHY: Hayes, L. N., *The Music of Ulysses Kay: 1939-63* (doctoral thesis, Madison, Wis., 1971); Southern, Eileen, *The Music of Black America* (N.Y., 1971); Thomson, Virgil, *American Music Since 1910* (N.Y., 1970); *American Composers Alliance Bulletin*, Fall 1957.

Kelley, Edgar Stillman, b. Sparta, Wis., April 14, 1857; d. New York City, November 12, 1944.

Like so many other American composers of the late 19th and 20th centuries who had lived and studied in Germany, Kelley was a voice of the German romantic movement. His music had considerable circulation in his time (though it has been almost completely neglected since his death), much acclaimed for the vividness of imagery in his programmatic works in which he was influenced by Richard Strauss and for his innovative use of orchestration and tone colors.

He was of New England ancestry, a descendant of William Kelley, who fought in the Revolutionary War, and of Thomas Bingham, who came from England to settle in Connecticut in 1642.

Kelley's mother was an excellent pianist. She gave him his first piano lessons when he was eight. When he was thirteen, Kelley became a piano pupil of Farwell W. Merriam, with whom he continued to study until 1874. That year he moved to Chicago. There, for the next two years, his teachers included Napoleon Ledochowsky (piano) and Clarence Eddy (harmony and counterpoint). His progress encouraged him to seek further musical education in Germany. In 1876 he entered the Stuttgart Conservatory, where, for two years, he was a pupil of Max Seifriz's (composition), Wilhelm Krüger's (piano) and Friedrich Finck's (organ). In 1878 he shifted to the Speidel Conservatory to study the piano with Wilhelm Speidel for two more years.

Upon graduating from the Speidel Conservatory and returning to the United States in 1880, Kelley settled in San Francisco, where he earned his living playing the organ both there and in Oakland, and teaching. He was also composing. His first opus was Theme and Variations, for string quartet (1880), followed by a number of other compositions, including the *Wedding Ode*, for tenor solo, men's chorus, and orchestra (c. 1882) and incidental music to *Macbeth*, for chorus and orchestra (1883–85). The overture to *Macbeth* became his first successful composition when it was introduced in Chicago by the Theodore Thomas Orchestra on August 3, 1883. A production of *Macbeth*, with all his incidental music, was mounted in San Francisco on February 12, 1885.

In 1890, Kelley came east, where he taught piano and theory in various schools including the New York College of Music (1891–92) and conducted a touring light opera company. One of its productions was his operetta *Puritania, or The Earl and the Maid of Salem* (1892); it opened at the Tremont Theater in Boston on June 9, 1892, and scored a huge success with a run of a hundred consecutive performances before going on tour. The libretto, by C.M.S. McLellan, was based on the Salem witch trials during colonial days.

On July 23, 1891, Kelley married Jessie M. Gregg, one of his piano pupils. She was an excellent musician who, in later years, distinguished herself as piano teacher, director of music at Western College for Women in Oxford, Ohio, and as president of the National Federation of Music Clubs. With her husband, she organized the Kelley Stillman Publishing Company for the publication of some of his compositions.

Kelley was back in San Francisco in 1892. Between 1893 and 1895 he was the music critic of the *San Francisco Examiner*. In 1893, he composed a Chinese suite for orchestra, *Aladdin*, written after hearing indigenous music in San Francisco's Chinatown. In his orchestration, Kelley used mandolins, muted trumpets, and oboes to simulate the sound of Chinese instruments. *Aladdin* was introduced in April 1894 by the San Francisco Symphony, the composer conducting.

Kelley left San Francisco in 1896 to establish a six-year residence in New York City. He taught piano and composition at the New York College of Music (1891–92), was a lecturer in the extension division of New York University (1896–1900), and served as acting professor of music at Yale University, substituting for Horatio W. Parker, who was on sabbatical leave (1900–1). In 1900, Kelley provided incidental music for William Young's drama *Ben Hur*, first produced in New York on October 1, 1900. The play, with Kelley's music, was heard in some six thousand performances throughout the English-speaking world. Kelley's incidental music for Chester Bailey Ferald's play *The Cat and the Cherub* was heard on June 15, 1901, when that play opened in New York.

Between 1902 and 1910, Kelley lived in Berlin, teaching piano and composition, assuming some engagements as conductor, and composing. In Berlin he wrote a Piano Quintet (c. 1905; Berlin, December 1905) and two string quartets.

Kelley and his wife left Berlin in 1910 to assume posts with the Western College for Women in Ohio. Kelley was lecturer in music theory, holding the first fellowship in musical composition ever awarded an American composer; his wife served as director of music. Concurrently with this appointment at Western College for Women, Kelley served as head of the composition department of the Cincinnati Conservatory of Music. He held both posts up to the time of his retirement in 1934.

Both assignments allowed him sufficient time for composition. It was since 1910 that Kelley completed the bulk of his best concert music, some inspired by American writers or American history, which led some of his contemporaries to consider him the successor of Edward MacDowell as America's leading composer. Symphony no. 2, *New England* (1913), had titles taken from Governor Bradford's *Mayflower* diary, its score utilizing American Indian songs, Puritan psalm tunes, and bird songs. The premiere took place at the Norfolk Festival in Connecticut (for which it was written) on June 3, 1913, the composer conducting. *Pilgrim's Progress* (1918), music for a miracle play with text by Elizabeth Hogkinson based on John Bunyan, for solo voices, chorus, children's chorus, organ and orchestra, became one of Kelley's best-known and most admired works. It was first heard on May 10, 1918, at the Cincinnati May Festival, after which it was performed by the New York Oratorio Society, also at festivals in America and England. An orchestral pantomime-suite, *Alice in Wonderland* (1919), based on Lewis Carroll, was premiered at the Norfolk Festival on June 5, 1919. A symphonic suite based on Edgar Allan Poe's *The Pit and the Pendulum*, first performed on May 9, 1925, at the Cincinnati Festival, was awarded first prize in a competition for new American compositions sponsored by the National Federation of Music Clubs. Symphony no. 1, subtitled *Gulliver—His Voyage to Lilliput*, though begun in 1893 was not completed until 1936; its initial hearing took place on April 9, 1937, in a performance by the Cincinnati Symphony under Eugene Goossens. Kelley's realistic tonal representation of galloping horses, battle scenes, and Gulliver in the act of falling asleep aroused amusement and admiration. Later in April, as part of a nationwide celebration commemorating Kelley's eightieth birthday with performances of his works, this symphony was heard on nationwide hookup performed by the NBC Symphony conducted by Walter Damrosch. In honor of this birthday, an Edgar Stillman Kelley Society was founded in 1937 to underwrite the publication of works by American composers.

Kelley received honorary degrees from Miami

University in Oxford, Ohio (1916), and the University of Cincinnati (1917). He was elected to membership in the National Institute of Arts and Letters. He was the author of *Chopin, the Composer* (1913) and *The History of Musical Instruments* (1925).

THE COMPOSER SPEAKS: The American composer should apply the universal principles of his art to the local and special elements of the subject matter as they appeal to him, and then, consciously or unconsciously, manifest his individuality, which will involve the expression of mental traits and moral tendencies peculiar to his European ancestry, as we find them modified by the new American environment."

PRINCIPAL WORKS: 2 symphonies (1893–1936, 1913); 2 string quartets (c. 1880, 1907).

Incidental Music to *Macbeth*, for chorus and orchestra (1883–85); *Phases of Love*, song cycle for voice and piano (1890); *Puritania*, comic opera (1892); *Aladdin*, Chinese suite for orchestra (1893); Incidental Music to *Ben Hur*, for chorus and orchestra (1900); Piano Quintet (c. 1905); *Pilgrim's Progress*, musical miracle play for vocal soloists, chorus, children's chorus, orchestra and organ (1918); *Alice in Wonderland*, pantomime suite for orchestra (1919); *The Pit and the Pendulum*, symphonic suite (1925). *Also*: choral works (including *The Flower Seekers; Confluentia, My Captain*).

BIBLIOGRAPHY: Howard, John Tasker, *Our American Music* (N.Y., 1946); King, Maurice R., "Edgar Stillman Kelley" (doctoral thesis, Tallahassee, Fla., 1970); *New York Times* (obituary), November 14, 1944; *Who's Who in America 1944–45*.

Kennan, Kent Wheeler, b. Milwaukee, Wis., April 18, 1913.

Kennan's best-known works are those composed relatively early in his career in a style that contains both neoromantic and impressionistic elements.

Although his parents were not musical, they encouraged and enjoyed the musical activities of their children at home. Kennan attended the Milwaukee Normal Training School and Riverside High School. During this period he studied piano privately with Addie Seldon Gay for some ten years and organ with Winogene Hewitt Kirchner for three.

In 1930 he entered the University of Michigan, majoring first in architecture and then in liberal arts. A particular interest in creative writing led to a Hopwood Award for a short story in 1932, and he also studied composition formally for the first time, with Hunter Johnson. Music having become the dominant interest, Kennan enrolled, in 1932, in the Eastman School of Music in Rochester, N.Y., where he studied composition with Howard Hanson and Bernard Rogers. He remained at Eastman until 1934 and returned in 1935–36 as a teaching assistant, ac-

quiring his bachelor of music degree in composition and theory in 1934 and his master's degree in composition in 1936.

In 1936 Kennan won the Prix de Rome in music and spent the following three years in residence at the American Academy in Rome. In 1938 he studied composition for a semester with Ildebrando Pizzetti at the Santa Cecilia Academy in Rome. These years, creatively the most productive of his life, yielded some of the compositions by which he became known and which have since been heard frequently in performances by major orchestras. His best-known work, *Night Soliloquy* (1936)—for flute with accompaniment of piano, or strings or wind ensemble— was first performed on October 18, 1938 (in the version for flute and strings), at an American Composers' Concert conducted by Howard Hanson in Rochester, N.Y.; Joseph Mariano was the soloist. Since then, this composition has appeared on the programs of most major orchestras in this country, including the New York Philharmonic under Ormandy, the NBC Symphony under Toscanini, the Philadelphia Orchestra under Toscanini and Ormandy, and the Houston Symphony under Stokowski. It was recorded by RCA Victor, Columbia, and Mercury Records. The title of the piece is intended merely to indicate the music's general mood and character rather than to suggest any specific scene or program. A critic for the *New York Times* described the work as "surprisingly beautiful," while the *New Yorker* called it "a happy introduction to an uncommonly gifted young composer."

Also highly successful was the Andante, for oboe and orchestra (1939). First performed in Rochester under Howard Hanson on January 21, 1941, it was subsequently heard at concerts of the National Orchestral Association under Leon Barzin in New York and by the Philadelphia Orchestra under Ormandy. Here again, the writing is nonprogrammatic; the mood in this case is predominantly somber, the idiom neoromantic.

Additionally, among the works Kennan completed in Italy were: Nocturne for solo viola and orchestra and *Il campo dei fiori* (descriptive of a Roman market), for solo trumpet and orchestra (both in 1938; both first performed in Rochester under Hanson on January 5, 1939; and both clearly influenced by early Stravinsky works); Symphony (1938; Rochester, 1939); *Dance Divertimento*, consisting of "Promenade," "Air de ballet" and "Jig" (1938–39), "Promenade," first performed in its entirety in Rochester, April 14, 1943, by the Eastman School Little Symphony under Frederick Fennell; and *Blessed Are They That Mourn*, for chorus and orchestra (1939; Rochester, New York, April 27, 1942).

Upon his return to the United States, Kennan taught theory and piano at Kent State University in Ohio (1939–40), then theory and composition at the University of Texas at Austin (1940–42). In 1942, during World War II, he enlisted in the armed forces, serving as bandsman and then bandleader with the U.S. Army Air Corps both in the United States and on Iwo Jima. *The Unknown Warrior Speaks* (1944), for a cappella men's chorus, was written for the Army Music School Chorus, was introduced in Washington in the spring of 1944 by that group under William Strickland, and was performed at the White House for Mrs. Franklin D. Roosevelt and her guests on March 3, 1944. Subsequent performances included some 180 by de Paur's Infantry Chorus during its national tours.

From 1947 to 1949 Kennan taught theory at Ohio State University in Columbus. In 1949 he returned to the University of Texas at Austin, where he has remained as a teacher of theory—and, for a time, in certain administrative capacities within the music department. During the summers of 1954 and 1956 he taught theory and composition at the Eastman School of Music.

Kennan's principal compositions in the late 1940s and early 1950s are in a somewhat Hindemithian neoclassical idiom. These include a Sonatina for piano (1946); Scherzo, Aria, and Fugato, for oboe and piano (1948); Theme with Variations, for organ (1952); and Sonata for Trumpet and Piano (1956), commissioned by the National Association of Schools of Music and first performed by Frank Elsass, trumpet, and the composer at an NASM convention in St. Louis in 1956.

Since the late 1950s Kennan has written little new music. Certain earlier works have been revised, among these a Concertino originally (1946) written for piano and orchestra and first performed by the composer and the Columbus Philharmonic under Izlar Solomon in 1948, then extensively reworked and rescored with accompaniment of wind ensemble in 1963. (Incidentally, this was the composer's only venture into what might be called "manufactured folk music.") Likewise, the Piano Sonatina (1946) and a single movement of an uncompleted sonata for piano (1942) were rewritten in 1979. Mainly, Kennan has devoted himself during those years to teaching and administrative duties and the preparation of several publications: *The Technique of Orchestration* (1952, revised 1970); *Counterpoint* (1959, revised 1972), *Orchestration Workbooks* I and II (1952, 1956), and *Counterpoint Workbook* (1959, revised 1972). The first two of these are widely used as texts.

THE COMPOSER SPEAKS: It seems ironic that in this day of "improved communications" the long-lamented gap between serious new music and the general American public appears to be as wide as ever—if not wider. Commercial television and radio are of virtually no help in this regard, since they are "big business" and feel that they must conform to mass taste in order to exist. Some commercial radio stations have programmed full-time classical music (though even that has included a little avant-garde

music). But their number has decreased enormously in the last decade. Happily, there is still some commercial recording of new works, but there, too, retrenchment is more often the order of the day.

Apparently our chief hopes in the face of this situation are noncommercial radio and television stations, including especially those of colleges and universities. Being generally unfettered by the need to turn a profit, these can make (and are already making) a splendid contribution to the dissemination of significant new music.

PRINCIPAL WORKS: *Night Soliloquy*, for flute with accompaniment of piano, or strings, or wind ensemble (1936); Nocturne, for viola and small orchestra (1938); *Il campo dei fiori*, for trumpet and orchestra (1938); Symphony (1938); Three Preludes, for piano (1939); *Sea Sonata*, for violin and piano (1939); *Blessed Are They That Mourn*, for chorus and orchestra (1939); Andante, for oboe and orchestra (1939); *Air de ballet*, for orchestra (1939); Concertino, for piano and orchestra (1946; revised for piano and wind ensemble 1963); Piano Sonata (1942, revised 1979); *The Unknown Warrior Speaks*, for a cappella men's chorus (1944); Sonatina, for piano (1946, revised 1979); Scherzo, Aria, and Fugato, for oboe and piano (1948); Two Preludes, for piano (1951); Theme and Variations, for organ (1952); Trumpet Sonata (1956).

BIBLIOGRAPHY: *BBDM; DCM; Who's Who in America, 1980–81.*

Kirchner, Leon, b. Brooklyn, N.Y., January 24, 1929.

However much Leon Kirchner has been influenced by Schoenberg and Berg, he has never permitted any system to control his creativity. And however much he may also have been influenced by Bartók, he has never been another master's shadow. Kirchner has developed a style uniquely his own, utilizing the fullest resources of 20th-century vocabulary in music that is romantic, rhapsodic, dramatic, lyrical, and generates the white heat of excitement. He received the Pulitzer Prize in music in 1970.

His parents were of Russian origin. Kirchner's childhood and early boyhood were spent in the Bronx, where, while attending public school, he began to study the piano at the age of six at the Diller-Quale School. In his ninth year, his family moved to Los Angeles, where, because of the depression years, piano study was suspended until he was fourteen. He then continued piano study with Richard Buhlig and John Crown and before long was beginning to make public appearances. Since his mother wanted him to become a physician, he entered the Los Angeles City College for a premedical course in 1936 after graduating from Roosevelt High School. While at college, he took courses in harmony and began composing, winning honorable mention for a piano piece in an intramural student composition contest when he was sixteen. His piano teacher, Crown, was so impressed with the promise of some of these early Kirchner pieces that he introduced him to Ernst Toch, who, in turn, encouraged the boy to give serious consideration to developing himself as a composer. Kirchner now enrolled in the University of California in Los Angeles to attend the composition class of Arnold Schoenberg. For further and more intensive training in composing he entered the University of California in Berkeley in 1938, majoring in music (as well as zoology) and studying theory with Albert Elkus and Edward Strickland. He received his bachelor of arts degree in 1940. For one year after that he returned to Schoenberg's class in Los Angeles to do graduate work, after which he was back at Berkeley to study composition further with Ernest Bloch and to try for the George Ladd Fellowship (Paris Prize). He won that fellowship in 1942 with a string quartet in Hindemith's neoclassic linear idiom. Since the war made it impossible for travel to Paris, Kirchner prolonged his stay in New York an additional year by joining the inactive reserve of the U.S. Army Signal Corps. Later, in 1943, he was called into active service, and in 1946 was discharged as lieutenant.

After leaving the armed forces, Kirchner returned to Berkeley to resume the study of composition with Sessions and in 1947 he was appointed lecturer of music. At the same time he taught composition at the San Francisco Conservatory. At this point he discarded everything he had composed up to now to start on a new footing, except for a composition for chorus and organ, *Dawn*, to a text by Federico García Lorca, which he had begun in 1943 while in the army but did not complete until after returning from the service in 1946; it was finally performed in New York in February 1949.

The work that Kirchner looks upon as his real beginnings as a mature composer is the Duo, for violin and piano (originally called Rhapsody), in 1947, performed at Berkeley in the year of its composition and then becoming his first work to be published. After a later performance, Aaron Copland said of it that it gave "the impression of a creative urge so vital as to burst all bonds of ordinary control."

In 1948, Kirchner took leave from Berkeley to concentrate on composition in New York after being awarded a Guggenheim Fellowship, which was renewed for an additional year. Under this fellowship, Kirchner wrote two works for piano, a Sonata (1948) and a *Little Suite* (1949). The sonata was first heard on May 19, 1949, at a concert of the Columbia University Composers Forum, which also presented *Duo*. The *Little Suite*, in a neobaroque structure (dedicated to his recent bride, Gertrude Schoenberg, a singer, whom he had married on July 8, 1949, and with whom he later had two children), was presented at a concert of the League of Composers in New York in April 1950. Both times the composer was the performing artist. These works were chromatic, percussive, strongly dissonant, and Bartókian in their rhythmic drive. A critic for the *New York Times* remarked that this music was "strong of line and structure, violent or moody . . . usually disturbing in its impact."

Kirchner's first acclaim outside on an elite circle of admirers came with the String Quartet no. 1 (1949), dedicated to Roger Sessions, which received its initial hearing in New York on March 26, 1950, at a concert of the League of Composers performed by the Juilliard Quartet, after which it received the New York Music Critics Circle Award as the best new chamber music work of the season. It was Bartókian in its dynamic power, tension, urgency, and unusual instrumental effects. "The work has its own immensely individual profile," remarked a critic for *Hi Fidelity*. "One feels it is music that *had* to be written, and one feels behind it the mind of a great composer." This quartet later won the Jeunesse Musicale Award at the festival of the International Society of Contemporary Music in Tel-Aviv.

In 1950, Kirchner received a citation from the National Institute of Arts and Letters. Between 1950 and 1954, Kirchner served as assistant and, later, full professor at the University of Southern California in Los Angeles. These years were creatively productive as Kirchner's strong individuality began to grow increasingly assertive. The later Kirchner style was now beginning to take shape: the use of dissonant harmonies, linear counterpoint, arhythmic patterns, and a declamatory melodic line to their fullest expressive potential within a nontonal style; a concern for the organic growth of each composition within structures in which classical order prevails; in which lyricism, expressivity, and personal intensity are the main impulses; in which the moods often change quickly and dramatically. Sinfonia in Two Parts (1951) is Kirchner's first large-scale composition for orchestra. Commissioned by Rodgers and Hammerstein for the League of Composers, it was introduced by the New York Philharmonic under Dimitri Mitropoulos on January 31, 1952. Years later, the Sinfonia brought Kirchner the International Koussevitzky Award. *Sonata concertante*, for violin and piano (1952), was first heard in November 1952 in New York performed by Tossy Spivakovsky and the composer and then recorded on a grant from the Fromm Music Foundation. The Concerto no. 1, for piano and orchestra (1953), commissioned by the Koussevitzky Music Foundation and the Library of Congress in Washington, D.C., was introduced by the composer and the New York Philharmonic under Mitropoulos on February 23, 1956; on a Naumburg Foundation grant, it was recorded the following morning. With this concerto, Kirchner first established his reputation in Europe, when it received its European premiere in Baden-Baden with the composer as soloist and Hans Rosbaud conducting. "It is music," a critic for the *New York Times* said, "that needs rehearing and study, not because it is so abstruse, but because it is packed with thought and feeling and written in a highly dissonant, structurally complex idiom. As . . . the more one listens, the more one discovers a firm design in the bewilderingly rich and emotionally vibrant substance of his music. . . . It is alive from the first bar to last and, for all its segmentation, it has rhythmic drive and structural continuity." The Piano Trio (1954), commissioned by the Elizabeth Sprague Coolidge Foundation, was the recipient of a Fromm Music Foundation recording grant; its premiere took place in New York in November 1954.

In 1954, Kirchner was appointed Luther Brusie Marchant Professor of Music at Mills College in Oakland, Calif. He held this post seven years, during which time he was also Visiting Slee Professor at the State University in Buffalo, N.Y. (1958) and a teacher of composition at the Berkshire Music Center at Tanglewood, Mass. (summers 1959, 1960), and pianist, conductor, and composer at the Marlboro Music Festival in Vermont (summer 1959). On a Fromm Music Foundation grant he completed Toccata, for strings and solo percussion (1955), the percussion handled by a three-man ensemble called upon to perform on drums, celesta, gong, tambourine, xylophone, and woodblock. Introduced by the San Francisco Symphony under Enrique Jorda in February 1956, it was later performed by the Boston Symphony with the composer conducting in Boston and Washington, D.C., and by the Symphony of the Air, conducted by Leopold Stokowski. This is a ten-minute work in four uninterrupted sections and is highly complex in rhythmic and metric structures, with an unflagging propulsion, but without sacrificing a virile lyricism.

With String Quartet no. 2 (1958), commissioned by the University of Michigan, Kirchner received his second New York Music Critics Circle Award after it had been introduced by the Lenox String Quartet in New York on November 23, 1959, in a concert sponsored by the Fromm Music Foundation. *Musical America* described it as "music of searing beauty, inspiration, and freshness." On a commission from the Chamber Music Society of Baltimore, Kirchner wrote the Concerto, for violin, cello, ten solo winds, and percussion (1960), which that society premiered in Baltimore on October 16, 1960.

Between 1961 and 1965, Kirchner was professor of music at Harvard University in succession to Walter Piston, and since 1965 has been its Walter Bigelow Rosen Professor. He returned to the Marlboro Music Festival in Vermont each summer between 1963 and 1973 as composer-in-residence, pianist and conductor, guiding there the Rockefeller Contemporary Music Program. In 1965, with several of his colleagues from the Marlboro Festival, he was sent by the State Department to tour Europe; in Paris he conducted a highly successful performance of Beethoven's *Choral Fantasy*. Kirchner further dis-

tinguished himself as conductor when he was musical director of the Boston Philharmonia between 1969 and 1971; of the Harvard Chamber Players since 1973; and of the Harvard Chamber Orchestra since 1978.

Kirchner wrote Piano Concerto no. 2 in 1963 on a commission from the Ford Foundation for Leon Fleisher, who introduced it in Seattle, Wash., with the Seattle Symphony on October 28, 1963, with the composer conducting. Fleisher repeated his performance in New York with the New York Philharmonic, the composer conducting, on December 6, 1964. It is in two movements, and differs from the earlier concerto in that it is shorter and more objective. "In outward form," Edward Downes wrote in his program annotation for the New York Philharmonic, "[it] shows a closer continuity with the Romantic traditions of the 19th century than with the older Classical models. . . . In its constant fluctuations of tempo (amounting almost to a structural principle), in its intricate rhythmic and metrical patterns, in its variety and refinement of tone color combinations, and in its powerful communication of subjective moods, the Concerto seems further related to the Romantic tradition."

Kirchner was awarded the Pulitzer Prize in music in 1967 for String Quartet no. 3 (1966), and its first performance given in New York by the Beaux-Arts String Quartet (for whom it was written) on January 27, 1967. This work represented for Kirchner a radical departure in methodology in that it was scored not only for string quartet but also for electronic sounds on tape amplified by two speakers. The electronic sounds are for the most part used with discretion until the end of the composition when they take center stage completely.

On a commission from the New York Philharmonic to commemorate its 125th anniversary, Kirchner wrote Music for Orchestra, but it was not heard until two years after the event—on October 16, 1969, just ten days after it had been completed. The composer conducted. A brilliantly orchestrated and strongly crafted bravura piece, Music for Orchestra is built from a spare germinal motive (the interval of the second) that is sounded at the beginning by the oboe. At the end of the composition, controlled improvisation is used as the speed is left to the wishes of the conductor. This work proved so successful that it was soon performed by the Philadelphia Orchestra, the Boston Symphony, the Los Angeles Philharmonic, the Chicago Symphony, and the Minnesota Orchestra, among other orchestras, before returning to the programs of the New York Philharmonic in October 1972, conducted by Pierre Boulez.

Some of the material in Music for Orchestra came out of an operatic score that Kirchner was then working on. He had been commissioned to write that opera in 1959 by the Fromm Music Foundation, but it was many years before he completed a version that satisfied him. He called it *Lily*, his own libretto being an adaptation of the first half of Saul Bellow's novel *Henderson, the Rain King*. But before it was completed, Kirchner used other materials from that score for a concert work, also named *Lily*, for violin, viola, cello, woodwind quintet, piano, and percussion. (1973). It was first performed in New York in March 1973. Then, on a year's leave of absence from Harvard, with a grant from the New York City Opera and as a composer-in-residence at the American Academy in Rome, Kirchner worked intensively on his opera. Most of it got written in 1975 in Rome, where he was senior resident fellow at the American Academy. It was completed in 1977 while Kirchner was a fellow at the Institute of Advanced Musical Studies at Stanford University in California. On April 14, 1977, the New York City Opera produced it with the composer conducting. Amplified sounds from recorded tapes were used in conjunction with a live orchestra. "Kirchner," wrote Royal S. Brown in *High Fidelity/Musical America*, "has come up with a deeply expressive score whose musically created tensions strike the listener with much greater impact than any of the verbal or scenic symbolism. . . . He masterfully alternates musical moods and atmosphere, showing an expressionist sensibility that has its match, perhaps, only in the work of Alban Berg."

In 1962, Kirchner was elected member of the National Institute of Arts and Letters and the American Academy of Arts and Letters. In 1976, he received the National Music Award from the music industry of America "in honor of extraordinary contribution to the development and performance of American music" and in 1977 Brandeis University in Waltham, Mass., presented him with its Creative Arts Award (Medal of Achievement). An all-Kirchner concert was heard in Pittsburgh on March 28, 1959, and another all-Kirchner concert, sponsored by the Fromm Music Foundation and the University of Chicago, was given in Chicago on May 3, 1961. In March 1977, a retrospective concert of Kirchner's music spanning a quarter century of his creativity was given in New York by the Performers Committee for 20th Century Music.

THE COMPOSER SPEAKS: It is my feeling that many of us, dominated by the fear of self-expression, seek the superficial security of current style and fad; worship and make a fetish of complexity, or with puerile grace denude simplicity. Idea, the precious ore of art, is lost in the jungle of graphs, prepared tapes, feedback and cold stylistic minutiae.

An artist must create a personal cosmos, a verdant world in continuity with tradition, further fulfilling man's "awareness," his "degree of consciousness," and bringing new subtilization, vision, and beauty to the elements of experience. It is in this way that Idea, powered by conviction and necessity, will create its own style and the singular, momentous structure capable of realizing its intent.

PRINCIPAL WORKS: 3 string quartets (1949, 1958, 1966); 2 piano concertos (1953, 1963).

Duo, for violin and piano (1947); Piano Sonata (1948); *Little Suite*, for piano (1949); "Of Obedience" and "The Runner," both for soprano and piano (1950); Sinfonia in Two Parts, for orchestra (1951); *Sonata concertante*, for violin and piano (1952); Piano Trio (1954); Toccata, for strings, six solo winds and percussion (1955); Concerto, for violin, cello, solo winds, and percussion (1960); *Words from Wordsworth*, for chorus (1966); Music for Orchestra (1969); *Lily*, for violin, viola, cello, woodwind quintet, piano, percussion, and voice (1973); *Lily*, opera (1977); Music for Flute and Orchestra (1978); *A Moment for Roger*, for piano (1978); Music for Flute and Orchestra (1981).

BIBLIOGRAPHY: *High Fidelity/Musical America*, January 1971; *Musical Quarterly*, January 1957; *New Yorker*, May 2, 1977; *New York Times*, February 21, 1960, March 11, 1973; *Time*, July 5, 1954.

Kohn, Karl, b. Vienna, Austria, August 1, 1926. American citizen, 1945.

First influenced by Bartók, Stravinsky, and Hindemith, Kohn later became interested in atonality, the twelve-tone system, and aleatory procedures. His works since the early 1960s have been athematic and chromatic, utilizing chords, figurations, and textures that evoke the music of the past. "This conscious but spontaneous attempt to integrate the past with the present," he says, "proved to be a turning point and has played a dominant role in my compositional approach of the past two decades."

His father, a textile salesman, was an excellent amateur violinist, and his mother, a competent pianist. Both encouraged Karl in his early musical interests. He was six when he began studying the piano with Alice Löwinger-Feldstein, who remained his teacher until 1939. At the same time he attended four years of primary school and two and a half years of gymnasium (high school); at the gymnasium he played the timpani in the school orchestra. "The most important influence on my early years," he says, "was at the age of thirteen to survive imminent destruction in Nazi-occupied Vienna by being able to immigrate to the United States and be transplanted into the New World at the end of 1939."

On coming to the United States, the family settled in Goshen, N.Y. There Kohn attended Goshen Central School (1940–43) and, after the family moved to the nearby city, was graduated from Middletown (N.Y.) High School, in 1944. In both places he participated in the performances of the various school groups by playing the oboe, bassoon, horn, and piano.

In 1940, on a scholarship, he entered the New York College of Music in New York City, studying piano with Carl V. Werschinger and conducting with Julius Prüwer during the next four years. In 1944, he was enrolled in Harvard University, but his studies were interrupted a year later when Kohn was called into military service during World War II. For a year he served as noncommissioned bandmaster of the 297th Army Grand Forces band on Tinian in the Marianas.

Separated from military service in 1946, Kohn returned to Harvard. The next three years were spent studying theory and composition with Walter Piston, Irving Fine, Randall Thompson, and Edward Ballantine; he received the bachelor of arts degree, *summa cum laude*, in 1950. Two days after this, on June 23, 1950, he married Margaret Sherman. She is a gifted pianist who had then just graduated from Radcliffe College. Since her marriage, she has taught piano, appeared in concerts with her husband, specializing in 20th-century music, and, with him, raised two daughters.

In 1950, Kohn was appointed teacher of composition, theory, music history, and piano at Pomona College and Claremont Graduate School in Claremont, Calif. He has remained there since then, having been named Thatcher Professor of Music and composer-in-residence in 1973. During the summers of 1954, 1955 and 1957 he was on the music faculty of Berkshire Music Center at Tanglewood, Mass. In 1957 he was appointed to the board of directors of the Monday Evening Concerts in Los Angeles, which presented concerts of mixed repertoire devoted to rarely heard old as well as new music, and since 1967 he has been the director of its Ensemble I concerts.

His first adult works, completed in the 1950s, reflected his musical training in Harvard by favoring an American neoclassicism that leaned towards the harmonic and rhythmic idiom of Bartók and linear contrapuntal writing of Hindemith. These works included *Sinfonia concertante*, for piano and orchestra (1951; Claremont, Calif., April 8, 1952); *The Red Cockatoo*, for chorus and piano on Chinese texts translated by Wytter Bynner (1954; Cambridge, Mass., March 29, 1955); *Five Pieces*, for piano (1955; Boston, March 18, 1958); *Quartet*, for horns (1957; Los Angeles, June 13, 1958); and *Castles and Kings*, an orchestral suite for children (1958; Claremont, March 22, 1959).

In 1954–55, on leave from Pomona College, Kohn was teaching fellow at Harvard while completing requirements for a master of arts degree in 1955. Still on leave, he was able, in 1955–56, to go to Finland as a faculty Fulbright Research Scholar in composition. "That year in Finland," he recalls, "aroused an intensive involvement with my at least geographically Viennese ancestry: atonality, twelve-tone procedures and the current developments in the multiserialism evolved from that heritage." These influences were reflected in several compositions between 1958 and the first part of the 1960s: *Three Scenes*, for orchestra (1958–60), which was introduced by the Los Angeles Philharmonic under Alfred Wallenstein on May 5, 1965; *Divertimento*, for flute, oboe, clarinet, and bassoon (1959; Boston, March 28, 1960), which had been commissioned by the Harvard Musical Association; *Serenade*, for piano and wind quintet (1962; Los Angeles, November 5, 1962); and *Concerto mutabile*, for piano and chamber orchestra (1962; San Francisco, March 18, 1963) in which aleatory practices are involved. "My music," he explains, "had become more intense, fragmentary, and less vertical in conception.

In 1961–62 Kohn was awarded a Guggenheim Fellowship and a grant of the Howard Foundation administered by Brown University, enabling him to spend a sabbatical year from Pomona College in Holland. The Wig Distinguished Professorship Award and another Pomona College Sabbatical grant brought him to London in 1968–69. A Mellon Foundation grant in the humanities made it possible for him to take a semester's leave in 1974, and two fellowship grants from the National Endowment for the Arts and a second Wig Distinguished Professorship award at Pomona allowed him to spend the year of 1975–76 in Claremont composing. In 1979 he received a third fellowship grant from the National Endowment for the Arts.

In 1960, he wrote Rhapsody, for piano, which he introduced on November 12, 1960, in New York. This work made use of traditionally derived scale patterns and figurations within a predominantly chromatic context. By the middle 1960s, he had come to the last stage of his creative development in which past and present techniques were merged. This trend became apparent in *Capriccios*, for harp, cello, flute, clarinet, and piano (1962; Los Angeles, November 5, 1962). Here, at times, reminiscences from the past are direct and specific by borrowing, reworking, or modifying materials taken from earlier music into a kind of parody or collage. More often, however, the references have been just oblique allusions to characteristics of past styles, their elements of harmony, melody, rhythm, and texture.

Characteristic of such "reminiscences" are *Introductions and Parodies*, for clarinet, horn, bassoon, string quartet, and piano (1967; Pasadena, Calif., November 15, 1970), which borrowed material from Mendelssohn's Violin Concerto; *Reflections*, for clarinet and piano (1970; Pasadena, May 16, 1971) which developed fragments from Mahler and Alban Berg; *Souvenirs* I, for violin and piano (1971; N. Y., April 5, 1979) which referred to "remembrance of things past," as the composer has explained, "as well as being a souvenir for Rafael Druian, the concertmaster of the Cleveland Orchestra, who had left for New York after a two-year stay in Los Angeles; *Souvenirs* II, for oboe and harp (1976; St. Louis, January 18, 1977); *The Prophet Bird*, for ten instruments (1976; San Francisco, September 30, 1976); and *Son of Prophet Bird*, for harp (1977; Boston, June 22,

1977). *Souvenirs* II recalled the past not by specific borrowings from older music but by tangential references to a 19th-century harmonic idiom and the ingenuous use of running scale figurations and brilliant passage work typically associated with the harp. *The Prophet Bird*—Concert Music II for chamber ensemble—owes its title to, and develops quotations from, one of Robert Schumann's piano pieces. *Son of Prophet Bird* is a "paraphrase" that drew its musical material almost entirely from the harp part of the earlier composition.

Between 1966 and 1977, Kohn produced a series of chamber music compositions for various solo instruments and piano carrying the collective title of *Encounters*. While in the first of the *Encounters* for flute (or piccolo) and piano, the title of the work was intended also to honor the occasion of its first performance in the Pasadena Art Museum's *Encounter Series*, it refers more specially to the form and character of the music—the dialogue and dramatic action between the instruments, and how, with their characteristic motifs and figurations, they confront and respond to each other. In subsequent *Encounters* for various instruments (horn, violin, oboe, bassoon, and cello) and piano, Kohn has attempted to present each "solo" instrument in its most idiomatic language, to bring out some of its most natural and characteristic qualities of sound and figuration.

In 1974 and 1978 he completed two sets of *Paronyms*, the first for flutes and piano (Oberlin, Ohio, October 12, 1974) and the other for saxophone (one player) and piano (Los Angeles, April 30, 1979). A paronym is a word derived from another or from the same root. In his *Paronyms* Kohn quoted and integrated excerpts from pieces he had previously written, including a portion of *Encounters* V (1973); segments of a Hugo Wolf song are also recalled.

In *Centone*, for orchestra (1973; Claremont, July 27, 1973), Kohn abandoned recollections or quotations. *Centone* is Italian for "patchwork quilt." In this composition, musical materials from the reservoir of at least a thousand years of Western music are selected, retrieved, recycled and reshaped. Segments and fragments appeared throughout the work in different juxtapositions as if in a patchwork quilt.

Innocent Psaltery, colonial music for an orchestra of symphonic winds and percussion (1975; Evanston, Ill., February 20, 1977), was composed in fulfillment of a fellowship grant by the National Endowment for the Arts in its Bicentennial Composer/Librettist Program. The three movements of this work made use of musical sources from the Sternhold and Hopkins Psalter (published in London in 1624) and compositions by the 18th-century American composers John Tufts, William Billings, and Francis Hopkinson. *Waldmusik*—a concerto for clarinet and orchestra (1979)—is a lyrical work in which the solo instrument provided rhapsodic commentary to an orchestra of winds, piano, and strings in which oboes, bassoons, and horns predominate. The integration of traditional horn calls and fanfares recalling their characteristic classical usage with a rich harmonic idiom suggests a bucolic mood that evoked the German title, meaning "forest music."

THE COMPOSER SPEAKS: An attempt to take a retrospective look at my music impels me to refer to two significant interrelated aspects: idea and style. The first of these is clearly the more crucial since it deals with inventiveness, vivid imagination, and sense of balance and taste. The force and persuasiveness of a work depends largely on the composer's creativity and musical vision. These determine how acutely he is able to shape and refine the basic materials of music into viable and satisfying formal structures. Style refers to the language in which he speaks, the idiom he fashions from the environment of his inherited musical tradition. It seems to me presumptuous and unnecessary to call attention to matters that relate to idea, in the hope that his aspect will be made clear by the energy and vitality of the music itself. . . .

Whether or not a composer chooses to probe or discuss his artistic role by facing, as a critical observer, the inevitable issue of "language" and style, his task remains what it has always been: to develop his own hybrids from the plants closest and nearest to him. i.e., the music with and in which he himself grew up. However, during the last century of massive publication of printed music, and particularly in recent decades since the spectacular development of sound recordings and radio, what was the "old-time" composer's neatly fenced and clearly defined garden plot of his musical heritage has become a vast botanical garden with a multiplicity of available "roots" from an enormous range of chronological and geographic strata. For better or for worse, and for composer as well as his listeners, the phenomenon has brought about the new dimensions of "choice," not unlike the often vexing confrontation with the bountiful delights of the supermarket, that emblem of our contemporary culture. . . .

It is hard to imagine how this new pattern towards continuous absorption of the whole available past is likely to be reversed, except by cataclysmic changes perhaps too dreadful to contemplate—changes that would push us back into more isolated, locally sustained, and self-centered cultures like those that prevailed in earlier civilizations. At least for the foreseeable future, therefore, the process of recycling and reshaping of musical materials that come from an enormous and inexhaustible international reservoir, and its new implications for a music resonant with the spirit of our time, appears as a most natural and likely basis for our art.

PRINCIPAL WORKS: *Encounters* I–VI, for various solo instruments and piano (1966–77); 3 rhapsodies, for piano (1960, 1971, 1977).
The Red Cockatoo, cycle of songs on Chinese texts,

for chorus and piano (1954); Concert Music, for twelve wind instruments (1956); Quartet, for horns (1957); *Three Descants from Ecclesiastes*, for chorus and brass or piano (1957); *Three Goliard Songs*, for a cappella male chorus (1958); *Castles and Kings*, orchestral suite for children, also for piano four hands (1958); *Three Scenes*, for orchestra (1958–60); Divertimento, for flute, oboe, clarinet, and bassoon (1959); *Sensus spei*, for chorus with piano or instrumental ensemble (1961); Five Bagatelles, for piano (1961); Serenade, for wind quintet and piano (1962); Capriccios, for harp, cello, flute, clarinet, and piano (1962); *Concerto mutabile*, for piano and orchestra or chamber ensemble (1962); Partita, for piano (1963); *Kaleidoscope*, for string quartet (1964); *Sonata da camera*, for alto flute, clarinet, and piano (1964); *Interludes*, for orchestra (1964); Fantasia, for organ (1964); *Leisure and Other Songs*, for voice and piano (1965); *Episodes*, for piano and orchestra (1966); Preludes and Fantasia, for organ (1968); *Recreations*, for piano four hands (1968); Intermezzo, for piano and strings (1969); Impromptus, for eight wind instruments (1969); *Esradas—Anthems and Interludes for piano solo, chorus and orchestra* (1970); *Reflections*, for clarinet and piano (1970); Variations for Horn and Piano (1971); *Souvenirs* I, for violin and piano (1971); *Only the Hopeful*, for a cappella solo voices and male solo voice (1972); Trio, for violin, horn and piano (1972); *Bits and Pieces*, for piano (1973); *Centone*, for orchestra (1973); *Hal'lu et Adonai*, for cantor and organ (1973); *Also the Sons*, anthem for vocal soloists, chorus and organ (1973); Horn Concerto (1974); *Paronyms* I, for flutes and piano (1974); *Innocent Psaltery*, colonial music for orchestra of symphonic winds and percussion (1975); *The Prophet Bird*, for chamber ensemble (1976); Quintet, for two trumpets, horn, trombone, and tuba (1976); *Souvenirs* II, for oboe and harp (1976); Serenade II, for concert band (1977); *Son of Prophet Bird*, for harp (1977); *From a Journal*, Part I, for piano (1977); *Paronyms* II, for saxophone and piano (1978); *Waldmusik*, concerto for clarinet and orchestra (1979).

BIBLIOGRAPHY: *BBDM; DCM; Musical Quarterly*, April 1963; *Perspectives of New Music*, Fall-Winter, 1963; *Who's Who in America, 1980–81*.

Kohs, Ellis Bonoff, b. Chicago, Ill., May 12, 1916.

In his music, Kohs has attempted to reconcile classic-romantic, tonal, and serial procedures.

Both his parents were musical, his mother being a competent amateur violinist whose playing constituted Kohs's first remembered musical impressions. He began taking lessons when he was eight with Irmengard Horn, who remained his teacher for about two years. From 1926 to 1928 he attended the San Francisco Conservatory. He still recalls how much pleasure he derived those days from accompanying his mother's violin playing on the piano. When he was twelve, the family moved to Brooklyn, N.Y. While attending James Madison High School, where he played timpani in the school orchestra, he continued his music study at the Institute of Musical Art in New York with Adelaide Belser (1928–33). In 1933 he was back in Chicago, a student at the University of Chicago (1933–38) majoring in composition as a student of Carl Bricken's and receiving his master of arts degree in 1938. Later that year he returned to New York to spend the next year at the Juilliard School of Music on a fellowship, a student of Bernard Wagenaar's in composition and Olga Samaroff in musical pedagogy.

Kohs continued his postgraduate musical training at Harvard University (1939–41), where he studied composition with Walter Piston and musicology with Hugo Leichtentritt and Willi Apel, and, in 1940–41, attended Stravinsky's seminar. During the summer of 1940 he was employed as lecturer in music at the University of Wisconsin in Madison.

While at Harvard he completed his String Quartet no. 1 (1940), which, a decade later, writing in the *San Francisco Examiner*, Alexander Fried called "remarkable," adding: "Writing in a moderately modern vein, Kohs handled the difficult quartet form on a large scale with plenty of ideas and with unflagging life and surety. . . . The music is resourceful in its variety of sound and effect. It has expressive character." Kohs also wrote his first work for orchestra—and at the same time his first concerto, a form he would later favor in several important works—the Concerto for Orchestra (1941), which, when introduced at the festival of the International Society for Contemporary Music at Berkeley, Calif., with Werner Janssen conducting on August 9, 1942, was the only work in the entire festival by a native American in army uniform. This concerto was successfully repeated in San Francisco by the San Francisco Symphony under the composer's direction in February 1943, at the invitation of Pierre Monteux.

Between 1941 and 1946, during World War II, Kohs served in the armed forces first as a chaplain's assistant and organist and from 1943 to 1946 as a warrant officer band leader at Fort Benning, Ga., and an air force band leader at St. Joseph, Mo., and in Nashville, Tenn. While in uniform he produced two compositions in a satirical vein inspired by army life. *Life with Uncle Sam* (1942; San Luis Obispo, Calif., 1943), originally for band but later scored for orchestra, is a six-movement suite descriptive of six phases of army life. The respective movements were entitled: "Reveille," "Goldbrick," "First Sergeant and Little Joe," "Tactical March," "Mail Call," and "The First Morning of a Furlough." The Columbus Symphony in Ohio under Izler Solomon presented it on October 23, 1945, in a program selected entirely in a poll of servicemen and servicewomen throughout the world. *The Automatic Pistol*, for a cappella male chorus (1943; Washington, D.C., September 5, 1943), was a humorous composition taking its text verbatim from the United States Army military service manual, which describes in detail how to disassemble a pistol.

Upon his separation from military service in 1946, and with an Alice M. Ditson Fellowship from Columbia University, Kohs was appointed assistant professor of music at Wesleyan University in Connecticut (1946–48). During the summers of 1946 and of 1947 he was also an instructor at the Kansas City Conservatory. Between 1948 and 1950 he was associate professor of music at the College of the Pacific at Stockton, Calif. In 1950 he was appointed associate professor at the School of Music of the University of Southern California in Los Angeles, where he rose to full professorship in 1952 and in 1966 was made chairman of the theory department.

On February 27, 1947, Kohs's *Legend*, for oboe and string orchestra (1946), was introduced in Columbus, Ohio. "The title was not intended to imply that a literary narrative is involved," the composer explained, "but is rather metaphorical in character." Two other works in the 1940s were in a concerto structure. He wrote a Cello Concerto in 1947, premiered in Los Angeles on November 25, 1952, and a Chamber Concerto, for viola and string nonet (1949; Berkeley, Calif., December 13, 1949) which the violinist Ferenc Molnar had commissioned and recorded for Columbia Records in 1953.

Another structure to which Kohs was partial in the 1940s, and to which he returned in subsequent years, was the variation form. First came Passacaglia, for organ and strings (1946), which E. Power Biggs commissioned and performed with a chamber orchestra conducted by William Strickland over the facilities of CBS radio on May 26, 1946. After that followed Piano Variations (1946) and *Variations on L'homme armé*, for piano (1947). In 1956 he wrote Variations, for recorder, and in 1962 he produced an ingenious exercise in variation writing with *Studies in Variation*. The last of these is a four-part work, the first for woodwind quintet, the second for piano and strings, the third for piano alone, and the fourth for solo violin. The material for all four parts is the same and recurs in the same order, but with each appearance the rhythm, dynamics, texture, and special effects change chameleonlike. "As an ambitious work," reported Albert Goldberg in the *Los Angeles Times*, "Mr. Kohs's work is probably unique. Countless composers have produced variations of one kind or another, but we think of none who had utilized the variation principle on such a large and complicated scale." All four works were produced at a concert of the International Society for Contemporary Music in Los Angeles on May 5, 1963.

On a commission by Pierre Monteux, the musical director of the San Francisco Symphony, Kohs completed Symphony no. 1 in 1950, premiered by Monteux and his orchestra on January 3, 1952. Writing

in the *San Francisco Chronicle*, Alfred Frankenstein described it as "rich in ideas . . . remarkable for its high-spirited humor, its melodiousness, and its lithe, sparkling texture both harmonic and orchestral." Symphony no. 2, for chorus and orchestra, followed six years later, the result of a commission from the Fromm Music Foundation and the University of Illinois in Urbana, where it was given its world premiere on April 13, 1957, Robert Shaw conducting.

By the mid-1950s, Kohs had evolved the style that would henceforth identify his music. It is harmonically dissonant, largely contrapuntal, and employs Bartókian asymmetric rhythms and variable meters; the structure is clearly defined and the texture pellucid. For the most part, his writing generates power but it is also capable of meditative repose and lyrical eloquence. When, on occasion, he employs the twelve-tone system, he modifies it radically to meet the demands of the composition at hand, often using the row as a motivically unifying element.

Such a modified form of twelve-tone writing characterizes his only work for the operatic stage: *Amerika*, an opera with his own libretto based on the novel by Kafka. Three rows were used, each a variant of the others. One is designed to suggest minor modality, one major, one chromatic. An abridged concert version was heard in Los Angeles on May 19, 1970.

In 1961, Kohs reactivated and became chairman of the Los Angeles Chapter of the International Society for Contemporary Music. In 1966 he was appointed director of the Institute for Music in Contemporary Education (Western Region), an activity of the Contemporary Music Project administered through the Music Educators National Conference. In 1968–69 he was the president of the Los Angeles Chapter of the National Association for American Composers and Conductors.

Kohs is the author of *Music Theory, a Syllabus for Teachers and Students*, two volumes (1961); *Musical Forms: Studies in Analysis and Synthesis* (1976); and *Musical Composition: Projects in Ways and Means* (1978). Two of Kohs's concert works were evolved from the last of these texts: *Calumny*, for voice, flute, horn, timpani, and cello (1978; Los Angeles, November 7, 1978), based on a text from Beaumarchais's *The Marriage of Figaro*, and the Concerto for Percussion Quartet (1979; Los Angeles, November 12, 1979). Both works employ serial procedures in a mixed tonal-atonal context.

THE COMPOSER SPEAKS: I believe that a truly creative composer dedicates his life to the pursuit of some goal other than that of simply making a living. For me, that pursuit has always been to explore the neglected middle of the road, the main trunk of the historical musical tree rather than to play games or to experiment on a far-out limb. My road is not that of the avant-garde but rather that of the assimilator of everything (or anything) that is most relevant to what I wish to communicate. Old forms *may* be reborn, apparently incompatible styles *can* be reconciled. I try to learn from the successes and failures in history, and from my own experiences. I insist on being *myself* and not joining a group because it is fashionable. Above all, I see my music as my modest thanks to the life forces for having provided me with a "voice" to "sing my song."

PRINCIPAL WORKS: 2 symphonies (1950, 1956); 2 string quartets (1940, 1948).

Concerto for Orchestra (1941); *Legend*, for oboe and string orchestra (1946); *Etude in Memory of Bartók*, for piano (1946); Passacaglia, for organ and strings (1946); Piano Variations (1946); Cello Concerto (1947); *Variations on L'homme armé*, for piano (1947); Psalm 25, for chorus and orchestra or organ (1947); Capriccio, for organ (1948); Sonatina, for violin and piano (1948); Toccata, for harpsichord or piano (1948); *Fantasy on La, Sol, Fa, Re, Mi*, for piano (1949); Chamber Concerto, for viola and string nonet (1949); ten two-voice Inventions and one for three-voice, for piano (1950); *Fatal Interview*, five songs for voice and piano (1951); Clarinet Sonata (1951); *Three Chorale Variations on Hebrew Hymns*, for organ (1952); *Lord of the Ascendant*, for eight solo dancers, seven solo voices, chorus, and orchestra (1955); Variations, for recorder (1956); Psalm 23, for four vocal soloists and chorus (1957); Piano Sonata no. 1 (1957); Brass Trio (1957); *Three Songs from the Navajo*, for a cappella chorus (1957); *Three Greek Choruses*, for a cappella women's chorus (1957); *Three Medieval Latin Songs*, for a cappella male chorus (1957); *Four Orchestral Songs*, for voice, percussion, harp and strings (1959); *Studies in Variations*, in four parts: Part I, for woodwind quintet; Part II, for piano and strings; Part III, for piano; Part IV, for solo violin (1962); Suite for Cello and Piano (1964); Sonata for Snare Drum and Piano (1966); *Amerika*, opera (1969); Duo for Violin and Cello (1971); *Calumny*, for bass-baritone, flute, horn, cello and timpani (1978); Concerto for Percussion Quartet (1979).

BIBLIOGRAPHY: *BBDM; DCM*; Ewen, David, *American Composers Today* (N.Y., 1949); *American Composers Alliance Bulletin*, Autumn 1956, autobiographical sketch entitled "Thoughts from the Workbench"; *Composers of the Americas*, vol. 15, (Washington, D.C., 1970).

Kolb, Barbara, b. Hartford, Conn., February 10, 1939.

The first American woman to win the Prix de Rome in music composition, Barbara Kolb is a composer who has never favored any specific idiom, evolving a style of her own combining tonal, aleatoric, serial, electronic, and textural elements, occasionally with a leaning toward impressionistic experiences.

Her father was a pianist, organist, composer of popular songs, and director of WTIC, a radio station in Hartford. Neither parent wanted Barbara to become a professional musician, hoping she would favor either commercial art or nursing. As far as she herself was concerned, her primary activities at first centered around the visual arts. At Hartford Public High School (1952–56) her art teacher recommended her for a scholarship to art school. But by then Kolb realized that her talent in music was greater than it was in art, since music always came easily to her, while art required continual effort. She had begun to study the clarinet when she was eleven with William Goldstein, who remained her teacher through her years in high school and college. At New Park Avenue Grammar School, from which she graduated in 1952, she took part in all its musical activities. And in high school she wrote words and music for the class song and was the recipient of several awards in music at her graduation.

Upon graduating from high school, she received a full scholarship for the study of clarinet at the Julius Hartt College of Music of the University of Hartford. She remained there seven years (1957–64), combining clarinet study with Louis Speyer with that of composition with Arnold Franchetti. She earned her bachelor of arts degree there, *cum laude*, in 1961, and her master of music degree in composition three years later. Summers of 1960, 1964, and 1968 were spent at the Berkshire Music Center at Tanglewood, Mass., for the study of clarinet and composition with Lukas Foss and Gunther Schuller, both of whom were to become powerful influences in her later development. Between 1964 and 1966 she continued clarinet lessons with Leon Russianoff.

Among her earlier compositions is *Rebuttal*, for two clarinets (1964), a freely chromatic composition in which the two clarinets engage in a free-flowing dialogue before reaching for independent lines. The writing is light and witty, and pervaded with charm. Its comparatively traditional ways are further pursued in *Chansons bas*, for voice, harp and two percussions (1965: N.Y., April 1965); *Figments* for flute and piano (1966); and *Three Place Settings*, for narrator, clarinet, violin, double bass, and percussion (1968; N.Y., 1968).

On a Fulbright Fellowship, Kolb spent the year of 1966–67 in study in Europe. The years of 1969–71 she lived in Rome at the American Academy as the recipient of the Prix de Rome.

Her first commission came from the Fromm Music Foundation and resulted in the writing of *Trobar clus* (1970), for thirteen instrumentalists. The title comes from a medieval Provençal poetic form that foreshadowed the rondeau, but her composition is a wordless poem. The instrumentalists are divided into four groups, and the work, cyclic in structure, is built from various statements, each self-sufficient yet carrying the implication of continuation. The timbres are subtly varied, exploring contrasts between plucked strings and sustaining ones. When *Trobar clus* was given its world premiere in Tanglewood on August 29, 1970, Tom Willis of the *Chicago Tribune* reported: "Miss Kolb is an exceptionally cunning manipulator of musical texture, as able to negotiate the intricacies of a palindromic tone as to find idiomatic timbres for her carefully selected group of strings, brass, percussion, and harpsichord. But the importance of this work lies not in its structure but in its effect."

Kolb wrote *Soundings* (1972) on a commission from the Koussevitzky Music Foundation to celebrate its thirtieth anniversary. She originally scored this work for a chamber ensemble of eleven players and prerecorded tape, the tape providing those parts that are played live in the orchestral version. In its original scoring it was first heard on October 27, 1972, at a concert of the Chamber Music Society of Lincoln Center in New York, Gunther Schuller conducting. "Soundings" is a technique to ascertain the depth of water by measuring the time between the sending of a signal and the return of its echo. Kolb came upon the title only after she had written most of the music. When *Soundings* was first performed, Kolb came to realize that the end music was neither long nor well structured enough and that this material called for orchestral treatment. She rewrote *Soundings* as an orchestral work in 1972, its first performance given by the New York Philharmonic under Pierre Boulez on December 11, 1975. She revised it again in 1977, this version given by the Boston Symphony under Seiji Ozawa on February 16, 1978. Ozawa thought so highly of this composition that he decided to feature it on his tour to Japan with the Boston Symphony in March 1978 in Osaka and Tokyo, with Kolb traveling with the orchestra. This final version is scored for three orchestras (replacing channels of taped music in the original chamber music composition) requiring two conductors. Fragmented and insistently repetitive melodies and overlapping rhythmical patterns abound. But as Richard Dyer noted in the *Boston Globe*, "[Kolb] used procedures to make a piece that has a beginning, a middle, and an end, something that to atmosphere, texture, and color adds destination. The music makes sense and leaves mysteries."

In 1971, Barbara Kolb received a Guggenheim Fellowship. A second one came in 1976, enabling her to spend that year in Paris. In 1973 she was given an award by the National Institute of Arts and Letters and in 1975 and again in 1977 the Creative Artists Public Service Awards. In 1973 she received a grant from the Ford Foundation to study electronic music at Mills College in Oakland, Calif.; that summer she was resident composer at the Marlboro Music Festival in Vermont. From 1973 to 1975 she was assistant professor of music at Brooklyn College in Brooklyn, N.Y.; in 1975 she was composer-in-residence at the American Academy in Rome; and in 1978 she served as visiting professor of composition and analysis at Temple University in Philadelphia. She has received grants from the National Endowment for the Arts in 1972, 1974, 1977, and 1979.

She wrote *Musique pour un vernissage* (for flute, violin, viola, and guitar) in 1976–77 for the opening of an exhibition of paintings by Pierre Jacquemon in Paris in March 1977, where it was first heard with the composer conducting. The music was intended to simulate one of Erik Satie's "musique d'ameublement" compositions, serving as background music while visitors strolled around the exhibit. The instruments were distributed throughout the gallery so that, as visitors moved about, they could hear the music in different perspectives. Since then, *Musique pour un vernissage* has been heard as a concert piece, its American premiere taking place at the Kennedy Center for the Performing Arts in Washington, D.C., on February 3, 1979, Leon Fleischer conducting. The composer informs us that the purpose for which this composition was originally written is reflected in the way "various textures of the piece weave in and out: instruments come to the fore to introduce a new pattern or series of notes, then fade into the background to let another idea emerge from another part of the ensemble." One of these ideas is a brief and conscious recollection from Debussy's *La mer*. Toward the end of the work a three-minute section coalesces the varied textures into a single, gradually changing set of patterns.

Between 1972 and 1975, Kolb served as trustee of the American Academy in Rome, and in 1978 she received the alumna of the year award from the University of Hartford (Hartt School of Music).

THE COMPOSER SPEAKS: Recognizing one's own personality is probably the single, most essential ingredient to the development of an artist and may very well take an entire lifetime to achieve. The more an individual develops a consciousness of what he is, of himself, the more he's able to transform what comes into him and integrate it into some substance or energy which is also creative.

For as long as I can remember, I've been interested in and influenced by poetry and the visual arts and through these art forms have somehow developed as a composer. Since 1970 my thoughts on composition have focused on the development of layers of sound which emerge and disappear from a sound matrix, much like a kind of confused perspective in painting. For example: the development of lines and "motivic" ideas are treated similarly to objects in space which either gradually or suddenly collide. In painting terms it would be like a time when the figure/ground relationship is very clear and simple and a time when the figure/ground relationship becomes all interwoven and mixed up. As a fine painter and dear friend, James Herbert, once stated: "You must paint things clearly enough and there is nowhere to go except to make them more complicated. Then you make them too complicated and you clarify them again." In musical terms it would be compared to several parts sounding at once, resulting in a dimension of depth, an idea distributed in space, a union of parts expressing the idea rather than one part.

If one has something to say one must have ideas, and the beauty of expressing an idea that can't be expressed in any way but sound continues to be a source of stimulation for me. Perhaps the expression of love is the same.

PRINCIPAL WORKS: *Three Place Settings*, for narrator, clarinet, violin, double bass, and percussion (1968): *Crosswinds*, for alto saxophone and winds (1968); *Trobar clus*, for thirteen instruments (1970); Toccata, for harpsichord and tape (1971): *Soundings*, for eleven players and prerecorded tape, also for three orchestras and two conductors (1972); *Frailties*, for tenor, four-channel tape, and orchestra (1972); *Spring*River*Flowers*Moon*Night**, for two pianos and tape (1974): *Looking for Claudio*, for solo guitar and tape (1975); *Appello*, for solo piano (1975–76); *Musique pour un vernissage*, for flute, violin, viola, and guitar (1976–77); *Songs before an Adieu*, for flute doubling alto flute, guitar, and voice (1977–79); *Chromatic Fantasy*, for narrator, alto flute, oboe, soprano, saxophone, muted trumpet, electric guitar and vibraphone (1979); *Three Lullabies*, for solo guitar (1980); *The Point That Divides the Wind*, for organ and four percussionists (1981).

BIBLIOGRAPHY: *DCM; Classical Music* (London), June 30, 1979.

Korngold, Erich Wolfgang, b. Brünn, Austria, May 29, 1897; d. Hollywood, Calif., November 29, 1957. American citizen, 1943.

"I am and always will be an opera composer," Korngold said in the mid-1940s. "I think that's my fate." While an opera brought him international fame, he also produced symphonic literature and scores for Hollywood films with which screen music acquired an altogether new dimension through his music-dramatic and symphonic approaches. Despite the onrush of new idioms and techniques around him, Korngold remained throughout his career, and in whatever medium he chose, a child of German neoromanticism, walking in the footsteps of Wagner, Mahler, and particularly Richard Strauss.

He was the younger of two sons of Dr. Julius Korngold, one of Vienna's most influential music critics (*Neue Freie Presse*). Erich Wolfgang's precocity was so extraordinary that comparisons with the child Mozart were inevitable; he bore the name "Wolfgang" with honor. His father was his first teacher in piano; by the time Erich was five, he and his father were playing four-hand piano reductions of the classics. Subsequent teachers included Robert

Fuchs, Karl Weigl, Hermann Grädener, and Alexander Zemlinsky. Korngold was only ten when he played his cantata *Gold* for Mahler, who forthwith pronounced him to be a "genius" and arranged for him to study with Zemlinsky. He completed his Piano Sonata no. 1 when he was eleven, and it was published. At thirteen, his pantomime with music, *Der Schneemann* (1909), orchestrated by Zemlinsky, was given a command performance for Emperor Franz Josef at the Vienna Royal Opera on October 4, 1910, Franz Schalk conducting. It proved such a sensation that it was staged in forty Viennese and German opera houses. In 1910 he wrote a Piano Trio and his Piano Sonata no. 2, among other works. When the Piano Trio (which was published) received its first public performance in Vienna in the year of its composition, the pianist in the performing group was Bruno Walter. Artur Schnabel was so taken with the Piano Sonata no. 2 that he performed it all over Europe, and many years later could still speak of it as "a most amazing piece." When this sonata was introduced in London in 1910, one English critic wrote: "To pretend that Korngold is as learned as Reger or Richard Strauss is unnecessary, but in the matter of sheer invention, he is already their equal. His precocity is marvelous." Rudolph Ganz introduced this sonata to America in New York in 1912–13. More than half a century later, in 1975, when it was recorded, the distinguished concert and recording pianist Glenn Gould called it an "astonishingly mature work . . . the blueprint for what might well have been one of the better symphonic essays of its time." Its dramatic and pictorial writing as well as its skillful cyclic structure led a critic for *Stereo Review* to consider it "a . . . prophecy of his film style."

Upon becoming acquainted with young Korngold's first works for orchestra—*Schauspiel Ouverture* (1911) and Sinfonietta (1912)—Richard Strauss said: "One's first reaction that these compositions are by an adolescent boy are those of awe and fear; this firmness of style, this sovereignty of form, this individual expression, this harmonic structure . . . it is really amazing."

All these works, written in boyhood, were so sure in technique, so astutely contrived, and so appealing in melodic and harmonic interest that a rumor was circulated in Vienna that this may be the voice of the son but surely the hand is that of the father; also that his father's importance as a critic was responsible for the music of a mere boy being given such important performances by major artists. But all such rumors had no real basis in fact.

Under the spell of Richard Strauss's sensuality of harmonic, melodic, and instrumental writing, Korngold completed two one-act operas between 1915 and 1916. *Der Ring des Polykrates* was a comedy, and *Violanta* was a tragedy vivid with erotic implications. In 1957, Bruno Walter recalled: "The experience of hearing him [Korngold] play and sing for me the two one-act operas which I was going to perform at the Munich Opera House will remain unforgettable. One could have compared his interpretation of his works on the piano to the eruption of a musical dramatic volcano, if the lyric episodes and graceful moments had not also found their insinuating expression in his playing." Both operas were premiered at the Vienna Royal Opera on March 28, 1916. A decade later, on November 5, 1927, *Violanta* came to the United States at the Metropolitan Opera in New York.

During World War I, Korngold served in the Austrian army for two years. He was not engaged on the battle front, but was recruited to play the piano for military personnel. The first music Korngold wrote after leaving military service was the incidental music to *Much Ado about Nothing*, produced at Vienna's Burgtheater in 1919.

Between 1919 and 1922, Korngold was the conductor of the Hamburg Opera. This was when he completed the opera upon which his fame as composer achieved international proportions and fulfilled the high promises of his prodigy years: *Die tote Stadt*, given a dual premiere in Hamburg and Cologne on December 4, 1920, and a giant success in both theaters. Paul Schott's libretto, based on a Belgian novel by George S. Rodenbach, was concerned with a widower who, obsessed with memories of his dead wife, falls in love with a dancer who resembles her and whom he murders in one of the opera's dream sequences. Still in the image of Richard Strauss, with some additional traits of Wagner (even a quotation from *Die Walküre*), Puccini and Mahler, the score Korngold produced had searing dramatic impact, its lyric pages soaring over a consummately masterful orchestral background. One of its arias, "Marietta's Lied," or "Marietta's Lute Song," has become more famous in the concert hall than in the opera house. The success of the opera's premiere soon led to performances throughout Europe on some eighty different stages, and in less than a year it was brought to the Metropolitan Opera (November 19, 1921) in a performance in which Maria Jeritza made her American debut. In the *New York Times*, Richard Aldrich called it "the product of no mean talent in musical composition, of a real fertility of invention, of a genuine melodic gift, of a highly developed technical skill in the treatment of material, the laying out of the larger proportions, and the mastery of detail." *Die tote Stadt* was successfully revived many times including in Munich in 1956, in the Vienna Volksoper in 1967, and by the New York City Opera in 1975. It was also recorded in its entirety in Munich.

Korngold's next opera, *Das Wunder der Heliane* (1927; Hamburg, October 7, 1927), failed to approximate the success of *Die tote Stadt*. In the 1920s, Korngold also produced some concert music, but his primary efforts were directed in resuscitating, rescor-

ing, and getting produced operettas by Johann Strauss II, notably *A Night in Venice* in 1923 and *Cagliostro in Vienna* in 1925, and assembling a collection of little-known Strauss compositions for a new operetta called *Waltzes from Vienna* (which came to New York as *The Great Waltz* on September 22, 1934). In addition, in 1929, Korngold initiated a collaboration with the distinguished German stage director Max Reinhardt by providing music for some of his productions, one of which was a memorable revival of Johann Strauss's *Die Fledermaus*.

On April 30, 1924, Korngold married Luise von Sonnenthal; they raised two sons. In 1930, the president of Austria awarded him the honorary title of professor. From 1930 to 1934, Korngold taught opera, composition, and conducting at the Music Academy in Vienna.

Korngold first came to the United States late in 1934 at the invitation of Max Reinhardt to adapt Mendelssohn's music for Reinhardt's screen production of *A Midsummer Night's Dream*, released in 1935. This was the beginning of Korngold's career as a composer for the screen that lasted two decades. He contributed scores for nineteen more films, and won Oscars from the Academy of Motion Picture Arts and Sciences for *Anthony Adverse* (1936), *The Adventures of Robin Hood* (1938), and *The Sea Wolf* (1941). Korngold also wrote notable scores for *Captain Blood* (1935), *The Prince and the Pauper* (1937), *Juarez* (1939), *The Private Lives of Elizabeth and Essex* (1939), *The Sea Hawk* (1940), *King's Row* (1941), *The Constant Nymph* (1943), and *Deception* (1946). Regarding each motion picture as a libretto, Korngold brought to his screen assignments an operatic approach calling for the fullest resources of his dramatic and technical gifts in capturing every essential nuance of action, mood, and background as well as fulfilling the visual and transitional requirements of each film. In so doing, Korngold ushered in a new age for screen music, something well appreciated while he was working in Hollywood and even more so in 1972 and 1973 when, posthumously, two record albums of his best screen music were successfully released. Reviewing these recordings in *High Fidelity*, Royal S. Brown wrote: "Everything here is stamped not only with Korngold's totally distinct style but also with the period from which it grew. A great deal of Korngold's music is often bigger—intentionally so—than the film, for it is frequently the music that provided almost single-handedly the esthetic emotion that supplements the dramatic emotion. From this point of view, the warm, often sumptuous romanticism of Korngold's writing could not be more appropriate. The scores . . . abound in extraordinary lyrical richness." Korngold himself was fully appreciative of the high quality of his screen music. He lifted material from four motion picture scores (*Anthony Adverse*, *The Prince and the Pauper*, *The Private Lives of Eliz-*

abeth and Essex, and *Another Dawn*) for Concerto for Violin and Orchestra (1945), which Jascha Heifetz and the St. Louis Symphony introduced on February 15, 1947, and a musical episode for cello from *Deception* for his Concerto for Cello and Orchestra (1946).

Between his first visit to Hollywood and 1939, Korngold returned periodically to Vienna. He was frustrated in his efforts to get his new opera, *Die Käthrin* (1938), produced at the Vienna State Opera. It was mounted by the Royal Opera in Stockholm (and none too successfully) on October 7, 1939. The rising tide of nazism in Europe, combined with the need for a warmer climate for an ailing son, persuaded Korngold to abandon Austria and plant permanent roots in the United States, where he became a citizen. His home was in the Toluca Lake district of North Hollywood, which he left in 1942 and 1944 for New York to conduct operetta performances with the New Opera Company of New York.

His fame as composer of concert works and operas was now in a sharp delcine, first because he was identified most often as a commercial composer for motion pictures and also because the lush romanticism and sentiment of his lyricism and harmonic writing seemed an anachronism in a musical age of new sounds and new idioms.

His father's death in California in 1945 led Korngold to reevaluate his life in 1946. He decided to spend his remaining years working solely on concert music. He regarded his imminent fiftieth birthday as a "turning point," adding: "I look back on my life and I see three periods. First I was a prodigy, then a successful opera composer in Europe until Hitler, and then a movie composer. Fifty years is very old for a child prodigy. I feel I have to make a decision now, if I don't want to be a Hollywood composer for the rest of my life." In 1946 he turned down a lucrative new contract from Warner Brothers. After that he concentrated on writing his concertos for the cello and the violin, and a symphony (1950). The concertos had a negative response. Writing in the *New York Times*, Olin Downes referred to one of them as "a Hollywood concerto . . . commonplace in its thoughts. . . . The melodies are ordinary and sentimental in character; the facility of the writing is matched by the mediocrity of the ideas." The symphony had to wait fifteen years after Korngold's death to be heard, in Munich, Germany, on November 27, 1972, performed and later recorded by the Munich Philharmonic conducted by Rudolf Kempe.

Korngold's disappointments sent him back to Vienna in 1949 for a year of residence, but there, too—the scene of his early victories—he was a composer who had outlived his reputation. When *Die Käthrin* was finally given at the Vienna State Opera in 1950, it lasted six performances and was dropped.

Korngold suffered his first heart attack that year (1950). Six years later, now back in Hollywood, he was victimized by a stroke. His death in a Hollywood hospital came only a few hours after he had been seized by a second heart attack at his home.

PRINCIPAL WORKS: 3 string quartets (1922, 1935, 1945); 3 piano sonatas (1908, 1910, 1922).

Der Schneemann, pantomime with music (1909); Piano Trio (1910): *Fairy Pictures*, for piano (1910); *Schauspiel Ouverture* (1911); Violin Sonata (1912); Sinfonietta, for orchestra (1912); *Der Ring des Polykrates*, one-act opera (1915); *Violanta*, one-act opera (1916); Incidental music to *Much Ado about Nothing* (1918); *Sursum Corda*, symphonic overture (1919); *Die tote Stadt*, opera (1920): *Sinfonie Overture*, for orchestra (1921); Piano Quintet (1922); Concerto for Piano, Left Hand (1923); *Das Wunder der Heliane*, opera (1927); *Die Käthrin*, opera (1938); Four Shakespeare Songs, for voice and piano (1940); *Psalm*, for solo voice, chorus and orchestra (1941); Violin Concerto (1945); *Die stumme Serenade*, comedy with music (1946); Cello Concerto (1946); Five Songs, for voice and piano (1947); *Symphonic Serenade*, for string orchestra (1947); Symphony in F-sharp minor (1950); *Sonnet to Vienna*, for voice and piano (1952); Theme and Variations, for orchestra (1953).

BIBLIOGRAPHY: Carroll, B. G., "The Operas of Erich Wolfgang Korngold" (doctoral thesis, Liverpool, 1975); Korngold, L., *Erich Wolfgang Korngold* (Vienna, 1967); Thomas, Tony, *Music for the Movies* (Cranbury, N. J., 1973); *High Fidelity*, February 1973; *New York Times*, October 25, 1942, October 27, 1946, November 30, 1957 (obituary); *New Yorker*, April 14, 1975; *Dictionary of American Biography*, supplement 6.

Koutzen, Boris, b. Uman, Russia, April 1, 1901; d. Mt. Kisco, N.Y., December 10, 1966. American citizen, 1929.

In his music, Koutzen carried on the traditions of the Russian romantic school of the late 19th century. His writing was basically polyphonic. He was successful in realizing a spontaneous and direct emotional appeal. Some of his compositions were inspired by American history and folk music.

His father, Leo Koutzen, was a violinist who headed a music shcool in Uman. He was Boris's first violin teacher. As a child, Boris enjoyed improvising and playing music by ear. At six he was composing. One of these pieces, a waltz, was arranged by his father for band and was performed in the city park. The urge to create remained vital from then on. In 1910, the family moved to Cherrson, where his father became head of the violin department of the music school of the Imperial Music Society. There,

Boris continued to study the violin with his father. By the time he was eleven, Boris was able to make a public appearance with orchestra in a performance of the Mendelssohn Violin Concerto.

In 1918, the Koutzens established permanent residence in Moscow. A few weeks after their arrival, Boris Koutzen won a competition for the post of first violinist of the State Opera House Orchestra. He was also engaged for the violin section of the Koussevitzky Concerts conducted by Serge Koussevitzky. At the same time, between 1918 and 1922, he was a student at the Moscow Conservatory, where composition was studied with Reinhold Glière and violin with Leo Zetlin. "Glière's approach," Koutzen once recalled, was "most valuable in crystallizing the student's style, since he believed in uninhibited writing unrestricted by any theoretical consideration. He devoted much time to musical analysis rather than abiding by the rules derived by theoreticians." One of Koutzen's compositions, a string quartet, was performed at the conservatory. It made such a favorable impression on Ippolitov-Ivanov, one of the conservatory's renowned professors, he advised Koutzen to take a trip to Europe to expand his musical experiences. When the conservatory council passed a resolution giving Koutzen permission to leave the country, he left for Germany in 1922, spending a year and a half mostly in Berlin. He gave a violin recital, made some recordings, absorbed many new musical experiences, but did almost no composing.

He left Germany in 1923 for the United States, henceforth to be his permanent home and the land of his citizenship. Soon after his arrival, he joined the violin section of the Philadelphia Orchestra, with which he remained for five years. On June 3, 1924, he married Inez Merck, a professional pianist. Both their children became concert artists—George as cellist and Nadia as violinist. Between 1925 and 1962, Boris Koutzen was head of the violin department of the Philadelphia Conservatory.

His official debut as composer took place on April 1, 1927, when the Philadelphia Orchestra, under his own direction, presented the premiere of his *Poème-Nocturne, Solitude*, which was described by Samuel L. Laciar in the *Philadelphia Public Ledger* as "the work of a highly gifted musician."

Koutzen resigned from the Philadelphia Orchestra in 1928 to devote himself more fully to composition and to advance himself as a concert violinist through appearances in recitals. His most important composition up to that time, and one of his most successful, was his first with an American identification. It was a tone poem for orchestra, *Valley Forge* (1931), inspired by his visit to that historic place. His aim, as he explained, was not to "illustrate a sequence of historical events but to convey the impressions of one visiting Valley Forge today. As the panorama unfolds, majestic and serene, one's thoughts turn to the human drama of the past: to the unwavering fortitude shown in the face of every deprivation, to the

slow return of spiritual strength which turned the tide to victory and culminated in renewed courage and great rejoicing." *Valley Forge* had to wait nine years for performance, being introduced in New York by the National Orchestral Association under Leon Barzin on February 19, 1940. But it was subsequently given frequent hearings, principally by the Cleveland Orchestra and the NBC Symphony, and in 1944 it received the Juilliard Publication Award. Later works by Koutzen with American subjects were the concert overture *From the American Folklore* (1943), which the Pittsburgh Symphony Orchestra under William Steinberg introduced on April 5, 1957, and the String Quartet no. 3 (1944). In both, American folk songs provided not only basic materials but even the overall stylistic substances. "I sought to capture the atmosphere which the American legends, ballads, songs and so forth, create, for one who submits to their spell," Koutzen said.

Koutzen's New York debut as composer took place with his Piano Sonatina (1931), whose premiere was given in New York at a concert of the League of Composers on March 6, 1934. The Barrère-Salzedo-Britt Trio gave the initial hearing of Trio, for flute, cello, and harp (1933), on May 8, 1934, in New York, and on March 12, 1935, the National Orchestra Association under Barzin introduced the Concerto for Five Solo Instruments and String Orchestra (1934).

Between 1937 and 1945, Koutzen was a violinist with the NBC Symphony, Arturo Toscanini musical director. Koutzen served as associate professor of music at Vassar College in Poughkeepsie, N.Y., from 1944 to 1966, and from 1958 until his death he was the conductor of the Chappaqua Chamber Orchestra in Chappaqua, N.Y., which he had organized.

Awards came to him in 1944 for two compositions. For the String Quartet no. 2 (1936), which was heard at the Coolidge Festival in San Francisco, he received the Society for the Publication of American Music Award, and for Music for Saxophone, Bassoon and Cello (1940), he earned recognition from the American Composers Alliance and Broadcast Music, Inc. (BMI).

Important performances of subsequent works brought Koutzen further recognition. His Violin Concerto (1946) was first performed by the Philadelphia Orchestra under Eugene Ormandy, with Nadia Koutzen as soloist, on February 22, 1952; *Morning Music,* for flute and string orchestra (1948), was premiered at a concert of the New York Philharmonic on April 19, 1951; the Viola Concerto (1949) was introduced in New York on February 13, 1955; and a one-act opera, *The Fatal Oath*, which he had begun in 1938 but did not complete until 1955, received its world premiere in New York on May 25, 1955—libretto by the composer based on Balzac's *La grande Bretèche*. Reviewing the premiere of this opera in the *New York Times*, Howard Taubman wrote: "Mr. Koutzen employs what may be called an old-fashioned international style. He uses his orchestra for color and dramatic effect, and he does not hold up his story for set arias. . . . Give him credit . . . for being shrewd where theatrical values are concerned."

Koutzen suffered a heart attack after conducting a dress rehearsal concert of the Chappaqua Chamber Orchestra, and he died the next day.

THE COMPOSER SPEAKS: I have only one complex in composition, and that is to avoid having complexes. I am intensely interested in many new tendencies in musical thinking, but I am never impressed by abstract logic unrelated to the musical impressions new works produce on me as a listener. In my own quest for new paths, I am chiefly concerned with the realization of my musical ideas, believing that the idiom the composer chooses should be dictated by these ideas. Whatever complexities my works possess, these are merely the tonal base for each given work, but its effect on the listener must be that of spontaneous expression. My sin, however, is to create music of the greatest possible simplicity.

PRINCIPAL WORKS: 3 string quartets (1932, 1936, 1944), 2 violin sonatas (1929, 1951).

Poème-Nocturne, Solitude, for orchestra (1927); Piano Sonatina (1931); *Valley Forge,* tone poem for orchestra (1931); Trio, for flute, cello, and harp (1933): Concerto, for flute, clarinet, bassoon, horn and string orchestra (1934); Concerto for Five Solo Instruments and Orchestra (1939); Symphony in C (1939); Music for Saxophone, Bassoon and Cello (1940); Concert Piece, for cello and strings (1943): *Holiday Mood,* for violin and piano (1943); *From the American Folklore,* concert overture (1943): Sonata for Two Pianos (1944); *Duo concertante,* for violin and piano (1944); Violin Concerto (1946); Sinfonietta, for orchestra (1947); Piano Trio (1948); *An Invocation,* for women's voices and orchestra (1948); *Morning Music,* for flute and string orchestra (1948): Viola Concerto (1949); Sonata, for violin and cello (1952); *Eidolons,* poem for piano (1953); *Landscape and Dance,* for woodwind quintet (1953); *The Fatal Oath,* one-act opera (1938–54); Divertimento, for orchestra (1956); Concertino, for piano and string orchestra (1957); Rhapsody, for band (1959); *You Never Know,* one-act opera (1960); *Fanfare, Prayer, and March,* for orchestra (1961); *Elegiac Rhapsody,* for orchestra (1961); *Words of Cheer to Zion,* for chorus (1962): *Melody with Variations,* for violin or clarinet and piano (1964); Pastorale and Dance, for violin and piano (1964); Concertante, for two lutes and orchestra (1965); Music for Violin Alone (1966).

BIBLIOGRAPHY: Ewen, David, *American Composers Today* (N.Y., 1949); Howard, John Tasker, *Our Contemporary Composers* (N.Y., 1941): *New York Times,* December 12, 1966 (obituary); *Who's Who in America, 1966–67.*

Kraft, Leo, b. Brooklyn, N.Y., July 24, 1922.

After exploring the potentials of a tonal diatonic idiom, often with a strong American flavor, Kraft turned to a richer and more chromatic idiom. Since 1963 his chromatic language has remained his natural mode of expression. In addition, the electronic medium has added another dimension to his work.

Though neither of his parents was a professional musician, both were musical. His father had a small but select collection of operatic records, among the first music that young Kraft heard. His mother sang for many years in the choir of the Laurelton Jewish Center, as did Kraft in his teens. His early musical training consisted of piano lessons, which were intermittent. Later he was to study piano with Louise Kirschner, an experience he describes as having been of inestimable profit.

After graduating from Far Rockaway High School in Far Rockaway, N.Y., in 1940, Kraft entered Queens College, in Queens, N.Y. During the next five years his study of music—composition and theory specifically—began in earnest with Karol Rathaus, an all-important influence in his early development. Kraft was graduated from Queens College in 1945, with a bachelor of arts degree, *magna cum laude,* with a major in music. On May 16, 1945, he married Amy Lager, then a music student and later a psychologist; they raised two sons.

With the intention of pursuing advanced studies in composition, Kraft came to Princeton University in 1945. During the next two years he worked there with Randall Thompson. Kraft received his master of fine arts degree in 1947. That year Kraft joined the music faculty of Queens College, where he has remained ever since. He served as chairman of the department from 1959 to 1961 and has held the rank of full professor since 1973.

When he left graduate school, Kraft's music was involved partly with the American idiom associated with Aaron Copland and William Schuman and partly with elements of Igor Stravinsky and Paul Hindemith. It was written in a language of extended tonality, incorporating American rhythms. An early Overture, for orchestra (1947), received its premiere in Jamaica, N.Y., on March 19, 1949, and that same year was awarded the Queens College Golden Jubilee Prize. During the next few years his main works included the String Quartet no. 1 (1950; N.Y., February 19, 1951), a *Short Suite,* for flute, clarinet, and bassoon (1951; Queens, N.Y., May 23, 1952), a Concerto, for flute, clarinet, trumpet, and strings (1951; N.Y., March 28, 1954), and *A Proverb of Solomon,* for chorus and small orchestra (1953).

In 1954, Kraft was awarded a Fulbright Fellowship, which made it possible for him to spend a year of study in Paris with Nadia Boulanger.

The culmination of a period in Kraft's creative growth, which had begun with his graduate student days, came in 1958 with Partita no. 1, for piano, and Variations for Orchestra. The Variations were built on a broad theme in four phrases, successively stated by strings, by winds, by brass with a violin counter-melody, and finally by brass and strings answering each other. Six variations followed, sometimes with new ideas starting the variations and sometimes with new ideas combined with the material from the basic theme. Variations for Orchestra was introduced by the Cincinnati Symphony under Max Rudolf on December 10, 1960. Successive reworkings of the piece led to a revised version performed for the first time on October 26, 1975, in Great Neck, N.Y.

After the completion of the Partita and the Variations for Orchestra Kraft began to feel the limitations of the rather straightforward musical language he had adopted in the 1940s. Attracted by the wealth of resources he had gradually discovered, and particularly impressed with the music of Elliott Carter, Kraft began to work out a musical language with greater expressive potential. The key work in this transition was the String Quartet no. 2 (1959; N.Y., March 25, 1961). Chromaticism continued to be a basis of Kraft's style in several works that followed, notably, Three Pieces for Orchestra (1963), which was introduced by the Cincinnati Symphony under Max Rudolf on May 8, 1965; Trios and Interludes, for flute, viola, and piano (1965) and Concerto no. 2, for thirteen players (1966); as well as for numerous later compositions.

In 1967, Kraft spent a semester at Columbia University studying electronic music with Vladimir Ussachevsky. His interest in electronic music dates from that time. Kraft's concern is to combine live and electronic sounds, contrasting the essential character of each and yet letting each influence the other. The first such work was *Eyre and Yse*, for chorus and tape (1967). Later works include *Dialogues*, for flute and tape (1968; N.Y., March 9, 1968) and *Antiphonies*, for piano four hands and tape (1971; N.Y., October 22, 1971).

Among Kraft's subsequent significant works are the following: *Line Drawings*, for flute and percussion (1972; N.Y., January 7, 1973), which Donal Henahan in the *New York Times* described as "a five-movement piece marked by mercurial flights of witty sustained dialogue"; Eight Choral Songs to texts by Moses Ibn Ezra, its world premiere taking place at a concert of the League of Composers–International Society of Contemporary Music in Carnegie Hall, N.Y., on February 10, 1977; *Diaphonies*, for oboe and piano (1975; N.Y., March 24, 1976); Partita no. 4, for violin, double bass, flute, clarinet, and piano (1975; Boston, Mass., May 10, 1977); *Dialectica*, for flute, clarinet, violin, cello, and tape (1976; Baltimore, Md., January 30, 1977), commissioned by the Chamber Music Society and written on a grant from the National Endowment for the Arts,

which, as the composer explains, is a musical argument among the four musicians not only soloistically and in various instrumental combinations but also in violent discourse with the sounds on the tape; and the Concerto for Piano and Fourteen Instruments (1978; N.Y., May 6, 1979).

In addition to his post at Queens College, Kraft was a member of the music faculty at the Cantor's Institute of New York (1962–66). He has served as president of the American Music Center (1976–78), vice-president of the College Music Society (1970–72), and a member of the board of directors of the International Society for Contemporary Music (1973–78). He is the author of *A New Approach to Ear Training* (1967) and *Gradus: An Integrated Approach to Harmony, Counterpoint, and Analysis* (1976). In collaboration with Sol Berkowitz and C. Frontrier he wrote *A New Approach to Sight Singing* (1960), and in collaboration with Allen Brings and others, *A New Approach to Keyboard Harmony* (1979).

THE COMPOSER SPEAKS: I think that we live in a very exciting and variegated musical era. Out of the enormous number of possibilities available I have chosen to follow a certain line of development growing out of earlier 20th-century practices that appeal to me. I keep my ear and mind open to what's new in music and keep trying to incorporate new acquisitions into my stream of musical thought. It is pointless to be overly concerned about the artistic value of one's own work, either in the eyes of the present audience or from the viewpoint of some imaginary future audience. The point is to do today's job as well as possible.

PRINCIPAL WORKS: 3 string quartets (1950, 1959, 1966).

Concerto no. 1, for flute, clarinet, trumpet, and strings (1951); *A Proverb of Solomon*, for chorus and small orchestra (1953); Variations for Orchestra (1958); Partita no. 1, for piano (1958); Partita no. 2, for violin and viola (1961); *When Israel Came Forth*, Psalm 114, for chorus (1961); *Four English Love Songs*, for voice and piano (1961); Five Pieces, for clarinet and piano (1962); Fantasy, for flute and piano (1963); Partita no. 3, for wind quintet (1964); *Statements and Commentaries*, for piano (1965); Trios and Interludes, for flute, viola and piano (1965); Concerto no. 2, for thirteen players (1966); *Dialogues*, for flute and tape (1968); Concerto no. 3, for cello, wind quintet, and percussion (1968); Harpsichord Sonata (1968); *Spring in the Harbor*, chamber cycle for soprano, flute, cello, and piano (1969); *Dualities*, for two trumpets (1970); *Sestina*, for piano (1971); *Antiphonies*, for piano four hands and tape (1971); *Line Drawings*, for flute and percussion (1972); Eight Choral Songs, for chorus (1974); *Diaphonies*, for oboe and piano (1975); Ten Short Pieces, for piano (1976); *Dialectica*, for flute, clarinet, violin, cello, and tape (1976); *Toccata giocosa*, for clarinet, cello, percussion, and piano (1976); Three Pieces, for saxophone and piano (1978); Concerto for Piano and Fourteen Instruments (1978); *Strata*, for eight instruments (1979); *Conductus Novum*, or *The Revenge of Perotinus*, for trombone quartet (1979).

BIBLIOGRAPHY: *BBDM; DCM; Who's Who in America, 1980–81.*

Kraft, William, b. Chicago, September 6, 1923.

Among the avant-gardists who have been attracted to percussion music, Kraft is the only one who has spent many years as a percussionist with a major symphony orchestra. His performing experiences have helped him to uncover new sounds, timbres, and effects, thereby broadening the horizon of percussion music.

When he was three his family moved to San Diego, where, while attending Grant Elementary School, he received his first lessons in music: piano lessons with a Mrs. Palmer begun when he was five. Piano lessons were continued in Los Angeles in the early 1930s with Vera Heifetz, and in the latter part of the 1930s in San Diego with Arthur Frazer; at the same time Kraft began studying drums with Myron Collins. Between 1938 and 1943, Kraft played piano and drums and made arrangements for various jazz groups.

In 1941, Kraft graduated from San Diego High School. For one year he attended the San Diego State College, and in the fall of 1942 he enrolled at the University of California in Los Angeles, when he also studied drums with Murray Spivack. Drafted into the army in 1943, during World War II, Kraft served as pianist, percussionist, and arranger for various air force bands in the United States, France, and Germany. While still in service, he attended Cambridge University in England for courses in musical theory and score reading, the latter with Boris Orr. Released from military duty in 1946, Kraft earned his living playing piano and drums with jazz groups. At the same time he continued to study drums with Spivack while taking lessons in composition from Charles Marsh and orchestration from Arthur Lange.

Attendance at the Berkshire Music Center at Tanglewood, Mass., during the summer of 1948, changed the course of his life. Studying composition informally with Irving Fine, auditing the conducting class of Leonard Bernstein, and playing the timpani in the opera orchestra convinced him that from this point on he must devote himself to serious musical endeavors solely. Realizing that still more intensive study was essential, he entered Brooklyn College, in Brooklyn, N.Y., that fall, at the same time studying percussion with Morris Goldenberg. The following spring he transferred to Columbia University, there

to supplement his academic curriculum with classes in composition with Henry Cowell, Normand Lockwood, Jack Beeson, and Otto Luening, as well as in orchestration, conducting, harmony, counterpoint, music history, and aesthetics. In 1949–50 he received further instruction in percussion from Goldenberg and studied timpani with Saul Goodman. As a Columbia undergraduate, Kraft organized the Columbia Chamber Concerts to perform compositions of university students; served as an extra percussionist with the Metropolitan Opera orchestra; and, during the summers, was percussionist for the San Diego Summer Symphony.

In 1951, Kraft graduated with a bachelor of arts degree, *cum laude*. On June 6, 1951, he and Betty Lou Fox were married. They made their home in New York City and within the next decade had two sons. Upon receiving his bachelor's degree, Kraft went on to graduate school at Columbia, twice under the Anton Seidl Fellowship, earning his master of arts degree in 1955. During the first half of that year he conducted the orchestra for *Ondine*, a stage play by Jean Giraudoux with incidental music by Virgil Thomson, which opened on Broadway on February 16, 1954.

In 1954, Kraft was appointed percussionist for the Dallas Symphony. This was the dawn of a long and successful career as symphony orchestra percussionist and timpanist. In the fall of 1955, he assumed a similar post with the Los Angeles Philharmonic, moving on to the timpani in 1963 when Zubin Mehta became musical director, and in 1968 was made Mehta's assistant conductor. While fulfilling his duties with the Los Angeles Philharmonic, Kraft organized the First Percussion Quartet in 1956, which, within a few years, became the Los Angeles Percussion Ensemble. Since its beginnings, Kraft functioned regularly as performer and conductor of its Monday Evening Concerts until 1970, when he restricted himself exclusively to conducting.

Kraft looks upon his Theme and Variations for Percussion Quartet (1956), in which four players perform on twenty-seven instruments, as the true beginnings of his visible career as a composer; it was premiered by the percussion section of the Los Angeles Philharmonic at one of its youth concerts during the 1956–57 season. This was the first of a number of works for percussion completed in 1958. Among others were: Suite for Percussion (Los Angeles, November 6, 1961); Nonet, for brass and percussion (Los Angeles, October 13, 1958); *Three Miniatures*, for percussion and orchestra (Los Angeles, February 14, 1959). Here his rhythmic writing was virtuosic in its intricacy and variety while a gift for effective colorations and unusual sonorities was already in evidence. In the Nonet and the *Three Miniatures*, Kraft combined his creativity in writing for percussion with the twelve-tone technique, to which he remained partial in many of his later works.

With two compositions in the early 1960s, Kraft reached back to the baroque era. One was Concerto Grosso (1961; San Diego, March 22, 1963). Here, for his *concertino*, Kraft selected the violin, flute, cello, and bassoon. All the material was derived from a thematic statement in a modified row presented by the *concertino* in the opening measures. The second baroque work was *French Suite*, for solo unaccompanied percussion (1962), modeled after the keyboard *French Suites* of Johann Sebastian Bach. However, Kraft's Concerto Grosso departs from the baroque keyboard suite by using "multiple percussion" as a solo instrument—in this instance the "multiple percussion" being low tenor drum, field drum, low and high snare drums, low and high bongos, and low and high suspended cymbals.

Jazz references are found in Concerto for Four Percussion Soloists and Orchestra (1964), written in memory of Edgard Varèse; its world premiere was given by the Los Angeles Philharmonic under Zubin Mehta on March 10, 1966. Jazz appears even more prominently in *Configurations* (1966) and *Contextures* (1967). The first is a concerto for four percussion players and a jazz orchestra in which jazz becomes an equal partner to symphonic music (Los Angeles, December 13, 1966). *Contextures*, subtitled "Riots—Decade '60," is a multimedia composition commissioned by the Los Angeles Philharmonic. It was introduced by that orchestra under Zubin Mehta on April 4, 1968. On October 23, 1980, the Chicago Symphony presented it under Henry Mazer's direction. In this work, the composer depicted "the correspondence between the fabric of music and the fabric of society," as he himself has written, in which "social aspects are translated into musical techniques." The first movement called for a color film which projected abstract patterns interrupted by stills of the summer riots in American cities in 1967 on a large screen to the rear of the stage. The fourth and fifth movements utilized a film of Reginald Pollack's paintings on segregation, violence, and other social problems of the mid-1960s. A solo violin and snare drum presented a jazz interlude at the end of the first movement, and an offstage quartet was heard at the close of the entire work.

Since 1966 Kraft has produced several compositions bearing the collective title of *Collage*. The first two *Collages* are called *Games*. The first Game, *Collage* I (1969), was scored for an orchestra of twenty-six players divided into two antiphonal groups of thirteen each and consisted of eight "games." One was a game of chance in which each percussionist had a large variety of cells playable in any order. In another game, the conductor chose the time to begin the game. Game five was chess, and game eight, poker. Commissioned by the Encounters Committee to celebrate the opening of the Pasadena Art Museum, *Games: Collage* I was for wind orchestra and four percussion (1969). *Tintinnabulations: Collage* III (1974), however, dispensed with the game concept.

Though scored for full orchestra, it was intended to explore the characteristics of bells and the sensations aroused when one is surrounded by a world of bells.

On a Guggenheim Fellowship in 1968, Kraft completed *Triangles*, a concerto for percussion and ten instruments, introduced in Los Angeles in 1969. The title *Triangles* comes from the fact that percussion instruments were arranged in two triangles facing each other, to the left of the conductor, and a third percussion group, also in a triangle, to the conductor's right. The accompanying instruments were also placed in triangles—the winds and brass to the conductor's left and the strings to the right.

Between 1966 and 1978, Kraft completed eight instrumental works entitled *Encounters*. Each was intended to demonstrate how a traditional instrument can be treated in a novel sonic way: where a solo instrument is juxtaposed with a tape recording or percussion, the two parts are thoroughly integrated rather than having the tape or percussion serve as a background. *Encounters* III and IV (1971, 1972) each gave a descriptive account, with some humorous intent, of certain tenets of war (Strategy, Truce of God—a medieval practice—and Tactics). *Encounter* III was subtitled "duel" for trumpet and percussion, and *Encounter* IV was a "duel" for trombone and percussion. *Encounter* VII (1977-78)—in opposition to *Encounters* III and IV with their war orientation—was a nonvocal work utilizing antiwar poems as text. Each of the five sections, except for the opening, began by quoting in Morse code the first words of a specific poem before progressing to its musical setting. The Morse code was woven into the musical fabric as a parameter.

A major work that does not concern itself primarily with percussion is the Concerto for Piano and Orchestra (1972-73; Los Angeles, November 21, 1973), written on a commission from the pianist Mona Golabek on a grant from the Ford Foundation. Kraft explains that this music was based "largely on timbres as well as being what I call lyrical. I don't mean lyrical in the 19th-century melodic sense, but lyrical in the sense of being expressive." He also explains that his aim was "to tie the medium of the piano concerto in with the nature of 20th-century music, as well as to tie it in with the nature of *my* music . . . [and] to explore the bottom and top registers of the piano."

In commemoration of the American bicentennial, and on a commission from the Los Angeles Master Chorale, Kraft completed the writing of *The Innocents: The Witch Trial at Salem* (1976), text by Barbara Kraft. Since the Los Angeles Master Chorale did not get to perform it, due to a dispute over the funding of copying costs, this work was first given by the West Coast Division of the International Society for Contemporary Music on October 18, 1976. It was scored for four vocal quartets, mixed chorus, four percussion, and a harmonium (or celesta), with the four vocal quartets designated as "The Afflicted," "Magistrates," "Clergy," and "The Accused," and the chorus as the "Populace."

Andirivieni, a Concerto for tuba with three chamber groups and orchestra (1977; Los Angeles, January 26, 1978)—written on a grant from the National Endowment for the Arts on a commission from Zubin Mehta for his last season with the Los Angeles Philharmonic—was the composer's attempt to expand and extend his *Encounters* II (for solo tuba) into a concerto. "I became fascinated by the possibility of creating a musical structure wherein the character of the tuba would constantly change through interreactions and other instruments would come and go," Kraft explains. "Thus the structure of *Andirivieni*, which means 'coming and going.'"

Kraft and Betty Lou were divorced in 1959, and on June 15, 1960, he married Barbara Lenore Schauerte, with whom he had a daughter; they were divorced in 1979.

Kraft received a second Guggenheim Fellowship in 1972 and a Rockefeller Foundation scholarship for residency in Italy in June 1973. He has been a member of the music faculty at the University of Southern California since 1963: lecturer in percussion (1963–65 and 1967–68), instructor in percussion for individuals (1966–67), and visiting professor in composition (1977–78). He has also been composer and conductor-in-residence at Redlands University in California (1972) and the University of North Carolina in Greensboro (1975). He is a member of the board of directors of the American Music Center and chairman of the International Society for Contemporary Music, West Coast Chapter.

In 1981, the Los Angeles Philharmonic appointed Kraft composer-in-residence, coordinator of all contemporary-music activities, and, by having him present lecture-demonstrations, the orchestra's contemporary music ambassador to the city. He is also called upon to screen and audition contemporary works for possible performance by that orchestra. Kraft also directed the premiere season of the New Music Group in Los Angeles in 1981–82.

THE COMPOSER SPEAKS: Character is perhaps the most important term to me. It establishes the identity of a piece and its composer. Within its world are the elements of construction, idea-concept-purpose, idiom, technique and personality—all of which should be fundamental, consistent, and all pervasive, yet subservient to the whole. It matters little to me whether the composer approaches each piece as an end in itself or as a part of a large all-embracing vision.

PRINCIPAL WORKS: Theme and Variations for Percussion Quartet (1956); Suite for Percussion (1958); *Three Miniatures*, for percussion and orchestra (1958); Nonet, for brass and percussion (1958); Concerto Grosso (1961); *American Carnival Overture* (1962); *French Suite*, for solo unaccompanied percussion (1962); Concerto for Four Percussion Soloists and Orchestra (1964); Double Trio, for piano, prepared piano, amplified guitar, tuba, and two percussion (1965); *Mobiles*, for three different groups of instruments (1965); *Configurations:* Concerto for Four Percussion Soloists with Jazz Orchestra (1966); *Momentum*, for percussion (1966); *Encounters* II, for solo tuba (1966); *Morris Dance*, for percussion (1967); *Contextures:* "Riots—Decade '60," a multimedia production (1967); *Games: Collage* I, for eight horns, six trumpets, six trombones, two tubas, and four percussion (1969); *Games: Collage* II, for wind orchestra and voices (1970); *Cadenze* I, for flute, oboe, clarinet, horn, violin, and viola (1971); *Encounters* III, "duel" for trumpet and percussion (1971); *Encounters* IV, "duel" for trombone and percussion (1972); Piano Concerto (1972–73); *In Memoriam Igor Stravinsky*, for violin and piano (1972–74); *Tintinnabulations: Collage* III, for orchestra (1974); *Due Imagistes*, for six percussion and a reciter (1974); *Requiescat*, for piano (1975); *Encounters* I, for solo percussion and magnetic tape (1975); *Encounters* V: "Homage to Scriabin," for cello and percussion (1975); *Encounters* VI: Concertino for Roto-toms and Percussion Quartet (1976); *The Innocents: The Witch Trial at Salem*, for four vocal octets, mixed chorus, four percussion and harmonium or celesta (1976); *Dream Tunnel*, for narrator and small orchestra (1976); *Andirivieni*, concerto for tuba, three chamber groups, and orchestra (1977); *Ombra*, for piano (1977); *Encounters* VII, for two percussion (1977–78); *Encounters* VIII, for solo percussion (1978); *Luminescences*, for piano (1979); *The Sublime and the Beautiful*, for tenor and six players (1980); *Dialogues and Entertainments*, for wind ensemble (1980).

BIBLIOGRAPHY: *BBDM; DCM; Chicago Symphony Program Notes*, October 23, 1980.

Krenek, Ernst, b. Vienna, Austria, August 23, 1900. American citizen, 1945.

During the more than six decades of Krenek's creativity, which produced over two hundred and twenty-five compositions in virtually every form, his style has undergone numerous transformations. His works since the early 1920s up to the present time represent a veritable cross-section of 20th-century music. But almost from his beginnings he was the constant seeker of wider horizons; and always he has been the consummate craftsman in full command of every style he adopted.

Son of an Austrian army officer, Krenek revealed signs of creativity when he was five by composing little melodies. He began receiving instruction at the piano when he was six. Between 1911 and 1919 he attended gymnasium (high school). In 1916, he entered the Vienna Academy of Music, where for the next four years he was Franz Schreker's pupil in composition. At the same time he attended the University of Vienna for the study of philosophy, history of music and art (1919–21). As Schreker's student, Krenek wrote several works, among which was a Double Fugue, for piano (1918), his Violin Sonata no. 1 (1919) and his Piano Sonata no. 1 (1919), in which an ardor, "in the exalted romantic style of my teacher, Franz Schreker," was combined with elements of Max Reger's contrapuntal mannerisms.

In 1918, during World War I, Krenek was called into military service in the artillery with the Austrian army. After the war, when Schreker left Vienna in 1920 to become director of the Academy of Music in Berlin, Krenek followed him there, remaining his pupil for another three years. He was becoming increasingly productive, writing in that time his first three symphonies (1921, 1922, 1922), his first three string quartets (1921, 1921, 1922), *Symphonic Music*, for nine instruments (1922), his Piano Concerto no. 1 (1923), and two operas. *Symphonic Music* was introduced at the Donaueschingen Festival on July 10, 1922. His first two operas were *Die Zwingburg*, in one act, to a text by Franz Werfel (1922), and a three-act comedy, *Der Sprung der Schatten* (1923), text by the composer, in which he made his first attempt to introduce a quasi-jazz idiom into his writing. The former opera was produced in Berlin on October 26, 1924, and the latter, in Frankfurt on June 19, 1924. What these works reveal is a breaking away from the neoromanticism to which he had thus far been addicted. Having come in Berlin into personal contact with some of its progressive musicians (Busoni, Artur Schnabel, and Herman Scherchen, among others), Krenek was finding and exploring new paths through atonality.

In 1918, he married Anna Mahler, daughter of the composer Gustav Mahler, but they were divorced two years later. Between late in 1923 and 1925, Krenek resided in Zurich, Switzerland, from where he embarked on visits to France and Italy. Now become interested in Stravinsky and Milhaud, Krenek began seeking in his own music a more abstract style within a neoclassical framework. This tendency first became discernible in Concerto Grosso no. 2, for orchestra (1924–25); Symphony, for brass and percussion (1924–25); and Five Pieces, for piano (1925).

Between 1925 and 1927 Krenek was the assistant to Paul Bekker, first at the State Theater at Cassel and then in Wiesbaden, both in Germany, serving as coach, conductor, and at times as composer of incidental music for several productions. This affiliation intensified his interest in the musical theater. At this time, he wrote *Orpheus und Eurydike* (1923), an atonal opera to an expressionist text by Oskar Kokoschka. It was produced in Cassel on November 27, 1926.

In 1926, Krenek completed a satirical opera to his own text, utilizing a racy subject for his libretto and a score spiced with pseudo-jazz idioms, one of the ear-

liest European operas to employ jazz. He called it *Jonny spielt auf*, his aim, as he said, being to interpret the rhythms and atmosphere of modern life in an age of technical science. Jonny was a Negro violinist-bandleader who gets involved with white women and ends up bestriding the globe of the world playing a jazz tune as the people around him dance corybantically to its infectious rhythms. Introduced in Leipzig on February 10, 1927, it proved such a sensation that within a few years of the premiere it was produced in more than a hundred European theaters and was translated into eighteen languages. A year and a half after its premiere, it was introduced to the United States at the Metropolitan Opera House on January 19, 1929. At that time, W. J. Henderson, in the *New York Sun*, referred to it as "a pretty good musical comedy with some outstanding moments," adding: "Krenek does not confine his burlesque attacks to opera; all conventions of music are his target. . . . The grand opera music is frequently dissonant in the approved style of the day and there are some peppery instrumental combinations." *Jonny spielt auf* was first sung in English when it was revived for the first time since 1929 in a concert performance in Boston in May 1978.

Made financially secure by the success of *Jonny spielt auf*, Krenek was now able to devote himself exclusively to composition. In 1928, he married Berta Hermann, an actress, settling in Vienna, his home for the next decade. There, in 1930, he became a contributor to the *Frankfurter Zeitung*, and later *Wiener Zeitung*. He combined literary efforts with lectures and appearances as accompanist in recitals of his songs, in addition to composing.

The city of Franz Schubert's birth initially inspired in Krenek a return to early 19th-century romanticism. In that style, he wrote the opera *Leben des Orest* (1928–29), a modern-day adaptation by the composer of the Greek legend in which jazz appears in a work of his for the last time. It was produced in Leipzig on January 19, 1930, and its American premiere came on November 14, 1975, in Portland, Oreg. Romantic, too, are the String Quartet no. 5 (1930) and the song cycle for voice and piano *Reisebuch aus den Österreichischen Alpen* (1929–30), modeled after Schubert's *Die Winterreise*.

But Vienna soon affected Krenek's music in quite a different way. Krenek, the onetime atonalist, was drawn into the circle of the Viennese school of twelve-tone composers. The twelve-tone idiom of Schoenberg and Webern now led Krenek to reject romanticism for musical expressionism. The transition from romanticism to the twelve-tone system was made with the song cycle *Gesänge des späten Jahres*, for voice and piano (1931). His first completely twelve-tone work was the opera *Karl V* (1930–33), with a historical text by the composer in which the hero tries to justify his past deeds before the tribunal of the Lord. It was commissioned by the Vienna State Opera, which removed it soon after it had gone into rehearsal due to Nazi influence, which had already penetrated the opera house. It was finally staged in Prague on June 15, 1938. After that, for the next quarter of a century, Krenek continued using the twelve-tone idiom extensively but not exclusively. Works like the Piano Concerto no. 3 (1946; Minneapolis, Minn., November 22, 1946) and Symphony no. 5 (1949; Albuquerque, N.M., March 16, 1950), for example, are basically atonal rather than twelve-tonal.

Krenek paid his first visit to the United States in 1937 as a member of the touring Salzburg Opera Guild. After the Nazi invasion of Austria, Krenek (though an Aryan) felt he could return to that country no longer. In 1938 he found a new home in the United States, becoming a citizen. He initiated his American career as educator by serving as professor of music at Vassar College in Poughkeepsie, N.Y. (1939–42). From 1942 to 1947 he was head of the department of music and later, dean, at Hamline University in St. Paul, Minn. During those and subsequent years he made numerous appearances as lecturer or visiting professor at universities and colleges throughout the United States, including the universities of Michigan, Wisconsin, and New Mexico, the University of California in Los Angeles, and the Chicago Musical College. In addition, he made numerous tours as conductor-pianist, one such on April 1, 1947, in an all-Krenek program at the University of Chicago.

In 1947, Krenek planted his roots in southern California, initially in Los Angeles, ultimately in Palm Springs. In August 1950 he married Gladys Nordenstorm, an American composer born in Minnesota. American experiences, settings, and subjects provided him with fresh material for some of his compositions. *I Wonder As I Wander*, for orchestra (1942), was a series of seven variations on a North Carolina folk song of the same name which he had heard in a recording by John Jacob Niles. "I wanted," Krenek said, "to unfold the feeling of tragic loneliness and passionate devotion by which the solitary wanderer 'under the sky' is animated." It received its world premiere on December 11, 1942, Dimitri Mitropoulos conducting the Minneapolis Symphony. *The Santa Fe Time Table*, for a cappella chorus (1945), set a text enumerating the railroad stops between Albuquerque and Los Angeles. The opera *Dark Waters* (1950; Los Angeles, May 2, 1951) had for its setting a river barge in southern California waters. *Scenes from the West*, "four impressions for high school orchestra" (1952–53), were tone pictures of "Pageant in Paso Robles," "Hermosa Hills," "Moon Over Monterey," and "Fresno Ferris Wheel." *Der goldene Bock* (1963–64; Hamburg, June 16, 1964), a "fantastic opera," placed the legendary story of the Argonauts partly in America by having Jason recover the Golden Fleece from the American Indian on Route 66.

In one of his first major works written in the United States, the *Lamentatio Jeremiae Prophetae*, for chorus (1941), Krenek indulged in his interest in musicomathematics. In subsequent works—Piano Sonata no. 4 (1948) and in a varied form in the *Sestina* (1957)—he evolved the "principle of rotation," which he would use in several subsequent works. This principle, Charles Boone explains, "provides for the formation of serial variants through the systematic change of the pitches of a given series with their adjacent pitches. An example using a numerical series is: given series 1-2-3-4-5-6-4; first rotation,1-3-2-5-4-6; second rotation, 3-1-5-2-6; and so forth." This principle is pursued successfully in the String Quartet no. 7 (1943); *Pentagram*, for woodwind quintet (1952); and *Spiritus Intelligentiae Sanctus* (1956). Krenek's first works to employ electronic means were *Kette, Kreis, und Spiegel*, tone poem for orchestra (1957), and *Fibonacci-Mobile*, for string quartet, two pianos, and "coordinator" (1965; Hanover, N.H., July 7, 1965).

By 1957, with *Sestina*, for voice and instrumental ensemble, introduced in New York on March 3, 1958, and set to one of Krenek's poems, he passed on to serialism. "Its instrumental writing," reported Howard Taubman in the *New York Times*, "is almost as fragmented as Anton Webern's. . . . In its strange and eerie timbres, its ejaculations of sound and its weird vocal line with its wide skips, it manages to hold the attention firmly. . . . It has evocative force." From the mid-1960s on, Krenek modified his use of serialism to allow for greater freedom of technique and expressivity and for improvisatory passages. On occasion, he also exploited the resources of electronics. He has remained prolific through the years. His later works include the comic opera *Sardakai* (1969–70; Hamburg, June 27, 1970) and a TV play entitled *Bottled Message from Paradise* (1973), both to Krenek's texts using the fictitious island of Migo-Migo as setting; the *Anniversary Cantata*, for speaker, two soloists, chorus, and orchestra (1974–75)—text by Krenek with interpolations of quotations by other writers—written for and introduced at the Berlin Festival in September 1975; *They Knew What They Wanted*, a setting of three English stories, for narrator, oboe, piano, percussion, and electronic tape (1977), introduced in New York in November 1978; and *The Dissembler*, a monologue for baritone and chamber orchestra with Krenek's own text (1978), commissioned and introduced by the Chamber Music Society of Baltimore on March 11, 1979.

Krenek was awarded the Prize of the City of Vienna (1955), the Great Austrian State Prize (1963), the Order of Merit for Science and Art from Austria (1975), and the Goethe Plaque from Hessen, Germany (1978). He also received the Cross of Merit from the Federal Republic of Germany. He was appointed an honorary citizen of Minnesota (1965) and he has received honorary doctorates in music from Hamline University in St. Paul, Minn. (1944), the

University of Mexico (1965), and the New England Conservatory in Boston (1976) among others. His seventy-fifth birthday was commemorated with a week-long festival of his works at Palm Springs, Calif., and in Minneapolis/St. Paul, Minn. In April 1979, an eight-day Krenek festival, comprising a dozen concerts, lectures by eminent scholars, and an exhibition of Krenek paintings, photographs, manuscripts, and memorabilia was held in Santa Barbara, Calif. The compositions heard spanned nearly six decades, from his 1921 String Quartet no. 1 to his 1978 *The Dissembler*. A Krenek archive was established at the University of California in San Diego in 1977.

Krenek's literary output embraces not only libretti for his operas, texts for vocal works and music criticism, but also poetry, drama, and sundry essays. He is the author of such books as *Music, Here and Now* (1939), *Studies in Counterpoint* (1940), *Self-Analysis* (1948), *Exploring Music* (1966), and *Horizons Circle* (1974). *Self-Analysis* is only a portion of an autobiography Krenek completed in 1950. He deposited the manuscript in the Library of Congress in Washington, D.C., with the instruction that it not be made public until fifteen years after his death.

THE COMPOSER SPEAKS: Looking back over the evolution of my musical style, I am not astonished that even benevolent observers became confused and vacillating in their faith. Whenever they thought I had comfortably settled down in some stylistic district I was not at the expected place the next time, and the business of classifying had to start all over again.

My apparently aimless meandering through the styles was explained handsomely by some of my critics as unscrupulous opportunism. Plausible as it seems, this interpretation takes in no account the small detail that I seemed to embrace almost each of these styles just when it was utterly impractical to do so, as seen from worldly viewpoints. If I should venture an explanation myself (whatever such a subjective view may be worth) I would say that I have been striving at an ever freer and more incisive articulation of musical thought. Liberation of this thought from harmonic conventions and rhythmic patterns, preparation of a new, genuinely polyphonic way of thinking which makes full and conscious use of the tremendous experience of tonality appear to me as guiding factors in my present endeavors.

PRINCIPAL WORKS: 7 string quartets (1921–44); 6 piano sonatas (1919–51); 5 sonatinas, for piano (1920); 5 symphonies (1921–49); 4 piano concertos (1923–50); 2 concerti grossi (1921); 2 suites, for piano (1924); 2 violin concertos (1924, 1954); 2 sonatas for solo violin (1925, 1942).

Orpheus und Eurydike, opera (1923); Suite, for clarinet and piano (1924); Concertino, for flute, violin, harpsichord and string orchestra (1924); Symphonie, for brass and percussion (1924–25); Five Pieces, for piano (1925); *Jonny spielt auf*, opera (1925–26); *Three Lively Marches*, for orchestra (1926); *Potpourri*, for orchestra (1927); *Kleine Symphonie*, for orchestra (1928); *Leben des Orest*, opera (1928–29); *Reisebuch aus den Österreichischen Alpen*, song cycle for voice and piano (1929); *Karl V*, opera (1930–33); Theme and Variations, for orchestra (1931); *Little Music*, for wind orchestra (1931); *Eight Column Line*, ballet (1939); Symphonic Piece, for string orchestra (1939); *Little Concerto*, for piano and organ with chorus and orchestra (1940); *Tarquin*, opera (1940); *Lamentatio Jeremiae Prophetae*, for chorus (1941); Sonatina, for flute and viola (1942); *I Wonder As I Wander*, for orchestra (1942); *Hurricane Variations*, for piano (1944, orchestrated as *Tricks and Trifles*, 1945); *The Sante Fe Time Table*, for a cappella chorus (1945); Eight Piano Pieces (1946); *Symphonic Elegy*, for strings (1946); *What Price Confidence?*, opera (1946); *In Paradisum*, motet for women's a cappella voices (1946); Viola Sonata (1948); String Trio (1948); *George Washington Variations*, for piano (1950); *Pallas Athene weint*, opera (1950); *Parvula Corona Musicalis ad Honorem J. S. Bach*, for string trio (1950); Double Concerto, for violin, piano, and orchestra (1950); Concerto for Harp and Chamber Orchestra (1951); Concerto for Two Pianos and Orchestra (1951); *Medea*, for contralto and orchestra (1951–52); Sinfonietta, for string orchestra (1952); Cello Concerto (1953); Suite, for flute and string orchestra (1954); Capriccio, for cello and chamber orchestra (1955); *Eleven Transparencies*, for orchestra (1954); Seven Light Pieces, for string orchestra (1955); Suite, for clarinet and string orchestra (1955); *The Bell Tower*, opera (1955–56); *Spiritus Intelligentiae Sanctus*, oratorio, for voice and electronic tape (1956); *Kette, Kreis, and Spiegel*, for orchestra (1956–57); *Sestina*, for soprano, violin, guitar, clarinet, trumpet, and percussion (1957); *Hexaeder*, six pieces for chamber ensemble (1958); *Missa Duodecim Tonorum*, for chorus and organ (1958); *Quaestio Temporis*, for orchestra (1958–59); Six Motets, for chorus (1959); *Flute Piece in Nine Phases*, for flute and piano (1959); *From Three Make Seven*, for orchestra (1960–61); *5 + 1*, Alpbach Quintet, ballet (1962); *San Francisco Sequence*, for electronic tape (1963); *Der goldene Bock*, opera (1963–64); *Quintina*, for soprano, chamber ensemble, and electronic tape (1965); *Der Zauberspiegel*, TV opera (1966); *Glauber und Wissen*, oratorio for solo voices, chorus, and orchestra (1966); *Horizont unkreist*, for orchestra (1967); *Instant Remembered*, for voice, chamber orchestra, and tape (1967); *Fivefold Enfoldment*, for orchestra (1969); *Sardakai*, comic opera (1969–70); *Gib uns den Frieden*, Mass for vocal soloists, chorus, instruments, and organ (1969–70); *Kitharaulos*, for oboe, harp, string orchestra or electronic tape, the electronic tape version retitled *Aulokithara* (1971); Two *Time Songs*, for soprano and string quartet (1972); *Bottled Message from Paradise*, play for television with electronic tape (1973); *Late Harvest*, cycle of songs for baritone and piano (1973); *Rebellion and Rejection*, for orchestra (1974); *Anniversary Cantata*, for speaker, two soloists, chorus, and orchestra (1974–75); *Four Winds Suite*, for organ (1975); *Dream Sequence*, for symphonic band (1975–76); *They Knew What They Wanted*, for narrator, oboe, piano, percussion, and electronic tape (1976–77); *The Dissembler*, monologue for baritone and chamber orchestra (1978); Concerto for Organ and String Orchestra (1978).

BIBLIOGRAPHY: Austin, William W., *Music in the Twentieth Century* (N.Y., 1966); Ewen, David, (ed.), *The Book of Modern Composers*, 2nd ed. (N.Y., April 1950); Knessl, Lothar, *Ernst Krenek* (Vienna, 1967); Krenek, Ernst, *Selbstdarstellung*, or *Self-Analysis* (Zurich, 1948); Machlin, Joseph, *Introduction to Contemporary Music*, revised ed. (N.Y., 1979); Rogge, Wolfgang, *Ernst Krenek* (Hamburg, 1970); *High Fidelity/Musical America*, October 1965; *New York Times*, May 1, 1960.

Kreutz, Arthur, b. La Crosse, Wis., July 25, 1906.

American folk music, and jazz particularly, are predominant in Kreutz's best compositions, the style reflecting and incorporating the language of past and present.

Music was a continual presence in the Kreutz home. Arthur's father, Rudolph S. Kreutz, was a violinist in the St. Paul Symphony and a director of theater orchestras. He and other members of the immediate family gathered for Saturday evening musicales. The father began teaching Arthur the violin when the boy was seven. In a few years Arthur was able to participate in family concerts, and when he was thirteen he played violin in his father's theater orchestra. "Most violinists aspire to play like Kreisler and Heifetz," he says, "and on hearing their early recordings [1918] so did I. But for me there was another 'fiddler,' named Joe Venuti, who with his solid bow arm and classic tradition bridged the gap between classic music and jazz. We listened to his recordings in Madison, Wis., in the late 1920s. So I threw away the notes and improvised my way through fifteen years of jazz. I played with stage bands, in nightclubs, and at campus dances at the University of Wisconsin in Madison, doubling violin and banjo."

Despite the boy's involvement with music, his father advised him to pursue a career in science. After graduating from La Crosse Central High School in 1923, Kreutz attended the University of Wisconsin majoring in chemical engineering, and in 1930 received his bachelor of science degree. But he elected not to pursue that profession. In 1928 and again in 1931 he toured Europe with a jazz group. In 1932–33 he attended the Royal Conservatory in Ghent,

Belgium, studied violin with Henri Gadeyne, played it with the Ghent Symphony, and received a diploma in violin as well as the *Premier Prix avec la plus grand distinction*.

Returning to the United States in 1933, he spent the next two years studying music at the University of Wisconsin, concentrating on violin and composition with Cecil Burleigh. While employed as an instructor of music in the public school system (1936–38) he conducted the Madison Federal Symphony. Between 1939 and 1940 he taught acoustics, conducting, and instruments at Teachers College, Columbia University, in New York, where he received a master of arts degree in music education in 1940. While teaching at Georgia State College at Milledgeville the same year, he was awarded the Prix de Rome in composition, subsequently becoming a fellow of the American Academy.

In 1939, Kreutz composed *Paul Bunyan*, a dance poem for orchestra, the first of many works displaying American background and interest. Its second movement, "Winter of the Blue Snow," performed independently of the rest of the work, brought him his first success as a composer. It was introduced over WNYC radio in New York, June 15, 1941, conducted by Fritz Mahler; received the National Association of American Composers and Conductors Publication Award (1941); and was programmed by Désiré Defauw, conducting the Chicago Symphony on January 13, 1944.

Paul Bunyan is one of two works which brought Kreutz the Prix de Rome. The other, Music for Symphony Orchestra (1940), was first heard on June 16, 1940, performed by the NBC Symphony under Frank Black over the NBC network. When the first concert performance took place on March 22, 1945, with Kreutz conducting the New York Philharmonic, the *Musical Leader* commented: "Mr. Kreutz shows decided talent and understanding in the handling of his material. He has attempted an unusual method of development which gives one the feeling of rhythmic vitality in a short melodic line."

Kreutz received the Prix de Rome in 1940, but because of the war, spent the two-year fellowship in New York. On September 4, 1942, he married Blanche Wurdach Harper. They were divorced in 1947. From 1948 to 1954 he was assistant professor of music at the University of Texas in Austin, teacher of theory and composition, conductor of the university orchestra, and music director of the University Opera Company.

In 1942, he was commissioned by Martha Graham to compose music for the ballet *Litany of Washington Street* (also titled *Land Be Bright*), produced at the Civic Opera House in Chicago on March 8, 1942. Originally for piano, Kreutz scored it for orchestra when the ballet was choreographed by Shirley Dodge at the University of Texas on April 26, 1944.

In 1944, Kreutz received a Guggenheim Fellowship which was renewed in 1945. Under these fellowships he completed the Violin Concerto no. 1 (1944), premiered at the University of Wisconsin on August 1, 1948, and *Symphonic Sketch* (1945; Berkeley, Calif., August 1, 1946), based on three American folk tunes, "Kentucky Moonshiner," "The Little Brown Jug," and "Suckin' through a Straw."

Kreutz composed and directed the incidental music for the American National Theater and Academy (ANTA) production of *Hamlet* at the annual presentation of the Shakespeare tragedy in the courtyard of Kronborg Castle, in Elsinor, Denmark (June 17, 1949). *Scenes from Hamlet* (1949) is a concert work for orchestra based on this incidental music. He also contributed the incidental music to two theater productions in New York: *The Wanhope Building* (February 19, 1947) and *E=MC²* (June 15, 1948).

Kreutz served on the faculty at Teachers College, Columbia University, in New York (1946–52); joined the faculty of Brooklyn College in Brooklyn, N.Y., for one year (1947–48); was composer-in-residence and instructor at the Rhode Island State College (summer of 1946) and at the University of Wisconsin (summer of 1947). He became a member of the faculty at the University of Mississippi at Oxford in 1952, where he remained professor until his retirement in 1972.

In 1950 he married the novelist and librettist Zoë Lund Schiller. They wrote and produced *Acres of Sky* (1950), a ballad opera commissioned by Governor McMath and the University of Arkansas, Fayetteville, Ark., for the opening of the Fine Arts Center on November 16, 1950. It was again produced at the Brander Matthew Theater at Columbia University, N.Y., on May 7, 1952. *The University Greys* (1954), a two-act opera, was commissioned by the University of Mississippi and produced under the direction of the authors at the university on March 15, 1954. Later it was presented on WMC-TV Memphis, Tenn., on May 8, 1954. *Sourwood Mountain*, a one-act folk opera (1958), was premiered at the University of Mississippi, January 8, 1959, and presented at the Music Educators National Conference Convention at Roanoke, Va., on April 4, 1959.

Jazz has been the prime influence upon Kreutz. Among his most important jazz-oriented compositions are *Dixieland Concerto* (1949), commissioned and introduced by the Little Orchestra Society under Thomas Scherman in New York on January 14, 1950, and *Quartet Venuti* for string quartet (1954), premiered at the University of Mississippi by the New Music String Quartet. Both works received the Mississippi Education Television Award in January 1969. The finest works in this style are *Jazzonata* no. 1 (1961) and Variations, both for violin and piano, in which Kreutz incorporated his own personal style of jazz fiddling. In this category is the *"Sinfonia" Violin Concerto*, for violin and orchestra (1964), commissioned by the National Music Fraternity, Phi Mu

Alpha Sinfonia, introduced by Kreutz in a violin-piano adaptation at the first regional meeting of Phi Mu Alpha at Abilene, Tex., on April 15, 1966.

A documentary on Kreutz was filmed in 1978 at Raymond, Miss., for television distribution. For this film, Kreutz composed *Concertino in Blue*, for violin and orchestra (1978).

THE COMPOSER SPEAKS: I have never had an urge to invent a new musical language. My compositions proceed from early experience in jazz and serious music. It is difficult to find or create a new emotional area in music, but jazz offers this opportunity. Dixieland jazz is extroverted, exuberant, carefree, and happy. It seemed to me the only really new mood that has happened to music in the last century.

PRINCIPAL WORKS: 3 violin concertos (1944, 1955, 1965); 2 *Jazzonatas*, for violin and piano (1961, 1970).

Paul Bunyan, dance poem for orchestra (1939); Music for Symphony Orchestra (1940); *Litany of Washington Street*, ballet (1942); *American Dances*, for orchestra (1942); Symphony no. 2 (1943); Three Shakespeare Songs, for soprano and chamber orchestra (1943); Four Robert Burns Songs, for soprano and chamber orchestra (1943); *Symphonic Sketch*, for orchestra (1945); *New England Folksing*, for chorus and orchestra (1946); *Mosquito Serenade*, for string orchestra (1947); Clarinet Concerto (1947); *Dixieland Concerto*, for clarinet, trumpet, trombone, and orchestra (1949); *Scenes from Hamlet*, for orchestra (1949); *Dance Concerto*, for violin and orchestra (1950); *Acres of Sky*, ballad opera (1950); *The University Greys*, opera (1954); *Symphonic Jam Session* (1954); *Quartet Venuti*, for string quartet (1954); *Sourwood Mountain*, folk opera (1958); Variations, for violin and piano (1964); Piano Concerto (1970); Saxophone Quartet (1977); *Song and Dance*, for oboe and string quartet (1977); *Concertino in Blue*, for violin and orchestra (1978).

BIBLIOGRAPHY: Ewen, David, *American Composers Today* (N.Y., 1949); Reis, Claire, *Composers in America* (N.Y., 1947).

Kubik, Gail Thompson, b. South Coffeyville, Okla., Spetember 5, 1914.

In 1952, at the age of thirty-eight, he was the youngest composer ever to win the Pulitzer Prize in music. Kubik's music has been described as neoromantic. He has experimented with some of the avant-garde styles (one movement from his *Scenario for Orchestra* has a distinctly Webernlike texture). His functional music for radio, television, and theatrical films has experimented with orchestral colors and textures that are available to the composer familiar with all of the new acoustical devices of the electronic laboratory. Kubik's style shows the influences of his extensive work in the "mass audience" field. Clarity of sonority and texture, an uncomplicated directness of expression make his work readily accessible. Many of his scores have been inspired by American personalities and legends; he has made extensive use of native American folk music.

His father was of American birth but Bohemian descent, and his mother, of English-Irish origin, was a concert singer who studied with Ernestine Schumann-Heink in Kansas City. "I can remember mother dragging me along when I was six or seven years old on the train to Kansas City—two hundred miles away—as a kind of protection and bodyguard," Kubik recalls. He and his brothers were all given piano lessons in their early boyhood. "We were all practicing when everyone else was out playing baseball, that sort of thing."

When Kubik was fifteen, he was awarded a four-year scholarship to the Eastman School of Music in Rochester, N.Y. As he was still in high school, the scholarship was conditional on the young composer's parents allowing him to come to Rochester, to complete there his last two years of high school and at the same time to start his four-year course at the Eastman School. There, Kubik studied the violin with Samuel Belov, composition with Bernard Rogers and Edward Royce, and theory with Irving McHose, gaining the degree of bachelor of music in 1934 "with distinction" (with a major in both violin and composition). From 1930 on, and for the next seven years, he played the violin with the Kubik Ensemble (voice, violin, cello, and piano), of which his two brothers and his mother were members, and which gave public concerts throughout the Middle West.

Composition began to become a serious endeavor in his years at the Eastman School. Among these earlier works—all, as the composer himself says, the student works of a conservative—were the Piano Trio (1934), which won first prize in a national contest held by the Sinfonia Honorary Music Fraternity; Violin Concerto no. 1 (1934), in which he himself appeared as soloist when it was premiered on January 2, 1938, in Chicago with Izler Solomon conducting, after which it was performed with orchestras in Rochester and New York City; and *Variations on a 13th-Century Troubadour Song*, for orchestra (1935).

Between 1934 and 1935, Kubik taught violin and conducted the orchestra at Monmouth College in Illinois. At the same time, in 1935–36, again on a scholarship, he continued music study at the American Conservatory of Music with Scott Willits (violin) and Leo Sowerby (composition), which led to a master's degree in music in 1936. In 1936–37 he taught violin and conducting at Dakota Wesleyan University in Mitchell, S.D.; in 1937–38 he attended Harvard, studying composition there with Walter Piston. (It was during his year with Piston that Nadia Boulanger became interested in his music, remaining its strong champion until her death in 1979.) From

1938 to 1940, Kubik was on the music faculty of Teachers College at Columbia University in New York. In 1938, he completed one of his earliest concert works rooted in American folklore: *In Praise of Johnny Appleseed*, for bass-baritone, chorus, and orchestra, inspired by that American pioneer and orchardist who became a hero of legends.

In 1940, Kubik was appointed staff composer and music-program adviser for the National Broadcasting Company in New York. This was the first time a composer of serious musical attainments was employed on the permanent staff of a major radio network. In this post he wrote music for several radio productions, including the Smithsonian Institution's *The World Is Yours* series and the *Great Plays* and *Elizabethan Drama* series. One of his most ambitious radio scores was *Puck: A Legend of Bethlehem*, based on a poem by Mary B. Dupree, for narrator, strings, and winds (1940), premiered over the NBC network on December 29, 1940.

In 1942, his music for a motion picture documentary, *The World at War*, earned him a citation from the National Association for American Composers and Conductors for "the best documentary score of the year." He had not, however, abandoned concert music. *Scherzo for Large Orchestra* (1940) received the Chicago Symphony Golden Jubilee Award. His Violin Concerto no. 2 (1940) captured the first prize in the Jascha Heifetz competition sponsored by Heifetz and the publishing house of Carl Fischer, Inc. Kubik's Sonatina for Violin and Piano (1941) received the Society of Publication of American Music Award in 1944, and was featured by Ruggiero Ricci on his concert tours.

On the strength of *The World at War*, Kubik was appointed director of music for the Office of War Information Bureau of Motion Pictures in 1942. In 1943, during World War II, Kubik joined the air force. Eventually holding the rank of staff sergeant, he was occupied both in the United States and in England with the writing and conducting of scores for the U. S. Air Force First Motion Picture Unit. Among his best-known documentary scores was that for *The Memphis Belle* (1943), directed by William Wyler, which received the New York Film Critics Award in 1944. Kubik then recast this music as a concert work for narrator and orchestra under the title of *Memphis Belle: A War Time Episode* (1944).

Kubik remained in military service until 1946. In that time he completed a major work for orchestra utilizing American folk music: *Folk Song Suite* (1941–45). Here he utilized the cowboy tune "Whoop-ti-yi-yo" for the first movement, two hymns by William Billings ("When Jesus Wept" and "Chester") for the second, and Stephen Foster's "De Camptown Races" for the third. The first movement was done on a commission from the Columbia Broadcasting System and was introduced over that radio network on April 8, 1941, Bernard Herrmann conducting; the third movement was commissioned by the BBC in London, which introduced it on March 30, 1944 (while the composer was stationed in London as a member of the U. S. Air Force).

While still in uniform, Kubik was awarded a Post-Service Fellowship by the Guggenheim Foundation, the first such wartime fellowship given by that foundation. Upon his discharge from the air force in 1946, Kubik replaced Ernst Toch that summer as guest professor of composition at the University of Southern California in Los Angeles. He came to New York later that year where he was commissioned to write the music for a folk opera, *A Mirror for the Sky* (1946). Its book and lyrics were by Jessamyn West; Raoul DuBois designed the sets; and John Houseman acted as consultant. It was based on the life of the American ornithologist and artist John Audubon. (Almost three decades later, on a grant from the National Endowment for the Arts, Kubik conducted a concert performance of this opera in Kansas on April 7, 1976.)

Still in 1946, Kubik contributed the score for a ballet for dance band and folk singer, *Frankie and Johnny*, following it in the next few years with the Symphony in E-flat (1947–49), *Spring Valley Overture* (1947), and scores for the motion pictures *The Miner's Daughter* (1950) and *Gerald McBoing-Boing* (1950). The music to *The Miner's Daughter* later served as the basis for a one-act curtain raiser, *Boston Baked Beans*, for soprano, bass-baritone, and instrumentalists (1950), premiered at a concert of the League of Composers in New York on March 9, 1952. *Gerald McBoing-Boing*, an animated cartoon, won an Oscar from the Academy of Motion Picture Arts and Sciences in 1951 and, in the same year, the British Institute Award. Kubik's score for *Gerald McBoing-Boing*, having been written before the film was made, became a concert work for narrator, percussion, and nine instruments without difficulty and was performed by a dozen or so major American symphony orchestras as well as in Europe.

Awarded the Prix de Rome in 1950 and 1951, Kubik was able to spend three years at the American Academy of Rome. In Rome he served as guest lecturer at the Santa Cecilia Academy in 1952. One of the compositions completed at this time was the *Symphony concertante*, for piano, viola, trumpet, and orchestra (1951), commissioned and introduced by the Little Orchestra Society, conducted by Thomas Scherman on January 7, 1952, in New York. "It is a brilliant piece because of its strident (but not at all inelegant) orchestration," said Virgil Thomson in the *New York Herald Tribune*. "It is a neoclassic work of angular tunes and insistently thematic textures, with widely spaced intervals (or else, by contrast, closely spaced ones) both harmonically and melodically disposed. It recalls with vigor the musical ideas of 1925 in making no appeal by sweetness of tone or grace of line. Its structure is rhythmically

rather than harmonically or emotionally determined." A sensitive balance between a symphonic and a popular style was maintained, with the jazz idiom utilized symphonically in sophisticated orchestration and rhythmic procedures. It was with this composition that Kubik gained the Pulitzer Prize in music in 1952.

Altogether, from 1950 to 1967, Kubik remained in Europe thirteen years (returning to the United States between 1955 and 1959), devoting himself to conducting, lecturing, and composing. His music became more complex in its vertical arrangements and more intricate in rhythm; for his thematic material he now favored short motives which were rarely developed but which he transformed through intervallic and rhythmic changes. But in this process he did not relinquish his style's accessibility or communicability. His Symphony no. 2, written in Paris between 1953 and 1955, is an excellent example of this development.

For motion pictures he provided the music for William Wyler's *The Desperate Hours*, starring Fredric March and Humphrey Bogart (1955), which he rewrote for orchestra with a two-piano obbligati as *Scenario for Orchestra* (1957). It was given its first performance in Palermo in 1959, the composer conducting. When Dimitri Mitropoulos commissioned him to write a symphonic work, Kubik responded with Symphony no. 3 (1956), where he incorporated melodic material previously employed in scores of three of his documentary World War II films. "Whereas in the film scores these tunes were at best 'bit players' contributing to the mood and atmosphere of the total dramatic story," Kubik explains, "in the Symphony they are leading characters, occupying the center of the stage and acting out musicodramatic roles that are every bit as real to the composer as were the flesh and blood creations to the writer of these . . . documentary films." But the symphony had no specific program, concerning itself technically with the working out of the musical ideas. The New York Philharmonic under Mitropoulos introduced it on February 28, 1957. "Mr. Kubik knows how to keep his material in motion," reported Howard Taubman in the *New York Times*, "and he knows how to build excitement." In the *Saturday Review*, Irving Kolodin said: "He has a strong sense of orchestral combinations, a knack for putting his choirs and components together in a novel-sounding way."

Subsequent to his return to the United States in the fall of 1967, after his prolonged stay in Europe, Kubik served as visiting professor at Kansas State University, in Manhattan, Kan., in 1968. There he received a commission from the University and its President to write *A Record of Our Time*, "a protest piece" for narrator, chorus, vocal soloist, and orchestra (1970). This work, the composer says, "sums up my feelings about some aspects of the 20th century which put in doubt, so it seems to me—and to many of us—the values of contemporary Western civilization: the Jewish Holocaust, our lack of concern about social injustices in America, our tragic involvement in Vietnam, the cancerous racism . . . which helped to tear the country apart." Working in collaboration with the American novelist Harvey Swados, Kubik assembled an omnibus text drawn from the Bible, Mark Twain, Yeats, Vanzetti, John Jay Chapman, and the words of a Negro spiritual. *A Record of Our Time* was introduced in Manhattan, Kan., performed by the Minnesota Orchestra, George Trautwein conducting and Ray Milland serving as narrator, on November 11, 1970. Its West Coast premiere followed on October 30, 1976 with Roger Wagner conducting the Los Angeles Master Chorale.

Among Kubik's subsequent compositions are *Scholastics*, for a cappella chorus (1972), based on five medieval poems, which was commissioned by the Claremont University Center of the Claremont Colleges and premiered by the Four College Choir under John Lilley in Claremont in March 1973; and *Magic, Magic, Magic*, a three-movement work for chamber chorus and chamber orchestra (1976) written for the Texas bicentennial celebration and given its world premiere in San Antonio on April 25, 1976. The concluding section of the latter work was built around a chilling primitive chant, "Exu-Zin-Ho," heard in Brazil.

In 1966, Kubik lectured at Oxford University in England. He has also appeared as guest lecturer for UNESCO in Paris and in Budapest. Since 1970 he has been composer-in-residence at Scripps College in Claremont, Calif. He was awarded an honorary doctorate in music from Monmouth College in 1955. Kubik was married four times: to Jessie Louise Mayer on April 5, 1938; Joyce Mary Scott-Paine, on December 21, 1946; Mary Gibbs Tyler, on April 9, 1952; and Joan Allred Sanders on September 1, 1970. All marriages ended in divorce.

THE COMPOSER SPEAKS: One of the important problems facing the contemporary composer, a problem not faced by the composers of any other era, is his relationship to the mass audience, reaching out to it with a music that is intelligible and which "communicates" but which involves no compromise in the basic creativity of his idiom. The composer either solves this problem and contributes his fair share of sounds to films, radio, television, recordings, school music, or he ignores the problem altogether and continues to write music on the basis of a composer-audience relationship which numbers listeners at most in the few thousands and not in the millions. This ivory-tower premise, of course, has much to recommend it. There is no question that involved, complex thinking in music demands from its audience a background which approaches the keenness of think-

ing and maturity brought by the composer to his musical expression. Obviously, there always will be a need for this kind of music, this kind of art. There is the music which shows the composer completely unfettered. And it is only when the creative artist works with complete freedom that you have the widest possible range of emotional expression.

Admittedly, writing a piece which will make sense to ten million people and more imposes restrictions upon the composer. It is my contention, however, that those restrictions are essentially technical in nature and need not involve the slightest esthetic compromise. Instead of using a musical language which involves "long words" it seems to me possible to express the same *idea* with "short words." It is the *idea* which is expressed that is important, and as long as that *idea* is expressed with no watering down of the composer's style I see no reason why it must be necessarily concluded that a simplified musical speech is, a priori, routine, banal and uncreative.

PRINCIPAL WORKS: 3 symphonies (1949, 1955, 1956); 2 violin concertos (1934, revised 1936; 1940, revised 1951).

In Praise of Johnny Appleseed, for bass-baritone, chorus, and orchestra (1938, revised 1961); *Choral Profiles, Folk Song Sketches*, for chorus (1938); *Scherzo for Large Orchestra* (1940); *Puck: A Legend of Bethelehem*, radio music for narrator, strings, and winds (1940); Piano Sonatina (1941); Violin Sonatina (1941); *Folk Song Suite*, for orchestra (1941–45); *Litany and Prayer*, for men's chorus, brass, and percussion (1943–45); *Frankie and Johnny*, ballet for dance band and singer (1946); *A Mirror for the Sky*, folk opera (1946); Piano Sonata (1947); *Spring Valley Overture*, for orchestra (1947); *Soliloquy and Dance*, for violin and piano (1948); *Gerald McBoing-Boing*, for narrator, percussion, and nine instruments (1950); *Fables in Song*, for voice and piano (1950–59); *Boston Baked Beans*, "opera piccola" (1950); *Symphony concertante*, for piano, viola, trumpet, and orchestra (1951, revised 1953); *Thunderbolt Overture*, for orchestra (1953); *Scenario for Orchestra* (1957); Sonatina, for clarinet and piano (1959); Divertimento no. 1, for thirteen players, no. 2, for eight players (1959); *Scenes for Orchestra* (1962); *Intermezzo: Music for Cleveland*, for piano (1967); *A Christmas Set*, for chamber chorus and chamber orchestra (1968); *Prayer and Toccata*, for organ and chamber orchestra (1968); *Five Theatrical Sketches* (Divertimento no. 3), for piano trio (1970–71); *A Record of Our Time*, a "protest piece" for narrator, chorus, vocal soloist, and orchestra (1970); *Scholastics*, for a cappella chorus (1972); *Five Birthday Pieces*, for two recorders (1974); *Magic, Magic, Magic*, for chamber chorus and chamber orchestra, originally entitled *Texas Grimorium* (1976).

BIBLIOGRAPHY: *DCM*; Ewen, David, *American Composers Today* (N.Y., 1949); Reis, Claire, *Com-*

posers in America (N.Y., 1947); *Who's Who in America, 1978–79.*

Kupferman, Meyer, b. New York City, July 3, 1926.

A prolific and versatile composer, Kupferman has favored the varied styles and idioms of 20th-century music, including neoclassicism, the twelve-tone technique, electronic music, aleatory processes and jazz. Occasionally, he has employed non-Western scales, such as the six-note scale of South Africa, the pentatonic scale as found among the Balinese, and the eight-note symmetrical scale.

His father, who came from Rumania, was the musical member of the family. Though self-taught, he played several instruments and had a pleasant singing voice. Strongly conscious of his Judaic heritage, he transferred some of his own interest in Jewish ritual, religion, even the mysticism of the Kabbalah, to his son. This Jewish consciousness, so early implanted in the boy, was further heightened by attendance at religious services where the chanting of the congregation remained a strong impression. "My father," Kupferman recalls, "taught me many Rumanian songs. I loved the clarinet style of old Rumanian folk music and it made an impact on my compositions later on." From his mother, who had come from Russia, he learned to love Russian-Yiddish songs.

Kupferman was ten when he started taking lessons on the clarinet with Louis Levy, continuing these with Abram Klotsman and Robert Rohman, as well as some study of the piano with Joel Newman. Composition began when he was thirteen with some jazz arrangements and continued a year later with the writing of some impressionistic piano pieces. But he never received formal instruction, learning the craft through a long period of trial-and-error apprenticeship. While attending the High School of Music and Art in New York, he played the clarinet in the school band and orchestra, and wrote a string quartet, a passacaglia for chorus, and a wind sextet, among other compositions. The last of these was performed in 1942 at a students' concert at the high school that drew the attention of Virgil Thomson, who reviewed it for the *Herald Tribune* and spoke of the composition's "moderate but wholly neat and charming French impressionism." Upon graduating from the high school in 1943, Kupferman attended Queens College, Queens, N.Y., for two years. On June 16, 1948, he married Sylvia Kasten, with whom he had a daughter.

During the latter half of the 1940s, Kupferman played the clarinet in jazz groups, and at various night spots, an experience which, in later years, he would carry over into many of his compositions. He gained further experiences as a musician during those apprentice years by working for a number of modern-dance groups and by serving in 1946–48 in

the dual role of codirector and performer with the New York Chamber Music Society, which gave weekly concerts over WNYC, the municipal radio station in New York City. In 1947–48 he was director of the Bolton Music Festival at Bolton Landing, N.Y.; in 1948 he wrote the music for five documentary films on China; and in 1949–50 he was a member of Composers' Workshop, an experimental group that gave readings to new music.

Kupferman first attracted attention as composer with a charming one-act opera, *In a Garden* (1948), libretto by Gertrude Stein, throwing a nostalgic and tender backward glance at childhood. This little opera was introduced in New York on December 29, 1949. Soon afterward it became a favorite with opera workshops throughout the United States, was performed by the After Dinner Opera Company at the Edinburgh Festival in Scotland in 1950, and toured Europe under the sponsorship of Amerika Haus. The opera was largely responsible for bringing Kupferman the first annual La Guardia Award for Best Achievement in Music in New York City.

By 1948, Kupferman had discovered and become fascinated with the twelve-tone system, which he began using in such compositions as Variations for Piano (1948), *Libretto, for orchestra* (1948), a one-movement Piano Concerto (1948), and Chamber Symphony (1950). But then, as later, twelve-tone writing was only one of several different styles Kupferman favored. Divertimento, for orchestra (1948), had suggestions of jazz within an atonal structure and in a neoclassical style. *Little Symphony* was also neoclassical, but clearly tonal. Divertimento, Chamber Symphony, and *Little Symphony* were all commissioned by the Daniel Saidenburg Little Symphony, which introduced the Divertimento on February 15, 1950, and the Chamber Symphony on February 11, 1951, both in New York. Another notable composition of this period was *Trio concertante*, for flute, clarinet, and violin (1948), heard at a Composers Forum concert at Columbia University in New York on October 30, 1955, when Lester Trimble, in the *New York Herald Tribune* described it as "a miracle of instrumental blending."

In 1951, Kupferman was appointed to the music faculty of Sarah Lawrence College in Bronxville, N.Y. Since then he has taught composition and chamber music there, formed a student orchestra in his early years, and later founded and directed the Sarah Lawrence Improvisation Ensemble, for which he wrote a number of compositions. In addition to giving concerts, this ensemble has participated in performances by the Joseph Papp Shakespeare Festival and in various experimental theaters and dance companies.

Kupferman's principal works of the 1950s included the Symphony no. 4 (1955), which was commissioned, performed (on January 27, 1956), and recorded by the Louisville Orchestra in Kentucky under Robert Whitney; several operas, among them *Doctor Faustus Lights the Lights* (1952), to a libretto by Gertrude Stein; a children's opera, *Draagenfut Girl* (1958), libretto by the composer, based on the Cinderella fairy tale, commissioned by Sarah Lawrence College, where it was introduced on May 8, 1958; and a good deal of chamber music.

Many of Kupferman's compositions since 1961 come under the collective title of *Infinities*; some other works, however, though carrying various other titles, can also be characterized as "Infinities." *Infinities* 1 (1961), for solo flute, exploited "echo timbres," a device originating with Kupferman in which a solo flute is pitted against the reacting amplified sounds of the strings of two pianos (without performers). Echo timbres is an effect found in several later *Infinities*. Since 1961 Kupferman has written about forty such works. Some are for solo instruments with or without accompaniment. Some are for various combinations of instruments. *Infinities* 4 is a song cycle for soprano solo without accompaniment, and *Infinities* 6 (1962) is a cantata for vocal soloists and chorus, both to texts by Rimbaud. *Infinities* 12 (1965) is for chamber orchestra, *Infinities* 14 (1965) is for trumpet and chamber orchestra, *Infinities* 26 (1968) is for string orchestra. All compositions in this series are based on a single twelve-tone row with this difference: The idea here is to explore the possibilities of one tone row over a period of years to see the melodic and harmonic results as the row became a really deep-rooted source (rather than a superficial string of notes, as it had often been during the past periods). Nevertheless the *Infinities* cover a wide gamut of style and technique, some including aleatory processes, some electronic devices, some jazz, some Judaica. Jazz is found in *Jazz Infinities* 3, for saxophone and drums (1961); in *Infinities* 5 (1962), a concerto for cello and jazz band; in *Infinities* 8 (1964), for jazz quartet (performed throughout the world of music by the Claremont Quartet); and in *Infinities* 26, subtitled "Moonchild and the Doomsday Trombone" (1968), for voice, oboe, and chamber and jazz ensembles. All these works are successful in combining jazz with serialism.

Judaica appears in *Infinities* 18, "The Judgement" (1966). This is an "opera" for voices alone (a taped chorus replacing the orchestra), text by Paul Freeman based on the Bible. Its conception, the composer reveals, "may have been inspired by my childhood memories of chanting male voices and the total absence of instruments in the orthodox synagogue." Four choruses of different size are here combined with choruses heard on prerecorded tape transmitted to the audience through twenty-four loudspeakers placed in various parts of the auditorium. The voice of God appears solely on tape.

Among Kupferman's notable later works are *Tunnels of Love*, a jazz concerto for clarinet, bass, and drums (1970; N.Y., May 22, 1971); *In the Garden of*

My Father's House, for clarinet and violin (1972), where the composer recalls his youth when he listened to his father sing and would respond by playing the same tune on the clarinet; *The Possessed* (1974), Kupferman's first completely electronic score, in which he collaborated with the composer Joel Spiegelman, a ballet whose text was based on the mystical East European legend of the "dybbuk" written for and choreographed by Pearl Lang; *Abracadabra Quartet*, for string trio and piano (1976; N.Y., December 5, 1976), the title alluding to the "special sense of magic" which his father introduced to the composer with his explanations of Jewish rituals and mysticism and whose writing was further stimulated by the composer's visit to places of Jewish historic interest in Prague in 1975.

In some of his compositions, Kupferman employed a method he designated as "mirror-tape gestalt." The idea came to him one day when he heard a soprano sing along with her own prerecorded tape. A duality of timbre suggested itself to Kupferman as the soprano pitted her voice against the tape in different entries and overlays of sound. Kupferman's first use of this method was *Refractions*, for cello and tape (1962). It was later used effectively in *The Judgement* (*Infinities* 18); in *Illusions*, for oboe and tape (1968); in *Superflute* for flute and tape (1972); in the Concerto for Cello, Tape and Orchestra (1974; White Plains, N.Y., May 1976), which had been commissioned by the National Endowment for the Arts and recorded under a grant from the Ford Foundation. What Kupferman enjoyed in this mirror-tape technique was the provocative contradictions it posed, such as tonality against atonality, the live performance against prerecorded sound. "I enjoy the kind of psychological explosions that occur when you hear contradictory things."

On April 3, 1979, Kupferman's *Sound Objects* IV, V and VI, for clarinet and piano (1978), was introduced at a New York concert in which Kupferman offered not only his own works but also that of some of his friends'. These "sound objects" represented to the composer "musical dream images" similar to feelings and images experienced following a dream. "*Sound Objects* combines playful moods and figurations with darker, more poetic currents," reported Joseph Horowitz in the *New York Times*. "Drawing on his long affinity for jazz, Mr. Kupferman has prominently incorporated languorous reveries and syncopated rhythms. But these and other familiar-sounding elements are altered by tart juxtapositions, as well as by the frequent urgency of their deployment. It adds up to a provocative idiom—fanciful but never frivolous."

Having divorced his wife, Sylvia, in 1969, Kupferman married Pai-Fen Chin, an artist and dancer, on July 24, 1973. In 1975, Kupferman was the recipient of a Guggenheim Fellowship, enabling him to travel to Europe, where he appeared as a clarinetist in a program of his works for Amerika Haus broadcast over the Frankfurt Radio, made some recordings, and worked on an opera, *Prometheus*, libretto by the composer, based on Goethe and completed in 1977. That year, his *Fantasy Sonata*, for violin and piano—which marked the beginning of his "gestalt" approach to compositional form and which he had written in 1970 on a commission from the Library of Congress in Washington, D.C.—was used as the background music for a ballet, *O Thou Desire Who Art about to Sing*, choreographed by Martha Graham and performed by her company in June 1977. Since 1977, Kupferman has been composer-in-residence during the summers at the California Music Center in Palo Alto, California. In 1981, the American Academy and Institute of Arts and Letters presented Kupferman with an award of $5,000 and a grant for the recording of one of his compositions.

THE COMPOSER SPEAKS: For me, exclusivity in music in any one stylistic area for an extended period of time, makes me restless or uncomfortable. I do not believe there is, or ever was, a European style; I do feel, however, that the particular way I handle any musical statement always has my personal stamp. People who know my early music and my recent works claim that they can always determine the Kupferman personality in the rhythms, or in the harmonics, texture or melodic tunes. Also, my music is often very passionate and forceful—a kind of explosive expression that requires an audience in order to survive. I say this because I lament the fact that American audiences have, to a large extent, turned away from contemporary music.

After experimenting for many years with the rich resources and techniques available to the 20th-century composer I came to the conclusion that a *mixed* stylistic method was the only right direction for me. A return to melodic and harmonic materials—in a fresh new approach—also seemed in order. As a result, the "gestalt" form, which I began to employ in works dating from the early 1970s, offered me the opportunity to bring together all kinds of hitherto "unmixable musics" and create an expressive structural design that could be enjoyed on many levels. The truth is that I really started doing this sort of thing long ago—mixing jazz with twelve-tone symphonic music, for example, or tonal melodies with atonal harmonies, cogent use of titles, associations, and program-note materials. If I choose to give my listener a clue about an image that haunted my mind while I composed a certain work it may help him understand it better and achieve a deeper level of comprehension. Images, feelings, stories, poems, ideas, names of people or legendary figures, religious themes, geometric forms, colors, abstractions, etc., have provided me with interesting opportunities for titles or notes. Also, the idea or title has a strong

shaping impact on the complex crucible of mixed materials I enjoy composing with.

PRINCIPAL WORKS: 7 symphonies (1950–74); 2 piano concertos (1948, 1978).

Concerto, for eleven brass instruments (1948); *Libretto*, for orchestra (1948); Divertimento, for orchestra (1948); *In a Garden*, one-act opera (1948); Chamber Symphony (1950); Concerto for Two Solo Pianos (1950); *Doctor Faustus Lights the Lights*, opera (1952); Sonata for Two Solo Pianos (1956); Woodwind Quintet (1958); Variations, for orchestra (1958); *Sonata on Jazz Elements*, for piano (1958); String Quartets nos. 4 and 5 (1959); *Infinities* 1, for solo flute (1961); *Infinities* 2, for solo viola (1961); Concerto for Cello and Jazz Band (1962); *Refractions*, for cello and tape (1962); *Infinities* 4, for solo soprano (1962); *Infinities* 5, for solo cello (1962); *Infinities* 6, cantata for vocal soloists and chorus (1962); *Infinities Fantasy*, for piano (1962); *Infinities* 8, for jazz string quartet (1964); *Infinities* 12, for chamber orchestra (1965); *Infinities* 14, for trumpet and chamber orchestra (1965); *Infinities* 17, for piano four hands (1965); *Infinities* 18, for solo harp (1966); *The Judgement*, "opera" for voices and taped chorus (1966); *Infinities* 19, for oboe and piano (1967); *Infinities* 22, for trumpet and piano (1968); *Infinities* 24, for string orchestra (1968); *Moonchild and the Doomsday Trombone*, for oboe and jazz band (1968); *Persephone*, ballet (1968); *Madrigal*, for brass quartet (1970); *Fantasy Sonata*, for violin and piano (1970); *Diaries of a Tarot Player*, for harp and bass (1971); *The Last Blue Zeppelin*, for horn and cello (1972); *In the Garden of My Father's House*, for clarinet and violin (1972); *Thoughts*, for piano (1972); *Second Thoughts*, for piano (1972); *Symphony of the Yin-Yang*, for orchestra (1972); *The Celestial City*, for piano and tape (1973); *Sonata Mystikos*, for piano (1973); *The Possessed*, ballet score for magnetic tape (1974); *Li-Po*, for soprano and four instruments (1974); Concerto for Cello, Tape and Orchestra (1974); *Symphony Brevis* (1975); Four Quartets, for sixteen solo voices (1975); *Prometheus*, for six percussion players (1975); *Prometheus Profundus*, for chorus, brass, and percussion (1975); *Abracadabra Quartet*, for piano and string trio (1976); *Passage*, for string orchestra (1976); *Forms for a Duo*, for violin and piano (1976); *Perspective*, for piano (1976); Violin Concerto (1976); *Five Little Zeppelins*, for piano (1976); *Prometheus*, opera (1977); *Infinities* 27, for flute and guitar (1977); *The Red King's Throw*, for clarinet, cello, piano, and percussion (1977); *Zarathustra's Rhapsody*, for violin, piano, vibes, and bass (1977); *Masada*, a chamber symphony for flute, clarinet, cello, bass, piano, and violin (1977); *Adjustable Tears*, three jazz songs for soprano, clarinet, and bass (1977); Concerto for Six Instruments and Orchestra (1978); *Sound Objects*, I and III, for trumpet, tuba, and piano (1978); *Sound*

Objects IV and VI, for clarinet and piano (1978); *Infinities* 29, for wind quintet (1978); *Sound Objects* VII for guitar and harp (1978); *Sound Objects* VIII, for clarinet, viola and bass (1978); *A Heroic Infinities*, for solo cello (1978); *Three Nietzsche Songs*, for soprano, flute and piano (1978); *Poseidon*, for brass quintet (1979); *Kierkegaard*, for 4 tubas (1979); *A Nietzsche Cycle*, for soprano, horn and piano (1979).

BIBLIOGRAPHY: *BBDM; DCM; Musical Quarterly*, October 1963.

L

Labunski, Felix Roderick, b. Ksawerynów, Poland, December 27, 1892; d. Cincinnati, Ohio, April 28, 1979. American citizen, 1941.

Labunski's style is grounded in the traditions of the Russian and Polish romantic school. It is a blend of harmonic and contrapuntal writing often based on scales of his own invention derived from those of Polish folk music which in turn had their origin in old Roman Catholic modes. His music is tonal, diatonic, and sometimes modal.

He was born to a musical family. His father, a successful civil engineer, sang publicly, and his mother played the piano, often accompanying her husband at his concerts. A younger brother, Witold, became a prominent pianist, composer, and teacher.

From his earliest years, Felix Labunski was interested in music, hearing it constantly at home and being given important stimulation and direction by his mother. Regular piano instruction began when he was eight, and later the same year he made his first attempt at composition which, he says, "did not arouse any serious consideration in my family." Within a few years he was playing four-hand arrangements of operas and symphonies with his brother, Witold, and frequently attended performances of symphonic music, operas, and ballets.

Upon graduating from a private high school in Moscow, Labunski, on his father's urging, entered the Polytechnic Institute in St. Petersburg to prepare for a career as architect. Labunski followed these studies for four years. He also took lessons on the piano with Roch Hill. World War I interrupted his academic and musical education as he was called into military service. When the war ended and Labunski was ready to resume the study of architecture, the outbreak of the revolution in Russia interfered. During these years he was composing all the time, mainly pieces for the piano, though up to that time he had had no sound theoretical training.

In 1920, Glazunov became interested in Labunski's piano music and encouraged him to think seriously of devoting himself to composition. When in 1921, in Warsaw, Labunski joined other members of his family who had been dispersed by the revolution in Russia, he came to the firm decision to desert architecture and concentrate on music. With this in mind, he began studying theory with Lucian Marczewski in Zakopane in 1922, and one year later he took a course in harmony with Witold Maliszewski at the Warsaw Conservatory.

He came to Paris in 1924 with the hope of becoming Maurice Ravel's pupil, but on discovering that Ravel accepted no students, he entered the École Normale de Musique, where for the next three years he studied counterpoint, fugue, and compositon with Nadia Boulanger and orchestration with Paul Dukas. He also took private lessons in musicology with Georges Migot. In 1927, in Paris, Labunski helped organize the Young Polish Musicians in Paris to encourage Parisian-based Polish musicians with scholarships and performances. From its founding until 1929 he was its secretary; in 1929–30, vice-president; and from 1930 to 1933, president. Through this society, Labunski met Paderewski in 1928, who not only became a patron of this organization but also provided Labunski with a scholarship for the continuation of his studies at the École Normale.

Success came to Labunski with his first orchestral work *Triptyque champêtre* (1931), a three-movement suite which received second prize in a competition among Polish composers in Warsaw. Upon being introduced by the Warsaw Philharmonic under Gregor Fitelberg in 1931, it was soon performed in major cities in Poland as well as in Paris, Liège, Brussels, Helsinki, Chicago, and Montreal. Equally successful was *The Birds,* for soprano and orchestra (1934), performed in Paris, Monte Carlo, Brussels, and in cities in France and Poland.

On July 22, 1933, in London, Labunski married Dorothea Boit-Giersach, an American-born sculptress and painter who subsequently gave exhibitions under the name of Labunska. Their only child, a son, was born a year later. One year after his marriage, Labunski returned to his native Poland, becoming head of the classical division of the Polish Radio, an office he held for two years and in which he was responsible for introducing to Poland a number of American compositions. During these two years, his String Quartet no. 1 (1934) was introduced by the Tritone Quartet in Paris, and Divertimento, for flute and piano (1936), by René le Roy at a concert of the Société nationale de musique in Paris.

In 1936, Labunski came to New York for what he originally planned to be a short visit but which turned out to be permanent American residence and citizenship. He continued living in New York for the next nine years. One of his first major works completed in the United States was Symphony no. 1 in G minor (1937), written as a tribute to the land of his adoption even though it had no specific program. He followed this with the score for a ballet, *God's Man* (1937).

In 1940–41, he joined the faculty at Marymount College at Tarrytown-on-the-Hudson as professor of counterpoint, musical analysis, and composition. During the next few years he appeared as guest lecturer at numerous universities and colleges including New York University, Columbia University, Vassar College, and the Curtis Institute of Music. He was also heard in recitals of his own piano music. Between 1940 and 1944 he was a member of the board of directors of the American section of the International Society for Contemporary Music in New York. Among his compositions during these years were *Threnody,* for piano (1941), in homage to Paderewski, and Suite for Orchestra (1941). The latter, one of his most successful works, was inspired by Polish folk songs and dances, though the thematic material is entirely Labunski's. It was introduced at the festival of the International Society for Contemporary Music at Berkeley, Calif., on August 2, 1942, after which it was heard on programs of the New York Philharmonic, the Cincinnati Symphony, and the Chicago Symphony. "It has a contemporary flavor that's distinctive," reported Mary Leighton in the *Cincinnati Enquirer.* "It has originality and individual style. More than that, it is music that sounds—music that is highly expressive in a positive idiom aimed to rise above its novelty into the realm of inspired music rather than being a new idiom for its own sake."

Labunski left New York in 1945 to come to Cincinnati and join the faculty of the Cincinnati College Conservatory. When this Conservatory was merged with the University of Cincinnati, Labunski retained his post, retiring in 1964 as professor emeritus.

His most important works after settling in Cincinnati included: Variations, for orchestra (1947), its world premiere given by the Cincinnati Symphony; Symphony in D (1954), which, in 1962, was beamed by short-wave radio to the United States from Warsaw; *Elegy,* for orchestra (1954; *Cincinnati,* May 11, 1955); *Images of Youth,* a cantata for children's chorus, vocal soloists, and orchestra (1956), first heard on May 11, 1956, at the Cincinnati May Festival; *Symphonic Dialogues* (1960), commissioned by Max Rudolf, a one-movement work in cyclical form inspired by Arthur Schnitzler's play *Reigen* and first performed by the Cincinnati Symphony under Rudolf on February 9, 1961; and *Primavera,* for orchestra (1973), commissioned by Thomas Schippers for the Cincinnati Symphony, which introduced it on April 19, 1974.

In 1959, within a single month, four Labunski compositions received world premieres: the Piano Sonata no. 2 (1957) by Claude Kahn in Paris on April 8; Nocturne, for orchestra (1957), in Cincinnati on April 9; Pastorale and Dance, for oboe and piano (1958), in Cincinnati on April 21; and the Mass, for treble voices (1958), in Ashland, Ky., on April 29.

In 1951, Labunski was awarded the Huntington Hartford Fellowship and an honorary doctorate from Chicago Musical College. He was given the Alfred Jurzykowski Foundation Award in 1969, a National Endowment for the Arts grant in 1973–74, and in 1974 the Ohioan Citation Award for distinguished contributions as composer.

THE COMPOSER SPEAKS: I believe in well-defined melody, symmetrical, well-balanced form, and economy of means in achieving ultimate results.

PRINCIPAL WORKS: 2 symphonies (1937, 1954); 2 string quartets (1934, 1962).

Triptyque champêtre, for orchestra (1931); *The Birds,* for soprano and orchestra (1934); Divertimento, for flute and piano (1936); *God's Man,* ballet (1937); Suite for Orchestra (1941); *Threnody,* for piano (1941); *Song Without Words,* for soprano and strings (1946); Variations, for orchestra (1947); *There Is No Death,* cantata, for chorus and orchestra (1950); *Elegy,* for orchestra (1954); *Xaveriana,* fantasy for two pianos and orchestra (1956); Divertimento, for flute, oboe, clarinet, and bassoon (1956); *Images of Youth,* cantata for children's chorus, soloists, and orchestra (1956); Nocturne, for orchestra (1957); *Ave Maria,* motet, a cappella chorus (1957); Piano Sonata no. 2 (1957); Mass, for treble voices and organ (1958); Pastorale and Dance, for oboe and piano (1958); *Diptych,* for oboe and piano (1958); Two Madrigals, for a cappella chorus (1960); *Symphonic Dialogues,* for orchestra (1960); *Canto di aspirazione,* for orchestra (1963); Five Polish Carols, for organ (1966); *Polish Renaissance Suite,* for orchestra (1967); *Salut à Nadia,* for brass (1967); *Intrada festiva,* for brass (1968); Music for Piano and Orchestra (1968); *Salut à Paris,* ballet suite for orchestra (1968); *Primavera,* for orchestra (1973).

BIBLIOGRAPHY: *DCM;* Ewen, David, *American Composers Today* (N.Y., 1949); *Who's Who in America, 1978–79.*

Laderman, Ezra, b. Brooklyn, N.Y., June 29, 1924.

Laderman has worked within traditional structures, modified for his artistic needs, and has adopted a style with neoromantic overtones. Yet he is thoroughly modern in the strength and vigor of his discordant harmonies, declamatory lyricism, and occasional deflections into atonality and electronics.

While attending the High School of Music and Art in New York City he wrote a Piano Concerto (1940) that won a prize. During World War II he served as technical sergeant in the American armed forces, a time that saw the writing of a symphony, *Leipzig,* which was introduced in Wiesebaden, Germany, in 1945. From 1946 to 1950 he attended Brooklyn College in Brooklyn, N.Y., receiving a bachelor of arts degree in 1950, and from 1950 to 1952 he studied with Otto Luening (composition), Douglas Moore (opera), and Paul Henry Lang (musicology) at Columbia University, where he received his master of arts degree. He also studied composition privately with Stefan Wolpe. While still at Columbia he married Aimlee H. Davis (who subsequently became a research biologist), with whom he had three children.

In 1955 he was awarded a Guggenheim Fellowship (which he received again in 1958 and in 1964). Compositions in the latter part of the 1950s gave indications of growing creative maturity: sonatas for flute and for clarinet (1957), for violin (1958–59), his String Quartet no. 1 (1958–59), and his first two operas, *Jacob and the Indians* (1956–57; Woodstock, N.Y., July 24, 1957), and *Sarah* (1958; N.Y., November 30, 1958).

Laderman was appointed to the music faculty of Sarah Lawrence College in Bronxville, N.Y., in 1960, where he remained a year, a time in which he completed a children's opera, *The Hunting of the Snark* (1960), based on a story by Lewis Carroll (N.Y., March 25, 1961), an oratorio, *The Eagle Stirred* (1960–61), and a Violin Concerto (1963). From his song cycle, *Songs for Eve,* to poems by Archibald MacLeish (1962–63), comes "The Riddles," since become one of his most frequently heard compositions.

In 1963, Laderman received the Prix de Rome. At the American Academy in Rome he wrote Symphony no. 1 (1964) and String Quartet no. 2 (1964–65; Washington, D.C., May 8, 1965). Upon returning to the United States, Laderman spent another year as professor at Sarah Lawrence College (1965–66)— summers as staff composer at the Bennington Composers Conference in Vermont in 1967 and 1968— before assuming the post of professor of composition and composer-in-residence at the State University of New York at Binghamton, N.Y., in 1971, where he remained until 1979. Meanwhile he contributed an effective score to the motion picture *The Eleanor Roosevelt Story* (1965), winner of an Oscar as the year's best documentary film; he adapted its main theme into a concert work for chamber orchestra.

Two major works by Laderman were stimulated by his interest in the state of Israel. The emotional impact of the Six Days' War led to the writing of *From the Psalms* (1967–68), for soprano and piano, text derived from material taken from twenty psalms. In a new version, scored for soprano and five instruments, it was heard in New York on January 12, 1977, when Harold C. Schonberg in the *New York Times* called it "the hit of the evening. Mr. Laderman has set the Biblical texts in an austere manner;

the harmonies are bleak and powerful. . . . The vocal line is declamatory. This is a competent piece of craftsmanship." Symphony no. 3, *Jerusalem* (1973), was commissioned by CBS-TV to commemorate the twenty-fifth anniversary of the founding of the state of Israel. Each of its four movements ("Beginning," "Exile," "Longing," and "Return") presented a different stage in the history of the Jewish people climaxed by the triumphant birth of the state. First introduced in Jerusalem in 1973, this symphony received its American premiere over the CBS-TV network on April 3, 1977, in celebration of the Passover holiday. In this work, Laderman's writing is neoromantic with frequent use of chromaticisms and atonality.

A one-act opera, *And David Wept* (1970), was still another Laderman work of Hebraic content and interest. CBS-TV commissioned it and, with choreography by José Limon and a cast including Sherrill Milnes and Rosalind Elias, presented it on its television network in 1971. Joe Darion's libretto reached into the Bible for the story of King David and his emotional involvement with Bathsheba, wife of the general Uriah, who is dispatched by King David to battle and death. Laderman's score skillfully combined speech (over an instrumental accompaniment) and song, the song consistently tonal and lyrical with an occasional suggestion of popularism. The first staged production of this opera came a decade later, in New York, on May 31, 1980.

Among Laderman's later works, *Elegy,* for solo viola (1973), is one of his most lyrical and emotional, and the opera *Galileo Galilei* (1978) is structurally the most ambitious and stylistically the most dramatic. *Elegy,* the composer's lament on the death of his mother, was commissioned by the violist Toby Appel, who introduced it in New York on February 17, 1974. Subsequently Laderman rewrote it as *Other Voices,* for three violas, to be performed by a single solo instrumentalist, the other two parts dubbed in on tape (CBS-TV, March 20, 1977). *Galileo Galelei* was first produced in Binghamton, N.Y., on February 3, 1979. This was an extension and a rewriting of an oratorio, *The Tragedy of Galileo* (1967; CBS-TV, May 14, 1967). Both the oratorio and the opera had librettos by Joe Darion that touched upon various episodes in Galileo's life in which he came to grips with the church authorities and which was climaxed by a trial before the Inquisition when, under torture, Galileo was forced to recant his beliefs. Laderman's score was an astute fusion of tonal and atonal writing, of lyrical ariosos and powerful speechlike declamations, always conscious of and meeting the demands of Darion's high-tensioned, dramatic text. "The actual writing and scoring display a most experienced composer, and some of the choral writing is magnificent," said Harold C. Schonberg in the *New York Times.* He concluded: "His score will occupy an honorable place in the annals of American opera." In *High Fidelity/Musical America,* a critic noted that "the most important addition to the oratorio, in a scene where the women in Galileo's life—daughters, mistress, prostitutes—variously accuse him of heartlessness and forgive him, achieves the revised opera's most sustained flights of melody and harmonic beauty."

Commemoration of the American bicentennial, and a commission from the Columbus Symphony Orchestra in Ohio, led to the writing of *Columbus,* a monologue for solo bass and orchestra (1975) which the Columbus Symphony under Evan Whalon premiered on October 10, 1975. The text was an adaptation of material from a play by Nikos Kazantzakis. For the Alard String Quartet, Laderman produced his String Quartet no. 5 (1976), with the world premiere following four years later in a performance by that group in New York on November 24, 1980. Baroque and classical procedures are followed in this long, three-movement composition which combines baroque-type dance forms, a sonata-form movement and a finale consisting of a theme and ten variations. "All this," reported Peter G. Davis in the *New York Times,* "is carried out with Mr. Laderman's customary skill. Yet the piece digests the style of so many early 20th-century composers so smoothly that it finally ends up sounding anonymous." On a commission from the New Music for the Young Ensembles, Inc., Laderman completed *Cadence,* for double string quartet, two flutes, and double bass (1978); it was introduced in New York on October 23, 1979. This is a work, said Joseph Horowitz in the *New York Times,* "of Bergian richness [which] superbly juxtaposes shimmering flute sounds with the warmth of massed strings." Laderman's Piano Concerto no. 3 (1978) had its world premiere in Washington, D.C., early in May 1979 and was heard in New York on May 14, 1979. A traditional three-movement work, tonal and lyrical, this concerto neatly fuses the neoromanticism of Rachmaninoff with post-Webern expressionism. "Although the form of the concerto's first movement is to move through a series of variations towards a rapprochement between the two styles," noted a critic for *High Fidelity/Musical America,* "the composer's bias seems unquestionably to be on the tonal, lyric side in this work. The concerto . . . is broadly scored with titanic piano writing."

On Christmas Eve, 1979, Laderman's *Mass for Cain* (1979), for solo voices, chorus, two pianos, and organ, subsequently orchestrated, received its world premiere at the Riverside Church in New York; this performance was telecast by CBS-TV. An orchestral work, *Summer Solstice,* which the Saratoga Performing Arts Center in New York had commissioned, was given its first hearing on August 15, 1980, in Saratoga, in a performance by the Philadelphia Orchestra conducted by Michael Tilson Thomas.

Laderman completed several notable concertos between 1979 and 1980. One of these was for violin and orchestra which Elmar Oliveira (for whom it was written) introduced on December 12, 1980, as soloist with the Philadelphia Orchestra, the composer conducting. As the composer has explained, this is "a work that moves easily into and out of tonality. In fact, the opening D-flat-G-flat cadence proclaims a tonal center with clear conviction. The cadence is the beginning of a thematic statement that is the central motivating force of the first movement." Of the other two movements, the composer has this to say: "A controlled, enigmatic introduction opens the second movement. The solo violin's entrance changes that feeling completely and unfolds a long lyric line that becomes the centerpiece of the art that spans this movement. . . . The third movement is in the form of a rondo. Again the juxtaposition of contrasting elements is evident. A triplet rollicking theme, a running figuration, an expressionistic soaring line that is superimposed on the initial material, a middle section that explores with drama and irony expressed through various types of pizzicato—all create a rich and colorful texture, building to a buoyant, exhilarating conclusion."

The Concerto for String Quartet and Orchestra (1980) was written for the Alard String Quartet, the ensemble that presented the world premiere in Pittsburgh on February 6, 1981, as soloists with the Pittsburgh Symphony conducted by André Previn. As the composer has written, this composition represented for him a challenge to create "an atmosphere wherein the sound of the quartet remained true unto itself while it achieved an aggregate soloistic personality." A spirited first movement Allegro is followed by a reflective Andante of great sobriety, and the work concludes with a dramatic and rhythmic Allegro. As had been the case with the Violin Concerto, the work moves flexibly in and out of tonality.

Laderman's Symphony no. 4 (1980) received its world premiere on October 22, 1981, Carlo Maria Giulini conducting the Los Angeles Philharmonic.

Laderman was president of the American Music Center between 1973 and 1976. He resigned as professor of composition and composer-in-residence at the State University of New York in Binghamton to become director of the music program of the National Endowment for the Arts in Washington, D.C., in 1979.

PRINCIPAL WORKS: 6 string quartets (1958–80); 4 symphonies (1964–81); 3 piano concertos (1957–78); 2 violin concertos (1963, 1979); 2 piano sonatas (1952, 1956).

Jacob and the Indians, opera (1956–57); Flute Sonata (1957); Clarinet Sonata (1957); *Sarah,* one-act opera (1958); Theme, Variations, and Finale, for four winds and four strings (1957); Violin Sonata (1958–59); *Goodbye to the Clowns,* opera (1959–60); *Stanzas,* for chamber orchestra (1960); *The Eagle Stirred,* oratorio, for solo voices, chorus, and orchestra (1960–61); *Songs for Eve,* song cycle for voice and piano (1962–63); Nonette (1963); *Shadows Among*

Us, opera (1956–69); *Magic Prison*, for two narrators and orchestra (1967); *Satire: Concerto for Orchestra* (1967); *The Tragedy of Galileo*, oratorio for solo voices, chorus, and orchestra (1967); *From the Psalms*, song cycle for soprano and piano, also for soprano and instruments (1967–68); *And David Wept*, one-act opera (1970); *Elegy*, for solo viola, also for viola with two violas dubbed on prerecorded tape (1973); *Momenti*, for piano (1973); *Celestial Bodies*, for flute and string quartet (1975); *Columbus*, monologue for bass and orchestra (1975); Twenty-five Preludes, for organ (1975); *Galileo Galilei*, opera (1978); *Cadence*, for double string quartet, two flutes, and bass viol (1978); *Mass for Cain*, for solo voices, chorus, two pianos, and organ, also for voices and orchestra (1979); Violin Concerto (1979); *Summer Solstice*, for orchestra (1980); Concerto for String Quartet and Orchestra (1980); Viola Concerto (1980).

BIBLIOGRAPHY: *BBDM*; *DCM*; *High Fidelity/Musical America*, March 1980; *New York Times*, May 25, 1980; *Who's Who in America, 1980–81*.

La Montaine, John, b. Chicago, Ill., March 17, 1920.

Winner of the Pulitzer Prize in music in 1959, La Montaine is the composer of a wide range of undertakings: symphonic, chamber ensemble, ballet, opera, choral, and solo works. His influences are also wide-ranging: medieval, classical, romantic, diatonic, dodecaphonic and serial, hymn. folk song, and jazz. The chief characteristic of all his works is their appeal to the broad public rather than to the specialist in any of these fields. Some of his major works utilize bird calls and animal sounds.

His mother was a pianist whose performances of hymns became John's first musical experience. He began studying the piano when he was five, his earliest teachers including his neighbors and after that Muriel Parker and Margaret Farr Wilson. In spite of the fact that his piano study was intensive, and that he made a debut as pianist in Bloomington, Ind., when he was eleven, he never aspired to be a virtuoso but almost from his musical beginnings aimed to become a composer.

Between 1935 and 1938, he attended the American Conservatory of Music in Chicago, where he studied theory with Stella Roberts. Then, at the Eastman School of Music in Rochester, N.Y. (1938–42), he studied the piano with Max Landow and composition with Howard Hanson and Bernard Rogers. He received his bachelor of music degree in 1942.

During World War II, La Montaine served in the U.S. Navy (1941–46). While in uniform, he continued piano study with Rudolph Ganz at the Chicago Musical College. Upon his discharge from military service La Montaine resumed music study at the Juilliard School of Music (composition with Bernard Wagenaar) and subsequently at the American Conservatory in Fontainebleau in France with Nadia Boulanger. He was writing music all this time, his first published work being a Toccata, for piano, followed by Four Songs, for soprano, piano, and violin or flute (op. 2), Piano Sonata (op. 3), and *Invocation*, for voice and piano (op. 4), all essentially romantic, yet each possessing an identity of its own.

The first work of his maturity was *Song of the Rose of Sharon*, op. 6, a song cycle performed uninterruptedly, for soprano and orchestra, text taken from the Song of Solomon. This work waited eight years for its premiere, which took place in Washington, D.C., on May 31, 1956, sung by Leontyne Price as soloist with the National Symphony under Howard Mitchell. This work was subsequently performed extensively both in the United States and abroad and was recorded by Eleanor Steber.

From 1950 to 1954 La Montaine was pianist and celestist of the NBC Symphony Orchestra, of which Arturo Toscanini was then musical director. La Montaine's creative output during this time was comparatively meager. In 1958, on commission from the Ford Foundation, he went to work on a Piano Concerto (op. 9), written in memory of his sister. This was the most ambitious creative project up to that time. It was a success of major dimensions when it was introduced by Jorge Bolet and the National Symphony under Howard Mitchell on November 25, 1958, in Washington, D.C. In 1959 it was awarded the Pulitzer Prize in music and in 1962 a grant from the American Academy of Arts and Letters to finance its recording. Soon after its premiere, the concerto was featured at the concerts of the Boston Symphony, the Cincinnati Symphony, and the San Francisco Symphony, among other orchestras.

A Guggenheim Fellowship in 1959, which was extended for a second year, enabled La Montaine to devote himself to the study of medieval literature and music. His aim was to compose a trilogy of liturgical operas based on medieval miracle plays. This project, delayed by a severe illness, was initiated in 1960 with the first of the trilogy, *Novellis, Novellis*, dealing with the Annunciation and the birth of Jesus. It was introduced in Washington, D.C., on December 24, 1961. Under a grant from the Martha Baird Rockefeller Foundation it was later heard in New York, and since has been given somewhere in the United States every year.

In 1960, La Montaine won the Rheta Sosland Chamber Music Competition with the String Quartet, op. 16, which makes extensive use of inversion of thematic materials and motivic development. One year later he became the first composer ever commissioned to write music for a presidential inauguration. That was the *Overture: From Sea to Shining Sea*, which the National Symphony under Howard Mitchell performed on January 20, 1960, at the inaugural concert for President and Mrs. John F. Kennedy.

La Montaine was visiting professor of composition at the Eastman School of Music in 1961, and composer-in-residence at the American Academy in Rome in 1962.

On a farm in Mt. Kisco, N.Y., in 1963, La Montaine first became fascinated with bird calls. This interest eventually sent him to foreign places, including Africa, India, Nepal, and New Guinea. As a result of the study of bird calls and animal sounds he began incorporating them into his compositions. The first of these was *Birds of Paradise*, op. 34, first performed in April 1964 in Rochester, N.Y., by the Eastman Rochester Symphony under Howard Hanson. Gerald Arpino choreographed this music for the Joffrey Ballet in 1966, and under the title of *Nightwings* it was produced in New York on September 7, 1966. Another and more complex work utilizing bird and animal sounds was the *Mass of Nature*, op. 37, for narrator, chorus, and orchestra, which, though completed in 1966, was not performed until May 26, 1976, in Washington, D.C. At that concert two related works using the same thematic material were also heard, the already-mentioned *Birds of Paradise*, and *Te Deum*, op. 35, for narrator, chorus, wind orchestra, and percussion, forming a trilogy the composer has designated as *Sacred Service*.

La Montaine was able to proceed with the second and third operas of his liturgical trilogy in 1966 through a grant from an anonymous benefactor. *Shephardes Play*, op. 38, once again using the original text of a medieval miracle play, was premiered in Washington, D.C., on December 24, 1967, and in 1968 it was televised nationally over the ABC-TV network when it received the Sigma Alpha Iota Television Award as the year's best musical program over television. The third opera was *Erode, the Greate*, op. 40, given its world premiere in Washington, D.C., on New Year's Eve, 1969.

What the composer himself regards as one of his most significant works is *Wilderness Journal*, op. 41, a symphony for bass-baritone, organ, and orchestra that he wrote on commission from Mrs. Jouett Shouse for the opening of the Kennedy Center in Washington, D.C., and the dedication of the Filene Organ which she had donated. Every part of every bar of the fourteen movements in *Wilderness Journal* is based on the same twelve-tone theme. "The structural means employed are intended as a grand metaphor suggesting the unity of nature, the variety of its forms, its wealth of organic relationships . . . and above all the logic of its structure, everywhere present beneath the sensuous beauty of surface," the composer explains. Bird calls and other sounds of nature are predominant. The premiere took place at the Kennedy Center on October 10, 1972, with Donald Gramm as vocal soloist, Paul Callaway, organist, and the National Symphony under Antal Dorati.

Commissioned by the Institute for the Arts and Humanistic Studies of Pennsylvania State University to prepare a work commemorating the American bicentennial, La Montaine completed a documentary opera-extravaganza *Be Glad Then, America*, op. 43, subtitled "A Decent Entertainment from the Thirteen Colonies." The text, by the composer, was taken from the speeches, letters, journals, newspapers, and broadsides of colonial America, tracing the events leading to the signing of the Declaration of Independence. The Boston Tea Party is enacted at the close of the first act; the Battle of Lexington ends the second act; and the third act closes with the singing of William Billings's "Chester," one of two Billings anthems used in this score, the other being "An Anthem for Fast Day." The chorus represented "we the people." Principal characters included King George, a town crier, a folk singer, the Muse of Liberty and one singer who was called upon to play eight different American patriots. The world premiere, given in Pittsburgh on February 6, 1976, was "a triumph at first hearing," as Paul Hume reported in the *Washington Post*. A television documentary, tracing the opera from its writing stage to its production, was telecast by the Public Broadcasting Service over its nationwide network on July 4 and 10, 1977, and again in July 1978.

In 1977, at a time when his vision was severely diminished due to cataracts making the writing of ambitious scores impossible, La Montaine entered a new phase of his productivity by writing hymns. This phase was initiated when he was commissioned by the Hymn Society of America to compose Three Hymns and an Anthem. Upon completing this work, La Montaine was fired with the ambition of writing an entire hymbook. *The Whittier Service*, op. 42-A, for chorus, organ, and guitar, based on texts of John Greenleaf Whittier, was a step in this direction.

Some of La Montaine's later works were written for the flute. The most significant of these is the Concerto for Flute and Orchestra, op. 48, which received its world premiere at the American Music Festival in Washington, D. C., in April 1981.

La Montaine has served as visiting professor of composition in several universities, including the University of Utah in Salt Lake City, and Whittier College in California. At the latter institution he held the Nixon Chair as the Nixon Distinguished Scholar in 1977, Whittier College being President Nixon's alma mater. The Eastman School presented La Montaine with its Distinguished Alumni Award.

THE COMPOSER SPEAKS: The world can offer no adventure greater than being a composer. You are always at the frontier of your own possibilities; you are always traveling into the unknown future you are creating. The hazard of performers, publishers, critics, friends, and the public surround you and make every forward step a new peril. You achieve nothing if you do not dare to lay your life on the line with every new undertaking. When you dare to take a long voyage into the unknown, you may discover a new continent. But even if you do not, the journey itself is the greatest of rewards.

PRINCIPAL WORKS: (*Note*: The composer is reluctant to pinpoint any of his works with the year of composition, thus the exact year of each is hard to come by. He prefers to indicate the chronological order of his works with opus numbers, a procedure followed throughout the biography and in the following listing.)

Songs of the Rose of Sharon, biblical cycle for soprano and orchestra or piano, op. 6; Cello Sonata, op. 8; Piano Concerto, op. 9; *Ode*, for oboe and orchestra, op. 11; Six Sonnets of Shakespeare, for voice and piano, op. 12; Sonnets, for orchestra, op. 12-A; *Songs of Nativity*, for a cappella chorus, op. 13; *Fuguing Set*, for piano, op. 14; Three Poems by Holly Beye, for voice and piano, op. 15; String Quartet, op. 16; *Six Dance Preludes*, for piano, op. 18; *Jubilant Overture*, for orchestra, op. 20; *God of Grace and God of Glory*, for chorus and organ, op. 22; *Wonder Tidings*, for vocal soloists, chorus, harp, and percussion, op. 23; Quartet for Woodwinds, op. 24-A; *Fragments from the Song of Songs*, biblical cycle for soprano and orchestra, op. 29; *Overture: From Sea to Shining Sea*, for orchestra, op. 30; *Novellis, Novellis,* liturgical opera, op. 31; *A Summer's Day*, sonnet for orchestra, op. 32; *Canticle*, for orchestra, op. 33; *Birds of Paradise*, for piano and orchestra, op. 34; Three Psalms, for chorus and small orchestra, op. 36; *Mass of Nature*, for narrator, chorus, and orchestra, op. 37; *Shephardes Playe*, liturgical opera, op. 38; *Incantation for Jazz Band*, op. 39; *Erode the Greate*, liturgical opera, op. 40; *Wilderness Journal*, for bass-baritone, organ, and orchestra, op. 41; *Conversations*, for violin, viola, and flute, op. 42; *The Whittier Service*, for chorus, organ, and guitar, op. 42-A; *Be Glad Then, America*, a "documentary opera-extravaganza," op. 43; *Overture: An Early American Sampler*, op. 43-A; *The Nine Lessons of Christmas*, for vocal soloists, narrator, chorus, harp, and percussion, op. 44; *Canonic Variations*, for flute and clarinet, op. 47; Flute Concerto, op. 48; *Come into My Garden* and *My Beloved, Let Us Go Forth*, for flute and piano (also flute and orchestra), op. 49, nos. 1 and 2.

BIBLIOGRAPHY: *BBDM; DCM; Who's Who in America, 1978–79.*

Lee, Dai-Keong, b. Honolulu, Hawaii, September 2, 1915.

Drawing upon his unusual personal heritage as a Hawaiian American born of Chinese parentage, Lee has succeeded in synthesizing the musical soul of Polynesia in his first successful compositions in which he realized a kind of Pan-American Americanism. Consequently, in style and content, Lee's output reflects the spirit, exuberant energy, and af-

firmation of Polynesia with brisk driving rhythms, open harmonies, and sonorous textures. By combining the neoprimitive tetratonic scale of early Polynesia with that of the 16th-century modes, he has succeeded in discovering a language of his own.

Musical from childhood, Lee began studying the piano when he was nine. He does not remember the name of his first piano teacher but he does recall studying theory with Vern Waldo Thompson at Kokokahi for several summers in the 1930s. This led to further studies with George W. Andrews, who had retired as dean of Oberlin College to become organist of the Central Union Church in Honolulu. During his high school days, Lee played trumpet in a band, piano for local dances, and the French horn in the Honolulu Symphony Orchestra under Fritz Hart. It was Hart who introduced Lee's first orchestral piece, *Valse pensieroso*, with the Honolulu Symphony Orchestra in 1936. Lee recalls that his first piece sounded like a mixture of Sibelius and Stravinsky.

After three years at the University of Hawaii, he decided to make music his career. In 1937 he left for New York, becoming a scholarship student with Roger Sessions. In 1938 he was awarded a three-year fellowship in composition at the Julliard School of Music to study under Frederick Jacobi, and following his graduation in 1941, still another fellowship which brought him to the Berkshire Music Center at Tanglewood, Mass., for further composition study with Aaron Copland.

Out of this came two compositions for orchestra: *Prelude and Hula* (1939) and *Hawaiian Festival Overture* (1940). Both utilized the Polynesian tetratonic scale in combination with the 16th-century modes. Albert Stoessel introduced *Prelude and Hula* over the NBC radio network on July 20, 1941, with the Chautauqua Orchestra; Dean Dixon premiered it in New York on August 7, 1941, with the New York Philharmonic. Lee revised the work a few months later, the new version premiered on January 18, 1942, by Hans Kindler and the National Symphony, who also recorded it. "The music," reported a critic in the *Washington Post*, "has an intrinsic charm and imaginative poetry beneath its surface of harmonic sophistication." *Hawaiian Festival Overture* had started out as the third movement of the Hawaiian legend suite *Naupaka*, which was heard at the Juilliard School in 1942. Extracting the third movement and adapting it into an overture, Lee retitled it the *Hawaiian Festival Overture*, which Efrem Kurtz premiered with the New York Philharmonic in the summer of 1942. Major orchestras throughout the United States performed it under Fritz Reiner, Eugene Goossens, Saul Caston, Leopold Stokowski, William Steinberg, and Dimitri Mitropoulos, the last of whom featured it during his tour with the Minneapolis Symphony in 1942–43. A critic in the *St. Paul Pioneer Press* wrote: "Perhaps the most important thing about the *Hawaiian Festival Overture* is that it presents a new aspect of creative music in

America. . . . There are primitive melodic patterns of several kinds, ranging from delicately insinuating pizzicatti in the basses to the good lusty wham on the drums."

Other compositions of this period included a one-act opera, *The Poet's Dilemma*, produced at the Juilliard School on April 12, 1940, and Introduction and Allegro for Strings (1941), commissioned by the CBS radio network, where it received its first performance on November 15, 1941, Howard Barlow conducting. On a commission from Richard Bales, Lee prepared Introduction and Scherzo (1941), which Bales introduced on November 6, 1941, with the Philadelphia Little Symphony in Philadelphia. For the CBS British American Music Festival, Lee wrote the *Golden Gate Overture*, originally called *Essay for Orchestra* (1942), premiered on March 13, 1942, over the CBS network. During the summer of 1941, while studying with Copeland, Lee wrote his first major work, Symphony no. 1 in One Movement. "Copland," Lee reveals, "was a strong influence in pointing the way to further exploitation of harmonic and rhythmic possibilities."

In 1942, during World War II, Lee enlisted in the armed forces, serving with the advance echelon of the Fifth Air Force in the Southwest Pacific Theater. During the tour of duty in New Guinea, Lee completed *Pacific Prayer* (1943). "I wanted this composition to express the hopes of the fighting men in the Pacific for a just end to the war and a better postwar world." Leopold Stokowski and the New York City Symphony introduced it on March 12, 1944. A few months later, on a furlough, Lee appeared as guest conductor of the Sydney ABC Symphony Orchestra presenting his *Pacific Prayer* and the world premiere of Symphony no. 1.

In 1945, Lee received the first of two Guggenheim Fellowships (the second coming six years later). He revised his Symphony no. 1, separating it into three movements. Structurally, it was neoclassical and stylistically, modal and occasionally diatonic. It anticipated the idiom Lee would favor for many of his subsequent compositions. An earlier version was premiered by Howard Hanson and the Eastman-Rochester Philharmonic in 1947, the definitive one conducted by Leon Barzin and the National Orchestra Association in New York on January 5, 1951. "The music does move forward," Virgil Thomson said in the *New York Herald Tribune*, "and it moves in response to the composer's will. That will seems to demand that music express his thought, his own real personal and private universe. . . . It sings and it declaims. What it sings and what it declaims is pure poetry and not borrowed attitudes." In 1946 Lee also wrote *East and West*, a choral piece promoting tolerance for American racial minorities; it was commissioned by the Inter-Racial Singers, who introduced it in New York on June 3, 1946. A Violin Concerto (1947), commissioned by Albert Metz, was premiered by Joan Field in Washington, D. C., on September 29, 1957, with the National Gallery Orchestra conducted by Richard Bales.

In 1950–51 Lee attended Columbia University to study composition with Otto Leuning, with special emphasis on musical prosody. Commissioned by the Blackfriars Theater of New York, Lee completed a three-act opera, *Open the Gates*, text by Robert Payne, based on the life of Mary Magdalene, which was produced in New York on February 22, 1951. On March 13, 1952, Pierre Monteux premiered Lee's Symphony no. 2 (1952) with the San Francisco Symphony Orchestra. Alfred Frankenstein wrote in the *San Francisco Chronicle* that "it was a well-made work with a particularly effective slow movement in the Copland tradition." A year later, Lee composed the musical score for the Broadway success *Teahouse of the August Moon*, which opened on October 15, 1953. A symphonic suite adapted from this music was premiered in Boston by the Boston Pops under Arthur Fiedler.

Two one-act operas followed, pointing the new direction toward which Lee was traveling in the musical theater: to the kind of *Zeitkunst* made famous by Kurt Weill and Carl Orff. This tendency in Lee was culminated with *Ballad of Kitty Barkeep* (1979), libretto by Robert Healey, a drastic revision of one of two one-act operas. Meanwhile, Lee had been involved with some concert music. *Polynesian Suite*, for orchestra (1958), was premiered by the Honolulu Symphony Orchestra under George Barati on January 29, 1961. *Mele Olili*, or *Joyful Songs* (1960), was a scenic cantata for vocal soloists, chorus, and orchestra. It consisted of seven Hawaiian chants of premissionary time, two of which had to be deleted from the score because Hawaiian scholars objected to one of them as being too sacred and the other as too salacious. *Canticle of the Pacific* (1968), for chorus and orchestra—an extension of the earlier *Pacific Prayer*—was a symphonic prayer for world peace based on a Vietnamese children's song and a Buddhist chant. It received its world premiere on November 10, 1969, in a performance by the Tulsa Philharmonic directed by Franco Autori.

THE COMPOSER SPEAKS: I believe music is a language of feeling. The creation of music has always been and still is a mystery to me. Sometimes, after I hear a piece of music I composed many years ago, I wonder how it all came about.

I do not have the immortality syndrome; all I ask is that my music communicate.

PRINCIPAL WORKS: 2 symphonies (1941–42, revised 1946; 1952); 2 Polynesian Suites, for orchestra (1958, 1960).

Prelude and Hula, for orchestra (1939); *Hawaiian Festival Overture*, for orchestra (1940); Introduction and Allegro (1941); Introduction and Scherzo, for strings (1941); *Golden Gate Overture*, for chamber orchestra (1941); *Pacific Prayer*, for orchestra

(1943); Violin Concerto (1947, revised 1955); *Incantation and Dance*, for violin and piano (1948); Piano Sonatina (1949); *Open the Gates*, opera (1951); *Teahouse of the August Moon*, symphonic suite (1954); *Mele Olili*, scenic cantata for vocal soloists, chorus, and orchestra (1960); *Canticle of the Pacific*, for solo voices and orchestra (1969); *Noa Noa*, musical play (1972); *Ballad of Kitty the Barkeep*, musical play (1979); *Jenny Lind*, musical play (1979).

BIBLIOGRAPHY: Ewen, David, *American Composers Today* (N.Y., 1949); Thomson, Virgil, *American Music Since 1910* (N.Y., 1970); *Who's Who in America 1978-79*.

Lees, Benjamin, b. Harbin, China, January 8, 1924. American citizen, 1931.

"The tools of composition are everywhere for everyone to use," Lees has written, "and I have employed them all from a simple triad to controlled chaos." Through the years, Lee has maintained a consistent posture. He is partial to a lucid texture within clearly defined structures and he avoids far-out avant-garde idioms.

He was born to Russian parents. He was eighteen months old when his family settled in San Francisco. There, when he was six, he began studying the piano with K. I. Rodetsky. In this he was encouraged by both parents, though neither was especially musical; but later, they did what they could to discourage him from becoming a professional musician. At Roosevelt Junior High School (1934–37) and George Washington High School (1938–39), both in San Francisco, Lees sang in the school chorus and gave performances on the piano in the assembly. When he was sixteen, the Lees family moved to Los Angeles, which remained Lees's home up to the time of World War II. For four years he studied the piano privately with Marguerite Bitter. As a student at Alexander Hamilton High School (1939–41) he once again was a participant in the school's musical activities.

He was graduated from high school in 1941. The next four years he served in the U. S. Army, during World War II, initially in the Signal Corps and later on with a mobile radar unit training in the swamps of Florida in preparation for action in the Pacific. He never saw overseas duty. Upon his discharge from military service he returned to Los Angeles, where, in need of money, he took a job with the Metro-Goldwyn-Mayer studios in a nonmusical capacity. This enabled him to pay for music lessons on the outside without burdening his family. By the end of 1945 he was ready for formal training in composition and, in 1946, he enrolled in the University of Southern California in Los Angeles, studying composition and theory with Halsey Stevens and Ingolf Dahl, counterpoint and theory with Ernst Kanitz, and canon and fugue with Richard Donovan (1945–48). In 1948 he married Leatrice Banks (with whom he has

a daughter). By the end of 1948 he decided to leave the University of Southern California to begin private studies in composition with George Antheil (1949–53). "Those years of advanced study," Lees recalls, "marked a turning point in my life." It was Antheil who encouraged him to become a composer. As Antheil's pupil, Lees completed his first two piano sonatas (1949, 1950), a Sonata for Two Pianos (1951), his first work for orchestra, *Profile for Orchestra* (1952; NBC radio, April 18, 1954), and *Declamations*, for string quartet and piano (1952; Oklahoma City, Okla., April 26, 1956).

Between 1950 and 1952, Lees was employed as piano accompanist for the Eugene Loring Ballet School in Los Angeles, and he completed four seven-minute scores for short animated films. He left Los Angeles in 1953 to come to New York, where he wrote the Piano Concerto no. 1 (1954–55), which was introduced in Vienna, Austria, on April 26, 1956, and then was given performances in Helsinki, Geneva, and Paris. Recognition of his blossoming creative talent came in 1953 with the Fromm Music Foundation Award for the String Quartet no. 1 (1952); in 1954, with a Guggenheim Fellowship; in 1955, with the Norma Copley Award for overall achievement in music; and in 1956, with a Fulbright Fellowship. The Fulbright Fellowship brought Lees to Finland for composition. For the next six years he remained in Europe, partly in Paris, partly in Vienna, partly in Genoa, and partly traveling and absorbing musical and cultural experiences. "In Vienna, where I lived for over a year, I met some of the avant-garde composers just coming on the scene. In Genoa, I lectured on American music. The French experience was highlighted by my friendship with the painters Marcel Duchamp, Renée Magritte, and Man Ray, and with composers Henri Sauguet, Henri Dutilleux, André Jolivet, and Darius Milhaud. Primarily, Europe was a refuge, so to speak, where I seemingly did little else save write and refine my craft."

In major works completed in Europe, Lees crystallized a style that was his own and immediately recognizable. It combined discipline, economy, emotional expressivity, and rhythmic drive. His Symphony no. 2 (1957), which was commissioned by the Louisville Orchestra in Kentucky, was introduced by that organization under Robert Whitney on December 3, 1958. George Szell, musical director of the Cleveland Orchestra, was so impressed with it that he performed it not only in Cleveland but also on tour, the final performance given in Carnegie Hall in New York. "My career began after the critics hailed the work and the brilliant performances given by Szell and his orchestra in the season of 1959–60."

The Violin Concerto (1958), which Henryk Szeryng premiered with the Boston Symphony under Erich Leinsdorf on February 8, 1963, was classic in spirit and structure, but diverged from the classical concerto in that it had two slow movements instead of one, with one of them utilizing only a basic theme (instead of two) which underwent various transformations. When the Concerto for Orchestra, no. 1 (1959; Rochester, N.Y., February 22, 1962) was first heard in November 1972 in New York, John Rockwell in the *New York Times* described it as "unabashedly tonal [with] the formal procedures conventional, and the writing throughout lovingly idiomatic, with that for percussion downright fresh." *Visions of Poets* (1961) was a large-scale dramatic cantata for soprano, tenor, chorus, and orchestra using Walt Whitman's poems as text. It was written on commission for the dedicatory concert of a new opera house in Seattle, Wash., on May 15, 1962, Milton Katims conducting. Writing in *Musical America*, Tom Wendel reported that it "invokes the historical imagination with its vision of the past. It continues with a sensuous realization of the present and closes with a vision of the future. The musical settings for these verses were lean, terse, and remarkably imaginative with a vigor and integrity that mark the piece as a major work." *Spectrum*, for orchestra (1964), was commissioned by Milton Katims for the Musical Arts Society of La Jolla, Calif., where it was given its premiere on June 21, 1964. "The title," the composer explains, "refers to the rather strange colors in this composition achieved by various timbres and textures."

In 1958, Lees was the recipient of the UNESCO Award in Paris, and shortly after that of the Sir Arnold Bax Medal. In 1963, he finally returned to the United States. For the next two years, he was visiting professor at the Peabody Conservatory in Baltimore (to which he returned for an additional two-year period in 1966–68). From 1964 to 1968 he was professor of music at Queen's College in Queens, New York.

In 1963, on a Ford Foundation grant, Lees composed the traditional but ambitiously structured Piano Sonato no. 4 for Gary Graffman, who introduced it in New York on April 3, 1964. For Graffman, on commission, Lees also wrote the Piano Concerto no. 2 (1966), a neoclassically oriented work in a modified classical form but with harmonic, rhythmic, and motivic materials rooted in Bartók and Prokofiev. Its first performance was given on March 15, 1968, by Gary Graffman and the Boston Symphony conducted by Leinsdorf. "It possesses two attributes inseparable from . . . high distinction: a musical impulse and sound substance. It is, to my hearing, neither contrived nor constructed; it is composed, which is to say, evolved with purpose and integrity from a productive premise," wrote Irving Kolodin in *Saturday Review*. Between these two piano works came the important Concerto for String Quartet and Orchestra (1964), which the Kansas City Symphony commissioned and introduced on January 19, 1965, after which it was featured prominently by several other major American orchestras.

In 1967, Lees toured the Soviet Union on an invitation of the State Department of the United States. He wrote Symphony no. 3 in 1968 on a commission from the Detroit Symphony, which premiered it under Sixten Ehrling's direction on October 23, 1968. One of the novel instrumental features here was the inclusion of a tenor saxophone (a modern instrument being pitted against a classical one—the orchestra). With percussion accompaniment, it is heard in a slow interlude to begin each of its three movements. When he wrote this symphony, Lees had in mind the modern electronic age of computers, satellites, and space explorations, and in his music he tried to seek out some meaning in time of such social and scientific upheaval.

Between 1970 and 1972 Lees was composer-in-residence at the University of Wisconsin in Milwaukee; in 1974, resident composer at the International Piano Festival Institute at Round Top, Tex.; and in 1976–77, visiting professor at the Juilliard School of Music.

Since 1970, Lees has relaxed neither his creative productivity nor the high standards of achievement which he has always set for himself. *The Trumpet of the Swan*, for narrator and orchestra (1971), was commissioned by William Smith, who conducted its premiere with the Philadelphia Orchestra on May 13, 1972. Its whimsical text, derived from a tale by E. B. White, found its counterpart in an infectiously charming, witty, and lyrical score. Etudes, for piano and orchestra (1974), was commissioned by the Albritton Foundation for the pianist James Dick, the artist who premiered it on October 28, 1974, with the Houston Symphony under Lawrence Foster. Fast and slow passages, rhythmic and lyrical ones, were continually contrasted in these five etudes. "In this particular piece," noted Irving Lowens in the *Washington Star-News*, reporting from Houston, "there seems to be an underlying sense of malaise, a hint of suppressed anger, that makes it peculiarly a product of the United States in 1974."

In commemoration of the American bicentennial, Lees completed three major works. Passacaglia, for orchestra (1975), was commissioned by the National Symphony Orchestra of Washington, D. C., which, under Antal Dorati, introduced it on April 13, 1976. Paul Hume, in the *Washington Post*, called it "one of the finest and most impressive scores Lees has created. . . . The music has power and lyric beauty." Variations, for piano and orchestra (1975), commissioned by the Music Teachers National Association for its one hundredth anniversary as well as for the American bicentennial, was first offered on March 31, 1976, by Eugene List with the Dallas Symphony under Louis Lane. And Concerto for Woodwind Quintet and Orchestra (1976), a commission of the Detroit Symphony, was programmed by that orchestra under Aldo Ceccato's direction on October 7, 1976. Toward the end of this composition, each member of the woodwind quintet is given an opportunity to display, solo, his virtuosity in a series of five cadenzas continually punctuated by rhythmic thrusts from the orchestra.

THE COMPOSER SPEAKS: I compose because I must—just as I must eat, live, breathe, love. . . . When I compose, I express myself, so perhaps in that sense one could call my music expressive. I consider music generally to be expressive of the composer's feelings. . . . By trying to master form thoroughly I have arrived at the point where I can experiment on an intelligent and intelligible level with new forms. In my compositions I consider form on a par with expression.

PRINCIPAL WORKS: 4 piano sonatas (1949–63); 3 symphonies (1953, 1958, 1968); 3 string quartets (1952, 1955, 1980); 2 piano concertos (1955, 1963); 2 violin sonatas (1953, 1972).

Profile, for orchestra (1952); *Declamations*, for string orchestra and piano (1952); Toccata, for piano (1953); Fantasia, for piano (1954); *Ten Kaleidoscopes*, for piano (1954); *Three Variables*, for wind quartet and piano (1955); *The Oracle*, music drama (1955); *Divertimento burlesca*, for orchestra (1957); Violin Concerto (1958); Concerto for Orchestra (1959); *Concertante breve*, for oboe, two horns, piano, and strings (1959); *Epigrams*, for piano (1960); *Visions of Poets*, dramatic cantata, for soprano, tenor, chorus, and orchestra (1961); Oboe Concerto (1963); *Spectrum*, for orchestra (1964); *Silhouettes*, for wind instruments and percussion (1967); *Odyssey*, for piano (1970); *Medea of Corinth*, for vocal solo and wind quintet (1971); *The Gilded Cage*, comic opera (1972); *The Trumpet of the Swan*, for narrator and orchestra (1972); *Collage*, for string quartet, woodwind quintet, and percussion (1972); Etudes, for piano and orchestra (1974); *Labyrinth*, for wind ensemble (1975); Variations, for piano and orchestra (1975); Passacaglia, for orchestra (1975); Concerto for Woodwind Quartet and Orchestra (1976); *Dialogue*, for cello and piano (1976); Viola Concerto (1977); *Staves*, song cycle for soprano and piano (1978); *Mobiles*, for orchestra (1980).

BIBLIOGRAPHY: *NGDMM*; Ewen, David, *Composers Since 1900* (N. Y., 1969); *Tempo*, Spring-Summer 1959, Spring 1963, June 1975; *Who's Who in America, 1980–81*.

Lockwood, Normand, b. New York City, March 19, 1906.

Lockwood has integrated into his writing many of the musical language constructional devices of the 20th century but without sacrificing a personal profile.

His father was a violinist, teacher, and the conductor of the School Community Orchestra at the School of Music at the University of Michigan in Ann Ar-

bor; his mother, a violinist, played in the school orchestra and the school faculty string quartet without being on the faculty. From his earliest years, Normand Lockwood was imbued with music. When he was ten, while attending elementary school at Ann Arbor, he began studying piano with Otto J. Stahl, who also worked theory into these lessons. Stahl was the first to encourage Lockwood to write music, and in his earliest compositions Lockwood was assisted in the notation by his father. From 1920 on, Lockwood took piano lessons with his uncle Albert Lockwood, who had an important influence on his early musical growth. Theory and formal analysis were pursued in classes at the School of Music at the University of Michigan with Stahl, Beryl Fox Bacher, and Earl Vincent Moore.

Lockwood's academic education ended in 1924 after two years at Ann Arbor High School. Later that year his uncle took him on an extended trip through Europe, finally depositing him in Rome, where he stayed on alone. In Rome, Lockwood studied composition for one year (1924–25) with Ottorino Respighi. Study of composition then continued with Nadia Boulanger in Paris (1926–27, 1928–29, and on and off between 1930 and 1932). "It was with her," he says, "that my training really began to take place and, it would seem, took hold." Meanwhile, on September 2, 1926, Lockwood married Dorothy Sanders, with whom he raised three children. She died in 1978.

On the strength of an orchestral work, *Odysseus* (1927), which the Chicago Symphony under Frederick Stock introduced at the May Festival in Ann Arbor in 1928 and which the composer subsequently withdrew, Lockwood was awarded the Prix de Rome, which brought him to the American Academy in Rome (1929–31). He returned to the United States in 1932 to become assistant professor of theory and composition at Oberlin College in Ohio, where he remained for the next thirteen years, having been promoted to associate professorship in 1937. In that time he wrote a good deal of chamber music: seven string quartets between 1933 and 1938, the third of which (1935) was the recipient of the Society for the Publications of American Music Award; Piano Quartet (1936); a Trio, for flute, viola, and harp (1940), which was commissioned by the Elizabeth Sprague Coolidge Foundation; and *Nine American Folk Songs*, for string quartet (1941). He also wrote a Symphony (1934) and a major work for unaccompanied chorus with text by Walt Whitman, *Out of the Cradle Endlessly Rocking* (1939), which received the G. Schirmer World's Fair Prize in 1939. All were tonal and diatonic, their lyric flow not arrested by the intrusion of controlled dissonances.

In 1943 Lockwood was engaged by CBS radio in New York to write music and make arrangements for some of its productions, including *Columbia Workshop, Studio One* and *The Squibb Show* between 1943 and 1951. In 1943 he was also awarded the first of two Guggenheim Fellowships, which was extended for an additional year in 1944. One year later, while lecturing on music at Columbia University (1945–52) Lockwood completed writing his first opera, *The Scarecrow* (1945), libretto by the composer's wife, based on a play by Percy MacKaye, which was written on a commission from the Alice M. Ditson Fund of Columbia University. There, its world premiere took place on May 19, 1945. In 1947, Lockwood was presented with the Ernest Bloch Prize for his oratorio *The Birth of Moses* (1947).

Lockwood received an award in music from the National Institute of Arts and Letters in 1945. Between 1945 and 1953 he was a faculty member at the School of Sacred Music at the Union Theological Seminary in New York. During those years he was also a faculty member of Westminster Choir College in Princeton, N.J. (1948–50), visiting professor at Queens College in Queens, N.Y. (1950–51), and a member of the faculty at the School of Music at Yale University (1950–51).

In 1951, on a commission from CBS radio, Lockwood wrote Concerto for Organ and Brasses for the organist E. Power Biggs, who introduced it over the CBS radio network on April 27, 1952. In 1951, Lockwood also completed *Memories of President Lincoln* (*Elegy to a Hero*), which Indiana University in Bloomington commissioned and then premiered on February 10, 1952. Lockwood followed these with *Prairie*, for chorus and orchestra (1952), based on Carl Sandburg's poems, written on a commission from Thor Johnson and the University of Michigan Musical Society. Though it received only a single performance—that of its world premiere on May 3, 1953, by the Philadelphia Orchestra and the University Choral Union conducted by Thor Johnson at Ann Arbor—it inspired such high praise that the limelight was now focused on Lockwood. Though it was written in a demonstrably American folk idiom, it did not resort to quotations, and Lockwood revealed "enough individuality to make it interesting, appealing and excitable," reported Harvey Taylor in the *Detroit Times*. In the *New York Times*, Olin Downes called the writing "sincere, melodic and substantial in workmanship," and in the *Ann Arbor News*, Louise Cuyler said, "Lockwood is both a sensitive composer and a practical craftsman, a combination which makes him articulate and comprehensible to a remarkable degree."

Other significant compositions in the 1950s included two oratorios and the Clarinet Quintet. One of these oratorios, *Children of God*, for five soloists, chorus, children's chorus, and orchestra (1956), was commissioned jointly by the Department of Worship and Arts of the National Council of Churches and Berea College of Kentucky. The text was arranged from the Revised Standard Version of the Bible by Clara Chassell Cooper, sections chosen by Professor Cooper to point up the theme of brotherhood. The Cincinnati Symphony and Berea College Communi-

ty Choir under Thor Johnson introduced it on February 1, 1957. "While the work is written in eighteen sections," wrote George Lynn in the *Bulletin of American Composers Alliance*, "it has the natural rise and fall of a large piece, the episodes serving only to move it on. Lockwood chooses to abandon certain stereotyped positions of the chorus in the oratorio tradition and turns to 'using' it to aid the progress of the dramatic moment."

The other oratorio was *Light Out of Darkness*, for baritone, chorus, and orchestra (1957), text taken from the letters of Paul and from the Psalms; it was commissioned by the Buffalo Philharmonic. The Clarinet Quintet (1959), a commission of the Cleveland Chamber Music Society, was premiered by that group in Cleveland on June 1, 1960.

Since 1960, Lockwood has continued producing compositions in all media, including three operas. *Early Dawn*, libretto based on a play by Russell Porter, was produced in Denver on August 1, 1962; *The Inevitable Hour* (originally billed as *The Hanging Judge*), libretto by Russel Porter, in Denver in March 1964; and *Requiem for a Rich Young Man*, a one-act opera to a libretto by Donald Sutherland, on November 24, 1964.

Recent major works for orchestra include a Piano Concerto (1974), Symphony for Strings (1976), and Symphony, for large orchestra (1979).

Lockwood was head of the music department at Trinity University in San Antonio, Tex., from 1953 to 1955. In 1957–58 he was visiting faculty member at the University of Oregon, and in 1960–61 at the University of Hawaii. After serving as visiting faculty member at the University of Denver during the summer of 1969, Lockwood was appointed associate professor of music and composer-in-residence there in 1961. He remained at the University of Denver until 1974, when he retired as professor emeritus.

In 1971, Lockwood received the Governor's Award in Music from the Colorado Council of Arts and Humanities. He was awarded an honorary doctorate in music from Berea College in Kentucky (1973) and an honorary doctorate of humane letters from the University of Denver (1979), and the Marjorie Peabody Waite Award in 1981. In 1981, the American Academy and Institute of Arts and Letters cited Lockwood for continuing achievement and integrity in his art.

THE COMPOSER SPEAKS: Ideally in music one should look for a vehicle sufficiently abstract to allow the listener to move around in it as he would in traversing, exploring an area of terrain. Mood, however, is the great magnet. Where it exists it draws the listener to itself and conveys to him its properties. It can afford pure pleasure. It can arouse emotions of joy, sorrow, dislike, hatred. It can establish sheer indefinable beauty. It can raise monotony to a level of impressive impact. It can generate responses of physical movement. For some it evokes pictures, Nature.

Also, alas, it can be so overly busy with itself (music, that is) as to create boredom.

To be anything, music—with or without words—must have character, definition, discernible delineation, otherwise it is Muzak. Untold quantities by every composer of every century sound repetitious, cliché-ridden, as much alike as avant-garde fun and games. Since the production line probably makes this inevitable, it is all the more reason to give composing one's personal attention.

PRINCIPAL WORKS: *Out of the Cradle Endlessly Rocking*, for a cappella chorus (1939); Trio, for harp, flute, and viola (1940, revised 1978); *Nine American Folk Songs*, for string quartet (1941); *The Scarecrow*, opera (1945); *Mary Who Stood in Sorrow*, for soprano and orchestra (1946); *Le chateau*, overture for orchestra (1949); *Carol Fantasy*, for chorus, occasional solo parts, and orchestra (1949); *Memories of President Lincoln* (*Elegy for a Hero*), for chorus (1951); Concerto no. 1, for organ and brass (1951); *Prairie*, for chorus and orchestra (1952); *I Hear America Singing*, for chorus and piano (1953); *Children of God*, oratorio for five vocalists, chorus, children's chorus, and orchestra (1956); *Light Out of Darkness*, oratorio for baritone, chorus, and orchestra (1957); Clarinet Quintet (1959); *Early Dawn*, opera (1961); *The Wizard of Balazar*, opera (c. 1962); *The Inevitable Hour*, opera (c. 1963); *Requiem for a Rich Young Man*, one-act chamber opera for four vocalists and nine instruments (1964); Sonata-fantasy, for accordion (1964); *The Dialogue of Abraham and Isaac*, for tenor and piano (1964); Oboe Concerto (1966); *From an Opening to a Close*, for wind instruments and percussion (1967); *Choreographic Cantata*, for chorus, organ, percussion, and dance (1967); *Shine, Perishing Republic*, for chorus, brass, violas, organ, and percussion (1968); Concerto for Organ and Orchestra (1970); *Fantasie*, for piano (1971); Oboe Concerto (1973); Piano Concerto (1974); *Four Excursions*, for four string basses (1976); *Valley Suite*, for violin and piano (1976); Mass, for children and orchestra (1976); Symphony for Strings (1976); *Life Triumphant*, for chorus, brasses, and flutes (1976); Concerto no. 2, for organ and brasses (1977); *To Margarita Debayle*, song cycle for voice and piano (1977); *Donne's Last Sermon*, for chorus and organ (1978); Four Songs, cycle for soprano, violin, and piano (1979); Symphony, for large orchestra (1979); *Panegyric*, for string orchestra and horn (1979); *Songs of Sappho*, for young women's singing group, piano, flute, tambourine, and choreography (1979); Organ Preludes (1979–80).

BIBLIOGRAPHY: *BBDM*; *DCM*; Ewen, David, *American Composers Today* (N.Y., 1949); *American Composers Alliance Bulletin*, volume 6, no. 4, 1957; *Who's Who in America, 1980–81*.

Loeffler, Charles Martin Tornow, b. Mulhouse, Alsace, January 30, 1861; d. Medfield, Mass., May 19, 1935. American citizen, 1887.

The forty-four years Loeffler lived in the United States left no vestige of Americanism on his writing (except for one or two negligible items in a jazz idiom toward the end of his life). The bulk of his music, and the works by which he was recognized as one of America's foremost composers of his time, is Gallic in spirit and personality, exquisitely fashioned in every detail, poetic, evocative, primarily in a postimpressionist idiom but, in some works, also sounding the modal speech of Gregorian chant.

He was one of three surviving children of Karl Valentin Immanuel Loeffler, a playwright who wrote the music for his own comedies, the author of several books, for some of which he used the pseudonym of Tornow (which Loeffler in later years added to his own name) and a political activist who spent several years in a Prussian prison. Charles Loeffler's brother, Erich, became a cellist with the Boston Symphony, and their sister, Helen, was a concert harpist. When Charles was still a child, the family moved to Smjela, in the province of Kiev, in Russia, where the father had been engaged to work for the government. In his eighth year, Loeffler received the gift of a violin, on which he was given lessons by a German musician who spent summers in Smjela. After several years in Russia, the Loefflers went to live in Debrecen, Hungary, the father having acquired a post as teacher in the Royal Agricultural School. By 1875, Loeffler had come to the decision to become a concert violinist. With this in mind, he came to Berlin in 1875, where he studied violin with Eduard Rappoldi, who prepared him for studies with Joseph Joachim. Joachim was sufficiently impressed with young Loeffler to invite him to assist in performances of chamber music at his home. In addition to the violin, Loeffler studied theory with Friedrich Kiel and the Bach motets with Woldemar Bargiel. From Berlin, Loeffler went on to Paris to study violin with Joseph Massart and counterpoint and composition with Ernest Guiraud.

For one season, Loeffler was a violinist with the Pasdeloup Orchestra in Paris. Then, in 1879, he was engaged for the private orchestra of the Russian baron, Paul von Derweis, at his palaces in Nice and near Lugano. When the baron died, in 1880, and his musical ménage was disbanded, Loeffler decided to come to the United States. He arrived in July 1881, making America his permanent home and the country of his citizenship.

In 1881–82, on a letter of recommendation from Joachim, Loeffler was engaged by Leopold Damrosch for his symphony orchestra. When the Boston Symphony was founded in 1882, Loeffler was appointed its second concertmaster. The twenty-week season of the Boston Symphony allowed him to accept other engagements for the rest of the year. In the spring of 1883 he toured with the Theodore Thomas Orchestra. Summers of 1883 and 1884 were spent in Paris for further study of the violin with Hubert Léonard.

In Boston, Loeffler at first shared the concertmaster's desk with Bernhard Listenmann, then with Franz Kneisel. During the two decades Loeffler was thus employed, the stage of the Boston Symphony became a platform launching premieres of some of his most significant compositions. *The Nights in the Ukraine*, a suite for orchestra based on Gogol's *Evenings on a Farm near Kinia*, was the first of two works in which Loeffler reached back into memories of three years of boyhood in Russia and tapped the veins of Russian folk music. He wrote the work in 1891, and on November 20 of that year the Boston Symphony introduced it. *Fantastic Concerto*, for cello and orchestra (1893), was heard in Boston on February 2, 1894; *Divertimento*, for violin and orchestra (1894), on January 4, 1895; the two versions of *La morte de Tintagiles*, a dramatic poem for orchestra inspired by Maeterlinck—the first (1897) for two viole d'amore and orchestra, and the other (1900) for one viola d'amore and orchestra—were given respectively on January 8, 1898, and February 16, 1901; *La villanelle du diable*, a tone fantasy for organ and orchestra (1901), inspired by a poem by Rollinat, on April 11, 1902; the rhapsodic *Poem*, for orchestra (1901), based on the fifth poem in Paul Verlaine's *La bonne chanson*, first heard on April 11, 1902, and then in a new orchestration, on November 1, 1918.

In 1903, Loeffler resigned from the Boston Symphony to devote himself exclusively to composition. His masterwork, and his most frequently heard composition, came three years later in its definitive form. *A Pagan Poem*, for orchestra, suggested by parts of the eighth eclogue of Virgil, in which a Thessalian girl employs an incantation and magic spells to bring back her deserted lover, originated in 1901 as a work for chamber orchestra. In 1903, Loeffler rewrote it for two pianos and three trumpets, but finally in 1906 rescored it for full orchestra. The last is the version that has become famous after being premiered by the Boston Symphony under Karl Muck on November 22, 1907. This tone poem does not follow its literary source programmatically but, instead, provides an impressionistic picture of the moods and emotions the poem evokes. "The music of *A Pagan Poem*," wrote the distinguished Boston critic, Philip Hale, "is highly imaginative. Its pages are pages of beauty and passion. The strangeness of the opening is not forced or experimental. . . . A dolorous theme, broadly and nobly thought, is sung by the English horn. The spell works." Hale also spoke of this music as "serene," but glowing with a "cool fire that is more deadly than fierce, panting flame."

On December 8, 1910, Loeffler married Elise Burnett Fay. At their home, a farm in Medfield, Mass., Loeffler lived for the remainder of his life the existence of a semirecluse. In several major works that followed, Loeffler combined his impressionism with the modal style of Gregorian chant, of which he had long been a student. In *Hora Mystica*, for men's chorus and orchestra (1916)—written for the Norfolk (Conn.) Festival of 1916 and performed by the Boston Symphony under Muck on March 2, 1917—"the mood is one of religious meditation and adoration of nature," the composer explained. Old church modes derived from plainchant are also found in *Music for Four Stringed Instruments* (1917) and *Canticum Fratria Solis* (1925). Both are pervaded with deep religious feeling and mysticism. The quartet—written in memory of an American aviator, Victor Chapman, who was a fatality of World War I—opens with a motto theme ("*Resurrexi*") which recurred throughout the composition. *Canticum Fratris Solis*, a setting for solo voice and chamber orchestra of St. Francis's *Canticle of the Sun*, was commissioned by the Elizabeth Sprague Coolidge Foundation and received its world premiere at the first festival of chamber music at the Library of Congress in Washington, D. C., on October 28, 1925.

In 1923, Loeffler reverted for a second time since his early *The Nights in the Ukraine* to the Russian folk and church tunes he had heard as a boy. *Memories of My Childhood (Life in a Russian Village)*, a tone poem for orchestra, sought, as the composer said, "to express by this music what still lives in the heart and memory of those happy days." In this score, he remembered the strains of a Russian peasant song, a Russian Litany prayer, and some Russian dance music. "The closing movement of the tone poem," the composer added, "commemorates the death of Vasinka, an elderly Bayan, or storyteller, singer, maker of willow pipes upon which he played tunes of weird intervals." In 1924, this tone poem was awarded the Chicago North Shore Festival Prize and on May 30, 1924, it was premiered by the Chicago Symphony in Evanston, Ill., Frederick Stock conducting.

Loeffler's last major work was *Evocation*, for speaking voice, women's chorus, and orchestra (1930). It was written on commission for the concert dedicating Cleveland's new concert auditorium, Severance Hall, on February 5, 1931. For his text, Loeffler went to T. W. Mackail's *Selected Epigrams of the Greek Anthology*. "The imagined form of this music is to tell the building of a beautiful temple to the Muses," Loeffler noted in the published score. To a program annotator he added: "The very beginning of the music, namely the fugue out of which grows the one most important theme a few pages on, suggested itself to me on account of its harmonically chaotic theme, alike, I imagined, to the matter which in confusion marked the beginning of the fine temple of music which the architects had in mind." Lawrence Gilman, in the *New York Herald Tribune*, called this music "radiant, serene, Hellenic, [speaking] with irresistible effect the thought of a mind which has never forgotten that the ultimate ritual of the spirit is the worship of that loveliness which is outside of time." *Evocation* received the Juilliard Publication Award.

In 1906, Loeffler was nominated officer of the French Academy by the French government and in 1919 he was appointed chevalier of the French Legion of Honor and was presented with the Gold Medal of the National Institute of Arts and Letters. Yale University in New Haven awarded him an honorary doctorate in music in 1926. He was a member of the American Academy of Arts and Letters.

Following his death by heart attack, his widow presented the Library of Congress with his manuscripts, letters, and other memorabilia. Since he and his wife were childless, she left the Loeffler estate to the French Academy and the Paris Conservatory. Loeffler was the author of *Violin Studies for the Development of the Left Hand* (1936).

PRINCIPAL WORKS: *The Nights in the Ukraine*, suite for violin and orchestra (1891); *Fantastic Concerto*, for cello and orchestra (1891); String Sextet (1893); Divertimento, for violin and orchestra (1894); *La mort de Tintagiles*, dramatic poem originally for two viole d'amore and orchestra (1897), revised for one viola d'amore and orchestra in 1900; *La villanelle du diable*, tone fantasy for orchestra (1901); *Poem*, for orchestra (1901); Four Melodies, for voice and piano (1903); Two Rhapsodies, for oboe, violin, and piano (1905); Four Poems, for voice and piano (1906); *A Pagan Poem*, originally for chamber orchestra, then for large orchestra (1901–6); *The Wind among the Reeds*, for voice and piano (1909); *Hora Mystica*, for orchestra and men's chorus (1915); *Beat! Beat! Drums!*, for unison men's chorus, three saxophones, brass, drums, and two pianos (1917); Music for Four Stringed Instruments (1917); *Five Irish Fantasies*, for voice and orchestra (1921); *Memories of My Childhood*, for orchestra (1923); *Canticum Fratris Solis*, for voice and chamber orchestra (1925); *The Reveller*, for voice, violin, and piano (1925); *Clowns*, for jazz orchestra (1927); *Evocation*, for women's voice and orchestra (1930); *Also*: Octet, for two clarinets, two violins, viola, cello, double bass and harp.

BIBLIOGRAPHY: *NGDMM*; Gilman, Lawrence, *Nature in Music and Studies in Tone Painting* (N.Y., 1914); Howard, John Tasker, *Our American Music* (N.Y., 1946); Locke, R., "Charles Martin Loeffler: His Life and Works" (doctoral thesis, Rochester, N.Y., 1959); *Musical Quarterly*, July 1925, July 1935; *New York Times* (obituary), May 20, 1935.

Lombardo, Robert, b. Hartford, Conn., March 5, 1932.

The composer of over one hundred and twenty-five compositions, Lombardo has shown a preference for small, heterogeneous combinations, or for voice and small mixed ensemble. Within a tightly organized structure he brings an individualized treatment of rhythm and dissonant counterpoint together with a rich lyricism.

Son of Sicilian immigrants, neither of whom was musical, Lombardo began studying the clarinet when he was thirteen with Sebastiano Cassarino. While attending Weaver High School in Hartford (1947–50) he played the clarinet not only in the school band but also in the orchestra of the Hartt College of Music. He expected to major in clarinet at college, but a lung injury forced him to give up that instrument in his last year of high school. Since he was still bent on a career in music he entered Hartt College of Music at the University of Hartford in 1950 as a composition major, even though up to then his creative efforts had produced just two short movements for string trio in the style of Mozart and a handful of popular songs, the last of these written under the stimulation of having played the clarinet and saxophone in jazz bands. At Hartt College he studied composition with Isadore Freed and orchestration and counterpoint with Arnold Franchetti. "Although I did not begin composition study as such with Franchetti until 1954," Lombardo recalls, "this man was to have a profound influence on my development throughout my college education and for several years afterwards." In 1954 Lombardo earned his bachelor of music degree, *cum laude*, and a year later his master in music degree.

During the summer of 1956, Lombardo continued his music study at the Berkshire Music Center at Tanglewood, Mass.: orchestration with Aaron Copland and composition with Goffredo Petrassi. That fall he went to Italy, where he was a composition student with Guido Turchi, and early in 1957 he went on to Florence, where he stayed through the summer working on a commission from the Fromm Music Foundation which resulted in the writing of a Quintet, for winds (1957), whose premiere was given at Tanglewood in 1958. The fall of 1957 found him in Berlin, enrolled at the High School for Music as a student of composition of Boris Blancher's. Upon his return to the United States, in 1958, he went for his postgraduate studies to the University of Iowa, in Iowa City, studying composition there with Philip Bezanson (in addition to teaching theory between 1959 and 1961) and acquiring a doctorate in music in 1961. During these years of music study he did not neglect composition. Among his works at this time were: Five Songs, for mezzo-soprano and cello (1959), heard first at the International Music Festival at Bilthoven on September 8, 1959, and Aria and Allegretto, for orchestra (1959), performed over the Hilversum Radio on September 9, 1959, both in Holland; and *I due orfani,* a dramatic dialogue for soprano, alto, and chamber ensemble (1959) featured at the Bilthoven Music Festival in September 1960.

Between 1962 and 1963, Lombardo was composer-in-residence on grants from the Ford Foundation in two public school systems: at Hastings-on-Hudson in New York and Colorado Springs in Colorado. On still another Ford Foundation grant, he spent the summer of 1962 attending the session of the Santa Fe Opera. In 1963–64 he was on the music faculty of his alma mater, the Hartt College of Music, and in 1964 he joined the Chicago Musical College of Roosevelt University as composer-in-residence and professor of composition, where he has remained since then.

His most important composition up to this point came in 1964, prompted by the death of John F. Kennedy. It was *Threnody for Strings*, a deeply emotional and lyrical composition which was introduced by the Cincinnati Symphony under Max Rudolf on May 8, 1965. When the Chicago Symphony under Carlo Maria Giulini performed it almost a decade later (October 19, 1972), Robert C. Marsh, in the *Sun-Times*, saluted Lombardo "for writing a work that has both substance and immediate appeal"; and in the *Daily News*, Bernard Jacobson praised it for "the logic with which it grows out of three germinal ideas and for its way of evoking every precise consciousness of grief without resort to conventional breast-beating." Jacobson added: "Lombardo has the ability to wield intricately chromatic material into textures of an openness and resonance usually associated with plainer diatonic styles of harmony. . . . His string writing . . . sounds with an authority that compasses telling effects through apparently simple strokes."

In 1964, Lombardo was awarded a Guggenheim Fellowship. Taking a leave of absence from Roosevelt University, he returned to Florence. There, on March 27, he married Kathleen Knudsen, a poet and dramatist. In addition to becoming the mother of his two children, Kathleen Lombardo also served as poet and librettist for many of her husband's compositions. In Florence, to her libretto, Lombardo worked upon an opera, *Savanarola*, which he did not complete. Back in the United States in 1966, he wrote *Dialogues of Lovers*, for soprano, baritone, and chamber ensemble, on a commission from the Koussevitzky Music Foundation; it was introduced at the University of Chicago, Ralph Shapey conducting, on December 4, 1966. That year he received a commission from the Chicago Musical College for a one-act chamber opera, *The Sorrows of a Supersoul* (1967), produced in Cincinnati on March 11, 1971, at the Music Educators National Conference and later that month at Roosevelt University. His wife provided the texts for both works.

In Memoriam, for bassoon and string trio (1967)—the entire work based on a five-note chromatic scale from which all melodic and harmonic shapes derived—was written in memory of the composer's father. It was first performed in Chicago in the winter of 1968. *Aphorisms*, for orchestra (1968), was introduced in Chicago on April 22, 1970, and *Climbing for Tree Frogs*, love songs for soprano and harpsichord (1969), text by Kathleen Lombardo, was premiered in Chicago on February 27, 1970.

A program devoted exclusively to Lombardo's music—including the world premiere of *Fourplay*, for violin, bassoon, percussion, and harpsichord (1969)—was heard at Roosevelt University on January 13, 1971. It covered Lombardo's productivity from 1958 through 1969. In reviewing this concert, Bernard Jacobson, in the *Chicago Daily News*, described Lombardo's style as follows: "His harmonic language is freely chromatic, and his method of developing material frequently postserial. The general sound of his music is neat, intricate, involuted—you could call it 'small bones.' But the spirit it reveals is anything but small: humanity, and a singularly rich, sensitive humanity at that, is always to be felt beneath the skillfully polished surface."

In 1973, Lombardo was commissioned by Mr. and Mrs. Lee A. Freeman to write a work for the Fine Arts Quartet. This led to the String Quartet no. 2 (1974), which the Fine Arts Quartet introduced in Chicago on May 18, 1975. The cello is here used as the focal instrument for the presentation of intensely felt and vividly harmonized thematic material. "The introspective musical moods shift and grow through the two continuous movements," reported Louise Kenngott to the *Milwaukee Journal*, "and finally end in fragments and questions." On a research grant from Roosevelt University, to a libretto by his wife, Lombardo completed a one-act opera on ecology (on vanishing animals), *The Dodo* (1975), first produced on September 27, 1979, at the Lincoln Park Zoo in Chicago. *Down the Rabbit Hole*, also composed in 1975, was a multimedia production for voices, actors, dancers and film, text by Kathleen Lombardo, which was commissioned by Columbia College in Chicago and performed there on February 27, 1976. On a grant from the National Endowment for the Arts, Lombardo completed *Sicilian Lyric*, for timpani solo, percussion, and orchestra (1976), whose main melody was taken from an old Sicilian folk tune. Lombardo received a second grant from the National Endowment for the Arts in 1980 to compose an opera.

In 1977, Lombardo adapted the music of Scott Joplin and composed original music of that period for a ragtime musical called *Joplin*, for which his wife wrote both the book and the lyrics. It was presented at the St. Nicholas Theater in Chicago in 1976.

THE COMPOSER SPEAKS: In each line of music that I compose, whether it is of primary or secondary importance, written for viola, snare drum, or any other instrument—pitched or nonpitched—my concern is to make it "sing." It is the melodic counterpoint that gives shape to my work. I want each performer to feel he or she is contributing something important and interesting to the overall form, much in the same way characters in a drama, by their interaction with one another, create the essence of a play.

PRINCIPAL WORKS: 2 string quartets (1960, 1974).

Movement, for violin solo (1958, revised 1973); *I due orfani*, for soprano, alto, and chamber ensemble (1959); Five Songs, for mezzo-soprano and cello (1959); Fantasy, for piano (1960); *Orchestral Fantasy* (1962); Solo Cantata, for baritone, and chamber orchestra (1963); *Three Italian Poems*, for narrator, flute, percussion, and bass (1964); Piano Variations (1964); *Threnody*, for string orchestra (1964); *Variations on a Lyric Theme*, for solo percussionist (1965); *Song for Morpheus*, for soprano and vibraphone (1965); *Cinque piccoli pezzi*, for violin and piano (1965); *Dialogues of Lovers*, for soprano, baritone, and nine instruments (1966); *Three Cinquains*, for alto, flute, bassoon, vibraphone, and bass (1966); *A War Ballad*, for female speaking voice and cello (1966); *In Memoriam*, for bassoon, violin, viola, and cello (1967); *Sorrows of a Supersoul*, one-act chamber opera (1967); *Program Notes*, for soprano, flute, bass clarinet, vibraphone, and bass (1968); *Aphorisms*, for orchestra (1968); *Climbing for Tree Frogs*, for soprano, flute, oboe, clarinet, marimba, harp, viola, and bass (1969); Largo, for string quartet (1969); *Fourplay*, for violin, bassoon, one percussion, and harpsichord (1969); *Selected Shorts*, for piano (1970); *Fantasy Variations* no. 1, for cello solo (1970); *Fantasy Variations* no. 2, for harpsichord solo (1972); *Fantasy Variations* no. 3, for violin solo (1972); *Aria and Fragments*, for cello and harp (1973); *Dark Pastorale*, for guitar (1973); *The Dodo*, one-act opera (1975); *Down the Rabbit Hole*, multimedia production (1975); *Frosted Window: Variations on White*, for soprano, bassoon, percussion, and viola (1975); Duo Variations, for trumpet and harp (1977); *Sicilian Lyric*, for timpani solo, percussion, and orchestra (1977); *Erogenous Zones*, for soprano, flute, alto flute, piccolo, and percussion (1978); *Mesto*, for bassoon and strings (1978); *Blues*, for cello alone (1978); Fantasy with Variations, for bassoon and harpsichord (1979); *Why Not?*, for two tubas (1979); *Piano mezzo piano*, for trombone and timpani (1979); *Songs to Kandinsky*, song cycle for soprano, clarinet, and viola (1980); *Cantabile*, for alto saxophone and vibraphone (1980).

BIBLIOGRAPHY: *DCM*; Anderson, E. Ruth (ed). *Contemporary American Composers* (Boston, 1976).

Lopatnikoff, Nikolai, b. Reval, Estonia, March 16, 1903; d. Pittsburgh, Pa., October 7, 1976. American citizen, 1944.

Throughout his career, Lopatnikoff remained faithful to the neoclassic and neobaroque tendencies of Hindemith and of Stravinsky's middle creative period. Except for one or two instances, he was a composer of instrumental music whose architecture was compact, texture transparent, polyphony resourceful and economical, tonality comparatively free and a melodic gift that had Russian overtones.

He started studying the piano and composition in his native city in childhood. When the family moved to St. Petersburg in 1914, he entered the St. Petersburg Conservatory, where he studied theory and composition with Alexander Zhitomirsky and piano with Sacharoff. At the same time, he received his academic education in high school. With the outbreak of revolution in Russia in 1917, the family moved to Finland. There Nikolai's academic education was continued in the local schools and music at Helsinki Conservatory (1918–20), where he studied theory with Eric Furuhjelm. In 1920, Lopatnikoff came to Germany to continue the study of composition with Ernst Toch, Hermann Grabner, and Willy Rehberg. In 1921, he entered the Technological College in Karlsruhe, majoring in engineering; he graduated with an engineer's diploma in 1928. While still a college student he married Nora Laschinsky on August 17, 1926; she died two decades later, in July 1945.

During his years at college, Lopatnikoff began to attract attention and interest in his music, beginning with his String Quartet no. 1 (1920), which was performed in Karlsruhe in the year of its composition, and continuing with his Piano Concerto no. 1 (1921), heard initially on November 3, 1925, in Cologne, and Introduction and Scherzo, for orchestra (1927), with which Lopatnikoff made his American debut as composer when the Boston Symphony under Serge Koussevitzky introduced it on April 27, 1928.

Once he left Technological College with his diploma, Lopatnikoff decided he preferred devoting his life to composition. Before long, he was making notable progress. His String Quartet no. 2 (1928) received the Belaiev Prize. Symphony no. 1 (1928), introduced at the German Music Festival at Karlsruhe on January 9, 1929, was awarded the German Radio Corporation Prize in 1930. When this symphony was given by the Berlin Philharmonic under Bruno Walter soon after its premiere, the critic of *Börsen Zeitung* said: "Here are to be met qualities rare in new music: youthfulness, invention which has élan, powerful directness and which without pretentiousness looks at the world in a frank and knowing way." The distinguished Berlin critic Alfred Einstein described this music in the *Tageblatt* as "Asiatic folklore, stark rhythms, raw sevenths and sequences of seconds, but a symphonic poster style of such raciness, in contrast to which the German symphonic style seems 'leathern.'" The American premiere of this symphony followed in 1930 in Detroit with Ossip Gabrilowitsch conducting the Detroit Symphony, and not long after that the work was programmed by the Philadelphia Symphony under Stokowski and then by the New York Philharmonic.

In 1931, Lopatnikoff made his home in Berlin.

For the next two years he served on the board of the Berlin section of the International Society for Contemporary Music. In Berlin, he wrote his Piano Concerto no. 2 (1930), which was introduced in Düsseldorf on October 16, 1930, where it scored a major success which was repeated when it was heard at the festival of the International Society for Contemporary Music in Vienna on June 16, 1932. Reporting from Vienna to the *Neues Nachrichten* in Leipzig, Adolph Aber described this concerto as "a work of magnificent clarity and thematic significance, revealing a sure knowledge of the piano and its effects. . . . The work as a whole is stamped with an individual style and personality." Here the robustly rhythmic and the linear style that would henceforth characterize Lopatnikoff's music became crystallized. In Berlin, Lopatnikoff also worked upon a three-act opera, *Danton* (1930), which was never staged, but excerpts from which were given by the Pittsburgh Symphony under William Steinberg on March 25, 1967.

With the rise of the Third Reich in Germany, Lopatnikoff left the country for Helsinki, where, through the intervention of Sibelius, he was given a residence permit. After that, London was his home for six years, during which he made numerous appearances as composer-pianist.

With the imminence of war in Europe, Lopatnikoff came to the United States in 1939 for permanent residence and new citizenship. In 1942–43 he taught composition at the Hartt College of Music in Hartford, Conn., and in 1943–45 he was head of the theory department at the Westchester Conservatory in White Plains, N.Y. In 1945 he was appointed associate professor of composition at the Carnegie Institute of Technology in Pittsburgh, where he became professor in 1948 and, upon his retirement in 1969, professor emeritus.

In the United States, Lopatnikoff became increasingly productive and in so doing began to accumulate major successes. Symphony no. 2 (1939) was given its world premiere in Boston on December 22, 1939, by the Boston Symphony conducted by Serge Koussevitzky, and the Violin Concerto (1941) was premiered by the same orchestra and conductor, with Richard Burgin as soloist, on April 17, 1942. Sinfonietta (1942), which used the classic structure of the concerto grosso and whose final movement was enlivened with Russian-type dance melodies, received its world premiere over the CBS radio network on April 27, 1942, Howard Barlow conducting, and then was heard at the festival of the International Society for Contemporary Music at Berkeley, Calif., on August 2, 1942. After it was performed by the Pittsburgh Symphony under Fritz Reiner on April 9, 1948, a critic for the *Post-Gazette* said: "The whole work has entity and unity and is unacademic in its free and easy scholasticism." *Opus Sinfonicum* (1942), described by the composer as "a kind of abstract symphonic poem, free in form," was awarded the first prize in the Cleveland Orchestra competition commemorating its twenty-fifth anniversary, in which 151 compositions were judged, and was given its first hearing by that orchestra under Erich Leinsdorf on December 9, 1943. The Piano Sonata in E (1943; N.Y., January 29, 1944) revealed, said Alexander Borovsky in the *New York Times*, "the mature conception of a master. The end movements have a vigorous rhythm and are rich in witty details, while in the middle movement the passionate expressiveness does not blur the epical background of a characteristic Russian scene with its endless steppes." Concertino for Orchestra (1944), which the Koussevitzky Music Foundation had commissioned (and whose middle-movement "Elegietta" was written in memory of Mrs. Koussevitzky), was premiered by the Boston Symphony under Koussevitzky on March 2, 1945. *Variations and Epilogue*, for cello and piano (1946)—written as a memorial to the composer's wife upon her then recent death—was heard first on January 17, 1947, in New York, performed by Raya Garbousova and Erich Itor Kahn. Meanwhile, in 1945, Lopatnikoff was awarded a Guggenheim Fellowship. (A second followed eight years later.)

After 1950, Lopatnikoff's most important works included two more symphonies—no. 3 (1954), introduced by the Pittsburgh Symphony under Steinberg on December 10, 1954, and no. 4 (1972), commissioned by the Pittsburgh Symphony, which gave its premiere under Steinberg on January 21, 1972; Concerto for Two Pianos and Orchestra (1950), which Vronsky and Babin, as soloists with the Pittsburgh Symphony under Victor Bakaleinikoff, presented for the first time on December 7, 1951; Divertimento, for orchestra (1951), written on commission from the Musical Arts Society of La Jolla, Calif., where it was first given on August 19, 1961, Nikolai Sokoloff conducting; *Variazioni concertanti*, for orchestra (1958), written on a grant from the Pittsburgh Bicentennial Association and heard on November 7, 1958, performed by the Pittsburgh Symphony under Steinberg; Music for Orchestra (1958), commissioned by the Louisville Orchestra in Kentucky, which performed the premiere on January 14, 1959, Robert Whitney conducting; *Festival Overture* (1960), on a commission from the Pittsburgh Plate Glass Company, with its world premiere taking place in Detroit as a salute to the United States auto industry on October 12, 1960, with Paul Paray conducting the Detroit Symphony; and Concerto for Orchestra (1963), its premiere given by the Pittsburgh Symphony under Steinberg on April 3, 1964.

On January 27, 1951, Lopatnikoff married his second wife, the former Sara Henderson Hay. He received a grant and special citation from the National Institute of Arts and Letters in 1953, and a decade later was elected to its membership. In 1966 he received a grant from the National Endowment for the Arts.

THE COMPOSER SPEAKS: I am an advocate of no theories at all regarding music, but only of creative values. I fear more than anything else the danger of academicism and dogmatism in the musical art.

PRINCIPAL WORKS: 4 symphonies (1928–1972); 3 string quartets (1920, 1928, 1955); 2 piano concertos (1921, 1930).

Sonata, for piano, violin, snare drum (1926); Introduction and Scherzo, for orchestra (1927); Cello Sonata (1928); *Danton*, opera (1930); Piano Trio (1936); *Two Russian Nocturnes*, for orchestra (1939); Violin Concerto (1941); Opus Sinfonicum (1942); Sinfonietta, for orchestra (1942); Piano Sonata (1943); Concertino, for orchestra (1944); *Variations and Epilogue*, for cello and piano (1946); Concerto for Two Pianos and Orchestra (1951); Divertimento, for orchestra (1951); *Variazioni concertanti*, for orchestra (1958); *Music for Orchestra* (1958); *Festival Overture*, for orchestra (1960); Concerto for Orchestra (1963); *Divertimento da camera*, for chamber group (1965); *Melting Pot*, ballet (1975).

BIBLIOGRAPHY: *DCM;* Ewen, David, *Composers Since 1900* (N.Y., 1969); Reis, Claire, *Composers in America* (N.Y., 1947); Thomson, Virgil, *American Music Since 1910* (N.Y., 1970); *Who's Who in America, 1976–77.*

Lourié, Arthur Vincent, b. St. Petersburg, Russia, May 14, 1892; d. Princeton, N.J., October 12, 1966. American citizen, 1947.

Early in his career in Russia, Lourié was an *enfant terrible* who had experimented with quarter tones, nontonal music, new forms, and even anticipated by several decades graphic notation. He then rejected his extreme modernism for neoclassicism. His later works were filled with religious mysticism, their idiom rooted in the modes of Gregorian chant. However much his music has been neglected since his death, he was performed widely and significantly in his lifetime.

Lourié's later preoccupation with early church ritual music had its beginnings when, as a child, he was raised in a devout Greek Orthodox household. He received some training at the piano with private instructors while attending elementary and high school in St. Petersburg. In 1909, he entered the St. Petersburg Conservatory, where he remained seven years and received diplomas in composition and piano. (The information found in many reference books that he dropped out of the conservatory early and was largely self-taught in music after that is erroneous.) At the same time he attended the University of St. Petersburg for the study of philosophy and aesthetics. As a conservatory student he composed some piano music—*Préludes fragiles, Synthèses,* and three piano sonatinas—that were neoromantic, strongly influenced by Scriabin.

As a young man, Lourié moved in a circle of Russian intellectuals—writers, painters as well as musicians—all artist-revolutionaries. They directed Lourié to innovative practices in his music. He now produced compositions in an ultrachromatic idiom with quarter tones within amorphous structures. During this period he composed *Forms in Air* (1915), subtitled "Sound Script," in which, influenced by Picasso, he devised a graphic notation that simulated cubistic designs.

When the Bolsheviks came to power in Russia, Lourié was appointed chief of the music department of the Commissariat for Public Instruction. In this post, which he retained between 1918 and 1922, he antagonized many of his more conservative musical colleagues with his extremism. He called them "petit bourgeoisie" and condemned them for not being *en rapport* with new ideologies. The feud grew so bitter that a document was published trying to heal the wounds of both parties in this struggle. Ostensibly it supported Lourié's position, but at the same time it adopted a much more orthodox position that severely undermined Lourié's prestige. Disenchanted, Lourié left the Soviet Union for good in 1922, and in 1923 he came to Paris, which remained his home for the next eighteen years. Between 1923 and 1940 he pursued the career of a concert pianist in Europe. He married Elizabeth Comtesse Belevsky and became a close friend of Serge Koussevitzky, who was to become a staunch champion of his music.

In Paris, influenced by Stravinsky, Lourié embraced neoclassicism. He now favored 18th-century structures and a style that was austere in its simplicity and transparency and thoroughly objective. This new neoclassic approach became evident in the *Dithyrambes*, for flute (1923), the Toccata and the Gigue, both for the piano (1927), and the *Sinfonia dialectica* (1930). The last of these was introduced by the Philadelphia Orchestra under Leopold Stokowski on April 18, 1931, and then was brought to Boston by the Boston Symphony under Koussevitzky on December 1, 1933.

Religion, and with it the liturgical music of the past, began influencing him in the late 1920s, and continued in some of his subsequent major works. The *Sonata liturgique* (1928), for alto voice and small wind orchestra, used old church modes and plainchant within medievallike formalized structures. He continued in this direction with the *Concerto spirituale*, for chorus, double basses, piano, and organ (1929), whose world premiere took place in New York on March 26, 1930, in a performance of the Schola Cantorum, to become the first work by Lourié to be heard in the United States. The Boston Symphony under Koussevitzky performed it on January 2, 1931.

In 1935, Lourié completed the score for an opera-ballet which was planned for production at the Paris Opera in 1939–40. This was *The Feast during the Plague*, to a text by the composer based on Pushkin's

Dramatic Scene, with interpolations of excerpts from the poets of the Latin decadence. "Naturally," the composer explained, "I have no intention of illustrating in my music the 'plague' or 'catastrophe.' I have thought only of the psychological implications of the subject. My task was purely musical, its tendency, lyrical, colored perhaps by the anguish of a dark moment and the disintegration of a culture once secure. This anguish, with its threats and presentiments, was already felt in the atmosphere while I was working on the score." Though *The Feast during the Plague* went into rehearsal, it was not produced in Paris. The invasion of Paris by the Nazis put an end to the project.

One year after completing *The Feast during the Plague* Lourié wrote one of his most deeply religious compositions, *Kormatschaia* (Symphony no. 2). The title comes from the Greek Orthodox liturgical verse in which the Virgin is described as a "guiding mother" and is made the symbol of Russia itself. On the score, a motto of Michaelangelo appears: "Remember that thou livest, and go thy way." The work consists of ten variations, *without* a theme, and the style is modal. To Virgil Thomson the unifying factor in this symphony is "a state of mind." This symphony was introduced on November 7, 1941, by the Boston Symphony under Koussevitzky.

The invasion of Paris by the Nazis brought Lourié to the United States in 1941 for permanent residence and a new citizenship. One of his first major tasks in America was to arrange the score for *The Feast during the Plague* into a six-movement suite for chorus and orchestra, the first and fourth movements of which were death marches, the last two movements also entirely instrumental, and the second movement calling for a chorus in a setting of a Latin text by Petrarch in which the dialogue is carried on by alternate four-part choruses accompanied by brass and drums. He completed this suite in 1943, and on January 5, 1945, it was premiered by the Boston Symphony under Koussevitzky.

For many years, Lourié resided in New York, where, in addition to composing, he involved himself with literary endeavors by writing for leading journals articles not only on music but also on politics and aesthetics. In 1947, he joined the Russian section of The Voice of America. In his last years, he lived in Princeton, N.J. His productivity as a composer slackened greatly in America and his works were now few and far between. But in 1961 he completed a three-act opera, *The Blackamoor of Peter the Great*—libretto by the composer based on Pushkin—which was never produced.

THE COMPOSER SPEAKS: Melody, the touchstone of all music, held its proper domination in the last century, but in this one has been buried under complexities of harmony and rhythm. When a modern composer attempts to use a melody, he does so not from a genuine impulse of song, which is the birthright of true music, but under a conscious effort towards stylization or methodological constructivism. Composers have been even ashamed to be caught writing an obviously melodic phrase. I believe that this sense of shame may be explained by the fact that melody (any melody) is apt to reveal some intimate truth, the genuine psychological and spiritual substances of its maker. Melody discloses the nature of the subject, not the object.

PRINCIPAL WORKS: 3 string quartets (1921–24); 2 symphonies (1930, 1936).

La naissance de la beauté, cantata for soprano, chorus of six sopranos, and piano (1922); *Dithyrambes*, for flute (1923); Toccata and Grand Gigue, both for piano (1927); *Sonata liturgique*, for voice and small orchestra (1928); *Concerto spirituale*, for chorus, double basses, piano, and organ (1929); *Procession*, for two women's voices and piano (1934); *La flute à travers le violon*, for flute and violin (1935); *The Feast during the Plague*, opera-ballet (1935), arranged in 1943 into a suite for chorus and orchestra; *El Cristo crucificado ante al mar*, for voice and piano (1938); *De Ordinations Angelorium*, for chorus and five brass (1942); *Concerto da camera*, for violin and string orchestra (1947); *The Mime*, for clarinet (1956); *The Blackamoor of Peter the Great*, opera (1961).

BIBLIOGRAPHY: Ewen, David, *American Composers Today* (N.Y., 1949); Sabaneyev, Leonid, *Russian Composers* (N.Y., 1927); Schwarz, Boris, *Music and Musical Life in the Soviet Union, 1917–1970* (N.Y., 1972); *New York Times*, March 23, 1930; *Ramparts*, January 1965; *Who's Who in America, 1966–67*.

Lucier, Alvin b. Nashua, N.H., May 14, 1931. In the avant-garde movement in music, Lucier has struck new ground, totally revolutionizing existing concepts of music. Since 1965 he has made a series of works that explore the physical properties of sound and the acoustic characteristics of architectural spaces as musical material. He often uses preexisting electronic technology to uncover new sound sources—brain waves, echoes, room resonances, for example—and in doing so finds it unnecessary to use written musical language or formal structures based on scales, intervals, tonality, and serialism. "My method of composition," he explains, "consists in studying a particular phenomenon until I understand it; experimenting with it empirically, in real situations; then in trying to think of beautiful ways of using it in a musical performance. I regard music as a means of putting people into harmony with nature."

His father, an attorney, former mayor of Nashua, and a member of the Governor's Council of New Hampshire, played the violin, and his mother, the piano. There was always music at the Lucier home, including pickup orchestras for parties and impromptu four-part singing around the dinner table. Lucier's boyhood interest in music was stimulated by listening to recordings of such jazz greats as Duke Ellington, Count Basie, and Stan Kenton; but not until he was fifteen years old did he discover classical music, particularly the symphonies of Beethoven, the Schoenberg Serenade, and some of Virgil Thomson's *Portraits*, also through recordings. From 1940 to 1945 he studied the piano and drums sporadically. At Nashua High School he sang in the glee club and played snare drum in the band. At that time he came under the influence of Elmer ("Pop") Wilson, director of music for Nashua schools, who encouraged him in music by selecting him occasionally to be student conductor of the Nashua High School Band and Glee Club. He graduated from Nashua High School in 1949 as president of his senior class, after which he did a year of post-graduate study at the Portsmouth Abbey (then Priory) school where he became interested in Gregorian chant. In 1950 he entered Yale University. During the next four years he studied theory with Howard Boatwright; composition, conducting, and orchestration with Richard Donovan; composition with David Kraehenbuhl and Quincy Porter; and music history with Bruce Simonds.

Upon acquiring his bachelor of arts degree at Yale in 1954 he went on to the Yale School of Music. For the next two years he studied theory with David Kraehenbuhl and advanced composition with Quincy Porter in addition to conducting Yale's Apollo Glee Club (1955–56). In New Haven, Lucier taught theory and percussion at the Neighborhood Music School (1954–57).

He dropped out of Yale School of Music in 1956, worked for two years at odd jobs around the country, and in 1958 resumed music study at Brandeis University at Waltham, Mass. There he studied theory and composition with Arthur Berger, Irving Fine, and Harold Shapero, receiving a master of fine arts degree and the Samuel Wechsler Award in 1960. During the summers of 1958 and 1959 he attended the Berkshire Music Center at Tanglewood, Mass., for the study of composition with Lukas Foss and orchestration with Aaron Copland. There he was awarded the Jack E. Lund Commission for a new work.

In 1960 he went to Italy on a Fulbright Fellowship, spending that summer at the Benedetto Marcello Conservatory in Venice in the fugue and composition class of Giorgio Federico Ghedini. He then settled in Rome for two years, receiving intermittent private instruction in composition from Boris Porena. While living in Rome he met pianist-composer Frederic Rzewski, who became a strong musical influence and lifelong friend and with whom, during the summer of 1961, he drove to Darmstadt, Germany, to sit in on David Tudor's piano class.

In 1962 Lucier returned to the faculty of Brandeis where, until 1969, he taught music theory and conducted the Choral Union and Chamber Chorus, which devoted much of its time to the performance of new music. On July 25, 1965, he married visual artist Mary Denman Glosser in Cambridge, Mass.; they had one child, a daughter, and were divorced in 1979.

Except for *Action Music for Piano* (1962; Rome, June 7, 1962), and a few other minor items, Lucier did little composing up to 1965. As he explains: "I had lost confidence in the musics of my education. Post-Webern serialism . . . seemed florid and complex enough to be obsolete, and the tape music of that period seemed to be only an extension of that language. I felt the need for a new idea." He came upon that "new idea" when Edmond Dewan, a physicist, suggested to him that he explore the possibilities of making music with brain-wave equipment. "As I started learning to generate alpha to make sound," Lucier says," I began experiencing a sensibility to sound and its production, different from that of the other musics based on ideas of tension, contrast, conflict, and other notions of drama. To release alpha, one has to attain a quasimeditative state while at the same time monitoring its flow. One has to give up control to get it."

In 1965, Lucier completed Music for Solo Performer (Waltham, Mass., May 5, 1965), in which amplified alpha brain waves detected by medical electrodes attached to the scalp of a human performer activated a variety of percussion instruments. It marked the first use of brain waves in music.

In 1969, Lucier left Brandeis to join the faculty of Wesleyan University in Middletown, Conn. He became full professor of music in 1978 and chairman of the music department in 1979. He has also taught at the Harvard Summer School of Education, has been Regents Lecturer in Music at the University of California at Santa Barbara, and has made numerous appearances as lecturer in universities, colleges, and art centers throughout the United States and Europe. In August of 1979 he married Wendy Wallbank Stokes of Denver, Col.

In 1967, Lucier made his first tour of Europe as a member of the Sonic Arts Union, which he had cofounded in 1966 with composer-performers Robert Ashley, David Behan, and Gordon Mumma, for the presentation of their works. This was followed two years later, in 1969, by a one-month, fifteen-concert European tour, with other tours abroad in succeeding years. Since 1973 he has given numerous solo concerts as well as radio broadcasts and installations of his work in the United States and Europe. From 1973 to 1978 he was music director of the Viola Farber Dance Company.

Lucier received several grants and awards during the 1970s. In 1972, he was awarded a grant from the New York State Council on the Arts for the development of a multimedia production, *The Queen of the*

South (Brooklyn, N.Y., March 19, 1972). Two years later he received a Rockefeller Foundation grant to participate in the Composers Recording Project at Mills College in Oakland, Calif., and in 1977 earned a Composer-Librettist Award from the National Endowment for the Arts.

Lucier has contributed the music for two stage productions: *Fire!*, produced on Broadway in 1968, and the American Shakespeare production of *King Henry V* at Stratford, Conn., in 1969.

He has contributed articles and scores to several periodicals and books. In the spring of 1980 the Wesleyan University Press published his book *Chambers*, written in collaboration with Douglas Simon, consisting of fourteen musical scores of his major works from 1965 to 1977, accompanied by twelve interviews that discuss and illuminate these works.

Each of Lucier's works is usually based on an acoustical or natural phenomenon. The goal of the work and the activity of the performance lie in the exploration of that phenomenon. The physical setup, suggestions, and tasks for the performers are usually described in a written prose score. "The idiom I use," Lucier explains, "is almost always live performance with electronics, often acoustical test equipment—pulse-wave generators, sine-wave oscillators, for example. Sometimes I use devices from other technologies, such as vocoders, solar panels, computers or biomedical equipment including brainwave amplifiers and galvanic skin sensors."

Several works from 1967 to 1970 are specifically concerned with the articulation of architectural spaces by sound. In *Shelter* (1967; Waltham, Mass., February 21, 1967), for example, high-gain vibration pickups are attached to the walls, floors, and ceilings of a building to pick up and filter through the structural materials purposeful or environmental sounds. In *Vespers* (1968; Ann Arbor, Mich., February 10, 1968), performers play Sondols (Sonor-dolphin), hand-held pulse generators, to produce echoes which reflect off surfaces in the environment, and make acoustic signatures of enclosed spaces; *Vespers* is in the repertoire of the Merce Cunningham Dance Company accompanying the dance *Objects* (Brooklyn, N.Y., November 10, 1970). Time and space are directly related; durations are directly proportional to distances between sound sources and reflective surfaces. *Chambers* (1968; N.Y., January 15, 1968), on the other hand, started simply as a work for blown conch shells but was later expanded to include any small or large resonant chambers that could be made to sound. "I thought of them as rooms within rooms which impinge their acoustic characteristics upon each other." In *"I am sitting in a room"* (1970; N.Y., March 24, 1970), several paragraphs of human speech are recycled through a room by means of a pair of tape recorders to amplify by repetition the resonant frequencies common to both the original recording and those implied by the room. And in *Quasimodo, the Great Lover* (1970; Clinton, N.Y., November 4, 1970) sounds sent over long distances by means of microphone-amplifier-loudspeaker systems capture and carry the acoustic characteristic of the spaces through which they travel.

More recent works have had to do with the properties of sound itself, rather than how it acts in space. *Still and Moving Lines of Silence in Families of Hyperbolas* (1974; Paris, France, October 18, 1974) is an exploration of standing waves and related phenomena. *Outlines of Persons and Things* (1975) uses sound waves to create diffractive patterns around opaque objects, producing silhouettes "which may be perceived directly with one's ears, or through loudspeakers which shift, enlarge, and amplify the images." In *Music on a Long Thin Wire* (1977; Potsdam, N.Y., March 27, 1977) metal wire is explored, extended fifty feet or more across a performance space, and made audible for listeners. *Directions of Sounds from the Bridge* (1978; N.Y., February 11, 1978) and *Shapes of the Sounds from the Board* (1979; N.Y., June 18, 1979) explore the directionality of sound flow from musical instruments.

In 1979, Lucier began working on a series of *Solar Sound Systems* for public places. Each system, consisting of packages of electronic music modules, amplifiers and loudspeakers, is completely solar powered. The generation, propagation, and quality of the music is determined by the intensity of the sun's rays at any given moment in time.

Alan Sondheim, in *Ear* magazine, describes Lucier's work as "a series of breakdowns, fragmentations, and recombinations. The performer may become one with the performance space; the performer/space together may constitute the music. All of this fragmentation, however, is reassembled into a unity through the transcendence of the music itself, which often consists of slow transforms, changing directions, harmonics and so forth—a music often rich in overtones . . . and always rich in timbres . . . In Lucier's work . . . the reassembling occurs naturally and joyfully; the music is beautiful, exciting, and calming. One learns to *listen*, 'listen from the beginning.' The experience is memorable."

THE COMPOSER SPEAKS: I was brought up to believe that my interests in the world are purely "artistic" and that any scientific endeavor was beyond me. I never thought I could fix anything; I could never understand how a radio worked, for example. I was never very successful in physics, or any science class, for that matter. I always thought that the world was divided into two kinds of people, poets, and practical people, and that while the practical people ran the world, the poets had visions about it. I felt the scientific point of view only skimmed the surface; artists were really the brightest people on earth. Now I realize there is no difference between science and art.

My first approach to music was that "artistic" one, but I wasn't very successful at it. I could never settle down enough to learn to play the piano very well, though I did compose several successful student pieces for conventional instruments. I didn't get inspired until I started investigating simple natural occurrences. Some composers find inspiration in words, in setting texts to music, or in politics, or drama, or in more abstract relationships, but I can't seem to get into those. I don't seem to be interested in the ensemble idea either, everybody playing together. I wish I were. I seem to be a phenomenologist in some ways; I would rather discover new sound situations than invent new ways of putting materials together. Whenever I think of changing direction, of making something more popular or attractive to a larger audience, I lose interest very quickly, so I follow my instincts and continue making pieces with brain waves, echoes, room resonances, vibrating wires, and other natural phenomena, and I try to put people into harmonious relationships with them.

PRINCIPAL WORKS: *Action Music for Piano* (1962); Music for Solo Performer, for amplified brain waves and percussion (1965); *Whistlers*, electromagnetic disturbances in the ionosphere (1967); *Shelter*, electronic sensing of environmental sounds (1967); *North American Time Capsule*, for voices and vocoder (1967); *Chambers*, moving large and small resonant environment (1968); *Vespers*, acoustic orientation by means of echolocation (1968); *The Only Talking Machine of Its Kind in the World*, for stutterer and tape delay system (1969); *Memory Space*, environmental mimicry for orchestra (1970); "*I am sitting in a room*," for voice and electromagnetic tape (1970); *Quasimodo, the Great Lover*, long-distance sound transmission (1970); *The Duke of York*, for voice(s) and synthesizer (1971); *Gentle Fire*, for synthesizer and related equipment (1971); *The Queen of the South*, for players, responsive surfaces, strewn material, and closed-circuit television system (1972); *RMSIMI, The Bird of Bremen Flies through the Houses of the Burghers*, computer-controlled sound environment (1972); *Still and Moving Lines of Silence in Families of Hyperbolas*, for singers, players, dancers, and unattended percussion (1974); *Outlines of Persons and Things*, for microphones, loudspeakers, and electronic sounds (1975); *Bird and Person Dying*, for performer with microphones, amplifiers, loudspeakers, and sound-producing object (1975); *Tyndall Orchestrations*, for female voice, sensitive flame, players with bunsen burners and glass tubes, and recorded birdcalls (1976); *Music on a Long Thin Wire*, for audio oscillators and electronic monochord (1977); *Directions of Sounds from the Bridge*, for stringed instrument, audio oscillator, and sound-sensitive lights (1978); *Ghosts*, for loudspeakers and performer with sound-sensitive light (1978); *Clocker*, for performer with galvanic skin response sensor, audio digital delay system, amplified clock, and loudspeakers (1978); *Solar Sounder*, electronic music system powered and controlled by sunlight, in collaboration with John Fullemann (1979); *Job's Coffin*, for

performer with amplified chest of drawers (1979); *Shapes of the Sounds from the Board*, for amplified piano (1979).

BIBLIOGRAPHY: *BBDM; DCM; Ear* magazine, December 1978–January 1979; *High Fidelity/Musical America*, June 1978; *Musical Quarterly*, April 1979.

Luening, Otto, Clarence, b. Milwaukee, Wis., June 15, 1900.

Luening's prolific output since 1915 traverses a wide gamut of styles: near serial, aleatoric, linear, polytonal, and atonal. Acoustic studies led him to what he calls "acoustical harmony" based on different combinations from the harmonic series used as norms from which chords and new scale structures could be formed. This approach eventually led him to compose electronic music for which he is perhaps best known. As one of the earliest pioneers, he used tape for musical compositions, first processing manmade sounds, and eventually combining these with natural and electronically produced sounds on tape with live performers. Together with Vladimir Ussachevsky he composed *Rhapsodic Variations* (1854), the first work to combine live performers (a symphony orchestra) with tape-recorded sound.

Luening came from a rich musical background. His father, Eugene Luening, who had studied at the Leipzig Conservatory, was prominent as pianist, composer, and conductor in the Midwest, and was music director of the Milwaukee Music Society for more than thirty years, performing great oratorios in which Otto's mother, Emma Luening, often joined in the soprano section. Otto's maternal grandfather, William Jacobs, was an excellent amateur singer who sang the leading tenor roles in eight operas performed in Milwaukee.

Otto was four when his father began giving him piano lessons, which he continued only sporadically; by the time Otto was six he was composing. While his family lived on a farm in Wauwatosa, he attended public school there, and later in Madison, Wis., through seventh grade. When he was twelve years old his family left the United States, settling in Munich, Germany, where his father became prominent as a music teacher. In 1915, Otto Luening entered the Akademie der Tonkunst in Munich, where he studied theory with Anton Beer-Walbrunn, flute with Alois Schellhorn, and piano and organ with Josef Becht. On March 27, 1916, Otto Luening made his concert début as flutist in Munich. Meanwhile, in 1914–15, he worked as an orderly with wounded soldiers at the American Red Cross Hospital in Munich.

In 1917, just before America became involved in World War I, Luening went to Zurich to complete his musical education at the Municipal Conservatory (1917–20), concentrating on flute, conducting, and composing and studying with Philip Jarnach and Volkmar Andreae. At the University of Zurich in 1919–20 he audited the seminar in abnormal psychology directed by Professor Paul Eugene Bleuler, the teacher of Carl Jung. In 1918–19, Luening was also an actor in the English Players, a company that had James Joyce as business manager. Busoni became interested in Luening's compositions, gave him private lessons, and introduced him to the world of electronic sound production. Busoni's progressive and innovative concepts about music were a significant influence in Luening's development as an iconoclast composer. During the years of 1917–20, Luening first played percussion and then flute in the Zurich Tonhalle Orchestra and the Municipal Opera Orchestra. In 1917, he made his conducting debut in Zurich, directing a Viennese operetta. Later that year he conducted the Tonhalle Orchestra in Grieg's Piano Concerto, with Ernst Weilemann as soloist. The year of 1917 also marked the time in which Luening's Violin Sonata no. 1 and two songs for tenor and piano were first performed at the Zurich Conservatory. His early works—including the Sextet (1918; Zurich, April 30, 1921) and his String Quartet no. 1, with clarinet obbligato (1919; Berlin, March 1924)—were then considered radical in idiom and were sometimes atonal, polytonal, linear, contrapuntally complex, and harmonically dissonant, but with tonal passages used as contrast.

Luening returned to the United States in 1920, settling in Chicago for the next few years, supporting himself by playing the flute in a motion picture theater orchestra, teaching, arranging, and conducting choral societies. In Chicago he helped organize the American Grand Opera Company, serving as its music director; it specialized in presenting operas in the English language, and in 1922 offered the first all-American opera (Cadman's Shanewis).

Luening's compositions during these years in Chicago were quite controversial and remained so for several decades. His Trio, for violin, cello, and piano (1921; Chicago, October 10, 1922), was received favorably by some critics but one of them wrote that the Trio was not music. For a short while Luening studied Bernhard Ziehn's theories of harmony and contrapuntal techniques with Wilhelm Middelschulte, the foremost authority on Bach at that time. These studies had a strong influence on Luening's composing, particularly in his Introitus, for organ (1921; South Bend, Ind., July 17, 1921), the Violin Sonata no. 2 (1922; Rochester, N.Y., 1927), Choral Fantasy, for organ (1922; South Bend, Ind., 1922) and Music for Orchestra (1923; N.Y., May 23, 1978).

Additional works composed during these Chicago years included a Trio, for soprano, flute, and violin (1924; N.Y., March 18, 1957), in which only pitches are given in the last movement, leaving the choice of rhythms, dynamics, phrasing, and entrances to individual performers. His Symphonic Poem (1924; Rochester, N.Y., November 25, 1925), which was

recorded in 1955 and retitled Symphonic Fantasia no. 1, combined all of the practices he had developed in his earlier works. It was propelled by an abundant lyricism and an expressive romanticism controlled by a well-balanced overall gestalt, or form, that characterizes most of his subsequent music.

He came to Rochester, N.Y., in 1925, serving for the next three years as coach and executive director of the Eastman School of Music Opera Department. In Rochester, he also served first as assistant conductor, then as conductor, of the Rochester American Opera Company. On April 19, 1927, he married Ethel Codd, a concert singer, with whom, between 1928 and 1941, he toured the United States and Canada in joint recitals. They were divorced in 1959. On September 5, 1959, Luening married Catherine Johnson Brunson.

In 1928, Ethel and Otto Luening spent a year in Cologne, Germany, concertizing and composing. In 1929–30 he conducted concerts over the radio in New York and was musical director of Broadway productions until he resigned, after having been awarded a Guggenheim Fellowship in 1930 (extended an additional year in 1931). These consecutive fellowships enabled him to work on an opera, Evangeline, to his own libretto which closely followed selected scenes from Longfellow's narrative poem. Luening completed his opera in 1932 and received for it the David Bispham Medal a year later. He continued to revise it during the next decade and a half. Then, with the aid of a grant from the Alice M. Ditson Fund, the opera was produced at Columbia University in New York on May 5, 1948, the composer conducting and Teresa Stich-Randall in the title role. The highly lyrical score is colored by Acadian folk songs and dances, Swedish hymns, Indian music, and Catholic church music in its arias, choral scenes, dances, and instrumental interludes, giving it an eclectic American folk identity.

Between 1932 and 1934, Luening was the associate professor of music at the University of Arizona in Tucson, and from 1934 to 1964 he was chairman of the music department at Bennington College in Vermont, where, from 1939 to 1941, he was also music director of the Bennington School of the Arts.

Two Symphonic Interludes, for orchestra—contrasts in moods and tempo—was introduced by the New York Philharmonic under Hans Lange on April 11, 1936. A Suite, for string orchestra (1937), was heard first on September 12, 1937, at Saratoga, N.Y. Prelude to a Hymn Tune, based on a hymn by the 18th-century composer William Billings, was premiered by the New York Philharmonic Chamber Orchestra conducted by the composer on February 1, 1937. All these works go further along the paths of structure and idiom that Luening was establishing.

Luening served as Joline Associate Professor of Music, and was often chairman of the music department, of Barnard College in New York from 1944 to

1964. From 1944 to 1959 he was also the musical director of the Brander Matthews Theater at Columbia University, where, among many other works, he conducted the world premiere of Menotti's *The Medium* (May 8, 1946) and Virgil Thomson's *The Mother of Us All* (May 12, 1947). In 1946, Luening received an award from the National Institute of Arts and Letters, to which he was given a life appointment in 1952 and of which he was vice-president in 1953.

One of his most successful works during this period was *Pilgrim's Hymn*, for chamber orchestra (1946), which, as the composer explained, "bears a certain relationship, in feeling, to the music of William Billings." After its first hearing at the Yaddo Festival in Saratoga, N.Y., on September 14, 1946, Luening adapted it for large orchestra by a proportional doubling of the wind instruments to balance the larger string choir. The new version was premiered by the New York Philharmonic under Leopold Stokowski on January 24, 1949.

In 1949, Luening joined the faculty of philosophy at Columbia University, where he held seminars in composition, retaining this post up to the time of his retirement as professor emeritus in 1968. In 1959 he helped found, and from 1959 on (with Milton Babbitt and Ussachevsky) was codirector of, the Columbia-Princeton Electronic Music Center at Columbia University; in 1966–70 he was music chairman at the School of the Arts at Columbia. In 1971–73 he was professor of composition at the Juilliard School of Music.

Luening first became active in manipulating sound through the tape recorder in 1952 when he composed *Fantasy in Space*, with flute sounds played by him and transformed on magnetic tape. It was given its initial hearing at the first public performance in the United States of electronic music on October 28, 1952, in New York by Leopold Stokowski. This program included two other electronic pieces by Luening, both written in 1952: *Low Speed* and *Invention*. From this point on, Luening continued experimenting with electronic music, often using his own flute playing as the original sound source, and sometimes collaborating with Ussachevsky.

Rhapsodic Variations, for orchestra and tape (1954), written with Ussachevsky—the first work to combine live performers with sounds produced on tape—was commissioned by the Louisville Orchestra in Kentucky, which introduced it on March 30, 1954. It was the success of this work, and the repercussions it had throughout the world of music, that led to the formation of the Columbia-Princeton Electronics Music Center five years later. When *Rhapsodic Variations* was performed in Amsterdam on December 13, 1961, a critic for *Die Nieuwe Dag* wrote: "In our opinion, it seems to be a morganatic marriage, the assemblance of these two dissimilar sound units; the electronic novelties should not be seen as an expansion and enrichment of the rules of

harmony and melody, but as a newly discovered territory hardly to be overlooked, where the human mind is going to express itself in a completely different way, according to different standards, that the sounds of nature made possible not long ago. *Rhapsodic Variations* created a spatial effect which associates itself completely with mind and the development of this time."

Without abandoning music for conventional instruments, to which Luening continued to contribute a sizable repertoire, he has continued to experiment with and to exploit the sources of electronic music, with or without the collaboration of live performers. On November 18, 1954, *A Poem in Cycles and Bells*, for tape and orchestra, written with Ussachevsky, was introduced by the Los Angeles Philharmonic under Alfred Wallenstein, and on March 31, 1960, the New York Philharmonic under Leonard Bernstein presented the world premiere of *Concerted Piece for Tape Recorder and Orchestra* (1960), also a collaboration with Ussachevsky. Televised at one of Bernstein's Youth Concerts, it brought the name of the composer and the medium to national prominence. Without Ussachevsky's collaboration, Luening produced *Synthesis*, for tape and orchestra (1960; Erie, Pa., October 22, 1963); *Sonority Canon*, for four solo flutes and thirty-three flutes on tape (1962); *Fugue and Chorale Fantasy*, for organ with electronic doubles (1972), among other works. A ballet, *Of Identity*, was composed with Ussachevsky in 1955 on a commission from the American Mime Theater, which introduced it that year with Paul Curtis's choreography. *Theater Piece* no. 2, for tape, voice, brass, percussion, and narrator (1956), written without collaboration, was produced with choreography by Doris Humphrey and José Limon in New York on April 20, 1956, the composer conducting. In collaboration with Ussachevsky, Luening also contributed electronic music for the Orson Welles production of *King Lear* at the City Center in New York (January 12, 1956) and to Margaret Webster's Theater Guild production of Bernard Shaw's *Back to Methuselah* (March 5, 1958).

Among Luening's later nonelectronic compositions, the following are worthy of attention: *Wisconsin Suite: Of Childhood Tunes Remembered*, for orchestra (1955); *Lyric Scene*, for flute and strings (1958; Johnston, Vt., August 23, 1972); *Fantasia*, for string quartet and orchestra (1969; N.Y., 1971); *Introduction and Allegro*, for trumpet and piano (1971; N.Y., March 13, 1972); *Eight Tone Poems*, for two violas (1971; Albany, N.Y., January 27, 1972); *Sonority Forms*, for orchestra (1973; North Bennington, Vt., October 14, 1973); and *A Wisconsin Symphony* (1975), commissioned by the Milwaukee Symphony Orchestra, which introduced it under Kenneth Schermerhorn on Janaury 4, 1976.

In August 1960, Luening was the U.S. delegate to the International Composers Conference at the Stratford Festival in Ontario, Canada. He was com-

poser-in-residence at the American Academy of
Rome in 1958, 1961, and 1965. In 1963 he received
an honorary doctorate in music from Wesleyan University in Middletown, Conn. In 1965, he was cited
by the Wisconsin State Assembly and House of Representatives for outstanding achievements in and contributions to education and music. That year he returned to Munich, where, in commemoration of his
sixty-fifth birthday, he was given a reception by the
mayor of Munich in the Rathaus and his Trio, for
flute, violin and piano, was performed at the High
School for Music on July 13. In the United States,
the year of 1966 brought him a citation from the
National Association of Composers and Conductors,
and an appointment from Phi Beta Kappa as visiting
scholar to give lectures in more than thirty colleges
and universities over a three-year period, as a result
of which he was elected to honorary membership.
When, in May 1970, Luening was participant in
concerts commemorating the tenth anniversary of the
founding of the Columbia-Princeton Electronic Music Center, American Composers Alliance presented
him with its Laurel Leaf "for distinguished achievement in fostering and encouraging American music."
In 1972 he received the Thorne Music Fund Award
and two years later his third Guggenheim Fellowship.

Through the years he has been affiliated with numerous organizations promoting new music and
American composers. In 1940 he was a founder of
American Music Center, serving as its chairman
from 1940 to 1960. Between 1945 and 1951 he was
president of the American Composers Alliance, of
which he was a founder. He was a member of the
Educational Advisory Board of the Guggenheim
Foundation between 1964 and 1970, and from 1968
to 1974 he was president of Composers Recordings,
Inc., which he had founded together with Oliver
Daniel and Douglas Moore in 1954.

Luening received honorary doctorates from the
University of Wisconsin in Madison (1976), the
Wisconsin Conservatory of Music in Milwaukee
(1979), and Columbia University (1981); a medal
from the Wisconsin Academy of Sciences, Arts and
Letters (1976); and a citation from the Wisconsin
State Assembly (1976), his second such. He is the
author of an autobiography, *The Odyssey of an
American Composer* (1980).

THE COMPOSER SPEAKS: Nothing could be more misleading than to pretend that composers are everything in the world of music. They are not. They
merely create and write music. As always, popular
composers are doing reasonably well. They always
have and always will. But one can hazard a guess
that there are at least fifteen hundred composers
writing "standard" music, that is to say, concert,
operatic, church, and experimental music of various
kinds. Of these, one-third at the most have active
publishers or are connected with one of our licensing
and collection societies. The remaining thousand,
many of them young people, are in limbo. They have
no chance of making professional connections because their works have not been tried out, and no
chance of having their works tried out because they
have no professional connections. The result is that
some of them stop their composing careers before
they have even begun them. This represents a waste
of considerable proportions. All of these composers
have had long training and some of them have perhaps won some of our prizes and fellowships, though
there are not enough of these around.

What is to be done with this "lost battalion" of
young composers? The schools and the colleges responsible for developing our young composers teach
them our musical heritage and show them the broad
stream of music as it reaches us from the past. This
stream includes not only music which was immediately successful and functional, but also music which
was in its time new and strange and which furnished
the ideals for what was then the music of the future,
which we now admire as the music of the past. Music
with qualities somewhat more subtle than the merely
functional has ever been necessary to prevent stagnation and deadly routine from getting the upper hand.
Teaching people how to write music that will definitely be successful is just as impossible as to teach to
them how to always beat the stock market. . . .

Today we have the greatest possibilities in scope
and style of musical composition in the entire history
of music. Not only do we have the whole sweep of
music history before us, but also many new inventions to enlarge our horizons. If a composer chooses,
he can write not only according to the regular scales
but microtonically. He can write in the tempered
scale or in just intonation, or according to the Hindu
scale of twenty-two notes to the octave, or, as Harry
Partch has done so brilliantly, fragment the octave
into forty-three tones.

PRINCIPAL WORKS: 5 suites for solo flute (1947–69);
4 *Symphonic Fantasias* (1924–80); 3 sonatas for violin solo (1958, 1968, 1970–71); 3 string quartets
(1919, 1923, 1928).

Concertino, for flute, harp, celesta, and strings
(1923); Trio, for flute, violin, and soprano (1924);
The Soundless Song, for soprano, string quartet,
flute, clarinet, piano, dancers, and lights (1924);
Symphonic Poem, for orchestra (1924); Serenade, for
three horns and string orchestra (1927–28); *Evangeline*, opera (1928–33, revised 1947); *Two Symphonic
Interludes* (1935); *Fantasia Brevis*, for clarinet and
piano (1936); *Prelude to a Hymn Tune*, for chamber
orchestra (1937); *Fuguing Tune*, for flute, oboe,
clarinet, bassoon, and horn (1941); Suite, for cello
and piano (1946); *Pilgrim's Hymn*, for chamber orchestra, also for large orchestra (1946); Three Nocturnes, for oboe and piano (1951); *Legend*, for oboe
and strings (1951); *Kentucky Concerto*, for orchestra
(1951); Bassoon Sonata (1952); *Fantasy for Space*,

Low Speed, Invention, all three for flute on tape (1952); *Incantation*, on tape, composed with Ussachevsky (1952); Trombone Sonata (1953); *A Poem in Cycles and Bells*, for tape and orchestra, with Ussachevsky (1954); *Rhapsodic Variations*, for orchestra and tape, with Ussachevsky (1954); *Wisconsin Suite: Of Childhood Tunes Remembered*, for orchestra (1955); *Of Identity*, ballet music for tape, with Ussachevsky (1955); *Theater Piece* no. 2, for tape, voice, brass, percussion, and narrator (1956); Serenade, for flute and strings (1957); Bass Viol Sonata (1958); *Lyric Scene*, for flute and strings (1958); *Synthesis*, for orchestra and tape (1960); *Gargoyles*, for violin and tape (1961); *Sonority Canon*, for four solo flutes and thirty-three flutes on tape (1962); *Diffusion of Bells, Electronic Fanfare*, for tape, both in collaboration with Halim El Dabh (1962–65); *Moonflight*, for flute on tape (1967); *Fantasia*, for string quartet and orchestra (1969); Eight Tone Poems, for two violas (1971); Fugue and Chorale Fantasy, for organ and electronic doubles (1972); *Sonority Forms*, for orchestra (1973); *A Wisconsin Symphony* (1975); Triadic Canons, for two violins and flute (1975); *Fantasies on Indian Music*, for flute solo (1977); *Potawatomi Legends*, for chamber orchestra (1979).

BIBLIOGRAPHY: Ewen, David, *American Composers Today* (N.Y., 1949); Luening, Otto, *The Odyssey of an American Composer* (N.Y., 1980); Schwartz, Elliott, *Electronic Music* (N.Y., 1973); Thomson, Virgil, *American Music Since 1910* (N.Y., 1970); *American Composers Alliance Bulletin*, Autumn 1953; *New York Times*, June 15, 1980; *Who's Who in America, 1980–81*.

Luke, Ray Edward, b. Fort Worth, Tex., May 30, 1928.

Luke is not a disciple of any particular style or technique of composing but rather is committed to an amalgamation of all techniques available to him. As a result, his style has changed gradually, though regularly, as he absorbed new practices into his own technique and attempted to use them in unique ways. His music is imaginative in the use of timbres and sonorities.

The only musician in the family was his mother, who played piano occasionally, but both parents were strongly supportive when, early in his life, Luke began revealing an interest in music. He was a boy soprano who sang extensively in school, church, and community events. He started studying the piano with Wayne McNeeley when he was five, and trumpet with G. R. Carson three years later. In Fort Worth's public schools, Luke played the trumpet in the orchestra and band and sang in the chorus. At fourteen he started playing the trumpet professionally in jazz groups and dance bands.

Upon graduating from Polytechnic High School in

Fort Worth in 1945, Luke entered Texas Christian University. There he continued studying the piano with Keith Mixon and trumpet with Joe Cinquemani, while taking courses in theory, composition, and orchestration with Ralph Guenther and arranging and instrumental ensembles with Leon Breeden. Breeden not only encouraged him in all his performing endeavors but trained him as an arranger, an activity which for some years remained Luke's sole creative outlet. While attending Texas Christian University Luke played the trumpet with the Fort Worth Opera Orchestra (1947–49) and with the Fort Worth Symphony when it gave concerts from time to time. He was also doing a considerable amount of arranging for dance bands. Attempts at composition were sporadic and tentative. "I arranged so easily, scored so easily," he recalls, "that I always felt I should be able to compose, but I had little incentive. I wasn't around anybody who was composing. I suppose I could have done some composing for the piano, but I was interested in ensemble work, and I didn't know where to begin. I started some compositions but never completed them."

He received his bachelor of music degree in 1949 and his master of music degree in theory one year later, his master's thesis being a modern adaptation and arrangement of *No Song, No Supper*, an opera by the 18th-century English composer Stephen Storacc. In 1949–50, Luke was director of instrumental music in the public schools of Granbury, Tex.; in 1950–51 he held a similar post in Atlantic Christian College in Wilson, N.C., and, from 1951 to 1962, at East Texas State University in Commerce, Tex.

On April 11, 1952, Luke married Virginia Faye Smith, an elementary grade schoolteacher with whom he raised two children. Five years later, he entered the Eastman School of Music in Rochester, N.Y., for postgraduate work in theory and composition. He remained there three years, studying theory with A. I. McHose, and composition with Bernard Rogers. "I entered as a theory major and hoped to compose," he says, "but I felt I had no background for it. My background was in arranging and scoring for band and orchestra, but at Eastman they thought I should enter an advanced class in orchestration and also composition. I discovered these two classes had the same teacher, Bernard Rogers. I told Dr. Rogers I thought I was in the wrong class. He told me to write something for the next class. When he saw it he threw it in the wastebasket and asked me to try again. I did, and he insisted that I stay with the class. By the end of the year, he insisted I become a composition major. I finally decided to stay in the theory program but to write my theses as a composition major. Studying with Rogers at Eastman proved my awakening as a composer."

While attending Eastman he wrote background music for ten dramatic productions telecast over the Canadian TV network. He also completed several apprentice compositions, some chamber music, *Two*

Miniatures for Orchestra (1957), Suite, for orchestra (1958–59), and *Epilogue*, for orchestra (1958), all performed in Rochester; *Two Miniatures* on August 12, 1957, and the Suite on April 15, 1958, both conducted by Howard Hanson, and the *Epilogue* conducted by Frederick Fennell on April 12, 1958. For his doctor of philosophy degree in theory and composition, which Luke received in 1960, he submitted as thesis his Symphony no. 1 (1959), introduced in Rochester on March 26, 1959, under Hanson. That symphony was one of two works selected by the Fleischer Collection in Philadelphia, a free library that makes scores available for performance; (the other work was the Suite). It was through the Fleischer Collection that this symphony came to the attention of Guy Fraser Harrison, the conductor of the Oklahoma City Symphony. Harrison conducted a performance of this symphony with his orchestra on March 27, 1960. "That really started the long chain of performances. He took my works sight unseen. You had the feeling with him that the important thing was that he perform the work, not that he judge it. He gave first-class performances and I think he assumed that performance would be the composer's best teacher." With the Oklahoma City Symphony, Harrison presented the world premieres of Luke's Symphony no. 2 (1961) on February 3, 1963, and Symphony no. 3 (1963) on February 21, 1964.

In 1962, Luke was appointed professor of composition at Oklahoma City University in Oklahoma, where he has remained since. At Oklahoma City, in addition to his teaching assignments, Luke began developing himself as a conductor: with the university orchestra and opera, of which he had been musical director since 1962; as musical director and conductor of the Oklahoma City Lyric Theater (1963–67); as associate conductor of the Oklahoma City Symphony (1968–73); as music director and interim resident conductor of the Oklahoma City Symphony (1973–74); and, until 1978, as principal guest conductor of that orchestra.

From 1965 on, Luke intensified his efforts at composition, producing major works within traditional structures but developing a personalized harmonic and rhythmic idiom. The Oklahoma City Symphony under Harrison continued to provide him with an important showcase by presenting the world premieres of his Bassoon Concerto (1965) and *Fanfare for Symphonic Winds and Percussion* (1967), both of which it commissioned; *Symphonic Dialogues*, for violin, oboe, and orchestra (1965), commissioned by Catherine Paulu; and Suite no. 2, for orchestra (1967). The last of these won first prize in the Oklahoma Symphonic Composition Competition in 1967.

Luke's Piano Concerto (1968) brought him international recognition when it was awarded first prize in the prestigious Queen Elisabeth of Belgium International Composition Competition in 1969, the only time an American has captured this honor up to this present writing. The Piano Concerto was introduced in Brussels by L'Orchestre National de Belgique, conducted by Michaël Gielen, with Claude-Albert Coppens as soloist on November 26, 1969, and on October 18, 1970, it was given its American premiere by John Ogdon as soloist with the Oklahoma City Symphony under Harrison. In the *Oklahoman*, John Acord III called it "a vital modern work. . . . The most clashing dissonances do not disturb the ear. They are well planned to add weight as sonority and the resulting cacophony of sound is orderly and euphonious in the end result. The work is tremendously exciting both from a harmonic standpoint and the basic rhythmic structure."

After that, commissions led to the writing of some of his most important works. *The Incantation*, for cello, harp, and strings (1968), commissioned by Paul Maxwell, was introduced in January 1969 by Robert Marsh and the Oklahoma City Symphony under Harrison. Symphony no. 4 (1970), commissioned by the Oklahoma City Symphony, was premiered by that orchestra under Harrison on March 30, 1970. *Compressions for Orchestra* (1972), one of his most important compositions—a commission from Guy Fraser Harrison and the Oklahoma City Symphony—received its first hearing on January 9, 1973. *Compressions 2*, for orchestra (1973), was commissioned by Texas Christian University, its premiere given by the Fort Worth Symphony under John Giordano on November 9, 1973; *Tapestry*, a one-act ballet, was written for the Ballet Oklahoma, which produced it in collaboration with the Oklahoma City Symphony, the composer conducting, on May 8, 1975; and Septet, for wind and strings (1979), was commissioned by the Oklahoma City Chamber Players, who gave the first performance on July 22, 1979.

Luke's opera *Medea* (1978)—libretto by Carveth Osterhaus, based on the tragedy of Euripides—won first prize among fifty entries in a contest sponsored jointly by the Rockefeller Foundation and the New England Conservatory in Boston for American operas. Its world premiere took place in Boston on May 3, 1979, the composer conducting. "The music is complex, difficult to perform and of such harmonic language that Luke at times must use his own terms on the score," reported W. U. McCoy to the *Sunday Oklahoman*. "But it is not at all difficult on the emotional level for the listener; its effect is inescapably powerful and immediate. . . . The vital, brilliant music set the stage for scenes and moods with swift, unerring, compressed strokes; it supported, buoyed, built, and carried the story line forward, never taking over but always a part of the organic whole with the action and libretto, and those musical lines and carefully wrought vocal lines were eminently singable."

In 1970, Luke was named Oklahoma Musician of the Year by Governor Dewey Bartlett, and in 1973, Texas Christian University named him Distinguished Alumnus. In 1974, Luke received the Sigma

Alpha Iota Community Service Award, and in 1979, the Oklahoma Governor's Arts Award was presented to him by Governor George Nigh.

THE COMPOSER SPEAKS: The composer is certainly a lonely figure in 20th-century society in the United States. Suffering the sophistication gap between composer and audience as well as enduring a preponderance of critics with narrow taste and limited understanding, he must continue to compose with few prospects of major performances (and with inadequate professional remuneration).

We must hope that history will document the last two decades of the 20th century in the United States as a time in which a fantastic array of techniques was assimilated into a language through which great compositions might emerge. We must also hope that opportunities for composers to hear their music performed will increase and that their endeavors will become more important to the concert and recital repertoire.

PRINCIPAL WORKS: 4 symphonies (1959–70); 2 Suites, for orchestra (1958, 1967); 2 *Compressions*, for orchestra (1972, 1973).

Two Miniatures for Orchestra (1957); *Epilogue*, for orchestra (1958); Suite for Twelve Orchestral Woodwinds (1962); *Five Miniatures*, for piano (1964); Bassoon Concerto (1965); Two Odes, for mezzo-soprano, flute, and piano (1965); *Symphonic Dialogues*, for violin, oboe, and orchestra (1965); String Quartet (1966); *Fanfare for Symphonic Winds and Percussion* (1967); Piano Concerto (1968); *The Incantation*, for cello, harp, and strings (1968); *Symphonic Songs*, for mezzo-soprano and orchestra (1968); *Four Dialogues*, for organ and percussion (1970); *Sonics and Metrics*, for concert band (1970); *Concert Overture for Orchestra: Summer Music* (1970); Trio, for flute, clarinet, and piano (1974); *Tapestry*, ballet (1975); *Design*, for concert band (1976); *Medea*, opera (1978); Septet, for winds and strings (1979); *Epitaphs*, for twelve mixed voices (1979).

BIBLIOGRAPHY: *Sunday Oklahoman*, July 15, 1978; *International Who's Who in Music*, 8th ed., 1977.

Lyon, James, b. Newark, N.J., July 1, 1735; d. Machias, Me., October 12, 1794.

With Francis Hopkinson and William Billings, Lyon belongs with America's earliest native-born composers. He wrote odes, psalms, and anthems for the church and one or two secular songs, of which only ten items are now extant.

He was a descendant of Henry Lyon, who came to the New World in 1649, settling first in Milford, Conn., and then in Newark, N.J. When James was nine, his father died, leaving him to be raised by guardians. Beyond this, nothing is known of his childhood and boyhood. As a young man he entered the College of New Jersey, then in Newark. When, in 1756, this college moved to Princeton (subsequently to become Princeton University), Lyon followed it there, graduating with a bachelor of arts degree in 1759. The commencement exercises on September 26 included Lyon's *Ode to Peace,* believed to be his first composition to be publicly performed. "It is a very early, if not the earliest, specimen of American Commencement-odes," wrote O. G. Sonneck in his book on Lyon, "as such a very early monument of secular music in our country and consequently a strong weapon against the prevalent but incorrect theory that secular music had no stronghold in the colonies previous to the end of the eighteenth century."

Some months after these commencement exercises, Lyon came to Philadelphia, where he taught in a singing school while attending the College of Philadelphia. Once again, on May 23, 1761, commencement exercises included a Lyon composition. In Philadelphia, in 1761, Lyon published an anthology of psalm tunes, anthems, and hymns "from the most approved Authors, and some entirely new, in two, three or four parts and the whole adapted to the Use of Churches and Private Families." He called it *Urania* and it included seven of Lyon's own compositions: settings of Psalms 8, 23, 95, and 104, settings of two verses from the Sternhold and Hopkins psalter, and an anthem taken from Psalm 150. *Urania* proved so popular that it enjoyed new editions in 1767 and 1773; a facsimile edition was published in New York in 1973.

When Lyon received his master of arts degree at Princeton in 1762, the commencement, on September 29, concluded with an entertainment entitled *The Military Glory of Great Britain.* Here, five speakers glorified the deeds of Wolfe, Amherst, and Albermarle. It opened with an orchestrally accompanied chorus entitled "Britannia's Glory" after which choruses were interspersed between sections of dialogue and monologues. When *The Military Glory of Great Britain* was published in Philadelphia in 1762, no author of text or composer was identified. There lingers a suspicion that Lyon contributed at least some of the numbers, and possibly the entire text and score. Though no incontrovertible evidence has surfaced as to Lyon's authorship, when *The Military Glory of Great Britain* was resurrected in a concert presentation in New York by the Federal Music Society on May 16, 1979, with a full orchestra of antique instruments, James Lyon was named as its author.

Lyon was ordained a Presbyterian minister by the synod of New Brunswick, N.J., in 1764. One year later he accepted a pastorate in Nova Scotia where, on February 18, 1768, he married Martha Holden. His income in Halifax and Onslow in Nova Scotia was so meager that he was not able to take care of his family properly. He left his post in 1771, and in 1772 found a new and better-paying assignment in the newly founded town of Machias in Maine. For a while there he supplemented his church income by operating a salt distillery on Salt Island near Machiasport. Except for two brief intermissions (in 1773 and again in 1783–85) he remained in Machias until his death.

He was an ardent supporter of the American Revolution. In 1775 he dispatched a letter to George Washington outlining plans for conquering Nova Scotia, and offering his services since he knew that territory so well. The offer was politely rejected.

In Machias, Lyon continued composing. One of his contemporaries, Philip Vickers Fithian, mentions in his diary that he met Lyon in Cohansie, N.J., and that Lyon informed him he was about to publish "a new book of tunes which are to be chiefly of his own compositions." No trace of this book has been found and in all probability it was never published. At Andrew Adgates's Uranian Concerts in Philadelphia, two Lyon pieces were performed: an anthem based on Psalm 18 on May 4, 1786, and "Friendship Thou," a secular song, on April 12, 1787.

Following the death of his first wife (date not known), Lyon married a second time: the former Sarah Skillen on November 24, 1793.

THE COMPOSER SPEAKS: ["Directions for Singing" in the preface to *Urania*]: 1. In learning the 8 notes, get the assistance of some person well acquainted with Tones and Semitones.

2. Choose that part which you can sing with the greatest Ease, and make yourself Master of that first.

3. Sound all high Notes as soft as possible, but low ones hard and full.

4. Pitch your Tune so that the highest and lowest Notes may be sounded distinctly.

PRINCIPAL WORKS: (*all vocal*): *Ode to Peace* (c. 1759); Settings for Psalms 9, 23, 95, 104, two verses from Sternhold and Hopkins, and an anthem from Psalm 150, all collected in *Urania* (published in 1761); two secular songs, "A Marriage Hymn" and "Friendship Thou" (c. 1787); Psalm 17 (c. 1788); Psalm 19 (c. 1792).

BIBLIOGRAPHY: Chase, Gilbert, *America's Music* (N.Y., 1955); Edwards, G. T., *Music and Musicians of Maine* (Portland, Me., 1928); Howard, John Tasker, *Our American Music* (N. Y., 1946); Metcalf, F. J., *American Writers and Compilers of Sacred Music* (N.Y., 1925); Sonneck, O. G., *James Lyon, Patriot, Preacher, Psalmodist* (Washington, D.C., 1905).

M

MacDowell, Edward Alexander, b. New York City, December 18, 1860; d. New York City, January 23, 1908.

MacDowell was America's first composer of major stature of concert music, the first American composer whose best concert works have remained in the concert repertoire. A romanticist in the traditions of Mendelssohn and Grieg, MacDowell excelled as a miniaturist, as producer of cameos for the piano that often drew their inspiration and subject matter from American landscapes and other natural beauties and occasionally from the supernatural world of elves, gnomes, and witches. His lyrical and harmonic gifts were abundant; his craftsmanship, impeccable; his taste, immaculate; and his sense of structural symmetry and balance, exquisite.

He was born the third and youngest child to a cultured and financially secure household. His father, a prosperous businessman of Scottish origin and a Quaker, had a talent for painting; late in his youth he had been deflected by his parents from art to business. Edward MacDowell's mother, who was Irish, also had an appreciation of the arts, though no special talent in any direction. Both parents proved sympathetic and responsive when the child Edward began revealing a marked talent for drawing, an interest in writing poems and inventing fairy tales, a passion for reading, and a gift for music. When, in his eighth year, he expressed a desire to study the piano, his parents recruited Juan Buitrago, a friend of the family, to give him lessons. Additional lessons and coaching came from Teresa Carreño, the foremost woman virtuoso of her day. Then a three-year period of intensive training at the piano with Paul Desverine followed. All this took place while MacDowell was receiving his academic education at New York City public schools and, from 1870 to 1876, at a private French school. When he was thirteen his mother took him on an extended trip throughout Europe to broaden his intellectual horizon.

He received the *Billet de satisfaction* (diploma of graduation) from the French private school in January 1875, which described him as "a good pupil; leaves behind him . . . an excellent character in conduct and lesson; and much regret for his withdrawal." His academic education was now over, and from this time on his studies were confined to music. By 1876, his mother had become determined to dispatch her son to Europe for intensive training in music. In the company of Buitrago, he arrived in

Paris in 1876. At first he was an auditor in Augustin Savard's class in harmony. Then, on February 8, 1877, he was admitted to the conservatory to receive his training in piano with Antoine-François Marmontel, and solfège with Marmontel's son. The following October MacDowell won a full scholarship.

MacDowell's ambition was to become a concert pianist, and to advance himself in that direction he continued his training in Germany. In 1878 he left Paris to spend a brief period as a pupil of Siegmund Lebert at the Stuttgart Conservatory, which dissatisfied him. He spent the year of 1878–79 studying composition and theory privately with Louis Ehlert in Wiesbaden. Then, in 1879, he entered Hoch's Conservatory in Frankfurt, continuing his piano study there with Karl Heymann. Though he also received instruction in advanced composition from Joachim Raff, the conservatory's director, and in counterpoint and fugue from Franz Böhme, MacDowell's ambition in music still rested solely on the piano. But in 1880 he had a change of heart. On a challenge from Raff that he prepare for the composition class something more ambitious than mere exercises, MacDowell produced his first mature composition, *First Modern Suite*, for piano (1881) on the basis of which Raff encouraged the young student to begin thinking seriously of composition. Raff also suggested to MacDowell he send this work to Franz Liszt in Weimar who, in turn, was sufficiently impressed to recommend it for performance at a concert of the Allgemeiner Deutsche Musik Verein in Zurich on July 11, 1882, where it was well received. (This was not the first time that MacDowell and Liszt crossed paths. On a visit to Wiesbaden, Liszt had heard MacDowell participate in a two-piano transcription of one of Liszt's tone poems on June 9, 1879).

When Heyman retired from his teaching post at Hoch's Conservatory in 1880, he recommended MacDowell as his successor, a choice that met with Raff's complete agreement. But in the end MacDowell was turned down because he had not yet had enough teaching experience. He found another post at the Darmstadt Conservatory as head of its piano department. The hours were long, the duties arduous, the pay insufficient. MacDowell's problems were compounded by the necessity of spending a considerable amount of time commuting from Frankfurt to Darmstadt, though he used this travel time to good advantage by devoting it to his compositions, including the *Second Modern Suite*, for piano (1882). The strain, however, took its toll on his health and in 1882 he withdrew from the Darmstadt Conservatory to set himself up in Frankfurt as a teacher of piano to private pupils and to devote himself more assiduously to composition. That year he completed the writing of his Piano Concerto no. 1 in A minor.

In 1882, MacDowell went to Weimar to visit Liszt, bringing with him the manuscript of his piano concerto. Liszt proved cordial, and when he went through the concerto, with Eugèn d'Albert playing the orchestral accompaniment on a second piano, he proved highly enthusiastic. Liszt also used his influence to find MacDowell a publisher—the powerful house of Breitkopf und Härtel—which released MacDowell's first two *Modern Suites*. This was his first music to get into print.

Nature and the world of the supernatural began to influence his music in 1883–84 with the writing of *Two Fantastic Pieces* (one of which was a "Witches' Dance") and *Forest Idyls* (whose movements included a dance of the dryads, the play of nymphs, a tone painting of a forest stillness, and a reverie), both for the piano.

In June 1884, MacDowell returned briefly to the United States to marry Marian Griswold Nevins on July 9, in Waterford, Conn. His plan then was to support his wife by playing and teaching the piano, but his bride had other plans. Convinced that her husband's destiny lay in composition, she placed at his disposal an inheritance of five thousand dollars she had recently received, so that they might return to Germany for several years and allow MacDowell to develop himself creatively. After a brief honeymoon in London and Paris, they returned to Frankfurt. There, using Liszt as his inspiration, MacDowell completed his first tone poem, and his first composition exclusively for orchestra, *Hamlet and Ophelia* (1885). Later that year, the MacDowells moved to Wiesbaden, where they purchased a small cottage. The next three years were probably the happiest in MacDowell's life, as he began to experience a growing strength and assurance as composer and started to get some recognition. *Hamlet and Ophelia* proved an extraordinary success in performances in Darmstadt, Wiesbaden, Baden-Baden, Sonderhausen, and Frankfurt. And even the United States was beginning to hear his music, Teresa Carreño having performed some of his piano pieces at her recitals since August 4, 1883, when she presented a movement from the *First Modern Suite* in Saratoga, N.Y., and March 8, 1884, when she was heard in the complete *Second Modern Suite* in Chicago. He found another stout American supporter in the conductor Frank Van der Stucken, who performed in New York the last two movements of the Piano Concerto no. 1 with Adele Margulies as soloist in March 1885. (The premiere of the complete concerto took place in Vienna on April 17, 1898.) In 1886, Van der Stucken gave the American premiere of the "Ophelia" sec-

tion of *Hamlet and Ophelia*, and in 1887 the "Hamlet" section.

Nurtured by these successes and by his wife's tireless encouragement and enthusiasm, MacDowell became increasingly productive. In 1886 he completed his Piano Concerto no. 2 in D minor and his second orchestral tone poem, *Lancelot and Elaine*, and in 1887, several songs, including a cycle, *From an Old Garden*.

In 1888, the MacDowells decided to return permanently to the United States. They made their home in Boston. Initially, there were some setbacks. MacDowell hoped to support himself by teaching composition, but found that the only pupils available to him were in piano instruction. He wanted to devote himself as much as possible to composition but soon realized that if he were to get piano pupils he would have to make numerous appearances as pianist to become better known. But it was not long before he found enthusiastic audiences. He made his American debut as pianist-composer in Boston on November 19, 1888, when, as assisting artist to the Kneisel Quartet, he performed three movements of his *First Modern Suite* (besides participating with the Kneisels in a presentation of Karl Goldmark's Piano Quintet). On December 10, he introduced several more of his piano works at Boston's Apollo Club. On March 5, 1889, he himself was heard in the world premiere of Piano Concerto no. 2 with Theodore Thomas conducting the New York Philharmonic. Writing in the *New York Tribune,* Henry E. Krehbiel called it "a splendid composition, so full of poetry, so full of vigor, as to tempt the assertion that it must be placed at the head of all works of its kind produced by either a native or adopted son of America. But . . . it can stand by itself and challenge the heartiest admiration for its contents, its workmanship, and its originality of thought." MacDowell performed his concerto in Boston with the Boston Symphony under Wilhelm Gericke on April 12, 1889, and on July 12, 1889, he repeated his performance at an all-American concert at the Paris Exposition in France.

His strongest ally in the United States to lift him to the top echelon of American composers was the Boston Symphony. Following its performance of the Piano Concerto no. 2, it offered *Lancelot and Elaine* on January 10, 1908, Arthur Nikisch conducting; *Hamlet and Ophelia*, on January 28, 1893; Suite no. 1, for orchestra (1891), on October 16, 1895 (following its world premiere at the Worcester Festival in Massachusetts on September 24, 1891); *Lamia* (1888), a tone poem inspired by Keats, on October 23, 1908; and the *Indian Suite* (Suite no. 2), for orchestra (1895), MacDowell's last work for orchestra and one of his rare excursions into musical nationalism, for which he had little sympathy, in New York on January 23, 1896, a world premiere.

All this while MacDowell was cultivating the garden for which he had the inimitable "green thumb":

short mood and nature pictures for piano. The famous *Woodland Sketches* (1896), a suite of ten such tonal portraits, included two of his most famous piano pieces, which became staples in the light classical repertoire, "To a Wild Rose" and "To a Water Lily." His piano poems, as John F. Porte wrote in his biography of the composer, "are absolutely responsive to elemental moods, unaffected in style and yet distinguished, free from the commonplace. Speaking with a personal note that is inimitable, they are mature nature poems of an exquisitely charming order, beautiful not only for their outward manifestations, but for the deeper significance they give to their source of inspiration."

MacDowell was also working in the larger structure of the piano sonata. The first such was the Sonata in G, subtitled *Tragic* (1892), which the distinguished critic James Gibbons Huneker called "the most marked contribution to solo sonata literature since Brahms' F minor Sonata." MacDowell's Piano Sonata no. 2 in G minor, *Eroica* (1895), was programmatic music whose source was the legends of King Arthur and the Round Table. MacDowell produced two more sonatas in the first years of the 20th century. The Sonata in D minor, *Norse* (1899), drew its inspiration from the Nibelungen sagas. Sonata in E minor, *Celtic* (1900), was based on Irish folk tales. These last two were described by their composer as "more of a 'bardic' rhapsody on the subject than an attempt at acutal presentation of it, although I have made use of all the suggestions of tone-painting in my power—just as the bard would have reinforced *his* speech with gesture and facial expression."

In contemplating MacDowell's piano music—the large works as well as the small—Lawrence Gilman, the eloquent critic, wrote: "He was one of the most individual writers who ever made music—as individual as Chopin, or Debussy or Brahms, or Grieg. His manner of speech was utterly untrammeled, and wholly his own. Vitality—an abounding freshness, a perpetual youthfulness—was one of his prime traits; nobility—nobility of style and impulse—was another. The morning freshness, the welling spontaneity of his music, even its moments of exalted or passionate utterance, was continually surprising: it was music not unworthy of the golden ages of the world."

MacDowell's deeply poetic nature expressed itself just as felicitously within the song form. Some of his best songs are found in a set of four for voice and piano to his own lyrics, op. 56 (1898): "Long Ago," "The Swan Bent Low to the Lily," "A Maid Sings Light," and "As the Gleaming Shadows Creep." Among his other distinguished songs are "Thy Beaming Eyes," from *Six Love Songs* (1890), poem by W. H. Gardner; "Confidence," from Eight Songs, op. 47 (1893), poem by the composer; "Constancy," from Three Songs, op. 58 (1899), poem by the composer; and "Fair Springtide" and "To the Golden Rod," from Three Songs, op. 60 (1901), poems by the composer.

When Columbia University in New York established a music department in 1896 it summoned MacDowell, whom it then described as "America's foremost composer," to be its head. With high-minded purpose MacDowell threw all his energies into the task of creating for America a new standard of music education. But it was not long before disenchantment set in. At first compelled to teach all the music courses (before he was given an assistant), which were attended by the indifferent and the inept as well as by those with a smattering of brilliance, he found the teaching chores a drudgery he detested. Finally, he became enmeshed in red tape and bureaucracy each time he tried opening new horizons for music education. It was all a sad mistake, the critic Henry T. Finck wrote, to "harness Pegasus." Escape from his frustrations and conflicts came during the summers at his farm in Hillcrest, in Peterboro, N.H., which he and his wife purchased in 1896. It became for him a haven for rest, the contemplation of nature, and, in a log cabin, for composing. Some of his best piano pieces were written there, including the already mentioned *Woodland Sketches* as well as *Fireside Tales* and *New England Idyls* (1902).

During his initial years at Columbia University, MacDowell was the conductor of the Mendelssohn Glee Club in New York for two seasons. In 1899 he was made president of the newly organized American Society of Musicians and Composers, devoted to furthering the cause of American music. He resigned from this post in February 1900 after conflicts with the board of directors, and the organization itself expired soon after that. In 1902–3, during a sabbatical leave from Columbia University, MacDowell made an extensive and highly successful tour of the United States, following it with appearances in England.

He returned to his academic duties at Columbia University in 1903, a tired, restless, and depressed man. He found a new president at its head, Nicholas Murray Butler, who rejected MacDowell's plans for the creation of a comprehensive department of fine arts. In the face of this opposition, MacDowell tendered his resignation in January 1904. The incident was blown up by the press into a *cause célèbre* which created considerable bitterness and played havoc with MacDowell's sensitive nervous system.

He went back to teaching the piano privately and, hopefully, to assign more time to composition. But shortly before Easter, 1904, he was knocked down by a hansom cab in a New York City street, which resulted in severe back pains. His health was now on the downgrade, and his nervous system was beginning to show signs of damage. By December 1905 he could no longer walk, and by late 1907 he had a complete mental collapse due to brain damage. In his last years he was totally withdrawn, oblivious of his surroundings and of those near him, looking through glazed eyes that showed no sign of comprehension. His death came at his home in the Westminster Hotel in New York. He was buried on a hilltop on his farm in Peterboro, commanding a view he dearly loved.

Following his death, funds were raised for a Mac-Dowell Memorial Association to which MacDowell's widow deeded her farm in Peterboro. It has since become a summer colony where, at minimal cost, creative artists could work undisturbed in separate cottages. Until her death in 1958, Mrs. Mac-Dowell scrupulously supervised the running of the colony.

In 1960, MacDowell became the first composer of concert music and the second composer in any field to be elected to the Hall of Fame at New York University. (His predecessor in music was Stephen Foster.) At the Hall of Fame, a bust of MacDowell, the work of Paul Jennewin, was unveiled in October 1964 during ceremonies in which MacDowell's music was performed. An Edward MacDowell Chair in music has been established at Columbia University

MacDowell's critical essays were collected and edited by W. J. Baltzell in *Critical and Historical Essays* (1912, reprinted 1969).

THE COMPOSER SPEAKS: The high mission of music . . . is neither to be an agent for expressing material things; nor to utter pretty sounds to amuse the ear; nor a sensuous excitant to fire the blood; nor a sedative to lull the senses. It is a *language*, but a language of the intangible, a kind of soul-language. It appeals directly to the *Seelenzustände* it springs from, for it is the natural expression of it, rather than, like words, a translation of it into stereotyped symbols which may or may not be accepted for what they are intended to denote by the writer. . . .

Painting is primarily an art of externals . . . for that art must touch its audience through a palpable delineation of something more or less material; whereas music is the stuff dreams are made of. . . . The successful recognition of this depends not only upon the susceptibility of the hearer to delicate shades of sensation, but also upon the receptivity of the hearer and his power to accept freely and unrestrictedly the mood shadowed by the composer. Such music cannot be looked upon objectively. To those who would analyze it in such a manner it must remain an unknown language; its potency depends entirely upon a state of willing subjectivity on the part of the hearer.

PRINCIPAL WORKS: 4 piano sonatas (1892–1900); 2 piano concertos (1882, 1886); 2 suites for orchestra (1891, 1895); 2 *Modern Suites*, for piano (1881, 1882).

Forest Idyls, for piano (1884); *Hamlet and Ophelia*, tone poem for orchestra (1885); *Lancelot and Elaine*, tone poem for orchestra (1886); *From an Old Garden*, cycle of six songs for voice and piano (1887); Six Idyls after Goethe, for voice and piano (1887); Six Poems after Heine, for voice and piano (1887);

The Saracens and *The Lovely Alda*, two tone poems for orchestra (1887–88); Romance, for cello and orchestra (1887); *Lamia*, tone poem for orchestra (1888); *Étude de concert* in F-sharp, for piano (1887); Twelve Studies, Books I and II, for piano (1890); *Two Northern Songs*, for chorus (1891); Twelve Virtuoso Studies, for piano (1894); *Woodland Sketches*, suite for piano (1896); Three Choruses, for men's voices, op. 52 (1897); *Two Songs from the 13th Century*, for men's voices (1897); Two Choruses, for men's voices, op. 53 (1897); *The Witch*, for men's chorus (1897); *War Song*, for men's chorus (1898); *Sea Pieces*, suite for piano (1898); Four Songs, for voice and piano, op. 56 (1898); *Six Love Songs*, for voice and piano (1890); Eight Songs, for voice and piano, op. 47 (1893); Three Songs, for voice and piano, op. 58, (1899); *Summer Wind*, for women's chorus (1902); *Fireside Tales*, suite for piano (1902); *New England Idyl*, suite for piano (1902); Three Songs, for voice and piano, op. 60 (1901).

BIBLIOGRAPHY: Brown, Abbie Farwell, *The Boyhood of Edward MacDowell* (N.Y., 1927); Brown, R. W., *Lonely Americans* (N.Y., 1929); Gilman, Lawrence, *Edward MacDowell: A Study* (N.Y., 1908, reprinted 1969); Lowens, M. M., "The New York Years of Edward MacDowell" (doctoral thesis, Ann Arbor, Mich., 1971); MacDowell, Marian, *Random Notes on Edward MacDowell and His Music* (Boston, 1950); Matthews, J. B., *Commemorative Tribute to MacDowell* (N.Y., 1922); Page, E., *Edward MacDowell: His Work and Ideals* (N.Y., 1910); Porte, J. F., *Edward MacDowell* (London, 1922); *Musical America*, February 15, 1955; *Musical Courier*, February 1, 1955; *Musical Quarterly*, January 1915; *Stereo Review*, December 1967.

Martino, Donald James, b. Plainfield, N.J., May 16, 1931.

The winner of the Pulitzer Prize in music in 1974, Martino is a twelve-tone composer with a difference. He views that system as a set of principles to build upon and develop. Consequently, he never adheres to a totally organized serialism. His modified use of twelve tonalism does not preclude dramatic imagination, expressive warmth, and an infectiously lyrical content.

His father was of Italian, his mother of German, extraction and neither was musical. However, Donald's maternal grandfather had been a professional choral conductor in Basel, Switzerland.

At Evergreen School, a grade school in Plainfield, Martino received some lessons on the clarinet. Participating in a performance of a march with the school band was his first indication that he wanted to be a musician. At Plainfield High School he was first clarinetist of its band and orchestra. At the same time, he was solo clarinetist with the New Jersey All

State Band and Orchestra and during his last two years in high school he played the clarinet in the Plainfield Symphony and in several jazz groups. His first compositions date from this period.

His aim, initially, was to become a professional clarinetist. But while attending Syracuse University in Syracuse, N.Y., on a scholarship (1948–52) he studied composition with Ernst Bacon, who encouraged him to devote himself to composition rather than to the clarinet. Such stimulation led to the writing of a number of compositions between 1949 and 1951, including his first two string quartets (1950, 1951), *Folk-song Suite*, for cello and piano (1950), a Clarinet Sonata (1951) and a Piano Sonata (1951). String Quartet no. 2 was premiered on February 19, 1952, at Syracuse University and was awarded a Student Composer Award from Broadcast Music, Inc. (BMI). These early works, traditional in idiom, revealed a strong melodic and dramatic feeling.

From Syracuse University, Martino went on to do graduate work at Princeton University (1952–54), where he entered with a fellowship to major in history but soon changed to composition. At Princeton he studied composition with Milton Babbitt and Roger Sessions, both of whom were influential on his creative growth. From Babbitt he learned "to prevision a work," and Sessions introduced him to Arnold Schoenberg's music and the twelve-tone system. The compositions Martino produced at Princeton, however, were more influenced by Bartók and jazz than by Babbitt and Sessions. These works included the String Quartet no. 3 (1953), a Cello Concerto (1954), and *Set for Clarinet* (1954). The last of these was first performed in the year of its composition at Princeton and subsequently received numerous public performances elsewhere.

A number of early honors gave him initial recognition, among these being a scholarship from the Koussevitzky Music Foundation (1953–54) and, in 1954, awards from the National Federation of Music Clubs and a second Student Composers Award from BMI.

On September 5, 1953, Martino married Mari Rice; their only child, Anna Maria, was born a decade later. (The Martinos were divorced in 1968.) After receiving his master of fine arts degree in music from Princeton in 1954, Martino was awarded the first of two successive Fulbright Fellowships, enabling him to continue his study of composition in Florence, Italy, with Luigi Dallapiccola, Italy's foremost serialist. It was through Dallapiccola that Martino first became interested in using the twelve-tone system as a way of controlling the chromaticisms which had begun to dominate his style.

Martino emerged as a twelve-tone composer in 1957 with *Contemplations for Orchestra* (1957), commissioned by the Paderewski Fund, and the Quartet for Clarinet and Strings (1957), which received the Pacific Award in 1961. *Contemplations* had to wait almost a decade for its first performance,

on August 19, 1965, at the Berkshire Music Center at Tanglewood, Mass., conducted by Gunther Schuller. The Clarinet Quartet was introduced in New York on February 15, 1958.

With the *Piano Fantasy* (1958), premiered in New York by William Masselos on March 13, 1960, Martino began to depart from the rigid concept that only a single twelve-tone set should govern a composition. The Trio, for violin, clarinet and piano (1959; N.Y., March 13, 1960), exemplified, as Eric Salzman reported in the *New York Herald Tribune*, "a kind of careful serialism, but elegantly worked out and purified into a kind of remarkable crystalline beauty." This trio represented American music at the Festival of the International Society for Contemporary Music in Amsterdam on June 13, 1963.

Back from Italy, Martino found teaching posts at the Third Street Settlement School in New York (1956–57) and at Princeton University (1957–59). Since neither post paid enough to support him adequately, he also played the clarinet in jazz bands, for which he made special arrangements and wrote functional pieces, and tried his hand at popular songwriting. In 1958 he provided the score for a motion picture, *The Lonely Crime*.

With an appointment as assistant professor of music at Yale University in 1959, he had the financial security to be able to concentrate on composition. He remained at Yale until 1969, after having received a Morse Academic Fellowship in 1965, and a promotion to associate professorship one year later. During his years at Yale he also taught composition at the Berkshire Music Center (1965–67, 1969) and at the Yale Summer School of Music and Art (1960, 1961).

His full maturity as composer, and an expanding recognition of his talent, arrived with his works in the 1960s. First came the *Two Rilke Songs*, for mezzo-soprano and piano (1961; New Haven, Conn., February 25, 1963), in which Martino's now modified use of the twelve-tone idiom was combined with a pronounced lyricism. These songs were influenced by, without being imitative of, Robert Schumann and aspired to carry on the tradition of the German lied into American vocal music. Concerto for Wind Quintet (1964; Tanglewood, Mass., May 17, 1964)—commissioned by the Fromm Music Foundation at Tanglewood—was a complex twelve-tone work in which each of its five principal sections contained duos, trios, quartets, and quintets (for flute, oboe, clarinet, French horn, and bassoon); the five sections are separated by cadenzalike solos framed by an introduction and a coda. In the Piano Concerto (1966), commissioned by the New Haven Symphony, which introduced it in March 1966, Martino employed the union of two different twelve-tone sets. One set is determined for the piano part; the other for the orchestra. The piece explores the interrelation of these two sets. The sets gradually transform into each other as do the sentiments or emotions they represent. In *Notes*, Arthur Custer called it a "busy, rhapsodic composition . . . a stunning work made of texture and mood, of fluid tempos and dramatic contrasts." *Mosaic*, for large orchestra (1967), was commissioned by the University of Chicago for the Chicago Symphony, its premiere taking place on May 26, 1967, Jean Martinon conducting.

In 1964, Martino received a Creative Arts Citation from Brandeis University in Waltham, Mass. In 1967 he was awarded the first of two Guggenheim Fellowships (the second in 1973) and a grant from the National Institute of Arts and Letters. He was appointed chairman of the composition department of the New England Conservatory in 1969, where he remained eleven years. In 1980 he was appointed professor of music at Brandeis University. In the 1970s, he was also visiting lecturer of music at Harvard (1971), Koussevitzky Composer-in-Residence at the Berkshire Music Center (1973), and he held a residency at the Johnston State College in Vermont (summer 1978).

Martino's second marriage took place on June 5, 1969, to Lora Harvey, then a music student who later became a teacher of mathematics in high school and the mother of Martino's son, Christopher James.

The Pulitzer Prize came in 1974 for *Notturno*, for flute, clarinet, violin, cello, and piano (1973), written on commission from the Naumburg Foundation and first heard on May 15, 1973, at a concert of Speculum Musicae in New York. This is a romantic work intended to portray, as the composer informs us, "night moods rather than night sounds." "The first thing you notice about *Notturno*," wrote Michael Steinberg in the *Boston Globe*, "is its sure writing for the instruments. . . . I sensed in *Notturno* an uncommon dramatic imagination, but also an equally uncommon mastery in matters of pacing and transition wherewith to project this nocturnal theater of the soul."

On a commission from the Paderewski Fund, Martino completed one of his most ambitious compositions in 1974, the *Paradiso Choruses*, which used textual material from *The Divine Comedy*. This work was scored for chorus, children's chorus, fourteen vocal soloists, an orchestra, and electronic tapes. Its world premiere took place in Boston on May 7, 1975, a performance that was recorded live, a release selected by *Record World* as the year's best recording of a contemporary work. In *High Fidelity/Musical America*, a critic described this composition as follows: "Basically the work is a great static hymn of praise occasioned by Dante's Journey to Paradise with Beatrice as his guide. There, he is blessed with the Beatific Vision and surveys the ten regions of Heaven plus the ascension of sanctified souls from Purgatorio. The music is tremendously lush, dense, and complex. . . . Martino's writing is crazily difficult, too, with many extra-terrestrial high notes for the seven soloists and enormous competition from the massed forces of choir and orchestra."

Martino was elected membership to the American Academy and Institute of Arts and Letters in 1981.

THE COMPOSER SPEAKS: If we have talent for music we learn the techniques of composition with relative ease. That is, we learn the techniques that others before us have set forth, although we learn them as though they were part of some collective intention. But each composer's *technique* sprang from his special musical ideals and if the aggregate of these techniques is to be somehow transformed into our *techniques* we must find a music that is only ours to sing. When we realize this need, then learned techniques are of no avail and *technique* comes hard to us. For at this moment we attempt to forge a unique expression not so much from the fruits of our talent but from our creative being and from our will. And when we finally "get it all together," so to speak, we discover that *technique* is the natural servant of one's intention— that no task, however formidable it might have seemed had it been posed as an examination question devised by someone else, is formidable if we devise it. (I think that one reason why teachers are "better" than students is that teachers devise the problems and hence have the answers. Another reason is that for the most part students are not yet clear as to which problems are proper to pose.) My argument, then, is that at least in one sense the rules of composition do not exist a priori; they are forged anew by each composer from the core of his musical intention. To talk of that intention is impossible. For it has no language other than the language of sound by which it originally expressed itself. It does not translate! Without such a language, to talk of technique is idle. Technique is an inseparable component of the style to which it belongs and, therefore, is inseparable from the creative body and the talent from which it is drawn. Talent, style, creativity, and the like are things we hope we have and attempt with each new work to reaffirm. But there is no satisfactory measure of these things. Perhaps there are as many measures as there are men of talent, creativity, and will.

PRINCIPAL WORKS: 3 string quartets (1950, 1951, 1953); 2 cello concertos (1954, 1972).

Clarinet Sonata (1951); Piano Quartet (1951); Violin Sonata (1952, revised 1954); *Set for Clarinet* (1954); Prelude and Fugue, for brass and percussion (1953); Sinfonia, for orchestra (1953); *Portraits*, a secular cantata for mezzo-soprano, bass-baritone, chorus, and orchestra (1955); *Contemplations for Orchestra*, originally entitled *Composition for Orchestra* (1956); Clarinet Quartet (1957); *Piano Fantasy* (1958); Trio, for violin, clarinet, and piano (1958); Two Rilke Songs, for mezzo-soprano and piano (1961); *Fantasy Variations*, for violin (1962); Piano Concerto (1966); *Mosaic*, for large orchestra (1967); *Pianissisimo*, a sonata for piano (1970); Seven Piano Pieces, for chorus and optional keyboard (1972); *Notturno*, for flute, clarinet, cello, percussion, and piano (1973); *Paradiso Choruses*, for vocal soloists, children's chorus, adults' chorus, tape, and orchestra (1974); *Ritorno*, for community orchestra, also concert band (1975); Triple Concerto, for clarinet, bass clarinet, contrabass clarinet, and chamber orchestra (1977); *Impromptu for Roger*, for piano (1977); Quodlibets II, for flute solo (1980); Fantasies and Impromptus, for piano (1980).

BIBLIOGRAPHY: *BBDM; DCM*; BMI, *The Many Worlds of Music*, Issue 2, 1974; *Boston Sunday Globe*, May 12, 1974; *High Fidelity/Musical America*, September 1974; *Who's Who in America, 1980–81.*

Mason, Daniel Gregory, b. Brookline, Mass., November 20, 1873; d. Greenwich, Conn., December 4, 1953.

For almost half a century, Mason filled a triple role in American music: as educator, writer on music, and composer. He distinguished himself in all three capacities, and in all three he stood on the bulwark of 19th-century German romanticism, fighting the onslaughts of 20th-century "modernism." Brahms was his ideal, and as composer, Mason remained frankly and unashamedly a Brahmsian romantic, in the vanguard of those right-wing American composers who preferred living in the past to looking into the future. Because he was a thoroughly skillful craftsman with an elegant harmonic and melodic idiom, his works were frequently and significantly performed when he was alive. Because he lacked individuality, they have since lapsed into comparative discard.

He was one of four sons of Henry Mason, cofounder of the piano manufacturing company of Mason and Hamlin. The Mason family boasted other prestigious musicians. Daniel Gregory's grandfather was Lowell Mason, distinguished organist, conductor, and composer of hymns, the most famous of which was "Nearer My God to Thee." His uncle was the eminent pianist and teacher William Mason. Other Masons were publishers, teachers, or concert performers. Consequently, professional musicians were omnipresent in the Henry Mason household and they were always making music. "It was because I heard music daily from piano, organ, glee club or music box," Daniel Gregory Mason recalled in his autobiography, *Music in My Time and Other Reminiscences*, "it was because my family entertained musicians and discussed their problems . . . it was for all these environmental reasons that music became for me so early the most vivid thing in the world." Music lessons on the piano began with Nellie Coolidge when Daniel was seven. In the same year he made his first effort at composition in emulation of a brother who was then writing songs for the Hasty Pudding Club shows at Harvard University. Then, while attending boarding school in Boston in 1890, Mason studied composition privately with Ethelbert Nevin.

In 1891, Mason entered Harvard University for an academic degree. There he attended music classes of John Knowles Paine, finding them so dull that for a time he lost interest in all musical activity except writing some music for an operetta produced by the Hasty Pudding Club. The first concert work that he later allowed to be published was written in 1894: *Birthday Waltzes for Piano*.

After receiving a bachelor of arts degree in 1895 and spending that summer in a walking trip through Europe with the poet-dramatist William Vaughn Moody, Mason settled in Boston to concentrate on music study: piano with Clayton Johns and composition with George Chadwick. In 1895 he wrote Romance and Impromptu for piano, whose only interest lies in the fact that the Romance section was Mason's first piece of music to get a public performance, when Edward Burlingame Hill performed it in Cambridge on March 18, 1898.

In the fall of 1895, Mason came to New York to continue music study there with Arthur Whiting (piano) and Percy Goetschius (composition). In New York, Mason supported himself by lecturing on music and teaching; he helped organize the first classes in adult education in music sponsored by the board of education. In 1902, Mason's first book, *From Grieg to Brahms* (a gathering of articles he had been writing for the magazine *Outlook*), was published, becoming one of the earliest books on music by an American designed for lay consumption to enjoy wide distribution.

Between 1902 and 1904, Mason was a member of the faculty of Princeton University. His compositions at that time were few and far between. "I was going through that long dark tunnel in my life," Mason recalled. He remembered those years as "a baffling, interminable, and sometimes unendurable period of trial and error—especially error. They were my first conscious facing of the agonizing alternative between the two horns of the dilemma: writing-plus-livelihood versus music-minus-livelihood-but-plus-happiness." His entire output consisted of a few songs and an *Elegy*, for piano, the latter written in 1899 in memory of his friend Philip Henry Savage, a poet. As it turned out, *Elegy* became Mason's first successful composition. Ossip Gabrilowitsch introduced it in Berlin on April 8, 1908, and then performed it intermittently at other recitals in Europe and America, where it was well received by audiences and critics, although some critics in Germany did not fail to detect in this music echoes of Schumann and Brahms.

On October 8, 1904, Mason married his sister-in-law, Mary Lord Taintor Mason. With her two younger children, they set up permanent residence in New York City. Publication of two more books on music for the layman—*Beethoven and His Forerunners* (1904) and *The Romantic Composers* (1906)—

serving as editor of a music magazine called *Masters in Music,* delivering occasional lectures at Chicago University, and conducting a teaching session at Harvard Summer School, all brought him the financial ability to devote himself intensively to composition for the first time. He made his initial experiments at writing chamber music with a Violin Sonata (1907–08; Orange, N.J., February 2, 1912) and a Piano Quartet (1909–11), which members of the Kneisel Quartet, supplemented by Gabrilowitsch, introduced in Boston on December 1, 1914. All this music was, as Mason himself acknowledged "shamelessly Brahmsian."

In 1905, Mason joined the music faculty of Columbia University where he remained more than three and a half decades. Feeling the need for more technical instruction in composition, he took leave from the university in 1913 to spend the year in France, studying composition there with Vincent d'Indy. The technical assurance he gained from d'Indy together with an appreciation of French restraint and refinement which put a curb to his overflowing romanticism, led to the writing of his Symphony no. 1 in C minor (1913–14), which was introduced by the Philadelphia Orchestra under Leopold Stokowski on February 18, 1916. Frederick Stock, conductor of the Chicago Symphony, thought so highly of it that he performed a revised version on two successive seasons, in January 1925 and April 1926, and in the latter year the New York Philharmonic presented it in New York under Josef Stransky and somewhat later Ossip Gabrilowitsch introduced it to Detroit. A Clarinet Sonata, which Mason had begun in 1912 but did not complete until 1915, and which was premiered in New York December 18, 1915, became one of the first two compositions issued by the newly founded Society for the Publication of American Music in 1920. *Russians* was a cycle of five songs for baritone and orchestra to poems by Witter Bynner based on incidents and even actual phrases used by Russian peasants as described by Stephen Graham in *Undiscovered Russia.* Mason wrote the first song in 1915 and the other four in 1917. The entire cycle was given its premiere by Reinald Werrenrath, baritone (to whom it was dedicated), and the Chicago Symphony under Eric De Lamarter on November 15, 1918. *String Quartet on Negro Themes* (1918–19), in which "Deep River" is quoted together with several other spirituals, received its first hearing by the Flonzaley Quartet in Detroit on January 5, 1920. This quartet was one of Mason's earliest compositions to reflect his interest in American nationalism.

After that, Mason did his most successful writing for the orchestra. The works that gained the widest and the most significant circulation were *Chanticleer,* "a festival overture," and Symphonies nos. 2 and 3.

The score of *Chanticleer* (1926) bears a motto that heads Thoreau's *Walden:* "I do not propose to write an ode to dejection, but to brag as lustily as the chanticleer in the morning, standing on his roost, if only to wake up my neighbors." The crow of the cock was heard first in trumpet at the opening of the composition, recurred intermittently throughout the piece and brought the work to its conclusion. After the Cincinnati Symphony under Fritz Reiner introduced it on November 23, 1928, *Chanticleer* was given numerous performances by other major American orchestras.

Symphony no. 2 in A major (1928–29) was also premiered by the Cincinnati Symphony under Reiner—on November 7, 1930. After that, it was performed by the New York Philharmonic under Bruno Walter on February 19, 1932. Lawrence Gilman said of it in the *New York Herald Tribune:* "There is feeling in this music and there is strength—a masculine security and control. Above all, there is admirable power of organization: out of the long and remarkably articulated theme of the Andante, the matter of the slow movement is evolved. . . . This is writing of a sort which has, for the most part, disappeared from the music that is characteristic of our time. It is music of brain and sinew; it is clear-eyed; it is sure-footed."

Symphony no. 3, *A Lincoln Symphony* (1935–36), whose first performance was given on November 17, 1937, by the New York Philharmonic under John Barbirolli, is a four-movement portrait of "the great Emancipator." In the first movement, "The Candidate from Springfield," Lincoln's Springfield years were described in music that quoted a popular tune of that day. The second movement, "Massa Linkum," told of the black man's adoration of the president; one of its themes is a slave song. The lighter side of Lincoln, his wit and jests, were suggested by the third-movement scherzo, "Old Abe's Yarns," and the finale, "1865," was a threnody for the passing of an American immortal. A unifying element in this symphony was a three-note motive identifying Lincoln: a descending fifth followed by an ascending tenth. In various guises it appeared throughout the work. "Lincoln," says Burnet C. Tuthill in the *Musical Quarterly,* "is portrayed in varying moods by different developments of his motive: his inner struggle . . . contemplation . . . rough gaiety . . . and poignant sorrow."

Mason was promoted to assistant professorship at Columbia University in 1910 and to associate professorship four years later. In 1929 he was named MacDowell Professor and appointed chairman of the department. He withdrew from his executive duties in 1940, but continued teaching for another two years when he retired as professor emeritus. In 1925, he delivered a series of lectures at Northwestern University in Evanston, Ill. He received an honorary doctorate in literature from Tufts University in Medford, Mass. (1929) and honorary doctorates in music from Oberlin College in Ohio (1931) and the University of Rochester, in Rochester, N.Y. (1932). He was a member of the National Institute of Arts and Letters.

In addition to three titles already mentioned, Mason was the author of: *The Appreciation of Music* (1907), *The Orchestral Instruments and What They Do* (1909, reprinted 1971), *A Guide to Music* (1909), *A Neglected Sense in Piano Playing* (1912), *Great Modern Composers* (1916), *Short Studies of Great Masterpieces* (1917), *Contemporary Composers (1918)*, *Music as a Humanity and Other Essays* (1921), *From Song to Symphony* (1924), *Artistic Ideals* (1925), *The Dilemma of American Music* (1928, reprinted 1969), *The Chamber Music of Brahms* (1933), *Music in My Time and Other Reminiscences* (1938, reprinted 1970), and *The Quartets of Beethoven* (1947). In addition, he was a prolific contributor of articles on music to leading American literary and musical journals.

THE COMPOSER SPEAKS: Music is of all arts proverbially the most emotional. In comparison with literature, for instance, it compensates for an inferior power in dealing with specific detail by a deeper eloquence in the presentation of fundamental moods and attitudes. Its penetration to the profoundest levels of our consciousness is akin to that of philosophy, but it expresses emotionally, as Schopenhauer recognized more fully than most philosophers, what philosophy only formulates intellectually. In so far, then, as our contemporary music has turned a cold shoulder upon emotion, it has repudiated its most essential quality and foregone its supreme advantage. . . .

Partly effect, partly, in turn, cause of this ban on emotion is the extraordinary development among our modern sophisticates of the purely intellectual, or the pseudointellectual, exploration of music, replacing the emotional experience of it; music, it has been said, used to be made to be enjoyed, but now it is made to be discussed.

In place of this innocence, this fecund naïveté, we find in ultramodernism a sterile sophistication, a restless itch for formulas. Music can no longer be just music; it must be atonal, or polytonal or polyrhythmic, or impressionistic or symbolistic. It is even the fashion now to make it to specifications. . . . Indeed, your genuine modernist composer cannot write three notes without equipping them with three paragraphs of explanatory comment.

PRINCIPAL WORKS: 3 symphonies (1913-14, revised 1922; 1928-29, 1935-36).
Elegy, for piano (1899, revised 1940); Violin Sonata (1907-08, revised 1944); Piano Quartet (1909-11); *Pastorale*, for violin, clarinet, and piano (1909-12); *Country Pictures*, for piano (1908-12, revised 1942); Passacaglia and Fugue, for organ (1912); Clarinet Sonata, or Sonata for Violin (1912-15, re-

vised 1945); Scherzo-Caprice, for chamber orchestra (1912-16); *Russians*, five songs for baritone and orchestra or piano (1916, revised 1937); Intermezzo, for string quartet (1916, revised 1937); *String Quartet on Negro Themes* (1918-19, revised 1930); Prelude and Fugue, for piano and orchestra (1919); *Three Silhouettes*, for piano, also for cello and piano (1921); *Songs of the Countryside*, for vocal soloists, chorus, and small orchestra (1923); *Variations on a theme of John Powell*, for string quartet (1924-25); Divertimento, for two pianos, also for woodwind quintet (1926); *Chanticleer*, a "festival overture" for orchestra (1926); *Fanny Blair*, folk-song fantasy for string quartet (1927); Serenade, for string quartet (1931); *Suite after English Folk-Songs*, for orchestra (1933-34); Prelude and Fugue in C minor, for string orchestra (1939); *Variations on a Quiet Theme*, for string quartet (1939); *Nautical Lays of a Landsman*, five songs for baritone and piano (1941); Two Chorale Preludes, for organ, on hymn tunes of Lowell Mason (1941); *Soldiers*, song cycle for baritone and piano (1948-49).

BIBLIOGRAPHY: Klein, Sister Mary Justina, *The Contribution of Daniel Gregory Mason to American Music* (Washington, D.C., 1957); Lewis, R. B., "The Life and Music of Daniel Gregory Mason" (doctoral thesis, Rochester, N.Y., 1959); Mason, Daniel Gregory, *Music in My Time and Other Reminiscences* (N.Y., 1938); Dictionary of American Biography, supplement 5; *Musical Quarterly*, January 1948; Who's Who in America, 1952-53.

Mayer, William, b. New York City, November 18, 1925.

Mayer's music is lyrical and rhythmic, organized in a rather free tonal framework and transparent in timbres. Two contrasting moods—ethereal and satiric—are often present in the same work. He is particularly drawn to vocal writing in choral and operatic media on the one hand and to wind instruments and piano on the other.

His father, an investment broker, was an amateur violinist who often took his son to concerts. His mother, Dorothy Ehrich, was a writer of children's books. Piano study for William Mayer began when he was seven and continued with George Morgan at the Taft Prep School in Watertown, Conn., which he attended between 1940 and 1943. At Yale University (1944-48) he studied theory with Richard Donovan. College work was interrupted in 1944 for two years of military service with the Army Counterintelligence Corps during World War II (1944-46). But in 1946 Mayer was back at Yale to complete the requirements for a bachelor of arts degree in 1948. While at Yale, motivated by his love for show music and particularly that of Jerome Kern, he made his first attempts at composition by writing popular songs.

During the summer of 1949, Mayer was at the Juilliard School of Music in New York, where one of his teachers in composition was Roger Sessions. Mayer's composing efforts now began taking a more serious turn with the writing of some compositions for the voice, the piano and for strings, many stylistically reminiscent of Ravel.

Between 1949 and 1952, Mayer went to the Mannes School of Music in New York to continue study of theory and composition with Felix Salzer, in both of which areas he received diplomas in 1952. On December 26, 1950, he married Meredith Nevins, a visual artist, with whom he had three children, one of whom, Steven, is a concert artist. Two summers (1951 and 1952) were spent at the Bennington Composers Conference in Vermont. While at the Mannes School, his compositions included a String Quartet (1952), one of whose movements, rewritten as Andante for Strings (1956), was first heard at the American Music Festival in New York on January 1958, Maurice Peress conducting. In 1952, Mayer studied composition privately with Otto Luening; later (1960) he was a student in conducting of Izler Solomon at the Aspen Music School in Colorado.

Mayer's first composition to get a significant hearing was *Essay*, for brass and winds (1953) which was commissioned by Robert Nagel and the New York Brass and Wind Ensemble. It was introduced over New York's radio station WNYC in February 1953 during its annual American Music Festival. When, a quarter of a century later, it was presented in New York by the American Brass Quintet and the Dorran Woodwind Quintet (January 9, 1979), Allen Hughes, writing in the *New York Times*, called it "delightfully tuneful and uncomplicated . . . all . . . devoid of wind-instrument clichés."

The *Essay* was a tonal, consonant work within a classical design. Individual characteristics of the instruments were exploited rather than their ensemble attributes. Mayer retained but expanded his sense of tonality in other compositions of the 1950s, of which these are the most notable: *Angles*, for piano (1956), introduced by Ray Lev in New York in the year of its composition; Concert Piece, for trumpet, strings, and percussion (1955), which received its initial hearing in New York on January 21, 1957 in a performance by Robert Nagel and the Little Orchestra Society under Thomas Scherman; a dramatic ballet for children, *Hello, World!* (1956) described as "a trip around the world with music," for singer, narrator, dancers and orchestra, commissioned and introduced by the Little Orchestra Society under Scherman, its premiere taking place in New York on November 10, 1956, and since performed frequently by major American orchestras; *Overture for an American*, for orchestra (1958), commissioned by the Theodore Roosevelt Centennial Observance Committee, and premiered in Chautauqua, N.Y., in 1958, Walter Hendl conducting; *Two Pastels*, a neoimpressionistic work for orchestra (1959), suggested by two uniden-

tified lines of poetry and heard first at Carnegie Hall on February 12, 1961, when Richard Korn conducted the Orchestra of America, then, in a revision, by the Cincinnati Symphony under Max Rudolf in 1967, and in 1971 recorded by the Minnesota Orchestra under a Ford Foundation grant; and the Piano Sonata (1959), which received its first hearing in 1959 performed by Jack Chaiken, then featured by William Masselos in his recitals and in a recording. This sonata is less diatonic than some of its immediate predecessors—it even suggests serialism—but it is no less communicative. "Mayer's full-scale conception is pungent with contrast—of moods, of textures, and of meanings," reported a critic for *American Record Guide* in commenting upon the Masselos recording. "Its three movements . . . have rhapsodic ingredients but not the sort to destroy strength of design. . . . Mayer's Sonata denotes sound, potent musical architecture."

Two widely performed, large-scale compositions by Mayer were written and performed in the early 1960s. Out of the ballet *The Snow Queen* (1963)—based on the tale by Hans Christian Andersen—came the orchestral suite *Scenes from the Snow Queen*, which the Minnesota Orchestra premiered in 1966 and which was later performed by the Philadelphia Orchestra and, as a ballet production, at a concert in New York by the Little Orchestra Society conducted by Thomas Scherman. The opera *One Christmas Long Ago* (1961) was introduced at Ball State Teachers College in Muncie, Ind., in 1962, and two years later was given a performance by the Philadelphia Orchestra.

On a commission from the New York Brass Quintet, Mayer composed his first major work for this combination, Brass Quintet (1964), one of his most important and successful works up to this time; its second movement, "Elegy," has often been performed separately. The New York Brass Quintet introduced the entire quintet in New York in 1965.

A searching work of quite a different order is *Octagon*, a concerto for piano and orchestra (1965–66), its world premiere given in New York by the American Symphony Orchestra conducted by Leopold Stokowski with William Masselos, soloist, on March 21, 1971. In *Music Journal*, Robert V. Weinstein described it as "a shattering, bold, and strangely beautiful piece of music. . . . Structurally, it is fascinating. Mayer maintains two basic levels: the orchestra for the most part works as an integrated unit, thwarting and cruelly antagonizing the piano with its dissonant jabs, runs, and syncopated counter movements. As soon as a lyric passage appears, it is immediately transformed, taking on a new stature. Like a crystal assuming different shapes before your eyes, *Octagon* changes its hue and intensity as each part quickly passes. . . . A central facet of *Octagon* is the rapid alternation of the gentle and the abrasive."

Spring Came Forever (1975) and *Dream's End*

(1976) are among Mayer's most significant works of the 1970s. The former, a cantata for mezzo-soprano, tenor, baritone, triple chorus, and orchestra, was commissioned by the New York Choral Society, which gave the first performance at the Lincoln Center for the Performing Arts in New York on May 16, 1975. The text was based on poems by James Stephens and Vachel Lindsay and excerpts from the Song of Songs. The eight-movement *Dream's End*, for oboe, clarinet, French horn, violin, cello, and piano (1976), was commissioned by the Michigan Council of the Arts and was first performed by members of the Detroit Symphony on May 2, 1976. This is one of the composer's more complex and dissonant pieces, but sophistication and lightness of touch are not absent. Since the premiere, this work has been given by several other chamber-music groups including the St. Paul Chamber Orchestra, which recorded it.

Messages, for flute, string trio, and percussion (1971), is another of Mayer's successful chamber music works. It was commissioned by the flutist Paul Dunhel, who introduced it in New York the year of its composition. A delicate work, whose four movements are entitled "Wind," "Touch," "Wood," and "Light," it is one of Mayer's most evocative compositions.

For two years, beginning with 1969, Mayer worked at the Columbia-Princeton Electronic Music Center in New York. He used its facilities to write parts of his most ambitious composition on a grant from the National Endowment for the Arts; a full-length opera, *A Death in the Family* (1979), libretto by the composer, based on two Pulitzer Prize-winning works, James Agee's novel of the same name, and Tad Mosel's dramatic adaptation entitled *All the Way Home*.

Most of Mayer's noncomposing career has been divided between writing numerous articles on contemporary music for the United States Information Agency, and major newspapers and magazines, and, beginning with 1966, serving for thirteen years as a member of the board of Composers Recording Incorporated (CRI), becoming chairman of its board in 1978. In 1966, a year in which he received a Guggenheim Fellowship, Mayer taught composition and orchestration at Boston University. Since then, he has often delivered lectures at American schools, conservatories and universities, including Columbia University and the Juilliard School of Music.

THE COMPOSER SPEAKS: A composer's vision, shared with others, can be infinitely valuable in this world. It gives the listener a new sense of wholeness. The composer, in giving shape and form to what previously were formless and dimly perceived emotions, gives the listener a sharpened awareness of the depth of his own nature. Internal divisions dissolve as he renews contact with the deepest corners of his being, which so often elude him because of their intangible and subtle aspects. It's as if there were amorphous feelings trapped within us in unreachable terrain. Their lack of definition holds them prisoner. It is the composer, in giving them shape, who sets them free. And just as the separate compartments within the listener become one, so his isolation from other human beings is transcended in this sharing of the composer's vision."

PRINCIPAL WORKS: *Essay*, for brass and winds (1954); Concert Piece, for trumpet, strings, and percussion (1955); *Celebration Trio*, for flute, clarinet, and piano (1955); *Hello, World!*, children's ballet, for singer-narrator and orchestra (1956); *Angles*, for piano (1956); Andante for Strings, adapted from the slow movement of the String Quartet (1956); *Country Fair*, for brass (1957); *Overture for an American*, for orchestra (1958); *One Christmas Long Ago*, opera (1961); *Snow Queen*, ballet (1963); Brass Quintet (1964); *Brief Candle*, micro-opera for small chorus and chamber orchestra (1965); *Always, Always Forever Again*, for soprano, flute, and piano (1965); *Octagon*, piano concerto, for piano and orchestra (1965–66); *Eight Miniatures and News Items*, for soprano and seven instruments (1968); *Letters Home*, for chorus and orchestra (1968); *Khartoum*, for soprano and four instruments (1968); *Eve of St. Agnes*, for vocal soloists, chorus, and orchestra (1969); *Lines on Light*, for women's voices and piano (1970); *Messages*, for virtuoso flute, violin, viola, cello, and percussion (1971); *Two News Items*, for soprano and seven instruments (1972); Toccata, for piano (1972); *Spring Came on Forever*, cantata for mezzo-soprano, tenor, baritone, triple chorus, and orchestra (1975); *Dream's End*, for oboe, clarinet, violin, cello, French horn, and piano (1976); *La belle dame sans merci*, for tenor and chorus (1976); *A Death in the Family*, opera (1979); *Enter Ariel*, for soprano, clarinet, and piano (1980).

BIBLIOGRAPHY: *DCM*; Anderson, E. Ruth (ed.), *Contemporary American Composers* (Boston, 1976); Siegmeister, Elie (ed.), *The New Music Lover's Handbook* (N.Y., 1973).

McBride, Robert Guyn, b. Tucson, Ariz., February 20, 1911.

McBride is a popularist who has drawn deeply from the well of his experiences as a church, theater and dance band musician and from his southwest heritage which brought him into close contact with Mexican folk music. He has also been a functional composer who has often written music tailor-made for specific occasions and for practical teaching purposes. He has always demonstrated an unusual gift for reaching out to and winning the interest of audiences on many different levels. To his writing he has brought an engaging sense of humor and, despite the levity of some of his quixotic titles, a seriousness of artistic purpose.

He was born into a musical family. His father was an organist; his brother played the trumpet and French horn: his older sister was accomplished both as organist and singer. While attending grade school in Tucson, McBride began playing the clarinet without formal instruction. It was not long before he became a member of a trio in which his father was pianist and his brother the trumpeter and which gave concerts at the Trinity Presbyterian Church in Tucson. At Tucson High School, from his freshman year on, McBride occupied the first clarinet chair in the school band which was conducted by W. Arthur Sewell who was the first to interest McBride in becoming a composer. One of McBride's earliest pieces was the *Ninety-first Division March*, for which he wrote the melody and which Sewell arranged for band and performed at the annual high school band concert.

While still in high school, from his fifteenth year on, McBride played the clarinet professionally in movie theater pit bands. He continued this up to the time of his graduation from high school in 1928. McBride now hoped to end his academic education and to continue developing his career as a theater clarinetist. But his mother insisted he continue his schooling long enough to fulfill the requirements for a degree as a teacher of music in the public schools. Between 1928 and 1935 McBride attended the University of Arizona in Tucson. During summer vacations he began receiving his first formal training in oboe with Henri De Busscher (1933). He also took piano lessons with Audrey Camp Clampitt and Eleanore Altman (1932–35). He now played the oboe as well as clarinet, saxophone and piano in various jazz performances in the 1930s. Between 1928 and 1935 he was a clarinetist and oboist with the Tucson Symphony.

At the university, McBride was a student in composition of Otto Luening's. "He oriented me toward more serious music," McBride recalls, "and he was excellent in bringing out a student's artistic potential." Under Luening's guidance McBride produced his first compositions to gain national attention. *Mexican Rhapsody*, for orchestra (1934), was premiered in a two-piano arrangement in Tucson in 1935 before being heard as an orchestral composition in 1936, when it was performed in Rochester, N.Y., under Howard Hanson. *Mexican Rhapsody* not only received numerous performances by major American orchestras but also was choreographed by Thelma Bieracree and was presented as a ballet in Rochester, once again with Hanson conducting, on April 29, 1938. *Fugato on a Well-known Theme* (1935) was introduced in Tucson on May 7, 1935, after which it was successfully performed by the Boston Pops under Arthur Fiedler, as well as by other American orchestras, and was recorded by RCA Victor. The "well-known theme" was a tune McBride had heard newsboys whistle in the street, but he never identified it further. *Prelude to a Tragedy*, for orchestra (1935), received its world premiere in New York in a per-

formance by the New York Philharmonic under Hans Lange on November 20, 1935. On his tour of South America as conductor in 1940, Lazare Saminsky featured it frequently on his programs.

McBride received his bachelor of music degree at the University of Arizona in 1933, and his master's degree in music two years later. After giving a demonstration in composition at the National Teachers Convention in Pasadena, Calif., during the summer of 1935, he was appointed to the music faculty of Bennington College in Vermont in 1935, where for the next eight years (on and off) he taught theory and the wind instruments. During the summer of 1937 he also taught theory and wind instruments also at the Concord (Mass.) Summer School.

On a commission from the League of Composers, McBride wrote *Workout*, for chamber orchestra (1936), in which, in a jaunty jazz style, he recreated his own adventures playing jazz when each performer would take up the refrain and "go with it." It was broadcast over the radio network of the Columbia Broadcasting System in 1936. "It is a virtuoso, idiomatic, and urbane piece of modern writing," wrote Miles Kastendieck in a New Haven newspaper, "which has a claim to originality and considerable distinction for its clever writing and its witty rhythmic construction." When, in April 1936, a complete program of McBride's work was heard in New York at a Composers Forum Laboratory concert, a critic for the *New York Times* singled out the common denominator of McBride's music of this period as "restless and exuberant rhythms, acrid harmonies, good humor, speed. Tender or contemplative moods are quite foreign to his nature. In this direction . . . *Prelude to a Tragedy* presages deeper thought and feeling."

In 1937, McBride was awarded a Guggenheim Fellowship. This gave him the time to orchestrate his music for the ballet *Show Piece*. With choreography by Eric Hawkins, it was presented by the Ballet Caravan on December 12, 1937, at the New York Center Theater, Erno Rapee conducting. The suite from this ballet was subsequently performed by the Philadelphia Orchestra directed by Leopold Stokowski in 1937 and the American Youth Orchestra under Stokowski in 1941.

On June 21, 1941, McBride married Carol Haines, a music student at Bennington College who had been his pupil. They raised two children. Soon after his marriage, McBride left on a Latin American tour as a member of a woodwind quintet sponsored by the League of Composers which sent him winging some 17,000 miles. In 1942, McBride received an award from the American Academy of Arts and Letters "for developing a new American idiom." That new American idiom could be found not only in the popularist works already commented upon but also in such jazz-oriented items for the concert hall as *Swing Stuff*, for clarinet and orchestra (1938); *In the Groove*, for flute and piano (1942); and *Jam Session*, for woodwind quintet (1941), the last of which earned him first prize in a publication contest sponsored by the Composers Press. In this group belongs, also, the score for *Punch and Judy*, which he wrote on commission, in 1943, for Martha Graham who introduced it in New York in December 1943. That year, six dances from this work were performed by the composer and Gregory Tucker in a two-piano arrangement during their tour of the United States for the Association of American Colleges, and McBride conducted a suite from it with the Boston Pops in May 1945.

Leaving Bennington College in 1945, McBride came to New York. There, for the next dozen years, he was deeply involved writing functional film scores for Jack Shaindlin, including *The March of Time* newsreels, and for Triumphs Films, of which he was the musical director, as well as for radio.

In his concert music he continued tapping popular veins within ambitious structures, notably: *Concerto for Doubles* (1947), introduced by Al Gallodoro and the Paul Whiteman Orchestra; *Variety Day*, a concerto for violin and orchestra (1948), inspired by a reading of the theatrical trade weekly *Variety*, whose movements were subtitled with Variety-type headings: "Sock 10-G," "Lush Pix Nix," and "B. O. Hypo"; and a ballet, *Jazz Symphony* (1953).

In 1957, McBride returned to the city of his birth, where he has since made his home. That year he joined the music faculty of the University of Arizona as associate professor. He was elevated to full professorship in 1960, and in 1976 he retired. At the university, between 1963 and 1967, he was the oboist of the University of Arizona Woodwind Quintet. In 1960 he received the University of Arizona Award of Merit.

His return to his roots stimulated the writing of compositions reflecting his southwestern ambience. Some were once again on Mexican subjects whose music sprang from Mexican folk song idioms: *Panorama of Mexico* (1960), *Sunday in Mexico* (1963), and the score to the ballet *Brooms of Mexico* (1973). Some were inspired by the geography of America's other rural districts, such as the *Hill-Country Symphony* (1963), *Country Music Fantasy* (1964), and the *Folksong Fantasy* (1973). Some were functional pieces for a specific need, occasionally slanted for children. Some were in the whimsical vein he had long exploited which had "tang, laughter and impudence," as a critic for the *New York Times* once described such pieces.

THE COMPOSER SPEAKS: It is true that I do not care much for discussions about music. I would rather write some, arrange some, try to play some, copy some parts or just listen. Our word "clinic," when applied to music, is a mistake; our word "analysis" is overdone. Do we eternally have to be examining the art under a microscope? Could we not just enjoy it or

hate it? And for composers I believe it is important to remember that even Mozart told the young Beethoven to take heed of his audience. The audience will make its adjustments eventually, and the composer might as well make his adjustments now.

It seems to me we are often overeager and overpretentious in our explanation and analysis of music. Can you explain or analyze a magnificent tree or a beautiful sunset? I think we can explain or analyze the techniques of an art work, we can discuss the component parts of its structure, but the more we pull it to pieces, the further we get away from the real thing. Call it inspiration or the divine spark if you please, but I feel that no amount of analysis can "explain away," for example, Beethoven's Fifth Symphony or the Fifth Symphony of Shostakovich. Perhaps herein lies the difference between science and art. Science perhaps endeavors to rationalize the universe. Art does not.

PRINCIPAL WORKS: *Mexican Rhapsody*, for orchestra (1934); *Fugato on a Well-known Theme*, for orchestra (1935); *Prelude to a Tragedy*, for orchestra (1935); *Workout*, for oboe and piano, also for chamber orchestra (1936); Oboe Quintet (1936); Prelude and Fugue, for string quartet (1936); *Show Piece*, ballet, also suite for orchestra (1937); *Swing Stuff*, for clarinet and piano (1937); *Tarry Delight*, for voice and piano (1939); *In the Groove*, for flute and piano (1940); *Jam Session*, for woodwind quintet (1941); *Punch and Judy*, ballet, (1943); *Sherlock Holmes Suite*, for band (1945); Aria and Toccata, for violin and piano (1946); *Concerto for Doubles*, for saxophone and orchestra (1947); *Variety Day*, concerto for violin and orchestra (1948); *Jazz Symphony*, ballet (1953); *Fantasy on a Mexican Christmas Carol*, for orchestra (1955); *Pumpkin Eater's Little Fugue*, for string orchestra, and also large orchestra (1955); *Pioneer Spiritual*, for orchestra (1956); *String Foursome*, for string quartet (1957); *Five Winds Blowing*, for wind quintet (1957); *Memorial*, for organ (1958); Vocalise, for chorus and piano four hands (1959); *Panorama of Mexico*, for orchestra (1960); *Sunday in Mexico*, for wind symphony (1963); *Hill-Country Symphony*, for wind symphony (1964); *Country Music Fantasy*, for wind symphony (1965); *Symphonic Melody*, for orchestra (1968); *Brooms of Mexico*, ballet (1970); *Folksong Fantasy*, for orchestra (1973); *The Golden Sequence*, for chorus and organ (1974); *1776 Overture*, for piano four hands (1975); *Improvisation*, for boys' chorus (1976); *Light Fantastic*, for orchestra (1976–77); *Sportsmusic*, for band (1976–77).

BIBLIOGRAPHY: *BBDM*; *DCM*; Ewen, David, *American Composers Today*; *American Composers Alliance Bulletin*, vol. 8, no. 1, 1958; *Arizona Music News*, Fall 1976; *Who's Who in American Music*, *1980–81*.

McDonald, Harl, b. near Boulder, Col., July 27, 1899. d. Princeton, N.J., March 30, 1955.

McDonald was at his best writing orchestral compositions that remembered his early years in the Southwest and were influenced by the "Hispanic-Indian Anglo-Saxon combination of the Mexican border region," to use his phrase. His language was, for the most part, conventional, making a direct and instant appeal to audiences through its emotion and, in his programmatic writing, through his vivid pictorialism.

He was born on his father's cattle ranch in the high Rockies above Boulder, and his early years were spent on a stock farm in El Selano in southern California, then in the cattle ranch country of San Jacinto. Both parents were musical. His father was a competent performer on the piano and the French horn, and his mother was a talented singer of lieder. She gave Harl his first piano lessons when he was four, introduced him to harmony one year later, and encouraged him when he made his first efforts to write music when he was seven. A significant influence on his early musical development was the Mexican songs he heard around him, and his first composition was a set of dances for the piano in which he used Mexican rhythms and Mexican-type melodies.

Since he was displaying unusual responsiveness to music, his mother broadened his musical horizon by having him take lessons on the violin and French horn as well as the piano. When his father objected to his preoccupation with music, Harl McDonald, then in his teens, left home for Los Angeles, where he played the French horn with the Los Angeles Philharmonic. The study of music now continued with Vernon Spencer, Ernest Douglas, and Jorslaw de Zielinski.

After taking some music courses at Redlands University in California (1917–18), and serving for several months in the U.S. Army in 1918, during World War I, McDonald entered the University of Southern California for a full academic course of study, acquiring a bachelor of music degree in 1920. For a year after that he earned his living as piano accompanist for various artists and teaching music privately. His free hours belonged to composing. Three of his early orchestral pieces were performed in Los Angeles in 1920, one of them by the Los Angeles Philharmonic conducted by Walter Henry Rothwell; and another, a piano concerto, was heard in 1920 at a concert of the San Francisco Symphony with the composer as soloist and Alfred Hertz conducting.

Prizes for a Suite, for orchestra, by the Federation of Music Clubs, and for a ballet suite, for orchestra, by the Ballet Association in conjunction with the Los Angeles Philharmonic, enabled McDonald to go to Europe in 1921 for further study at the Leipzig Conservatory, with Augustus Steiner and Robert Teichmuller. In Germany he completed his first composition in which he felt he outgrew his apprenticeship.

It was an orchestral tone poem, *Mojave*, based on Indian legends of California, its music descriptive of the Mojave desert. The orchestra of the Berlin State Opera under August Steiner introduced it in 1922 and later that year it was heard in London in a performance conducted by Albert Coates. On the strength of this work, McDonald was invited to serve as lecturer on music at the Académie Tournefort in Paris in 1922.

After returning to the United States late in 1922, McDonald spent the next two years as a free-lance musician, making appearances as concert pianist and piano accompanist, doing editorial work, and teaching privately. He joined the faculty of the Philadelphia Musical Academy in 1924 where he remained two years. In 1925 he married Eleanor Gosling who brought him two sons from an earlier marriage and with whom he subsequently had two daughters. He joined the music department of the University of Pennsylvania in 1926, first as lecturer, then as assistant professor, professor and, from 1935 to 1939, chairman of the department.

During his years at the university, McDonald conducted five different choral societies in Philadelphia: the University Men's Glee Club, the Choral Society, the Women's Club, the A Cappella Chorus and the Mendelssohn Club, four of which made periodic appearances with the Philadelphia Orchestra. For a decade, he was the organist and music director of the parish of the Church of the Holy Apostles in Philadelphia, one of the largest units of the American Episcopal Church. Additionally, on a Rockefeller Foundation grant, he spent the years between 1930 and 1933 doing research in acoustics and sound measurement of instrumental and vocal tunes. His findings were published in a monograph, *New Methods of Measuring Sound* (1935), written collaboratively with O. H. Schuck; this publication earned McDonald election to the scientific fraternity, Sigma Xi.

Despite such varied activities, composition was not neglected. Between 1931 and 1932 McDonald completed two piano trios, a Fantasy, for string quartet, and the *Festival of the Workers*, for orchestra, the last of which became his first work to be premiered by the Philadelphia Orchestra (which would henceforth introduce many of his subsequent compositions) when Leopold Stokowski conducted it on April 16, 1934. Later that year, on November 16, the same orchestra and conductor presented the premiere of McDonald's Symphony no. 1, *The Santa Fe Trail* (1932), with which the composer realized his first major success. It was widely represented on programs of major American orchestras in addition to being recorded by RCA Victor. An evocative programmatic symphony, it was a graphic tonal canvas on which, with melodies and rhythms rooted in American folk music, McDonald recalled his boyhood days in the Southwest. "I heard many of the old men describe their experiences in the early days when they came to the new country," he explained. "With few words and long periods of silence, they painted pictures so vivid that they must remain clear in my mind as long as I live." This symphony sought to capture "something of the spirit and experiences of those pioneers." The first movement, "The Explorers," described the westward movement of the early settlers across the desert towards Spanish settlements. The life and spirit of these Spanish settlements were captured in the second-movement scherzo, frequently with musical patterns of a pronounced Hispanic identity. The third movement, "The Wagon Trails of the Pioneers," represented the Hispanic, Nordic, and American Indian influences that combined to build up the Southwest.

The Hispanic presence is also found in McDonald's Symphony no. 2 (1934), in the scherzo, which is a rhumba. This movement acquired considerable popularity on symphony and "pop" programs and in a recording by RCA Victor. But the rest of the symphony is concerned with the economic and social upheaval and the highly charged emotional climate of the early 1930s. This is the reason McDonald subtitled the work *Reflections on an Era of Turmoil.* "In the midst of effortless production," MacDonald said, "I came face to face with breadlines, hunger, labor, strife and the final intervention of the federal government. . . . This was also an age that had an almost insatiable appetite for gaiety and entertainment." To project this era more effectively, McDonald made one of his rare excursions into discordant harmonies. Throughout the opening, second, and closing movements there was considerable gravity and at times even bitterness. The first movement opened with a solemn introduction which led into a frenetic depiction of the tensions of the times. The slow movement was a melancholy reflection by the composer on the somber events. The third-movement rhumba was, by contrast, an expression of the era's feverish search for gaiety and pleasure. The symphony ended with macabre music. Almost in a prophetic mood, as the composer looked into the future, he saw marching men file by and, as they passed, he saw that theirs were the faces of the dead. Leopold Stokowski and the Philadelphia Orchestra introduced this symphony on October 4, 1935.

The Philadelphia Orchestra, sometimes under Stokowski, more often under Eugene Ormandy, continued to promote significant McDonald premieres in the 1930s. The most significant of these works were: *Three Poems on Traditional Aramaic and Hebrew Themes* (1935; December 18, 1936); Concerto for Two Pianos and Orchestra (1936; April 2, 1937), in which Jeanne Behrend and Alexander Kelberine were soloists; Symphony no. 4 (1937; April 8, 1938); Suite for Harp and Orchestra (1940; January 17, 1941), Edna Phillips soloist. Two major McDonald premieres, however, were not heard first in Philadelphia during this period. *San Juan Capistrano*, two

nocturnes for orchestra (1938), was given its first hearing on October 30, 1939, by the Boston Symphony under Serge Koussevitzky. In two movements sharply contrasted in mood and tempo, this music brought up two scenes in the little mission community of Capistrano, near the Mexican border of California, one of them entitled "The Mission," the other, "The Fiesta." *The Legend of the Arkansas Traveler* (1939), a "humoresque" for orchestra, was premiered over the CBS radio network in a broadcast emanating from Detroit over the Ford Radio Hour on March 3, 1940, with Eugene Ormandy conducting the Ford Symphony.

In 1934, McDonald was named to the board of directors of the Philadelphia Orchestra. From 1939 until his death he was general manager of the orchestra. World War II inspired the writing of several timely compositions. Among these were *Overture 1941*, for orchestra (1941); *Bataan*, a tone poem for orchestra (1942; Washington, D.C., April 3, 1942); and *My Country at War*, for orchestra (1943; Indianapolis, Ind., January 8, 1944). McDonald's most significant work after the war was *The Saga of the Mississippi*, a two-section tone poem for orchestra (1945–47) which Eugene Ormandy and the Philadelphia Orchestra introduced on April 9, 1948. The first movement, "Prehistoric Mississippi," was vaguely modal to suggest antiquity; the second, "Father of Waters," prefigured an Indian ceremony, as a quasi-Gregorian chant identified the French and Spanish priests who navigated the Mississippi and a Canadian Indian fishing call in an altered rhythm and harmony represented the black field hands and the roustabouts at the river's banks.

THE COMPOSER SPEAKS: I do not believe that nationalism in music has any purpose as an aim in itself. The use of native source material is valuable to the composer in that it tends to discourage artificiality, and helps him to maintain emotional poise in harmony and humanity. . . .

Many of us have had the good fortune to have spent some of our formative years in close association with some of the highly individual forms of native music. . . . It is true that these many types never have been fused into a true national form or style. Neither have the people of this country become one people, except in certain matters of temper, spirit and habits.

As an expression of this temper and spirit, jazz is our nearest approach to a completely native art. But our people are drawn from many races and the music of our country must be drawn from many sources.

I would suggest that the composer who would benefit from native source material had best give his attention to the music of his locale or racial group. He need not necessarily confine himself to it, but he should remember that there are surprising numbers of undiscovered gold mines in people's back yards."

PRINCIPAL WORKS: 4 symphonies (1932–37); 2 piano trios (1931, 1932).

Festival of the Workers, tone poem for orchestra (1932); Fantasy, for string quartet (1932); *String Quartet on Negro Themes* (1933); *Three Poems on Traditional Aramaic and Hebraic Themes* (1935); Concerto for Two Pianos and Orchestra (1938); *Miniature Suite*, for orchestra (1938); *San Juan Capistrano*, two nocturnes for orchestra (1938); *Legend of the Arkansas Traveler*, for orchestra (1939); *Chameleon Variations*, in the style of ten composers, for orchestra (1940); *From Childhood*, suite for harp and orchestra (1940); *Overture 1941*, for orchestra (1941); *Bataan*, tone poem for orchestra (1942); *My Country at War*, suite for orchestra (1943); Violin Concerto (1943); *Song of the Nations*, for soprano and orchestra (1945); *Saga of the Mississippi*, for orchestra (1945–47); Two Concert Pieces, for orchestra (1947); *Children's Symphony*, on familiar nursery rhyme tunes (1950); *God Give Us Men*, for voices and orchestra (1950).

BIBLIOGRAPHY: Goss, Madeleine, *Modern Music Makers* (N. Y., 1952); Howard, John Tasker, *Our Contemporary Composers* (N. Y., 1941); *Musical America*, March 10, 1944; *Who's Who in America, 1954–55*.

McKay, George Frederick, b. Harrington, Wash., June 11, 1899; d. Stateline, Nev., October 4, 1970.

A romantic who worked within traditional structures and in a conservative idiom, McKay was at his best in compositions descriptive of the regional backgrounds of the Pacific Northwest where he spent most of his life.

After attending the University of Washington in Seattle, where he studied composition with Wood, he enrolled in the Eastman School of Music in Rochester, N.Y., a student of composition of Selim Palmgren's and Christian Sinding's. When McKay received his bachelor of music degree there in 1923, he was in its first graduating class in composition. Later that year, on August 23, he married Frances Martha Greene, with whom he had four children.

Between 1923 and 1926, McKay taught music in public schools in Greensboro, N.C., and Lead, S.D. A Violin Sonata (1923) and *April Suite*, for piano (1924), both in a postromantic style to which he would henceforth be partial, were his earliest mature works. In 1925, his first orchestral work, *A Short Symphony*, subtitled "From a Mountain Town," or "From the Black Hills," became his first work to be stimulated by the geography of the Northwest. Its first movement became Sinfonietta no. 1 (1925), which was selected in a national competition for performance at the first American Music Concert in Rochester, N.Y., on May 1, 1925. Fabien Sevitzky

conducted it with the Peoples Symphony in Boston on October 21, 1934.

In 1926–27, McKay was on the music faculty of the State Teachers College in Kirksville, Mo. He joined the music faculty of the University of Washington in Seattle in 1927 (from this time on he would live in the Northwest without interruption) where his Sonatina, for clarinet and strings (1929), arranged from his Sonata for Clarinet and Harmonium (1929), was introduced on February 23, 1932. At the university, McKay was promoted to associate professor in 1938 and to full professor in 1944, retaining his professorship there until his retirement in 1968. During those years, he was guest professor at the University of Southern California during the summers of 1938 and 1939, and at the University of Michigan in the summer of 1943.

In 1930, his Woodwind Quintet won honorable mention in a contest sponsored by the National Broadcasting Company. One year later he composed *Fantasy on a Western Song*, introduced in Rochester, N.Y., on May 3, 1933, and, in a 1935 revision, by the Seattle Symphony conducted by the composer on November 11, 1935. Other major orchestral works with an American identity followed, the most significant of which were: *Prairie Portrait* (1932), premiered by the San Francisco Symphony under Paul Lemay on September 4, 1941, over the Mutual radio network; *Harbour Narrative*, for orchestra (1934); *Pioneer Epic*, for orchestra (1935; Oakland, Calif., February 17, 1942), originally the third act of the American ballet, *Epoch* (1935); *American Street Scenes*, for clarinet, trumpet, saxophone, bassoon, and piano (1935); *Westward*, for orchestra (1935); *Symphonic Prelude in an American Idiom*, for symphonic band (1937); *Port Royale, 1861*, a suite for strings (1939) based on three Negro songs collected in the Port Royale Islands in South Carolina in 1861; and *To a Liberator*, a tone poem written as a tribute to Abraham Lincoln on commission from Fabien Sevitzky who introduced it with the Indianapolis Symphony on March 15, 1940.

McKay received first prizes in contests sponsored by the American Guild of Organists and the Northern California Harpists Association. He was also awarded the Harvey Gaul Prize. In 1951 he was commissioned to write his Symphony in commemoration of the Seattle Centennial.

PRINCIPAL WORKS: 4 sinfoniettas (1925–42).

A Short Symphony, "From a Mountain Town," or "From the Black Hills (1925); *Lyric Poems*, for ten instruments (1928); Sonata for Clarinet and Harmonium, also Sonatina for Clarinet and Strings (1929); Woodwind Quintet (1930); Piano Trio (1931); *April Poem*, for string quartet, flute and piano (1931); *Fantasy on a Western Folk Song* (1931, revised 1933); *A Prairie Portrait*, for orchestra (1932); *Five Dramatic Moods*, for chamber orchestra (1933); Cello Sonata (1933); *Harbour Narrative*, for orchestra (1934); *Epoch*, an American ballet (1935); Pastorale, for women's voices and strings (1935); *Pioneer Epic*, originally act three of *Epoch*, for orchestra (1935); *American Street Scenes*, for clarinet, trumpet, saxophone, bassoon, and piano (1935); *Symbolic Portrait*, for orchestra (1935); *Westward*, for orchestra (1935); *Machine Age Blues*, for orchestra (1935); String Quartet (1936); *Bravura Prelude*, for brass ensemble (1936); *Symphonic Prelude in an American Idiom*, for symphonic band (1937); Sonata for Organ and piano (1937); *Port Royale, 1861*, folksong suite for strings (1939); Violin Concerto (1940); *To a Liberator*, tone poem for orchestra (1940); *Introspective Poem*, for strings (1940); Cello Concerto (1942); Symphony (1951).

BIBLIOGRAPHY: *BBDM;* Howard, John Tasker, *Our Contemporary Composers* (N.Y., 1941); *Who's Who in America, 1968–69.*

McPhee, Colin Carhart, b. Montreal, Canada, March 15, 1901; d. Los Angeles, Calif., January 7, 1964. American citizen.

McPhee was a pioneer in recreating Indonesian music for the Western world, and one of its foremost exponents. Some of his major works drew their idioms and instruments from Balinese music.

He received his early musical training in his native Montreal and continued it at the Peabody Conservatory in Baltimore, Md., where he studied composition with Gustav Strube and from which he graduated in 1921. For the next three years he received further instruction on the piano in Toronto from Arthur Friedheim. At that time he completed a Piano Concerto (1923), which scored a major success when he introduced it in Canada as soloist with the Toronto Symphony in 1924. Later in 1924, he left for Paris for the study of composition with Paul Le Flem and piano with Isidor Philipp (1924–26).

Returning to the United States in 1926, he made his home in New York, for a time studying composition there with Edgard Varèse. Later in the 1920s, his early compositions were getting a hearing at concerts promoting new music by such organizations as the League of Composers, International Composers Guild and the Copland-Sessions Concerts. His most important work of this period was the Concerto for Piano and Wind Octet (1928), introduced in Boston under the direction of Nicolas Slonimsky on March 11, 1929. This work represents McPhee's tendency at the time to employ economy of means and formalism. Following a revival of this work in New York in 1954, Peggy Glanville-Hicks wrote in the *Herald Tribune*: "The McPhee Concerto is surely one of the classics of the 20s; its three movements expound instrumental and acoustic originality that—although colored by the ear—is highly personal, highly expert."

In scores written in the early 1930s for two experimental films—*H₂O* and *Mechanical Principles*—McPhee went on from his early neoclassicism to a music more complex in materials, structure, and rhythms and in which he began employing such then advanced techniques as polytonality and polyrhythm. Since writing this concerto, McPhee aspired, as he himself explained, "to express through music an emotion resulting from contact with daily life—its noise, rhythms, energy, and mechanical daring. . . . I have no more definite, concrete idea in mind than the construction of logical music whose rhythms derive from mechanics, whose tonal structure, while orderly and complete, is as complex as the structure of a large bridge."

A new creative vista opened up for him in 1931 when he heard some French recordings of music performed by gamelan orchestras of Java and Bali. He became so fascinated with the percussive sonorities of gongs, metallophones, drums, and cymbals, and the unique rhythmic patterns of Indonesian music, that he decided to make a pilgrimage to Bali to study this music firsthand. In 1933, immediately after his marriage to Jane Belo, an ethnologist, he left for Bali for what he expected would be a six-month visit. Before long, however, he and his wife decided to build a house for themselves on the island. They adopted an eight-year-old houseboy named Samphi and stayed on for six years. McPhee now became the first Westerner to study Balinese music with native teachers and the first Westerner to perform native instruments in Balinese gamelan orchestras. Additionally, he was responsible for bringing about in Bali a revival of interest in the older forms of traditional Balinese music.

McPhee left the island briefly in 1936 to visit Mexico on an invitation of Carlos Chávez. In Mexico, McPhee wrote his most celebrated composition, *Tabuh-Tabuhan* (1936), which incorporated Balinese percussion instruments into the traditional symphony orchestra and which used the pentatonic scale, the block polyphonic structure of rhythms, and melody devoid of harmony, all characteristic of Indonesian music. The first performance of *Tabuh-Tabuhan* took place in Mexico City in 1936 with Chávez conducting the National Orchestra of Mexico. After that it was performed by many major symphony orchestras. When Leopold Stokowski conducted it in New York in October 1953, Virgil Thomson in the *Herald Tribune* called it "a brilliant and striking work. . . . Its themes and rhythms are all authentic (and very beautiful), its sounds and structure nearly so. . . . The whole piece is a delight for bright sounds, lively rhythms and lovely tunes." After a performance in Cleveland in December 1957, Herbert Elwell in the *Cleveland Plain Dealer* called it "a sensuous experience in Indonesian exoticism . . . a remarkable assimilation by a Westerner of Eastern sonorities and rhythms." In 1954, *Tabuh-Tabuhan* received an award from the American Academy of Arts and Letters citing its "unprecedented combination of traditional Indonesian music with Western orchestral techniques which has produced original music of great distinction." In 1956, in commemoration of the eleventh anniversary of the United Nations, it was heard there in a performance by the New York Philharmonic under Hugh Ross.

The imminence of World War II brought McPhee back to the United States in 1939. In 1940 he provided incidental music for a New York revival of Eugene O'Neill's *The Emperor Jones* starring Paul Robeson. During World War II he served as consultant for the Office of War Information. After the war, the United Nations commissioned him to write music for several documentary films. From 1958 until his death, McPhee was a member of the faculty at the Institute of Ethnomusicology at the University of California in Los Angeles.

In addition to his Balinese music—which included the tone poem *Bali* (1936) and the *Balinese Ceremonial Music*, for two pianos (1940)—McPhee produced Western music, including three symphonies (1955, 1957, 1962), the second of which, *Pastoral*, was commissioned, introduced, and recorded by the Louisville Orchestra in Kentucky; *Transitions*, for orchestra (1954), which the Koussevitzky Music Foundation had commissioned; and Nocturne, for orchestra (1958), commissioned by the Contemporary Music Society and introduced in New York under Leopold Stokowski's direction. The exoticism of the East still clung to McPhee's writing in the Nocturne. Its style was partly impressionistic, partly modal, but with persistent recollections of Balinese gamelan percussiveness.

During his last twenty years—aided by two Guggenheim Fellowships and grants from the Huntington Hartford Foundation, the Bollingen Foundation and the National Institute of Arts and Letters—McPhee worked on a study of Balinese music. He completed it just a few weeks before his death. Under the title of *Music in Bali* it was published posthumously in New Haven in 1966. McPhee was also the author of a book of Balinese reminiscences, *A House in Bali* (1956), and a children's book about Bali, *A Club of Small Men* (1946). For a decade (1935–45) McPhee contributed a column, "Scores and Records" to *Modern Music*.

McPhee's marriage ended in divorce. Their adopted son, Samphi, became one of the most famous dancers of Bali; he toured the United States in 1952 with a Balinese group.

THE COMPOSER SPEAKS: I have always felt that musical expression, like good prose, increases in eloquence as the composer, through long training and the widest possible musical experience, attains a personal and deceptively simple style. I am a conservative, inasmuch as I believe that sound, well-balanced structure, rhythmic and metric vitality, and carefully planned continuity are the main factors which prevent a work from deterioration with age, provided

the musical material itself is stated in terms of fresh and interesting resonance. I learned much about this during my years in Bali and Java, where traditional music forms, combined with sensuous orchestration of the gamelan, form the basis for a musical art which even now continues to enchant men, women and children in every walk of life.

PRINCIPAL WORKS: 3 symphonies (1930, 1957, 1962).

Piano Concerto (1923); Sonatina, for 2 flutes, clarinet, trumpet and piano (1925); Concerto for Piano and Wind Octet (1928); *Sea Shantey Suite*, six Scottish airs for baritone, men's chorus, two pianos and six timpani (1929); *Invention, Kinesis*, both for piano (1930); *From the Revelation of St. John the Divine*, for men's chorus, two pianos, two trumpets, and timpani (1935); *Bali*, tone poem for orchestra (1936); *Tabuh-Tabuhan*, toccata for orchestra (1936); *Balinese Ceremonial Music*, for two pianos (1940); *Four Iroquois Dances*, for orchestra (1944); *Transitions*, for orchestra (1954); Nocturne, for orchestra (1958); Concertino for Wind Orchestra (1959).

BIBLIOGRAPHY: Cowell, Henry (ed.), *American Composers on American Music* (Stanford, Calif., 1933); McPhee, Colin, *A House in Bali* (N.Y., (1946); Thomson, Virgil, *American Music Since 1910* (N.Y., 1970); *New York Times* (obituary), January 8, 1964.

Mennin, Peter (originally **Mennini, Peter**), b. Erie, Pa., May 17, 1923.

Mennin's prime importance as composer rests on his orchestral music, and particularly with his symphonies. In his early works, the writing is somewhat tonal and bitonal, largely polyphonic, with sustained melodic lines and irregular assymetric rhythmic motives, often within structures of ambitious dimensions. The musical language has more recently developed more complexly without, however, losing the earlier distinguishing features.

He is one of two sons of Italian-born parents; his older brother, Louis Mennini, has also distinguished himself as composer. Their father, a businessman, loved music and flooded his home with the sounds of great music through recordings. Peter Mennin cannot remember a time when he was not committed to music. In fact, he learned to read music before he could read or write, since his piano teacher, Tito Spampani, insisted he learn solfeggio before taking lessons at the keyboard. Peter Mennin was five when these lessons began, and at seven he composed for the piano his first piece of music. When he was eleven, he made an attempt to write a symphony.

Upon graduating from Strong Vincent High School in 1940, Mennin entered Oberlin Conservatory in Ohio, where he remained a year (1940–41), studying composition with Normand Lockwood. As an Oberlin student, Mennin completed his Symphony no. 1 (1941), his String Quartet no. 1 (1941), as well as a choral work and some songs.

In 1942, during World War II, he joined the U.S. Army Air Force. After basic training, he was assigned to the officers' candidate school in Florida. Upon being discharged from military service in 1943 he resumed music study, entering the Eastman School of Music in Rochester, N.Y., where he remained four years, studying composition with Bernard Rogers and Howard Hanson and orchestration with Rogers. Even while he was studying, he was creatively productive, and even had his first taste of success. One of the movements of his Symphony no. 2 (1944) became the first winner of the George Gershwin Memorial Award and, as *Symphonic Allegro*, was introduced by the New York Philharmonic under Leonard Bernstein on March 27, 1945. The symphony, as a whole, was awarded the Bearns Prize of Columbia University in 1945. Another student work, *Folk Overture*, for orchestra (1945)—so-called because of the simple folklike thematic material—became his first composition to get wide hearings from American symphony orchestras. After being introduced in Rochester, N.Y., in 1945 with Hanson conducting, it was performed by the National Symphony Orchestra in Washington, D.C., on November 28, 1945 (and in several of its subsequent seasons), and the New York Philharmonic on January 19, 1946. Symphony no. 3 (1946), with which Mennin realized his greatest success up to that time, was premiered by the New York Philharmonic under Walter Hendl on February 27, 1947, after which it received a recording grant from the Naumburg Foundation. In his review in the *New York Herald Tribune*, Virgil Thomson called the symphony "an accomplished work, in the sense that its shape holds together and that its instrumentation is professional. Its expressive content is eclectic, ranging from a Sibelius-like sadness to a syncopated animation suggestive of William Schuman."

Mennin received both his bachelor of music and master of music degrees at the Eastman School in 1945, and his Ph.D. two years later. The summer of 1946 was spent at the Berkshire Music Center at Tanglewood, Mass., studying conducting with Serge Koussevitzky. That year Mennin received an award from the American Academy of Arts and Letters.

Between 1947 and 1958 Mennin taught composition at the Juilliard School of Music in New York. On August 28, 1947, he married Georganne Bairnson, a violinist who had just graduated from the Eastman School of Music. Following her marriage she surrendered her own career to devote herself to her husband and the raising of their two children.

In 1948, Mennin received a Guggenheim Fellowship (a second to follow eight years later), and in 1950 the University of Rochester presented him with a centennial citation for distinguished service to mu-

sic. Two more symphonies came between 1948 and 1950. Symphony no. 4, subtitled *The Cycle*, for chorus and orchestra (1948), was commissioned and premiered in New York by the Collegiate Chorale, Robert Shaw conducting, on March 18, 1949. Virgil Thomson, in the *Herald Tribune*, said: "The symphony's force lies . . . in its treatment of the choir as a section of the orchestra capable of rivalry with the instrumental body in loudness and in musical interest. I don't think I've ever heard a choral symphony in which the vocal and instrumental forces are so well equilibrated in the whole expressive achievement. He has really composed them, conceived them as cooperating toward a single end. . . . He has resolved a hitherto unsolved problem and created by that fact a musical work of genuine originality." Symphony no. 5 (1950) was commissioned by the Dallas Symphony, which introduced it on April 2, 1950, under Walter Hendl's direction. Describing this work, the composer said: "Each of the movements has its own basic character and achieves contrast within itself through the musical materials and textures rather than from change in tempo. . . . The basic aim of this work is expressivity. Therefore, there is a great emphasis placed on the broad melodic line, and little use of color for color's sake. Orchestrally speaking, the colors used are primary rather than pastel in quality. Hence, the work as a whole is a direct assertive and terse communication." Outside the realm of orchestral music, Mennin produced String Quartet no. 2 in 1951, whose world premiere was given by the Juilliard String Quartet in New York on February 24, 1952, and which emerged as a winner of first prize in the Columbia Records Chamber Music competition.

Concertato no. 2, *Moby Dick*, for orchestra (1952), has become one of Mennin's most often performed shorter works for orchestra. It was written on a commission from the Erie (N.Y.) Philharmonic in celebration of the centenary of that city, and its first performance took place there on October 20, 1952, Fritz Mahler conducting. In this work, Mennin had no intention of creating programmatic music descriptive of the Melville novel; rather, he sought to express the emotional impact the novel had had upon him. As the mold into which to pour such emotion, Mennin chose the baroque structure of the "concertato," which may be identified as a miniature concerto for orchestra pitting a small group of solo instruments against a larger orchestral body (in the manner of a concerto grosso), with antiphonal writing provided by contrasting groups. Mennin described this music as follows: "The composition opens very quietly with a sustained note in the first violins against which a characteristic harmonic idea is introduced by the woodwinds. This is then used many times in variation throughout the work. Aside from several new ideas which are introduced in the Allegro, the introductory section contains most of the materials of the whole work. The diversity and contrast in the ideas themselves preempt the kind of growth they will receive, and the expansion and development unfolds along purely musical lines."

Commissions by major musical organizations led to the writing of other significant works in the 1950s: from the Louisville Orchestra in Kentucky for Symphony no. 6 (1953), premiere on November 17, 1953, Robert Whitney conducting; from the Coolidge Foundation to honor the thirtieth anniversary of the League of Composers, for *Sonata concertante*, for violin and piano (1956), first performance given by Ruggiero Ricci in Washington, D.C., on October 19, 1956; from the Juilliard School of Music for the Cello Concerto (1956), premiered by Leonard Rose and the Juilliard School of Music Orchestra under Jean Morel on February 19, 1956; from the Cleveland Orchestra commemorating its fortieth anniversary, for the Piano Concerto (1957), its first hearing coming on February 27, 1958, in a performance by Eunice Podis and the Cleveland Orchestra under George Szell.

Mennin left the Juilliard School in 1958 to become director of the Peabody Conservatory in Baltimore, where his innovations to help young conductors (American Conductors Project) and young opera singers (Peabody Art Theater) gained nationwide attention. In the fall of 1958, Mennin participated in the first cultural exchange of composers with the Soviet Union at the invitation of the U.S. State Department. He served as a member of the advisory panel of the United States Information Agency in 1961. One year later he was appointed president of the Juilliard School of Music, a post he has retained with distinction since that time. In 1964 he served on an advisory committee for the arts for the State Department. He was composer-in-residence at the Hopkins Center Congregation at Dartmouth College in New Hampshire during the summer of 1966, when several of his major works were heard at three festival concerts. In 1967, he was elected an officer and treasurer of the National Institute of Arts and Letters, and in 1968 he was made president of the National Music Council.

Orchestral music continued to dominate Mennin's creativity after 1960. There are two more symphonies, his seventh and eighth. Symphony no. 7, *Variations Symphony* (1963), was commissioned by George Szell for the Cleveland Orchestra and was first heard in Cleveland on January 23, 1964. A one-movement work made up of five major sections, this symphony has little relationship to the traditional methods of variation, but uses the techniques resulting from the overall structural and dramatic concept. In the *New York Times*, Harold C. Schonberg described this music as "brisk-busy, energetic, brilliantly scored and even exuberant." Symphony no. 8 (1973), introduced by the New York Philharmonic under Daniel Barenboim on November 21, 1974, is programmatic in that each of its four movements represents a biblical text: I. "In Principio"; II. "Dies Irae"; III. "De Profundis"; IV. "Laudate Dominum." But, as Harold C. Schonberg noted, these were just "clues to the emotional nature of the music rather than an attempt to tell a story."

Other orchestral works, but not in the symphonic structure, included the *Canto for Orchestra* (1963), commissioned by the Association of Women's Committees for Symphony Orchestras, which received its initial hearing at its biennial convention in San Antonio, Tex., on March 4, 1963. This is a lyrical work described by the composer as "a dramatic elegy." The term "canto" is not used here to signify a part of an epic poem but to suggest that the orchestra is given an opportunity "to sing." *Sinfonia capricciosa*, a commission of the National Symphony Orchestra in Washington, D.C. (1980) was introduced by that organization, with Mstislav Rostropovich conducting, on March 10, 1981. "As its title implies," Mennin explains, "*Sinfonia capricciosa* has many capricious moments, many sharp changes, and more contrasting sections than the usual symphony." Mennin subsequently completed a Flute Concerto (1981) for the flutist, Julius Baker.

Two major vocal works were also written since 1960. *Cantata de Virtute*, for tenor, baritone, narrator, chorus, children's chorus and orchestra (1968–69) was commissioned by Max Rudolf for the Cincinnati May Festival, where it was first heard on May 2, 1969. Mennin's original plan in writing this work was to make a musical adaptation of *The Pied Piper of Hamelin*, based on Browning's poem. Upon realizing that its medieval subject matter was pertinent to modern problems, Mennin broadened his conception by adding to parts of Browning other materials; the Latin text of Psalm 117; two 13th-century poems elaborating the basic conception; and an adaptation of the *Missa pro Defunctis*. The completed work became a secular cantata about morality, that term being used in its broadest meaning. "The music is clearly dramatic," the composer explains, "and, when the conception demands, theatrical." To achieve proper crowd effects, Mennin had to devise approximate notation for several of the sections.

Voices, for mezzo-soprano, percussion, piano, harp, and harpsichord (1976), based on poems by Thoreau, Melville, Walt Whitman, and Emily Dickinson, was commissioned by the Chamber Music Society of Lincoln Center in New York, which gave the premiere performance on March 28, 1976, with Frederica von Stade as soloist. Here the composer's aim, as he said, was "to conceive musical settings that would bring out and strengthen the mystical and spiritual qualities of the metaphysical images. The basic thrust of these poems is in creating new worlds to see, and new visions that seem invisible to the prosaic eye. . . . The choice of poems . . . was subject to the musical images they evoked from the composer. There is a common thread in each of them that made these particular choices inevitable. The instrumentation was chosen for its possibilities to enhance the imagery and varies from poem to poem." The percussion ensemble included such pitched instruments as tubular bells, glockenspiel, vibraphone, antique cymbals and timpani, while the unpitched percussion included bellplates, suspended cymbals, tam-tams, bongos, tom-toms, and timbales.

In addition to offices already mentioned, Mennin has been a member of the board of directors of the American Music Center, of the Composers Forum and of the Walter W. Naumburg Foundation. He has served as member of the Lincoln Center Council, on the advisory committee to the American Society of Composers, Authors, and Publishers (ASCAP) and on the evaluating panel for the New York State Council on the Arts. He has been awarded honorary doctorates by the University of Chicago, Oberlin College, the University of Wisconsin, the University of Heidelberg (in Germany), Temple University and the Peabody Conservatory.

THE COMPOSER SPEAKS: I have become increasingly reluctant to make analyses of my works. . . . In a sense, I feel that it is inappropriate for the composer—who has been looking inward during the creation of the work—to have to explain merely the compositional technique without the emotional involvement with the content of musical ideas that created the urgency to make the work come into being. Compositional techniques are merely tools of the creative impulse and are uninteresting in themselves, except to the musician who, with score in hand, wants to study the music in detail at a later date. Actually, it is difficult in the extreme for a composer to analyze his work dispassionately—or should be.

Also in recent times it has become prevalent that highly detailed explanations accompany the performances of a new work. The practice of analysis and "evaluation" has so increased that one sometimes wonders if the music itself will become obsolete.

To do justice to an intricate structure, a full-length analysis would have to be offered. The device of "hitting the high points" seems to the composer to be somewhat superficial. He feels that the listener should rather concentrate, at a first hearing, on the sound and its expressive development, rather than on any elements of compositional technique.

PRINCIPAL WORKS: 8 symphonies (1941–73); 2 string quartets (1941, 1951).
Concertino, for flute, strings, and percussion (1944); *Folk Overture*, for orchestra (1945); Fantasia, for string orchestra (1947); Divertimento, for piano (1947); *Settings of Four Chinese Poems by Kiang Kang Hu*, for a cappella chorus (1948); Five Piano Pieces (1949); Partita, for piano (1949); *The Christmas Story*, cantata for soprano, tenor, chorus, brass, timpani, and strings (1949); Violin Concerto (1950); Canto and Cantata, for piano (1950); Concertato,

Moby Dick, for orchestra (1952); *Sonata concertante*, for violin and piano (1956); Cello Concerto (1956); Piano Concerto (1957–58); *Canto for Orchestra* (1963); Piano Sonata (1963); *Cantata de Virtute*, for tenor, baritone, narrator, chorus, children's chorus, and orchestra (1968–69); Sinfonia, originally entitled *Symphonic Movements*, for orchestra (1970); *Voices*, for mezzo-soprano, percussion, piano, harp, and harpsichord (1976); *Reflections of Emily*, for chorus of treble voices, piano, harp, and percussion (1978); *Sinfonia capricciosa*, for orchestra (1980); Flute Concerto (1981).

BIBLIOGRAPHY: *DCM;* Thomson, Virgil, *American Music Since 1910* (N.Y., 1970); *High Fidelity/Musical America*, March 1976, November 1980; *Juilliard Review*, Spring 1954; *New York Times*, March 21, 1971; *Saturday Review*, February 26, 1955; *Who's Who in America, 1980–81.*

Mennini, Louis Alfred, b. Erie, Pa., November 18, 1920.

His musical expression does not consciously adhere to any particular trend or idiom, though his early mature works revealed an interest in contrapuntal and at times modal writing. His best works are straightforward, with energetic rhythmic drive, lyrically flowing counterpoint and a highly developed sense of melody.

He is the older brother (by three years) of Peter Mennin, the distinguished composer and educator. Both were sons of a businessman who was passionately interested in music and whose collection of recordings was the source of their earliest musical experience. Louis Mennini studied the piano and theory with Tito Spampani (1929–31), and at nine started composing. Upon graduating from the Strong Vincent High School in Erie in 1938, he received a thorough musical training at Oberlin Conservatory in Oberlin, Ohio (1939–42), where he studied composition with Normand Lockwood.

World War II interrupted his studies. For three years (1942–45) he served as sergeant in the U.S. Army Air Force in England. At the request of General Doolittle, he spent a month touring as musician with the USO through Germany, the Netherlands, and Belgium. Upon his discharge from the armed forces, he spent three years at the Eastman School of Music in Rochester, N.Y. (1945–48), studying composition with Bernard Rogers and Howard Hanson, at the same time serving as teaching fellow in orchestration (1946–48). These were the years when he completed his first mature works, and the first to gain significant performances. They included an Andante (1947) and *Allegro energico* (1948), both for orchestra and both introduced in Rochester in the year of their composition. Both reflected Mennini's interest in the music of the 16th and 17th centuries in regard to their polyphonic structure. The *Allegro en-*

ergico was in modal style and quoted a Gregorian chant, *Kyrie Orbis Factor*. Both compositions were performed by the Philadelphia Orchestra conducted by Evan Whallon on December 3, 1948. The Philadelphia Orchestra under Eugene Ormandy performed another early Mennini work for orchestra, this one more lyrical and harmonic than contrapuntal, the *Arioso* for strings (1948) on December 1, 1950.

Mennini received his bachelor of music degree at the Eastman School in 1947, and his master of music degree in 1948, both in composition. In 1948–49 he taught composition and orchestration at the University of Texas in Austin. Between 1949 and 1965 he was professor of composition and orchestration at the Eastman School where, in 1961, he earned his Ph.D. in music, once again in composition. On June 16, 1956, he married Charlene White, a professional cellist; they had three sons (one deceased).

In 1949, Mennini received a grant from the American Academy of Arts and Sciences and the National Institute of Arts and Letters. In the 1950s he was given two commissions from the Koussevitzky Music Foundation. The first led to the writing of a Sonatina, for cello and piano (1952), for the Library of Congress in Washington, D.C., where it was introduced in 1952 by Gregor Piatigorsky and performed by Donald McCall at his debut in New York in October 1956. The second produced a highly successful one-act chamber opera, *The Rope* (1955), libretto by the composer based on Eugene O'Neill's grim one-act play. (This was Mennini's second one-act chamber opera. The first, *The Well*, to his own libretto, had been produced in Rochester, on May 8, 1951, and was subsequently performed at several American colleges and universities.) *The Rope* was introduced at the Berkshire Music Center at Tanglewood, Mass. (for which it was written), on August 8, 1955. In his report to the *New York Herald Tribune*, Francis D. Perkins wrote: "The music's individual style has no unblended elements and no doctrinaire touches; pungent dissonance appears at times for an expressive purpose but is not characteristic. . . . There are a few spoken passages, but in most of the score the singers are given a flexible lyric speech with occasional more fully defined melodic episodes and a few arias which in most cases arise spontaneously from the general musical texture. The instrumental score . . . is expertly written; there is color and expressive significance, a knowledge of how to use a particular timbre or combination of timbres to meet the dramatic requirements of the moment."

The strength of lyricism and the skill in orchestration found in this opera were also revealed in several important orchestral works written in the early 1960s. The Symphony no. 1, *Da chiesa* (1960), was commissioned by the Mary Biddle Duke Foundation for the orchestra of Duke University, which introduced it in Durham, N.C., on March 15, 1963. His second symphony, *Da festa* (1963), was written on commission from the Erie Sesquicentennial Committee, its premiere presented by the Erie Philharmonic under James Sample on September 7, 1963. *Tenebrae* (1963) was the result of a commission from Edward B. Benjamin for a piece of "tranquil music," and was premiered by the New Orleans Symphony on March 5, 1963.

In 1965, Mennini was appointed dean of the School of Music at the North Carolina School of the Arts in Winston-Salem, the first state-sponsored art school in the United States. He retained this post six years while also serving as its acting president from December 1966 to June 1967. Upon leaving the North Carolina School of the Arts in 1971, Mennini spent two years in Florence, Italy. He returned to the United States in 1973 to become chairman of the music department at Mercyhurst College in Erie, Pa., a post he has retained since that time. In Erie he has also served as vice-president of the Erie Philharmonic Board of Directors, on the music advisory committee of the Pennsylvania Council on the Arts and, from 1977 on, as director of the d'Angelo Young Artists Competition. He has conducted a weekly radio program over station WQLN-FM entitled *Composer's Choice*. In 1978 he was the recipient of the Composer of the Year Award of the Lancaster Symphony in Pennsylvania, and in 1979 he was given a grant from the National Endowment for the Arts to write an opera.

THE COMPOSER SPEAKS: A composer should not *primarily* be concerned with a method or technique of composition. Any truly creative artist will be able to express himself through his particular medium (poetry, painting, and so forth) if what he has to say is of primary importance. I have found that those who restrict themselves to a particular "technique" are generally the most "romantic" when they describe their "technique."

PRINCIPAL WORKS: 2 symphonies (1960, 1963).

Andante, for strings (1947); Violin Sonata (1947); *Allegro energico*, for strings (1948); *Arioso*, for strings (1948); *Overture Breve*, for orchestra (1949); *Cantilena*, for orchestra (1950); Canzona, for chamber orchestra (1950); *The Well*, one-act chamber opera (1951); Sonatina, for cello and piano (1952); *The Rope*, one-act chamber opera (1955); *Credo*, for orchestra (1955); String Quartet (1961); *Tenebrae*, for orchestra (1963); Concerto Grosso (1975).

BIBLIOGRAPHY: *BBDM*; Anderson, E. Ruth, *Contemporary American Composers* (Boston, 1976); *New York Herald Tribune*, August 7, 1955.

Menotti, Gian Carlo, b. Cadegliano, Italy, July 7, 1911.

Menotti is Italian not only by birth but also by citizenship. But he spent so many of his formative and mature years in the United States, wrote so many of his operas in America, and had so many of them premiered there that he can justifiably be numbered with American composers. His principal medium is opera, in which he has achieved extraordinary successes, including two Pulitzer Prizes in music, in 1950 and 1955. Through the opera house, the Broadway theater, motion pictures, television, radio, and phonograph recordings he has reached a larger audience than any opera composer in the 20th century. In his operas as in his citizenship, he never broke ties with his native land. In comic opera he carries on the traditions of Italian opera buffa, and in serious works he has inherited the *verismo* style from Puccini. Menotti is the total theater man, who always writes his own librettos, often serves as his own casting and stage director, and personally involves himself in every detail of production. As a composer he is an eclectic who, on the one hand, can be eloquently lyrical, romantic, even sentimental, and consistently consonant and who, on the other hand, can provide his writing with the strong fiber of harmonic discords, polytonality, and song-speech.

He was born to an affluent, cultured, and locally influential family, the sixth of ten children. His father became wealthy in an export-import business with South America. His mother sang, played the piano, became a painter when she was sixty-two, and taught herself to play the guitar two years after that. "Every day," Menotti recalls, "in the long winter my mother taught the villagers to sing Gregorian chants." Since both parents were musical, their children were early given music instruction. Their performances of chamber music, and concerts of four-hand piano music by his mother and aunt, were Menotti's first remembered musical experiences. He was four when his mother began teaching the piano. At six he composed some songs, several to erotic verses by D'Annunzio. Menotti was equally fascinated by the theater, appearing in plays at the grade school in Cadegliano, which he attended for five years. At home, he would put on productions with a puppet theater he had acquired when he was nine, writing his own plays and doing his own costuming and scenic designs.

When he was about ten his family moved to Milan. There he attended high school for two and a half years ("a great bore," he described it). He also went to the Verdi Conservatory for the study of composition, harmony, and piano (1923–27). Going to opera performances for the first time at La Scala provided so much stimulation that when he was twelve he wrote a complete opera, *The Death of Pierrot*, to his own text. This one, and a second opera based on Hans Christian Andersen's *The Little Mermaid* four yeats later, were subsequently destroyed.

A beautiful boy and highly gifted, he was the spoiled darling of the Milan salons. He became a problem child who refused to become seriously involved with music study and who shirked his class-room responsibilities. When his mother consulted Arturo Toscanini about her son, he strongly advised her to leave Milan and the idolatry it lavished on the boy, and go to the United States for the continuation of his musical education.

When Menotti was fourteen, his father died, leaving his business in South America in a state of disorganization. His mother took Menotti with her to Colombia to straighten out the affairs. After that, they came to New York (1927), then, with a letter of introduction from Tullio Serafin, proceeded to Philadelphia to try to gain admittance for the boy at the Curtis Institute. Menotti played some of his pieces for Rosario Scalero, teacher of composition at Curtis, who then offered to obtain for him a scholarship if he promised to mend his former indolent ways. Menotti promised and, as Scalero says, "he abided by his agreement." "One rainy afternoon," Menotti recalls, "I saw my mother off at the Broad Street Station. Both of us wept. For the first time in my life, I was left alone without family or friends. I remember my terror." To make matters worse, he did not know a word of English.

He remained at Curtis six years (1927–33), studying composition with Rosario Scalero and piano with Vera Resnikoff. "I was a puzzle to my teachers. I had to learn in my own way or not at all. I had to develop a private technique. I had to fashion my own instruments, my own weapons, so to speak." He was rapidly learning to speak English by going to the movies four times a week. And he was beginning to make friends, one of whom was a classmate, Samuel Barber.

In his student compositions, Menotti was writing in emulation of the German romantics, Brahms particularly, his interest in Brahms having been awakened by Barber's enthusiasm. In this vein, Menotti wrote *Variations on a Theme of Schumann*, for piano (1931), which received the Lauber Composition Prize. Schubert was another influence at this time. "Schubert taught me to express myself simply." Then, because Scalero emphasized the study of baroque music, Menotti became so fascinated with it that everything he now wrote was polyphonic.

He graduated from Curtis Institute with honors in 1933. That winter he spent in Vienna, and it was there that the idea for his first adult opera was germinated. He began working on a one-act opera buffa set in Milan and involving its characters in the kind of amatory intrigues with which he himself as a boy had become acquainted in Milanese salons. He called his little opera *Amelia Goes to the Ball* (1936), prepared his own libretto in Italian, and adopted the established opera buffa format of arias, duets, ensemble numbers, and set pieces. The text was frivolous—a heroine who is ready and willing to see her husband go to prison for attacking her lover so that she can go to the ball with the police officer. And in his music, as well, Menotti was flippant, with a score that was exuberantly melodic, buoyed by an infectious lightness of touch and spirit. *Amelia Goes to the Ball* was produced at the Curtis Institute, with Fritz Reiner conducting, on April 1, 1937, Menotti's Italian libretto translated into English by George Mead. The opera was received so enthusiastically that in less than a year, on March 3, 1938, the Metropolitan Opera presented it, retaining it in its repertoire the following season. In the *New York World-Telegram*, Pitts Sanborn described it as an "agreeable example of modern Italian opera . . . conceived in the great comic line of *The Marriage of Figaro, The Secret Marriage, The Barber of Seville, Don Pasquale* and *Falstaff.*"

Menotti's success brought him a commission from the National Broadcasting Company for an opera written expressly for radio transmission. Menotti responded with another one-act opera buffa, this time with an American setting: *The Old Maid and the Thief* (1939). Like its predecessor, both libretto and score were farcical, ebullient, and briskly paced. This opera was heard over the NBC radio network on April 22, 1939, and on February 11, 1941, in Philadelphia, it was staged for the first time.

Another commission had far less happy consequences. For the Metropolitan Opera Menotti wrote his first tragic opera, *The Island God* (1941), to an allegorical text. Produced on May 20, 1942, it was a fiasco. Menotti himself conceded that in writing an opera with grand dimensions he was out of his depth. "In it I tackled a subject too heroic for my kind of music. It was then that I realized that the first duty of an artist is to know his limitations. My vein was not heroic." After four performances the opera was removed from the repertoire and Menotti withdrew the work from further circulation, though he did permit some of the orchestral episodes to be heard in the concert hall.

Depressed by his failure, Menotti secluded himself at "Capricorn," a house he had then just acquired in Mount Kisco, N.Y., which he would share with Samuel Barber for the next three decades. He temporarily abandoned writing opera for music in other media. For the piano virtuoso Rudolf Firkusny he wrote a Piano Concerto (1943), his first adult instrumental composition, and Firkusny introduced it with the Boston Symphony on November 2, 1943. Menotti here tried to recreate the spirit of 18th-century harpsichord music in a work Olin Downes in the *New York Times* called "a clear, melodic, exhilarating piece of music." Then on a commission from Ballet International he composed a score for the ballet *Sebastian* (1944) to his own melodramatic scenario set in Venice in the 1600s. With choreography by Edward Caton, it was produced in New York on October 31, 1944. On May 27, 1957, it was successfully revived in New York with new choreography by Agnes de Mille. A suite extracted by the composer from this score became popular at concerts.

In 1941, Menotti was appointed to the composition department at the Curtis Institute to introduce a course on Dramatic Forms, new in the curricula. He remained on the composition faculty at Curtis for the next seventeen years. From Curtis Institute he received an honorary bachelor of music degree in 1945, and from the American Academy of Arts and Sciences and the National Institute of Arts and Sciences he received a grant that same year. In 1946, he was awarded a Guggenheim Fellowship.

During that fellowship, and with a grant from the Alice M. Ditson Fund of Columbia University, Menotti went to work on a new tragic opera though in a more modest format and with more economical means than he had used in *The Island God*. It was *The Medium* (1945) to Menotti's own macabre text, "a tragedy," as Menotti described it "of a person caught between two worlds, the world of reality which she cannot wholly comprehend, and the supernatural world which she cannot believe." The heroine, Madame Flora, is a fraudulent medium who is compelled to reveal her quackery to her clients after she has felt a ghostly hand seizing her throat. Her panic leads her to drink, which in turn invokes a stupor during which she murders the dumb Gypsy boy who had been her helper, and with whom her daughter, Monica, had been in love. This stark drama was developed for the most part in music that was discordant and polytonal. Expressive song-speech was used for the medium, while gentler melodic pages were reserved for the daughter. Menotti's uncommon gift for musical characterization, for atmospheric tone painting, and for the presentation of melodramatic theater with vivid realism here came into focus for the first time; they would remain his identification as an opera composer from this point on.

So successful was *The Medium* when it was introduced at Columbia University on May 8, 1946, that, on May 1, 1947, it was brought to Broadway for a seven-month run, coupled with an amusing trifle for two characters, *The Telephone* (1946), which had been introduced in New York on February 18, 1947. Within a few years, *The Medium* received more than one thousand performances in the United States and Europe; was recorded; was made into a motion picture (1951); and went on a European tour in 1955 under the auspices of the State Department.

In *The Medium*, Menotti proved his mastery of *verismo* operatic theater, and he proved it decisively again with *The Consul* (1949), his first full-length adult opera. It was inspired by the reading of a newspaper account of a European woman committing suicide because she could not get a visa to the United States. Using an unidentified police state as his setting in the present day, Menotti built his libretto around the character of Magda, who, hounded and victimized by the secret police, makes a futile attempt to gain a visa for a foreign land to which her husband, an underground freedom fighter, had fled. In this she is continually frustrated, sees her half-starved child die in his sleep and her returning husband imprisoned. Her only escape from a repressive society is in suicide. Here, as elsewhere, Menotti proved he could create stark, musical theater; and here, as elsewhere, he demonstrated an uncanny gift at providing light as contrast to shade. At times dissonant and atonal, *The Consul* is, at other times, expansively lyrical (Magda's second act aria, "To This We've Come"), tender and sensitive (the grandmother's lullaby to the child, "I Shall Find for You Shells and Stars"), and even popular (the French tune heard on a phonograph when the opera opens).

The Consul opened on Broadway (after tryouts in Philadelphia beginning on March 1, 1950) on March 15, 1950, and was a triumph. The final curtain inspired an ovation, and the following day the critics reflected the audience enthusiasm in their reviews. Writing in the *New York Times*, Olin Downes said: "He has produced an opera of eloquence, momentousness, and intensity of expression unequaled by any native composer," and in the *Herald Tribune*, Virgil Thomson described it as "music drama of great power." *The Consul* brought Menotti his first Pulitzer Prize in music together with the Drama Critics Award. In 1951 it was produced in London, Hamburg, Munich, Zurich, Berlin, Vienna, and at La Scala in Milan, becoming the first American opera ever produced by the La Scala Company. Everywhere it was acclaimed except Milan, where left-wing groups, regarding *The Consul* as an indictment of Communist countries, staged a demonstration, while patriotic Italians also denounced it because they resented Menotti making his home permanently in the United States. Once again *The Consul* became the center of a political storm in Italy in 1972 when it was scheduled for performance at the Florence May Music Festival. Luigi Nono, the left-wing Italian composer, refused to permit his own opera *Intolleranza* to be produced at the festival since he regarded *The Consul* as a "squalid product of the cold war and anti-Sovietism," and left-wing groups in Florence vociferously joined him in his denunciations.

On the heels of *The Consul* came an opera totally different in character and mood, and another giant success for its composer. Commissioned by the National Broadcasting Company to write a television opera, Menotti completed a Christmas musical play, *Amahl and the Night Visitors* (1951), which was televised on December 24, 1951. This was the first opera ever written expressly for television; the first opera written through sponsorship by a commercial organization; and the first opera in America to become a holiday institution. For years it was the custom for NBC to present it at Christmas time, and in 1978 it was given an entirely new production. It was also produced successfully on the stage, the first time at Bloomington, Ind., on February 21, 1952, then, the same year, at the New York City Center; in 1953 at the Florence May Music Festival conducted by Leopold Stokowski; at the Hamburg State Opera in 1968–69; and in Geneva and Rome in 1971–72.

In this opera, Menotti strayed far from the field of *verismo*. In preparing his text, Menotti was stimulated by *The Adoration of the Magi*, the painting of the Flemish master, Hieronymous Bosch. The text tells the tale of Amahl, a crippled boy, who turns over to the Three Wise Men, en route to the Manger in Bethlehem, his crutches as a gift to the Holy Child. Because of his generosity he is able to walk again. Simplicity of style and directness of approach here become the essence of Menotti's musical style, be it in the expressive recitatives often of lyrical quality, the ingenuous tune Amahl pipes when the opera opens, the radiant pastoral a cappella chorus of the shepherds, or the infectious melody to which the young people dance to entertain the Kings.

The religious feeling permeating *Amahl and the Night Visitors* was also omnipresent in *The Saint of Bleecker Street* (1954), the opera with which Menotti received his second Pulitzer Prize in music as well as the Drama Critics and the Music Critics Circle awards. This was Menotti's first opera with an American setting: Bleecker Street in the Italian quarter of New York City. The heroine is a religious mystic who receives the stigmata on her palms and in the exaltation of being accepted by the Church as the Bride of Christ falls dead. The high tension of this text is captured in a score gripping for its dramatic realism and spiritual in its religious fervor, with lighter moments interjected with dance tunes and even humorous ditties. After its world premiere on Broadway on December 27, 1954, it went to La Scala in Milan on May 8, 1955, and in 1956 was telecast over BBC in London.

Menotti returned to a present-day European background in *Maria Golovin* (1958), which was commissioned by the National Broadcasting Company to represent American culture at the Brussels Exposition where it was introduced on August 20, 1958. The action takes place in a town near a European frontier a few years after "a recent war." The heroine is the wife of a prisoner-of-war she has not seen in many years. When he is released from prison and returns, he finds his wife living with a blind maker of bird cages. The blind man makes a futile attempt to kill his rival, misses, but lives with the delusion that he has permanently separated his beloved from her husband. "From the atmospheric prelude . . . to its effective end," wrote Irving Kolodin in the *Saturday Review*, "the ideas are strong and fresh. Moreover, Menotti's flow is cleverly diverted into some channels and areas he has not previously been able to navigate, in conversational vocal exchanges while the orchestra carries the melodic undercurrent." When *Maria Golovin* received its American premiere on November 5, 1958, on Broadway, it had so little audience appeal that it managed to survive only five performances. Early in 1959 it was televised by the National Broadcasting Company and soon after that was presented by the New York City Opera. Menotti revised the opera a few years later, the new version first presented in Washington, D.C., on January 22, 1965.

In 1958, Menotti became the founder of the Festival of Two Worlds in Spoleto, Italy, whose artistic destinies he has directed each summer since that time. The first time a Menotti opera was produced there was during the summer of 1968 when *The Saint of Bleecker* Street was presented. Two decades after the Spoleto festival had been created, Menotti inaugurated its counterpart in the United States, Spoleto U.S.A., at Charleston, S.C., which opened on May 25, 1977.

In the early 1960s, Menotti became the first non-French composer since Verdi to be commissioned for an opera by the Paris Opéra. For that company he wrote *The Last Savage* (1963), calling it "a satire of contemporary life," which was premiered not at the Paris Opéra but at the Opéra-Comique, on October 21, 1963. Here, for the first time since *Amelia Goes to the Ball*, Menotti wrote his libretto in Italian; it was translated into French for the premiere. Poorly received by Parisian critics, *The Last Savage* was revised and presented in an English translation for its American premiere at the Metropolitan Opera on January 23, 1964. (Only when the opera was produced in Venice later in 1964 was the original Italian libretto used.) A satire on the foibles of modern civilization—with sardonic looks at cocktail parties, avant-garde composers and painters, beatniks, and other facets of life in the early 1960s—*The Last Savage* described the efforts of an American anthropologist to search in India for "the Abominable Snowman" or "the last savage," and her emotional involvement with the maharajah. Since she refuses to marry the maharajah until she finds her "last savage," the maharajah contrives to have his stable boy assume the role. The structure is the French opéra bouffe, with its formal arias, duets, and other set numbers, something which met with little favor with the New York critics, who dismissed the entire opera as unworthy of Menotti's talent. Ethan Madden, in *Opera in the Twentieth Century*, called it a "fiasco of anti-American drivel."

Menotti did not write an opera of the dimensions of *The Last Savage* for another seven years, but he did not abandon opera totally, concentrating on more intimate works, more economically realized. These included his second opera for television, *Labyrinth* (1963), produced over the NBC television network (which had commissioned it) on March 3, 1963; a dramatic cantata, *The Death of the Bishop of Brindisi* (1963), commissioned by the Cincinnati May Music Festival, which gave its premiere on May 18, 1963; and *Martin's Lie* (1964), a one-act opera set in medieval England, commissioned by CBS-TV, its first hearing given at the Bath Festival in England on June 3, 1964, then telecast by CBS on January 24, 1965.

Menotti returned to full-length opera with *The Most Important Man* (1970), which the New York City Opera produced on March 12, 1971. Touching

on a racial problem, this opera is set in an apartheid community, probably in Africa, where a black scientist creates the formula capable of making him the world's most powerful man. He refuses to turn over this formula to the white community and, when compelled to do so, destroys it and is shot in the process. The critics attacked both the libretto and the music. In the *New York Times*, for example, Harold C. Schonberg said "most of it is more soap opera than opera," and in *High Fidelity/Musical America*, George Movshon wrote: "This paper-cutout of a libretto was colored by numbers with a wash of music to match, a sort of peanut-butter score, homogenized and utterly disposable."

Such hostility embittered Menotti. For some years now he had been upset by the reaction of some critics to his work: critics who felt that, creatively speaking, he had frozen himself into a posture that made any further progress impossible; that he was continually repeating himself; that with him, more often than not, theatrical effect takes precedence to musical content. The reaction of the critics to both *The Last Savage* and *The Most Important Man* led him to spill his resentment in a letter to the *New York Times* on his sixtieth birthday. "I hardly know of another artist who has been more consistently damned by the critics. Even those critics who have defended my music have done so (with two or three exceptions) condescendingly, or apologetically. Recently, a well-known New York critic wrote that he was 'ashamed' of liking my music. The insults that most of my operas had to endure through the years would make a booklet as terrifying as *Malleus Maleficarum*."

Menotti now spoke seriously of abandoning opera for good. But important commissions made him change his mind. For the Ninth International Congress of Anthropological and Ethnological Science convention in Chicago he wrote *Tamu-Tamu* (1973), a chamber opera introduced on September 5, 1973. The first-night audience liked what it heard and showed enthusiasm, but the critics were of another mind, calling the orientalism of Menotti's music "a fake" or remarking that "the silliness of *Tamu-Tamu*'s mundane moments undermine the seriousness of its most dramatic, philosophical segmants." *The Hero* (1976), a comic opera commissioned by the Lyric Opera Company of Philadelphia, which produced it on June 1, 1976, in commemoration of the American bicentennial, was hardly better received. This was a comedy about a small-town citizen who has slept for ten years and is about to break the world's record. He is awakened by his girlfriend's kiss, then defies the conspiracy of his neighbors to have him return to sleep to make that record. "It's a gentle and good-humored indictment of contemporary society's self-satisfaction and greed," Menotti explained, "and of those leaders who, in order to protect their own interests, choose the mediocre, the expedient and glorify the innocuous—the man who is asleep and thus cannot bother anyone." Throughout the text there were satirical allusions to present-day aberrations and foibles: pop art, chicken-à-la-king luncheons, exploiters, Watergate, doctored tapes, the mouthings of politicians, scatological humor and so on. "Musically," noted Robert Jacobson in *Opera News*, "it is as if Menotti is the one who slept through the decades, for he has not progressed a whit from *Amelia*." *The Hero* was given its New York premiere on December 10, 1980, by the Juilliard American Opera Center.

On a commission from the San Diego Opera to honor Beverly Sills on her fiftieth birthday and her imminent retirement as an opera singer, Menotti completed *La Loca* in 1979. Beverly Sills assumed the title role when it received its first performance on June 3, 1979, in San Diego and again when it reached the New York City Opera on September 16, 1979. This was Menotti's first full-scale opera on a historical subject, his first to use characters that once lived rather than those of his imagination. The heroine, Juana of Castile, in 15th-century Spain, goes mad after her husband, her father, and her son try to seize control of her throne and contrive to have her incarcerated for almost fifty years. But if the new opera (the first written expressly for Beverly Sills) was a triumph for the singing star, it was hardly that for Menotti. "Even among Mr. Menotti's operas, *La Loca* is weak," said Harold C. Schonberg in the *New York Times*. "*La Loca* is almost a caricature of his derivative Puccini style." In *Newsweek*, Hubert Saal called the libretto "implausible, vulgar, and mawkish," and maintained that the music "consisted of long spells of dry recitative, sparsely orchestrated, with an occasional oasis where Verdi, Puccini, and Prokofiev drank before him."

Despite Menotti's lifetime preoccupation with opera, he did not altogether neglect concert music, in which he revealed the same communicability with audiences through an outpouring of lyricism on the one hand and dramatic power on the other that characterized his best operas. The Piano Concerto of 1945 has already been mentioned. The most significant concert works to follow were: the tone poem *Apocalypse* (1951; Pittsburgh, October 19, 1951); the Violin Concerto (1952), which Efrem Zimbalist introduced with the Philadelphia Orchestra on December 5, 1952, Eugene Ormandy conducting; the song cycle *Canti della lontananza*, for soprano and piano (1967), premiered by Elisabeth Schwarzkopf on March 19, 1967; the *Triple Concerto a tre*, for three solo instruments and orchestra (1970)—commissioned by the Samuel Rubin Foundation for the twenty-fifth anniversary of the United Nations—introduced by the American Symphony under Stokowski on October 6, 1970; *Landscapes and Remembrances*, a cantata for vocal soloists, chorus, and orchestra (1975), based on the composer's own autobiographical lyrics tracing his arrival and experiences in the United States, first performed on May 14, 1976, by the Milwaukee Symphony; and Menotti's Symphony no. 1 (A minor), *The Halcyon* (1976), a neoclassic work in which Menotti recalled the halcyon days of his youth, a commission of the Saratoga Performing Arts Center in Saratoga, where it was introduced by the Philadelphia Orchestra under Eugene Ormandy on August 4, 1976.

Menotti provided Samuel Barber with the libretti for his operas *Vanessa* and *Antony and Cleopatra*. Menotti's stage play (without any music) *The Leper* was first produced on April 22, 1970, in Tallahassee, Fla. In 1973, Menotti left "Capricorn" in Mount Kisco to make a new home for himself at Yester House, a baronial castle on seventy-two acres in Lothian, Scotland, where he spends most of the year with his legally adopted son, Francis ("Chip") Phelan. Menotti's seventieth birthday was saluted at Spoleto: U.S.A. between May 22 and June 7, 1981, with productions of several of his most important works, including a revival of *The Last Savage* on May 22.

THE COMPOSER SPEAKS: One may ask why, if opera is a valid and vital form, it hasn't stimulated more successful contemporary contributions to the theater. Most modern composers blame their failures on the librettos, but I am afraid that the fault more often lies with the music. Opera is, after all, essentially music, and such is the ennobling or transfiguring power of music that we have numerous examples of what safely could be labeled awkward plays transformed into inspiring operas. We have, however, no single example of a successful opera whose main strength is the libretto. I have often been accused of writing good librettos and mediocre music, but I maintain that my librettos become alive or illuminated only through my music. Let anyone read one of my texts divorced from its musical setting to discover the truth of what I say. My operas are either good or bad; but if their librettos seem alive or powerful in performance, then the music must share this distinction.

One of the reasons for the failure of so much contemporary opera is that its music lacks immediacy of communication. Theater music must make its point and communicate its emotion at the same moment the action develops. It cannot wait to be understood until after the curtain comes down. Mozart understood this, and there is a noticeable difference in immediacy between some of his symphonic or chamber music styles on the one hand and his operatic style on the other. Many contemporary composers seem to fear clarity and directness, perhaps because they are afraid of becoming obvious. To quote Goethe: "We must not disdain what is immediately visible and sensuous. Otherwise we shall be sailing without ballast."

PRINCIPAL WORKS: *Amelia Goes to the Ball*, one-act opera buffa (1936); *The Old Maid and the Thief*, one-act opera (1939); *Sebastian*, ballet (1944); Piano Concerto (1945); *The Medium*, opera (1945); *The*

Telephone, one-act opera (1946); *Errand into the Maze*, ballet (1947); *The Consul*, opera (1949); *Apocalypse*, tone poem for orchestra (1951); *Amahl and the Night Visitors*, one-act television opera (1951); Violin Concerto (1952); *The Saint of Bleecker Street*, opera (1954); *The Unicorn, the Gorgon and the Manticore*, ballet-opera (1956); *Maria Golovin*, opera (1958); *Labyrinth*, one-act television opera (1963); *The Death of the Bishop of Brindisi*, cantata, for mezzo-soprano, baritone, children's chorus, adult chorus, and orchestra (1963); *The Last Savage*, opera (1963); *Martin's Lie*, one-act church opera (1964); *Canti della lontananza*, cycle of songs for soprano and piano (1967); *Help! Help! the Gobolinks*, children's opera (1968); *Triple Concerto a tre*, for three solo instruments and orchestra (1970); *The Most Important Man*, opera (1970); *Tamu-Tamu*, opera (1973); *Landscapes and Remembrances*, cantata for four vocal soloists, chorus, and orchestra (1975); *The Hero*, opera (1976); Symphony no. 1 in A minor, *The Halcyon* (1976); *The Egg*, one-act opera (1976); *The Trial of the Gypsy*, one-act opera for treble voices and piano (1978); *O Pulchritudo*, Mass for solo voices, chorus, and orchestra (1978); *La Loca*, opera (1978); *Chip and His Dog*, one-act children's opera (1980).

BIBLIOGRAPHY: Ewen, David (editor), *The New Book of Modern Composers*, revised ed. (N.Y., 1961); Gruen, John, *Menotti: A Biography* (N.Y., 1978); *Holiday*, June 1963; *New Yorker*, May 4, 1963; *New York Times*, September 16, 1973, April 17, 1974; *New York Times Magazine*, May 19, 1950; *Opera News*, May 1977; *Theatre Arts*, September 1951; *Time*, May 1, 1950.

Mills, Charles, b. Asheville, N.C., January 8, 1914.

Very early in his career, Mills invented his own neobaroque idiom. His style has always been consistently classical. The earlier diatonic period has made a gradual transition to the use of dodecaphonic principles.

He is descended from early settlers of North Carolina who had come to that state in the 17th century. His paternal ancestors (named Mills) were presented with a land grant by Charles II of England. His parents, of whom he was the only child, were of English and Scotch-Irish lineage. Both were musically inclined. His father played the piano; his mother, besides singing in a church choir, played piano and mandolin proficiently. Soon after his birth, his family moved to Spartanburg, S.C., where he was raised by his mother. His father, George Clair Mills, who had enlisted in World War I, was seriously wounded in action in France. Returning, he spent his last decade in a government hospital.

In Spartanburg, Mills attended grammar school. "By then, many musical influences made an impres-

sionable dent in my consciousness," he recalls. "I well remember beautiful folk songs sung by mountaineers who could neither read nor write, and excitingly rhythmic and moving spirituals that workers in the cotton fields sang with perfect spontaneity and unaffected zest." Literature and graphic arts were his main interests at grammar school; as an extracurricular activity, he was a boy alto in the choir of Converse College. Later, at Spartanburg High School, he became a sports enthusiast, playing football and running on the track team. He was also an honor student.

When he was about fifteen, music began assuming a major role in his life. A self-taught pianist, he acquired sufficient facility to be able to memorize some sonatas and shorter works and to make an intensive study of Beethoven's music. Hearing a recital by Paderewski became an important stimulant in developing his enthusiasm for the piano. He also made an effort to study and practice composition, once again without formal instruction, "but without the grace of an Apollonian attitude about counterpoint, harmony, and theory," he says. "I had a feeling then that these subjects were dryly academic and stifling to what I considered the 'Dionysian freedom' of inspiration and imagination." He persisted in such an attitude all the time he remained in Spartanburg, where, from the time he was seventeen until he moved to New York, he earned a living by playing saxophone, clarinet, and flute in dance bands. He was self-taught in all these instruments.

Following his first marriage, he came to New York in 1933, spending several years at the Greenwich Music School for his first formal musical education. This took place mainly with Max Garfield, who put him through the paces of a thorough study of harmony and counterpoint. During this period, Mills wrote two symphonies and a suite for string orchestra (both either totally withdrawn or sectionally incorporated into later works) and a slow movement for string quartet (1935) which he came to designate as his first opus.

Between 1935 and 1937, he studied composition with Aaron Copland. A Sonatina for Flute and Piano, and a Sonata for Flute and Piano, both written in 1937, were performed that same year in New York. Between 1937 and 1939 he continued to study composition with Roger Sessions and from 1939 to 1941 with Roy Harris. "Having a sound contrapuntal equipment already, I thoroughly enjoyed the somewhat disconcerting erudition of Sessions, whose compositions I had studied with interest and profit. My work with Harris served to reinforce my natural inclinations to compose first and 'doctor up' details later."

Mills was now composing prolifically. The works of this period included his first two string quartets (1939, 1942); his first two violin sonatas (1940, 1941); his first two symphonies (1941, 1942); his first two cello sonatas (1940, 1942); and his Piano

Trio (1941). John Kirkpatrick introduced the Piano Sonata no. 1 at a concert of the League of Composers in New York, broadcast over the municipal radio station WNYC in 1941, and Claudio Arrau presented the Piano Sonata no. 2 during his tour of South America in 1944. In all of these works Mills was the strict classicist, faithful to the sonata form (though subject to modifications), always creatively diatonic, occasionally in a neobaroque idiom. When the Violin Sonata was first heard in New York, Arthur Berger wrote in the *Herald Tribune*: "His earlier, ascetic, neo-Bachian style is now colored by a more curved and gracious line, resulting in an interesting and workable blend of romantic and neoclassic forces of contemporary music."

On April 29, 1943, a concert of Mills's chamber music was heard in Detroit performed by Morris and Sylvia Hochberg and several assisting artists. "From this severe test of the one-man exhibit," reported Paul Rosenfeld, in *Modern Music*, "Mills's music emerged in its originality. It is plainly a thing of deep moods and of aristocratic, reticent, even dry subjective sentiment; finely melodic, with frequently recitative-like textures achieved by continuous melodic outgrowths. It is definitely diatonic, but sharpened by bold transparencies in chord progressions, and exquisitely idiomatic. . . . Mills's music is further distinguished by a quality which, in all reverence, causes one to associate pages of it with the music by the mighty Bach. This is the trait of piety, religiosity, devotion."

From 1939 to 1947, Mills was a critic for *Modern Music*. In 1944, his String Quartet no. 3 (1943) was awarded the Roth String Quartet Prize.

On March 14, 1944, Mills was baptized according to the rite of the Roman Catholic Church (he was born Protestant), a conversion reflected in many of his compositions. During 1945, for example, he composed *Thirty Penitential Preludes*, for piano solo; *The Fourth Joyful Mystery*, for two violins and piano; *Sacred Canticle* no. 4, "The Canticle of the Sun," for voice and piano. But the year of 1945 saw the writing of many works that were nonreligious. These included four piano sonatinas, three sonatinas for violin solo, and the score for a modern dance work, *John Brown*, choreographed by Eric Hawkins. This work, performed by Hawkins and Will Hare, was given its premiere by Martha Graham's Modern Dance Company on May 16, 1945, in New York.

Many of Mills's best compositions came in the 1950s. Theme and Variations, for orchestra (1951), was introduced on November 8, 1951, by the New York Philharmonic under Dimitri Mitropolous, who had commissioned it. Olin Downes, in the *New York Times*, reported that this piece "made a strong impression because of the forthrightness, virility and color of the music. . . . The theme sings and foliates in expressive ways. The fugue is written with conviction and direction and the instrumentation is expert." Following this premiere, this work was per-

formed by the Cleveland Orchestra under George Szell in 1953 and by the Cincinnati Symphony under Max Rudolf in 1959–60. In the spring of 1954, *The Ascension Cantata* for a cappella chorus with tenor solo (1953–54) was awarded the first prize of the Church of Ascension, New York City, and given its premiere performance there. *Prologue and Dithyramb*, for string quartet (1951), which the Cleveland Chamber Music Society commissioned and introduced, was transcribed for full string orchestra in 1954 and in that version was introduced in New York with Jonel Perlea conducting on March 8, 1955; it was subsequently performed by the Radio Orchestra of Zurich, Switzerland, Jacques Monod conducting. During the American bicentennial year, it was played on all leading radio stations in North and South Carolina as part of the Exxon Parade of American Music. Ross Parmenter in the *New York Times* described it as follows: "The prologue is a slightly mournful opening that moves slowly and flowingly. The dithyramb is lively and rhythmically intricate." A Concertino, for oboe and strings (1956), was commissioned by the oboist Harold Gomberg. *Crazy Horse Symphony* (1958), written in tribute to the Sioux Indian Chief named Chief Crazy Horse, was given its first hearing in Cincinnati on November 28, 1958, Max Rudolph conducting the Cincinnati Symphony. In the *Cincinnati Enquirer*, Arthur Darack called it "a good symphony. . . . The work is serious, has a firm but somewhat cool and distant melodic element and a hot-blooded harmonic and rhythmic undercurrent, as befits a bold warrior. It is music that 'takes' instantly, though it is not exactly old hat. But it is not high hat either; that is, it does not indulge in any obscure academic combinations or any unusual pretensions toward what it is not."

In 1952, Mills was awarded a Guggenheim Fellowship. He served as acting chairman of the composition department at the Manhattan School of Music in New York (1953–54). During many of the subsequent years he devoted one day each week to give private instruction in composition to talented students. In 1957 he contributed the music for an art film *On the Bowery*, which won grand prizes from both the Edinburgh and Venice film festivals.

Without totally abandoning his former diatonic style or classical approach, Mills has shown increasing interest in dodecaphony in his later compositions. Among the more important of his later works are: Piece for Recorder, Flute and Strings (1964), aired on a CBS-TV program dealing with creativity called "Inspiration"; *In a Mule Drawn Wagon*, for full string orchestra (1968), written in memory of Martin Luther King; Sonata no. 4, for violin and piano (1970; Detroit, May 22, 1974); Sonata no. 5, for violin and piano (1975); *Symphonic Ode*, for string orchestra (1976), written on a grant from the National Endowment for the Arts in commemoration of the American bicentennial; Sonata no. 6, for violin and piano (1977); and Symphony no. 5, for string orchestra (1980), which is a completely serial work in all four movements. The last of these was also composed under a grant from the National Endowment for the Arts.

THE COMPOSER SPEAKS: My method of composition varies from piece to piece but certain fundamental work habits in the creative process remain unchanged. I first decide what kind of piece I want to write (a sonata-allegro, theme and variations, fugue, rondo or other) and choose the tonality. All of my music is tonal, even my serial works. When this is clear I'm ready to start some detailed work which occurs in four consecutive steps. At first I do pencil sketches of thematic materials (themes, subjects, harmonies, contrapuntal treatments, etc.). Then I make a pencil version of the composition in compressed form (two or more staves resembling a piano reduction). After that comes the final score in pencil, for full orchestra (or whatever), followed by the ink score for use.

Workshop items like the above, factual as they may be, are seldom able to expose the highly personal mysteries of the creative process. For example, unless one is a Mozart, the work patterns must undergo numerous revisions in certain compositions to arrive at a version that approximates one's search for a particular perfection of detail. Any composer worth his salt must study Beethoven's sketches and learn to apply an equal measure of love and patience to his own musical needs.

And every composition will disclose its own laws and nature which must be perceived and discovered. Composers always need to change and grow, and to expand their craft constantly. Who knows what unforeseen demands the next work will require? Spiritual techniques have a large place in the total arsenal of musical skills, and require as much practice and polish as the less subtle uses of vocal and instrumental writing. As Schoenberg asked: "Does the work contain an idea?," and as Beethoven taught: "Music should strike fire from the hearts of men."

If I am asked by a student: "What is the highest and most important element in music," I answer, "Melody."

PRINCIPAL WORKS: 11 piano sonatinas (1942–45), of which only 1, 3, 4, 6, and 9 are available; 6 violin sonatas (1940–77); 5 string quartets (1939–59); 5 symphonies (1940–80); 3 sonatinas for violin solo (1945); 2 suites for solo violin (1942, 1944); 2 cello sonatas (1940, 1942); 2 piano sonatas (1941, 1942).

Piano Trio (1941); Chamber Concerto, for ten instruments (1946); *John Brown,* music for modern dance (1945); *Thirty Penitential Preludes,* for piano (1945); *Sacred Canticle* no. 4, "Canticle of the Sun," for voice and piano (1945); *The Fourth Joyful Mystery,* for two violins and piano (1946); English horn Sonata (1946); Piano Concerto (1948); *Concerto ser-*

eno, for woodwind octet (1948); Theme and Variations, for orchestra (1951); *Prologue and Dithyramb,* originally for string quartet, also for strings (1951); Toccata, for orchestra (1952); Prelude and Fugue, for orchestra (1953); *The Ascension Cantata,* for a cappella chorus, with tenor solo (1954); "The True Beauty," madrigal for a cappella solo voices (1953); Concertino, for oboe and strings (1956); *The First Thanksgiving,* cantata for chorus and organ (1956); *The Centaur and the Phoenix,* for jazz ensemble (1960); *Summer Song,* for jazz ensemble (1960); Serenade for Winds and Strings (1961); Brass Quintet (1962); *The Brass Piano,* for brass sextet (1964); *Paul Bunyan Jump for Jazz Quintet* (1964); *In a Mule Drawn Wagon,* for full string orchestra (1968); Prelude and Allegro, for violin and piano (1966); *Sonata da chiesa,* for tenor recorder and harpsichord (1972); *The Five Moons of Uranus,* for tenor recorder and piano (1972); *Symphonic Ode,* for string orchestra (1976); *Duo Dialogue,* for tenor recorder and organ (1976).

BIBLIOGRAPHY: *BBDM;* Ewen, David, *American Composers Today* (N.Y., 1949).

Moevs, Robert Walter, b. La Crosse, Wis., December 2, 1920.

Though Moevs's music has changed through the years, it reveals a logical evolution. Under the Boulez influence he has become a modified serialist who has evolved a compositional technique he calls "systematic chromaticism," whereby various pitches of a tone row are exhausted but not according to a rigid process.

His maternal grandfather was the mayor of La Crosse for some twenty years. Moevs's mother was the musician in the family. She was a good amateur pianist and was the one who gave him his first piano lessons. Moevs's principal piano teacher in La Crosse, however, was Don Jonson, a one-armed pianist who had been personally assisted by Paderewski. At grade and high schools in La Crosse, Moevs served as pianist for choral groups and performances of operettas and small orchestras. Additionally, he presented concerts as a pianist after giving his first recital in 1929 at State Teachers College.

In 1938, he entered Harvard University where, during the next four years, on a scholarship, he studied composition with Walter Piston, orchestration with Edward Burlingame Hill and choral writing with Archibald T. Davison, and received his bachelor of arts degree, *cum laude,* in 1942. He served his compositional apprenticeship during these college years by writing songs, chamber music, his first orchestral work, Passacaglia (1941), and *Peace,* for a cappella women's chorus to his own English text (1942).

Between 1942 and 1947, during World War II, Moevs was a pilot in the U.S. Air Force, serving as officer in the U.S. Military Mission to the Allied Control Commission in Rumania from February 1945 until the dissolution of that commission in October 1947. While still in service, Moevs attended the Écoles d'art at Fontainebleau in France in 1946, studying composition there with Nadia Boulanger. When, as first lieutenant, he was discharged from military service in 1947, he continued to study composition with Nadia Boulanger at the Paris Conservatory, which he attended for four years. In Paris his *Youthful Song*, for voice and piano (1940–51) to an original text was performed in 1951 (and again heard in Rome in 1954 and Cambridge in 1955). Among other works completed in Paris were *The Bacchantes*, for a cappella chorus (1947), first performed in Paris in 1949, Nadia Boulanger conducting; the ballet, *Endymion* (1948); a piano sonata (1950), privately commissioned, introduced by the composer in Paris and performed by Beveridge Webster in Town Hall, New York, in December 1952, with other performances following in many cities in Europe and the United States; Overture for Orchestra (1950; Wisconsin, July 20, 1963); and *Fantasia sopra un motivo*, for piano (1951), introduced in New York on February 12, 1962, and then given frequent hearings in major cities in Europe and the United States.

In 1952, Moevs completed two major works. *Canta Sacra*, to a Latin text from the Easter liturgy, was commissioned by the Creative Concerts Guild of Boston and was introduced there by the Chorus Pro Musica on March 24, 1953, after which it was performed in New York on April 15, 1955, under Margaret Hillis's direction, and in Rome in May 1955 by the Italian Radio Chorus. On still another commission, this one from the Koussevitzky Music Foundation, he wrote Fourteen Variations for Orchestra, which, after being introduced in New York in the fall of 1955, was performed by the Symphony of the Air conducted by Leonard Bernstein on April 6, 1956, was given five times by the Boston Symphony in 1957, again with Bernstein conducting, when it was also broadcast over the NBC radio network, and by the National Orchestra of Colombia in 1959.

In 1951–52, Moevs was back at Harvard to earn his master degree in music. Later in 1952 he was awarded the Prix de Rome for a three-year residence at the American Academy in Rome. In Bologna, on October 1, 1953, he married Maria Teresa Marabini, an archaeologist who, after raising their two children, became professor of Italian and archaeology at Douglass College at Rutgers University in New Brunswick, N.J. One of the works Moevs completed in Italy was Three Symphonic Pieces (1954–55), which the League of Composers had commissioned for the fortieth anniversary of the Cleveland Orchestra and which that orchestra under George Szell introduced on April 10, 1955.

Moevs was appointed instructor of music at Harvard in 1955. He remained at Harvard until 1963, having risen to the post of assistant professor in 1957, serving as director of undergraduate studies between 1958 and 1960, and as curator of the Ancient Instruments Collection. In 1956 he received an award from the National Institute of Arts and Letters.

With String Quartet (1957), first performed by the Claremont Quartet at Harvard University on February 17, 1960, Moevs began to develop his technique of intervallic control complemented by, or worked out against, balanced pitch distribution. "This duplex consideration," he explains, "brought about a systematic chromaticism that I have found more musically sensitive than the determinism of orthodox serialism." This quartet, as Bruce Archibald wrote in *Musical Newsletter*, "is 'neo-classic' and 'tonal' in ways similar to the middle Bartók quartets, four and five especially. Each of the four arch-shaped movements attains a shattering climax: the drama of the third movement in particular."

He developed and refined his technique in a work that created such furor when it was introduced by the Boston Symphony under Richard Burgin on February 13, 1960, that it was reported on the front pages of Boston newspapers. This composition was *Attis*, Part I, for tenor solo, chorus, percussion, and orchestra (1958) to a Latin text by Catullus, which the Boston Symphony and Charles Munch had commissioned under a Ford Foundation grant. "If the audience had been French and the year 1913," reported Harold Rogers in the *Christian Science Monitor*, "the world premiere . . . would have caused a greater scandal that that of Stravinsky's *Le sacre du printemps*." Rogers then went on to describe the work. "*Attis*, as a piece of musical architecture is made up of elements of awe-inspiring design. Fierce tensions are built by moving gigantic chords chromatically, either in parallel or contrary motion. Brasses growl, bite and snarl. Tempos remain largely in flux, breathing, one might say, when breath is needed. Percussion is earthy, exotic, maddening. All these elements are employed to create a mood of violent paganism, a tonal illustration in the most vivid terms possible of the ancient book rites of a cult dedicated to the worship of Attis and Cybele. . . . He chose a strong subject on which to paint a shocking scene and what is more he did it with stupefying success." *Attis*, Part II, was written in 1963; the full score was completed in 1980.

In the Concerto for Piano, Orchestra, and Percussion (1960), commissioned by Andrew Heath, Moevs proved once again, as he had done in *Attis*, that he was no cerebralist whose compositional processes were rigidly controlled by a system. This was music made compellingly dramatic by its variety of sonoric and rhythmic effects and by the inexorable logic of its structure. A three-note progression and a rhythmic pattern heard at the beginning served as the embryo out of which the entire composition grew. In its first version, this concerto was performed on March 26, 1961, by the Connecticut Symphony and the Manhattan Percussion Ensemble conducted by Jonel Per-lea. In 1968, using the original material, the compos-er prepared a new polymetric version with amplified instruments; random elements were then introduced that ultimately disintegrated all but the underlying structure. After further changes in 1977, the concerto received its first performance on June 15, 1978, by the Milan RAI Orchestra, Zoltan Pesko conducting and Daniel Rivera soloist. The American premiere followed in New York on April 20, 1981, performed by Wanda Maximilien and The Orchestra of the Twentieth Century conducted by Arthur Weisberg.

Moevs was composer-in-residence at the Ameri-can Academy in Rome in 1960–61. In 1963–64, he was the recipient of a Guggenheim Fellowship. In 1964 he left Harvard to become assistant professor at Rutgers University, where he has remained since that time, having been elevated to full professorship in 1968, New Brunswick Chairman of Music in 1974, and graduate director in 1977.

Between 1963 and 1970, Moevs's three most sig-nificant compositions were *Et Occidentem Illustram* (1964), *Musica da camera* I (1965), and *A Brief Mass* (1968). The first of these, for chorus and or-chestra, was commissioned by Rutgers University for its bicentennial celebration, and its premiere was given by the Boston Symphony and the Rutgers Uni-versity Choir conducted by Erich Leinsdorf on Feb-ruary 24, 1967. The text is partly Latin, from the commission of the Dutch Reformed church to Theo-dore Frelinghuysen in 1755 to go to Holland to raise money for the seminary (the future Rutgers) and partly from Dante's *Inferno*, Canto 26 (the exhorta-tion of Ulysses). "Moevs had devised an exciting dec-lamation for these words," said Michael Steinberg in the *Boston Globe*. "They are given in small units that become smaller and more widely separated as the work goes on. Much of the choral writing is sharply, almost percussively, declamatory, but Moevs also makes a grand and expressive effect with long sustained lines. . . . All this is underlined, surrounded, articulated by imagnatively conceived orchestral writing. . . . *Et Occidentem Illustram* is a strong and gripping work of considerable individu-ality. It is also entrancing as a piece of virtuoso writ-ing for chorus and orchestra."

Musica da camera I, for chamber ensemble, was written for and first performed by the Contemporary Chamber Ensemble in New York on April 11, 1966, and then presented by the New York Philharmonic at a Boulez "Encounter" concert on October 29, 1971. The composer explains that this work begins with Henry James's *The Turn of the Screw*, with its country-park setting in the afternoon, a place of ap-parent serenity but also of mysterious foreboding, whose stillness is interrupted only by the call of a bird. The music was made up of twelve sections, each averaging about a minute. Sections VIII to XII were inversions, or the pitch complements, of sections I–V in reverse order, an inverted mirror image, somewhat

condensed. Section VII actually telescoped section VI, arriving at the climactic point when the percus-sion reached the foreground. Only at the beginning and the end were all twelve pitches heard. Through-out the work each pitch absents itself from one or another section to generate a migrating negative cen-ter.

A Brief Mass, scored for chorus, organ, vibra-phone, guitar and double bass, was written for the National Meeting of Catholic Commission on Intel-lectual and Cultural Affairs held at Rutgers on May 1, 1969. Bruce Archibald said that it was "a very accessible work, not simply in that it delights the ear and conveys a quiet solemnity but in that its pitch content can be studied with the ear as well as the mind." What Archibald said of *Et Occidentem Illus-tram* applies equally to this later work. "Distinctive to this work . . . is the sense of tradition, a sense of shape and line that is not a radical departure but a continuity of Western music from Josquin to Bach to Stravinsky. There is no break with the past."

Among Moevs's later works is *Main-Traveled Roads*, for orchestra (1973), which is really an exten-sion of the Three Symphonic Pieces of 1954–55. Moevs took this title from that of a collection of sto-ries by the Wisconsin writer Hamlin Garland, but Moevs was not concerned with a geographical or lit-erary road but a musical one, especially that built by the great musical masters of the past. Here Moevs sought a rapprochement between the musical past and the present. Material common to both eras was given serialized patterns. Commissioned by the Wis-consin American Revolution Bicentennial Commis-sion, *Main-Traveled Roads* was written for the Mil-waukee Symphony Orchestra, which first performed it on February 9, 1974, with Kenneth Schermerhorn conducting.

Ludi Praeteriti: Games of the Past, for two pianos (1976; New Brunswick, N.J., October 16, 1976), is a curiosity among Moevs's later compositions in that the composer here adapted a systematic chromaticism to 18th-century procedures. The main intervallic material was heard in the introductory Adagio. Out of this grew a theme and three countersubjects which were manipulated in the typical ways of imitation, canon, inversion, augmentation, mirror, stretto. The music gradually worked its way from the lowest to the highest register. "It is an old game," the compos-er says, "but it is a game that can plumb deeper sub-strata." *Crystals*, for solo flute (1979), used transpo-sitions of a symmetrical nonoctave scale that ex-tended over the entire range of the instrument. The Piano Trio (1981), commissioned by the Naumburg Foundation, was premiered on April 28, 1981, in New York by the New Arts Trio.

Moevs was a member of the jury for the Prix de Rome in composition in 1956 and 1962, and in 1960–61 he was on the executive committee of the American section of the International Society for Contemporary Music. He was also a founding member of the American Society of University Composers. In 1978 he received the Stockhausen International Prize in composition in Italy for his new version of the Piano Concerto. He has made numerous appearances as concert and ensemble pianist in the United States and Europe, often in performances of his own music.

THE COMPOSER SPEAKS: Intervallic control has been of paramount importance, for both expressive and stylistic purposes, in my music from the very beginning. In works prior to the String Quartet (1957), tonal centers are firmly established. Later, the choice of intervals, while remaining strictly determined, becomes more flexible and insistence on tonal centers shifts to an equalized, or balanced, distribution of the two chromatic pitches. The first step was already taken in 1949 with the canon of the Piano Sonata. From the String Quartet on, it led with increasing evidence to a new amalgam of interval and pitch which I call systematic chromaticism. This process reached maturity in two choral works, *Itaque Ut* (1959) and *Et Nunc Reges* (1963).

PRINCIPAL WORKS: Piano Sonata (1950); *Fantasia sopra un motivo,* for piano (1951); *Pan: Music for Solo Flute* (1951); *Cantata Sacra,* for baritone solo, men's chorus, flute, four trombones, and timpani (1952); Fourteen Variations, for orchestra (1952); Three Symphonic Pieces (1954–55); String Quartet (1957); *Attis* I, for tenor solo, chorus, percussion, and orchestra (1958); *Itaque Ut,* for a cappella chorus (1959); Concerto for Piano, Orchestra, and Percussion (1960; second polymetric version 1968–1977); *Variazioni sopra una melodia,* for viola and cello (1961); *Et Nunc Reges,* for women's chorus, flute, clarinet, bass clarinet (1963); *Attis* II, for soprano and tenor soli, chorus, percussion, and orchestra (1963); *Et Occidentem Illustram,* for chorus and orchestra (1964); *Musica da camera* I, for chamber ensemble (1965); *A Brief Mass,* for chorus, organ, vibraphone, guitar, and double bass (1968); *Heptachronon,* for solo cello (1969); *B-A-C-H, Es ist genug,* organ prelude (1970); *Phoenix,* for piano (1971); *Musica da camera* II, for chamber ensemble (1972); *Main-Traveled Roads,* Symphonic Piece no. 4 (1973); *The Aulos Player,* for soprano solo, two choruses and two organs (1975); *Ludi Praeteriti: Games of the Past,* for two pianos (1976); *Una collana musicale,* for piano (1977); *Epigram,* for voice and piano (1978); *Crystals,* for solo flute (1979); Piano Trio (1981).

BIBLIOGRAPHY: *BBDM; DCM; Musical Newsletter,* April 1971; *Who's Who in America, 1980–81.*

Moore, Douglas Stuart, b. Cutchogue, N.Y., August 10, 1893; d. Greenport, Long Island, N.Y., July 25, 1969.

Moore consistently favored a 19th-century Teutonic style that was tonal, consonant, lyrical, occasionally polymodal, whose only concession to modernism was in the use of discords for contrast. His strength lay in works whose subject matter was indigenously American, to which he provided a rhythmic and melodic language modeled after American popular, folk, military, and even hymnal music, but without resorting to actual quotations except in rare instances. Moore received the Pulitzer Prize in music in 1951.

He was a descendant of Thomas Moore, who had come to Long Island from Connecticut in 1640 to found the township of Southold, the oldest English-speaking settlement in New York State. For nine generations after that the Moores were inhabitants of Long Island. The house where Douglas Moore was born in Cutchogue remained his residence until his death.

His parents were literary people, his father, Stuart Hull Moore, the editor of one of America's earliest women's magazines (*Ladies World*). His mother, Myra Drake Moore, a descendant of both Miles Standish and John Alden, was also an editor. As a child, Moore showed such interest in his mother's piano playing that she soon turned him over to a local teacher. Though he detested exercises and was lax about practicing, he kept at the piano well through his boyhood years. His early academic schooling took place mainly at the Hotchkiss School in Long Island. There he met and became a friend of Archibald MacLeish's. Without having received any training in music theory, Moore set a few of MacLeish's poems to music in 1910, his earliest compositions.

In 1911, Moore entered Yale University for a liberal arts course. For the first three years his sole activity in music there was to write popular songs. One of these, "Naomi, My Restaurant Queen," written when he was a freshman, became his first piece of music to be published. After that he wrote school songs. "Good Night, Harvard," a football song, became popular with Yale students.

In his third year at Yale, Moore entered the harmony class of David Stanley Smith, and that same year he was able to write incidental music for a college production of *Quentin Durward,* which earned the praise of Horatio Parker, professor of composition at Yale. On Parker's encouragement, Moore attended his composition class during Moore's last undergraduate year. It was mainly because of Parker's influence that Moore began to nurse the ambition to become a musician. Upon receiving the bachelor of arts degree in 1915, Moore spent an additional two years at Yale in postgraduate work, mainly to continue the study of composition with Parker. In 1917, Moore received his bachelor of music degree.

That year, after America's entry into World War I, Moore enlisted in the navy, serving as lieutenant junior grade aboard the U. S. S. *Murray.* To entertain his "buddies" he would write popular songs, some of them with ribald lyrics. One of these, "Destroyer Life," gained considerable circulation among navy men.

With a modest inheritance from his father, who died just before the end of the war, Moore was able to continue music study in Paris following his discharge from military service in 1919. He spent a year attending the Schola Cantorum, studying composition with Vincent d'Indy and organ with Charles Tournemire. In 1920, he made a brief return to the United States to marry Emily Bailey on September 16, 1920, with whom he subsequently had two daughters. Then, for an additional year, he was back in Paris, this time to study composition with Nadia Boulanger.

In 1921, Moore was appointed organist, lecturer, and director of musical activities at the Art Museum in Cleveland. During the four years he held this post he also was organist at Adelbert College at Western Reserve University (1923–25), and a composition student of Ernest Bloch's at the Cleveland Institute in 1924. Moore's first concert work in a design larger than the song form came during this period, when four art masterpieces in the museum provided him with the subject for an orchestral suite, *Four Museum Pieces* (1922). He originally wrote it for organ before transcribing it for orchestra, conducting its premiere performance in 1924 with the Cleveland Orchestra.

Friendship with the poet Vachel Lindsay gave him a new direction in his music. It was Lindsay who encouraged him to seek out American scenes and life as material for composition. Moore's first significant attempt to create musical Americana came with his orchestral suite, *The Pageant of P. T. Barnum* (1924), introduced by the Cleveland Orchestra on April 15, 1926, with which Moore realized his first success. Here Moore described Barnum's boyhood ("Boyhood in Bethel"), simulating the sounds of country bands and fiddles, since this was the music with which young Barnum was most familiar. In the second movement, "Joyce Heath" (Joyce Heath being a 160-year-old black woman who was Barnum's first attraction), Moore interpolated a reminder of the spiritual "Nobody Knows De Trouble I've Seen." For another Barnum attraction, "General and Mrs. Tom Thumb," American military music was parodied in the third section. The sounds of flute recalled Jenny Lind, one of Barnum's most sensational attractions. The suite ended with "Circus Parade" in boisterous music rich with the sounds of a calliope. "Moore paints in brilliant colors the American scene of the 1860s without resorting to period stylization or naïve archaism," wrote James Rogers in the *Cleveland Plain Dealer*. "He has recreated the charming simplicity and warm humor and spirit of the Currier and Ives prints."

In 1925, Moore became affiliated with the American Laboratory Theater in New York. For that group he prepared incidental music for *Much Ado*

about Nothing (November 18, 1927), and Robert Sherwood's *The Road to Rome* (January 31, 1927). Paul Rosenfeld was so impressed with these scores that he was led to inquire in his book *An Hour with American Music* (1929) whether Moore "is not the most competent and tasteful composer of incidental music among Americans."

Later in 1925, on the strength of *The Pageant of P. T. Barnum*, Moore received a Pulitzer traveling fellowship enabling him to make a return visit to Europe. In 1926, he was appointed instructor of music at Columbia University. During the next quarter of a century his classes influenced an entire generation of music students as he rose to assistant professorship in 1926, associate professorship in 1928, was head of the music department in succession to Daniel Gregory Mason between 1940 and 1962, and MacDowell Professor of Music from 1943 to 1962. In 1960, the Society of Older Graduates cited him as "a great teacher." Moore retired in 1962, becoming professor emeritus, but for some years after that he continued to give courses in music appreciation.

Moby Dick, a tone poem for orchestra (1928), and *Overture on an American Tune*, for orchestra, originally named *Babbitt* (1931), were two more Moore compositions in which he tapped American subjects. But Moore also began writing music in a nonprogrammatic, nonfolkloristic vein, developing a style that was at times polymodal, at times passingly dissonant, but which never neglected the melodic and rhythmic line. His first attempt at writing chamber music was the Violin Sonata (1929). He followed this with his first symphony, "A Symphony of Autumn" (1930), and his only String Quartet (1933).

In 1934, Moore was awarded a Guggenheim Fellowship. Taking leave from Columbia, he now completed his first opera, *White Wings* (1934–35). It was based on Philip Barry's play about the resistance of street cleaners, raised in the age of the horse, to the burgeoning importance of the automobile. Introduced on February 9, 1949, in Hartford, Conn., by the Opera Department of the Julius Hartt School of Music fourteen years after it was written, it was described by Allen Bole in the *New York Times* as "full of charm, color, even beautiful nonsense. Moore . . . had provided an intelligent, agreeable score, conventional in content and orchestration, but never dull."

Moore's first successful opera came several years later. It was *The Devil and Daniel Webster* (1938), a one-act work with libretto by Stephen Vincent Benét based on his own short story (which was also used for a distinguished motion picture released in 1941 starring Walter Huston and Edward Arnold). This was a New England fantasy with Faustian overtones. Its principal character, a New Hampshire farmer, sells his soul to the devil to get enough money to marry the girl he loves. When the devil, in the body of a Boston attorney, comes to claim the soul, Daniel Webster uses his eloquence before a jury of traitors and blackguards of the distant past to save the farmer. Moore called this a folk opera because "it is legendary in its subject matter and simple in musical expression," as he explained. "We have tried to make an opera in which the union of speech, song and instrumental music will communicate the essence of the dramatic story, enhanced but not distorted." In the *American Scholar* Alfred J. Frankenstein agreed that Moore and Benét had succeeded. He called his opera "as artful, eloquent and effective a statement of the principles of American democracy as has ever been written." The first production was given in New York City on May 18, 1939, Fritz Reiner conducting.

Before undertaking his next opera, Moore completed a number of major concert works and a powerful score for a documentary film. The latter was *Power and Land* (1940), which Moore subsequently adapted into an orchestral suite, *Farm Journal* (1947), which was commissioned by the Little Orchestra Society and performed by that organization under Thomas Scherman on January 19, 1948. Among other concert works of this period were: *Village Music*, a suite for small orchestra (1941), premiered in New York on December 18, 1941, Dean Dixon conducting; a tone poem, *In Memoriam* (1943), written in memory of the young who died in World War II, given its first performance in Rochester, N.Y., on April 27, 1944, and then heard at a concert of the New York Philharmonic under Artur Rodzinski in January 1945; *Prayer for the United Nations*, for alto solo, chorus, and orchestra (1943), text by Stephen Vincent Benét using words by President Franklin D. Roosevelt, written for the Treasury Department; and most significantly the Symphony no. 2 in A major (1945). That symphony, dedicated to Stephen Vincent Benét, received its first performance in Paris on May 5, 1946, under Robert Lawrence's direction, with an American premiere following in Los Angeles on January 16, 1947, conducted by Alfred Wallenstein. Soon after, the symphony was heard in New York performed by the NBC Symphony under Wallenstein on May 17, 1947; it received honorable mention from the Music Critics Circle Award. Bruno Walter conducted it with the New York Philharmonic in a performance on February 19, 1948. Moore explained that this symphony, his most ambitious work for orchestra, was "an attempt to write in clear, objective, modified, classical style, with emphasis upon rhythmic and melodic momentum rather than upon sharply contrasted themes or dramatic climaxes. There is no underlying program, although the mood of the second movement was suggested by a short poem by James Joyce which deals with music heard at the coming of twilight."

Moore returned to the music-dramatic stage in 1950 after an eleven year absence. In all that time he had failed to find a libretto capable of arousing and feeding his musical imagination. He finally came upon such a text in O. E. Rölvaag's novel, *Giants in the Earth*, describing the settling of the Dakotas by Norwegians. It had, Moore said, "everything—an American theme (and I liked the Norwegian overtones, too), drama, sweep, touches of humor." Arnold Sundgaard prepared the libretto, and under the sponsorship of the Columbia Theater Associates at Columbia University the opera was introduced on March 28, 1951. Here Moore once again made use of a formal structure which allowed for opulent arias, choral pages, an abundance of concert pieces and dance sequences. In the concerted pieces, said Olin Downes in the *New York Times*, "Mr. Moore has written dexterously and to the point. And there are moments when the orchestra takes a hand, paints a scene, as in the fine opening stages of the score, with the horn solo and musical implication of the distances of the boundless plain." A decade later, composer and librettist revised their opera.

Despite the fact that *Giants in the Earth* received the Pulitzer Prize in music in 1951, it was not Moore's most successful opera. That prestige must go to *The Ballad of Baby Doe* (1956), commissioned by the Koussevitzky Music Foundation to honor the centennial of Columbia University. Its premiere took place in Central City, Col., on July 7, 1956, after which it acquired permanence in the American operatic repertoire through numerous revivals. John Latouche's libretto (written in prose) was based on history during the gold rush days of the late 19th-century in Leadville, Col. Baby Doe is a blond beauty from Wisconsin who marries a silver baron. When he is made destitute by the panic of 1893, she remains faithful to him, ending up alone in an impoverished shack on the outskirts of a worthless mine her husband has left her, where she freezes to death in 1935. Moore filled his opera with singable melodies and graceful ensemble numbers sometimes popular in style, sometimes in a folk vein, and sometimes operatic, with supple, well-spaced dramatic recitatives in which the speech patterns of the period are gracefully recreated, all supported by a rich orchestral foundation. In the *New Yorker*, Winthrop Sargeant called it "a sort of declaration of independence—independence from all the fashionable highbrow fiddle-faddle and mysterious technical mumbo-jumbo that during the past forty years have tended to reduce the art to a feeble caricature of itself. Mr. Moore . . . has renounced all this practically learned clutter and returned to fundamentals. . . . The result is a completely enchanting work of art—one that points to a bright future in which people will attend contemporary opera not out of grim sense of cultural duty but simply because it is so infectious that they can't bear to stay away." On April 3, 1957, *The Ballad of Baby Doe* was produced by the New York City Opera with Beverly Sills in the title role, the first of many revivals by that company. The Santa Fe Opera presented it in Berlin and Belgrade in 1961.

Though Moore's later operas never duplicated the

triumph of *The Ballad of Baby Doe*, they continued to reveal his skill in producing American operas with melodic scores pleasurable to the ear and effective in recreating atmospheric backgrounds, developing moods and characterizations, and realizing highly effective theater. *The Wings of the Dove* (1961), text by Ethan Ayer, based on the Henry James novel, was written on a grant from the Ford Foundation and produced by the New York City Opera on October 12, 1961. *Carrie Nation* (1966)—libretto by William North Jayme, based on the life of the early 20th-century prohibitionist and hatchet-carrying crusader—was written for the centenary celebration of the University of Kansas in Lawrence, where it was premiered on April 28, 1966 (Kansas having been the state where Carrie Nation first launched her crusade against alcohol and where she ultimately died). The New York City Opera first produced it on March 28, 1968. Between these two operas, Moore, in one of his occasional indulgences into functional music, wrote a delightful one-act satire on radio and television "soap operas" to a libretto by Arnold Sundgaard, called *Gallantry*; CBS-TV produced it over its network on August 30, 1972, fourteen years after it had been premiered in New York on March 15, 1958.

In 1941, Moore was elected member of the National Institute of Arts and Letters, serving as its president from 1945 to 1953. In 1946 he was made member of the board of directors of the American Academy in Rome. From 1959 to 1962 he was president of the American Academy of Arts and Letters. He was also director of the American Society for Composers, Authors, and Publishers (ASCAP). Moore received honorary doctorates in music from Cincinnati Conservatory (1946) and the University of Rochester (1947), and an honorary doctorate in humane letters from Yale (1955).

Moore made numerous appearances as a guest conductor of major American orchestras. He was the author of *Listening to Music* (1932) and *From Madrigal to Modern Music* (1942).

THE COMPOSER SPEAKS: I feel very strongly that we are all of us overconscious today of the problem of idiom or esthetics. Most of us compose under the deathly fear of being either not modern enough or too modern. Too many of us worry about whether our music is properly a reflection of America, or suitably international, in order to please whatever faction impresses us most. The particular ideal which I have been striving to attain is to write music which will not be self-conscious with regard to idiom, and will reflect the exciting quality of life, tradition, and country which I feel all about me. . . .

If we happen to be romantically inclined, if we like a good tune now and then, if we still have a childish love for atmosphere, is it not well for us to admit the fact and try to produce something which we ourselves like?

PRINCIPAL WORKS: 2 symphonies (1930, 1945).

The Pageant of P. T. Barnum, suite for orchestra (1924); *Moby Dick*, tone poem for orchestra (1928); Violin Sonata (1929); *Overture on an American Tune*, originally entitled *Babbitt* (1931); String Quartet (1933); *White Wings*, chamber opera (1935); *The Headless Horseman*, one-act high school opera (1936); *The Devil and Daniel Webster*, one-act opera (1938); *Dedication*, for chorus (1938); *Dirge* (Passacaglia), for organ, 1939; *Village Music*, suite for small orchestra (1941); Wind Quintet (1942); *Three Divine Sonnets of John Donne*, for voice and piano (1942); *In Memoriam*, tone poem for orchestra (1943); *Prayer for the United Nations*, for alto solo, chorus and orchestra (1943); *Down East Suite*, for violin and piano or orchestra (1944); *Three Shakespearean Songs*, for voice and piano (1944); Clarinet Quintet (1946); *Farm Journal*, suite for chamber orchestra (1947); *The Emperor's New Clothes*, one-act opera for children (1948); *Giants in the Earth*, opera (1950); *Cotillion*, suite for orchestra (1952); Piano Trio (1953); *The Ballad of Baby Doe*, opera (1956); *Gallantry*, one-act television comic opera (1957); *The Wings of the Dove*, opera (1961); *The Greenfield Christmas Tree*, for vocal solos and chorus (1962); *Carrie Nation*, opera (1966).

BIBLIOGRAPHY: Ewen, David, *Composers Since 1900* (N.Y., 1969); Goss, Madeleine, *Modern Music Makers* (N.Y., 1952); Reagan, D. J., "Douglas Moore and His Orchestral Works" (doctoral thesis, Washington, D.C., 1972); *Modern Music*, May 1943; *Musical America*, August 1963; *New York Times*, July 1, 1962, July 28, 1969 (obituary).

Moross, Jerome, b. Brooklyn, N.Y., August 1, 1913.

American popular and folk idioms are basic to Moross's style, which has been consistently diatonic and consonant, gracious and readily assimilable in its lyricism, and strong-fibered in its rhythmic vigor.

He was a musical prodigy who could play the piano by ear when he was five. By the time he was eight, he was composing. For many years he studied the piano with Albert von Doenhoff. Moross was equally precocious in his academic schooling, graduating from De Witt Clinton High School when he was fifteen. As a high school student he played the piano at avant-garde concerts, performing music by Ives, Antheil, Schoenberg, and Ornstein, among others. Between 1929 and 1932 he attended New York University, where he studied with Philip James, Vincent Jones, and others. There, his friendship with such fellow students as Bernard Herrmann and Arthur Berger helped to open up for him the world of avant-garde music. They became part of a circle of young creative musicians known as the Young Composers Group and under the guiding ministrations of

Aaron Copland expanded their knowledge of new music.

During his senior year at New York University, Moross held a fellowship for the Juilliard School of Music, attending both schools simultaneously. At Juilliard, where he studied composition with Bernard Wagenaar, Moross had his first public performance. It came on February 13, 1932, in New York when Bernard Herrmann conducted the premiere of *Paeans*, for orchestra (1931). Henry Cowell thought so highly of it that he published the score in the New Music Edition of which he was editor. *Paeans* was the last of Moross's purely atonal and microtonal pieces he had been writing since he was sixteen. Later in 1931 Moross wrote *These Everlasting Blues*, for voice and chamber orchestra, an early example of Moross's interest in popularism; it was introduced early in 1933, Nicolas Slonimsky conducting.

Upon graduating from New York University in 1932 with the degree of bachelor of science in music education, Moross began supporting himself by playing the piano professionally and writing functional music for ballets and the theater. In 1934 he wrote the score for *Paul Bunyan*, a ballet introduced by Charles Weidman, and for a Broadway politically conscious revue, *Parade*, produced by the Theater Guild on May 20, 1935. Out of the score of *Parade* came an orchestral composition, *Biguine* (1934), premiered in New York over the CBS radio network on November 21, 1934, John Green conducting, before it was heard in the Broadway revue. *Biguine* was also published in New Music Edition.

Through Oscar Levant, Moross met George Gershwin, who invited him to play the piano in the pit orchestra of *Porgy and Bess* when it was nearing the end of its New York run in the spring of 1936 and to continue in that capacity when that folk opera went on a six-week tour. When *Porgy and Bess* was produced on the West Coast, Moross was engaged as assistant conductor and pianist, and to help train the principals, during the summer following Gershwin's death in 1937.

In 1937, Moross was commissioned by Ruth Page, the dancer, to prepare the music for the ballet *American Pattern* (1937), performed by her at the Chicago Opera in December 1937. For Ruth Page and the Federal Theater, Moross followed this score with the music for another ballet, *Frankie and Johnny* (1938), produced in New York in 1945. "*Frankie and Johnny*," Moross explains, "was a very early attempt to utilize voices and dancers, an idea I elaborated upon in subsequent ballets where the chorus and solo singers moved and performed simultaneously with the dancers." This score, in an intriguing popularist style, has become one of Moross's greatest successes. The ballet entered the repertoire of the Ballet Russe de Monte Carlo and the score has been performed by numerous orchestras at symphony concerts.

In 1938, on a commission from the Columbia Broadcasting System, Moross completed a new work for orchestra, *A Tall Story*, introduced over the CBS radio network on September 25, 1938, Howard Barlow conducting. On August 28, 1939, Moross married Hazel Abrams, then a stand-in for Sylvia Sidney in motion pictures. In February 1940 the Morosses moved to Hollywood, Calif., with their infant daughter (their only child). For the ensuing decade, Moross was busily engaged making orchestrations for the film music of such famous Hollywood composers as Franz Waxman, Adolph Deutsch, Frederick Hollander, and Hugo Friedhofer, among others. Escape from such routine, functional commitments came in the writing of his Symphony (1941–42), given its premiere in Seattle, Wash., on October 18, 1943, conducted by Sir Thomas Beecham and soon afterward performed by the Los Angeles Philharmonic under Alfred Wallenstein. This symphony had started out as a commission from CBS radio for a short orchestral piece. In fulfilling this commission, Moross composed a work based on the famous hobo tune "Midnight Special." Convinced that it required other music around it, Moross made it the third movement ("Invention") of his four-movement symphony, changing the very fast tempo of the song into a very slow melodic line.

Between 1945 and 1946, Moross wrote the music for three one-act ballet operas, all of the scenarios by John Latouche: *Willie the Weeper*, *The Eccentricities of Davy Crockett*, and *Riding Hood Revisited*. Together with an earlier ballet opera, *Susanne and the Elders*, which he had written in 1940–41 to a scenario by John Latouche, these were gathered under the umbrella of *Ballet Ballads*. They were first produced on May 9, 1948, on Broadway.

In 1947 and again in 1949, Moross received Guggenheim Fellowships. During the second, he took a recess from his Hollywood chores to write the music for an opera, *The Golden Apple* (1949–50). John Latouche's satirical text transferred the Homeric legend to the American town of Angel's Roost, where Ulysses became an American soldier home from the Spanish-American War; Penelope, his wife; and Helen, a farmer's daughter in love with Paris, a traveling salesman. The story moved briskly in song, lyrics, pantomime, and in the dances conceived by Hanya Holm. Out of this score came the song "Lazy Afternoon," the high point of the opera and a success outside of it. *The Golden Apple* opened Off Broadway on March 11, 1954, where it received accolades from the critics. Robert Coleman in the *New York Daily Mirror* called it "quite the most original and imaginative work of its kind to blaze across the theatrical horizon in many a moon." This success carried the opera into the Broadway sector five weeks later, where it was given the Drama Critics Award as the year's best musical.

In 1953, on a commission from Ruth Page, Moross completed writing one of his best scores, for the ballet *The Last Judgment*. Though never produced as a ballet, *The Last Judgment* received performances at symphony concerts. After that, the history of the Civil War in the form of a minstrel show became the material for a popular-styled opera, *Gentlemen, Be Seated!* (1955–56), libretto by Edward Eager. Its world premiere took place at the City Center in New York on October 10, 1963, Emerson Buckley conducting. This opera opened with a minstrel-show walk-around. Throughout the minstrel-show, the characters of Mr. Interlocuter, Mr. Tambo and Mr. Bones were present. The score was replete with songs and dance routines together with humor lifted from the joke books of that period. Several songs from this opera have been frequently heard in the concert hall, principally "Have You Seen Him," "I Can't Remember," and "Shiloh."

By 1950, Moross was able to give up the commercial orchestrations in Hollywood to write original film scores. The most successful motion pictures with his background music were: *The Proud Rebel* (1958), starring Alan Ladd and Olivia de Haviland; *The Big Country* (1958), starring Gregory Peck, become a film classic; *The Cardinal* (1963); *The War Lord* (1965), starring Charlton Heston; and *Rachel, Rachel* (1968). In 1965, Moross extracted the material from five of his film scores spanning the years from 1952 to 1965 for an orchestral concert suite, *Music for the Flicks*.

Since the mid-1960s, Moross, in his concert music, concentrated on chamber music, producing a number of sonatinas for various instruments between 1966 and 1970, and a Sonata, for piano duet with string quartet (1975). Within a larger format were a one-act opera, *Sorry, Wrong Number* (1974–77), based on the famous radio play by Lucille Fletcher, which was made into a motion picture starring Barbara Stanwyck, and a Concerto for Flute with String Quartet (1978), in all of which he continued to favor a style influenced by American popular idioms. The Sonata, for piano duet with string quartet, and the Concerto for Flute, with String Quartet, received their premiere performances in a recording released by Varèse-Sarabande in August 1979. In reviewing this recording for *High Fidelity/Musical America*, Irving Lowens wrote: "The two lively works . . . show him to be something of an American Poulenc, with the same crystal-clear handling of odd instrumental combinations, the same engagingly light touch, the same neatness and wit, the same spontaneous vigor. Then again, the simple, diatonic melodies and pervasive American rhythms give a curious, clean, outdoorsy feeling reminiscent of Copland in his folklike moods."

THE COMPOSER SPEAKS: In my teens I was interested in sounds per se, as so many composers are today. By my late twenties I found myself interested in communicating with my audience, and I still feel that way. I do feel that a composer should write not only to put down on paper what he feels, but in such a way that his audience experiences his emotions anew. It is a popular cliché to say that diatonic music and classical form are dead, but I disagree. In addition, the composer must reflect his landscape and mine is the landscape of America. I don't do it consciously, it is simply the only way I can write. It would be impossible for me to write in the so-called international style which has nothing to do with my experiences.

PRINCIPAL WORKS: *Paeans*, for orchestra (1931); *Those Everlasting Blues*, for voice and chamber orchestra (1932); *Biguine*, for orchestra (1934); *Paul Bunyan*, ballet (1934); *American Pattern*, ballet (1937); *Frankie and Johnny*, ballet (1937–38); *A Tall Story*, for orchestra (1938); *Guns and Castinets*, ballet (1939); *Ballet Ballads*: I. *Susanna and the Elders*, II. *Willie the Weeper*, III. *The Eccentricities of Davy Crockett*, IV. *Riding Hood Revisited* (1940–46); Symphony (1941–42); *Recitative and Aria*, for violin and piano (1943); *Variations on a Waltz*, for orchestra (1946); *The Golden Apple*, opera (1949–50); *The Last Judgment*, ballet (1953); *Gentlemen, Be Seated!*, opera (1955–56); *Music for the Flicks*, suite for orchestra (1965); Sonatina, for clarinet choir (1966); String Bass Sonatina (1967); Sonatina, for brass quintet (1968); Sonatina, for woodwind quintet (1970); *Sorry, Wrong Number*, one-act opera (1974–77); Sonata, for piano duet and string quartet (1975); Concerto for Flute with String Quartet (1978).

BIBLIOGRAPHY: *DCM*; Ewen, David, *American Composers Today* (N.Y., 1949); Reis, Claire, *Composers in America* (N.Y., 1947); *Who's Who in America, 1978–79*.

Moss, Lawrence Kenneth, b. Los Angeles, Calif., November 18, 1927.

As a student at the Eastman School of Music and later at the University of Southern California, Moss was considered by some of his teachers as too "radical" in his compositional methods, while in more recent years as a university professor some of his students regard him as too conservative. The truth lies midway between the two viewpoints. Without aligning himself to any "school" of composition, nor to the avant-garde movement, Moss has successfully utilized atonality, bitonality, a polyphony of "time effects" or moods and a modified form of the twelve-tone idiom. At the same time, without entering the camp of the neoclassicists, he has respected the values of the past. His writing has a strong lyricism, rhythmic energy, concentration of thought, and skillful structure.

His mother was a prominent artist who at one time was part owner of the avant-garde gallery, "Ferus," in Los Angeles, and his father was a successful lawyer. Though neither was trained in music, both loved it deeply; his father was the principal patron of the renowned series of contemporary music in Los Angeles called "Monday Evening Concerts." Both parents were highly supportive when young Moss began revealing an interest in music and sought to make it his career.

He began piano lessons when he was six. His first piano teacher was Rose Robinson, a friend of the family's. Later teachers included Beatrice Grosbayne and especially Victor Auer, with whom he worked through his undergraduate years. At John Marshall High School he first became interested in composition due to the influence of Morris Hutchins Ruger, a composer on the faculty who taught classes in harmony and composition. Among Moss's earliest influences were the traditional German composers, Brahms and Schumann particularly, as well as Sibelius, whose works he early came to know well through his father's library of recordings.

After graduating from high school in 1945, Moss attended Pomona College for one year (1946-47) and the University of California in Los Angeles for an additional year (1948-49) where he earned his bachelor of arts degree. In 1949 he studied composition with John Vincent. In an evening course with Ernst Krenek at Los Angeles City College he first became acquainted with twelve-tone music. In 1949-50 he attended the Eastman School of Music at Rochester, N.Y., where he studied composition with Bernard Rogers and Howard Hanson. Then, at the University of Southern California, which he reentered in 1951, he came under the influence of Leon Kirchner, his teacher in composition, and Ingolf Dahl, with whom he studied orchestration and conducting. His student years saw the production of a Suite, for orchestra (1950), a Fantasia, for piano (1952), and a Trio, for flute, violin, and cello (1953), the last of which received first prize in the National Federation of Music Clubs Contest in 1953. Stylistically, the Fantasia was heavily indebted to Kirchner; the Trio reflected the work he had done with Dahl.

As the recipient of a Fulbright Fellowship in 1953-54, Moss spent a year in Vienna, where, as he puts it, "I finally got the 'German' side of my psyche out of my system." He further reveals: "Ostensibly, I was in Vienna to work with Karl Schiske, the chief teacher of composition at the Akademie at the time. However, when I found that 'composition' would be rather dull exercises, I switched to conducting under Hans Swarowsky and others. At the same time, I continued to write on my own—including my Ph.D. thesis, a symphony—and to go to many operas and concerts as well as systematically visit all the homes and haunts of Viennese composers I could find." For a year and a half after that (1954-56) Moss served in the U.S. Army, stationed in Frankfurt, Germany, where he served as translator.

Between 1956 and 1958, Moss was an instructor of music at Mills College in Oakland, Calif. In 1957 he received his doctorate in music at the University of Southern California. On March 29, 1958, he married Graydon Hindley, then employed in the radiation laboratory of the University of California at Berkeley; they became the parents of four children.

In 1958, on the first of two Guggenheim Fellowships, Moss went to Italy, a trip which, he says, "I think as much as any event in my life formed my music." There he worked on a one-act comic opera, *The Brute* (1960), libretto by Eric Bentley based on a play by Chekhov. It was first produced on July 15, 1961, by the Yale Opera Workshop at Norfolk, Conn., and in 1970 was chosen to represent the United States at the International Youth Festival at Bayreuth, Germany. In the *New York Herald Tribune*, Eric Salzman spoke of it as follows: "The setting, cast in a light, delicate chromatic vein, has wit and line that sketches, accents, juxtaposes, and moves along with good humor and attractive brushed-in color. . . . An elegant, clever, and well-worked musical tale of great charm."

From 1960 to 1965, Moss was professor of music at Yale University; from 1965 to 1969 associate professor. He returned to Italy in 1964 on a Morse Fellowship from Yale to concentrate on writing a second opera, *The Queen and the Rebels* (1965), a three-act work with libretto by the composer based on Ugo Betti's play. It was given a partial performance (two acts, with a two-piano accompaniment) under Gunther Schuller's direction, and staged by Nathaniel Merrill, at Central City, Col., on August 14, 1972.

The decade between *The Queen and the Rebels* and Moss's next dramatic work, *Unseen Leaves* (1975), marks his emerging maturity as a composer. The more "traditional" Kirchner idioms give way to a synthesis of new influences (Webern, Dallapiccola, Debussy, electronic music) and new structural procedures.

A second Guggenheim Fellowship, in 1968, was once again spent in Italy, this time to work on two compositions: *Ariel*, for voice and orchestra (1969), which was commissioned by the Morse Foundation for the New Haven Symphony, and *Elegy*, for two violins and viola (1969), written in memory of his brother.

In 1969, Moss was appointed professor of music and chairman of the division of composition and theory at the University of Maryland, where he has remained since that time. In the 1970s, Moss became interested in electronic music, whose resources he tapped into ambitious multimedia productions. *Unseen Leaves* (1975), for soprano, oboe, magnetic tape, slides, and lights to a text by Walt Whitman, was written on a grant from the National Endowment for the Arts and given its world premiere at the Contemporary Music Forum at Washington, D.C., on October 20, 1975. In the *Washington Post*, Alan Kriegsman called it "an evocative collage. . . . Lawrence Moss has succeeded remarkably well in finding a fresh voice of his own. The work sounded impressively resourceful and imaginative." In reviewing a recording of this work, Robert Morgan in *High Fidelity/Musical America* found that Moss used "electronic sounds in interesting and subtle ways. The tape part is closely integrated . . . with the live music. . . . The structure . . . is clear and yet unpredictable." *Nightscape* (1978) was a multimedia production scored for soprano, instruments, dancer, tape, and slides, introduced on November 20, 1978. Other of Moss's works to employ electronics include *Auditions*, for woodwind quintet and tape (1971), first performance by the Dorian Quartet at a concert of the Chamber Music Society of Baltimore on January 28, 1973; *Evocation and Song*, for alto sax and tape (1972), first heard on June 4, 1972, at the American Music Festival in Washington, D.C.; and *Omaggio* II, for piano four hands and tape (1977), premiered on October 14, 1977.

Since 1970, Moss's most important works dispensing with magnetic tape were: *Paths*, for orchestra (1971), commissioned by the University of Chicago Symphony, which gave the premiere performance on May 22, 1971; Fantasy, for piano (1973), first performance in Washington, D.C., on March 11, 1973; and, most significantly, the String Quartet no. 2 (1975), commissioned by the Chamber Music Society of Baltimore to commemorate the American bicentennial, introduced by the Composers Quartet in Baltimore on January 25, 1976, and after that recipient of first prize in international competitions in Evian, France, and São Paulo, Brazil. *Symphonies*, for brass quintet and chamber orchestra (1977), was commissioned by the Annapolis Brass Quintet, which, with the collaboration of the American Camerata for New Music, gave the first performance in Annapolis on April 2, 1977.

In 1970, Moss received the Creative and Performing Arts Award from the University of Maryland; in 1978, his second grant from the National Endowment for the Arts; and in 1978 a General Research Board Grant from the University of Maryland.

THE COMPOSER SPEAKS: I find that in my most recent music I am trying to focus on what started me off in the first place—the expressive power of music—and at the same time to structure this music in ways which owe less and less to preordained schemes and more and more to the intuitive. Ideas well up from the subconscious, are channeled, focused by technique and artistic experience, and then continually processed and modified by the subconscious (this happens during time away from the work), to emerge as the finished composition when intuition says that nothing more can be done, that creative energies will be better spent on the next piece. The intensity of this struggle to be born often leaves me with a certain disgust for the new work—it seems so far short of the mark! Later, of course, I revise this opinion, and usually find that I prize just those portions, just those ideas, where I can remember the dictates of my sub-

conscious flowed most freely, where the anxious "I"—the willful, self-conscious artisan—was silent, and the mysterious, preverbal "me"—likened to Everyman—took over.

PRINCIPAL WORKS: 3 string quartets (1958, 1975, 1980).

Song of Solomon, for chorus and piano (1956); Violin Sonata (1959); *The Brute*, one-act comic opera (1960); *Scenes for Small Orchestra* (1961); *Four Scenes*, for piano (1961); *Three Rilke Songs*, for soprano and piano (1963); *Music for Five*, for brass quintet (1963); *Remembrances*, for eight instruments (1964); *The Queen and the Rebels*, opera (1965); *Omaggio* I, for piano four hands (1966); *Patterns*, for flute, clarinet, viola, and piano (1967); *Exchanges*, for two trumpets, trombone, two flutes, oboe, and percussion (1968); *Ariel*, for soprano and orchestra (1969); *Elegy*, for two violins and viola (1969); *Timepiece*, for violin, piano, percussion (1970); *Paths*, for orchestra (1970); *Auditions*, for woodwind quintet and magnetic tape (1971); *Evocation and Song*, for alto saxophone and magnetic tape (1972); Fantasy, for piano (1973); *Exercise*, for chorus and magnetic tape (1973); *Unseen Leaves*, multimedia production for soprano, oboe, magnetic tapes, slides, and lights (1975); *B. P., A Melodrama*, for trombone and piano (1976); *Symphonies*, for brass quintet and chamber orchestra (1977); *Omaggio* II, for piano four hands and magnetic tape (1977); *Little Suite*, for oboe and harpsichord (1978); *Nightscape*, a multimedia production for soprano, flute, clarinet, violin, percussion, dancer, tape, and slides (1978); Ballad, for piano (1978); *Hands Across the C*, for piano and tape (1979); *Omaggio* III, for eight flutes (1979); *Flight*, for brass quintet (1979); *Tubaria*, a "melodrama" for bass-baritone and tuba (1980).

BIBLIOGRAPHY: *BBDM*; *DCM*; *Who's Who in America, 1980–81*.

Mumma, Gordon, b. Framingham, Mass., March 30, 1935.

Though Mumma has written notated music for conventional instruments, he is best known for his intensive involvement with electronics. In addition to producing much studio-composed electronic compositions, he is one of the earliest composers utilizing live electronic music. He is the creator of "cybersonic" music in which acoustical and electronic media are controlled by circuits which integrate compositional and performing aspects of musical sound. He has also been a collaborator in the creation and development of multimedia art, including "Manifestations: Light and Sound," "Space Theater," and the Pepsi-Cola Pavilion at Expo '70 in Osaka, combining light, sound, and the projection of images.

Neither of his parents were professional musicians. His father, a manufacturer of specialized materials and packaging for retail commerce, enjoyed playing the harmonica and the cornet and was a collector of classical records through which Gordon received his earliest musical experiences. The only professional musician in the family was a distant relative, Archie A. Mumma, a violinist and composer of songs and piano pieces.

Both Gordon Mumma and his sister (who has become an excellent cellist and teacher of music) were encouraged by their parents when first they demonstrated an interest for music, "though during my childhood," Mumma says, "I suspect they had different aspirations for my career." Mumma began studying the French horn while attending junior high school in Hinsdale, Ill. "Hinsdale," he recalls, "had an extraordinary public school music program. My progress as a horn player was sufficiently rapid that I played in the high school orchestra there while still in junior high." In 1947, Mumma moved to Ferndale, Mich. There, in addition to continuing his horn lessons, he began studying the piano. "The teachers were very supportive of my interests, and encouraged my parents to find a first-rate horn teacher for me. That teacher, with whom I studied all through high school, was Kenneth Schultz of the Detroit Symphony."

Mumma was in his late teens when electronic music first began fascinating him. At that time, his father acquired a new phonograph for the newly introduced long-playing record, turning over his old machine to his son. "It became," Mumma says, "the victim of experimentation, resulting in my development of a primitive understanding of transducers, electronic amplification, and electronic shock. The local library supplied me with books of electrical subjects for budding boy engineers."

While attending Interlochen, a music camp in northern Michigan during the summer of 1949, Mumma began composition studies with Homer Keller. Mumma also became acquainted with the first oscilloscope in action through Roderick Dean Gordon, a musical acoustician on that faculty. "By his disciplined approach to the subject, he established the legitimacy of my pursuit of it. He introduced me to magnetic recording." Back home soon after that, one of his neighbors, a physician who played the bassoon, introduced him to radio-frequency electronics.

Mumma returned to the Interlochen camp each summer through 1952. "I had one extraordinary piano teacher there with whom I studied Bartók's *Mikrokosmos*. He was George Exon." In 1952 Mumma left high school without completing the normal four-year course to enroll in the University of Michigan for the continuation of his study of composition with Homer Kelly, who was on the faculty, and to major in theory and composition. At the university, Mumma began composing music and sound effects (through two tape recorders and sound-effects records) for plays produced by the university's theater department. "My success at making electronically generated music with these tape recorders was probably due to a precarious balance between my knowledge of some aspects of electronic circuitry."

Finding his involvement with the innovative performance arts and music composition more fulfilling than his work at the university, Mumma left it in 1954 to continue his musical activities in the cultural periphery of Ann Arbor. His interest in and knowledge of electronic music was enhanced in 1965 when he acquired disc recordings of *musique concrète* from France, electronic compositions from Cologne, and Ussachevsky's early electronic pieces. In 1958, with Robert Ashley, Mumma founded an electronic music studio in Ann Arbor—the Cooperative Studio for Electronic Music—with which he remained involved until 1966, by which time the studio was taken over by the university. By 1958, Mumma had written some notated instrumental and vocal pieces with which he was at least partially satisfied. They tended to be quite chromatic, with a notable equality between the twelve notes of the scale, his major preoccupation being with experimentation with serial counterpoint, often with considerable rhythmic complexity. But his major interest was in electronics. By 1958 he also produced his first large-scale electronic composition—music for an Ann Arbor production of Ionesco's *The Bald Soprano*. Other compositions for magnetic tape came soon thereafter, notably, Sinfonia, for twelve instruments and magnetic tape (1958-60; Ann Arbor, March 4, 1961), *Vectors* (1959), *Densities* (1960), *Mirrors* (1960), and *Epoxy* (1961). Then, as later, his electronic music was involved with a fairly large range of sound densities, and as wide a dynamic range as he could get on to magnetic tape.

Meanwhile, in 1957, with the collaboration of Robert Ashley and Milton Cohen (the latter an artist), Mumma embarked on his first experiments in a new esthetic medium they called "Manifestations: Light and Sound," subsequently come to be known as "Space Theater." These were series of Performances given every Tuesday night during the late 1950s in a large studio in Ann Arbor. They involved both notated and improvisational procedures, and an intersection of complex light-image projection with taped and electronic music. In a report of some of these performances to the *Illustrated Weekly of India*, Padma Hejmadi described them as follows: "There is no warning of what lies ahead as one takes one's chair and the lights go off—except perhaps the anticipation of an unknown experience. Then in the darkness there is a stab of light—maybe a clear, intense red—appearing on the screen (to the accompaniment of an equally clear, equally intense impact of sound), which widens into abstract images of color and light (as the music begins to unfold its theme), moving across the surfaces, breaking as one screen ends and reappearing on the next one, gaining depth here and complexity there (as the music, too, acquires corresponding timbre and overtones)—altogether an integrated pattern of sight and sound."

This series continued for about two years and out of it developed the specific production called "Space Theater." The "Space Theater" production was invited to the Twenty-seventh Music Biennale in Venice, where it was produced on September 11, 1964, at the Teatro la Fenice under the title of "*Teatro dello spazio, luce e suono*" (come to be known as Music for the Venzia Space Theater). This was a composition for four-channel tape, and other electronic apparatus, involving sculpture, dancers, light projections, and live instrumentalists.

Between 1960 and 1966, Mumma was codirector of the ONCE festival and the ONCE group at Ann Arbor for the presentation of electronic music. In 1962–63, Mumma was research assistant for the department of acoustics and seismics at the Institute of Science and Technology at Ann Arbor. During this period he developed an expertise in seismology by studying tape recordings of earthquakes and nuclear explosions. In 1963, Mumma produced his first work using cybersonic procedures and circuitry: *Medium Size Mograph*. This is the only one of Mumma's six *Mographs* to use modification, and the score of the piece includes both the musical notation and the first electronic circuit diagram. This work is also apparently the first published musical score with a musically and electronically functional circuit, released in Canada in 1964.

Mumma came to New York in 1966, the city of his permanent residence for the next decade. Between 1966 and 1974 he was composer and performing musician for the Merce Cunningham Dance Group, and since 1966 composer and performing musician with the Sonic Arts Union, which specialized in the presentation of live electronic music. In 1969–70 he served as consulting artist and engineer for Experiments in Art and Technology, Inc. During the summer of 1974 he was visiting lecturer at the Ferienkürse für Neue Musik in Darmstadt, Germany. In January 1975 he was on the faculty of Cuarto Curoso Latino Americano de Música Contemporánea in Cerro del Toro in Uruguay and, in January 1977, of the Sexto Curso Latino Americano de Música Contemporánea in Buenos Aires. Throughout the decade he made numerous other appearances as visiting lecturer on the theater arts and music, or composer-lecturer, at various American universities, including Brandeis University in Waltham, Mass. (1968), the University of Illinois in Urbana (1969–70), University of California in Berkeley (summer 1971), Dartmouth College in Hanover, N.H., (summer 1972), University of California in Santa Cruz (1973–75) and Wesleyan University in Middletown, Conn. (summer 1974). In 1975 he was appointed professor of music at the University of California in Santa Cruz.

Mumma's first significant work engaging a cybersonic console was *Le Corbusier*. This was one of the few pieces by Mumma for a large instrumental ensemble. Two instruments (a violin and a double bass) had their sounds cybersonically modified. These two instruments, to which he referred as a "cybersonic concertante" had an honest "concertant" relationship (in the traditional baroque musical sense) with the rest of the ensemble. He wrote it in 1965 for the Southern Methodist University in Dallas, Tex., where it was introduced on February 13, 1965. This composition was followed by one of Mumma's most successful works: *Mesa*, composed for the Merce Cunningham Dance Company on a grant from the National Endowment for the Arts. Written for live electronic performance and a cybersonic bandoneon (the bandoneon being a member of the organ family resembling an accordion), *Mesa* received its world premiere at St. Paul de Vence in France on August 6, 1966, with David Tudor performing on the bandoneon and the composer officiating at the cybersonic console. In commenting on a recording of this composition in his book, *Electronic Music*, Elliott Schwartz commented: "We hear an amazing assortment of buzzes, noise components, vibrato states, modulations and reverberations." Also for the Merce Cunningham group, Mumma created *Telepos*, on a grant from the Rockefeller Foundation, in which the dancers were equipped with telemetry belts and accelerometers; the first performance took place in Brooklyn, N.Y., on February 2, 1972.

Another of Mumma's highly successful works is *Hornpipe*, for French horn and cybersonic sounds (1967), which received a highly successful hearing at the Burdock Festival, in Royalton, Vt., in August 1969. The French horn is seldom played in the traditional way; for example, a bassoon reed replaces the usual French horn mouthpiece. This allows for a more complex harmonic distribution than the horn can normally produce. Writing in *Tempo*, Tim Souster said: "In *Hornpipe* he concentrates on the use of different kinds of feedback as a means of building up a sustained electronic texture out of discontinuous instrumental sound. Such was the sophistication of the gadgetry that different kinds of feedback seemed to be emerging from different speakers equidistant from the horn—a technical impossibility, one would have imagined. Mumma's music was certainly interesting, but the work was particularly remarkable for the creative possibilities it brings about. It is clear that the sophisticated extension of a conventional instrument has far greater potential than isolated sound-producing machines (such as the echo detector) whose application is necessarily limited."

Mumma's later electronic compositions included *Cybersonic Cantilevers* (1973), written on a grant from the New York State Council on the Arts. This work, which called for public participation, was given its premiere in Syracuse, N.Y., On May 18, 1973. *Some Voltage Drop* (1974), described as "variable duration theatre with electronic music implementation," was given its initial hearing at the Festival d'automne in Paris, France, on October 1, 1974.

"Like much of his music," said Tom Johnson in *Village Voice*, "this is not a set composition so much as a set of materials. Everything changes and develops from performance to performance." *Passenger Pigeon: 1776–1976* (1976) was first presented on February 3, 1977, at the State University of New York in Albany. This is Mumma's sole live performance piece with a relatively standard keyboard oriented analog synthesizer. It is a "cybersonic analog electronic synthesizer" because he added cybersonic control circuitry to the synthesizer. *Earheart: Flights, Formations & Starry Nights*, written in 1977 for the Portland Dance Theater on grants from the National Endowment for the Arts and the Oregon Arts Commission, received its world premiere in Portland on September 9, 1977, *Echo-BCD* (1978), also composed for the Portland Dance Theater, was premiered on October 15, 1978. *Pointpoint* (1979), commissioned by the Oregon Arts Council, for the Cirque Studio in Portland, was introduced on March 14, 1980.

In recent years Mumma has also written notated music for conventional instruments, notably a series of short pieces for harpsichord—*Eleven-Note Pieces and Decimal Passacaglia* (1979) and a larger work, *Los desaparecidos*, "for solo clavichord with electronic aggrandizement." Commenting on *Los desaparecidos*, the composer says: "The title suggests something about the structure of the piece: in the process of their development the themes mysteriously disappear." He then adds: "I'm composing for clavichord and harpsichord because of the challenge of defined limited resources for which there is a living tradition of virtuoso performers. And, even in competition with extravagant electronic apparatus, the clavichord remains the most efficient of expressive keyboard instruments."

Mumma has contributed music for various television and film documentaries both in the United States and abroad. His writings on electronic music have appeared in numerous scholarly journals and anthologies.

THE COMPOSER SPEAKS: Music, for me, has always been primarily a performance-oriented art. What interests me particularly about live-electronic music is that it is an interactive art, either with other people, or with electro-acoustic circuitry, or both. One of the claims for electronic music is that the composer can control everything. That's probably not true in any circumstances, but I'm uneasy with the political and philosophical implications of such an idea. My personal interest is with matters of *influence* rather than *control*. In my live-electronic work I explore the influences and interactions between myself and other people and the electro-acoustic circuitry which is our "instrument." Quotation marks should be around "instrument" because it means "environment" as much as it refers to the object for making sound. Though much of my music exists only as music composed with magnetic tape, and heard on recordings or broadcasts, for me the process of composing in the electronic music studio is very much of a live-performance experience.

PRINCIPAL WORKS: Sinfonia, for twelve instruments and magnetic tape (1958–60); *Mographs*, six compositions for various combinations of pianos and pianists (1962–68); *Megaton for Wm. Burroughs*, for ten electronic acoustic and communication channels (1963); *Music for the Venezia Space Theater*, four-channel magnetic tape with live electronic music (1964); *The Dresden Interleaf 13 February 1945*, quadraphonic electronic music on magnetic tape (1965); *Le Corbusier*, for orchestra, organ, magnetic tape, and cybersonic concertante (1965); *Mesa*, live electronic music with cybersonic bandoneon (1966); *Hornpipe*, for French horn and cybersonic sounds (1967); *Beam*, for violin, cybersonic modification and digital control (1969); *Conspiracy* 8, for digital computer with up to eight performers (1970); *Ambivex*, phantom myoelectrical telemetering system with pairs of performing appendages (1971); *Telepos*, for dancers with telemetry belts and accelerometers (1971); *Cybersonic Cantilevers*, for cybersonic music system with public participation (1973); *Some Voltage Drop*, variable duration theater with electronic music implementation (1974); *Passenger Pigeon, 1776–1976*, live-performance cybersonic analog electronic music synthesizer (1976); *Equale: Zero Crossing*, for violin, flute, clarinet, saxophone, bassoon, cello, and bandoneon (1976); *Earheart: Flights, Formations & Starry Nights*, ballet (1977); *Echo-BCD*, ballet (1978); *Pointpoint*, ballet (1979); *Eleven-Note Pieces and Decimal Passacaglia*, for harpsichord (1979); *Los desaparecidos*, for solo clavichord with electronic aggrandizement (1980).

BIBLIOGRAPHY: *DCM*; Hitchcock, H. W., *Music in the United States: A Historical Introduction* (Englewood Cliffs, N.J., 1969); Schwartz, Elliott, *Electronic Music* (N.Y., 1973); Thomson, Virgil, *American Music Since 1910* (N.Y., 1970); *Who's Who in America, 1980–81*.

N

Nabokov, Nicolas, b. near Lubcha, Minsk, Russia, April 17, 1903; d. New York City, April 6, 1978. American citizen, 1939.

"When I left Russia," Nabokov said late in his life, "all of my musical instincts remained Russian. I am an old-fashioned Russian composer." He might have been the cosmopolitan who had moved freely, frequently and actively in such world centers as Paris, Berlin, Rome, and New York, but in the final analysis he remained a composer rooted in his homeland. His lyricism, which was copious, grew out of the melodies and tonalities of Russian folk and church music, and at times his subjects were often just as Russian. To his writing, in addition to his gift for melody, he brought an elegant orchestration and frequently powerful dramatic thrusts.

He was born in a castle in the northwest corner of White Russia near the Lithuanian border to a distinguished family. His grandfather was a minister of justice who legislated toward the abolition of serfdom in Russia; one of his uncles was a liberal member of the Duma (the Russian parliament); and his cousin, Vladimir Nabokov, became an eminent writer. Nicolas Nabokov began to study the piano as a child in his native town. In 1911 his family moved to Saint Petersburg, where he attended the Imperial Lyceum. In 1917, soon after the outbreak of the revolution, the Nabokovs came to Yalta. There for the next three years, Nabokov studied composition with Vladimir Rebikov. In 1920, Nabokov left Russia for Germany, attending the Academy of Music in Stuttgart (1920–22), then the High School of Music in Berlin as a composition student of Paul Juon (1922–23). After that, for a brief period, he studied privately with Ferruccio Busoni.

In 1923, Nabokov left Berlin for Paris. For three years (1923–26) he attended the Sorbonne, from which he received an academic degree. Between 1926 and 1933 he lived mainly in Paris, but at times also in Germany, supporting himself by teaching languages and literature privately. At the same time he initiated his career as a composer with several works including his first piano sonata (1926).

On a commission from Serge Diaghilev, the founder and artistic director of the Ballet Russe de Monte Carlo, Nabokov created his first successful composition. It was music for a ballet-oratorio, entitled *Ode, or Meditation at Night on the Majesty of God as Revealed by the Aurora Borealis* (1928). Scored for soprano, alto, tenor, bass, chorus, and orchestra, this

was music meant to be sung and played as well as danced to. Boris Kochno wrote the scenario; the sung text came from poems by Lomonosov; the choreography was realized by Leonid Massine; and the principal dancers were Danilova, Lifar, and Massine. In his score, Nabokov reached back to the nationalist operas of Glinka. The ballet score comprised a dozen separate arias together with recitatives, duets, choruses, and instrumental interludes. In spite of the overall simplicity and economy of Nabokov's musical approach, "the nakedness, far from being a mark of poverty," as André Schaeffner wrote, "becomes the expression of force—the strength of a young composer who already knows the value of direct emphasis, and of the constant presence in music of song." Both at its premiere in Paris on June 6, 1928, and at its first performance in London the following July 9, this ballet was a success of such dimensions that the hitherto totally unknown Nabokov was carried into the limelight.

He followed this success with his Symphony no. 1, *Lyrique* (1929), which was first performed on February 16, 1930, in Paris with Pierre Monteux conducting; the following fall (October 31) it was introduced to the United States by the Boston Symphony under Serge Koussevitzky. Then came a cantata, *Job*, for two tenors, two baritones, bass, and chorus (1933), in which Nabokov reached back stylistically to 15th- and 16th-century monodies. Soon after it was introduced in Paris in the year of its composition, it was heard in Mexico City, conducted by José Iturbi, and received its American premiere at the Worcester Festival in Massachusetts in 1934.

Nabokov immigrated to the United States in 1933 on an invitation from the Barnes Foundation to give a series of lectures on European music in Merion, Pa. In the United States, Nabokov was commissioned to write another ballet score for the Ballet Russe de Monte Carlo, this time on an American subject, *Union Pacific*. Archibald MacLeish provided a scenario describing the episodes in the building of that railroad. Adapting himself to an American theme, Nabokov here produced a score with an American (rather than Russian) identity in which he quoted such American tunes as "Pop Goes the Weasel," "Butcher Boy," "Lady Gay," and a cakewalk, "Monsieur Banjo." *Union Pacific*, with choreography by Leonid Massine, was so well received when it was introduced in Philadelphia on April 6, 1934, that the company kept it in its repertoire for several years, performing it throughout the United States and in Europe.

After living in New York for a year and a half, devoting himself to composing, teaching, and writing, Nabokov joined the music faculty of Wells College in Aurora, N.Y., in 1936 where he remained for the next five years. In Aurora, Nabokov wrote a String Quartet (1937), music for a production of Milton's *Samson Agonistes* (1938), performed at Wells College on May 14, 1938, and his Symphony no. 2, *Biblica* (1940). The last of these was a programmatic symphony, religious in feeling, occasionally Hebraic in musical personality, and generously spiced with such 20th-century idioms as polyrhythms and polytonality for dramatic effects. The entire score was developed from two principal themes heard early in the first movement, and last movement came as a summation of what had previously transpired. Each of the four movements was based on a section of the Bible, carrying with it an identifying title: I. "Ecclesiasticus (Wisdom)"; II. "Solomon (Love)"; III. "Absalom (Fear)," and IV. "Hosannah (Praise)." "There is considerable oriental color in the score," said Olin Downes in the *New York Times*. "The material comes indirectly from many sources. It is strikingly integrated." Dimitri Mitropoulos conducted the premiere performance with the New York Philharmonic on January 2, 1941.

Together with the Symphony no. 2 in 1940, Nabokov completed a piano sonata, and one year later, a bassoon sonata. Then came a hiatus of several years when he devoted himself primarily to major activities outside composition. Between 1941 and 1944 he taught music at St. John's College in Annapolis, Md. In 1944, during World War II, the U.S. Army called upon him to serve as a civilian with the morale division of the Strategic Bombing Survey in Europe. For two and a half years under this assignment, Nabokov filled the posts of deputy chief of film, theater, and music control for Germany, coordinator of interallied negotiations for information media, and special adviser on cultural and Russian affairs to Ambassador Robert D. Murphy.

Nabokov was back in the United States in 1947. For one year he worked for the State Department, helping to establish and becoming the first chief of the Russian Broadcast Unit of the Voice of America. He was also busy composing again. On a commission from the Koussevitzky Music Foundation he wrote a three-part elegy for voice and orchestra, *The Return of Pushkin* (1947), whose text was based on verses by Pushkin describing that poet's impressions on returning in 1835 to his family estate from which he had been banished in his youth. "I was attracted to this poem in particular," Nabokov explained, "when I returned to Europe with the United States armed forces and revisited places where I had lived before." In form, Nabokov explained further, he attempted "to combine Russian song with the larger instrumental forms. The whole structure . . . is essentially

tonal, and the voice is treated as a melodic instrument." The Boston Symphony under Koussevitzky introduced it on January 2, 1948. The same orchestra and conductor also introduced another major Nabokov work on March 2, 1951: *La vita nuova*, for soprano, tenor, and orchestra (1950). A third Nabokov vocal work was *Symboli chrestiani*, for baritone and orchestra (1953), text in Greek and Latin derived from early Christian sources. It was commissioned by the Louisville Orchestra, which introduced it, with William Pickett as soloist, in Kentucky on February 15, 1956, after which it was featured at the Venice Festival in September 1956.

In addition to these vocal compositions, Nabokov completed a Cello Concerto subtitled *Les hommages* (1953), premiered in Philadelphia on November 6, 1953, and a two-act opera, *The Holy Devil* (1958), libretto by Stephen Spender based on the life of Rasputin, which the Kentucky Opera Association introduced in Louisville on April 16, 1958. This opera, greatly expanded and revised, and renamed *Rasputin's End*, was first produced in Cologne, Germany, on November 27, 1959, under the German title *Der Tod des Grigori Rasputin*. The influence of Tchaikovsky and Mussorgsky was found in many of the arias and choral numbers, but elements of popularism were also encountered in a two-step popular French tune (heard through a phonograph loudspeaker) and a ragtime-style dance. But extended passages were based on a twelve-tone row.

From 1947 to 1952, Nabokov taught composition at the Peabody Conservatory in Baltimore, Md. In 1952, he was back in Europe, serving as secretary general of the Congress for Cultural Freedom, in which capacity he organized three festivals: "Masterpieces of the 20th Century" in Paris in 1952; "Music in our Times" in Rome in 1954; and "East-West Music Encounter" in Tokyo in 1961. Between 1963 and 1966 he was cultural adviser to Mayor Willy Brandt of West Berlin, and from 1963 to 1968, artistic director of an annual Festival of the Arts in West Berlin. In 1969, he was artistic director of the Teheran Festival in Iran. Meanwhile, in June 1967, Nabokov paid his first return visit to his native land in half a century, on an invitation from the Ministry of Culture and the Union of Soviet Composers.

Nabokov's principal compositions in the 1960s were: a score to the ballet *Don Quixote* (1964–65), choreography by George Balanchine, produced in New York in August 1965; his Symphony no. 3, subtitled *A Prayer* (1967), its premiere given by the New York Philharmonic under Leonard Bernstein on January 4, 1968; and the *Prelude, Four Variations and Finale on a Theme by Tchaikovsky*, for cello and orchestra (1968), first performed on January 5, 1972, by Mstislav Rostropovich as soloist with the Philadelphia Orchestra. The Symphony no. 3, commissioned by the New York Philharmonic for its 125th anniversary, is of particular importance. It was inspired by the prayer of Pope John XXIII pleading for forgiveness "for our blindness in not recognizing the beauty of His chosen people, the Jewish people, for our fault in the suffering inflicted upon them over the centuries, and for our having crucified Him a second time in their flesh." One of the three melodies Nabokov "approximated" rather than quoted directly was a Hasidic tune he had heard an old Hasid sing to him during his boyhood days in Russia. A second "approximated" melody was a Catholic hymn of oriental origin; and a third theme was taken from Stravinsky's *Requiem Canticles.*

Nabokov's last major work was his opera, *Love's Labor Lost* (1970), libretto by W. H. Auden and Chester Kallman based on the Shakespeare comedy. It received its world premiere at the Théâtre de la Monnaie in Brussels on February 7, 1973, and on September 13, 1973, it was performed by the Deutsche Oper in West Berlin during the Berlin Music Weeks. In contrast to Nabokov's earlier opera on Rasputin, which was a musical drama, *Love's Labor Lost* had a light, often satirical score. Time and again, Nabokov digressed from a more serious attitude to poke fun at such varied subjects as twelve-tone composers, American popular "crooning" songs of the 1930s, Stravinsky's neoclassicism, the *Zeitkunst* of Kurt Weill and Bertolt Brecht, and even Indian music. In the last, he used a "prepared" cello (just as John Cage prepares a piano) with paper and a loudspeaker to make it sound like a sitar.

Nabokov was a lecturer on esthetics at the New York State University in Buffalo in 1970–71. From 1970 to 1973 he was composer-in-residence at the Aspen Institute for Humanistic Studies in Colorado and in 1972–73 he was a lecturer on music at New York University.

Nabokov married Dominique Cibiel, a photographer, in 1970. She was his fourth wife. From earlier marriages, all of which ended in divorce, he had three sons.

In 1973, Nabokov received the Commander's Cross of the German Order of Merit from the Federal Republic of Germany. Nabokov was the author of two books of reminiscences: *Old Friends and New Music* (1951) and *Bagazh: Memoirs of a Russian Cosmopolitan* (1975). He also wrote *Igor Stravinsky* (1964).

THE COMPOSER SPEAKS: I do not belong to any school of aesthetic ideology, but I suppose that, quite beyond my conscious control, the music that comes out of my mind and my heart belongs to a generation of composers and sounds Russian to foreigners. I like to invent melismatic patterns that enter readily into the secret folds of a listener's memory.

PRINCIPAL WORKS: 3 symphonies (1929, 1940, 1967); 2 piano sonatas (1926, 1940).

Ode, ballet-oratorio, for soprano, alto, tenor, bass, chorus, and orchestra (1928); Piano Concerto (1932); *Collectionneur d'échoes,* for soprano, chorus, and nine percussion (1932); *Job,* cantata, for two tenors, two baritones, bass, and chorus (1933); *Union Pacific,* ballet (1933); *La vie de Polichinelle,* ballet (1934); String Quartet (1937); Bassoon Sonata (1941); *The Return of Pushkin,* for high voice and orchestra (1947); Flute Concerto (1948); *La vita nuovo,* for soprano, tenor and orchestra (1950); Cello Concerto, *Les hommages* (1953); *Symboli christiani,* for baritone and orchestra (1953); *The Last Flower,* symphonic suite (1957); *Rasputin's End,* opera (1958); *Four Poems by Boris Pasternak,* for baritone and orchestra (1959); *Studies in Solitude,* for orchestra (1961); *Five Poems by Anna Akhmatova,* for voice and orchestra (1964); *Don Quixote,* ballet (1964–65); *The Wanderer,* ballet (1966); *Prelude, Four Variations and Finale on a Theme by Tchaikovsky,* for cello and orchestra (1968); *Love's Labor Lost,* opera (1970).

BIBLIOGRAPHY: Nabokov, Nicolas, *Bagazh: Memoirs of a Russian Cosmopolitan* (N.Y., 1975); Nabokov, Nicolas, *Old Friends and New Music* (N.Y., 1951); *High Fidelity/Musical America,* April 1968, April 1, 1973; *Intellectual Digest,* April 1973; *Modern Music,* November-December 1934.

Nordoff, Paul, b. Philadelphia, Pa., June 4, 1909; d. Herdecke, West Germany, January 18, 1977.

Though in his earlier years he was a crusader for the new departures in music and for American composers of radical musical tendencies, their influence on his own music was nonexistent. He preferred traveling the conservative route by writing tonal, consonant, highly lyrical, and often romantic music within traditional structures. After 1960, Nordoff's career in musical therapy for handicapped children displaced that of composer.

His music instruction began with private piano lessons with local teachers, and gained momentum in 1923 at the Philadelphia Conservatory, where for four years he studied with Hendrik Ezerman, who was the first to recognize his talent. From his fourteenth year on, and for the next two decades, Nordoff taught piano privately. Upon Ezerman's death, Nordoff continued piano study with Olga Samaroff at the Philadelphia Conservatory. Upon receiving his bachelor of music degree in 1927, and his master of music degree in 1932, he went to the Juilliard School of Music on two fellowships, one in composition and the other in piano, even though at that time Juilliard had a ruling not to give more than one fellowship in a major subject. Composition was studied with Rubin Goldmark and piano with Mme. Samaroff. As a Juilliard student, Nordoff composed *Prelude and Three Small Fugues,* for two pianos (1930), which he subsequently orchestrated, the orchestral version introduced in St. Louis by the St. Louis Little Symphony in 1936.

In 1933 Nordoff graduated from Juilliard *cum laude*. That year he received the Bearns Prize for composition from Columbia University and the first of two Guggenheim Fellowships, the second coming in 1935. These fellowships gave him an opportunity to travel in Europe and to intensify his efforts as composer. *Secular Mass*, for chorus and orchestra (1934) to a text by Walter Prude, was Nordoff's first composition to get a major performance when the Minneapolis Symphony under Eugene Ormandy introduced it in 1936. Ormandy thought so highly of this work that he performed it again in April 1938 with the Philadelphia Orchestra. A Piano Concerto (1934), introduced in Holland by the Groningen Orchestra, received its American premiere in 1938 with the composer performing it with the National Symphony in Washington, D.C., Hans Kindler conducting.

Together with several outstanding young musicians of Philadelphia and New York, Nordoff organized a Modern Chamber Music Concerts series in Philadelphia in 1937–38. At its concert on February 24, 1938, Nordoff presented the premiere of his Piano Quintet (1936), which, as a critic for the *Philadelphia Public Ledger* reported, "scored a great success." The critic added that this work "revealed a high musical content and demonstrated in its three movements definite endowment and imagination. . . . It was a delight to find a young modern composer who does not disdain a discernible and graceful melodic line and who is concerned with writing music rather than intellectual or psychological theses and whose craftsmanship indicates sound training and intelligent conception of instrumentation." This quintet brought its composer a Pulitzer Traveling Fellowship in 1940.

In addition to concert works, Nordoff completed at this time his first opera *Mr. Fortune* (1936–37) to a libretto by Walter Prude based on Sylvia Townsend Warner's novel *Mr. Fortune's Maggot*. Nordoff also contributed the incidental music to *Romeo and Juliet* when it opened on Broadway on December 23, 1935, starring Katherine Cornell, and to Bernard Shaw's *St. Joan*, again with Katherine Cornell, which came to Broadway on March 9, 1936.

Between 1938 and 1943, Nordoff was head of the composition department at the Philadelphia Conservatory. His Suite, for orchestra (1938), was premiered by the St. Louis Symphony under Vladimir Golschmann on December 6, 1940, and his one-act comic opera, *The Masterpiece* (1940), with libretto by Franklin Brewer, was produced in Philadelphia on January 24, 1941.

In 1945, Nordoff married Sabina Zay, a eurythmist. They raised three children. Stimulated by his wife's profession, Nordoff composed, in 1944, *That Was the True Light That Lighteth Every Man That Comes into the World*, for speaking chorus, solo speakers, singers, eurythmy, and instruments, and in 1945 music for a cantata, with a eurythmic ballet,

The Sun. This was not the first time Nordoff had written music for ballet, nor the last. In 1937 he had composed music for *Every Soul Is a Circus*, presented in 1939 by Martha Graham and her company. He subsequently provided scores on commission for Doris Humphrey and Agnes De Mille. In the theater, his incidental music to *Anthony and Cleopatra* with Katherine Cornell was heard when that play opened on Broadway on November 26, 1947.

Between 1945 and 1949, Nordoff was assistant professor in the Fine Arts Course of Basic College at Michigan State University in East Lansing. In the fall of 1949 he was appointed assistant professor of music at Bard College in Annandale-on-Hudson, N.Y., where he remained until 1959, serving as full professor from 1953 on. During these years a number of important commissions brought him further significant exposure as composer. Two came from the Louisville Orchestra in Kentucky: *Lost Summer*, for mezzo-soprano and orchestra (1949), using as text some unpublished poems by Sylvia Townsend Warner, first performed on January 31, 1951, by that orchestra under Robert Whitney with Nan Merriman as soloist; and *Winter Symphony* (1954), introduced by the Louisville Orchestra under Whitney on May 15, 1955. Additionally, Nordoff wrote the Concerto for Violin, Piano, and Orchestra (1948) for Eugene List and Carroll Glenn, who, as soloists with the Indianapolis Symphony under Fabien Sevitzky, gave its first performance on January 5, 1952; *Little Concerto*, for violin, viola, cello, and bass (1950), first heard in 1950 at a concert of the Little Orchestra Society in New York under Thomas Scherman for whom it was written; *Lyric Sonata*, for violin and piano, written in 1952 on a grant from the Olga Samaroff Foundation and performed in her memory in New York on May 9, 1952; *Dance Sonata*, for flute and piano (1953), composed for Claude Monteux and performed by him in New York on October 6, 1953; and *Tranquil Symphony* (1955), commissioned by Edward B. Benjamin, and given its world premiere in New Orleans on March 14, 1965.

Nordoff was the recipient of a Ford Foundation Faculty Fellowship in 1954, and an honorary doctorate in music from Combs College of Music in Philadelphia in 1958.

In 1959, Nordoff resigned from Bard College to go to England to prepare himself as a musical therapist for handicapped children. Combs College awarded him the degree of Bachelor of Music Therapy in 1960. From this point on, musical therapy became his life's work and composition came to an end, his last major work being the *Gothic Concerto*, for piano and orchestra (1959). From September 1961 until April 1962, he worked at the Institute of Logopedics at Wichita, Kans., where he helped train an assistant in a method he had developed with Clive Robbins for using music as therapy for handicapped children. In May 1962, the National Institute of Health gave a grant to the department of child psychiatry of the University of Pennsylvania to make possible the continuation of his methods with autistic children. Nordoff directed this project for three years. Concurrently, he was employed as teacher-consultant for the Special Education Division of the Board of Public Education, a project in which he and Robbins worked with retarded trainable children and their teachers. After that, Nordoff worked as musical therapist for brain-damaged and mentally retarded children in Finland, Germany, and England, among other countries. In this capacity he was lecturing fellow of the American Scandinavian Foundation in 1967–68. The Goldie Leigh Hospital in London opened a Nordoff Music Therapy Center based on principles he had developed.

Nordoff was the author of *Music Therapy for Handicapped Children* (1971) and *Music Therapy in Special Education* (1971).

THE COMPOSER SPEAKS: Truth in music depends partly on a balance between the elements of which it is composed—the melodic element naturally expressive, "original" and clear; yet the whole without false sentiment nor dominated by intellectual theories.

I am convinced the *the* new career for composers is musical therapy for retarded and handicapped children. It is a challenge for the composer to explore the limitless possibilities for therapy that live in every element of music. That challenge led me to musical experiences and discoveries that I never dreamt existed. This seems to me to be a career in keeping with the political, emotional and moral developments in which we are living today.

PRINCIPAL WORKS: 2 symphonies (1954, 1955); 2 piano concertos (1932, 1959); 2 string quartets (1932, 1935); 2 violin sonatas (1932, 1952).

Prelude and Three Small Fugues, for two pianos, also for orchestra (1930); *Variations on a Bavarian Dance Theme,* for piano, also for orchestra (1933); *Secular Mass,* for chorus and orchestra (1934); Piano Quintet (1936); *Mr. Fortune,* opera (1936–37); *Every Soul Is a Circus,* ballet (1937); Suite, for orchestra (1938); *The Masterpiece,* one-act comic opera (1940); *Salem Shore,* ballet (1943); *That Was the True Light That Lighteth Every Man That Comes Into the World,* for speaking chorus, solo speakers, singers, eurythmy and instruments (1944); *The Sun,* cantata with eurythmy, ballet, 1945; Concerto for Violin, Piano, and Orchestra (1948); *Lost Summer,* for mezzo-soprano and orchestra (1949); *Little Concerto,* for violin, cello, and bass (1950); *Dance Sonata,* for flute and piano (1953); *The Frog Prince,* for narrator and orchestra (1954); more than 150 songs.

BIBLIOGRAPHY: *DCM;* Howard, John Tasker, *Our Contemporary Composers* (N.Y., 1941); Reis, Claire, *Composers in America* (N.Y., 1947); *Who's Who in America, 1976–77.*

O

Oliveros, Pauline, b. Houston, Tex., May 30, 1932.

Oliveros, who considers herself as a radical in the sense of returning to the root or fundamentals, has passed through various stages which sometimes overlapped and sometimes blended before ending. The first stage was traditional. This was followed by improvisational electronic, theatrical, meditational, conceptual and political music, moving into what she calls "software for people" in which audiences are often invited to participate in the performance. Her materials have come from four major sources: all the music she ever heard; all the sounds of the natural world including her own inner biological sounds; all the sounds of the technical world; and all the sounds from her imagination. Her music is the result of the processing of such materials, interacting with traditional ways as well as the new ways made possible by technology.

Both her grandmother and mother were teachers of the piano. Her mother initiated her to music with piano instruction when she was five. She later studied the violin with William Sydler (1941–42) and accordion with Marjorie Harrigan (1944–45). Musical sounds were a basic part of her early life through hearing her grandmother and mother play and teach and through music heard on the phonograph and radio. She responded as sensitively to nonmusical sounds as to musical ones. "My childhood in a rural part of Texas," she recalls, "sensitized me to sounds of the elements and animal life. There was wind and rain, cows, chickens and animal life. I loved to hear them. There were only occasional motor noises, not the constant drone we experience in cities today." In listening to the radio, she was even more fascinated by static and the whistling sounds produced between stations than by the music itself.

Her musical world began expanding in the 1940s with the development of long-playing records. She would spend hours listening to a single record and then write down the melody so she could play it on her accordion. At James S. Hogg Junior High School in Houston (1944–46) she was director of the school band, and from the time she was sixteen she appeared publicly as an entertainer by playing the accordion. She expanded her musical horizon by studying the French horn with J. M. Brandstetter (1947–49).

She graduated from Reagan High School in Houston in 1949. Between 1949 and 1952, she attended the University of Houston, where she started studying composition with Paul Koepke and majored in accordion with Willard Palmer. Her first compositions—a Wind Quintet and *Song*, for horn and harp—came when she was nineteen. At that time, as she says, "I had not the slightest notion of the existence of so many different manifestations or phenomena one recognized as music," having been raised solely on Western European classical and romantic music (especially piano and orchestral literature), popular music, jazz, and country and western. "I only vaguely understood that there was other music."

She left the university without getting a degree after three years. In 1952 she came to San Francisco. There she attended San Francisco State College (1954–57), earning a bachelor of arts degree in 1957 with composition as major. She took a year of postgraduate work before deciding to quit the university because it interfered with composition. For the first time she came into contact with "new" music and the young, adventurous musicians who were creating it. A six-year period of the study of composition privately with Robert Erickson followed. Erickson reinforced her interest in sound quality, encouraged her to improvise her way through composition rather than rationalize, and introduced her to the concept of organic rhythm, that is, rhythm that shifts, expands, contracts, and is not periodic in the metrical sense.

In 1957, she joined several San Francisco avant-garde composers in creating group improvisations. "We simply sat down and played together without prior discussion, recorded and listened to the results," she says. "At first we were amazed at the spontaneous organization in the music. . . . We all felt our hearing expanded by the simple process of throwing oneself into spontaneous music making, getting immediate feedback in the form of the recording, and discussion of the process and results."

Oliveros made an important discovery in 1958 through technology. She put a microphone in her window and recorded the sound environment. Only then did she come to realize that though she had been listening carefully during that recording she had not heard all the sound the tape had captured. "From that moment, I determined that I must expand my awareness of the entire sound field. I gave myself the seemingly impossible task of listening to everything all the time. Through this exercise, I began to hear the sound environment as a grand composition."

With such newly developed perceptual skills, she began to hear tones as composites: She heard the overtone structure and partials at will instead of always resolving the tones to single pitches. Since she was a French horn player she began tuning consciously to the overtones as she changed from pitch to pitch. This exercise deepened her continuing interest in sound quality and the ambiguity between pitch and sound. Her subsequent electronic music reflected these interests.

Recognition as a composer came to her for the first time with Variations for Sextet, for flute, clarinet, trumpet, horn, cello, and piano (1960), in which she was influenced by the motivic fragmentation and concision of Anton Webern. In 1960 it was introduced in San Francisco and in 1961 it received the Pacifica Foundation National Prize. "It doesn't aim to be melodious," wrote Alexander Fried in the *San Francisco Examiner*. "Rather it presents its tone patterns in pointillist spurts, murmurs, splashes, and meaningful frames of abstract sound." Alfred J. Frankenstein, in the *San Francisco Chronicle* considered it "the most remarkable work I have heard by any of the younger American composers."

In 1962, Oliveros was awarded the Foundation Gaudeamus Prize in Bilthoven, Holland, for *Sound Patterns*, for chorus (1962), as the best foreign work. It was distinguished by its lack of any text and for the overall electronic/orchestral sound of the chorus produced by vocal sounds of an abstract nature. Precise control of pitch was abandoned to gain the possibility of complex clusters of sound. Thus *Sound Patterns* became one of the first compositions to explore vocal sounds in this way by a 20th-century composer.

Meanwhile, in 1961, in association with Morton Subotnick and Ramon Sender, Oliveros helped develop the San Francisco Tape Music Center, the first electronic music studio in that area. Four years later, the center received support from the Rockefeller Foundation. It was moved to Mills College in Oakland, Calif., in 1966 with Oliveros becoming its director. As a result of experiments at the Center, Oliveros began producing tape-recorded music, some of which was heard at a concert of improvised music in San Francisco on March 24, 1962, in collaboration with several of her colleagues. Alfred J. Frankenstein in the *Chronicle* referred to the music heard at this performance as "stimulating sounds too new to be named." He added: "While the musicians are busy, mostly with percussive sounds, and the two others were acting and singing and what not, Ramon Sender was taping the goings-on, and the taped sounds came back often in greatly altered forms, on speakers located at various points in the hall. As a result, the past of this improvisation became a part of its present, and this use of the past as both substance and subject for improvisation in the present seems to me to be a most remarkable idea."

Oliveros continued to develop and elaborate upon the ideas and activities heard in this germinal program up to about 1967. In 1967, she was appointed to the music faculty of the University of California in San Diego, where she has stayed since then as assistant professor of composition on the music faculty (1969–78) and, since 1978, full professor. Before leaving for San Diego, she ended her fifteen-year stay in San Francisco with a twelve-hour "Tape-a-thon: Electronic Music by Pauline Oliveros," on July 22, 1967, a program of compositions in which she presented most of her electronic music. This represented for her the end of an era.

Oliveros's interests now widened again, this time to include visual, kinetic and dramatic elements in her music as well as electronic sounds. Three representative works of this period are *Pieces of Eight*, a theater piece for wind octet and tape (1965), which contains the seeds of many of her later works; *Theater Piece for Trombone Player*, for garden hose instruments (constructed by Elizabeth Harris) and tape (1966), written on commission for the trombonist Stuart Dempster; and *I of IV*, a two-channel purely electronic piece (1966; Oakland, Calif., January 1967), which is a solo studio improvisation in real time.

Pieces of Eight, reported Arthur Bloomfield in the *San Francisco Examiner*, "unwound amidst a concatenation of alarm clocks, cuckoo clock, cash register, and assorted glissandos, burps and bellows from an ensemble of eight performers who looked rather more plausible than they sounded." As part of the overall whimsy, the oboist entered in a fur-lined parka which he removed, then unpacked his instrument, sounded an eight-second whirling cadenza, and put on his parka again and stalked off. There was a solo for a cash register. A bust of Beethoven was paraded up and down the aisles.

In *Theater Piece for Trombone Player*, the sonic elements are an arrangement of an improvised vocabulary and mixed on tape in a sequence by the composer, while the soloist has specific instructions for improvising with tape. He is called upon to light and extinguish candles on a dark stage, to scrape the strings of a piano, bark like a dog, and perform on several lengths of garden hose each of which is fitted with a trombone mouthpiece. Through these garden hoses, lawn sprinklers were set into operation, cigarette smoke was exhaled, and sounds were reproduced while the performer whirled one of the hoses overhead.

In *I of IV* the composer elaborated a strong mental sonic image as she became the medium or channel through which she could observe the emerging improvisation.

As she became increasingly concerned with theatrical and visual materials as part of her music, Oliveros began producing works in which the visual elements were as important as the musical ones and in which the musicians were actors, often assuming bizarre and absurd theatrical roles. In *Night Jar*, a theater piece for viola d'amore (1968), the performer for whom it was written on commission (Jacob Glick) came on the stage dressed in white tie and tails to perform acts of legerdemain with cards, coins, and cigarettes. *The Wheel of Fortune*, a theater piece for solo clarinet (1969; Seattle, Wash., October 14, 1970), commissioned by William O. Smith, combined mime, magic, and music as Tarot cards are read. The performer was surrounded by eight yellow flashing beacons in front of slides of Tarot cards. "Smith alternately whipped small cards from his sleeve, delivered random verbiage about the significance of a sieve or the symbolism of a shoe, performed magic tricks and finally sat down among the beacons and improvised a piece on his clarinet," as Stephanie Miller noted in the *Seattle Post Intelligence*. *Aeolian Partitions*, a theater piece for flute, clarinet, violin, cello, and piano (1969), was created from a photograph of the Aeolian Players, for whom it was written. Oliveros used this pictorial medium to create in her music descriptive and idiosyncratic traits of each player. This piece also called for a number of "extra" performers to serve as page turners and piano movers, to sweep the floor, carry a transistor radio across the stage, and so forth.

After that, Oliveros's interest in the total act and environment of performance caused her work to change considerably, though the base remained the same. In 1970 she began exploring ritual and ceremony, and looking for ways of composing for despecialized performers. *Meditation on the Points of the Compass*, for chorus and percussion (1970; Bloomington, Ill., March 19, 1971), commissioned by David Mott for the Illinois Wesleyan Choir, was the beginning of her "ceremonial" works. Here, the audience is included in performing specific materials. Twelve soloists intoned texts of their own independent choice according to special rules. Soloists were chosen for differences in ethnic origin who articulated chosen texts in their respective native languages. The usual relationship of audiences to performer was broken by a special circular seating arrangement with the chorus surrounding the audience and the soloists in the center of the circle.

That year (1970), Oliveros formed an ensemble of ten women devoted to the exploration of meditative states of consciousness and their relationship to performance practice. This led to the writing of such works as *Sonic Meditations* I–XII (1971–72), for voices, instruments and unspecialized performers, parts of which were later incorporated into an "evening ritual" entitled *Phantom Fathom* (1972) of mixed-media events including meditations and an exotic potluck dinner (1972; Long Beach, Calif., July 19, 1972). "The instructions," Oliveros explains, "are intended to induce altered states of consciousness with slow-moving, richly textured sonic events. Anyone may participate with immediate results but these meditations are meant for repetition by a group over a long period of time. Our program consists of training in advance a portion of the poten-

tial audience in a workshop, then instructing in writing all persons who come to the program in how to participate. No one is a spectator."

In January 1973, Oliveros began a three-month tenure as faculty fellow in the Project for Music Experiment funded by the Rockefeller Foundation at the University of California in San Diego. She worked two hours a day with twenty people doing relaxation, meditation exercises, and experimenting with "sonic meditations." "I was no longer interested in making the electronic music and theatrical pieces I had become known for," Oliveros informs us. "The simplicity of my new approaches appeared to be opposed to the performance practices my friends knew and loved. I completely abandoned notation for oral tradition. I went underground and worked alone." *Sonic Meditation* I–XI, for voices, instruments and unspecified performers (1971–72), *Sonic Images*, an auditory fantasy designed to trigger auditory imagination in the participants (1972), and *Sonic Meditations* XII–XXV (1973) were representative of her earlier works involving sonic meditations.

On a Guggenheim Fellowship (1973–74), a commission from the Center for Creative and Performing Arts at the State University of New York at Buffalo, and a grant from the National Endowment for the Arts, Oliveros produced *Crow Two: A Ceremonial Opera* (1974; La Jolla, Calif., March 6, 1975). This was a combination of meditations both new and old (the old derived from the various *Sonic Meditations*). Oliveros was now beginning to compose *with* her meditations, combinations of meditations varying from performance to performance, depending on the circumstances.

Later in 1974, in Berlin, during the Metamusik Festival, Oliveros led a ten-day seminar in Sonic Meditations and, with her ensemble, performed a program of her works in October 1974. More personal works involved her after that. *Rose Mountain Slow Runner* (1975; De Kalb, Ill., October 1975) was a meditation which she sang and played on her accordion. "I set myself the task, after establishing an accordion drone, of singing long tones until the tones seemed to change of their own accord. At least part of the performance is unheard by the audience because I am listening mentally to tonal changes which do not occur. The results are felt or perceived in some other mode than auditory. The effect generally is reported to be deep relaxation."

Oliveros has received numerous grants from the University of California at San Diego to pursue her various researches. She has been visiting professor, guest-in-residence, lecturer, performer, and conductor of workshops in numerous colleges and universities throughout the United States. In 1977, she received first prize from the city of Bonn in Germany during its annual Beethoven Festival for *Bonn Feier*, an environmental theater piece originally entitled *Link* for specialized and unspecialized performers (1971), commissioned by Palomas College in San

Marcos, Calif., where it was introduced as *Link* on May 5, 1971. She is vice-president of the Institute for the Study of Attention at Solana Beach in California. She holds third Kyu Black Belt in Shotokan-style Karate.

THE COMPOSER SPEAKS: All of music speaks to me as music, no matter how diverse, no matter what its function might be, no matter how apparently simple or complex, no matter how it affects me emotionally, or intellectually, and no matter what its origin, whether human, animal, artificial, or extraterrestrial. No matter how much I might like or dislike something I hear, I cannot deny that it is music. Above all I believe passionately that I must respect each music in terms of its own context. For me this is one of the first steps in learning to understand and to interact appropriately with any music alien to my own culture. If nothing else, music in any of its multitudinous manifestations is a sign of life. Sound *is* intelligence. . . .

I believe that humanity has been forced to the edge of a new frontier by the accelerating rate of change instituted by technology. This frontier is the exploration of consciousness. A commonality might be found in the sensory and attention processes which enable humans to perceive, organize, interpret, and interact with the intelligence that is music. It is no longer sufficient to dwell only on the music, the perceiver must be included. The analysis, understanding, and possible expansion of such sensor and attention processes, as distinguished from the content or results, with and without the aid of technology will greatly influence the future of music. I believe that through the exploration of (human) consciousness, we will reach a new understanding of what music can be, and how we can, and do, interact with it."

PRINCIPAL WORKS: Variations for Sextet, for flute, clarinet, trumpet, horn, cello, and piano (1960); *Sound Patterns*, for chorus (1961); Trio, for flute, piano, and page turner (1961); Trio, for trumpet, accordion, and string bass (1961); *Time Perspectives*, for four-channel tape (1961); *Seven Passages*, for two-channel tape, mobile, and dancer (1963); *Five*, for trumpet and dancer (1964); *Apple Box Orchestra*, for ten performers, amplified apple boxes, and small sound sources (1964); *Apple Box*, for two performers, amplified apple boxes and small sound sources (1964); *Light Piece for David Tudor*, for four-channel tape, amplified piano, and prismatic lighting effects (1965); *Before the Music Ends*, for two-channel tape and dancer (1965); *Pieces of Eight*, a theater piece for wind octet and tape (1965); *George Washington Slept Here*, for amplified violin, film, projections, and tape (1965); *A Theater Piece*, for fifteen actors, film projection, and tape (1965); *Winter Light*, for two-channel tape, mobile, and figure (1965); *Cat o' Nine Tails*, a theater piece for mimes with two-channel tape (1965); *Theater Piece for Trombone Player*, for garden hose instruments constructed by Elizabeth Harris and tape (1966); *The C(s) for Once*, for trumpets, flutes, voices, organ, and tape delay system (1966); *I of IV*, for two-channel tape (1966); *II for IV*, for two-channel tape (1966); *Hallo*, a theater piece for instruments, tape delay system, amplified piano, mimes, and light projections (1966); *Circuitry*, for five percussionists, voltage-controlled light score, and light events (1968); *Mills Bog*, for two-channel tape (1968); *Alien Bog*, for two-channel tape (1968); *Night Jar*, a theater piece for viola d'amore player (1968); *Festival House*, a theater piece for orchestra, mimes, light, film and slides (1968); *Double Basses at Twenty Paces*, a theater piece for two string bass players, conductor/referee, seconds, two-channel tape, and slide projection (1968); *AOK*, for accordion, eight country fiddlers, chorus, conducts, and tape delay system (1969); *The Dying Alchemist Preview*, for narrator, violinist, trumpet, piccolo, percussion, and slide sequence by Lynn Lonidier (1969); *The Wheel of Fortune*, a theater piece for clarinet soloist (1969); *Aeolian Partitions*, a theater piece for flute, clarinet, violin, cello and piano (1969); *Music for Expo '70*, for accordion, two cellos, and three voices (1970); *To Valerie Solanis and Marilyn Monroe in Recognition of Their Desperation*, for orchestra or chamber orchestra, electronic music system, and lighting (1970); *Meditation on the Points of the Compass*, for chorus and percussion (1970); *Sonic Meditations* I–XI, for voices, instruments and unspecialized performers (1971); *Bonn Feier*, formerly *Link*, an environmental theater piece for specialized and unspecialized performers (1971); *Post Card Theater*, multimedia events for unspecialized performers (1972); *Phantom Fathom*, an evening ritual, mixed-media events including meditations on an exotic potluck dinner (1972); *1000 Acres*, for string quartet (1972); *Dialogue with Basho*, a written sonic meditation (1972); *Sonic Images*, an auditory fantasy designed to trigger auditory imagination in the participants (1972); *Sonic Meditations* XII–XXV (1973); *Phantom Fathom* II, a ceremonial participation evening (1973); *Crow Two*, a ceremonial opera (1974): *Rose Mountain Slow Runner*, for voice and accordion (1975); *Willow Brook Generations and Reflections*, for winds, brass, and vocalists (1976); *The Yellow River Map*, a ceremonial meditation for a group of fifty or more people (1977); *King Kong Sings Along*, for chorus (1977); *Rose Moon*, a ceremonial for chorus and percussion (1977); *The Witness*, for virtuoso instruments (1978); *El relicario de los animales*, for soprano and twenty instruments (1979); *Carol Plantamura*, for voice and twenty instruments (1979); *Gone with the Wind, 1980*, for assorted ensembles (1980).

BIBLIOGRAPHY: *BBDM*; *DCM*; Schwartz, Elliott, *Electronic Music* (N.Y., 1973); *High Fidelity/Musical America*, June 1975; *Music Educators Journal*,

Ornstein

484

February 1975, March 1975; *New York Times*, May 25, 1980.

Ornstein, Leo, b. Kremenchug, Russia, December 11, 1892. American citizen.

Ornstein was one of America's first avant-gardists. In the second decade of the 20th century, his piano music aroused shock and denunciation in many quarters, and enthusiastic admiration from a few, for its unresolved discords, tone clusters, and amorphous structures. He has never stopped composing, but little of what he has written has gained circulation. A recent revival of interest in Ornstein has focused exclusively on the compositions of his rebellious youth, and one or two major works of his early manhood, while leaving his later music virtually untouched.

His father, Abraham Ornstein, was a synagogal cantor in Kremenchug. When Leo Ornstein was three, he received his first piano lessons from him. Additional piano study took place during Ornstein's childhood with Vladimir Puchalski in Kiev. Though the boy revealed unmistakable talent, his father refused to allow intensive study until the boy's uncle intervened. When Ornstein was ten, he played for Josef Hofmann, then touring Russia, who was impressed by his talent and recommended him for admission to the St. Petersburg Conservatory. While attending the conservatory, Ornstein coached singers of the St. Petersburg Opera.

Anti-Semitism in Russia drove the Ornstein family to the United States in 1907; from then on this remained the country of Ornstein's residence and citizenship. At the New England Conservatory in Boston, Ornstein studied the piano with Bertha Feiring Tapper. He continued his musical studies in New York at the Institute of Musical Art, where he was a student of composition of Percy Goetschius's. At the same time he completed his academic education at the Friends Seminary.

He began composing in 1910. With his first piece for the piano, *Impressions of Notre Dame*, written during a visit to Paris, he broke every rule he was taught. "The music I composed did not evolve consciously," he has explained. "It was there and I wrote it down." He followed this piece with the even more dissonant *Wild Men's Dance* (1912), which became his most notorious composition, and the *Dwarf Suite*, for piano (1913).

His debut as concert pianist took place in New York on March 5, 1911. From then on he concertized extensively throughout the United States, appearing not only in recitals but also as guest artist with American major orchestras. In 1913 he made his first tour of Europe, with appearances in London, Paris, Norway, and Denmark, besides delivering lectures on music at the Sorbonne in Paris and at Oxford in England. His recital in London on March 27, 1914, was billed as a "concert of futuristic music" in which he featured his own Piano Sonata (1913) together with some other of his piano works. One unidentified critic said of the sonata that it sounded like "four spasms of mental anguish too great to be borne." In Oslo, a Norwegian critic said Ornstein's music "transformed the hall into a dental parlor." He returned to the United States early in 1915 to give a series of concerts in which he featured 20th-century music by Debussy, Ravel, Schoenberg, and Scriabin as well as Ornstein. His piano playing inspired unqualified admiration; he was generally accepted as one of the most brilliant virtuosos of his time. But his own music met a far different reception. Reviewing Ornstein's recital of "modern music" in New York on December 5, 1915, Richard Aldrich in the *New York Times* said of three Ornstein piano compositions that they sounded not "as brass and tinkling cymbals, for there might be something musical in them, but sound and fury, signifying nothing. The three are distinctly differentiated, it is true; but they seem to be simply different ways of making noises that range from the merely disagreeable to the actually intolerable. We have no doubt that so conscientious and highly accomplished a performer as Mr. Ornstein played the notes of *Wild Men's Dance* exactly as he wrote them down and published them; but the effect would not be appreciably different to most ears if fistfuls of notes were recklessly pounded upon the instrument by an unskilled person in the same rhythms."

But within a few years, voices were beginning to be heard in praise of Ornstein. Frederick H. Martens considered Ornstein important enough to write his biography in 1918. "In his case," wrote Martens, "youth lends him the fiery energy, the passionate concentration, the intense belief in his aims and ideals which inform the musical maturity of his inspiration with so triumphant an accent of sincerity, so eloquent a feeling of truth." James Gibbons Huneker, the distinguished critic in New York, referred to Ornstein as "the only true-blue, genuine Futurist composer alive." Paul Rosenfeld, spokesman for new music, wrote: "Leo Ornstein is sure of reaching the high heaven of art which he seemed and still seems bound for."

Ornstein continued concertizing extensively until 1933. In that time, he introduced his own Piano Concerto (1923) as soloist with the Philadelphia Orchestra conducted by Leopold Stokowski on February 13, 1925. Here, and in his chamber music a few years later—Piano Quintet (1927) and String Quartet (1929)—he continued to be dissonant, but a romantic element began to intrude into his writing which softened whatever shock his cacophonies might have aroused with audiences now more inured to such innovations. From this time on, Ornstein's music was heard with less frequency—though his orchestral *Nocturne and Dance of the Fates* (1936), commissioned by the League of Composers, received a major premiere by the St. Louis Symphony under Vladimir Golschmann on February 12, 1937. Then, for several decades, his works disappeared totally from the music scene.

Despite his successes as a piano virtuoso, Ornstein decided to retire in 1933. "One beautiful day I decided not to stand the incessant practicing and the incessant traveling. So I gave up concerts." He turned to teaching composition and piano, first at the Zeckwar Hahn School and after that at the Ornstein School of Music in Philadelphia. He also gave courses in music at Temple University in Philadelphia. By the rest of the music world outside Philadelphia, he was forgotten as well as neglected.

But, beginning with the 1970s, a revival of interest in Ornstein's music began taking place. It started with several recordings: the Piano Quintet, the orchestral *Nocturne and Dance of Fates*, and an album of his piano pieces. Reviewing the last of these in March 1977, a critic for *High Fidelity* said it revealed "a dominant, innovative, unruly personality, capable of drawing incredibly angry and volcanic sounds from the piano." Michael Sellers was the pianist who performed the music in this album. He also revived Ornstein's music in the concert hall. On December 11, 1976, in New Haven, Conn., he gave the first performance of Ornstein's Piano Concerto since its premiere a half century earlier. In reporting from New Haven to the *New York Times*, Harold C. Schonberg found this work to be eclectic. "It starts with Rachmaninoff-like gestures, goes into a Bartókian kind of dissonance, explores a type of nationalism that suggests the Near East and Hasidic elements, mixes romantic pianism with percussive figurations out of Prokofiev. As a period piece it is fascinating."

On December 13, 1918, Ornstein married Pauline Mallet-Prévost, a pianist he had known from his childhood days. In 1923, Ornstein was one of the founders of the League of Composers, of which he became a board member. Since his retirement as teacher in 1955, Ornstein has lived in New Hampshire, Arizona, and Florida before settling down in a small mobile house in Brownsville, Tex. His late works are varied in style, since he comes to each new work with a fresh viewpoint. Sometimes his writing is atonal and structurally complex, and sometimes conservative, romantic and simple in design and materials.

Ornstein was presented the Marjorie Waite Peabody Award by the American Academy and National Institute of Arts and Letters in 1975.

THE COMPOSER SPEAKS: How easy it is to become a victim to one's own style. You begin to imitate yourself. I have tried to go my own way, not worrying about style or fashion. What I hear, I put down. . . .

Fame never had much meaning or appeal to me. It was not worth it. If my music has any value, it will be picked up and played. If it has not value, it deserves its neglect."

PRINCIPAL WORKS: 2 string quartets (1929, 1976).
Impressions of Notre Dame, for piano (1910); *Wild Men's Dance*, for piano (1912); *Dwarf Suite*, for piano (1913); Piano Sonata (1913); *Suicide in an Airplane*, for piano (1913); *Moods*, for piano (1914); *The Fog*, tone poem for orchestra (1915); Cello Sonata (1916); *Impressions of Chinatown*, for piano, also for orchestra (1917); *Poems of 1917*, suite of ten pieces for piano (1917); Violin Sonata (1917); *Three Russian Choruses*, for a cappella chorus (1921); Piano Concerto (1923); Two Nocturnes, for orchestra (1924); Piano Quintet (1927); Five Songs, for voice and orchestra (1929); *Hebraic Fantasy*, for violin and piano (1929); *Pantomime Ballet* (1930); *Lysistrata*, suite for orchestra (1930); Preludes, for cello and piano (1931); Symphony (1934); Five Songs, for voice and piano, or orchestra (1935); *Six Water Colors*, for piano (1935); *Nocturne and Dance of the Fates*, for orchestra (1936); Nocturne, for clarinet and piano (1952); Ballade, for saxophone and piano (1953); Twenty Waltzes, for piano (1955–68); Intermezzo, for flute and piano (1958); Prelude and Allegro, for flute and piano (1958); Tarantella, for piano (1958); *Prelude and Minuet in Antique Style*, for flute and clarinet (1960); *Some New York Scenes*, for piano (1971); *A Morning in the Woods*, for piano (1971); *Fantasy Pieces*, for viola and piano (1972); *Biography in Sonata Form*, for piano (1974); *Valse diabolique*, for piano (1978).

BIBLIOGRAPHY: Martens, Frederick H., *Leo Ornstein: The Man, His Ideas, His Work* (N.Y., 1918); Rosenfeld, Paul, *Musical Portraits* (N.Y., 1920); Van Vechten, Carl, *Music and Bad Manners* (N.Y., 1916); *Musical Quarterly*, April 1918; *New York Times*, March 14, 1976; *Notes*, June 1975.

P

Paine, John Knowles, b. Portland, Me., January 9, 1839; d. Cambridge, Mass., April 25, 1906.

Time has all but extinguished Paine's music, but not his significance in the history of American music. Above and beyond his contributions as a music educator who pioneered the first music courses in an American college and chartered the course of so many important American musicians, Paine was, as composer, the first American to distinguish himself as a symphonist; the first American whose works received repeated performances by major musical institutions; and the first American composer to gain respect and admiration abroad. Some historians go so far as to say he was America's first composer of consequence of concert music. But his music was far from being American. Totally subservient to the style, structures, heritage, and artistic directions of the German romantics, he was an echo of Mendelssohn, Schumann, and Joachim Raff, which is probably the reason why his music, with one or two exceptions, has become silent in the 20th century.

His American ancestry reached back to the 17th century, to Thomas Payne, who settled in Yarmouth, Mass. Paine's more immediate family background included musicians. His grandfather, John K. H. Paine, built the first organ in Maine and his father, Jacob Small Paine, was the conductor of a local band and owner of a music store in Portland. Of his five children, John was the only one to show talent for music. He was placed under the solid instruction of Hermann Kotschmar, an organist, with whom he made such progress that a career in music became assured. When he was eighteen, Paine made a notable debut as organist in Portland. One year later he came to Berlin, Germany, to continue his music study at the Academy of Music: organ with Karl August Haupt, composition and orchestration with Friedrich Wilhelm Wieprecht, singing with Gustav Wilhelm Teschner. After three years at the academy, Paine achieved success as an organ virtuoso with recitals in Berlin and other German cities, and in London, acclaimed particularly for his performances of the music of Johann Sebastian Bach.

When he returned to the United States in 1861 he gave an organ recital in Portland, following it with performances in Boston, where he settled permanently later that year. In Boston he was appointed organist of West Church but one year later he left this post to become director of music at Harvard University, serving as both organist and choir director at Appleton Chapel. At this time he became a pioneer in music education in colleges by delivering at Harvard lectures on musical forms (accepting no salary). These attracted only a few students, since they offered no college credits, and were soon dropped. But in 1870 he again offered his teaching services without salary for classes in harmony and counterpoint. This time, in spite of severe opposition, music education took hold at Harvard. In 1873, Paine was made assistant professor in music and two years later he became full professor, the first professorship in music given by any American university. He remained in Harvard's music department thirty years.

He returned to Germany in 1866 to tour for a year as organist. In 1867 in Berlin, he directed a performance of his first major composition, Mass in D, for vocal soloists, chorus and orchestra (1867), which was successful at a concert of the Singakademie attended by the Crown Princess Victoria. This is one of the few works by Paine to enjoy revivals in the United States many years later, first in a performance at the New England Conservatory in Boston in 1972, conducted by Gunther Schuller. To Peter G. Davis, in a review in the *New York Times*, the recording of this Mass was "an amazing accomplishment for a composer in his 20's and something of a miracle for an American in 1860." Davis went on to describe the Mass as "a work of singular power, beauty, breadth and technical sophistication . . . [without] one carelessly written measure, no moment of flagging invention. The melodic inspiration is often of haunting loveliness, the harmonic language strikingly original yet always natural, the choral, solo, and orchestral writing wonderfully assured and unceasingly expressive."

Major works after the Mass gave Paine a position of first significance among American composers of his generation. These compositions included an oratorio, *St. Peter* (1872), whose premiere he directed in Portland before it was performed, a year later, by the Handel and Haydn Society of Boston. In 1875, he completed the first of two symphonies in C minor, which he called "the turning point in my career," and which L. C. Elson in *The History of American Music* described as an "epoch-making work." It was introduced in Boston in January 1876 by the Theodore Thomas Orchestra, conducted by Thomas. Thomas then commissioned Paine to write *Centennial Hymn,* for chorus and orchestra (1876), which he performed in Philadelphia in 1876 in commemoration of the American centennial. Two orchestral compositions inspired by Shakespeare were also completed in 1876: *Overture to As You Like It* and the tone poem *The Tempest*. An impressive success came with the Symphony no. 2 in A, the *Spring Symphony* (1879). When it was given its initial performance in Boston on March 10, 1880, with Theodore Thomas conducting, it received an unusual demonstration of enthusiasm. According to a contemporary report, men shouted, women waved their handkerchiefs and John S. Dwight (the esteemed Boston critic and publisher of a music magazine) stood on his seat and expressed his delight by opening and shutting his umbrella. Modeled closely after Joachim Raff's *Spring Symphony*, written one year earlier, this was a programmatic work in which the first movement described the passing of winter, the second-movement Scherzo was a "May-Night Fantasy," the third-movement Adagio, a tonal picture of "A Romance of Springtime," and the Finale, a paean to "The Glory of Nature."

Another substantial success came with Paine's incidental music to Sophocles' *Oedipus Tyrannus*, produced at the Sanders Theater in Cambridge on May 17, 1881, the first classical revival projected on such an ambitious scale in America. Paine's score, which he himself conducted, consisted of a prelude, six male choruses, and a postlude. In 1904, this music received a gold medal in Berlin at an international concert during ceremonies unveiling a monument to Wagner.

Paine continued to compose prolifically up to the end of his life. A tone poem, *An Island Fantasy* (1888), was inspired by two paintings by J. Appleton Brown of the Isles of Sholes in New Hampshire. Daniel Gregory Mason pointed up Paine's indebtedness to the German romantics by saying in *The Dilemma of American Music* that this composition supposedly inspired by New Hampshire's Isle of Sholes was "artistically speaking . . . within easy sailing distance of Mendelssohn's *Hebrides*." *Song of Promise*, a cantata for soprano, chorus, and orchestra (1888), was successfully performed by Theodore Thomas at the Cincinnati Festival of 1888. *Hymn of the West*, a cantata for vocal soloists, chorus, and orchestra, was written in 1903 for the St. Louis Exposition where it was introduced that year and repeated a year later by the Handel and Haydn Society in Boston.

In or about 1900, Paine completed his only opera, *Azara*, on which he had been laboring for several years. He wrote his own text based on the medieval poem *Aucassin and Nicolette*. The opera never received a stage production but in 1903 it was given a concert presentation with piano accompaniment in Boston, and four years later another concert performance in Boston, this time with orchestra, in a performance of the Cecilia Society, B. J. Lang conducting. *Moorish Dances* from this score became

popular at symphony concerts after being introduced by the Boston Symphony on March 9, 1900. By that time, the Boston Symphony had performed Paine's compositions about twenty times.

Paine resigned from Harvard in 1905 to devote himself completely to composition. His death from pneumonia came one year later; his last work, a tone poem for orchestra, *Lincoln*, was left unfinished.

Paine received the honorary degree of master of arts from Harvard in 1869, and an honorary doctorate in music from Yale in 1890. In 1896, he was one of the founders of the American Guild of Organists. At Harvard, the music building bears his name as does a traveling fellowship.

He was the author of *The History of Music to the Death of Schubert*, published posthumously in 1907. Before then, in 1885, *Harvard Lecture Notes* was published in Boston.

PRINCIPAL WORKS: 2 symphonies (1875, 1879).
String Quartet (c. 1859); *Four Character Pieces*, for piano (1866); Mass in D, for vocal soloists, chorus, and orchestra (1867); *St. Peter*, oratorio, for solo voices, chorus, and orchestra (1872); Piano Trio (c. 1875); Violin Sonata (1875, revised 1905); Romanza and Scherzo, for cello and piano (c. 1875); *Four Characteristic Pieces*, for piano (1876); *Centennial Hymn*, for chorus and orchestra (1876); *As You Like It*, concert overture for orchestra (1876); *The Tempest*, tone poem for orchestra (1876); *Music to Oedipus Tyrannus*, for chorus and orchestra (1881); *Phoebus Arise*, cantata for vocal soloists, chorus, and orchestra (1882); *The Realm of Fancy*, cantata for vocal soloists, chorus, and orchestra (1882); *The Nativity*, cantata for vocal soloists, chorus and orchestra (1883); *Song of Promise*, cantata for soprano, chorus, and orchestra (1888); *An Island Fantasy*, for orchestra (1888); *Columbus March and Hymn*, for orchestra (1893); *Azra*, opera (c. 1900); Incidental Music to *The Birds* (1901); *Hymn of the West*, for vocal soloists, chorus and orchestra (1903).

BIBLIOGRAPHY: *NGDMM;* Chase, Gilbert, *America's Music* (N.Y., 1955); Edwards, G. T., *Music and Musicians of Maine* (Portland, Me., 1928); Howard, John Tasker, *Our American Music* (N.Y., 1946); Roberts, K. C., "John Knowles Paine" (doctoral thesis, Ann Arbor, Mich., 1962); Spalding, Walter Raymond, *Music at Harvard* (N.Y., 1935); *Dictionary of American Biography*, vol. 7; *Who Was Who in America*, vol. 1, 1897–1942.

Palmer, Robert Moffett, b. Syracuse, N.Y., June 2, 1915.
Palmer's style has been aptly described by one of his former students, Richard Monaco. "Renaissance polyphony and American jazz have influenced his preferred textures and rhythms. He has kept his early commitment to tonality as a basic organizing

formal principle, and within this framework has evolved a harmonic language which is both sensitive and sinewy. Those who know his music will immediately think of its energetic rhythms; but it is in the balance between these rhythms and the lyricism of the melody and harmony which has created a place for his music in the repertory of our time."

Palmer is a tenth-generation descendant of Walter Palmer of Stonington, Conn. His father, personnel director of a woodwork equipment manufacturer, had a serious interest in music, and his mother had been a trained pianist. Hearing his father sing light classics to his wife's piano accompaniment, listening to recordings of music by the Russian Five, Debussy, and Ravel and to operatic arias and to piano literature produced on piano rolls—all this was Palmer's early initiation to good music. "Those evenings of music," he recalls, "go back to my earliest years and were of the utmost importance to me." His mother was his first piano teacher, lessons beginning when he was twelve. While attending Central High School in Syracuse (1930–34) he studied piano further, as well as violin and theory at the Music School Settlement in that city. During these school years he played the violin in a string ensemble and in a small symphony orchestra.

A scholarship in piano brought him to the Eastman School of Music in Rochester, N.Y., in 1934. One year later he changed his major from piano to composition, which he studied with Bernard Rogers and Howard Hanson. In 1938 he received his bachelor of music degree and, in 1939, his master of music. During the summer of 1939 he studied composition privately with Roy Harris in New York, and the summer of 1940 was spent at the first session of the Berkshire Music Center at Tanglewood, Mass., on a scholarship for the study of composition with Aaron Copland. "Also of importance," Palmer says, "were some informal visits to the home of Quincy Porter in Poughkeepsie, N.Y., during the period of 1936–39 when Porter was teaching at Vassar. His music, along with that of Harris and Copland, was quite meaningful to me, particularly Porter's unique harmonic language and lyric melody and the intricate rhythmic writing of his 1930 Violin Sonata." Under such influences Palmer produced such compositions as his String Trio no. 1 (1937); his Piano Sonata no. 1 (1937–38), introduced by John Kirkpatrick in New York on March 26, 1940; *Poem*, for violin and chamber orchestra (1938), first heard in Rochester, N.Y., on October 20, 1938, Howard Hanson conducting; and his String Quartet no. 1 (1938–39), premiered in New York in 1939 by the Walden String Quartet.

On May 25, 1940, Palmer married Alice Frances Westcott, with whom he had two daughters. Between 1940 and 1943 he taught composition, theory, and piano at the University of Kansas, at Lawrence. Since 1943 he has been a member of the music faculty at Cornell University in Ithaca, N.Y., where he

has taught composition and advanced courses in theory and in 1976 was named Given Professor of Music Composition. In 1955–56 he also held the George A. Miller chair as professor of composition at the University of Illinois in Urbana and in summer of the same year taught at the University of Michigan in Ann Arbor. Through the years he has served as visiting composer to colleges and universities throughout the United States.

He first attracted interest as composer with several commissioned works. They were polyphonically inclined, influenced mainly by the English school of the Tudor period. As he explained at the time, his prime interest was "in a totally organic music with great purity and sensitiveness of texture . . . [with] a balance between individual lines, evolving a succession of vertical structures and the form as a whole." The formal structure of these early works were evolved "from the older static conceptions of polyphonic form to newer dynamic ones which fulfill the need for greater plasticity within a frame of order."

The first of these commissions came in 1940 from the Columbia Broadcasting System and the League of Composers. It resulted in the writing of Concerto for Small Orchestra (1940). In 1943, on commission from the Koussevitzky Music Foundation, he completed the String Quartet no. 2. In 1945 he was commissioned by Dimitri Mitropoulos and the Minneapolis Symphony to write his first successful work for orchestra: Variations, Chorale, and Fugue (1947), introduced in Ithaca, N.Y., on April 18, 1954. One of his most successful chamber-music compositions of his earlier years was the Piano Quartet(1947), which was premiered by John Kirkpatrick and members of the Walden Quartet at the Library of Congress in Washington, D.C., soon after its composition. When it was revived in Washington, D.C., two decades later (March 12, 1970), Robert Evett, writing in the *Evening Star*, said: "This is one of the most engrossing works of a superb American composer. . . . The most conspicuous characteristic of his music . . . is a kind of nervous rhythmic propulsiveness. . . . At its premiere . . . it was a triumph. It was a triumph again last night." The major orchestral work of this period was Symphony no. 1, begun in 1953 and completed a year or so later. Palmer revised this symphony in 1979 and it was first heard in Ithaca, N.Y., on December 9, 1979.

He continued for the most part to favor a polyphonic texture and modern evolvements of classical structures through the first half of the 1950s. Many of these works were also written on commission: the Piano Quintet (1950), from the Elizabeth Sprague Coolidge Foundation and heard first in 1951 performed by the Juilliard String Quartet with Erich Itor Kahn in Washington, D.C.; the first version of the Clarinet Quintet (1952), from the Quincy (Ill.) Society of Fine Arts, which introduced it in Quincy in 1953; String Quartet no. 3 (1954), from the Stanley Commission of the University of Michigan, where it was heard for the first time on July 12, 1955; the chamber cantata *Of Night and the Sea*, for soprano, alto, tenor, and baritone soli and eleven instruments (1956; Urbana, Ill., 1957), from the Fromm Music Foundation.

Beginning with the Sonata for Violin and Piano (1956; Urbana, Ill., 1956) he began reaching to the new directions being explored by European composers and at the same time searching for an expanded harmonic and tonal language. His music was now becoming more intense and inward.

In his later works he greatly expanded his rhythmic as well as harmonic and tonal language, while extending the range of expression. From then on he has moved between this later more complex stylistic pole and the earlier open and "American" one.

In 1965, Cornell University and the Lincoln Center for the Performing Arts commissioned him to write an orchestral work commemorating the centenary of Cornell University. He responded with *A Centennial Overture*, which the New York Philharmonic under George Cleve introduced at the Lincoln Center for the Performing Arts on March 12, 1965, a taped version of which was broadcast over a nationwide radio network of CBS on April 8, 1965. Symphony no. 2 (1966), written on a commission from the Ithaca High School Symphony, was given its first hearing on April 2, 1967, in Ithaca, N.Y. The Piano Concerto (1968–70), begun in Rome while the composer was on sabbatical leave from Cornell, was premiered in Ithaca on November 5, 1972. *Organon* II, for string orchestra (1975), was first heard on April 4, 1975, in a performance by the Rochester Philharmonic under David Zinman. *Portents of Aquarius (Visions and Prophecies)* for narrator, chorus, and organ (1975), was given for the first time on May 11, 1975, in Ithaca; and the Piano Sonata no. 3 (1978–79) received its world premiere in London on June 5, 1979, performed by Ramon Salvatore, who had commissioned it.

In 1946, Palmer was given a Grant of Recognition by the Academy of Arts and Letters. He received a Guggenheim Fellowship in 1952, and a second one—together with a Fulbright Research Grant for Italy—in 1960–61. In 1980 he was the recipient of a grant from the National Endowment for the Arts.

THE COMPOSER SPEAKS: I feel that my language, and its range of expression, has evolved and widened with each phase. I feel much as a recent British playwright who said: "I like the discipline of the classic conventions." I have rethought and recreated older principles like the sonata structure and the fugue. Since my music is essentially tonal, though in increasingly complex ways, these are natural for me. I feel I can never exhaust their possibilities, nor those of the standard instrumental and vocal media."

PRINCIPAL WORKS: 11 *Epigrams*, for piano (1958–1967); 4 string quartets (1939–59); 3 piano sonatas (1939, 1948, 1979); 2 symphonies (1953–58, revised 1979; 1966); 2 piano quartets (1947, 1973).

Variations, Chorale and Fugue, for orchestra (1947–54); Chamber Concerto no. 1, for violin, oboe, and string orchestra (1949); Piano Quintet (1950); Viola Sonata (1951); Quintet for Winds (1951); Clarinet Quintet (1952, revised 1964); *The Trojan Women*, for women's chorus, winds, and percussion (1955); *Of Night and the Sea*, chamber cantata, for vocal soloists and eleven instruments (1956); Violin Sonata (1956); *Evening Music*, for piano (1956); Sonata for Piano, four hands (1952–57); Piano Trio (1958); *Memorial Music*, for chamber orchestra (1959–60); *Organon* I, for flute, clarinet, violin, and cello (1961–77); *Nabuchodonosor,* dramatic oratorio for vocal soloists, male chorus, symphonic brass, and percussion (1960–64); *A Centennial Overture*, for orchestra (1965); *Epithalamion*, for organ (1966); *Choric Song and Toccata*, for wind ensemble (1968); Piano Concerto (1968–70); Trumpet Sonata (1971–72); *Organon* II, for string orchestra (1975); *Portents of Aquarius (Visions and Prophecies)*, for narrator, chorus, and organ (1975); Cello Sonata (1976–78); *Transitions*, for piano (1977); *Carmina Amoris*, song cycle for soprano, viola, clarinet, and piano (1978).

BIBLIOGRAPHY: *DCM;* Ewen, David, *American Composers Today* (N.Y., 1949); *Musical Quarterly*, January 1956; *Who's Who in America, 1980–81.*

Parker, Horatio William, b. Auburndale, Mass., September 15, 1863; d. Cedarhurst, Long Island, N.Y., December 18, 1919.

Parker was most distinguished for his choral music, particularly on religious texts. His remarkable polyphonic skill and solidity of architectonic structures are the fruits of his Germanic training and his reverence for the Teutonic musical heritage. His writing was also affected by the sobriety and restraint of English church music. But he had a voice of his own, in the incandescence and spirituality of his music, and the grace of his expression.

He traced his American ancestry, on his father's side, to Deacon Parker, who settled in New England in 1635. His father was an eminent architect. His mother, who was of German birth, was a scholar of Greek and Latin, a poet and a translator who provided him with some of his texts, and a trained pianist who had studied at the High School of Music in Munich and subsequently became a teacher of the piano. One of his uncles was a professor of Latin at Dartmouth College for twenty-five years. The student concerts his mother gave at their home, the four-hand transcriptions for piano of orchestral classics which she performed with her husband and the choir singing at the Episcopal church in Auburndale were Horatio Parker's earliest musical experiences. But until he was fourteen he showed no signs of being particularly attracted to music. His entire academic schooling took place in a private school at Newton, near Auburndale. Music study began when he was fourteen, when his mother taught him piano and organ. Initially he was not a responsive student, but hearing one of his mother's students perform one day became a stimulus for emulation. He now began applying himself to music assiduously, and as he did so, his love for it mounted. Piano lessons were continued in Boston with John Orth while theoretical studies took place with Stephen A. Emery (harmony) and George Chadwick (composition). "As my pupil," Chadwick later recalled, "he was far from docile. In fact he was impatient with the restrictions of music form and rather rebellious of counterpoint and fugues. But he was very industrious and did his work well." By the time Parker was fifteen he wrote *Under the Window*, a setting of fifty verses by Kate Greenway. At sixteen he was serving as organist in a church in Dedham, Mass., and somewhat later at St. John's Church in Roxbury.

On Chadwick's advice and urging, Parker left for Germany in 1882 to spend the next three years at the High School of Music in Munich, where he was subjected to severe contrapuntal and structural discipline by Josef Rheinberger, his professor in organ and composition at the High School for Music. Under Rheinberger's watchful eye, Parker composed a good deal of music: songs, choral pieces, overtures, a symphony, a string quartet and two cantatas. The cantatas were *The Ballad of a Knight and His Daughter*, for chorus and orchestra (1884; Munich, July 7, 1884), text by Leopold Graf zu Stolberg, and *King Trojan*, for solo voices, chorus and orchestra (1885; Munich, July 15, 1885), text by F. A. Muth. *Venetian Overture* and Scherzo in G, both for orchestra, written in 1884, were introduced in Munich in 1884; Symphony in C minor (1885), was premiered on May 11, 1885 in Munich; String Quartet in F (1885) was given its initial hearing in Detroit on November 29, 1887. At the High School of Music, Parker met and fell in love with one of its piano students, Anna Plössl, who was then not yet sixteen.

Though he was held in highest esteem at the High School of Music, particularly by Rheinberger, Parker decided to leave the school in 1885 without waiting for his graduation or the diploma to which he was entitled. He returned to Boston where he opened a piano studio, but found few candidates. He then occupied a post as teacher of music at St. Paul's School in Garden City, Long Island, supplementing this income with a salary as organist at the St. Luke's Church in Brooklyn, N.Y. Now in an economic position to marry, he returned to Germany during the summer of 1886 and on August 9, married Anna Plössl at the Frauenkirche in Munich. They raised three daughters.

While making his home first in Garden City and then in New York City, Parker continued to teach at St. Paul's until 1890. During this period he also held a number of posts: as church organist, principally at

the Holy Trinity Church in New York (1888–93); and as teacher of composition at the National Conservatory in New York of which Antonín Dvořák became director in 1892. For his various church posts, Parker produced a library of practical music for the church, including services, anthems, and hymns. "They combine in a curious way respect for tradition . . . with an escape from dullness which is the distinguishing mark of much of the older music of this type," Chadwick wrote. "It is English but with ingratiating admixture of New World buoyancy." He also produced two successful concert works: *Count Robert of Paris*, an orchestral concert overture (1890; N.Y., December 10, 1890) and *Dream-King and his Love* (1891; N.Y., March 30, 1893), a cantata for tenor, chorus, and orchestra that received the National Conservatory prize in 1893.

Just before he resigned his posts at both St. Paul's and Holy Trinity Church, Parker completed a work that brought him international fame and is recognized as the most important choral music written by an American up to that time and which to this day is accepted as the composer's magnum opus. It was *Hora Novissima* (1893), for chorus and orchestra, to the text "Rhythm of the Celestial Country," a 12th-century Latin poem by Bernard de Morlaix, a monk of Cluny, translated by Parker's mother. It was written for the Church Choral Society in New York, which presented the world premiere on May 3, 1893, where it proved so successful that one year later it was heard in Boston performed by the Handel and Haydn Society and in Cincinnati, conducted by Theodore Thomas during the city's festival. On September 14, 1899, Parker conducted it at the Three Choirs Festival in Worcester, England, the first time an American composition was heard there. Comprising eleven numbers, including solos for soprano, contralto, tenor, and bass, a quartet for four voices, an a cappella chorus and four accompanied choruses, *Hora Novissima* was exalted music in which Parker's choral style was finally fully developed. David Stanley Smith, distinguished teacher, composer and a pupil of Parker, later wrote: "The melody and partwriting are particularly fascinating, and the sentiment, which lies midway between the celestial and the human, responds naturally to the feeling of the thoughtful listener."

Upon leaving his posts at St. Paul's School and the Holy Trinity Church in 1893, Parker settled in Boston to become organist and choirmaster of Trinity Church. One year later he received an honorary master of music degree from Yale University and was appointed professor of music at Yale where he remained until his death. As Battell Professor of Music, he taught composition and music history, at the same time organizing the curriculum Yale would retain for several decades. In 1904 he was made dean of the School of Music. In New Haven, Parker organized a local orchestra which, in time, became affiliated with the university and then was expanded into the New Haven Symphony. He also directed Euterpe, a women's chorus, and later an oratorio society. For his first six years at Yale he combined his teaching duties there with his organ obligations at Trinity Church in Boston. In time, commuting between the two cities became too arduous, particularly since Parker was beginning to suffer from rheumatism that afflicted him for the rest of his life. He replaced his organ post in Boston with one nearer to New Haven. He later also conducted two choral societies in Philadelphia, the Eurydice Club for women and the Orpheus Club for men.

In spite of his commitments in three different cities, there was no interruption in his creative productivity. He wrote major works not only for chorus but for orchestra and the operatic stage. *Cáhal Mór of the Wine-Red Hand*, a rhapsody for baritone and orchestra (1893), text by James Clarence Morgan, was introduced by the Boston Symphony under Wilhelm Gericke on March 29, 1895. *The Legend of St. Christopher*, a dramatic oratorio for solo voices, chorus, orchestra, and organ (1897), text by Parker's mother, was given its first performance on April 15, 1898, by the New York Oratorio Society under Walter Damrosch after which it was heard in Bristol and London in England. *A Northern Ballad*, tone poem for orchestra (1899), received its initial hearing on December 29, 1899, in a performance of the Boston Symphony under Gericke. *A Wanderer's Psalm*, a cantata for solo voices, chorus, and orchestra (1900), was written on commission for the Three Choirs Festival at Hereford, England, where it was introduced on September 13, 1900. *A Star Song*, a lyric rhapsody for solo voices, chorus, and orchestra (1901), was awarded a $500 prize by the Paderewski Fund and was premiered at the Norwich Festival in England on October 23, 1902. Concerto for Organ and Orchestra (1902) was given its first hearing at a concert of the Boston Symphony on December 26, 1902, Wilhelm Gericke conducting and the composer at the organ.

On sabbatical leave from Yale, Parker and his family went to Munich where he worked on *Greek Festival Hymn*, for chorus and orchestra (1901), to a text by Thomas Dwight Goodell, which had been commissioned to commemorate the bicentennial of Yale University. He interrupted that sabbatical to return to New Haven to conduct the premiere performance at Yale in October 1901. While abroad that year, he was awarded, in 1902, an honorary doctorate in music by Cambridge University in England. In 1904, in the United States, he was elected membership to the American Academy of Arts and Letters.

In a contest sponsored by the Metropolitan Opera Association in New York, Parker was the recipient of the first prize of $10,000 for his first opera, *Mona* (1910). The libretto by Brian Hooker had a British setting during the Roman occupation; its heroine was a British princess who was emotionally involved with the invading Roman governor. When the Metropolitan Opera produced it on March 14, 1912, with Louise Homer in the title role, *Mona* became only the third opera by an American to be presented by that company. It was not successful, lacking both dramatic and melodic interest, and burdened rather than profiting from the influences of Wagner and Richard Strauss. Nevertheless, in the *New York Times*, Richard Aldrich did speak of the work's "remarkable musicianship" and its "many elements of beauty, strength, and originality." *Mona* was dropped from the Metropolitan Opera repertoire after that one season and has not been heard since.

Parker's second opera, *Fairyland* (1914)—text again by Brian Hooker—was the winner of a $10,000 first prize, this time in a contest of the National Federation of Music Clubs. Its world premiere took place in Los Angeles on July 1, 1915. This, too, was a failure and, like its predecessor, has lapsed into oblivion. As Walter Henry Hall, the choral conductor and organist, wrote: "His ventures into opera, while they proved his complete mastery of musical material, also showed that his greatest gift was in the direction of pure choral music."

On June 16, 1916, Parker's music to *Cupid and Psyche* (1916), a three-act masque by John Jay Chapman, was performed at Yale University on June 16, 1916, to commemorate the founding of the Yale School of Fine Arts. During World War I, in 1918, Parker wrote a song for voice and orchestra, "The Red Cross Spirit Speaks," to lyrics by John Finley, which Louise Homer introduced in Carnegie Hall, New York. Parker's last composition, *A.D. 1919* (1919), was also a child of the war, a cantata for soprano solo, chorus and orchestra to a poem by Brian Hooker in memory of the men of Yale who died in conflict. Parker himself conducted the premiere performance during the Commencement exercises at Yale on June 15, 1919. This plangent lament was not only Parker's swan song but also his own requiem. He died of pneumonia at his daughter's home in Long Island a half year later. A memorial service, including performance of several of his works, was held at Yale on February 15, 1920.

Several revivals of long-neglected Parker works helped to focus attention of present-day audiences on his talent. *Vathek* (1903), an orchestral tone poem inspired by a novel by W. Backford, had to wait more than sixty years for its premiere, which took place not in a concert hall but in a 1967 recording by the Royal Philharmonic of London, conducted by Karl Krueger. It was first performed in a concert auditorium on April 2, 1978, in New York. In 1978, Parker's Sonata in E-flat, for organ (1908), was recorded by William Osborne, and on December 14, 1979, in New York, the secular ballad, for chorus and orchestra, *King Corn the Grim* (1907; Norfolk, Conn., June 4, 1908), received its first performance in half a century.

THE COMPOSER SPEAKS: In the making of music there

are three functions, equally indispensable, that of the composer, who conceives and creates the music, that of the performer who reproduces the composer's ideas and gives it to the hearer, and that of the listener which is equally indispensable to the other two, for music needs to be heard as well as composed and performed to fulfill its mission.

Now the composer is the only real producer of music. All performers are reproducers, and although we hear of a singer creating a new role, it may be doubted if it ever transcends the mental picture of the original creator. The work of the performer is a great and indispensable function with wide opportunity for originality, and it is as necessary as that of the composer. Heaven forbid that composers should reproduce their own works, especially their vocal works!

The duties of listeners are also well defined and indispensable. Unheard music is like unpainted pictures. An intelligent attitude toward performer and composer stimulates both—in fact is the only incentive for continued effort. I emphasized the need of intelligence in listeners. Passive suffering of music is not the way to acquire merit or understanding. Merely to let music trickle in and out of one's ears is not a more permanently profitable pleasure than that of drinking soda water, or having one's back scratched. Nothing remains, for effort is needed.

The mind is colored by what passes through it, but most of all by what is retained. It is the intellect rather than the senses or the emotions which stops up leaky minds, and helps them understand and retain what they hear. For this reason, listeners must be cultivated to perform their duties—the composer and the performer can do only half the work.

PRINCIPAL WORKS: String Quartet in F (1885); *King Trojan*, cantata for solo voices, chorus and orchestra (1885); *Count Robert of Paris*, concert overture for orchestra (1890); *Dream-King and His Love*, cantata for tenor, chorus and orchestra (1891); *Hora Novissima*, oratorio for solo voices, chorus, and orchestra (1893); *Cáhal Mór of the Wine-Red Hand*, rhapsody for baritone and orchestra (1893); String Quintet (1894); Suite, for violin and piano (1894); *The Legend of St. Christopher*, oratorio for solo voices, chorus, orchestra, and organ (1897); *A Northern Ballad*, tone poem for orchestra (1899); *A Wanderer's Psalm*, cantata for solo voices, chorus and orchestra (1900); *Greek Festival Hymn*, for chorus and orchestra (1901); *A Star Song*, lyric rhapsody for solo voices, chorus, and orchestra (1901); Concerto for Organ and Orchestra (1902); *Vathek*, tone poem for orchestra (1903); *The Shepherd's Vision*, a Christmas cantata for solo voices, chorus and organ (1906); *King Corn the Grim*, ballad for chorus and orchestra (1907); Sonata in E-flat, for organ (1908); *Mona*, opera (1910); *Collegiate Overture*, for orchestra with male chorus (1911); *Seven Greek Pastoral Scenes*, for solo voices, women's chorus, harp, and strings or pi-

ano (1912); *Fairyland*, opera (1914); *Morven and the Grail*, oratorio for solo voices, chorus and orchestra (1915); *Cupid and Psyche*, masque (1916); Introduction and Fugue, for organ (1916); *The Dream of Mary*, morality for solo voices, children's chorus, chorus, congregation, organ and orchestra (1918); *A.D. 1919*, for soprano solo, chorus, and orchestra (1919). *Also*: numerous songs; pieces, sketches and compositions for organ; anthems, hymns, and services for chorus and organ.

BIBLIOGRAPHY: *NGDMM*; Chadwick, George W., *Horatio Parker* (N.Y., 1921); Kearns, W. K., "Horatio Parker, 1863–1919: A Study of his Life and Music" (doctoral thesis, Urbana, Ill., 1965); Mellers, Wilfrid, *Music in a New Found Land* (N.Y., 1965); Semler, Parker Isabel and Underwood, Pierson, *Horatio Parker: A Memoir for His Grandchildren Compiled from Letters and Papers* (N.Y., 1942); *Musical America*, October 25, 1929; *Musical Quarterly*, April 1930; *Dictionary of American Biography*, vol. 7; *Who Was Who in America*, 1897–1942.

Parris, Robert, b. Philadelphia, Pa., May 21, 1924.

Parris's music, says Nicolas Slonimsky, "is distinguished by strong formal structure and tonal cohesion; when pragmatically justifiable, he applies serialistic technique with deliberate circumspection." His writing ranges from the lyrical to the percussive, from the atmospheric to the fantastic and humorous.

Both parents were musical, though the father was totally untrained, and the mother only slightly so on the piano. She began teaching her son the notes on the piano when he was about four. But serious piano study did not begin until his twelfth year with Dolores Sewer (and later David Sokoloff) followed by instruction in theory one year later with William Hapich. Subsequent piano study took place with Joseph Schwarz at the Philadelphia Academy. Although he wrote some music during this time, he was, for the time being, more interested in performing music. This changed when he was nineteen. After being graduated from Central High School in 1941, he attended the University of Pennsylvania (1941–46). There he received his bachelor of science degree in musical education in 1945, and his master of science degree a year later. By the time he was nineteen, he was writing music steadily.

In 1946 he entered the Juilliard School of Music in New York on a scholarship, studying composition first with Peter Mennin and later with William Bergsma. As a Juilliard student he wrote Three Songs, for baritone, celesta, and piano (1947), to the text of Tagore's *The Gardener*, and some chamber music that included his String Trio no. 1 and his String Quartet no. 1, both in 1948.

After graduating from Juilliard in 1948, Parris held his first teaching post at the State University of

Washington, in Pullman, Wash. (1948–49) Dissatisfied with what he described as "the musical wilderness" in Pullman, he returned to New York in 1949 to teach piano and coach singers. The summers of 1950 and 1951 were spent at the Berkshire Music Center at Tanglewood, Mass., studying composition with Jacques Ibert and Aaron Copland. At Tanglewood, his *Harlequin's Carnival*, for orchestra (1948), was introduced during the summer of 1951, the composer conducting. During this period (1951) he was also a composition student of Otto Luening's at Columbia University.

Later in 1951, on a Fulbright Fellowship, Parris went to Europe, continuing the study of composition with Arthur Honegger at the École normale de musique in Paris (1952–53). After returning to the United States in 1953 he settled in Washington, D.C., where he taught piano, composition, and harpsichord, wrote music criticism for the *Washington Post* (1958–61), and was a member of the music faculty of the University of Maryland in College Park (1961–63). In 1964 he was appointed head of the theory department at George Washington University in Washington, D. C. He has remained there since then, first as associate professor (1968) then full professor (1976). He has combined his classroom duties with public performances as pianist and harpsichordist and with the writing of occasional music reviews for the *Washington Star*.

While continuing to produce chamber music in the early 1950s, including his String Trio no. 2 (1951) and his String Quartet no. 2 (1952), Parris broadened the scope of his creativity with the completion of his Symphony no. 1 (1952) and a Piano Concerto (1954), the latter introduced in Washington, D. C., on March 21, 1954, with the composer as soloist. His first success came with the Concerto for Five Kettledrums and Orchestra (1955) with which his mature style can be said to have become fully crystallized. It was successfully introduced by Fred Begun and the National Symphony Orchestra under Howard Mitchell in Washington, D. C., on March 25, 1958. Here the composer demonstrated that gift for brilliant virtuoso writing for solo instruments that he would reveal in so many of his later works: in Trio for Clarinet, Piano, and Cello (1959; Washington, D. C., January 11, 1960), written on a grant from the Hans Kindler Foundation; the Viola Concerto (1956; Washington, D. C., May 20, 1971); Violin Concerto (1959); Flute Concerto (1964); Trombone Concerto (1964; Washington, D. C., September 19, 1964); Concerto for Percussion, Violin, Cello, and Piano (1967; Washington, D. C., October 3, 1967); and *The Phoenix*, a concerto for kettledrums and orchestra (1969) which was introduced by the Detroit Symphony under Sixten Ehrling on January 2, 1970.

Commenting on the Trombone Concerto, Paul Hume wrote in the *Washington Post*: "The opening movement (Nocturne) has about it the feeling of an eerie fantasy in which the strings sustain, usually on high harmonics, a single chord. . . . Clearly the Nocturne is one filled with weird phantoms. At its conclusion we are, however, precipitated into a running fire of figures (Perpetual Motion)." In the *Washington Star*, Theodore Price had this to say about the Concerto for Percussion, Violin, Cello, and Piano: "Any labels would do it a disservice; for its means of developing motifs, investigating textures, and sound continuity are complex. . . . It presents to the listener a multitude of musically interesting ideas. Purely from the rhythmic stance it is perspicacious: rhythmic phrase structures achieve a high level of continuity within themselves and exploitation with the scope of a single movement. And 'continuity' is also the mot juste . . . for its sonority spectrum."

Outside concerto literature Parris's subsequent major works include *The Book of Imaginary Beings*, *Walking Around*, and two works written on commission from the National Endowment for the Arts. *The Book of Imaginary Beings* (1972), scored for chamber ensemble and percussion, was premiered in Washington, D. C., on May 7, 1972. In reviewing a recording of this work for *Stereo Review*, David Hall spoke of Parris's "ability to weave brilliantly colorful yet tautly knit tonal tapestries for chamber ensemble." He added: "His musical bestiary is fanciful, at times wildly colorful, occasionally terrifying and also genuinely funny." In the sixth movement, Parris gave an amusing parody of Saint-Saëns's "The Swan" from *The Carnival of Animals*. *Walking Around* is a chamber cantata for men's voices and instruments (1973), a setting of a poem by Pablo Neruda. It was introduced in Washington, D. C., on May 27, 1973. The two works commissioned by the National Endowment for the Arts are *Angels*, for orchestra (1974; Albany, N. Y., March 14, 1975), originally entitled *The Messengers*; and *Rite of Passage*, for clarinet solo, electric guitar, piano, celesta, harp, percussion, cello, and bass (1978).

On May 18, 1974, Parris married Anna Elkes in Columbia, Md. They have a daughter.

THE COMPOSER SPEAKS: "At the moment, contemporary musical thought seems to be quiescent, recovering from about thirty-five years of frantic innovative activity. Some of that activity was a gratuitous overreaching for specious originality; some of it was honest ferment, fed by serious social changes and technological development. While waiting around for the next stylistic invention, some composers are reverting to 19th-century materials, with which, it seems to me, they must have felt most comfortable all along. Not that there is anything odd about that. Almost everyone is still being nurtured on music since 1700 or so, and will continue to be until the concert repertoire dictates a change in educational materials. But the educational materials mold those who maintain the museum pieces of the concert repertoire. And so the malignant circle continues to turn on itself, separating by an always increasing distance the composer from what would be, in a society whose values were less secular, his potential audience.

One can understand, therefore, why some composers, however wrong-headed, are quoting Beethoven and wanting to be Mahler. History has been pushed too far, too fast; as if in retaliation it has slid back a bit.

Another shove into the future is the last thing contemporary thought needs at this point. Now is the time for composers to swear off avant-gardes (they are all gone for a while) and arrière-gardes (until time learns to move backwards they are illusory anyway) and find only the true, the most difficult, originality—the one that lies within our own psyches.

PRINCIPAL WORKS: 2 string quartets (1951, 1954); 2 string trios (1948, 1951).

Symphony (1952); Sonatina, for winds (1954); Piano Concerto (1954); Fantasy and Fugue, for solo cello (1954); Concerto for Five Kettledrums and Orchestra (1955); Sonata for Violin and Harpsichord, or piano (1956); Viola Concerto (1956); Three Passacaglias, for soprano, harpsichord, violin, and cello (1957); Viola Sonata (1957); Quintet, for flute, oboe, bassoon, violin, and cello (1957); Violin Concerto (1958); Trio, for clarinet, cello, and piano (1959); *Mad Scene*, for soprano, two baritones, and chamber orchestra or piano (1960); *The Leaden Echo and the Golden Echo*, for baritone and orchestra (1960); *The Raids: 1940*, for soprano, violin, and piano (1960); Cadenza, Caprice, and Ricercar, for cello and piano (1961); *Lamentations and Praises*, for brasses and percussion (1962); Sinfonia, for brass quintet (1963); Flute Concerto (1964); Trombone Concerto (1964); Concerto for Percussion, Violin, Cello, and Piano (1967); *The Phoenix*, concerto for timpani and orchestra (1969); *The Book of Imaginary Beings*, for chamber ensemble and percussion (1972); *Walking Around*, chamber cantata for men's voices, clarinet, violin, and piano (1973); *Angels*, for orchestra, originally entitled *The Messengers* (1974); *Dreams*, for soprano and chamber orchestra (1976); *Rite of Passage*, for clarinet solo, electric guitar, and chamber orchestra (1978); *Cynthia's Revells*, for baritone and piano or guitar and piano (1979); *Three Lyrics by Ben Jonson*, for baritone and piano (1979).

BIBLIOGRAPHY: *BBDM*; *DCM*; *Who's Who in America, 1980–81*.

Partch, Harry, b. Oakland, Calif., June 24, 1901; d. San Diego, Calif., September 3, 1976.

Partch's world of avant-garde music was of his own making. He rejected not only the traditions, techniques, ideologies, methods, and instruments of Western music but even those of his fellow musical rebels. He had no interest in serialism, indeterminacy, or electronic music. He had to devise his own aesthetics, create his own scales based on just intonation, concoct his own harmonic language based upon the use of the seventh and eleventh partials of the overtone series, and manufacture his own instruments capable of playing such music. He regarded music not as a self-sufficient art by itself but as one element in a multifaceted art, an art that was part magic and part ritual, an art that removed itself from present-day society, an art that consisted of words, dance movements, miming, even slapstick, as well as music, an art that had to be seen as well as heard. Whatever ties he had to the past were to ancient rather than to Western culture.

He was the son of Presbyterian missionaries in China who abandoned their religious calling and settled in America in nonreligious occupations. Both parents were musical. His father collected and performed on various instruments. His mother—a reporter, teacher, and dedicated suffragette—sang and played the organ. In Arizona near the Mexican border, where the family came to live when Harry was still a child, he began learning to play the reed organ, mandolin, cornet, violin, and harmonica by himself when he was about six. Conscious of his intense interest in music, his mother began giving him some instruction on the piano. By the time Partch was fourteen he was composing music.

During his early adolescent years, he lived in New Mexico. There he studied music with private teachers. He soon grew so impatient with their conservative attitudes toward music that he decided to forego further lessons and go his own way in music, which he did from that point on. The same thing happened to his academic schooling. When he graduated from Albuquerque High School he decided he was through with the classroom and schoolroom curriculum. From then on his education came from going to libraries, reading, and studying textbooks without outside help. The influences that helped to mold his future musical identity were many, varied, and unusual. He enumerated them as follows: public libraries, Yaqui Indians, Chinese lullabies, Hebrew chants for the dead, Christian hymns, Congo puberty rites, Chinese music bells in San Francisco, lumber yards, junk shops, and *Boris Godunov*.

To support himself, he played the piano and organ in motion picture theaters for silent films. He also worked at a variety of jobs, such as those of a migrant fruit picker, teacher, and proofreader for a newspaper. All this time he was writing music for traditional instruments in a traditional style. By the time he was twenty-four he had become so stifled by the limitations imposed upon his musical thinking and writing by established methods and precedents that he stopped writing altogether. Six years later he destroyed everything he had ever written. When he resumed writing music in 1930 he had permanently broken all ties with Western music and embarked on his solitary journey to new destinations. He had become interested in just intonation in place of the

Western tempered scales and started experimenting with microtones. Since such music required special instruments, he set for himself the task of building them. Between 1928 and 1930 he constructed an "adapted viola" with an elongated neck which had to be played like a cello and which was able to sound thirty-seven stops to an octave. By the early 1930s he composed a work for his viola using microtones in which is reflected that fascination for the Orient he had acquired early in boyhood by listening to his mother sing Chinese songs and by attending Chinese operas in San Francisco. This work was *Seventeen Lyrics by Li-Po*, (1930–33), settings of poems by an 8th-century Chinese poet. The voice part consisted of a series of spoken or chanted incantations in pentatonic phrases to a microtonal background provided by his "adapted viola." Two other works of these years used similar approaches: *Potion Scene from Romeo and Juliet* and *By the River of Babylon*.

A grant from the Carnegie Corporation of New York in 1934 made it possible for him to go to England to study the history of intonation at the British Museum. When he returned to the United States in 1935, the country was deep in an economic depression. Unable to find a way of earning a living, Partch spent the next eight years as a hobo. He rode the rails and learned at firsthand about American geography, backgrounds, customs, peoples, regional idiosyncracies and social problems. At the same time he was collecting materials he would use in later compositions. He also expended a good deal of thought in clarifying for himself the kind of music he was interested in writing, and intermittently he turned his hand to the building of new musical instruments. In 1935 he adapted the Hawaiian-type guitar for six to ten strings. In 1938 he began to work on a seventy-two string kithara, a six-foot instrument shaped like the ancient Greek lyre. He was also writing some music for his instruments. Tapping his experiences as a hobo, he completed *Barstow* (1941), subtitled "Eight Hitchhiker Inscriptions from a California Highway at Barstow, California." The text was the graffiti scribbled by hitchhikers, and the music was chanted above an exotic, microtonal instrumental accompaniment.

He was employed as a lumberjack in the West in 1943 when he was awarded a Guggenheim Fellowship, which was extended for a second year in 1944. This provided him with the financial independence he needed to end his hobo life and to devote himself more intensely to his musical endeavors. Once again dipping into the well of his hobo experiences, he wrote *U. S. Highball: A Musical Account of a Transcontinental Life* (1943), for chorus and instruments; it received its world premiere in New York on April 22, 1944. Here, as he explained, his aim was to point up "the disintegration of urban civilization and the pathos of the outcasts' search for the spring of life." The text, narrated or chanted by a hobo called Mac, consisted of the names of railway stations, slogans on billboards, and Partch's own random thoughts as he wandered around the country. In his background music, for his own invented instruments, Partch recreated railroad noises while fragments of hillbilly music and popular tunes were woven into the overall texture. In 1950, Partch rewrote this work to include some newly manufactured instruments. In 1943, among other compositions, Partch wrote *The Letter*, "a depression message from a hobo to a friend" for voices and an instrumental ensemble.

Between 1944 and 1947, Partch was a research associate at the University of Wisconsin in Madison on a grant. He spent those years building more new instruments: Harmonic Canon I, with overlapping sets of forty-four strings and a movable bridge for each string, allowing for all kinds of microtonal patterns; the Chromelodeons, adapted reed organs with forty-three tones to the octave; and the diamond marimba consisting of thirty-six spruce blocks over redwood resonators arranged in diagonal rows to permit the sounding of an arpeggiolike chord with the single sweep of the mallet. In Wisconsin, he completed writing a book upon which he had been at work since 1928, elaborating on his ideas about his new music and his aims: *Genesis of Music*, published in 1949, and reissued in 1973.

His third Guggenheim Fellowship came in 1950, providing him with further funds for the development of his new music. By the early 1950s, Partch had perfected his tonal system: a forty-three microtonal scale. In the building of instruments he had become increasingly adventurous. Cloud-Chamber Bowls consisted of the tops and bottoms of pyrex carboys (acquired from the University of California Radiation Laboratory), suspended from a six-foot-high frame and struck with a mallet to produce bell-like tones. Spoils of War was a percussion instrument made of artillery shells, cloud-chamber bowls, bellows, a 1912 auto horn and a "whang gun." The Marimba Eroica consisted of four long wooden blocks on resonators played with heavy padded mallets. The Boo (bamboo marimba) had sixty-four bamboo cylinders played with felted stick to give forth a dry, percussive sound with one enharmonic overtone. Additionally, he constructed a new type of kithara and Harmonic Canon. Not only did he concoct picturesque names for his instruments but he also adorned some of them with fanciful decorations, such as African masks.

In 1951, Partch turned to the theater, beginning with *Oedipus*, the Yeats translation of the Sophocles drama *Oedipus Rex*. Because he could not find actors with the necessary musical sophistication, Partch, for the time being, had to abandon microtonal writing for traditional scales, all the better to promote some of his new ideas. The precise tone, rhythm, and inflection of the speaking parts were meticulously determined by the composer. "The music," Partch said, "is conceived as an emotional saturation that is the particular province of dramatic music to achieve. My idea has been to present the drama expressed by the language, not to obscure it, whether by operatic aria or symphonic instrumentation. Hence in the critical dialogue the music enters almost insidiously." *Oedipus* was first produced on March 14, 1952, at Mills College in Oakland, Calif. In the *San Francisco Chronicle*, Alfred Frankenstein wrote: "The score vastly enhanced the ominous tension of the tragedy." But *Time* found that it was "mostly what Hollywood called Mickey Mouse music—the tempo coinciding with the movement and speech. The orchestra produced cacophonous sounds sometimes reminiscent of a movie soundtrack for a Chinese street scene. The best thing about it is it seldom got in the actor's way."

On commission from the Fromm Music Foundation and the University of Illinois, Partch completed a second dramatic work, the satirical *The Bewitched* (1955), modeled after the Japanese Kabuki Theater *Noh* play. Partch here sought "for release—through satire, whimsy, magic, ribaldry—from the catharsis of tragedy," as he said. "It is an essay toward the miraculous abeyance of civilized rigidity." A group of lost clown-musicians appears as principal characters to destroy 20th-century mechanization and intellectualism. "They are primitive in their outspoken acceptance of magic as real," Partch explained, "reclaiming an all-but-lost value for the exploitation of their perception." Episodes provided a clue to the composer's dramatic intent through their titles, such as "A Soul Tortured by Contemporary Music Finds a Harmonic Alchemy," and "The Cognoscenti Are Plunged into a Demonic Descent with Cocktails," and "Visions Fill the Eyes of the Defeated Baseball Team in a Shower Room." *The Bewitched* featured a whole armory of Partchian instruments: Cloud-Chamber Bowls, Spoils of War, Marimba Eroica, Boo, Surrogate Kithara, Harmonic Canon, Chromelodian. "The musicians who play the instruments are not merely accompanists to the drama of the piece," said Eric Salzman in reviewing the recording for *Stereo Review*. "They are protagonists. In addition to contributing to the visual impact of these extraordinary constructions by playing them on the stage, the instrumentalists also form a vocal Chorus of Lost Musicians who experience various uncommon misadventures of modern life." Viewing *The Bewitched* as a whole, Salzman called it "a remarkable example of Partch's ritual music-theater. . . . He deals with the paradoxes and banalities of contemporary life in terms of magical and spiritual transformation. And his theater, again like his music, is antispecialized, antitragic, and very much conceived as an antidote to the ills and woes of technological civilization." After Partch had spent some six months in training students to play his instruments, *The Bewitched* was presented on March 26, 1957, at the University of Illinois in Urbana; three years later it was produced at the Juilliard School of Music in New York.

Revelation in the Courthouse Park (1960) was a contemporary version of Euripides' *The Bacchae*, the setting transferred from ancient Thebes to a modern-day park. Dionysius became a Hollywood Elvis Presley type of star named Dion, and the present-day ritual of worshiping singing heroes was celebrated with Hollywood-style music, parodies of the popular song. "The open stage is dark," explained Peter Yates in *High Fidelity/Musical America* when *Revelation* was performed at the University of Illinois at its premiere on April 11, 1961, "but we see at each side . . . unusually shaped instruments . . . The musicians enter . . . and the lights go on among the instruments. . . . At the rear of the hall, a brass band breaks out, and uniformed musicians march down the aisle led by four girls twirling batons. Here is the homecoming of Dion, the folk hero from Hollywood. He is greeted with squeals and yells, and the whole chorus, gathering around him on the stage, breaks into a chant, song, shouting, and dance, to the dark, heavy tones of the marimbas, the throb and glitter of the plucked strings."

On a commission from the University of Illinois, Partch completed a fourth drama, the farcical *Water, Water*, described as an "American ritual," first produced on March 9, 1962, at the University of Illinois. It consisted of eleven prologues and nine epilogues, separated by an intermission. On the left side of the stage stood a disk jockey, alderman, a lady mayor, and a baseball commentator in an American city called Santa Mystiana. On the right was an open countryside. What transpired was a duel between man and nature. Man was symbolized by a huge dam controlling the water supply; nature's ultimate victory, by torrential floods that destroy the city.

Delusion of the Fury: A Ritual of Dream and Delusion (1966) was judged by Tom Johnson in *High Fidelity/Musical America* to be the apex of Partch's works in the theater. "It is almost as if Partch's earlier works had been simply a preparation for this one. For here his many invented instruments, his ideas about the voice, his theatrical concepts, and his highly sophisticated harmonic and textural devices all converge in one authoritative statement." Act I, in which the hero is an enlightened ghost, was based on the Japanese *Noh* play; Act II, with a deaf and near-sighted judge as hero, was an adaptation of an Ethiopian folk tale. Partch elaborates: "Act I treats with death and with life despite death. Act II treats with life and with life despite death." The work was prefaced by an *Exordium* performed by several Partchian instruments evoking the world of the Orient.

Partch's music was also used in motion pictures: in *Windsong* (1958), a study of nature, shown at the Brussels Exposition of 1958, and *Rotate the Body in All Its Planes* (1961), a film about gymnastics. Three films were about Partch himself. *Music Studio, Harry Partch* (1958) showed Partch performing on the ten instruments he had used in *Windsong*. *The Music of Harry Partch* was produced by KEBS-TV, a television station at the San Diego State College in California. In 1972, a new television film about Partch was produced, entitled *The Dreamer Remains*.

Sporadic performances in the eastern states and recordings of Partch's music on his own label (Gate V) and by one or two small companies were unable to make Partch and his music known to America at large. Outside a small sphere in the West, where he made his home and where a handful of his admirers had for some time made him into something of a cult, his name was as unknown to the general public as his theories, innovations, and music.

An important break from this obscurity came on September 8, 1968, when a concert of his works was given at the Whitney Museum of American Art in New York, combined with an exhibition of his instruments. By providing a cross-section of what he had written through the years, this program offered an opportunity for eastern United States to evaluate his work. "It was plain," reported Theodore Strongin in the *New York Times*, "that Mr. Partch is fanciful, whimsical and a philosopher. . . . It is even plainer that in the best sense he has never grown up. *Petals* and *Exordium* have a kind of wide-eyed simplicity, a lack of disillusion that is unaffected by the oversophisticated musical practices." About *And on the Seventh Day Petals Fall on Petaluma* (1963–64), Strongin added: "Each episode seemed a segment of some far-off continuous music that reveals itself to us only at moments of hearing. It is an amiable, even funny piece."

In 1966, Partch received an award from the National Institute of Arts and Letters and the Nealie Sullivan Award from the San Francisco Art Institute.

THE COMPOSER SPEAKS: The rebelliously creative act is also a tradition, and if our art of music is to be anything more than a shadow of its past, the traditions in question must periodically shake off dormant habits and excite themselves into palpable growth.

Much has been said about expressing one's own time. Nothing could be more futile or downright idiotic. The prime obligation of the artist is to transcend his age, and therefore to show it in terms of the eternal mysteries.

PRINCIPAL WORKS: *Seventeen Lyrics by Li-Po* (1930–33); *Barstow* (1941); *Dark Brother* (1943); *The Letter* (1943); *San Francisco Newsboy Cries* (1943); *U. S. Highball* (1943); *Two Settings from Finnegans Wake* (1944); *Intrusions* (1949–50); *Electra and Percussion Dances* (1949–52); *Oedipus* (1951); *The Bewitched* (1955); *Music Studio* (1958); *Revelation in the Courthouse Park* (1960); *Rotate the Body in All Its Planes* (1961); *Ballad for Gymnasts* (1961); *Water, Water* (1962); *And on the Seventh Day Petals Fell on Petaluma* (1963–64).

BIBLIOGRAPHY: Ewen, David, *Composers of Tomorrow's Music* (N. Y., 1971); Larrabee, E. (editor), *American Panorama* (N.Y., 1957); Partch, Harry, *Genesis of a Music* (Madison, Wis., 1949); Yates, Peter, *Twentieth Century Music* (N.Y., 1967); *Hi-Fi Stereo Review*, February 1961; *High Fidelity*, July 1963; *High Fidelity/Musical America*, November 1975; *New York Times*, September 9, 1968; *Saturday Review*, November 27, 1971.

Pasatieri, Thomas, b. New York City, October 20, 1945.

As one of America's most successful composers of opera, Pasatieri has been more a voice of the past than of the present or future. He is in the image of the 19th-century Italian bel canto composers in the ease with which he writes operas to order, in tailoring his principal roles to specific singers, in his love for and command of the voice for which he often writes soaring lyrical passages (with a preference for female voices), and in his insistence on writing his operas for the pleasure of audiences rather than for fellow composers or critics. His operas are derivative from the *verismo* styles of Puccini and Menotti.

From his boyhood days, Pasatieri was interested in both theater and music. He was always involved in theatrical productions at the St. Francis Prep School in Flushing, N.Y., which he attended from 1958 to 1960, and at Sewanhaka High School where he produced and directed a performance of Jerome Kern's musical *Leave It to Jane* for the graduation exercises in 1962. Piano lessons were begun when he was seven with Vera Wels, and were continued with her for the next nine years. Two years after these lessons were started he was already making public appearances as pianist in New York City. These performances continued until 1965, and in time were supplemented by chores as conductor. Without any preliminary training, he initiated his composing career when he was fourteen with songs and pieces for the piano. One year later, he attended a lecture by Nadia Boulanger, then in New York. After the lecture he sent her a batch of his compositions. She found the works so meritorious that she encouraged him to keep sending his music, which she corrected and commented upon in a continuous exchange through the mails.

A scholarship in 1961 brought Pasatieri to the Juilliard School of Music. There he sang in the choir, gave piano recitals, and received training in theory and composition from Vincent Persichetti and Vittorio Giannini. The latter was the first to arouse his interest in opera. With Giannini's encouragement and under his watchful eye, Pasatieri wrote both libretto and music for his first opera, *The Trysting Place* (1964) based on a Booth Tarkington story. Nothing much came from this student effort, which was soon discarded, but it whetted Pasatieri's appetite for writing operas. While occupied with the tasks of coaching singers and playing the piano at vocal lessons in order to learn what he could about the voice, Pasatieri completed a second opera, *The Flowers of Ice* (1965). This, too, was never produced and was soon abandoned.

In his nineteenth year, Pasatieri attended the music school at Aspen, Colo., to continue the study of composition with Darius Milhaud. It was there that one of his operas was produced for the first time: *The Women*, a one-act opera to his own libretto, heard on August 20, 1965, and winner of the Aspen Festival Prize. "The audience reaction was tremendous," he recalled, "and that hooked me on opera—the whole experience was so exciting."

Pasatieri was now writing prolifically, sometimes two or three operas a year, beginning to work on a new one before the ink was dry on the manuscript of its predecessor. A satiric one-act opera, *La divina* (1965), was produced at the Juilliard School on March 16, 1966, and *Padrevia* (1966), also in one act, was performed at Brooklyn College, in Brooklyn, N.Y., on November 18, 1967. His first three-act opera came in 1967: *The Penitentes*, a searing dramatic work with libretto by Anne Howard Bailey about a sect of New Mexican Indians in which one of its members is chosen to reenact the Crucifixion. It took seven years for this opera to get heard, at Aspen on August 3, 1974.

In 1965, Pasatieri received the bachelor of arts degree at Juilliard, following it with his master's degree in 1967, and his doctorate (the first one conferred by that school for composition) in 1969. In 1967 he served on the music faculty of North Carolina School of the Arts in Siena, Italy. He taught composition at the Juilliard School between 1967 and 1969 and at the Manhattan School of Music from 1969 to 1971. Since then, he has conducted master classes in opera and composition at colleges and universities throughout the United States.

Recognition came first with *Calvary* (1971), a setting of a play by W. B. Yeats. Following its premiere in Bellevue, Wash., in April 1971 it was extensively performed in churches throughout the United States. His first success outside the limited boundaries of Aspen, the Juilliard School or churches came about through television. Commissioned by the National Education Television, Pasatieri completed in 1972 the score for *The Trial of Mary Lincoln*, libretto by Anne Howard Bailey, based on the trial in Chicago in which Mary Lincoln, widow of the president, was declared insane. Telecast over the National Education Television network on February 14, 1972, the opera took full advantage of the television medium by employing flashbacks, dissolves, voice-overs, and other television devices to enhance the dramatic action and provide keen psychological insight into the personality of Mary Lincoln. "He writes melody which can be sung," wrote Harriet Johnson in her review in the *New York Post*. "He is knowledgeable about what the voice can do and sensitive in his style to its

needs and possibilities. In *The Trial of Mary Lincoln*, he uses a kind of endless melody, song speech which propels itself forward as the emotions rise and carries us along too. The instrumental background is sometimes almost too rich."

The Trial of Mary Lincoln, his first commissioned work, was followed by many other commissions. For the Seattle Opera in Washington he wrote *The Black Widow* (1972), successfully produced on March 2, 1972. The composer wrote his own libretto, basing it on *Duos madres*, a novella by Miguel de Unamuno about a Spanish woman so obsessed with the desire for a child that she compels her lover to marry somebody else so that she can appropriate their child for herself. *The Seagull* (1974) was mounted by the Houston Opera in Texas, which had commissioned it, on March 5, 1974 (a day designated by the mayor of Houston as "Pasatieri Day"). Kenwood Elmslie adapted the Chekhov drama. Text and music became, in the words of Olin Chism in the *Dallas Times*, "a soaring piece of lyrical theater." *Ines de Castro* (1976)—libretto by Bernard Stambler, concerned with love, political intrigues, and murder in 14th-century Portugal—was composed for the Baltimore Opera in Maryland to commemorate its silver jubilee and was first performed there on May 31, 1976; but its world premiere took place in Aspen, Colo., on April 1, 1976. *Washington Square* (1976)—Kenwood Elmslie's libretto based on Henry James's *Portrait of a Lady*—was written at the request of the Michigan Opera in Detroit to celebrate the American bicentennial; it was mounted on October 1, 1976. *Before Breakfast* (1977) is a one-act opera written on a commission from the National Endowment for the Arts for a television operatic production starring Beverly Sills. Her retirement as an opera singer forced a change of plans. She decided to produce it at the New York City Opera of which she had become director, the first performance taking place on October 9, 1980. Its libretto, by Frank Corsaro, was based on a short tragic play by Eugene O'Neill about a woman whose unhappy marital life sends her husband to suicide. In all these operas, Pasatieri's gift for writing for the voice, his pronounced dramatic talent, and inordinate capability of communicating with audiences at first hearing were always evident. As Hubert Saal said in *Newsweek*: "The young composer was born to write dramatic and vocal music. It pours out of him—for the orchestra, for the voices, in one diverse lyrical outburst after another, tonal and atonal, always suited to the characters who sing them." *Before Breakfast*, however, is much more dissonant than Pasatieri's previous operas, "partially because," the composer explains, "the language is so astringent—you can't set these words in a bel canto fashion." To the accusation of some of his colleagues and critics that he was, in his overall operatic output, too old-fashioned and too commercial for serious artistic consideration, Pasatieri countered by saying: "I want to express myself in whatever way works, tonally or dissonantly. Because my music is tonal, I am accused of not being serious. What's avant-garde, what's conservative in the perspective of history?"

Pasatieri brought his talent for writing for the voice to the concert hall as well as to the theater. Thomas Stewart and Evelyn Lear (distinguished husband and wife concert and operatic team) were so impressed with Pasatieri's vocal writing that they invited him to write a concert work for them. He responded with a song cycle, *Heloise and Abelard*, for soprano, baritone, and piano (1971), which they introduced in New York on December 11, 1971. The following April, Patricia Brooks featured four Pasatieri songs at the Lincoln Center for the Performing Arts in New York. *Rites de passage*, for voice and chamber orchestra (1974), on a text by Lloyd Phillips, was introduced at Fort Lauderdale, Fla., in March 1974; *Three Poems of James Agee*, for voice and piano (1974), sung by Shirley Verrett, received its premiere in New York in April 1974; *Permit Me Voyage* (1976), a cantata for soprano, chorus, and orchestra to poems by Agee, was first performed by Catherine Malfitano in Connecticut on April 13, 1976; and *Day of Love*, for voice and piano (1978), was heard first on February 25, 1979, presented by Frederica von Stade at a recital at the Lincoln Center for the Performing Arts in New York.

Among the awards and scholarships Pasatieri gathered were the Richard Rodgers Scholarship, the Marion Freschi Prize, the Brevard Festival Prize, the George A. Wedge Prize, and the Irving Berlin Fellowship.

THE COMPOSER SPEAKS: I'm interested in people. Otherwise why write an opera? . . . Since I am a theater composer, whatever works—the best music I can write *for that moment*—is what I will write. But first of all, it has to be good music, and always music that is beautiful to sing. . . .

I'm writing for an audience. I want to bring joy with my music. I would rather please a real audience than please five other composers sitting in a room.

PRINCIPAL WORKS: *Heloise and Abelard*, for soprano, baritone and piano (1971); *Calvary*, one-act religious music drama (1971); *The Trial of Mary Lincoln*, television opera (1972); *The Black Widow*, opera (1972); *Rites de passage*, for voice and chamber orchestra (1974); *The Seagull*, opera (1974); *Signor Deluso*, one-act opera buffa (1974); *The Penitentes*, opera (1974); *Three Poems of James Agee*, for voice and piano (1974); *Ines de Castro*, opera (1976); *Washington Square*, opera (1976); *Permit Me Voyage*, cantata for soprano, chorus, and orchestra (1976); two piano sonatas (1976); *Before Breakfast*, one-act opera (1977); *Day of Love*, for voice and piano (1978); *The Three Sisters*, opera (1979).

BIBLIOGRAPHY: *High Fidelity/Musical America*,

March 1972; *New York Times Magazine*, March 26, 1976; *Opera News*, March 4, 1972; *Who's Who in America, 1980-81*.

Perle, George, b. Bayonne, N.J., May 6, 1915.

Perle was one of the first American composers to become interested in serialism, but he was always critical of Schoenberg's system because it did not seem to him to offer a coherent means of organizing the harmonic dimension of twelve-tone music. Through certain radical modifications of Schoenberg's system, Perle derived a systematic approach to twelve-tone harmony. In Perle's view, the seemingly disparate styles of posttriadic music share common structural elements, elements which collectively imply a new tonality, as "natural" and coherent as the major-minor tonality of the past. This is the basis of most of his music between 1939 and 1969 and all of it since 1969.

His parents had immigrated to the United States from Russia just before World War I. Neither parent had any musical training but both loved music; his mother was a particularly significant influence in his early musical growth. When Perle was about six his family acquired a piano. Hearing a relative play Chopin and Liszt on this instrument was Perle's first vivid musical recollection. "These pieces," he says, "used to put me into a strange and terrifying trance of which no one—not even my mother—had the slightest inkling." Perle's cousin was his first piano teacher, while subsequent piano instruction continued with various teachers in the localities where the Perles made their home. From his beginnings as a music student, his prime interest lay in composition in which, initially, he was self-educated through the analysis and dissection of piano pieces he was practicing.

He received his academic education in elementary schools and at the John Marshall High School in Chicago. During these years he continued to study piano at the Chicago College of Music, at the same time receiving there his first formal instruction in harmony. Between 1935 and 1938 he attended DePaul University in Chicago, studying composition there with Wesley La Violette. He was composing all the time, but in 1939 he destroyed much of what he had written. The sole survivors were *Pantomime, Interlude and Fugue* and *Classic Suite*, both for piano, and *Triolet* and *Molto adagio*, both for string quartet, all written in 1937–38.

Initiation into the posttonal music of Schoenberg and Alban Berg in the late 1930s forced him to re-evaluate everything he had written. "I was fully aware of the disintegration of the traditional harmonic and tonal system before I found out about the works of Schoenberg," he says. "But my first five minutes with Berg's *Lyric Suite* at the piano was like a revelation (in the literal biblical sense)." In 1939,

Perle started writing a string quartet based on an altogether original concept of the compositional implication of the twelve-tone row, but he soon found it necessary to abandon this piece until he could think through the problems of set structure. As he later wrote: "I considered the possibility of constructing special sets whose linear adjacencies would present a coherent pattern, sets more likely to suggest consistent harmonic procedures than does the general set." One of Perle's earliest works based on his special method was *Two Rilke Songs*, for voice and piano (1941), which were recorded in 1979 by Bethany Beardslee and the composer.

Perle studied composition privately with Ernst Krenek between 1939 and 1941. During this period, in 1940, he married his first wife, Laura Slobe; they were divorced in 1952. In 1942, Perle earned his master of music degree at the American Conservatory of Music in Chicago. Between 1943 and 1946, during World War II, Perle served in the U. S. Army, stationed in both the European and Pacific theaters of operation. When the war in the Pacific ended, he was sent with the army of occupation to Japan before being discharged in February 1946.

He initiated a long and eventful career as teacher in 1948 by serving as lecturer on music at the College of the City of New York. Between 1949 and 1957 he was on the music faculty of the University of Louisville in Kentucky, as instructor in composition and music history. He was also on the music faculty of the University of California at Davis between 1957 and 1961. In 1956 he received his doctorate in musicology at New York University, having studied music history there with Gustave Reese and Curt Sachs. On August 11, 1958, Perle married Barbara Phillips, an English-born sculptress, with whom he raised two adopted daughters and a son by Barbara's first marriage.

In 1961 Perle was appointed assistant professor at Queens College of the City University of New York. He was elevated to professorship in 1963 and full professorship in 1966. He has held visiting positions on the faculties of the Juilliard School of Music (1963), the University of Southern California (summer of 1965), Yale University (1965–66), the Berkshire Music Center at Tanglewood, Mass. (1967 and 1980), the State University of Buffalo (1971–72), the University of Pennsylvania (1976 and 1980) and Columbia University (1979).

Between 1941 and 1969, Perle produced several works that may be said to be more "freely" or "intuitively" conceived than those based on his special method. This represented an independent line of development going back to the so-called atonal music that preceded Schoenberg's formulation of his twelve-tone system in 1922–23, but which, like all of Perle's music, is much involved with tone centers and harmonic structure and very different in its thematic and rhythmic character from the music of preserial "atonality." In such a style we find the Quintet for

Strings (1958), scored for extra viola, which Perle considers to be one of his best works up until his String Quartet no. 7 (1973); it was introduced in San Francisco on February 19, 1960. The three wind quintets (1959, 1960, 1967) also reflect the same approach. But other works between 1941 and 1969, and all since 1969, are in his "postdiatonic tonality" idiom.

Two of Perle's widely performed compositions were introduced at a concert of the Composers' Showcase in New York on May 10, 1962: *Monody* no. 1, for solo flute (1960), performed by Samuel Baron, who also recorded it, and Serenade no. 1, for solo viola and chamber orchestra (1962), with Walter Trampler as soloist and Arthur Weisberg conducting. In reviewing the recording of *Monody* no. 1 in *Stereo Review*, Eric Salzman called it a "lively and engaging little masterpiece of the medium." The five-movement Serenade, as Donal Henahan reported in the *Chicago Daily News*, "achieved a variety in expression and sound that contemporary music too often ignores in its preoccupation with organizational techniques. . . . The composer enlivened matters at one point with a jazz interlude, then explored the varieties of music experience inherent in the solo viola's insistence on one note, while the others went other, more colorful ways."

Three Movements, for orchestra (1960), was premiered at the Festival of the International Society for Contemporary Music in Amsterdam on June 14, 1963. Reporting from Amsterdam to the *Christian Science Monitor*, Everett Helm wrote: "Vertical relationships are carefully planned and thought out to create some fascinating harmonies. The piece displayed an admirable feeling for nicely balanced form, orchestral color, and texture. It was agreeable music, well written and expressive." Three Movements was given its first American hearing on March 7, 1965, in a performance by the Chicago Symphony under Jean Martinon and was recorded by the Royal Philharmonic Orchestra of London under David Epstein in 1974.

On a commission from Irving Ilmer for a composition for violin and viola, on both of which Ilmer was adept, Perle wrote the five-movement Partita, for violin and viola (1965), which Ilmer introduced in Chicago on April 23, 1965. The opening Prelude is for viola, followed by an Allemande (violin), Courante (viola), Sarabande (violin), and Finale (violin). String Quartet no. 5 (1960, revised 1967) received its initial performance at Tanglewood on August 13, 1967, at the Festival of Contemporary American Music sponsored by the Fromm Music Foundation and the Berkshire Music Center. Michael Steinberg, in the *Boston Globe*, called it "the most innovatory work of the festival, but one that had particular pleasure for being so personal and so new." Serenade no. 2, for chamber orchestra (1968), commissioned by the Koussevitzky Music Foundation for the Library of Congress in Washington, D. C., was premiered there by the Contemporary Chamber Ensemble under Arthur Weisberg on February 28, 1969. *Sonata quasi una fantasia*, for clarinet and piano (1972), which Robert Laneri and the composer introduced in Buffalo, N.Y., on March 19, 1972, was a demanding virtuoso piece with extraordinarily difficult rhythmic interrelations between the two instruments, and exploiting multiphonics and harmonics for the clarinet.

One of Perle's most significant chamber music works is the String Quartet no. 7 (1973), whose premiere was given by the Cleveland Quartet (which had commissioned it) in Buffalo, N.Y., on March 19, 1974. Reviewing this composition in the British journal *Musical Times*, Paul Griffiths described it as "eloquent testimony to the range and coherence" of Perle's twelve-tone tonality. "The main impression, thanks to the skill with which Perle balances phrase against phrase, section against section, is one of genial musical discourse."

Perle is also at the peak of his creative powers in *Songs of Praise and Lamentation* (1974), for solo voices, chorus, and orchestra, structurally his most ambitious work to date. It was commissioned by the Dessoff Choirs with grants from the New York State Council of the Arts and several others; its world premiere took place in New York on February 18, 1975. Each of its three movements uses a different text in a different language. Lines from Psalm 18, in Hebrew, were found in the first movement, and four of Rilke's *Sonnets to Orpheus*, in German, in the second. The third movement consisted of three Renaissance deplorations, the first a lamentation in French on the death of Binchois by Ockeghem, the second a lamentation in French on the death of Ockeghem by Josquin and the third a lamentation on the death of Josquin by Vinders. All these are incorporated within Perle's own musical setting of John Hollander's text in English with Latin refrains. A work of poetic beauty and a sensitivity to word settings and rich in atmospheric writing, this composition rises to heights of eloquence in the concluding movement.

Few of Perle's compositions received such an immediate and consistently enthusiastic reception as his Six Etudes, for piano (1976), which Morey Ritt premiered in Boston on October 29, 1976, as part of the "World Music Days" of the International Society for Contemporary Music. A number of critics described these etudes as the outstanding work heard at the thirteen concerts of this festival. Paul Hume of the *Washington Post* even wrote that the etudes were "among the finest works for piano written in a generation."

On June 19, 1978, at Princeton, N.J., Bethany Beardslee presented the premiere of *Thirteen Dickinson Songs*, for soprano and piano (1978), which Perle wrote on a commission from the National Endowment for the Arts. These songs convey the motifs of remembrance, autumn, and death. In *Keynote*, Mark Swen wrote: "One never loses Dickinson's voice as it moves from the awestruck emotions of childhood through wistful midlife sentiments to poignant thoughts about death. The music sets the mood, heightens the drama, underscores the emotion, and subtly conforms to the poetic meter."

Perle completed a Concertino, for piano, winds, and timpani, in 1979 on a commission from the Fromm Music Foundation. Morey Ritt and the Contemporary Chamber Players of the University of Chicago under Ralph Shapey presented the premiere in Chicago on April 27, 1979. "I have no hesitation calling the ten-minute Concertino a small Perle of great price," wrote John von Rhein in the *Chicago Tribune*. "Throughout, the composer's language remains distinctly his own: clean and lively and invigorating, without an ounce of fat. Twelve-tone elements are involved but they are shrewdly used to sustain a solidly tonal flavor."

Perle wrote *A Short Symphony* in 1980, and it received its world premiere at the Berkshire Music Festival at Tanglewood, Mass., on August 16, 1980, with Seiji Ozawa conducting the Boston Symphony. In the *New York Times*, Harold C. Schonberg called it "a throwback to the atonal world of Alban Berg. . . . In this three-movement, seventeen-minute long symphony he evoked the composer of *Lulu* and *Wozzeck*."

Perle was awarded Guggenheim Fellowships in 1966 and 1974. Between 1968 and 1970, he was president of the United States section of the International Society for Contemporary Music, and in 1966 he was the cofounder and has since served as director of the International Alban Berg Society. Perle is a world authority on Berg and his music, a field in which he has done valuable research which has shed new and significant light on Berg's life and music.

In 1977, Perle received an award from the National Institute of Arts and Letters, and in 1978 he was elected to membership in the American Academy and National Institute of Arts and Letters. He is the author of *Serial Composition and Atonality* (1977), *Twelve-Tone Tonality* (1977), and *The Operas of Alban Berg*, vol. 1 (1980), as well as numerous articles on various aspects of 20th-century music, but most notably on twelve-tone music and its composers. On several occasions his writings won the Deems Taylor Award from the American Society of Composers, Authors, and Publishers (ASCAP).

THE COMPOSER SPEAKS: It would never occur to anybody that the music of Bach or Chopin or Mozart or Brahms must remain inaccessible to people who haven't the technical competence to read a treatise on tonal harmony. Neither does the accessibility of my music depend on the listener's competence to read my treatise on twelve-tone tonality. A good deal of "advanced" music today is obscure and difficult to comprehend. Mine isn't, and I think this is largely due to the concepts of pitch organization that are at the basis of my music, even though any *theoretical* explanation of these concepts is bound to be difficult. After all, very few people are prepared to deal with a simple text on tonal harmony, and it hasn't made tonal music inaccessible to them.

PRINCIPAL WORKS: 7 string quartets (1939–73); 3 wind quintets (1959, 1960, 1967); 2 sonatas for solo violin (1959, 1963).

Two Rilke Songs, for voice and piano (1941); Piano Sonata (1950); Quintet, for strings (1958); Three Movements, for orchestra (1960); *Monody* no. 1, for solo flute (1960); Serenade no. 1, for viola and chamber ensemble (1962); *Monody* no. 2, for double bass solo (1962); *Short Sonata*, for piano (1964); Partita, for violin and viola solos (1963); Six Bagatelles, for orchestra (1965); Cello Concerto (1966): Serenade no. 2, for strings (1968); Toccata, for piano (1969); Suite in C, for piano (1970); *Sonata quasi una fantasia*, for clarinet and piano (1972); *Songs of Praise and Lamentation*, for vocal soloists, chorus, and orchestra (1974); Etudes, for piano (1976); *Thirteen Dickinson Songs*, for soprano and piano (1978); Concertino, for piano, winds, and timpani (1979); *A Short Symphony* (1980).

BIBLIOGRAPHY: *DCM; NGDMM; American Composers Alliance Bulletin,* September 1962; *Musical Quarterly,* April 1971, July 1975; *New York Times,* October 5, 1980; *Who's Who in America, 1980–81.*

Persichetti, Vincent, b. Philadelphia, Pa., June 6, 1915.

There is no stylistic common denominator to Persichetti's large output in virtually every medium. Throughout his career he has carefully steered a course that avoided any extremes of right or left, yet was wide enough to encompass and synthesize elements of classicism, romanticism, and moderation. Expansive lyricism on the one hand and motivic germinal materials on the other, together with skillful polyphony and subtle and often complex rhythmic and metric patterns, are all used for statements producing an art uniquely his.

Persichetti's father came to the United States from Italy at the age of twelve, and Persichetti's mother was born in Germany and brought to America as an infant. Neither was musical, but both were supportive of Vincent's musical interests from childhood onwards. He revealed his precocity for music early. "I always liked music," he recalls, "and set about learning it as quickly as possible." Piano study began when he was about six at the Combs Conservatory in Philadelphia with Warren E. Stanger, who remained his teacher for a decade. Later, at Combs, Persichetti received grounding in theory and composition from Russell King Miller (whom he regards as one of the most potent influences on his musical development), while continuing piano study with Gil-

bert Reynolds Combs (1931–34) and Alberto Jonas (1934–36). When Persichetti was eleven, he began studying the organ with Stanger (1926–31). Later on, he also received instruction in double bass from William Geiger (1929–31) and tuba (1934–35).

He was already a professional musician by the time he was eleven, serving as piano accompanist and as a staff member of a radio station, and playing double bass in local orchestras. At twelve he gave organ recitals; at fifteen, became an organist and musical director of St. Mark's Reformed Church in Philadelphia; and at sixteen he was appointed organist of the Arch Street Presbyterian Church, a post he retained for twenty years, later combining it with that of director. He was also receiving his academic education in Philadelphia's public schools, in one of which he played the double bass in the school orchestra.

All the while, he was composing music, "some secretly, because my teachers didn't approve, and some of it openly in the style and structure of 19th-century composers which they favored." Two early works were neoclassic serenades, the first for ten instruments and the other for piano, both completed in 1929. The latter was performed by the composer in Philadelphia on December 21, 1929, but the former had to wait twenty-three years to be heard, being introduced at San Angelo College in Texas on April 11, 1952, performed by the New York Wind Ensemble.

Upon receiving his bachelor of music degree from Combs College in 1936, Persichetti studied conducting with Fritz Reiner at the Curtis Institute of Music in Philadelphia (1936–38), receiving his diploma in 1938. Then, while serving as head of the composition department at Combs College between 1937 and 1941, he attended the Philadelphia Conservatory of Music on scholarships, where he continued studying piano with Olga Samaroff (1937–39) and composition with Paul Nordoff (1938–40). When, one day, he came to Olga Samaroff's piano class unprepared for his lesson, he placed on the piano the music of a Bach organ prelude he happened to have with him at the time and transcribed it at sight. Olga Samaroff liked it and encouraged him to get it down on paper. Somehow, the transcription fell into the hands of Eugene List, concert pianist, who performed it in New York, where it was praised by one of the critics. A publisher (Elkan-Vogel) accepted it, and Persichetti's first opus made its appearance.

On June 3, 1941, Persichetti married Dorothea Flanagan, a trained pianist, who became the mother of his two children as well as a performer of his piano compositions, annotator of his major works, and his fellow artist in presenting concerts of two-piano music, or four-hand piano music, of contemporary interest.

Dissatisfied with the music he had written before 1938, Persichetti discarded practically everything he had written except for the two serenades. He now started out on a new footing, less inclined to be subservient to the rules he had learned at the conservatory and freer in his use of tonality, harmony, and rhythm. Several compositions in 1939 represented his emancipation from his past. These included his first two piano sonatas, two volumes of *Poems*, for the piano, and his String Quartet no. 1. A Concertino for Piano and Orchestra followed in 1941 (Rochester, N.Y., October 23, 1945); and, in 1942, came his first two symphonies (the first of which was introduced in Rochester on October 21, 1947, Howard Hanson conducting), and the *Dance Overture*, for orchestra, which received the Juilliard Publication Award in 1943 and was premiered in Japan on February 7, 1948, by the Tokyo Symphony Orchestra.

As a composer, he began gaining recognition in Philadelphia in 1943 with two world premieres and one local premiere of works written in 1943. The two world premieres arrived on the same day—April 20, 1945—when the Philadelphia Orchestra under Eugene Ormandy, with Robert Grooters as soloist, introduced *Fables*, for narrator and orchestra, and when the Curtis Quintet presented the Pastoral, for woodwind quintet. The local premiere came with the Piano Sonata no. 3 later the same year, which the composer had introduced at the Colorado Springs Fine Arts Festival in Colorado on August 13, 1943, where it received first prize and became his second publication. *Fables* used six of *Aesop's Fables* for its text, in which the speaking part was treated as an instrument. In this music, as the composer explained, he sought an "emotional parallel of the ageless tales and the text as an integral part of the music; no certain instrument is assigned to any one character, but rather a musical equivalent is given the underlying meaning of the fables." In *Modern Music*, Rafael Druian called the Pastoral "bright music, cleanly scored, achieving even in its five-part contrapuntal texture a nice balance between the characteristic variety of the individual instruments and the unity of the ensemble" and the Piano Sonata as "a substantial work built entirely upon a chorale motive [moving] from a tragic 'Declaration' to a memorial-like 'Episode' and culminating in the 'Psalm,' a hope for peace and a hymn of praise."

In 1941, Persichetti received his master's degree in music at the Philadelphia Conservatory, and for three weeks in 1943 he studied composition with Roy Harris at Colorado College. In 1942, Persichetti was appointed head of the composition department at the Philadelphia Conservatory, where he remained for the next twenty years and where he received his doctorate in music in 1945. Since 1947 he has been a member of its composition faculty, head of that department from 1963 to 1973. He has also taught at the Juilliard School of Music in New York since 1947, to become one of America's most influential and scholarly teachers of composition. From 1952 on, Persichetti was an editorial consultant for his publisher, Elkan-Vogel, later on director of publications.

For his String Quartet no. 2 (1944; Colorado Springs, Colo., August 18, 1945) Persichetti was awarded the Blue Network Prize by the National Broadcasting Company in 1945. *The Hollow Men*, for trumpet and orchestra (1944), acquired a secure place in the symphonic repertoire after its initial hearing in Germantown, Pa., on December 12, 1946; it owes its inspiration to poems by T. S. Eliot. Poems by e. e. cummings provided texts for the *e. e. cummings Songs* (1945), for soprano and piano, which Phyllis Curtin premiered in Philadelphia on May 17, 1948.

Persichetti emerged as one of America's significant symphonists with the Symphony no. 3 (1943), first performed on November 21, 1947, by the Philadelphia Orchestra under Ormandy. He had begun planning it as far back as 1942. The first movement, marked "Somber," was developed from the dotted-note figure that established a dark mood. This mood lightened with the second movement, "Spirited," which was dominated by a dance theme. The third movement, "Singing," was highlighted by a mobile melody for English horn. In the fourth movement, "Fast and Brilliant," a rapid theme received variation treatment from each of the orchestral sections, sometimes alone, sometimes in combination with the others. The symphony's opening sombre theme serves as the motive for a chorale in the bass with which the symphony ends.

Persichetti's most important symphonies after that were the fourth, fifth, seventh, and ninth, each of which entered the repertoires of major orchestras. Symphony no. 4 (1951) was introduced on December 17, 1954, by the Philadelphia Orchestra under Ormandy. Persichetti wrote it at a time when he was also creating *Harmonium*, a song cycle for soprano and piano (1951; N. Y., January 20, 1952). "It was a refreshing breather after the big cycle," the composer's wife has revealed, "and the symphony came easily and quickly. The composer scarcely remembers writing it; it was almost an automatic act. Its music is bright and light, and its form is tight and classic in feeling. It winks at Mozart and Mussorgsky and opens with Haydnesque introduction."

The Symphony no. 5 (1953) was the result of a commission from the Louisville Orchestra, which, under Robert Whitney's direction, gave the premiere performance in Kentucky on August 28, 1954. The Philadelphia Orchestra under Ormandy presented it in 1959, and since then it has been successfully performed by numerous American and European orchestras. Here, as in several other major compositions by this composer, a one-movement structure is employed. The entire work is based on a single principal idea which was first heard in the violas and was evolved through five basic tempos. The composer explained: "During the opening Sostenuto the melodic and harmonic potentialities of the opening line are explored. The second section converts the various aspects of the growing material into a driving Allegro.

The following Adagio and Andante sections bring fresh lyricism through complete thematic transformation. The final Allegro pushed toward the arrival of thematic aspects of the symphony in a conclusion of a triple counterpoint and rhythmic insistence."

Symphony no. 7, *Liturgic* (1958), was written on commission from the St. Louis Symphony for its eightieth anniversary and was presented by that orchestra under Eduard von Remoortel on October 24, 1959. Music of deep religious consciousness, this symphony drew all of its material for its five distinct and continuous movements from Persichetti's *Hymns and Responses for the Church Year* (1955; Philadelphia, October 7, 1956).

Symphony no. 9, *Janiculum* (1970), also in a single movement, was premiered by the Philadelphia Orchestra under Ormandy on March 5, 1971. It was written while the composer was in Rome during his second Guggenheim Fellowship (the first having come early in 1958), where he was so fascinated by the tolling bells of the Chiesa di San Pietro and Gianicolo that he reproduced these sounds at the symphony's opening and closing. The symphony is concerned with Janus, the god, after whom the *Janiculum* was named, and Janus's two faces, symbolizing the opposites and conflicts of life. In her review in the *New York Post*, Harriet Johnson described this symphony as follows: "Section I opens delicately, followed by long sweeps of melody which are abandoned too soon. Section III features the oboe, 'the female aspect.' Section IV closes in what Persichetti considers to be a 'fast-driving rush to a code of affirmation.' There are stops and starts to indicate the nature of Janus."

Symphony no. 6 (1956; St. Louis, Mo., April 16, 1956) is for band. Since its premiere it has been given hundreds of performances, becoming Persichetti's most frequently heard symphony.

A prolific composer, Persichetti produced numerous works other than symphonies. Since he is also a composer who has maintained his creativity on a consistently high level of excellence and integrity, only a random sampling of such other works can be singled out for brief attention. Commissioned by Martha Graham to write music for a ballet, Persichetti completed *King Lear*, a septet for woodwind quintet, timpani, and piano (1948), which was used for the ballet *The Eye of Anguish*, first presented by the Martha Graham company in Montclair, N.J., on January 31, 1949. The six-movement Serenade no. 5, for orchestra (1950; Louisville, Ky., November 15, 1950), was commissioned by the Louisville Orchestra. One of the composer's most frequently performed band compositions, Divertimento for Band (1950)—written for and introduced by the Goldman Band in New York on June 16, 1950—first became popular in a Mercury recording conducted by Frederick Fennell. Since then it has been performed hundreds of times annually by American bands. A highly significant chamber music work, Quintet no.

2, for piano and strings (1954), was the result of a commission from the Koussevitzky Music Foundation and received its premiere in Washington, D.C., on February 4, 1955. In a single movement it is constructed from germinal material (a falling motive in the fourth measure) heard in the nonvibrato first violin passage before being set into motion by various tempo changes. A commission from the Juilliard School of Music led to the writing of one of Persichetti's largest solo works for the piano, the Sonata no. 10 (1955), its first performance given by Josef Raieff during the fifteenth anniversary festival of American music at the Juilliard School on February 20, 1956. This is still one more product of the composer's interest in one-movement forms derived from a germinating source motive (a descending figure in thirds in this instance). This same process—the single movement built on a single principal idea which undergoes continuous transformation of character and tempo—is encountered in the String Quartet no. 3 (1959), which the Alabama String Quartet premiered in Tuscaloosa on April 9, 1959.

The Piano Concerto (1962) is one of the composer's major works for solo instrument and orchestra. It was written on a commission for the virtuoso Anthony di Bonaventura, who was the soloist when the work received its initial hearing on August 2, 1964, at the Congregation of the Arts at the Hopkins Center of Dartmouth College in Hanover, N.H. "It is a brilliant bravura work, sprinkled with moments of unpressured reflectiveness," reported a critic to the *New York Times* from Hanover. "As a whole, it is spacious in scale, sharp in detail."

The Creation (1969) is, structurally, one of Persichetti's most ambitious compositions, and contextually one of his most exalted works. It is in a massive design (consuming more than an hour to perform), scored for four vocal soloists, chorus, and orchestra; the Juilliard School of Music had commissioned it and performed it first on April 17, 1970. The text was prepared by the composer based loosely on Genesis, and supplemented by a variety of quotations from poetic, mythological, and scientific sources. "The result," wrote Raymond Ericson in the *New York Times*, "is contemporary, larger in dimension and implication than the terse Biblical story and mystical." Ericson goes on to describe this work: "The music is conceived in a near-symphonic pattern, moving through two dramatic movements. . . . For all the drama in it, the score is basically lyrical. . . . The contrasting kinds of melodies, which are usually made up of small chromatic figurations for the chorus and large-intervalled melodies for the soloists, are always affecting, often poignant. . . . The work ends with a kind of mysterious indecisiveness as if the Creation itself held only a mysterious meaning."

String Quartet no. 4 (1972) was subtitled *Parable X* because, since 1965, the composer had been producing a series of compositions under the collective title of *Parable* for various solo instruments or combinations of instruments (ten other "parables" came between 1972 and 1978). By "parable" the composer inferred a one-movement "story" in which an instrument or group of instruments is allowed to develop an identity through melody. In the String Quartet, Persichetti quotes fragments from the earlier scores in a work characterized by sharp contrasts of mood, tempo, and timbre, and which ends elegaically. Written for the Alard Quartet, it was first performed by that group in University Park, Pa., on February 28, 1973; the Juilliard String Quartet brought it to New York on April 16, 1974.

In 1973, Persichetti and one of his compositions became a *cause célèbre* that brought both to the front pages of the nation's newspapers. He had been commissioned by the Presidential Inaugural Committee to write a composition for performance at Richard Nixon's second Inaugural concert by the Philadelphia Orchestra on January 19, 1973. Persichetti was given, as text, excerpts from Abraham Lincoln's Second Inaugural Address. This choice met with the disapproval of the Inaugural Committee since President Lincoln's comments on the Civil War, which he described as a "mighty scourge," proved embarrassing to the administration at the time when the Vietnam War was polarizing the country. Consequently, Persichetti's composition—*A Lincoln Address*, for narrator and orchestra (1972)—was summarily deleted from the Inaugural Concert program. It was heard later that month, on January 25, performed by the St. Louis Symphony under Walter Susskind, with William Warfield, narrator. Borrowing materials from his own Symphony no. 7 and *Hymns and Responses*, Persichetti here produced music in a comparatively conservative idiom that had great sobriety, poignancy, and optimism.

Among Persichetti's most consequential works since 1973 are the *Auden Variations*, for organ (1977), and the Concerto for English Horn and String Orchestra (1977). The *Auden Variations* is the composer's most extended work for solo organ. Leonard Raver performed the premiere presentation on July 14, 1978, at the International Contemporary Organ Music Festival in Hartford, Conn. (which had commissioned it) and where Persichetti was featured composer. The variations are based on an original hymn from the composer's *Hymns and Responses*, which had used as text a segment from a poem by W. H. Auden—hence the title of the organ work.

The Concerto for English Horn and Orchestra was one of several works commissioned by the New York Philharmonic for its solo players. Thomas Stacy was the soloist when the New York Philharmonic under Erich Leinsdorf premiered it on November 17, 1977. "This concerto," said Harold C. Schonberg in the *New York Times*, "reflects the current trend of contemporary composers to write music that means something to an audience. If anything it is an Im-

pressionistic work, although the score does contain sections where Mr. Persichetti demonstrates that the writing of the previous decade is not unknown to him. The first movement is a fantasy . . . and, indeed, the whole work could well have been called a fantasy." This work began in a reflective mood and ended with a dance episode and was at turns lyrical and declamatory in order to demonstrate the expressive gamut of the solo instrument. As a transition between the second and third movements, a quotation from Rossini's *William Tell Overture* is briefly interpolated. In September 1978, this concerto received the First Kennedy Center Friedheim Award for the best orchestral work premiered that season.

In 1948, Persichetti received a grant from the National Academy of Arts and Letters to which he was elected member in 1965. He earned a citation from the Italian government (1959), a Naumburg Foundation grant (1960), the Symphony League Award (1964), a grant from the National Foundation on the Arts and the Humanities (1966), a third Guggenheim Fellowship (1973), and the Creative Arts Award from Brandeis University in Maltham, Mass. (1975). He has been awarded honorary doctorates from Baldwin-Wallace College in Berea, Ohio (1966), Bucknell University in Lewisburg, Pa. (1970), Combs College in Philadelphia (1970), Millikin University in Decatur, Ill. (1974), and Peabody Conservatory in Baltimore (1974). Between 1964 and 1967 he was adviser to the Ford Foundation and the Music Educators National Convention. During the summer of 1978, through the American Society of Composers, Authors, and Publishers (ASCAP), Persichetti represented the United States at the International Composers Meeting in the Soviet Union and Armenia.

From 1952 on, he has been visiting composer, lecturer, and performer at more than two hundred colleges, universities, and other educational institutions throughout the United States. At Arizona State University in Tempe, where he was visiting composer in 1979, a festival of his compositions was presented over a two-week period.

Persichetti is the author of *Twentieth Century Harmony* (1961), and coauthor with Flora R. Schreiber of *William Schuman* (1953).

THE COMPOSER SPEAKS: I tend to amalgamate the sounds around me and press them into the clay of the shaping object. I prefer to say more about less and less about more. An exciting collection of musical segments creates a newsreel of random shots of unrelated landscapes. I work for completeness in the architecture of all I compose. I avoid sudden flamboyance and momentary pleasure if it does not contribute to the overall design and dramatic purpose. I have no reason to try to please or entertain the listener. I know what I want to say because that thought means something to me. I can find validity in my music only when it is right for me. If I don't speak as a human to the listener, I do not have the right to take the time of the audience.

PRINCIPAL WORKS: 13 serenades, for various instrumental groups (1929–63); 11 *Parables*, for solo instruments or combinations of instruments (1965–78); 11 piano sonatas (1939–65); 9 symphonies (1942–70); 6 piano sonatinas (1950–54); 4 string quartets (1939–72); 2 piano quintets (1940, 1954).

Magnificat, for chorus and piano (1940); Suite for Violin and Cello (1940); Sonata for Solo Violin (1940); Concertato for Piano and String Quartet (1940); Sonata for Two Pianos (1940); Piano Concertino (1941); *Dance Overture*, for orchestra (1942); Pastoral, for woodwind quintet (1943); *Fables*, for narrator and orchestra (1943); *The Hollow Man*, for trumpet and string orchestra (1944); *King Lear*, septet for woodwind quintet, timpani and piano (1948); *Two cummings Choruses*, for women's voices (1950); Divertimento for Band (1950); *Fairy Tale*, for orchestra (1950); *Harmonium*, song cycle for soprano and piano (1951); Harpsichord Sonata (1951); Sonata for Solo Cello (1952); Concerto, for piano four hands (1952); *Parades*, for piano (1952); *Hymns and Responses for the Church Year*, for chorus (1955); *Song of Peace*, for male chorus and piano (1959); *Infanta Marina*, for viola and piano (1960); Mass, for a cappella chorus (1960); Organ Sonata (1960); Piano Concerto (1962); Stabat Mater, for chorus and orchestra (1963); Te Deum, for chorus and orchestra (1963); *Spring Cantata*, for women's chorus and piano (1963); *Winter Cantata*, for women's chorus, flute and marimba (1964); *Masques*, for violin and piano (1965); *Masquerade*, for band (1965); *Celebrations*, for chorus and wind ensemble (1966); *Choral Prelude: Turn Not Thy Face*, for band (1966); *The Pleiades*, for chorus, trumpet, and string orchestra (1967); *The Creation*, for soprano, alto, tenor, baritone, chorus, and orchestra (1969); *Night Dances*, for orchestra (1970); *A Love*, for women's a cappella chorus (1971); *O Cool Is the Valley*, poem for band (1971); *A Lincoln Address*, for narrator and orchestra (1972); *Glad and Very*, for chorus and piano (1974); *Auden Variations*, for organ (1977); Concerto for English Horn and String Orchestra (1977); *Mirror Etudes*, for piano (1978); *Dryden Liturgical Suite*, for organ (1979); Three Toccatinas, for piano (1979).

BIBLIOGRAPHY: *American Composers Bulletin*, no. 2, 1954; *ASCAP in Action*, Spring 1980; *Diapason*, Spring 1979; *Juilliard Review*, Spring 1955; *Musical Quarterly*, April 1957, October 1961; *Philadelphia Sunday Bulletin*, April 12, 1970; *Saturday Review*, December 2, 1961.

Phillips, Burrill, b. Omaha, Nebr., November 9, 1907.

In his earlier years as composer, Phillips was pre-occupied with American themes. His first successes came with programmatic compositions reflecting his fascination for everything "in the American grain." Later compositions have been more abstract and less ostensibly national. They are preponderantly lyrical and dramatic in an idiom that is atonal, rhythmically free, and formally dependent on context whether the music is totally abstract or based on a text.

The family came to Denver when Phillips was three, and he was raised and educated there for the next twenty-one years. His mother, who played the piano well, saw to it that he begin lessons early. "I had the standard boy's resentment at being required to practice an hour a day," he recalls. "It became more interesting to me about the time I was seven years old when I discovered I had absolute pitch and also that I could invent more interesting music of my own than the music teacher assigned for study." By the time of his adolescence he was able to find a piano teacher, Louise Philips, who recognized his talent for composition and provided him with opportunities to perform his pieces at recitals. During his high school years in Denver, Phillips played the piano in the school orchestra and wrote the school song.

By the time he graduated from high school in 1924, he had arrived at the decision to concentrate on music study. That year he entered the Denver College of Music, where he studied theory and composition with Edwin Stringham (the director of the college) and piano with Francis Hendricks. Since the Phillips family could not afford to finance his education, he supported himself by holding various jobs, including working weekends in a grocery store, taking on full-time employment on a dairy farm, and subsequently by giving private lessons in piano and harmony. When he was eighteen he was hired as part-time announcer and studio pianist for a local radio station where much of the music he played had to be read at sight. "The sink-or-swim atmosphere of this kind of music-making soon became a delight to me. . . . It also widened my knowledge of music literature and stood me in good stead later when I was teaching composition."

Marriage, which brought with it the necessity of earning a living for two, ended his studies at the Denver College of Music before he could get a degree. This marriage took place on November 17, 1928, to Alberta Mayfield, a violinist and writer; in years to come she provided him with texts for many of his compositions in addition to giving birth to and raising their two children. They spent the first three years of marriage teaching the violin and piano privately and in classes in southern Colorado and northern New Mexico.

A partial scholarship, and savings enough to provide several months of subsistence, brought Phillips to Rochester, N.Y., in 1931 for admission to the Eastman School of Music. There, he studied composition and orchestration with Bernard Rogers and Howard Hanson. Phillips earned his bachelor of music degree in 1932 and his master of music degree one year later. In 1933, he was appointed to the music faculty of the Eastman School, where he remained for sixteen years as teacher of theory and composition.

During his initial years there as faculty member he wrote his first major work for orchestra: a three-movement suite, *Selections from McGuffey's Reader* (1933), which was introduced in Rochester, N.Y., on May 3, 1934, Howard Hanson conducting. The first stimulus in writing this music came from seeing Grant Wood's painting *The Midnight Ride of Paul Revere*, which challenged Phillips to try translating this subject into musical terms. Reading Oliver Wendell Holmes's *The Wonderful "One-Hoss Shay"* and Longfellow's *The Courtship of Miles Standish* provided him with two more subjects. In this suite, the composer used a richer harmony, more decisive rhythms and a more singing style than he had favored in his earlier apprentice works.

American subjects continued to provide Phillips with material and inspiration during the next decade: *Courthouse Square*, for orchestra (1935; Rochester, N.Y., April 1936), which Leopold Stokowski and the Philadelphia Orchestra performed on April 16, 1937; *Play Ball* (1937), music for a ballet produced in Rochester on April 29, 1938; *American Dance*, for bassoon and strings (1940; Rochester, April 25, 1940); and, most significantly, *Tom Paine*, an overture for orchestra (1946). The last of these was commissioned by the Koussevitzky Music Foundation. Here, as the composer has explained, he intended "to convey in clear, forceful terms a kind of music I feel is characteristic of our day—strong, open, large-minded, with roots in native soil. It was not intended to illustrate the biography of Tom Paine but seeks to be in phase with the spirit of the man." The composer further described the music: "In structure it is simple: two main themes, separated by subsidiary ideas, contrapuntally treated, and prefaced by a fanfare fugue. The conclusion is a massive canon ending in a full orchestral cadence." *Tom Paine* was given its premiere at the Columbia University Festival of American Music in New York on May 17, 1947, performed by the NBC Symphony under Alfred Wallenstein. It was subsequently featured by several major American symphony orchestras.

All this time, Phillips was also producing a considerable amount of abstract music without any American affiliation. These included the *Sinfonia concertante*, for orchestra (1935; Rochester, April 3, 1935); his String Quartet no. 1 (1940), which the Galimir Quartet introduced at a concert of the League of Composers in New York on October 4, 1941; Piano Concerto (1942; Rochester, May 6, 1943); *Three Satiric Fragments*, for orchestra, (1941; Rochester, May 21, 1941); and Scherzo, for orchestra (1944), commissioned by the League of Composers, which was introduced in New York on March 8, 1945, with

Leopold Stokowski conducting the New York City Symphony.

In 1942, Phillips received the first of two Guggenheim Fellowships. He spent the first in New York, composing. In 1944, the American Academy of Arts and Letters gave him its award. In 1947, Phillips wrote the music to a one-act chamber opera buffa for which his wife, Alberta Phillips, provided the text: *Don't We All*, first produced in Rochester on May 9, 1949.

Phillips left the Eastman School in 1949 to become professor of music at the University of Illinois in Urbana. There he taught theory and composition for the next fifteen years, serving as chairman of that division between 1957 and 1960. For this university's Fine Arts Festival, which took place once every two years, Phillips wrote, on commission from the Fromm Music Foundation, a major choral work, *The Return of Odysseus*, for baritone, narrator, chorus, and orchestra (1956), text provided by his wife. Robert Shaw conducted the premiere performance in Urbana on March 11, 1957, and later recorded it; this work was featured at the Centennial Celebration of the University of Chicago in 1967.

Commissions led to the writing of other works. These included: Concerto Grosso, for string quartet and orchestra (1949), premiered by the Walden Quartet in Ithaca, N.Y., in 1951; *A Bucket of Water*, for chorus and piano (1952), commissioned by the Pittsburgh International Festival of Contemporary Music and heard first in November 1952; the Triple Concerto, for viola, clarinet, piano, and orchestra (1952), written for and introduced by the Quincy Society of Fine Arts in Quincy, Ill., in 1953; String Quartet no. 2 (1958), which the Elizabeth Sprague Coolidge Foundation had commissioned and which received it first hearing at the Library of Congress in Washington, D.C., by the Paganini String Quartet in spring 1960.

The second Guggenheim Fellowship, in 1961, and a Fulbright grant as Lecturer brought Phillips to Europe. He lectured on American music at the University of Barcelona, then spent nine months in Paris, working on *Perspectives in a Labyrinth*, for three string orchestras (1962), which he completed two years later. "I met no Parisian musicians or composers. Indeed I made no attempt to. Paris to me meant visiting all the medieval landmarks that I could find . . . and walking through Notre Dame de Paris every day if possible."

In 1964, Phillips completed writing an unusual work—Canzona III, for seven instruments "and a poet." "My idea was, if different composers have traditionally set the same text, why not write music to which different poets could write different texts." The verse for the first performance in Urbana on May 9, 1964, was written by the composer's wife. The second performance was as music for dance, mounted at the East-West Festival in Honolulu in 1965, and the third performance, to still a newer text, was broadcast over WNYC, the municipal radio station of New York City, in 1970.

Phillips resigned from the University of Illinois in 1964 to devote more time to composition. But teaching was not totally abandoned. He was visiting composer at the East-West Center of the University of Hawaii (1965) and visiting professor at the Eastman School of Music (1965-66), the Juilliard School of Music (1968-69) and Cornell University (1972-73). In 1965 he wrote *Soleriana concertante*, for orchestra, for the Festival of Contemporary Art at the University of Hawaii; this was composed in homage to the 18th-century Spanish composer, Antonio Soler, and its premiere was performed by the Honolulu Symphony under George Barati on April 16, 1965. As visiting professor to the Eastman School, Phillips completed the Sonata in Two Movements, for violin and harpsichord (1965; Rochester, March 18, 1966). During his visiting professorship at Juilliard he was commissioned to write a score for the dancer José Limon. *La piñata* (1968-69; N.Y., April 16, 1969) was the result, based on Mexican children's songs furnished him by Limon.

In 1976, Phillips and his wife received a grant from the National Endowment for the Arts for the writing of a full-length opera, *The Unforgiven* (1980).

THE COMPOSER SPEAKS: I look upon music as an art founded on expert craftsmanship. The craft is learned through practice and constant watchfulness. The art's origin and impact are mysterious, but I suspect what is operating here has something to do with the ability of evoking magic through the medium of tone in a time framework. Poetry I consider the nearest parallel, with its rhythms and forms that give heightened intensity to its content.

PRINCIPAL WORKS: 4 piano sonatas (1942-60); 2 string quartets (1940, 1958).

Selections from McGuffy's Reader, suite for orchestra (1933): *Sinfonia concertante*, for orchestra (1935); *Courthouse Square*, for orchestra (1935); Trio, for three trumpets (1937); *Play Ball*, ballet (1937); Music for Strings (1938); Concert Piece, for bassoon and string orchestra (1940); *Three Satiric Fragments*, for orchestra (1941); Violin Sonata (1941); Piano Concerto (1942); *Step into My Parlor*, ballet (1942); *Declaratives*, for female voices and small orchestra (1943): Toccata, for piano (1944); Scherzo, for orchestra (1944); *Set of Three Informalities*, for piano (1945); Three Divertimenti, for piano (1946); *Tom Paine*, concert overture for orchestra (1946); *Scena*, for chamber orchestra (1946); Cello Sonata (1946); Partita, for piano, violin, viola, and cello (1947); *Don't We All*, one-act chamber opera buffa (1947); Concerto Grosso, for string quartet and orchestra (1949); Divertimento, for orchestra (1950); *A Bucket of Water*, for chorus and piano (1952); Triple Concerto, for viola, clarinet, piano, and orchestra (1952); *Four Figures in Time*, for flute and piano (1952); *Music for This Time of Year*, thirty-two pieces for all possible ensembles of the instruments of the woodwind quintet (1954); *The Return of Odysseus*, for baritone, narrator, chorus, and orchestra (1956); Serenade, for piano four hands (1956); Nine Motets, for a cappella chorus (1958); *Sinfonia brevis*, for organ (1959); *Five Various and Sundry*, for piano (1961); *Perspectives in a Labyrinth*, for three string orchestras (1962); Canzona III, for seven instruments, piano, "and a poet" (1964); Organ Sonata (1964); Five Pieces, for woodwind quintet (1965); *Soleriana concertante*, for orchestra (1965); Sonata in Two Movements, for violin and harpsichord (1965); Quartet, for oboe and strings (1967); *Theatre Dances*, for orchestra (1967); *That Time May Cease*, for men's chorus and piano (1967); Canzona IV, for soprano and three instruments (1967); Quartet, for oboe and strings (1967); *La piñata*, dance for chamber orchestra (1968); Fantasia, for concert band (1968); Canzona V, for solo piano and mixed chorus (1971); *Yellowstone, Yates, and Yosemite*, for tenor saxophone and concert band (1971); *Eve Learns a Little*, duo cantata for soprano and piano, with four winds (1974); *Huntingdon's 2's and 3's*, for flute, oboe, and cello (1975); *The Recesses of My House*, for soprano, clarinet, percussion, and piano (1977); *Scena da camera*, for viola and piano (1978); *The Unforgiven*, opera (1980).

BIBLIOGRAPHY: *DCM*; Ewen, David, *American Composers Today* (N.Y., 1949); Reis, Claire, *Composers in America* (N.Y., 1947); *Music Clubs Magazine*, Winter 1970-71; *Who's Who in America, 1980-81*.

Pinkham, Daniel Rogers, b. Lynn, Mass., June 5, 1923.

As a performer on harpsichord and teacher of early music, Pinkham was early drawn to baroque structures and a polyphonic style, sometimes in large religious choral works. He later became interested in the twelve-tone technique, which he used in personal ways, always at once tonal and lyrical. Since 1970 he has worked with electronic music. His compositions have always been characterized by strong formal design, rhythmic clarity, and colorful and sometimes novel instrumentation.

He was born to a prominent family in Lynn, Mass., the great-grandson of Lydia E. Pihkham, founder of the medicine company that carries her name, of which his father was a sometime president. Daniel Pinkham began taking piano lessons when he was five, and it was not long after that that he was composing music. "I was always writing little tunes and trying to peddle them," he recalls. For his academic education he went to Phillips Academy in Andover (1937-40), where he was able to study harmony and organ with Karl F. Pfatteicher. Then, at

Harvard University (1940–44), his musical training continued in classes in composition and theory with Walter Piston, Aaron Copland, A. Tillman Merritt, and Archibald T. Davison. Summers of 1941, 1946, and 1947 were spent at the Berkshire Music Center at Tanglewood, Mass. There he continued to study composition with Samuel Barber and Arthur Honegger. Additional study of the organ took place privately with E. Power Biggs (1947) and composition with Nadia Boulanger (1941, 1946), and he began to master the harpsichord with private study with Jean Chiasson (1940–41), Putnam Aldrich (1941–42), and Wanda Landowska (1946).

He received his bachelor of arts degree at Harvard in 1943 (the degree coming one year early because of the accelerated war-years plan), and his masters degree in art one year later. He joined the faculty of the Boston Conservatory of Music in 1946. In that year, and in a few to follow, he became influenced in his compositions by the neoclassical works of Stravinsky, producing several in classical structures to which he brought not only contrapuntal skill but also clarity of texture, conciseness of speech, and a flair for unusual sonorities. All this became apparent in his Clarinet Sonata (1946), Concertino for Organ and Strings (1947), Three Motets, for women's chorus and instruments (1948), and *The Garden of Artemis* (1948; Cambridge, Mass., 1948). The last of these, Pinkham's most ambitious composition up to that time, was a chamber opera with libretto by Robert Hillyer, which had been commissioned by Fanny Peabody Mason and which Warren Storey Smith, noted Boston critic, described as a "thoroughly ingratiating work." By virtue of the talent of such works, Pinkham received a Fulbright Fellowship in 1950.

While thus involved creatively, Pinkham was also developing himself as a harpsichordist and teacher. In 1948 he joined Robert Brink in forming the Brink-Pinkham violin and harpsichord duo, which performed extensively throughout the United States and Canada and, under the sponsorship of the State Department, made two tours of Europe in 1952 and 1954. Beginning with 1950, and for the next decade, Pinkham was making appearances as harpsichordist with the Boston Symphony both in concerts and recordings. In 1951 he was appointed special lecturer on music history at Simmons College in Boston, becoming associate in harpsichord at Boston University a year after that. Since 1958 he has been the music director of King's Chapel in Boston, and since 1959 professor at the New England Conservatory in Boston, where he was later made chairman of the department of the performance of early music. He also gave a series of lecture-recitals at the summer school at Darlington Hall in Devon, England (1954), and in 1957–58 was visiting lecturer at Harvard University.

In commenting upon the influences brought to bear on his growth as composer, Pinkham has singled out his lifetime contact with performers. "I am

most happy when writing for a specific performance," he explains. "I have always been interested in making music technically accessible, and delight in trying to achieve sonorities by combining instruments in a way that is at once idiomatic for the individual performer and yet new in ensemble sound."

Concerto for Solo Harpsichord and Celesta (1954), premiered in New York on November 18, 1955, was regarded by Warren Storey Smith as typical of Pinkham's compositions of this period. "For all its modernity of timbre, contemporary rhythmic and tonal structure, the impress of the Baroque is there, thanks alike to the celesta and the way the harpsichord is employed. The first and third movements ('Prelude' and 'Canzona') are 'busy' and wholly impersonal. More expressive by far is the 'Ricercare,' which might have been labeled a *fuga a tre voci*. Here we are confronted with Pinkham's skill as a contrapuntist. . . . Tonal brilliance and rhythmic energy characterize the final Canzona."

The baroque influence is still present in the Partita for Harpsichord (1958), in which each of its six principal divisions is dedicated to a different master of that instrument. The baroque influence can also be found in several major religious choral works of the late 1950s and early 1960s, though the dissonant writing is more predominantly linear than chordal. These choral works include the *Wedding Cantata*, for chorus and piano or chamber orchestra (1956), text taken from the Song of Songs; the *Christmas Cantata (Sinfonia Sacra)*, for chorus and two brass choirs (1957); Te Deum, for two-part chorus (1959), which was commissioned by the Southern New England Unitarian Council and premiered in Boston in 1960; and the *Easter Cantata*, for chorus and instruments.

While a twelve-tone row is suggested in the Piano Concertino of 1950, in the first dozen notes of the second movement, Pinkham did not make that technique basic to his style until much later in the 1950s. But he was never a strict adherent of the Viennese dodecaphonists, preferring always to harmonize his twelve-tone row, and to use the row with considerable expressivity while seeking unusual sonoric and instrumental effects. This style was crystallized in the early 1960s in his two symphonies (1960, 1964), the first introduced by the Orquesta Sinfonica in Mexico City in June 1961, and the second receiving its first hearing on November 23, 1964, in Lansing, Mich.; in the Concertante, for organ, celesta, and two percussion (1962); in Requiem, for alto, tenor, and chorus (1963); and in *Signs of the Zodiac*, for orchestra and optional speakers (1964; Portland, Me., November 10, 1964), to poems by David McCord.

Pinkham became interested in electronic music by 1970. "No one was more surprised than I to discover that I was able to embrace this medium," he says. "I found that I could use the material in a personal way, still bringing into play the bright colors and timbres that have fascinated me and that I first heard in acoustical instruments such as the harpsichord, the guitar and tuned percussion and, in particular, the glockenspiel." He has never been interested in music solely for tape because he regards it still in the infancy of technology and the timbres of most of the readily available electronic tones boring and too predictable. He is excited, however, about combining the sounds of conventional instruments and voices with tape. In addition to many small pieces for clarinet and tape, organ and tape, mezzo-soprano and tape, and such, Pinkham has used electronic music in such larger works as *To Troubled Friends*, for string orchestra and tape (1972), *Daniel in the Lions' Den*, for narrator, tenor, bass, baritone solos, two pianos, timpani, and percussion (1973), *Four Elegies*, for tenor solo, chorus, small orchestra, and tape (1975), which uses poems by various 17th-century English poets as texts, and *Garden Party*, a comic opera (1976), using excerpts from the Bible for its libretto, together with other material by Norma Ferber, Mrs. M. A. Kidder, and others.

In *Daniel in the Lions' Den* there is, for Pinkham, an increased concern for the dramatic values and theatrical effects, which characterizes some of Pinkham's later works, most notably *Passion of Judas* (1976), which followed the traditions of the medieval mystery plays. Scored for narrator, five solo voices, chorus, and five instruments—text taken from the Bible, poems by Norma Farber and James Wright and a play by R. C. Norris—*Passion of Judas* can be staged in the chancel of a church as well as in the concert hall. It was introduced at the National Presbyterian Church in Washington, the composer conducting, in 1976.

Pinkham received a Ford Foundation grant in 1962. He was awarded the honorary degree, doctor of letters, by Nebraska Wesleyan University, and honorary doctorates in music from Adrian College in Adrian, Mich. (1977), and from Westminster Choir College in Princeton, N.J. (1979). He is a fellow of the American Academy of Arts and Sciences. Pinkham never married.

THE COMPOSER SPEAKS: When writing a song (or even a symphony) the work at hand only reflects one or at best a few facets of any thoughts on music and these cannot be translated into words. Be that as it may, I can confess a certain sympathy for François Couperin who wrote in *L'art de toucher le clavecin* that he preferred music which touched him to that which surprised him.

PRINCIPAL WORKS: 2 symphonies (1961–63); 2 sonatas for organ and strings (1953, 1954).

The Garden of Artemis, chamber opera (1948); Violin Concerto (1950); Concertino, for small orchestra with piano obbligato (1950); Concerto for Harpsichord and Celesta (1953); Concertante no. 1, for violin and harpsichords soli, strings, and celesta (1954); *Wedding Cantata*, for optional soprano and tenor solo and chorus with piano or small orchestra (1956); *Christmas Cantata*, for chorus and brass choirs (1957); Concertante no. 2, for violin and strings (1958); Divertimento, for oboe and strings (1958); Te Deum, for two-part chorus and instruments (1959); *Angelus ad Pastores*, for a capella women's chorus and instruments (1959); Five Canzonets, for a cappella women's chorus (1959); *Easter Cantata*, for chorus, brass, and percussion (1960–61); *Three Songs from Ecclesiastes*, for voice and piano or string quartet or orchestra (1960); *The Reproaches*, for chorus and orchestra (1960); Concertante, for organ, celesta, and two percussionists (1962); Requiem, for alto, tenor, chorus, and instruments (1963); *Eight Poems of Gerard Manley Hopkins*, for baritone and viola (1964); Concertante, for organ, brass, and percussion (1964); *Signs of the Zodiac*, for optional speaker and orchestra (1964); Stabat Mater, for soprano and chorus (1964); *Letters from St. Paul*, for organ and piano (1965); *Eclogue*, for flute, harpsichord and handbells (1965); *Jonah*, for narrator, solo voices, and orchestra (1966); *St. Mark Passion*, for vocal soloists, chorus, and small orchestra (1967); *Lamentation of Jeremiah*, for chorus and small orchestra (1967); *Martyrdom of St. Stephen*, for chorus and guitar (1967); Brass Trio (1970); *Ascension Cantata*, for chorus, winds, and percussion (1970); *In the Beginning of Creation*, for chorus and tape (1970); Organ Concerto (1970); *Lessons*, for harpsichord (1971); *The Other Voices of the Trumpet*, for trumpet, organ and tape (1971); *The Troubled Friends*, for chorus, string orchestra, and tape (1972); *Safe in Their Alabaster Chamber*, for mezzo-soprano and piano (1972); *Daniel in the Lions' Den*, for narrator, solo voices, chorus, two pianos, instruments, and tape (1973); *Liturgies*, for organ, timpani, and tape (1974); *The Passion of Judas*, for solo voices, chorus, instruments, and organ (1976); *Blessings* for organ (1977); *Charm Me Asleep*, nine songs on old English texts for voice and guitar (1977); *Masks*, for harpsichord and chamber ensemble (1977); *Epiphanies*, for organ (1978): *Miracle*, for flute and organ (1978): *Proverbs*, for organ (1979); *Transitions*, for voice and bassoon or piano (1979); Serenades, for trumpet and wind ensemble (1979); *When God Arose*, for vocal soloists, organ, harpsichord, and percussion (1979).

BIBLIOGRAPHY: DCM; Johnson, M., "The Choral Works of Daniel Pinkham" (doctoral thesis, Iowa City, Ia., 1966); *American Composers Alliance Bulletin*, vol. 10, no. 1, 1961; BMI, *The Many Worlds of Music*, Winter 1976.

Piston, Walter Hamor, b. Rockland, Me., January 20, 1894: d. Belmont, Mass., November 12, 1976.

Two Pulitzer Prizes in music and two awards from the New York Music Critics Circle point in the

Piston

direction where Piston's greatest strength as composer lay: orchestral music. His more than forty years of creativity concentrated on instrumental music—chamber music as well as orchestral—producing only two choral works as his sole compositions for voice and one ballet as his single contribution to the stage. Though he absorbed atonal and discordant practices into his writing, and toward the end of his career was trying to come to terms with twelve-tone music, he was basically a traditionalist who was partial to tonal and diatonic processes, was comfortable in classic structures, and whose style was deeply grounded in the polyphonic art of Bach and the developmental methods of Beethoven. His music was always masterfully structured, usually broadly and expressively lyrical, and for over four decades maintained a consistency of approach and ideology.

Except for his paternal grandfather, a sailor named Antonio Pistone, Piston was of Yankee extraction. Pistone had come from Italy, married a Penebscot Yankee and settled in Rockland, Me., where he Americanized his name by dropping its final "e." Piston was one of four children; neither parent was musical.

When Piston was ten, his family moved to Boston. There he attended the Mechanic Arts High School, where he studied mechanical drafting, woodwork, blacksmithing, and machine-shop work, graduating in 1912. During that summer he worked as a draftsman for the Boston Elevated Railway. His interest in the visual arts brought him to the Normal Art School in 1912, where he concentrated on drawing and painting. While there, he began studying the violin and piano. His principal teachers were Harris Shaw (piano) and Julius Theodorowicz, Winternitz and Fiumara (violin).

He was graduated from Normal Art School in 1916. One year later, during World War I, he enlisted in the navy. Stationed at the Massachusetts Institute of Technology, he served as a member of the Aeronautics Division band, playing the saxophone, which he had learned within several days while in service by studying a textbook. "The only battle I took part in," he once recalled, "was the Battle of Charles River."

Upon his discharge from military service, Piston decided to specialize in music. While earning his living playing the violin in hotels, restaurants and dance halls, he entered Harvard University in 1919 as a special student in Archibald T. Davison's class in counterpoint. One year later he enrolled in the music school of Harvard University, where he spent the next four years studying counterpoint, composition, harmony, and orchestration. He became conductor of the Pierian Sodality, the Harvard student orchestra, and in his last year was an assistant to Archibald T. Davison. He received his bachelor of arts degree in 1924, *summa cum laude*, with membership in Phi Beta Kappa. Meanwhile, on September 14, 1920, he married Kathryn Mason, a gifted

artist whom he had met when both were students at the Normal Arts School.

On a John Knowles Paine Traveling Fellowship from Harvard, Piston spent two years in Europe (1924–26), attending the École normale de musique as a student of composition of Paul Dukas, and studying composition privately with Nadia Boulanger. In Paris, in 1926, Piston completed a Piano Sonata and Three Pieces, for flute, clarinet, and bassoon, both of which were performed, the latter at a concert of the Société independente de musique. Speaking of the Three Pieces, which in time was recorded, Klaus George Roy wrote in *Stereo Review*: "This . . . is a fully formed and individual creation, with all those fingerprints that mark it as belonging uniquely to this composer's style: conciseness, lyricism, wit, a certain spikiness, an assured direction and a satisfying design."

Returning to the United States in 1926, Piston and his wife settled in Belmont, Mass., where they maintained their home up to the time of the composer's death. In 1926, he joined the music faculty of Harvard University, where he remained for thirty-four years: assistant professor from 1926 to 1938, associate professor from 1938 to 1944, full professor from 1944 to 1959. In 1951 he was named the Walter W. Naumburg Professor of Music when that chair was endowed, and when he retired in 1960, he became professor emeritus. He brought to the classroom, together with musical scholarship, humanity, wit, and empathy with each talented student whatever direction he was taking, which made Piston one of the most significant musical educators of his time.

Serge Koussevitzky, music director of the Boston Symphony, influenced Piston to write for the orchestra. Once Piston did so, the Boston Symphony became a forum where many of his major orchestral works were heard, eleven of them premieres, some of which it commissioned. Piston's first orchestral work was *Symphonic Piece* (1927), introduced by the Boston Symphony on March 23, 1928, Koussevitzky conducting. This was followed by Suite no. 1, for orchestra (1929), its premiere taking place on March 29, 1930, with the composer conducting the Boston Symphony, and the Concerto for Orchestra (1933), once again introduced by the Boston Symphony under the composer's direction, in Cambridge, Mass., on March 6, 1934. In these three works, as in his later ones, a compromise was reached between conventional means and a modern harmonic, rhythmic, and tonal vocabulary within classical structures which the composer adapted pliantly to his needs. When the Concerto for Orchestra was given in New York in February 1935, W. J. Henderson remarked in the *New York Sun*: "Mr. Piston has made a work which will add to his repute. It is music of his time, vigorous, compact, straightforward, firmly knit. . . . He writes with a mastery of the basic principles of form, a clean and fluent logic of development and clear-cut devising always easy to follow. . . . It is made with well-placed boldness and assurance."

In the Concerto for Orchestra, Piston reverted to the concerto grosso structure of the baroque era. He once again used a baroque structure as well as baroque polyphony in Prelude and Fugue, for orchestra (1934). This was commissioned by the League of Composers and was first performed in Cleveland on March 12, 1936, with Artur Rodzinski conducting the Cleveland Orchestra.

In 1935, Piston received a Guggenheim Fellowship. He spent that year in Paris writing a Piano Trio (1935) on a commission from the Elizabeth Sprague Coolidge Foundation. It was premiered at the Library of Congress in Washington, D.C., by the Kroll-Britt-Sheridan Trio on October 30, 1935. Two major works were completed in the United States in 1937: Concertino for Piano and Orchestra, commissioned by the Columbia Broadcasting System and first performed on June 20, 1937, over the CBS radio network by Jesús Maria Sanromá and the CBS Symphony conducted by the composer; and Piston's first involvement with the symphonic form—a field he would dominate for the remainder of his life—Symphony no. 1, first performed on April 8, 1938, by the Boston Symphony under the composer's direction.

The flashes of wit that occasionally contributed luster to his compositions, and which provided the concertino with so much of its sheen, were predominant in the work with which Piston gained national prominence and which turned out to be his sole excursion into the world of ballet as well as one of his rare attempts at programmatic writing. This work was *The Incredible Flutist* (1938), whose scenario was provided by the dancer Hans Wiener. The ballet was introduced by the Hans Wiener Dancers at a concert of the Boston Pops, Arthur Fiedler conducting, on May 30, 1938. Its central character is a flutist who, upon arriving in a village with the circus, uses the necromantic powers of his flute to charm snakes and women and who inspires a wave of romance among the villagers. Throughout his score, Piston translated ballet sequences with a trenchant wit and a vivid imagery. The symphonic suite made up of twelve episodes from the ballet score became one of the composer's most frequently performed compositions; it was first heard in Pittsburgh on November 22, 1940, with Fritz Reiner conducting the Pittsburgh Symphony.

Piston's first New York Music Critics Award came in 1944 with his Symphony no. 2 (1943), a commission from the Alice M. Ditson Fund of Columbia University. The National Symphony Orchestra under Hans Kindler gave the first performance in Washington, D.C., on March 5, 1944, after which it was heard at the concerts of the Boston Symphony (which also broadcast it over the NBC radio network), the New York Philharmonic, the Cincinnati Symphony, the Cleveland Orchestra, the NBC Sym-

phony, the Pittsburgh Symphony and the Philadelphia Orchestra besides getting recorded. "In this symphony," reported Noel Straus in the *New York Times*, "he is again the master craftsman, while at the same time he has managed to invest the content with a wealth of mood and meaning. . . . There is character and strength in the score. It is closely knit and eloquent in each of its three movements. . . . Moreover, in this opus, no display of involved counterpoint, for its own sake, obtains, and the simplification of means results in a new fund of genuine expressiveness."

The wide emotional range and the technical assurance of the Symphony no. 2 are again encountered in Symphony no. 3 (1947), which, commissioned by the Koussevitzky Music Foundation, was given its premiere by the Boston Symphony Orchestra under Koussevitzky on January 9, 1948. It is here that Piston earned Pulitzer Prize in music for the first time (as well as the Horblit Award in Boston). Piston's second Pulitzer Prize arrived thirteen years and four symphonies later, with the Symphony no. 7 (1960), written for the Philadelphia Orchestra, which introduced it under Eugene Ormandy on February 10, 1961. In writing the latter work for the Philadelphia Orchestra, Piston kept in mind and ear the luscious tone of that distinguished organization by continually emphasizing lyric, sonoric, and expressive values over the dramatic.

Of Piston's other symphonies, no. 4 (1950) came about through a commission by the University of Minnesota to celebrate its centenary and was introduced by the Minneapolis Symphony under Antal Dorati on March 30, 1951. It entered the repertoire of the Boston Symphony the following October, after which it was performed by most of America's major orchestras. This symphony was even more strongly melodic and more spontaneous in expression than its three predecessors. As the composer revealed in commenting on this work: "My music is becoming more relaxed, I think; more flowing, less angular and nervous. I feel a greater sense of ease in the Fourth Symphony than I have ever felt before. . . . About that first long melody (the *dolce espressivo* theme in the first violins with which the symphony opens) I felt strongly that I was following it wherever it was going, instead of pushing it along." Symphony no. 5 (1954) was written on commission for an American Music Festival at the Juilliard School of Music planned for 1955. But it was not heard there until February 24, 1956, Jean Morel conducting. Symphony no. 6 (1955) was composed on commission to honor the seventy-fifth anniversary of the Boston Symphony, which premiered it in Boston on November 25, 1955, before performing it extensively in the United States, Europe, and the Soviet Union and recording it. Symphony no. 8 (1965), Piston's last such work and one of the first in which he made a slight obeisance to the twelve-tone row, was commissioned by the Boston Symphony and its music director Erich Leinsdorf, its first performance taking place on March 5, 1965. What Piston said so simply about the Seventh Symphony applies with equal validity to the Eighth. They were composed "with no intent other than to make music to be played and listened to."

Piston's Concerto for Viola and Orchestra (1957) brought him his second New York Music Critics Circle Award. It was written for Joseph Pasquale, the first violist of the Boston Symphony, who offered the premiere with the Boston Symphony under Charles Munch on March 7, 1958. This is one of several Piston concertos for a solo instrument and orchestra. It had been preceded by the Violin Concerto no. 1 (1939; N.Y., March 18, 1949) and was followed by Concerto for Two Pianos and Orchestra (1959; Hanover, N.H., July 4, 1964); Violin Concerto no. 2 (1960; Pittsburgh, Pa., October 28, 1960); Concerto for Clarinet and Orchestra (1967; Hanover, N.H., August 6, 1967); and Piston's last composition, Concerto for String Quartet, Wind Instruments, and Percussion (1976; Portland, Me., October 26, 1976). Though not in concerto form, the Variations, for cello and orchestra (1966), is one of Piston's major works for solo instrument and orchestra. It was commissioned and introduced by Mstislav Rostropovich in New York on March 2, 1967. Earlier, in 1964, his String Quartet no. 5 (1962) brought Piston his third award from the New York Music Critics Circle.

Works for orchestra outside the periphery of the symphony and the concerto have also had their healthy measure of success. These are some of the most notable: Prelude and Allegro, for organ and strings (1943; CBS radio, August 8, 1943), composed for E. Power Biggs and his Sunday morning organ recitals in Boston; Symphonic Suite no. 2, written in 1947 on a commission from the Dallas Symphony, which gave the first performance under Antal Dorati's direction on February 29, 1948; Toccata, for orchestra (1948), written as an orchestral showpiece for the American tour of the Orchestre National de France and receiving its initial presentation at Bridgeport, Conn., on October 14, 1948, Charles Munch directing; Three New England Sketches (1959; Worcester, Mass., October 23, 1959), three nostalgic pieces ("Seaside," "Summer Evening," and "Mountains") in which the composer described "impressions, reminiscences, even dreams that pervaded the otherwise musical thoughts of one New England composer"; Symphonic Prelude (1960), the result of a commission from the Association of Women Committees for Symphony Orchestras for its biennial conference in Cleveland, where it received its first hearing on April 20, 1961, George Szell conducting the Cleveland Orchestra; Lincoln Center Festival Overture (1962; N.Y., September 25, 1962), written for the opening week ceremonies at the Lincoln Center for the Performing Arts in New York; and Ricercare (1967), written on commission from the New York Philharmonic for its 125th anniversary, premiered on March 7, 1968, Leonard Bernstein conducting.

Piston's skill in instrumental writing, in bringing out to the full both the expressive and the virtuoso qualities of the instruments he worked with, together with his gift for communicating on a personal basis with his audiences, made him also a significant contributor to chamber music literature. Through the years he produced a rich repertory of compositions for various combinations of instruments, many of them commissioned by instrumental groups or for specific performances. As Ross Parmenter wrote in the *New York Times* after hearing an evening of Piston's chamber music in New York in March 1961: "What he has to say is at the heart of his music. There is little distracting external style to obscure its essential content. . . . As one followed the interweaving strands of the various instrumental voices, one did not worry whether the harmonies were traditional or not. In fact, one was struck by how right they were for what they expressed. And such was the beauty of the craftsmanship that one got the impression that every note, every effect, came out exactly the way the composer wanted it."

In 1938, Piston was elected to membership in the National Institute of Arts and Letters and to the American Academy of Arts and Sciences in 1940. He received the Dickinson College Arts Award for outstanding achievement in music in 1966, and the MacDowell Medal in 1974. He was awarded eight honorary doctorates, including that in music from Harvard University in 1952. He was decorated Officer dans l'Ordre des Arts et Lettres by the French government in 1969. Two years later he was presented with an award for "Excellence in the Arts" by the Governor of Vermont. Piston was the author of *Harmonic Analysis* (1933), *Harmony* (1941), *Counterpoint* (1947), and *Orchestration* (1955).

THE COMPOSER SPEAKS: It is not one of my aims to write music that will be called modern, nor do I set out to compose according to any particular style or system. I believe my music is music of today in both manner and expression, since I am inevitably influenced by the art, thought, and daily life of the present. . . . It is the business of the composer to have knowledge of all new features to be found in the music of other composers and to keep alive his own inquisitiveness and alertness for the discovery of fresh sounds, or new uses for familiar sounds. These he will absorb selectively according to his taste, along with traditional elements of musical speech, into what will ultimately become his personal style.

The self-conscious striving for nationalism gets in the way of the establishment of a strong American School of composition and even of significant individual expression. If composers will increasingly strive to perfect themselves in the art of music and will follow only those paths of expression which seem to them the true way, the matter of a national school will take care of itself. And who can predict the time of its coming? Some say it is already here. Some say it has been here since the turn of the century. Others feel that it will take time to show the true significance of the enormous development of these recent years. But the composer cannot afford the wild-goose chase of trying to be more American than he is.

PRINCIPAL WORKS: 8 symphonies (1937–65); 5 string quartets (1933–62); 2 violin concertos (1939, 1960); 2 suites for orchestra (1928, 1947).

Symphonic Piece (1927); Concerto for Orchestra (1933); Prelude and Fugue, for orchestra (1934); Piano Trio (1935); Concertino, for piano and chamber orchestra (1937); *The Incredible Flutist*, ballet, also suite for orchestra (1938); Viola Sonata (1939); *Carnival Song*, for men's chorus and brass (1938); Violin Sonata (1939); Sinfonietta, for orchestra (1941); Quintet, for flute and strings (1942); Passacaglia, for piano (1943); Prelude and Allegro, for orchestra (1943); Partita, for violin, viola, and organ (1944); Sonatina, for violin and harpsichord (1945); Divertimento, for nine instruments (1946); Toccata, for orchestra (1948); Piano Quintet (1949); Duo, for viola and cello (1949); Fantasy, for English horn, strings, and harp (1952); Serenata, for orchestra (1956); Viola Concerto (1957); *Psalm and Prayer of David*, for women's chorus and seven instruments (1958); Concerto for Two Pianos and Orchestra (1959); *Three New England Sketches*, for orchestra (1959); *Symphonic Prelude* (1961); *Lincoln Center Festival Overture* (1962); Capriccio, for harp and string orchestra (1963); *Variations on a Theme by Edward Burlingame Hill*, for orchestra (1963); String Sextet (1964); Piano Quartet (1964); Variations, for cello and orchestra (1966); Clarinet Concerto (1967); Ricercare, for orchestra (1967); Fantasia, for violin and orchestra (1970); Duo, for cello and piano (1973); Concerto for String Quartet, Wind Instruments, and Percussion (1976).

BIBLIOGRAPHY: Copland, Aaron, *The New Music: 1900–1960* (N.Y., 1968); Daniel, Oliver, and others, *Walter Piston* (N. Y., 1964); Ewen, David (ed.), *The Book of Modern Composers* (N. Y., 1943); Goss, Madeleine, *Modern Music Makers* (N. Y., 1952); Lindenfeld, H. N., "Three Symphonies of Walter Piston: an Analysis" (doctoral thesis, Ithaca, N. Y., 1975); *High Fidelity/Musical America*, August 1974; *New York Times*, May 2, 1961, November 14, 1976 (obituary); *Stereo Review*, April 1970.

Porter (William), Quincy, b. New Haven, Conn., February 7, 1897; d. Bethany, Conn., November 12, 1966.

Porter was the recipient of the Pulitzer Prize in

music in 1954. Most of what Porter has written does not seek sustenance in any descriptive programs, poetic texts, or varied ideologies. He was basically an instrumental composer of absolute music within classical structures. His goal of a flowing melody almost consistently stepwise and with very closely knit continuity of sections was something he learned by studying the motets of Orlando de Lasso. But his musical equipment, deeply rooted though it was in polyphonic practices of the past, also included many of the harmonic, tonal, and rhythmic accoutrements of the 20th century. His music was so masterfully realized, had such inevitability of flow, was so uninhibited that it gave the impression of having been written spontaneously though, in truth, the writing of each major work cost him considerable time, effort and struggle.

On both sides of his family he was descended from early American settlers. One of his ancestors was Jonathan Edwards, the theologian of colonial times. Both his grandfather and father were professors at Yale University. His father, Reverend Frank Chamberlin Porter, a minister, was affiliated with the Yale Divinity School.

Porter received his preliminary academic education at Hopkins Grammar School in New Haven. While there, he began studying the violin when he was ten, and from 1913 to 1920 continued these studies privately with Herbert Dittler. Upon graduating from Hopkins Grammar School in 1914, Porter entered Yale University, where he studied composition with Horatio Parker and David Stanley Smith. As a Yale undergraduate he gave recitals for the Red Cross with Bruce Simonds, pianist, and revived and conducted the Yale Orchestra.

He received his bachelor of arts degree at Yale in 1919. In 1920 he attended the Schola Cantorum in Paris for the study of violin with Lucien Capet and composition with Vincent d'Indy. Upon his return to the United States, he resumed his music studies at the Yale School of Music, where his talent was recognized with the winning of the Osborne and Steinert prizes in composition. When the American Prix de Rome was instituted in 1921, he entered a Violin Concerto, which he described as "very Brahmsian" in style and structure; it received honorable mention.

After earning his bachelor of music degree at Yale in 1921, Porter settled in New York, where he was employed as violinist in the Capitol Theater Orchestra on Broadway. In New York he studied composition privately with Ernest Bloch. When Bloch was made director of the Cleveland Institute of Music in 1922, Porter continued to study with him there. From 1923 to 1928 (and again in 1930–31) Porter was a member of the faculty of the Cleveland Institute as a teacher of theory. During his first six years in Cleveland he played the violin with the Ribaupierre Quartet, which gave concerts regularly in the Cleveland area, including a complete cycle of Beethoven's string quartets, and the Cleveland premiere of Bloch's Piano Quintet no. 1. This association with the Ribaupierre Quartet encouraged him to write chamber music, a field which he would henceforth cultivate richly, including his first two string quartets (1923, 1925), his Violin Sonata no. 1 (1926) and a Piano Quintet (1927). He also produced an orchestral work—the *Ukrainian Suite*, for string orchestra (1925)—which was published and which outlived its premiere in Rochester, N.Y., on May 1, 1925, to find performances with several major orchestras.

On December 21, 1926, Porter married Lois Brown, a violinist, with whom he had two children, one of whom, William Lyman Porter, became an architect. In 1928, having been awarded a Guggenheim Fellowship, Porter and his wife went to Paris, where they remained three years. The chamber music Porter completed in Paris contained, as Howard Boatwright has written, "the prototypes of the melodic, rhythmic and textural devices which were later on to typify the more mature Porter." These works included the Sonata no. 2, for violin and piano (1929), which was his first work to get published by virtue of a Society for the Publication of American Music Award and the first to get recorded; a Clarinet Quintet (1929); a Piano Sonata (1930), written for Beveridge Webster; and the third and fourth string quartets (1930, 1931). The Clarinet Quintet, the Piano Sonata, and the String Quartet no. 3 were introduced at Salle Pleyel in Paris on February 18, 1931, at which time the French critic Felix Raugel spoke of their "remarkable thematic content, the significant conciseness of thematic development and the true beauty of the sonoric forms." The String Quartet no. 4, said Alfred Frankenstein in the *San Francisco Chronicle*, "like the composer's third quartet . . . is very beautifully made, full of sound sense and authentic personality. . . . He can be melodious without being hackneyed. The slow movement . . . seems on first hearing to be one of the finest lyric episodes in recent chamber music."

When his three-year stay in Paris ended in 1932, Porter was appointed professor of music at Vassar College in Poughkeepsie, N.Y., where he also conducted the Vassar Orchestra. If the Paris years brought the first fulfillment of his chamber music style, the Vassar years saw a similar development in his symphonic writing. *Poem and Dance* (1932), which Porter wrote on commission from the Cleveland Orchestra summer concerts, was introduced in Cleveland on June 24, 1932, the composer conducting. More significant still was the Symphony no. 1 (1934), recipient of honorable mention in the American Composer Awards in 1936, its premiere given by the New York Philharmonic on April 2, 1938, under the composer's direction. "The texture of the music is firmly woven," reported Lawrence Gilman in the *New York Herald Tribune*, "the idiom mildly contemporary, the flavor quite dry. . . . His thematic patterns are intricate, and they are adroitly

designed and evolved. But the emphasis is rather on elaborate and subtle counterpoint and rhythm. . . . Here the work of the composer is deft and ingenious." *Dance in Three-Time*, for chamber orchestra (1937), received its first hearing in St. Louis on July 2, 1937, performed by the St. Louis Little Symphony (which had commissioned it) under Hans Lange.

In 1938, Porter succeeded Frederick Converse as dean of the New England Conservatory in Boston and from 1942 to 1946 he was its director. On October 30, 1943, Porter received the Elizabeth Sprague Coolidge medal for "eminent service to chamber music." When this presentation was made—at the Founders' Day concert at the Library of Congress in Washington, D.C.—the Coolidge Quartet presented the premiere of Porter's String Quartet no. 7 (1943), written on commission for this occasion. Rudolph Elie, Jr., in the *Boston Herald*, did not hesitate to call this work "one of the most significant pieces in the form yet produced by an American composer. Of great dignity, even nobility of expression, it is nonetheless warm and graciously melodic and it speaks quickly and eloquently, yet always personally."

Further honors came to Porter in 1943–44 with his election to membership in the National Institute of Arts and Letters and the award of an honorary doctorate in music from the University of Rochester in New York.

Porter was appointed professor of music at Yale University in 1946. At that time he was given an honorary master of arts degree by the university. He remained at Yale until his retirement as professor emeritus in 1965, having served as Battel Professor of Theory and Music between 1960 and 1965 as well as master of Pierson College from 1958 on. In New Haven, the Porters occupied the house in which Porter had been born and raised.

His most important compositions after 1966 included two concertos, the String Quartet no. 8, and the Symphony no. 2. The Viola Concerto (1948) was introduced by Paul Doktor and the CBS Symphony conducted by Dean Dixon in New York on May 16, 1948—"a work of felicity and charm, of melodious pleasure, and rich delectable colors," Alfred Frankenstein called it in the *San Francisco Chronicle*. Porter's other concerto brought him the Pulitzer Prize. Written in Florence, Italy, between November 1952 and March 1953, on a commission from the Louisville Orchestra while Porter was on sabbatical leave from Yale, it originally was a concerto for two pianos and orchestra and as such was introduced in Kentucky on March 17, 1954, with Dorothea Adkins and Ann Monks as soloists. This well-integrated one-movement composition was, as Howard Boatwright has written, "an expression of the same psychological atmosphere and approach to musical materials which characterize most other pieces by Porter, except that in this case there is a new polyphonic emphasis, a more brilliant treatment of the orchestra, and a more powerful emotional expression than in any other work except the also recent String Quartet no. 8. This is, in other words, not just typical Porter, but a real masterpiece in the kind of idiom which he has established for himself." Three simple motives form the material, appearing in various transformations of tempo and mood throughout the composition. After winning the Pulitzer Prize, Porter came to the conclusion that this work was not really a virtuoso piece for the two solo instruments, that the two instruments were inextricably involved with the orchestra in equal artistic partnership. This is the reason he now called it *Concerto concertante*.

String Quartet no. 8 (1950) came between the two concertos, the result of a commission from the University of Michigan for the Stanley Quartet, which introduced it an Ann Arbor in 1950. Though in three movements, each with a different tempo, this work is in actuality a single integrated work in which one idea flows into another through the three movements. "The work has the sound of a masterwork," said Paul Hume in the *Washington Post* after it had been performed in Washington, D.C., by the Juilliard Quartet in March 1951.

Porter's Symphony no. 2 (1962) was commissioned by the Louisville Orchestra, which, under Robert Whitney, presented the world premiere in Kentucky on January 14, 1964.

Porter was one of the founders of the American Music Center in 1939, and elected chairman of its board of directors in 1958. He was the vice-president of the National Association of Schools of Music in 1941 and member of its commission on curricula from 1942 to 1947. From 1954 until his death he was the treasurer of the National Institute of Arts and Letters. He received an honorary doctorate in music from the University of Michigan in 1954. After his retirement from Yale in 1965 Porter lived in Bethany, Conn., eight miles north of New Haven, where he died of a stroke.

THE COMPOSER SPEAKS: There are so many branches of the musical art with which the would-be composer should acquaint himself that it is impossible to mention them all. He should gather as much knowledge of music as he can from as many good musicians as he is able to get in touch with: from other composers, from performers on as many different instruments as possible, from historians, from conductors. He should hear as much music as he can, with a keenly critical mind. He must broaden, rather than narrow his base as a musician. He will keep discovering constructive principles which appear to him and which he can use, perhaps in an individual way. And he should make a point of making friends with those implicated in other branches of art. He may get new insight into the solution of his own problems through a discussion with some painter, sculptor, etcher or a writer or a poet, thereby freeing himself from a con-

sideration of the blinding mass of small detail with which he is involved in his own work.

If we grant that he has been given his tools, and has acquired a wide base as a musician, how does he go about writing American music? My feeling is that he makes no conscious effort whatever to be American, but that he writes whatever seems to ring the bell most resonantly to his own musical consciousness. If he has been brought up in this country he will be influenced by his environment to write in certain ways; listeners who hear his music may find that these ways of writing music strike a sympathetic note. There may be something fresh in his music which rings true to the listener.

PRINCIPAL WORKS: 10 string quartets (1923–65); 2 symphonies (1934, 1962); 2 violin sonatas (1928, 1929).

Ukrainian Suite, for string orchestra (1925); Piano Quintet (1927); Clarinet Quintet (1929); Piano Sonata (1930); Sonata for Solo Viola (1930); *Poem and Dance*, for orchestra (1932); *Dance in Three-Time*, for orchestra (1937); Quintet, for flute and strings (1940); Music, for strings (1941); Canon and Fugue, for organ (1941); *Fantasy on a Pastoral Theme*, for organ and string orchestra (1942); Six Miniatures, for piano (1943); Horn Sonata (1946); *String Quartet on Slavic Themes* (1947); Four Pieces, for violin and piano (1947); Viola Concerto (1948); *Fantasy*, for cello and small orchestra (1950); *The Desolate City*, scena for baritone and orchestra (1950); *Concerto concertante*, for two pianos and orchestra, originally Concerto for Two Pianos and Orchestra (1953); *New England Episodes*, suite for orchestra (1958): Harpsichord Concerto (1959); Concertino for Wind Symphony (1959); Divertimento, for woodwind quintet (1960); *Symptoms of Love*, song cycle for voice and piano (1961); Quintet, for harpsichord and strings (1961); *Wedding Music for Damaris*, for brass, strings, and soprano (1962); *Overture on Three American Folk Tunes*, for orchestra (1963);

BIBLIOGRAPHY: Howard, John Tasker, *Our Contemporary Composers* (N.Y., 1941); Machlis, Joseph, *Introduction to Contemporary Music*, revised ed. (N.Y., 1979); Thomson, Virgil, *American Music Since 1910* (N.Y., 1970); *American Composers Alliance Bulletin*, vol. 6, no. 3, 1957; *Modern Music*, Winter 1946; *New York Times*, November 12, 1966 (obituary); *Who's Who in America, 1966–67.*

Powell, John, b. Richmond, Va., September 6, 1882; d. Charlottesville, Va., August 15, 1963.

Powell's music, which followed traditional romantic paths, was rooted in American folk sources. His most famous composition drew stimulus from the American Negro, but most of Powell's other major works were based musically on Appalachian folk songs, ballads, and dances of Anglo-Saxon origin which he learned from Cecil Sharp's collections and in which he did valuable research. Using such material, his writing became modal in its harmonic and melodic structures.

His mother, Rebecca (Leigh) Powell, an excellent pianist, was descended from Nicholas Lanier, court musician to Charles I of England and an ancestor of the American poet Sidney Lanier. Powell's father was headmaster of a girl's school in Richmond. John Powell's interest in music revealed itself early and received encouragement from his mother. He began studying piano in early boyhood with his sister, Mrs. J. S. Brockenbraugh, with whom he made such excellent progress that before long he was placed in the more experienced hands of Frederick Charles Hahr, a pupil of Liszt, who taught Powell harmony as well as piano. At the same time, Powell received his academic education in public schools in Richmond and completed it at the University of Virginia, where he received his bachelor of arts degree in 1901.

By the time he graduated, he knew he wanted to develop himself as a musician. Over the objections of his father, he went to Vienna in 1902. There for the next five years he studied piano with Leschetizky, three of those years also spent in lessons in composition with Karel Navrátil. In December 1907, Powell made his debut as concert pianist in Berlin by appearing as soloist with the Tonkünstler Orchestra. This performance proved so successful that a concert tour followed, bringing him to Berlin, Paris, London, and Budapest, the first of many tours in the next seven years. In some of these recitals, Powell began featuring his own piano music, which included *In the South*, a suite (1906); Variations and Double Fugue (1906): *At the Fair*, a suite (1907); and his three piano sonatas—*Sonate psychologique*, *Sonate noble*, and *Sonata teutonica*, all three completed between 1907 and 1913, though some of them took many years to develop. His writing at that time was influenced by German postromanticism with its concern for huge structures, programmatic ideologies, and richly textured harmonic and sonoric patterns. The *Sonata teutonica* (1913)—which Benno Moiseiwitsch introduced in London in 1914—has particular interest for us today, since it was edited and revived more than half a century later by Roy Hamlin Johnson on a grant from the National Endowment for the Arts and performed by him publicly and in a recording released in 1977. He reduced it from its former one-hour length to three-quarters of an hour; this sonata appeared to Irving Lowens, reviewing it in *High Fidelity/Musical America*, as "superb and totally convincing. There is a grandeur and an almost orchestral scope and sound to the sonata reminiscent of Liszt in his more effective moments."

Just before the outbreak of World War I, Powell returned to the United States to launch his American career as concert pianist. He soon came to be numbered with the leading American-born pianists of his time, a reputation he enhanced during the next two decades with extensive tours.

He soon also established his reputation as composer by turning for his subjects and musical style to the American scene. His first success—and as it turned out, his greatest—came with the tone poem *Rapsodie nègre*, for piano and orchestra (1917), which had been inspired by a reading of Joseph Conrad's *Heart of Darkness*, and written at the request of Modest Altschuler, conductor of the Russian Symphony Orchestra in New York. In this work Powell sought to interpret the American Negro in music. As described by John Tasker Howard in *Our American Music*, it "begins and ends on a primal note, pagan, orgiastic; the idealization that creeps in the middle section cannot maintain itself against the primitive instinct. The work is intense in a fervor that rises to fury." Its world premiere took place in New York on March 23, 1918. From then, and for the next decade and more, it became a staple in American symphonic literature, widely performed by major orchestras in the United States and Europe. When the New York Symphony toured Europe in 1920, its conductor, Walter Damrosch, invited Powell to appear as guest artist with that orchestra in performances of this composition. Almost a decade later, in 1929, it was still receiving over fifty performances in New York City alone.

Powell continued to use the American Negro as subject and inspiration for a few more compositions. The most significant after the *Rapsodie nègre* was *Sonate virginianesque*, for violin and piano (1919), a picture of plantation life in Virginia before the Civil War, its music derived from several Negro song and dance themes. Here blacks are depicted in their uninhibited gaiety and humor ("In the Quarters"), in a romantic interlude ("In the Woods"), and as entertainers for their white Virginian masters ("At the Big House"). The last of these movements utilized themes based on Virginia reels revealing Powell's now growing interest in the American folk music of Virginia.

Some of Powell's most important works henceforth drew their musical and programmatic materials from his native Virginia and its folk ballads and dances. Virginian folk music is richly tapped in the orchestral overture *In Old Virginia* (1921). *Natchez on the Hill*, for orchestra (1931; Worcester Festival, Mass., 1931), used three fiddle tunes heard in the Appalachian mountains region. "The three folk tunes," explains John Tasker Howard, "are attached to each other in a novel pattern, somewhat akin to rondo form, but with a third theme taking the place of a recurrence of the first theme." Following its premiere, *Natchez on the Hill* was frequently heard at symphony concerts and over the radio. *A Set of Three*, an orchestral suite (1934), was also based on Virginia folk tunes. The first movement utilized "Snowbird on the Ashbank," the second, "Green Willow," and the third, a number of folk dance melodies. Individual movements of this suite received numerous hearings before the work as a whole was introduced in February 1940 by the New York Philharmonic Orchestra.

The influence of Virginia folk music of Celtic origin is omnipresent in Powell's Symphony in A (1946), which was commissioned by the National Federation of Music Clubs. It was introduced by the Detroit Symphony Orchestra on April 23, 1947. Each of its four movements, as the composer explained, typified "one of the major segments of folk music tradition, namely, the country dance, the folk song, the ballad and ritual dance."

On April 25, 1928, Powell married Louise Burleigh. Later the same year he made an extended tour of Europe as concert pianist. Powell continued to concertize for a quarter of a century after that. On November 1, 1938, he commemorated the twenty-first anniversary of his American virtuoso career with a Carnegie Hall recital in New York, the proceeds from which went to the purchase of rare letters by Jefferson for presentation to the library of the University of Virginia.

Powell was the organizer of the State Choral Festival and a prime mover in the annual White Top Mountain Folk Festival, both in Virginia. Outside music, his main interest was astronomy. He was a member of the Société Astronomique de France and the discoverer of a comet. He was also a member of the National Institute of Arts and Letters.

THE COMPOSER SPEAKS: I believe thoroughly in the dignity and worth of American folk music. I don't think it is reasonable to be ashamed of such tunes from the American frontier as "The Mississippi Sawyer." . . . As for jazz, it is already a worn-out and limited style. It is a weak and elementary way of saying things, as I see it, which need a far richer and more adaptable speech than it is able to give.

PRINCIPAL WORKS: 3 piano sonatas (1907–13); 2 violin sonatas (1919, 1925).

Violin Concerto (1914); *Rapsodie nègre*, tone poem for orchestra (1917); *In Old Virginia*, overture (1921); *At the Fair*, for solo piano, also for orchestra (1925); *From a Loved Past*, for violin and piano (1930); *Natchez on the Hill*, for orchestra (1931); *A Set of Three*, for orchestra (1935); *Five Virginian Folk Songs*, for baritone and piano (1937); Symphony in A (1946). *Also:* 2 piano concertos; *Judith and Holofernes*, opera; String Quartet.

BIBLIOGRAPHY: Ewen, David, *American Composers Today* (N.Y., 1949); Howard, John Tasker, *Our American Music* (N.Y., 1946); Reis, Claire, *Composers in America* (N.Y., 1947); *Who's Who in America, 1962–63.*

R

Rachmaninoff, Sergei Vassilievitch, b. Oneg, Novgorod, Russia, April 1, 1873; d. Beverly Hills, Calif., March 28, 1943. American citizen, 1943.

The revolution had taken Rachmaninoff out of Russia, but nothing could ever take Russia out of Rachmaninoff. To the end of his days he remained a *Russian* composer, faithful to the Russian romantic movement of the 19th century. His music was Tchaikovsky's legitimate, recognizable offspring in the amplitude of its plangent melodies, rhapsodic sonorities, resonant harmonies, and melancholy statements. Rachmaninoff's style changed little from the days of his youth. Where he was innovative and *sui generis* was not in uncovering new techniques or devising a new language, but in using, with a craftsmanship, subtlety, sophistication, and expressivity that have few parallels in 20th-century music, those he had been taught in the conservatory.

His ancestry was musical. His great-grandfather had been a violinist and the founder of an orchestra and chorus. His grandfather, a pupil of John Field's, was an excellent pianist and the composer of published music. Rachmaninoff's father, Vassili, was a wealthy landowner who had retired from military service to become a dilettante. He played the piano constantly and was skilled at improvisation; one of his melodies was used by Rachmaninoff in 1911 for a piano polka. Rachmaninoff's mother, Lubov, was a trained pianist; and his young cousin, Alexander Siloti, became a distinguished pianist and conductor.

Rachmaninoff was five when his mother began giving him piano lessons. His academic education was assigned to private tutors and governesses. He made such progress at the piano that before long he was turned over to Anna Ornazkaya, a graduate of the St. Petersburg Conservatory, with whom he studied for three years. Two early musical experiences affected him deeply and were never forgotten. One was listening to his sister, Yelena, sing Tchaikovsky's music; the other was the music he heard in church.

His father aspired to make him an army officer, but his mother had other ideas, insisting that he be trained for a career in music. When Sergei was nine, the problem of his future was resolved through an economic disaster that struck the household due to the father's reckless extravagances and speculation. The Rachmaninoffs were forced to auction off their estate at Oneg to pay off debts and move into an apartment in St. Petersburg. At that time his father deserted the family for good. With paternal interfer-

ence thus removed, Sergei was free to enter into the St. Petersburg Conservatory on a scholarship in 1882, where he studied paino with Vladimir Demiansky and harmony with Alexander Rubets. Lack of home discipline and guidance spoiled him into indolence and irresponsibility which made him avoid classroom studies and practicing the piano. He would wander aimlessly about the city stealing rides on trolley cars or he would go roller skating. Despite his inborn musicality he did so poorly at school that he was compelled to alter the marks he brought home. When asked to perform on the piano he would pass off his own improvisations as compositions by Chopin and other masters he had failed to study assiduously. At the end-of-term examinations in 1885 he failed all his general subjects. Karl Y. Davidov, the director of the conservatory, had no hesitancy in describing him as not only incorrigibly lazy but also lacking in talent.

Alexander Siloti, Rachmaninoff's twenty-two-year-old cousin and already a pianist of repute, advised a change of scene for him: Moscow, where the boy could be placed under the autocratic discipline of Nicolai Zverev of the Moscow Conservatory. This proved the right prescription. For three years, beginning with 1885, Rachmaninoff lived with and studied under Zverev, whose ruthless regime proved providential in the molding of this great musician. Through Zverev, Rachmaninoff attended performances of theater, opera, and concerts. What impressed the boy most deeply was a series of recitals Anton Rubinstein was giving, covering the history of piano literature. The young Rachmaninoff also had opportunities to perform as pianist at Zverev's open-house Sundays attended by leading Moscow musicians. "I cannot adequately describe," Rachmaninoff later recalled, "what a spur to our ambition was this opportunity . . . and to listen to their kindly criticism—nor what a stimulus it was to our enthusiasm."

By 1888, Rachmaninoff was ready to assume the full curriculum at the conservatory. There he continued piano study with Siloti and composition and harmony with Taneiev and Arensky. Probably as homework for his composition classes, Rachmaninoff wrote a number of compositions early in 1887: a Scherzo for Orchestra and three Nocturnes and other pieces for piano. As a conservatory student, he had his first opportunity to meet Tchaikovsky, whom he idolized then as later. At one of his examinations,

Rachmaninoff played his own *Song without Words* to a jury that included Tchaikovsky and received kind words of encouragement from the master.

Rachmaninoff was now a shining light at the conservatory. As one of his fellow students, Alexander Goldenweiser, recalled many years later: "Rachmaninoff's musical gifts . . . surpassed any others I have ever met, bordering on the marvelous, like those of Mozart in his youth. The speed with which he memorized new compositions was remarkable. . . . It was his practice to memorize everything he heard, no matter how complicated it was."

Rachmaninoff graduated from the conservatory as pianist with honors in 1891, but he remained an additional year to receive a diploma in composition. In July 1891, he completed his Piano Concerto no. 1, the first movement of which he introduced in Moscow on March 17, 1892. One of his fellow students, Mikhail Nubnik, played in the student orchestra when this movement was premiered. He recalled: "The melodic part of the concerto did not astonish me, but I was impressed by the freshness of its harmony, the free writing, and the easy mastery of its orchestration." This concerto, over which hovered Tchaikovsky's shadow, became Rachmaninoff's first published work, his talent having attracted the interest and support of Karl Gutheil, who remained his publisher until Gutheil's death. Rachmaninoff revised the concerto drastically in 1917 and from then on often featured it at his appearances with orchestras in Europe and the United States.

Several more of his compositions were heard when he made his first formal concert appearance as composer-pianist on January 18, 1892, in Moscow: a Piano Trio and a Prelude, for cello and piano, both written in 1892 for that performance. Later that year, he wrote and published Five Pieces, for piano, op. 3. Here we find the composition that would soon make Rachmaninoff a household name in Russia and which, since that time, has remained one of his most popular pieces for the piano: the Prelude in C-sharp minor, which he himself introduced in Moscow on September 28, 1892, in a recital that Rachmaninoff always looked back upon as his real beginnings as a piano virtuoso.

For his graduation in composition from the conservatory in 1892, he was assigned to write a one-act opera, *Aleko*, libretto adapted from Pushkin's poem *The Gypsies*. Rachmaninoff completed his score in seventeen days, the music highly derivative of Tchaikovsky's opera *The Queen of Spades*. *Aleko* was so highly esteemed by the conservatory committee, which included Tchaikovsky, that it unanimously recommended for Rachmaninoff the highest honor the conservatory could bestow on a student, the Great Gold Medal, which had previously been presented just twice. When *Aleko* was produced at the Bolshoi Theater in Moscow on May 9, 1893, it was an unqualified success. Tchaikovsky, who was in the audience, gave an open demonstration of his enthu-

siasm and the rest of the audience responded in kind. Writing in *Arise*, Semyon Kruglikov said: "He has a feeling for the stage and an almost perfect understanding of the human voice, and he is endowed with the fortunate capacity for melody. . . . As the work of an eighteen-year-old composer, as the work of a student, *Aleko* is beyond all praise."

Once out of the conservatory, Rachmaninoff proceeded to advance his career as pianist with appearances in recitals and with orchestras throughout Russia. By 1895, he was generally acknowledged to be one of Russia's foremost pianists, well on his way toward the imperial position among virtuosos that he would henceforth occupy. On October 12, 1897, he made his first appearance as conductor in Saint-Saëns's *Samson and Delilah* in Moscow. When he made his debut in London in 1898 he appeared for the first time in the triple role of conductor-composer-pianist by performing his Piano Concerto no. 1 and conducting his composition *The Rock*, a fantasia for orchestra (1893; Moscow, March 20, 1894) based on a poem by Chekov. In years to come, both in Europe and the United States, he would have ample opportunity to present himself as composer-conductor-pianist at single concerts.

The death of Tchaikovsky in 1893 was a blow that led Rachmaninoff to sublimate his grief in the writing of *Trio élégiaque*, for violin, cello, and piano, inscribed "to the memory of a great artist." This Trio was the opening work of the first concert devoted entirely to Rachmaninoff's music; it took place in Moscow on January 31, 1894. The other compositions performed that evening were the Fantasia, for two pianos (1893), which was so well received that it had to be repeated; the Five Pieces, for piano, op. 3; and the newly composed Seven Pieces, for piano, op. 10 (1894); as well as two songs and two pieces for cello. The piano works were all performed by Rachmaninoff himself.

Still in his twenties, Rachmaninoff was enjoying substantial success in the three areas of music in which he was involved. But there was also a disaster that almost destroyed him physically and emotionally and threatened to bring his career to a standstill. It came with the world premiere of Symphony no. 1 (1895), taking place in St. Petersburg on March 15, 1897, conducted by Alexander Glazunov. The performance was so poor that much of the music was unrecognizable. Rachmaninoff himself was aware not only of the bad presentation his symphony was getting but also of its many artistic defects. He ran out of the concert hall and wandered about the streets in a daze. "The despair that filled my soul would not leave," he recalled later. "My dreams of a brilliant career lay shattered. My hopes and confidence were destroyed. . . . This was the effect of my own symphony on myself. When the indescribable torture of this performance had at last come to an end, I was a different man." The critics offered little solace. They referred to the work as "modernist trash" and lamented its "poverty of themes and sickly perversity of harmony."

The manuscript of this symphony was for many years considered lost until a two-piano version was discovered in the Soviet Union after Rachmaninoff's death, leading to a search for the orchestral parts, which were finally located in the library of the Leningrad Conservatory. On March 19, 1948, this symphony was reintroduced in Philadelphia with Eugene Ormandy conducting the Philadelphia Orchestra. At that time it was esteemed as little better than a talented apprentice work, hardly anticipatory of the composer's later creative powers for orchestra.

After completing and publishing *Six Moments musicaux*, for piano, op. 16 (1896), Rachmaninoff wrote little for the next four years, mired as he was in overwhelming depression and self-doubt that made work difficult and at times impossible; the few works he completed at that time were of little consequence. He later recalled that these years were "the most difficult and critical period of my life." His relatives prevailed on him to seek the help of Dr. Nikolai Dahl, a specialist in neurology, before he became involved in the therapeutic values of hypnosis and autosuggestion. Rachmaninoff began treatments in January of 1900 and by summer he made such progress that he was beginning to compose again. His most ambitious project was a new piano concerto, the Piano Concerto no. 2 in C minor (1901). Even before the work was finished, two of its movements were performed by the composer in Moscow on December 15, 1900, Siloti conducting. "It's been long since the walls of the Nobility Hall reverberated with such enthusiastic, storming applause," reported a critic for *Russkaya Muzkalnaya Gazeta*. "This work contains much poetry, beauty, warmth, rich orchestration, healthy, and buoyant creative power." The entire concerto was premiered by the composer in Moscow on October 27, 1901. It enjoyed a success far beyond anything Rachmaninoff had experienced up to this time, a triumph that was repeated when it was given in St. Petersburg the following March 28, performed by Siloti, with Arthur Nikisch conducting. Since that time, with its opulent outpouring of sensuous and at times sentimentalized melodies, its emotional excesses and rhapsodic moods, it has become a strong favorite with audiences, one of the most beloved of all Rachmaninoff's larger works, and certainly one of the most popular piano concertos ever written.

This success gave Rachmaninoff the reassurance he needed to advance himself as composer. In 1901, in addition to the Second Piano Concerto, he completed the Suite no. 2, for two pianos (first performed in Moscow on November 24, 1901), and the Sonata in C minor, for cello and piano, one of his chamber music masterworks, which was premiered in Moscow on December 2, 1901. In 1902, he composed a set of twelve songs, op. 21, which included such Rachmaninoff song classics as "Fate" (based on the opening notes of Beethoven's Fifth Symphony),

"How Fair This Spot," and "Lilacs." In 1903, he wrote the *Variations on a Theme by Chopin* and a set of ten preludes for piano, op. 23, the premieres of both given by the composer in Moscow on February 10, 1903. Between 1903 and 1905 he completed two operas: *The Miserly Knight* (1903–4), based on a drama by Pushkin, and *Francesca da Rimini* (1904–5), libretto by Modeste Tchaikovsky derived from Dante's *Inferno*. Rachmaninoff conducted the premieres of both operas at the Bolshoi Theater on January 11, 1906.

His personal life had also come to a peaceful resolution as a result of his sessions with Dr. Dahl. On April 29, 1902, he married his second cousin, Natalie Satina, a piano graduate of the Moscow Conservatory; they had two daughters.

Between 1904 and 1906, Rachmaninoff was the conductor of the Bolshoi Theater in Moscow, where he was acclaimed for his performances of Russian operas. The pressure of these conducting duties and the disturbances of a crowded social calendar made him neglect composition, except for a cycle of fifteen songs, op. 26, completed between August 14 and September 5, 1906. This group included several more Rachmaninoff gems, among these being "Before My Window," "Christ Is Risen," and "To the Children."

To find more leisure and time for composition, he decided in late 1906 to resign his post in the opera house and to find a new and more peaceful life for himself in Dresden, Germany, where he stayed for the next three years. There he completed three major symphonic compositions. Symphony no. 2 (1907), a work of introspective and melancholy beauty, revealed a growing mastery of symphonic structure and thematic developments. It was introduced on February 8, 1908, in Moscow, the composer conducting, when it received the Glinka Prize. *The Isle of the Dead* (1909) was a tone poem inspired by a grim painting by Arnold Böcklin depicting a cliff surrounded by ghostly cypresses to which approaches a boat bearing a flag-draped coffin and a single mourner. In his music, the composer revealed a more mature gift in conveying to music atmosphere, background, and brooding pictorial images. In this work he quoted the somber strains of the Dies Irae, which he would use again in several later compositions. The first performance of *The Isle of the Dead* was heard in Moscow on May 1, 1909, the composer conducting.

A third masterwork of these Dresden years was the Concerto no. 3, for piano and orchestra (1909), which he was writing for his upcoming first tour of the United States. He made his American debut as pianist with a recital in Northampton, Mass., on November 4, 1909. His first American appearance as conductor followed on November 8, when he directed Mussorgsky's *A Night on Bald Mountain*, and, for the first time in America, was filling the tripartite role of composer-conductor-pianist. On November

28, as soloist with the New York Symphony under Walter Damrosch, he gave the world premiere of his new concerto, a work that showed significant advances over its highly popular predecessor in cohesion of structure, in evolving secondary episodes from primary themes through rhythmic or melodic transformations, in the stronger interrelationship between solo instrument and orchestra, and in the growing richness and expressivity of his harmonic language.

Just before his American tour ended, he was offered the conductorship of the Boston Symphony. He was also given contracts to return the next year for another extended American tour as pianist. He turned a deaf ear because he had found his American experiences too debilitating of his nervous and physical energies. Returning to Russia, he spent the next four years touring that country and Europe as pianist, and in conducting orchestral concerts in Moscow with the Philharmonic Orchestra.

He spent the years of World War I in Russia, frequently giving concerts for soldiers and refugees, and composing mostly songs and piano pieces. In December 1917, having been disturbed by the excesses of the Bolshevik revolution in Russia, he left for a tour of Scandinavia with just a few hundred rubles in his pocket and some personal belongings in a suitcase. He was never to return to his native land. For one year he made his home in Scandinavia and, from 1918 to 1935, in Switzerland, on the banks of Lake Lucerne. He spent those years touring extensively as piano virtuoso, having by now become a box-office as well as artistic attraction of the first magnitude. He returned for his second tour of the United States in December 1918. When he gave his recital in Carnegie Hall, New York, on December 21, Richard Aldrich, in the *New York Times*, called him "a master etcher on the keyboard," adding: "The oldsters were reminded of von Bülow. The same cold white light of analysis, the incisive touch, the strongly marked rhythms, the intellectual grasp of the musical ideas and the sense of the relative importance in phrase-groupings proclaimed that Rachmaninoff is a cerebral, not an emotional, artist."

Between 1917, when he left Russia to become an expatriate, and the time he made America his home eighteen years later, Rachmaninoff's principal works were the Piano Concerto no. 4 in C minor (1926), which he introduced with the Philadelphia Orchestra on March 18, 1927, Leopold Stokowski conducting; the *Variations on a Theme by Corelli* (1910; Montreal, Canada, October 12, 1931), based on the theme from Corelli's *La folia* sonata; and the *Rhapsody on a Theme by Paganini*, for piano and orchestra (1934), the composer's last work for piano and orchestra, its premiere taking place in Philadelphia on November 6, 1936, with Stokowski conducting the Philadelphia Orchestra and the composer, soloist. The *Rhapsody* is one of Rachmaninoff's most frequently heard large compositions, second in popularity only to the Piano Concerto no. 2, and one of his unqualified master-

works. The theme, which was the germ from which the entire work grew, came from Paganini's Caprice no. 24, for solo violin, which was the source for a series of twenty-four variations of changing melodic, rhythmic, and harmonic interest. In three of these variations, Rachmaninoff quoted the Dies Irae, finally using it in conjunction with fragments of the Paganini theme to bring the work to its rousing conclusion.

In 1935, he left Switzerland to find a new home in the United States. He resided first in New York City, and from February 1, 1943, in Beverly Hills, Calif., where he spent his last months. He was in poor health in his last years, and a man who keenly suffered from a poignant nostalgia for his native land. Nevertheless he continued to compose, his major productions in the United States being his Symphony no. 3 in A minor (1936), which the Philadelphia Orchestra under Stokowski premiered on November 6, 1936, and the *Symphonic Dances*, for orchestra (1940), its first performance given by the Philadelphia Orchestra under Eugene Ormandy on January 3, 1941. He was also concertizing as a pianist. He was on a new tour of the United States when he collapsed in New Orleans on February 8, 1943, and was taken back to his home in California, where he died of melanoma. Everything Rachmaninoff ever recorded as pianist, conductor, and participant in chamber music performances was collected in a five-album, fifteen-disk set by RCA and released in 1973 to commemorate the centenary of his birth.

THE COMPOSER SPEAKS: I feel like a ghost wandering in a world grown alien. I cannot cast out the old way of writing, and I cannot acquire the new. I have made intense efforts to feel the musical manner of today, but it will not come to me. Unlike Madame Butterfly with her quick religious conversion, I cannot cast out my musical gods in a moment and bend the knees to the new ones. I have always felt that my own music and my reactions to all music remained spiritually the same, unendingly obedient in trying to create beauty. . . .

The new kind of music seems to come not from the heart but from the head. Its composers think rather than feel. They have not the capacity to make their music "exult," as Hans von Bülow called it. They meditate, protest, analyze, reason, calculate, and brood but they do not "exult." It may be that they compose in the spirit of the times; but it may be, too, that the spirit of the times does not call for expression in music. If that is the case, rather than compile music that is thought and not felt, composers should remain silent and leave contemporary expression to those authors and playwrights who are masters of the factual and literal, and do not concern themselves with soul states.

PRINCIPAL WORKS: 24 preludes for piano (1892–

1910); 15 *Etudes-Tableaux* for piano (1911–17); 4 piano concertos (1891–1926); 3 symphonies (1895, 1907, 1936); 2 piano trios (1892; 1893, revised 1907, 1917); 2 piano sonatas (1907, 1913); more than 80 songs (1893–16).

Aleko, one-act opera (1892); Five Pieces, for piano, op. 3 (1892); *The Rock*, orchestral fantasy (1893); Seven Pieces, for piano, op. 10 (1893–94); Suite no. 2, for two pianos (1900–1); Sonata in C minor, for cello and piano (1901); *Spring Cantata*, for baritone, chorus, and orchestra (1902); *Variations on a Theme by Chopin*, for piano (1902–3); *The Miserly Knight*, opera (1903–5); *Francesca da Rimini*, opera (1904–5); *The Isle of the Dead*, tone poem for orchestra (1909); *Liturgy of St. John Chrysostom*, for a cappella chorus (1910); *The Bells*, tone poem for solo voices, chorus, and orchestra (1913); *Three Russian Songs*, for chorus and orchestra (1926); *Variations on a Theme by Corelli*, for piano (1931); *Rhapsody on a Theme by Paganini*, for piano and orchestra (1934); *Symphonic Dances*, for orchestra (1940).

BIBLIOGRAPHY: Bertenson, Sergei, and Leyda, Jay, *Sergei Rachmaninoff* (N.Y., 1956); Culshaw, John, *Rachmaninoff: The Man and His Music* (London, 1949); Lyle, Watson, *Rachmaninoff: A Biography* (London, 1939); Norris, G., *Rachmaninoff* (London, 1974); Satin, Sophia, *In Memory of Rachmaninoff* (N.Y., 1946); Seroff, Victor, *Rachmaninoff* (N.Y., 1950); Threlfall, R., *Sergei Rachmaninoff: His Life and Music* (London, 1973); *Journal of the American Musicological Society*, Spring 1968; *Musical Quarterly*, January, April 1944; *New York Times*, April 1, 1973; *Stereo Review*, May 1973; *Tempo* (London), Rachmaninoff Issue, Winter 1951–2.

Read, Gardner, b. Evanston, Ill., January 2, 1913.

Read's musical output covers a wide area: almost one hundred fifty compositions in all forms and in a variety of styles. Just as he has consistently refused to subscribe to avant-gardism, so he has scrupulously avoided any one school or idiom. He has spoken in a romantic, neoclassical, quasi-impressionistic, and, at times, folk or popularist language. He has been basically tonal, at the same time bringing to his writing polyharmonic, polytonal, and polyrhythmic processes which make his music very much of the 20th century. Whatever direction he travels, it is with the sure footing of a superb craftsman and a musician of the highest ideals.

He was the youngest of three children of music-loving parents, his mother a concert pianist. Though Read did not receive his first music instruction until he was fifteen, he was involved in making music as a boy by singing in the choir of St. Luke's Episcopal Church in Evanston between 1921 and 1923. At Evanston Township High School, which he entered

in 1928, he majored in music. At the same time he began to study music privately: piano with Lora M. Bell (1928–1932) and organ with Archer Lambuth (1928–1930); he also took private composition lessons at the School of Music at Northwestern University in Evanston, Ill. His first composition was a piece entitled *Motion Picture Incidental Music* (1928–1930), fifty pieces for piano or organ interpreting changing episodes in silent films. By the time he graduated from high school in 1932 he had written eighteen compositions, including the senior song for the graduation class.

During the summers of 1932 and 1933 he received scholarships to the National Music Camp in Interlochen, Mich. There he studied conducting with Vladimir Bakaleinikoff, as well as harp, and had two of his orchestral compositions performed: *The Lotus Eaters* (1932) on August 12, 1932, and *The Painted Desert* (1932–33) on July 28, 1935.

On scholarships Read attended the Eastman School of Music in Rochester, N.Y., between 1932 and 1937, studying composition with Bernard Rogers and Howard Hanson, conducting with Paul White, and piano with Jerome Diamond. Read received his bachelor of music degree in 1936, and in 1937, while at the Eastman School on a graduate fellowship, the degree of master of music, with a major in composition. At Eastman, Read wrote several compositions that were performed publicly, all basically romantic in concept and traditional in structure and technique. These included *Sketches of the City*, a symphonic suite inspired by Carl Sandburg (1933; Rochester, N.Y., April 18, 1934), which received the Juilliard School of Music Publication Award in 1938; Four Nocturnes, for contralto and chamber orchestra (1933–34; Rochester, April 3, 1935); Fantasy, for viola and orchestra (1935; Rochester, April 22, 1937); and Prelude and Toccata, for small orchestra (1936; Rochester, April 29, 1937). The last of these was Read's first major success, enjoying more than forty performances in the United States and South America besides receiving the Juilliard School of Music Publication Award in 1941. A success of another dimension came with his Symphony no. 1 in A minor (1934–36). It won first prize in the American Composers Competition sponsored by the New York Philharmonic, which introduced it on November 4, 1937, John Barbirolli conducting. A critic for the *New York Herald Tribune* said of it: "The musical ideas are well defined, he is well acquainted with the orchestra and its possibilities, and in addition to many measures revealing a richly colored and impressive use of the hues of the instrumental palette, the symphony has passages of appealing lyric eloquence."

On a commission from the Ravinia Festival Committee in Illinois, Read completed Passacaglia and Fugue, for orchestra (1938), a transcription of a work for organ he had written two years earlier. This was one of several compositions in which the composer revealed pronounced neobaroque tendencies and an exceptional technique in polyphonic structure. Its world premiere was given at the festival by the Chicago Symphony Orchestra under Artur Rodzinski on June 30, 1938.

In 1938, Read was awarded the first of two successive Cromwell Fellowships for travel abroad. He spent these years visiting Europe and the Near East, receiving some instruction in composition from Ildebrando Pizzetti in Rome and visiting Jean Sibelius in Finland. Following his return to the United States in 1940, Read became professor of composition at the National Music Camp in Interlochen that summer. On September 17, 1940, he married Margaret Vail Payne, who was then employed in public relations and with whom he had a daughter. During the summer of 1941 he studied composition with Aaron Copland on a fellowship at the Berkshire Music Center at Tanglewood, Mass. That fall, he was appointed head of the composition department at the St. Louis Institute of Music, where he remained two years. Between 1943 and 1945, he was head of the composition department at the Kansas City Conservatory of Music, and from 1945 to 1948 he headed the composition and advanced theory departments at the Cleveland Institute of Music.

In 1942 Read won the Paderewski Prize for Symphony no. 2 in E-flat minor (1937–42), whose premiere was given on November 26, 1943, by the Boston Symphony Orchestra conducted by the composer. This was a powerful and individual work whose sonoric and dynamic interest and astute harmonic and polyphonic techniques took precedence over formal melodic content. Other compositions of the 1940s contributed further to his now rapidly growing stature among American composers of the period. One of these was *Night Flight*, for orchestra (1936–42; Rochester, April 27, 1944). Though inspired by the novel of the same name by Antoine de Saint-Exupéry, it made no effort to be programmatic or realistic. "I have sought," the composer explained, "to express the loneliness and mysterious beauty of the space in which these [early mail] planes fly." A radio-beam signal was simulated by a constantly reiterated note. "This is an attractive experiment," wrote Bernard Rogers in *Modern Music*, "showing a resourceful hand and an alert mind."

Two of Read's compositions in the 1940s are of special interest because they drew their material and inspiration from American folk or popular sources. *First Overture* (1943), recipient of the Composers Press Publication Award in 1949, was a brisk, almost jazzy orchestral piece which quoted a little-known song of Stephen Foster's ("The Glendy Burk"), and the Negro spiritual "Don't Be Weary, Traveler." It was commissioned by Fabien Sevitzky and the Indianapolis Symphony and was introduced on November 6, 1943. *Pennsylvaniana* (1947) was an orchestral suite utilizing folk songs of western Pennsylvania, one in each of the three movements:

"Dunlap's Creek," "I'm a Beggar," and "John Riley." Commissioned by the Pittsburgh Symphony, it was premiered on November 21, 1947, with Fritz Reiner conducting.

Between 1946 and 1948, Read worked on Symphony no. 3, in which his skill in polyphonic writing once again came strongly to the fore. Its opening movement was a Passacaglia, followed by a second-movement *sotto voce* scherzo. The concluding third movement opened with a chorale which led into a giant fugue based on the opening-movement Passacaglia theme before the chorale and Passacaglia theme were joined contrapuntally and climactically. This symphony waited fourteen years to be heard. On March 2, 1962, it was finally given by the Pittsburgh Symphony under William Steinberg. According to Ralph Lewando, writing in the *Christian Science Monitor*: "It is a work of creative worth and vibrancy. In three movements, it has melody and invention, saying much without being prolix. Mr. Read's ideas flow. Their development is attractive. Tonal and rhythmic contrasts abound—effects to be expected since the composer is an expert craftsman in full command of instrumental form and technique." It received the Sheil Publication Award in 1963.

In 1948, Read became professor of composition and music theory at the School for the Arts at Boston University. From 1950 to 1952 he was chairman of its department of theory and composition, and, from 1952 until his retirement in 1978, composer-in-residence and professor of composition. In that time he was also guest instructor at Simmons College in Boston (summer 1951) and Harvard University Extension Courses (1957–58) and visiting professor at the University of California in Los Angeles (1966). Between 1950 and 1960 he was the editor of the Birchard-Boston University Contemporary Music Series and from 1953 to 1960 host and commentator on the weekly radio program in Boston *Our American Music*, which he had initiated. He made two trips to Mexico to lecture on American music and conduct under special grants by the Department of State. In 1962 he was awarded an honorary doctorate in music from Doane College in Nebraska.

Read has continued to be prolific not only in orchestral music but in other media as well. Many of his works were the results of commissions, for example, *Toccata giocosa*, for orchestra (1953), written at the request of the Louisville Orchestra, which introduced it in Kentucky under Robert Whitney on March 13, 1954; *Vernal Equinox*, for orchestra (1955), a commission from the Brockton Symphony Orchestra in Massachusetts, introduced on April 12, 1955; the String Quartet no. 1 (1956–57), commissioned by the Kindler Foundation and premiered by the Classic Quartet in Washington, D.C., on January 6, 1958.

Symphony no. 4 was written between 1951 and 1959, and received its first hearing on January 30, 1970, with Erich Kunzel directing the Cincinnati

Symphony. The Cleveland Orchestra, conducted by Lorin Maazel, revived it on April 10, 1980. The composer describes it as "basically a study of orchestral trills and unusual harmonic and melodic spacings, the tonal texture being predominantly polyharmonic. The symphony was designed first and foremost as an emotional expression, not an intellectual one, in spite of its interrelated thematic construction, elaborate contrapuntal techniques, and unusual orchestrational devices." Henry S. Humphreys, writing in the *Cincinnati Enquirer*, found it to be "replete with beautiful lyrical passages and soaring powerful buttressed climaxes. . . . From the opening section of the first movement—with its expressive divided cello passage—to the sunburst of its biggest full-orchestra climax and its well-crafted ending, the hand of a top-notch tone poet is evident."

Read provides the following brief analysis of his four symphonies: "Symphonies 1, 3 and 4 are cyclical in that thematic ideas from their initial movements appear in one guise or another in succeeding movements. The passacaglia first movement of Symphony no. 3, for example, forms the basis for the fugue in the final movement, while the chordal structure of the scherzo movement is transformed to become the opening chorale of the last movement. Further similarities—and differences—between the four symphonies include the first and fourth both ending quietly and in a somber mood while the second and third finish with a blaze of full orchestra. Symphony no. 1 requires the largest orchestra of the four while no. 4 relies on the standard symphonic ensemble, but minus harp and keyboard instruments. Nonetheless, all differences aside, the one factor linking all four symphonies is their prevailing mood of romanticism, of emotional expression taking precedence over intellectualism, in spite of elaborate formal and complex thematic relationships."

Outside the field of instrumental music, Read completed two large works that are of special significance. One was an oratorio, *The Prophet*, for narrator, chorus, alto, and baritone solos, and orchestra, written in 1960 while the composer was resident fellow at the Huntington Hartford Foundation in Pacific Palisades, Calif. The work, with text by Kahlil Gibran, was divided into three sections: Love, Marriage, and Children; Joy and Sorrow, Reason and Passion, Pain; and Teaching, Beauty, and Death. The first and third sections were subdued as they interpreted the biblical, philosophical and mystical nature of the text. The middle part was dramatized by discordant harmonies and complex rhythmic patterns. The words of the Prophet were assigned to the narrator with surrounding music providing comment. "The music," noted a critic for *High Fidelity/Musical America*, "comments straightforwardly on the text—swelling to the great fortissimos (with organ) when the sentiment becomes 'profound,' suggesting a kind of exotic orientalism."

Read's second major work since 1960 is the opera *Villon* (1965–67), a three-act, eleven-scene work to a libretto by James Forsyth. The story deals with the criminal escapades and tragic love affairs of France's great lyric poet François Villon. Though thoroughly modern in its harmonic and rhythmic language, the music also evoked the spirit of 15th-century Paris. In addition, the score utilized some unusual taped effects, in particular a montage of the bells of Paris, which served as prelude to the opera. The title role demands a tenor of exceptional musical abilities and stamina, as he appears in every one of the opera's eleven scenes.

Read is the author of *Thesaurus of Orchestral Devices* (1953), *Music Notation: A Manuel of Modern Practice* (1964), *Contemporary Instrumental Techniques* (1976), *Modern Rhythmic Notation* (1978), and *Style and Orchestration* (1979).

THE COMPOSER SPEAKS: It seems to me that our culture, past and present, is the inspired way that creative minds transmute ordinary materials into art. Let us use, as an example of such ordinary materials, an unabridged dictionary.

Our Merriam-Webster has some 550,000 entries; but in itself it is not literature, and unless it is used by an artist it cannot be said to be part of our national culture. Yes, a poet like Robert Frost can arrange a half-dozen words into a deceptively simple line so freighted with meaning that it will have philosophers haggling over it for a decade. . . .

The paint in an artist's tube, the pipes of an organ, the vocal cords of a tenor, the stone or clay or metal in the countryside—these are not part of our national culture until they have been disciplined and transformed by an artist's imagination.

The result of this miraculous transformation of earth's materials to sculpture or architecture; of words to literature; of sounds to music; the transmutation of such familiar activities as entering and leaving and walking and talking, to drama and dance—this result is the rich assemblage of arts we call our culture.

PRINCIPAL WORKS: 4 symphonies (1934–59); 4 *Sonoric Fantasias*, for various instrumental combinations (1957–75); 2 piano sonatas (1932–33, 1945).

The Painted Desert, for orchestra (1932–33); *Sketches of the City*, suite for orchestra (1933); Four Nocturnes, for voice and orchestra (1933–34); *Three Satirical Sarcasms*, for piano, also for orchestra (1934–35); Suite, for string quartet (1935); Fantasy, for viola and orchestra (1935); *From a Luṱe of Jade*, for voice and piano, also orchestra (1935–36); Passacaglia and Fugue, for organ, also orchestra (1936); *Night Flight*, for orchestra (1936–42); Piano Quintet (1937–45); Cello Concerto (1939–45); *Pan e Dafni*, for orchestra (1940); *First Overture for Orchestra* (1943); *Quiet Music*, for strings (1946); *Threnody*, for flute and piano (1946); Partita, for small orchestra (1946); *A Bell Overture*, for orchestra (1946);

Pennsylvaniana, suite for orchestra (1946–47); *Sonata Brevis,* for violin and piano (1948); Suite, for organ, also for orchestra (1948–49); *Eight Preludes on Old Southern Hymns,* for organ (1950); *Toccata giocosa,* for orchestra (1953); *Vernal Equinox,* for orchestra (1955); String Quartet (1956–57); *Los Dioses aztecas,* for percussion ensemble (1958); *The Prophet,* oratorio, for narrator, baritone, alto, chorus, and orchestra (1960); *Six Preludes on Old Southern Hymns,* for organ (1960); *Five Polytonal Etudes,* for piano (1961–64); *Chants d'auvergne,* for chorus and chamber ensemble (1962); *Villon,* opera (1965–67); *Haiku Seasons,* for four speakers and instrumental ensemble (1970); *A Christmas Ballad,* for a cappella chorus (1973); Piano Concerto (1975–79); *The Hidden Lute,* for soprano and instrumental ensemble (1975–79); *Invocation,* for trombone and organ (1977); *Galactic Novae,* for organ and percussion (1977–78); *Diabolic Dialogue,* for double bass and timpani (1978–79).

BIBLIOGRAPHY: *BBDM; DCM;* Ewen, David, *Composers Since 1900* (N.Y., 1969); Pavlakis, Christopher, *The American Music Handbook* (N.Y., 1974); Reis, Claire, *Composers in America* (N.Y., 1947); Thomson, Virgil, *American Music Since 1910* (N.Y., 1970); *Cleveland Symphony Program Notes,* April 10, 1980; *Who's Who in America, 1978–79.*

Reich, Steve Michael, b. New York City, October 3, 1936.

The roots of Reich's avant-gardism stretch into many directions: to the 12th-century Notre Dame organum school of Leonin and Perotin, to Johann Sebastian Bach, to Bartók, Stravinsky, and Webern, and to the jazz of the 1950–65 vintage; to electronic music and to notated music for traditional instruments; to the resources of Western music and to the kind of motivic fragmentation, rhythms, and sonoric effects of West African drumming, Balinese gamelan music, and cantillation (chanting) of the Hebrew scriptures. His compositions have been variously called "minimal music," or "phase music," or "pulse music." The common denominator is emphasis on rhythm, continuous repetition of melodic patterns with minuscule canonic variation, minute metric adjustments, and the deployment of subtle changes of harmonic rhythm. After 1973, Reich began using such clearly defined techniques within a more harmonically and timbrally enriched context—a step into the more traditional Western concerns for harmony and orchestration.

Reich's first experience with music came when he was about three by listening to his mother sing the popular songs of the day to her father's piano accompaniment. Reich's mother, June (Sillman) Carroll, had been a popular-song lyricist who had performed her own songs in Broadway musicals. When Steve was about seven, he began receiving piano lessons

from the first of several private teachers. Called upon to perform at a Carnegie Hall recital, he grew so nervous that he refused to take any more piano lessons. But by the time he was fourteen, having heard and become fascinated with such variegated works as Stravinsky's *The Rite of Spring,* Bach's *Brandenburg Concertos,* the jazz music of Charlie Parker and Miles Davis and the drumming of Kenney Clarke, he was motivated to return to music study. Soon after entering Mamaroneck High School in Mamaroneck, N. Y., in 1950, Reich began a three-year period of study of rudimental snare drumming with Roland Kohloff (who subsequently became principal timpanist with the New York Philharmonic). "My drumming studies at the age of fourteen were undoubtedly one of my most important early musical influences. The combination of tastes for Stravinsky, Bach, and jazz coupled with my early training as a drummer has persisted as a basic musical outlook in my compositions ever since," he says.

In 1953, upon graduating from high school, Reich entered Cornell University in Ithaca, N. Y. During his college years he played trap drums with jazz combos and with dance bands performing at fraternity parties and Black Elk Dances. Though he majored in philosophy (specifically the later philosophy of Ludwig Wittgenstein), Reich took courses in music: history of music (including some examples of Balinese gamelan music), formal analysis of classical music, and a class in the formal analysis of jazz. One of his music professors at Cornell, William Austin, was the first to encourage him to become a composer. "I felt that, perhaps, not having become an accomplished composer by the age of seventeen, I might be a little too late." Nevertheless, in his senior year at Cornell, he arrived at the decision to abandon philosophy for music. In June 1957 he graduated from Cornell with a bachelor of arts degree with honors in philosophy, and had been accepted as a graduate student in philosophy at Harvard University. Reich turned down graduate work in philosophy to come to New York for the private study of composition with Hall Overton for a year and a half. "He was an excellent teacher," Reich recalls. "His use of Bartók's *Mikrokosmos* as a model for simple compositions introduced me to the modes and to canonic writing, techniques that have proved to endure in my compositions over the years."

Between 1958 and 1961, Reich attended the Juilliard School of Music in New York, studying composition with Vincent Persichetti and William Bergsma. Persichetti helped Reich analyze the so-called free atonal style of Webern's Five Movements, for string quartet, from a traditional harmonic viewpoint. During these years at Juilliard, Reich spent numerous evenings playing the drums with friends and listening to and absorbing jazz, and particularly the music of John Coltrane.

In 1961, Reich left New York for California, enrolling as a graduate student at Mills College in

Oakland. During the next two years he continued his study of composition with Darius Milhaud and Luciano Berio. With Berio, Reich studied the twelve-tone and serial tecnhiques, but Reich's concern for tonality and harmonic interest made it impossible for him to subscribe to the strict dictates of the Viennese School. "If you want to write tonal music, why don't you write tonal music?" Berio asked him. This question proved useful in making Reich aware of his own priorities at a time when tonality and steady pulse were not in fashion.

At Mills College, Reich served as graduate assistant in music in 1962–63. Though he heard African music several years earlier, Reich first became interested in the African music system through A. M. Jones's *Studies in African Music*, which Gunther Schuller had recommended to him.

After receiving his master of arts degree in music at Mills College in 1963, Reich settled in San Francisco. There he wrote music for the San Francisco Mime Troupe and presented concerts at the San Francisco Tape Music Center. Determined to be a performer in his own compositions, he formed a five-man ensemble specializing in free and controlled improvisation. For this unit he wrote *Pitch Charts* (1963), which gave all the players the same notes to play but with a free rhythm. After less than a year of the ensemble's existence, Reich came to feel that its efforts with improvisation seemed fruitless. He disbanded the group and returned to fully notated scores.

Electronic music now engaged his interest. Music for Piano and Tape (1964) was introduced at the San Francisco Tape Music Center in January 1965 with the composer at the piano with tape. While supporting himself by driving a taxicab, Reich taped over ten hours of the sounds of the streets and the voices of passengers which, in 1965, became *Livelihood* (San Francisco, January 1965), a three-minute sound collage.

His first major work in which the phase-shifting technique is first discovered, *It's Gonna Rain* (1965; San Francisco, January 1965), is a taped speech composition using the voice of a black Pentecostal minister preaching about the Flood. Its first movement takes the continually repeated three-word, four-syllable phrase in two voices from unison, gradually moving out of phase with itself, and about seven minutes later back into unison with itself. The second movement takes a much longer speech loop and superimposes it on itself finally in eight voices all out of phase with each other producing a musical sound of cosmic dissolution. *It's Gonna Rain* was recorded by Columbia Masterworks in 1969. *Come Out* (1966; N. Y., April 1966) is also a taped speech piece which repeats for thirteen minutes and hundreds of times the five spoken words of a black boy trying to avoid police brutality in Harlem in 1966. The words are "Come out to show them." These words were recorded on two channels, "first in

unison, then with Channel 2 slowly beginning to move ahead. As the phrase begins to shift, a gradually increasing reverberation is heard which slowly passes into a sort of canon or round. Eventually, the two voices divided into four, and then into eight." *Come Out*, released by Columbia Records in 1967, became Reich's first recorded composition. Reviewing that release in *High Fidelity/Musical America*, Alfred Frankenstein wrote: "Long before the voices divide, the sound has lost all resemblance to speech. The sibilants come to sound like maracas, and the whole takes on a curiously savage, yet stern and impersonal character; it is an astounding and most impressive piece."

In 1965, Reich left the Bay Area of San Francisco to return to New York. There, in 1966, with Art Murphy, pianist (a friend from Juilliard) and Jon Gibson, soprano saxophonist (a friend from San Francisco), he formed an ensemble to perform his own compositions. Joined by James Tenney and Philip Corner, this group gave its first major concerts at Park Place Gallery on March 17, 18, and 19, 1967, the first time Reich's "live phase music" was being heard. This happened with a composition named *Piano Phase* (1967), originally for two pianos but heard at this concert in a four-piano version.

The method employed in *Violin Phase*, for violin and prerecorded tape, or for four violins (1967; N.Y., April 1969), illustrates Reich's phase-music technique. The basic violin pattern and its superimpositions are prerecorded on tape. The solo violinist first phases (by gradually accelerating) ahead of the tape and then selects those patterns written in the score, or some he himself selects, and reinforces them on his instrument, creating an ingenious aural kaleidoscope. When Andrew Porter heard *Violin Phase* a decade after it was composed, he explained in the *New Yorker* how the listener inadvertently becomes a participant in the performance. "The soloist shares or guides the listener's perceptions. When he ceases, their ears continue to trace the indicated new melody or motif; a figure in the sonic carpet is discerned for a while, and then gradually fades as the patterns alter. *Violin Phase* is a work that seems to make its auditors concerned participants in what is happening. Reich's music has a joyful, very attractive surface. There is substance beneath."

In 1968, Reich began evolving pulse music. He explains: "I had the idea that if a number of single tones were all pulsing at the same tempo, but with gradually shifting phase relations, a great number of musical patterns would result. If the tones were all in phase [struck at the same time], a pulsing chord would be heard. If the tones were slowly shifted just a bit out of phase, a sort of rippling broken chord would be heard which would gradually change into a melodic pattern, then another, and so on. If the process of phase shifting was gradual enough, then minute rhythmic differences would become clearly audible. A given musical pattern would then be heard to change into another with no alteration of pitch, timbre, or loudness, and one would become involved in a music which worked exclusively with gradual changes in time." To realize such pulse music, Reich felt the need to devise an electronic instrument "that would be both an instrument in itself, and also a phase variable metronome enabling several performers to work together." With the help of Larry Owens of the Bell Laboratories, and David Flooke, both electrical engineers, Reich created the "phase-shifting pulse gate." In April 1969 he used it for the first time at a concert at the New School for Social Research in New York in a composition called *Pulse Music* (1969). A second performance of *Pulse Music* in a more elaborate form took place at the Whitney Museum of American Art in New York on May 27, 1969. Soon after that, Reich felt that the device was musically uninteresting in performance because of its electronic, stiffly "perfect" nature and he abandoned it. "I felt very clearly then," he says, "that I did not wish to have any involvement with electronic music again."

But the musical idea inherent in that musical device was carried over to live musicians in *Four Organs* for four electric organs and maracas (1970; N. Y., May 7, 1970), consisting exclusively of the lengthening of the individual tones within a single chord. Here the increasing durations come directly from the pulse-width control of the phase-shifting pulse gate. *Four Organs* was performed by the composer with members of the Boston Symphony under Michael Tilson Thomas in Boston on October 8, 1971. This performance was repeated at Carnegie Hall on January 18, 1973, to tumultuous boos and bravos. Writing of this performance in *Music and Musicians*, John Rockwell said: "To these ears it is one of Reich's best and most emotionally rewarding efforts, in which elements of a single chord are stretched out into a kind of gothic arch of cadential effects, and time is played with in a manner ultimately as complex as Elliott Carter's initially more complex metrical manipulations."

Immediately after completing *Four Organs*, Reich composed another work for four electric organs, *Phase Patterns* (1970; N. Y., May 7, 1970). The performers are called upon to drum on their keyboards, each hand playing certain notes throughout the piece more or less without change alternating up and down, left, right, left, left, right, left, right, right, which in Western rudimental drumming is called a paradiddle. "The idea of drumming on the keyboard," Reich says, "comes out of my limitations as a keyboard player together with my studies of rudimental drumming as a child. Though the cause is partially one of physical limitation, the effect is of a new approach to the keyboard. I now look at all keyboard instruments as extraordinary sets of tuned drums." This work was performed by Reich's ensemble under the sponsorship of Pierre Boulez at a New York Philharmonic "Prospective Encounter"

concert in New York on October 29, 1971. Writing of *Phase Patterns* in the *New York Times*, Donal Henahan observed: "As in all Reich's music, it is impossible to predict from looking at the simple score the variety of sonorities and kaleidoscopic rhythmic pulsations that can grow out of such tiny cells. And yet there is a primitive directness retained throughout."

Between 1969 and 1971, Reich was instructor in new and electronic music at the School of Visual Arts and at the New School for Social Research, both in New York. A grant from the Special Projects Division of the Institute for International Education in the summer of 1970 made it possible for him to attend the Institute for African Studies in Accra, Ghana, for the study of African drumming with Gideon Alorworye, a master drummer of the Ewe tribe. While in Ghana, Reich gave no thought to his own music, preferring to devote himself solely to his work as a student. "After returning to New York and enthusiastically resuming work on my own music, I found that I did not wish either to return to Africa or to continue my studies. . . . Since I had no desire to become either an African drummer or an ethnomusicologist, or a composer of 'African-style' music, it became difficult to see where else further studies could lead me." If his African studies had any influence upon him and his music, it was not, he says, through imitation or assimilation but through confirmation. "It confirmed my intuition that acoustic instruments could be used to produce music that was genuinely richer in sound than that produced by electronic instruments, as well as confirming my natural inclination toward percussion." Producing electronic music on tapes was now for him a thing of the past.

In 1970, Reich's ensemble became a quintet, and in 1971 it expanded to twelve musicians and singers, from which time it was called Steve Reich and Musicians. This group has made numerous tours of the United States and Europe in performances of Reich's music, often under grants by the New York State Council of the Arts, the National Endowment for the Arts, and the Martha Baird Rockefeller Foundation.

Between fall 1970 and fall 1971, Reich worked on the longest piece of music he had thus far attempted, requiring an hour and half for performance. He called it *Drumming*, a four-part work played without pauses, for four pair of tuned bongo drums, three marimbas, three glockenspiels, two women's voices, and piccolo, plus male voices and whistling (N. Y., December 3, 1971). "*Drumming* in the context of my own music," Reich says, "is the final expansion and refinement of the phasing process, as well as the first use of four new techniques: the process of gradually substituting beats for rests (or rests for beats) within a constantly repeating rhythmic cycle; the gradual changing of timbre while rhythm and pitch remain constant; the simultaneous combination of instruments of different timbre; and the use of the human voice to become part of the musical ensemble by imitating the exact sound of the instruments." In the *Soho News*, Josef Bush said: "My thoughts on the first hearing of . . . *Drumming* was that it was music of such space, scope, and effect that it would be completely conceivable to hope it would be performed out of doors, on mountain tops, in jungles, beside vast bodies of water, and in our National Forests. It is music which evokes a serenity of sound without stultifying the intellect with false sentiment, and literary allusion, no matter how well meant."

After *Drumming* and the composition that followed it—*Clapping Music* (1972; N. Y., April 27, 1973)—Reich abandoned the gradual phase-shifting process he had employed since 1965. *Clapping* sought to produce music that required no instruments, but only the human body. It called for two clapping performers, one repeating the same basic pattern throughout, while the second moved abruptly after a number of repeats from unison to one beat ahead until he was back in unison with the first performer. *Six Pianos* (1973; N. Y., May 1973) resulted from a long-held ambition to write a piece of music for all the pianos in a piano store, an idea that was finally realized in a New York store in the fall and winter of 1972–73. Since too many pianos produced a thick, unmanageable sound, Reich reduced his concept to a work for six small spinet pianos or small grands. "It begins with three pianists all playing the same eight-beat rhythmic pattern," Reich explains, "but with different notes for each player. Two of the pianists then begin in unison to gradually build up to the exact pattern of one of the pianists already playing. First by playing the notes of his fifth beat on the seventh beat of their measure, then, his first beat on their third beat, and so on until they have constructed the same pattern with the same notes, but two beats out of phase. This is the same process of substituting beats for rests as appears for the first time in *Drumming*." Another piece in which a simple pattern is permitted to grow spontaneously into many patterns played by different instruments is *Music for Mallet Instruments, Voices, and Organ* (1973; N. Y., May 12, 1973) scored for four marimbas, two glockenspiels, vibraphone, three women's voices, and electric organ. This score was used for a ballet, *Marimba*, first produced by the Lar Lubovitch Dance Company in New York in April 1981.

A new approach to rhythm, harmony, instrumentation, and structure is encountered in *Music for 18 Musicians* written between May 1974 and March 1976. For Reich, this work represented a new method as to the number and distribution of the instruments (violin, cello, two clarinets doubling bass clarinet, four women's voices, four pianos, three marimbas, two xylophones, and a vibraphone without motor). All instruments are acoustical, the use of electronics limited to microphones. The harmonic movement here plays a more significant role than in any-

thing Reich had written up to this time. Rhythmically, the composition called for two basically different kinds of time occurring simultaneously—the first a regular rhythmic pulse in pianos and mallet instruments that continues throughout the piece, the second, the rhythm of the human breath in the voice and wind instruments. Structurally, this work is based on a cycle of eleven chords played at the beginning and repeated at the end. "What's here," said Hubert Saal in *Newsweek*, "is explored to the hilt with subtle, hypnotic variations, in exotic colors and fascinating rhythms." *Music for 18 Musicians* was premiered by Steve Reich and Musicians at Town Hall, New York, on April 24, 1976. The ECM recording sold twenty-five thousand albums in its first year, something believed to be without precedent for new music.

On a commission from the Holland Festival, and as a recipient of a Guggenheim Fellowship, Reich completed *Music for a Large Ensemble* in 1978, its world premiere taking place at the Holland Festival in June 1979 with Reinbert de Leeuw conducting the Netherlands Wind Ensemble. This was one of three compositions heard on an all-Reich program at Carnegie Hall, New York, performed by Steve Reich and Musicians (and Guest Artists) on February 19, 1980, a concert made possible by grants from the New York State Council of the Arts, the Department of Cultural Affairs of New York City, and the National Endowment for the Arts. The hall was sold out, and the outburst of enthusiasm from the audience (many of whom were youngsters) suggested how strongly Reich was becoming something of a cult. This evening, *Music for a Large Ensemble*, was an American premiere, as was Octet (1979), the latter the result of a commission from Radio Frankfurt in Germany, over whose facilities it was first heard on June 21, 1979, in a performance by the Netherlands Wind Ensemble under Reinbert de Leeuw. The third and final work on the program was a world premiere: Variations for Winds, Strings, and Keyboard. A version for full symphony orchestra was commissioned by the San Francisco Symphony, which introduced it on May 14, 1980, in San Francisco, Edo de Waart conducting. Reich feels that with these variations a "markedly new harmonic, formal, and timbrel material [enters] into my music. The constant yet slow harmonic change (there are no repeat markings in the score), the slow recurrence of materials from variation to variation, and the scoring for oboes, flutes, full brass, strings, acoustic and electric keyboards, all give this piece a sound quite different from my earlier music. The variations are on an harmonic progression somewhat in the manner of a chaconne, but with considerably longer harmonic progressions than the four or eight bar progressions customarily found in the chaconne."

In commenting on the all-Reich Carnegie Hall concert, Nicholas Kenyon, in the *New Yorker*, described it as "an extraordinary experience: exhiliarating, engrossing, hypnotizing, disorienting. . . . The listener is confronted by what seems at first like a fixed mass of sound whirling around a static center. The rhythmic shapes, the volume, the repeating flashes of melody seem unchanging. But as one is drawn into the music's state of suspended animation, one begins to hear that things are changing all the time. Patterns are developing and their relationships are being modified; the resulting shapes are different. The loud, bright sounds that give the music its momentum become only a background to the intricate, shifting structure that gives it its real life."

During the summer of 1973, Reich studied Balinese gamelan semar pegulingan with a Balinese teacher at the American Society for Eastern Arts Summer Program at the University of Washington in Seattle and during 1976–77 he studied traditional forms of Hebraic cantillations both in New York and Jerusalem. In 1974, he was artist-in-residence in Berlin at the invitation of DAAD. (Deutsche Akademische Austauschdienst), and in 1979 he received a second grant from the Rockefeller Foundation. On May 30, 1976, he married Beryl Korot, an artist; they have a son, Ezra. Reich has another son from a previous marriage.

THE COMPOSER SPEAKS: For me, the most important aspect of a piece of music, mine or someone else's, is its emotional-intellectual effect on performers and listeners. I find it basically impossible to separate the emotional and intellectual aspects of a piece of music.

Though my music may have a recognizable sound, this is due not to a set of particular techniques or influences, but to my intuitive musical choices. In composing music, it isn't what you do, it's how you do it.

PRINCIPAL WORKS: *It's Gonna Rain*, for tape (1965); *Come Out*, for tape (1966); *Piano Phase*, for two pianos or two marimbas (1967); *My Name Is*, for three or more tape recorders, performers, and audience (1967); *Violin Phase*, for four violins or violin and tape (1967); *Pendulum Music*, for three or more microphones, amplifiers, loudspeakers, and performers (1968); *Four Organs*, for four electric organs and maracas (1970); *Phase Patterns*, for four electronic organs (1970); *Drumming*, for four pair of tuned bongo drums, three marimbas, three glockenspiels, two women's voices, and piccolo, plus optional male voice and whistling (1971); *Clapping Music*, for two musicians clapping (1972); *Six Pianos* (1973); *Music for Mallet, Instruments, Voices, and Organ*, for four marimbas, two glockenspiels, vibraphone, and three women's voices, and electric organ (1973); *Music for Pieces of Wood*, for five pair of tuned claves (1975); *Music for 18 Musicians*, for violin, cello, two clarinets doubling bass clarinet, four women's voices, four pianos, three marimbas, two xylophones, vibra-

phone, and maracas (1976); *Music for a Large Ensemble*, for flute, two clarinets, two soprano saxophones, two women's voices, four trumpets, two pianos (four hands), two marimbas, two xylophones, two vibraphones, two violins, two violas, two cellos, and two double basses (1978); Octet, for two clarinets doubling with bass clarinet, flute, and piccolo (or alternately two clarinetists and two flutists), two pianos, two violins, viola, and cello (1979); Variation for Winds, Strings, and Keyboards, also for full orchestra (1979); *My Name Is*, ensemble portrait for chamber group (1980); *Tehillim*, psalms for chorus (1981).

BIBLIOGRAPHY: Reich, Steve, *Writings About Music* (Halifax, Nova Scotia, 1974); *New York Arts Journal*, no. 17, 1980; *New York Times*, October 24, 1971; *San Francisco Symphony Program Notes*, May 14, 1980; *Virtuoso*, June 1981; *Who's Who in America, 1980–81*.

Reinagle, Alexander, b. Portsmouth, England, 1756, baptized April 23; d. Baltimore, Md., September 21, 1809.

For almost a quarter of a century, Reinagle was a pivotal force in the early musical life of Philadelphia—as an instrumentalist, vocalist, teacher, concert and theater manager, and composer. The four piano sonatas he wrote there in or about 1790 are the most important such works written in America up to that time.

His father, Joseph Reinagle, was an Austrian-born musician who played the trumpet. During Alexander's boyhood, his family moved from Portsmouth to Edinburgh, Scotland, where he received music instruction from Raynor Taylor. In time, Reinagle developed into an outstanding virtuoso of the violin and the harpsichord. On April 9, 1770 he made what is believed to have been his first public appearance by performing the harpsichord at Edinburgh's Theatre Royal. In Glasgow, several years later, he taught the harpsichord. He subsequently made his home in London. It is probable that his friendship there with John Christian Bach was the stimulus for his own first attempts at composition. In London, Reinagle wrote and published *Twenty-four Short and Easy Pieces*, for the pianoforte (his first opus) in or about 1780. He followed it with his second opus, *A Second Set of Short and Easy Lessons*, for pianoforte (c. 1781), *A Select Collection of My Most Favorite Scot Tunes with Variations, for harpsichord* (c. 1782) and *Six Sonatas for the Pianoforte: With an Accompaniment for the Violin* (1783).

In 1784, Reinagle visited Lisbon, where, on January 8, 1785, he gave a concert jointly with his brother Hugh, a cellist. A week later, Alexander Reinagle gave a command performance for the royal family. About this time, while touring the Continent, he visited Hamburg and befriended Karl Philipp Emanuel

Bach, whose fame and music had made a profound impression on him. When his brother died, Alexander Reinagle returned to London and became there a member of the Royal Society of Musicians.

On June 9, 1786, Reinagle arrived in the United States, where he made his home for the remainder of his life. His first stop was New York, where he hoped to establish himself as a teacher of the violin, harpsichord, and piano, and where, on July 20, he gave a concert, appearing in the triple role of vocalist-pianist-cellist. Failing to make much headway in New York, he proceeded to Philadelphia later the same year. Before long he had established himself there as one of its most active and versatile musicians. In 1786 he helped to revive the "City Concert" (which had been discontinued for a time) and managed it until 1794 in annual series of subscription concerts. He made numerous appearances as a virtuoso of the harpsichord and piano in Philadelphia, New York, Baltimore and Boston, earning high praise for his musicianship. One of his contemporaries, John R. Parker, described his playing in *The Euterpeiad* as follows: "He never aimed at excessive execution, but there was sweetness of manner—nay, in the way he touched the instrument I might add, there was a sweetness of tone, combined with exquisite taste and neatness [that] produced unusual feelings of delight." In 1787, in Philadelphia, Reinagle gave the first public performance in America of music for piano four hands when, with a colleague, he performed a four-hand sonata by Haydn.

In or about 1790, in Philadelphia, Reinagle composed four piano sonatas with which he made his most significant claim as composer. Though obviously derivative of Karl Philipp Emanuel Bach and Haydn, these works represented an altogether new standard for piano-sonata writing in America. Gilbert Chase, in *America's Music,* says of them: "They reveal a fresh and lively invention, resourcefulness in development and figuration, a fine feeling for structure and proportion, and a capacity for sustained lyric expression in the Adagios." These four sonatas were never published, but the manuscripts are in the Library of Congress in Washington, D.C.

Two orchestral works by Reinagle were heard in 1791 at the "City Concert": *Miscellaneous Quartett* and *New Miscellaneous Quartett.*

In 1792, Reinagle was appointed manager of a new theatrical company formed in Philadelphia. Its first production, at the New Theater, was Samuel Arnold's opera, *The Castle in Andalusia,* on February 17, 1794. In its first six seasons this company offered seventy-five productions. Reinagle remained manager up to the time of his death. Through the years he contributed a considerable amount of incidental music, overtures, and accompaniments to its various productions. Among these were *Slaves in Algiers* (1794), *The Sicilian Romance* (1795), *The Volunteers* (1795), *Columbus* (1797), *The Savoyard* (1797), *The Italian Monk* (1798), *The Gentle Shep-*

herd (1798), *Pizarro* (1800), and *The Castle Spectre* (1800). Little of this music is extant.

Toward the end of his life, Reinagle was working on his most ambitious composition: a secular oratorio based on Milton's *Paradise Lost* in which spoken narrative replaced recitatives. He did not live to complete it and what he had committed to paper has disappeared.

On September 20, 1803, Reinagle married Anna Duport. They had one daughter, born after Reinagle's death. This was a second marriage. From the first one—the name of his wife and the date of that marriage not known—he had two sons.

PRINCIPAL WORKS: 6 sonatas for piano with a violin accompaniment (1783); 4 sonatas for piano (c. 1790).

Miscellaneous Quartett (c. 1791); *New Miscellaneous Quartett* (c. 1791); *Concerto on the Improved Piano with Additional Keys* (1794); *Preludes in Three Classes,* for piano (1794); *Rosa,* for voice and piano (c. 1794); *America, Commerce, and Freedom,* for voice and piano (c. 1794); *Masonic Overture,* for orchestra (1800).

BIBLIOGRAPHY: Chase, Gilbert, *America's Music* (N.Y., 1955); Horton, C. A., *Serious Art and Concert Music for Piano in the One Hundred Years from Alexander Reinagle to Edward MacDowell* (Chapel Hill, N.C., 1965); Howard, John Tasker, *Our American Music* (N.Y., 1946); Sonneck, O. G., *Early Concert Life in America* (N.Y., 1915); *Musical Quarterly,* January 1932; *Dictionary of American Biography,* vol. 8.

Riegger, Wallingford Constantin, b. Albany, Ga., April 29, 1885; d. New York City, April 2, 1961.

He was one of the first Americans to use atonality and after that the twelve-tone system, but he never confined himself to any single idiom. Much of his writing was polyphonic, sometimes within such baroque structures as the canon, passacaglia, and fugue; some of it was romantic; some was neoprimitive in its use of multiple rhythms and frequent meter changes or unusual meters. To a consummate mastery of technique he brought a subtlety of intellectual processes and high-minded purpose that made him a figure of reverence among many of his colleagues, though the general public failed to give him his due until almost the end of his life.

He was one of two sons of musical parents. They came to southern Georgia from Indianapolis, where the mother had acquired local fame as pianist and the father had been concertmaster of a small orchestra at fourteen and later choir director of a leading church. Soon after their marriage, they came to Albany, the father acquiring there a lumber mill. When this burned down in 1888, the parents decided to return to Indianapolis. There, at an early age, Wallingford

Riegger began studying violin. Soon after that he received some instruction in harmony and piano from his mother.

When he was fifteen, his family came to New York, where his father opened a plumbing supply business. In New York, Riegger changed from violin to cello so that a string quartet could be organized within the family circle. For several years, weekly rehearsals of string quartet music took place in the Riegger household. "Those Sunday afternoon quartet rehearsals," he once recalled, "were among my most enjoyable musical experiences."

His father expected him to enter his business, but any such decision was temporarily postponed when, on graduating from high school in 1904, Riegger was awarded a scholarship to Cornell University. He stayed there a year, having by this time come to the irrevocable decision to develop himself as a musician. In 1905, he entered the Institute of Musical Art in New York, specializing in cello with Alvin Schroeder and studying composition with Percy Goetschius. In 1907, Riegger received his bachelor of music degree, a member of the Institute's first graduating class. A year later he left for Germany to enroll in the Academy of Music in Berlin. During the next three years he studied cello with Robert Hausmann and Arnold Hekking and composition with Max Bruch and Edgar Stillman Kelley. At the same time he played cello in one orchestra, viola in another, belonged to several chamber music groups and attended one hundred fifty orchestral concerts and rehearsals during his first season in Berlin, listening to performances conducted by Arthur Nikisch, whom he idolized, and Richard Strauss, among others. Riegger broadened his cultural horizons by reading the German classics, studying philosophy, and visiting art museums. His training, academic as well as musical, was, in his words, "intensive, extensive, and expensive."

In 1910, Riegger made his debut as conductor in a concert of the Blüthner Orchestra, directing symphonies by Brahms and Tchaikovsky, and a cello concerto by Saint-Saëns, entirely from memory, a practice not customary at that time. Though his performance was praised, lack of funds compelled him to end his German visit that year. Returning to New York, he married Rose Schramm on June 17, 1910, whom he had met and befriended in high school; they raised three daughters. To support his wife, he became cellist in the St. Paul Symphony Orchestra (1910–13), concurrently taking on other performing assignments with hotel and motion-picture-theater orchestras.

His ambition to become a conductor sent him back to Germany in 1913. During the first two years of World War I, he served as assistant conductor in Würzburg and Königsberg, and for the season of 1916–17 he directed the Blüthner Orchestra in Berlin. In all his appearances, Riegger continued to conduct without a score.

In 1917, just three days before America entered World War I, Riegger was back in the United States. Failling to find a conducting post, he compromised by accepting a job as teacher of theory and cello at Drake University in Iowa (1918–22). In 1924–25 he was a faculty member of the Institute of Musical Art in New York.

At this time, he also began giving increasing consideration to composition, which until now he had done more or less sporadically, in a Germanic neoromantic idiom. His first work to gain attention, however, was in a quasi-impressionistic vein: the Piano Trio in B minor (1920). Though it received the Paderewski Prize and the award of the Society for the Publication of American Music (it became Riegger's op. 1), it did not receive a hearing until a decade later, in New York on March 21, 1930. When this composition was recorded in 1960, Eric Salzman said of it: "It is an enormously competent and professional work in a thoroughly unoriginal style. There is certain faded elegance in the Fauré-like contours, the old-fashioned gestures, and the attractive instrumental writing."

Still in a somewhat impressionist style was *La belle dame sans merci*, for vocal soloists and chamber orchestra (1923), based on the poem by Keats. It received the Elizabeth Sprague Coolidge Award (the first time it was given to a native American) and was premiered at the Coolidge Festival in Pittsfield, Mass., on September 19, 1924, the composer conducting.

But a radical change of style was soon to take place with Riegger. Beginning with Rhapsody, for orchestra (1926), Riegger began employing atonality (though only partly in this work). "I felt," Riegger explained, "the need to express musical ideas for which the older techniques were inadequate. I found the new atonal idiom, with its fresh possibilities in sonority and rhythm, creatively stimulating, and more expressive of the feelings I wished to convey in music." Rhapsody received its first hearing on October 29, 1931, with Erich Kleiber conducting the New York Philharmonic.

From a partial use of atonality, Riegger passed on to completely atonal writing in *Study in Sonority,* for strings (1927), for ten violins or any multiple of ten. This was Riegger's most novel and complex work up to this time. He wrote it as a functional piece for the student orchestra of Ithaca Conservatory in Ithaca, N.Y., whose faculty he had joined in 1926, and where he stayed two years. "What there was of the student orchestra had a tendency to melt away at the summer session," Riegger revealed. "Sick and tired of cuing in for missing instruments, I decided to write something for the only instrument of which I was sure to have enough—violins. It was to be something quite simple, but it turned out differently. After the shock of the first few chords, the students—professedly—got a kick out of it. We gave it three performances all told (the first on August 11, 1927), including one encore." Leopold Stokowski performed it with the Philadelphia Orchestra on March 30, 1929, using forty strings. Writing in the *San Francisco Argonaut,* Henry Cowell found that this music "explores many new possibilities of sonorous combinations of violins," adding: "Riegger establishes a new and self-invented dissonance as a tonic chord, from which the music proceeds, and to which it returns. He also establishes another dissonance as a dominant chord, which always resolves to the tonic. In this way he induces a logic which the ear can readily follow, though the material is very complex. Emotionally, the work soars like the choiring of angels in the altissimo register of ten fiddles."

When Riegger left Ithaca Conservatory in 1928, he settled permanently in New York City. For a number of years he earned his living by making hundreds of choral arrangements (publishing them under various pen names) as well as doing other chores for publishers. In New York, Riegger became involved with the avant-garde composers of the time (Henry Cowell, Charles Ives, Carl Ruggles, Edgard Varèse), was stimulated by their advanced thinking, and joined them in forming groups for the presentation of new music, including the Pan American Association of Composers.

Under such stimuli, Riegger, as composer, went on from atonality to twelve-tone music, beginning with *Dichotomy,* for chamber orchestra (1931–32), introduced at a concert of the Pan American Association in Berlin on March 10, 1932, Nicolas Slonimsky conducting. This was one of the earliest examples of twelve-tone writing by an American-born composer. Riegger avoided the strict discipline of the Viennese school, using the twelve-tone row for coherence and departing from it when expressivity and variety demanded. "The basic idea," Henry Cowell explained in the *Musical Courier,* "is a dual one consisting of two free melodies set in the old question-answer relationship. Two different tone rows, one of eleven tones, the second of thirteen (ten different tones, three of which recur) are used at first as a mere contrapuntal background for the two main melodies introduced at the beginning of the piece, but they are developed consistently in true twelve-tone technique, and finally come to dominate the work in the passacaglia that closes it."

Riegger's admiration of Martha Graham aroused his interest in the modern dance in 1930. Between 1930 and 1939 he confined his composing almost exclusively to ballets (usually on themes of social protest) choreographed by such leading figures in the world of modern dance as Martha Graham, Doris Humphrey, Anna Sokolow, and Charles Weidman. Much of this music, he said, "was of necessity episodic in structure" with the result that only a small fraction of it could be adapted for concert performances. One that successfully made this transition was *New Dance,* which he had written in 1935 for Doris Humphrey and which he adapted for two pianos, for violin and piano, for band, and for sympho-

ny orchestra; the symphonic version was given its premiere on January 30, 1942, in a performance by the Pittsburgh Symphony under Fritz Reiner. Riegger used other ballet music episodes in his symphonies nos. 3 and 4.

By the end of the 1930s, Riegger was once again producing music solely for concert performance. His String Quartet no. 1 (1938–89; Saratoga, N.Y., September 8, 1940) was a twelve-tone composition "full of vigorous and beautiful dissonance," as Elliott Carter described it in *Modern Music.* "The music is straightforward; tone clusters are hammered out, yet the texture remains transparent. Emotional balance and formal clarity are always maintained." Two orchestral compositions in the early 1940s favored polyphony and baroque structures over the twelve-tone technique, while at the same time remaining thoroughly modern in harmonic, rhythmic, and tonal idioms. Canon and Fugue, for strings (1941)—later transcribed for full orchestra—was premiered at the festival of the International Society for Contemporary Music at Berkeley, Calif., on August 1, 1942. Passacaglia and Fugue (1942) was heard first in Washington, D. C., on March 19, 1944, performed by the National Symphony under Hans Kindler.

Riegger's greatest success came with Symphony no. 3 (1946–47), which had been commissioned by the Alice M. Ditson Fund. Following its introduction in New York at the annual Festival of Contemporary American Music at Columbia University in New York on May 16, 1948, it received the New York Music Critics Circle Award and an award of the Naumburg Foundation for a recording (the first for a major Riegger composition). Fugal passages were found in all four movements, the last of which is a passacaglia and fugue, while an arbitrarily arranged twelve-tone row was the source of the first-movement material, and some music Riegger had written in 1936 for a Doris Humphrey ballet (*With My Red Fires*) was interpolated into the second movement. Riegger revised this symphony twice, the final version heard in New York on December 7, 1964. At that time, Louis Biancolli, writing in the *World-Telegram,* said of it: "This is Riegger at his most individual. The idiom is spare and knotty, the development original and compact, the finale fugue an intellectual teaser to performer and listener."

Riegger's Symphony no. 4 (1957), commissioned by the Fromm Music Foundation, was more tonal and lyrical than its preccessor. "This is a symphony which has both head and heart appeal," reported the Boston critic Cyrus Durgin, "and whose texture ranges from free-flowing melody to grinding dissonance, with a good amount of mild and tonal harmony in between." The highlight of the symphony was the second movement, where Riegger used some of the music he had written in 1936 for a Martha Graham ballet, *Chronicle.* Since the ballet dealt with the Spanish Civil War, this music had a Spanish identity and was tragic in its overtones. The symphony was introduced at the Festival of Contemporary Arts at the University of Illinois in Urbana on April 12, 1957.

Riegger's seventy-fifth birthday was celebrated in 1960 with performances of his major works by significant organizations, including the New York Philharmonic under Leonard Bernstein which performed the Variations for Piano and Orchestra (1952–53; Louisville, Ky., February 13, 1954). An all-Riegger concert was given by the Kansas City Philharmonic (the composer conducting) and another was heard in New York at a concert of the Contemporary Music Society.

In 1936, Riegger joined the music faculty of the Metropolitan Music School in New York, where he was subsequently made president. In 1948 he served as president of the U.S. Section of the International Society for Contemporary Music; he also served for a time as vice-president and was member of the board of directors of the American Composers Alliance, which he had helped to organize. He received honorary doctorates in music from Cincinnati Conservatory (1925) and Bard College in Annandale, N.Y. (1961). In 1960 he was given the Award of Merit from the National Association of Composers and Conductors and, in 1961, just before his death from unsuccessful brain surgery, the Creative Arts Award from Brandeis University in Waltham, Mass.

THE COMPOSER SPEAKS. Personally, I prefer that music, the most abstract of all the arts, be divorced from literary or dramatic connotations. In listening to program music, I find no pleasure in making the expected associations, although the music per se may give me keen pleasure.

While I do not claim that the possibilities of the major, minor, and modal tonalities have been exhausted, I believe that the greatest music in this idiom has probably been written. On the other hand, specially invented tonalities, atonality, and polytonality open up vast fields as yet but little explored. . . .

My musical ideas come intuitively, though generally only after a conscious seeking. At first they may seem satisfactory, even "inspired," but in the course of time often reveal shortcomings to an aroused critical sense, or, properly speaking, to a critical sense that for some unexplained reason functions well only after a lapse of time. In the many retouchings, complete rejections, and fresh beginnings which I find necessary, the three factors of talent—"inspiration," aesthetic feeling, and purely objective reasoning—work together, corroborating or contradicting one another. The final arbiter is aesthetic feeling, or a satisfied sense of fitness of the material, of balance between unity and variety, of the relation of the parts to one another and to the work as a whole.

PRINCIPAL WORKS: 4 symphonies (1944–57); 3 string quartets (1938–39, 1945–47, 1948).

Piano Trio (1920); *An American Polonaise,* for orchestra (1923); *La belle dame sans merci,* for vocal soloists and chamber orchestra (1923); Rhapsody, for orchestra (1926); *Study in Sonority,* for ten violins or any multiple of ten (1927); Suite, for solo flute (1929); Three Canons, for flute, oboe, clarinet, and bassoon (1930); Fantasy and Fugue, for organ and orchestra (1931); *Dichotomy,* for chamber orchestra (1931–32); Scherzo, for orchestra (1932); Divertisement, for flute, harp, and cello (1933); *New Dance,* for orchestra (1935); Canon and Fugue, for orchestra, also for strings (1941); Passacaglia and Fugue, for orchestra, also for band (1942); *New and Old,* twelve studies for piano (1944); *Who Can Revoke,* for chorus and piano (1948); Music for Brass Choir (1948–49); *In Certainty of Song,* cantata for vocal soloists, chorus, piano, or chamber orchestra (1950); Piano Quintet (1951); Music for Orchestra (1951); Nonet, for brass (1951–52); Woodwind Quintet (1952); Sextet, for piano and winds (1952); Concerto for piano and woodwind quintet (1952); Variations for Piano and Orchestra (1953); *Dance Rhythms,* for orchestra (1955); Preamble and Fugue, for orchestra (1956); Movement, for two trumpets, trombone, and piano (1957); *Festival Overture* (1957); Variations for Violin and Orchestra (1959); Sinfonietta, for orchestra (1959); Duo for piano and orchestra (1960).

BIBLIOGRAPHY: Machlis, Joseph, *Introduction to Contemporary Music,* revised ed. (N. Y., 1979); Rosenfeld, Paul, *Discoveries of a Music Critic* (N. Y., 1936); Schmoll, Joseph B., "An Analytical Study of the Principal Instrumental Compositions of Wallingford Riegger" (doctoral thesis, Evanston, Ill., 1954); Thomson, Virgil, *American Music Since 1910* (N. Y., 1970); *American Composers Alliance Bulletin,* November 1956; *Hi Fi/Stereo Review,* April 1968; *Musical America,* December 1, 1948; *Musical Quarterly,* January 1950, July 1961; *New York Times,* April 9, 1961.

Rochberg, George, b. Paterson, N.J., July 5, 1918.

Between 1952 and the mid-1960s, Rochberg was a dedicated serial composer. As such he produced works of arresting individuality and interest that brought him deserved prominence. But by the mid-1960s he had come to the conclusion that serialism restricted his expressivity. Turning his back on it, and stimulated and inspired by Mahler, he now sought to make his music speak of human experience. Thus he turned to "tonal gravities" by becoming a neoromantic, writing in an often tonal idiom, with only occasional excursions into the well of music's past, sometimes in imitation of and sometimes in direct quotation from the masters.

Rochberg was a one-year-old infant when his family moved to Passaic, N. J., where he was raised, attended its public schools, and began music study. He received his first piano lessons when he was ten from Kathleen Hall. After two years, in which time he made his first tentative attempts at composition, he continued to study piano with Julius Koehl (1930–33). When Rochberg was fifteen, he started playing piano with various jazz groups in northern New Jersey. His interest in popular music led him to write popular songs, but at the same time he was also producing art songs and some pieces for the piano.

Upon graduating from Passaic High School in 1935, Rochberg entered the Montclair State Teachers College, earning his bachelor of arts degree four years later. His direction in music was aimless, the idea of becoming a full-time composer far from his mind. But in 1939 he played some of his music for a vocal coach and teacher at the David Mannes School of Music in New York, who was responsible for bringing him a scholarship to that school. There, between 1939 and 1942, Rochberg studied theory and composition with Hans Weisse, Leopold Mannes, and George Szell. As a student, Rochberg wrote songs and piano music, tried his hand at chamber and orchestral music, and started but never finished a one-act opera. He performed his *Variations on an Original Theme*, for piano (1941), at a student concert.

After marrying Gene Rosenfeld on August 18, 1941, he made his home in New York City, where their son, Paul, was born three years later. During his first few months in New York, Rochberg taught the piano privately. In 1942, during World War II, he was inducted into the army and was wounded in action in the European theater of operations.

When he was discharged from military service during the summer of 1945, Rochberg entered the Curtis Institute of Music in Philadelphia. There, he studied composition with Rosario Scalero and Gian Carlo Menotti. *Songs of Solomon*, for voice and piano (1946), became his first music to be published, and the first to be performed in a concert hall when David Lloyd introduced it in Philadelphia in 1947 and repeated it in New York a year later.

In 1947, Rochberg earned his bachelor of music degree at Curtis. From 1948 to 1954 he taught harmony, counterpoint, form, and analysis at Curtis. In that time he fulfilled the requirements for a master of arts degree at the University of Pennsylvania (1949), submitting as thesis an orchestral suite he had written in 1946.

The music Rochberg wrote during the next few years betrayed the influence Hindemith, Bartók, and Stravinsky had on him. *Night Music*, for orchestra (1948), won the Gershwin Memorial Award and received its world premiere in New York in April 1953 with Dimitri Mitropoulos conducting the New York Philharmonic. Rochberg interpolated *Night Music* into his five-movement Symphony no. 1 (1949) as a second movement. When he subsequently revised this symphony, he deleted it (together with a Capric-

cio movement) to make it a three-movement work which the Philadelphia Orchestra under Eugene Ormandy introduced on March 29, 1958.

A Fulbright Fellowship, together with one from the American Academy in Rome, brought Rochberg to Italy in 1950. Reevaluation of what he had thus far composed led him to the conviction that his writing needed the discipline of serialism. His thinking in this direction received reinforcement through his personal associations with Luigi Dallapiccola, Italy's foremost dodecaphonic composer.

Upon his return to the United States in 1952 (when a daughter was born), Rochberg resumed his teaching duties at Curtis. At the same time he assumed an editorial post with Theodore Presser, which he retained for eight years. The first major work he completed following his return was String Quartet no. 1 (1952), whose idiom was basically Bartókian. After being premiered by the Galimir Quartet in New York in January 1953, it received the Society for the Publication of American Music Award in 1956.

Rochberg's first composition in a dodecaphonic idiom came later in 1952: Twelve Bagatelles, for piano, which he introduced in New York in 1953 and which later was widely performed by pianists. Twelve years after these bagatelles were written, Rochberg orchestrated them, renaming the work *Zodiac*. The Cincinnati Symphony under Max Rudolf introduced it on May 8, 1965.

For the next eleven years following the bagatelles, Rochberg continued to favor serialism, though he often modified it to meet his artistic needs. Chamber Symphony, for nine instruments, came in 1953; *David, the Psalmist*, for tenor and orchestra, to a Hebrew text followed in 1954; *Duo concertante*, for violin and cello, in 1955–56. Describing the Chamber Symphony, the composer said: "Everything in the work is drawn from a single twelve-tone row. The problem was to find a way to employ a total chromatic palette, melodic and harmonic, on a large scale true to what the term 'symphony' had come to mean after Beethoven, without losing a sense of proportion, continuity, growth. The language is contemporary but the adherence to concepts of logic of musical discourse is traditional. The emotional tone of the work is dark, intense. It ends on a note of resignation which, despite the generally assertive character of the music, seems quite appropriate." The Cleveland Orchestra under George Szell gave the first performance on February 26, 1959, and in 1962 the symphony received the Naumburg Recording Award.

The serial technique continued to be Rochberg's basic creative tool for a number of years after that. He wrote *Dialogues*, for clarinet and piano, in 1956, on a commission from the Koussevitzky Music Foundation, and Erich Simon premiered it in New York in 1958. The *Cheltenham Concerto* for small orchestra (1958)—so-called because it was commissioned

by the Cheltenham Arts Center in Pennsylvania—
was first heard on June 10, 1959, in Philadelphia,
after which it was presented at the festival of the
International Society for Contemporary Music in
Rome (June 10, 1959) and won first prize in the
Italian International Society for Contemporary Music Competition. String Quartet no. 2 (1959–61), for
voice and string quartet, utilizing as text an elegy by
Rilke, was given its premiere in Philadelphia in 1962
and then recorded through a grant from the National
Institute of Arts and Letters. *Time Span* I (1960)
was a symphonic movement first heard in St. Louis
on October 22, 1960, and then, in a revision now
titled *Time Span* II, on January 19, 1964, with the
composer conducting the Buffalo Philharmonic.
Rochberg's last composition to use serialism was the
Piano Trio (1963), written for and introduced by the
Nieuw Amsterdam Trio in Buffalo in 1964.

Between 1960 and 1968, Rochberg was chairman
of the music department at the University of Pennsylvania in Philadelphia. In 1962 he received an honorary doctorate in humane letters from Montclair
State College, and in 1964 an honorary doctorate in
music from the Philadelphia Musical Academy.

The year of 1965–66 was a period of temporary
creative silence for Rochberg brought on by the death
of his son, Paul, from a brain tumor. But by 1966
Rochberg had finally come to realize that the only
way he could face living any longer was by composing. This tragedy, and the one-year cessation of writing, led Rochberg once again to reassess what he had
already accomplished. At this juncture he decided to
abandon serialism permanently and to seek out for
himself a new expressivity by returning to the romantic and emotional values of the past.

He returned to composing with *Black Sounds*
(1966), music for winds, piano, and percussion, written as music for a ballet which the Lincoln Center for
the Performing Arts in New York had commissioned
for a telecast over National Educational Television.
With choreography by Anna Sokolow, and under the
title of *The Act*, it was seen over the NET network
on September 24, 1966. The same year it was
awarded the Prix Italia.

In *Music for the Magic Theater*, for small orchestra (1965)—title and subject matter taken from Herman Hesse's *The Wolf of the Steppes*—Rochberg began a practice of quoting the music of others which
he would pursue in some of his subsequent compositions. Written on commission from the University of
Chicago to commemorate its seventy-fifth anniversary, and heard for the first time on January 24, 1967,
this score recalled horn passages from Mahler's
Symphony no. 9 and the Adagio from Mozart's Divertimento in B-flat (K. 287) from the past, and some
music of Stockhausen and Edgard Varèse from the
20th century. To Alexander L. Ringer, in a feature
article on Rochberg in the *Musical Quarterly*, this
work "represents George Rochberg in the full hardwon glory for that complete independence from the

past which is given only to those who have so fully
absorbed it that it has ceased to burden the present,
showing instead the way to the future."

Rochberg was invited as guest composer to the
Berkshire Music Center at Tanglewood, Mass., in
1966. He earned a Guggenheim Fellowship for the
second time in 1966–67. In 1969 he was guest composer at Temple University College of Music in
Philadelphia and in 1970 guest composer at the
Oberlin Festival of Contemporary Music at Ann Arbor, Mich. Concurrently, at the University of Pennsylvania, where he had been chairman of the music
department, he served as professor of composition
and theory between 1968 and 1976, was appointed
composer-in-residence in 1976, and, in 1978, was
named first Annenberg Professor of the Humanities.

Rochberg aligned himself once again with music's
past through quotations in the Symphony no. 3
(1966–69), for double chorus, chamber chorus, soloists, and large orchestra, which the Juilliard School
of Music commissioned and performed on November
24, 1970. Using Latin and German texts formerly set
to music by such masters as Heinrich Schütz and
Johann Sebastian Bach impelled Rochberg to quote
some of the music of these composers as well as material borrowed from Beethoven, Mahler, and Charles
Ives. Structurally, this symphony also looked backward in time by employing such baroque structures
as chorales and fugues. "Rochberg treats the composed music of the Western classic masters in his
own free way," wrote James Felton in the *Philadelphia Inquirer*, "infusing separate passages with an
indescribable emotional tension built up again and
again, often with a brilliant handling of the material."

When Rochberg does not quote the music of other
composers he sometimes emulates their styles. This
happened in String Quartet no. 3 (1972), in which
he assumed some of the identifying mannerisms of
Beethoven, Brahms, Mahler, and Bartók. Rochberg
described this music as "primarily ironic in tone and
spirit . . . a music which left behind obvious modernisms, a music which relied almost entirely on basic simple genres and structures and direct and uncomplicated gestures." The Concord Quartet, which
commissioned it, presented the world premiere in
New York on May 15, 1972; its recording was selected by *Stereo Review* as record of the year. "This is
the finest work I've heard this season and maybe in
years," wrote Jack Heimenz in *Stereo Review*. "It's
a masterpiece, through and through."

The Concerto for Violin and Orchestra (1974) is
another work of prime importance. It was written on
a grant from the National Endowment for the Arts
and on commission from the Pittsburgh Symphony
and its musical director, William Steinberg, in memory of Donald Steinfirst, a Pittsburgh music critic.
Due to Steinberg's illness, the baton was turned over
to Donald Johanos on April 4, 1975, with Isaac

Stern as soloist. After this performance Rochberg revised the concerto, and the new version was given numerous hearings throughout the United States and Europe.

In writing his concerto, Rochberg deliberately set out to work within the traditions of violin concerto writing ranging from Mozart through Bartók and Schoenberg. In five movements, the concerto was divided into two sections, three movements in the first (Introduction, Intermezzo, and Fantasia) and two in the second (Intermezzo and Epilogue). The composer described this work as follows: "Movements 1, 3, 5 share ideas in common although each has its own emotional and structural character. Movements 2 and 4 are essentially different from each other despite their common designation as 'Intermezzi': 2 is a kind of burletta, 4 a kind of berceuse (lullaby) combined with scherzando-like material which bears close relation to some ideas in 2." This music was basically tonal, consistently lyrical and romantic and very much in the 19th-century mood and instrumental technique. "In this work," wrote Harriet Johnson in the *New York Post*, "the composer turns to an elegiac outpouring of melody linked to tonality. Sections end on one tone and the final chord is a triad in which the mellifluous third is obvious. There are also countless bristling, complex dissonant passages which recur intermittently to remind us of life's chaos and tragedy. . . . The music is deeply felt and is a welcome addition to the repertory because . . . it lets the violin really sing and sing a lot."

In celebration of his sixtieth birthday in 1978, Rochberg wrote for the Concord Quartet a set of three string quartets (nos. 4, 5, 6), intended for performance on the same evening. These works bear the collective title of *Concord Quartets*. Traditional forms were employed (rondo, fugue, fantasia, serenade); quotations from Beethoven's String Quartet in G minor, op. 18, no. 2 and from Pachelbel's celebrated canon appeared in the final movement of the Sixth Quartet; string quartet styles from Haydn to Schoenberg were explored. "Each of the *Concord Quartets* is a substantial work on its own," reported Harold C. Schonberg in the *New York Times*. "One thing is immediately apparent: there is nothing about the resources and sonority of the string quartet that Mr. Rochberg does not know. . . . Throughout the *Concord Quartets* are striking ideas, moments of passion and beauty, and the feeling of a composer defiantly striking out in opposition to today's more fashionable musical trends. Mr. Rochberg has skill and imagination."

All three of the *Concord Quartets* were premiered on the same evening, January 20, 1979, at the University of Pennsylvania by the Concord Quartet. That ensemble repeated its performance at the Santa Fe Chamber Music Festival in July 1979 where a "Rochberg Week" was celebrated with Rochberg in residence. On September 16, 1979, the String Quar-

tet no. 4 was singled out from the set to receive the second annual Kennedy Center Friedheim Award for composition of the best new American instrumental work.

In *Octet, a Grand Fantasia* (1980), a one-movement composition, Rochberg sought to arrive at "a fusion of atonal harmonic means with the directionality of tonal principles derived from the major-minor system."

This was Rochberg's first conscious attempt "to realize this further enlargement." This work was commissioned by the Chamber Music Society of Lincoln Center, which introduced it in New York on April 25, 1980. The basic material is presented in the piano following an opening flourish, with each of the instruments given an opportunity to take center stage in a solo or in duets: the composition ends with a piano solo.

Rochberg was composer-in-residence at the Testimonium in Jerusalem (1970–71), the Aspen Conference of Contemporary Music in Colorado (summer 1972) and at the Grand Teton Festival in Wyoming (summer 1974).

THE COMPOSER SPEAKS: There can be no justification for music, ultimately, if it does not convey eloquently and elegantly the passions of the human heart. Who would care to remember the quartets of Beethoven or Bartók if they were merely demonstrations of empty formalisms? What claim would Chopin have on us if he had merely given us the abstractions of gesture and motion through time? Debussy was being celebrated only a few years ago as one of the patron saints of pure instrumental timbre as a compositional virtue. How he would have writhed to be reduced to the size of his idolators! More recently, interest has been shown in Varèse's penchant for symmetry. All well and good; but one could hardly claim that this describes or explains in any meaningful way the passion, bite and force of his rhetoric, the real reason we value him. The insistence by all on ignoring the dramatic, gestural character of music, while harping on the mystique of the minutiae of abstract design for its own sake, says worlds about the failure of much new music. Like mushrooms in the night, there has sprung up a profusion of false, half-baked theories of perception, of intellection, of composition itself. The mind grows sterile, and the heart small and pathetic.

PRINCIPAL WORKS: 7 string quartets (1952–80); 4 symphonies (1948–76).

Book of Songs, for voice and piano (1937–69); *Night Music,* for orchestra (1948); Twelve Bagatelles, for piano (1948), orchestrated in 1964–65 under the title of *Zodiac: Chamber Symphony,* for nine instruments (1953); *Canto Sacro,* for small orchestra (1954); *David, the Psalmist,* for tenor and orchestra (1954); *Serenate d'Estate,* for six instruments (1955); *Dialogues,* for clarinet and piano (1956); *Sonata*

Fantasia, for piano (1956); *Cheltenham Concerto*, for small orchestra (1958); *Bartókiana*, for piano (1959); *Blake Songs*, for soprano and chamber ensemble (1961); *La bocca della verità*, for violin and piano (1962); *Time Span* I and II, for orchestra (1960–62); Piano Trio (1963); *Apocalyptica*, for wind ensemble (1964); *Contra Mortem et Tempus*, for violin, flute, clarinet, and piano (1965); *Black Sounds*, music for the ballet *The Act* (1965); *Music for the Magic Theater*, for fifteen players (1965); *Nach Bach*, fantasia for harpsichord or piano (1966); *Passions According to the 20th Century*, for vocal solos, speakers, chorus, and instruments (1967); *Cantes flamencos*, for baritone and piano (1969); Eleven Songs, for voice and piano (1969); *Songs in Praise of Krishna*, for voice and piano (1970); *Sacred Songs of Reconciliation* (*Mizmor l'Piyus*), for bass-baritone and chamber orchestra (1970); *Fifty Caprice Variations*, for violin and piano (1970); *Carnival Music*, for piano (1971); Fantasies, for voice and piano (1971); *Electrikaleidoscope*, for amplified ensemble (1972); *Ricordanza*, for cello and piano (1972); *Imago Mundi*, for orchestra (1973); *Ukiyo-e* (*Pictures of the Floating World*), for solo harp (1973); *Behold, My Servant*, for a cappella chorus (1973); *Phaedra*, monodrama for mezzo-soprano and orchestra (1973–74); Violin Concerto (1974); *Transcendental Variations*, for string orchestra (1975); Piano Quintet (1975); *Partita Variations*, for piano (1976); *Songs of Inanna and Dumuzi*, for alto and piano (1977); *Ukiyo-e* II (*Slow Fires of Autumn*), for flute and harp (1978–79); *Book of Contrapuntal Pieces*, for keyboard instruments (1979); Viola Sonata (1979); Septet, for flute, clarinet, horn, violin, viola, cello, and piano (1980); *Octet, a Grand Fantasia*, for flute, clarinet, horn, violin, viola, cello, double bass, and piano (1980); Cello Quintet (1980); *The Confidence Man*, opera (1981).

BIBLIOGRAPHY: *NGDMM*; *Musical Quarterly*, October 1966, January 1972; *Newsweek*, February 19, 1979; *New York Times*, May 28, 1972; *Who's Who in America, 1980–81*.

Rogers, Bernard, b. New York, February 4, 1893; d. Rochester, N.Y., May 24, 1968.

Biblical and esoteric subjects, and paintings of both the Eastern and Western worlds were sparks that often ignited Rogers's creative imagination. Though he did not hesitate to use modern harmonic and subtly complex rhythmic language and unconventional sonorities to dramatize his writings, he was for the most part a conservative whose music was deeply rooted in traditional practices and structures.

Until he was sixteen, Rogers had little interest in music, though piano lessons began when he was twelve. His first passion was art, and though his father wanted him to become an architect, his own ambition lay in painting. While attending New York City elementary and high schools he spent his spare time working with paints and canvases. He left school when he was fifteen to work for Carrère and Hastings. He first became interested in music through a friend who played the violin and took him to his first concert. Soon after that Rogers started taking lessons on the violin. His first teacher in composition was Arthur Farwell. He also studied theory with Hans van den Berg. For a time, after graduating from high school, he tried to fulfill his father's ambition for him by studying architecture, but he soon dropped these studies to concentrate on music. In 1913, he became a critic for *Musical America*, continuing to work for that journal as critic and editor for nine years.

As a composition student of Ernest Bloch's in New York, Rogers wrote his first orchestral composition, *The Faithful* (1918). His first important performance came with its orchestral successor, *To the Fallen*, a tone poem written in 1918 as a tribute to those who died in World War I; it was introduced by the New York Philharmonic Orchestra on November 13, 1919. On the strength of this composition, Rogers was awarded the Pulitzer Traveling Fellowship from Columbia University which enabled him to travel in Europe in 1919. Between 1919 and 1921, he attended the Institute of Musical Art in New York, studying theory and composition there with Percy Goetschius. His talent brought him the Loeb Prize in 1920. After leaving the institute, Rogers went to Cleveland to continue to study with Bloch. For a student ensemble of the Cleveland Institute of Music of which Bloch was director, Rogers composed *Soliloquy* no. 1, for flute and string orchestra (1922), "an attempt," as he explained, "to write music of a serious character which could be performed by young musicians." After being introduced in Rochester in 1926, *Soliloquy* no. 1 was programmed by several important American orchestras.

While on a visit to Kent, England, in 1924–25, Rogers composed his Symphony no. 1, which he subtitled *Adonais*. This was a two-movement work of romantic intensity in which the influence of Bloch and the late 19th-century Russian romanticists was strongly felt. This composition, which had its premiere in Rochester, N.Y., on April 29, 1927, helped bring him a Guggenheim Fellowship that year and was extended for a second year. Having just completed a year of teaching composition at the Julius Hartt School of Music in Hartford, Conn. (1926–27), Rogers returned to Europe for a two-year stay, studying composition with Frank Bridge in London and Nadia Boulanger in Paris. During this period he wrote his first large choral composition, his first work on a biblical subject and one of his first compositions in which he freed himself from earlier constricting influences to develop his own melodic, rhythmic, harmonic, and instrumental vocabulary. That work was *The Raising of Lazarus*, for solo voices, chorus, and orchestra (1928). Here, as Howard Hanson has written, Rogers "uses the voice in a completely lyrical sense foreign to many contemporaries. This is true not only in the solo passages such as the poignant 'Song of Martha' but also in the mighty concluding chorus. Here we have a fusion of rhythm, orchestral, and vocal color, dramatic urgency with diatonic melodic writing."

In 1929 Rogers was appointed instructor at the Eastman School of Music in Rochester, N.Y. He remained a member of its faculty for thirty-six years as teacher of orchestration and composition, and for many years as chairman of the department, retiring in 1967.

Almost all of his major works in the 1930s had their first hearing in Rochester. These included the lyric drama *The Marriage of Aude* (1930) on May 22, 1931, winner of the David Bispham Medal. Most of the other works performed in Rochester were orchestral, usually conducted by Howard Hanson. The most important were *Three Japanese Dances* (1932; May 3, 1934); *Two American Frescoes* (1934; January 16, 1936); Symphony no. 3 (1936; October 27, 1937); *The Supper of Emmaus* (1936; April 29, 1937), based on Rembrandt's painting; Fantasy, for flute, viola and orchestra (1938; April 25, 1938); *Soliloquy* no. 2, for bassoon and orchestra (1938; October 18, 1938); and *Colors of War* (1939; October 25, 1939). Another significant orchestral work was introduced by the Cincinnati Symphony under Eugene Goossens on March 24, 1940: *The Song of the Nightingale* (1939) based on a tale of Hans Christian Andersen.

Rogers reached once again to biblical subjects for his most significant works of the 1940s. The idea of writing an orchestral composition about Salome and her celebrated dance came to the composer from Flaubert's story, *Herodias*, and from paintings by Gustave Moreau. *The Dance of Salome* (1940) was first performed in Rochester during the Festival of American Music on April 25, 1940, and then was presented by several major American orchestras including the Cleveland Orchestra on April 2, 1942. An unusual array of percussion instruments that included the tam-tam, castanets, gourd, vibraphone, xylophone, and anvil together with the more usual percussion instruments, and novel sonoric and instrumental efforts, brought this work an oriental character.

Another biblical work, *The Passion*, an oratorio for solo voices, chorus, and orchestra (1942), is generally regarded as Rogers's most famous and most important composition. "I have not been able to understand the long neglect of this world-subject [the Passion] by composers," Rogers said, "and it has seemed to be right to attempt a setting, using the contemporary musical language in which all the resources of the modern palette might be applied. I considered this subject for about ten years. . . . The work is divided into six broad sections, beginning with the entry into Jerusalem and culminating with the Resurrection. The aim throughout was towards concision, vivid color, and the exploration of all the rich tonal resources that the subject justifies. Treated thus, the work becomes a continuous tense fabric of emotional change and growth, with a deep emphasis upon the spiritual feeling which music is so well fitted to subserve." Excerpts were heard first at the Festival of American Music in Rochester in 1942, Hanson conducting. The complete oratorio was given at the Cincinnati May Festival on May 12, 1944, under Eugene Goossens's direction. "Rogers approaches the gigantic problem of setting the Passion in a highly personal, subjective, deeply reverent spirit," wrote Howard Hanson. "He has poured into it the full resources of his creative ability and it is, as a consequence, far removed from the conventional. An intensely dramatic, emotional work, it embodies a strong personal reaction. It is conceived in the spirit of the East rather than of the West, suggesting the barbaric colors of the Orient. A work of startling power, it is an important milestone in contemporary choral writing."

In the opera *The Warrior* (1944), the Bible is once again tapped, this time in Norman Corwin's libretto based on the story of Samson and Delilah. The Metropolitan Opera produced it on January 11, 1947, a performance that was heard nationwide through a live radio broadcast. Though the opera was poorly received by the critics, which sealed its fate as far as many further productions were concerned, it received the Alice M. Ditson Award from Columbia University.

The death of an American president, rather than the Bible, was the inspiration of the orchestral elegy *In Memory of Franklin Delano Roosevelt* (1946). It was first performed by the New York Philharmonic under Artur Rodzinski on April 11, 1946, before an audience that included eight delegate heads of the United Nations. "Mr. Rogers has composed with genuine and admirable simplicity," reported Olin Downes in the *New York Times*. "If there is a place where reticence has a special value and appropriateness, it is here. The music starts from a little germinal beginning and expands in a logical way, and seems at the end to return to the tonal center from which it came. This style of development is . . . perfectly in accordance with the nature of the musical motive and the expressive purpose with which it is used."

On May 18, 1950, at Indiana University in Bloomington, Rogers's one-act opera *The Veil* (1950) was produced; it was performed in New York City on October 26, 1954. This is a macabre opera with libretto by Robert Lawrence set in an English madhouse in the early 19th century.

Other late works include a biblical cantata, for solo voices, chorus, and orchestra, *The Prophet Isaiah* (1950; Rochester, 1963); *Dance Scenes*, for orchestra (1953), which the Louisville Orchestra commissioned and introduced on October 28, 1953; Symphony no. 5, subtitled *Africa* (1958; Cincinnati, 1958); and *Apparitions*, for orchestra and wind ensemble (1967; Cincinnati, 1967), inspired by Flaubert's *The Temptation of St. Anthony*.

Rogers was married twice. His first wife was Anne Thacher, whom he married in June 1934 and with whom he had a daughter. His wife died in October 1935. On August 27, 1938, Rogers married Elizabeth Mary Clark.

In 1947 Rogers was elected to membership in the National Institute of Arts and Letters. He received an honorary doctorate in music from Valparaiso University in Indiana (1959) and an honorary doctorate in humane letters from Wayne State University in Detroit (1962). He was awarded a Fulbright grant in 1953, the Lillian B. Fairchild Award in 1962, and commissions from the Juilliard School of Music, the Ford Foundation and the Koussevitsky Music Foundation. Rogers is the author of *The Art of Orchestration* (1949).

THE COMPOSER SPEAKS: In composing I follow what I believe to be the procedure of the painter. I try to rough out the first sketch as quickly and intensely as possible. After that, the problem is one of separating the wheat (if any) from the chaff. A constant and painful process of revision is necessary before a work is finished; in some cases, the final product shows only slight resemblance to the initial sketch. In other words, the action is from big to little, from the whole to its parts, and from the first play of emotion to the later checks and influences of the mind.

PRINCIPAL WORKS: 5 symphonies (1926–58).

Soliloquy no. 1, for flute and strings (1922); *The Raising of Lazarus*, for solo voices, chorus, and orchestra (1928); *Prelude to Hamlet*, for orchestra (1928); *The Marriage of Aude*, lyric drama (1930); *Exodus*, sacred poem for solo voices, chorus, and orchestra (1932); *Three Japanese Dances*, for orchestra (1932); *Two American Frescoes*, for orchestra (1934); *Once Upon a Time*, five fairy tales for small orchestra (1935); *The Supper of Emmaus*, for orchestra (1936); Fantasy, for flute, viola and orchestra (1938); *Soliloquy* no. 2, for bassoon and string orchestra (1938); *The Colors of War*, for orchestra (1939); *The Song of the Nightingale*, for orchestra (1939); *The Dance of Salome*, for orchestra (1940); *The Plains*, "landscapes for orchestra" (1940); *The Passion*, oratorio for solo voices, chorus, and orchestra (1943); *Invasion*, for orchestra (1943); *The Warrior*, opera (1944); *Characters from Hans Christian Andersen*, for orchestra (1944); *In Memory of Franklin Delano Roosevelt*, elegy for orchestra (1946); *A Letter from Pete*, cantata for solo voices, chorus, and orchestra (1947); *Amphitryon*, symphonic overture (1947); *The Prophet Isaiah*, cantata for solo voices, chorus, and orchestra (1950); *The Veil*, one-act opera (1950); *Leaves from the Tale of*

Pinocchio, for narrator and chamber orchestra (1951); Psalm 68, for baritone and orchestra (1952); *Portrait*, for violin and orchestra (1952); *Dance Scenes*, for orchestra (1953); String Trio (1953); *The Nightingale*, opera (1954); Fantasia, for horn, timpani, and string orchestra (1954); *The Silver World*, for flute, oboe, and strings (1956); *The Musicians from Bremen*, for narrator and thirteen instruments (1958); *Variations on a Song of Mussorgsky*, for orchestra (1960); Violin Sonata (1962); *Apparitions*, for orchestra and wind ensemble (1967); *Dirge for Two Veterans*, for chorus and piano (1967); Psalm 114, for chorus and piano (1968).

BIBLIOGRAPHY: Cowell, Henry (ed.), *American Composers on American Music* (Stanford, Calif., 1933); Ewen, David, *American Composers Today* (N.Y., 1949); Goss, Madeleine, *Modern Music Makers* (N.Y., 1952); *Modern Music*, March–April 1945; *Musical Quarterly*, April 1947; *Opera News*, January 6, 1947; *Who's Who in America, 1966–67*.

Rorem, Ned, b. Richmond, Ind., October 23, 1923.

Rorem has long been recognized as America's foremost composer of art songs, of which he has written some three hundred in addition to some twenty song cycles. He has been highly acclaimed in other media as well, one of his orchestral works receiving the Pulitzer Prize in 1976.

Of Norwegian ancestry, Rorem was one of two children of Dr. Clarence Rufus Rorem, a medical economist and a member of the faculty at Earlham College in Richmond, Ind. His mother, née Gladys Miller, has long been affiliated with the Society of Friends and involved in various civil rights movements. His background was, in his own words, "upper middle-class, semibohemian but with a strong Quaker emphasis." When he was an infant, his family moved to Chicago. There, he attended nursery school through high school at the University of Chicago and began piano lessons with Margaret Bonds, who introduced him to the music of Debussy and Ravel which, from then on, made him a Francophile and inspired him to become a composer. In his boyhood he also showed a literary bent by writing stories, poems, and a diary which he has continued until today. "When I was young," he recalls, "it was a toss-up whether I would be a composer or a writer, so I became a little of both."

At fifteen, he began formal training in harmony at the American Conservatory in Chicago with Leo Sowerby. (Additional study of composition took place with Max Wald at the Chicago Musical College during the summer of 1941.) Between 1940 and 1942 Rorem attended the School of Music at Northwestern University. For one year after that he was Gian Carlo Menotti's student in composition and orchestration and Rosario Scalero's in counterpoint and composition at the Curtis Institute in Philadelphia on a scholarship.

Rorem came to New York in 1944. He attended the Juilliard School of Music, studying composition with Bernard Wagenaar and receiving his bachelor of science degree in 1946 and his master of art degree in 1948. At the Berkshire Music Center at Tanglewood, Mass., during the summers of 1946 and 1947, he studied composition with Aaron Copland. In New York he also studied privately with Virgil Thomson while serving as copyist. Both Copland and Thomson became fairly important influences in Rorem's growth.

In 1946, Rorem began writing songs as much (as he has said) from a love for words as from a love of music. One of these, "The Lordly Hudson," to a poem by Paul Goodman, was voted by the Music Library Association the best published song of 1948. He also wrote Overture in C, for orchestra (1948), which was awarded the George Gershwin Memorial Award and was premiered in May 1948 by the New York Philharmonic under Mishel Piastro.

In the spring of 1949, by way of Paris, Rorem went to live in Morocco. It was there, he says, that his career as a composer really began. "There was no diversion. The best influence for a composer is four walls. The light must come from inside. When it comes from outside, the result is postcard music." In a prolific outburst, he now produced the score to a ballet, *Melos* (1949), which was awarded the Prix de Biarritz in 1951 and his first opera, *A Childhood Miracle*, libretto by Elliott Stein based on a story by Nathaniel Hawthorne, which had to wait three years for performance (N.Y., May 10, 1955). Several song cycles included *Flight for Heaven* to poems by Robert Herrick (1950); *Six Irish Poems* to poems by George Darley (1950), broadcast over the French radio in a performance by Nell Tangeman in July 1951; *Cycle of Holy Songs* to biblical texts (1951); and *To a Young Girl* to poems by William Butler Yeats (1951), performed first in Hyères on April 13, 1951. Symphony No. 1 and Piano Concerto no. 2, both completed in 1950, were among his more important early instrumental works. The first was introduced by Julius Katchen on French radio in the spring of 1954, and the latter in Vienna in February 1951 conducted by Jonathan Sternberg. If the style and structure of these compositions follow traditional paths, a personal note is struck through grace, simplicity, economy, and a certain Spartan-Americanism mixed on a palette with logical Gallic sensuousness. In 1950, Rorem was the recipient of the Lili Boulanger Prize for composition.

On a Fulbright Fellowship in 1951–52, Rorem studied composition with Arthur Honegger in Paris. Rorem remained there for the next seven years. He found a generous patron in the Vicomtesse Marie Laure de Noailles, at whose 18th-century mansion he resided, and received musical stimulation from his friendship with Francis Poulenc, Georges Auric, and Darius Milhaud. Creatively, he was more productive than ever. His style, still influenced by the contemporary French composers, took on increasing refinement and, thanks to an elegant sense for texts in English, acquired a recognizable panache. He continued writing songs and song cycles, now revealing a fresh and more subtle response than heretofore to his various poetical texts and an uncommon gift in finding the musical *mot juste* for every nuance of each textual line or phrase. Sometimes, to heighten the emotional climate, he would have the voice sing without accompaniment; other times, the accompaniment provided contrasts to the soaring lyric line through dissonant harmonies, intervallic leaps, and melismatic phrasing. The cycle *Poèmes pour la paix*, based on medieval French texts (1953), was selected for performance by the International Center for Musical Documentation at its festival in Paris in November 1954.

In addition to songs, he wrote Piano Sonata no. 2 (1950), which Julius Katchen introduced in Paris in February 1951 and then recorded; the scores of two ballets, *Ballet for Jerry* (1951) and *Dorian Gray* (1952), the latter in collaboration with the actor Jean Marais and first mounted in Barcelona; *Design for Orchestra* (1953), which the Louisville Orchestra in Kentucky had commissioned and which, under Robert Whitney, introduced it on May 28, 1955, and then recorded; *The Poet's Requiem*, for soprano solo, chorus, and orchestra (1954–55), meditations on death using quotations from Kafka, Rilke, Mallarmé, Cocteau, Freud, Gide, and Paul Goodman, first performed by Margaret Hillis Concert Choir on February 15, 1957, in New York City; and Symphony no. 2 (1956), commissioned by Nikolai Sokoloff and the Musical Arts Society of La Jolla, Calif., its first performance given in La Jolla on August 5, 1956. A concert of Rorem's works was heard in Paris in 1953, and in 1954 he was given the Eurydice Choral Award for his *Five Prayers for the Young*. Rorem's experiences in Paris between 1951 and 1955 were detailed in a diary entitled *The Paris Diary of Ned Rorem*, published in New York in 1966.

Rorem was back in the United States in 1957, the year in which he received his first Guggenheim Fellowship and a grant from the American Woodwind Ensemble for Sinfonia, for woodwinds and percussion (1956). In 1959–61 he was composer-in-residence at the State University of New York in Buffalo and in 1966–67 he held a similar post at the University of Utah in Salt Lake City.

His tone poem *Eagles* (1958) was premiered by Eugene Ormandy and the Philadelphia Orchestra on October 23, 1959, and was chosen by Leopold Stokowski when he first conducted the Boston Symphony on August 21, 1964. It was inspired by Walt Whitman's *A Dalliance of Eagles*, of which it is a free interpretation, intended, as the composer said, "to relate in tone the calm of the poet's country stroll inter-

rupted from outside by an intense sensual distur-
bance which ultimately subsides leaving the dreamer
alone again—but not quite." Leonard Bernstein,
conducting the New York Philharmonic, introduced
Rorem's Symphony no. 3 (1957–58) on April 16,
1959, which Jay S. Harrison in the *New York Herald Tribune* described as "a warmhearted outgoing
number that makes no pretense at hiding its alternating sentiments of high joy and nostalgic regret" and
which everywhere was "lavish, luscious, and luxe."
Eleven Studies for Eleven Players (1959–60), commissioned by the Slee Foundation of Buffalo University, was first heard on May 17, 1960, at the university with the composer conducting.

In these compositions, and in those that followed,
Rorem was the "first successful modern romanticist," as Dillard Gunn once described him. Rorem,
who regards himself as a conservative, was interested
in pure lyricism, emotion, beautiful sounds, all produced with restraint, immaculate taste, and a consummate mastery of technique. "After ten years of
chattering every known musical speech," he wrote in
Paris Diary, "of imitating now one and then another
school, of wanting to become famous by writing like
the famous, I decided now to write again the way I
did at the age of eleven when I knew no one: my
music from the heart with my own influences."
Though modern idioms are not absent—such as
polytonality, discords, altered chords, a modified
form of serialism—Rorem has consistently refused to
write "new" music for the sake of being "new," and
so he has scrupulously avoided aleatory or electronic
practices and even a nontonal idiom.

In the 1950s and early 1960s Rorem contributed
incidental music to several plays on and off
Broadway, among these being two by Tennessee
Williams, *Suddenly Last Summer* (January 1, 1958)
and *The Milk Train Doesn't Stop Here Anymore*
(January 1, 1964). From his incidental music to the
former he drew two sections for his *Eleven Studies
for Eleven Instruments*: "Bird Call" and "The Diary."

Significant commissions were responsible for several of Rorem's major works in the 1960s. *Poems of
Love and the Rain* (1962–63), for mezzo-soprano
and piano, was a cycle of seventeen songs to poems by
W. H. Auden, Emily Dickinson, Howard Moss, and
Theodore Roethke, among others, commissioned by
the Ford Foundation. In this cycle, Rorem employed
a "mirror sequence," whereby each song (with the
exception of the ninth) received two different musical
treatments. Regina Safarty, mezzo-soprano, for
whom this cycle was written, gave the first performance in Madison, Wis., on April 12, 1964, with the
composer at the piano; they also recorded it. A commission from the New York State Opera, with an
assisting grant from the Ford Foundation, resulted in
the two-act opera, *Miss Julie* (1964–65), in which
Kenward Elmslie's libretto was based on August
Strindberg's play. It was first performed by the New

York City Opera on November 4, 1965. In this
opera, Rorem combined his skill and experience in
writing for the voice with a sure instinct for powerful
drama. *Miss Julie* was revived by the New York Lyric Opera on April 5, 1979, shortened and otherwise
altered. *Sun,* eight poems for voice and orchestra
(1967), to words by Byron, Blake, Shakespeare,
Whitman, and others, was commissioned by the Lincoln Center Fund for the Lincoln Center Festival of
1967 in New York, its first performance given by the
New York Philharmonic under Karel Ancerl, with
Jane Marsh, soloist, on July 1, 1967. *Letters from
Paris* (1966), commissioned by the Koussevitzky
Music Foundation, was a setting of nine prose extracts from Janet Flanner's *Paris Journal,* scored for
chorus and small orchestra, and dedicated to the
memory of Serge and Natalie Koussevitzky; its premiere was given in Ann Arbor, Mich., on April 25,
1969. Concerto in Six Movements, for piano and orchestra (1969), was commissioned by the Music Associates of Aspen for Jerome Lowenthal, who gave
the first performance in Pittsburgh as soloist of the
Pittsburgh Symphony under William Steinberg on
December 3, 1970.

In addition to these compositions, mention should
also be made of two other notable works of the 1960s:
Lions, for orchestra (1963), which the Detroit Symphony under Sixten Ehrling introduced on October
28, 1965; and *Lovers,* a narrative in ten scenes, for
harpsichord, oboe, cello, and percussion (1964), first
performed by Sylvia Marlowe in New York on December 15, 1964, and then used as the background
music for a ballet by Glen Tetley, produced in 1966
on the National Educational Television network.

The commissions accumulated further in 1974–75
when, in that year, Rorem was called upon to write
no less than seven works to commemorate the American bicentennial. The most lengthy of these was *Air
Music* (1974), which Thomas Schippers and the
Cincinnati Symphony asked for, was composed with
an assist from a grant by the National Endowment
for the Arts and introduced in Cincinnati on December 5, 1975. It is this work that brought Rorem the
Pulitzer Prize in music in 1976. This composition is
subtitled "Ten Variations," but the variations Rorem had in mind were those used by dancers. "The
variations," he explains, "are on each other rather
than on an initial statement, for there is no theme
proper. The movements share traits (shapes, hues,
rhythms, tunes) but this resemblance is more that of
cousins than siblings." Three of the ten sections are
for full orchestra, the seven others requiring only
small instrumental groups. An epigraph from Wilhelm Heinse on the title page of the published score
provided an explanation for the overall title (other
than the fact that the composer had previously written *Water Music,* for orchestra in 1966; *Day Music,*
for violin and piano in 1971; and *Night Music,* for
violin and piano in 1972; and thus was partial to still
another kind of *Music* composition). The epigraph

reads: *"Music touches the nerves in a particular manner and results in a singular playfulness, a quite special communication that cannot be described in words. Music represents the inner feeling in the exterior air. . . ."*

For the Saratoga Performing Arts Center in New York, on commission, Rorem completed an eight-part orchestral suite named *Sunday Morning* in 1977 and the Philadelphia Orchestra under Eugene Ormandy performed it there on August 25, 1978. The piece was inspired by Wallace Stevens's poem "Sunday Morning," of which the music is a nonliteral, dreamlike recollection. This was not the first time Rorem has been inspired by Stevens, having previously written *Last Poems of Wallace Stevens* for soprano, cello, and piano (1971–72; N.Y., November 13, 1972).

Ned Rorem's fiftieth birthday was celebrated in New York on November 25 and 26, 1973, with two concerts of his works at Alice Tully Hall. One of these, on November 26, was a world premiere: *Bertha*, a one-act opera (1968–69) with text by Kenneth Koch, a satire on politics and war, Shakesperean dramas about kings and contemporary civilized barbarism. This opera is of modest proportions enlisting only a piano for accompaniment and six singers to assume both the sixteen solo roles and the chorus.

Rorem received a second Guggenheim Fellowship in 1978. A year later he was voted membership to the American Academy and Institute of Arts and Letters. In 1981 he received a fellowship from the National Endowment for the Arts.

Rorem has made numerous concert tours as accompanist with various singers, notably Donald Gramm and Phyllis Curtin, in concerts devoted entirely to American songs, half of each program consisting of Rorem's own songs. In 1980, Rorem was appointed codirector (with David Loeb) of the undergraduate department in composition at the Curtis Institute of Music, which had been dormant for many years. As composer-in-residence at the Santa Fe Music Festival in New Mexico, Rorem attended the world premiere of his *The Santa Fe Songs,* for baritone and piano quartet (1980) during the summer of 1980.

In addition to his first book, *The Paris Diary of Ned Rorem,* he has written *New York Diary* (1967), *Music from Inside Out* (1967), *Music and People* (1969), *Critical Affairs* (1970), *Pure Contraption* (1973), *The Final Diary: 1961–1972* (1974), and *An Absolute Gift: A New Diary* (1978). *Critical Affairs* and *Final Diary* received the ASCAP–Deems Taylor awards in 1971 and 1975 respectively.

THE COMPOSER SPEAKS: I am never *not* working, yet I never catch myself in the act. At the end of each year, I've somehow produced around an hour of music, and that hour is not a few sheets of penciled whole notes, but hundreds of pages of inked orchestration. Work is the process of composing—making it up as it goes along, which is the only precise description since Homer. The action is at once so disparate and so compact that the actor is unaware, which is doubtless why I "never mind myself," etc.

I know my worth, yet that worth lies in past works which now lead their own life and no longer concern me. I feel unprotected, and, in spite of dear friends, alone. I no longer smoke, drink, carouse, or go to parties. Sugar is my sole vice and reading my joy. My mind is on work, or released elements, twenty-four hours a day, which accounts for the egocentricity of all artists and hides them from their own vulnerability.

My music is a diary no less compromising than my prose. A diary nevertheless differs from a musical composition in that it depicts the moment, the writer's present mood which, were it inscribed an hour later, could emerge quite otherwise. I believe that composers notate their moods, they don't tell the music where to go—it leads them. . . . Why do I write music? Because I want to hear it—it's as simple as that. Others may have more *talent,* more sense of *duty.* But I compose just from necessity, and no one else is making what I need.

PRINCIPAL WORKS: 3 symphonies (1949, 1956, 1957–58); 3 piano concertos (1950, 1951, 1969); 3 piano sonatas (1949, 1952, 1954).

Overture in C, for orchestra (1949); Violin Sonata (1949); *Six Irish Poems,* for voice and orchestra (1950); *Cycle of Holy Songs,* for voice and piano (1951); *A Childhood Miracle,* opera (1952); *Poèmes pour la paix,* song cycle for voice and piano (1953); Six Songs, for high voice and orchestra (1953); *Design for Orchestra* (1953); *Eight Poems of Whitman,* for voice and piano (1954); *The Poet's Requiem,* for chorus and orchestra (1954–55); Sinfonia, for woodwinds and percussion (1956); *The Robbers,* opera (1958); *Eagles,* for orchestra (1958); *Pilgrims,* for string orchestra (1958); *Eleven Studies for Eleven Players* (1959–60); Trio, for flute, cello, and piano (1960); *King Midas,* cycle for voice and piano (1960–61); *Poems of Love and the Rain,* song cycle for mezzo-soprano and piano (1962–63); *Lions,* for orchestra (1963); *Lovers,* narrative for harpsichord, oboe, cello, and percussion (1964); *Miss Julie,* opera (1964–65); *Hearing,* cycle for medium voice and piano (1965–66); *Letters from Paris,* for chorus and small orchestra (1966); *Water Music,* for violin, clarinet, and chamber orchestra (1966); *Sun,* for soprano and orchestra (1967); *Bertha,* one-act opera (1968–69); *Three Sisters Who Are Not Sisters,* opera (1969); *War Scenes,* for baritone and piano (1969); *Fables,* six mini-operas (1970); *Ariel,* for voice, clarinet, and piano (1971); *Day Music,* for violin and piano (1971); *Night Music,* for violin and piano (1972); *Last Poems of Wallace Stevens,* for voice and piano (1971–72); *Little Prayers,* for soprano, baritone, chorus, and orchestra (1973); *Missa Brevis,* for solo voices and a cappella chorus (1973); *Air Music,* for orchestra (1974); *Assembly and Fall,* tone poem for orchestra (1975); Eight Etudes, for piano (1975); *Book of Hours,* for flute and harp (1976); Serenade, for voice, viola, violin, and piano (1976); *Sky Music,* ten pieces for solo harp (1976); *A Quaker Reader,* eleven pieces for organ (1976); *Romeo and Juliet,* for flute and guitar (1976); *Women's Voices,* eleven songs for soprano and piano (1976); *Sunday Morning,* for orchestra (1977); Concerto for Cello, Piano, and Orchestra (1979); *The Nantucket Songs,* for soprano and piano (1979); *The Santa Fe Songs,* for baritone and piano quartet (1980); *After Reading Shakespeare,* for solo cello (1981); Quintet for clarinet, bassoon, violin, cello, and piano (1981).

BIBLIOGRAPHY: Rorem, Ned, *The Paris Diary of Ned Rorem* (N.Y., 1967); ibid., *New York Diary* (N.Y., 1967); ibid., *Final Diary: 1961–1972* (N.Y., 1974); ibid., *An Absolute Gift: A New Diary* (N.Y., 1978); *ASCAP Today,* Spring 1978; *High Fidelity/Musical America,* August 1976; *New York Times,* May 30, 1976; *People,* August 21, 1978.

Rózsa, Miklós, b. Budapest, Hungary, April 18, 1907. American citizen, 1946.

However prolific, successful, and gifted Rózsa has been through the years as a composer of motion-picture music, his concert music is by no means a subsidiary activity. His concert works are deeply embedded in the soil of Hungarian folk songs, whose melodic, rhythmic and harmonic characteristics are readily recognizable. As is the case with Magyar folk songs, Rózsa's abundant lyricism is either pentatonic or modal, with a strong elegiac undercurrent. And in line with Magyar folk dances it is characterized by rapidly varying rhythms and time signatures, syncopations and motor energy.

His father was a wealthy industrialist and his mother, a trained pianist. They owned a country estate at the foot of the Matra Mountains, where Miklós was born. There, in childhood, Rózsa was subjected to his first important musical influence: the Magyar folk songs of that region. "This music," he recalls, "was all around me. I'd hear it in the fields when the peasants were at work. I'd hear it emanating from festivities in the village as I lay awake at night." In time he felt impelled to perpetuate this music by putting it down on paper and later on by incorporating some of it (in his earliest compositions).

Rózsa began studying the violin when he was five with Lajos Berkovitz, a pupil of Jenö Hubay's. Before long, Rózsa supplemented this instruction with lessons on the viola and piano. By the time he was eight, he was performing in public: dressed up as the boy Mozart, he performed a movement from a Mozart violin concerto and led a children's orchestra in the *Toy Symphony* (a work long erroneously as-

cribed to Haydn). Rózsa was also beginning to compose.

For all Rózsa's obvious talent for music, his father was determined to have him become a professional man and saw to it that he received a thorough academic education. Music, however, remained a significant preoccupation at school. At the Budapest High School he organized matinees of "modern music" which featured the works of such Hungarian contemporaries as Bartók, Kodály, and Dohnányi. Rózsa was elected president of the school's Franz Liszt Society, which, in 1925, presented him with its first prize for a trio, for flute, oboe, and cello, based on a patriotic tune called "The Sunset."

With the secret determination to concentrate on music, Rózsa left Budapest for Leipzig in 1925, entering the university ostensibly to advance his academic education and to major in chemistry, but also to take a course in musicology with Theodor Kroyer and to continue his studies of composition at the Leipzig Conservatory. He soon found a strong ally for his musical ambitions in his composition teacher, Hermann Grabner, who, in turn, successfully prevailed upon Rózsa's father to allow the young man to study music full time at the conservatory. While attending the conservatory, Rózsa had one of his works, a Piano Quintet in F minor (1928), performed publicly. One of the members of that audience was Karl Straube, cantor of the Thomaskirche, who was so impressed by this composition that he recommended Rózsa to the prestigious Leipzig publishing house of Breitkopf and Härtel, which gave him a contract and forthwith released his first publications: a Trio and a Piano Quintet. These were followed by the publication of *Variations on a Hungarian Peasant Song,* for violin and piano; Rhapsody, for cello and orchestra, and *North Hungarian Peasant Songs and Dances,* for violin and piano, all completed in Leipzig in 1929. His Violin Concerto no. 1 (1929) was performed in Leipzig on March 27, 1929, by Ruth Meister with Heinrich Labe conducting.

In the conservatory, Rózsa was often called upon to substitute for Grabner in his composition classes. Then, when Rózsa received his conservatory diploma, *cum laude,* in 1929, he served for a while as Grabner's assistant.

Following a concert of Rózsa's chamber music at the École Normale de Musique in Paris on May 13, 1932, Rózsa decided to make Paris his permanent home. This was the year in which his first published work for orchestra, Serenade, op. 10, for small orchestra (1932), was performed by the Budapest Philharmonic on October 25 under the direction of Ernst von Dohnányi and received the praise of Richard Strauss. Several other prominent conductors became interested in him, one of whom was Bruno Walter, who suggested that Rózsa write for him a new work for orchestra. Rózsa complied with Theme, Variations, and Finale (1933), which was introduced in Duisburg on October 9, 1934, and then performed in Budapest under the direction of Charles Munch. It was a success, and within a few years was heard not only throughout Europe but also in the United States, the American premiere taking place in Chicago on October 28, 1937, with Hans Lange conducting the Chicago Symphony. This work was on the program when the twenty-five-year-old Leonard Bernstein made his unscheduled and sensational debut as conductor by substituting for the ailing Bruno Walter at a concert of the New York Philharmonic on November 14, 1943. The theme from which the variations were built was in the style of a Hungarian folk song. Eight variations and a finale in folk-dance style followed. Reviewing the New York Philharmonic concert, Olin Downes reported in the *New York Times* that the Theme, Variations, and Finale "brought down the house."

On December 22, 1934, a concert of music by Arthur Honegger and Miklós Rózsa was given at the Salle Debussy in Paris. Less than two years later, Rózsa came to London to attend the premiere of his ballet *Hungaria* (1935), the score based on Hungarian folk melodies; it was performed by the company of Anton Dolin and Alicia Markova at the Duke of York Theater.

In 1937, Rózsa was engaged to write the music for *Knight without Armour,* a motion picture starring Marlene Dietrich and Robert Donat, produced in London by Alexander Korda. After contributing a second score, for the motion picture *Thunder in the City* (1937), Rózsa was made a member of the Korda staff as its official composer. Between 1937 and 1942 he provided the music for seven additional Korda films, the most notable of which were *The Four Feathers* (1938), *The Thief of Bagdad* (1940), *Lady Hamilton* (1941), and *The Jungle Book* (1942). *Lady Hamilton* was released in the United States under the title of *That Hamilton Woman.*

During this eventful affiliation with Korda, Rózsa wrote, in 1938, a new successful work for orchestra, *Three Hungarian Sketches (Capriccio, pastorale e danza)*, its premiere given at an international music festival in Baden-Baden, Germany, on March 31, 1939. For his musical endeavors in concert music, Rózsa was awarded the Franz Joseph Prize of the city of Budapest in 1937, and a second time in 1938, the highest honor Hungary could bestow on a composer.

While *The Thief of Bagdad* was in early stages of production, World War II broke out in Europe. With new funds provided by United Artists in America, the production was transferred to Hollywood in the spring of 1940. Miklós Rózsa now came to the United States to make his home in Los Angeles for the rest of his life and to become active as a composer of music for American films. On August 31, 1943, he married Margaret Finlason, the former secretary to

Gracie Fields; they raised two children. From 1945 to 1965 he was on the music faculty of the University of California in Los Angeles.

The last time Rózsa wrote music for Korda was *The Jungle Book,* whose score he adapted as a concert work for narrator and orchestra, which was premiered by the Los Angeles Philharmonic in 1948 and whose recording became Rózsa's first to be released in the United States. From 1942 on, he continued to work for the screen, most of the years for MGM, but frequently for other studios as well. Up to 1980 he either wrote the original music or did the scoring for about eighty films. The most important were: *Double Indemnity* (1944), *A Song to Remember* (1945), *The Lost Weekend* (1945), *Spellbound* (1945), *The Killers* (1946), *A Double Life* (1948), *Quo Vadis* (1951), *Lust for Life* (1956), *Ben Hur* (1959), *El Cid* (1960), *The V.I.P.'s* (1963), *The Private Life of Sherlock Holmes* (1970), *Providence* (1977), *Fedora* (1978), *The Private Files of J. Edgar Hoover* (1978), *The Last Embrace* (1978), and *Time after Time* (1979). For his music to *Spellbound, A Double Life,* and *Ben Hur* he was awarded Oscars from the Academy of Motion Picture Arts and Sciences, and for *Providence* he was given a César by the French Académie. He is perhaps most often remembered for his music to *Spellbound,* in which he made significant use of electronic music to suggest hysteria, terror, or madness. Rózsa adapted this score as a concert composition named *Spellbound Concerto,* for piano and orchestra (1958), which he recorded. For his contribution to motion pictures he received the Award of Merit from the National Association of Composers and Conductors (1943), and in 1956 the Los Angeles Conservatory of Music presented him with an honorary doctorate in music. He was a member of the music faculty of the University of Southern California for two decades (1945–65). From 1955 to 1965, Rózsa served as president of the Screen Composers Association and in 1957–58 he was president of the Los Angeles chapter of the National Association of American Composers and Conductors.

Despite his intensive preoccupation with the screen, Rózsa never neglected concert music. His Concerto for String Orchestra (1943) was successfully introduced by the Los Angeles Philharmonic on December 28, 1944. String Quartet (1950), when premiered in Los Angeles by the Compinsky Quartet in the year of its composition, led Albert Goldberg to say in the *Los Angeles Times:* "It is conceived on broad lines, employs the four stringed instruments in an orchestral fashion and maintains a consistent interest throughout." Jascha Heifetz commissioned him to write a violin concerto, which Heifetz introduced in Dallas with the Dallas Symphony Orchestra under Walter Hendl on January 25, 1956. John Rosenfield in the *Dallas Morning News* described the concerto as a composition of "unfailing spontaneity . . . dramatic excitement and everything else to insure it being heard often in seasons to come," while in the *Saturday Review,* Mildred Norton said it "proved to be that rarest of concert phenomena—a new work that is instantly accessible without being in any way trite." (In 1970, Rózsa used some of the material from this violin concerto in his score for the motion picture *The Private Life of Sherlock Holmes.*) *The Vintner's Daughter* for orchestra (1952), a series of twelve variations on a French folk song, was premiered by the Philadelphia Orchestra under Eugene Ormandy in 1956. The same conductor and orchestra also introduced *Notturno ungherese* (1964) on April 17, 1964, a work commissioned for the Philadelphia Orchestra by Edward N. Benjamin, music which the composer described as a "nostalgic nightpiece harking back to the memories of my childhood in Hungary." On September 22, 1966, the Chicago Symphony under Jean Martinon gave the first hearing to *Sinfonia concertante,* for violin, cello, and orchestra (1966). On April 6, 1967, Leonard Pennario, pianist, and the Los Angeles Philharmonic under Zubin Mehta were heard in the first performance of the Piano Concerto (1968). Pennario once again was the soloist when this concerto was featured by the Hague Philharmonic under Willem van Ooterloo during its American tour in 1969. Later major works include Concerto for Cello and Orchestra (1971), written for Janos Starker, first heard on October 6, 1971, at the Berlin Festival; *Tripartita,* for orchestra (1972), whose first American performance was given by the National Symphony under Antal Dorati in Washington, D.C., on October 12, 1976; *Toccata capricciosa,* for cello solo and orchestra (1976); and Concerto for Viola and Orchestra (1978).

In 1974, Rózsa made his first return to his native land in more than four decades to direct a concert of his own music. He has also been active as conductor of his own music throughout Europe, the United States and in recordings.

THE COMPOSER SPEAKS: I believe in the formal and architectural values of the classics, but on the other hand I speak my own musical language. I do not avoid dissonances if I can use them as intensification of my artistic expression and I am not afraid of consonant writing either when it suits my purpose. I never have any programmatic, literary or ideological associations in my music, as I believe music is a strong enough art to create its own abstract forms, expressing nothing else but the feelings of its creator. The years of my youth spent in the Hungarian countryside made a lasting influence on my musical style, and I endeavor to create a Hungarian symphonic music which tries to go deeper than just adapting the superficial characteristics of Hungarian folk music.

PRINCIPAL WORKS: Trio-Serenade, for violin, viola, and cello (1927, revised 1974); Piano Quintet (1928); *Variations on a Hungarian Peasant Song,* for violin and piano (1929); Rhapsody, for cello and or-chestra (1929); *North Hungarian Peasant Songs and Dances,* for violin and orchestra, or violin and piano (1929); Duo, for violin and piano (1931); Duo, for cello and piano (1931); Variations, for piano (1932); Bagatelles, for piano (1932); Serenade, for small orchestra (1932, revised 1946); Theme, Variations, and Finale, for orchestra (1933, revised 1943); *Three Hungarian Sketches,* for orchestra (1938); *Jungle Book Suite,* for narrator and orchestra (1942); Concerto for Strings (1943, revised 1957); *Kaleidoscope,* for orchestra, also for piano (1945); *To Everything There Is a Season,* motet for chorus with organ ad libitum (1946); *Hungarian Serenade,* for small orchestra (1948); String Quartet (1950); Sonatina, for solo clarinet (1951); *The Vintner's Daughter,* variations for orchestra (1952); Violin Concerto (1953); *Overture to a Symphony Concert,* for orchestra (1957); *Spellbound Concerto,* for piano and orchestra (1958); *Ben Hur Suite,* for orchestra (1959); *Notturno ungherese,* for orchestra (1964); *Sinfonia concertante,* for violin, cello, and orchestra (1966); *The Vanities of Life,* motet for chorus with organ ad libitum (1967); Piano Concerto (1968); Cello Concerto (1971); *Tripartita,* for orchestra (1972); Psalm 23, for chorus with organ ad libitum (1972); *Toccata capricciosa,* for orchestra with cello solo (1976); *Three Chinese Poems,* for chorus (1977); Viola Concerto (1978).

BIBLIOGRAPHY: Ewen, David, *American Composers Today* (N.Y., 1949); Palmer, Christopher, *Miklós Rózsa: A Sketch of His Life and Work* (London-Wiesbaden, 1975); Thomas, Tony, *Music for the Movies* (Cranbury, N.J., 1973); *Who's Who in America, 1978–79.*

Rudhyar, Dane (originally **Chennevière, Daniel**), b. Paris, France, March 23, 1895. American citizen, 1926.

Rudhyar has been described as a "Renaissance man." In addition to being a composer and pianist, he is a painter, poet, author, mystical philosopher, astropsychologist, and orientalist. In his music he was an early avant-gardist whose unresolved discords and polytonal and polyrhythmic writing made him an *enfant terrible* in the early decades of the 20th century. By his own admission, he has been influenced by Debussy, the neoprimitive Stravinsky, the late Liszt, and the late Scriabin. Rudhyar's music, not unlike Scriabin's, springs from inner experiences conditioned by metaphysical and theosophical concepts.

He was born to a middle-class family, his father, Leon Chennevière, being the owner of a small factory. Rudhyar's mother taught him to read notes on musical staves when he was still a child. He was seven when he started taking piano lessons at a small music school in Paris. He made sufficient progress to be able, before long, to perform at student concerts even though he disliked practicing and preferred spending time with books rather than music. He also failed to show much enthusiasm for solfeggio and harmony when these were taught him when he was about twelve.

Just before his thirteenth birthday he underwent a serious operation that permanently undermined his health while strengthening his spiritual resources, making him look increasingly more inward. He recovered sufficiently to continue his academic studies at the lycée, where he earned his baccalaureate at the age of sixteen, a year ahead of schedule. Soon afterward, he met and befriended a young art student who introduced him to the world of art as well as to the works of Nietzsche. Nietzsche's concept of life cycle so fascinated Rudhyar that only three months after he had first become acquainted with that philosopher's works he began writing a book outlining his own concepts of the cyclic development of civilization.

For about three and a half years he did not touch the piano. But a mounting appreciation of Debussy's music, intensified after a hearing of *Pelléas et Mélisande,* and a strong experience with the music of Borodin and Mussorgsky brought Rudhyar back to music. His musical appetite thus aroused, he now found ways of sneaking into auditoriums to listen to orchestral rehearsals, pocket scores in hand. This is the way he learned orchestration (in which he never received any formal instruction). Other lessons in theory were acquired in 1913 when he audited some classes at the Paris Conservatory and, later, when he briefly took a correspondence course in counterpoint.

In a postromantic style, Rudhyar began composing pieces for the piano. The first to get published was *Prière d'un enfant triste* (1912) followed by *Lament* and *Death March,* the three later gathered into a piano suite called *Three Poems.* Additionally, Rudhyar wrote a book, *Claude Debussy and the Cycle of Musical Civilization,* part of which was published in 1913. Debussy praised it and this led to a meeting with the master.

Rudhyar was now writing reviews for a Parisian journal which made it possible for him to attend concerts regularly for the first time. The premiere of Stravinsky's *The Rite of Spring* on May 29, 1913, had a cyclonic impact upon his musical thinking.

Because of frail health, Rudhyar was exempt from military service during World War I. For a few months in 1915 he worked as a secretary to the distinguished sculptor Auguste Rodin. At this time, Rudhyar became interested in an abstract, ritualistic type of dance-drama initiated by Valentine de Saint-Point called metachory (meaning "beyond dance") which applied recited poetry, colored lights, incense, and geometrical patterns flashed on a backdrop. For the esoteric dance performances, Rudhyar wrote *Vision végétale* and the three *Poèmes ironiques,* all for orchestra (1914–15).

A small inheritance enabled him to come to the United States in November 1916. On April 4, 1917, a festival of metachory was given at the Metropolitan Opera House in New York at which Rudhyar's music was heard, conducted by Pierre Monteux. The performance was a dismal failure as the audience found the new dance form and Rudhyar's music obscure and mystifying; nor was it in any mood to appreciate the new and totally unfamiliar performance on the evening of the day in which America declared war on Germany.

Rudhyar now moved away from metachory. He spent his time in the library studying oriental music and philosophy and Western occultism, which not only brought him new intellectual interests but a new identity for which he felt impelled to discard the name with which he was born for Dane Rudhyar. For a short period in 1918 he lived in Canada, where he lectured and gave readings of his own poems, some of which were gathered into a volume entitled *Rhapsodies,* published in Canada in 1918. In Canada, Rudhyar met the French-Canadian pianist, Alfred Laliberté, who introduced him to the music of Scriabin, which impressed him deeply for its interior psychic quality and its chord building.

During the summer of 1918, he wrote, as Debussy had done before him, the *Trois chansons de Bilitis,* for voice and piano, on words by Pierre Louÿs and *Mosaics,* a suite of eight pieces for the piano describing several phases of Christ's life, influenced by the late Liszt and in a sense evoking the future early works of Messiaen. But some critics felt that the works that came after that—*Dithyrambs,* for piano but later orchestrated (1919); the tone poem *Soul Fire,* for orchestra (1920); *Syntony* no. 1, *To the Real,* for orchestra (1919–21); and *Syntony* no. 2, *Surge of Fire,* for orchestra (1921), were unmistakably Scriabinesque. "They stem directly from the later sonatas and poems of the mystic Muscovite," wrote Paul Rosenfeld. "Rudhyar inherits the coolly aristocratic idiom built on Scriabin's 'natural' scale and overtones; finds the climate of music at the pitch of ecstasy; and recovers the Russian's erotically surging form. . . . The mantle of the mystic is upon him, too, through fascination with the Absolute . . . and a tendency to identify himself with it."

Though *Soul Fire* received a first prize of $1,000 in a contest sponsored by the Los Angeles Philharmonic, it was denied performance because it was regarded as "too modern." *Surge of Fire*—now scored for three pianos and a dozen other instruments, the pianos a basic element of the orchestration—was first heard on October 22, 1925, at the initial concert of the newly formed New Music Society in Los Angeles. "There were moments in this music," a critic wrote for the *Los Angeles Times,* "when a sensitive listener could feel the ruthless tearing of inner fibers immediately followed by an assuagement of beautiful sounds as comforting as a caress." *To the Real* received its world premiere in Paris on February 21, 1932, Nicolas Slonimsky conducting.

Mrs. Christine Wetherill Stevenson, a Philadelphian, founder of the Art Alliance and a theatrical producer, commissioned Rudhyar in 1920 to write the music for the *Pilgrimage Play* (based on the life of Christ), which she wrote and directed and which was to be performed in Hollywood, Calif. The first performance took place in July. Two years later Rudhyar wrote a second score for a new version of the *Play*.

After 1922, Rudhyar went into a two-year period of creative silence as far as composing went. He earned his living by playing bit parts in silent movies; appearing twice a day as Christ on the stage of Graumann's Egyptian Theater in a prologue for the Cecil B. De Mille silent movie *The Ten Commandments*; and with a friend opened on Hollywood Boulevard the first shop importing Indonesian artifacts. In his free time he wrote articles on political, sociological, and musical subjects. All this time he was becoming increasingly involved in oriental philosophy and music. Out of his studies of Eastern music came, in 1925, a long work, *The Rediscovery of Music* (still unpublished), and a shorter one, *The Rebirth of Hindu Music,* published in Madras, India, in 1928.

He returned to composing in 1924 with the first of the *Four Pentagrams,* for piano (1924–26), each consisting of five sections with each bearing its own title; these pieces were originally named *Moments,* and under that title were performed by the composer at a concert of the International Composers Guild in New York in December 1925, at a performance of the New Music Society in Los Angeles on December 11, 1926, and in a number of lecture-recitals given by Rudhyar. Tonality was abandoned and new piano resonances (which Rudhyar called tone substance) were explored here and in the piano music that followed in rapid succession. Between 1924 and 1929, he wrote seven *Tetragrams,* for piano, an eighth having preceded them in 1920, and a ninth to come in 1967. Each had four untitled sections. "They try," explained Leyla Rael in her unpublished book on Rudhyar, "to evoke various phases of deep processes of human transformation." *Three Paeans,* for piano (1925), premiered in New York by Richard Buhlig on May 6, 1928, was described by John J. Becker in the *South Bend News Times* as "tremendously conceived and for me indescribably beautiful . . . beautiful in their inherent content and beautiful in their logical upbuilding." Of *Granites,* for piano (1929), which Rudhyar himself introduced in Carmel, Calif., Henry Cowell wrote: "His style is built on piling up of resonant harmonies . . . his music has power, and can exert at times the very magical hypnotism he desired for it. He is a leader in his field." *Granites* became one of Rudhyar's most frequently performed compositions after the pianist William Masselos discovered it in the 1940s and performed it at his concerts.

Rudhyar wrote very little music between 1930 and 1949. After the depression and his first marriage he became deeply involved in an attempt to reformulate astrology according to new concepts—a field in which he became an authority and produced a number of books, including *The Astrology of Personality* (1936), which has become something of a classic in its field. He published a small magazine, *Hamsa,* and a mimeographed course of ten lessons, *Liberation Through Sound.* He wrote several volumes on philosophy and a good deal of poetry, some of which was published under the titles *Toward Man* and *White Thunder.* Abstract painting also became a major preoccupation from 1942 to 1952, for which he demonstrated an uncommon gift and which led to a number of important exhibitions.

A third creative phase in music began unfolding in 1949 with *Tripthong,* for piano and orchestra (1949); a Piano Quintet (1950), subsequently revised and rescored for chamber orchestra and renamed *Dialogues; Solitude* (1950), a string quartet version of one of his *Tetragrams,* whose premiere was given in 1951 by the New Music Quartet; and *Thresholds* (1954–55), an orchestral trilogy whose orchestration was long delayed but was completed in 1975 by George Champion in consultation with the composer.

Between 1959 and 1963, Rudhyar spent most of his time in Europe writing and giving lectures, but by the end of 1963 he was back in the United States, permanently settled in California. His later works, in addition to the already mentioned ninth *Tetragram* (1967), included two "tone rituals" for piano, *Transmutation,* in seven movements, and *Theurgy,* in five movements, both completed in 1976 after he and his new wife moved to establish residence in Palo Alto. These are two of his finest compositions. The move spurred a major resurgence of Rudhyar's musical creativity. He composed several other piano works, transformed *Tripthong* into a much longer work for piano and orchestra, wrote *Nostalgia* for an instrumental group (premiered in New York in 1979 by Relache), and two string quartets *Advent* and *Crisis and Overcoming,* recorded by the Kronos Quartet in 1979.

"Rudhyar's music," writes Leyla Rael, "is neither intellectually conceived nor abstract and formalistic. It is, in the real sense of the term, 'concrete,' or, as we might say today, 'experiential.' It is born of an immediacy of feeling-response in which the whole human being—the living person—is involved. It aims at producing immediate reactions to the whole being of the hearer. Ideally it should rouse in him or her almost 'occult' energies, a new vision, a new sense of livingness. . . .

"Rudhyar's music is seed music; it is evocative—just as are his paintings, his poems, and even his metaphysics and transpersonal astrology. All these modes of creative expression, as Rudhyar uses them, seek first of all to shake loose from their traditional thinking, feeling, and modes of interpersonal relating the persons to whom they are addressed. This is the first phase of the process, the deconditioning phase. As this occurs, the now disengaged and 'dis-committed' consciousness (and nervous system) of the hearer can open up a new realm of possible relating, thinking, and feeling-responses. Deconditioning, however, is not enough. It must lead to a state of receptivity for positive new values; and these should be 'evoked' by what the music implies and suggests."

Rudhyar was a charter member of the International Composers Guild, the California New Music Society, and the Pan American Association, the last formed in 1928 to promote new American and Latin-American music in the United States and abroad. In 1976 and 1977 he received grants from the National Endowment for the Arts and in 1978 he was the recipient of the Marjorie Peabody Waite Award from the American Academy and Institute of Arts and Letters. He was married four times: to Malya Contento on June 9, 1930 (divorced 1945); to Eya Fechin on June 27, 1945 (divorced 1954); to Gail Tana Whittall on March 27, 1964 (divorced 1976); and to Leyla Rael on March 31, 1977. He had no children.

Rudhyar's eighty-fifth birthday was remembered on March 20, 1980, in New York at a concert of the League of Composers–International Society for Contemporary Music, in which three of his piano compositions were given: *First Pentagram, Second Pentagram,* and *Granites.* "As these 1920s pieces indicate . . . he had vivid musical ideas in those days," wrote Allen Hughes in the *New York Times,* "and fused them into somewhat exotic forms that are still durable and satisfying despite their unconventionality."

THE COMPOSER SPEAKS: My works are not formalistic; they do not include the technical development, distortion, and inversion of themes or like procedures. They are essentially spontaneous exteriorizations of peak experiences; they are as condensed as seeds are. Melody and harmony are inseparably united in my most characteristic works, for the melody is an emergence from the resonant substance of the tones, or else a pure song evoking subtle harmonic resonances. It is not descriptive music in any sense, but it is evocative—as, in my opinion, any great art should be. . . . Western music is, alas, but too often "score music," to be seen rather than to be heard. A technical musician can hear with his eyes following an invisible score; he recognizes intellectually the themes of the "rows," admiring the skill with which they are developed. To me this has nothing to do with real tone-experience which should be the foundation and aim of music, no more than a discussion between intellectuals or a typical college course has anything to do with the existential realities of the process of living, growing, and dying—with the immediate experience of reality.

PRINCIPAL WORKS: (*Note:* Because so many earlier works were incorporated into later ones and because many titles have in later years been changed, confusion exists about the exact titles and dates of compositions of Dane Rudhyar. The following is a present-day listing prepared by the composer.)

Three Poems, for piano (1912–14); *Four Symphonic Poems,* "for the metachory," for orchestra (1914–19); *Trois poèmes tragiques,* for contralto and piano (1918, revised 1977); *Mosaics,* for piano (1918); Three Melodies, for flute and piano and cello accompaniment (1918); *Trois chansons de Bilitis,* for contralto and harp (1918); *Dithyrambs,* for piano, also for orchestra (1919); Three Poems, for violin and piano (1919–20); *Syntony* no. 1, *To the Real,* for orchestra (1919–21); *Unfoldment,* for orchestra (1920); *Spanish Rhythms,* "for a dance drama," for piano (1920); *Nine Tetragrams,* for piano (1920–67); *The Warrior,* tone poem for piano and orchestra (1921); *Syntony* no. 2, *The Surge of Fire,* tone poem for orchestra (1921); *Nazaria,* "scenic music for the *Pilgrimage Play,*" for orchestra, also for piano (1922); *Catharsis,* for piano (1923); *Three Paeans,* for piano (1925); *Five Stanzas,* for string orchestra (1926); Sinfonietta, for orchestra, transcribed from a piano sonatina (1928); *Granites,* for piano (1929); *Commune,* for baritone or mezzo-soprano and piano (1939–40); *Three Invocations,* for baritone and piano (1939–40); *Dialogues,* transcription of a piano quintet, for orchestra (1950–57); *Solitude,* for string quartet, transcribed from *Tetragram* no. 4 (1951); *Thresholds,* for piano (1954–55), orchestrated in 1975 by George Champion; *Transmutation,* for piano (1976); *Theurgy,* for piano (1976); *Poems of Youth,* trilogy for orchestra (1976–77); *Encounter,* "dramatic sequence" for piano and orchestra (1977); *Cosmic Cycle,* trilogy for large orchestra (1977).

BIBLIOGRAPHY: Cowell, Henry (ed.), *American Composers on American Music* (Stanford, Calif., 1933); Morang, A., *Dane Rudhyar, Pioneer in Creative Synthesis* (N.Y., 1929); Rosenfeld, Paul, *An Hour with American Music* (N.Y., 1929); "Dane Rudhyar: a Brief Biography," an anonymous booklet Berkeley, Calif., 1972); *Human Dimensions* (Rudhyar Issue), vol. 4, no. 3; *Who's Who in America, 1980–81.*

Ruggles, Carl Sprague (originally **Ruggles, Charles Sprague**), b. Marion, Mass., March 11, 1876; d. Bennington, Vt., October 24, 1971.

In a life span that reached the patriarchal age of ninety-five, Ruggles produced less than ten compositions. But the best of these is music of such exalted character that Ruggles's place in the Pantheon of American composers is assured. He was an American pioneer in the writing of linear, chromatic, asymmetrical music. His compositions are discordant, high-tensioned, with an incandescent intensity; at the same time he was noble, rhapsodic, and at times mystical. Each of his works is chiseled to perfection, each a remarkable exercise in organization, concentration, Spartan economy, and luminous sound.

He was descended from New England whalers and seafaring people. His mother was a trained vocalist whose singing was Ruggles's earliest musical memory. His desire to collaborate in this music making led him, when he was six, to try to construct a violin from a cigar box so that he might provide her singing with an instrumental background. A real violin was presented to him not long after that, upon which he learned to play by ear before receiving formal instruction from a local teacher, George Hill. By the time he was nine he was performing for summer visitors to Cape Cod, among these being President and Mrs. Cleveland.

His ambition to become a shipbuilder sent him to Boston during his teenage years to study ship design. But, in Boston, these plans were ultimately abandoned as Ruggles turned to more intensive music study: violin with Felix Winternitz and composition with Josef Claus. In the fall of 1903 Ruggles enrolled for special music study at Harvard University, entering the composition and theory classes of John Knowles Paine and Walter Spalding. It was at this time, spurred on by his enthusiasm for German music, that he decided to replace his Yankee given names of Charles Sprague with the Teutonic one of Carl.

In 1907, Ruggles went to Winona, Minn., where for a time he taught in a local school. In 1908, he founded the Winona Symphony, which he conducted for the next four years. In Winona, on April 27, 1908, he married Charlotte Snell, a professional singer from New England, who often appeared as soloist with the Winona Symphony; they had a son. To support his family Ruggles played the violin in theater orchestras. During his years in Winona he composed some music, but everything he wrote at this time was later destroyed.

In 1917, the Ruggles family came East, settling in New York. Ruggles soon affiliated himself with the avant-garde composers in New York and became active in such organizations promoting new music as the International Composers Guild, which he helped organize in 1921, and in 1928 with the Pan American Association.

A song for voice and orchestra, "Toys" (1919), written for his son, Micah, on his fourth birthday, was Ruggles's first composition he allowed to survive. This was homophonic music with an extended melodic line. In his next work, *Men and Angels*, for five trumpets and bass trumpet (1920), Ruggles remained homophonic and melodic, but at the same time he was moving vigorously toward atonality and dissonance. *Men and Angels* was Ruggles's first composition to get an important hearing when it was introduced at the first concert of the newly organized International Composers Guild in New York on December 17, 1922. It represented the United States at

the festival of the International Society for Contemporary Music in Venice on September 8, 1925. In 1938, Ruggles took a portion of *Men and Angels,* scoring it for four trumpets and three trombones, all muted. Now called just *Angels* it was introduced in Miami, Fla., on April 24, 1939. When *Angels* was heard in New York on February 27, 1949, Virgil Thomson in the *Herald Tribune* called it an "extraordinary and secretly powerful work." He added: "The texture of it is chromatic secundal counterpoint. Its voices, non-differentiated as to expressive function, are woven together by thematic imitation. The dissonance-tension is uniform throughout, hence, in the long run, harmonious, though that tension carries the maximum of dissonances possible to seven voices. Complete avoidance of the dramatic and the picturesque gives to the work a simplicity and a nobility rare in the music of our times. Its plain nobility of expression and the utter perfection of its workmanship place Ruggles as one of the century's masters."

Men and Mountains, for chamber orchestra (1924), is more dissonant still as Ruggles becomes increasingly atonal. The title comes from a line by William Blake reading: "Great things are done when men and mountains meet." The rugged individuality of this music and the discords, searing to ears not yet attuned to such harmonic excesses, caused considerable discontent when it was heard for the first time in New York on December 7, 1924. But a decade later, when Ruggles rescored it for large orchestra and it was given a new hearing—at a concert of the New York Philharmonic conducted by Hans Lange on March 19, 1936—the unresolved discords and atonality had begun to be a familiar language. The response, consequently, was more enthusiastic. Reviewing the new version in the *Herald Tribune,* Lawrence Gilman said of it: "Mr. Ruggles is well suited to set Blake to music. . . . The wild gigantic, tortured symbols of Blake's imagination, his riotous and untrammeled excursions in the world behind the heavens are all of a piece with Mr. Ruggles's thinking. There is a touch of the apocalyptic, the fabulous, and his fantasies. . . . He is a master of a strange, torrential and perturbing discourse."

With *Portals* (1925), originally for thirteen strings but revised three years later for string orchestra, Ruggles moved on from homophony to a stark, complex linear style. This linear idiom, and a conciseness and economy, would henceforth identify Ruggles's music. He never doubled a note in the harmony, and never repeated a note nor its octave in either the melody or the inner parts until the other seven to nine notes had been sounded. The inspiration for *Portals* was a Walt Whitman quotation: "What are those of the known, but to ascend and enter the unknown?" The first version of *Portals* was premiered in New York on January 24, 1926; the second, again in New York, on October 26, 1929.

During this period Ruggles was also hard at work

on an opera, *The Sunken Bell*, for which he himself prepared a libretto based on Gerhart Hauptmann's drama. He labored on it, on and off, for eight years. The Metropolitan Opera scheduled a premiere date, but before it arrived Ruggles had become so convinced that the opera had little merit that he tore up the manuscript.

It took Ruggles five years to complete *Sun-Treader*, for large orchestra (1931–32), which is often singled out as his finest composition. The quotation Ruggles used for his point of departure came from Robert Browning: "Sun-treader, light and life be thine forever." Nicolas Slonimsky conducted the premiere performance in Paris on February 25, 1932. Four years later, on April 22, 1936, it was heard at the festival of the International Society for Contemporary Music in Barcelona and after that in Berlin. But America did not get to hear it until three decades later, when it was given in Maine on January 24, 1966, by the Chicago Symphony under Jean Martinon as part of Ruggles's ninetieth birthday celebration. "Craggy, rangy, it is all contained power," Theodore Strongin said of it in the *New York Times*. "Its concentrated, close-knit dissonant lines surge and recede and finally rise to an apotheosis of a close."

In 1937, Ruggles came to Miami to become a member of the faculty of the School of Music at the University of Miami as instructor of music and to give seminars on modern composition. He remained in Miami a decade. His only composition in that time was *Organum*, for large orchestra (1945), its first performance given by the New York Philharmonic, Leopold Stokowski conducting, on November 24, 1949.

One of the reasons for the paucity of Ruggles's output—above and beyond the fact that he always worked slowly, was always revising what he had written, and was never in a hurry to begin a new work when he had finished an older one—is the fact that in or about 1935, while on vacation in Jamaica, Ruggles became interested in painting abstract canvases. Painting from then on was no dilettante hobby but an all-consuming interest to which he applied himself with total dedication. Except for a single musical work produced in 1958—*Exaltation*, for "congregation in unison"—Ruggles was through with composing; but he remained a painter—and a talented one—until the end of his life.

In the 1940s, Ruggles found a patron in Harriet Miller (to whom he dedicated some of his works). She first came to know him when he gave her some art lessons. A friendship developed which led to her subsidizing Ruggles for the remainder of his life. Permanently freed of the necessity of earning a living, Ruggles left Miami to divide his home between a hotel room in New York and a summer place in Arlington, Vt., the Vermont place being an old schoolhouse he had converted into living quarters and a large studio. When Ruggles's wife died in 1957, he

abandoned New York City permanently to spend all his time in seclusion at his Arlington home which, after his death, was designated as a musical landmark.

Both during his lifetime and since, Ruggles has been a composer more often written about and praised than performed. Few if any composers of his stature have been represented on major concert programs so infrequently as he. Nevertheless, on his ninetieth birthday, a two-day Ruggles festival took place at Bowdoin College in Brunswick, Me., where his music was played, his works and his place in American music evaluated in lectures and discussions, and his paintings were exhibited. The composer himself was too feeble to attend, and thus he was unable to be present for the American premiere of *Sun-Treader*, which he had never heard performed. A retrospective concert of Ruggles's music was heard at Columbia University in New York on February 19, 1976, to commemorate the centenary of his birth. The program spanned his career from the early *Angels*, through *Evocations*, for piano, which he had written between 1935 and 1942 and then in 1942 transcribed for orchestra (premiere of orchestral version in New York on February 3, 1971), and up to the 1949 *Organum*. At intermission time, a slide show of his paintings was presented.

In 1980, CBS Masterworks released an album of all of Ruggles's compositions, performed by the Buffalo Philharmonic conducted by Michael Tilson Thomas.

The honors bestowed on him were as sparse as were performances of his masterworks. The National Association of Composers and Conductors presented him with an award for his creative achievement in 1953, and, one year later, Ruggles was elected member of the National Institute of Arts and Letters. In 1966, he earned the Koussevitzky International Recording Award.

THE COMPOSER SPEAKS: Music which does not *surge* is not great music. In all works, there should be the quality we call mysticism. All the great composers have it.

PRINCIPAL WORKS: *Angels*, for four trumpets and three trombones, originally entitled *Men and Angels*, for five trumpets and bass trumpet (1920, 1939); *Vox Clamans in Deserto*, cycle for voice, chorus, and orchestra (1923); *Men and Mountains*, for orchestra (1924); *Portals*, for string orchestra (1925, revised 1941, 1953); *Sun-Treader*, for orchestra (1931–32); *Evocations*, for piano, also for orchestra (1935–42, revised 1954); *Polyphonic Composition*, for three pianos (1940); *Organum*, for large orchestra (1949); *Exaltation*, for "congregation" in unison and organ (1958).

BIBLIOGRAPHY: Archabal, N.M., "Carl Ruggles: Composer and Painter" (doctoral thesis, Minneapolis, 1975); Cowell, Henry, *American Composers on American Music* (Stanford, Calif., 1933); Harrison, Lou, *About Carl Ruggles* (Yonkers, N.Y., 1946); Rosenfeld, Paul, *An Hour with American Music* (N.Y., 1929); Thomson, Virgil, *American Music Since 1910* (N.Y., 1970); *Musical Quarterly*, October 1932; *New York Times*, October 12, 1958, October 24, 1971 (obituary); *Score*, June 1955.

Rzewski, Frederic Anthony, b. Westfield, Mass., April 13, 1938.

As an avant-gardist, Rzewski has touched virtually all the bases: electronics, improvisation, multimedia productions, postserialism. In his latest works he has evolved into a postromanticist whose equipment, as Alan Rich has written in *New York*, includes "elegance and delicacy of sound, an extraordinary command of rhythm that now and then brushes against some of the more interesting new jazz people . . . a way of using simplistic harmonies in a thoroughly original way." Some of his later works reflect his left-wing social and political thinking.

He was born to Polish parents. After receiving his early musical training at the piano mainly with Charles Mackey in Springfield, Mass., Rzewski entered Harvard University in 1954. There he studied composition with Walter Piston, counterpoint with Randall Thompson, and orchestration with Claudio Spies, graduating *magna cum laude* with a bachelor of arts degree in 1958. For the next two years he attended Princeton University for graduate work, studying philosophy and Greek literature as well as composition with Milton Babbitt and Claudio Spies. At Princeton, Rzewski served as Woodrow Wilson Fellow (1958–59) and teaching fellow (1959–60). He earned a master of fine arts degree in 1960.

Between 1957 and 1960, Rzewski's compositions were mainly for the piano in which advanced tonal and harmonic resources were used. These works included a set of preludes (1957); *Poem* (1959); Sonata, for two pianos (1959); and *Study* (1960).

Beginning with 1960, and for the next few years, Rzewski made numerous appearances as a concert pianist in contemporary works in which a formidable technique was matched by interpretative insight. As Nicolas Slonimsky commented amusingly: "He is . . . a granitically overpowering piano technician, capable of depositing huge boulders of sonoristic material across the keyboard without actually wrecking the instrument."

On a Fulbright Fellowship, Rzewski spent the years between 1960 and 1962 in Italy, where he was highly active in its progressive music movement. From 1963 to 1965 on a Ford Foundation grant, he was artist-in-residence in West Berlin. During this period he served as member of the faculty of the Cologne Courses for New Music (1963, 1964), to which he returned in 1970. In 1966, Rzewski was an associate of creative and performing arts at the State University of New York in Buffalo.

As a composer he was extending his horizons by producing a large-scale chamber music work, the Octet, for flute, clarinet, trumpet, trombone, violin, double bass, piano, and harp (1961–62), and by embarking on his early experiments. Among his first innovative works were *Self-Portrait*, "for one person and any sounds"; *Composition for Two*, for any two instruments; and *Speculum Dianae*, for any eight instruments, all in 1964. He was also beginning to work with electronics and multimedia productions: *Zoologischer Garten*, for magnetic tape (1964), and *Projector Piece*, for any two groups of musicians with dancers and slide projectors (1966).

Rzewski resided in Rome from 1966 to 1971. There he helped organize Musica Electtronica Viva (MEV), a group involved with experimental improvisation and live electronic performances for whom he composed *Work Songs*, using prose texts (1967–69), and his greatest success up to that time, *Plan for Spacecraft* (1968), both for improvising groups. Other major works during his Rome years included *Portrait*, for actor, lights, slides, film, photoresistors, and six tapes (1967); *Impersonation*, an audiodrama for two soloists, four stereo tape machines, and "mixer" (1967); *Symphony for Several Performers* (1968); and *Les moutons de Panurge,* for any number of melody instruments (1969).

Rzewski spent the summer of 1969 at the Berkshire Music Center at Tanglewood, Mass., on a Fromm Music Foundation fellowship. In 1971, he established his home in New York City, where he remained for the next few years before returning again to Rome. In New York he gained further prominence as a performer at avant-garde concerts and as composer. One of his most important works after settling in New York had a social-conscious context. He called it *Coming Together*, a work for speaker and instrumental octet (1972) inspired by the tragic uprising at Attica prison in New York in 1971. For his text Rzewski used a letter by one of its prisoners who was subsequently killed by a law-enforcement official. When *Coming Together* was performed in Brooklyn, N.Y., on April 6, 1979, John Rockwell said of it: "This is a piece that uses motoric repetition to suggest the tension, boredom, and passion of Attica prison before, during, and after the 1971 uprising. The piano and electric guitar form the basis of the ostinato, the other instruments either accent the music sharply or overplay it with softer, more flowing lines. It's a major work of this sort of music."

Rzewski composed two important works for the piano for Ursula Oppens on commission. *The People United Will Never Be Defeated!* (1975) is a set of thirty-six variations on the Chilean song "El pueblo unido jamás sera vencido!" Four Pieces, for piano (1977), is something of a sequel, though no popular song is used here. But, as the case had been with the earlier work, echoes of Spanish-American idioms are sounded. In these Four Pieces, a single melody predominates, occurring throughout, but each time in a different setting. When Four Pieces was performed by Ursula Oppens in Boston on December 12, 1979, Ellen Pfeiffer said in *High Fidelity/Musical America* they "present a luminous clarity of design as well as a riveting theatricality. The composer . . . obviously possesses a deep understanding of the resources of the keyboard, and he exploits those resources to the fullest. He makes use of the widest extremes of dynamics, of pitches, of textures. He makes extreme demands on the pianist's technique. And he colors everything with his own unmistakable and occasionally off-the-wall personality. His music doesn't sound as if anyone else could have written it." *Down by the Riverside* is still another impressive piece for the piano, its first performance taking place in New York on December 16, 1979.

On a commission from the New Hampshire Symphony, Rzewski completed *Long Time Man* in 1979, its world premiere given by that orchestra under James Bolle's direction at Dartmouth College in Hanover, N.H., on March 8, 1980. This work, for piano and orchestra, consists of twenty-four variations on the prison song "It Makes a Long Time Man Feel Bad," which Pete Seeger, the folk singer, had discovered and recorded in the 1950s. This song is heard at once in solo trombone. "Thereafter," reported Christian Wolff in *High Fidelity/Musical America*, "its melodic and rhythmic elements are fragmented, overlayed and reconstituted. The feeling of the song is somehow sustained and at the same time transformed into a music which sounds completely contemporary."

In 1972–73, Rzewski was a member of the music faculty of the New Lincoln School and, in 1973, of the Turtle Bay Music School, both in New York. In 1972 he received commissions from the New York State Council of the Arts and the Berlin Festspiel.

He has also been given a grant by the National Endowment for the Arts.

PRINCIPAL WORKS: Octet, for flute, clarinet, trumpet, trombone, violin, double bass, piano, and harp (1961–62); Requiem, for chorus and chamber ensemble (1963–67); *Composition for Two*, for any two instruments (1964); *Speculum Dianae*, for any eight instruments (1964); *Self-Portrait*, for one person and any sounds (1964); *Nature morte*, for instruments and five percussion groups (1964); *Zoologischer Garten*, for magnetic tape (1965); *Projector Piece*, for any two groups of musicians with dancers and slide projectors (1966); *Plan for Spacecraft*, for improvising group (1967); *Portrait*, for actor, lights, slides, film, photoresistors, and seven tapes (1967); *Impersonation*, audiodrama for two soloists, four stereo tapes, and "mixer" (1967); *Work Songs*, for improvising group (1967–69); *Symphony for Several Performers* (1968); *Les moutons de Panurge*, for any number of melody instruments (1969); *Last Judgment*, for trombone (1969); *Monuments*, for voice and piano (1970); *Old Maid*, for soprano and chorus (1970); *Falling Music*, for piano and tape (1971); *Coming Together*, for speaker and instruments (1972); *Second Structure*, for improvising group (1973); *Struggle*, cantata for bass and chamber orchestra (1974); *No Place to Go but Around*, variations for piano (1975); *The People United Will Never Be Defeated!*, for piano (1975); Thirteen Instrumental Studies (1977); Four Pieces, for piano (1977); *Song and Dance*, for vibraphone, double bass, bass clarinet and flute (1977); *Down by the Riverside*, for piano (1979); *Long Time Man*, for orchestra and piano (1979); *Moonlight and Memories*, for trombone and six instruments (1980).

BIBLIOGRAPHY: *BBDM*; *DCM*; Anderson, E. Ruth, *Contemporary American Composers* (Boston, 1976).

S

Salzman, Eric, b. New York City, September 8, 1933.

Salzman is an avant-gardist turned music-theater composer. Since the 1960s his work in multimedia and music-theater forms have gradually evolved into a concern for the creation of a new American music theater. Influences from media, technology, and the American vernacular are blended into an approach that incorporates layers of experience and style. He characterizes his work in this direction as being in the traditions of Charles Ives and Kurt Weill. These works are all through-composed, involving "cross-overs" or syntheses of elements from modern and avant-garde music and theater, the pop vernacular, traditional music, and even opera.

The theater is an inherited passion since Salzman's maternal grandfather was a song-and-dance man in the Yiddish theater and his mother wrote songs for the musical theater for many years in addition to directing a children's theatrical company for which she wrote the music. His father, Samuel Salzman, is a psychologist. Eric Salzman began his musical education on the violin at the age of seven; in piano he has been basically self-taught. When he was eleven, he discovered the minuets that Mozart wrote at the age of five or six and Salzman came to the conclusion that he could do equally well. From 1947 to 1951 he studied composition with Morris Lawner, principal composition instructor at the High School of Music and Art in New York City. While attending Forest Hills High School in Queens, N.Y. (1946–50), Salzman played violin in the school orchestra (which he also conducted briefly) as well as in a number of symphonic and chamber organizations in the New York metropolitan area.

Between 1950 and 1954 he attended Columbia University. There, his musical studies continued with Otto Luening, Vladimir Ussachevsky, and Jack Beeson. At Columbia he wrote music for several productions of the Columbia Players, a Suite for Violin and Piano, on American Indian themes (1953), and a song cycle, *cummings Set* (1953–54), both of which were performed in New York within a year of their composition.

He graduated from Columbia in 1954 with a bachelor of arts degree and honors in music. Between 1954 and 1956 he studied composition and theory with Roger Sessions and Milton Babbitt at Princeton University, earning the degree of master of fine arts. On December 24, 1955, Salzman married Lorna Jackson, who ultimately became a leading environmentalist and mid-Atlantic representative of the Friends of the Earth; twin daughters, their only children, were born in 1960.

A Fulbright Fellowship made it possible for Salzman to spend two years in Europe (1956–58) for the study of composition with Goffredo Petrassi at the Santa Cecilia Academy in Rome and to attend courses of avant-garde music as a scholarship student of Hermann Scherchen's, Karlheinz Stockhausen's, and Luigi Nono's in Darmstadt, Germany.

Salzman's music in the 1950s was in a kind of rhythmic expressionist style into which the influence of Ives and Edgard Varèse intruded. These works included String Quartet (1955); Flute Sonata (1956); Inventions, for orchestra (1957–58); and Partita, for solo violin (1958).

When he returned to the United States in 1958, Salzman became a music critic for the *New York Times,* where he remained for four seasons. In 1962–63 and again from 1968 to 1972 Salzman was music director of a noncommercial New York radio station, WBAI-FM, where he founded the "Free Music Store" and produced many contemporary-music programs including original works and productions. Between 1963 and 1966 he was music critic for the *New York Herald Tribune,* partially interrupted by a year in Europe (1964–65) on a Ford Foundation grant. In 1966 he began a two-year stay as assistant professor of music at Queens College in New York and an association as a critic with *Stereo Review* which has continued until the present day.

In Praise of the Owl and the Cuckoo, a cycle of Shakespearean poems for soprano, guitar, and chamber ensemble (1963–64), was a transition work between Salzman's earlier instrumental compositions and the later vocal and theatrical works. His first dramatic piece to deal with ideas about art and technology in a changed musicodramatic form came between 1964 and 1967 when he wrote *Foxes and Hedgehogs,* for four soloists, two instrumental groups, and sound systems to texts of John Ashbery. After its initial production on November 30, 1967, in New York, a radio version was widely broadcast throughout Europe. In 1972 it was performed by Pierre Boulez with the BBC Symphony in London and in 1977 by the Brooklyn Philharmonic under Lukas Foss.

The Peloponnesian War (1967–68), music for an evening-long dance-mime-theater work for solo dancer, choreographed and performed by Daniel Nagrin, received its premiere in Brockport, N.Y., in 1968 and toured widely in North America. *Feedback* (1968) is a multimedia participatory environmental work with visuals by Stan Vanderbeek. A modular structure with multichannel and spatial, audiovisual elements, is structured to involve the participation of local instrumental, vocal, dance, media, and theater forces. It was first performed at Colgate University in Hamilton, N.Y., in 1968 and was subsequently realized at various other American colleges and universities, in Buenos Aires, Argentina, and on a tour of many leading South American cities. A television version was broadcast throughout New York State in 1972. *Can Man Survive?* (1968–69) is a multimedia environmental work commissioned for the centennial of the American Museum of Natural History in New York on the theme of the environmental crisis. It was on display at the museum between 1969 and 1971; in 1969–70 a radio version was broadcast on WBAI in New York. "The essential effect of the score, as it were," reported Michael Steinberg from New York to the *Boston Globe*, "is in its overall form, and that represents a highly effective use of only partially determined form. What you hear depends partly on a combination of chance and choice (both the composer's and the visitor's). It is a question of whereabouts in the sound loop you tune in, how quickly you move through the exhibit and how long you choose to stay at any particular point in it, how selectively and intently you listen, where in each 'room' you stand, which determines the balance between the sound track for that space and what you overhear from adjacent spaces. These collisions between neighboring sound tracks are also calculated to become progressively more violent. In a sense, then, the viewer makes his own composition as he walks."

The Nude Paper Sermon (1969)—commissioned and recorded by Nonesuch Records—is a dramatic concert work for actor, Renaissance instruments, chorus, and electronics to texts of Wade Stephenson (Stephen Wade) and John Ashbery. In his review of the recording for *Stereo Review*, Don Heckman described this work as follows: "*The Nude Paper Sermon* consists, in effect, of a series of musical segments—instrumental solos and ensembles, choral passages, vocal solos and duets, sound effects, and the like—interrupted by and interspersed with a running narration. . . . The effect is not unlike the world of mass media suddenly gone wild, with a text that is sometimes specific, sometimes absurd, interrupted by whistling sounds, effects, electronics and voices." Its first performance and recording with actor Stacy Keach, directed by Joshua Rifkin, took place in New York in 1969. Subsequently, it toured the United States and Canada with Paul Hecht as actor-narrator, was given a new production at the Claremont Festival in Pomona, Calif., in July 1974, and, in a special version, was broadcast throughout

Canada through the facilities of the Canadian Broadcasting Company. "Salzman," wrote Alan Rich in *New York*, " has put together a work which comes off as a keen, rather harrowing reflection of a great many contemporary sociopolitical concerns. His piece covers a lot of ground."

In 1970 Salzman founded Quog Music Theater, which became the principal focus of his work in ensuing years. *Ecolog* (1971) was created with Quog Music Theater for the Artistic Television Workshop of WNET-TV in New York through whose facilities it was broadcast several times in 1971. *Saying Something* (1972) and *Biograffiti* (1972–73) were music-theater productions with Quog of a largely improvisatory nature and were performed at the annual New York avant-garde festival, the WBAI "Free Music Store," Space for Innovative Development, the Kitchen, Washington Square Methodist Church, and other locations in New York and elsewhere. *Lazarus* (1973) represents a return to written-out music theater in a simplified form. First presented at Washington Square Methodist Church in New York in 1973, it was based on a 12th-century music drama, telling the same events from a medieval and a contemporary point of view. It was restaged at La Mama Theater in New York in 1975 and subsequently toured in the United States and in Europe.

In 1975, Salzman began a series of words-and-music theater opera collaborations with Michael Sahl, a classmate of his at Princeton and himself a composer and pianist with a background in contemporary, pop and film music. Their first collaboration, *The Conjurer* (1974), was presented in 1975 by Joseph Papp in his Public Theater in New York with Tom O'Horgan directing. *Stauf,* "an American Faust" (1976), was produced in New York on May 28, 1976. In this new Faustian version, the protagonist is Stauf, a man combining "country virtue and city brains" who is determined to do good, joins a commune, and is perverted into corruption by a pair of gods who lead him to join Goodworks, Inc. This plot, said Raymond Ericson in the *New York Times*, "is a strong enough springboard for the songs, dances and dialogue scenes . . . the overall tone . . . is satiric, although in a search for variety it becomes compassionate and melodramatic at times. . . . The songs are cast in popular forms, jazz, blues, ballads, corporate hymns, and they are very good songs, often extended with the freedom with which thoroughly trained composers are capable."

In 1978 Sahl and Salzman were in residence at Pratt Institute in Brooklyn where their production *Noah* (1978) was introduced on February 10, 1978. Salzman explains that at the beginning of this work Noah is a "supercologist who sees the flood coming; a kind of do-it-yourself, homesteader type trying to make a living in a society whose values he doesn't believe in." He faces the contemporary problem of "how to survive without compromising yourself in a corrupt society." When the floods descend on Atlantis City, Noah signs a covenant with God and lands in New Atlantis populated by Indians, where he becomes a tycoon and dies in his 600th year. "What makes this unconventional stew work," said Peter G. Davis in the *New York Times*, "is the wildly eclectic but always sophisticated musical score. . . . The music . . . is wonderfully inventive, whether pop or bump-and-grind, old-time psalmody, Handelian aria, Wagnerian declamation, or just unaffectedly sweet lyricism. All of it is handled with such skill and imagination that each stylistic reference comes up sounding fresh and new."

While in residence at the Hunter Center for Lifelong Learning in 1978–79, Salzman and Sahl wrote and produced *The Passion of Simple Simon* in 1979. The characters here step out of the day's news and are treated satirically—from David Berkowitz through Mick Jagger. "It would be easy to dismiss *Simple Simon* merely as a smart-aleck satire of today's pop-culture stereotypes," wrote Alan Rich in *New York*. "What elevated the work for me was the degree to which both Salzman and Sahl have come to control their material; there are some deep, disturbing elements below the surface here, and some marvelous observations."

After *the Passion of Simple Simon*, Salzman and Sahl collaborated in writing an opera buffa, *Civilization and Its Discontents* (1980). It won the Prix Italia and was recorded by Nonesuch.

Although the mixture of musical and performance styles remains a major feature at such recent music theater (or theater opera) works, their evolution is strongly in the direction of greater simplicity, directness and dramatic form. The orchestrations of these operas have as much in common with a pop ensemble as with a classical or modern music group and the singers and vocal styles employed range from pop and theater to modern music and opera.

Since 1978, Salzman has broadcast extensively for National Public Radio, including a weekly program, *Five Minutes with Eric Salzman*. He has taught and lectured in the Institute for Studies in American Music at Brooklyn College in Brooklyn, N.Y. He has also become a producer for Nonesuch Records. He is the author of *Twentieth Century Music: An Introduction* (1967, revised 1974), and, with Michael Sahl, of *Making Changes: A Practical Guide to Vernacular Harmony* (1977), in addition to numerous articles to publications both in the United States and abroad, not only on music and the arts but also on the environment, natural history and conservation.

THE COMPOSER SPEAKS: The time has come to re-establish the age-old connection between live musical evolution and theater. . . . The new music theater really is opera—*dramma per musica*, theater through music, as Monteverdi put it. . . . The music may be an amalgam of popular, classical, theatrical, and modernist elements; the question is not style but veracity, dramatic truth. The music carries not only the mood and inner feeling but character and conflict. The interaction of drama and music lifts the most difficult of musical ideas out of the abstract and makes it immediate; at the same time it can also take the simplest and most familiar of pop clichés and give it new and even profound meaning. . . . Concert music has become too abstract, too detached from the mainstream of contemporary life. In theater, music is never merely an end in itself but part—the essential part in the new music theater—of a larger meaning. It's not what you do but how and why—and how well—you do it.

PRINCIPAL WORKS: String Quartet (1955); Inventions, for orchestra (1957–58); *In Praise of the Owl and the Cuckoo*, for soprano, guitar, and chamber ensemble (1963–64); *Foxes and Hedgehogs* (Verses and Cantos), for four soloists, two instrumental groups, and sound system (1964–67); *Queens College*, "an academic overture" for tape (1966); *Larynx Music*, for voice, guitar, and four-channel tape (1966–67); *The Peloponnesian War*, a mime-dance theater production for dancer (1967–68); *Feedback*, a multimedia participatory environmental work (1968); *The Nude Paper Sermon*, tropes for actor, ensemble of Renaissance instruments, chorus, electronic apparatus, and tape (1969); *Can Man Survive?*, a multimedia environmental work (1968–69); *Ecolog*, "a media poem" (1971); *Helix*, for voices, percussion, clarinet, and guitar (1971); *Voices*, an a cappella "radio opera" (1971); *Saying Something*, a music-theater program (1972); *Biograffiti*, a music-theater evening (1972–73); *Lazarus*, a music drama of the 12th and late 20th centuries (1973); *Fantasy on Lazarus*, for string orchestra (1974); *The Conjuror*, "fable in music of the posttechnological age," with Michael Sahl (1974); *Accord*, for accordion solo with optional singing and acting (1975); *Stauf*, "an American Faust," a music-theater or theater-opera work, with Michael Sahl (1976); *Noah*, a music-theater work, with Michael Sahl (1978); *The Passion of Simple Simon*, theater opera, with Michael Sahl (1979); *Civilization and Its Discontents*, opera buffa, with Michael Sahl (1980).

BIBLIOGRAPHY: *BBDM; DCM;* Thomson, Virgil, *American Music Since 1910* (N.Y., 1970); *Stereo Review*, April 1977.

Saminsky, Lazare, b. Vale-Hotzulovo, near Odessa, Russia, November 8, 1882; d. Port Chester, N.Y., June 30, 1959. American citizen, 1926.

As one of the founders of the Hebrew Folk Song Society in Russia in 1913, as a research scholar who went on an ethnological expedition to seek out the religious chants of Georgian and Persian Jews in Transcaucasia, and as the musical director of Temple Emanu-El in New York for thirty-four years, Saminsky's involvement in Hebrew music was wide and deep. As a composer of concert and religious music with a Hebraic identity he was a germinal force. But he was also the composer of much nonethnic orchestral music which was performed by some of the world's greatest orchestras. In this he was the romantic, bringing to his writing a rich instrumental, harmonic and polyphonic fabric, technical mastery, fresh approaches to tonality and structure, and a rich funded lyricism that often found its source in Hebrew music.

He was born to a middle-class family. His father (a devotee of the theater and literature) was a successful merchant in Odessa, where, for generations, the Saminskys had been merchant patricians. His mother was the musician in the family who played the piano well. Lazare Saminsky's early academic education took place at the Emperor Nicholas II Lyceum of Commerce in Odessa (1893–99). Academically, he was so precocious that at seven he could speak French and German, at sixteen wrote a commentary on Spinoza's *Ethics*, and at nineteen translated Descartes's *Meditations de Prima Philosophia* from Latin to Russian. In music, he began improvising songs when he was five. But musical instruction did not begin until his fifteenth year, when he received his first piano lessons; that same year he was writing compositions for the piano. His first serious study of theory took place at the Music School of Odessa during the winter of 1903–4.

Financial distress having struck the Saminsky family in 1902, Lazare was forced to earn his living for the next two years as private tutor and as a teacher of Latin and mathematics in Moghileff, in southern Russia. In the fall of 1905, he was admitted to the Moscow Philharmonic Conservatory, but a half year later was expelled and exiled from Moscow for having joined revolutionary circles and taking part in political demonstrations. He went to St. Petersburg (Petrograd) in 1906 to pursue academic and musical studies concurrently. Between 1906 and 1909 he attended the University of St. Petersburg, where he majored in mathematics and philosophy; during the summer of 1907 he published an essay on "Critical Analysis of Neogeometrical Conceptions and Generalizations." From 1906 to 1910 he was also a student at the St. Petersburg Conservatory, in the classes of Rimsky-Korsakov and Liadov in composition and Nicholas Tcherepnine in conducting. Saminsky made his conducting debut in 1907–8 with the St. Petersburg University Chorus and Orchestra; in 1908, he composed a string quartet (since lost); and on October 30, 1908, he made his first appearance as composer-conductor with a performance of his choral work *Ode to Mendelssohn* in St. Petersburg.

As a conservatory student he joined several of his colleagues, in the fall of 1908, to form the Hebrew Folk Song Society for research in and promotion and publication of authentic Hebrew music. He was its first secretary (1908–09) and, intermittently, between 1909 and 1916, he was chairman of its art and publication committee. Some of his compositions of this period were markedly influenced by his work with Hebrew music. His first ethnic compositions included the *First Hebrew Song Cycle*, for voice and piano, and *Hasidic Dance*, for violin and piano, both written in 1909, the latter published by the Hebrew Folk Song Society.

In December 1909, Saminsky made his professional debut as conductor with a performance of Glinka's *Russlan and Ludmilla* at the St. Petersburg Opera, and in April 1910, he conducted the premiere of his orchestral Overture in F (1908).

Upon graduating from the conservatory in 1910, Saminsky spent a year in military service in the Caucasus, where he first became acquainted with religious chants of the ancient tribes of Israel. Upon his return to the Caucasus as a civilian in 1913, he was commissioned by the Baron Horace de Guinzburg ethnological expedition to do further research in this field. In 1912–13 he was assistant music editor of *Russkaya Molva*, published in St. Petersburg.

On February 20, 1913, he was invited by Serge Koussevitzky to conduct the Koussevitzky Orchestra in Moscow in the premiere of his own *Vigiliae*, a triad of "poems for orchestra" inspired by texts by three Russian poets (1910–11). This work, though recognizably influenced by Wagner and Richard Strauss, represented an important step forward for the composer toward a music more cosmopolitan than his Hebraic efforts. From this time on, he would faithfully cultivate both fields.

Early within this ethnic fold were *Two Hebraic Lullabies*, for voice and string quartet (1914); *Four Sacred Choruses* (1913–14); *Second Hebrew Song Cycle*, for voice and piano (1913–15); *The Lament of Rachel*, a one-act ballet (1913) based on the biblical story of Rachel, Jacob, and Leah, scenario prepared by the composer; and *The Vision of Ariel*, a three-act opera-ballet (1916), libretto by the composer. *The Lament of Rachel* represented his first successful experiment using Hebrew chants and synagogal cantillations. This was material he would tap again and again in his later important Hebraic compositions, since he was vigorously opposed to the existing tendencies to incorporate Jewish domestic songs and foreign Germanic and Italian musical materials and styles into the writing of Hebrew music.

At the same time, during these years, he consciously withdrew from any Hebraic associations in writing *The Verlaine Song Cycle*, for voice and piano (1913); *Orientalia*, an orchestral suite (1913) in which he tapped non-Hebraic Georgian folk melodies; the Symphony no. 1, *Symphony of the Great Rivers* (1914), first heard on February 25, 1917, in St. Petersburg at a concert of the State Opera Orchestra conducted by the composer; and Symphony no. 2, *Symphony of the Summits* (1918), world premiere in Amsterdam on November 16, 1922, Willem Mengelberg conducting the Concertgebouw Orchestra. Both symphonies carry poetical quotations written by the composer to suggest the overall mood and atmosphere of the music rather than provide any specific program. Symphony no. 1 was inspired by the awesome sight of snow-capped Caucasian mountains. "Despite some old influences still in evidence," wrote Joseph Yasser in *Lazare Saminsky*, "the first symphony is a definite turning point in Saminsky's activity in that it reveals certain undeniable characteristics of which only faint suggestions could be found in preceding . . . orchestral compositions." These characteristics included the originality and freedom of the symphonic structure, the unusual tonality designed by the composer as (E-frimoll) a term he coined to designate a free minor mode, a free flowing polyphony, and a richly textured orchestration. Symphony no. 2, written in the woods of western Georgia (Russia), showed greater refinement in orchestration and polyphony, and is in the "free-major mode" of "H-fridur," another term coined by the composer. "This tonality," Yasser says, "in some way predetermines the serene 'mountain' mood of this symphony which is in this respect the opposite of the pessimistic 'Symphony of Great Rivers.' It is also more ecstatic than the latter and its religious pathos does not lack a subtle Chassidic strain."

Between 1915 and 1917, Saminsky was professor of composition and the conductor of symphony concerts in Tiflis. He spent the winter of 1916–17 on a concert-lecture tour of several Russian cities. In 1917–18 he was the director of the People's Conservatory in Tiflis.

The years between 1918 and 1920 were Saminsky's *Wanderjahre*. In Constantinople in January 1919 he lectured on Hebrew music; he traveled through Syria and Palestine between March and April 1919 giving lecture-recitals on Hebrew music; between May and September 1919 he lived in Paris; and, beginning with fall 1919, he spent more than a year in England, lecturing at universities in London, Oxford, and Liverpool on Russian, oriental, and Hebrew music, conducting choral concerts and a ballet season at the Duke of York Theatre.

In December 1920 he immigrated to the United States for permanent residence and citizenship. He made his American debut as composer-conductor on December 20, 1921, when he led the American premiere of *Vigiliae* with the Detroit Symphony at the invitation of Ossip Gabrilowitsch. His New York debut as composer-conductor came one year later, on February 5, 1922, when he directed the American premiere of his early *Four Sacred Choruses* at a concert of the Society of Friends of Music. Fragments of *The Lament of Rachel* were given by the Boston Symphony under Pierre Monteux on March 3, 1922, and on March 18, 1923, the New York Philharmonic presented the American premiere of Symphony no. 2, the composer conducting. Saminsky was also heard as a lecturer on "Music of the Russian Orient" at Harvard University in 1922.

On April 22, 1923, Saminsky married Lillian Morgan Buck, an American-born poet descended from old colonial and English families. Four years later, Saminsky was appointed musical director of Temple Emanu-El, a post he held with distinction for thirty-four years. In this office, in March 1936, he inaugurated and conducted the first Three Choir Festival at the Temple, which henceforth would be an annual event in New York, presenting choral music old and new. The tenth anniversary of these festivals was celebrated in 1945 with a series of concerts devoted to "A Hundred Years of American Music."

In New York, Saminsky became a vigorous participant in the promotion of new music, particularly new American music. In 1922 he was elected member of the executive board of the International Composers Guild, from which he (and five other directors) resigned a year later in protest to what they regarded as the comparatively conservative posture of the guild, to help form the more progressive League of Composers, of which Saminsky became a director. In 1923 he was elected member of the jury of the American section of the International Society for Contemporary Music.

All such activity did not deflect him from composing music abundantly in all forms, Hebraic and non-ethnic. Three religious services represent the cream of the Hebraic crop: *Sabbath Evening Service* (1925), *Sabbath Morning Service* (1925–28), and the *Holiday Service* (1927–29), all for cantor, chorus, and organ. With these came the opera-ballet *The Daughter Jeptha* (1928). His major works of nonethnic content or style were: Symphony no. 3, *Symphony of the Seas* (1924), introduced by the Colonne Orchestra in Paris, the composer conducting, in June 1925, and first heard in the United States on November 4, 1927, when Fritz Busch led a performance with the New York Symphony Society; Symphony no. 4 (1926; Berlin, April 19, 1929); *Venice*, a "poem serenade" for small orchestra (1927; Berlin, May 9, 1928); Symphony no. 5, with chorus, *Jerusalem, City of Solomon and Christ* (1929–30; N.Y., April 29, 1958); an Italian orchestral suite for small orchestra; *Ausonia* (1930; Florence, Italy, February 24, 1935); *Three Shadows*, poems for orchestra (1936; N.Y., February 6, 1936); *Pueblo: A Moon Epic*, for orchestra (1936), commissioned by the League of Composers and introduced in New York on February 17, 1937, by the National Symphony Orchestra under the composer's direction; and Requiem, for vocal soloists, chorus, and orchestra (1945), written in memory of his then recently deceased wife, its premiere given in New York on May 20, 1946. "His creative gifts are subtle and manifold; his musical speech is active and vibrant, yet with a secret tenderness in it," the distinguished French critic Émile Vuillermoz said of Saminsky's vast output.

Saminsky was the author of *Music of Our Day* (1932), *Music of the Ghetto and the Bible* (1934), *Living Music of the Americas* (1949), *Physics and*

Metaphysics of Music and Essays on the Philosophy of Mathematics (1957), and *Essentials of Conducting* (1958). He edited *Anthology of Hebrew Sacred and Traditional Songs,* for cantor, soloists, chorus, and organ (1948), and *A Song Treasury of Old Israel,* for voice and piano (1951). He also completed an autobiography in 1959, *Third Leonardo: Autobiography,* which was never published.

Saminsky's appearances as guest conductor and lecturer throughout the United States and Europe remained extensive up to the end of his life. In 1926 he was elected honorary member of the Royal Academy in Florence, Italy, for contributions "to modern art." On February 1, 1948, he married his second wife, Jeniffer Gandar, an American pianist.

THE COMPOSER SPEAKS: Nothing characterizes the music of our day better than its diseases as they sharpen the expression in so peculiar a way. These debilities are abuse of nourishment or underfeeding, the monotony of wealth or of penury. The aesthetic will and imagination of our day's composer—the city dweller, *par excellence*—suffer both from the putrefying luxury of tonal riches and from their unrelatedness. This is followed by a revulsion to tonal luxury and by greed for another extremity. A characteristic of clinical pictures!

The music of our time swings frantically from abuse of harmonic and orchestral color to conscious or instinctive rebarbarization.

Swamped by means, methods, proceedings or strangled by forced simplification, trying to stem the befuddling luxury with the device of *l'art dépouillé,* art stripped to the bone—our music has come to the point of simulating the scarecrow. . . .

As yet, we are not fully conscious of the sins of our aesthetic aspect; or perhaps we dare not confess to these sins.

All the brave doctrines of our day cannot veil the fact that the composer of the modern era lives in exceptional servitude to two strong agents, the means and the market.

PRINCIPAL WORKS: 5 symphonies (1914–32); 3 *Hebrew Song Cycles,* for voice and piano (1909, 1913–15, 1923).

Vigiliae, triad of poems for orchestra (1910–11); *Orientalia,* for orchestra (1913); *Four Sacred Choruses* (1913–14); *The Prophet,* cantata, for voice and orchestra (1916); *The Lament of Rachel,* ballet (1913; revised 1920); *The Vision of Ariel,* opera-ballet (1916); *Ten Hebrew Folk Songs and Dances,* for piano (1922); *Hasidic Suite,* for violin or cello and piano (1923); *Songs for Three Queens,* for voice and piano (1924); *Sabbath Evening Service,* for cantor, chorus, and organ (1925, revised 1927); *Six Songs of the Russian Orient,* for voice and piano (1925–26); *The Gagliarda of a Merry Plague,* opera-ballet (1924); *Sabbath Morning Service,* for cantor, chorus, and organ (1925–28); *Holiday Service,* for cantor,

chorus, and organ (1927–29); *Litanies of Women,* for mezzo-soprano and chamber orchestra (1925); *Venice,* a "poem serenade" for small orchestra (1927); *Ausonia,* "Italian pages," for small orchestra (1930); *To a New World,* for orchestra (1932); *Three Shadows,* for orchestra (1936); *Julian, the Apostate Caesar,* opera (1933–38); *Stilled Pageant,* for orchestra (1935); *Newfoundland Air,* for chorus and piano or organ (1935); *Pueblo: A Moon Epic,* for orchestra (1936); *East to West,* for violin and piano, also for violin and orchestra (1937); *Eon Hours,* concerto for four voices and four instruments (1938); *From American Poetry,* two choruses (1939–40); *Rye Septet,* for flute, clarinet, French horn, piano, violin, viola, cello with voice (1942); *Rhapsody on Dunlap's Creek,* for chamber orchestra (1944); Requiem, for vocal soloists, chorus, and orchestra (1945); *A Sonnet of Petrarch,* for three women's voices and three instruments (1947); *Western Psalm,* for mixed chorus, piano, and/or organ (1948); *Five Petalled Flame,* for chorus and orchestra (1949).

BIBLIOGRAPHY: De Paoli, Domenico (and others), *Lazare Saminsky: Composer and Civic Worker* (N.Y., 1930); Reis, Claire, *Composers in America* (N.Y., 1947); Rothmüller, Aron Marko, *The Music of Jews* (N.Y., 1934); Weisser, Albert, *The Modern Renaissance of Jewish Music, Events and Figures* (N.Y., 1954); *Who's Who in America, 1958–59.*

Schelling, Ernest Henry, b. Belvedere, N.J., July 26, 1876; d. New York City, December 8, 1939.

Schelling's compositions sounded so pleasant, were so neatly structured, and, when programmatic, so vividly graphic that their appeal was immediate. At least three of his orchestral works had important and repeated hearings when he was alive. But because his music lived in the romantic past, totally unaware that the world of music was changing in the 20th century, and because it lacked a personal profile, its success proved ephemeral.

He was the youngest of three children of Felix Schelling, a native of Switzerland, a philosopher, and theosophist who had been trained in music, had done some composing, and at one time was the director of the St. Louis Conservatory. Ernest Schelling's mother was of English birth. The three children were given their earliest music training by their father. Of the three, Ernest proved to be the musical prodigy. He made his first public appearance at the age of four and a half at the Academy of Music in Philadelphia. When he was six he was taken to Europe for comprehensive training as pianist: in Paris with Georges Mathias and Moritz Moszkowski; in Basel, Switzerland, with Hans Huber; in Vienna with Leschetizky. After one of his concerts in Vienna he was kissed by Brahms, and he performed for and was adulated by some of Europe's crowned heads.

Neuritis of the hands when he was sixteen seemed

to doom all hopes for a career as a virtuoso. Schelling returned to the United States for an academic education but after a period at the University of Pennsylvania in Philadelphia he dropped out. He spent the next four years teaching the piano.

With an improvement in his physical condition, Schelling decided on another effort at developing himself as a concert pianist. Paderewski, then in Philadelphia for a concert appearance, heard him play and was so impressed that he invited Schelling to study with him as his only pupil. Schelling did so for four years (1898–1902), gave a concert which was not successful, and became so discouraged that he sought refuge in a monastery for a few months. He emerged in 1903 to try his luck again on the concert stage. This time he was received so well that he went on an extended concert tour of Europe and South America, giving 186 concerts in eighteen months. He was back in the United States for his American debut as an adult, which took place in Boston as soloist with the Boston Symphony in February 1905. At that time he did not show to his best advantage because of an inflamed tendon of the right hand. But following his first New York recital on April 5, 1905, Richard Aldrich could say in the *New York Times*: "Through it all there was the note of sincerity and seriousness and fine and deep poetic feeling. There was sentiment in it that never lapsed into sentimentality and while his playing is continent in the expression of emotion and passion, it is not reserved but gives full utterance to a music nature that has felt much and gained understanding of much." One year later, Aldrich wrote that Schelling was "an artist of deeply poetic nature . . . and of a wide range of sympathy and expression . . . with a tone of fullness and beauty." From this point on, and for almost a decade afterwards, Schelling's appearances as pianist in the United States and abroad placed him with the most successful piano virtuosos of his time.

He had been composing music, mainly pieces for the piano, from his early youth on. His first compositions to receive major performances were for the orchestra, and revealed an indebtedness to Brahmsian romanticism in its luxuriant melodic content and rich-textured harmonic and instrumental structures. *Légende symphonique* (1904) was introduced by the Philadelphia Orchestra conducted by Leopold Stokowski on October 31, 1913. *Suite fantastique*, for piano and orchestra (1905–06), was premiered by the Concertgebouw Orchestra of Amsterdam, Holland, on October 10, 1907, with the composer at the piano and Willem Mengelberg conducting; three years later it was successfully performed by the Berlin Philharmonic. *Impressions from an Artist's Life*, Schelling's first highly successful composition, followed in 1913. This was a set of variations on a theme in which each variation described one of the composer's friends. It was given its initial hearing on December 13, 1915, by the Boston Symphony con-

ducted by Karl Muck. "Mr. Schelling," wrote Herbert F. Peyser at the time, "has written with cleverness, ingenuity, frequently picturesqueness of fancy and adroitness of expression." These variations were extensively performed by major orchestras. It was the first work by an American composer ever conducted by Arturo Toscanini when he presented it with the New York Philharmonic on March 14, 1929.

Just before World War I, a return of neuritis forced Schelling to terminate his concert appearances. When America became involved in the war, he enlisted in the army, seeing overseas duty from October 1917 to April 1920, rising to the rank of major. France decorated him with the Legion of Honor and the United States, in 1923, with the Distinguished Service Cross. Schelling was also decorated Commander Alphonso XII in Spain and made Officer of the Polonia Restitute in Poland.

The war, and the disenchantment that followed, was his motivation for writing his most famous composition, the orchestral fantasy *A Victory Ball* (1922). "I had come back from Europe still very much under the impression of the cataclysm," Schelling explained, "much troubled for the future, and was amazed to find that so few seemed to remember what the war really had meant, with its sacrifice of life and youth." While in this mood, he read Alfred Noyes's poem "A Victory Ball," describing a ball celebrating victory over the enemy while shadows of war victims hover nearby. To open his fantasy, Schelling quoted two army bugle calls, "Call to Arms" and "Charge," to usher in the Vision of War. There followed suggestions of a polonaise, a fox trot, a tango, and a waltz, interrupted by war calls from trumpets, a fragment of the Dies Irae in brasses, the bagpipings of Scottish highlanders and the treading of marching men. The work ended with the sounding of "Taps." *A Victory Ball* was given its world premiere by the Philadelphia Orchestra under Leopold Stokowski on February 23, 1923, following which it was heard at orchestral concerts throughout the United States.

Though Schelling never repeated a success of such dimensions, three more of his compositions were significantly exposed. For Fritz Kreisler he wrote the Concerto for Violin and Orchestra (1916), introduced by Kreisler with the Boston Symphony Orchestra on October 17, 1916. Divertimento, for string quartet and piano (1925), was successfully premiered and promoted by the Flonzaley Quartet, with the composer at the piano. *Morocco*, a symphonic tableau (1927), was given its first performance on December 10, 1927, by the New York Philharmonic, the composer conducting.

An injury to his hands incurred during an automobile accident in 1919 put a permanent end to Schelling's career as a virtuoso. He now turned to the baton. He served as the conductor of the Baltimore Symphony Orchestra between 1935 and 1938, and though he made numerous guest appearances with

American and European orchestras his fame as conductor rested primarily on his work with children's concerts where he came to be known as "Uncle Ernest." He initiated children's concerts for the New York Philharmonic on January 26, 1924, and remained their conductor until his death. He also gave children's concerts in Philadelphia, Boston, Cincinnati, Los Angeles, and San Francisco.

Schelling was twice married. His first wife was Lucie Howe Draper, whom he married on March 3, 1905. After her death in 1938 he married Helen Huntington ("Peggy") Marshall, a niece of Mrs. Vincent Astor, in August 1939. Schelling received an honorary doctorate in music from the University of Pennsylvania in 1928.

PRINCIPAL WORKS: *Légende symphonique*, for orchestra (1904); *Suite fantastique*, for piano and orchestra (1905–6); *Impressions from an Artist's Life*, for piano and orchestra (1913); Violin Concerto (1916); *A Victory Ball*, for orchestra (1922–23); Divertimento, for string quartet and piano (1925); *Morocco*, "symphonic tableau" (1927); Tarantella, for chamber orchestra, originally for string quartet (1936). *Also*: Violin Sonata; pieces for piano (Romance, Theme and Variations, Gavotte, *Fatalisme*, *Two Morceaux*, etc.).

BIBLIOGRAPHY: Ewen, David, *American Composers Today* (N.Y., 1949); Howard, John Tasker, *Our American Music* (N.Y., 1946); *Dictionary of American Biography*, Supplement 2; *New York Herald Tribune Magazine*, December 7, 1930; *New York Times*, December 9, 12, 1939; *Who Was Who, 1897–1942*.

Schoenberg, Arnold Franz Walter, b. Vienna, Austria, September 13, 1874; d. Los Angeles, Calif., July 13, 1951. American citizen, 1941.

It is doubtful if any composer had more decisive impact on the musical thought of the 20th century than Schoenberg. To few in music history has it been given the destiny to change the world of music as he had found it. Schoenberg was one of the chosen. He developed a new musical doctrine that broke with the past in favor of a new truth in which composers everywhere became believers. That doctrine is the twelve-tone system (dodecaphony), which he did not invent. Before him, Joseph Mathias Hauer devised a system based on "tropes," a tonal pattern in which themes were developed to the twelve tones of the chromatic scale without any note being repeated; this was the foundation upon which Schoenberg built his own structure. He developed the system with such technical skill, inexorable logic, mathematical precision, and creative imagination that it, and Schoenberg's name, have become virtually synonymous. Toward the end of his life, Schoenberg modified and sometimes even abandoned his method to bring political and human values to musical abstraction, making it a vehicle for emotion and drama denied to much of his earlier twelve-tonal masterworks.

He was the oldest of three children born to nonmusical orthodox Jewish parents of modest means, his father being a small-time shoe merchant. (Arnold Schoenberg converted to Lutheranism in 1898.) At eight, he was enrolled in the Realschule in Vienna, where, in addition to his academic education, he started taking violin lessons. After that he taught himself to play the cello. Without any knowledge of composition or theory he was writing music when he was twelve, mostly duets for the violin which he performed with his teacher. Despite his facility with music, he harbored no ambition at the time to become a professional musician.

When he was sixteen his father died, necessitating that Arnold help support the family. He left the Realschule in the sixth grade (ending his academic education permanently) to become a bank clerk. He continued to study the violin and cello with private teachers, one of whom was his friend Oskar Adler, participated in chamber music performances, and wrote some more compositions. He showed one of his works to Alexander Zemlinsky, who became so convinced of the boy's talent that he took him into his household almost like an adopted son. From Zemlinsky, Schoenberg received some training in counterpoint, the only formal instruction in theory he ever received. Schoenberg now played the cello in an orchestra Zemlinsky conducted and, in 1895, joined an amateur chorus.

His first composition of even passing consequence was the String Quartet in D major (1897), introduced one year later in Vienna. Schoenberg never assigned to it an opus number and it is not numbered among his string quartets; for a long time the manuscript was considered lost, but in time Schoenberg recovered it, and it was heard for the first time anywhere since 1898 in Washington, D.C., on February 8, 1952. In the late 1890s Schoenberg wrote numerous songs which were gathered in his first three opuses. Some of the songs were an echo of Brahms, though they revealed enough originality of melodic and harmonic thought to make them unpalatable to the audience. Wagner soon replaced Brahms as Schoenberg's composer for emulation. And it is the voice of Wagner, not Brahms, that we hear in Schoenberg's first successful composition and his first retained in the permanent repertoire. This was *Verklaerte Nacht*, or *Transfigured Night* (1899), originally for string sextet, but best known in its transcriptions for chamber orchestra (1917) and full orchestra (1943). As a sextet it was introduced in Vienna by the Rosé Quartet, expanded to six players at a concert of the Wiener Tonkünstlerverein in Vienna on March 18, 1902, and, for the most part, was well received (though one contemporary critic maintained that "it sounded as if someone had smeared the score of *Tristan* while it was still wet").

Verklaerte Nacht was programmatic music—something unusual for a chamber music composition—based on Richard Dehmel's opening poem in the collection "Weib und Welt." A moonlight walk by a man and woman is described during which the woman confesses she is bearing a child that is not his; the man listens, forgives, embraces her; they resume their moonlight walk, love having brought redemption. The composition is in five sections, the first, third, and fifth of which are tonal descriptions of the moonlit night and the emotions of the man and the woman; the second part, the woman's sad confession; the fourth, the man's compassionate reply. The atmosphere of the entire work was immediately projected in the introductory theme in the highest positions of the violins. The subject of redemption through love, the richly textured harmonic and contrapuntal structures, the sensuous melodic content, the chromaticisms, the passionately surging climaxes were all deeply rooted in Wagner. Many years after it was written and first performed, the music of *Verklaerte Nacht* was used for the ballet *Pillar of Fire*, choreography and scenario by Anthony Tudor, first produced in New York on April 8, 1942.

On October 7, 1901, Schoenberg married Zemlinsky's sister, Mathilde, with whom he had two children. The necessity to earn a living sent him to Berlin the following December, where he worked as conductor in a cabaret, "Überbrettl," and taught at the Stern Conservatory. In Berlin, Schoenberg completed *Pelleas und Melisande* (1902–03), based on Maurice Maeterlinck's play, written after Debussy's opera of the same name had been introduced in Paris. Though the whole-tone scale is found in the concluding pages of Schoenberg's score, the music is a luxuriant postromantic product in the idiom of Wagner and Richard Strauss rather than impressionistic; and it is elaborately contrapuntal. It was comparatively well received when introduced in Vienna on January 26, 1905, even though Ludwig Karpath in *Die Signale* called the score "not merely filled with wrong notes . . . but in itself is a fifty-minute-long protracted wrong note. . . . What else may hide behind this cacophony is impossible to ascertain."

In Berlin, Schoenberg completed two parts of a monumental score he had begun writing in 1899. It was the *Gurre-Lieder*, a work not only in a Wagnerian idiom but also of Wagnerian dimensions. It was scored for an orchestra of one hundred and forty musicians that included twenty-five woodwinds (among them, eight flutes), twenty-five brass (with ten horns), a greatly enlarged percussion (including chains), four harps, together with an eight-part chorus, three men's choruses, five vocal soloists, and a narrator. Special note paper of forty-eight staves had to be devised for Schoenberg to accommodate all his voices and instruments. For his text Schoenberg used nineteen poems by Jens Peter Jacobsen. It describes the love of King Waldemar I of Denmark for Tove,

to whom he presents the gift of a castle. When the queen of Denmark murders Tove, the king rejects God. The work ends with the vision of Death and the chorus singing a hymn to the rising sun. "The Song of the Wood Dove," in which the dove laments Tove's death to its forest friends, is a melodic highlight of the score that almost sounds as if it had arisen from the pages of *The Ring of the Nibelungs*. The final chorus and overall orchestration was not completed until 1911.

After receiving the Franz Liszt Stipend in Berlin in 1902, and briefly holding a post as teacher of composition at the Stern Conservatory, both made possible through the intercession of Richard Strauss, Schoenberg returned to Vienna in July 1903 to divide his energies between composition and teaching. Alban Berg and Anton Webern became his pupils in 1904; they were the nucleus of a small group of students who became Schoenberg's disciples and formed a Viennese "school" of music guided by the new principles Schoenberg was now slowly beginning to formulate. In March 1904, with Zemlinsky, Schoenberg organized the Vereinigung schaffender Tonkünstler for the performances of new music in Vienna, and it was there that the already mentioned *Pelleas und Melisande* received its first hearing.

One of the reasons the score of *Gurre-Lieder* lay unfinished for so many years was that in the 1900s Schoenberg was beginning to move in a totally new direction in his music, away from the kind of postromanticism he had favored in the first two parts of the *Gurre-Lieder*. He had become convinced that postromanticism had come to a dead end. He rejected the gargantuan musical structures, the grandiloquent language, the pretentious aims of Wagner and his followers. Schoenberg's artistic goal was now a music less emotional and more objective, less elaborate and more concise and precise. To achieve such aims he felt impelled to desert old concepts of melody, harmony, consonance, and tonality. His thinking became further crystallized through the acquaintance with the paintings of Oskar Kokoschka, one of the earliest Viennese expressionists, who produced on canvas what Schoenberg was seeking for music: an austere, unrepresentational art of distorted images and designs divorced from a world of reality.

Schoenberg made his first move into the future with the *Kammersymphonie* no. 1, for fifteen solo instruments (1906), in which tonality was treated freely to give the impression of atonality though not yet realizing it; in which unresolved discords replaced consonance; in which melodic and harmonic elements were built on the intervals of fourths and fifths rather than thirds; and in which each solo instrument was allowed independence of movement within the overall contrapuntal scheme. When *Kammersymphonie* was first heard—on February 8, 1907, in Vienna—it provoked outrage and denunciation. Schoenberg rescored it for full orchestra in November 1922 and again in 1935; the last version was premiered in Los Angeles on December 17, 1935, the composer conducting.

Once he had set his course, Schoenberg would not retreat. In the finale of String Quartet no. 2 in F-sharp minor with voice (1907–08)—text by Stefan George—the break with the past became total as the tonal center is completely eliminated to realize the first piece of atonal music ever written. "With the first notes, corresponding to the words 'I feel the air of other planets,' " wrote W. W. Cobbett in his *Cyclopedic Survey of Chamber Music*, "the hearer is at once in a new tone world." Schoenberg's orchestral version of this string quartet, still with voice, was introduced by the Boston Symphony Orchestra under Erich Leinsdorf in April 22, 1965.

In 1908, with the fifteen-song cycle to the poems from Stefan George's *Das Buch der hängenden Gärten*, "I have for the first time succeeded in approaching an ideal of expression and form that has been in my mind for years," Schoenberg said, adding: "I am obeying my inner compulsion which is stronger than my upbringing." After that came Three Pieces, for piano, op. 11 (1909), Schoenberg's first completely atonal composition, succeeded by the totally atonal Five Pieces for Orchestra op. 16 (1909). The Five Pieces was introduced in London on September 3, 1912, Henry J. Wood conducting. "Modern intellect has advanced beyond mere elementary noise; Schoenberg has not," said the critic of the *London Morning Post*. Five Pieces was once again received with hostility when it was introduced in the United States by the Boston Symphony under Karl Muck on December 18, 1914. But when it was given one of its later rare revivals in the United States—in the fall of 1948 at a concert of the New York Philharmonic under Dimitri Mitropoulos—Virgil Thomson called it, in the *Herald Tribune*, "among the more celebrated works of our century. . . . It deserves every bit of its worldwide prestige and none of its worldwide neglect."

Erwartung (1909) was Schoenberg's first work for the stage, an expressionist one-act monodrama for soprano and large orchestra. All that transpires in Marie Pappenheim's text is that a woman searches for her lover in the forest and finds him dead, the victim of her rival. In place of action we get a minute-to-minute development of the woman's inner emotion, along the lines of Freudian psychoanalysis. "Schoenberg adopted a new approach," wrote Abraham Skulsky in *Musical America*. "The purely musical elements . . . are as original as its dramatic form. Schoenberg breaks radically not only with the set patterns of clear-cut recitative and aria, but also with the unifying principle of leitmotiv. For the first time in the history of modern music there appears a structure in which no thematic elements are repeated. This procedure gives the music extreme variety and continuous invention." *Erwartung* did not get heard until fifteen years after it was written: at the festival of the International Society for Contempo-

rary Music in Prague on June 6, 1924, sung by Marie Gutheil-Schroder and conducted by Zemlinsky. The American premiere was a concert version by the New York Philharmonic under Mitropoulos on November 15, 1951, followed by America's first staged version in Washington, D. C., on December 28, 1960.

A counterpart to *Erwartung* is Schoenberg's second stage work, the one-act opera *Die glückliche Hand* (1910–13)—world premiere in Vienna on October 14, 1924, and the American premiere in Philadelphia on April 11, 1930, Leopold Stokowski conducting. The composer wrote his own text in which a man, lying on a darkened stage, is held captive by the paw of a mythological monster. A chorus laments the fact that the man is trying to achieve the unattainable. When monster and chorus disappear, the man goes through a series of tableaux in search of a woman representing power and wealth. He meets only frustrations and ends up once again the monster's victim. "In this drama," wrote the Belgian critic Paul Collaer, "the destiny of life in its entire span is condensed into a few decisive and supreme moments. There is no realism here, either, and we are transported into that dream state which reflects the almost visionary state Schoenberg lived in for the whole period from 1910 to 1914. . . . The music is even more unreal than *Erwartung* and is lit with almost heavenly colors. . . . [It] achieves, even more completely than *Erwartung*, the ideal of dramatic expression: all emotion is confined to the spirit."

The severity with which Schoenberg's music was rejected in Vienna drove him back to Berlin in 1911. There he was employed as teacher of composition at the Akademie für Kunst and as lecturer on aesthetics at the conservatory. In Berlin he completed one of his most celebrated and provocative works, *Pierrot lunaire*, a song cycle for speaking voice, piano, and five instruments (1912), in which his abstract writing reached its ultimate realization, an art totally removed from extramusical connotations. An identifying tonality is altogether dispensed with; the style is intense and concentrated; unresolved discords predominate. For the voice, Schoenberg devised the *Sprechstimme* or *Sprechgesang* (song-speech), a declamation in which the pitch is indicated rather than sung, with the voice swooping from one interval to the next. The voice becomes just another instrument in the ensemble.

Pierrot lunaire is a setting of twenty-one symbolist poems by Albert Guiraud, Pierrot symbolic of men's varied whims, moods, and emotions. But Schoenberg's music seems to have a life of its own, independent of the text it is setting—as remote, obscure, and abstract and tantalizing as the poems themselves but without providing any literal representation of the words. Because of this music's complexity and newness, forty rehearsals were needed before it was performed. When it was finally brought to the public—in Berlin on October 16, 1912—a riot ensued in the audience comprising laughter, catcalls, shouts of dis-approval, and even fist fights. "If this is music," wrote Otto Taubman in the *Börsen Courier*, "then I pray my Creator not let me hear it again." Later critics, however, accepted it as an unqualified mas-terwork, "the most striking and influential work of this period," according to Aaron Copland. "The har-monic daring of the work has no precise precedent in any other music; it bespeaks an extraordinarily keen aural imagination. Out of the few instruments called for, Schoenberg extracts an incredible variety of in-strumental imagery—and with the greatest economy of means. . . . The poems . . . have faded; nev-ertheless, with these poems as pretext, Schoenberg created a phantasmagoria that has retained its fresh-ness."

It is understandable why, when the now-com-pleted *Gurre-Lieder* received its world premiere on February 23, 1913, in Vienna to an audience that arose to cheer, Schoenberg should have regarded this, his first real triumph, with contempt. The public, which for some years now had been attacking him with almost unmatched ferocity, was now embracing him for a work he considered an anachronism. He refused to take a bow from his seat in the audience and, when summoned, refused to come to the stage. "For years, those people who cheered me tonight re-fused to recognize me," he said in explanation. "Why should I thank them for appreciating me now?"

With the outbreak of World War I, Schoenberg returned to Vienna. He was called twice to military service, from December 1915 to September 1916 and from July to October 1917. Because of his age he was assigned only to garrison duty in Vienna. During this period he taught music at the Seminary for Com-position, which he founded in 1915. Once out of uni-form, Schoenberg made his home in the Viennese suburb of Mödling, where he taught composition and was surrounded by his disciples. His wife, Mathilde, with whom he had two children, died in 1923. On August 26, 1924, he married Gertrud Kolisch, sister of the violinist Rudolf Kolisch who had been one of his pupils. Of their three children, a daughter, Nu-ria, became the wife of the avant-garde composer Luigi Nono.

Between 1918 and 1933 Schoenberg spent part of the year in Vienna and part of it in Berlin. In Vien-na, in 1918, he formed the Society for Private Mu-sical Performances, an organization devoted to concerts of the music of Schoenberg and his followers at concerts from which critics were banned and where applause was forbidden. In Berlin, in 1925, he received the lifetime appointment of professor of composition at the Prussian Academy of Art in succession to Ferruc-cio Busoni, an appointment abruptly terminated when the Nazis came to power.

The years of World War I, which had interrupted Schoenberg's creative output, brought reevaluation and self-analysis. Schoenberg now felt that atonality had been an invitation to anarchy, that what he now needed was the discipline of a new set of principles, a new method, to replace the older ones. Thus he em-braced and developed the twelve-tone system. He used a twelve-tone row for the first time in the con-cluding movement (a waltz) in Five Pieces, for piano, op. 23 (1923) and in the fourth movement of his Serenade, for instruments, op. 24 (1923). The first work entirely in the twelve-tone system was the Suite, for piano, op. 25 (1924). After that, the twelve-tone system became basic to his major compo-sitions: String Quartet no. 3 (1927; Vienna, Septem-ber 19, 1927); Variations for Orchestra (1928; Ber-lin, December 2, 1928); Piano Pieces op. 33a (1929); Violin Concerto (1936; Philadelphia, December 6, 1940); Piano Concerto (1942; N. Y., February 6, 1944); and *Kammersymphonie* no. 2 (1939; N.Y., December 15, 1940).

With the rise of nazism in Germany, Schoenberg left for Paris in May 1933. There, as a gesture of sympathy with the persecuted Jews of Germany, he went through a religious ceremony in which he re-turned to the religion of his birth. Then, on October 31, 1933, he came to the United States, where he was to live the rest of his life, and became a citizen. He spent a few months in Brookline, Mass., while hold-ing a post as teacher of composition at the Malkin School of Music in Boston. Then his chronic asthma made him seek a warmer climate. In 1934 he found a new, and his last, home in Brentwood, Calif. In 1935 he was professor of music at the University of South-ern California and between 1936 and 1944 he held a similar post at the University of California in Los Angeles. Subsequently, until a month before his death, his teaching was confined solely to a few pri-vate students.

The tragic political developments first in Germany and then in Austria, which led him to renounce his German past (to the point where he insisted upon Anglicizing his name from Schönberg to Schoenberg) and the Lutheranism to which he had been con-verted, had an overwhelming impact on the music he would henceforth write. Its insularity was shattered and so was its total abstraction. Schoenberg now sought to make his music the voice of his newly found political and religious convictions as well as an ex-pression of his inner torment. He would now turn to the writing of such Hebraic works as *Kol Nidre* (the prayer intoned on the eve of the Day of Atonement when Jews expiate their sins), scored for speaker, chorus, and orchestra (1938). In 1951 he resumed work on a biblical opera, *Moses und Aron*, which he had begun writing in 1930 and then laid aside, but which he did not live to finish. This opera, based on a single twelve-tone row, is one of Schoenberg's crown-ing masterworks. It was introduced, in its incomplete state, in a concert version over the Hamburg radio in Germany on March 12, 1954; then was given suc-cessful stage presentations in Europe's principal cit-ies including performances at Covent Garden in London, where it scored a major success before receiving its American premiere on November 30, 1966, in Boston. The distinguished Austrian critic Hans F. Redlich said of it: "Its very sound—mysterious, visionary, frenzied, triumphant in turns—is as unique as its mixture of elements of opera, oratorio, and cantata, serving together in the transmission of a tremendous religious experience. When the music ebbs away prematurely at the end of Act II—with Moses despairing of his vocation in a moving passage combining instrumental melody and *Sprech-stimme*—an artistic and a human experience has reached its consummation which may well represent to future generations the musical highwater mark of this century."

In addition to his racial compositions, Schoenberg produced two major politically oriented compositions. *Ode to Napoleon*, for speaking voice, piano, and string orchestra (1942), a setting of Byron's poem of that name, denounced dictatorship and praised democratic freedom. It was premiered by the New York Philharmonic under Artur Rodzinski on November 23, 1944. *A Survivor from Warsaw*, a cantata for narrator, men's chorus, and orchestra to his own text (1947; Albuquerque, N.M., November 4, 1948), was inspired by the heroism of the Jews in the ghetto of Warsaw in resisting the Nazi war machine with primitive weapons for a month before annihilation. Though both works are basically in the twelve-tone system, it is used with freedom and resiliency to allow for human and dramatic values, and at times even for programmatic writing.

Though he was receiving important performances and honors in the United States, Schoenberg's memories of past attacks continued to embitter him. When, in 1944, his seventieth birthday was celebrated in the United States with nationwide tributes and performances, including several all-Schoenberg concerts, his response to some of their sponsors was: "For many years I have resigned myself to the fact that I cannot hope for a full and appreciative understanding of my work—for what I have to say as a musician." In 1947 he was given a Special Award of Distinguished Achievement by the National Institute of Arts and Letters, to which he replied acidly that such honor belonged more rightfully to his many enemies since it was they who made him famous. One year later, he was upset to discover that Thomas Mann, in his novel *Doktor Faustus*, used a twelve-tone composer as central character. Even though Mann took pains to explain in an introductory statement that the twelve-tone system was the property of Arnold Schoenberg and that passages in the novel dealing with musical theory were taken from Schoenberg's treatise *Harmonielehre* (1911, published in the United States in 1947 under the title of *Theory of Harmony*), Schoenberg angrily accused Mann of "stealing my literary property . . . ascribing my creation to another person which, in spite of being fictitious, is represented as a living man."

But, after 1948, he began to grow mellow. He was now able to accept tributes from his native city of Vienna gracefully and even spoke of returning to Austria, though this never materialized. And he warmly welcomed the worldwide recognition he received on his seventy-fifth birthday.

Throughout his life, Schoenberg was excessively superstitious, particularly pertaining to the number thirteen, which he regarded as an evil omen because he had been born on the thirteenth of the month. When he was seventy-five he was convinced that this was his last year since the numbers seven and six add up to thirteen. He did die that year, death arriving thirteen minutes before midnight on the thirteenth of July. His last work was an incomplete setting of a psalm.

A year after his death, a street in Vienna was named after him. On the centenary of his birth, his ashes were brought back to Vienna (June 5, 1974) for burial in the city's Central Cemetery. At that time, a Schoenberg Congress was convened in Vienna for lectures, seminars, concerts, and an exhibition. A tablet was affixed to his home in Mödling, now become a museum. In the United States posthumous honors included a three-program festival of his music at the University of Southern California in Los Angeles and the opening of a Schoenberg Institute on the campus on February 20, 1979. Even before that dedication, a publication, *Journal of the Arnold Schoenberg Institute*, was launched in 1976 under the editorship of Leonard Stein.

In addition to *Theory of Harmony*, Schoenberg was the author of *Models for Beginners in Composition* (1942) and *Style and Idea* (1950).

THE COMPOSER SPEAKS: What I did was neither revolution, nor anarchy, but evolution. . . . My music must be listened to in the very same way as is any other music—forget the theories, the twelve-tone method, the dissonance, and so forth, and may I add: If possible, try to forget the composer too. I once said in a lecture: "A Chinese poet talks Chinese, but what does he say?" To this I add: It is my private business to write in this or that style, to use one or another method—this should not be of interest to the listener. But I do want my mission to be understood and accepted.

PRINCIPAL WORKS: 4 string quartets (1905–36); 2 *Kammersymphonien* (1906, 1940).

Verklaerte Nacht, for string sextet, also for chamber orchestra and large orchestra, op. 4 (1899); *Gurre-Lieder*, for speaker, vocal soloists, eight-part chorus, three men's choruses and orchestra (1901–11); *Pelleas und Melisande*, tone poem for orchestra, op. 5 (1902–03); *Friede auf Erden*, for chorus, op. 13 (1907); Fifteen Songs, for voice and piano, op. 15, (1908); Five Pieces, for orchestra, op. 16 (1909, revised 1949); *Erwartung*, one-act monodrama, op. 17 (1909); Three Pieces, for piano, op. 11 (1909); *Die glückliche Hand*, one-act drama with music, op. 18

(1910–13); Six Small Piano Pieces op. 19 (1911); *Pierrot lunaire*, melodrama for *Sprechstimme* and instruments, op. 21 (1912); *Die Jacobsleiter*, incomplete oratorio (1913); Four Songs, for voice and orchestra, op. 22 (1914–15); Five Pieces, for piano, op. 23 (1924); Serenade, for instruments with baritone, op. 24 (1924); Suite for Piano op. 25 (1924); Quintet, for flute, oboe, clarinet, horn, and bassoon, op. 26 (1924); Four pieces, for chorus, op. 27 (1925); *Three Satires*, for chorus, the first two a cappella, the third with instruments, op. 28 (1925); Variations, for orchestra, op. 31 (1926–28); Suite, for two clarinets, bass clarinet, violin, viola, cello, and piano, op. 29 (1927); Piano Piece op. 35a (1929); Six Pieces, for men's chorus, op. 35 (1930); *Moses und Aron*, incomplete opera (1930–51); Piano Piece op. 33b (1932); Violin Concerto op. 36 (1936); *Kol Nidre*, for speaker, chorus, and orchestra, op. 39 (1938); Variations and Recitative, for piano, op. 40 (1940); Piano Concerto op. 42 (1941); *Ode to Napoleon*, for speaker, strings, and piano, op. 41 (1942); Theme and Variations, for orchestra, op. 43 (1943); *A Survivor from Warsaw*, cantata for narrator, chorus, and orchestra, op. 46 (1947); Fantasia, for violin and piano (1949); *Dreimal tausend Jahre*, for a cappella chorus, op. 50a (1949).

BIBLIOGRAPHY: Armitage, Merle (ed.), *Arnold Schoenberg* (N.Y., 1937); Ewen, David (ed.), *The New Book of Modern Composers*, revised ed. (N.Y., 1961); MacDonald, Malcolm, *Schoenberg* (London, 1977); Newlin, Dika, *Schoenberg Remembered: Diaries and Recollections* (N.Y., 1980); Reich, Willi, *Schoenberg* (N.Y., 1971); Rosen, Charles, *Arnold Schoenberg* (N.Y., 1975); Stein, Erwin (ed.), *Letters of Arnold Schoenberg* (London, 1974); Stuckenschmidt, H. H., *Arnold Schoenberg: His Life, World and Work* (London, 1976); *High Fidelity/Musical America*, August 1971, September 1974; *Musical Quarterly*, October 1944, October 1951, April 1978; *New York Times* (obituary), July 15, 1951; *New York Times Magazine*, September 11, 1949; *Saturday Review*, January 30, 1960; *Stereo Review*, September 1974.

Schuller, Gunther, b. New York City, November 22, 1925.

On August 27, 1957, Schuller coined the phrase "third stream" to identify a musical style combining contemporary classical forms with jazz improvisation, jazz vocabulary, and jazz instrumentation. In that style, he produced a number of major works, including an opera. But many of his important compositions are not jazz oriented, but derive their techniques from the atonality of the Viennese school and subsequently from post-Webern serialism as well as Stravinsky and such early influences as Scriabin and Ravel. The most important influences to give shape and direction to Schuller's music are jazz, Schoen-

berg, Stravinsky, and Milton Babbitt. Some of Schuller's most significant works owe their subject matter to great paintings, and some of their titles reflect styles in painting.

He was born to a family of professional musicians. His paternal grandfather had been a bandmaster and music teacher in Germany, and his father, Arthur Schuller, was violinist with the New York Philharmonic for forty-two years. Gunther Schuller was one of two sons. When he was seven, he was sent off to Germany, where he spent four years in a private boarding school near Erfurt, in what is now East Germany (1932–36). In his twelfth year he was enrolled in the St. Thomas Church Choir School in New York City, where he appeared as boy soprano and spent three years (1937–40) studying, along with regular academic courses, harmony and counterpoint with T. Tertius Noble, as well as the flute and, later, the French horn. At twelve, he made his first attempts at composition. He continued his academic education in the city public schools and at Jamaica High School in Jamaica, Queens, N.Y., while also attending the Manhattan School of Music for courses in theory and counterpoint and further study of the French horn with Robert Schulze. By 1942, when he left Jamaica High School and the Manhattan School of Music, both his academic and musical education were over. From then on, he was entirely self-taught in both areas.

Schuller was sixteen when he made his professional debut as musician by filling a chair in the French horn section of the New York Philharmonic, in the first concert hall presentation of Shostakovich's Symphony no. 7, the *Leningrad*, on October 14, 1942. In January 1943 he was engaged as second French horn for the touring orchestra of the Ballet Theater conducted by Antal Dorati. In the fall of 1943, as principal French horn player, he joined the Cincinnati Symphony then led by Eugene Goossens.

Two significant developments in Cincinnati opened up new musical vistas for Schuller. On April 16, 1945, Schuller made his official debut as composer by performing his own Concerto for French Horn and Orchestra no. 1 (1944) with the Cincinnati Symphony under Goossens. And, in 1943, Schuller heard for the first time a live performance by Duke Ellington. He was so fascinated by this concert and soon became so interested in many of the great bands of this period that he began making symphonic arrangements of Ellington's music for the Cincinnati Symphony "pop" concerts. Though this enthusiasm for Ellington never waned (in 1955, Schuller composed *Symphonic Tribute to Duke Ellington*), other jazz influences were soon absorbed, particularly those of Charlie Parker, Dizzy Gillespie and the new bebop movement. In 1950, Schuller was playing the French horn in a nine-man ensemble led by Miles Davis, with whom he recorded *Birth of the Cool*. Another significant jazz affiliation was the one with John Lewis, jazz pianist, and his Modern Jazz

Quartet, for which Schuller wrote a number of jazz compositions and arrangements. He also recorded with numerous other jazz ensembles such as those of Gil Evans and Lalo Schifrin.

While in Cincinnati, Schuller taught horn at the Cincinnati College of Music and the Cincinnati Conservatory of Music (which subsequently merged). One of the students in voice and piano at the college was Marjorie Black. They were married in New York City on June 8, 1948, and raised two sons, both of whom became jazz musicians.

Between 1945 and 1959, Schuller played the French horn in the orchestra of the Metropolitan Opera, occupying the first desk for nine of those years. While serving in that orchestra, he was intensifying his efforts at composition, producing three chamber music works in 1947–48 (Quartet, for four double basses; *Fantasia concertante*, for three oboes and piano; and Trio, for oboe, horn and viola) together with *Symphonic Study*, for orchestra, which was introduced in Cincinnati in 1948 and later revised for a slightly reduced orchestra. In these works, as well as in *Atonal Studies in Jazz*, for winds and jazz drums (1948), he was beginning to assume an atonal idiom.

His first significant success came with Symphony for Brass and Percussion (1950), one of Schuller's early twelve-tone works, which attempted to fuse an advanced harmonic language and dissonant counterpoint with classical forms and structures. After it was introduced by Leon Barzin in New York in 1950 at a concert of the International Society for Contemporary Music, it was given its first major performance in 1956 by the New York Philharmonic under Dimitri Mitropoulos, and its European premiere at the Salzburg Festival in Austria in 1957. *Dramatic Overture* (1951) was performed in Darmstadt, Germany, in the spring of 1957. Recitative and Rondo, originally for violin and piano (1953), then, in 1955, scored for violin and orchestra, was given its orchestral world premiere ten years later in Holland with Bruno Maderna conducting and its American premiere by the Chicago Symphony conducted by Seiji Ozawa at the Ravinia Festival. String Quartet (1957) was commissioned by the Fromm Music Foundation for the 1957 Festival of Contemporary Arts at the University of Illinois in Urbana, the last movement incorporating some brief aleatory and improvised sections.

Schuller continued to use jazz elements in some of his concert music. He followed the already mentioned *Symphonic Tribute to Duke Ellington* of 1955 with *12 by 11* (1955) and *Transformation* (1956), both for chamber jazz groups, and Concertino, for jazz quartet and orchestra (1959). The last of these was introduced by the Baltimore Symphony Orchestra in 1959 with the collaboration of the Modern Jazz Quartet.

Schuller was also moving more and more toward innovation and experiment. *Spectra*, for orchestra (1958), written (like all his works since 1950) in the twelve-tone idiom, advanced structurally and acoustically to new directions. It was commissioned by Dimitri Mitropoulos and the New York Philharmonic, which introduced it on January 14, 1960. It represented the United States at the festival of the International Society for Contemporary Music in Cologne, Germany, on June 12, 1960. "The title, *Spectra* (suggesting an analogy with the color spectrum)," the composer explained, "refers to the use of various color series as an important all-pervading structural element of the work. This is in terms of Schoenberg's concept of *Klangfarbenmelodie* (literally, tone-color-melody)—the concept of a melody undergoing a number of color or timbre changes during its course." Structurally, the work was as unconventional in that its one-movement format had, as Schuller said, "no preconceived formal mold into which the music could be formed. In terms of form, the work literally unfolded itself." The other innovation was of a "physical-acoustical nature." He now devised a seating plan which divided the orchestra into registered groups as well as allowing the new color and sonoric possibilities of the modern orchestra to be manifested spatially. The orchestra was split up into seven groups, five of various chamber music size, capable of performing as independent units or to be joined with a larger entity. The alto flute, for example, was placed in front of the orchestra while the tuba, four horns, and contrabassoon were put to the right of the conductor. High woodwinds replaced the usual strings at the conductor's left. This new arrangement made possible the creation of spatial or stereophonic effects which caused "sounds literally to travel from one side of the stage to the other" and to incorporate "into the very structure of the work (not as mere effects) antiphonal ideas." Writing in *Saturday Review*, Irving Kolodin remarked: "Whether to the palate or the ear, the proof of the pudding is in the tasting: and Schuller's musical upside-down cake had a distinctive flavor of its own."

Between 1951 and 1959, Schuller taught French horn at the Manhattan School of Music. He resigned both from the school and from the Metropolitan Opera Orchestra, in 1959, to concentrate on composition. His first major work following his retirement also became one of his most successful: *Seven Studies on Themes of Paul Klee*, for orchestra (1959), commissioned jointly by the Minneapolis Symphony, the Ford Foundation, and the American Music Center. Its premiere was given by the Minneapolis Symphony under Antal Dorati on November 27, 1959. After that, it was programmed by about seventy-five orchestras, many presenting it twice. Each of the seven pieces, the composer informs us, "bears a slightly different relationship to the original picture from which it stems. Some relate to the actual design, shape, or color of the painting, while others take the general mood of the picture of its title as a point of departure." In *Antike Harmonien* (*Antique Harmonies*) Schuller recreated sonorically Klee's amber, ochre, and brown colors and the varied blocklike shapes from which the picture was built. *Abstraktes Terzett* (*Abstract Trio*) was played entirely by only three instruments as any given time, the three instruments changing color from the bright hues of the woodwinds, through the grainier texture of muted brass and bassoon, to the dark colors of low woodwinds and tuba. *Kleiner blauer Teufel* (*Little Blue Devil*) was a perky, blues-oriented jazz piece, Schuller's subjective musical impression of the geometrically conceived head in Klee's painting. *Die Zwitschermaschine* (*The Twittering Machine*) was given a pointillistic musical representation. *Arabische Stadt* (*Arabian Town*) incorporated authentic Tunisian scales and other Arabic elements. *Ein unheimlicher Moment* (*An Eerie Moment*) is, in Schuller's music, a play on the words of the title rather than a literal description of the pen drawing. In *Pastorale*, which Klee subtitled "Rhythms," several rhythmic-melodic shapes occurred in various registers and speed levels as the lyric mood of the music was maintained with pastorallike dialogue between the clarinet and French horn. "It has been said of Klee's works that it has a 'childlike freshness,'" wrote Herbert Elwell in the *Cleveland Plain Dealer* after this work was performed by the Cleveland Orchestra. "That is exactly what the music possessed. To me it was fascinating in its clarity and simplicity of texture, its humor, its total lack of platitude, and its variety of moods and colors."

In 1960, Schuller received the Creative Arts Award from Brandeis University in Waltham, Mass., and an award from the National Institute of Arts and Letters. He was given a Guggenheim Fellowship in 1962 which was extended for an additional year in 1963. In 1962, he was the musical director of the first International Jazz Festival, held in Washington, D.C., under the sponsorship of the music committee of President John F. Kennedy's People-to-People Program. Between 1963 and 1965, he conducted a series of concerts in New York entitled *Twentieth-century Innovations*, sponsored by the Carnegie Hall Foundation. These concerts were devoted exclusively to new and twentieth-century music, turning out to be the progenitor of many of the contemporary groups subsequently populating the musical scene in New York; many of the conductors and performers who played leading roles in this arena in later years performed under Schuller's leadership in those path-breaking concerts. He also broadcast a weekly series of 153 programs over the New York FM radio station WBAI entitled *Contemporary Music in Evolution*. This series was subsequently repeated over seventy-seven radio stations of the National Association of Educational Broadcasters. In 1963, Schuller was chosen as the acting head of the composition department at the Berkshire Music Center in Tanglewood, Mass., by Erich Leins-

dorf and Aaron Copland, succeeding the latter as head. In 1969 Schuller became artistic codirector of musical activities there and in 1972, full director. In 1964 he received the Darius Milhaud Award for his score to the Polish-made motion picture *Yesterday in Fact*, which he wrote while on a State Department visit to Poland. On a grant from the Ford Foundation in 1965 he participated in its artists-in-residence program in Berlin. Between 1964 and 1967 he was also associate professor of music at Yale University in New Haven. In 1966 he was the recipient of the Boston Symphony Horblit Award.

During the 1960s, Schuller was extraordinarily prolific in his output of major compositions, almost all of them written on commission. In 1960, on a commission from the Coolidge Foundation, he completed Music for Brass Quintet, introduced at the Library of Congress in Washington, D.C., in January 1961. Schuller returned to third-stream music with *Variants* (1960), for a jazz quartet consisting of a vibraphone, piano, double bass, and drums as well as orchestra. This music in which jazz was merged with twelve-tone music for a jazz ballet was choreographed by George Balanchine, who commissioned it. It was successfully produced in New York by the New York City Ballet on January 4, 1961. The jazz quartet was placed on the stage with the dancers, while the orchestra was in the pit, both conducted by the composer. *Contrasts,* for woodwind quintet (1961), became the first composition ever commissioned from an American by the modern music festival at Donaueschingen, in Germany, where it was premiered on October 22, 1961, Hans Rosbaud conducting. *Composition in Three Parts*, for orchestra (1962), was written for the Minneapolis Symphony, which first performed it on March 29, 1963, under the composer's direction. Though played without interruption, it is in three sections, each exploring and emphasizing a different kind of musical continuity and compositional technique. The first part was primarily based on the technique of rhythmic fragmentation; the second was principally linear and melodic; and the third combined essential characteristics of the two earlier parts. A symphony (1964), which the Dallas Symphony commissioned, received its first performance under Donald Johanos's direction on October 29, 1964. Writing in the *Musical Quarterly*, Irving Lowens called it "the product of a creative mind of the highest order. It is at its best when it is most approachable through the ears alone. And it is a pretty convincing demonstration that melody and the most advanced serial techniques are by no means incompatible." With *American Triptych: Studies in Texture*, for orchestra (1964), Schuller once again translated visual arts into musical sound in music combining serialism with jazz. Three abstract paintings were selected: *Four Directions* by Alexander Calder, *Out of the Web* by Jackson Pollock, and *Swing Landscape* by Stuart Davis. The first performance took place in New Orleans on March 9, 1965, the composer conducting. When the Cincinnati Orchestra under Max Rudolf brought this work to New York, Harold C. Schonberg had this to say of it in the *New York Times:* "The work, short and snappy—the three movements take only a little over twelve minutes—is in Mr. Schuller's easy-to-take serialism, complete with jazzy effects. It is all very smart, very cute, composed with a sure hand, beautifully orchestrated. Mr. Schuller is a pro." *Diptych,* for brass quintet and orchestra (1966), was an adaptation of a similarly titled piece written in 1964 on commission from the New York Brass Quintet under the sponsorship of the music department of Cornell University and scored for brass quintet and band. In its orchestral garb, it was introduced by the Boston Symphony on March 31, 1967. In two contrasting movements, *Diptych* reaches a climactic point with a jazz-oriented section. *Triplum* I, for orchestra (1967), was commissioned by the Lincoln Center for the Performing Arts in New York for the New York Philharmonic, the first performance taking place on June 28, 1967, Leonard Bernstein conducting. Written as it was for the New York Philharmonic, *Triplum* I exploited the orchestra's distinctive sound textures and virtuosity. "It is the pitting of various orchestral choirs against each other that forms the basis of the score," reported Raymond Ericson in the *New York Times.* "The details are worked out with great complexity, yet the structure is easy to follow as the brass, woodwind, or string sections of the orchestra are brought into prominence, functioning alone or in contrast to each other. . . . On a single hearing, *Triplum* was impressive as a dazzler for the ear and a vehicle for the New York Philharmonic." For the opening of Powell Symphony Hall, the new home of the St. Louis Orchestra, Schuller wrote, on commission, *Fanfare for St. Louis* (1967), its first performance taking place on January 24, 1968.

Schuller's most provocative work in the 1960s was his third-stream opera *The Visitation,* which he wrote for the Hamburg Opera in Germany at the request of its director, Rolf Liebermann. For his libretto (which Schuller wrote) he went to Kafka's surrealistic novel *The Trial,* but transplanted the setting to the United States and used American Negroes as principal characters. The central protagonist is an American university student who is not accepted by white people and rejected by his own race; who is also victimized by his own sensuality, persecuted for crimes he is not aware of committing; is brought to trial in a kangaroo court out to destroy him; and in the end is lynched. For this story, Schuller produced a score that leans on jazz for support. A seven-piece jazz ensemble is a supplement to the full orchestra. The opera opens with a recording of Bessie Smith singing the blues, "Nobody Knows You When You're Down and Out." There are sprinklings of gospel songs and nightclub sequences. But the score is basically serial, and the prevailing melodic line is more a modern atonal style than that of the blues,

spirituals, or Negro ballads. The world premiere in Hamburg on October 12, 1966, was a triumph, inspiring a twenty-two-minute ovation, about fifty curtain calls, and a rhapsodic response from the critics. Although American critics and audience were far less responsive when the visiting Hamburg Opera brought *The Visitation* to the United States on June 28, 1967, in New York, the opera was handsomely received in its first American production—by the San Francisco Opera in October 1967—when the critic of the *San Francisco Chronicle* said: "The opera made impressive impact and established itself as an important work." *The Visitation* was produced for television by the BBC in London in 1969.

In 1966, Schuller was appointed president of the New England Conservatory in Boston. There, in 1972, he formed and directed the New England Conservatory Ragtime Ensemble, which gave concerts of ragtime music throughout the United States and became a prime mover in the revival of ragtime in the early 1970s; their recording of Scott Joplin's *The Red-Back Book* sold more albums in the United States in the first six months of circulation than any classical release and earned a Grammy from the National Academy of Recording Arts and Sciences. Schuller was also responsible for the orchestration of Joplin's opera *Treemonisha,* whose premiere Schuller conducted with the Houston Opera on May 23, 1975, with subsequent performances in Washington, D.C., and New York. His arrangements of several Joplin rags were used in the motion picture *The Sting.* In April 1974, Schuller conducted students of the New England Conservatory in a Special Jazz Heritage Concert at the Smithsonian Institution in Washington, D.C., as a tribute to Duke Ellington on his seventy-fifth birthday.

Schuller's most important works since 1970 have included the following: *Museum Piece,* for an ensemble of Renaissance instruments and orchestra (1970), a centennial commission from the Boston Museum of Fine Arts, which the Boston Symphony and the Collegium Musicum of the New England Conservatory introduced on December 11, 1970, William Steinberg conducting; *Capriccio stravagante* (1972), a "fun piece" inspired by the 17th-century Carlo Farina work of the same title, written on commission for the sixtieth anniversary of the San Francisco Symphony, which gave the initial presentation on December 1972, Seiji Ozawa conducting; *Triplum* II, for orchestra (1974), a transliteration of the early classical sinfonia concertante concept featuring three different solo trios in its three movements, commissioned and introduced by the Baltimore Symphony under Sergiu Comissiona on February 26, 1975; Concerto no. 2, for orchestra (1976), commissioned by the National Symphony in Washington, D.C., for the commemoration of the American bicentennial, and premiered under Antal Dorati's direction on October 12, 1976; the Violin Concerto (1976; Lucerne, Switzerland, August 25, 1976), commissioned by the Eastman School of Music and performed by Zvi Zeitlin and the Lucerne Festival Orchestra conducted by the composer; *Deaï* for two orchestras (1978), in which Mozart is quoted, commissioned by the Boston Symphony, whose first performance was given in Tokyo on March 17, 1978, by the Boston Symphony and the Tokyo Symphony conducted by Seiji Ozawa and the composer; Concerto for Contrabassoon and Orchestra (1978; Washington, D.C., January 16, 1979), the first concerto ever written for that instrument, commissioned by the National Symphony of Washington, D.C., and first performed by that orchestra under Mstislav Rostropovich with Lewis Lipnick, soloist; and Octet (1979), a work using the same instrumentation as Schubert's Octet, commissioned by the Chamber Music Society of Lincoln Center in New York, its world premiere given on November 2, 1979. In these works, Schuller modified his serialism to incorporate analogues to earlier melodic and harmonic values and forms.

Schuller was named winner of the Columbia University Alice M. Ditson Conductors Award in 1970 for noteworthy contributions to 20th-century American music. He received the Rodgers and Hammerstein Award in 1971, and honorary doctorates in music from Northwestern University in Boston (1967), the University of Illinois in Urbana (1968), Colby College in Waterville, Me. (1969), Williams College in Williamstown, Mass. (1975), New England Conservatory (1978), and Rutgers University in New Brunswick, N.J. (1980). He was elected to membership in both the National Institute of Arts and Letters and the American Academy of Arts and Letters, and, in 1980, to the American Academy and Institute of Arts and Letters. In 1975 he founded the publishing house of Margun Music whose philosophy reflects Schuller's own broad musical interests, with publication goals covering the entire spectrum of music from ethnic and vernacular musics, medieval and Renaissance music, to jazz and ragtime-oriented concert works. His book *Early Jazz: Its Roots and Musical Development* (1968), recipient of the ASCAP-Deems Taylor Award in 1970, was acclaimed as one of the most authoritative and penetrating works on the subject. He was also the author of *Horn Technique* (1962).

Schuller's appearances as guest conductor of major orchestras both in the United States and abroad in traditional programs as well as in new music, and as lecturer at leading colleges and universities, have been extensive. In 1977, he retired as president of the New England Conservatory.

THE COMPOSER SPEAKS: I have never been able, even in my teen years, to accept the widespread notion that categories of music should be kept segregated and that inherent *qualitative* evaluations could be attributed to them. Unfortunately, most musical institutions, be they educational or performing, divide the musical spectrum *vertically* into many different categories and labels of musical styles, concepts, periods, and schools. And amongst these, most people and most institutions pick one (or at the most two) which they consider worthy of their attention. Thus some people—performers, educators, and consumers—will regard classical music, for example, as inherently superior to other forms of music such as jazz or various kinds of ethnic or vernacular musics from around the world. Conversely, some people have only ears for popular music and wouldn't be caught dead, for example, in an opera house or listening to a Renaissance motet. Still others think that only baroque music is valid fare for their musical appetites and consider contemporary music and even late romantic music as quite worthless. One could continue enumerating the countless variables in the perception of this musical spectrum, but it always comes to the same thing: that one kind of music or another is considered inherently superior to the others.

My philosophy on the other hand views the musical spectrum *horizontally*. That is to say, to quote Gioacchino Rossini's old witticism: "There are only two kinds of music—good and bad." For me there is creativity of the highest order to be found in *all* musics, just as by the same token all musics are capable of inferior or lesser products. Thus a Beethoven symphony, a great Charlie Parker blues improvisation, and an African drum ensemble of master drummers are, as creative and listening experiences, all of equal value and validity. Quality is not dependent upon the label a music may carry or a category it may typify, but rather on the talent and genius of the individual creator.

For me, music is one totality. indivisible—except as to quality. My publishing company carries the motto: "All musics are created equal." Which, of course, is not to say that they *are* all equal; just that they are inherently equal and all capable of the highest quality of human artistic expression.

PRINCIPAL WORKS: 2 horn concertos (1944, 1978); 2 concertos for orchestra (1966, 1976); 2 *Triplum*, for orchestra (1967, 1974).

Symphony for Brass and Percussion (1949–50, revised 1964); Fantasy, for unaccompanied cello (1951); *Dramatic Overture*, for orchestra (1951); Five Pieces, for five horns (1952); Quartet, for flute and strings (1953); Recitative and Rondo, for violin and piano, also for violin and string orchestra (1953); *12 by 11*, for chamber orchestra and jazz group (1953); *Contours*, for chamber orchestra (1956); Music for Violin, Piano, and Percussion (1957); String Quartet (1957); Woodwind Quintet (1958); *Fantasy Quartet*, for four cellos (1958); *Spectra*, for orchestra (1958); Concertino, for jazz quartet and orchestra (1959); *Seven Studies on Themes of Paul Klee*, for orchestra (1959); Capriccio, for tuba and orchestra (1960); *Variants*, ballet (1960); Music for Brass Quintet (1961); *Contrasts*, for woodwind quintet and orchestra (1961); Piano Concerto

(1962); *Composition in Three Parts*, for orchestra (1962); Symphony (1964); *American Triptych: Three Studies in Textures*, for orchestra (1966); *The Visitation*, opera (1966); *Colloquy*, for two pianos and orchestra (1966); *Diptych*, for brass quintet and orchestra (1966); *Fanfare for St. Louis*, for orchestra (1967); *Aphorisms*, for flute and string trio (1967); Double bass Concerto (1968); *Shapes and Designs*, for orchestra (1968); *Museum Piece*, for Renaissance instruments and orchestra (1970); *The Fisherman and His Wife*, one-act children's opera (1970); *Concerto da camera*, for nine instruments (1971); *Capriccio stravagante*, for orchestra (1972); *Tre invenzione*, for chamber ensemble (1972); *Poems of Time and Eternity*, for chorus and chamber orchestra (1972); Three Nocturnes, for orchestra (1972); *Four Soundscapes*, for orchestra (1974); Violin Concerto (1975–76); *Triptyque*, for organ (1976); *Deaï*, for two orchestras (1978); Contrabassoon Concerto (1978); *Sonata serenata*, for chamber orchestra (1978); Octet (1979); Trumpet Concerto (1980).

BIBLIOGRAPHY: Ewen, David, *Music Since 1900* (N.Y., 1969); Machlis, Joseph, *Introduction to Contemporary Music*, revised ed. (N.Y., 1979); Thomson, Virgil, *American Music Since 1910* (N.Y., 1970); BMI, *The Many Worlds of Music*, Winter 1976; *High Fidelity/Musical America*, April 1976; *Musical Quarterly*, April 1965; *New York Times*, September 6, 1970; May 29, 1977; *New Yorker*, December 9, 1961; *Saturday Review*, November 12, 1966.

Schuman, William Howard, b. New York City, August 4, 1910.

Though it was with a choral work with orchestra that Schuman became the first composer to win a Pulitzer Prize when that award in music was initiated in 1943, and though he subsequently produced other choral works of distinction, his significance and fame rest most securely on the foundation of his orchestral work. For all the complexity of his musical thought and technique, Schuman's music makes an inescapable impact through the varied sonoric effects, motor energy, majestic sweep of melodic line, expressiveness of his often elaborate and at times linear contrapuntal texture and the clarity of his architectonic structure. Some of his compositions spring from such native American sources as William Billings, Charles Ives, baseball, and American melorhythms.

He is the second child and only son of parents of German-Jewish descent, born in New York City. His father, an executive in a printing firm, was originally named Schumann, but he shortened it to Schuman. William Howard Schuman was named after William Howard Taft, president of the United States when Schuman was born. Except for Sunday evening music making at his home, consisting of singing light-opera selections and listening to Caruso

and Efrem Zimbalist recordings, Schuman's childhood interest in or association with music was minimal. He began violin lessons at the age of eleven with Blanche Schwarz because he was eager to play Beethoven's Minuet in G in the orchestra of P.S. 165 in Manhattan. He later attended the Speyer Experimental Junior High School in New York, a school for superior students. His main interests were baseball and the theater; at Speyer Junior High School he combined both interests by writing and having performed a play in which one of the characters was an athlete. He avoided practicing the violin when he could, but he did enjoy participating as violinist in his family's music sessions.

In 1925 he entered George Washington High School where he was taught to play the double bass (because the school lacked one). "They gave me an instrument, a room and a self-instruction book," he recalls, "and by the end of the year I was playing in a contest for New York City school orchestras. In fact, since I was the *only* double bass player in the New York City schools, I played in every one of the orchestras, doing nineteen performances in a row of the *Oberon* Overture."

In high school, he formed the Billy Schuman and his Alamo Society Orchestra, a jazz band which performed at dances, weddings, bar mitzvahs, and proms. In addition to playing the violin and banjo with this group he sang the vocals, wrote the arrangements (which he taught the players by rote), and served as business manager. He was also beginning to write some popular music, his first piece being a violin tango, *Fate,* written in 1926 at a boys' camp in Maine. This was followed by a score for a musical comedy produced at camp, two numbers from which were published. Later on, with Frank Loesser (then also a neophyte songwriter) producing the lyrics, Schuman provided music for about forty songs, one of which "In Love with the Memory of You," was Loesser's first published song.

When he graduated from George Washington High School in February 1928, Schuman enrolled in New York University School of Commerce, planning to prepare himself for a business career. During this time he wrote copy for an advertising agency and worked as a salesman for a printing house. One day (April 4, 1930) his sister induced him to go with her to a concert of the New York Philharmonic, his first experience in hearing good music in a public auditorium. "That concert literally changed my life," he has said. "I was astounded at seeing the sea of stringed instruments, and everybody bowing together. The visual thing alone was astonishing. But the sound! I was overwhelmed. I had never heard anything like it." The very next day, he decided he wanted to become a composer. He left New York University, determined never to return, telephoned the advertising agency that employed him saying he was through, and walked into the Malkin School of Music seeking to learn how to become a composer.

He was advised to study harmony with Max Persin. Persin combined harmony lessons with analyses of musical scores and the styles of different composers, which opened for young Schuman the world of great music. "I could see," Persin later said, "there was something burning there." Before long, Schuman supplemented these harmony lessons with the study of counterpoint with Charles Haubiel. At the same time, he continued writing popular songs, making arrangements for jazz bands, and on one or two occasions even serving as a song plugger in Tin Pan Alley. There were also a few tentative attempts at serious composition: "God's World," an art song (1932), and Four Canonic Choruses to poems by Tennyson, Sandburg, Edna St. Vincent Millay, and Countee Cullen (1932–33; N.Y., May 3, 1935).

In 1933, Schuman entered Teachers College at Columbia University to prepare himself for a teaching profession. He received his bachelor of science degree in 1935 and a master's degree in 1937. During the summer of 1935, he studied conducting at the Mozarteum in Salzburg, Austria.

In the fall of 1935 Schuman became a member of the music faculty and, from 1938 on, director of the chorus at Sarah Lawrence College in Bronxville, N.Y. He retained this teaching post for a decade. During his first year at Sarah Lawrence College, on March 27, 1936, he married Frances Prince, with whom he had been in love for more than four years, and with whom he later raised a son and a daughter.

Between 1936 and 1938, Schuman studied composition with Roy Harris, initially at the Juilliard School of Music and later privately. As Harris's pupil, and with Harris in attendance, Schuman received his first public performance in New York on October 21, 1936, when his Symphony no. 1 (1935) and String Quartet no. 1 (1936) were introduced and the Four Canonic Choruses was performed, only the last of which was well received. Harris's interest in polyphonic music of the baroque era and in medieval modes directed Schuman's interest in contrapuntal writing; Schuman was also impressed with Harris's polyharmonic thinking. Such Harris influences can be detected in Schuman's Symphony no. 2 (1937), introduced at a WPA concert in New York on May 25, 1938. Aaron Copland, who was in the audience, was so impressed with it that he induced Serge Koussevitzky to perform it with the Boston Symphony in February 1939. The audience and the Boston critics rejected it vigorously, with the sole exception of Moses Smith who countered the unfavorable response with this comment in the *Boston Evening Transcript*: "Dr. Koussevitzky, far from having made a mistake in placing it on one of his programs, is actually disclosing to Boston audiences a genuine American talent."

Since Schuman himself was strongly dissatisfied with his first two symphonies and his First String Quartet, he withdrew them, together with several other works, from further performances. By this gesture he was liberating himself from an all too slavish adherence to the Roy Harris polyphonic and polyharmonic methods in favor of his own style, placing a greater emphasis on melody and rhythm. A work with a marked American identity (still partly contrapuntal) now became his first composition to stay alive in the repertoire. It was the *American Festival Overture* (1939), composed for and introduced at the Festival of American Music with Serge Koussevitzky conducting the Boston Symphony on October 6, 1939, under the auspices of the American Society of Composers, Authors, and Publishers (ASCAP). The first three notes of this overture were a recollection of Schuman's boyhood on New York City streets since they simulated the "call to play" of his friends (shouted on the syllables "wee-awk-eee"). "This call," the composer has explained, "very naturally suggested itself for a piece of music being composed for a very festive occasion. From this it should not be inferred that the overture is program music. In fact, the idea of the music came to my mind before the origin of the theme was recalled. The development of this bit of 'folk material' then is along purely musical lines." The entire middle part of the overture is a fugue. The overture was so well regarded at its premiere in Boston that it was soon performed by other major orchestras in America as well as being recorded.

In 1939, Schuman received the first of two consecutive Guggenheim Fellowships. His creativity now went into high gear. He wrote String Quartet no. 3 (1939) on the first commission ever awarded jointly by the League of Composers and Town Hall in New York; the Coolidge Quartet introduced it in New York on February 27, 1940. *This Is Our Time* (1940), a secular cantata for chorus and orchestra to a text by Genevieve Taggard, was premiered at the Lewisohn Stadium in New York on July 4, 1940, Alexander Smallens conducting. Most significant of all in the early 1940s was the Symphony no. 3 (1941), first performed by the Boston Symphony under Koussevitzky on October 17, 1941. It is with this work that Schuman emerged as an important American symphonist. In two parts, each subdivided into two sections, the symphony reached back to baroque structures since the first part consisted of a passacaglia and fugue and the second of a chorale and toccata. But to his polyphonic writing Schuman now brought a dynamic rhythmic power together with his former expressiveness, henceforth to be a hallmark of so much of his writing. When the Boston Symphony brought the work to New York, Olin Downes wrote in the *New York Times*: "This symphony is full of talent and vitality, from first to last, and done with an exuberance and conviction on the part of the composer that carry straight over the footlights. . . . Although couched in 18th-century contrapuntal forms or molds . . . in its pages the old bottle was filled with a new exhilarating wine. The chosen formula did not prevent the young composer from writing lusty, audacious, surefooted music." The New York Music Critics Circle, then in its first year, presented it with its first award as the year's best orchestral work, and the *New Yorker* called Schuman "the composer of the hour by virtue of the popular and critical success of his Third Symphony." The symphony was soon programmed by most of America's major orchestras, and it has since remained vital in the American symphonic repertoire, with significant recordings by the New York Philharmonic under Leonard Bernstein and the Philadelphia Orchestra under Eugene Ormandy.

Symphony no. 4 was completed just a few months after the third, still in 1941, and its world premiere was given on January 22, 1942, performed by the Cleveland Orchestra under Artur Rodzinski.

In 1941, the National Association of Composers and Conductors presented Schuman with its Award of Merit. Two years later, the National Institute of Arts and Letters also gave Schuman its award. On January 13, 1943, an all-Schuman concert was given in Town Hall, N.Y., at which his Piano Concerto (1942) was premiered by Rosalyn Tureck and the Saidenberg Sinfonietta, conducted by Daniel Saidenberg. Two months after that, the national limelight was focused more brilliantly than ever on Schuman with the winning of the first Pulitzer Prize in music. It was given to *A Free Song,* Schuman's second secular cantata (1942), this time setting three poems from Walt Whitman's *Drum Taps,* for chorus and orchestra, music that owed its inspiration to World War II. The Boston Symphony, supplemented by the Harvard Glee Club and Radcliffe Choral Society, all conducted by Koussevitzky, presented the premiere performance on March 26, 1943. This was a sonorically brilliant, rhythmically propulsive composition in which Schuman once again demonstrated his skill in contrapuntal writing with a giant fugue that opened the second part.

Prayer in Time of War, for orchestra (1943), was another composition written under the impact of the war. This was a deeply moving, unprogrammatic composition whose title, as the composer then said, was "merely some indication of the kind of feeling that went into the composition. . . . *Prayer* is not only introspective, it can also be demanding—shrieking for help." When the Pittsburgh Symphony gave the first performance on February 26, 1943, with Fritz Reiner conducting, it bore the title of *Prayer 1943.* A new symphony, his fifth, called *Symphony for Strings,* was also a product of 1943. It was commissioned by the Koussevitzky Music Foundation and received its first hearing on November 12, 1943, with Koussevitzky conducting the Boston Symphony. Sheila Keats, writing almost twenty years later in *Stereo Review,* described it as "one of Schuman's most original and attractive works. Deliberately denying himself the easy road to brilliance provided by winds, brass, and percussion, Schuman relies on

his musical materials alone to create variety and drama within the context of a string orchestra. Exploiting in full the strings' generic lyric possibilities, he writes long singing lines which stand out in relief from the imaginative rhythmic and percussive passages. Schuman's linear approach is ideally suited to the string group, and he is extremely imaginative in his demands for a variety of sonorities."

Schuman terminated his affiliation with Sarah Lawrence College in 1945. For a brief period that year he was the director of publications at G. Schirmer, leaving to become president of the Juilliard School of Music. He continued to serve Schirmer as chief adviser of publications for the next seven years. At Juilliard, Schuman's remarkable gifts as educator and administrator came into sharp focus. Under his far-sighted, progressive leadership, Juilliard became one of the world's great conservatories. He overhauled the curriculum to embrace a program of instruction that included dance, literature, sociology, even race relationships. He instituted major festivals and premieres, developed an important opera company, and founded one of the world's most distinguished chamber music ensembles, the Juilliard String Quartet.

In spite of such taxing responsibilities, and the drain they made on his time and energies, Schuman refused to relegate composing to a minor status in his life. As he put it at the time: "If I'm a composer, I must write music." In fact, he opened for himself a new area of creativity by producing music for ballets: *Undertow* (1945), for Anthony Tudor, produced by the American Ballet Theater in New York on April 10, 1945; *Night Journey* (1947), on a commission from the Elizabeth Sprague Coolidge Foundation and mounted at Cambridge, Mass., at the Harvard University Symposium on Music Criticism by Martha Graham and her company on May 3, 1947; and *Judith* (1949), commissioned by the Louisville Orchestra for Martha Graham and first performed by the Louisville Orchestra under Robert Whitney, with Martha Graham, in Kentucky on January 4, 1950. The last of these brought Schuman his second New York Music Critics Circle Award. His major concert works during these years with the Juilliard included the Violin Concerto (1947), which Isaac Stern and the Boston Symphony under Charles Munch introduced on February 10, 1950, and which Schuman revised in 1954 and again in 1958–59; symphonies nos. 6 and 7, the sixth (1948) commissioned by the Dallas Symphony Orchestra League and premiered by the Dallas Symphony under Antal Dorati on February 27, 1949, and no. 7 (1960), a commission of the Koussevitzky Music Foundation for the 75th anniversary of the Boston Symphony, which, under Munch, performed it for the first time on October 21, 1960; String Quartet no. 4 (1950; Washington, D.C., October 28, 1950), commissioned by the Elizabeth Sprague Coolidge Foundation to honor the 150th anniversary of the founding of the

Library of Congress; *Credendum,* for orchestra, subtitled "An Article of Faith" (1955; Cincinnati, Ohio, November 4, 1955), written for the U.S. National Commission for UNESCO through the Department of State; *New England Triptych* (1956; Miami, Fla., October 28, 1956), commissioned and first conducted by André Kostelanetz, a work based on three hymns by the 18th-century American composer William Billings; and *Song of Orpheus,* a fantasy for cello and orchestra (1961; Indianapolis, Ind., February 17, 1962), based on one of Schuman's own songs, "Orpheus with His Lute" (1944), written for Leonard Rose on a Ford Foundation commission. "If there is more of one ingredient than another in the rich mixture of William Schuman's music," wrote Flora Rheta Schreiber and Vincent Persichetti in their Schuman biography published in 1954, "it is the strong-fibered energy that generates a constant boil of motion. There is motion stirred by boldness and intensity, movement that pushes forward resourcefully and seriously and beneath even the quietest pages a restless current that will eventually surface in a rush."

When Schuman resigned as president of the Juilliard School in 1962, it was to assume a no less exciting executive post as president of the Lincoln Center for the Performing Arts in New York: a giant complex eventually comprising theaters, opera houses, concert halls, a library of performing arts, and the Juilliard School of Music. It opened with a concert of the New York Philharmonic under Leonard Bernstein on September 23, 1962. Schuman retained this office until 1969.

His first major composition after becoming Lincoln Center president was Symphony no. 8 (1962), commissioned by the New York Philharmonic for its opening season at Lincoln Center, where it was heard on October 4, 1962, Leonard Bernstein conducting. It provided further confirmation, if such were any longer needed, that Schuman had become one of America's leading symphonists. A critic for *Musical America* reported: "What a work it is! The opening is ominous with subterranean chords tolling out a dirge that is exemplary in its scoring. It is a keen lament, all sorrow and genuine tragic . . . and even when it turns fast there is a sadness to its melodic gestures. The second movement, too, is pensive and brooding, and it is full of deep thoughts. . . . The third movement is exciting, elaborately and melodically disjunct, but always with a purpose. . . . The work ends with a climax . . . a roar . . . that does enormous credit to its creator."

Schuman completed two more symphonies after that. He titled Symphony no. 8 *Le fosse ardeatine* (1968) after a cave in Rome in which 335 Italians (Christians and Jews) were slain by the Nazis on March 24, 1944, in reprisal for the killing of 32 German soldiers by the Italian underground. Schuman and his wife visited that cave in 1967. "The mood of my symphony," he says "especially in its opening

and closing sections, is directly related to emotions engendered by this visit. But the entire middle section, too, with its various moods of fast music, much of it far from somber, stems from the fantasies I had of the variety, promise and aborted lives of the martyrs. . . . The work does not attempt to depict the event realistically. . . . My reason for using the title is not, then, musical but philosophical." This symphony was written on a commission from the friends of Alexander Hilsberg (onetime concertmaster and assistant conductor of the Philadelphia Orchestra) and on January 10, 1969, Eugene Ormandy conducted the Philadelphia Orchestra in its premiere performance. It is in three sections played without pause: "Anteludium," dominated by a melody heard first at the opening in muted violins and cellos; "Offertorium," the bulk of the work, in which moods change from the playful to the dramatic; "Postludium," in which the symphony's opening melody is heard again but in slower tempo, followed by recollections of music of the "Offertorium" and culminating in an emotional climate that serves as a kind of summation.

Symphony no. 10 (1975) is titled *American Muse,* written, the composer says, as a dedication "to our country's creative artists, past, present, and future." The National Symphony of Washington, D.C., and its music director, Antal Dorati, commissioned it to commemorate the American bicentennial, the premiere taking place on April 6, 1976. An important stimulus for its writing was Schuman's reexamination of a choral work he had written in 1937, *Pioneers!,* based on Walt Whitman, which had been introduced by the Westminster Festival Choir in Princeton, N.J., on May 23, 1937. "Experiencing again its optimism was precisely what I needed to get me started on my symphony. Optimism is, after all, an essential ingredient in understanding America's beginnings. To be sure, the spirit of optimism one expressed in his middle sixties is as removed from that of his middle twenties as are today's complexities from those of colonial times. The symphony reflects these differences. Between the outer movements is the largely contemplative second movement, and while variegated facets of the first and third movements surely cannot be described as exclusively optimistic, I trust that, over all, the music emerges as an expression of affirmation." The symphony opens with a subject Schuman had used thirty-nine years earlier in *Pioneers!* and it recurs in overlapping statements in the third movement.

Other works by Schuman since the early 1960s also merit attention. *Variations on America* (1963) was an orchestral adaptation of Charles Ives's organ treatment of the national ballad "America." It was commissioned by Broadcast Music Incorporated (BMI) to celebrate its twentieth anniversary and was first performed on May 20, 1964, with André Kostelanetz conducting the New York Philharmonic. *Amaryllis Variations,* a set of variations on an Old

English round, for string trio (1964), was written at the request of the Elizabeth Sprague Coolidge Foundation to commemorate the centenary of the birth of its founder; the New York String Trio introduced it at the Library of Congress in Washington, D.C., on October 31, 1964. *The Witch of Endor* was a ballet (1965) commissioned by Martha Graham, who introduced it with her company in New York on November 2, 1965. *In Praise of Shahn,* a canticle for orchestra (1969), was a tribute to the distinguished artist Ben Shahn, written on commission from his friends shortly after his death; it was introduced by the New York Philharmonic under Bernstein on January 29, 1970. In his music, Schuman aspired to reflect two characteristics of Shahn's nature, his "unabashed optimism and a searching poignancy." Since Shahn used to enjoy listening to a friend sing folk songs from the Eastern European and Jewish heritage, Schuman sought to include these feelings in his score, developing them contrapuntally to create a harrowing tension. *Concerto on Old English Rounds,* for solo viola, women's chorus and orchestra (1973), was a Ford Foundation commission for the violist Donald McInnes. Four rounds form the basis of the concerto: "Amaryllis," "Great Tom Is Cast," "Who'll Buy My Roses?" and "Come, Follow Me." "He has twisted the elements to suit himself," reported Harold C. Schonberg in the *New York Times.* "There are some beautiful things in this viola concerto, especially at the quiet opening and closing. Here and there, there is a modal feeling or a deliberate archaism, but Mr. Schuman has not set out to be quaint. . . . Altogether characteristic of the composer were the motoric sections—those fast-moving passages, often punctuated by pungent brass combinations found in so much of Mr. Schuman's music." Donald McInnes was soloist with the Boston Symphony conducted by Michael Tilson Thomas on November 29, 1974, when the concerto was premiered. *The Young Dead Soldiers* (1975) was written in commemoration of the American bicentennial on a commission by the National Symphony Orchestra of Washington, D.C., and its music director, Antal Dorati, and they gave the first performance on April 6, 1976. This is a fifteen-minute "lamentation," a setting of a poem by Archibald MacLeish for soprano, French horn, eight woodwinds, and nine strings, written, according to Raymond Ericson in the *New York Times,* "with unerring taste, evoking a strong sentiment but never sliding into sentimentality."

Schuman retired as president of Lincoln Center in 1969 to devote himself to composition, to serve as consultant to various enterprises, and to commit himself to eleemosynary projects. The last of these involved being a director of the Chamber Music Society of Lincoln Center and of the Koussevitzky Music Foundation and of the Naumburg Foundation, and chairman of the MacDowell Colony in Peterborough, N.H. He has also served on the advisory panel of the U.S. Cultural Presentation Programs, the music panel of the National Endowment for the Arts, music adviser of the U.S. Information Agency, and vice-chairman of the U.S. delegation of UNESCO International Conference of Creative Artists.

Among the many honors and awards he has accumulated through the years (above and beyond those already mentioned) are the following: Columbia University Bicentennial Anniversary Award (1957); the first Brandeis University Creative Arts Award (1957); Citation of Merit from the State University of New York in Buffalo (1963); Brandeis Medal for distinguished service to higher education (1965); Handel Medallion from the City of New York (1967); Finley Award of the University of the City of New York (1968); the Edward MacDowell Medal "for exceptional contribution to the arts" (1971); and the Boston Symphony Horblit Award (1980). He has been awarded twenty-three honorary doctorates in either music or humane letters. Among them are those from the University of Wisconsin (1952), Columbia University (1954), Colgate University (1962), Dartmouth College (1962), New York University (1962), Northwestern University (1963), Fordham University (1967), the University of Rochester (1972), and the University of the State of New York in Buffalo (1974). He is a member of the National Institute of Arts and Letters and an honorary fellow of the Royal Academy of Music in London.

Schuman was composer-in-residence at the Aspen Festival in Colorado during the summer of 1980. There, on August 4, his seventieth birthday was celebrated with a special program of his works. This was just the first of many tributes celebrating his seventieth year. The following fall America's foremost orchestras performed many of his major compositions in his honor.

THE COMPOSER SPEAKS: A composition must have two fundamental ingredients—emotional vitality and intellectual vigor.

Techniques constitute the objective working methods of art. In the mature artist, they are distinguishable from the creative act. In our time, however, techniques are discussed at such length and with such partisanship that often they seem to be viewed as ends in themselves. The only test of a work of art is, of course, in the finished product and not in the process of its making. Furthermore, we know that adherence to a particular school of thought or esthetic predilection cannot, in and of itself, guarantee quality. Works of merit in our time, as in times past, have been composed through a variety of approaches and techniques encompassing the gamut of known devices, plus the invention of new ones. . . .

The composer's job is to be faithful to his gifts by composing the best music of which he is capable. No discussion of his work or championing of his esthetic in any way alters his final product. The continuing flow of the art of music through the centuries and the possibility, however modest, that his music may enter the stream, is sufficient reward.

PRINCIPAL WORKS: 10 symphonies (1935–78); 4 string quartets (1936–50).

American Festival Overture, for orchestra (1939); *This Is Our Time,* secular cantata for chorus and orchestra (1940); *Requiescat,* for women's chorus and piano (1942); *Holiday Song,* for chorus and piano (1942); Piano Concerto (1942); *A Free Song,* secular cantata for chorus and orchestra (1942); *Prayer in Time of War,* for orchestra (1943); *Undertow,* ballet (1945); *Night Journey,* ballet (1947); Violin Concerto (1947, revised 1954, 1958–59); *Judith,* choreographic poem for orchestra (1949); *Voyage,* five pieces for piano (1953); *Credendum,* "article of faith," for orchestra (1955); *New England Triptych,* three pieces after William Billings, for orchestra (1956); *Carols of Death,* for a cappella chorus (1958); *A Song of Orpheus,* for cello and orchestra (1961); *Amaryllis Variations,* for string trio (1964); *The Witch of Endor,* ballet, (1965); *In Praise of Shahn,* for orchestra (1969); *Declaration Chorale,* for a cappella voices (1971); *Voyage,* for orchestra (1971); *Concerto on Old English Rounds,* for viola, women's chorus, and orchestra (1973); *The Young Dead Soldiers,* for soprano, French horn, and seventeen instruments (1975); *Casey at the Bat,* a baseball cantata adaptation of the 1953 one-act opera, *The Mighty Casey,* for vocal soloists, chorus, and orchestra (1976); *In Sweet Music,* for voice, flute, viola, and harp (1978); *Three Colloquies,* for French horn and orchestra (1979); *Time to the Old,* for soprano and piano (1980).

BIBLIOGRAPHY: Ewen, David (ed.), *The New Book of Modern Composers,* revised ed. (N.Y., 1967); Goss, Madeleine, *Modern Music Makers* (N.Y., 1952); Schreiber, Flora Rheta, and Persichetti, Vincent, *William Schuman* (N.Y., 1954); BMI, *The Many Worlds of Music,* Winter 1976; *High Fidelity/Musical America,* August 1980; *Musical Quarterly,* January 1945; *New York Times,* January 28, 1970, November 28, 1975, August 3, 1980; *Saturday Review,* November 1, 1947, *Stereo Review,* June 1974.

Schwantner, Joseph, b. Chicago, Ill., March 22, 1943.

He was the recipient of the Pulitzer Prize in music in 1979. In his earlier compositions he explored serial techniques. Later works, though often not abandoning serialism, revealed a new interest in tonal materials and a style that synthesized and drew upon the vast palette of past and present music, both Western and non-Western, all within the context of a defining personal style.

Neither of his parents was particularly musical, but Joseph Schwantner revealed an interest in music from childhood on. His first involvement in music came while he was attending Warren Palm School, a grade school in Hazelcrest, Ill., where he was asked by a teacher to join the school orchestra. He studied tuba with A. Anderson and was soon able to play that instrument in the school ensemble. In 1957, he entered Thornton Township High School in Harvey, Ill. He studied the guitar privately with Robert Stein, a friend, at first learning folk guitar before moving to classical literature. In high school, he studied theory and musical history, played tuba in the school band, and guitar in jazz ensembles. He started composing when he was about thirteen "so that I'd have things to play on my guitar." Before long, he was making arrangements and writing pieces for various jazz bands, large and small, in which he was performing. One of his jazz compositions, *Offbeat,* won the National Band Camp Award in 1959.

Between 1961 and 1964 he attended the Chicago Conservatory College, studying composition with Bernard Dieter, his first such teacher and a man who had a pronounced influence on his early musical growth. Under his watchful eye, Schwantner wrote his first concert work for orchestra, *Sinfonia Brevis* (1963).

After graduating from the conservatory with a bachelor of music degree in 1964, Schwantner pursued postgraduate studies in music at Northwestern University School of Music in Evanston, Ill. (1964–68). As a major in composition, he studied with Anthony Donato and Alan Stout. Recognition of Schwantner's talent was not slow in coming. In 1965, his Concertino, for alto saxophone and three chamber ensembles (1964), which was performed at Northwestern University in May 1965, brought him his first Broadcast Music Incorporated (BMI) Student Composers Award. A second such award came in 1966 for *Diaphonia Intervallum* (1965), for alto saxophone, flute, piano, and strings, which the Eastman Musica Nova performed in Rochester in 1967. Andrew Frank in *Notes* described as " a lovely and, in places, an almost pastoral type of composition [which] should gain a place in the repertoire of major contemporary music chamber ensembles. Schwantner is a masterful composer who possesses a sure technique and a highly refined sense of timing and proportion." This composition also earned the Bearns Prize at Columbia University in 1967, was published and subsequently recorded. In 1966, Schwantner also received the William T. Faricy Award for Creative Music, and in 1967 a third BMI Composers Student Award, the latter, for *Chronicon,* for bassoon and piano (1967), which was premiered at the Festival of Contemporary Music at Tanglewood, Mass., on August 15, 1968. In these early compositions, Schwantner was a serialist.

Schwantner married Janet Elaine Rossate, an executive secretary, on August 21, 1965, with whom he had two children. In 1966, he was awarded the master of music degree at Northwestern. For the next two years he was teaching assistant in music theory there while fulfilling requirements for a doctorate in music, received in 1968. For one year (1968–69) he taught music theory and composition both at the Chicago Conservatory College and the Pacific Lutheran University in Tacoma, Wash., and in 1969–70 he was assistant professor of theory at Ball State University in Muncie, Ind. In 1970 he joined the faculty of the Eastman School of Music, where he has since remained: assistant professor of composition and theory (1970–73); assistant professor of composition from 1975; and full professor in 1980. Through the years, he has made numerous appearances as guest composer and lecturer at American universities and colleges. In 1975, while on leave from the Eastman School, he served as lecturer on music at the University of Texas in Austin and guest composer and lecturer at the University of Houston; in April 1979 he was composer-in-residence at Wolf Trap Farm for the Performing Arts in Vienna, Va. Later in 1979 he was guest composer and lecturer at Yale University and the University of Michigan at Ann Arbor. In 1970, he received the first Charles Ives Scholarship in music from the National Institute and the American Academy of Arts and Letters.

Schwantner began adopting a more tonal framework while at the same time exploring new resources in timbres and sound textures and experimenting with aleatory practices, with *Consortium* I, for violin, viola, cello, flute, and clarinet (1970). He wrote it for Musica Viva in Boston, which gave the premiere performance on September 23, 1970, on a program where it was heard twice, as the opening and closing number of the first half. *Consortium* II, for six instruments (1971), was also written for the Boston Musica Viva, its first performance taking place in Cambridge, Mass., on February 7, 1972, after which it was presented in London, Hamburg, and Cologne. Commenting on *Consortium* II in the *Quincy Patriot Ledger*, David Noble said: "A brilliant outburst of metallic percussion showed Schwantner being quite serious and quite beautiful . . . but an undertone of musical satire lingered in the corners of his witty muscular writing."

Schwantner regards *In Aeternum*, for cello and four players (1973), as a key piece in his creative evolution. A twelve-tone composition, this is a fascinating study in sonorities and sound textures, since the orthodox instruments are combined with exotic sounds produced by rubbing the fingers on half-filled wine glasses, dipping gongs in washtubs of water, and scraping metallic percussion instruments with violin and cello bows. Such effects proved no mere gimmicks but the means of realizing eerie, haunting, shimmering effects, skillfully synchronized with the more formal sounds of the usual instruments. Musica Viva, for whom it was written, gave the first performance in Cambridge, Mass., on February 26, 1973. It then became one of Schwantner's most widely performed compositions, receiving over forty performances by the Contemporary Chamber Ensemble in 1974–75.

Schwantner continued to combine a twelve-tone idiom with experimental sonic effects in *Shadows* II, for baritone and eight players (1973; Cambridge, Mass., March 4, 1974), a setting of Kenneth Rexroth's *One Hundred Poems from the Japanese,* and in *Elixir*, for flute and five players (1974; Great Barrington, Mass., October 3, 1975), subtitled "Consortium VIII." The latter was written on a grant from the National Endowment for the Arts. Novel sounds are produced in *Shadows* II by lowering vibrating triangles into buckets of water; and in *Elixir* by striking small cymbals (crotales) with string bows and rubbing wet fingers on the rims of crystal glasses. When *Elixir* was first performed in New York on May 19, 1978, at a League of Composers–International Music Society for Contemporary Music concert, the program notes explained: "The employment of the multiple instrumentation increases the articulative, gestural, and timbral possibilities available to the performers in the ensemble and provides a more expansive sonic landscape to support and surround the important virtuosic flute playing. The resulting ensemble, with its increased sonorous resources, provides interesting dramatic and expressive musical possibilities." *Elixir* was extensively performed by Musica Viva in Europe during a tour in 1976, and it was selected by the U.S. section of the International Society for Contemporary Music for performance at the World Music Days in Helsinki, Finland, on May 9, 1978. Schwantner was able to attend that performance on a Martha Baird Rockefeller grant.

Schwantner wrote *Autumn Canticles*, for piano trio (1974; Laramie, Wyo., July 1974), on a commission from the William P. Coe Meritag Commission in American Music for the Western Arts Festival, and it was written under a grant from the Creative Artists Public Service Program of the New York State Council on the Arts. The title refers to a series of five ancient Chinese poems, all dealing with various aspects of autumn. While there is not much of programmatic intent or purpose, these poems did provide a rich reservoir of moods, feelings, and ideas that stimulated and intensified the compositional process. This work was widely performed in Europe in 1976 by the Western Arts Trio. *Canticle of the Evening Bells*, for flute and twelve players (1975), was commissioned by Arthur Weisberg and the Contemporary Chamber Ensemble, which first performed it on February 19, 1976, in New York. Here the flute is pitted against the highly diverse instrumental ensemble (some of whose members are required to double on glass crystals, bowed crotales, and play bowed vibes) and exploits the full timbral sonic resources of the ensemble. A commission from the Naumburg Foundation for the Jubal Trio led to the writing of *Wild Angels of the Open Hills*, for soprano, harp, and flute (1977; N.Y., February 2, 1977). In addition to requiring each performer to play on multiple instruments, all players are called upon to whistle, narrate, whisper, and sing. This work consists of a cycle of five songs, text taken from a collection of poems by Ursula LeGuin. "The poems," the composer says, "struck an immediate and deep responsive resonance within me and I became excited by the dramatic and musical possibilities envisaged by the poem's vivid imagery. The work's title is taken from the first line of the opening poem. . . . While each song is a separate entity with its own definite identity, they all share common musical ideas and materials."

On a grant from the National Endowment for the Arts, Schwantner completed *and the mountains rising nowhere* for Donald Hunsberger and the Eastman Wind Ensemble, which premiered it in Rochester, N.Y., on February 28, 1977. It is scored for amplified piano, six percussionists, winds, and brass together with seven glass crystals and a glass harmonica played by the oboist. The title comes from a poem by Carol Adler and "while the work is not specifically programmatic, the poem nevertheless acted as the creative impetus for the composition and provided for me an enigmatic, complex and powerful imagery creating a wellspring of musical ideas and feelings in sympathetic resonance with the poem."

The Pulitzer Prize in music came in 1979 for *Aftertones of Infinity*, for orchestra (1978), a commission of the American Composers Orchestra; the world premiere took place at the Lincoln Center for the Performing Arts in New York on January 29, 1979. The composer derived some of his basic musical materials from an earlier work, *Wild Angels of the Open Hills*. Once again the composer is innovative, requiring woodwind players to double on musical glasses and calling on various orchestral members to vocalize "with a pure, delicate, childlike quality . . . like a distant ethereal choir." The composition ebbs away with the members of the orchestra humming.

In 1978, Schwantner was awarded a Guggenheim Fellowship. That year he completed *Sparrows* for the 20th-Century Consort, on a grant from the National Endowment for the Arts; the world premiere took place in Washington, D.C., on March 18, 1979, after which it was recorded under the sponsorship of the Smithsonian Institution. This is a setting of fifteen haiku by Issa, the first and last of which speak of sparrows. This is music in which the composer began developing a more accessible style in contrast to earlier complex and dissonant texture, music more readily assimilable on first hearing. Passages of quasi-Renaissance polyphony are intoned by the instrumentalists at key points. This score also includes a dancelike interlude and toward the end embarks on an extended contrapuntal passage. But the earlier experiments with aural coloration by having cymbals struck and bowed by string players and requiring instrumentalists to sing have not been abandoned. Dark timbres of string sound are produced through the technique of scordatura. "The solo vocal writing," reported Paul Hume in the *Washington Post*, "is designed to heighten the composer's purpose of creating 'a series of dream states.' He achieves his purpose in music of exquisite sounds and images."

THE COMPOSER SPEAKS: My notions about music are naturally reflected in my work, and those notions, values, and musical issues change as the work changes, thus requiring new responses and solutions to compositional problems. This for me is a way of living my life, with each new work further defining that search for a personal voice—a voice that is an evolving continuum that seeks its identity through a compositional impulse which becomes an exciting journey filled with eager expectations of confronting the unknown. The journey raises questions that find their ultimate solution in the compositional process—a process with a multiplicity of seemingly infinite possibilities that totally engages my ear, mind, and spirit.

PRINCIPAL WORKS: Nonet, for piano and chamber ensemble (1964); Concertino, for alto saxophone and three chamber ensembles (1964); *Diaphonia Intervallum* (1965); *Entropy*, for soprano, saxophone, bass clarinet, and cello (1966); *Chronicon*, for bassoon and piano (1966); *Enchiridion*, for violin and piano (1968); *August Canticle*, for orchestra (1968); *Consortium* I, for violin, viola, flute, and clarinet (1970); *Consortium* II, for six instruments (1971); *Modus Caelestis*, for twelve flutes, twelve strings, three percussionists, piano, and celeste (1972); *In Aeternum*, for cello and four players (1973); *Shadows* II, for baritone and eight players (1973); *Autumn Canticles*, for violin, cello, and piano (1974); *Elixir*, "Consortium VIII," for flute and five players (1974); *Canticle of the Evening Bells*, for flute and twelve players (1975); *Etherea*, for flute, horn, piano, percussion, and contrabass (1976); *and the mountains rising nowhere*, for amplified piano, wind, brass, and percussion (1977); *Wild Angels of the Open Hills*, for soprano, harp, and flute (1977); *Aftertones of Infinity*, for orchestra (1978); *Sparrows*, for soprano and eight players (1979); *Music of Amber*, for flute, alto clarinet, violin, cello, piano, and percussionist (1979); *Wind Willow, Whisper*, for flute, clarinet, violin, cello, and piano (1980); *First Morning of the World*, for percussion group and wind ensemble (1980); *Through Interior Worlds,* for chamber group (1980).

BIBLIOGRAPHY: BMI, *The Many Worlds of Music*, Winter 1976, issue 2, 1979; *High Fidelity/Musical America*, December 1979; *Who's Who in America, 1980–81*.

Schwartz, Elliott, b. Brooklyn, N.Y., January 19, 1936.

In many of his compositions, Schwartz has been stimulated by timbres of instruments singly or in combinations. He is also excited by the variables of performance (what might be called theater); the placement of players, movement by players (or audience), lighting, speaking, or "acting" by instrumentalists, audience participation, and so forth. He enjoys using improvisation by performers, usually in the area of synchronization (building up textures from tiny fragments) rather than in choice of pitch. He has also composed pieces quite free in their overall shapes, the form being assembled by the players. Many of his works involve instruments with tape, the tape part sometimes made on a synthesizer or entirely put together as a collage of edited scraps. In all this, he is primarily fascinated by the use of loudspeakers as one more variable for performance. The placement of loudspeakers, their theatrical "magic" and their relation to human perception interest him much more than any specific sounds coming out of them.

His father was a physician who had played the violin as a young man, and his mother, a New York City grade school teacher, was an excellent amateur pianist. It was she who gave him his first piano lessons when he was about seven. "My interest in music was always high," he recalls, "and it remained very high because it turned out that I was very good at piano playing, accompanying, improvising, and so forth, all of which was ridiculously easy for me to do and won me instant recognition and approval. Naturally, I stayed with it." He also started composing at about the same time. "I loved composing because I loved the *look* of music on the page. The calligraphy must have been very exciting. All the childish scores of mine I can find are covered with lots of big black notes, beams, rests, clefs, etc—and virtually unplayable."

His next two piano teachers, as it turned out, were not piano teachers at all. For a time he studied piano with Benedict Gordon, an elderly Russian violinist who has once been Nathan Milstein's teacher. After that, Schwartz continued piano lessons with Mrs. Jennie Glickman, who had formerly taught theory. Since all of Mrs. Glickman's piano pupils were required to attend classes in theory and composition, Schwartz was now able to receive his first such instruction. "My pieces started to become 'ear' music instead of 'eye' music after I began studying with Mrs. Glickman."

When he was about fourteen he acquired his first significant piano teacher in Alton Jones, a member of the faculty at the Juilliard School of Music. Schwartz was probably Jones's youngest pupil. He continued studying with Jones up to the time he went to college. At P.S. 253, from which he graduated in 1949, and Abraham Lincoln High School, both in Brooklyn, N.Y., Schwartz was active in music: as pianist, accompanist, and, whenever needed, arranger. But in spite of such involvement in and talent for

music, he was convinced at the time that he did not want to make a career in it. His main interests in high school were writing, literature, philosophy and mathematics; and, in the back of his mind was the intention of ultimately following in his father's footsteps and becoming a physician. In fact, when he entered Columbia University in 1953, it was as a premedical student. But he managed to add a considerable amount of music to the prescribed premedical curriculum by taking some music literature courses with Douglas Moore and Otto Luening, among others, and studying theory and composition with Luening, Jack Beeson, and William Mitchell. In his senior year, Schwartz decided against medicine as a career and spent his last year in college solely with music courses. Then, having majored in chemistry, he was graduated from Columbia with a bachelor of arts degree in 1957.

Since he had not taken sufficient music courses at Columbia to warrant recognition as a bona fide music major, Schwartz was ineligible for any formal graduate work in composition. He compromised by enrolling in the graduate program in music education at Teachers College in Columbia, at which time he continued studying composition with Luening and Beeson and served as a graduate assistant to Howard A. Murphy. At the same time, at Teachers College, he resumed piano lessons with Thomas Richner. During his last year, he studied composition privately with Paul Creston.

In 1958, Schwartz received his master of arts degree, and in 1962 his doctorate in education, both at Teachers College, his doctoral thesis being a study of the symphonics of Vaughan Williams. Meanwhile, in 1960, he was appointed instructor of music at the University of Massachusetts in Amherst, where he remained four years, and on June 26, 1960, he married Dorothy Feldman, who had then just graduated from Smith College and was beginning graduate work in art; they raised two children.

He was composing music all the time. His earliest apprentice works were totally influenced by the German-Austrian-Central European instrumental tradition of the 18th and 19th centuries. "We could have been living in Vienna, for all the music I ever heard those years was traditional. I had no interest in jazz, or 'pop' songs, or *any* music for voices. American music then was to me *Rhapsody in Blue*, a bit of Copland, and a record of Varèse that I discovered in the early 1950s." But in his later years in high school he had discovered French and English music and had fallen in love with it. During his college and graduate school years, his compositions began to reflect the styles of Satie, Poulenc, Saint-Saëns, Vaughan Williams, and Gustav Holst: Romance, for basso and piano (1961); Sonata for Violin and Double bass (1961); *Symphony in Two Movements*, for orchestra (1961); and Trio, for flute, clarinet, and cello (1962). The symphony was introduced at the American University Festival in Washington, D.C., on May 26,

1961, and a year and a half later (December 2, 1962) was performed by the Oklahoma City Symphony conducted by Guy Fraser Harrison. Schwartz has since withdrawn this work.

Schwartz's final powerful educational influence came about after he left graduate school. Beginning with the summer of 1961 and continuing for five summers after that, he attended the Bennington Composers Conference in Vermont, where he came into contact with such progressive-thinking American composers as Henry Brant, Stefan Wolpe, Ralph Shapey, and Barney Childs, with styles Schwartz had never known existed, such as total serialism, aleatoric music, multimedia productions, happenings, and so forth. "I was fascinated by chance, 'theater,' the use of improvisation, and I was given the opportunity to have my own music read and criticized by the best free-lance performers of eastern United States. I discovered that I had a knack for handling orchestral sonorities. Bennington really completed my musical education."

Still another important influence was brought to bear on his musical development between 1960 and 1964, the painter John Goodyear, his colleague at the University of Massachusetts. Goodyear was active in "pop" and "op" movements, interested in accidental, randomly arrived at environmental art, and was the first person Schwartz had met who took John Cage seriously and could articulate why. "My music changed a good deal during the early sixties, partly because of Goodyear and partly because of the Bennington summers." This change could be first detected in Quartet, for oboe and strings (1963; Bennington, Vt., August 1965), which, in 1966, was performed by the New York Chamber Soloists during a tour of Europe; Music for Orchestra, with electronic tape (1964; Portland, Me., December 7, 1965), Schwartz's first experiments in combining taped sounds with instruments; Concert Piece, for wind quintet, four strings, and percussion (1965; N.Y., April 11, 1966); and Soliloquies, for flute, clarinet, violin, and piano (1965; Brunswick, Me., May 1965). In these chamber music works, Schwartz was already revealing that interest in timbres of various instruments that he would henceforth continue to explore successfully in a large repertoire of compositions for solo instruments and combinations of instruments.

In 1964, Schwartz was appointed assistant professor of music at Bowdoin College in Brunswick, Me., where he has remained since that time, serving as associate professor from 1970 to 1975, full professor since 1975, and department chairman between 1975 and 1978. At Bowdoin he was also acting director of its Summer Music School (1968–75), codirector of the Bowdoin Music Press since 1966, and, from 1965 on, director of an annual contemporary music festival where, in 1966, a festival of Carl Ruggles's music was probably responsible for a renaissance of that composer's works. Schwartz combined his activities at Bowdoin with appearances as guest composer, lecturer, and pianist at leading colleges and universities in the United States, Canada, and England; in many of these places he presented "one-man" shows of all-Schwartz concerts.

By the latter half of the 1960s he was moving into those areas in which he was to become most involved: "theater pieces" requiring improvisation, audience participation, structures shaped by the performers, antiphonal space, and electronic music. Elevator Music (1967; Brunswick, Me., January 6, 1967) called for at least twelve players in a sixteen-or-more-story building. The performers (on any instrument) were stationed at elevator doors of a high-rise building while the audience was riding in the elevators up and down. Magic Music, for orchestra, piano, and "other sounds" (1967, Portland, Me., February 13, 1968), was basically a piano concerto in which the piano becomes an object for worship by the orchestra musicians; they leave their seats, come to the piano, strum into its strings, blow into it, and so forth. Following its premiere in Maine, Magic Music was performed in 1969 by the Indianapolis Symphony under Thomas Briccetti and, in 1973, by the Rhode Island Philharmonic under Francis Madeira. The central moment in Island (1970) occurred when all the house lights went out. The tape used here combined BBC weather forecasts, Coney Island carnival noises and harmonica folk tunes for theatrical impact. Island was premiered by the Utrecht Symphony Orchestra under Paul Hupperts at the Gaudeamus International Music Week in Rotterdam, Holland, on September 18, 1970, at which time Schwartz received second prize from the festival; it was subsequently presented by several American orchestras including the Minnesota Orchestra in Minneapolis. In various other pieces—notably in Signals, for trombone and contrabass (1968; N.Y., March 18, 1970); Septet, for voice, piano and five other players (1969); Music for Prince Albert, for piano and two tapes (1969; N.Y., March 19, 1970); Eclipse III, for chamber orchestra (1975; Center Harbor, N.H., August 4, 1974)—the performers were required to speak, whisper, scream, and sometimes move about as well. Performers were even given latitude in assembling the overall design of a composition, though Schwartz controlled the outcome in subtle notational ways in compositions such as the Septet; Options I, for trombone, tape, and percussion (1969); and Options II, for clarinet, tape, and percussion (1971).

Many of Schwartz's pieces involve instruments plus tape. The tape part of Extended Oboe, for oboe and tape (1974), was made on a synthesizer. That of Memorabilia, for cello and tape (1970), is a collage of edited scraps. Grand Concerto, for piano and tape (1973; Sacramento, Calif., January 11, 1974), and Extended Clarinet, for clarinet and tape (1974), used instrumental material "processed" by a synthesizer. Often the live player or players must be synchronized tightly to the tape part as in Music for Prince Albert and in *Prisms*, for organ and tape (1974). At times, the player can improvise freely against a fixed tape as in *Grand Concerto* and *Extended Oboe*, while at other times the tape part itself may have to be "performed" in an improvisatory way by an assistant, as in *Options* I and II, and *Music for Prince Albert*. In other pieces, the soloist must make his or her own tape out of the instrumental sounds according to instructions. This is found in *Dialogue* no. 2, for clarinet and tape (1967); *Mirrors*, for piano and tape (1973); and *Ziggurat*, for flute and tape (1976).

In the 1970s Schwartz became increasingly interested in composing a body of music for performance by amateurs—school children, beginning students, audiences—in which the textures and situations of the "new music" can be experienced firsthand with little traditional skill or rehearsal time. One such work is *Music for Soloist and Audience* (1970), in which the soloist can perform any instrument or instruments he or she may desire, while the audience is divided into four groups (each with its own conductor) producing specified vocal and percussive sounds. Other similar works designed for performance by "nonmusicians" include: *A Dream of Bells and Beats*, for piano, audience performers (radios, metronomes, music boxes), audience chorus, and alarm clocks (1977); *Pentagonal Mobile*, for piano and four-channel tape or five grand pianos (1977; Hartford, Conn., November 20, 1977); and *California Games*, for four to six players (including one percussion), audience, tape deck, performers, and audience chorus (1978; La Jolla, Calif., April 12, 1978). "In this," the composer says, "I have been influenced heavily by experiments in Europe and the process pieces of Steve Reich, Fred Rzewski, and others in the United States. The period I spent improvising publicly with jazz virtuoso Marion Brown (1972–75) was very helpful here and so were many of the guests who have appeared at the Bowdoin College festivals including Morton Subotnick and William Bolcom."

Schwartz received travel and research grants from the Ford Foundation during the summers of 1969 and 1971–72, enabling him to tour and do research in Europe. In 1970 he received the Maine State Award in the Arts and Humanities, and in 1974, and again in 1976, composition grants from the National Endowment for the Arts. In 1974 he was a delegate to the International Conference on New Musical Notation at Ghent, Belgium, and in 1980 he was given a Rockefeller Foundation Study Center residence fellowship in Bellagio, Italy. From 1976 to 1978 he was elected to a three-year term as member of the board of directors of the American Music Center.

Schwartz is the author of *The Symphonies of Ralph Vaughan Williams* (1964), *Electronic Music: A Listener's Guide* (1975) and *Music: Ways of Listening* (1980), as well as coeditor, with Barney Childs, of *Contemporary Composers in Contemporary Music* (1967). His articles on music have appeared extensively in music journals in the United States, England and Sweden.

THE COMPOSER SPEAKS: A music performance takes place not in the abstract, but in a real setting of some sort: a small room, a large hall, an outdoor garden, a cathedral, a restaurant, the interior of an automobile (through loudspeakers), and so on. Listeners are influenced by space, most likely in a subconscious way. Our traditional concert hall seating assumes but one kind of spatial arrangement: the audience seated in rows, all facing in one direction towards a raised stage on which musicians stand or sit. Furthermore, neither group (audience or players) moves or speaks during the performance. Compare that with: (a) a marching band parading down Main Street, U. S. A., the spectators lined up on both sides of the street with the musicians moving between them; or (b) a medieval banquet in which music, juggling, conversation, food, and laughter intermingle randomly; or (c) the aristocratic 19th-century "salons" of Paris, at which Chopin and Liszt played their piano compositions amidst the tinkle of glasses and cups, whispered gossip, guests arriving late or leaving early.

Recording creates its own unique spaces and makes any kind of music available for any situation. The very private world of the clavichord can be entered into by two hundred students in a lecture hall; a mighty Mahler symphony for hundreds of performers can be summoned up for one "private" listener walking the beach with a transistor radio or driving a car or taking a bath. Such situations are no longer rare. More music is being heard, and by more people, in an electro-acoustic state than in its "natural" form. Listeners should be aware of the inherent ambiguity of recorded performance, the illusion of the concert hall or cathedral being shrunk to the dimensions of a table-model radio or stereo system. Remember that our surroundings create a unique "performance space" for the recording: Loudspeakers or headphones can be located (literally) *anywhere*, in a rowboat or 30,000 feet up in the sky. When we wear a copy of the Mona Lisa on a T-shirt, or see a Rembrandt on a television screen, the visual image is surrounded by our furniture and the pictures on the walls; so, too, with Berlioz's *Symphonie fantastique* heard during a lunch-table conversation.

PRINCIPAL WORKS: Music for Orchestra, with electronic tape (1964); *Soliloquies*, for flute, clarinet, violin, and piano (1965); Concert Piece, for ten players (1965), *Texture*, for chamber orchestra (1966); *Dialogue* no. 1, for contrabass solo (1966); *Aria* no. 2, for violin and drums (1966); *Elevator Music*, for at least twelve players and a 16 +-story building (1967); *Music for the Ascension*, for chorus, organ, narrator, and percussion (1967); *Magic Music*, for orchestra, piano, "and other sounds" (1967);

Divertimento no. 2, for two horns and two keyboard players (1968); *Signals*, for trombone and contrabass (1968); *Areas*, for instrumental ensemble and dancers (1968); *Music for Napoleon and Beethoven*, for trumpet, piano, and two tapes (1969); *Music for Prince Albert*, for piano and two tapes (1969); Septet, for voice, piano, and five other players (1969); *Voyage*, for brass, wind, and percussion (1969); *Mini-Concerto*, for flute, oboe, violin, viola, and cello (1969); *Rip*, for trumpet, horn, trombone, and tape (1970); *Island*, for orchestra (1970); *Memorabilia*, for cello and tape (1970); *Music for Audience and Soloist* (1970); *Dream Overture*, for orchestra and recorded orchestra (1971); Octet 1971, for winds, strings, and keyboard (1971); *Eclipse* I, for ten players (1971); *The Decline and Fall of the Sonata*, for violin and piano (1972); *Telly*, for nine wind and percussion players, television sets, radio, tape (1972); *Eclipse* II, for band with auxiliary instruments (1973); *Mirrors*, for piano and tape (1973); *Grand Concerto*, for piano and tape (1973); *The Harmony of Maine*, for synthesizer and orchestra (1974); *Extended Oboe*, for oboe and tape (1974); *Extended Clarinet*, for clarinet and tape (1974); *Prisms*, for organ and tape (1974); *Cycles and Gongs*, for organ, trumpet, and tape (1975); *Eclipse* III, for chamber orchestra (1975); *Five Mobiles*, for flute, organ, harpsichord, and tape (1975); *Archeopteryk*, for trombone and piano (1976); *Ziggurat*, for flute and tape, tape made by performer (1976); *Janus*, for piano and orchestra (1976); *A Bowdoin Anthology*, for narrator, instruments, and tape (1976); *Pentagonal Mobile*, for piano and four-channel tape, also for five grand pianos (1977); Chamber Concerto no. 1, for contrabass and fifteen players (1977); Chamber Concerto no. 2, for clarinet and nine players (1977); Chamber Concerto no. 3, for piano and small orchestra (1977); *A Dream of Bells and Beats*, for piano, audience performers, audience chorus, and alarm clocks (1977); *California Games* for four to six players (including one percussion), audience performers and audience chorus (1978); *Scatter*, for twelve players (1979).

BIBLIOGRAPHY: *BBDM; DCM.*

Serly, Tibor, b. Losonc, Hungary, November 25, 1901; d. London, England, October 8, 1978. American citizen, 1909.

Serly devised a new tonal system called Modus Lascivus which he used in some of his most important later works. But several of these later compositions, as well as significant earlier ones, were rooted in Hungarian folk music, either through direct quotations or through the assimilation of melodic and rhythmic idioms suggestive of Hungarian folk songs and dances.

His father, Lajos Serly, was a composer and the conductor of the Budapest National Light Opera, and his mother, Hermina Barany, was a professional singer. When Tibor was four, his family immigrated to the United States, settling in New York, where they founded and performed with a Hungarian musical theater troupe. In New York, Tibor attended the city grade schools, bringing his academic education to an end after the eighth grade. When he was six, he began receiving music instruction from his father, both on violin and piano. At fourteen he attended the Von Ende School in New York for violin instruction. At that time he was already able to perform regularly during the weekends with the troupe in which his parents were appearing. At sixteen he became a regular member of the violin section of the Russian Symphony in New York. Further music study took place at the Institute of Musical Art in New York with A. W. Lilienthal and Rubin Goldmark. Serly began writing music and getting it performed while he was still in his adolescence.

In 1922 he returned to his native land to complete his musical education at the Royal Academy of Music in Budapest, where he studied orchestration with Hans Koessler and Leo Weiner. During the next three years he studied the violin with Jenö Hubáy and composition with Zoltán Kodály. As a student at the academy, he wrote a Violin Sonata (1923) and his string quartet no. 1 (1924), both traditional in structure and romantic in style. He graduated from the academy in 1925 with highest honors in both violin and composition; at his graduation a concert of his compositions was given.

He returned to the United States in 1925. For about a year he earned his living playing violin in jazz bands, vaudeville, speakeasies, and with hotel orchestras. Soon after his return, through his friendship with several young avant-garde American writers and poets, he came to know the literary work of James Joyce. From Joyce's *Chamber Music* he selected four poems ("Sleep Now," "Gentle Lady," "All Day," and "Silently She's Combing Her Long Hair") to set to music for soprano and chamber orchestra (1926), the music always subtly responsive to the different texts. These songs received their first public performance on March 4, 1936, in Philadelphia, during an evening devoted entirely to Serly's chamber and vocal music in which his string quartet no. 1 was included. "Mr. Serly," commented Samuel L. Lacier in the *Philadelphia Evening Ledger* at the time, "is a modernist in thought and style and does not disdain to use modern harmonization where it will give the effect which he desires, although he does not carry this feature of his compositions to disagreeable extremes and in some instances does not use it at all."

While continuing to advance his career as a composer after 1926, Serly initiated a long and eventful career as a member of symphony orchestras by joining in 1927–28 the viola section of the Cincinnati Symphony, then conducted by Fritz Reiner. From

1928 to 1937 he was a violist with the Philadelphia Orchestra under Leopold Stokowski.

During his first year in Philadelphia, Serly completed writing his first major work, a Viola Concerto (1929), "as practice material for myself" and to fill a need for a major virtuoso work for that instrument. The Hungarian folk music is here encountered in the affecting slow movement where the profuse arabesques were derivative of certain parlando-type melodies found in Hungarian folk songs expressing lamentation. The Hungarian folk song was also strongly assertive in Serly's Symphony no. 1, for large orchestra (1931), particularly in the eloquently lyrical second-movement Adagio. Both the Viola Concerto and the Symphony no. 1—as well as *Six Dance Designs*, for large orchestra (1933)—were given their world premieres at an all-Serly concert in Budapest on May 13, 1935, the composer conducting. Writing in *New Hungary*, Geza Haics said: "This music is daring and guides us in new paths to beauties felt but yet unseen. It does not grip you because it is a mellowed, ripened fruit. Quite the contrary, it grips you with its throbbing seed of youthful genius. Serly's originality and ingenuity are most striking in his treatment of the orchestra where each phrase speeds straight to the mark. His orchestra is rich, sonorous and powerful." *Six Dance Designs* was performed by the Philadelphia Orchestra under the composer's direction in May 1936, and the Symphony no. 1 by the same orchestra under Eugene Ormandy on January 15, 1937. In commenting on the symphony when the Philadelphia Orchestra brought it to New York, Winthrop Sargeant said: "The work . . . seemed to have both substance and individuality. Its style, which shows a natural debt to the Hungarian school, avoids the more obvious formulas of the modernists and leaves room for forthright melodic writing. . . . It is a work of distinct promise."

Symphony no. 2, for woodwinds, brass, and percussion, in two movements (1931), was polyphonic music that avoided harmonic support. Each instrument (second and third instruments included) had its independent melodic line. Chords, when they did occur, were only incidental; in no part were chords or harmonies used to gain additional sound value. Thus, the effects achieved by way of color or instrumentation were the direct consequences of contrapuntal combinations meeting and crossing through various registers rather than through orchestration. Strings were dispensed with because the composer felt their intense overtones would tend to obscure the clarity of the contrapuntal voices.

With the *Sonata concertante*, for string orchestra, specifically with a string quartet solo in the last movement (1935–36; Chautauqua, N.Y., August 1944), the complexity of polyphonic structure and the discreet dissonances of earlier works were replaced by a more transparent texture, a well-sounding consonance that placed its emphasis on lyricism,

and strict classical structure. This simpler and more consonant approach was further pursued in Serly's music for the ballet *The Mischianza Ball* (1936–37), which Catherine Littlefield commissioned for the Philadelphia Ballet, scenario based on the British occupation of Philadelphia during the Revolutionary War, from whose score the composer extracted two orchestral suites; in the orchestral tone poem *The Pagan City* (1938), a popularist composition based on a melodic theme of John Klenner's, a popular-song composer; and *American Elegy*, for orchestra (1945: Chautauqua, N.Y., 1948), in which "Taps" and "The Battle Hymn of the Republic" were quoted.

On October 2, 1936, Serly married Alice Sands, a social worker. They had no children and were divorced in 1962. In 1937–38, Serly served as violist in the NBC Symphony, which had been founded for Arturo Toscanini as musical director and which gave weekly concerts over the NBC radio network. When Toscanini resigned from the NBC Symphony in 1938, Serly withdrew from performing in orchestras to devote himself henceforth more completely to composition, to travel to Europe to conduct major orchestras in his works, to lecture, and to write.

In the mid-1940s, Serly began developing his own tonal "discovery": Modus Lascivus, or Enharmonicism. This was a new concept in composition which reached beyond the diatonic and chromatic language of the 19th century, in which all known consonances and dissonances were resolved. The language of harmony was expanded from fourteen basic chords to eighty-two, all founded on the interval of the third, and were then combined both vertically and horizontally, each commencing on the note C. The consonant harmonies were based on the traditional thirds, and the dissonant ones from the notes left out in the construction of those chords. To put theory into practice, Serly planned a series of eighty-two etudes for the piano, one etude on each harmonic structure. He worked on this project between 1946 and 1960, completing only forty of these etudes. He then discontinued the project to work on a number of larger works in Modus Lascivus. The world premiere of the forty etudes was given in New York on May 4, 1977, performed by Miriam Molin, who, on June 18, 1964, became Serly's second wife.

The first large-scale composition in Modus Lascivus was a three-movement Piano Sonata (1947), which Miklos Schwalb introduced in Carnegie Hall, New York, in 1947. "The score," said Louis Biancolli in the *World Telegram*, "seemed to cling almost strictly to sonata form. . . . Rhythmically, the scene breezed along at a crisp pace, and crisp was the word, too, for the sequences and groupings of notes. In fact, of all the brash new vogues of music writing, Tibor Serly's was among the easiest to take. If this be dissonance, let's have more of it. Precious little sounded harsh in the makeup of style and idiom."

Major works in Modus Lascivus following the Piano Sonata were: Suite, for two pianos (1946); Sonata for Solo Violin (1947; N.Y., November 17, 1947; Concerto for Two Pianos and Orchestra (1948–52; Syracuse, N.Y., March 4, 1965); Concerto for Trombone and Orchestra (1952; Chautauqua, N.Y., August 17, 1952), written for and introduced by Davis Schuman; *Lament*, for string orchestra, written between 1953 and 1958 in homage to Béla Bartók, which was introduced over the Budapest radio in 1960; *Concertino 3 Times 3*, for piano and orchestra (1964–65; Syracuse, N.Y., January 13, 1967); multidimensional music made up of three different compositions, a concertino for piano solo, a concertino for orchestra alone, and, when played simultaneously, a concertino for piano and orchestra; and *The Pleiades*, a cantata for vocal soloists, chorus, and orchestra (1975; Portland, Ore., May 6, 1978), a composition dominated by a five-note plainsong motive with which it opens.

Serly's output of works, other than those in Modus Lascivus, remained prolific for the remainder of his life. Some reached back to his Hungarian origins: Rhapsody, for viola and chamber orchestra (1946–48; N.Y., February 27, 1948), based on some Hungarian folk songs Béla Bartók had harmonized; Trio, for violin, piano, and taragato—the taragato being a Hungarian woodwind instrument with a mournful sound akin to the clarinet—which was written in 1949 and introduced in New York on November 7, 1949; and Three Variations, for symphonic band (1969), based on an old Hungarian folk song which became the melodic source for the variations. A few of Serly's compositions were of American rather than Hungarian identity. These included the *American Fantasy of Quodlibets*, for orchestra (1959; Seattle, Wash., 1973), which made use of several popular American tunes; and the *Musical Play of Ancient Mississippi Folksong-Ballads*, for small orchestra, chorus, and solo singers, which Serly had begun writing in the 1930s but did not complete until 1975.

Serly's many years of friendship with and admiration for Béla Bartók had a powerful impact on his own musical thinking and writing. He paid his respects to Bartók in ways other than the writing of the already mentioned *Lament*. In 1942, Serly orchestrated for piano and strings some of the pieces from Bartók's *Mikrokosmos Suite*, a suite of children's pieces for piano, and in 1943 more pieces from this suite, for orchestra. Between 1945 and 1948 he reconstructed, completed, and scored Bartók's Viola Concerto, left unfinished by Bartók's death, and in 1945 he developed the concluding seventeen measures of Bartók's Third Piano Concerto. Serly subsequently orchestrated ten pieces from Bartók's early piano music for chamber orchestra (1966) and arranged six Bulgarian dances from Bartók's *Mikrokosmos* (1973). Serly was also the first conductor to record Bartók's orchestral music and has lectured on Bartók's music.

On December 1, 1976, Serly received the George Washington Award from the American-Hungarian Foundation for his distinguished service to music. He was the author of *A Second Look at Harmony* (1965) and *Modus Lascivus: A New Concept in Composition* (1975). Just before his death, he had completed the third book, *A Rhetoric of Melody*, in collaboration with Norman Newton.

THE COMPOSER SPEAKS: I am convinced that after most of the blustering efforts of the avant-garde have passed into limbo, there will arise a genuine new music, much of which can be read at sight by the average orchestra musician, and yet sound as intricate as the most extreme pointillistic dodecaphony.

PRINCIPAL WORKS: 2 symphonies (1931, 1932).

Viola Concerto (1929); *Innovations*, for two harps and string orchestra (1931–33); *Six Dance Designs*, for large orchestra (1933–34); *Transylvania Suite*, for chamber orchestra (1935); *Sonata concertante*, for string orchestra with string quartet (1935–36); *The Pagan City*, tone poem for orchestra (1938); *The Mischianza Ball*, ballet, also two suites for orchestra (1936–37); *Ex Machina*, ballet, for small orchestra (1943); *American Elegy*, for orchestra (1945); Piano Sonata, in Modus Lascivus (1946); Sonata for Solo Violin, in Modus Lascivus (1947); Rhapsody for Viola and Chamber Orchestra (1946–48); Trio, for clarinet (or taragato), violin, and piano (1949); Two-Piano Concerto (1948–52); Trombone Concerto, in Modus Lascivus (1952); *Lament*, for string orchestra, in Modus Lascivus (1953–58); Concerto for Violin and Wind Symphony (1955–58); *Symphonic Variations for Audience and Orchestra* (1956); *String Symphony in Four Cycles* (1956); *Little Christmas Cantata*, for audience and small orchestra (1957); *American Fantasy of Quodlibets*, for orchestra (1959); Forty Piano Etudes, in Modus Lascivus (1946–60); *Concertino 3 Times 3*, for piano solo and orchestra, in Modus Lascivus (1964–65); *Anniversary Cantata on a Quodlibet*, for voices and small orchestra (1966); *Chorale in Three Harps*, in Modus Lascivus (1967); *Stringometrics*, for violin and harp (1968); Adagio and Scherzo, for solo flute, in Modus Lascivus (1968); *Consovowels no. 1*, for solo soprano, in Modus Lascivus (1968); *Three Variations on an Old Hungarian Song*, for symphonic band (1969); *Consovowels no. 2*, for soprano and clarinet, in Modus Lascivus (1970); *Consovowels no. 3*, for soprano and clarinet, in Modus Lascivus (1971); *Fantasy for Three Harps on a Double Quodlibet* (1972); Canonic Fugue, in ten voices on ten tones for strings, in Modus Lascivus (1972); *Cast Out*, ballet, for small orchestra (1973); *Threnody*, for four cellos, also four horns (1973); *Consovowels nos. 4 & 5*, for soprano and violin, in Modus Lascivus (1974); *Musical Play on Ancient Mississippi Folksong-Ballads*, for vocal soloists, chorus, and small orchestra (1975); *The Pleiades*, cantata, for solo voices, chorus, and orchestra (1975); Music for Four Harps and String Orchestra (1977).

BIBLIOGRAPHY: *BBDM*; Anderson, E. Ruth, *Contemporary American Composers* (Boston, 1976).

Sessions, Roger Huntington, b. Brooklyn, N.Y., December 28, 1896.

The subtlety and intricacy of Sessions's musical thought and the complexity of his contrapuntal, harmonic, and rhythmic structures may have alienated a segment of the general music public. But, at the same time, they have won for him the highest approbation of his colleagues and critics. Few American composers are regarded more highly by the elite in music than he; he has often been spoken of as a "composer's composer." Once he had discarded the romantic style of his early adulthood, Sessions adopted an idiom that was discordant, linear, and high-tensioned, from which he advanced to serialism, which he fashioned to his own creative needs. His thought processes are not easy to follow but once followed and understood they leave the hearer, as Alfred Frankenstein, the critic, once wrote, "rather breathless." The Pulitzer Prize committee recognized his unique status in American music in 1974 by presenting him with a special citation for his contributions.

He was descended from colonial New England ancestry. His mother, Ruth Huntington Sessions, the daughter of a bishop, came from a long line of New England ministers and free thinkers. She was an excellent pianist who had been trained at the Leipzig Conservatory. When Roger was four, his family returned to New England, settling in Hadley, Mass. From his fifth year on, he studied piano with local teachers. He showed an unusual response to music early; even as an infant he was able to reproduce in perfect pitch and time the songs he heard. He made such progress with his piano studies that in 1908 his mother decided to become his teacher. A year later, inspired by hearing some of Wagner's music at an orchestral concert, Sessions wrote an opera, *Lancelot and Elaine*, based on Tennyson's *Idylls of the King*. When, in 1910, he heard his first opera—Wagner's *Die Meistersinger*, performed in Boston by the visiting Metropolitan Opera, Arturo Toscanini conducting—he decided he wanted above all else to become a composer.

His early academic education took place at the Kent School, an Episcopal preparatory school in Connecticut, where he was a brilliant student, graduating with highest honors. Though only fourteen, he entered Harvard University in 1911, where he took courses in music with Edward Burlingame Hill, and wrote for and then edited the *Harvard Review*. He enriched his musical experiences at this time by attending the concerts of the Boston Symphony as well as performances of opera and chamber music. In 1913 he made his first contact with "modern" music through some of Schoenberg's piano pieces, which he

learned to play, and Stravinsky's *Petrouchka*, both of which had a powerful impact on him.

After receiving his bachelor of arts degree at Harvard in 1915, Sessions spent two years doing graduate work at the Yale School of Music. As a composition student of Horatio Parker's, he wrote a movement for a Violin Sonata (1916) and the first movement of a symphony (1917), which, under the title of *Symphonic Prelude*, was performed at Yale School of Music and brought him the Steinert Prize.

In 1917, having received the bachelor of music degree at Yale, Sessions became an assistant in the music department of Smith College in Northampton, Mass., serving as instructor between 1917 and 1921. During this period he studied privately with Ernest Bloch in New York. When, in 1921, Bloch became the head of the Cleveland Institute of Music in Ohio, Sessions followed him there, continuing to study with Bloch until 1922, and from 1921 to 1925 assisting Bloch as the school director besides teaching classes in theory. Under Bloch's watchful eye, Sessions composed a seven-part score emulating Bloch's rhapsodic style: incidental music for Andreyev's allegorical play *The Black Maskers* (1923), produced at Smith College in June 1923. From this music Sessions extracted four sections ("Dance," "Scene," "Dirge," and "Finale") as a symphonic suite, also named *The Black Maskers*, with which he realized his first success as a composer. "In its original form," Sessions has written, "the music, composed in seven separate numbers, formed an almost continuous accompaniment to the action of the play . . . conceived throughout as an expression of certain moods felt behind the incidents of the play, rather than as their descriptive counterpart. . . . The four numbers which have been retained contain all the most significant musical material of the work, and have been somewhat reshaped to permit of performance apart from the play." After the suite was introduced by the Cincinnati Symphony under Fritz Reiner on December 5, 1930, it was performed by several major American orchestras including the Philadelphia Orchestra under Leopold Stokowski. In *America's Music*, Gilbert Chase described this work as "extremely brilliant orchestration, emotionally powerful in its dramatic expression, [and] rich in texture."

When Bloch resigned as director of the Cleveland Institute of Music in 1925, Sessions also decided to leave. With funds supplied by his father, Sessions now made his first trip to Europe, where (except for a few sporadic interruptions) he remained for eight years, subsidized by two consecutive Guggenheim Fellowships (1926, 1927), a Walter Damrosch Fellowship at the American Academy in Rome (1928-31), and a Carnegie Fellowship (1931-32). His most ambitious composition up to that time was written in Europe in 1926-27, the Symphony in E minor, in which Bloch's influence was replaced by that of the neoclassical Stravinsky. In *An Hour with American Music*, published in 1929, Paul Rosenfeld said of it that it was "eminently 'music for every day' in the spirit of *Renard* and *L'histoire du soldat*, and as such distinguished from all preceding pieces of American music, predominantly exalted and grandiose in their conceptions. One doesn't feel the temple-dome over it. It seems to live in the atmosphere of weekdays, serious, sober but never ritualistic. There are no hot clashing colors, no heavy emphasis, no Wagnerian intensifications and ardors and exaltations in this symphony. The material is stark and the outline strong. Sessions's polytonality and polyphony are uncompromising, and sometimes harsh." When the Boston Symphony under Serge Koussevitzky introduced it on April 22, 1927, Sessions returned to the United States to attend the performance. The symphony represented the United States at the festival of the International Society for Contemporary Music in Geneva, Switzerland, on April 6, 1929. Three decades later it was first recorded, at which time Eric Salzman, in the *New York Times*, noted: "All the earmarks of Sessions's mature style are present . . . in sound and concept: the big orchestration, the large-scale constructive ideas with a brilliant sense of line, flow, and continuity."

Sessions returned to the United States for another stay in 1928. At that time he joined Aaron Copland in forming the Copland-Sessions concerts in New York, which, during the next three years, presented programs of new music. Subsequently, Sessions further promoted modern music as a member of the board of the League of Composers, to which he was appointed in 1933 and, from 1934 to 1942 he was the president of the United States section of the International Society for Contemporary Music, and from 1953 its co-chairman with Aaron Copland.

Other compositions completed in Europe were: two chorale preludes for organ (1926), introduced in New York by Joseph Yasser in December 1927; Pastorale, for flute solo (1929; Paris, 1929); a Piano Sonata (1930; Bad Hamburg, Germany, May 1931), which Aaron Copland called "a cornerstone upon which to base an American music"; and *On the Beach at Fontana*, for voice and piano (1930).

Sessions was brought back permanently to the United States in 1933 by the rise of Nazism in Germany. He supported himself in several teaching posts; at the Malkin School of Music in Boston (1933), the Boston University College of Music (1933–35), the Dalcroze School in New York (1933–34), and the New Jersey College of Women (1935–37), as well as teaching composition privately. In 1935 he joined the music faculty of Princeton University, remaining there a decade, first as instructor (1935–37), then as assistant professor (1937–40), and finally as associate professor (1940–44). During the summers of 1935, 1936, and 1938 he conducted summer courses in composition at the University of California at Berkeley. While there, on November 26, 1936, he married Elizabeth Franck, with whom he had two children, one of whom, John, became a

professional cellist. (This was Sessions's second marriage, his first, in 1920, having been to Barbara Foster.)

One of the first major works he completed after returning to the United States was the Concerto for Violin and Orchestra in B minor (1935), which he had begun writing in Europe in 1931. This was more chromatic, more linear, more dissonant than the symphony; twelve-tone elements were introduced in the last movement. In his orchestration, Sessions dispensed with violins in order to emphasize the role of the solo instrument. The wind section was expanded and the string writing enriched by subdividing the violas and cellos. The first performance, in a violin and piano version, was given by Serge Kotlarsky and the composer at the New School for Social Research in New York in 1935; the first performance with orchestra took place on January 8, 1940, in Chicago with Robert Gross, violinist, and the Illinois Symphony conducted by Izler Solomon. Twenty-four years after it was written, the Violin Concerto was heard in New York for the first time, at a concert of the New York Philharmonic conducted by Lenoard Bernstein with Tossy Spivakovsky, soloist; and almost a decade after that it was finally recorded (Paul Zukofsky, soloist). Writing in *Modern Music*, not long after the concerto was first performed, Arthur Berger said: "It is in such a grand scale that it has a unique place not only in Sessions's output but in all of American music."

Sessions grew increasingly complex and dissonant in his contrapuntal and harmonic writing, and his exercise of the twelve-tone technique became more extended in String Quartet no. 1 (1936). It was commissioned by Mrs. Elizabeth Sprague Coolidge, was written during Sessions's second visit to Berkeley, and was first performed in April 1937 by the Coolidge String Quartet in Washington, D.C. Sessions's mature style was fully crystallized in Symphony no. 2 (1944–46) which he himself has come to regard as "a kind of milestone in my work . . . a point towards which I had been moving in a number of my previous works . . . and one which forms, as it were, a point of departure for the music I have written since." It was commissioned by the Alice M. Ditson Fund of Columbia University. The death of President Franklin Delano Roosevelt while Sessions was hard at work on this symphony affected him deeply and was reflected in the elegiac and contemplative moods of the Adagio and also in the turbulent parts of the first and last movements. At its first performance—on January 9, 1947, in San Francisco, with Pierre Monteux conducting the San Francisco Symphony—the audience was apathetic, largely due to the work's high-tensioned dissonant contrapuntal textures and highly complicated harmonic and rhythmic structures. In the *San Francisco Chronicle*, Alfred Frankenstein called it "a complex of forceful and fruitful ideas which can be studied for a long time before they yield all their secrets." On June 9,

1948, this symphony was heard at the festival of the International Society for Contemporary Music in Amsterdam. After the work was performed by the New York Philharmonic under Dimitri Mitropoulos (January 12, 1950) it received the New York Music Critics Circle Award and a Naumburg Foundation grant for a recording.

Sessions's first completed opera, *The Trial of Lucullus*, in one act (1947), was produced at Berkeley, Calif., on April 18, 1947. The text, by Bertold Brecht, was a denunciation of war and tyranny. "In setting the text," the composer said, "I have been guided . . . by my strong convictions first that opera can become once more, as it has so often been in the past, a vital dramatic medium; that music and drama are essential ingredients which must be welded into an ensemble in which neither is subservient to the other, and both, essential elements of an indissoluble whole; and finally that opera is, first of all, vocal music and that characterization becomes stereotyped and one dimensional if it is entrusted mainly to instruments." The expressive declamatory style of Sessions's lyricism through which he realized not only dramatic power but penetrating characterization was particularly noteworthy.

When Sessions left Princeton in 1944, he returned to the University of California in Berkeley to spend the next eight years teaching composition. As a Fulbright Fellow he was at the Accademia Luigi Cherubini in Florence, Italy, in 1952–53. Returning to the United States in 1953, he assumed the post of William Shubael Conant Professor of Music at Princeton University, retaining this post for twelve years before his retirement. Meanwhile, in 1958, he was one of several American composers sent by the State Department to the Soviet Union as part of a cultural exchange program to participate in performances of some of his works, which were highly acclaimed. He was back at the University of California as Ernest Bloch Professor in 1966–67 and in 1968–69 he was Charles Eliot Norton Professor at Harvard University. From 1965 on, he also taught composition at the Juilliard School of Music, and in 1971 he was visiting professor of composition at the University of Iowa in Iowa City.

In the 1950s, Sessions further absorbed serialism into his writing, but without adhering to the strict principles set down by that system. His writing remained dissonantly contrapuntal, densely structured, but without sacrificing the fluid movement of the lines. String Quartet no. 2 came in 1951. *Idyll of Theocritus*, for soprano and orchestra (1954), which set Theocritus' Idyll no. 2 from *The Sorceress*, was commissioned by the Louisville Orchestra in Kentucky, which introduced it under Robert Whitney's direction on January 14, 1956. The Piano Concerto (1956) was commissioned by the Juilliard School of Music for its Festival of American Music and presented first on February 10, 1956, by Beveridge Webster. Symphony no. 3 (1957), a commission from

the Koussevitzky Music Foundation, was heard for the first time on December 6, 1957, performed by the Boston Symphony under Charles Munch. Symphony no. 4 (1958) was written to celebrate the centennial of the state of Minnesota and was given its first performance on January 2, 1960, by the Minneapolis Symphony under Antal Dorati.

Sessions's full-length opera *Montezuma* took more than two decades to grow from its initial planning stages to completion. Structurally, this is Sessions's most ambitious work, and stylistically, it is one of his most difficult compositions to comprehend and appreciate at first hearing. He first harbored the idea, in the 1930s, of making an opera about the 16th-century Aztec emperor and the Spanish conquest of Mexico by Cortez and his legions, and G. A. Borghese completed a libretto for him in 1941. Since Sessions found this libretto too long and discursive, he lost interest in the project until the late 1950s when, with the librettist now dead, he set himself the task of rewriting and condensing the text. The next three years were spent in the preparation of his score, which was finally completed in 1963. The opera was produced by the Deutsche Oper in West Berlin (with the support of the U. S. State Department) on April 19, 1964, when it was received with mixed reactions. In *Musical America*, Heinz Joachim said: "The work is not so much an opera as it is epic music theater. . . . Without dramatic action, the historical material is treated as a monumental chronicle. . . . The harsh and austere sound of the score surprisingly complements the exotic coloration and the sacerdotal rigidity of the scenery." Following the American premiere—in Boston on March 31, 1976—John Rockwell, reporting for the *New York Times*, maintained that the "prevailing impression one is left with . . . is of high-minded seriousness. The libretto . . . deals with the utmost solemnity of a collision of two barbaric cultures and the need for a 'compact universal.' Mr. Sessions's music is a deliberately ecumenical blend of styles . . . the basic idiom . . . is the sort of personalized serialism to which Mr. Sessions moved with ever greater decisiveness after his early neoclassical days. . . . At its best, the music reaches out overtly to a general audience. But on a first full hearing, it seems too convoluted, crabbed and complex, for its own operatic good." From this score, Sessions extracted four orchestral sections for a symphonic suite.

Sessions completed five more symphonies after 1958. No. 5 (1964) was commissioned by Eugene Ormandy and the Philadelphia Orchestra, and was introduced in Philadelphia on February 7, 1964. Symphony no. 6 (1966) was the result of a joint commission from the New Jersey Symphony and the state of New Jersey to commemorate the 300th anniversary of that state, the first performance taking place in Newark on November 19, 1966, although the first movement had previously been performed by the same orchestra on January 19, 1966. Symphony no. 7 (1967) was premiered in Ann Arbor, Mich., on October 1, 1967. Symphony no. 8 (1968) was written on commission to commemorate the 125th anniversary of the New York Philharmonic, which gave the premiere on May 2, 1968, William Steinberg conducting. Symphony no. 9 (1978) was a commission from the Syracuse Symphony in New York, its premiere presented by that orchestra under Frederick Prausnitz in January 1980. "It is a tough, dense score," said Nicholas Kenyon in the *New Yorker*, "and as with so much of Sessions's music, difficult to like at first hearing. But something compels one to listen, and to listen hard . . . the most striking aspect of the music is its constant state of flux, its perturbed restlessness."

Like Hindemith before him, Sessions produced one of his most important works by setting to music Walt Whitman's elegy on the death of Abraham Lincoln, *When Lilacs Last in the Dooryard Bloom'd* (1970). This is a cantata for solo voices, chorus, and orchestra, commissioned by the University of California in Berkeley to celebrate the centenary of its founding; but it was also written in memory of Martin Luther King, Jr., and Robert F. Kennedy. Like other significant compositions by Sessions, this is music not readily understood or appreciated with a single hearing. As Andrew Porter said in *Stereo Review*, commenting upon its recording: "Its 'song'—or so I found—is not evident at the start; it takes time to sort out the background from the foreground, to learn the themes. . . . But then, when the work suddenly falls into place, one is amazed that one did not respond at once to its vigorous, lucid progress and its full-throated passionate lyricism." *When Lilacs Last in the Dooryard Bloom'd* was given its initial hearing at Berkeley on May 23, 1971. Sir Georg Solti conducted it with the Chicago Symphony in 1976, and subsequently Seiji Ozawa with the Boston Symphony, the latter performance being the one that was recorded.

Since 1970, other important Sessions works include the *Three Biblical Choruses*, for chorus and chamber orchestra (1971–72; Amherst, Mass., February 8, 1975), commissioned by Amherst College for its sesquicentennial, though first performed four years after that event; the Concerto for Violin, Cello, and Orchestra (1971; N. Y., November 5, 1971); and the Concertino, for chamber orchestra (1971–72; Chicago, April 4, 1972).

A three-day festival of Sessions's music was held at Northwestern University School of Music in Evanston, Ill., between January 27 and 29, 1961, under the sponsorship of the Fromm Music Foundation, when eight of his major works were heard under the composer's direction. A retrospective concert of Sessions's music covering a quarter of a century of his creativity was heard in New York City in October 1961 honoring his sixty-fifth birthday; his seventy-first birthday was celebrated (belatedly) in New York on March 3, 1968, with an all-Sessions concert;

and his eighty-fifth birthday was commemorated (again belatedly) with a Sessions concert in New York on March 28, 1981, spanning his creative years between 1923 and 1966. Previously, on February 7, 1973, a half century of Session's music was presented at Columbia University. In February 1975, a weekend festival of Sessions's compositions (as well as lectures and round-table discussions) was held at Amherst, Mass., at which time his *Three Biblical Choruses* was premiered.

Sessions received the Creative Arts Award from Brandeis University in Waltham, Mass. (1958); was made honorary life member of the International Society of Contemporary Music (1959); was elected member of the Academy of Arts in West Berlin, Germany (1960) and the Academy of Fine Arts in Buenos Aires (1965); and was awarded the Gold Medal of the MacDowell Association (1968). He has been an honorary life member of the National Institute of Arts and Letters since 1938, and a member of the American Academy of Arts and Letters. He has received honorary doctorates from Wesleyan University (1958), Rutgers University (1962), Harvard University (1964), Brandeis University (1965), the University of Pennsylvania (1966), the New England Conservatory (1967), the University of California in Berkeley (1967) and the Cleveland Institute of Music (1975).

Sessions is the author of the *Musical Experience of Composer, Performer and Listener* (1950), *Harmonic Practice* (1951), *Reflections on the Music Life in the United States* (1952), and *Questions About Music* (1970). His essays were collected in *Roger Sessions on Music*, edited by E. T. Cone (1979).

THE COMPOSER SPEAKS: Let us, then, put away childish things, or rather, more seriously and more accurately, let us put away childish attitudes toward things that are of a truly deadly seriousness. Nationalism or nativism in music may seem a far cry from political nationalism . . . [but] believe me, this is the most dangerous of yearnings. It is on the basis of precisely such yearnings that dangerous illusions such as that of the master race are born, even though they develop by slow and almost imperceptible degrees, from apparently harmless and even well-intentioned beginnings.

So when one hears, as every one constantly does today, of positions for which only native Americans need apply, or when one hears even the slogan "play American music," the only adequate reaction is a shudder of apprehension, and the only adequate response is a redoubled effort to fight this poison. Aside from the overwhelming human menace which such slogans or programs carry with them, they carry a deadly danger to American music; and by implication, a fundamental offense to American musicians. For the implication is clearly that American music cannot endure honest competition even when the scales are heavily weighted, as they inevitably are, in their favor. It implies that music by American composers is tainted by reason of its origin, and that as inferior music it needs to be "protected."

PRINCIPAL WORKS: 9 symphonies (1927–78); 3 piano sonatas (1930, 1946, 1968); 2 string quartets (1936, 1951).

Three Chorale Preludes, for organ (1925); *The Black Maskers*, symphonic suite (1928); Violin Concerto (1935); *From My Diary*, for piano (1940); Duo, for violin and piano (1942); *The Trial of Lucullus*, one-act opera (1947); Violin Sonata (1953); *Idyll of Theocritus*, for soprano and orchestra (1954); Mass, for unison chorus and organ (1955); Piano Concerto (1956); String Quartet (1958); Divertimento, for orchestra (1960); *Montezuma*, opera (1963); Psalm 140, for soprano and organ, or orchestra (1963); Six Pieces, for cello (1966); *When Lilacs Last in the Dooryard Bloom'd*, cantata for vocal soloists, chorus, and orchestra (1970); Rhapsody, for orchestra (1970); *Three Biblical Choruses*, for chorus and chamber orchestra (1971); Concerto for Violin, Cello, and Orchestra (1971–72); Concertino, for chamber orchestra (1971–72); Five Pieces, for piano (1974–75).

BIBLIOGRAPHY: Copland, Aaron, *The New Music: 1900-1960* (N.Y., 1968); Cowell, Henry (ed.). *American Composers on American Music* (Stanford, Calif., 1933); Liebowitz, Herbert A. (ed.), *Musical Impressions: Selections from Paul Rosenfeld's Criticisms* (N.Y., 1969); Machlis, Joseph, *Introduction to Contemporary Music*, revised ed. (N.Y., 1979); *High Fidelity/Musical America*, July 1976; *Musical America*, September 1957; *Musical Quarterly*, April 1946, July 1959, July 1961; *New York Times*, April 14, 1968; *Newsweek*, May 13, 1968, March 22, 1981; *New Yorker*, May 16, 1977; *Saturday Review*, June 28, 1954; *Time*, May 10, 1968.

Shapero, Harold Samuel, b. Lynn, Mass., April 29, 1920.

Shapero's first successes as composer came with instrumental music within classical structures concerned with the preservation of musical values and qualities associated with the classical period. His writing is characterized by a highly expressive lyricism, a vigorous and at times complex harmonic and rhythmic language learned from the music of Stravinsky and Copland, with an occasional intrusion of jazz. His most recent compositions employ electronic, serial, and tonal material freely combined.

Both parents were music lovers who owned an extensive record collection (from which Harold acquired his initial experiences in music) and who were in regular attendance at the concerts of the Boston Symphony. "I certainly owe a great deal to my mother," he has said, "who possesses amazing innate musicality and encouraged my musical career from

the beginning." He began studying piano when he was seven, and at nine made his first attempt at composition with a mazurka for piano. While attending Newton High School in Massachusetts (1934–37) he formed a jazz band for which he wrote arrangements. When he discovered he did not know how to modulate, he decided to seek formal instruction in theory. In 1936, he began studying harmony, counterpoint, and composition with Nicolas Slonimsky. With this preliminary training he was able to write some piano compositions (influenced by Debussy).

He entered Harvard University in 1937, where he majored in music, studying composition with Walter Piston and, in his junior year, he played some of his compositions for Stravinsky, who was Charles Eliot Norton Professor of Music at Harvard in 1939–40. While still a freshman, Shapero spent six months of composition study with Ernst Krenek at the Malkin Conservatory in Boston on a scholarship. Krenek introduced him to atonality and the twelve-tone system. Under Krenek's guidance, Shapero wrote a string trio in the twelve-tone technique "actually working with its complexities before I had acquired a clear knowledge of academic harmony." While at Harvard, he spent summers (1940, 1941) at the Berkshire Music Center at Tanglewood, Mass., studying composition with Paul Hindemith. At Harvard his talent was recognized with the winning of the Knight Prize in 1939 and 1940.

In 1941 he graduated from Harvard with a bachelor of arts degree, *magna cum laude*, and with membership in Phi Beta Kappa. During his college years he wrote several chamber music works, including *Three Pieces for Three Pieces*, for flute, clarinet, and bassoon (1938), a Trumpet Sonata (1939), and a String Quartet (1940). The Trumpet Sonata and *Three Pieces for Three Pieces* received their first performances in New York in 1940 at concerts of the League of Composers. His first composition for orchestra, *Nine Minute Overture* (1940), was introduced by the CBS Orchestra under Howard Barlow over the CBS radio network on June 8, 1941, and brought him the American Prix de Rome. Because World War II had started, Shapero was unable to go to Rome. Instead, on a grant from the Weyman Fund, he studied composition with Nadia Boulanger at the Longy School in Cambridge, Mass. (1942–43). "The impressions made by Boulanger's presentation of classical literature (most importantly the Beethoven quartets) proved to be of considerable significance to me in these years." While studying with Boulanger, he worked as an arranger for Benny Goodman's swing band, but in 1943 Shapero resigned to devote himself to composition. "This was a decisive break with jazz and popular culture," he says. In 1944 he completed three piano sonatas and in 1945, the Serenade in D, for string orchestra. The first movement of the Serenade brought him the Gershwin Memorial Award and the complete five-movement work won the Bearns Prize, both in 1945 and, in 1946, a

Guggenheim Fellowship, which was extended for a second year. Leonard Bernstein, conducting the Rochester Philharmonic, introduced the first movement of the Serenade in New York on March 16, 1946. Meanwhile, in 1943, Shapero received the Naumburg Foundation Award and in 1944 the Paine Traveling Fellowship from Harvard, the latter enabling him to come to New York to advance his career further as composer.

While spending the summer composing at the MacDowell Colony in Peterboro, N.H., in 1945, Shapero met Esther Geller, an artist. They were married in Boston on September 21 of that year. In addition to raising a daughter, she has developed her career as artist and teacher in the Boston area, her encaustic paintings, watercolors, and prints being represented in many American museum collections.

On a commission from the Koussevitzky Music Foundation, Shapero wrote the *Symphony for Classical Orchestra* (1947), his most successful work up to that time. Here, he used the forces of the classical orchestra within a classical structure (movements I, II, and IV are in sonata form), in a neoclassic idiom reminiscent of Stravinsky. Leonard Bernstein conducted the premiere performance with the Boston Symphony on January 30, 1948, following which it was performed by the Cleveland Orchestra under George Szell, and the Adagietto movement by the New York Philharmonic under Bernstein and at the Berkshire Music Festival at Tanglewood. In the *Boston Post*, Henry S. Lawton described the work as "a skillfully wrought work . . . full of syncopated effects and offbeat entrances in a harmonic setting sometimes pungent." Another commission—from the Houston Symphony in Texas—led to the writing of *The Travellers*, a concert overture (1948), premiered by the Houston Symphony under Efrem Kurtz on February 28, 1949.

A Fulbright Fellowship and a second Prix de Rome, both in 1949–50, brought Shapero to Rome, where he wrote the Concerto for Orchestra (1950). That summer he served as Lecturer at the Salzburg Seminar in American Studies in Austria. After his return to the United States, Shapero was appointed, in 1951, to the music faculty of Brandeis University in Waltham, Mass., where he became associate professor in 1956, chairman of the music department between 1966 and 1969, and, since then, full professor, as well as director of the electronic music program. He returned to Italy in 1961–62 on a second Fulbright Fellowship and, in 1970–71, was composer-in-residence at the American Academy in Rome.

In 1955, on a commission from the Louisville Orchestra in Kentucky, Shapero simplified and shortened the second movement of the Concerto for Orchestra, now calling it *Credo*, for orchestra. It was first heard on October 19, 1955, Robert Whitney conducting, and then recorded. On a commission from the American Jewish Tercentenary Committee, he wrote a Hebrew cantata, *Until Night and Day*

Shall I Cease (1955), for solo voices, chorus, trumpet, flute, violin, harp, and organ, to poems by Jehuda Halevi. In 1960, commissioned by the Ford Foundation, he wrote the Partita, for piano and small orchestra, which Seymour Lipkin introduced with the Detroit Symphony under Paul Paray in 1961.

Since 1967, Shapero has worked with electronic music, producing a number of works for synthesizer and piano. He has collaborated with Melville Clark and David Luce, engineers, in developing a new synthesizer, the Orchestron, which can duplicate electronically and with great precision the sounds of all familiar orchestral instruments.

THE COMPOSER SPEAKS: I feel that if my music has some originality, beauty, and invention, it will be sufficient, whatever the labels applied. Though I am no enemy of the "new," the avant-garde music of the last twenty years has in a large part been an unnatural, ignorant, and often hideous farce. The excitement of physical sound has too often masked intellectual, moral, and aesthetic chaos.

PRINCIPAL WORKS: Sonata, for piano, four hands (1940); String Quartet (1940); Violin Sonata (1942); Three Sonatas, for piano (1943–44); Serenade in D, for string orchestra (1945); *Symphony for Classical Orchestra* (1947); Variations in C minor, for piano (1947); Piano Sonata in F minor (1948); Concerto for Orchestra (1950); *Until Night and Day Shall I Cease*, Hebrew cantata for solo voices, chorus, trumpet, flute, violin, and organ (1955); *Credo*, for orchestra, a simplification of the second movement of Concerto for Orchestra (1955); *Lyric Dances*, ballet (1956–58); Partita, for piano and small orchestra (1960); Three Improvisations in B, for synthesizer and piano (1968); Three Studies in C-sharp, for synthesizer and piano (1969); Four Pieces in B-flat, for synthesizer and piano (1970); *Two Hebrew Songs*, for tenor, strings, and piano (1978).

BIBLIOGRAPHY: *DCM*; Ewen, David, *American Composers Today* (N.Y., 1949); Goss, Madeleine, *Modern Music Makers* (N.Y., 1952); *Who's Who in America, 1970–71*.

Shapey, Ralph, b. Philadelphia, Pa., March 12, 1921.

Shapey calls himself a serial composer, though he uses any technique, method, or discipline necessary in the creation of a work of art. His compositions are one-fabric works, that is, his materials go through a metamorphosis from movement to movement; one is always able to trace the materials of each movement back to their original source. His writing is often strongly contrapuntal, intense in its lyricism, and occasionally romantic in feeling. "In his music," Bernard Jacobson once wrote in the *Chicago Daily*

News, "every detail is worked out with an almost ferocious intellectual power."

He received his academic education in Philadelphia's public schools while pursuing his musical studies. Violin lessons began when he was seven and a half, and when he was about nine he wrote a Mozartlike piece for violin. He played in the school orchestra and made successful appearances as a prodigy. His subsequent violin study took place with Emmanuel Zetlin and was supplemented by the study of composition with Stefan Wolpe, who made Shapey more knowledgeable of the twelve-tone technique, with which Shapey was already acquainted.

Between 1938 and 1942, Shapey was assistant conductor of the Philadelphia National Youth Administration. During World War II, Shapey served in the U.S. Army (1942–45) in units stationed in the South and Southwest. While in uniform, in the summer of 1942, he conducted the Philadelphia Orchestra at Robin Hood Dell as the winner in the Philadelphia Finds Contest. During his service in the army, he wrote in 1946–47 his String Quartet no. 1, Piano Sonata no. 1, and a Piano Quintet, all in a modified twelve-tone idiom, highly chromatic, bordering on serial technique. He continued producing chamber music for the next few years. In 1949 he wrote String Quartet no. 2, with which his career as composer was launched. The Juilliard String Quartet introduced it on March 27, 1950. Then, in 1951, he wrote a work for orchestra, Fantasy (1951), which received honorable mention in the George Gershwin Memorial Competition. Dimitri Mitropoulos, who made the final decision, revealed that Shapey's composition was in fact the best and deserved first prize but had to be turned down because its performance would have required an inordinate amount of rehearsal time.

In 1953, Shapey received the Frank Huntington Beebe Award for travel abroad. While in Florence, Italy, he completed the work that brought his talent to greater public attention. It was the Concerto, for clarinet and chamber group. This was a serial composition in which the full row does not appear until the middle movement. It was introduced by the New York Philharmonic Chamber Society, Shapey conducting, with Stanley Drucker as clarinet soloist, on March 20, 1955. It was selected as one of two compositions representing the United States at the festival of the International Society at Strasbourg, France, on June 9, 1958.

On October 28, 1957, Shapey married Vera Klement Shapiro, a painter, with whom he had a son. They were divorced in 1977. In 1958–59 he completed a significant trilogy of orchestral compositions bearing the overall title of *Testament to Man,* in which his personalized serial style and some of his innovative practices come into full focus. They were *Ontogeny* (1958); *Invocation,* a concerto for violin and orchestra (1959); and *Rituals* (1959). *Ontogeny* and *Rituals* were introduced by the Chicago Symphony conducted by the composer on May 12 and May 26, 1966, respectively; *Rituals* earned the Naumburg Recording Award in 1966. *Invocation* was heard first on May 25, 1968, in Chicago. In all these works, the symphony orchestra was subdivided into smaller orchestral segments distributed in a novel arrangement on the stage. There were seven smaller groups in *Ontogeny* and eight in *Rituals.* (One of the eight in *Rituals* was a trio of saxophones to whom aleatory passages were assigned.) Germinal, fragmentary, Webernlike material was developed step by step in each of the sections until its full potential had been realized. Donal Henahan wrote of *Ontogeny* in the *Musical Quarterly:* "Several unitary ideas predominate, each one handled like a building block: a stabbing trumpet fanfare, rhythmic patterns of triplets, a cantus firmus, tone clusters, and the like. Much use is made of antiphonally treated percussion. . . . [Shapey's] music sounds like a vision of chaos, but it is ordered right down to the last subdivided thirty-second note." In *Rituals,* the twelve-tone row and Webernlike fragments are ordered into well-sounding blocks of sounds. "The music," Bernard Jacobson wrote in the *Chicago Daily News,* "bursts from the loudspeakers with positively explosive force. . . . It is a work of violently expressive character. But beneath the jagged gestures, there is a lyricism that puts the music—for all its thoroughly contemporary harmonic language—firmly in the late-romantic tradition . . . Shapey is one of the authentic geniuses in today's creative world." In *Invocation,* as Jacobson later wrote in the *Daily News,* "the proliferating textures serve to further the communication of a vibrant, white-hot lyricism . . . . The Concerto is full of stimulating ideas and new, exciting, beautiful sounds."

In 1959–60, Shapey received a grant from the Italian government for a visit to that country which he rejected because it had been denied to his wife, Vera Klement. That year (1960), on a commission from the Fromm Music Foundation, he wrote *Dimensions,* for soprano and twenty-three instruments. Bethany Beardslee and an ensemble conducted by the composer introduced it at a Fromm Music Foundation concert in New York on May 13, 1961. In *Incantations,* for soprano and ten instruments (1961)—which Bethany Beardslee and an ensemble conducted by the composer premiered in New York on April 22, 1961—the vocal part makes up three-fourths of the entire composition. In both works no literary text is used, just vowel sounds that, as Allen Hughes noted in the *New York Times,* result in "one of the most searing, terrifying, and altogether extraordinary compositions this listener has heard . . . a composition of abstract expressionism that seems to lay bare the most secret and elemental doubts, yearnings, ferments, and despairs of the human soul trapped in the chaos of the urban jungle. The shattering blare of street and machine, the crazy din of the cabaret, the frenzied rush that won't slow down—all are there.

And against all, a lone human voice cries out—wondering, questioning, imploring."

In 1962, Shapey was given the Creative Arts Award by Brandeis University in Waltham, Mass., as well as the Edgar Stern Family Fund Award and the William and Noma Copley Foundation Award; and in 1966 he was the recipient of an award from the National Institute of Arts and Letters. Meanwhile, in 1963–64, he was a member of the music faculty at the University of Pennsylvania. In 1964, he was appointed assistant professor of music at the University of Chicago, where, since 1969, he has been full professor. At the university, with a grant from the Rockefeller Foundation, he organized and has since conducted the Contemporary Chamber Players in concerts of new, provocative music. His imaginative and innovative programs, and his exceptional skill in bringing this music to life led Martin Bernheimer, the critic of the *Los Angeles Times*, to refer to him as "the Toscanini of the coherent farout." Shapey has also made numerous guest appearances as conductor with major symphony orchestras.

As a composer, Shapey remained productive through the 1960s. He wrote Partita-Fantasy, for cello and sixteen players, in 1967 on a commission from the Koussevitzky Music Foundation as a companion piece to the Partita, for violin and thirteen players he had written one year earlier, on commission from the University of Chicago. *Songs of Ecstasy*, commissioned by the Fromm Music Foundation, was scored for soprano, piano, percussion, and tape (1967; Chicago, May 23, 1969)—the live soprano pitted against her own voice on the tape. Its text was derived from the Genesis, Walter Benton's *This Is My Beloved*, Shakespeare's *As You Like It*, and the last three lines from James Joyce's *Ulysses*. This was music expressing the emotions of sexual union but elevating it to a spiritual plane.

In 1969, Shapey announced that he would no longer make any of his compositions available for performance. He had also decided not to compose any longer and even thought of burning everything he had written. He would not provide a reason for such total withdrawal, regarding it as too personal, and, in a way, philosophic. He made it clear, however, that he had no grievance against audiences (many of whom, he said, were "surprisingly receptive to my music") nor to critics, one of whom, Bernard Jacobson, had called his output "the finest and most substantial body of music of any American composer of our times." Yet it was obvious that there was much about the musical establishment that disturbed him. Though recognized as a creative force of singular importance in American music, not one of his works had been published by 1969; every work of his that had been performed came about through his own contrivance and arrangement, with none of the major orchestras or musical organizations seeking out his music for performance on their programs; and precious little of what he had done had been recorded.

He ended his silence, and the moratorium against performance of his works, with a major religious composition: *Praise* (1971), an oratorio for bass-baritone, chorus, and orchestra. This was a Hebrew service which took its text from the Old Testament and the Union Prayer Book and was written in a monodic, chantlike style but in a thoroughly atonal and twelve-tone idiom. Shapey dedicated this work to "all descendants of Abraham, Isaac, and Jacob" and sent a copy to Israel to honor that country on its twenty-fifth anniversary. After that, he produced several more significant works. String Quartet no. 7 (1971–72) was written on a commission from the Fromm Music Foundation and was a response, as he said, "for my deep love for Beethoven's last quartets." It was introduced in Chicago on April 22, 1977. Its first movement is a series of interludes and fantasias, each interlude derived from the opening section while the fantasias were developmental images of material from the interludes. *The Covenant*, for soprano and sixteen players, and tape (1977; Chicago, April 14, 1978), was written to commemorate the thirtieth anniversary of the birth of Israel and was concerned with the present-day crisis in faith. "It is meant for all humankind—to walk upright, in dignity, in the image of—as One," the composer explained. "*The Covenant*," wrote Andrew Porter in the *New Yorker*, "is not absolute music. Its composer would expect his listeners to be moved, to consider their own thoughts and feelings about Israel's history, about Israel today, about its policies and actions. . . . During the music, the listeners are moved to share Shapey's own thoughts as proclaimed, given shape, by his urgent vital music, and to share his larger vision of life that has some meaning in it." Putting the word of God and the prophet Isaiah in the voice of a soprano might come as a shock, but, as Andrew Porter noted, "only at first; then it becomes clear that voice and words arise out of and make articulate the deeper, full-voiced imagery." For this work, Shapey found his text in the Bible and in the works of several Jewish poets.

On May 17, 1978, in New York, at a concert of the International Society for Contemporary Music, Robert Black gave the world premiere of Thirty-one Variations, for piano (1972–73), which has since come to be known as the "Fromm Variations," being dedicated to Paul Fromm. In the *New Yorker*, Andrew Porter spoke of it as "a rich, thoroughly and almost ruthlessly exhaustive, imposing composition." Another such set, Twenty-one Variations, for piano (1978), was commissioned by Abraham Stokman, who introduced it in New York on January 20, 1979. This is a one-fabric work in four sections. Each section has its own set of variations—all variations derived from the opening statement; one variation is linked to the next until the final resolution comes in the twenty-first variation, serving as the coda.

In 1979, on a commission from the Elizabeth

Sprague Coolidge Foundation for the Library of Congress in Washington, D.C., Shapey wrote *Song of Songs* I, for soprano, fourteen players, and tape. That year he received the Laurel Leaf Award from American Composers Alliance and was resident composer at the Berkshire Music Center at Tanglewood.

Shapey's sixtieth birthday was commemorated in Chicago on June 2, 1981, with an all-Shapey concert.

THE COMPOSER SPEAKS: Great art is a miracle. My true antecedents are Bach, Beethoven, Brahms. I bemoan that I cannot write works like they did, but they too were men of their day, and would surely write differently had they lived now.

After all, what is music? We are trying to make real an abstract thing, which is sound itself as it moves in time and space. I have asked myself, "What is it that is going to ground this one into one's memory pattern?" until I arrived at my concept of "the graven image." This abstract thing, sound, must be made to seem so concrete that you can practically hold it in your hand. It must be unforgettable. This is what Mozart and Beethoven understood.

I insist that the listener bring his brain to a concert. I am trying to write unforgettable music. You might hate it, but you are not going to forget it.

PRINCIPAL WORKS: 7 string quartets (1946–72).

Fantasy, for orchestra (1951); Symphony no. 1, for orchestra (1952); Cello Sonata (1953); Sonata-Variations for piano (1954); Concerto, for clarinet and chamber group (1954); Piano Trio (1953–55); *Challenge: The Family of Man*, for orchestra (1955); Mutations, for piano (1956); *Walking Upright*, eight songs for female voice and violin (1958); *Ontogeny*, for orchestra (1958); *Invocation*, concerto for violin and orchestra (1959); *Rituals*, for orchestra (1959); *Evocation*, for violin with piano and percussion (1959); *Soliloquy*, for narrator, string quartet, and percussion (1959); *Movements*, for woodwind quintet (1960); *Five*, for violin and piano (1960); *Dimensions*, for soprano and twenty-three instruments (1960); *Incantations*, for soprano and ten instruments (1961); *Discourse*, for four instruments (1961); *Convocation*, for chamber group (1962); Chamber Symphony, for ten solo players (1962); Brass Quintet (1963); *Configurations*, for flute and piano (1965); String Trio (1965); Partita, for solo violin (1966); Partita, for violin and thirteen players (1966); *Poems*, for viola and piano (1966); Partita-Fantasy, for cello and sixteen players (1967); *Deux*, for two pianos (1967); *Songs of Ecstasy*, for soprano, with piano, percussion, and tape (1967); *Reyem*, or *Musical Offering*, for flute, violin, and piano (1967); *Praise*, oratorio, for bass-baritone, double chorus, and chamber group (1971); Thirty-one Variations, for piano (1972–73); *Song of Eros*, for soprano, symphony orchestra, and tape (1975); *The Covenant*, for

soprano, sixteen players, and tape (1977); Twenty-one Variations, for piano (1978); *Trilogy: Song of Songs* I, II, III, for soprano, bass, fourteen instruments and tape (1979–81); Evocations II, for cello, piano, and percussion (1979); Movements for Wind Quintet (1981).

BIBLIOGRAPHY: *DCM*; Mellers, Wilfrid, *Music in a New Found Land* (N.Y., 1964); Salzman, Eric, *Twentieth Century Music* (N.Y., 1967); *New York Times*, May 8, 1977, July 9, 1979, May 10, 1981; *Who's Who in America, 1980–81*.

Shepherd, Arthur, b. Paris, Idaho, February 19, 1880; d. Cleveland, Ohio, January 12, 1958.

By reason of his wholly English ancestry and his early years in the Rocky Mountain region of the American West, Shepherd had a natural predilection for a folk-music type of melody that had continuous flow and often was modal in character. This is romantic music with which he first became famous. His later works demonstrated an increasing concern for free, clear contrapuntal textures and a plastic rhythmic syntax. Throughout his career, he showed little concern for stylistic or idiomatic experimentation.

He was one of ten children; two of his brothers also became professional musicians, one as a pianist, the other as a violinist. The parents, both of English birth, had immigrated to the United States in 1877 as English converts to Mormonism. They were musical, the mother being a trained singer, and the father a performer on the reed organ. Arthur Shepherd's earliest musical experiences came from hearing the reed organ played at home and the singing of part songs and English glees by his parents and their relatives.

"I early learned to read at sight," Shepherd once recalled. "*How* I have never known." As a boy he was a member of a fife and drum band, then played the cornet with a brass band and sang with the Bear Lake State Choir. His father gave him lessons on reed organ and piano before turning him over to more experienced piano teachers, first George Haessel, then Otto Haenisch. Shepherd made such progress with Haenisch that, on the teacher's encouragement and with the father's full support, Arthur was despatched to Boston when he was twelve to enter the New England Conservatory. There he received a thorough musical training, primarily from Charles Dennée (piano), Samuel W. Cole (solfeggio), Benjamin Cutter (harmony), and later Carl Faelten (piano), Percy Goetschius (harmony), and George Chadwick (composition). Because of his natural facility for sight-reading, Shepherd was much in demand as piano accompanist, which enabled him to acquire familiarity with a wide range of music literature. He graduated from the New England Conservatory in 1897, with a silver seal of honor on his diploma, after having been president of his class.

When his conservatory training was completed, his family decided to move from their home base in Idaho to Salt Lake City, where, the father felt, greater opportunities were available for the musical development of his three musical sons. Shepherd decided to join his family there. From 1897 to 1908, he earned his living in Salt Lake City teaching harmony and counterpoint, serving as pianist and as musical director of the Salt Lake Theater, playing the organ in churches, and, for four or five years, conducting the Salt Lake City Symphony. In 1901 he married Hattie Hooper Jennings. They had four children, one of whom died in infancy.

In 1901, Shepherd wrote *Ouverture joyeuse* which, in December 1905, won the initial Paderewski Prize and which previously (1903) had been introduced by the Russian Symphony Orchestra under Modest Altschuler in New York. It was subsequently performed by the New York Symphony under Walter Damrosch. After that, as Shepherd said, "it was placed on the shelf, where it has remained in abysmal obscurity." Another composition written in Salt Lake City was his Piano Sonata no. 1 (c. 1907), whose folklike American melodies represented a departure from Shepherd's earlier eclecticism rooted in 19th-century French and Russian romanticism. This is a work, as William S. Newman said of it in the *Musical Quarterly,* "that displays a surging youthful drive and precocious command of the-then newest harmony." In 1909 this sonata won a prize in a contest of the National Federation of Music Clubs.

One of Shepherd's activities in the beginning of the 20th century, and extending for a five-year period, was to participate in the publishing venture of the Wa-Wan Press which Arthur Farwell had founded in 1901 to promote American music. Shepherd's first publications were issued by this press: Theme and Variations (c. 1903), Mazurka (1905), and Prelude (1905), all for piano.

In 1909, Shepherd left Salt Lake City to live and work in Boston. That year, the National Federation of Music Clubs once again presented him with its prize, this time for the song "The Lost Child," which was a number in the cycle Five Songs (1909; Grand Rapids, Mich., 1909) on poems of James Russell Lowell. In Boston, Shepherd taught piano and harmony and conducted the orchestra at the New England Conservatory. Outside the conservatory he directed the Musical Arts Society (a women's choral group) for three years and the St. Cecilia Society for two years more. His creative output at this time was somewhat sporadic as he was passing through a transition period, away from his former European-oriented romanticism to his subsequent personalized style. He produced some piano pieces and songs; a cantata for baritone, chorus, and orchestra, *The City of the Sea* (1913), text by William Bliss, which won a prize from the National Federation of Music Clubs

in 1913 and that year was performed by the Chicago Symphony under Frederick Stock at the annual conference in Chicago of that Federation; an orchestral overture, *The Festival of Youth* (1915), performed by the St. Louis Symphony under Max Zach in the year of its composition; and *Fantaisie humoresque,* for piano and orchestra (1916), premiered at the New England Conservatory on February 8, 1918, with Lee Pattison as soloist and the composer conducting. Shepherd revised this last-named work, retitling it Fantasia; as such it was performed by the Cleveland Orchestra with Heinrich Gebhard, pianist, on November 18, 1920, and soon after that by the Boston Symphony.

On July 13, 1918, during World War I, Shepherd enlisted in the army. He spent eight months at the front as the bandmaster of the 303rd Field Artillery Regiment, seeing action in the battles of the Toul Sector.

Upon his discharge from military service, he returned to Boston to resume his teaching activities at the New England Conservatory. He completed a highly successful composition for orchestra, *Overture to a Drama,* in 1919. It received a notable premiere in Cleveland five years after it was written, on March 27, 1924, with the composer conducting the Cleveland Orchestra. After that it was performed by that orchestra under Nikolai Sokoloff on tour, and during the 1949–50 season was revived by the Cleveland Orchestra under George Szell, receiving favorable audience and critical response.

Here is how Richard Loucks describes *Overture to a Drama* in his biography of Shepherd: "The opening theme is a long line which, by avoiding cadences, stretches out to fifteen measures, not without phrase delineation but certainly with little correspondence to customary relationships between antecedent and consequent phrases. The mood is energetic, the effect virile. Wild Straussian shapes are flung out by the horns and the harmony is shot through with extensive chromatic deviations that eventually plunge back into a rock-solid A minor. The second subject, quiet, feminine, expressive, begins with a slowly arpeggiated seventh chord similar to Debussy's flaxen-haired maiden but harmonized by Romantic augmented sixths. Out of these materials Shepherd developed a sonata form of considerable scope, drama, and conviction."

Domestic problems which led to divorce in 1919 made Shepherd seek a change of scene. In 1920 he came to Cleveland on an invitation of Nikolai Sokoloff, conductor of the Cleveland Orchestra, to serve as his assistant. Between 1920 and 1926, Shepherd worked under Sokoloff, in addition to which he played piano, led a chorus, conducted children's concerts, and served as the orchestra's program annotator. When, in 1927, he severed his affiliation with the Cleveland Orchestra, he became for a short period that year a lecturer on music appreciation at Cleveland College of Western Reserve University. In 1928 he was appointed professor of music there, remaining twenty-two years and resigning in 1950 as professor emeritus. From 1928 to 1931 he was the music critic of the *Cleveland Press*. Meanwhile, on May 27, 1922, he married his second wife, Grazella Puliver, with whom he had a son.

His most important compositions in Cleveland were *Triptych,* for string quartet and voice (1925; Columbus, Ohio, 1926), based on three poems from Tagore's *Gitanjali;* his first major work with a distinct American identity, his Symphony no. 1, *Horizons* (1927); and the Piano Sonata no. 2 (1930; Cleveland, Ohio, 1930), whose slow movement (a theme and variations) reflected Shepherd's interest in melodies with a strong Celtic cast. The symphony is the most important of these, indeed, one of Shepherd's finest works. Four cowboy songs were developed here: "The Old Chisholm Trail," "The Dying Cowboy," "The Dogie Song," and "The Lone Prairie." "The Western spirit is the real thing here, not stimulated," says William S. Newman. "When he writes about the West it is because he has known its epic qualities. When he uses Western tunes it is because they really appeal to him." *Horizons* was first performed on December 15, 1927, Nikolai Sokoloff conducting the Cleveland Orchestra. It was repeated in Cleveland in 1929 and 1930 and was programmed by other major American orchestras besides being heard in Paris, Prague, Berlin, and Warsaw. It was the recipient of a publication award of the Juilliard Foundation.

These are Shepherd's most important compositions after 1930: *Choreographic Suite on an Exotic Theme,* for orchestra (1930)—based on *Exotic Dance,* for piano, written two years earlier—premiered by the Cleveland Orchestra on October 22, 1931; *The Song of the Pilgrims,* a cantata for tenor, double chorus, and orchestra, with text by Rupert Brooke (1932; Cleveland, summer 1936) in which the plainsong *Orbis Factor* was quoted; Symphony no. 2 (1938), first heard on March 7, 1940, in Cleveland, and performed by the Boston Symphony in November 1940, the composer conducting on both occasions; the Piano Quintet (1940; Cleveland, January 31, 1941), one of the composer's own favorite works; *Praeludium Salutatorium for Divers Instruments* (1942), for seven instruments, commissioned by the League of Composers and performed by an ensemble of the New York Philharmonic in New York on December 27, 1942; *Fantasia on Down-East Spirituals* (1946), based on four native American white spirituals from a collection gathered by George Pullen Jackson and Cecil Sharpe, written on commission for the tenth anniversary of the Indianapolis Symphony, which introduced it under Fabien Sevitzky on November 2, 1946, before the Minneapolis Symphony under Dimitri Mitropoulos took it on an extensive national tour in 1948–49; Violin Concerto (1946); and *Variations on an Original Theme,* for orchestra (1952; Cleveland, April 9, 1953).

"It was to his disadvantage," writes Richard Loucks, "that he could not or would not promote his music more effectively. It was probably within his power to write so that his music would attract more attention—he had, perhaps, exaggerated notions of musical and personal integrity. Probably many obstacles to success resulted from an overstrict, uncompromising adherence to an outmoded idea of the right, the true, the beautiful. Nevertheless, he believed in himself and in his music. He spoke when he felt something had to be said, and it was evidently more important to him that his works accurately reflect his views on art than that they spread his name in concert halls far and wide. To him, notes represented more than tunes and scintillating harmonies. Shepherd's notes spoke the language of his heart and soul, and the thoughts they uttered are true to his whole philosophy and being."

Shepherd received an honorary doctorate in music from Western Reserve in 1937 and in 1941 he was elected to membership in the National Institute of Arts and Letters. He is the author of *The String Quartets of Beethoven* (1937).

THE COMPOSER SPEAKS: Tradition. What is there about this word that is so provocative? What do we mean when we employ it in conversation and in writing? Is it a derogatory epithet or is it the acknowledgment of some recognizable achievement?

One hears the phrase such and such a work is "in the great tradition," one hears also the phrase, such a person is a "slave to tradition."

Now by connotation and implication "tradition" is inseparable from our noblest concepts. God Himself is our greatest tradition. Truth is traditional; our habits of speech, food, clothing, are traditional, our Democratic Ideals are traditional. Great works of art are the means of establishing tradition. . . .

The connotations of the word are preponderantly good and constructive. And yet it seems inherent in human destiny to contest and battle, resist and break away from traditional practices.

This is particularly observable in the realm of art. But the apparent strife is basically nothing more than the normal operation of the laws which govern growth and change. So, I think we may assume that a "traditionalist" is one who creates with an awareness of his heritage and an awareness of doctrine and discipline.

PRINCIPAL WORKS: 4 string quartets (1933–55); 3 *Exotic Dances,* for piano (1928, 1941, 1941); 3 capriccios, for piano (1948, 1941, 1943); 3 *Eclogues,* for piano (1948–49); 2 symphonies (1927, 1938); 2 piano sonatas (1907, 1930).

Ouverture joyeuse, for orchestra (1901); *The City in the Sea,* cantata for baritone, chorus, and orchestra (1913); *The Festival of Youth,* overture for orchestra (1915); *Fantaisie humoresque,* for piano and orchestra (1916, revised as Fantasia, for piano and orchestra); Violin Sonata (c. 1917); *Overture to a Drama,* for orchestra (1919); *Triptych,* for string quartet and voice (1925); *Choreographic Suite on an Exotic Theme,* for orchestra, based on *Exotic Dance* no. 1, for piano (1930); *The Song of the Pilgrims,* cantata for tenor, double chorus, and orchestra (1932); *A Ballad of Trees and the Master,* for a cappella chorus (1934); *Invitation to the Dance,* for chorus and orchestra, also for chorus and two pianos (1936); *Fantasia concertante on "The Garden Hymn,"* for organ, also for orchestra (1939); Piano Quintet (1940); *Praeludium Salutatorium for Divers Instruments,* for flute, oboe, horn, bassoon, violin, viola, cello (1942); *Hilaritas,* overture for concert band (1942); Divertissement, for wind quintet (1943); Psalm 42, for vocal quartet, chorus, and orchestra (1944); *Fantasy Overture on Down-East Spirituals,* for orchestra (1946); Violin Concerto (1946); *Variations on an Original Theme,* for orchestra (1952); *A Psalm of Mountains,* for chorus and orchestra (1956).

BIBLIOGRAPHY: Ewen, David, *Composers Since 1900* (N.Y., 1969); Howard, John Tasker, *Our American Music* (N.Y., 1946); Loucks, Richard, *Arthur Shepherd—American Composer* (Provo, Utah, 1980); *Musical Quarterly,* April 1950; *Who's Who in America, 1956–57.*

Shifrin, Seymour, b. Brooklyn, N.Y., February 28, 1926; d. Boston, Mass., September 26, 1979.

In his mature work Shifrin commands an original rhetoric characterized by subtle and complex effects of phrasing. Apparent irreconcilables are frequently yoked together—long lines of fragmentary interjections, metrical regularity, and rhythmic dislocation. Shifrin avoids the precompositional pitch structures favored by many contemporary composers and, as a result, his harmony is apt to seem unpredictable at first hearing but it is always placed in the service of specific phrase shape.

The son of a businessman, Shifrin began his music studies with piano lessons when he was six. At the High School of Music and Art in New York, which he attended from 1940 to 1944, he took courses in theory and composition. One of his youthful compositions performed at the high school was heard by William Schuman, who was so impressed that he offered Shifrin a scholarship to study composition privately with him. After two years of such study, Shifrin entered Columbia University in 1944, where he received his bachelor of arts degree in 1947, with election to Phi Beta Kappa, and, in 1949, his master of arts degree in composition after having studied composition with Otto Luening. *Two Early Songs,* for soprano and piano, to poems by Rainer Maria Rilke, was composed in 1947, followed by Sonata for Cello and Piano and Music for Orchestra in 1948; the former was introduced over New York's municipal radio station, WNYC, in February 1948. In 1947–48 Shifrin was awarded the Seidl Fellowship in Composition at Columbia University and, in 1950, the Bearns Prize, also from Columbia University, for his String Quartet no. 1 (1949).

On June 6, 1947, Shifrin married Miriam Levine, a pianist and teacher; a son was born in 1953 and a daughter in 1961. In 1949–40 Shifrin was lecturer in music at Columbia University and in 1950–51 at the College of the City of New York. On a Fulbright Fellowship in 1951 he spent a year in Paris studying composition with Darius Milhaud. When Shifrin returned to the United States in 1952 he was appointed to the faculty of the University of California at Berkeley, where he taught until leaving for Brandeis University in 1966.

An early composition that attracted widespread attention was the Chamber Symphony (1952–53). This was to some degree a tonally oriented composition with those peculiarly truncated phrases Shifrin would later favor. The talent Shifrin revealed in this work brought him a Fromm Music Foundation Award in 1953. The Serenade for Five Instruments (1954) was written on commission from the Juilliard School of Music for a festival of contemporary music celebrating its fiftieth anniversary. The first performance took place in New York on February 17, 1956. "It is a work of pronounced originality not readily identifiable with the style of any teacher or school," wrote Andrew Imbrie in the *Musical Quarterly.* "One is fascinated by the highly expressive and exposed melodic shapes, interrelated in a supple and elastic rhythmic context. . . . In expression, the work is both economical and manysided; its gesture is aristocratically direct."

In 1956 Shifrin received the first of two Guggenheim Fellowships. This made it possible for him to go to Zurich, Switzerland, where he composed one of his most important and ambitious works, a setting of four *Sophoclean Odes,* for chorus and orchestra. It remains a remarkable essay in "extended" tonality in which a 19th-century sensibility animates a 20th-century language without embarrassment or archaism.

In 1957 he was the recipient of a grant from the National Institute of Arts and Letters and by the end of that year he was already described in *Time* as "one of the most significant of America's younger composers," whose music was "free of today's playthings, yesterday's sanctorums, and tomorrow's sensationalisms." He went a long way toward justifying such a tribute in 1958 with his most successful composition up to that time, the Three Pieces for Orchestra, which had been commissioned by Rodgers and Hammerstein through the League of Composers-International Society for Contemporary Music for the Minneapolis Symphony Orchestra. That orchestra, under Antal Dorati, gave the first hearing in Minneapolis on January 8, 1960. Shifrin described the first piece as "enunciatory and celebrative in nature . . . meant to serve as Introduction. . . . The slow, lyric middle part evolves from a hushed, delicate texture in winds and percussion instruments . . . the third piece begins with a terse, compact statement of four germinal ideas central to the movement . . . meant to be cumulative in its growth." Writing in a St. Paul newspaper, John H. Harvey said in reviewing the premiere performance: "Mr. Shifrin is gifted, resourceful and imaginative. His musical speech is original without seeming to strain to be so. His work has fascinating textures and closely woven designs using short, punchy motives."

In 1959 Shifrin was presented with the Creative Arts Award from Brandeis University in Waltham, Mass. He spent the year of 1959–60 in Rome and Paris on his second Guggenheim Fellowship. In 1961 he received the Copley Foundation Award.

With *The Modern Temper,* for piano, four hands (1959), and the String Quartet no. 2, Shifrin began to abandon tonal references while further developing his technique of disintegration and fragmentation of thematic, rhythmic, and textural elements of a compositional statement. In reviewing the Second String Quartet for *Perspectives in New Music,* David Lewin spoke of the contrasting play of the two textures. "One of these, characterized by sustained melodic lines in one or more instruments, I shall call 'lyric.' The other I shall call 'terse,' and in it the instruments participate in a fragmentary way, throwing out melodic or motivic bits, siolated notes or double stops."

On commission from the Berkeley Chamber Singers, Shifrin completed *Odes of Shang* (1962), for chorus, piano, and an elaborate body of percussion instruments that included such esoteric items as drums from India, pitched cow bells from Greece, pitched wood blocks, cymbals of assorted sizes from the Orient, wood and glass chimes from Japan in addition to claves, castanets, maracas, and glockenspiel from the West. The text comes from the oldest known anthology of Chinese poetry, the Confucian *Book of Odes,* which Ezra Pound translated into English in 1958. Shifrin indicated that some of the percussion instruments were to be played by the singers in order "to invoke the tribal and ceremonial nature of the text" as well as to give the singing "a more percussive quality," but this practice has not proved feasible. The work has two parts. The first is a ceremonial call to worship celebrating youth and fecundity; the second involved concillation with age, the offerings of sacrifice. Shifrin's technique of alternating a flowing melodic line in the chorus with fragmented material in the piano is found in the second part. A two-line musical and textural refrain ends each of the two parts. "His style is harmonically quite free," wrote Alan Rich in *New York,* "but strongly propelled by a masterful use of dissonant counterpoint. His music is full of energy, emotionally rather tense, yet colored with extreme delicacy." For his "meritorious contribution to orchestral literature" Shifrin received the Boston Symphony's Hor-

blit Award in 1963. Two commissions that year resulted in the writing of two significant works. For the Fromm Music Foundation, he completed *Satires of Circumstance,* a setting of three poems by Thomas Hardy, for mezzo-soprano and six instruments (1964). "It is Hardy's sense of irony that attracted me to his texts," Shifrin said. With its complicated phrasing and its stark opposition of flowing lyric line to terse, epigrammatic statement, *Satires* may be said to initiate a new phase of Shifrin's career.

The one-movement String Quartet no. 3 (1966), commissioned by the Koussevitzky Music Foundation and the Library of Congress, was premiered by the Juilliard String Quartet in Washington on March 30, 1967. This is a three-section work which, as Shifrin explained, "generates from its opening measures; from a series of expanding relationships grow consequent lines and harmonies."

A year later (1967) he completed String Quartet No. 4, commissioned by the Fine Arts Foundation of Chicago for the Fine Arts Quartet and first performed in Chicago on April 10, 1967. In view of Shifrin's life-long concern with phrasing, the scherzo is an unexpected essay in string textures with a minimum of articulations. *In Eius Memoriam* (1968) has been one of Shifrin's most widely performed compositions. Scored for flute, clarinet, violin, cello, and piano, it recalls some of the gestures of *Satires,* but accommodated to the genre of the short piece by a device of pitch circularity whereby each phrase turns back to its beginning. In 1970, Shifrin completed *Chronicles,* a cantata for chorus, soloists, and orchestra, based on Old Testament texts that move in a connected way from the public statements of the Book of Chronicles to the private lyricism of Job. This work was chosen by the International Society for Contemporary Music for performance by the Boston Symphony Orchestra at the World Music Days in 1976.

In 1966 Shifrin left the University of California to become professor of music at Brandeis University, where he remained to the time of his death. The significance of two of his earlier works was recognized in 1970 when *Satires of Circumstance* received the Koussevitzky International Recording Award and the Walter Naumburg Award came for the recording of Three Pieces for Orchestra (which, two years later, earned another Koussevitzky International Recording Award).

The works of Shifrin's last years are among the finest he produced. String Quartet no. 5 (1972), commissioned by the Stanley Quartet of the University of Michigan, attempts in a radical way to devise an alternative to the "crisis" preocedures of traditional music. In the second movement, the juxtaposition of disparate materials is carried to an extreme; fragmentary interjections are contrasted with Beethovenian breadths of unusually static harmony, and the movement closes with a connected lyrical line. One of Shifrin's most austere compositions is the short piano piece *Responses* (1973), which presents a harmony governed by the gradual unfolding of the circle of fifths. In the Piano Trio (1974), composed for the Francesco Trio, Shifrin came to feel that his complex and restless style could even accommodate literal repetition. *A Renaissance Garland* (1975; N.Y., January 23, 1978), commissioned by the Naumburg Foundation for the Boston Camerata, is a setting of poems by Sir Thomas Wyatt, Sir Philip Sidney, Shakespeare, and an anonymous Tudor poet for soprano, tenor, lute, recorders, bass viol, percussion. *The Nick of Time,* for flute, piccolo, clarinets, piano, violin, cello, bass, and percussion (1978), was written on a grant from the National Endowment for the Arts and was performed in New York on May 18, 1978. Shifrin's last composition, completed while he was fatally ill, Five Songs, for soprano and piano, shows no loss of intensity; the harmonic language, utterly personal as always, has a density and richness akin to the early music of Schoenberg.

Shifrin was a member of the board of the Koussevitzky Music Foundation, the National Advisory Board of American Composers Alliance, and the editorial board of *Perspectives of New Music.*

THE COMPOSER SPEAKS: While finding my own way, I should like not to give up anything that has ever been won in the way of subtlety, richness, and complexity; yet I retain a taste for the simple and the vernacular. The qualities I value in music have to do with strong intent, the interaction of the small and the large, and the will to make whole what seems disparate. What I hope continues to evolve in my work is a highly inflected, plain, elegant language.

PRINCIPAL WORKS: 5 string quartets (1949–72).
Cello Sonata (1948); Music for Orchestra (1948); Composition for Piano (1950); Chamber Symphony (1952–53); Serenade for Five Instruments (1954); *Trauermusik,* for piano (1956); *Cantata for Sophoclean Choruses,* for chorus and orchestra (1957–58); Three Pieces for Orchestra (1958); *The Modern Temper,* for piano, four hands (1959); *Give Ear, O Ye Heavens,* for chorus and organ (1959); Concert Piece for Solo Violin (1959); Fantasy for Piano (1961); *Odes of Shang,* for chorus, piano, and percussion (1963); *Satires of Circumstance,* for mezzo-soprano and six instruments (1964); *In Eius Memoriam,* for flute, clarinet, violin, cello, and piano (1967–68); Duo, for violin and piano (1969); *Chronicles,* for three male soloists, chorus, and orchestra (1970); *Responses,* for piano (1973); Piano Trio (1974); *A Renaissance Garland,* for soprano, tenor, lute, recorders, bass viol, and percussion (1975); *The Nick of Time,* for flute, piccolo, clarinets, piano, violin, cello, bass, and percussion (1978); Five Songs, for soprano and piano (1979).

BIBLIOGRAPHY: *BBDM; DCM; Who's Who in America, 1978–79.*

Shulman, Alan, b. Baltimore, Md., June 4, 1915.

Contrasting elements can be found in Shulman's compositions. Some have strong Hebraic feeling while others incorporate elements of jazz. Shulman is basically a traditionalist to whom melodic interest, well-sounding harmonic and instrumental textures, clearly conceived structures, and expressivity are of prime importance.

He was one of three children in a musical family. His father, a pharmacist, played the flute; his mother was a trained singer; an older sister played the piano; an older brother was a violinist. Shulman's father died when Alan was one and a half years old and his mother supported the family by teaching and supervising the drug store of her late husband. Since she wanted to have a piano trio in the family, she directed Alan Shulman to the cello when he was eight. After receiving some instruction from a local teacher, he entered the Peabody Conservatory in Baltimore, where he studied the cello with Bart Wirtz and theory and harmony with Louis Cheslock. While still young, Shulman was a member of the Shulman Trio, which performed in several Baltimore theaters and over the radio, where it became a pioneer in promoting radio commercials. Shulman's formal academic education was sporadic. Since his mother was a licensed teacher, she received permission from the superintendent of schools to tutor her children privately. Shulman supplemented the lessons his mother taught him by devouring books borrowed from the local public library.

When Shulman was thirteen, his family moved to Brooklyn, N.Y. He enrolled in Erasmus Hall High School so that he might be eligible for a New York Philharmonic Scholarship. He stayed at Erasmus Hall for a year and a half, where he played in the school orchestra. In 1929 he left high school to take out working papers because he had to help support his family and he wanted to serve his orchestral apprenticeship as cellist with the National Orchestral Association conducted by Leon Barzin (1929–32). On a New York Philharmonic Scholarship, he was able to continue his cello studies with Joseph Emonts and harmony with Winthrop Sargent. At the same time he attended the Brooklyn Boys' Continuation School (soon to become known as Brooklyn Vocational High School), from which he graduated in 1932, bringing his formal academic education to an end. On his graduation, the Women's Roosevelt Association awarded him a medal for conspicuous service to the school that year. The school presented him with a certificate of merit for distinguished service to the community in 1935.

In 1932, a fellowship brought him to the Juilliard School of Music. During the next five years, his musical studies covered the cello with Felix Salmond, counterpoint and composition with Bernard Wagenaar, and orchestral training with Albert Stoessel. While at Juilliard, he made popular arrangements for sponsored musical programs over the radio. He also made his official debut as composer when *Chinese Nightingale*, a play based on a Hans Christian Andersen story, with incidental music by Shulman, was produced in New York on October 5, 1934. A critic for *Variety* described Shulman's music as possessing "humor, mood, and taste."

Between 1934 and 1938, Shulman was cellist with the Kreiner String Quartet, which performed chamber music over the CBS radio network. Upon graduating from Juilliard in 1937, Shulman joined the cello section of the NBC Symphony, which had just been founded for Arturo Toscanini. Shulman remained with this orchestra from 1937 to 1942. During this period he studied cello privately with Emanuel Feuermann (1939) and composition with Paul Hindemith. Between 1940 and 1942, Shulman was the principal arranger for Wilfred Pelletier, director of the Metropolitan Auditions of the Air. During World War II, Shulman was in the U.S. Maritime Service (1942–45). Following his discharge, he earned his living for several years writing scores for several documentary films. In 1946 he arranged music for Columbia record releases by Risë Stevens, Robert Weede, Irra Petina, and Marjorie Lawrence. He was back in the cello section of the NBC Symphony in 1948 for an additional six years. In 1938, he was cofounder and, from 1938 to 1954, cellist of the Stuyvesant Quartet, which specialized in contemporary music.

Shulman's first successful concert work was Theme and Variations (1940), originally for viola and piano, and subsequently rewritten for viola and orchestra. In its first version, it was introduced by Emanuel Vardi and Vivian Rivkin in New York on February 17, 1941. The orchestral adaptation was premiered by the NBC Symphony on a short-wave broadcast to South America on March 11, 1942, with Emanuel Vardi once again the soloist and Frank Black conducting. The work then entered the standard viola repertoire and received numerous performances from leading violists and orchestras. After it was performed by Milton Preves with the Chicago Symphony under Hans Lange on December 16, 1943, Felix Borowski said in the *Chicago Sun*: "Alan Shulman wrote gratefully and, on occasion, brilliantly, for the instrument. He knew its strongest points and made a great show with them; but he knew the orchestra as well, and caused it to be more than a mere background."

Shulman wrote Pastorale and Dance, for violin and orchestra, in 1944, for his brother, Sylvan, then concertmaster of the American Broadcasting Symphony. Sylvan Shulman and the American Broadcasting Symphony introduced it over the ABC radio network in July 1944. The Pastorale movement was dominated by a plaintive melody which returned in a lively dance movement that followed, the dance described by its composer as "an American tarantella."

On September 17, 1946, Shulman married Sophie Pratt Bostelmann, a progressive music educator. They first met in 1934 at the Juilliard School of Music where she then studied the piano with Olga Samaroff, graduating in 1938. All of their four children have become musicians, two professionally, one other with a doctorate in musicology, and the fourth engaged in music management.

For Leonard Rose, then first cellist of the New York Philharmonic, Shulman wrote a Cello Concerto (1948), which Rose premiered with that orchestra on April 13, 1950, Dimitri Mitropoulos conducting. There is a Hebraic feeling throughout this work; and since it was completed soon after the establishment of the state of Israel, Shulman dedicated this work "to the people of Israel." "Its lines are chromatic and return on themselves in the near-East style," wrote Virgil Thomson in the *New York Herald Tribune*. "Its harmony is lachrymose, but solid withal. Its colors are dark and a little muddy, but sometimes they glow. . . . This is a personal work and full of feeling, some of which projects handsomely, particularly an animated passage in the second movement and a tranquil movement at the very end." Still another Shulman work inspired by Israel was *Threnody*, for strings quartet (1950), dedicated to Israel's fallen soldiers. The NBC String Quartet gave it its first hearing over the NBC radio network on February 26, 1950. Between these two Israel-oriented works, Shulman completed an orchestral composition in a much lighter, jazzlike vein, and a more infectious mood. It was the Waltzes, for orchestra (1949), whose world premiere took place on November 15, 1949, with Milton Katims conducting the NBC Symphony over the NBC radio network.

The Laurentian Mountains of northern Canada were the inspiration for a significant orchestral work: *A Laurentian Overture* (1951), first performance heard on January 17, 1952, at a concert of the New York Philharmonic conducted by Guido Cantelli. To capture the spirit of this majestic Canadian setting, Shulman modeled his own melodic material after French-Canadian folk songs. In the *New York World-Telegram*, Robert Bagar described this music as "lively, extremely well orchestrated, dotted with folkish material and cleverly varied in its tonal coloring," while in the *New York Times* Olin Downes spoke of it as "contagiously high-spirited and boldly and mischievously made."

Notable Shulman compositions since then include: *Top Brass*, for twelve brass instruments, a work in a jazz idiom (1958; Portland, Ore., April 25, 1958); Theme and Variations, for cello and chamber orchestra (1966; Westchester, N.Y., March 17, 1967); *Elegy*, for cello octet (1971; N.Y. October 19, 1971), written in memory of Felix Salmond; and *Four Diversions*, for cello quartet (1974). The last of these was first heard on April 6, 1975, at an all-Shulman concert in New York celebrating his sixty-fifth birthday.

Between 1962 and 1969, Shulman was a member of the Philharmonia Trio, and since 1972, of the Haydn Quartet. He has also frequently participated in chamber music concerts with many of America's foremost ensembles. He has taught cello at Sarah Lawrence College (1964), the Juilliard School of Music (1965), St. University of New York, College at Purchase (1974–75), and he has directed the summer Chamber Music School at Johnson State College in Vermont (1975) and the University of Maine Summer Chamber Music Workshop at Orono (1978). In 1972 he was composer-in-residence at the New England Festival at Mt. Hermon–Northfield Schools in Massachusetts. Since its founding in 1956, he has been a member of the board of directors of the Violoncello Society, serving as its president from 1967 to 1972 and as vice-president in 1979.

THE COMPOSER SPEAKS: In my youth, I was tremendously taken by French impressionists. Subsequently, I have been influenced by many national schools. I feel that the fewer notes I put into a score, the better I like it. I do not approve of the school that camouflages a paucity of musical ideas under a barrage of orchestration. I also feel that there is too much "intellectual" music being written today. That doesn't mean that one should necessarily "write down" to an audience; it means that the lay person (who represents the majority of music lovers) wants an aural satisfaction which will arouse his emotions; he must have something to grasp and retain—namely, a tune.

PRINCIPAL WORKS: Theme and Variations, for viola and piano, also viola and orchestra (1940); Suite, on American folk songs, for violin and piano (1944), Pastorale and Dance, for violin and orchestra (1944); Cello Concerto (1948); Waltzes, for orchestra (1949); *Threnody*, for string quartet (1950); Suite, for solo cello (1950); *A Laurentian Overture*, for orchestra (1951); Suite, for solo viola (1953); *Suite Miniature*, for eight celli (1955); Theme and Variations, for cello and chamber orchestra (1966); *Kol Nidre*, for cello and organ, also for cello and orchestra (1970); *Elegy*, for cello octet (1971); *Four Diversions*, for cello quartet (1974).

BIBLIOGRAPHY: *BBDM;* Anderson, E. Ruth, *Contemporary American Composers* (Boston, 1976); Ewen, David, *American Composers Today* (N.Y., 1949).

Siegmeister, Elie, b. New York City, January 15, 1909.

The half century of Siegmeister's continuous creativity has produced numerous works in virtually every medium of music. His compositions range from the highly complex to the simplest, covering a wide variety in theme and expressive character, always strongly communicative. His *oeuvre* can be divided into three stages. In the first, dissonance and intense dramatic elements were juxtaposed with American motives. In the second, folk and jazz materials and long melodic lines emerged to the fore, with dissonance and complex techniques relegated to the background. In his third stage—a synthesis of the first two on another level—his works became more closely and subtly interwoven. His music of this period is characterized by intensity, freedom of personal expression, a certain wildness, greater concentration, and improvisational spontaneity. In all three stages, his works reveal firmly grounded architecture. His use of such traditional structures as the symphony, the sonata, the concerto, the string quartet, the opera, the song—and such time-honored frameworks as the sonata form, the fugue, the theme and variations—make his music a logical continuation of the past. His excursions into dissonance and atonality, complex rhythmic and metrical structures, and frequent tapping of the resources of jazz make his very much the voice of the 20th century, and specifically of 20th-century America.

Both his parents, of whom he was the second son, were of Russian-Jewish background, the father, Dr. William Siegmeister, being a surgeon. When Elie was five, the family moved to Brooklyn, N.Y., where he was raised and educated, and where he was to live for four decades. In his seventh year, his parents acquired a piano, and soon thereafter he was given his first lessons. "I report without regret," he has written, "that I was no *Wunderkind*. For, music study being what it was in those days (endless hours of practicing exercises, isolation from normal life) I found it repugnant to my instincts as a boy." While attending the Brooklyn grade schools, his interests lay in enjoying the companionship of friends on the city streets, playing baseball on sandlots, playing chess, and doing problems in mathematics. When Elie was twelve his father began taking him to performances of the New York Philharmonic and the Metropolitan Opera, including the unforgettable experiences of hearing *Aïda* and later *Tristan und Isolde* for the first time. All this ignited a flame that remained incandescent from then on. "I began to run to every concert and opera I could scrape up fifty cents to hear." By the time he was fourteen he could identify the leading motives in the Wagnerian music dramas and had become a passionate admirer of Beethoven and Tchaikovsky. A year later he acquired in the Viennese-born Emil Friedberger a warmly sympathetic piano teacher who could not only perfect his technique but also open new musical horizons by analyzing for him the masterpieces of the keyboard repertoire.

At Boys High School, in Brooklyn, Siegmeister was continually in the topmost scholastic echelon. There he distinguished himself as a member of the mathematics and chess teams, both of which enjoyed championship status among city high schools, and as president of the physics club. He was only fifteen when he graduated from Boys High. Between 1924 and 1927 he continued his academic education at Columbia University, at first majoring in philosophy and psychology, but then transferring to music and studying composition with Seth Bingham. At the same time (1926) he took counterpoint lessons privately with Wallingford Riegger. For Bingham's classes, Siegmeister wrote a sonata and fugues, "but my heart wasn't in them." More to his liking was a sardonic song based on Wallace Stevens's poem "Rosenbloom Is Dead" (1926). "When friends went around chanting its refrain, I knew I was a composer."

In 1927, Siegmeister graduated from Columbia, *cum laude*, with membership in Phi Beta Kappa. That year he went to Paris for further music study. He remained there four and a half years as a private pupil of Nadia Boulanger's, also studying at the École normale de musique, where he received a diploma in 1931. Meanwhile, on January 15, 1930, he married Hannah Mersel. She was a young American psychologist and teacher who was running a nursery school in Paris along the principles of advanced modern education and who had studied piano and music theory at New York University. They raised three daughters. One of them, Nancy, became a concert violinist who, with her husband, the pianist Alan Mandel, has given numerous premieres and performances of Siegmeister's music.

In Paris, Siegmeister wrote some chamber music, including a Nocturne, for oboe and piano (1927); *Saturday Night*, for violin and piano (1929, later rearranged and published as *Contrasts*, for bassoon and piano); four *Robert Frost Songs* (1930); and two *William Blake Songs* (1932). Theme and Variations no. 1, for piano (1932), revealed a highly dissonant harmonic idiom and austere melodic line quite advanced for its time and totally independent of the neoclassic style then current in the Boulanger circle. He now looks back upon this work as his first "completely achieved, personal piece."

When he returned to the United States in 1932, to settle in Brooklyn, he brought together several progressive young musicians who, calling themselves the Young Composers Group, gave a concert of new American music at the New School for Social Research in New York City on January 15, 1933. Here, Siegmeister's music had its initial hearing in New York. "Behold!" he recalls, "the critics came and wrote not unfavorable reviews. Performances by various musical groups followed, and gradually my music began to get around." Among the important works of this period was *The Strange Funeral in Braddock*, for voice and piano, a dramatic, highly dissonant narrative of the death of a steelworker. Henry Cowell gave the young composer encouragement by publishing the song in the prestigious *New Music Quarterly* series and followed this by arranging the performance of his first orchestral work,

American Holiday (1933), in New York in 1934.

In the depression days of the early 1930s, Siegmeister began to grow increasingly impatient with the music performed by the "uptown" elite organizations for the sole delectation of musical sophisticates. To reach out to a wider audience, he formed and conducted a chorus made up of working people and students ("their enthusiasm was greater than their note-reading ability") which gave concerts in empty lofts and abandoned stores for an admission price of twenty-five cents. As a composer, he was also beginning to think in terms of a music that was more socially aware and more readily communicative than the harmonically complex works he had been writing. His discovery of the music of Charles Ives now pointed out to him a new direction: music with an American identity, rooted in folk and popular music, deriving its themes and inspiration from American people, heartland, and traditions. In 1934, Aunt Molly Jackson, from Harlan, Ky., introduced Siegmeister to a rich repertoire of American folk songs which made such a deep impression on him that he began an intensive study of America's native music in various parts of the United States. In addition to writing them down, Siegmeister now began assimilating the melodic and rhythm elements of American folk ballads and tunes into his own style. This led him to seek a greater simplicity and directness of expression in such works as *John Henry*, for tenor solo and a cappella chorus (1935); *Abraham Lincoln Walks at Midnight*, for chorus and orchestra (1937), to the poem by Vachel Lindsay; *Funnybone Alley* (1941), fourteen children's songs to poems of Alfred Kreymborg; and *Doodle Dandy of the U.S.A.* (1942), music for a children's play by Saul Lancourt, which ran on Broadway and toured the country for two years. Much of this music achieved an infectiously tuneful simplicity.

In 1939, Siegmeister organized, and from 1940 to 1945 conducted, the American Ballad Singers, a pioneer group that toured the United States bringing then little-known American folk music to concert audiences in large and small towns. These were also the years when he realized his first success with orchestral compositions of a pronounced American identity. Originally conceived as a theater work, *Ozark Set* (1943) found its definitive form as a four-movement suite suggesting scenes in the life of the Ozark Mountain people as they rose at dawn, shouted and stamped exuberantly at a camp meeting, lolled about in the open fields on a lazy afternoon, and participated in a Saturday night square dance. It was first performed on November 7, 1944, by the Minneapolis Symphony under Dimitri Mitropoulos and was then heard at concerts of many American and foreign orchestras. When it was performed in the Soviet Union on July 3, 1945, by the Moscow State Philharmonic, the distinguished Soviet critic Grigory Schneerson said of it: "The music is expressive and colorful, combining the simplicity of folk songs and square dances with intricately woven harmonies and original and daring instrumentation." In June 1972, *Ozark Set* was heard over the Dutch radio in Hilversum.

The American countryside inspired Siegmeister's music for the next two years. *Prairie Legend: A Midwestern Set* (1944), starting as a work for band written on commission, was then orchestrated, This is a three-movement suite suggesting the pioneer ox drivers who first settled the Midwest; the quiet beauty of a harvest evening; and the gaiety and tumult of a country fair. In the last movement a phrase from Stephen Foster's "De Camptown Races" appears. Leopold Stokowski, conducting the New York Philharmonic, gave the premiere performance on January 18, 1947. *Wilderness Road*, for orchestra, another mood picture of the Midwest (1944), was premiered by the Minneapolis Symphony under Mitropoulos on November 9, 1945. In addition to his music for orchestra, Siegmeister also produced *American Sonata* (among many other works), for piano (1944). While its melodic material was basically the composer's own, he incorporated fragments of three folk songs: "The Saint's Delight," "Sistern and Brethren," and "The Promised Land."

Public interest in Siegmeister was focused more strongly than ever on November 25, 1945, when Arturo Toscanini conducted the premiere of *Western Suite* (1945) at a concert of the NBC Symphony over the NBC radio network. In the *New York Herald Tribune*, Virgil Thomson called its material "of the highest beauty; and its treatment is full of sound sense as well as skill. Its moods run from the tenderest sentiment to the roughest roughhouse, and all are convincing. It is outdoor music with air in it and horses around it. It is written with love and with gusto. Also with an experienced folklorist's judgment."

In conjunction with his researches into American folk music, Siegmeister arranged and edited *A Treasury of American Song* (1940) an anthology of folk songs, to which Olin Downes provided part of the text. And it was with American folk music that Siegmeister made his first important bow in the theater: with *Sing Out, Sweet Land*, a play with music (text by Walter Kerr and Edward Eager) which came to Broadway as a Theatre Guild production starring Alfred Drake and Burl Ives on December 27, 1944; its score consisted largely of American folk ballads which Siegmeister had adapted and orchestrated.

Without abandoning a native quality in his compositions, Siegmeister began by early 1946 to feel the need to compose "something broader and more personal; to dig deeper, as it were, below the surface of our American life and character." With this in mind, and at the invitation of Stokowski, Siegmeister completed his Symphony no. 1 in 1947, and the conductor performed it first with the New York Philharmonic on October 30, 1947. In classical form, this symphony—which Siegmeister said "deals with the spirit, the struggle, the hope of man"—employed

original melodic ideas that still had a marked folk character, with some sections carrying the feeling of American popular song and dance.

While busily engaged with his activities as a composer, Siegmeister felt the need to pass on his experiences to young people, teaching for various periods in the 1930s and 1940s at Brooklyn College in Brooklyn, N.Y., and the New School for Social Research and the Metropolitan Music School in New York City. In 1948 he was visiting professor at the University of Minnesota in Minneapolis. In 1949, he was appointed to the music faculty of Hofstra University in Hempstead, N.Y. In addition to his professorial duties he conducted the Hofstra Symphony Orchestra between 1953 and 1965. In 1965 he founded, and in 1965–66 conducted there, the Pro-Arte Orchestra. From 1966 to 1976 he was composer-in-residence, retiring as professor emeritus in 1976.

As a composer, he entered a new area in 1951 by writing his first opera, *Darling Corie*. This is a one-act opera with text by Lewis Allan based on the life of the mountain people of the southern Appalachians to a story drawn from the ballad of the same name. First produced at Hofstra University on February 18, 1954, the opera was televised by the Canadian Broadcasting Company on March 21, 1956. *Darling Corie* brought Siegmeister two commissions for operas in the 1950s. *Miranda and the Dark Young Man*, libretto by Edward Eager (1955; Hartford, Conn., May 9, 1956), is a one-act comic opera with lyrical overtones, a Shavian parody on traditional romantic opera. *The Mermaid in Lock No. 7* (1958), libretto by Edward Mabley, is a dreamlike fantasy in *Singspiel* style which comments sardonically on commercial music, its score interweaving complex harmonies, recitatives, songs, arias, blues, and ensemble numbers in juxtaposition of serious and popular music. It was first produced in Pittsburgh on July 20, 1958; in January 1972 it was performed in a Flemish translation in Antwerp, Belgium.

In the 1950s, Siegmeister began to move away from the folk-music style toward a more introspective music in classical structures which better reflected his own personal experiences and deeper feelings. This new approach led him to combine diatonic melodic lines with chromatic harmonies, long flowing passages with short, pithy motives. "Mingled feelings involved mingled techniques," he once explained. "Music is what it is, and a man's writing is himself."

Symphony no. 2 (1950), premiered in New York on February 25, 1952, is a work of striking contrasts—now lyrical, now dramatic. Siegmeister said it represented "one man's thoughts,—the search for love, the struggle against violence, and the belief in the human," but it is not in any sense programmatic. Reviewing the symphony in the *New York Herald Tribune*, Virgil Thomson wrote: "Its songful material is of the utmost beauty. Its constant eruptions of violence are a source of buoyancy. Its tone is serious and its emotional content is all the more real." Symphony no. 3 (1957; Oklahoma City, Okla., February 8, 1959) represented a departure from its two predecessors by being a one-movement work based on a free variation rather than the sonata principle. Its music grew out of three short motives; an elemental five-note pattern at the opening; an upward reaching chromatic figure; and a four-note "wedge" theme at the peak of the first climax. Out of these ideas four contrasting sections emerged; in the fourth part, cool jazzlike figurations for piano and the clarinet appear. Jazz was featured even more prominently in the Concerto for Clarinet and Orchestra (1956; Oklahoma City, February 3, 1956) with a perky, dancelike second movement and a deep blues in the third. "The music laughs at times," the composer says, "and at times is barbed and prickly. In the last movement the feeling of a struggle mounts in persistent rhythms—until, finally, a clear triumphant passage is reached. Jazz, emerging from the people, is seen by the composer as an affirmative life-breathing statement."

In the 1960s, Siegmeister's writing became increasingly concentrated, subtler in sonorities, lighter in texture; its harmonic structures became more intricate and adventurous. He was in full command of his technique and means. Elements of lyricism, energy, wildness—consistently a part of Siegmeister's writing since the 1950s—characterize the String Quartet no. 2 (1960; Hempstead, N.Y., January 28, 1961), which was performed by many quartets throughout the country. Concerto for Flute and Orchestra (1960; Oklahoma City, February 17, 1961) was one of Siegmeister's most expressive and reflective scores up to that time. *I Have a Dream* (1967; Long Beach, N.Y., April 16, 1967) is a powerful, deeply moving cantata for narrator, baritone, chorus, and orchestra in which Edward Mabley's text was based on Martin Luther King's speech at a civil rights march in Washington, D.C., in August 1963 calling for the brotherhood of races. Symphony no. 4 (1967–70) opens unorthodoxly with a long cello solo. After that, the composer explains, "the themes appear, entwine, interrupt each other, enact various evolutions." In the second movement, lively pointillistic rhythms are suddenly interrupted by snatches of popular music—ragtime, old tunes, a children's song. The finale opens with a dissonant attack which is then expanded and developed multitonally and polyrhythmically. The symphony's first performance was given by the Cleveland Orchestra under Lorin Maazel on December 6, 1973. Writing in the *Long Island Press*, Byron Belt said: "The work is conceived on a grand scale with a somber opening and a stirring finale, a sardonic scherzo and a soaring Andante of special power and beauty."

One of Siegmeister's most ambitious works, structurally and artistically, is his opera *The Plough and the Stars,* performed in its first version in St. Louis on May 15, 1963. The text by Edward Mabley was based on Sean O'Casey's drama of the Irish uprising against the British in 1916 and its impact on both the fighting men and the poor Irish in Dublin's slums. Siegmeister's score ranges from the folk and the popular to the abstract, from Broadway show music to modern operatic idioms. Text and music made for (as a critic for the *St. Louis Globe-Democrat* noted) "powerful musical theater . . . [and] intense dramatic utterance." A revised version of the opera was produced by the Louisiana State University on March 16, 1969, followed on May 13, 1970, by its European premiere (and actually its first *professional* production) at the Grand Theatre in Bordeaux, France, the first American opera ever produced by that company and, as far as is known, by any major opera company in France.

With Siegmeister's high station in American music firmly established by 1970, he did not lack commissions which, in turn, resulted in compositions of prime interest. His Symphony no. 5, *Visions of Time* (1971), was written for the Baltimore Symphony. Under Sergiu Comissiona's direction it was introduced by that orchestra at the Kennedy Center for the Performing Arts in Washington, D.C., on May 2, 1977. In a somewhat unusual structure consisting of two short movements followed by two longer ones, Siegmeister's symphony reflected on the nature of time through quotations by Thoreau, Bernard Shaw, Thomas Mann, and William Faulkner. Writing in the *Baltimore Sun*, Elliott W. Galkin said of it: "With its novel neo-impressionistic passages, the textures light and airy, the sound of the various percussion instruments bright and shimmering, there are also some wonderful melodic moments, surprisingly expressive in Nineteenth Century romantic terms— epic passages written for unison celli, and poignantly eloquent lines for the French horn combined with the English horn. This symphony is also a magnificent exercise in rhythmic variety, for the musical motion seems to be an incessant state of flux, constantly modified in its metrical transformations."

On a commission from the National Gallery of Art in Washington, D.C., Siegmeister completed the Concerto for Piano and Orchestra (1974). The first performance, on December 3, 1976, was given by Alan Mandel and the Denver Symphony conducted by Brian Priestman. This concerto, the composer explained, "embodies dissonances, tone clusters, crossrhythms in many sections; in others, clear melodic and contrapuntal meaning, even triads; but more important than this technical jargon is what the music says in its pianistic and orchestral colors, lines and sound combinations."

Three commissions from the Shreveport Symphony in Louisiana to commemorate the American bicentennial led to the writing of an orchestral suite, a ballet, and an opera. The first was *Shadows and Light*, "homage to five paintings" (1974–75; November 9, 1975). The five paintings (Albert Ryder's *Night Ship*, Paul Klee's *All Around the Fish*, Léger's *The Great Parade*, Degas's *Blind Woman Ar-*

ranging Flowers, and Van Gogh's *Starry Night*) find a sensitive, evocative response in five movements. The Cleveland Orchestra under Maazel gave it six performances during the 1979–80 season. The ballet *Fables from the Dark Wood* (1976; April 25, 1976) used as scenario five symbolic stories from a volume of Creole folk tales compiled by Alcée Fortier in 1895. The opera, in three acts, was *Night of the Moonspell* (1974–76; November 14, 1976). Edward Mabley's libretto derived freely from Shakespeare's *A Midsummer Night's Dream.* In this robust, bubbling comic opera, the scene is changed from a very Elizabethan Athens to the forest and bayou country of Louisiana in the Mardi Gras season. Shakespeare's aristocrats have been transformed into plantation dwellers, his "mechanicals" into Cajun workmen, his fairies into blacks. In *Opera News,* a critic said: "The composer has a Puccinian sense of the dramatic. The supporting fabric of sound has sheen, bite, and bounce, and the singers are provided with soaring, expressive melodies."

Once again to honor the American bicentennial, Siegmeister completed a light orchestral piece in an American idiom: the Double Concerto, for violin, piano, and orchestra (1976), subtitled *An Entertainment.* It was commissioned by Isidore and Ann Saslav, who premiered it with the Baltimore Symphony under Comissiona in Columbia, Md., on June 25, 1976.

Through the years, concerts devoted exclusively to Siegmeister's music have been presented in New York, Boston, London, Paris, and elsewhere, particularly in honor of his sixty-fifth and seventieth birthdays. At the Contemporary American Composers Festival of the University of Bridgeport in Connecticut on March 16–17, 1978, four concerts of Siegmeister's works covering half a century of his music were given. That summer, Siegmeister was the first composer-in-residence at the Brevard Music Center in North Carolina, where, once again, several programs of his music were presented.

Siegmeister was the founder of the American Composers Alliance of the American Music Center (1938), was its vice-president (1964–67) served as vice-president of the Composers and Lyricists Guild (1965–68), was founder of the Kennedy Center's National Black Music Competition and Colloquium (1979–80), and is a member on the board of directors of the American Society of Composers, Authors, and Publishers (ASCAP) (1977–   ).

Siegmeister wrote the score for a major motion picture, *They Came to Cordura,* starring Gary Cooper and Rita Hayworth (1959). He is the author of *Invitation to Music* (1961) and *Harmony and Melody* (1966). In addition to *A Treasury of American Song* (1940) he edited *Work and Song* (1944) and *The Music Lover's Handbook* (1943). He revised and expanded the latter book into the *New Music Lover's Handbook* (1973).

In 1978, at the age of sixty-nine, Siegmeister was presented with a Guggenheim fellowship and an award from the American Academy and Institute of Arts and Letters. The citation from the Academy and Institute read in part: "His music is always highly charged, admirably crafted, and is deeply rooted in the life of the people as well as in his own profound emotional experiences."

THE COMPOSER SPEAKS: I see artists around us dominated by fear and mezmerized by technology, which have led them to turn away from the central subject of art: the human being. Afraid to deal with this basic matter of all art, they retreat into theory, pedantry, and academicism. In literature we have the antinovel, in the theater the antiplay, in music the antimelody. In all this there is a perpetual coldness; one listens in vain for an unselfconscious human voice.

Today there are few in contemporary music to sing of compassion, understanding, and beauty of men's travail in these times. I think such composers will come; they are bound to come. Perhaps they are here now, but their voices are lost in the outcry of relentless publicity, the pressures of the cultists and machinemen. Never before has the concertgoer been so brainwashed by long technical analyses exposing a new "system" in front of every piece of music. Today, every composer must find a new catchword or jump on the latest bandwagon of an organized cabal if he wants to impress the critics or the "new music" establishment.

Haven't we had enough of authoritarian voices in art, as in life? Can't we have a little independence in music, a little less of "thou shalt" and "thou shalt not"?

A man's work should not be judged by whether it contains sixteen tones or forty or two; whether it uses a fistful of notes, or just tonic and dominant; whether he belongs to one school or another, or to no school. All possibilities are open to the poetic mind not hedged in by rules and systems. Let us have freedom to experiment, or not to experiment, recognizing that the "latest thing" in music this year may be pretty stale next year. Let us have a little open air, a song or dance, a human cry of sorrow or rejoicing. Let music be honest craftsmanship and speech between man and man.

PRINCIPAL WORKS: 5 symphonies (1947–71); 5 violin sonatas (1951–71); 3 string quartets (1935, 1960, 1973); 4 piano sonatas (1944–80); 2 theme and variations, for piano (1932, 1967).

American Holiday, for orchestra (1933); *The Strange Funeral in Braddock,* for voice and piano, also for orchestra (1933); *Abraham Lincoln Walks at Midnight,* for chorus and orchestra (1937); *Johnny Appleseed,* for chorus and piano (1940); *Doodle Dandy of the U.S.A.,* theater music (1942); *Ozark Set,* suite for orchestra (1943); *Prairie Legend,* for orchestra, also for band (1944); *Wilderness Road*, for orchestra (1944); *Sing Out, Sweet Land*, play with music (1944); *Western Suite*, for orchestra (1945); *Sunday in Brooklyn*, for orchestra, also for piano (1946); *Lonesome Hollow*, for orchestra (1946); *Summer Night*, for orchestra (1947); *From My Window*, suite for orchestra, also for piano (1949); *Darling Corie*, one-act opera (1952); *For My Daughters*, eight songs for voice and piano (1952); Divertimento, for orchestra (1953); *Miranda and the Dark Young Man*, one-act opera (1955); Clarinet Concerto (1956); *The Mermaid in Lock No. 7*, one-act opera (1958); Flute Concerto (1960); *Theater Set*, for orchestra (1960); *The Plough and the Stars*, opera (1963, revised 1969); *Madam to You*, six songs for voice and piano (1964); *In Our Time*, for chorus and orchestra or piano (1965); Sextet, for brass and percussion (1965); *American Harp*, for solo harp (1966); *Dick Whittington and His Cat*, for narrator and orchestra (1966); *Songs of Experience*, five songs for voice and piano, also for voice, viola, and piano (1966); *I Have a Dream*, cantata for narrator, baritone, chorus, and orchestra (1967); *Five Fantasies of the Theater*, for orchestra (1967); *The Face of War*, five songs for baritone and orchestra, also piano (1968); *Five cummings Songs*, for soprano and piano (1970); *Six cummings Songs*, for baritone and piano (1970); *On This Ground*, for piano (1971); *Songs of Innocence*, for voice and piano (1972); *A Cycle of Cities*, for soprano and tenor solos, chorus, and orchestra (1974); Piano Concerto (1974); *Shadows and Lights, Homage to Five Paintings*, for orchestra (1975); *Fables from the Dark Wood*, for orchestra (1976); Double Concerto (*An Entertainment*), for violin, piano, and orchestra (1976); *Night of the Moonspell*, opera (1976); *Declaration*, for brass and timpani (1976); *Front Porch Saturday Night*, for band (1977); *A Set of Houses*, for piano (1977); *City Songs*, for chorus and piano (1977); Violin Concerto (1978); *Summer*, for viola and harp (1978); *Introduction to the Problems of Philosophy*, five songs for voice and piano (1979); *The Marquesa of O.*, opera (1980).

BIBLIOGRAPHY: Ewen, David, *Composers Since 1900* (N.Y., 1969); Schneerson, Grigory, *Portraits of American Composers* (Moscow, 1977); Siegmeister, Elie (ed.). *The New Music Lover's Handbook*, two autobiographical sketches (N.Y., 1973); Thomson, Virgil, *American Music Since 1910* (N.Y., 1970); *Music Journal*, January 1973; *NATS Bulletin*, January–February 1979; *Newsday*, January 26, 1972; *New York Times*, January 7, 1976; *St. Louis Literary Supplement*, November, 1976.

Sims, Ezra, b. Birmingham, Ala., January 16, 1928.

Sims's mature career as a composer began with twelve-tone music, from which he quickly moved on to music using the same technique on materials no longer rigorously limited to the form of the twelve-tone row, to electronic music and on to his current microtonal music using scales made up of mixed quarter, third, and fifth tones, and transposable to any of the seventy-two pitches his notation can describe within the octave (much as can the diatonic scale throughout the twelve-note chromatic gamut). He has designed an electronic keyboard which, through application of computer logic and microprocessor technology, is capable of producing this scale in all its transpositions as well as any temperament or just tuning of up to thirty-six pitches in the octave (seventy-two, in the larger version). To his music he brings not merely new sonoric textures and tonal structures but at times also a wry sense of humor and whimsy.

His father was in civil service in Birmingham, and his mother a record librarian in a hospital; neither was particularly musical. Ezra Sims began music study early, receiving his first instruction in reading notes from Florette Cohn, and his first piano lessons from local teachers. While attending grade schools and the Woodlawn High School in Birmingham, he participated in school music activities by performing in the orchestras, choruses, and operettas. He began composing when he was about fourteen. His first public performance came with a short piece for piano and orchestra presented by the Woodlawn High School Orchestra in 1944. "After that, I wrote the usual string of juvenile and student pieces which received local performance."

Upon graduating from Woodlawn High School in 1944, Sims entered Birmingham Southern College. There, on scholarships, he majored in mathematics and received his bachelor of arts degree in 1947 with a secondary-school teaching certificate. While at college, he was also a student at the Birmingham Conservatory of Music (1945–48), again on scholarships, studying theory and composition with G. Ackley Brower and Hugh Thomas. Singing in Thomas's class, Sims says, "formed my sense of phrasing and made me open to the variety of pitch." Between 1950 and 1952 he studied composition with Quincy Porter at the School of Music at Yale University, earning his bachelor of music degree in 1952. In 1953 at the U.S. Army Language School he was given a diploma in Mandarin Chinese. In 1956, after having attended Mills College for two years, where he held a teaching fellowship, and having studied composition there with Darius Milhaud and Leon Kirchner, he was awarded his master of arts degree. He spent the summer of 1960 studying composition with Aaron Copland at the Berkshire Music Center at Tanglewood, Mass., on a Crofts scholarship, where he was awarded the Sagalyn Prize in composition. "During all these years of undergraduate and graduate work, I held, of course, the requisite set of jacket-blurb jobs:

schoolteacher, steelworker, mail clerk, choir director, display designer, and so forth." Between 1958 and 1962 (and again from 1965 to 1974) he worked as programmer and cataloguer at the Harvard University music library.

Sims's first works as a mature composer were in a twelve-tone idiom. *Chamber Cantata on Chinese Poems*, for tenor and chamber ensemble (1954) used for its text several Mandarin poems dealing with the seasons, and was sung in Chinese. "Unlike native settings of language," the composer says, "which either ignore the speech tones of the words or use various conventions to represent them, the voice line of the cantata mirrors them directly." Its first performance took place at a concert of the Composers Forum in New York on October 31, 1959. Six years later it was recorded and this release was reviewed in *Hi Fi Stereo Review* by a critic who wrote: "It is . . . full of pretty instrumental sound and quite fetching expressivity and lyricism in its vocal line. The music gives pleasure."

Sims continued adapting the twelve-tone idiom to his own requirements in several more works in the 1950s. These included a Mass, for a cappella chorus (1955); *Masque*, for chamber orchestra (1955), for a ballet produced in San Francisco in 1957 with choreography by Welland Lathrop; Sonatine, for piano (1957), which used the same tone row as the Mass; Two Folk Songs, for baritone and piano (1958; N.Y., March 11, 1972), which was based on the American folk tunes "Charles Guiteau" and "Streets of Laredo"; *Grave Dance*, for piano (1958), a serial treatment of "Streets of Laredo"; and String Quartet (1959; N.Y., March 20, 1960). In the third movement of this string quartet, Sims felt compelled for the first time to experiment with microtonal writing, though this was still done tentatively. This quartet was premiered at a concert of "Music in Our Time."

Sims's first composition that was almost consistently in quartertones was *Sonate concertante*, consisting of *5 Sonatine* (for oboe, viola, cello, and doublebass) and *5 Sonate* (for string quartet). The sonatinas and the sonatas can be played separately (in which case the five sonatas become Sims's second string quartet, though not officially numbered as such) or as an octet. The octet form of this work was first heard at a concert of "Music in Our Time" in New York on April 16, 1961, Ralph Shapey conducting. Sims's Third String Quartet (1962; N.Y., 1965), written on a grant from the Endicott Fund, was his last work exclusively in quartertones.

In 1962, Sims received a Guggenheim Fellowship. That year (1962–63) he was an observer and composer at the Electronic Music Studio, NHK, in Tokyo. There he composed the electronic portions (the instrumental sections being written by a Japanese composer) of the incidental music for *Sakoku*, a Japanese play telecast in Tokyo on April 28, 1963.

Sims's first collage was *In Memoriam Alice Haw-thorne*, for reciter, tenor, baritone, and instruments (1967; Boston, January 28, 1977). This is a three-part work on texts by Edward Gorey. In "Introduction and Litany" the speaker and singers presented an alphabet in counterpoint to a little march quoted from Carl Maria von Weber's *Konzertstück*. In the second part, "Passion," the spoken narrative is "The Object Lesson" and the sung duets are drawn from "The Listening Attic." The concluding section, "Antiphon and Coda," once again quotes the Weber *Konzertstück* was well as the song "Listen to the Mocking Bird," while "The Nursery Frieze" is shouted by the voices, word by word in permutated rotation.

Since 1968, Sims has been music director of the New England Dinosaur in Boston. Beginning with 1968 he began producing tapes for dance and theater—largely tape collage and/or *musique concrète*. For choreography by Toby Amour he created, among others, *Antimatter* (N.Y., June 16, 1968) and *McDowell's Fault*, or *The Tenth Sunday after Trinity*, both in 1968, and *Where the Wild Things Are* (1973; N.Y., October 31, 1973). In 1970 he produced *Real Toads*—*musique concrète* for Cliff Keuter's choreography (N.Y., April 9, 1970).

Without the benefit of any choreography he completed *Commonplace Book*. This was *musique concrète* made up of "twenty-four beer cans, with two orchestral quotes, a radio preacher, an angry dog, and a Concord midnight." The initial percussion was produced by the destruction of a beer can by flexion, that sound slowed down, edited, and superimposed on itself. The choruses were beer cans being rubbed, that noise lowered until it functioned as vowel formants. The ragtime piano was those beer cans dropped, the sound lowered in pitch, and edited. *Commonplace Book* was introduced at a "Music Here and Now" concert at the Museum of Fine Arts in Boston on January 30, 1973.

At the Massachusetts Institute of Technology (Artificial Intelligence Laboratory) and the University of Pennsylvania, Sims worked with Stephen Smoliar on and with his Euterpe System, encoding and reproducing a computer realization of *From an Oboe Quartet*, for oboe, violin, viola, and cello in 1971. Sims considers this composition his first "reasonably clear exposition of my subsequent language."

String Quartet no. 2 (1962) (1974) was written as a kind of capricious response to an error in Nicolas Slonimsky's *Baker's Biographical Dictionary of Musicians* in which Slonimsky listed among Sims's works a "String Quartet no. 2 (1962)" which did not exist, his second quartet being the *5 Sonate* of his *Sonate concertante* written in 1961. Sims, therefore, decided to set the record straight by writing a piece with that name to fulfill a commission from Boston Musica Viva. As if to compound the whimsy, but actually as yet another exemplification of the work's concern for the ratio 5:4, he wrote it not for a string quartet but for a quintet of three strings and two winds. Complicating things further, Sims wrote his work not in the usual twelve-tone scale but in an interim version of his microtonal one. Boston Musica Viva premiered this work in Boston late in February 1976. "The unusual scale put a strain on one's hearing for a couple of minutes," reported David Noble in the *Quincy Patriot Ledger*, "but after a while the notes that had sounded off-center and 'intellectual' became dramatic, even exciting in the harmonic web Sims had built."

His next work in this microtonal idiom, *Elegie—nach Rilke*, for soprano and instruments (1976) on a text drawn from the tenth of Rilke's *Duino Elegies*, was also premiered by the Boston Musica Viva—in Cambridge, Mass., on November 16, 1976, with Elsa Charlston soloist. It was commissioned by the Goethe Institute of Boston. The word setting ranges from barely abstracted speech (precisely notated as to pitch) through speech-biased song, on through fully abstracted lyricism to the complete abstraction of wordless cantilena. To Richard Ruell in the *Boston Globe*, *Elegie* "seemed a perfect fitting of words to technique. . . . Though there is a high dissonance level to the music, the instrumental textures are bracing, lucid ones, and through plain, solid rhythms they communicate a kind of frayed nerve-end brightness. Sims pushes the voice to its limits, but it's not obtusely inconsiderate writing; it's simply extreme and it makes no bones about it."

On January 16, 1978, Dinosaur Annex performed in Boston a concert of Ezra Sims's music in celebration of his fiftieth birthday. The program ranged from his compositions of the 1950s to two world premieres: *Aeneas on the Saxophone* (1977) to a text by Osbert Lancaster, for vocal quartet and instruments, and *Yr Obed*[l] *Serv*[l] (1977), for a chamber instrumental ensemble, both microtonal works written expressly for this concert.

From 1976 to 1978, Sims was a member of the theory faculty at the New England Conservatory in Boston. He received fellowships from Cambridge Arts Council in 1975 and 1976, fellowships from the National Education Association in 1976 and 1978, and an Artists Fellowship from Massachusetts in 1979. In 1977 he was guest composer at the Contemporary Music Festival at Wesleyan University in Illinois. He has lectured and conducted seminars at various colleges and universities in the United States as well as at Warwick University in Coventry, England, and International Christian University in Tokyo.

THE COMPOSER SPEAKS: In others, and in their works, what I value most, I think, is a high heart, a merry soul, and a knowledge of grief—these and the discipline, depth, and skill to make of all these things something fine and flawless. From myself, I have to take what I can get.

I think I can claim a position, however humble, in the mainstream of Western musical style. I think there is and always has been a strong and structurally coherent affective element in my stuff. I'm in no way, so far as I can tell, a revolutionary. I've used a variety of techniques in a fairly smooth progress and perhaps not inconsistent style on my way to my current one. I write microtonal music because that's how my art works, what it demands; if I didn't, it would permit me to write nothing else (with any of that real delight that makes composing worth doing). I consider what I write as being unquestionably tonal. I can't say that I consider myself in any way to have *returned* to tonality, having never to my knowledge abandoned it.

PRINCIPAL WORKS: 3 string quartets (1959, 1961, 1962, as well as one labeled a string quartet, actually a quintet for 3 strings and 2 winds, 1974).

Chamber Cantata on Chinese Poems, for tenor and chamber ensemble (1954); Mass, for small a cappella chorus (1955); *Masque*, ballet, for chamber orchestra (1955); Cello Sonata (1957); Sonatine, for piano (1957); *Grave Dance*, for piano (1958); Two Folk Songs, for baritone and piano (1958); *Brief Glimpses into Contemporary French Literature*, for four countertenors and piano (1958); *Music for Kubla Khan of Coleridge*, no. I, for reciter, gamelan, and chamber ensemble, no. II, for reciter and tape collage (1958); String Quartet (1959); Three Songs, for tenor and orchestra (1960); *Sonate concertante*, for string quartet, oboe, viola, cello, and double bass (1961); *Buchlein for Lyon*, for piano (1962); *In Memoriam Alice Hawthorne*, for reciter, tenor, baritone, French horn, four clarinets, and marimba, four hands (1967); *Antimatter*, ballet, for tape collage (1968); *McDowell's Fault*, or *The Tenth Sunday after Trinity*, tape collage (1928); *Alec*, ballet, tape collage/*musique concrète* (1968); *A Frank Overture, Four Dented Interludes and Coda*, ballet, tape collage/*musique concrète* (1969); *Commonplace Book*, or *A Salute to Our American Container Corp.*, *musique concrète* (1969); *Pastorale*, ballet, *musique concrète* (1970); *Clement Wenceslaus Lothaire Nepomucene, Prince Metternich In Memoriam*, ballet, combine tape (1970); *Elina's Piece*, electronic/*musique concrète* (1970); *From an Oboe Quartet*, for oboe, violin, viola, and cello, computer realization (1971); *Ground Cover*, ballet, combine tape (1972); *Museum Piece*, collage (1972); *Wall to Wall*, collage/*musique concrète* (1972); *Thirty Years Later*, *musique concrète* (1972); *Where the Wild Things Are*, ballet, combine tape (1973); *Second Thoughts*, for one, two or many double basses, with or without magnetic tape (1974); *The Temptations at the Siege of Air and Darkness*, for voices, piano, and optional instruments (1975); Oboe Quartet, includes the 1971 *From an Oboe Quartet* (1975); *After Lyle*, *musique concrète* (1975); *The Owl and the Pussycat*, ballet, for bass voice, chromatic harmonica, and electric guitar (1975); *Elegie—nach Rilke*, for soprano and instruments (1976); *Celebration of Dead Ladies*, for voice and instruments

(1976); *Yr Obed^l Serv^l*, for chamber ensemble (1977); *Aeneas on the Saxophone*, for vocal quartet and instruments (1977); *Twenty Years After*, for violin and clarinet (1978); *Come Away*, for mezzo-soprano and instruments (1978); *Midorigaoka*, for two violins, two violas, and cello (1978); *—and as I was saying . . .* for viola solo (1978); *All Done from Memory*, for violin solo (1980).

BIBLIOGRAPHY: *BBDM; DCM;* Anderson, E. Ruth, *Contemporary American Composers* (Boston, 1976).

Skilton, Charles Sanford, b. Northampton, Mass., August 16, 1868; d. Lawrence, Kans., March 12, 1941.

Skilton was a romanticist who worked with traditional structures and idioms while trying to achieve American nationalist music through compositions on American-Indian subjects, utilizing the melodies and rhythms of American-Indian tribal music. He also wrote works exploring other areas of American style.

He received his early musical training at the piano with local teachers in Northampton, and his early academic education in its public schools. While attending Yale University, he wrote his first compositions, which included a cantata, *The Burial of Moses*, and incidental music (choral as well as instrumental) for a production of *Elektra* at Smith College in Northampton in 1889.

After graduating from Yale with a bachelor of arts degree in 1889, Skilton spent two years as instructor of languages at Siglar's Preparatory School in Newburgh, N.Y. (1889–91). He left this school for music studies in Germany, attending the Academy of Music in Berlin from 1891 to 1893 as a student in composition with Woldemar Bargiel and organ with Albert Heinz. Following his return to the United States, he served as director of music at Salem Academy and College in North Carolina (1893–96), at the same time conducting the Salem Philharmonic. He left Salem in 1896 to come to New York, continuing his study for the next two years at the Metropolitan College of Music: organ with Harry Rowe Shelley and composition with Dudley Buck and Otis Boise. A Violin Sonata (1897) won a prize from the Music Teachers National Association.

From 1897 to 1903, Skilton was director of music at the State Normal School in Trenton, N.J. In 1903 he was appointed professor of organ and theory at the University of Kansas, in Lawrence, retaining this post for the remainder of his life and serving as Dean of its School of Fine Arts between 1903 and 1915.

The music he wrote up until the middle of the second decade of the 20th century—some of which received prizes from the Kansas Federation of Music Clubs—was indebted to the style and structures of the German romantic school. Then, in 1915, an American Indian offered to introduce him to the American-Indian tribal music in return for harmony lessons. This native American music so impressed Skilton that he went to Haskill Institute, a government-subsidized school for American Indians in Lawrence, to explore American-Indian music in depth.

His first composition to use native American-Indian music was also his most successful: *Two Indian Dances*—"Deer Dance" and "War Dance"—originally (1915) for string quartet, then orchestrated a year later. The orchestral version was introduced by the Minneapolis Symphony under Emil Oberhoffer on October 29, 1916. After that, *Two Indian Dances* had over five hundred performances by fifty symphony orchestras in the United States and in nine foreign countries. Almost as successful was his *Suite Primeval* (1920), consisting of four tribal Indian melodies: "Sunrise Song" (Winnebago), "Gambling Song" (Rogue River in Oregon), "Flute Serenade" (Sioux), and "Moccasin Game" (Winnebago). *Suite Primeval* was premiered by the Minneapolis Symphony under Oberhoffer on November 13, 1921, and then was programmed by several other major American orchestras.

Skilton produced several other successful compositions on American-Indian subjects. *American Indian Fantasy* (1920) was a work for organ that he transcribed for orchestra and cello obbligato nine years later. As an orchestral work it was premiered at Interlochen, Mich., on August 14, 1937, Vladimir Bakaleinikov conducting. Violin Sonata no. 2 in G minor was a two-movement composition built on two American-Indian melodies: "Autumn Night" and "Shawnee Indian Hunting Song." Skilton transcribed both movements for orchestra in 1930, the first of which was given its first performance on December 11, 1930, with Ossip Gabrilowitsch conducting the Detroit Symphony. "Widely performed in its day," said Gilbert Chase in *America's Music*, "his Indianizing music, superficial and conventional, has for us now solely the interest of a period piece, demonstrating the 'picture postcard' school of 'native music.' "

Two operas were also about the American Indian. *Kalopin* (1927) was an allegorical three-act opera to his own text which was based on the legendary explanation by Chickasaw and Chotonow Indians for the New Madrid earthquake of 1811: punishment meted out to the Chickasaw chief, Kalopin, for going to another tribe for his bride. Though it was never produced, it was awarded the David Bispham Medal in 1930. *The Sun Bride*, a one-act radio opera, was premiered over the NBC radio network on April 17, 1930. Its libretto (written by the composer) was concerned with the sun worshipping beliefs of Pueblo Indians of Arizona. Into this score, Skilton interpolated the music of his "Sunrise Song" from the *Suite Primeval*. "Exotic themes," wrote John Tasker Howard in *Our American Music*, "help to bring out the Indian locale and story, and in spite of a conventional melodiousness, the Indian atmosphere is effectively suggested."

Other works by Skilton tapped American veins other than the Indian. The cantata *The Witch's Daughter* (1918) was a musical dramatization of Whittier's poem about Salem witchcraft. *The Guardian Angel* (1925) was an oratorio whose text spoke of the early Moravian settlers in North Carolina. *Ticonderoga* was a cantata for male voices (1933) based on Robert Louis Stevenson's poem of the same name dealing with the French and Indian War.

On a sabbatical leave from the University of Kansas, Skilton spent the year of 1937–38 in Europe (mostly in Vienna), where he completed String Quartet in B minor, his last major chamber music composition. His last work was *Zoo fantastique*, a set of songs for soprano and piano.

Skilton married Maude H. Grignard on December 30, 1903; they had two daughters and a son. In 1933, Skilton received an honorary doctorate from Syracuse University in New York State. He was fellow of the American Guild of Organists—dean of its Kansas Chapter in 1915. Skilton was the author of *Symphonic Forms* (1927).

PRINCIPAL WORKS: 2 violin sonatas (1897, 1922). *Two Indian Dances,* originally for string quartet, also for orchestra (1916); *Three Indian Sketches,* for piano (1918); *The Witch's Daughter,* cantata for solo voices, chorus, and orchestra (1918); *Sioux Flute Serenade,* for trio (1920); *Suite Primeval,* for orchestra (1920); *American Indian Fantasy,* originally for organ, also for orchestra with cello obbligato (1920); *Suite East and West,* for orchestra (1921); *The Guardian Angel,* oratorio for solo voices, chorus, and orchestra (1925); *Legend,* for orchestra (1927); *Kalopin,* opera (1927); *The Sun Bride,* one-act radio opera (1930); *From Forest and Stream,* twelve songs for treble voices (1930); Overture in F major, for orchestra (1931); *Ticonderoga,* cantata for male chorus and orchestra (1932); *The Day of Gayomir,* opera (1936); String Quartet in B minor (1938); *Zoo fantastique,* for voice and piano (1940).

BIBLIOGRAPHY: Ewen, David, *Composers Since 1900* (N.Y., 1969); Howard, John Tasker, *Charles Sanford Skilton* (N.Y., 1929); Reis, Claire, *Composers in America* (N.Y., 1947); *Who's Who in America, 1940–41.*

Smit, Leo, b. Philadelphia, Pa., January 12, 1921.

In the earliest works of his maturity, in the 1940s, Smit passed through an American phase in which some of his works were inspired by American subjects and many were stylistically influenced by Aaron Copland. During the next decade, he passed through a neoclassical period in which he became partial to pellucid contrapuntal textures and an objective approach. Subsequently, his music became marked by integration of various styles and techniques and by the mingling of free and controlled meters.

Both his parents were of Russian birth. His father, Kolman Smit, was a professional violinist who at different stages of his career was a member of the Philadelphia Orchestra and the NBC Symphony, among other orchestras. Leo Smit received his first instruction in music (piano and theory) when he was five from his father. Between 1927 and 1929, he studied piano privately with Martha Lantner, Joseph Wissof, and Bert Shefter. Smit spent three months in 1929 at the Moscow Conservatory on a scholarship, studying piano with Dmitri Kabalevsky. Back in New York in 1930, he was awarded the Music Week Association gold medal for piano and theory. Between 1930 and 1932, on a scholarship, he attended the Curtis Institute of Music in Philadelphia, a piano student of Isabelle Vengerova's. After that, still on scholarships, he studied piano privately with José Iturbi (1933–35) and composition with Nicolas Nabokov (1935). During these student years he orchestrated the first movement of Brahms's D-minor Violin Sonata, arranged Mozart's D-minor Piano Concerto (K. 466) for piano and string quartet, and Wagner's *Siegfried Idyll* for piano four hands. His first original composition was "Zvay" ("Two"), a song for soprano and piano written in 1935 to a Yiddish poem by Mani Leib which was chromatic and expressionistic in idiom.

When he graduated from junior high school in New York in 1933, Smit continued his academic education through private tutoring with Dr. Abraham Breslau and Sidney Meyers, and received a New York State Regents high school diploma in 1935. His formal education ended in 1941 at St. John's College in Annapolis, Md., where, as guest student-teacher, he attended classes, lectures, and seminars.

In 1936–37, Smit was pianist with George Balanchine's American Ballet Company, an association that brought him into personal meetings with Igor Stravinsky, whose influence would subsequently be reflected in Smit's neoclassicism. Between 1935 and 1939, Smit completed several compositions that followed traditional structural patterns: all were diatonic but at times bordered on the exotic. These included Septet, for woodwind and brass (1936); *Hebraic Heritage,* for piano solo (1938), a set of dances for which Julia Levien provided the choreography; and *The Rime of the Ancient Mariner,* for speaker and piano (1939), based on Samuel Taylor Coleridge's poem.

Smit made his debut as concert pianist in Carnegie Hall in New York, on February 17, 1939. This was followed a year later by an American tour. Between 1953 and 1955 he toured Europe and in 1967–68 he performed extensively throughout Latin America under the auspices of the U.S. Department of State in programs featuring American music. In addition to performances in recitals and in recordings, he was heard as guest performer with major orchestras both in the United States and abroad, most notably in 20th-century concertos. Smit has also appeared as conductor.

In 1947–48, he was the official pianist of the New York City Symphony, of which Leonard Bernstein was then music director. In 1947, Smit was administrator of artists and repertoire for Concert Hall Society Records. Between 1947 and 1949 he was a member of the music faculty at Sarah Lawrence College in Bronxville, N.Y.

He arrived at creative maturity with Sextet, for clarinet, bassoon, and strings (1940). The 1940s, Smit's "American period," saw the writing of *Virginia Sampler* (1947), a ballet commissioned by the Ballet Russe de Monte Carlo. Its world premiere took place in New York on March 4, 1947, choreography by Valerie Bettis. Smit revised this ballet score in 1960. This was also the period of several notable works for piano. Among these were the *Five Pieces for Young People* (1947), *Rural Elegy* (1948), *Seven Characteristic Pieces* (1949), and Variations in G (1949).

In 1950, Smit received a Fulbright Fellowship in piano and a Guggenheim Fellowship in composition. During an extended stay in Italy in 1950–51, he completed a setting for four solo voices, two oboes, bassoon, two horns, and string quartet of seven poems by Anthony Hecht, *A Choir of Starlings* (1951). He conducted its premiere at a concert at the American Academy in Rome on Christmas Eve, 1951. After his return to the United States, his orchestral overture *The Parcae* (1953) was premiered by the Boston Symphony under Charles Munch on October 16, 1953. This work was ultimately withdrawn to become part of the final section of the opera *The Alchemy of Love* (1969). In 1953, Smit was honored with the Boston Merit Award.

Smit's first major success as composer arrived with his most ambitious composition up to that time, the Symphony no. 1 in E-flat, which had been commissioned by the Koussevitzky Music Foundation for the thirtieth anniversary of the League of Composers. The Boston Symphony under Charles Munch introduced it on February 1, 1957. Though somewhat influenced by Stravinsky and Copland, this neoclassical music was personalized in its melodic, rhythmic and contrapuntal idiom. "The texture is fresh and strong and exceptionally melodic considering the times," reported Rudolph Elie in the *Boston Globe*. When the Boston Symphony brought the symphony to New York a few days later, Howard Taubman in the *New York Times* wrote: "It was written with directness and clarity. His first movement has a slow introduction which, in mood and utility, has an almost classic profile. The main part of the movement takes thematic material stated in the introduction and manipulates it with brightness and dexterity. . . . In the slow movement, Mr. Smit is almost Brahmsian in his broad, singing theme which has a long line and a strong romantic inclination. The three variations and coda sustain the mood. . . . The scherzo is feathery and transparent in the instrumentation. And the finale, in sonata form, moves with color and vivacity." The symphony brought Smit the New York Music Critics Circle Award.

Smit's neoclassical period continued with the Capriccio, for string orchestra (1958), introduced at the Ojai Festival in California on May 23, 1958, Aaron Copland conducting. The term *capriccio* is here used in its 17th-century meaning, denoting a work that incorporates such characteristic elements as fugal structure, variation form, and quoted material. Though played without interruption, it is in three parts beginning with a fugal Ricercar; continuing with an Introduction, Theme, and Variations in which the theme comes from Tchaikovsky's ballet *The Sleeping Beauty* (Smit wrote the capriccio in homage to Tchaikovsky); and ending with an Epilogue that returned to the first subject of the Ricercar. *Academic Graffiti*, for voice, clarinet, cello, piano, and percussion (1959), is a witty setting of a collection of humorous or gossipy quatrains about famous or notorious men and women of history by W. H. Auden. This music often parodies the styles of composers of the past. "A specific percussion instrument," the composer explains, "is 'leit-motifed' with its accompanying 'hero,' sometimes incongruously, like the alpine cow bell for shy urbane Henry Adams, and then, fittingly, like the tinkling triangle in the fetal lullaby for Sören Kierkegaard."

Between 1957 and 1963, Smit was head of a piano department at the University of California in Los Angeles. During this period he served on the board of directors of the "Monday Evening Concerts" in Los Angeles (1959–63). In the fall of 1962 he was visiting Slee Professor of music at the State University of New York in Buffalo. Since 1963 he has held a professorship in music there. The *Buffalo Evening News* presented him with its Man of the Year Award in 1969. In 1978, Smit was visiting Artist Certificate at Harvard University.

Since 1961, Smit has been producing compositions integrating earlier styles and techniques with music whose individual profile is characterized by rhythmic momentum, colorful sonorities, strong-fibered lyricism. The six-movement Symphony no. 2 (1965), commissioned by Dr. Norman Rosenthal, was introduced by the Buffalo Philharmonic, the composer conducting, in 1965. Concerto for Orchestra and Piano, first performed on November 24, 1968, by the Buffalo Philharmonic under Lukas Foss with the composer at the piano, was described by one Buffalo critic as "an ode to Nature." Writing in the *Buffalo Evening News*, John Dwyer said: "It's a kind of old-fashioned work by a composer acutely alive to his world but also enamored of its traditions." A witty interpolation of a quotation from Beethoven's *Sonata pathetique* added spice to the vigorous proceedings. In 1980, Smit revised this work by adding a new first and last movement and changing the title to Concerto for Piano and Orchestra.

Smit's three-act opera, *The Alchemy of Love* (1969), libretto by Sir Fred Hoyle, is described as a "space fable." It deals with incidents on planet 197/43 which bear an uncomfortable similarity to events transpiring on this earth. Smit used material from this score for *Four Kookaburra Marches*, for orchestra (1971; Istanbul, Turkey, February 10, 1973). The kookaburra is a large Australian kingfisher noted for his hysterical laugh. "In the opera and the Marches," Smit says, "the kookaburra symbolically replaces the biblical rooster whose crowing points at man's age-old talent for betrayal. The kookaburra's infectious laughter smacks of the pettiness and cruelty of Homo Sapiens' blundering on earth, while heralding the day when man abandons himself to his intelligence and love of life."

Since 1970, Smit's most important compositions have included the *Caedmon*, "after the Venerable Bede," to an English-Latin text by Anthony Hecht, for three solo voices, male chorus, and orchestra (1972; Buffalo, December 10, 1972); *Copernicus: Narrative and Credo* (1973; Washington, D.C., April 22, 1973), commissioned by the National Academy of Sciences through the Copernicus Society of America to commemorate the 500th birthday of Nicolaus Copernicus, a work for narrator, chorus, and nine instruments to an English-Italian-Latin text by Sir Fred Hoyle; *At the Corner of the Sky* (1976; Buffalo, May 16, 1976), commissioned by St. Paul's Cathedral in Buffalo, scored for men and boys' choir, solo flute, and oboe, and using as text North American Indian poetry translated by Jerome Rothenberg; *In Woods*, for oboe, harp, and percussion (1978); and *Scena cambiata*, for trombone, viola, and cello (1980).

THE COMPOSER SPEAKS: The frightening but inspiring task confronting the composer is to make something intelligible out of unformed beginnings.

Anyone who has looked at the awesome struggles recorded in Beethoven's sketchbooks will be conscious of the miracle of musical creation. All composers share in this process, varied only by degrees of mental concentration and physical energy.

That aspect of music which makes ordinary listeners turn towards each other with smiles of wonder reflects the beauty of the composer's signature and is beyond the scope of analytical thought. If inspiration is the right word, then it must be the gift all composers pray and work for.

PRINCIPAL WORKS: 2 symphonies (1955, 1965).

Sextet, for clarinet, bassoon, and strings (1940); *Yerma*, ballet (1946); *Virginia Sampler*, ballet (1947; revised 1960); *Five Pieces for Young People*,

for piano (1947); *Vi Shum-Roo*, for cantor, chorus, and organ (1947); *Rural Elegy*, for piano (1948); *Seven Characteristic Pieces*, for piano (1949); Variations in G, for piano (1949); *A Choir of Starlings*, for four solo voices and ten instruments (1951); Three Romances, for mezzo-soprano and piano (1952); *Fantasy: The Farewell*, for piano (1953); *Four Madrigals for a Roman Lady*, for a cappella chorus (1955; revised 1965); *Sonata in One Movement*, for piano (1955); Four Motets, for voice and instruments (1955); Capriccio, for string orchestra (1958, revised 1974); *Academic Graffiti*, for voice and instruments (1962); *A Transient View*, for a cappella chorus (1967); Concerto for Orchestra and Piano (1968), revised in 1980 as Concerto for Piano and Orchestra; *The Alchemy of Love*, opera (1969); *Channel Firing*, for baritone and piano (1970); *Myopia: A Night*, for baritone and instruments (1971); *Caedmon*, for three solo voices, male chorus, and orchestra (1972); *Copernicus: Narrative and Credo*, for narrator, chorus and nine instruments (1973); *Lizzie in Wonderland*, for harp solo (1974); *Three Christmas Tree Carols*, for chorus and eight instruments (1974); *Songs without Words*, for wind quintet (1975); *A Mountain Eulogy*, for narrator and piano, also narrator and orchestra (1975); *At the Corner of the Sky*, for men's chorus, boys' chorus, flute, and oboe (1976); *In Woods*, for oboe, harp, and percussion (1978); *Magic Water*, one-act opera (1979); *Scena cambiata*, for trombone, viola, and cello (1980); *Cock Robin*, for soprano, piccolo and percussion (1980); *Delaunay Pochoirs*, for cello and piano (1980).

BIBLIOGRAPHY: *BBDM*; *DCM*; Anderson, E. Ruth, *Contemporary American Composers* (Boston, 1976).

Smith, David Stanley, b. Toledo, Ohio, July 6, 1877; d. New Haven, Conn., December 17, 1949.

Though Smith's music is often harmonically and contrapuntally dissonant, he was basically a traditionalist who favored classical structures and whose writing, at its best, was poetic and dramatic. In the *Musical Quarterly*, Burnet C. Tuthill described Smith's style as "sensitive, sometimes dynamic, often very subtle. . . . It is always logical even in its most rhapsodic moments. . . . The passages that suggest the obvious or the commonplace are very rare." Smith was at his best in instrumental music and most particularly in chamber music, to which he confided his most personal, intimate, touching, and winning sentiments.

His father, W. H. H. Smith, a businessman of Scottish descent, was a self-taught organist and the composer of anthems and hymns who performed on the organ in Toledo's churches as an avocation. His mother, Julia Welles (Griswold) Smith, who was of New England ancestry, was a trained singer. Since

David Smith's two brothers and a sister also sang, they often joined their mother in family vocal concerts accompanied by their father on a small pipe organ. These performances represented David Stanley Smith's introduction to music.

David began receiving piano lessons with local teachers in Toledo while still young. As a high school student, he taught himself harmony by studying a music theory textbook. At the same time he received some instruction in counterpoint from Arthur Kortheuer.

A performance of Horatio Parker's *Hora Novissima* at the Cincinnati May Festival made such a deep and lasting impression on him that when Smith entered Yale University in 1895 for academic studies he attended Parker's classes in music history and composition. After his freshman year, financial reverses in the family compelled Smith to leave Yale. But he was back in 1897, and in 1900 he received his bachelor of arts degree, all the while attending Parker's classes. As a Yale student, Smith played organ in several New Haven churches. He was also composing seriously: an orchestral Overture in E-flat (1898); an unnumbered String Quartet (1899); and *Ode for Commencement* (1900), sung at his graduation ceremony.

When he graduated from Yale, Smith was encouraged by Parker to go to Europe, not so much for study as to come into contact with and absorb European musical influences. Smith spent the year of 1901–2 in London, Munich, and Paris. "During this period, I was able to hear much music and visit art galleries consistently." He did study composition with Ludwig Thuille in Munich and organ with Charles-Marie Widor in Paris. He also produced some choral works together with an orchestral tone poem, *Darkness and Dawn* (1901).

After his return to the United States, he reentered Yale, working under Horatio Parker and receiving his bachelor of music degree in 1903. At the commencement exercises Smith performed his own Prelude, Chorale, and Fugue, for organ and orchestra (1903), which he had submitted as the thesis for his degree. In 1903 Smith was appointed instructor of music at Yale. There, from 1909 to 1916, he was assistant professor; from 1916 to 1925, full professor; from 1920 to 1940, dean of the School of Music, and from 1925 to 1946, Battell Professor of Music. In 1914 he was visiting lecturer on music at the University of California in Berkeley. Between 1936 and 1946 he was also associate fellow of Berkeley College at Yale. When, in 1945, he retired as professor emeritus, he continued giving courses in theory as Battell Professor until the end of his life. While teaching at Yale, Smith earned his master of music degree in 1916. From 1920 to 1946 he was a conductor of the New Haven Symphony Orchestra, sole conductor for most of that time.

Smith's earlier compositions were conventional in harmonic and contrapuntal idiom, romantic in spirit, and highly lyrical with long, flowing melodic phrases. His String Quartet no. 1 in E minor (1906) was performed by the Kneisel Quartet soon after it was written. His Symphony no. 1 in F minor (1910) was introduced by the Chicago Symphony under Frederick Stock in 1912. His first successful composition was *Prince Hal* (1912), a concert overture inspired by Shakespeare's *Henry V*, which was performed by several major American orchestras after being introduced in New Haven in December 1912. "It is a brilliant piece," wrote Burnet C. Tuthill. "It has dash and an admixture of sly humor; there are rousing climaxes and a crashing close. . . . The scoring is rich and sonorous and of colorful variety; the themes are tuneful and easy to remember without being too obvious or commonplace." In 1914, Smith wrote his only opera, *Merrymount*, which was never produced; this was two decades before Howard Hanson wrote an opera on the same subject and with the same title.

Smith personalized his musical speech in the 1920s by moving away from romanticism, sentimentality, and rousing climaxes toward a subtle and carefully thought-out language in which dissonance was used increasingly for contrast and dramatic effect and a powerful musical expression and exuberance were becoming ever more assertive. The personal characteristics of his subsequent thought and method can first be encountered in the single-movement String Quartet no. 3 in C (1920). It is sometimes labeled the *Gregorian Quartet* because it introduced the plainsong *Jesu Corona* with a simple modal harmonization. Dissonance became more prominent in the String Quartet no. 6 in C (1934). "The melodic line governs the writing," Tuthill explains. "Suspensions are resolved only to find that at the time of resolution the harmony has moved on to a new chord of which the note of resolution forms no part. In the counterpoint, a melodic line does not give way to avoid consecutive sevenths or augmented octaves." Smith's most important and successful string quartet was the no. 8 in A (1936), introduced at the Coolidge Festival at the Library of Congress in Washington, D.C., on April 14, 1940. Even more poetic and thoughtful than before has Smith's language become in this work, which ends in an unconventional way of fading pianissimo on the supported dominant degree in the second violin, "an expression of a true poet in sound," said Tuthill.

Smith's major works for orchestra—all characterized by masterful craftsmanship and instrumentation—received important performances. Symphony no. 3 (1928) was introduced by the Cleveland Orchestra with the composer conducting on January 8, 1931. Symphony no. 4 in D minor (1937) was performed first on April 14, 1939, by the Boston Symphony under the composer's direction. *Epic Poem*, for orchestra (1926), was premiered by the Boston Symphony on April 12, 1935, the composer conducting. One of his most popular works, *1929—A Satire*

(1932), was heard first in a performance by the New York Philharmonic on November 15, 1933. The tone poem for orchestra, *Credo* (1941), was given its premiere by the New York Philharmonic in November 1941, Bruno Walter conducting.

Smith married Cora Deming Welch, daughter of a New Haven banker, on December 6, 1913; they raised an adopted son. Smith received honorary doctorates in music from Northwestern University in Evanston. Ill. (1918) and the Cincinnati Conservatory of Music in Ohio (1927). He was a member of the National Institute of Arts and Letters and the American Academy of Arts and Letters, and fellow of the American Guild of Organists.

PRINCIPAL WORKS: 10 string quartets (1905–44); 5 symphonies (1910–49); 2 violin sonatas (1924, 1945); 2 piano sonatas (1929, 1940); 2 violin concertos (1933, 1942).

Prince Hal, concert overture for orchestra (1912); *Merrymount*, opera (1914); *Rhapsody of St. Bernard*, for vocal soloists, chorus, and semichorus (1915); *Sonata pastorale*, for oboe and piano (1918); *Four and Twenty Little Songs*, for voice and piano (1919); *Poem of Youth*, for orchestra (1920); *Fête galante*, for flute and orchestra (1921); *Epic Poem*, for orchestra (1926); *Cathedral Prelude*, for organ and orchestra (1926); Piano Quintet (1927); *Vision of Isaiah*, for soprano, tenor and orchestra (1927); Cello Sonata (1928); String Sextet (1931); *Scenes from a Tragedy*, for violin and piano (1932); *Tomorrow*, concert overture for orchestra (1932); *1929—A Satire*, for orchestra (1932); Viola Sonata (1934); *Songs of Three Ages*, song cycle for soprano and piano (1936); *Requiem*, "poem" for violin and orchestra (1939); Clarinet Sonata (1941); *Credo*, poem for orchestra (1941); *Triumph and Peace*, poem for organ (1943); Four Pieces, for strings (1943); *The Apostle*, tone poem for orchestra (1944); *Small Sonata*, for two violins (1945); *The Ocean*, for bass, chorus, and orchestra (1945).

BIBLIOGRAPHY: Ewen, David, *American Composers Today* (N.Y., 1949); Howard, John Tasker, *Our American Music* (N.Y., 1946); Reis, Claire, *Composers in America* (N.Y., 1947); *Musical Quarterly*, January 1942; *Who's Who in America, 1948–49*.

Sowerby, Leo, b. Grand Rapids, Mich., May 1, 1895. d. Port Clinton, Ohio, July 7, 1968.

Sowerby was the first composer to be awarded the American Prix de Rome; subsequently he was the recipient of the Pulitzer Prize in music. He was a versatile composer whose music covered many genres and styles. He wrote abstract music and programmatic music; ecclesiastical music and music grounded in American popular and folk idioms. He was a classicist (often using such baroque forms as the passaca-

glia, chaconne and fugue), a romanticist, and a modernist who was prolix in his use of dissonance.

His father was English, his mother Canadian. Since his mother died when Sowerby was four, he was raised from his seventh year on by a stepmother who directed him to music. Piano lessons began in his seventh year with Mrs. Frederick Burton, who remained his teacher up to the time he graduated from elementary school. When he was eleven he taught himself theory by studying a textbook, and soon after that he started composing.

In 1909, his family moved to Chicago. There, while attending Englewood High School, he continued music study with Authur Olaf Andersen (theory) and Calvin Lampert and Percy Grainger (piano). At fifteen, he received some lessons on the organ from Lampert, but from that time on, as organist, he was self-taught.

Sowerby made his debut as composer in 1913 when his Concerto for Violin and Orchestra was written for and performed at an all-American concert by the Chicago Symphony, organized by Glenn Dillard Gunn, the Chicago critic who was a staunch supporter of American music. Sowerby's debut as pianist came four years later at the Norfolk (Conn.) Festival. After that, he made numerous appearances as concert pianist both in recitals and as guest artist with orchestras.

Sowerby's first two published compositions were released through the auspices of the Society for the Publication of American Music. Those works were a Woodwind Quintet (1916) and Serenade, for string quartet (1917), the latter written as a birthday gift to Elizabeth Sprague Coolidge and introduced at the Berkshire Music Festival in Massachusetts in 1918. On January 17, 1917, Sowerby presented in Chicago a program of his own works which included three world premieres of compositions completed between 1916–17: Piano Concerto no. 1 (in which he was the soloist), Cello Concerto no. 1, and two smaller items for orchestra which became his first successes. One of these was *The Irish Washerwoman*, an adaptation of an 18th-century Irish jig. The other, the orchestral scherzo *Comes Autumn Time*, inspired by a poem by Bliss Carman, acquired a place in the American symphonic repertoire. It originated as a piece for organ and as such was introduced in Chicago on October 28, 1916, by Eric de Lamarter, for whom it had been written. Frederick Stock, conductor of the Chicago Symphony, heard this performance and was so taken with Sowerby's composition that he asked Sowerby to orchestrate it. The orchestral version, introduced by the Chicago Symphony under Stock, took place on October 29, 1920. Another orchestral work by Sowerby was introduced by the Chicago Symphony under Frederick Stock, for whom it was written, on February 15, 1918: *A Set of Four*, subtitled "A Suite of Ironics" (1917).

In December 1917, during World War I, Sowerby enlisted in the U.S. Army. He served for fifteen months in England and France, first as a performer of the clarinet and than as bandmaster of the 332nd Field Artillery Band, rising from the rank of private to that of first lieutenant.

Upon his discharge from the army, Sowerby revised his Piano Concerto no. 1, the new version introduced in Chicago on March 5, 1920. On the strength of this work and several other compositions—including Trio, for flute, viola, and piano (1919); *The Edge of Dreams*, a song cycle to a text by Mark Turbyfill (1920); Violin Sonata no. 1 (1921); and Symphony no. 1 (1921; Chicago, April 7, 1922)—Sowerby became the first recipient of the American Prix de Rome in 1921 when it was first established. He had not applied for it, but was selected when the compositions submitted by other composers proved unsatisfactory. For three years, Sowerby lived at the American Academy in Rome, working on compositions. Two received significant performances in Rome: *Ballad of King Estmere*, for two pianos and orchestra (1922), on April 8, 1923, with Albert Coates conducting, and *From the Northland* (1922), impressions of landscapes of the Lake Superior country, originally for piano and then orchestrated, introduced on May 27, 1924, and winner of the Society for the Publication of American Music Award.

Sowerby returned to the United States in 1924. Soon after reestablishing himself in Chicago he produced some compositions rooted in American folk and popular idioms. *Money Musk*, originally for piano (1917) but orchestrated in 1924, was a country dance in American folk style. For the popular band leader Paul Whiteman Sowerby wrote two pieces for jazz band, *Syncopata* and *Monotony* (1924, 1925), which were premiered in Chicago on October 11, 1925. *Pop Goes the Weasel* (1927) was an adaptation of the familiar folk tune for flute, oboe, clarinet, and horn.

In 1932, Sowerby was appointed to the faculty of the American Conservatory in the department of composition, retaining this post until 1962, most of that time as head of the department. In 1934 he fulfilled the requirements for a master of music degree at the conservatory. While meeting his teaching obligations, Sowerby was also involved as organist and choirmaster of St. James Episcopal Cathedral in Chicago (1927–62), for which he produced a rich library of ecclesiastical music for chorus and also for organ in a neobaroque idiom.

Many of Sowerby's concert compositions of the 1920s were mainly in a French romantic style, sensitive in mood, transparent in texture, and long-breathed in their lyricism. *Medieval Poem*, for organ and orchestra (1926), which was commissioned by the National Association of Organists, was first heard on April 20, 1926, in a performance by the Chicago Symphony, with the composer at the organ and Eric de Lamarter conducting; Symphony no. 2 (1926–27) was introduced by the Chicago Symphony under Frederick Stock on March 29, 1929; *Prairie*

(1929), a programmatic tone poem for orchestra inspired by the poem of Carl Sandburg, was given its first performance on August 11, 1929, at Interlochen, Mich., with the composer conducting, and then performed by the Boston Symphony under Serge Koussevitzky on March 11, 1932. In the *New York Herald Tribune*, Lawrence Gilman called it "virile, poetic, imaginative. There is in it something of the sweep and largeness and mysteriousness of earth, sky and light—something timeless and elemental."

A variety of styles ranging from the consonant to the dissonant, from the classic to the romantic, can be found in Sowerby's most important compositions after that. "I have been accused by right-wingers of being too dissonant and cacophonous," he said, "and by the leftists of being old-fashioned and derivative." Be that as it may, there was no gainsaying that to whatever style or idiom he addressed himself, he was always the sure craftsman, an artist of immaculate taste. He did not lack for significant performances. The Boston Symphony, under Serge Koussevitzky, with Joseph Brinkman as soloist, premiered the Piano Concerto no. 2 (1932) on November 30, 1936. A major work for organ and orchestra—Concerto in C major (1937)—was given its first hearing by the Boston Symphony under Koussevitzky with E. Power Biggs as soloist, on April 22, 1938. When the Philadelphia Orchestra under Ormandy, and with Biggs again as soloist, revived this work in Philadelphia on September 27, 1963, and then brought it to New York, Harold C. Schonberg said of it in the *New York Times*: "The score is in three movements, and it is a lively, old-fashioned virtuoso concerto with cadenzas and everything. There is in it a strong strain of England, and especially in the third movement one thought of Delius. . . . In a work like this, no problems are posed. None are intended. One can relax and enjoy a conservative piece of writing." More advanced in harmonic and rhythmic procedures was the Symphony no. 3 (1940), which the Chicago Symphony had commissioned for its fiftieth anniversary and which introduced it on March 6, 1941.

Sowerby was given the Society for the Publication of American Music Award for the fourth time in 1943 for his Clarinet Sonata (1938). In 1944 he received the Pulitzer Prize in music for *The Canticle of the Sun*, a cantata for chorus and orchestra (1944) which used as text the canticle of St. Francis of Assisi as translated into English by Matthew Arnold. Introduced in New York on April 16, 1945, it was described by Robert A. Simon in the *New Yorker* as "a colorful and finely wrought work." Sowerby followed this with the Symphony no. 4 (1947), perhaps his most important symphony. It was introduced by the Boston Symphony under Koussevitzky on January 7, 1949. Though not literally programmatic, Sowerby intended this to be a portrait of a large, sprawling city. "Perhaps I had Chicago in mind, for it is my town," he explained. "In writing the work, I was trying to picture the excitement and gusto of the way of life in such a town, its noise and glamour, its eagerness and bigness, if you like. Then there are quieter and even more dismal aspects of it. One may find a sense of loneliness which everyone who knows a large city knows only too well, the disappointment and the frustration which go with the bigness and uncouthness of the place."

On a commission from the Indianapolis Symphony and its music director, Fabien Sevitzky, Sowerby wrote *Fantasy Portraits*, for orchestra (1953), introduced in Indianapolis on November 21, 1953. Another commission—this one from the Louisville Orchestra in Kentucky—led to the writing of the orchestral tone poem, *All on a Summer's Day* (1954), first performance in Louisville on January 8, 1955, Robert Whitney conducting.

In 1957, on a commission from the Washington Cathedral in Washington, D.C., Sowerby wrote an ambitiously structured anthem for chorus and orchestra, *The Throne of God*, using the Revelations as text. It was first heard on November 18, 1957, at the cathedral. Five years later, Sowerby left Chicago to settle in Washington, D. C., where he founded the College of Church Musicians, affiliated with the Washington Cathedral, of which he was dean until the end of his life.

Sowerby received an honorary doctorate in music from the University of Rochester in 1934, and a year later he was elected to membership in the National Institute of Arts and Letters. He was made honorary fellow of Trinity College in London, England (1957), and of the Royal School of Church Music in Croydon, England (1963), the first American to be thus honored. In 1963 he was presented to Her Majesty Queen Elizabeth II.

PRINCIPAL WORKS: 5 symphonies (1921–64); 3 violin sonatas (1922, 1944, 1959); 2 piano concertos (1916, revised 1919; 1932); 2 cello concertos (1917, 1934); 2 organ concertos (1936, 1967); 2 string quartets (1923, 1935).

Comes Autumn Time, scherzo for orchestra (1916); *The Irish Washerwoman*, for orchestra (1916); Quintet, for flute, oboe, clarinet, bassoon, and horn (1916); Serenade, for string quartet (1917); *A Set of Four*, "Suite of Ironics," for orchestra (1917); Trio, for flute, viola, and piano (1919); *The Edge of Darkness*, song cycle for voice and piano (1920); Cello Sonata (1921); *From the Northland*, originally for piano, also for orchestra (1922); *Ballad of King Estmere*, for 2 pianos and orchestra (1922); *The Vision of Sir Launfal*, for chorus and orchestra (1925); *Medieval Poem*, for organ and orchestra (1926); *Prairie*, tone poem for orchestra (1929); *Florida*, suite for piano (1929); *Organ Symphony* (1930); Passacaglia, Interlude, and Fugue, for organ (1931); Suite, for organ (1937); *Theme in Yellow*, for orchestra (1938); Clarinet Sonata (1938); *Forsaken of Men*, cantata for chorus and orchestra (1939); *Concert Overture*, for orchestra (1941); *Poem*, for

viola with organ and orchestra (1941); *Song of America*, for chorus (1942); *Canticle of the Sun*, cantata for chorus and orchestra (1942); *Classic Concerto*, for organ and strings (1944); Trumpet Sonata (1945); *Ballade*, for English horn and organ (1949); Canon, Chacony, and Fugue, for organ (1949); *Christ Reborn*, oratorio for solo voices, chorus, and orchestra (1950); *Whimsical Variations*, for organ (1950); Concert Piece, for organ and orchestra (1951); Trio, for violin, viola, and cello (1952); Suite, for organ, brass and timpani (1953); *Fantasy Portrait*, for orchestra (1953); *All on a Summer's Day*, tone poem for orchestra (1954); Fantasy, for trumpet and organ (1954); *The Throne of God*, for chorus and orchestra (1957); Suite, for piano (1959); *Bright, Blithe and Brisk*, for organ (1962); Piano Sonata (1964); *Solomon's Garden*, for chorus and orchestra (1965); Passacaglia, for organ (1967).

BIBLIOGRAPHY: Ewen, David, *Composers Since 1900* (N.Y., 1969); Goss, Madeleine, *Modern Music Makers* (N.Y., 1952); Howard, John Tasker, *Our Contemporary Composers* (N.Y., 1946); Huntington, R. M., "A Study of the Musical Contributions of Leo Sowerby" (doctoral thesis, Los Angeles, 1957); Reis, Claire, *Composers in America* (N.Y., 1947); *Musical Quarterly*, April 1938; *Who's Who in America, 1966–67*.

Spiegelman, Joel Warren, b. Buffalo, N.Y., January 23, 1933.

Before reevaluating his music in the middle 1960s, Spiegelman was a neoclassicist, influenced by Stravinsky. He then became principally a composer of electronic music who dedicated himself to developing live electronic performances. Other than electronic, his music, at various times, has been dodecaphonic, classical, mystical, dissonant, romantic, and astral. His style is a dialectic where diverse elements—appropriate to each other, and sometimes seemingly inappropriate to each other—are synthesized into a greater whole.

Both his parents were of Russian birth, his father being a physician who practiced in Buffalo, N. Y. His mother was a trained pianist and his father began studying cello after the age of fifty. One of Joel Spiegelman's great-uncles on his father's side, William Nissenson, had been a member of the Russian Imperial Opera and later of the Metropolitan Opera, as well as a cantor, for many years. Nissenson's son, Harold, was a violinist with the Buffalo Philharmonic.

Stimulated and guided by his mother, "who was an inspiration to me," Joel Spiegelman began taking lessons on piano when he was ten with Otto Hager. Spiegelman's progress was so rapid that within three years he mastered several piano concertos by Mozart and Beethoven and a large repertoire of other piano classics. As a prodigy, he gave a recital in Buffalo on

January 27, 1946, when Benno Rosenheimer said, in *Musical America*, that "he played with the confidence of a mature artist, displaying an exceptionally fine tone and surprising technique." On July 16, 1946, he was soloist with the Buffalo Philharmonic in a performance of Liszt's *Hungarian Rhapsody*, a performance which Rosenheimer described in *Musical America* as "a revelation." Each year after that, Spiegelman appeared as solo pianist with the Buffalo Civic Symphony in outdoor park concerts. He also made numerous appearances over radio and television. In 1949 he won the annual concerto audition at the National Music Camp at Interlochen, Mich.—the highest award the camp could give—which entitled him to appear with the camp orchestra in a performance of the first movement of MacDowell's Piano Concerto no. 2.

His academic education took place in Buffalo public schools and at Bennett High School (1946–49). "I did not participate in too many school musical activities," he recalls. "I was looked upon as the local *Wunderkind* and was not often in the swing of mainstream student action."

Between 1946 and 1949 he studied piano simultaneously with Beth Wolanek in Buffalo and Mona Bates in Toronto, Ontario. All this while, his musical horizon was being extended through attendance at concerts of the Buffalo Philharmonic, the Chamber Music Society, and recitals by visiting world-famous virtuosos. "These concerts had an enormous impact on me," he says. "The composer that affected me most those days was Beethoven. I wanted to know everything I could about his music, all of it, and about the man himself. I gobbled up sonatas, quartets, concertos, symphonies, and so on, as if they were the Divine Word—which they are."

Upon graduating from Bennett High School in 1949, Spiegelman attended for one year the Yale School of Music in New Haven in the classes of Howard Boatwright (theory), Hugo Kortschak (chamber music), and Ellsworth Grimman (piano). At the University of Buffalo (1950–53) he received the bachelor of arts degree. He spent the year of 1953–54 at the Longy School of Music in Cambridge, Mass., studying harmony and harpsichord with Melville Smith, counterpoint with Hubert Lamb, piano with Gregory Tucker, and keyboard harmony with Luise Vosgerchian. In 1954 he came to Brandeis University in Waltham, Mass., spending the next two years there in the study of theory and composition with Harold Shapero, Irving Fine, and Arthur Berger. In 1954 he made his debut as harpsichordist at Harvard University and on October 25, 1955, he gave his first Boston piano recital. From 1962 to 1964 he was the harpsichordist of the Camerata of the Boston Museum of Fine Arts.

Upon receiving his master of fine arts degree at Brandeis in 1956, Spiegelman was awarded a French government grant enabling him to go to Paris. At the Paris Conservatory he was Nadia Boulanger's pupil in piano accompaniment (1956–57) and her private student in theory, composition, piano, and analysis (1956–60).

Between 1956 and 1957 he made many appearances as a concert pianist and harpsichordist in Poland, France, Israel, and Yugoslavia. On June 29, 1958, at the opening concert of the music festival at Royaumont, France, Spiegelman conducted the world premiere of his Serenade, subtitled *Ouverture de saison* (1958), scored for two flutes, two harps, celesta, and piano.

Returning to the United States in 1960, Spiegelman reentered Brandeis University for musicological studies with Kenneth Levy and Caldwell Titcomb. Between 1961 and 1966 he taught harpsichord, piano, harmony, counterpoint, and baroque keyboard music at Brandeis, serving as instructor in 1964 and assistant professor from 1964 to 1966. Concurrently, he taught harmony at the Longy School of Music in Cambridge (1961–62) and theory, composition, piano, harpsichord, and chamber music at the Cummington School of the Arts in Massachusetts (summers of 1962 and 1963). For a production of *Medea* by Euripides at Brandeis, he provided a score that marked his first attempt at the production of electronic music.

Spiegelman spent the summer of 1964 at the Slavic Institute of Indiana University in Bloomington studying Russian intensively. He received a travel grant from the Inter-University Committee in 1965–66, on a cultural exchange plan, to visit the Soviet Union and do research in 18th-century Russian keyboard and avant-garde Soviet music. In the Soviet Union, Spiegelman gave four harpsichord recitals, two each in Moscow and Leningrad. He brought back with him a repertoire of Russian music, new and old, which he introduced in concerts of Russian music in Boston, Buffalo, and New York.

That visit to the Soviet Union led Spiegelman to take stock of the music he had thus far written, mainly in the neoclassical idiom, and caused him to turn to new directions. Soon after his return, he wrote *Kousochki*, or *Morsels*, five small pieces for piano, four hands, loosely in the twelve-tone technique. The work had been inspired by his visit to Vladimir and Szdal, two 12th-century Russian towns, where he had been fascinated by the bell sounds from the cathedrals. In both the conventional way of playing the piano and by plucking the strings on the soundboard, the varied sonorities of sounding church bells were simulated. Jean and Kenneth Wentworth introduced this work on January 17, 1967, in New York. "It suggests," said Michael Steinberg in the *Boston Sunday Globe*, "the technique of using small musical germs that recur in various lights through the five sections. . . . Its bell evocations are just one aspect of the resourceful piano writing."

In 1966, Spiegelman was appointed teacher of composition and harpsichord at Sarah Lawrence College in Bronxville, N.Y., where he has remained since that time, becoming professor in 1966, and chairman of the music department from 1970 to 1972. He also directed the school's Collegium Musicum and, since 1970, its Studio for Electronic Music and Experimental Sound Media.

As a composer he was becoming increasingly involved with electronic music. In 1969, he wrote the music for a ballet which utilized an electronic score—*The Eleventh Hour*; it had been commissioned by the Ingram Merrill Foundation of New York and produced at Sarah Lawrence College in 1970. On a commission from Temple Emanu-El of Yonkers, N.Y., he wrote, in 1970, *Sacred Service*, for cantor, choir, reader, and electronic tape. *They*, in 1970, was an electronic score commissioned by the National Education Television Playhouse for the production of a play of that title by Marya Mannes in 1970. *Réponse à Goya* (1970), which used texts by Dylan Thomas and Robert Vosnesensky, was scored for flute, double bass, synthesizer, and electric harpsichord, with the audience participating. *Daddy*, text by Sylvia Plath (1972), was scored for reader, soprano, flute, oboe, conga drums, and ARP synthesizer. *Bachlike*, for soprano, flute, oboe, synthesizer, and jazz drums, came in 1972. *Réponse à Goya*, *Daddy*, and *Bachlike* were introduced in the year of composition at Sarah Lawrence College. *Midnight Sun*, for solo oboe and four-channel tape (1976), was premiered in New York in November 1976. When *Midnight Sun* was heard again in New York on September 25, 1979, Raymond Ericson said of it in the *New York Times*: "This is in flavor highly romantic. On the tape are oboe sounds that seem to be calling to the live soloist, and the former are joined by burbling electronic noises that suggest a contemporary *Forest Murmurs*. This Wagnerian feeling is enhanced by the intense and lovely melodies played by the live oboist. It is extraordinarily haunting."

Spiegelman was also productive outside the field of electronics, in compositions that traversed a wide gamut of styles and idioms. These included *Astral Dimensions*, originally named *Chamber Music*, for piano, violin, viola, cello, and percussion (1973; N.Y., November 1973); Fantasy no. 2, for string quartet (1974; Eugene, Oreg., 1977); and *A Cry, a Song, and a Dance*, for string orchestra (1978). Speaking of *Astral Dimensions*, in which tonal and atonal writing was combined, Spiegelman said that it was more than a piece of music; it was an adventure in thinking. "I would rather leave it unexplained. Although I wrote it in three months, it took me six years to find the title. This work has a special spiritual meaning for me. I feel that I made a large leap to a place of synthesis and growth, a place that I never saw before or that I ever knew existed."

A retrospective concert of Spiegelman's music was heard in New York on September 25, 1979, covering his productivity from *Kousochki* to *Midnight Sun* and representing the evolution of a style that merged tonality, electronics, and musical realism.

In 1970, Spiegelman founded and directed the New York Electronic Ensemble, which gave concerts of electronic music. In 1976 he became the artistic director of the New Russian Chamber Orchestra (originally called Strings in Exile), which he had founded to preserve the traditions of Russian string playing by employing Russian émigré musicians from the Soviet Union. This ensemble has given numerous performances throughout the United States under the auspices of the New Russian Music Society, a nonprofit corporation in New York.

Spiegelman received awards from the American Philosophical Society (1965) and the American Society of Composers, Authors, and Publishers (ASCAP) in 1968, 1969, and 1970. On November 18, 1979, in New York, he married Galina Finkelstein, an assistant director at the Georgian State Film Studio in Tiflis, who had immigrated to the United States in 1977 with her son. This was Spiegelman's second marriage. His first wife, Gail Carol Voelker, whom he had married in 1954 and with whom he had three children, he divorced in 1972, taking custody of the children.

THE COMPOSER SPEAKS: I consider all past traditions as a giant palette of musical information to be drawn upon at the moment of creation. One's life experience, tradition, roots, and general culture all feed into the making of a composer. In my case, these factors play a strong role in determining the "tone" of my music and influence the way I hear sounds being put together.

Probably the elements of ethos and culture interacting with my psychological history have provided me with the emotional "stuff" from which comes my own particular expressivity. Most important is a constantly growing awareness of our connection to the cosmic powers around us and a striving to get closer to our Creator.

PRINCIPAL WORKS: 2 fantasies, for string quartet (1963, 1974).

Ouverture de saison, or Serenade, for two harps, two flutes, piano, and celesta (1958); *Two Hebrew Motets*, for chorus (1960); *Kousochki*, for piano, four hands (1966); *Phantom of the Opera*, for chorus and bells (1968); *The Eleventh Hour*, an electronic ballet (1969); *Sacred Service*, for cantor, choir, reader, and electronic tape (1969); *Flashback*, for guitar solo (1970); *They*, an electronic score for a television production (1970); *Réponse à Goya*, for flute, double bass, audience, synthesizer, and electronic harpsichord (1970); *Outtakes In*, for solo electronic harpsichord (1971); *Daddy*, for reader, soprano, flute, oboe, conga drums, and ARP synthesizer (1972); *Bachlike*, for soprano, flute, oboe, synthesizer, and jazz drums (1972); *Three Miniatures*, for clarinet and piano (1972); *Astral Dimensions*, for piano, percussion, violin, viola, and cello, originally entitled *Chamber Music* (1973); *The Possessed*, ballet

(1975); *Midnight Sun,* for solo oboe and four-channel tape (1976); *A Cry, a Song, and a Dance,* for
string orchestra (1978); *A Memory,* for clarinet and
cello (1980).

BIBLIOGRAPHY: *BBDM*; *DCM*; *Boston Sunday
Globe,* February 6, 1966.

Starer, Robert, b. Vienna, Austria, January 8,
1924. American citizen, 1957.

Starer has written for many different musical media and in many forms. Though some of his most
important works are dodecaphonic, his eclecticism
and restless search for various idioms of expression
have led him in many directions. His writing is
marked by a motor-driven rhythmic energy, dramatic power, incisiveness, compelling and personalized
lyricism, and striking sonoric effects.

Born to a well-to-do family, Robert Starer was
raised in early childhood by a governess who, upon
discovering he had perfect pitch, began giving him
piano lessons when he was four. After further piano
study with local teachers, at thirteen Starer entered
the Vienna State Academy, where he studied piano
with Victor Ebenstein. At the same time, his academic schooling took place in high school, where he
majored in Greek and Latin.

When the Nazis invaded and annexed Austria in
1938, the Starers were in danger of their lives, since
the father was a known Zionist. Through Emil
Hauser, founder of the Budapest String Quartet
(since become director of the Jerusalem Conservatory), Robert Starer, age fourteen, was brought to Palestine for admission to the Jerusalem Conservatory
on a scholarship. Separated from his family, Starer
made his home in Jerusalem, studying composition
at the conservatory with Joseph Tal and receiving
instruction in Near Eastern music, including lessons
on the oud (an oriental version of the lute). He became so fascinated with the oud that he wrote a composition for it synthesizing Eastern and Western musical styles. But the other music he was writing at the
time was solely Western. Between 1941 and 1943,
Starer was employed as staff pianist by the Palestinian radio. Now self-supporting, he married Johanna
Herz on March 27, 1942. She was a soprano who
was also a student at the Jerusalem Conservatory.
Their only child, a son, was born in 1954. One year
after his marriage, Starer's opposition to nazism
drove him to enlist in the British air force during
World War II. His activities in the service were more
musical than military; he gave numerous concerts for
the troops at the various battlefronts of the Middle
East. When not thus occupied, he spent his time
composing. One of the works written while he was in
the air force was Fantasy for Strings (1945), in a
postromantic style. It was introduced by the Palestine Philharmonic conducted by George Singer on
March 11, 1947. When this Fantasy was heard in
New York in 1949, Noel Straus described it in the
New York Times as "rich textured, deeply expressive
music that had something to say and said it with fervor, originality, and conviction."

Following his discharge from military service in
1946, Starer continued his musical education at the
Juilliard School of Music in New York on a scholarship. He was so successful in his entrance examinations that he was admitted on a postgraduate level to
study composition with Frederick Jacobi. After receiving his diploma in 1949, he was appointed to the
faculty of the Juilliard School, remaining there until
1975. As a Juilliard student he supported himself by
being a piano accompanist for singers and instrumentalists. But most of his efforts were concentrated
on composition. When his Piano Concerto no. 1
(1947) was premiered on February 21, 1949, with
the composer as soloist, Carter Harman wrote in the
New York Times that it was "glittering with atmosphere, pounding with energy and impossible to label
with a 'school.' It held fascination, both for itself and
the potentialities of its composer." Those potentialities were slowly becoming realized with the Concertino, for two voices, or for violin and piano (1948;
N.Y., March 19, 1949); Prelude and Dance, for orchestra (1949; N.Y., April 29, 1949); Symphony no.
1 (1950), whose premiere was heard in Tel Aviv on
May 7, 1953 with Erich Leinsdorf conducting the
Israel Philharmonic; and *Kohelet* (*Ecclesiastes*), a
major work for vocal soloists, chorus, and orchestra
(1952; N.Y., February 20, 1953).

With the Piano Concerto no. 2 (1953), Starer began to realize a personalized style in which modern
harmonic and rhythmic idioms were brought within
classical structures. Its first performance took place
on July 17, 1956, in Cincinnati, with David Bar-
Illan soloist with the Cincinnati Symphony conducted by Thor Johnson. The classical concerto form
continued to interest Starer in the *Concerto à tre,* for
piano, trumpet, trombone, and strings (1954; N.Y.,
November 22, 1954), a 20th-century adaptation of
the baroque concerto grosso form; and the Concerto
for Viola, Strings, and Percussion (1958; Geneva,
Switzerland, July 3, 1959), which received its American premiere on December 10, 1959, at a concert of
the New York Philharmonic under Leonard Bernstein, with William Lincer soloist. "Starer's sense of
musical continuity and his bent for tonal expression
remain unusual," Irving Kolodin said of this concerto in the *Saturday Review,* while Jay S. Harrison
in the *New York Herald Tribune* described it as "a
lovely, haunting work . . . genuinely touching."

The Concerto for Viola, Strings, and Percussion
was written in Vienna in 1958 while Starer was the
beneficiary of a Guggenheim Fellowship. After his
return to the United States he was made a member of
the composition faculty at the New York College of
Music (1959–60). On March 4, 1960, a concert devoted exclusively to his music was given in New

York, covering eleven years of his creativity. "One of the most notable things that emerged," said a critic for the *New York Times*, "was a striking and original harmonic sense. . . . All the music is firmly tonal in conception, and the harmonic palette ranges from simple triads to big sounds chock-full of notes and intervals. The sense of originality grew out of the way the composer was able to go from the simple to the complex and back again, meaningfully and without getting involved in serious contradictions. This also seemed to work for and within the tonal implications of the music."

In 1962–63, Starer served on the music faculty of the Jewish Theological Seminary, and from 1962 to 1964 he was on the board of directors of the American Music Center. He was appointed professor of music at Brooklyn College, in Brooklyn, N.Y., in 1963 (the year in which he received his second Guggenheim Fellowship), a post he has retained since then with intermittent interruptions. In 1964 he was awarded a Fulbright predoctoral research grant.

Beginning with 1960, Starer widened his creative horizons by writing music for the ballet. His first such score was for *The Story of Esther*—music scored for ten instruments—which he wrote for the dancer Anna Sokolow, who introduced it over the CBS-TV network on March 15, 1960. *The Dybbuk* (1960), starring Herbert Ross and Nora Kaye, was first produced on September 20, 1960, at the Berlin Festival in West Germany. *Samson Agonistes*, originally called *Visionary Recital* (1961), and *Phaedra* (1962) were produced by Martha Graham and her company in New York, the first on April 16, 1961, and the other on March 4, 1962. In later years, Starer wrote the music for two more Martha Graham ballets: *The Lady of the House of Sleep* (1968; N.Y., June 1968) and *Holy Jungle* (1974; N.Y., April 27, 1975). Starer adapted his ballet score of *Samson Agonistes* into a symphonic work (1963) which the Cincinnati Symphony premiered under Max Rudolf's direction on May 8, 1965. In this music, Starer turned to twelve-tone writing by using two twelve-tone rows, though not with the rigid discipline of the Viennese school. From this point on, Starer continued to write dodecaphonic music, though not exclusively. In *Mutabili, Variants for Orchestra* (1965), which the Pittsburgh Symphony premiered on October 28, 1966, under William Steinberg, each of the five variants developed a mutation of a single twelve-tone row, stated by the strings in the first variant and repeated after the fifth. In the second variant, the row became the basis of a Scherzo; in the third, of a lyrical melody; in the fourth, it was broken up to become an ostinato figure; and in the fifth it appeared in various chords derived from the row to punctuate a melody in the violins. The twelve-tone technique can also be found in Starer's first full-length opera, *Pantagleize* (1967)—the composer's libretto based on a play by Michel de Ghelderode—which was produced in Brooklyn, N.Y., on April 7, 1974; and in *Six Variations with*

Twelve Tones, for orchestra (1967; Newark, N.J., March 28, 1968).

On October 30, 1970, the Pittsburgh Symphony under William Steinberg presented the first performance of Starer's Symphony no. 3 (1969). "My symphony," the composer explained, "has nothing in common with the classical symphony in terms of key relationships. What it did retain from the classical concept is the principle of statement of ideas, development, transformed restatement and conclusion. . . . I have also retained the four-movement sequence which here represents four basic human moods or attitudes: I. Introspective, Dramatic, Intense; II. Light, Humorous, Jocose; III. Lyrical, Contemplative; and IV. Dancelike, Rhythmically straightforward." The first movement was built from a motive stated at the opening by the oboe. In the second movement "I have deliberately sought out the rhythmic simplicity and directness which the young look for in music, often outside the concert halls, and without which the music really does become emasculated." Long-arched melodies were prominent in the third movement, while the fourth focused on clear and simple rhythms in duple time. This last movement is the first piece of music without a single meter change that the composer had written in many years.

Since 1970, Starer's major works have included his Piano Concerto no. 3 (1972), which had been commissioned for David Bar-Illan, who introduced it on October 9, 1974, with the Baltimore Symphony conducted by Sergiu Comissiona; *The Last Lover*, a musical morality play for vocal soloists and instruments (1974; Caramoor, N.Y., August 2, 1975), with Gail Godwin's libretto based on the legend of St. Pelagia, a 4th-century courtesan who decides to impersonate a monk and is accused of impregnating a nun; *Journals of a Songmaker*, for baritone, soprano, and orchestra (1975), written on a grant from the National Endowment for the Arts and premiered by the Pittsburgh Symphony under William Steinberg on May 21, 1976; *The People, Yes*, for chorus and orchestra (1976; Binghamton, N.Y., December 4, 1976), text by Carl Sandburg, written for the Bicentennial Commission of Broome County, N.Y., and the Binghamton, N.Y., Junior League to commemorate the American bicentennial; and *Voices of Brooklyn*, for narrator, vocal soloists, and symphonic band (1980), introduced in Brooklyn, N.Y. on May 16, 1981, and written to commemorate the fiftieth anniversary of Brooklyn College in New York.

THE COMPOSER SPEAKS: If I were to sum up my views on music I would say that I make music because it is what I enjoy the most and I do believe in music as an expression of the human soul and a communication between people.

PRINCIPAL WORKS: 3 symphonies (1950, 1951, 1969); 3 piano concertos (1947, 1953, 1972).

Fantasy, for string orchestra (1945); String Quartet (1947); Concertino, for two voices or for violin and piano (1948); *Five Miniatures*, for brass (1948); Prelude and Dance, for orchestra (1949); *Kohelet (Ecclesiastes)*, for baritone, soprano, chorus, and orchestra (1952); *Concerto à tre*, for piano, trumpet, trombone, and strings (1954); *The Intruder*, one-act opera (1956); Concerto for Viola, Strings, and Percussion (1958); *Ariel: Vision of Isaiah*, for soprano, baritone, chorus, and orchestra, or piano and organ (1959); *The Story of Esther*, ballet (1960); *The Dybbuk*, ballet (1960); *Samson Agonistes*, ballet (1961); Prelude and Rondo giocoso, for orchestra (1961); *Phaedra*, ballet (1962); *Samson Agonistes*, a symphonic portrait (1963); *Mutabili, Variants for Orchestra* (1963); *Joseph and His Brethren*, cantata for narrator, soprano, tenor, baritone, chorus, and orchestra or organ (1966); *I'm Nobody*, for a cappella chorus (1967); *Sabbath Eve Service*, for baritone or tenor, soprano, alto, chorus, and organ (1967); *Six Variations with Twelve Tones*, for orchestra (1967); Concerto for Violin, Cello, and Orchestra (1967); *Pantagleize*, opera (1967); *The Lady of the House of Sleep*, ballet (1968); *On the Nature of Things*, for a cappella chorus (1968); *Images of Man*, for soprano, mezzo-soprano, tenor, baritone, and chorus (1973); *Stone Ridge Set*, for piano (1973); *Mandala, Profiles in Brass* (1974); *The Last Lover*, musical morality play, for vocal soloists and instruments (1974); *Holy Jungle*, ballet (1974); *Journals of a Songmaker*, for baritone, soprano, and orchestra (1975); *The People, Yes*, for chorus and orchestra (1976); Piano Quartet (1977); *Transformation*, song cycle for voice and piano (1978); *Apollonia*, opera (1978); *Voices of Brooklyn*, for narrator, vocal soloists, and symphonic band (1980).

BIBLIOGRAPHY: *DCM*; *New York Times*, April 1, 1973; *Pittsburgh Symphony Program Notes*, October 11, 1968; *Who's Who in America, 1980–81*.

Stein, Leon, b. Chicago, Ill., September 18, 1910.

During half a century of composing music, Stein has refused to align himself with any movements in vogue at any given time, nor has he been a slave to the musical past, preferring always to steer a middle course between conservatism and radicalism.

His parents, as children, emigrated from their native Ukraine. The father, a tailor and furrier, had an excellent tenor voice; as a young man he was soloist with the synagogue choir, and at times officiated as cantor. From him, the child Leon acquired his first taste of and love for music. Leon began studying violin when he was ten. In 1922 he entered the American Conservatory in Chicago, where, for the next five years, he continued his violin studies with Herbert Butler. Upon graduating from Sabin Grade School in 1923 and Crane Technical High School in 1927,

Stein attended Crane Junior College for two years, studying theory there with Robert Comer Jones and graduating as salutatorian of his class. During the years that followed, he studied composition by himself, making sufficient progress to gain, in 1930, a scholarship to the DePaul University School of Music, where he served as concertmaster in its symphony orchestra. When he graduated from the School of Music in 1931 with a bachelor of music degree, he was given the first prize for Suite for String Quartet. In 1931 he was appointed instructor at the DePaul University School of Music, where he remained until his retirement forty-seven years later, rising from instructor to full professor, then serving as chairman of the departments of theory and composition and director of the graduate division between 1948 and 1966, and as dean from 1968 to 1976. During his first year at DePaul, he founded, and for twelve years directed, the DePaul Chamber Orchestra, and in 1955 he became conductor of the school's symphony orchestra. Through the years, he held several other conducting posts with orchestras near or in Chicago and made guest appearances in the United States and Canada.

Prior to receiving his master's degree in music at DePaul in 1935, Stein continued his music studies with Leo Sowerby and Wesley La Violette in composition and Eric de Lamarter in orchestration. Under the auspices of the Chicago Symphony he was awarded a fellowship in conducting with Frederick Stock and Hans Lange (1937–40). In 1949, Stein earned his Ph.D. at the DePaul school, his dissertation being *The Racial Thinking of Richard Wagner* (1950), which received high critical acclaim. Meanwhile, on October 31, 1937, he married Anne Helman, and they raised two sons in Chicago.

In 1944–45, during World War II, Stein was a petty officer with the U.S. Navy. While in uniform, he conducted the Concert Orchestra and Band at the Great Lakes Naval Training Station and composed and arranged music for the regular internationally broadcast radio programs *Meet Your Navy* and *On the Target*.

Though Stein did intensive research in Jewish music from 1930 on, and was head of the Institute of Music at the College of Jewish Studies in Chicago between 1952 and 1957, only a small portion of his compositions are of ethnic Jewish interest. One of these brought Stein his first success as an orchestral composer: *Three Hasidic Dances* (1941), its world premiere taking place in Chicago on April 13, 1942, with Izler Solomon conducting the Illinois Symphony. Here Stein successfully captured the fervor and ecstasy of Hasidic worshipers in music with the strong syncopations, marked rhythms, and frequent repetitions and improvisations encountered in Hasidic chants. These Dances were recorded by Thor Johnson and the Cincinnati Symphony and provided the music for a ballet performed by the Pearl Lang Dance Group in New York and Montreal.

The core of Stein's creativity can be found in five string quartets (all recorded in a single set by the Chicago Symphony String Quartet) and in four symphonies which range over a forty-year period. His String Quartet no. 1 was completed in 1933 (Chicago, December 12, 1933), and his Symphony no. 1 in 1940. From his beginnings as a mature composer, Stein refused to make a fetish of any idiom, nor was he overly concerned about technical virtuosity. He took whatever material from the past or present that was serviceable to his development of a style that, as one program annotator (Edward Barry) described it, was "assertive and often vehement . . . [with] abrupt changes in dynamics, shifting meters, free structuring of movements, atonality, innovative tone colorings." Perhaps the most eloquent and atmospherically the most evocative of his five quartets is the last (1967), whose premiere was given in Chicago on April 5, 1968. This composition was inspired by the poetry of Dylan Thomas. Each of its four movements bears a motto from a Thomas poem, while the fifth movement (preceded by a recitative for solo cello and some funeral music) is a setting for soprano and string quartet of the poem "And Death Shall Have No Dominion." The music of this final movement was used for a ballet produced in South Bend, Ind., on September 30, 1977.

Symphony no. 2 (1942; N.Y., February 18, 1951) was the winner of the Charles Cohen American Composers' Commission Award Contest. Peggy Glanville-Hicks in the *New York Herald Tribune* described it as music of "considerable power" whose themes are "developed naturally from the feeling and imagination rather than from mechanical procedures." Symphony no. 4 (1977), winner of the Elkart Symphony International Competition Award in Indiana, was premiered by the Elkart Symphony on December 12, 1977. Two shorter works also received prizes: *Triptych on Three Poems of Walt Whitman*, for orchestra (1943; Chicago, March 29, 1949), the American Composers' Commission Award; and *Symphonic Movement* (1950; Midland, Mich., November 2, 1955), the Midland Foundation National Contest Award.

Among Stein's subsequent major compositions is *Then Shall the Dust Return*, for orchestra (1971), title taken from a passage in Ecclesiastes. It was first performed at Orchestra Hall, Chicago, by the DePaul University Symphony under the composer's direction on March 6, 1974. Reviewing the performance, Edward Barry, the Chicago music critic, wrote: "This purely instrumental work . . . is a deeply serious reflection on life and death—rich on long, passionate phrases, and in tone colorings of a quiet splendor. The brasses, in particular, speak with a solemn, almost apocalyptic, eloquence."

Stein's most frequently performed works include seven compositions for saxophone and various ensemble combinations, five commissioned by Cecil Leeson and two by Brian Minor.

In 1960, Stein's complete works were presented by the Americans for a Music Library in Israel to the three major libraries of Israel. In July 1978, Stein was invited to Israel as opening speaker at a special convocation commemorating the thirtieth anniversary of the Rubin Academy in Jerusalem, where, on two previous visits to Israel, he had served as consultant.

On the occasion of Stein's retirement as dean of the DePaul School of Music in 1976 he received the Distinguished Alumni Award. Upon retiring from the faculty in 1978, a concert of his music was performed at the university on April 28, covering thirty years of his productivity from 1931 to 1961. His seventieth birthday was celebrated with a program of his works in Chicago on January 27, 1980, that included the world premiere of Quintet, for harp and string quartet (1977). On February 4, 1979, Stein, now dean emeritus, was given the highest faculty honor DePaul University could bestow, the Via Sapientiae Award. Previously, he had received an Award of Merit from the National Federation of Music Clubs (1966).

In addition to *The Racial Thinking of Richard Wagner*, Stein is the author of *Structure and Style* (1962) and *Anthology of Musical Forms* (1962) as well as numerous articles on music.

THE COMPOSER SPEAKS: I believe the most important function of music is meaningful communication. Musical composition is the transmutation of *experience*, in its broadest sense, into auditory patterns. The content of music, however, is neither "*emotion*" nor "*experience*," but the esthetic equivalent of both, achieved through this transmutation. A composer is, therefore, an individual who thinks creatively in terms of sonic symbols.

A musical composition as a work of art is a revelation of a reality beyond direct experience, a revelation made possible through the insight and intuition of its creator. The composer is simply the medium through which the idea is given embodiment in palpable form. Once he realizes that there is a certain inevitability in the nature and direction of his work, the composer is content to leave the matter of evaluation to the future and simply do what he must.

PRINCIPAL WORKS: 5 string quartets (1933–67); 4 symphonies (1940–74).

Prelude and Fugue, for orchestra (1935); Passacaglia, for orchestra (1936); Sinfonietta, for string orchestra, (1938); Violin Concerto in A (1939); *Exodus*, ballet (1939); *Doubt*, ballet (1940); *Three Hasidic Dances*, for orchestra (1941); Twelve Preludes, for violin and piano (1942–49); *Triptych on Three Poems of Walt Whitman*, for orchestra (1943); *Great Lakes Suite*, for small orchestra (1944); *A Festive Overture*, for orchestra (1950); Trio, for three trumpets (1953); *The Lord Reigneth*, cantata for tenor, women's chorus, and orchestra (1953); *The Fisher-*

man's Wife, one-act opera (1954); Rhapsody, for solo flute, harp, and string orchestra (1954); *Deirdre*, one-act opera (1956); Toccata no. 2, for piano (1957); Adagio and Rondo ebraico, for orchestra (1957); Quintet, for solo saxophone and string quartet (1957); Sextet, for solo saxophone and woodwind quintet (1958); Quartet for Trombones (1960); Sonata for Solo Violin (1960); Suite for Saxophone Quartet (1962); Saxophone Sonata (1967); Trio, for clarinet, saxophone, and piano (1969); Phantasy, for solo saxophone (1970); Suite, for wind quintet (1970); *Then Shall the Dust Return*, for orchestra (1971); Brass Quintet (1975); Quintet, for harp and string quartet (1977); Cello Concerto (1977); *Duo concertante*, for violin and viola (1978); Suite for solo flute (1978); Suite, for string trio (1980).

BIBLIOGRAPHY: *BBDM*; Reis, Claire, *Composers in America* (N.Y., 1947); *Who's Who in America, 1980–81.*

Stevens, Halsey, b. Scott, N.Y., December 3, 1908.

Stevens's music has a strongly affirmed tonic allegiance. Though advanced rhythmic, metrical, and harmonic idioms are employed, far-out avant-garde practices are avoided and serial procedures are used only rarely. His works favor scales of mixed modal types (with free use of chromatics) or gapped or arbitrary (e.g., octotonic) scales; sharply defined rhythms, often motoric in fast movements, irregular meters and asymmetrical forms; nonfunctional harmonies with all elements governed by melodic necessities; and chords built in all intervals ranging from triads to secundal "clusters."

Neither parent was a musician. Halsey's father, a merchant and farmer, was entirely unmusical, and his mother, while interested in music, was totally untrained. "My mother (whose mother had come from Kentucky) and my paternal grandmother (of Pennsylvania Dutch stock) had a substantial store of folk songs which I heard very early," he recalls. "In my early days (through high school) I very often went to square dances, which were undergoing a kind of revival at the time, and became thoroughly indoctrinated with the fiddle tunes that accompanied the quadrilles, Virginia reels, and other traditional square dances." Formal instruction in music did not begin until he was about nine, when he began studying piano and took a weekly course in theory. At the Homer Academy in Homer, N.Y., where he received his academic education between 1915 and 1926, he was not involved in any of its musical activities. But he was beginning to compose in or about 1920, mostly piano pieces and songs, all derivative of the composers whose music he had studied.

In 1926, he entered Syracuse University in New York State. There, between 1928 and 1931, he studied piano with George Mulfinger and composition

with William H. Berwald, receiving his bachelor of arts degree in 1931.

Between 1931 and 1935, the years of the economic depression, Stevens was occupied with various musical tasks such as teaching (privately), accompanying, writing for local newspapers, and playing the organ and directing choirs in churches. "This was not a very productive time," he says, "and most of the music written then has long since been withdrawn."

He returned to Syracuse University in 1935 to continue his music studies for an additional two years and to serve as instructor of music. Between 1937 ad 1941 he was associate professor of music at Dakota Wesleyan University in Mitchell, S.D. During this period, on September 2, 1939, in Iowa City, he married Harriett Elizabeth Merritt, an artist and teacher, especially in ceramics; their three children were born in 1943, 1946, and 1948. From 1941 to 1946, Stevens was professor of music and director of the College of Music at Bradley University (later renamed Bradley Polytechnic Institute) in Peoria, Ill. He took leave of absence from there in 1943 to serve for three years in the U.S. Naval Reserve during World War II. While in uniform, he attended the University of California in Berkeley in 1944, studying composition with Ernest Bloch.

He first attracted interest as composer in the 1940s with works that were tonal, basically diatonic, though with chromatic excursions, and which depended for their coherence upon the devices of pedal point, ostinato, and canon. Some of these earlier works were in the field of chamber music. Suite, for clarinet (or viola) and piano (1945), was introduced in Saratoga, N.Y., on September 14, 1946. Quintet, for flute, string trio, and piano (1945), which had its premiere in Middlebury, Vt., on August 30, 1946, received the publication award of the Society for the Publication of American Music in 1948. Reviewing the Quintet in the *New York Herald Tribune*, Alfred Frankenstein described it as "a work of extraordinary refinement in texture build, and melodious expressiveness, and beautifully conceived in terms of the bright, special coloring obtainable with its combination of instruments."

In 1945, Stevens completed writing his Symphony no. 1, sketches for which had been begun as early as 1938. The San Francisco Symphony, with the composer conducting, introduced it on March 7, 1948, and on March 3, 1950, the Los Angeles Philharmonic, again under the composer's direction, premiered a revised version. A one-movement composition based on four thematic ideas, this symphony, in the words of Alfred Frankenstein in the *San Francisco Chronicle*, "projects and encloses a complete and complex set of ideas, is large and eloquent in conception, has thrust and weight and power." After the Los Angeles performance, Mildred Norton in the *Los Angeles Daily News* wrote: "The music holds your interest throughout. It never slackens." She further found in this music "a convincing ingredient of personal expression, and this, added to a fertile invention and feeling for form, lends the present work an integrity." This symphony was subsequently recorded by the Japan Philharmonic conducted by Akeo Watanabe.

During the spring semester of 1946, Stevens was professor of music at the University of Redlands in California. He was appointed assistant professor of music at the University of Southern California in Los Angeles in 1946, where he remained thirty years: associate professor in 1948, full professor in 1951, chairman of the composition department between 1948 and 1974, composer-in-residence between 1972 and 1976 and, since 1976, professor emeritus. During these years he was also visiting professor at Pomona College in Claremont, Calif. (spring 1954), the University of Washington in Seattle (summer 1958), Yale University (1960–61), the University of Cincinati (summer 1968) and Williams College in Williamstown, Mass. (winter 1969). Additionally, he appeared extensively as lecturer between 1950 and 1977 in over sixty American and European colleges and universities. At the same time, Stevens was a prolific writer of articles of music for various notable journals, is the author of *The Life and Music of Béla Bartk* (1953) and the program annotator for the Los Angeles Philharmonic (1946–51) and the Coleman Chamber Concerts in Pasadena, Calif. (1967–).

For the Vermont Symphony, Stevens wrote *A Green Mountain Overture* (1948), the first performance heard in Burlington, Vt., on August 7, 1948. This work was, as Paul A. Pisk noted in an article on Stevens in the *Bulletin of the American Composers Alliance*, "a sparkling, vivid piece . . . based on three motives: the first diatonic, almost dancelike in spite of the changing meter, the second lyric and very expressive, the third chordic. The transparency of the orchestral writing is remarkable." Stevens revised this overture in 1953, the premiere taking place in Tallahassee, Fla., on March 20, 1954, the composer conducting.

The Violin Sonata (1947–48; Los Angeles, 1948) represents a transition to Stevens's mature and fully crystallized style. Dissatisfied with much that he had been writing thus far, Stevens was creatively silent for two years. The emergence of the style he would henceforth favor could first be detected in String Quartet no. 3 (1949; Bloomington, Ind., January 17, 1951). This work Stevens also transcribed in 1955 for string orchestra as Allegro and Adagio; in this form its first performance was given by the San Francisco Chamber Orchestra on May 24, 1957.

Sonata for Horn and Piano (1953; Los Angeles, March 16, 1953) received in 1954 the publication award of the National Association of College Wind and Percussion Instructors. Septet, for clarinet, horn, bassoon, two violas, and two cellos (1957), was commissioned by the Fromm Music Foundation and the

University of Illinois and was premiered in Urbana, Ill., on March 3, 1957.

Two significant works for orchestra resulted from commissions from the Louisville Orchestra in Kentucky. The first was *Triskelion* (1953; February 27, 1954). The title, describing a three-branched figure radiating from a center, referred to the work's structure, whose beginning, Pisk explains, "creates a feeling of monumental serenity. However, it is followed by an Allegro moderato in vivid dance rhythm. . . . The slow movement is a testimonial for the melodist Stevens. . . . Most of it emphasizes tender, ethereal tone colors. The Finale . . . returns to exuberant accentuated dance rhythms in ever-changing meter. *Triskelion*, as a whole, seems to be a milestone in the development of Stevens's musical personality."

The second Louisville commission led to the writing of *Sinfonia breve* (1957; November 10, 1957). "The modifier 'breve' should not mark this symphony as a slight or a lightweight piece," wrote Walter Arlen in the *Los Angeles Times*. "It only indicates that the work is concise, lean, and without repetitious padding. The music is thoroughly symphonic and unmistakably American. The three movements are craggy, rugged, serious, rhythmically questing, in orchestration brassily sonorous."

The Ballad of William Sycamore, for chorus and orchestra (1955)—text by Stephen Vincent Benét—is one of Stevens's few works suggesting American folk tunes (mainly those he had heard as a boy) but without resorting to direct quotation. This work was commissioned by the University of Southern California in Los Angeles to celebrate its seventy-fifth anniversary; the first performance took place on October 6, 1955, in Los Angeles, Ingolf Dahl conducting. "In adapting it for chorus and orchestra," wrote Wallace Berry in the *Musical Quarterly*, "Stevens makes every use of the poem's direct, intrinsic form and suggestiveness. Excessively literal word painting is avoided but Stevens does not hesitate to let the atmosphere, and on occasion the specific connotations of verse, pour into his music."

Symphonic Dances (1958), commissioned by the San Francisco Symphony, received its premiere under Enrique Jorda on December 10, 1958. "It has a large design, complexity, and thrust beyond the implications of its title," reported Alfred Frankenstein in the *San Francisco Chronicle*. "It possesses a restrainedly nostalgic slow movement, and its outer movements have that electrically scintillating quality, produced by a very knowing mixture of harmonic and instrumental means."

Folk elements are to be found in many of Stevens's compositions since 1950, though not usually of American origin, an exception being the already mentioned *Ballad of William Sycamore*. Hungarian, Portuguese, Swedish, Slovakian, are some of the sources the composer has tapped. Stevens's interest in such folk music may be partly explained by his enthusiasm for the music of Béla Bartók. However, the temptation to seek other stylistic Bartókian influences in Stevens should be avoided. Some of Bartók's rhythmic and metric practices can be encountered in some early Stevens music *before* he came to know Bartók's music. Indeed, the motivation for his researches into Bartók came from the discovery that what he himself was writing had striking coincidences with Bartók's work.

In 1960, Stevens received the Friends of Harvey Gaul Award; in 1961, a citation and recording grant from the National Institute of Arts and Letters; and in 1964–65 a Guggenheim Fellowship (a second Guggenheim Fellowship came in 1971–72). In 1966 he was awarded an honorary doctorate (Litt.D.) from Syracuse University. As a Rockefeller Foundation Resident Scholar he spent a part of 1972 at Villa Serbelloni, in Bellagio, Italy. A Distinguished Faculty Award came from the University of Southern California in Los Angeles in 1973; a grant from the National Endowment for the Arts in 1976 for the writing of the Concerto for Viola and Orchestra (1976); and in 1978, the Abraham Lincoln Award of the American Hungarian Foundation.

Stevens has remained a prolific composer through the 1960s and 1970s, writing in all forms and all media except opera, ballet, and electronic music. Performances of his music have been given throughout the United States and in over forty foreign countries. In addition to the 1976 Viola Concerto, the cream of this later crop includes: Magnificat, for chorus and string orchestra or piano, or organ (1962; Chicago, March 12, 1963); Concerto for Cello and Orchestra (1964; Los Angeles, May 12, 1968); Te Deum, for chorus and brass septet, organ, and timpani (1967, Statesboro, Ga., November 4, 1967), commissioned by the Georgia Southern College for the dedicatory concerts of the Foy Fine Arts Center; *Threnos: In Memoriam Quincy Porter*, for orchestra (1968; New Haven, Conn., November 1968), commissioned by the New Haven Symphony through a grant from the William Inglis Morris Trust for Music; Concerto for Clarinet and String Orchestra (1969; Denton, Tex., March 20, 1969), commissioned by Friends and Students of Lee Gibson, the clarinetist who introduced it; *Quintetto "Serbelloni,"* for woodwinds (1972; Los Angeles, March 16, 1972); Double Concerto, for violin, cello, and string orchestra (1973; Los Angeles, November 4, 1973), commissioned by the Alchin Fund of the University of Southern California; and *Songs from the Paiute*, for chorus, four flutes, and timpani (1976; Furnace Creek, Calif., December 18, 1976). Casting a *coup d'oeil* over Stevens's overall productivity, Wallace Berry said it reveals "a capacity for communicative and moving expression—warmth, plaintiveness, exuberance or a trenchant irony that provoke and compel attention."

THE COMPOSER SPEAKS: No composer, I think, is capable of evaluating his significance in his own time, and certainly none can predict the fate of his music in the future. I write, as I believe most artists rreate, first for my own satisfaction and out of the great need I feel to take the stubborn materials of music and make them malleable, combine them into a convincing entity. Beyond that, I do think of the potential listener—naturally the ideal listener, open-minded and intelligent—but I have rarely if ever modified what I have wanted to write because of possible adverse listener reaction. One cannot reach the entire mass of humanity with any one offering, and music is far from the "universal language." But, I hope, and I have been assured by numerous listeners, that the music I write, fashionable or unfashionable, simple or complex, is capable of giving pleasure to some few people. Any future reward is an added bonus.

PRINCIPAL WORKS: Symphony no. 1 (1941–45); Quintet, for flute, string trio, and piano (1945); Suite, for clarinet or viola and piano (1945); Piano Sonata no. 3 (1947–48); *A Green Mountain Overture*, for orchestra (1948); Bassoon Sonato (1949); String Quartet no. 3 (1949); *Three Hungarian Folk Songs*, for viola and piano (1950); *Six Millay Songs*, for voice and piano (1950); Viola Sonata (1950); *Four Songs of Love and Death*, for voice and piano (1951–53); Six Preludes, for piano (1951–56); Horn Sonata (1952–53); *Triskelion*, for orchestra (1953); Partita, for harpsichord or piano (1953–54); Trumpet Sonata (1953–56); Piano Trio No. 3 (1954); Sonatina, for solo harp (1954); Four Short Pieces, for orchestra (1954); Suite, for solo violin (1954); Three Short Preludes, for organ (1954–56); Adagio and Allegro, for string orchestra, transcription of String Quartet no. 3 (1955); *The Ballad of William Sycamore*, for chorus and orchestra (1955); *Sonatine piacevole*, for alto recorder or flute and harpsichord or piano (1955–56); *Sonetto del Petrarca*, for voice and piano (1956); *Sinfonia breve*, for orchestra (1956–57); Sonata, for solo cello (1956–58); Septet, for clarinet, bassoon, horn, two violas, and two cellos (1957); Five Pieces, for orchestra (1958); *Symphonic Dances*, for orchestra (1958); Divertimento, for two violins (1958–66); *Two Shakespeare Songs*, for voice, flute, and clarinet (1959); *A Testament of Life*, for tenor, bass, chorus, and orchestra (1959); Suite, for viola and piano (1959); Trio, for winds and/or strings (1959); *Ritratti, Portraits for Piano* (1959–60); Sonatina, for bass tuba or trombone and piano (1960); Fantasia, for piano (1961); *Cuatro canciones*, for voice and piano (1961); Magnificat, for chorus and string orchestra (1962); Three Pieces, for organ (1962); *Twelve Slovakian Folk Songs*, for two violins (1962); Cello Concerto (1964); *Siete canciones*, for voice and piano (1964); Cello Sonata (1965); *Eight Yugoslavian Folk Songs*, for piano (1966); *Six Slovakian Folk Songs*, for harp (1966); *Campion Suite*, for chorus (1967); Te Deum, for chorus, brass septet, organ, and timpani (1967); *Chansons courtoises*, for chorus (1967); *Threnos: In Memoriam Quincy Port-*

er, for orchestra (1968); Concerto for Clarinet and String Orchestra (1969); Eight Canons, for two violins or violin and viola (1969); Oboe Sonata (1971); Quintetto "*Serbelloni*," for woodwinds (1972); Double Concerto, for violin, cello, and string orchestra (1973); Viola Concerto (1976); *Songs from the Paiute*, for chorus, four flutes, and timpani (1976).

BIBLIOGRAPHY: *BBDM*; *DCM*; Murphy, James, "The Choral Music of Halsey Stevens" (doctoral thesis, Lubbock, Tex., 1980); *Bulletin of the American Composers Alliance* vol. 4, no. 2, 1954; *Musical Quarterly*, July 1968; *Who's Who in America, 1980-81*.

Still, William Grant, b. Woodville, Miss., May 11, 1895; d. Los Angeles, Calif., December 3, 1978.

Sometimes called "the dean of Afro-American composers," Still was one of the foremost symphonic and operatic voices of the black people. In music that was consistently consonant, lyrical, immediate in its emotional or dramatic appeal, at times refined and at other times sensuous, Still gave musical interpretation to racial subjects. He rarely resorted to ethnic quotations, preferring to shape his own melodic and rhythmic material in the mold of Negro folk music. He is credited with having written the first successful symphony by a black man and the first opera by a black man to be performed by a significant company. As a conductor of his own music, he was the first black man to direct a major American orchestra (the Los Angeles Philharmonic at the Hollywood Bowl in 1936) and a major southern symphony orchestra (the New Orleans Philharmonic in 1955).

He was born to and raised in a comfortable middle-class family. Both parents were college graduates and teachers. His father, a cornetist and leader of a local band, was instructor of music at the Agricultural and Mechanical College of Alabama. When he died, during William's infancy, the mother moved to Little Rock, Ark. There she remarried and took a teaching job in high school, which she retained until her death in 1927. Still's earliest musical experience was listening to his maternal grandmother sing spirituals and hymns. Another important early influence was his stepfather, who brought music into the home by singing and by purchasing recordings of operatic arias. He often took William to concerts and musical productions, and was supportive when the boy showed an interest in making music. Still's first instruction in music came while he attended grade school through violin lessons from a local teacher.

When Still was sixteen, he entered Wilberforce University in Ohio, specializing in the sciences; his mother wanted him to become a physician. Still did not neglect music. He learned to play oboe and clarinet by himself, then formed a string quartet in which he played violin. He also performed in and made arrangements for the college band, and did some composing; a concert of his music was presented at college.

With music soon to become his prime interest, he dropped out of college to play in various dance bands in Columbus, Ohio, including one led by W. C. Handy, for which Still wrote arrangements. Then he decided to finish his schooling at Wilberforce University, receiving his bachelor of science degree in 1915. That year he married Grace Dorothy Bundy; after raising three children, they were divorced.

Still spent the first two years of his married life playing oboe and cello with various dance orchestras and in vaudeville theaters. At one period in 1916 he worked in W. C. Handy's publishing company in Memphis.

On his twenty-first birthday, Still received a small legacy from his father, making it possible for him to resume music study at Oberlin College in Ohio (1917-18). He had to leave the school in 1918, during World War I, to serve in the navy, first as mess attendant and then as a performer of the violin in the officers' mess. When he was discharged from military service in 1919, he came to New York to advance himself as a musician. Meeting failure, he decided to return to Oberlin College. There, his teachers raised a fund to provide him with a scholarship for the study of composition with George W. Andres, theory with F. J. Lehmann, and violin with Maurice Kessler.

Leaving Oberlin in 1921, Still joined the orchestra of the black revue *Shuffle Along*, which played in New York and on the road. When this company came to Boston, Still studied composition privately with George W. Chadwick for four months (who refused to accept any payment for this instruction, though Still could now afford it). Still then came to New York to play jazz with various black groups and to serve as director of the Black Swan Phonograph Company. Between 1923 and 1925 he studied composition privately with Edgard Varèse, whose influence on him was reflected in Still's leaning at the time toward the kind of dissonance then favored by "modern" composers. This can be found in *From the Land of Dreams*, for three voices and chamber orchestra (1924)—the voices appearing not as solos but as part of the orchestral texture—which received its first performance at a concert of the International Composers' Guild in New York on February 8, 1925, Vladimir Shavitch conducting. Also dissonant was *Darker America*, for chamber orchestra (1924), which received a publication award from the Eastman School of Music in Rochester, N.Y., and was given its initial hearing at another concert of the International Composers' Guild in New York on November 28, 1926, under the direction of Eugene Goossens. "There is no doubting the man's power," said a critic for *Musical Courier* after hearing *Darker America*, "and his music on this particular occasion was like a bright spot amid a lot of muddy grime."

Levee Land, a cycle of songs for voice and instruments (1925), was music of a different character, employing as it did jazz idioms. Florence Mills presented the premiere at a concert of the International Composers' Guild on January 24, 1926, Eugene Goossens conducting. A critic for the *New York World* described this music as "curious and elemental . . . plaintive in part, blue, crooning and sparkling with humor."

Still soon began to disavow so-called modern practices for the simpler harmonic and melodic approaches and the more romantic and lyrical writing he would henceforth favor: music drawing its materials from ethnic and popular sources and sometimes from his own experiences. Such a style is found in *From the Black Belt* (1926), a seven-movement suite for orchestra whose first performance was heard on March 20, 1927, with Georges Barrère conducting the Barrère Little Symphony in New York. This style was developed further in music to two ballets. *La Guiablesse* (1927) had a scenario by Ruth Page based on a tale by Lafcadio Hearn, set in the West Indies island of Martinique. This ballet was first produced at the Festival of American Music in Rochester, N.Y., on May 5, 1933, Howard Hanson conducting, and Thelma Biracree, solo dancer. Three solo dances from this score were assembled into a suite that was performed by several American orchestras after its premiere in Rochester, N.Y., on May 5, 1933. *Sahdji* was a choral ballet (1930), scenario by Alain Locke and Richard Bruce, based on an African tribal subject. Once again Thelma Biracree was solo dancer and Howard Hanson was the conductor when this ballet was first produced on May 22, 1931, in Rochester. When this score was recorded some forty-five years later, Paul Kresh, writing in *Stereo Review*, said: "There may not be a single note of authentic African music in it, yet this colorful score chants and surges persuasively to its muscular denouement."

Still's first recognition as a black composer came in 1928 when he received the second Harmon Award given annually to those making the most significant contributions to Negro culture in America. To such contributions Still added the *Afro-American Symphony* in 1930, perhaps his most successful composition and the first important symphony on a racial subject by a black man. (This was not Still's first symphony, however. That one was *Africa* [1928], performed in 1930 and then permanently withdrawn by the composer.) "I knew I wanted to write a symphony; I knew it had to be an American work; and I wanted to demonstrate how the blues, so often considered a lowly expression, could be elevated to the highest musical level." He had been gathering materials for *Afro-American Symphony* in a sketchbook for several years, shaping his melodic ideas to the idiom of the blues. A blues melody, first heard in English horn over a simple harmonic accompaniment, dominated the first movement, and recurred as subordinate material in later movements. Each of the four movements was prefaced by a quotation from a poem by Paul Laurence Dunbar to suggest the emotion of the music; but the symphony was not programmatic. The world premiere of the symphony was given under Hanson's direction in Rochester on October 29, 1931; two years later, Hanson conducted it in Berlin, Stuttgart, and Leipzig. It was also heard in Budapest, Paris, and in several cities in England and Panama, as well as in performances by several major American orchestras, and was recorded by Columbia Records in 1974.

From the late 1920s and into the 1940s, Still was a successful arranger for popular musicians, among these being Paul Whiteman, Sophie Tucker, Don Voorhees, and Artie Shaw. (Artie Shaw's recording of "Frenesi," one of his greatest disk successes, used Still's arrangement.) Still also worked as arranger and conductor for radio for all three networks and after that for television. In addition, he provided orchestrations for several Broadway musical productions.

While one hand was thus deeply involved with commercialism, the other was just as busily engaged creating symphonic and operatic music, most of it inspired by his race. A Guggenheim Fellowship in 1934–35 provided him with the opportunity to relax from his commercial efforts and devote himself to the writing of an opera, *Blue Steel* (1935). The libretto was the work of Carlton Moss and Bruce Forsyth, in which the hero is a black worker in Birmingham and the subject is the conflict between African voodooism and modern American values. Still's score absorbed jazz, spirituals, and Negro religious music.

Significant concert works came later, in the 1930s. *Kaintuck* (*Kentucky*), for piano and orchestra (1935), music redolent of the Old South, was commissioned by the League of Composers; it received its first performance (in a two-piano version) at a Pro Musica concert in Los Angeles on October 28, 1935, and (for piano and orchestra) in Rochester, N.Y., on January 16, 1936. *Lenox Avenue* (1937) was commissioned by CBS and performed as a work for narrator, chorus, and piano over the CBS radio network on May 23, 1937. This score, stripped of the narrator, was used for a ballet describing street scenes in New York's Harlem, with scenario by Verna Arvey. *Symphony in G minor* (1937) was intended as a sequel to the *Afro-American Symphony*. Where the latter was intended to speak for the black man of Africa, the G-minor Symphony touched upon the Negro of the 1930s. The Philadelphia Orchestra under Leopold Stokowski presented the world premiere on December 19, 1937. Linton Martin, in the *Philadelphia Inquirer*, spoke of it as music "of absorbing interest, unmistakably racial in thematic material and rhythms and triumphantly articulate in expressions of moods ranging from the exuberance of jazz to brooding wistfulness."

In 1939, Still received the Rosenwald Fellowship.

That year he married Verna Arvey, writer and critic, who had provided him, and would henceforth continue to do so, with many of the texts or scenarios for his operas, ballets and other compositions (in addition to bearing two more of their children). She assisted in the writing of a libretto, originally conceived by Langston Hughes, for Still's first opera to be performed: *Troubled Island* (1938). Its theme was the search for human freedom as symbolized by the story of Jean Jacques Dessalines, the liberator and first emperor of Haiti. In this music, Still incorporated two native Haiti melodies, a voodoo theme in the first movement and a merengue in the last; but all the other musical material was his own, though retaining the personality of Haitian native music, tailored to meet the demands of subject and locale. *Troubled Island* waited almost a decade for performance, being produced on March 31, 1949, by the New York City Opera (the first time the opera of a black man was given by an important opera company). "There is enough that is broadly melodious," wrote Olin Downes in his review in the *New York Times*, "enough that supplied dramatic movement on the stage, enough of operatic architecture to make the opera as a whole entertaining." For this opera, the National Association of American Composers and Conductors presented Still with its citation in 1949.

In 1940, Still completed still another full-length opera that was ultimately produced: *A Bayou Legend*. Verna Arvey provided him with a libretto inspired by an authentic legend of the Biloxi region during the 19th century in which a young man falls in love with a spirit: the jealousy of a young girl leads her to accuse him of witchcraft, a crime for which he is killed by the primitive villagers. This story was told with disarming simplicity by the librettist, and Still's music matched such a script with a graceful outpouring of singable melodies, sensitively textured orchestration, and an unsophisticated projection of drama and emotion. Opera/South in Mississippi presented the world premiere on November 15, 1974, followed by a production in Los Angeles on February 13, 1976, and a television presentation over the facilities of the Public Broadcasting Service on June 15, 1981.

Still's nonoperatic works of the early 1940s reflected not only his omnipresent racial consciousness but also his social awareness and the impact that World War II had upon him. One of his most deeply affecting compositions was an attack on racial bigotry and intolerance and a plea for the brotherhood of man: *And They Lynched Him on a Tree* (1940), a structurally ambitious work for narrator, contralto, black chorus, white chorus, and orchestra, text by Katherine Garrison Chapin; it was heard first on June 25, 1940, at the Lewisohn Stadium in New York, Artur Rodzinski conducting. *Plain-Chant for America*, for baritone, orchestra, and organ (1941)—text again by Katherine Garrison Chapin—was a stirring patriotic work written on commission for the centennial of the New York Philharmonic, which, under John Barbirolli's leadership, introduced it on October 23, 1941. *In Memoriam: The Colored Soldiers Who Died for Democracy*, for orchestra (1943), was written on commission from the League of Composers. Following its premiere on January 5, 1944, by the New York Philharmonic under Rodzinski, it was performed by many major orchestras in the United States and abroad. *Poem for Orchestra* (1944) was inspired by the concept of a spiritually reborn world following the desolation of the war years. Written on commission from the Kulas Fund in Cleveland for the Cleveland Orchestra, it was premiered on December 7, 1944, Rudolph Ringwall conducting.

Other works of the early 1940s did not deal with racial, social, or war-oriented themes. *Old California*, for orchestra (1941; Los Angeles, October 30, 1941), was a capsule musical history of the state of California from its Indian beginnings. *Festive Overture* (1944) was a submission to a competition sponsored by the Cincinnati Symphony for a short work celebrating the orchestra's fiftieth anniversary. It was awarded first prize by the unanimous decision of the jury. The Cincinnati Symphony under Goossens gave the first performance on January 19, 1945, and not long after that Leopold Stokowski conducted several performances with the New York Philharmonic.

Still wrote several more symphonies after the one in G minor. Symphony no. 3 (1945) was discarded by the composer. Symphony no. 4, *Autochthonous* (1949; Oklahoma City, Okla., March 18, 1951), represented the varied spirits of the American people—now optimistic and energetic, now pensive, now humorous, and now expressing the love of mankind. In 1958, Still wrote a completely new Symphony no. 3 to replace the one he had withdrawn, titling it *The Sunday Symphony*. Symphony no. 5 (1945) was a total revision of the withdrawn Symphony no. 3 to become a glorification of the beauties, energy, kindness, and justice of the Western Hemisphere, hence its title *Western Hemisphere*. Oberlin College Orchestra in Ohio, under Robert Baustian, celebrated Still's seventy-fifth birthday (somewhat belatedly) with the world premiere of Symphony no. 5 on November 9, 1970, with a program devoted exclusively to Still's music. Another all-Still program was given in Los Angeles to honor the composer when he turned eighty.

The Peaceful Land, for orchestra (1960), won first prize in a competition sponsored jointly by the National Federation of Music Clubs and the Aeolian Music Foundation for a composition honoring the United Nations; Fabien Sevitzky and the University of Miami Symphony gave the first performance in Florida on October 22, 1961. Two years later, on May 11, 1963, the same orchestra and conductor—with soloists and chorus—presented the world premiere of Still's one-act opera *Highway 1, USA* (1962), in which Verna Arvey's libretto was set in a filling station near a highway and focused on an incident in the life of an American family. This little opera was revived in New York on December 3, 1977.

Still received the Phi Beta Sigma Award, the Freedom Foundation Award, and a citation from the Los Angeles Council and County Board, all in 1963; an award from the Association for the Preservation of the Arts in Washington, D.C., in 1968; a scroll from the American Society of Composers, Authors, and Publishers (ASCAP) for his "extraordinary" contributions to music and his "greatness, both as an artist and a human being" in 1976. The William Grant Still Community Arts Center, a facility of the Municipal Arts Department in Los Angeles, was dedicated on March 11, 1976.

Still was awarded an honorary master of music degree from Wilberforce University in 1936. Four other institutions of higher learning presented him with honorary doctorates in music: Howard University in Washington, D.C. (1941), Oberlin College in Ohio (1947), the New England Conservatory of Music in Boston (1973), and Peabody Conservatory in Baltimore (1974); Bates College in Lewiston, Me., awarded him an honorary doctor of law degree in 1971 and Pepperdine University in Malibu, Calif., an honorary doctor of fine arts degree in 1973.

THE COMPOSER SPEAKS: For years it became the fashion to write thus and so, and those who did not follow the fashion slavishly were disparaged. Their music was sneeringly termed popular and reactionary. Many people claimed to be seeking a musical Messiah, who would shed light on the contemporary musical situation, but whenever anyone dared to speak out, he was met head-on by the pronouncement of the dominant group.

Mathematical formulae were often used by certain leading contemporary composers as a basis for musical creation. . . . The intellect usually took precedence over the emotions, and while intellect is necessary to musical creation, it should be no more than subordinate to inspiration. Even when some of the composers spoke or wrote of the importance of inspiration, it was not always apparent in their works.

The demand for inspired music has had its effect, however. Some composers, long steeped in the intellectual tradition, have felt the need to respond in some measure and have devised long statements to describe and justify their methods. Nonetheless, words cannot disguise the basic qualities of music. Simply saying something is devout and spiritual does not make it so. Simply declaring that a succession of notes is a melody does not make it a melody, nor a few odd beats a recognizable rhythm.

These things the public senses intuitively because the public is, after all, the final judge of what will live and what will not live. It resents being forced, it refuses to be intimidated. Just as the spark of freedom burns in the hearts of people all over the world, whether they are free men or oppressed, so does the inner love of beauty, and so does the public appreciation of all that is worthy in the arts.

PRINCIPAL WORKS: 5 symphonies (1928–49); 4 folk suites, for various instruments (1962).

Levee Land, for voice and orchestra (1925); *From the Black Belt*, for orchestra (1926); *Log Cabin Ballads*, for orchestra (1927); *La Guiablesse*, ballet (1927); *Sahdji*, choral ballet (1930); *Blue Steel*, opera (1935); *Kaintuck*, for piano and orchestra (1935); *Dismal Swamp*, tone poem for orchestra (1936); *Lenox Avenue*, for narrator, chorus, and piano, also ballet (1937); *Troubled Island*, opera (1938); *And They Lynched Him on a Tree*, for narrator, contralto, black chorus, white chorus, and orchestra (1940); *A Bayou Legend*, opera (1940); *Caribbean Melodies*, for solo voices, chorus, piano, and percussion (1941); *Plain-Chant for America,* for chorus and orchestra (1941); *Old California*, for orchestra (1941); *A Southern Interlude*, opera (1942); Suite, for violin and piano (1943); *In Memoriam: The Colored Soldiers Who Died for Democracy*, for orchestra (1943); *Poem for Orchestra* (1944); *Festive Overture*, for orchestra (1944); *From the Delta,* for band (1945); *Incantation and Dance*, for oboe and piano (1945); *Pastorela*, for violin and piano (1946); *Archaic Ritual*, for orchestra (1946); *Wood Notes*, for orchestra (1947); *Danza de Panama*, for string quartet (1948); *From a Lost Continent,* for piano and orchestra (1948); *Songs of Separation*, for voice and piano (1949); *Costaso*, opera (1949); *A Psalm for Living*, for chorus and orchestra (1954); Rhapsody, for soprano and orchestra (1955); *Ennaga*, for harp solo and orchestra, also for chamber orchestra and piano (1956); *An American Scene*, for orchestra (1957); *Four Indigenous Portraits*, for string quartet and flute (1957); *Minette Fontaine*, opera (1958); *Lyric String Quartet* (1960); *Patterns*, for chamber orchestra (1960); *The Peaceful Land*, for orchestra (1960); *From the Hearts of Women*, song cycle for voice and piano (1961); *Highway 1, USA*, one-act opera (1962); *Vignettes*, for oboe, bassoon, and piano (1962); Preludes, for string orchestra (1962); *Folk Suite*, for band (1963); *Miniature Overture*, for orchestra (1963); *Choreographic Prelude*, for string orchestra (1970).

BIBLIOGRAPHY: Arvey, Verna, *William Grant Still* (N.Y., 1939); Mass, Robert Bartlett (ed.), *William Grant Still: And the Fusion of Cultures in American Music* (Los Angeles, 1975); Southern, Eileen, *The Music of Black Americans: A History* (N.Y., 1971); *Arkansas Historical Quarterly*, Winter 1965; *Black Perspectives in Music* (Still issue), May 1975; *Music*, Spring 1964; *Who's Who in America, 1978–79.*

Stokes, Eric, b. Haddon Heights, N. J., July 14, 1930.

Stokes's lively, creative imagination has covered a wide area. Some of his music is spatial, and some of it is aleatory. He has ingeniously integrated electronic sounds with those of a live orchestra, and he has juxtaposed light with music, and opera with films. In a few of his works the audience has been included as an active participant. Much of what he has written is in the vein of Charles Ives, not only in its use of musical collages but also in its evocation of various aspects of Americana and its frequent excursions into whimsy, grotesquerie, and tomfoolery, but always with an ear to life's seriocomic paradox.

Stokes's mother came from a musical family, her father having been the concertmaster of the Crystal Palace Orchestra in London, and her uncle, a cellist in the Boston Symphony. Though she had no musical training and was musically illiterate, she was singing much of the time, and this was Eric Stokes's first musical recollection. Singing was also important to Stokes from his early boyhood. He sang with the boys' choir and later with the regular church choir at St. Mary's Episcopal Church in Haddon Heights from 1937 to 1948. In Haddon Heights High School he was a member of the chorus, for which he sometimes wrote compositions. Other forms of musical activity included piano lessons with Evelyn White (1939–46) and theory with Frederick Happich (1947–48).

He completed his academic education at Lawrence College (1948–52) in Appleton, Wis., where he received further instruction in music from James Ming and attained his bachelor of music degree in 1952. That year he was called into military service. For two years he was an instructor at Fort Eustis in Virginia. "That was a shock," he recalled. "Suddenly I was deprived of so much I had taken for granted. I understood my need for serious, intensive training, and I recognized my ambition. But all that had to wait."

Discharged from military service in 1954, he resumed his music study at the New England Conservatory in Boston, a pupil in composition of Carl McKinley's. While there, Stokes composed some chamber music, including a Trio, for harpsichord, flute, and violin (1956; Boston, June 12, 1956); a Cello Sonata (1956; Boston, December 17, 1957); and Duets, for flute and clarinet (1957; Boston, December 17, 1957). This early music was centered on a tonal lyrical style that was quite out of step with the twelve-tone and serial approaches then becoming popular in academic circles. He was a resident fellow at Villa Montalvo, the mansion in Saratoga, Calif., of former senator Phelan, converted to an art colony, during the summers of 1957 and 1958. There he composed *Smoke and Steel* (1957–58), for tenor, men's chorus, and chamber orchestra which the tenor Frederick Jagel introduced with the New England

Conservatory Orchestra conducted by Roger Voisin on May 14, 1958. A Divertimento, for chamber orchestra (1959), won first prize at the Music-Drama Festival at Lawrence College, where it was premiered on March 13, 1960, Kenneth Blyer conducting.

On June 20, 1959, Stokes married Cynthia Schuyler Crain, a flutist. (A daughter was born in 1963, a son two years later.) They established their home in Minneapolis. There, from 1959 to 1963, Stokes was in attendance at the graduate school of the University of Minnesota, studying composition with Paul Fetler and being awarded his Ph.D. in music in 1963. Meanwhile, in 1961, he had become an instructor in the music faculty of that university, where he has remained since: assistant professor in 1963, associate professor in 1973, and full professor since 1977. In the early 1960s, with Thomas Nee, he founded the Here Concerts in Minneapolis for the presentation of new music. In 1970 he founded and became the director of the First Minnesota Moving and Storage Warehouse Band, a new music ensemble at the university, and that year he planned and initiated the electronic music program at the university, serving as director of the electronic music laboratory since that time.

The influence of Charles Ives began to grow assertive in *A Center Harbor Holiday* (1963), a concerto for tuba and orchestra in which Stokes presented a tonal picture of a New England summer's day. It was commissioned by the New Hampshire Festival, where it was heard for the first time in July 1963. Almost four years later (April 26, 1967) the Minneapolis Symphony performed it under Stanislaw Skrowaczewski. In the *Minneapolis Star*, John K. Sherman described it as an "orchestral picture of great charm and humor, opening with dawn sounds, working up to a festive parade section and ending with fireworks and visible flag-waving by the orchestra members." Ivesian, too, was *Three Sides of a Town* in evoking the scenes of a small town in music carrying folk and popular echoes. Written in 1964, it received its initial hearing on October 7, 1964, in a performance by the Civic Orchestra of Minneapolis under Thomas Nee; subsequently, it was programmed by the Minneapolis Symphony on three different occasions by three different conductors.

Sonatas, for string orchestra (1966) was commissioned by the Netherlands Chamber Orchestra in Holland and given its premiere in Monnikendam, Holland, on July 11, 1970, David Zinman conducting. This is spatial music in an antiphonal style with the string orchestra distributed into three groups directed by three conductors between the stage and the auditorium. "But the work is by no means a gimmicky composition," said Peter Altman in the *Minneapolis Star*, "only interested in striving for stereophonic effects. Its calm, soft lines and deep hues are hypnotically relaxing. . . . It is a short work and a very beautiful one which creates a strong mood."

Stokes's first opera (actually a multimedia production) was *Horspfal* (1967–68), title combining the syllables from "horse opera" and Wagner's *Parsifal*. This is a collage opera combining singing, instrumental music, pantomime, and cinema in the telling of the sad fate of the American Indian at the hands of the white man, in a libretto by Alvin Greenberg. "*Horspfal* is my *Boris Godunov* in the one clear parallel that the hero is not who he seems to be on first thought," the composer explained in a letter to the conductor Dennis Russell Davies. "In *Boris* the true hero (i.e., Victim—sufferer) is 'Mother Russia' and her surrogate, the masses of Russians singing folk songs in the Forest of Kromy. So then, by analogy and parallel in *Horspfal*, the true hero is not the Indian but the terribly patient and enduring land, his Bed. My Indian is almost closely analagous to Mussorgsky's 'Fool' from whom the crowd steals his penny and of whom they make fun while cries out for 'Mother Russia.' " A huge bed was symbolic of the Indian homeland which was invaded by the white man until no room existed any longer for the Indian. "An outrageous jolly blasphemy," reported Harold Blumenfeld in the *St. Louis Sunday Post Dispatch*. "*Horspfal* exposes the varicose linings of the American Dream. It never overtly editorializes but leaves it to the viewer to react ad libitum in glee or scandalized shock." Stokes's score once again recalled Ives in the way in which old-fashioned tunes, hymns, tape noises, and instrumental interjections create a skillful collage of sounds. "Perhaps the prime importance of *Horspfal*," Blumenfeld adds, "lies in the fact that it is the first opera to make use of the full gamut of cinematic possibilities—not just in terms of actual film sequences . . . but because the entire work is conceived and realized in the staged equivalents of superimposure, fade and wash; fast and slow motion; the split screen and the still." *Horspfal* was successfully produced in New York on May 26, 1971.

On the Bedlands—Parables, for orchestra (1972), which the St. Paul Philharmonic Society of Minnesota commissioned and then introduced on March 6, 1972, with Sydney Hodkinson conducting, utilized spatial music together with the integration of prerecorded sound on tape with orchestral music. This work ends with off-stage drum sounds which become increasingly louder and then explosive as musicians enter the auditorium and march down the aisle to the drum beats. On February 13, 1978, *On the Bedlands—Parables* was performed in New York by the American Composers Orchestra under Dennis Russell Davies. Writing in the *New York Times*, Peter G. Davis said: "For all the rigorous compositional control, this brief atmospheric work makes its point primarily through the evocative power of crunching clusters, twittering strings, wailing electronics and thwacked bass drums. The piece may not be much more than a collection of sound effects, but when used so cleverly they are hard to resist."

The Continental Harp and Band Report, for orchestra (1974–75), is one of Stokes's most Ivesian and most winning compositions. He wrote it on commission for the inaugural season of the Minnesota Symphony at its new home, Orchestra Hall, where it was first heard on March 4, 1975, with Skrowaczewski conducting. It is made up of nine pieces reflecting many different aspects of Americana, past and present. The composer explains: " 'Continental' refers to early American prototypes; 'Harp' is both sacred and profane; and the 'Band Report' is addressed to the people." The nine pieces can be played as a complete unit, or they can be performed as separate compositions, or in any order of any combination of these pieces the conductor may desire. One requirement, however, must be fulfilled: 'The Triumph of Time', inspired by a painting by Pieter Breughel, must always be the final movement to any combination of the other parts." The score is headed with a quotation from Hart Crane's poem "The Bridge," while another quotation provides the stimulus for the first section, "Brooklyn Bridge." Unique effects and textures give the work a singular personality. In the third part, "No Deposit—No Return," the orchestra is split into four ensembles, each playing in its own meter and tempo. Here the orchestration includes an old washboard made of corrugated tin and played upon with a large wooden spoon. In the fourth section, "Toccata, Captain Smith, His Tucket," all instruments are "touched"—trombonists thump their mouthpieces with the palms of the hands; percussionists rap their fingernails on the drums; and so forth. Pantomime enters into the sixth section, "A Shopping Center Xmas Eve" with the introduction of a mime as a frustrated salesclerk. "In all," commented Andrew Porter in the *New Yorker*, "it lasted about forty minutes, and was a stimulating sequence of entertainment, ingenuity, and poetic musing."

In the opera *The Jealous Cellist* (1976–77)—written on a grant from the National Endowment for the Arts for the Minnesota Opera—the audience is invited to become part of the cast. This opera was so designed by its authors that it could readily be performed in high school and community auditoriums, with community musical groups asked to participate by singing and playing whatever they wished at specified moments in the opera. In this libretto, by Alvin Greenberg, science fiction invades opera as a cellist is separated from the rest of the orchestra when it changes places with a revolutionary army by way of a space warp. Stokes divided his instrumental ensemble into three units, one backstage, on stage right, and a supplementary percussion and keyboard group at stage left, led by two conductors. It is, as Roy M. Close said of the opera in the *Minneapolis Star* after it had been premiered by the Minnesota Opera Company on February 2, 1979, "an amalgam of a lot of things, including some distinct Savoyard echoes and ends at a pep rally . . . [containing] plenty of lively tunes, several amusing episodes and a few moments of inspired nonsense."

Symphony(s), Book I (1979) is a four-movement work, designated Book I because other movements (or pieces) were being planned by the composer. It is, the composer explained, "a collection of separate movements which may be performed in various groups of three or four or more at any time. Any such set of these pieces is then one of the Symphony(s)." Book I was given its world premiere at the Cabrillo Music Festival in California on August 31, 1979.

With *The Phonic Paradigm* in 1980, the first of several similar works, Stokes veered in a new direction. He rejected the fixed concept of how music should be written, what its personnel should be, and where it should be heard. Holding that all sounds enjoy the inalienable right to proceed from any point of the compass "out of any height or depth however near or far as soever called forth by their composers or any other compelling life force," Stokes began to use a native grammar in which noninstitutionalized sonic resources play a major part. They include such things as ice, leaves, stone, seed pods, scissors, cutlery, zippers, gloves, files, hunters' wild animal calls, glass, springs, and so forth. Each movement of *The Phonic Paradigm* is centered on one or a few of these natural inflections and puts into practice some of their conjugations. Stokes conceives this music for performance in "true sound galleries," which will be stripped of institutional prejudices.

Stokes has received grants or fellowships from the Martha Baird Rockefeller Foundation, the Ford Foundation, the McMillin Fund, all in 1969–70, for study and travel. In 1975 he was the recipient of a grant from the Jerome Foundation and in 1979 a $10,000 fellowship from the Minnesota State Arts Board.

THE COMPOSER SPEAKS: I write what I like and I hope others will like it too. That's the only meaningful thing that can be said as far as an explanation of my music is concerned.

How I make my music, out of which sounding elements or by whatever organizing principles I realize the finished work—all of that is my private concern. How others listen to it is theirs.

I hope they won't undo my work by trying to figure out how I composed it. The methods I use in any piece are only a means to an end. The result comes about only in performance. I hope my listeners will join in somewhat like dancers join in with the music, giving themselves up to it body and soul. It is the sounding immediacy that counts. To be attuned to that is the greatest understanding I know.

We and the musicians must be willing to make mistakes, to experiment. We should try black-out concerts, audiences and performers in motion, hidden performers, unusual architecture like bridges and lobbies and cellars, all kinds of spatial effects in music, listening devices somewhat like sunglasses for the ears, audience responses and opportunities to contribute to the musical sounds, too.

PRINCIPAL WORKS: 2 divertimentos, for chamber orchestra (1959, 1960).

Smoke and Steel, for tenor, men's chorus, and chamber orchestra (1957–58); *A Celebration for the Saint*, for chamber orchestra (1961); *A Center Harbor Holiday*, for orchestra (1963); *Three Sides of a Town*, for orchestra (1964); *Gnomic Commentaries*, for chamber ensembles (1964–66); Music for String Quartet (1966); Sonatas, for chamber orchestra (1966); *Horspfal*, opera (1967–68); *Expositions on Themes by Henry David Thoreau*, for chamber ensemble (1970); *When This You See, Remember Me*, for twelve voices (1970); *Circles in a Round*, for piano and tape (1971); *On the Bedlands—Parables*, for orchestra (1972); *Of the Mountains, of the Past, the Shifting Lights Call to Remembrance the Music*, for chorus, band, and orchestra (1972); *Lampyridae*, for chamber orchestra (1973); *Five Verbs of Earth Encircled*, for chamber orchestra (1973); *The Continental Harp and Band Report*, for wind orchestra (1974–75); *Variations on a Space and a Quiet*, for chamber orchestra (1974); *The Whole Note*, for indeterminate instruments (1974); *Nights and Lights*, for voice and piano (1977); *Inland Missing the Sea*, nine songs for soprano, tenor, baritone, and instruments (1977, revised 1979); *The Spirit of Place Among People*, for orchestra and participating audience (1977); *Harp, or Orpheus in Clover*, a microopera birthday celebration (1977); *The Jealous Cellist*, opera (1976–77); *Symphony(s)*, for orchestra (1979); *What Eve Sang*, for chorus and handbells (1980); *Anwatin Winter Set*, for winds, brass, strings, percussion, and piano (1980); *The Phonic Paradigm* (1980).

BIBLIOGRAPHY: Anderson, E. Ruth, *Contemporary American Composers* (Boston, 1976); *Minnesota Program Notes*, March 5, 1975; *New Yorker*, March 24, 1975.

Stout, Alan Burrage, b. Baltimore, Md., November 26, 1932.

Despite the fact that some of Stout's important works have had a prolonged period of gestation, he has been a prolific composer who has produced over a hundred compositions. In different works, and sometimes in the same work, his musical style spans the polar points between Gregorian plainchant (in a modern adaptation) and serialism and microtonal music. Some of his works have been developed from graphs, scientific charts, and meteorological readings. But for all such excursions into esoterics, Stout's best works are basically conservative in their concern for well-sounding sonorities and emotional and dramatic content.

Concurrently, while receiving his academic education at Johns Hopkins University in Baltimore between 1950 and 1954, from which he received his bachelor of science degree in 1954, he was musically trained at the Peabody Conservatory, where he studied composition with Henry Cowell. Intermittently, from 1951 to 1956, he also studied composition privately with Wallingford Riegger in New York. Stout's String Quartet no. 1 (1952–53); *Solemn Prelude*, for trombone and organ (1953); Two Hymns, for tenor and orchestra (1953); and Three Hymns, for orchestra (1954), were among the compositions of his student years. The last of these waited two decades for its premiere, which finally took place on September 27, 1972, in a performance by the Baltimore Symphony under Sergiu Comissiona.

On a Danish government grant, Stout spent the year of 1954–55 in Copenhagen in the study of composition with Vagn Holmboe. Following Stout's return to the United States he was employed as librarian at the Baltimore Enoch Pratt Free Library (1958). At the same time, in 1958–59, he concluded his study of composition with John Verrall at the University of Washington in Seattle, where he also took courses in Swedish, and from which he received a master of arts degree in music in 1959. Between 1959 and 1962 he was employed in the music department of the Seattle Public Library.

Stout was productive as a composer throughout the 1950s with music that hewed to traditional lines both structurally and stylistically. His principal works of those years included five additional string quartets (1952–59); *Two Ariel Songs*, for soprano and chamber orchestra (1957); *Die Engel*, for soprano, flute, piano, percussion, and brass (1957); a Clarinet Quintet (1958); and his Symphony no. 1 (1959). Two works of major dimensions were first seminated in those years, though they had to wait some time for full fruition. One of these was the Symphony no. 2, the earliest sketches of which dated back to 1951. When, fifteen years later, the Ravinia Festival Association in Illinois commissioned him to write a work through a grant from the Illinois Arts Council, he finally brought this symphony to its completion. The first performance took place on August 4, 1968, with Seiji Ozawa conducting the Chicago Symphony. This is a three-movement work further subdivided into thirteen sections, played without pause. The subsections, as the composer explained, "relate to each other freely, in an arch shape, around the center of the work, the Trio ostinato. Large-scale relations in this piece are achieved through tempo and texture, rather than through thematic development." Such advanced idioms as tone clusters and quarter tones are used from time to time; at certain places, the strings are divided into as many as sixty-two individual parts. "The extramusical ideas behind this piece," the composer adds, "are a fascination with the paintings of Hieronymus Bosch, and two quotations from the Mass for the Dead—as a superscript, 'Libera Me Domine de Morte Aeterna,'

and a postscript: 'Pax Domini Sit Semper Vobiscum.' "

The symphony was scored for an immense orchestra and is the largest-scaled work Stout had produced up to that time. More ambitious still in structural dimension is the *Passion*, for soloists, chorus, and orchestra, which takes more than two hours to perform. Stout began this work in 1953 and continued it in 1962–63 with a series of motets for the liturgy of Passion Week and Good Friday. Most of the music was written by 1969. It was finally completed in 1975 on a commission from the Chicago Symphony with a grant from the National Endowment for the Arts, and the world premiere took place on April 15, 1976, Margaret Hillis conducting. The text came partly from the gospel narratives from St. Matthew and St. John and partly from excerpts from the Roman Catholic liturgy for Passiontide, from the Ordinary of the Mass and from Te Deum Laudamus, all sung in Latin. "It is a work," said Arrand Parsons in the program book of the Chicago Symphony, "which assimilates history in its utilization of liturgy, Gospel narrative, and musical elements from medieval plainsong to the present in a single contemporary style that is dramatic, almost operatic, as well as a lyric outpouring of an inner musical conviction." This eclectic score included plainsong, elaborate contrapuntal textures, choral whispering. As in the Passions of Bach, motets were interpolated to comment on the action, while the chorus carried the principal burden of the work with instrumental passages providing descriptive interludes. A male trio sang Christ's lines, but the other three singers were not assigned any specific biblical identification. "Stout fashions his church Latin text into curtains and tapestries of sound," wrote Thomas Willis in the *Chicago Tribune*. "Like a sonic borealis, they expand and contract as needed, supplying intimate but still objective commentary on an emotion-laden event, creating towering climaxes at the peak points of action, or providing canopies of tightly woven, often contrapuntal sheets of sound against which other portions of the action can take place."

The year of 1962 was a time of exceptional creativity for Stout. It saw the completion of Symphony no. 3, for soprano, male chorus, and orchestra, the writing of which had begun in 1959. In addition, other notable works included *Movements*, for violin and orchestra (Fish Creek, Wis., August 17, 1966); the Tenth String Quartet, *Canticum Canticorum*, for soprano and chamber ensemble; Suite for Flute and Percussion; *Christmas Poem*, for soprano and chamber ensemble; and *George Lieder*, for baritone and orchestra. The last of these was a cycle of songs based on the mystical and transcendental love poems from Stefan George's *Das neue Reich*. Stout revised this work in 1965 and 1970. The first performance of the final version took place on December 14, 1972, by the Chicago Symphony conducted by Sir Georg Solti, with Benjamin Luxon soloist. "It is music," wrote

Robert C. Marsh in the *Chicago Sun-Times*, "that places a vocal line above constantly shifting textures. The work is, indeed, a study in texture and color rather than rhythm and melody."

Since 1963, Stout has been a professor in theory and composition at the School of Music at Northwestern University in Evanston, Ill. In 1968 he was visiting lecturer on music at Johns Hopkins University in Baltimore; in 1973, visiting professor of music at State College of Music in Stockholm, Sweden; in 1974, visiting professor of composition at the Berkshire Music Center at Tanglewood, Mass.; and in 1975 visiting professor of music at the University of Minnesota in Minneapolis under the auspices of the American Choral Foundation and at the Yale University Summer School of Music and Art.

In 1970, Stout was commissioned by the Chicago Symphony to write a work commemorating the orchestra's eightieth anniversary. In Sweden, while on leave from Northwestern University, he completed this assignment in December 1970 with Symphony no. 4, for chorus and orchestra, and on April 15, 1971, the world premiere took place in Chicago with Solti conducting the Chicago Symphony. In its basic design, Stout emulated Witold Lutoslawski's Symphony no. 2, a two-movement work whose two parts were entitled *Hesitant* and *Direct*. Stout's symphony is in four movements, but the two middle ones are similar to Lutoslawski's symphony, the *Hesitant* movement becoming a *Quaderno* and the *Direct* becoming a Rondo. The *Quaderno* is preceded by an overture featuring string sounds that recur throughout the work, by a four-part chorale, and by a cadenza for alto flute and percussion. The Rondo is followed by a *Lament* in which the bass trombone quotes a Gregorian phrase followed by the chorus, speaking, chanting, and at times whispering a text in Latin from the Lamentations of Jeremiah. The score, wrote Arrand Parsons in the *Chicago Symphony Program Book*, "utilizes the musical language of this day without following any single line. Expressive and dramatic use of sound and sonorous groups is the principal motivating force in the music; a wide range of densities and textures is to be found organized in a way which may best be described as architectonic. Orchestral clusters of sound often serve as the foundation for the projection of thematic elements. The Symphony is of a sectional nature, but with a continuity running from beginning to end, often punctuated by floods of sound, and with a sensitive orchestration which gives coherence to the whole." The *Quaderno* section is, in the composer's description, "a collection of events" which contains all the symphony's basic materials and which could conceivably be ordered in a different way. "The ordering I chose is based upon psychological intuition, and the manner of events growing into or out of previous events possibly owes more to electronic music than to conventional symphonic music." In this symphony, Stout quotes passages from several of his other compositions including Suite for Flute and Percussion and parts of the Passion upon which he was then still at work.

On another commission, this one from the Fromm Music Foundation, Stout completed a second significant work in 1970, Nocturne, for narrator, contralto, and chamber ensemble, first presented on November 10, 1970, at a concert of the International Society for Contemporary Music in Chicago, Easley Blackwood conducting. On April 16, 1971, Recitative, Capriccio, Recitative, and Aria, for oboe, harp, and percussion (1967), was premiered in Chicago on a program of Contemporary Concerts, Inc., performed by the University of Illinois Percussion Ensemble. At the International Society for Contemporary Music concert in Chicago on April 12, 1976, Stout's Sonata for Two Pianos (1975), which had been commissioned by that organization as a memorial to its founder, was introduced by the two-piano team of Philips and Renzulli.

PRINCIPAL WORKS: 10 string quartets (1952–62); 4 symphonies (1956–70).

Three Hymns, for orchestra (1954); Intermezzo, for English horn, percussion, and strings (1954); *Two Ariel Songs*, for soprano and chamber orchestra (1957); *Pietà*, for string bass and orchestra (1957); *Die Engel*, for soprano, flute, piano, percussion and brass (1957); Clarinet Quintet (1958); Ricercare and Aria, for strings (1959); *Serenity*, for solo cello, bassoon, percussion, and strings (1959); Eight Chorale Preludes, for organ (1960); *Elegiac Suite*, for soprano and strings (1961); Laudi, for soprano, baritone, and orchestra (1961); *Triptych*, for horn and organ (1961); *Christmas Poem*, for soprano and chamber ensemble (1962); Suite for Flute and Percussion (1962); *George Lieder*, for baritone and orchestra (1962–70); Varianti, for piano (1962); Fantasia, for piano (1962); Movements, for violin and orchestra (1962); *Prologue*, oratorio, for solo voices, chorus, and orchestra (1964); Toccata, for saxophone and percussion (1965); Music for Oboe and Piano (1966); Cello Sonata (1966); Suite, for piano (1967); *Studies in Densities and Duration*, for organ (1967); Music for Flute and Harpsichord (1967); Three Chorale Preludes, for organ (1967); *Fem Sanger*, song cycle for voice and piano (1967); Recitative, Capriccio, and Aria, for oboe, harp, and percussion (1967); Two Movements, for clarinet and string orchestra (1968); *Dialogo per la Pascua*, for solo voices, chorus, harp and string septet (1970); Nocturnes, for narrator, contralto, and chamber ensemble (1970); *Fanfare for Charles Seeger*, for orchestra (1972); *Pulsar*, for three brass choirs and timpani (1972); Suite for Saxophone and Organ (1973); *O Altitudo*, for soprano, women's chorus, solo flute, and instrumental ensemble (1974); *Passion*, for vocal soloists, chorus, and orchestra (1975); Sonata for Two Pianos (1975); Waltz, for piano (1977); *Studies in Timbres and Interferences,* for organ (1977); *Nimbus,* for strings (1979).

BIBLIOGRAPHY: *BBDM; DCM; NGDMM: Chicago Symphony Program Book,* April 5, 1976; *Who's Who in America, 1980–81.*

Strang, Gerald, b. Claresholm, Alberta, Can., February 13, 1908. American citizen, 1914.

As Arnold Schoenberg's teaching and editorial assistant, Strang has been greatly influenced by the twelve-tone master, but he has never been a strict and confirmed dodecaphonist. Strang's writing has been atonal, polyrhythmic, and contrapuntal, and only occasionally, and with modifications, twelve-tonal. Since 1963 his entire output has been either electronic or computer music.

His father, a mortgage banker, played the piano and repaired reed organs as a young man; his mother taught piano and played organ in church. His family came to the United States in 1908, settling in Grant Falls, Mont. Music study began with piano lessons when Gerald was seven. At ten he started studying violin, and at thirteen, organ. Upon graduating from the Principia Junior College in St. Louis (1924–26) he entered Stanford University in California, where he majored in philosophy with a minor in foreign languages (1926–28), earning his bachelor of arts degree in 1928, *cum laude.* Prior to completing his academic studies at Stanford, he did not seriously consider music as a vocation.

The study of composition and counterpoint began in 1928 at the University of California at Berkeley, where his teachers were Edward G. Stricklen and Glen Haydon. On September 27, 1930, he married his first wife, Clara Weatherwax, a poet and later a novelist, with whom he had a son (deceased at the age of fifteen). Six weeks with a private group in counterpoint study took place with Charles Koechlin in Oakland, Calif., during the summer of 1930. The first composition of his adult years was *Mirrorrorrim,* for piano (1931), the title referring to "mirror" in mirror spelling. This was followed by a Sonatina, for solo clarinet (1931–32).

From 1935 to 1940, Strang was the managing editor of *New Music Edition.* He worked as a teaching assistant to Arnold Schoenberg at the University of California in Los Angeles (1936–38), the beginning of a relationship which proved to be the most significant influence in Strang's musical life. That relationship continued from 1936 to 1950, when Strang worked as Schoenberg's amanuensis and as editor of some of his theoretical works.

In 1938, Strang was appointed to the music faculty of the Long Beach City College in California. He remained there until 1958, the last four years as chairman of the music department. He left his teaching post temporarily in 1942 to work for three years in the engineering department of the Douglas Aircraft Company in California.

Upon the death of his wife, Clara, in 1958, Strang married Eileen Kelly, a professional cellist, on December 26, 1958.

In 1942, Strang completed his most ambitious composition up to that time, and the first work with which he realized success: Symphony no. 1. Here, his writing became more tonal, more faithful to classical structural relationships and less chromatic than some of his earlier works. The slow movement, Intermezzo, which had previously been conceived as part of an unfinished Suite for Chamber Orchestra and which had first been performed in Los Angeles on April 14, 1937, was heard at a concert of the Los Angeles Philharmonic under Otto Klemperer on February 8, 1939, after which it was broadcast nationally by the Columbia Broadcasting System. Commenting on this work in *Modern Music* in 1942, Lazare Saminsky said: "Both the opening section and the symphony's Scherzo are closely knit thematically in spite of a certain caprice in the layout. A nature still and deep is mirrored in the serene Andante. The orchestral sonorities are of delicate coloring and not heavily massed."

In 1945, Strang returned to the University of Southern California to study composition with Ernst Toch and acquire his doctorate in music in 1948, submitting as his thesis Symphony no. 2 (1947).

His main works of the 1940s and 1950s used melodic and contrapuntal techniques of twelve-tone music with modal-sounding rows, and quartel harmony was emphasized. These compositions included Concerto Grosso, for orchestra (1951; Los Angeles, December 4, 1951); Concerto, for cello accompanied by piano, flute, oboe, clarinet, and bassoon (1951; Los Angeles, February 11, 1952); and Variations for Four Instruments (1956; Baton Rouge, La., April 10, 1957). When the Cello Concerto was repeated on May 17, 1958 in Los Angeles, Albert Goldberg, in the *Los Angeles Times,* called it "a fairly conventional piece, for it has a clear, formal structure, recognizable tunes and definite rhythms. The woodwind background provides some interesting textures and the things the solo cello is called upon to do lie well within the limits of possibility and are reasonably grateful."

Since 1950, Strang has been involved in the design of music facilities. He pioneered studio-type construction, including extensive use of recording facilities at Long Beach City College in 1951. Since then he has been employed as acoustical consultant on over forty such projects, including auditoriums, churches, and music facilities of many colleges and universities.

Between 1958 and 1965, Strang was professor of music at San Fernando Valley State College in California, chairman of its music department from 1958 to 1963. From 1965 to 1969 he was professor of music at the California State College at Long Beach, Calif., as well as chairman of its music department for three years (1965–69).

Strang became interested in computer music in 1963, from which time on, this was the sole area of his musical creativity. His first such compositions were COMPUSITIONS nos. 2 and 3, computer music on tape. (No. 1 was never completed.) He worked with electronic and computer music at the Bell Telephone Laboratories in New Jersey in 1963 and again in 1969, and since 1964 at the University of California in Los Angeles, where from 1969 to 1974 he was lecturer in electronic music. During this period his computer-synthesized pieces were called COMPUSITIONS and his electronic pieces, SYN-THIONS.

Strang has written articles on computer music for various technical journals and anthologies. He was the editor of Arnold Schoenberg's *Fundamentals of Composition*, published in 1967.

THE COMPOSER SPEAKS: Two main motives have dominated my entire composing life: (1) Challenge, and critical evaluation of most of the basic assumptions of musical theory and esthetics; and (2) experimental search of other and hopefully better ways of accomplishing musical objectives. Typical questions that occupied me: Why a fixed, regular pulse as a base for rhythmical organization? At which levels of rhythmic organization, and within what range of rates? For what reason do we need predetermined fixed pitches (apart from the mechanics of instrument making)? Could we make music without fixed repetitive pitches? Why twelve pitches per octave? Why equally spaced pitches? To what degree does musical comprehension depend on repetition? What kinds of similarities are perceived as repetitions at what levels of complexity?

I'm sure I must have considered at least a hundred such questions at one time or another, and concluded that every basic assumption needs to be reconsidered and either verified, modified, or discarded.

My devotion to electronic and computer music during the last twenty years has enabled me to explore a lot of these matters experimentally, for example: synthetic scales of equal and unequal intervals and numbering more and less than twelve; random intervals and note-length, continually changing timbre.

This preoccupation with the scientific and theoretical fundamentals influenced my choice of musical materials, but my compositional methods and objectives remained close to those of Schoenberg—primarily thematic and melodic; contrapuntal; evolving through the interplay of repetition, contrast, and variations. I've always written as economically as possible, hence most of my music is short. I prefer to say what I have to say as briefly and expressively as possible, then quit.

PRINCIPAL WORKS: COMPUSITIONS nos. 2 through 10, computer music on tape (1963–73); SYNTHIONS nos. 1 through 9, electronic synthesis on tape (1969–72); 2 symphonies (1942, 1947).

Percussion Music for Three Players (1935); Intermezzo, for orchestra (1937); Three Pieces, for flute and piano (1937); *Overland Trail*, for orchestra (1943); Divertimento, for four instruments (1948); Violin Sonata, also for clarinet (1949); *Three Excerpts from Walt Whitman*, for chorus (1950); Concerto Grosso (1951); Concerto, for cello and five instruments (1951); Sonata, for solo flute (1953); Variations for Four Instruments (1956); *Every Night, Every Morn*, for chorus (1960).

BIBLIOGRAPHY: *BBDM*; *DCM*; Mitchell, Alan Berman, "Gerald Strang: Composer, Educator, Acoustician" (master's thesis, Long Beach, Calif., 1977).

Stravinsky, Igor, b. Oranienbaum, Russia, June 17, 1882; d. New York City, April 6, 1971. American citizen, 1945.

For half a century, Stravinsky's giant stature dominated the world of music. He produced some of the crowning and most enduring masterworks of 20th century music. Additionally, he exerted an influence upon three generations of composers that had few parallels. Three times in his career he changed direction radically, and each time he was followed. He first came to fame (or notoriety) as a neoprimitive who released the dynamic forces of rhythm, meter, and percussion. "More than anyone else," Satie said of him at the time, "he has freed the musical thought of today." Then, in rejection of his neoprimitive style, he embraced neoclassicism. In his last phase, neoclassicism was rejected for serialism, modeled after Webern. "His example," Erich Walter White wrote, "has been a stimulus and a challenge to musicians and music lovers everywhere in the world."

On both sides of his family he came from landed gentry. He was the third of four sons of Feodor Stravinsky, one of Russia's most distinguished bass-baritones, a leading artist of the renowned Russian Imperial Opera in St. Petersburg. Feodor was descended from the Polish counts of Soulina. Stravinsky's mother, Anna Kholodovsky, was Little Russian.

Soon after Igor's birth, the family moved from Oranienbaum to an apartment in St. Petersburg. Stravinsky's childhood was unhappy, since he was in constant fear of his autocratic father, disliked his two older brothers, and had little more than a perfunctory relationship with his mother. The household servants were the only ones to give him some measure of sympathy and affection. Since Stravinsky's father did not look kindly on music as a profession for his son, Igor's early signs of musicality were ignored. As an infant in his nursery, Igor loved listening to his father rehearse his roles in a nearby study. At two, Igor sang in perfect pitch and rhythm a folk song he had just heard. He was entranced at his first visit to the Imperial Opera, when he was about eight, for a performance of Tchaikovsky's ballet *The Sleeping Beauty.* But not until he was nine did he begin to get piano lessons, first from Mlle. A. P. Snetkova and then from Mlle. L.A. Kashperova. He was also given some instruction in harmony by Feodor Akimenko.

At the gymnasium (high school) in St. Petersburg, Stravinsky was, by his own admission, a lackadaisical student, a loner who made few friends. Music was his prime interest. Once he had acquired some proficiency at the piano, he was continually improvising, making transcriptions or sight-reading the scores of Russian operas he found in his father's well-stocked library. Most of his spare time he spent backstage at the Imperial Opera, listening to rehearsals. Despite such enthusiasm, he was no prodigy, either in his piano studies or in his tentative attempts at composition.

Since his parents did not esteem his musical efforts highly, they were more determined than ever, once he graduated from the gymnasium, that he find a career elsewhere. They selected law for him. For that purpose he entered the University of St. Petersburg in 1901. "I probably did not hear more than fifty lectures in all that time," he later recalled. His time was spent mainly with music. He studied harmony with a private teacher whom he regarded as thoroughly incompetent. By himself, he learned counterpoint through a textbook and, also mostly without benefit of formal instruction, developed his pianism further.

In the summer of 1902, in Heidelberg, Germany, Stravinsky performed for Rimsky-Korsakov some of his juvenilia. Rimsky-Korsakov advised that more study in harmony and counterpoint was called for, recommending that this take place with private teachers rather than in a conservatory, and suggested he come to him intermittently for advice and guidance. "Although in my ingenuousness I was somewhat downcast over the lack of enthusiasm the master had for my efforts at composition," Stravinsky later wrote, "I found some comfort in the fact that he had nevertheless advised me to continue my studies and so demonstrated his opinion that I had sufficient ability to devote myself to a musical career. This comforted me."

While continuing to attend the university, Stravinsky took some lessons in theory from Vassili Kalafati, but most of what he learned at this time continued to come autodidactically. He broadened his musical experiences through associations with young progressive musicians both at Rimsky-Korsakov's home and through a musical society specializing in the performance of French music, where he came to know and admire the music of Dukas, Franck, and Debussy, among others. In 1903-1904, Stravinsky wrote a piano sonata, some of whose sketches he

showed to Rimsky-Korsakov. The master thought enough of them to offer to teach Stravinsky orchestration. This was the beginning of a teacher-pupil relationship lasting three years that had a far-reaching impact on Stravinsky's musical development at the time. These lessons took place twice weekly, each lasting a little more than an hour. Sometimes, at Rimsky-Korsakov's weekly musicales, Stravinsky's pieces were performed.

Now convinced that music, and not law, was to be his life work, Stravinsky left the university in 1905. On January 23, 1906, he married his cousin, Catherine Gabrielle Nossenko, his beloved childhood playmate. (They had four children, one of whom, Soulima, became a concert pianist and another, Theodore, a painter.) Stravinsky now made his home on an estate in Volhynia, owned jointly by his young wife and his sister-in-law. There, except for periodic visits to St. Petersburg, he stayed for the next few years, devoting himself to composition. By 1907 he had completed his first two opuses: op. 1, Symphony in E-flat, which echoed with the voices of Tchaikovsky and Rimsky-Korsakov; and op. 2, *La faune et la bergère,* a song cycle to poems by Pushkin for mezzo-soprano and orchestra, partly influenced by Debussy. These became Stravinsky's first works to get performed, both at a Belaiev concert in St. Petersburg on February 5, 1908. Six years later, Stravinsky revised his symphony, the new version being heard for the first time on April 2, 1914, in Montreux, Switzerland, Ernest Ansermet conducting.

Between 1907 and 1908, Stravinsky wrote two more orchestral works: *Scherzo fantastique* and *Feu d'artifice,* or *Fireworks.* The former was premiered in St. Petersburg on February 6, 1909; the latter, also in St. Petersburg, on June 17, 1908. When, almost half a century later, Stravinsky conducted a performance of the *Scherzo fantastique,* he "was surprised to find that the music did not embarrass me. The orchestra 'sounds,' the music is light in a way that is rare in the compositions of the period, and there are one or two quite good ideas in it." *Feu d'artifice,* a brilliant exercise in orchestration (with an occasional reminder of Dukas's *L'apprenti sorcier*) was written for the imminent marriage of Rimsky-Korsakov's daughter. Stravinsky despatched his manuscript to his teacher as a surprise but it never reached the master's hands—nor was he able to attend the premiere performance—because he was then fatally ill. He died four days after the concert. In his biography of Stravinsky, Alexandre Tansman regards *Feu d'artifice* as Stravinsky's first composition to reveal his future direction. "There arises a new personality which, when viewed in perspective, already seems clearly Stravinskyan. . . . The melody, the harmony and the rhythm, as well as the symphonic treatment, already indicate the characteristics of the future author of *The Rite of Spring* in their embryonic stage. The themes are incisive, abrupt. . . . A new harmony manifests itself as well as a conception towards tonal and diatonic polarization. The rhythm brings about pauses, abrupt foreshortenings, and a certain explosiveness such as had seldom been heard until then."

The concert of February 6, 1909, at which the *Scherzo fantastique* was introduced and where *Feu d'artifice* was given a fresh hearing, changed Stravinsky's destiny. In attendance was Serge Diaghilev, the supreme dilettante of the arts, who had organized an exhibition of Russian art in 1906, a season of Russian music in 1907, another of Russian opera in 1908 (with *Boris Godunov,* starring Chaliapin, introduced to France) all in Paris. By the winter of 1909, Diaghilev was on the eve of a new artistic adventure: the organization of the Ballet Russe, gathering under one umbrella Russia's foremost ballet artists. With his uncommon gift for detecting genius in the raw, Diaghilev sensed that in Stravinsky he had found a young musician able to write the music the company would need. Diaghilev had Stravinsky orchestrate two pieces by Chopin for *Les Sylphides,* which the Ballet Russe mounted in Paris on June 2, 1909, during its inaugural season. This was Stravinsky's initiation in writing for the ballet theater, an area in which he was soon to achieve both greatness and world prestige.

Stravinsky's next assignment for the Ballet Russe was an original score for *L'oiseau de feu,* or *The Fire-Bird,* in 1910. This was based on a Russian legend about Ivan Tsarevitch who, with the magic property of a feather from the Fire-Bird and with the help of the Fire-Bird itself, destroys the dreaded Kashchei and his castle and frees the captive maidens. With choreography by Michel Fokine, settings by Bakst and Golovin, and with Fokine, Mme. Fokina and Karsavina as principal dancers, *L'oiseau de feu* was first performed on June 25, 1910, in Paris, becoming the most resounding success of that Ballet Russe season. In this score, Stravinsky was a composer still derivative of Rimsky-Korsakov (*Le coq d'or* particularly), but the borrowed language had now become transmuted into something so new and revolutionary that it marked the dawn of a new musical era. The unusual sonoric effects (such as the harmonic glissandi in the Introduction), the discordant harmonies, the ever-changing rhythms and meters, the demoniac frenzy of "The Dance of the Kashchei" all sounded a new voice in 20th-century modernism. After a final curtain, Debussy rushed backstage to embrace Stravinsky, almost as if to hail a successor. "Mark him well," Diaghilev said of Stravinsky prophetically. "He is a man on the eve of celebrity." From this ballet score, Stravinsky extracted three orchestral suites (1911, 1919, 1946), the second of which has become a staple in the orchestral repertoire.

The tie that bound him to his teacher, Rimsky-Korsakov, was broken with Stravinsky's next ballet score, *Petrouchka* (1911)—but not yet his tie to his motherland. This new score retained its Russian identity in the carryovers from Russian folk music, some of which is quoted. The subject of the ballet is also Russian, since Petrouchka is a puppet in a Russian carnival who falls in love with the carnival ballerina and is killed by his rival, a Moor. In his vividly pictorial and at times sardonic score, Stravinsky's discords have become increasingly explosive; polytonality was introduced (F-sharp-major arpeggio combined with a C-major arpeggio to form the "Petrouchka chord"); the longer lyric line of some of the pages of *L'oiseau de feu* was replaced by motives strung together loosely; fresh orchestral sonorities were produced (such as the accordion sound of the opening section) and new colors superimposed by the piano, xylophone, high piccolo, and celesta. This was the "music of the future" that inspired the futurist Marinetti to parade the streets of Rome with a banner reading: "Down with Wagner! Long Live Stravinsky!"

Petrouchka—choreography by Michel Fokine and with Karsavina and Nijinsky as principal dancers—was another giant success for the Ballet Russe when introduced in Paris on June 13, 1911. The orchestral suite derived from the ballet score was to become one of Stravinsky's best-loved and most frequently performed compositions. "*Petrouchka,*" wrote Guido Pannain in *Modern Music,* "fell like a meteor upon the comfortable Strauss-dominated musical world of the pre-war twentieth century. The triumphant, crystal-clear technique [Stravinsky] displayed in this ballet was like a flash of light in a murky wilderness. The harmonies and rhythms of the dance music created a dramatic atmosphere which fermented, which quivered with suppressed energy."

Stravinsky's neoprimitive style achieved its apotheosis with *Le sacre du printemps,* or *The Rite of Spring* (1913), subtitled "Scenes from Ancient Russia." This ballet came about through a "vision" Stravinsky had in which he saw a girl dancing herself to death in a sacrificial pagan rite. With the collaboration of Nicholas Roerich, Stravinsky worked out a ballet scenario describing barbaric dances and primitive rituals in pagan Russia climaxed by the sacrifice in which a female performs a corybantic dance, whirling to her death. Excruciating tensions were realized by the continuous repetition of brief diatonic themes set against discordant harmonies; by the displaced accents, the complex polymeters and polyrhythms; the unleashing of orchestral timbres, with an importance given to percussion it had never known before this. This was "music of the Fauve," a term applied to Stravinsky's neoprimitivism after the canvases of wild beasts so popular in Paris at the time.

The world premiere of *Le sacre du printemps* on May 29, 1913 (choreography by Nijinsky), inspired one of the greatest scandals in the history of musical performances. A few minutes after the ballet started, the theater became charged with electric excitation, and sparks of dissension slowly developed into a conflagration. "A certain part of the audience," wrote Carl van Vechten in *Music After the Great War,* "was thrilled by what it considered to be a blasphemous attempt to destroy music as an art and, swept away with wrath, began, very soon after the rise of the curtain, to make cat-calls and to offer audible suggestions as to how the performance should proceed. The orchestra played unheard except occasionally when a slight lull occurred. The young man seated behind me in a box stood up during the course of the ballet to enable him to see more clearly. The intense excitement under which he was laboring betrayed itself when he began to beat rhythmically on the top of my head with his fists. My emotion was so great that I did not feel the blows for some time." In the ensuing pandemonium—the exchange of shouts, insults, spitting, fisticuffs—little of the music was heard. In later performances, with the shock of its newness somewhat worn off, *Le sacre du printemps* could take its rightful place among the classics in the modern ballet repertoire. Away from the theater, it became a monument in 20th-century symphonic music, the orchestral score of which was heard for the first time in a concert hall on April 5, 1914, in Paris, conducted by Pierre Monteux, the same man who had directed the world premiere of the ballet. "*Le sacre,*" wrote Cecil Gray, the English musicologist, "is one of the most conspicuous landmarks in the artistic life of our period." The fiftieth anniversary of the premiere of *Le sacre* was celebrated in Paris on May 29, 1963, with Pierre Monteux conducting the concert suite, inspiring a fifteen-minute ovation.

Still in the neoprimitive style were *Le rossignol,* or *The Nightingale,* and *Les noces,* or *The Wedding.* The former, based on a fairy tale by Hans Christian Andersen, has three different versions: first as an opera inspired by Rimsky-Korsakov's *Le coq d'or* (1914; Paris, May 26, 1914); then as a concert work for orchestra (Geneva, Switzerland, December 6, 1919); and finally as a ballet in the repertoire of the Ballet Russe (Paris, February 2, 1920). *Les noces* (1917) is a cantata with dancers—text by Stravinsky derived from poems by Kirievski. With Bronislava Nijinska's choreography, it was premiered by the Ballet Russe in Paris on June 13, 1923. Described as "Russian choreographic scenes," this work consisted of four tableaux descriptive of a Russian wedding ritual. The score called for solo voices, chorus, four pianos, and seventeen percussion instruments (the singers placed in the orchestra pit). "The ballet," wrote H. G. Wells in response to the unfavorable reception *Les noces* received in London in 1920, "is a rendering in sound and vision of the peasant soul, in its gravity, in its deliberate and simple-minded intricacy, in its subtly varied rhythms, in its deep undercurrent of excitement."

World War I compelled Stravinsky to redesign his formerly ambitious structures along more economical and practical lines. Many opera and ballet companies had suspended operations. Ambitious operas and ballets calling for a large company and orchestra had no chance of getting produced. This state of affairs persisted in the first postwar years in a war-ravaged, poverty-stricken Europe. Stravinsky consequently came to realize that if he was to be heard at all it could only be with works making the most limited demands on production facilities. And so, in 1918, he completed an intimate ballet requiring only three dancers, a narrator, and seven accompanying instruments. He called it *L' histoire du soldat,* or *The Soldier's Tale* ("a narrative ballet in five scenes to be read, played and danced") with text by C. F. Ramuz and choreography by Ludmilla Pitoev. Its first production took place on September 28, 1918, in Lausanne, Switzerland. This was a heterogeneous score including a march, tango, waltz, chorale, and—innovative for that time—ragtime. In fact, the seven instruments Stravinsky used, and the way he wrote for the clarinet, cornet, trombone, and piano, recalled the Dixieland jazzband of 1916. Stylistically, *L' histoire du soldat* was a move from complexity to comparative simplicity; from subjectivity to objectivity; from neoprimitivism to classical procedures. Stravinsky made this move again with *Pulcinella,* a ballet with song (1919; Paris, May 15, 1920) in which his own music was an adaptation of what was said to be recently rediscovered melodies by the early-18th-century Italian composer Pergolesi, though some authorities regard this supposed Pergolesi material to be spurious.

Between 1914 and 1920, Stravinsky lived in Switzerland. In 1920 he established permanent residence in France, initially on the outskirts of Paris, later within the city. France remained his homeland for the next two decades; in 1934 he became a French citizen.

Having thus left his native country, seemingly for good, Stravinsky also freed himself artistically from Russian influences. After *Mavra*—a one-act opera buffa with text by Boris Kochno based on Pushkin's "The Little House of Kolomna" (1922; Paris, May 18, 1922), he lost all interest in Russian subjects and Russian folk music as sources for his compositions, preferring to work along more cosmopolitan lines within classic structures. In his music he replaced the dynamic forces of his former neoprimitivism with precision, economy, transparency, and symmetry in which contrapuntal procedures took precedence over rhythm and which became absolute in its strict avoidance of the pictorial or the programmatic.

This total break with his own artistic past in favor of neoclassicism was foreshadowed in *Symphonies of Wind Instruments* (1920; London, June 19, 1921), written in memory of Debussy. The word "Symphonies" in the title connotes the sounding together or the harmony of sounds rather than a classical symphonic structure. Here, the color possibilities of various wind instruments treated in groups were exploited.

With Stravinsky, neoclassicism came into full maturity with the Octet, for winds (two each of bassoons, trombones, and trumpets, and one flute and clarinet), which he completed in 1923 and which was introduced at a Concerts Koussevitzky on October 18, 1923, the composer conducting (the first time Stravinsky introduced his own works). "The Octet," the composer explained, "is a musical object. This object has a form that is influenced by the musical matter with which it is composed. . . . My Octet is not an 'emotive' work but a musical composition based on objective elements which are sufficient in themselves. The aim I sought . . . is to realize a musical composition through means that are emotive in themselves. These emotive means are manifested in the rendition by the heterogeneous play of movements and volume. . . . This sort of music has no other aim than to be sufficient in itself." Thus Stravinsky pronounced his neoclassic credo. To those long accustomed to, and now adherents of, his neo-primitive music, the Octet came as a shock almost as volcanic as the one *Le sacre* had produced. These Stravinsky admirers were now confronted with what Aaron Copland described as "a new universalistic ideal for music, based on classical forms and contrapuntal textures, borrowing his melodic material eclectically from all periods, yet fusing the whole by the indubitable power of his personality. . . . With the writing of the Octet, he completely abandoned realism and primitivism of all kinds and espoused the cause of objectivism in music."

Stravinsky remained faithful to neoclassicism for a quarter of a century. In this idiom he produced masterworks with which his imperial station in 20th-century music remained unchallenged. The best of these works are: Concerto for Piano and Wind Instruments, a recreation of the baroque concerto grosso structure and style but with the unusual instrumentation of winds supplemented by double basses and timpani (1924; Paris, May 22, 1924); *Oedipus Rex,* an opera-oratorio that could be presented in concert version or staged (1927; Paris May 30, 1927), text by Jean Cocteau translated into Latin based on Sophocles, the score calling for a narrator in 20th-century attire appearing at intermittent periods to explain the action; *Apollon Musagète* (1927–28; Washington, D. C., April 27, 1928), a classic ballet with scenario by Stravinsky and Adolph Bolm, which Elizabeth Sprague Coolidge had commissioned for a modern music festival at the Library of Congress; the ironic *Capriccio,* for piano and orchestra (1929; Paris, December 6, 1929); *Symphonie des psaumes,* or *Symphony of Psalms,* for chorus and orchestra (1930), written for the fiftieth anniversary of the Boston Symphony but introduced in Brussels on December 13, 1930, Ernest Ansermet conducting, one week before Koussevitzky directed it in Boston; the Violin Concerto in D major (1931; Berlin, October 23, 1931), written for and introduced by Samuel Dushkin; *Perséphone,* a melodrama with text by André Gide (1934), commissioned by the dancer Ida

Rubinstein, who premiered it in Paris on April 30, 1934; *Jeu de cartes,* or *Card Game,* a ballet in "three deals" (1936; N.Y., April 27, 1937), scenario by Stravinsky and M. Malaieff and choreography by George Balanchine; Symphony in C major (1940; Chicago, November 7, 1940), Stravinsky's first such work in thirty-five years, written on commission to commemorate the fiftieth anniversary of the Chicago Symphony; Symphony in Three Movements (1945; N.Y., January 24, 1946), a work independent of formal symphonic structure but conceived as Ingold Dahl explains, "as the succession of clearly outlined locks, or planes, which are unified and related through the continuity of a steadily and logically evolving organic force"; Mass, for men's chorus, boys' chorus, and ten wind instruments (1948; Milan, Italy, October 27, 1948), the composer's first liturgical composition, which stylistically looked back upon the early contrapuntal Flemish school; the ballet *Orpheus* (1948; N.Y., April 28, 1948), choreography by George Balanchine, scenario following closely the Greek classic tale of Orpheus and Euridice; and the opera, *The Rake's Progress.*

The Rake's Progress was Stravinsky's last neoclassic masterpiece, and his most important work for the operatic stage. Inspired by lithographs of the same title by Hogarth and using a libretto by W. H. Auden and Chester Kallman, Stravinsky completed this opera in 1951, its world premiere, an event of international importance, taking place at the Festival in Venice, Italy, on September 11, 1951. Structurally, Stravinsky reverted to the classic operas of Handel, Gluck, and most particularly Mozart, using the classic operatic patterns of arias, recitatives, ensemble numbers, choruses, and extended finales. A chamber orchestra eliminated trombones, but included a harpsichord for the accompaniment of the recitatives. But for all its 18th-century leanings, it remained a voice of the 20th century in Stravinsky's discordant harmonies, elastic rhythms, complex in their mutations of duple and triple meters, and astringent lyricism. In portraying the degeneration and regeneration of a rake, Stravinsky's music covered a wide gamut of emotion ranging from wit and farce to passion and tragedy. In *Music and Letters,* Colin Mason called it "the greatest and most important neo-classic work that has as yet been produced." Nicolas Nabokov, writing in the *New York Herald Tribune,* described it as "an unquestioned masterpiece whose Mozartian dimensions and transparent beauty have not been matched by any other work for the lyric theater in the last half century." The American premiere of *The Rake's Progress* took place at the Metropolitan Opera on February 14, 1953.

Stravinsky made his American debut by appearing as guest conductor of the New York Philharmonic on January 8, 1925, the start of his first extended American tour. He returned for other American tours during the next decade and a half. Then, with the outbreak of World War II, he came to the United States in September 1939 to serve as the Charles Eliot Norton lecturer on the poetics of music at Harvard University (1939–40). With the death of his wife, Catherine, in 1939, Stravinsky married Vera de Bossett Sudekine, a dancer, on March 9, 1940, in Bedford, Mass. They made their home in Beverly Hills, Calif. There, in 1948, they were joined by Robert Craft, a brilliant musician and journalist, who became Stravinsky's right hand, assumed many of the obligations and responsibilities that fell to the daily life of a world-famous personality, assisted Stravinsky at rehearsals, concerts, and readings, and faithfully recorded Stravinsky's conversations in six volumes. These were: *Conversations with Igor Stravinsky* (1958), *Memories and Commentaries* (1959), *Expositions and Developments* (1962), *Themes and Episodes* (1967), *Retrospections and Conclusions* (1969), and *Themes and Conclusions* (1972), the last of these gathering material from two earlier volumes.

After World War II, Stravinsky made frequent guest appearances as conductor of his own works throughout the United States and Europe. One of these, in 1962, brought him for the first time to Israel and to his Russian homeland after an absence of almost half a century. He conducted his first concert in Moscow on September 26, 1962, before making other appearances in the Soviet Union. Though during his expatriation the Soviet Union had denounced him and his music, his return was that of a conquering hero, a source of infinite delight to the Russian people and to Stravinsky himself. "I am certain," wrote Robert Craft in his diary, "that to be recognized and acclaimed as a Russian in Russia, and to be performed there, has meant more to him than anything else in the years I have known him."

Stravinsky remained abundantly productive in the United States, initially with a long string of neoclassic compositions that have already been enumerated earlier. In old age, he abandoned neoclassicism for dodecaphony. Initially, he worked only tentatively with the twelve-tone system in *Cantata on Four Poems by Anonymous English Poets,* for soprano, tenor, female chorus, and instrumental quintet (1952; Los Angeles, November 11, 1952) and in Septet, for piano and string and wind instruments (1953; Washington, D. C., January 23, 1964). *Canticum Sacrum ad Honorem Sancti Marci Nominis,* for tenor, baritone, chorus and orchestra—a sacred cantata written in 1955 on commission from the Venice Festival and first heard there on September 13, 1956, at St. Mark's Basilica, the composer conducting—was Stravinsky's first composition in which parts were in a strict serial technique (the three middle sections). In *Threni,* "Lamentations of the Prophet Jeremiah," for solo voices, chorus, and orchestra (1958; Venice, September 23, 1958), Stravinsky once again used serialism in just three of five sections. His last compositions were predominantly serial. *A Sermon, a Narrative and a Prayer,* for contralto, narrator, and chorus (1961), was commissioned by Paul Sacher and

the Basle Chamber Orchestra, who introduced it on February 23, 1962. The composer described this work as a "meditation of the New Testament virtue of hope" and as a "personal expression of faith." The first part was based on St. Paul's sermon on the nature of hope; the second was an account in Acts of Stephen's martyrdom, pointing up the virtue of action; and the third was a setting of Thomas Dekker's "Foure Birds of Noah's Ark." In the *New York Times,* Peter Heyworth called this composition "one of the most impressive examples of twentieth-century religious art." *Abraham and Isaac* (1963; Jerusalem, August 23, 1964) was a sacred ballad for baritone and chamber orchestra with a Hebrew text written on commission from Israel for its fourth annual music festival in Jerusalem. Variations for Orchestra was written in 1964 in memory of Aldous Huxley and was introduced by the Chicago Symphony under Jean Martinon on April 17, 1965, when it was performed twice in a single evening (at the composer's request). Stravinsky's last work, *Requiem Canticles,* for vocal quartet, chorus, and orchestra (1966; Princeton, N.J., October 8, 1966) was written on commission from Princeton University, where it was introduced under Robert Craft's direction. Three of its movements were instrumental, while the other five were settings for chorus and orchestra of texts from the Latin Requiem.

A victim of poor health, after 1967 Stravinsky was able only to attempt to orchestrate two preludes and fugues from Bach's *Well-Tempered Clavier.* In 1969, embittered that Los Angeles did not pay him and his music the homage he felt he deserved, he found a new home in New York, first in a hotel, then in a spacious apartment overlooking Central Park. He occupied that apartment only one week before dying of a heart attack. As he had requested, he was buried on the island of San Michele off Venice; during the burial services, his *Requiem Canticles* was performed.

However much he may have felt toward the end of his life that Los Angeles had neglected him, he could have no complaint about the way the world had continually honored him through the years. Among the more prestigious awards he was given were the Busoni Prize (1950), the gold medal of the National Institute of Arts and Letters (1951), the gold medal of the Royal Philharmonic Society of London (1954), the Sibelius Gold Medal, given only once every five years (1955), the Sonning Foundation International Prize (1959), the Sibelius Prize of $27,000 by the Finnish Fund for Arts and Sciences (1963), and the Canada Council Medal (1967).

His eightieth birthday, in 1962, inspired Stravinsky festivals through the Western world. On that occasion he was invited by President and Mrs. John F. Kennedy to dine at the White House and to receive a gold medal from the secretary of state, Dean Rusk, at ceremonies held at the State Department. Almost four years later, between June 30 and July 23, 1966, the New York Philharmonic presented a ten-concert Stravinsky festival at the Lincoln Center for the Performing Arts and at about the same time Columbia Records announced it had embarked on a project to record, under Stravinsky's personal supervision, everything the composer had written. Following Stravinsky's death, the New York City Ballet offered, in New York, a Stravinsky festival between June 18 and 25, 1972, in which thirty-two ballet productions were mounted, twenty-one of them premieres, all to Stravinsky's music. A two-month Stravinsky festival of eleven concerts covering all of his orchestral, chamber music, and solo works was held in Paris in the fall of 1979.

THE COMPOSER SPEAKS: The public cannot and will not follow me in the progress of my musical thought. What moves and delights me leaves them indifferent and what still continues to interest them holds no further attraction for me. For that matter, I believe that there was seldom any real communion of spirit between us. If it happened—and it still happens—that we liked the same thing, I very much doubt whether it was for the same reasons. . . . Their attitude certainly cannot make me deviate from my path. I shall most assuredly not sacrifice my predilections and my aspirations to the demands of those who, in their blindness, do not realize that they are simply asking me to go backwards. It should be obvious that what they wish for has become obsolete for me, and that I could not follow them without doing violence to myself. But, on the other hand, it would be a great mistake to regard me as an adherent of *Zukunftsmusik*—the music of the future. Nothing could be more ridiculous. I live neither in the past nor in the future. I am in the present. I cannot know what tomorrow will bring forth. I can only know what the truth is for me today. That is what I am called upon to serve and I will serve it in all humility.

PRINCIPAL WORKS: 3 symphonies (1905–7, 1940, 1945).

Scherzo fantastique, for orchestra (1908); *Feu d'artifice,* for orchestra (1908); *L'oiseau de feu,* ballet, also three suites for orchestra (1910); *Petrouchka,* ballet, also orchestral suite (1911; revised 1946–47); *Le sacre du printemps,* ballet, also orchestral suite (1913); *Le rossignol,* opera, orchestral suite and ballet (1914; revised 1962); *Renard,* a burlesque chamber opera (1915); *Les noces,* cantata-ballet (1917); *L'histoire du soldat,* opera-ballet (1917); *Pulcinella,* ballet and orchestral suite (1920); *Symphonies of Wind Instruments* (1920); *Mavra,* one-act opera buffa (1921); Octet, for wind instruments (1923, revised 1952); Concerto for Piano and Wind Instruments (1924); Piano Sonata (1924); *Oedipus Rex,* opera-oratorio (1927); *Apollon Musagète,* ballet (1927–28); *Le baiser de la fée,* ballet (1928); Capriccio, for piano and orchestra (1929); *Symphonie des psaumes,* for chorus and orchestra (1930); Violin

Concerto in D major (1931); *Duo concertante,* for violin and piano (1932); *Suite italienne,* for cello and piano (1933); *Perséphone,* melodrama for narrator, tenor chorus, children's chorus, and orchestra (1934); Concerto for two solo pianos (1935); *Jeu de cartes,* ballet (1937); *Dumbarton Oaks,* concerto for sixteen instruments (1938); *Danses concertantes,* for orchestra (1942); *Norwegian Moods,* for orchestra (1942); *Ode,* for orchestra (1943); *Scènes de ballet,* for orchestra (1944); Sonata, for two pianos (1944); *Ebony Concerto,* for clarinet and orchestra (1946); Concerto in D major, for strings (1946); *Orpheus,* ballet (1947); Mass, for men's voices, boys' voices, and ten instruments (1948); *The Rake's Progress,* opera (1951); *Cantata on Poems by Anonymous English Poets* (1952); Septet, for piano, string and wind instruments (1952); *Three Songs from William Shakespeare,* for mezzo-soprano and instruments (1953); *In Memoriam Dylan Thomas,* for tenor, two tenor trombones, two bass trombones, and string quartet (1954); *Canticum Sacrum ad Honorem Sancti Marci Nominis,* for tenor, baritone, chorus, and orchestra (1955); *Agon,* ballet (1957); *Threni,* Lamentations of Jeremiah, for vocal soloists, chorus, and orchestra (1957); Movements, for piano and orchestra (1959); *Epitaphium,* for flute, clarinet, and harp (1959); *Monumentum Pro Gesualdo,* for instruments (1960); *Noah and the Flood,* biblical spectacle (1962); *Abraham and Isaac,* for baritone and orchestra (1962); Variations, for orchestra (1964); *Elegy for J. F. K.,* for baritone or mezzo-soprano, and three clarinets (1964); *Requiem Canticles,* for contralto, bass, chorus, and orchestra (1966).

BIBLIOGRAPHY: Craft, Robert, *Chronicles of a Friendship* (N.Y., 1972); Dobrin, Arnold, *Igor Stravinsky: His Life and Times* (London, 1970); Horgan, Paul, *Encounters with Stravinsky* (N.Y., 1972); Lang, Paul Henry (ed.), *Stravinsky: The Composer and His Works* (London, 1966); Libman, Lillian, *And Music at the Close: Stravinsky's Last Years* (N.Y., 1972); Routh, Francis, *Stravinsky* (London, 1977); Stravinsky, Th., *Catherine and Igor Stravinsky: A Family Album* (N.Y., 1974); Stravinsky, Vera, and Craft, Robert, *Stravinsky* (N.Y., 1975); Stravinsky, Vera, and Craft, Robert (eds.), *Stravinsky: In Pictures and Documents* (N.Y., 1978); Tansman, Alexandre, *Stravinsky* (N.Y., 1959); White, Eric Walter, *Stravinsky, The Composer and His Works,* revised ed. (Berkeley, 1980).

Musical Quarterly, Stravinsky issue, July 1962; *Saturday Review,* May 29, 1971; *Tempo* (London), Stravinsky issue, summer 1967.

Stringham, Edwin John, b. Kenosha, Wis., July 11, 1890; d. Chapel Hill, N. C., July 1, 1974.

In earlier compositions, Stringham experimented with dissonant harmonic and contrapuntal idioms.

His later, and successful, works were consonant, sometimes spiced with jazz condiments, and favoring rhythmic counterpoint combining three or four patterns, and masses of orchestral color and sound.

During his boyhood, he revealed a talent for both music and science. When he was sixteen, he invented a wireless set, an accomplishment publicized by the Associated Press, encouraging scientists to visit him, and bringing him an invitation from the University of Wisconsin to use its laboratories. Music study began early in boyhood with lessons on the violin, on which he made notable progress. Upon completing his preliminary schooling in Kenosha, he earned a scholarship to the School of Music of Northwestern University in Evanston, Ill., where he received a bachelor of music degree in 1914. That year he completed *Three Panels*, for piano, which he orchestrated in 1915, when it was performed by the American Symphony Orchestra; revised in 1924, it was performed in Rochester, N.Y., on May 17, 1928. His later study of composition took place with E. Stillman Kelley at the Cincinnati Conservatory, where he was given a doctorate in pedagogy in 1922.

Between 1914 and 1916, Stringham taught violin at North Shore School of Music in Chicago, and in 1914–15 he was director of the Grand Forks School of Music in Grand Forks, S.D. On August 26, 1916, he married Alta Morrill Potts, with whom he had a son, Edward MacDowell Stringham, named after the eminent American composer.

A breakdown in his health compelled Stringham to leave the north and live in New Mexico from 1916 to 1919 for rehabilitation. In 1919, he established residence in Denver, Colo. There, he organized, in 1920, the Denver College of Music, serving as its dean for the next nine years. From 1919 to 1929 he was the music critic of the *Denver News* and *Denver Post*, and from 1922 to 1929, chairman of the music board of the Colorado State Board of Education. His orchestral compositions of this period emphasized a "modern" idiom, the most important of which were *Visions*, an orchestral tone poem (1924) whose premiere was given by the Denver Symphony Orchestra in 1926, and *The Ancient Mariner* (1927), inspired by Coleridge's poem, which was introduced by the Denver Symphony on March 16, 1928.

On a scholarship, Stringham came to Rome in 1929 to attend the Royal Academy of Music, studying composition with Ottorino Respighi. In Italy, Stringham completed his Symphony no. 1 in B-flat minor, titled *Italian*, a programmatic work in neoromantic style. The Minneapolis Symphony under Henri Verbrugghen premiered it on November 15, 1929, at which time *Musical America* referred to it as "a most appealing work."

Recollections of Italy were the inspiration of Nocturne no. 1, for orchestra (1931), first performance taking place in Rochester, N.Y., on December 9, 1937, Howard Hanson conducting. This was a programmatic composition whose warp and woof were constructed or generated out of a single theme. "I have tried," the composer explained, "to express the passing moods of the early evening at dusk. . . . I was reliving my visits to the Pincio, overlooking the city of Rome, towards the direction of St. Peter's, experiencing again the feelings that the scene aroused in me by the view and life of the city before me and in the park about me. It is at sunset, or a little after, and the sacred, profane, and sentimental expressions of life intermingle, pass in parade, and eventually fade into the falling darkness and only nostalgia remains." Nocturne became Stringham's first success, receiving performances from several major American orchestras, including the New York Philharmonic on January 20, 1935.

Stringham wrote two other excellent Nocturnes after that. The second (1935) was for woodwinds, horns, and harp. A third (1939) was again for orchestra. Where the first orchestral Nocturne had been programmatic and pictorial, the second for orchestra was introspective—a dreamlike mood picture at nighttime. "It is interesting to note," the composer explained, "that the generating theme, out of which the entire Nocturne is built, does not appear until just before the climax which leads to a restatement of the opening section." The second orchestral Nocturne was introduced in 1939 by the Chicago Symphony.

In 1930, Stringham and his family settled in New York City. While engaged as professor of composition at the School of Sacred Music at the Union Theological Seminary (1932–38) he was on the music faculty of Teachers College at Columbia University (1930–38) and the Juilliard School of Music (1930–45). At the same time, he was the music editor of the Carl Fischer Publishing Company (1930–31) and of the American Book Company (1932–39), and was a member of the board of directors (as well as editor) of Music Press, Inc. (1939–46). During the summer of 1936 he received the Cromwell Traveling Fellowship for a visit to Germany. In 1938 he was called upon to found the music department at Queens College in Queens, N.Y., where he served as chairman of the music department until 1946 and as full professor between 1944 and 1946. In 1941 he organized the first music festival featuring the music departments of the four city colleges in New York. He received a year's leave-of-absence from Queens College in July 1945 to become divisional head of the U.S. Army University at Biarritz, France. After leaving Queens College in 1946, he was visiting professor at the University of California in Los Angeles in 1946–47, and the University of Texas in 1947–48. In 1948, Stringham went into retirement in Chapel Hill, N.C., where he lived up to the time of his death.

One of Stringham's major works in the 1940s was the *Fantasy on an American Folk Tune*, for violin and orchestra (1941), which was commissioned by Fabien Sevitzky and the Indianapolis Symphony, the world premiere taking place in Indianapolis in 1943.

The entire composition was based on the Negro spiritual "Nobody Knows De Trouble I've Seen," though this melody is not heard until the very end. The work abounds in the popular American rhythms of ragtime, the Charleston and the drag.

Stringham was awarded an honorary doctorate in music from the Denver College of Music in 1928. He was the author of *Listening to Music Creatively* (1943); coauthor, with Carl and Betty Carmer, of *America Sings* (1943); and with H. A. Murphy of *Creative Harmony and Musicianship* (1951).

PRINCIPAL WORKS: 2 nocturnes, for orchestra (1932, 1939).

Visions, tone poem for orchestra (1924); *The Ancient Mariner*, for orchestra (1927); *Springtime*, overture for orchestra (1927); *Danses exotiques*, for orchestra (1938); Symphony no. 1, *Italian* (1929); *Pilgrim Fathers*, for a cappella chorus (1931); *Dream Song*, for soprano, two altos, and piano (1933); String Quartet in F minor (1935); Nocturne, for woodwinds, horns, and harp (1935); *Ave Maria*, for a cappella chorus (1937); *Fantasy on an American Folk Tune*, for violin and orchestra (1942); *Longing*, for women's voices (1944); *Tears*, for chorus (1946); *Childe Roland*, symphonic narrative (1947).

BIBLIOGRAPHY: Ewen, David, *American Composers Today* (N.Y., 1949); Howard, John Tasker, *Our American Music* (N.Y., 1946); Reis, Claire, *Composers in America* (N.Y., 1947); *Who's Who in America, 1974–75*.

Subotnick, Morton, b. Los Angeles, Calif., April 14, 1933.

With some exceptions, when he favored post-Webern serialism Subotnick has devoted himself primarily to electronic music, to multimedia productions requiring electronic processes, and to compositions he calls "ghost pieces" recruiting magnetic tape.

His first musical experiences came from hearing his father play the mandolin, impressions that proved so durable that the mandolin, or simulated mandolin sounds, can be found in some of his adult compositions. His first lessons in music were on piano from his mother, but in time he concentrated on clarinet, which he studied with Franklin Stokes (1947–51). Composition began when he was eleven, while attending Canfield Elementary School in Los Angeles (1940–45). But in composition and theory he was initially self-taught through the study of masterpieces of music and copying them down note by note. As a student at North Hollywood High School (1949–51) he first became interested in avant-garde music by learning the twelve-tone technique from the school's harmony teacher, Joel Harry. When Subotnick graduated from high school, he wrote the music

for a graduation stage production in which the influence of Charles Ives (whom he had now come to admire) was omnipresent in the use of multiple rhythms, fragmented themes, polytonality, and unresolved discords.

After a year at the University of Southern California in Los Angeles in 1951, where he studied composition with Leon Kirchner, Subotnick played clarinet with the Denver Symphony Orchestra. A three-year period of military service followed (1953–56). While in the service, stationed at the Presidio in San Francisco, he traveled, weekends, to Los Angeles to study clarinet with Mitchell Lurie (1953–54) and to continue to study composition with Kirchner.

Discharged from the army in 1956, Subotnick returned to Denver, where he attended its university, completing the requirements for a bachelor of arts degree in 1956, majoring in literature. He then was back in San Francisco. At Mills College in Oakland, he continued to study composition with both Kirchner and Darius Milhaud, earning a master of arts degree in 1959. During this time he played clarinet with the San Francisco Symphony on a substitute basis.

Between 1959 and 1965, Subotnick was involved in the musical avant-garde movement in San Francisco, particularly as founder and from 1959 to 1965, as director of the San Francisco Tape Music Center. He was instructor of music at Mills College (1959–62) where he was cofounder of the Mills College Performing Group for the presentation of new music by young composers, and from 1961 to 1967 he was the musical director of the Ann Halperin Dance Company.

His first adult compositions date from 1959: two serenades for various instruments, strongly influenced by post-Webern serialism. The second serenade, for clarinet, horn, piano, and a percussionist who played the insides of the piano, was heard at the Venice Biennale in Italy on April 16, 1963.

After 1960, Subotnick abandoned serialism to experiment with electronic music and with new kinds of musical performances enlisting the collaboration of films, game plays, abstract theater, light shows, and rituals. Since he considered the way concerts were being given in auditoriums obsolete, he sought to effect an intimate relationship among composer, performer, and audience through the introduction of game elements and occasionally through forms of audience participation. With these ideas in mind, he completed four works collectively entitled *Play!* between 1964 and 1966 which combined the sounds of traditional instruments with those produced on magnetic tape, and used them for pantomimes, films, and various rituals. *Play!* 4 (1966) was a multimedia production calling for theater, films, light shows, games, and chance processes, which was performed both in Seattle, Wash., and in New York City in 1966.

In 1967, Subotnick transferred his activities to New York. For one season he was the musical director of the Repertory Theater at the Lincoln Center for the Performing Arts. He then filled the post of master artist at the School of the Arts at New York University (1966–69) and director of electronic music at the Electric Circus Discothèque in Greenwich Village (1967–69). In 1967 he became the first composer to write an electronic composition exclusively for a recording. This work was *Silver Apples of the Moon*, for magnetic tape, which Nonesuch Records commissioned and which has since become a classic of electronic music; it subsequently served as a musical background for ballets produced by such companies as the Netherlands Ballet and the Ballet Rambert of London. Commenting on *Silver Apples* in the *Sunday Oregonian*, Robert Lindstrom wrote: "Subotnick's music constantly has a thread of continuity which helps the listener follow the line of the musical thought. . . . In *Silver Apples*, the device is rather simple. A melody, which is more than slightly oriental, progresses in a more or less stream-of-consciousness manner while punctuated with a variety of electronic beeps, clicks and cork-pops. The continuity of the 'flute' melody aids the listener in understanding the more random, less accessible, aspects of the music."

Subotnick followed *Silver Apples* with several other electronic compositions written directly for recordings: *The Wild Bull* (1967), *Touch* (1969), *Sidewinder* (1970), *Four Butterflies* (1971–71), and *Until Spring* (1974). All were distinguished not only by unusual sonorities and sound effects produced on the modular synthesizer Donald Buchler had designed for Subotnick in San Francisco but also by dramatic contrasts between deep silences and Gargantuan climaxes, and between powerful windswept passages and lyrical thrusts.

Four Butterflies was Subotnick's first work to use butterflies (with the three stages of larva-cocoon-butterfly) as a basic aesthetic and philosophic metaphor for a series of compositions. He explains his "butterfly" theory in the following way: "The butterfly is viewed as: 1. a symmetrical form—WING-BODY-WING; 2. a metaphoric process—larva, pupa, and imago (butterfly)—the identified image of the larva. The symmetrical view provides all the external and internal 'shaping' qualities. The metaphoric view essentially says that at all levels the three-part form (wing-body-wing) will progress in such a way that the first wing will be larva-like, the body will be pupa-like (transformations will be taking place but hidden from the viewer), and the final wing will be the Butterfly or imago—the idealized self-image of the original material."

This butterfly metaphor was used in two of Subotnick's significant works for orchestra. *Two Butterflies*, for amplified orchestra (1974), written on a grant from the National Endowment for the Arts, was introduced by the Los Angeles Philharmonic under Zubin Mehta on April 7, 1975. This work, the composer explains, is divided into two sections (or "butterflies"). The first is made up of WING A–BODY ("noise" transformed) and WING B. The second section (or butterfly) consists of WING A (identical performance but transformed by the addition of ten violins with contact microphones)—BODY ("music" transformed)—WING B (again an identical performance transformed by the addition of the violins). The orchestra is split into several groups of instruments, some amplified, some modifying the amplified sound by altering up or down in pitch from a sixteenth of a tone into a minor third. "For those who like to ponder the merits of intellectualism over emotionalism (or vice versa), this was, indeed, a provocative occasion," wrote Melody Peterson in *High Fidelity/Musical America*. "One admired the adroit ordering and coloristic display of amplified and timbrally modified instruments, of violas and cellos tuned at quarter tone variance from one another, of claps and whispers, delicate trilling, bow tapping, keyclicking and the like."

Before the Butterfly (1974–75) was one of six works commissioned by the National Endowment for the Arts from six leading American composers to commemorate the American bicentennial, each work performed by six of America's leading orchestras. It received its world premiere in Los Angeles on February 26, 1976, Zubin Mehta conducting the Los Angeles Philharmonic. In this work, the composer sought to present "the idea of emergence, or more precisely, the moment before emergence—the moment before transformation—the moment before breaking free—before change—*Before the Butterfly*," as the composer said. Each of the three sections, he goes on to explain, "makes its own move 'to become' and each draws from the preceding movement the most emergent qualities as its basis or starting point." Coloristic effects and timbres are enhanced not only through electrification but also through such devices as glittering fast glissandi on the violins ending with the performers tapping their instruments with their bows, popping sounds on other string instruments, and by having the violinists play their instruments as if they were mandolins in simulation of mandolin sounds. A critic for *Horizon* called *Before the Butterfly* "one of the freshest and most innovative works to appear in years." He added: "Subotnick mixes natural sounds with distorted ones to coax haunting colors from the orchestral palette. He has devised a system of fifteen interlocking microphones that can distort natural sounds as they are being produced by orchestral players. The distorting power is activated when the soloists from two groups play into the mikes at the same time. Why one instrument can modify the pitch of another is baffling; but there is no question that it works. Subtle nuances conjure up the microtonal blur of insects at night. Tiny quartertone slidings hint at the stirrings within a cocoon. Genuine artistry is at play. . . . Subotnick approaches the orchestra with extraordinary virtuosity and vitality and in the process molds it into a very personal instrument."

In the late 1970s, Subotnick veered into a new direction by writing a series of compositions for solo instruments and tape which he designated as "ghost pieces." These are works in which the tape serves solely as a "ghost score," containing information which triggers other electronic equipment that modifies instrumental sounds as they are being played. Thus the soloist provides his own electronic accompaniment. The electronic modifications include the capacity to change pitch, timbre, volume, and the directionality of the sounds. The electronic tape specifies its own set of attacks and rhythms, adding another whole dimension into the sound of instruments and voices. Among these "ghost pieces" are *Liquid Strata*, for piano (1977), introduced at the Ojai Music Festival in California on June 11, 1977; *Wild Beasts*, for trombone and piano (1978); *Passages of the Beasts*, for clarinet (1978); *The Life of Histories*, for voice and clarinet (1978); and *The Last Dream of the Beast*, for voice (1978; N.Y., March 2, 1979); and *Axolotl*, for cello (1980). A complete program of Subotnick's "ghost pieces" was given in New York on March 2, 1979.

Subotnick was visiting professor of music at the University of Maryland (1968–69) and the University of Pittsburgh (1969–70). He was appointed associate dean at the California Institute of the Arts in Valencia, Calif., in 1969. Since 1972 he has directed its electronic music studio and was chairman of its music department in composition. He received a Guggenheim Fellowship in 1975 and a $4,000 award from the American Academy and Institute of Arts and Letters in 1979.

He was married three times. His first marriage, to Linn Pottle in 1954, produced a son and a daughter. Following his divorce in 1970, he married Doreen Nelson in 1976. After his divorce two years later, he married Joan La Barbara, composer, music critic, and vocalist, on December 18, 1979.

PRINCIPAL WORKS: Serenade no. 1, for flute, clarinet, vibraphone, cello, piano, and mandolin (1959); Serenade no. 2, for clarinet, horn, piano, and percussionist (1959); *Mandolin*, for viola, tape, and film (1962); *The Tarot*, for flute oboe, trumpet, trombone, three percussion, piano, viola, bass, tape, and "choreographed conductor" (1963); Prelude no. 3, for piano and electronic sounds (1964); *Play!* 1, for woodwind quintet, piano, tape, and film (1964); *Play!* 2, for orchestra, conductor, and tape (1964); *Play!* 3, for mime, tape, and film (1965); *Play!* 4, for four game players, two conductors, four musicians, tape, and two films (1965); Serenade no. 3, for flute, clarinet, violin, piano, and tape (1965); Prelude no. 4, for piano and electronic sounds (1966); *Silver Apples of the Moon*, for tape (1966); *Realities* 1–2, for

tape (1967); *The Wild Bull*, for tape (1967); *Misfortune of the Immortals: A Concert*, for woodwind quintet (1969); *Touch*, for tape (1969); *Sidewinder*, for tape (1970); *A Ritual Game*, for electronic sounds on tape, lights, dancer, four game players, and "no audience" (1970); *Four Butterflies*, for tape (1971–72); *Two Butterflies*, for amplified orchestra (1974); *Until Spring*, for tape (1974); *Before the Butterfly*, for orchestra (1974–75); *Liquid Strata*, "ghost piece" for piano and electronic sounds (1977); *The Wild Beasts*, "ghost piece" for trombone and piano (1977); *Passages of the Beast*, "ghost piece" for clarinet (1978); *A Sky of Cloudless Sulphur*, for electronic tape (1978); *Sky with Clouds*, for electronic tape and voice-actuated (1978); *Two Life Histories*, "ghost piece" for voice and clarinet (1978); *The Last Dream of the Beast*, "ghost piece" for voice (1978); *Ice Flow*, for tape (1978); *Parallel Lines*, for solo piccolo and chamber ensemble (1979); *Place*, for orchestra (1979); *Axolotl*, "ghost piece" for cello (1980).

BIBLIOGRAPHY: *DCM*; Schwartz, Elliott, *Electronic Music* (N.Y., 1975); *Music Journal*, January 1970; *Notes on Arts*, January–February 1979; *Who's Who in America, 1980–81*.

Surinach, Carlos, b. Barcelona, Spain, March 4, 1915. American citizen, 1959.

For all its dissonances and modern percussiveness, Surinach's music is deeply grounded in flamenco song and dance. Many of his major works use the eight-tone scale of flamenco music as well as its intervallic structure.

His mother, of Austro-Polish extraction, was a trained pianist who had won first prize at the Royal Conservatory of Madrid. She was responsible for Surinach's early musical upbringing. Not only did she give him piano lessons until he was thirteen but she also took him to performances of opera and ballet. When he was fourteen, Surinach continued his piano study with José Caminals at the Caminals Academy of Music in Barcelona, where he remained seven years and received a thorough theoretical training. Since Surinach's father, a stockbroker, insisted that Carlos receive an academic education, the boy attended elementary school and received the six-year course of the baccalaureat.

After leaving the Caminals Conservatory in 1936, Surinach studied composition privately for three years with Enrique Morera in Barcelona. Since these were the years of the Spanish Civil War, he was required to do office work for the army in uniform, a preoccupation that left him a considerable amount of free time to study scores and do composing. One of his compositions at this time was *Tres canciones*, for voice and piano or small orchestra (1939), on texts by Federico García Lorca and Antonio Mached, in which the influence of Spanish music can already be detected. This was his first composition to be published.

In November 1940, on an Alexander von Humboldt Fellowship, Surinach came to Düsseldorf, Germany—this, in spite of World War II—to study composition with Hugo Balzer and several teachers at the Robert Schumann Conservatory. He then went to Berlin to become a "master student" in composition of Max Trapp's at the Academy of Fine Arts. The war notwithstanding, Berlin was rich with musical activity. Hearing performances of Richard Strauss's *Salome* and *Elektra*, Carl Orff's *Carmina burana* and Heinrich Sutermeister's opera, *Romeo and Juliet*—among many other works—provided a powerful stimulus to his musical growth. But when he took to writing his own music, it was Spanish music, not German, that was his inspiration. In Berlin he wrote a Piano Sonatina (1941), Piano Quartet (1941) and *Sinfonia-Passacaglia*, for large orchestra (1942; Barcelona, April 8, 1945), in all of which he made tentative efforts to make use of the eight-note flamenco scale.

Surinach returned to Barcelona in the spring of 1942. For a time, he was assistant conductor at the Gran Teatro del Liceo Opera House, and conductor of orchestral concerts. He broadened the scope of his conductorial activities after the end of World War II by performing throughout Western Europe. Temporarily, composition assumed a subsidiary role. But he did manage to complete the scores of a ballet, *Monte Carlo*, which was produced on May 2, 1945, by the Ballets de Paul Goube in Barcelona, and of a one-act opera, *El mozo que casó con mujer brava*, produced in Barcelona on January 10, 1948. More significant was the Symphony no. 2 (1949; Paris, January 26, 1950). When, a few years later, this symphony was televised in the United States, Peggy Glanville-Hicks wrote in the *New York Herald Tribune*: "The clarity in musical thought and in instrumentation is a joy to follow. Each department of the orchestra seems to follow its typical nature. . . . The first movement is spare to a point of starkness, but manages to include both delicacy and intimacy within its lean polyphony. The slow movement, original in its very bones, presents the flamenco meditation and in its terrifying high-strung intensity in modern abstract form, while the third and final movements . . . are gay and buoyant, even brash in their use of popular Hispanic traditions."

Between 1947 and 1950, Surinach made his home in Paris, where he conducted several major French orchestras. He came to the United States in 1950, establishing permanent residence and becoming an American citizen. Initially, he earned his living in New York by composing jingles for television commercials, but before long he became involved as conductor and composer. At two concerts of contemporary chamber music that he conducted at the Museum of Modern Art in New York in May 1952, he introduced, on May 5, his own *Ritmo jondo*, for clar-

inet, trumpet, and percussion (1952). An enlargement of this score was used for the ballet *Deep Rhythm* about a year later (April 15, 1953), choreography by Doris Humphrey and presented by José Limón and his company. In 1954 on a commission from the Louisville Orchestra, he wrote *Sinfonietta flamenca* (1954), its world premiere given in Kentucky under Robert Whitney's direction on January 9, 1954. The Louisville Orchestra under Whitney also presented the premiere of *Feria mágica*, an orchestral overture (1956) on March 14, 1956, when William Mootz in the *Louisville Courier-Journal* called it "a triumph . . . a wildly exciting piece of music. . . . The piece is an explosive Spanish fiesta—brief, dazzling and gaudy." In 1956, Surinach also completed Concertino for Piano, Strings and Cymbals, a commission from MGM Records, which the MGM Orchestra, under the composer's direction, with William Masselos as soloist, introduced in New York on February 9, 1957. Two ballets used this last score effectively: *La Sibila*, by the John Butler Dance Company at the Festival of Two Worlds at Spoleto, Italy, on July 3, 1959, and *Celebrants*, by the Bath-Sheba Dance Company of Israel in Tel Aviv on November 25, 1963.

In addition to having his concert music used by ballet companies, Surinach was also highly active writing original ballet scores. Several were choreographed by Martha Graham and presented by her company. *Embattled Garden* (1958) was commissioned by the Bethsabee de Rothschild Foundation and was introduced in New York on April 3, 1958, after which it was given more than five hundred performances. *Acrobats of God* (1960) was performed by the Martha Graham Company in New York on April 27, 1960; this, too, was given some five hundred performances. *Chronique* (1974), based on poems by St. John Perse, was seen in New York on April 19, 1974, and *The Owl and the Pussycat* (1978), scenario developed from Edward Lear's poem, was mounted by Martha Graham at the Metropolitan Opera House on June 26, 1978.

In addition to his music for Martha Graham, Surinach provided scores for other notable dance groups. The most important ballets were *David and Bath-Sheba* (1960), which CBS-TV commissioned and which was introduced over that television network with choreography by John Butler on May 15, 1960 and whose music was used for another ballet, *A Place in the Desert*, produced at Sadler's Wells in London on July 25, 1961; *Feast of Ashes* (1962), commissioned by the Rebekah Harkness Foundation and premiered by the Robert Joffrey Ballet in Lisbon on November 30, 1962, then given eighteen performances by the same company in the Soviet Union; *Agathe's Tale* (1967), commissioned by the Dance Festival of Connecticut College, first presented on August 12, 1967, by the Paul Taylor Dance Company in New London, Conn.; *Suite espagnole* (1970), mounted on October 6, 1970, by the Harkness Ballet in Barcelona; and *Bodas de sangre* (1978), written for and introduced by the Oklahoma School of Drama, Department of Dance, in Norman, Okla., on April 25, 1979.

These are among Surinach's most important concert works since 1960: *Symphonic Variations* (1963; Phoenix, Ariz., May 25, 1963); *Melorhythmic Dramas*, an orchestral suite (1966) which the Detroit Symphony, conducted by Sixten Ehrling, introduced at the Meadow Brook Festival, which had commissioned it, in Rochester, Mich., on August 16, 1966; *Missions of San Antonio*, a five-part symphonic canticle for male chorus and orchestra with texts in Latin from medieval Spanish prayers (1968; San Antonio, Tex., January 25, 1969); *Piano Concerto* (1974), written for Alicia de Larrocha, who introduced it on November 13, 1974, as soloist with the Minnesota Orchestra under Stanislaw Skrowaczewski; and Concerto for Harp and Orchestra (1978; Grand Rapids, Mich., February 15, 1979). The flamenco eight-tone scale is used prominently in these works. In addition, Surinach orchestrated seven pieces of Albéniz's *Iberia Suite*, for piano, which were performed by the Philadelphia Orchestra under Eugene Ormandy.

Surinach was visiting professor of composition at the Carnegie-Mellon University of Pittsburgh (1966–67) and adjunct professor of music at Queens College of the City University of New York (1974–76). He was awarded by Great Britain the Arnold Bax Medal (1966) and Spain named him knight commander of the Order of Isabella of Castile (1972).

THE COMPOSER SPEAKS: The principles of my music, since it was well established in 1952, have never changed. Some choreographers, however, have told me that it is not the Spanish style that fascinates them, but the musico-theatrical power. A self-analysis has induced me to emphasize more freely these effects, particularly through orchestral devices and contrasts. All these works though, I believe, are different from one another because each composition has its own raison d'être.

PRINCIPAL WORKS: Symphony no. 2 (1949); *Ritmo jondo*, for chamber orchestra (1953); *Sinfonietta flamenca*, for orchestra, also for band (1954); *Fandango*, for orchestra (1954); *Doppio concertino*, for violin, piano, and chamber orchestra (1954); Concertino, for piano, strings, and cymbals (1956); *Feria mágica*, overture for orchestra (1956); *Embattled Garden*, ballet (1958); *David and Bath-Sheba*, ballet (1960); *Acrobats of God*, ballet (1960); Guitar Sonatina (1960); *Four Tonadillas*, for voice and chamber orchestra (1961); *Apasionada*, ballet (1961); *Tres cantares*, for voice and piano (1961); *Feast of Ashes*, ballet (1962); *Cantata of St. John*, for chorus and percussion (1962); *Celebrants*, ballet (1963); *Symphonic Variations*, for orchestra (1963); *Songs of the Soul*, for a cappella chorus (1964); *Drama jondo*,

overture for orchestra (1965); *Los renegados*, ballet (1965); *Flamenco Meditations*, song cycle for voice and piano (1965); *Venta quemada*, ballet (1966); *Melorhythmic Dramas*, for orchestra (1966); *Agathe's Tale*, ballet (1967); *Missions of San Antonio*, for orchestra (1968); *Suite espagnole*, ballet (1970); *Via crucis*, for chorus, guitar with optional timpani (1971); *Prayers*, for voice and guitar (1972); *Las trompetas de los Serafines*, for orchestra (1973); *Chronique*, ballet (1974); Piano Concerto (1974); String Quartet (1974); *The Owl and the Pussycat*, ballet (1978); Harp Concerto (1978); Concerto for String Orchestra (1978).

BIBLIOGRAPHY: *DCM*; Chase, Gilbert, *The Music of Spain*, revised ed. (N.Y., 1959); BMI, *The Many Worlds of Music*, Winter 1976.

Sydeman, William Jay, b. New York City, May 8, 1928.

To an interviewer for the *New York Times*, Sydeman described himself as "a musical hybrid, split between the traditional urge to 'say something' and the 20th-century materials which have so long been associated with impersonality and abstraction. I wed a traditional esthetic to a contemporary technique." That technique has been basically atonal, polytonal, and occasionally serial, aleatory, and electronic.

The son of a Manhattan stockbroker, Sydeman began taking piano lessons in early boyhood, continuing its study with private teachers while attending Hunter College Elementary School and Blair Academy. Composing began when he was seventeen. "From then on I kept on composing music four hours a day, six days a week." Since he planned a career in business rather than music, he entered Duke University in Durham, N.C., in 1944 to study business administration. While there, providing the score for a college musical convinced him that music, not business, had to be his ultimate goal. With this in mind, he left Duke University after a year. From 1946 to 1951 he attended the Mannes College of Music in New York, studying theory and composition with Felix Salzer and Roy Travis. His music study was then interrupted by a two-year period in the U.S. Army (1951–52), after which he returned to Mannes College to complete requirements for a bachelor of science degree in 1955 and to study composition privately with Roger Sessions in 1954–55. Sydeman spent the summer of 1955 at the Berkshire Music Center at Tanglewood, Mass., to continue this study. He returned to Tanglewood the following summer to study composition with Goffredo Petrassi. Between 1958 and 1959 Sydeman studied composition with Arnold Franchetti at the Hartt College of Music at Hartford, Conn., earning his master of music degree there in 1958. In 1959, he joined the faculty of the Mannes College of Music as a teacher of composition, remaining there eleven years.

Everything that Sydeman had composed up to 1955, and some of what he wrote between 1955 and 1958, was destroyed as he embarked upon a new creative course that embraced ultramodern harmonic and tonal processes. In 1955, he completed a String Quartet: his First Woodwind Quintet; a Quartet for Clarinet, Violin, Trumpet and Double bass; *Japanese Songs*, for soprano and two violins, to poems from the Japanese; and *Reflections Japanese*, for female chorus, again to Japanese poems. With *Orchestral Abstractions*, for chamber orchestra (1958), he began arriving at stylistic maturity. Its premiere took place in New York on January 10, 1962, at a concert of the Orchestra of America under Richard Korn, and was subsequently recorded by the Louisville Orchestra. "*Orchestral Abstractions*," reported *Time*, "was jagged in profile, strong in rhythm and color, the solo instruments, particularly the brasses in the last movement, in fascinating juxtaposition with a curtain of translucent strings. The effect suggested flashes of pigment seen through swiftly running water." This was followed by the *Concerto da camera* no. 1, for viola and chamber ensemble (1958), introduced in New York on May 7, 1960. This was a partly serial work, with "the kind of tense misterioso atmosphere," said a critic for the *New York Times*, "that is so often found in Schoenberg and Berg." In the *Herald Tribune*, Lester Trimble described Sydeman's idiom in this *Concerto da camera* as "full of fresh and original sounds; his sense of form and organization is delicate and accurate; and the instrumentation is finesse itself. The concerto was compelling at every moment and left one with a sense of having heard something important." In 1960, the concerto received the Pacifica Foundation Award. A second and third *Concerto da camera*, these two for violin and instruments, followed in 1961 and 1965 respectively. Both were written for Max Polliakoff and introduced at Polliakoff's *Music in Our Time* concerts in New York; the second, on February 5, 1961, and the third on May 5, 1965.

With fifteen premieres between 1960 and 1962—five of them in January 1962—Sydeman was gaining recognition as one of the most significant and frequently performed of the younger generation of American composers. The National Institute of Arts and Letters recognized this fact when it presented him with a citation in May 1962 in which his music was described as "clearly conceived, colorful and cleanly contrapuntal . . . the honest and straightforward music of an outstanding young talent." Among the major works premiered during this two-year period (above and beyond the already-mentioned *Orchestral Abstractions* and the *Concerto da camera* nos. 2 and 3) were the following: Concert Piece, for chamber orchestra (1960; N.Y., July 27, 1960); Duo, for violin and cello (1960; N.Y., March 9, 1961); Woodwind Quintet no. 2 (1961; N.Y., April 3, 1962) Trio, for violin (or oboe), viola and piano (1961; N.Y., November 18, 1961); Piano So-

nata (1961; N.Y., January 29, 1962); and Music for Flute, Viola, Guitar, and Percussion (1962; N.Y., February 6, 1963). Much of this is twelve-tone music with modifications. Discussing a recording of the Music for Flute, Viola, Guitar, and Percussion, a writer for *Musical Quarterly* said: "The immediate expressive impact of the piece is so fresh and strong that one forgets to check whether it is twelve-tone or not—a healthy sign. It is by far the most appealing, best proportioned, most enjoyable among the more recent compositions by Sydeman heard by this reviewer."

Sydeman's most important work for orchestra up to that time was the *Study for Orchestra* no. 2 (1963), which received its world premiere in Boston on November 22, 1963, with the Boston Symphony conducted by Erich Leinsdorf. A one-movement work, it was made up of four sections preceded by an introduction and continuing with the first and third sections slow and lyrical, the second and fourth, dramatic. "The style partakes largely of twelve-tone techniques," said Alan Rich in the *New York Herald Tribune*, "but of the rather conservative side of the school. . . . Some of the orchestral writing has the open, delicate quality of Webern's music, but the resemblance is on the surface. Sydeman's atonality is a good deal more romantic than was Webern's, and a good deal more accessible. The new work . . . has a fine sense of flow and direction. Its materials are extremely attractive and so is the orchestral sound." The Boston Symphony under Leinsdorf repeated their performance at the Berkshire Music Festival in August 1964 during a five-day festival of contemporary American music; it was the only avant-garde composition on the program. On October 15, 1965, the Boston Symphony under Leinsdorf premiered *Study for Orchestra* no. 3 (1965). Once again a four-section work in one movement, the new *Study* proved particularly interesting in its handling of the orchestral choirs and in its expressive sonorities, to which an enlarged percussion battery added dramatic interest. On the strength of these two compositions, Sydeman was presented with the Boston Symphony Merit Award in 1964 and the Koussevitzky Music Foundation Award two years after that.

Between these two *Study* compositions came *The Lament of Elektra*, for alto, five small choruses, and a chamber orchestra, requiring four conductors (1964), to a text by Sophocles. It was commissioned by Samuel Wechsler for the Festival of American Music at Tanglewood, where its first performance took place on August 10, 1964. "Theatrical might be a good word for *Elektra*," reported Howard Klein in the *New York Times* from Tanglewood, "for the effect is extremely dramatic."

During the summer of 1966, Sydeman traveled to Czechoslovakia, Rumania, and Bulgaria, lecturing on American music under the auspices of the U. S. State Department Cultural Exchange Program. While in Prague, he attended a performance of his

Study no. 2 at the Prague Spring Festival performed by the Czech Philharmonic conducted by Leinsdorf. Returning to the United States, Sydeman left for the Congregation of the Arts at Hopkins Center at Dartmouth College for the world premiere of his Music for Viola, Winds and Percussion on August 7, which the Hopkins Center Festival had commissioned.

On a commission from Mrs. Ruth Kaufmann, Sydeman wrote *In Memoriam—John F. Kennedy*, for narrator and orchestra (1966); the Boston Symphony under Leinsdorf, with E. G. Marshall as narrator, first presented it on November 4, 1966. For his text, the composer drew material from Ecclesiastes, a poem by Stephen Spender, some of President Kennedy's speeches, and comments about President Kennedy by Theodore Sorensen and Arthur M. Schlesinger, Jr. "The text," the composer said, "is not only integral to the general form and 'sonority' of the work, but it is the basic element of the work, with which the music functions to clarify, delineate or make dramatically more effective." In his score, Sydeman quoted from the Funeral March of Beethoven's *Eroica Symphony*, the reason being that Erich Leinsdorf had played it in memory of President Kennedy on the same program that he had performed Sydeman's *Study for Orchestra* no. 2 and "it is impossible for me to think of the tragedy without recalling this movement." A suggestion of "The Star-Spangled Banner" was interpolated.

Sydeman's *Malediction*, for tenor, speaking actor, string quartet, and electronic tape (1970), is a curiosity. It was commissioned by the Chamber Music Society of Lincoln Center in New York, and its first performance was given by that group on February 6, 1971. As described in *High Fidelity/Musical America*: "A big black box was wheeled onstage by a freaky looking individual sporting scruffy beard, shades and leather jacket. He stepped behind the box and lifted up two flaps on top. Out popped another gentleman, a tenor soloist, who began chanting a long parody of excommunication from Laurence Sterne's novel *Tristram Shandy*. The hipster frequently interrupted with irreverent remarks, but each time the tenor resumed his sermon with increased fervor. . . . There's something to be said for any new music which is received with such a hefty chorus of boos and bravos at a time when most premieres provoke only audience apathy."

THE COMPOSER SPEAKS: If I engage in any form of serialism it is never as an end in itself, but as a means of ordering my musical material discreetly, so as to sound sensible. If I utilize some aleatoric procedures, it is because a specific musical problem I have encountered during the course of composition is best solved by improvisatory methods. If my "sound" or rhythmic vocabulary is contemporary, it is because the cliché offends me as much as the world of creative imagination delights me.

If I had lived a hundred years ago, I would probably have written like Schumann, but I think that if Schumann were living now, he would write as I do.

PRINCIPAL WORKS: 12 duos, for various instruments and piano (1959–71); 3 studies for orchestra (1959, 1963, 1965); 3 fantasies, for various solo instruments (1959, 1961, 1963); 2 woodwind quintets (1955, 1961); 2 *concerti da camera,* for violin and chamber orchestra (1959, 1961).

Concertino, for oboe, piano, and string orchestra (1956); *Fanfare and Variations*, for brass quintet (1957); Divertimento, for flute, clarinet, bassoon, and string quartet (1957); *Concerto da camera*, for viola and chamber orchestra (1959); Music for Low Brass, for three trombones (1958); *Orchestral Abstractions*, for orchestra (1958); Seven Movements, for septet (1958); Variations, for piano (1958); Concert Piece, for French horn and string orchestra (1959); Quintet, for clarinet, French horn (or trombone), piano, percussion, and double bass (1960); Concert Piece, for chamber orchestra (1960); Piano Sonata (1961); Trio, for violin (or oboe) viola and piano (1961); Quartet, for oboe, violin, viola, and cello (1962); *Homage to L'histoire du soldat*, for instrumental group (1962); Music for Flute, Viola, Guitar, and Percussion (1962); Quartet, for violin, flute, double bass, and percussion (1963); *Lament of Elektra*, for alto, three choruses and chamber orchestra (1964); Fantasy and Two Epilogues, for flute, violin, cello, and piano (1964); *Oecumenicus*, concerto for orchestra (1964); *The Affectations*, for trumpet and piano (1965); Fantasy Piece, for harpsichord (1965); *In Memoriam —John F. Kennedy*, for narrator and orchestra (1966); Music for Viola, Winds, and Percussion (1966); Sonata for Solo Violin (1966); *Texture Studies*, for wind quintet (1966); Concerto, for piano four hands, chamber orchestra, or electronic sounds on tape (1967); *Projections* no. 1, for amplified violin, tape, and slides (1968); *Texture Studies*, for orchestra (1969); Trio, for bassoon, bass, clarinet and piano (1969); *Malediction*, for tenor, speaking actor, string quartet, and electronic tape (1970); *Full Circle*, for three solo voices, clarinet, trombone, percussion, and organ (1971); Duo, for percussion (1971); Duo, for violin and double bass (1972); *Trio montagnana*, for clarinet, cello, and piano (1972); *Five Movements*, for winds (1973); Duo, for two clarinets (1975); Fugue, for string quartet (1975); Duo, for two horns (1976); *Eighteen Duos*, for two violins (1976); *The Last Orpheus*, for two flutes (1976); Duo, for clarinet and saxophone (1977); Duo, for xylophone and vibraphone (1977).

BIBLIOGRAPHY: *DCM*; Reich, Nancy B. (ed.), *Catalogue of the Works of William Sydeman*, 2nd ed. (N.Y., 1968); *New York Times*, November 21, 1966; *Time*, January 19, 1962.

T

Talma, Louise Juliette, b. Arcachon, France, October 31, 1906.

A highly productive and well-esteemed composer for some four decades (sometimes described as "the dean of women composers"), Talma began her mature years as composer as a neoclassicist who favored tonal and contrapuntal procedures. She subsequently embraced serialism, but without abandoning either tonality or lyricism, using it as a tool and skillfully incorporating it with other methods.

Both her parents were American, and both were professional musicians. Her father was a pianist, and her mother, Alma Cécile Garrigues, an opera singer. Since Louise's father died when she was an infant, she was raised only by her mother, who began giving her piano lessons when Louise was five, took her frequently to concerts, and carefully nurtured and developed her early interest in music. Upon graduating from Wadleigh High School in New York in 1922, Talma continued her undergraduate academic education at Columbia University (1923–30), majoring in chemistry. At the same time, at the Institute of Musical Art in New York, she studied theory with George Wedge, ear training with Helen Whitley and Franklin Robinson, counterpoint and fugue with Percy Goetschius and composition with Howard Brockway (1921–30). There, her creative talent was recognized with the winning of the Isaac Newton Seligman Prize for composition for three consecutive years (1927–29) for three student chamber-music works: a piano quartet, a piano quintet, and a string quartet modeled after Brahms, Scriabin, and Debussy, respectively. But her ambition at that time was to become a concert pianist, for which she received encouragement in 1927 by winning first prize in an Eastern Interstate Piano Competition conducted by the National Federation of Music Clubs.

When she was twenty-one she began earning her living by teaching piano, but without interrupting her academic or musical education. Summers between 1926 and 1935 were spent in France studying piano with Isidor Philipp. In France, her piano playing brought her the Pleyel Prize in 1927 and the Presser Prize in 1928. In 1928, she entered the composition class of Nadia Boulanger in Fontainebleau, returning each summer after that for many years to continue studying with her. On the advice and encouragement of Boulanger, Talma arrived at the decision, in 1935, to devote herself to composition rather than to the piano. Ending her studies with Isidor Philipp, she concentrated on her work with Boulanger each summer until 1939 (after that returning in 1949, 1951, and 1961). During the summers between 1936 and 1939, Talma taught solfeggio at Fontainebleau, the only American employed there. Nadia Boulanger proved to be a profound spiritual as well as musical influence on her. Through her teacher, Talma became deeply involved with the religious teachings of the Catholic Church. In 1934, she was converted to Catholicism (having been born a Protestant) and she has remained religious ever since.

After two years of teaching theory and ear training at the Manhattan School of Music in New York (1926–28) Talma joined the music faculty of Hunter College in New York, becoming full professor in 1952 and, after September 1976, professor emeritus and distinguished visiting professor. In 1931, Talma earned a bachelor of music degree at New York University and, two years later, a master of arts degree at Columbia University.

Because her time and energies had been occupied with studying and teaching, Talma's career as a mature composer did not begin to take wing until she was thirty-three, though one of her earlier works, *La belle dame sans merci*, for baritone solo and women's chorus, based on Keats, had won the Bearns Prize at Columbia for composition in 1932. Her composing career began in earnest in 1938 when *The Hound of Heaven*, for tenor and small orchestra—text, the poem by Francis Thompson—received the Stovall Prize. Talma won this prize a second time a year later with *In Principio Erat Verbum*, for chorus and organ, which was introduced on January 30, 1950, in New York.

Her career as composer gained momentum in the early 1940s with *Carmina Mariana*, for two sopranos and piano (1943; N.Y., January 21, 1946); a Piano Sonata (1943), which she herself introduced at a League of Composers concert in New York on January 21, 1945; Toccata, for orchestra (1944), which was premiered by the Baltimore Symphony under Reginald Stewart on December 20, 1945, and years later recorded in a performance by the Tokyo Philharmonic under William Strickland; and *Terre de France*, a song cycle for soprano and piano (1943–45); N.Y., January 27, 1946). The last, written in homage to France, was a setting of nostalgic texts by Cardinal du Bellay, Charles d'Orléans, and Joan of Arc.

In 1946, Talma was the recipient of a Guggenheim Fellowship which was renewed a year later. (She was the first woman to be awarded two such fellowships.) Thus aided financially, she was able to devote herself to the completion of her most ambitious composition up to this point; a large-scale oratorio in a neoclassical idiom, *The Divine Flame*, oratorio for mezzo-soprano, baritone, chorus, and orchestra. Its text was taken from the Bible and the missal. Excerpts (the solo portions) received their initial hearing on February 14, 1950, at Harvard University with the composer at the piano. Other neoclassical vocal works followed in the late 1940s, leading to the award of Prix d'excellence de composition from the French government in 1951 on Nadia Boulanger's recommendation.

Talma's direction as a composer changed in 1952 through the hearing of a twelve-tone quartet by Irving Fine. This music made such an impression on her that she started to correspond with Fine, receiving from him instruction in the use of the twelve-tone row. She wrote Piano Sonata no. 2 (1955; N.Y., February 13, 1959) to unite tonal and serial elements in a single work, all of whose movements employed such a procedure in one form or another. Writing in the *New Haven Register*, Gordon Emerson described this sonata as "a rare jewel. In common with all her mature music, it owes no debt to any particular stylistic predisposition, though it utilizes dissonance freely, is generally tonal . . . and frequently lyrical and during Allegros just as frequently jazzily spontaneous and free without sounding at all like jazz."

Her most successful work represented just such a marriage of twelve-tone music with tonality and lyricism. This was the three-act opera, *The Alcestiad* (1955–58), text by Thornton Wilder based on the Greek legend of Alcestis. (This was the first opera written to a Wilder libretto.) The last ten months of the work were done in Rome on a Senior Fulbright Research Grant. The world premiere took place not in the United States but Germany, the first opera by an American woman to be mounted by a major European company. That premiere—on March 1, 1962, at the Frankfurt Opera—was a major success, a twenty-minute ovation following the final curtain. Each of its subsequent seven performances was virtually sold out. "Talma's score," reported a correspondent to *Time*, "which frequently employed the twelve-tone row, was aglow with curving lyric lines but avoided any hint of romantic lushness, was sometimes reminiscent of Stravinsky. The lightly modern music at no point obscured the text, at many points sharply illuminated it, as in the moving second-act farewell duet of Alcestis . . . and Admetus." *The Alcestiad* brought its composer the Marjorie Peabody Award from the National Institute of Arts and Letters with a citation reading: "To Louise Talma, whose personal, highly controlled and beautifully shaped music has gained a new cogency and dramatic

effectiveness in the opera she has made of Thornton Wilder's *The Alcestiad*." Other prestigious honors came in 1963, though not specifically for this opera, but nevertheless influenced by its success: the Sibelius Medal for composition from the Harriet Cohen International Awards in London, the first time it was received by a woman; the award of the National Association of American Composers and Conductors; and another from the National Federation of Music Clubs.

A commission from the Koussevitzky Music Foundation led to the writing of *All the Days of My Life* (1963–66), cantata for tenor, clarinet, cello, piano and percussion, which used a biblical text together with a quatrain discovered in a trench in Tunisia in 1943. The Contemporary Chamber Ensemble conducted by Arthur Weisberg presented the world premiere on November 25, 1966, at the Library of Congress in Washington, D.C. This was music basically in a Stravinskyan style in its rhythmic and metric complexity, dramatic contrasts, and vivid declamatory writing.

In spring of 1966, Talma took sabbatical leave from Hunter College through an award from the National Endowment for the the Arts. That year (1966–67) she completed *A Time to Remember*, a five-section composition for three choruses and orchestra which used a text taken from speeches by John F. Kennedy in addition to biblical and literary quotations. Its premiere took place in New York on November 25, 1966. "The work," said Allen Hughes in the *New York Times*, "has a ceremonial quality and is both tasteful and dignified. The music, uncomplicated, is easy to listen to. It comes to a climax in 'Last Day' over a relentless drumbeat."

Three poems on the nature of existence and death by Shakespeare, Marlowe, and Donne provided Talma with the text for *The Tolling Bell*, a triptych for baritone and orchestra (1967–69). The title came from John Donne's famous line: ". . . and therefore never send to know for whom the bell tolls; it tolls for thee." This work was commissioned by the MacDowell Club of Milwaukee for its sixtieth anniversary, and its world premiere took place on November 29, 1969, in a performance by the Milwaukee Symphony under Kenneth Schermerhorn, with William Metcalf, vocal soloist. The first and third parts are meditative, while the middle one, by contrast, is agitated and dramatic.

Voices of Spring, for chorus and strings (1973), is one of Talma's most important compositions of the 1970s. It owed its inspiration to the news on January 28, 1973, that peace was coming to Vietnam. Seeking to express the "resurgent and universal yearning of the human soul for peace on this earth," as she put it, she reached for her text to the Bible, the missal, St. Francis of Assisi and Gerard Manley Hopkins. On February 10, 1974, the first performance took place in Philadelphia, Louis Salemno conducting.

On a commission from the International Society

for Contemporary Music to celebrate the seventieth birthday of the pianist Beveridge Webster, Talma wrote *Textures*, for piano (1977), premiered by Webster in New York on March 17, 1978. In the *New York Times*, Harold C. Schonberg described it as a "bravura work in contemporary style. The dissonances stem from Bartók and Copland, the writing is steely and effective; the pianistic layout, knowledgeable."

When Talma was made Samuel Simons Sanford Fellow at Yale University in March 1976, she received a medallion. At the same time, a concert of her works was presented on March 26, featuring selections from *The Alcestiad*, the Second Piano Sonata, together with Six Etudes, for piano (1953–54; N.Y., April 18, 1955), and the Violin Sonata (1962; N.Y., February 13, 1963). "Her music," Gordon Emerson said in the *New Haven Register*, "ranges from the competent to masterfully crafted, is borne of unquestionable taste and refinement and . . . approaches genuine brilliance." Almost a year later, on February 5, 1977, the fiftieth anniversary of Talma's affiliation with Hunter College was commemorated with another program of her works, this time in New York, covering her productivity from *Terre de France* of 1945 to *Summer Sounds*, a quintet for clarinet, two violins, viola and cello (1969–73; Nelson, N.H., July 24, 1974). That February, Hunter College made her a member of the President's Circle.

In 1974, Talma was elected member to the National Institute of Arts and Letters (the first woman to receive this honor). Later that year, the National Endowment for the Arts presented her with a fellowship grant.

Talma was the Clark Lecturer at Scripps College in Claremont, Calif., in March 1976 and visiting professor at the University of Iowa in Iowa City in April 1979. She has been a member of the board of directors of the League of Composers, the International Society for Contemporary Music, the Fontainebleau Arts Association, the American Music Center, charter member of the American Society of University Composers, and corporate member of the Edward MacDowell Association. She is the author of *Harmony for the College Student* (1966) and coauthor, with James S. Harris and Robert Levin, of *Functional Harmony* (1970).

THE COMPOSER SPEAKS: Music must first of all give pleasure to the ear. No mere fulfillment of a scheme, be it a form, a set, a parameter, a mix or whatever can suffice. It must have that intangible something which leads people to say: "This is beautiful, expressive, moving, etc." When Debussy, while still a student at the Paris Conservatory, was asked by Émile Rety what rules he observed, he replied: "My pleasure." And Schoenberg writes in "Heart and Brain in Music": "I believe that a real composer writes music for no other reason than that it pleases him." And Mozart, dear Mozart, writes in a letter to his father, September 26, 1781: "Music, even in its most terrible situations, must never offend the ear, but must please the hearer or in other words must never cease to be music." To all of which I say Amen.

PRINCIPAL WORKS: 2 piano sonatas (1943–45). *Terre de France*, song cycle for soprano and piano (1943–45); Toccata, for orchestra (1944); *Alleluia in Form of Toccata*, for piano (1945); *The Divine Flame*, oratorio for mezzo-soprano, baritone, chorus, and orchestra (1946–48); Two Sonnets, for baritone and piano (1946–50); *Pastoral Prelude*, for piano (1949); *The Leaden Echo and the Golden Echo*, for double chorus, soprano solo, and piano (1950–51); *Song and Dance*, for violin and piano (1951); *Let's Touch the Sky*, three songs for chorus, flute, oboe, and clarinet (1952); Six Etudes, for piano (1953–54); String Quartet (1954); *La corona*, seven songs for a cappella chorus (1954–55); Three Bagatelles, for piano (1955); *The Alcestiad*, opera (1955–58); Passacaglia and Fugue, for piano (1955–62); "Birthday Song," for tenor, flute, and viola (1960); Violin Sonata (1962); *All the Days of My Life*, cantata for tenor, clarinet, cello, piano, and percussion (1963–65); *Dialogues*, for piano and orchestra (1963–64); *A Time to Remember*, for chorus and orchestra (1966–67); *The Tolling Bell*, triptych for baritone and orchestra (1967–69); *Summer Sounds*, quintet for clarinet, two violins, viola, and cello (1969–73); *Voices for Peace*, for chorus and strings (1973); *Sound Shots*, twenty short pieces for piano (1944–74); *Have You Heard? Do You Know?*, divertimento for soprano, mezzo-soprano, tenor, and instrumental ensemble; *Celebration*, for chorus and orchestra (1976–77); *Textures*, for piano (1977); Psalm 84, for a cappella chorus (1978); *Deidam*, for tenor and chamber orchestra (1979).

BIBLIOGRAPHY: *DCM*; Goss, Madeleine, *Modern Music Makers* (N.Y., 1952); *New York Post*, March 1, 1974; *New York Times*, February 4, 1977; *SoHo News*, January 25, 1979; *Who's Who in America, 1980–81*.

Taylor, Clifford b. Avalon, Pa., October 20, 1923. Taylor reveals that "my music has always, in one way or another, found its expression in the harmonic dimension of the medium, although in widely varying degrees of emphasis." It has also always depended on a clear, objective forming process. His works between 1957 and 1973 (greatly influenced by Roger Sessions's text *Harmonic Practice*) were chromatic in an almost totally linear and dodecaphonic idiom. Since 1973 both of these tendencies have merged into a more unified musical expression, more harmonically resonant and consequently more clearly tonal. Jazz has always been, and without conscious effort, a natural commonplace in his musical thought.

His mother, who played the piano, saw to it that Clifford Taylor received music instruction early. In his boyhood, he studied violin first with Jean Zimmerman, with occasional supervision by Paul Sladek. When Taylor was in the eighth grade in Jackson Elementary School in Bellevue, Pa., he received the opportunity to join the violin section of the senior high school orchestra. At Bellevue High School, which he attended from 1936 to 1941, he came under the influence of Robert H. Ruthart, the conductor of the high school orchestra, who gave him important musical direction.

After graduating from high school, Taylor attended Carnegie-Mellon University in Pittsburgh for two years (1941–43). For two and a half years after that, he traveled through much of the non-Western world, particularly Africa, China, India and Burma, the result of his enlistment in the U. S. Army, which assigned him to service in an entertainment unit. During these travels, he recalls, "I saw and came to understand the life there in both micro- and macro-cosmic dimension because of the nature of my living conditions and the easy day-to-day relationship with all levels of people, the small village railway stations, the rural life in the south of China, the large cities in both the Far East and the Arab world, conversations and marketplaces, wealthy Parsi homes in Bombay, and so forth. Considering my age at the time, the impact of such experience cannot be dismissed."

He resumed his musical education at the Carnegie-Mellon University in 1945, studying clarinet with Domenico Caputo, violin with Gösta Andreasson, and composition with Nikolai Lopatnikoff. From that university he received, in 1948, a bachelor of fine arts degree in music and one in composition. That year, on September 26, 1948, he married Louise Kemp, a pianist and teacher. They have three children.

Between 1948 and 1950, Taylor attended Harvard University. There—where his principal teachers were Paul Hindemith, Walter Piston, Randall Thompson, A. Tillman Merritt, G. Wallace Woodworth, and Irving Fine—he earned the degree of master of arts in music in 1950. During those years, in addition to his work at Harvard, he studied clarinet with Rosario Mazzeo. The summer of 1950 was spent at the Berkshire Music Center at Tanglewood, Mass., in the advanced orchestra and in chamber music performance.

In 1950, he was appointed to the department of music at Chatham College in Pittsburgh. He spent the next dozen years there, serving initially as lecturer, then instructor, and after that as assistant professor (1954–61), associate professor (1961–63) and Buhl Associate Professor of the Humanities (1962–63). Additionally, he was chairman of its music department in 1959–60 and from 1960 to 1963 he directed the Advanced Developments of Contemporary Music Concerts, which he had founded. At that col-

lege he was given an endowment grant for creative work by the Buhl Foundation in 1958.

His early compositions comprised some songs; Symphony for Organ; Adagio and Allegro, for woodwinds; a Violin Sonata; and Theme and Variations, for orchestra. The Violin Sonata (1952) won the Friends of Harvey Gaul Prize in 1955 and was introduced in Pittsburgh in the spring of that year; between 1956 and 1957 it received several significant performances at Oberlin, Cincinnati, Cleveland, and throughout Pennsylvania. Theme and Variations (1952) was entered in a composers' contest conducted by the National Symphony Orchestra in Washington, D. C., to commemorate its twenty-fifth anniversary. It won first prize and was introduced under Howard Mitchell's direction in 1956. One year later, it was performed by the Pittsburgh Symphony under William Steinberg. This symphony, with its melodic-rhythmic interplay and controlled modality, reflected an influence that Roy Harris had upon him in those years, when Roy and Johana Harris joined the faculty of Chatham College and a warm friendship developed.

In 1958 Taylor was participating composer at the Bennington Composers Conference at Bennington College in Vermont. His String Quartet no. 1 (1960) was selected from one hundred forty compositions for the Rheta A. Sosland Prize in 1964, after having been heard in Kansas City on October 25, 1963. It was then performed at the Composers' Forum in Philadelphia by the Paul Zukofsky Quartet in 1966 and, in 1967, by the Lenox String Quartet in Pittsburgh and elsewhere. In the *Musical Quarterly*, Arthur Custer called it "an engaging and highly effective composition . . . characterized by a Bartókian textural thickness. . . . It is a work of great rhythmic vitality, moving from climax to climax with very little relief. . . . Taken in sum, Taylor's quartet must be considered a forceful and evocative composition."

Taylor's Symphony no. 2 (1955), one of his most important works, is a one-movement composition in four designated sections. The Philadelphia Orchestra, conducted by William Smith, premiered it on December 16, 1970. "The essence of the musical expression in this piece is line (e.g., melodic continuity) and not static timbral effects in dramatic juxtapositions," the composer explains. Three ideas, heard at the outset, are worked out significantly throughout the symphony. "It is complex thought," the composer goes on to say, "but it is 'sung' in the true sense of the word. The feelings expressed are sometimes volatile, even distraught, but at the best of all of it is a joy and, hopefully, a confidence in the nature of life itself, of the intense interaction of human concerns and needs worked out in a fabric which is part of our present world as it is being shaped." In his review in the *Philadelphia Inquirer*, Daniel Webster wrote: "For all its density of idea, the score remains one of considerable transparency. Mountains of sound develop at times, through which single voices, excellently fit to the instrument involved, sing clearly. It is full of lyricism; at the same time it moves through opaque, gruff periods. He achieves some orchestral effects which are notable by themselves. . . . The music is uncompromising and sometimes seems leathery, but the clarity of the instrumental lines keeps the direction apparent and the variety of sound keeps it alive."

Taylor left Chatham College in 1964 to become assistant professor of music and composition and chairman of the composition department at Temple University in Philadelphia. Since 1969 he has been full professor. He has also been conductor and director of the Contemporary Players and Singers, which has presented provocative programs of new music since 1967, and in 1968 he established—and has since been director of—its electronic music studio. On various occasions, the university has presented him with research fellowships and grants, including one in 1974 for study and travel in Belgium, France, Italy, England, Austria, and Germany.

Taylor's most important later works include a Piano Concerto (1974), written on a grant from the National Endowment for the Arts; a one-act opera, *The Freak Show* (1973–74), libretto by Edward Lind; Concerto no. 2, for strings and soloists (1977; Philadelphia, March 6, 1978); Concerto no. 3, for strings and soloists (1978; Philadelphia, January 14, 1980); String Quartet no. 2 (1978); and Symphony no. 3 (1978). When the Concerto no. 2, for strings and soloists, was premiered, with the composer conducting, Tom Di Nardo described it in the *Philadelphia Evening Bulletin* as "typically rhapsodic, with repeated statements of a haunted, restless theme over constantly changing harmonic patterns, dense string writing. . . . Impassioned, strong and yet vulnerable, especially in the central elegiac section, taut and intense throughout, but not relentless, this stark, gripping and beautiful work's interplay was moving."

THE COMPOSER SPEAKS: I believe we are now at the point of the time and growth in this country particularly, but in Western Europe as well, when we can produce didactic artifacts out of a humanistic view of life in the Western world. We no longer need to be obscure for want of artistic definition, and to this purpose we should establish the differences between scientific-technological enterprise and art in its historical Western definition. They are not the same at all. Our thinking, our feeling, and our beliefs can be articulated in didactic terms, in understandable forms. For myself, my effort and concern is to speak musically to an essential quality of life, humanistically directed and expressively related through *idea,* articulated musically, which relies on the total interplay of musical elements, including the harmonic condition, but not overindulgent of it, as it defines the music of Western culture.

PRINCIPAL WORKS: 3 symphonies (1958, 1965, 1978); 2 concertos, for strings and soloists (1977, 1978); 2 string quartets (1960, 1978).

Violin Sonata (1952); Piano Sonata (1952); Theme and Variations, for orchestra (1952); Chaconne, for orchestra (1956); Concerto Grosso, for string orchestra (1957); *Commencement Suite*, for chorus and orchestra (1958); Fantasia and Fugue, for piano (1959); Trio, for clarinet, cello, and piano (1959–60); Concert Duo, for violin and cello (1961); *Sacred Verses*, for vocal soloists, chorus, and orchestra (1961); Nine Studies, for piano (1962); Concerto, for organ and chamber orchestra (1963); *A Pageant of Characters from William Shakespeare*, for vocal soloists and chorus (1964); *Sinfonia seria*, for concert band, flute, and baritone horn (1965); Duo, for alto saxophone and trombone (1965); Serenade, for percussion ensemble (1967); *Movement for Three*, for violin, cello, and piano (1967); *Parabolic Mirrors*, for tape (1971); Five Poems, for oboe and five brasses (1971); *Quattro liriche*, for mezzo-soprano and orchestra (1971); Thirty Ideas, for piano (1973); *The Freak Show*, one-act opera (1973–74); Piano Concerto (1974); *Thirty-six More Ideas*, for piano (1976).

BIBLIOGRAPHY: *BBDM*; Anderson, E. Ruth, *Contemporary American Composers* (Boston, 1976).

Taylor, Joseph Deems, b. New York City, December 22, 1885; d. New York City, July 3, 1966.

As one of America's outstanding music critics and commentators, Deems Taylor was always an articulate proponent of new music, new composers, and new idioms. As a composer, he was of another mind, avoiding any semblance of so-called modernism, not to mention avant-gardism, preferring to write music that was traditional in structure and style, romantically conceived, lyrical, concerned with the expression of atmosphere and emotion. He was at his best when his music leaned on a story, libretto, or program.

Though he demonstrated enough interest in music to compose a waltz for piano when he was ten, Taylor's musical training was spasmodic and fragmentary. He began piano lessons when he was eleven and discontinued them eight months later; resumed them again for a few months in 1899 and never took another lesson. He studied theory privately with Oscar Coon during the summer of 1908 and again for several months in 1912–13. Beyond that, he was entirely self-taught. His academic education, however, was more formal and thorough, beginning with elementary schools and continuing at the Friends School and the Ethical Culture School, all in New York. Upon graduating from the Ethical Culture School in 1902, he entered New York University, intending to prepare himself for a career in architecture, a plan soon frustrated by his overall ineptitude in mathematics. He pursued the regular arts course and received his bachelor of arts degree in 1906. At college, he wrote the music for four campus shows, one of which, *The Echo*, was produced on Broadway on August 17, 1910, starring Bessie McCoy.

Soon after his graduation, Taylor toured the vaudeville circuit in a comedy act. He turned from the stage to editorial work in 1906, with *Nelson's Encyclopedia*. He then worked on the editorial board of the *Western Electric News* between 1912 and 1918 and was assistant editor of the Sunday section of the *New York Tribune* in 1916, for which, during World War I, he served as war correspondent in 1916–17. In 1917, he married his first wife, Jane Anderson, from whom he was divorced a few years later. Between 1917 and 1919 he was associate editor of *Collier's Weekly*.

Without any formal instruction in composition or orchestration, he wrote a tone poem for orchestra, *The Siren Song* (1912), which received a prize from the National Federation of Music Clubs. It had to wait a decade for its performance in New York on July 18, 1922. In 1913, a song, "Witch Woman," became Taylor's first piece of music to be published. In 1914, he completed two ambitious cantatas: *The Chambered Nautilus*, for chorus and orchestra, using Oliver Wendell Holmes's poem as text, and *The Highwayman*, for baritone, women's voices and orchestra, poem by Alfred Noyes.

Taylor's first successful composition was *Through the Looking Glass*, a suite based on the nonsense fairy tale by Lewis Carroll. Taylor wrote it originally in 1917–19 for chamber orchestra, and as such it was premiered by the New York Chamber Music Society on February 18, 1919. Subsequently, Taylor rescored it for full orchestra (1921–22), this version getting its first hearing at a concert of the New York Symphony Society conducted by Walter Damrosch in Brooklyn, N. Y., on March 10, 1923. After that, it received performances by many major American symphony orchestras. Throughout this work, Taylor displayed a fine gift for pictorial writing: the chatter of the talking flowers; the portrait of Jabberwock, and the fugal description of the battle against that monster; and the two contrasting themes describing the White Knight as he conceived himself and as he really was.

Through the Looking Glass was followed in 1919 by *Portrait of a Lady*. It was commissioned by the New York Chamber Society. Taylor rewrote it completely in 1923 and in its definitive version it was introduced in New York on February 3, 1925.

In 1921, Taylor initiated his fruitful career as music critic with the *New York World*. During the next four years he proved himself a trenchant, discerning, and often witty reviewer. While in this service, he channeled his musical creativity into the Broadway theater by composing incidental music for nine plays, including Molnar's *Liliom* (March 20, 1922) and

Beggar on Horseback by Marc Connelly and George S. Kaufman (February 12, 1924.) The latter contained an extended musical pantomime in a quasi-impressionist style entitled *A Kiss in Xanadu*, which was occasionally heard at orchestral concerts.

By 1925, Taylor had decided to concentrate his efforts on composition. He resigned from the *World* to work on an orchestral tone poem, *Jurgen* (1925), inspired by the satirical novel of James Branch Cabell, which Walter Damrosch had commissioned for the New York Symphony Society. In this music, Taylor once again revealed his skill at musical characterization and in translating programmatic images into tones. The work was premiered in New York on November 19, 1925.

A year later, the Metropolitan Opera commissioned Taylor to write an opera. Taylor enlisted the collaboration of one of America's distinguished poets, Edna St. Vincent Millay, to prepare a poetical libretto. Using the setting of tenth-century England, she devised *The King's Henchman*, a tale (reminiscent of *Tristan and Isolde*) which involved King Eadgar in a romance with a Devon princess, Aelfrida, only to be betrayed by his best friend, Aethelwold, who falls in love with and marries her. When the treachery is uncovered, Aethelwold dies by his own hand. Taylor's music, like Millay's text, was far removed from American associations, the romantic score carrying frequent reminders of Wagner and Debussy. While *The King's Henchman* opened no new worlds for opera, it provided an evening of theatrical and musical charm, with Taylor's music at its best in its occasional simulation of English folk songs and in the lyricism and emotion of the love music of the first and second acts. When *The King's Henchman* was produced on February 17, 1927, it was received enthusiastically. Lawrence Gilman, in the *Herald Tribune*, went so far as to maintain that it was "the best American opera we have ever heard." In the *New York Times*, Olin Downes wrote: "The remarkable thing is Mr. Taylor's degree of success, the communicative and sensuous quality of his music, and, above all, the direct and unaffected manner of his composing." The opera was the most successful work by an American produced by the Metropolitan up to this time, achieving a record for American operas by receiving fourteen performances in three seasons. When the Columbia Broadcasting System was launched in the fall of 1927, a one-hour abridgement of the opera was presented on its inaugural program, an event also marking Taylor's debut as a radio commentator.

The success of *The King's Henchman* brought Taylor a second commission from the Metropolitan Opera. Once again, the text chosen was not American: *Peter Ibbetson*, the famous novel of George Du Maurier which Taylor himself adapted into a libretto with the assistance of Constance Collier. Taylor completed this score in 1930, and the opera was produced on February 7, 1931. It was heard sixteen times in four seasons, establishing a new record for an American opera at the Metropolitan Opera. As in *The King's Henchman*, the score was of European orientation, including, as it did, interpolation of French folk songs and serving the text best in European-styled postromantic episodes as in the waltzes of the first act and the dream music of the third. "He had assembled a very affecting drama with slow music, and some fast music, too," reported Olin Downes in the *New York Times*. "It is the slow music which, in scenes of irresistible pathos, touches the heart." *Peter Ibbetson* was revived on July 22, 1961, by the Empire State Music Festival in New York. Taylor assembled two orchestral suites from his score which were performed by major orchestras. The first suite was introduced on March 18, 1938, by the Indianapolis Symphony under Fabien Sevitzky; the second on January 7, 1940, by the Baltimore Symphony conducted by Howard Barlow.

Taylor returned to music journalism in 1927 by becoming the editor of *Musical America* for one year. In 1931–32 he was the music critic of the *New York American*. Beginning with 1931, when he appeared as commentator for a series of programs on the history of opera over the NBC Radio network, Taylor was radio's most prominent music commentator, serving the Metropolitan Opera Saturday afternoon broadcasts and from 1936 to 1943 the Sunday afternoon broadcasts of the New York Philharmonic. He also made numerous appearances as master of ceremonies or as a guest on major radio programs including the popular *Information Please*, where his wit was matched by his musical wisdom. Out of these radio commentaries came three best-selling books: *Of Men and Music* (1937), *The Well-Tempered Listener* (1940), and *Music to My Ears* (1947). Additionally, Taylor was the author of *Some Enchanted Evenings: The Story of Rodgers and Hammerstein* (1953) and *The One Track Mind* (1957); editor of the revised edition of *The Music Lover's Encyclopedia* (1939); and author of the descriptive notes for *A Treasury of Gilbert and Sullivan* (1941) and *A Pictorial History of the Movies* (1943). In 1940, he did the commentary for the Walt Disney animated cartoon motion picture, interpreting musical masterworks, *Fantasia*.

In the 1940s and 1950s, Taylor's Symphonic works included *Marco Takes a Walk*, a set of variations for orchestra (1942; N.Y., November 14, 1942); *A Christmas Overture* (1943; N.Y., December 23, 1943), and *Elegia*, (1944; Los Angeles, January 4, 1945). His later operas were: *Ramuntcho* (1937; Philadelphia, February 10, 1942), libretto by the composer, based on Pierre Loti's novel set in the Basque country and making effective use of Basque folk songs; and *The Dragon* (1958; N.Y., February 6, 1958), a fantasy based on an Irish play by Lady Gregory.

Crippled by arthritis, Taylor was forced to halt his activities in the late 1950s. One of his last public appearances took place in Miami in December 1963, when he attended a performance of an orchestral suite from *Peter Ibbetson*, which Fabien Sevitzky had arranged and conducted.

Between 1933 and 1966, Taylor was a member of the board of directors of the American Society of Composers, Authors, and Publishers (ASCAP), and from 1942 to 1948 he was its president. Following his death, ASCAP honored his memory by initiating the annual Deems Taylor Awards for outstanding writing on music. Taylor was the recipient of honorary doctorates in music from New York University (1927), Dartmouth College (1939), the University of Rochester (1939), the Cincinnati Conservatory (1941), and Syracuse University (1944).

Taylor's second wife was Mary Kennedy, an actress, whom he married on July 11, 1921. They had a daughter (Taylor's only child) and were divorced in 1934. On April 17, 1945, Taylor married Lucille Little, a twenty-year-old costume designer; this marriage was annulled in 1952.

THE COMPOSER SPEAKS: I have an idea that music is the one art that can be enjoyed by someone who has no technical training whatsoever. We hardly realize, I think, how much technical training we bring to our appreciation of the other arts. . . . What gives music its universal appeal is the very fact that it is at the same time the most subtle and intangible and the most primitive of all arts. It makes its primary appeal through the ear, directly to the nerve centers. It doesn't have to be translated, and it doesn't have to be understood to make its impression. It can make a dog howl, and silence a crying baby. Its intellectual appeal is secondary, and is the result, and not the cause, of its emotional appeal.

In other words, a person who knows nothing about its technique or history, who cannot define a phrase or a bar or a sonata or a symphony, can derive genuine pleasure from listening to music—provided only that he isn't tone deaf. And such a listener has no need to apologize to anyone for his technical ignorance. That is not to say that if you appreciate the structure and finer points of a given composition you won't enjoy it more than the completely ignorant listener. But the enjoyment must come first, if the technical knowledge is to do good. . . .

For never forget: no pronunciamento, no comment on music—no, not even mine—is anything but somebody's opinion. There are no abstract truths in art: and that is why opinions are worthless if they are merely handed down. To have any value, they must be exchanged.

PRINCIPAL WORKS: *The Chambered Nautilus*, cantata for chorus and orchestra (1914); *The Highwayman*, cantata for women's voices and orchestra (1914); *Through the Looking Glass*, suite for chamber orchestra, also for full orchestra (1917–19); *Portrait of a Lady*, rhapsody for eleven instruments

(1920; revised 1923); *Circus Day*, "eight pictures from memory," for jazz orchestra, also for full symphony orchestra (1925); *Fantasy on Two Themes*, for orchestra (1925; revised 1943); *The King's Henchman*, opera (1926); *Peter Ibbetson*, opera (1930); Suite, for string orchestra (1934); *Ramuntcho*, opera (1937); *Processional*, for orchestra (1941); *Marco Takes a Walk*, variations for orchestra (1942); *A Christmas Overture*, for orchestra (1943); *Elegia*, for orchestra (1944); *Restoration Suite*, for orchestra (1950); *The Dragon*, opera (1957).

BIBLIOGRAPHY: Ewen, David, *Composers Since 1900* (N.Y., 1969); Howard, John Tasker, *Deems Taylor* (N.Y., 1927); *New York Times*, February 11, 1940, July 3, 1966 (obituary); *New Yorker*, June 6, 1925; *Newsweek*, January 29, 1940; *Saturday Review*, November 27, 1937.

Tcherepnin, Alexander, b. St. Petersburg, Russia, January 21, 1899; d. Paris, France, September 29, 1977. American citizen, 1958.

The full meaning of the word "eclectic" comes into play when we consider Tcherepnin's music. Early in his career he combined postromanticism with Prokofiev-influenced "grotesquerie," from which he advanced to polyphonic textures and neoclassicism. Much of his music reflected the influence of Georgian folk music of the Caucasus and the Orient. His last works involved complex polytonal and choral structures, with occasional suggestions of atonality and serialism. In the process of assimilating such disparate elements, he evolved his own techniques, notably the nine-tone scale (a semitone, a whole tone, and a semitone repeated three times), a new contrapuntal technique he called "interpunctus" (interpoint), and the combination of different rhythms contrapuntally. Nicolas Slonimsky has described Tcherepnin's interpunctus method as a technique "in which pairs of conjugated contrapuntal voices enter a vacancy between another pair of contrapuntal parts without overlapping." But whatever style or idiom he adopted, Tcherepnin was always the masterful technician, a composer of substance.

He was the son of Nicolas Tcherepnin, distinguished Russian composer and conductor, and of Maria Benois Tcherepnin an accomplished pianist, niece of the famous stage director Alexander Benois. From his childhood, Alexander Tcherepnin responded enthusiastically to the musical activities of his family. "There was plenty of music paper around our home," he once recalled. "I observed how my father was writing his scores and tried to do the same while alone." Noticing her son's interest, his mother began teaching him notation when he was about five, at the same time starting him on piano lessons. "So it happened that I learned how to write music and how to notate my musical ideas before I learned how to write, even before I learned the alphabet." He was composing all the time: a comic opera when he was twelve, a ballet score at thirteen, piano sonatas at fourteen. Such music had the ardor and sentiment of 19th-century Russian romanticism. But at the same time it was marked by unexpected intervallic leaps, chords in unorthodox relationships, and spicy discords young Tcherepnin had borrowed from Prokofiev. Tcherepnin's father, while always ready to advise and give him criticism, never provided him with any formal instruction in theory and composition.

When Tcherepnin was fourteen, he gave a piano recital in St. Petersburg featuring several of his own compositions. His academic education took place in schools in St. Petersburg between 1908 and 1917. Upon graduating from high school in 1917, he entered the St. Petersburg Conservatory. For one year he studied the piano there with Nicolai Sokolov and harmony with Kohiliansky. With the outbreak of the revolution in Russia, the Tcherepnin family left St. Petersburg for Tiflis in Georgia, where the father became director of the conservatory. In Tiflis, Alexander took courses in philosophy at the university and resumed his music study with private teachers: piano with Ter-Stepanova and composition with Thomas de Hartmann. During his four years in Tiflis, Tcherepnin gave piano recitals, wrote music criticism for newspapers, composed his Piano Sonata no. 1 (1918), *Ode*, for cello and piano (1919), Eight Preludes, for piano (1919–20), and his Piano Concerto no. 1 (1920), among sundry other compositions. He also contributed scores for various theatrical productions, at the same time serving as conductor. The folk music of Georgia, which he now came to know and love, would make inroads into his creativity within a few years.

When the revolution spread to the Caucasus, the Tcherepnins once again uprooted themselves and made their way to Paris, establishing permanent residence there in 1921. Tcherepnin now attended the Paris Conservatory for a year, completing his musical training with Isidor Philipp (piano) and Paul Vidal (counterpoint).

Upon leaving the conservatory in 1922, Tcherepnin initiated his professional career as composer-pianist by making his debut in London in a program made up exclusively of his own music. One year later, he made his Monte Carlo debut with the premiere of his Piano Concerto no. 1. After that, his appearances as composer-pianist covered most of Europe.

As composer, he outgrew his indebtedness to Prokofiev to arrive at a personalized identity by tapping the resources of Georgian music. He did this successfully with *Rhapsodie géorgienne*, for cello and orchestra (1922), which, without quoting any folk materials directly, was derived from the rhythmic, melodic, and harmonic idioms of Georgian folk songs and dances. André Hekking was the cello soloist when it was introduced in Bordeaux, France, early in 1924.

Tcherepnin came even more strongly into the limelight in 1923 with the music for the ballet *Ajanta's Frescoes*. Anna Pavlova, the distinguished ballerina, had commissioned him to prepare this score, using materials she had gathered in India. On September 10, 1923, she introduced *Ajanta's Frescoes* at Covent Garden in London, achieving such success with it that she featured it on a world tour and then retained it in her permanent repertoire. This work was also produced by various other ballet companies in central Europe.

By the early 1920s, Tcherepnin had devised and begun to make significant use of his nine-tone scale, found in the Piano Concerto no. 2 (1923), in which he was soloist at its world premiere in Paris on January 26, 1924; also in the *Concerto da camera*, for flute, violin, and chamber orchestra (1924). After the *Concerto da camera* had been introduced in 1925 in Donaueschingen, Germany, Hermann Scherchen conducting, it was awarded the Schott International Prize.

Tcherepnin completed his first opera, *Ol-Ol*, in 1925, preparing his own libretto based on Andreyev's *The Days of Our Lives*. "The text," wrote Willi Reich, Tcherepnin's biographer, "is a lively picture of student and soldier life in old Russia. To this material, Tcherepnin added some striking music." After the opera's successful premiere in Weimar, Germany, on January 31, 1928, it was revised and produced in Vienna, Prague, Bratislava, and New York.

Tcherepnin paid his first visit to the United States in 1926. While vacationing in Islip, Long Island, he completed Symphony no. 1 in E (1927), of which the nine-tone scale is again the spine. Its Scherzo movement was unorthodox in that it employed percussion instruments exclusively. The symphony received its first hearing in Paris at a Concert Colonne on October 29, 1927, Gabriel Pierné conducting. Its United States premiere took place in 1951 with Walter Handl conducting the Dallas Symphony.

His international fame was further enhanced during the next few years with significant performances. *Magna Mater*, for orchestra (1926-27), was first heard in Munich on October 30, 1930; two years later, on December 9, 1932, it received its American premiere at a concert of the Boston Symphony. *Le violoncelle bien temperé* (1926), twelve preludes for cello and piano (two of which enlisted the service of drums), was first given in Paris in 1926 and on March 23, 1927, in Berlin. A second opera, *Die Hochzeit der Sobeide* (1929-30), libretto by Hugo von Hofmannsthal, was produced in Vienna on March 17, 1933, and an orchestral suite from that score was heard later that year in Berlin. The composer presented the premiere of his Piano Concerto no. 3 (1932) in Paris on February 5, 1933. *Danses russes*, for orchestra (1933), had its world premiere in Omaha, Neb., on February 15, 1934, before being heard in Paris and Munich a year later.

Tcherepnin embarked on a world tour as composer-pianist in 1933, returning to the United States in 1934 for his first coast-to-coast tour. Between 1934 and 1937 he made four consecutive trips to the Orient, becoming deeply involved in oriental music. The impact of the Orient on his own music was soon reflected in the piano etudes (1935), written in the pentatonic scale. In China and Japan, Tcherepnin taught numerous Chinese and Japanese composers, and in Tokyo he founded the Collection Tcherepnin for the publication of new Japanese music. In 1937 he married Lee Hsien-Ming, a Chinese concert pianist. Of their three sons, two—Serge and Ivan—became experimental composers.

The outbreak of the Sino-Japanese War brought Tcherepnin back to the United States for a one-year stay. He returned to Paris in 1938, remaining there throughout the years of World War II. After the liberation of Paris, he gave numerous concerts for American troops in France. His tours of Europe were resumed after the end of the war.

He was back in the United States in 1948. That summer he gave master classes in piano playing and composition at the San Francisco Music and Art Institute. In 1949, he was appointed to the piano and composition faculty at De Paul University in Chicago. During some of those years he also conducted summer master classes at the Salzburg Mozarteum in Austria and at the Académie International d'Eté in Nice, France. He withdrew from all teaching assignments in 1964 to devote himself more fully to composition and to appearances as lecturer, conductor and pianist. From 1948 until his death he maintained residences in the United States (in New York City after 1964) and Paris, but his citizenship became American.

On March 20, 1952, Tcherepnin's Symphony no. 2 in E-flat (1947-51), which had been commissioned by the Associated Music Publishers, was premiered by the Chicago Symphony, Rafael Kubelik conducting. When this symphony was performed by the Louisville Orchestra in March 1964, William Mootz wrote in the *Louisville Courier-Journal*: "It is a work of enormous self-assurance and strives for eloquence without being self-conscious about it. . . . The symphony's first movement opens on a mood of numb pain and ends with a cry of anguish. The second is cloaked in stoic grief. With a pulsing tattoo from the timpani, however, the third movement embarks on a brilliant toccata that throbs with life. Hailed by a proclamation from the brass, the last theme surges to a climax that, with its pealing themes, seems to be awakening the world to the dawn of a new chance."

Some of Tcherepnin's works of the 1950s were oriental in character. His third opera, *The Farmer and the Fairy* (1952), libretto by Siao Yu based on an old oriental fable, was given its world premiere at Aspen, Col., on August 13, 1952; in 1960 it was awarded the David Bispham Medal. In her review in

Musical America, Quaintance Eaton wrote: Tcherepnin has employed the pentatonic scale for his fable, exemplifying, as he says, an uncomplicated way of life. . . . To tell the simple story, the composer has devised a set of songs connected by orchestral tissue of the colorful texture provided by a large percussion section, used in the five-tone manner, which gives oriental flavoring throughout, plus the occasional Slavic reference that seems to be inescapable. The narrative is sometimes humorous. . . . The Tcherepnin opera provided considerable visual amusement." The Orient is also encountered in *Lost Flute*, a cycle of seven songs for narrator and orchestra, on poems translated from the Chinese (1955; San Francisco, 1955).

The nine-tone scale, the individual polyphony he called interpunctus—together with polytonal writing, serial chromatic patterns, oriental colorations, and a quotation from a Russian church chant—are to be found in Symphony no. 4 in E (1957), written on commission from the Boston Symphony and its music director Charles Munch, the premiere taking place on December 5, 1958. The orientalism is suggested in tone colorings of the first movement; serial chromatics are encountered in the second movement as transitions between different sections; a Russian church chant is heard as cantus firmus in the liturgical-sounding third movement with which the symphony ends. Cyrus Durgin in the *Boston Globe*, called this "a work of large stature, solid substance, much imagination in melody and harmony, and, above all, original. It is the work of an expert in the use of counterpoint and employs every instrument for coloring purposes, and makes everything sound." Robert Taylor, in the *Boston Herald*, added: "Few contemporary works are more accessible at first hearing, display such a natural and clear development of musical thought, and so sweet and serene a melodic texture." This symphony was awarded the prestigious Glinka Prize, which, in earlier years, had gone to Rimsky-Korsakov, Scriabin, Glazunov, and Tcherepnin's father, among other Russian masters.

Two of Tcherepnin's most successful works of the 1960s were written between 1963 and 1964. Piano Concerto no. 5 (1963) was composed on a commission from the Berlin Festival Weeks. The composer was the soloist when it was first performed on October 13, 1963, in West Berlin. Serenade, for string orchestra (1964), was commissioned by the Zurich Chamber Orchestra in Switzerland. Under the direction of Edmond de Stoutz, this orchestra offered the premiere at the Venice Biennale on September 11, 1965, after which de Stoutz conducted it on his tours in Germany, Austria, Holland, Italy, and Switzerland. This five-movement composition presents one idea after another without resorting to development or repetition.

Tcherepnin paid his first return visit to his native Russia in almost half a century in May 1967, appearing in recitals, in performances of his Piano Concerto no. 2, and in chamber music concerts in Moscow, Leningrad, and Tiflis. "The reception everywhere was touching by its cordiality and spontaneity," he wrote in a personal communication to this writer. "In Leningrad I visited the apartment in which I lived with my dear parents from the age of seven until I was nineteen and felt as if I never have left—so familiar and unchanged it all seemed to me. This open door to the country of my origin is more than stimulating. It somehow closes a circle: Leningrad, Tiflis, Paris, New York, Paris, Tiflis, Leningrad!"

Tcherepnin was the editor of *An Anthology of Russian Folk Music* (1966). He completed Mussorgsky's unfinished score for the opera *The Marriage*, which was produced in Essen, Germany, on September 14, 1937. In 1953 he was awarded an honorary doctorate in music from Roosevelt University in Chicago; in 1968 he was decorated Chevalier des Arts et Lettres by the French Ministry of Culture; and in 1974 he was elected to membership in the National Institute of Arts and Letters.

THE COMPOSER SPEAKS: Music never stops working in me. It is as if musical sounds were part of my blood circulation. In fact, I cannot separate myself from music. I love it above all, just as I love human beings. It is through music that I communicate with people. The concert stage is like a church for me, the place where I can serve my religion—which is music—and thus accomplish my mission towards human beings.

PRINCIPAL WORKS: 6 piano concertos (1920–65); 4 symphonies (1927–57); 3 cello sonatas (1924, 1924, 1926); 2 string quartets (1922, 1926); 2 piano sonatas (1918, 1961).

Ten Bagatelles, for piano, or piano and orchestra (1913–18); *Ode*, for cello and piano (1919); *Feuilles libres*, for piano (1920–24); Five Arabesques, for piano (1921); Nine Inventions, for piano (1921); Three Pieces, for chamber orchestra (1922–25); Violin Sonata in F major (1922); *Rhapsodie géorgienne*, for cello and orchestra (1922); *Two Novelettes*, for piano (1922); *Six études de travail*, for piano (1923); *Ajanta's Frescoes*, ballet (1923); *Concerto da camera*, for flute, violin, and chamber orchestra (1924); *Ol-Ol*, opera (1925); Piano Trio (1925); *Le violoncelle bien temperé*, twelve preludes for cello and piano (1926); *Message*, for piano (1926); *Magna Mater*, for orchestra (1927); *Élégie*, for violin and piano (1927); Piano Quintet (1927); *Die Hochzeit der Sobeide*, opera (1930); *Entretiens*, for piano (1930); Concertino, for violin, cello, piano, and strings (1931); Duo, for violin and cello (1932); *Danses russes*, for orchestra (1933); *Étude pour piano sur le gamme pentatonique* (1936); *Trepak*, ballet (1937); *Suite géorgienne*, for piano and string orchestra (1938); Sonatina, for bassoon or saxophone and piano or orchestra (1939); Trio, for flutes

(1939); Quartet, for flutes (1939); *La légende de Razin*, ballet (1941); *Les douze*, for narrator and chamber orchestra (1945); *Déjeuner sur l'herbe*, ballet (1945); *Le jeu de la Nativité*, cantata for vocal soloists, chorus, strings, and percussion (1945); *La colline des fantômes*, ballet (1946); *La femme et son ombre*, ballet (1948); *The Farmer and the Fairy*, opera (1952); Twelve Preludes, for piano (1953); Harmonica Concerto (1953); Suite, for orchestra (1953); *Lost Flute*, cycle of seven songs for narrator and piano (1954); Eight Piano Pieces (1955); Divertimento, for orchestra (1957); *Georgiana*, suite for orchestra (1959); *Vom Spass und Ernst*, folk song cantata for voice and strings (1964); Serenade, for string orchestra (1964); Suite, for harpsichord (1966); Mass, for three equal a cappella choruses (1966); *The Story of Ivan the Fool*, cantata for narrator, vocal soloists, chorus, and orchestra (1968); *Six Liturgical Songs*, for a cappella chorus (1969); *Musica Sacra*, for string orchestra (1972).

BIBLIOGRAPHY: Ewen, David, *Composers Since 1900* (N.Y., 1969); Reich, Willi, *Alexander Tcherepnin*, revised ed. (Bonn, Germany, 1970); Thomson, Virgil, *American Music Since 1910* (N.Y., 1970); *New York Philharmonic Program Notes*, February 1969; *Tempo* (London), January 1969.

Thompson, Randall, b. New York City, April 21, 1899.

Thompson once explained that there were two sides to his creativity, one which was nationalism, and the other the eclecticism that drew some of its idioms and stylistic mannerisms from the music of the past. But whether he writes on an American subject, or about the American environment, or to an American text on the one hand, or abstract music on the other, his is American music rather than music by an American, thoroughly indigenous in its lyricism, the energy of its rhythmic drive, its occasional salty humor and sardonic moods or its equally occasional exploitation of popular music. Though most famous for his choral music, Thompson has also been an eminently successful composer of symphonies and string quartets.

He was of New England descent, both his parents born in Augusta, Maine. His father was an English teacher at Lawrenceville School in New Jersey, then headmaster of Roxbury Latin School in Massachusetts; his mother was an accomplished pianist, though she never gave concerts. Randall Thompson's first instruction in music came with piano lessons from the family housekeeper while the parents were away. Academic studies were pursued at Miss Fine's School at Princeton, N. J., for four years, then at Lawrenceville School. At the latter place, he received some singing lessons from Howard Wood, "who taught me music of real quality, such as Handel arias." As a member of the school glee club he was

one of two boy sopranos capable of negotiating high C, which became a feature of those concerts. His most important early music teacher, and the one he regards as the principal influence in his musical life, was Francis Cuyler Van Dyck, an organist who was a superior Bach performer, and for whom young Thompson often served as page turner. "He taught me to tune the organ and had me play the organ for the school choir." When Van Dyck fell ill and died, Thompson was called upon to play the organ for daily and two Sunday services. In his last year at the Lawrenceville School, he was employed as the school organist. Meanwhile, in his third school year, he composed a hymn and a Christmas carol, the latter in the Aeolian mode.

Upon graduating from Lawrenceville School in 1916, Thompson was headed for Amherst College, which most of his family had attended. But because there was little music there in those days, and on the advice of his friends, he went instead to Harvard University. There he pursued an academic course while attending the composition and theory classes of Walter Spalding, Edward Burlingame Hill, and Archibald T. Davison, among others. "Their musical influence on me was of the greatest importance. It was Archibald T. Davison who was the ultimate choral influence in my life." Thompson received his bachelor of arts degree in 1920 and his master of arts, "with highest honors," two years later. In 1920–21 he studied composition privately with Ernest Bloch in New York.

In 1922, Thompson composed *Pierrot and Cothurnus*, an orchestral prelude suggested by Edna St. Vincent Millay's one-act poetical drama *Aria da Capo*. It was responsible for bringing him the Prix de Rome and a three-year residence in Rome, where it was introduced at the Santa Cecilia Academy on May 17, 1923, the composer conducting. In Rome, he wrote, among other works, a Piano Sonata (1923; Rome, January 15, 1924); a Piano Suite (1924; Rome, May 16, 1925); *Five Odes of Horace,* for male voices (1924; Lauro, Italy, May 16, 1925); a symphonic prelude, *The Piper at the Gates of Dawn* (1924; Rome, May 29, 1924). In Venice he made sketches for his first symphony. In these compositions his stylistic individuality was slowly being developed.

After returning to the United States in 1925, Thompson made his home in Greenwich Village, N.Y. In 1926, he wrote incidental music for the revues *The Grand Street Follies* (June 25, 1926) and *The Straw Hat Revue* (October 14, 1926). On February 26, 1927, he married Margaret Quayle Whitney, who had studied painting at the Philadelphia College of Art; they raised four children.

Between 1927 and 1929, Thompson was assistant professor of music, organist, and choir director at Wellesley College in Massachusetts. His most important compositions during those years were *Jazz Poem,* originally for piano (1927), then transcribed for piano and orchestra (1928), the orchestral version premiered in Rochester, N. Y., on November 27, 1928, with the composer at the piano and Howard Hanson conducting; and Symphony no. 1 (1929; Rochester, February 20, 1930).

In 1929, Thompson was lecturer on music at Harvard University. That year, on a Guggenheim Fellowship (which was renewed for a second year in 1930), he worked on his Symphony no. 2, with which he won his first major success. He completed it in 1931, its first performance taking place in Rochester, N. Y., on March 24, 1932, Hanson conducting. After that it became one of the most successful symphonies by an American written up to that time, receiving several hundred performances in the United States and Europe. For this symphony, Thompson disavowed any program "either literary or spiritual," maintaining that all he wanted to do was to "write four contrasting movements, separate and distinct, which together should convey a sense of balance." Parts had a strong American profile, as in the elegiac second movement in which the principal melody had the sound and emotion of a Negro spiritual, and in the third-movement Vivace, alive with jazz rhythm and blueslike thematic material. When it was conducted in New York by Leonard Bernstein, Olin Downes said in the *New York Times:* "There are pages which . . . owe something of their wit, twist and rhythmical caprice to jazz, but the popular elements are absorbed in the refined and distinctive expression of an original composer. . . . The score in the sum of it is one in which the composer fights free of European derivations and does so without the ostentation and pretentiousness of the fellow who shouts, 'Just see how American I can be.' This is the score of a musician of sincerity and taste."

As guest conductor of the A Cappella Singers and the Dessoff Choirs, and as conductor of the Madrigal Choir and Supervisor's Chorus at the Juilliard School, all in New York (1931–32), Thompson's interest was focused more sharply than ever on choral music. In 1932, he wrote *Americana,* for chorus and piano (or orchestra). This was a satirical setting of a text using material from H. L. Mencken's column in the *American Mercury* about American inanities; the five-part Thompson composition touched upon fundamentalism, spiritualism, temperance, capital punishment, and optimism. It was premiered in New York by the A Cappella Singers, with the composer conducting, on April 3, 1932.

His first choral masterwork was *The Peaceable Kingdom* (1936), for a cappella chorus, commissioned by the League of Composers for its twenty-fifth anniversary and introduced on March 3, 1936, in Cambridge, Mass., conducted by G. Wallace Woodworth. The inspiration was a painting of the same title by the 19th-century artist Edward Hicks, interpreting the spirit of the prophecies of Isaiah. The painting showed William Penn making peace with the Indians on the one side and Isaiah's depiction of the lion lying down with the lamb on the other. Thompson used Biblical texts from Isaiah. Simplicity of means and clarity of structure contributed to the overall eloquence, as Thompson revealed a consummate skill in contrapuntal writing. The music was dramatically dissonant when the text spoke of the fury of the Lord and the destruction He wrought.

Alleluia, for a cappella chorus (1940), is one of the most celebrated works in American choral literature; Serge Koussevitzky commissioned it for the opening-day ceremonies of the first session of the Berkshire Music Center at Tanglewood, Mass. Thompson's text was the single word "Alleluia" (even as Mozart had done in the motet, *Exsultate, Jubilate,* K. 165). "So sure was Thompson's technique," wrote G. Wallace Woodworth, "so expert his craftsmanship, and so masterly his grasp of the true genius of choral singing, that despite a blueprint of unique limitations, he had created one of the noblest pieces of choral music in the 20th century." G. Wallace Woodworth conducted the premiere performance at Tanglewood on July 8, 1940.

The Testament of Freedom, for men's voices and piano (or orchestra), came two years later. This was the time of World War II, and Thompson's intention was to write a song of praise to a free democracy, using as text four passages from the writings of Thomas Jefferson in honor of the 200th anniversary of his birth. Consciously striving to make his music and its message reach as large an audience as possible, Thompson used the simplest of means. The chorus often sang in unison and, when divided, its music lacked the complexity of a simple hymn. The orchestra utilized only conventional harmonic schemes as the foundation on which the vocal music rested, and was never assertive. "The influences are apparent," noted Elliot Forbes in the *Musical Quarterly,* "one from the Renaissance, the other from the Baroque. But to this we must add the influence of American folk expression." *The Testament of Freedom* (with piano accompaniment) was first presented at the University of Virginia (which Jefferson had founded) on April 13, 1943, a concert broadcast throughout the United States over the CBS radio network and transmitted by short wave to the armed forces overseas by the Office of War Information. The first orchestral version was given by the Boston Symphony on April 6, 1945.

There were areas other than choral music cultivated by Thompson in the 1940s. Virgil Thomson called Thompson's String Quartet no. 1 in D minor (1941) "one of the lovely pieces our country has produced, that any country has produced in this century." The Coolidge Quartet gave the premiere in Washington, D.C., on October 30, 1941, when it received the Elizabeth Sprague Coolidge Prize. Thompson's only opera, *Solomon and Balkis,* followed a year later, a one-act work with libretto by the composer, based on Rudyard Kipling's *The But-*

terfly That Stamped. "The opera is full of humor of two kinds," wrote Elliot Forbes. "The first is a literal interpretation of a specific action in musical terms. . . . The second kind of humor is the mimicking of the dramatic recitative of the 17th and 18th century. . . . *Solomon and Balkis* is an effective work of art because it combines humor with beauty. The last is achieved, as always in Thompson's music, first of all through a fine sense of melodic line. . . . All the characteristics of his music for the voice are here: a completely vocal line; an enhancement of the meaning of the words through the line . . . a natural rhythmic equivalent in music to the pronunciation of a given word; and lastly an agreement in relative value between phrases of the text and their musical counterparts." This little opera was first heard in New York in a radio performance over CBS on March 29, 1942. Its first staged production followed in Cambridge, Mass., on April 14, and was given in New York the following December.

The decade of the 1940s ended for Thompson with the writing of another powerfully conceived and eloquently realized symphony: no. 3 in A minor (1949), which the Alice M. Ditson Fund of Columbia University had commissioned five years earlier. It was first heard at the annual Festival of Contemporary American Music at Columbia University in New York on May 15, 1949, the CBS Symphony conducted by Thor Johnson. Soon after that, it was performed by the Cleveland Orchestra, the Boston Symphony, and other major American symphonic organizations. The symphonic structure was classical, with the first and last movements in sonata form; the second, a modified rondo; and the third, a theme and variations. To it Thompson brought, as Noel Straus reported in the *New York Times,* "nobility, real depth of feeling," with each of the movements carrying "a definite message. . . . Tragic in its implications, this was music that was at once markedly sincere, spontaneous and moving." The four movements were "welded into a logical unity which made the symphony one of Mr. Thompson's major creations to date."

Between 1932 and 1935, Thompson, on a grant from the Carnegie Corporation, was director of the College Music Study for the Association of American Colleges. Thompson was lecturer on music at Wellesley College (1936–37), professor of music at the University of California in Berkeley (1937–39), director of the Curtis Institute of Music in Philadelphia (1939–41), director of the music division of the School of Fine Arts at the University of Virginia (1941–46), professor of music at Princeton University (1946–48), and from 1949 to 1965 professor, then Walter Bigelow Rosen Professor, at Harvard University (the first to hold this chair) as well as chairman of the music department from 1952 to 1957. Thompson retired as professor emeritus in 1965.

From 1950 on, Thompson continued producing music in every area except opera. *A Trip to Nahant,* a fantasy for orchestra (1954), commissioned by the Koussevitzky Music Foundation, was premiered by the Philadelphia Orchestra on March 18, 1955, Eugene Ormandy conducting. Requiem, for double a cappella chorus (1958), was performed at the University of California at Berkeley (which had commissioned it) on May 22, 1958. *The Nativity According to St. Luke,* a sacred drama for solo voice, chorus, chamber orchestra, organ, and bells (1961; Boston, December 12, 1961) was a commission from Christ Church in Cambridge. *The Passion According to St. Luke* (1965; Boston, March 28, 1965), an oratorio for vocal soloists, chorus, and orchestra, was introduced by the Handel and Haydn Society of Boston. String Quartet no. 2 (1967; Boston, April 17, 1967) was written for the Harvard Music Association. *The Place of the Blest,* a cantata for female voices and chamber orchestra (1969) written for St. Thomas's Church in New York, was given its first performance on March 2, 1969, in New York. *A Concord Cantata* (1975), written for the bicentennial of Concord, for voice and orchestra, was premiered in Concord, Mass., on May 2, 1975. *Five Love Songs,* for baritone, chorus, and string quintet (1978), was first heard on August 8, 1978, in Estes Park, Colo.

Thompson was a member of the United States section of the International Society for Contemporary Music (1934–35); a member of the executive board of the League of Composers (1939–41) and on its board of directors (1945–48); member of the National Institute of Arts and Letters, of which he was vice-president in 1939; and of the American Academy of Arts and Sciences. He was decorated Cavaliere Ufficiale al Merito della Repubblica Italiana by the government of Italy in 1958. He was awarded honorary doctorates in music by the University of Rochester in New York (1933) and the University of Pennsylvania (1969). Thompson is the author of *College Music* (1935).

THE COMPOSER SPEAKS: A composer's first responsibility is and always will be to write music that will reach and move the hearts of his listeners in his own day. . . . Literal and empty imitation of European models must be rejected in favor of our own genuine musical heritage in its every manifestation, every inflection, every living example.

PRINCIPAL WORKS: 3 symphonies (1929, 1931, 1949); 2 string quartets (1941, 1967).

Piano Sonata (1923); *The Wind in the Willows,* string quartet (1924); Suite, for piano (1924); *Five Odes of Horace,* for male voices (1924); *Jazz Poem,* originally for piano, also for piano and orchestra (1927–28); *Americana,* for chorus and piano, or orchestra (1932); *The Peaceable Kingdom,* for a cappella chorus (1936); Tarantella, for men's voices and piano (1938); Suite, for oboe, clarinet, and viola (1940); *Alleluia,* for a cappella chorus (1940); *Solo-*

mon and Balkis, radio opera (1942); *The Testament of Freedom,* for men's voices and piano or orchestra (1943); *The Last Words of David,* for chorus and piano or orchestra (1949): *A Trip to Nahant,* orchestral fantasy (1955); *Mass of the Holy Spirit,* for a cappella chorus (1955); *Ode to the Virginian Voyage,* for chorus and orchestra (1956); Requiem, for double a cappella chorus (1958); *Frostiana,* seven choruses for men's, women's, and mixed voices with piano or orchestra (1959); *The Nativity According to St. Luke,* for vocal soloist, chorus, and chamber orchestra, organ and bells (1961); *The Passion According to St. Luke,* for vocal soloists, chorus, and orchestra (1965); *The Place of the Blest,* cantata for treble voices and piano or chamber orchestra (1969); Twenty Chorale Preludes, Four Inventions, and a Fugue, for organ (1970); *Wedding Music,* suite for string quartet (1971); *The Mirror of St. Anne,* for double chorus (1972); *Fare Well,* for a cappella chorus (1973); *A Concord Cantata,* for chorus and orchestra (1975); *Five Love Songs,* for baritone, chorus, and string quintet (1978).

BIBLIOGRAPHY: *DCM;* Howard, John Tasker, *Our American Music* (N.Y., 1946); Machlis, Joseph, *Introduction to Contemporary Music,* revised ed. (N.Y., 1979); Thomson, Virgil, *American Music Since 1910* (N.Y., 1970); *Boston Symphony Program Notes,* March 31, 1950; *Modern Music,* No. 19, 1942; *Musical Quarterly,* January 1949; *Who's Who in America, 1980–81.*

Thomson, Virgil Garnett, b. Kansas City, Mo., November 25, 1896.

Winner of the Pulitzer Prize in music in 1949, Thomson is a sophisticated and eclectic composer who has assimilated different styles of the past and present, the popular as well as the serious, without sacrificing his own identity. He has never subscribed to any system, but he has been sympathetic to many avant-garde movements. He has generally chosen to speak with music that is simple in technique, full of well-sounding tunes, direct in emotional or pictorial appeal, fundamental in structural logic. But this is a simplicity that comes from consummate technical skill, articulateness, and discrimination. When he engages voices, he has shown an exceptional gift in adapting American speech inflections to musical declamation.

He was the younger of two children, with both their parents tracing their ancestry back to colonial days. Neither parent was musical; the father, a postal clerk, was tone deaf. But Virgil's musicality was a phenomenon from earliest childhood. When he was five, his cousin, Lela Garnett, gave him his first piano lessons. She soon turned him over to local piano teachers, all incompetent, but none capable of arresting his mounting interest in music. "I took my place quite early as a child performer," he has recalled in

his autobiography. "I was precocious, good-looking, and bright. My parents loved me for all these things and for being their man-child. My sister, eleven years older, looked on me almost as her own [child]. My relations were pleased at my being able to read and sing songs and remember things. So with all this admiration around (and being, in spite of the praise, not wholly spoiled) I early seized the center of the stage and until six held it successfully. By the time I was eleven, I had a gluttonous musical appetite." After hearing his first public concert at twelve—a recital by Paderewski of which Thomson "remembered everything, literally every note, including the false ones"—he began going to all the major concerts that he could hear in Kansas City. And at that time he initiated a professional career in music by serving as substitute organist at the Calvary Baptist Church in Kansas City. But music was not his only interest. From the time, at the age of six, that he saw his first stage production, he was a theater aficionado; he also revealed an unusual gift for words.

Upon graduating from Irving School in 1908, in Kansas City, where he had been a top student, he entered Central High School. At this time he came under the musical influence of Robert Leigh Murray, the tenor soloist of the Calvary Baptist Church. Realizing how thoroughly inadequate Thomson's musical training had been up to that time, Murray became "the mentor of my musical progress. He saw to it that I did have proper lessons and eventually that I earned money to pay for them. He also taught me to play his accompaniments and paid me at commercial rates for doing so." With Murray's guidance, Thomson now acquired his first accomplished piano teacher, Moses Boguslawski, who was succeeded by two others equally competent, Rudolf King and E. Geneve Lichtenwalter, paying for these lessons by working as a page in a public library. Thomson also branched out in his music studies with lessons in harmony with Gustav Schoettle and organ with Clarence Sears; the latter soon had Thomson assist him at Sunday services. All this took place while Thomson was a consistently "grade-A" student at high school, from which he graduated in 1914.

One year later, he went to junior college, which had just been founded (Kansas City Polytechnic Institute and Junior College). There he helped form a literary society and to found a literary journal. He earned his keep by working as organist in a Methodist church in Westport, a suburb of Kansas City.

Even before America's entry into World War I, Thomson—eager for military action—enlisted in the National Guard Regiment in January 1917. His first nine months of service were with that regiment, the 129th Field Artillery, in which Harry Truman was captain of Company D. Subsequently, Thomson was trained at the Pilots' Ground School at the University of Texas (School of Military Aeronautics) and finally at an air service school for radio officers at Columbia University in New York. Commissioned second lieutenant in the Military Aviation Service, he was finally given overseas orders in September 1918, but the armistice two months later kept him in the United States.

When he was discharged from the armed forces in 1918, Thomson had come to two fixed decisions: to complete his education at Harvard University and to make music his profession. Thomson was able to go to Harvard with funds borrowed from a Mormon church, though he was not a member of that faith. In Boston, he took piano lessons privately with Heinrich Gebhard. After his first semester in Harvard, Thomson was appointed instructor there on an Elkan Naumburg Fellowship, and organist at the North Easton Unitarian Church. In July 1920, his first known composition was written. It was a song, "Vernal Equinox," for soprano, to a poem by Amy Lowell. It was followed the same year by a second song for soprano, "The Sunflower" (poem by William Blake) and *De Profundis*, for a cappella chorus.

In 1921, Thomson toured Europe as a member of the Harvard Glee Club. He was allowed to remain in Paris for a year to study with Nadia Boulanger on a John Knowles Paine Traveling Fellowship from Harvard (the first ever given to an undergraduate) and a scholarship from the École Normale de Musique.

Back at Harvard in 1922, he resumed his academic and musical studies—the latter with Walter Spalding, Archibald T. Davison, Wallace Goodrich, and Edward Burlingame Hill—receiving his bachelor of arts degree in 1923. A Juilliard Fellowship then enabled him to come to New York in 1923, where he studied composition with Rosario Scalero at the David Mannes School of Music and conducting with Chalmers Clifton. In New York, Thomson wrote some vocal music, a *Missa Brevis*, for voices, and *Two Sentimental Tangos*, for orchestra.

Once again on an Elkan Naumburg Fellowship, Thomson was back in Harvard in 1924–25. At the same time, he initiated his career as a writer on musical subjects with contributions to the *American Mercury* and *Vanity Fair*.

In September 1925, Thomson decided to return to Paris. Except for intermittent short visits to the United States, he remained there fifteen years. After November 1927 his home was a converted top story at 17 Quai Voltaire on the Left Bank. The Friday evenings there saw a continuous convocation of the intellectual elite of Paris when the wine, food, conversation, and music were all superlative. His personal intellectual circle comprised not only the leading French composers of the time (including Milhaud, Auric, Honegger and Poulenc) but also Jean Cocteau, Scott Fitzgerald, André Gide, Pablo Picasso and, most important as far as his own career in music was concerned, Gertrude Stein. They all had a decisive influence on his intellectual growth. Musically, perhaps, he was most strongly affected by

Erik Satie, whose "everyday music" struck a responsive chord with Thomson's own aims to write a simple, communicable music. The witty and at times satirical and often music-hall–oriented pieces by members of the "French Six" also had their impact. In February 1926, Thomson completed the ironic and extremely dissonant *Sonata da chiesa*, for clarinet, trumpet, viola, horn, and trombone, whose three movements consisted of a "Chorale," "Tango," and "Fugue." The following April, Thomson made his first setting of a Gertrude Stein text, "Susie Asado," for soprano and piano. Between 1927 and 1928, other Gertrude Stein texts were used for his music, including *Capital Capitals*, for four men's solo voices and piano (1927), a conversation among four cities in Provence. In 1928, Thomson completed *Symphony on a Hymn Tune*, which he had begun two years earlier. The hymn which recurred in one form or another throughout the four movements was "How Firm a Foundation," an old Scottish melody in the pentatonic scale; a subsidiary melodic subject was the children's hymn "Yes, Jesus Loves Me." In using hymns as the basis of his symphony, Thomson aimed to invoke the atmosphere of American farm life in the 19th century. Its musical style had such folklorish overtones that Paul Rosenfeld once compared the symphony to a Currier and Ives print. The premiere of the symphony took place two decades after it had been written: on February 22, 1945, with the composer conducting the New York Philharmonic.

During the year of 1928, Thomson wrote his first opera, the work that made him famous. This was *Four Saints in Three Acts*, for which Gertrude Stein had provided an obscure, dadaistic text made up of unintelligible words or intelligible words and phrases which, together, seemed to have no comprehensibility. This text was later given a scenario by Maurice Grosser. In keeping with the opera's conscious incongruities, the work was in four acts and not in three, and the cast consisted not of four saints but more than twenty. Incongruous, too, was placing an all-black cast into a Spanish setting. Further compounding these incongruities was Thomson's score, which was not in a dissonant, polytonal and avant-garde idiom, but thoroughly tuneful, with melodies derived from folk and church sources. The harmonic language was almost rudimentary, the overall style consistently witty. Such music gave meaning and purpose and sometimes even intelligibility to Gertrude Stein's alogical text.

Its world premiere took place in Hartford, Conn., on February 8, 1934. It was the project of a group calling itself the Society of Friends and Enemies of Modern Music, of which Thomson was the musical director for the three years of its existence. "By the consistency, high quality and painstaking preparation of all the contributing elements, it showed, as only the ballets of Diaghilev had shown, that the Wagnerian ideal, divested of its Victorian eroticophilosophic paraphernalia, could still be realized," wrote Kathleen Hoover in *Virgil Thomson: His Life and Music.* "And this close union of the arts was achieved by the most difficult means: everything in it was of contemporary design. No shade of the easy-ways-out known in the lyric theater jargon as 'tradition' dimmed its bright workmanship. The decor was pop art at its most imaginative. Cellophane, crystal, feathers, seashells, lace and brilliant colors such as the American stage had never seen before—nor has since then—went into this confection of a visionary Spain. The illumination brought to the scene, in turn, dawn, noontide, dusk and the white light of Heaven itself. The singers, holding their tutored poses with an exaltation all their own, might have served as models for El Greco or Zurbaran. The dancers blended saintly abandon with attitudes of the classic ballet. And the score achieved the ever-astonishing feat of transcending the limitations of its libretto: its tunefulness and bounce dispelled perplexity over the cryptic text; its gravity, glinting with blithe overtones, evoked both the mystical strength and the native gaiety of lives devoted in common to unworldly ends."

The success in Hartford made a New York production a foregone conclusion. *Four Saints in Three Acts* opened a six-week engagement on Broadway on February 21, 1934. Later that year the opera was awarded the David Bispham Medal. Since then, it has remained a classic of the American operatic theater, recorded, broadcast over radio, and frequently revived both in the United States and Europe.

His suddenly won fame with *Four Saints in Three Acts*, combined with his lifelong love for the stage, now established Thomson on Broadway. For the Federal Theater of the Works Progress Administration, he wrote the incidental music to a production of *Macbeth* with an all-Negro cast, directed by Orson Welles, which opened at the Lafayette Theater on April 9, 1936. Later in the 1930s, Thomson's music was heard in productions of *Hamlet*, starring Leslie Howard (November 10, 1936), and *Anthony and Cleopatra*, starring Tallulah Bankhead (November 10, 1937). For the ballet stage, Thomson provided the score for *Filling Station*, the first successful ballet on an American subject and the first written for and performed exclusively by Americans. With scenario by Lincoln Kirstein, it was produced on January 6, 1938, in Hartford, Conn., by the Ballet Caravan. Thomson also wrote music for the screen. On commissions by the United States Farm Security Administration, he wrote background music to two documentaries by Pare Lorenz: *The Plough That Broke the Plains* (1936) and *The River* (1937). Thomson adapted both these scores into symphonic suites, the one from *The Plough That Broke the Plains* becoming one of his most frequently performed symphonic compositions.

In spite of his preoccupation with the theater, films, and ballet, Thomson did not neglect concert music. His major works in the 1930s included Stabat Mater, for soprano and string quartet (1931); Symphony no. 2 (1931; Seattle, Wash., November 7, 1941), which was an orchestration of his first piano sonata; two string quartets (1932); and several *Portraits*, for various instruments or combinations of instruments or orchestra, in which he gave tonal characterizations of friends and acquaintances, having him or her sit for him as he composed as they might have sat for an artist's portrait. He had begun writing such portraits in 1927, one of which, for solo violin, was "Miss Gertrude Stein as a Young Girl." He continued to write them through the years; among those who were thus portrayed were Aaron Copland, Eugene Ormandy, Mayor Fiorello H. LaGuardia, Dorothy Thompson, and Pablo Picasso.

With the German occupation of France, Virgil Thomson left Paris during the summer of 1940 to reestablish himself permanently in the United States. His home from then on was at the Chelsea Hotel in New York, which became another salon similar to the one he had known on Quai Voltaire. In 1940, he was appointed successor to Lawrence Gilman as music critic of the *New York Herald Tribune*. For the next fourteen years, he contributed to that paper perceptive, witty, opinionated, and often controversial music reviews and feature articles which had an urbanity and an insight all their own. "As a writer, he has done more for contemporary music than any man of his time," noted Jay Harrison in *Musical Magazine*. As music critic, he became the founder, in 1941, of the New York Music Critics Circle for the presentation of annual awards to the most important works heard each season in New York; it was dissolved in 1965.

His most important work in the 1940s was his second opera, *The Mother of Us All*, text by Gertrude Stein, again with a scenario by Maurice Grosser. Thomson wrote it on commission from the Alice M. Ditson Fund of Columbia University, completing it in 1947, and seeing it produced for the first time on May 7, 1947, in New York. The libretto no longer confined itself to the incomprehensibility of *Four Saints in Three Acts* in the presentation of a political fantasy based on the career of Susan B. Anthony, pioneer in the women's suffragette movement. The play was full of anachronisms and symbolism, with irrelevant asides, its cast of characters including Ulysses S. Grant, Lillian Russell, Daniel Webster, Andrew Jackson, Anthony Comstock and others, as well as "Gertrude S." and "Virgil T." The humorous or satiric thrusts of this text were not lost upon Thomson, who once again produced a tuneful, witty, thoroughly American score filled with melodic reminiscences of marches, waltzes, dance tunes, sentimental songs and revival hymns. "That there was no trouble in understanding the text," Francis D. Perkins reported in the *Herald Tribune*, "could be credited . . . to Mr. Thomson's skill in its musical investiture. . . . Mr. Thomson showed a remarkable ability to present English words flexibly and lyrically. Here again his music supports and enhances the text; the score as a whole shows a remarkable mastery and successful solution of the often vexatious problems of recitative and lyric declamation in English." As had been the case with its eminent operatic predecessor, *The Mother of Us All* has become an American operatic classic. Since its premiere it has had several thousand performances in American opera houses, churches, colleges, and various semi-professional groups; it has been recorded, a release selected by *Stereo Review* as record of the year. Reviewing that recording for *High Fidelity/Musical America* in 1977, Conrad L. Osborne spoke of it as "a fine, rare and sophisticated art work . . . one of the six or eight works of the American musical theater that have both true artistic stature and proven popular appeal." As a symphonic suite, *The Mother of Us All* was first heard on January 17, 1950, in Knoxville, Tenn., after which it was performed by many leading American symphony orchestras.

Another notable success was achieved with music for the documentary film, *Louisiana Story* (1948), produced by Robert Flaherty, describing the impact of an oil development project in Louisiana on a French-speaking family as viewed through the eyes of a twelve-year-old boy. Thomson's score adapted folk songs and dances of the Acadian region which he had discovered in *French Folk Songs* edited by Irene Therese Whitfield. On the soundtrack, Thomson's music was performed by the Philadelphia Orchestra under Eugene Ormandy. For this music, Thomson received the Pulitzer Prize in music, the only time this award has been presented for a motion picture score. The symphonic suite *Louisiana Story*, in four movements, which the Philadelphia Orchestra under Ormandy premiered on November 26, 1948, is another of Thomson's orchestral scores that has found permanence in the American symphonic repertoire. A second suite from this film score, containing seven other sections, is called *Acadian Songs and Dances*.

Between 1947 and 1952, Thomson completed three tone pictures for orchestra, more sophisticated in technical approaches and more impressionistic in style than much of his earlier music. The first was *The Seine at Night* (1947; Kansas City, Mo., February 24, 1948), which the composer described as a "landscape piece, a memory of Paris and its river as viewed nocturnally from one of the bridges to the Louvre," its principal melody, which represented the river, appearing in three different orchestral colorations. *Wheatfield at Noon* (1948) was commissioned by the Louisville Orchestra, which gave the first performance on December 7, 1948, in Kentucky, the composer conducting. This was a series of free variations on a theme containing all twelve tones of the chromatic scale arranged in four mutually exclusive triads. *Sea Piece with Birds* (1952; Dallas, Tex., December 10, 1952) was "an attempt to portray the undertow of the sea," the composer says, "the surface tension of the waves and the flight of the birds as they sail back and forth above the sea."

Thomson resigned as music critic of the *Herald Tribune* in 1954 to concentrate on composition and to expand his activities as conductor, lecturer, and teacher. That same year, he toured Europe as conductor. In 1960 he was awarded a Guggenheim Fellowship. From the early 1960s on he filled various university posts. In 1963 he was Visiting Slee Professor of Music at the University of Buffalo in New York; in 1965, Regents' Professor at the University of California in Los Angeles; in 1966-67, Visiting Mellon Professor of Music at Carnegie Institute of Technology in Pittsburgh; and in 1968, Visiting Dorrance Professor at Trinity College in Hartford, Conn. In the 1970s, he was composer-in-residence at the University of Bridgeport in Connecticut (1972); Trinity College in Hartford, Conn. (1973); Claremont College in California (1974); Dominican College in San Rafael, Calif. (1974); Otterheim College in Westerville, Ohio (1975); and the University of California in Los Angeles (1976). He was artist-in-residence at the California State University at Fullerton in 1975.

Thomson's third opera, *Lord Byron* (1968), is one of the most significant works of his later years. He wrote it on commission from the Koussevitzky Music Foundation for the Metropolitan Opera. When the Metropolitan Opera failed to mount it, it was given its world premiere by the Juilliard American Opera Center in New York on April 13, 1972. In his libretto, which utilizes excerpts from Byron's works, Jack Larson covered Byron's life in flashbacks after an opening scene in which Londoners mourn Byron's death as his body is being brought back from Greece. What follows are recollections of Byron's early successes as poet, his sexual adventures including the love affair with his half-sister, frustrated marriage and definitive abandonment of England for the European continent. The opera ends as it had begun, with the return of Byron's body to London. Shades of poets long dead, and their statues from Poets' Corner in Westminster Abbey, led by Shelley, welcome Byron back into their fold. Thomson's music tapped English and Irish folk traditions and quoted from such varied sources as "Believe Me If All Those Endearing Young Charms," "Auld Lang Syne," "Ach du lieber Augustin," and "La Marseillaise." The ballet music and the instrumental interlude were particularly interesting; and so was the remarkably idiomatic writing for the voice. Patrick J. Smith wrote in *High Fidelity/Musical America*: "Thomson's music continues as accomplished as in his earlier operas—chameleon, flowing, very 'conservative,' conjunct and highly lyric with lots of pastiche writing." In the *New Yorker*, Andrew Porter said: "Thomson has the gift to be simple; his notes come down where they ought to be, in the place just right. But his simplicity is not artless, but careful, refined and purified, by a process that has not destroyed its zest."

These are some of Thomson's later concert works of special interest. The Concerto for Cello and Orchestra (1950) was written as a tribute to the cellist Luigi Silva, but it was Paul Olefsky who performed it when it was introduced by the Philadelphia Orchestra under Ormandy on March 24, 1950. Thomson intended it as a self-portrait. American hymnology plays an important role in this score. The second movement is a set of variations on the southern hymn tune "Death, 'Tis a Melancholy Day"; in the third movement another hymn, "Yes, Jesus Loves Me," is quoted. The Concerto for Flute, Harp, Strings, and Percussion (1950) is a portrait of the painter Roger Baker. Its world premiere took place at the Biennale in Venice on September 18, 1954. Thomson's lifelong interest in liturgical music was again reflected, but more ambitiously than before, in the nine-section *Missa Pro Defunctis*, for double chorus and orchestra (1960; Potsdam, N. Y., May 14, 1960). Waltzes, the tango, progressive jazz idioms, and boogie-woogie are carried into this religious framework, "placed on the side of the angels," as John Gruen wrote in *Musical America*, "and . . . given reverential status." Symphony no. 3 (1972; N.Y., December 26, 1976) was an orchestration of String Quartet no. 2. *Cantata on Poems of Edward Lear*, for soprano, baritone, chorus, piano, and chamber orchestra (1973; Towson, Md., November 18, 1973), is a setting of five Lear nonsense poems: "The Owl and the Pussycat," "The Jumblies," "The Pelican Chorus," "Half an Alphabet," and "The Akond of Swat." Thomson put these jingles, as he explained, "into musical conventions so far removed from the poetic ones involved that the contrast is in itself a joke, another joke, if you will, but one which does not ask for laughter."

Thomson continued to be a prolific contributor of incidental music for the theater in the 1950s. Among the productions for which he provided music were: Truman Capote's *The Grass Harp* (April 27, 1953); *Ondine*, starring Audrey Hepburn and Mel Ferrer, and directed by Alfred Lunt (February 18, 1954); *King John* and *Measure for Measure*, directed by John Houseman for the American Shakespeare Festival Theater at Stratford, Conn. (June 1956); *Othello*, starring Alfred Drake; *The Merchant of Venice*, starring Katharine Hepburn, and *Much Ado About Nothing*, starring Katharine Hepburn and Alfred Drake, once again at the Shakespeare Festival Theater (June 1957). Thomson also contributed the background music for the motion picture *The Goddess* (1958).

Thomson's accumulation of honors is commensurate with the lofty station he has occupied in American music for half a century. He was decorated as officer of the French Legion of Honor (1947) and elected to membership in the National Institute of Arts and Letters and to the American Academy of Arts and Letters (1959). He was awarded the National Institute of Arts and Letters gold medal (1966); the Creative Arts Award from Brandeis University in Waltham, Mass. (1968); the Handel Medallion of the City of New York (1971); the Henry Hadley Medal of the National Association for American Composers and Conductors (1972); and the Edward MacDowell Medallion (1977). His honorary degrees include doctor of fine arts, from Syracuse University in New York (1949), University of Missouri in Columbia (1971), and Roosevelt University in Chicago (1968); doctor of letters, from Rutgers University in New Brunswick, N. J. (1956); doctorates in music, from New York University (1971), Columbia University (1978), and the Kansas City Conservatory (1980); and doctor of humane letters, from Johns Hopkins University in Baltimore, Md. (1978).

The city of Thomson's birth, Kansas City, honored its native son on his eighty-fourth birthday in October 1980 with a week-long festival devoted to some of his principal works, including excerpts from his operas. A television documentary on his life was then previewed before receiving national coverage over the facilities of Public Broadcasting Service network on December 27.

Thomson is the author of *The State of Music* (1939), *The Musical Scene* (1945), *Virgil Thomson*, an autobiography (1966), *Music Reviewed—1940–1954* (1967), and *American Music Since 1910* (1970). In his advanced age, Thomson decided to turn over his library and literary possessions to educational institutions. Johns Hopkins University received two thousand books on music; New York University, five hundred books together with paintings; the Manhattan School of Music, a fabulous collection of recordings. The largest collection of all went in 1979 to Yale University: an accumulation of his music manuscripts (10,000 pages) and 125 boxes of correspondence.

THE COMPOSER SPEAKS: Persons unprepared by training to roam the world of music in freedom but who enjoy music and wish to increase that enjoyment are constantly searching for a key, a passport that will hasten their progress. There is none, really, except study. And how far it is profitable to spend time cultivating talent where there is no vocation, every man must decide for himself. But if there is any door-opener to taste, it is knowledge. One cannot know whether one likes a work unless one has some method beyond mere instinct for tasting it. The ways to taste a piece of music are to read it in score or to follow it in performance. And it is quite impossible to follow unfamiliar kinds of music without an analytical method, a set of aids to memory that enables one to discern the pattern of what is taking place. . . .

How can anybody really know anything about

music, beyond its immediate practice or perception, least of all what he likes? Learning is a precious thing and knowing one's mind is even more so. . . . Those who think themselves most individual in their likings are most easily trapped by the appeal of chic, since chic is no more than the ability to accept trends in fashion with grace, to vary them ever so slightly, to follow a movement under the sincere illusion that one is being oneself.

In the long run, such freedom as anybody has is the reward of labor, much study, and inveterate wariness. And the pleasures of taste, at best, are transitory, since nobody, professional or layman, can be sure that what he finds beautiful this year may not be just another piece of music to him the next. The best any of us can do about any piece, short of memorizing its actual sounds and storing it away intact against lean musical moments, is to consult his appetite about its immediate consumption, his appetite and his digestive experience. And after consumption, to argue about the thing interminably with all his friends. "De gustibus disputandum est."

PRINCIPAL WORKS: 12 *Portraits*, for orchestra (1937–44); 5 albums of *Portraits*, for piano (1929–45); 4 piano sonatas (1929–40); 3 symphonies (1928, 1931, 1976); 2 string quartets (1931–32).

Capital Capitals, for two tenors, two baritones, and piano (1927); *Four Saints in Three Acts*, opera (1927–28); Violin Sonata (1930); Stabat Mater, for soprano, string quartet, or orchestra (1931); *Seven Choruses from the Medea of Euripides*, for women's voices (1934); *Missa Brevis*, for women's voices (1934); *The Plough That Broke the Plains*, incidental music for film, also suite for orchestra (1936); *The River*, incidental music for film, also suite for orchestra (1937), *Filling Station*, ballet, also suite for orchestra (1937); Ten Etudes and Nine Etudes, for piano (1940–51); Sonata, for solo flute (1943); *The Mother of Us All*, opera (1947); *The Seine at Night*, for orchestra (1947); *Wheatfield at Noon*, for orchestra (1948); *Louisiana Story*, incidental music for film, also two suites for orchestra, the second entitled *Acadian Songs and Dances* (1948); *A Solemn Music*, for band (1949); *Four Songs to Poems by Thomas Campion*, for mezzo-soprano and piano or clarinet, viola, and harp (1951); *Five Songs from William Blake*, for baritone and piano, or orchestra (1951); *Sea Piece with Birds*, for orchestra (1952); Kyrie, for chorus (1953); Concerto, for flute, strings, harp, and percussion (1954); *Old English Songs*, for baritone and piano (1955); Mass, for solo voice or unison chorus with piano or orchestra (1960); *Missa Pro Defunctis*, for men's and women's choruses and orchestra (1960); *A Joyful Fugue*, for orchestra (1962); *Praises and Prayers*, for mezzo-soprano and piano (1963); *Autumn*, concertino for harp, strings, and percussion (1964); *The Feast of Love*, for baritone and orchestra (1964); *The Nativity as Sung by the Shepherds*, for vocal soloists, chorus, and orchestra

(1967); *Shipwreck and Love Scene from Byron's Don Juan*, for tenor and orchestra (1967); *Lord Byron*, opera (1967–68); *Cantata on Poems of Edward Lear*, for soprano, baritone, chorus, and piano (1973–74); *Family Portrait*, for two trumpets, French horn and two trombones (1974); *Parson Weems and the Cherry Tree*, ballet (1975).

BIBLIOGRAPHY: Copland, Aaron, *The New Music: 1900–1960* (N.Y., 1966); Hoover, Kathleen, and Cage, John, *Virgil Thomson: His Life and Music* (N.Y., 1959); Thomson, Virgil, *Virgil Thomson* (N.Y., 1966); *ASCAP Today*, January 1972; *High Fidelity/Musical America*, November 1971; *Musical Quarterly*, April 1949; *New York Times*, March 21, 1971, January 9, 1972, April 9, 1972, April 25, 1976; *New Yorker*, January 17, 1977; *Opera News*, July 1976.

Thorne, Francis Burritt (Jr.), b. Bay Shore, N.Y., June 23, 1922.

His music has been the synthesis of two primary influences of his childhood and teenage years: jazz and Wagnerian chromaticism. Melodic lines are often long and expressive in slow movements while the fast music often runs in legato eighth-note lines with off-beat surprise accents. Serial techniques as well as jazz elements were extensively utilized before Thorne began moving toward a more natural stream-of-consciousness lyricism.

He was born into a family in which music was an influential presence. His father, Francis Burritt Thorne, Sr., a stockbroker, was an amateur ragtime pianist, an interest he shared with his aunt. The maternal grandfather was Gustave Kobbé, for many years music critic of the *New York Herald* and the author of *The Complete Opera Book*. Kobbé, a passionate enthusiast, brought the love of Wagner's music into the Thorne household. In childhood, the younger Francis Thorne would listen to his father's ragtime playing from a crouching position under the piano. He would then try to pick out these tunes on the piano. Symphonic and operatic music on the phonograph—especially that of Beethoven and Wagner—and attendance at concerts and opera performances contributed a broader dimension to his boyhood musical experiences. There were some piano lessons at this time. While attending Pomfret School, a private preparatory school (1934–39), Thorne sang in the school choir. Otherwise, his musical education was temporarily arrested. During his teenage years, his musical activities consisted of playing jazz, in which he was self-taught. He entered Yale University for an academic course in 1939. There he soon shifted to theory and composition as his major, in defiance of his parents' wishes, and attended classes in composition with Richard Donovan and Paul Hindemith. Studies with Hindemith were, as far as he himself was concerned, "a disaster," so much so that he would not resume serious study of composition for another eighteen years, in which time jazz remained his prime musical interest. Thorne maintains that in his early years at Yale he learned far more by singing with, and making arrangements for, the Whiffenpoofs than from Hindemith.

In 1942, Thorne received his bachelor of arts degree, in theory of music, at Yale, and on December 8 of the same year he married Ann Cobb, his childhood sweetheart who was then a college student and with whom he has had three daughters. For three years, during World War II (1943–45) he served in the U.S. Navy, as commanding officer of a subchaser in the Atlantic, Caribbean, and Pacific theaters of operation. Upon his separation from military service, he went to work as credit analyst at the Bankers Trust Company in New York (1946–50) and after that was customer's man at Harris, Upham & Company in New York (1950–54). For twelve years he took piano lessons with Claude Gonvierre, Geraldine Farrar's accompanist.

Deciding in 1955 to abandon the world of finance for music, Thorne worked as jazz pianist at Julius Monk's Upstairs at the Downstairs (1955–57) and at the Hickory House restaurant (1955–58), both in New York. In 1958 he took his family to Florence, Italy where he rented a villa and aspired to study music seriously. He had hoped to be a pupil of Luigi Dallapiccola's, the Italian dodecaphonist, but at that time Dallapiccola had just left for the United States. A chance meeting brought him into contact with David Diamond, then living in Florence. Two years of intensive study of composition with Diamond followed. "Diamond was not only a terrific teacher," Thorne says, "but he was finally my real mentor and inspiration as far as serious musical composition was concerned."

In 1958, Thorne composed *Broadway and 52nd Street*, a jazz work for two pianos, which became his first piece of music to get performed when Whittemore and Lowe introduced it in Butte, Mont., in 1958. A Sonatina, for two solo violins, followed in 1959, his String Quartet no. 1 in 1960, and Symphony in One Movement, for large orchestra, in 1961, among other compositions.

Thorne looks back upon *Elegy for Orchestra* (1962–63) as the real beginning of his mature career as composer. It was also his first work to gain recognition. Written in memory of his parents, this is a work in tripartite form with dramatically changing moods and contrasting rhythms; sounds of jazz were skillfully interpolated, without seeming to be either an intrusion or an irrelevancy in an elegiac composition. *Elegy* was first performed professionally on November 19, 1964, by the Philadelphia Orchestra conducted by Eugene Ormandy. In the *Philadelphia Bulletin*, Max de Schaunesee said: "It . . . slowly progresses in plangent accents with an unmistakable refinement of feeling and scoring. It is deeply felt and effective."

That concert by the Philadelphia Orchestra brought Thorne back to the United States after a six-year absence. He once again worked as jazz pianist, this time at Goldie's in New York and various other places. He completed the writing of his Symphony no. 2 in 1964, its first performance given on May 4, 1967, by the Kansas City Philharmonic under Robert Baustian in Lawrence, Kans. On January 5, 1968, the Minneapolis Symphony, conducted by Stanislaw Skrowaczewski, performed Thorne's *Burlesque Overture* (1963–64) in which Thorne arrived at a synthesis of serialism and jazz. John K. Sherman, in the *Minneapolis Star*, called it "clever, madcap and witty with slapstick percussion and rowdy dissonance. . . . The total effect was rather fragmented, with quick-changing episodes." The premiere of this work had taken place in Turku, Finland, on July 29, 1966, William Strickland conducting.

In 1965, tapping his cousin's ample financial resources, Thorne founded the Thorne Music Fund, serving as its president all of its nine years. Its aim was to provide financial assistance to deserving innovative composers. The initial grant—a three-year fellowship of $10,000, payable at $300 a month—went to Ben Weber. Thorne's grants were soon increased to $15,000. By 1967, the fellowship spent $65,000 a year, both on three-year fellowships and on commissions for special works.

In 1968 Thorne was the recipient of a fellowship from the National Institute of Arts and Letters. His principal works following his Piano Concerto no. 1 (1966) included *Lyric Variations* I, for large orchestra (1966–67; Buffalo, N.Y., September 24, 1967); *Six Set Pieces*, for thirteen players (1967; Chicago, January 23, 1970); *Double Concerto*, for viola, double bass, and orchestra (1967–68); and *Sonar Plexus*, for electric guitar and orchestra (1968; New Haven, Conn., January 17, 1970).

In 1968, Thorne returned to Florence for an additional three-year stay, teaching at the Villa Schifanoia and playing jazz at Ruby's nightclub. These years saw the writing of a number of significant compositions. *Liebesrock*, for three electric guitars and orchestra (1968–69), was called by Lester Trimble in *Stereo Review*, "an unusual piece by a very unusual composer. To say that he is 'marching to a different drummer' would be an understatement. In a period of post-Webern-like astringency, he aims here for textual bulk and opaque (though resonant) sonorities. In an era when quotations à la Ives have ceased to be fashionable, he uses them with deliberation and evocativeness. In a decade when jazz has become past tense to rock, he incorporates jazz, or the spirit of jazz, into his music and spices it up with, of all things, electric guitars! 'Surrealist' probably comes closer to describing this programmatic piece. I find it impressive for its originality of viewpoint and its intensity."

Between 1969 and 1972, Thorne was executive director of the Walter W. Naumburg Foundation, and from 1972 to 1975 executive director of Lenox Arts Center. He has been executive director of American Composers' Alliance since 1975. In 1976 he was the founder—and since 1976, president—of the American Composers' Orchestra in New York. Between 1971 and 1973 he was on the music faculty of the Juilliard School of Music in New York.

In the 1970s, Thorne produced two additional sets of *Lyric Variations*, two new symphonies, and three concertos, among major productions. *Lyric Variations* II (1971–72; N.Y., April 10, 1972) was scored for woodwind quintet and percussion, and *Lyric Variations* III (1972; N.Y., February 17, 1973) for piano, violin, and cello. Symphony no. 3 (1969), for string orchestra and percussion, was introduced in New York in October 1971 by the Manhattan Orchestra under Anton Coppola, and Symphony no. 4 (1977) was first heard at the Cabrillo Music Festival in California (which had commissioned it) in August 1978, Dennis Russell Davies conducting. Of his three new concertos, the Concerto no. 2, for piano and orchestra (1974), was introduced on April 5, 1975, by the St. Paul Chamber Orchestra, which had commissioned it, Dennis Russell Davies serving as piano soloist with John De Main conducting. The Chamber Concerto for Cello and Ten Instruments (1974–75) was premiered in New York, performed by The Group of Contemporary Music (for which it was written), Andrew Thomas conducting, on April 28, 1975. The Concerto for Violin and Orchestra (1975–76) was given its first performance by Romuald Tucco at the Cabrillo Music Festival, Dennis Russell Davies conducting, in August 1976. In these works the composer's concern for heightened expressiveness, lyric beauty, and rhythmic vitality superseded his former interest in serialism and jazz.

The Festival of Contemporary Music presented by the Juilliard School of Music at the Lincoln Center for the Performing Arts in New York in February 1981 offered the world premiere of Thorne's *The Eternal Light* (1980). This is a setting of Canto XXIII of Dante's *Paradiso* for soprano and large orchestra. In *The New Yorker*, Nicholas Kenyon described it as "by turns rhapsodic and passionate, skittish and ironic, visionary and tranquil." He added: "The music was always resourceful, always ear-catching."

Thorne was the recipient of grants from the National Endowment for the Arts in 1974, 1976, and 1979, and from the Contemporary Music Society in 1968 and 1979.

THE COMPOSER SPEAKS: I firmly believe that the influence of jazz (Afro-American) music is more significant in the 20th century than Schoenberg's serialism. I believe the works thus influenced of Stravinsky, Copland, Bernstein, Milhaud, Bartók, et al., will survive the crabbed serialist works (with a few exceptions) because of the fresh rhythmic vitality and urgency of communication.

PRINCIPAL WORKS: 4 symphonies (1961–77); 3 string quartets (1960, 1967, 1975); 2 piano concertos (1966, 1974).

Elegy for Orchestra (1962–63); *Burlesque Overture*, for orchestra (1963–1964); *Rhapsodic Variations*, for piano and orchestra (1964–65); Ricercare and Coda, for piano (1965); *Lyric Variations* I, for large orchestra (1966–67); *Six Set Pieces*, for thirteen players (1967); Double Concerto, for viola, double bass, and orchestra (1967–68); *Song of the Carolina Low Country*, for chorus and orchestra (1968); *Sonar Plexus*, for electric guitar and orchestra (1968); *Chamber Deviations*, for clarinet, double bass, and percussion (1968); *Liebesrock*, for three electric guitars and orchestra (1968–69); Songs and Dances, for cello, keyboard, and percussion (1969); *Antiphonies*, for four groups, winds, and percussion (1969–70); "A Mad Wriggle," for madrigal group (1970); *Simultaneities*, for brass, five electric guitars, and percussion (1971); *Quintessence*, for the Modern Jazz Quartet and orchestra (1971); *Lyric Variations* II, for woodwind quintet and percussion (1971–72); Piano Sonata (1972); *Evensongs*, for flute, harp, percussion, and celesta (1972); *Fanfare, Fugue, and Funk*, for three trumpets and orchestra (1972); *Lyric Variations* III, for piano, violin, and cello (1972); *Cantata Sauce*, for mezzo-soprano, baritone, and eight players (1972); Two Pieces for Organ, with percussion (1973); *Songs of the Great South Bay*, for soprano and piano (1974); *After the Teacups*, ballet (1974); Chamber Concerto, for cello and ten instruments (1974–75); Violin Concerto (1975–76); *Head Music*, for clarinet, cello, and piano (1975); Grand Duo, for oboe and harpsichord (1976); *Echoes of Spoon River*, ballet (1976); *Five Set Pieces*, for saxophone quartet (1976); *Love's Variations*, for soprano, flute, and piano (1976–77); *Spoon River Overture*, for orchestra (1976–77); *A Lovesong Waltz*, for solo piano (1977); Divertimento, for flute and chamber orchestra (1979); Duo Sonata, for two bassoons (1979); *The Eternal Light*, for soprano and large orchestra (1980).

BIBLIOGRAPHY: *BBDM, DCM*; *New York Times*, December 11, 1967; *Who's Who in America, 1980–81*.

Toch, Ernst, b. Vienna, Austria, December 7, 1887; d. Los Angeles, Calif., October 1, 1964. American citizen, 1940.

Toch's music represents a compromise between modern idioms and postromanticism. His best works, for all their digressions into 20th-century harmonic, tonal, or percussive innovations, are basically lyrical, emotional, dramatic, or programmatic. However modern in style and spirit, they never forgot their debt to 19th-century Germanic and Austrian romanticism. He received the Pulitzer Prize in music in 1956.

There were no musicians in his family. His father, a dealer in unprocessed leather, was opposed to his son's preoccupation with music, determined that Ernst prepare himself for some profession. Much of Toch's early involvement with music was done secretly. His initial contact with it came in his grandmother's pawn shop where he saw a piano for the first time and forthwith tried to produce a melody. Soon after that he learned to read music by following the printed sheets used by an amateur violinist performing at his house. Sounds, the nonmusical as well as the musical, always fascinated him. "I can remember as a child listening to the stone cutter while he was making cobblestones and taking great pleasure from different qualities which the ear perceived each time the hammer struck a fresh blow. I can also remember playing tunes for hours on the wooden boards of graduated lengths which formed the gate to our country garden in Vienna."

His first attempt at composition came when he was six. After that, most of what he learned about music was done autodidactically. As a boy, he purchased the pocket scores of Mozart's ten string quartets. In order to learn them better, he copied them out painstakingly, thereby acquiring an insight into classical structure and style. "Mozart not only replaced for me every living teacher," Toch once said, "but outdid them all." Inspired by Mozart, and without any formal instruction, Toch proceeded to write string quartets of his own while attending elementary school and the gymnasium in Vienna. By the time he was seventeen, he had completed six string quartets, as well as other chamber music pieces, some piano compositions, a Scherzo for orchestra, and a piano concerto that has been lost, all of these very Brahmsian in style. In 1905, one of his schoolmates at the gymnasium brought Toch's String Quartet no. 6 in A minor to the attention of Arnold Rosé, who introduced it in Vienna with the Rosé String Quartet in 1905.

Complying with his father's wishes that he become a doctor, in 1906 Toch entered the University of Vienna, where he spent the next three years aimed at a degree in medicine. He did not abandon composition, completing String Quartet no. 7 in G major (1908), some duos for two violins (1909), and several pieces for piano. One of his compositions won the prestigious Mozart Prize, an international competition for young composers, in 1909, bringing with it a four-year stipend and a one-year fellowship at Frankfurt Conservatory of Music in Germany. Leaving behind him all further intentions of pursuing medicine, Toch left Austria to settle in Germany. At the Conservatory, he studied piano with Willy Rehberg and composition with Ivan Knorr (1910–13). In 1910, Toch won the Mendelssohn Prize and the first of four consecutive annual Austrian State

prizes. He received the Mendelssohn Prize again in 1913, the year in which he was appointed professor of composition at the Academy of Music in Mannheim.

With the outbreak of World War I, Toch served in the Austrian infantry, seeing action in the front lines in the Italian Alps. Except for *Spitzweg Serenade* (1917), a pastoral string trio written in the trenches, Toch's creativity came to a temporary halt. During one of his furloughs, on July 23, 1916, he married Alice Babette (Lilly) Zwack, daughter of a banker; they raised one child, a daughter. Then, through the influence of several important Austrian musicians, Toch was transferred from the fighting front to behind the lines in Galicia, where he remained until the war's end.

Upon his discharge from military service, Toch came to Heidelberg, Germany. There he resumed his academic education at the university, specializing in philosophy and earning his Ph.D. in 1921. That year he returned to Mannheim to resume his teaching duties at the Academy of Music for the next seven years. His five-year cessation from composition ended in 1919 with the writing of the String Quartet no. 9 in C major, in which, rebelling against the influence Brahms had had upon him, Toch struck new ground by adopting the dissonant, polytonal, and atonal techniques favored by the young German musical iconoclasts. Introduced in Mannheim soon after it was written, it aroused considerable controversy and disapproval. But for Toch, the writing of such music was "indeed . . . refreshing, an inner need to get away from the overemotional type of music. . . . It was as refreshing as a plunge into cold water on a tropical summer day." This is the style he adhered to for many of his works during the next few years.

In the 1920s, Toch extended his compositional activities into musical media other than the chamber music to which, up to now, he had been partial. His success brought him to the forefront of composers in Germany. *Die chinesische Flöte*, for soprano and chamber orchestra (1922), was introduced in Frankfurt on June 24, 1923 (and heard in Boston on March 7, 1932). Five Pieces, for chamber orchestra (1924), represented Germany at the festival of the International Society of Contemporary Music in Prague, Erich Kleiber conducting, on May 15, 1925. Emanuel Feuermann was the soloist when Toch's Cello Concerto (1924) was first heard on June 17, 1925, at the German Tonkünstlerfest in Kiel, singled out by the German critic Hugo Leichtentritt as "the most remarkable work heard at the festival." Most significant was the Piano Concerto no. 1 (1926), premiered by Walter Gieseking in Düsseldorf on October 8, 1926, Hans Weisbach conducting. Reviewing it in the London musical publication *Chesterian*, L. Dunton Green wrote: "Toch is firmly rooted in the great tradition of German classicists and romanticists; but his spirit is thoroughly modern, unsentimental (but by no means unfeeling) and immensely dynamic. . . . It will rank in the course of time with the great piano concertos of musical literature." Soon after the premiere performance, the concerto was heard in Berlin; was a feature of the festival of the International Society for Contemporary Music in Frankfurt on July 3, 1927; and received its American premiere in Chicago on February 3, 1928. Highly successful, too, was a charming one-act opera, *Die Prinzessin auf der Erbse* (1927; Baden-Baden, Germany, July 17, 1927); Benno Eikan's libretto was based on the Grimm fairy tale *The Princess and the Pea*.

In 1929, Toch transferred his home from Mannheim to Berlin. His continuous interest in innovation was reflected in a novel choral composition entitled *Fuge aus der Geographie* (1930), first heard on June 17, 1930, at the Berlin Festival of New Music. Here the chorus speaks its part rhythmically and fugally in a recitation of names of exotic places. On several later occasions, Toch again employed spoken choruses in his works, including one named *Valse* (1961) in which clichés at a cocktail party are recited in three-quarter time.

Early in 1932 Toch was invited by the American Pro Musica Society to tour the United States in performances of his piano and chamber music. On March 25, 1932, Toch was soloist with the Boston Symphony, conducted by Serge Koussevitzky, in a performance of his Piano Concerto no. 1. The program included the American premiere of Toch's *Bunte Suite*, for orchestra (1928; Frankfurt, February 22, 1929).

Back in Berlin later in 1932, Toch worked on his Piano Concerto no. 2 (sometimes also known as Symphony for Piano and Orchestra). With the menacing shadow of nazism hovering over Germany, the premiere of this concerto in Berlin in 1933 was disrupted by Nazis and could not get heard; its scheduled publication was canceled. Toch realized the time had come for him to make an escape. He was permitted by the Nazis to leave the country to represent Germany at a musicological convention in Florence, Italy, in April, 1933. Toch never returned to Berlin. Instead, he went to Paris, and from Paris he made his way to London, where his Second Piano Concerto was premiered on August 20, 1934, the composer as soloist, Sir Henry J. Wood conducting.

In the fall of 1934, Toch came to the United States for permanent residence, settling first in New York, where he taught composition at the New School for Social Research. One of his first works written in the United States also became one of his most successful: the orchestral variation-fantasy on the Westminster Chimes, *Big Ben* (1934), which was inspired by the tolling bells of Big Ben in London on a foggy evening while the composer crossed Westminster Bridge. "The theme," the composer said, "lingered in my

imagination for a long while and evolved into other forms, somehow still connected with the original one, until, finally, like the chimes themselves, they seemed to disappear into the fog from which they had emerged. I have sought to fix this impression in my variation-fantasy." The "Big Ben" theme is heard first slightly disguised. Variations of changing moods follow, culminating in a fugue; the composition ends with the sounds of the Westminster chimes. Readily assimilable in its atmospheric and programmatic writing, this work proved so successful when introduced in Cambridge, Mass., on December 20, 1934, by the Boston Symphony under Richard Burgin that within the next few years it was programmed by most major American orchestras.

Highly communicable, too, and frequently performed, was another orchestral composition completed in New York: *Pinocchio: A Merry Overture*, based on Carlo Collodi's famous story of the wooden puppet whose nose grew longer whenever he lied. Otto Klemperer and the Los Angeles Philharmonic gave the first performance on December 10, 1936.

In 1936, Toch went west to make a new home in the Los Angeles area, initially at Pacific Palisades and after that, in 1958, in Santa Monica. The influence of George Gershwin brought him a commission from Warner Brothers to do the scoring for a film. That project never materialized but another came from Paramount studios: the writing of background music for *Peter Ibbetson*, starring Gary Cooper (1935). This began a ten-year association with motion pictures in which Toch provided music for ten additional films. Among these were *Outcast* (1937), *The Cat and the Canary* (1939), *Ladies in Retirement* (1941), *None Shall Escape* (1944), *Address Unknown* (1944), and *The Unseen* (1945).

In spite of his preoccupation with commercial music, Toch produced one of his most significant chamber music works during his first year in California: the Piano Quintet (1938). It was commissioned by Elizabeth Sprague Coolidge, and its world premiere was heard in Pittsfield, Mass., on September 23, 1938, performed by the Roth Quartet with the composer at the piano. To each of the four movements, Toch assigned a descriptive title to suggest the varied moods: I. The Lyrical Part; II. The Whimsical Part; III. The Contemplative Part; and IV. The Dramatic Part. Stylistically, this work—as well as the String Trio (1936) which had preceded it—reverted to the advanced harmonic and tonal idioms of Toch's music of the twenties. Here, as Nicolas Slonimsky wrote in his liner notes to the recording, "Toch displays his best qualities of sustained rhythmic drive, romantic and elegiac melody, lucidity of contrapuntal technique, economy and richness of harmony and—last but not least—his practical knowledge of instrumental writing." The piano part assumed an independence from the four stringed instruments, often heard antiphonally. "The piano is projected to the foreground," Slonimsky adds, "when massive sonorities or percussive statements are required, and the strings, solo or in combination, enter when a lyric utterance is made. Both groups participate in rhythmic passages in which a maximum of motoric energy is extracted from the music."

The complexity of Toch's style discouraged audience enthusiasm as well as performances and delayed publication for both the String Trio and the Piano Quintet for almost a decade. "This unresponsiveness of American audiences to the modernist style," wrote Lawrence Weschler in his introduction to Toch's *The Shaping Forces of Music*, "is surely one reason (the osmosis of Hollywood film scoring being another) for the slow bending of Toch's creative production during the late thirties and forties into a more harmonic and tonal idiom." This trend can be detected in the *Cantata of the Bitter Herbs*, for narrator, vocal soloists, chorus, and orchestra (1938), text taken partly from the Bible (Psalm 126) but mostly from the *Haggadah* of the Hebrew Passover services.

The rising power of Nazi Germany in Europe in the final years of the 1930s, the outbreak of World War II, and Toch's own later failures to achieve the kind of recognition he had once enjoyed, were all depressants that arrested the flow of his music. Though he had produced thirty-five works between 1919 and 1933, he completed only eight between 1933 and 1937, and just one work between 1938 and 1945. "Disappointments and sorrows render me frustrated and lonesome," he wrote to a friend in 1943. "I become somehow reluctant to go on writing if my works remain more or less paper in desks and on shelves." Instead he turned to teaching composition, first privately and then, from 1940 to 1948, at the University of California in Los Angeles. In 1944 he was a guest lecturer at Harvard University.

By the second half of the 1940s—and in spite of a heart attack in 1948—creative rebirth began taking place, beginning with the String Quartet no. 12 (1946), which bore a motto from a poem by Eduard Mörike: "I do not know what it is I mourn for—is it unknown sorrow; only through my ears can I see the beloved light of the sun." *Hyperion*, a dramatic prelude for orchestra based on Keats, came a year later, having been commissioned by the Kulas Fund of Cleveland; its first hearing took place on January 8, 1948, with George Szell conducting the Cleveland Orchestra.

The further renewal of Toch's creative strength became intensified with the writing of three symphonies. These, said Lawrence Weschler, "should be interpreted as a musical triptych, the sustained outpouring of a single course in Toch's deeply religious and humanistic experience of the late Forties." Symphony no. 1 (1949–1950) carried a motto from Luther: "Although the world with devils filled should threaten to undo us, we will not fear, for God has willed his truth to triumph through us." Written during a visit to Vienna, this symphony was first

heard there on December 20, 1950. Symphony no. 2 (1951; Vienna, January 11, 1952) was not only dedicated to Albert Schweitzer but, as the composer once said, was "dictated" by him. Symphony no. 3 (1955), Toch's masterwork in symphonic form, brought him the Pulitzer Prize in music in 1956, and one of the greatest successes he was to enjoy in the United States. Commissioned by the American Jewish Tercentenary Committee of Chicago, it was given its world premiere on December 2, 1955, by the Pittsburgh Symphony under William Steinberg before receiving performances by major orchestras in the United States and Europe. A quotation from Goethe's *The Sorrows of Werther* in the published score suggests the mood of the entire work: "Indeed am I but a wanderer, a pilgrim on earth?—what else are you?" Lyricism contrasts with dramatic fire within a structure which, as the composer explained, is, in each of the three movements, in the nature of a "ballistic curve with an initial impulse, a steady line, and then a decline." Innovation is found in orchestration that included two backstage sound-producing instruments creating noises. One is a tank of carbon dioxide creating a hissing sound through a valve; the other, a wood box in which croquet balls were set into motion by a rotating crank to create a novel percussive effect. "It must not be assumed," wrote a critic for *Musical America*, "that the symphony is merely a trick piece depending upon instrumental novelties for its effects. The odd instruments are used sparingly, though not timidly, nor just for textural reasons and they fit artistically into the general orchestral design. The music as a whole has a nostalgic oriental quality. It is tonal and substantially melodic with a good deal of emotional expressiveness."

However innovative the orchestration of Symphony no. 3 was—and though, in String Quartet no. 13 (1953), a twelve-tone row is used in the final movement—most of the music that Toch wrote in the 1950s was more concerned with lyrical and emotional interest than with experimentation. This proved true of his melancholy and brooding Symphony no. 4 (1957), written as a memorial to Mrs. Miriam MacDowell, widow of Edward MacDowell, and commissioned by the Women's Association of the Minneapolis Symphony, the orchestra that introduced it on November 22, 1957, under Antal Dorati. The pensive *Notturno* (1953) is another case in point. Commissioned by the Louisville Orchestra in Kentucky, it was premiered on January 2, 1954, under Robert Whitney; also the elfin *Peter Pan*, a "fairy tale" (1956; Seattle, Wash., February 13, 1956), which the Koussevitzky Music Foundation had commissioned.

In most of his subsequent concert works, Toch favored fantasialike structures in preference to rigid classical forms. The one-movement Symphony no. 5, for example, is a rhapsodic poem titled *Jephta* (1961; Minneapolis, November 22, 1964), in which four solo violins (in one place increased to six) are prominently featured within a flexible structure that begins briskly and ends pianissimo. "I would not know how to account for this structure," Toch said. "The form to be achieved, I would say, is inherent in the musical substance, follows the laws of its motive intent and becomes identical with it." In the last two symphonies (1963, 1964), and two sinfoniettas, one for string orchestra (1964) and the other for wind orchestra (1964)—all in Toch's last year—"the lyric line breaks free of all restrictions," says Lawrence Weschler. "The orchestration becomes leaner and clearer partly perhaps because of the pressure of the relentless passage of time."

Toch's final years were marked by a remarkable productivity. "Never in my life has writing come as easily to me as it does now," he told a friend. "I am writing myself empty." Though he spent much of the time between 1950 and 1958 in Vienna and Switzerland, his death, from cancer of the stomach, came in a Los Angeles hospital.

In 1954, Toch was visiting composer at the Berkshire Music Center in Tanglewood, Mass. He was elected member of the National Institue of Arts and Letters in 1957, and in 1963 he received the Cross of Honor for Science and Art from the Austrian government. An Ernst Toch Archive of his manuscripts, books, and memorabilia was founded in 1974 at the University of California in Los Angeles. He was the author of *Die Melodielehre* (1923) and *The Shaping Forces in Music* (1948).

THE COMPOSER SPEAKS: A great number of contemporary composers do not any longer acknowledge the force of musical substance. Instead they claim entirely different basic principles as motivation for music and for their own music. In these discussions there is an undercurrent of references to the "atomic" age we live in, which, with its tremendous implications, calls for, as they hold, the fundamentally new forms of expression that are pouring forth abundantly. Is this not, I wonder, oversimplification?

As biological, psychological beings we are unchanged, untouched. We are functioning as we ever did, breathing; our hearts still so made that their beat is subject to our emotions, halting from joy and horror, recording all the antonyms of human existence, love and hate, jubilation and despair, struggles, winning and losing; with senses so made as to carry images to the store of our memories, to take delight and enchantment from what we name beauty; with a mind so made as to reflect not only on, say, atomic fusion, but also on what happens in ourselves, to gather and grasp and express what it perceives from the outside and from within, forging it all into one in the white heat of a human universe.

It is here that music and language take their origin, are fed, sustained, given impulses and change of direction, receiving ever new status and balance, a universe indeed, rising from chaos, not much affected by our strivings into the universe of the stars, but strongly formed according to its own laws.

Because we hold in common the enormous wealth of elemental properties and inner experiences—phenomenally integrated in the tissue of our expressive reactions—we find language and music to be communicative to the highest degree. Expression drawn from the common pool communicates forcefully, does impart its law (depending, of course, on the potential of the one who tells and the one who listens) and therefore can be "understood." Thus only can art become valid to multitudes of passionate participants.

All attempts at the construction of "esperantos," perfectly logical forms of languages, have failed. Art being a living language, all its inconsistencies, irregularities and random ways have their part in it, and it is our part to let organic processes grow, even if we cannot account for them.

PRINCIPAL WORKS: 13 string quartets (1902–53); 7 symphonies (1950–64); 2 piano concertos (1925, 1932); 2 violin sonatas (1912, 1928).

Die chinesische Flöte, for soprano and chamber orchestra (1922); *Burlesken Suite*, for piano (1923); *Tanz Suite*, for small orchestra (1923); Five Pieces, for chamber orchestra (1924); Cello Concerto (1925); *Wegwende*, opera (1925); Two Divertimenti, for string orchestra (1926); *Die Prinzessin auf der Erbse*, one-act opera (1927); *Komödie*, for orchestra (1927), *Egon und Emilie*, opera (1928); Piano Sonata (1928); *Bunte Suite*, for orchestra (1928); Cello Sonata (1929); *Gesprochene Musik*, for speaking chorus (1930); *Fuge aus der Geographie*, for speaking chorus (1930); *Der Fascher*, opera (1930); *Das Wasser*, cantata for narrator, vocal soloists, chorus, and chamber orchestra (1930); *Kleine Theater Suite*, for orchestra (1931); Fifty Etudes, for piano (1931); Music for Orchestra with Baritone (1932); *Big Ben*, variation-fantasy for orchestra, (1934, revised 1936); *Pinocchio: A Merry Overture* (1935); String Trio (1935); Piano Quintet (1938); *Cantata of the Bitter Herbs*, for narrator, vocal soloists, chorus, and orchestra (1938); *Poems to Martha*, for voice and strings (1943); *Profiles*, for piano (1946); *Ideas*, for piano (1946); *Hyperion*, dramatic overture for orchestra (1947); *The Inner Circle*, for six a cappella choruses (1953); *Notturno*, for orchestra (1953); *There Is a Season for Everything*, for mezzo-soprano and instruments (1953); *Vanity of Vanities*, for soprano, tenor, and instruments (1954); *Divisions*, for piano (1956); Sonatinetta, for piano (1956); *Peter Pan*, fairy tale for orchestra (1956); *Phantoms*, for narrator, women's speaking chorus, and orchestra (1957); Five Pieces, for wind (1959); Sonatinetta, for flute, clarinet, and bassoon (1959); *Valse*, for speaking chorus and percussion (1961); *Reflections*, for piano (1961); Sonata, for piano four hands (1962); *The Last Tale*, a Scheherazade one-act opera (1962);

Three Impromptus, for violin, cello, and viola (1963); *Three Pantomimes*, for orchestra (1963–64); Quartet, for oboe, clarinet, bassoon, and viola (1964); Sinfonietta, for string orchestra (1964); Sinfonietta, for wind orchestra (1964).

BIBLIOGRAPHY: Ewen, David, *Composers Since 1900* (N.Y., 1969); Johnson, C., "The Unpublished Works of Ernst Toch" (doctoral thesis, Los Angeles, 1973); Toch, Ernst, *The Shaping Forces in Music*, biographical introduction by Lawrence Weschler, revised ed. (N.Y., 1975); Weschler, Lawrence, *Ernst Toch: 1887–1964* (Los Angeles, 1974); *Musical Quarterly*, October 1938; *New York Times* (obituary), October 3, 1964; *Who's Who in America, 1964–65*.

Tremblay, George Amedée, b. Ottawa, Canada, January 14, 1911. American citizen, 1939.

Tremblay has been a staunch adherent of twelve-tone music, but with different works he has either modified or revised the system to meet the specific artistic demands of a given composition.

His father, Amedée Tremblay, was a professional pianist, organist, and composer. George was only three when he began to extemporize on a little portable reed organ given him by a priest at the basilica where his father was organist and general music director. Still in his childhood, guided by his father, Tremblay learned to duplicate the sounds of Debussy on the piano. "I astounded everyone who would ask me to play my impressions of Debussy, as they called it. This music seemed quite natural to me, although to my listeners it seemed remote and incomprehensible."

When he was eight, Tremblay was invited to play the piano for Sir Wilfred Laurier, prime minister of Canada, and his family at their official residence. The following Sunday, Tremblay performed the piano publicly for the first time by giving a recital with his father at the pipe organ at the basilica, his performance consisting solely of improvisations. "This is a skill which I continued to develop, and it has served me well—both for myself and my students in our communication with one another. I have often performed in this capacity at concerts and festivals of contemporary music."

Though he received some instruction on piano and organ from his father, his formal musical training was haphazard, because "lessons" were emphasized whereas he preferred "making music." He says: "My education was widespread. Half the time, I didn't know whether I was teaching or being taught. To say that one is self-taught is an unwarranted conceit, it seems to me, since one learns and is taught from everyone and everything."

In 1920, the Tremblay family moved from Canada to the United States, initially settling in Salt Lake City in Utah, where the father had become organist and choir director of the Cathedral of St. Madeleine. In 1923, the family transferred its home to San Diego, Calif. There, young Tremblay became infatuated with jazz at the seaside ballroom at Mission Beach, an interest that has remained with him ever since and which occasionally penetrated into some of his later compositions. In San Diego he was also affected by the sight of the ocean and the ships anchored in the harbor. "The far vision across the sea instilled in me the feeling for the long line, which has become such an integral part of my thinking." He remembers still one other influence in San Diego: a public school teacher whose name he now remembers only as Miss Powell, who taught him to read books and how to learn.

In 1925, the family came to Los Angeles, his father now assuming the post of first organist and choir director of the new Church of St. Vincent. In Los Angeles, Tremblay's musical life acquired a new dimension. "I studied every book on music in the new Central Library of Los Angeles, which had just been completed, and it was at this time also that I became intensely interested in motion pictures, which made a lasting impression on me."

He met David Patterson, author of *Tone Patterns,* in 1927. For the next five years, Tremblay was his pupil in harmony, counterpoint, and composition. This was a period during which Tremblay made a number of successful public appearances as composer-improviser in Los Angeles, San Diego, and Oakland. In 1934 he studied composition with Arnold Schoenberg, whose influence on Tremblay's musical development was decisive and permanent. Tremblay's first major work, the String Quartet no. 1 (1936), was in a strict twelve-tone technique. It received its first performance in Los Angeles from the New Motive String Quartet at a concert of contemporary music sponsored by the New Motive group. Tremblay's next composition, Prelude and Dance, for piano, was written for a friend, the writer and painter Verabel Champion, who became his wife on July 10, 1937. Prelude and Dance was introduced by John Crown on December 6, 1940, in Los Angeles.

In 1938, at the request of Gerald Strang, then editor of *New Music,* Tremblay completed two piano sonatas which were published in *New Music* in January 1939. W. L. Landowski gave them their premiere performance on March 15, 1939, over the Paris radio in France, and Maurice Zam introduced them to the United States over the radio in Hollywood, Calif., later that year.

By the time of Pearl Harbor, Tremblay had become a celebrity in Los Angeles, but not because of his compositions nor even for his improvisations. "I was reputed to know every musical piece ever written," he explains, "though this, of course, was a gross exaggeration. Nevertheless, I was selected as a permanent member of a changing panel on a weekly evening radio quiz show, *Are You Musical?* in Los Angeles. This show lasted two years, ending shortly before Pearl Harbor. That made me an instant Hollywood celebrity. I came in contact with theatrical people as a result of this experience: producers, directors, writers, actors, and composers. These events shaped the direction and the course of my role in the evolution of motion picture music."

In 1940, Theodore Norman, violinist, commissioned Tremblay to write a work for string quartet for a projected children's concert in Beverly Hills. Tremblay filled this assignment by writing *Modes of Transportation,* which the McCarthy Peet String Quartet first performed publicly on December 14, 1940, before recording it. It consisted of three parts respectively entitled "The Mayflower," "The Covered Wagon" and "The Iron Horse." Writing in *Modern Music,* Lazare Saminsky reported that *Modes of Transportation* revealed the pliancy of Tremblay's musical nature. " 'The Covered Wagon' movement shows a striking tone-painting talent. 'The Mayflower,' reveals the same pictorial inventiveness. Very remarkable are the means by which Tremblay tone-paints the crude wooden vessel, its sea struggle and woes; yet the frank, noble elegy that closes the movement rests on a far higher plane."

Instead of adhering rigidly to a twelve-tone row in *Modes of Transportation,* Tremblay used three symmetrically constructed eight-tone scales, the better to impart an impressionistic character. When Schoenberg heard this composition, he was intrigued by the serialization of the three scales, and by the harmonization by chords with notes duplicating those in the melody. This prompted Schoenberg to use a similar technique in his own *Ode to Napoleon,* where he used a row of two symmetrical hexachords similar to the three scales of *Modes of Transportation.*

Modes of Transportation influenced motion picture music. The new sounds of this composition were so often imitated and recreated by film composers that these sounds came to be known as "the Hollywood eight" (an eight-note chord constructed of alternate minor and major seconds).

Another widely performed Tremblay composition of this period was the Wind Quintet (1940), one of two short wind quintets Tremblay had written at the request of Adolph Weiss. It was introduced at a concert of the League of Composers in Los Angeles on March 19, 1941, and on May 24 of the same year was broadcast over the radio facilities of CBS. On the basis of this composition Saminsky, in *Modern Music,* described Tremblay's music as "dark and stern . . . and it is strikingly personal. Atonalists are notoriously alike—all gray. But in spite of its atonal loam, Tremblay's grim and whimsical speech reminds of no other. His music couples an excellent logic with a draconian austerity. This trait is indeed the one that relates his mind to Schoenberg as a parallel, not as a derivative."

The death of Tremblay's brother at Bataan on Easter morning of 1942 led to the writing of *In Memoriam,* a string quartet which the Norman Quartet premiered the following summer at the University of California in Los Angeles. In a greatly revised version it was one of the compositions performed by the Vertchamp Quartet at a concert of "Evenings on the Roof" in Los Angeles on December 3, 1945. In *Modern Music,* Ingolf Dahl called it "a deeply moving piece even to those who do not know that the war has had a very direct and personal bearing on it. . . . The precarious balance between program (expression) and musical form (system) is very beautifully achieved. . . . His music has a strong, poignant face of its own and it will become known."

Symphony in One Movement was written during the closing years of World War II, the final score being completed in the spring of 1949. Like all of Tremblay's major works up to this time, it was composed in a serial technique but, as the composer explains, a technique "especially created for its particular realization. For this piece I evolved a definite harmonic system from the subsidiary aspects of the basic tone row. . . . The row is sometimes treated as a block sound rather than in numerical sequence. Certain tones of the basic series may be repeated indefinitely within the block without regard for the specific designated number of the notes in the series." This symphony is divided into three sections of the classical sonata form: exposition, development, and recapitulation, the exposition preceded by an extended introduction in which all the material of the composition is presented. Before receiving its public premiere, the symphony was recorded in Hamburg, Germany. The concert premiere was given by the Los Angeles Philharmonic under Zubin Mehta on April 28, 1966.

Among Tremblay's more significant works in the 1950s were the Quintet, for wind instruments (1950); the Serenade, for twelve instruments (1955); and the Quartet, for piano and strings (1958). The wind-instrument quintet was introduced by the Los Angeles Woodwinds on May 10, 1953. To Walter Arlen, writing in the *Los Angeles Times,* "the three movements of this quintet are engrossing, inventive and skillfully written essays in a clear and meaningful language, and it is of no import whether or not the composer adhered to the twelve-tone or any other method of composition for the music conveyed its message on its own account." Serenade was first presented on October 14, 1957, in Los Angeles, at the "Monday Evening Concerts" series, David Raksin conducting. This twelve-tone jazz work in several movements "is one of the most attractive and certainly one of the most melodiously successful new works by an American composer that I have heard in several years," wrote Peter Yates in *Arts and Architecture.* About the Quartet for piano and strings, whose premiere was given by the Chamber Arts Quartet in

Los Angeles on January 13, 1963, Walter Arlen said in the *Los Angeles Times:* "For the most part it exposes fresh and imaginative ideas that are treated with musical impulse, sound knowledge of instrumental techniques and a feeling for concise form."

In 1965, Tremblay founded in Los Angeles the School for the Discovery and Advancement of New Serial Techniques. This school also provided film and television composers with a center for consultation and for experimental studies. Since 1965, Tremblay devoted so much time to teaching that there was a relaxation to his creativity, but several consequential works were written, notably a Sonata, for double bass and piano (1967); a Sonata, for bassoon and piano (1969); and Symphony no. 3 (1970).

In 1965, Tremblay and his wife, Verabel, were divorced, and on August 8, 1969, he married Patricia Hedberg Elwell, who had been his student in piano and composition; she is a talented painter. For some years after that, Tremblay suffered a series of illnesses; two heart attacks; a bout with cancer in 1971; and a serious liver ailment. His teaching and creative schedule was greatly affected. But with a partial restoration of his health and energy by 1978 he was able to resume his activities both as teacher and composer. He worked on the completion of two new symphonies and a multimedia piece for the theater about the myth of the Phoenix.

Tremblay is the author of *The Definitive Cycle of the Twelve-Tone Row* (1974).

THE COMPOSER SPEAKS: The most important attributes of music are melody, sound structure and completeness. All sounds are valid; there are no bad sounds. There are only different sounds, or brighter or darker sounds. But consistency is imperative for clarity. . . .

There is no experimentation in art, since the work is its own reality. Where the artist leaves off is the finality; therefore it cannot be an experiment. Since everything has form, selection is the responsibility of the composer.

PRINCIPAL WORKS: 4 string quartets (1936–64); 3 symphonies (1949, 1952, 1970); 3 piano sonatas (1938, 1938, 1957).

Prelude and Dance, for piano (1936); *Modes of Transportation,* for string quartet (1940); Quintet, for wind instruments (1950); Serenade, for twelve instruments (1955); Piano Quartet (1958); Piano Trio (1959); *Epithalamium,* for nine instruments and percussion (1960); Quartet, for oboe, clarinet, bassoon, and viola (1964); String Trio (1964); Viola Sonata (1966); Duo, for viola and piano (1966); Double bass Sonata (1967); Sextet, for flute, oboe, clarinet, bass clarinet, bassoon, and tenor saxophone (1968); Bassoon Sonata (1969).

BIBLIOGRAPHY: *DCM*; Chase, Gilbert, *America's Music,* revised ed. (N.Y., 1966); Reis, Claire, *Composers in America* (N.Y., 1947); Swan, Howard, *Music in the Southwest* (San Marino, Calif., 1952); Yates, Peter, *Twentieth Century Music* (N.Y., 1967).

Trimble, Lester Albert, b. Bangor, Wis., August 29, 1923.

Disregarding the prevailing winds of musical trends, "schools," and systems, Trimble has consistently sailed in his own direction, achieving a compositional and structural logic of his own.

In childhood he came to love good music through recordings and radio broadcasts, and by appearing as vocal soloist on church programs. He was seven when he started taking piano lessons. At nine, he received his first instruction on violin, since then become his favorite performing instrument. In Pittsburgh, where his family moved when Lester was ten, he became a violin student of Robert Eicher's. Through Eicher, over a period of several years, Trimble came to know the entire basic literature of chamber music as permanent member of a string quartet ensemble performing regularly at Eicher's home. At the same time, when Trimble was sixteen, and without any formal instruction but the lessons learned by reading theoretical texts, Trimble made his first attempt at composition by writing pieces for violin and piano and, in 1942, completing a string quartet.

That year (1942), at the outbreak of World War II, he joined the army air force. After a year of service he was hospitalized for months with rheumatoid arthritis. While in the hospital, he sent some of his compositions to Arnold Schoenberg, then teaching at the University of Southern California, in Los Angeles. Schoenberg replied with an encouraging letter as well as advice (a letter included in a book of Schoenberg's correspondence edited by Erwin Stein). Released from the air force in 1944, Trimble entered the Carnegie Institute of Technology in Pittsburgh as a violin student, but one semester later he changed his major to composition which he studied with Nikolai Lopotnikoff for the remainder of Trimble's undergraduate and postgraduate years. As an undergraduate, Trimble also studied composition with Darius Milhaud at the Berkshire Music Center in Tanglewood, Mass. (summer of 1947), and on July 5, he married Mary Constance Wilhelm, an art student.

In 1948, Trimble received the bachelor of arts degree at Carnegie Institute, together with membership in Phi Beta Kappa, and in 1949, his master of arts degree. For two years after that he taught music at the Pennsylvania College for Women (now Chatham College) in Pittsburgh. Between 1949 and 1951 his career as a mature composer began to unfold with the writing of his String Quartet no. 1 (1950; N.Y., May 8, 1955) and Symphony in Two Movements (1951; N.Y., April 14, 1964), both distinctive for the clarity of their structure and the ingenuity of thematic growth. The String Quartet received the award of the Society for the Publication of American Music. Reviewing its premiere, a critic for the *New York Times* said: "One was struck by the sense of abundance in Mr. Trimble's work. He has a richer melodic gift than most, a delight in complex and vigorous rhythms, the ability to invent new sonorities without striving for far-fetched effects, and considerable emotional intensity. His swift music has life, which is a rare quality. And the slow movement . . . is beautiful." When the symphony was heard in Washington, D. C., performed by the National Symphony Orchestra in 1965, Paul Hume reported in the *Washington Post:* "Written with the specific intention of avoiding the customary structure of the sonata form, the symphony, in two connected movements, is a sophisticated score in which unusually congenial ideas are announced in a texture that remains constantly clear. Trimble avoids not only the usual symphonic form but also any hint of rhetoric or weightiness."

The year of 1951–52 was spent in Paris for the study of composition with Arthur Honegger at the École Normale de Musique, with Milhaud at the Paris Conservatory, and privately with Nadia Boulanger. In 1952, Trimble returned to the United States, making his home in New York. While employed as music critic for the *New York Herald Tribune* for the next eight years, and writing criticism and articles for various other newspapers and journals, he completed several compositions in which his creativity ripened into maturity: Concerto for Winds and Strings (1953; Copenhagen, Denmark, September 26, 1956); *Four Fragments from the Canterbury Tales* (1955; N.Y., April 20, 1958), recipient of an award from the American Academy of Arts and Letters and a citation from the National Institute of Arts and Letters in 1961; *Sonic Landscape,* for orchestra (1957), commissioned by the Pittsburgh Symphony, which introduced it as *Closing Piece* on February 7, 1958, while in its revision as *Sonic Landscape* it was first heard at the Inter-American Festival in Washington, D. C., on June 30, 1968, Walter Hendl conducting the National Symphony; and an opera, *Boccaccio's "Nightingale,"* text by George Ross based on the *Decameron* (1958–62), written on a grant from the Alice M. Ditson Fund. These compositions were influenced by Germanic (or Beethovenian) concepts of thematic and formal unity while the instrumental coloring was mainly derived from the French school. But the style was thoroughly modern in harmonic and rhythmic independence, in sonic interest, and in the strong thrust of the melodic line.

Trimble was composer-in-residence and lecturer at the Bennington Composers Conference at Bennington College in Vermont in 1959. (He returned there six years later as head of the composition department.) Between 1960 and 1962 he was general manager and editor of a newsletter of the American Music Center. In 1964 he received a Guggenheim Fellowship. He was lecturer and senior composer at the Composers Conference at Duke University in Durham, N. C., in 1967. On a Rockefeller Foundation grant he filled the post of composer-in-residence with the New York Philharmonic on Leonard Bernstein's invitation in 1967–68. He attended the Columbia-Princeton Music Center in 1969–70 for the study of techniques in electronic music. Since 1971 he has been on the faculty of the Juilliard School of Music. In 1973 he was composer-in-residence at Wolf Trap in Virginia (the first such there), and in 1974 he received the Creative Artists Public Service Award from the New York State Council of the Arts.

Trimble's admiration for President John F. Kennedy was reflected in three compositions in the 1960s. In 1964 he wrote the *Kennedy Concerto,* for two solo violins and chamber ensemble, its premiere given on April 27, 1964, in New York. *In Praise of Diplomacy and Common Sense,* for baritone, male speaking chorus, two speaking soloists and percussion (1965; N.Y., May 6, 1965) touched on the Kennedy assassination in an overall text made up of current events. It received the Martha Baird Rockefeller recording grant in 1970. And, in 1968, the *Duo concertante,* for two violins and orchestra, commissioned by the Meadow Brook Festival in Rochester, Mich., was introduced by the Detroit Symphony under Sixten Ehrling on August 10, 1968. This score was based on the *Kennedy Concerto* and was subtitled "To a Great American." It quoted the authentic Irish version of "Hail to the Chief" (rather than its derivative, "The Presidential March"); once again, in remembrance of Kennedy's Irish ancestry, an Irish folk dance was introduced. The work ended perfunctorily with the same abruptness with which Kennedy's life ended. "The work's reference points seem to be Alban Berg and Charles Ives," said Jay Carr in the *Detroit News,* "in the agitated and atmospheric flavor of the music, the atmosphere being largely that of brooding introspection, Ives in the incisive, virtuosic variations on 'Hail to the Chief.' . . . Trimble's new work has plenty of individual character of its own. It is marked by a clean, spare, plangent flavor, both in the orchestral writing and in the lines for the two solo instruments, and is an impressive, distinguished piece of writing."

Symphony no. 2 (1966–67), commissioned by the Koussevitzky Music Foundation, is structurally one of Trimble's most ambitious works. It was introduced in Lisbon with Igor Buketoff conducting, on April 25, 1969, during a week-long festival of American music. "We were certainly in the presence of a sincere work," wrote Joao de Freitas Branco, a leading Lisbon music critic, "not just another composition fabricated by the yard. And we particularly liked the passage where the highest point of the discourse was attained by a means opposite to what is common: that is, by decreasing the intensity instead of increasing it. In this respect, the percussion instruments were employed in an extremely clever and subtle way."

After 1970, Trimble began traveling in a new direction, stylistically and structurally, by writing a series of instrumental compositions collectively called *Panels*. Here the composer's aim was to depart from the traditional structures through an abstract format made up of many short, independently composed and unchanging episodes or modules (Trimble called them "events"), juxtaposed and overlaid to produce a powerful sonic and rhythmic impact. This method had been suggested to the composer by Jackson Pollock's abstract paintings. *Panels* I, for ten players (1969), was given its premiere in New York in March 1971, the composer conducting, was repeated at a festival of American music at Tanglewood, Mass., under Gunther Schuller on August 16, 1972, and was recorded under a Ford Foundation Recording Grant. *Panels* II, for thirteen players (1971–72; N.Y., November 13, 1972), commissioned by the Thorne Music Fund, adopted an aleatory practice (as had been the case with *Panels* I) by permitting the performers or conductor to decide just how to juxtapose the various modules and their dynamics. *Panels* III, for six players (1973–78), was introduced at an all-Trimble concert of the League of Composers-International Society for Contemporary Music in New York on May 20, 1979. *Panels* IV, for sixteen players (1973–74; N. Y., October 27, 1978), was written for a television ballet that never materialized but has been heard without the dancing. String Quartet no. 3 (1973–75) is *Panels* V, a commission from the National Endowment for the Arts. *Panels* VI, subtitled "Quadraphonics," was scored for percussion quartet (1974–75; N. Y., February 7, 1975). *Panels* VII (1975) is Serenade, for nine players. It was commissioned by the Chamber Music Society of Lincoln Center in New York, which introduced it on April 23, 1976. *Panels for Orchestra*—an expansion of *Panels* IV—was commissioned by the National Endowment for the Arts and premiered by the Milwaukee Symphony on December 16, 1976, Kenneth Schermerhorn conducting.

THE COMPOSER SPEAKS: In my music I am not so concerned with geometric formulations, which I find rigid, as I am with the interactions and intersections of sonic lines and masses within controlled formal situations. Someone . . . likened a piece of mine to James Joyce, and I was pleased to have that said, because I am consciously, and to a greater and greater extent, working with the layerings of sonic materials and with the idea of montage and of the interpretation of massive textures. It seems to me that it is in this area that some of the greatest possibilities for future composition lie. One does not have to give up all ideas of vertical coherence, in an expanded harmonic or tonal sense. Nor does he have to give up any more control than he wishes over the acoustical and expressive results of his technical procedures.

PRINCIPAL WORKS: 7 *Panels,* for various combinations of instruments (1969–75); 3 string quartets, the third being *Panels IV* (1950, 1955, 1975); 2 symphonies (1951, 1966–67).

Concerto for Winds and Strings (1953); Violin Concerto (1954, revised 1976); *Four Fragments from the Canterbury Tales,* for soprano, harpsichord, flute, and clarinet (1956); *Sonic Landscape,* for orchestra, originally entitled *Closing Piece* (1957–58); *Allas Myn Hertes Queene,* for a cappella male chorus, or male chorus with chamber ensemble (1959); *Boccaccio's "Nightingale,"* opera (1962); *Five Episodes,* for orchestra, also for piano solo (1962); *Kennedy Concerto,* for two solo violins and chamber ensemble (1964); *In Praise of Diplomacy and Common Sense* (1965); *Petit Concert,* five interludes and arias, for soprano, harpsichord, violin, and oboe (1966); *Notturno,* for string orchestra (1967); *Duo concertante* for two violins and orchestra, based on the *Kennedy Concerto* (1968); *The Mistress of Bernal Frances,* for soprano and piano (1971); *Solo for a Virtuoso,* for solo violin (1971); *A Whitman's Birthday Broadcast with Static,* for soprano and piano (1972); Music for Solo Trumpet (1974); *Portrait of Juan de Pereja,* for piano (1974); *Panels for Orchestra* (1976); Fantasy, for solo guitar (1977); Harpsichord Concerto (1979).

BIBLIOGRAPHY: *BBDM; DCM; Who's Who in America, 1980–81.*

Tuthill, Burnet Corwin, b. New York City, November 16, 1888.

As a composer, Tuthill was a late bloomer. His first compositions (except for some schoolboy efforts) came when he was forty-four. Once he started composing in earnest, his output became prolific, most of it instrumental and all of it conservative in its structural and idiomatic approaches. A modern use of church modes—and the harmonic juxtapositions these modes created—and original rhythmic patterns are his identifying traits.

His father, William Burnet Tuthill, the architect of Carnegie Hall in New York, was an amateur cellist. He met his wife, Henrietta Corwin, while he was singing in a church choir at the Calvary Baptist Church in New York, where she was organist. In 1895, when Burnet was seven, a string quartet ensemble was formed at the Tuthill home whose weekly playing over a period of many years was a decisive influence in the boy's early musical development.

Except for some study of the piano until he was twelve with his mother and Mary Barrow, Burnett

Tuthill received no formal musical training until comparatively late in life. However, he managed to acquire enough ability at notation and harmonization in his boyhood years to write his own piano exercises offering and solving specific rhythmic problems. Visiting a display of musical instruments at the Metropolitan Museum of Art when he was fourteen interested him in wind instruments, and a desire to play one of them was born. Soon after that, hearing a performance of Brahms's Clarinet Quintet aroused his fascination for the clarinet. After four lessons on that instrument with the first clarinetist of the New York Philharmonic, Tuthill was able to play the final twenty measures of the first movement of the Brahms Clarinet Quintet when it was performed at a family musicale. Subsequently, Tuthill received instruction on the clarinet from Henri Leon LeRoy.

Between 1898 and 1905, Tuthill received his academic education at the Horace Mann School in New York. There, with the help of a classmate, Morris Ernst (who became a distinguished attorney), he formed an orchestra. The limited number of instruments available made it necessary for Tuthill to make arrangements of existing orchestral literature, his knowledge of orchestration acquired from the study of Berlioz's treatise. When Tuthill was a senior at the Horace Mann School, he was recruited to play the clarinet in the Columbia University Orchestra. Then, as a student at Columbia University between 1905 and 1909, he served as the orchestra's student conductor (1908–9) and then as faculty conductor (1909–13). In 1909, having majored in chemistry, he received his bachelor of arts degree at Columbia, and in 1910, his master of arts degree. Among his rare attempts at composition at college was a Scherzo, for three clarinets (1909).

Between 1910 and 1922, Tuthill pursued a successful career in the real estate business. All that time, music was an avocation, but one he followed actively. He was librarian and member of the board of directors of the Oratorio Society of New York from 1909 to 1916, and its assistant conductor between 1914 and 1916; he conducted the People's Chorus Union of New York from 1912 to 1915; with the Young Men's Symphony Orchestra of New York he was first clarinetist (1911–17); and he was assistant conductor and librarian of the New Chorale Society in New York (1916–18) and conductor of the Plandome Singers in Long Island (1919–22). His most significant involvement with music during these years was the founding in 1919 of the Society for the Publication of American Music. During the half century of its existence, in which time it issued some eighty-five compositions, Tuthill served as its treasurer.

On January 1, 1917, Tuthill married his first wife, Helen Hersey, soprano. She died in 1928. From this marriage there was a daughter. On August 9, 1930, Tuthill married Ruth Wood, a violist, with whom he had a second daughter. Tuthill abandoned the business world to become a professional musician in July 1922, when he was appointed general manager of the Cincinnati Conservatory of Music, a post that required business as well as musical background. He spent the next eight years in this office. At the same time, he served as conductor of its chorus and of the Girls Glee Club at the University of Cincinnati. In 1924, he helped form, and from then until 1959 was general secretary of, the National Association of Schools of Music, which was responsible for the establishment of accreditation for American colleges.

During the summers of 1929 to 1937, Tuthill was a member of the faculty of the National Music Camp in Interlochen, Mich. He began an intensive period of composition study with Sidney Durst at the Cincinnati College of Music in 1930, acquiring a master's degree in music five years later.

His first serious attempts at composition came in 1932 with *Benedicte,* for eight-part chorus, which became his first composition to get published, and *Fantasy Sonata,* for clarinet and piano, which was introduced at the Berkshire Festival of Chamber music in Massachusetts on September 20, 1934. During the next two years he produced some chamber and orchestral music, the most important of which was *Bethlehem,* a pastorale for orchestra, which was written at the request of Eugene Goossens, conductor of the Cincinnati Symphony. "The piece attempts no detailed depiction of the Bible story," the composer explained. "The pastoral melody which is its basis, however, inevitably parallels in the imagination the transcendent story of Bethlehem." First performed at Interlochen, Mich., on July 22, 1934, the composer conducting, it was soon thereafter heard in Rochester, N. Y., Cincinnati, St. Louis, Cleveland, and Chicago. James G. Heller, the Cincinnati composer and the program annotator for the concerts of the Cincinnati Symphony, described it as "the evocation of a single mood. It has the simplicity and the strange tang of a shepherd of Palestine, blowing his oaken pipe on the Judean hills. It winds upward out of the unaccompanied pastoral lines into the richness of the Adoration and ends in the sudden ecstasy of worship."

The rhapsody, *Come Seven* (1934–35), received its world premiere at a concert of the St. Louis Symphony, the composer conducting, on February 19, 1944. This work, the composer has said, made no attempt at a "musical description of the well-known gutter game, but rather a sort of plea, through the name, to the Muse, to bless with reasonable success my attempt to compose in seven rhythms. However, the spell of the game seems to have made it necessary to end the piece with an 11-8 measure."

In the fall of 1935, Tuthill was called to Southwestern College in Memphis to organize its music curriculum. He was head of its music department until 1959. In 1935 he also became a member of the faculty of the Memphis College of Music, filling the post as its director from 1937 to 1959. As part of his activities in Memphis, he organized a school orchestra in 1937 which, even before its initial concert, became the Memphis Symphony Orchestra. Tuthill was its conductor for eight years. On these programs, some of Tuthill's early major works for orchestra were introduced. Among these were Symphony in C (1940) on March 10, 1942, and *Big River,* for soprano, women's chorus and orchestra (1942). The latter was a setting of James Gould Fletcher's poetic tribute to the Mississippi River. At the premiere, on March 21, 1943, Fletcher read his poem just before Tuthill's composition was heard. "The complexities of the rhythms, the variations of the spirit depicting the changing vistas traversed by the Mississippi River, the spiritual elevation of the unaccompanied prayer, give *Big River* a dramatic quality of sustained interest," reported Natilee Posert in the *Memphis Commercial Appeal.*

An earlier successful orchestral work was given its first hearing not in Memphis but in Rochester, N. Y., on October 30, 1936. It was the tone poem *Laurentia* (1936), in which the composer quoted the French-Canadian song "Isabeau, s'y promène."

In the spring of 1945, at the close of World War II, Tuthill was recruited by the War Department to organize the music branches of two army universities set up in England and France for the reeducation of men awaiting demobilization. After securing faculties for both schools, Tuthill proceeded to England as chief of the fine arts section of the Shrivenham American University, returning home the following December.

Tuthill's Suite, for band (1946), won first prize in the Columbia University band competition in 1947 and was first performed in Rochester, N. Y., on May 2, 1947, Frederick Fennell conducting, after which it received repeated hearings from various university bands. Before the decade ended, Tuthill completed a Clarinet Concerto (1948; Memphis, Ala., March 1950) and *Rowdy Dance,* for orchestra or band (1948; Indianapolis, Ind., January 1949). Since then he has produced a large library of concertos for various solo instruments and of chamber music, as well as many shorter works for orchestra or band, and choral music. *Flute Song,* for flute, strings, and two horns (1954), was given its world premiere in Tuscaloosa, Ala., where the *Rhapsody,* for clarinet and orchestra (1964), was also premiered, on April 20, 1956. Among his major vocal works were Requiem for two vocal soloists and orchestra (1960); Magnificat, for three vocal soloists and organ or piano (1968); and *Thanksgiving Anthem,* for chorus (1971). All were classically structured and all remained faithful to traditional harmonic, contrapuntal and melodic practices.

Tuthill received honorary doctorates in music from the Chicago Musical College (1943) and Southern University at Memphis (1972). He is the author of an autobiography, *Recollections of a Musical Life: 1900–1974* (1974).

THE COMPOSER SPEAKS: I have always been a protagonist for the contemporary composer, and I have tried to study all the new music that has been written. All this study does not convince me that the effort to get away from the classic forms and principles has created a new art that will stand the test of time. For atonality, I have no use, nor for harmony that is merely distortion.

PRINCIPAL WORKS: *Bethlehem,* pastorale for orchestra (1934); *Come Seven,* rhapsody for orchestra (1935); Clarinet Quintet (1936); Divertimento, in classic style, for wind quartet (1936); *Laurentia,* tone poem for orchestra (1936); *Overture brilliante,* for band (1937); Viola Sonata (1937); Violin Sonata (1937); Alto Saxophone Sonata (1939); Symphony in C (1940); *Big River,* for soprano, women's chorus and orchestra (1942); Oboe Sonata (1945); *Elegy,* for orchestra (1946); Suite, for band (1946); Clarinet Concerto (1948); *Rowdy Dance,* for orchestra or band (1948); Trumpet Sonata (1950); *Family Music,* for flute, two clarinets, viola, and cello (1952); Psalm 120, for chorus (1952); String Quartet (1953); *Flute Song,* for flute, strings, and two horns (1954); Rhapsody, for clarinet and orchestra (1954); Quintet, for piano and four clarinets (1957); Processional, for band (1958); Psalm 104, for chorus (1959); Requiem, for two vocal soloists and orchestra (1960); *Six for Bass,* for double bass and piano (1961); *Rondo concertante,* for two clarinets and band (1961); Gloria in D, for unison chorus and organ (1962); Concerto for Double bass and Winds (1962); Flute Sonata (1963); *Trombone Trouble,* for three trombones and orchestra or band (1963); Concerto for Tenor Saxophone and Orchestra (1963); *Communion Service,* for unison chorus and organ (1966); Saxophone Quartet (1966); Trombone Concerto (1967); Fantasia, for tuba and band (1968); Magnificat, for women's chorus and piano or organ (1968); Tenor Saxophone Sonata (1968); *Two Essays,* for brass quintet (1969); *Thanksgiving Anthem,* for chorus (1971); *Service Chants for Episcopal Service,* for chorus (1971–72); Caprice, for guitar (1972); *Ten Tunes,* for tuba (1973); Tuba Concerto (1975).

BIBLIOGRAPHY: Ewen, David, *American Composers Today* (N.Y., 1949); Tuthill, Burnet Corwin, *Recollections of a Musical Life: 1900–1974* (Memphis, 1974); *Who's Who in America, 1948–49.*

U

Ussachevsky, Vladimir Alexis, b. Hailar, Manchuria, China, November 3, 1911. American citizen, 1937.

Ussachevsky is one of the most significant pioneers in the production of electronic music and one of its most potent generative forces. He was a founder and has served as director of the Columbia-Princeton Electronic Music Center for more than twenty years. He has supplied the ideas and encouraged the development of several specialized electronic studio instruments which provided the means of expanding techniques for sound transformation. With the collaboration of Otto Luening, he composed the first work to combine live performers (in this instance a symphony orchestra) with tape-recorded sound. His many electronic works have explored extensively a variety of timbres, transformations, and alterations of musical sounds, and rhythmic patterns new to music.

He was born in China, the youngest of four children, to parents who settled in Manchuria soon after the Russo-Japanese War. All members of the family were musical. The father, Alexei, a colonel in the Russian army, was an amateur entrepreneur of musical and theatrical events. The mother, Maria Mihailovna (Panoff), was a trained pianist and a successful piano teacher. One of Vladimir's sisters played the violin and another sister and brother became professional pianists. There was, consequently, always good music at the Ussachevsky home provided not only by the performances of the children and their mother's pupils but also by the frequently spontaneous sessions of choral singing of popular Russian folk and Gypsy music. Vladimir Ussachevsky began playing piano at the age of six, receiving instruction at home. As a boy, he was a psalm reader and altar boy in the Greek Orthodox Church. "The most important and still apparent influence," he recalls, "was the opportunity to hear twice weekly an excellent church choir singing the entire repertoire of Russian sacred music, both traditional and that of the 19th-century Russian masters from Tchaikovsky to Gretchaninoff and Rachmaninoff."

His world of music long remained circumscribed. Not until he was sixteen did he hear, through recordings, any orchestral music by Europeans, and not until he was nineteen did he hear or play any music by Johann Sebastian Bach. But Ussachevsky did a good deal of improvising, supplying background music for silent movies and playing in popular ensembles in nightclubs. During dance breaks, he wrote his first composition, in 1930, a short piece for the piano, solidly harmonic, with a melodic line of romantic profile. It remained untitled.

Just before his eighteenth year, in 1930, he joined his mother and brother in the United States, settling in California. His first private piano teacher there was Clarence Mader, who introduced him to Bach's Inventions and to articulate piano playing, and supplemented piano study with lessons in composition. Between 1931 and 1933, Ussachevsky attended Pasadena Junior College in California, where he was a student in harmony and music history. Composing was a peripheral endeavor. His first orchestral work, a set of variations on a theme of another student, was written at this time. Its first performance was responsible for bringing Ussachevsky a scholarship to Pomona College in California in 1933. During the next two years he studied strict counterpoint, analysis and composition with Walter Allen and Gordon Sutherland. He also won a first prize in a piano competition. In his senior year, a recital of his music was given at the college, a program that consisted of *Classical Suite*, for piano, two movements from a violin sonata, and his first choral work, *Praise Be to the Lord in Heaven*.

Upon receiving his bachelor of arts degree at Pomona College in 1935, Ussachevsky entered the Eastman School of Music in Rochester, N.Y., for a four-year period in which he studied composition first with Edward Royce and with Howard Hanson and Bernard Rogers, and then theory with Burrill Phillips. In 1936, he earned his master of music degree, and in 1939, his Ph.D. in composition. His most important student work was *Jubilee Cantata*, for large chorus, baritone solo, narrator, and symphony orchestra, written in 1938 at the invitation of Pomona College to celebrate its fiftieth anniversary. In February 1938 it was introduced at Pomona College with Robert Shaw (later to become the distinguished conductor) as narrator and Kenneth Fisk conducting. After that, in the spring of 1938, under Howard Hanson's direction, it was heard over the NBC radio network. Writing in *Modern Music*, Elliott Carter said of it: "This was a very well-planned setting of selections from the Bible—arranged to form an exhortation to youth to have faith in God. From the dramatic and formal point of view, it was unusually effective with convincing sincerity and musicality." *Jubilee Cantata* was in a tonal, neoromantic style rooted in the music of the Russian masters of the late 19th century and in that of the Russian Orthodox Church, but also influenced by Stravinsky's *Symphony of Psalms* and Howard Hanson. This was the style to which Ussachevsky remained faithful for the next decade, though in later works modernizing his language with dissonant polychordal harmonies.

In 1940–41, Ussachevsky attended Claremont College in California for courses in music education leading to a teacher's certificate. Between 1940 and 1942 he was a substitute and probationary music teacher in the Los Angeles and Pasadena public school system. In 1940–41 he was also assistant choral conductor to Richard Lert with the Pasadena Civic Chorus Association.

In 1942, Ussachevsky was inducted into the U.S. Army, where his knowledge of Chinese and Russian eventually made him valuable to the Intelligence Division. While serving in the army, he received intensive training in a Far Eastern Specialized Program at the University of Washington in Seattle. On February 26, 1943, in Tacoma, Wash., he married Elizabeth Denison Kray, who was studying and working for the University of Washington, and who subsequently became executive director of the Academy of American Poets in New York.

Upon completing his training at the University of Washington, Ussachevsky was assigned by the War Department to Washington, D. C., as a research analyst. He continued in this capacity for an additional year in the State Department upon his discharge from the armed forces in 1944.

Returning to civilian life, Ussachevsky taught music and political science at the Putney School in Putney, Vt. (1946–47). In 1947, he was appointed to the music faculty of Columbia University in New York as lecturer. He has remained there since then, rising to the post of assistant professor in 1954, associate professor in 1957, and full professor in 1964. In 1970–71 and again in 1973–74 and from 1975 to 1980 he was composer-in-residence at the University of Utah in Salt Lake City.

As composer, Ussachevsky continued pursuing his neoromantic tendencies until 1952. Intermezzo, for piano and orchestra (1951)—formerly a movement from a piano concerto—was premiered at Bennington College in Vermont in 1951. On May 5, 1952, this work was heard at Columbia University on the Composers' Forum series together with the premiere of *Two Autumn Songs on Rilke's Texts*, for soprano and piano (1952). In his report on that concert for the *New York Herald Tribune*, Virgil Thomson said: "Mr. Ussachevsky's music . . . showed a sweetness all its own and a genuineness of proportion, and honest relation of feeling to form, that won your reviewer's hard heart." That program ended with Ussachevsky's earliest experiment with electronic music, piano sounds distorted by a tape recorder. "These," Thomson continued, "were utterly charming and . . . delighted the audience no end."

Ussachevsky first became actively interested in sound transformation when he purchased a tape recorder for the Columbia Music Department and began finding out what could be done with this machine beyond its normal use. He knew "very little about the tape recorder and nothing of what anyone else might have been doing with it as a creative tool," as he said. He continued to experiment and in 1951 completed two compositions for tape alone: *Transposition, Reverberation, Composition* and *Underwater Valse*.

The first public performance in the United States of electronic music (other than Ussachevsky's brief and tentative exhibition at the May 5, 1952, concert) took place at the Museum of Modern Art in New York on October 28, 1952, presented under the auspices of Broadcast Music, Inc. (BMI), with Leopold Stokowski providing a preliminary comment. On that program, the premiere performance of Ussachevsky's *Sonic Contours* (1952) was given. This was a piece exploiting the resources of piano sounds by means of a tape recorder and other electronic devices. Ussachevsky explains: "In this process of composition on the tape recorder, the components were created first by combining various sound patterns, and then superimposing them on each other." Other than the piano, the only sounds used, though briefly, were human voices. Recalling that concert in *Horizon* magazine years later, David Randolph said: "The first sound to emerge from the machine was a low rumble suggesting the sound of the very lowest notes on the piano. . . . A chord was struck, but no sooner had the sound begun than it was immediately cut off in a manner that could never be achieved by any pianist. For the next seven minutes, the audience listened to a composition made possible by electronic manipulation of the sounds of the piano, joined at a few spots by the sounds of human voices. With this hearing (I hesitate to use the word 'performance') of Vladimir Ussachevsky's *Sonic Contours*, the tape recorder made its official bow in the United States."

Since 1952, Ussachevsky has devoted himself almost exclusively to experimenting and composing in the electronic medium. In 1953 with the collaboration of Otto Luening, he created *Incantation for Tape Recorder*, which was first heard in the fall of 1953 in a broadcast over the CBS radio network, introductory remarks made by Stokowski. In 1954, once again with Luening, Ussachevsky completed the first work ever written combining tape recorder with live instruments: *Rhapsodic Variations*, for orchestra and tape recorder, commissioned by the Louisville Orchestra, which introduced it under Robert Whitney's direction in Kentucky on March 20, 1954. "The two composers . . . in this joint, avant-garde venture . . . have created a substantial work of music—experimental as to means, but fully formed and expressive in its final product," wrote Lester Trimble in the *New York Herald Tribune*. "It is full of the newest sounds, of great enveloping winds and other-worldly chirps, often tremblingly brilliant, and continuously integrated with orchestral textures of the most forthright clarity. It has an expressive life, too, strangely evocative of emotional states in the past tense. They are like profound experiences relived in one's memory—a remembered happiness, and amazingly secure with its new materials." This work received numerous performances following the premiere, some by established symphony orchestras both in the United States and abroad.

Ussachevsky continued to work productively with Luening for a number of years after that, producing electronic music not only for the concert stage but also for ballet, the theater, and television. *Ballet of Identity* (1954) was commissioned by the American Mime Theater. For the concert stage, Ussachevsky and Luening produced, among other works, *A Poem in Cycles and Bells*, for tape recorder and orchestra (1954), its first performance given by the Los Angeles Philharmonic under Alfred Wallenstein on November 22, 1954. *Concerted Piece for Tape Recorder and Orchestra*, which the New York Philharmonic had commissioned, was introduced by that orchestra under Leonard Bernstein over television (CBS) on March 31, 1960. This telecast served to focus the limelight of national interest not only on electronic music but also on its two principal producers, Luening and Ussachevsky. For the theater, they provided taped sounds for the Orson Welles production of *King Lear* at the New York City Center (January 12, 1956) and for Margaret Webster's production of *Back to Methuselah* for the New York Theater Guild (March 26, 1958). For television (in addition to several lesser efforts in the 1950s) they provided the first completely electronic score written for that medium (in collaboration with Pril Smiley) for *The Incredible Voyage*, a documentary narrated by Walter Cronkite over the CBS-TV network on October 13, 1965.

Most of Ussachevsky's creative work, however, was done without collaboration. In *A Piece for Tape Recorder* (1955) Ussachevsky combined purely electronic sounds with diversified sounds from a piano, gong, cymbal, kettledrum, organ, and jet-plane noise, all altered, modified, and transformed through changes of tape speed and the use of multiple recorded techniques. "The sounds of the piano and of the jet are used in an episodic manner," Ussachevsky says, "and give dynamic punctuation to an otherwise slowly evolving sound texture. The remaining sounds take the secondary role of background accompaniment. Here the aim was "to achieve a large, assymetrical arch, both in dynamics and pitch." This piece was written for the "Music in Our Time" concerts in New York, where it was first heard in 1956. *Studies in Sound Plus* (1958) are three short compositions based on electronic and instrumental materials with timbres changed by internal rearrangement of frequency components. *Creation—Prologue and Interlude*, for four choruses, live and prerecorded so-

loists, and tape (1941; N.Y., May 9, 1961) was based on Akkadian and Latin texts in which the composer sought to exploit the contrast between the archaic quality of Akkadian and the sound of classical Latin by assigning to each text a different musical characterization. An English text is used as well. Together with two later movements—*Conflict* for tape (1971, revised 1975) and *Epilogue: Spell of Creation*, for chorus and electronic accompaniment (1971)—the above composition forms a part of an unfinished oratorio, *Creation. Of Wood and Brass* (1965; N. Y., April 19, 1965). It drew its title from materials used in its composition: a half dozen or so notes on a trombone, several patterns on a xylophone, and a single stroke on a Korean gong. To gain an absolute maximum of timbre transformations while removing the final sound materials as far as possible from the original quality of the instrumental sounds, Ussachevsky used several machine and tape manipulative techniques which he had developed, at the same time creating a complex rhythmic polyphony.

In 1968, Ussachevsky began incorporating the possibilities of sound synthesis by means of computers. *Computer Piece* no. 1 (1968)—first heard in June 1968 at a Ussachevsky concert at the Instituto Torquato di Tella in Buenos Aires, where Ussachevsky was in brief residence—used the GE-635 computer in several different manners: preparing material of electronic and nonelectronic character; converting this material into digital form and depositing it in the computer's memory; extracting the material negatively; providing instructions for pitch transpositions and imposition of various levels of dynamics. A separate program generated certain purely electronic sounds by means of a program called "Music 5," which had originated in the Bell Telephone laboratories. Both programs were then translated into patterns recorded on magnetic tape with additional manipulation and final arrangement done outside of the computer through the use of a conventional electronic music studio. This composition was subsequently combined with a specially made film first shown on January 21, 1970, at the Whitney Museum in New York, Called *Two Images of a Computer*, which was part of an Electronic Music and Mixed Media evening on the Composers' Showcase Series.

The sound materials in *Conflict* (1971; Salt Lake City, Utah, May 10, 1971) were obtained from transformed sounds of musical instruments, some developed on a synthesizer, and some randomly generated electronic signals by programming a computer to produce asymetrically distributed sharply attacked pitches. *Conflict* describes the final battle between two Babylonian deities: the goddess Tiamat, who had the appearance of a dragon and symbolized the sea, and Marduk. In the cosmic battle, Tiamat is defeated by Marduk to music that describes the struggle realistically.

Ussachevsky used electronic music with humorous

intent in *Colloquy for Symphony Orchestra, Tape Recorder, and Various Chairs* (1976). It was heard first in the Mormon Tabernacle in Salt Lake City on February 20, 1976, on the opening program of the annual festival of contemporary music sponsored by the University of Utah and performed by the Utah Symphony under the direction of Maurice Abravanel. Here is how Lowell Durham, for *High Fidelity/Musical America* described it: "The score juxtaposes conventional with preprocessed tape sounds; its scenario is a conversation between orchestra, tape recorder, and conductor. The very considerable spoken dialogue is partially versified by the Poet X. J. Kennedy. After conversing, pleading, and demonstrating its right to orchestral membership—by approximating orchestral sounds for producing contrasting timbres—the tape recorder woos and wins the orchestra. The piece culminates in a happy 'marriage' with the composer's transformed voice saying, 'Thank you kindly!'—which sparked spontaneous applause."

In 1959—with Luening, Milton Babbitt, and Roger Sessions—Ussachevsky founded the Columbia Princeton Electronic Music Center on a grant from the Rockefeller Foundation; since its beginnings, Ussachevsky has served as chairman of the Committee of Direction. He has appeared several times on national network television programs over NBC and CBS and as soloist with symphony orchestras. His appearances as lecturer have been extensive throughout the United States and abroad in over one hundred and fifty universities and other educational institutions. He has given informal presentations of his electronic works in Great Britain, France, the Soviet Union, and, in 1979, in Peking and Shanghai in the People's Republic of China. The American State Department sponsored his tour of South America in lecture-demonstrations during the summer of 1968; at that time he presented six seminars on electronic music at the Instituto Torquato di Tella in Buenos Aires. In March and April of 1969 he once again was chosen by the State Department, this time to serve as an American delegate to the Inter-American festival of Contemporary Music in Rio de Janeiro. In July 1968 he was an American delegate to the Yugoslav-American Seminar in Music.

For his contributions to electronic music he has frequently been honored in various ways. In 1957 he received the first of two Guggenheim Fellowships, the second following three years later. He was presented with an award from the National Institute of Arts and Letters (1962), grants from the National Endowment for the Arts (1966, 1974, 1975), and the Creative Artists Public Service Program grant (1973). Recognition of his achievements as a writer on electronic music for various publications came in 1979 with a National Endowment for the Humanities grant for research in the twenty-five-year period between 1946 and 1971, particularly in the area of the structural aspects and aesthetics of electronic mu-

sic. The University of Rochester, in New York, awarded him a Distinguished Alumnus Award (1973). That year (1973), Ussachevsky also was elected to membership in the National Institute of Arts and Letters, and in 1974 he received an honorary doctorate from Pomona College.

Ussachevsky has composed two electronic scores for motion pictures: for George Tabori's full-length adaptation of Jean-Paul Sartre's *No Exit*, starring Viveca Lindfors (1962), and for a forty-five-minute abstract film produced by Lloyd Williams, *Line of Apogee* (1967).

Between 1952 and 1959, he supervised the publication of the *New Music Quarterly*, an important music journal established in the 1920s by Henry Cowell. Ussachevsky was president of the American Composers' Alliance between 1968 and 1970, and a board member of the Composers Recording, Inc. (CRI), where he still serves on the advisory panel. He has also been a member of the board of directors of the Edward MacDowell Colony, Inc., the Alice M. Ditson Fund Committee, and on the editorial board of the musicological journal, *Perspectives of New Music*.

THE COMPOSER SPEAKS: Because my present interest in composing for the electronic medium is so real and all-important to me, I find myself quite detached from my pre-electronic efforts in musical composition. It would be pretentious to claim the possession of clairvoyance about one's own future, and yet, even during those years when musical composition grew to be a compelling force in my life, I did not find full satisfaction in my creative efforts and was restless to find something of a different nature that might lie beyond. Likewise, I felt no desire to have my earlier works published or to have them available for performance, except when the condition of commission made it necessary. Thus, numerous piano compositions, several orchestra scores, a potential suite from a movie score, etc., are quietly gathering dust. The few preelectronic works which I am mentioning have had performances and were kindly received and can be referred to as evidence that I have not sprung up as a full-grown apostle of musical mechanization. Curiously, I have the feeling that some day, perhaps soon, I shall resume some composition for conventional instruments. But I must first respect a clear realization that much still needs to be explored in the electronic medium and that so little has yet been shown of its vast potential that, for me at least, there is indeed very little time to spare creatively on anything else. It is my conviction that the new world of sound now available is a legitimate expansion of musical resources.

PRINCIPAL WORKS: *Jubilee Cantata*, for large chorus, baritone solo, narrator, and symphony orchestra (1938); Psalm 24, for chorus and organ or seven brass instruments (1948); Intermezzo, for piano and orchestra, a movement from a piano concerto (1951); *Transposition, Reverberation, Composition*, for tape (1951); *Underwater Valse*, for tape (1951); *Two Autumn Songs on Rilke's Text*, for soprano and piano (1952); *Sonic Contours*, transformed piano and voices on tape (1952); *Incantation for Tape Recorder*, for tape, with Otto Luening (1953); *Rhapsodic Variations*, for tape recorder and orchestra, with Otto Luening (1954); *A Poem in Cycles and Bells*, for tape recorder and orchestra, with Otto Luening (1954); *Piece for Tape Recorder* (1955); *Metamorphosis*, for tape (1956); *Studies in Sound, Plus*, originally just *Studies in Sound*, for tape (1958); *Concerted Piece for Tape Recorder and Orchestra*, with Otto Luening (1960); *Wireless Fantasy*, for tape (1960); *Creation—Prologue and Interlude*, for four choruses, prerecorded basses, mezzo-soprano, soprano, and tape (1961); *Of Wood and Brass*, for tape (1965); *Computer Piece* no. 1 (1968); *Epilogue: Spell of Creation*, for mixed chorus and electronic accompaniment (1971); *Conflict*, made from combined computer and concrete materials on tape (1971); *Missa Brevis*, for chorus and brass ensemble (1973); *Colloquy for Orchestra, Tape Recorder, and Various Chairs*, (1976); *Celebration for String Orchestra and Electronic Valve Instrument* (1980).

BIBLIOGRAPHY: *BBDM; DCM; NGDMM;* Schwartz, Elliott, *Electronic Music* (N.Y., 1973); *Who's Who in America, 1980–81.*

V

Van Vactor, David, b. Plymouth, Ind., May 8, 1906.

Though Van Vactor's music looked backward to such classical structures as the chaconne, passacaglia, fugue, concerto grosso, symphony, and concerto, he was a 20th-century voice in his sonoric, rhythmic, tonal, and harmonic methods. His works represent a harmonious and effective marriage of past with present values, producing a library of instrumental literature in a personalized style.

He came from early American stock, his boyhood lived in northern Indiana. In Argos, he received his first lessons on the flute from the town barber in early boyhood. He became sufficiently adept at that instrument to play in the town band, a contact which was largely responsible for his subsequent interest in writing march music.

For a long time, Van Vactor had no intention of becoming a professional musician, choosing medicine as a future vocation. He spent three years taking premedical courses at Northwestern University in Evanston, Ill. (1924–27), before entering its School of Music, where he studied flute with Arthur Kitti and composition with Felix Borowski, Arne Oldberg, and Albert Noelte. He began showing interest in composition in 1927-28 with the production of several songs for voice and piano and a Chaconne, for strings, the latter introduced in Rochester, N.Y., on May 17, 1928, Howard Hanson conducting.

Upon receiving his bachelor of arts degree in 1928, Van Vactor became convinced that his future lay with music rather than medicine. To continue his musical training, he went to Vienna in 1928, spending a year at the academy as a pupil of Franz Schmidt's (composition) and Josef Niedermayr's (flute). One of Van Vactor's compositions, completed in 1929, was *Five Small Pieces for Large Orchestra*, which received its premiere at Ravinia Park, Ill., on July 5, 1931, Eric De Lamarter conducting.

In 1931 he was engaged as a flutist with the Chicago Symphony Orchestra, retaining this post thirteen years. He married Virginia Landreth (with whom he had two children) on May 28, 1931. That summer (1931) was spent in Paris in the study of composition with Paul Dukas at the École Normale de Musique and flute with Marcel Moyse at the Paris Conservatory.

Several talented compositions followed his return to Chicago. The Concerto for Flute and Orchestra (1932) was given its first performance on February 26, 1933, in Chicago with Caroline Solfronk, soloist, and Eric De Lamarter conducting. An orchestral composition, *The Masque of the Red Death* (1932), inspired by Edgar Allan Poe, was awarded honorable mention in the Gustavus Swift Competition in Chicago in 1935; Quintet, for flute, two violins, viola and cello (1932), received the Society for the Publication of American Music Award. With his own Passacaglia and Fugue in D minor, for orchestra (1933), Van Vactor made his debut as conductor, appearing with the Chicago Symphony Orchestra at the Century of Progress Exposition on July 28, 1934. He was again conductor when, on June 20, 1937, his *Overture to a Comedy* no. 1 (1934) was premiered by the Chicago Symphony. Concerto Grosso, for three flutes, harp and orchestra (1935), was commissioned by Frederick Stock and the Chicago Symphony, Stock conducting the initial performance on April 24, 1935.

In 1935 Van Vactor was awarded the master of music degree by Northwestern University, where, between 1936 and 1947, he was a member of the music faculty. In 1939 he received the Frederick Stock Conducting Scholarship, remaining Stock's only protégé until the conductor's death in 1942.

Van Vactor had been a traditionalist in his early compositions and he remained so with the works of the late 1930s and early 1940s that carried him further into the national limelight. These included: Five Bagatelles, for strings (1938; Chicago, February 7, 1938); Symphony no. 1 in D (1937), winner of first prize in a competition sponsored by the New York Philharmonic, which, under the composer's direction, introduced it on January 18, 1939; Symphonic Suite (1938; Ravinia Park, Ill., July 21, 1938); Divertimento, for small orchestra (1939; Ravinia Park, July 8, 1939); Concerto for Viola and Orchestra (1940; Ravinia Park, July 13, 1940); *Overture to a Comedy* no. 2 (1941; Indianapolis, Ind., March 14, 1941), the first of several works commissioned by Fabien Sevitzky and the Indianapolis Symphony, and winner of the Juilliard Publication Award in 1942; *Variazioni solenne*, originally entitled *Gothic Impressions* (1941; Chicago, February 26, 1942); *Fanfare for Orchestra* (1943; Indianapolis, January 23, 1943), a salute to Russia during World War II; and *Music for the Marines*, for orchestra (1943; Indianapolis, March 27, 1943).

In 1941 Van Vactor was asked to direct the North American Woodwind Quintet, an ensemble which toured Central and South America that year under the auspices of the League of Composers in New York. Two years later Van Vactor resigned from the Chicago Symphony to become flutist and assistant conductor of the Kansas City Philharmonic for the next four years. During this period he also conducted the Kansas City Allied Arts Orchestra (1945–47), which he had founded to perform works for chamber orchestra, with emphasis on contemporary music. He was head of the department of theory and composition at the Conservatory of Music in Kansas City (1943–47).

In the summer of 1945 Van Vactor was invited by the government of Chile to serve as guest conductor of the Orquesta Sinfonica de Chile, and to be visiting professor at the University of Chile. Among the creative fruits of this Chilean visit were a Sonatina, for flute and piano (1945), Cantata, for treble voices and orchestra (1947) and, in 1945, the first sketches of *Suite for Orchestra on Chilean Folk Tunes.* This last-named work made extensive use of four authentic Chilean folk dances of the 18th and 19th centuries. The four movements are *"El cuándo," "El aire," "Zamacueca: Negro querido,"* and *"Zapateo."* Van Vactor did not complete this composition until 1963, when it was introduced by the Knoxville Symphony in Tennessee, the composer conducting, on February 12. This music was subsequently also used for a ballet with choreography by Irma Witt (Knoxville, April 19, 1963).

Van Vactor embarked on his third tour of Latin America under the auspices of the American State Department in 1946, performing and conducting his own music and that of other North American composers in Brazil and Chile. In 1947 he left Kansas City to assume the posts of conductor of the Knoxville Symphony Orchestra and professor of music at the University of Tennessee.

In 1957 Van Vactor received a Guggenheim Fellowship which enabled him to work on his Symphony no. 3 in C (1958). Its world premiere was given by the Pittsburgh Symphony, William Steinberg conducting, on April 3, 1959. A Fulbright Research grant in 1957–58 brought him to Frankfurt, Germany, for the study (under controlled conditions) of the comparative reaction of school children to educational concerts. As a part of this study, he conducted the Jugend Symphonie Orchester in Frankfurt. His conclusions from this experiment were set forth in the book *Every Child May Hear,* written in collaboration with Katherine Davis Moore (1960).

In his later compositions, Van Vactor set his music "in sophisticatedly enhanced tonalities," as Nicolas Slonimsky has written, "and sparked with ingenuous atonalities." On the latter point, the composer has cited Schoenberg's comment, "I'd rather be called amoral than atonal." Among the more significant of his works in the 1960s and 1970s were the *Sinfonia breve,* for orchestra (1964; Indianapolis, October 30, 1966); Symphony no. 4, *Walden,* for chorus and or-

chestra, which used a text from Thoreau (1969; Knoxville, March 1, 1971); Requiescat, for string orchestra (1970); Andante and Allegro, for saxophone and orchestra (Muncie, Ind., December 16, 1973); and *Episodes—Jesus Christ,* for double chorus and orchestra (1977; Knoxville, April 25, 1978), written during Van Vactor's first year of retirement. The last of these, one of the composer's major works for chorus, used a text prepared by his daughter, Raven Harwood, derived from the four Gospels (chiefly the fourth), and from Acts, Romans, I Corinthians, and I Timothy, though not in the order found in the Scriptures and with occasional changes to favor the singing voice.

In 1965, on his fourth visit to South America, Van Vactor was artist-in-residence at Santiago, Chile, at the request of the U.S. Department of State. In the course of that visit he conducted twelve orchestral concerts and made numerous solo appearances. Van Vactor's appearances as conductor of American and foreign orchestras have been extensive. In 1950 he received Northwestern University's Alumni Merit Award. In 1975 he was named composer laureate of Tennessee.

THE COMPOSER SPEAKS: I've been unusually fortunate in my life as a musician. Having had many opportunities to learn, I've tried to profit from my situations most of the time. I have been blessed with good health and abundant energy—things that contribute so much to one's success, and to the development of real devotion to any profession.

PRINCIPAL WORKS: 6 symphonies (1937–80); 2 *Overtures to a Comedy* (1934, 1941); 2 string quartets (1940, 1949).

Five Small Pieces for Large Orchestra (1929); *The Play of Words,* ballet (1931); *The Masque of the Red Death,* for orchestra (1932); Flute Quartet (1932); Flute Quintet (1932); Flute Concerto (1932); Passacaglia and Fugue in D minor, for orchestra (1933); Suite, for two flutes (1934); *Das Nachtlied,* for soprano and strings (1935); Concerto Grosso, for three flutes, harp, and orchestra (1935); Symphonic Suite, for orchestra (1938); Five Bagatelles, for strings (1938); Divertimento, for small orchestra (1939); Viola Concerto (1940); *Adagio mesto,* for strings (1941); *Variazioni solenne,* originally entitled *Gothic Impressions,* for orchestra (1941); Credo, for chorus and orchestra (1941); String Trio (1942); Fanfare for Orchestra (1943); *Music for the Marines* (1943); Flute Sonatina (1945); Recitative and Saltarello, for orchestra (1946); Pastorale and Dance, for flute and strings (1947); *Three Dance Scenes,* for orchestra (1947); Introduction and Presto, for strings (1947); Cantata, for treble voices and orchestra (1947); Suite, for bassoon and contrabassoon (1948); Prelude and March, for orchestra (1950); Violin Concerto (1951); Eight Choruses, on texts from "A Shropshire Lad," for a cappella chorus (1953); *The New Light,*

Christmas cantata for solo voices, chorus, and orchestra (1954); Fantasia, Chaconne, and Allegro, for orchestra (1956); Suite, for woodwind quintet (1959); *Children of the Starrs* for violin and piano (1960); *Christmas Songs for Young People*, for chorus and orchestra (1961); Suite, for trumpet and orchestra (1961); Five Pieces, for piano (1962); Brass Octet (1962); *Suite on Chilean Folk Tunes*, for orchestra (1963); Passacaglia, Chorale, and Scamper, for band (1964); *Sinfonia breve*, for orchestra (1964); *Economy Band* no. 1, for trumpet, trombone, and percussion (1966); Music for Woodwinds (1966–67); Four Etudes, for winds and percussion (1968); Sarabande and Variations, for brass quintet and strings (1968); *Economy Band* no. 2, for horn, tuba, and percussion (1969); Requiescat, for strings (1970); Tuba Quartet (1971); Andante and Allegro, for alto saxophone and strings (1972); *Episodes—Jesus Christ*, for double chorus and orchestra (1977); Fanfare and Chorale, for concert band (1977); *The Elements*, for concert band (1978); Processional, for chorus, winds, and percussion (1979).

BIBLIOGRAPHY: *DCM*; Ewen, David, *American Composers Today* (N.Y., 1949); Howard, John Tasker, *Our Contemporary Composers* (N.Y., 1946); Reis, Claire, *Composers in America* (N.Y., 1946); *Who's Who in America, 1980–81*.

Varèse, Edgard (Edgar) Victor Achille Charles, b. Paris, France, December 22, 1883; d. New York City, November 6, 1965. American citizen, 1926.

Varèse's adult creative output consists of less than a dozen compositions, most of minor dimensions. Such a crop may be sparse, but it has nurtured and helped to develop several generations of avant-garde music. Varèse was a visionary who rejected the existing concepts and techniques governing Western music; dispensed with traditional rhythmic, thematic, harmonic, contrapuntal, constructional, and structural processes. He regarded sound (or, to use his own term, "sound organization") as an end in itself, the intrinsic part of musical structure, determining the progress of a musical composition. Initially, he searched for new effects and sound qualities from traditional instruments by exploring the extremes in sonorities, applying unusual performing techniques, combining instruments unorthodoxly, and giving percussion instruments solo importance. Then, becoming aware that pitched instruments had their limitations, he resorted to nonmusical instruments of indeterminate pitch. In the end, he sought out electronic possibilities. He was abused with ridicule, attack, and laughter when his works were first heard, then ignored for a decade or two after that. But he lived long enough to see himself recognized and honored as a musical prophet and as a patron saint of avant-gardists throughout the musical world who,

through him, found a new direction for their own experiments.

Edgard was the eldest of five children whose father was a native of Piedmont; the mother was born in Paris. The father, an engineer, was a tyrannical despot who abused his wife and children psychologically and physically. Edgard feared and hated him from the earliest years. This hatred grew to fanatical dimensions as the years passed and left its imprint on Varèse's personality, in his nervous disorders, combustible fits of temper, depressions, and contempt for authority. When his mother died at the age of thirty-one (Varèse was then fourteen) she begged him on her death bed: "Protect your brothers. Your father is an assassin."

Several weeks after he was born, probably because of domestic friction between the parents, Varèse was sent off to Le Villars in Burgundy, where he was raised for several years by his maternal grandfather, Claude Cortot, who gave him the love and sympathy denied him by his own father. At Le Villars, Varèse spent a pleasant childhood. In later years he kept returning to Le Villars to replenish his spirits.

As a child there, he was already fascinated by sounds: train whistles heard from a distance, the splashing of the waters of the river Saone, or the sound of the wind. When he acquired a mandolin, he stretched the strings in different ways trying to realize new, strange sound effects. "Ever since I was a boy," Varèse recalled in later years, "most music sounded to me terribly enclosed, corseted, one might say. I liked music that explodes in space."

In his boyhood, he was forced to leave Le Villars to return to his parents' home in Paris so that he could attend public school, which he detested. During the summer of 1893, the Varèse family moved to Turin, Italy. There, when he was eleven, Varèse taught himself to compose music, and when he was twelve, he wrote an opera, *Martin Pas*, based on Jules Verne's love story. Since his father was determined that Edgard become an engineer, all formal instruction in music was denied. When the boy was found at the piano, his father made it inaccessible by locking the instrument and covering it with a black shroud.

As preparation for a career in engineering, Varèse attended the Institute Technique in Turin, a high school where he specialized in mathematics and science, for both of which he showed unusual aptitude. Music, however, was not denied. Somehow, in Turin, he managed to hear his first orchestral concert, an unforgettable event because the program included Debussy's *Prélude à l'après-midi d'un faune*; from that time on Debussy became one of his favorites. When Varèse was seventeen, his grandfather took him for a visit to the Paris Exposition, where he heard his first opera, Massenet's *Manon*. That year, Varèse also managed to receive his first formal instruction in music by studying harmony and counterpoint secretly with Giovanni Bolzoni, director of the

Turin Conservatory, paying for his lessons with money he earned in his father's office.

After the death of Varèse's mother in 1897, his father remarried. Six years later, Varèse broke permanently and totally with his father when, in a fit of rage at seeing him physically attack his stepmother, Edgard thrashed the old man and left home, returning to Paris to shift for himself, supporting himself at first by working as a copyist. Freedom brought exhilaration, but with it appalling poverty. Sometimes he had to sleep under the arcades of the Louvre and at other times, when he had a place to live in, he did not have the price of food.

But he was now able to devote himself completely to music. Through his cousin, Alfred Cortot (then already famous as conductor in Paris and subsequently achieving world renown as a piano virtuoso) Varèse gained admission to the Schola Cantorum in 1904 for the study of composition, orchestration and conducting with Vincent d'Indy, counterpoint and fugue with Albert Roussel and medieval and Renaissance music with Charles Bordes. To pay for his tuition he worked as the school librarian. In 1905, Varèse was accepted as a student at the Paris Conservatory in Widor's master class in composition. While attending the conservatory, he began demonstrating an increasing interest in physicists. Through one of them (Wronsky) he came upon a definition of music which, he said, "seemed suddenly to throw light on my gropings toward a music I sensed could exist. . . . He defined music as the corporealization of the intelligence that is sound. It was a new and exciting conception to me, the first that started me thinking of music as spatial—as moving bodies of sound in space, a conception I gradually made my own. . . . I studied Helmholtz and was fascinated by his experiments with sound, which he described in his *Physiology of Sound*. Later I made some experiments of my own and found I could obtain parabolic and hyperbolic curves of sounds which seemed to me the equivalent of the parabolas and hyperbolas in the visual domain."

In his second year at the conservatory, Varèse organized a chorus of working men and women which, under his direction, gave concerts at the Château du Peuple under the auspices of the Université Populaire du Faubourg Saint-Antoine. In addition to his conducting chores, he was also involved in composing. Among the compositions completed in 1905 were two for large orchestra, *Trois pièces* and *Le prélude à la fin d'un jour*, followed one year later by *Rapsodie romaine*, also for orchestra. He made a bid for the Prix de Rome in 1904 but failed; but one year after that he was awarded a stipend, the Bourse Artistique of the city of Paris.

At the conservatory, Varèse met Suzanne Bing, then a student of acting. They were married in Paris on November 5, 1907. Their only child, a daughter named Claude, after Varèse's beloved grandfather, was born three years later. When, in 1913, Suzanne

decided to pursue a career as an actress, they decided to separate permanently as a prelude to divorce later that year.

By 1908, Varèse felt he had had his fill of the schoolroom and academic studies. He left the conservatory under a cloud, having been ejected following a fiery exchange of ideas with Gabriel Fauré, then the conservatory's director. Varèse was also eager to leave Paris. "I left Paris," he later explained, "out of disgust with all the petty politics, to escape from myself, to get away from bourgeois ideas."

He now made his home in Berlin for seven years (1908–15). In Berlin, he worked as copyist and gave private lessons; founded, in 1909, and conducted the Symphonischer Chor, which, in addition to giving concerts, participated in several Max Reinhardt productions, including those of *Faust* and *A Midsummer Night's Dream*; came into contact with and gained the moral support of Richard Strauss, Romain Rolland, Ferruccio Busoni, and Hugo von Hofmannsthal. Von Hofmannsthal provided Varèse with a generous monthly stipend in 1910 besides giving him permission to adapt his play *Oedipus und die Sphinx* into an opera. That opera was never completed, but Varèse did write several orchestral works. One of them, *Bourgogne* (1907), a tribute both to the region where he had spent such a happy childhood and to his grandfather, was introduced in Berlin on December 15, 1910, at a concert of the Blüthner Orchestra conducted by Josef Stransky. Though romantic in style and spirit, with orchestration influenced by Richard Strauss, it was rejected by audience and critics because of its outlandish dissonances. One critic, Bruno Schrader, called it "infernal noises, the music of cats," while another insisted it was "even worse than Schoenberg."

All this while Varèse was continuing to study the physics of sound and to formulate for himself the aesthetics of sound organization. But he conceived unpitched musical sound, however much it was free of the tempered system, as artistic in purpose to be produced within a creative format. Thus he rejected the "noises" in musical composition promoted by the Italian futurist composer, Luigi Russolo, who, in 1913, issued the manifesto *The Art of Noises*, and invented noise-making instruments. Varèse felt that futurists like Russolo were promoting noise as an end in itself and not as a part of an overall artistic scheme. "Italian futurists," Varèse wrote in protest, "why do you merely reproduce the vibrations of our daily life only in their superficial and distressing aspects?"

On January 4, 1914, Varèse appeared as the guest conductor of the Czech Philharmonic in Prague in a program of 20th-century French music that included the first concert presentation of Debussy's *Le martyre de Saint Sébastian*. The critic of the *Prager Tageblatt* said of Varèse: "The nobility of his manner, the precision and clarity with which he conducts and which makes it immediately clear that Varèse knows what he wants, all held the orchestra under his spell and immediately captivated the audience." That concert had been planned as the first of a European tour, but World War I disrupted that plan. Instead of further pursuing a career as conductor, Varèse returned to Paris to be mobilized in the French army in April 1915. He was stationed with the Twenty-fifth Staff Headquarters in Paris as a bicycle messenger. After six months, following a siege with double pneumonia, he was demobilized.

He came to the United States in December 1915 planning a visit of just several weeks. He stayed seven years before paying a return visit to Paris, adopted the United States as his new homeland, and in time became an American citizen. On April 1, 1917, he made his American conducting debut with a performance in New York of Berlioz's Requiem, performed as a memorial to the war dead of all nations, those of the enemy included. "Mr. Varèse," said a critic for the *New York Evening Mail*, "seemed to possess the inspiration of genius." On March 17, 1918, Varèse conducted a guest performance with the Cincinnati Symphony, and in 1919 he founded the New Symphony Orchestra in New York to promote 20th-century music, its first concert (which was badly reviewed) taking place on April 11, 1919. When, one season later, the directors of the orchestra insisted that its artistic policy be changed to place less stress on the moderns, Varèse resigned as its conductor. In 1921, with Carlos Salzedo, Varèse brought into existence the International Composers' Guild, the first American organization devoted entirely to 20th-century music. Its initial concert, on December 17, 1922, offered some music by Carl Ruggles as well as works by Honegger and Ravel. During the six years of its existence, the International Composers' Guild performed works by fifty-six composers from fourteen countries, including the American premieres of Schoenberg's *Pierrot lunaire*, Stravinsky's *Les noces*, and Berg's Chamber Concerto. After the guild passed out of existence, Varèse organized the Pan American Association of Composers in New York in 1928 to give performances to music of North and Latin American composers both in the United States and abroad.

In the fall of 1918, Varèse met Louise Norton (who, in later years, became famous for her translations of French literature into English). Soon after their meeting they set up house together. In 1925 they acquired a house on Sullivan Street in New York's Greenwich Village which remained their home until the death of Varèse.

By 1920, all the music Varèse had written in Europe had either been lost, burned in a fire in Berlin, or destroyed by the composer. His career began anew in the United States with *Amériques* (1920–21), originally scored for an orchestra of one hundred and forty instruments, but subsequently reduced to more normal dimensions. *Amériques* was Varèses first work to explore the new world of sound experiences

he had so long envisioned. Its large complement of percussion (twenty-one instruments performed by ten executants) included, with the usual instruments, a whip, a siren, and a string drum simulating a "lion's roar." Varèse adopted the title *Amériques* not for its geographic implications, as he explained, "but as symbolic of discoveries—new worlds on earth, in the sky, or in the minds of men." He said further: "This composition is the interpretation of a mood, a piece of pure music absolutely unrelated to the noises of modern life. . . . The use of strong musical effects is not simply my rather vivid reaction to life as I see it, but it is the portrayal of a mood in music and not a sound picture." Paul Le Flem, distinguished French critic and composer, described this music as follows: "There are two densities at work above all in *Amériques*: the orchestra proper and its stimulant, the percussion. The role of the percussion is not to provide rhythmic punctuation or to accentuate certain cadences, but to penetrate into the masses of instrumental sound, to lend them special and varied vibrations. The percussion element will thus be sometimes deep, sometimes flexible and light, the rhythm explosive and nervous." *Amériques* did not get performed until five years after it was written, when the Philadelphia Orchestra under Leopold Stokowski introduced it on April 9, 1926, in its original large-scale orchestration. Boos, catcalls, laughter, hisses, were the audience response both in Philadelphia and New York, and the critics were hardly kinder. In the *New York Post*, Stokowski's former wife, Olga Samaroff, wrote: "Mr. Stokowski . . . could scarcely have done anything more detrimental to the cause of modern music than to produce a work like *Amériques*," and in the *New York World*, Samuel Chotzinoff thought that this music was descriptive of "the progress of a terrible fire in one of our larger zoos."

Varèse's first composition to get heard in the United States was *Offrandes*, for soprano and chamber orchestra (1921), which included eight percussion instruments. It was given its premiere on April 23, 1922, in New York, before getting heard in Berlin and Paris. This work, in two separate sections, is a setting of poems by Vicente Huidobro and José Juan Tabalda. "They are vital pieces," reported a critic for *Musical America* about Varèse's music, "experimental in a certain sense, the music of an artist who knows and admires Arnold Schoenberg."

The critics were far less receptive to other Varèse compositions heard soon after that. *Hyperprism*, for nine wind instruments and eighteen percussion devices (1922–23; N.Y., March 4, 1923) reminded Olin Downes in the *New York Times* of "election night, a menagerie or two and a catastrophe in a boiler factory." In the *New York Sun*, W. J. Henderson said: "Bully Bottom in his proudest moments could not have given such imitations of the roaring of the lion, the shrieking of the wind, the shattering of the hailstones and the swearing of distracted menagerie."

(On the other hand, when Leopold Stokowski conducted *Hyperprism* with the Philadelphia Orchestra on November 7, 1924, Paul Rosenfeld, one of Varèse's first and most staunch supporters, wrote in the *Dial*: "Varèse has done, undoubtedly, as much with the aural sensations of contemporary nature as Picasso with the purely visual ones.") About *Octandre*, for seven winds and double bass (1923; N.Y., January 13, 1924)—an "octandre being a flower with eight stamens—W. J. Henderson in the *Sun* said it was "a ribald outbreak of noise . . . it shrieked, it grunted, it chortled, it moved, it barked—and it turned all eight instruments into contortionists." To Ernest Newman, the English critic serving a guest season with the *New York Post*, *Intégrales*, for small orchestra and percussion (1925; N.Y., March 1, 1925) sounded "a good deal like a combination of the early morning in Mott Haven freight yards, feeding time at the zoo and a Sixth Avenue trolley rounding a curve, with an intoxicated woodpecker thrown in for good measure." *Arcana*, for large orchestra, including five choirs of percussion (1927), which the Philadelphia Orchestra under Stokowski premiered on April 8, 1927, "plunged the listener into a morass of sound which seemingly had little relation to music," wrote Oscar Thompson in *Musical America*. "There was no mercy in its disharmony, no pity in its succession of screaming, clashing discord."

In these works, abstract in design, developmental forms were abandoned; melodies were replaced by repeated notes or fragments; harmonies became densities of timbre and sound; effects were achieved through a process of accumulation; pitch no longer served as a fundamental factor of musical expression; rhythm, meter, dynamics, timbre were elevated to places of equal importance and percussion no longer served the subsidiary role of accentuation and emphasis but became basic to the overall creative scheme; spatial effects (which first came to existence with *Intégrales*) were explored. "In revealing his own universe of sound with the creation of *Offrandes*, *Hyperprism* and *Octandre*," wrote Fernand Ouellette in his biography of the composer, "Varèse was not only appearing for the first time in all the originality of his genius, he was also causing music as a whole to take an immense leap forward. Another beacon had been lighted to continue the great chain of musical tradition. The cause of music could never be the same again after 1924. A mutation had taken place. *Hyperprism*, for example, that black diamond, will always inflict a lasting wound on those who know how to hear, on those who are able to encompass its tragic dimension, on those who allow themselves to be lacerated by the cries that pierce its silences."

The music of *Octandre* was used for *Trend*, in 1937, a ballet choreographed by Hanya Holm which received the *New York Times* award as the year's best dance production. Music from *Octandre* and *Intégrales* was heard in the ballet *Octandre*, choreographed by Richard Tanner and produced by the New York City Ballet in 1971. Martha Graham used the music of *Intégrales* for her ballet *Shapes of Ancestral Wonder*.

One of Varèse's most complex use of rhythm, meter, and percussive sonority came with *Ionisation* (1931; N. Y., March 6, 1933). This was one of the earliest works ever written exclusively for percussion—thirteen percussionists performing on forty-three instruments that included two sirens and various instruments of Varèse's own invention producing sibilant or friction noises. Novel colors were produced by tapping on or beating special metal and wooden objects, by pounding tone clusters on the piano, by striking tubular chimes. What Varèse was trying to realize here was the kind of sounds later realizable through electronics. Already in 1926, Varèse had become interested in electronic music when he began a ten-year period of working with Leon Theremin, the Russian engineer who invented the space-controlled electronic instrument bearing his name. Then Varèse became involved with *Ondes musicales* or *Ondes Martenot*, an electronic instrument utilizing a keyboard invented by Maurice Martenot of France. He used it for the first time in 1929 when *Amériques* was performed in Paris as a substitute for sirens, which were unavailable in that city. Two "Ondes musicales" are found in *Ecuatorial* (1934: N. Y., April 15, 1934).

Between 1936 and 1947, Varèse was creatively silent. He spent his time traveling, teaching at the Arsuan School of Fine Arts in Santa Fe (1937), lecturing at various universities, including the University of Southern California in Los Angeles (1939), visiting electronic studios and, in 1940, founding and directing the New Chorus in New York for the presentation of baroque music (the organization later changing its name to Greater New York Chorus). In the 1940s, his music was rarely performed. Those who remembered him regarded him as a strange relic of a turbulent period of musical revolt in the United States.

The growth of electronic music in the early 1950s made him creatively alive again, for through these developments he was able to realize sound textures and timbres he had imagined but which were beyond the scope of the pitched or unpitched instruments he had used in the 1920s and 1930s. He spent several years in the early 1950s in Paris doing research on *musique concrète*, which experimented with new sounds on magnetic tape by accelerating or slowing down the rotating tape, or combining on one tape sounds recorded on two or more other tapes. In 1953, Varèse was presented with an Ampex tape recorder, which he began using for tape interpolations into a composition he was then creating, *Déserts*. Completed in 1954, it was scored for orchestra and two tracks of "organized sounds" on magnetic tape and was introduced in Paris on December 2, 1954. Electronic sounds were introduced three times in this work. Percussions, in complex rhythmic patterns, served as the transition from the music of wind instruments to the sounds on magnetic tape. "The thematic material has been abstracted to the barest figures of one or two repeated notes and intervals," a critic wrote for *High Fidelity/Musical America*. "The patterns of rhythm, accent, dynamics and sonority have achieved equal importance and actually emerge with 'thematic' significance. And all these powerfully imagined instrumental sounds dovetailed with the taped interludes through skillful use of percussion. The percussion mediates, so to speak, between the sophisticated, complex, pitched close sounds of the wind and the primitive, open, limitless power of the sounds on tape. Out of this opposition grows a good deal of the strength and the shape of the work."

In 1958, Varèse prepared *Poème électronique* for Le Corbusier's Philips Pavilion at the Brussels International and Universal Exposition in Belgium. This work consisted of tracks of organized sounds on magnetic tape projected spatially through some four hundred loudspeakers. The music was intended to accompany the display of lights devised by Le Corbusier flashed on the pavilion ceiling, but no attempt was made to create any relationship between lights and music. A concert performance (for two or three tapes) was given in New York on November 9, 1958.

During the last decade of his life, Varèse was finally accorded the accolades, the recognition, the honors, and the performances he deserved. The house of G. Ricordi undertook the publication of all his works in 1956. Columbia Records released a volume of his works in 1960. At an all-Varèse concert in New York on May 1, 1961, he was given a standing ovation, proof—as Ross Parmenter commented in the *New York Times*—of the extent "to which Mr. Varèse has won his points. These people accepted him as a modern master." Further ovations attended other Varèse performances, including all-Varèse concerts heard in New York and Paris to honor him on his eightieth birthday. At one of these—a retrospective concert in New York on March 31, 1965, conducted by Ralph Shapey—the four Varèse compositions performed covered thirty-four years of his creativity. "Just as there is tremendous might in his music," reported Theodore Strongin in the *New York Times*, "whether of 1924 or 1958, so there is tremendous gentleness. There is also palpability. At times, Mr. Varèse's sounds are like physical objects, almost able to be touched, torn or exploded. They caress, cajole—and above all have a sense of natural life."

In 1962, Varèse received the Creative Arts Award from Brandeis University in Waltham, Mass., and was elected member of the Swedish Academy. He became the first recipient of the Koussevitzky International Recording Award (1963) and he was presented with the Edward MacDowell medal (1965). He was a member of the National Institute of Arts and Letters.

Varèse produced an electronic score, *La Procession de verges* (1955) for a documentary film, *Around and About Joan Miró* produced by Thomas Bouchard. A documentary on Varèse was produced posthumously for distribution over television.

THE COMPOSER SPEAKS: There has always been misunderstanding between the composer and his generation. The commonplace explanation of this phenomenon is that the artist is in advance of his time; but this is absurd. The fact is that the creative artist is representative in a special way of his own period, and the friction between himself and his contemporaries results from the fact that the masses are by disposition and experience fifty years out of date.

Nothing has changed fundamentally, or is likely to change. Methods of expression, however, have changed and must change. . . .

Just as the painter can obtain different intensity and gradation of color, the musician can obtain different vibrations of sound, not varying, ultimately, from vibration to vibration.

In order to exploit the art of sound (i.e., music) we shall require an entirely new medium of expression. We certainly should not forget forthwith the pianoforte and all the arbitrary mechanical restrictions which it has imposed. . . .

Music is antiquated in the extreme in its medium of expression compared with the other arts. We are waiting for a new notation—a new Guido d'Arezzo—when music will move forward at a bound.

PRINCIPAL WORKS: *Amériques*, for large orchestra (1920–21); *Offrandes*, for soprano and chamber orchestra (1921); *Hyperprism*, for nine wind instruments and percussion (1922–23); *Octandre*, for flute, clarinet, oboe, bassoon, horn, trumpet, trombone, and double bass (1923); *Intégrales*, for small orchestra and percussion (1923–25); *Arcana*, for large orchestra (1926–27); *Ionisation*, for thirteen percussionists (1931); *Ecuatorial*, for brass instruments, two *Ondes Martenot* and percussion (1933); *Densité 21.5*, for solo flute (1936); *Étude pour espace*, for chorus, two pianos, and percussion (1947); *Déserts*, for wind instruments and two tracks of magnetic tape (1950–54); *Poème électronique*, for magentic tape (1958); *Nocturnal*, for soprano and bass, chamber orchestra and percussion, completed by Chou Wen-chung (1961).

BIBLIOGRAPHY: Boretz, Benjamin, and Cone, Edward T. (eds.), *Perspectives on American Music* (N.Y., 1971); Ouellette, Fernand, *A Biography of Edgard Varèse* (N.Y., 1968); Peyser, Joan, *The New Music* (N.Y., 1971); Rosenfeld, Paul, *An Hour with American Music* (Philadelphia, 1929); Thomson, Virgil, *American Music Since 1910* (N.Y., 1970); Varèse, Louise, *Varèse: A Looking Glass Diary*, vol. 1, 1883–1928 (New York, 1972); *Juilliard Review*, Fall 1954; *New York Times*, February 21, 1965, November 14, 1965; *Perspectives of New Music*, Spring–Summer 1966, Fall–Winter 1966.

Verrall, John Weedon, b. Britt, Iowa, June 17, 1908.

In many of his compositions between the late 1940s and the early 1950s, Verrall adopted a nine-note scale, an adaptation of the Phrygian mode. He subsequently arrived at a more simplified style, modal in harmony, extensively contrapuntal, occasionally incorporating principles of the baroque concerto form.

His father, a U.S. Treasury tax agent, had sung as a boy soprano in a church choir in England. John Verrall first became interested in the piano when he was eleven by hearing his older brother practice the sonatas of Haydn. Soon after that, John started the study of the piano with Mrs. John Anderson. Without instruction in composition, he began writing short piano pieces at the age of twelve. In his last year in grade school in Britt, which he attended between 1915 and 1922, he accompanied on the piano many of the singing classes. That year (1922) he met Sergei Rachmaninoff, who had come to Ames, Iowa, to give a concert. Rachmaninoff examined some of Verrall's compositions, found them promising, and recommended that he study with Daniel Prothero, who became Verrall's first teacher in composition (1922–23).

In 1923, the family moved to Minneapolis, Minn. At Washburn High School there (1923–27) Verrall was the piano accompanist for the school chorus and student conductor of its orchestra. Upon being graduated from high school, he attended the Minneapolis College of Music (1928–31), where he studied the cello and composition with Engelbert Roentgen, theory with Edmund Langlais, and piano with Gabriel Zsigmondy, and received his bachelor of music degree in 1932. During that time he also attended the Royal College of Music in London, England, for six months (1928–29) as a piano student of Frank Merrick's, who helped him develop a contrapuntal style. Between September 1930 and January 1931 he was at the Liszt Conservatory in Budapest, where he acquired a keen sense for orchestral color from his teacher in composition, Zoltán Kodály. In 1932 Verrall completed a Sonata, for cello and piano, which became his first work to get published. Between 1932 and 1934 he studied piano and composition with Donald Ferguson at the University of Minnesota in Minneapolis, acquiring a bachelor of arts degree there in 1934.

In 1934 he was appointed instructor of theory and music history at Hamline University in St. Paul, Minn., where he was promoted to assistant professor in 1940 and associate professor in 1941. He married Margaret Larawa, a school teacher, on January 1, 1935. The summer of 1938 was spent at the Berkshire Music Center at Tanglewood, Mass., in the study of composition with Aaron Copland. "Copland" he recalls, "gave me an appreciation of texture, solid but varied form and above all he helped to make me more self-critical."

His first adult compositions were completed in 1939. Divertimento, for clarinet, horn, and bassoon, and Symphony no. 1, the latter introduced on January 16, 1940, by the Minneapolis Symphony under Dimitri Mitropoulos. "The thing that impressed me most about the Verrall symphony," wrote Johann S. Egilsrud in the *Minneapolis Journal*, "was the remarkable firmness and many deviations from strict diatonic harmony, the dissonances were sensible, intelligent and structurally sound. Every movement has direction." String Quartet no. 1 (1940) was premiered by the Coolidge Quartet in Minneapolis on November 5, 1941. "Simplicity and earnestness of the work as a whole, taut rhythmic ingenuities of the second movement and a springy fugue finale—these were evidences of a compositional authority that grows steadily more impressive," was John K. Sherman's reaction in the *Minneapolis Star Journal*.

During the summer of 1940, Verrall was Roy Harris's student in composition at Colorado College in Colorado Springs. "Harris helped me develop a feel for long-line melodies and a more expressive relationship between melody and its supporting harmonies." The influence of Harris could be found in two orchestral works which Dimitri Mitropoulos premiered. One was *Portrait of Man* (1940), a suite for orchestra inspired by passages from the Bible, heard at a concert of the Minneapolis Symphony on March 14, 1941. The other was Concert Piece for Strings and Horn (1940), a revision and enlargement of an earlier sinfonietta for string orchestra; Mitropoulos conducted this work with the New York Philharmonic on January 8, 1941.

A strong Bartokian influence affected Verrall in the writing of chamber music in the early 1940s: in the Trio, for two violins and viola (1941); the Sonata, for horn and piano (1941); and the String Quartet no. 2 (1942). The last of these was premiered by the Coolidge String Quartet in Springfield, Mass., on March 8, 1943.

In 1942, Verrall left Hamline University to become assistant professor of theory and history at Mount Holyoke College in South Hadley, Mass. He remained there four years, though not without interruption since twenty-one of those months were spent in the American armed forces during World War II as cryptographer with the Signal Corps (1943–45). While in uniform, Verrall completed Serenade for Five Wind Instruments (1944), which the Army Air Forces Wind Quintet introduced in Washington, D.C., in November 1944.

In 1945, Verrall studied composition with Frederick Jacobi at the Institute of Musical Art in New York. One year later, Verrall was awarded a Guggenheim Fellowship, at which time he completed his Violin Concerto (1946). In 1947–48 he was employed as an editor at the New York publishing house of G. Schirmer. Verrall came to the University of Washington in Seattle as assistant professor of theory in 1948, becoming associate professor in 1950 and full professor in 1966. He retired as professor emeritus in 1973. During the summer of 1964 he held the D. H. Lawrence Fellowship at the University of New Mexico in Taos.

In 1948, Verrall adopted the nine-tone scale as a basic creative tool in the "Night Visions" section of *Dark Night of St. John*, for chamber orchestra, inspired by *The Dark Night of the Soul of St. John*, given its first hearing in Seattle on August 2, 1949, Stanley Chapple conducting. The nine-tone scale is also found in (among other works) the String Quartet no. 3 (1943; Philadelphia, March 12, 1954) and String Quartet no. 4 (1948; Seattle, Wash., May 22, 1949); *The Cowherd and the Sky Maiden*, an opera with libretto by Esther Shepherd based on a Chinese legend (1951; Seattle, January 17, 1952); Piano Sonata (1951; Seattle, August 22, 1952); and *The Wedding Knell* (1952), a one-act opera based on a grotesque tale by Nathaniel Hawthorne which was premiered in Seattle on December 5, 1952, when it received the Seattle Centennial Opera Award. In reviewing this opera for the *Seattle Times*, Louis R. Guzzo reported that "the score sustains the mood of the story in astonishing fashion. It must be said that Verrall creates a mood that cannot be forgotten soon."

After abandoning the nine-tone scale, Verrall's writing became modal. "But this modal harmony is not of the folksy or antique variety," said James Neale in the *American Composers Alliance Bulletin*. "This is finely wrought, mature art music, often with lengthy melodic lines and characteristic instrumental figurations. Aeolian and Dorian are the favored modes." This is the style first encountered in String Quartet no. 6 (1956; Seattle, May 28, 1956), Sonatina for Cello and Piano (1956), Nocturne, for bass clarinet and piano (1956; Indianapolis, February 8, 1960), and *Portrait of Saint Christopher*, tone poem for orchestra (1956), the last of which was introduced by the Seattle Symphony under Milton Katims on October 22, 1956.

Verrall's most important later works include a Piano Concerto (1960; Vancouver, British Columbia, November 8, 1960); String Quartet no. 7 (1961; Bloomington, Ind., March 14, 1968); Nonet, for winds and strings (1969; Seattle, March 4, 1971); Sonata for Flute and Piano (1972), which received an award from the National Flute Association as an outstanding flute composition; Variations and Adagio, a quintet for strings, wind, and piano (1975; St. Paul, March 9, 1975), written on a grant from the National Endowment for the Arts; *Radiant Bridge*, an orchestral tone poem (1975), commissioned and premiered by the Port Angelus Symphony in the state of Washington (February 1, 1976); *Eusebius Remembered*, a sonata for horn and piano (1977), premiered in Seattle on February 5, 1978; and a song cycle, *Songs of Nature*, to poems by John Gracen Brown (1979; Los Angeles, May 4, 1980).

A retrospective concert of Verrall's music was given at the University of Washington in Seattle on May 31, 1973, covering thirty years beginning with the First Sonata for Viola and Piano (1939) and ending with the Nonet.

Verrall is the author of *Fugue and Invention in Theory and Practice* (1966) and *Basic Theory of Scales, Modes, and Intervals (1969)*.

THE COMPOSER SPEAKS: I have always been interested in the relationship between design elements and the meaning to be expressed, so that form to me is a matter of total relationship rather than a geometric sequence of separate ideas. Thus, the basic elements of music, out of which I unfold my meanings are sound-silence, direction and distance, duration, thickness or thinness of texture, tone color, dynamic intensity, tensions and their relaxation, and then melody, harmony, and rhythm, which are end results, not the basic materials of the creative process.

PRINCIPAL WORKS: 7 string quartets (1941–61); 3 symphonies (1939, 1943, 1966); 2 violin sonatas (1950, 1956); 2 horn sonatas (1942, 1977); 2 viola sonatas (1939, 1963); 2 serenades, for wind quintet (1944, 1950).
Portrait of Man, tone poem for orchestra (1940); Concert Piece for Strings and Horn (1940); Violin Concerto (1946); Prelude and Allegro, for strings (1948); *Dark Night of St. John*, for orchestra (1949); *The Cowherd and the Sky Maiden*, opera (1951); Piano Sonata (1951); Piano Quintet (1953); *The Wedding Knell*, one-act opera (1954); *Portrait of St. Christopher*, tone poem for orchestra (1956); Cello Sonatina (1956); Oboe Sonata (1956); *Autumn Sketches*, for piano (1956); Nocturne, for bass clarinet and piano (1956); Passacaglia, for band (1958); Piano Concerto (1959); Septet, for winds (1966); Viola Concerto (1968); Nonet, for winds and strings (1969); Flute Sonata (1972); *Radiant Bridge*, tone poem for orchestra (1975); *Songs of Nature*, song cycle for voice and piano (1979).

BIBLIOGRAPHY: *BBDM; DCM; American Composers Alliance Bulletin*, vol. 7, no. 4, 1958.

W

Wagenaar, Bernard, b. Arnhem, Netherlands, July 18, 1894; d. York Harbor, Maine, May 19, 1971. American citizen, 1927.

Wagenaar's music was molded by both Germanic and French influences: Germanic in the solidity and clarity of its architectural structures and in a postromantic style reminiscent of Mahler and Richard Strauss; French in its occasional neoclassical orientation and in its harmonic language. His music was readily digestible. Some of it was marked by a light and graceful touch and a discreet use of popularism.

His father, Hendryk Wagenaar, was a professional musician. Bernard Wagenaar received music instruction on both violin and piano while attending private schools in Arnhem for his academic education. Between 1909 and 1914, he attended the Utrecht Conservatory; an intensive training in music included violin with Gerard Veerman, piano with Mme. Veerman-Bekker, and composition with Johan Wagenaar. When his studies were completed, he spent the next six years teaching music privately at Arnhem and conducting chorus and lesser orchestras in the Netherlands.

In 1920 he immigrated to the United States for permanent residence and citizenship. Willem Mangelberg, then the conductor of the New York Philharmonic, engaged him for its violin section, where he remained two years (1921–23), at the same time also performing for that orchestra on the harpsichord, organ, and celesta.

He began receiving performances for compositions completed in the early 1920s. *Three Songs from the Chinese,* for voice, flute, and harp (1921), over which hovered the shadow of Mahler, was introduced in 1925 at a concert of the Society of Friends of Music in New York, after which it was performed by the Schola Cantorum in New York and by various other musical groups in the United States and Europe besides being transmitted by special broadcast from Holland to the East Indies. *From a Very Little Sphinx,* song cycle for voice and piano (1921), using poems by Edna St. Vincent Millay as text, entered the repertoire of the distinguished concert soprano Povla Frijsh.

Wagenaar resigned from the New York Philharmonic in 1923 to devote more time to composing. Between 1925 and 1927 he taught composition, fugue, and orchestration at the Institute of Musical Art in New York, and from 1927 to 1968 at the Juilliard School of Music.

His Violin Sonata (1925), which was performed by several virtuosos, received the Society for the Publication of American Music Award in 1928, and his Piano Sonata (1927) was introduced at the Copland-Sessions Concert in New York, also in 1928. Even more significant hearings for his orchestral music came soon after. Willem Mengelberg, conducting the New York Philharmonic, presented the premiere of Wagenaar's Symphony no. 1 (1926) on October 7, 1928. Divertimento no. 1, for orchestra (1927), was commissioned by Artur Bodansky and the Society of Friends of Music, but its world premiere was given by the Detroit Symphony, Ossip Gabrilowitsch conducting, on November 28, 1929. After that it was programmed by several other major American orchestras including the Cincinnati Symphony, the Minneapolis Symphony and the National Symphony in Washington, D.C., besides being transmitted several times over the radio, once in a special international broadcast; it was also the recipient of the Eastman School Publication Award. Sinfonietta, for orchestra (1929), received its initial hearing on January 16, 1930, with Willem Mengelberg conducting the New York Philharmonic. This work, which enjoyed significant performances in the United States and western Europe, was selected as the only work to represent the United States at the festival of the International Society for Contemporary Music in Liège, Belgium, on September 4, 1930. The "neo-Beethovenian idiom, vigorous and dramatic," which Nicolas Slonimsky, in *Music Since 1900,* found in this Sinfonietta characterizes the other two orchestral works as well. The romantic sentiments, partly Mahlerian, were expressed concisely and convincingly; the orchestration was richly textured in the vein of Richard Strauss; the harmonization, in its free chromaticism over a solid diatonic bass, was French. "Characteristic are the building up of a highly organized structure from several short motives," wrote Donald Fuller in *Modern Music,* "the motored urge of fast passages, and constantly alive orchestration."

On September 11, 1931, Wagenaar married Irene Chadwick, with whom he had two children. About a year later, came Wagenaar's greatest success as composer up to then, when Arturo Toscanini, conducting the New York Philharmonic, gave the premiere of

Symphony no. 2 on November 10, 1932. In this work, Wagenaar adopted such then modern practices as atonality and polytonality. Writing in the *Musical Standard* of London, Leigh Henry said: "In his Second Symphony, Wagenaar emerges with the freedom of the creative artist who has mastered his means of expression and is no longer self-conscious about them. The slow movement, especially, is startlingly and essentially lyrical, being laid out 'after the manner of the nocturne.' I feel that in this Second Symphony Wagenaar has contributed something vital to contemporary music and something to which it would be difficult to attach the label of this or that modern school, in spite of its modernity in the best sense."

Wagenaar's Symphony no. 3 followed the Second by four years. It was completed in 1935, premiered by the Philadelphia Orchestra on January 23, 1937, and recipient of the Juilliard Publication Award. In the *New York Herald Tribune*, Virgil Thomson called it "elegant, eloquent, eclectic . . . authoritative, cultured, worldly, incisive without profundity, brilliant without ostentation." Symphony no. 4 (1949), in five movements, was first performed on December 16, 1949, by the Boston Symphony, the composer conducting. Wagenaar said of it: "The 'inspiration' for the composing of this piece was the desire to say what I wanted to say about shaping orchestral sounds into a, formally speaking, rather compact version of the compound musical construction known as a 'symphony.' The movements are mostly short, therefore. . . . The construction of the first movement is that of a modified Sonata-Allegro form; that of the second has been based upon a 'Song with two Trios'; that of the third movement is one written in a continuous line, while that of the adagietto is ternary and that of the Finale in a binary form."

For the Barrère-Salzedo-Britt Trio, Wagenaar produced still another successful orchestral work, the Triple Concerto, for flute, harp, cello, and orchestra (1935). After it was introduced by the Barrère-Salzedo-Britt Trio as soloists with the Philadelphia Orchestra under Eugene Ormandy on March 17, 1938, this work was broadcast over the NBC radio network in May 1941 in a performance sponsored by the International Society for Contemporary Music. This was music in a vein lighter than that of the symphonies. As Olin Downes noted in the *New York Times*: "He appeared to be writing a concerto that aimed, in a modern artistic way, to please. He wrote to entertain, and he produced an art work of value. He did not sacrifice his standards in so doing."

Another work in an infectiously light style was the two-act opera *Pieces of Eight* (1944), libretto by Edward Eager based on an old New England legend. In the style of a *Singspiel*, this opera included spoken dialogue as well as recitatives, together with bountiful arias and ensemble numbers which often made sly references to or quotations from composers of the past. Introduced in New York on May 9, 1944, it became the first composition to win the Alice M. Ditson Award from Columbia University.

Some of Wagenaar's most important works after that resulted from commissions. For the Hendrik Willem Van Loon Scholarship Fund Concert of the Netherlands American Foundation he wrote *Song of Mourning*, for orchestra (1944), which Hans Kindler first performed on December 5, 1944, in New York with the National Symphony Orchestra of Washington, D.C. Concert Piece, for orchestra (1954), was commissioned and introduced by the Louisville Orchestra in Kentucky, Robert Whitney conducting. *Preamble*, for orchestra (1955), was a commission of the Juilliard School of Music for its fiftieth anniversary, the first performance taking place on February 10, 1956, Jean Morel conducting. The Koussevitzky Music Foundation commissioned the writing of String Quartet no. 4 (1960).

Wagenaar was a member of the executive committee of the American section of the International Society of Contemporary Music and the Society for History of Music of the Netherlands. He was decorated officer of Orange-Nassau in the Netherlands.

PRINCIPAL WORKS: 4 symphonies (1926–49); 3 string quartets, a fourth withdrawn (1931, 1936, 1960); 2 divertimentos, for orchestra (1927, 1953).

From a Very Little Sphinx, for voice and piano (1921); *Three Songs from the Chinese,* for voice harp, and piano (1921); Violin Sonata (1925); Piano Sonata (1927); Sinfonietta, for orchestra (1929); Cello Sonatina (1934); Triple Concerto, for flute, cello, harp, and orchestra (1935); Violin Concerto (1940); *Fantasietta on British-American Ballads,* for chamber orchestra (1940); Concertino, for eight instruments (1942); *Feuilleton,* for orchestra (1942); *Song of Mourning,* for orchestra (1944); Ciacona, for piano (1948); *Five Tableaux,* for cello and orchestra (1952); *Preamble,* for orchestra (1955); *Four Vignettes,* for harp (1965).

BIBLIOGRAPHY: Ewen, David, *American Composers Today* (N.Y., 1949); Howard, John Tasker, *Our Contemporary · Composers* (N.Y., 1946); Reis, Claire, *Composers in America* (N.Y., 1947); *Modern Music,* June 1944; *Who's Who in America, 1970–71.*

Walker, George, b. Washington, D. C., June 27, 1922.

In his early works, Walker was concerned with a strong rhythmic movement and a pronounced lyricism within clear formal structures. Since 1968, his writing has been characterized by rhythmic fluidity suggested by rapidly changing meters, complex sonorities, disjunct lines, and pointillistic effects. Diverse material distilled from ethnic and popular sources are sometimes embedded in the compositional fabric, but are seldom discernible.

He was the son of a physician. Study of the piano began when he was five. He received his academic education in the public schools of Washington, D. C., graduating from Dunbar High School in 1937. As a high school student of fourteen, Walker gave his first public recital as a pianist at Howard University, in Washington.

Between 1937 and 1941, Walker received an intensive training in music at Oberlin College in Ohio. There he studied piano with David Meyer, organ with Arthur Poister, and composition with Normand Lockwood, receiving his bachelor of music degree in 1941. His music studies were then continued at the Curtis Institute of Music in Philadelphia (1941–45) with Rudolf Serkin (composition), Gian Carlo Menotti (orchestration), and Gregory Piatigorsky and William Primrose (chamber music). In Piatigorsky's classes Walker often served as pianist. In 1945 he received from the Curtis Institute the award of a piano recital in Town Hall, N.Y., which took place on November 13, 1945. That year, on December 4, 1945, he was also the winner of the Philadelphia Orchestra Youth Audition, which brought him a guest appearance with the Philadelphia Orchestra, Eugene Ormandy conducting, in a performance of the Rachmaninoff Piano Concerto no. 3.

His first talented composition was *Lyric for Strings* (originally entitled *Lament for Strings*), written in 1946 as a memorial for his grandmother. It was introduced on March 24, 1947, by the National Gallery Sinfonietta in Washington, D. C., Richard Bales conducting. When it was heard in New York in 1977 in a performance by the New York Philharmonic, Paul Freeman conducting, Irving Lowens, reporting to the *Washington Star*, described it as a "bittersweet, transparent, beautifully textured piece . . . very touching and attractive." In 1946, Walker also completed his String Quartet no. 1.

He spent the summer of 1947 at the American Conservatory at Fontainebleau, France, studying the piano with Robert Casadesus. Walker's career as a pianist was launched in 1950 when he began the first of several tours of the United States and Europe that continued for three years. In 1953, he completed the first of his piano sonatas, its initial performance taking place in Washington, D. C., on January 27, 1957. In 1953–54, Walker was instructor of music at Dillard University in New Orleans. Between 1955 and 1957, he completed his music studies at the Eastman School of Music in Rochester, N.Y., receiving an artist's diploma and the degree of doctor of musical arts in 1957, his doctoral thesis being his Piano Sonata no. 2 (1957).

A Fulbright Fellowship in piano and a John Hay Whitney Fellowship in composition made it possible for Walker to return to Paris in 1957 to resume piano study with Robert Casadesus in Fontainebleau.

Between 1957 and 1959 he also studied composition privately with Nadia Boulanger. During this period his most important compositions were the Concerto for Trombone and Orchestra (1957) and *Address for Orchestra* (1959). The Trombone Concerto was premiered on January 17, 1957, in Rochester, N. Y., Howard Hanson conducting, with Porter Pondexter soloist. In reviewing a recording of this work for *High Fidelity/Musical America*, Kenneth Furie called it "a tremendous contribution to the meager trombone literature, a bold virtuoso vehicle of considerable melodic and rhythmic power that speaks with a deeply personal voice." *Address for Orchestra* is a three-movement work, an excerpt from which ("Passacaglia") was introduced on February 3, 1968, by the Atlanta Symphony under Paul Freeman, and which since that time has had numerous performances apart from the rest of the work. The entire composition had its first hearing at the Mons Festival in Belgium, James De Preist conducting, on October 22, 1971. After that, it was heard in Berlin in 1972 and received its American premiere in Baltimore on January 16, 1974.

Upon returning from Paris, Walker made his home in New York City, where he married Helen Siemens, a concert pianist, on July 23, 1960. (They were divorced in 1975.) In New York he became active as instructor of piano at the Dalcroze School of Music (1960–61) and at the New School for Social Research (1961), where he gave a course on aesthetics. He was also involved as concert pianist, beginning with a successful return recital in Town Hall, N.Y., on March 3, 1960, when he presented the New York premiere of his Piano Sonata no. 2 (1957).

In 1961 he was appointed instructor on the music faculty at Smith College in Northampton, Mass., remaining there seven years, in 1968 promoted to associate professorship. In 1961 he completed a symphony, the premiere of which was heard in Boulder, Colo., on March 17, 1969. *Gloria in Memoriam*, for chorus and orchestra (1963), became his first composition to get published. In 1963 Sonata for Two Pianos, a version of his Piano Sonata no. 2, received the Harvey Gaul Prize. *Perimeters*, for clarinet and piano (1966), was premiered by Leroy Johnston at the Juilliard School of Music in New York in the year of its composition. String Quartet no. 2 (1968), premiered in New York on September 5, 1968, by the New England Festival Chamber Players, was a serial composition, the writing of which, said Raymond Ericson in the *New York Times*, was "delicate, clear-textured and fluid, sensitive to the need for dramatic phrases as contrasts and highlight." *Antiphonys*, a composition for chamber orchestra (1968), was featured at the Bennington Composers Conference, where it received its world premiere on August 14, 1968.

Since 1969, Walker has been professor of piano and theory at Rutgers University in New Brunswick,

N.J. Between 1974 and 1978 he was adjunct professor of music at Peabody Conservatory in Baltimore and in 1975–76 he was Distinguished Professor of Music at the University of Delaware in Newark, Del.

One of Walker's most substantial successes as composer came with his Piano Concerto (1975), written on a grant from the National Endowment for the Arts. Its first performance was given on May 23, 1975, by the Minnesota Symphony, Paul Freeman conducting. The first movement is in classical structure, while the third employs such baroque forms as toccata and fugue; the lyrical second movement is a tribute to Duke Ellington. When the New York Philharmonic presented a week-long "Celebration of Black Composers" in 1977, Walker's Piano Concerto was called by Irving Lowens in the *Washington Star* the "blockbuster of the evening . . . full of poetry and pyrotechnics for both soloist and orchestra." In the *Saturday Review*, Irving Kolodin said: "He [Walker] emerged from the convocation not merely as a leader of his black colleagues but as one of the ablest composers in the American community, occupying a place between the older circle of Copland-Schuman-Carter and the younger coterie of Crumb-Wuorinen-Druckman. He addresses himself confidently to his problem, possesses a sure sense of direction and works energetically toward his objective."

On a commission from the Musical Arts Association of Cleveland in observance of the American bicentennial, and on a fellowship from the Rockefeller Foundation, Walker completed *Dialogus*, for cello and orchestra, in 1976. The Cleveland Orchestra conducted by Lorin Maazel, with Stephen Geber as soloist, presented the world premiere on April 22, 1976. This work opens and closes with a huge cluster of notes from which a lyric line is drawn by the cello. Klaus G. Roy's program notes for the Cleveland Orchestra describe this work further: "In the course . . . the cello alternates statements which are lyrical and rhythmically propulsive. The title *Dialogus* (a Latin form of the Greek *dialogos*, or dialogue) suggests the use of material between the soloist and the orchestra which is sometimes complementary but more often not; soloist and orchestra appear much of the time to proceed along independent directions. Because of its frequently pointillistic usage, the orchestra does not consistently 'support' or 'agree with' the soloist. The composer likens the solo cello at times to a 'voice in the forest' surrounded by things which are not directly related to what it has to say."

In 1978, on a commission from the Kennedy Center for the Performing Arts and the violinist Sanford Allen, Walker wrote Sonata no. 2, for violin and piano. Allen gave the premiere in Washington, D. C., on March 30, 1979. The first movement has a rhapsodic quality, the second is in the perpetual-motion

style of a toccata, and in the third movement a segment of the spiritual "Let Us Break Bread Together" is quoted.

On February 12, 1981, the New York Philharmonic conducted by Zubin Mehta gave the world premiere of Walker's *In Praise of Folly*, for orchestra (1980).

Walker received grants from Rutgers University Research Council in 1970, 1971, and 1973. He was honored with a citation from the University of Rochester Alumni in 1960 and an Alumni Achievement Award from the Eastman School of Music (1975).

THE COMPOSER SPEAKS: Musical composition is for me a selective organizational process which reflects a concern for all the elements that constitute a musical statement in Western terms. Although color has played a more important part in recent orchestral works, I do not feel that it justifies a dominant role. I feel that music may not be capable of expressing anything specific, as Stravinsky asserts; but it can and does suggest a content that must be revealed before a sense of communication evolves between the composer and his audience. To this end must the composer's craft be honed without sacrificing his personal taste and standards.

PRINCIPAL WORKS: 3 piano sonatas (1953, 1957, 1975); 2 string quartets (1946, 1967); 2 violin sonatas (1958, 1978).

Lyric for Strings, originally *Lament for Strings* (1956); Cello Sonata (1957); Trombone Concerto (1957); Three Lyrics, for Chorus (1958); *Address for Orchestra* (1959); Symphony (1961); *Spatials*, for piano (1961); Psalm 96, for chorus (1963); *Gloria in Memoriam*, for chorus and orchestra (1963); *Perimeters*, for clarinet and piano (1966); *Antiphonys*, for chamber orchestra (1968); *Music for Three*, for violin, cello, and piano (1970); *Spektra*, for piano (1971); Variations, for orchestra (1971); *Spirituals*, for orchestra (1974); *Five Fancies*, for clarinet and piano, four hands (1975); Piano Concerto (1975); Music for Brass (1975); Three Spirituals, for voice and piano (1975); *Dialogus*, for cello and orchestra (1976); Mass, for chorus and orchestra (1977); *In Praise of Folly*, for orchestra (1980); Cello Concerto (1981).

BIBLIOGRAPHY: *BBDM*; Southern, Eileen, *The Music of Black Americans* (N.Y., 1971); *Cleveland Orchestra Program Notes*, April 22, 1976.

Ward, Robert Eugene, b. Cleveland, Ohio, September 13, 1917.

The strong American profile of so many of Ward's compositions comes from his interest in American folk music and jazz. He is a modernist who does not disavow expressive, strong-fibered lyricism, emotion, or dramatic interest. From his earliest works he favored rhythmic variety, austere contrapuntal textures, well-sounding though at times dissonant harmonies and a lyric line of heroic dimension. He was awarded the Pulitzer Prize in music in 1962.

He was one of five children, his father, the owner of a moving and storage company. Singing in school and church choirs and in the chorus of operetta productions, and the study of harmony in Cleveland's public schools, represented Ward's earliest musical experiences. He then studied piano from 1933 to 1935 with Ben Burtt and made his first attempts at composing music.

He was graduated from John Adams High School in Cleveland in 1935. Between 1935 and 1939 he attended the Eastman School of Music, in Rochester, N. Y., the first year as a double major in composition and public-school music, the latter for practical reasons. The following fall, he dropped public-school music to concentrate on composition, which he now studied with Bernard Rogers, Howard Hanson, and Edward Royce. Several of his compositions written at that time were publicly performed. *Fatal Interview*, for soprano and orchestra (1937), a setting of two poems by Edna St. Vincent Millay, was premiered in Rochester, N. Y., in the year of its composition, Howard Hanson conducting. In April 1938, *Slow Music*, for orchestra (1937)—which he had planned as a movement for a symphony he never finished—was also introduced in Rochester under Hanson. Andante and Scherzo, a composition for string quartet (1937) which he orchestrated, was heard first in Detroit in July 1941 in the orchestral version. *Ode*, for orchestra (1939), was given its initial hearing in Rochester under Hanson in 1939.

After receiving the bachelor of music degree at Eastman School in 1939, Ward earned a fellowship in composition for the Juilliard School of Music in New York. During the next two years he continued his music studies there with Frederick Jacobi (composition), Albert Stoessel and Edgar Schenkman (conducting) and Bernard Wagenaar (orchestration). While attending the Juilliard School, Ward served on the music faculty of Queens College in Queens, N. Y., (1940–41) and wrote reviews and articles for *Modern Music*. During the summer of 1941 he was Aaron Copland's student in composition at the Berkshire Music Center at Tanglewood, Mass.

As a Juilliard student, Ward completed writing Symphony no. 1 (1941), his first successful large work. Contrapuntal structures were here combined with the sonata-allegro form in the first movement; the second movement consisted of two themes with variations; and the third movement was a scherzo-finale. The symphony was first performed on May 10, 1941, at the Juilliard School, the composer conducting, after which it was heard in Denver, Rochester, New York City, Baltimore, Washington, D. C., and elsewhere, in addition to becoming the recipient of the Juilliard Publication Award in 1942. After a

performance in New York in 1952, John Briggs said in the *New York Times* that it was a "thoughtful work, constructed with great care." The *Washington Times-Herald* said: "It is concise, logical in development, significant in idea, virile in mood and exciting in its several climaxes."

During World War II, Ward served in the American armed forces (1942–46). The first phase of army life consisted of writing music for and playing in an all-soldier revue, *The Life of Riley*. Following a period of study at the Army Music School in Fort Myer, Va., he was assigned to the Seventh Infantry Division, first as regimental, then as divisional, bandleader. He and his band received a citation for outstanding service. In addition to his duties with the army band, he organized a jazz ensemble that performed for the servicemen. "The years in the army proved beneficial musically," he recalls, "in that I came into close contact with several phases of musical activity which otherwise I might never have had." He was decorated with the Bronze Star for meritorious service during a Japanese attack on Attu in the Aleutian Islands.

While stationed in Hawaii, he composed Adagio and Allegro for orchestra (1943). Ward revealed that this music reflected his moods at the time. "They varied between despair at all the implications of the war (and later resignation toward them as I came to feel that armed strife was but the violent phase of a struggle that was continuous) and moments of greater hope and courage." He also conceded that in writing this work, he was influenced by Tchaikovsky and Sibelius on the one hand, and by Hindemith and Hanson on the other. Adagio and Allegro was initially performed on May 20, 1946, in New York by the National Orchestral Association, Leon Barzin conducting; on February 4, 1951, it was heard in Baltimore with the composer conducting the Baltimore Symphony.

In Leyte and Okinawa, Ward made sketches for *Jubilation: An Overture*, for orchestra, but it was not completed until 1946 after his discharge from the army. This is one of Ward's first successful attempts to incorporate jazz and popular dance rhythms into serious music. It was introduced by the National Orchestral Association in New York under Leon Barzin on May 20, 1946 (on a program that also included the Adagio and Allegro). Later that year, on November 21, it was performed by the Los Angeles Philharmonic under Alfred Wallenstein. In the *Times-Herald* in Washington, D. C., Glenn Dillard Gunn described it as "brilliant, compact and expertly wrought."

While still in uniform, Ward received the Alice M. Ditson Fellowship from Columbia University in 1944. On June 19 of that year he married Mary Raymond Benedict, with whom he has five children.

Upon being demobilized on March 1, 1946, with

the rank of warrant officer, Ward returned to Juilliard School to conclude his music study and receive his certificate in May 1946. In 1946 he was also the beneficiary of a grant from the National Institute of Arts and Letters.

Between 1946 and 1948 Ward gave courses in music at Columbia University, and from 1946 to 1956 he was on the music faculty of the Juilliard School of Music (assistant to the president from 1954 to 1956). He was director of the Third Street Settlement Music School in New York City (1952–55) and conductor of the Doctors Orchestral Society of New York (1949–55).

National recognition as composer came with Symphony no. 2 (1946–47). Here again Ward incorporated jazz melodies and idioms. The first movement opened with a jazz tune that was then developed fugally with bold accents. The beautiful song of the second movement had the style of a blues, and the third movement was enlivened by popular dance tunes. The composer described this symphony further as follows: "The first movement includes both a traditional sonata form and a fugue, the slow movement is more akin to an aria of the baroque period than the later classical slow movement, and the finale is a rondo of dance tunes with variations." The National Symphony under Hans Kindler introduced it in Washington, D. C., on January 25, 1948. After that it was heard on programs of several other American orchestras including the Philadelphia Orchestra under Eugene Ormandy on January 27, 1950. When the Philadelphia Orchestra performed it in New York, Virgil Thomson, in the *New York Herald Tribune*, said: "It is exuberant and warm, also boisterous. . . . The life in it comes, I think, from the rhythm which is never plodding, and also from a certain naturalness in the melodic content. . . . The melodic matter is frankly popular in character, the harmony suggestive of commercial 'richness'. . . . His good humor, his easy-going, if somewhat assertive, buoyancy of spirit and his shameless acceptance of standard 'American-way-of-life' feelings do have their charm."

Ward received a Guggenheim Fellowship in 1950, which was renewed for an additional year. Commissions in the 1950s led to the writing of various compositions. *Jonathan and the Gingery Snare*, for narrator, small orchestra, and percussion (1950)—the story of a boy in search of a pet who found more pets than he had bargained for—was written for a young people's concert of the New York Philharmonic, which premiered it, under Igor Buketoff, on February 4, 1950. This work was designed to highlight the percussion instruments, which, with the normal contingent, included castanets, a siren, wood blocks, ratchet, and a peanut whistle. For the Friends of Music of Dumbarton Oaks in the District of Columbia, Ward wrote Symphony no. 3, for small orchestra (1950), which the Dumbarton Oaks Orchestra under

the composer introduced on March 31, 1950. *Sacred Songs for Pantheists*, for soprano solo and orchestra (1951), was commissioned and first performed by the Quincy Society of Fine Arts in Quincy, Ill., and *Euphony*, for orchestra (1954), by the Louisville Orchestra in Kentucky, Robert Whitney conducting. For its thirtieth anniversary, the Juilliard School called upon Ward to write Fantasia for Brass Choir and Timpani (1956). In all these works Ward demonstrated an ever-increasing interest in a strong lyric line and in a more subtly complex texture of polyphony and orchestration.

On a commission from the Musical Arts Society of La Jolla, Calif., Ward wrote Symphony no. 4 (1950), introduced on August 3, 1968. When this symphony was heard in New York in March 1959, Winthrop Sargeant, writing in the *New Yorker*, called it "a sturdy, well-constructed and agreeably melodious composition, exhibiting a mastery of contrapuntal lines (with an especially fine sense of how to keep the bass line moving), a feeling for structural climax that depended neither on noise nor on superficial tricks of orchestration, and invention of a kind that was neither banal nor irritatingly doctrinaire." Ward revised this symphony two decades later, the first performance of the new version being heard in Albany, N.Y., on May 3, 1980.

When Ward left the Juilliard School of Music in 1956, he was appointed executive vice-president and managing editor of Galaxy Music Corporation and of Highgate Press. He remained with both organizations until 1967, becoming a director of Galaxy Music and Highgate Press in 1965.

The 1950s witnessed the completion of Ward's first opera, *Pantaloon* (1956), libretto by Bernard Stambler based on Andreyev's play *He Who Gets Slapped*. Its first performance was given by the Columbia University Opera Workshop in New York on May 17, 1956. When the New York City Opera revived it on April 12, 1959, the opera's title reverted to the one Andreyev had used. Adopting a comparatively conservative stance that placed considerable emphasis on song, whether for the voice or orchestra, Ward here produced a score that always remembered, as Howard Taubman noted in the *New York Times*, "that his central obligation is to keep the line of the drama taut. His musical setting has pace and contrasts. It gives the principle singers a chance to sing and to reveal character; in the orchestra, it provides colorful atmosphere and often underlines the action with considerable power."

With *The Crucible* (1961), Ward developed into a powerful and significant musical dramatist. This opera boasted a tautly structured and strongly projected libretto by Bernard Stambler adapted (almost intact) from Arthur Miller's drama of lust, superstition, revenge, bigotry and jealousy during the Salem witch trials of 1692 in New England. Ward wrote this opera on a commission from the Ford Foundation, and its world premiere took place in New York on October 26, 1961, in a production by the New York City Opera. Impressed by what he described as "the rich orchestration" of Miller's language, Ward placed emphasis on the voice over the orchestra, using for his orchestral background a modest ensemble comprised of paired winds, four horns, two trumpets, two trombones, strings, and percussion. The voice carried the drama, sometimes in arias and ensemble numbers, but most often in a powerful declamatory, or parlando, style, much of which drew its identity from New England psalmody and hymnology. In the *Saturday Review*, Irving Kolodin described Ward's lyricism as "a kind of melodic sing-song, with the orchestra a source of commentary contrast. When appropriate, the vocal line flames into a strain of song not unrelated to the psalmody characteristic of the time and place." In his review in the *New Yorker*, Winthrop Sargeant called Ward's music "dignified and nowhere banal. It is continuously expressive and it intensified all the nuances of the drama, from anguish and despair to heroic nobility. . . . He has created an imposing work that will, I suspect, take its place among the classics of the standard repertory."

When first produced by the New York City Opera, *The Crucible* was given a rousing ovation after the final curtain. The opera went on from there to win the Pulitzer Prize and the New York Music Critics Circle Award, both in 1962. In 1963 a performance of *The Crucible* at the Hessisches Staatstheater and on television in Wiesebaden, Germany, made Ward the first American to direct the German premiere of an American opera. Since 1963 it has been given notable revivals.

Ward wrote other full-length operas after *The Crucible. The Lady from Colorado* (1964), in a light, almost operetta vein, was commissioned by the Central City Opera Association which presented the world premiere in Central City, Colo., on July 3, 1964, where all scheduled thirteen performances were sold out. Bernard Stambler's libretto was based on a novel by Homer Croy, set in the mountain town of Elkhorn, Colo., in the late 19th century. Some of the musical numbers were in praise of Colorado, one of which, "Out Here in Colorado," proved the hit of the production. Sandor Kallai, writing in the *Kansas City Star*, felt that the opera caught "the spirit and the lawless excitement of the old West" and that Ward's score had "an absolute abundance of singable melody and earthy humor."

Though the New York City Opera had commissioned *Claudia Legare* (1977), the world premiere was given by the Minnesota Opera in St. Paul on April 14, 1978. While reaching to Ibsen's *Hedda Gabler* for a text, Bernard Stambler transferred the setting to Charleston, S.C., and the time of the Reconstruction following the Civil War. The characters bore American names (which the composer and the librettist found in old Charleston city directories),

each character a counterpart for that found in Ibsen. Mindful of the time and setting, Ward incorporated into his score the popular Civil War Song of the South "The Bonnie Blue Flag" and provided music for "No Surrender," a hymn of that period of which only the words have survived. But, as Harold C. Schonberg reported from St. Paul to the *New York Times*, "for the most part, the musical language is completely neutral in that it tries to address itself to states of mind and emotion rather than to local color. The approach is gently lyric." Most of the vocal members were in the parlando style Ward had used so effectively in *The Crucible*. "They are," said John H. Harvey in the *St. Paul Sunday Pioneer Press* of the vocal numbers, "by turns attractive and well-charged dramatically and always are eminently singable." The large orchestra which Ward employed as background "skillfully and effectively creates atmosphere," Harvey adds. "It heightens the dramatic moments and is also unobtrusively supportive when the focus is on the vocal lines."

In his most important concert works since 1960, as in his operas, Ward skillfully uses modern melodic, harmonic, rhythmic, and linear techniques to extend his expressivity and to provide dramatic interest and contrasts. But communicability is never sacrificed. *Festive Ode*, for orchestra (1966), which was commissioned by the Women's Symphony League in Milwaukee for the Milwaukee Symphony, was received so enthusiastically when it was premiered under Harry John Brown's direction on October 3, 1966, that it had to be repeated. Walter Monfried in the *Milwaukee Journal* said of it that it had "that flavor and aroma, that jauntiness of rhythm, that mark the best of Foster and Ives and Copland and Gershwin." The Piano Concerto (1968), commissioned by the Powder River Foundation, Inc., had its initial performance at the Inter-American Festival in Washington, D.C., on June 19, 1968, with Howard Mitchell conducting the National Symphony and Marjorie Mitchell soloist. To commemorate the American bicentennial, and coincidentally the twenty-fifth anniversary of the Oratorio Singers of Charlotte, N.C., Ward wrote his Fifth Symphony, *Canticles of America*, for narrator, soprano, baritone, chorus, and orchestra (1976), on grants from the Mary Reynold Babcock Foundation, the Mark Duke Biddle Foundation, and Mr. and Mrs. E. Yandle. The composer, in collaboration with his wife, prepared a text drawn from poems by Walt Whitman and Henry Wadsworth Longfellow as well as segments from American history and biography. Text and music—music consisting of quotations and recollections—expressed the development of the spirit of America through the years. "In the melodies of the symphony," the composer explains, "the listener will, I suspect, be aware of the influence of the music I came to know in my youth as a boy soprano in every kind of church and school performance and later as a band leader during

World War II." In the *Charlotte Observer*, Richard Maschal said: "The work is as American as apple pie, full of the spirit of our sweet country—its vastness, humor, strength, good nature, and, yes, its naïveté and its long painful struggle to fulfill its ideals."

When Ward resigned from his executive posts with the Galaxy Music and Highgate Press in 1967, he was made chancellor of the North Carolina School of the Arts in Winston-Salem. He withdrew as chancellor in 1975, but from 1975 to 1977 he remained with the school to teach composition. In 1978 he was visiting professor of composition at Duke University in Durham, N.C., and one year later he joined its faculty as professor of composition and was named the Mary Duke Biddle Professor of Music. Ward has been the guest composer, conductor, and lecturer on many college and university campuses over the years. In April 1980 he was guest composer at the American Festival at DePauw University in Greencastle, Ind., where his works for orchestra, chorus and band were performed over the course of several days.

In 1963 he was honored with a weekend of concerts of his music, lectures, and festivities in Sioux City, Ia. He received a third Guggenheim Fellowship in 1966, an honorary doctorate of fine arts from Duke University in 1972, and an honorary doctorate of music from Peabody Conservatory in Baltimore in 1975. That year he also was recipient of the Fine Arts Award from the state of North Carolina.

Ward was president of the American Composers' Alliance in 1955–56, following which he served on its board of directors. He has also been a board member of the Composers Recording Inc. (CRI), the Alice M. Ditson Advisory Committee of Columbia University, the Martha Baird Rockefeller Fund for Music, the American Symphony League, and the National Opera Institute. In addition, he has been panelist for the National Endowment for the Arts and the National Endowment for the Humanities, and a trustee of the Moravian Music Foundation. Ward has made numerous appearances as guest conductor in the United States and abroad performing his own works.

THE COMPOSER SPEAKS: At a time when listeners have been besieged, bothered, and bewildered by verbal explanations, apologia, and sales pitches for every kind of music, there is a strong temptation to remain silent altogether and trust that the simple hearing of one's music will amply justify and explain its existence. For those with an interest in aesthetics, however, the general point of view behind all of my work may be illuminating. In the first place I see my creative work not only as an urgent and rewarding part of my life but also as a desirable and social function. It involves the freedom to produce whatever my fantasy dictates. I recognize, however, that the listener has a parallel and equal freedom to accept or reject

my work. I ask only that he give that work an open-minded hearing. . . .

All depends on the sensibility, the individuality, and the genius of the composer. Those are rare qualities, the presence of which is most clearly evident in music which speaks as simply as possible, and the absence of which no amount of edifice and complexity will hide.

PRINCIPAL WORKS: 5 symphonies (1941–76).
Jubilation: An Overture, for orchestra (1946); *Night Music*, for chamber orchestra (1949); *Jonathan and the Gingery Snare*, for narrator and orchestra (1949); Violin Sonata (1950); *Sacred Songs for Pantheists*, for soprano and orchestra (1951); *Euphony*, for orchestra (1954); *He Who Gets Slapped*, opera, originally entitled *Pantaloon* (1956); Fantasia for Brass and Timpani (1956); *Earth Shall Be Fair*, for soprano, children's chorus (or soprano solo), adult chorus, orchestra, and organ (1960); *Divertimento*, for orchestra (1960); *The Crucible*, opera (1961); *Hymn and Celebration*, for orchestra (1962); *The Lady from Colorado*, opera (1964); String Quartet (1965); *Sweet Freedom's Song*, cantata for narrator, soprano, baritone, chorus, and orchestra (1965); *Festive Ode*, for orchestra (1966); *Antiphony*, for wind instruments (1967); Piano Concerto (1968); *Canticles of America*, for narrator, soprano, baritone, chorus, and orchestra (1976); *Abstractions*, for band (1977); *Claudia Legare*, opera (1977); *Three Celebrations of God in Nature*, for organ (1980); *Abelard and Heloise*, opera (1980); *Sonic Structures*, for orchestra (1980); *Minutes Till Midnight*, opera (1981–82).

BIBLIOGRAPHY: *DCM*; Ewen, David, *Composers Since 1900* (N.Y., 1969); Thomson, Virgil, *American Composers Since 1910* (N.Y., 1970); *American Composers Alliance Bulletin*, May 1962; BMI, *The Many Worlds of Music*, Winter 1976; *Composers of America*, vol. 9, 1963; *New York Times*, September 30, 1973; *Who's Who in America, 1980–81*.

Ward-Steinman, David, b. Alexandria, La., November 6, 1935.

Ward-Steinman's restless and innovative creative imagination has conducted him into such avant-garde pastures as electronic and aleatory music; multimedia productions involving film, videotape, and slide projectors in various combinations; arcane and Far Eastern sound textures; and music for "fortified" piano, which he developed from Cage's "prepared piano." Some of Ward-Steinman's earlier works were in the "third-stream" movement involving jazz with techniques and structures of advanced concert music; when his writing was not overtly jazz-based, it often reflected his background in jazz through kinetic rhythms, syncopations, polyrhythms, improvisation options, and so forth.

His father, Irving Ward-Steinman, is an attorney who has also been engaged as painter, radio commentator and book reviewer; his mother, Daisy Ward-Steinman, was a songwriter and a teacher of piano and organ (in her own studio and in public schools), who later became a music supervisor, since retired. "There was always something musical going on at home," recalls David Ward-Steinman, "and all kinds of sheet music around. I was encouraged to sight-read, browse, and explore, which I did with great curiosity and enthusiasm." Between 1941 and 1950, he studied with his mother not only piano but also theory and notation. While in the second grade in elementary school he supplemented this study with lessons on the clarinet. "Practicing," he says, "was never a chore because it was always geared to something I wanted to learn."

While attending Bolton High School in Alexandria, he added the saxophone to the instruments he was learning to play. When he was sixteen, he appeared as piano soloist with the New Orleans Symphony in a performance of his own works. He played the clarinet in the high school band and the piano for the school chorus (for which he also made arrangements), besides organizing a dance band for extracurricular activities, which he led from the piano. Between 1951 and 1952, his piano study continued with John T. Venettozzi, who took over where his mother had left off, broadening his repertoire and technique considerably. A summer at the National Music Camp at Interlochen in 1952 provided him with his first opportunity to study with a composer, Homer Keller. "From then on there was no question that composition was what I wished to devote my life to."

Venettozzi was instrumental in getting a scholarship for Ward-Steinman for the Florida State University in Tallahassee in 1953. There, during the next four years, he studied composition with John Boda and piano with Edward Kilenyi, and in 1957 received his bachelor of music degree, *cum laude*. During those college years he went to the Indian Hill Music Workshop in Stockbridge, Mass. (summer 1954), on a Charles Ives Scholarship, where he studied composition with Wallingford Riegger, and in the summer of 1956 he studied composition further with Darius Milhaud at the Aspen Music School in Colorado. In 1956–57 he wrote his first works, other than student compositions: a Piano Sonata and Three Songs, for clarinet and piano. In reviewing a recording of both compositions for *Arizona Quarterly*, Barney Childs said: "Both . . . are fine examples of what can be done by a fresh look at the 'mainstream' tonal vocabulary. The music often is affirmative, forthright, optimistic; the bright portions are full of air and light and the darker outlines are clean shadow, not the pathological darkness of self-dramatization and personal distortion."

On December 28, 1956, in Jacksonville, Fla., Ward-Steinman married Susan Diana Lucas, a flutist and music teacher; they raised two children. In 1957–58 he attended the University of Illinois in Urbana. As a student of composition of Robert Kelly's he gained his master of music degree in 1958. The summer of 1957 was spent at the Berkshire Music Center at Tanglewood, Mass., as a composition student of Milton Babbitt's. Ward-Steinman returned to the University of Illinois in 1959 in continuation of his study of composition, this time with Burrill Phillips and Gordon Binkerd. Two years later, he was awarded the doctor of music arts degree there. On a McKinley Memorial Musical Fellowship from the University of Illinois in 1958–59 he studied composition privately with Nadia Boulanger in Paris, an important turning point in his musical development. "I was not at all anxious to join the burgeoning ranks of the 'Boulangerie,'" he recalls. "But I met Boulanger during her visit to Southern Illinois University at Carbondale when two works of mine were performed, and, in a session with her later, she so impressed me with her perception and insight, catching things that my previous teachers had missed, and that I had begun to believe were not really weaknesses, that I was bowled over. She was like an external musical conscience, going immediately to the secret places that one worries about but that no one else seems to notice. And I'm so glad she did. She made an enormous difference in the way I approached music and in my compositional work habits. Her standards were higher than mine had ever been before and, indeed, higher than my previous teachers' expectations. It was exhilarating to find myself working at such a level with someone who seemed to understand everything immediately and to care passionately about the 'rightness' of every single note, every single detail in a piece."

That year with Boulanger was culminated with the writing, in Paris, of Symphony no. 1 (1959). It was first heard at a concert of the San Diego Symphony in California on December 4, 1962. That symphony later won two national prizes, one from Broadcast Music, Inc. (BMI), and the other (the Bearns Prize) from Columbia University. In 1960–61, back at the University of Illinois, Ward-Steinman became involved in the study of electronic music with Lejaren A. Hiller.

The year of 1961 began with an engagement on the music faculty of the San Diego State College in California, (now San Diego University) that lasted more than two decades. He was assistant professor the first four years, associate professor between 1965 and 1968, and full professor since 1968. In 1968 Ward-Steinman was named one of two outstanding professors of the year by the board of trustees of California State College, selected from nine thousand faculty members of nineteen state colleges.

From the early 1960s on, Ward-Steinman based most of his music on (or had it derive from) cluster harmony in one way or another, with melodic ideas being spun out of the clusters through octave displacement and other permutations. In such an idiom we find his first successful work, the Prelude and Toccata, for orchestra (1962; Albuquerque, N.M., March 21, 1963). "The treatment of the various orchestral choirs," the composer has explained, "is mostly independent and antiphonal with great concern for color and sonorities." All the material of its two movements was an outgrowth of a subject first presented as a trombone solo at the opening of the Prelude. This theme passes through various sections of the orchestra, frequently built up into impressive climaxes.

After that came the Concerto no. 2, for chamber orchestra (1962), commissioned by Daniel Lewis and the Sherwood Hall Orchestra of La Jolla and introduced in San Diego on March 3, 1963. "The concerto," Lawrence McGillvery said in the *California Light* of La Jolla, "has throughout its length brilliant orchestral color and vivid and exciting surface." *Fragments from Sappho*, for soprano, flute, clarinet, and piano (1962–65; La Jolla, April 29, 1965), in which the Sappho text was translated by Mary Barnard, was, in the opinion of Alfred Frankenstein in *High Fidelity*, "the best setting of old Greek texts since Debussy's *Chansons de Bilitis*. . . . The setting . . . ricochets off the text in brilliant fashion."

All the music he had written up to this time, the composer says, was in one way or another preparation for the writing of a seventy-minute oratorio, *Song of Moses*, for narrator, soprano, two tenors, baritone, chorus, and orchestra (1963–64). Commissioned by San Diego State College for its eight-hundred-voice chorus, it received its world premiere in San Diego on May 31, 1964, with Gregory Peck as narrator. "The Moses of my imagination is the Moses of Michelangelo," the composer says. "I have tried to convey musically the power, majesty, and charisma of the man as he is to me: the most fascinating and intriguing figure in the Old Testament." Both the tragedy of Moses' forbidden entry into the Promised Land and his heroism in accepting his fate are emphasized. Structurally, the work is divided into a prologue, five parts and an epilogue, twenty-four numbers in all, each part covering some portion of the Moses epic. The work begins with a quiet prologue in which the dying Moses sees the Promised Land from Mount Nebo. Moses' story is then told in flashback, arriving at a climax of concentration and intensity in the central "Battle" and "Heresy" sections, and ending as quietly as it had begun, with the death of Moses, the chorus of the prologue returning. Narrator and chorus throughout the work are catalytic agents for what transpires, serving the same function as the chorus in Greek drama. A large orchestra, with a percussion section of twenty-five different instruments including an autoharp, is used, the instrumentation varying with each number. In the "Dance of the Golden Calf," a pagan atmosphere is evoked through third-stream jazz highlighting a solo for alto saxophone. Alan M. Kriegsman in the *San Diego Union* praised the score for its "ingenious strokes, such as the vivid depiction of the plagues, the use of jazz for the raucous irreverence of the Golden Calf scene, the women's voices converging in unison to symbolize the submerging of Pharaoh's host by the Red Sea and innumerable points in the scoring."

Western Orpheus (1964), a radical transformation of the classic Orpheus legend, is a ballet with choreography by Richard Carter, successfully produced by the San Diego Ballet (which commissioned it) for its opening presentation at the new San Diego Civic Theater on February 26, 1965. Here, as in *Song of Moses*, the score is eclectic, at turns lyrically tender and dramatically strident, employing neoromantic idioms on the one hand, third-stream jazz on the other. Unusual effects are realized in the orchestration by such esoteric instruments as the Japanese koto (to simulate the stage sounds of the guitar) or by striking the strings of the piano with mallets. In the *San Diego Union*, Kriegsman described this music as "dazzling in its immediate impact. . . . Ward-Steinman's score, with its quilted moods and persistent unifying threads, appears to generate every gesture and motif of Carter's evocative dance designs."

The Cello Concerto (1966), commissioned by cellist Edgar Lustgarten, is partially in a serial technique with a feeling of tonality not altogether absent. Cluster harmonies as a generative-structural device are explored, with melodic lines and counterpoint from source-clusters derived through freely serial permutations. The composer's aim in this work was to capture in music the visual images inspired by Mark Rothko's paintings. "I envisioned the cello moving in that sound-space, dynamic against static sheets of sound—the color blocks—that shimmer iridescently," the composer says. Its world premiere was given in Tokyo on June 13, 1967, with Milton Katims conducting and Lustgarten as soloist. This was followed by the American premiere in Seattle the following December, performed by the Seattle Symphony conducted by Katims and once again with Lustgarten as soloist.

The use of the koto in the orchestration of *Western Orpheus* is one of several instances in which the Orient has influenced Ward-Steinman's music. Another work in which his interest in the Orient is reflected is *The Tale of Issoumbochi* (1968; San Diego, April 18, 1968), a setting of a Japanese fairy tale for narrator, soprano, and chamber ensemble, libretto prepared by the composer's wife, Susan Lucas. Though no specific Japanese instruments or musical motives are used, the Orient is evoked through some use of pentatonic scales, parallel fourths and fifths, delicate timbres, and exotic instrumental effects, with celesta clusters often providing an interplay. (A decade later, during the summer of 1977, Ward-Steinman spent several weeks in Hong Kong acquiring some Chinese instruments and taking some basic instruction in them.)

Ward-Steinman took a two-year leave of absence from San Diego State University between 1970 and 1972 to serve as composer-in-residence for the Tampa Bay area in Florida on a grant from the Ford Foundation and the Music Educators National Conference Contemporary Music Project. These years saw an opening up for him of a new world of creativity through the tapping of the sources of electronic music for magnetic tape or synthesizer with two sister works: *Antares* (1971) and *Arcturus* (1972). Both works were scored for a Putney Electronic Music Synthesizer and a large orchestra with an expanded percussion section that included such esoteric items as water gong, wind chimes, sandpaper blocks and five kinds of cymbal (in *Antares*), and water gong, bowed tam-tam, brake drum, roto-toms and a grand piano with claves placed on the strings and played upon with mallets (in *Arcturus*). *Antares* additionally requires the services of a gospel choir. The names of both works, we learn from the program notes of the Chicago Symphony, "were suggested by the composer's interest in cluster-sonorities, independent of over-lapping time streams, exploding galaxies of sound and 'free-fall' elements suspended in time." The Putney synthesizer is a small unit consisting of a separate keyboard, a control board with dials, switches, and a grid by which different channels can be combined and amplified through speakers. In both works aleatory processes were used. *Antares* was introduced in Tampa on April 22, 1971, with Irwin Hoffman conducting the Florida Gold Coast Symphony. *Arcturus* was commissioned by Irwin Hoffman for his engagement as guest conductor of the Chicago Symphony, which premiered it in Chicago on June 15, 1972.

The fortified piano was another area in which Ward-Steinman experimented with new sound textures. As in John Cage's prepared piano, a fortified piano requires various items to be inserted between the strings of a piano (washers, screws, rubber wedges, and so forth). In addition, solid wood cylinders are laid on the strings and the strings are struck with mallets, brushed lightly with a wire brush or plucked with the fingers. *Sonata for Fortified Piano*, Ward-Steinman's first major solo work of the kind, was written in 1972 and introduced in Tampa, Fla., on June 23, 1972. He has also used the fortified piano in conjunction with other instruments, as in *The Tracker*, for clarinet, fortified piano, and tape (1976; Fullerton, Calif., November 12, 1976), winner of a recording award from the American Society of University Composers.

Kaleidoscope (1971) and *Nova* (*Collage '72*), the latter for sound/color film and synthesizer (1972; Tampa, March 25, 1972), are among Ward-Steinman's early multimedia productions. *Kaleidoscope* called for videotape for TV, sound-color films, musicians and synthesizer, magnetic tape, and integral video-camera work. It was televised through the facilities of WTVT in Tampa on December 5, 1971, and then given a live performance, also in Tampa, on March 25, 1972. *Tamar* (1970–77) is a three-act multimedia drama based on Robinson Jeffers's prose poem of that name set in the Carmel–Monterey–Big Sur region of California around the time of World War I. The libretto is by William J. Adams. Speaking of *Tamar*, the composer says: "It is the most ambitious work I've ever undertaken. . . . Like *Song of Moses*, a decade earlier, it is a kind of stylistic summing-up of things I've been exploring and working with since then, except that there are no exotic references to non-Western music. Some of it reaches back to the idiom of *Moses*, and some of it looks forward, in its use of electronic music, special instrumental effects, multimedia aspects."

On a number of occasions, in the 1970s, Ward-Steinman was invited to serve as composer-in-residence at various schools and universities in the United States. In 1970, he was a postdoctoral visiting fellow of music at Princeton University. With the collaboration of his wife, Ward-Steinman is the author of the two-volume *Comparative Anthology of Musical Forms* (1976).

In 1965, Ward-Steinman received the Ernst von Dohnányi Citation "for excellence in performance or composition" from Florida State University in Tallahassee.

THE COMPOSER SPEAKS: I write for myself and that mythical other—anyone who is capable of understanding and enjoying the music. This isn't really an ivory-tower attitude, but I have never "written down" to an audience—I respect their potential too much. But there are too many different audiences, and audiences are notoriously capricious, so I never write for a specific audience.

So I write initially to please myself, even when I am working on a commission, and hope others will be interested. I do enjoy writing for specific performers and ensembles, and trying to find fresh things for them to say. I often try to involve the performers more directly and personally through, for example, improvisation options or alternate routes through a score, and sometimes through a maximally individualized polyphony where each performer may have his own tempo, meter, rhythms, and pitch material for part of the time. I never relinquish control over the macrostructure of a piece, however, when these options are part of a piece.

But, I think music ought to communicate something to an attentive audience even on first hearing—and without resort to the paraphernalia of program notes, elaborate analyses, or biographical anecdotes. I believe that each work should employ its own standards by which is it meant to be perceived and judged. A piece is finished only when my imagination cannot improve it.

PRINCIPAL WORKS: 2 concertos, for chamber orchestra (1961, 1963).

Piano Sonata (1956–57); Quintet, for brass (1958–59); Symphony (1959); Concerto Grosso, for combo and chamber orchestra (1960); *Psalms of Rejoicing*, for a cappella chorus (1960); Prelude and Toccata, for orchestra (1962); *Fragments from Sappho*, for soprano, flute, clarinet, and piano (1962–65); *Song of Moses*, oratorio for narrator, soprano, two tenors, baritone, chorus, and orchestra (1963–64); *Western Orpheus*, ballet (1964); Cello Concerto (1964–66); *These Three*, ballet (1966); *Jazz Tangents*, for wind ensemble or band (1966–67); *The Tale of Issoumbochi*, for narrator, soprano, instruments, and percussion (1968); *Montage*, for woodwind quintet (1968); *Tamar*, multimedia music drama (1970–77); *Rituals*, for dancers and musicians (1971); *Antares*, for gospel choir, tape or synthesizer, and orchestra (1971); *Kaleidoscope*, multimedia videotape production (1971); *Raga for Winds* (1971–72); *Arcturus*, for tape or synthesizer and orchestra (1972); *Nova (Collage '72)*, for sound/color film and tape or synthesizer (1972); *Sonata for Fortified Piano* (1972); *Scorpio*, for wind ensemble (1975–76); *The Tracker*, for clarinet, fortified piano and tape (1976); *Brancusi's Brass Beds*, for brass quintet (1977); *Toccata for Synthesizer and Slide Projector* (1978); *Bishop's Gambit*, for wind ensemble (1979); *And in These Times*, Christmas cantata for narrator, vocal soloists, chorus, and chamber ensemble (1979–80); *Intersections*, for fortified piano and tape (1981).

BIBLIOGRAPHY: *DCM*; BMI, *The Many Worlds of Music*, June 1970; *Pan Pipes of Sigma Alpha Iota*, May 1966; *San Diego Magazine*, December 1962, May 1964, April 1965.

Weber, Ben Brian, b. St. Louis, Mo., July 23, 1916; d. New York City, May 9, 1979.

Weber belongs with America's early composers of twelve-tone music. Within structures of tonal music he employed a basically contrapuntal twelve-tone technique but with tonal implications. "Two polarities exist in this music," writes Carl Sigmon in the *Dictionary of Contemporary Music*. "The first, in the 1940s and early 50s, is characterized by the declarative statements, jaunty rhythms and an air of exuberance and wit. The second, appearing increasingly in more recent works, is characterized by a greater emotional reserve. These latter works tend to be longer and to incorporate increased contrapuntal manipulation, denser harmonic textures and larger instrumental forces.

He was born while his mother was visiting St. Louis; until seven, he was raised in Louisville, Ky.

Then his family moved to Chicago, where he attended its public schools. He received little musical instruction in his earlier years as, for many years, it was assumed that he was heading for a career in medicine. For one year (1934–35) he attended the University of Illinois in Urbana for premedical studies. Then, deciding he preferred music to medicine, he enrolled in 1937 in the De Paul University in Chicago for training in piano, voice, and theory. At the time he aspired to a career in musical education. But this was renounced in favor of composition after Weber received encouragement and guidance from Arnold Schoenberg, whom he visited in Los Angeles in 1940, and from the pianist Artur Schnabel. From this point on, Weber was self-taught as a composer. His earliest compositions included some works for the piano; Five Pieces, for cello and piano (1941); his String Quartet no. 1 (1942); his String Trio no. 1 (1943); and two violin sonatas and a Cello Sonata.

In 1945, he came to New York, which remained his home. He earned his living by music copying and by giving private lessons in composition and orchestration. During these first years in New York, he wrote sparingly, his main efforts being the String Trio no. 2 (1946); *Aubade*, for flute, harp, and cello (1950); and music for a ballet, *The Pool of Darkness*, scored for six instruments. In spite of such slim pickings, his talent attracted the interest of colleagues and critics as well as, in 1950, the first of two Guggenheim Fellowships and an award from the National Institute of Arts and Letters.

Weber's career as composer went into high gear in the early 1950s. Symphony in Four Movements, for baritone and chamber ensemble (1951) on poems by William Blake, was introduced in New York on October 28, 1952, and subsequently was recorded for CRI with Leopold Stokowski conducting. When String Quartet no. 2 (1951) was premiered in New York on September 23, 1951, Theodore Strongin, in the *Herald Tribune*, described it as "full of graceful corners and flickering angles through which its warm, strong nature appears. Its quick-silvery tricks are never isolated; they are always disclosing something about an entity, not a moment." Both of these works were in a twelve-tone idiom which he temporarily abandoned in Two Pieces for String Orchestra (1952), whose world premiere took place in New York in a performance by the Clarion Concerts Orchestra, Newell Jenkins conducting, on February 9, 1960. These "two pieces" are basically a single work since the second one is the first in reverse. A reviewer for *Musical America* called it the best composition on the program and "one of Mr. Weber's most expressive creations." This is one of several contemporary American works which the Clarion Concerts Orchestra, sponsored by the U.S. State Department, performed in the Soviet Union, as well as in Bulgaria and Rumania, between September and November 1965.

In 1953, Weber received his second Guggenheim Fellowship together with the first Thorne Music Foundation grant ever given. He became one of two Americans selected to write music for the Convegno Musicale in Rome in 1954, responding with the Concerto for Violin and Orchestra (1954). That year, on a commission from the Louisville Orchestra in Kentucky, and on a grant from the Rockefeller Foundation, he completed Prelude and Passacaglia, for orchestra, performed first by the Louisville Orchestra on January 1, 1955, then by the New York Philharmonic under Dimitri Mitropoulos. "This is solid music," said Paul Henry Lang in the *New York Herald Tribune*, "dignified, and altogether free of tentative frivolities one so often encounters in would-be contemporary music." *Rapsodie concertante*, a twelve-tone work for viola and orchestra (1957), was written on a commission from Walter Trampler, violist, and MGM Records. This work was heard in New York in 1961 on a program that also included Weber's *Chamber Fantasy*, for violin solo and six instruments (1959). In the *Rapsodie concertante*, the melodic materials were developed in the manner of a fantasia, the materials often appearing in other instruments in contrast to the solo viola, the part for solo viola cast in an extended lyric line with contrasts of register and over a colorful musical background. Lester Trimble, in reviewing this work for *The Nation*, called Weber "one of the most meticulous craftsmen in the country, a 12-tonist of Romantic bent who, despite the complexity of his technical equipment, seeks always to express and to communicate. Though his music is evanescent and mysterious in color, due to his manner of orchestrating the intricate mesh of lines, which makes it up at any given moment, it is always warm. . . . While his techniques are almost entirely contrapuntal, the result is a *corpus* of considerable amplitude, and a strongly defined melodic flow."

Characteristic of Weber's full creative maturity is his Piano Concerto (1961), which the Ford Foundation Program for the Humanities had commissioned for the pianist William Masselos, who gave the first performance on March 25, 1961, in New York with the New York Philharmonic, Leonard Bernstein conducting. Though this composition was organized from a twelve-tone unit, the initial theme sidesteps the twelve-tone row by having the single note "C" repeated four times; at the same time a feeling of tonality prevails throughout the entire work. "Mr. Weber," said Harold C. Schonberg in his review in the *New York Times*, "has evolved an entirely personal style. At first hearing, the concerto impressed as strong, confident and beautifully worked out." Schonberg also said: "Ben Weber is an American composer who belongs to no school as such. He writes modern music that sounds conservative . . . and he writes twelve-tone music that sounds tonal. But whatever he writes has workman-

ship and strength, and a good measure of individuality, too. All these characteristics were encountered in . . . his Piano Concerto."

The Ways, a song cycle for soprano, tenor, and piano (1964), is a work combining serialism with the romantic traditions of Schubert and Schumann; its first hearing took place at a concert of "Music in Our Time" in New York on April 12, 1964. *Dolmen*, for winds and strings (1964)—first performed on December 16, 1964—is an elegy centered on a twelve-tone row. ("Dolmen" is a Breton word for a megalithic monument.) Three major orchestral works were completed between 1967 and 1973: *The Enchanted Midnight* (1967); *Concert Poem*, for violin and orchestra (1970); and *Sinfonia Clarion*, for orchestra (1973; N.Y., February 26, 1974).

From 1965 on, Weber was a member of the faculty in the department of composition at the New York College of Music. He received a grant from the Koussevitzky Music Foundation in 1967. In 1968 he became the first recipient of a grant from the newly organized Phoebe Ketchum Thorne Fellowship, a three-year subsidy totaling $10,000. For many years, Weber was an active member on the boards of the International Society of Contemporary Music and the American Composers' Alliance, serving as president for the latter organization in 1959. He also served as a judge for BMI (Broadcast Music Inc.) Student Composers Awards. He was a life member of the National Institute of Arts and Letters.

THE COMPOSER SPEAKS: My use of "techniques with twelve-tones"—i.e., serial music—has been consistent over a period of . . . years, and most of what I and some others consider to be my most important works is accomplished within these means. It is very broad, not unlike the language itself. I am not an experimenter primarily, though one does this as a matter of living concern, but I feel much more that I am an exponent of musical art with deep reference to the past, and with great respect for the best accomplishments of all those times. Not losing patience with the present, I hope to have some part in preparing the future for those who must follow me. We are so ambivalent in these times that I feel one must cultivate responsibility more than outside forces can encourage.

PRINCIPAL WORKS: 2 string quartets (1941, 1951); 2 string trios (1943, 1946).

Fantasia, for piano (1950); *The Pool of Darkness*, ballet (1950); *Episodes*, for piano (1950); *Aubade*, for flute, harp, and cello (1950); Symphony in Four Movements, for baritone and chamber orchestra (1951); Two Pieces, for string orchestra (1952); *Colloquy*, for brass septet (1953); Serenade, for harpsichord, flute, oboe, and cello (1953); Four Songs, for soprano or tenor with solo cello (1953); Violin Concerto (1954); Prelude and Passacaglia, for orchestra

(1954); Concertino, for flute, oboe, clarinet, and string quartet (1955); Serenade, for strings (1955); *Rapsodie concertante*, for viola and orchestra (1957); *Chamber Fantasy*, for violin solo and six instruments (1959); Piano Concerto (1961); Nocturne, for flute, celesta, and cello (1962); *The Ways*, song cycle for soprano, tenor, and piano (1964); *Dolmen*, an elegy for winds and strings (1964); *The Enchanted Midnight*, for orchestra (1967); *Concert Poem*, for violin and orchestra (1970); *Sinfonia Clarion*, for orchestra (1973); *Consort*, for wind quintet (1974); Three Capriccios, for cello and piano (1977).

BIBLIOGRAPHY: *DCM; Composers of America*, vol. 9, 1963; *New York Times*, March 19, 1961, May 9, 1979 (obituary); *Who's Who in America, 1980–81*.

Weill, Kurt, b. Dessau, Germany, March 2, 1900; d. New York City, April 3, 1950. American citizen, 1943.

When he was in his twenties, Weill first attracted attention as an expressionist composer favoring a discordant, partly atonal style slanted for sophisticated audiences. Then he deserted the ivory tower to come down to the people and become one of the most significant exponents of *Zeitkunst,* or "contemporary art," then becoming a popular-styled aesthetic cult in Germany. As an exponent of *Zeitkunst,* Weill broke away from the musicodramatic aesthetics of Wagner and Richard Strauss to devise, with his literary collaborator Bertolt Brecht, a new stage art form, baptized *Songspiel,* derived from the old Austrian and German *Singspiel*. At the same time, Weill allied himself with still another movement in Germany in the 1920s which went one step further in bringing music to the masses: *Gebrauchsmusik,* or "functional music," music created expressly for radio, motion pictures, and schools. In the United States, Weill distinguished himself in the Broadway musical theater, becoming one of its most successful and significant practitioners. He who had once carried opera into the popular musical theater now succeeded in lifting the popular musical theater into the opera house.

The Weill family was one of the oldest in Europe, reaching back to the 14th century. Many of its members were distinguished rabbis, beginning with Jacob Weill, who was ordained in Nuremberg in 1427. Kurt Weill was the third of four children of Albert Weill, a rabbi, cantor, and composer of synagogal music, and Emma Ackerman Weill, an amateur pianist whose father, Aaron Ackerman, was also a rabbi and composer of liturgical music. The parents expected their sons to enter the rabbinate. In his early years, Kurt received from his father a thorough religious education, but he also was given some instruction on the piano by his mother. It was not long before music completely superseded religion in his interests. Stimulated by the operatic performances he attended at the Ducal Court Theater in Dessau, Weill tried writing an opera based "on an old German play about knights and ladies" when he was about ten. By the time he was fourteen, he was composing songs which have survived, one of which was called "A Folk Tune," using a poem by Arno Holz. Locally, young Weill became known as a *Wunderkind*. He attracted the interest and support of Duke Frederick, who had him teach his youngest daughter the piano, hired him as rehearsal pianist for the singers at the Ducal Theater and invited him to perform at a benefit concert at the palace.

Weill did not receive any instruction in composition until he was fifteen, when he became a pupil of Albert Bing's, associate musical director of the court theater. Bing was responsible for changing Weill's direction in music from that of a piano virtuoso to that of a composer. On Bing's encouragement, Weill left Dessau for Berlin in 1918 to enter the Academy of Music and continue his study of composition with Engelbert Humperdinck while also studying conducting with Rudolf Krasselt. There, Weill was president of the student council and composed an orchestral tone poem, *The Lay of the Love and Death of Cornet Christopher Rilke,* the music carrying reminders of Mahler and early Schoenberg. It was performed at the school and earned him a Felix Mendelssohn Foundation Scholarship for further study. After a single semester, the scholarship notwithstanding, Weill decided to leave the academy to launch his professional career. For a short period in 1919 he was a coach at the Dessau Opera, and in 1920 he was appointed staff conductor at the Ludenscheid Civic Opera in Westphalia, where he led both serious and light operas. "This is where I learned everything I knew about the stage," he recalled years later. After one season in Ludenscheid, Weill spent the summer conducting a men's chorus in Leipzig.

Between 1919 and 1920, Weill completed a number of compositions including String Quartet in B minor, a Cello Sonata, and a one-act opera, all of which, for all their occasional lapses into dissonance, were in the romantic tradition of Schubert and Brahms.

Weill returned to Berlin in December 1920. During the next three years he was a student in Ferruccio Busoni's master class in composition. Under Busoni's guidance, Weill began developing his compositional style, which, while still derivative, began to show a personal approach in the freedom of the tonality and in the resources of dissonant harmonic and contrapuntal idioms then favored by the young progressive composers in Germany. Among these works were Symphony no. 1 (1921); Divertimento, for small orchestra and male chorus (1922); and *Sinfonia Sacra (Fantasia, Passcaglia and Hymnus)* for orchestra (1922). The symphony was never performed in Weill's lifetime. The score, lost for many years, was recovered in 1957 and was finally performed for the first time over the Hamburg radio, conducted by Wilhelm Schuyhter. A decade later it was edited by David Drew, a version performed on October 25, 1978, when it received its American premiere and was recorded. This is a one-movement composition strongly influenced by Beethoven, Liszt, Mahler, Richard Strauss, and early Schoenberg. In the *New Yorker,* Andrew Porter called it "a turbulent, wonderfully inventive piece. . . . There seems to be an eventful program, part political, part religious—visions of violence, victory and peace—just below the surface." In the *New York Post,* Richard M. Sudhalter found that "now and then during the symphony, bits of purely melodic felicity peered forward to the collaboration with Brecht and to the American musicals of later years."

An assignment in 1922 to write music for a children's ballet, *Die Zaubernacht,* for a visiting Russian dance company, was Weill's first break with expressionist writing. Slanting his music for a young audience, Weill assumed a simple, direct, and melodious style. First performed on November 18, 1922, in Berlin, the composer conducting, it was received so enthusiastically that Weill came to realize how to reach out to large and receptive audiences within the theater with simplified techniques. Weill thought well enough of this music to use some of it for an orchestral piece, Quodlibet, for orchestra (1923), whose premiere was conducted by his teacher, Albert Bing, in Coburg, Germany, on February 6, 1926.

But it was to be a few years before Weill stood ready to abandon expressionist music for a more popular approach. Stimulated by Hindemith's early quartets, Weill wrote the dissonant String Quartet op. 8 (1923), using material from his Symphony no. 1. *Frauentanz* (1923), a cycle of seven songs based on medieval German poems for soprano and instrumental accompaniment, was almost completely atonal. It acquired a major showcase when it was performed at the festival of the International Society for Contemporary Music in Salzburg, Austria, on August 6, 1924. On the strength of this work Weill received a ten-year contract with the powerful Viennese publishing house of Universal Editions.

In December 1923, Weill graduated from Busoni's master class. A few months later he wrote for Joseph Szigeti Concerto for Violin and Wind Orchestra (1924), in which traces of Stravinsky can be discerned together with those of Hindemith and Schoenberg (as well as fleeting suggestions of jazz). Szigeti never performed it. At its premiere on June 11, 1925, in Paris, the violinist was Marcel Darrieux and Walter Straram conducted. The approbation of critics and audience led to other performances of this concerto, which became one of Weill's most successful concert works up to this time. On June 23, 1926, it represented Germany at the festival of the International Society for Contemporary Music in Zurich. Its

first American performance took place in March 1955, performed by Anahid Ajemian as soloist with the Indianapolis Symphony, Izler Solomon conducting.

The year of 1924 was significant for Weill on two counts other than the writing of the Violin Concerto. He became acquainted and planned a collaboration with the German expressionist dramatist Georg Kaiser. And, through Kaiser, he met Karoline Blamauer, a Viennese singer, dancer, and diseuse who had played a part in Weill's *Zaubernacht* and who had officially adopted her stage name of Lotte Lenya. While working with Kaiser, Weill had opportunities to get to know her better. They were married on January 28, 1926.

The collaboration of Weill and Kaiser carried Weill for the first time as a composer into the opera house. This opera was the one-act *Der Protagonist* (1926), in which Kaiser's surrealistic text had for its central character an actor in a touring troupe in Elizabethan England who confuses the stage with real life and ends up committing murder at one of his performances. Once again, as in the children's ballet, Weill communicated with the audience with music whose main appeal rested on melodious vocal numbers and concerted pieces. Weill employed two orchestras for this opera, a larger one for the pit and a smaller one in the gallery on the stage to accompany one of the ballets. Introduced at the Dresden Opera on March 26, 1926, Fritz Busch conducting, this little opera was acclaimed, receiving thirty-five curtain calls, and then ten more for Weill himself. Oskar Bie, an eminent German music critic, called it the perfect fusion of text and music. Other performances throughout Germany followed inevitably.

This success brought Weill a commission from the Kroll Opera in Germany for a new stage work. This time he used a text by Ivan Goll, *The Royal Palace* (title originally in English), which was introduced on March 2, 1927. This was an experimental opera with an Italian resort hotel as the setting in which the heroine, bored with the attentions of her fawning admirers, ends her life in the nearby lake. Music and drama were here combined with pantomime and film. Though a failure, this was an important step in Weill's development as a composer for the popular theater because here, for the first time, he used recognizable jazz motives only hinted at in some of his earlier works.

Success returned to Weill with the resumption of his collaboration with Kaiser: with *Der Zar lässt sich photographieren,* set in a Parisian photographic studio. Conspirators take over the studio for the purpose of assassinating a visiting Czar. Jazz and other popular musical idioms are used freely; one of the musical highlights was a tango sequence with erotic implications. Always the restless seeker for innovation, Weill used a male chorus throughout the opera, placed in the orchestra pit, to comment on the stage proceedings. First presented in Leipzig on February 18, 1928, it proved so successful that it was soon produced in eighty German theaters. When the intellectual elite in Germany accused Weill of "selling out" to the box office, he replied: "I want to reach the real people, a more representative public than any opera house attracts. I write for today. I don't care about writing for posterity."

The new concept of "songplay" became realized when Weill started collaborating with Bertolt Brecht, the Marxist German poet and dramatist whose politically oriented writings were generously coated with irony and cynicism. The term songplay (*Songspiel*) was adapted from *Singspiel*, the 18th-century German form of light opera in which spoken dialogue was combined with light songs sometimes of folklike character. For Weill and Brecht, songplay was not just a play on a word. It connoted that in their operas, song was to be the basic ingredient; and the songs, using consciously conceived banal texts, were to be popular in nature. "Weill had written relatively complicated music of a mainly psychological sort," Brecht explained in referring to Weill's operatic works before their collaboration, "and when we agreed to set a series of more or less banal song texts he was making a courageous break with a prejudice which the solid bulk of serious composers stubbornly held." They first began working together when Weill decided to set to music a group of five Brecht poems from *Hauspostille*, a satire on capitalist society about an imaginary American boomtown free of moral or ethical values called Mahagonny. *Mahagonny Songspiel* (or "*kleine Mahagonny*" as it came to be known to distinguish it from the later expanded operatic version) was introduced at the Music Festival in Baden-Baden on July 18, 1927. The score was a rich amalgam of jazz, blues, music hall tunes, folk songs, marching melodies, ballads, and parodies. "Alabamy Song" (title originally in English) was intended as a parody of a Tin Pan Alley ballad (this melody was the work of Brecht rather than Weill). "Benares Song" used nonsense dialogue in pidgin English set to jazz fragments. Throughout the composition, sophistication was combined with a conscious naïveté, artistic intent with lowbrowism. At its premiere, it caused shock and dismay on the one hand, and enthusiastic excitement on the other. The difference of opinions in the audience expressed in catcalls, laughter, and shouts of approval caused a scandal in the theater surpassed only by that attending the premiere of Stravinsky's *The Rite of Spring* in Paris a decade earlier. One of the members of that Baden-Baden audience was Aaron Copland, who later wrote: "In the last analysis, dramatic effectiveness had been the point. It was a novel dramatic idea that had called the tune, and with this had come a novel combination of musical ones. In the context, even touches of banality were allowed; for banality, along with melody itself—both banished for a time

from the 'serious' musical stage—was now being welcomed back with a newfound sense of humor." H.W. Heinsheimer, the Viennese publisher and writer, has since said: "Nothing like it had ever been tried by a serious composer, and it had the effect of a bombshell."

An even greater bombshell was to explode on the German cultural scene in the late 1920s with the next Weill-Brecht collaboration: *Die Dreigroschenoper*, or *The Threepenny Opera* (1928). John Gay's 18th century ballad opera *The Beggar's Opera,* on which it was freely based—transferred in time to the early 20th century in a fantasy Soho—provided Brecht with ample opportunities to speak about the social and political corruption of German life in the 1920s in a cynical and at times bitter libretto. Weill's score was a cloth of many colors: a mock chorale, a canon, a tango-ballad, the blues, a shimmy, ragtime, jazz, ballads, operalike arias and choruses. The opening night—August 31, 1928, in Berlin—found the audience at turns puzzled and amused by what it was hearing, unable to decide whether all this was opera or operetta or parody or tongue-in-cheek spoof. Lotte Lenya, who played the role of Jenny the Prostitute, the role that made her a star, described what transpired that evening: "Up to the stable scene the audience seemed cold and apathetic, as though convinced in advance that it had come to a certain flop. Then, after the 'Kanonen Song,' an unbelievable uproar went up, and from that point on it was wonderfully, intoxicatingly clear that the public was with us. However, late the next morning, while we were waiting for the first reviews, there persisted a crassy unreality about what had happened, nobody quite dared to believe in our success. Nor did the reviews confirm it for us—they were decidedly mixed." Some reviews were uninhibited in their enthusiasm. In the *Berliner Börsen Courier,* Herbert Ihering maintained that this opera "proclaims a new world in which the frontiers of tragedy and humor are eradicated. . . . Brecht has torn language, and Weill music, from their isolation. Once more we listen to speech on the stage that is neither literary nor shopworn, and music that no longer works with threadbare harmonies and rhythms." Those not in accord with the opera's social and political views called it "class-conscious Bolshevism" or "Bolshevist madness."

What happened after that had few parallels in the history of the German theater. The city, and then the entire country, was swept by a *Dreigroschenoper* fever. As Lotte Lenya goes on to say: "In the streets no other tunes were whistled. A *Dreigroschenoper* cafe was opened where no other music was played." In its first year, the opera was given more than four thousand times in over one hundred German theaters; in five years it was seen ten thousand times in Central Europe, translated into eighteen languages. It was made into a German-language motion picture, produced by G. W. Pabst. Weill adapted some of the principal melodies from the opera into a suite for wind orchestra: *Kleine Dreigroschenmusik* (1928) whose premiere was conducted by Otto Klemperer (who asked for it) in Berlin on February 7, 1929. On the fiftieth anniversary of the opera's premiere in 1978, productions sprouted throughout Europe.

When first produced in the United States, on Broadway, on April 13, 1933, *The Threepenny Opera* was such a failure that it had to close down after only thirteen performances. But a revival, Off Broadway, on March 10, 1954—text modernized by Marc Blitzstein but with Weill's music left intact— was a monumental success. It ran Off Broadway then on Broadway for six years, totaling 2,500 performances. Two national companies toured the United States in 1960 and 1961. Its most famous ballad, "Mack the Knife" or "Moritat," became such a hit song that it was recorded in some fifty versions, selling well over ten million disks. "As a theater work," Brooks Atkinson wrote in the *New York Times,* "*Threepenny Opera* is a triumph of style, the . . . music, the austere technique, the callous attitude towards characters and story are all of a piece. What you feel in the theater is not the emotional experience of the characters, but the coldness of the minds of composer and author. 'Malice' is too active a word to describe their point of view. It is more like a sardonic acceptance of evil as the law of the land. As citizens of pre-Hitler Germany they doubtlessly reflected the cynicism of a particular time and place." Harold C. Schonberg, also in the *New York Times,* said of the opera that it "holds its own as one of the more significant works of the century. . . . The composer never wrote more evocative, brilliant and imaginative music."

In 1929, Weill and Brecht collaborated on *Happy End* (original title in English), a songplay intended as a sequel to *Der Dreigroschenoper.* It was produced on September 2, 1929, and was a failure. The setting is Chicago in 1915. A Salvation Army lass is bent on reforming a group of gamblers only to fall in love with one of them. (This theme is similar to the later Damon Runyan story, *The Idyll of Sarah Brown,* which was made into the successful Frank Loesser musical *Guys and Dolls.*) *Happy End* contained some excellent Weill music, including "The Bilbao Song" (which, with new English lyrics, became an American hit in 1951), "Surabaya Johnny," and "Sailor's Tango." Nevertheless, *Happy End* lay neglected for about forty years after its unsuccessful premiere before the first revival in Germany. It received its American premiere in New Haven, Conn., on April 6, 1972. At that time, Mel Gussow, in the *New York Times,* called Weill's score "a rich, smoky evocation of Chicago in 1915, full of laments, hymns, anthems and calls to social revolution." In 1974, *Happy End* was successfully produced in London and on May 16, 1977, it was revived on Broadway.

Weill and Brecht collaborated on two productions in 1930. They expanded the *Mahagonny Songspiel* into a three-act opera renamed *Aufstieg und Fall der Stadt Mahagonny* (1929). It instigated riots when introduced simultaneously in Leipzig and Frankfurt on March 9, 1930. In Leipzig, Nazis provoked a scandal in the theater where stink bombs were dropped, denunciatory shouts sounded, and fistfights ensued. Things went just as badly in Frankfurt, where, during a fight in the audience, one man was shot and killed. That management decided to discontinue further performances. Three other German houses that had planned productions abandoned the project and two others gave only token performances before calling it a day.

Brecht's text was irreverent, at times salacious, iconoclastic, continually calculated to provoke shock. *Mahagonny* was a mythical city in Alabama in whose wilderness three stranded convicts, fleeing from the law, decided to build a new kind of society where people could do whatever they wished without regard to morality or ethics; where freedom was limited only to the law of supply and demand; where anything was pardonable except the lack of money. All this, in Brecht's hands, became symbolic of the corruption, decadence, hypocrisy, and immorality of the Weimar Republic. H. H. Stuckenschmidt, the eminent Berlin critic, remarked that the opera was "a document of its times." The best songs of *Mahagonny Songspiel* were carried over into the opera, with the addition of a new successful number, "Havana Song."

The American premiere of *Aufstieg und Fall der Stadt Mahagonny (The Rise and Fall of the City of Mahagonny)* took place in New York on March 4, 1970. The Metropolitan Opera revived it with extraordinary success on November 16, 1979, one of these performances getting telecast nationally, live from the stage, on November 16, 1979. "The music is fantastic," wrote Clive Barnes in the *New York Times* in 1970. "Erotic, melodious, childlike yet sinister. It has a musical innocence, and charms as potent and as poignant as poisoned chocolates. In style it stretched back to Mahler, and forward to the Beatles and the Who. It is beautiful and lingers, lingers, lingers."

With their second production in 1930, Weill and Brecht produced *Gebrauchsmusik,* one of the earliest school operas written by a major composer. It was *Der Jasager,* based on a Japanese *Noh* play. Neither Brecht nor Weill was a newcomer in writing functional art. This cult of simplicity slanted for a large general public (with which Hindemith became identified) was one of which Brecht had long been a leading theoretician; and in the late 1920s, Weill had written functional music for the radio. *Der Jasager* was performed in more than five hundred schools in Germany. Many years later, Weill could look back on this music as one of the scores he cherished most.

Weill's last two operas produced in Germany were written without the benefit of Brecht's collaboration. They were *Die Burgschaft* (1932; Berlin, March 10, 1932), libretto by Casper Neher, based on a parable by Herder; its first important revival in post-Hitler Germany took place at the Berlin Festival in October 1957. *Der Silbersee*, "a winter's tale," had a text by Georg Kaiser that was part fantasy and part realism. Its opening had been scheduled simultaneously for eleven German opera houses on February 18, 1933. In each of these theaters the opera had to close down the following morning due to Nazi interference. Nazi hostility to Weill and Brecht reached a pont of no return with one of the opera's principal songs, "The Ballad of Caesar's Death," a bitter indictment of Hitler. The American premiere of *Der Silbersee (Silverlake)* was given by the New York City Opera on March 20, 1980.

The sudden closing of *Der Silbersee* at its premiere in Germany had been accompanied by an official Nazi announcement that from that moment on all the works of Kurt Weill (*"der Kulturbolschewist"*) would forever be banned in Germany. Learning from a friend that the Gestapo was about to arrest him, Weill made his escape from Germany on March 21, 1933. For the next two years, the Weills made their home in Louveciennes, outside Paris. In France, Weill contributed the music to *Die sieben Todsünden,* a song-ballet with choreography by George Ballanchine, scenario by Bertolt Brecht (Brecht's last joint work with Weill) starring Tilly Losch. It was produced in Paris by Les Ballets on June 7, 1933. The Opera Theater of St. Louis revived it on June 4, 1980, for its American premiere. Weill also provided the score for *Marie Galante,* a musical play with text by Jacques Duval, which opened in Paris on December 22, 1934. One of its finest songs, "J'attends un navire," was taken over by the French Resistance fighters during World War II. In addition to these stage works, Weill also completed in Paris Symphony no. 2 (1934). Bruno Walter, as guest conductor of the Concertgebouw Orchestra, introduced it on October 11, 1934, in Amsterdam, and subsequently performed it in Vienna and New York. It was recorded several decades later both by the Leipzig Gewandhaus Orchestra under Edo de Waart and the BBC Symphony under Gary Bertini. In Andrew Porter's review of these recordings in *High Fidelity/Musical America,* he described the work as "a neoclassical symphony in three movements for a classical orchestra. . . . The textures are clear and 'rational.' . . . The melodies and harmonies show procedures familiar from Weill's stage works." Following a revival in New York on November 25, 1979, conducted by Julius Rudel, Joseph Horowitz called it "an irresistible concoction nourished by the vitality and diversity of Weimar culture, as well as shadowed by its grim dissolution."

Weill was brought to the United States in the fall of 1935 by Max Reinhardt, the distinguished Austrian-born stage director. Reinhardt, who was preparing for New York *The Eternal Road,* a pageant tracing the history of the Jewish people written by Franz Werfel, invited Weill to write the music. From this year on until his death, the United States remained Weill's home and, from 1943 on, the country of his citizenship.

Since *The Eternal Road* suffered numerous postponements, and did not get produced until January 7, 1937, Weill's American debut did not take place with this pageant, but with a Broadway musical satire, *Johnny Johnson,* a scathing antiwar play by Paul Green to which Weill contributed seven songs so skillfully integrated with the play that *Johnny Johnson* may well be considered Broadway's first musical play as distinguished from musical comedy. It opened on November 19, 1936, and closed after only sixty-eight performances.

Success for Weill on Broadway was not long in coming. Its first appearance (a comparatively modest one) was with *Knickerbocker Holiday,* text and lyrics by Maxwell Anderson, the score yielding one of Weill's most substantial American song hits, "September Song." Greater box-office successes followed, firmly establishing Weill as one of Broadway's major creative figures: *Lady in the Dark* (January 23, 1941), text by Moss Hart and lyrics by Ira Gershwin; *One Touch of Venus* (October 7, 1943), text by S. J. Perelman and Ogden Nash and lyrics by Nash; and *Love Life,* book and lyrics by Alan J. Lerner (October 7, 1948).

In two musicals, Weill brought operatic dimensions to the Broadway musical theater. They were: *Street Scene* (January 9, 1947), described as "a folk play with music," text by Elmer Rice based on his own Broadway play of the same name; and *Lost in the Stars* (October 30, 1949), "a musical tragedy" with book and lyrics by Maxwell Anderson based on Alan Paton's novel, *Cry the Beloved Country.* Both musicals were produced and several times revived by the New York City Opera as part of its regular repertoire (as well as by other American opera companies). A New York City Opera performance of *Street Scene* was televised live nationally from its stage on October 27, 1979.

Despite his involvement with the Broadway musical theater—and with motion pictures, for which he produced original scores for *Blockade* (1938) and *Where Do We Go from Here?* (1945)—Weill did not completely desert so-called serious musical endeavors. His most significant such effort was *Down in the Valley.* This is a one-act American folk opera for schools with text by Arnold Sundgaard, written on commission from the School of Music of Indiana University in Bloomington where it was first heard on July 15, 1948. The score is rich with lyrical solo numbers for the voice together with dramatic passages for a chorus that serves as a commentator of and a participant in the drama. Five folk songs from the Kentucky Mountain region were interpolated:

the title song, "The Lonesome Dove," "The Little Black Train," "Hop Up, My Ladies," and "Sourwood Mountain."

At the time of his death, caused by a heart attack, Weill was working with Maxwell Anderson on a musical based on *Tom Sawyer*, never completed. Since Weill's death, his widow had been actively involved in the recital halls, theaters, on recordings and over television, performing her husband's songs. "A Kurt Weill Cabaret," was an evening of Weill music presented by Martha Schlamme and Alvin Epstein in nightclubs and college campuses for several years before they brought it to Broadway in November 1979. "Berlin to Broadway" was another collection of Weill's greatest songs, produced Off-Broadway on October 1, 1972.

In eulogizing Weill soon after his death, Virgil Thomson in the *New York Herald Tribune* singled him out as "probably the most original single workman in the whole musical theater, internationally considered, during the last quarter of a century. He was an architect, a master of music-dramatic design, whose structure, built for function and solidity, constitutes a repertory of models that have not only served well their original purpose but also had a wide influence on composers as examples of procedure."

THE COMPOSER SPEAKS: Ever since I started working for the theater I have considered myself a theater composer. I believe that the musical theater is the highest, the most expressive and the most imaginative form of theater, and that a composer who has a talent and a passion for the theater can express himself completely in this branch of musical creativeness. Through my work for the theater I have arrived at the conclusion that the distinction between "serious" and "light" music is one of the misconceptions of the Wagnerian period in music. The only distinction we should make is the one between good and bad music. I believe that new forms of musical theater can be developed in close connection with the living theater and the fundamental ideas of our time, and that these new forms can take the place of the traditional opera or operetta. Most of my own works for the theater in Europe and in this country have been experiments in different forms of musical theater. Broadway seems to me a perfect place to develop a musical theater which, in time, will become to this country what opera is to Europe.

PRINCIPAL WORKS: 2 symphonies (1921, 1934). String Quartet op. 8 (1923); Quadlibet, for orchestra (1923); Concerto for Violin and Wind Orchestra (1924); *Der Protagonist*, a one-act opera (1925); *Der neue Orpheus*, cantata for soprano, solo violin, and orchestra (1925); *Royal Palace*, one-act opera (1926); *Der Zar lässt sich photographieren*, one-act opera buffa (1927); *Mahagonny*, songspiel, song cycle (1927); *Die Dreigroschenoper*, play with music (1928); *Kleine Dreigroschenmusik*, for orchestra (1928); *Das Berliner Requiem*, cantata for male voices and wind orchestra (1928); *Der Lindberghflug*, or *The Lindbergh Flight*, radio cantata for vocal soloists and orchestra (1929); *Aufstieg und Fall der Stadt Mahagonny*, or *The Rise and Fall of the City of Mahagonny*, opera (1929); *Happy End*, comedy with music (1929); *Der Jasager*, school opera (1930); *Die Burgschaft*, opera (1931); *Der Silbersee*, or *The Silverlake*, a "winter's tale" (1932); *Die sieben Todsünden*, song-ballet (1933); *The Eternal Road*, dramatic oratorio for solo voices, chorus, and orchestra (1935); *The Ballad of Magna Carta*, radio cantata for solo voice, chorus, and orchestra (1939); *Three Walt Whitman Songs*, for voice and piano (1942); *Kiddush*, for cantor, chorus, and organ (1946); *Street Scene*, musical play (1947); *Down in the Valley*, one-act folk opera (1948); *Lost in the Stars*, "a musical tragedy" (1949).

BIBLIOGRAPHY: Kowalke, K. H., "Kurt Weill in Europe" (doctoral thesis, New Haven, 1979); Sanders, Ronald, *The Days Grow Short: The Life and Music of Kurt Weill* (N.Y., 1980); *ASCAP Today*, March 1970; *Dictionary of American Biography*, supplement 4; *New York Times*, April 4, 1950 (obituary), April 9, 1950, October 10, 1964; *Opera News*, December 1, 1979; *Tomorrow*, March 1948.

Weinberger, Jaromir, b. Prague, Czechoslovakia, January 8, 1896; d. St. Petersburg, Fla., August 8, 1967. American citizen, 1948.

Weinberger's music reflected two cultures. His earlier works (following his apprentice years) were influenced by the aesthetics and idioms of Smetana and Dvořák, and were grounded in the folk songs, dances, and lore of his native land. After he had become an American, he was creatively stimulated by American literature, backgrounds, visual sensations, and ideologies. In both phases he was a traditionalist and a romanticist, faithful to diatonic and tonal practices, fastidiously scrupulous to avoid the newer, advanced techniques and styles and ever concerned with sound structures, well-sounding harmonic and orchestral language, and emotional responses that sprang from the heart.

He was descended from peasant stock. Most of his early years, particularly during the summers, were spent on his grandparents' farm south of Prague. There, he first heard and came to love Bohemian folk songs and dances which the villagers performed around the town fountain and the songs of gooseherds plying their trade. Weinberger began receiving formal instruction in composition during his youth while attending the Prague Conservatory, where his teachers included Jaroslav Křicksa, Karel Hoffmeister and Vitězslav Novak (composition and theory), and Karel Stecker (organ). Weinberger's boyhood compositions were imitative of Debussy and Ravel.

While still at the conservatory, Weinberger destroyed everything he had written up to this point. Rejecting impressionism, he embraced the music of Smetana and Dvořák, as Bohemian folk music and lore began absorbing his interest. One of his first works revealing this new orientation, and his first work to get widely heard, was *Marionette Overture*, for orchestra, written when he was seventeen, recipient of a number of performances in Europe.

Feeling the need for further music instruction, Weinberger went to Leipzig in 1915, where he studied composition privately with Max Reger. His pantomime, with music, *The Abduction of Eveline*, was produced in Vienna in 1917. Five years later, he met with his greatest success up to then with *Overture to a Knightly Play* (1922), based on an old Czech folk tale about an errant knight. To recreate this character and the Bohemian ambiance, Weinberger made plentiful use of old Bohemian melodies. After this work was introduced in Vienna in 1923, it was given numerous performances throughout Europe.

Weinberger paid his first visit to the United States in 1922. At that time he became professor of composition at Ithaca Conservatory in New York. He returned four years later to Czechoslovakia to devote himself to conducting and teaching in Bratislava and Eger.

The international limelight was focused on Weinberger with his folk opera *Schwanda, the Bagpipe Player* (1927), text by Milos Karesi based on a legend by Josef Tyl. Part fantasy and part realism, and rich in folkloric traditions, the opera told the story of Schwanda, a farmer, who is lured away from his wife to the court of Queen Ice-Heart where he delights everybody with his wonderful bagpipe playing and wins the heart of the Queen; in the end he is reconciled with his wife. Drawing deep from the well of Bohemia's folk music, Weinberger created a score that was infectiously melodious, rhythmically spirited, and harmonically and orchestrally colorful. When first performed on April 27, 1927, at the Prague Opera, *Schwanda* was not a success. But a year and a half later, on December 16, 1928, it was produced in Breslau, Germany, translated into German by Max Brod and bearing the German title of *Schwanda, der Dudelsackpfeifer*. It aroused enormous enthusiasm among many Germans who found it a refreshing antidote to the new experimental or decadent operas to which they were then continually subjected. This success in Breslau was the beginning of the opera's triumphant march throughout the world of music. Within four years it had been produced over two thousand times on a hundred stages in Central Europe, translated into fourteen languages. On November 7, 1931, it received its American premiere at the Metropolitan Opera. In 1934 it was produced at Covent Garden in London, and in 1935 in Buenos Aires. After the American premiere, Pitts Sanborn wrote in the *New York World Telegram* that the opera boasted a "score overflowing with catchy music. . . . The music is eclectic and by no means radical. . . . Reminiscences of Smetana (above all of Smetana), of Wagner and of Bohemian folk song are many. But Weinberger uses them with no little skill and the score as a whole has verve, impetuosity and an engaging tunefulness."

Two orchestral excerpts from this opera became Weinberger's most frequently performed orchestral compositions. They are the "Polka" and "Fugue," the climax of the fugue repeating the main melody of the polka contrapuntally with the fugue subject. First heard in Halle, Germany, on February 9, 1930, "Polka" and "Fugue" was then programmed by major orchestras throughout Europe and the United States, the first American hearing taking place at the Lewisohn Stadium in New York on August 4, 1930.

Bohemian nationalism is to be found in two of Weinberger's orchestral works in 1929. *Christmas Overture*, for orchestra and organ, quoted three Bohemian Christmas songs of the festival of Epiphany (Koledy) inspired by old Bohemian folk tales. The overture was introduced in Munich on November 7, 1929. *Six Bohemian Songs and Dances* was premiered in Darmstadt on March 10, 1930.

Weinberger's second opera was *Die geliebte Stimme* (1930), first produced on February 28, 1931, in Munich in the German language. This was followed by an opera with an American setting based on an American story: *The Outcasts of Poker Flat* (1931), libretto derived from Bret Harte. It was first produced on November 19, 1932, in Brünn. This is one of Weinberger's earliest compositions to use some indigenous American musical material: rhythms of old American dances. Weinberger's last opera written and produced in Europe before his migration to the United States was *Wallenstein* (1936), a lyric tragedy based on Schiller used by the composer as an allegory on resistance to the Nazis, heard first in Vienna on November 18, 1937.

The eminent Czech-born musicologist Paul Nettl made the following appraisal of Weinberger's operas. "In examining these operas we can trace the path of Weinberger's artistic development. Though *Schwanda* is strongly influenced by Czech legendary time, and *Die geliebte Stimme* followed the patterns of Czech-Yugoslavic folklore, the two succeeding works already depart from the canons of style dictated by folklore tendencies. In *Outcasts of Poker Flat*, a new dramatic principle is introduced and developed. We have in this work a combination of opera and melodramatic portrayal: that is, realistic dialogue is spoken while, on the other hand, emotional outbursts of the leading characters are portrayed musically, both of these being accompanied by the orchestra, to which is entrusted the task of describing the psychological situation and painting a background. By way of this experiment Weinberger arrived (in his *Wallenstein*) at a new form of dramatic technique which is quite novel in essentials though it has roots in older models. Where Wagner uses the leitmotiv to accompany the various characters as they appear on the stage, Weinberger uses definitely formed motives to characterize specific emotional situations."

When the Sudeten territory of Czechoslovakia fell to the Nazis in 1938 following the Munich agreement, presaging the seizure of that country by the Third Reich, Weinberger left his native land never to return. He was on the French Riviera, in Juan les Pins, during the summer of 1938 when he saw a newsreel in which the king of England was visiting a boys' camp where he was serenaded with the singing of "Under the Spreading Chestnut Tree," by the English composer Sterndale Bennett. This song so pleased Weinberger that he decided to use it for a concert work for orchestra in variation form, portraying historic English scenes, English backgrounds and landscapes. One variation paid tribute to 18th-century English madrigalists, another to the "Dark Lady" of Shakespeare's sonnets, and a third to a chapter in Dickens's *Pickwick Papers*. The "Pastorale" variation described the English countryside, and "The Highlanders" had a Scottish identity by simulating the sounds of bagpipe music. *Under the Spreading Chestnut Tree* did not get written until after Weinberger had come to the United States in 1939 for permanent residence and citizenship; its first performance was given by the New York Philharmonic under John Barbirolli on October 12, 1939."

Once having become an American, Weinberger proceeded to seek out American subjects for his compositions. "I now feel," he said at the time, "that to compose Czech music is to cultivate a patch of ground too limited and restricted. That was very good when my viewpoint on cosmic matters was limited." *Prelude and Fugue on "Dixie"* (1939) was commissioned by the San Antonio Symphony, which, under Max Reiter, gave the first performance on April 12, 1940. Other Weinberger orchestral works were based on works by American writers (Weinberger had been a passionate reader of American literature from boyhood days): from Edgar Allan Poe in *The Raven*, for cello and orchestra (1940), and *The Devil in the Belfrey*, for violin and orchestra (1940); from Washington Irving in *The Legend of Sleepy Hollow*, a suite for orchestra (1940), whose premiere was given by the Detroit Symphony under Victor Kolar on November 21, 1940. A great American president was the inspiration for his *Lincoln Symphony* (1941; Cincinnati, October 17, 1941). The sounds of popular music can be heard in Concerto for Saxophone and Orchestra (1940).

There was a brief, nostalgic return to Bohemian folk music and lore in the *Czech Rhapsody*, for orchestra (1941; Washington, D.C., November 5, 1941). But, after 1940, Weinberger's music had neither a Bohemian nor an American identity, but aimed at cosmopolitanism and a more universal language. *A Bird's Opera* (1941; Detroit, November 13, 1941) was a symphonic fantasy descriptive of animal life in a barnyard. *Preludes réligieuses et profanes*, for orchestra (1953), was introduced in Rotterdam in 1955, and the premiere of *Five Songs from Des Knaben Wunderhorn* (1962) was featured at the Festival Weeks in Vienna in 1962.

Weinberger spent his last years in St. Petersburg, Fla., in frustration, bitterness and melancholia. With provocative new styles and techniques in music seizing the limelight and capturing performances, Weinberger's music (now looked upon as old-fashioned) was being neglected. Regarding himself as a forgotten composer, he committed suicide through an overdose of pills. He was survived by his wife, the former Jana Lembergerova.

THE COMPOSER SPEAKS: In my music as in my politics I have grown from a nationalist into an internationalist. Though I was born a Czech, and though I have always felt my native sources deeply, I now am a cosmopolitan, a citizen of the world, rather than of one country. I dream of the time when national boundaries and racial hatreds—all lines of demarcation which separate people and keep them apart—will be removed once and for all. I dream of a Europe in which different races and nationalities live side by side in freedom and harmony. Dreaming of such things, I can no longer compose music that has restricted boundary lines. I can no longer speak of any one country in my music, even though that country is that of my birth. I must speak to all people everywhere, and in an idiom that they will understand.

I now feel that music should be humanitarian in its approach and message; it should be universal in scope. To achieve this is to attain the highest realm of true art. The day of nationalistic music is over; music should now aspire to be international, speaking to, and of, all races, creeds and countries.

PRINCIPAL WORKS: *Marionette Overture*, for orchestra (1913); *Overture to a Knightly Play*, for orchestra (1922); *Schwanda, the Bagpipe Player*, folk opera (1926); *Six Bohemian Songs and Dances*, for orchestra (1929); *Die geliebte Stimme*, opera (1930); *The Outcasts of Poker Flat*, opera (1931); Passacaglia, for organ and orchestra (1931); *A Bed of Roses*, light opera (1934); *Wallenstein*, lyric tragedy (1936); *Prelude and Fugue on "Dixie,"* for orchestra (1939); Timpani Concerto (1939); *Under the Spreading Chestnut Tree*, variations for orchestra (1939); *Song of the High Seas*, for orchestra (1940); *The Raven*, for cello and orchestra (1940); *A Devil in the Belfry*, for violin and orchestra (1941); *A Bird's Opera*, for orchestra (1941); *The Legend of Sleepy Hollow*, suite for orchestra (1941); *Czech Rhapsody*, for orchestra (1941); *Ecclesiastes*, for soprano, baritone, chorus, and organ (1945); *Preludes réligieuses et profanes*, for orchestra (1953); *Aus Tirol*, for orchestra (1960);

Five Songs from Des Knaben Wunderhorn, for voice and orchestra (1962).

BIBLIOGRAPHY: *BBDM*; Ewen, David, *Composers Since 1900* (N.Y., 1969); Machlis, Joseph, *Contemporary Music*, revised edition (N.Y., 1979).

Weisgall, Hugo David, b. Ivančice, Czechoslovakia, October 13, 1912. American citizen, 1926.

Though Weisgall has written important concert works for voice, the area in which he has achieved his greatest success has been opera. He has effectively used resources of atonal and twelve-tonal writing. A highly vocal declamatory style often contrasted with dramatic song (but avoiding *Sprechstimme*), an expressive harmonic language derived from preserial atonal procedures, a fluent contrapuntal technique, intricate motivic developments, and propulsive rhythms make up some of the musical equipment which he brings for keen psychological insights into character, subtle changes of mood and atmosphere, and compelling dramatic interest.

Weisgall was descended from several generations of synagogal cantors and composers. His father, Adolph Joseph Weisgal, sang in light opera before he gave up that career to become a cantor in Ivančice. An uncle, Meyer W. Weisgal, on the other hand, became famous as a communal leader, Zionist, and president of the Weizmann Institute of Science in Israel.

The elder of two sons, Hugo was early influenced in music by his father. When Hugo was four he became a regular member of the synagogue choir and, after receiving his early instruction at the piano, sometimes served as accompanist for his father's singing of lieder. In his childhood, Hugo Weisgall also made his first tentative attempts at composition.

In 1920, the composer's immediate family immigrated to the United States, settling a year later in Baltimore, Md. There he attended elementary school and completed his high school education at the Baltimore City College in 1929. The theater was an early love. In his boyhood he concocted a play about the Knights of the Round Table which he (as King Arthur) and his friends enacted. Later on, in his backyard, he recreated the story of Robinson Crusoe.

His academic education—which continued on an undergraduate level at Johns Hopkins University between 1929 and 1931—was combined with music study on a Boise scholarship at the Peabody Conservatory (1927–32): piano with Florette Gorfine and Alexander Sklarevski, and theory with Louis Cheslock. During his early manhood, Weisgall made a number of appearances as actor in small repertory companies. He subsequently embarked on a professional career as singer.

In 1931, he completed a Piano Sonata in F-sharp minor and *Four Impressions*, for voice and piano, on

poems by Amy Lowell, Rilke, and Humbert Wolfe, which received the Bearns Prize from Columbia University. Both works were romantic, the songs betraying the influence of Mussorgsky. Weisgall put foot into the musical theater for the first time with a one-act opera, *Night* (1932), based on a play by Sholem Asch, following this with a second one-act opera, *Lilith* (1934). All these works have since been withdrawn from circulation.

Between 1931 and 1942, Weisgall was musical director of Har Sinai Temple Choir in Baltimore. In 1933 he was made member of Phi Beta Kappa at Johns Hopkins University. After leaving the Peabody Conservatory in 1932 he began, in 1933, an eight-year period of intermittent private study of composition with Roger Sessions. Weisgall was conductor of the Y-Alliance String Orchestra from 1936 to 1938. At the same time, on a scholarship, he attended the Curtis Institute of Music in Philadelphia (1936–39) as a student in composition of Rosario Scalero's and in conducting of Fritz Reiner's. At Curtis, he received a diploma in conducting and a traveling fellowship to Italy in 1938 and a diploma in composition in 1939. He was back at Johns Hopkins to complete his academic education from 1937 to 1940, and in the latter year he received his Ph.D. in German literature without ever having earned either a bachelor of arts or master of arts degree.

Four Songs, for voice and piano (1934), to poems by Adelaide Crapsey, became Weisgall's first work to be published. The first three of these songs are diatonic and consonant, but the fourth is more dissonant, pointing to Weisgall's future development. A Hebraic choral work, *Mi Chomocho*, for baritone, chorus, and organ (1937), became his first work to get a major hearing when it was performed at the Three Choir Festival in New York, Lazare Saminsky conducting, on March 25, 1938. *Quest*, in 1938, was a romantic ballet which the Baltimore Ballet had commissioned and premiered on May 17, 1938, the composer conducting. An orchestral suite derived from this score was introduced by the New York Philharmonic under John Barbirolli on March 21, 1942. Weisgall wrote a second ballet score for the Baltimore Ballet, *One Thing Is Certain* (1939), first produced on February 25, 1939. Fugue and Romance, for two pianos (later transcribed for string orchestra) came out of this score, the orchestral version premiered on March 19, 1947, with the composer conducting the Prague Chamber Orchestra in Czechoslovakia.

Some of his compositions in the early 1940s were well received by the critics. *Hymn*, for chorus and orchestra (1941), with a liturgical text taken from the service for the Day of Atonement, was first performed on March 28, 1942, in Baltimore, Stanley Chapple conducting. Weldon Wallace, in the *Baltimore Sun*, said of it: "The choral writing is original and beautifully adapted to the words. . . . The phrases have intelligent outline and order, and there is not that feeling of chaos that many present-day works seem to convey." Overture in F (*American Comedy*), for orchestra, was given its first performance on July 29, 1943, in London with the composer conducting the BBC Orchestra. The eminent British critic Ralph Hill called it in *The Listener* "brilliant and clearly designed . . . the product of an alert and refined mind. The music is intended to suggest an American spirit of comedy and gaiety, a spirit somewhat tempered but not subdued by the events of our time."

On December 28, 1942, Weisgall married Nathalie Shulman, a physiologist who came from a highly musical family. They have two children. During World War II, in 1942, Weisgall enlisted in the U. S. Army. He served first as assistant military attaché to the Allied Governments in Exile in London (1943–45) and later as cultural attaché to the American embassy in Prague (1946–47). In 1945 he was awarded the Czechoslovakian Military Medal and decorated with the Order of the White Lion, first class, also from Czechoslovakia.

His war experiences led to the writing of *Soldier Songs*, for baritone and orchestra (1944–46), dramatic settings of nine poems by various poets including Siegfried Sassoon, e. e. cummings, Wilfred Owens, Robert Graves, and Karl Shapiro, which lay bare the horror of war and the bitter disenchantment it brings. Here Weisgall's idiom is harmonically dissonant, and the melodic line is often more declamatory than lyrical; occasionally a popular element (in the manner of Mahler) is introduced. "Throughout this cycle," wrote George Rochberg in *American Composers Alliance Bulletin*, "flickers the picture of youth destroyed by the brutal stupidity of the iron god of war and the opposite image of society proud that its youth is fighting to preserve hearth and home." This cycle waited almost a decade for performance, receiving its first performance (with piano) in New York on April 26, 1954, from Grant Garnell. A revised version in 1965 with orchestral accompaniment, commissioned by Peter Herman Adler for the Baltimore Symphony, was first heard on March 30, 1966. In *Notes*, Henry Woodward wrote: "The music is powerful, even crude, in its super-abundance of material and abrupt shifts from one accompaniment figure to another, but it is coherent nonetheless, and compels attention by sheer force of musical and poetic imagination."

While serving as cultural attaché in Prague, Weisgall composed music for another ballet, *Outpost* (1947), commissioned by the National Theater of Prague. Weisgall's wife provided a scenario set in the American West. Music from this ballet was premiered by the National Symphony of Washington, D.C., on January 11, 1950, the composer conducting.

While abroad, Weisgall made numerous appearances as conductor of major orchestras in London, Brussels, and Prague, and of Italian operas in Prague. He turned down offers for a permanent conducting assignment in Europe to return to the United States in 1948 following his discharge from the armed forces. That year he received a Ditson Fellowship in composition from Columbia University. In Baltimore, Weisgall earned his living as musical director for the synagogue and by teaching and coaching music privately. He also involved himself in a variety of other musical activities. Between 1948 and 1951 he was instructor of composition at the Cummington School of the Arts in Massachusetts and was director of the Baltimore Institute of Musical Arts. From 1951 to 1957 he was lecturer on music at Johns Hopkins University, where he conducted its orchestra between 1952 and 1958. In 1952 he founded the Hilltop Musical Company, which he directed for three years. Since 1952 he has been chairman of the faculty of the Cantors Institute and the College of Music of the Jewish Theological Seminary in New York.

Weisgall made important inroads in his career as opera composer with two one-act operas completed between 1950 and 1952. *The Tenor* (1950) was economically conceived for six singers and a chamber orchestra with single winds. The libretto, by Karl Shapiro and Ernst Lert, was based on Frank Wedekind's psychological drama *Der Kammersinger*. Weisgall's style here is more chromatic and atonal than anything he had thus far written. Dramatic effectiveness is realized by the contrast between declamation and an outpouring of lyricism. Two brief quotations from *Tristan und Isolde* are interwoven into the musical fabric. An interesting trait new to Weisgall appears in this opera: "punctuation material," which Bruce Saylor in *Musical Quarterly* described as "short epigrammatic musical ideas that in various guises form bridges between large sections or highlights and particular dramatic action." The world premiere of *The Tenor* took place in Baltimore on February 1, 1952. (It has since been recorded.) In 1952, Weisgall wrote another one-act opera, *The Stronger*, in which Richard Hart's libretto was derived from a play by August Strindberg. This is a "vocal monologue" or "monodrama" for one soprano (and one silent female role) set in a cocktail lounge. "His music," said Richard F. Goldman of this opera in *Musical Quarterly*, "is continuously interesting and appropriate and manages strikingly to sustain pace and dramatic force." The Hilltop Musical Company of Baltimore gave the first performance (with piano) on August 9, 1952. The premiere with orchestra followed in January 1955 at Columbia University, Siegfried Landau conducting.

Weisgall achieved prominence as opera composer with his first full-length work, *Six Characters in Search of an Author* (1956), commissioned by the Alice M. Ditson Fund of Columbia University. Denis Johnston's libretto was adapted from Luigi Pirandello's symbolical tragic-comedy which fluctuates between illusion and reality. Projected on several levels, the opera moved flexibly from the emotional to the intellectual, from the fantastic to the satiric, from the dramatic to the comic. "Constant changes of mood and involved interwoven situations result in an opera which is almost breathless in pace," wrote Abraham Skulsky in *Etude*. "Weisgall uses all the possible operatic forms; every type of technique of singing and of ensemble is present. There is no rest, for the planes are changing in such rapid succession that one cannot dwell on any given situation. Weisgall's music itself presents all varieties of mood and expression, but is stylistically strong and personal. It has great rhythmic vitality, expressive chromatic lyricism, and rare contrapuntal ingenuity." First produced on April 26, 1959, by the New York City Opera, it returned to the same stage the following season and then was featured on this company's five-week tour.

Without relinquishing his post at the Jewish Theological Seminary, Weisgall served as instructor of composition at the Juilliard School of Music in New York from 1957 to 1968 and as associate professor of music at Queens College in Queens, N.Y., from 1961 on. (In 1980 he was named there Distinguished University Professor.) In 1959–60 he was Distinguished Visiting Professor of Music at Pennsylvania State University at University Park, Pa.

Purgatory (1958) is a one-act opera for two singers and a chamber orchestra in which William Butler Yeats's allegory of youth, age, and motherhood was set to music, word for word. Its first performance was heard at the Library of Congress in Washington, D.C., on February 17, 1961. This is a dissonant, occasionally dodecaphonic, opera (Weisgall's first attempt to adapt the twelve-tone technique). In its two-part successor, *Athaliah* (1963)—libretto by Richard F. Goldman based on the Racine tragedy—the composer turns to a neoclassical idiom. This opera was commissioned by Thomas Scherman and the Little Orchestra Society, who premiered it in concert form in New York on February 17, 1964. On a Ford Foundation grant, Weisgall's next opera was *Nine Rivers from Jordan* (1968), a musical tragedy of guilt and redemption during World War II, text by Denis Johnston. In it, Bruce Saylor says, "Hugo Weisgall's entire musical, dramatic, philosophical and personal experience converge. . . . The opera is cinematographically conceived; real and symbolic events are juxtaposed as the action shifts quickly among various World War II fronts. . . . It is for the most part through-composed, but prominent arias, ensembles and symphonic movements merge with the continuous flow." When introduced by the New York City Opera on October 9, 1968, this opera was a failure, an experience that proved so traumatic that for the next eight years Weisgall made no further attempts at writing operas. Instead he concentrated on vocal music for the concert stage. *Fancies and Inventions* (1970; Baltimore, November 1, 1971) is a song cycle for baritone and five instruments using Robert Her-

rick's "The Hosperides" as text; it was commissioned by the Chamber Society of Baltimore. *End of Summer* (1970), another song cycle, this time for tenor and chamber ensemble, was one of the numbers on an all-Weisgall concert in New York on November 17, 1974. *Translations*, seven songs for mezzo-soprano and piano (1972), was commissioned by Shirley Verrett. *A Song of Celebration*— text by John Hollander—is a cantata for two vocal soloists, chorus, and orchestra written in 1976 for the centenary of the founding of Johns Hopkins University and was premiered in Baltimore on February 20, 1976.

On April 22, 1976, Weisgall returned to the opera stage when *Jenny/or The Hundred Nights* (1976) was produced at the Juilliard American Opera Center in New York. This is a one-act opera based on a *Noh* play by Yukio Mishima, libretto by John Hollander. The setting is London's Kensington Gardens at the turn of the present century. "What appears in Weisgall's music is, first of all, that he works in his chosen idiom with great skill," said Alan Rich in *New York*, "and also that he has the gift, denied to many of today's composers on the fringes of progressivism, of making voices serve drama. *Jenny* is, in terms of shape and continued impact, Weisgall's best stage work to date."

From 1950 to 1960, Weisgall was vice-president of American Composers Alliance and from 1963 to 1973 was president of the American Music Center. He received the Guggenheim Fellowship three times (1955, 1959, 1966) as well as a grant from the National Institute of Arts and Letters (1954) and a commission from the Koussevitzky Music Foundation (1961). In 1966–67 he was composer-in-residence at the American Academy in Rome, Italy. In 1973 he was awarded an honorary doctorate in music from Peabody Conservatory and, in 1976, the degree of doctor of humane letters from the Jewish Theological Seminary. He was elected to membership in the National Institute of Arts and Letters in 1975. His appearances as conductor have been extensive both in the United States and abroad.

THE COMPOSER SPEAKS: Manifestos should properly belong to the young. At that stage you can easily make statements which later may either be forgiven or forgotten. All that I want to say is that it's a damn tough job writing music. I suppose it always has been. I try to do the best I can at all times. I think I am as self-critical as one can be and still be able to continue writing. I feel that I may have something to say in opera, but in that most difficult and formless form in which the vagaries of taste and fashion play so large a part, the going is lonely and not easy. I try to be as direct and communicative as possible—on my own terms. I never deliberately confound an audience, I have never written down to it, nor do I ever coddle it. I don't, however, believe in making matters too easy—either emotionally or intellectually. The things I consider important are perhaps neither too pleasant nor too simple. Though I want to reach an audience, I never pretty things up nor can I ever oversimplify.

PRINCIPAL WORKS: *Quest*, ballet (1938); *One Thing Is Certain*, comedy ballet (1939); *Hymn*, for chorus and orchestra (1941); Overture in F (*American Comedy*), for orchestra (1942, revised 1943); *Soldier Songs*, for baritone and orchestra (1944–46, revised 1965); *Outpost*, dance legend (1947); *The Tenor*, one-act opera (1950); *The Stronger*, one-act opera (1952); *A Garden Eastward*, cantata for high voice and orchestra (1952); Two Madrigals, for high voices and piano (1955); *Six Characters in Search of an Author*, opera (1956); *Purgatory*, one-act opera (1958); *Evening Prayer for Peace*, for a cappella chorus (1959); *Athaliah*, opera (1963); *Graven Images*, for piano or woodwind quintet, or for woodwind quintet and trumpet (1966); Psalm 29, for solo voice, unison or two-part chorus, and piano or organ (1966; revised 1971); *Nine Rivers from Jordan*, opera (1968); *Fancies and Inventions*, song cycle for baritone and five instruments (1970); Seven Songs, for mezzo-soprano and piano (1972); *Translations*, song cycle for voice and piano (1972); *End of Summer*, for tenor, oboe, and three strings (1974); *A Song of Celebration*, for soprano, tenor, chorus, and orchestra (1975); *Jenny/or the Hundred Nights*, one-act opera (1976); *The Golden Peacock*, seven popular songs from the Yiddish, for voice and piano (1977); *Liebeslieder*, four songs for voice with interludes (1979); *The Gardens of Adonis*, opera (1980).

BIBLIOGRAPHY: Balkin, A., "The Operas of Hugo Weisgall" (doctoral thesis, St. Louis, 1971); Ewen, David, *Composers Since 1900* (N.Y., 1969); Machlis, Joseph, *Introduction to Contemporary Music*, revised ed. (N.Y., 1979); Thomson, Virgil, *American Music Since 1910* (N.Y., 1970); *American Composers Alliance Bulletin*, vol. 7, no. 2, 1958; *Etude*, December 1956; *Musical Quarterly*, April 1973; *New York Times*, April 18, 1976; *Who's Who in America, 1980–81*.

Weiss, Adolph A., b. Baltimore, Md., September 12, 1891; d. Van Nuys, Calif., February 20, 1971.

He was one of the first American composers to use the twelve-tone technique and to spread knowledge about it in America at a time when it was still either unknown or misunderstood. He remained a faithful disciple of Schoenberg's throughout his career, but not without bringing to his writing a strong personal identity and approach. "While many dabblers in row technique deal in a watered-down version of Schoenberg's music," Henry Cowell has written, "Weiss, like Berg and Webern, used the technique to enhance his own creative tendencies. These include a strong

sense of the lyrical, the poetic, the curve of beauty of the phrase. There is always a sense of unity and of direction in each movement. Dramatic and melodic ideas were well contrasted, but his personal sense of musicality always predominated."

Both his parents were of German origin. His father, a factory worker, played clarinet and bassoon in a symphony orchestra and conducted a choir. "Father was cruelly strict with his three boys," the composer recalled. They had to practice violin or piano every day after school from four to five o'clock. From the time the boys were six, eight and nine years respectively, the family reading-circle consumed three hours every Sunday morning with the reading and translating of German and English books such as Darwin's *Voyage of the Beagle* and John William Draper's *Conflict between Religion and Science*."

Weiss supplemented the study of violin and piano with lessons on the bassoon, which became his favored instrument. While attending public schools he played bassoon in school and church orchestras. When he was sixteen, he became first bassoonist of the Russian Symphony in New York, of which Modest Altschuler was conductor. When that orchestra went on a world tour, Weiss left high school, ending his formal academic education permanently. After that he played bassoon in the orchestra of the touring Ben Greet Players in productions of Shakespeare in 1908; in 1909 was bassoonist of the New York Philharmonic, then conducted by Gustav Mahler; and from 1910 was bassoonist for many years with the New York Symphony under Walter Damrosch.

While working in orchestras, he extended his musical knowledge with private lessons in theory with C. C. Mueller and Abraham Lilienthal, and with Cornelius Rybner and Frank Edwin Ward at Columbia University. In 1916 Weiss moved to Chicago to play bassoon with the Chicago Symphony. At this time he studied composition with Adolph Weidig and Theodore Ötterstrom. Among the compositions he was then writing, the only one to survive was Songs for Soprano (1916–18) and Fantasie, for piano (1918).

He left Chicago in 1921 to come to Rochester, N.Y., to fill the posts of bassoonist with the Rochester Philharmonic conducted by Eugene Goossens and Albert Coates and at the Eastman Theater (a motion picture house), and to coach singers at the Eastman School Opera Department. Weiss's *I segreti*, for large orchestra (1923), based on Goethe's *Die Geheimnisse*, was introduced in Rochester, Howard Hanson conducting, on May 1, 1925.

In 1925, Weiss went to Europe to study with Arnold Schoenberg, entering his master class in composition at the Akademie der Künste in Berlin, to become the first American to become Schoenberg's pupil. This affiliation with Schoenberg aroused Weiss's interest in the twelve-tone technique as a tool of composition. In that idiom he wrote two string quartets (1925, 1926), the second of which was performed by the New World String Quartet in New York in 1929; Chamber Symphony for Ten Instruments (1927), performed in Berlin under the auspices of the Akademie der Künste under Josef Rüfer and introduced to New York in 1930 under Nicolas Slonimsky's direction; and Twelve Preludes, for piano (1927), first performed in San Francisco in 1925 by Richard Buhlig.

Weiss was back in New York in May 1927. Between 1928 and 1932 he was secretary of the Pan American Society of Composers, serving as its conductor for a number of concerts featuring only premieres of new music at the New School for Social Research in 1927–28. In 1930, he also helped organize in New York the Conductorless Orchestra, in which he played bassoon and for which he was chairman of the program committee. One of the compositions performed at its concerts (February 21, 1930) was Weiss's *American Life* (1928), a scherzo for large orchestra in jazz, atonal, and dodecaphonic idioms which Olin Downes in the *New York Times* called "an intriguing novelty, cleverly done." Nicolas Slonimsky featured this work with the Pan American Society in Paris on June 6, 1931.

American Life was soon followed by Seven Songs for Soprano and String Quartet (1928), to poems by Emily Dickinson, performed by the New World Quartet with Mary Bell at the New School for Social Research and then recorded for New Musical Quarterly Recordings by the same artists soon after that. *Sonata da camera*, for flute and viola (1929; N. Y., January 16, 1930), was a twelve-tone piece in which, as the composer explained, "the original, the inverted, the retrograde forms are used without transposition." *The Libation Bearers* (1930), based on Aeschylus, was a choreographic cantata, for dancers performing on the stage while chorus, vocal soloists, and orchestra were placed in the pit; its music was written, though freely, in a modal style.

On the strength of *The Libation Bearers*, Weiss was awarded a Guggenheim Fellowship in 1931. With his wife, the former Agnes Henrietta Erpenbach (whom he had married on October 27, 1926), he spent the next year in Italy and Spain, writing the Piano Sonata (1932; N.Y., 1933) and *Sketches for "David,"* an opera in rhythmic declamation (1931), which he never completed.

Soon after his return to the United States in 1933, Weiss completed writing his most important orchestral work, Theme and Variations (1933), the first performance of which was given by the San Francisco Symphony under Pierre Monteux in 1936, and which was subsequently recorded. "I know of no American twelve-tone piece that is as eloquent as this," wrote Alfred Frankenstein in *High Fidelity* magazine. A critic for *American Record Guide* described this work as follows: "He codifies his music by polyphonic interest, plus a liberal view of twelve-tone technique. The handling of the contrapuntalism and expressive shifting harmonies requires a composer not only with a keen intellect but with an astute sense for the creative balance. The piece has real personality."

Except for the Suite for Orchestra (1938) Weiss confined himself to chamber music compositions in the 1930s and 1940s. The String Quartet no. 3 (1932), a Violin Sonata (1941), Passacaglia, for horn and viola (1942), Sextet, for winds and piano (1947), Trio, for clarinet, viola, and cello (1948), and Concerto, for bassoon and string quartet (1949), are the most important works of this period.

In 1941, Weiss traveled through South America with the American Wind Quintet, a tour sponsored by the Rockefeller Foundation. Two of Weiss's works were heard on these programs: Quintet, for flute, oboe, clarinet, bassoon, and horn (1931), and *Petite Suite*, for flute, clarinet, and bassoon (1939).

Among Weiss's most significant later works are a series of duos, trios, quartets, and quintets for any combination of flute, oboe, clarinet, bassoon, and horn called *Vade Mecum*, the first of which was written in 1951; Concerto, for trumpet and orchestra (1951); Trio, for flute, violin, and piano (1955); Five Fantasies, for violin and piano, based on Gagaku (Japanese court music), commissioned by a member of the International Cultural Exchange Association in Tokyo and completed in 1956; Tone Poem for Brass and Percussion (1957); and Rhapsody, for four French horns (1957).

In 1955, Weiss received a grant from the National Institute of Arts and Letters. Weiss lived the last decades of his life in Los Angeles, where, in the 1950s, he was bassoonist with the Los Angeles Philharmonic, then directed by Alfred Wallenstein; Weiss toured the Orient with that orchestra in 1956.

PRINCIPAL WORKS: 3 string quartets (1925, 1926, 1932).

I segreti, for orchestra (1923); Chamber Symphony for Ten Instruments (1927); Twelve Preludes, for piano (1927); *American Life*, for orchestra (1928); Seven Songs, for soprano and string quartet (1928); *The Libation Bearers*, choreographic cantata, for soloists, chorus, and orchestra (1930); Quintet for Winds (1931); Piano Sonata (1932); Theme and Variations, for orchestra (1933); Suite, for orchestra (1938); *Petite Suite*, for flute, clarinet, and bassoon (1939); Violin Sonata (1941); Passacaglia, for horn and viola (1942); Ten Pieces for Low Instruments and Orchestra (1943); *Ode to the West Wind*, for baritone, viola, and piano (1945); *Protest*, for two pianos (1945); Sextet, for winds and piano (1947); Trio, for clarinet, viola, and cello (1948); Concerto for Bassoon and String Quartet (1949); *Vade Mecum*, for various ensembles of wind instruments (1951); Trumpet Concerto (1952); Trio, for flute, violin, and piano (1955); Five Fantasies, based on Gagaku for violin and piano (1956); Tone Poem for Brass and Percussion (1957); Rhapsody, for four French horns (1957).

BIBLIOGRAPHY: *DCM;* Howard, John Tasker, *Our Contemporary Composers* (N.Y., 1941); Reis, Claire, *Composers in America* (N.Y., 1947); *American Composers Alliance Bulletin*, vol. 7, no. 3, 1958; *Who's Who in America, 1970–71.*

Wernick, Richard Frank, b. Boston, Mass., January 16, 1934.

He won the Pulitzer Prize in music in 1977. Though in some of his later works he used electronic devices and occasionally a modified twelve-tone technique, Wernick never affiliated himself with the avante-garde movement. Using the resources of 20th-century harmonic and contrapuntal practices, and a modern concept of lyricism, he preferred working within a tonal framework and well-defined structures. His aim, as he once explained, has always been "to make sense to the ear."

His first significant experience in music came when he was eleven, hearing Bartók's Concerto for Orchestra. "It excited me so much I think I resolved right then and there to become a composer," he recalls. One year later he began piano lessons, to which he took none too enthusiastically. He began showing interest in composing music after he had begun studying theory with Henry Lasker at Newton High School in Newton, Mass. Several years later, Lasker urged him to study composition with Irving Fine. Since Fine was then on the music faculty of Brandeis University in Waltham, Mass., Wernick enrolled there in 1951 after graduating from high school. In addition to Fine, his teachers in composition at Brandeis University included Arthur Berger and Harold Shapero. Two compositions written by Wernick between 1953 and 1955 were among his first to get public performances: a String Quartet (1953), performed in Jordan Hall in Boston in March 1953, and Four Pieces, for string quartet (1955), first heard at Brandeis University in April 1955.

While attending Brandeis, Wernick spent the summers of 1954 and 1955 at the Berkshire Music Center in Tanglewood, Mass., studying composition with Aaron Copland, Ernst Toch, and Boris Blacher, and conducting with Leonard Bernstein and Seymour Lipkin. Upon graduating from Brandeis in 1955 with a bachelor of arts degree, Wernick continued studying composition on a teaching fellowship with Leon Kirchner at Mills College in Oakland, Calif. Kirchner was the first to introduce him to the atonal and twelve-tonal techniques of the Viennese school. Mills College provided Wernick with his first opportunity to develop himself as conductor with performances of music by Britten and Pergolesi. During his years at Mills, he also received hearing for two of his compositions: Divertimento, for viola, cello, clarinet, and bassoon (1956), performed by the Mills College Chamber Players in May 1956 and *From Tulips and Chimneys* (1956), a song cycle for baritone and orchestra to poems by e. e. cummings,

performed at the University of Utah in Salt Lake City in June 1956.

While at the Berkshire Music Center, Wernick met and fell in love with Beatrice Messina, a bassoon student there. They were married on July 15, 1956, and have raised three sons. After receiving his master of arts degree at Mills College in 1956, Wernick left for Winnipeg, Canada, becoming, one year later, a composer-in-residence with the Winnipeg Ballet, where he was also music director of ballet performances for a full season. For this company, on commission, he wrote two ballet scores: *The Twisted Heart* (1957), introduced on November 27, 1957, and *Fête brilliante* (1958), premiered on January 13, 1958. He combined activities with the Winnipeg Ballet with those of musical director and composer-in-residence with the Canadian Broadcasting Corporation, for whom, on commission, he wrote scores for two more ballets: *The Emperor's Nightingale* (1958; April 1958) and *Queen of Ice* (1958; May 1958).

The Wernicks left Canada in 1958 to settle in New York for the next six years. He taught composition privately and, from 1959 to 1962, at the Metropolitan Music School. He further supported himself by writing a good deal of functional music for documentary and industrial films and for television, as well as incidental music for Off-Broadway productions. His score for *Music for the Nativity: Ballet for Television* was produced over the CBS television network on January 1, 1961, choreography by John Butler.

A Ford Foundation grant in 1962 sent Wernick to Bay Shore, Long Island, where he wrote music for public schools during the next two years. Among his most important student-oriented works were *Hexagrams*, for chamber orchestra (1962; Kiamesha Lake, N.Y., December 4, 1962), and String Quartet no. 1 (1963; Bay Shore, L. I., December 5, 1963). A tape recording of this quartet was chosen by Norman Dello Joio for presentation at the annual meeting of the International Society of Music Educators in Budapest, Hungary, in August 1964.

By 1964, Wernick had come to the realization that if he was to develop himself as a composer of concert music, he would have to abandon the kind of functional assignments that had thus far occupied him. To help him in this direction, he turned to teaching music in universities as a means of livelihood. In 1964–65 he was instructor of music at the State University of New York in Buffalo, where he was called upon to serve as coordinator of the department of music and of the Center of the Creative and Performing Arts. In 1965, he was appointed instructor of music at the University of Chicago, becoming assistant professor in 1966 and, from 1965 to 1968, conducting the University of Chicago Orchestra.

Wernick looks back to *Stretti*, for clarinet, violin, viola, and guitar (1964), as his first mature work, since this was the first time he felt he had under control the techniques he had thus far learned and was able to use them to achieve his own musical identification. This work, commissioned by Sherman Friedland, clarinetist, was introduced in Buffalo, N.Y., by members of the Center of the Creative and Performing Arts at the State University on April 25, 1965, this performance repeated in New York two days later. Another work commissioned the same year (1964) was *Music for Viola d'Amore*, written for the viola virtuoso Walter Trampler, who first performed it in April 1965 in Buffalo.

Haiku of Bashō, for soprano, flute, clarinet, violin, double bass, two percussion, piano, and tape (1968), is Wernick's earliest successful work to combine electronic sounds with live instruments. The Contemporary Chamber Players of the University of Chicago gave the first performance in Chicago on March 1, 1968, repeated it in New York on March 22, and at the Ravinia Festival in Illinois on July 1.

Since 1968, Wernick has been a member of the music faculty at the University of Pennsylvania in Philadelphia. He was promoted to associate professorship in 1969, was chairman of the music department between 1969 and 1974, and became full professor in 1976. For two of those years (1968–70) he conducted the University of Pennsylvania Symphony Orchestra.

Wernick's *A Prayer for Jerusalem* (1971), for mezzo-soprano and percussion (the percussionist required to play the xylophone, vibraphone, and various antique instruments), is one of his most significant works up to this time. Its text, in Hebrew, is a setting of five verses from Psalm 122, and the musical score is based on the opening phrase of Bach's chorale, "Es ist genug." Following its first performance at the University of Pennsylvania in the spring of 1972, with Jan DeGaetani, soloist, and Matthew Hopkins, percussionist, it received in 1976 the Naumburg Recording Award. When it was performed for the first time in New York in May 1978, John Rockwell, in the *New York Times*, said it sounded "like studied Hebraic cantilena," adding: "The cold proclamations of the percussion set against the emotive passion of the singer makes for an interesting contrast."

The anguish, bitterness, and frustration attending Americans everywhere during the Vietnam War led Wernick to write a major work on commission for the Composers' Forum in Philadelphia. It was *Kaddish-Requiem, a Secular Service for the Victims of Indo-China* (1971), scored for mezzo-soprano, violin, flute, clarinet, cello, piano, two percussionists, and magnetic tape. It was first performed in the year of its composition in Philadelphia. The work is in three uninterrupted sections. In the first, a few notes from "All Flesh Is Like Grass" from Brahms's *A German Requiem* were quoted. The composer explains: "In a time when flesh and grass can be recklessly devastated by napalm and defoliants, the simplicity and beauty of the biblical image becomes tinged with a cruel and bizarre cynicism. This is reflected musical-

ly by the use of brief and disjointedly recomposed portions of the Brahms as an ironic and nagging commentary throughout the first movement." The second part is a musical collage reproducing on tape the singing of the traditional Hebrew prayer for the dead, the *Kaddish*, superimposed on the sounds of two worshipers intoning the words, and set off by two instrumental interludes based on portions of Lassus's two-voice motet *Sancti mei*. The third part is a setting for mezzo-soprano of the traditional Latin Requiem Aeternam, with instrumental interludes based on Palestrina's *Veni Spiritus*. "This is fervent music," wrote Elliott W. Galkin in the *Baltimore Sun*, "obviously deeply felt, an expression of the composer's indignant reaction to the tragedies of the Indochinese War."

Wernick composed *Songs of Remembrance*, four songs for shawm, English horn, oboe, and mezzo-soprano, in 1973–74 at the request of the singer Jan DeGaetani as a surprise birthday gift for her husband, Philip West. The shawm is the 18th-century predecessor of the oboe and was used here because West occasionally performed on it at his concerts of old music. "It struck me," Wernick explains, "that the sonority of this wonderful medieval-Renaissance instrument would fit in very well with the aesthetic of a contemporary work." All four songs were based on a single four-note motive made up of intervals of the minor second, the perfect fifth, and the minor sixth, in both ascending and descending configurations. The texts—taken from Horace, Virgil, Pythagoras, and Robert Herrick—were chosen to mourn the death from leukemia of the daughter of one of Wernick's good friends, and the work as a whole was intended, the composer says, "as a memoriam of her tragically brief life."

On a Guggenheim Fellowship in 1976, Wernick completed *Visions of Terror and Wonder*, for mezzo-soprano and orchestra, with which he won the Pulitzer Prize in music in 1977. Its text, sung in Hebrew, Arabic, and Greek, was taken from the Old and the New Testament and the Koran. *Visions of Terror and Wonder* was commissioned by the Aspen Music Festival in Colorado, and written on a grant from the National Endowment for the Arts, its world premiere taking place in Aspen on July 19, 1976, with Jan DeGaetani as vocal soloist and Richard Dufallo conducting. This work, said Joseph Horowitz in the *New York Times* when it was introduced to New York on March 18, 1979, is a "colorful evocation of the biblical Middle East. . . . There are abrupt, staccato fanfares for muted trumpets; shrill, chattering choruses for massed woodwinds; and gaudy sprays of spangles and glitter from the percussion department. The vocal line incorporates chantlike ornaments, presumably based on liturgical modes."

Since the winning of the Pulitzer Prize, Wernick's most significant compositions have been Introits and Canons, for chamber orchestra (1977; N.Y., January 13, 1978) and *A Poison Tree*, for instrumental quintet (1979; Syracuse, N.Y., January 20, 1980). The former is in a dissonant, polyphonic style within such baroque structures as the canon, chaconne and passacaglia among other forms. Scored for a chamber orchestra, a string quartet is placed on the left of the conductor, a wind quartet on his right, and the percussion instruments (played by a single performer) lined up in the back. *A Poison Tree*, using the William Blake poem of the same title, is music with sardonic overtones and occasional excursions into parody. It was written specifically for the Da Capo Chamber Players, who introduced it. When this group performed it for the first time in New York on April 28, 1980, Donal Henahan in the *New York Times* described it as follows: "Beginning with violent instrumental clashes, it moved on to a glummer section in which the soprano, Neva Pilgrim, declaimed William Blake's . . . poem about the deadly power of hate. Vaguely reminding one of Schoenberg's *Verklärte Nacht* or *Erwartung* in its confessional attitude as well as its dark texture, the Wernick piece had absorbing moments."

Wernick has made numerous appearances as a conductor. He has been musical director of the Penn Contemporary Players since 1968, was conductor of the Swarthmore College Orchestra in Pennsylvania in 1979, and in May 1979 was called upon by Eugene Ormandy to conduct the Philadelphia Orchestra in a performance of George Crumb's *Star-Child*.

THE COMPOSER SPEAKS: To live and work in a world of music is one of the great privileges that life can bestow. Music is the most profound of all the arts; it moves and elevates us as no other human endeavor can. The musical impulse—the impulse to "sing"— is common to all humanity and, although it is undoubtedly a mistake to characterize it as a "universal language," the resonances that music touch are resonances that we all share.

PRINCIPAL WORKS: 2 string quartets (1963, 1972–73).

Stretti, for clarinet, violin, viola, and guitar (1964); Music for Viola d'Amore (1964); *Lyrics from IxI*, for soprano, vibraphone, marimba, and contrabass (1966); *Haiku of Bashō*, for soprano, flute, clarinet, violin, and double bass, two percussionists, piano, and tape (1967); *Moonsongs from the Japanese*, for soprano and two prerecorded tracks of soprano voice (1972); Cadenzas and Variations II, for solo violin (1970); *Kaddish-Requiem*, for mezzo-soprano, violin, flute, clarinet, cello, piano, two percussionists, and magnetic tape (1971); *A Prayer for Jerusalem*, for mezzo-soprano and percussion (1971); Variations III, for solo cello (1972); *Songs of Remembrance*, four songs for mezzo-soprano, shawm, English horn, and oboe (1974); *Visions of Terror and Wonder*, for mezzo-soprano and orchestra (1976); *Contemplations of the Tenth Muse*, Book I, for soprano and

piano (1977); Introits and Canons, for chamber ensemble (1977); Partita, for solo violin (1978); *Contemplations of the Tenth Muse*, Book II, for soprano and piano (1978); *A Poison Tree*, for soprano and chamber ensemble (1979); *And on the Seventh Day*, a Sabbath evening service for cantor and two percussion (1980).

BIBLIOGRAPHY: *DCM; High Fidelity/Musical America*, August 1977; *New York Times*, May 8, 1977; *Who's Who in America, 1980–81*.

Whithorne, Emerson (originally **Whittern, Emerson**), b. Cleveland, Ohio, September 6, 1884; d. Lyme, Conn., March 25, 1958.

Whithorne's orchestral compositions had highly significant performances during his lifetime. His works embraced a wide gamut of styles. He was one of America's earliest composers to simulate machine sounds. Some of his compositions were inspired by oriental subjects and texts and were stylistically modeled after oriental music. Still others were stimulated by American scenes and backgrounds, occasionally using American Negro or jazz rhythms. Though he long favored programmatic writing, for which he demonstrated a particular flair, his later works were mostly absolute music.

He retained the name with which he was born (Whittern) until 1918, when he legally adopted and permanently retained the original family name of his paternal grandfather. His given name was derived from Ralph Waldo Emerson, a distant relative. Emerson Whithorne was of Dutch-English and Scottish-Irish descent. One of his ancestors was Thomas Whythorne, the 16th-century English composer of vocal music.

Whithorne's introduction to music came at the home of his paternal grandmother where three of his granduncles gathered regularly to perform chamber music. When he was ten, Whithorne expressed an interest in learning to play an instrument. Since his father frowned upon music as a career, he objected to formal lessons for his son. But, encouraged by his mother, Whithorne took piano lessons secretly with James H. Rogers and did his practicing away from home. Rogers was eventually able to convince Whithorne's father that the boy had talent and should be allowed to pursue a musical career without interference. When Whithorne was fifteen, he initiated his professional career by appearing for two seasons as concert pianist at the Ohio Chautaugua summer circuit.

On Rogers's urging, Whithorne went to Vienna in 1904, continuing there his music study with Leschetizky (piano) and Robert Fuchs (theory and composition). Between 1905 and 1907 he studied piano further with Artur Schnabel.

In 1907, Whithorne married Ethel Leginska, then a young pianist, later to become celebrated both as pianist and conductor. They made their home in London. For two years Whithorne was his wife's impresario for her concerts in Germany. In London, Whithorne also became active as the music critic of *Pall Mall Gazette* and as a teacher of piano and theory. At the same time he did considerable research in Chinese and Japanese music at the British Museum.

He began attracting interest as composer in London through his incidental music for Lawrence Irving's successful production in London of *Typhoon*, and by providing English dance music for the Shakespeare Ball organized by Lady Randolph Churchill for the Shakespeare Memorial Theatre Fund. At the same time he was writing his first concert works. The *Gate of Memory*, for piano (1908), was a set of musical impressions of pictures by Dante Gabriel Rossetti. Whithorne's first work for orchestra was *The Rain* (1912), in which the oriental pentatonic scale was used to simulate the sounds of falling raindrops; it received its premiere performance on February 22, 1913, in Detroit. *Greek Impressions*, for string quartet (1914), used authentic Greek melodies. *On a Lute of Jade* (c. 1914) was a cycle of songs using translations from the Chinese as text for music that was Chinese oriented.

Whithorne and Ethel Leginska separated in 1912. (Divorce followed four years later.) In 1915, Whithorne returned to the United States, settling in St. Louis, where for five years he was editor of the Art Publication Society of St. Louis. In 1920, he came to New York. For two years he was vice-president of Composers' Music Corporation devoted to the publication of music by young composers. From 1922 on, he devoted himself exclusively to composition.

One of his first pieces written in New York was also one of the earliest examples of machine music. It was a work for piano entitled *The Aeroplane* (1920), which he orchestrated in 1925. The orchestral version received its first hearing in Birmingham, England, on January 30, 1926, with Adrian Boult conducting the Birmingham City Orchestra.

Success came with *New York Days and Nights*, a programmatic and often realistic suite descriptive of the sights, sounds, and experiences of the great metropolis. The titles of its respective movements provided a clue to their programmatic intent: "On the Ferry," "Chimes of St. Patrick's," "Pell Street," "A Greenwich Village Tragedy," and "Times Square." The sounds of horns and whistles and the rhythm of a ferry in motion were recreated in the first movement. In the second, the bells of St. Patrick's chime the strains of the Dies Irae. The third is highlighted by a piquant Chinese tune and the fiddling of an aged Chinaman. The fourth is a somber picture of "a strange region of highly dramatized lives, of mockery and jest . . . [where] an episode becomes an epic [and] from a trysting burgeons a tragedy." The finale, through jazz idioms and sprightly syncopations, evokes the bustle, noise, and colors of the Great White Way. *New York Days and Nights* was first written as a piano suite in 1922, when it was successfully performed and promoted by various concert pianists, including E. Robert Schmitz. On August 5, 1923, this piano suite represented the United States at the first Festival of the International Society for Contemporary Music, in Salzburg, Austria, performed by the composer. Whithorne orchestrated it in 1923. A partial performance of the orchestral suite (the second, third, and fifth movements) was heard in Paris on June 24, 1923, and the entire work was introduced on July 30, 1926, at the Sesquicentennial International Exposition, performed by the Philadelphia Orchestra conducted by Alexander Smallens. After that, numerous American orchestras programmed it, and it was further heard extensively in motion picture theaters and in special arrangement for jazz band.

The eclecticism Whithorne had already revealed was further developed in his most important works, all in the 1920s and 1930s. *Saturday's Child* (1926), "an episode in color," was a cycle of songs for mezzo-soprano, tenor, and small orchestra using as text poems from Countee Cullen's *Color*. Its first performance took place in New York on March 13, 1926, at a concert of the League of Composers, and then was heard sixteen times within the next year and a half. In this work, and in a second song cycle to Cullen's poems—*The Grim Troubadour*, for baritone and piano (1927)—Whithorne's writing was influenced by Negro spirituals. "The poetry is the authentic outpouring of the Negro," wrote John Tasker Howard in his brochure on Whithorne, "somewhat on the defensive, and yet taking pride in his color. In setting them, Whithorne has reflected the racial traditions, the love of the dance, the intense rhythmic feeling of the black man." In his incidental music to *Marco Millions*, first produced on January 9, 1928, on Broadway, Whithorne reverted to the oriental style of earlier compositions. In several concert works from which all ethnic or racial leanings are absent, he produced music that was romantic and atmospheric, thoroughly modern in harmonic, rhythmic, and polytonal language. *Poem*, for piano and orchestra (1926), was premiered by Walter Gieseking and the Chicago Symphony under Frederick Stock on February 4, 1927. In the *New York Sun*, W. J. Henderson regarded it as "a work of vigor and fine logical development." *Fata Morgana* (1927) and *The Dream Pedlar* (1930) were atmospheric tone poems, the first premiered by the New York Philharmonic on October 11, 1928, and the second by the Los Angeles Philharmonic under Artur Rodzinski on January 15, 1931. In the *Christian Science Monitor*, Winthrop P. Tryson said of *Fata Morgana*: "Here is a rich blending and careful balancing of sonorities. Here is tone-painting of high color and at the same time of skillful draftsmanship. Here is perspective, and here is light and shade. Here, too, is modern feeling." The Violin Concerto (1928–31) received its first hearing in Chicago with Jacques Gordon, soloist, and the Chicago Symphony directed by Stock, on November 19, 1932.

Some of Whithorne's works were evocative of American landscapes and backgrounds. *Moon Trail*, which had originated as a piece for the piano in 1930, was orchestrated in 1933; the orchestral version was heard for the first time on December 15, 1933, with Serge Koussevitzky conducting the Boston Symphony. *El Camino Real*, a suite for piano (1937), was a picture of the old California mission, San Juan Capistrano. *Sierra Morena* (1938), a tone poem inspired by Spanish bandits hiding in the mountains of Sierra Morena, was first performed on May 7, 1938, over the NBC radio network with Pierre Monteux conducting. Two symphonies, however, were devoid of any programmatic implications. Both were introduced by the Cincinnati Symphony under Eugene Goossens: the first (1929) on January 12, 1934, and the second (1937) on March 19, 1937, with the Second Symphony receiving the Juilliard Foundation Publication Award. W. J. Henderson's description in the *Sun* of another of Whithorne's compositions applied equally to the two symphonies. "There is a general leaning toward modernity, a determined shattering of the long melodic line, an intermixture of persistently chromatic modulations, jarring rhythms, and sometimes stealing the characteristic syncopations of ragtime and many passages in which sheer ugliness seems to have been and certainly has been attained."

In 1932, Whithorne married his second wife, the former Jane Reynolds. Whithorne was an active member of the board of directors of the League of Composers in New York.

THE COMPOSER SPEAKS: I believe our music of the 20th-century has dealt too much with mutable things as opposed to eternal things. We have put too much faith in intelligence alone, mistaking cerebral commotion for inspiration. The intellect has its important functions, but for creation is required plus intellect, will or choice, direct perception or intuition and spirit—that which resides in the most sacred precincts of the unconscious. It is for us to keep contact with life, drawing from it all that is useful to us, and yet in solitude to plumb deep into that vital essence we call our soul. Thus shall great music be made by music makers.

PRINCIPAL WORKS: 2 symphonies (1929, 1937).

The Rain, for orchestra (1912); *Greek Impressions*, for string quartet (1914); *To a Lute of Jade*, song cycle for voice and piano (c. 1914); *Adventures of a Samurai*, suite for orchestra (1919); *New York Days and Nights*, for orchestra, originally for piano (1922–23); *Sooner or Later*, ballet (1925); Piano Quintet (1926); *The Aeroplane*, for orchestra, originally for piano (1925); *Saturday's Child*, song cycle for mezzo-soprano and small orchestra (1926);

Poem, for piano and orchestra (1926); *The Grim Troubadour*, song cycle for baritone and piano (1927); *Fata Morgana*, tone poem for orchestra (1927); String Quartet (1930); *The Dream Pedlar*, tone poem for orchestra (1930); Violin Concerto (1928–31); *Fandango*, for orchestra (1931); *Moon Trail*, tone poem for orchestra (1933); *El Camino Real*, suite for piano (1937); *Sierra Morena*, tone poem for orchestra (1938); *Stroller's Serenade*, for string orchestra (1944).

BIBLIOGRAPHY: Ewen, David, *American Composers Today* (N.Y., 1949); Howard, John Tasker, *Emerson Whithorne* (N.Y., 1929); Reis, Claire, *Composers in America* (N.Y., 1947); *Modern Music*, January–February 1931; *Who's Who in America, 1956–57*.

Wolpe, Stefan, b. Berlin, Germany, August 25, 1902; d. New York City, April 4, 1972. American citizen, 1944.

It is not easy to put Wolpe's music in a convenient pigeonhole. He had a lifetime fascination for jazz and ragtime—and in the 1920s he aligned himself with the artistic cults of *Zeitkunst* (contemporary art) and *Gebrauchsmusik* (functional music) in Berlin—but he was in no sense a popularist. During his stay in Palestine, his music became involved with the ethnic idioms of Yemenite, Arab, and Palestinian music, but he was not a nationalist composer. The twelve-tone system was all-important in his creative development, yet he was never a confirmed dodecaphonist; his serialism, when used, was freely contrived to include small groups of pitches instead of a complete twelve-tone row. His most important music was a compromise between triadic tonality and atonality, with triadic and nontriadic chords moving to distant relationships in a process Wolpe referred to as "decomposition of tonality." He favored complex contrapuntal and at times linear textures, asymmetrical rhythms, dissonant harmonies, and the principles of variation. For all its complexity and density, his music was arresting for its expressive lyricism, dramatic power, infectious moods, and poetic feelings.

His father was Russian and his mother Hungarian; neither of them was musical; both tended to discourage Stefan's preoccupation with music since they hoped he would become a businessman. His academic education took place between 1908 and 1919 in grade schools in Berlin and at the Mommsen Gymnasium, from which he graduated in 1919.

He early revealed his interest in music, following instruction in piano and theory when he was fifteen, and from the first what attracted him most were new sounds and rhythms. As he recalled in an interview with Joan Peyser in the *New York Times*: "For my *bar mitzvah* in Berlin, I received an electrical toy, a miniature motor that could accelerate the speed of my other toys. The ability to change tempi interested me intellectually. I experimented with my fists on the piano, doing to Chopin and Bach what the motor did to my railroad train and car."

By the time he was fifteen, he had composed a complete opera, an octet for wind, and numerous piano pieces, all this with no formal instruction. Not until he became a pupil of Alfred Richter's in 1916 did he receive formal lessons in counterpoint. "The sounds he recommended I found boring and stupid. Finally, he threw me out. This made my father feel righteous."

During 1918–19, Wolpe left home to join up with a group of young painters, writers, and philosophers then wandering about Germany. He supported himself by working as an errand boy, gardener, and at several other occupations. All this while he continued composing music wherever he could find a resting place: in railway stations, on streets, under stairways. Between 1919 and 1924 he formalized his music study through attendance at the Academy of Music in Berlin. There he studied composition with Otto Taubman, Paul Juon, and Franz Schreker. Private study of composition with Ferruccio Busoni, begun in 1920, pleased him more. "For the first time I found someone adequate to myself." In 1920, he also initiated a five-year period of study with Hermann Scherchen, who thought highly enough of some of Wolpe's juvenilia to get them published in the journal *Melos*.

But these early works did not please Wolpe. When he was twenty-one he destroyed everything he had thus far composed in order to start his composing career anew. He now assumed the harmonically dissonant, linear, and occasionally atonal style then in favor among young progressive composers in Europe. Among his earliest works in this advanced idiom were Duo, for two violins (1923); Andante in C minor, for piano (1924); *Five Hölderlin Songs*, for contralto and piano (1924); and Piano Trio (1924). During these years he undertook a comprehensive study of musical analysis by himself, at which time the music of Arnold Schoenberg began to make a deep impression on him.

As a radical socialist, Wolpe wrote music for some of Bertolt Brecht's socially and politically oriented plays. Wolpe's social consciousness made him aware of folk and popular idioms and, as he said, "of the gap between music as an artistic language and the music of the people." Thus he became involved with *Zeitkunst*, that cult in Berlin in the late 1920s and early 1930s which treated timely, popular subjects in an easily assimilable style slanted for popular consumption. In such a vein Wolpe wrote two operas: *Schöne Geschichten* (1927–29), a group of farcical sketches for actors, singers, chorus, and jazz orchestra, and *Zeus und Elida* (1928), in a jazz idiom. At the same time, Wolpe affiliated himself with organizations promoting functional music *(Gebrauchsmusik)* by writing simple pieces for school choruses and amateurs, background music for films, incidental

music for the theater and popular-styled songs and hymns that had wide circulation. Functional, too, were *The Passion of Man* (1930), text by Ludwig Benn, for tenor alto, chorus, and orchestra; *On the Education of Man* (1931) to his own text, for chorus and orchestra; and March and Variations, for two pianos (1932–33). The last of these was heard at a concert of the League of Composers in New York in 1940. "In these works," Wolpe explained, "I was able to adhere to my own standards of composition, at the same time infusing into my works the warmth and dignity of a people's music."

In 1933, with the rise of nazism in Germany, Wolpe visited Vienna to study composition with Anton Webern. Under the influence of his dodecaphonic style, Wolpe produced Five Pieces for Orchestra (1934) and *Four Studies on Basic Rows*, for piano (1935–36). "This," he said, "matured me for a return to atonal music, a form of expression which had always corresponded to the innermost demands of my nature." Hitler's rise to power in Germany made Wolpe *persona non grata* in the Third Reich, first because he was a Jew, then because of his pronounced leftist political leanings and finally because of his collaboration with the "degenerate" Bertolt Brecht. Wolpe's return to Germany was not to be contemplated. After brief visits to the Soviet Union and Rumania, he came to Palestine in 1934, where he stayed for four years, was head of the composition department and taught theory at the Jerusalem Conservatory. "There my innate love for folk music was revived. Oriental music with all its unique characteristics attracted me very much. I undertook to interpret the folklore of Palestine and to write songs to texts by Bialek, the Bible, as well as many choral and chamber works." He made an intensive study of Arabic, Yemenite and other Palestinian folk music, much of which he arranged for voice and piano, some of whose materials he incorporated into his compositions. But in addition to works derived from folk sources he also produced distinctive chamber music with no ethnic affiliation in which he continued developing an atonal style. These included Concerto for Eight Instruments (1936–37) and Sonata for Oboe and Piano (1938).

Wolpe came to the United States in 1938 to make it his new and permanent home. In some of his works of his early American years he continued to develop the ethnic idioms he had evolved in Palestine, including an important score for a ballet in 1942, *Man from Midian*, commissioned by the dancer Eugene Loring, scenario based on the story of Moses. He was also revealing new approaches, beginning with *Unnamed Lands*, a cantata for chorus and orchestra (1940), using poems by Walt Whitman as text. Here he worked with the seven tones of the diatonic scale which he would use in some of his subsequent compositions. "This work," Wolpe explained, "marked the use of all possible kinds of homogeneous chord structures as well as the use of heterogeneous chord structures." Another new feature in *Unnamed Lands* was the organization of "the musical space in a different way," Wolpe said. "This technique led to the divisions and subdivisions of this space, the total result being a new interconnection of sound layers, a new fluidity in the way these structures flow in space. New principles of thematic evolution came into being. Thematic contents were unfolded in a continuous variation. This work is marked by a constant resurgence of thematic material through a chain of developments on ever-changing levels, comparable to a thematic spiral."

Between 1943 and 1945, Wolpe completed several songs dealing with social problems. "In these works," he informed us, "I aimed to achieve simplicity and directness in the expression of the chromatic material I have been using for years." Other compositions of this period were less concerned with elementary approaches than with dramatic expressiveness and subtlety of thought. *Encouragements* was a series of piano pieces written between 1943 and 1947 seeking to express the pathos, heroism, and chaos attending the years of World War II. To his Quartet, for saxophone, trumpet, percussion, and piano (1950), Wolpe carried his love for jazz idioms, though complexly structured. Later concert works were extremely complicated and dense in structure and idiom, chromatically conceived along serial lines. The difficulties they posed both for the players and audiences discouraged performances. When Leonard Bernstein saw the manuscript of the Symphony no. 1 (1955–56)—a commission from Rodgers and Hammerstein through the League of Composers–International Society of Contemporary Music—he was sufficiently impressed to schedule its premiere for a New York Philharmonic concert. But he advised the composer to rewrite it in more practical terms. When the work was finally performed (January 16, 1964) Bernstein assigned the baton to Stefan Bauer-Mengelberg since Bauer-Mengelberg was a mathematician as well as musician and for this reason Bernstein felt he was better equipped to cope with the symphony's intricacies. (Even so, only two-thirds of the symphony was given, since the entire work could not be prepared properly in time.) Wolpe described this music as "a structured field of pitches, the various tones standing in relation to one another that the composer views as an analogue to those of physical bodies in a force field. The successive elaborations of the material result when these relations of the tones are in some way disturbed and at times restored. . . . There are treatments of complexity and of simplicity, of tension and of calm, of animation and of ebbing activity." In his review in the *New York Times*, Harold C. Schonberg wrote: "Complex and difficult the work certainly is. Mr. Wolpe . . . has composed a serial work for full orchestra that goes far beyond anything the Viennese dodecaphonists have attempted. The two movements . . . are tremendously dense examples of to-

tal musical organization, fragmented in texture, void of melody (at least in the accepted sense), completely dissonant, composed so the entire work is derived from the twelve notes of the initial row. . . . Whether or not the ear can take in the multiple relationships of the musical organizations—probably no ear can; the eye is needed to see the actual writing—it was apparent that Mr. Wolpe was completely in charge of his materials."

Between 1946 and 1948 Wolpe taught composition at the Settlement School in Philadelphia. He then became professor of composition at the Contemporary Music School in New York (1948–52), the Philadelphia Academy of Music (1949–52), and Black Mountain College in North Carolina (1952–56). Between 1957 and 1968 he headed the music department at C. W. Post College in Long Island, N.Y.

In 1964 Wolpe was stricken with Parkinson's disease, which in time immobilized him, making such physical movements as talking, writing, and even reading difficult. Despite his infirmity, he continued to teach both privately and at C. W. Post College, where he was named adjunct professor in 1968, and at the David Mannes College of Music, to which he was appointed in 1968. He was able to attend a concert of his works at Columbia University on February 16, 1972, receiving an ovation from his many pupils and admirers. Another commemorative concert was planned to honor his seventieth birthday but he did not live to attend it. It took place in New York in April 1972 as a "memorial concert" covering thirty years of his creativity from the Oboe Sonata of 1938 to the String Quartet of 1969. "While each composition contains the composer's customary energetic vitality and sharply chiseled rhetoric," wrote Peter G. Davis in the *New York Times*, "the Quartet and the Violin Sonata (1949) are deeply impressive for their expressive eloquence and passionate stylistic purity."

Despite the infrequency with which his works were given major presentations through the years, Wolpe did not lack recognition from prestigious organizations. He was given awards from the American Academy of Arts and Letters (1949), the Rothschild Foundation (1953), the Fromm Music Foundation (1960), the Thorne Music Fund (1965, 1966, 1967, 1968), and the Brandeis University Creative Arts Award (1966). He was the recipient of fellowships from the Fulbright Foundation (1956) and the Guggenheim Foundation (1962). The New York Music Critics Circle presented him with a citation (1963), and he was given the Koussevitzky International Recording Award (1970). The New England Conservatory in Boston awarded him an honorary doctorate. Wolpe was a member of the American Academy of Arts and Letters and the National Institute of Arts and Letters.

He was married three times: to Olga Okuniewska, a painter, in July 1927 (with whom he had a daughter, Katharina, who became a concert pianist); to Irma Schoenberg, a Rumanian pianist, in April 1934; and to Hilda Morley, a poetess, in December 1948.

THE COMPOSER SPEAKS: In that universe of organic possibilities there are no codes of selection, not even preferences. Observe the patterns of intentional order. Is one better than another? Also observe the combined patterns of intentional and nonintentional order. Can one say one is better than the other?

Who is going to rule over the sequences of a hundred released simultaneities? . . . How serious must be the intersecting passages when each of the goals is an honest and exposed one! There is a formal pathos in an ashtray, on an old wall, on a cluttered table, in the junk store, on a beach with stones, and shells, and the foot writing in the sand, and the theater of shifting positions of bathers, and the motions of waves, and the deadened meaning of interchasing voices, and pieces of cheese and the newspaper flying off, and an observer shaking off the pains of change, and the hetero-coincidences of the guideless, total-proportional world.

But what offering of profusions, recessions, interception, interstices, intermixtures, interpositions, inter—in—inter—out— ex—off! What sequences of fleeting fields, of intervals of haps-happenings! which all render the total scope within the total field. And each of the single happenings has each digested the total field, and comprehends its own singular totality of aspects.

The supreme eye, the supreme ear grasps the whole! The singular situation, supporting the never-vanishing axes of the whole, is alien to itself, yet, inside the whole, its identity is deeply proven and vivified. It is the unfolding of adjacent opposites. A world where all the aspects are available to themselves in any given stretch of a continuum of time or in its instant conversion into the all-inclusive moment.

PRINCIPAL WORKS: 2 string quartets, an early one discarded (1926, 1969); 2 chamber pieces, for fourteen players (1964, 1965-66); 2 pieces, for solo violin (1964, 1966).

Piano Sonata (1924); *Hölderlin Lieder*, for contralto and piano (1924; revised 1935); Piano Trio (1925); Clarinet Sonata (1925); *Schöne Geschichten*, opera for actors, singers, marionettes, chorus, and chamber orchestra (1927-29); Music for Flute, Viola, and Cello (1927); *Zeus und Elida*, one-act burlesque for five voices and instruments (1928); Five Characteristic Marches, for piano (1929-34); *The Passion of Man*, cantata, for tenor, contralto, chorus, and orchestra (1930); *On the Education of Man*, cantata, for chorus and orchestra (1931); March and Variations, for two pianos (1932-33); Five Pieces, for orchestra (1934); Three Pieces, for chorus (1934); *Four Studies in Basic Rows*, for piano

(1935-36); *Two Palestinian Songs*, for contralto and piano (1936); Duo, for oboe and clarinet (1936); Concerto, for eight instruments (1936-37); Passacaglia, for orchestra (1937); *Two Ancient Chinese Epitaphs*, for chorus and drums (1937); *Ten Songs from the Hebrew*, for voice and piano (1938); Oboe Sonata (1938); Dances, for orchestra (1938); *Zemach Suite*, for piano (1939); *Unnamed Lands*, cantata, for chorus and orchestra (1940); Toccata, for piano (1941); Sonata in One Movement, for violin and piano (1941); *Man from Midian*, ballet (1942); *Encouragements*, for piano (1943-47); Clarinet Quartet (1944); Trio, for clarinet, violin, and cello (1945); Two Studies, for piano (1948); Violin Sonata (1949); Quartet, for trumpet, tenor saxophone, percussion, and piano (1950); *Enchantments*, for piano (1950-53); Seven Pieces, for three pianos (1950-51); Oboe Quartet (1955); Symphony (1955-56, revised 1964); Quintet, for clarinet, horn, cello, harp, and piano, with voice (1956-57); Piece in Two Parts, for flute and piano (1969); *For Piano and Sixteen Players* (1960-61); *Street Music*, for baritone, oboe, clarinet, cello, and piano (1963-68); Cantata, for voices and instruments (1963-68); Trio, for flute, cello, and piano (1964); Solo Piece, for trumpet (1966); String Quartet (1969); Concerto for Bass Clarinet and Piano (1968-69); *Broken Sequences*, for piano (1969); *From Here on Farther*, for clarinet, bass clarinet, violin, and piano (1969); Concerto for Trumpet and Chamber Ensemble (1969); *Form*, for piano (1969).

BIBLIOGRAPHY: *NGDMM*; Ewen, David, *American Composers Today* (N.Y., 1949); Machlis, Joseph, *Introduction to Contemporary Music*, revised ed. (N.Y., 1979); Sucoff, Herbert, "Catalogue and Evaluation of the Works of Stefan Wolpe" (master's thesis, Queens, N.Y., 1969); *The Listener* (London, September 1968); *Modern Music*, Winter 1946; *New Republic*, January 6, 1941; *New York Times*, April 4, 1972 (obituary).

Wuorinen, Charles, b. New York City, June 9, 1938.

Wuorinen received the Pulitzer Prize in music in 1970. He is a serialist composer, though he has modified and expanded that vocabulary by adopting individual practices. He has also successfully incorporated electronic sounds into major works.

His parents were of Finnish descent; his father, Charles Peter Wuorinen, was a professor of history and later chairman of the history department at Columbia University in New York. Without having received any music lessons, Wuorinen made his first attempts at composition when he was five. While attending Trinity School in New York for his academic education, he continued to compose. He now received some piano lessons from local teachers, then training in composition from Jack Beeson and Vladimir Ussachevsky. When he was fifteen, Wuorinen received the Young Composers Award from the New York Philharmonic. Between 1953 and 1956 he produced a repertoire of music for the piano and chamber ensembles together with his first two works for orchestra, *Into the Organ Pipes and Steeples* and Music for Orchestra, both completed in 1956.

Upon his graduation from Trinity School in 1956, Wuorinen was enrolled in Columbia University. There, while pursuing an academic course, the study of composition was continued with Otto Luening. Wuorinen supported himself through college by working as a piano accompanist and recording engineer, by singing countertenor parts in church choirs, and by earning the Alice M. Ditson Fellowship (1959) and the Arthur Rose Fellowship (1960). He spent four consecutive summers during his undergraduate years at the Bennington Composers Conference in Vermont on scholarships. His output of compositions during these years was prolific, including a Piano Sonata (1959), three symphonies (1958, 1959, 1959), three *concertante* (one for violin and orchestra in 1958; another for harpsichord, oboe, violin, viola, and cello in 1959; and a third for oboe, violin, and piano, also in 1959). All this music was influenced by Stravinsky and Varèse. It generated momentum and explosive power contained and controlled within original structures. Rhythmic dynamism and the use of fragmentary motives were strongly evident, and occasionally his writing was atonal. When the Piano Sonata no. 1 and the *Triptych*, for violin, viola, piano, and percussion (1957)—the latter calling on the pianist to play on the strings of his instrument with mallets—were heard at a concert of the Composers' Forum in New York in April 1961, Allen Hughes reported in the *New York Times*: "The two works heard . . . were imaginatively and skillfully wrought. He is an atonalist who manages to keep his music buoyant and who has an ear for interesting timbres." Wuorinen's compositional talent was recognized at Columbia when he was awarded the Bearns Prize in 1958, 1959, and 1961. Additionally, he was the recipient of the Broadcast Music Inc. (BMI), Student Composition Award in 1959 and 1961 (and again in 1962 and 1963) and the Lili Boulanger Memorial Award in 1961 and again in 1962.

In 1961, Wuorinen received his bachelor of arts degree at Columbia together with membership in Phi Beta Kappa. Two years later, he acquired his master of arts degree at Columbia on a Regents College Teaching Fellowship. He joined the music faculty of Columbia University in 1964 as lecturer and instructor, becoming assistant professor a decade and a half later. In addition to his teaching assignments at Columbia, he conducted the Group for Contemporary Music, which he had founded with Harvey Sollberger in 1962, probably the first campus ensemble in the United States devoted to new music and works of young, unknown composers.

In his music in the early 1960s, Wuorinen began to incorporate extensions and expansions of the twelve-tone system as Milton Babbitt had articulated and developed it on the foundation of the Schoenberg twelve-tone practice. Wuorinen's Trio no. 2, for flute, cello, and piano (1962), Piano Variations (1963), Flute Variations I (1964), and Chamber Concerto, for flute and ten players (1964)—the last commissioned by the Fromm Music Foundation for a festival of new music at Tanglewood in Massachusetts—were all significant steps in his early development as a serialist. The Chamber Concerto, following its performance by the Group for Contemporary Music at Columbia University in November 1975, drew the following comment from Theodore Strongin in the *New York Times*: "The work showed that in the hands of a strong-minded individual, post-Webern serialism is a language not a fashion. Mr. Wuorinen uses the language carefully, but with great force."

Interested in electronic music by Ussachevsky, Wuorinen used it for the fist time in *Consort from Instruments and Voices*, for magnetic tape in 1961. *Orchestral and Electronic Exchanges* (1965) combined the orchestra with magnetic tape. It received its world premiere at the French-American Festival of the New York Philharmonic on July 30, 1965, in New York, Lukas Foss conducting. Writing in the *New York World Telegram and Sun*, Robert Jacobson said: "Charles Wuorinen provided a study in sonic limits, in tension and release. . . . Both orchestra and tape use the twelve-tone scale, with the tape often sounding very instrumental. This is a fascinating sound experience."

In Duo for Violin and Piano (1966–67), Wuorinen applied the principle of correlating pitch and time relations known as the "time point system." Wuorinen explains: "The time point system is a direct expression in temporal terms of the relationships that generate the twleve-tone system. Like the twelve-tone pitch system, it is enormously broad in scope and implication." This system is found in many of Wuorinen's works of this period.

In 1967, Wuorinen received an award from the American Academy of Arts and Letters, in 1968 a Guggenheim Fellowship, and in 1969 the Ingram Merrill Fellowship. One of his most important electronic compositions was completed in 1969: *Time's Encomium* (1969), for synthesized sound and processed synthesized sound. He wrote it on commission from Nonesuch Records, after working for a year at the Columbia-Princeton Electronic Music Center in New York with the RCA Mark II Synthesizer. In *Time's Encomium* the sounds of traditional instruments were simulated together with those only a Synthesizer could produce. "Metaphorically," the composer said, "the listener stands in the midst of this synthesized music, which presents itself to him with maximal clarity, and stretching away from him, becoming more and more blurred in detail, through various transformations, from the slightly altered to the unrecognizable." In his review of the recording, Alfred J. Frankenstein called it "a wonderful work. . . . My own reaction to it is that it is a genuinely mighty score, full of new worlds and galaxies of sound, magnificent in its size, its spacious implication, and the grandeur of its form." *Time's Encomium* was awarded the Pulitzer Prize in music in 1970 (the first time the award was given to a composition written expressly for a recording). Subsequently, Wuorinen rewrote this composition for orchestra.

In 1970, Wuorinen was presented with the Creative Arts Award Citation in music from Brandeis University in Waltham, Mass. In 1971, because he had been denied tenure and because Columbia University had decided to withdraw its support from the Group for Contemporary Music, Wuorinen resigned angrily from the university faculty. He now joined the Manhattan School of Music. Both before and after 1971 he made numerous appearances both as lecturer and visiting composer-in-residence in numerous American colleges and universities, including Princeton University (1967–68), the New England Conservatory in Boston (1968–69), University of Iowa in Iowa City (1970), and the University of Southern Florida (1971).

If, as professor, he felt rejected by Columbia University, he did not lack recognition elsewhere. The Guggenheim Foundation presented him with a second fellowship in 1972, and the Phoebe Ketchum Thorne Foundation with an honorary award in 1973. In 1978 he received the Creative Artists Public Service Award and the Arts and Letters Award of Finlandia Foundation. Paterson State College in Wayne, N.J., awarded him an honorary doctorate in music.

Wuorinen has remained highly prolific since 1970, and he has lacked neither significant performances nor accolades from critics. When his String Quartet no. 1 (1971) was performed in New York by the Fine Arts Quartet (which had commissioned it) in the winter of 1973, Irving Kolodin noted in *Saturday Review/World* that this was "another work of quality. . . . Its special characteristic is that the participants are not so much performers as they are protagonists. It projects a musical dramaturgy. . . . He loves sonority, esteems dynamic contrasts as a means of capturing the attention of the listeners, recognizes that tonal drama must partake of emotion shared as well as expectations aroused." *Speculum Speculi*, for flute, oboe, bass clarinet, contrabass, piano, and percussion (1972), which the Naumburg Foundation had commissioned for the Speculum Musicae ensemble, was introduced in New York by that group on February 21, 1973. In the *New York Times*, Allen Hughes found it to be "full of energy. . . . Its jots and jolts of woodwind color and drum beats, melodic fragments, contrasts of register and many other elements come together in a vivid musical fabric that insists, quite successfully, on

the integrity of its form and the importance of its existence."

Two significant concertos made effective use of electronic amplification for their respective solo instruments. *Concerto for Amplified Violin and Orchestra* (1972), a commission from the Fromm Music Foundation for a festival of contemporary music at Tanglewood, received its world premiere August 4, 1972, at a concert of the Boston Symphony under Michael Tilson Thomas with Paul Zukofsky, soloist. "The solo violin amplification," explained Michael Steinberg in the *Boston Globe*, "involves a few special effects such as shuddery electronic reverberations around a pizzicato, but mostly it is simply functional, meant to let the solo carry one voice in the polyphonic web of Wuorinen's buoyantly violent discourse." The Piano Concerto no. 2, for amplified piano and orchestra (a Baldwin ED-1 Concert Electropiano was used) was composed in 1973 on a grant from the National Endowment for the Arts and was introduced by the composer and the New York Philharmonic under Erich Leinsdorf on December 6, 1974. In a single movement, this concerto placed the full burden of its musical message on the piano rather than have the orchestra share prominently in the proceedings; the orchestra was used basically only as a doubling, a reflection and variation of the soloist's music. Antiphonal writing was used extensively, transmitted through loudspeakers on the stage and in the auditorium. This work is written entirely in $\frac{4}{4}$ time without a single change of meter, its expanse including a wide variety of tempos as well as frequent *accelerandi* and *ritardari*. A twelve-tone set (three diminished seventh chords) which underlies the entire work never appears explicitly but rather serves in various ways to control the large unfolding and indirectly to produce the notes.

By the middle 1970s, Wuorinen considerably expanded his vocabulary through modifications of the twelve-tone technique. He put it this way: "For the previous fifteen years or so I had used a composition method that resulted in a certain predictable sound. . . . My approach to composition now became somewhat more intuitive. The music ideas are as highly organized as they ever were. However, my use of twelve-tone sets is more a matter of dividing them into segments and using them as content groups. . . . I don't find it as necessary to justify verbally every note in its relationship to the rational framework." Since this is what Stravinsky tried to do in his last works, Wuorinen (commissioned jointly by Buffalo Philharmonic and the Ojai Festival in California) paid tribute and expressed his indebtedness to that master by writing a fifteen-minute orchestral work, *A Reliquary for Igor Stravinsky* (1975). Mme. Stravinsky gave Wuorinen the last, unfinished fragments on which Stravinsky had been working at the time of his death: some charts and a half dozen extremely brief sketches ranging in length from one measure to two lines. Wuorinen used this for his basic material, combining it with his own music composed with the Stravinsky series and in his spirit. *A Reliquary for Igor Stravinsky* is in three large parts. The first five minutes is in the Stravinsky manner; the second is a variation on the first in the Wuorinen manner, interrupted by an independent lament by the violin over tolling chords in piano, harp, and chimes; the third is a reprise of the Stravinsky material ending with a coda recalling the manner in which Stravinsky closed such works as the *Symphony of Psalms, Appolon Musagètes, Orpheus,* and *Requiem Canticles.* "Taken as a whole," remarked Joseph Horowitz in the *New York Times,* "*A Reliquary* has a tragic commemorative cast that is most impressive." The world premiere took place at the Ojai Festival on May 30, 1975.

The W. of Babylon (1975) was Wuorinen's first opera—or, as the composer preferred to designate it, a "baroque burlesque." (His only earlier stage work was a masque, *The Politics of Harmony,* in 1967). Renaud Charles Bruce's text, set in 17th-century France, was, as the composer informs us, a "risqué (not to say indecent) set of sexual permutations involving personages of the lesser French and Italian nobility, about 1685." The central characters are a lascivious marquise and her lecherous club-foot cousin; a Chinese princess; four homosexuals and a pretty boy; and the Spirit of Moral Sensibility, a speaking role, who, at the end of the opera, descends from the roof of a half shell to denounce the participants. "It is lewd in every syllable," the composer says further. "It has, however, naturally redeeming social value: it touches briefly upon youth, age, love, hate, despair, hope, resignation, reconciliation, and other minor themes of human concern." In his through-composed music there are allusions, references, implications, and imitations (though no actual quotes) of older operatic practices of Mozart, Purcell, Verdi, and Wagner. But this is no collage of styles, nor is it in any way a parody. This opera was given its first hearing through the presentation of some of its scenes by the Group of Contemporary Music in New York on December 15, 1975.

Tashi Concerto, in five movements, exists in two versions. In 1975, Wuorinen wrote it as chamber music work for clarinet, violin, cello, and piano, intending it for the chamber music ensemble calling itself Tashi. In this form it was conceived to display the virtuosity of Tashi, who presented the world premiere in New York on February 18, 1976. A version for the same four instruments and orchestra was prepared by the composer in 1976 and introduced by the Cleveland Orchestra with the Tashi group as soloists on October 13, 1976, the composer conducting. Describing the orchestral version, the composer says: "The first, third, and last movements are for soli with orchestra and constitute slices of a single continuity; the second and fourth movements are interludes for the soloists alone. . . . Although the exter-

nal or large shape of the piece is made in the usual way, and though the notes still are formed out of materials of the twelve-tone system, the immediate foreground, the gestural shapes, the lines and colors of the work are intuitive responses to the boundaries set in the large by the overall form of the work, and in the small by the growth and flowering of notes from twelve-tone roots." In her review in the *Cleveland Plain Dealer,* Wilma Salisbury described this music as erupting "in violent outbursts of sonic energy. The thorny . . . work shoots out in jagged lines, dense textures, sharp accents and loud dynamics. Brilliantly organized within a tight rhythmic structure the dramatic music assaults the ear drums, tenses the nerves and ties the stomach in knots."

A grant from the National Endowment for the Arts in 1976 led to the writing of Wuorinen's most expansive and ambitious work for percussion, the *Percussion Symphony,* completed in 1976 for the New Jersey Percussion Ensemble, who introduced it in Somerville, N. J., in January 1978 and then recorded it. Calling for twenty-four percussion players, "its scope and intent are symphonic," the composer says, "a large-scale single structure spanning the three movements. . . . Between adjacent main movements are 'entr'actes' which are two different transcriptions (different in tempo, instrumentation and 'key') of the chanson 'Vergine bella' by Guillaume Dufay. These light-textured interludes afford a contrast to the massive main movements and—though not directly related musically to the chief substances of the work—still share certain melodic characteristics, especially with the last movement." In a review of the recording, a critic for the *American Record Guide* said: "This is music in the typical Wuorinen manner: tough, uncompromising, intellectual, distant. Even so, it is music which grows on you with repeated hearings. The first time through, all is chaotic. The second time, things begin to fall in place. And the third time it really comes alive. . . . The variety and clarity of sound are enchanting. Particularly effective are the endings to all three movements where the continuity increases and really striking conclusions are achieved."

A symphony of far different character is the *Two-Part Symphony* (1978), once again in the neo-Stravinsky style of *A Reliquary for Igor Stravinsky.* This work represented the United States at the International Rostrum of Composers/UNESCO meetings in Paris in 1980, following its premiere on December 11, 1978, in New York by the American Composers Orchestra conducted by Dennis Russell Davies.

THE COMPOSER SPEAKS: It is my absolute conviction that the vast bulk of hostility to new music would pass if genuinely representative performances of the works were available to those listeners who are now averse. And, given adequate time for preparation, the sometimes opposition of orchestral players to the confidence-destroying rupture of their regular routine by the introduction of the musically unfamiliar would also inevitably be diminished. . . .

We must once more firmly assert the difference between art and entertainment, a reassertion made mandatory in the face of present tendencies to deny the effort to draw real pleasure from works of art, to say that the casual popular and the serious artistic are the same, to refuse a hierarchy of values, to equalize, to homogenize, to relevantize. Entertainment entertains because it requires nothing from the receiver. Art is itself because it demands an active relation with him who perceives it. He cannot just "appreciate" it; he must himself create the work's meaning.

PRINCIPAL WORKS: 4 *concertante*, for various solo instruments and orchestra (1957–59); 3 piano trios, for flute, cello, and piano (1961, 1962, 1972); 3 symphonies (1958, 1959, 1959); 2 piano concertos (1966, 1973); 2 string quartets (1971, 1979); 2 piano sonatas (1969, 1976); 2 sets of cello variations (1970, 1975); 2 sets of flute variations (1963, 1968).

Triptych, for violin, viola, and percussion (1957); *Alternating Currents*, for chamber orchestra (1957); *Dr. Faustus Lights the Lights*, for narrator and instruments (1957); Three Pieces, for string quartet (1958); *Spectrum*, for violin, brass quintet, and piano (1958); *Trio concertante* (1959); *Musica Duarum Partium Ecclesiastica*, for brass quintet, piano, organ, and timpani (1959); Flute Sonata (1960); *Madrigale spirituale*, for tenor, baritone, two oboes, two violins, cello, and contrabass (1960); *Turetzky Pieces*, for flute, clarinet, and contrabass (1960); *Concertone*, for brass quintet and orchestra (1960); *Symphonia Sacra*, for tenor, baritone, bass, two oboes, two violins, contrabass, and organ (1961); *Consort from Instruments and Voices*, for magnetic tape (1961); *Tiento sobre Cabezon*, for seven instruments (1961); *Evolutio Transcripta*, for orchestra (1961); Octet, for flute, clarinet, horn, trombone, violin, cello, contrabass, and piano (1962); *The Prayer of Jonah*, for voices and string quintet (1962); Chamber Concerto, for cello and ten players (1963); Piano Variations (1963); Composition, for violin and ten instruments (1964); Chamber Concerto, for flute and ten players (1964); *Super Salutem,* for male voices and instruments (1964); *Orchestral and Electronic Exchanges*, for orchestra and tape (1965); *Janissary Music*, for percussion (1966); *Harpsichord Divisions*, for harpsichord (1966); *John Bull: Salve Regina Versus Septem,* for chamber ensemble (1966); Duo for Violin and Piano (1966–67); *The Politics of Harmony*, masque (1967); String Trio (1968); *Contrafactum*, for orchestra (1969); *Time's Encomium*, for synthesized sound and processed synthesized sound, also for orchestra (1969); *Ringing Changes*, for percussion ensemble (1970); Chamber Concerto, for tuba, twelve winds, and twelve drums (1970); *A

Message to Denmark Hill, for baritone, flute, cello, and piano (1970); *A Song to the Lute in Musicke*, for soprano and piano (1970); Canzona, for twelve instruments (1971); *Grand Bamboula*, for string orchestra (1971); Harp Variations, for harp, violin, viola, and cello (1972); Bassoon Variations, for bassoon, harp, and timpani (1972); Violin Variations (1972); *On Alligators*, for eight instruments (1972); *Speculum Speculi*, for flute, oboe, bass clarinet, contrabass, piano, and percussion (1972); *Concerto for Amplified Violin and Orchestra* (1972); *Grand Union*, for cello and drums (1973); *Arabia Felix*, for flute, bassoon, violin, electric guitar, vibraphone, and piano (1973); *Mannheim, 87.87.87*, for unison chorus and organ (1973); *An Anthem for Epiphany*, for chorus, organ, and trumpet (1974); Fantasia, for violin and piano (1974); *A Reliquary for Igor Stravinsky*, for orchestra (1975); *Tashi*, for clarinet, violin, cello, and piano; also for clarinet, violin, cello, piano and orchestra (1975); *The W. of Babylon*, opera (1975); *Hyperion*, for twelve instruments (1976); *Percussion Symphony*, for twenty-four players (1976); *The Winds*, for eight wind instruments (1977); *Fast Fantasy*, for solo cello (1977); *Archangel*, for bass trombone and string quartet (1977); Six Songs, for two voices, violin, and piano (1977); Wind Quintet (1977); Six Pieces, for violin and piano (1977); *Ancestors*, for chamber ensemble (1978); *Two-Part Symphony*, for orchestra (1978); *Joan's*, for chamber ensemble (1980); *"ng. c,"* for orchestra (1980); *The Celestial Sphere*, sacred oratorio for chorus and orchestra (1980); *Archaeopteryx*, for bass trombone (1980).

BIBLIOGRAPHY: Machlis, Joseph, *Introduction to Contemporary Music*, revised ed. (N.Y., 1979); Thomson, Virgil, *American Music Since 1910* (N.Y., 1970); BMI, *The Many Worlds of Music*, Winter 1976; *Esquire*, July 1972; *High Fidelity/Musical America*, September 1970; *New York Times*, June 7, 1970, August 8, 1971, February 13, 1977.

Wykes, Robert Arthur, b. Aliquippa, Pa., May 19, 1926.

Wykes has avoided using rubrics or labels to identify his music. In general, he has sought clarity of voices and mood and a precision in notation that provides the performer with all the information he needs before his eyes. Wykes's early style was basically lyric in intent, consonant and tonal. After some percussively aggressive works in the 1960s, he has returned to a basically lyric metaphor.

Though no one in his family was musical, Robert Wykes began revealing intense responses to music when he was about six. His earliest sources of music stimulation came from hearing the choir in church, the choral singing in public school, and a variety of compositions over radio and on the home player piano. He started studying flute when he was nine with A. D. Davenport as part of the public school music program in Aliquippa. Within a year, Wykes was playing the flute in the senior high school band and orchestra conducted by Davenport. Wykes continued studying flute with Davenport up to the time he entered the Saturday Morning Music Classes of the Carnegie Institute in Pittsburgh (now Carnegie-Mellon University) in 1942, where, for two years, he took private lessons in flute with Victor Saudek. Wykes also received instruction in harmony from Davenport (1941) and piano from Ruth Ault (1942). Between 1943 and 1944 he studied jazz arrangements with Max Adkins and piano with Homer Oxenhirt.

In 1943, Wykes won the Pittsburgh Young Artists Contest, which entitled him to appear as piano soloist with the Pittsburgh Little Symphony in a performance of a Mozart concerto. In January 1944 he entered the Eastman School of Music in Rochester, N.Y., under a wartime accelerated plan allowing him a high school diploma after completing one semester of the bachelor of music program. During this period he remained at the Eastman School just three months since, in July 1944, during World War II, he was drafted into the army. As a member of the 421st Combat Infantry Regiment he saw action overseas until the end of the European phase of operations. When combat ended in Europe, and while still in uniform, he played in and made arrangements for the 314th Armed Service Bands, and in September 1943 he entered the so-called G.I. Universities, assigned to Biarritz, France, where he studied composition with Cecil Effinger.

He was back at the Eastman School in the fall of 1946, studying composition with Burrill Phillips and Wayne Barlow, orchestration with Bernard Rogers, theory and harmony with Donald White, and flute with John Thomas. The summer of 1946 was spent at the Colorado College in Colorado Springs in the renewal of composition study with Effinger and with lessons in conducting from Nicolas Slonimsky. Wykes received his bachelor of music degree (with honors) and master of music degree in June and August of 1949 respectively.

On February 12, 1949, in Rochester, Wykes married Rosalyn Faye Koplowitz, then a voice student at the Eastman School. While later developing herself as a singer and promoting a professional career, she helped raise three children.

Wykes first emerged as a mature composer in 1949 with Divertimento, for small orchestra, which the St. Louis Symphony under Leigh Gerdine introduced in the fall of 1955. This was followed by Concert Overture, for orchestra (1951), premiered in Austin, Tex., on March 23, 1953, at the Southwestern Symposium of Contemporary Music, and *The Prankster* (1951), a chamber opera for soprano, baritone, and piano to his own libretto, introduced in

Bowling Green, Ohio, on January 12, 1952. These compositions were tonal, with a strong emphasis on lyricism.

Between 1950 and 1952, Wykes played flute with the Toledo Symphony in Ohio and was a member of the music faculty at Bowling Green State University in Bowling Green, Ohio. From 1952 to 1955 he was on the music faculty of the University of Illinois in Urbana. There he continued to study composition with Burrill Phillips together with musicology with John Ward and the Heinrich Schenker method of musical analysis with Hubert Kessler. In 1955, Wykes earned his doctor of musical arts degree at the university. Since 1955 he has been on the music faculty at Washington University in St. Louis, where, in 1965, he was elevated to full professorship. Between 1963 and 1967 he was flutist with the St. Louis Symphony, and from 1966 to 1969 with the Studio for New Music in St. Louis.

A number of commissions, beginning with two in 1959, led to the writing of several compositions responsible for drawing increased attention to his music. *Density* III (1959), commissioned by Washington University, was first performed on January 8, 1960, by the St. Louis Symphony, Leigh Gerdine conducting; it became a United States entry in music at the Biennale in Paris in 1961. For the Washington University Band, Wykes wrote Concertino for Piano and Chamber Orchestra (1959), the first performance taking place in St. Louis in Spring 1959. Commissioned by the Paderewski Foundation of Boston, Wykes completed Piano Quintet in 1961, its premiere given in St. Louis on May 18, 1961. For New Music Circle of St. Louis he wrote in 1961 the Suite, for soprano and three woodwinds, to a poem by Lloyd Frankenburg consisting of a vocalise, interlude, song, interlude, and vocalise; the first performance was heard in St. Louis in April 1961. Concertino for Flute, Oboe, Piano, and Strings (1963; Detroit, April 1963) was commissioned by the Detroit Little Symphony, and *Wave Forms and Pulses,* for orchestra (1964; University City, Mo., May 2, 1964), by the University City Symphony. Eleazar de Carvalho, conductor of the St. Louis Symphony, commissioned *The Shape of Time,* for orchestra (1965; St. Louis, April 2, 1965), and *Letter to an Alto Man,* for chorus and orchestra, to a poem by Donald Finkel (1967; St. Louis, May 19, 1967).

Many of the works Wykes wrote after 1965 have for their central theme the metaphor of a conflict between (or contrasts of) static, unchanging sounds, some of which have surface motion but no movement, and sounds which do move (modulate). "These contrasts exist in nature," he says, "which I dearly love, and in human life, which I also love dearly." Using this metaphor are such compositions as the already mentioned *The Shape of Time* and *Letter to an Alto Man,* together with *Density* IV, for solo harp (1969; St. Louis, January 1969); Fantasy, for solo flute (1970; Washington, D.C., August 1970); *Excerpen-*

dium, for brass and voices (1970; Honolulu, July 15, 1970); and *Toward Time's Receding,* for orchestra (1972). The last of these was commissioned in 1972 by the Mark Twain Bancshares, Inc., and its world premiere was given by the St. Louis Symphony under Walter Susskind on April 7, 1972. In the score, the title is hand-lettered, and the letters of the first word become progressively larger while those of the last diminish in size. "The semantic and graphic content of this title explain the macro form of the work exactly," the composer says. "Three parts (words) resulting from two pauses (spaces) in the ongoing flow of sound. A very simple form. . . . In Part I, musical events move towards a central moment. In Part II (time measured by a regular pulse) these events continue and then begin to recede (Part III) into silence." When the Philadelphia Orchestra, under Leonard Slatkin, performed this composition in Philadelphia on April 2, 1976, James Felt said in the *Evening Bulletin* that it "uses the full modern orchestra expressively with many haunting lyrical passages and outbursts of fluid rhythm, fascinating in itself. One felt structure under the silvery incense showered by the piano and high-pitched percussion, including two glockenspiels and vibraphone."

Structurally, Wykes's most ambitious composition is the oratorio, *The Adequate Earth* (1976), for two male narrators, baritone, three choruses, and orchestra, written on a grant from the National Endowment for the Arts on a commission from the St. Louis Symphony. This is a sixty-six-minute setting of poems by Donald Finkel about Antarctica, which the poet had visited as a guest of a scientific expedition. "The prominence that Wykes assigns to Finkel's verses," explains Frank Peters in the *St. Louis Post-Dispatch,* "is made clear in many ways. . . . The concert piece revolves around . . . the poem so attentively that it appears more a musical paragon than an oratorio. Finkel used a collage system, embodying numerous quotations from explorers' journals and other Antarctic documents in his poem. This effect of voices heard from here and there, then and now, moved Wykes towards his elaborate distribution of vocal parts among right, left, and middle choruses and three soloists. Fidelity to the flow of speech likewise led him to lay out a rhythmic structure of great complexity. There are frequently changes of meter from measure to measure, cross rhythms within measures where voices overlap, and an avoidance of distinct beats or pulses at almost every point. Tempo changes are fairly frequent and Wykes adjusts tempos within phrases by offbeat rhythmic groupings, e.g., three quarter notes in the first half of a four-four bar. There are very few measures without a vocalization of the text in some form, and hardly any place where the orchestra overrides the text with a big statement of its own."

The world premiere took place in St. Louis on February 5, 1976, with the poet and William Warfield as narrators, Samuel Timberlake, baritone, and

the St. Louis Symphony and Washington University Choruses conducted by Gerhardt Zimmerman. "Wykes' musical treatment . . . was ingenious, propulsive, finely crafted and free of posturing," wrote Frank Peters in the *St. Louis Post-Dispatch.* "The work was the most talked about piece of new music to be done in St. Louis for at least a decade. It brought out literary and visual-art types who don't usually attend concerts. Without administering musical shocks (Wykes' style was quiet, reflecting the sombre, spacious character of the poem, and conservative, by avant-garde standards). *Adequate Earth* stirred interest, debate, feelings of frustration, disappointment and approval, in contrast with the polite indifference that usually greets new music performances."

On a commission from the St. Louis Symphony for its bicentennial season, Wykes composed the four-movement *A Lyric Symphony* in 1980, its world premiere given under Leonard Slatkin's direction on May 10, 1980. Whereas Wykes's works since 1965 generally used melodies almost as incidental "objects" within a musical environment, *A Lyric Symphony* concentrated its prime interest on its lyric content. The melodic materials, the composer explains, were "present each in its own due time and place, and then developed before being heard a final time. Thus on the most grand level of form there are four movements each with its one set of tunes." The only pause in the work comes between the second and third movements. In his review in the *St. Louis Globe Democrat,* James Wierzbieki said: "It states its terms directly at the outset . . . and then . . . builds a well-balanced structure on what is essentially a very simple melodic idea. It's much like the classical music of the late 18th century in that, although it's filled with pleasant little surprises, the expectations it stirs up are almost always fulfilled. *A Lyric Symphony* was one of five compositions performed by the Curtis Symphony Orchestra under Lukas Foss on September 28, 1980, at the Kennedy Center in Washington, D.C., in a program comprising those major orchestral works by Americans that had been selected as nominees for the third annual Friedheim Award at Kennedy Center.

Wykes has provided the music for some highly significant documentary films. *Children Without* was nominated for an Oscar by the Academy of Motion Picture Arts and Sciences in 1964. *Monument to the Dream* was featured at the Venice Film Festival in 1968. *Robert Kennedy Remembered* won Oscar and Cindy awards in 1969. *A Special Kind of Morning* was nominated for an Emmy by the National Academy of Television Arts and Sciences. The San Francisco International Film Festival Prize for the best entry in its catagory, together with the Christopher Award of the Columbia Festival, came to *The Journey of Lyndon Johnson,* a film prepared in 1974 for the Johnson Library in Austin, Tex.; the Cine (Council on International Non-Theatrical Events)

Golden Eagle and the Silver Plaque of the Chicago Film Festival were awarded to *The Eye of Jefferson,* produced for the National Gallery of Art in Washington, D.C., in 1977; and the Cine Golden Eagle Award was given to *John F. Kennedy: 1917–1963,* filmed in 1979 for the Kennedy Library in Boston. Additionally, he composed incidental music for Tennessee Williams's *Eccentricities of a Nightingale,* a score commissioned by the Loretto-Hilton Repertory Theater in St. Louis for its production in April 1977, and fourteen songs for Addie Walsh's adaptation of Mark Twain's *The Prince and the Pauper,* mounted in St. Louis in June 1980.

THE COMPOSER SPEAKS: However much the surface characteristics of my music might change, its substance has been and will remain my subjective, nonverbal thoughts about sound, silence, and a myriad of personal experiences wrestled into an objective, self-sufficient work—a composition. This process of making my subjective thoughts into a verifiable object is the means by which I can best understand music, which remains for me one of humankind's most enchanting mysteries. A life's time seems to me not too long to spend at such an endeavor.

PRINCIPAL WORKS: Divertimento, for small orchestra (1949); Concert Overture, for orchestra (1951); *The Prankster,* chamber opera for soprano, baritone and piano (1951); *Dance Overture,* for orchestra (1955); Flute Sonata (1955); Concerto for Eleven Instruments (1956); *Four American Indian Lyrics,* for chorus (1957); String Sextet (1958); Piano Quintet (1959); *Density* III, for orchestra (1960); Suite, for soprano and three woodwinds (1961); *Points and Excursions,* for brass quintet (1962); Concertino for flute, oboe, piano and strings (1963); *Horizons,* for orchestra (1964); *Wave Forms and Pulses,* for orchestra (1964); *The Shape of Time,* for orchestra (1965); *Letter to an Alto Man,* for chorus and orchestra (1967); *Cheirality,* for string quartet (1970); *Excerpendium,* for voices and brass (1970); Fantasy, for solo flute (1970); *Resonances,* for orchestra (1971); *Toward Time's Receding,* for orchestra (1972); *A Shadow of Silence,* for a cappella chorus (1973); Fantasy no. 2, for piano (1974); A Choral Fantasy, for female voices (1976); *Adequate Earth,* oratorio for two male narrators, baritone, three choruses, and orchestra (1976); *A Lyric Symphony* (1980).

BIBLIOGRAPHY: *BBDM*; Anderson, E. Ruth, *Contemporary American Composers* (Boston, 1976); *St. Louis Post-Dispatch,* February 1, 1976.

Y

Yardumian, Richard, b. Philadelphia, Pa., April 5, 1917.

Yardumian's music is written in an original tonal idiom with a unique twelve-tone organization which has evolved from early impressionistic influences through a period of basically homophonic free chromaticism. Since 1954 it has been fused with techniques of medieval and Renaissance modality and baroque polyphony. The later works, as well as some of the earlier ones, are characterized by the use of Armenian folk and liturgical melodies and Catholic liturgical chants. His commitment to his religious beliefs has strongly influenced both the content of his works and his approach to composition and its function in society.

Yardumian is the youngest of ten children of Armenian parents. His father, Rev. Haig Yardumian, escaped to Bulgaria during the persecution of Armenians with a price on his head; in 1906 he brought his family to America. His mother, Lucia (Atmian) Yardumian, was a teacher and an amateur organist. Richard Yardumian's academic education took place in Philadelphia's public schools, at the William Cullen Bryant Grammar School (1923–31) and West Philadelphia High School (1931–35). Though he received no formal instruction in music until his early twenties, his fascination for it reached back to childhood, to the Armenian folk songs his parents sang. Western music was also a significant part of his early experiences. From time to time, students of Curtis Institute—colleagues of his brother, Elijah, who studied piano there with Isabelle Vengerova and Josef Hofmann—would give informal concerts at the Yardumian home. But the most significant impact came from hearing his brother practicing and playing the classics. "When I was eleven," Yardumian recalls, "I took on myself to imitate my brother at the piano when he was away from the house, and succeeded for many years in concealing what I was doing. Somehow I managed some of the Beethoven sonatas and those Bach preludes that did not have too many formidable polyphonic stumbling blocks." Thus he first learned to play piano without receiving lessons. When he was fourteen, he began composing piano pieces of his own, still without benefit of any instruction. The "Lullaby" in his later *Armenian Suite* was composed at that time. "Though many handicaps developed by those years of secret self-study," he says, "so did valuable self-reliance." When he was nineteen, Yardumian wrote *Sea* (1936), a prelude for piano, which he played for José Iturbi. By good chance, Leopold Stokowski overheard this performance. Both men encouraged Yardumian to continue with his self-study. He did this at the Free Library in Philadelphia, where he listened to recordings with score in hand, copied out scores, and studied theoretical texts. During this period of intense self-study he composed his first work for orchestra—six of the seven movements of *Armenian Suite* (1936–37), based on authentic Armenian folk songs he had learned in his early years. The seventh-movement finale was added seventeen years later (1954), and the Philadelphia Orchestra under Eugene Ormandy introduced the complete suite on March 5, 1954. After its premiere, the work was widely performed elsewhere, including the use of one of its themes as signature music by the Voice of America for its news broadcasts behind the iron curtain.

On January 9, 1937, Yardumian married Ruth Elsie Seckleman, who had worked with Leopold Stokowski since 1932 to promote his new concept of Youth Concerts. The Yardumians raised a family of thirteen children. From 1939 to 1961 Yardumian earned his living teaching piano privately at his home in Bryn Athyn, Pa. In 1937 he became a member of The Lord's New Church (a Swedenborgian church in Bryn Athyn), which strongly influenced his life and thought and to which he has devoted much of his time. Since 1939 he has been musical director of the church and member of the church board of directors; was secretary from 1940 to 1957; and from 1957 to 1980 was president of its board of directors.

Finally, at twenty-two, Yardumian began some formal music studies. During the years of 1939 to 1942 he studied harmony with W. F. Happich, counterpoint with H. Alexander Matthews, and piano with George F. Boyle. In 1947 he studied conducting with Pierre Monteux, who was influential in Yardumian's movement toward polyphonic composition. After that, Yardumian intensified his research in the ancient and medieval modal systems and polyphonic techniques.

During World War II, Yardumian served in the U.S. Army, received his training at Camp Wheeler, Ga., and was later stationed in Manila in the Philippines. Before entering the army he completed *Desolate City,* for orchestra (1943–44), which consists of two sections, "Desolation" and "Renaissance." The first section, bearing the collective title of *Desolate*

City, was premiered by the Philadelphia Orchestra under Eugene Ormandy on April 6, 1945, while Yardumian was stationed at Camp Wheeler. Though dedicated to "the Desolate Cities of the War," this piece was intended not as an atmospheric portrait of a war-ravaged city but, as the composer explained, was "directed more specifically to the inner life of each man, not necessarily as to what he does, but as to why he does what he does." "Renaissance," the second movement, was given its world premiere in November 1976 with Louis Vyner conducting the Lancaster Symphony in Pennsylvania.

This first performance in 1945 was the beginning of an association between Yardumian and the Philadelphia Orchestra and Eugene Ormandy which had a far-reaching impact both on his creative growth and on his developing recognition. The Philadelphia Orchestra and Eugene Ormandy presented ten Yardumian world premieres, nearly one hundred performances of his various works, and four Columbia recordings. Yardumian enjoyed the status of composer-laureate with that orchestra from 1949 to 1964, with the privilege of associating with Ormandy and the orchestra during rehearsals, recording sessions, and concerts, and acting as consultant in various capacities, including preparations for transcontinental and international tours.

From Yardumian's works of the late 1940s, the Philadelphia Orchestra under Ormandy gave initial hearings to Psalm 130, for tenor and orchestra (1947; April 15, 1955), and two movements from the Violin Concerto (1949; March 30, 1951). In the Psalm, the composer sought to create the musical portrait of two worlds: the spiritual or eternal and the natural or temporal, and the open communication between them. An introductory section sets the scene as a night in ancient Israel, where the psalmist David sings in his tent. The main section of the movement consists largely of a statement and development of two main themes: the rising euphonium solo, which represents man ascending to God, and the following outburst of the trumpets, representing the spirit of God descending to man. A return to the introductory material initiates the closing section, with variations and development of the opening vocal solo.

The two movements of the Violin Concerto took shape while Yardumian was touring Holland by car in August 1948 and were completed several months later. Anshel Brusilow, violinist, was the soloist for the premiere performance. When, some years later, Yardumian revised the concerto, he added a third-movement Allegro, the new version receiving its initial hearing on November 11, 1960, with Brusilow again as soloist. The composer's original twelve-note concept is used in this concerto. His system is not related to the Viennese twelve-tone row, and it is ultimately tonal. Rather, the twelve-tone structures are built of thirds on alternating white and black keys of the piano. This principle provides the basis for melodic and harmonic material used in freely conceived traditional forms.

After completion of this concerto, Yardumian's music evolved toward a union between 16th-century modal techniques and his 20th-century twelve-note concept. In *Cantus Animae et Cordis* he became thoroughly polyphonic and consistently modal. This work originated in 1954, as a string quartet on a commission from the Stringart Quartet, which introduced it in Philadelphia on April 3, 1955. At Ormandy's suggestion, Yardumian rescored it for string orchestra during the summer of 1955, its premiere given by the Philadelphia Orchestra under Ormandy on February 17, 1956. Inspired by passages in the writings of Emanuel Swedenborg on the spiritual conflict of good and evil and the regeneration of man, this work is based on two main themes as settings of "Eli, Eli, Lama Sabachtani" (Psalm 22:1).

Yardumian once again reached to his concept of modal writing as applied to structures of the baroque era in Passacaglia, Recitatives and Fugue (1957), a concerto for piano and orchestra in three movements. It was commissioned for the piano virtuoso Rudolf Firkusny, who was the soloist when the Philadelphia Orchestra under Ormandy gave it its first hearing on January 3, 1958, and has been recorded in three separate albums by three different virtuosos.

In 1957 Edward F. Benjamin commissioned Yardumian to write a composition for his "Quiet Music" project. Between January and March 1958, Yardumian completed *Choral Prelude: "Veni, Sancte Spiritus."* The Philadelphia Orchestra under Ormandy first presented it on April 13, 1959, and then recorded it.

As his concept of his twelve-note technique developed further, Yardumian composed two symphonies. Symphony no. 1 was commissioned by Eugene Ormandy. Its first movement and a small section of the third were written in 1950. The second movement, in a style combining medieval modes with his twelve-note cycle, and a complete reworking of the third movement followed eleven years later. The entire work was first heard on December 1, 1961, with Ormandy conducting the Philadelphia Orchestra. Inspired by the biblical story of Noah and the Great Flood, the symphony bore the following titles for its three movements: "Legend," "Aria," and "March." The composer's aim was not to produce program music, but to have the music make the listener become part of the drama. The symphony opens with a "Creation" motif in solo horn. Most of the first and third movements is built from one or another form of this motif, either as a major theme or as an architectural detail.

The Old Testament also serves as a source for Symphony no. 2, *Psalms,* for middle voice and orchestra, of which the Philadelphia Orchestra under Ormandy, with Lili Chookasian as vocal soloist, gave the first hearing on November 13, 1964. The first movement is the Psalm 130, for orchestra, which the composer had written in 1947. The second movement was added in 1964, consisting of a prelude and a fugue based on lines from Psalms 95, 27, 24, together with the entire Psalm 121. An original theme and a quotation of a chorale tune are introduced in the prelude. These become the main themes of the fugue and are treated along with their countersubjects much in the manner of the last of the fugues in Bach's *The Art of the Fugue.*

Other organizations besides the Philadelphia Orchestra have featured premieres of later Yardumian works. The Mass, *Come, Creator Spirit,* for middle voice, two choruses, and chamber orchestra (1966)—based on the familiar Gregorian chant *Veni, Creator Spiritus*—was commissioned by Fordham University to commemorate its 125th anniversary and was premiered at the Lincoln Center for the Performing Arts in New York on March 31, 1967, with Anshel Brusilow conducting the Chamber Symphony of Philadelphia. The oratorio *The Story of Abraham* (1970–73), a commission of the Maryville College in Maryville, Tenn., for its sesquicentennial, is a mixed-media work with text from Genesis 12–15, calling for vocal soloists, chorus, and orchestra. André Girard's original hand-painted 70mm film depicting the story is projected synchronously throughout the performance. The world premiere was given by the London Symphony, Elyakum Shapiro conducting, at the English Bach Festival in London on May 4, 1972. The American premiere was given in Maryville, Tenn., on May 18, 1972, by the Dallas Symphony under Anshel Brusilow.

Two Chorale Preludes for orchestra (*Jesu, meine Freude* and *Nun komm der heiden Heiland*), written in 1976 for organ but orchestrated two years later, received their premiere on March 29, 1979, by the Denver Symphony under Brian Priestman. A third prelude, *Ee Kerezman* ("Resurrection"), originating as an organ piece in 1976 and orchestrated in 1979, was first performed as an orchestral work on April 27, 1980, by the Michigan Chamber Orchestra in Detroit, Mich., with Andrew Massey conducting.

In commenting on Yardumian's music, the musicologist Hans Moldenhauer described it as "a true reflection of the composer's spiritual and emotional temperament, tending toward contemplation and meditation. . . . Long sections of Yardumian's music are pervaded by mysticism and religious fervor. . . . Yardumian's handling of tonal and formal idioms and techniques . . . is always filtered through, and tempered by, an abiding sense for that which is lasting, a clairvoyance for the timeless and, therefore, a reverence for that which has endured through the ages."

In 1975, Yardumian received the Lancaster (Pa.) Symphonic Award, and in 1976 the Gold Medal

Award from the Armenian Bicentennial Commemoration Committee. He was awarded an honorary doctorate of sacred music by Maryville College (1972) and an honorary doctorate in music from Widener College in Chester, Pa. (1978). He has served as a member of the board of directors of the Philadelphia Chamber Orchestra, which he helped found in 1965, trustee of the Philharmonia Orchestra in Philadelphia, and vice-president of the Grand Teton Symphony Music Festival, as well as being the cofounder of the Chamber Symphony of Philadelphia (1967).

THE COMPOSER SPEAKS: To whom does the contemporary composer address himself when he goes to put his notes on score paper? And from out of what? Does he direct his mind out to professionals? To his peers? To critics? To prevailing traditions of the time? Or does he look up to something higher—inward—deeper, but in common with the audience, something worth singing about: community, country, church, God, any high objective or aspiration that the composer has in common with the audience?

A higher objective helps put the ego in its proper place. I am not saying suffocate or kill the ego. Just don't let it dominate the scene! To put it another way: self-assurance comes from having things in their right order; to put in the first place the common aspirations or higher objectives that a composer has with the audience, and in second place the hope that he is thought well of by them as well as by the professionals.

PRINCIPAL WORKS: 3 symphonies (1950–61, 1947–64, 1981).

Armenian Suite, for orchestra (1937–54); Symphonic Suite, for orchestra (1939); *Three Pictographs,* for orchestra (1941); *Desolate City,* for orchestra (1943–44); Psalm 130, for solo voice and orchestra, also the first movement of Symphony no. 2 (1947); Violin Concerto (1949–60); *Cantus Animae et Cordis,* for string quartet, also for string orchestra (1954–55); Passacaglia, Recitatives, and Fugue, piano concerto (1957); *Chorale-Prelude: Veni, Sancte Spiritus,* for orchestra (1958); Mass, *Come, Creator Spirit,* for contralto, two choruses, and chamber orchestra (1966); *The Story of Abraham,* oratorio for solo voices, chorus, and orchestra with film (1970–73); Two Chorale Preludes, for organ, also orchestra (1978); *Poem: To Mary in Heaven,* for voice and orchestra (1978); *Ee Kerezman,* choral prelude, for organ, also chamber orchestra (1979).

BIBLIOGRAPHY: *BBDM*; Anderson, Ruth E., *Contemporary American Composers* (Boston, 1976); *Who's Who in America, 1980–81.*

Z

Zador, Eugene, b. Bátaszék, Hungary, November 5, 1894; d. Hollywood, Calif., April 4, 1977. American citizen, 1944.

From his beginnings and up to his last works, Zador adhered to his own artistic credo of writing only that music that moved him personally, using only those techniques which he had mastered early in his career and which best served his messages. He never submitted to styles or idioms in fashion, had no interest in any of the advanced innovations in vogue. Consequently, he was sometimes regarded as an "old-fashioned composer," and if by "old-fashioned" we mean a respect for solidity and clarity of architectonic structure, total mastery of harmonic and contrapuntal resources, inordinate skill in instrumentation and a high degree of expressivity, then he was certainly that. Some of his best-known compositions were molded after idioms and the spirit of Hungarian gypsy folk tunes, but most others lack Hungarian identity and are notable either for their vivid atmospheric and pictorial writing or, at other times, for their gaiety and wit.

He was the seventh of eight children, his father a schoolteacher in Bátaszék, and some years later owner of a small leather factory. When Eugene Zador was six, the family moved to the town of Pec, where his piano lessons were initiated. Before long he was composing piano pieces influenced by Schumann. Later on, in Budapest, he heard a composition by Richard Strauss for the first time. "I came under his spell," he recalled.

He received his academic education in public schools in Pec, but his mind seemed to be on music all the time. "One day, my French teacher saw that I was composing in class and, being a kind and sympathetic man, he stopped teaching until I finished the piece." In Pec, Zador began studying composition with the head of the local conservatory under whose supervision he kept producing music.

In 1911, Zador came to Vienna for further study of composition. There he studied for two years with Richard Heuberger. Then he was Max Reger's composition pupil in Leipzig. "Heuberger," Zador later said, "was a mediocre composer but a good teacher; Reger was a mediocre teacher but a good composer." In Leipzig, Zador also took courses in musicology with Hermann Abert and Arnold Schering. In 1921, Zador completed his study of musicology with Fritz Volbach at the University of Münster, earning his Ph.D. after submitting a dissertation on the development of the tone poem from Liszt to Richard Strauss. During these years, Zador wrote music reviews for a Hungarian paper in Pec. In 1918, he completed writing his first mature work for orchestra, *Bánk Bán*, a tone poem over which hovered the shadow of Richard Strauss, and which received its first performance one year later in Budapest. *Variations on a Hungarian Folksong*, Zador's first successful composition to derive its stylistic identity from Hungarian folk music, was premiered on February 9, 1927, in Vienna.

Between 1922 and 1928, Zador was a member of the music faculty at the Vienna Conservatory. He wrote his first symphony, the *Romantic*, in 1922, and two operas between 1923 and 1928: *Diana* and *The Isle of the Dead*, both produced by the Budapest Royal Opera, the former on December 22, 1923, and the latter on March 29, 1928.

In 1928, Zador left the conservatory to devote himself completely to composition, while still maintaining residence in Vienna. That year he completed writing a new opera, *The Inspector General*, libretto by the composer based on Gogol's comedy satirizing the corruption of middle-class Russian officialdom in the 19th century. This opera had to wait more than forty-three years to get performed. When it was finally produced (in an English translation by George Mead) in Los Angeles on June 11, 1971, it was warmly received for its rich lyricism gently touched with a Slavic brush, and for Zador's flair for portraying not only characterization but also comic and tragicomic situations in music and his uncommon gift for colorful orchestration.

If the acceptance of *The Inspector General* was belated, that of two orchestral works between 1933 and 1934 was immediate and remained permanent. Rondo (1933) was acclaimed when it was first performed in Vienna in 1934 by the Vienna Symphony conducted by Kurt Pahlen. After that, performances were heard throughout Europe. In *Essays in Musical Analysis*, Donald Francis Tovey said of it: "It admirably represents the style of a master who, being versed in every form of classical technique, has devised a pleasantly humorous modus vivendi with every modern tendency that does not display a conscientious objection to mastery." *Hungarian Caprice* (1935) was even more successful. Once again tapping the rhythmic and melodic treasures of Hungarian folk music, but without resorting to actual quotation, Zador here produced a vivacious score that won

worldwide appreciation. The Budapest Philharmonic under Carl Schuricht gave the premiere performance in Budapest on February 1, 1935. Since
then, it was given hundreds of performances both in
Europe and the United States by major orchestras.
This composition went a long way to establish Zad-
or's fame internationally, as did the winning of the
Hungarian National State Prize for his Piano Quintet (1933). Aware of his growing artistic stature, the
Royal Academy of Music in London conferred on
him the honorary title of professor, and the New
York College of Music awarded him an honorary
doctorate in music, both in 1935.

On February 15, 1936, the Budapest Royal Opera
presented the world premiere of Zador's opera, *Asra*,
and on February 8, 1937, the Budapest Philharmonic under Hans Kanppertsbusch gave the first
performance of Symphony no. 3, the *Dance Symphony*. Following the *Anschluss* in 1938, Zador left Austria to immigrate to the United States. For about a
year he lived in New York, working as an orchestrator for the *Ford Radio Hour*. His one-act opera-oratorio *Christoph Columbus* (1939) was produced in
New York on October 8, 1939. When this work was
revived in Los Angeles on October 12, 1971, Orrin
Howard wrote in the *Los Angeles Times*: "As an
oratorio, it makes its point by way of Zador's expressive, skillfully written music, his colorful orchestration and, above all, the composer's winning purpose-
fulness. . . . Melodies abound—simple ones be-
fitting the circumstances; vocal lines are eminently
singable; harmonies are pleasantly pungent." In
1977, this work was recorded on a Ford Foundation
grant.

In 1941, Zador's Symphony no. 4, *Children's
Symphony* (1941), was premiered in New Orleans.
Though not specific in its programmatic writing, it
suggested in three of its four movements a fairy tale,
marching soldiers, and a day on the farm, preceded
by a first-movement Allegro in sonata form without
any programmatic indications. Two decades later, in
an extensive revision, this symphony was successfully
performed in its new version on October 17, 1960, in
Los Angeles. Since that time it has been heard more
than a hundred times in the United States, Europe,
Israel, and the Philippines.

From 1960 on, until his death, Zador made his
home in Hollywood, Calif. There he became an
American citizen, and from 1940 to 1963 was employed to score the music for about 120 motion pictures. For three films, he orchestrated the music of a
composer who received Oscars from the Academy of
Motion Picture Arts and Sciences: in 1945 for *Spellbound*, in 1947 for *A Double Life*, and in 1959 for
Ben Hur, music of all three composed by Miklós
Rózsa. On November 9, 1946, in Geneva, Switzerland, Zador married Maria Steiner; they raised a son
and a daughter.

Inspired by Thomas Mann's biblical trilogy *Joseph and his Brethren*, Zador completed an orches-

tral triptych, *Biblical Scenes*, originally named *Biblical Triptych* (1943). Though the composer originally
intended concentrating on the character of Joseph, he
soon expanded the idea to include David and the
Apostle Paul. "The music," Zador explained, "does
not follow the events in detail; it rather endeavors to
depict them in large contours and symbolic moods."
The opening movement, "Joseph," portrayed Joseph
as the symbol of Innocence. This is followed by "David," dominated by the music of the harp (symbol of
David) and pastoral melodies for the oboe. The final
movement portrayed "Paul" as the relentless perse-
cutor of Christ, and described his spiritual transformation and the triumph of Christ's teachings. The
world premiere was heard on December 9, 1943, in
Chicago. "You have succeeded admirably in doing
with musical notes that which I attempted to do with
words," Dr. Mann wrote to Zador, "namely to unite
primitive, oriental sound with modern sensibility and
understanding."

Some of Zador's later works drew their stylistic
details and personality from Hungarian folk music,
as had been the case with so many of his earlier
works. Divertimento, for strings (1954)—commissioned by and introduced at the La Jolla Music Festival in California in July 1955, Nikolai Sokoloff
conducting, before it was performed by the Philadelphia Orchestra under Eugene Ormandy on April 5,
1957—was "a musical entertainment" abounding
with Hungarian folk rhythms and folklike tunes or
their derivatives. *Elegie*, for orchestra (1960), was
commissioned by Edward B. Benjamin for his project
to encourage "quiet music," its premiere given on
November 11, 1960, by the Philadelphia Orchestra
under Ormandy. Primarily elegiac, though occasionally dramatic as well, this music was once again in a
pronounced Hungarian style, the reason Zador had
originally planned to call it *The Hungarian Plains*.
Rhapsody, for orchestra (1961; Los Angeles, February 5, 1961), was, as the composer said, "highly
colored by Hungarian folk style with the rhapsodic
rhythm and gypsylike figures of the clarinet suggesting Hungarian dance patterns."

Other late Zador music reflected a facet of Zador's
creativity other than Hungarian nationalism, notably his effervescent sense of humor, love of gaiety,
and infectious good spirits. All this could be found in
A Christmas Overture, for orchestra (1961; Glen-
dale, Calif., December 17, 1961); *Five Contrasts*, for
orchestra (1963; Philadelphia, January 8, 1965);
Variations on a Merry Tune (1964; Birmingham,
Ala., January 12, 1965); and *Festival Overture*, for
orchestra (1964). The last of these was written on
commission for the opening of the Los Angeles Music Center, at which time it was performed by the Los
Angeles Philharmonic conducted by Zubin Mehta
(December 10, 1964). This overture was revised in
1967 to include an organ, a version first performed
on December 8, 1967, by the Philadelphia Orchestra
under Ormandy.

Zador's last full-length opera was *The Scarlet Mill* (1967), libretto by George Jellinek based on a story by Ferenc Molnar. It received its first production on October 26, 1968, in Brooklyn, N. Y. Six years later, to commemorate Zador's imminent eightieth birthday, it had its West Coast premiere (February 6, 1974). An amusing parable, this opera told of the effort to corrupt a man, a paragon of virtue, with a machine devised by a professor in hell, a devil's disciple. The victim is a young peasant who has all the desirable virtues. But he is corrupted by the temptations of greed, gambling, adultery, and other vices. In the end, however, the young man returns penitently to his wife and child, believing that all his experiences had been just a dream. "Zador," reported Albert Goldberg in the *Los Angeles Times*, "has composed a well-crafted score that supports the subject matter amiably. The music is graphically descriptive, always singable, often agreeably melodic in its echo of native Hungarian idioms, and expertly orchestrated. It is even adventurous at times in its free employment of appropriate dissonances." The better to realize Hungarian sounds and colors, Zador incorporated into his orchestration the Hungarian gypsy zitherlike instrument, the cimbalom, as well as a vibraphone and a keyed theremin.

Zador's last works included some for unusual (or as he liked to call them "underprivileged") instruments: Concerto for Trombone and Orchestra (1966; Rochester, Mich., July 20, 1967); Rhapsody, for cimbalom and orchestra (1969; Los Angeles, November 2, 1969); *Fantasia hungarica*, for double bass and orchestra (1970); and Concerto for Accordion and String Orchestra with Percussion (1972). Some major works, however, were for the more usual instruments: Music for Clarinet and Strings (1970); Duo Fantasy, for two cellos and string orchestra, with harp and timpani (1971; Riverside, Calif., December 1973); Suite, for horn, strings, and percussion (1972); and Concerto, for oboe and string orchestra (1975).

THE COMPOSER SPEAKS: As in every art, music is in permanent revolution, so every composer should be acquainted with avant-garde elements. Each generation has experimental periods which, in a way, may characterize the life of the time. Nobody can ignore this evolution. After listening to all styles, the young composer can and will develop his own. Composers with vision and imagination want to escape conventionality and clichés.

The style can be called neoromantic, neoclassic, impressionistic, atonal, bitonal, or serial. The title can be "Structure," "Density," or "*Zeitmasse*." So long as it has musical substance, showing organic unity and musical maturity, it is good music.

But there is no easy way—no shortcut—in musical education. Nobody can disregard the heritage of the great masters. I believe strongly in education and esthetics, and first of all in faith and conviction of crea-

tion. Young composers must go through the regular school of learning, through harmony and counterpoint and orchestration.

Even a "contemporary" work must be practically written. There is no reason to be complicated unless it is important to the work, certainly not simply for the sake of complication. The technique of the composer is like digesting food. Compositional technique is to me as important as the knowledge of the alphabet to the writer. Every great composer had great technical knowledge.

PRINCIPAL WORKS: 4 symphonies (1922–41).

Variations on a Hungarian Folk Song, for orchestra (1918); *The Inspector General*, opera (1928; revised 1970); Chamber Concerto, for strings, two horns, and piano (1930); Piano Quintet (1933); Rondo, for orchestra (1934); *Hungarian Caprice*, for orchestra (1935); *Asra*, opera (1935); *Christoph Columbus*, opera-oratorio (1939); *Czardas Rhapsody*, for orchestra (1940); Pastorale and Tarantella, for orchestra (1941); *Biblical Scenes*, for orchestra (1943); *Elegie and Dance*, for orchestra (1954); Divertimento, for strings (1955); Fugue-Fantasia, for orchestra (1958); *Elegie*, for orchestra (1960); Rhapsody, for orchestra (1961); Suite, for brass (1961); *A Christmas Overture*, for orchestra (1961); *Cantata tecnica and Scherzo domestico*, for chorus (1962); *Ode to Peace*, for orchestra (1962); *In Memoriam*, for orchestra (1962); *Variations on a Merry Tune*, for orchestra (1963); *The Remarkable Adventure of Henry Bold*, for narrator and orchestra (1963); *Five Contrasts*, for orchestra (1963); *Triptych*, chorales for chorus (1964); *Festival Overture*, for orchestra (1964); *The Virgin and the Fawn*, one-act opera (1963); *Dance Overture*, for orchestra (1965); *Miniature Overture*, for orchestra (1965); *The Magic Chair*, one-act opera (1965); Trombone Concerto (1966); Aria and Allegro, for strings and brass (1966); *The Scarlet Mill*, opera (1967); Rhapsody, for cimbalom and orchestra (1969); Music for Clarinet and Strings (1970); *Studies for Orchestra* (1970); *Fantasia hungarica*, for double bass and orchestra (1970); Duo Fantasy, for two cellos, strings, and harp (1971); Suite, for woodwind quintet (1972); Accordion Concerto (1972); Suite, for harp, horn, strings and percussion (1972); Brass Quintet (1973); *Fantasy on Themes from The Inspector General*, for orchestra (1973); *The Judgment*, for three solo voices, women's chorus, brass ensemble, and percussion (1974); *Yehu*, a Christmas legend (1974), Oboe Concerto (1975); *Hungarian Scherzo*, for orchestra (1975); *Song of the Nymph Called Echo*, for soprano, women's chorus, and piano (1975).

BIBLIOGRAPHY: Ewen, David, *Composers Since 1900* (N.Y., 1969); Tovey, Donald Francis, *Essays in Musical Analysis,* vol. 6 (London, 1939); Zador, Leslie, *Eugene Zador: A Catalogue of His Works* (San Diego, Calif., 1978).

Appendix

An Index of Programmatic Titles

AOK (Oliveros)
Apartment House 1776 (Cage)
Apasionada (Surinach)
Aphorisms (Lombardo)
Aphorisms (Schuller)
Aphrodite (Chadwick)
Apocalypse (Menotti)
Apocalyptica (Rochberg)
Apollonia (Starer)
Apollon Musagète (Stravinsky)
Apostle, The (Smith)
Apotheosis of Achaeopterix, An (Hiller)
Apotheosis of This Earth (Husa)
Appalachian Spring (Copland)
Apparitions (Crumb)
Apparitions (Rogers)
Appello (Kolb)
Apple Box (Oliveros)
Apple Box Orchestra (Oliveros)
après-midi d'un Summer Meeting, L' (Ghent)
April Poem (McKay)
Aquarelles (Gretchaninoff)
Arabia Felix (Wuorinen)
Arcadian Symphony (Bristow)
Arcana (Varèse)
Archaeopteryx (Wuorinen)
Archaic Aggregates (Dlugoszewski)
Archaic Ritual (Still)
Archaic Timbre Piano Music (Dlugoszewski)
Archangel (Wuorinen)
Archeopteryk (Schwartz)
Archers, The (Carr)
Arcturus (Ward-Steinman)
Ardent Song (Hovhaness)
Areas (Schwartz)
Arevakal (Hovhaness)
Aria and Fragments (Lombardo)
Aria and Hymn (Diamond)
Aria sinfonico (Dahl)
Arie da capo (Babbitt)
Ariel (Moss)
Ariel (Rorem)
Ariel Songs (2) (Stout)
Ariel: Vision of Isaiah (Starer)
Arithmetic Points (Dlugoszewski)
Arjuna (Symphony no. 8) (Hovhaness)
Armenian Dance (Dubensky)
Armenian Rhapsodies (Hovhaness)
Armenian Suite (Yardumian)
Arms That Have Sheltered Me (Branscombe)
ARP (Hannay)
Articles of Faith (Gottlieb)
Artik (Hovhaness)
Artist, The (Cheslock)
Ascension Cantata (Pinkham)
Ascension Cantata, The (Mills)
Ascension Sonata, The (Burleigh)
As of a Breeze (Dello Joio)
As Quiet As (Colgrass)
Asra (Zador)

Assembly and Fall (Rorem)
Assyrian Prayers (Jacobi)
As the Prophets Foretold (Franco)
Astral Dimensions (Spiegelman)
As You Like It (Castelnuovo-Tedesco)
As You Like It (Paine)
"At Dawning" (Cadman)
Athaliah (Weisgall)
Atlantis (Brant)
Atlantis (Cowell)
Atlantis (Feldman)
Atlas Eclipticalis (Cage)
Atonement of Pan, The (Hadley)
At the Corner of the Sky (Smit)
At the Crossroads (Gretchaninoff)
At the Fair (Powell)
At the Tomb of Charles Ives (Harrison)
Attis I-II
Aubade (Fletcher)
Aubade (Weber)
Aucassin and Nicolette (Castelnuovo-Tedesco)
Auden Variations (Persichetti)
Auditions (Moss)
August Canticle (Schwantner)
Aulokithara (Krenek)
Aulos (Kay)
Aulos Player, The (Moevs)
Aurelia, the Vestal (Fry)
Aureole (Druckman)
Aurora Borealis (Cadman)
Aurora Borealis (Hadley)
Ausonia (Saminsky)
Aus Tirol (Weinberger)
Autobiography for Strings (Amram)
Autochthonous (Symphony no. 4) (Still)
Autumn (Thomson)
Autumnal (Harbison)
Autumn Canticles (Schwantner)
Autumn Evening and Evening Ebb (Huston)
Autumnmusic (Erb)
Autumn Sketches (Verrall)
Available Forms I-II (Brown)
Ave atque Vale (Converse)
Ave Maria (Labunski)
Ave Maria (Stringham)
Ave Rota (Jacobi)
Aviation Suite (Grofé)
Axolotl (Subotnick)
Azra (Paine)

Baal Shem Suite (Bloch)
Babar the Elephant (Berezowsky)
Babbitt (Moore)
Bacchae (Albert)
Bacchanal (Cadman)
Bacco in Toscana (Castelnuovo-Tedesco)
B-A-C-H, Es ist genug (Moevs)
Bachlike (Spiegelman)
Background Music (Felciano)

Bacontana (Franco)
Badlands (Benson)
baiser de la fée, Le (Stravinsky)
Baker's Dozen, A (Behrens)
Balanced Naked Flung (Dlugoszewski)
bal des blanchisseuses, Le (Duke)
Bali (Eichheim)
Bali (McPhee)
Balinese Ceremonial Music (McPhee)
Balladen (D. Harris)
Ballad for Gymnasts (Partch)
Ballad of Baby Doe, The (Moore)
Ballad of King Estmere (Sowerby)
Ballad of Kitty Barkeep (Lee)
Ballad of Magna Carta, The (Weill)
Ballad of New England (Burleigh)
Ballad of Trees and the Master, A (Chadwick)
Ballad of Trees and the Master, A (Shepherd)
Ballad of William Sycamore, The (Stevens)
Ballet Ballads (Moross)
Ballet in E (Haieff)
Ballet mécanique (Antheil)
Ballet of Flowers (Hadley)
Bal masqué (Beach)
Bamboula (Gottschalk)
Bananier, Le (Gottschalk)
Banjo, The (Gottschalk)
Banshee, The (Cowell)
Baobab (Ghent)
Baroque Variations (Foss)
Barstow (Partch)
Bartókiana (Rochberg)
Bataan (McDonald)
Batoula (Josten)
Battle of Trenton (Hewitt)
Battle Overture (Hewitt)
Bayonne Barrel and Drum Company, The (Childs)
Bayou Legend, A (Still)
Beaded Leaf, The (Benson)
Beam (Mumma)
Beat! Beat! Drums! (Loeffler)
Beat Hunt, The (Beeson)
Beatrice (Hoiby)
Beauty and the Beast (Giannini)
Beauty and the Beast (Haieff)
Beauty Music I-III (Dlugoszewski)
Bed of Roses, A (Weinberger)
Before Breakfast (Pasatieri)
"Before My Window" (Rachmaninoff)
Before the Butterfly (Subotnick)
Before the Music Ends (Oliveros)
"Be Glad Then, America" (La Montaine)
Behold, My Servant (Rochberg)
Behold the Earth (Brant)
Behold the Man (Gillis)
Behold, the Star (Dawson)
belle dame sans merci, La (Converse)
belle dame sans merci, La (Mayer)
belle dame sans merci, La (Riegger)
Bell Overture, A (Read)

Bells, The (Rachmaninoff)
Bells of Circumstance, The (Branscombe)
Bells of Zion, The (Franco)
Bell Tower, The (Krenek)
Belshazzar (Hadley)
Beloved Son (Brubeck)
Ben Hur (incidental music) (Kelley)
Ben Hur Suite (Rózsa)
Beowulf (Flagello)
Berliner Requiem, Das (Weill)
Bermuda Triangle (Harbison)
Bertha (Rorem)
Best Wishes, U.S.A. (Colgrass)
Bethlehem (Tuthill)
Betrothal, The (De Lamarter)
Between Categories (Feldman)
Bewitched, The (Partch)
Beyond Silence (Anderson)
Bianca (Hadley)
Biblica (Symphony no. 2) (Nabokov)
Biblical Scenes (Zador)
Bi-Centurion (Gutchë)
Big Ben (Toch)
Big River (Tuthill)
Biguine (Moross)
Bilby's Doll (Floyd)
Billy the Kid (Copland)
Binding, The (Adler)
Biograffiti (Salzman)
Biography in Sonata Form (Ornstein)
"Bird, The" (Billings)
Bird and Person Dying (Lucier)
Birds, The (Labunski)
Birds, The (incidental music) (Paine)
Birds of Paradise (La Montaine)
Bird's Opera, A (Weinberger)
Birthday Music (Karlins)
Birthday of the Infanta, The (Carpenter)
Birthday of the Infanta, The (Castelnuovo-Tedesco)
Birthday Pieces (5) (Kubik)
Birthdays (George)
Bishop's Gambit (Ward-Steinman)
Bits and Pieces (Kohn)
Blackamoor of Peter the Great, The (Lourié)
Black and White Song (Bacon)
Black Angels (Crumb)
Black, Brown, and Beige (Ellington)
Black Host (Bolcom)
Black Maskers, The (Sessions)
Black November Turkey, A (Corigliano)
Black Orchid, The (De Lamarter)
Black Salt, Black Provender (Bergsma)
Black Sounds (Rochberg)
Black Widow, The (Pasatieri)
Blatant Hypotheses (Bergsma)
Blehris (Finney)
Blennerhasset (Giannini)
Blessed Are They That Mourn (Kennan)
Blessings (Pinkham)
Blind Man's Cry (Eaton)

Blood Moon (Dello Joio)
Blue Flame, The (Hovhaness)
Blue Is the Antecedent of it (Hiller)
"Blue Rondo à la Turk" (Brubeck)
Blues (Lombardo)
Blue Steel (Still)
Blue Symphony (Elwell)
Boccaccio's "Nightingale" (Trimble)
bocca della verità, La (Rochberg)
Bohemia (Heinrich)
Bold Island Suite (Hanson)
Bonn Feier (Oliveros)
Book of Esther, The (Castelnuovo-Tedesco)
Book of Hours (Rorem)
Book of Imaginary Beings, The (Parris)
Book of Jonah, The (Castelnuovo-Tedesco)
Book of Ruth, The (Castelnuovo-Tedesco)
Book of Songs (Rochberg)
Books of Hours and Seasons (Harbison)
Book, The (Argento)
Boor, The (Kay)
"Bossa Nova U.S.A." (Brubeck)
Boston Baked Beans (Kubik)
Bottled Message from Paradise (Krenek)
Bounty of Athena, The (Clarke)
Bowdoin Anthology, A (Schwartz)
Bowdoin Hymn (Berezowsky)
Bowling Again with the Champs (Childs)
B.P., A Melodrama (Moss)
Branches (Chihara)
Brancusi's Brass Beds (Ward-Steinman)
Brass Piano, The (Mills)
Bravo Mozart! (Argento)
Bravura Prelude (McKay)
Brazen (Ghent)
Break, Break, Break (Dawson)
Breaking Heart, The (Fry)
Brennen on the Moor (James)
Bret Harte (James)
Bridesmaid's Song (Branscombe)
Bridge, The (Carter)
Brief Candle (Mayer)
Brief Elegy (Kay)
Brief Glimpses into Contemporary French Literature (Sims)
Brigg Fair (Grainger)
Bright, Blithe and Brisk (Sowerby)
Broken Consort, A (Austin)
Broken Sequences (Wolpe)
Broken Troth (Cole)
Brooms of Mexico (McBride)
Brothers, The (Antheil)
Browning (Ives)
Brute, The (Moss)
Buchlein for Lyon (Sims)
Bucket of Water, A (Phillips)
Builders, The (Britain)
Bunte Suite (Toch)
Buoyant Overture, A (Diamond)
Burchfield Gallery (Gould)

Burgschaft, Die (Weill)
Burlesca (Flagello)
Burlesken Suite (Toch)
Burlesque Overture (Thorne)
Burma (Eichheim)
Burmese Pwe (Eichheim)
Burning House, The (Hovhaness)
By Blue Ontario (Bacon)
By the Rivers of Babylon (Partch)
By the Rivers of Babylon (Amram)
Byways (Bacon)

Cabeza de Vaca (Antheil)
Cabildo (Beach)
Cactus Rhapsody (Britain)
Cadence (Laderman)
Cadenze I (W. Kraft)
Caedmon (Glanville-Hicks)
Caedmon (Smit)
Café Society (Grofé)
Cáhal Mór of the Wine-Red Hand (Parker)
Calder Piece (Brown)
Caledonian Frolic, The (Carr)
California (Converse)
California Games (Schwartz)
California Suite, A (Jacobi)
Caligula (Haieff)
Call of the Plains (Goldmark)
Calumny (Kohs)
Calvary (Pasatieri)
Camino Real, El (Whithorne)
campo dei fiori, Il (Kennan)
Canciones españolas (Bowles)
Candide (Bernstein)
Candide (Castelnuovo-Tedesco)
Can Man Survive? (Salzman)
Canonic Variations (La Montaine)
Cantata de Virtute (Mennin)
Cantata for Easter (Effinger)
Cantata for Sophoclean Choruses (Shifrin)
Cantata of St. John (Surinach)
Cantata of the Bitter Herbs (Toch)
Cantata on Poems of Edward Lear (Thomson)
Cantata Sacra (Moevs)
Cantata Sauce (Thorne)
Cantata tecnica and Scherzo domestico (Zador)
Cantes flamencos (Rochberg)
Canticle (La Montaine)
Canticle for Christmas (Giannini)
Canticle of Freedom (Copland)
Canticle of the Evening Bells (Schwantner)
Canticle of the Martyrs (Giannini)
Canticle of the Night (Alexander)
Canticle of the Pacific (Lee)
Canticle of the Sun (Boatwright)
Canticle of the Sun (Sowerby)
Canticles of America (Ward)
Canticles of the Sun (Beach)
Canticle to the Sun (R. Harris)

Canticum Fratris Solis (Loeffler)
Canticum Sacrum et Honorem Sancti Marci Nominis (Stravinsky)
Canti della lontananza (Menotti)
Cantilena (Mennini)
Cantilever II (Dlugoszewski)
Canto di aspirazione (Labunski)
Canto for Orchestra (Mennin)
Canto Sacro (Rochberg)
Cantus Animae et Cordis (Yardumian)
Canyon (Britain)
Canzona seria ("A Hamlet Monologue") (Josten)
Capital Capitals (Thomson)
Capital of the World (Antheil)
Capitoline Venus, The (Key)
Capriccio mexicano (Duke)
Capriccio on Five Notes (Hoiby)
Capriccio stravagante (Schuller)
Caprichos de Goya (Castelnuovo-Tedesco)
Capricorn Concerto (Barber)
Captain Jinks of the Horse Marines (Beeson)
Cardillac (Hindemith)
Caribbean Melodies (Still)
Carillon (Britain)
Carissima (Gaburo)
Carmel Concerto (Carpenter)
Carmilla (Johnston)
Carmina Amoris (Palmer)
Carnival Fantasy (Branscombe)
Carnival Music (Rochberg)
Carnival Scene, A (Bird)
Carnival Song (Piston)
Carol Fantasy (Lockwood)
Carol on Twelfth Night, A (Bergsma)
Carol Plantamura (Oliveros)
Carols of Death (Schuman)
Carrie Nation (Moore)
Casey at the Bat (Schuman)
Castles and Kings (Kohn)
Castle Spectre, The (incidental music) (Reinagle)
Cast Out (Serly)
Cat and the Mouse, The (Copland)
Catharsis (Rudhyar)
Catharsis: Open Style for Two Improvisational Ensembles, Tape and Conductor (Austin)
Cathedral Music (Albert)
Cathedral Prelude (Smith)
Cat o' Nine Tails (Oliveros)
Catskill Songbook, A (Cazden)
Cave of the Heart (Barber)
Cave of the Winds (Dett)
Celebrants (Surinach)
Celebration (Hannay)
Celebration (Karlins)
Celebration (Talma)
Celebration for String Orchestra and Electronic Valve Instrument (Ussachevsky)
Celebration for the Saint, A (Stokes)
Celebration in Praise of Earth (Bassett)
Celebration of Dead Ladies (Sims)

Celebrations (Alexander)
Celebrations (Persichetti)
Celebration Trio (Mayer)
Celestial Bodies (Laderman)
Celestial Mechanics (Crumb)
Celestial Sphere, The (Wuorinen)
Celestial Vision, The (Creston)
Celtic Set (Cowell)
Celtic Songs (Gilbert)
Cenotaph (Hiller)
Centaur and the Phoenix, The (Mills)
Centauri, 17 (Bazelon)
Centennial Hymn (Paine)
Centennial Ode (Donato)
Centennial Overture, A (Palmer)
Center Holiday, A (Stokes)
Centering (Brown)
Centone (Kohn)
Central Park in the Dark (Ives)
Ceremonies I-IV (Chihara)
Ceremony (Brant)
Ceremony of Allegiance (Gillis)
Chacona (Davidovsky)
Challenge (R. Harris)
Challenge: The Family of Man (Shapey)
Chamber Cantata on Chinese Poems (Sims)
Chamber Deviations (Thorne)
Chambered Nautilus (Beach)
Chambered Nautilus, The (J.D. Taylor)
Chamber Fantasy (Weber)
Chamber Music (Colgrass)
Chamber Music (Spiegelman)
Chambers (Lucier)
Chamber Symphony (Imbrie)
Chameleon Variations (Bergsma)
Chameleon Variations (McDonald)
Changes (Bergsma)
Channel Firing (Smit)
Chanson of the Bells of Oseney (Donovan)
Chanson sombre (Hannay)
Chant (Colgrass)
Chant (Crawford)
Chant d'amour (Herbert)
Chanticleer (Mason)
Chant of Darkness, A (Clapp)
Chant of 1942 (Creston)
Chants d'auvergne (Read)
Chants élégiaques (Gretchaninoff)
Character Pieces after Omar Khayyam (4) (Foote)
Characters from Hans Christian Andersen (Rogers)
Chariot Jubilee (Dett)
Chariots (Kay)
Charles IX (Gottschalk)
Charleston Rhapsody (Bennett)
Charmes (D. Harris)
Charm Me Asleep (Pinkham)
château, Le (Lockwood)
Chaumont (James)
Cheap Imitation (Cage)
Chef d'orchestre/Calder Piece (Brown)

Columbus (Herbert)
Columbus (Laderman)
Columbus (incidental music) (Reinagle)
Columbus March and Hymn (Paine)
Columbus Overture (Bristow)
Come Away (Sims)
Come, Creator Spirit (Yardumian)
Comedy Overture on Negro Themes (Gilbert)
Come into My Garden (La Montaine)
Come Out (Reich)
Comes a Day (Amram)
Comes Autumn Time (Sowerby)
Come Seven (Tuthill)
Coming of the King, The (Gillis)
Coming Together (Rzewski)
Commedia (Bolcom)
Commemoration (Beeson)
Commencement Suite (C. Taylor)
Comments on This World (Custer)
Committee, The (Doran)
Commonplace Book, or A Salute to Our American Container Corp. (Sims)
Communion Service (Tuthill)
Complaint of Logan the Mingo Chief, the Last of His Race (Heinrich)
Composition for Two (Rzewski)
Composition in Three Parts (Schuller)
Compressions (Luke)
COMPUSITIONS 2-10 (Strang)
Computer Canada (Hiller)
Computer Music for Percussion and Tape (Hiller)
Computer Piece (Ussachevsky)
Concatenata (Clarke)
Concatenations (Bazelon)
Concertant (Erb)
Concerted Piece for Tape Recorder and Orchestra (Ussachevsky)
Concertino 3 Times 3 (Serly)
Concertino in Blue (Kreutz)
Concertmaster (Colgrass)
Concert Music (Karlins)
Concerto arabesque (Becker)
Concerto da camera (Castelnuovo-Tedesco)
Concert of Man Rooms and Moving Space (Dlugoszewski)
Concerto for Amplified Violin and Orchestra (Wuorinen)
Concerto for Doubles (McBride)
Concerto for Tap Dancer and Orchestra (Gould)
Concerto in Slendro (Harrison)
Concerto italiano (Castelnuovo-Tedesco)
Concerto lirico (Berezowsky)
Concerto lirico (Franco)
Concerto mutabile (Kohn)
Concertone (Wuorinen)
Concert on Old English Rounds (Schuman)
Concerto romantico (Glanville-Hicks)
Concerto sacro (Josten)
Concerto sereno (Mills)
Concerto spirituale (Lourié)

Concerto symphonique (Bloch)
Concert Overture (Sowerby)
Concert Overture for Orchestra: Summer Music (Luke)
Concert Poem (Weber)
Conclave (Brant)
Concord Cantata, A (Thompson)
Concord Psalter, The (Epstein)
Concord Quartets (Rochberg)
Condemned, The (Blitzstein)
Condemned Playground, The (Gideon)
Conductus Novum, or The Revenge of Perotinus (L. Kraft)
Confession, The (V. Fine)
Confidence Man, The (Rochberg)
Configurations (W. Kraft)
Configurations (Shapey)
Confinement (Harbison)
Conflict (Ussachevsky)
Confluentia (Kelley)
Confrontation (Bergsma)
Confrontation (Hannay)
Congo, The (Cheslock)
Congo, The (Donato)
Conjuror, The (Salzman)
Connections (Anderson)
Connotations for Orchestra (Copland)
Consort (Weber)
Consort from Instruments and Voices (Wuorinen)
Consortium I-II (Schwantner)
Consovowels 1-5 (Serly)
Conspiracy 8 (Mumma)
Contemplations (Flagello)
Contemplations (Jacobi)
Contemplations of the Tenth Muse (Wernick)
Continental Harmony, The (Billings)
Continental Harp and Band Report, The (Stokes)
Continuance, A (Childs)
Contours (Schuller)
Contrafactum (Wuorinen)
Contra Mortem et Tempus (Rochberg)
Contrasts (Blumenfeld)
Contrasts (Davidovsky)
Contrasts (Schuller)
Conversations (La Montaine)
Convocation (Shapey)
Copernicus: Narrative and Credo (Smit)
Coplas (Castelnuovo-Tedesco)
Corinthians XIII (Creston)
Coriolanus (Castelnuovo-Tedesco)
corona, La (Talma)
Corpus Christi (Green)
Correspondences (Babbitt)
Corroborée (Brown)
Cortège (Elwell)
Cosmic Christ, The (Haubiel)
Cosmic Cycle (Rudhyar)
Cosmic Mist Symphony (Britain)
Costaso (Still)
Cotillion (Moore)

Count Robert of Paris (Parker)
Country Fair (Mayer)
Country Gardens (Grainger)
Country Idyls (Hill)
Country Music Fantasy (McBride)
Country Pictures (Mason)
Courthouse Square (Phillips)
Court of Hearts, The (Daniels)
Covenant, The (Shapey)
Coventry's Choir (Branscombe)
Cowboy Rhapsody (Britain)
Cowboy Rhapsody (Gould)
Cowboy Song (Jones)
Cowherd and the Sky Maiden, The (Verrall)
"Cradle Song" (Gretchaninoff)
Cradle Will Rock, The (Blitzstein)
Crasis (Felciano)
"Creation" (Billings)
Creation (Gruenberg)
Creation, The (Persichetti)
Creation—Prologue and Interlude (Ussachevsky)
Creations (Corigliano)
Creation Symphony (Burleigh)
Creator, The (Cowell)
Credendum (Flagello)
Credendum (Schuman)
Credo (Mennini)
Credo (Shapero)
Credo (Smith)
Creole Mystery, A (Beeson)
Creole Rhapsody (Ellington)
Crisis, The (Fletcher)
Cristo crucificado ante al mar, El (Lourié)
Cross-Currents (Bazelon)
Cross Sections and Color Fields (Brown)
Crosswinds (Kolb)
Crow Two (Oliveros)
Crucible, The (Ward)
Crucifixion, The (Gillis)
Crucifixion of Christ, The (Fry)
Cry, a Song, and a Dance, A (Spiegelman)
Cry of Clytaemnestra, The (Eaton)
Cryptics (Haubiel)
Crystals (Moevs)
C(s) for Once, The (Oliveros)
Cuban Overture (Gershwin)
Cues from the Little Clay Cart (incidental music)
   (Avshalomov)
Cumberland Concerto (R. Harris)
Cupid and Psyche (Parker)
Cursive (Chou)
Cuthbert Bound (Hiller)
Cybersonic Cantilevers (Mumma)
Cycle, The (Symphony no. 4) (Mennin)
Cycle of Cities, A (Siegmeister)
Cycle of Holy Songs (Rorem)
Cycles and Gongs (Schwartz)
Cyclotron Stew (Austin)
Cynthia's Revells (Parris)
Cyprus Serenades (3) (Fuleihan)

Cyrano de Bergerac (Damrosch)
Cyrano de Bergerac (Effinger)
Czardas Rhapsody (Zador)
Czech Rhapsody (Weinberger)

Dance (Glass)
Dance, A (Becker)
Dance Calinda (Kay)
Dance Cantata (Glanville-Hicks)
Dance Concerto (Kreutz)
Dance Energies (Green)
Dance Figure (Becker)
Dance Grotesque (Britain)
Dance in Place Congo, The (Gilbert)
Dance in Three-Time (Porter)
Dance of Life, The (De Lamarter)
Dance of Salome, The (Rogers)
Dance of the Mah Jongg Pieces (Clarke)
Dance Overture (Creston)
Dance Overture (Persichetti)
Dance Overture (Wykes)
Dance Preludes (6) (La Montaine)
Dancer of Fjaard, The (Branscombe)
Dance Rhythms (Riegger)
Dance Scenes (Rogers)
Dance Set (Green)
Dances from the Southwest (Fletcher)
Dances from Woodland (Cazden)
Dance Sonata (Green)
Dance Sonata (Nordoff)
Dance Symphony (Copland)
Dance Variations (Gould)
Dandelion Wine (Imbrie)
Daniel (Bristow)
Daniel in the Lions' Den (Pinkham)
Daniel Jazz (Gruenberg)
"Danny Deever" (Damrosch)
Danse orientale (Dubensky)
Danses exotiques (Stringham)
Danses russes (Tcherepnin)
Dante's Farewell (Flagello)
Danton (Lopatnikoff)
Danton and Robespierre (Eaton)
Danza (Gottschalk)
Danza de la muerte (Clarke)
Danza de la vida (Clarke)
Danza de Panama (Still)
Danza mexicana (Bowles)
danze del Re David, Le (Castelnuovo-Tedesco)
Daoma, or The Land of the Misty Water (Cadman)
Daphne (Bird)
Dark and the Light, The (Chou)
Dark Brother (Partch)
Dark Dancers of the Mardi Gras (Cadman)
Dark Hills, The (Fletcher)
Dark Music (Bolcom)
Dark Night of St. John (Verrall)
Dark Pastorale (Lombardo)

Dark River and Distant Bell (Hovhaness)
Dark upon the Harp (Druckman)
Dark Virgin, The (Benson)
Darling Corie (Siegmeister)
Daughter Jeptha, The (Saminsky)
David (Cheslock)
David and Bath-Sheba (Surinach)
David, the Psalmist (Rochberg)
"David's Lamentation" (Billings)
Dawn (Farwell)
Dawning of Music in Kentucky, The, or The Pleasure of Harmony in the Solitudes of Nature (Heinrich)
Day in the Country, A (Fry)
Day Music (Rorem)
Day of Gayomir, The (Skilton)
Day of Love (Pasatieri)
Day's No Rounder Than Its Angles, The (Beeson)
Dead March and Monody (Carr)
Deaï (Schuller)
"Death and General Putnam" (Damrosch)
Death in the Family, A (Mayer)
Death of Bishop of Brindisi, The (Menotti)
Death of the Machines (Antheil)
Death Spreads His Gentle Wings (Bauer)
Death Valley Suite (Grofé)
Décalage (Bolcom)
December (Brant)
December 8 (Gaburo)
Declamation (Flagello)
Declamations (Lees)
Declaration (Behrens)
Declaration (Gould)
Declaration (Siegmeister)
Declaration Chorale (Schuman)
Declarations (Goeb)
Declaratives (Phillips)
Decline and Fall of the Sonata, The (Schwartz)
Dédicaces (Duke)
Dedication (Moore)
Dedication Ode (Chadwick)
Dedications for Piano (Green)
Deep Blue Devil's Breakdown, The (Dahl)
Deep Forest (Daniels)
Deep Nocturne (Grofé)
Deep South Suite (Ellington)
Defense of Corinth, The (Carter)
Definition, A (George)
Deidam (Talma)
Dierdre (Stein)
Dierdre of the Sorrows (Becker)
Déjà vu (Adler)
Déjà vu (Colgrass)
Déjeuner sur l'herbe (Tcherepnin)
De Kooning (Feldman)
Delaunay Pochoirs (Smit)
Delicate Accidents in Space (Dlugoszewski)
Delphic Serenade, A (Bennett)
Denmark Vesey (Bowles)

Densité 21.5 (Varèse)
Densities (Dlugoszewski)
Density (Wykes)
De Ordinations Angelorum (Lourié)
De Profundis (Barlow)
Derivations, for Clarinet and Jazz Band (Gould)
desaparecidos, Los (Mumma)
Descant (Cheslock)
Descant Nocturne (Harbison)
Descants from Ecclesiastes (3) (Kohn)
Déserts (Varèse)
Design for Orchestra (Rorem)
Design for Radio (Donovan)
Designs (String Quartet no. 3) (Hannay)
Desolate City (Yardumian)
Desolate City, The (Daniels)
Desolate City, The (Porter)
Despite and Still (Barber)
De-Tonations (Bazelon)
Deux (Shapey)
Devil and Daniel Webster, The (Moore)
Devil in the Belfry, A (Weinberger)
Diabelskie Skrzypce (Hiller)
Diabolic Dialogue (Read)
Dialectica (L. Kraft)
Dialogo per la Pascua (Stout)
Dialogue (Lees)
Dialogue of Abraham and Isaac, The (Lockwood)
Dialogues (Gould)
Dialogues (L. Kraft)
Dialogues (Rochberg)
Dialogues (Rudhyar)
Dialogues (Talma)
Dialogues and Entertainments (W. Kraft)
Dialogues of Lovers (Lombardo)
Dialogue spirituale (Alexander)
Dialogue with Basho (Oliveros)
Dialogus (Walker)
Diaphonia Intervallum (Schwantner)
Diaphonic Suites (Crawford)
Diaphonies (L. Kraft)
Diaries of a Tarot Player (Kupferman)
Dichotomy (Riegger)
Dick Whittington and His Cat (Siegmeister)
Die Natali (Barber)
Dies Natalis (Hanson)
Diffusion of Bells, Electronic Fanfare (Luening)
Digression (Daniels)
Dimensions (Shapey)
Dingle Hill (Cazden)
Dioses aztecas, Los (Read)
Diotima (Harbison)
Diptych (Flagello)
Diptych (Franco)
Diptych (Labunski)
Diptych (Schuller)
Directions of Sounds from the Bridge (Lucier)
Dirge (Moore)
Dirge for Two Veterans (Rogers)

Disappointment, The (Adler)
Discourse (Shapey)
Discourse I-II (Donato)
Discussion (Amram)
Dismal Swamp (Still)
Dissembler, The (Krenek)
Dithyrambos (Ghent)
Dithyrambs (Lourié)
Dithyrambs (Rudhyar)
Divan of Moses-Ibn-Ezra (Castelnuovo-Tedesco)
Diversion (Dello Joio)
Diversion (Fletcher)
Diversions (Hoiby)
Divertimento burlesca (Lees)
Divertimento da camera (Beversdorf)
Divertiments for Electronic Violin and Computer Bass (Ghent)
divina, La (Pasatieri)
Divine Flame, The (Talma)
Divinely Superfluous Beauty, Natural Music (Huston)
Divinity (Brant)
Divisions (Toch)
Dixieland Concerto (Kreutz)
Doctor Faustus Lights the Lights (Kupferman)
Dr. Faustus Lights the Lights (Wuorinen)
Dr. Franklin (Bacon)
Dr. Heidigger's Fountain of Youth (Beeson)
Dodo, The (Lombardo)
Doina (Alexander)
Dolmen (Weber)
Domain of Huraken, The (Farwell)
Donne's Last Sermon (Lockwood)
Don Quixote (Nabokov)
Don't Be Weary, Traveler (Dett)
Don't We All (Phillips)
Doodle Dandy of the U.S.A. (Siegmeister)
Double Basses at Twenty Paces (Oliveros)
Double Crossings (Bazelon)
Doubles (Custer)
Doubt (Stein)
Dove of Peace, The (Damrosch)
Dover Beach (Barber)
Dover Beach (Boatwright)
Dover Beach (Cone)
Down by the Riverside (Rzewski)
Down East Suite (Moore)
Down in the Valley (Weill)
Down the Rabbit Hole (Lombardo)
Downtown (Dubensky)
Downtown Blues for Uptown Halls (Gottlieb)
Down with the Drink (Jones)
Drag and Run (Donato)
Dragon Suite (J.D. Taylor)
Drake's Dream (Chadwick)
Drama jondo (Surinach)
Dramatic Essay (Doran)
Dramatic Fanfare for 1970 (Bazelon)
Dramatic Moods (5) (McKay)

Dramatic Movement (Bazelon)
Dramatic Overture (Etler)
Dramatic Overture (Schuller)
Dramatic Overture, A (Hannay)
Dramatic Overture, or Under the Red Robe (Herbert)
Dramatic Poem (Clapp)
Dream-King and His Love (Parker)
Dream Music (Bolcom)
Dream Net, The (Benson)
Dream of Audubon, The (Diamond)
Dream of Bells and Beats, A (Schwartz)
Dream of Mary, The (Parker)
Dream Overture (Schwartz)
Dream Pedlar, The (Whithorne)
Dreams (Antheil)
Dreams (Parris)
Dreamscape (V. Fine)
Dream's End (Mayer)
Dream Sequence (Krenek)
Dream Song (Stringham)
Dream Tunnel (W. Kraft)
Dresden Interleaf 13 February 1945, The (Mumma)
Driftwood (Chihara)
Drouth (Britain)
Drum Dance (Effinger)
Drumlin Legend, A (Bacon)
Drumming (Reich)
Drums of Africa (Britain)
Drum Taps (Imbrie)
Drunkards, The (Aitken)
Dryden Liturgical Suite (Persichetti)
Dry Weather Legend (Bennett)
Dual (Babbitt)
Dualites (Ghent)
Dualities (L. Kraft)
Dude Ranch (Gillis)
Due Imagistes (W. Kraft)
due orfani, I (Lombardo)
Duke of Sacramento, The (Dello Joio)
Duke of York, The (Lucier)
Dumbarton Oaks (Stravinsky)
Dunkirk (Damrosch)
Duo concertante (Dahl)
Duo Dialogue (Mills)
Duo Forms (Haubiel)
Durations (Feldman)
Dwarf Suite (Ornstein)
Dyad (Alexander)
Dyad (Fletcher)
Dybbuk (Bernstein)
Dybbuk, The (Starer)
Dying Alchemist Preview, The (Oliveros)
Dying Poet, The (Gottschalk)
Dying Soldier, The (Fry)
Dynamic Motion (Cowell)
Dynamisms (Barlow)
Dynamite Tonight! (Bolcom)

Ennaga (Still)
Entelechy (Ghent)
Enter Ariel (Mayer)
Entertainment Piece (Berger)
Entretiens (Tcherepnin)
Entropy (Schwantner)
Eon Hours (Saminsky)
Epic Poem (Britain)
Epic Poem (Smith)
Epigram (Moevs)
Epigrams (Eaton)
Epigrams (Lees)
Epigrams (Palmer)
Epigrams and Hymn (Kay)
Epigraph (Dello Joio)
Epilogue: Spell of Creation (Ussachevsky)
Epilogue to Profiles in Courage: J.F.K. (R. Harris)
Epimethus U.S.A. (Gutchë)
Epiphanies (Pinkham)
Epiphany (Jones)
Episode (Donato)
Episodes (2) (Gilbert)
Episodes (Kohn)
Episodes (Weber)
Episodes—Jesus Christ (Van Vactor)
Epitaph (Duke)
Epitaph (V. Fine)
Epitaph for the Young American Soldier (Adler)
Epitaphium (Stravinsky)
Epitaphs (Alexander)
Epitaphs (Luke)
Epitaphs from Robert Burns (Gideon)
Epithalamion (Palmer)
Epithalamium (Fuleihan)
Epithalamium (Tremblay)
Epoch (McKay)
Epochs (Haubiel)
Epos (Donovan)
Equale: Zero Crossing (Mumma)
Erode the Greate (La Montaine)
Erogenous Zones (Lombardo)
Eros and Death (Brunswick)
Eroscapes (Blumenfeld)
Errand into the Maze (Menotti)
Erwartung (Schoenberg)
Escenas campestres (Gottschalk)
Eskaton (Doran)
Esradas (Kohn)
Essay (Mayer)
Essays (3) (Barber)
Essence (Blumenfeld)
Etcetera (Cage)
Etchmiadzin (Hovhaness)
Eternal Light, The (Thorne)
Eternal Road, The (Weill)
Etherea (Schwantner)
Et Nunc Reges (Moevs)
Etruscan Concerto (Glanville-Hicks)
Etude Fantasy (Corigliano)
Etude in Memory of Bartók (Kohs)

Étude pour espace (Varèse)
Étude pour piano sur le gamme pentatonique (Tcherepnin)
Etude Primitive (Symphony no. 1) (Becker)
Études australes (Cage)
Euphony (Ward)
Euphrosyne (Converse)
Evangeline (Burleigh)
Evangeline (Fry)
Evangeline (Luening)
Eve Learns a Little (Phillips)
Evening Music (Palmer)
Evening Piece (R. Harris)
Evening Prayer for Peace (Weisgall)
Evensong (Effinger)
Evensongs (Thorne)
Event: Synergy II (Brown)
Eve of St. Agnes (Jacobi)
Eve of St. Agnes (Mayer)
Everybody Incorporated (Brant)
Everyday Sounds for e.e. cummings (Dlugoszewski)
Everyman's Handyman (Beeson)
Every Night, Every Morn (Strang)
Every Soul Is a Circus (Nordoff)
Evocation (Loeffler)
Evocation (Shapey)
Evocation and Song (Moss)
Evocations (Avshalomov)
Evocations (Bloch)
Evocations (Dello Joio)
Evocations (Ruggles)
Evocations of Slovakia (Husa)
Evolution (Farberman)
Evolutio Transcripta (Wuorinen)
Excerpendium (Wykes)
Excerpts from a Diary (Epstein)
Exchanges (Moss)
Excursions (Bazelon)
Excursions (4) (Lockwood)
Exercise (Moss)
Exile (Symphony no. 1) (Hovhaness)
Ex Machina (Serly)
Exodus (Rogers)
Exodus (Stein)
Exotic Dance (Shepherd)
Expansions (Blumenfeld)
Expositions on a Theme by Henry David Thoreau (Stokes)
Extended Clarinet (Schwartz)
Extended Oboe (Schwartz)
Extensions (Feldman)
Exultate Deo (Daniels)
Eyepiece (Custer)

Fable of the Hapless Folktune (De Lamarter)
Fables (Aitken)
Fables (Bacon)
Fables (Persichetti)
Fables (Rorem)

Fables from the Dark Wood (Siegmeister)
Fables in Song (Kubik)
Face of War, The (Siegmeister)
Facets (Kay)
Facsimile (Bernstein)
Faculty Meeting (Doran)
Fadograph of Yestern Scene (Barber)
Fairyland (Parker)
Fairy Pictures (Korngold)
Fairy Scherzo (Daniels)
Fairy Tale (Persichetti)
Fairy Thorn, The (Hadley)
Fall, The (Diamond)
Falling Music (Rzewski)
Fall of the House of Usher, The (Hill)
Fall River Legend (Gould)
False Faces (Barlow)
False Relationships and Extended Ending (Feldman)
Family Album (Gould)
Family Music (Tuthill)
Family Portrait (Thomson)
Fancies (Epstein)
Fancies and Inventions (Weisgall)
Fancy for Five (Imbrie)
Fancy Free (Bernstein)
Fandango (Surinach)
Fandango (Whithorne)
Fanfare (Dubensky)
Fanfare and Variations (Sydeman)
Fanfare for Charles Seeger (Stout)
Fanfare for St. Louis (Schuller)
Fanfare for Symphonic Winds and Percussion (Luke)
Fanfare for the Common Man (Copland)
Fanfare for the New Atlantis (Hovhaness)
Fanfare for the Two Hundredth (Huston)
Fanfare, Fugue, and Funk (Thorne)
Fanfare on Chow Call (Eaton)
Fanfare, Prayer, and March (Koutzen)
Fanfare Prelude (Clapp)
Fanfare '76 (Creston)
Fanny Blair (Mason)
Fantaisie humoresque (Shepherd)
Fantaisie symphonique (Cole)
Fantasia (Luening)
Fantasia Brevis (Luening)
Fantasia concertante on "The Garden Hymn" (Shepherd)
Fantasia hungarica (Zador)
Fantasia quasi una sonata (Bauer)
Fantasia sopra un motivo (Moevs)
Fantasia tragica (Becker)
Fantasie (Lockwood)
Fantasies on Indian Music (Luening)
Fantasietta on British-American Ballads (Wagenaar)
Fantastic Concerto (Loeffler)
Fantasticks, The (Herrmann)

Fantasy for Space, Low Speed, Invention (Luening)
Fantasy for Three Harps on a Double Quodlibet (Scrly)
Fantasy in Delft, The (Gilbert)
Fantasy on a Mexican Christmas Carol (McBride)
Fantasy on an American Folk Tune (Stringham)
Fantasy on a Pastoral Theme (Porter)
Fantasy on a Western Folk Song (McKay)
Fantasy on Irish Folk Motives (Gideon)
Fantasy on Japanese Woodprints (Hovhaness)
Fantasy on La, Sol, Fa, Re, Mi (Kohs)
Fantasy on My Mother's Name (Karlins)
Fantasy on Themes from The Inspector General (Zador)
Fantasy Overture on Down-East Spirituals (Shepherd)
Fantasy Pieces (Ornstein)
Fantasy Portrait (Sowerby)
Fantasy Quartet (Schuller)
Fantasy Sonata (Kupferman)
Fantasy Tales (Bolcom)
Fantasy: The Farewell (Smit)
Fantasy Variations on a Theme of Youth (Hanson)
Fantôme (Hannay)
Far-East Suite (Ellington)
Fare Well (Thompson)
Farewell of Hiawatha, The (Foote)
Farewell to Pioneers (R. Harris)
Farmer and the Fairy, The (Tcherepnin)
Farm Journal (Moore)
Fascher, Der (Toch)
Fast Fantasy (Wuorinen)
Fatal Interview (Kohs)
Fatalisme (Schelling)
Fatal Oath, The (Koutzen)
Fata Morgana (Whithorne)
"Fate" (Rachmaninoff)
Father Abraham (Haubiel)
Father of Waters, The (Cadman)
Faun, The (De Lamarter)
Faust (Becker)
Fear (Blitzstein)
Feast during the Plague, The (Lourié)
Feast of Ashes (Surinach)
Feast of Life, The (Behrens)
Feast of Light, A (Adler)
Feast of Love, The (Thomson)
Federal Overture, A (Carr)
Feet First (Doran)
femme et son ombre, La (Tcherepnin)
Fem Sanger (Stout)
Feria mágica (Surinach)
Fern Hill (Corigliano)
Festival Fugues (Green)
Festival House (Oliveros)
Festival Jubilate (Beach)
Festival Mass (Brubeck)
Festival of Pan (Converse)

Festival of the Workers (McDonald)
Festival of Youth, The (Shepherd)
Festival Overture (Cowell)
Festival Overture (Gretchaninoff)
Festival Overture (Lopatnikoff)
Festival Overture (Riegger)
Festival Overture (Zador)
Festival Prelude (Branscombe)
Festival Suite (Ellington)
Festival Trumpets (Hannay)
Festive Music (Gould)
Festive Ode (Husa)
Festive Ode (Ward)
Festive Overture (Creston)
Festive Overture (Still)
Festive Overture, A (Stein)
Fête galante (Smith)
Feuerwerk (Brant)
Feuilles libres (Tcherepnin)
Feuilles mortes (Gretchaninoff)
Feuilleton (Wagenaar)
Fiddler's Jig (Cowell)
Fiesta (Fuleihan)
Fiesta de la Posada, La (Brubeck)
Fighting Men, The (Chadwick)
Filling Station (Thomson)
Final Alice (Del Tredici)
Final Ingredient, The (Amram)
"Fireflies" (Beach)
Fire Fragile Flight (Dlugoszewski)
Fire Garden, The (Brant)
Fire in Cities (Brant)
Fireside Tales (MacDowell)
Fireworks for the Profane Waltzers (Antheil)
First Construction (Cage)
First Fantasy (Austin)
First Morning of the World (Schwantner)
First Principles (Feldman)
First, Second, Third Construction (Cage)
First Thanksgiving, The (Mills)
Fisherman and His Wife, The (Schuller)
Fisherman's Wife, The (Stein)
Fission (Erb)
Fission (Ghent)
Five (Oliveros)
Five (Shapey)
Five Acre Pond (Gillis)
Five and Ten Cent Store Music (Brant)
Five Anniversaries (Bernstein)
Five Considerations (Childs)
Five Contrasts (Zador)
Five Days (Creston)
Five Episodes (Trimble)
Five Fancies (Walker)
Five Fantasies of the Theater (Siegmeister)
Fivefold Enfoldment (Krenek)
Five Fragments (Johnston)
Five Greek Lyrics (Bauer)
Five Indian Sketches (Burleigh)

Five Kings (incidental music) (Copland)
Five Little Zeppelins (Kupferman)
Five Miniatures (Starer)
Five Mobiles (Schwartz)
Five Moons of Uranus, The (Mills)
Five One Page Twelve-tone Pieces, The (Cheslock)
Five Petalled Flame (Saminsky)
Five Pieces for Young People (Smit)
5 + 1 (Krenek)
Five Portraits (Kay)
Five Portraitures of Two People (Anderson)
Five Set Pieces (Thorne)
Five Short Colloquies (Chanler)
Five Small Pieces for Large Orchestra (Van Vactor)
Five Stanzas (Rudhyar)
Five Tableaux (Wagenaar)
Five Variations on a Popular Theme (Gruenberg)
Five Various and Sundry (Phillips)
Five Verbs of Earth Encircled (Stokes)
Five Winds Blowing (McBride)
Flamenco Meditations (Surinach)
Flaming Brand, The (Clapp)
Flashback (Spiegelman)
Flashbacks (Colgrass)
fleurs d'automne, Les (Gretchaninoff)
fleurs du mal, Les (Gretchaninoff)
Flicks (Gottlieb)
Flight (Bacon)
Flight (Moss)
Flight of the Eagle, The (Converse)
Flivver Ten Million (Converse)
Florida (Sowerby)
Flower and the Hawk (Floyd)
Flower-Fed Buffaloes, The (Harbison)
Flower Music for Left Ear in a Small Room (Dlugoszewski)
Flower Seekers, The (Kelley)
Flower Wagon (Daniels)
flute à travers le violon, La (Lourié)
Flute Piece in Nine Phases (Krenek)
Flute Song (Tuthill)
Flute Song, The (Britain)
Fog, The (Ornstein)
Folio (Brown)
Folk Fantasy for Festivals (R. Harris)
Folk Overture (Mennin)
Folksong Fantasies (Green)
Folksong Fantasy (McBride)
Folk Song for Orchestra (Foss)
Folk-Song Mass (Chihara)
Folk Song Suite (Kubik)
Folk Song Suite (R. Harris)
Folk-Song Symphony (Symphony no. 4) (R. Harris)
Folk Suite (Still)
Fontana Mix (Cage)
For a Bust of Erik Satie (V. Fine)
Forces (Bassett)

From the Muses (Burleigh)
From the Northland (Sowerby)
From the Prophet Nehemiah (Jacobi)
From the Psalms (Laderman)
From the Revelation of St. John the Divine (McPhee)
From These States (Bacon)
From the Steeples and the Mountains (Ives)
From This Earth (R. Harris)
From Three Make Seven (Krenek)
Frontiers (Creston)
Front Porch Saturday Night (Siegmeister)
Frosted Window: Variations on White (Lombardo)
Frostiana (Thompson)
Fruit of Love, The (Hannay)
Fugal Fanfare (Brubeck)
Fugato on a Well-known Theme (McBride)
Fuge aus der Geographie (Toch)
Fuguing Set (La Montaine)
Fuguing Tune (Luening)
Fuji (Hovhaness)
Full Circle (Sydeman)
Full Moon in March (Harbison)
Fun and Faith of William Billings, The (Bennett)
Furama (Flagello)
Gaelic Symphony (Beach)
Gaelic Symphony (Cowell)
Gagliarda of a Merry Plague (Saminsky)
Galactic Novae (Read)
Galactic Rounds (Felciano)
Galileo Galilei (Hoiby)
Galileo Galilei (Laderman)
Gallantry (Moore)
gallina, La (Gottschalk)
Gallop (Jones)
Gambit for Dancers and Orchestra (Johnston)
Games (W. Kraft)
Game That Two Can Play, A (Clarke)
Garden Eastward, A (Weisgall)
Garden Is a Lovesome Thing, A (Bauer)
Garden of Artemis, The (Pinkham)
Garden of Eden (Bolcom)
Garden of Mystery, The (Cadman)
Gardens of Adonis, The (Weisgall)
Gargoyles (Luening)
Gates of Justice, The (Brubeck)
Gazebo Dances (Corigliano)
geliebte Stimme, Die (Weinberger)
Gemini (Gutchë)
General William Booth Enters into Heaven (Ives)
General William Booth Enters into Heaven (James)
Generation with the Torch (Beversdorf)
Genghis Khan (Gutchë)
Gentle Fire (Lucier)
Gentleman Desperado, The (Effinger)
Gentlemen, Be Seated! (Moross)
Gentle Shepherd, The (incidental music) (Reinagle)
Gently, Lord, Oh Gently Lead Us (Dett)

Geod (Foss)
Geography of Noon (Dlugoszewski)
Geometry of Circles (Glass)
George Washington Slept Here (Oliveros)
George Washington Variations (Krenek)
Georgiana (Tcherepnin)
Gerald McBoing-Boing (Kubik)
Gertrude, or Would She Be Pleased to Receive It? (Johnston)
Gesprochene Musik (Toch)
Ghosts (Lucier)
Giants in the Earth (Moore)
Gib uns den Freiden (Krenek)
Giddy Puritan, The (De Lamarter)
Gift of the Magi, The (Gillis)
Gilded Cage, The (Lees)
Gilgamesh (Berezowsky)
Giorno dei morti (Elwell)
Gitanjali (Alexander)
Gitanjali (Carpenter)
Give and Take (Clarke)
Give Ear, O Ye Heavens (Shifrin)
Glad and Very (Persichetti)
Glances (Brubeck)
Glauber and Wissen (Krenek)
Glittering Gate, The (Glanville-Hicks)
Gloriai in the Five Official Languages of the United Nations (Clarke)
Gloria in Memoriam (Walker)
Glossolalia (Felciano)
Glyphs (Fletcher)
Gnomic Commentaries (Stokes)
God Give Us Men (McDonald)
God Is Our Refuge (Boatwright)
God of Grace and God of Glory (La Montaine)
God of the Expanding Universe (Felciano)
God's Man (Labunski)
Gods of the Mountain, The (Farwell)
Gold and the Senor Commandante (Bergsma)
Golden Apple, The (Moross)
Golden Broom (Ellington)
Golden Bubble, The (Childs)
goldene Bock, Der (Krenek)
Golden Gate Overture (Lee)
Golden Gate Symphony (Clapp)
Golden Legend (Cowell)
Golden Peacock, The (Wiesgall)
Golden Sequence (McBride)
Golden Shore, The (Childs)
Goliard Songs (3) (Kohn)
Gondla (Duke)
Gone with the Wind, 1980 (Oliveros)
Goodbye to the Clowns (Laderman)
Gossips (Dubensky)
Gothic Concerto (Nordoff)
Gothic Impressions (Van Vactor)
Gothic Variations (Haubiel)
Goutelas Suite (Ellington)
Grand Bamboula (Wuorinen)
Grand Canyon Suite (Grofé)

Heroic Infinities, A (Kupferman)
Heroic Piece (Cole)
Heroic Piece (Diamond)
Heroic Poem (Britain)
Heroic Symphony (Clapp)
He Who Gets Slapped (Ward)
Hex (Ghent)
Hexaeder (Krenek)
Hexagon (Erb)
Hexapoda (Bennett)
Hiawatha (Goldmark)
Hiawatha's Wooing (Cole)
Hidden Lute, The (Read)
Hieroglyphics 3 (Brant)
Highwayman, The (Bird)
Highwayman, The (J.D. Taylor)
Highway 1, USA (Still)
Hilaritas (Shepherd)
Hill-Country Symphony (McBride)
Hill of Dreams (Gruenberg)
Hill Rhapsody, A (Clapp)
Hill Songs 1-2 (Grainger)
Historiettes au crépuscule (Bloch)
Histrionics (Adler)
Hiver–Printemps (Bloch)
Hobgoblin (Chadwick)
Hochzeit der Sobeide, Die (Tcherepnin)
Hodograph I (Brown)
Hölderlin Lieder (Wolpe)
Holiday for Four (Green)
Holiday Mood (Koutzen)
Holidays (Ives)
Holiday Service (Saminsky)
Holiday Song (Schuman)
Hollow Men, The (Cone)
Hollow Men, The (Persichetti)
Hollywood (Bennett)
Hollywood Ballet (Grofé)
Hollywood Suite (Cadman)
Hollywood Suite (Grofé)
Holofernes (Gutchë)
Holy City, The (Hovhaness)
Holy Jungle (Starer)
Holy Star, The (Daniels)
Holy Week Liturgy (Haieff)
Homage à Chopin (Behrens)
Homage à Mendelssohn (Cheslock)
Homage aux Frères Marx (Brant)
Homage to Haydn (Dello Joio)
Homage to Iran (Cowell)
Homage to Ives (Brant)
Homage to L'histoire du soldat (Sydeman)
Homecoming (Austin)
hommages, Les (Nabokov)
Hoofprints (Gottlieb)
Hooligan, The (Beversdorf)
Hootenany, The (Bacon)
Hora Mystica (Loeffler)
Hora Novissima (Parker)
Horizons (Wykes)

Horizont unkreist (Krenek)
Horn of Plenty (R. Harris)
Hornpipe (Mumma)
Horse Eats Hat (incidental music) (Bowles)
Horspfal (Stokes)
Horton Hatches the Egg (Gottlieb)
Hound of Heaven, The (Gideon)
Hour Glass, The (I. Fine)
Hour of Delusion, An (Bennett)
How Beautiful Is Night (Behrens)
"How Fair This Spot" (Rachmaninoff)
How Long, O Lord (Avshalomov)
HPSCHD (Cage)
HPSCHD (Hiller)
Hsiang Fei (Gutchë)
Huckleberry Finn Goes Fishing (Cadman)
Hudson River Suite (Grofé)
Hum-Drum Heaven (George)
Humoresque on Negro-Minstrel Tunes (Gilbert)
Hungarian Caprice (Zador)
Hungarian Folk Songs (3) (Stevens)
Hungarian Scherzo (Zador)
Hungarian Serenade (Rózsa)
Hungarian Sketches (3) (Rózsa)
Huntingdon's 2's and 3's (Phillips)
Hurricane Variations (Krenek)
Hyas Illahee (Creston)
Hydraulis (Bolcom)
Hydrogen Jukebox, The (Gaburo)
Hylas and Nymos (Glanville-Hicks)
Hymn (Jones)
Hymn (Weisgall)
Hymn and Celebration (Ward)
Hymn for Pioneers (Hanson)
Hymn of the Nativity, A (Hoiby)
Hymn of the West (Paine)
Hymns and Fuguing Tunes (Cowell)
Hymns and Responses for the Church Year (Persichetti)
Hymn to the Ancients (Burleigh)
Hymn to the Night (Donovan)
Hymn Tune Set for Two Pianos (Green)
Hymnus (Cole)
Hyperion (Toch)
Hyperion (Wuorinen)
Hyperprism (Varèse)

I Am a Mynstrel (Jones)
"I Am the Rose of Sharon" (Billings)
IBM Symphony (Giannini)
"I Can't Remember" (Moross)
Icarus (Gutchë)
Ice Flow (Subotnick)
Idealized Indian Themes (Cadman)
Ideas of Order (Berger)
Idioms (Huston)
Idiots First (Blitzstein)
Idyll of Theocritus (Sessions)
If Music Be (Farberman)

I Hate Music: Five Kid Songs (Bernstein)
I Have a Dream (Siegmeister)
I Hear America Singing (Lockwood)
I Hear an Army (Del Tredici)
"I Know a Little Garden Patch" (Foote)
Illegible Canons (Bergsma)
I'll Never Turn Back (Dett)
Illuminations (Albert)
Illusion Quartet (Burleigh)
Illustrated Alice (Del Tredici)
Image of Man (Colgrass)
Images (Babbitt)
Images (Barlow)
Images and Textures (Bassett)
Images of Man (Starer)
Images of Youth (Labunski)
Imaginary Landscapes 1–4 (Cage)
Imago Mundi (Rochberg)
Imitation (Albert)
Immigrants, The (Converse)
Immortal Autumn (Finney)
Immortal Combat (Brant)
I'm Nobody (Starer)
Impersonation (Rzewski)
Importance of Being Earnest (Castelnuovo-Tedesco)
Impressions for Oboe (Farberman)
Impressions from an Artist's Life (Schelling)
Impressions from Life (Huston)
Impressions from the Odyssey (Jacobi)
Impressions of Chinatown (Ornstein)
Impressions of Notre Dame (Ornstein)
Imprints on Ivory and Strings (Bazelon)
Impromptu for Roger (Martino)
Improving Songs for Anxious Children (Carpenter)
Improvisation (McBride)
Improvisations (Donato)
Improvisations for Orchestra and Jazz Soloists (Austin)
In a Boat (Elwell)
In Aeternum (Schwantner)
In a Garden (Kupferman)
In a Glass of Water (Bergsma)
In America (Duke)
In a Mule Drawn Wagon (Mills)
In Bohemia (Hadley)
Incantation (Luening)
Incantation, The (Luke)
Incantation and Dance (Lee)
Incantation and Dance (Still)
Incantation for Jazz Band (La Montaine)
Incantation for Tape Recorder (Ussachevsky)
Incantations (Shapey)
In Celebration (Floyd)
In Celebration of Golden Rain (Felciano)
In Celebration: Toccata for the Sixth Day (Bergsma)
In Certainty of Song (Riegger)
Incredible Flutist, The (Piston)
Indiana Homecoming (Beeson)

Indian Dances (Jacobi)
Indian Lullaby (Herbert)
"Indian Piper" (Bauer)
Indian Serenade (Converse)
Indian Snake Dance (Burleigh)
Indian War Council, The (Heinrich)
Indices (Brown)
Indigenous Portraits (4) (Still)
In Eius Memoriam (Shifrin)
Ines de Castro (Pasatieri)
Inevitable Hour, The (Lockwood)
Infanta Marina (Persichetti)
Infernal Machine, The (Chihara)
Infinities (Kupferman)
Infinity (Karlins)
Inflexions (Davidovsky)
Inland Missing the Sea (Stokes)
In Memoriam Alice Hawthorne (Sims)
In Memoriam Dylan Thomas (Stravinsky)
In Memoriam Igor Stravinsky (W. Kraft)
In Memoriam: J.F. Kennedy (Austin)
In Memoriam—John F. Kennedy (Sydeman)
In Memoriam Malcom X (Anderson)
In Memoriam: The Colored Soldiers Who Died for Democracy (Still)
In Memory of . . . (Gottlieb)
In Memory of a Summer Day (Del Tredici)
In Memory of Franklin Delano Roosevelt (Rogers)
In Midwood Silence (Glanville-Hicks)
In Music's Praise (Hadley)
Inner Circle, The (Toch)
Innerness (Ghent)
Innocent Psaltery (Kohn)
Innocents, The: The Witch Trial at Salem (W. Kraft)
In Nomine (Jones)
Innovations (Serly)
In Old Virginia (Powell)
In Our Time (Siegmeister)
In Paradisum (Krenek)
In Praise of Diplomacy and Common Sense (Trimble)
In Praise of Folly (Walker)
In Praise of Johnny Appleseed (Kupik)
In Praise of Music (Argento)
In Praise of Shahn (Schuman)
In Praise of the Owl and the Cuckoo (Salzman)
Inscape (Copland)
Inscriptions at the City of Brass (Avshalomov)
Inscriptions from Whitman (Kay)
Insects (Gruenberg)
In Space (Bergsma)
Inspector General, The (Zador)
Inspiration Waltzes (Dett)
In Springtime (Daniels)
Instant Remembered (Krenek)
Instants in Form and Movements (Dlugoszewski)
In Sweet Music (Schuman)
In Tall Grass (Crawford)
Intégrales (Varèse)

Intensity (Huston)
Interbalance I–VI (Childs)
Interface I (Custer)
Interlude (Dawson)
Interludes (Kohn)
Intermezzo and Complement (Dubensky)
Intermezzo: Music for Cleveland (Kubik)
Intermissions (Feldman)
Intermission–Ten Minutes (Gillis)
Inter-Planetary Aleatoric Serial Factory, The (Hannay)
Interplay (Gould)
Intersections (Feldman)
Intersections (Ward-Steinman)
Intervals (Anderson)
Intervals (Feldman)
In the Beginning of Creation (Pinkham)
In the Beginning Was the Word (Hovhaness)
In the Bottoms (Dett)
In the Country (Bauer)
In the French Manner (Haubiel)
In the Garden of My Father's House (Kupferman)
In the Gateway of Ispahan (Foote)
In the Greenwood (Daniels)
In the Groove (McBride)
In the Mode of Shang (Chou)
In the Mountains (Foote)
Intrada (Adler)
Intrada festiva (Labunski)
Intradas and Interludes (Husa)
Introductions and Goodbyes (Foss)
Introduction to the Problems of Philosophy (Siegmeister)
Introspection (Behrens)
Introspective Poem (McKay)
Intruder, The (Starer)
Intrusions (Partch)
Invasion (Rogers)
Invention (McPhee)
Inventions on a Motive (Colgrass)
Invisible Fire, The (Effinger)
invitation au voyage, L' (Corigliano)
Invitation to the Dance (Shepherd)
Invocation (Read)
Invocation (Shapey)
Invocation, An (Koutzen)
Invocation and Dance (Creston)
Invocations (3) (Rudhyar)
Invocation to Isis (Fuleihan)
In Wonderland (Del Tredici)
In Woods (Smit)
I, Odysseus (Aitken)
Ionisation (Varèse)
Iowa Concerto (Goeb)
Irish Suite (Cowell)
Irish Tune from County Derry (Grainger)
Irish Washerwoman, The (Sowerby)
Iron Flowers (Creston)
Iroquois Dances (4) (McPhee)
Isaiah's Prophecy (Creston)

Isaura de Salerno (Gottschalk)
Island (Schwartz)
Island Fantasy, An (Paine)
Island of the Fay, The (Gilbert)
Islands Suite (Fuleihan)
Israel Symphony (Bloch)
Is There Survival? (Hovhaness)
Italian Monk, The (incidental music) (Reinagle)
Italian Symphony (Symphony no. 1) (Stringham)
Itaque Ut (Moevs)
It's Gonna Rain (Reich)
I've Got the Tune (Blitzstein)
I Was with Him (Elwell)
I Will Praise Thee O Lord (Converse)
I Wonder As I Wander (Krenek)

Jack and the Beanstalk (Greenberg)
Jack Frost in Midsummer (Hill)
Jack's New Bag (Childs)
Jacob and the Indians (Laderman)
Jacobowsky and the Colonel (incidental music) (Bowles)
Jade Garden, The (Bassett)
Jager's Adieu, The (Heinrich)
Jam Session (McBride)
Janabar (Hovhaness)
Janiculum Symphony (Persichetti)
Janissary Music (Wuorinen)
Janus (Creston)
Janus (Schwartz)
Japanese Dances (3) (Rogers)
Japanese Nocturne (Eichheim)
Jardin publique (Duke)
Jasager, Der (Weill)
Java (Eichheim)
Jazzettes (Gruenberg)
Jazzonatas (Kreutz)
Jazz Poem (Thompson)
Jazz Suite (Gruenberg)
Jazz Symphonietta (Antheil)
Jazz Symphony (McBride)
Jazz Tangents (Ward-Steinman)
J. B., Larry and . . . (Austin)
Jealous Cellist, The (Stokes)
Jehovah and the Ark (Bacon)
Jekyll and Hyde Variations (Gould)
Jenny Lind (Lee)
Jenny/or the Hundred Nights (Weisgall)
Jeremiah Symphony (Bernstein)
Jersey Hours (Kay)
Jerusalem, City of Solomon and Christ (Symphony no. 5) (Saminsky)
Jesse James (Hiller)
jeu de la Nativité, Le (Tcherepnin)
Jewel Merchants, The (Cheslock)
Jewels of Lake Tahoe (Britain)
Jibbenainosay (Bristow)
Jig Theme and Six Changes (Green)
Joan's (Wuorinen)

Lysistrata (Brunswick)
Lysistrata (Clarke)
Lysistrata (Ornstein)

Ma Barker (Eaton)
Macbeth (Bloch)
Macbeth (incidental music) (Kelley)
Machinations (Brant)
Machine Age Blues (McKay)
Machine Music (Hiller)
Madam to You (Siegmeister)
Made by Hand (Doran)
Madeleine (Herbert)
Mme. Press Died Last Week at 90 (Feldman)
Mlle. Modiste (Herbert)
Mad Empress Remembers, A (Cadman)
Madras Sonata (Hovhaness)
Madrigal (Kupferman)
Madrigal for a Bright Morning (Barlow)
Madrigali spirituali (Wuorinen)
Mad Scene (Parris)
Magic Chair, The (Zador)
Magic Dragon, The (Custer)
Magicians, The (Austin)
Magic, Magic, Magic (Kubik)
Magic Music (Schwartz)
Magic Prison (Laderman)
Magic Water (Smit)
Magna Mater (Tcherepnin)
Magnificat (Dello Joio)
Magnolia Suite (Dett)
Mahagonny (Weill)
Maine Scene (Childs)
Main-Traveled Roads (Moevs)
"*Majesty*" (Billings)
Makrokosmos I-IV (Crumb)
Malay Mosaic (Eichheim)
Malediction (Sydeman)
Malta (Hiller)
mancenillier, Le (Gottschalk)
Manchega (Gottschalk)
Mandala, Profiles in Brass (Starer)
Mandolin (Subotnick)
mandragola, La (Castelnuovo-Tedesco)
Man from Midian (Wolpe)
Manila Te Deum (Damrosch)
Mannheim, 87.87.87 (Wuorinen)
Man without a Country, The (Damrosch)
Man with the Blue Guitar (Benson)
MAP (Foss)
Maples (Branscombe)
Maple Sugaring (Bacon)
Marching As to War (Clarke)
Marching Song of Democracy, The (Grainger)
March! March! (Farwell)
March of the Hungary Mountains (Donato)
Marco Takes a Walk (D. Taylor)
Marginal Intersection (Feldman)
Maria Golovin (Menotti)

Maria Malibran (Bennett)
Maria Theresa (Heinrich)
Marienleben, Das (Hindemith)
Marionette Overture (Weinberger)
Markheim (Floyd)
Marquesa of O., The (Siegmeister)
Marriage, The (Gretchaninoff)
Marriage at the Eiffel Tower, The (Harrison)
Marriage Counselor, The (Doran)
"*Marriage Hymn, A*" (Lyon)
Marriage of Aude, The (Rogers)
Marriage with Space, A (Becker)
Mars Ascending (Haubiel)
Marshall's Medium Message (Hannay)
Martin's Lie (Menotti)
Martyrdom of St. Stephen (Pinkham)
Martyr's Elegy, The (Finney)
Mary Who Stood in Sorrow (Lockwood)
Masada (Kupferman)
Mask of Night, The (Argento)
Mask of Night, The (Benson)
Masks (Pinkham)
Masonic Overture (Reinagle)
Masque (Jones)
Masque (Sims)
Masque of Angels, The (Argento)
Masque of the Red Death, The (Van Vactor)
Masque of the Wild Man, The (Glanville-Hicks)
Masquerade (De Lamarter)
Masquerade (Persichetti)
Masques (Persichetti)
Mass for All Souls (Clarke)
Mass for Cain (Laderman)
Mass in English (Huston)
Mass in Honor of St. Mark (James)
Mass in Honor of the Eucharist (Dello Joio)
Mass in Honor of the Sacred Heart (Becker)
Mass of Nature (La Montaine)
Mass of the Holy Spirit (Thompson)
Mass of the Pictures (James)
Mass to the Blessed Virgin (Dello Joio)
Master Builder, The (Brunswick)
Masterpiece, The (Nordoff)
Mastodon (Heinrich)
Mathis der Maler (Hindemith)
Mavra (Stravinsky)
Maypole Lovers, The (Cole)
"*May the Word of the Lord*" (Amram)
Maze, The (Austin)
McDowell's Fault or, *The Tenth Sunday after Trinity* (Sims)
McKonkey's Ferry (Antheil)
Mechanisms (Antheil)
Medea (Barber)
Medea (Farberman)
Medea (Krenek)
Medea (Luke)
Medead, The (Giannini)
Medea of Corinth (Lees)
Medieval Latin Songs (3) (Kohs)

Music for Six (Donovan)
Music for Small Centers on Piano (Dlugoszewski)
Music for the Ascension (Schwartz)
Music for the Dance (Druckman)
Music for the Flicks (Moross)
Music for the Magic Theater (Rochberg)
Music for the Marines (Van Vactor)
Music for the Mass (Babbitt)
Music for the Theater (Copland)
Music for the Venezia Space Theater (Mumma)
Music for This Time of Year (Phillips)
Music for Three (Walker)
Music for Two Violinists (Jones)
Music for Voices (Glass)
Music from The Stone Harp
Music Hall (Jacobi)
Musicians from Bremen, The (Rogers)
Music in Contrary Motion (Glass)
Music in Eight Parts (Glass)
Music in Fifths (Glass)
Music in Miniature (Billings)
Music Inn Suite (Farberman)
Music in Similar Motion (Glass)
Music in the Mine (Dett)
Music in Twelve Parts (Glass)
Musicke for Christening (Fletcher)
Music of Amber (Schwantner)
Music on a Long Thin Wire (Lucier)
Music on a Quiet Theme (Bergsma)
Music Studio (Partch)
Music to an Imaginary Ballet (Gruenberg)
Music to Oedipus Tyrannus (Paine)
Music with Changing Parts (Glass)
Musique d'amateurs (Husa)
Musique pour un vernissage (Kolb)
Mutability (I. Fine)
Mutabili, Variants for Orchestra (Starer)
Mutations for Orchestra (Felciano)
My Beloved, Let Us Go Forth (La Montaine)
My Captain (Kelley)
My Country at War (McDonald)
"My Days Have Been So Wondrous Free" (Hopkinson)
My Ends Are My Beginnings (Babbitt)
My Heart's in the Highlands (Beeson)
My Heart's in the Highlands (incidental music) (Bowles)
"My Land" (Gretchaninoff)
My, My, My, What a Wonderful Fall (Gaburo)
My Name Is (Reich)
Myopia: A Night (Smit)
My People (Ellington)
My River (Bacon)
My Shadow and I (Eichheim)
Myshkin (Eaton)
My Son, My Enemy (V. Fine)
Mysteries (Bolcom)
Mysterious Marriage, The (Hewitt)
Mysterious Mountain, The (Symphony no. 2) (Hovhaness)

Mystery, The (Floyd)
Mystery Flower of Spring (Colgrass)
Mystic Trumpeter, The (Converse)
Mystic Trumpeter, The (Dello Joio)
Mystic Trumpeter, The (Hanson)
Mystique (Bloch)
Mythical Beats (Brant)

Nabuchodonsor (Palmer)
Nach Bach (Rochberg)
Nachtlied, Das (Van Vactor)
Nagooran (Hovhaness)
naissance de la beauté, La (Lourié)
Naked Carmen, The (Corigliano)
Naked Flight Nageire (Dlugoszewski)
Naked Point Abyss (Dlugoszewski)
Naked Quintet (Dlugoszewski)
Naked Swift Music (Dlugoszewski)
Nantucket Songs, The (Rorem)
Nara (Benson)
Narrative (Finney)
Natchez on the Hill (Powell)
Nation of Cowslips, A (Argento)
Native American Portraits (Amram)
Nativity, The (Paine)
Nativity According to St. Luke, The (Thompson)
Nativity as Sung by the Shepherds, The (Thomson)
Natoma (Herbert)
Nature (Bacon)
Nature morte (Rzewski)
Nausicaa (Glanville-Hicks)
Nautical Lays of a Landsman (Mason)
Nazarene, The (Gillis)
Nazaria (Rudhyar)
Negro Folk Symphony (Dawson)
Negro Rhapsody, A (Gilbert)
Negro Work Song (Dawson)
Neither (Feldman)
Ne m'oubliez pas (Gretchaninoff)
neue Orpheus, Der (Weill)
Never (Gaburo)
New and Old (Riegger)
New Dance (Riegger)
New England Chronicle (Donovan)
New England Episodes (Porter)
New England Folksing (Kreutz)
New England Idyl (MacDowell)
New England Overture, A (Alexander)
New England Prospect (Erb)
New England Psalm Singer, The (Billings)
New England Sketches (3) (Piston)
New England Triptych (Schuman)
Newfoundland Air (Saminsky)
New Frontiers (Beversdorf)
New Land, New Covenant (Hanson)
New Light, The (Van Vactor)
New Orleans Suite (Ellington)
New People (Colgrass)

New Piece Loops (Brown)
New Song, A (Hopkinson)
New World a-Comin' (Ellington)
New Year's Service for Young People (Gottlieb)
New York Days and Nights (Whithorne)
New York Profiles (Dello Joio)
New York Times—August 30, 1964 (Farberman)
New York World's Fair Suite (Grofé)
"ng. c" (Wuorinen)
Niagara (Bristow)
Niagara (Fry)
Niagara Falls Suite (Grofé)
Ni bruit, ni vitesse (Foss)
"Nickel under My Foot, The" (Blitzstein)
Nick of Time, The (Shifrin)
"Night" (Gretchaninoff)
Night (Johnston)
Night before Christmas, The (Gillis)
Night Conjure-Verse (Del Tredici)
Night Creature (Ellington)
Night Dances (Persichetti)
Night Fantasies (Carter)
Night Flight (Read)
"Night Has a Thousand Eyes, The" (Foote)
Night in Bethlehem, A (Daniels)
Nightingale (Colgrass)
Nightingale, The (Rogers)
Nightingale and the Two Sisters, The (Grainger)
Night in Old Paris, A (Hadley)
Night Jar (Oliveros)
Night Journey (Schuman)
Night Music (Crumb)
Night Music (Rochberg)
Night Music (Rorem)
Night Music (Ward)
Night of the Four Moons (Crumb)
Night of the Moonspell (Siegmeister)
Night of the Raccoon (Colgrass)
Night of the Tropics (Gottschalk)
Night Piece (Jacobi)
Night Piece, A (Foote)
Night Piece and Dance (Jacobi)
Nights and Lights (Stokes)
Nightscape (Moss)
Nights in the Ukraine, The (Loeffler)
Night Soliloquy (Kennan)
Night Song (Barlow)
Night Song (Benson)
Night Voices (Epstein)
Night Waltz (Bowles)
Nine Lessons of Christmas, The (La Montaine)
Nine Moods (Gruenberg)
Nine Rivers from Jordan (Weisgall)
—1963 (Symphony no. 9) (R. Harris)
Nine Tetragrams (Rudhyar)
90th Psalm, The (Chihara)
Nissan (Britain)
Noah (Salzman)
Noah and the Flood (Stravinsky)
Noa Noa (Lee)

Nobilissime Visione (Hindemith)
Noblest Game, The (Diamond)
Nocturnal (Varèse)
Nocturne and Dance of the Fates (Ornstein)
Nocturne in Hollywood (Castelnuovo-Tedesco)
Noël (Chadwick)
No for an Answer (Blitzstein)
Noiseless, Patient Spider, A (Dahl)
Nomads (Brant)
No Man Is an Island (Clarke)
Noneto (Davidovsky)
No Place to Go but Around (Rzewski)
Nordic Symphony (Hanson)
Norge (Clapp)
North American Time Capsule (Lucier)
North and West (Hanson)
Northern Ballad, A (Parker)
Northern Lights (Donato)
North Hungarian Peasant Songs and Dances
  (Rózsa)
Norwegian Moods (Stravinsky)
Nostalgic Songs of Earth (Becker)
Nostalgic Waltzes (Finney)
Notes in the Silence (Bassett)
Notre Dame de Paris (Fry)
Notturno (Toch)
Notturno (Trimble)
Notturno ungherese (Rózsa)
nouvelle Heloïse, La (Haieff)
Nova (Collage '72) (Ward-Steinman)
Novara (Brown)
Novela (String Quartet no. 9) (Bolcom)
Novellis, Novellis (La Montaine)
Novo Odo (Harrison)
Now Tilting Naked (Dlugoszewski)
Nuances (Haubiel)
Nude Paper Sermon, The (Salzman)
Numbers (Feldman)
Nunc Sanctis Nobis Spiritus (Boatwright)
Nunsch-Nunschi, Das (Hindemith)
Nuns of Perpetual Adoration (Hill)
Nun's Priest's Tale, The (Finney)
Nuptial Scene (Adler)
Nymph and Satyr (Hanson)

O Altitudo (Stout)
Ocean, The (Hadley)
Ocean, The (Smith)
O Cool Is the Valley (Persichetti)
Octagon (Mayer)
Octandre (Varèse)
Octoroon Ball, The (Castelnuovo-Tedesco)
Octet, a Grand Fantasia (Rochberg)
Octocelli (Fletcher)
Ode for Orchestra (Elwell)
Ode for St. Cecilia's Day (Josten)
Ode, or Meditation at Night on the Majesty of God
  as Revealed by the Aurora Borealis (Nabokov)
Odes of Shang (Shifrin)

Ode to Freedom (Hovhaness)
Ode to Music (Hadley)
Ode to Music (Hopkinson)
Ode to Napoleon (Schoenberg)
Ode to Peace (Lyon)
Ode to Peace (Zador)
Ode to Pothos (Etler)
Ode to the Memory of James Bremner (Hopkinson)
Ode to the Milky Way (Duke)
Ode to the Morning of Christ's Nativity (Diamond)
Ode to the New Earth (Hadley)
Ode to the Sacred Memory of Our Late Gracious Sovereign George II (Hopkinson)
Ode to the Virginian Voyage (Thompson)
Ode to the West Wind (Argento)
Ode to the West Wind (Weiss)
Ode to Truth (R. Harris)
Ode to Zion (Jacobi)
Odyssey (Lees)
Oecumenicus (Sydeman)
Oedipus (Partch)
Oedipus Rex (Stravinsky)
Of a Feather (Bacon)
Offrandes (Varèse)
Of Hartford in a Purple Light (D. Harris)
Of Identity (Luening)
Of Love (Dlugoszewski)
Of Man's Moralitie (Avshalomov)
Of Mice and Men (Floyd)
Of New Horizons (Kay)
"*Of Obedience*" (Kirchner)
Of Night and the Sea (Palmer)
Of Pioneer Women (Green)
Of Place (Childs)
Of Saints and Sinners (Adler)
Of Shadows Numberless (Gideon)
Of the Mountains, of the Past, the Shifting Lights Call to Remember the Music (Stokes)
Of Wood and Brass (Ussachevsky)
Oh, Friends! (Hannay)
O'Higgins of Chile (Cowell)
Ohioana (Haubiel)
Ohio River Suite (Bennett)
Ojos Criollos (Gottschalk)
Old American Country Set (Cowell)
Old California (Still)
Old Chisholm Trail, The (Effinger)
Old English Songs (Thomson)
Old Maid (Rzewski)
Old Maid and the Thief, The (Menotti)
Old Man's Love Song (Farwell)
Omaggio I–III (Moss)
Omaggio a Boccherini (Castelnuovo-Tedesco)
Ombra (W. Kraft)
O Moment's Reflection (Imbrie)
On Alligators (Wuorinen)
On American Themes (Green)
On a Quiet Theme (Gaburo)
Once Upon a Time (Rogers)

One Christmas Long Ago (Mayer)
105 Degrees West (Effinger)
135th Street (Gershwin)
One Man (Johnston)
I of IV (Oliveros)
One Thing is Certain (Weisgall)
1000 Acres (Oliveros)
Ongaku (Cowell)
Only Jealousy of Emer, The (Harrison)
Only Talking Machine of Its Kind in the World (Lucier)
Only the Hopeful (Kohn)
Onomtopeosis (Etler)
On the Beach at Night (Bergsma)
On the Beach at Night (Imbrie)
On the Bedlands—Parables (Stokes)
On the Death of a Spanish Child (Cazden)
On the Education of Man (Wolpe)
On the Highway (Dubensky)
On the Morning of Christ's Nativity (Jones)
On the Nature of Things (Brant)
On the Nature of Things (Starer)
"*On the Steppe*" (Gretchaninoff)
On the Town (Bernstein)
On the Waterfront (film score) (Bernstein)
On This Ground (Siegmeister)
Ontogeny (Shapey)
Ontonagon Sketches (Britain)
On Variations (D. Harris)
Open House (Bolcom)
Openings of the Eye (Dlugoszewski)
Open Road, or *Western Dance, The* (Harrison)
Open Style (Austin)
Open the Gates (Lee)
Opera Cloak, The (Damrosch)
Operation Flabby Sleep (Childs)
Opposites (Clarke)
O Pulchritudo (Menotti)
Opus 51 (V. Fine)
Oracle, The (Lees)
Oracles (Bolcom)
Oratorio of the Pilgrim Fathers (Heinrich)
Oratorio of Understanding, The (Huston)
Orchestra (Felciano)
Orchestral Abstractions (Sydeman)
Orchestral and Electronic Exchanges (Wuorinen)
Orchestral Fantasy (Lombardo)
Orchestral Radiant Ground (Dlugoszewski)
Orchestral Sketches (Elwell)
Orchestral Songs (4) (Kohs)
Orchestra Structure for the Poetry of Everyday Sounds (Dlugoszewski)
Ordering of Moses, The (Dett)
Organon I–II (Palmer)
Organ Symphony (Sowerby)
Organum (Ruggles)
Orientale (Dubensky)
Orientale Suite (Hadley)
Orientalia (Saminsky)
Oriental Impressions (Eichheim)

Pilate (Hovhaness)
Pilgrimage (Floyd)
Pilgrim Fathers (Stringham)
Pilgrim Psalms (Finney)
Pilgrims (Rorem)
Pilgrims, The (Chadwick)
Pilgrim's Hymn (Luening)
Pilgrims of Destiny (Branscombe)
Pilgrim's Progress (Kelley)
Pilgrim Vision, A (Carpenter)
Pinocchio: A Merry Overture (Toch)
Pioneer (Cole)
Pioneer Epic (McKay)
Pioneers (Haubiel)
Pioneer Spiritual (McBride)
Pioneers Symphony, The (Clapp)
Pipe of Desire, The (Converse)
Piper of Hamelin, The (Flagello)
Pirate, The (Gilbert)
Pirates' Island (Daniels)
"Pirate Song, The" (Gilbert)
Pit and the Pendulum, The (Kelley)
Pizarro (Hewitt)
Place (Subotnick)
Place of the Beast, The (Thompson)
Plain-Chant for America (Still)
Plains, The (Donato)
Plains, The (Rogers)
Plan for Spacecraft (Rzewski)
Planta-Tholoi (Huston)
Plastic Surgery (Austin)
Platero y Yo (Castelnuovo-Tedesco)
Play! 1-4 (Subotnick)
Play Ball (Phillips)
Play of Words, The (Van Vactor)
Playthings of the Wind (Alexander)
Pleasure Dome of Kubla Khan, The (Griffes)
Pleiades, The (Persichetti)
Pleiades, The (Serly)
Plough and the Stars, The (Siegmeister)
Plough That Broke the Plains, The (Thomson)
Pocahontas (Carter)
Pocket Encyclopedia of Orchestral Instruments,
 The (Fletcher)
Pocket Size Sonata, A (Behrens)
Poem (Creston)
Poem (Griffes)
Poem (Husa)
Poem (Sowerby)
Poem (Whithorne)
Poem and Dance (Porter)
Poème dramatique (Gretchaninoff)
Poème électronique (Varèse)
Poème élégiaque (Gretchaninoff)
Poème-Nocturne, Solitude (Koutzen)
Poèmes d'automne (Bloch)
Poèmes pour la paix (Rorem)
Poem for Orchestra (Still)
Poem in Cycles and Bells, A (Luening)
Poem in Cycles and Bells, A (Ussachevsky)

Poem in October (Corigliano)
Poem of Youth (Smith)
Poem on His Birthday (Corigliano)
Poems (Shapey)
Poems for Music (Barlow)
Poems of Love and the Rain (Rorem)
Poems of 1917 (Ornstein)
Poems of Time and Eternity (Schuller)
Poems of White Stone (Chou)
Poems of Youth (Rudhyar)
Poems to Martha (Toch)
Poem: To Mary in Heaven (Yardumian)
Poetical Sketches (Hill)
Poet in the Desert, The (Jacobi)
Poet's Requiem, The (Rorem)
Pointpoint (Mumma)
Points and Excursions (Wykes)
Points on Jazz (Brubeck)
Points West (Clarke)
Point That Divides the Wind, The (Kolb)
Poison Tree, A (Weiss)
Polish Dance (Cheslock)
Polish Renaissance Suite (Labunski)
Political Power (Harrison)
Political Suite (Dubensky)
Politics of Harmony, The (Wuorinen)
Polychromatics (Gruenberg)
Polyphonica (Cowell)
Polyphony (Berger)
Ponteach (Hiller)
Pool of Darkness, The (Weber)
Poor Richard (Finney)
Pop-Pourri (Del Tredici)
Porgy and Bess (Gershwin)
Portals (Ruggles)
Portents of Aquarius (Visions and Prophecies)
 (Palmer)
Portfolio for Diverse Performers and Tape, A
 (Hiller)
Portrait (Husa)
Portrait (Rogers)
Portrait (Rzewski)
Portrait of a Frontier Town (Gillis)
Portrait of a Lady (D. Taylor)
Portrait of Carlos Chávez (Beversdorf)
Portrait of Juan de Pereja (Trimble)
Portrait of Man (Verrall)
Portrait of St. Christopher (Verrall)
Portraits (Haubiel)
Portraits (Martino)
Portraits (Thomson)
Portrait Suite (Kay)
Port Royale, 1861 (McKay)
Poseidon (Kupferman)
Possessed, The (Kupferman)
Possessed, The (Spiegelman)
Postcard from Morocco (Argento)
Post Card Theater (Oliveros)
Postman's Knock (Glanville-Hicks)
Post-Partitions (Babbitt)

Puck: A Legend of Bethlehem (Kubik)
Pueblo: A Moon Epic (Saminsky)
Pulsar (Stout)
Pumpkin Eater's Little Fugue (McBride)
Punch and Judy (McBride)
Punchinello (Herbert)
Purgatory (Weisgall)
Puritania (Kelley)
Purple Roofed Ethical Suicide Parlor (Erb)
Pursuing Happiness (George)
Pushmataha—A Venerable Chief of a Western Tribe of Indians (Heinrich)
Pygmalion Overture (Britain)
Pyknon (Anderson)
Pyramids of Giza (Britain)
Pyramids of Giza, The (Fuleihan)

Quadra (Fletcher)
Quadrants: Event/Complex (Austin)
Quaestio Temporis (Krenek)
Quaint Events (Del Tredici)
Quaker Reader, A (Rorem)
Quarter-tone Piano Pieces (3) (Ives)
Quartet (Green)
Quartet Euphometric (Cowell)
Quartet Four (Austin)
Quartet in Open Style (Austin)
Quartet Plus (Foss)
Quartet Romantic (Cowell)
Quartet Three (Austin)
Quartet Venuti (Kreutz)
Quasimodo, the Great Lover (Lucier)
Quebec (Branscombe)
Queen and the Rebels, The (Moss)
Queen Helena (Gruenberg)
Queen of the South, The (Lucier)
Queens College (Salzman)
Queens Obsession, The (Green)
Quentin Durward (incidental music) (Moore)
Quest (R. Harris)
Quest (Weisgall)
Question of Summer, A (Childs)
Questo fu il carro della morte (Castelnuovo-Tedesco)
Quick Dichotomies (Dlugoszewski)
Quiet City (incidental music) (Copland)
Quiet Evening (Effinger)
Quiet Lodging, The (Chadwick)
Quiet Music (Alexander)
Quiet Music (Read)
Quiet Piece—for a Violent Time, A (Bazelon)
Quintessence (Farberman)
Quintessence (Huston)
Quintessence (Thorne)
Quintet Concerto (Kay)
Quintet for Groups (Johnston)
Quintetto "Serbelloni" (Stevens)
Quintina (Krenek)
Quodlibet Montagna (Avshalomov)

Rabbi Akiba (Feldman)
Race of Life, The (V. Fine)
Radiant Bridge (Verrall)
Raga for Winds (Ward-Steinman)
"Raggy Waltz" (Brubeck)
Ragpicker's Love (Bauer)
Raids, The: 1940 (Parris)
Rain, The (Whithorne)
Rain Down Death (Becker)
Rain Music (Chihara)
Raising of Lazarus, The (Rogers)
Rajah (Dubensky)
Rake's Progress, The (Stravinsky)
Ramuntcho (D. Taylor)
Rapsodie concertante (Weber)
Rapsodie nègre (Powell)
Raptures (Ashalomov)
Rapunzel (Harrison)
Raquel (Gutchë)
Rasputin's End (Nabokov)
Rat Riddle (Crawford)
Raven, The (Dubensky)
Raven, The (Gillis)
Raven, The (Weinberger)
Realities 1-2 (Subotnick)
Realm of Fancy, The (Paine)
Rebellion and Rejection (Krenek)
Recesses of My House, The (Phillips)
Recitative and Aria (Moross)
Reconnaissance (Erb)
Recordare (Foss)
Record of Our Time, A (Kubik)
Re-Creation (Anderson)
Recreations (Kohn)
Red Clay (Britain)
Red Cockatoo, The (Kohn)
Red King's Throw, The (Kupferman)
Redwood (Chihara)
Reflections (Babbitt)
Reflections (Beversdorf)
Reflections (Kohn)
Reflections (Toch)
Reflections of Emily (Mennin)
Reflux (Karlins)
Refractions (Kupferman)
Regina (Blitzstein)
Registrar, The (Doran)
Reisebuch aus den Österreichischen Alpen (Krenek)
Rejoice (R. Harris)
Rejoice and Sing (R. Harris)
Relata I-II (Babbitt)
relicario de los animales, El (Oliveros)
Reliquary for Igor Stravinsky, A (Wuorinen)
Remarkable Adventure of Henry Bold, The (Zador)
Remembrance (Bassett)
Remembrance (Benson)
Remembrance (Flagello)
Remembrances (Moss)

Reminiscences (Dubensky)
Reminiscing in Tempo (Ellington)
Renaissance Garland, A (Shifrin)
renegados, Los (Surinach)
Renga (Cage)
Réponse à Goya (Spiegelman)
Reproaches, The (Pinkham)
Requiem, The (Symphony no. 4) (Hanson)
Requiem and Resurrection (Hovhaness)
Requiem Canticles (Stravinsky)
Requiem for a Rich Young Man (Lockwood)
Requiescat (W. Kraft)
Requiescat in Pace (Adler)
Resonance (Wykes)
Responses (Shifrin)
Restoration Suite (D. Taylor)
Resurgam (Hadley)
Resurrection of Don Juan, The (Argento)
Reticulation (Erb)
Return and Rebuild the Desolate Places (Hovhaness)
Return of Odysseus, The (Phillips)
Return of Pushkin, The (Nabokov)
Reuben, Reuben (Blitzstein)
Reunion (Cage)
Revelation in the Courthouse Park (Partch)
Revelation Is Not Sealed (Clarke)
Revelation of St. John the Divine (Argento)
Revelations of St. Paul (Hovhaness)
Revelation Symphony (Burleigh)
Reveller, The (Loeffler)
Reyem (Shapey)
Rhapsodality Band (Custer)
Rhapsodality Brass! (Custer)
Rhapsodality Brown! (Custer)
Rhapsodic Fantasy (Colgrass)
Rhapsodic Variations (Luening)
Rhapsodic Variations (Thorne)
Rhapsodic Variations (Ussachevsky)
Rhapsodic géorgienne (Tcherepnin)
Rhapsody in Blue (Gershwin)
Rhapsody in Red and White (Cheslock)
Rhapsody of Dances, A (Fletcher)
Rhapsody of St. Bernard (Smith)
Rhapsody on a Russian Theme (Gretchaninoff)
Rhapsody on a Theme by Paganini (Rachmaninoff)
Rhapsody on Dunlap's Creek (Saminsky)
Rhumbando (Britain)
Rhymes from the Hill (Gideon)
Rhythm Gallery (Gould)
Rhythmicana (Cowell)
"Rialto Ripples" (Gershwin)
Richard Cory (James)
Ricordanza (Rochberg)
Rider, The (Daniels)
Riding Hood Revisited (Moross)
Riding the Wind (Chou)
Rilke (Blumenfeld)
Ring des Polykrates, Der (Korngold)

Ringing Changes (Wuorinen)
———*Ringings* (Gaburo)
Ring of Time, A (Argento)
Riolama (Piano Concerto no. 1) (Bacon)
Rip (Schwartz)
riposo, Il (James)
Rip Van Winkle (Bristow)
Rip Van Winkle (Chadwick)
Rip Van Winkle (Flagello)
Rissolty Rissolty (Crawford)
Rite of Passage (Parris)
Rites de passage (Pasatieri)
Rites in Tehnochtitlàn (Gutchë)
Ritmo jondo (Surinach)
Ritorno (Martino)
Ritratti, Portraits for Piano (Stevens)
Ritual Game, A (Subotnick)
Rituals (Shapey)
Rituals (Ward-Steinman)
Rivals, The (Eichheim)
River, The (Ellington)
River, The (Thomson)
RMSIMI, The Bird of Bremen Flies through the Houses of the Burghers (Lucier)
Robbers, The (Rorem)
Robin Hood (Hewitt)
Rock, The (Beversdorf)
Rock, The (Rachmaninoff)
Rock Crusher, The (Donato)
Rock of Liberty, The (Cole)
Rodeo (Copland)
Roma: A Theater Piece in Open Style (Austin)
Romance with a Double Bass (Dubensky)
Roman Sketches (4) (Griffes)
Romantic Ode (V. Fine)
Romantic Piece (Blitzstein)
Romantic Symphony (Symphony no. 2) (Hanson)
Romanza (Creston)
Romeo and Juliet (incidental music) (Nordoff)
Romeo and Juliet (Rorem)
Romeo and Juliet Suite (Diamond)
Rondo capriccioso (Gutchë)
Rope, The (Mennini)
Rosa (Reinagle)
Rose (Johnston)
Rose for Emily, A (Hovhaness)
Rose Moon (Oliveros)
Rose Mountain Slow Runner (Oliveros)
Rose of Avontown, The (Beach)
Rota (Barlow)
Rotate the Body in All Its Planes (Partch)
Rothko Chapel (Feldman)
Rouge Bouquet (Becker)
Round a Common Center (Foss)
Rounds (Diamond)
Rowdy Dance (Tuthill)
Royal Invitation, or Homage to the Queen of Tonga (Argento)
Royal Palace (Weill)
Rubâiyât (Hovhaness)

Rübezahl (Bird)
Ruby, The (Dello Joio)
Rudolph Gott Symphony (Farwell)
"*Runner, The*" (Kirchner)
Running Colors (Goeb)
Rural Elegy (Smit)
Russian Bells (Dubensky)
Russian Nocturnes (2) (Lopatnikoff)
Russians (Mason)
Rye Septet (Saminsky)

Saadia (Jacobi)
Sabbath Evening Service (Jacobi)
Sabbath Evening Service (Saminsky)
Sabbath Eve Service (Starer)
Sabbath Morning Service (Saminsky)
Sabi Music (Dlugoszewski)
Sack of Calabasas, The (Fletcher)
Sacred Canticle no. 4 ("Canticle of the Sun")
   (Mills)
Sacred Service (Bloch)
Sacred Service (Spiegelman)
Sacred Service for Sabbath Eve (Amram)
Sacred Service for Sabbath Morning (Gideon)
Sacred Service for the Sabbath Eve (Castelnuovo-
   Tedesco)
Sacred Songs for Pantheists (Ward)
Sacred Songs of Reconciliation (Mizmor l'Piyus)
   (Rochberg)
Sacred Verses (C. Taylor)
Sacrifice, The (Converse)
Sadhana (Creston)
Sadness (Barber)
Safe in Their Alabaster Chamber (Pinkham)
Safie (Hadley)
Saga of the Mississippi (McDonald)
Saga of the Prairie (Copland)
Sahdji (Still)
St. Francis (Hindemith)
Saint Francis of Assisi (Britain)
St. Joan (incidental music) (Nordoff)
St. Lawrence Suite (Gould)
St. Luke Christmas Story, The (Effinger)
St. Mark Passion (Pinkham)
Saint of Bleecker Street, The (Menotti)
St. Peter (Paine)
Saints' Wheel (Haieff)
St. Vartan (Symphony no. 9) (Hovhaness)
Salammbô's Invocation to Tanith (Gilbert)
Salem Shore (Nordoff)
Salome (Hadley)
Salomone Rossi (Foss)
salón México, El (Copland)
Salut à Nadia (Labunski)
Salut à Paris (Labunski)
Salute to Youth (R. Harris)
Salve, Festa Dies (Daniels)
Samson (Goldmark)
Samson Agonistes (incidental music) (Nabokov)
Samson Agonistes (Starer)

Samuel Chapter (Harbison)
Sancti Spiritus (Gretchaninoff)
San Francisco Newsboy Cries (Partch)
San Francisco Sequence (Krenek)
San Francisco Suite (Grofé)
San Juan Capistrano (McDonald)
San Luis Rey (Britain)
Santa Claus, a Christmas Symphony (Fry)
Santa Fe Saga (Gould)
Santa Fe Songs, The (Rorem)
Santa Fe Time Table (Krenek)
Sappho (Glanville-Hicks)
Saraband for the Golden Goose (Clarke)
Saracens, The (MacDowell)
Sarah (Laderman)
Sardakai (Krenek)
Sassafras (Bacon)
Satire, A (Smith)
Satire: Concerto for Orchestra (Laderman)
Satires (Bolcom)
Satires of Circumstance (Shifrin)
Satirical Sarcasms (3) (Read)
Satiric Dances (Dello Joio)
Satiric Fragments (3) (Phillips)
Saturday Night at the Firehouse (Cowell)
Saturday's Child (Whithorne)
Saturn (Hovhaness)
Saturnale (Britain)
Satyagraha (Glass)
Saul (Castelnuovo-Tedesco)
Saul and the Witch of Endor (Glanville-Hicks)
savane, La (Gottschalk)
Savoyard, The (incidental music) (Reinagle)
Saws (Bacon)
Sayings in Our Time (Hannay)
Sayings of the World (Franco)
Saying Something (Salzman)
Scarecrow, The (Lockwood)
Scarlet Letter, The (Damrosch)
Scarlet Letter, The (Giannini)
Scarlett Mill, The (Zador)
Scatter (Schwartz)
Scena (Phillips)
Scena cambiata (Smit)
Scena da camera (Phillips)
Scenario for Orchestra (Kubik)
Scènes d'Anabase (Bowles)
Scènes de ballet (Stravinsky)
Scenes for Orchestra (Kubik)
Scenes for Small Orchestra (Moss)
Scenes from a Tragedy (Smith)
Scenes from Hamlet (Kreutz)
Scenes from Shir Ha-Shirim (Davidovsky)
Scenes from the Louvre (Dello Joio)
Schauspiel Ouverture (Korngold)
Schelomo (Bloch)
Scherzi musicale (Kay)
Scherzo diabolique (Hadley)
Scherzo fantastique (Bloch)
Schiller (Heinrich)

Short Overture to an Unknown Opera (Gillis)
Short Symphony (Copland)
Short Symphony (Cowell)
Short Symphony, A ("From a Mountain Town,"
    or "From the Black Hills") (McKay)
Shout for Joy (Gottlieb)
Show Piece (McBride)
Shropshire Lad, A (Duke)
Sicilian Limes (Argento)
Sicilian Lyrics (Lombardo)
Sicilian Romance, The (incidental music)
    (Reinagle)
Sidewinder (Subotnick)
sieben Todsünden, Die (Weill)
Siege of Tripoli, The (Carr)
Sierra Morena (Whithorne)
Sights and Sounds (Bennett)
Signals (Schwartz)
Sign Here (Doran)
Signor Deluso (Pasatieri)
Signs of the Zodiac (Pinkham)
Sign Sounds (Brown)
Silbersee, Der (Weill)
Silent Noon (Cone)
Silent Paper Spring and Summer Friend Songs
    (Dlugoszewski)
Silhouettes (Lees)
Silhouettes (3) Mason)
Silhouettes, San Francisco (Hadley)
Silver Apples of the Moon (Subotnick)
Silver Pilgrimage (Symphony no. 15) (Hovhaness)
"Silver Shield, The" (Duke)
Silver World, The (Rogers)
Simfony from Simfonies (Harrison)
Simultaneities (Thorne)
Sinbad the Sailor (Converse)
Sinfonia breve (Bloch)
Sinfonia breve (Van Vactor)
Sinfonia capricciosa (Mennin)
Sinfonia Clarion (Weber)
Sinfonia da camera (Barlow)
Sinfonia Sacra (Hanson)
Sinfonia seria (C. Taylor)
Sinfonica da Pacifica (Glanville-Hicks)
Sinfonietta flamenca (Surinach)
Singing Master's Apprentice (Billings)
Sing Out, Sweet Land (Siegmeister)
Sinister Resonance (Cowell)
Sinner Man (Boatwright)
Sioux Flute Serenade (Skilton)
Sir Gawain and the Green Knight (Felciano)
Sister Beatrice (Gretchaninoff)
Sisters (film score) (Herrmann)
sito de Zaragoza, El (Gottschalk)
Six Characters (Clarke)
Six Characters in Search of an Author (Weisgall)
Six Dance Designs (Serly)
Six for Bass (Tuthill)
Six from Ohio (Etler)
Six Pianos (Reich)

Six Set Pieces (Thorne)
Sixty (Brant)
Six Variations with Twelve Tones (Starer)
Six Winter Evening Tales and Tone Poems
    (Brunswick)
Skating on the Sheyenne (Finney)
Skeleton in Armor, The (Foote)
Sketches in Black and White (Beeson)
Sketches of the City (Read)
Sky Music (Rorem)
Sky of Cloudless Sulphur, A (Subotnick)
Skyscrapers (Carpenter)
Sky with Clouds (Subotnick)
Slava! (Bernstein)
Slaves in Algiers (incidental music) (Reinagle)
Slow Dance (Avshalomov)
Slow Dusk (Floyd)
Slow Piece (Finney)
Slumber Music and Serenade (Cheslock)
Small Sonata (Smith)
Smoke and Steel (Donovan)
Smoke and Steel (Stokes)
Snowflakes (Gretchaninoff)
Snow Goose, The: A Legend of World War II
    (Becker)
Snow Queen (Mayer)
Snow Queen, The (Gaburo)
Sojourner and Mollie Sinclair, The (Floyd)
Solari (Haubiel)
Solar Sounder (Lucier)
Soldiers (Mason)
Soldier Songs (Weisgall)
Soldiers on the Town (Berezowsky)
Solemn Music, A (Thomson)
Soleriana concertante (Phillips)
Soliloquies (Bassett)
Soliloquies (Schwartz)
Soliloquy (Corigliano)
Soliloquy (Eaton)
Soliloquy 1-2 (Rogers)
Soliloquy (Shapey)
Soliloquy and Dance (R. Harris)
Soliloquy and Dance (Kubik)
Soliloquy of a Bhiksuni (Chou)
Solitary Dancer, The (Beeson)
Solitude (Rudhyar)
Solitude in the City (Donato)
Solo for a Virtuoso (Trimble)
Solomon and Balkis (Thompson)
Solomon's Garden (Brant)
Solomon's Garden (Sowerby)
Solo Requiem, A (Babbitt)
Some New York Scenes (Ornstein)
Something New for the Zoo (Hoiby)
Something of the Sea (Benson)
Some Voltage Drop (Mumma)
Sonar Plexus (Thorne)
Sonata canonica (Castelnuovo-Tedesco)
Sonata da camera (Childs)
Sonata da camera (Dahl)

Sonata Fantasia (Rochberg)
Sonata for Fortified Piano (Ward-Steinman)
Sonata for Microtonal Piano (Johnston)
Sonata for Two (Johnston)
Sonata liturgique (Lourié)
Sonata Mystikos (Kupferman)
Sonata on Jazz Elements (Kupferman)
Sonata pastorale (Dahl)
Sonata pastorale (Smith)
Sonata piccola (Jones)
Sonata seria (Dahl)
Sonata teutonica (Powell)
Sonate noble (Powell)
Sonate psychologique (Powell)
Sonate sauvage (Antheil)
Sonatine piacevole (Stevens)
Sonetti romani (Gretchaninoff)
Sonetto del Petrarca (Stevens)
Song and Dance (Kreutz)
Song and Dance (Rzewski)
Song and Dance (Talma)
Song at Evening, A (Converse)
Songfest (Bernstein)
Song for Morpheus (Lombardo)
Song for St. Cecilia's Day, A (Boatwright)
Song for Warriors, A (Fletcher)
Song in Summer (Gillis)
Song of America (Sowerby)
Song of Anguish, The (Foss)
Song of Bethlehem (Brubeck)
Song of Celebration, A (Weisgall)
Song of Consolation, A (Cole)
Song of Deborah, The (Huston)
Song of Democracy, The (Hanson)
Song of Eros (Shapey)
Song of Faith (Carpenter)
Song of Faith, A (Gruenberg)
Song of Freedom (Carpenter)
Song of Gratitude, A (Cole)
Song of Honor (Fletcher)
Song of Human Rights (Hanson)
Song of Innocence (Blumenfeld)
Song of Isaiah (Epstein)
Song of Jael (Daniels)
Song of Moses (Ward-Steinman)
Song of Mourning (Wagenaar)
Song of Occupations, A (R. Harris)
Song of Orpheus, A (Schuman)
Song of Peace (Persichetti)
Song of Promise (Paine)
Song of Solomon (Moss)
Song of Songs, The (Castelnuovo-Tedesco)
Song of Songs, Which is Solomon's, The (Gottlieb)
Song of the Carolina Low Country (Thorne)
Song of the Future (James)
Song of the High Seas (Weinberger)
Song of the Nations (McDonald)
Song of the Night (James)
Song of the Nightingale, The (Rogers)
Song of the Nymph Called Echo (Zador)

Song of the Pilgrims, The (Shepherd)
Song of the Sea (Converse)
Song of the Viking, The (Chadwick)
Song of Welcome (Beach)
Song of Youth, A (Clapp)
Songs about Spring (Argento)
Songs at Parting (Bacon)
Songs before an Adieu (Kolb)
Songs, Drones and Refrains of Death (Crumb)
Songs for Eve (Alexander)
Songs for Eve (Laderman)
Songs for R.P.B. (Eaton)
Songs for Three Queens (Saminsky)
Songs from Drum Taps (3) (Hanson)
Songs from Housman (Cone)
Songs from the Catskills (Cazden)
Songs from the Navajo (3) (Kohs)
Songs from the Paiute (Stevens)
Songs from the Silence of Amor (Barlow)
Songs in Praise of Krishna (Rochberg)
Songs of Abelard (Dello Joio)
Songs of A.E. Housman (Glanville-Hicks)
Songs of Ecstasy (Shapey)
Songs of Elfland (Daniels)
Songs of Eternity (Bacon)
Songs of Experience (Antheil)
Songs of Experience (5) (Harbison)
Songs of Experience (Siegmeister)
Songs of Freedom, Love, and War (Custer)
Songs of Inanna and Dumuzi (Rochberg)
Songs of Innocence (George)
Songs of Innocence (Siegmeister)
Songs of Loneliness (Gottlieb)
Songs of Love and Death (4) (Stevens)
Songs of Motherhood (5) (Floyd)
Songs of Nativity (La Montaine)
Songs of Nature (Verrall)
Songs of O (Benson)
Songs of Our Time (V. Fine)
Songs of Praise and Lamentation (Perle)
Songs of Remembrance (Dello Joio)
Songs of Remembrance (Wernick)
Songs of Sappho (Lockwood)
Songs of Separation (Still)
Songs of the Countryside (Mason)
Songs of the Great South Bay (Thorne)
Songs of the Rose of Sharon (La Montaine)
Songs of the Russian Orient (6) (Saminsky)
Songs of the Season (Custer)
Songs of the Soul (Surinach)
Songs of the Spirit (Franco)
Songs of Three Ages (Smith)
Songs of Voyage (Gideon)
Songs of Youth and Madness (Gideon)
Songs to Kandinsky (Lombardo)
Songs without Words (Smit)
Song to the Lute in Musicke, A (Wuorinen)
Song without Words (Labunski)
Sonic Contours (Ussachevsky)
Sonic Images (Oliveros)

Storm Overture (Hewitt)
Story of Abraham, The (Yardumian)
Story of Esther, The (Starer)
Story of Ivan the Fool, The (Tcherepnin)
Straits of Magellan, The (Feldman)
Strange Funeral in Braddock, The (Siegmeister)
Stranger, The (Weisgall)
Strange Tenderness of Naked Leaping (Dlugos-
  zewski)
Strata (Johnston)
Strata (L. Kraft)
Streams (Benson)
Streams in the Desert (Hanson)
Street Music (Wolpe)
Street Scene (Weill)
Streets of Pekin (Hadley)
Stretti (Wernick)
String Foursome (McBride)
Stringometrics (Serly)
String Quartet on Negro Themes (Mason)
String Quartet on Negro Themes (McDonald)
String Quartet on Slavic Themes (Porter)
String Symphony in Four Cycles (Serly)
Stroller's Serenade (Whithorne)
Structure (Hannay)
Structures (Feldman)
Struggle (Rzewski)
Studies for Orchestra (Zador)
Studies in Densities and Duration (Stout)
Studies in Solitude (Nabokov)
Studies in Sound, Plus (Ussachevsky)
Studies in Timbres and Interferences (Stout)
Study in Sonority (Riegger)
Subito (Gaburo)
Sublime and the Beautiful, The (W. Kraft)
Suchness Concert (Dlugoszewski)
Suchness with Radiant Ground (Dlugoszewski)
Such Sweet Thunder (Ellington)
Suffolk Harmony, The (Billings)
Suicide in an Airplane (Ornstein)
Suite after a Notebook of 1762 (Jones)
Suite after English Folk Songs (Mason)
Suite ancienne (Hadley)
Suite Anno, 1600 (Dubensky)
Suite Billings (Hannay)
Suite East and West (Skilton)
Suite espagnole (Surinach)
Suite fantastique (Jacobi)
Suite fantastique (Schelling)
Suite for Microtonal Piano (Johnston)
Suite for Nine Concerts (Dlugoszewski)
Suite for Symphonic Suite (Harrison)
Suite géorgienne (Tcherepnin)
Suite hebraïque (Bloch)
Suite in Folk Style (Goeb)
Suite italienne (Stravinsky)
Suite modale (Bloch)
Suite nello stile italiano (Castelnuovo-Tedesco)
Suite of Prayers (Franco)
Suite of Serenades, A (Herbert)

Suite on Chilean Folk Tunes (Van Vactor)
Suite on Danish Folksongs (Grainger)
Suite passacaille (Haubiel)
Suite Primeval (Skilton)
Suite romantique (Herbert)
Suite sinfónica para "El payaso" (Davidovsky)
Suite symphonique (Bloch)
Suite Thursday (Ellington)
Sumare (Fletcher)
Summer (Clapp)
Summer (Siegmeister)
Summer and Smoke (incidental music) (Bowles)
Summer and Smoke (Hoiby)
Summer Divertimento (Bolcom)
Summer Fancies (Cole)
Summer Festival Overture (Hannay)
Summer in Valley City (Finney)
Summer Night (Siegmeister)
Summer's Day, A (La Montaine)
Summer Seascape (Hanson)
Summer Solstice (Laderman)
Summer Song (Mills)
Summer Sounds (Talma)
Summerspace (Ixion) (Feldman)
Summer Stock (Adler)
Summer Wind (MacDowell)
Sun (Rorem)
Sun, The (Nordoff)
Sun and Warm Brown Earth (Branscombe)
Sun Bride, The (Skilton)
Sunday Costs Five Pesos (Haubiel)
Sunday in Brooklyn (Siegmeister)
Sunday in Mexico (McBride)
Sunday Morning (Rorem)
Sunday Sing Symphony (Green)
Sunday Symphony, The (Symphony no. 4) (Still)
Sunset Trail, The (Cadman)
Sunshine Sonata, The (Cazden)
Sun Splendor (Bauer)
*Sun, the Soaring Eagle, the Turquoise Prince, the
  God, The* (Bergsma)
Sun-Treader (Ruggles)
Supernatural Songs (Albert)
Super Salutem (Wuorinen)
Supper of Emmaus, The (Rogers)
Supplication, Revelation, and Triumph (Franco)
Surrealist (Duke)
Sursum Corda (Korngold)
Survivor from Warsaw, A (Schoenberg)
Susanna and the Elders (Moross)
*Suspension ". . . at the still point of the turning
  world, there the dance is . . ."* (Green)
Swallows of Sanangan, The (Feldman)
Sweet Bye and Bye, The (Beeson)
Sweet Freedom's Song (Ward)
*Sweet Was the Song the Virgin Sang: Tristan Re-
  visited* (Bergsma)
Swift and Naked (Dlugoszewski)
Swift Music (Dlugoszewski)
Swing Set (Anderson)

Swing Stuff (McBride)
Sycophantic Fox and the Gullible Raven, The (Donato)
Sylvania (Beach)
Symbolic chrestiani (Nabokov)
Symbolic Portrait (McKay)
Symbolist Studies (Farwell)
Symphonia Brevis (Gideon)
Symphonia Sacra (Wuorinen)
Symphonia serena (Hindemith)
Symphonic Allegro (Mennin)
Symphonic Aria (Flagello)
Symphonic Dances (Stevens)
Symphonic Dialogue (Labunski)
Symphonic Dialogues (Luke)
Symphonic Elegy (Krenek)
Symphonic Fantasias (Luening)
Symphonic Interludes (2) (Luening)
Symphonic Jam Session (Kreutz)
Symphonic Melody (McBride)
Symphonic Metamorphosis on Themes of Carl Maria von Weber (Hindemith)
Symphonic Ode (Copland)
Symphonic Ode (Mills)
Symphonic Odes (Alexander)
Symphonic Piece (Gilbert)
Symphonic Poem (Luening)
Symphonic Prelude (Cole)
Symphonic Prelude in an American Idiom (McKay)
Symphonic Serenade (Korngold)
Symphonic Sketch (Kreutz)
Symphonic Sketches (Chadwick)
Symphonic Songs (Luke)
Symphonic Suite (Fletcher)
Symphonic Variations for Audience and Orchestra (Serly)
Symphonie concertante (Bazelon)
Symphonie on G (Harrison)
Symphony Amphitryon 4 (Blumenfeld)
Symphony Brevis (Kupferman)
Symphony for Classical Orchestra (Shapero)
Symphony for Strings (Josten)
Symphony for Strings (Symphony no. 2) (Schuman)
Symphony for Voices (R. Harris)
Symphony: In Memoriam Theodore Roosevelt (Giannini)
Symphony in One Movement (Barber)
Symphony in Steel (Grofé)
Symphony Intermezzo (Britain)
Symphony in Variation Form (Haubiel)
Symphony: 1933 (Symphony no. 1) (R. Harris)
Symphony No. 5½ (Gillis)
Symphony of Chorales (Foss)
Symphony of Faith (Gillis)
Symphony of Free Men (Gillis)
Symphony of Madrid (Custer)
Symphony of Overtures (Erb)
Symphony of Spirituals (Gould)

Symphony of the Great Rivers (Symphony no. 1) (Saminsky)
Symphony of the Seas (Symphony no. 3) (Saminsky)
Symphony of the Summits (Symphony no. 2) (Saminsky)
Symphony of the Yin-Yang (Kupferman)
Symphony(s) (Stokes)
Symphony: The Oregon (Avshalomov)
Symptoms of Love (Porter)
Synchronisms 1-8 (Davidovsky)
Synchrony (Cowell)
Syntagm III (Brown)
Synthesis (Luening)
SYNTHIONS 1-9 (Strang)
Syntony no. 1, To the Real (Rudhyar)
Syntony no. 2, The Surge of Fire (Rudhyar)
Syringa (Carter)
Syzygy (Del Tredici)

Tabasco (Chadwick)
Tableaux (Babbitt)
Tableaux vivants (Austin)
Table d'hôte (Grofé)
Tabloid (Grofé)
Tabuk—Tabuhan (McPhee)
Take 5 (Childs)
Taking of T'ung Khan, The (Avshalomov)
Tale of a Syrian Night (Duke)
Tale of Issoumbochi, The (Ward-Steinman)
Tale of the Sun Goddess Going into the Stone House (Hovhaness)
Tales of Our Countryside (Cowell)
Tales of Power (Colgrass)
Talin (Hovhaness)
Tamar (Huston)
Tamar (Ward-Steinman)
Taming of the Shrew, The (incidental music) (Bazelon)
Taming of the Shrew, The (Clapp)
Taming of the Shrew, The (Giannini)
Tammany (Hewitt)
Tam O'Shanter (Chadwick)
Tamu-Tamu (Menotti)
Tanz Suite (Toch)
Taos Portraits (Behrens)
Tapestry (Glanville-Hicks)
Tapestry (Luke)
Tarot, The (Subotnick)
Tarquin (Krenek)
Tarry Delight (McBride)
Tartar Song and Dance (Dubensky)
Tashi (Wuorinen)
Tears (Stringham)
Te Deum for All Mankind (Flagello)
Tefilot Sheva (Gottlieb)
Tehillim (Reich)
Teisho (V. Fine)
Telephone, The (Menotti)

Telephone and Birds (Cage)
Telepos (Mumma)
Tell Me Where Is Fancy Bred (Imbrie)
Telly (Schwartz)
Tempest, The (Diamond)
Tempest, The (Paine)
Temple Dances (3) (Franco)
Temple of Minerva, The (Hopkinson)
Temptations at the Siege of Air and Darkness, The (Sims)
Tender Land, The (Copland)
Tender Theatre Flight Nageire (Dlugoszewski)
Tenebrae (Mennini)
Tennessee Variations (Effinger)
Tenor, The (Weisgall)
Ten Tunes (Tuthill)
Terre de France (Talma)
Tertullian Overture (Eaton)
Terza rima (Clarke)
Testament of Life, A (Stevens)
Testimony to a Great City (Symphony no. 2) (Bazelon)
Texas Grimorium (Kubik)
Texture (Schwartz)
Texture Studies (Sydeman)
Thalia (Chadwick)
Thanatopsis (Creston)
Thanksgiving Anthem (Tuthill)
Thanksgiving Overture, A (George)
Thanksgiving Psalm from the Dead Sea Scrolls, A (Cowell)
That Time May Cease (Phillips)
That Was the True Light That Lighteth Every Man That Comes into the World (Nordoff)
Theater of the Universe (Colgrass)
Theater Piece (Cage)
Theater Piece (Luening)
Theater Piece, A (Oliveros)
Theater Piece for Trombone Player (Oliveros)
Theater Set (Kay)
Theater Set (Siegmeister)
Theatre Dances (Phillips)
Theatrical Sketches (5) (Kubik)
Theme in Yellow (Sowerby)
Then Shall the Dust Return (Stein)
There Is a Season for Everything (Toch)
There Is a Time (Dello Joio)
There Is No Death (Labunski)
These Are the Times That Try Men's Souls (Clarke)
"*These, My Ophelia*" (Chanler)
These Three (Ward-Steinman)
Theurgy (Rudhyar)
They (Spiegelman)
They Knew What They Wanted (Krenek)
They Too Are Exiles (V. Fine)
They, Too, Went t' Town (De Lamarter)
Thinker, The (Bauer)
Third Construction (Cage)
Thirteen Clocks, The (Avshalomov)

Thirteen Ways of Looking at a Blackbird (Foss)
Thirty Ideas (C. Taylor)
Thirty-six More Ideas (C. Taylor)
Thirty-two Piano Games (Finney)
Thirty Years Later (Sims)
This Is Our America (Gillis)
This Is Our Time (Schuman)
This Is the Garden (Blitzstein)
This Sacred Ground (Diamond)
This We Believe (Effinger)
Those Everlasting Blues (Moross)
Thoughts (Kupferman)
Thoughts on Rilke (Eaton)
Thoughts Provoked on Becoming a Prospective Papa (Gillis)
Three Against Christmas (Imbrie)
Three Brothers (Colgrass)
Three Candle Blessing (Gottlieb)
Three Celebrations of God in Nature (Ward)
Three Colloquies (Schuman)
Three Impressions (Bauer)
Three Inventories of Casey Jones (Green)
Three Moods for Dancing (Barlow)
Three Mysteries (Creston)
Three Narratives (Creston)
Three Observations (Daniels)
Three Pictographs (Yardumian)
Three Pieces about Marches (George)
Three Place Settings (Kolb)
Three Places in New England (Ives)
Three Prayers (Franco)
Three Protests (Ives)
Three Rituals (Hiller)
Three Satires (Schoenberg)
Three Scenes (Cheslock)
Three Scenes (Kohn)
Three Shades of Blue (Grofé)
Three Shadows (Saminsky)
Three Sides of a Town (Stokes)
Three Sisters, The (Pasatieri)
Three Sisters Who Are Not Sisters (Rorem)
Three Sonnets from "Fatal Interview" (Gideon)
Three Studies in Four (Finney)
Three Variables (Lees)
Three Variations on an Old Hungarian Song (Serly)
Threni (Stravinsky)
Threnody for Love (Haubiel)
Threnody I (Igor Stravinsky: In Memoriam) (Copland)
Threnody: The Funeral of Youth (Beversdorf)
Threnody II (Beatrice Cunningham: In Memoriam) (Copland)
Thresholds (Rudhyar)
Throne of God, The (Saminsky)
Through Interior Worlds (Schwantner)
Through the Looking Glass (D. Taylor)
Thunderbird (Cadman)
Thunderbolt Overture (Kubik)
Ticonderoga (Skilton)

Variations on a Familiar Theme (Farberman)
Variations on a Hebrew Dance Theme (Gottlieb)
Variations on a Hungarian Folk Song (Zador)
Variations on a Lyric Theme (Lombardo)
Variations on a Memory (Finney)
Variations on a Merry Tune (Zador)
Variations on an Irish Theme (R. Harris)
Variations on an Original Theme (Shepherd)
Variations on a Quiet Theme (Mason)
Variations on a Song of Mussorgsky (Rogers)
Variations on a Space and a Quiet (Stokes)
Variations on a Theme by Alban Berg (Finney)
Variations on a Theme by Chopin (Rachmaninoff)
Variations on a Theme by Corelli (Rachmaninoff)
Variations on a Theme by Edward Burlingame Hill (Piston)
Variations on a Theme of John Powell (Mason)
Variations on a Waltz (Moross)
Variations on I Got Rhythm (Gershwin)
Variations on L'homme armé (Kohs)
Variations on Obiter Dictum (Karlins)
Variations Symphony (Symphony no. 7) (Mennin)
Variazioni (Crumb)
Variazioni concertanti (Lopatnikoff)
Variazioni solenne (Van Vactor)
Variazioni sopra una melodia (Moevs)
Variety Day (McBride)
Vasco (Fuleihan)
Vathek (Parker)
Veil, The (Rogers)
Venice (Gould)
Venice (Saminsky)
Veni Creator Spiritus (Daniels)
Venta Quemada (Surinach)
Vent-ures, Three Pieces for Symphonic Wind Ensemble (Epstein)
Venus and Mercury (Huston)
Verlaine Moods (2) (Gilbert)
Vernal Equinox (Read)
Verticals Ascending (Brant)
Vertical Thoughts (Feldman)
Vespers (Lucier)
Vestiges (Cowell)
Via crucis (Surinach)
Vibrations (Eaton)
vie antérieure, La (Blumenfeld)
vie de Polichinelle, La (Nabokov)
Vigilante (Becker)
Vigiliae (Saminsky)
Vignettes (Still)
Viking's Last Voyage, The (Chadwick)
Village Music (Moore)
villanelle du diable, La (Loeffler)
Villon (Read)
Vintage Alice (Del Tredici)
Vintner's Daughter, The (Rózsa)
Viola in My Life, The (Feldman)
Violin Phase (Reich)
violoncelle bien temperê, Le (Tcherepnin)
Virgil's Dream (Colgrass)

Virgin and the Fawn, The (Zador)
Virginia City: Requiem for a Ghost Town (Grofé)
Virginia Sampler (Smit)
Virgin Island Suite (Ellington)
Vi Shum-Roo (Smit)
Vision and Prayer (Babbitt)
Vision of Ariel, The (Saminsky)
Vision of Columbus, The (Herbert)
Vision of Isaiah (Smith)
Vision of Isaiah, The (Adler)
Vision of St. Joan (Haubiel)
Vision of Sir Launfal (Cadman)
Vision of Sir Launfal, The (Sowerby)
Visions (Stringham)
Visions of Poets (Lees)
Visions of Terror and Wonder (Wernick)
Visions of Time (Symphony no. 5) (Siegmeister)
Visitation of Christ (Beversdorf)
Vistas (Barlow)
vita nuovo, La (Nabokov)
Vitebsk (Copland)
Vito de Sancto Hieronymo (Brant)
Vivaldi Gallery (Gould)
Vivre-Aimer (Bloch)
Voice in the Wilderness, A (Bloch)
Voice of My Beloved, The (Daniels)
Voice of Philomel (Chadwick)
Voices (George)
Voices (Mennin)
Voices (Salzman)
Voices for Peace (Talma)
Voice from Elysium (Gideon)
Voices of Brooklyn (Starer)
Voices of Darkness (Barlow)
Voices of Faith (Barlow)
Voices Within (Albert)
voix reconnue, La (Blumenfeld)
Volpone (Antheil)
Volpone (Gruenberg)
Volunteers, The (incidental music) (Reinagle)
Vom Spass und Ernst (Tcherepnin)
Vox Balaenae (Crumb)
Vox Cathedralis (Haubiel)
Vox Clamans in Deserto (Ruggles)
Voyage (Corigliano)
Voyage (Schulman)
Voyage (Schwartz)
voyage â Cythère (Blackwood)
Voyage 4 (Brant)
Voyage of Edgar Allan Poe, The (Argento)
Voyages (Bergsma)
Voyages (Blumenfeld)
Voyages (George)
Voyaging (Piano Concerto no. 2) (Bacon)

Wait for the Promise of the Father (Barlow)
Waking, The (Adler)
Waldmusik (Kohn)
Walker through the Walls, The (Donato)